ILLUSTRATED DAVIS DICTIONARY OF THE BIBLE

THE OLD-TIME GOSPEL HOUR EDITION

Color Illustration Credits:

Holy Land Photographs—Moore & Associates
Section of Maps—Thomas Nelson & Sons, Ltd.
Royal Publishers, Inc.

Illustration Credits:

American Baptist Assembly, 324
American Bible Society, 355, 845, 846, 847
The Berlin Museum, 72 (top, l)
Boston Museum of Fine Arts, 204 (top)
The British Museum, 71 (bottom), 72 (top and bottom, r), 109, 132, 187, 201 (bottom), 290 (top r and center), 544, 585, 695 (coins), 734, 858. 635, 636, 637 from Barnett's *Illustrations of Old Testament History*. Used with permission of The British Museum.
The Brooklyn Museum, 628 (top)
E. Leslie Carlson, 116
Ecce Homo Orphanage, 41
Lee C. Ellenberger, 341, 667, 746
Ewing Galloway, 106, 268, 304, 468, 813
H. Gokberg, 224
B. Goudis, 291 (top, l)
Israel Information Service, 8, 54, 87, 113, 124, 256, 415 (bottom), 432, 593, 598, 672, 768, 772, 792, 793, 801, 811
Jewish Theological Seminary of America, The Library, 120, 760
John Knight, 50, 105, 130, 135, 259, 386, 464, 475, 478, 542, 588, 651, 735, 757, 803, 804, 834, 856
Levant Photo Service, 11, 47, 48, 79, 93, 97, 162, 165, 177, 178, 179, 222, 257, 258, 270, 290 (top, l), 311, 335, 342 (middle and bottom), 343 (bottom), 344, 347, 364, 366 (bottom), 372, 389, 393, 394, 453, 516, 525, 554, 578, 579, 606 (middle), 607 (middle and bottom), 631, 679, 682, 691, 694, 695, 707, 709, 730, 731, 747, 794, 795, 822 (top), 851, 860, 866

Louvre Museum, 32, 202 (bottom), 203 (top, r), 565, 812
Matson Photo Service, 7, 40, 71 (top), 199, 315, 342 (top), 343, (top and middle), 366 (top), 386, 387, 391, 395, 450, 592, 653, 674 (bottom), 678, 708, 771, 797, 810
The Metropolitan Museum of Art, 202 (top, r), 204 (bottom), 290 (bottom, l), 503, 527, 543
R. H. Mount, Jr., 798, 769
National Aeronautics and Space Administration, 767
The National Museum, Naples, 111, 185
The Oriental Institute of the University of Chicago, 25, 28, 72 (bottom, l), 74, 202 (top, l), 203 (bottom and top, l), 205, 209, 458, 530, 617, 742
Palestine Archaeological Museum, 674 (top), 675
Philadelphia University Museum, 303, 508, 839
Religious News Service, 86, 397, 414 (top), 599, 607 (top, l), 637 (bottom, l), 642
Sculpture Masterworks, 461
UNESCO, 201 (top)
University of Michigan, Kelsey Museum of Archaeology, 606 (bottom)
University of Michigan, Library, 871
Three Lions, Inc. 266, 647, 648, 785
Trans World Airlines, 434, 756
Giovanni Trimboli, 706
Turkish Information Office, 606 (top, l)
Bastiaan Van Elderen, 189, 805
Howard F. Vos, 108, 208, 628 (bottom), 822 (bottom), 868
Helen Wace, 290 (bottom, r)
Zion Research Library, 762

ISBN: 0-87836-001-8

Printed in the U.S.A.

FOREWORD

As important as Webster's Dictionary is to the high school student, so is the Bible dictionary to the Bible student. A Bible-believing Christian needs three basic tools to become a Bible student. First, he needs a good study-reference edition of the Scriptures. Secondly, he needs a good concordance. I usually recommend *Strong's Exhaustive Concordance of the Bible.* Thirdly, he needs a good Bible dictionary. I usually recommend *Davis Dictionary of the Bible.*

In order to fully understand what the Word of God has to say, we must study it thoroughly. A Bible dictionary and a concordance enable us to do this. As you read your Bible, verse by verse, and word by word, use your concordance to look up reference Scriptures and your dictionary to look up any unfamiliar words.

This *Davis Dictionary of the Bible* was chosen by the Old-Time Gospel Hour because it is the best and can be a blessing to you. If it is properly used, it will greatly enhance your study of the Bible.

Jerry Falwell, Pastor
Thomas Road Baptist Church

PUBLISHER'S PREFACE TO NEW PRINTING

This edition has been published in cooperation with Baker Book House under a special arrangement with the Board of Christian Education of the Presbyterian Church of the U.S.A. This edition gives the dictionary a new look, as well as a new dimension. The addition of almost 50 pages of photo reports and substitution of photographs for most of the line drawings, and the addition of 32 pages of four-color material effectively supplement the text. Of this, 16 pages are devoted to views of the Holy Land; and there are 16 pages of four–color maps.

We are happy to perpetuate this great work.

ROYAL PUBLISHERS, INC.
NASHVILLE, TENNESSEE 37203 U.S.A.

PREFACE

THIS Dictionary covers the canonical books of the Old and New Testaments, in both the Authorized and Revised Versions, together with the First Book of the Maccabees in the Revised Version. The Cambridge edition of 1857, minion 24mo, has been the standard of reference for the canonical books of the Authorized Version. The inclusion of one book of the Apocrypha, and only one, was determined by its unique intrinsic worth, the First Book of the Maccabees being conspicuous among the apocryphal writings for its value to the historian and the biblical student as throwing much light upon an important period of Jewish history between the death of Ezra and Nehemiah at the close of the Old Testament dispensation and the birth of Christ, which inaugurated a new order of things. The other books of the Apocrypha have by no means been neglected: they have been laid under constant contribution, and their available material has been employed; but it was not deemed desirable to devote an article to every proper name, or to register very divergent spelling, which occurs in these writings.

The book aims to be a dictionary of the Bible, not of speculation about the Bible. It seeks to furnish a thorough acquaintance with things biblical. To this end it has been made a compendium of the facts stated in the Scriptures, and of explanatory and supplementary material drawn from the records of the ancient peoples contemporary with Israel.

The variations in the orthography of Scripture proper names have been noted in the respective articles. Neither the Authorized Version nor the Revised Version is thoroughly consistent. When several methods of spelling the same name exist, the choice will depend upon individual taste. The writer may perchance prefer one orthography, the reader another. There may also be circumstances which make a rare spelling preferable in particular cases. The reader may rest assured that no form has been admitted to the pages of the Dictionary which is not supported by authority.

The pronunciation of anglicized Scripture proper names is still in a chaotic state. In the majority of names the syllabification and accentuation have never been settled. Even the systems of pronunciation most in vogue are unnecessarily inconsistent. A chief reason for this is that the pronunciation has been so largely based on the forms which the Greek and Latin translators gave to the Hebrew names. These translators did not transliterate the names in accordance with any fixed rule; and, as a result, names of similar formation and pronunciation in Hebrew appear in different forms in the Greek and Latin; and often, when quite similar in appearance in English, retain the divergent Greek or Latin pronunciation. In many cases this is intolerable. The present work follows in the main the system of Webster in the division into syllables and the position of the accent. The departures are confined almost exclusively to certain classes of words. The pronunciation adopted is always supported by good authority, and is in the interest of consistency. When once the syllables and the accent of the anglicized biblical name have been determined, its correct pronunciation in the mouth of every person of true English instinct follows as a matter of course. The letters are sounded as they would be under similar circumstances in an ordinary English word. The exceptions are that the g is soft in only one name, Bethphage (pronounced Beth'pha-je), and ch is always hard and sounded like k, except in Rachel and cherub. The latter word is scarcely an exception, for it is not a proper name. The proper name Cherub, a place in Babylonia, is pronounced according to rule (Ke'rub).

The meaning of proper names has been given whenever it is known. The cases are many where it has been necessarily omitted or stated cautiously. Even where there is no note of caution, the reader must be on his guard; for although the general signification of the name may be perfectly clear, the shade of meaning which lent the name flavor among those who bestowed it may elude discovery. Judah means an object of praise; but it might be an expression either of thankfulness on the part of the parents to God, or satisfaction in the child; either God or the child might be thought of as praiseworthy. Jehovah-jireh means Jehovah doth see; but the special sense may be, Jehovah doth provide.

In regard to the modern names of places in Palestine, the orthography of the Palestine Eplloration Fund has been adopted, except that the elevated comma is employed to represent the Arabic consonant alif, and the inverted comma to represent the guttural ain; compare ALPHABET. This is the rule; but occasionally, for special reasons, the etymology is more fully indicated by the diacritical points conventionally used by Semitists.

Persons are genealogically described as far as possible according to the method of registration which was employed by the Hebrews, namely, by the tribe, family, and father's house.

In the preparation of the Dictionary the author has had the cooperation of his colleagues the Reverend Professors Benjamin Breckinridge Warfield, D.D., LL.D., and George Tybout Purves, D.D., LL.D., who have furnished the articles pertaining to New Testament introduction and several others on important subjects. To each of these articles the initials of its author are appended.

J. D. D.

AUGUST 17, 1898.

PREFACE TO THE FOURTH REVISED EDITION

THE DICTIONARY has been subjected to a revision, pervasive yet unobtrusive, in order to incorporate material gathered by biblical research during the past decade and a half. Purposely the book has not been increased in size, nor has the pagination been changed.

J. D. D.

AUGUST 25, 1924.

COLOR ILLUSTRATIONS

The Holy Land (8 pages of photographs) ....following page 248

The Holy Land (8 pages of photographs) ....following page 440

MAPS   Page

Probable Location of Mount Ararat 50

Ancient Babylon 71

Ancient Egypt 202

Jerusalem 387

Philistine Cities and Areas of Expansion 638

Qumran Area of the Dead Sea 674

The Sinai Peninsula 767

COLOR MAP SUPPLEMENT

The Fertile Crescent 1

The Land of Promise 2

The Ancient Near East (1500 to 600 B.C.) 3

The Empire of Alexander 3

The Wandering in the Wilderness 4

The Settlement in Canaan 5

Judah 6

Palestine in the Time of the Early Monarchy 7

The Divided Monarchy 8

Palestine in the Time of the Maccabees 9

Jerusalem 10

Palestine in New Testament Times 11

The Journeys of St. Paul 12

Paul's Journey to Rome 13

Paul's First, Second, and Third Missionary Journey 13

The Middle East and Holy Land at Present 14

Jerusalem at Present 15

The Exodus 16

Assyrian Empire 16

Babylonian Empire 16

Persian Empire 16

A DICTIONARY
OF THE BIBLE

Aa′ron [etymology doubtful. The name possibly means bright, shining].

The brother of Moses and his senior by three years (Ex. vii. 7). He was a descendant of Levi through Kohath and Amram (Ex. vi. 14–27). As we do not read of perils attending his infancy, it may be inferred that he was born before the promulgation of the nefarious Egyptian edicts dooming the Hebrew male children to death. He was younger than his sister Miriam (q. v.). He married Elisheba, daughter of Amminadab and sister of Nahshon, of the tribe of Judah, who bore him four sons, Nadab, Abihu, Eleazar, and Ithamar (Ex. vi. 23; Num. iii. 2). When Moses at Horeb was called to stand forth as the deliverer of his oppressed countrymen, and, wishing to escape the mission, complained that he was "slow of speech, and of a slow tongue," God repelled the objection, and said, "Is not Aaron the Levite thy brother? I know that he can speak well." Aaron was forthwith instructed to go out and meet Moses in the wilderness. He did so. The brothers met and embraced each other (Ex. iv. 10–16, 27). Returning to Egypt, they gathered together the elders of Israel and intimated to them the approaching deliverance (29–31). Aaron acted as the spokesman and agent of Moses and carried the rod in the first interviews with the elders and with Pharaoh, and during the first three plagues (iv. 30; vii. 2, 9, 19 [by the command of Moses and hence Moses' act, xvii. 5]; viii. 5, 16). But soon afterwards Moses partly dispensed with the agency of Aaron, and thenceforth, whenever the rod was used symbolically, it was in the hand of Moses himself (ix. 23; x. 13, and cp. 22; xiv. 16, 21; xvii. 5; Num. xx. 11). Aaron and Hur supported Moses' arms during the battle with Amalek (Ex. xvii. 12). When the covenant between Jehovah and Israel was entered into at mount Sinai, the ceremony of its ratification was concluded, as usual, by a common meal spread for the contracting parties. Aaron and two of his sons with Moses and seventy elders of Israel were appointed to partake of this meal as the legal representatives of the nation and to behold the vision of the God of Israel at the ceremony (Ex.

xxiv. 1, 9, 10). During the prolonged stay of Moses in the mount, the people became impatient at the absence of their leader and turned to Aaron with the demand that he make them gods to go before them. Aaron weakly yielded and made the golden calf (Ex. xxxii.). According to instructions which Moses received, Aaron and his sons were to fill the office of priest. Accordingly, after the tabernacle had been completed, and was ready for actual services to begin, Aaron and his four sons were solemnly consecrated to the priesthood by being anointed with oil and clothed in splendid typical official vestments (Ex. xxviii.; xl. 13–16; Lev. viii.). Aaron was thus the first high priest, an office which he filled for nearly forty years. Shortly after leaving Sinai, he joined with Miriam in finding fault with Moses for having married a Cushite woman (Num. xii. 1–16). The rebellion of Korah was directed as much against the exclusive priesthood of Aaron and his sons as against the civil authority of Moses. The divine appointment of Moses and Aaron to their respective offices was attested by the destruction of the rebels; and Aaron's right to the priesthood was further and specially vindicated by the budding of the rod taken for Levi and inscribed with Aaron's name (Num. xvi. and xvii.). Toward the close of the journey in the wilderness, when the people were encamped for the second time at Kadesh, Aaron and Moses dishonored God by their conduct when they smote the rock. For this sin they were denied the privilege of entering the promised land (Num. xx. 1–13). Soon afterwards, when the Israelites were encamped at Moserah, by divine direction Aaron was led by Moses up mount Hor and stripped of his sacred vestments, which were transferred to his son Eleazar. There he died, at the age of one hundred and twenty-three years. The nation publicly mourned for him thirty days (Num. xx. 23–29; xxxiii. 37–39; Deut. x. 6). See PRIEST and HIGH PRIEST.

Aa′ron-ites, in the Hebrew text simply Aaron, the name being used collectively.

The priestly descendants of Aaron (1 Chron xii. 27; xxvii. 17, A. V.).

A-bad'don [destruction, ruin]
1. Destruction, ruin (Job xxxi. 12); the place of the dead, synonymous with the grave (Ps. lxxxviii 11), Sheol (Job xxvi 6; Prov. xv. 11, R. V), and death (Job xxviii 22)
2. A name of the angel of the abyss, who is called in Greek Apollyon (Rev. ix 11)

A-bag'tha.
One of the seven chamberlains of the Persian king Ahasuerus (Esth i. 10). These chamberlains, guardians of the harem, ministered in the presence of the king (i. 10, 11). They were eunuchs, as the Hebrew title denotes and custom required ; and hence were probably foreigners and liable to bear foreign names.

Ab'a-nah, R. V., in A. V. **Abana** ; in margin of R. V Amanah (q. v.), of A. V. Amana [The name probably means stony].
One of the two rivers of Damascus ; presumably the more important, for Naaman, of that city, mentions it first (2 Kin. v 12). It is probably the Barada, the Chrysorrhoas of classical writers, which rises in a large blue pool of unfathomable depth on the high plain south of Zebedâny on Anti-Lebanon, twenty-three miles from Damascus, rushes in a southeasterly course down the mountain, and then, turning eastward, runs along the north wall of the city, to be lost finally in an inland lake, the middle one of three existing. It flows sluggishly through the plain, but on its passage through Damascus it has a rapid course. Nine or ten branches are taken from it, yet it flows on deep and broad. It is the chief cause of the beauty and fertility of the plain of Damascus.

Ab'a-rim [those beyond].
A region east of the Jordan, so named by people living west of the river. Jeremiah mentions Lebanon, Bashan, and Abarim in this order, from north to south (Jer. xxii. 20, R. V.; in A. V., "passages"). The Israelites encamped in this region shortly before crossing the Arnon (Num. xxi. 11). In it the Reubenites were granted lands (xxxii. 2, 37). The mountains of Abarim denote the bluffs which overlook the Dead Sea and Jordan valley from the east. On these heights the Israelites encamped before they moved down to Shittim by the Jordan (xxxiii. 47–49). From a peak of the range Moses looked across at the promised land (Deut. xxxii. 49; xxxiv. 1).

Ab'ba [Aramaic, father].
A term borrowed from childhood's language to express filial address to God (Mark xiv. 36; Rom. viii. 15; Gal. iv. 6). The corresponding Hebrew word is Ab; it is common in compound proper names in the forms Ab and Abi, as Abimelech, Abner or Abiner, Eliab.

Ab'da [Aramaic, servant, probably meaning servant of God].
1. The father of Adoniram (1 Kin. iv. 6).

2. A Levite, the son of Shammua (Neh. xi. 17). See OBADIAH 12.

Ab'de-el [servant of God].
The father of Shelemiah (Jer. xxxvi. 26).

Ab'di [servant of, a contraction of servant of God].
1 A Levite of the family of Merari. He was the son of Malluch, and father of Kishi (1 Chron. vi. 44). The Abdi of 2 Chron. xxix. 12 seems to be the same man
2. Son of a certain Elam (Ezra x. 26).

Ab'di-el [servant of God].
A Gadite, resident in Gilead (1 Chron. v. 15).

Ab'don [servile].
1. The son of Hillel, a native of Pirathon, in the tribe of Ephraim He judged Israel, or a portion of it, eight years, and is the eleventh judge in the order of enumeration. He had forty sons and thirty sons' sons, who rode on as many ass-colts—a sign of rank in days when the Hebrews did not yet have horses. He was buried in his native place (Judg. xii. 13–15).
2. Head of a father's house of Benjamin, a son of Shashak, dwelling in Jerusalem (1 Chron viii. 23, 26, 28).
3. A Benjamite, the firstborn of Jehiel of Gibeon and an ancestor of king Saul (1 Chron. viii. 30, ix 35, 36) See KISH 2.
4. An official of king Josiah (2 Chron. xxxiv. 20); see ACHBOR.
5. A town in the territory of Asher, given, with its suburbs, to the Levites of the Gershon family (Josh. xxi. 30, 1 Chron. vi. 74). Abdon is perhaps identical with the ruins of 'Abdeh, ten miles north of Acre.

A-bed'ne-go [servant of Nego, probably the same as Nebo]
The name given by the prince of the eunuchs at Babylon to Azariah, one of the three faithful Jews, afterwards miraculously saved from the fiery furnace (Dan. i. 7; iii. 12–30; 1 Mac. ii. 59).

A'bel, I. [breath, vapor; applied to Abel apparently from the shortness of his life; or perhaps the name means son]
A younger son of Adam, and by calling a shepherd. Abel was a righteous man (Mat. xxiii. 35; 1 John iii. 12); one of the Old Testament worthies whose conduct was controlled by faith (Heb. xi 4). He offered to God a lamb from his flock, which was accepted. It was not the kind of offering, but the character of the offerer that God respected. As brought by Abel, the offering showed the surrender of the heart to God. The offering of the best further revealed the sense of obligation and gratitude to God as the sole bestower of the good, to whom all thanks were due. It expressed the consciousness in the offerer of entire dependence upon God for daily blessing and the desire for the continuance of God's favor. In one in whom the sense of sin was deep, it set forth the entire dependence of the sinner upon

God's unmerited mercy. Cain's character was different from Abel's; and being rejected he at the promptings of envy slew Abel (Gen. iv). The ultimate ground of Abel's acceptance by God was the atoning blood of Christ.

A'bel, II. [a grassy place, a meadow].
1. The same as Abel-beth-maachah (2 Sam. xx. 14, 15, 18).
2. In 1 Sam. vi. 18 it is apparently an erroneous reading for 'Eben, stone; see R. V.

A'bel-beth-ma'a-cah and **Abel of Beth-maacah**, in A. V. written Maachah [Abel, i. e. Meadow near Beth-maacah].
A fortified town in the tribe of Naphtali (2 Sam. xx. 15; 1 Kin. xv. 20), famous for prudence, or for its adherence to Israelite customs (2 Sam. xx. 18; cp. Greek text). Sheba fled thither when his revolt against David failed. Joab prepared to assault the town to capture him, but a "wise woman" after conference with Joab agreed to have the rebel slain, and thus saved the town (14–22). Ben-hadad seized it and other towns when Asa of Judah sought his aid against Baasha of Israel (1 Kin. xv. 20). In 734 B. C. Tiglath-pileser captured it, and carried off its inhabitants to Assyria (2 Kin. xv. 29). Its site is probably marked by Abl, a village west of the Jordan on a knoll overlooking the valley, 12 miles north of the Huleh and opposite Dan. The Derdâra flows by the mound on the west. Girded by a well watered, fertile plain, it merits its name Abel-maim, meadow of waters (2 Chron. xvi. 4).

A'bel-cher'a-mim [meadow of vineyards].
A place east of the Jordan to which Jephthah pursued the Ammonites (Judg. xi. 33, R. V.).

A'bel-ma'im. See ABEL-BETH-MAACAH.

A'bel-me-ho'lah [meadow of dancing].
A town, apparently in the Jordan valley, where Elisha was born (Judg. vii. 22; 1 Kin. iv. 12; xix. 16). It was fixed by Jerome ten Roman miles south of Scythopolis, the Scripture Bethshean. Conder places it at 'Ain Helweh.

A'bel-miz-ra'im. See ATAD.

A'bel-shit'tim [meadow of acacias]. See SHITTIM.

A'bez, in R. V. **Ebez** [whiteness, tin].
A town of Issachar (Josh. xix. 20). Not identified.

A'bi. See ABIJAH 7.

A-bi'a. See ABIJAH.

A-bi'ah [Jehovah is a father].
The Hebrew name is usually rendered Abijah in the English version of the Old Testament, with but two exceptions in E. R. V. (1 Chron. ii. 24; vi. 28), and always so in A. R. V. See ABIJAH.

A-bi-al'bon [fath r of strength].
One of David's mighty men (2 Sam. xxiii. 31. The Septuagint supports the reading Abiel

in this passage, which is the name he bears in 1 Chron. xi. 32.

A-bi'a-saph, or **Ebiasaph** [father of gath ering, perhaps in the sense of removing reproach].
A descendant of Levi through Korah (Ex. vi. 16, 18, 21, 24; 1 Chron. vi. 23; ix. 19).

A-bi'a-thar [father of abundance].
A priest, the son of Ahimelech, of the line of Eli. On the slaughter by Doeg at the instance of king Saul of the priests at Nob, Abiathar escaped, carrying the ephod with him; and, as was natural, cast in his lot with David (1 Sam. xxii. 20-23). When David at length ascended the throne, Zadok and Abiathar apparently shared the high-priesthood between them (cp. 1 Chron. xv. 11, 12; 2 Sam. xv. 24 seq.; xv. 35, etc.). The mention of Ahimelech, son of Abiathar, as priest with Zadok in 2 Sam. viii. 17, is regarded by some as a copyist's error, whereby the names of father and son were transposed. But the number of allusions to Ahimelech, the son of Abiathar, as priest, is so great that an error is improbable (1 Chron. xviii. 16, Septuagint; xxiv. 3, 6, 31). A simpler explanation is that, since Abiathar was becoming quite old (he was about seventy years of age at the time of Absalom's revolt), his son and legal successor assumed the burdensome priestly functions and was called priest, as Phinehas served during the lifetime of Eli and was called priest (1 Sam. i. 3; ii. 11). The aged Abiathar remained faithful to the king during Absalom's rebellion, and rendered the fugitive monarch great service (2 Sam. xv. 24, 29, 35, 36; xvii. 15; xix. 11); but when later Adonijah sought to wrest the succession to the throne from Solomon, Abiathar cast his priestly influence with the military influence of Joab, another old man, in favor of the attractive aspirant (1 Kin. i. 7). Though this attempt failed, he again favored Adonijah after David's death (1 Kin. ii. 12-22). For this he was deposed from the high-priesthood, and Zadok, a priest of approved loyalty, but of the other branch of the Aaronic family, was put into his place (1 Kin. ii. 26, 35). His deposition involved that of his sons Ahimelech and Jonathan; and thus the rule of the house of Eli came to an end, according to prophecy (1 Sam. ii. 31-35). The passage in 1 Kin. iv. 4 probably refers to the time immediately prior to his deposition. Abiathar is alluded to by our Lord in the New Testament (Mark ii. 26).

A'bib [an ear of corn].
The month which the Hebrews were directed to make the first of the year in commemoration of their departure from Egypt (Ex. xii. 1, 2; xiii. 4). Harvest began in it. The feast of unleavened bread or the passover fell during the month (Ex. xii. 1 seq.; xxiii. 15; Deut. xvi. 1). The Jewish months following the moon and ours being fixed, the two cannot be made exactly to correspond.

Abib most nearly approaches our month of March, though in some years its end moves some distance into our April. After the captivity the name Abib gave place to Nisan (Neh. ii. 1; Esth. iii. 7). See YEAR.

A-bi′da, in A. V. once **Abidah** (Gen. xxv. 4) an inconsistency from which the original edition of A. V. is free [father of knowledge].

A descendant of Abraham through Midian (Gen. xxv. 4; 1 Chron. i. 33).

A-bi′dan [father of a judge, or the father judgeth].

The representative prince of the tribe of Benjamin in the wilderness. His father's name was Gideoni (Num. i. 11; ii. 22; vii. 60, 65; x. 24).

A-bi′el [father of strength, or God is a father].

1. A Benjamite, the father of Kish and of Ner, and the grandfather of Saul and of Abner (1 Sam. ix. 1; xiv. 51). See KISH 2.

2. An Arbathite, one of David's mighty men (1 Chron. xi. 32), called in 2 Sam. xxiii. 31 Abi-albon (q. v.).

A-bi-e′zer [father of help].

1. A descendant of Manasseh through Machir, and founder of a family (Josh. xvii. 2; 1 Chron. vii. 18); abbreviated in Num. xxvi. 30 to Iezer (A. V. Jeezer). The judge Gideon belonged to this family (Judg. vi. 11).

2. Collectively, the family of Abiezer (Judg. vi. 34; viii. 2).

3. One of David's heroes (2 Sam. xxiii. 27; 1 Chron. xi. 28; xxvii. 12).

A-bi-ez′rite.

One belonging to the family of Abiezer (Judg. vi. 11, 24; viii. 32). In Num. xxvi. 30 abbreviated, and R. V. has Iezerite, A. V. Jeezerite; but the spelling should rather be Iezrite to accord with the Hebrew and be consistent with Abiezrite.

Ab′i-gail, in R. V. once **Abigal** [perhaps, father of exultation].

1. The wife of Nabal. She was a woman of good understanding, and of a beautiful countenance, and on the death of her first husband became one of David's wives (1 Sam. xxv. 3, 14–44; xxvii. 3; 2 Sam. ii. 2). When the Amalekites captured Ziklag they took her captive, but she was rescued by her husband after he had defeated the enemy (1 Sam. xxx. 5, 18). She bore to him a son called Chileab (2 Sam. iii. 3) or Daniel (1 Chron. iii. 1)

2. A sister of David (1 Chron. ii. 16); not, however, a daughter of Jesse, but of Nahash (2 Sam. xvii. 25, in R. V. Abigal). She was the mother of Amasa.

Ab-i-ha′il [father of strength]. In the Hebrew text the *h* is a different letter in the name of the men and in that of the women. The difference is commonly attributed to an arly misreading of the text.

1. A Levite of the family of Merari (Num. iii. 35).

2. Wife of Abishur (1 Chron. ii. 29).

3. A Gadite (1 Chron. v. 14).

4. Wife of king Rehoboam and a descendant of Eliab, David's brother (2 Chron. xi. 18).

5. Father of queen Esther (Esth. ii. 15).

A-bi′hu [He, *i. e.* God, is father].

A son of Aaron. He shared in the privileges, in the sin, and in the fate of Nadab the eldest son, and like him died childless (Ex. vi. 23; xxiv. 1; xxviii. 1; Lev. x. 1–7; Num. iii. 2).

A-bi′hud [probably, father of praiseworthiness].

A descendant of Benjamin through the family of Bela (1 Chron. viii. 3).

A-bi′jah, in A. V. of O. T. four times **Abiah** (1 Sam. viii. 2; 1 Chron. ii. 24; vi. 28; vii. 8), in A. V. of N. T. **Abia** [Jehovah is a father].

1. The wife of Hezron, a man of the tribe of Judah (1 Chron. ii. 24, A. R. V.). See ABIAH.

2. A descendant of Aaron. His family had grown to a father's house in the time of David, and was made the eighth of the twenty-four courses into which David divided the priests (1 Chron. xxiv. 1, 6, 10). See 8 below.

3. A descendant of Benjamin through Becher (1 Chron. vii. 8).

4. The younger son of Samuel, appointed by his father a judge in Beersheba, but who proved corrupt (1 Sam. viii. 2; 1 Chron. vi. 28). See ABIAH.

5. A son of Jeroboam. While yet a child he fell dangerously sick. Jeroboam sent his queen in disguise to the prophet Ahijah, who had predicted that he should obtain the kingdom, to inquire what the issue of the sickness would be. The prophet recognized the queen, notwithstanding her disguise, denounced judgment against Jeroboam for his apostasy from Jehovah, and added that the child would die at once, and that alone of all that household he would obtain honorable burial, because in him was found some good thing toward the Lord God. All came to pass as the seer had foretold (1 Kin. xiv. 1–18).

6. The name given in Chronicles to the son and successor of Rehoboam, called in Kings Abijam (2 Chron. xii. 16; xiii. 1–xiv. 1); see ABIJAM.

7. The mother of Hezekiah (2 Chron. xxix. 1). In 2 Kin. xviii. 2 she is called with great brevity Abi.

8. A chief of the priests who returned with Zerubbabel from Babylon (Neh. xii. 4, 7). Possibly he was a representative of the old course of Abijah, but the connection cannot be established, and in view of Ezra ii. 36 seq. is not probable. In the next generation, a father's house among the priests bore this name (Neh. xii. 17). The father of John the Baptist belonged to this family (Luke i. 5).

9. A priest who, doubtless in behalf of a

father's house, signed the covenant in the days of Nehemiah (Neh. x. 7).

A-bi'jam [possibly, father of the sea].

The son and successor of Rehoboam on the throne of Judah. His mother's name was Maacah, a descendant of Absalom (1 Kin. xv. 2; 2 Chron. xiii. 2). He sinned after the manner of his father, and had not a heart true to Jehovah. The kings of Judah had not yet become reconciled to the revolt of the ten tribes, and Abijam continued the war with Jeroboam which his father had waged (1 Kin. xv. 6, 7). According to 2 Chron. xiii. 3, compared with 2 Sam. xxiv. 9, the whole population "able to go forth to war" was under arms. In the slaughter which accompanied the warfare, half a million men of Israel were slain (2 Chron. xiii. 16-20). Abijam had fourteen wives, twenty-two sons, and sixteen daughters (2 Chron. xiii. 21). He reigned three years, and died, leaving his son Asa to succeed him in the kingdom (1 Kin. xv. 1-8; 2 Chron. xiv. 1). Abijam is called in Chronicles Abijah.

Ab-i-le'ne [Greek 'Abilene, so called from Abila, its capital, and that again probably from the Semitic 'abel, a meadow].

A tetrarchy near Anti-Lebanon. Its capital Abila lay upon the Barada, 18 or 20 miles N. W. from Damascus, in part upon the site of the modern village of es - Suk. There is a romantic gorge, with a Roman road cut in the cliff, a cemetery, a number of tall pillars, a stream below and the so-called "tomb of Abel" above. The local tradition that Abel was buried here doubtless originated in the similarity of sound between Abel and Abila. Of the formation of the tetrarchy Josephus makes no mention. In Luke iii. 1 it is referred to as separate from the tetrarchy of Philip, and as governed by Lysanias in the fifteenth year of Tiberius. Likewise an inscription at Abila, dating from the reign of Tiberius, mentions Lysanias as tetrarch of Abilene at that time. Some years later the two tetrarchies are still distinct; for Caligula, 790 A. U. C., bestowed the "tetrarchy of Philip," now dead, and the "tetrarchy of Lysanias" upon Herod Agrippa, the Herod of the book of Acts (Antiq. xviii. 6, 10), and Claudius confirmed to him "Abila of Lysanias" (xix. 5, 1).

There was an Abila in Peræa, east of Gadara, but it is not mentioned in Scripture.

A-bim'a-el [composition of the name still unknown].

A name in the genealogy of Joktan. It may denote a person, a tribe, or a locality, and is to be sought in Arabia (Gen. x. 28; 1 Chron. i. 22).

A-bim'e-lech [father of the king].

1. The personal name or official title of a king of Gerar, at whose court Abraham attempted to pass Sarah off as his sister (Gen. xx. 1-18). The king and the patriarch at a

later period entered into a covenant with each other (xxi. 22-34).

2. A king of the Philistines at Gerar, at whose court Isaac attempted to pass off Rebekah as his sister, and with whom he also, like his father, at last formed a covenant (Gen. xxvi. 1-33).

3. The son of the judge Gideon by a concubine. This woman was a native of Shechem, where her family had influence. One natural penalty of polygamy is that the sons by one mother tend fiercely to quarrel with those by another; and Abimelech, obtaining assistance from his mother's relatives, killed seventy sons of his father on one stone at Ophrah, the native city of the family. One son only, Jotham, escaped from the massacre. Then Abimelech was elected king of Shechem. Before he had ruled three years he and his subjects were at variance, and his throne, founded in blood, had begun to totter. A plot against him was formed by Gaal. It came to the ears of Zebul, Abimelech's second in command. Gaal was defeated and driven out of Shechem, the city being afterwards destroyed and sowed with salt. A thousand men and women who had taken refuge in its tower were burnt to death. When Abimelech shortly afterwards was besieging Thebez, he was mortally wounded by a millstone dropped on his head from the city wall by a woman. Regarding it as dishonorable to be killed by a female, he ordered his armor-bearer to draw his sword and slay him, which he did (Judg. ix. 1-57).

4. See ACHISH.

5. A priest, a son of Abiathar (1 Chron. xviii. 16). The spelling is doubtless a copyist's error for Ahimelech. The Septuagint reads Ahimelech; see also 1 Chron. xxiv. 6, etc.

A-bin'a-dab [father of liberality].

1. A man of Kiriath-jearim, who when the ark was sent back by the Philistines, gave it accommodation in his house, where it remained until the reign of David. A son of Abinadab was consecrated to act as its custodian (1 Sam. vii. 1, 2; 2 Sam. vi. 3; 1 Chron. xiii. 7).

2. The second son of Jesse and an elder brother of David (1 Sam. xvi. 8; xvii. 13).

3. A son of Saul, killed with his father in the battle of Gilboa (1 Sam. xxxi. 2).

4. Father of a son-in-law of Solomon and tax-gatherer for the region of Dor (1 Kin. iv. 11, A. V.). See BEN-ABINADAB.

A-bin'o-am [father of sweetness or grace].

The father of Barak (Judg. iv. 6; v. 12).

A-bi'ram [legitimate variant of Abram. For meaning see ABRAHAM].

1. A Reubenite, a brother of Dathan and fellow conspirator with Korah (Num. xvi.).

2. The firstborn son of Hiel, who rebuilt Jericho (1 Kin. xvi. 34). His death, when its foundations were laid, in part fulfilled a curse pronounced by Joshua (Josh. vi. 26).

A-bish'ag [perhaps, father of wandering].

A beautiful girl from Shunem, employed to

attend upon king David when he was old and declining in vitality (1 Kin. i. 1–4). Adonijah wished to marry her after David's death, and made application for the needed permission to Solomon, who not merely refused his request, but interpreted it to mean an insidious claim for the crown, and put him to death (1 Kin. ii. 13–25).

A-bish′a-i and **Abshai** (1 Chron. xviii. 12 margin) [possessor of all that is desirable].

A son of David's sister Zeruiah, and brother of Joab and Asahel (2 Sam. ii. 18; 1 Chron. ii. 15, 16). When David found Saul and his followers asleep, Abishai asked permission to kill the king; but David would not sanction his doing harm to "the Lord's anointed" (1 Sam. xxvi. 5–9). He served under Joab in David's army (2 Sam. ii. 18; x. 10). When Abner, fleeing from the battle at Gibeon, was compelled to kill Asahel, the two brothers of the latter, Joab and Abishai, pursued the homicide, but without effect (2 Sam. ii. 18–24). He was loyal to David during the revolts of Absalom and Sheba (2 Sam. xvi. and xx). He desired to slay Shimei for cursing David, even when Shimei asked forgiveness (2 Sam. xvi. 9; xix. 21). He was one of David's mighty men who had lifted up his spear against three hundred and slain them (2 Sam. xxiii. 18; 1 Chron. xi. 20). He defeated the Edomites also in the valley of Salt, slaying eighteen thousand of them and garrisoning their country (1 Chron. xviii. 12, 13). He succored David in the fight with Ishbi-benob (2 Sam. xxi. 16, 17).

A-bish′a-lom. See ABSALOM.

A-bish′u-a [father of salvation].
1. A Benjamite of the family of Bela (1 Chron. viii. 4).
2. The son of Phinehas the priest (1 Chron. vi. 4, 5, 50; Ezra vii. 5).

A-bi′shur [father of a wall].
A man of Judah, family of Hezron, house of Jerahmeel (1 Chron. ii. 28, 29).

A-bi′tal [apparently, father of dew, perhaps in the sense of refreshment].
One of David's wives. Her son was Shephatiah (2 Sam. iii. 4; 1 Chron. iii. 3).

A-bi′tub [father of goodness].
A Benjamite, son of Shaharaim by his wife Hushim (1 Chron. viii. 8–11).

A-bi′ud [the Greek form, probably, of Hebrew Abihud].
A member of the royal line of Judah (Mat. i. 13). The name is omitted in 1 Chron. iii. 19.

Ab′ner [father of light]. A legitimate variant form, Abiner, is used in the Hebrew text of 1 Sam. xiv. 50, and in the margin of some editions of the English version.
The son of Ner, king Saul's uncle. During the reign of that monarch Abner was commander-in-chief of the army (1 Sam. xiv. 51). He first became acquainted with David when that youth offered to meet Goliath in combat (1 Sam. xvii. 55–58). On the death of Saul,

Abner availed himself of the tribal feeling adverse to Judah, and turned it to the advantage of the house to which he was related by blood, and to which he had owned allegiance. He proclaimed Saul's son Ish-bosheth king at Mahanaim (2 Sam. ii. 8). During the war between the house of Saul and David which followed, in an interview which he held at Gibeon with Joab, David's commander-in-chief, Abner proposed what he seems to have intended for a tournament between twelve young men picked from Ish-bosheth's supporters and as many taken from the followers of David, but mutual animosities converted the mimic combat into a real battle; and the two armies being drawn into the struggle, that which Abner led was defeated with great slaughter (12–32). During the retreat from this battle Abner was pertinaciously followed with hostile intent by Asahel, one of Joab's brothers, and after repeatedly warning him off, had at last to strike him dead in self-defence (18–24). Soon afterwards Abner had a serious charge brought against him by Ish-bosheth, which so irritated him that he intimated his intention of transferring his allegiance to David, and was as good as his word. First he sent messengers to David, and then sought an interview with him, and was graciously received. But Joab, believing or pretending to believe that Abner had come simply as a spy, went after him, invited him to a friendly conversation, and stabbed him dead. The ostensible reason for this assassination was revenge for the death of Asahel, who, however, had died in fair fight. An unavowed motive probably was fear that Abner might one day displace him from the command of David's army. The king was justly incensed against the murderer, and conspicuously showed the people that he had no complicity in the crime. He attended the funeral, lamented the unworthy fate of the prince and great man who had fallen in Israel, and finally left it in charge to his successor to call Joab to account for the crime (iii. 6–39; 1 Kin. ii. 5). Abner had at least one son, Jaasiel (1 Chron. xxvii. 21), and seems to have had a regard for the house of God, for he dedicated to it some of the spoils which he had taken in battle (xxvi. 28).

A-bom-i-na′tion of Des-o-la′tion.
Idolatry with its blighting effect upon man, its degradation of the divine ideal, and its violent outward, as well as its less visible insidious, opposition to the kingdom of God. To Daniel was revealed: "For the half of the week, he shall cause the sacrifice and the oblation to cease; and upon the wing of abominations shall come one that maketh desolate" (ix. 27, R. V.): "and they shall profane the sanctuary, even the fortress, and shall take away the continual burnt offering, and they shall set up the abomination that maketh desolate" (xi. 31, R. V.); and "from the time that the continual burnt offering shall be taken

away, and the abomination that maketh desolate set up, there shall be a thousand two hundred and ninety days" (xii. 11, R.V.). These prophecies depict outstanding features of the development of the kingdom of God, which are typical for all time. A notable fulfillment of xi. 31, which the Jews were quick to discern, was the stoppage of the daily sacrifice by Antiochus Epiphanes in June, 168 B. C., and the erection on the brazen altar of an idolatrous one, on which sacrifices were offered to Jupiter Olympius (1 Mac. i. 54; vi. 7; 2 Mac. vi. 2; Antiq. xii. 5, 4; 7, 6). But the prophecy of the abomination of desolation was not exhausted by this fulfillment. The prophecy belongs to Messianic times (Dan. ix. 27), and yet more generally to the conflict of the kingdom of God until its final triumphant establishment (xii. 7, 11 with vii. 25-27; cp. xii. 2). Christ reiterated the prophecy, enjoining those to flee to the mountains who should see the abomination of desolation, spoken of by Daniel the prophet, standing in the holy place (Mat. xxiv. 15, etc.).

A'bra-ham, at first **Abram** [in Hebrew, Abram denotes exalted father; the change to Abraham appears to consist merely in strengthening the root of the second syllable, in order to place increased emphasis on the idea of exaltation].

Son of Terah, progenitor of the Hebrews, father of the faithful, and the friend of God (Gen. xi. 26; Gal. iii. 7-9; Jas. ii. 23). The name was in vogue among the Semites of Babylonia at least two generations before the reign of Hammurabi, who is commonly believed to be Amraphel of Gen. xiv.

Is Abraham a tribal name? Is he the personification of a tribe? The justification for raising this question is the fact that many names in the genealogical registers of the Hebrews denote tribes and not individuals (Gen. x.; xxv. 1-4). It is not always easy, at times it is impossible, to decide whether a people or a person is meant. But it is important to note, further, that a tribal name and history often include persons whose deeds are recorded in the name of the tribe and as the acts of the tribe (see CHRONOLOGY I. 3). Noah, for example, may be the name of a tribe; but if so, in the narrative of the flood it denotes likewise an individual member of that tribe, who was saved with his family in the ark. In the case of Abraham, Gen. xi. 26, 27, and the first ten verses of the twelfth chapter might readily be read as the story of a tribe's origin and migration, in fact, it does recount the movement of a sheik and his people; the separation of Abram and Lot might also be tribal, and so too the treaty with Abimelech. But though the tribal ele-

Ruins at Ur of the Chaldees, Abraham's early homeland.

Traditional well of Abraham at Beer-sheba.

ment may enter into the narrative, the history is not exclusively tribal. The majority of the deeds recorded in it cannot be explained as tribal movements without violence and improbable interpretations. They are the acts of an individual (Gen. xv. 1-18; xvi. 1-11; xviii. 1-xix. 28; xx. 1-17; xxii. 1-14; xxiv.). Moreover, the passages just cited belong to the earliest literature of Israel, as all schools of criticism agree; and during all the centuries that followed the Hebrews themselves regarded Abraham as an individual (Is. xxix. 22; xli. 8; li. 2; Jer. xxxiii. 26; Ezek. xxxiii. 24; Mat. viii. 11).

I. *Chronology.*—1. *His life before his arrival in Canaan*, 75 years. In his early life Abraham dwelt with his father and his brethren in Ur of the Chaldees. He married Sarai, his half-sister. After the death of his brother Haran, he, his wife, and Lot his nephew migrated, under the headship of Terah, from Ur to go to the land of Canaan (Gen. xi. 27–31). The motive which led the family to change its habitation is not stated in Gen. xi. Josephus inferred from the narrative that Terah was actuated by a desire to escape from associations which reminded him of the son who had died (Antiq. i. 6, 5). It has also been suggested that the migration of the family may have been prompted by the wish to better their condition in a new and freer country, or have been incited by political disturbances in Chaldea, such as an invasion of the Elamites. Stephen understood Gen. xii. 1 to refer back to this time, and to be the initial command, given while the family was yet in Ur, for he says: "God appeared unto Abraham, when he was in Mesopotamia, before he dwelt in Haran" (Acts vii. 2, R. V.). Stephen's interpretation is countenanced by Gen. xv. 7 and Neh. ix. 7; although these passages might refer to God's providence. All the various causes suggested may have coöperated; and the natural motives may have been the means providentially employed by God to persuade the party to obey the heavenly vision. The family departed from Ur and, taking the customary route, followed the Euphrates toward the northwest. On reaching Haran, the party temporarily abandoned the purpose of journeying to Canaan and took up residence where they were. When Abraham was 75 years old, he departed from Haran to go to Canaan. This move may have been due to God's will as revealed by him in Ur, or to a command now first received. Stephen, as already said, adopts the former interpretation and the wording of the details in Gen. xii.1 well suits, with our present meager knowledge of the community at Haran, this explanation. The departure is related after the record of Terah's death. It does not follow, however, from this that Abraham tarried at Haran until his father died. The narrator as usual concludes what he has to say of Terah before taking up the detailed history of Abraham. Still it is a plausible conjecture that Abraham did tarry so long; for the same party that left Ur now, with the exception of Terah, leaves Haran: and this also is the interpretation of Stephen. But if so, Abraham was born when Terah was at least 130 years old, and not 70, as is often unnecessarily inferred from Gen. xi. 26. In this passage Abraham is mentioned first, either because he was the firstborn and born in Terah's 70th year, or else, if he was a younger son and born after Terah's 70th year, because he was the progenitor of the chosen people (cp. Gen. v. 32 with ix. 22, 24). From Haran Abraham went to Canaan. What route did he take? Probably the road by way of Damascus, for a great highway led from Mesopotamia past that city to Canaan; and later mention is made of Abraham's steward, Eliezer of Damascus. Abraham did not stop long at any place along the way, but properly speaking journeyed continuously; for he was 75 years old when he left Haran, and he spent ten years in Canaan before he took Hagar to wife (Gen. xvi. 3), and he was 86 years old when Hagar bore Ishmael (16); so that not more than a year elapsed between the departure from Haran and the arrival in Canaan.

I. 2. *Unsettled life in Canaan*, at most 10 years. He encamped at Shechem (Gen. xii. 6), at Beth-el (8), journeyed to the south country (9), and was driven by famine into Egypt. In Egypt, through fear for his life, he represented Sarah merely as his sister (10–20). He returned to the south country (xiii. 1), was again at Beth-el (3). He and Lot now separated on account of their increasing possessions. Lot chose the plain of the Jordan (5–12). Abraham afterwards moved his tent to the oaks of Mamre at Hebron (18).

I. 3. *Residence at the oaks of Mamre*, at least 15, perhaps 23 or 24 years. Abraham is in treaty with the Amorite chieftains of the vicinity (Gen. xiv. 13), pursues Chedorlaomer (1–16), is blessed by Melchizedek (17–24). The promise of an heir is given him and is believed; and the promise of Canaan as an inheritance is confirmed by covenant (xv.).

Birth of Ishmael (xvi.). After an interval of 13 years (16; xvii. 1), the promise is unfolded. Man's attempt to fulfill God's promise does not alter God's intention; not the bondwoman's child, but the free woman's; not the child of the flesh, but the child of promise. On this occasion the covenant sign of circumcision is appointed, and the name Abram is changed to Abraham (Gen. xvii.). Sodom is destroyed (xviii. and xix.).

I. 4. *Residence in the south country*, some 15 years during the childhood of Isaac. Sarah taken to the court of Abimelech (Gen. xx.). When Abraham is 100 years old, Isaac is born, and a little later Ishmael is expelled (xxi. 1–21). At a well owned by Abraham, Abimelech and he conclude a treaty, and Abraham names the well Beer-sheba (22–34). When Isaac was somewhat grown (xxii. 6; Josephus conjectures 25 years, Antiq. i. 13, 2), Abraham's faith was put to an open test by the command to sacrifice his only son. In obedience to this command, he and Isaac repaired to the mountains of Moriah, when a ram was graciously substituted for Isaac. They returned to Beer-sheba (xxii. 1–19).

I. 5. *Again at Hebron*, after an uneventful interval of 20 years. Here Sarah died, aged 127 years (Gen. xxiii).

I. 6. *Probably in the south country with Isaac*, about 38 years. After the death of Sarah, when Abraham was 140 years old (xxiv. 67; xxv. 20), he sends to Mesopotamia to obtain a wife from his own people for Isaac. Rebekah is brought back and meets Isaac at Beer-lahai-roi, perhaps 'Ain Muweileh (xxiv). That Abraham took Keturah to wife is next recorded (see KETURAH). Abraham died, aged 175 years, and was buried in the cave of Machpelah (xxv. 1–9).

II. *The size of the community under Abraham.* Abraham departed from Haran with his wife, his nephew, and the souls that they had acquired (Gen. xii. 5), and in Canaan he obtained additional servants by purchase, by gift and doubtless by birth (xvi. 1; xvii. 23, 27; xviii. 7; xx. 14). He was rich in flocks and herds and their necessary accompaniment, menservants and maidservants (xii. 16: xiii. 2, 7; xxiv. 32, 35, 59; xxvi. 15). He led 318 trained men, born in his house, to the rescue of Lot (xiv. 14). He was recognized by the neighboring chieftains as a mighty prince (xxiii. 6), with whom they do well to make alliances and conclude treaties (xiv. 13; xxi. 22 seq.). Yet when deprived of the aid of his allies, as when he went to sojourn in Egypt, his sense of insecurity triumphed over his better self, and he repressed part of the truth in regard to Sarah. He desired peace and was a man of peace (xiii. 8), yet like many other hardy settlers would in time of need brave hardship and danger and do battle for relatives and friends (xiv).

III. *The religious belief of Abraham.* His nearer ancestors served other gods (Josh. xxiv. 2). Their worship was at least corrupted by the prevalent animism of Babylonia, which assigned a spirit to every object in nature, and which led to the conception of eleven great gods besides innumerable minor deities. The great gods were the deities of the majestic and impressive objects in nature: of the sky, of earth's surface, of the ocean and all subterranean waters; of the moon, the sun, and the storm; and of the five planets visible to the naked eye. The gods were powerful, were active in nature, bestowed special care on favorite individuals and communities, heard and answered prayer. Abraham's faith was distinguished from the belief of the great majority of his contemporaries of whom we have any knowledge, in that Abraham believed in God the almighty (Gen. xvii. 1), the everlasting (xxi. 33), the most high (xiv. 22), the possessor or maker of heaven and earth, i. e. the actual and lawful Lord of all (ibid., xxiv. 3), the righteous Judge, i. e. the moral governor of all the earth (xviii. 25); and in accordance with the faith of his contemporaries, Abraham believed in this God as the disposer of events, who seeth and taketh knowledge of what occurs on earth, and who giveth and withholdeth as he will. In this faith Abraham obeyed, worshiped, and guarded the honor of God. How came Abraham by this faith? 1. Reason lent its aid, as it still helps the intelligent Christian. Polytheists have often arrived at henotheism; and there are traces of henotheism among Abraham's countrymen in Babylonia. A clear, logical mind, such as Abraham exhibits, would tend to pass from henotheism to monotheism. Melchizedek had come to worship the most high God, possessor of heaven and earth; and his religious conceptions and practices called forth profound recognition from Abraham. Monumental evidence seems to show that occasionally an individual among the Assyrians and Babylonians arrived at a speculative belief in the unity of God, but without influencing the people at large. It is no more unique for Abraham to believe in one God, Lord over all, than for Hosea or Amos to do so. 2. The religious inheritance, which he received from his forefathers, aided Abraham. In support of this source of religious information may be urged, (a) the reasons for believing in a primitive revelation: (b) the existence of the line which began with Adam and included such true worshipers of God as Seth (see Gen. iv. 26), Enoch, and Noah; and (c) the historical fact of the transmission to the Hebrews of traditions like that of the creation and the flood. 3. Special revelation was granted to Abraham by dreams, visions, and theophanies (xii. 7; xv. 1, 12, 17; xvii. 1; xviii. 1, 2: xxii. 1, 2). Theophanies are as conceivable in Abraham's time as is the manifestation of Christ at a later age.

IV. *Harmony between the Hebrew record and contemporary history.* 1. *The language of Canaan.* Before the conquest of the country by the Israelites under Joshua not a few places and persons bore Semitic names. Abimelech and Urushalim, *i. e.* Jerusalem, were in vogue.

IV. 2. *The narrative of Abraham fits into Egyptian history.* Biblical chronological data place the arrival of Abraham in Canaan about 645 years before the Exodus. This date explains at once Abraham's willingness to go to Egypt when famine prevailed in Canaan and his kindly reception by Pharaoh. for the date of his journey falls within the period when Asiatics, the so-called shepherd kings, held the throne of Egypt. The biblical data place not only Abraham's visit to the Nile country, but also the descent of Jacob and his sons to Egypt, within the period of the shepherd rule: a strong confirmation both of the chronological data and of the authenticity of the narrative.

IV. 3. *The narrative fits into Babylonian history.* (1.) About the time assigned by the Hebrew record to Abraham and the invasion of the west, the populous plain at the mouth of the Tigris was ruled by an Elamite dynasty. (2.) Under the Elamite sovereign vassal kings exercised sway, as described in Genesis. (3.) The Babylonian kings in preceding centuries and during this period made expeditions into the far west and often held Canaan in subjection (cp. Lugalzaggisi, Sargon, Gudea, Kudurmabug probably, Hammurabi, and Ammisatana). (4.) Chedorlaomer, the name assigned to the king of Elam, is a genuine Elamite name. Chedor, *i. e.* Kudur, is constantly used in the composition of Elamite royal names, and Laomer, *i. e.* Lagamar, is the name of an Elamite god. Thus the Hebrew record gives an accurate and somewhat detailed picture of the political condition of Babylonia as well as of Canaan. On the theory, generally accepted, that Amraphel, king of Shinar, is identical with Hammurabi, who was king of Babel from about 2123 to 2080 B. C., a valuable synchronism is afforded with the life of Abraham (Gen. xiv. 1, 13), and the date of Abraham is established within narrow limits.

A'bra-ham's Bo'som.
The Jews fondly thought of being welcomed by Abraham, Isaac, and Jacob to Paradise (4 Mac. xiii. 17); and of having fellowship with Abraham, even resting as it were on his breast (Luke xvi. 22). In the rabbinical speech of the third century A. D., to say that a person was sitting in Abraham's bosom meant that he had entered Paradise.

A'bram (Gen. xi. 26–xvii. 5). See ABRAHAM.

A-bro'nah, in A. V. **Ebronah** [a passage, or opposite].
A station of the Israelites in the wilderness, apparently north of Ezion-geber (Num. xxxiii. 34, 35).

Ab'sa-lom and **Abishalom** (1 Kin. xv. 2, 10) [father of peace].

1. The third son of David, king of Israel. He was born in Hebron, and had for his mother Maacah, the daughter of Talmai, king of Geshur, in Aram (2 Sam. iii. 3). He was of faultless form, and had long, fine hair, of which he was inordinately vain. His beauty was shared by his sister Tamar, who so fascinated her half-brother Amnon that he criminally dishonored her, for which two years afterwards he was treacherously assassinated at the instance of Absalom, whose guest he was at the time. Though Absalom was his father's favorite, his crime was too gross to be overlooked even by his indulgent parent. He had to go into exile, and remained three years with his maternal connections in Geshur, and two more at Jerusalem, before he was allowed to return to the

Tomb of Absalom.

court or see his royal father. He soon afterwards deliberately set himself to win the hearts of the people away from the king his father, and when the plot was ripe, repaired, under false pretences, to Hebron, and raised the standard of rebellion. The perfection of his bodily frame marked him out for rule of the highest kind. Probably he had heard that Solomon was to succeed David, and considered the arrangement unfair to himself, as he was the elder of the two brothers, and, unlike Solomon, was by the mother's as well as the father's side of royal blood. Whether or not he was aware that it was by the divine choice, as recorded in 1 Chron. xxii. 7–10, that Solomon was designated to the sovereignty, is less certain; if he did know it, then in a theocracy like the Jewish, the enormity of his rebellion was further heightened. It is noticeable, in connection with this point, that the priests and Levites sided with David, and brought him much moral as well as material support; but the mass of

the people seem to have gone against him, and he had to escape with a few faithful followers from Jerusalem to save his life. Of David's two chief counselors, the abler one, Ahithophel, had gone over to Absalom; the other, Hushai, was faithful to David, and went after the fugitive king. David sent him back to Jerusalem to pretend adherence to Absalom, and thwart the counsel of Ahithophel. When the time arrived for offering advice to Absalom, Ahithophel astutely recommended that he should be allowed to take 12,000 men that very night and follow David before David recovered from his depression. He would kill only the king, and the people would then come over to Absalom. Before the scheme was carried out, Hushai was asked if he adhered to it, and of course he raised objections, and proposed a rival scheme of his own, so preposterous that it does not say much for Absalom's penetration that he did not see it was meant to effect his ruin. Hushai counseled long delay, a course which would really tend to make Absalom weaker and David stronger. He flattered Absalom's self-conceit by proposing that he should be commander, which would give the army a poor leader. When victory was achieved, which he assumed to be a certainty, he provided that there should be extensive and unnecessary bloodshed, a serious political blunder as well as a great crime. Hushai's absurd scheme, however, recommended itself to Absalom and the people, and Ahithophel, seeing that it was all over with the rebellion, went home and committed suicide. Hushai, understanding that the danger was not yet over, sent David counsel immediately to cross the Jordan, which he did. Absalom and the rebel army were beginning to revert to the policy of Ahithophel; and ultimately a compromise was made between his plan and that of Hushai, i. e. hostilities should be immediate, but Absalom should be the commander-in-chief. The battle took place in the wood of Ephraim, apparently near Mahanaim, where David was then residing. The rebel host, undisciplined and badly led, went down at once before David's veterans, handled by three skillful commanders. When the rout took place, Absalom, riding furiously on a mule, got his head entangled among the spreading branches of an oak, great disservice being done him by the long hair of which he was so vain. The animal ran away, leaving him hanging helplessly, but alive. Joab, one of the three commanders, thrust three darts through the heart of the unhappy prince, and ten of Joab's immediate followers surrounding him completed the slaughter. David had given express directions that Absalom should not be injured, and on hearing of his death he gave himself up to excessive grief (2 Sam. xiii. 1–xix. 8). Absalom was buried near the place where he died, in a pit under a great cairn of stones. He had reared for himself a pillar at Jerusalem to keep his name in remembrance (xviii. 17, 18). What is now called Absalom's tomb is in the valley of the Kidron. In the beginning of the fourth century A. D., however, it seems to have been regarded as the tomb of Hezekiah (Bordeaux Pilgrim), but scarcely in agreement with 2 Chron. xxxii. 33. The decorations of the monument date from the Greco-Roman period, but the chamber itself may be older. According to the title, Ps. iii. was composed by David during Absalom's rebellion; perhaps also Ps. vii.

2. Father of Mattathias and probably of Jonathan, captains of the Jewish army under the Maccabees Jonathan and Simon (1 Mac. xi. 70; xiii. 11; Antiq. xiii. 5, 7; 6, 4).

Ab'shai. See ABISHAI.

A-bu'bus.

Father of that Ptolemy who was the governor of the district about Jericho (1 Mac. xvi. 11, 15).

A-byss' [bottomless].

Hades, the place of the dead (Rom. x. 7, R. V.); in particular the dwelling of evil spirits, presided over by Apollyon, that is, Satan (Rev. ix. 11; xvii. 8; xx. 1–3, in A. V. bottomless pit; cp. Luke viii. 31, in A. V. the deep).

A-ca'ci-a. See SHITTAH.

Ac'cad.

An ancient city in the land of Shinar and one of four towns which constituted the original kingdom of Nimrod (Gen. x. 10). It is also mentioned by Nebuchadnezzar called the First, who reigned at Babylon about 1150 B. C. (VR 56, 50). The name was extended to denote a district called the land of Accad. This district, at one period at least, embraced northern Babylonia, adjacent to Assyria, and included within its bounds the cities of Babylon and Cutha.

Ac'co, in A. V. ACCHO [hot sand].

A city on a small promontory of the coast of Palestine, about 25 miles south of Tyre. The town looks across the bay of its own name to mount Carmel, about 8 miles to the south. It was assigned to the tribe of Asher, but was not occupied by the Hebrews (Judg. i. 31). In the time of Hoshea it submitted to Shalmaneser, king of Assyria (Antiq. ix. 14, 2); and it suffered from the same nation in the reign of Ashurbanipal. A century or so before Christ its name was changed to Ptolemais, in honor of one of the early Ptolemies. It acquired importance politically as the key of Galilee and as a seaport at the end of commercial routes to Decapolis and Arabia (1 Mac. v. 15, 21, 55; x. 1; Antiq. xiii. 12, 2 seq.). Jonathan Maccabæus was treacherously slain there (1 Mac. xii. 48; Antiq. xiii. 6, 2). A large number of Jews found a home within its walls (War, ii. 18, 5), and a Christian community early grew up here. On his last journey to Jerusalem, Paul spent a day here with the brethren (Acts xxi.

7). Later the town became the seat of a Christian bishop. The Arabs restored the old name, which the Franks corrupted into Acre. It was taken in A. D. 1191 by Philip Augustus, king of France, and Richard I., king of England. From A. D. 1229 it was held by the Knights of St. John, and was often called in consequence St. Jean d'Acre. Prior to 1799 it was strongly fortified by Jezzar Pasha, who ruled with energy, but with such cruelty that he was nicknamed "the Butcher." In that year it was attacked by Napoleon, who was baffled, and at once began his retreat from Syria. Jezzar's victory was largely due to English sailors, who had been landed to give him aid. In 1832 it was wrested from the Turkish sultan by one of his subjects, Ibrahim Pasha, son of Mohammed Ali, the ruler of Egypt. On November 3, 1840, it was bombarded by the British and Austrian fleets, until the day was decided by the explosion of the powder magazine, which caused the death of from 1700 to 2000 Egyptian soldiers. The place was given back to the sultan, under whose rule it still remains. It is now a walled town, with a single land gate at the southeast angle and a sea gate leading to the shipping in the harbor. Its ramparts, injured by the bombardment of 1840, have not been repaired. Its inhabitants number about 8000. Grain and cotton are exported.

Ac'cos [Greek form of Hakkoz (1 Chron. xxiv. 10)].

The priestly family Hakkoz, probably (1 Mac. viii. 17).

Ac-cur'sed.

Anything on which a curse has been pronounced, devoting it to destruction (Josh. vi. 18; vii. 1, 11, 13, 15; xxii. 20). See ANATHEMA.

A-cel'da-ma. See AKELDAMA.

A-cha'ia.

Originally a state of Greece situated in the northern part of the Peloponnesus (now the Morea), and comprehending Corinth and its isthmus. After Greece had been conquered by the Romans, the emperor Augustus Cæsar divided that country with the adjacent regions into two provinces, Macedonia and Achaia. The latter comprehended the whole of the Peloponnesus, with continental Greece S. of Illyricum, Epirus, and Thessaly. Corinth was the capital, and was the residence of the proconsul by whom the province was ruled. It is in the second or comprehensive sense that the word Achaia is used in the New Testament (Acts xviii. 12, 27; xix. 21; Rom. xv. 26; 2 Cor. i. 1; ix. 2; 1 Thess. i. 7, 8).

A-cha'i-cus [belonging to Achaia].

A Christian who came with two others from Corinth to Paul (1 Cor. xvi. 17).

A'chan and **Achar** [trouble; or, he has troubled].

A son of Carmi, of the house of Zimri, family of Zerah, tribe of Judah. At the capture of Jericho he appropriated to his own use and hid in his tent a Babylonish garment and a wedge of gold, part of the spoil of Jericho, which had been devoted to utter destruction. He thereby troubled Israel. His transgression led to the defeat of the Israelites before Ai. Lots were then cast to discover the culprit who had brought on the catastrophe, and Achan was pointed out as the individual. He made confession of his guilt, but this did not avert his fate. He was stoned to death in the valley of Achor (Josh. vii. 1–26; xxii. 20; 1 Chron. ii. 7).

A'char. See ACHAN.

A'chaz. See AHAZ.

Ach'bor [a mouse].
1. The father of Baal-hanan, king of Edom (Gen. xxxvi. 38; 1 Chron. i. 49).
2. The son of Michaiah and father of Elnathan. He was a trusted officer at the court of Josiah (2 Kin. xxii. 12, 14; Jer. xxvi. 22; xxxvi. 12). Called Abdon in 2 Chron. xxxiv. 20.

A'chim [Greek, from Hebrew Jachin or Jakim, Jehovah will establish].
An ancestor of Jesus in the line of Joseph, who lived after the exile (Mat. i. 14).

A'chish [Philistine name, meaning is unknown].
The son of Maoch and the king of Gath, to whom David twice fled during the time that he was persecuted by Saul (1 Sam. xxi. 10–15; xxvii. 1–12; xxviii. 1, 2; xxix. 1–11). He is probably the Achish who was king of Gath at the beginning of Solomon's reign: for the latter was the son of Maachah, a name which is radically identical with Maoch the father of the Achish already known. The reign of about fifty years required by this assumption is not extraordinary (cp. among many others the reigns of Uzziah and Manasseh). Achish survived his contemporary, David, at least three years (1 Kin. ii. 39). In the title of Ps. xxxiv. he is called Abimelech, which appears to have been an official designation of the Philistine kings as Pharaoh was a title of the Egyptian monarchs.

Ach'me-tha [Median *Hangmatâna*].
A city in the province of the Medes. When the Jews asserted that Cyrus had issued a decree permitting them to build the temple, their adversaries sent to Babylon to inquire if the document were in existence. Darius ordered an investigation. The house of the archives where the treasures were laid up in Babylon was first searched, but in vain. The quest was continued in Achmetha in the province of the Medes, and the decree was found in the palace (Ezra v. 6–vi. 2). There is no reason to doubt that Achmetha was Ecbatana, the capital of Media, the summer residence of the Persian kings, and a treasure city (Herod. i. 98; iii. 64: Xenophon, Cyropæd. viii. 6, 22). It is the modern Hamadan.

A'chor [trouble].
The valley near Jericho where the unhappy Achan was stoned to death (Josh. vii. 24–26; Is. lxv. 10; Hos. ii. 15). It lay south of Jericho, for it formed part of the northern boundary of Judah (Josh. xv. 7), whereas Jericho was a city of Benjamin.

Ach'sah, in A. V. once **Achsa** (1 Chron. ii. 49), an inconsistency from which the original edition of A. V. was free [a leg-band, an anklet].
A daughter of Caleb, son of Jephunneh, who promised her in marriage to anyone who should capture Kirjath-sepher. Othniel, his younger brother or half-brother, took the town, and received the maiden. At her request her father gave her the upper and nether springs (Josh. xv. 16–19; Judg. i. 12–15; 1 Chron. ii. 49). See DEBIR.

Ach'shaph [fascination].
A royal city of Canaan (Josh. xi. 1), captured by Thothmes III; also by Joshua (xii. 20). It stood on the boundary of the territory of Asher (xix. 25).

Ach'zib or Che'zib, as it was with equal correctness pronounced by the Hebrews [deceitful].
1. A town of southern Palestine eventually included in Judah (Gen. xxxviii. 5; Josh. xv. 44; Mic. i. 14). Probably the same place as Chozeba (1 Chron. iv. 22). It is commonly identified with ruins at the spring 'Ain Kezbeh, which is apparently a corruption of the old name.
2. A town on the seacoast of Asher (Josh. xix. 29), from which the Canaanite inhabitants were not driven out (Judg. i. 31). It yielded to Sennacherib in 701 B. C. It was known as Ekdippa to the Greeks and Romans (War i. 13, 4); and has been identified as Zib, eight and a half miles north of Acre.

Acts of the A-pos'tles, The.
The fifth book of the N. T. The common title, which is as old as the second century, does not mean that the book relates all the acts of the apostles. Its purpose was to show the establishment by the Spirit through the apostles of gentile Christianity. At first Peter and afterwards Paul are most prominent; but frequently the apostles as a body are represented as taking action (Acts i. 23–26; ii. 42; iv. 33; v. 12, 29; vi. 2; viii. 1, 14; xv. 6, 23). The book is addressed to a certain Theophilus, probably a gentile Christian of distinction. The author refers (i. 1) to a previous treatise by him concerning the life and teachings of Christ, which was clearly our Third Gospel, because (1) it was addressed to Theophilus; (2) it consists of a narrative of Christ's life and teaching until his ascension (Luke xxiv. 51); (3) it presents the ministry of Christ with special reference to its universal mission, which would naturally be the point of view adopted by the author of The Acts; (4) the vocabulary and style of the two books are notably alike. Further,

while the author does not name himself in either book, he uses the first person plural in certain portions of the narrative of Paul's journeys (Acts xvi. 10–17; xx. 5–xxi. 18; xxvii. 1–xxviii. 16), and by this intimates that he was a companion of the apostle; that he joined him on his second journey at Troas and accompanied him to Philippi, again rejoined him at Philippi in the third journey and went with him to Jerusalem, and traveled with him from Cæsarea to Rome. The earliest tradition of the post-apostolic age assigns both the Third Gospel and The Acts to Luke, and the allusions to Luke in Paul's epistles accord with the above references to his movements in The Acts, while no other of Paul's known companions will fit into them. From Col. iv. 14, Philem. 24, we learn that Luke was with Paul in Rome, and no mention of him occurs in epistles written when, according to The Acts, its author was not with the apostle. Moreover, the use of medical terms (see Hobart, *The Medical Language of St. Luke*) and the classical elements in his style, as well as his evident acquaintance with the Roman world, indicate that the author was an educated man such as a physician would be likely to be. There should be no doubt, therefore, that Luke wrote both the third Gospel and The Acts. The purpose of The Acts has been already stated. Chap. i. recounts Christ's last interviews with the apostles through forty days, his promise of the Spirit and his command to preach to all the world (ver. 8), followed by his ascension and the actions of the disciples until Pentecost. Then follows an account of the church in Jerusalem after Pentecost (ii. 1–viii. 3), in which certain representative facts are described (the first conversions, the first opposition, the first discipline, the first persecution, the first organization, the first martyrdom), and, after each, a brief notice of its effect upon the Church (see ii. 41–47; iv. 23–37; v. 11–16, 41, 42; vi. 7; viii. 1–3). Here Peter is most prominent, though the first martyr and the man who prepared for the following period was Stephen. Next we have an account of the transition of the Church to a missionary religion, offering salvation by faith alone to all men (viii. 4–xii. 25). Here five significant events are described: (1) Philip's work in Samaria and the Ethiopian steward's conversion (viii. 4–40); (2) Saul's conversion and earliest preaching (ix. 1–30); (3) Peter's missionary work in Syria, leading to the conversion of Cornelius and the conviction of the Church that the gospel was for gentiles (ix. 31–xi. 18); (4) the founding of the gentile church of Antioch, a new center for further gentile work (xi. 19–30); (5) the Herodian persecution whereby the Jewish state finally repudiated Christianity (xii.). Then follows the establishment of Christianity, chiefly through Paul, in the principal centers of the empire (xiii. to the end). This was done in three great journeys: the first,

to Cyprus and the interior of Asia Minor (xiii.; xiv.), led to the Council of Jerusalem (xv. 1–35), when the standing in the Church of uncircumcised gentiles was formally recognized; the second, to Macedonia and Greece (xv. 36–xviii. 22); the third, to Ephesus as well as Greece (xviii. 23–xx. 3), followed by Paul's last visit to Jerusalem (xx. 4–xxi. 26), where he was arrested, and, after defending himself before the Jews, Felix, Festus, and Agrippa, and after two years' imprisonment in Cæsarea (xxi. 27–xxvi. 32) was sent, on his appeal to the emperor, to Rome (xxvii. 1–xxviii. 16), where he preached for two years (xxviii. 17–31). Many think that The Acts was written just at the close of these "two years" (*i. e.* A. D. 63). Others think Luke ended there because his object was attained in bringing Paul, as an apostolic preacher, to Rome, or because he intended to write a third book descriptive of later events, and that The Acts should be dated a few years later than 63. The remarkable historical accuracy of The Acts has been proved by modern research (see *e. g* Ramsay's *Church in the Roman Empire*). Its harmony with Paul's epistles has been much debated and successfully defended. It is written with much artistic power, and supplies the information necessary to explain the rise of Christianity as a universal religion during the thirty-three years from the death of Christ covered by its narrative. G. T. P.

Ad′a-dah [holiday, festival].
A town on the extreme south of the tribe of Judah (Josh. xv. 22). It has not been identified, unless Adada is a misreading of 'Ar'ara (cp. Septuagint). See AROER 3.

A′dah [as a Hebrew word, means adornment, beauty].
1. One of Lamech's wives, and mother of Jabal and Jubal (Gen. iv. 19–21, 23).
2. One of Esau's wives, daughter of Elon, the Hittite (Gen. xxxvi. 2, 4); in Gen. xxvi. 34 called Bashemath. Double names are frequent among men; and it is stated that women in the East more frequently adopt new names than do men, and are apt to alter their name if they re-marry or change their religion.

A-da′iah [Jehovah has adorned].
1. A man of Bozkath, father of Josiah's mother (2 Kin. xxii. 1, R. V.).
2. A Levite descended from Gershom (1 Chron. vi. 41, 42).
3. A priest, descended through Jeroham from Malchijah (1 Chron. ix. 12; Neh. xi. 12).
4. A Benjamite, son of Shimhi (1 Chron. viii. 21).
5 and 6. Two men descended from Bani, each of whom was induced to put away his foreign wife (Ezra x. 29, 39).
7. A son of Joiarib (Neh. xi. 5).
8. Father of Maaseiah (2 Chron. xxiii. 1).

A-da′li-a.
One of Haman's ten sons (Esth. ix. 8).

Ad′am [human being, meaning etymologically either ruddy or formed].

1. The first human being. Mankind was made, as were all other created things, by God (Gen. i. 26) ; and was made male and female (27 ; Mat. xix. 4–6), the man being first formed, then the woman (Gen. ii. 7, 20–23 ; 1 Tim. ii. 13). Like other animals and later men, his body was formed of the ordinary materials of the universe and life was granted by God (Gen. ii. 7 ; cp. 19 ; vi. 17 ; vii. 22 ; Job x. 8–12 ; xxvii. 3 ; xxxiii. 4). He was made in the image of God (Gen. i. 26, 27). Paul describes the similarity as consisting in knowledge, or, more completely, in knowledge, righteousness, and true holiness (Eph. iv. 22–25 ; Col. iii. 9, 10). Mankind was invested with dominion over the inferior animals (Gen. i. 26–28) ; was exhorted to be fruitful and to multiply, and replenish the earth, and subdue it (28) ; and shared in the approval when God pronounced that everything which he had made was very good (31).

Adam, the first of mankind, was placed with Eve in the garden of Eden to dress it and keep it in order. A command was laid upon him, in the nature of a covenant of life and death (Gen. ii. 16, 17). On his transgression, sentence of death was passed upon him, toil and undesired results were annexed to labor, and he was expelled from the garden (iii. 1–24 ; 2 Esdr. iii. 4–7, 21, 22). Afterwards he had children, Cain, Abel, and, when he was 130 years old, Seth. He lived 800 years more, at last dying at the age of 930. See CHRONOLOGY. Paul draws a double parallel between Adam and Christ, calling our Lord the last Adam (Rom. v. 12–21 ; 1 Cor. xv. 22, 45).

2. A city in the Jordan valley beside Zarethan (Josh. iii. 16). Its identification with ed-Dâmieh on the western bank of the river, less than a mile below the mouth of the Jabbok and eighteen miles above Jericho, must be received with caution.

Ad′a-mah [soil].

A fenced city of Naphtali (Josh. xix. 36). The Palestine surveyors place it at ed-Dâmieh, five miles southwest of Tiberias.

Ad′a-mant [in Greek, unconquerable].

An extremely hard metal or mineral, especially the diamond. It is the traditional rendering of the Hebrew *Shamir*, a hard substance compared with flint and the stony heart (Ezek. iii. 9 ; Zech. vii. 12), and used to point graving tools (Jer. xvii. 1, where it is rendered "diamond").

Ad′a-mi [human], in R. V. **Adami-nekeb** [perhaps, Adami of the pass].

A frontier town of Naphtali (Josh. xix. 33), called Adam of the pass, in distinction probably from Adam of the ford (cp. Josh. iii. 16) ; perhaps the ruin ed-Dâmieh, five miles S. W. of Tiberias, at the mouth of a pass on the old caravan route from Gilead to Acre. Conder, however, suggests the ruined village of Admah on the table-land midway between

Tiberias and Beth-shean, and overlooking the Jordan from the west. See NEKEB.

A′dar, I. [perhaps, amplitude].

A town of Judah, better written Addar (q. v.).

A′dar, II. [Assyro-babylonian *adaru* and *addaru*, probably dark, cloudy].

The later name of the twelfth month of the Jewish year, borrowed by the Jews from the Babylonian calendar during the exile (Ezra vi. 15 ; Esth. iii. 7, 13 ; ix. 15). It extended from the new moon in February to that in March. See YEAR.

Ad′a-sa.

A town near Beth-horon (1 Mac. vii. 40, 45, cp. 39 ; Antiq. xii. 10, 5), at the junction of the two main lines of advance on Jerusalem from the north.

Ad′be-el [perhaps, a miracle of God].

A tribe descended from Ishmael (Gen. xxv. 13 ; 1 Chron. i. 29). In the eighth century before Christ a tribe called Idiba′il dwelt in northern Arabia, at no great distance from the frontier of Egypt.

Ad′dan or **Addon** ; the pronunciation with a, which appears to be Aramaic or Babylonian, being exchanged for its regular Hebrew modification [Babylonian, native form and meaning unknown].

A place in Babylonia from which people who could not prove their Israelitish descent went to Palestine after the captivity (Ezra ii. 59 ; Neh. vii. 61).

Ad′dar [perhaps, largeness].

1. A town of Judah, on the southern boundary line of Palestine (Josh. xv. 3, in A. V. written Adar ; and Num. xxxiv. 4). In the latter passage it is called Hazar-addar, *i. e.* village of Addar. Sea HEZRON, 1.

2. A Benjamite. See ARD.

Ad′der.

The rendering of four Hebrew words, referring probably to four distinct species of venomous snake.

1. *Sh⁽ᵉ⁾phiphon*, the creeper. Probably the *Vipera cerastes*, the Horned Sand-snake of Arabia and Egypt. At Thebes it was regarded as sacred (cp. Herod. ii. 74). It is a venomous viper, three to six feet long, of a gray color, and with a horn above each eye. It hides in the sand, and may well be the serpent which bites the horses' heels so that the rider falls backward (Gen. xlix. 17).

2. *Pethen*, a species of serpent incapable of being affected by the voice of the snakecharmer, and therefore called the deaf adder (Ps. lviii. 4, 5). It is very venomous (xci. 13). It is the asp of Deut. xxxii. 33 ; Job xx. 14, 16 ; and Isaiah xi. 8. Probably the *Naja haje* of Egypt ; see ASP.

3. *′Akshub* (Ps. cxl. 3). In the Septuagint and in the quotation in Rom. iii. 13 it is translated "asp." Bochart considers it the Common Adder (*Pelias berus*), and Colonel

Hamilton Smith the Puff Adder of the Cape Colonists, *Vipera arietans*, but there is as yet no certainty as to the identification.

4. *Siph'oni* (Prov. xxiii. 32), translated in Is. xi. 8; xiv. 29; lix. 5, cockatrice or basilisk; see these words.

Ad'di [a Greek form of Iddo].
An ancestor of Christ who lived several generations before Zerubbabel (Luke iii. 28).

Ad'don. See ADDAN.

A'der. See EDER.

Ad'i-da. See ADITHAIM and HADID.

A'di-el [ornament of God].
1. A Simeonite (1 Chron. iv. 36).
2. A priest, son of Jahzerah (1 Chron. ix. 12).
3. Father of the supervisor of David's treasuries (1 Chron. xxvii. 25).

A'din [soft, delicate].
Founder of a family, members of which returned from Babylon with Zerubbabel (Ezra ii. 15) and Ezra (viii. 6). Its chief signed the covenant made by Nehemiah to serve Jehovah (Neh. x. 16).

Ad'i-na [delicate].
A Reubenite, one of David's military officers (1 Chron. xi. 42).

Ad'i-no.
One of David's mighty men, an Eznite; the same as Josheb-basshebeth (2 Sam. xxiii. 8 A. V., and A. V. margin and R. V.). The verse as it stands is defective. Luther and most modern interpreters change the text, altering the words "Adino the Eznite" to accord with 1 Chron. xi. 11.

Ad-i-tha'im [perhaps, double booty-town].
A town in the lowland of Judah (Josh. xv. 36). Sometimes identified with Adida, but Adida is rather Hadid.

Ad'lai [justice, or possibly justice of Jehovah].
Father of a herdsman of David (1 Chron. xxvii. 29).

Ad'mah [perhaps, redness].
One of the cities of the plain (Gen. x. 19; xiv. 2, 8) which was destroyed with Sodom and Gomorrah (Gen. xix. 25, 28, 29; Deut. xxix. 23; Hos. xi. 8).

Ad'ma-tha [Persian name of doubtful meaning].
One of the seven princes of Persia and Media under Ahasuerus (Esth. i. 14). See PRINCE.

Ad'na [Aramaic, pleasure].
1. A priest, head of the father's house Harim in the second generation after the exile (Neh. xii. 15).
2. A son of Pahath-moab, induced by Ezra to divorce his foreign wife (Ezra x. 30).

Ad'nah [pleasure].
1. A Manassite who joined David at Ziklag (1 Chron. xii. 20).

2. A man of Judah, of high military rank under Jehoshaphat (2 Chron. xvii. 14).

A-do'ni-be'zek [lord of Bezek].
A king of Bezek, conquered by the warriors of the tribe of Judah, who inflicted on him a cruel mutilation. This he regarded as a divine requital for similar cruelties perpetrated by him on seventy kings (Judg. i. 4–7).

Ad-o-ni'jah [Jehovah is lord].
1. A son of David by Haggith, one of his wives. He was the fourth son born to the king at Hebron (2 Sam. iii. 2, 4). He was a goodly, probably meaning a handsome, young man, and apparently his father's next favorite after Absalom. Blinded by foolish fondness, David never rebuked him for a misdeed. When David was stricken in years Adonijah attempted to seize the throne. He was doubtless aware of his father's intention that Solomon should be king (1 Kin. i. 13; 1 Chron. xxiii. 1; xxviii. 5); but since the first and third born sons of David, and probably the second born also, were dead, Adonijah as the eldest remaining son doubtless felt that he had a claim to the crown, although neither law nor custom required the succession to go to the eldest. He won Joab to his cause, who, he hoped, would bring with him the army; and Abiathar, the priest, who, he expected, would bring with him the priests and the Levites. But Zadok the priest, Benaiah, commander of the royal bodyguard, and Nathan the prophet he did not gain. He invited his partisans to a great open-air feast at the stone of Zoheleth by the fountain of Rogel, and had himself proclaimed king. But Solomon had been divinely chosen to be the successor to David; and Bath-sheba, Solomon's mother, supported by Nathan the prophet, waited on the aged king to remind him of his promise concerning Solomon, report the proceedings of Adonijah, and ask instructions. Promptly, by David's order, Solomon was proclaimed king; the open-air feast came to an abrupt termination, the guests took to flight, and Adonijah sought asylum at the altar (1 Kin. i. 5–50). Solomon pardoned him for the time; but when Adonijah asked that the maid Abishag be given him to wife and thereby justified the belief that he was again aiming at the kingdom, Solomon ordered that he be put to death (vs. 51–53; ii. 13–25).
2. One of the Levites whom Jehoshaphat sent to instruct the people of Judah (2 Chron. xvii. 8).
3. For Neh. x. 16, see ADONIKAM.

Ad-o-ni'kam [the Lord arises].
Founder of a family, members of which returned from Babylon both with Zerubbabel and with Ezra (Ezra ii. 13; viii. 13; Neh. vii. 18). The head of this family, apparently, sealed the covenant in Nehemiah's time (Neh. x. 16), but is called Adonijah.

Ad-o-ni′ram [the Lord is exalted].

An officer who was over the tribute during the reigns of David and Solomon. He was the son of Abda, and was called also Adoram (2 Sam. xx. 24) and Hadoram (2 Chron. x. 18). When the ten tribes revolted, Rehoboam sent him to treat with the rebels, who, however, instead of listening to him, stoned him to death (2 Sam. xx. 24 ; 1 Kin. iv. 6 ; xii. 18 ; 2 Chron. x. 18).

A-do′ni-ze′dek, in A. V. **Adonizedec** [lord of righteousness].

A king of Jerusalem who, on learning that Ai had been captured by the Israelites, and that the Gibeonites had made peace with Joshua, formed a confederacy with four other Amorite kings to punish Gibeon. He and his confederates were defeated, taken, and slain (Josh. x. 1-27). In the Septuagint called Adonibezek.

A-dop′tion.

The act of taking a stranger to be one's own child, as in the case of Moses and Esther (Ex. ii. 10 ; Esth. ii. 7).

In the N. T. the word is used to denote :

1. The choice by Jehovah of the Jewish nation to be his special people (Rom. ix. 4).

2. The reception of all true Christians to be in a special sense the sons of God (Gal. iv. 5 ; Eph. i. 4). The spirit of adoption enables us to feel to God as children to a loving father. It is distinguished from the spirit of bondage, which compels one to feel to him as a slave to a master (Rom. viii. 14-21).

3. The redemption of the body ; its deliverance from sin, pain, and death in the glorified state (Rom. viii. 23).

A-do′ra. See ADORAIM.

Ad-o-ra′im [perhaps, two mounds].

A city of Judah fortified by Rehoboam (2 Chron. xi. 9). It is probably identical with Adora, shortened into Dora, a town of the interior, near Idumæa, and after the exile reckoned as belonging to the latter country (Antiq., xiii. 9, 1 ; 15, 4 ; xiv. 5, 3 ; War, i. 2, 5 ; 1 Mac. xiii. 20). Since Robinson's researches, it is identified with Dura, a village on a hillside five miles west of Hebron.

A-do′ram. See ADONIRAM.

A-dram′me-lech [god Adar is king].

1. A deity to whom the colonists of Samaria, who had been brought from Sepharvaim, burnt their children in the fire (2 Kin. xvii. 31). The god Adar was the sun worshiped under a particular attribute.

2. A son of Sennacherib. With another brother he murdered his father, and afterwards escaped to Armenia (2 Kin. xix. 37 ; Is. xxxvii. 38).

Ad-ra-myt′ti-um.

A maritime city in Æolia. Under the Romans it belonged to the province of Asia. The vessel in which Paul embarked at Cæsarea for Rome was a ship of Adramyttium, about to sail to the places on the coast of Asia (Acts xxvii. 2).

A′dri-a.

A part of the Mediterranean (Acts xxvii. 27). The name was derived from the commercial town of Adria on the lower Po, and in the narrowest sense it denoted only the neighboring part of the sea. But the name was extended to include the expanse of sea as far as the extreme southern points of Greece and Italy (Ptolemy iii. ; Pausanias, Eliac. v. ; Procopius, Bell. Vand. i. 14).

A′dri-el [flock of God].

A Meholathite, to whom Saul gave his daughter Merab in marriage, though he had previously promised her conditionally to David (1 Sam. xviii. 19).

A-dul′lam [enclosure].

A town in the Shephelah, in the territory of Judah, mentioned between Jarmuth and Socoh (Josh. xv. 35). It was in existence, inhabited by Canaanites, as early as the time of Jacob (Gen. xxxviii. 1, 2). A petty king ruled over it at the time of the conquest (Josh. xii. 15). It was fortified by Rehoboam (2 Chron. xi. 7), continued to flourish in the time of Micah the prophet (Mic. i. 15), and was inhabited after the exile (Neh. xi. 30 ; 2 Mac. xii. 38). In its vicinity was the cave which David at one period of his wanderings made his headquarters, and whither his father and his brethren and many other adherents went down to join him (1 Sam. xxii. ; 2 Sam. xxiii. 13 ; Antiq. vi. 12, 3). M. Clermont-Ganneau is possibly right in hearing an echo of the name still lingering in Aid el-Miyeh. This name belongs to a hill which is crowned with a fortress and has caves in its sides. The hill stands on the south side of a ravine at its junction with the southern extension of the valley of Elah (es-Sunt), and is about two miles from the place where the fight took place between David and Goliath.

A-dul′ter-y.

1. In a special sense, sexual intercourse of a married man with a female not his wife, or that of a married woman with a man not her husband. Polygamy, with inferior wives and concubines, is not adultery. Under the Mosaic law adultery was punished with death (Lev. xx. 10).

2. In a general sense, all sexual impurity in thought, word, or deed, or whatever tends thereto. This is the sense in the seventh commandment, interpreted on the principles of the Sermon on the Mount (Ex. xx. 14 ; Deut. v. 18 ; Mat. v. 27, 28).

3. Figuratively, the worship of false gods or other infidelity to the covenant with Jehovah (Jer. iii. 8, 9 ; Ezek. xxiii. 37, 43 ; Hos. ii. 2-13), God claiming our undivided affections, as a husband does the undivided regard of the woman who has sworn him fidelity.

A-dum′mim [red objects].

The ascent of Adummim is a pass leading up from the Jordan valley to the hill country

The boundary beteen Judah and Benjamin passed near it (Josh. xv. 7; xviii. 17), and the shortest and most traveled road from Jerusalem to Jericho ran through it. According to Jerome, the name belonged to a hamlet, which in his day was lying in ruins, and which was still called Maledomim, apparently the full Hebrew phrase Ascent of Adummim. Jerome ascribes the origin of the name to the blood frequently spilled there by robbers (cp. Luke x. 30); but it more probably arose from the red marl of the neighborhood. An echo of the name is still heard in Tala'at ed-Dumm, Ascent of Blood, the name given to a hill and fortress half way between Jerusalem and Jericho, and to the wady which the road follows downward.

Æ'ne-as [Latin from N. T. Greek *Aineas,* classic Greek *Aineias;* the name of a Trojan hero].

A man at Lydda bedridden eight years with palsy. His restoration by the power of the risen Jesus resulted in large increase of the Church in that region (Acts ix. 32–35).

Æ'non [Greek, probably from Aramaic *'ênavan,* fountains].

A village, or merely a locality of perennial springs, near Salim, where John at one time at least baptized because there was there much water (or, as in Greek, many waters) (John iii. 23). The site has not been identified. But according to Jerome, Ænon and Salim were situated in the Jordan valley, eight Roman miles south of Scythopolis. The names have ceased to be heard. Measurement indicates either the place now called ed-Deir, in the neighborhood of which are seven springs and extensive ruins, or Umm el-'Amdan, hard by on the east, or the ruins and spring at the base of Tell Ridghah, which, however, is only seven Roman miles from Scythopolis.

The modern map can, indeed, show villages bearing the names of 'Ainun and Salim. A town called Salim is situated four miles east of Shechem, on an extensive plateau south of the wady Far'ah. 'Ainun is a ruin on the eastern slope of the wady Tubas, about ten miles northeast of Shechem and four miles north of the Far'ah valley. The objection to identifying 'Ainun with Ænon mentioned by John is that 'Ainun is not near Salim. The villages are distant from each other about eight miles, and the great wady Far'ah lies between. 'Ainun is but little farther from the important city of Shechem than from Salim, and is more closely connected with Shechem by road. Rejecting 'Ainun, one thinks of the plentiful waters of the Far'ah valley but three miles distant from Salim, or even the two living springs which supply Salim with water; but a place of fountains near this Salim would be in Samaria, and it is scarcely probable that John the Baptist was laboring among the Samaritans (cp. Mat. iii. 5; x. 5; Luke iii. 3).

The only other site proposed, which offers any attractions, is Shilhim, in the Septuagint Seleeim, in the wilderness in the extreme south of Judah, near which was a place called Ain (Josh. xv. 32); but Ain is constantly connected with Rimmon and not with Shilhim.

Ag'a-bus [meaning is uncertain].

A Christian prophet of Jerusalem. He went to Antioch and predicted a great famine which took place in the days of the emperor Claudius (Acts xi. 28; see Antiq. xx. 2, 6; 5, 2). When Paul passed through Cæsarea on his last journey to Jerusalem, Agabus, who was there, bound his own hands and feet with Paul's girdle, and announced that this would be done also to the owner of the girdle when he reached the capital (Acts xxi. 10, 11).

A'gag [perhaps, flaming].

Whether Agag was a title of the kings of Amalek, as Pharaoh was for those of Egypt, or was a recurring name in the royal line, is unknown. Specially

1. A king of Amalek whose greatness was alluded to by Balaam (Num. xxiv. 7).

2. The king of Amalek slain by Samuel, after he had been spared by Saul (1 Sam. xv. 9–33).

A'gag-ite.

An appellation given to Haman, the great enemy of the Jews (Esth. iii. 1, 10; viii. 3–5). Its reference to his Amalekite descent (Antiq. xi. 6, 5, and see AGAG) is extremely doubtful.

A'gar. See HAGAR.

Ag'ate [named from a river in Sicily near which the agate abounded].

A precious stone composed of various kinds of colored quartz, especially of amethyst, chalcedony, and jasper. Two Hebrew words are so rendered:

1. *Kadkod,* which means sparkling (Is. liv. 12; Ezek. xxvii. 16, in A. V.). This characteristic ill accords with the agate, which in its natural state is wanting in lustre; hence the R. V. translates it Ruby, and the margin of the A. V. Chrysoprase.

2. *Sh⁾bo;* perhaps from *shabah* to lead captive, or less probably from Sheba, from which it may have been brought. It was the middle stone in the third row of gems on the high priest's breastplate (Ex. xxviii. 19; xxxix. 12).

Age.

1. The time counted by years, or more precisely by years, months, and days, that one has lived in the world. Extraordinary age is ascribed to men in the registers of Gen. v. and xi., dwindling as the genealogy becomes more particular as it approaches Abraham; see CHRONOLOGY. Abraham died at the age of 175 (Gen. xxv. 7), and his wife Sarah at 127 (xxiii. 1), Isaac at 180 (xxxv. 28), Jacob at 147 (xlvii. 28), Joseph at 110 (l. 26), Moses at 120 (Deut. xxxiv. 7), and Joshua at 110 (Josh. xxiv. 29). The ordinary length of human life is reckoned at 70 years, or, by reason of strength, 80 years, in the prayer of Moses (Ps. xc. 10). David died an old man at 70 (2

Sam. v. 4 ; 1 Kin. ii. 11). Veneration for old age is inculcated in the Bible (Lev. xix. 32 ; Prov. xx. 29), and old age itself is considered a blessing (Ex. xx. 12 ; Deut. v. 16).

2. A frequent rendering in the N. T. of the Greek *Aiōn*, the later Latin *Æon:*

(*a*) A certain specified period of the world's history, past or to come (1 Cor. x. 11, in A. V. world ; Eph. ii. 7 ; iii. 9 ; Col. i. 26 ; Heb. vi. 5—all R. V.). More frequently it signifies an indefinitely long period of time, eternity past or to come ; "unto the ages" being equivalent to "forever" (cp. text and margin of R. V. of Luke i. 33 ; Rom. i. 25 ; ix. 5 ; xi. 36 ; Heb. xiii. 8), or "for evermore" (2 Cor. xi. 31). "The age of the ages" is "for ever and ever" (Eph. iii. 21). "Unto the ages of ages" is also "for ever and ever" (Gal. i. 5 ; Phil. iv. 20 ; Rev. i. 18).

(*b*) The world literally (Heb. i. 2, R. V. margin) ; or figuratively (Mat. xiii. 22 ; Luke xvi. 8 ; xx. 34 ; Rom. xii. 2 ; 1 Cor. i. 20 ; ii. 6, 7, 8 ; 2 Cor. iv. 4 ; Gal. i. 4 ; 2 Tim. iv. 10 ; Titus ii. 12—all R. V., margin). The connecting link between *a* and *b* is when the world means the duration of this world (Mat. xii. 32 ; xiii. 40 ; xxiv. 3), and of that to come (Mark x. 30 ; Luke xviii. 30 ; Heb. ii. 5).

(*c*) The course of the world (Eph. ii. 2, R. V., text and margin).

Ag′e-e [perhaps, a fugitive].

A Hararite, the father of one of David's mighty men (2 Sam. xxiii. 11).

Ag′ri-cul-ture.

The cultivation of the soil. The word does not occur in Scripture, but the idea does ; and the analogous term husbandry is found both in the O. T. and N. T., while husbandman is common. Adam was expected to dress the garden of Eden (Gen. ii. 15) ; Cain cultivated the soil (iv. 2) ; Noah planted a vineyard (ix. 20) ; and Isaac sowed (xxvi. 12). Agriculture was in an advanced stage among the ruling race in the delta of the Nile at the time of the sojourn of the Israelites in Egypt. Cereals of various kinds were cultivated and exported (Gen. xli. 49, 57 ; xliii. 2). Wheat, rye, or rather spelt, and barley, are mentioned, besides which there were crops of flax (Ex. ix. 31, 32). The crops cultivated by the Israelites were sometimes summed up as corn and wine (Gen. xxvii. 37 ; Ps. iv. 7). If a third agricultural product was named it was generally olives (Deut. vi. 11). When the enumeration was more ample, the list was increased to "wheat, barley, vines, fig-trees, pomegranates, and olives" (viii. 8), not to speak of honey, which was from wild bees (cp. also xi. 14 ; xii. 17). To this list Isaiah adds fitches (Is. xxviii. 25, 27), and Ezekiel beans, lentils, and millet (Ezek. iv. 9). The Israelites had ploughs drawn by oxen (1 Kin. xix. 19 ; Is. ii. 4), and pruning-hooks, sickles, etc. (ibid. ; Deut. xvi. 9 ; Joel iii. 13, etc.). The purpose now effected by rotation of crops was carried out by letting the land lie fallow during the seventh year (Ex. xxiii. 10, 11).

As a rule, good crops were reaped, and they would have been so to a larger extent had proper attention been paid to the storing of water in reservoirs, so that absence of rain should not result, as it generally did, in famine. Agriculture and the keeping of flocks and herds continued, through all the period of scriptural history, the staple industries of Palestine, which was not to any considerable extent a commercial land.

A-grip′pa. See HEROD.

A′gur [garnered, hired, or collector].

Son of Jakeh, and author of the maxims contained in Proverbs xxx. (see ver. 1).

A′hab [a father's brother].

1. A king of Israel, and son and successor of Omri. He began to reign about 874 B. C., in the thirty-eighth year of Asa, king of Judah (1 Kin. xvi. 29). He married an idolatress of masculine temperament, Jezebel, the daughter of Ethbaal, king of Sidon. She worshiped Baal, and her husband being weak and irresolute, she ruled over him, and made him also a Baal-worshiper (30–33). This was a revolution in the national religion of Israel. When Jeroboam set up the two golden calves, he still desired to worship Jehovah nominally, using them as helps for the purpose. But Ahab, under Jezebel's influence, wholly gave up the adoration of Jehovah, Baal being a rival god. The intolerant Jezebel did not stop with Ahab's perversion, but attempted to force the whole people to adopt her faith. The prophets of Jehovah were sought out and slain. Only a remnant escaped, being hidden in a cave by a high functionary, Obadiah. Now, however, appeared the most formidable prophet known in the history of Israel, Elijah the Tishbite. He was sent to Ahab to predict years of drought and famine as the punishment of Ahab's sin. Toward the close of the drought, which lasted three years and six months (1 Kin. xviii. 1 : Luke iv. 25 ; Jas. v. 17), Elijah, by the divine command, again confronted Ahab, and demanded that the prophets of Baal and he should meet on the top of mount Carmel and submit the question between them to a decisive test. The meeting took place ; Jehovah vindicated himself by sending fire from heaven to consume Elijah's sacrifice. By direction of the prophet the people who had witnessed the event and acknowledged Jehovah took the 450 prophets of Baal and 400 prophets of the Asherah down to the brook Kishon, and slew them. Jezebel, on learning what had been done, uttered imprecations against herself if Elijah were alive by the morrow. The prophet, fearing for his life, fled to mount Horeb. God sent him back with the charge to anoint Hazael to be the king of Damascus and the scourge of idolatrous Israel, Jehu to be the king of Israel to supplant the family of Ahab and put down the worship of Baal by the power of the state, and Elisha to be prophet to destroy idolatry

by moral suasion. The cup of iniquity of Ahab and Jezebel was made full to over-flowing by the affair of Naboth's vine-yard. About this time Ahab had won a victory over Ben-hadad of Damascus, king of Syria, and had permitted that poten-tate, who had been captured, to escape with a treaty. The approach of Shalmaneser, king of Assyria, led to an alliance between the king of Damascus, Ahab of Israel, and other neighboring kings, to resist the in-vader. Ahab furnished 2000 chariots and 10,000 infantry. The allies were defeated at Karkar, in the district of Hamath. in 854 B. C. The war with Damascus was soon after-wards renewed, and Ahab, taking advantage of a visit from Jehoshaphat, king of Judah, proposed a joint expedition for the recovery of Ramoth-gilead, beyond Jordan. The prophets of Baal spoke well of the enterprise. Micaiah, the only prophet of Jehovah ob-tainable, foreboded the death of Ahab. The man of doom resolved to go into the battle disguised, while proposing that the king of Judah should put on his royal robes, thus becoming a mark for every missile. But a certain man drew a bow at a venture and smote Ahab between the joints where the plates of his armor met. Ahab died that evening, and the siege of Ramoth-gilead was raised. Ahab's chariot and armor were washed in the pool of Samaria, the dogs, as Elijah had predicted, licking his blood. Ahab died after a reign of twenty-two years, and was succeeded by his son Aha-ziah (1 Kin. xvi. 29–xxii. 40 ; 2 Chron. xviii. 1–34).

2. A lying and immoral prophet, a son of Kolaiah. Jeremiah predicted that Nebu-chadnezzar, king of Babylon, would roast him in the fire (Jer. xxix. 21–23).

A-har'ah.
A son of Benjamin, probably the founder of a family (1 Chron. viii. 1), who is called Ehi (Gen. xlvi. 21) and Ahiram (Num. xxvi. 38).

A-har'hel [possibly, strength hath tarried].
A son of Harum, founder of a family which was enrolled in the tribe of Judah (1 Chron. iv. 8).

A'has-ai. See AHZAI.

A-has'bai [perhaps a foreign name].
A Maacathite, the father of Eliphelet, one of David's heroes (2 Sam. xxiii. 34).

A-has-u-e'rus [from Persian *Khshaya*, king].
1. The father of Darius the Mede (Dan. ix. 1). See DARIUS.
2. A Persian king, the husband of Esther (Esth. i. 2, 19 ; ii. 16, 17). Ahasuerus is Khshayarsha, whom the Greeks called Xerxes. The book of Esther tells of his sensuality, his fickleness, his lack of fore-thought, his despotism, and his cruelty. Greek history presents essentially the same picture of Xerxes (Herod. vii. 35, 37 ; ix. 107).

He was the son of Darius Hystaspis, whom he succeeded on the Persian throne, 486 B. C. His mother was Atossa, the daughter of Cyrus. In the second year of his reign he subdued the Egyptians, who had revolted against his father Darius. After about four years' preparation, he led an immense host to invade Greece ; but fled back to Persia on seeing his great fleet defeated (480 B. C.) by a much smaller number of Greek ships at Salamis. The next year (479 B. C.) his gen-eral, Mardonius, whom he had left behind with an army, allowed his camp at Platæa to be forced by the Greeks, when such a slaugh-ter ensued as rendered the Persian invasion hopeless. In 466, after a reign of twenty years, Xerxes was murdered by two of his courtiers, and was succeeded on the throne by his son, Artaxerxes Longimanus. Xerxes is probably again mentioned as Ahasuerus in Ezra iv. 6, where the author completes the history of Samaritan machinations at the Persian court against the Jews, resuming in ver. 24 the narrative which he interrupted at ver. 5. The older interpreters thought that Ahasuerus in this passage referred to Cam-byses, son of Cyrus ; but there is no evidence that Cambyses was ever called Ahasuerus.

A-ha'va.
A locality in Babylonia, doubtless to the north of Babylon (Ezra viii. 15). It serves to indicate the river or canal in its vicinity on which Ezra assembled the people who pro-posed to go to Jerusalem with him (vii. 28 with viii. 31). It appears to have been dis-tant about nine days from Babylon (vii. 9 ; viii. 15, 31). On mustering the Jews who were present and finding no Levites, except priests, among them, Ezra sent for and se-cured a number of these ministers for the house of God. Here also a fast was kept, and the protection of God supplicated for the journey.

A'haz, in A. V. of N. T. **Achaz** [he has sustained].
1. A king of Judah who was probably pro-claimed king about 741 B. C., when 20 years old, and who succeeded his father Jotham about 734 B. C. He was an idolater, causing his son to pass through the fire, and sacri-ficing and burning incense on high places and under green trees (2 Kin. xvi. 3, 4). He was unsuccessfully besieged in Jerusalem by the army of Rezin, king of Syria, and Pekah, king of Israel (5 ; Is. vii. 1). In connection with this crisis, before the invading force arrived, Isaiah was sent to exhort him to rely upon Jehovah and not call in foreign aid. He did not believe, and refused to ask a sign. Thereupon the prophet uttered the celebrated prophecy relative to the birth of Immanuel (Is. vii. 1–16) ; see IMMANUEL. Ahaz turned to Tiglath-pileser, king of Assyria, and pur-chased his aid with the treasures of the tem-ple and the palace. Tiglath-pileser marched to his assistance. The approach of the Assyr-

ians seems to have led Rezin and Pekah to raise the siege of Jerusalem. Tiglath-pileser attacked Philistia, overran Samaria, took Damascus and slew Rezin, and connived at the murder of Pekah and enthronement of Hoshea as king of Israel. With other vassals of Assyria, Ahaz went to Damascus to do homage to Tiglath-pileser (2 Kin. xvi. ; 2 Chron. xxviii. ; Assyrian inscriptions). While there he admired a heathen altar, and had a facsimile of it made at Jerusalem. Ahaz died about the year 726 B. C., after reigning 16 years, and left his son Hezekiah to ascend the throne. Hosea, Micah, and Isaiah prophesied during the whole of Ahaz's reign, zealously witnessing for Jehovah (Is. i. 1 ; vii. 1–16 ; Hos. i. 1).

Ahaz is mentioned on the Assyrian monuments by the name *Yauhazi,* corresponding to the Hebrew Jehoahaz, the full form of Ahaz. Ahaz means "He has sustained," while Jehoahaz signifies "Jehovah has sustained."

2. A descendant of Jonathan (1 Chron. viii. 35, 36 ; ix. 42).

A-ha-zi′ah [Jehovah hath sustained].

1. A king of Israel who was apparently placed on the throne when his father Ahab marched with the allies against Shalmaneser in 854 B. C. He succeeded his father on the latter's death. His entire reign lasted only two years (1 Kin. xxii. 40, 51). He joined with Jehoshaphat in fitting out ships of Tarshish to go to Ophir for gold ; but the vessels were wrecked at Ezion-geber. Ahaziah proposed a second attempt; but Jehoshaphat, warned by a prophet, declined (1 Kin. xxii. 48, 49 ; 2 Chron. xx. 35–37). After the death of Ahab, Moab rebelled ; but Ahaziah took no steps to reduce it to subjection (2 Kin. i. 1 ; iii. 5). Ahaziah fell through a lattice in his palace, and was seriously injured. He sent to consult Baal-zebub, the god of Ekron, as to the result. Elijah intercepted the messengers, and sent them back with the message that the injury would prove fatal (2 Kin. i. 2–17). Ahaziah left no son to succeed him, so the throne passed over to his brother Jehoram (17).

2. A king of Judah, who began to rule the kingdom in 843 B. C. (2 Kin. ix. 29), apparently during his father's sickness (2 Chron. xxi. 18, 19), and succeeded his father Joram or Jehoram the next year (2 Kin. viii. 25). He was then twenty-two years old, and reigned only a year. His mother, Athaliah, was his evil genius (2 Chron. xxii. 3). He went with Joram, king of Israel, to fight with the Syrians at Ramoth-gilead. Joram returned to Jezreel wounded, and Ahaziah paid him a visit, was with him during the revolt of Jehu, and was killed with him by that ruthless soldier (2 Kin. viii. 25–29 ; ix. 16–29 ; 2 Chron. xxii. 1–10). By a reversal of the constituent parts of his name, he is called Jehoahaz in 2 Chron. xxi. 17. "Azariah" in 2 Chron. xxii. 6 has probably arisen from

Ahaziah through corruption of the text.

Ah′ban.

A man of Judah, family of Hezron, house of Jerahmeel (1 Chron. ii. 29).

A′her [another].

A Benjamite (1 Chron. vii. 12). R. V. margin identifies him with Ahiram. See AHARAH.

A′hi [brother of, or a brother is (Jehovah)].

1. Chief of the Gadites in Gilead in Bashan (1 Chron. v. 15).

2. An Asherite, son of Shamer, of the family of Beriah (1 Chron. vii. 34).

A-hi′ah. See AHIJAH.

A-hi′am.

One of David's mighty men (2 Sam. xxiii. 33).

A-hi′an [perhaps. brotherly].

A Manassite of the family of Shemida (1 Chron. vii. 19).

A-hi-e′zer [brother of help].

1. Son of Ammishaddai, and head of the tribe of Dan in the wilderness (Num. i. 12 ; ii. 25 ; vii. 66).

2. A man of Gibeah who joined David at Ziklag (1 Chron. xii. 3).

A-hi′hud [probably, brother of praiseworthiness, or a brother is the praiseworthy one].

1. The prince representing the tribe of Asher on the commission to divide the land (Num. xxxiv. 27).

2. Head of a father's house in Geba of Benjamin (1 Chron. viii. 7).

A-hi′jah, in A. V. sometimes **Ahiah** (viz. 1, 3, 6) [brother of, or a brother is Jehovah].

1. A Benjamite apparently, who assisted Gera in carrying off inhabitants of Geba (1 Chron. viii. 7).

2. A man of Judah descended through Jerahmeel (1 Chron. ii. 25).

3. A son of Ahitub, and great-grandson of Eli. He at one time in the reign of Saul performed the functions of high priest at Gibeah (1 Sam. xiv. 3, 18). He was elder brother of Ahimelech, or possibly that priest himself under another name.

4. A Pelonite, one of David's mighty men (1 Chron. xi. 36).

5. A Levite who in David's reign was over the treasures of the tabernacle and the dedicated offerings (1 Chron. xxvi. 20; but see R. V. margin).

6. A scribe in Solomon's reign (1 Kin. iv. 3).

7. A prophet belonging to Shiloh, who, meeting Jeroboam. rent his own garment in twelve pieces, and directed Jeroboam to take ten, as an indication that he should be king over ten tribes (1 Kin. xi. 29–39). After Jeroboam had become king, he sent his queen disguised to the now aged and half-blind prophet to inquire whether their child who was sick would recover. Ahijah recognized her under her disguise, and predicted that the child would die (xiv. 1–18). He committed his prophecies to writing (2 Chron. ix. 29).

8. The father of Baasha, klng of Israel (1 Kin. xv. 27, 33).

9. A chief of the people who set his seal to the covenant to keep the law of God (Neh. x. 26, in R. V. irregularly Ahiah).

A-hi′kam [brother of him who riseth, or a brother hath appeared].

Son of Shaphan and a prince of Judah (2 Kin. xxii. 12). He protected Jeremiah when priests and false prophets demanded Jeremiah's death (Jer. xxvi. 24). He was the father of Gedaliah (2 Kin. xxv. 22).

A-hi′lud [perhaps, brother of one born, or brother of the son].

Father of the recorder Jehoshaphat (2 Sam. viii. 16 ; xx. 24 ; 1 Kin. iv. 3), and quite likely one with the father of Solomon's purveyor Baana (1 Kin. iv. 12).

A-him′a-az [brother of irascibility].

1. Father of Ahinoam, Saul's wife (1 Sam. xiv. 50).

2. A son of Zadok, high priest in David's time. He and Jonathan, Abiathar's son, maintained communication between David and the loyal party in Jerusalem during Absalom's rebellion (2 Sam. xv. 27, 36 ; xvii. 20). He was the first to bring David intelligence of the victory over Absalom (xviii. 19-30). It may have been he who was afterwards Solomon's purveyor in Naphtali (1 Kin. iv. 15).

A-hi′man [brother of a gift].

1. A son of Anak, and probably founder of a famiiy of Anakim (Num. xiii. 22), stalwart men (33 ; see GIANT), driven from Hebron by Caleb (Josh. xv. 14 ; Judg. i. 10).

2. A Levite who acted as porter of the house of God (1 Chron. ix. 17).

A-him′e-lech [brother of a king].

1. A son of Ahitub, and chief priest at Nob. David, fleeing from Saul, but pretending to be on the king's business, being in great want of food, received from him the show-bread, which, by the law, was a perquisite of the priests. He also obtained the sword which had formerly belonged to Goliath (1 Sam. xxi. 1-9 ; in Mark ii. 26 the event is dated in the time of Abiathar, Ahimelech's son). Doeg the Edomite reported the occurrence to Saul, who, interpreting it as a proof that Ahimelech and the other priests were treacherous, gave orders that they should be slain. One inhabitant of Nob—Abiathar, a son of Ahimelech—escaped from the massacre (1 Sam. xxi. 7 ; xxii. 7-23 ; title of Ps. lii.).

2. The son of the Abiathar who escaped from the slaughter at Nob, and the grandson of Ahimelech, son of Ahitub. He was one of two high priests during David's reign (2 Sam. viii. 17 ; 1 Chron. xxiv. 3, 6, 31). Abimelech in 1 Chron. xviii. 16 is probably a copyist's error for Ahimelech.

3. A Hittite, and follower of David (1 Sam. xxvi. 6).

A-hi′moth [brother of death].

A Levite, a son of Elkanah (1 Chron. vi. 25).

A-hin′a-dab [brother of liberality].

Solomon's purveyor in Mahanaim (1 Kin. iv. 14).

A-hin′o-am [brother of grace].

1. Saul's wife, a daughter of Ahimaaz (1 Sam. xiv. 50).

2. A woman of Jezreel, one of David's wives (1 Sam. xxv. 43 ; xxvii. 3), taken captive at Ziklag by the Amalekites (xxx. 5). She was the mother of Amnon (2 Sam. iii. 2).

A-hi′o [fraternal].

1. A son of Abinadab and brother of Uzzah. The two drove the cart on which David was taking the ark to Jerusalem (2 Sam. vi. 3, 4).

2. A Benjamite, son of Elpaal (1 Chron. viii. 14).

3. A Benjamite, son of Jehiel by his wife Maachah (1 Chron. viii. 29, 31 ; ix. 35, 37).

A-hi′ra [brother of evil].

A son of Enan, and head of the tribe of Naphtali during the early journeyings in the wilderness (Num. i. 15 ; ii. 29 ; vii. 78 ; x. 27).

A-hi′ram [exalted brother, or brother of the high one].

A Benjamite, founder of a family (Num. xxvi. 38). Aharah (1 Chron. viii. 1) doubtless represents the same name ; and Ehi (Gen. xlvi. 21) is either an abbreviation or more probably a corruption, as the last syllable of Ahiram was easily overlooked by a copyist by reason of the recurrence of similar Hebrew letters in the two following names.

A-his′a-mach [brother of support].

A Danite, the father of the craftsman Aholiab (Ex. xxxi. 6).

A-hish′a-har [brother of the dawn].

A man descended from Benjamin through Jediael and Bilhan (1 Chron. vii. 10).

A-hi′shar [brother of a singer].

An official who was over Solomon's household (1 Kin. iv. 6).

A-hith′o-phel [brother of folly].

A resident of Giloh in southwestern Judah, one of David's counselors (2 Sam. xv. 12), father of one of David's mighty men (xxiii. 34), and perhaps the grandfather of Bathsheba (xi. 3 with xxiii. 34). So unerring was his sagacity that his advice was "as if a man had inquired at the oracle of God" (2 Sam. xvi. 23), but he was morally untrustworthy. Absalom found him ready to betray David, and to point out how he might be destroyed. When Absalom preferred the absurd counsel of Hushai, who was secretly in David's interest, Ahithophel, foreboding that it was therefore all over with the rebellion, committed suicide (2 Sam. xv. 12, 31-34 ; xvi. 15 ; xvii. 23), offering thus a strange O. T. type of Judas, both in his treachery and his fate.

A-hi′tub [brother of benevolence].

1. A son of Phinehas, and grandson of Eli (1 Sam. xiv. 3), and father of Ahimelech, the priest (xxii. 9).

2. A son of Amariah, and father of Zadok, the priest (2 Sam. viii. 17; 1 Chron. vi. 7, 8).

3. A later priest in the same family, son of another Amariah, and grandfather of another Zadok, also a priest (1 Chron. vi. 11, 12; Neh. xi. 11).

Ah′lab [a fat, fertile place].

A town within the territory of Asher, but from which that tribe did not drive out the Canaanite inhabitants (Judg. i. 31). Gush Halab of the Talmud, the Giscala of Josephus, five miles northwest of Safed on the road to Tyre, lies too far eastward to have been within the territory of Asher. Not unlikely Ahlab is a textual corruption of Mahlab, a town on the coast between Achzib and Tyre.

Ah′lai [O that!].

A descendant, namely a daughter of Sheshan (1 Chron. ii. 31, 34), and perhaps an ancestress of Zabad (xi. 41).

A-ho′ah [heat].

A Benjamite of the family of Bela (1 Chron. viii. 4); perhaps Ahijah (7). See AHOHITE.

A-ho′hite.

A descendant of Ahoah (2 Sam. xxiii. 9, 28; 1 Chron. xi. 12, 29).

A-ho′lah. See OHOLAH.

A-ho′li-ab. See OHOLIAB.

A-hol′i-bah. See OHOLIBAH.

A-hol-i-ba′mah. See OHOLIBAMAH.

A-hu′mai [perhaps, brother of water].

A man of Judah, family of Hezron, house of Caleb (1 Chron. iv. 2 with ii. 18, 19, 50).

A-huz′zam, in A. V. **Ahuzam** [possession].

A man of Judah, son of Ashhur, of the family of Hezron (cp. 1 Chron. iv. 5, 6 with ii. 24).

A-huz′zath [possession].

A friend of Abimelech, king of Gerar, in Isaac's time (Gen. xxvi. 26). See FRIEND OF THE KING.

Ah′zai, in A. V. **Ahasai** [possession, or perhaps clear-sighted].

A priest descended from Immer through Meshillemoth (Neh. xi. 13); probably not the person called Jahzerah in 1 Chron. ix. 12, but a different link in the genealogy.

A′i, in A. V. in Genesis **Hai**, with retention of the Hebrew article [ruins]. Aija and Aiath (Neh. xi. 31; Is. x. 28) are feminine forms of the word.

1. A town east of Beth-el and near Bethaven, with a valley on its north (Gen. xii. 8; Josh. vii. 2; viii. 11). It lay north of Michmash, if Aiath is the same as Ai, as is in every way probable (Is. x. 28); a location which excludes such sites as el-Hai, half a mile southeast of Michmash, and a name, moreover, radically different from Ai. Its site was apparently near the modern Deir Diwan, on the ancient road between Michmash and Beth-el, about midway between the two places. Three-quarters of a mile northwest of Deir Diwan is the ruin et-Tell, the heap (cp. Josh.

viii. 28); and one-third of a mile south, and less definitely in the gardens extending one-half mile southwestwardly to el-Kadeirah, is the ruin el-Haiyan. Each of these three sites has its advocates. The name Haiyan, it may be noted, is an entirely different word from Ai, and Josephus' name for Ai scarcely forms the connecting link, for the Greek texts of the historian do not show the nominative case Aina. At first Ai was unsuccessfully attacked by Joshua (Josh. vii. 2-5). When it was found that the defeat was caused by the sin of Achan. and when he had suffered for it, Ai was again attacked, and this time was taken by stratagem. Its inhabitants, numbering about 12,000, were slaughtered, its king was hanged on a tree, and the city was burned (vii.–viii.). It lay in ruins until some time after the account in Joshua was written (viii. 28), but ultimately was rebuilt (Is. x. 28; Ezra ii. 28).

2. A city of the Ammonites, apparently not far from Heshbon (Jer. xlix. 3).

A-i′ah, in A. V. once **Ajah** [bird of prey].

1. A Horite, son of Zibeon and brother of Anah (Gen. xxxvi. 24; 1 Chron. i. 40).

2. The father of Rizpah, Saul's concubine (2 Sam. iii. 7; xxi. 8, 10, 11).

A-i′ath. See AI.

A-i′ja. See AI.

Ai′ja-lon, in A. V. occasionally **Ajalon** [place of harts].

1. A village of the Shephelah, near a valley (Josh. x. 12; 2 Chron. xxviii. 18), mentioned as Aialuna in letters of the fifteenth century before Christ, found at Tell el-Amarna. It corresponds to Yalo, a village thirteen miles northwest of Jerusalem, on a low spur, looking northward over a beautiful plain. It was assigned to the tribe of Dan, but they did not expel the Amorite inhabitants (Judg. i. 34, 35). Aijalon was designated to be a Levitical city for the Kohathites (Josh. xxi. 20, 24; 1 Chron. vi. 69). After the secession of the ten tribes, it was included in Benjamin, and was fortified by Rehoboam (1 Chron. viii. 13; 2 Chron. xi. 10); but in the time of Ahaz it was captured by the Philistines (xxviii. 18).

2. A place in the tribe of Zebulun, where the judge Elon was buried (Judg. xii. 12). Exact site unknown. The ruin Jallun, nine and a half miles east of Acre and one and a half miles southwest of Mejd el-Kerum, seems too far north for Zebulun, and like 'Ailut, another proposed site two and a half miles by road northwest of Nazareth, is a radically different word.

Ai′je-leth hash-Sha′har, in A. V., with omission of the Hebrew article, **Aijeleth Shahar** [hind of the dawn].

Probably a tune, to which the chief musician was directed to set the twenty-second Psalm (Ps. xxii. R. V., title).

A'in [an eye, and a natural spring].

1. The sixteenth letter of the Hebrew alphabet, originally in outline an eye. English *O* comes from the same source, but is used as a vowel, whereas ain is a consonant of peculiar guttural sound. In anglicizing Hebrew names which contain ain, the letter is sometimes not represented at all, at other times it appears as *g*, rarely through the Greek as *h*. In the original, ain stands at the beginning of the words Amalek, Eli, Gomorrah, and perhaps Heli. It heads the sixteenth section of Ps. cxix., in which section each verse of the Hebrew begins with this letter.

2. A place on the northern boundary-line of Palestine west of Riblah (Num. xxxiv. 11).

3. A town in the territory of Judah, toward Edom and near Rimmon (Josh. xv. 32; 1 Chron. iv. 32), and as it were forming one town with it (Neh. xi. 29). It was transferred with Rimmon to Simeon, and assigned to the priests who resided with that tribe (Josh. xix. 7; xxi. 16; but see ASHAN). It is identified with extensive ruins at Bir Khuweilfeh, a large well of perennial water about three-quarters of a mile north of the probable site of Rimmon.

A'jah. See AIAH.

Aj'a-lon. See AIJALON.

A'kan. See JAAKAN.

A-kel'da-ma, in A. V. **Aceldama** [field of blood].

A parcel of ground known as the potter's field. The priests purchased it with the thirty pieces of silver which Judas cast down in the temple. They designed it to be a burial place for strangers (Mat. xxvii. 7); and, as it was intended for a cemetery, it was named the field of sleep (*akeldamach*, Acts i. 19, Greek; other authorities, however, such as the fifth century codex C, the Syriac, and the Ethiopic, have *akeldama* or its equivalent). The argument has, indeed, been pressed that the Greek form *akeldamach* is a mere unessential variation of *akeldama*, field of blood. But the case where a Greek *chi* represents a final *aleph* is extremely rare. An isolated instance is the form of *Seirach* for the Aramaic *Sira'*, in the name of Sira, who was the father of the author of Ecclesiasticus (Ecclus. l. 27). Probably, therefore, the form *akeldamach* stands for Aramaic *ḥªḳal dᵉmak*, field of sleep; but this sound is very like that of *ḥªḳal dᵉma'*, field of blood, and was too suggestive of the latter to escape the popular fancy. Hence the plot of ground by a play upon this name, and as bought with the price of blood, and because Judas hanged himself in it, was popularly called the field of blood, *akeldama* (Mat. xxvii. 8; Acts i. 19). Peter alludes to Judas as acquiring the field (Acts i. 18, 19). Probably he does not mean that it was purchased by Judas in person, but by the priests with Judas' ill-gotten money. The traditional site, dating from the time of Jerome in the fourth century, is on the southern side of the valley of Hinnom. This identification is not improbable, for the locality is one which can furnish potter's clay, and has long been surrendered to burial purposes. Many crusaders were subsequently buried there. Its modern name is Hakk ed-Dumm.

Ak'kub [cunning, artful].

1. A descendant of Shecaniah through Elioenai (1 Chron. iii. 21, 24).

2. A Levite who founded a family of temple porters known by his name (1 Chron. ix. 17; Ezra ii. 42; Neh. viii. 7; xi. 19; xii. 25).

3. One of the Nethinim (Ezra ii. 45).

Ak-ra-bat-ti'ne.

A place in Idumæa (1 Mac. v. 3), probably Akrabbim.

A-krab'bim, in A. V. once **Acrabbim** (Josh. xv. 3) [scorpions].

An ascent on the southeast frontier of Judah near the southern point of the Dead Sea, and not far from the desert of Zin (Num. xxxiv. 4; Josh. xv. 3; Judg. i. 36). Apparently, the boundary between Canaan and Edom on leaving the Dead Sea followed wady el Fikreh.

Al'a-bas-ter [without a handle (labas); or else derived from a place called Alabastrum].

The material of which the cruse was made from which Jesus was anointed at Bethany (Mat. xxvi. 7; Mark xiv. 3 ; cp. Luke vii. 37). Alabaster commonly denotes massive gypsum of a fine-grained variety, white in color, and delicately shaded. Being more easily worked than marble, it can be made into columns or turned on the lathe into cups, boxes, basins, or vases. Anciently alabaster denoted any stone suitable for working into such utensils. Most of the extent ancient ointment flasks are made of a light gray, translucent limestone.

A-la'meth. See ALEMETH.

A-lam'me-lech. See ALLAMELECH.

Al'a-moth [maidens].

A musical term (1 Chron. xv. 20; Ps. xlvi. title). It probably refers to maiden or treble voices.

Al'ci-mus.

A high priest appointed by Antiochus Eupator (2 Mac. xiv. 3, 7; Antiq. xii. 9, 7), confirmed by Demetrius I. in 162 B. C. (1 Mac. vii. 5–9), and installed by Bacchides at the head of an army (10–20). He was entirely Greek in sympathy, and was abhorred by the Jews. He was driven out of Palestine by Judas Maccabæus (21–25); but was brought back by Bacchides (ix. 1), and destroyed the inner wall of the temple, 160 B. C. (54). His sudden death soon afterwards was regarded by the Jews as a punishment for the impious act (55, 56).

Al'e-ma.

A town in Gilead (1 Mac. v. 26), conjectured to be Beer-elim (Is. xv. 8).

Al'e-meth, in A. V. once **Alameth, the** Hebrew pronunciation, in this instance, due merely to the position occupied by the name in the sentence (1 Chron. vii. 8) [covering].

1. A Benjamite, descended through Becher (1 Chron. vii. 8).

2. A descendant of king Saul (1 Chron. viii. 36 ; ix. 42).

3. A town (1 Chron. vi. 60). See ALMON.

Al'eph.

The first letter of the Hebrew' alphabet. The English letter *A* has the same origin ; but the Hebrew letter is a consonant, having no representative in the speech of the English people. In the spelling of Hebrew names in the English versions it does not appear. It is the initial letter, for example, in the original of the words Edom, Ophir, and Ur.

Aleph stands at the head of the first section of Ps. cxix. in many versions, since in the original each verse of the section begins with this letter.

Al-ex-an'der [defending men].

1. Alexander the Great, king of Macedonia, who followed his father Philip (1 Mac. i. 1). He began to reign 336 B. C. After quelling disturbances at home, he crossed the Hellespont to attack the Persians, whom he met and defeated at the Granicus, and again at Issus on the northeastern corner of the Mediterranean Sea. After the battle of Issus, Alexander took Damascus, which contained great treasure, and Sidon, and laid siege to Tyre. From there he sent to the Jewish high priest Jaddua, demanding his allegiance and supplies for his army. Jaddua refused on the ground of being subject to the Persian king. Angry at this answer, Alexander set out in person for Jerusalem as soon as he had reduced Tyre. According to Josephus, the Jews were in terror at his approach, but Jaddua threw open the gates and went in full priestly robes to meet the conqueror, who fell at his feet in worship of the God whom Jad-

Silver Drachma of Alexander the Great found at the Treasury, Persepolis, Iran.

dua represented. He explained that before he left Macedonia he had seen in a dream the Deity in the garb of this high priest, and had been promised victory over Persia. He granted the Jews many special privileges (Antiq. xi. 8, 5). From Palestine he went on to Egypt, where he founded Alexandria ; he then returned through Palestine to Persia, where he overthrew the Persian king Darius. After further conquests he died in Babylon in 323 B. C., aged 33. After his death, his generals made some show of holding the empire for his infant son, his widow and brother being set up as regents. But dissensions soon arose among the generals. All the members of Alexander's family were made away with, and the ruling generals were reduced from seven to four ; these four then assumed the title of king, and founded four royal houses— Ptolemy in Egypt, Seleucus in Syria, Antipater in Macedonia, and Philetærus in Asia Minor.

In the first division of Alexander's empire, before the final reduction to four kingdoms, Syria and Palestine formed an independent satrapy under Laomedon, but they were soon annexed to Egypt by Ptolemy I, Lagi. This rich province was coveted also by others, and was twice taken by Antigonus, another of Alexander's generals, who was then master of the greater part of Asia Minor, but in the final partition into four kingdoms after the battle of Ipsus it passed into Egyptian hands, and remained so from that time, 320 B. C., until 203 B. C., when it became part of the Syrian kingdom of Antiochus the Great.

2. Alexander Balas, a pretender, who claimed to be the son of Antiochus Epiphanes. By the help of Ptolemy, king of Egypt, whose daughter Cleopatra he married, he reigned over Syria 150–146 B. C. He proved incapable of holding the kingdom and, betrayed by Ptolemy, was easily driven out by Demetrius II. He made treaties with Jonathan Maccabæus, and sued for the help of the Jews (1 Mac. x. 1, 18–20 ; Antiq. xiii. 2, 1 ; 4, 8).

3. A son of Simon of Cyrene (Mark xv. 21).

4. A leading man at Jerusalem when Peter and John were tried there (Acts iv. 6).

5. A defender brought forward by the Jews during the tumult at Ephesus (Acts xix. 33).

6. One who made shipwreck of his faith, blasphemed, and was excommunicated by Paul (1 Tim. i. 19, 20) He perhaps was the same as Alexander the coppersmith, who did the apostle and his associates much injury (2 Tim. iv. 14, 15).

Al-ex-an'dri-a [named after its founder].

A city founded by Alexander the Great, in the year 332 B. C., on the north coast of Egypt, of which it was designed to be the Greek metropolis. A site was fortunately selected west of the mouths of the Nile, and the Mediterranean current which sweeps from the west carries the mud of the river away from the harbor and prevents silting.

The city was built on a tongue of land lying between the Mediterranean Sea and lake Mareotis, and connected by a mole with the isle of Pharos, on which there was a celebrated lighthouse. The city was admirably situated for commercial purposes. It became the great port for the export of Egyptian wheat, cargoes destined for Rome being carried direct to Puteoli, unless unfavorable winds compelled the vessels to coast along Asia Minor (Acts xxvii. 6; xxviii. 11–13; Philo, in Flac. v.). It was also the mart of interchange between the Orient and the Occident. The city flourished greatly under the Ptolemies, and subsequently under the Romans, until it extended along the coast fifteen miles by a breadth of one. During the time that the old Roman empire was dominant, Alexandria was considered the second city of the empire, having a population of 600,000 or 700,000. Its inhabitants were drawn from many nationalities, Greeks, Egyptians, Jews, Romans, who used the Greek language as the medium of communication. The different peoples occupied, as a rule, different quarters of the city. The Jews resided in the northeastern part, enjoyed equal rights with the other citizens, and were governed by their own ethnarch (Antiq. xix. 5, 2; War, ii. 18, 7). The Ptolemies founded a museum with a renowned library of several hundred thousand volumes, and the city was looked upon as one of the greatest intellectual centers in the world. The translation of the Hebrew Scriptures into Greek was begun in Egypt, probably in this city, in the third century, and completed by the second century, B. C. Here, too, the spirit of Greek philosophy permeated Judaism, and exegetes like Philo arose who excessively allegorized Scripture. The Jews of Alexandria had their own synagogue in Jerusalem, and were among the persecutors of Stephen (Acts ii. 10; vi. 9); but the teaching of John the Baptist and the knowledge of Jesus also gained entrance into Alexandria, and under God produced such men as Apollos (Acts xviii. 24, 25). Tradition ascribes the planting of the Christian Church in Alexandria to the evangelist Mark. In the early Christian ages the city was the seat of a celebrated Christian catechetical school with such teachers as Clement and Origen, and the home of bishops like Hesychius and Athanasius. In A. D. 616, Chosroes II., king of Persia, took Alexandria, and in 640 it was captured by Amrou, the general of Omar I., the Arab caliph. With the exception of a few brief intervals, it has since remained under Mohammedan government. The French, under Napoleon I., captured it in 1798, but were driven out by the British in 1801, after which it reverted to the Mohammedans. On July 11, 1882, the Alexandrian forts were bombarded by the British fleet, and the British occupation of Egypt began. In that year Alexandria contained 227,064 inhabitants.

Al'gum. See ALMUG.

A-li'ah. See ALVAH.

A-li'an. See ALVAN.

Al-lam'me-lech, in A.V. **Alammelech** [perhaps, king's oak].

A village of Asher (Josh. xix. 26). The wady el-Melek, which drains the waters of the plain of el-Buttauf into the Kishon opposite mount Carmel, may possibly echo the name.

Al-le-lu'ia. See HALLELUJAH.

Al-le'meth. See ALMON.

Al'lon [an oak].

A Simeonite, descended from Shemaiah (1 Chron. iv. 37).

In Josh. xix. 33 Allon is not a proper name, as in A. V., but a common noun, the oak or terebinth of Bezaanannim (Judg. iv. 11, R. V.; where in A. V. plain should be oak). See ZAANANNIM.

Al'lon-bac'uth, in A. V. **Allon-bachuth** [oak of weeping].

An oak near Bethel under which Deborah, Rebekah's nurse, was buried (Gen. xxxv. 8).

Al-mo'dad.

A people descended from Shem through Joktan (Gen. x. 26; 1 Chron. i. 20). They doubtless settled in the south of Arabia.

Al'mon [something hidden].

A village within the territory of Benjamin, assigned to the priests (Josh. xxi. 18). In 1 Chron. vi. 60 it is called Alemeth, or, following the traditional Hebrew pronunciation more closely, Allemeth. Both names have the same origin and meaning, and differ merely in outward form. Its site is the ruin 'Almit, a low, naked mound between Geba and Anathoth.

Al'mon-dib-la-tha'im [probably the district included between Almon and Diblathaim].

A station of the Israelites between the Arnon and Shittim (Num. xxxiii. 46); probably identical with Beth-diblathaim.

Alm'ond.

A tree and its fruit (Gen. xliii. 11; Ecc. xii. 5), called in Hebrew *Shaked*, the awaker, probably because it is the first tree to blossom in the spring. It is the *Amygdalus communis* of botanists, a tree about 20 feet high, originally, it is believed, from Barbary, but now introduced into many lands. In Palestine it is found on Lebanon, Hermon, and in most of the region beyond Jordan. The town of Luz in the hill country of Ephraim derived its name from the almond. The tree grew also in Mesopotamia (Gen. xxx. 37, R. V.). There are two varieties, the bitter and the sweet; the former has white flowers, the latter roseate. Almonds were sent by Jacob to the Egyptian dignitary (Gen. xliii. 11). The cups on the branches of the golden candlestick were modeled after almond blossoms (Ex. xxv. 33, 34). When the rod marked with Aaron's

name budded it brought forth almond blossoms (Num. xvii. 8). The rod of an almond
tree, which Jeremiah saw in his earliest vision, signified Jehovah's wakefulness (Jer. i.
11, 12). The white hairs on the head of the
aged are probably compared to the white
flower of the bitter almond tree (Ecc. xii. 5).

Al'mug, in 2 Chron. **Algum** [perhaps from
Sanscrit *valgu, valgum* (Lassen, Max Müller)].
A timber brought in abundance by sea
from Ophir during the reign of Solomon. It
was used to make pillars or balustrades, as
also harps and psalteries (1 Kin. x. 11. 12; 2
Chron. ix. 10, 11). According to Josephus, it
resembles the wood of the fig tree, but is
whiter and shines more (Antiq. viii. 7, 1).
It is commonly believed to be sandal wood,
the *Santalum album* of botanists, and the type
of the order *Santalaceæ*. The tree is small,
much-branched, in aspect somewhat resembling a myrtle, a native of India and the
eastern islands. If found on Lebanon (2
Chron. ii. 8) it must have been introduced
there. The wood, which is odoriferous, is
burnt to perfume temples and private houses
both in India and China. It is well adapted
for the purpose for which it was used by
Solomon.

Al'oes.
Not the botanical genus *Aloe*, consisting of
succulent plants belonging to the order *Liliaceæ*, and furnishing a bitter purgative medicine. The chief value of the scriptural plant
is evidently its fragrance (Ps. xlv. 8; Prov.
vii. 17; Song iv. 14). It seems to be *Agallocha*, called in various Indian dialects *agar,
agaru,* and *agru,* of which the Hebrew words
'ᵃhalim and *'ᵃhaloth* are probably a corruption. The species *Aquilaria agallocha* grows in
Sylhet, in the east of Bengal, and at Tennas-
serim, in the Eastern Peninsula. It is a large
tree, having alternate lanceolate leaves, a
leathery calyx, no petals, ten stamens, and
a two-celled seed-vessel. The wood contains
a resin, and an essential oil, which constitutes
the perfume for which it is prized in the East.
It is the lign-aloes of Num. xxiv. 6, and the
aloes of John xix. 39, one of the kinds of
spice with which Nicodemus designed to
anoint the body of our Lord.

A'loth [yielding milk].
A place of which, according to the Hebrew
text, the name may just as well be Bealoth,
known only as constituting with Asher one
of the twelve districts from which Solomon
drew provisions (1 Kin. iv. 16).

Al'pha.
The first letter in the Greek alphabet; derived from the Phœnician, and corresponding to the Hebrew letter Aleph. Omega is
the last letter of the Greek alphabet. "I am
Alpha and Omega" means "I am the first
and the last" of beings (Rev. i. 8, 11; xxi. 6;
xxii. 13; cp. Is. xliv. 6).

Al'pha-bet [from Greek *Alpha, Beta,* the
first two letters of the Greek alphabet].
The letters used in writing or printing a
language, these being arranged in a conventional order. The English alphabet is borrowed from the Latin, which in turn came
from the Greek. The Greek was derived
from the Phœnician; the tradition that Cad-
mus brought letters into Greece, if not true
in its details, being yet essentially historical. The Phœnicians, Hebrews, Moabites,
and Aramæans used a common alphabet at
least as early as the eighth century B. C. Its
use in Phœnicia as early as 1200 B. C. has
been established by French archæologists
excavating at Gebal. In their original form
these letters were pictures of familiar objects,
bore the names of these objects, and had the
initial sound of these words; thus, Gimel
had the sound of g and depicted a camel,
which was called *gamalu.* The names of the
several letters in the Hebrew alphabet and
the order in which they are arranged have
long been familiar to the English reader,
from their having been used to mark the
divisions of the 119th Psalm. The R. V. gives
in addition the later forms of the letters
themselves, *i. e.* the square characters introduced after the beginning of the Christian
era. It will be seen that they are twenty-
two in number. The Hebrew Bible has other
alphabetical psalms than the 119th, though
the fact is not ascertainable from the English
versions; see PSALMS and LAMENTATIONS.
To transliterate the Hebrew letters is to substitute for them as nearly as possible the
equivalent Roman characters. There are
different methods of transliterating some of
the letters. In the present work Aleph is
represented by the smooth breathing ' and
Ain by the rough breathing ', Heth by ḥ,
Teth by ṭ, Jod when a consonant by y,
Tzaddi by ṣ, Koph by ḳ, Shin by sh. The
other letters require neither explanation nor
diacritical point. In the N. T. two letters
of the Greek alphabet are mentioned, Alpha,
the first, and Omega, the last. In translating
this alphabet, Epsilon is represented by ĕ,
Eta by ē, Theta by th, Xi by x, Omikron by
ŏ, Upsilon by u, Phi by ph, Chi by ch, Psi by
ps, and Omega by ō.

Al-phæ'us [perhaps, transient].
1. The husband of one of the Marys, and
father of James the less and Joses (Mat. x. 3;
Mark xv. 40). He was scarcely Clopas, in
A. V. Cleophas (John xix. 25, with Mark xv.
40), for Clopas cannot be shown to be, like
Alphæus, a Greek modification of the Hebrew
name *Halpay.* See JAMES 2.
2. The father of Levi or Matthew (Mark ii.
14; cp. Mat. ix. 9).

Al'tar.
An elevated structure on which incense is
burned or sacrifice offered to the deity. It
might be a mound of earth; or a huge stone
or a platform built of several stones, dressed
or undressed; or an object of similar shape

Pottery incense stand or altar discovered at Meggido, thought to be used in Canaanite religious rites.

made of metal. In patriarchal times, worshipers reared altars wherever they pitched their tents or had special occasion to sacrifice to God (Gen. viii. 20; xii. 7; xxii. 9; xxxv. 1, 7; Ex. xvii. 15; xxiv. 4). The fundamental law of the Hebrew altar, which was embodied in the theocratic covenant and was given at Sinai before the tabernacle was built, enjoined

the erection of an altar of earth or stone wherever Jehovah should manifest himself. This law was the primary warrant for the altars at the tabernacle and temple, where Jehovah's presence continually was, and for the transient altars and sacrifices on occasions of theophanies (Judg. ii. 5, etc.).

The tabernacle had two altars: 1. The *brazen altar* or *altar of burnt offering*, which stood in the outer court and directly in front of the door of the tabernacle. It was 5 cubits square and 3 high. It consisted of a hollow frame of acacia wood overlaid with brass, and it was furnished with rings and staves that it might be transported from place to place. On its upper corners were projections called horns. It was without steps, but had a ledge round about it, midway between the bottom and the top for the priests to stand on. It was probably intended to be filled with earth. All sacrifices were offered at this altar. Its position at the very threshold taught distinctly that man has no access to Jehovah except as a sinner atoned for by blood (Ex. xxvii. 1–8; xxx. 28; xxxviii. 30; xl. 29; cp. 1 Kin. i. 50; Ps. cxviii. 27). 2. The *golden altar*, or *altar of incense*, which stood in the holy place before the veil that hung before the mercy seat. It was a cubit square and two cubits high, and was made of acacia wood overlaid with gold, with a border of gold about its top, horns at its corners, and two golden rings at each side for staves. Incense of prescribed ingredients, lighted by fire from the brazen altar, was burned on it morning and evening when the light of the candlestick was seen to. It symbolized the obligatory and acceptable adoration of God by his people (Ex. xxx. 1–10, 28, 34–37; xl. 5; cp. Heb. ix. 4 and 1 Kin. vi. 22; Lev. xvi. 18, 19). When Solomon's temple was built, the new brazen altar had nearly four times the dimensions of the old (1 Kin. viii. 64; 2 Chron. iv. 1). A new golden altar was also made (1 Kin. vii. 48; 2 Chron. iv. 19).

These were the only permanent altars on which sacrifices or incense could be acceptably offered (Deut. xii. 2, 5, 6, 7). But the rearing of altars and offering of sacrifice in other places where God manifested himself was authorized by the fundamental law; and the privilege was embraced, as for example, by the Israelites at Bochim, by Gideon, by Manoah (Judg. ii. 1–5; vi. 20-25; xiii. 15–23). And Joshua erected an altar on mount Ebal to serve for a single occasion. As the twelve tribes of Israel were assembled there for a national function, and the ark of the covenant was present, this altar was for the time being the national altar (Josh. viii. 30–35), and quite in the spirit of the Deuteronomic legislation (Deut. xxvii. 5-8). The law of the altar was necessarily in abeyance twice. 1. When God forsook the tabernacle and the ark was in the hands of the Philistines, or in dreaded seclusion at Kirjath-jearim, there was no place where Jehovah manifested himself (Ps. lxxviii. 60-64; 1 Sam. vi. 20-vii. 4). Samuel, as the prophet and representative of Jehovah, erected an altar at Ramah and sacrificed in several places (1 Sam. vii. 9, 17). Out of the confusion of worship caused by the capture of the ark, the domination of the Philistines, and the political complications connected with Saul and David, there arose and continued for a time two high priests and two altars, the original altar at the original tabernacle and a new altar near the ark in Jerusalem (1 Kin. iii. 2, 4, 15; 2 Chron. i. 3-6). 2. When the Ten Tribes revolted, the pious Israelites of the north who were debarred the pilgrimage to Jerusalem were compelled either to abstain from worshiping Jehovah by sacrifice, or else to erect local altars. They chose in some instances the latter alternative (1 Kin. xviii. 30, 32; xix. 10).

After the exile, at a time when the insistence of Deuteronomy upon one central, national altar had long been known, the Jews who were living at Yeb in Upper Egypt in the sixth century before Christ, and in the second century before Christ those Jews dwelling near Leontopolis, ventured to build in each of these places a local temple to Jehovah and to erect an altar and offer sacrifices on it to the God of heaven (Elephantine papyri; Antiq. xiii. 3, 1; War, vii. 10, 2 and 3).

Altars were not always intended for sacrifices or for the burning of incense; the two and a half tribes who settled east of the Jordan built an altar designed to be a memorial of their affinity in blood to the other tribes, who crossed the river (Josh. xxii. 10-34).

Al-tash'heth, in A. V. less accurately **Altaschith** [do not destroy].

A compound word occurring in the titles of Psalms lvii., lviii., lix., and lxxv., all R. V. It probably refers, like Aijeleth Shahar, to the name of some Hebrew melody to the tune of which those psalms were to be sung.

A'lush [tumult of men].

An encampment of the Israelites between Egypt and mount Sinai (Num. xxxiii. 13, 14).

Al'vah or **A-li'ah** [high, tall, thick]. For variation in spelling perhaps cp. VAU.

A duke of Edom, descended from Esau (Gen. xxxvi. 40; 1 Chron. i. 51). He probably bears the name of his district (43).

Al'van or **A-li'an** [high, tall]. For variation in form perhaps cp. VAU.

A Horite (Gen. xxxvi. 23; 1 Chron. i. 40).

A'mad [people of duration or, better, station, domicile].

A frontier village of Asher (Josh. xix. 26). Not identified.

A'mal [labor, sorrow].

An Asherite, son of Helem (1 Chron. vii. 35).

Am'a-lek.

Son of Eliphaz, Esau's son, by his concubine Timna (Gen. xxxvi. 12); or, collectively, the Amalekites (Ex. xvii. 8; Num. xxiv. 20; Deut. xxv. 17; Judg. v. 14, etc.).

Am'a-lek-ites.

The descendants of Esau (Gen. xxxvi. 12). For a long time they were centered about Kadesh-barnea. In this neighborhood they dwelt at the time of the exodus (Num. xiii. 29; xiv. 25). The territory occupied by them was visible from the mountains of Abarim (Num. xxiv. 20; Deut. xxxiv. 1-3). They were among the foremost people of their time in that part of the world (Num. xxiv. 20). A writer after the era of the exodus, referring to ancient events which occurred in that region, could speak proleptically of the country of the Amalekites. Hence in the narrative of the campaign of Chedorlaomer and his allies in this region, it is said that these eastern invaders "came to Kadesh and smote," not the Amalekites (as one would expect the writer to say, after the manner of his context, had that people been in existence), but in guarded phrase "all the country of the Amalekites" (Gen. xiv. 7). From their center near Kadesh, the people roamed and their camps radiated. They harassed the rear of the Israelites soon after the Hebrews had left Egypt and entered the wilderness; and at Rephidim on the west of Sinai they engaged with Israel in battle and were defeated. Because of their hostility to Israel, their utter destruction was authorized (Ex. xvii. 8-16; Deut. xxv. 17-19). A year later, when Israel had reached Kadesh, and in defiance of God attempted to push northward into Canaan, the Amalekites opposed and repulsed them (Num. xiv. 43-45). About that date perhaps or later, their name became attached to a hill district in Ephraim (Judg. xii. 15; cp. v. 14). Soon after the time of Moses and Joshua, they aided Eglon, king of Moab, to wrest Jericho from the Israelites; and a few generations later they were allied with the Midianites in oppressing northern Israel (Judg. iii. 13; vi. 3, 33). Evidently they had been working their way eastward, in friendly intercourse with other inhabitants of the desert; and in Saul's time their bands were found roaming through a stretch of perhaps five or six hundred miles of wilderness from the border of Egypt, near their original seat, to Havilah, a designation which includes northern central Arabia (1 Sam. xv. 7; xxvii. 8). They suffered crushing defeat from Saul, their king was captured and slain, and they presently disappear from Hebrew history.

A'mam [perhaps, collection or conjunction].

A village of Judah in the southland (Josh. xv. 26).

Am'a-na [firmness, a treaty].

The mountains of Anti-Lebanon, doubtless those in which the Abanah or, as it is also called, Amanah takes its rise (Song iv. 8).

Am-a-ri ah' [Jehovah hath said or promised].

1. Son of Meraioth, a priest descended from Phinehas (1 Chron. vi. 7).

2. A priest in the same high-priestly line of descent, a son of Azariah (1 Chron. vi. 11; Ezra vii. 3).

3. A chief of the priests, who returned from Babylon with Zerubbabel (Neh. xii. 2, 7). A father's house bore his name in the next generation (ver. 13).

4. A priest, doubtless head of a father's house, who sealed the covenant in Nehemiah's time (Neh. x. 3).

5. A man who had taken a foreign wife, whom Ezra made him divorce (Ezra x. 42).

6. A man of Judah, family of Perez (Neh. xi. 4).

7. A son of Hezekiah, and an ancestor of the prophet Zephaniah (Zeph. i. 1, R. V.).

8. A chief priest in Jehoshaphat's time (2 Chron. xix. 11).

9. A Levite, descended through Kohath and Hebron (1 Chron. xxiii. 19; xxiv. 23).

10. An assistant distributor of the freewill offerings of God in Hezekiah's time (2 Chron. xxxi. 14, 15).

Am'a-sa [a burden].

1. The son of David's half-sister Abigail and Jether an Ishmaelite (1 Chron. ii. 17). He was Joab's cousin (2 Sam. xvii. 25). Absalom appointed Amasa captain of his army (ibid.). After Absalom's defeat and death, Amasa was forgiven by David and appointed commander-in-chief in supersession of Joab (2 Sam. xix. 13). On the breaking out of the revolt headed by Sheba, Amasa received orders to have an army in readiness to start in three days. He was behind his time; and Abishai was sent with troops, among whom Joab was, after Sheba. The two companies united at Gibeon; and Joab, under pretext of greeting Amasa with a kiss, stabbed him (2 Sam. xx. 1-13). Compare AMASAI 2.

2. A prince of Ephraim and son of Hadlai. When captives from Judah were being carried off by the Israelite army under Pekah, he aided in securing their release (2 Chron. xxviii. 12).

Am'a-sai [burdensome].

1. A Levite of the Kohathite family, descended through Abiasaph and an ancestor of Heman the singer (1 Chron. vi. 35). Amasai in ver. 25 is perhaps a different person of the same family and name, but descended from the brother of Abiasaph (Ex. vi. 24).

2. A chief who early joined David and at one time was a prominent captain (1 Chron. xii. 18). Perhaps he was David's nephew Amasa.

3. A Levite who blew a trumpet before the ark in David's reign (1 Chron. xv. 24).

4. A Kohathite whose son aided in the religious revival in Hezekiah's reign (2 Chron. xxix. 12).

Am'a-shai, in R. V. **Amashsai** [perhaps, two variant spellings of Amasai combined].

A priest, the son of Azareel. He lived in Jerusalem, at Nehemiah's request (Neh. xi. 13).

Am-a-si'ah [Jehovah hath borne].

A son of Zichri, and high military officer under Jehoshaphat (2 Chron. xvii. 16).

Am-a-zi'ah [Jehovah is strong].

1. A king of Judah who, about 804 B. C., at the age of twenty-five years, undertook the conduct of the government in behalf of his father Joash, who had become incapacitated by reason of sore disease. On the murder of his father in 802 B. C., he succeeded to the throne (2 Kin. xiv. 1; 2 Chron. xxiv. 25-27). When he found himself firmly established in power, he put the murderers of his father to death; but spared their children, in conformity with the principle laid down on the subject in the Mosaic law (Deut. xxiv. 16). He hired 100,000 Israelitish mercenaries to accompany him on an expedition against the Edomites, but at the command of a man of God he dismissed them and, taking the forces of Judah alone, defeated the Edomites in the Valley of Salt and captured their capital, Selah. But he brought back idols of the Edomites, and set them up for his gods. The dismissed Israelites on their way home plundered the cities of Judah north of Beth-horon. Amaziah, following bad advice, challenged Jehoash, king of Israel, to fight, but he was defeated in a battle at Beth-shemesh, taken prisoner, and carried to Jerusalem. Part of the wall of Jerusalem, his capital, was broken down by Jehoash, and treasure and hostages were taken by him to Samaria. About the year 787 B. C. a conspiracy was formed against Amaziah in Jerusalem. He fled to Lachish, but twelve years later was sought out there and murdered. He reigned twenty-nine years (2 Kin. xiv. 1-20; 2 Chron. xxv. 1-27).

2. A Simeonite (1 Chron. iv. 34).

3. A Levite of the family of Merari (1 Chron. vi. 45).

4. Priest of Beth-el, who tried to silence the prophet Amos (Amos vii. 10-17).

Am'ber.

The hardened or fossilized resin of a now extinct pine tree (*Pinus succinifer*) allied to the Norway spruce or to the Silver fir. That it was originally fluid is plain from the fact that it is found to enclose numerous remains of plants and of insects. The pines producing it grew in the southeastern part of what is now the bed of the Baltic Sea, and it is still picked up on the southern shore of that sea. It was regarded as a gem, and early became an object of commerce over regions very remote from the Baltic Sea. It is generally yellow, and that is the color of amber referred to in Ezek. i. 4, 27; viii. 2, A. V., E. R. V. and margin of A. R. V. It is mentioned on the margin of Ex. xxviii. 19, R. V.

A'men' [firm, established].
1. Jesus, as the faithful and true One (Rev. iii. 14; cp. Is. lxv. 16, R. V. margin).
2. An interjection, "So be it," "May it be" as has been asked, said, promised, or threatened (Mat. vi. 13; Deut. xxvii. 16–26; 2 Cor. i. 20). To render it more emphatic, it is sometimes redoubled (Num. v. 22). Jesus begins many of his sayings with this word, which is then translated "verily." This idiom is peculiar to nim.

Am'e-thyst [the Hebrew name suggests dream-stone].
A precious stone, believed to be intended by the Hebrew name for the last gem in the third row on the Jewish high priest's breastplate (Ex. xxviii. 19; xxxix. 12). The amethyst formed the twelfth foundation of the New Jerusalem (Rev. xxi. 20). It is a glassy, clear, purple or bluish violet variety of quartz, the color, it is believed, being produced by manganese. The Hebrews could obtain it in Edom, Egypt, Galatia, or Cyprus; but finer specimens came from India and Spain.

A'mi. See AMON I, 3.

A-min'a-dab. See AMMINADAB.

A-mit'tai [truthful].
The father of Jonah the prophet (2 Kin. xiv. 25; Jonah i. 1).

Am'mah [mother of anything in a figurative sense; beginning, foundation].
A hill near Giah, on the road from Gibeon through the wilderness to the Jordan (2 Sam. ii. 24; cp. 16, 29). Exact situation unknown.

Am'mi [my people] (Hos. ii. 1).

Am'mi-el [one of the family, or a devoted ally, is God].
1. Son of Gemalli, and representative of the tribe of Dan on the commission to spy out Canaan (Num. xiii. 12).
2. A man of Lo-debar. and father of Machir (2 Sam. ix. 4, 5; xvii. 27).
3. A son of Obed-edom (1 Chron. xxvi. 5).
4. Father of Bath-sheba (1 Chron. iii. 5); see ELIAM.

Am-mi'hud [kinsman of praiseworthiness, or an ally is the praiseworthy one].
1. An Ephraimite, descended through Tahan, and father of Elishama (Num. i. 10; 1 Chron. vii. 26).
2. A man of Simeon, and father of Shemuel (Num. xxxiv. 20).
3. A man of Naphtali, and father of Pedahel (Num. xxxiv. 28).
4. Father of Talmai, king of Geshur (2 Sam. xiii. 37). In the Hebrew text the name is written with ḥ and r instead of h and d, but is traditionally pronounced Ammihud.
5. A descendant of Judah through Perez (1 Chron. ix. 4, R. V.).

Am-mi'hur [perhaps, kinsman of nobility]. See AMMIHUD 4.

Am-min'a-dab, in A. V. of N. T. **Aminadab** [the people or kinsman is generous].
1. A man of Judah, family of Hezron, house of Ram (1 Chron. ii. 10). He was the father of Nahshon, the prince of Judah (Num. i. 7), father-in-law of Aaron the priest (Ex. vi. 23), and an ancestor of David (Ruth iv. 19; Mat. i. 4; Luke iii. 33).
2. A Levite, family of Kohath, house of Uzziel. He was head of his father's house in David's reign (1 Chron. xv. 10, 11; cp. Ex. vi. 18, 22).
3. A Levite, family of Kohath (1 Chron. vi. 22). The genealogies of Kohath, however, regularly have the name Izhar in this place (vs. 37, 38; Ex. vi. 18, 21, 24), so that Amminadab is probably either another name of Izhar or a corruption of the genealogy.

Am-min'a-dib [my princely willing people, or the people is generous].
If a proper name, which is doubtful, then it is some one famous for his chariots (Song vi. 12; cp. text and margin).

Am'mi-shad'dai [an ally or kinsman is the Almighty].
A Danite, father of Ahiezer (Num. i. 12; ii. 25).

Am-miz'a-bad [the kinsman hath endowed].
A son of David's mighty man Benaiah (1 Chron. xxvii. 6).

Am'mon [pertaining to the nation].
An adjective which paraphrases the name of Ben-ammi, Lot's younger son, ancestor of the Ammonites (Gen. xix. 38).

Am'mon-ites.
A people descended from Ben-ammi, Lot's second son (Gen. xix. 38). They dispossessed the Zamzummim of the territory between the Arnon and the Jabbok (Deut. ii. 20, 21; iii. 11); but were in turn driven out by the Amorites and compelled to keep on the border of the eastern desert, with the upper Jabbok as their western boundary (Num. xxi. 24; Deut. ii. 37; Judg. xi. 13, 22). For having joined the Moabites in hiring Balaam to curse the Israelites, they were excluded from the congregation of the Lord to the tenth generation (Deut. xxiii. 3–6). They aided Eglon, king of Moab, in subjugating a portion of the Israelites (Judg. iii. 13). In the time of Jephthah they again oppressed the Israelites east of Jordan (Judg. x. 6, 9, 18). Just before Saul became actual king, Nahash, the Ammonite king, besieged Jabesh-gilead. Saul came to the assistance of the beleaguered citizens, and totally defeated Nahash (1 Sam. xi. 1–11). Nahash befriended David; doing this, perhaps, because both were enemies of Saul. On the death of Nahash, David sent an embassy to his son, Hanun; but the ambassadors were insulted, and war supervened.

In the first campaign, the confederate Syrians and Ammonites were defeated by the Israelites, led by Joab and Abishai (2 Sam. x. 1–19; 1 Chron. xix. 1-19). In the second, the Israelites captured Rabbah, the Ammonite capital (2 Sam. xi., xii.; 1 Chron. xx. 1-3). Solomon took several Ammonite women as wives (1 Kin. xi. 1). In the time of Jehoshaphat Moabites, Ammonites, and Edomites unsuccessfully invaded Judah (2 Chron. xx. 1-30). To Uzziah and Jotham the Ammonites sent tribute (xxvi. 8; xxvii. 5). Ammonites joined with others in vexing Jehoiakim (2 Kin. xxiv. 2); and after the fall of Jerusalem, they frustrated the attempt of the Jews to form a new community (xxv. 25; Jer. xl. 11–14). As inveterate enemies of Israel, they were denounced by the prophets (Jer. xlix. 1-6; Ezek. xxi. 20; xxv. 1-7; Amos i. 13-15; Zeph. ii. 8-11). They opposed the rebuilding of the walls of Jerusalem by the returned exiles (Neh. iv. 3, 7); yet intermarriages between them and the Israelites took place, which were censured by Ezra and Nehemiah (Ezra ix. 1, 2; Neh. xiii. 23-31). Judas Maccabæus, under strong provocation, made war against them (1 Mac. v. 1-8). They are mentioned as late as the second Christian century. Their chief deity was Milcom, another designation of Molech (1 Kin. xi. 7, 33). In the time of Jephthah they were worshiping Chemosh, the Moabite god (Judg. xi. 24).

Am′non [faithful].

1. A son of David by Ahinoam, the Jezreelitess; born at Hebron while that was his father's capital. He behaved scandalously to Tamar, his half-sister, and was in consequence murdered by her full brother Absalom (2 Sam. xiii. and iii. 2; 1 Chron. iii. 1).

2. A son of Shimon, registered with the tribe of Judah (1 Chron. iv. 20).

A′mok [deep].

A chief of the priests who returned from Babylon with Zerubbabel (Neh. xii. 7). In the next generation a father's house bore this name (ver. 20).

A′mon, I. [security or handicraftsman].

1. Governor of the city of Samaria under Ahab (1 Kin. xxii. 10, 26).

2. A king of Judah who at the age of twenty-two succeeded his father Manasseh. He followed his father's bad example. In two years his servants murdered him in his palace. The people of the land put the murderers to death, and placed his son Josiah on the throne (2 Kin. xxi. 19-26; 2 Chron. xxxiii. 21-25).

3. One of the class known as the children of Solomon's servants (Neh. vii. 59); called Ami in Ezra ii. 57.

A′mon, II. [Egyptian *Amen*, the hidden one, the unseen being].

The chief divinity of Thebes, named after him No-amon, the capital of Upper Egypt (Jer. xlvi. 25, R. V.; Nah. iii. 8, R. V.). The

The Egyptian God Amon.

Hyksos were expelled from Egypt under his ensign, and he consequently became head of the pantheon, and was called the successor of Ra. He was represented as wearing two plumes of hawk's feathers, a disk, and a red cap.

Am′o-rites [commonly explained as "mountaineers," but this explanation is questionable].

One of the tribes who occupied Canaan before the conquest of the country by the Hebrews (Gen. x. 16; xv. 21; Ex. iii. 8). At the time of Abraham, they dwelt at least on the western shore of the Dead Sea and back on the mountain (Gen. xiv. 7, 13). Even then they were the most powerful tribe in the hill country, and their name was used as synonym for the inhabitants of that region generally (xv. 16), if not, as later when their power had further increased, for the inhabitants of Canaan generally (xxxiv. 2 with xlviii. 22; Josh. vii. 7; ix. 7 and xi. 19 with 2 Sam. xxi. 2; Judg. vi. 10; Amos ii. 10). At the time of the exodus they were still in the hill country (Num. xiii. 29; Deut. i. 7, 19, 20, 44; they could of course be called Canaanites, Num. xiv. 45); but before this date they had carried their conquests to the east of the Jordan (Num. xxi. 26-30), and taken possession of the land from the Arnon to mount Hermon and from the wilderness to the Jordan (Deut. iii. 8; iv. 48; Josh. ii. 10; ix. 10

Judg. xi. 22). At this time they occupied the entire hill country west of Jordan from Jerusalem to Hebron, and westward to and inclusive of the Shephelah (Josh. x. 5, 6) as far north as Aijalon and even the territory of Ephraim (Judg. i. 35; Josh. xi. 3; xiii. 4). For their wickedness they were devoted to destruction; but a strong remnant remained in the land after the conquest (Judg. i. 35; iii. 5), with whom in Samuel's day there was peace (1 Sam. vii. 14), and who with other survivors of the earlier races were made bondservants by Solomon (1 Kin. ix. 20, 21; 2 Chron. viii. 7).

A'mos [burden; burden-bearer].

1. A prophet, a citizen of Tekoa, in the territory of the tribe of Judah, about six miles south of Bethlehem (Amos i. 1). He belonged to the humbler class. He was a herdsman; one of a number of shepherds who had their home at Tekoa, but doubtless spent their lives out in the wilderness that extends from the village eastward to the Dead Sea, engaged in raising and tending sheep. In some sheltered spot in this wild region, down on the lower level toward the sea, he found further humble employment as a dresser of sycomore trees (i. 1; vii. 14, 15). From the acquaintance which he displays with distant places and events, it seems probable that he had driven sheep or carried hides and wool as far as Egypt and Damascus. Although a man of Judah, he was called to prophesy in the kingdom of the ten tribes. He appeared at Beth-el, then the king's sanctuary and a royal house, which still had within it one of the two golden calves reared by Jeroboam I. as objects of worship (viii. 14; Hos. viii. 5, 6; x. 5). Amos spoke with such freedom and faithfulness against the sins of the king and the people that Amaziah, the idolatrous priest at Bethel, sent word to king Jeroboam II. that Amos was conspiring against him in his own kingdom (Amos vii. 10). The time and circumstances of Amos' death are unknown.

Amos knew God as omnipotent, the God of creation and providence, the sovereign ruler of individuals and nations, inflexible in justice, whose power reaches unto sheol and who knows the thoughts of men. And Amos was a shrewd observer of men and manners, and able to reflect upon what he saw, and to generalize and look at it in its relation to God.

The prophecy of Amos is a fine example of pure Hebrew style. The diction is simple, and yet the speech is dignified and impressive. The prophet uses imagery with moderation, but with effect; and he has coined not a few striking phrases that have gained currency in modern speech (e. g. iii. 3, 6 iv. 11, 12; vi. 1). Amos is not so tender in his entreaty or so full of feeling as Hosea is at times, who belonged to the people among whom he labored; but there is a certain air of aloofness about Amos, natural enough in a prophet from another tribe and kingdom, and he pronounces the impersonal judgment of one whose ties of blood are not close with the people whom he addresses.

The book of Amos is the third of the minor prophets. Amos prophesied after the time of Hazael and Benhadad (i. 4), in the days of Uzziah, king of Judah, and in the days of Jeroboam, son of Joash, king of Israel, two years before the earthquake (i. 1; vii. 10; cp. Zech. xiv. 5), and probably while the kingdom was at its greatest extent (Amos vi. 14; cp. 2 Kin. xiv. 25). He uttered his message before Hosea delivered the discourses embodied in Hos. iv.–xiv.: for the social and religious condition of Israel, as reflected in the pages of Amos, seems not to be so desperate as Hosea depicts during the years of assassination, conflict, and misrule which ensued on the death of Jeroboam II.; and Amos does not, like Hosea in chaps. iv.–xiv., allude to the Assyrian invasions, probably because they had not begun.

The theme of the prophecy is the judgment of the Lord (i. 2; cp. Joel iii. 16); and the book consists of three parts: 1. Introductory (i.–ii.). 2. Three discourses (iii.–vi.), followed by a series of five visions (vii.–ix. 7). These first two parts of the book are denunciatory, and each subdivision ends with the announcement of judgment to come. 3. Promissory (ix. 8–15). 1. In the introductory section (i. 2–ii. 16) the prophet denounces judgment upon six neighboring gentile nations, upon Judah, and finally upon Israel. The first seven denunciations are embraced in seven stanzas of precisely the same structure, are opened and closed in the same way, and are linked to the introductory denunciation of Israel, to which they lead up, by the familiar opening formula. The argument seems to be: If these heathen nations are to be punished, how much more should Judah be, which has sinned against light; and if Judah is punished, how much more should Israel be, which has sinned more deeply. 2. Denunciation of Israel occupies the body of the book (iii. 1–ix. 7). There are three discourses, each beginning with the formula "Hear this word" (iii. 1; iv. 1; v. 1), followed by five visions. In the first vision devouring locusts are seen; but at the prayer of the prophet God forgives Israel and ends the work of devastation. In the second vision fire is seen, which devours the waters and would have destroyed the land; but again at the prophet's prayer God makes the evil to cease. Perhaps an actual invasion of locusts occurred during the ministry of the prophet Amos, and was followed by a season of intense heat and the resulting drought (cp. JOEL). At any rate the two visitations represent every past judgment which has befallen Israel; the locusts denoting destructive invaders, either devouring insects or hostile armies, and the fire being a symbol of God's righteous indignation burning against sin. Most probably Amos sees in these visions the past calamities, upon which he has already discoursed, which were sent to warn Israel and were checked by God's grace, but failed to bring the nation to repentance (iv. 6-11). Therefore the people must prepare to meet their God in judgment (iv. 12); and the third vision, that of the plumbline, shows that a desolating judgment is certain to come and is according to rectitude (vii. 7-9). At this point the prophet was interrupted by the priest of Beth-el, and forbidden to prophesy; but he resumes his recital. In the fourth vision a basket of summer fruit is seen, indicating that Israel is ripe for judgment, yea, in God's sight is already plucked (viii. 1-3). In the fifth vision Jehovah is seen standing beside the altar, doubtless that at Bethel (cp. iii. 14), and commanding to smite and slay; showing that the order is being issued for the judgment to begin (ix. 1-4). 3. The prophecy concludes with promises (ix. 8-15): the exile only a sifting (8-10); restoration of the royal house of David to its former glory (11); extension of the kingdom over Edom and other heathen nations (12); restoration of Israel from captivity (13-15).

The text of Amos has been transmitted in excellent condition. The genuineness of several passages, however, especially of ii. 4, 5; iv. 13; v. 8, 9; ix. 5, 6 and 8ᵇ-15, has been questioned. Against the genuineness of ii. 4, 5, it is urged, first, that the thought and diction are Deuteronomic; and, secondly, that the indictment against Judah is conventional and general in contrast with the specific charges brought against the other nations. But 1. The Deuteronomic features, seen in the references to the rejection of the law of Jehovah, failure to keep his statutes, and walking after other gods, are found in the writings of contemporaries of Amos and earlier (Ex. xv. 26; xviii. 16; Is. v. 24; Hos. ii. 7, 15; iv. 6). 2. Regarding the indictment, it has the formal structure of each arraignment in the series, and it is so far specific as that disobedience to Jehovah's commands and idolatry are conceptions definite enough in prophetic thought to be specific charges (cp. Is. i. 2-4; Hos. viii. 1; Jer. i. 16; ii. 4-8). And 3. These two verses (Amos ii. 4, 5) cannot be removed, and the accusation against Judah omitted, without altering the nature of the argument and disturbing its progress (Driver, Joel and Amos, p. 117; Vos, Presb. and Ref. Rev., ix. 226). The three passages, iv. 13; v. 8, 9; and ix. 5, 6, of which also the genuineness has been called in question, are descriptive of Jehovah; and they are rejected on the theory, first, that the doctrine of God which finds expression in these verses does not become prominent in Hebrew literature until the period of the exile; secondly, such ejaculations in praise of Jehovah's power are in the manner of the later style

of Is. xl.-lxvi.; and, thirdly, two of these passages, iv. 13 and ix. 5, 6, are not closely connected with the argument of the context, while v. 8, 9 actually interrupts it. The reply is made: 1. It is true that these passages "might be omitted without causing a perceptible gap; but the same is true of a great number of passages whose genuineness is doubted by none. In all three places they serve to lend force to the prediction of judgment by declaring the transcendent greatness of him whose the judgment is" (Vos, loc. cit., p. 227). 2. "The ejaculatory form of the appeal, especially at critical points of the prophet's discourse, is 'not surprising under the general conditions of prophetic oratory'" (Driver quoting Robertson Smith), and 3. "The doctrine of Jehovah's lordship over nature is in agreement with Amos' teaching elsewhere (iv. 7ff.; vii. 1, 4; ix. 3)" (Driver); and, it may be added, with teaching that antedates the prophecy of Amos and found, for example, in Gen. ii.-viii.; xi.; xviii.; Ex. vii.-xiv. Of the promises of good, with which the book closes, ix. 8ᵇ-15, it has been asserted that the passage can scarcely have been the original conclusion of Amos' vision of judgment, because it differs from the rest of the prophecy in phraseology, conception, and outlook. It is, of course, a matter of small moment whether it was written by Amos at the time he penned the visions or later. No ground has been found for rejecting its genuineness. The prophets frequently annexed to the prediction of judgment a prophecy of hope. The godly needed encouragement, and it was necessary to show the congruity between the overwhelming judgment and God's long-standing promise of the stability of David's throne and the perpetuity and triumph of God's kingdom on earth.

2. An ancestor of Christ (Luke iii. 25).

A'moz [powerful, brave].

The prophet Isaiah's father (Is. i. 1, etc.).

Am-phip'o-lis [a city pressed on all sides].

A city of Thrace, situated at the mouth of the Strymon on a bend of the river. It was founded by the Athenians in the fifth century B. C., and called Amphipolis because nearly surrounded by the river. Under the Romans it was the chief town of Macedonia prima. It was on the Via Egnatia, thirty-three miles southwest of Philippi, and Paul accordingly passed through it while traveling by that road from Philippi to Thessalonica (Acts xvii. 1). It is now called Empoli or Yamboli, is about three miles from the sea, and has a village, Neokhorio or Jeni Keui (New Town), on part of its site.

Am-pli-a'tus, in A. V. **Am'pli-as** [enlarged].

A Christian of Rome to whom Paul sent salutation (Rom. xvi. 8).

Am'ram, I. (1 Chron. i. 41). See HEM-DAN.

Am'ram, II. [perhaps, inexperience].

1. A Levite, son of Kohath, husband of Jochebed and founder of the father's house of the Amramites, who in the time of Moses numbered approximately two thousand males (Num. iii. 17, 19, 27, 28). He was an ancestor of Aaron and Moses, and lived to the age of 137 years (Ex. vi. 20; for form of expression cp. Gen. xlvi. 16–18, 19–22, 23–25; Mat. i. 5, 6, 8, 11).

2. A son of Bani, induced by Ezra to put away his foreign wife (Ezra x. 34).

Am'ram-ites.

The descendants of Amram, constituting a subdivision of the Levites (Num. iii. 27; 1 Chron. xxvi. 23).

Am'ra-phel.

King of Shinar, ally of Chedorlaomer in the invasion of the west (Gen. xiv. 1, 9).

The name is unlike that of Hammurabi or Ammurabi [or, in Amorite, Ammurawih (Luckenbill)], who became king of Babel about 2123 B. C. and reigned at least forty-three years. At first he held sway over a small district only; but about the thirtieth year of his reign he wrested Larsa from the Elamites, and made himself lord of all Babylonia. He sought the welfare of his subjects; repaired old canals and cut new ones in order to bring fertility to both northern and southern Babylonia, strengthened fortifications, embellished and erected temples, superintended the administration of justice and codified the laws of the land. He richly deserved the title which he gave himself, father to his people. Hammurabi is the earliest known codifier of law; the first name in the list which includes Moses and Justinian and Napoleon. He was doubtless himself a legislator; but beyond enacting legislation, he discerned the importance of collecting the laws of the realm which pertained to the social life of the people, grouping the related ones, and giving them the widest publicity.

These ancient laws of Babylonia bear a close resemblance to the enactments in the Book of the Covenant by which justice was administered in Israel (Ex. xx. 23–xxiii. 33; cp. xxiv. 7). Not only are they codified, like the later body of Hebrew legislation (see THEOCRACY), but they are like many of those Hebrew statutes in beginning with the word "if." Besides this outward likeness, there is material resemblance. In twenty-four or twenty-five instances the two bodies of legislation treat of the same injury to person or property. This coincidence is, of course, not surprising, since just these mishaps and misdeeds occur in every community of men and must receive notice in any code of laws dealing with civil life. It is more remarkable that in so many instances the same classes of people, particularly the less fortunate members of society, were regarded by both Babylonians and Israelites as possessing rights that could be recognized by the state. But what is most remarkable is that in fourteen instances at least the Babylonian and Hebrew law imposes the same, or practically the same, penalty for the same offence. To a remarkable degree the two peoples shared the same conception of justice. It is not probable that the Hebrew legislator had the laws of Hammurabi before him; but it is certain that Israel inherited from some source the conceptions of justice and the judicial customs which existed among the Babylonians in the days of Hammurabi. See MOSES.

Am'u-let.

Anything worn as a protection against sorcery. It often serves at the same time as an ornament (Is. iii. 20, R. V.; cp. Gen. xxxv. 4).

Am'zi [robust].

1. A Levite, a descendant of Merari (1 Chron. vi. 46).

2. A priest of the course of Malchijah (Neh. xi. 12, R. V.).

A'nab [probably, fruitful in grapes].

A town in the mountains of Judah (Josh. xi. 21; xv. 50). Two ruins still bear the name; one is twelve miles southwest of Hebron, and the more extensive is one and a half miles farther southwest.

A'nah [perhaps, hearkening to, granting].

A tribe of Horites (Gen. xxxvi. 20, R. V.), organized under a chief (29). The tribe bore the name of its progenitor, who was descended from Zibeon and expanded to a branch tribe (20, 24). Anah discovered warm springs in the wilderness (24). From this circumstance he probably received the name Beeri, man of the well (2 with xxvi. 34, where, if Hittite does not include Hivite, the two names may be confused; for in the Septuagint of xxvi. 34 Elon is a Hivite, but in the Hebrew text a Hittite). A daughter of the tribe, traced back also to Zibeon, became a wife of Esau (xxxvi. 2, 14, 25). Daughter of Zibeon (2, 14) may refer to Oholibamah; an emendation of the Hebrew text from bt, daughter, to bn, son, of Zibeon would not affect the foregoing statements. Many interpreters, however, discern three persons of the name—a woman (2, 14) and two men (20, 25, 29 and 24).

An-a-ha'rath [possibly, nostril or pass].

An ancient town (Thothmes' list) on the frontier of Issachar (Josh. xix. 19). Possibly en-Na'ûrah, five miles N. E. of Jezreel, echoes the name. The location suits.

A-na'iah [Jehovah hath answered].

One who stood by Ezra when he read the book of the law to the people (Neh. viii. 4), and who afterwards sealed the covenant to serve God (x. 22).

A'nak [the long neck (with definite article, Num. xiii. 22, 28, but not 33)].

Collective name of the Anakim (Num. xiii. 22 with Deut. i. 28), who possibly, though not necessarily, were descended from Arba (Josh. xiv. 15 with xv. 13).

.An′a-kim ; A. V. has **Anakims**, using both the Hebrew and the English plural ending.

A stalwart race, connected with the Rephaim (Num. xiii. 33 ; Deut. ii. 10, 11, 21). Three families of them settled at Hebron (Num. xiii. 22), and others were found in neighboring towns and elsewhere throughout the hill country (Josh. xi. 21 ; xv. 14 ; cp. Rephaim, xvii. 15, R. V.). They were cut off by the Israelites in the general campaign under Joshua (Josh. x. 36, 39 ; xi. 21), and particularly at Hebron, on the allotment of the land, by Judah under Caleb (xiv. 12 ; xv. 13–19 ; Judg. i. 10–15). A remnant was left in Gaza, Gath, and Ashdod, in the Philistine country (Josh. xi. 22). The giant, Goliath of Gath, was probably one of the Anakim.

An′a-mim.

An Egyptian tribe, of which nothing is known (Gen. x. 13 ; 1 Chron. i. 11).

A-nam′me-lech [god Anu is king, or Anu-king].

One of the deities worshiped by the people of Sepharvaim, a city of Babylonia (2 Kin. xvii. 31). Anu was god of the sky. When Sepharvites were brought to colonize Samaria, they burnt their children in the fire to him, worshiping Anu as Molech was worshiped.

A′nan [a cloud, or he hath covered].

One who with Nehemiah sealed the covenant to worship Jehovah (Neh. x. 26).

A-na′ni [cloudy, or covered hath (God)].

A son of Elioenai (1 Chron. iii. 24).

An-a-ni′ah [Jehovah hath covered].

1. The father of Maaseiah (Neh. iii. 23).

2. A town of Benjamin (Neh. xi. 32). Despite the difference in spelling, it is commonly identified with Beit Hanina, about three miles north of Jerusalem toward Gibeon.

An-a-ni′as [Greek form of Hananiah, Jehovah hath been gracious].

1. A disciple of Jerusalem who, with his wife Sapphira, sold a piece of land, and taking a portion of the price, laid it at the apostles' feet (Acts v. 1 seq.). The Christian community held all things common. There was none among them that lacked ; for as many as were possessors of lands or houses sold them and laid the price at the apostles' feet, and distribution was made unto each, according as any one had need. No one was under obligation to do this (ver. 4), and the end proposed did not demand that all property be sold, but forbade it. Property was sold as need required. Ananias brought part of the proceeds, and laid it at the apostles' feet ostensibly as the whole. Peter rebuked him for having lied unto the Holy Ghost, and he fell down and expired ; as did his wife Sapphira, when, coming in three hours afterwards, in ignorance of what had taken place, she repeated her husband's falsehood, and had the same doom foretold her by Peter.

2. A Christian at Damascus who was informed in a vision of Saul's conversion, and sent to restore his sight and admit him to the Christian Church by baptism (Acts ix. 10–18).

3. A high priest appointed by Herod, king of Chalcis, about A. D. 48 (Antiq. xx. 5, 2). Four years later he was sent to Rome by the governor of Syria to answer for violence done by the Jews to the Samaritans, but he was acquitted through the influence of Agrippa, and returned to Jerusalem (Antiq. xx. 6, 2 and 3 ; War ii. 12, 6 and 7). Jonathan, former high priest, was politically associated with him. In the year 58, Paul was arraigned before Ananias, and he appeared against the apostle before the procurator Felix (Acts xxiii. 2 ; xxiv. 1). Jonathan, his colleague, was now murdered, and about the year 59, toward the close of Felix's administration, Ananias himself was deposed by Agrippa (Antiq. xx. 8, 5 and 8 ; War ii. 13, 3). He appears to have resided on the southwestern hill of Jerusalem, in the upper city, near the palace of the Asmonæans. He was murdered in the year 67 (War ii. 17, 6 and 9).

A′nath [a hearkening, a granting].

Father of the judge Shamgar (Judg. iii. 31 ; v. 6).

A-nath′e-ma [anything devoted].

In the N. T., a person or thing devoted to destruction. It corresponds to the Hebrew *Herem* (Rom. ix. 3, R. V. ; 1 Cor. xii. 3, R. V. and margin of A. V. ; Gal. i. 8, 9, R. V. ; see Lev. xxvii. 28, 29 ; Josh. vi. 17 ; vii. 1, R. V.).

A-nath′e-ma Mar-an-ath′a [Greek, one devoted to destruction, and Aramaic *Maran 'atha*, the Lord cometh].

One accursed at the coming of the Lord (1 Cor. xvi. 22, A. V.). R. V. regards Maran atha as a distinct sentence.

An′a-thoth [answered prayers ; or perhaps, as the name of a town, the plural of Anath, who was a goddess (cp. Beth-anath, and the plural, Ashtaroth)].

1. Head of a father's house of Benjamin, family of Becher (1 Chron. vii. 8).

2. Head and representative of the men of Anathoth, who in their name sealed the covenant to worship Jehovah (Neh. x. 19).

3. A city in the territory of Benjamin, assigned to the priests (Josh. xxi. 18 ; 1 Chron. vi. 60). It was the home of Abiathar the high priest (1 Kin. ii. 26), and the birthplace of Jeremiah, and the prophet's life was also endangered here (Jer. i. 1 ; xi. 21). The town was repeopled after the exile (Ezra ii. 23). It was twenty stades distant from Jerusalem (Antiq. x. 7, 3). Its site is represented by the modern 'Anata, which is about 3 miles northeast of Jerusalem. It was once a fortified town. Portions of the wall still remain, built of large hewn stone, apparently ancient.

An′a-thoth-ite, in A. V. **Anethothite, Anetothite**, and **Antothite**.

A native or inhabitant of Anathoth (2 Sam. xxiii. 27 ; 1 Chron. xi. 28 ; xxvii. 12).

An'drew [manliness].

The brother of Simon Peter, of Bethsaida on the sea of Galilee (John i. 44). By vocation he was a fisherman like his brother (Mat. iv. 18; Mark i. 16-18), and with his brother had a house at Capernaum (Mark i. 29). He was a disciple of John the Baptist, but being directed by John to Jesus as the Lamb of God, he obtained an interview with Jesus and became convinced that Jesus was the Messiah. Forthwith he found his brother and induced him to visit Jesus (John i. 35-42). He was afterwards called to permanent fellowship with Jesus (Mat. iv. 18, 19; Mark i. 16, 17; cp. John vi. 8), and appointed an apostle (Mat. x. 2; Mark iii. 18; Luke vi. 14; Acts i. 13). He joined with his brother and James and John in inquiring regarding the destruction of the city and temple, and the second advent of Christ (Mark xiii. 3, 4), and with Philip he presented the request of the Greeks to Jesus (John xii. 22). Nothing trustworthy is known of his subsequent life. According to tradition, he suffered martyrdom in Achaia by crucifixion on a cross shaped like the letter **X**. This is now called St. Andrew's Cross. It is also related that a ship bearing two relics of him was wrecked in a bay of Scotland, afterwards called St. Andrew's Bay. The mariners who reached the shore introduced the gospel into the region. St. Andrew, therefore, became the patron saint of Scotland, and gave name to St. Andrew's town. His festival is kept by the Greek and Roman churches on the 30th of November. In the Church of England it has become customary on that day to preach on the subject of missions. The Acts of St. Andrew, an alleged gospel from his pen, is spurious.

An-dro-ni'cus [conquering men].

A Jewish Christian, and once fellow-prisoner of Paul, to whom at Rome Paul sent greeting (Rom. xvi. 7).

A'nem [two fountains].

A town in the territory of Issachar, given with its suburbs to the sons of Gershom (1 Chron. vi. 73). Probably a corruption of the text out of En-gannim (Josh. xxi. 29; cp. xix. 21).

A'ner.

1. An Amorite, resident at Mamre, and one of Abraham's confederates in the battle with with the eastern kings (Gen. xiv. 13, 24).

2. A town of Manasseh west of the Jordan. It was given with its suburbs to the Kohathites (1 Chron. vi. 70). In Josh. xxi. 25, R. V., Taanach appears in its stead. Either name, as it stands in the text, might easily be misread as the other.

An'e-thoth-ite or **Anetothite.** See ANATHOTHITE.

An'gel [messenger, envoy].

1. A celestial being a little higher in dignity than man (Ps. viii. 5; Heb. ii. 7). They are spiritual beings (Heb. i. 14), and they neither marry nor are given in marriage (Mat. xxii. 30). From their worship of God as well, probably, as from their nature they are called, at least in poetry, sons of God (Job i. 6; xxxviii. 7); and from their character, holy ones (Job v. 1, R. V.; Ps. lxxxix. 5, 7, R. V.). Their office is denoted by the term angel. In the later books differences among angels in rank and dignity are implied, for there are archangels (chief angels), as well as those of a more ordinary kind (1 Thess. iv. 16; Jude 9). This twofold distinction does not seem to be all. Both among fallen angels and angels unfallen there are thrones, dominions, principalities, and powers (Rom. viii. 38; Eph. i. 21; iii. 10; Col. i. 16; ii. 15). Cherubim and Seraphim seem also to belong to the angelic order. The inanimate powers of nature, by which the ordinary economy of the universe is carried on, are God's messengers (Ps. civ. 4, R. V.); but pestilence and death, when acts of the divine government, are represented as under angelic charge (2 Sam. xxiv. 16; 2 Kin. xix. 25; Zech. i. 7-17). Unseen they encamp round about them that fear God (Ps. xxxiv. 7; Gen. xxviii. 12; xlviii. 16; 2 Kin. vi. 17; Is. lxiii. 9). The angel of the Lord came in human form to Abraham, Hagar, and Lot, to Moses and Joshua, to the Israelites at Bochim, to Gideon and Manoah. An angel came to Elijah and to Daniel. Angels are fittingly prominent in the history of Jesus, announcing his birth and that of his forerunner, heralding his advent to the shepherds, ministering unto him after his victory over temptation and in the garden (Luke xxii. 43, a passage omitted in many old copies), and bearing tidings to his disciples at the resurrection and ascension. An angel also aided Peter and stood by Paul. The names of some angels or archangels are mentioned, namely, Gabriel (Dan. viii. 16; ix. 21; Luke i. 19, 26), and Michael (Dan. x. 13, 21; xii. 1; Jude 9; Rev. xii. 7). The Apocrypha adds Raphael and Uriel; see MICHAEL 11. The old Persians and the modern Parsees have recognized the existence of angels of different rank and assigned names to some of them.

While any angel sent to execute the commands of God might be called the angel of the Lord (2 Sam. xxiv. 16; 1 Kin. xix. 5, 7), yet mention is made of an angel, and under the circumstances one is justified in always thinking of the same angel, who is distinguished from Jehovah, and yet is identified with him (Gen. xvi. 10, 13; xviii. 2-4, 13, 14, 33; xxii. 11, 12, 15, 16; xxxi. 11, 13; Ex. iii. 2, 4; Josh. v. 13-15; vi. 2; Zech. i. 10-13; iii. 1, 2), who revealed the face of God (Gen. xxxii. 30), in whom was Jehovah's name (Ex. xxiii. 21), and whose presence was equivalent to Jehovah's presence (Ex. xxxii. 34; xxxiii. 14; Is. lxiii. 9). The angel of the Lord thus appears as a manifestation of Jehovah himself, one with Jehovah and yet different from him. See THEOPHANY.

2. The representative of a church; but whether this is the board of elders which directed the affairs of the local church, or the pastor, or a celestial being of the angelic order watching over the church, is by no means clear (Rev. i. 20; ii. 1, 8, 12, 18; iii. 1, 7, 14).

A'ni-am [sighing of the people].

A Manassite, family of Shemida (1 Chron. vii. 19; cp. Num. xxvi. 32).

A'nim [a contraction of "*yanim*, fountains].

A town in the hill country of Judah, mentioned immediately after Eshtemoh (Josh. xv. 50). It is apparently identical with the ruin Ghuwein, about eleven miles south of Hebron and three south of Semûa, *i. e.* Eshtemoh.

An'ise.

An umbelliferous plant (*Pimpinella anisum*) somewhat like caraway in appearance, occasionally cultivated in the East for its seeds, which are used as a seasoning and as a carminative. The English versions render the Greek word *anēthon* (Mat. xxiii. 23) in the text by anise, on the margin by dill. The latter is *Anethum graveolens* of the same order (umbelliferous) as anise, resembles anise in appearance and properties, and is more commonly grown in gardens.

An'kle Chain.

A chain binding together the two ankles of a female, so as to compel her to take short steps, and, especially when they were combined with anklets, to make a tinkling sound when she walked (Num. xxxi. 50; Is. iii. 20, both R. V.; in A. V. called simply chains and ornaments of the legs).

Ank'let.

An ornament for the ankles, consisting of metallic or glass rings, and corresponding to bracelets on the wrists. Anklets are often worn by boys as well as women in the East (Is. iii. 18, R. V.; in A. V. called tinkling ornaments about the feet): see ANKLE CHAIN.

An'na [Greek form of Hannah, grace].

A widow, daughter of Phanuel of the tribe of Asher. Her married life had lasted seven years. At the age of eighty-four she visited the temple daily, and was there when the infant Jesus was brought to be dedicated. A prophetess, she recognized and proclaimed him to be the Messiah (Luke ii. 36–38).

An'nas [a Greek form of Hananiah, Jehovah hath been gracious].

A high priest at Jerusalem, as was Caiaphas, in the year when John the Baptist began his ministry (Luke iii. 2), it is thought about A. D. 26. He is called Ananos by Josephus, which is nearer the Hebrew form of the name than is Annas. He was appointed high priest about A. D. 7 by Quirinius, governor of Syria, and was deposed by the procurator of Judæa, Valerius Gratus, about A. D. 16. Each of his five sons became high priest, and he was father-in-law of the high priest Caiaphas (Antiq. xviii. 2, 1 and 2; John xviii. 13). Although Annas was no longer officiating

high priest when Jesus was arrested, he was yet the most influential priest and still bore the title (Luke iii. 2; Acts iv. 6), and to him Jesus was first taken (John xviii. 13), and after being examined by him was sent bound to Caiaphas (24). When Peter and John were subsequently arrested, Annas was prominent among their examiners (Acts iv. 6).

A-noint'.

To pour oil upon the head, or in any other way apply it to a person, or to a thing. Among the Jews there were an ordinary, a sacred or official, and a medical or surgical anointing. The ordinary anointing was simply a matter of the toilet (2 Sam. xii. 20; Dan. x. 3; Mat. vi. 17). The anointing of the head with oil in the time of Jesus was extended, as an act of courtesy, also to guests (Luke vii. 46). The official anointing was conferred on prophets, priests, and kings. Elijah the prophet was directed to anoint Elisha, his successor (1 Kin. xix. 16). Aaron the high priest, and those who followed him in the same office, were anointed with a holy consecrating oil (Ex. xxviii. 41; xxix. 7; xxx. 30; xl. 13, 15). Saul (1 Sam. ix. 16; x. 1), David (xvi. 1, 12, 13; 2 Sam. ii. 7; iii. 39, etc.), Solomon (1 Kin. i. 34), Hazael of Syria (xix. 15), Jehu (16), Jehoash (2 Kin. xi. 12), and others, were anointed kings. Messiah and Christ mean the Anointed One. Jesus the Christ was anointed by the Spirit to be prophet, priest, and king. Of things, the altar (Ex. xxix. 36; xl. 10), and the tabernacle (xxx. 26; xl. 9), the laver, etc. (xl. 9–11), were also anointed. The medicinal or surgical anointing, not necessarily with oil, was a customary remedy applied to the sick and wounded (Is. i. 6; Luke x. 34; Rev. iii. 18). The Christian places reliance, not in the natural means in themselves, but in God who works through the means and renders them effectual (Jas. v. 14, 15).

Ant.

Any hymenopterous insect of the family *Formicidæ*. They are social insects like bees and wasps, to which they are not remotely akin. The species are numerous and widely diffused, the larger members, however, occurring in the tropics. The ant is held up as an example of industry and forethought, industriously providing food in summer and gathering grain in harvest (Prov. vi. 6–8; xxx. 24, 25). That the ants of Palestine store food on which to live in winter is not expressly asserted in Proverbs, but it is clearly stated in similar Arabic maxims. Dr. Thomson states that the ants of Palestine are great robbers of grain in harvest. Sykes in 1829 found an ant in India, at Poonah, storing grain, and called it *Atta providens*. Moggridge witnessed similar forethought exercised by certain ants in the south of Europe, and McCook by ants in Texas.

An'te-lope.

An animal, believed to be mentioned in Deut. xiv. 5 and Is. li. 20, R. V. It was captured in nets, and was ceremonially fit for food. Targum, followed by A. V., renders wild ox; probably meaning the bubale, *Antilope bubalis*, of Egypt and Arabia, classed by the Arabs with wild oxen. In the Greek versions and the Vulgate, the word is generally rendered oryx, which refers to the *Antilope leucoryx*. This animal has horns which are long, slender, conical, and with ringlike ridges round. The animal is white, with the exception of a long tuft of hair under the throat, which is black. It is a native of Sennaar, Upper Egypt, and Arabia, and is said to be found in Syria.

An-tho-thi'jah, in A. V. **Antothijah** [answers of Jehovah].

A Benjamite descended through Shashak (1 Chron. viii. 24).

An'ti-christ [Greek *antichristos*, against or instead of Christ].

The word antichrist may mean, as the etymology shows, an enemy of Christ or a usurper of Christ's name and rights. The former was probably its primary meaning, though the other idea was also attached to it. In the N. T. St. John alone uses the term (1 John ii. 18, 22; iv. 3; 2 John 7). From 1 John ii. 18, R. V., we learn that the Christians had been taught that "Antichrist" would appear in "the last hour," *i. e.* before the second advent of Christ. While not denying that Antichrist would be a single person, John lays stress on the spirit to be embodied in him, and declares that already many antichrists had come. The substance of the antichristian spirit. he says, is denial that Jesus is the Christ or the real incarnation of the Son of God, by which is meant not only denial of the doctrine, but moral antagonism to its religious implications. This opposition was already appearing in the Church in the persons of false teachers and false disciples, for Antichrist arises out of nominal Christianity itself. But while John alone uses the term, the doctrine it taught elsewhere. Jesus himself not only warned his apostles of "false Christs" (Mat. xxiv. 5, 23, 24; Mark xiii. 21, 22)—by which, however, he meant primarily Jewish Messianic pretenders—but plainly intimated that apostasy would arise within the Church (see parables of tares, ten virgins, Mat. vii. 22, 23; xxiv. 12, etc.). Paul more fully teaches (2 Thes. ii. 3-12) that before the second advent "the man of lawlessness" (R. V.) must be revealed, "who opposeth and exalteth himself above all that is called God, or that is worshiped," and "in the temple of God" (= probably the Church) claims to be God (to usurp the place of God). Paul, too, like John, represents this as the culmination of a process of apostasy (ver. 7; see, too, 1 Tim. iv. 1). Many interpreters also see in the "beast" of Rev. xiii. a further description of Antichrist. Thus the N. T. declared that Christian history would not be a pure development of goodness and truth, but that within Christendom apostasy would arise, develop, have many

representatives, and finally culminate in Antichrist proper (= either a person or an institution, perhaps both), of which the essential spirit would be antagonism to Christ and the impious claim of that allegiance from man's mind and life which is alone due to God and his Son. In different periods, various apostasies have seemed to believers to be Antichrist, and have more or less embodied the antichristian principle; but doubtless the full manifestation of Antichrist is yet to come, and will precede and be destroyed at the second advent of the Lord.   G. T. P.

An'ti-och [pertaining to Antiochus].

1. The metropolis of Syria under the Macedonian Greek dynasty (1 Mac. iii. 37 et passim), founded about 300 B. C. by Seleucus Nicator, and named by him after Antiochus, his father. It was situated on the southern side of the Orontes, about twenty miles from its mouth, the river being navigable up to the city. Mount Casius approached it closely on the south, and the Amanus mountains were not far off on the west, whilst in front lay the valley of the Orontes, five or six miles across. The city became large and numerously inhabited. It remained the capital when the Roman province of Syria was erected in 64 B. C. Its population was gentile, but also with not a few Jews (Antiq. xii. 3, 1; War vii. 3, 3). Christians who fled from Jerusalem to avoid the persecution which arose upon the martyrdom of Stephen preached the gospel here, addressing at first only Jews who spoke the Aramaic tongue, then those who spoke Greek. Barnabas was despatched from Jerusalem to aid the work. After laboring there for a while he fetched as a coadjutor Paul from Tarsus. For a whole year these two great evangelists made the city the sphere of their labors, and taught much people. The disciples were called Christians first in Antioch (Acts xi. 19-26). Further reinforcements arrived in the persons of prophets (27). From Antioch Paul and Barnabas were sent on a missionary journey (xiii. 2). On its completion they returned to the city (xiv. 26). The disciples at Antioch kept up active intercourse with the brethren at Jerusalem. In time of famine, they sent relief to them (xi. 28-30), and they submitted the question regarding the circumcision of gentile converts to a council at Jerusalem (xv.). The second missionary journey of Paul, like the first, commenced with a departure from Antioch (35, 36), to which Paul returned, this time by the way of Cæsarea (xviii. 22). At Antioch Paul withstood Peter to the face because of his vacillating conduct with regard to the gentile converts (Gal. ii. 11). The city remained great, and the Church went on to develop while the Roman empire stood. In A. D. 538 Chosroes, the Persian king, took and destroyed it. It was rebuilt by the Roman emperor Justinian. In A. D. 635 it was taken by the Saracens, from whom it passed in 1084

to the Turks. Except between 1098 and 1269, when it was the seat of a Christian kingdom founded by the crusaders, it has remained in Mohammedan hands. It has been all along very liable to earthquakes, one of which, occurring in 1822, damaged Justinian's walls. The place, still called 'Antâkia, is now unimportant.

2. A town in Asia Minor, also founded by Seleucus Nicator and named after his father,

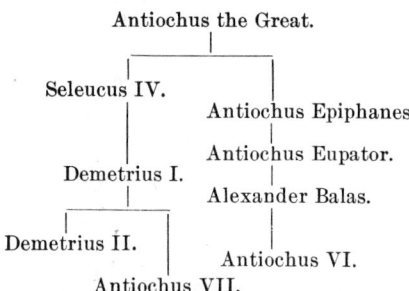

Antioch in Syria.

Antiochus. It was situated in Phrygia, near the borders of Pisidia, and was accordingly designated Antioch toward Pisidia and Pisidian Antioch to distinguish it from Antioch in Syria. It was included within the Roman province of Galatia, and was the center of the civil and military administration of the southern part of the province. Jews dwelt there, and had a synagogue (Acts xiii. 14; cp. Antiq. xii. 3, 4). Barnabas and Paul visited it on their first missionary journey (Acts xiii. 14-52; xiv. 19-21; 2 Tim. iii. 11). In 1833 Arundel identified the ruins of this Antioch near the modern town of Yalabatch.

An-ti′o-chus [withstander, endurer].

1. ANTIOCHUS III., surnamed the Great, king of Syria and sixth ruler of the Seleucidan dynasty, father of Seleucus IV. and Antiochus Epiphanes (1 Mac. i. 10; viii. 6-8). He reigned from 223 to 187 B. C. He attempted to wrest Cœlesyria, Phœnicia, and Palestine from Ptolemy IV., but was defeated at Raphia 217 B. C. After the death of Ptolemy he renewed the attempt and was successful, gaining the decisive battle of Paneas in 198. He invaded Europe, but his victorious career was terminated at Thermopylæ. On his retreat he was decisively defeated at Magnesia in Asia in 190. By the terms of peace he was obliged to send twenty hostages to Rome, including his son, and pay an enormous tribute. While plundering a temple in Susiana he was murdered by a mob. The Seleucidan line was continued as follows:

```
                  Antiochus the Great.
                           |
              ┌────────────┴────────────┐
        Seleucus IV.
              |                  Antiochus Epiphanes.
              |                           |
              |                  Antiochus Eupator.
        Demetrius I.                      |
              |                  Alexander Balas.
      ┌───────┴───┐                       |
 Demetrius II.    |            Antiochus VI.
            Antiochus VII.
```

2. ANTIOCHUS E-PIPH′A-NES, the eighth ruler of the house of Seleucidæ, 175-164 B. C. (1 Mac. i. 10; vi. 16). He passed fifteen years of his life as a hostage at Rome (1 Mac. i. 10). He was an energetic prince who extended and strengthened his kingdom, but enraged his subjects by religious intolerance. He stirred up the Jews by robbing the temple and setting up a statue of Jupiter in the holy of holies. He also pulled down the walls of Jerusalem, commanded the sacrifice of swine, forbade circumcision, and destroyed all the sacred books that could be found. It was these outrages which induced the revolt of the Maccabees (1 Mac. i. 41-53). He died between Elymais and Babylon, shortly after receiving news of the Jewish revolt (vi. 1-16).

3. ANTIOCHUS EU'PA-TOR, son of the above. As a minor he reigned two years under the regency of Lysias (1 Mac. vi. 17–63). He was slain and succeeded by Demetrius Soter.

4. ANTIOCHUS VI., the young child of the pretender Alexander Balas. He was set up as king by the general Tryphon, who used him merely as a cloak for his own ambition, and slew him as soon as he felt himself established, 142 B. C. (1 Mac. xi. 39, 40, 54 ; xiii. 31, 32).

5. ANTIOCHUS VII., brother of Demetrius II., who reigned in the stead of Demetrius during his imprisonment by Arsaces, 138–128 B. C. He defeated Tryphon (1 Mac. xv. 1, 10–14), made first a treaty with Simon Maccabæus, but afterwards repudiated his help and tried to rob the temple. His attempt was frustrated by John and Judas Maccabæus (1 Mac. xvi. 1–10).

6. A Jew known only as being the father of the councilor Numenius (1 Mac. xii. 16).

An'ti-pas [contraction of Antipater].

1. A Christian who suffered martyrdom at Pergamos, in Asia Minor (Rev. ii. 12, 13).

2. Son of Herod the Great ; see HEROD 2.

An-tip'a-ter [in place of or like the father]·

1. A Jew, son of Jason. He was a councilor, and one of two ambassadors sent by Jonathan and the elders to Rome to renew the alliance (1 Mac. xii. 16 ; Antiq. xiii. 5, 8). His father was perhaps the Jason who had formerly gone on a similar mission (viii. 17).

2. Father of Herod the Great (Antiq. xiv. 7, 3).

An-tip'a-tris [belonging to Antipater].

A town founded by Herod the Great, in the fertile plain of Caphar Saba, on the site of that village, near the mountains, and called after Antipater, his father. It was surrounded by a river (Antiq. xiii. 15, 1 ; xvi. 5, 2 ; War i. 4, 7 ; 21, 9). It lay on the Roman military road between Jerusalem and Cæsarea, forty two Roman miles from the former city and twenty-six from the latter. The old name lingers under the modern form Keîr Saba, and its site is commonly sought at this village ; but the conditions of the site are in all other respects fulfilled by Wilson and Conder's location of it at Ras el 'Aîn, at the junction of the old Roman road from Jerusalem with that from Ramleh through Lydda to Cæsarea. From the base of the mound that covers the site the river 'Aujah gushes forth a full-sized stream. It was the limit of Paul's journey the first night while he was being taken as a prisoner from Jerusalem to Cæsarea (Acts xxiii. 31). See APHEK, 2.

An-to'ni-a, Tow'er of [pertaining to Antonius].

A castle connected with the temple at Jerusalem. It presumably occupied the site of the stronghold Birah, which appertained to the temple and was restored by Nehemiah (Neh. ii. 8). John Hyrcanus built the tower, and he generally dwelt in it and kept the priestly

Model of the Fortress of Antonia.

vestments there, for he was entitled to wear them (Antiq. xv. 11, 4 ; xviii. 4, 3). Until the time of Herod the Great it was known as the Baris, but Herod repaired it at vast expense, and fortified it more firmly than before in order that it might guard the temple, and named it Antonia in honor of Marc Antony (Antiq. xviii. ; War i. 21, 1 ; v. 5, 8 ; Tacitus, Hist. v. 11). It was situated at the northwestern corner of the temple area, on a rock fifty cubits in height, the highest point in the neighborhood (War vi. 1, 5). Its presence there prevented the area from being foursquare (War vi. 5, 4). The fortress had the amplitude and form of a palace, with chambers, courts, barracks, and baths. Its walls rose forty cubits above the rock on which they rested. At the corners were turrets, three of which were fifty cubits high, while the fourth, which overlooked the temple, was seventy cubits (cp. Antiq. xx. 5, 3 ; War vi. 2, 5). It was separated by a deep trench from the hill Bezetha (War v. 4, 2), but was connected with the northern and western cloisters, at the junction of which it stood, with gates for the guards and a staircase (Acts xxi. 35 with 37 ; 40 with xxii. 24), and with the inner temple at its eastern gate by a subterranean passage (Antiq. xv. 11, 7), which seems to have existed in the Baris as built by Hyrcanus (Antiq. xiii. 11, 2). Over the temple end of this underground passage Herod erected a tower. The arrangement was intended to afford him a way of escape in case of a popular sedition. In the castle a Roman legion was stationed, which stood on guard in the cloisters, especially during the Jewish festivals, to prevent any excesses on the part of the populace (Antiq. xviii. 4, 3 ; War v. 5, 8). The castle was finally demolished by order of Titus in A. D. 70 (War vii. 1, 1 ; cp. vi. 2, 7 : 5, 4 ; 9, 1 and 4).

The most tragic event in the history of the

castle occurred during the reign of Aristobulus, son of Hyrcanus. The king lay sick in one of its chambers. His beloved brother Antigonus, returning from the war, hastened clad in armor and accompanied by his military escort to the temple to offer prayers for the recovery of the king. The act was misrepresented to Aristobulus; but he summoned his brother to his bedside, with the request that he come unarmed, and ordered soldiers to lie in the underground passage and slay him if he appeared in armor. The queen suppressed the message in part, and contrived to have Antigonus informed that the king desired to see his splendid armor. Suspecting nothing, he entered the passage clad in mail and was murdered. The deed was reported to the king, and the shock brought on a hemorrhage. A slave bore away the vessel in which the blood had been caught, but stumbled on the spot where Antigonus had been slain. The blood of the two brothers mingled on the floor. A cry of horror ran through the palace, and roused the king to inquire the cause. When he learned what had occurred he was filled with an agony of remorse and instantly expired (Antiq. xiii. 11).

Paul, when rescued from the infuriated mob who had dragged him out of the temple, was carried into this castle, and on the way was allowed to address the people from the stairs (Acts xxi. 30 seq.).

An-to-thi'jah. See ANTHOTHIJAH.

An'toth-ite. See ANATHOTHITE.

A'nub [joined together].
A man of Judah, son of Hakkoz (1 Chron. iv. 8, R. V.).

Ape.
A quadrumanous animal. The Hebrew word *Ḳoph*, which is rendered ape, is probably generic and includes apes, which are without tails, and monkeys, which possess them. In Greek *kêpos* denotes a monkey of Ethiopia. In Malabar and Sanscrit *kapi* or *kefi* signifies a monkey. There is no genuine ape either in Malabar or in any other part of India. If the animals which were brought to Palestine by the vessels that went to Ophir for gold (1 Kin. x. 22; 2 Chron. ix. 21) came from India, they were a tailed monkey, perhaps that called *Hanuman* (*Semnopithecus entellus*), which is common throughout India, and is worshiped as a god.

A-pel'les.
An approved Christian at Rome to whom Paul sent a salutation (Rom. xvi. 10).

A-phær'e-ma.
A government district which in the time of Jonathan Maccabæus was separated from Samaria, annexed to Judæa, and placed under the authority of the high priest (1 Mac. xi. 34; cp. x. 30, 38). The name is thought to be a Greek corruption of Ephraim, and to designate the most southern part of Samaria (cp. John xi. 54).

A-phar'sach-ites or **Apharsathchites.**
A tribe from beyond the Euphrates, settled by Asnapper in Samaria (Ezra iv. 9; v. 6).

A-phar'sites.
An eastern tribe, transplanted by Asnapper to Samaria (Ezra iv. 9).

A'phek [strength].
1. A city apparently north of Zidon (Josh. xiii. 4), and hence commonly identified with Afka, the ancient Aphaca, twenty-three miles northeast of Beirut. Being so far north, it is scarcely the same as Aphek, variant Aphik, which was situated within the territory of Asher, but not cleared of its Canaanite inhabitants (Josh. xix. 30; Judg. i. 31).
2. A town in the plain of Sharon (Josh. xii. 18, Greek text), at the source of the 'Aujah, at Râs el-'Ain (War ii. 19, 1). Perhaps it was here that the Philistines encamped before the first battle with Israel at Ebenezer. Shiloh was within twenty-five miles (1 Sam. iv. 1, 12). See ANTIPATRIS.
3. A town apparently between Shunem and Jezreel. The Philistines pitched at Shunem, but soon discovered that the Israelites had occupied the heights of Gilboa. From Shunem they advanced to Aphek, and thence to Jezreel, where they attacked the Israelites who had descended to the spring at Jezreel, forcing them back to their former position on Gilboa and completing the slaughter on that mountain (1 Sam. xxviii. 4; xxix. 1, 11; xxxi. 1). Probably it is the town Apku mentioned by Ashurbanipal, king of Assyria, as "on the border of Samaria," and, by implication, on the military road to Egypt. It may also be the town of Aphek to which Benhadad advanced with the intention of giving battle to Ahab, and to which he and his army retreated after his defeat, and where a wall fell and 27,000 of his soldiers were killed (1 Kin. xx. 26–30); and it may also be the town where Joash, king of Israel, should, according to prophecy, smite the Syrians till they were consumed (2 Kin. xiii. 14–19). The situation presupposed in the narratives is fully met by a town west of the Jordan in the plain of Jezreel. Still the Aphek referred to in these two passages may be the town of that name beyond Jordan, about three miles east of the sea of Galilee, on the highway between Damascus and Beth-shean, and now represented by the village of Fik.

A-phe'kah [strong place, fortification].
A town in the hill country of Judah (Josh. xv. 53); probably not the same as Aphek 2.

A-phi'ah [perhaps, refreshed, revivified].
An ancestor of king Saul (1 Sam. ix. 1).

A'phik. See APHEK 1.

Aph'rah, in R. V. Beth-le-Aphrah [dust].
A town (Mic. i. 10), site unknown.

Aph'ses. See HAPPIZZEZ.

A-poc'a-lypse [disclosure, revelation].
A name frequently given to the last book of the Bible. See REVELATION.

A-poc′ry-pha [Greek *apokrupha*, hidden things, used by ecclesiastical writers for (1) matters secret or mysterious ; (2) of unknown origin, forged, spurious ; (3) unrecognized, uncanonical].

The name generally given to the following sixteen books : 1 and 2 Esdras, Tobit, Judith, The Rest of Esther, The Wisdom of Solomon, Ecclesiasticus, Baruch, with the Epistle of Jeremiah, The Song of the Three Holy Children, The History of Susanna, Bel and the Dragon, The Prayer of Manasses, 1, 2, 3, and 4 Maccabees. Sometimes the number is limited to fourteen, 3 and 4 Maccabees being omitted.

Unlike the books of the O. T., which are in Hebrew, with the exception of a few verses in Aramaic, the apocryphal productions are in Greek, though at least Judith, Ecclesiasticus, Baruch i.-iii. 8, and 1 Maccabees were originally written in Hebrew. The Jewish church considered them uninspired, and some of their writers disclaim inspiration (Prologue to Ecclesiasticus ; 1 Mac. iv. 46 ; ix. 27 ; 2 Mac. ii. 23 ; xv. 38). They are not found in the Hebrew canon ; they are never quoted by Jesus ; and it cannot with certainty be affirmed that the apostles ever directly allude to them. The early churches permitted them to be read for edification, and recommended them to the catechumens for study, but rejected them from the canon, their decision carrying authority during the middle ages, as it does now with the various Protestant churches. Thus the Church of England in the sixth of the Thirty-nine Articles published in 1562 calls the apocryphal treatises books which "the Church doth read for example of life and instruction of manners ; but yet doth it not apply them to establish any doctrine." The Westminster Confession of 1643 declares, as a matter of creed, that "The books, commonly called Apocrypha, not being of divine inspiration, are no part of the canon of Scripture, and therefore are of no authority in the Church of God, or to be any otherwise approved or made use of than other human writings." The Council of Trent at its sitting on April 15, 1546, declared eleven of the sixteen apocryphal books to be canonical, enumerating Tobit, Judith, Wisdom, Ecclesiasticus, Baruch, and the two books of Maccabees, and adding The Rest of Esther to the canonical Esther, and incorporating the History of Susanna, the Story of the Three Holy Children, and the History of Bel and the Dragon with Daniel. The Council pronounced an anathema against anyone who ventured to differ from it in opinion. This has since regulated the belief of the Roman Catholic Church. The Apocrypha was introduced into the English version by Coverdale in 1535, and was included in king James' version, but began to be omitted as early as 1629. When inserted, it was placed between the O. T. and N. T. A controversy on the subject was carried on between the years 1821 and 1826, which resulted in the exclusion of the Apocrypha from all Bibles issued by the British and Foreign Bible Society.

1. 1 Es′DRAS. Esdras is simply the Greek form of Ezra, and the book narrates the decline and fall of the kingdom of Judah from the time of Josiah, the destruction of Jerusalem, the Babylonian captivity, the return of the exiles, and the share taken by Ezra in reorganizing the Jewish polity. In some respects it amplifies the biblical narrative, but the additions are of doubtful authority. It is followed by Josephus, A. D. 93 (cp. 1 Esdras iii. 1-iv. 44 with Antiq. xi. 3, 2-8, etc.). How much earlier than his time it existed, there is no evidence to show. Nor is its author known.

2. 2 Es′DRAS. This is in quite a different style from 1 Esdras. It is not a history, but is a religious treatise, much in the style of the Hebrew prophets. Its kernel, consisting of chapters iii.-xiv., purports to record seven revelations granted to Ezra in Babylon, several of which took the form of visions : the woman that mourned (ix. 38-x. 56), the eagle and the lion (xi. 1-xii. 39), the man that rose from the sea (xiii. 1-56). The author of these chapters is unknown ; but he was evidently a Jew, full of affection for his people (Jesus in vii. 28 is wanting in the oriental versions). Since the vision of the eagle, which is expressly based on the prophecy of Daniel (2 Esdr. xii. 11), seems to refer to the Roman empire, a date from about A. D. 88 to about A. D. 117, is generally accepted. A date later than A. D. 200 is precluded by the citation of v. 35 in Greek by Clement of Alexandria, with the preface "Esdras the prophet says." The first two and the last two chapters of 2 Esdras (i., ii., xv., xvi.) are additions. They are lacking in the oriental versions and in a majority of the best Latin manuscripts. They date from a time after the Septuagint was in circulation, for the Minor Prophets are arranged in the order of the Greek version (i. 39, 40). Chapters i. and ii. abound in reminiscences of the New Testament and justify the rejection of Israel and the substitution of the Gentiles (i. 24, 25, 35-40 ; ii. 10, 11, 34) ; and accordingly were written by a Christian, not unlikely a Christian Jew.

3. To′BIT. This is a narrative of a certain pious Naphtalite, Tobit by name, who has a son Tobias. The father loses his eyesight. The son, dispatched to obtain payment of a debt to Rages in Media, is led on by an angel to Ecbatana, where he makes a romantic marriage with a widow, who still remained a virgin, though she had been married to seven husbands, all of whom had been killed by Asmodeus, the evil spirit, on their marriage day. Tobias, however, is encouraged by the angel to become the eighth husband of the virgin-widow, and escapes death by burning the inner parts of a fish, the smoke of which puts the evil spirit to flight. Then he cures his father's blindness by anointing

the darkened eyes with the gall of the fish which had already proved so useful. Tobit is manifestly a moral tale, and not serious history. The most probable date of the publication is about 350 B. C., or from 250 to 200 B. C.

4. JU′DITH. A narrative professing to be a history of the way in which Judith, a Jewish widow, in order to deliver her people, insinuated herself into the good graces of Holofernes, an Assyrian commander in chief, then besieging Bethulia, and seizing his sword when he was asleep, cut off his head. The narrative contains misstatements, anachronisms, and geographical absurdities. It is doubtful if there is any truth in the story, which may possibly have been suggested to the author by the narrative of Jael and Sisera (Judg. iv. 17-22). The first distinct reference to the book is in an epistle of Clement of Rome, about the end of the first century A. D., but it may have existed as early as 175 to 100 B. C., say four or six hundred years after the event it professed to record. By that time to say that Nabuchodonosor, apparently Nebuchadnezzar, reigned in Nineveh, instead of Babylon (Judith i. 1), would not look so erroneous as it would to a contemporary of the great king.

5. THE REST OF THE CHAPTERS OF THE BOOK OF ES′THER, which are found neither in the Hebrew nor in the Chaldee. The canonical Esther ends with a short tenth chapter of three verses. The apocryphal production adds ten verses more, and six chapters (xi.–xvi.). In the Septuagint this supplementary matter is distributed in seven portions through the text, and does not interrupt the history. It amplifies parts of the Scripture narrative, without furnishing a new fact of value, and it often contradicts the history as contained in the Hebrew. The common opinion is that the book was the work of an Egyptian Jew, and that he wrote about the time of Ptolemy Philometor, 181-145 B. C.

6. THE WIS′DOM OF SOL′O-MON. This is an ethical treatise in commendation of wisdom and righteousness, and in denunciation of iniquity and idolatry. The passages which point out the sin and folly of image-worship recall those on the same theme in the Psalms and Isaiah (cp. Wisd. xiii. 11-19 with Ps. cxv. ; cxxxv. 15-18; and Is. xl. 19-25; xliv. 9-20). It is remarkable to what extent the author, in referring to historical incidents illustrative of his doctrine, limits himself to those recorded in the Pentateuch. He writes in the person of Solomon ; says that he was chosen by God as king of his people, and was by him directed to build a temple and an altar, the former on the model of the tabernacle. He was a man of genius and of piety, his religious character being sustained by his belief in immortality. He lived apparently between 150 and 50 B. C., and possibly between 120 and 80 B. C. Though never formally quoted or in any way referred to in

the N. T., yet occasionally both the language and the trains of thought in the N. T. somewhat resemble those in the book of Wisdom (Wisd. v. 18-20 with Eph. vi. 14-17; Wisd. vii. 26 with Heb. i. 2-6 ; and Wisd. xiv. 13-31 with Rom. i. 19-32).

7. EC-CLE-SI-AS′TI-CUS, called also the Wisdom of Jesus, the Son of Sirach. This is a comparatively long work, extending to fifty-one chapters. In chap. l. 1-21 great commendation is bestowed on Simon, the high priest, the son of Onias, probably the pontiff of that name who lived between 370 and 300 B. C. ; and the work may, therefore, have been written as early as 290 or 280 B. C. It was originally in Hebrew. The author, Jesus, son of Sirach, of Jerusalem (Ecclus. l. 27), was the grandfather or, taking the word in its wider sense, remoter ancestor of the translator. The translation was made in Egypt "in the eight-and-thirtieth year" "when Euergetes was king." The reference is either to Ptolemy III., surnamed Euergetes, who was king of Egypt from 247 to 222 B. C., or to Ptolemy Physcon, who was likewise surnamed Euergetes, and who reigned from 169 to 165 and 146 to 117 B. C. The great theme of the work is wisdom. It is a valuable ethical treatise, in places reminding one of the books of Proverbs, Ecclesiastes, and parts of Job, in the canonical Scriptures, and of the Wisdom of Solomon in the Apocrypha. It is generally quoted as Ecclus., to distinguish it from Ecc.—that is, Ecclesiastes.

8. BA′RUCH, with the Epistle of Jeremiah. Baruch was Jeremiah's friend. The first five chapters are made nominally to emanate from Baruch, while the sixth is headed "The Epistle of Jeremiah." After an introduction describing the origin of the work (Baruch i. 1-14), the book of Baruch falls naturally into three divisions : 1. Israel's confession of sin and prayer for forgiveness and restoration to favor (i. 15-iii. 8). This part bears evidence of having been written originally in Hebrew. The use to be made of it, according to the introduction (i. 14), also suggests that the language was Hebrew. It is generally dated fully three centuries before Christ. 2. Exhortation to return to the fountain of wisdom (iii. 9-iv. 4), and 3. Encouragement and promise of deliverance (iv. 5-v. 9). These two latter sections, from the quality of the Greek, are believed to have been written in that language. They show, too, resemblances to the Septuagint. It is disputed whether the similarity between chap. v. and Psalm of Solomon ix. indicates that the chapter was based upon the psalm, and hence written after A. D. 70 ; or that both writings rest independently on the Septuagint. The Epistle of Jeremiah warns the Jews in exile against Babylonian idolatry. Perhaps it was written about 100 B. C.

9. THE SONG OF THE THREE HO′LY CHIL′- DREN was designed to fit into the canonical Daniel between iii. 23 and 24. Its author and

exact date are unknown. (Cp. verses 35–68 with Ps. cxlviii.)

10. THE HISTORY OF SU-SAN′NA. This is also an apocryphal addition to Daniel, showing how the prophet sagaciously discovered an accusation against Susanna, a godly woman, to be a malignant slander. Its author and date are unknown.

11. THE IDOL BEL AND THE DRAG′ON. Yet another apocryphal addition to the canonical book of Daniel. The prophet proves that the priests of Bel and their families ate the food offered to the idol ; and he kills a dragon, for which, a second time, he is put into a lions′ den. Author and date unknown.

12. THE PRAYER OF MA-NAS′SES, king of Judah, when he was holden captive in Babylon (cp. 2 Chron. xxxiii. 12, 13). Author unknown ; date probably the first century B. C.

13. THE FIRST BOOK OF THE MAC′CA-BEES. A historical work of great value, giving an account of the Jewish war of independence, under the Maccabee family of Levites in the second century B. C. ; see ANTIOCHUS 2 and MACCABEE. Its author, whose name is unknown, was evidently a Jew belonging to Palestine. Two opinions exist as to its date : the one places it between 120 and 106 B. C., the other, on better grounds, between 105 and 64 B. C. It was doubtless translated into Greek from a Hebrew original.

14. THE SECOND BOOK OF THE MAC′CA-BEES is professedly an abridgment of the large work of Jason of Cyrene. It is concerned chiefly with Jewish history from the reign of Seleucus IV., 175 B. C., to the death of Nicanor in 161 B. C. It is much less valuable than the first book, and the author has a love of the marvelous which diminishes the credibility of his narrations, though they contain a good deal of truth. The book was written after 125 B. C., and before the destruction of Jerusalem in A. D. 70.

15. THE THIRD BOOK OF THE MAC′CA-BEES refers to events before the war of independence. The leading incident is the attempt of Ptolemy IV. Philopator in 217 B. C. to penetrate into the holy of holies, and his subsequent persecution of the Jews in Alexandria. It was written shortly before or shortly after the beginning of the Christian era. It has even been dated as late as A. D. 39 or 40.

16. THE FOURTH BOOK OF THE MAC′CA-BEES is a moral treatise advocating the mastery of the passions, and illustrating its teaching by examples of constancy under suffering, drawn from Maccabæan times. It was written after 2 Maccabees and before the destruction of Jerusalem.

Ap-ol-lo′ni-a [pertaining to Apollo, the youthful god of music, song, soothsaying, archery, etc.].

A town of Macedonia, on the Egnatian Way, thirty Roman miles west of Amphipolis.

Paul passed through it as he journeyed to Thessalonica (Acts xvii. 1).

Ap-ol-lo′ni-us [pertaining to Apollo.]

1. An official under Antiochus Epiphanes, who was sent to Judæa to collect tribute, and who treacherously ordered a massacre at Jerusalem (1 Mac. i. 29–32 ; 2 Mac. v. 24–26 ; cp. iv. 21). He became governor of Samaria (Antiq. xii. 5, 5). He was defeated and slain by Judas Maccabæus (1 Mac. iii. 10 ; Antiq. xii. 7, 1).

2. Governor of Cœlesyria, whom Demetrius II. made general of his army. He was defeated in battle by Jonathan Maccabæus at Ashdod (1 Mac. x. 69–85). Less credibly, Josephus speaks of him as on the side of Alexander Balas (Antiq. xiii. 4, 3 and 4).

A-pol′los [a modification of Apollonius or Apollodorus].

A Jew born at Alexandria, eloquent and learned, and deeply versed in the O. T. Scriptures. He became a disciple of John the Baptist, and zealously taught concerning the Messiah, though knowing only the baptism of repentance. While itinerating in Asia Minor for this purpose, he met at Ephesus, Aquila and Priscilla, who instructed him more fully ; and the brethren wrote letters of introduction for him to the brethren in Achaia. On arriving in Greece, he helped the Christians, publicly confuting the Jews, and showing from the Scriptures that Jesus is the Christ (Acts xviii. 24–28). The disciples with whom Paul soon afterwards fell in at Ephesus, who knew only John's baptism, and had never heard that there was a Holy Ghost, were probably converts of Apollos (xix. 1–7). Apollos' preaching at Corinth raised a party in the church at that place (1 Cor. i. 12 ; iii. 4, 5, 6, 22 ; iv. 6). But Paul had all confidence in him, and urged him to revisit Corinth (xvi. 12). He also enjoined Titus to help Apollos, apparently then in or on his way to Crete (Titus iii. 13). It is thought by many scholars that Apollos was the writer of the Epistle to the Hebrews.

A-pol′ly-on [destroying, a destroyer].

The angel of the abyss (Rev. ix. 11). The Greek synonym of Abaddon.

A-pos′tle [one sent forth, a messenger, an ambassador (John xiii. 16, R. V. margin)].

1. One of the men selected by Jesus to be eye-witnesses of the events of his life, to see him after his resurrection, and to testify to mankind concerning him (Mat. x. 2–42 ; Acts i. 21, 22 ; 1 Cor. ix. 1). They were chosen in succession at a very early period of the Saviour's public life. First came Andrew and his brother Simon, the well-known Simon Peter (Mat. iv. 18–20 ; x. 2 ; Mark i. 16–18 ; Luke vi. 14 ; John i. 35–42) ; then apparently James and John, sons of Zebedee (Mat. iv. 21, 22 ; x. 2 ; Mark i. 19, 20 ; Luke vi. 14) ; then seemingly Philip and Nathanael, named also Bartholomew (John i. 43–51) ; and sub-

sequently six more, viz., Matthew, called also Levi (Mat. ix. 9–13; Mark ii. 14–17; Luke v. 27–32); Thomas; James the son of Alphæus; Simon the Zealot or Cananæan; Judas, the brother of James; and Judas Iscariot (Mat. x. 1–4; Mark iii. 16–19; Luke vi. 13–16; Acts i. 13, all R. V.). The apostles were regarded as illiterate men by the higher Jewish dignitaries who had before them Peter and John (Acts iv. 13). All they seem to have meant was that the apostles had received elementary rather than higher education. Jesus gave great attention to their spiritual training: yet to the last they failed to understand his mission, believing that he was about to set up a temporal rather than a spiritual kingdom (Mat. xx. 20–28; Mark x. 35–45; Acts i. 6); they slept in the hour of his agony in the garden (Mat. xxvi. 40), and held aloof all the day of his death on the cross (Mat. xxvi. 56; Mark xiv. 50). They were often called disciples or pupils (Mat. xi. 1; xiv. 26; xx. 17; John xx. 2). Peter, James the son of Zebedee, and John, seem to have possessed a clearer comprehension of the teacher's instructions and a higher appreciation of him than the others. On three different occasions they were singled out from the rest for special privilege. They were in the room at the raising from the dead of Jairus' daughter (Mark v. 37; Luke viii. 51); they were present at the transfiguration (Mat. xvii. 1; Mark ix. 2; Luke ix. 28), and were in the garden of Gethsemane during the agony (Mat. xxvi. 37; Mark xiv. 33). Peter, though rash and impetuous in speech, was constitutionally the best fitted to lead. He is generally mentioned first, but not always (Gal. ii. 9). John was the disciple whom Jesus peculiarly loved (John xix. 26; xx. 2; xxi. 7, 20). Thomas was scrupulous as to evidence, but yielded when the proof he sought was complete. Judas proved a traitor, who, betraying his divine Lord to death for lucre's sake, and then repenting, committed suicide. The step taken to fill his place showed that the number of the apostles, fixed originally at twelve, required, for a time at least, to be kept at that figure; the reason probably was that there might be as many apostles as there were tribes of Israel. Two men possessing the necessary qualifications were put forward, the one Joseph, called Barsabas and Justus, and the other Matthias. The lot fell upon Matthias, who was consequently elected in Judas' room (Acts i. 15–26; cp. with ver. 20, Ps. cix. 8). The descent of the Holy Spirit on the day of Pentecost produced a spiritual transformation of the apostles, fitting them for the great work to which they were called, the evangelization of the world (Acts ii. 1–47). To this they at once addressed themselves, Peter and John taking the lead (iii. 1–v. 42; ix. 32–xii. 18). James was also zealous, for he became so obnoxious to the Jewish authorities that they slew him with the sword (Acts xii. 2). Paul

was divinely chosen and called for the arduous work of preaching the gospel to the gentiles (Acts ix. 1–31; xxii. 5–16; xxvi. 1–20). He had not itinerated with Jesus whilst our Lord was on the earth; but he possessed the apostolic qualification of having seen Jesus after his resurrection. On the way to Damascus Jesus appeared to him and spoke to him, changing his hostility into passionate devotion. He was able to say "Am I not an apostle? Have I not seen Jesus Christ our Lord?" (1 Cor. ix. 1). Paul was a highly educated man, and able to address cultured audiences of the gentiles at Athens, Rome, and elsewhere. Nor did his intellectual acquirements lead him away from his proper work. His labors were so abundant that the record of them fills about half the book called The Acts of the Apostles. Where the several apostles labored, how they lived, and how they died, is in most cases known only by the doubtful evidence of tradition. One matter, however, and an all-important one, is placed by tradition on a secure foundation, namely, that no second Judas appeared among them; all were faithful to the end; and some at least, if not even the majority, sealed their testimony to Jesus with their blood.

2. The word is occasionally applied in a less restricted sense in the N. T. to men of apostolic gifts, graces, labors, and successes. It is so notably of Barnabas, who was sent forth with Paul (Acts xiii. 3; xiv. 4, 14). Similarly one still meets with such expressions, as Judson the Apostle of Burmah. The name is applied also to Jesus, in Heb. iii. 1.

Ap'pa-im [the nostrils].
A man of Judah, family of Hezron, house of Jerahmeel (1 Chron. ii. 30, 31).

Ap'phi-a.
A Christian woman, probably the wife of Philemon (Philemon 2).

Ap'pi-i Fo'rum [market place of Appius].
A town in Italy, about forty-three Roman, or thirty-nine and a half English, miles from Rome, on the celebrated Appian Way from Rome to Capua. Its ruins exist near Triponti. Paul was met at this town by Christians from Rome, when he was being brought a prisoner to the capital (Acts xxviii. 15).

Ap'ple.
A tree and its fruit (Song ii. 3; viii. 5; Prov. xxv. 11), the rendering of the Hebrew *Tappuaḥ*. *Tappuaḥ* seems akin to the Arabic *tuffâḥ*, meaning an apple, and the one referred to in the O. T. is probably our English apple tree *Pyrus malus*, which Thomson found growing splendidly at Askelon in the Philistine country. The name may have included the quince as well. Tristram believes that the apricot is meant. The apple tree is enumerated with the vine, the fig tree, the pomegranate, and the palm tree, as one of the chief trees cultivated (Joel i. 12). There were

several towns called Tappuah—in the low
land (Josh. xv. 34), near Hebron (53), and
on the border of Ephraim and Manasseh
(xvii. 8), where doubtless many apple trees
grew.

The apple of the eye is the eyeball or
pupil (Deut. xxxii. 10; Ps. xvii. 8; Lam.
ii. 18; Zech. ii. 8). For apple of Sodom, see
VINE.

Aq'ui-la [eagle].

A Jew, born in Pontus, who with his wife,
Priscilla, lived for a time at Rome, but had
to leave that city when the emperor Claudius
commanded all its Jewish inhabitants to depart. He removed to Corinth, where he
worked at his craft, tentmaking. Paul, who
was of the same occupation, lodged with him
at Corinth, and formed a high opinion of him
and his wife (Acts xviii. 1–3). They were
his fellow-passengers from Corinth as far as
Ephesus, on his way to Syria (Acts xviii. 18,
19). In the First Epistle to the Corinthians,
the two join Paul in sending salutations from
Asia, i. e. probably from Ephesus (1 Cor. xvi.
19). At Ephesus they met Apollos, and instructed him more completely in Christian
doctrine (Acts xviii. 26). Afterwards they
seem to have returned to Rome, for Paul sends
them salutations in his letter to that church
(Rom. xvi. 3). But they must again have
left it, for in the apostle's second Epistle to
Timothy, written from Rome, salutations are
sent them anew (2 Tim. iv. 19).

Ar [city].

One of the chief cities of Moab, more fully
called Ar of Moab (Isa. xv. 1). It lay on the
northern boundary of Moab (Num. xxi. 15;
Deut. ii. 18), in the midst of the Arnon valley
(Num. xxii. 36; Deut. ii. 36; Josh. xiii. 9).

The Greeks connected the name with Ares,
the god of war, the Roman Mars, and called
it after him Areopolis, city of Mars. The
Jews and others in the early Christian centuries named it Rabbath Moab, or simply
Rabbah, i. e. capital, of Moab. It was destroyed by earthquake, probably in A. D. 342,
and the name Areopolis was transferred to
another Rabbah, about ten miles south on
the plateau.

A'ra.

A man of Asher (1 Chron. vii. 38).

A'rab [ambuscade].

A village in the hill country of Judah
(Josh. xv. 52). Cp. ARBITE.

Ar'a-bah [arid region, desert].

1. The geographical name of that great depression of the land in which are found the
sea of Galilee, the Jordan, and the Dead Sea
(Josh. xi. 2; xii. 3, R. V.). The name apparently belonged also to the extension of the
valley to the Red Sea (Deut. ii. 8, R. V.). In
A. V. the word is translated, being generally
rendered by plain, but also by wilderness or
desert (Amos vi. 14; Ezek. xlvii. 8).

2. The same as Beth-arabah (Josh. xviii. 22).

A-ra'bi-a [Greek form of Arabic 'arab,
arid region].

In modern geography the most westerly of
the three great peninsulas in Southern Asia.
It is bounded on the east by the Persian Gulf

Arab housewife returning from market.

and the Gulf of Oman, on the south by the
Indian Ocean, and on the west by the Red
Sea. Northward it projects triangularly and
passes insensibly into the Syrian desert. Its
length from north to south is about 1500
miles; its average breadth from east to west,
about 800; its area about 1,139,000 square
miles. It consists mainly of an elevated
table-land called Nejd, highest along the west
and south near the coast, and sloping on the
north toward the Syrian desert. It is separated from the coast by a low-lying sandy
region, the western portion of which is called
Hejaz, the southwestern and southern Yemen,
and the eastern, Oman, Hejr, and Bahrein.
Arabia lies athwart the enormous belt of
desert, commencing near the Atlantic Ocean
with the Sahara, and extending through
Chinese Tartary, almost to the Pacific Ocean.
Arabia is consequently largely desert. Among
the Hebrews the name Arabian denoted the
inhabitants of the desert portion (Jer. iii. 2),
whether near Babylonia or Ethiopia (Is. xiii.
20; 2 Chron. xxi. 16), often as distinguished
from the prominent settled tribes (Jer. xxv.
24; Ezek. xxvii. 21). Eventually Arabia
came to denote the entire peninsula (Acts ii.
11; Gal. i. 17; iv. 25; cp. 2 Chron. ix. 14).
Ptolemy, the geographer of Alexandria who
wrote in the second century A. D., divided
the country into three regions: Arabia Felix,
the Happy or Fertile; Arabia Petræa, the
Stony; and Arabia Deserta, the Desert. Arabia Felix was of indefinite extent. Arabia
Petræa, having for its capital Petra, was the

district between the Red and the Dead Seas; and Arabia Deserta the projecting angle on the northern boundary, sometimes called the Syrian desert. The streams are few and small, none navigable. The geology is little

The Minæan kingdom was ultimately superseded by the Sabæan, the scriptural kingdom of Sheba. Arab tribes often came into contact with the Hebrews (Gen. xxxvii. 28, 36; Judg. vi.–viii.). Solomon bought from the Arabs gold, silver, and spices (2 Chron. ix. 14). Jehoshaphat received tribute from them in flocks of sheep and goats (xvii. 11). In the reign of Jehoram, Arabs with other marauders plundered Jerusalem (xxi. 16). They were after-

Arab shepherds tending their sheep.

known, but gold and precious stones were obtained. The feature of the botany is the prevalence of aromatic plants, some of them furnishing valuable spices. Of its birds the most noted is the ostrich; of its quadrupeds the camel, the Arab horse, and the wild ass. The country was settled by Semites (Gen. x. 26–29; xxv. 2–4; 13–15), as physiognomy, traits, and language evidence; in part also by Hamites (Gen. x. 6, 7). As early as the time of the sojourn of the Israelites in Egypt, there existed in southern Arabia a civilized power, the Minæan kingdom, with its capital at Ma'in, about thirty miles to the north of Mariaba. The names of thirty-three Minæan kings have been recovered. Even the Minæans used the familiar Semitic alphabet.

wards defeated by Uzziah (xxvi. 7). Isaiah and Jeremiah denounced judgments against their race (Is. xxi. 13–17; Jer. xxv. 24), and both used the wandering Arab in their poetic illustrations (Is. xiii. 20; Jer. iii. 2). Arabs were hired allies of the Syrians against Judas Maccabæus (1 Mac. v. 39). There were Arabs present on the day of Pentecost (Acts ii. 11), and Paul sojourned for a time in Arabia, before commencing his apostolic work (Gal. i. 17). The scantiness of water, the courage of the Arabs, and their wandering life, prevented even the greatest of the ancient empires from conquering Arabia and holding it in subjection. Both Judaism and Christianity had rooted themselves in Arabia when, in the seventh century of the Christian era, Mohammed arose. Before his death (A. D. 632) his faith was everywhere dominant throughout the peninsula, and in a century more the Saracens, issuing thence, had put in danger the civilization and faith of the whole Christian world.

A-ra′bi-an.
One of the Arab race ; a native or inhabitant of Arabia (2 Chron. xvii. 11).

A′rad [wild ass].
1. A town on the border of the south country and the wilderness of Judah (Num. xxi. 1 ; Josh. xii. 14 ; Judg. i. 16). The site is marked by Tell 'Arad, on a barren-looking eminence sixteen miles south of Hebron. Its king fought against the Israelites when they were at mount Hor and took some of them captive ; but the Israelites roused themselves to new trust in God, and devastated the territory of the king, and eventually he himself or his successor was vanquished by Joshua (ibid.).
2. A Benjamite, descended through Beriah (1 Chron. viii. 15).

Ar′a-dus. See ARVAD.

A′rah [wayfarer].
1. Founder of a family, members of which returned from Babylon with Zerubbabel (Ezra ii. 5 ; Neh. vii. 10).
2. An Asherite, a son of Ulla (1 Chron. vii. 39).

A′ram.
1. A person, or collectively a people, descended from Shem, who inhabited the region known as Aram (Gen. x. 22, 23 ; 1 Chron. i. 17).
2. The plain occupied by the Aramæans, extending from the Lebanon mountains to beyond the Euphrates, and from the river Sagur on the north to Damascus and beyond on the south. The prophet Amos speaks of the Aramæans as dwelling from Damascus to Beth-eden ; in other words, from Lebanon on the southwest to mount Masius on the northeast (i. 5). Several districts were distinguished :
(1) A′RAM-NA-HA-RA′IM, *i. e.* Aram of the two rivers, referring either to the Euphrates and Tigris, or, more probably, to the Euphrates and Chabur. It is commonly believed that in this region Paddan-aram was situated, Paddan being identified with the place near Haran called Tell Faddan (Gen. xxviii. 5 and xxiv. 10, 47, R. V.). This is the Aram where the patriarchs dwelt before they went to Canaan, where the ancient cities of Haran and Nisibis stood, where later Edessa the noted seat of Syrian culture arose ; the Aram which the Hebrews speak of as "beyond the river" (2 Sam. x. 16).
(2) A′RAM-DA-MAS′CUS. The Hebrews during almost, if not quite, the entire period of their kingdom, found Aramæans in Damascus (2 Sam. viii. 5, R. V. margin ; 1 Kin. xv. 18). The city became eventually the center of Aramæan influence west of the Euphrates,

and waged intermittent warfare with the northern Israelites during their entire existence as a separate kingdom.
(3) A′RAM-ZO′BAH. In the days of Saul, David, and Solomon, another powerful Aramæan kingdom flourished west of the Euphrates, namely the kingdom of Zobah (1 Sam. xiv. 47 ; 2 Sam. viii. 3 ; cp. 2 Chron. viii. 3), called Aram-zobah by Hebrew writers (2 Sam. x. 6). At one time its dominion extended as far as the borders of Hamath on the northwest (1 Chron. xviii. 3 ; 2 Sam. viii. 10) ; had Damascus to the south or southwest, for one of its towns, Berothai, was situated between Hamath and Damascus (2 Sam. viii. 5 and 8 with Ezek. xlvii. 16), and during this prosperous period probably exercised sway well toward the Euphrates on the east and the Hauran on the south.
(4) A′RAM-MA′A-CAH lay east of the Jordan within the contemplated bounds of Israel, hard by mount Hermon (Josh. xii. 5 ; xiii. 11). From the description of Abel, which belonged to the tribe of Naphtali, as "Abel [in the neighborhood] of Beth-maacah," it may be inferred that Maacah extended as far west as the Jordan.
(5) GE′SHUR in Aram was a small kingdom not far from Maacah, and like it east of the Jordan, near mount Hermon, and within the territory allotted to Manasseh (Deut. iii. 14 ; 2 Sam. xv. 8, R. V. margin, with xiii. 37).
(6) A′RAM-BETH-RE′HOB (2 Sam. x. 6). The location is uncertain. If identical with the place mentioned in Num. xiii. 21 and Judg. xviii. 28, it was near both Maacah and Dan.
3. A descendant of Asher (1 Chron. vii. 34).
4. A Greek form of Ram, the father of Amminadab (Mat. i. 3 ; Luke iii. 33 ; and R. V. margin). See ARNI.

Ar-a-ma′ic or the **Ar-a-mæ′an** or **Aramean Language.**
A Semitic language spoken in Aram. It was written with the same alphabet as the Hebrew, and differs from this language chiefly in the system of vocalization and in the structure of a few grammatical forms. Before the inscriptions revealed that the Babylonian vernacular was Assyrian, Aramaic was incorrectly called Chaldee, a term not yet obsolete. Aramaic was used by Laban (Gen. xxxi. 47, R. V. margin) ; it is seen in the proper names Tabrimmon, Hazael (1 Kin. xv. 18, R. V. ; xix. 15), and Mari'; it is found in inscriptions as early as the time of Shalmaneser and Sargon, showing that it was used by traders at Nineveh ; it became the international language of business and diplomacy (2 Kin. xviii. 26, R. V. margin) ; it was used by Jeremiah to state an address to idols (x. 11, R. V. margin), and by Daniel and Ezra for certain portions of their books ; it was adopted by the Jews who returned from Babylonia, and in the time of Christ was spoken by large numbers of the Jews colloquially (see HEBREW), and also by neighbor-

ing nations. The Hebrew Scriptures were translated into it; the Targum of Onkelos, a pupil of Gamaliel, comprising the Law and the Prophets, was the first work of the kind and a fine version. Syriac is a dialect which developed out of the Aramaic.

A'ram-beth-re'hob. See ARAM 2 (6).

A'ram-i'tess.
A woman of Aram (1 Chron. vii. 14).

A'ram-ma'a-cah. See ARAM 2 (4).

A'ram-na-ha-ra'im. See ARAM 2 (1).

A'ram-zo'bah. See ARAM 2 (3).

A'ran [wild goat].
A descendant of Dishan or offshoot of that Horite tribe (Gen. xxxvi. 28; 1 Chron. i. 42).

Ar'a-rat.
A mountainous country north of Assyria, centering about the elevated plateau of the Araxes. In the time of Jeremiah it was the seat of a kingdom apparently adjacent to

the boundary line between Russia and Turkey. It has two peaks, one higher than the other. The loftier one rises 17,260 feet above the level of the ocean, more than 10,000 feet above the table-land on which it stands, and 3000 above the line of perpetual snow. The ascent is so difficult and laborious that the Turks call Ararat Aghri Dagh, or the Painful Mountain. Its summit was long deemed inaccessible, but it was at length reached by Parrot in 1829, and in 1850 by Col. Khoelzko and his party of sixty, while they were engaged on the trigonometrical survey of Trans-Caucasia.

A-ra'thes, in A. V. **Ariarathes.**
King of Cappadocia from 162 to 131 B. C., surnamed Philopator (1 Mac. xv. 22).

A'ra-rite.
So R. V., following the present Hebrew text, once in 2 Sam. xxiii. 33, where A. V. has Hararite as in the corresponding passage, 1 Chron. xi. 35.

A-rau'nah.
A Jebusite who possessed a threshing floor on mount Moriah. David purchased the floor in order to erect there an altar to Jehovah that the plague then raging might be stayed (2 Sam. xxiv. 18–25; 1 Chron. xxi. 15–28). The place afterwards became the site of Solomon's temple (2 Chron. iii. 1). Araunah is called Ornan in Chronicles, Urnah or Ornah in the Hebrew text of 2 Sam. xxiv. 16, and yet differently in ver. 18. It is difficult to determine which was the original form of the name. Araunah has the most foreign look.

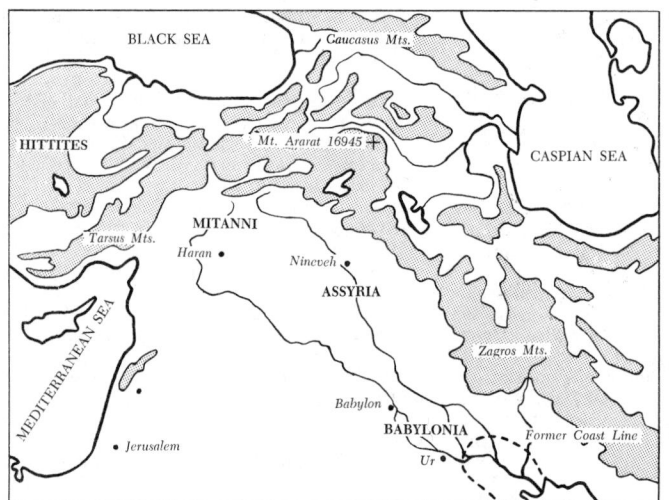
Probable location of Mt. Ararat.

those of Minni and Ashkenaz (Jer. li. 27). When the sons of Sennacherib killed their father they escaped into the land of Ararat, which the A. V. happily identifies with Armenia (2 Kin. xix. 37; Is. xxxvii. 38). On one of the mountains of Ararat, it is not stated which, the ark of Noah rested (Gen. viii. 4). The Assyrian cuneiform account of the flood implies a mountain near the country of Urtu, northeast of Babylonia. Perhaps the name Ararat (Urarṭu) and Urṭu have been confounded. Traditions with respect to the resting place of the ark attach themselves to various mountains in western Asia; but by mount Ararat is now meant a noble mountain almost midway between the Black Sea and the Caspian, and not far from

Ar'ba, in A. V. once **Arbah** [four, or, perhaps, the croucher (with article, Gen. xxxv. 27)].
Father or greatest man of Anak (Josh. xiv. 15; xv. 13). He founded, or gave name to, Kirjath-arba, the city later known as Hebron, or else he derived his title from the town (Josh. xiv. 15; Judg. i. 10). See HEBRON.

Ar'bath-ite.
An inhabitant of Beth-arabah (2 Sam. xxiii. 31; 1 Chron. xi. 32).

Ar-bat'ta, in A. V. **Arbattis.**
A locality near Galilee (1 Mac. v. 23). The readings of the name vary greatly in the manuscripts, and it is uncertain what place is meant.

Ar-be′la.

A place (1 Mac. ix. 2); according to Josephus, the well-known town of the name in Galilee (Antiq. xii. 11, 1), now Irbid. See BETH-ARBEL.

Ar′bite.

A native of Arab, in the hill country of Judah (2 Sam. xxiii. 35, possibly a variant reading of 1 Chron. xi. 37).

Ar-che-la′us [leading the people, a chief].

The elder one of two sons whom a Samaritan wife bore to Herod the Great, the younger one being Antipas, afterwards Herod the Tetrarch (Antiq. xvii. 1, 3). With his brother Antipas and his half-brothers Herod and Philip, he received his education at Rome. While there Antipater, a half-brother of his, falsely accused him and Philip of plotting to murder their common father; but Archelaus and Philip were acquitted, and the crime which the accuser had alleged against others being brought home to himself, he was put to death (Antiq. xvi. 4, 3; xvii. 7, 1; War, i. 31, 2 ;o 32, 7). Herod died immediately afterwards, 4 B. C.; and when his will, which had been altered a few days previously, was opened, it was found that the greater part of the kingdom was left to Archelaus, though tetrarchies had been cut out of it for Antipas and Philip, and some cities reserved to Herod's sister Salome (Antiq. xvii. 8, 1). But at that time the Jewish kingdom stood to imperial Rome in the relation of a protected state. Archelaus therefore prudently abstained from ascending the throne till he had solicited permission from Augustus, the Roman emperor, and he resolved to start at once for the metropolis to urge his suit in person (8, 4). But before he could leave, an unhappy incident occurred. A number of people, who conceived that they had a grievance, wished it redressed by strong measures then and there. Their demand was clearly premature, but they would take no denial; and when they could not have their way, they rioted at the passover, till, sorely against his will, for he wished to gain popularity, Archelaus had to put down the sedition by military force, 3000 people losing their lives. In consequence of this, a deputation of Jews was dispatched to Rome, to urge the emperor not to allow Archelaus to obtain the kingdom. His younger brother, Herod Antipas, also appeared as his rival, petitioning that he, in place of Archelaus, might be made king. The emperor confirmed Herod's will in its essential provisions. Archelaus obtained the larger portion of the kingdom, but only with the title of ethnarch or ruler of a people, which was inferior to that of king (Antiq. xvii. 8, 1; 9, 7; 11, 5). His rival Antipas was given only a tetrarchy. Soon after this, Joseph and Mary returned with the infant Jesus from Egypt. They might consider that the queller of the passover riot was not a man over-tender of human life, and that it was only common

prudence for them to turn aside to Galilee so as to keep out of his jurisdiction (Mat. ii. 22). A parable of our Lord himself seems to refer to the circumstances attending the accession of Archelaus. "A certain nobleman," we read, "went into a far country to receive for himself a kingdom, and to return" (Luke xix. 12). "But his citizens hated him, and sent a message after him, saying, We will not have this man to reign over us" (14). If the reference is really to Archelaus, then another verse may be history rather than parable. "But those mine enemies, which would not that I should reign over them, bring hither, and slay them before me" (27). Quite in keeping with this view, Josephus says that Archelaus used not only the Jews but the Samaritans barbarously, out of resentment for their old quarrels with him. Both nationalities, therefore, sent embassies to Rome to complain of his cruelty. They succeeded in their object. In the ninth year of his government, about A. D. 6, he was deposed, and banished to Vienne, in Gaul, while his wealth was put into the emperor's treasury (War ii. 7, 3).

Ar′che-vites.

Babylonians, inhabitants of Erech. A body of them were settled by Asnapper in Samaria after the ten tribes had been carried captive (Ezra iv. 9).

Ar′chi. See ARCHITE.

Ar-chip′pus [master of the horse].

A Christian at Colosse who approved himself as a champion of the gospel, was intimate with Philemon, and an office-bearer in the church (Col. iv. 17; Philem. 2).

Ar′chite, in A. V. once **Archi,** the Hebrew form.

A member of a Canaanite tribe of the same name, or else a native or inhabitant of a village known as Erech. The border of the Archites was on the boundary between Ephraim and Benjamin, west of Bethel, where the fountain 'Arîk and the wady 'Arîk are found (Josh. xvi. 2). Hushai, David's faithful counselor, was an Archite (2 Sam. xv. 32).

Arc-tu′rus [the Bear-ward].

A large and bright star, which the Greeks and Romans called by this name, meaning the keeper of the Bear, because in its course through the heavens it always kept behind the tail of Ursa Major, or the Great Bear. In the A. V. of Job. ix. 9 and xxxviii. 32 it is the translation of the Hebrew 'Ash or 'Ayish. But 'Ash is not Arcturus, which looks very solitary in the sky, while the 'Ayish of Job (xxxviii. 32) has sons or bright stars near it in the heavens. It is not the Bear-keeper but probably the Bear itself, and is so rendered in the R. V. The Arabs call it Na'sh, a bier. There are in it seven bright stars. The four constituting the irregular diamond seem to the Arabs to resemble a bier carrying a corpse, while the three stars constituting the Bear's tail appear to them to be the children of the deceased person, walking behind the bier to the place of interment.

Ard.

A son of Bela and grandson of Benjamin (Gen. xlvi. 21 ; Num. xxvi. 38 and 41 with 40). He gave name to a family of the tribe of Benjamin (ibid.). The person called Addar in 1 Chron. viii. 3 is probably he. The variation in form is probably due to a copyist's transposition of two letters very similar in Hebrew, or to his confusion of Hebrew d and r. The latter error is especially frequent, and is quite intelligible ; see under DALETH.

Ar'don.

A man of Judah, family of Hezron, house of Caleb (1 Chron. ii. 18).

A-re'li.

A son of Gad, and founder of a family (Gen. xlvi. 16 ; Num. xxvi. 17).

Ar-e-op'a-gite.

A judge of the court of Areopagus (Acts xvii. 34).

Ar-e-op'a-gus [hill of Ares].

1. One of the lower hills on the west of the acropolis of Athens. It was consecrated to Ares, the god of war. It is a narrow, naked ridge of limestone rock, running from northwest to southeast, and terminating abruptly over against the acropolis, or citadel of Athens. This southeastern end was crowned by several altars ; and rises 50 or 60 feet above the valley separating it from the acropolis, which is much the higher of the two hills. Ares corresponding to the Roman Mars, Areopagus is the same as Mars' hill.

2. The supreme court of Athens, which met on the hill called Areopagus to pass sentence. It was constituted of venerable and eminent citizens. The seats of the judges and others connected with the court are still seen hewn in the rock ; and toward the southwest there is a flight of steps descending to the market place. It was before the Areopagus that Paul pleaded his own cause and that of Christianity, and the philosophic character of his discourse arose from his vivid consciousness that he was addressing some of the most intellectual men in the most intellectual city in the world.

During judicial trial the court sat in its official chamber on the market place, and adjourned to the hill to pass formal sentence. It has been argued that Paul made his defence in the chamber of justice and not on the hill, before the Areopagus and not on the Areopagus (Curtius). Recent studies of Aristotle, however, lead to the conclusion that cases of heresy were not subject to the jurisdiction of this court (Manatt), and the narrative in The Acts militates against the supposition that Paul's discourse was a formal defence in a trial before the court (Conybeare and Howson). It appears, therefore, that Paul addressed an informal gathering of

philosophers on the Areopagus (Acts xvii. 16 seq.).

Ar'e-tas [Greek form of ḥareṭhaṭh].

More than one king of Arabia Petræa, during the time that it was occupied by the Nabatæan Arabs, bore this name. Among others,

1. A contemporary of the high priest Jason, about 170 B. C. (2 Mac. v. 8).

2. Father-in-law of Herod the Tetrarch. When Herod prepared to divorce his daughter in order to marry Herodias, Aretas declared war against Herod and totally defeated his army in A. D. 36. The Romans took Herod's part, and Vitellius was dispatched to chastise Aretas, but the death of the emperor Tiberius put an end to the expedition (Antiq. xviii. 5, 1–3). It was about A. D. 39 or 40, during the reign of Caligula, or perhaps in 36, that Aretas for a brief period held Damascus (2 Cor. xi. 32).

A-re'us. See ARIUS.

Ar'gob [a heap of stones or clods].

1. A region of Bashan, included within the dominions of Og, and marching on Geshur and Maacah. It contained sixty fenced cities, besides the nomad encampments taken by Jair (Deut. iii. 4, 13, 14 ; Josh. xiii. 30 ; 1 Kin. iv. 13) ; see HAVVOTH-JAIR. The Targum indicates the district of Trachonitis, but this region lies too far to the east. Josephus identifies a portion of it with Gaulonitis (Antiq. viii. 2, 3 with 1 Kin. iv. 13). It probably corresponded in part to the region between the eastern slope of northern mount Gilead and the Lejjah.

2. A man assassinated along with Pekahiah, king of Israel, by Pekah, who aspired to the throne (2 Kin. xv. 25).

A'ri-a-ra'thes. See ARATHES.

A-ri'dai.

A son of Haman (Esth. ix. 9).

A-rid'a-tha.

A son of Haman (Esth. ix. 8).

A-ri'eh [lion].

A man assassinated along with king Pekahiah, Argob, and others, by Pekah, the son of Remaliah (2 Kin. xv. 25).

A'ri-el [lion of God].

1. A Moabite (2 Sam. xxiii. 20, R. V.).

2. A name of Jerusalem, symbolical of the strength it possesses through God (Is. xxix. 1, 2, 7). A slightly different form would signify the hearth of an altar.

3. A chief of the Jews who were with Ezra at the river Ahava (Ezra viii. 16).

Ar-i-ma-thæ'a [Latin and Greek modification of Ramah, height].

The town from which the councilor Joseph came, who obtained permission of Pilate to take away the body of Jesus and give it honorable interment in his own new sepulcher (Mat. xxvii. 57–60; Mark xv. 43 ; Luke xxiii. 51–53; John xix. 38). Arimathæa is the Greek form of Ramah, but which town of that name is intended is uncertain. Ramleh near Lydda is out of the question; for it was not built until the beginning of the eighth century A. D. The name occurs in 1 Mac. xi. 34 (cp. Antiq. xiii. 4, 9) as belonging at that period to Samaria.

A'ri-och [servant of the moon-god].

1. King of Ellasar, who was confederate with Chedorlaomer on his invasion of the Jordan valley (Gen. xiv. 1, 9). A king of Larsa called Eriaku, son of Kudurmabug, ascended the throne about 2166 B. C. Larsa, probably Ellasar, his capital, is now represented by the mounds of Senkereh, a little to the southeast of Erech.

2. Captain of the king's guard at Babylon under Nebuchadnezzar (Dan. ii. 14, 15). It pertained to the office to execute sentences of death (24).

A-ri'sai.

A son of Haman (Esth. ix. 9).

Ar-is-tár'chus [best ruling].

A Macedonian of Thessalonica who was with Paul at Ephesus, and in the riot was seized by the mob and probably dragged into the theater; but he seems not to have been seriously injured (Acts xix. 29). On the apostle's return from Greece, whither he had gone from Ephesus, Aristarchus accompanied him from Troas to Asia (Acts xx. 4, 6). He was subsequently his fellow-voyager to Rome (xxvii. 2; cp. Philem. 24), as also at one time his fellow-prisoner (Col. iv. 10).

Ar-is-to-bu'lus [best advising].

1. A celebrated Jewish philosopher at Alexandria (2 Mac. i. 10).

2. A Christian, to whose household at Rome Paul sent salutations (Rom. xvi. 10).

A-ri'us, in A. V. **Areus.**

King of Sparta (1 Mac. xii. 20; Antiq. xiii. 5, 8), probably the first of the name, who reigned from 309 to 265 B. C.

Ark.

A chest, box, or vessel of similar shape.

1. Noah's ark was the rude vessel which Noah was divinely ordered to construct, and in which he floated about when the deluge was on the earth. If the cubit, in terms of which the dimensions of the ark are stated, was the ordinary cubit of 18 inches, then the length of the ark was 450 feet, the breadth 75 feet, and the height 43 feet. The *Great Eastern* steamship was 674 feet long, 77 feet broad, 58 feet deep, and had a gross tonnage of 22,500 tons. The ark was made of gopher, probably cypress, wood, and rendered watertight by being daubed inside and outside with bitumen. It had lower, second, and third stories. A door in the side afforded ingress and egress. A window, probably a cubit in height, extended, with slight interruptions, all around the vessel. A rooflike covering protected the inmates from rain and sun (Gen. vi. 14–viii. 19; Mat. xxiv. 38; Luke xvii. 27; Heb. xi. 7; 1 Pet. iii. 20). The ark was designed for the accommodation of Noah, his family, and the animals which were selected to be preserved.

Dr. Howard Osgood, in *The Sunday School Times* for Feb. 6, 1892, discusses the question whether every species of animals, as they are now classified by naturalists, could have found accommodation in the ark. The highest estimate of the number of species of land mammalia is 290 above the size of the sheep, 757 from the sheep to the rats, and 1359 of the rats, bats, and shrews. The average size is about that of the common cat. Allowing five square feet of deck room as amply sufficient for a cat, two of each species of mammalia could find room on two-thirds of one deck of the ark, with its 33,750 square feet of surface. The representatives of 10,000 species of birds, 979 of reptiles, 1252 of lizards, and 100,000 of insects could easily be placed on the remaining third of the deck, leaving the other two decks for storing food.

2. The infant Moses' ark, made for his reception when he was exposed upon the Nile, was a basket composed of papyrus leaves or stems, or both, plaited together, and rendered watertight by a coat of bitumen (Ex. ii. 3–6).

3. The Ark of the Covenant or Testimony was the central object of the tabernacle. It was a chest 2½ cubits long, 1½ cubits broad, and the same in depth; made of acacia wood, and overlaid within and without with pure gold. A rim or moulding of gold encircled it at the top. At the bottom were two golden rings on each side, through which poles of acacia wood overlaid with gold were put for the purpose of carrying the ark about. It was covered by a lid of solid gold which was called the mercy seat. Two cherubim of gold stood on this cover, of one piece with it, one at each end, spreading their wings on high so as to overshadow it, and facing each other, but looking down toward the mercy seat. They were symbols of the presence and unapproachableness of Jehovah who, as King of Israel in the midst of his people, dwelt between the cherubim, uttered his voice from between them, and met the representative of his people there (Ex. xxv. 10 seq.; xxx. 6; Num. vii. 89; 1 Sam. iv. 4). It was made specially as a receptacle for the Testimony, on the tables of stone (Ex. xxv. 21; xxxi. 18; Deut. x. 3, 5), and it was placed in the holy of holies (Ex. xxvi. 34). Afterwards a pot of manna, Aaron's rod that blossomed, and the book of the law were put beside the ark (Ex. xvi. 34; Num. xvii. 10; Deut. xxxi. 26; Heb. ix. 4), but were removed during the times of confusion (1 Kin. viii. 9). The ark was placed in charge of the Kohathite Levites (Num. iii. 29–31; iv. 4–15). The priests, who were Levites and of the family of Kohath, bore it themselves on occasions of special solemnity (Josh. iii. 3; vi. 6; viii. 33; 2 Sam. xv. 24, 29; 1 Kin. viii. 3). It went before the Israelites when they left mount

Sinai (Num. x. 33); either in the van or, as
the expression may denote, like a king in
the midst of his troops, leading and directing the march, while the priests who accompanied it signaled the orders of Jehovah
(x. 5, 6, 8; and for the phraseology Ex. xxxii.
1; Deut. iii. 28; x. 11; xxxi. 3ᵇ). It went
in advance of the people into the Jordan and
halted, where the stream ceased to flow, until
the tribes had done crossing to the other side
(Josh. iv. 9–11). It was carried in the midst
of the host for seven days round Jericho before the walls of the city fell down (vi. 1–20).
From Gilgal by Jericho it was removed to
Shiloh (1 Sam. iii. 3). Having been taken in
Eli's time to the field of battle, as a talisman
which was expected to work wonders in the
contest with the Philistines, it was captured
by the enemy (1 Sam. iv. 1–22), but was soon
afterwards sent back into the Hebrew territory (v. 1–vi. 11). It was successively at
Beth-shemesh, where the inhabitants looked

Bas relief of the Ark of the Covenant found in
ruins of an ancient synagogue in Capernaum.

into it and were punished (vi. 12–20; see
BETH-SHEMESH); at Kirjath-jearim (vii. 1,
2); and at Perez-uzzah, where Uzzah was
struck dead for touching it (2 Sam. vi. 1–11;
1 Chron. xiii. 1–14; cp. Num. iv. 15, 19, 20).
Thence it was taken by David to Jerusalem
(2 Sam. vi. 12–23), being now borne by men
(13) who, if the custom in Israel before and
during the reign of David was followed, were
priests or priests assisted by other Levites
(Josh. iii. 3, 13; iv. 9; vi. 4, 6; 2 Sam. xv.
24, 25, 29), as the Chronicler states (1 Chron.
xv. 1–15). At Jerusalem it was put in a temporary tabernacle erected for it by David
(2 Sam. vi. 17; vii. 1, 2; 1 Chron. xvi. 1, 4–6,
37–43). Later it was placed in the holy of
holies in Solomon's temple (1 Kin. viii. 1–9).
Josiah refers to it (2 Chron. xxxv. 3), but the
meaning is obscure. It disappeared when
Jerusalem was destroyed by Nebuchadnezzar, and has not been reported since.
Sacred chests were in use among other

peoples of antiquity. They were employed
by the Greeks and Egyptians, and served as
receptacles for the idol, or for symbols of the
deities, or for other sacred objects.

Ark'ite.

A tribe descended from Canaan (Gen. x.
17; 1 Chron. i. 15). According to Josephus
they founded the Phœnician city Arke, the
modern 'Arka, about twelve miles north of
Tripoli, in Syria (Antiq. i. 6, 2). This town
is mentioned as Arkatu by Thothmes III.
about 1600 years before Christ.

Ar-ma-ged'don, in R. V. Har-Magedon
[mountain of Megiddo].

A prophetic battlefield where the kings of
the whole world gather together unto the
war of the great day of God (Rev. xvi. 16).
The name is framed with evident reference
to the sanguinary contests which took place
near the town of Megiddo; the first, that in
which Sisera and the Canaanites were defeated at the waters of Megiddo (Judg. v. 19),
the second, that which resulted in the death
of Ahaziah, king of Judah, at Megiddo (2
Kin. ix. 27), and the third, that in which king
Josiah was killed when in conflict with the
army of Pharaoh-necho (2 Kin. xxiii. 29;
Zech. xii. 11). The historical associations
with Megiddo in the past were seized upon
by the prophet to supply a speaking name
appropriate in a description of the future
sorrows and triumphs of God's people.

Ar-me'ni-a. See ARARAT.

Arm'let.

An ornament like a bracelet, but surrounding the arm higher up than the wrist (Ex.
xxxv. 22, R. V.). There were armlets among
the spoil of the Midianites (Num. xxxi. 50,
R. V.). In parts of the East an armlet, generally studded with jewels, is worn by kings
as one of the insignia of royal authority (cp.
2 Sam. i. 10).

Ar-mo'ni [pertaining to the palace].

One of Saul's sons by his concubine Rizpah.
He was slain by the Gibeonites to satisfy justice (2 Sam. xxi. 8–11).

Ar'mor.

Covering worn to protect the person against
offensive weapons (Eph. vi. 11). It consisted
of—1. The shield. Shields were used by all
nations of antiquity. The Israelites employed a larger and a smaller kind (1 Kin.
x. 16, 17). The larger kind, translated shield,
buckler, target, belonged to the heavy armed
spearmen and lancers (1 Chron. xii. 8, 24, 34;
2 Chron. xiv. 8). The smaller shield, rendered shield or buckler, was carried by archers
(1 Chron. v. 18; 2 Chron. xiv. 8). Shields
were of various shapes—round, oval, and oblong. They were commonly made of several
thicknesses of leather or of wood covered
with leather (cp. Ezek. xxxix. 9), which was
oiled to keep it glossy and pliable, and to protect it against the wet (Is. xxi. 5). They were
sometimes covered with brass (Antiq. xiii.

12, 5), or made entirely of brass (1 Kin. xiv. 27, probably), or even of beaten gold (1 Kin. x. 17; 2 Chron. ix. 16; 1 Mac. vi. 2, 39). Bronze shields were often two or three feet in diameter. Sometimes a shieldbearer accompanied a warrior into battle (1 Sam. xvii. 7). 2. Helmets were made of leather and eventually of iron and brass (1 Mac. vi. 35). They were known to Egyptians, Philistines, Assyrians, Babylonians, Persians (1 Sam. xvii. 5; Jer. xlvi. 4; Ezek. xxiii. 23, 24; xxvii. 10). Helmets of brass were in occasional use among the Israelites and Philistines as early as the time of Saul (1 Sam. xvii. 5, 38). Uzziah armed his troops with helmets and coats of mail (2 Chron. xxvi. 14). 3. The breastplate or properly coat of mail, as it is sometimes rendered, covered the breast, back, and shoulders. It was made of leather, quilted cloth, linen (Herod. iii. 47), brass, or iron (1 Sam. xvii. 5; Rev. ix. 9), and even gold (1 Mac. vi. 2). There were joints in it or between it and the adjacent armor (1 Kin. xxii. 34). Scale-armor coats were worn by Goliath, and chain coats by the soldiers of Antiochus Eupator (1 Sam. xvii. 5, Hebrew; 1 Mac. vi. 35, Greek). 4. Greaves, consisting of thin plates of metal, were occasionally worn to protect the front of the leg below the knee (1 Sam. xvii. 6); and sometimes, 5. Laced boots set with nails (Is. ix. 5, R. V. margin). For offensive weapons, see the several articles.

Ar'my.

The army of Israel consisted originally of infantry only (Num. xi. 21; 1 Sam. iv. 10; xv. 4), composed of spearmen, slingers, and archers. It included all the able-bodied men of the nation—all the males from 20 years old and upward, able to go forth to war, being enrolled for service (Num. i.; 2 Sam. xxiv. 9). The Levites were not numbered in the wilderness for military service; but they might bear arms, if the occasion arose (Num. i. 48–50; 1 Chron. xii. 26–28 with 23). The number of men reported as participating in various battles is sufficiently large to include the greater part of the adult male population of the region. For military operations of no great magnitude, each tribe furnished its quota of warriors (Num. xxxi. 4; Josh. vii. 3; Judg. xx. 10); but inroads of the enemy were naturally met by all the manly spirits seizing their weapons to defend their firesides. In time of national peril messengers were sent throughout all the coasts of Israel to summon the men of war by the sound of the trumpet, by proclamation, or by symbolic act, to come to the rescue (Judg. vi. 34, 35; xix. 29; 1 Sam. xi. 7).

The militia of Israel was organized on the basis of the political divisions. The military and political units alike were the thousand, a term apparently interchangeable with father's house (Ex. xii. 37; Num. i. 2, 3, 16, 46;

Judg. vi. 15; 1 Sam. x. 19, 21; xvii. 18). A chieftain of Judah was accordingly often an *'alluph* or chiliarch (Zech. ix. 7; xii. 5), as were the chiefs of Edom (Gen. xxxvi.; Ex. xv. 15). For both political and military purposes the thousands were divided into hundreds (Ex. xviii. 25; Num. xxxi. 14, 48; 2 Sam. xviii. 1; 2 Chron. xxv. 5), and fifties (Ex. xviii. 25; 1 Sam. viii. 12; 2 Kin. i. 9; cp. Num. i. 25), and tens (Ex. xviii. 25; cp. Num. xxvi. 7). The actual number composing a father's house or thousand necessarily varied constantly, according to natural law; and it is probable that the "thousand" was usually very much smaller than the technical name indicates (cp. the varying numbers in legion and regiment). Each of these divisions was under its own officer (Num. xxxi. 14; Judg. xx. 10; 1 Sam. viii. 12; 2 Kin. i. 9; xi. 4; 2 Chron. xxv. 5). The commander-in-chief and the officers formed a council of war (1 Chron. xiii. 1; cp. 2 Kin. ix. 5, 13).

The first traces of a standing army in Israel are found in the reign of Saul. He retained three thousand men of all Israel to hold the Philistines in check (1 Sam. xiii. 2), and impressed any men of marked valor whom he saw (xiv. 52). David increased the army, and organized it into twelve divisions of twenty-four thousand footmen each (1 Chron. xxvii.), and Solomon added a large force of chariots and horsemen, which he distributed in the cities throughout his kingdom (1 Kin. ix. 19; x. 26; cp. iv. 26; 2 Chron. ix. 25). The successors of these three kings of all Israel continued to bestow attention on the organization and equipment of the host, as Jehoshaphat (2 Chron. xvii. 13–19), Amaziah (xxv. 5, 6), Uzziah (xxvi. 11–15), Judas Maccabæus (1 Mac. iii. 55). See WAR.

Ar'nan [agile].

Founder of a family, presumably of the lineage of David (1 Chron. iii. 21).

Ar'ni.

Ram, the father of Amminadab (Luke iii. 33, R. V.; cp. Ruth iv. 19). The Hebrew name Ram generally appears in the Greek translation of the Old Testament as APPAN or APAM; and APNEI, which is found in important texts of Luke, may be a mere corruption.

Ar'non [murmuring, noisy; or, perhaps, quickly moving].

A river which anciently formed the boundary between the Amorite country on the north and that of the Moabites on the south (Num. xxi. 13, 26), and at a later period between the tribe of Reuben on the north and again Moab on the south (Deut. iii. 8, 16; Josh. xiii. 16). It had fords (Is. xvi. 2). Its valley is the deep chasm of the Wady Môjib. The stream is perennial, formed by the junction of three smaller tributaries, and falls into the Dead Sea. It is fringed by oleanders, the vegetation of its banks is exuberant, and its waters are full of fish.

A'rod or **Ar'o-di.**

A son of Gad, and founder of a family (Gen. xlvi. 16; Num. xxvi. 17).

Ar'o-er [naked, nakedness; or juniper thicket].

1. A town on the right or northern bank of the river Arnon. It was the southern point of the. Amorite kingdom ruled by Sihon (Deut. ii. 36; Josh. xii. 2; Judg. xi. 26), and afterwards of the tribe of Reuben (Josh. xiii. 16); but it was fortified and occupied by Gadites (Num. xxxii. 34). It was taken by Mesha, king of Moab (Moabite Stone, 26). It fell into the hands of Hazael, king of Syria (2 Kin. x. 33; 1 Chron. v. 8). In the time of Jeremiah it belonged to Moab (Jer. xlviii. 19). It is now called 'Ara'ir, and is a desolate heap just south of Dibon and a little east of the Roman road which runs north and south through Moab.

2. A city in Gilead on the frontier of Gad; before, that is east of, Rabbah, doubtless Rabbath Ammon (Josh. xiii. 25; and perhaps Judg. xi. 33). Site unknown.

3. A village of Judah, to which David sent spoil after his victory over the Amalekites who had pillaged Ziklag (1 Sam. xxx. 28). Its ruins lie in the wady 'Ar'ara, twelve miles southeast of Beer-sheba.

If Aroer in Is. xvii. 2 is a proper name, and not a common noun meaning nakedness, ruin, the phrase in which it stands may be rendered "the cities of Aroer," and interpreted as the suburbs of the Gadite Aroer; or "the cities Aroer," the two Aroers east of the Jordan being used representatively for all the cities of the region.

Ar'o-er-ite.

A native or inhabitant of Aroer (1 Chron. xi. 44, where the reference is probably to Aroer 3).

Ar-pach'shad, in A. V. **Arphaxad** [etymology unknown; the latter part of the name, if separable, is contained in Chaldea].

A son of Shem (Gen. x. 22, 24; 1 Chron. i. 17, 18, both R. V.). He was a remote ancestor of Abraham, was born two years after the flood, at the age of 35 begat Shelah, and died 403 years afterwards, at the age of 438 (xi. 10-13, R. V.). Arpachshad is not necessarily a person. The structure of these genealogical registers, apparent at a glance, is such that the name may be that of a tribe or land, of which the people were descended from that son of Shem born two years after the flood. Arpachshad was long identified with the mountainous country on the upper Zab north and northeast of Nineveh, called by the Greek geographers Arrapachitis, and by the Assyrians Arabcha. But this identification fails to account for the final syllable, shad.

Ar'pad, in A. V. twice **Arphad.**

A city, generally coupled in the O. T. with Hamath, from which, consequently, it was not far distant (2 Kin. xviii. 34; xix. 13; Is.

x. 9; Jer. xlix. 23). It has been placed at Tell Erfâd, 13 miles north of Aleppo. It was a place of importance, and was subjected to repeated visitations from the Assyrians. It saw the army of Rammannirari in 806 B. C., and of Ashurnirari in 754; it was besieged and taken by Tiglath-pileser 742-740; and an uprising of cities which included Arpad was suppressed by Sargon in 720.

Ar-phax'ad. See ARPACHSHAD.

Ar'sa-ces.

King of Persia and Media (1 Mac. xiv. 2, 3; xv. 22), from 174 to 136 B. C. He was the sixth of the name, but is better known as Mithridates I. of Parthia. His rule extended far beyond the bounds of Media and Persia. He conquered Asia from the Hindu Kush to the Euphrates and raised the Parthian kingdom to an empire.

Ar-tax-erx'es [possessor of an exalted kingdom].

The third son of Xerxes and his successor on the Persian throne, 465 B. C. He is called Longimanus, the Longhanded. This epithet is generally interpreted literally, but Dr. John Wilson considers that it is figurative, and means only that Artaxerxes had a widely-extended dominion. He was led to forbid building at Jerusalem (Ezra iv. 7), but afterwards permitted it (vi. 14). The older interpreters understood the king referred to to be the Pseudo-Smerdis, i. e. a Magian impostor called Gomates, who pretended to be Smerdis, brother of the deceased Cambyses, and reigned as such for seven months in the year 521 B. C., until the fraud was discovered and he was put to death. But see remarks under AHASUERUS. In the seventh year of his reign (458 B. C.) Artaxerxes allowed Ezra to lead a great multitude of exiles back to Jerusalem (Ezra vii. 1, 11, 12, 21; viii. 1). In the twentieth year of his reign (445 B. C.) he permitted Nehemiah to make his first journey to the Jewish capital, and rebuild the walls of the city (Neh. ii. 1, etc.). In the thirty-second year of his reign (433-432 B. C.) he allowed Nehemiah, who had returned for a little to Persia, to revisit Jerusalem, and become governor of the restored city and the adjacent country (xiii. 6). Artaxerxes died in the year 425 B. C.

Ar'te-mas [gift of Artemis].

A companion whom Paul thought of sending on an errand to Titus (Tit. iii. 12).

Ar'te-mis.

The Greek goddess of hunting, corresponding to the Roman Diana (Acts xix. 24, R. V., margin); see DIANA.

A-rub'both, in A. V. **Ar'u-both** [the lattices].

A place mentioned in connection with Socoh and Hepher; hence probably in the southwest of Judah (1 Kin. iv. 10).

A-ru'mah [perhaps, a height].

A village near Shechem, once the residence

of Abimelech (Judg. ix. 41). It has been supposed to be identical with Rumah (2 Kin. xxiii. 36), and has been placed doubtfully at el-'Ormeh, 6 miles southeast of Shechem, which, however, is spelled with a different initial letter.

Ar'vad [wandering].

A place which, in Ezekiel's time, furnished mariners and valiant defenders of the stronghold of Tyre (Ezek. xxvii. 8, 11). It is the island of Aradus near the coast of Phœnicia, now called er-Ruad (1 Mac. xv. 23).

Ar'vad-ite.

One of the inhabitants of Arvad. They were reckoned to Canaan (Gen. x. 18 ; 1 Chron. i. 16).

Ar'za [delight].

The steward of king Elah's house in Tirzah (1 Kin. xvi. 9).

A'sa [physician].

1. A Levite, son of Elkanah who lived in a village of the Netophathites (1 Chron. ix. 16).

2. A king of Judah who ascended the throne in the twentieth year of Jeroboam, king of Israel. He was son of Abijam and grandson of Rehoboam. His mother (really his grandmother) was Maacah, daughter of Absalom (1 Kin. xv. 9–10, cp. 2). His reign began with ten years of peace (2 Chron. xiv. 1). He took away the male prostitutes out of the land, abolished the idols of his predecessors, and removed his grandmother from her position of queen-mother, because she had made an image for an Asherah (1 Kin. xv. 9–13 ; cp. xiv. 22–24 ; 2 Chron. xiv. 1–5 ; xv. 16). He also destroyed the strange altars, the high places, and the sun images throughout Judah (2 Chron. xiv. 3–5) as fully as he was able (cp. 1 Kin. xxii. 46 ; 2 Chron. xix. 4) ; but, though his own heart, the people still occasionally sacrificed to Jehovah on high places (1 Kin. xv. 14 ; 2 Chron. xv. 17). His kingdom was invaded by the Ethiopian Zerah, at the head of an enormous host of Africans, but by the help of Jehovah he defeated them, and drove them from the land (2 Chron. xiv. 9-15). In the fifteenth year of his reign, encouraged by the prophet Azariah, he completed the religious reformation, restored the altar of burnt offering at the temple, and induced the people to renew the covenant with Jehovah (xv. 1–15). In the thirty-sixth [sixteenth] year of his reign (see CHRONOLOGY), Baasha, king of Israel, invaded Benjamin and fortified Ramah on the main road from Jerusalem to the north. Asa, finding himself too weak to capture Ramah and reopen the road, took the temple treasures, and hired Ben-hadad, king of Damascus, to attack Baasha. Ben-hadad invaded the northern portion of the Israelite kingdom, compelling Baasha to withdraw from Ramah. Asa took the building materials which Baasha had gathered at Ramah and fortified Geba and

Mizpah. The prophet Hanani reproved the king for his worldly policy, after his experience of God's help at the time of the Ethiopian invasion. Asa resented the interference of the prophet, putting him in prison (1 Kin. xv. 16–22 ; 2 Chron. xvi. 1–10). In the thirty-ninth year of his reign he became diseased in his feet. In his distress he sought help from the physicians, but not from the Lord (1 Kin. xv. 23 ; 2 Chron. xvi. 12). In his latter days he was not so true to Jehovah as in his earlier life. He died in the forty-first year of his reign, and was buried with royal honors in a sepulcher which he had made for himself in the city of David.

As'a-hel [God hath made].

1. Son of David's sister Zeruiah, and brother of Joab and Abishai (1 Chron. ii. 16) ; noted for valor and fleetness (2 Sam. ii. 18 ; xxiii. 24). He was in the army of David ; and in the rout of Ishbosheth's troops at Gibeon, he pursued Abner, their commander, in the desire to kill him. Abner, after vainly warning him to desist, in self-defence gave him a mortal thrust (ii. 12–23). His death occurred before David became king of all Israel ; yet when David organized the army in twelve divisions, the fourth was assigned to Asahel and Zebadiah his son after him (1 Chron. xxvii. 7). The form of the statement is peculiar. It may denote that the command of the division for the fourth month was vested in the house of Asahel, being exercised by his son who was now the head of the house. Perhaps the new organization perpetuated an earlier arrangement, only on a larger scale.

2. One of the Levites employed by Jehoshaphat to teach the people the law (2 Chron. xvii. 8).

3. An overseer of the temple in the reign of Hezekiah (2 Chron. xxxi. 13).

4. Father of a certain Jonathan (Ezra x. 15).

A-sa'iah, in A. V. twice **As-a-hi'ah** (2 Kin. xxii. 12, 14) [Jehovah hath made].

1. A Simeonite prince (1 Chron. iv. 36).

2. A Levite, head of the family of Merari in David's time (1 Chron. vi. 30 ; xv. 6, 11).

3. A man of Judah, son of Baruch, and head of the family of Shelah at the time of the return from the captivity (1 Chron. ix. 5). He was known also by the synonymous name Maaseiah (Neh. xi. 5).

4. An officer whom Josiah sent with others to the prophetess Huldah to inquire of the Lord about the things which he had heard from the Law found by Hilkiah (2 Kin. xxii. 12, 14 ; 2 Chron. xxxiv. 20).

A'saph [collector ; or He hath gathered or removed reproach].

1. A Levite, the son of Berachiah, of the Gershomite family (1 Chron. vi. 39, 43). With Heman and Ethan, he sounded cymbals before the ark during its removal from the house of Obed-edom to the city of David (xv. 16-19). He was then assigned the per-

manent office of sounding cymbals at the service (xvi. 4, 5, 7); and when the service was finally and fully arranged, of the three families permanently charged with the music and song and instructed in the art, his family, with him at the head, was one (xxv. 1–9). Their position was on the right (vi. 39). The family often receives mention (2 Chron. xx. 14; xxix. 13). A hundred and twenty-eight, all of them singers, came back from Babylon (Ezra ii. 41; Neh. vii. 44), and conducted the psalmody when the foundations of Zerubbabel's temple were laid (Ezra iii. 10). Twelve psalms, viz. the 50th and the 73d to the 83d, both inclusive, are attributed in the titles to the family of Asaph (cp. 2 Chron. xxix. 30). The 50th belongs to the second book of psalms; the others constitute the bulk of the third book. In them the usual name of the deity is God, rather than Jehovah. Asaph, like the other chief singers, is called a seer (2 Chron. xxix. 30; cp. xxxv. 15 and 1 Chron. xxv. 5).

2. Father of Hezekiah's recorder (2 Kin. xviii. 18).

3. Keeper of the king's park in Palestine under Artaxerxes Longimanus, king of Persia (Neh. ii. 8).

4. In 1 Chron. xxvi. 1 read Ebiasaph (cp. ix. 19).

A-sar′a-mel, in A. V. **Saramel.**
Perhaps a title of Simon Maccabæus, *Sar ′am ′el*, prince of the people of God; or more probably, since the word is preceded by a preposition, it stands for *ḥᵃṣar ′am ′el,* the court of the people of God, the forecourt of the temple (1 Mac. xiv. 28).
The suggestion has also been made that "in Asaramel" represents the Hebrew sentence: There was no prince of the people of God. The historian states that there was no civil governor at the side of the high priest.

As′a-rel, in A. V. **A-sar′e-el** [God hath bound].
A son of Jehaleleel (1 Chron. iv. 16).

As-a-re′lah. See ASHARELAH.

As′ca-lon (1 Mac. x. 86). See ASHKELON.

As′e-nath [Egyptian *Snat,* belonging to the goddess Neith].
Daughter of Poti-phera, priest of On, wife of Joseph and mother of Manasseh and Ephraim (Gen. xli. 45, 50–52; xlvi. 20).

A′ser. See ASHER.

Ash.
The rendering in the A. V. of the Hebrew *′Oren* in Is. xliv. 14. The wood of the tree was suitable for use in making idols. A tree which the Arabs call *′arân* is said by one of their writers to grow in Arabia Petræa, and is described as having thorns and producing bunches of bitter berries. This imperfect description recalls the mountain ash, and the name *′arân* may be connected with *′oren.* But by *′oren* the Seventy understood the fir tree. Jerome renders it pine. R. V. accordingly

translates the word by fir tree, and places ash on the margin. The Syrian fir (*Pinus halepensis*) is perhaps intended, which flourishes on the mountains of Palestine, and is occasionally found as far south as Hebron. See FIR.

A′shan [smoke].
A town in the lowland, allotted to Judah, afterwards transferred to Simeon and assigned with its suburbs to the Levites (Josh. xv. 42; xix. 7; 1 Chron. iv. 32; vi. 59). In the present text of Josh. xxi. 16 or 1 Chron. vi. 59 Ashan and Ain have become confounded through the misreading of one letter. Ashan is apparently identical with Cor-ashan, in A. V. Chor-ashan, smoking furnace (1 Sam. xxx. 30), where many manuscripts and versions have Bor-ashan, smoking pit.

Ash-a-re′lah, in A. V. **Asarelah** [upright toward God].
A son of Asaph (1 Chron. xxv. 2). Called in ver. 14 Jesharelah, a word having the same meaning.

Ash′be-a [let me call as witness].
A descendant of Shelah, of the tribe of Judah. The members of the family wrought fine linen (1 Chron. iv. 21).

Ash′bel [perhaps, a secondary form of Eshbaal, man of the Lord].
A son of Benjamin and founder of a tribal family (Gen. xlvi. 21; Num. xxvi. 38; 1 Chron. viii. 1).

Ash′che-naz, See ASHKENAZ.

Ash′dod, in N. T. **Azotus** [a fortified place, a castle].
One of the five chief Philistine cities, ruled over by a lord, and seat of the worship of Dagon (Josh. xiii. 3; 1 Sam. v. 1 seq.; vi. 17; 1 Mac. x. 83; xi. 4). Anakim remained in it after the conquest of Canaan by the Hebrews (Josh. xi. 22). It was assigned to Judah (xv. 46, 47), but was not possessed by that tribe. The ark of God was carried to Ashdod by the Philistines after they captured it at Ebenezer, and was placed in the temple of Dagon (1 Sam. v. 1–8). A judgment falling on the inhabitants, the ark was transferred to Gath (6–8). Uzziah broke down the walls of Ashdod (2 Chron. xxvi. 6). The Tartan or Assyrian commander-in-chief under Sargon besieged it with success (Is. xx. 1). In the time of the Assyrian kings, from Sargon to Esarhaddon, Ashdod was ruled by an official called king by the Assyrians. Psammetichus, king of Egypt, utterly destroyed it about 630 B. C., after a siege which, according to Herodotus (ii. 157), lasted twenty-nine years. Only a remnant survived (Jer. xxv. 20; cp. Zeph. ii. 4; Zech. ix. 6). Its inhabitants were among those who opposed the rebuilding of the walls of Jerusalem, and they spoke a different language from the Israelites of that day; nevertheless some of the returned Jews married women of Ashdod (Neh. iv. 7; xiii. 23, 24). The city was twice besieged and partially destroyed

by the Maccabees (1 Mac. v. 68; x. 84), but was rebuilt by the Romans about 55 B. C. In N. T. times it was called Azotus (Acts viii. 40).

Philip preached the gospel from this place as far as Cæsarea (Acts viii. 40). The city became eventually the seat of a bishop. Its approximate site is the mud village of Esdûd on the eastern slope of a low, round knoll, among sycomore trees and prickly pears, 9 miles northeast from Ascalon, 3 from the Mediterranean, and about midway between Jaffa and Gaza.

The text of 1 Mac. ix. 15, which mentions mount Azotus, is uncertain.

Ash'dod-ite, in A. V. once **Ashdothite.**

A native or inhabitant of Ashdod (Josh. xiii. 3; Neh. iv. 7).

Ash'doth-ite. See preceding article.

Ash-doth-pis'gah, in R. V. slopes of Pisgah, in A. V. once springs of Pisgah.

The slopes of Pisgah east of the Dead Sea, which face the west (Deut. iii. 17; iv. 49; Josh. xii. 3; xiii. 20).

Ash'er, in A. V. of N. T. **Aser**, in imitation of the Greek form [happy].

1. The eighth son of Jacob, and the second by Zilpah, Leah's maidservant (Gen. xxx. 12, 13; xxxv. 26). His blessing given by Jacob on his deathbed is thus worded, "Out of Asher his bread shall be fat, and he shall yield royal dainties" (Gen. xlix. 20). That of Moses, "Let Asher be blessed with children; let him be acceptable to his brethren, and let him dip his foot in oil. Thy shoes shall be iron and brass; and as thy days, so shall thy strength be" (Deut. xxxiii. 24). He had four sons, Jimnah, Ishuah, Isui, and Beriah; and a daughter named Serah (Gen. xlvi. 17; 1 Chron. vii. 30).

2. The tribe of which Asher, the son of Jacob, was the progenitor. As assigned, its territory extended on the north to the northern boundary of Palestine, and on the south reached to the south of Carmel, a length of about 60 miles. On the east it was bounded by the territories of Zebulun and Naphtali, and on the west by the Mediterranean (Josh. xix. 24-31). But from Tyre, Sidon, Accho, and other strong places the Asherites did not expel the Canaanite inhabitants (Judg. i. 31, 32). The failure of the Asherites to capture and occupy the Phœnician plain along the sea left them only the inland hill-country, except near Carmel. This was well adapted for the culture of the olive, so that the inhabitants might dip their feet in oil (cp. Deut. xxxiii. 24).

3. Asher may possibly denote a town also, east of Shechem (Josh. xvii. 7); perhaps Teiâsîr, about 11 miles northeast of Shechem on the road to Bethshean.

A-she'rah, plural **A-she'rim**, masculine, and **Asheroth**, feminine [upright or uniting, or less probably, bringing fortune].

A word uniformly translated grove in the A. V., but a grove of trees would not be brought out of the temple (2 Kin. xxiii. 6). It was something upright made of wood (Ex. xxxiv. 13), originally, perhaps, the trunk of a tree with the branches chopped off, and was regarded as the wooden symbol of a goddess Asherah, who like Ashtoreth, was the type of abounding fertility (Ex. xxxiv. 13, R. V. margin). It was erected beside the altar of Baal (Judg. vi. 25, 28, R. V.). The prophets of the Asherah in Ahab's time were, with those of Baal, slain by Elijah at the river Kishon (1 Kin. xvi. 33; xviii. 19-40, both R. V.). Women wove hangings for an Asherah in the temple (2 Kin. xxiii. 7, R. V.), and Josiah, as part of his religious reformation, brought out the idolatrous symbol and burnt it at the brook Kidron (6).

A-she'rim. See preceding article.

Ash'er-ite.

A member of the tribe of Asher (Judg. i. 32).

A-she'roth. See ASHERAH.

Ash'hur, in A. V. **Ashur** [blackness].

Son of Hezron by his wife Abiah. He was enrolled with the house of Caleb, was head or ancestor of the inhabitants of Tekoa, and had two wives and seven children (1 Chron. ii. 24; iv. 5-7).

Ash'i-ma.

A divinity worshiped by the people of Hamath (2 Kin. xvii. 30).

Ash'ke-lon, in A. V. sometimes **Askelon** [starting point, migration].

One of the five leading Philistine cities each ruled by a lord (Josh. xiii. 3). It was situated in a valley on the Mediterranean seashore (Jer. xlvii. 5, 7), 12 miles north of Gaza, and was the seat of the worship of Derceto, a goddess with the body of a fish, whose temple and lake lay to the east of the city. It was captured by the tribe of Judah in the time of the judges (Judg. i. 18), but soon reverted to its old rulers (xiv. 19; 1 Sam. vi. 17). It was to have its inhabitants, all but a remnant, cut off and made desolate, apparently by a Pharaoh in Jeremiah's time (Jer. xlvii. 1, 5, 7; Zeph. ii. 4, 7; cp. also Zech. ix. 5). Ashkelon was twice taken by Jonathan Maccabæus (1 Mac. x. 86; xi. 60). It was the birthplace of Herod the Great, and the residence of his sister Salome. In the conflicts during the procuratorship of Florus the city was attacked by the Jews and set on fire (War ii. 18, 1); but not long afterwards the citizens retaliated and butchered 2500 in their midst (ii. 18, 5). In A. D. 1270, the sultan Bibars destroyed it and filled the harbor with stones. Its site lies within a natural amphitheater formed by a ridge of rock, with the open side to the sea. The wall ran along the top of the ridge. The soil is fertile, producing large apples, sycomore figs, etc. The onion called shallot, or eschalot, came at first from Ashkelon; hence its name.

Ash'ke-lon-ite; in A. V. **Eshkalonite**, following partly the traditional Hebrew pronunciation and partly the obsolete spelling, Eshkalon.

An inhabitant of Ashkelon (Josh. xiii. 3).

Ash'ke-naz, in A. V. twice **Aschenaz**.

The eldest son of Gomer (Gen. x. 3; 1 Chron. i. 6). The name, whether originally that of a person or country or tribe, denoted a people of the race of Gomer. In the time of Jeremiah they dwelt in the neighborhood of Ararat and Minni, that is, near eastern Armenia (Jer. li. 27).

Ash'nah [strong].

1. A village in the lowland of Judah near Zorah (Josh. xv. 33, R. V.).

2. Another village of Judah, but farther south (Josh. xv. 43). Exact site unknown.

Ash'pe-naz.

The master of the eunuchs at Babylon during Nebuchadnezzar's reign (Dan. i. 3).

Ash'ri-el. See ASRIEL.

Ash'ta-roth [plural of Ashtoreth (q. v.)].

1. In connection with the plural of Baal, a general designation for all the false gods of the neighboring nations and their idols; or better, to judge from Gen. xiv. 5 and 1 Sam xxxi. 10, the old Canaanitish plural of eminence whereby the goddess Ashtoreth was honorably spoken of in the plural number.

2. A town of Bashan, ancient (Thothmes' list), seat of the worship of the goddess Astarte, and capital of Og (Deut. i. 4, in A. V. Astaroth; Josh. ix. 10). Some of the ancient inhabitants were giants, Og himself being of the number (Josh. xii. 4; xiii. 12). The place fell to the lot of Machir, the son of Manasseh (31), but became a Levitical city, inhabited by the children of Gershom (1 Chron. vi. 71). Uzzia, one of David's mighty men, was connected with the town (xi. 44). Its site is commonly identified with Tell 'Ashterah, which agrees with the statement of Eusebius that the town was distant 6 Roman miles from Edrei. This tell stands on a hill in the midst of a well-watered, grassy plain. See ASHTEROTH-KARNAIM.

Ash'te-rath-ite.

A native of Ashtaroth (1 Chron. xi. 44).

Ash'te-roth-kar-na'im [two-horned Ashtaroth]. In A. V. written as two words.

A place smitten by Chedorlaomer on his expedition against the cities of the plain (Gen. xiv. 5, R. V.). Its name suggests that the inhabitants specially worshiped the horned moon. Probably Ashteroth-karnaim is the full name of Ashtaroth. and it may be the place known centuries later as Karnaim, which is mentioned in connection with cities of Gilead and in which Atargatis was worshiped (1 Mac. v. 26, 36, 43; 2 Mac. xii. 26). This goddess, whose true name according to Strabo was Athara, was the Syrian nature deity corresponding to Ashtoreth. It is to be remembered that the physical features ascribed to Carnion in 2 Mac. xii. 21 do not

agree with Tell 'Ashterah, the commonly accepted site of Ashtaroth.

Ash'to-reth [a binding together, union].

Astarte, a Phœnician goddess, partly evolved, perhaps, from admiration for the planet Venus, but symbolizing also the soft radiance of the moon; cp. Ashteroth-karnaim. Her worship was early established at Sidon, hence she is called the goddess or the abomination of the Zidonians (1 Kin. xi. 5, 33; 2 Kin. xxiii. 13). It was in vogue east of the Jordan in the days of Abraham (Gen. xiv. 5). As early as the times of the judges it had spread to the Hebrews (Judg. ii. 13; x. 6). It was also practiced in Philistia (1 Sam. xxxi. 10). Solomon in his old age gave it the support of his great name (1 Kin. xi. 5; 2 Kin. xxiii. 13). The pronunciation of the name as Ashtoreth instead of Ashtareth is believed to express the loathing felt for idolatry, by conforming the sound to that of *bosheth*, shame (cp. ISHBOSHETH).

Ash'ur. See ASHHUR.

Ash'ur-ite.

A people belonging to the kingdom of Ishbosheth (2 Sam. ii. 9). They are enumerated between Gilead and Jezreel. Vulgate and Syriac have Geshurites.

Ash'vath.

An Asherite, family of Heber, house of Japhlet (1 Chron. vii. 33).

A'si-a.

The continent east of Europe and Africa (Herod. iv. 36–40). The name was employed in a narrower sense for the kingdom of the Seleucidæ (1 Mac. viii. 6; xi. 13), which embraced Syria and extensive regions west of the river Halys. When the Romans transferred most of these western districts, Mysia, Lydia, and Phrygia, to Eumenes II., king of Pergamos, the name was used by them for the kingdom of Pergamos, and when this kingdom was appropriated by them in 133 B. C., they added Caria and a strip of coast to it and formed the province of Asia (Acts vi. 9; xxvii. 2; 1 Pet. i. 1; Rev. i. 4, 11). Pliny, however, distinguishes between Phrygia and Asia (v. 28). So do Paul and others (Acts ii. 9, 10; xvi. 6). The names of the incorporated districts were not abandoned; and Paul, who was traveling along but outside of the borders of Asia, mentions being at a point over against Mysia (Acts xvi. 7, R.V.), in which Pergamos was situated, one of the cities of Asia (Rev. i. 4, 11). The province was at first governed by proprætors, but in 27 B. c. it was made senatorial and so continued for 300 years, being governed by proconsuls (cp. Acts xix. 38, R. V.). Its capital was Ephesus. In the N. T. Asia always denotes the Roman province (Acts xix. 10, 22, 26, 27; xx. 4, 16, 18; xxi. 27; xxiv. 18; xxvii. 2; 1 Cor. xvi. 19; 2 Cor. i. 8; 2 Tim. i. 15).

A'si-arch [chief of Asia].

Member of a college of deputies who were

annually appointed by various towns of the province of Asia to conduct a festival and games in honor of the Roman emperor. The festivities took place yearly at one of the several cities which had the honor in succession. The asiarchs were chosen each year, but in time formed an influential body in the towns, and often secured the reëlection of their members. The asiarchs of Ephesus were friends to Paul (Acts xix. 31, R. V. marg.).

A-si-de'ans. See HASIDÆANS.

A'si-el [God hath made].
A Simeonite (1 Chron. iv. 35).

As'ke-lon. See ASHKELON.

As-mo-næ'an [Greek *'Asamōnaios*, from Hebrew *Hashman*, opulent].
A descendant of Hashman, a priest of the family of Joarib and ancestor of the Maccabees (Antiq. xii. 6, 1; cp. 1 Mac. ii. 1; 1 Chron. xxiv. 7). The title Asmonæan is commonly employed in Jewish literature to designate the family from Mattathias to Herod the Great and Aristobulus (Antiq. xiv. 16, 4; xx. 8, 11).

As-mo-næ'ans, Pal'ace of the.
A palace in Jerusalem erected by the Asmonæan princes, opposite the western court of the temple, on an elevation which commanded a view of the city and the sanctuary (Antiq. xx. 8, 11). It stood near the Xystus and overlooked it (ibid.; War ii. 16, 3). It is probably the royal palace which was reckoned one of the two fortresses of Jerusalem, the Baris being the other, and in which Herod the Great resided before the erection of his palace in the upper city (Antiq. xiv. 13, 9; xv. 3, 7; 8, 4 and 5). This latter building excelled it in magnificence and as a fortress. So late as A. D. 60 the last prince of the Herodian house used it as a residence, Agrippa II., the king Agrippa of Acts xxv. 13 (Antiq. xx. 8, 11; War ii. 16, 3). It was probably the palace burnt by the seditious Jews at the beginning of the war with the Romans (War ii. 17, 6).

As'nah [a bramble].
One of the Nethinim, some of whose descendants returned from the captivity at Babylon (Ezra ii. 50).

As-nap'per, in R. V. **Osnappar.**
A high Assyrian dignitary called great and noble who settled various foreign tribes in Samaria (Ezra iv. 10). He seems to have been either Esar-haddon or one of his officials (cp. 2 and 10). The name is supposed by some to be a rude Aramaic form of Ashurbanipal, the son of Esar-haddon, who from about 671 B. C. or later was his associate, and from 668 B. C. his successor on the Assyrian throne, and reigned until about 626 B. C. Ashurbanipal records that he penetrated Elam, took Susa the capital, and carried off many of the inhabitants to Assyria (cp. Ezra iv. 9, 10). His father, Esar-haddon, had conquered Egypt. Rebellion occurred among the petty rulers,

and assistance was rendered them by the able Tirhakah. To suppress this revolt, Ashurbanipal conducted two campaigns, in which on the whole he was successful, though Egypt was lost at last. In the later campaign, about 664 B. C., Thebes, then known as No, was captured and plundered (cp. Nah. iii. 8–10). He had relations first friendly, but afterwards the reverse, with Gyges, the usurping king of Lydia; see GOG. He had to crush a rebellion of his own brother, the ruler of Babylon. He had a war with the Minni. By the Greeks, who called him Sardanapalus, he was considered effeminate. Modern scholars regard his memory with gratitude on account of the splendid library which he brought together. He had copyists incessantly at work not merely transcribing Assyrian books, but translating works of value from the so-called Accadian and other tongues. Part of this library has been recovered, and it is from it that we derive most of our acquaintance with the Assyrian empire and its kings.

Asp [a round shield, which the serpent when coiled up resembles].
The rendering of the Hebrew word *Pethen* in Deut. xxxii. 33; Job xx. 14, 16; and Is. xi. 8, and of the Greek *Aspis* in Rom. iii. 13. With some inconsistency *Pethen* is rendered not asp but adder in Ps. lviii. 4 and xci. 13. *Pethen* is a species of snake (Ps. lviii. 4), venomous (Deut. xxxii. 33), dwelling in holes (Is. xi. 8); probably *Naja haje*, which is found in Egypt and Palestine, is the asp of the Greeks and Romans, is of the same genus as the deadly cobra of India, and is generally used by the snake-charmers in their performances. It has a hood which it dilates when about to strike its prey.

As'pa-tha.
A son of Haman (Esth. ix. 7).

As'phar.
A reservoir in the wilderness of Tekoah (1 Mac. ix. 33).

As'ri-el, in A. V. once **Ashriel** [probably, vow of God].
A descendant of Manasseh and founder of a family (Num. xxvi. 31; Josh. xvii. 2).

Ass.
The genus called by zoölogists *Asinus*, containing the several species and varieties of asses, wild or domesticated. The ass genus belongs to the family *Equidæ* or Horses. Three asses are mentioned in Scripture.
1. The wild ass, called in Hebrew *'Arod*, the fugitive. It is poetically described in Job xxxix. 5–8, where, however, there is mention also of the common wild ass of Syria, and is named also in Dan. v. 21. If distinct in species from the common wild ass, it is probably *Asinus onager*, which is found in the Sahara and in Arabia, where it was once common, but is now more rare. It occasionally visits the Hauran. It is the progenitor of the domestic ass.

2. The wild ass of Syria (*Asinus hemippus*); Hebrew *Pere'*, the leaper, occurring in Job xxiv. 5; xxxix. 5; Ps. civ. 11; Is. xxxii. 14, and Jer. xiv. 6. It is rather smaller than the onager. Tristram mentions that enormous herds of them often enter the Armenian mountains in summer. They are found at all times in Northern Arabia, Mesopotamia, and Syria, occasionally entering Northern Palestine. They are the species represented on the Ninevite sculptures.

3. The domestic ass (*Asinus asinus*), the Hebrew *Ḥᵃmor*. It is a sub-species descended from the onager. It is obstinate and typical of stupidity. But on the other hand the ass is strong, easily fed, patient, and forgiving. Its faults are mainly produced by the cruel bondage imposed upon it by its human taskmaster. The ass was early domesticated. Abraham had asses (Gen. xii. 16) on which he rode (xxii. 3), so had Jacob (xxx. 43). They were used also for burden-bearing (xlix. 14; Is. xxx. 6), for ploughing, etc. (Deut. xxii. 10). White asses were deemed fit for persons of rank (Judg. v. 10), as they still are in Palestine. Jesus showed his lowliness, and at the same time the spirit of the earlier kings, by rejecting horses and riding on an ass in his triumphal entry into Jerusalem (Zech. ix. 9; Mat. xxi. 5).

As-sas'sins [Greek *sikarioi*, daggermen]. Ruffians who terrorized Judæa, A. D. 50–70. Their organization was formed in order to assert liberty from the Romans and recognize no master save God. They carried a small sword hidden beneath the cloak; and, mingling with the multitude at the festivals, stabbed those who were marked for destruction. They even formed bands and pillaged villages (Acts xxi. 38, R. V.; Antiq. xx. 8, 10; War vii. 10, 1). Cp. ZEALOT.

As'shur, in A. V. twice **Assur** [probably originally *A-ushar*, watered plain (Delitzsch), or from the local deity Ashur, the good (Schrader)]. Pronounced Ash'ur.

A people descended from Shem (Gen. x. 22), and the country which they inhabited (Ezra iv. 2, A. V.; Ezek. xxvii. 23). See ASSYRIA.

As-shu'rim.

A people, doubtless of Arabia, descended from Dedan, and more remotely from Abraham by Keturah (Gen. xxv. 3). The like name borne by an individual mentioned in the Minæan inscription throws little or no light on this tribe. The Ashurites, named after Gilead in 2 Sam. ii. 9, are almost certainly different, as is also Asshur, that is Assyria, in Ezek. xxvii. 23.

As-si-de'ans. See HASIDÆANS.

As'sir [captive].
1. A descendant of Levi through Korah, born in Egypt (Ex. vi. 24; 1 Chron. vi. 22).
2. A descendant of the preceding (1 Chron. vi. 23, 37).
3. A son of king Jeconiah (1 Chron. iii. 17). The name does not appear in R. V. The

revisers regard it as an adjective descriptive of Jeconiah, and translate it "the captive;" but there is no definite article in the present Hebrew text, and there was none in the text used by the Seventy. His name suggests that Assir was born in captivity. This accords with other indications. Jeconiah was 18 years old when carried off to Babylon, and in the enumeration of the members of his family deported with him, no children are mentioned (2 Kin. xxiv. 8–15). Assir did not succeed to the royal title; the right to the throne passed to Shealtiel (q. v.).

As'sos.

A seaport town of Mysia, now called Beiram, not far from Troas (Acts xx. 13, 14).

As'sur. See ASSHUR.

As-syr'i-a [Greek modification of Asshur (q. v.)].

A country on the river Tigris (Gen. ii. 14, R. V. margin). It was originally the district dominated by the town of Asshur, the ruins of which have been found at Kalah Shergat, on the western bank of the Tigris, about 60 miles below Nineveh. With the growth of the city's power and dominion, the name came to denote the region compassed by the Gordyæan mountains of Armenia on the north, the ranges of Media on the east, and the little Zab river on the south. Westward it extended a short distance from the Tigris into Mesopotamia. This district is the Assyria proper of history, but the name was often given to the extensive empire conquered and ruled by the Assyrians. The inhabitants were Semites (Gen. x. 22), who derived their culture from Babylonia, and probably originally emigrated thence. They became powerful enough under king Tukulti-adar, about 1300 B. C., to subjugate Babylonia, and thenceforth during 700 years they were, with brief interruptions, the leading power in the east. Tiglath-pileser I., about 1120 to 1100 B. C., raised the kingdom into the most extensive empire of the age. Under his successors it greatly declined, its decadence leaving a void which permitted the kingdoms of David and Solomon to reach their widest limits. Ashur-naṣirpal (885 to 860) by his conquests restored the prestige of the empire. He erected a palace in the northwestern part of Calah, and made that ancient town (Gen. x. 11) the capital. He was succeeded by his son Shalmaneser, who reigned from about 860 to 825, and was the first Assyrian king to come into conflict with the Israelites; see AHAB and JEHU. The later kings were Pul, known also as Tiglath-pileser, 745–727; Shalmaneser, 727–722; Sargon, 722–705; Sennacherib, 705–681; Esar-haddon, 680–668; and Ashurbanipal, 668–626 (see ASNAPPER).. Minor kings followed. In 612 probably, or in 606 B. C. Medes, Babylonians, and their allies captured Nineveh, the capital, and by 606 had put an end to the Assyrian empire. When at the height of its power in the seventh century B. C., Assyria held sway over Babylonia, parts of Media, Armenia, Syria, Cyprus, Arabia, and Egypt. The kings of Israel mentioned in the Assyrian inscriptions are Ḥumri (Omri), Aḥabbu (Ahab), Yaua (Jehu), Minihimmu (Menahem), Pakaḥa (Pekah), and Ausi' (Hoshea). The kings of Judah so mentioned are Yauhazi (Ahaz), Hazakiyau (Hezekiah), and Minasi (Manasseh). The identification of Azriyau with Azariah, i. e., Uzziah, is no longer generally accepted.

The Assyrian religion was borrowed from that of Babylon, except that Ashur, the presiding god of the city of Asshur, became the chief deity of Assyria. It was animistic nature-worship. Every object and phenomenon in nature was believed to be animated by a spirit. The great gods, after Ashur, were the prominent objects of nature. They were eleven in number, in two triads and a pentad. Chief were Anu, heaven, Bel, the region inhabited by man, beast, and bird, and Ea, terrestrial and subterranean waters. Next in order were Sin, the moon, Shamash, the sun, and Ramman, god of the storm. Then came the five planets. There were innumerable other deities, some of whom were merely different aspects of the foregoing. Subordinate gods often attained eminence as patrons of important towns.

Excavations in the Assyrian palaces, begun by the Frenchman Botta in 1843, followed immediately by the Englishman Layard, and then, after a time, by George Smith of the British Museum, Rassam, and others, have made the Assyrian empire, which was little more than a myth to the classic nations of antiquity, to us a great reality.

The language spoken by the Assyrians and the kindred people in Babylonia was of the Semitic family and closely allied to the Hebrew. An alphabet was not used. The language was written in characters which expressed syllables, not single letters or sounds. These signs were impressed on clay by a stylus, each impression having the shape of a wedge or arrow, whence the writing is called cuneiform. The characters were originally pictures of objects, but in time assumed conventional forms which often bore no resemblance to the original object.

As'ta-roth. See ASHTAROTH 2.

As-trol'o-gers.
1. The rendering of the Hebrew words *Hobᵉre shamayim*, dividers of the heavens. They are mentioned with stargazers (Is. xlvii. 13). There is no question that these were astrologers who divided the heavens into certain mansions, with the view of tracing the course of the planets through each of them, in the vain hope of being able to tell fortunes and predict future events. Though their failure was complete, yet the careful study of the heavens which astrologers found needful led to the gradual growth of the sublime science of astronomy.

2. The rendering in A. V. of the Hebrew and Aramaic words *'Ashshaphim* (Dan. i. 20), *'Ashᵉphin* (ii. 27), and *'Ashᵉphayya* (iv. 7; v. 7), all translated in the R. V. "enchanters." See ENCHANTMENT and ENCHANTER.

A-sup'pim [collections, stores].
A building for storing temple goods, which stood near the southern gate of the outer court (1 Chron. xxvi. 15, 17); hence R. V. renders the word by storehouse.

A-syn'cri-tus [incomparable or unlike].
A Christian at Rome to whom Paul sent a salutation (Rom. xvi. 14).

A'tad [a plant, *Rhamnus paliurus*, or Christ's thorn].
The great company, which was bearing the body of Jacob from Egypt to the sepulcher at Hebron, after making a detour, perhaps to avoid the Philistines and Edomites, halted at the threshing-floor of Atad, east of the Jordan, and made a mourning for seven days. The Canaanites saw and called the place Abel-mizraim, Meadow, or with slightly altered pronunciation, Mourning of Egypt. The procession afterwards entered Canaan (Gen. l. 9-13).

At'a-rah [a crown, a diadem].
A wife of Jerahmeel (1 Chron. ii. 26).

At'a-roth [crowns, diadems].
1. A town east of the Jordan, rebuilt by the tribe of Gad (Num. xxxii. 3, 34). It was taken from the men of Gad by Mesha, king of Moab (Moabite Stone, 10, 11). Its name is generally supposed to be preserved in the ruins 'Attârûs, on the western slope of Jebel 'Attârûs, three or four miles east of Machærus. The mountain is some miles south of Heshbon, which is in the tribe of Reuben; but the territories of Reuben and Gad, like those of Judah and Simeon, were much commingled. The ruins consist of unwrought stones, lying in heaps; ranges of broken walls; remains of foundations, large caverns, and circular cisterns. The old citadel was an hour's walk from the town, than which it is lower, but more isolated.

2. The same as Ataroth-addar (Josh. xvi. 2).

3. A town on the border of Ephraim, not far from Jericho. Apparently different from Ataroth-addar (Josh. xvi. 7).

4. A village, apparently in Judah (1 Chron. ii. 54). The name should include the four words that follow in A. V. and be written as in R. V., Atroth-beth-joab.

At'a-roth-ad'dar, in A. V. once **Ataroth-addar** [crowns of Addar].
A village on the southern frontier of Ephraim (Josh. xvi. 5), on the boundary line between that tribe and Benjamin, west of Luz and near the hill that lieth on the south side of the nether Beth-horon (xviii. 13). Not identified. 'Atara, 3½ miles south of Bethel, on the road leading to Jerusalem, is much too far east.

A'ter [shut].

1. A man called, by way of distinction, Ater of Hezekiah, ninety-eight of whose descendants returned from Babylon after the captivity (Ezra ii. 16 ; Neh. vii. 21).

2. A porter (Ezra ii. 42 ; Neh. vii. 45).

A'thach [a lodging-place].

A village in the south of Judah, to which David sent some of the spoil of Ziklag (1 Sam. xxx. 30). Perhaps it is Ether (Josh. xv. 42 ; xix. 7), kaph and resh being confused by a scribe.

A-tha'iah.

A man of Judah, son of Uzziah, of the family of Perez (Neh. xi. 4) ; scarcely the same as Uthai (1 Chron. ix. 4).

Ath-a-li'ah [Jehovah has afflicted or is exalted].

1. The wife of Jehoram, king of Judah, a daughter of Ahab and granddaughter of Omri (2 Kin. viii. 18, 26 ; 2 Chron. xxi. 6 ; xxii. 2). She possessed the masculine courage of her mother Jezebel, and was equally unscrupulous in shedding blood. When her son, king Ahaziah, was slain by Jehu, she killed all the sons of the murdered monarch excepting one infant, Joash, who was stolen away by his aunt, Jehosheba. Then seizing the throne, she reigned six years, at the end of which a priestly insurrection took place in favor of Joash. Attempting to quell it, she was dragged from the temple courts and killed at the carriage entrance of the palace (2 Kin. xi. 1–16 ; 2 Chron. xxii. 1–xxiii. 21).

2. A Benjamite of the house of Jeroham (1 Chron. viii. 26).

3. A man of the father's house of Elam (Ezra viii. 7).

Ath'a-rim.

The way of the Atharim was not far from the town of Arad, and was the route followed by the Israelites as they journeyed from Kadesh by way of mount Hor in order to enter Canaan (Num. xxi. 1, R. V.). The meaning of the name has not been established.

Ath-e-no'bi-us.

A commissioner sent by Antiochus Sidetes to Simon Maccabæus. He belonged to the privileged class known as friends of the king (1 Mac. xv. 28).

Ath'ens.

The capital of Attica, one of the Greek states. The city became the center of enlightenment in science, literature, and art for the ancient world. It grew up around the rocky hill called Acropolis (top or highest point of the city), and covered the smaller hills and intervening valleys on the northeast side of the Gulf of Ægina, between the small river Ilissus on the east and south, and the Cephisus a little to the west. Athens was about 5 miles from the sea. Its commercial port was Piræus, with which the city when in its glory was connected by long walls. The navy anchored close by at Phaleron.

Tradition says that Athens was founded by Cecrops about 1556 B. C., that it sent fifty ships to the Trojan war, and that it was ruled by kings till about 1068 B. C. The supreme authority was afterwards vested in archons. Two celebrated legislators are spoken of ; Draco, about 621 B. C., whose name has become proverbial for pitiless severity, and Solon, about 594 B. C., a wiser man, whose laws were more humane. In 490 B. C. the Athenians, supported by the Platæans, gained the great victory at Marathon against the generals of Darius Hystaspis, king of Persia. In 480 Athens had to be abandoned to his son and successor, Xerxes, but the great naval battle at Salamis gained by the Greeks compelled the invader to withdraw. The city was, however, burnt in 479 B. C. by his general, Mardonius. The glory gained by the Athenians in the Persian war led to the establishment of a small empire, with Athens for its capital and a powerful fleet rather than a large army for its support. About 444 B. C. the power of Pericles, an able democratic leader, became very great. The good feature of his enlightened government was the erection of many beautiful public buildings in Athens. Literature also greatly flourished under his administration. In 431, while he yet lived and ruled, the Peloponnesian war began, which ended by the surrender of Athens to the Spartans in 404. The city afterwards went through various political vicissitudes, though the intellect and knowledge of its inhabitants rendered them influential, whatever changes took place. Four great schools of philosophy—Platonic, Peripatetic, Epicurean, and Stoic—flourished here and attracted numerous students, not only from Greece, but also later from Rome. The city was taken by the Roman general Sulla in 86 B. C., and was still subject to the Romans when Paul was there. Altars "to an unknown god" were found in the city and at the harbor Phaleron (Acts xvii. 23 ; Pausanias i. 1, 4 ; Philostratus, vit. Apol. 6, 2). Mars' Hill, on which Paul delivered his celebrated discourse, was a short distance west of the Acropolis (Acts xvii. 15–xviii. 1 ; cp. also 1 Thes. iii. 1). Athens subsequently came into the hands of the Goths, the Byzantines, and other temporarily dominant races, ending with the Turks. Since the establishment of the modern Greek kingdom, in A. D. 1828, Athens has become the capital not merely of Greece, since A. D. 1835, but of the Hellenic race throughout the world.

Ath'lai [afflicted or exalted].

A man who was induced by Ezra to divorce his foreign wife (Ezra x. 28).

A-tone'ment [at-one-ment, the making of those one in feeling who before were at variance].

1. Reconciliation between persons or beings at variance (Rom. v. 11, A. V.).

2. That which produces this reconciliation,

specially an expiatory sacrifice designed to have that effect (Ex. xxx. 16 ; Lev. iv. 20, 26, 31, 35). This is the sense in which the word atonement is now commonly used.

A-tone′ment, Day of.

The annual day of humiliation and expiation for the sins of the nation, when the high priest offered sacrifices as an atonement for the sanctuary, the priests, and the people (Lev. xvi. ; xxiii. 26–32 ; Num. xxix. 7–11). It was observed on the tenth day of the seventh month by abstinence from daily labor, by a holy convocation, and by fasting. It was the only fast enjoined by the law. It was "the fast" (Acts xxvii. 9 ; Antiq. xiv. 4, 3). On that day the high priest laid aside his official ornaments, and clad in simple white linen sacrificed a bullock as a sin offering for himself and the priests. Taking a censer of live coals from off the altar, he entered the holy of holies and burned incense that the smoke might cover the mercy seat above the law. He then fetched the blood of the slain bullock and sprinkled it on the mercy seat and on the floor. This completed the atonement for the priesthood. He took the two goats provided by the nation and cast lots upon them. One he slew as a sin offering for the people, brought its blood within the veil, and sprinkled it as before to make atonement for the holy of holies. By similar rites he made atonement for the holy place and the altar of burnt offering. He now took the remaining goat, placed his hands on its head, and confessed over it the sins of the people. Typically the sins of the people were "laid on its head," it was made the sin bearer of the nation, and laden with guilt not its own was sent away into the wilderness ; see AZAZEL. The high priest resumed his official raiment, offered his burnt offering and that of the people, and likewise the fat of the sin offering. The flesh of the bullock and the goat were carried without the camp and burned. The Epistle to the Hebrews points out that this entry of the high priest into the most holy place, once a year, and not without blood, foreshadowed the entrance of Jesus, the great high priest, once for all into heaven, having purchased for us eternal salvation (Heb. ix. 1–12, 24–28).

At′roth. See ATROTH-SHOPHAN.

At′roth-beth-jo′ab [crowns of the house of Joab].

A village, apparently in Judah (1 Chron. ii. 54, R. V.). In A. V. the name is cut asunder.

At′roth-sho′phan [crowns of Shophan].

A town rebuilt by the Gadites (Num. xxxii. 35, R. V.). Site unknown. In A. V. incorrectly represented as two towns.

At′tai [perhaps, opportune].

1. A man of Judah whose descent through his mother was from Jerahmeel and Hezron, but whose father was an Egyptian slave (1 Chron. ii. 34–36).

2. A Gadite who came to David at Ziklag (1 Chron. xii. 11).

3. A son of Rehoboam by his queen Maacah (2 Chron. xi. 20).

At-ta-li′a [pertaining to Attalus].

A city on the seacoast of Pamphylia, built by Attalus Philadelphus, king of Pergamos, 159–138 B. C., and now called Antali or Adal. Paul sailed thence to Antioch on his first missionary journey (Acts xiv. 25).

At′ta-lus.

King of Pergamos, either Attalus II., Philadelphus, or his nephew Attalus III., who succeeded his uncle in 138 B. C. (1 Mac. xv. 22).

Au-gus′tan Band, in A. V. **Augustus′ Band.**

A cohort of Roman soldiers, apparently named after the Roman emperor Augustus (Acts xxvii. 1).

Au-gus′tus [venerable, august].

The personal name of the first Roman emperor, called in the N. T. Cæsar Augustus. See CÆSAR.

A′va. See AVVA.

A′ven [emptiness, nothingness, an idol].

1. The Egyptian city On, called by the Greeks Heliopolis (Ezek. xxx. 17). The Hebrew consonants of On and Aven are the same, though the vowels differ. The pronunciation has been intentionally modified by the prophet to express his contempt for the idolatries of the city.

2. A name applied by Hosea to Bethel as no longer the house of God, but now a house of idolatry (Hos. x. 8) ; see BETH-AVEN.

3. A town, apparently, which served to designate a valley in the kingdom of Damascus (Amos i. 5) ; probably Heliopolis, now Baalbec, which like the Egyptian On was a seat of the sun-worship (cp. 1 above).

A-ven′ger of Blood.

One who inflicts punishment on a murderer, thus vindicating the majesty of the law, "Whoso sheddeth man's blood, by man shall his blood be shed" (Gen. ix. 5, 6 ; Num. xxxv. 31). When civil life is regulated, this duty is undertaken by courts of justice. Of old, however, the Semitic nations, like the ancient Greeks, Germans, and Slavs, acted to a large extent on the system of each injured man being his own avenger. When murder or accidental homicide took place, the nearest relative of the victim was expected to avenge his death, and was called the avenger of blood. He slew the murderer or the unintentional homicide, without any preliminary trial to settle the actual facts of the case. Then, very probably, the nearest relative of the second man slain murdered the avenger of blood, and a blood feud was established. The Mosaic legislation introduced modifications into the system which destroyed its worst features. Cities of refuge were established, and any one killing a man and fleeing to one of those cities was granted a fair trial, and was not put to death unless he had committed actual murder (Num. xxxv. 19, 21, 24. 27; 2 Sam. xiv. 11). The A. V. reads, Revenger of blood. See CITIES OF REFUGE.

A'vim and Avims. See AVVIM.

A'vites. See AVVITES.

A'vith [ruins].

An Edomite city, the native place of king Hadad (Gen. xxxvi. 35; 1 Chron. i. 46). Exact site unknown.

Av'va, in A. V. **A'va.**

A city of the Assyrian empire, in or northwest of Babylonia, from which people were brought to help to colonize Samaria. Their gods were Nibhaz and Tartak (2 Kin. xvii. 24, 31). It is doubtless the place called Ivvah in 2 Kin. xviii. 34; xix. 13, R. V.

Av'vim, in A. V. **A'vims** and **A'vites** and, as name of the town, **A'vim.**

1. The aborigines of the Philistine country about Gaza. All save a small remnant were destroyed by the Caphtorim, afterwards called Philistines (Deut. ii. 23; Josh. xiii. 3).

2. A town of Benjamin, perhaps the same as Ai (Josh. xviii. 23).

Av'vites, in A. V. **A'vites.**

1. The same as Avvim (Josh. xiii. 3).

2. People of Avva (2 Kin. xvii. 31).

A'zal. See AZEL.

Az-a-li'ah [Jehovah hath spared].

Son of Meshullam and father of Shaphan the scribe (2 Kin. xxii. 3).

Az-a-ni'ah [Jehovah hath given ear].

A Levite, father of Jeshua (Neh. x. 9).

Az'a-rel, in A. V. **A-zar'e-el,** once **A-zar'-a-el** (Neh. xii. 36) [God has helped].

1. A Levite who joined David at Ziklag (1 Chron. xii. 6).

2. A singer in David's time (1 Chron. xxv. 18). In ver. 4 he is called Uzziel (as king Azariah was also known as Uzziah), and is recorded as of the lineage of Heman.

3. A son of Jeroham, the chief of the tribe of Dan (1 Chron. xxvii. 22).

4. A man whom Ezra persuaded to divorce his foreign wife (Ezra x. 41).

5. A priest of the father's house of Immer (Neh. xi. 13).

6. A musician of priestly descent (Neh. xii. 36).

Az-a-ri'ah [Jehovah hath helped].

1. A man of Judah, family of Zerah, house of Ethan (1 Chron. ii. 8).

2. A Levite, family of Kohath, line of Izhar, and an ancestor of Samuel the prophet and Heman the singer (1 Chron. vi. 36; perhaps, 2 Chron. xxix. 12).

3. One of Solomon's officials, son of the high priest Zadok (1 Kin. iv. 2) and brother of Ahimaaz.

4. Grandson of Zadok and son of Ahimaaz. He was in the line of high-priestly succession (1 Chron. vi. 9).

5. Son of Nathan, and hence probably Solomon's nephew (2 Sam. v. 14), who was over Solomon's twelve tax-collectors (1 Kin. iv. 5).

6. A prophet, son of Oded, who encouraged king Asa to persevere in national religious reformation (2 Chron. xv. 1–8).

7. Two sons of king Jehoshaphat (2 Chron. xxi. 2). The recurrence of the same name in the family is surprising. It may be due to an early corruption of the text; or, if the text is correct, to a difference of mother, the two boys being half-brothers (cp. the Herods). It cannot be explained by the theory that the younger was named after a deceased elder brother, for the two seem to have been alive together and to have been put to death at the same time.

8. A man of Judah, family of Hezron, house of Jerahmeel (1 Chron. ii. 38, 39). His grandfather was Obed (38); hence he was perhaps the captain Azariah, son of Obed, who assisted in overthrowing Athaliah and placing Joash on the throne (2 Chron. xxiii. 1).

9. Another captain, son of Jeroham, who aided in overthrowing Athaliah (2 Chron. xxiii. 1).

10. A prince of Ephraim, son of Johanan, who aided in persuading the soldiers of Pekah's army to release the captives of Judah (2 Chron. xxviii. 12).

11. A king of Judah, known also as Uzziah (cp. 2 Kin. xv. 1 with 2 Chron. xxvi. 1); see UZZIAH. The belief is no longer generally held that he is the Azriyau mentioned in the inscriptions of Tiglath-pileser.

12. A high priest (1 Chron. vi. 10), probably he who rebuked Uzziah for encroaching on the priest's office (2 Chron. xxvi. 17–20). Perhaps he was still officiating in Hezekiah's reign (xxxi. 10, 13), but probably the pontiff of the latter reign was another priest of the name Azariah; see HIGH PRIEST.

13. A Levite, family of Merari, who assisted in purifying the temple in Hezekiah's reign (2 Chron. xxix. 12).

14. A high priest, son of Hilkiah and father of Seraiah, not long before the exile (1 Chron. vi. 13, 14; perhaps ix. 11). See SERAIAH 12.

15. A son of Hoshaiah and an opponent of the prophet Jeremiah (Jer. xliii. 2).

16. The Hebrew and original name of Abednego (Dan. i. 7; 1 Mac. ii. 59).

17. A prominent person, probably prince of Judah, who marched in the procession at the dedication of the wall of Jerusalem (Neh. xii. 32, 33).

18. A son of Maaseiah, who had a house at Jerusalem in Nehemiah's time, and repaired the wall in its immediate vicinity (Neh. iii. 23, 24).

19. One of those, apparently Levites, who explained to the people the law which Ezra read (Neh. viii. 7).

20. A priest, doubtless head of a father's house, who in the days of Nehemiah sealed the covenant to keep separate from foreigners and observe the law of God (Neh. x. 2).

21. A descendant of Hilkiah who was inter

of the house of God after the exile (1 Chron. ix. 11); see, however, SERAIAH 12.

Besides these, a king of Israel (not Uzziah) is called Azariah in 2 Chron. xxii. 6, but this seems a copyist's error for Ahaziah, which is given in the next verse (2 Chron. xxii. 6, 7; cp. 2 Kin. viii. 29).

Az-a-ri'as [Greek form of Azariah].

One of two men appointed by Judas Maccabæus to chief authority in Judæa during his absence (1 Mac. v. 18), but who were defeated by Gorgias (56–60).

A'zaz [strong].

A Reubenite, line of Joel (1 Chron. v. 8).

A-za'zel [probably for *'azalzel*, in the sense of dismissal or dismissed, separated one].

The word occurs originally in one passage only (Lev. xvi. 8, 10, 26, R. V.); see ATONEMENT, DAY OF. The data for determining its meaning are meager and insufficient, being confined as yet to etymology, exegesis of the passage, and general biblical teaching. Numerous interpretations have been proposed, but they are conjectures more or less satisfactory. The word has been interpreted both impersonally and personally, as meaning—1. A place: a solitary desert (Jonathan, Jerome); 2. A goat: the departing goat (Jewish revisers of the Septuagint; Vulgate); scape-goat, the goat that is allowed to escape (A. V.); 3. An abstract noun: utter removal or dismissal (Bähr, Winer, R. V.); 4. A personal being: (*a*) some demon of the wilderness (Stade); (*b*) a fallen angel who seduces men to evil (Book of Enoch vi. 7; viii. 1 et passim), later identified with Sammael; (*c*) an epithet applied to the devil (Origen, Hengstenberg, Oehler, Kurtz, Keil; see Milton, *Paradise Lost* i.).

Either of two interpretations is satisfactory: 1. To regard the word as an abstraction. Aaron shall cast lots upon the goats, "one lot for the Lord and the other lot for dismissal," and shall send the goat, upon which the latter lot falls, away "as a dismissal to the wilderness." The idea of the escaped goat is virtually preserved by this interpretation. 2. To regard the word as an epithet of the devil, the apostate one. Those who are laden with sin belong to the devil. The objection to this interpretation is that Satan is nowhere mentioned in any part of the Pentateuch. The serpent indeed is, but it is not certain that the devil was as yet recognized as the possessor and actuator of the serpent of the temptation.

Az-a-zi'ah [Jehovah is strong].

1. A harper for religious service during the reign of David (1 Chron. xv. 21).

2. Father of a prince of Ephraim in David's reign (1 Chron. xxvii. 20).

3. An overseer of the temple in the reign of Hezekiah (2 Chron. xxxi. 13).

Az'buk.

Father of a certain Nehemiah, contempo-

rary, but not identical with the celebrated governor of that name (Neh. iii. 16).

A-ze'kah [a field dug by a hoe and set out with new vines].

A town in the lowland, near Socoh, to which the kings besieging Gibeon were driven by Joshua (Josh. x. 10, 11). It was assigned to Judah (xv. 35). Goliath and the Philistines encamped near it (1 Sam. xvii. 1). It was fortified by Rehoboam (2 Chron. xi. 9), besieged by Nebuchadnezzar (Jer. xxxiv. 7), and it existed after the exile (Neh. xi. 30) between Eleutheropolis and Jerusalem, nine Roman miles from the former town, hence perhaps at Tell Zachariyeh.

A'zel; in A. V. once **A'zal** (Zech. xiv. 5), a Hebrew pronunciation sometimes employed when the word stands at a pause in the sentence (as in text of 1 Chron. viii. 38, but not of ix. 44, R. V.) [perhaps, noble].

1. A descendant of Jonathan, Saul's son (1 Chron. viii. 37, 38; ix. 43, 44).

2. Probably a hamlet; and if so, it lay to the east of Jerusalem (Zech. xiv. 5). Perhaps identical with Beth-ezel.

A'zem. See EZEM.

Az'gad [strong of fortune, or the god Gad is strong].

Founder of a family, members of which returned from Babylonia with both Zerubbabel and Ezra (Ezra ii. 12; viii. 12). Its representative sealed the covenant (Neh. x. 15).

A'zi-el. See JAAZIEL.

A-zi'za [robust].

A man whom Ezra induced to divorce his foreign wife (Ezra x. 27).

Az'ma-veth [death is strong].

1. A Barhumite, one of David's mighty men (2 Sam. xxiii. 31).

2. A Benjamite, whose sons came to David at Ziklag (1 Chron. xii. 3).

3. The son of Adiel. He was over David's treasures (1 Chron. xxvii. 25).

4. A son of Jehoadah and descendant of Jonathan, Saul's son (1 Chron. viii. 36).

5. A village in the vicinity of Jerusalem, near Geba. Forty-two of its inhabitants returned from the Babylonian captivity (Ezra ii. 24). Some singers resided on its fields (Neh. xii. 29). Called also Beth-azmaveth (Neh. vii. 28). Its site is perhaps Hizmeh, midway between Geba and Anathoth.

Az'mon [robust].

A place on the southern boundary of Canaan, to the west of Kadesh-barnea and near the brook of Egypt (Num. xxxiv. 4, 5; Josh. xv. 4, R. V.). Exact site unknown.

Az'noth-ta'bor [the ears, *i. e.* slopes or tops, of Tabor].

A place on the boundary of Naphtali, evidently near mount Tabor (Josh. xix. 34).

A'zor.

An ancestor of Christ who lived after the exile (Mat. i. 13, 14).

A-zo'tus. See ASHDOD.

Az'ri-el [help of God].

1. A chief man of the half tribe of Manasseh, east of the Jordan (1 Chron. v. 24).

2. A Naphtalite of David's time, father of Jerimoth (1 Chron. xxvii. 19).

3. Father of Seraiah of Jeremiah's time (Jer. xxxvi. 26).

Az'ri-kam [help against an enemy, or help hath arisen].

1. A son of Neariah (1 Chron. iii. 23).

2. A son of Azel, and descendant of Jonathan, Saul's son (1 Chron. viii. 38 ; ix. 44).

3. A Levite, descended from Merari (1 Chron. ix. 14).

4. The governor of the palace under king Ahaz. He was killed by an Ephraimite, Zichri (2 Chron. xxviii. 7).

A-zu'bah [forsaken or desolation].

1. A wife of Caleb (1 Chron. ii. 18, 19).

2. A daughter of Shilhi and mother of Jehoshaphat (1 Kin. xxii. 42).

A'zur. See AZZUR.

Az'zah. See GAZA.

Az'zan [strong].

Father of Paltiel, prince of Issachar in the days of Moses (Num. xxxiv. 26).

Az'zur, in A. V. twice **A'zur** [helpful].

1. Father of Hananiah the false prophet (Jer. xxviii. 1).

2. Father of Jaazaniah (Ezek. xi. 1).

3. One of those who, with Nehemiah, sealed the covenant (Neh. x. 17).

B

Ba'al [master, lord, possessor].

1. A sun-god, exhibiting different aspects of the solar energy, the center of whose worship was Phœnicia, whence it spread to the neighboring countries. Baal was adored on high places in Moab as early as the days of Balaam and Balak (Num. xxii. 41). In the time of the judges he had altars within the country of the Israelites (Judg. ii. 13; vi. 28–32), and when king Ahab married Jezebel, the daughter of Ethbaal, king of the Sidonians, the worship of Baal almost supplanted that of Jehovah. The life and death struggle between the two religions culminated on mount Carmel when the prophet Elijah met the priests of Baal (1 Kin. xvi. 31, 32; xviii. 17–40). Though it ended in the slaughter of the priests of Baal, yet they soon swarmed anew until crushed by Jehu (2 Kin. x. 18–28). About this time, the worship of Baal received new impulse in Judah through the influence of Jezebel's daughter, Athaliah, wife of Jehoram (2 Chron. xvii. 3; xxi. 6; xxii. 2). On her overthrow, the temple of Baal at Jerusalem was pulled down, the altars and images were destroyed, and Mattan, the chief priest, slain before the altar (2 Kin.

xi. 18). After a time the worship of Baal was revived in both Israel (Hos. ii. 8; iv. 13) and Judah. Ahaz made molten images for the Baalim (2 Chron. xxviii. 2). Hezekiah, indeed, wrought a reformation, but Manasseh erected altars to Baal (2 Kin. xxi. 3). Josiah destroyed the vessels of Baal at Jerusalem, and made the public worship of Baal for the time to cease (xxiii. 4, 5). Jeremiah frequently denounced it, as did other prophets (Jer. xix. 4, 5). The worship of Baal was accompanied with lascivious rites (cp. 1 Kin. xiv. 24), the sacrifice of children in the fire by parents (Jer. xix. 5), and kissing the image (1 Kin. xix. 18; Hos. xiii. 2). Baal was often associated with the goddess Ashtoreth (Judg. ii. 13), and in the vicinity of his altar there was often an Asherah (Judg. vi. 30; 1 Kin. xvi. 32, 33, both R. V.). Baal must not be confounded with the Babylonian Bel, though both were sun-gods.

2. A Reubenite, house of Joel, who lived before the captivity of the ten tribes (1 Chron. v. 5, 6).

3. A Benjamite, son of king Saul's ancestor Jeiel (1 Chron. viii. 30; ix. 35, 36, 39, R. V.).

4. A village of Simeon (1 Chron. iv. 33); the same as Baalath-beer (q. v.).

Ba'al-ah [mistress].

1. A town better known as Kirjath-jearim (Josh. xv. 9).

2. A hill in Judah, between Ekron and Jabneel (Josh. xv. 11).

3. A town in the south of Judah (Josh. xv. 29); apparently the same as the Simeonite town Balah (Josh. xix. 3) or Bilhah (1 Chron. iv. 29). Site unknown.

Ba'al-ath [mistress].

A village of the original territory of Dan (Josh. xix. 44), near Gezer (Antiq. viii. 6, 1). Solomon fortified it (1 Kin. ix. 18; 2 Chron. viii. 6).

Ba'al-ath-be'er [possessor of a well].

A town on the boundary line of the tribe of Simeon. Called simply Baal (1 Chron. iv. 33), and apparently known also as Ramah and Ramoth of the South (Josh. xix. 8; 1 Sam. xxx. 27, R. V.). Site unknown.

Ba'al-be'rith [lord of a covenant; i. e. the god who enters into a covenant with his worshipers].

A designation under which in the time of the judges Baal was worshiped at Shechem, where he had a temple (Judg. viii. 33; ix. 4). Sometimes he was spoken of as El-berith, the covenant-keeping god (Judg. ix. 46, R. V.; where A. V. partly translates the name).

Ba'al-e, or rather, as in R. V., **Baale Judah** [a construct form, probably singular, Baal of Judah].

A town of Judah, the same as Baalah and Kirjath-baal and Kirjath-jearim (2 Sam. vi. 2; cp. 1 Chron. xiii. 6; Josh. xviii. 14). See KIRJATH-JEARIM.

Ba'al-gad [lord of fortune].

A place at the foot of mount Hermon, in the valley of Lebanon, where apparently Gad, the god of fortune, was worshiped. It constituted the extreme northern limit of Joshua's conquests (Josh. xi. 17; xii. 7; xiii. 5). It can scarcely be identified with either Banias or Baalbek.

Ba'al-ha'mon [place of a multitude].

A place where Solomon had a vineyard (Song viii. 11). Its identity with Balamon, a town near Dothan (Judith viii. 3), which Gesenius suggested, is extremely doubtful in view of the variant spelling Belbaim, Belmaim, Abelmaein (iv. 4; vii. 3).

Ba'al-ha'nan [the Lord is gracious].

1. Son of Achbor and king of Edom (Gen. xxxvi. 38; 1 Chron. i. 49).

2. Custodian of the olive and sycomore trees under king David (1 Chron. xxvii. 28).

Ba'al-ha'zor [lord of a village].

A place beside Ephraim (2 Sam. xiii. 23). Gesenius suggested Hazor in Benjamin (Neh. xi. 33). Another view is that it was at Tell 'Aṣûr, 4½ miles north-northeast of Bethel; but the two names are quite different etymologically.

Ba'al-her'mon [Baal or lord of Hermon].

A mountain marking the northwestern limit of the half tribe of Manasseh east of Jordan, and situated south or southwest of mount Hermon proper (Judg. iii. 3; 1 Chron. v. 23). The comparison of Josh. xiii. 5 with Judg. iii. 3 is not sufficient to establish its identity with Baal-gad.

Ba'al-i [my master] (Hos. ii. 16).

Ba'al-im [Hebrew plural of Baal].

The sun-god Baal as worshiped under different aspects by the nations neighbor to Israel, or the old Canaanite plural of eminence instead of the singular number (Judg. ii. 11; iii. 7: viii. 33; x. 10; 1 Sam. vii. 4; xii. 10). Often coupled with Ashtaroth (q. v.).

Ba'a-lis.

A king of the Ammonites who reigned shortly after Nebuchadnezzar's capture of Jerusalem (Jer. xl. 14).

Ba'al-me'on [lord of Meon or habitation].

An old Amorite city on the frontiers of Moab, known fully as Beth-baal-meon (Num. xxxii. 38; Ezek. xxv. 9; both forms on Moabite Stone 9, 30). It was assigned to the Reubenites and rebuilt by them (Num. xxxii. 38; in ver. 3 called Beon; Josh. xiii. 17; 1 Chron. v. 8). It was held by Mesha, king of Moab (Stone 9, 30), and was in possession of the same people in the sixth century B. C. (Ezek. xxv. 9; and Jer. xlviii. 23, where it is abbreviated to Beth-meon). It was still a considerable town in the time of Jerome, who gives its distance from Heshbon as 9 Roman miles. The ruins, now called Ma'în, lie in the northern Moabite territory, 4 miles southwest of Medeba. Tristram describes them as occupying the crests and sides of four adjacent hills, one being evidently the site of the central city, connected with the rest by a causeway. There are remains of foundations, walls, streets, arches, carved stones, caverns and cavernous dwellings, wells, and cisterns.

Ba'al-pe'or [lord of Peor].

A Moabite deity worshiped with impure rites on the top of mount Peor. The Israelites, when encamped at Shittim, felt attracted by it, and so sinned that a plague broke out among them, and was not stayed till a slaughter had been ordered of the chief transgressors (Num. xxv. 1–9; Ps. cvi. 28; Hos. ix. 10).

Ba'al-per'a-zim [place of breaking forth].

A place near the valley of Rephaim where David gained a victory over the Philistines (2 Sam. v. 18–20; 1 Chron. xiv. 9–11; cp. Is. xxviii. 21).

Ba'al-shal'i-shah, in A. V. **Baal-shalisha** [lord of Shalishah, a third part].

A village from which bread and corn of the firstfruits were brought to Elisha when he was at Gilgal, on the mountains, seven and a half miles north of Bethel (2 Kin. iv. 42–44). The gift was brought to Gilgal because a school of the prophets was there. Jerome and Eusebius call Baal-shalishah Beth-shalishah, and describe it as situated 15 Roman miles to the north of Lydda. Conder locates it at the present village of Kefr Thilth on the lower hills of Ephraim, 16 English miles northeast of Lydda and 13½ miles northwest of Gilgal. The distance and etymology favor the identification. Cp. 1 Sam. ix. 4.

Ba'al-ta'mar [lord or possessor of a palm].

A place in Benjamin where the Israelite army took their stand when about to assail Gibeah (Judg. xx. 33). Exact site unknown.

Ba'al-ze'bub [lord of the fly].

The name under which the sun-god Baal was worshiped at Ekron as the producer of flies, and consequently able to defend against this pest. Ahaziah, king of Judah, applied to him for a revelation (2 Kin. i. 6, 16). See BEELZEBUB.

Ba'al-ze'phon [lord of watchfulness, scarcely Baal of the north or place of Typhon].

A place which was over against the Israelites while they were encamped beside Pi-hahiroth, between Migdol and the sea, just before they crossed through the sea (Ex. xiv. 2, 9). So also in Num. xxxiii. 7, Pi-hahiroth is said to be before Baal-zephon. Site disputed.

Ba'a-na, in A. V. once **Baanah** (1 Kin. iv. 16) [Aramaic form of Baanah].

1. Solomon's purveyor for the southern district of the plain of Jezreel from Megiddo to the Jordan. He was a son of Ahilud and probably brother of Jehoshaphat the recorder (1 Kin. iv. 12; cp. ver. 3).

2. Solomon's purveyor for Asher and vicinity. He was a son of Hushai, not unlikely

of that Hushai who was the friend and adviser of David (1 Kin. iv. 16).

3. A certain Zadok's father (Neh. iii. 4).

Ba'a-nah.

1. A Benjamite, brother of Rechab, and leader of a predatory band. Although the brothers belonged to the tribe of Saul, they nevertheless murdered his son Ish-bosheth, and thus were partly instrumental in turning the kingdom to David. They carried the head of the murdered man to David at Hebron in expectation of a reward ; but David had them put to death as criminals (2 Sam. iv. 1–12).

2. A Netophathite, father of Heled, one of David's worthies (1 Chron. xi. 30).

3. One of Solomon's purveyors. See BAANA.

4. A Jew who returned from Babylon with Zerubbabel (Ezra ii. 2; Neh. vii. 7). It was probably the representative of his family who sealed the covenant in Nehemiah's time (x. 27).

Ba'a-ra [perhaps stupidity].

A wife of Shaharaim (1 Chron. viii. 8).

Ba-a-se'iah.

A Levite, descendant of Gershom and ancestor of Asaph the singer (1 Chron. vi. 40).

Ba'a-sha.

Son of Ahijah, of the tribe of Issachar, who conspired against Nadab, the son and successor of Jeroboam I., king of Israel. When Nadab was directing the siege of Gibbethon, then in the hands of the Philistines, Baasha murdered him and all Jeroboam's descendants, thus fulfilling the judgment denounced against his house (1 Kin. xvi. 7; cp. Acts ii. 23). Then the assassin ascended the throne of Israel in the third year of Asa, king of Judah, and fixed his capital at Tirzah (1 Kin. xv. 25–xvi. 4). He carried on a long war with Asa. He began to fortify Ramah to blockade the northern frontier of Judah, but was diverted from his purpose by the invasion of his kingdom by Benhadad, king of Damascus, whom Asa hired (1 Kin. xv. 16–21; 2 Chron. xvi. 1–6). Baasha continued the calf-worship begun by Jeroboam, and the prophet Jehu threatened him and his house with Jeroboam's fate. He died after a reign of 24 years, and was buried in Tirzah. His son Elah succeeded him (1 Kin. xv. 34–xvi. 6).

Ba'bel [gate of God].

A city in the plain of Shinar. It is first mentioned after the flood. It was the beginning of Nimrod's kingdom, *i. e.* probably the earliest and chief seat of his power (Gen. x. 10). In the English versions the word Babel occurs in this passage and xi. 9 only, being rendered Babylon in all later notices.

The tower of Babel was begun shortly after the flood. Those who planned its erection hoped to establish a renowned center and prevent the danger of their being scattered over the earth. There is neither building-stone nor lime on the alluvial plain of Shinar, so bricks were used in place of stone in building this tower, and for mortar bitumen was employed, abundant supplies of which were found at Hit, about 140 miles higher up the river. The plan of the builders, however, was not carried out, for those erecting the tower were visited with a punishment which instantly or soon produced difference of dialect and the withdrawal of men to new regions. Hence the city was called Babel, place of God's judgment (see GATE). To describe the event the Hebrew writer selected the word *balal*, which bears some resemblance in sound to Babel (Gen. xi. 1–9). This confusion of tongues is recorded in the midst of a section of the book of Genesis devoted to the Semites (x. 21–xi. 26), and may, therefore, have been an incident of Semitic, and not of universal, history. It may have originated dialects among the Semites only (xi. 1 is equally true on this interpretation) ; have occurred after the rise of the family of Eber, and be echoed in the name Peleg (x. 25); see PELEG. A groundless tradition identifies the tower of Babel with the Birs Nimrûd, at Borsippa, about 7 miles from the center of Babylon. But if the unfinished tower was ever put to use afterwards, it was more likely perpetuated by the temple-tower Etemenanki, north of the great temple of Marduk, in the city of Babylon itself.

Although work on the tower ceased, yet the place was not wholly deserted. In after years it was the home of a great community. See next article.

Bab'y-lon [Babel, Assyrian *Bab-ilu*, with the Greek ending *on*].

1. The capital of the Babylonian empire. Its first mention in the Hebrew Scriptures is in Gen. x. 10, with three other places, as the beginning of Nimrod's kingdom (cp. Is. xxiii. 13). There the tower of Babel (q. v.) was undertaken and the consequent confusion of tongues took place (Gen. xi. 1–9). The city became the mistress of Babylonia under king Hammurabi, about the middle of the twentieth century B. C. (see AMRAPHEL), and henceforth was the political and religious center of the country. It reached the height of its glory in the sixth century B. C., under Nebuchadnezzar, who did much for it, rendering it the largest and most splendid capital of his time. The old palace stood on the eastern bank of the Euphrates. This royal residence was enlarged by Nebuchadnezzar to twice its original size, by an addition on the north, and then had the river on the west and a canal on the north and the south, while the eastern side and a magnificent gateway stood upon the great Procession Street, which came from the temple of Marduk, about half a mile to the south. Nebuchadnezzar built another palace a mile and a half to the north of the older one, on an artificial hill whose terraced sides were

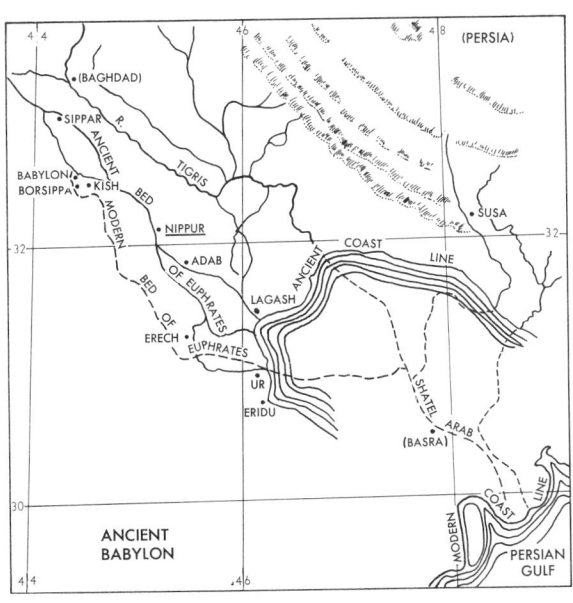

Babylon today is a waste area. These are remains of the city walls. Excavators have been able to trace the streets of the city and the walls of the buildings.

Clay model of a sheep's liver, inscribed as a guide to Babylonian diviners. This model, found in Southern Babylonia, dates from about 1700 B.C.

Above: A one mina weight which dates back [to] the time of Nebuchadnezzar. Sixty shekels ma[de] a maneh (mina) and sixty manehs equalled [a] talent (biltu).
Left: Facade from the throne room of Nebucha[d]nezzar.
Below: Kudurra (boundary) stone from the tim[e] of Nebuchadnezzar I (12th century B.C.). Symbo[ls] of major deities were inscribed on such ston[es] to discourage their removal. The boundary ston[e] publicized grants which the king made to priva[te] citizens. This stone grants land rights to Ritta[-] Marduk, a district governor, from Nebuchadnezz[ar] I.

This painting by Maurice Bardin shows the two parts of the city of Babylon linked by a bridge set on boat-shaped piers. A massive double wall protected the city proper.

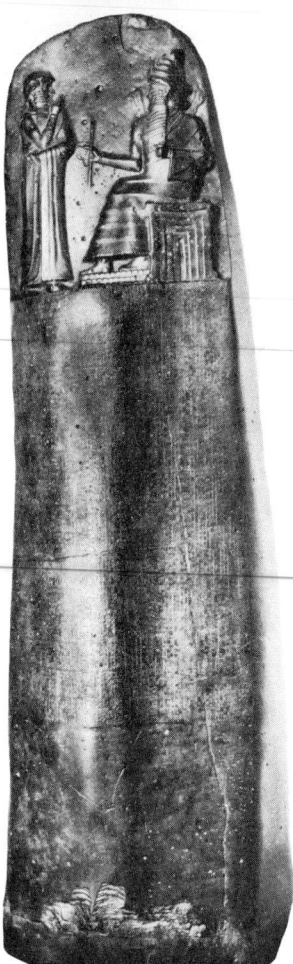

An impression of a cylinder seal from the Old Babylonian Period — the eighteenth or nineteenth century B.C. The text reads: "Manum the Diviner and Servant of the god Enki."

This stele of the Code of Hammurabi contains the longest Babylonian inscription ever found. The top portion shows Hammurabi receiving laws from Shamash, the Sun-god. The remainder of the stele, written in archaic Babylonian cuneiform, is divided into three main parts: the dedication to Shamash, the law code in detail, and the epilogue. This pillar, nearly eight feet high, is of back diorite stone and dates back to 1723 B.C. It was discovered on the site of the acropolis at Susa in 1901 by the French archaeologist, M. J. de Morgan.

From the ninth century B.C., this stone tablet records the rebuilding by Nabu-apal-iddina of the Temple of Shamash, the Sun-god at Sippar, Babylonia.

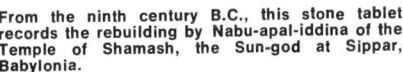

Babylon 604-561, B.C. This painting by Maurice Bardin of ancient Babylon shows a procession moving along Marduk's Way and entering the precincts of Nebuchadnezzar's palace through the Ishtar Gate. The lush growth of the hanging gardens is shown in the upper right.

probably covered by the famous hanging gardens. Herodotus, who flourished about 443 B. C., states that Babylon, which he presumably visited, was a square, each side being 120 stades, or about fourteen miles, in length. This measurement yields an area of nearly 200 square miles, and includes Borsippa in the city limits. Ctesias, also an eyewitness, wh flourished about the year 400 B. C., makes each side of the square about 90 stades, or the length of the four sides together 360 stades or 42 miles, in which case the area would slightly exceed 100 square miles. The city was surrounded by a wall (Jer. li. 58), or rather double walls (Herod. i. 181). Without was a deep and broad moat. Between the two walls, all around the square, was a space in which no houses were allowed to be built. Within the circuit of the inner wall were many gardens, orchards, and fields. These counted much for area, but added little to the population of the city. Herodotus says that the walls were 50 royal cubits broad, or about 85 English feet; and the height 200 royal cubits, about 335 English feet. Quintus Curtius, about A. D. 40, gives the breadth at about 32 English feet; and Clitarchus (as reported by Diodorus Siculus) and Strabo make the height 75 feet. These writers state the circuits variously, from 365 to 385 stades. The city had a hundred gates of bronze, twenty-five on each side. From these there ran broad streets at right angles to the walls, thus dividing the whole area into squares. The Euphrates flowed through the midst of the city, dividing it into two portions. Along each bank of the river there was a continuous quay. A wall separated the quay from the city; but it was pierced by twenty-five gateways, from each of which a sloping descent led to the water's edge. There were ferryboats, a bridge, and even a tunnel. The walls, quays, palaces, temples, and private edifices were built of brick; the cement or mortar was bitumen (cp. Gen. xi. 3). The timber of the houses, which were two, three, and four stories high, was of palm wood (Herod. i. 178–186).

In 520–19 B. C., and again in 514, Babylon revolted against Darius Hystaspis, but on both occasions it was subdued, and the last time was dismantled. Its decay was hastened by Seleucus Nicator, who conquered the city in 312 B. C., and made large use of its materials in building the new capital, Seleucia, on the banks of the Tigris.

The Scripture prophecies regarding Babylon have been fulfilled (Is. xiii.; xiv. 1–23; xxi. 1–10; xlvi. 1, 2; xlvii. 1–3; Jer. l. and li.). Jeremiah (li. 37, cp. l. 26) said that it should become heaps, and mounds are all that remain of it now. They commence about 3½ miles above the village of Hillah, and extend northward slightly above 3 miles, by 2 from east to west, lying chiefly on the eastern side of the river. The three most notable mounds are now called by the Arabs the Babil, the Kasr, and the Amran mounds. They lie east of the river, and in a section of the old city which, at some period of history, was a triangular area bounded by the river and two walls. These walls were practically straight, met in almost a right angle toward the east, and measured two and three miles in length. The southern mound, Amran, marks the site of Marduk's temple. The central one, Kasr, covers the remains of the old palace and a temple of the goddess Belit, which stood farther to the east and was separated from the palace by the Procession Street. The mound Babil, in the north, is the site of Nebuchadnezzar's northern palace.

2. The mystic Babylon of Revelation xiv. 8; xvi. 19; xvii., xviii., is the city of Rome, which stood on seven hills (cp. xvii. 3, 5, 6, 9, 18).

Bab-y-lo'ni-a.

A region of western Asia which had Babylon for its capital. It is sometimes called, in whole or in part, Shinar (Gen. x. 10; xi. 2; Is. xi. 11), and sometimes land of the Chaldeans (Jer. xxiv. 5; xxv. 12; Ezek. xii. 13). It was bounded on the north by Mesopotamia, the dividing line between the two running from near Hit on the Euphrates to a little below Samarah on the Tigris. The boundary is a natural one, separating the slightly elevated plain of secondary formation on the north from the low-lying alluvium brought down by the Euphrates and the Tigris on the south. Babylonia is bounded on the east by the mountains of Elam, east of the river Tigris, on the south by the Persian Gulf, and on the west by the Arabian desert. In ancient historic times the area was about 25,000 square miles, but the northern part of the Persian Gulf is being gradually filled with alluvium, so that now the district is 430 miles long by 185 broad at the widest part, and contains 30,000 square miles. The deep, rich, alluvial soil, artificially irrigated, was of almost matchless fertility. Cushites were early in the country (Gen. x. 8–10), and likewise the Semites. Cities were built, notably Ur (xi. 28), Larsa (cp. xiv. 1), Erech, Babel, Accad (x. 10), Cuthah (2 Kin. xvii. 24), and Nippur. These towns were sometimes independent kingdoms, at other times under one monarch. The Cushite Nimrod early united four under his sway. Sargon of Agade, who was a Semite by race or had adopted the Semitic language, held the entire region under his rule about 3750 B. C. But his dominion and that of his son Naram-sin extended far beyond Babylonia, and reached to the Mediterranean Sea. Two millenia before Christ Kudurnanhundi descended from Elam and conquered Babylonia. To this Elamite dynasty Chedorlaomer probably belonged (Gen. xiv. 1). But the Elamites were at length defeated, and an end was put to their rule in Babylonia by Hammurabi. Several generations later the Cosseans established themselves in the country. About the sixteenth century B. C., the officials of Palestine used the Babylonian script and language in their correspondence with the Egyptian court. About 1270 B. C. the Assyrians under Tukulti-adar subjugated Babylonia, which for the next 700 years remained a second-rate power, though occasionally casting off the Assyrian yoke. Nabonassar achieved independence in 747 B. C. The country was reconquered by Tiglath-pileser about 731 B. C.; then, after successive revolts, by Sargon in 709 B. C., by Sennacherib in 703 B. C., by Esarhaddon in 680 B. C., and by Ashurbanipal in 648 B. C. During this period Merodach-baladan twice occupied the throne, once from 721 to 709, and again in 704 or 703. In 625 B. C., Babylonian independence was finally secured by Nabupaluṣur, known to the Greeks as Nabopolassar, who was probably an official under the Assyrians. The Assyrian empire was threatened by Medes and restless Babylonians. Aided by the Chaldeans, Nabopolassar took possession of Babylon, proclaimed independence from Assyria, and allied himself with the Medes, and laid the foundations of what soon developed into the great Babylonian empire. He reigned from the year 625 to 605 B. C. Nineveh had been captured and destroyed by 606 B. C., and in the partition of its empire the share of Nabopolassar was Susiana, the valley of the Euphrates, Syria, and Palestine, which were annexed to the Babylonian empire. But the claim of Babylonia to the country west of the Euphrates was disputed by Pharaoh Necho, king of Egypt, and Nabopolassar sent his son Nebuchadnezzar to protect the Babylonian interests. Nebuchadnezzar totally defeated Necho at the battle of Carchemish, fought 605 B. C., and pushed westward in order to follow up his victory, but he was recalled to Babylon by the news of his father's death. He ascended the throne in 605 B. C., and reigned nearly forty-four years. Under him the Babylonian empire reached the farthest limits to which it ever attained; and almost all its engineering and architectural achievements were carried out under his direction. Jerusalem was captured and destroyed by him, and the people of Judah carried into captivity; see NEBUCHADNEZZAR. On his death in 562 B. C., he was succeeded by his son Evil-merodach, who befriended the captive Jehoiachin (2 Kin. xxv. 27; Jer. lii. 31). After a reign of two years (562-560 B. C.) Evil-merodach was put to death by conspirators, headed by Neriglissar, husband of a daughter of Nebuchadnezzar. Neriglissar, who was probably the military officer Nergal-sharezer who took part in the siege against Jerusalem (Jer. xxxix. 3, 13), then ascended the throne and reigned four years and a half, dying early in 556 B. C. His son and successor, Labashi-marduk, a mere boy, was clubbed to death a few months later. The conspirators against the boy-king

then invested one of their number, Nabona'id, with the sovereignty. In the seventeenth year of his reign, 539 B. C., Cyrus the Persian entered Babylon, terminating the Babylonian empire; see CYRUS. From the Persians the domination of the country was wrested by Alexander the Great, by his victories in 333 and 331 B. C. Since then the territory on the Lower Euphrates has passed from the Greeks successively to the Romans, the Parthians, the Persians again, and finally to the Mohammedans. After the fall of Jerusalem in A. D. 70 Babylonia became, and for centuries remained, a seat of Jewish schools devoted to the study and interpretation of the law. The country at present is comparatively unproductive, but under firm and enlightened rule would be one of the most fertile regions in the world.

Ba'ca [a balsam tree, so named from its shedding, as it were, tears of gum; possibly also a noun meaning weeping].
A valley in Palestine (Ps. lxxxiv. 6), so called from the balsam trees which grew in it; possibly the valley of Rephaim, where such trees were found (2 Sam. v. 22, 23, R. V. margin). Perhaps, however, the expression is figurative, as the Greek and Syrian translators believed, like "valley of the shadow of death," and denotes any vale of tears.

Bac'chi-des.
A Syrian general sent by Demetrius I. at the close of 162 B. C. to place Alcimus in the high priesthood, and to subjugate rebellious Judah (1 Mac. vii. 8-20). The next year he defeated Judas and Jonathan Maccabæus; but his third campaign, which he undertook in 157 B. C., was not successful, and he returned discouraged (ix. 1-57, 59-72).

Badg'er.
The rendering of the Hebrew word *Taḥash* in the A. V. (Ex. xxvi. 14; xxxv. 7; Num. iv. 25; Ezek. xvi. 10). It was an animal. Its skin was used for the outer covering of the tabernacle, and for sandals. Tristram says that the common badger, *Meles vulgaris*, is not rare in the hilly and wooded parts of Palestine, but it does not seem to be alluded to in the Bible. See SEAL, I.

Bæ'an.
Probably a Bedouin tribe which made predatory incursions (1 Mac. v. 4). Blau has, however, suggested that it may be the name of the place which is called Bajaa in the inscription at Karnak, and which was situated in the region indicated by the narrative.

Bag'pipe.
The rendering on the margin of the R. V. of the Aramaic *Sumphoneya* in Dan. iii. 5, 7, 10, 15. The texts of the A. V. and R. V. translate it dulcimer. *Sumphoneya* is apparently from the Greek *sumphonia*, symphony, unison of sounds. The bagpipe is known in Italy by the name sambogna, and in Asia Minor as sambonya, names which recall *sumphoneya*. The instrument is used also

in Egypt and Arabia, where it consists of a leathern bag in which two pipes are inserted, one for inflating the bag, the other for playing upon with the fingers.

Ba-ha′rum-ite.
An inhabitant of Bahurim (1 Chron. xi. 33).

Ba-hu′rim [young men].
A village near the mount of Olives, on the road from Jerusalem to the Jordan (2 Sam. xvi. 5). It is mentioned repeatedly in the history of David. Thence came Shimei, who cursed him, and in a well there Jonathan and Ahimaaz hid when pursued by the partisans of Absalom (2 Sam. iii. 16; xvi. 5; xvii. 18; xix. 16; 1 Kin. ii. 8). There is reason to believe that it was on or near the old road that ran from Jerusalem to the Jordan through the wady Rûâbeh, and stood either at the ruins a mile and a half northeast of Jerusalem and the same distance south of Anathoth or else half a mile to the southeast on the ridge.

Ba′jith. See BAYITH.

Bak-bak′kar.
A Levite (1 Chron. ix. 15).

Bak′buk [a flagon].
One of the Nethinim, and founder of a family, members of which returned from the captivity (Ezra ii. 51; Neh. vii. 53).

Bak-bu-ki′ah [effusion of Jehovah].
1. A Levite resident of Jerusalem, and in high office immediately after the exile (Neh. xi. 17).
2. A Levite, perhaps representative of the family of the earlier Levite of this name, who served as gatekeeper of the temple in Nehemiah's time (Neh. xii. 25).

Ba′laam [perhaps, devouring].
A diviner (Josh. xiii. 22; cp. Num. xxiv. 1), son of Beor, and resident at the town of Pethor, on the Euphrates (Num. xxii. 5), in Aram, in the hill country of the east (xxiii. 7; cp. Deut. xxiii. 4). The Hebrew text of Num. xxii. 5 describes Balak as sending to Balaam "to the land of the children of his people," meaning Balak's native land or, better, Balaam's. The Samaritan and Syriac, reading 'ammon for 'ammo, have "land of the children of Ammon"; but Balaam is nowhere else connected with the Ammonites, not even in Num. xxxi. 8. This diviner recognized Jehovah as the god of Israel (xxiii. 21), and as one at least of his own gods (xxii. 18; but the Greek version reads merely "Jehovah God"). Balak, king of Moab, sent an embassy to him, consisting of elders of Moab and Midian, offering him reward to place the Israelites under a ban (Num. xxii. 5–7). He answered that he could not do so without the consent of Jehovah, the God of Israel. Consent was, of course, refused. Balak dispatched more honorable negotiators, not elders, but princes. Balaam replied that not for a house full of gold and silver would he go beyond the word of Jehovah. Impor-

tuning God for permission, he was allowed to go with the men, on condition of uttering only the words that God put into his mouth. On the way an angel of the Lord with drawn sword, visible to the ass on which Balaam rode, but not to its rider, thrice disputed his progress. The ass refused to go forward. When beaten it spoke (Antiq. iv. 6, 3; 2 Pet. ii. 15). Finally, Balaam himself was permitted to see the angel, and learn the peril he was in. He offered to turn back, but was allowed to go forward, on the same stringent condition as before. Balak met him on the banks of the Arnon, and conducted him to Kiriath-huzoth, probably the same as Kiriath-aim, on the conspicuous eminence near by north of the Arnon. The next morning the two, accompanied by the princes of Moab, went northward to the high places of Baal, from which lofty spot part of the camp of Israel at Shittim was visible (Num. xxii. 8–41, R. V.). After sacrifices on seven altars, Balaam went alone to a bare height. There the word of the Lord came to him. He returned to Balak, and under the irresistible power of God blessed the people he had been invited to curse (xxiii. 1–12). Balak was disappointed, but held to the idea that, as long as Balaam saw but a part of the camp, perhaps he might be able to curse the Israelites. He took Balaam to the top of Pisgah and sacrificed as before; but the only result was fresh blessing instead of cursing (13–26). A third attempt was made from the top of Peor, on the ridge north of Nebo. Not merely was there blessing, but the utterance ended with the prophecy of a star out of Jacob, and a scepter out of Israel that should sway over Moab and Edom. Balak in anger dismissed Balaam without conferring on him the intended honor (xxiii. 27–xxiv. 25). Balaam, however, before quitting the country, suggested that if the Israelites could be seduced into the idolatry and the impurity of the worship practiced in Baal-peor, they would come under Jehovah's curse. The evil counsel was followed. In the war waged by the Israelites to execute vengeance on the Midianites for this deed, Balaam was slain (xxxi. 8, 16). Various other O. T. books and some of the N. T. writers refer to Balaam's character and fate (Deut. xxiii. 4, 5; Josh. xxiv. 9, 10; Neh. xiii. 2; Mic. vi. 5; 2 Pet. ii. 15; Jude 11; Rev. ii. 14).

Ba′lac. See BALAK.

Bal′a-dan [a son he hath given]. The name is abbreviated by omission of the name of some god who bestowed the son.
Father of Merodach-baladan (Is. xxxix. 1).

Ba′lah. See BAALAH 3.

Ba′lak, in A. V. of N. T. **Balac** [emptying].
A Moabite king, son of Zippor, who lured Balaam from Pethor to curse Israel (Num. xxii.–xxiv.; Josh. xxiv. 9; Judg. xi. 25; Mic. vi. 4. 5; Rev. ii. 14).

Bald Lo'cust.

The rendering of the Hebrew Sal'am, consumer. An unknown species of locust or grasshopper (Lev. xi. 22). There is nothing in the Hebrew etymology to suggest that the animal had a bald appearance.

Balm, Balm of Gil'e-ad.

The rendering of the Hebrew word Sori, ooze, a vegetable product obtained especially in Gilead (Gen. xxxvii. 25; Jer. viii. 22; xlvi. 11), and exported from Palestine (Gen. xxxvii. 25; Ezek. xxvii. 17). It was used as an ointment for the healing of wounds (Jer. ii. 8). It was once strongly believed, and still is by many, that the balm of Gilead was opobalsamum, a greenish-yellow oily resin of the consistency of honey, to which wonderful healing virtues were attributed. It comes from a tree, Balsamodendron opobalsamum or gileadense, belonging to the order Amyridaceae (Amyrids). It is from six to eight feet high. But the identification of the opobalsamum with the balm of Gilead is rendered doubtful by the fact that the tree producing it is not now found in Gilead, even in gardens, and there is no proof that it ever existed in that locality. It is a native of Arabia and Nubia, and hence is often called the balm of Mecca. On the margin of R. V. (Gen. xxxvii. 25) the word is rendered by mastic, Pistacia lentiscus, a bushy evergreen tree, about twelve feet high. It grew in Palestine (Pliny 14, 25). The transparent. pale yellow, fragrant gum was used for incense and, when dissolved in water. as an ointment; while oil obtained from the bark, leaves, and berries was used as a medicine. Josephus mentions a plant bearing very precious balsam as cultivated at Jericho, but he does not give details sufficient for its identification (Antiq. xiv. 4, 1; xv. 4, 2: War i. 6, 6). Nor can it be examined now, for it has been extinct, it is believed. since the time of the crusades.

Bal'sam Tree.

The rendering of Hebrew Baka' on the margin of Ps. lxxxiv. 6; 2 Sam. v. 23, 24; 1 Cron. xiv. 14, 15 in R. V. The plant grew near Jerusalem. The Arabs apply the name to a bush which grows near Mecca, resembles the balsam (see BALM), and has a white, acrid sap.

Ba'mah [high place] (Ezek. xx. 29). See HIGH PLACES.

Ba'moth [high places].

An encampment of the Israelites north of the Arnon, probably an abbreviation of Bamoth-baal (Num. xxi. 19).

Ba'moth-ba'al [high places of Baal].

A place north of the Arnon. probably that at which the Israelites temporarily encamped. to which Balak took Balaam, and whence the plains of Moab were visible (Num. xxi. 19; xxii. 41 R. V. margin). It was within the limits of the tribe of Reuben (Josh. xiii. 17; where it is named between Dibon and Beth-baal-meon). It is believed to be one of the peaks of the long ridge of 'Attarus on the south bank of the Zerka Ma'in.

Ba'ni [built].

1. A Gadite, one of David's mighty men (2 Sam. xxiii. 36). Textual criticism is still unable to determine the text of this verse and of 1 Chron. xi. 38. One or both may need revision.

2. A descendant of Judah through Perez (1 Chron. ix. 4. R. V.).

3. Founder of a family, members of which returned from Babylonia with Zerubbabel (Ezra ii. 10). Some of them took foreign wives (x. 29). The family's representative sealed the covenant (Neh. x. 14). Called also Binnui (Neh. vii. 15).

4. A Levite of the family of Merari (1 Chron. vi. 46).

5. A Levite who lived before the return from exile, of the sons of Asaph and hence of the family of Gershom (Neh. xi. 22).

6. A Levite, father of Rehum (Neh. iii. 17); perhaps he who took a prominent part at the feast of tabernacles in Ezra's time (Neh. viii. 7; ix. 4, 5), and in behalf of his house sealed the covenant (x. 13).

7. A Levite (Neh. ix. 4). As the name is mentioned twice in ver. 4 and only once in ver. 5, it is perhaps once corrupt in ver. 4.

8. Founder of house or family (Ezra x. 34), among whose descendants was a person also named Bani (38).

Bank and **Bank'er**.

Not only was money loaned by a man to his neighbor as a private transaction, but money-lending was a regular business. The banker sat at his table (Luke xix. 23), received money on deposit, allowed interest on it (ibid.; Mat. xxv. 27), and loaned it to others on pledge or mortgage (cp. Neh. v. 3, 4). A branch of the banking business was money-changing. For a small commission the broker exchanged money of one denomination for that of another. as shekels for the half-shekels needed to pay the temple tax; or gave coins current in the country for foreign money, as a Hebrew shekel for Roman denarii and Greek drachmas (Mark xi. 15; John ii. 15). See LOAN.

Baptism.

The rite of washing with water as a sign of religious purification and consecration.

Among the Jews, as elsewhere, such washings were frequent; some prescribed in the O. T. (e. g. Ex. xxix. 4; xxx. 20; xl. 12; Lev. xv.; xvi. 26, 28;

Baptismal font excavated from the large Byzantine Church in Tekoa. Made of pinkish semi-meta-morphosed limestone which has the appearance of marble, it is one of the finest baptistries in existence.

xvii. 15; xxii. 4, 6; Num. xix. 8) and others the product of later custom (see Mark vii. 3, 4; Heb. vi. 2). Many believe also that in Christ's time, as certainly was the case later, proselytes to Judaism were baptized. Hence, John, the Forerunner, when sent to call Israel to repentance, was directed by God (John i. 33) to administer baptism to those who accepted his message. His rite is called "the baptism of repentance unto remission of sins" (Mark i. 4, R. V.). Recipients of it thereby acknowledged their sins and professed their faith that through the coming Messiah they would be forgiven. Jesus sought baptism partly to express his sympathy with John's work, partly to dedicate himself to his own work, and partly to express his assumption of the sins of men.

Christians have differed, even from earliest times, as to the mode of baptism and as to those who are entitled to this rite.

A large and influential segment of Protestantism insists that immersion is the only valid mode of baptism. It is their contention that the word baptizo invariably means immersion, and that there can be no question that the form of baptism used by the apostles and the early church was complete immersion. Baptism is primarily a symbol of identification with Christ in His burial and resurrection (Col. ii. 11, 12). Then the mode should correspond as nearly as possible to that symbol; hence, immersion. As to the subjects of baptism, only believers are entitled to the rite. The Scriptures indicate that instruction (Matt. xxviii. 19), repentance (Acts ii. 38), and faith (Acts ii. 41; viii. 12; xviii. 8; Gal. iii. 26, 27) should precede baptism. This can only be true of believers; hence, believers baptism.

There are those who maintain that baptism may be by affusion or aspersion (sprinkling) and that it may and ought to be administered to children of believers. Those who hold this position state their case as follows. While the word baptism is derived from a verb, baptizo, which means etymologically to immerse, this does not prove that immersion was the mode always practiced nor that it is necessary. In fact, instances occur where the word plainly does not mean immerse (e.g. Luke xi. 38. in English version "wash" and probably Mark vii. 4). The Scriptures nowhere prescribe the mode. In the post-apostolic times both immersion and affusion were used. This variation still persists. The Eastern Churches, the Baptists, as well as various other groups still practice immersion, the Latin Church generally uses affusion, while most Protestants use affusion or aspersion. Probably the mode varied even in apostolic times. According to

Christ's command, it is to be administered in the name of the Trinity. The church from the earliest times (it is claimed) has administered baptism also to children who have sponsors to care for their Christian nurture. Those who adhere to the infant baptism position believe that it is certainly Scriptural to do this to children of believers. They hold that Paul expressly teaches (Gal. iii. 15-29) that believers in Christ are under the gracious provisions of the covenant which God made with Abraham. Under that covenant circumcision was administered to children as a sign of their participation in the relationship in which their parents stood to God. It is upon this basis that they believe that the children of Christian believers have a similar right to baptism.

The phrase "baptized for the dead" (1 Cor. xv. 29) is difficult to explain. It probably either means "baptized with a view to the world of the dead into which we are going," or refers to a custom of baptizing one person in place of another who has died, a custom which Paul might cite for his argument without approving. G.T.P.

Bar-ab'bas [son of a father].
A robber who had made an insurrection in which he had committed murder. He was a notable prisoner when Jesus was arrested. Pilate, anxious that Jesus should be released, offered the Jews the option of releasing Jesus or Barabbas, and they chose Barabbas (Mat. xxvii. 16, 17, 20, 21, 26).

Bar'a-chel [God has blessed].
A Buzite, father of Elihu, Job's friend (Job xxxii. 2, 6).

Bar-a-chi'ah, in A. V. **Barachias**, the Greek modification of the Hebrew name [Jehovah hath blessed].
Father of that prophet, Zachariah, who was slain between the temple and the altar (Mat. xxiii. 35). See ZACHARIAH.

Ba'rak [lightning].
An Israelite, belonging to the city of Kedesh-naphtali, who at the command of Deborah the prophetess, called together 10,000 men of Naphtali and Zebulun, with whom he routed Sisera, Jabin's commander-in-chief, and destroyed his army (Judg. iv. 1-24; v. 1, 12; Heb. xi. 32).

Bar-ba'ri-an.
1. Originally one who did not speak the Greek language. The phrase Hellenes and barbarians embraced all nations (cp. Rom. i. 14). There being nothing offensive in the word, the Romans and the Jews were content to be called barbarians.
2. Later, one who did not belong to the cultivated Hellenic race (cp. Col. iii. 11).

3. One who spoke an unintelligible foreign tongue (1 Cor. xiv. 11).

Bar-hu′mite.
Probably a misreading of Baharumite (2 Sam. xxiii. 31 with 1 Chron. xi. 33).

Ba-ri′ah [fugitive].
A descendant of Shecaniah (1 Chron. iii. 22).

Bar-je′sus. See ELYMAS.

Bar-Jo′nah, in A. V. **Bar-jona.**
A surname of the apostle Peter (Mat. xvi. 17); probably meaning "son of John" (John i. 42; xxi. 15–17, R. V.), for the Hebrew word from which John is derived is occasionally written in Greek in a form not distinguished from the Greek of Jonah (cp. various Greek texts of 2 Kin. xxv. 23; 1 Chron. vi. 9, 10; xii. 12; xxvi. 3; Ezra viii. 12; 1 Esdras ix. 1, 23).

Bar′kos [painter].
One of the Nethinim, who founded a family, members of which returned from the captivity (Ezra ii. 53; Neh. vii. 55).

Bar′ley.
A cereal grain, called by the Hebrews Se‘orah, the hairy, bristling thing, and by the Greeks Krithai, and largely cultivated in Palestine (Ruth i. 22), Egypt (Ex. ix. 31), and the adjacent regions, and made into cakes or loaves (Judg. vii. 13; John vi. 9). The several barleys belong to the genus Hordeum. They are cereal grasses, with the spikelets, which are in threes, on opposite sides of the rachis or flower axis, so as to form a two-sided spike. Ten species are known, of which Tristram found six in Palestine, one of them, Hordeum athaburense, from mount Tabor, being peculiar to the Holy Land. That now cultivated in Palestine is chiefly Hordeum distichum, which has only the central floret fertile, the two side ones being abortive.

Bar′na-bas [son of prophecy, especially of prophesying which takes the form of exhortation or consolation].
The surname of Joses, a Levite of Cyprus, who early converted to Christianity, sold his land and laid the price at the feet of the apostles in Jerusalem (Acts iv. 36, 37). When the Christians of Jerusalem were afraid to receive the new convert Paul, Barnabas spoke in his behalf, and removed their apprehensions (ix. 27). On the report reaching Jerusalem that Christians of Cyprus and Cyrene had been proclaiming the gospel with great success to Greeks as well as to Jews at Antioch of Syria, the Church sent Barnabas thither, and he aided in the work (xi. 19–24). From Antioch he went to Tarsus and brought back Saul (xi. 22–26). Later the two were dispatched to carry alms to their brethren at Jerusalem, then suffering from famine (27–30). Returning with John Mark to Antioch (xii. 25), they were sent forth by the church on a mission to the gentiles (xiii. 2). They visited Cyprus, and went thence to Perga,

Antioch in Pisidia, Iconium, Lystra, and Derbe. At Lystra at Paul's command a cripple walked; and the inhabitants concluded that Barnabas was the supreme god Jupiter, and that Paul, since he was the chief speaker, was Mercury, the messenger of the gods (xiii. 3–xiv. 28). Having returned to Syria, they were sent by the church of Antioch to the council of Jerusalem. Barnabas spoke, as did Paul (xv. 1, 2, 12). At the close the two were commissioned to carry the decrees of the council to the churches in Syria and Asia Minor (22–31). After further labors at Antioch (35), Paul proposed a second missionary journey. Barnabas desired to have with him his relative, John Mark (Col. iv. 10). Paul objected, as John Mark had withdrawn from the work on the former tour. After sharp contention, the two evangelists separated and went different ways. Barnabas with Mark sailed again to Cyprus, while Paul went on to Asia Minor. But their mutual affection did not cease. Paul, in his epistles, speaks in a friendly way of Barnabas (1 Cor. ix. 6; Gal. ii. 1, 9, 13; Col. iv. 10), and yet more so of John Mark, about whom the quarrel arose (2 Tim. iv. 11).

Bar-sab′bas, in A. V. **Bar′sa-bas** [son of Sabba (?)].
1. The surname of the Joseph who stood candidate for the apostleship against Matthias (Acts i. 23).
2. The surname of the Judas who was sent to Antioch as a delegate of the metropolitan church with Paul, Barnabas, and Silas (Acts xv. 22).

Bar-thol′o-mew [son of Tolmai].
One of the twelve apostles (Mat. x. 3; Mark iii. 18; Luke vi. 14; Acts i. 13). As in the first three of these passages the name of Bartholomew immediately follows that of Philip, and nearly does so in the fourth, Bartholomew was probably the surname of Nathanael, who was led to Christ by Philip (John i. 45, 46).

Bar-ti-mæ′us [son of Timæus].
A blind man healed by Jesus at Jericho (Mark x. 46).

Ba′ruch [blessed].
1. A scribe, member of the family of Neriah, and a friend of Jeremiah (Jer. xxxvi. 26, 32; cp. Antiq. x. 9, 1). In the fourth year of Jehoiakim, he wrote the prophecies of Jeremiah at the prophet's dictation (xxxvi. 1–8). In the following year he publicly read them on the fast day (10), and afterwards before the princes, who took possession of the roll (14–20). The king, on hearing the opening sentences, burnt the roll and ordered the seizure of the prophet and the scribe, but they escaped (21–26). Baruch made a new copy with additions (xxxvi. 27–32). In the tenth year of Zedekiah, during the siege of Jerusalem, Jeremiah bought a field at Anathoth from his uncle and, being at the time a prisoner,

placed the deed in the charge of Baruch and testified that the land should again be possessed by Israel (xxxii. 6–16, 43, 44). Baruch was taken with Jeremiah to Egypt (Jer. xliii. 1–7). For the book bearing the name of Baruch, see APOCRYPHA.

2. Son of Zabbai. He repaired part of the wall of Jerusalem (Neh. iii. 20). He is perhaps the person of that name who sealed the covenant (x. 6).

3. A man of Judah, of the Shilonite family (Neh. xi. 5).

Bar-zil'la-i [made of iron].

1. A wealthy Gileadite of Rogelim, east of the Jordan. He showed David princely hospitality, sending him and his army food and other necessaries while the fugitive king was at Mahanaim during Absalom's rebellion (2 Sam. xvii. 27–29). After the victory, Barzillai escorted David over the Jordan, and was invited to become a member of the king's household and court at Jerusalem, but he excused himself on account of his great age —eighty years. It was therefore arranged that his son Chimham should go in his stead (xix. 31–40).

2. A Meholathite, whose son Adriel married Saul's daughter Michal (2 Sam. xxi. 8).

3. A priest who married a daughter of Barzillai the Gileadite, and assumed his father-in-law's name (Ezra ii. 61 ; Neh. vii. 63).

Bas'ca-ma.

A town east of the Jordan near which Jonathan Maccabæus was put to death, and where for a time he was buried (1 Mac. xiii. 23 ; and Antiq. xiii. 6, 6, where it is called Basca).

Bas'e-math, in A. V. **Bashemath**, once **Basmath** (1 Kin. iv. 15) [fragrance].

1. One of Esau's wives, daughter of Elon the Hittite (Gen. xxvi. 34) ; in xxxvi. 2 called Adah. See ADAH.

2. One of Esau's wives, a daughter of Ishmael and sister of Nebaioth (Gen. xxxvi. 3, 4, 13, 17) ; in xxviii. 9 called Mahalath.

3. A daughter of Solomon and wife of his tax collector for Naphtali (1 Kin. iv. 15).

Ba'shan [broad, open land].

A region east of the Jordan. Its location and extent in O. T. times is best learned from its cities. Within its bounds were Golan, north of the Yarmuk (Deut. iv. 43), Edrei and Ashtaroth (Deut. i. 4), Salecah on the southern slope of the Jebel Hauran (Deut. iii. 10; Josh. xiii. 11, both R. V.). That is to say, it extended southeastwardly from the neighborhood of the upper Jordan to the border of the Arabian desert south of the Hauran mountain. It marched on the north with Geshur and Maacah (Josh. xii. 5 ; see ARAM), and contained "the region of the Argob," famous for sixty cities high-walled (Deut. iii. 4, 5 ; 1 Kin. iv. 13). So large a number is not incredible. In the mountainous parts of the country there are still at least one hundred deserted cities and villages, many of

them built of basalt and with basaltic doors (Porter, *Cities of Bashan*). Josephus identifies Bashan with Gaulonitis and Batanea (Antiq. iv. 5, 3 with 1 Kin. iv. 13 ; and ix. 8, 1 with 2 Kin. x. 33). In the days of Abraham it was occupied by a people of especially large and powerful build, known as Rephaim (Gen. xiv. 5). The last king of this race was Og, who was defeated and slain at Edrei by the Israelites in the time of Moses (Num. xxi. 33–35 ; Deut. iii. 1–7). Bashan was assigned to the half tribe of Manasseh (Deut. iii. 13). It is a broad, fertile plateau, of volcanic formation, and well adapted for pasture. It was celebrated for its cattle (Ps. xxii. 12 ; Ezek. xxxix. 18 ; Amos iv. 1), and for its breed of sheep (Deut. xxxii. 14). It was celebrated also for its oak trees (Is. ii. 13 ; Ezek. xxvii. 6 ; Zech. xi. 2). Forests of evergreen oak still survive.

Ba'shan-ha'voth-ja'ir ; rightly separated by R. V., which renders "he called them, even Bashan, after his own name, Havvoth-jair" (Deut. iii. 14). See HAVVOTH-JAIR.

Bash'e-math. See BASEMATH.

Bas'i-lisk.

The rendering of the R. V. of the Hebrew *Ṣepha'* and *Ṣiph'oni*, a venomous serpent living in a hole (Is. xi. 8). It deposits eggs, from which its young are hatched (lix. 5). It is insensible to the charmer's arts (Jer. viii. 17). The marginal rendering is adder, except in Prov. xxiii. 32, where adder is used in the text. Except in the last case, the A. V. translates the word by cockatrice.

Ba'sin, formerly spelled **Bason.**

A portable vessel for holding water for washing and other purposes (John xiii. 5).

In the English version the word is used for bowls and dishes of various kinds, especially for—

1. A small vessel, in Hebrew *'Aggan* (Is. xxii. 24, rendered cup), used for wine (Song vii. 2, rendered goblet) and other liquids (Ex. xxiv. 6).

2. A shallow vessel, in Hebrew *Saph*, used for domestic purposes (2 Sam. xvii. 28) and to receive the blood of sacrifices (Ex. xii. 22). They were employed in the temple (Jer. lii. 19, R. V. cups ; 2 Kin. xii. 13, A. V. bowl, R. V. cup).

3. A large bowl, in Hebrew *Mizraḳ*, used in the tabernacle and temple, especially in ministrations at the great altar (Num. iv. 14), to hold the meal offering (Num. vii. 13, rendered bowl), and to receive the blood of sacrifices (Zech. ix. 15 with xiv. 20, rendered bowl). It was made of gold, silver, or brass, and burnished (Ex. xxvii. 3 ; Num. vii. 84, rendered bowl : 1 Kin. vii. 45, 50). Revelers sometimes drank wine from such vessels (Amos vi. 6, rendered bowl).

Bas'ket.

Baskets of different sizes, shapes, and construction were in use, and various names were employed for them. As ancient sculptures and relics show, and as the etymology denotes, they were woven open or close, were made of the fiber or leaves of the palm tree or of rushes, reeds, twigs, or ropes, tapered at the top or at the bottom, were shallow or deep, ornamented with colors or plain, small enough to be carried in the hand, or so large that they were carried on the shoulder or head or borne on a pole between two men. They were employed for carrying fruit (Deut. xxvi. 2; Jer. vi. 9; xxiv. 2; Amos viii. 2, where in each passage a different Hebrew word is used); for carrying bread, cakes, and flesh (Gen. xl. 17; Ex. xxix. 2, 3; Lev. viii. 2; Judg. vi. 19; Mark viii. 19, 20, where still another Hebrew and two Greek names occur); for carrying clay to the brickyard and earth for the building of embankments (Ps. lxxxi. 6, R. V.; see illustration under EGYPT).

Bas′math. See BASEMATH.

Bat.

The rendering of the Hebrew word *'a̱talleph*. It was classed with fowls, and was ceremonially unclean (Lev. xi. 13, 19; Deut. xiv. 11, 12, 18). It hides itself from observation in dark places (Is. ii. 20). The reference is pretty clearly to the bat order, of which Tristram enumerates seventeen species as occurring in Palestine. The bat is not a bird, but is a quadruped, covered with hair instead of feathers, having teeth instead of a bill, and suckling its young instead of laying eggs. Nor is its "wing" a flying apparatus of the bird type; it is an unfeathered membrane connecting the fore and hind legs.

Bath.

A Hebrew measure of capacity used for measuring liquids (1 Kin. vii. 26, 38; 2 Chron. ii. 10; iv. 5; Ezra vii. 22). It was the tenth part of a homer, and corresponds to the dry measure ephah in capacity (Ezek. xlv. 10, 11, 14).

Bath′ing.

In the warm climate of the East frequent bathing is a necessity. The daughter of Pharaoh bathed in the Nile (Ex. ii. 5). The Egyptians wore linen garments, constantly fresh-washed, and their priests washed themselves in cold water twice every day and twice every night (Herod. ii. 37). Egyptians, Hebrews, and Syrians washed the dust of the road from their feet when they tarried at a house (Gen. xviii. 4; xix. 2; xxiv. 32; xliii. 24; John xiii. 10). If the Israelites contracted ceremonial defilement, they bathed the body and washed the raiment (Lev. xiv. 8; xv. 5; xvii. 15; Num. xix. 7, 8), either in running water (Lev. xv. 13), at a fountain (Judith xii. 7, 9; cp. John ix. 7), in a river (2 Kin. v. 10), or at home in court or garden (2 Sam. xi. 2, 4; cp. Susanna 15). They washed and anointed themselves and put on their best garments for gala and court attire and on putting away mourning (Ex. xl. 12, 13; Ruth iii. 3; 2 Sam. xii. 20; Judith x. 3; Mat. vi. 17). The priests washed their hands and feet before entering the sanctuary or burning

an offering on the altar (Ex. xxx. 19-21). The high priest bathed at his inauguration and on the day of atonement before each act of propitiation (Lev. viii. 6; xvi. 4, 24). In the time of Christ, the Jews washed their hands before eating, and washed or sprinkled themselves on coming from the market (Mark vii. 3, 4). At this time also, when Greek and Roman customs had gained entrance among the Jews, there were public baths. The warm springs at Tiberias, Gadara, and Callirrhoe, near the eastern shore of the Dead Sea, were resorted to for health (Antiq. xvii. 6, 5; xviii. 2, 3). The fish ponds connected with the palace at Jericho were used for bathing and swimming (Antiq. xv. 3, 3).

Bath-rab′bim [daughter of many people].

One of the gates of Heshbon (Song vii. 4).

Bath-she′ba [daughter of an oath].

Daughter of Eliam, and wife of Uriah the Hittite; thus perhaps the daughter of one, as she was the wife of another, of David's mighty men. She is the woman with whom David so shamefully sinned, and who, after the removal of her husband, became the wife of David and mother of Solomon (2 Sam. xi. 3, 4; xii. 24; 1 Kin. i. 11). When Adonijah was preparing to usurp the kingdom, Bathsheba, supported by the prophet Nathan, appealed to David in favor of her own son Solomon, the result being that Adonijah's enterprise was thwarted (1 Kin. i. 11-53), and himself ultimately put to death (ii. 13-25).

Bath′-shu-a [daughter of riches or salvation].

1. The daughter of Shua (as the name is rendered in A. V.) and wife of Judah (1 Chron. ii. 3; see Gen. xxxviii. 2, 12, both R.V.).

2. The text of 1 Chron. iii. 5 refers to the mother of Solomon as Bath-shua, the daughter of Ammiel. Bath-shua is probably merely a misreading of Bath-sheba, due to a partial effacement of the Hebrew letter beth. The Septuagint has here the usual form for Bathsheba.

Bav′vai, in A. V. **Ba′vai**.

A son of Henadad, who superintended the repair of part of the wall of Jerusalem (Neh. iii. 18).

Ba′yith, in A. V. **Bajith** [the house]. The Hebrew text has the definite article.

A Moabite town or temple (Is. xv. 2).

Bay Tree.

The rendering in the A. V. of the Hebrew *'Ezraḥ* in Ps. xxxvii. 35. The plant referred to by the translators is *Laurus nobilis,* a tree thirty, forty, or more feet high, with lance-shaped evergreen aromatic leaves, inconspicuous flowers, and cherry-like fruits. Tristram met with it on Carmel, Tabor, and in Gilead. The R. V. renders *'Ezraḥ* "a green tree in its native soil," which, of course, tends to flourish better than a transplanted and, perhaps, a sickly exotic. The same Hebrew word is used in Lev. xvi. 29; xviii. 26, for a native as distinguished from a man from another country.

Baz′lith or **Baz′luth** [nakedness]. Either form is in itself legitimate.

One of the Nethinim and founder of a family, members of which returned from captivity (Ezra ii. 52; Neh. vii. 54).

Bdell′ium.

The rendering of the Hebrew *B⁰dolaḥ*, a substance of the same color as manna (Num. xi. 7), and found like gold and the onyx stone or the beryl in the land of Havilah (Gen. ii. 12). The Greeks gave the name *bdellion* to a transparent, waxy, fragrant gum obtained from a tree in Arabia, Babylonia, India, and Media. The best came from Bactria. As gold, the onyx, and the beryl, belong to the mineral kingdom, *b⁰dolaḥ* may perhaps also. The Septuagint translates it in Gen. ii. 12 *anthrax*, the carbuncle, ruby, and garnet; and in Num. xi. 7, *krustallos*, rock crystal.

Be-a-li′ah [Jehovah is Lord].

A Benjamite warrior who came to David at Ziklag (1 Chron. xii. 5).

Be′a-loth [literally mistresses, possessors].

1. A village in the extreme south of Judah (Josh. xv. 24). Site unknown.

2. A locality in the vicinity of the tribe of Asher, perhaps known by this name (1 Kin. iv. 16, R. V.). See ALOTH.

Bean.

Beans were used for food (2 Sam. xvii. 28), and occasionally, especially during famine, were mixed with grain and made into a coarse bread (Ezek. iv. 9). The common bean, *Vicia faba*, is still known in Palestine by the O. T. name for bean.

Bear.

The Syrian bear (*Ursus syriacus*) is of a yellowish-brown color, and, unless pressed by necessity, lives chiefly on vegetable food. But all bears are dangerous when meddled with (Is. xi. 7; Amos v. 19), especially when robbed of their whelps (2 Sam. xvii. 8; Prov. xvii. 12; Hosea xiii. 8). Though now almost confined to Lebanon, on the west of the Jordan, and Hermon, Gilead, and Bashan, on the east of the river, it anciently roamed over the land (cp. Prov. xxviii. 15). David killed one in the vicinity of Bethlehem (1 Sam. xvii. 34), and near Bethel two she bears, which came out of the woods, tore in pieces forty-two young persons who mocked Elisha (2 Kin. ii. 24).

The bear of Dan. vii. 5, commissioned to devour much flesh, was the Medo-Persian empire, one of four successive empires of the world. The four beasts of Daniel are combined in one beast in Rev. xiii. 2, to symbolize all the power of the world. The feet are bear's feet.

For the constellation Bear, see under ARCTURUS.

Beard.

The beard was cherished as the badge of manly dignity. Its neglect was an outward sign of mental aberration (1 Sam. xxi. 13) or of affliction (2 Sam. xix. 24). As a mark of mourning it was customary to pluck it out or cut it off (Ezra ix. 3; Is. xv. 2; Jer. xli. 5; Herod. ii. 36). The king of the Ammonites grievously insulted David's ambassadors when, among other acts, he shaved off one half of their beards (2 Sam. x. 4, 5; cp. Herod. ii. 121, 4). The ancient Egyptians shaved the head and the face, but often wore a false beard. They let the hair and beard grow as a sign of mourning (Herod. ii. 36). Hence Joseph, when released from prison, shaved the beard in order to appear before Pharaoh (Gen. xli. 14). The practice of shaving off the corners of the beard (Lev. xix. 27; Jer. ix. 26; xxv. 23, both R. V.) was probably a heathenish sign, as the Arabs shaved the side of the face between the ear and the eye in honor of their god Orotal (Herod. iii. 8).

Beast.

1. A mammal, not man, as distinguished from a fowl of the air and a creeping thing (Gen. i. 29, 30). The wild beasts are distinguished from domesticated animals (Lev. xxvi. 22; Is. xiii. 21, 22; xxxiv. 14; Jer. l. 39; Mark i. 13).

2. Any of the inferior animals, including reptiles and birds, as distinguished from man (Ps. cxlvii. 9; Ecc. iii. 19; Acts xxviii. 5). In this sense there was a distinction drawn under the Mosaic law between ceremonially clean and unclean beasts.

3. Figuratively, a fierce destructive power. Four successive empires, beginning with the Babylonian, are thus symbolized in Dan. vii. The four beasts, combined into a composite monster, represent the power of the world in Rev. xiii. 1–10, with its seat transferred from Babylon to Rome, xvii. 3–18. A beast with lamb's horns represents false prophecy (xiii. 11–18), which is a ravening wolf in sheep's clothing. The beasts of Rev. iv. 6–9 of the A. V. are very properly altered to "living creatures." in the R. V.

Be′bai.

The founder of a family, some of whose members returned from the captivity (Ezra ii. 11; viii. 11; Neh. vii. 16).

Be′cher [young camel].

1. A son of Benjamin (Gen. xlvi. 21; 1 Chron. vii. 6). His descendants were apparently too few at the beginning to form a tribal family, at least they found no place in the registry of families (Num. xxvi. 38; 1 Chron. viii. 1–6), but they ultimately increased to nine fathers' houses, inhabiting Anathoth and other towns in the territory of Benjamin and mustering 20,200 men (1 Chron. vii. 8, 9).

2. A son of Ephraim, and founder of a family (Num. xxvi. 35; reference to Becher lacking in the Septuagint). He is not mentioned among the sons of Ephraim in 1 Chron. vii. 20–27. Perhaps the children of Becher

the Benjamite were not so few in numbers
during the sojourn in Egypt as has been supposed, but were principally identified with
Ephraim, perchance through a marriage of
Becher with Sheerah, and hence their family
as a whole, but not all the fathers' houses,
were enrolled with Ephraim.

Be-co′rath, in A. V. **Be-cho′rath** [primo-
geniture].

A Benjamite, an ancestor of king Saul (1
Sam. ix. 1).

The identification of Becorath with Becher
(1 Chron. vii. 6) is groundless. Becorath was
son of Aphiah, the son of a Benjamite, whereas Becher was the son of Benjamin himself.

Bed.

An article of domestic furniture to sleep
upon. The poor and travelers often slept on
the ground, using their upper garment as a
covering (Gen. xxviii. 11; Ex. xxii. 26). A
bed might be no more than a rug or mat,
easily bundled up and carried away (Mat. ix.
6). But beds raised from the ground were
early in existence (2 Kin. i. 4, 6; iv. 10), with
bedsteads of wood, or of iron (Deut. iii. 11),
or among the wealthy of ivory (Amos vi. 4),
with silken cushions (Amos iii. 12, R. V.)
and rich coverings (Prov. vii. 16; Judith
x. 21).

Be′dad [separation].

The father of Hadad, king of Edom (Gen.
xxxvi. 35; 1 Chron. i. 46).

Be′dan.

Apparently a Hebrew judge, ruling between Gideon and Jephthah, and distinguished enough to rank with them and with
Samuel (1 Sam. xii. 11). No such personage
is mentioned in the Book of Judges. Four
theories have been proposed in explanation.
1. Bedan ruled Israel, though no record of
his administration is found in the Book of
Judges. 2. Bedan means in Dan, or is a contraction of Ben-Dan, son of Dan, and is equivalent to Samson. Better is 3. Bedan is the
judge Jair; for a person called Bedan is registered in 1 Chron. vii. 14–17 as a descendant of Gilead, the son of Machir, the son of
Manasseh; and Jair the judge was a Gileadite,
and belonged to the villages named from Jair,
a descendant of Machir (1 Chron. ii. 21, 22).
Bedan's descent from Manasseh differed from
that of Jair who captured and named the
villages; but this fact does not prevent Bedan from representing the descendants and
the district of Jair the conqueror, and being
officially called Jair. Best is 4. Bedan is an
early misreading for either Abdon (Judg. xii.
13) or for Barak, which is found in the Septuagint, Syriac and Arabic versions (cp. Heb.
xi. 32).

Be-de′iah.

A son of Bani, who was induced by Ezra to
put away his foreign wife (Ezra x. 35).

Bee.

An insect which makes honey (Judg. xiv.

8, 18). It is compared to an army (Is. vii
18) chasing man (Deut. i. 44), or surrounding
him (Ps. cxviii. 12). As Canaan was a land
flowing with milk and honey (Ex. iii. 8; cp.
Gen. xliii. 11; Ezek. xxvii. 17), bees must
have been there in large numbers. Their
nests were in rocks (Ps. lxxxi. 16) and in
woods (1 Sam. xiv. 25), especially in Judah
(Ezek. xxvii. 17; cp. Mat. iii. 4).

Be-e-li′a-da [the Lord hath known, i. e.
kindly regarded].

A son of king David, born at Jerusalem (1
Chron. xiv. 7). During his lifetime he may
have been called by the alternate name
Eliada. God hath known; at any rate, when
the word Baal became distasteful on account
of idolatrous associations, the Hebrew historians were apt to write Eliada instead of
Beeliada (2 Sam. v. 16; 1 Chron. iii. 8).

Be-el′ze-bub.

The prince of the demons (Mat. x. 25; xii.
24; Mark iii. 22; Luke xi. 15, 18, 19), whom
Jesus identifies with Satan (Mat. xii. 26;
Mark iii. 23; Luke xi. 18). The spelling
Beelzebub differs but slightly from Baalze-
bub, god of Ekron. The Greek text, however, has Beelzebul. The common explanation is that, with the view of insulting the
Ekronite god and his worshipers, the Jews
wished to make $z^e bub$, fly, into $zibbul$ or $zebel$,
dung. But as in Hebrew $z^e bul$ means habitation, Baalzebul may signify lord of the habitation, and the notion of insult falls to the
ground. Jesus played upon this meaning of
the name in Mat. x. 25. The notion of insult
also falls on the plausible supposition that
Beelzebul was merely a Greek modification
of Beelzebub, adopted because the pronunciation was for the Greeks easier to the tongue
and more pleasant to the ear.

Be′er [a well].

1. A station of the Israelites on the confines of Moab, at which a well was dug by
the leaders of Israel with their staves or under their official supervision (Num. xxi. 16–
18); possibly the same as Beer-elim.
2. A place to which Jotham fled from his
brother Abimelech (Judg. ix. 21). Situation unknown. Eusebius discriminates it from
Beeroth in Benjamin, and locates it eight
Roman miles to the north of Eleutheropolis,
i. e. Beit Jibrin, in the maritime plain. But
Josephus says that Jotham fled to the mountains (Antiq. v. 7, 2).

Be-e′ra [a well].

An Asherite, family of Heber (1 Chron.
vii. 37).

Be-e′rah [a well].

A prince of the Reubenites, who was carried captive by Tiglath-pileser, king of Assyria (1 Chron. v. 6).

Be′er-e′lim [well of heroes or of trees].

A village of Moab (Is. xv. 8); possibly the
same as BEER 1.

Be-e′ri [man of a well].

1. A Hittite, father of Judith, one of Esau's wives (Gen. xxvi. 34). See ANAH.

2. Father of the prophet Hosea (Hos. i. 1).

Be′er-la-hai′-roi [the well dedicated to the Living One who seeth me].

A well in the wilderness, between Kadesh and Bered on the road to Shur, where Hagar learned that Jehovah watched over her (Gen. xvi. 7, 14). The Bedouin identify it with 'Ain Muweileh, about twelve miles to the west of Kadesh.

Be-e′roth [wells].

1. A Gibeonite town (Josh. ix. 17), assigned to the Benjamites (xviii. 25). The inhabitants were Hivites (ix. 7) or Horites (Greek text), who fled to Gittaim and settled there (2 Sam. iv. 3). The murderers of Ish-bosheth, and an armorbearer of Joab's, were Beerothites (iv. 2; xxiii. 37); and men of Beeroth returned from Babylonia after the exile (Ezra ii. 25). The common identification is with el-Bireh, a village on a rocky hill with copious flowing water at its foot, nearly nine miles north of Jerusalem. Eusebius locates Beeroth on the road to Nicopolis or rather Neapolis (Jerome), perhaps at Tell en-Naṣbeh.

2. Beeroth of the children of Jaakan; wells on the borders of Edom, belonging to the tribe of Jaakan (Deut. x. 6). See JAAKAN.

Be-e′roth-ite, once **Berothite.**

A native or inhabitant of Beeroth (2 Sam. iv. 2; xxiii. 37; 1 Chron. xi. 39).

Be′er-she′ba [well of seven]. The pres-ence of the word seven in the name was a constant reminder that a covenant had been sworn to.

A well dug by Abraham in the wilderness adjacent to the Philistine country, and where he and the king of Gerar made a covenant not to molest each other. This well had already been an object of strife between their respective herdsmen. Accordingly Abraham gave Abimelech seven ewe lambs as a witness of the Hebrew title, and to further preserve the memory of the transaction, called the well Beer-sheba (Gen. xxi. 22–32). He also planted there a tamarisk tree, and called on the name of Jehovah, the everlasting God (33, R. V.). Abraham resided for many years at this place. Then he went to Hebron, and afterwards sojourned at Beer-lahai-roi. During the absence of the Hebrews from this part of the wilderness, the Philistines filled up the wells; but when Isaac came into authority he returned to this district and began to reopen them. While at Beer-sheba, engaged in clearing out that well also, the king of Gerar came and made a covenant with him, as he or his predecessor had done with Abraham. The Philistine and his companions had scarcely departed, when Isaac's servants announced that they had reached water. As in former like cases, Isaac piously revived the old name, calling the well Shibah, the feminine form of the numeral *sheba*', thus confirming and preserving the name Beer-sheba (xxvi. 32, 33, R. V.). It was from this well that Jacob started on his journey to Haran (xxviii. 10), and there he sacrificed on his way to Egypt (xlvi. 1–5). A town ulti-

A view of modern Beer-sheba.

Archaeologists have discovered underground silos dating back to 4000 B.C. near Beer-sheba. Calcinated grains of wheat, barley, and lentils were found inside these storage silos.

mately rose in the vicinity of the well (Josh. xv. 28). It was situated in the extreme south of Judah (Josh. xv. 28; 2 Sam. xxiv. 7; 2 Kin. xxiii. 8), though allotted to the Simeonites (Josh. xix. 1, 2; 1 Chron. iv. 28), and was also the southern limit of Palestine, so that the expression became proverbial, "from Dan to Beer-sheba," i. e. from the extreme north to the extreme south of the Holy Land (Judg. xx. 1 et pas.). Samuel's sons were judges in Beer-sheba (1 Sam. viii. 2). Elijah passed through it on his way to Horeb (1 Kin. xix. 3). It was inhabited after the captivity (Neh. xi. 27, 30). Edward Robinson found two deep wells, still called Bîr es-Seba', on the northern side of a wide watercourse or bed of a torrent, wady es-Seba'. And several others have since been discovered. The larger of the wells described by Robinson was found to be 12½ feet in diameter and 44½ deep, to the surface of the water, 16 feet at the lower part being cut through solid rock.

Be-esh'te-rah [house or temple of Astarte].

The same place as Ashtaroth (cp. Josh. xxi. 27 with 1 Chron. vi. 71). This contraction of Beth-ashterah is like that of Beth-shan to Beisan.

Bee'tle. See CRICKET.

Be'he-moth [probably derived from Egyptian p-ehe-mau, water ox, and modified by the Hebrews into bᵉhemoth, a plural of excellence denoting an animal which possesses in a high degree the attributes of bᵉhemah, a beast].

A large animal described by Job. It eats grass like an ox. Its body is thick and massive, with bones like bars of iron and a tail which it moves like a cedar. It is amphibious, sometimes feeding with other quadrupeds upon the mountains, and sometimes lying in fens, among reeds, or under willows or apparently in flooded rivers (Job. xl. 15-24; R. V. margin "hippopotamus"). It is probably the hippopotamus of the Nile (Hippopotamus amphibius). This has an unwieldy body eleven or twelve feet long, a large clumsy head, short stout legs. with four feet bearing toes. The gape of its mouth is enormous and the tusks of formidable size. It feeds on green corn, grass, and young shrubs. In ancient times it descended the Nile; but it was hunted for its valuable skin, teeth, and flesh, and it was also taken in considerable numbers to Rome for exhibition in the circus. Now, therefore, these animals are extinct in Egypt, though found on the Upper Nile.

Be'ka, in A. V. **Be'kah** [division, half].

Half a shekel (Ex. xxxviii. 26). The value was about 16.8 pence or 33 cents. It was used for weighing the precious metals (Gen. xxiv. 22). See WEIGHTS.

Bel [lord].

Title of the patron god of Babylon (Is. xlvi. 1; Jer. l. 2; li. 44; Bel and Dragon 3-22; Herod. i. 181), whose proper name was Marduk or, as pronounced by the Hebrews, Merodach. He was a sun-god, the sun of early day and of spring; and he was regarded as the son of Ea, god of the ocean and other terrestrial waters. His festival was celebrated in the spring, at the beginning of the year. Because the sun in this aspect exerts such potent influence in nature, and because he was their tutelary divinity, the men of Babylon paid him supreme worship and ascribed to him the loftiest attributes. He was not originally numbered among the chief gods by the people on the lower Tigris and Euphrates, but grew in importance with the increasing power and renown of the city of Babylon.

Another Bel, god of the region between earth and sky, and grouped in a triad with Anu, heaven, and Ea, was one of the eleven great gods.

Be'la, in A. V. once **Be'lah** (Gen. xlvi. 21) [devouring, destruction].

1. A king of Edom, whose father's name was Beor (Gen. xxxvi. 32).

2. A Reubenite chief (1 Chron. v. 8).

3. A son of Benjamin, and founder of a family (Gen. xlvi. 21 ; Num. xxvi. 38).

4. One of the cities of the plain, the same as Zoar (Gen. xiv. 2, 8).

Be'li-al [worthlessness, wickedness].

Ungodliness (Ps. xviii. 4, R. V.). The phrase "men of belial" is a Semitic circumlocution, in default of the appropriate adjective, for ungodly men (Deut. xiii. 13). Belial is personified in 2 Cor. vi. 15.

Bell.

Small golden bells, alternating with ornaments in the form of pomegranates, were attached to the lower part of the official blue robe of the high priest in order to send forth a sound that might be heard in the temple for a memorial of the children of Israel, that he die not (Ex. xxviii. 33. 34 ; Ecclus. xlv. 9). A string of flat pieces of brass was hung around the neck of horses, or a single bell was suspended from their throat (Zech. xiv. 20 ; cp. Judg. viii. 21). In either case the tinkling kept the horses together at night, and made it easy to find a strayed beast.

Bel'lows.

An instrument for blowing the fire of a smelting furnace (Jer. vi. 29 ; Iliad xviii. 470). As used by the ancient Egyptians. the bellows consisted of a pair of leather bags, fitted into a frame, from each of which a pipe extended to the fire. They were worked by the feet, the operator standing upon them with one under each foot, and pressing them alternately while he pulled up the exhausted skin with a string which he held in his hand. A double pair was used for each furnace.

Bel-shaz'zar [Babylonian *Bel-shar-uṣur,* Bel protect the king].

A king of the Chaldeans, who reigned a part at least of three years (Dan. viii. 1), apparently as co-regent of his father (v. 16, 29, by implication), and was slain on a memorable night (30). According to contemporary Babylonian records, he was the eldest son of Nabuna'id and grandson of Nabubalatsuikbi, the wise prince and mighty potentate (1 R. 68 No. 4 ; 69, ii. 26 ; V R. 63, i. 16 ; 65, i. 9). The Babylonian queen, probably Nabuna'id's wife, and Belshazzar himself, and Daniel

his contemporary speak of Nebuchadnezzar as Belshazzar's father (v. 11, 13) ; and his father Nabuna'id, speaking of himself, mentions "the kings, his fathers." It is quite possible that Belshazzar was descended, through his mother at least, from Nebuchadnezzar ; but the words spoken of Belshazzar that night at court may also be explained by the broad usage of the word father for a predecessor in the same office. Nebuchadnezzar speaks of Naramsin, who reigned three thousand years before him, as "the king, the ancient father," although doubtless no blood relationship existed between them. Sargon, king of Assyria, like Nabuna'id a usurper, speaks of being endowed with understanding beyond "the kings, my fathers" (Cylinder 48). Delegates from the Ionian cities urged Seleucus Nicator to adhere to the policy of his "ancestors," *progonoi,* although but one ancestor of his sat upon the throne (Bevan, House of Seleucus, I. 161). In the court parlance of the day Belshazzar was Nebuchadnezzar's son, politically his descendant, his successor on the throne.

In 555 B. C., the first year of his father's reign, he was occupying a house in Babylon ; and had taken into his own establishment, it would seem, two at least of the servants who had belonged to the household of the late king Nergalsharuṣur. During the years that his father remained in Tema, Belshazzar was with the army which was quartered in the district of Accad, to the north of Babylon and on the southern frontier of Assyria (Annals ii. 5–23). The king's son, as his title uniformly is, not only had nominal or actual command of the troops, but also represented his father in certain religious, administrative, and domestic duties. Not far from the military camp in Accad was the city of Sippar ; and again and again the documents certify to his gift of sheep and oxen to the temples at Sippar as an offering of the king, and even of a tongue of gold as a present to the sun-god.

The inscriptions which were written at Ur by order of Nabuna'id to commemorate his restoration of the temple of the moon-god are peculiar and significant because the king. after praying for himself, invariably adds a petition for Belshazzar. "As for me, Nabuna'id king of Babylon, deliver me from sin against thy great divine nature and grant unto me length of days. And concerning Belsharuṣur my firstborn, the offspring of my body, his heart also fill thou with awe of thy great divinity, that he may never indulge in sins. With abundance of days let him be satisfied."

The Persians under Cyrus' general Ugbaru, written Gubaru also, entered Babylon on the 16th day of Tammuz, the fourth month. 539 B. C. They boasted that they had taken the city without a battle. Nabuna'id was seized, and a guard of shield-bearers was stationed at the gates of the great sanctuary Esaggila for two weeks (Annals iii. 16, 17). The city was held by a foreign army, but the commercial documents of the time indicate no interruption of business and no feeling of financial insecurity. Property was bought and sold at Babylon and the transactions were duly recorded; money was loaned, bills payable were given, and houses were taken as security. Documents continued even to be dated by the regnal year of Nabuna'id, notwithstanding his arrest. Indeed, it would seem that beyond the restriction of Nabuna'id's liberty, the royal family was not molested nor its goods seized. Belshazzar even made a gift of money out of the king's substance to the sun-god at Sippar. It was not until the third day of the eighth month that Cyrus made his triumphal entry into Babylon (Annals iii. 18), and in the princely palace placed the seat of sovereignty (Cylinder 23). About a week later, on the night of the eleventh, an important event took place. The inscription is slightly defaced, and several of the written characters are rendered doubtful; but recent expert opinion declares that the word son is clear and certain (Pinches, Delitzsch, Hagen). On this reading the record states that "on the eleventh of Marchesvan, in the night, Gubaru upon . . . killed the son of the king." On that night, then, Belshazzar was slain. No bodily injury was done to his father Nabuna'id. On the contrary, according to Berosus, although Nabuna'id was deprived of the crown and deported from Babylonia, he was kindly treated by Cyrus, who granted him estates in Carmania, in southern Persia (contra Apion. i. 20), and endowed him with the government of the province (Eusebius, Chron. i. 10, 3). The feast which Belshazzar gave to a thousand men of rank (Dan. v. 1) took place, on this reading of the text, earlier in the evening of the eleventh of Marchesvan. To judge from the contemporary records, it was quite possible for Belshazzar, after the city was occupied by the Persian troops, to give a great banquet, and to obtain cups of gold and silver for the purpose out of the storehouse in the temple of Marduk (v. 2; Ezra i. 7). Perhaps conspiracy was the motive of the feast. See CYRUS and DANIEL.

Bel-te-shaz'zar [Babylonian, *Balaṭsu-uṣur*, protect his life]. The name is abbreviated by omitting the name of the deity invoked.

The name given by the prince of the Babylonian eunuchs to the prophet Daniel (Dan. i. 7). Bel, the god of Nebuchadnezzar, was the deity invoked in the name (iv. 8).

Ben [son].

A Levite (1 Chron. xv. 18), but probably the name has erroneously crept into the text; cp. 20, 21.

Ben-a-bin'a-dab [son of Abinadab].

Son-in-law of Solomon and his purveyor in the region of Dor (1 Kin. iv. 11, R. V.).

Be-na'iah [Jehovah hath built].

1. A Levite, the son of Jehoiada of Kabzeel in Judah (2 Sam. xxiii. 20). His father was a priest (1 Chron. xxvii. 5). If the title here denotes a minister at the altar, Benaiah's father was probably the leader of the priests who joined the army which placed David on the throne (xii. 27). Benaiah was a valiant man, celebrated for having descended into a pit and killed a lion, for having slain two lion-like men of Moab, and, when armed only with a staff, for having met an Egyptian giant, wrested away his spear, and killed him with his own weapon (2 Sam. xxiii. 20, 21; 1 Chron. xi. 22, 23). He was over the Cherethites and Pelethites, David's bodyguard (2 Sam. viii. 18), and also commanded the military division for the third month (1 Chron. xxvii. 5, 6). He with the bodyguard remained faithful to David during Absalom's rebellion (cp. 2 Sam. xv. 18; xx. 23) and that of Adonijah (1 Kin. i. 10). By David's order he, at the head of the guard, escorted Solomon to Gihon, to be anointed king (38), and as chief of the guard he executed Adonijah (ii. 25), Joab (29–34), and Shimei (46). The death of Joab having left the office of commander-in-chief vacant, Benaiah was promoted to the same (35).

2. A Pirathonite, one of David's thirty mighty men of the second rank (2 Sam. xxiii. 30; 1 Chron. xi. 31). He commanded the military division for the eleventh month (xxvii. 14).

3. A Levite of the second degree who played the psaltery before the ark when it was escorted to Jerusalem, and afterwards in the tabernacle erected by David (1 Chron. xv. 18, 20; xvi. 5).

4. A priest who blew a trumpet in the company which escorted the ark to Jerusalem and afterwards in David's tabernacle (1 Chron. xv. 24; xvi. 6).

5. A Levite, descended from Asaph, and living before the reign of Jehoshaphat (2 Chron. xx. 14).

6. A Simeonite, possibly a contemporary of Hezekiah (1 Chron. iv. 36; cp. 41).

7. A Levite, an overseer of dedicated offerings in Hezekiah's reign (2 Chron. xxxi. 13).

8. Father of Ezekiel's contemporary, prince Pelatiah (Ezek. xi. 1, 13).

9–12. Four men, sons of Parosh, Pahathmoab, Bani, and Nebo, respectively, who were induced by Ezra to put away their strange wives (Ezra x. 25, 30, 35, 43).

Ben-am'mi [son of my people; a circumlocution for my kinsman, and equivalent to Ammon, kin].

Son of Lot's younger daughter, from whom sprang the Ammonite tribe (Gen. xix. 38).

Ben-de'ker [son of Deker].

Solomon's purveyor in Bethshemesh and some other towns (1 Kin. iv. 9, R. V.).

Ben'e-be'rak [sons of Berak].

A town of Dan (Josh. xix. 45), now Ibn Ibrâk, 4 miles east of Jaffa.

Ben'e-ja'a-kan. See JAAKAN.

Ben-ge'ber [son of Geber].
Solomon's purveyor in Ramoth-gilead (1 Kin. iv. 13, R. V.).

Ben-ha'dad [son of god Hadad; in the speech of Damascus, Bar-hadad].
King of Damascus, son of Tabrimmon and grandson of Hezion, and a contemporary of Baasha, king of Israel. When Baasha built Ramah to blockade the entrance into Judah from the north, Asa, king of Judah, hired Ben-hadad to break his treaty with Baasha and invade the kingdom of Israel. The army of Ben-hadad entered the territory of the ten tribes, captured the cities of Ijon, Dan and Abel-maacah, and ravaged the land west of the lake of Gennesaret. The diversion caused Baasha to withdraw from Ramah and terminate the blockade of the kingdom of Judah (1 Kin. xv. 18–21; 2 Chron. xvi. 1–6).

A king of Damascus, contemporary of Ahab. He besieged Samaria, but drove Ahab to desperation and forced him to battle by insulting demands, and was defeated. The next year Ben-hadad renewed the war, but sustained a still heavier defeat; but Ahab granted him conditions of peace (1 Kin. xx. 1–34). The arrival of a common enemy, Shalmaneser king of Assyria, in the west in 856 B. C. necessitated the preservation of the peace, and it continued three years (1 Kin. xxii. 1).

Ben-hadad's name was perhaps Benhadadezer, by the Israelites shortened to Benhadad, by the Assyrians to Adadidri, i. e., Hadadezer. Or else in 854 B. C. Ben-hadad was succeeded by Hadadezer, and the latter about 845 by another Ben-hadad. Hence the king of Syria in 1 Kin. xxii. 2—2 Kin. vi. 23, where his personal name is not given, may be Hadadezer. In 854 the king of Syria, aided by Ahab and other allies, stopped the Assyrian advance at Karkar near Hamath. In the following year, as is probable, in early spring Ahab lost his life in an attempt to wrest Ramoth-gilead from the king of Syria (1 Kin. xxii. 1–36). For some time the Syrians waged predatory warfare with the Israelites (2 Kin. v. 2; vi. 8–23). These hostilities were repeatedly interrupted by Shalmaneser's operations against Damascus in the years 850, 849, and 846.

A king of Damascus, contemporary with Ahab's son Jehoram (2 Kin. vi. 24; cp. iii. 1; viii. 28). Between 846 and 843 B. C., there being no Assyrians in the west to harass him, he invaded the territory of Israel and laid siege to Samaria; but his army, hearing a noise as of troops on the march, became panic-stricken and fled (vi. 24; vii. 8). Shortly afterwards he was murdered and succeeded by Hazael (viii. 15).

A king of Damascus, son of Hazael. In the reign of Jehoahaz, king of Israel, Hazael and then Ben-hadad oppressed the ten tribes (2 Kin. xiii. 3–13). But Joash, son of Jehoa-

haz, thrice defeated Ben-hadad and recovered the cities which the king of Damascus had wrested from Israel (22–25; cp. x. 32, 33). Other warfare of Ben-hadad's was with Zakar, king of Hamath (Pognon, Inscrip. sémit.).

The palaces of Ben-hadad are the palaces of Damascus (Jer. xlix. 27; Amos i. 4).

Ben-ha'il [son of strength, virtuous].
One of the princes sent by Jehoshaphat to teach in the cities of Judah (2 Chron. xvii. 7).

Ben-ha'nan [son of the kind one].
A son of Shimon, registered with the tribe of Judah (1 Chron. iv. 20).

Ben-he'sed [son of benevolence or of Hesed].
Solomon's purveyor in Aruboth (1 Kin. iv. 10, R. V.).

Ben'hur [son of Hur].
Solomon's purveyor in mount Ephraim (1 Kin. iv. 8, R. V.).

Be-ni'nu [our son].
A Levite who with Nehemiah and others sealed a covenant with Jehovah (Neh. x. 13).

Ben'ja-min [son of the right hand, i. e. of happiness].
1. The youngest of Jacob's twelve sons and full brother of Joseph. As Jacob was approaching Bethlehem, Rachel gave birth to Benjamin, but, dying named him Benoni, son of my sorrow. Jacob called him Benjamin (Gen. xxxv. 16–20); and was deeply attached to him, especially after losing Joseph, as son of his old age and child of beloved Rachel. Only reluctantly did he allow Benjamin to go to Egypt with the brothers; and Judah expressed the fear that if evil should befall Benjamin too, their father would die of grief (xliii. 1–17). Joseph also felt much affection for Benjamin (29–34; xliv. 1–34). Ultimately Benjamin had, besides other descendants, five sons and two grandsons, through whom he became the founder of families and a tribe in Israel (Gen. xlvi. 21; Num. xxvi. 38–41; 1 Chron. vii. 6–12; viii).

2. The tribe to which Benjamin gave origin, and the territory that it obtained. In the distribution of land at Shiloh, after Judah and Ephraim had received territory, the first lot came to Benjamin, who was assigned the district lying between those of Judah and Ephraim. Its northern boundary ran from Jordan through Beth-el to Ataroth-addar, south of nether Beth-horon. Its western border ran from this point to Kiriath-jearim. Its southern boundary went thence through the valley of the son of Hinnom, immediately south of Jerusalem, to the northern point of the Dead Sea. Its eastern limit was the Jordan (Josh. xviii. 11–20). The territory thus marked out extended from west to east about 28 miles, and from north to south about 12 miles. It was a hilly country, but extremely fertile (Antiq. v. 1, 22) and it was studded

with towns, the chief of which were Jerusalem, Jericho, Bethel, Gibeon, Gibeath, and Mizpeh (Josh. xviii. 21–28). The tribe early furnished Israel with a deliverer from foreign oppression (Judg. iii. 15). The tribe was nearly exterminated for protecting the guilty inhabitants of Gibeah (xix.–xxi.). Later it gave the first king to Israel, and long clung to the house of Saul (2 Sam. ii. 9, 15 ; 1 Chron. xii. 29). Even after David had become king of all Israel, Benjamites occasionally showed dissatisfaction (2 Sam. xvi. 5 ; xx. 1–22 ; Ps. vii. title) ; but a large part of the tribe remained true to the house of David when the ten tribes separated under Jeroboam (1 Kin. xii. 21), and shared the fortunes of Judah to the end (Ezra iv. 1). From this tribe sprang the apostle of the gentiles (Phil. iii. 5).

Two gates at Jerusalem bore the name of Benjamin. The upper or high gate of Benjamin was in the temple (Jer. xx. 2). For the other gate of Benjamin, see JERUSALEM II. 3.

3. A Benjamite, a son of Bilhan, family of Jediael (1 Chron. vii. 10).

4. A son of Harim, who had taken a foreign wife (Ezra x. 32).

Be'no [his son].
A descendant of Merari through Jaaziah (1 Chron. xxiv. 26, 27), if Beno is a proper name, as it seems to be in ver. 27.

Ben-o'ni [son of my sorrow].
The name designed by Rachel for the child whose birth was causing her death. But Jacob changed it to Benjamin (Gen. xxxv. 18).

Ben-zo'heth [son of Zoheth].
A descendant of Ishi, registered with the tribe of Judah (1 Chron. iv. 20). Perhaps, however, a name has dropped out of the text before this name. If so, the passage should be translated : " And the sons of Ishi, Zoheth and . . . . the son of Zoheth."

Be'on. See BAAL-MEON.

Be'or [a torch].
1. Father of Bela, king of Edom (Gen. xxxvi. 32 ; 1 Chron. i. 43).
2. Father of Balaam (Num. xxii. 5). Called in A. V. of 2 Pet. ii. 15 Bosor.

Be'ra [excellence].
A king of Sodom, defeated by Chedorlaomer and his confederates (Gen. xiv. 2).

Ber'a-cah, in A. V. **Berachah** [blessing].
1. A Benjamite who joined David at Ziklag (1 Chron. xii. 3).
2. A valley in Judah near Tekoa. Jehoshaphat gave it its name because he and his army there returned thanks to God for a great victory over the Ammonites, Moabites, and Edomites (2 Chron. xx. 26). The name still lingers as Bereikût, a ruin about 4 miles northwest of Tekoa, 6 miles southwest of Bethlehem, and a little east of the road from the latter village to Hebron.

Ber-a-chi'ah. See BERECHIAH.

Be-ra'iah [Jehovah hath created].
A son of Shimei (1 Chron. viii. 21, R. V.), descendant of Shaharaim who had his registry with Benjamin (8, 11–13).

Be're-a.
A town in Judæa near which Judas Maccabæus was slain (1 Mac. ix. 4). Not identified.

For Be-re'a, a city of Macedonia (Acts xvii. 10, A. V.), see BERŒA.

Ber-e-chi'ah, in A. V. once **Berachiah** (1 Chron. vi. 39) [Jehovah hath blessed].
1. A Levite, the father of Asaph, descended from Gershom (1 Chron. vi. 39 ; xv. 17).
2. A Levite, one of the four doorkeepers for the ark in David's reign (1 Chron. xv. 23, 24).
3. One of the chief men of Ephraim in the reign of Pekah. He took the part of the captives from Judah. He was a son of Meshillemoth (2 Chron. xxviii. 12).
4. A son of Zerubbabel (1 Chron. iii. 20).
5. A Levite, descended from Elkanah of Netophah (1 Chron. ix. 16).
6. A son of Meshezabel. His son repaired part of the wall of Jerusalem (Neh. iii. 4, 30).
7. Father of the prophet Zechariah (Zech. i. 1, 7).

Be'red [hail].
1. A place in the wilderness of Shur, to the west of Kadesh, and not far from Beer-lahairoi (Gen. xvi. 7. 14). Its exact locality has not been determined.
2. An Ephraimite, of the family of Shuthelah (1 Chron. vii. 20).

Be'ri [man of a well].
An Asherite, son of Zophah, family of Heber (1 Chron. vii. 36).

Be-ri'ah [perhaps, with an outcry, or in evil].
1. A son of Asher, and founder of a family (Gen. xlvi. 17 ; Num. xxvi. 44).
2. A son of Ephraim (1 Chron. vii. 23).
3. A Benjamite, head of a father's house among the inhabitants of Aijalon (1 Chron. viii. 13).
4. A Levite, a son of Shimei, the Gershonite (1 Chron. xxiii. 10). His sons were united with the children of his brother Jeush into one father's house (11).

Be'rite.
Apparently a people living near Abel-bethmaacah (2 Sam. xx. 14), but it is questionable if the present text is correct.

Be'rith. See BAAL-BERITH.

Ber-ni'ce [for *Pherenikē*, carrying off victory, victorious].
The eldest daughter of Herod Agrippa I. She was married to her uncle, Herod, ruler of Chalcis, who soon afterwards died. She was so much with her brother Agrippa that scandal arose in consequence. She tried to allay it by a marriage with Polemo, king of

Cilicia. She soon became tired of him, and, deserting him, returned to her brother Agrippa (Antiq. xx. 7, 3; War ii, 11, 5). She was with him when Paul made his defense before him (Acts xxv. 23; xxvi. 30). She afterwards became the mistress, first of Vespasian and then of Titus.

Ber'o-dach-bal'a-dan. See MERODACH-BALADAN.

Be-rœ'a, in A. V. **Be-re'a.**

1. A city of Macedonia, about 50 miles west of Thessalonica and 23 or 24 miles from the sea, where Paul preached on his first journey to Europe (Acts xvii. 10-14; xx. 4). It is now called Verria or Boor.

2. A Syrian city between Antioch and Hierapolis, where Menelaus was smothered in a tower of ashes (2 Mac. xiii. 4). An earlier name of the town survives in Aleppo, the designation Berœa, which was given by Seleucus Nicator, having had a transient existence.

3. See BEREA 1.

Be-ro'thah or **Ber'o-thai** [wells].

Berothah was a town situated between Hamath and Damascus (Ezek. xlvii. 16). It is probably identical with Berothai, a city which was once subject to Hadadezer, king of Zobah, but was captured by David and yielded him large booty in brass (2 Sam. viii. 8; in 1 Chron. xviii. 8 called Cun, in A. V. Chun; probably a corruption, for the Seventy read the noun *Mibhar*, of which the letters are much like those of Berothai). Site unknown.

Ber'yl.

1. The rendering of the Hebrew *Tarshish*, a precious stone brought doubtless from the place bearing the same name. It was the first stone of the fourth row on the Jewish high priest's breastplate (Ex. xxviii. 20; xxxix. 13; Song v. 14; Ezek. i. 16; x. 9; xxviii. 13; Dan. x. 6). None of these passages tells the color of the stone. On the margin of the R. V. of Song v. 14 *tarshish* is rendered topaz, and on that of Ex. xxviii. 20 chalcedony. The Septuagint renders the word by chrysolite in Ex. xxviii. 20; xxxix. 13; Ezek. xxviii. 13; and by *anthrax*, carbuncle, in Ezek. x. 9.

2. The Greek *Berullos* (Rev. xxi. 20), the eighth foundation of the wall of the New Jerusalem. The beryl is an earthy mineral, having as its chief constituents silica, alumina, and beryllium (glucinum). It may be colorless or aquamarine, bluish green, or various blues and violet, or yellow and brown. It is closely allied to the emerald. It is found in Siberia, India, Brazil, and in some parts of Great Britain.

Be'sai.

One of the Nethinim and founder of a family (Ezra ii. 49; Neh. vii. 52).

Bes-o-de'iah [in familiarity with Jehovah].

Father of Meshullam, who helped to repair a gate of Jerusalem (Neh. iii. 6).

Be'sor [perhaps coldness, or, possibly, haste].

A brook south of Ziklag (1 Sam. xxx. 9, 10, 21), perhaps the Nahr Ghazzeh, which rises near Beer-sheba and empties into the Mediterranean south of Gaza.

Be'tah [trust, confidence].

A city of Aram-zobah (2 Sam. viii. 8), probably to be read Tebah. Called Tibhath in 1 Chron. xviii. 8. Site unknown.

Be'ten [body, belly, or valley].

A village of Asher (Josh. xix. 25). Eusebius identified it with a village Beth-beten, 8 Roman miles east of Acre.

Beth.

The second letter of the Hebrew alphabet. Originally it was a rude representation of a dwelling, and from this circumstance it derives its name, which means a house. The English letter B has the same origin. Beth stands at the head of the second section of Ps. cxix. in many versions, in which section each verse begins with this letter.

The Hebrew letters, beth, caph, mem, and pe, or b, k, m, and p, have at different stages of their development been so similar as to cause readers some difficulty in distinguishing them, and open the way to misreadings; for example, they are written, in the order just named, on

Old Hebrew Coins	ꓘ	ꓴ	ꓴꓴ	ꓴꓴ	ꓴꓴ	ꓔ
Tomb of James 1st Century B.C.		ꓘ		ꓴ	ꓴ	
Synagogue at Kefr Bir'im	ꓘꓘ	ꓘ		ꓘ	ꓘ	
Palmyrene		ꓴ	ꓴ	ꓴ		ꓴ

Beth-ab'a-ra [house of the ford].

A place beyond Jordan at which John baptized (John i. 28, A. V.). The oldest manuscripts have Bethany, as now the R. V.; but Origen, not being able to find a place of this name, decided in favor of the reading Bethabara. If the correct reading be Bethabara, then the site is evidently at one of the numerous fords of the Jordan, and of these only one is now called Makhadet 'Abârah. It is a main ford of the river just above the place where the Jalud stream, flowing down the valley of Jezreel by Beisân, enters the Jordan. The traditional site, however, is east of Jericho.

Beth-a'nath [house of the goddess Anath].

An ancient fenced town (Thothmes' list) in Naphtali (Josh. xix. 35, 38), from which the Canaanites were not expelled (Judg. i. 33). Suitably located at the village of 'Anâta or 'Aînâta, 6 miles west of Kedesh.

Beth-a'noth [house of the goddess Anath].

A town in the mountains of Judah (Josh. xv. 59); commonly sought at Beit 'Ainûn, 1½ miles southeast of Halhul.

Beth'a-ny [house of the afflicted one; in Talmud, house of non-maturing dates].

1. A small town on the mount of Olives (Mark xi. 1; Luke xix. 29), about 15 furlongs from Jerusalem (John xi. 18) on the road to Jericho. Our Lord often lodged there (Mat. xxi. 17; xxvi. 6; Mark xi. 1, 11, 12; xiv. 3). It was the town of Lazarus, of Martha, and of Mary (John xi. 1; xii. 1), as well as of Simon the leper, in whose house one of the anointings of Jesus took place (Mat. xxvi. 6–13; Mark xiv. 3). From near the town Jesus ascended to heaven (Luke xxiv. 50, 51). It has been generally identified as the village of el-'Azirîyeh (Lazarus' village) on the eastern slope of the mount of Olives, southeast from Jerusalem. As a cave tomb with pottery and weapons reveals, the place was a settlement of the Canaanites before the Israelites conquered the country. To-day it is merely a small, wretched village. The houses of Simon and of Martha and Mary and the tomb of Lazarus, which are shown, should not be regarded as genuine. Instead of date palms, which may once have flourished here, are olives, figs, and pomegranates.

2. A place east of the Jordan, probably a village, where John was baptizing when Jesus returned from the temptation (John i. 28, R. V.; cp. x. 40). See BETHABARA.

Beth-ar'a-bah [house of the wilderness].

A village in the wilderness of Judah, on the boundary line between Judah and Benjamin (Josh. xv. 6, 61; xviii. 22). Called simply Arabah in xviii. 18; unless the reading of the Septuagint be correct, Beth-arabah instead of "the side over against the Arabah." Site not yet identified.

Beth-a'ram. See BETH-HARAM.

Beth-ar'bel [house of God's ambush].

A town destroyed by Shalman with horrible cruelty (Hos. x. 14). The best identification that has been proposed is with Arbela of Galilee (Antiq. xii. 11, 1; xiv. 15, 4; cp. 1 Mac. ix. 2), now Irbid, 4 miles west-north-west of Tiberias. There are many natural caverns in a limestone precipice, which have been connected by artificial passages cut through the rock, with defenses wherever access was possible. Herod the Great found these caverns the abode of robbers, whom he rooted out (War i. 16, 2–4).

Beth-a'ven [house of nothingness or idolatry].

1. A town in the territory of Benjamin, near Bethel (Josh. vii. 2), west of Michmash (1 Sam. xiii. 5: cp. xiv. 23), and on the border of a wilderness (Josh. xviii. 12). Not yet identified.

2. A name applied by Hosea contemptuously to Bethel after it had become a seat of idolatry (Hos. iv. 15; v. 8; x. 5).

Beth-az'ma-veth. See AZMAVETH.

Beth-ba'al-me'on. See BAAL-MEON.

Beth-ba'rah [perhaps for Beth-abarah, house of the ford].

A place on the Jordan, probably on the right bank (Judg. vii. 24).

Beth-ba'si.

A place in the wilderness (1 Mac. ix. 62), probably the wilderness of Tekoa (33). Josephus calls it Bethalaga (Antiq. xiii. 1, 5).

Beth-bi'ri, in A. V. **Beth-bir'e-i** [house of my creation].

A Simeonite town (1 Chron. iv. 31). The

Ruins at Bethany.

name is probably a corruption of Beth-lebaoth (cp. Josh. xix. 6).

Beth'-car [house of pasture, a place fit for grazing].

A place which is named to indicate the point to which the Philistines were pursued by the Israelites after the second and decisive battle of Ebenezer (1 Sam. vii. 11). The use of the word "under" seems to imply that it overlooked a plain.

Beth-da'gon [house of Dagon].

1. A village in the lowland of Judah (Josh. xv. 33, 41), apparently in the vicinity of Eleutheropolis. Not identified.

2. A town of Asher, on the frontier toward Zebulun (Josh. xix. 27). Not identified.

Beth-dib-la-tha'im [house of fig cakes].

A town on the tableland of Moab, territory once in possession of Israel (Jer. xlviii. 21, 22; Moabite Stone 30). Probably the same as Almon-diblathaim.

Beth-e'den. See EDEN 2.

Beth'-el [house of God].

1. A town of Palestine, west of Ai, south of Shiloh (Gen. xii. 8; Judg. xxi. 19), and near Michmash (1 Sam. xiii. 2). Abraham on his first journey into Palestine, and subsequently, pitched his tent near it (Gen. xiii. 3). The town was called Luz by the Canaanites; but Jacob called the name of the place close by, where he passed the night sleeping on the ground, Beth-el on account of the vision which he saw there, and he erected a pillar to mark the spot (Gen. xxviii. 19 seq.; xxxi. 13). The two are distinguished (Josh. xvi. 2); but the name Beth-el soon supplanted Luz as designation of the town. On the return of Jacob from Paddan-aram he went to Bethel, built an altar, and reaffirmed the name (Gen. xxxv. 1-15; Hos. xii. 4). The people of the town helped those of Ai in the second battle with Joshua (Josh. viii. 9, 12, 17). Later it was taken and its king slain (xii. 9, 16). It was assigned to Benjamin, and stood on the boundary line between that tribe and Ephraim (Josh. xvi. 2; xviii. 13, 22). It was entered and its Canaanite inhabitants were slain by the men of Ephraim when they were engaged in securing their recently acquired territory (Judg. i. 22 seq.). Its villages on the north of the boundary line belonged to Ephraim, and so perhaps did the town, as a result of this extermination of the Canaanites within its walls (1 Chron. vii. 28). When the Israelites were gathered at Mizpah near Gibeah to war against Benjamin, the ark was brought from Shiloh, 18 miles distant, to Beth-el, 8 miles off (Judg. xx. 1, 27). Thither the men of Israel repaired to ask counsel of God, and there they built a temporary altar and offered sacrifices (18, 26, R. V.). At the end of the war they came again to Beth-el, sat there before the Lord, built a new altar or repaired the old one, and offered sacrifices (xxi. 2-4, R. V.). When the regular ser-

vices of the sanctuary at Shiloh were suspended during the loss and seclusion of the ark, Beth-el was one of the places where Samuel judged Israel, and whither men went with their offerings to God (1 Sam. vii. 16; x. 3). Jeroboam fixed one of his calves there (1 Kin. xii. 29-33), and Beth-el became a great center of idolatry (1 Kin. xiii. 1-32; 2 Kin. x. 29). It was taken and temporarily held by Abijah (2 Chron. xiii. 19). Elijah passed through it (2 Kin. ii. 1-3), and it was from Beth-el that the youths came who mocked Elisha (23, 24). The prophets denounced it for its idolatries (Jer. xlviii. 13; Hos. x. 15; Amos iii. 14; iv. 4; v. 5, 6), and called it Beth-aven, house of naught (Hos. iv. 15; v. 8; x. 5). Amos was in danger in Beth-el for his bold preaching (Amos vii. 10-13). Josiah broke down its altars and its high places, and, as foretold, burned the bones of the priests taken from its sepulchers (2 Kin. xxiii. 4, 15-20). Some of its inhabitants returned from Babylon with Zerubbabel (Ezra ii. 28; Neh. vii. 32), the place again reverting to the Benjamites (xi. 31). In Maccabee times it was fortified by the Syrian Bacchides (1 Mac. ix. 50). In the Jewish war it was captured by Vespasian, later Roman emperor (War iv. 9, 9). The ruins, called Beitin, lie on the watershed of Palestine, about 11 miles north from Jerusalem. They are on the summit of a hill sloping to the southeast, and cover three or four acres. A range of hills trends to the southeast (cp. 1 Sam. xiii. 2). In the valley to the west is a broken reservoir, 314 feet long by 217 broad, with two brooks of living water. Two other brooks are in the vicinity. There are sepulchers cut in a low cliff. The country round is of gray stone or white chalk, with scant vegetable mould. As in Abraham's time, it is a pastoral region.

2. A town in the territory of Simeon (1 Sam. xxx. 27). See BETHUEL.

Beth-e'mek [house of the valley].

A town within the territory of Asher (Josh. xix. 27). Not identified.

Be'ther [separation, division].

Probably a common noun, describing certain mountains as cleft and rugged (Song ii. 17; cp. iv. 6; viii. 14); and not the town in Judah called Baither or Bethther (Josh. xv. 59, Greek), now Bittîr, six miles southwest of Jerusalem, where on the height above the village the Jews under Bar-cocheba made their last stand against the Romans, B. C. 135.

Be-thes'da [house of mercy].

Earlier manuscripts of the N. T. have other spellings, as Bethsaida, house of fishing, and Bethzatha, house of the olive.

A pool at Jerusalem, which was near the sheep gate and had five porches, that were sufficiently ample to accommodate a great multitude (John v. 2 seq.). Its waters were supposed to possess healing virtue. The fourth verse of the A. V., which mentions a periodic troubling of the waters, and ascribes it to an angel, is omitted in R. V. as being insufficiently supported by early texts. Tradition located Bethesda at the Birket Israel, north of the temple, or at an adjacent pool. The tradition was well founded, even if it ultimately went astray. 1. In A. D. 333 the Bordeaux pilgrim stated that there were two pools and five porches. 2. Early manuscripts, e. g. the Sinaitic, have Bethzatha, abbreviated Bezatha, instead of Bethesda. These words are apparently variations of Bezetha, the name of the quarter of the city north of the temple hill, and imply that the pool was in the Bezethan section of the city. 3. The pool was near the sheep gate, and the natural explanation of Neh. iii. determines the location of this gate to have been north of the temple area. 4. In the autumn of 1888 excavation in the northeast part of Jerusalem, in connection with the repair of the church of St. Anne, laid bare 100 feet northwest of that building a pool with five porches. A faded fresco on the wall depicts an angel and water, and shows that in the early Christian ages this pool was regarded as Bethesda.

Beth-e′zel [perhaps, house at the side].

A town of Judah or Samaria—it is uncertain which (Mic. i. 11). Perhaps identical with Azal, i. e. Azel (Zech. xiv. 5).

Beth-ga′dor [house of a wall].

A town of Judah (1 Chron. ii. 51). See GEDER.

Beth-ga′mul [house of perfection].

A Moabite town (Jer. xlviii. 23), possibly Jemail, east of Dibon.

Beth-gil′gal. See GILGAL 1.

Beth-hac′che-rem, in A. V. **Beth-hac′cerem** [house of the vineyard].

A town of Judah (Neh. iii. 14; Jer. vi. 1). Jerome knew a village Beta-charma. It was visible from Bethlehem where he resided, and was situated on a hill between Tekoa and Jerusalem. Accordingly its site has been sought at the Frank mountain, 3½ miles southeast of Bethlehem.

Beth-ha′ran and **Beth-ha′ram,** in A. V. **Beth-a′ram** [Beth-haram may signify place of the height].

A town in the Jordan valley, rebuilt by the children of Gad (Num. xxxii. 36; Josh. xiii. 27). Tristram well identified it with the mound called Beth-haran, in the plain east of the Jordan, opposite Jericho on the southeast. This mound must be distinguished from Tell er-Rameh, 3 miles farther up the wady to the east, the site of Betharamphtha, where Herod had a palace (Antiq. xviii. 2, 1; War ii. 4, 2; 9, 1).

Beth-hog′lah, in A. V. once **Beth-hogla** [house of the partridge].

A village of Benjamin on the boundary line between that tribe and Judah, and near the river Jordan (Josh. xv. 6; xviii. 19, 21). The name and site are found at 'Ain Hajlah, 4 miles southeast of Jericho.

Beth-ho′ron [house of hollowness].

Twin towns of Ephraim, 1¾ miles apart, but with a difference of 600 fee in altitude, on the boundary between Ephraim and Benjamin, built by a woman of Ephraim called Sherah (Josh. xvi. 3, 5; xviii. 13; 1 Chron. vii. 24). One of them was assigned as residence to the Levites of the family of Kohath (Josh. xxi. 22; 1 Chron. vi. 68). The towns lay in a mountain pass, on the ancient highway between Jerusalem and the plain, 12 Roman miles northwest of the capital. They controlled the pass, and were fortified by Solomon (2 Chron. viii. 5); but especially did the walls of the upper town engage military attention, for it occupied the more strategic position (1 Kin. ix. 17; 1 Mac. ix. 50; cp. Judith iv. 4). Up and down, past these towns, repeatedly surged the tide of war. The Amorites fled down this pass before Joshua (Josh. x. 10 seq.). The Philistines ascended it to make war with Saul (1 Sam. xiii. 18). Judas Maccabæus fought two battles here (1 Mac. iii. 15 seq.; vii. 39 seq.), and the army of Cestius Gallus, governor of Syria, was almost annihilated here by the Jews (War ii. 19, 8). The towns still exist under the names Beit 'Ur et-Tahta and el-Fôka.

Beth-jesh′i-moth, in A. V. once **Beth-jes′i-moth** [house of the wastes].

A town east of the Jordan, near Pisgah and the Dead Sea (Josh. xii. 3; xiii. 20; War iv. 7, 6). When the Israelites encamped at Shittim, it formed the southern limit of the camp (Num. xxxiii. 49). It was 10 Roman miles southeast of Jericho. Direction and distance indicate 'Ain es-Suwêmeh, and this name seems an echo of Jeshimoth. It was assigned to the Reubenites, but in the time of Ezekiel was in the hands of the Moabites (Josh. xiii. 20; Ezek. xxv. 9).

Beth-le-aph′rah. See APHRAH.

Beth-leb′a-oth [house of lionesses].

A town in the south of Judah, assigned to the Simeonites (Josh. xv. 32; xix. 6); see BETH-BIRI. Not identified.

Beth′le-hem [house of bread].

1. A town in the hill country of Judah, originally called Ephrath; hence, to distinguish it from a place of the same name in Zebulun, called also Bethlehem-judah and Bethlehem-ephrathah (Gen. xxxv. 19; Judg. xvii. 7; Mic. v. 2). Bethlehem is not mentioned among the cities assigned to Judah (Josh. xv.; see, however, ver. 59, Septuagint). But as a village it existed as early as the time of Jacob. Rachel died and was buried in its vicinity (Gen. xxxv. 16, 19; xlviii. 7). Its citizens were hospitable to the Levites (Judg. xvii. 7; xix. 1). A branch of Caleb's family settled in the town and attained to great influence (1 Chron. ii. 51, 54; cp. Ruth. iv. 20). It was the residence of Boaz, of Ruth (i. 19; iv. 9–11), doubtless of Obed (iv. 21, 22), and of Jesse, the father of David (Ruth iv. 11, 17; 1 Sam. xvi. 1, 4). As the birthplace and

ancestral home of David, it was the city of
David (Luke ii. 11). It was a walled town
as early as the time of David. It fell temporarily into the hands of the Philistines (2
Sam. xxiii. 14, 15). Rehoboam strengthened
its fortifications (2 Chron. xi. 6). Bethlehemites returned from captivity with Zerubbabel
(Ezra ii. 21; Neh. vii. 26). It was looked to
as the place where the Messiah should be
born (Mic. v. 2: Mat. ii. 5), and accordingly
when the fullness of time had come Jesus became incarnate at Bethlehem. In its vicinity
the annunciation to the shepherds took place
(Luke ii. 1–20). Thither the Magi went to
salute the newborn babe, and it was the infants of Bethlehem who were murdered by
Herod to make sure that among them he had
cut off the future king (Mat. ii. 1–18). There
has never been any doubt as to its site. It is
5 miles south of Jerusalem, at the modern
village of Beit Lahm, on the east and northeast slope of a long ridge, which to the west
is higher than the village. The town has
several gates. The houses are mostly small,
but well built. The inhabitants, who may
be 4000 or more, are mostly Christians belonging to the Greek Church. There are in
the vicinity vineyards, orchards of fig trees,
and olive trees. The fields, though stony,
produce grain abundantly, and at harvest
gleaning may be seen as it was in the days
of Ruth. A little east of the town is the
church built by Helena, the mother of Constantine, over the cave said to be the stable
in which the nativity took place. Half a
mile to the north of the town is the traditional tomb of Rachel. On the southern side
of the town is a valley running to the Dead
Sea, while almost at the walls on the east a
valley begins which joins the wady es-Surar or
vale of Sorek, and near by is also an upper
branch of the wady es-Sunt or vale of Elah
(cp. 1 Sam. xvii. 2).

2. A town with dependent villages within
the territory of Zebulun (Josh. xix. 15). It
seems to have been this Bethlehem which
gave birth to the judge Ibzan (Judg. xii.
8–10; cp. 11). It is believed to have been on
the site of the modern Beit Lahm, a small
and wretched village 7 miles northwest of
Nazareth.

Beth-ma′a-cah, in A. V. **Beth-maachah**
[house of Maacah].

A town near the foot of mount Hermon
(2 Sam. xx. 14, 15). See ABEL-BETH-MAACAH.

Beth-mar′ca-both [house of the chariots].

A town of the Simeonites (Josh. xix. 5; 1
Chron. iv. 31). Exact site unknown. Perhaps Madmannah was a chariot station, and
was spoken of by this name (Josh. xv. 31).

Beth-me′on. See BAAL-MEON.

Beth-mer′hak [house of removal].

Probably only a house beside the brook
Kidron, between Jerusalem and the mount
of Olives (2 Sam. xv. 17, R. V.). The margin

renders it the Far House; the A. V., a place
that was far off.

Beth-nim′rah [house of limpid fresh
water, or house of leopardess].

A town in the Jordan valley east of the
river, assigned to Gad and rebuilt by that
tribe (Num. xxxii. 36; Josh. xiii. 27). Eusebius and Jerome locate it 5 Roman miles to
the north of Livias, now Tell er-Rameh. At
the place thus indicated ruins bear the name
Nimrin. They lie amidst rich, well-watered
pasture land.

Beth-pa′let. See BETH-PELET.

Beth-paz′zez [house of dispersion].

A town within the territory of Issachar
(Josh. xix. 21). Exact site unknown.

Beth-pe′let; in A. V. **Beth-phelet** and
Beth-palet [house of escape].

A town in the most southerly part of Judah
(Josh. xv. 27; Neh. xi. 26). Exact site unknown.

Beth-pe′or [house of Peor].

A town near Pisgah. In the valley opposite
to it the Israelites had their main encampment, elsewhere referred to as in the mountains of Abarim, when their army was warring with Sihon and Og (cp. Deut iii. 29; iv.
46; with Num. xxi. 20; xxiii. 28; xxxiii.
47–49). In this valley Moses was afterwards
buried (Deut. xxxiv. 6). The town was assigned to the Reubenites (Josh. xiii. 20). According to Eusebius, it lay 6 Roman miles
above, that is in the mountains east of, Livias,
now Tell er-Rameh.

Beth′pha-ge [house of figs].

A village near Bethany, on or near the
road from Jericho to Jerusalem (Mark xi. 1;
Luke xix. 29). It probably stood between
Bethany and Jerusalem, not far from the
descent of the mount of Olives (Mat. xxi. 1;
John xii. 1, 12, 14), and near the old road
that crosses the mountain at the summit.

Beth-phe′let. See BETH-PELET.

Beth-ra′pha [house of Rapha, house of a
giant].

A family of Judah, or a town whose inhabitants belonged to that tribe (1 Chron. iv. 12).

Beth-re′hob [house of a street].

A town in the north of Palestine, by the
valley of the upper Jordan (Num. xiii. 21,
where it is called simply Rehob; Judg. xviii.
28). It was inhabited by Syrians, who joined
the Ammonites in a great war with David (2
Sam. x. 6). Robinson doubtfully located it
at the modern fortress of Hûnin commanding the plain of Huleh, in which Dan was
situated; but the location is improbable.

Beth-sa′i-da [house of hunting or fishing].

A town on the lake of Gennesaret, near
the Jordan, rebuilt by Philip the tetrarch,
and named by him Julias in honor of the
daughter of the emperor Augustus (Antiq.
xviii. 2, 1; Life 72). To this town, which
was on the other side of the sea (actually **at**

A view of Bethlehem from the suburb of Beit Sahur.

the northern end), Jesus withdrew on receiving news of the murder of John the Baptist (Luke ix. 10; cp. Mat. xiv. 13; John vi. 1). Going forth to a desert grassy place, apparently about 2 miles down the eastern side of the lake, he was followed by the multitude. In the evening he miraculously fed them. The disciples then entered into a boat to precede him "unto the other side to [or toward] Bethsaida" (Mark vi. 45, R. V.). During the evening and night, the disciples were in the midst of the sea distressed in rowing, for the wind was contrary unto them. Jesus came walking on the sea, and was taken into the boat. And when they had crossed over they came to the land unto Gennesaret (ver. 53). Do these statements, taken in connection with John's mention of "Bethsaida of Galilee" (xii. 21), imply another Bethsaida? Notable scholars, like Robinson, think so, and locate it, among other places, at 'Ain et-Tabighah, about 3 miles southwest of the mouth of the Jordan. But the existence of two towns of the same name on the same lake, and at most only a few miles apart, is so improbable that the words of the evangelists must be subjected to careful scrutiny to learn whether they require this assumption; and 1. The ultimate destination of the disciples was Capernaum (John vi. 17); but it was determined that they should sail "toward Bethsaida," keeping nearer the shore than the direct course to Capernaum would require (Thomson). 2. Even if their purpose was to make a stop at Bethsaida, it was proper to speak of going "to the other side to Bethsaida," for Josephus uses a similar expression for proceeding by boat from Tiberias 3¾ miles to Tarichæ. He "sailed over to Tarichæ" (Life 59, quoted by G. A. Smith). 3. Philip was of Bethsaida of Galilee (John xii. 21). Thomson suggests that any city built at the mouth of the narrow Jordan, as Bethsaida-Julias admittedly was, would almost necessarily have part of its houses or a suburb on the west bank of the river, which would be in Galilee. Peter, Andrew, and Philip were Galilæans and of Bethsaida. Thomson further suggests that probably the whole city on both banks of the river was ordinarily attached to Galilee. Geo. Adam Smith affirms that "the province of Galilee ran right round the lake." His opinion is based on Josephus' mention of a certain Judas, who belonged to Gamala in Gaulanitis, as a Galilæan (War ii. 8, 1 with Antiq. xviii. 1, 1).

Beth-she′an, or, contracted, **Beth′-shan** [house of quiet or restful security].

A city in the throat of the valley of Jezreel, situated on the southern side of the stream that flows from the great spring near Jezreel and at the point where the valley drops down three hundred feet to the level of the Jordan. The town was in existence as early as 1700 B. C. About 1300 B. C. Seti I of Egypt rendered aid asked of him, and also erected a fortress there. The inhabi-

tants of town and valley made themselves formidable by the use of chariots of iron (Josh. xvii. 16). Beth-shean with its dependent villages fell within the area of Issachar, but was given to the Manassites (Josh. xvii. 11; 1 Chron. vii. 29). They failed, however, to drive out the Canaanites, but were strong enough to make them pay tribute (Josh. xvii. 12–16; Judg. i. 27, 28). At the battle of Gilboa the town apparently sided with the Philistines, for after the defeat of Israel, the Philistines fastened the bodies of Saul and his sons to the wall of Beth-shean (1 Sam. xxxi. 10–13; 2 Sam. xxi. 12–14). It was called Scythopolis as early as the time of Judas Maccabæus. In several instances this name is written Σκυθῶν πόλις, city of the Scythians (Judg. i. 27, Septuagint; Judith iii. 10; 2 Mac. xii. 29); and it has been supposed that a remnant of the Scythian hordes settled here, who are said to have advanced through Palestine against Egypt in the latter half of the seventh century before Christ (Herod. i. 103, 105; Pliny, hist. nat. v. 16). The name Scythopolis may, however, be the echo of some Semitic word. In the first century A. D. the population of the city was predominantly gentile (2 Mac. xii. 30; War ii. 18, 1, 3, 4; Life 6), and the Jews consequently sacked it during the war with the Romans. The citizens retaliated by massacring the Jewish residents. Josephus says that it was the largest of the ten cities called Decapolis, apparently disregarding Damascus, possibly because the city on the Abanah was not at this moment a member of the league (War iii. 9, 7). It was the only one of the ten cities that lay west of the Jordan. It figured in history as late as the crusades. The Arab village on the site bears the old name in altered form, Beisân. At the city's greatest extent, in the Greco-Roman period, its walls must have been nearly three miles in circuit. The city was divided into three parts by two streams flowing through deep ravines. The earliest settlement was in the central section, which is almost surrounded by the two streams. The mound or tell of the early towns rises about 200 feet high, and at its top are traces of a thick wall which once enclosed the summit.

Beth-she′mesh [house of the sun].

1. A town of the lowland, in the vale of Sorek, 100 yards west of the spot now known as 'Ain Shems. It was a settlement of the Canaanites in very ancient times, on the main road from Ashkelon and Ashdod to Jerusalem. The name indicates a seat of the worship of the sun. At an early date it was surrounded by a lofty and massive wall, about 8 feet thick, enclosing a space about 675 feet from east to west and 500 feet from north to south. On the south side was the city gate, with an entrance 12 feet wide, and a passageway 30 feet long, not straight, but with a left and right turn, flanked by two bastions. The one on the left contained a small room, with a doorway on the east

side, commanding the entrance and forming a sort of guardroom. The town was under Egyptian rule in the 15th century B. C. The Philistines seized and occupied it. It was allotted to Judah, and stood on the boundary line of Judah and Dan (Josh. xv. 10; xix. 41, where the synonymous name Ir-shemesh is used). The Danites did not occupy it; and when provision was made for the tribe of Levi, it was given to the priests the sons of Aaron, and reckoned as set apart from the tribe of Judah (xxi. 16, cp. 9; 1 Chron. vi. 59). After the formation of the kingdom it was within Judah (2 Kin. xiv. 11). The people of Beth-shemesh, whither the kine brought the ark from Ekron, were largely of priestly family, and offered sacrifice; but profanely looking into the ark, they were smitten by a plague which carried off seventy persons (Antiq. vi. 1, 4). After the words seventy men there is the strange insertion in the Hebrew text, rendered suspicious by the absence of the conjunction, of the further words fifty thousand men (1 Sam. vi. 1–21, R. V.). At Beth-shemesh Joash, king of Israel, defeated Amaziah of Judah (2 Kin. xiv. 11; 2 Chron. xxv. 21). The Philistines took the town during the reign of Ahaz (xxviii. 16).

2. A town on the boundary of Issachar, between Tabor and the Jordan (Josh. xix. 22). It may be the fenced city of the tribe of Naphtali, from which, however, the Canaanites were not driven (Josh. xix. 38; Judg. i. 33).

3. An Egyptian city where the sun was worshiped (Jer. xliii. 13); doubtless On.

Beth-she'mite.

A native of Beth-shemesh (1 Sam. vi. 14, 18).

Beth-shit'tah [house of the acacia].

A town between the valley of Jezreel and Zererah in the Jordan valley (Judg. vii. 22, R. V.). The fact that it is coupled with Zererah, and not with Beth-shean, excludes its identification with Shutta.

Beth-su'ra. See BETH-ZUR.

Beth-tap'pu-ah [house of apples or similar fruit].

A town in the hill country of Judah (Josh. xv. 53), the modern village of Tuffûh, about 4 miles west of Hebron (cp. 1 Chron. ii. 43).

Be-thu'el [perhaps abode of God].

1. Son of Nahor by his wife Milcah. He was the father of Laban and Rebekah, and nephew of Abraham (Gen. xxii. 20, 22, 23; xxiv. 15, 29; xxv. 20; xxviii. 2, 5).

2. A town of the Simeonites (1 Chron. iv. 30; in Josh. xix. 4 Bethul). David sent thither part of the recaptured spoil of Ziklag (1 Sam. xxx. 27). In this latter passage it is called Bethel, a modified form of the name, more suggestive to the Hebrew ear. It seems to be the Chesil of Josh. xv. 30. Not identified. Possibly the small village of Beit Aûla, 6½ miles northwest of Hebron.

Be'thul. See BETHUEL 2.

Beth-zach-a-ri'as.

A town (1 Mac. vi. 32, 33), 70 stades or 8 miles from Bethsura (Antiq. xii. 9, 4). It is identified with the modern Beit Zakariya, 9 Roman miles by road north of Bethsura.

Beth'-zur, in Maccabees **Bethsura** [house of a rock].

A town in the hill country of Judah (Josh. xv. 58). It was fortified by Rehoboam (2 Chron. xi. 7). In Nehemiah's time half of its district was subject to Azbuk (Neh. iii. 16). In the Greek period the name was written Bethsura, and it was important as a frontier town toward Idumæa. Here Judas Maccabæus gained a great victory over the Syrian general Lysias (1 Mac. iv. 29; 2 Mac. xi. 5: xiii. 19, 22). The patriot leader afterwards fortified it (1 Mac. iv. 61; vi. 7, 26, 31). Want of food compelled the garrison to surrender it to the Syrians (49, 50). Its defenses were strengthened by Bacchides (ix. 52), but it was recaptured by Simon (xi. 65, 66; xiv. 7) and refortified (33). The name lingers in the ruins Beit Sûr, 4 miles to the north of Hebron.

Bet'o-nim [pistachio-nuts].

A town of Gad (Josh. xiii. 26). Not properly identified.

Beu'lah [married].

A name prophetically applied to the once forsaken land of Palestine when it was restored to God's favor and repeopled after the captivity (Is. lxii. 4).

Be'zai.

Founder of a family, some of whom returned from Babylon with Zerubbabel (Ezra ii. 17; Neh. vii. 23). A representative of the family signed the covenant of fidelity to Jehovah (Neh. x. 18).

Be'zal-el, in A. V. **Be-zal'e-el** [in the shadow (i. e. under the protection) of God].

1. A man of Judah, family of Hezron, house of Caleb, and a grandson of Hur (1 Chron. ii. 20); a skillful artificer raised up of God and appointed to work in gold, silver, copper, in the setting of precious stones, and the carving of wood for the furnishing of the tabernacle (Ex. xxxi. 1–11; xxxv. 30–35).

2. A son of Pahath-moab, induced by Ezra to put away his foreign wife (Ezra x. 30).

Be'zek [dissemination, sowing, plantation].

A town evidently in central Palestine, not a great distance from Jabesh-gilead (1 Sam. xi. 8, 11). Twin villages of this name existed in Eusebius' time 17 Roman miles from Shechem toward Beth-shean. Conder identifies the site with the ruin Ibzik, 13 miles northeast of Shechem. With this town may be identified Bezek mentioned in Judg. i. 4 seq., on the assumption that Adoni-bezek advanced southward with his forces to unite with the southern Canaanites, was met and repulsed by Judah and Simeon, and pursued to his capital.

Be′zer [gold or silver ore].

1. An Asherite, son of Zophah (1 Chron. vii. 37).

2. A city in the wilderness, on the plateau within the territory of Reuben. It was given to the Levites, and was one of the cities of refuge (Deut. iv. 43; Josh. xx. 8; xxi. 36; 1 Mac. v. 26). It afterwards came into the possession of Moab, and Mesha, king of Moab, fortified it (Moabite Stone 27). Not identified.

Be′zeth.

A place not far from Jerusalem, where Bacchides pitched his camp (1 Mac. vii. 19), the village of Beth-zetho or Berzetho (Antiq. xii. 10, 2), doubtless Bezetha, the northern suburb of Jerusalem. See JERUSALEM II. 3.

Bi′ble [Greek *Biblia*, books, ecclesiastical Latin *Biblia*]. It is believed that the Greek word *Biblia* was first applied to the sacred books by John Chrysostom, patriarch of Constantinople from A. D. 398 to 404.

Etymologically viewed, the Bible means "the Books," and that no qualifying adjective stands before the noun implies that these writings were regarded by those who used the term as forming a class by themselves and as superior to all other literary productions. They are uniquely and preëminently the books. The same view is suggested by the etymology of the word Scripture and Scriptures, and the fact is rendered all the more significant that both terms occur frequently with this implied meaning in the N. T. (Mat. xxi. 42; Acts. viii. 32). The term Bible is absent from the sacred page; it is of ecclesiastical origin. The plural term *Biblia* marks the important fact that the Bible is not a single book, but a great many. The words Bible and Scripture, on the other hand, being both in the singular number, emphasize the fact that, under the diversity of human authorship, there lies a wonderful unity, pointing to the operation of one directing Mind, which acted during more than a thousand consecutive years when these writings were being produced. The claims to divine authority made by Scripture are investigated by the science of Apologetics. The word is used in a Greek rather than in an English sense, and is, therefore, liable to be misunderstood. It is related that when George III. was told that Bishop Watson had published an *Apology for the Bible*, he drily remarked that he did not know before that the Bible required an apology. The bishop used the word "Apology" like the Greek *apologia*, to mean defense; and the science of Apologetics *defends* the Bible. A second science is that of Biblical Criticism. This is divided into Higher Criticism, which inquires into the origin and character of the several books, and seeks to determine by whom, under what circumstances, and with what design they were written; and Lower or Textual Criticism, which seeks, by the aid of the ancient manuscripts and versions, to bring the text of these

books to the highest practicable level of accuracy. Cp. APOCRYPHA, CANON. The science of Hermeneutics investigates the principles of interpretation, while Exegesis applies them. The contents of the Bible are then methodically arranged. It will be found when this is done that they touch geography, history, science, philosophy, ethics—in fact, nearly every department of human thought. Further, Biblical Theology investigates the doctrines of the Bible in their historical development, and Dogmatic or Systematic Theology seeks to arrange the doctrines into the system which is contained in Scripture, show their relation to each other and to other truths, and to state them with precision.

The Bible embraces the Old and the New Testaments or covenants. The O. T. was written in Hebrew, except a few passages in Aramaic, and the N. T. in Greek. For the several books of the O. T. and N. T., see the articles which bear their names; and for the versions of the Scripture into other tongues, see SAMARITAN, SEPTUAGINT, VERSIONS, and VULGATE.

Each of the sacred books on its original publication came forth without division into chapters or verses. The author of the present division into chapters is believed to have been either the Spanish cardinal Hugo or the British archbishop Langton, both of whom lived in the thirteenth century. The Jewish Masorites of the ninth century divided the O. T. into verses. The division of the N. T. into its present verses is due to Robert Stephens, who introduced them into the Greek and Latin N. T. which he published at Geneva in 1551; and they were adopted in the English version of the N. T. printed at Geneva in 1557. The whole Bible first appeared with its present chapters and verses in Stephen's edition of the Vulgate in 1555. The first English Bible to be thus divided was the Genevan edition of 1560 (see NEW TESTAMENT). They are not perfect. Regarding chapters, there is an imperfection in drawing the line between the i. and ii. of Genesis at the place where the separation is now made. Gen. i. should also include Gen. ii. 1–3, and chapter ii. begin at ii. 4, where "God" is succeeded by "the LORD God." Is. liii. should begin with lii. 13, and John vii. should take in also viii. 1. Regarding the verses, they are absolutely indispensable for the purpose of reference, but they should be ignored when one is following the thread of an argument or of a narrative. The R. V. enables one to do this easily, for it does not make the division into verses prominent; but greater accuracy of reference is secured by citing the number of the verse from the A. V.

The Bible has already been translated, in its entirety or in part, into more than seven hundred languages or dialects. It is not an exaggeration, when referring to the writers of the Bible, to adopt the language of the psalmist, meant originally for the

silent theological teaching of the starry sky:
"Their line is gone out through all the earth,
and their words to the end of the world (Ps.
xix. 4).

Bich'ri [youthful].
Father of the rebel Sheba (2 Sam. xx. 1).

Bid'kar.
A captain under Jehu (2 Kin. ix. 25).

Big'tha.
A chamberlain who ministered in the presence of Xerxes (Esth. i. 10).

Big'than or **Big'tha-na** [Persian and Sanscrit *Bagadâna*, gift of fortune].
A chamberlain, keeper of the palace door,
who conspired against king Xerxes (Esth. ii.
21 ; vi. 2).

Big'vai.
1. One of the leaders of the exiles who returned from Babylon with Zerubbabel (Ezra
ii. 2).
2. Founder of a family, of which some 2000
returned from Babylon with Zerubbabel (Ezra
ii. 14 ; Neh. vii. 19), and several score afterwards with Ezra (Ezra viii. 14).

Bil'dad.
A Shuhite, one of Job's friends (Job ii. 11),
who made three speeches to the patriarch
(viii., xviii., xxv.).

Bil'e-am [perhaps greed, consumption, destruction].
A town of Manasseh, west of the Jordan,
which was assigned to the Levites of the
family of Kohath (1 Chron. vi. 70) ; see
IBLEAM. In its stead Gath-rimmon appears
in the present Hebrew text of Josh. xxi. 25.
This latter name has probably been erroneously copied from the preceding verse. The
Septuagint (Vat. and Alex.) lends confirmation to this view.

Bil'gah [cheerful].
1. A descendant of Aaron. His family had
grown to a father's house in the time of David,
and was made the fifteenth course of the
priests (1 Chron. xxiv. 1, 6, 14).
2. A chief of the priests, perhaps representing the priestly course of this name, who
returned from Babylon with Zerubbabel (Neh.
xii. 5, 7). In the next generation a father's
house among the priests bore this name (ver.
18) ; cp. BILGAI.

Bil'gai [cheerful].
One of the priests who, doubtless in behalf
of a father's house, sealed the covenant in
the days of Nehemiah (Neh. x. 8) ; cp. under
the similar name BILGAH.

Bil'hah [perhaps bashfulness].
1. Rachel's maidservant, who, at her mistress' desire, became one of Jacob's secondary
wives. She was the mother of Dan and Naphtali (Gen. xxx. 1-8 ; 1 Chron. vii. 13). Ultimately she committed sin with Reuben (Gen.
xxxv. 22).
2. A Simeonite town (1 Chron. iv. 29). See
BAALAH.

Bil'han [perhaps bashful].
1. A Horite, son of Ezer (Gen. xxxvi. 27).
2. A Benjamite, family of Jediael, and himself the ancestor of several father's houses
(1 Chron. vii. 10).

Bil'shan.
One of the twelve chief men who returned
from Babylon with Zerubbabel (Ezra ii. 2 ;
Neh. vii. 7).

Bim'hal.
An Asherite, family of Beriah, house of
Japhlet (1 Chron. vii. 33).

Bin'e-a.
A son of Moza, a descendant of Jonathan,
Saul's son (1 Chron. viii. 37 ; ix. 43).

Bin'nu-i [built].
1. The head of a family, of which several
hundred returned from the captivity. His
name is also pronounced Bani (Ezra ii. 10 ;
Neh. vii. 15).
2 and 3. Two men, a son of Pahath-moab
and a son of Bani, each of whom was induced by Ezra to put away his foreign wife
(Ezra x. 30, 38).
4. A Levite who went from Babylon with
Zerubbabel (Neh. xii. 8). He was a son of
Henadad (x. 9). His son was one who received the silver and gold brought from
Babylon to the temple by Ezra (Ezra viii. 33),
and his family was represented at the building of the wall (Neh. iii. 24), and its representative sealed the covenant (x. 9).

Birds.
The Hebrews classed as birds all animals
which fly, including the bat and winged insects. Tristram enumerates 348 species of
birds as either indigenous or visitants to Palestine. Of these 271 belong to the Palæarctic
zone of Sclater—that to which most of the
European birds belong ; 40 to the Ethiopian,
and 7 to the Indian zone ; while 30, as far as
is known, are peculiar to Palestine itself.
The Ethiopian and Indian types are almost
exclusively confined to the Dead Sea basin,
but it is so depressed beneath the level of the
ocean that it is really a small tropical region
located in the midst of the temperate zone.
In the Mosaic law twenty or twenty-one birds
and, in the case of four of them, their flesh
are expressly named as unclean (Lev. xi. 13–
19 ; Deut. xiv. 11–20). The flesh and the eggs
of all clean birds were eaten (cp. Is. x. 14 ; Luke
xi. 12), but the only birds used for sacrifice
were turtle doves and young pigeons (Lev. i.
14). Doves were domesticated (Is. lx. 8), and
later, chickens. The cock is mentioned (Mat.
xxvi. 34), and the hen (xxiii. 37 ; Luke xiii. 34).
Wild fowl were hunted, among other ways, by
decoy birds (Ecclus. xi. 30), with snares (Amos
iii. 5), and with nets (Prov. i. 17). The migration of birds is referred to (Jer. viii. 7).

Bir'sha.
A king of Gomorrah who was defeated by
Chedorlaomer and his confederates (Gen. xiv.
2, 8, 10).

Birth'day.

The birth of a child, especially of a son, was a glad occasion, and was often celebrated by a feast (Jer. xx. 15; Antiq. xii. 4, 7). The anniversary of one's birth was celebrated by the Egyptians. and Persians (Gen. xl. 20; Herod. i. 133). Herod the tetrarch kept the anniversary of either his birth or his accession, it is debated which (Mat. xiv. 6).

Birth'right.

A certain right or privilege considered to belong to the firstborn son in a family, and which is not shared by his younger brothers. The eldest son ordinarily succeeded to his father's rank and position, as head of the family or tribe, and as representative of its prerogatives. He also inherited a double portion of his father's property, a right guaranteed to the firstborn even when his mother was the less loved of two wives (Deut. xxi. 17; cp. 2 Kin. ii. 9). A birthright might be sold to a younger brother, as Esau sold his birthright to Jacob (Gen. xxv. 29, 34; Heb. xii. 16). It might also be forfeited on account of misconduct (1 Chron. v. 1).

Bir'za-ith, in A. V. **Bir'za-vith** [openings, wounds]. The form in R. V. is the traditional reading, that in A. V. represents the consonants of the present text.

An Asherite, family of Malchiel; or possibly a town, meaning olive well (1 Chron. vii. 31).

Bish'lam.

A Persian official who joined in the complaint to Artaxerxes that the Jews were rebuilding Jerusalem (Ezra iv. 7).

Bish'op [a corruption of Latin *episcopus,* Greek *episkopos,* an overseer].

The Greek word is used in the Septuagint for an official overseer, whether civil or religious, as Eleazar the priest (Num. iv. 16). and officers of the army (xxxi. 14). In the N. T. the word occurs first in the exhortation of Paul to the elders or, as in the margin, presbyters of the church at Ephesus, when he said, "Take heed unto yourselves, and to all the flock, in the which the Holy Ghost hath made you bishops," or, as in the margin, "overseers" (Acts xx. 17, 28, R. V.). Here and elsewhere Paul identifies elders, presbyters, and bishops (Tit. i. 5–7). The terms are different designations for the incumbent of the same office. Elsewhere he distinguishes simply between bishop and deacon (Phil. i. 1; 1 Tim. iii. 1–8). Peter, using the verb *episkopeō,* exhorts the elders to tend the flock of God, "exercising the oversight, not of constraint, but willingly" (1 Pet. v. 2, R. V.). In the church of the N. T. the duties of the bishop were to care for the flock of God (Acts xx. 28; 1 Pet. v. 2). He was the shepherd, bearing rule and watching in behalf of souls, admonishing, encouraging, and supporting (1 Thes. v. 14; Heb. xiii. 17), and some among them labored in the word and in teaching (1 Tim. v. 17). His qualifications are enumerated in 1

Tim.iii.1–7 and Tit.i.7–9. A plurality of them existed in the church at Philippi, as in that of Ephesus (Phil. i. 1); and the college of presbyter-bishops ordained by the laying on of hands (1 Tim. iv. 14). In the church at Jerusalem the elders and apostles consulted together, and the decision of the council was given in the name of the apostles and elders (Acts xv. 6, 22; xvi. 4; xxi. 18); see ELDER. The name is applied figuratively to Jesus (1 Pet. ii. 25). A distinction, however, grew up very early in the Church between elder or presbyter and bishop. It appears in the second century, being mentioned in the epistles of Ignatius, who died in 107 or 116. According to the Roman Catholic Council of Trent in the sixteenth century, "Bishops, being the successors of the apostles. are placed by the Holy Ghost to govern the Church of God, and to be superior to their presbyters or priests." Roman Catholic opinion assumes that the apostles had a general supervision of the congregation, while the elders whom they had ordained had the local oversight; but as the congregations increased in number, the apostles ordained assistants whom they appointed their successors, to be overseers of the congregation in a district. Such were the angels of the seven churches (Rev. i. 20); see ANGEL. High Anglicans find the institution implied in the position of Jesus' brother James in the church at Jerusalem, in the angels of the seven churches, and in the work of Timothy and Titus. Paul did indeed exhort Timothy to tarry at Ephesus, order public worship, exhort and teach (1 Tim. i. 3 ff.); and Titus, whom Paul had before employed as a messenger to the Corinthians (2 Cor. xii. 18), he left in Crete to set in order things that were wanting, and to appoint elders, called also bishops, in every city (Tit. i. 5–7). But it is to be noted that Timothy was in the first instance ordained by presbytery (1 Tim. iv. 14), and there is not a trace in the N. T. of the apostles appointing any man to succeed them.

Bi-thi'ah [a daughter, in the sense of a worshiper, of Jehovah].

A daughter of Pharaoh and wife of Mered, a man of Judah (1 Chron. iv. 18). Her name indicates that she was a convert to the worship of Jehovah.

Bith'ron [cut, division, gorge].

A region, doubtless a valley, north of the Jabbok near Mahanaim (2 Sam. ii. 29).

Bi-thyn'i-a.

A country in the northwestern part of Asia Minor, bounded on the north by the Black Sea, on the south by Phrygia and Galatia, on the east by Paphlagonia and part of Phrygia, and on the west by Mysia. But its boundaries varied at different times. It was colonized by the Thyni or Bithyni from Thrace, in Europe, who conquered or drove out the Bebryces, its original inhabitants, and imparted to it their own name (Herod. vii. 75). Under the Persian empire it constituted a satrapy.

Nicomedes III. bequeathed it to the Romans
in 74 B. C. Paul and Silas attempted to enter Bithynia, but the Spirit suffered them not
(Acts xvi. 7). The gospel was carried thither
by other means. Peter was able to address
Christians of Bithynia in his first letter (1 Pet.
i. 1), and at the beginning of the second century Pliny the younger reported numerous
Christians there. Later still, in two of its towns,
Nicæa and Chalcedon, great councils of the
Church were held. It is a fertile country, in
which the vine is largely cultivated. In
various parts, especially in the chain of mount
Olympus, which runs along its southern boundary, there are forests of oak, interspersed with
beech trees, chestnuts, and walnuts.

Bit'tern.

The rendering in A. V. of the Hebrew word
Ḳippod, the one contracting or rolling itself
together; an animal frequenting ruins (Is.
xiv. 23; xxxiv. 11), which ascended to the
top of ruined doors or to window sills, and
thence made its voice heard (Zeph. ii. 14).
The bittern (*Botaurus stellaris*) is a long-
necked and long-legged wading bird, habitually frequenting pools of water, but not
likely to be heard giving voice from a ruined
window. The R. V. considers the animal to be
the porcupine, while Tristram identifies it as
probably the Scops Owl (*Scops giu*), a migrant
in Palestine for the summer months, breeding
in the walls of old ruins and in hollow trees.

Bi-tu'men.

Mineral pitch. There are three varieties
of it: (1) Earthy bitumen; (2) elastic bitumen, elaterite or mineral caoutchouc; (3)
compact bitumen or asphalt, asphaltum, or
Jew's pitch. In its appearance it resembles
common pitch. It sinks in water, is easily
melted, is very inflammable, and when set
on fire burns with a red smoky flame. It is
produced in the chemistry of nature by the
enclosure of vegetable matter in the crust of
the earth, so that it is in immediate contact
with water, while atmospheric air is quite
shut out. There is a pitch lake in Trinidad.
Bitumen or asphalt exists at or near the Dead
Sea. called, in consequence, by the Greeks
and Romans, Lake Asphaltites. It is found
also at Hit, on the Euphrates, above Babylon,
and in other places. Bitumen was the slime
with which the bricks used for the erection
of the tower of Babel were cemented (Gen.
xi. 3). The slime pits in which the defeated
kings of Sodom and Gomorrah fell were bitumen pits (xiv. 10).

Biz'i-o-thi'ah, in A. V. Biz-joth'jah [con-
tempt of Jehovah].

A town in the most southerly portion of
Judah (Josh. xv. 28). The text is suspicious.
Almost the same consonants would mean "its
daughters or suburbs" (Septuagint, cp. Neh.
xi. 27).

Biz'tha.

A chamberlain at the court of Xerxes (Esth.
i. 10).

Blain.

The rendering of the Hebrew *'ăba'bu'oth*,
pustules. It signifies a bleb, a bubble of matter, a blister full of serum arising upon the
skin. It would now probably be ranked under the skin disease called pemphigus. Blains
accompanied by boils is the disease which constituted the sixth of the ten plagues of Egypt
(Ex. ix. 8-11).

Blas'phe-my.

Defamatory or other wicked language directed against God (Ps. lxxiv. 10-18; Is. lii.
5; Rev. xvi. 9, 11, 21). Under the Mosaic
law it was punished by stoning (Lev. xxiv.
16). The charge of blasphemy was falsely
brought against Naboth (1 Kin. xxi. 10-13),
Stephen (Acts vi. 11), and our Lord (Mat. ix.
3; xxvi. 65, 66: John x. 36).
Blasphemy against the Holy Ghost consisted in attributing the miracles of Christ,
which were wrought by the Spirit of God, to
Satanic power (Mat. xii. 22-32; Mark iii.
22-30).

Blas'tus [a sprout or shoot, a sucker].

A palace functionary who had charge of
Herod Agrippa's bedchamber (Acts xii. 20).

Bless.

The three leading meanings which the verb
bless has in Scripture are:

1. To bestow divine favor and confer divine benefits (Gen. i. 22; ii. 3; ix. 1-7).

2. To adore God for his goodness and return
thanks (Ps. ciii. 1; and Mat. xxvi. 26; Mark
xiv. 22 with Luke xxii. 19 and 1 Cor. xi. 24).

3. To invoke God's favor on a person (Gen.
xxvii. 4, 27-29; 1 Chron. xvi. 2: Ps. cxxix.
8), including salutation and even the ordinary greeting, "Peace be to you" (1 Sam.
xxv. 5, 6, 14; 2 Kin. iv. 29).

Bless'ing.

Any advantage conferred or wished for.
Specially—

1. Favors, advantages, conferred by God,
and bringing pleasure or happiness in their
train (Gen. xxxix. 5; Deut. xxviii. 8: Prov.
x. 22, etc.).

2. The invocation of God's favor upon a
person (Gen. xxvii. 12).

3. A present, a token of good will (Gen
xxxiii. 11; Josh. xv. 19; 2 Kin. v. 15).

Blind'ness.

Blindness is extremely prevalent in the
east. Its main causes are smallpox, and especially ophthalmia. aggravated by peculiar
conditions, such as the perpetual glare of the
sun, the quantity of fine dust in the air, and
flies. Children are also sometimes born blind
(John ix. 1). Consequently blind beggars are
frequent (Mat. ix. 27; xii. 22; xx. 30; xxi.
14). Total or partial blindness may result
from old age (Gen. xxvii. 1; 1 Sam. iv. 15;
1 Kin. xiv. 4). The eyes of captives taken
in war were frequently put out by barbarous
victors, as by the Ammonites, Philistines, Assyrians, and Babylonians (Judg. xvi. 21: 1

Sam. xi. 2; 2 Kin. xxv. 7). In a few instances men were miraculously smitten with
temporary blindness (Gen. xix. 11; 2 Kin. vi.
18–22; Acts ix. 9; xiii. 11). The Mosaic law
inculcated the exercise of humanity toward
the blind (Lev. xix. 14; Deut. xxvii. 18).

Blood.

The vital fluid circulating through the
body, and conveyed by a system of deep-
seated arteries from the heart to the extremities, and by a system of superficial veins
back again to the heart. Arterial blood is
florid red, while venous blood is of a dark
purple or modena hue. The life is in the
blood (Lev. xvii. 11, 14); or the blood is the
life (Deut. xii. 23), though not exclusively
(Ps. civ. 30). The blood represented the life,
and so sacred is life before God that the blood
of murdered Abel could be described as crying to God from the ground for vengeance
(Gen. iv. 10); and immediately after the
flood the eating of the blood of the lower
animals was forbidden, although their slaughter for food was authorized (ix. 3, 4; Acts xv.
20, 29), and the law was laid down, "Whoso
sheddeth man's blood, by man shall his blood
be shed" (Gen. ix. 6). The loss of life is the
penalty for sin, and its typical vicarious surrender was necessary to remission (Heb. ix.
22), and so, under the Mosaic law, the blood of
animals was used in all offerings for sin, and
the blood of beasts killed on the hunt or
slaughtered for food was poured out and covered with earth, because withheld by God
from man's consumption and reserved for
purposes of atonement (Lev. xvii. 10–14; Deut.
xii. 15, 16). The "blood of Jesus," the "blood
of Christ," the "blood of Jesus Christ," or
"the blood of the Lamb," are figurative expressions for his atoning death (1 Cor. x. 16;
Eph. ii. 13; Heb. ix. 14; x. 19; 1 Pet. i. 2, 19;
1 John i. 7; Rev. vii. 14; xii. 11).

For revenger, or rather avenger, of blood,
see AVENGER.

Blood'y Flux. See DYSENTERY.

Blood'y Sweat. See SWEAT.

Bo-a-ner'ges [sons of tumult or thunder].

A name given by Jesus to James and John
on account of their impetuosity (Mark iii. 17;
cp. Luke ix. 54, 55).

Boar.

The rendering of the Hebrew *Hᵃzir*, when
it refers to wild swine, and especially to the
male of wild swine (Ps. lxxx. 13). When the
reference is to the domesticated animal, it is
rendered swine. The wild boar is three or
more feet long, not counting the tail. The
canine teeth project beyond the upper lip,
constituting formidable tusks, with which it
seeks to rip up its assailants. The female is
smaller than the male, and has smaller tusks.
The animal is still found in Palestine, especially in the ravines east of the Jordan, in
the valley near Jericho, in the swamps of the
waters of Merom, on Tabor, Lebanon, and

Carmel, and in the plain of Sharon.

Bo'az, in A. V. of N. T. **Bo'oz** [commonly
interpreted as meaning "In him is strength,"
but both spelling and accentuation are against
this explanation].

1. A wealthy and honorable Bethlehemite,
kinsman to the husband of Ruth the Moabitess. He respected the memory of the dead
by marrying Ruth after the decease of her
husband, and became ancestor of David and
of Christ (Ruth ii.–iv.; Mat. i. 5). Late Jewish tradition, destitute of all probability, identifies him with the judge Ibzan.

2. One of two pillars, that on the left, set
up in the porch of Solomon's temple (1 Kin.
vii. 15–22).

Boch'e-ru [firstborn].

A son of Azel and a descendant of Jonathan, Saul's son (1 Chron. viii. 38).

Bo'chim [weepers].

A place near Gilgal, where the Israelites
repented and wept under the rebuke of the
angel of the Lord for their disobedience of
God's commands (Judg. ii. 1–5). Its exact
site is unknown.

Bo'han [thumb].

1. A son of Reuben (Josh. xv. 6; xviii. 17),
unless Bohan is a common noun in these
passages.

2. The stone of Bohan, son of Reuben, or
the stone known as the Reubenite's thumb,
was a landmark on the boundary between
Judah and Benjamin, not a great distance
from the Jordan (Josh. xv. 6; xviii. 17).
Exact site unknown.

Boil.

An inflamed ulcer. It was inflicted along
with blains as the sixth plague of Egypt (Ex.
ix. 8–11; cp. Deut. xxviii. 27, 35). It was a
prominent symptom in leprosy (Lev. xiii. 18–
20). It constituted the main feature of Hezekiah's disease, which brought his life into
imminent danger (2 Kin. xx. 7; Is. xxxviii.
21). Job was smitten by Satan with boils
from head to foot (Job ii. 7). Ordinary boils
are common, in the warmer parts of the East,
during the rainy season. They are unsightly,
but are not dangerous. One type of boil,
however, the carbuncle, arising from poisoned
blood and eating away the flesh like an ulcer,
may terminate the life. This was probably
Hezekiah's disease. The application of a
poultice of figs would do it good, but the
rapid cure was due to God.

Bol'ster.

The usual Hebrew word which is rendered
bolster or pillow means simply at the head,
and the Greek word rendered pillow in A. V.
does not necessarily mean a cushion for the
head. Jacob, sleeping in the open field, took
a stone to support his head (Gen. xxviii. 11,
18). Jesus probably placed the leather cushion
of the steersman's seat under his head when
he lay down to sleep in the stern of the boat
(Mark iv. 38). Michal put some article of

A booth prepared for the Feast of Tabernacles.

goats' hair at the head of the teraphim which she laid in the bed to deceive the messengers who were sent to take David. She did this perhaps to give the appearance of human hair or of a covering laid over the sleeper (1 Sam. xix. 13).

Bon'net.

Originally a head dress for men (Ezek. xliv. 18), a sense which the word still retains in Scotland. Then it was applied to a head dress for women (Is. iii. 20). The R. V. renders it head tires and tires (q. v.).

Book.

Documents were early inscribed on clay or graven on stone. Skin or parchment and papyrus came into use at an early period also. When written on skin, a long document took the form of a roll with writing on one or both of its sides. Of this type of book there is a memorial in the word volume, Latin *volumen*, properly, something rolled up (Ps. xl. 7; Jer. xxxvi. 2; Ezek. ii. 9). Books are first mentioned as written by the Hebrews after the sojourn in Egypt, where written literature had existed for centuries (Ex. xvii. 14). The 39 books of the O. T. and the 27 of the N. T., which constitute the canon of Scripture, do not represent the entire literary activity of the Hebrews during the time embraced by the canon. There were, for example, the books of the Apocrypha. Later there were memoirs of Jesus (Luke i. 1). In the O. T. period there were two poetical books at least, the Book of the Wars of Jehovah and the Book of Jashar (Num. xxi. 14; Josh. x. 13). The events of the reigns of David and Solomon were recorded in the History of Samuel the Seer, the History of Nathan the Prophet, the History of Gad the Seer (1 Chron. xxix. 29; 2 Chron. ix. 29), and also in the Chronicles of King David, which apparently mark the beginning of the custom of keeping royal annals (1 Chron. xxvii. 24). The reigns of Solomon and Jeroboam found record in the Visions of Iddo the Seer (2 Chron. ix. 29), and Rehoboam's reign in the History of Shemaiah the Prophet and in the History of Iddo the Seer (xii. 15). The Chronicles of the Kings of Israel and the Chronicles of the Kings of Judah recorded the history of the two kingdoms from the time of Rehoboam and Jeroboam, until as late as the reign of Jehoiakim (1 Kin. xiv. 19, 29; 2 Kin. xxiv. 5; 2 Chron. xxxvi. 8); see KINGS. In addition to these works, there was quite a library in existence at the time when the books of Chronicles were written, consisting largely of monographs, of which not a few titles are cited (2 Chron. ix. 29; xiii. 22; xx. 34; xxiv. 27; xxvi. 22; xxxii. 32; xxxiii. 18, 19; xxxv. 25; see also Prov. xxv. 1; 1 Kin. iv. 32, 33).

Booth.

A rude habitation designed in most cases for a longer occupation than a tent, but not for permanence like a house. It was often formed with branches of trees. Jacob made booths at Shechem for his cattle, the place in consequence being afterwards called Succoth (Gen. xxxiii. 17). The keeper of a vineyard occupied a booth (Job xxvii. 18; Is. i. 8, R. V.), which during the vintage sheltered the owner and his friends. The Israelites were required to form booths of branches of trees, palm leaves, etc., and dwell in them for seven days at the feast of tabernacles. The booths at this harvest festival were a reminder of the vintage life; but with this recollection there was also to be associated the memory of their deliverance from Egypt, when they sojourned in the wilderness without permanent habitation (Lev. xxiii. 39–43; Neh. viii. 14).

Boo'ty.

The plunder of a conquered district or town. It consisted of everything of value—household goods, gold, silver, cattle, and captives to be used as slaves (Gen. xiv. 11, 12, 16; Num. xxxi. 9, 26–52; Josh. vii. 21). At the conquest of Canaan the Israelites were required to slay everything that breathed and to destroy all idols and places of idolatrous worship, but in foreign conquests they were bidden to slay the men only, and were authorized to take the remaining spoil (Num. xxxiii. 52; Deut. xx. 14–16). Exceptions were occasionally made when everything was devoted, the living to destruction, the goods to the treasury of the sanctuary, or when a certain portion of the spoil was dedicated to the Lord (Num. xxxi. 26–47; Josh. vi. 19; 1 Sam. xv. 2, 3). David made a law that the troops detailed to guard the baggage should share equally with those who engaged in the battle (1 Sam. xxx. 23–25).

Bo'oz. See BOAZ.

Bor'row.

To ask in loan. Did the Israelites, when the Egyptians urged them to leave the country, borrow goods from the Egyptians or obtain them as gifts? The word rendered borrow in A. V. of Ex. iii. 22; xi. 2; xii. 35, means simply ask (R. V.) or request, whether the object desired was to be returned (2 Kin. vi. 5) or not (Judg. v. 25; viii. 24); and the word translated lend (Ex. xii. 36, A. V.) is a form of the same verb, and means to grant a request or let one have what one asks (R. V.; cp. 1 Sam. i. 28).

Bos'cath. See BOZKATH.

Bo'sor.

1. A town of Gilead, Gilead being doubtless used in a broad sense (1 Mac. v. 26, 36); perhaps Bezer in the former territory of Reuben (Josh. xx. 8).

2. See BEOR.

Bos'o-ra.

A town of Gilead (1 Mac. v. 26, 28), either Bozrah in Edom or Bostra in Hauran.

Botch.

The rendering in A.V. of Deut. xxviii. 27, 35 of the Hebrew word elsewhere translated boil.

Bot'tle.

1. A hollow vessel of leather, or the hollow hide of an animal, used for holding liquids (Job xxxii. 19; Mat. ix. 17). See under BUTTER.

2. A small vessel of earthenware formed by potters, and which was capable of being broken (Jer. xix. 1, 10, 11). If any glass bottle is referred to in Scripture, it was probably a small lachrymatory for holding tears (Ps. lvi. 8).

Bow.

A weapon used for shooting arrows (2 Kin. vi. 22; 1 Chron. xii. 2). It was made of a strip of elastic wood or metal (2 Sam. xxii. 35; Job xx. 24), with a cord stretched between its two ends (Ps. xi. 2), and was held in the left hand (Ezek. xxxix. 3). It was used both in hunting and war (Gen. xxvii. 3; xlviii. 22). Its use was general among the nations of antiquity (1 Sam. xxxi. 3; 1 Kin. xxii. 34; Jer. xlvi. 9; xlix. 35). There were archers among the soldiers of Reuben, Gad, the half tribe of Manasseh, Ephraim, and especially Benjamin (1 Chron. v. 18; 2 Chron. xiv. 8; Ps. lxxviii. 9). The bow was carried by officers and soldiers on foot, in chariots, or on horseback (2 Kin. ix. 24). The archers carried the little shield and a sword (1 Sam. xviii. 4; 1 Chron. v. 18; 2 Chron. xiv. 8), and with the slingers constituted the light-armed troops.

The arrows were of cane or polished wood, and were carried in a quiver (Lam. iii. 13; Is. xlix. 2; Ezek. xxxix. 9). Their heads were made of iron, copper, or stone, and were sometimes poisoned (Job vi. 4).

Bowl. See BASIN.

Box.

1. A small case or vessel with a cover. In Scripture times they were used to hold oil, ointment, etc. (2 Kin. ix. 1; Mat. xxvi. 7).

2. The rendering of the Hebrew *Te'ash-shúr*, meaning a straight tree. Boat seats were made of it (Ezek. xxvii. 6, R. V.), and writing tablets (2 Esdr. xiv. 24). The box, fir, and pine were the glory of Lebanon (Is. lx. 13; on R. V. margin of Is. xli. 19 cypress). The box tree of Lebanon is *Buxus longifolia*, a small evergreen tree about 20 feet high.

Bo'zez [shining].

Of two crags near Gibeah, the northernmost, in front of Michmash (1 Sam. xiv. 4, 5). It overlooked the Wady Suweinit.

Boz'kath, in A. V. once **Bos'cath** [elevated, stony ground].

A town in the extreme south of Judah (Josh. xv. 39). Josiah's maternal grandfather, Adaiah, was of the place (2 Kin. xxii. 1). Exact site unknown.

Boz'rah [an enclosure, a sheepfold].

1. An important city of Edom (Gen. xxxvi. 33; 1 Chron. i. 44; Is. xxxiv. 6; lxiii. 1).

Filling a goatskin bottle with water at a public fountain.

Amos predicted that its palaces should be destroyed (Amos i. 12) ; and Jeremiah foretold its utter destruction (Jer. xlix. 13, 22). It was noted for its sheep (Mic. ii. 12). Burckhardt and Robinson located it at el-Buseira, a village of some fifty houses, about 18 miles southeast of the Dead Sea. This identification is generally accepted.

2. A city of Moab mentioned with Kerioth, Beth-meon, Dibon, and other towns of the plateau (Jer. xlviii. 24) ; probably the same as Bezer (in Septuagint, Bosor).

Brace'let.
An ornament for the wrist or for the arm, worn by both sexes (Ezek. xvi. 11). One was put on Rebekah's wrist by Abraham's servant (Gen. xxiv. 22). Bracelets were given by the Israelites in the wilderness to furnish gold or silver for the construction of the vessels of

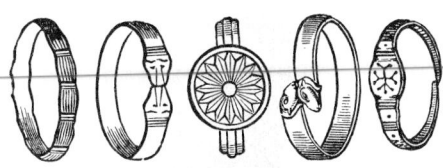

Egyptian bracelets.

the tabernacle (Num. xxxi. 50). Saul wore one, unless what he had on was rather an armlet (2 Sam. i. 10). For bracelet in A. V. in Gen. xxxviii. 18, 25, R. V. substitutes cord ; in Ex. xxxv. 22, brooches; and in Is. iii. 19, on the margin, chains.

Bram'ble.
The rendering of the Hebrew word *'Aṭad* in Judg. ix. 14, 15. The plant is named from its firmness. The R. V. renders it on the margin by thorn, and both versions so translate the word in Ps. lviii. 9. It is doubtless a variety of *Rhamnus*. The Septuagint and Vulgate render it by *Rhamnus*. This thorn is quite common in the warmer parts of Palestine, especially in the vicinity of the Dead Sea (cp. Gen. l. 10), in the Jordan valley, and about the Sea of Galilee. It is also found at Jerusalem. The *Rhamnus* is still called by the Arabs *'aṭad* or *nabk*, applying the name not only to Christ's Thorn (*Zizyphus spina Christi*), which takes its name from the tradition that the crown placed on Christ's head was made from its twigs, but apparently also to *Rhamnus paliurus*.

Branch.
A title applied to the Messiah as the off-spring of David (Jer. xxiii. 5 ; xxxiii. 15 ; Zech. iii. 8 ; vi. 12).

Brass.
The rendering of the Hebrew word *Nᵉḥosheth* and the Greek *Chalkos*. The margin of the R. V., however, at Gen. iv. 22 gives copper as a constant alternative. Copper was smelted from the ore dug from the ground (Deut. viii. 9 ; Job xxviii. 2). Traces of an-

cient copper works exist in Lebanon and in Edom. It was obtained notably in the peninsula of Sinai, in Cyprus, and in Meshech and Tubal (Ezek. xxvii. 13). Brass is an alloy of copper with from 28 to 34 per cent. of zinc. Unless accidentally associated with calamine, it does not occur in nature, but is an artificial product. The assertion used to be made that it was not known till it was accidentally formed by the running together of different melted metals when Corinth was burned, 146 B. C., by the consul Mummius. But vessels of brass have been found of much higher antiquity in Egyptian tombs. Bronze is another artificial product from copper, being an alloy of copper and tin. From copper and its alloys utensils were made : pots, shovels, basins, pans, spoons, snuffers (Ex. xxxviii. 3 ; Lev. vi. 28 ; Num. xvi. 39 ; Jer. lii. 18) ; armor, also, such as helmets, coats of mail, greaves, shields, spear points, and even bows (2 Sam. xxi. 16 ; xxii. 35, R.V. ; 2 Chron. xii. 10) ; fetters also, mirrors, city gates, musical instruments, idols, and in later times coins (Ex. xxxviii. 8 ; 2 Kin. xxv. 7, 13 ; Is. xlv. 2 ; Mat. x. 9 ; 1 Cor. xiii. 1 ; Rev. ix. 20). Where casting is spoken of, the metal was bronze. Thus were made the plating and railing for the altar, the lavers and the sea with its pedestal of oxen, and two magnificent pillars for the temple (1 Kin. vii. 41–46 ; 2 Chron. iv. 1–17).

Bra'zen Ser'pent.
The figure of a serpent, made of metal, and erected by Moses on a pole in the wilderness, that the Israelites who were bitten by fiery serpents might look at it with faith in God's promise to heal those who looked (Num. xxi. 8, 9). In after years the Israelites began to use it as an idol, and Hezekiah had it broken in pieces, contemptuously calling it Nᵉhushtan, that is to say, only a piece of brass (2 Kin. xviii. 4). Jesus in foretelling his crucifixion explained its spiritual significance by comparing it with the rearing of the brazen serpent (John iii. 14, 15).

Bread.
The bread in use among the Israelites consisted generally of small flat cakes of wheaten flour or, among the poor, of barley flour The grain was ground daily in a hand mill, and fresh bread baked every day. When this bread was to be eaten at once, it was often unleavened (Gen. xix. 3 ; 1 Sam. xxviii. 24), but the art of making leavened bread was also understood (Mat. xiii. 33). The show-bread which was edible after eight days was evidently leavened. The flour was made into a paste or dough by mixing with water, and might be leavened some time after mixing ; for example, at the first passover the dough was already mixed in the troughs, but not yet leavened when the order came to march (Ex. xii. 34).

The oven used by private families was a portable jar in which, after it had been heated, the loaves were laid or were stuck against the

Brickmaking in Egypt hasn't changed much through the centuries. A wooden frame is still used to form the wet clay into a brick. The frame is lifted and the process repeated for each brick. After the bricks are sun-dried they provide a rather sturdy building material in a land with a low annual rainfall.

sides, the cakes baked in this later fashion being very thin.

Besides the bread baked in the oven (Lev. ii. 4), cakes also were baked on a slightly concave pan put over a fire, these being something like pancakes (Lev. ii. 5). Bread was also baked on the heated hearth or on any hot stones after the ashes were swept aside (1 Kin. xix. 6). This kind was made especially when food was wanted in a hurry (Gen. xviii. 6). The Bedouin at present commonly bake by placing their loaves in a hole in the ground which has previously held a fire and then been cleared out. The hole is carefully covered and the bread allowed to bake all night. This method was probably well known to the Israelites. Baking was ordinarily done by the women (Gen. xviii. 6: 1 Sam. viii. 13; Lev. xxvi. 26; but Judg. vi. 19), and in large households by the slaves, but in the cities there were also bakers who sold bread (Jer. xxxvii. 21; cp. Hos. vii. 4, 6). In the second chapter of Leviticus is given a list of the different kinds of bread which were acceptable as offerings. In some places the word is applied to all kinds of food (Luke xi. 3).

Breast'plate.

1. A sacred article of dress worn by the Jewish high priest (Ex. xxviii. 15–30). See HIGH PRIEST.

2. Armor designed to protect the body in battle (Rev. ix. 9): see ARMOR. Figuratively, righteousness (Is. lix. 17; Eph. vi. 14; Wisd. v. 19), or faith and love, constitute a spiritual breastplate (1 Thes. v. 8).

Breth'ren of the Lord.

Their names are given in the gospels as James, Joseph or Joses, Simon, and Judas (Mat. xiii. 55, R. V.; Mark vi. 3). They appear in company with Mary (Mat. xii. 47–50; Mark iii. 31–35; Luke viii. 19–21), moved to Capernaum with her and Jesus and the latter's disciples at the beginning of Christ's ministry (John ii. 12), but are said not to have believed in Jesus even toward the close of his life (John vii. 4, 5). After the resurrection, however, they are found united with the disciples (Acts i. 14), and are afterwards mentioned as Christian workers (1 Cor. ix. 5). One of them, James (Gal. i. 19), became a

distinguished leader of the Jerusalem church (Acts xii. 17; xv. 13; Gal. ii. 9), and was the author of the epistle which goes by his name. In what sense they were Christ's "brethren" has been much disputed. In very early times they were regarded as the children of Joseph by a former marriage. The disappearance of Joseph from the gospels suggests that he had died, and may have been much older than Mary, and may have been previously married. This view is a possible one, but, in view of Mat. i. 25 and Luke ii. 7. not probable. In the fourth century Jerome proposed another view; viz., that they were Christ's cousins on his mother's side, the children of Alphæus (or Clopas) and Mary's sister of the same name. This is inferred mainly from a combination of Mark xv. 40 and John xix. 25 (the latter being thought to mention but three women), and from the identity of the names Alphæus and Clopas. On this view one (James the son of Alphæus) and perhaps more (Simon and Judas) of the apostles were Christ's brethren. But the apostles are distinguished from his brethren; the latter did not believe in him, and it is unlikely that two sisters had the same name. Another very old view was that they were cousins on Joseph's side, and some have even supposed they were the children of the widow of Joseph's brother (Deut. xxv. 5–10). But all these theories appear to have originated from a wish to maintain the perpetual virginity of Mary. That they were the children of Joseph and Mary, born after Jesus, is the natural view, and that Mary had other children is implied in Mat. i. 25; Luke ii. 7. This view explains also the constant association of "the brethren" with Mary.

G. T. P.

Brick.

A mass of clay tempered, made rectangular in shape, and hardened either by burning in a kiln (Gen. xi. 3) or by drying in the sun (Herod. ii. 136). They were of course sun-dried when the clay was mixed with straw (Ex. v. 7). Both bricks and tiles are often found stamped with names and inscriptions, from which we have derived much of our knowledge of those ancient times, as well as from the tablets of burnt clay specially prepared as documents in a similar way (cp. Ezek. iv. 1).

Brick bearing the name and inscription of Nebuchadnezzar.

Brick'kiln.

A kiln for enclosing bricks while they are being burned (2 Sam. xii. 31 and Nah. iii. 14, where R. V. margin translates brickmould; Jer. xliii. 9, in R. V. brickwork).

Bri'er.

The rendering of six distinct Hebrew words and of one Greek word.

1. *Barḳan* (Judg. viii. 7, 16); perhaps, as etymology suggests, so named because it grows in stony ground.

2. *Shamir*, bristling, prickly (Is. ix. 18; x. 17; xxvii. 4; xxxii. 13), such as springs up in abandoned vineyards (v. 6; vii. 23).

3. *Sirpad* (Is. lv. 13). Septuagint and Vulgate render it nettle.

4. *Sarab*, refractory (Ezek. ii. 6).

5. *Sillon* (Ezek. xxviii. 24; in ii. 6 rendered thorn).

6. *Ḥedeḳ* (Mic. vii. 4), used in hedges (Prov. xv. 19, where it is rendered thorn). The corresponding word in Arabic means the Eggplant, Mad-apple, Jew's-apple or Brinjal (*Solanum melongena*), one variety of which is thorny. It is a native of India and, it is believed, of Arabia. It is of the same genus as the potato, but the edible part is the fruit, which is much used in curries in the East.

7. Greek *Akantha*, a thorn or a prickly plant or thorny tree (Heb. vi. 8, A. V.).

Brig'an-dine.

A name for a coat of mail, composed of light thin-jointed scales, or of thin pliant plate armor (Jer. xlvi. 4; li. 3). The R. V. substitutes coat of mail.

Brim'stone.

Sulphur (Gen. xix. 24; Deut. xxix. 23).

Brook.

A small perennial stream, as the Kishon (1 Kin. xviii. 40) and the Jabbok (Gen. xxxii. 23, A. V.). Generally, however, in Scripture the word is used for a stream which flows in the rainy, winter season, but is dry in summer, as the brook of Egypt (Num. xxxiv. 5, R. V.; see RIVER), the Zered (Deut. ii. 13), and the Kidron (2 Sam. xv. 23; John xviii. 1, R. V.).

Broom.

A much-branched bush, with twiggy, nearly leafless, branches, and clusters of pinkish-white flowers, which grows in the Jordan valley and Arabia, and is common in the peninsula of Sinai (Job xxx. 4; 1 Kin. xix. 4). Its large root stalk is made into charcoal (Ps. cxx. 4). In the text of the last two passages in the R. V., and in all the three in the A. V., it is rendered juniper, but the Hebrew word corresponds to the still existing Arabic name for *Retama*, broom.

Broth'er.

1. A kinsman born of the same parents as the person to whom he is brother (Gen. xxvii. 6), or at least of the same father (xxviii. 2) or the same mother (Judg. viii. 19).

2. A man of the same near ancestry (as a nephew, Gen. xiv. 16), or of the same race or of a kindred nation (Deut. xxiii. 7; Neh. v. 7; Jer. xxxiv. 9).

3. An ally (Amos i. 9) or co-religionist (Acts ix. 17; 1 Cor. vi. 6; 2 Cor. ii. 13); often in the plural applied to Christian disciples (Mat. xxiii. 8; Rom. i. 13).

4. One of the male sex greatly beloved or politely addressed by the person who calls him brother (2 Sam. i. 26; 1 Kin. xx. 32).

5. Any man whatever, the common brotherhood of the human race being recognized (Gen. ix. 5; Mat. v. 22; xviii. 35).

Buck'ler. See ARMOR.

Buk'ki [abbreviation of Bukkiah].

1. Prince of the tribe of Dan and member of the commission for allotting the land (Num. xxxiv. 22).

2. A descendant of Aaron, in the high-priestly line of Phinehas (1 Chron. vi. 5, 51; Ezra vii. 4).

Buk-ki'ah [devastation sent by Jehovah].

A Levite, son of Heman, and head of the sixth of the twenty-four companies of twelve musicians each which David appointed for the service of the sanctuary (1 Chron. xxv. 4, 13).

Bul [growth].

The eighth month of the Jewish year (1 Kin. vi. 38). See YEAR.

Bull.

The male of the species called by naturalists *Bos taurus* (Job. xxi. 10; Ps. lxviii. 30; Is. xxxiv. 7; Jer. lii. 20); see Ox. A particularly strong and fierce breed of bulls existed in Bashan (Ps. xxii. 12).

The word *To'*, rendered wild ox and wild bull in A. V. (Deut. xiv. 5; Is. li. 20), is translated in R. V. by antelope (q. v.).

Bull'ock.

A young bull, though the Hebrew word is used once of an animal seven years old (Judg. vi. 25). Bullocks were used as draught animals bearing a yoke (Jer. xxxi. 18, A. V.), and were largely offered in sacrifice (Ex. xxix. 1; 1 Chron. xxix. 21).

Bul'rush [bull, i. e. a large, rush].
1. Hebrew *Gome'* (Ex. ii. 3; Is. xviii. 2, A. V.); papyrus (q. v.).
2. Hebrew *'Agmon.* The etymology suggests that it grows in swamps; and it is a low plant (Is. ix. 14; xix. 15), bows the head (lviii. 5), and was twisted into ropes (Job xli. 2, R. V. margin).

Bu'nah [prudence].
A descendant of Judah through Jerahmeel (1 Chron. ii. 25).

Bun'ni [built, erected].
1. A Levite who lived before the exile (Neh. xi. 15).
2. A Levite, contemporary of Nehemiah (Neh. ix. 4).
3. Representative of a family or father's house who sealed the covenant (Neh. x. 15).

Bur'den.
1. A heavy load to be borne; used in a literal or a figurative sense (Ex. xxiii. 5; Num. xi. 11, etc.).
2. An utterance or prophecy, in almost every instance denouncing heavy judgment on a place or people (Is. xiv. 28; xv. 1; Ezek. xii. 10; Hos. viii. 10; Nah. i. 1).

Bur'i-al.
Interment, the committal of a corpse to the ground, or its disposal in another reverential way. When a death occurred friends, especially women, hurried to the house and made loud lamentation (Mark v. 38). Mourners were even hired (Jer. ix. 17). The body was washed (Acts ix. 37), and wrapped in a cloth or closely bound in bands (Mat. xxvii. 59; John xi. 44). The wealthy added spices and perfumes (John xii. 7; xix. 39) or burned fragrant materials (Jer. xxxiv. 5). The body was carried upon a bier to the grave (2 Sam. iii. 31; Luke vii. 14). Burial was generally in a cave or in a sepulcher scooped horizontally in the rock (Gen. xxv. 9, 10; Mat. xxvii. 60). See MOURNING and SEPULCHER.

Burnt Of'fer-ing. See OFFERINGS.

Burnt Sac'ri-fice, the same as burnt offering. See OFFERINGS.

Bush.
1. The rendering of the Hebrew *Seneh* and Greek *Batos,* a thorny bush (Luke vi. 44). which Moses saw burning and from which Jehovah spoke (Ex. iii. 2, 3; Deut. xxxiii. 16; Mark xii. 26). Tristram believes it to have been the *Acacia vera* or *nilotica,* the Egyptian thorn. It is a withered-looking thorny tree, 12 feet high, with bipinnate leaves and white flowers. It grows throughout a large part of Africa, also in the Sinai Peninsula, and, in Palestine, on the shores of the Dead Sea. It yields the gum arabic of commerce, which naturally exudes in a nearly fluid state from the trunk and branches, hardening on exposure to the air.

2. Hebrew *Siah* (Job. xxx. 4, 7; and Gen. ii. 5, where it is rendered plant); a shrub large enough to afford some shade (Gen. xxi. 15, where it is rendered shrub).
3. Hebrew *Nahalol* (Is. vii. 19), rendered in the text of R. V. by pasture, and on the margin of the A. V. by commendable trees.

Bush'el.
The rendering of the Greek *Modios,* a dry measure containing more than two gallons (Mat. v. 15; Mark iv. 21). See MEASURE.

But'ler. See CUPBEARER.

But'ter.
In Scripture, curdled milk or curds (Gen. xviii. 8; Deut. xxxii. 14; Prov. xxx. 33; Is. vii. 15, 22). On margin of R. V. of Is. vii. 15 the translation is curds. Thomson says that neither the ancient nor the modern Orientals have made butter in our sense of the word. The butter given to Sisera by Jael was sour milk, called in Arabic *leben.* The butter, so called, of Prov. xxx. 33 is a production made in this way. A bottle formed by stripping off the entire skin of a young buffalo is filled with milk and then perseveringly kneaded or shaken by women. Then the contents are taken out, boiled or melted, and put into bottles of goats' skins. In winter it resembles candied honey, and in summer is mere oil.

Buz [contempt].
1. An Aramæan tribe, descended from a son of Nahor (Gen. xxii. 20, 21), and probably dwelling in Jeremiah's time near Dedan and Tema in Arabia (Jer. xxv. 23).
2. A Gadite, founder of a tribal family or house (1 Chron. v. 14).

Bu'zi [descendant of Buz].
Father of the priest and prophet Ezekiel (Ezek. i. 3).

Buz'ite.
One belonging to the Arabian tribe of Buz (Job. xxxii. 2).

C

Cab, in R. V. **Kab** [a hollow vessel].
A Hebrew measure of capacity for dry articles (2 Kin. vi. 25). It held, according to Rabbinical tradition, the sixth part of a seah or one hundred and eightieth part of a homer.

Cab'bon [a cake, or perhaps a binding].
A village of Judah in the lowland (Josh. xv. 40). Perhaps identical with Machbenah (1 Chron. ii. 49). The radical letters are the same and the location is suitable.

Ca'bul [perhaps, fettered land; proverbial for hard, dry land which produces no fruit].
1. A town of Asher (Josh. xix. 27; Life 43, 45). It is still known as Kabûl, a village 9 miles east-southeast of Acre.
2. A district of Galilee, that is, of the northern part of the territory of Naphtali, for the

most part inhabited by people other than Israelites (Is. ix. 1). It contained twenty towns,
which Solomon presented to Hiram, king of
Tyre, in return for services rendered in connection with the building of the temple.
Hiram was displeased with the gift, and
therefore called the region Cabul (1 Kin. ix.
13). Hiram thus apparently rejected the
proffered compensation as inadequate, and
returned the district to Solomon, who thereupon fortified the cities thus put back on his
hands, and caused Israelites to dwell in them
(2 Chron. viii. 2; Antiq. viii. 5, 3).

Cæ′sar.

The family name of a branch of the Julian
house or clan in Rome. According to Pliny
(7, 9), the first who bore the name was so
called *quod cæso mortuæ matris utero natus
fuerit.* Though it is traceable from 501 B. C.,
it did not gain extensive celebrity till it was
borne by Caius Julius Cæsar, who ranks with
Alexander the Great and Napoleon as one of
the three most remarkable conquerors the
civilized world has produced. On the assassination of Julius Cæsar, 44 B. C., his will requested his grandnephew Octavius, afterwards the emperor Augustus, to assume the
name of Cæsar. Tiberius, who succeeded
Augustus, and Caligula, Claudius, and Nero,
who followed in succession, were all entitled
by relationship to the great dictator to bear
the family name; the seven succeeding emperors—Galba, Otho. Vitellius, Vespasian,
Titus, Domitian, and Nerva—assumed it, so
that it is customary to speak of the twelve
Cæsars. From having been the name of one
mighty conqueror, and then of a series of
emperors, the name Cæsar became the type
or symbol of the civil power in general, and
it is continually used in this sense in discussions as to the relative domains of civil and
ecclesiastical rulers (cp. Mat. xxii. 17, 21;
Mark xii. 14, 16, 17; Luke xx. 22, 24, 25).

The name Cæsar is applied in the N. T. to:

1. AU-GUS′TUS CÆ′SAR, the first Roman
emperor (Luke ii. 1). In 43 B. C. he was
named one of the second triumvirate, Marc
Antony and Lepidus being the other two.
Lepidus was found incompetent and forced
to retire; and after the defeat of Antony
at Actium in 31 B. C. Augustus was sole
ruler of the Roman world, and was given
the title of emperor. It was in consequence
of a decree of Augustus that Joseph and
Mary went to Bethlehem to be taxed, at the
time of Christ's birth. Although Augustus
was not fond of the Jews, he favored them
from policy, and caused sacrifices to be made
daily in the temple at Jerusalem at his expense. He was friendly to Herod, recognizing that in him he had a valuable ally.
Cæsarea Philippi and Cæsarea by the Sea
were built in his honor by Herod. Augustus
died A. D. 14, in the sixty-seventh year of his
age.

2. TI-BE′RI-US CÆ′SAR, the second Roman

emperor (Mat. xxii. 17; Mark xii. 14; Luke
iii. 1; xx. 21, 22; John xix. 12), born 42 B. C.,
was the adopted son, also stepson and son-in-
law, of Augustus. He was of a morose and
gloomy temper, and spent a large part of his
reign in voluntary exile on the island of
Capri. During his reign Judæa was governed

Bust of Tiberius.

by Valerius Gratus and Pontius Pilatus. At
one time he banished the Jews from Rome,
but later recalled the edict, and gave them
redress for the severity of the provincial
governors. Tiberias, on the sea of Galilee,
was built in his honor by Herod Antipas. His
death was hastened by the hand of Caligula.
A. D. 37.

Coin with head of Claudius.

3. CLAU′DI-US, the fourth Roman emperor.
He was a weak, vacillating man, a nephew
of Tiberius. He was made emperor almost

against his will, and left the real power in the hands of unprincipled favorites. Herod Agrippa I. had been in Rome, and had assisted in his coronation, and in consequence was given the whole of Palestine as a mark of favor. In the beginning of his reign Claudius favored the Jews, and reinstated the Alexandrian Jews in their former privileges, but later he banished all Jews from Rome (Acts xviii. 2). He died A. D. 54, in the fourteenth year of his reign.

4. NE′RO, the fifth Roman emperor (Acts xxv. 12, 21 ; xxvi. 32 ; Phil. iv. 22). He was the adopted son of his predecessor Claudius, and secured his own position by poisoning his stepbrother Britannicus. Nero was a monster of lust and cruelty, though, perhaps, his crimes have been exaggerated. In the tenth year of his reign, A. D. 64, a great fire broke out at Rome, in large measure destroying three of the fourteen districts into which the city was divided. The emperor was believed, apparently on insufficient evidence, to have

Head of Nero.

been himself the incendiary, and was in consequence in danger of his life. To screen himself, he falsely accused the Christians of having caused the fire, and put many of them to cruel deaths, tradition adding that both Paul and Peter were among the sufferers. Nero is the "lion" of 2 Tim. iv. 17. Finding that he was deserted by his troops, and that he would soon be put to death, he anticipated his fate. Like Saul, he attempted suicide, and, failing, induced one of his supporters to complete the act of slaughter. He died A. D. 68, in the thirty-second year of his age and the fourteenth of his reign.

TITUS, son of Vespasian, and tenth Roman emperor. In A. D. 66 Vespasian was sent to Palestine to quell a revolt of the Jews, and Titus accompanied him. In 69, when Vespasian hurried from Judæa to Rome to secure the imperial office for himself, he left Titus in command of the army, and Titus conducted the siege of Jerusalem in A. D. 70 (War iii. 1, 3–vii. 3, 1) ; see JERUSALEM II. 3.

Coin with head of Titus.

Titus became emperor in 79 ; and died in 81, in the fortieth year of his age.

Cæs-a-re′a [pertaining to Cæsar].

A city on the coast of Palestine, about 23 miles south of mount Carmel. It was built by Herod the Great, on the site of a town called Strato's Tower. Twelve years, from 25 to 13 B. C., were spent in its erection. A sea mole was built of stones 50 feet long, 18 broad, and 9 deep. It was 200 feet wide, stood in 20 fathoms of water, and enclosed a harbor as large as that at Athens. The entrance to the artificial port was on the north, where there was a tower. The city was provided with a temple, a theater, and an amphitheater, and had a complete system of drainage. Herod named the place Cæsarea, after his patron Augustus Cæsar (Antiq. xv. 9, 6 ; War i. 21, 5, seq.). It was sometimes called Cæsarea of Palestine, or Cæsarea by the Sea, to distinguish it from Cæsarea Philippi. It became the Roman capital of Palestine. The gospel was carried thither by Philip the evangelist, who made it his residence (Acts viii. 40 ; xxi. 8). When Paul, soon after his conversion, was in danger of being murdered by the Jews of Jerusalem, his Christian brethren brought him down to Cæsarea, whence he sailed to his birthplace, Tarsus, in Asia Minor (ix. 30). It was at Cæsarea that the Roman centurion Cornelius lived, to whom Peter preached Christ, and that the calling of the gentiles took place (x. 1, 24 ; xi. 11). Herod Agrippa died at Cæsarea in A. D. 44 (Acts xii. 19, 23 ; Antiq. xix. 8, 2). Paul twice revisited the city, and found a church existing (Acts xviii. 22 ; xxi. 8, 16). He was afterwards taken thither as a prisoner (xxiii. 23, 33), and it was there that his trial before Festus and Agrippa took place (xxv. 1–4, 6–13). The population of the city was mixed, and race jealousies existed to such an extent that in the reign of Nero the Syrians made a wholesale massacre of the Jews, commencing the

Ruins of a Roman aqueduct at Caesarea.

troubles which culminated in A. D. 70 in the destruction of Jerusalem by Titus (War ii. 18, 1). In the second century A. D. Cæsarea became the residence of a bishop, who down to 451 was metropolitan of Palæstina Prima. In 195 a council was held there. A Christian school was established in the city, in which Origen taught and where Eusebius, afterwards bishop of Cæsarea, was educated. In 548 the Jews and Samaritans joined in assaulting the Christians. In 638 the city was captured by the Mohammedans. In 1102 it was taken by the crusaders, led by Baldwin I. Saladin retook it from them in 1189; the crusaders recovered it in 1191, but lost it to the sultan Bibars in 1265.

The ruins are of two periods. There is, first, the Roman town with mole and walls, a theater, hippodrome, temple, and aqueducts; and, secondly, the Crusading town with walls, a castle, a cathedral, a smaller church, and a harbor. The Roman wall extends 4800 feet from north to south, and 2700 from east to west. The harbor measures 540 feet across. A reef running into the sea is probably the old mole. Cæsarea is still called Kaisârieh.

Cæs-a-re′a Phi-lip′pi [Cæsarea of Philip, in distinction from Cæsarea of Palestine].

A city at the foot of mount Hermon, at the main source of the Jordan, and in the angle of a small plain, with hills on all sides except on the west. It has sometimes been identified with Baal-gad. The worship of the Roman god Pan long prevailed in the locality; and Herod the Great having built a temple of fine marble near the sacred spot, the place was called Paneas (Antiq. xv. 10, 3). The town was afterwards enlarged and adorned by Philip the tetrarch, and its name altered to Cæsarea in honor of the Roman emperor Tiberius Cæsar (Antiq. xviii. 2, 1; War ii. 9, 1). Jesus and his disciples visited it at least once, and it was there that the remark-

able conversation took place between him and Peter arising out of the question " Who do men say that I am?" (Mat. xvi. 13; Mark viii. 27). Agrippa II. still further embellished it, and changed the name to Neronias, to compliment the emperor Nero; but on the emperor's death the name speedily lapsed (Antiq. xx. 9, 4). After the destruction of Jerusalem Titus exhibited gladiatorial shows in this town also, one part of the spectacle being Jewish captives thrown to the wild beasts, or compelled to encounter each other in deadly warfare (War vii. 2, 1; 3, 1). Part of its fortifications still remain, and there are Greek inscriptions on the adjacent rocks. The town has dwindled to a small village called Banias, an alteration of its early name Paneas.

Cage.

A box or basket, Hebrew $K^{e}lub$, in which birds were kept, especially for purposes of decoy (Jer. v. 27; Ecclus. xi. 30). Sennacherib boasts of having shut up Hezekiah in Jerusalem like a bird in a cage.

Ca′ia-phas [depression].

Joseph Caiaphas, who was appointed to the high priesthood not earlier than A. D. 18 by Valerius Gratus, the Roman procurator and immediate predecessor of Pontius Pilate (Antiq. xviii. 2, 2). Caiaphas and his father-in-law Annas (John xviii. 13) were high priests when John the Baptist commenced his ministry (Luke iii. 2). Caiaphas proposed the death of Jesus, and, speaking of its import more significantly than he was aware, said: "It is expedient for us, that one man should die for the people, and that the whole nation perish not" (John xi. 49-53; xviii. 14). At his palace the council of chief priests, scribes, and elders was held to devise measures for the arrest of our Lord (Mat. xxvi. 3-5). When Jesus was apprehended, he was taken first to the palace of Annas, who sent him bound to

Caiaphas (John xviii. 24), whence he was led next to the prætorium of Pilate (28). Deeply responsible for the judicial murder of the innocent prisoner, Caiaphas afterwards took part in the trial of Peter and John (Acts iv. 6). In A. D. 36 he was deposed by Vitellius, the Roman president of Syria (Antiq. xviii. 4, 2).

Cain [fabrication, forged instrument, smith].
1. The elder brother of Abel, by calling an agriculturist. He brought of the fruits of the ground an offering to God, an implied acknowledgment of gratitude to God for the produce of the earth. But the heart of Cain was not right, and his offering was rejected. Then his character was revealed. He showed envy and anger, refused the exhortation to strive against sin, committed murder, denied his guilt; and when judgment was pronounced, gave no evidence of repentance for his sin, but only of fear of the punishment. Sent into exile, he lived in the land of Nod, eastward of Eden. He had a wife, one of the unnamed daughters or granddaughters of Adam. In early ages no impropriety existed or was felt in such a marriage (cp. Gen. xi. 27, 29; xx. 12). In his exile Cain built a fortified hamlet, and became the progenitor of a race which made considerable progress in the mechanical arts (Gen. iv. 1–25; 1 John iii. 12; Jude 11).
2. The progenitor of the Kenites. See KAIN.
3. A village in the mountains of Judah (Josh. xv. 57). Doubtfully located at the ruin Yukîn, 3 miles southeast of Hebron.

Cai'nan, in A. V. once **Kenan** (1 Chron. i. 2), as always in R. V. of O. T.
1. Son of Enos (Gen. v. 9–14; 1 Chron. i. 2; Luke iii. 37, 38).
2. Son of Arphaxad, and father of Shelah (Luke iii. 36, R. V.). The corresponding genealogy of Gen. xi. 12 has no Cainan; the Septuagint, however, has, and it was from the Septuagint that Luke quotes.

Ca'lah.
A city of Assyria, built by Nimrod or by people from his country, and forming part of that complex of cities which collectively were called by the Hebrews that great city (Gen. x. 11, 12; cp. Jon. i. 2). According to Ashurnasirpal (about 885–860 B. C.) it was built or rebuilt, embellished, and fortified by Shalmaneser, who reigned about 1300 B. C. Early in the ninth century B. C. it had fallen into decay, but was restored by Ashurnasirpal, who erected a palace and made the city the place of royal residence. Calah remained the favorite dwelling place of the Assyrian kings for more than one hundred and fifty years. Its ruins, now called Nimrûd, lie about 20 miles south of Nineveh.

Cal'a-mus [Greek *kalamos*, a reed, a cane].
The rendering of the Hebrew *Kᵉneh bosem*, reed of fragrance, and *Kaneh*, cane, reed, when an odorous variety is intended. The plant was sweet smelling (Song. iv. 14), a constituent of the anointing oil (Ex. xxx. 23),

and used in connection with sacrifice (Is. xliii. 24 and Jer. vi. 20, margin of R. V.). It was brought from a far country (Jer. vi. 20). The Tyrians obtained it apparently from Javan, the regions of western Asia Minor and Greece (Ezek. xxvii. 19). What came from Europe was probably the *Acorus calamus*, or common Sweet Sedge of England, an endogenous plant, with a spadix and spathe, akin to the Aroids, but belonging to the allied order of the *Orontiaceæ* or Orontiads. The rhizome or underground stem is aromatic. If an Indian plant is permissible, then the calamus was probably the *Andropogon calamus aromaticus*, a genuine grass, which, like its near ally, the Lemon Grass, *A. schœnanthus*, is highly scented.

Cal'col, in A. V. once **Chalcol** [sustenance, maintenance].
One of three sons of Mahol, each of whom was celebrated for wisdom (1 Kin. iv. 31; 1 Chron. ii. 6).

Cal'dron. See POT.

Ca'leb.
1. Son of Hezron, and brother of Jerahmeel (1 Chron. ii. 18, 42). A variant form of the name is Chelubai (ver. 9). In tribal registration, his posterity constituted a subdivision of the house of Hezron, family of Perez, tribe of Judah (1 Sam. xxv. 3; 1 Chron. ii. 3, R. V., seq.). Among his more immediate descendants were Hur, Aaron's associate, and Hur's grandson, the skilled artificer Bezalel (1 Chron. ii. 19, R. V., seq.).
2. Son of Jephunneh the Kenizzite and an elder brother of Othniel (Num. xxxii. 12, R. V.; Josh. xv. 17; 1 Chron. iv. 15, cp. 13). He was the head of a father's house of the tribe of Judah; was one of the twelve men sent to spy out the land of Canaan; was one of the two members of this commission who kept their faith in Jehovah, and forty years later took part in the conquest of Canaan; was, in fact, the first to speak for this minority of two (Num. xiii. 2, 6, 30; xiv. 6, 24, 38; Josh. xiv. 6, 14; 1 Mac. ii. 56). He was on the commission appointed by Moses before the conquest to distribute the land, and he represented, as before, the tribe of Judah (Num. xxxiv. 19). He was 85 years old when the conquest was completed (Josh. xiv. 7, 10). He received as his portion the town of Hebron (14), from which he expelled the Anakim by whom it had been previously occupied (xv. 13, 14); see HEBRON. He had also to do with the taking of the adjacent town of Kirjath-sepher, or Debir (15–19). The south of Caleb mentioned in 1 Sam. xxx. 14 was probably the south of the Hebron district or the vicinity of Debir.
In 1 Chron. ii. 49 (cp. 19, 42, 46) Achsah, the well-known daughter of Caleb the spy, is registered as daughter or descendant of Caleb the brother of Jerahmeel. To judge from this register, Caleb the son of Jephunneh and father of Achsah was descended from

the elder Caleb, and perhaps his concubine Maacah, and hence through Hezron and Perez from Judah. There are many details to be accounted for, and the ordinary difficulty of interpreting an ancient Hebrew genealogy is in this case greatly increased by the imperfect state of the text in 1 Chron. ii. and iv. The general explanation probably is that a member of the tribe of Kenizzites became identified with the Israelites by taking service with Judah before the Israelites went into Egypt, and he or his descendant married a woman descended from Judah through Perez. Various modifications of this general theory are possible. All genealogical and historical references, and the peculiarities of the register are satisfied by the assumption that shortly before the exodus Jephunneh the Kenizzite married a woman of the household of Caleb the brother of Jerahmeel, and by her had a firstborn son to whom was given the family name Caleb. This youth inherited the prerogatives of the family, and in time became head of the house and a chief of Judah. Jephunneh the Kenizzite took a second wife, by whom he had Othniel and Seraiah. Hence they are called sons of Kenez or Kenizzites, and are enrolled loosely with the tribe of Judah, and reckoned like Jephunneh as Kenizzites.

Ca'leb-eph'ra-thah, in A.V. Caleb-eph'ra-tah.

The community formed by the descendants of Caleb and his wife Ephrath (1 Chron. ii. 19, 24). The Septuagint had a slightly different text. If the present Hebrew text is correct, and the genealogy is here dealing strictly with persons, then Hezron, the father of Caleb, late in life married a grand-daughter of Manasseh. Their descendants were afterwards reckoned through the ancestress with the tribe of Manasseh, but in this register they are included with Hezron's descendants through Caleb and Ephrath. In this connection it is recorded that Hezron died in Caleb-ephrathah; that is, either in that part of Goshen where the branch of his family known as Caleb-ephrath resided, or in Palestine, whither Caleb had gone back from Egypt.

Calf.

A young bull or cow, *Bos taurus*. Calves were killed for food (Gen. xviii. 7) and for sacrifice (Heb. ix. 12, 19). Aaron made a golden image of a male calf that the people might worship Jehovah under this form (Ex. xxxii. 4; Ps. cvi. 19, 20; see also Neh. ix. 18). The young bull symbolized vigor, strength, and endurance (cp. Num. xxiii. 22); and the choice of this animal rather than another to represent God was favored also by the pomp of the bull worship in Egypt, where the Israelites had often seen the inhabitants adore the living bull Apis. On the division of the kingdom Jeroboam instituted the calf worship anew, setting up two calves, one at Beth-el and one at

Dan (1 Kin. xii. 29). He, too, had seen the Apis worshiped in Egypt while he was a refugee at the court of Shishak (1 Kin. xi. 40), but he was influenced more by the de-

Image of Apis, the sacred bull of Egypt.

sire to adhere to ancient traditions, for in recommending the calves he quoted the words of Ex. xxxii. 4.

Cal'neh.

A city of Babylonia, belonging to the kingdom of Nimrod (Gen. x. 10). A town of this name is also mentioned by Amos (Amos vi. 2). Not identified. Jerusalem Talmud, Eusebius, Jerome, indicate Ctesiphon east of the Tigris. Friedrich Delitzsch has suggested Kulunu.

Cal'no.

A city, probably in northern Syria, which the Assyrians cited as an example of the futility of offering resistance to Assyria (Is. x. 9).

Cal'va-ry [skull].

A place close to Jerusalem, but outside the city walls, where Christ was crucified, and in the vicinity of which he was buried (Mat. xxviii. 11; John xix. 17, 20, 41; Heb. xiii. 11–13). It appears to have been a conspicuous spot (Mark xv. 40; Luke xxiii. 49), and was perhaps near a highway (Mat. xxvii. 39). The name is derived from the Latin *calvaria*, more rarely *calvarium*, a skull (Luke xxiii. 33), corresponding to the Aramaic Golgotha (Mat. xxvii. 33; Mark xv. 22; John xix. 17, 41). Jerome supposed that the name arose from uncovered or unburied skulls; others have thought rather of a place of execution. The common explanation is that the name was due to the cranial shape of the rock or hillock, although the expression mount Calvary is modern.

The question of the site of the crucifixion is involved with that of the location of the sepulcher. The theory advanced by Fergusson, that the tomb was in the rock under the dome of the Mosque of Omar, has not obtained favor. Two sites contend for acceptance: 1. The church of the Holy Sepulcher, within the walls of the modern city. 2. The hill in which is Jeremiah's grotto, about 250 yards northeast of the Damascus gate. The church of the Holy Sepulcher has ancient tradition in its favor. Eusebius, born in Cæsarea about A. D. 264, is the earliest historian who gives any information on the subject. He states that impious men had covered the sepulcher with earth and built a temple to the goddess Venus over it, and that the place had long been given over to forgetfulness and oblivion. Constantine erected a church where the temple of Venus stood, and the site of Constantine's building is occupied by the present church of the Holy Sepulcher. Is this church on ground that was outside the second wall? This question can be decided only by costly excavation to determine the course of the second wall.

The theory that the hill above Jeremiah's grotto marks the site of Calvary is at present in the ascendant. It was suggested by Otto Thenius some thirty or forty years ago, and has been adopted or independently reached by other scholars, and greatly elaborated. This location unquestionably satisfies all the conditions of the problem. The hill in which is Jeremiah's grotto admittedly rises beyond the course of the second wall. The rounded summit of the hill, and the two hollow cave entrances beneath, present a striking resemblance to a skull. Its commanding position renders it visible from a distance. Near it was the great highway to the north. In the neighborhood are gardens and rock-hewn tombs. But no ancient tradition connects the crucifixion with this place.

Cam'el [borrowed from Semitic *gamal*].

The one-humped camel, which runs into two well marked varieties, the camel properly so called, which is a slow-going draught animal (2 Kin. viii. 9), and the dromedary, which is swift of foot (cp. Is. lxvi. 20, margin of R. V.). The two-humped Bactrian camel may be referred to in Tobit ix. 2. The camel has been called the ship of the desert, and its whole organization fits it to cross sandy wastes. It is a ruminating animal, but belongs to that aberrant portion of the *Ruminantia* in which, in place of the ordinary cloven hoof, the foot is enveloped in a hardened skin, enclosing the cushion-like soles, which can be spread out sidewise so as to adapt it to walk, without sinking deeply, over soft and yielding sand. Another adaptation is that in the walls of the paunch or first stomach there are two collections of water cells on which the animal can draw when no other water is procurable. Yet another adaptation is its ability to subsist on the poorest food. Even the hump is another adaptation. It is a storehouse of food, and becomes larger or smaller according as the camel is in good or in bad condition. The camel is stupid, illtempered, and sometimes vindictive; but its passive obedience and power of endurance render it very valuable. It is not now anywhere found wild, nor has it been known wild in historical times. Abraham and Jacob had camels (Gen. xii. 16; xxx. 43), and so had later nomads in the south of Palestine (1 Sam. xxvii. 9; 2 Chron. xiv. 15). The Ishmaelites who bought Joseph also had camels (Gen. xxxvii. 25). The camel was not, however, so much at home in Palestine, which is a hilly country, as in the Arabian and the African deserts (Ex. ix. 3; Judg. vi. 5; 1 Kin. x. 2; 1 Chron. v. 18–21). But it is still bred abundantly on the plains of Moab and in the south of Judæa. The milk was used (cp. Gen. xxxii. 15), but the animal was ceremonially unclean (Lev. xi. 4). From its hair a coarse cloth was woven, which was sometimes made into clothing (Mat. iii. 4) and used for tents. The burden was borne on the hump (Is. xxx. 6). When the camel is ridden, a saddle is commonly used, and sometimes a palanquin (cp. Gen. xxxi. 34). The Arabs commonly deck their camels' necks with ornaments (cp. Judg. viii. 21, 26).

Ca'mon. See KAMON.

Camp.

The station of an army or other body of people, where temporary structures are erected for their accommodation (Ex. xiv. 19; 1 Sam. iv. 5; xvii. 4; 2 Kin. vii. 7). Strict regulations were prescribed for the army of Israel in order to secure cleanliness in their camp (Deut. xxiii. 9–14). The arrangement of the camp of the migrating Hebrew nation, which was adopted for the journey through the wilderness, is described in Num. i. 47–ii. 34; iii. 14–39; cp. x. 11–28, and see SHITTIM.

Four camels pause for refreshment in the Valley of Ajalon.

It was, of course, absolutely regular only when the people were encamped on a broad, level plain. For the encampments of Israel during the journey through the wilderness, see WILDERNESS OF THE WANDERING.

Cam'phire [old form of English camphor; Greek *kaphoura*, Arabic *kafur ;* all from Malay *kapur*, chalk].

The rendering of the Hebrew word *Kopher* in Song i. 14; iv. 13, A. V. See HENNA.

Ca'na [place of reeds].

A village, more fully named Cana of Galilee, where Jesus wrought his first miracle, making water wine (John ii. 1–11), and healed the nobleman's son at Capernaum (iv. 46). Nathanael was of Cana (xxi. 2). Possibly the words "of Galilee" are added to this Cana to distinguish it from another in Cœlesyria (Antiq. xv. 5, 1). Josephus also mentions Cana of Galilee (Life 16, 71). The traditional site is Kefr Kenna, a village about 3¾ miles northeast of Nazareth, on the road to Tiberias. Robinson advocated the view, held by some inquirers in the Crusading period, that Cana of Galilee was at Kâna-el-Jelîl, which is the old name scarcely changed, about 8 miles north by east of Nazareth.

Ca'naan, in A. V. of N. T. twice **Cha'naan** [low, lowland].

1. Son of Ham and grandson of Noah; or better, the descendants of Ham who occupied Canaan and took their name from that country, and in whom the low traits manifested by their progenitor were strongly marked (Gen. x. 6, 15; Hos. xii. 7, margin). The continuance of Ham's character in a branch of his descendants had been prophesied by Noah, and the consequence of yielding to the bestial impulses had been foretold (Gen. ix. 18–27). In this passage the progenitor of the Canaanites is called Canaan proleptically by a late transmitter of the venerable prophecy. Wishing to indicate the forefather of the Canaanites among the sons of Ham, the narrator gives to their ancestor the name borne by his descendants, and by which he had come to be familiarly known, irrespective of the question whether it was his personal name or not.

2. A name probably given at first only to the low-lying coast line of Palestine to distinguish it from the neighboring hill country (Num. xiii. 29; Josh. xi. 3). Afterwards the name Canaan was extended first to the Jordan valley, and then to the whole of Palestine west of the river, and became one of the most common designations of the country inhabited by the Hebrews, though what they occupied was really the highland portion of Palestine and the Jordan valley, with little of the coast line (Gen. xi. 31; Num. xiii. 2).

The language of Canaan after the conquest of the country by the Israelites was Hebrew, the speech of the people of God (Is. xix. 18).

The Hebrews conquered Canaan under the leadership of Joshua after the death of Moses. The plan of the campaign included the establishment of a fixed camp at Gilgal. The site was on the east of Jericho, in the plain (Josh. iv. 19; v. 10). From it the Israelites *went up* to Ai and Gibeon (vii. 3; viii. 1, 3; x. 9). The advantages of this location for the camp of Israel were great. At Gilgal Joshua had no enemies in his rear, had water in abundance for the people, could draw supplies from the two tribes and a half which had settled in the country east of the Jordan, and had a safe place for hoarding spoil. The characteristic objects in this camp were the tabernacle (Josh. vi. 24; cp. ix. 23; xviii. 1; xxii. 19); the ark (iii. 17; vi. 11, etc. ; vii. 6); the altar (ix. 27; cp. xxii. 19, 28, 29); Eleazar the priest (xiv. 1; cp. 6), besides other priests (vi. 6, 12, etc. ; viii. 33); twelve stones which had been taken out of the bed of the Jordan and set up as a memorial of the passage of the river (iv. 20). Joshua's plan further included a preliminary campaign for the overthrow of the enemies which threatened the camp. He took Jericho, the outpost of Canaan, the mistress of the valley. Then he marched into the mountain, directly to the west, and overthrew Ai. This town lay at the head of the valley which emerged opposite Gilgal, and from it troops might be poured down against the camp. After this preliminary campaign he fulfilled the injunction of Moses to erect an altar on Ebal (Josh. viii. 30–35; Deut. xxvii.). According to Josephus, this solemnity was performed after the conquest of the entire country (Antiq. v. 1, 19). At this juncture ambassadors from the town of Gibeon appeared, with whom Joshua made a treaty without asking counsel of the Lord. It was an unfortunate step, as will be shown presently. Having obtained secure foothold in the country, Joshua proceeded to conquer Canaan in two campaigns. The alliance of the five kings determined the southern expedition (Josh. x.). The king of Jerusalem summoned the kings of Hebron, Lachish, Eglon, and Jarmuth to war against Gibeon; and Joshua was obliged to help those with whom he was in treaty. The five kings were routed, and fled down the pass of Beth-horon. Following up the victory, Joshua captured Makkedah, in or hard by the maritime plain, and pitched a temporary camp there; took Libnah, which was likewise in the plain; Lachish, where the king of Gezer also was defeated; and Eglon, where another temporary camp was fixed; and Hebron. From Hebron he turned and smote Debir, in the hill country. Thus the entire region included between Gibeon, Gaza, and Kadesh-barnea was smitten, and Joshua returned to Gilgal.

It was during this campaign that Joshua bade the sun to stand still (x. 12–15). This event occurred during a miracle period; see MIRACLE. But it is cited from the book of Jashar, which contained poems accompanied by remarks in prose. See SUN.

Having conquered the central region and the south, Joshua determined as a matter of

expediency, or under compulsion of the northern confederacy, to neglect the inconsiderable towns on the coast north of the Philistine
country, and to strike at the populous and
powerful north (Josh. xi.). With this end in
view, he undertook a northern campaign.
The king of Hazor was head of a confederacy of petty monarchs, and on hearing of
the Israelitish victories in the south he summoned the remaining kings of the country
to a united attempt to crush Joshua. The
allied armies met at the waters of Merom.
Joshua had reached the same neighborhood,
and he attacked them. He routed them, pursued the fugitives as far as Sidon toward the
northwest and eastward to Mizpeh. He then
returned, captured and burnt the town of
Hazor, and took the capitals of the other
petty kingdoms which had been in alliance.
In xi. 16–xii. 24 a summary of the conquest
is given.

The power of the Canaanites was broken
by these campaigns, but the inhabitants were
not wholly exterminated. Many of the natives remained. Important towns were left
in the possession of the Canaanitish population (xi. 13; xv. 63; xvi. 10, etc.); and even
where the destruction was most complete,
not a few of the people had escaped by flight
or hiding and, when the army of Israel withdrew (x. 43), they returned, rebuilt ruined
towns, and placed the wasted fields once
more under cultivation. Years afterwards,
when the tribes of Israel scattered over the
country in order to settle, they met with
sporadic resistance (Judg. i.; see HEBRON,
JOSHUA).

The time occupied in the conquest of Canaan was long, because not a city made peace
with Israel save the five cities of the Gibeonites (xi. 18, 19). It may be calculated with a
considerable degree of accuracy. From the
sending forth of the spies in the second year
(cp. Num. x. 11; xiii. 20; Deut. i. 2) to the
time of assigning the reconquest of Hebron
to Caleb when the land was about to be distributed was (Josh. xiv. 7, 10) 45 years; from
the sending forth of the spies to the crossing
of the Zered was (Deut. ii. 14) 38 years;
leaving for the conquest of the country, both
east and west of the Jordan, about 6 or 7 years.
From this is to be deducted the time consumed in the conquest of the eastern country and by the events at Shittim. The death
of Aaron (Num. xxxiii. 38) occurred in the
40th year, 5th month, 1st day, and the crossing of Jordan (Josh. iv. 19) in 1st month, 10th
day; leaving for the conquest of the country
of Sihon and Og, and for the events at Shittim, nearly 8 months, 9 days, of which period
the events at Shittim occupied about two
months (cp. Deut. i. 3, 4, with Josh. iv. 19;
Deut. xxxiv. 8; Josh. ii. 22, etc.; Ant. iv. 8,
49 and iv. 8, 1), leaving for the conquest of
western Palestine 5 or 6 years. Josephus assigns 5 years to this conquest (Antiq. v. 1, 19).

Three political blunders were committed

by Joshua: his making a treaty with the
Gibeonites; allowing the Jebusites to hold Jerusalem (Josh. xv. 63); and failure to dispossess the Philistines and control the country to
the sea. A study of the map shows that, as
a result of these mistakes, Judah and Simeon
were isolated from the rest of the nation.
The main road from Judah to the north was
commanded by the Jebusite stronghold at
Jerusalem, and was skirted for 10 miles on
the west by the settlements of the Gibeonites.
Between Jerusalem and Jericho on the east
was a tract of wild, rocky, uninhabited mountain land crossed east and west by impassable
gorges. From Jerusalem to the Mediterranean
Sea a strip of country stretched, which was
occupied by foreigners: first Gibeonites, next
Canaanites in Dan, then Philistines as far as
the sea. The consequences of this isolation
of Judah and Simeon were serious, distinctly
affecting the course of history in the years
that followed.

Was the extermination of the Canaanites
by the Israelites a justifiable act? The mere
matter of their dispossessing the Canaanites
presents no moral difficulties. This procedure
accorded with the spirit of the age. The Israelites doubtless had as much right to Canaan as had the inhabitants whom they drove
out. They despoiled despoilers. Nor does
the manner of warfare present moral difficulties, for the conduct of the Hebrews in
war compares favorably with the practices
of the time. Judged by the standards of
their own age, they were not bloodthirsty or
cruel. The Assyrians have pictured their own
wars. It was not infrequent for them to de-
capitate the inhabitants of captured cities,
and pile the heads in heaps; to crucify or
impale prisoners, pierce their eyeballs with a
spear, or flay them alive. In the battles of
Israel with the Canaanites there is record of
death, but not of torture. The moral difficulty connected with the extermination of
the Canaanites is that God commanded it.
God's character is involved. But it is to be
remembered that God had a twofold end in
view in the utter extermination by death and
expulsion which he commanded. It was
punitive (Gen. xv. 16; Lev. xviii. 25; Deut.
ix. 3, 4; xviii. 12) and preventive (Ex. xxiii.
31–33; xxxiv. 12–16; Deut. vii. 2–4). It was
to punish the Canaanites for their outrageous
wickedness, and to prevent them from con-
taminating the people of God. It is not asserted that the Canaanites were sinners above
all men that ever lived. Their personal morals
were perhaps not worse than those of other
heathen as described in Rom. i. The Canaanites were idolaters, they indulged in shameful and abominable vice, they went beyond
other nations in practicing human sacrifice.
It is appointed unto all men to die. God
holds nations as well as individuals responsible, and deals with them accordingly. He
doomed the nations of Canaan to extermination as a punishment for their wickedness,

and to prevent them from seducing the people of God. He had exterminated the wicked race of men in the days of Noah by the flood; he had swept away the iniquitous cities of the plain by an eruption, it would seem, of burning naphtha; he had overthrown Pharaoh and his host in the Red Sea; he had destroyed Korah and his rebellious crew by an earthquake and by fire. Now, instead of using the forces of nature to effect his punitory ends, he employed the Israelites as the ministers of his justice; as the public executioner, employed by the civil tribunal, is the minister of human justice. This truth was taught to the Israelites. They were informed that they were the instruments of divine justice. For these reasons the extermination of the Canaanites by the Israelites was just; the employment of the Israelites for the purpose was right; and in connection with the righteous judgment was an intention to benefit the world. The failure of the Israelites to carry out God's command fully was one of the great blunders which they committed, as well as a sin, and it resulted in lasting injury to the nation.

The distribution of the conquered territory on the west of the Jordan was made partly at Gilgal and partly at Shiloh, whither the tabernacle was removed (Josh. xiv. 1, 2, 6–xviii. 1, 2). It was conducted by Eleazar the priest, Joshua, and ten heads of fathers' houses (xvii. 4; cp. Num. xxxiv. 17, 18), and was made by lot (Josh. xviii. 6). The law to govern the distribution had already been enacted; namely, to the more numerous a larger inheritance, and wheresoever the lot falleth to any man (Num. xxvi.52–56; xxxiii. 54). The rabbis state that two urns were used; in one were placed tickets with the names of the tribes, and in the other were tickets with the names of the districts. A tribe was drawn and the district which it should possess. The size of the territory was then determined by the populousness of the tribe. Probably, however, the commission selected a district without narrowly defining its boundaries, and merely determined by lot what tribe should possess it; for—1. Compare the form of the question in Judg. i. 1. 2. This theory satisfies Num. xxxiii. 54. 3. Compare Josh. xviii. 1–10, where the land is first described in seven portions, and Joshua then cast lots for the tribes. 4. This theory also satisfies Josh. xix. 1, etc., where it is stated that at the final allotment the second lot came out for Simeon, the third for Zebulun, etc. 5. The districts were assigned for occupation, not as though determined by lot, but in regular order, building up the nation compactly as the allotment proceeded, and not leaping hither and thither. 6. Much was evidently left to the discretion of the supervisors. Caleb must have Hebron whether the lot of the main body of the tribe of Judah allowed him to settle in that neighborhood or not. Jacob's last wishes would be observed so far as the lot permitted (Gen.

xlix.), though the lot did not permit Zebulun to possess the seacoast, but his possession was doubtless adjusted as nearly as possible to the patriarch's desire. Mistakes were made and rectified. Before the allotment was completed—and it was not carried out in a day or a week—Judah reported that it had been granted too much territory. The surplus was accordingly added to the undistributed domain. The children of Joseph, on the other hand, informed Joshua that they had received too little land, and they asked and received more. It was intended, in accordance with Jacob's wish, that Ephraim and Manasseh should dwell side by side; hence the lot was not cast for them separately, but for them unitedly as the children of Joseph (Josh. xvi. 1, 4). In this manner the nation was compactly built up, the territory which lay nearest the camp being distributed first.

1. Southern hill country.	To Judah, 4th son of Leah.
2. Central hill country.	To Joseph, firstborn of Rachel.
3. Intervening hill country.	To Benjamin, 2d son of Rachel.
4. Part of the surplus of the southern hill country which Judah gave back.	To Simeon, 2d son of Leah.
5, 6. Territory bounding central hill country on the north.	To Zebulun, 6th son of Leah. / To Issachar, 5th son of Leah.
7. Adjoining seacoast.	To Asher, 2d son of Leah's maid.
8. Territory north of Issachar and Zebulon.	To Naphtali, 2d son of Rachel's maid.
9. Remaining part of Judah's surplus.	To Dan, 1st son of Rachel's maid.

Reuben, firstborn of Leah, Gad, son of Leah's maid, and half tribe of Manasseh, descendant of Rachel, had obtained lands east of the Jordan. These with Levi, son of Leah, did not participate in the distribution.

Ca′naan-ite.

1. An inhabitant of Canaan, especially one of Hamitic blood, although persons and tribes incorporated with the descendants of Ham in this region acquired the name. According as the geographical designation Canaan is used in its broader or its narrower sense, the word Canaanite has a broader or narrower signification. In the narrow sense, the Canaanites were the people of the coast and valleys (Gen. xv. 21; Josh. ix. 1). In the broad sense, they were the tribes enumerated in Gen. x. 15–19. The Canaanites were doomed to destruction on account of their sins (Deut. xx. 17). But the Israelites to a certain extent failed to carry out the injunction. They in many cases contented themselves with putting the Canaanite inhabitants to tribute (Judg. i. 27–36). Solomon levied on them a tribute of bondservice; in other words, made them perform forced labor (1 Kin. ix. 20. 21). The Canaanites eventually devoted them-

selves extensively to trade, and their name became synonymous with trader (Is. xxiii. 8).

2. A member of a Jewish patriotic party. See CANANÆAN.

Ca'naan-i'tess.

A woman of Canaan (1 Chron. ii. 3).

Ca-na-næ'an, in A. V. **Canaanite** [transliteration of the Aramaic word *kan'ân*, zeal].

A member of a Jewish patriotic party, which was also known by the synonymous Greek name Zealot (q. v.). Simon the apostle bore this epithet to distinguish him from Simon Peter (Mat. x. 4; cp. Luke vi. 15, R. V.).

Can'da-ce.

A queen of Ethiopia, *i. e.*, probably of Meroë, in southern Nubia. A eunuch of great authority at her court, when returning home from a visit to Jerusalem, where he had gone to worship, was converted to Christianity through the instrumentality of Philip the evangelist (Acts viii. 26–39). Strabo, Dion Cassius, and Pliny, all concur in stating that Meroë in the first century of the Christian era was governed by a succession of queens, each called Candace.

Candle. See LAMP.

Can'dle-stick.

A stand for a candle. That in the tabernacle was for lamps. It consisted of a base and a shaft with six branches, beaten out of solid gold, and it supported seven lamps. It stood on the south side of the sanctuary (Ex. xxv. 31–40; xl. 24; Lev. xxiv. 2–4). Pure olive oil was used in the lamps, and the light burned from evening to morning (Ex. xxvii. 20, 21; xxx. 7, 8; 1 Sam. iii. 3). According to Josephus, three of the lamps were allowed to burn by day (Antiq. iii. 8, 3). This continuous burning apparently symbolized the uninterrupted worship, even by night, and the unceasing emission of light, by the people of God (cp. Zech. iv.). This candelabrum was perhaps deposited in the temple (1 Kin. viii. 4). Solomon made ten candlesticks, five for the right and five for the left of the oracle (vii. 49; 2 Chron. iv. 7). They were carried away to Babylon (Jer. lii. 19). Zerubbabel had but one; this was carried off by Antiochus Epiphanes (1 Mac. i. 21). Replaced (iv. 49), it continued in use till the capture of Jerusalem by Titus, when it was taken to Rome, figured in Titus' triumph, and was sculptured on his arch (War vii. 5, 5).

Cane [from Hebrew *kaneh*, a reed].

The rendering of the Hebrew word *Kaneh* in Is. xliii. 24 and Jer. vi. 20. In both places on the margin of the R. V. it is rendered calamus, and so it is elsewhere translated in both versions, where a specific odorous cane is intended.

Seven-branched candlestick.

Can'ker-worm.

The rendering of the Hebrew *Yelek* in Joel and Nahum, and also in R. V. of Ps. cv. 34 and Jer. li. 27. In the two latter passages A. V. has caterpillar. It is a winged insect (Nah. iii. 16, R. V.), rough (Jer. li. 27), and very destructive to growing crops. As it is mentioned with the typical locust (Joel i. 4 ; Nah. iii. 15), which it resembles also in the numbers in which it appears (Joel ii. 25), it is probably a locust of some species or in some stage of development.

Can'neh.

A place, evidently in Mesopotamia, perhaps the same as Calneh (Ezek. xxvii. 23).

Can'on [reed, cane].

The meaning of the word was extended to denote : (1) any straight rod or bar, such as a rod or level used by masons in building ; (2) figuratively, anything which serves to regulate or determine other things, especially classical books ; a guide or model (Gal. vi. 16 ; Phil. iii. 16) ; (3) a type of Christian doctrine, the orthodox as opposed to the heterodox ; (4) the Scriptures viewed as a rule of faith and conduct. The word is Greek. It was first used in this fourth sense by the early fathers, but the idea denoted was ancient. A book entitled to a place in the Bible is called canonical ; one not so entitled, uncanonical ; and title to a place, canonicity.

THE OLD TESTAMENT CANON. Authoritative literature grew up by degrees and was carefully preserved. The ten commandments, written on tables of stone, Israel's constitution, were deposited in the ark (Ex. xl. 20). The statutes were recorded in the book of the covenant (xx. 23–xxiii. 33 ; xxiv. 7). The book of the law, written by Moses, was put by the side of the ark (Deut. xxxi. 24–26). Joshua added to the collection what he wrote (Josh. xxiv. 26). Samuel wrote the manner of the kingdom in a book, and laid it up before the Lord (1 Sam. x. 25). In the days of Josiah the book of the law of the Lord, the well-known book, was found in the temple and recognized by king, priests, prophets, and people, as authoritative and ancient (2 Kin. xxii. 8–20). Copies of the law were made (Deut. xvii. 18–20). Prophets committed their words to writing (*e. g.* Jer. xxxvi. 32), and they were acquainted with each other's writings and quoted them as authority (Is. ii. 2–4 with Mic. iv. 1–3). The law and the words of the prophets were recognized as authoritative, inspired by the Spirit of God, and jealously guarded by Jehovah (Zech. i. 4 ; vii. 7, 12).

The law of Moses, comprising the five books of Moses, circulated as a distinct portion of the sacred literature in the time of Ezra. It was in Ezra's hand (Ezra vii. 14), and he was a ready scribe in it (6, 11). At the request of the people, he read the book publicly to them (Neh. viii. 1, 5, 8). About this time also, before the schism between the Jews and Samaritans had become final, the Pentateuch was taken to Samaria. The arrangement of the minor prophets into a group of twelve is attested by Jesus, son of Sirach, as in vogue by the year 200 B. C. (Ecclus. xlix. 10). His language further suggests the great group of books—Joshua, Judges, Samuel, Kings, Isaiah, Jeremiah, Ezekiel, and the Twelve (xlvi.–xlix.)—which constitute the second division of the Hebrew canon. The existence of the threefold division of all the Scriptures into "the law, the prophets, and the others that have followed in their steps," or "the law, the prophets, and the other books," or, "the law, the prophecies, and the rest of the books," is attested as early as the year 132 B. C., and the existence of a Greek version of them at the same time ; for the grandson of Jesus, son of Sirach, states these things (Ecclus. prologue). Reference is made in a passage which dates from about 100 B. C. to "the sacred books which are now in our hands" (1 Mac. xii. 9). Philo Judæus, who was born at Alexandria in 20 B. C., and died there in the reign of Claudius, had the present canon, and quotes from nearly all the books while he cites nothing from the Apocrypha.

The N. T. refers to "the Scriptures" as a body of authoritative writings (Mat. xxi. 42 ; xxvi. 56 ; Mark xiv. 49 ; John x. 35 ; 2 Tim. iii. 16), as holy (Rom. i. 2 ; 2 Tim. iii. 15), and as the oracles of God (Rom. iii. 2 ; Heb. v. 12 ; 1 Pet. iv. 11) ; mentions a threefold division into "the law of Moses, and the prophets, and the psalms" (Luke xxiv. 44); and quotes from or refers to all the books except Obadiah and Nahum, Ezra and Nehemiah, Esther, Song of Songs, and Ecclesiastes. Josephus, a contemporary of the apostle Paul, writing about A. D. 100, and speaking for his nation, says : "We have but twenty-two [books], containing the history of all time, books that are justly believed in," or, according to the usual reading, "believed to be divine," and he speaks in the strongest terms of the exclusive authority of these writings, continuing : "From the days of Artaxerxes to our own times every event has indeed been recorded ; but these recent records have not been deemed worthy of equal credit with those which preceded them, on account of the failure of the exact succession of the prophets. There is practical proof of the spirit in which we treat our Scriptures ; for although so great an interval of time has now passed, not a soul has ventured either to add or to remove or to alter a syllable, and it is the instinct of every Jew, from the day of his birth, to consider these Scriptures as the teaching of God, and to abide by them and, if need be, cheerfully to lay down his life in their behalf" (against Apion, i. 8). Josephus states the contents of Scripture under three heads: (1) "Five belong to Moses, which contain his laws and the traditions of the origin of mankind till his death." (2) "From the death of Moses to Artaxerxes the prophets who were after

Moses wrote down what was done in their time in thirteen books." Josephus followed the arrangement of the Septuagint probably, and the enumeration of the Alexandrians. The thirteen books are probably Joshua, Judges with Ruth, Samuel, Kings, Chronicles, Ezra with Nehemiah, Esther, Job, Daniel, Isaiah, Jeremiah with Lamentations, Ezekiel, the Twelve Minor Prophets. (3) "The remaining four books contain hymns to God and precepts for the conduct of human life." These were doubtless Psalms, Song of Songs, Proverbs, Ecclesiastes.

So far facts. There was also a tradition current that the canon was arranged in the time of Ezra and Nehemiah. Josephus, as already cited, expresses the universal belief of his countrymen that no books had been added since the time of Artaxerxes—that is, since the time of Ezra and Nehemiah. An extravagant legend of the latter part of the first century of the Christian era (2 Esd. xiv.) grew out of the current tradition that Ezra restored the law and even the entire O. T. (21, 22, 40), of which the temple copies had been lost. It attests that the Jews of Palestine in that age reckoned the canonical books at twenty-four (24 + 70 = 94 ; vers. 44–46, R. V.). A passage of doubtful date and authenticity, perhaps penned about 100 B. C. (2 Mac. ii. 13), alludes to Nehemiah's activity in connection with the second and third divisions of the canon. Irenæus transmits the tradition thus : "After the sacred writings had been destroyed in the exile under Nebuchadnezzar, when the Jews after seventy years had returned to their own country, He in the days of Artaxerxes inspired Ezra the priest, of the tribe of Levi, to rearrange all the words of the prophets who had gone before, and to restore to the people the legislation of Moses." Elias Levita, writing in 1538, states the belief of his people in this wise : "In Ezra's time the twenty-four books were not yet united in a single volume. Ezra and his associates united them together and divided them into three parts, the law, the prophets, and the hagiographa." This tradition contains truth. Whether it can be accepted in every particular depends on the settlement of the date when certain books were written, such as Nehemiah and Chronicles.

The Pentateuch as the work of Moses, and as embodying the fundamental law of the nation, formed one division of the canon, and with chronological fitness occupied the first place in the collection. To the second division books written by the prophets were assigned, as the name and largely the contents indicate. The books were eight in number—Joshua, Judges, Samuel, and Kings, which came to be known as the former prophets, and Isaiah, Jeremiah, Ezekiel, and the Twelve, which were called the latter prophets. For Joshua, regarded as a prophet, see Ecclus. xlvi. 1. The nucleus of the third division consisted of sections of the books

of Psalms and Proverbs. They had two characteristics—they were poetry, and their authors were not official prophets. They attracted to themselves all other similar authoritative literature. The prayer of Moses (Ps. xc.), though written by a prophet, was placed in this division of Scripture because it is poetry. So, too, Lamentations, though written by a prophet, yet being poetry, likewise found place in the third division of the Hebrew canon. An additional reason existed for separating it from Jeremiah. It was read on the anniversary of the destruction of both temples, and hence was put with four other short books which were read on four other anniversaries, Song, Ruth, Ecclesiastes, and Esther. They constitute the five rolls or Megilloth. The book of Daniel was placed here because written by a man who, although gifted with prophecy, was not by office a prophet. In all probability Chronicles was written, not by a prophet, but by a priest ; hence it belonged in the third division of the canon. The mere fact of its late authorship does not account for its place in this division, for books and sections of books in this division were in existence before Zechariah and Malachi, which were put in the second division. It is proper to add that while the contents of the several divisions of the canon were fixed, the order of the books in the third division varied from time to time ; and even in the second division the Talmud knew Isaiah as standing between Ezekiel and the Minor Prophets. This order of the four prophetical books (Jeremiah, Ezekiel, Isaiah, and Minor Prophets), was evidently determined by size, the largest being placed first. As late as the close of the first century A. D., the right of several books of the third division to remain in the canon was discussed. The books were in the canon, none questioned that. The discussions concerned the contents of the books and difficulties in reconciling them with other books ; but the debates were probably mere intellectual displays. There was no intention of removing any book from the canon, but rather the purpose to establish its right to the place it already occupied. J. D. D.

CANON OF THE NEW TESTAMENT. The apostolic church received from the Jewish the belief in a written rule of faith. Christ himself confirmed this belief by appealing to the O. T. as the written word of God (e. g. John v. 37–47 ; Mat. v. 17, 18 ; Mark xii. 36, 37 ; Luke xvi. 31), and by instructing his disciples out of it (Luke xxiv. 45) ; and the apostles habitually refer to the O. T. as authoritative (e. g. Rom. iii. 2, 21 ; 1 Cor. iv. 6 ; Rom. xv. 4 ; 2 Tim. iii. 15–17 ; 2 Pet. i. 21). In the next place, the apostles claimed for their own teaching, oral and written, like authority with the O. T. (1 Cor. ii. 7–13 ; xiv. 37 ; 1 Thess. ii. 13 ; Rev. i. 3), and directed the public reading of their epistles (1 Thess. v. 27 ; Col. iv. 16, 17 ; 2 Thess. ii. 15 ; 2 Pet. i. 15 ;

iii. 1, 2), while revelations, given to the church through inspired prophets, were considered to form, with apostolic instruction, the foundation of the church (Eph. ii. 20). It was therefore both natural and right that the N. T. literature should be added to the Old, and thus the written canon of faith be enlarged. In the N. T. itself we may see this beginning to be done (1 Tim. v. 18; 2 Pet. iii. 1, 2, 16), and in the generations which followed the apostles, the writings which were known to have apostolic authority were gradually collected into the second half of the church's canon, and finally called the New Testament. For, from the beginning, the proof that a book had a right to a place in the canon was its *apostolicity*, by which was meant that it was bequeathed to the church with apostolic sanction, having either been written by an apostle or else guaranteed by one as authoritative. This, as we have said, was the apostolic doctrine; and evidence is abundant that, in the second and third centuries, this was the principle on which the N. T. collection was made. The complete collection, however, was formed slowly for various reasons. At first certain books were known only in some churches to be apostolic, and it was not until the whole body of believers throughout the Roman empire was united in one ecclesiastical consciousness that all the books, which in the several parts of the church were known to be apostolic, were universally accepted. The process of collection also did not at first have the incentive which it afterwards received through the rise of heresy and of spurious writings claiming apostolic authority. But, while the process of collection was slow, the books which in any church were accepted were regarded as canonical because apostolic. The teaching of the apostles was the rule of faith. Their works were read in public worship. Early in the second century we find them directly called Scripture (Ep. of Polycarp 12; Ep. of Barnabas 4). The books by Mark and Luke were received because stamped with the authority of Peter and Paul. Even commentaries began to be made upon them, and their statements and phraseology saturate the literature of the post-apostolic age. Then, as to the extent and rapidity with which the collection itself was made, the following facts are the most noteworthy. The four gospels were everywhere received from the beginning of the second century, while 2 Pet iii. 16 shows that its readers were already familiar with a collection of Paul's epistles. Very early we find the phrases "gospel" and "apostles" used to describe the two parts of the new collection. The evidence of the canonicity of The Acts likewise carries us back to the first half of the second century. Some books indeed were disputed in some sections of the church, but this only shows that their final acceptance was based on sufficient evidence. Finally it appears that the Syrian church in the second century received all our N. T. except Rev., Jude, 2 Pet., 2 and 3 John; the Roman church, all except Heb., Epp. of Pet., Jas., 3 John; the North African, all except Heb., 2 Pet., and perhaps James. These collections, however, only contained the books formally received in the respective churches, and do not prove that no other apostolic books were known. The remainder were in fact universally accepted in the course of the third century, though difference of opinion existed about some; and, when the age of councils came, our present N. T. canon appears in the lists as the accepted one. In the fourth century ten fathers and two councils have left lists of canonical books. Of these three omit Revelation, against which prejudice existed in some quarters, though earlier testimony to it is abundant. The rest give the N. T. as we have it.

In view of these facts it should be noted: (1) That while the collection of the N. T. into one volume was slow, the belief in a written rule of faith was primitive and apostolic. The history of the formation of the collection should not be thought to give the rise into authority of a written rule of faith. It only shows the stages by which the books rightly belonging to the canon were recognized and brought together. (2) Differences of opinion and usage, as to what books were canonical, and as to the degree of certainty with which a book could be received, appear in the writers and churches even of the second century. This fact, however, again only marks the stages by which the evidence for the books was gradually accepted by the church as a whole, and the carefulness of the primitive Christians in receiving books as apostolic. In like manner the occasional acceptance of spurious writings was corrected in due time. (3) The proof on which *we* should accept the several N. T. books as canonical is *historical evidence*. As to this, the judgment of the early church that our twenty-seven books are apostolic is entitled to acceptance unless it can be proved false. We should not, however, receive them merely because ecclesiastical councils decreed them canonical; nor, on the other hand, because of their contents. The question is one of historical evidence alone. (4) Finally, we note that the name *canon* is not known to have been applied to the collection of sacred books until the fourth century. But while this term, now universal, was not at first used, the thing denoted by it—viz. that the sacred books were the rule of faith—was, as we have seen, an apostolic doctrine.

G. T. P.

Can′ti-cles. See SONG OF SOLOMON.

Ca-per′na-um [village of Nahum or of consolation].

A town on the northwestern shore of the sea of Galilee, in the region of Zebulun and

Naphtali (Mat. iv. 13–16; cp. Luke iv. 31; John vi. 17–24). It was the seat of a tax-collector (Mark ii. 1, 14), and was apparently a Roman military post (Mat. viii. 5–13; Luke vii. 1–10). Our Lord at an early period of his ministry removed thither from Nazareth and made it so continually his headquarters that it came to be called his own city (Mat. ix. 1; cp. Mark ii. 1). It was there that he healed the centurion's palsied servant (Mat. viii. 5–13; Luke vii. 1–10), Peter's wife's mother when she was prostrate with fever (Mat. viii. 14–17; Mark i. 29–31), a demoniac (Mark i. 21–28; Luke iv. 31–37), a man sick of the palsy borne of four (Mark ii. 1–13; cp. Mat. ix. 1–8), a nobleman's son (John. iv. 46–54), and a number of other diseased people (Mat. viii. 16, 17; Mark i. 32–34; Luke iv. 23, 40, 41). The discourse recorded in John vi. 24–71, which followed on the feeding of the 5000, with many other addresses, was delivered in the synagogue at Capernaum or elsewhere in the town (Mark. ix. 33–50). It was at Capernaum also that Jesus called to the apostleship Matthew or Levi, as he was sitting at the receipt of custom (Mat. ix. 9–13; Mark ii. 14–17; Luke v. 27–32; cp. Mat. xvii. 24). Notwithstanding the teaching and works of Jesus its people did not repent, and Jesus predicted the utter ruin of the place (Mat. xi. 23, 24; Luke x. 15).

Capernaum is not mentioned in the O. T., and perhaps did not arise till after the captivity. Josephus was carried with bruised wrist from near Julias (not far from the spot where the Jordan enters the sea of Galilee) into a village named Cepharnome or Capernaum (Life 72).

Two spots contend for the distinction of being the site of Capernaum. They are about 2½ miles apart. The more northerly is called Tell Hum, and the more southerly Khan Minyeh or Minia. Each of them marks the site of a former town. At Capernaum, or near it, was a receipt of custom (Mark ii. 13, 14). If the object was the collection of toll from passing caravans, the tollhouse naturally stood close to the great trade route from Damascus to the Mediterranean seacoast and Egypt; and that location belongs preëminently to Khan Minyeh. But if the taxes were levied on the products of mills and the produce of the fields (cp. Luke xix. 2), the town was probably situated near the extensive water-power and celebrated wheat fields in the neighborhood of Tell Hum (Talmud). The fountain of Capernaum, from which the plain of Gennesaret was in part irrigated, and where coracin fish were and are found (War iii. 10, 8), was doubtless the abundant source at Tâbighah, midway between Khan Minyeh and Tell Hum. The locality is connected topographically with Tell Hum, not with Khan Minyeh. Mills doubtless stood there then as now; water was conducted thence to the plain by a canal, portions of which still remain; and a considerable town lay immediately to the north, the ruins of which include the site of Tell Hum and extend westward from the shore for at least 800 feet. The houses were largely of black basalt, while the ruins of a synagogue are of marble or fine limestone quarried in the mountains northwest of the place.

In the word Capernaum the first two syllables, Caper, represent the Hebrew word for village, and might well be supplanted by the Arabic *Tell*, mound, when the place became

Ruins of an ancient synagogue at Capernaum, dating back to the third century, B.C. It is possible that this is the site of the synagogue in which Jesus ministered.

a ruin. *Ḥum* in Arabic means "a herd of camels"; if Hebrew, it is probably part of the word Nahum. But Tell Hum is perhaps not an echo of Capernaum, but a corruption of Tanhum, the name of a Jewish rabbi who was buried there.

Caph, in A. R. V. **Kaph.**

The eleventh letter of the Hebrew alphabet. English K comes from the same source; but C and, especially before e and i, or when final, Ch are employed as its representative in anglicized Hebrew names. Caph stands at the head of the eleventh section of Ps. cxix., in which section each verse begins with this letter in the original. See BETH.

Caph-ar-sal'a-ma [village of Salem].

A town (1 Mac. vii. 31; Antiq. xii. 10, 4), perhaps the later Carvasalim, near Ramleh.

Ca-phen'a-tha. See CHAPHENATHA.

Caph'tor.

An isle or seacoast, from which the Philistines originally came (Jer. xlvii. 4; Amos ix. 7). The Philistines as a whole were Cherethites, that is, probably Cretans (1 Sam. xxx. 14; Ezek. xxv. 16; Zeph. ii. 5), and Caphtor was perhaps the island Crete. However, an Egyptian nome in the delta bore the name Kapet-hor. This word may be the original of Caphtor. If so, the ancestors of the Philistines went thence to Crete and later to Philistia, or they went thither from Crete and ultimately to Philistia.

Caph'to-rim; in A. V. once **Caphtorims** and once **Caphthorim.**

A tribe descended from the Egyptians (Gen. x. 14; 1 Chron. i. 12), and inhabiting Caphtor (Deut. ii. 23).

Cap-pa-do'ci-a.

A highland province of Asia Minor, bounded on the north by Pontus, on the south by Cilicia, on the east by Syria and Lesser Armenia, and on the west by Lycaonia. It produced excellent wheat and horses, but was regarded as a region of uncultivated minds and immoral practices. Worshipers from Cappadocia were present at the feast of Pentecost, rendered memorable by the descent of the Holy Spirit (Acts ii. 9). Some of the Dispersion to whom Peter addressed his first epistle sojourned in Cappadocia (1 Pet. i. 1).

Cap'tain.

As a military title, captain is generally in O. T. the rendering of the Hebrew word *Sar*. It is a broad designation for an official, whether he be the commander-in-chief of the army (Gen. xxi. 22; Judg. iv. 2; 1 Sam. xiv. 50; 2 Sam. x. 16), or the commander of a division of the army (2 Sam. xviii. 2 with 5), or part of a division (1 Kin. xvi. 9); an officer over 1000 men or 100 men or 50 men (Num. xxxi. 14, 48; 1 Sam. viii. 12; xvii. 18; xviii. 13; xxii. 7; 2 Sam. xviii. 1; 2 Kin. i. 9; Is. iii. 3); the commander of the king's body guard (Gen. xxxvii. 36; and 2 Kin. xxv. 8; Dan. ii. 14, where the word is *Rab*), or of a

post of sentries (Jer. xxxvii. 13, in Hebrew *Ba'al*). The word rendered captain in A. V. of Num. ii. is *Nasi'*, and denotes a tribal prince. *Ḳaṣin* is thrice rendered captain in A. V. (Josh. x. 24; Judg. xi. 6, 11), where it refers to leaders of the host; but the word is a general term for one with whom decision rests, and it is applied to civil rulers (Is. i. 10; iii. 6, 7; Mic. iii. 1, 9), whose duties included that of judging (Prov. vi. 7; xxv. 15, R. V. margin).

In N. T. the chief captain was a *chiliarchos*, a term which originally denoted the commander of 1000 men, but was used broadly for the commandant of a garrison, and as the equivalent of the Roman military tribune (John xviii. 12, R. V. margin). He was one of the general officers of a legion, and higher in rank than a centurion (Acts xxi. 31, 32, R. V. margin; xxii. 25). The captain of the guard at Rome (Acts xxviii. 16, A. V.) was a *stratopedarchos*, or commander of a legion, in this particular instance the chief officer of the legion known as the prætorian guard (R. V. margin). The captain of the temple was not a military officer, but the priest in command of the guard of Levites who kept watch at the temple (Acts iv. 1; v. 24, 26; Antiq. xx. 6, 2 with War ii. 12, 6; vi. 5, 3). Under him were subordinate officers of the several divisions of the guard (Luke xxii. 4, 52).

Cap-tiv'i-ty.

The state of being in bondage to enemies, especially in a foreign land. In O. T. times the Assyrians introduced, and the Babylonians adopted, the practice of making a wholesale deportation of at least the leading men belonging to each country which they conquered, and locating them in districts where they would be removed from familiar associations and patriotic memories, and would be under the eye of the central government. Deportation was generally resorted to as an extreme measure when other means failed. The stronger state was usually content with imposing tribute. The withholding of the customary tribute was treated as rebellion, and was punished by a military invasion and pillage of the country. If these harsh measures proved ineffective, resort was had to deportation.

Two principal captivities are mentioned in the Bible :

I. THE CAPTIVITY OF THE TEN TRIBES. As early as 842 B. C. Jehu paid tribute to Shalmaneser, king of Assyria. About 803 Rammannirari reports receiving tribute from the Israelites. But it was not until the reign of Tiglath-pileser, 745–727, that the Assyrians began emptying the land of the ten tribes of its inhabitants. That king received tribute from Menahem. In the reign of Pekah he captured cities of Naphtali and carried off the inhabitants to Assyria (2 Kin. xv. 29). He overran the country east of the Jordan and deported the Reubenites, Gadites, and half tribe of Manasseh to Mesopotamia (1

Chron. v. 26). By his connivance also Pekah was eventually slain and Hoshea placed on the throne. His successor Shalmaneser besieged Samaria, the city was taken in the accession year of Sargon, 722 B. C., and a large number of the inhabitants were transported to Mesopotamia and Media (2 Kin. xvii. 5, 6), and the rest were placed under tribute. This remnant, in alliance with Hamath and Damascus, presently attempted to throw off the Assyrian yoke; but Sargon crushed the rebellion and began introducing foreigners into Samaria, a process which his successors continued until a new and heterogeneous people occupied the former territory of the ten tribes. Some of the Israelites eventually returned to Jerusalem (Luke ii. 36), but most of them remained in the countries whither they had been carried, preserving their racial distinctions, continuing their religious observances, and visiting Jerusalem from time to time (Acts ii. 9; xxvi. 7).

II. THE CAPTIVITY OF JUDAH. Sennacherib has recorded that he removed 200,000 captives from Judah (cp. 2 Kin. xviii. 13). But by the captivity of Judah is meant the deportation of the people to Babylonia. Judah's captivity was predicted a century and a half before its occurrence (Is. vi. 11, 12; xi. 12), and Babylonia as the place was foretold by Micah (iv. 10) and Isaiah (xi. 11; xxxix. 6). The prophet Jeremiah announced that it should continue seventy years (Jer. xxv. 1, 11, 12). It was effected by Nebuchadnezzar. In 605 B. C., in the third or fourth year of Jehoiakim, according to the method of reckoning which one adopts, he came unto Jerusalem, took the vessels of the temple to Babylon, and carried off certain of the seed royal as captives (2 Chron. xxxvi. 2-7; Dan. i. 1-3). Seven years later he carried off Jehoiachin, the king's mother, wives, and 3000 princes, 7000 men of might and 1000 artisans (2 Kin. xxiv. 14-16). Eleven years later his army burned the temple, destroyed Jerusalem, and carried off the residue of the people, leaving only the poorest of the land to be vinedressers and husbandmen (2 Kin. xxv. 2-21). Five years after the destruction of the city, another batch was deported to Babylonia (Jer. lii. 30). In their exile the Jews enjoyed many privileges. They were permitted to build and occupy houses, keep servants, and engage in business (Jer. xxix. 5-7; Ezra ii. 65), and there was nothing to hinder them from rising to the highest positions in the state (Dan. ii. 48; Neh. i. 11). Their priests and teachers were with them (Jer. xxix. 1; Ezra i. 5), and they had the instructions and encouragement of Ezekiel (Ezek. i. 1). In 539 B. C. Daniel understood by the books that the captivity was to last for seventy years, and, as the time was drawing to a close, began to supplicate God for the restoration of divine favor to his people (Dan. ix. 2). In 538 Cyrus issued a decree authorizing the Jews to return to the land of their

fathers and rebuild the temple (Ezra i. 1-4), when about 43,000 of them embraced the opportunity (ii. 64). Many, however, preferred to remain in Babylonia and the east, and with the Israelites in Mesopotamia and Media formed part of what became known as the Diaspora (Zech. vi. 10; Acts ii. 9). See DISPERSION.

Carbuncle.

1. The rendering of Hebrew *Bareḳeth* and Bar*e*ḳath, shining like lightning. It denotes a gem (Ezek. xxviii. 13), and was the third stone in the first row of the high priest's breastplate (Ex. xxviii. 17). In both cases the margin of the R. V., following the Septuagint, the Vulgate, and Josephus, makes it an emerald.

2. The rendering of the Hebrew '*Eḳdaḥ*, blaze, sparkle. It denotes a precious stone (Is. liv. 12).

According to Dana three distinct minerals are called by Pliny carbuncles. They are the garnet, the ruby spinel, and the sapphire. The garnet specially included under Pliny's carbuncles is the precious or Oriental garnet or almandine. It is of a fine deep transparent color; the best are from Pegu. The ruby spinel is a spinel of a clear red or reddish color, transparent or translucent. For the sapphire, see the article.

Car'cas.

One of seven chamberlains who served in the presence of king Ahasuerus (Esth. i. 10).

Car'che-mish, in A. V. once Charchemish

(2 Chron. xxxv. 20).

The eastern capital of the Hittites, west of the Euphrates, at a ford of the river, and north of the confluence with the Sajur. Admirably situated for commercial purposes, it became very wealthy. The Assyrian king, Ashurnaṣirpal (885 to 860 B. C.) was about to assault it, but was bought off by the promise of rich tribute. In 717 B. C. it was captured by Sargon, and with it fell the Hittite empire (Is. x. 9). Pharaoh-necho, king of Egypt, was heavily defeated at Carchemish by Nebuchadnezzar in 605 B. C. (2 Chron. xxxv. 20; Jer. xlvi. 2). Its site is called Jerâbîs. It is on the western bank of the Euphrates, midway between Birejik and the mouth of the Sajur, about 200 miles northwest of Circesium. An artificial mound covers ruins. The human figures on the sculptured blocks have boots with upturned tips, which is believed to settle conclusively that they are of Hittite origin.

Ca-re'ah. See KAREAH.

Ca'ri-a.

A country at the southwestern point of Asia Minor. It was part of the territory conquered by the Romans from Antiochus the Great. The Roman senate bestowed it on the Rhodians, but released it again in 168 B. C. It was still a separate district in 139 B. C. (1 Mac. xv. 23), but it was finally incorporated in the province of Asia.

Car'ites. See CHERETHITES.

Car'mel [fruitful field, garden park].

1. A range of hills, about 15 miles long, connected by a chain of lower hills with the mountainous region of central Palestine and terminating in a promontory which juts into the Mediterranean (Jer. xlvi. 18), and constitutes the southern boundary of the bay of Acre. Near its southeastern end it is 1742 feet high, a little further onward it is 1715, and it gradually falls more and more, till at the northwestern top, which constitutes the promontory, it is only 556 feet high. The range constitutes the southwestern boundary of the valley of Esdraelon, through which the Kishon runs, and at one place that brook washes the northern slope of Carmel (1 Kin. xviii. 40). The summit of the range consists of a series of eminences with table-lands on their tops, sometimes bare and rocky, and sometimes covered with shrubs, especially the prickly oak and the juniper. The strata are of limestone, and there are caves on the sides of the mountain chain, though not on its summit. The view from its higher parts is fine. It is now called Jebel Kurmul. Carmel was on the southern boundary of Asher (Josh. xix. 26), within the limits of that tribe (cp. xvii. 11). On the top of Carmel Elijah brought to a decisive issue the question between Jehovah and the worship of Baal (1 Kin. xviii. 17–40), and from the top of the same range his servant saw the ascent from the Mediterranean of the little cloud like a man's hand which heralded the rain storm and the termination of the drought (41–46). Carmel was visited by Elisha (2 Kin. ii. 25; iv. 25). It is believed to have been anciently cultivated to the summit, with fruit trees in orchards or gardens, as its name imports, and as the fruitfulness ascribed to it indicates (Is. xxxiii. 9; xxxv. 2; Jer. l. 19). A forest, probably consisting chiefly of fruit trees, was in its midst (Mic. vii. 14). When in Song vii. 5 the lover says to the object of his affection, "Thine head upon thee is like Carmel," he probably means covered with luxuriant hair, as Carmel is with fruit trees. Amos prophesied : "The top of Carmel shall wither" (i. 2). There has long been a convent on mount Carmel, after which the Carmelite monks are named.

2. A town in the mountainous part of Judah (Josh. xv. 55; cp. 1 Sam. xv. 12; xxv. 2). The churlish Nabal's possessions lay in the vicinity (1 Sam. xxv. 2–40). The name is still retained in the modern Kurmul, a ruin about 7 miles south-southeast of Hebron. From this town one of David's wives hailed (1 Sam. xxx. 5), and also one of his mighty men (2 Sam. xxiii. 35).

Car'mi [vinedresser].

1. A son of Reuben, and founder of a tribal family (Gen. xlvi. 9; Ex. vi. 14; Num. xxvi. 6).

2. A descendant of Judah and father of Achan (Josh. vii. 1; 1 Chron. ii. 6, 7).

Car'na-im. See ASHTEROTH-KARNAIM.

Car'pen-ter.

The first mention of carpentry in the Bible as a distinct occupation is on occasion of carpenters being brought from Tyre to build David a palace (2 Sam. v. 11). Among carpenter's tools were the axe, saw (Is. x. 15), measuring line, plane, compass (xliv. 13), iron nails, hammers (Jer. x. 4; 1 Chron. xxii. 3). Joseph, husband of Mary, was a carpenter (Mat. xiii. 55), and Jesus in his youth worked at the same calling (Mark vi. 3).

Car'pus [the wrist].

A resident at Troas, with whom Paul left his cloak, for which he afterwards sent (2 Tim. iv. 13).

Car'riage.

That which is carried ; baggage (1 Sam. xvii. 22; Is. x. 28; 1 Mac. ix. 35, 39; Acts xxi. 15), heavy matters or goods (Judg. xviii. 21), a burden (Is. xlvi. 1). The place of the carriage (1 Sam. xvii. 20; xxvi. 5, 7, A. V. margin) was the enclosure formed by the carts which were used to transport goods for the army, and which were drawn up in a circle around the camp. In all passages R. V. has abandoned this obsolete sense of carriage and substituted the appropriate modern word.

Car'she-na [perhaps pillage of war, spoiler].

A prince of Persia at the court of king Ahasuerus (Esth. i. 14). See PRINCE.

Cart.

A wheeled vehicle employed in peaceful occupations, and distinguished from the chariot, which was used for state and war. It was made of wood (1 Sam. vi. 14), was either covered or uncovered (Num. vii. 3, where the Hebrew word is rendered wagon), was drawn by cattle (vii. 7; 1 Sam. vi. 7; 2 Sam. vi. 6), though horses occasionally dragged the threshing cart, it would seem (Is. xxviii. 28), and was used in threshing in lieu of a sledge (Is. xxviii. 27), for transporting goods (2 Sam. vi. 3), hauling grain (Amos ii. 13), and conveying persons (Gen. xlv. 19, rendered wag-

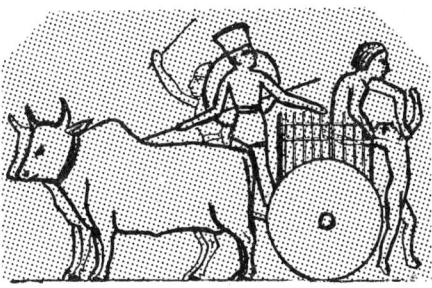

Ancient Egyptian cart.

on). In Egypt a cart was used like that which is now employed universally in western Asia, with two wheels of solid wood. Asiatic carts, including the one in which Jewish captive women of Lachish are riding on sacks of grain, are represented in Assyrian bas-reliefs as having two wheels with eight, six, or four spokes each and drawn by

Cart with women of Lachish.

oxen. They are also depicted as drawn by mules, or by two men.

Carv'ing.

The art of cutting letters, images, or ornamental designs in wood, stone, ivory, or other material. Bezaleel, a man of Judah, and Aholiab, a Danite, were gifted for this work, and wrought the carving for the tabernacle (Ex. xxxi. 1-7; xxxv. 30-35). There was carved work in Solomon's temple—flowers, palm trees, and cherubim (1 Kin. vi. 18, 29); in that of Zerubbabel (Ps. lxxiv. 6), and in the superior kind of domestic architecture (Prov. vii. 16).

Case'ment.

A sash which moves on a hinge; or part of a window, made movable by a hinge, so that it may be opened while the rest of the window remains shut (Prov. vii. 6, A. V.). But in Judg. v. 28 and in R. V. of both passages the Hebrew word is rendered lattice.

Ca-siph'i-a.

A place not far from the route between Babylon and Jerusalem, and in or near Babylonia (Ezra viii. 17).

Cas'lu-him.

A people descended from the Egyptians (or possibly only conquered and incorporated with them), and standing somewhere in the ancestral line of the Philistines (Gen. x. 14; 1 Chron. i. 12). Apparently they were the immediate ancestors of the Philistines. Perhaps they were the inhabitants of Casiotis, a district on the Mediterranean Sea extending from the eastern mouth of the Nile to Philistia.

Cas'phor.

A fortified town east of the Jordan, captured by Judas Maccabæus (1 Mac. v. 26, 36). In the latter verse A. V. gives the name as Casphon. Josephus calls it Casphoma (Antiq. xii. 8, 3).

Cas'sia.

1. The rendering of the Hebrew word Ḳiddah (Ezek. xxvii. 19). It denotes an aromatic wood, and was an ingredient of the anointing oil (Ex. xxx. 24). The translation cassia is supported by the Syriac version, the Targum, and the Vulgate. If correct, the word probably denotes a species of the wood. On the margin R. V. has costus. The *Costus* of

the ancients was discovered by Falconer to be a composite plant with purple flowers now called *Aplotaxis lappa*, growing in Cashmere from 8000 to 9000 feet above the sea level. It is exported to various countries, the valuable part being the root. The Chinese burn it in their temples for incense.

2. The rendering of the Hebrew word Ḳeṣi'ah. It is fragrant (Ps. xlv. 8). Cassia bark is derived from various species of *Cinnamomum*. See CINNAMON.

Cas'ta-net.

In the plural the rendering of the Hebrew Menaʿanʿim, moving to and fro (2 Sam. vi. 5, R. V.), a musical instrument which David and his subjects played. The margin, following the Vulgate, has sistra, and the A. V. cornets. Castanets are a pair of small spoon-shaped cymbals fastened to the thumb and beaten together by the middle finger. The word castanets is derived from *castanea*, a chestnut, two of these fruits being anciently attached to the fingers and beaten together. Castanets were employed in Greece and Rome as an accompaniment to hymns in honor of the goddess Artemis or Diana.

Cas'tle.

A fortified building or stronghold (Prov. xviii. 19). David took the Jebusite castle and converted it into his residence; and it was afterwards called the city of David (1 Chron. xi. 5, 7). Jehoshaphat built castles in the cities of Judah (2 Chron. xvii. 12; margin of A. V. palaces), and Jotham in its forests (xxvii. 4). The habitations of the descendants of Aaron (1 Chron. vi. 54), and probably those of the Ishmaelite chieftains and of the Midianites (Gen. xxv. 16; Num. xxxi. 10), were encampments (R. V.) and not castles (A. V.).

The castle which Nehemiah erected was presumably succeeded by the stronghold eventually known as Antonia, and in which Paul was confined at Jerusalem. See ANTONIA, TOWER OF.

Cas'tor and Pol'lux.

Two Greek and Roman divinities, born of the same mother, Leda, but by different fathers. Castor's father was Tyndareus, a Spartan king, while that of Pollux was Zeus, the Greek supreme god. By another account, however, Castor was also the son of Zeus. Castor was a great charioteer and horse-master, who was eventually killed in a fight. Pollux was a highly distinguished pugilist. His father Zeus offered him immortality, but he begged to be allowed to share it day and day about with the deceased Castor. The request was granted, and both brothers were worshiped, especially at Sparta, under the name of the Dioscuri, or sons of Zeus. They were regarded as the special protectors of distressed mariners. The Alexandrian vessel in which Paul sailed from Melita to Puteoli had for its sign or figurehead Dioskouroi. This the R. V. renders The Twin Brothers and the A. V., with more latitude, Castor and Pollux

(Acts xxviii. 11). The constellation Gemini (the Twins) is called after the affectionate brothers, and its two leading stars are named Castor and Pollux.

Cat'er-pil-lar.
The rendering of the Hebrew word Ḥasil, devourer. It is associated with the locust, and is a destroyer of vegetation (1 Kin. viii. 37 ; 2 Chron. vi. 28 ; Ps. lxxviii. 46 ; Is. xxxiii. 4 ; Joel i. 4 ; ii. 25). Probably a species of locust, or the common migratory locust in one stage of development (cp. Joel i. 4 ; ii. 25. margin of R. V.). For Ps. cv. 34 and Jer. li 27 of A. V., see CANKERWORM.

Cat'tle.
A comprehensive term used in the O. T. for domestic animals, large and small, for camels, horses, sheep, goats, oxen, and asses (Gen. xiii. 2 ; xxvi. 13, 14 ; xxx. 32, A. V. ; xxxi. 8, 9, 38, 41 ; xlvii. 16–18)

Cau'da. See CLAUDA.

Caul.
1. A net worn over the hair by Hebrew women (Is. iii. 18) ; rendered networks on the margin of both the R. V. and the A. V.
2. The lesser omentum, a layer of the inner lining of the cavity of the belly, partly enveloping the liver, as the greater omentum does the stomach (Ex. xxix. 13, 22 ; Lev. iii. 4, 10, 15).

Cave.
A hollow place or cavern in the side of a hill or in any similar situation. Caves tend to occur in all cliffs which are now or have at any former time been washed by sea waves ; they are, however, most numerous and largest in limestone countries, of which Palestine is one. Caves served as dwellings for the aborigines of mount Seir, as the name Horite indicates (Gen. xxxvi. 20). Even in later times they were used as temporary abodes, as by Lot and his daughters after the destruction of Sodom (xix. 30), and by Elijah 1 Kin. xix. 9). They often served as stables for cattle. They were natural tombs, and were constantly employed for burial purposes ; for example, the cave of Machpelah (Gen. xxiii. 1–20 ; xlix. 29) and the tomb of Lazarus (John xi. 38). In times of war and oppression they afforded a place of refuge (Judg. vi. 2 ; 1 Sam. xiii. 6 ; xxiv. 3–10 ; 1 Mac. i. 53 ; 2 Mac. vi. 11), the most noted being the caves at Makkedah (Josh. x. 16–27) and Adullam (1 Sam. xxii. 1 : 2 Sam. xxiii. 13).

Ce'dar.
A famous tree of Lebanon (1 Kin. v. 6), tall and stately (Is. ii. 13 ; Ezek. xvii. 22 ; xxxi. 3). It furnished a timber much prized in the construction of palaces and temples (2 Sam. v. 11 ; 1 Kin. v. 5, 6 ; vii. 1–12 ; Ezra iii. 7). From it pillars, beams, and planks were cut (1 Kin. vi. 9, 10, 18 ; vii. 2, 7) ; idols were hewn (Is. xliv. 14) ; masts were made for ships (Ezek. xxvii. 5). It is fragrant (Song iv. 11 ; Hos. xiv. 7), and it was used in ceremonial purifications (Lev. xiv. 4 ; Num.

xix. 6). The tree is evidently tne Cedar of Lebanon (Abies cedrus or Cedrus libani), is called 'erez in Hebrew, and bears the same name in Arabic, namely 'arz. It is a large tree of dome-shaped form, with long, spreading, contorted branches, evergreen leaves, and cones 3 to 5 inches long. It is wild on mount Taurus as well as in Lebanon. The little grove of trees on the latter range generally visited by travelers was long believed to be the only one ; but others have now been discovered on the back of the mountain. It is doubtful whether the Deodar of the Himalaya mountains is really a distinct species.

Ce'dron. See KIDRON.

Cel-o-syr'i-a. See CŒLESYRIA.

Cen'chre-æ, in A. V. Cenchrea [millet].
The eastern of the two ports of Corinth, that which gave access to the Archipelago. It was about 9 miles from the city. It was visited by Paul (Acts xviii. 18) ; and it possessed a Christian church, of which Phebe was a servant or deaconess (Rom. xvi. 1). The village of Kikries marks the site and preserves the old name a little changed.

Cen-de-bæ'us, in A. V. Cendebeus.
A general placed in command of the seacoast of Judæa by Antiochus VII. (1 Mac. xv. 38). He was routed by Judas and John, sons of Simon Maccabæus (xvi. 1–10).

Cen'ser.
A vessel for holding incense whilst it is being burned (Num. xvi. 6, 7, 39). The censers of the tabernacle were of brass (Lev. xvi. 12 ; cp. Ex. xxvii. 3, firepans) ; those of the temple were of gold (1 Kin. vii. 50 ; 2 Chron. iv. 22 ; Heb. ix. 4). The censers of the book of Revelation (viii. 3, 5) were also of gold.

Cen'sus.
An enumeration and registration of a people, conveniently made among the Hebrews according to tribe, family, and house (Num. i. 18), and in the wilderness probably based on the reports of the officers over thousands, hundreds, fifties, and tens (Ex. xviii. 25 ; cp. round numbers, Num. i. 21, 23, etc.). Besides enumerations of classes of the people, like that of the firstborn (Num. iii. 43), a formal census of all the Israelites of military age is recorded in the O. T. as having been taken on three different occasions. The first was taken at mount Sinai in the second month of the second year after they had left Egypt (Num. i). Omitting the Levites (47–54), there were of males above 20 years of age, and capable of bearing arms, 603,550 (45–47 ; xi. 21). The records of those who had recently paid tribute were probably used in making up the lists (Ex. xxxviii. 26). The Levites from one month old and upward were counted separately, and numbered 22,000 (Num. iii. 39). The second census was taken 38 years later at the camp at Shittim in the Moabite country at the close of the forty years' wandering. The number of men had altered but slightly

and now was 601,730 (Num. xxvi. 1-51). Levites 23,000 (xxvi. 62). The third census was
made by order of David, who found that there
were of fighting men in Israel 800,000, in
Judah 500,000 (2 Sam. xxiv. 1-9; cp. 1 Chron.
xxi. 1-6). About the same time the Levites,
from 30 years old and upward, numbered
38,000 (1 Chron. xxiii. 3). An enumeration
was made of the exiles who returned to Jerusalem from Babylonia with Zerubbabel (Ezra
ii.), and an enrollment was ordered by the
emperor Augustus for the Roman empire
shortly before the birth of Christ (Luke ii. 1;
see QUIRINIUS and THOUSAND).

Cen-tu′ri-on [from Latin *centum*, one hun-
dred].

An officer in the Roman army (Acts xxi.
32; xxii. 26), who at first commanded 100
soldiers and afterwards about that number
(cp. xxiii. 23). Two are mentioned by name
in the N. T.: Cornelius, stationed at Cæsarea,
through whom it was made evident that the

Roman centurion.

Holy Spirit is given to gentile believers not
less than to Jewish (Acts x.), and Julius, who

conducted Paul and other prisoners to Rome
and treated Paul kindly (Acts xxvii. 1, 3,
43). Two centurions, besides Cornelius, believed—one at Capernaum (Mat. viii. 5-13),
the other at the cross (xxvii. 54).

Ce′phas [Aramaic, rock or stone].

An appellation given by Jesus to the apostle Simon (John i. 42; 1 Cor. i. 12; iii. 22; ix.
5; xv. 5; Gal. ii. 9); from it his best-known
name Peter, which is the Greek equivalent of
Cephas, arose.

Chal-ced′o-ny [from *Chalkēdōn, Kalkēdōn*,
a town in Asia Minor where the mineral was
found].

A precious stone, the third foundation of the
wall of the New Jerusalem (Rev. xxi. 19). Chalcedony used to be regarded as a distinct species
of siliceous (flinty) mineral, but is now reduced
to a variety of the species quartz. It is hard,
its largest ingredient being silica. It is of a
waxy luster, and therefore much duller than
typical quartz. It is white-gray, brown, blue,
etc. It is not perfectly crystallized,
but often coats crystals of quartz. It
occurs massive, in veins, in nodules
of botryoidal form (*i. e.* resembling a
cluster of grapes), or in stalactites.
This stone, however, did not receive
the name chalcedony, it is believed,
until the Middle Ages, so that John,
it would seem, had a different stone
of Chalcedon in mind, perhaps the
Chalcedonian emerald or the Chalcedonian jasper which are mentioned
by Pliny (37, 18 and 37).

Chal′col. See CALCOL.

Chal-de′a [akin to Hebrew *Kasdim*, and perhaps meaning land of the
conquerors or of the Cushlanders].

Originally the southern portion of
Babylonia, at the head of the Persian
Gulf, but the designation was ultimately extended to the whole of the
alluvial plain stretching from above
Hit to the gulf. In the southern portion were situated Ur and Erech; in
the northern part Babylon, Cutha,
Sippara. There were other cities in
the country which are not mentioned
in the Scriptures or are not identified.

There is no evidence that the term
Chaldea included the plateau to the
north, in whole or in part. The
theory that it did is ultimately based
on the identification of the river
Chebar, which was in the land of the
Chaldeans (Ezek. i. 3), with the river
of Mesopotamia called by the Greeks
Chaboras. But this identification cannot be maintained; for the Hebrews
distinguished the two rivers by names
radically different, Kᵉbar and Habor.
Again, the presence of people called Chaldeans in the mountains of Kurdistan during the retreat of the ten thousand under

Xenophon (Anabasis iv. 3, 4, etc.), and of others in Pontus mentioned by Strabo (549) has been urged as proof that the primitive home of the Chaldeans was in Armenia. That theory seems now to be abandoned; partly doubtless because, although the Kurdish mountains and adjacent country were repeatedly traversed by the armies of Assyria during a period of seven hundred years, beginning in the fourteenth century B. C.. and the geographical notices in the records of these military expeditions are full and minute, yet there is no report of the Assyrians having found a people or country called Kaldu in all that region. If the people called Chaldeans by the classical writers referred to are properly named, and have any connection with the Chaldeans of the south, they are late immigrants, relics perhaps of the imperial army of Babylonia, rather than the original stock.

Chal-de'an, in N. T. Chaldæan.
A native or inhabitant of Chaldea. Chaldeans early entered Babylonia. By the 9th century B. C. they were firmly established on the shores of the Persian gulf, with Bit-yakin for their capital. Under Merodach-baladan they conquered Babylonia, but he was finally crushed by Sennacherib, king of Assyria. In 625 B. C. a Chaldean, Nabopolassar, founded the new Babylonian empire. The Chaldeans were now the dominant race, and doubtless possessed themselves of all offices of influence. So exclusively did they fill ecclesiastical positions at the capital that at Babylon their name became synonymous with priests of Bel-marduk (Herod. i. 181, 183). These priests were esteemed as possessors of wisdom (Dan. i. 4; ii. 2, 4).

Chal-dees'.
A variant form of Chaldeans used in the expression Ur of the Chaldees (Gen. xi. 31; Neh. ix. 7), and also sometimes in A. V. when there is no mention of Ur (2 Kin. xxiv. 2; xxv. 4-26; 2 Chron. xxxvi. 17; Is. xiii. 19).

Chalk'stone.
A stone taken from the limestone rocks which constitute a marked feature of Palestine (Is. xxvii. 9).

Chal'phi, in A. V. Calphi.
Father of Judas, one of the two captains who stood by Jonathan Maccabæus at Hazor (1 Mac. xi. 70).

Cham'ber-lain.
One who looks after the private chambers of a palace or mansion; as Blastus, who was over Herod's bedchamber (Acts xii. 20); or one who has charge of the treasure chamber, as Erastus, the treasurer of the city of Corinth (Rom. xvi. 23, A. V.; in R. V. treasurer). In the O. T. the word rendered chamberlain signifies eunuch, and is often translated so; see EUNUCH.

Cha-me'le-on [the ground lion].
A reptile which belongs to the same order as lizards, but, according to the present classi-

fication, not to the same group. The name is found in Lev. xi. 30. In R. V. it is the rendering of the Hebrew *Tinshemeth*, breathing, inflation (in A. V. mole), whereas in A. V. it represents the Hebrew word *Koah* (in R. V. land crocodile; see LIZARD). The lungs of the lizard are very large and, when expanded, render it semi-transparent. Its eyeballs protrude from the head, and are independent in their action, so that it can turn one eye up and the other down, or look in different directions and at different objects at the same time. It has also the faculty of changing its hue in accordance with the color of the objects about it or with its temper when disturbed. This power is due to the presence of clear or pigment-bearing cells in the skin, their contractions and dilatations being controlled by the nervous system. It lives in trees. Its feet are fitted for use as hands and its tail is prehensile, so that it is able to cling to the branches. It feeds upon insects which it captures by means of its long tongue covered at the end with a viscous substance.

Cham'ois.
The rendering of the Hebrew *Zemer*, leaper. The animal is ruminant. (Deut. xiv. 5). It is not the real chamois, which is a native of the European mountains from the Pyrenees to the Caucasus, but does not occur in Palestine.

Cham-paign' [open country] (Deut. xi. 30, A. V.). See ARABAH.

Cha'naan. See CANAAN.

Cha-phen'a-tha, in A. V. Caphenatha.
Apparently a portion of the eastern wall of Jerusalem, perhaps one of the towers or other mural fortifications (1 Mac. xii. 37), and possibly even the tower that stood out from the upper house of the king (Neh. iii. 25).

Chap'i-ter.
The capital, *i. e.* the head or uppermost part of a column, pillar, or pilaster (1 Kin. vii. 16). It can be varied in form and ornamentation, according to the order of architecture used in the building (Ex. xxxvi. 38; xxxviii. 17, 19; 1 Kin. vii. 19, 20).

Chap'man.
Originally a merchant; then a mere pedlar (2 Chron. ix. 14).

Char'a-shim [craftsmen], in R. V. Ge-har-ashim [valley of craftsmen].
A valley in Judah (1 Chron. iv. 14), inhabited after the exile by the tribe of Benjamin (Neh. xi. 35). Conder suggests the ruin Hirsha as an echo of the name, on the slope of a wady 1¾ miles southeast of Aijalon and 11 miles west-northwest of Jerusalem.

Char'che-mish. See CARCHEMISH.

Char'ger.
A large dish or platter. The name is appropriately used in the English version for the dish on which the head of John the Bap-

tist was brought to Herodias' daughter (Mat. xiv. 8), and for the silver dishes of 130 shekels' weight presented by the tribal princes at the dedication of the altar (Num. vii. 13). The Hebrew word rendered charger in the last passage denotes the golden dishes which stood on the table of showbread (Ex. xxvi. 29; Num. iv. 7).

Char'i-ot.

A two-wheeled vehicle, of various forms, drawn by horses (2 Sam. viii. 4), and used for military (Ex. xiv. 9; 1 Sam. xiii. 5), state (Gen. xli. 43; 2 Sam. xv. 1; 1 Kin. i. 5), and private purposes (Gen. xlvi. 29; 2 Kin. v. 9; Acts viii. 28). The bed was open behind, and rested on the axle without springs. The wheels were not clumsy, but consisted of felloes, spokes, and naves, and were often of metal (1 Kin. vii. 33). Chariots were but poorly adapted to the hills of Palestine, and were not much used, but they were common among the Canaanites in the valley (Josh. xvii. 16; Judg. iv. 3), and among the Egyptians (Is. xxxi. 1), Ethiopians (2 Chron. xvi. 8), Syrians (2 Kin. v. 9), Hittites (2 Kin. vii.

Royal Assyrian chariot.

6), and Assyrians (Nah. ii. 3, 4; iii. 2). The war chariots commonly carried a driver (2 Chron. xviii. 33), and occasionally a shield-bearer, besides the warrior himself. Probably among the Hebrews a third person, perhaps shieldbearer, sometimes occupied the chariot (2 Kin. ix. 25). The war chariot was at times constructed of iron or covered with iron plates (Josh. xvii. 16, 18; Judg. i. 19; iv. 3). The Persians armed the axles and sometimes the tongue with scythes. Cruel chariots of this sort were seen in Palestine in the Seleucidan period (2 Mac. xiii. 2). A four-wheeled vehicle may be intended in Rev. xviii. 13. See additional illustration under Bow.

Char'i-ty.

Love, often manifested by almsgiving. The charity described in 1 Cor. xiii. is not almsgiving, as is evident from ver. 3; it is love, charity in the broad sense, love toward all. It is so rendered by the R. V.

Char'ran. See HARAN.

Che'bar.

A river in the land of the Chaldeans, on the banks of which some of the Jewish exiles, including the prophet Ezekiel, were settled. It was there that the prophet saw several of his visions (Ezek. i. 1, 3; iii. 15, 23; x. 15, 20). It is not the river called by the Greeks Chaboras, which rises near Nisibis in upper Mesopotamia, and falls into the Euphrates at Circesium, for the Hebrew name of this river was Habor. The Chebar was a great canal, southeast of Babylon. These streams were known by the name nâr, river.

Ched-or-la'o-mer [Elamite, servant of the god Lagamar].

A king of Elam, who evidently held the sovereignty over Babylonia. In the days of Abraham, in alliance with Amraphel, king of Shinar, Arioch, king of Ellasar, and Tidal, king of Goiim, he made an expedition to the west and subjugated the country about the Dead Sea. The people of the plain served him twelve years and then revolted. The next year Chedorlaomer came with his allies and smote the region east of the Jordan from Bashan southward, the land of Edom to the head of the Red Sea, the country afterwards inhabited by the Amalekites, and the plain about the Dead Sea. This conquest gave him control of the caravan routes from Arabia past the head of the Red Sea to Egypt, Canaan, and the north. But he carried off Lot from Sodom. This induced Abraham to lead his numerous servants and his allied chieftains to the pursuit. They fell upon Chedorlaomer by night at Dan, put him and his followers to flight, and recovered the captives and the spoil (Gen. xiv. 1–16). It was not strange, even in those early days, for a Babylonian monarch to make an expedition to the countries on the Mediterranean sea. Long before the time of Abraham great kings, such as Lugal-zaggisi, Sargon, Gudea, had extended their conquests to the western sea or drawn supplies from that region.

Kudurmabug, the overlord of Babylonia, was an Elamite, and Eriaku, king of Larsa, was his son. Chedorlaomer's name, in its native form Kudurlagamar, proves that he was an Elamite, and his association with Arioch and the extent of his sway, strongly indicate that he was a member of this dynasty and a successor of Kudurmabug.

Cheese.

The curd of milk, coagulated, separated from the whey, and pressed (Job x. 10; cp. 1 Sam. xvii. 18; 2 Sam. xvii. 29). A valley at Jerusalem bore the name Tyropœon (War v. 4, 1), which in Greek means cheesemakers.

Che'lal [consummation, completion].

A son of Pahath-moab, whom Ezra induced to divorce his foreign wife (Ezra x. 30).

Che'lub [wicker basket; bird's cage].

1. A brother of Shuah, whose lineage is not traced, but who was entitled to registry in the tribe of Judah (1 Chron. iv. 11).

2. The father of David's officer over the cultivators (1 Chron. xxvii. 26).

Che-lu'bai. See CALEB 1.

Chel'u-hi, in A. V. **Chel'luh.**
A son of Bani, whom Ezra induced to divorce his foreign wife (Ezra x. 35).

Chem'a-rim, in text of A. V. **Chemarims.**
Priests of the high places (2 Kin. xxiii. 5, margin), of the calves at Bethel (Hos. x. 5, margin), and of Baal (Zeph. i. 4).

Che'mosh [probably subduer].
The god of the Moabites (Num. xxi. 29; Jer. xlviii. 46; Moabite Stone 3), worshiped in the same manner as was Molech, by the sacrifice of children as burnt offerings (2 Kin. iii. 27). His identity with Molech appears further from Judg. xi. 24, where the god of the Ammonites, who was Molech (1 Kin. xi. 7), is called Chemosh. Solomon erected a high place for him near Jerusalem (1 Kin. xi. 7), which was afterwards defiled by Josiah (2 Kin. xxiii. 13).

Che-na'a-nah [feminine of Canaan].
1. A Benjamite, family of Jediael (1 Chron. vii. 10).
2. The father of the false prophet Zedekiah who deluded Ahab (1 Kin. xxii. 11; 2 Chron. xviii. 10).

Chen'a-ni [firm].
A Levite who assisted in bringing the returned exiles to such a frame of mind that they agreed to enter into a covenant to worship Jehovah (Neh. ix. 4).

Chen-a-ni'ah [Jehovah is firm].
A chief of the Levites in David's reign, of the house of Izhar, who was appointed superintendent of the outward business, such as judging (1 Chron. xxvi. 29), and the transportation of the ark (xv. 22, 27, margin; in text, song).

Che-phar-am'mo-ni, in A. V. **Che-phar-ha-am'mo-nai** [village of the Ammonite].
A village of Benjamin (Josh. xviii. 24). Site unknown.

Che-phi'rah [village].
A city of the Gibeonites (Josh. ix. 17), allotted to the Benjamites (xviii. 26). It continued to exist after the captivity (Ezra ii. 25; Neh. vii. 29). Its site is the ruin Kefîreh, 8 miles west-northwest of Jerusalem.

Che'ran [possibly cither or lute].
A Horite, a son of Dishon (Gen. xxxvi. 26; 1 Chron. i. 41).

Cher'eth-ites, in A. V. once **Cherethims** [probably Cretans].
A nation or tribe inhabiting the Philistine country or its southern portion (1 Sam. xxx. 14; Ezek. xxv. 16; Zeph. ii. 5, 6). They may be identical with the Philistines who came from Caphtor (q. v.), or may represent a direct emigration from Crete. Some of them were members of David's bodyguard (2 Sam. viii. 18 with xxiii. 23; xv. 18). In three places the name Carite appears in their stead (2 Sam. xx. 23; 2 Kin. xi. 4, 19, both R. V.). It has been suggested that this name preserves the memory of Carian inhabitants of Crete, alluded to by classical writers.

Che'rith [cut, gorge].
A brook before Jordan, by which Elijah sojourned (1 Kin. xvii. 3, 5). Whether east or west of the Jordan is uncertain.

Cher'ub, plural **Cher'u-bim;** in A. V. **Cherubims.**
1. Guardians placed east of the garden of Eden to prevent the approach of our first parents to the tree of life after their expulsion from the garden (Gen. iii. 24). When the ark was constructed for the tabernacle, cherubim wrought of gold were placed facing each other, one at each side of the mercy seat, overshadowing it with their wings (Ex. xxv. 18–20; xxxvii. 7–9). They symbolized the presence and unapproachability of Jehovah, whose glory was manifested between them (Lev. xvi. 2), who thus dwelt in the midst of his people, and was present in the tabernacle to receive worship (Ex. xxv. 22; Lev. i. 1). Frequent reference is made to Jehovah dwelling between the cherubim (Num. vii. 89; 1 Sam. iv. 4; 2 Sam. vi. 2; 2 Kin. xix. 15; Ps. lxxx. 1; xcix. 1; Is. xxxvii. 16). Cherubim were also embroidered on the hangings of the tabernacle (Ex. xxvi. 1). For the grander temple Solomon had two gigantic cherubs made. The height was ten cubits, or about fifteen feet, and the expansion of their wings as many more. They were of olive wood, and were overlaid with gold (1 Kin. vi. 23–28; viii. 7; 2 Chron. iii. 10–13; v. 7, 8; Heb. ix. 5). Cherubs, with palm trees and open flowers, were also carved all round the walls of the temple (1 Kin. vi. 29). In a poem David represented Jehovah as riding upon a cherub and flying (2 Sam. xxii. 11; Ps. xviii. 10). Ezekiel had a vision of cherubs by the river Chebar. Each had four faces and four wings (Ezek. x. 1–22; cp. ix. 3), and since they seem to be identical with the four living creatures previously seen by the prophet, these four faces were those of a man, a lion, an ox, and an eagle (cp. i. 5–12 with x. 20, 21). They carried the throne of Jehovah (i. 26–28; ix. 3). Finally the apostle John in the apocalypse describes four living creatures, who had faces like those of the same four animals (Rev. iv. 6 9).

It is possible, though not yet proven, that the Assyrians had acquaintance with the same idea. Their winged, man-headed bulls have a certain external physical resemblance to cherubim as sometimes described in the Hebrew Scriptures; and they performed the same function, being placed at the entrance of palaces and temples where majesty dwelt. It is especially premature, however, to assert that the bulls of Assyria bore a name similar to that of the Hebrew cherubim.

The varying forms assumed by the cherubim

in art and poetic imagery show that they were symbols. But symbols of what? The flaming sword (Gen. iii. 24). and the darkness under Him who did ride upon a cherub and flew upon the wings of the wind (Ps. xviii. 10), have been cited as the main support of the theory that the cherub is in ultimate analysis the storm cloud. It is true that the cherubim might represent some power of nature, or all the powers of nature, as the servants of Jehovah and guardians of his abode. But the biblical writers represent the cherubim, symbolically at least, as animate beings with the intelligence of man, the strength of the ox, the courage of the lion, and the free motion of the eagle through the air. The facts at present obtainable indicate an order of. angels.

2. A place in Babylonia, from which certain persons came who could not prove their Israelite descent (Ezra ii. 59; Neh. vii. 61). Situation unknown. Pronounced *ke'rub*.

Ches′a-lon [trust, hope].
A town on the boundary line of Judah, on mount Jearim (Josh. xv. 10), commonly identified with the village of Kesla, 10 miles west of Jerusalem.

Che′sed [perhaps the noun from which *Kasdim*, Chaldeans, is derived].
A son of Nahor by his wife Milcah (Gen. xxii. 22).

Che′sil [a fool].
A village in the most southerly region of Judah (Josh. xv. 30); apparently called also Bethul and Bethuel.

Chest′nut. See PLANE.

Che-sul′loth [trusts, or perhaps the loins or slopes].
A town on the boundary line of Issachar (Josh. xix. 18), probably the same as Chislothtabor (q. v.).

Cheth, in R. V. **Heth and Hheth.**
The eighth letter of the Hebrew alphabet. English H, which developed out of the same original, and Ch, though neither is pronounced with the guttural sound of cheth, represent it in anglicized Hebrew names, as Haran, Chezib. It stands at the beginning of the eighth section of Ps. cxix. in several versions, in which section each verse begins with this letter.

Che′zib. See ACHZIB.

Chi′don [a javelin].
A name for the threshing floor at which Uzza was struck dead for touching the ark (1 Chron. xiii. 9). In 2 Sam. vi. 6 called Nachon. The difference of name has not been satisfactorily explained. Exact site unknown.

Chil′e-ab.
David's second son (2 Sam. iii. 3; where the Greek gives his name as Daluia[h], born at Hebron. His mother was Abigail. In 1 Chron. iii. 1 he is called Daniel.

Chil′i-on [a wasting away].
The younger son of Elimelech and Naomi (Ruth i. 2, 5).

Chil′mad.
A place which traded with Tyre, mentioned in connection with Sheba and Asshur (Ezek. xxvii. 23).

Chim′ham [longing].
The son of Barzillai the Gileadite. When the father was invited by David to Jerusalem, and declined the honor on account of his advanced age, Chimham was sent in his place (2 Sam. xix. 37, 38). He seems to have settled in the vicinity of Bethlehem and erected a caravansary (Jer. xli. 17).

Chin′ne-reth and **Chinneroth**, in A. V. once **Cinneroth** (1 Kin. xv. 20) [lute, harp].
1. A fortified city of Naphtali (Josh. xix. 35; Deut. iii. 17; and Thothmes' list).
2. The region around the city of Chinnereth (1 Kin. xv. 20; cp. also Josh. xi. 2), commonly identified with the plain of Gennesaret (Mat. xiv. 34).
3. The sheet of water adjacent to the fortified city and region of Chinnereth (Num. xxxiv. 11: Josh. xii. 3; xiii. 27; 1 Kin. xv. 20). In later times known as the lake of Gennesaret (Luke v. 1) and sea of Galilee or Tiberias (John vi. 1).

Chi′os.
An island, now called Scio or Chio, in the Greek Archipelago, at the entrance of the Gulf of Smyrna. It has Lesbos on the north and Samos on the south. It is about 32 miles long from north to south, 18 broad from east to west, and has an area of about 400 square miles. Paul's vessel passed it on his last voyage to Palestine (Acts xx. 15).

Chis′lev, in A. V. **Chisleu.**
The ninth month of the Hebrew year (Neh. i. 1; Zech. vii. 1; 1 Mac. i. 54). See YEAR.

Chis′lon [trust, hope].
Father of the prince of Benjamin in the time of Moses (Num. xxxiv. 21).

Chis′loth-ta′bor [the flanks of Tabor or the trust of Tabor].
A locality hard by mount Tabor, and a landmark on the boundary of Zebulun (Josh. xix. 12); probably the same as Chesulloth, a town on the border of Issachar (ver. 18). The two names are radically identical; they differ merely in the vocalization, and this difference of pronunciation is not supported by the Septuagint. Eusebius mentions a village Chasalus in the plain near mount Tabor. The place is commonly identified with the modern village of Iksâl or Ksâl, which stands on a low, rocky eminence west of Tabor.

Chith′lish, in A. V. **Kithlish.**
A village in the lowland of Judah (Josh. xv. 40).

Chit′tim. See KITTIM.

Chi'un.

A word occurring but once in the Hebrew Bible (Amos v. 26). It may denote the planet Saturn, known to the Syrians as Kewan or Kaivan, and which was looked upon as unpropitious. The A. R. V. translates it shrine.

Chlo'e [the first shoot of green grass].

A Christian woman, apparently of Corinth (1 Cor. i. 11).

Chor-a'shan. See ASHAN.

Cho-ra'zin.

A town mentioned along with Bethsaida and Capernaum, and probably, like them, near the sea of Galilee. Like the two other places, Chorazin had at times been the scene of the Saviour's preaching and beneficent miracles; but it failed to turn its spiritual privileges to account, and was doomed to suffer the penalty of its neglect (Mat. xi. 21; Luke x. 13). Eusebius, in the fourth century, said that it was 2 Roman miles from Capernaum. In 1842 the Rev. G. Williams believed that he had found it at Kerâzeh, about 2½ miles north of Tell Hum. The identification is now generally accepted. It is a little inland, in a side valley branching off from another one which goes down to the lake. The spot is marked by extensive ruins, including a synagogue.

Cho-ze'ba. See COZEBA.

Christ [Greek, anointed].

The Anointed One, a title corresponding to the Hebrew name Messiah, which denoted the anointed king of Israel, and, after Saul's reign, the royal son of David. The term was borrowed from the Septuagint, specially from Ps. ii. 2; Dan. ix. 25. When used in the N. T. it generally has the word *the* prefixed, and means the Messiah of O. T. prophecy (Mat. xvi. 16, 20; xxvi. 63; Mark viii. 29; Luke iii. 15; John i. 41). Sometimes *the* is omitted (Mat. xxvi. 68; John iv. 25).

Christ, though really used in the primary sense, is so constantly appended to Jesus, the distinctive personal name of our Lord, given from his birth, as virtually to constitute part of the proper name (John i. 17; Acts xi. 17; Rom. i. 1; v. 1; Philemon 1, etc.).

Chris'tian.

A follower of the Lord Jesus Christ. The name was first given at Antioch, about A. D. 43, and apparently by foes rather than friends (Acts xi. 26). Though destined ultimately to become universal, yet it took root so slowly that it is found only twice again in the N. T., once in the mouth of Agrippa II., when Paul preached repentance and remission of sins through Jesus and testified to the resurrection of Christ (Acts xxvi. 18, 23, 28), and once in a letter from Peter to comfort the faithful whose adherence to Christ brought persecution upon them (1 Pet. iv. 16).

Chronicles, Books of the.

Two historical books of the O. T. They are evidently the work of a single author, for they have unity of plan and purpose, and

Four Christian symbols are depicted here. The dove, the best known symbol for the Holy Spirit, is derived from the Gospel accounts of the baptism of Jesus. The Chi-Rho is the oldest monogram for Jesus Christ, formed by placing the Greek letters X (chi) and P (rho) together. These are the first two letters in the Greek word for Christ. The fish symbol was first a code used by Christians to avoid persecution and arrest. The Greek letters inside the fish are the first letters of the five Greek words which mean "Jesus Christ, Son of God, Saviour." The cross is the chief symbol of the church. More than fifty forms of the cross are used in Christian art.

are incomplete if one is sundered from the other. In fact they actually formed one book in the old Hebrew canon. The Septuagint translators divided them into two, and this division was finally admitted into printed editions of the Hebrew canon. The Hebrew name of the books is " Acts of the Days," i. e. of the Times. The Septuagint calls them *Paraleipomena*, or things left over. The title is unfortunate, since it incorrectly implies that the book was intended as a supplement, whereas it has an independent aim. The name Chronicles is derived from the title *Chronicon* applied to these writings by Jerome, who describes them as "a chronicle of the whole of sacred history."

The work naturally divides itself into two parts: 1. The genealogies, especially of Judah, Benjamin, and Levi, from the creation to the return from the Babylonian exile (1 Chron. i.-viii.), with a register of those who, probably before the exile, dwelt in Jerusalem (ix. 1-34). The transition to part second is afforded by means of the genealogy and death of Saul and Jonathan (ix. 35-x. 14). 2. History of the Israelites, more especially of Judah, from the accession of David to the return from the Babylonian exile (xi.-2 Chron. xxxvi.).

The abrupt conclusion of the work, and the identity of its closing verses with the opening verses of Ezra, have been thought to indicate that Chronicles and Ezra were originally one continuous history. But these verses are a quotation either in both Chronicles and Ezra from the same state document, or, more probably, in one book from the other. The books themselves never constituted one work. They are entirely different in plan, and ancient tradition never reckoned them as one. They may, however, have had one and the same author.

The first datum which bears on the question as to when the work was composed is found in the genealogies. The line of David is brought down to a date later than any other. The grandchildren of Zerubbabel are mentioned (1 Chron. iii. 19-21), consequently the work cannot have been composed a great while before the time of Ezra. It is, however, frequently affirmed that yet later descendants of Zerubbabel are registered, even the sixth generation after him (21-24). But there is not the shadow of proof that the families enumerated in verse 21, latter part, were descendants of Hananiah, son of Zerubbabel. Their descent and that of Shecaniah, whose posterity is given at considerable length (21-24), are not indicated. The phenomenon of unattached families is of common occurrence in these genealogies, and, when the text is not at fault, indicates that the family thus loosely catalogued belonged to the clan or tribe with which it is registered, though its connection is not traced. The four families enumerated in verse 21 belonged to the lineage of David, and were collateral with the royal line which descended through Hananiah, son of Zerubbabel. The other indications likewise point to the time of Ezra. The amount contributed toward the erection of the temple is stated in Persian coins, not in Greek (1 Chron. xxix. 7, R. V., darics), which indicates that the Greek empire had not supplanted the Persian when the work was composed. The designation of the temple as "the Birah," the castle or the palace (1 Chron. xxix. 1, 19), indicates a time not later than Nehemiah; for after his time "the Birah" denoted not the temple, but a structure erected by him (Neh. ii. 8, vii. 2, both R. V.), which came to be distinguished from the temple and all other buildings as the castle; · see ANTONIA, TOWER OF.

Ancient opinion was that Chronicles was written by Ezra. This tradition cannot be proved, and it is not vital that it should be. But there is no valid objection to it; and it is strengthened by peculiarities of language common to Chronicles and Ezra. These peculiarities have led most modern critics, even when influenced by the unwarranted interpretation of the genealogy in iii. 19-24 to assign a late date to Chronicles, nevertheless to hold that the two books in their present form are from the same hand.

Chronicles stands among the Hagiographa, the last division of the Hebrew canon, and not among "the prophets." This is evidence that the author was not a prophet; see CANON. The Masorites, followed as a rule by Spanish manuscripts, placed Chronicles first in order among the Hagiographa and immediately before the Psalms. In the printed editions of the Hebrew Bible, and in German and French manuscripts, it follows Ezra-Nehemiah, and is the last book in the division. This position it probably occupied at the time of Christ, for Zechariah is cited as the last [named] prophet who suffered a violent death (Mat. xxiii. 35; Luke xi. 51; cp. 2 Chron. xxiv. 20-22).

For the book of the chronicles of the kings of Israel, see KINGS, BOOKS OF THE.

Chro-nol'o-gy.

The nations of antiquity did not have a uniform system of chronology; nor did they entertain the same notions and feel the same need of an exact and unvarying chronological method as does the modern world. The Assyrians and Babylonians appear to have been confident of their ability to date events of remote antiquity; but, so far as known, they did not have an era serving as a fixed standard from which to reckon all occurrences, but named each year after a public official, and kept a list of these annual eponyms. An event having been dated by the eponymy in which it happened, its remoteness was readily ascertained by counting on the list or canon the number of eponyms that had intervened. In Babylonia, Assyria, Palestine, and Egypt, documents were frequently dated by the regnal year of the reigning monarch. Unfortunately the scribes did not always reckon uniformly; but under the same king some regarded the accession year as the first regnal year, while others considered the civil twelvemonth which followed the accession as the first year of the reign. Furthermore, a son was not infrequently associated with his father on the throne, and some scribes treated the first year of association with the father, and others the first year of sole reign, as the first regnal year. The deficient sense of chronology, estimated by modern conceptions, is seen in the fact that Josephus determines the duration of the kingdom of Israel by simply adding together the number of years that each king ruled, regardless of the fact that the reigns regularly overlapped one year, since the death of a king and the accession of his successor fell in the same year, and this year was apt to be reckoned to both reigns. Pursuing this method, he states that the kingdom of Israel lasted 240 years, 7 months, and 7 days (Antiq. ix. 14, 1); yet by other calculations, which he makes on the basis of the reigns of the kings of Judah, he implies that the period was 263 years (e. g. Antiq. x. 8, 5 with viii. 7, 8 and x. 9, 7). The same lack of a nice chronological sense appears in the fact that Josephus estimates the number of years that elapsed from the exodus to the founding of the temple at 592 (Antiq. viii. 3, 1), at other times at 612 (xx. 10; con. Apion. ii. 2), the Hebrew writer at 480 (1 Kin. vi. 1), and Paul apparently at about 574 (Acts xiii. 18–21 and 1 Kin. ii. 11; vi. 1). These diverse statements appear contradictory to the modern reader who lacks the historic sense and cannot divest himself of modern chronological conceptions; but they are accurate in the sense in which they were intended, and in which they were understood.

The era, as it is used in modern chronology, came into use at a comparatively late date. The exodus from Egypt served the Hebrews for a brief time as a point from which to reckon (Ex. xvi. 1; Num. ix. 1; x. 11; xxxiii. 38). The Romans dated all documents by the name of the consul in office, and later they added the regnal year of the emperor. Their historians began to date from the foundation of the city, A. U. C., but the custom did not arise until some centuries after the event. Varro's date for the founding of the city, 753 B. C., is generally accepted as the commencement of this era. The Greeks reckoned by periods of four years called Olympiads. The first began in 776 B. C., the year in which Corœbus was victor in the Olympic games. The Syrians used the Seleucidan era, beginning with October 312 B. C. It was used by the Jews in Maccabæan times (1 Mac. i. 10). The Mohammedans date from the Hegira, or flight of Mohammed from Mecca, in A. D. 622. The Jews use a world's

era, dating from the creation, which they place in the year 3760–61 B. C. Christian nations have adopted the birth of Christ as an era. At the beginning of the sixth century, the Roman abbot Dionysius in his Easter tables counted from the incarnation of the Lord. The abbot erred in his calculation of the date of Christ's birth, but the year which he fixed upon, A. U. C. 754, has been accepted as the commencement of the Christian era. The Christian era began, not with no year, but with a first year. Events which occurred within the civil year which included Christ's birth are dated in the first year.

Dates were placed in the margin of A. V. in 1701. They represent the chronological scheme of Usher, archbishop of Armagh, which he published in his *Annales Veteris et Novi Testamenti* in 1650–54. His work was careful and scholarly, and served a useful purpose for two centuries and a half. But it is inaccurate and obsolete. It gives only one of several possible arrangements. It is based in crucial points on Usher's private interpretation of disputed passages, in some of which he clearly erred, as has been proved in recent years. His system was worked out from the standpoint of modern chronological conceptions, and fails to do justice to the different notions which prevailed in antiquity. It was constructed without the invaluable aid of data which have been brought to light by modern research. But although Usher's system is obsolete, it cannot as yet be superseded by a complete and final scheme. A few dates are fixed, and the chronology of certain periods is established. Other dates are still under investigation or are awaiting disclosure from undiscovered ancient records. Much is tentative.

I. From the Creation of the World to the Birth of Abraham.

The data are furnished by the Hebrew records in Gen. v. 1–32; vii. 11; xi. 10–26. There are several possible methods of interpreting them, among which may be mentioned:

1. The genealogy was constructed by the ancient writers in the same manner that it would be framed by people of the present day.

Adam	having lived 130 years, begat
Seth,	who " " 105 " "
Enosh,	" " " 90 " "
Kenan,	" " " 70 " "
Mahalalel,	" " " 65 " "
Jared,	" " " 162 " "
Enoch,	" " " 65 " "
Methuselah,	" " " 187 " "
Lamech,	" " " 182 " "
Noah, in whose	600th year the flood came.
From the creation to the flood,	1656 years.

Noah	having lived 500 years, begat				
Shem,	who	"	"	100	"	"
Arpachshad	"	"	"	35	"	"
Shelah,	"	"	"	30	"	..
Eber,	"	"	"	34	"	"
Peleg,	"	"	"	30	"	"
Reu,	"	"	"	32	"	"
Serug,	"	"	"	30	"	"
Nahor,	"	"	"	29	"	"
Terah,	"	"	"	70	"	"

Abram, Nahor, and		
Haran,	890 years	after birth of Noah.
	290 "	after the flood.
	1946 "	after the creation.

The two years of Gen. xi. 10 are added to this result by Usher, according to whom Terah begat his sons 1948 years after the creation. On this interpretation Shem was not the eldest son of Noah, as is generally believed, born when his father was 500 years old (Gen. v. 32). But xi. 10 has another explanation. Interpreting the data of the genealogy as before, Noah having lived 500 years begat Shem, who having lived 100 years, begat Arpachshad. Arpachshad was thus born in the 601st year of Noah's life. He was born in the second civil year after the flood year, counting it the first. The flood year was the 600th of Noah's life (vii. 6, 11), the flood itself prevailing during five months of that year. Noah lived 350 full years after the flood year, counting it the first (ix. 28). In the flood year he was 599 years and some months old. As he lived 350 years longer, he died when he was 949 years and some months old, in the 950th year of his age (ix. 29). There are discrepancies between the Hebrew, the Septuagint, and the Samaritan Pentateuch. The Hebrew text is evidently the most accurate one with respect to dates. The Septuagint, probably on the ground that the long-lived antediluvians were not likely to beget a son while they were less than 150 years old, took the liberty of adding a century to the Hebrew date, where it was said that they had done so, as in the case of Adam, Seth, Enosh, Kenan, Mahalalel, and Enoch. The minor variations are that to Lamech the Alexandrian text and Lucian assign 188 + 565 = 753 years; and Lucian divides Methuselah's life into 167 + 802 = 969 years. The Samaritan Pentateuch, on the contrary, apparently on the ground that an antediluvian was not likely to have lived 150 years without begetting his first son, finding by the Hebrew text that Jared did so at 162, Methuselah at 187 (according to Lucian at 167), and Lamech at 182, cut the figures down to 62, 67, and 53. This reduced the total length of their lives, whereas the Septuagint had carefully balanced its additions to the first part of the lives by corresponding subtractions from the later part, so that the total length of each life

was the same in that version as in the Hebrew original, except in the case of Lamech. Similarly, in the case of the postdiluvian patriarchs who preceded Abraham, the Septuagint hesitates to allow them to beget a son till they were 100 years old. It adds 100 years to the ages at which sons were begotten by Arpachshad, Shelah, Eber, Peleg, Reu, and Serug, and 50 (Alexandrian manuscript and Lucian) to the time of life when Nahor begat Terah. After Arpachshad it inserts Kenan, and states that he begat Shelah when 130 years old. The Samaritan Pentateuch allows them to beget a son after 50; and in the case of Arpachshad, Shelah, Eber, Peleg, Reu, and Serug adds 100 years to the age assigned by the Hebrew text, and 50 years in the case of Nahor.

2. Or many links are omitted. As in other Hebrew genealogies, each member is said to have begotten his successor, although the latter may be a grandson or even remoter descendant; as in the royal genealogy given in Matthew, the three kings, Ahaziah, Joash, and Amaziah are passed over and Joram is said to have begotten Uzziah, his great-great-grandson (i. 8, R. V.; cp. the use of the verb "bare" in Gen. xlvi. 15, 18). Only prominent members of the line are enumerated, or else, as an aid to memory, a definite number is chosen; in Matthew groups of twice seven, in Genesis groups of ten.

Adam, at the age of 130 begat
Seth, who at the age of 105 begat
Ancestor of Enosh or Enosh himself.
Enosh, at the age of 90 begat
Ancestor of Kenan or Kenan himself.
Kenan, at the age of 70 begat
Ancestor of Mahalalel or Mahalalel himself.

According to this theory, the Hebrew records afford no basis for a chronology from Adam to Abraham. It assumes, further, that the age assigned to the patriarchs is that of their natural life. Adam lived 930 years. This extraordinary longevity is accounted for by the fact that sin, which has a physical effect and works disease and death, had only begun its malign influence on the race, and had not reached its normal hereditary power. The balance between man in a sinless state and man in the condition of sinner had not been attained.

3. Or the names denote an individual and his family spoken of collectively; as Israel denotes a patriarch and his descendants, Kain is used for the Kenites (Num. xxiv. 22, R. V.), David for the royal house (1 Kin. xii. 16). Sometimes the family takes its name from its progenitor or later leading member of the tribe; sometimes the name of the tribe or of the country it inhabits is applied to its chief representative, as to-day men are constantly addressed by their family name, and nobles are called by the name of their duchy or county. In Gen. x. the names in the gen-

ealogy are sometimes individuals, sometimes peoples, sometimes cities, sometimes countries; and in the pedigree of Abraham given in this chapter Arpachshad, whom Shem begat (x. 22), is apparently a country whose inhabitants were descendants of Shem, and this country produced Shelah (cp. bear, beget, firstborn in Gen. xxv. 2, 3; 12–16). The longevity is the period during which the family had prominence and leadership.

Adam,   1
  Family of Seth originated when Adam
    was 130 years old (v. 3).   130
  Adam and his direct line were at the
    head of affairs for 930 years (ver. 5),
    when they were superseded by
Family of Seth,   930
  In Seth, 105 years after it attained
    headship, the family of Enosh took
    its rise (ver. 6).   1035
  After being at the head of affairs for
    912 years (ver. 8), Seth was suc-
    ceeded by
Family of Enosh,   1842
  Ninety years after Enosh attained to
    headship there sprang from it the
    family of Kenan (ver. 9).   1932
  After Enosh had held the leadership
    815 years longer (ver. 10), Enosh
    gave place to
Family of Kenan,   2747
Family of Lamech,   6848
  Family which took its name from Noah
    originated,   7030
  Lamech is succeeded by
Family of Noah,   7625
  Shem, Ham, and Japheth born about   8125
  Flood,   8225
  Arpachshad originates,   8227
The race of Shem, as distinct from the
  other descendants of Noah, become
  preëminent,   8575

Hence the years from the creation of Adam to the flood were 8225, and from Adam to the death of Terah may be 11,571. This outline exhibits one application of the theory; but it must be remembered that at different points in the genealogy various interpretations are possible, which must be subject to individual preference until further data come to light.

II. From the Birth of Abraham to the Exodus.

How long after the flood Abraham was born cannot be determined from the biblical record, not even by the first method enumerated above and employed by Usher in interpreting the genealogy from Adam to Abraham, for the age of Terah at the birth of Abraham is not so stated in Gen. xi. 26, 32 as to be unquestionable; see Abraham. According to Usher, Abraham's birth occurred in 1996 B. C. The period from the birth of Abraham to the descent into Egypt can be measured:

Birth of Abraham to—
  "   "   Isaac   100 years (Gen. xxi. 5).
  "   "   Jacob   60 years (Gen. xxv. 26).
Jacob's age at de-
  scent into Egypt 130 years (Gen. xlvii. 9).
                        290 years.

The sojourn of the children of Israel in Egypt was 430 years (Ex. xii. 40, 41). But from what initial date is this period reckoned? From the covenant with Abraham (Gen. xv.), when he was between 75 and 85 years old (xii. 4; xvi. 3), as Usher and many others believe, or from the descent into Egypt? Probably from the latter event; see Egypt III. 3.

It is generally believed that Ramses II. was the Pharaoh of the oppression, and one of his successors, probably Mer-n-ptah (a name more familiar in the form Meneptah), was the Pharaoh of the exodus; see Egypt III. 8. The date of Ramses II. may be approximately fixed by the fact that Amen-hetep, or as the Greeks pronounced the name, Amenophis IV. of Egypt was a contemporary of Ashuruballit of Assyria. Tukulti-adar, fifth in descent from Ashuruballit, reigned, according to a statement of Sennacherib, about 1300 B. C. The fifth or sixth king on the throne of Egypt after Amenophis IV. was Ramses II., an indication that Ramses II. reigned about 1300 B.C. The date of Meneptah's reign was determined in the following manner: Menophres, apparently Meneptah, is the king in whose reign the Sothic period of 1460 years is said to have begun. According to Theon the astronomer, the Sothic period ended in A. D. 139. It began, therefore, in 1321 B. C. Hence Meneptah's reign included the year 1321. On the basis of these calculations for the date of the reigns of Ramses II. and Meneptah, the exodus has been provisionally fixed at about 1320. This date will be lowered about forty years if Dr. Mahler, astronomer at Vienna, proves to be correct in his opinion, founded on astronomical data, that Ramses II. reigned from 1348 to 1281 B. C.

III. From the Exodus to the Foundation of Solomon's Temple.

This interval was doubtless reckoned as twelve periods of forty years each (1 Kin. vi. 1), of which the first covered the sojourn in the wilderness (Ex. xvi. 35; Num. xiv. 33), six certainly, and probably eight, were allowed for the time of the judges proper, the oppression and rest being frequently included in the statement (Judg. iii. 11, 30—double period: v. 31; viii. 28; xiii. 1; and probably x. 1–4 and xii. 7–14), the high priesthood of Eli counted as one (1 Sam. iv. 18), Saul's reign probably as another (Acts xiii. 21), while David's reign made the twelfth (1 Kin. ii. 11). But the forty years are a round number, and not always exact. The periods enumerated were sometimes in whole or in part contemporary; see Judges. Jephthah speaks of the Israelites having occupied the country about Heshbon for 300 years (Judg. xi. 26), some seven periods of forty years. Josephus, reckoning in a different manner, estimates the time from the exodus to the temple at 592 or 612 years (Antiq. viii. 3, 1 ; xx. 10), while Paul, according to the received text, refers to the period of the judges as lasting about 450 years (Acts xiii. 20). As already pointed out, these diverse results do not contradict each other, although they do not agree. The variations are due to the different methods employed in calculating. The sum was not supposed to represent the exact duration of the period, as would a modern chronological statement. The length of the period cannot be given in modern terms until new data come to light.

IV. FROM THE FOUNDATION OF THE TEMPLE TO THE EXILE AND RETURN.

The temple was founded in the fourth year of Solomon (1 Kin. vi. 1). Solomon reigned forty years, and was succeeded by Rehoboam, on whose ascension of the throne the ten tribes revolted. The data obtained from both Hebrew and foreign sources may be arranged according to the following scheme. For discussion of the details, see the articles in this Manual which are devoted to the several kings, and a brief monograph on the chronology by Prof. Davis in the *Presbyterian and Reformed Review*, 1891, pp. 98–114. In general it may be remarked that this scheme recognizes the existence of co-reigns. They were common in the neighboring monarchies, and are proven in individual cases for the Hebrews. David when incapacitated by age for government, and in danger of having his throne

usurped, had Solomon made king (1 Kin. 1.). When Uzziah was compelled to seclude himself because he had become a leper, Jotham assumed the duties of royalty (2 Kin. xv. 5). The scheme further recognizes that among the Hebrews, as among neighboring nations, no fixed rule existed as to whether the accession year of a king or the civil year which followed should be counted as the first regnal year. Some recorders followed one method, others another. Examples might be multiplied; one will suffice. In Ptolemy's canon 604, the civil year following accession is treated as the first regnal year of Nebuchadnezzar. So it is by Josephus, Daniel, and Babylonian scribes, and in the record whence Jer. lii. 28–30 is taken. But Jeremiah himself and other Palestinian writers of the day numbered the accession year of Nebuchadnezzar his first year, synchronizing Jehoiakim 4 with Nebuchadnezzar 1, and Zedekiah 11 with Nebuchadnezzar 19. It will be observed, finally, that two events, the slaughter of Ahaziah of Judah and Jehoram of Israel by Jehu and the fall of Samaria, divide the history of the divided monarchy into three periods, each chronologically complete in itself. The dates of these two events are established. The chronology, therefore, of each of these periods must be settled by itself. Difficulties which arise in matters of adjustment affect only their own period, not the others.

This scheme is not offered as final in every particular. Slightly different arrangements of the data are possible at several points; for example, in the matter of Athaliah's usurpation. Such minor modifications, however, do not affect the chronology as a whole.

Judah Ref.	Name / Event	Judah yr.	B.C.	Israel yr.	Israel Name	Israel Ref.
1 K. 14 : 21.	Rehoboam.	1	931	1	Jeroboam.	1 K. 14 : 20.
		2		2		
2 C. 11 : 17.	Three years' godliness.	3		3		
		4		4		
1 K. 14 : 25.	Shishak's invasion.	5		5		
		6		6		
		17	915	17		
1 K. 15 : 1, 2 } 2 C. 13 : 1, 2 }	Abijam.	1		18		
		2		19		
1 K. 15 : 9, 10.	Asa ascends throne . . .	3		20		
	1st regnal year.	1		21		
2 C. 14 : 1.	Land quiet ten years.	2 1		22 1	Nadab.	1 Kin. 15 : 25.
		3 2		1	Baasha.	1 K. 15 : 28–33.
		4	908	2		
		10		8		
		11		9		
2 C. 14 : 9–15.	War with Zerah between years 11 and 14	12	900	10		
		13		11		
		14		12		
2 C. 15 : 10	Reformation.	15		13		
15 :19 } 16 : 1–2 } *	Buys aid of Benhadad against Baasha.	16		14		

* The dates 35 and 36 given in these verses in the Hebrew text were explained by the older commentators as reckoned from the commencement of the kingdom of Judah. The numbers are then correct. Modern interpreters generally regard the Hebrew text as corrupt, and read 15 or 25 and 16 or 26 for 35 and 36 respectively. They are doubtless right in doing so ; for the text of Chronicles has not been transmitted as carefully as it should have been, and the phrase "year of Asa" or other king always refers to his regnal year, and Baasha was dead before the 35th and 36th years of Asa.

Judah reference	Judah event	Judah yr	B.C.	Israel yr	Israel king / event	Israel reference
		25	887	23		
		26 1		24	**Elah.**	1 K. 16 : 8.
		27 . . . . . {2 / 1			. . Zimri (7 days).	1 K. 16 : 10, 15.
		28		2	**Omri.**	1 K. 16 : 15, 16.
		29		3		
		30		4		
		31 5			Omri prevails and reigns with undisputed authority. 1 K. 16 : 22, 23.	
		36	876	10		
LXX. 1 K. 16:28.	Jehoshaphat associated. 1 11					
		2..38 . . . .12..1			**Ahab.** { LXX. 1 K. 16:29. / Heb. do.	
2 C. 16 : 12.	Asa diseased.	3 39		2		
		4 40		3		
1 K. 22 : 41, 42.	**Jehoshaphat.** 5 41 4					
	1st year of sole reign.	1	870	5		
		2		6		
	Marries his first-born (	3		7		
2 K. 8 : 25, 26.	Jehoram to daugh- {	4		8		
2 C. 22 : 1.	ter of Ahab. (	5		9		
		15	856	19		
		16		20		
	Jehoram associated. . . 17 . . . . . 1 21				**Ahaziah.** Ahab, allied with Damascus, defeated by Shalmaneser near Hamath. Ob. 54.	1 K. 22 : 51.
		2..18 . . . . . 2..1..22			**Jehoram.** War with Moab.	2 K. 1:17; 3:1. 2 K. 3 : 4 seq.
		3 19		2		
		4 20		3		
		5 21	850	4	Shalmaneser at war with Damascus.	
2 K. 8 : 16, 17.	**Jehoram** sole king. 1 5				Shalmaneser at war with Damascus. 2 K. 6 : 24.	
		4		8	Shalmaneser at war with Damascus.	
		5		9	Ben-hadad besets Samaria. 2 K. 6 : 24.	
2 C. 21 : 18, 19.	Sorely diseased, hence	6		10	Benhadad murdered and succeeded	
2 K. 9 : 29.	Ahaziah made regent. . .7 11				by Hazael between 845-3.	
2 K. 8 : 25, 26.	**Ahaziah,** king. . .8 . . . . . {12				Jehoram slain by Jehu.	
	Slain by Jehu. {842				**Jehu** seizes the throne.	
2 K. 11 : 1-3.	**Joash,** sole surviving heir }				Jehu and Hazael pay tribute to	
	and legitimate king. }				Shalmaneser. III. R. 5, No. 6, 40-65.	
	In concealment for six }			1		
	years from Athaliah,		840	2		
	who usurped the			3	Shalmaneser at war	
	power.			4	with Hazael. Obelisk 102.	
				5		
				6		
2 K. 11 : 4; 12:1.	Placed on throne and Athaliah slain.	7 7				
					On account of Jehu's increasing age and incapacity for war,	
		21 21		1	**Jehoahaz** associated. Antiq. ix. 8, 5.	
		22	820	.2	and 2 K. 13 : 10, correcting ver. 1	
2 K. 12 : 6.	Renewed attempt to repair temple.	23		3	Hazael against Israel. 2 K. 10 : 32.	
		28		(28) 8	Jehoahaz alone. 2 K. 10 : 36.	
2 K. 12 : 17	Hazael against Gath and Jerusalem. When he departs, he leaves				Hazael continues to oppress Israel all the days of Jehoahaz. 2 K. 13 : 3, 22.	
2 Chron. 24 : 25.	Joash sorely diseased. 37 . . . . . 1 17				**Jehoash.**	2 K. 13 : 10.
2 K. 14 : 1.	**Amaziah** accordingly 1 2					
	undertakes the government.	2	803	3	[Bin-addu]-mari, king of Damascus, besieged by Ramman-nirari.	
	Joash slain and Amaziah sole king.	(40) 3		4	Moabites invade Israel. 2 K. 13 : 20. Jehoash victorious over Benhadad. 2 K. 13 : 25.	
Ant. ix. 9 : 3.	Defeated and his capital taken by Jehoash. }	14	791	15		
		15 16			**Jeroboam** ascends. 1st regnal year.	2 K. 14 : 23.
		16		1		
		17		2		
2 K. 14 : 19.	Conspired against.	18		3		

Reference	Event	Numbers		Assyrian / Notes
2 K. 14 : 21.	**Uzziah** or **Azariah** proclaimed by populace.	1 / 2	4 / 5	Ant. ix. 10, 3.
2 K. 14 : 17.	Amaziah survives Jehoash 15 years.			
2 K. 14 : 19.	Amaziah slain and Uz-(29) ziah supreme.	11 . . . . .14 / 12 775 15		
2 K. 14 : 22.	Builds Elath after death of Amaziah.			
2 K. 15 : 1.	In special sense "reigns."	. . . . .27 / 25 28		
2 K. 15 : 5.	Becomes leprous and	36 39 / 37 750 40		Earthquake hereabouts.
2 K. 15 : 32, 33.	**Jotham** conducts the government.	1 38} 41		Contemporary with Jotham.
				1 C. 5 : 17.
				Zechariah. 2 K. 15 : 8.
		2 (39)}		**Shallum.** 2 K. 15 : 13.
				Menahem ascends. 2 K. 15 : 17.
				1st regnal year.
		3	1	
		4	2	
		5 745	3	Pul, i. e. Tiglath-pileser, ascends throne of Assyria.
	Ahaz associated.	9	7	
		10 740	8	
		11	9	
		12	10	Menahem pays tribute to Pul.
				2 K. 15 : 19.
		13 (50)	1	**Pekahiah.** 2 K. 15 : 23.
		14	2	
	Uzziah dies and	15 (52)	1	**Pekah.** 2 K. 15 : 27.*
2 K. 15 : 32.	Jotham succeeds.	16 }	2	Tiglath-pileser captures Gaza.
2 K. 16 : 1, 2.	**Ahaz** alone.	8 }		
		9 733	3	Tiglath-pileser against Damascus.
		10		" " still against Damascus.
		11		Receives tribute from Ahaz.
		12 . (20) . 730 . .	1	**Hoshea.** 2 K. 15 : 30.
		13	2	2 K. 17 : 1.
2 K. 18 : 1, 2.	**Hezekiah** ascends.	14	3	
Ant. ix. 13, 1.	1st regnal year.	15 1	4	Tiglath-pileser succeeded by Shalmaneser.
	Ahaz dies.	16 2	5	
	Hezekiah sole king.	3	6	
2 K. 18 : 9; Ant. ix. 14, 1. }		4	7	Hoshea seeks an alliance with So of Egypt. 2 K. 17 : 4.
		5	8	
2 K. 18 : 10.		6 . . 722 . .	9	**Fall of Samaria.**
		7 721		1st year of **Sargon,** who had ascended the throne of Assyria in 10th month of the preceding year.
		720		Defeats Sibê, i. e. So, of Egypt.
		13 715		Assyrian troops in Samaria and Arabia. Tribute from Egypt.
2 K. 18 : 13; 2 C. 32 : 1-8; Is. 36 : 1. }	Sennacherib invades Judah.	14 714		Assyrian troops "subjugated Judah," perhaps under command of Sennacherib, probably end of 715 or beginning of 714. Nimr. tablet.
2 K. 20 : 1-6; Is. 38 : 1-8. }	Hezekiah sick.			
		15 713		
2 K. 20 : 12.	Receives embassy from	16 712		Judah tributary to Assyria (Octag. Cyl. 32-35). Merodach-baladan incites neighboring nations against Assyria.
Is. 39 : 1.	Merodach-baladan about this date.			
Is. 20 : 1.	Sargon against Ashdod.	17 711		Sargon against Ashdod.
		18 710		Sargon dethrones Merodach-baladan.
		23 705		**Sennacherib** ascends throne of Assyria.
2 K. 18 : 14 seq.	Besieged by Sennacherib.	27 701		Against Hezekiah and Jerusalem.
		28 700		
		29 699		
	Dies and			
2 K. 21 : 1.	**Manasseh** ascends throne. }	698		
	1st year.	1 697		
		2 696		

* Usher and the older chronologists assumed that anarchy prevailed for several years between the death of Pekah and the accession of Hoshea. Both the Hebrew and the Assyrian records, however, clearly indicate that no interregnum occurred, but that Hoshea slew Pekah and succeeded him on the throne. For the twenty years assigned to the reign of Pekah, see PEKAH.

Reference	Event	Yr	B.C.	Contemporary rulers
2 K. 19 : 37.		18	680	**Esarhaddon.** Receives tribute from Manasseh of Judah.
		30	668	**Ashurbanipal.**
		49	649	Assyrian garrison in Gezer.
2 C. 33 : 11.	Carried in chains to Babylon by the Assyrians, probably at this time.	50	648-7	Ashurbanipal captures Babylon and dethrones its king, who had incited peoples from Elam to the Mediterranean to revolt against Assyria. Receives tribute from Manasseh of Judah [about 647 (Schrader)]
		55	643	
2 K. 21 : 19	Dies and **Amon** ascends throne.		642	
	1st year.	1	641	
		2	640	
2 K. 22 : 1.	**Josiah.**	1	639	
		2	638	
2 C. 34 : 3.	Seeks Jehovah.	8	632	
2 C. 34 : 3.	Begins to purge nation.	12	628	
Jer. 1 : 1, 2.	Jeremiah begins.	13	627	
		14	626	
Jer. 25 : 1, 3.	13th Josiah to 4th Jehoiakim inclusive = 23 years.	15	625	**Nabopolassar.**
		30	610	~~**Necho,** king of Egypt.~~
2 K. 23 : 29.	Slain by Necho.	31	609	
2 K. 23 : 31.	**Jehoahaz** king 3 months.		608	
2 K. 23 : 36.	**Jehoiakim.**	1		
		2	607	
		3	606	
Jer. 25 : 1; 46 : 2. Ant. x. 6, 1.	He and Necho subjugated by Nebuchadnezzar.	4 . .	605	**Nebuchadnezzar.**
Jer. 36 : 9.	9th month, public fast. Jeremiah's roll burned.	5	604	2d or 1st year.
Ant. x. 10, 3. Dan. 2 : 1.	Two years *after* the destruction of Egypt Nebuchadnezzar dreams.	6 . .	603	3d or 2d year.
2 K. 24 : 1.	Having paid tribute to Neb. three years, rebels.	7 . .	602	4th year.
	Yields to Neb.	11		
2 K. 24 : 8–12. 2 C. 36 : 10.	**Jehoiachin,** 3 months. Goes captive to Babylon toward close of year.		. . 598	8th or 7th year.
2 K. 24 : 18.	**Zedekiah.**	1	597	
Jer. 51 : 59.	Visits Babylon.	4	594	**Psammetick II.** of Egypt.
2 K. 25 : 1. Jer. 32 : 1.	Jerusalem besieged.	9	589	**Apries,** king of Egypt. 18th or 17th of Nebuchadnezzar.
		10 . .	588	
2 K. 25 : 8, 9; Ant. x. 8, 5; C. Apion. i. 21.	Temple burned in 5th month.	11 . .	587	19th or 18th of Nebuchadnezzar.
Ezek. 33 : 21.	News reaches Ezekiel.			
Jer. 44 : 30.	Hophra, *i. e.* Apries, mentioned.			
Jer. 52 : 30. Ant. x. 9, 7.	Captives carried to Babylon 5th yr. *after* destruction of Jerusalem = 23d Neb.		 582	23d of Nebuchadnezzar.
			568	Nebuchadnezzar invades Egypt in 37th year of his reign.
2 K. 25 : 27.	37th year of Jehoiachin's captivity.		562	**Evil-merodach.**
			561	1st year.
			539	**Cyrus** takes Babylon.
2 C. 36 : 22, 23.	Rebuilding of temple authorized.		538	1st year.

Ezra 3 : 8.   Rebuilding begun in ⎫
C. Apion i. 21. 2d month, having re- |
             mained waste for 50 ⎬   537   2d year.
             years—*i. e.* 49 years |
             and 9 months.   ⎭

V. From the Return from Exile to the Birth of Christ.

Judæa under Persian rule.	539	**Cyrus** on throne of Babylon.
Zerubbabel leads back 42,000 Jews to Jerusalem.	538	
Foundation of the temple laid, but the work is soon interrupted.	537	
	529	**Cambyses.**
	521	**Darius Hystaspis.**
Haggai and Zechariah exhort the people to resume work on the temple.	520	
Temple completed in 12th month of 6th year, in the early spring.	515	
	490	Defeated by the Greeks at Marathon.
	486	**Xerxes,** called by the Jews Ahasuerus.
	480	Persians victorious at Thermopylæ, but defeated at Salamis.
	479	Persians defeated at Platæa.
	465	**Artaxerxes Longimanus.**
Ezra leads back 1755 Jews to Jerusalem.	458–7	
Nehemiah sent by Artaxerxes to Jerusalem in month Nisan.	445–4	
Repair of city wall begun on 3d day of 5th month, and completed on 25th of Elul, the 6th month.		
Nehemiah returns to the Persian court.	433–2	
	424	**Darius Nothus.**
	359	**Ochus.**
	338	**Arses** or Arogus.
	336	**Darius Codomannus.**
		Alexander ascends throne of Macedon.
	334	Alexander victorious at the Granicus.
	333	" " " Issus.
Alexander the Great visits Jerusalem, and is met by the high priest Jaddua.	332	
	331	Alexander defeats Darius at Arbela.
	330	Darius assassinated.
	323	Death of Alexander.
Judæa annexed to Egypt by Ptolemy Soter.	320	
He captures Jerusalem and plants colonies in Alexandria and Cyrene.		
	312	**Seleucus** founds the kingdom of the Seleucidæ.
	223	**Antiochus the Great.**
After the battle of Raphia, 217 B. C., Ptolemy Philopator sacrifices at Jerusalem. Being prevented from entering the holy of holies, he attempts to destroy the Jews in Alexandria.		
Antiochus takes Jerusalem.	203	
Scopas recovers Judæa for Egypt.	199	
Judæa annexed to Syria, being finally wrested by Antiochus from Egypt at the battle of Paneas.	198	
	190	Defeated by the Romans at Magnesia.
	175	**Antiochus Epiphanes.**
The high priest Onias removed, and Jason of the Grecian party put in office.	174	
Antiochus takes Jerusalem, massacres citizens, and defiles the temple.	170	
Antiochus orders an idolatrous altar to be erected on the temple altar and heathen sacrifices to be offered.	168	
The priest Mattathias raises the standard of revolt.		
The Maccabees. Judas placed in command.	166	
Defeats Gorgias.		
Defeats Lysias, and on 25th Chislev rededicates the temple.	165	
	164	Death of Antiochus and accession of **Antiochus Eupator.**
	162	**Demetrius I.**
Falls in battle, and is succeeded by Jonathan.	160	
	150	**Alexander Balas.**
	146	**Antiochus VI.** ascends the throne with the aid of his general Tryphon. Demetrius II. his rival.

	B.C.	
Jonatnan Maccabæus murdered by Tryphon, and succeeded by Simon.	143	
First year of the Freedom of Jerusalem and of Simon, high priest and captain.	142	Murder of Antiochus.
	138	**Antiochus VII.** regent until 128.
Simon murdered; succeeded by John Hyrcanus.	135	
Pompey takes Jerusalem.	63	
Julius Cæsar appoints Antipater procurator of Judæa.	47	
Assassination of Antipater.	44	Assassination of Julius Cæsar.
	43	
Parthians take Jerusalem and place Antigonus, the Maccabee, on the throne. The Roman senate, however, toward the end of the year appoint Herod to be king of Judæa.	40	
Herod takes Jerusalem, slays Antigonus, the last of the Maccabæan priest-kings, and becomes king of Judæa.	37	
	31	**Augustus** becomes Roman emperor.
Rebuilding of the temple begun.	19	
Birth of **Jesus Christ.** Close of	5	
or beginning of	4	
Death of Herod and division of the kingdom among his three sons, Archelaus receiving Judæa.		

VI. From the Death of Herod to the Destruction of Jerusalem.

The chronology of the life of Christ and of Paul is treated under the respective articles. The chronology of Paul's life hinges on the date of Festus' appointment to the procuratorship.

	B. C.	
On the death of Herod the Great his kingdom is divided among his three sons: Archelaus becomes king of Judæa; Herod Antipas, tetrarch of Galilee and Peræa; Philip, tetrarch of Ituræa and Trachonitis.	4	
	A. D.	
Deposition of Archelaus; Judæa and Samaria incorporated with the province of Syria, and placed under procurators. Coponius procurator.	6	
Marcus Ambivius procurator.	10	
	12	or, as some believe, 13. Tiberius associated with Augustus, receiving from the senate *imperium proconsulare* in all provinces.
Valerius Gratus fourth procurator.	14	Augustus dies Aug. 19th, and **Tiberius** is emperor.
Pontius Pilate procurator.	26	
Jesus begins his public ministry (Luke iii. 1, 23; cp. John ii. 20) probably early in	27	
Death of Philip the tetrarch. His tetrarchy is annexed to Syria.	33	
Pontius Pilate deposed by Vitellius, governor of Syria, and sent to Rome.	36	
Herod Antipas attends Passover at Jerusalem; Caligula appoints Herod Agrippa to be king of the tetrarchies of Philip and Lysanias, and sends Marullus to be procurator.	37	Tiberius smothered March 16th, and **Caligula** is emperor.
Herod Antipas banished to Gaul, and his tetrarchy given to king Herod Agrippa.	39	
Claudius makes Herod Agrippa king of Judæa and Samaria.	41	Caligula assassinated Jan. 24th, and **Claudius** becomes emperor.
Death of Herod Agrippa. Judæa again placed under procurators. Cuspius Fadus procurator.	44	
Tiberius Alexander, renegade Jew of Alexandria, procurator.	46	
Ventidius Cumanus procurator, probably jointly with Felix.	48	
Antonius Felix procurator.	52	Claudius expels the Jews and sorcerers and astrologers from Rome.
	54	Claudius dies of poison Oct. 13th, and **Nero** becomes emperor.
Porcius Festus succeeds Felix; but if the procuratorship of Felix be reckoned from A. D. 48, it is possible to date Festus' appointment in 55 or 56.	59 or 60	
Albinus procurator.	62	
Gessius Florus procurator.	64	Persecutions under Nero begin.

Outbreak of the Jewish war.

Destruction of Jerusalem.

66
68 Nero ends his life. **Galba** and **Otho** become emperors successively and die violent deaths.
69 **Vitellius** obtains the empire and is slain.
    Vespasian becomes emperor.
70

Chrys′o-lite, in A. V. **Chrysolyte** [Greek, gold stone].

A unisilicate mineral consisting mainly of magnesia and silica. There are two varieties of it, one precious, the other common. The former, which is transparent and of a pale yellowish-green, is brought from the Levant. It is disputed whether the chrysolite of Pliny and of the N. T. was a gold-colored chrysolite or a topaz. It constitutes the seventh foundation of the New Jerusalem (Rev. xxi. 20).

Chrys′o-prase, in A. V. **Chrysoprasus** [Greek, golden-green stone].

A variety of chalcedony of an apple-green hue, the color being produced by the presence of oxide of nickel. Its best-known locality is in Silesia. It constitutes the tenth foundation of the New Jerusalem (Rev. xxi. 20).

Chub. See CUB.

Chun. See BEROTHAI.

Church [probably from Greek, *kuriakon*, the Lord's house].

The rendering in the N. T. of the Greek *Ekklēsia*, which in the states of Greece meant the assembly of citizens summoned for legislative or other purposes (Acts xix. 32, 41, rendered assembly). The sacred writers use the word *ekklēsia* to denote an organized community acknowledging the Lord Jesus Christ as their supreme ruler, and meeting statedly or as opportunities offer for religious worship (Mat. xvi. 18; xviii. 17; Acts ii. 47; v. 11; Eph. v. 23, 25). As followers of Jesus arose in many different cities, the plural "churches" began to be employed, the Christian community in each separate locality being considered a church (Acts ix. 31; xv. 41; Rom. xvi. 4; 1 Cor. vii. 17; 1 Thes. ii. 14). Church is nowhere unequivocally used in the N. T. for the building in which any particular Christian community met. The Protestant doctrine of the church is that the church may exist without a visible form, because it is both invisible and visible. The invisible church is composed of all who are really united to Christ (1 Cor. i. 2; xii. 12, 13, 27, 28; Col. i. 24; 1 Pet. ii. 9, 10). It is not an external organization. Its members are known to God, though they cannot always be infallibly detected by the human eye, and many of them are in heaven or are yet to be born. The visible church consists of all who profess to be united to Christ.

The apostles occupied a peculiar position of authority (Acts v. 2; vi. 6; 1 Cor. xii. 28;

Eph. ii. 20; 2 Pet. iii. 2); but they were not the sole governing body, the elders or bishops also exercised rule (Acts xv. 2, 4, 6, 22, 23; 1 Tim. iv. 14; v. 17; 1 Pet. v. 1). The officers of the local churches were elders or bishops and deacons (Acts vi. 3; xiv. 23; xx. 17; 1 Tim. iii. 1, 8; Titus i. 5-9). The apostles sometimes appointed commissioners for special work (1 Tim. i. 3; Titus i. 5).

The public worship of the church was engrafted upon the synagogue service. It consisted of preaching (Mat. xxviii. 20; Acts xx. 7; 1 Cor. xiv. 19, 26-36), reading of Scripture (Jas. i. 22; Col. iv. 16; 1 Thes. v. 27; cp. Acts xiii. 15), prayer (1 Cor. xiv. 14, 16), singing (Eph. v. 19; Col. iii. 16; and cp. the hymns Eph. v. 14; 1 Tim. iii. 16), administration of the sacraments of baptism and the Lord's Supper (Mat. xxviii. 19; Acts ii. 41; 1 Cor. xi. 18-34), and almsgiving (1 Cor. xvi. 1, 2). When the spiritual gift was present, there were also prophesyings and tongues.

Chu′shan-rish-a-tha′im. See CUSHAN-RISHATHAIM.

Chu′za, in A. R. V. **Chuzas** [perhaps Aramaic *kuza′*, modest, or jug].

Herod the tetrarch's steward, whose wife Joanna ministered to the wants of Jesus (Luke viii. 3).

Ci-li′ci-a.

A province of Asia Minor, separated on the north by the Taurus mountains from Cappadocia, Lycaonia, and Isauria, and on the east by mount Amanus from Syria; bounded on the south by the Mediterranean, and on the west by Pamphylia. It was anciently divided into two portions, the western one, which was mountainous, called the Rough, and the eastern one, which was level, the Plain Cilicia. The chief town in the latter was Tarsus, the birthplace of St. Paul (Acts xxi. 39; xxii. 3; xxiii. 34). Cilicia formed part of the kingdom of Syria; and when in 148-7 B. C. Demetrius II. landed on its shores and set himself up for king of Syria, the bulk of its inhabitants supported him (1 Mac. xi. 14; Antiq. xiii. 4, 3). Jews from Cilicia disputed with Stephen (Acts vi. 9). The gospel reached it very early (xv. 23), planted apparently by Paul (ix. 30; Gal. i. 21). Afterwards, passing through it, he confirmed the churches which had been founded (Acts xv. 41). Subsequently on his voyage as a prisoner to Rome he sailed over the sea of Cilicia (xxvii. 5).

Cin′na-mon.

A fragrant wood (Song iv. 14; Rev. xviii. 13). It was an ingredient in the sacred anointing oil used in the consecration of Aaron and his successors (Ex. xxx. 23). It was used in after times to perfume beds (Prov. vii. 17). It is the aromatic bark of a tree, *Cinnamomum zeylanicum*, belonging to the laurel order, and cultivated in Ceylon, of which it is a native. The bark of the tree yields an essential oil, which is obtained from it by distillation. It is of a golden-yellow color, has an agreeable smell, and is used in perfumery. The tree has been grown in Arabia.

Cin'ne-roth. See CHINNERETH.

Cir-cum-cis'ion [a cutting around].

The initiatory rite into the covenant privileges of the family of God represented by Abraham and his descendants through Isaac, and the token of the covenant (Gen. xvii. 1–10, 21). As a rite of the religion of this people, it was instituted by God and enjoined upon Abraham, who was himself to be circumcised, as were all his male children and his male slaves, whether born in his house or bought with money. The act consists in removing the foreskin, and it was performed on the child by the father of the house or some other Israelite, and even by the mother (Ex. iv. 25; 1 Mac. i. 60). The proper time to carry out the rite was when the child was eight days old, but those born before the institution of the ordinance were to be circumcised at any time of life. Abraham was circumcised when he was 99, and Ishmael when 13 (Gen. xvii. 11–27). The rite was observed during the bondage in Egypt, but was neglected in the wilderness. Before the entry into Canaan, however, Joshua made knives of flint and circumcised the people (Josh. v. 2–9). By this time metal was known, but there is a strong conservatism in religion, and antique arrangements tend to remain after the necessity for them has passed away; so flint held its own against metal for centuries after the time that the former might have been superseded (cp. Ex. iv. 25). Foreigners who wished to become members of the commonwealth of Israel were required to submit to the rite, whatever their age might be (Gen. xxxiv. 14–17, 22; Ex. xii. 48). Shortly before the Christian era, the conquered Edomites and Ituræans were by force added thus to the Jewish nation (Antiq. xiii. 9, 1; 11, 3). Though there were other circumcised nations as well as the Hebrews, especially the Egyptians (con. Apion. ii. 14; Herod. ii. 104), and they as early as 3000 B. C., yet the Philistines, the Phœnicians, the Moabites, the Ammonites, the Syrians, the Assyrians, the Babylonians, and various other nationalities with whom the Jews were in contact were uncircumcised; so that the word "uncircumcised," as a term of reproach, meant almost practically (not etymologically) the same as heathen (Gen. xxxiv. 14; Judg. xiv. 3; xv. 18; 1 Sam. xvii. 26, 36; xxxi. 4; 2 Sam. i. 20; 1 Chron. x. 4; Ezek. xxviii. 10; xxxi. 18; xxxii. 19–32). "The circumcision,"

on the contrary, used in the N. T. meant the Jewish church and nation (Gal. ii. 8; Col. iv. 11). Circumcision was an act of religious purification (Herod. ii. 37), and in its full significance betokened the putting away of carnal lust (Col. ii. 11). To circumcise the heart is so to regenerate it that its irreligious obstinacy will disappear (Deut. x. 16), and it will be able and willing to love God with all its powers (xxx. 6). Circumcision is universal among the Mohammedans as well as the Jews.

Cis. See KISH.

Cis'tern.

A small artificial reservoir dug in the earth and enclosed by stone or brick work, or scooped in a rock to collect and retain rain water (Deut. vi. 11; Jer. ii. 13). Cisterns were very numerous in Palestine, as the populace was largely dependent upon rain water (cp. War iii. 7, 12, and 13; iv. 1, 8). In the cities they were constructed on the top of the towers of the city wall (War v. 4, 3). They were also excavated under the houses and in the courtyards (cp. 2 Sam. xvii. 18; Jer. xxxviii. 6), provided with bucket and windlass (Ecc. xii. 6), and supplied with water conducted to them from the roof. In the open country the mouth is closed with a large stone and frequently, especially in the wilderness, is covered with earth to conceal it.

Cit'y.

In Hebrew usage, a collection of permanent human habitations, whether few or numerous, especially if surrounded by a wall (Gen. iv. 17; xviii. 26; xix. 20; Num. xiii. 19; Josh. iii. 16; x. 39; xiii. 17; Judg. xx. 15; Luke ii. 4; xxiii. 51). Walled and unwalled cities are distinguished (Deut. iii. 5; Esth. ix. 19, Hebrew). Cities were built on hills (Josh. xi. 3; 1 Kin. xvi. 24; Mat. v. 14; War iii. 7, 7), where the situation rendered defense easy; and in fertile spots, where water and soil invited man to dwell. They were usually fenced with high walls, gates and bars (Num. xiii. 28; Deut. iii. 5; Josh. ii. 5, 15; vi. 5; Neh. iii. 3; Acts ix. 24, 25), and further defended by towers (Neh. iii. 1, 11, 25; War v. 4, 3). Walls of the thickness of 20 to 30 feet were not unusual. The gate was a massive structure, with a room over the gateway (2 Sam. xviii. 33). In time of need a guard was posted at the gate (2. Kin. vii. 10; Neh. xiii. 19), and a watchman was stationed on the roof of gatehouse or tower (2 Sam. xviii. 24; 2 Kin. ix. 17; War v. 6, 3). In open places at the gate public business was transacted, cases at law adjudicated, and markets held (Gen. xxiii. 10; Ruth iv. 1–11; 2 Sam. xv. 2; 1 Kin. xxii. 10; 2 Kin. vii. 1; Neh. viii. 1). The streets were as a rule narrow (Antiq. xx. 5, 3; War ii. 14, 9; 15, 5; v. 8, 1), but not always (2 Sam. xv. 1; 1 Kin. i. 5; Jer. xvii. 25); and some streets were devoted to bazaars

(1 Kin. xx. 34; Neh. iii. 31; Jer. xxxvii. 21).

Cit'y of Da'vid. See DAVID, CITY OF.

Cit'y of Mo'ab (Num. xxii. 36, R. V.). See AR.

Cit'y of Ref'uge.
Six Levitical cities designed to shelter the person who had accidentally committed manslaughter from the pursuit of the avenger of blood (Num. xxxv. 9–14; Ex. xxi. 13); see AVENGER. Moses appointed the three east of the Jordan: Bezer in the territory of Reuben, Ramoth-gilead in that of Gad, and Golan in Bashan in the tribe of Manasseh (Deut. iv. 41–43). After the conquest of Canaan, Joshua and the heads of the tribes designated the three west of the river, setting apart Kedesh in the territory of Naphtali, Shechem in Ephraim, and Kirjath-arba, which is Hebron, in the mountain of Judah (Josh. xx. 7). No part of Palestine was far from a city of refuge. To the nearest the manslayer fled. He might be overtaken on the way and slain by the avenger; but if he reached a city of refuge he was received into it and obtained a fair trial. If guilty of willful murder he was delivered to death. If he had slain a fellow creature by accident or in self-defense, actual or constructive, he was granted asylum in the city. If he left the city before the death of the high priest he did so at his own risk. On the death of the high priest he was at liberty to return to his home and enjoy the protection of the authorities (Num. xxxv.; Deut. xix.; Josh. xx.). The matter was between man and God; and the death of the high priest, who represented the people before God, closed a period of theocratic life (cp. the release at the year of jubilee).

Clau'da.
A small island off the southwest of Candia or Crete. Paul's ship ran under its lee when caught by the tempest off Crete (Acts xxvii. 16). It was also called Cauda (R. V. text) and Gaudos (Pliny, Hist. nat. iv. 42). The Greeks still call it Claudanesa, or Gaudonesi, which the Italians have corrupted into Gozzo.

Clau'di-a.
A Christian woman who joined Paul in sending a salutation to Timothy (2 Tim. iv. 21).

Clau'di-us. See CÆSAR.

Clau'di-us Ly'si-as.
A chiliarch or commander of 1000 men, who seems to have been the military tribune in charge of the whole garrison at Jerusalem. Each legion had as its officers six such tribunes. He resided in the castle of Antonia, and sent soldiers to rescue Paul from fanatical Jewish rioters. He gave orders that this unknown Jew be examined by scourging, but had him unbound on being informed of his Roman citizenship. Soon afterwards he frustrated a plot against Paul's life by sending him by night under military escort to Cæsarea to Felix, the Roman procurator (Acts xxii. 24–xxiii. 35).

Clean. See UNCLEAN ANIMALS, UNCLEANNESS.

Clem'ent [kind, merciful].
A Christian who labored along with Paul, apparently at Philippi (Phil. iv. 3). He may have been the same individual as the apostolic father, Clement of Rome.

Cle'o-pas.
One of the two disciples who journeyed to and from Emmaus on the evening of the Resurrection day (Luke xxiv. 18). Apparently not the same as Clopas or Cleophas, though some Christian fathers, not of early date, assumed the identity of the two.

Cle-o-pa'tra.
A name borne by many Egyptian princesses. One was daughter of Ptolemy VI. and wife of Alexander Balas (1 Mac. x. 57, 58). Her father afterwards took her from Balas and married her to Demetrius Nicator when he invaded Syria (xi. 12; Antiq. xiii. 4, 7). During the captivity of Demetrius in Parthia, she married his brother Antiochus VII. (Antiq. xiii. 7, 1; 9, 3; 10, 1). She had two sons by Demetrius; the elder she murdered, and then raised to the throne the younger, Antiochus VIII., called Grypus. As he was unwilling to gratify her ambitious designs, she attempted to make away with him by offering him a cup of poison, but was compelled to drink it herself, 120 B. C.

Clo'pas, in A. V. **Cle'o-phas.** See ALPHÆUS.

Cloth'ing.
Man at first went naked (Gen. ii. 25). The first clothing consisted of the skins of beasts (iii. 21). Subsequently the materials used for clothing were wool (xxxi. 19; Lev. xiii. 47; Job xxxi. 20), linen (Ex. ix. 31; Lev. xvi. 4), byssus, a fabric made of cotton or flax (Gen. xli. 42; Luke xvi. 19), silk (Ezek. xvi. 10, 13; Rev. xviii. 12), goats' hair (Rev. vi. 12), and camels' hair (Mat. iii. 4). The essential articles of the apparel of men and women were two: 1. An undergarment or tunic, commonly called coat, less frequently garment, in the English versions. It usually had short sleeves and reached nearly to the knees, though a longer form with sleeves of full length was in use (Gen. xxxvii. 3; 2 Sam. xiii. 18, R. V. margin). This tunic was sometimes woven without seam (John xix. 23, 24). It was confined at the waist by a girdle. 2. An upper garment or mantle (Ruth iii. 15, R. V.; 1 Kin. xi. 30; Acts ix. 39), a large, square piece of cloth, provided with tassels (Num. xv. 38; Mat. xxiii. 5). It was thrown over the left shoulder and brought over or under the right arm. The pendant ends were called skirts (Hag. ii. 12; Zech. viii. 23). The garment of hair worn by prophets (2 Kin. i. 8; Zech. xiii. 4) may have consisted of a sheepskin or goatskin (cp. Heb. xi. 37), but was more probably made of coarse camel's hair (cp. Mat. iii. 4). An occasional garment was worn between the tunic and the

mantle by men and women of distinction and officially by the high priest (Lev. viii. 7; 1 Sam. ii. 19; xviii. 4; xxiv. 4; 2 Sam. xiii. 18; 1 Chron. xv. 27; Job i. 20, margin). It was a long vestment, with or without sleeves, tied round with a girdle (Antiq. iii. 7, 4). The girdles, which confined the undergarments at the waist to prevent them as far as possible from impeding the action of the limbs, were made of leather, linen, or byssus (2 Kin. i. 8; Jer. xiii. 1; Ezek. xvi. 10); often elaborately wrought and richly decorated (Ex. xxviii. 39; xxxix. 29; Dan. x. 5; Rev. i. 13). The sword was worn in the girdle and money was carried there (Judg. iii. 16; 1 Sam. xxv. 13; Mat. x. 9, R. V. margin). When outside of a room they wore sandals, an imperfect shoe consisting of a sole of wood or leather (Ezek. xvi. 10), fastened to the bare foot by straps passing over the instep and around the ankle (Gen. xiv. 23; Is. v. 27; Acts xii. 8). Probably people commonly went bareheaded; still turbans were on occasion worn by both sexes (Job. xxix. 14, R. V. margin; Is. iii. 20; Ezek. xxiii. 15). The veil was worn by women in the presence of strangers (Gen. xxiv. 65; Song v. 7); but it was not uncommon for them to go with face unveiled (Gen. xxiv. 16; xxvi. 8; Judith x. 7, 14). By the Mosaic law a man was forbidden to wear a garment that pertains to a woman, and a woman to wear that belonging to a man (Deut. xxii. 5; cp. 1 Cor. xi. 6, 14).

Cloud.
As agents in connection with rain, clouds are the bearers of moisture (2 Sam. xxii. 12; Job xxvi. 8; xxxvii. 11; Ecc. xi. 3), and discharge it upon the earth (Judg. v. 4; Ps. lxxvii. 17). A cloud in the west was a harbinger of rain (1 Kin. xviii. 44; Luke xii. 54). The Pillar of Cloud was a miraculous cloud taking the form of a pillar, which moved in front of the Israelites in the wilderness to indicate to them the way along which God wished them to advance (Ex. xiii. 21, 22; Neh. ix. 19). When the evening was too far advanced for it to be seen, it shone with light as a pillar of fire. When God designed to show his presence to the Israelites he did it in the pillar of cloud (Num. xii. 5; Deut. xxxi. 15), and when he designed to trouble the Egyptians he looked at them with hostile gaze through the pillar of cloud (Ex. xiv. 24).

Cni'dus.
A city of Caria, on the southwest coast of Asia Minor, over against the isle of Cos, which is about 10 miles away. It was a Dorian colony. Extensive ruins exist at the spot, containing fine remains of Grecian architecture. A small island just off the coast, now joined to the mainland, constitutes a peninsula called Cape Crio. Paul's vessel passed near it during the voyage to Rome (Acts xxvii. 7).

Coal.
In Scripture this is not the mineral sub-stance coal, but charcoal made by burning wood. Hence we read of coals of juniper (Ps. cxx. 4). It was used to furnish warmth in winter (Is. xlvii. 14; John xviii. 18), for culinary purposes (Is. xliv. 19; John xxi. 9), and by the smith (Is. xliv. 12; liv. 16).

Coat. See CLOTHING and HIGH PRIEST.

Coat of Mail. See ARMOR.

Cock.
The male of the well-known domestic fowl *Gallus domesticus*. It is figured on the ancient Egyptian monuments. The cock is mentioned in the N. T. (Mat. xxvi. 34, 74, 75). Cock-crowing, as a portion of time, is the third watch of the night (Mark xiii. 35). See NIGHT.

Cock'a-trice [Old French *cocatrice*, a corruption of Latin *crocodilus*, a crocodile].
A fabulous monster, created by the fancy of Europeans, and reputed to be hatched from a cock's egg brooded by a serpent. The A. V. so renders the Hebrew word *Ṣiphʻoni* (Is. xi. 8; lix. 5; Jer. viii. 17), and *Ṣephaʻ* (Is. xiv. 29); but in Prov. xxiii. 32 it translates the word by adder. The R. V. everywhere alters it to basilisk, or in the margin to adder.

Cock'le.
The rendering of the Hebrew *Boʼshah*, malodorous plant (Job xxxi. 40). But the cockle, a plant which is found in grain fields and grows one or two feet high, does not have a bad smell. The margin has noisome weeds, which is a more exact rendering.

Cœl'e-syr'i-a, in A. V. **Celosyria** [hollow Syria].
The valley between the Lebanon and Anti-Lebanon mountains. It is watered by the two streams Orontes and Litany, which rise in the vicinity of Baalbek and flow in opposite directions. The term had, however, a wider application (1 Mac. x. 69). It included the western side of the Jordan valley as far as Bethshean (Antiq. xiii. 13, 2) and the region extending from Damascus southward through Trachonitis, Peræa, and Idumæa to the borders of Egypt (cp. Antiq. i. 11, 5). It was distinct from Phœnicia (2 Mac. iii. 5).

Col-ho'zeh [all-seeing one].
Father of Shallun and perhaps one with the father of Baruch (Neh. iii. 15; xi. 5).

Col'lege.
A mistranslation of the Hebrew word *Mishneh* in A. V. of 2 Kin. xxii. 14, and 2 Chron. xxxiv. 22. The word is correctly rendered "the second [part]" in Zeph. i. 10. In these passages R. V. has "the second quarter."

Col'o-ny.
A settlement of Roman citizens authorized by the senate, in conquered territory. The decree of the senate fixed the amount of land to be set apart for the colony, the manner in which it was to be distributed, and the burdens to be borne. Philippi was a colony (Acts xvi. 12). See PRAETOR).

Col'ors.

Colors are presented to the eye by nature (Esth. i. 6) and were early imitated. In Babylonia different clays were employed to produce orange, red, and yellow bricks. Bricks of blue were obtained by vitrifaction. The ancient Egyptians prepared colors from various metallic and earthy substances. The Hebrews dyed skins in various colors (Ex. xxv. 5), and wove and embroidered cloth out of threads of various hues (Ex. xxvii. 16; Judith x. 21). A reddish purple dye (Ex. xxvii. 16; 1 Mac. iv. 23; Acts xvi. 14) was obtained from the secretion of a species of shell fish, *Murex trunculus*, found in the Mediterranean. Blue (Num. iv. 7; Ezek. xxiii. 6) was obtained from another shell fish, *Helix ianthina*. Scarlet or crimson was made from an insect (Ex. xxv. 4; Is. i. 18). They used a vermilion pigment for decorating walls, beams, idols, and the like (Jer. xxii. 14; Ezek. xxiii. 14: Wisd. xiii. 14). In addition to these artificial coloring matters, allusion is made in the Bible to white (Gen. xlix. 12; Is. i. 18), black, including brown (Gen. xxx. 32; Song i. 6; Mic. iii. 6, R. V.), red (Gen. xxv. 25, 30; 2 Kin. iii. 22; Prov. xxiii. 31), reddish (Lev. xiii. 19), sorrel (Zech. i. 8; in A. V. speckled; margin, bay), greenish (Ps. lxvii. 13; in Eng. vers. yellow; Lev. xiii. 49).

Symbolism was connected with colors. The temple of the seven lights at Borsippa, in Babylonia, consisted of seven stages, each colored in a hue appropriate to the planet it represented. Beginning at the lowest stage, the succession of colors was black, orange, blood-red, gold, pale-yellow, blue, and probably silver, according with the planets Saturn, Jupiter, Mars, the sun, Venus, Mercury, and the moon. In the Scripture white is the constant emblem of purity (Mark xvi. 5; Rev. iii. 4; xix. 11, 14) and joy (Ecc. ix. 8). The white horse signifies victory in Rev. vi. 2. The black horse is typical of famine and death (5, 6). Red commonly typifies blood, in which is life, or war and carnage (4). Blue is the familiar color of the sky, and purple was worn by princes and the rich in their magnificence (Judg. viii. 26; Esth. viii. 15; Luke xvi. 19).

Co-los'sæ, in A. V. Colosse.

A city of southwestern Phrygia, in Asia Minor, lying on the river Lycos not far east of its confluence with the Meander. It was originally on the trade route from west to east and was a place of much importance (Herod. vii. 30; Xen. Anabasis I. ii. 6). But the road system was changed, and the neighboring cities of Laodicea and Hierapolis (Col. ii. 1; iv. 13), distant ten and thirteen miles respectively, surpassed it in position and wealth, and the importance of Colossæ declined. It was, however, like Laodicea, famous for its fine wool, and it retained municipal independence under the Romans. A Christian community grew up at Colossæ

under the ministrations of Epaphras and later of Archippus (Col. i. 7; iv. 17; Philem. 2). Of this church Philemon was an active member, and also Onesimus (Col. iv. 9; Philem. 2).

Co-los'si-ans, E-pis'tle to the.

An epistle written when the apostle Paul was a prisoner (iv. 3, 10, 18) probably at Rome during the two years of his first imprisonment there (Acts xxviii. 30, 31), though some believe that it was written from Cæsarea (Acts xxiii. 35; xxiv. 27). From Col. ii. 1 it appears evident that he had never himself preached at Colossæ; and i. 7 seems to imply that Epaphras had been the founder, or at least had assisted in the establishment of the Colossian church. The church may have been founded while Paul was laboring in Ephesus (Acts xix. 10). Epaphras had recently joined the apostle (i. 8), and his report of the condition of the church prompted the writing of the letter. It was sent by the hand of a certain Tychicus (iv. 7, 8), who was also intrusted with the letter to the Ephesians (Eph. vi. 21), written at the same time. With him went Onesimus (Col. iv. 9), who also bore the letter to Philemon, a resident of Colossæ, whose slave Onesimus had formerly been. The Archippus mentioned in Phile. 2, probably Philemon's son, is also mentioned in Col. iv. 17. The salutations which the letter contains (iv. 10-17) indicate that while Paul had not labored in Colossæ his friends had, and that he himself was well acquainted with some of the Colossians. In fact, Philemon was one of his converts (Phile. 19), made, perhaps, in Ephesus. The reports of Epaphras had shown that the Colossian Christians were threatened by false teachers, who seemed to have combined ritualistic, ascetic, and speculative tendencies. That they were Jewish appears from ii. 11, 16. But they were also ascetic (ii. 16, 20-23), a feature which may have come from the Jewish sect of Essenes. With this they united a mystic philosophy (ii. 8), which seems to have claimed superior knowledge of divine things (ii. 18) and to have introduced the worship of angels (ii. 18), thus infringing on the all-sufficiency and the supremacy of Christ. These false teachers, therefore, were different from the Judaizers whom Paul opposed in the Epistle to the Galatians. They represent a new form of error, and in certain respects appear as the forerunners of the Gnostics. They united with ritualism that theosophical tendency which was almost characteristic of oriental thought, and therefore demanded an immediate refutation by the apostle. The epistle naturally falls into four parts: (1) the introduction and thanksgiving (i. 1–8); (2) the doctrinal section (i. 9–iii. 4); (3) practical exhortations (iii. 5–iv. 6); (4) concluding salutations (iv. 7–18). The doctrinal section is of great importance. Beginning with a prayer for their growth in knowledge and holiness, he rises to a description of the preëminence of Christ in his relation to

God, the universe, and the church. Then in ch. ii. he sets forth Christ's preëminence as against the errorists, assuring believers of their completeness in him, since he has once for all triumphed over their spiritual foes, and nothing but union with him by faith is requisite for the full experience of salvation. As against asceticism he further urges, in his practical exhortations, to a spiritual morality and to social order. The epistle is, therefore, christological in character. It assumes the doctrines of salvation taught in previous epistles, but more explicitly states the pre-eminence of Christ's person and the sufficiency of his work. This epistle, together with Philemon and Ephesians, was probably written comparatively early in Paul's Roman imprisonment, perhaps in the early spring of A. D. 62. The Epistle to the Ephesians has many remarkable coincidences of language and thought with that to the Colossians, though their differences are equally note-worthy; see EPHESIANS. While evidently written at the same time, Ephesians presents a further unfolding of the truths which the specific needs of his Colossian readers led him to write to them.   G. T. P.

Com-men-ta′ry.
A Midrash or interpretation of history from the religious standpoint and its didac-tic exposition; as the prophet Iddo's com-mentary on the acts, ways, and sayings of king Abijah (2 Chron. xiii. 22, R. V.), and the commentary of the book of the kings, in which were set forth the burdens laid upon king Josiah and his rebuilding of the temple (xxiv. 27, R. V.).

Con-a-ni′ah, in A. V. twice **Cononiah** [Jehovah hath established].
1. A Levite who had charge of the tithes and offerings in Hezekiah's reign (2 Chron. xxxi. 12, 13).
2. A Levite of high station in the reign of Josiah (2 Chron. xxxv. 9).

Con′cu-bine.
In the Bible a secondary wife under the system of polygamy. Concubines were com-monly taken from among the purchased slaves or captives; as Hagar (Gen. xvi. 2, 3; xxi. 10), Bilhah (xxix. 29; xxxv. 22), Gideon's concubine (Judg. viii. 31; ix. 18). They could be more easily put away than a wife (Gen. xxi. 10-14), yet their rights were recog-nized and guarded by the Mosaic law (Ex. xxi. 7-11; Deut. xxi. 10-14).

Co′ney.
The coney of England is the rabbit; that of Scripture is probably the rock-badger (Lev. xi. 5). See ROCK-BADGER.

Con-gre-ga′tion.
In Scripture the word is used mainly for:
1. The body politic of Israel, including men, women, and children (Ex. xii. 3, 19, 47; xvi. 1, 22; Lev. iv. 13, 15; xxiv. 14; Num. i. 2; xiv. 1; xv. 26; xvi. 9; xx. 11; Judg. xx. 1).

2. An assemblage of the people, especially for religious purposes (1 Kin. viii. 14, 65; 2 Chron. xxx. 2, 4; Ps. xxii. 22, 25), or the community regarded as ever summoned and assembled for worship. In R. V. the word assembly is often preferred (Num. x. 7; xvi. 3; xix. 20; xx. 4; Josh. viii. 35; and so also sometimes in A. V. Judg. xx. 2), and in Acts xiii. 43 the word synagogue.
3. In A. V. the tabernacle of the congre-gation designates the tent of meeting (R. V.), the appointed place where Jehovah and his people met (Ex. xxvii. 21; cp. xxv. 22; xxix. 42; xxx. 36).

Co-ni′ah. See JECONIAH.

Con-o-ni′ah. See CONANIAH.

Con-se-cra′tion.
The act whereby a person or thing is dedi-cated to the service and worship of God. It includes ordination to a sacred office (Ex. xxix. 9), ordination to sacred service (Lev. viii. 33; 1 Chron. xxix. 5; 2 Chron. xxix. 31), and the setting apart of things from a common to a sacred use (Josh. vi. 19; 2 Chron. xxxi. 6).

Con-ver-sa′tion.
In the English versions the word conver-sation is used in its obsolescent sense and de-notes manner of life.
1. The rendering in the A. V. of the Greek words *Politeuō* and *Politeuma* (Phil. i. 27; iii. 20). The words refer to civil life, as is recog-nized by R. V. Christians are citizens of the heavenly kingdom and their daily civil con-duct should correspond with the teachings of the gospel of the kingdom.
2. The rendering, in many passages of the A. V., and even in R. V. of Ps. l. 23, of vari-ous words, especially of the Greek *Anas-trophē*. It means conduct, or mode of life, especially with respect to morals (Ps. xxxvii. 14; Eph. iv. 22; Heb. xiii. 5; 1 Pet. i. 15).

Con-vo-ca′tion.
A festival on which the Israelites were summoned to assemble together and when no servile work was allowed to be done. The holy convocations were every sabbath (Lev. xxiii. 1-3), the first and seventh days of the feast of unleavened bread (Ex. xii. 16; Lev. xxiii. 6, 7; Num. xxviii. 18, 25), Pentecost (Lev. xxiii. 15-21), the first and seventh days of the tenth month, the latter being the great day of atonement (Lev. xxiii. 24-28, 35; Num. xxix. 1), and the first and eighth days of the feast of tabernacles, which began on the 15th of the seventh month (Lev. xxiii. 34-36; Neh. viii. 18).

Co′os. See Cos.

Cop′per. See BRASS.

Cor. See MEASURES.

Cor′al.
A rendering of the Hebrew *Ra′moth*. It was highly prized (Job xxviii. 18; Prov. xxiv. 7, in E. V. "too high"), and was

brought to the markets of Tyre by Aramæan traders (Ezek. xxvii. 16). It was obtained in the Mediterranean and Red seas, and was made into beads and charms. Coral is properly the calcareous skeleton of certain animals of low organization, popularly but erroneously called coral insects. They are radiated animals, with a central mouth surrounded by fleshy limbs; and are either attached singly to a rock, or so bud from parents as to make a compound being of many half-distinct, half-united individuals. The carbonate of lime of which the coral skeleton is made is obtained from the sea water. The coral is often beautifully branched like a tree or shrub, whence these animals are often called Zoöphytes (Plant animals). Some species form great reefs.

Coral is also a marginal rendering of the Hebrew *Peninim*, rendered rubies in the text (Lam. iv. 7; Job xxviii. 18; Prov. iii. 15).

Cor-a′shan. See ASHAN.

Cor′ban [Hebrew *ḳorban*, offering].

An offering or oblation, either of a bloody or an unbloody sacrifice, given to God (Lev. i. 2, 3; ii. 1; iii. 1; Num. vii. 12–17; where the word occurs in the Hebrew text). A word *korbanas*, from the same root, is rendered in Mat. xxvii. 6 "treasury," and on the margin of the R. V. "sacred treasury." Corban is used for money or service dedicated to God (Mark vii. 11). The reprehensible practice arose of children giving no aid to parents needing their support, on the pretense that the money or service which would otherwise have been available for the parents had been dedicated to God, and that it would be sacrilege to divert it from this sacred purpose. Josephus relates that a clamorous mob beset the tribunal of Pontius Pilate when he took the sacred móney called Corban and expended it on aqueducts designed to improve the water supply of Jerusalem. This doubtless was a public benefit, but the Jews evidently thought that money once dedicated to God could never again be lawfully used for a secular purpose, however conducive to the public welfare (War ii. 9, 4).

Co′re. See KORAH.

Co-ri-an′der.

A plant, called in Hebrew *Gad*, which had white seeds (Ex. xvi. 31; Num. xi. 7). Very probably it was the Coriander (*Coriandrum sativum*), called in Punic *Goid;* a branched annual, with cut leaves, umbels of pink or white flowers, and a small globular fruit used to season dishes. It is wild in Arabia, northern Africa, and, perhaps, in southern Europe. In Palestine it is found in cultivated grounds and in the Jordan valley.

Cor′inth.

A city of Greece, on the narrow isthmus that connects the Peloponnesus with the mainland. At an early date a town grew up at the southern end of this neck of land on the plateau at the northern foot of the Acro-corinthus. This mountain is 1750 feet high, and its summit served as a citadel and as the site for a temple. The land traffic between the peninsula and the mainland was obliged to pass the town, and much of the commerce between Asia and the west was brought to its harbors and portage by the convenience of the water route afforded by the Salonic Gulf on the east of the isthmus and the Gulf of Corinth on the west. The town attracted Phœnician settlers, who made a purple dye from fish of the neighboring waters, introduced the manufacture of cloth, pottery, and armor, and established the impure worship of the Phœnician deities. At a later time emigrants from Attica became dominant. About 1074 B. C. the political supremacy passed to the Dorians. But the character of the inhabitants remained unchanged; they were commercial in spirit, unwarlike, luxurious, and licentious. Their immoral life gave rise and meaning to a verb "to corinthianize."

Except during the years 243–222 B. C., the Macedonians held the citadel from 335–197 B. C., when in 196 B. C. Greece was declared independent by the Romans. In 146 B. C., in consequence of rebellion against Rome, the Roman consul Mummius burned the city to ashes. The accidental fusing together of different metals during the conflagration is said to have led to the discovery of Corinthian brass. The city was rebuilt by Julius Cæsar shortly before his death in 44 B. C.; became the capital of the Roman province of Achaia, and was ruled by a proconsul. Paul reached Corinth probably in A. D. 52 and labored there for a year and a half. He lodged with Aquila and Priscilla, supported himself by tent-making, and preached Christ, first in the synagogue and then in the house of Justus. At length he was dragged before the tribunal of the proconsul Gallio, but was dismissed (Acts xviii. 1–18). After Paul's departure, Apollos continued the work (xviii. 24–28). On three several occasions later the apostle sent letters to the Corinthian church (1 Cor. v. 9). The Christian community continued to increase; and by the second century its bishop possessed great influence in the church at large. The capture of Constantinople by the Venetians and the crusaders in 1204 was followed by the surrender of Corinth. In 1446 the Turks took it, and in 1687 the Venetians retook it; the Turks capturing it again in 1715. In 1823 it joined in the successful great rebellion. In February, 1858, it was nearly destroyed by an earthquake, but has since been restored. It is now called Gortho.

Co-rin′thi-ans, E-pis′tles to the.

The First Epistle of Paul to the Corinthians was written during the apostle's long sojourn in Ephesus (xvi. 8, 9, 19; Acts xix.), probably early in A. D. 57. He had had much anxiety over the state of the Corinthian church, which he had founded a few years before. The Corinthians had written him a letter asking instructions on the subject of marriage and social purity, and he had replied (v. 9). This letter has not been preserved. Apparently also a deputation from Corinth had been sent to him (xvi. 17), and from other sources reports of divisions among them had reached him (i. 11). He had previously sent Timothy to Corinth by way of Macedonia (iv. 17; xvi. 10), but the later news moved him immediately to write this epistle. It is even thought by many that Paul himself made a brief unrecorded visit to Corinth from Ephesus for the purpose of exercising discipline in the church. This is inferred from 2 Cor. xii. 14; xiii. 1, where he speaks of being about to visit them a *third* time, though The Acts speaks of only one previous visit. Some have located this unrecorded visit before 1 Cor. was written; but, since that epistle does not allude to it, it should be placed between 1 and 2 Cor. But in 1 Cor. he takes up in order the practical and doctrinal points on which they needed instruction. The epistle is carefully written. It combines cogent doctrinal discussion, and skillful dealing with moral and ecclesiastical problems. It clearly reflects the actual conditions of the churches among the gentiles. Hence its great importance. The subjects discussed are, after the introductory salutation (i. 1-9):

1. The divisions in the church (i. 10-iv. 21). Factions had arisen, claiming to follow particular leaders, and doubtless characterized by special theological tendencies. He mentions a Paul-party, an Apollos-party, a Peter-party, and a Christ-party. Against them all he sets forth the dependence of all believers on Christ crucified, the inspired authority with which the gospel had first been preached to them, and the subordinate character of every one by whom it was administered, even though he were an apostle ; so that none should be the head of a party, but glory given to God in Christ alone.

2. The duty of exercising and honoring church discipline (v., vi.), especially in the case of offenders against purity, of which there had been one conspicuous example.

3. Directions on the subject of marriage and divorce (vii).

4. Directions concerning practical questions arising from contact with heathen society (viii.-xi. 1). These pertained especially to the eating of food which had been offered to idols ; in regard to which self-denial should control their liberty (viii.), even as he sought to have it do in his own life (ix.). While not needlessly inquiring as to the origin of the food they bought or ate, they should be careful not to seem to participate in recognition of the idol (x.).

5. Warnings against certain abuses in public worship (xi. 2-34) with respect to the prophesying of women and the administration of the Lord's Supper.

6. Directions as to the estimate, exercise and regulation, of miraculous gifts (xii.-xiv.).

7. Instruction concerning the doctrine of the resurrection of the dead, which some were disposed to doubt (xv.).

8. Directions about the collections being made for the saints in Judæa, and concluding remarks about his own movements and other personal matters (xvi.).

The Second Epistle to the Corinthians was written from Macedonia (ii. 13; vii. 5; ix. 2, 4) shortly after Paul left Ephesus (Acts xx. 1), and therefore in the summer or early autumn of A. D. 57. Timothy was now with him again (i. 1). Titus and another had recently been sent from Ephesus to Corinth (ii. 13; vii. 6, 7, 13, 14, 15; xii. 18) with directions to have the church immediately discipline an offender, probably the incestuous person of 1 Cor. v. 1, who had openly defied the apostle's authority and whose continued sin threatened the very stability of the church. Titus was to rejoin Paul at Troas, but the apostle, not finding him there, had gone on to Macedonia in great distress of mind. At last, however, Titus came with the good news that the Corinthians had disciplined the offender, and that the latter had humbly acknowledged his sin. Thereupon this epistle was written, and Titus, with two others (viii. 16-24), was sent back with it to Corinth. The epistle bears witness to the intense anxiety of the apostle lest the Corinthians should be false to him, and to the terrible strain he had been under because of their spiritual perils. It is the least methodical and the most personal of his epistles. It falls, however, into three main divisions: (1) i.-vii., in which, after grateful recognition of God's goodness to him even amid trial (i. 1-14), he vindicates himself from the charge of vacillation (i. 15-ii. 4), bids them not carry too far their zeal against the offender (ii. 5-11), and describes the spiritual (iii.), honest (iv. 1-6), suffering (iv. 7-18), hopeful (v. 1-9), solemn (v. 10, 11), Christ-impelled (v. 12-17) ministry of reconciliation (v. 18-21) with which, as a co-worker with God, he had been intrusted (v. 18-vi. 2), in which he had appeared himself (vi. 3-10), on the ground of which he appealed to them (vi. 11-18), and in their acknowledgment of which he found boldness and joy (vii.). (2) viii., ix., in which he treats of the collections for the Judæan saints and urges liberality. (3) x.-xii., in which he again gives a pathetic but confident testimony to his apostolic office and authority. He closes with a renewed warning against their besetting sins, and declares that if, when he comes to them, he find them uncorrected, he will exercise his authority upon them unsparingly.   G. T. P.

The last section of the epistle, chapters x.-xiii., is believed by many students of the New Testament to be a separate letter, or fragment of it, written by Paul soon after his return to Ephesus from his unrecorded visit to Corinth (see foregoing remarks introductory to the First Epistle). The mind of the apostle was not wholly relieved by that visit. He had come back to Ephesus anxious about the Corinthian church, and in his sorrow he wrote a letter. It is the letter of tears and anguish of heart, alluded to in passages which refer to events connected with the unrecorded visit (2 Cor. ii. 4; vii. 8–12). The section, 2 Cor. x.–xiii., so sad in tone and revealing the apostle's distress of mind, may be this sorrowful letter. But encouraging news from Corinth at length reached the apostle, brought by Titus. The offender had been disciplined. The hostility toward Paul, shown by a minority, had disappeared, and in its stead loyalty to him and growing affection reigned. Thereupon the apostle wrote the cheerful letter preserved in 2 Cor. i.–ix. The theory is, of course, interesting as a literary question (cp. Mark xvi. 9–20). It involves neither the genuineness of the epistle, as a whole or in its parts, nor its inspiration. But it is not the only tenable explanation of the facts in the case, as the analysis given in the former part of this article shows; and, if the last four chapters ever existed as a separate letter, it is strange, indeed, that no trace of the fact has been left in the history of the New Testament text.   J. D. D.

Cor'mo-rant.

1. The rendering of Hebrew *Shalak*, plunger; a bird ceremonially unclean (Lev. xi. 17; Deut. xiv. 17). It is probably the common cormorant (*Phalacrocorax carbo*), a large swimming bird of the Pelican family, but distinguished from the pelican by not having a pouch below the lower mandible. The common cormorant is widely distributed. In Palestine it lives on the Mediterranean coast and on the sea of Galilee. Its appetite is proverbial; and Tristram describes it as sitting on the snag of a tree where the Jordan enters the Dead Sea, and catching the fish while they are stupefied by being carried into the briny water. Another species, *Phalacrocorax pigmæus*, the Pygmy Cormorant, is found sparingly on the streams which flow through Palestine to the Mediterranean.
2. The rendering of Hebrew *Ka'ath* in text of A. V. (Is. xxxiv. 11; Zeph. ii. 14); see PELICAN.

Corn.

The generic name for the several cereal grasses cultivated in Palestine, and so staple that corn and wine stand figuratively for the entire vegetable produce of the fields (Gen. xxvii. 28; Deut. vii. 13, etc.). The chief were wheat, barley, spelt, and millet (Deut. viii. 8; and R. V. of Is. xxviii. 25 and Ezek. iv. 9).

Cor-ne'li-us.

A centurion of the Roman cohort called the Italian band. He lived at Cæsarea; and was a devout, charitable, God-fearing gentile On the ground of visions received by him and Peter, and the descent of the Holy Spirit upon him and his household when they believed, Peter baptized him. The descent of the Holy Ghost upon him was an event of prime importance in the early church. It marked the beginning of the calling of the gentiles and revealed that the Spirit is given to believers irrespective of nationality (Acts x. 1–48).

Cor'ner Stone.

A stone placed at the angle where two walls of a building meet, and helping to bind them together. Any stone in this position, from the foundation (Job xxxviii. 6; Is. xxviii. 16) to the roof (Ps. cxviii. 22; Zech. iv. 7), is a corner stone. Figuratively, Christ is the chief corner stone at the foundation (Rom. ix. 33; Eph. ii. 20; 1 Pet. ii. 6) and also the head of the corner (Mat. xxi. 42; 1 Pet. ii. 7).

Cor'net.

1. The rendering of the Hebrew *Shophar* in 1 Chron. xv. 28; 2 Chron. xv. 14; Ps. xcviii. 6; Hos. v. 8. Elsewhere, as in Lev. xxv. 9, it is translated trumpet (q. v.).
2. The rendering of the Hebrew *M^ena'an^eim* in 2 Sam. vi. 5, A. V. The R. V. renders the word castanets (q. v.).
3. The rendering of the Aramaic *Karna'*, corresponding to the Hebrew *Keren* in Dan. iii. 5, 7, 10, 15. It means a horn, and is so rendered in viii. 20. This instrument originally consisted of the hollow horn of some mammal; but later it was generally made of metal, and was curved, like many animals' horns, instead of being straight.

Cor-rup'tion, Mount of.

A hill to the east of Jerusalem (2 Kin. xxiii. 13; cp. 1 Kin. xi. 7). Solomon built altars on its southern side to the gods worshiped by his heathen wives. By common consent it is the southern portion of the mount of Olives. It is more familiarly known in tradition as the mount of Offense.

Cos, in A. V. Coos.

An island, now called *Stanko* or *Stanchio*, in the Archipelago off the coast of Caria in Asia Minor, in a gulf between Cnidus and Halicarnassus. It lies between Miletus and Rhodes, about a day's sail from the latter city (Acts xxi. 1; mentioned 1 Mac. xv. 23). It is about 21 miles long by 6 broad. Its principal city has been more than once seriously injured by earthquakes. Cos was celebrated for its wines, its ointments, and its purple dyes.

Co'sam.

A descendant of David through Nathan and an ancestor of Zerubbabel and Christ (Luke iii. 28).

Cot'ton.

The rendering of the Hebrew *Karpas* in the margin of the R. V. in Esth. i. 6. In the court of the royal palace at Shushan were hangings of fine white cotton and blue. The word which corresponds to *karpas* in Sanscrit, Persian, Armenian, and Arabic denotes cotton. Cotton is the bunch of threads surrounding the ripe seeds of the cotton plants. They belong to the genus *Gossypium*, which is one of the mallow order. The leaves have three or five lobes; the flowers, which are large and showy, and often of a yellow color, are surrounded by an outer involucre or calyx of three great leaves. The Indian cotton (*Gossypium herbaceum*) was early cultivated in Persia, and was probably that of Esther.

Coun'cil.

1. The Jewish governing body. The Persians granted to the Jews jurisdiction over their own affairs (Ezra vii. 25, 26; x. 14). After the fall of the Persian empire similar privileges were enjoyed by the Jews. A governing body arose and became known as *gerousia* or senate (Antiq. xii. 3, 3), and more fully as the senate of the nation (1 Mac. xii. 6). It was composed of elders (cp. xiv. 20). It represented the nation (xii. 3), and united with Jonathan, their high priest and leader, in making offensive and defensive alliance with the Spartans. Jonathan also called the elders of the people together and consulted with them about building strongholds in Judæa and increasing the height of the walls of Jerusalem (35; cp. further xiii. 36; xiv. 20, 28, and 47). Under Gabinius, proconsul of Syria, 57–55 B. C., Judæa was divided into five districts, each under a *sunedrion* or *sunodos*—i. e. assembly or sanhedrin (Antiq. xiv. 5, 4; War i. 8, 5). Henceforth the highest body at Jerusalem was called *sunedrion*, though not to the exclusion of *gerousia* or *boulē*. The arrangement, however, did not last long. In 47 B. C., Cæsar extended the jurisdiction of the sanhedrin of Jerusalem once more over all Judæa (cp. Antiq. xiv. 9, 3–5; War i. 10, 7). At the beginning of his reign Herod the Great put forty-five of its members to death (Antiq. xiv. 9, 4; xv. 1, 2), but did not abolish the council (xv. 6, 2). Under the Roman procurators, A. D. 6–66, its powers were extensive. According to Jewish authorities, it was composed of 71 members (cp. the mock council, War iv. 5, 4), and only Israelites whose descent was above question were eligible to membership. The seventy ordinary members corresponded, probably, to the seventy elders appointed by Moses to assist him as judges. The seventy-first member was the high priest, the official president of the body. It was the highest court, with power of life and death (Antiq. xiv. 9, 3 and 4; Mat. xxvi. 3, 57; Acts iv. 5, 6, 15; v. 21, 27, 34, 41; vi. 12, 15; vii. 1; xxiii. 2), though apparently it had no recognized authority to execute its sentence of death, but must submit its action to the review of the Roman authorities. It had the general administration of the government and of justice, so far as this was not exercised by the procurator and subordinate officials (cp. Acts xxii. 30). In the time of Florus, at least, the revenue was collected by the rulers and councilors, who dispersed themselves among the villages for that purpose (War ii. 17, 1). It had police at command and could make arrests on its own authority (Mat. xxvi. 47; Mark xiv. 43). Jesus was tried before the council (Mat. xxvi. 59; Mark xiv. 55; xv. 1: Luke xxii. 66; John xi. 47). It was before the council that Peter, John, and the other apostles were brought (Acts iv. 5, 6, 15; v. 21, 27, 34, 41) Stephen was taken before the council (Acts vi. 12), so also was Paul (xxii. 30; xxiii. 15; xxiv. 20). The sanhedrin was swept away at the destruction of Jerusalem.

2. A body of advisers selected by the highest Roman official of a province, in Judæa the procurator, to assist him in the administration of justice, before whom, with the official as president, cases were tried (Acts xxv. 12; Antiq. xvi. 11, 1 seq.; War ii. 16, 1).

Coun'cil House.

A building in Jerusalem west of the temple, near the gymnasium and adjoining the innermost city wall (War v. 4, 2). It was burned by the Romans under Titus in the course of their struggle for the possession of the city (vi. 6, 3). The council house was probably the place where the sanhedrin met: for 1. Its name in Greek was *bouleutērion*, and a member of the sanhedrin was called *bouleutēs* (Luke xxiii. 50, 51; cp. War ii. 17, 1). 2. The council is called by Josephus *sunedrion*—i. e. sanhedrin—and *boulē* indifferently (Antiq. xiv. 9, 3 and 4, with xx. 1, 2; War ii. 15, 6). 3. According to Jewish authorities, the sanhedrin met in the *lishkath haggazith* or chamber of the gazith, which probably denoted a chamber by the gymnasium. According to the Mishna, it is true, the *lishkath haggazith* was situated at the east corner of the court of the temple. But gazith means hewn, especially hewn stone (Ex. xx. 25; 1 Kin. vi. 36 et pas.); and as the chambers of the temple were largely constructed in this manner, the name gazith could not distinguish one from another. Now the council house stood near or adjoined the xystus or gymnasium; but xystos is the Greek equivalent of gazith, and is one of the words used in the Septuagint to translate gazith into Greek (1 Chron. xxii. 2; Amos v. 11). It can scarcely be doubted, therefore, that the xystos was called the gazith by one who chanced to be speaking Hebrew, and that the name *lishkath haggazith* meant the hall by the xystos (cp. Schürer, *Stud. u. Krit.*, 1878). Similar twin names are Christos, Messiah; Peter, Cephas; The pavement, Gabbatha; Place of a skull, Golgotha; Field of blood, Aceldama (John i. 41, 42; xix. 13, 17; Acts i. 19). This evidence is perhaps sufficient to override the fact that the chamber of the gazith is stated in the Mishna, as already mentioned, to have been within the court of the temple.

Coun'sel-or.

The seven counselors of Artaxerxes (Ezra) vii. 14) were probably the seven princes of Media and Persia who saw the king's face and sat first in the kingdom, and from whom the king sought advice (Esth. i. 14). These princes were perhaps the heads of the seven chief families of Persia (Herod. iii. 84).

Court.

An enclosed but uncovered area either connected with a private house and often containing a well (2 Sam. xvii. 18; Neh. viii. 16); or in a palace (1 Kin. vii. 8, 9, 12; Jer. xxxii. 2), in front of the royal apartments (Esth. iv. 11; v. 1; vi. 4) and sometimes containing a garden (i. 5); or around the tabernacle and temple (Ex. xxvii. 9; xl. 8; 1 Kin. vi. 36). As the area about the temple was divided (2 Kin. xxi. 5), the word is generally used in the plural (Ps. lxv. 4; lxxxiv. 2).

Cov'e-nant.

An agreement between two or more persons. Various covenants between man and man are mentioned in Scripture, but they are no longer important (Gen. xxi. 27, 32; 1 Sam. xviii. 3; xxiii. 18; 1 Kin. xx. 34). It is otherwise with those in which God condescended to be a covenanting party. His covenant with man is a free promise on his part, generally based upon the fulfillment of certain conditions by man. He made a promise of continued life and favor to man on condition of obedience, coupled with a penalty for disobedience (Gen. ii. 16, 17). He established a covenant with Noah, that Noah should be saved when the old world perished (vi. 18), and that there should be no other great deluge, the rainbow being the token of the covenant (ix. 12, 15, 16) ; with Abraham and his posterity, of which circumcision was to be the sign, to be their God and to give them the land of Canaan for an inheritance (xiii. 17; xv. 18; xvii. 2, 4, 7, 11, 13, 14, 19; 2 Kin. xiii. 23; 1 Chron. xvi. 15-18; Ps. cv. 9-11; Acts vii. 8; Rom. iv. 13, 17); with the Israelites as a nation, to continue to be their God and to grant national protection, of which a sign was to be the Sabbath (Ex. xxxi. 16), and the keeping of the ten commandments its condition (Deut. iv. 13, 23). This covenant was made at Horeb (Deut. v. 2; xxix. 1) and was renewed with the next generation on the plains of Moab (Deut. xxix. 1). There was a covenant with the Levites (Mal. ii. 4, 8), and one specially with Phinehas to give him and his descendants an everlasting priesthood (Num. xxv. 12, 13). There was a covenant with David that his posterity should forever occupy his throne (Ps. lxxxix. 20-28, 34; cp. 2 Sam. vii. 1-29 and 1 Chron. xvii. 1-27; 2 Chron. vii. 18; Jer. xxxiii. 21). In contrast with the covenant at Sinai, there was to be a new covenant, also with the Israelites, which was to

be of a more spiritual character than its predecessors (Jer. xxxi. 31-34; Heb. viii. 8-11), administered by the Spirit (John vii. 39; Acts ii. 32, 33; 2 Cor. iii. 6-9), based on faith (Gal. iv. 21-31), and designed for all nations (Mat. xxviii. 19, 20, Acts x. 44-47). Of this Christ is the Mediator (Heb. viii. 6-13; ix. 1; x. 15-17; xii. 24). With reference to it the Old and New Testaments would, perhaps, better have been called the Old and New Covenants.

The two tablets of stone on which were engraved the ten commandments, which were the fundamental law of God's covenant with Israel, were called the tables of the covenant (Deut. ix. 11), and the ark, in which these tables were deposited, was designated the ark of the covenant (Num. x. 33). The book of the covenant, prefaced perhaps by the ten commandments, consisted of the ordinances contained in Ex. xx. 22-xxiii. 33, which were written by Moses in a book, formally accepted by the Israelites, and ratified as a covenant between the Lord and his people (Ex. xxiv. 3-8); see THEOCRACY. Later the term is used as synonymous with the book of the law (2 Kin. xxiii. 2 with xxii. 8, 11) and included Deuteronomy (Deut. xxxi. 9, 26; 2 Kin. xiv. 6 with Deut. xxiv. 16).

Cow.

Cows were early domesticated. Egypt, Philistia, and Palestine, afforded excellent pasturage, and cows were kept in these lands (Gen. xli. 2; Deut. vii. 13; 1 Sam. vi. 7). Cows were herded by Abraham and his descendants (Gen. xii. 16; xxxii. 15). Their milk served for food (2 Sam. xvii. 29). They found use in concluding a covenant (Gen. xv. 9), in the ceremony attending the profession of innocence of a death caused by an undiscoverable murderer (Deut. xxi. 3), for a peace offering (Lev. iii. 1), for a sin offering for uncleanness arising from contact with the dead (Num. xix. 2; Heb. ix. 13), and in exceptional cases for a burnt offering (1 Sam. vi. 14).

Coz. See HAKKOZ.

Coz'bi [mendacious].

A daughter of Zur, prince of Midian. In the idolatrous rites to which the Midianites seduced Israel the woman was publicly taken by a prince of the Simeonites. Both were thrust through by Phinehas, son of the high priest, and shortly afterwards her father also was slain (Num. xxv. 6-8, 14, 15, 18; xxxi. 8).

Co-ze'ba, in A. V. Chozeba [deceitful].

A village in Judah, peopled chiefly by descendants of Shelah (1 Chron. iv. 22). It is generally believed to be the same as Achzib and Chezib. Conder, however, locates it at Kûeizîba, 5½ miles north-northeast of Hebron, at the head of Pilate's aqueduct to Jerusalem.

Crane.

Hebrew 'Agûr, a migratory bird which has a note like a chatter (Is. xxxviii. 14; Jer.

viii. 7). The crane is the type of a family of long-legged wading birds. It is a large and elegant bird, breeding in the north of Europe and of Asia, and migrating southward at the approach of winter. On these flights cranes go in large flocks of wedge-shaped form or in long lines. See SWALLOW 3.

Cre-a'tion.

The act or operation of God whereby he calls into existence what did not before exist. The verb always has God for its subject, and the result is an entirely new thing. God created the heavens and the earth (Gen. i. 1), aquatic and aërial life (21), man (27), the stars (Is. xl. 26), the wind (Amos iv. 13). He creates the clean heart (Ps. li. 10). Jehovah commanded and the heavens, with all their hosts, angels, sun, moon, and stars, and the waters that be above the heavens, were created (Ps. cxlviii. 5). He spake and it was done. Upon him all living creatures depend; his hand provides for them, his look preserves them, the hiding of his face destroys them, and his creative breath renews animate life on earth (Ps. civ. 27–30). God created the worlds by the Word, who is the Son (John i. 3; Eph. iii. 9; Col. i. 16; Heb. i. 2).

The designation creation is used specially for the original formation of the universe by God. In Genesis a general account of the creation of the universe is first given (i. 1–ii. 3), which is followed by a particular account of the formation of man and his surroundings (ii. 4–25). The general account describes six successive acts, or sometimes groups of logically related acts and processes, which were willed by God on as many days; see DAY 3. All facts at present available indicate that between the successive days long periods of time intervened. The omission of the definite article in the enumeration, one day and day second, instead of the first day, the second day, etc., is favorable to this view. And the parallel tradition, as preserved by the Babylonians, expressly refers to intervals between the successive acts of creation and assigns to them long duration.

The earliest extant form of the Babylonian account is found as the introduction to the myth of the sun-god Marduk's conflict with Tiamat the watery deep, represented as a she-dragon who has attempted to reduce the ordered universe to chaos. The tablet was inscribed about 650 B. C., but the tale itself can be traced much farther back. It states that—

At the time when on high the heaven announced not,
Below earth named not a name,
  [That is to say: When heaven and earth did not exist]
Then primeval ocean, their generator, [and]
Mummu Tiamat [the watery deep], the bearer of their totality,
United their waters as one;
When no field had been formed, no reed was to be seen.

At a time when none of the gods had been brought into existence,
When a name had not been named, destiny not determined,
Then were made the gods . . . .
The gods Lahmu and Lahamu were brought into existence
And grew up . . . .
Anshar [the host of heaven] and Kishar [the host of earth] were made . . . .
Many days passed by . . . .
God Anu [sky]. . . . .

Here the tablet is broken off, but this part of the tale has also been related by Damascius. He says: "The Babylonians assumed two principles of the universe, Tauthe and Apason [i. e. Tiamat the watery deep, and Apsu the primeval ocean]; making Apason the husband of Tauthe and naming her the mother of the gods. Of these two there was born an only-begotten son, Moymis. From these same another generation proceeded, Lache and Lachos. Then also from the same [original pair] a third generation, Kissare and Assoros; from whom sprang Anos [heaven], Illinos [earth's surface, with the atmosphere], and Aos [the waters of earth]; and of Aos and Dauke Belos [the sun of spring] was born, the fabricator of the world." In these narratives of creation the Babylonians fail to give God glory; but apart from this radical defect, these traditions of theirs preserve fundamentally the same account of the development of the world as the Hebrew prophet does. Stripped of polytheistic phraseology, the Babylonian tradition taught that the primeval universe was a chaotic watery mass (cp. Gen. i. 2). Out of this mass there proceeded not only Moymis and Lache and Lachos or Lahmu and Lahamu, who are doubtless natural objects or forces, but have not been identified as yet, but also by a series of generations, to use Damascius' figure (cp. Gen. ii. 4), the comprehensive heavens and the comprehensive earth (cp. Gen. i. 6–8), then sky and dry land and sea (cp. Gen. i. 9, 10), and then the sun (cp. Gen. i. 14). How natural objects, like the sky and the planets, came to be spoken of as gods is explained in the paragraph devoted to Assyrian and Babylonian religion in the article on ASSYRIA.

Before the Reformation scholars were uncertain whether the days of Gen. i. denote succession of time or are merely the distribution into logical groups of things created by one divine fiat (Augustine, de civ. dei, xi. 6 and 7). During the next 300 years the narrative was understood to mean that God created the universe in one week of seven consecutive days of twenty-four hours each. But geologists and astronomers alike became convinced that myriads of years had been required to produce the solar system and bring about the changes which the earth itself had undergone. When it became apparent that the geological claim for extended time rested on substantial grounds, Dr. Thomas Chalmers adopted the result and publicly declared in 1804 that "the writings of Moses do not fix the antiquity of the globe." Afterwards, in his *Evidences of Christianity*, published in 1813, he explained that many ages may have elapsed between the first act of creation described in Gen. i. 1, and the others commencing with verse 2. But was not a long period involved in the work of the six days themselves? In 1857 Hugh Miller in his *Testimony of the Rocks* interpreted the six days, as Cuvier of Paris had already interpreted them in 1798 in the preliminary discourse to his *Ossements Fossiles*, as being six geological ages; and traced the correspondence between the successive stages of creation as told in Gen. i. and as written in the rocks. So geology, in speaking of the carboniferous age, the age of fishes, the age of mammals, has named the dominating feature, but not denied it a humble origin in an earlier age.

The Hebrew narrative is marked by a symmetry and grouping, which may be plausibly explained as intentional arrangement. The chronological order has been observed in the main at least, but it remains to be discovered whether it has been followed in every detail. At any rate the works of the six days were more than six acts; God spake, to use a significant biblical term, eight times (vers. 3, 6, 9, 11, 14, 20, 24, 26), and on the third day the command went forth for both dry land and vegetation, on the fifth day for fish and for fowl, and on the sixth day for beast and for man. Moreover, the six days form two interrelated groups: the first day saw light, and the fourth day, the first of the second group, saw the luminaries; on the second day the waters were divided and the sky appeared, and on the second day of the other group fish were divinely willed in the waters and fowl to fly in the expanse of the sky; on the third day dry land and vegetation were decreed, and on the corresponding day of the second group land animals, including man, were made, and vegetation was granted them for food. The several works of creation have been logically distributed into six groups. Hence the fiat of the Almighty which called the dry land into being is not recorded alone, but with it is the command for vegetation. God contemplated the land as clothed with verdure. The two acts of the divine will are in reality and in purpose one, even though plant life possibly did not respond to the divine decree until the sun appeared. Yet, truly, vegetation of some form probably existed on the earth before the planet Mercury at least was flung from the whirling, contracting mass, and the sun, as man knows it, had been formed.

Creep'ing Thing.

Any animal which creeps (Gen. i. 24, 25), whether a land or a water reptile (vi. 7; Ps.

civ. 25), and whether crawling on the belly or creeping on four or more feet (Lev. xi. 41, 42).

Cres'cens [growing, increasing].

A Christian, who was for a time at Rome while Paul was a prisoner there, and then departed to Galatia or Gaul (2 Tim. iv. 10, R. V.).

Crete.

A large island in the Mediterranean, lying southeast of Greece, and now widely known as Candia. The Turks retain the old name in the modified form, Kiridi. It is about 160 miles long by 6 to 35 broad. It is traversed from east to west by a chain of mountains, of which mount Ida, near the center, is 8065 feet high. Homer speaks of its fair land, its countless men of different races, and its hundred cities (Il. ii. 649; Odys. xix. 174). The half-mythic legislator, Minos, lived in Crete, and the fabulous Minotaur was feigned to dwell there too. Crete was conquered by the Romans, 68–66 B. C. Many Jews settled in the island (Acts ii. 11; cp. 1 Mac. xv. 19–23, Gortyna being in Crete). Christianity was early introduced; and Titus was left there to arrange the affairs of the churches and to counteract Judaizing doctrine (Tit. i. 5, 10, 14). Paul sailed along its whole southern coast on his voyage to Rome (Acts xxvii. 7, 12, 13, 21). The Cretans were famous bowmen; but their moral reputation was bad, their unchastity and untruthfulness were proverbial (Tit. i. 12, and R. V. note). In A. D. 823 the island was conquered by the Saracens, who built a fort called Khandax, the Great Fortress, now corrupted into Candia, which, properly speaking, is the name of the capital only. The Greek emperor took the island from the Saracens in 961. From 1204 to 1665 the Venetians held it. Then the Turks regained possession. It secured autonomy in 1897.

Crib. See MANGER.

Crick'et.

The rendering in the text of the R. V. of the Hebrew *Hargol*, which belongs with grasshoppers and locusts, and which does not creep but leaps, is winged, and can be eaten (Lev. xi. 22). The chief leaping insects belong to three families of *Orthoptera*, viz. the grasshoppers, the locusts, and the crickets. The *hargol* almost certainly belongs to one of the three, though to which of them cannot now be determined. The crickets have long antennæ like the grasshoppers, but the wing-cases lie flat on the body instead of meeting over it like a roof. Among the few known species are the house cricket (*Gryllus domesticus*) and the field cricket (*G. campestris*). The A. V. renders *hargol* beetle, but the most typical species of the *Coleoptera*, or beetle order, are not leaping insects.

Cris'pus [curled].

The ruler of the Jewish synagogue at Corinth. After listening to Paul's reasonings, he with all his household believed in Jesus (Acts xviii. 8), and was one of the few persons whom Paul personally baptized (1 Cor. i. 14).

Croc'o-dile. See LEVIATHAN and LIZARD.

Cross.

This word does not occur in the O. T., but crucifixion was common among various nations of antiquity; see CRUCIFIXION. Cross is used in a figurative sense by Jesus (Mat. x. 38; xvi. 24). From the narrative of the crucifixion it is evident that the cross was of wood (Col. ii. 14), and was heavy, but still not too much so to be borne by a strong man (Mat. xxvii. 32; Mark xv. 21; Luke xxiii. 26; John xix. 17), and can scarcely, therefore, have been one of the massive structures which some painters depict. It was raised from the earth either before or after the victim had been affixed to it; probably, in most cases, before. Crosses are of three leading types: one, generally called the St. Andrew's cross, like the letter X; another like the letter T; and the third of the dagger form, †, with which we are so familiar. The cross of Christ was, probably, as artists believe, of the last-named type, which more easily than the others allowed the name, title, or crime of the victim to be affixed to the upper part (Mat. xxvii. 37; Mark xv. 26; Luke xxiii. 38; John xix. 19). Up to the death of Christ, and even after, the cross was evidently as much a name of horror and loathing as is the gallows now (John xix. 31; 1 Cor. i. 23; Gal. iii. 13; Phil. ii. 8; Heb. xii. 2; xiii. 13), so that to bear the cross meant to incur great reproach and obloquy; but after the crucifixion the more zealous followers of Jesus regarded the cross with wholly altered feelings. Paul gloried in the cross of Christ (Gal. vi. 14), by which he meant the atonement resulting from his crucifixion (Eph. ii. 16; Col. i. 20).

The pre-Christian cross of one form or another was in use as a sacred symbol among the Chaldeans, the Phœnicians, the Egyptians, and many other oriental nations. The Spaniards in the 16th century found it also among the Indians of Mexico and Peru. But its symbolic teaching was quite different from that which we now associate with the cross.

In the fourth century Rufinus, writing fifty years after the reputed event, relates that Helena, the mother of Constantine, was instructed in a vision to repair to Jerusalem and seek for the sepulcher of Christ. While there (A. D. 325) she found three crosses. These were shown to a sick woman. At the sight of the third she left her couch cured (Hist. eccl. i. 7, 8). Helena gave part of this cross to the city of Jerusalem, and sent the other

part to the emperor, who placed it within his statue, regarding it as the palladium of the empire. Eusebius, however, who flourished in the fourth century, and was a contemporary of Helena, and on terms of friendship with the imperial family, knew nothing of the story, which meets with no acceptance from modern scholars. It is believed that the practice was to burn, instead of to bury, the crosses on which real or alleged criminals had been crucified.

Crown.

1. An ornamental headdress worn as a badge of authority or dignity. Especially (1) The royal crown. It was generally a circlet of gold (Ps. xxi. 3), and was often studded with gems (2 Sam. xii. 30; Zech. ix. 16). Sometimes several crowns were combined or intertwined (vi. 11; 1 Mac. xi. 13). The crown which David took at Rabbah from the Ammonites probably belonged to the idol Malcam (2 Sam. xii. 30, R. V. margin). Its weight was a talent of gold, and in it were precious stones. The ordinary headdress of the Persian king (Esth. i. 11; vi. 8) was a stiff cap, probably of felt or of cloth, encircled by a blue and white band,

Crowns worn by royalty in ancient Egypt and Assyria.

which was the diadem proper. The royal crown of Assyria was a conical cap, sometimes tapering in a compound curve, but more frequently shaped like the modern Turkish fez, only higher and ending in a round blunt point. It was adorned with bands of wrought gold and jewels. The king is also represented wearing a simple fillet, and it is probable that this was a common custom, the crown royal being reserved for state occasions. In Egypt there were two royal crowns. The one for Upper Egypt was a high round white cap tapering to a knob; the crown for Lower Egypt was a flat-topped red cap, rising in a high point at the back and having a projection with a curled end springing diagonally toward the front. When the two kingdoms were united under one sovereign, he wore the two crowns combined, the crown of Lower Egypt being superimposed upon that of Upper Egypt. The Egyptian king is also frequently depicted with a band or diadem. The royal headdress, of whatever shape, is nearly always surrounded by the Uræus, the sacred serpent of the Egyptians, symbolizing power over life and death. See also illustrations under PHARAOH. The radiated diadem was a form of crown familiar to the Greeks and Romans and to the peoples under their influence. A crown or garland of some thorny plant was placed by the Roman soldiers around the temples of Jesus, with the twofold intention of torturing him and mocking his kingly claims (Mat. xxvii. 29). (2) The high priest's crown. It consisted of a golden plate (Lev. viii. 9), inscribed with the legend "Holiness to the Lord," and fastened on a lace of blue to the forefront of the miter (Ex. xxviii. 36, 37; xxix. 6). (3) The crown of victory (2 Tim. ii. 5; iv. 8; Heb. ii. 9). It might consist merely of a wreath of leaves or be made of metal.

2. Anything resembling a crown, as the border or moulding round about the ark, the table, and the altar (Ex. xxv. 11, 24, 25; xxx. 3, 4).

Cru-ci-fix′ion.

The act or operation of fixing a victim to a cross for the purpose of capital punishment. This was done either by tying his hands and feet to it, or in the more cruel way of fixing them to it by nails driven through their fleshy portions. This method of punishment existed in many ancient nations. Alexander the Great crucified a thousand Tyrians. According to Josephus, Cyrus introduced into his edict for the return of the Jews from Babylon a threat of crucifying anyone who attempted to prevent the missive from being carried into execution (Antiq. xi. 1, 3; 4, 6). Darius the Persian threatened this death, apparently, to those who refused obedience to his decrees (Ezra vi. 11). Antiochus Epiphanes crucified faithful Jews who would not abandon their religion at his bidding (Ant. xii. 5, 4), and Alexander Jannæus (War i. 4, 6) and the Pharisees crucified their enemies (War i. 5, 3). Among the Romans crucifixion was a penalty inflicted only on slaves, or on freemen who had committed the most heinous crimes; the ordinary Roman citizen was exempted from it by express legal enactment. The preliminary cruelties of scourging the victim (Mat. xxvii. 26; Mark xv. 15; John xix. 1), and then, when his body was lacerated, compelling him to bear his cross (xix. 17), were not rare (cp. the proverb, Mat. x. 38). Thus the Roman procurator Florus (War ii. 14, 9) and Titus, at least on one occasion, had those scourged first who were afterwards to be crucified. If the victim was simply tied to the cross, this was no injury sufficient to produce death, which did not take place till thirst and hunger had done their work; and this was sometimes the case even when the hands and feet were pierced by nails. If it was expedient on any ground to get rid of the victims before natural death had released them from their tortures, the end was sometimes hastened by breaking their legs, as was done in the case of the robbers crucified with Jesus (John xix. 31–33). Many Jews were crucified after Titus took Jerusalem (Life 75). Constantine abolished punishment by crucifixion in the Roman empire.

Cruse.

A small pot or jug used for carrying water during a journey (1 Sam. xxvi. 11; 1 Kin. xix. 6) and for holding oil (1 Kin. xvii. 12; Judith x. 5); a flask, such as were made of alabaster and used for holding ointment (Mat. xxvi. 7, R. V.). For cruse of honey (1 Kin. xiv. 3), a different word in Hebrew, the margin substitutes bottle; and the cruse of salt (2 Kin. ii. 20) was rather a dish.

Crys′tal.

1. The rendering of the Hebrew word Z⁰kukith, in A. V. of Job xxviii. 17. The R. V. makes it glass, since crystal occurs in the next verse. The corresponding word in Syriac is used for glass in Rev. iv. 6.

2. The rendering of the Hebrew Gabish, ice and crystal, another reputed product of cold (Job xxviii. 18; in A. V. pearl).

3. The rendering of the Hebrew word Ḳerah (Ezek. i. 22; cp. Ex. xxiv. 10). The R. V. has ice on the margin, which is an established meaning of the word (Job vi. 16; xxxviii. 29; Ps. cxlvii. 17).

4. The rendering of the Greek Krustallos (Rev. iv. 6 and xxii. 1). It is either ice or rock-crystal, which is quartz, transparent, and when pure colorless.

Cub, in A. V. Chub.

A people mentioned with Ethiopia, Put, and Lud (Ezek. xxx. 5, R. V.). The Seventy apparently read Lub, i. e. Libya.

Cu′bit [from Latin cubitum, an elbow, a cubit].

A measure of length based on the length of the forearm. The Babylonian cubit was 20.65 or 21.26 inches. The royal Babylonian cubit was longer than the common one by three finger-breadths (Herod. i. 178). The Egyptian cubit contained six hand-breadths or palms (ii. 149). The royal cubit was a palm longer and was equal to 20.64 inches, as appears from measuring sticks found in the tombs. The Hebrews also had two cubits, the common and perhaps older cubit (Deut. iii. 11; 2 Chron. iii. 3) and a cubit which was a hand-breadth longer than the common one (Ezek. xl. 5; xliii. 13). The table of Hebrew lineal measure is 4 fingers= 1 hand-breadth or palm; 3 hand-breadths= 1 span; 2 spans = 1 cubit (Ex. xxv. 10, with

Antiq. iii. 6, 5 ; Mishna, Chelim. xvii. 9). It is not unlikely that the royal Egyptian cubit and the cubit of Ezekiel were theoretically equal to the Babylonian cubit ; so that the common Hebrew cubit was 17.70 or 18.22 inches, or, if only three fingers shorter than the long cubit, 18.36 or 18.9 inches.

Cuck'oo, the A. V. has **Cuckow**, using the obsolete spelling [English, from the voice of the bird].

The rendering of the Hebrew *Shaḥaph*, emaciated bird, in the A. V. A bird ceremonially unclean (Lev. xi. 16 ; Deut. xiv. 15). The cuckoo, *Cuculus canorus*, is a well-known climbing bird, which, coming in spring from the south, on its annual. migration, remains till the fall of the year, being frequently heard, but rarely seen. The R. V., following the Septuagint translators, renders *shahaph* not cuckoo but seamew.

Cu'cum-ber.

The correct rendering of the Hebrew *Kisshu'*, a vegetable which the Israelites obtained while they were slaves in Egypt, and longed for when they could not have it in the wilderness (Num. xi. 5). It is *Cucumis chate*, which is very common in Egypt and somewhat sweeter than the common cucumber, *Cucumis sativus*. The cucumber was raised in gardens in Palestine (Is. i. 8 ; Baruch vi. 70), and both the species mentioned are grown there to-day.

Cum'min [from Hebrew *kammon*, Arabic *kammun*, Greek *kuminon*].

A cultivated plant sown broadcast and, when ripe, beaten with a rod to detach its seeds (Is. xxviii. 25, 27). It was one of the trifles of which the Pharisees were particular in paying tithes (Mat. xxiii. 23). Cummin is the *Cuminum cyminum* of botanists. a fennel-like plant bearing umbels of small white flowers. It was cultivated in Palestine for its seeds, which were eaten as a spice or relish with food. They are now in large measure superseded by caraway seeds, which are more agreeable to the taste and more nutritious.

Cun. See BEROTHAI.

Cup.

1. A small drinking vessel (2 Sam. xii. 3), of earthenware or metal (Jer. li. 7), held in the hand (Gen. xl. 11), and used for water (Mark ix. 41), or wine (Ps. lxxv. 8 ; Jer. xxv. 15). See BASIN.

2. Figuratively, the contents of the cup, whether pleasant or bitter : that which falls to one's lot (Ps. xxiii. 5 ; Is. li. 17 ; Jer. xvi. 7 ; Mat. xxvi. 39).

Cup'bear-er.

The official who poured drink into the cup and gave it to the king (Gen. xl. 9–14, where the Hebrew word is rendered butler ; Neh. i. 11 ; ii. 1, 2). The office was one of the most dignified in an oriental kingdom, and required moral trustworthiness in its occupant, lest he be bribed to present poisoned wine to the king (Antiq. xvi. 8, 1). It said much for the character of Nehemiah that he, a stranger and a foreigner, should have been appointed to such an office at the Persian court.

Cush [Hebrew *Kûsh*, Old Egyptian *Kash*, *Kesh*, and *Kish*, Ethiopia].

1. A son of Ham and his descendants collectively. They constituted five principal peoples, Seba, Havilah, Sabtah, Raamah, Sabteca, and were located in central and southern Arabia, except Seba, which is probably to be sought on the neighboring African coast (Gen. x. 6–8 ; 1 Chron. i. 8–10).

2. The land where the Cushites dwelt during any period. In Gen. ii. 13, R. V., the term denotes territory in the same great basin as the countries drained by the Tigris and Euphrates. In most or all other passages it designates Ethiopia in Africa (2 Kin. xix. 9 ; Esth. i. 1 ; Ezek. xxix. 10). Herodotus describes Asiatic Ethiopians in the army of Xerxes, who were different from the African Ethiopians (vii. 70). See EDEN 1.

3. A Benjamite, perhaps of Ethiopian descent (the Seventy read Cushi), who was a foe to David (Ps. vii. title).

Cu'shan [a name formed from Cush].

A country or its inhabitants mentioned in connection with Midian, and hence probably Arabia as occupied by Cushites (Hab. iii. 7 ; see CUSH). A reference is not apparent to Cushan-rishathaim (Judg. iii. 5), called Cushan by Josephus (Antiq. v. 3, 2).

Cu'shan-rish-a-tha'im, in A. V. **Chushan-rishathaim** [etymology and meaning unknown].

A king of Mesopotamia, who held the Israelites in subjection for eight years. Deliverance was achieved under the leadership of Othniel, Caleb's younger brother (Judg. iii. 5–11).

Cu'shi [an Ethiopian].

1. An ancestor of that Jehudi who lived in Jeremiah's time (Jer. xxxvi. 14).

2. Father of the prophet Zephaniah (Zeph. i. 1).

3. According to the A. V. one of the two men who carried David the news of the victory over his rebellious son Absalom ; but the Hebrew has " the Cushi," evidently meaning, as the R. V. renders it, " the Cushite," *i. e.* the Ethiopian. The actual name of the runner is unknown (2 Sam. xviii. 21-23, 31, 32).

Cush'ite.

An Ethiopian (Num. xii. 1, R. V. and margin of A. V. ; 2. Sam. xviii. 21, R. V.).

Cuth and **Cu'thah** [of doubtful meaning].

A city of Babylonia, often mentioned in connection with Babylon and Borsippa, and whose tutelary deity was Nergal. Colonists were brought from this place, among others, to Samaria after the deportation of the ten tribes (2 Kin. xvii. 24, 30). Its site is now fixed at the mounds of Tell Ibrahim, north-

The traditional tomb of Barnabas built on the site where he was martyred, a few miles from Salamis in eastern Cyprus.

west of Babylon.

Cym'bal [from Greek *kumbalon* (1 Cor. xiii. 1)].

A musical instrument (2 Sam. vi. 5; 1 Chron. xvi. 5), named in Hebrew from a root signifying to tinkle or clang. One form of the name is in the dual number, which implies that the instrument is of two distinct parts. This undoubtedly suggests cymbals, as the Septuagint renders the word, which are concave plates of brass (1 Chron. xv. 19), one form of them being nearly flat, another consisting of hollow cones designed to be clashed together for their sound. See Music.

Cy'press [from Latin *cupressus, cyparissus*, Greek *kuparissos*].

1. The rendering in A. V. of Is. xliv. 14 of the Hebrew word *Tirzah*, referring to the hardness of the wood. The R. V. translates it the holm tree.

2. The marginal rendering of the Hebrew *T'ashshur* in R. V. of Is. xli. 19; lx. 13. The text of both versions has box.

3. Rendering of *B'rosh*, margin R.V. See Fir. The Cypress, *Cupressus sempervirens*, is the type of the sub-order *Cupresseæ*, ranking under the order *Pinaceæ* (Conifers). About ten species of the genus *Cupressus* are known. The common cypress is an evergreen running into two well-marked varieties, one a tall tree 60 feet high with erect closely appressed branches, and the other smaller, with the branches spreading. The cypress is a native of Persia and the Levant. It is extensively planted in cemeteries of the East.

Cy'prus.

An island celebrated in the earliest ages for the richness of its mines of copper. It is situated in the northeastern part of the Mediterranean Sea, about 41 miles from the coast of Cilicia, 60 from Syria, and 238 from Port Said in Egypt. The more compact part of the island is 110 miles in length by 30 to 50 or 60 in breadth; besides which there runs from its northeastern extremity a narrow strip of land, 40 miles long by 5 or 6 broad, projecting from the rest of the island like a bowsprit from a ship. The area of Cyprus is about 3584 square miles. The island is mountainous, with intermediate valleys, which are at certain seasons unhealthy. The mountains yield copper, and the mines were at one time farmed to Herod the Great (Antiq. xvi. 4, 5). Its ancient inhabitants were Kittim, a branch of the Greek race (Gen. x. 4), but Phœnicians from the coast of Syria colonized the island. They built as their capital the town of Kition or Citium. Later other bodies of Greeks reinforced the original stock (cp. Herod. vii. 90), so that to this day about three-fourths of the population belong to that race. Cyprus was for a short time an imperial Roman province or part of one; but in the year 27 B. C. Augustus handed it over to the senate, and henceforth it was under a proprætor with the title of proconsul. Many Jewish communities existed in the island (1 Mac. xv. 23; Acts iv. 36). There were Christians connected with it before Stephen's martyrdom; and during the persecution which followed some of them returned to it, preaching the gospel (Acts xi. 19, 20). It was visited for missionary purposes, first by Barnabas and Paul (Acts xiii. 4), and afterwards by Barnabas and Mark (xv. 39). Paul sailed past it at least twice without landing (xxi. 3, 16: xxvii. 4). Since 1571 it has constituted a portion of Turkey, though by a treaty, dated June 4, 1878, Great Britain administers and holds it as a place of arms, while Russia retains Batoum and Kars. See Kittim.

Cy-re'ne.

An important Greek colonial city in North Africa, beautifully situated on a tableland many hundred feet above the sea level, and a few miles distant from the Mediterranean. It constituted one of five Greek cities called Pentapolis, situated in Libya Cyrenaica, now Tripoli. It is believed that it was founded by Dorians about the year 632 B. C. During the time of the Ptolemies, in the third century B. C., many Jews became resident in

Cyrene (con. Apion ii. 4; Antiq. xiv. 7, 2).
Simon, who was compelled to carry the cross
of Jesus, seems to have been a Cyrenian Jew
(Mat. xxvii. 32). Cyrenians joined with
Libertines and others in forming a synagogue
at Jerusalem (Acts vi. 9). Men of Cyrene early
became converts and preachers (xi. 20).
Among them was a certain Lucius, a prominent man in the church at Antioch (xiii. 1).
Extensive ruins of Cyrene still exist, now
called el-Krenna.

Cy-re'ni-us. See QUIRINIUS.

Cy'rus [Elamite and Persian, *K'ur'ush*].
A king twice named in the book of Isaiah
as anointed of God and predestined to conquer kings and fortified places, and set the
Jews free from captivity (Is. xliv. 28; xlv. 1–
14). Daniel, referring to the conquest of
Babylonia by the Medes and Persians, records
that during the night which followed a great
feast Belshazzar, the king of the Chaldeans,
was slain and Darius the Mede received the
kingdom (Dan. v. 30, 31). Darius was predecessor of Cyrus, or his regent, in Babylonia
(vi. 28). Ezra relates that Cyrus, king of
Persia, in the first year of his reign issued a
proclamation permitting the Jews to return
to their own land and rebuild the temple,
for the use of which he restored the sacred
vessels taken by Nebuchadnezzar (Ezra i.
1–11; v. 13, 14; vi. 3). Many of the Jews
embraced the privilege and returned to Jerusalem; but the work of rebuilding the sanctuary was greatly hindered by adversaries.
    According to Babylonian inscriptions, writ-
ten approximately at the time of the capture
of the city, Cyrus was a son of Cambyses,
grandson of Cyrus, great-grandson of Teispes,
all of whom reigned as kings of Ansan, a
designation which appears to denote eastern
Elam with Susa as its capital. About the
year 550 B. C., the sixth year of Nabuna'id
or Nabonidus, king of Babylon, Istuvegu or,
in Greek, Astyages, king of the people of
Manda, marched against Cyrus, but was betrayed by his own army and delivered into
the hands of Cyrus. Cyrus then took Ecbatana and carried its spoil to his own city.
In the month of Nisan, 547 B. C., Cyrus, now
called king of Persia, led the Persian army
across the Tigris near Arbela and carried his
conquest into the western country. According to Greek authorities, he conquered Lydia
about this time, taking Sardis and making a
prisoner of Crœsus, its king. In 539 B. C.,
the seventeenth year of Nabonidus, in the
month Tammuz, Cyrus met the Babylonians
in battle; on the 14th day he took Sippara
and Nabonidus fled. Two days later, on the
16th, Ugbaru or Gobryas, governor of Cyrus'
at the head of a detachment of Cyrus' army,
entered Babylon without fighting. Nabonidus
was afterwards captured at Babylon. On the
3d of Marchesvan Cyrus himself entered
Babylon, his governor Ugbaru proclaimed
peace to the province, governors were ap-

pointed, and an order issued for the restoration of many captive foreign idols to their
several native sanctuaries. About the 27th
of Adar the king's wife died. A public
mourning for her was observed for a week,
followed by religious services conducted by
Cambyses, son of Cyrus. Cyrus was succeeded by Cambyses in 529 B. C. So far the
inscriptions. According to Herodotus (i. 190,
191), Cyrus captured Babylon by turning the
waters of the Euphrates temporarily into a
lake excavated for the purpose, and then entering from the nearly dry bed of the river
by the gates which had been left open on the
night of a festival while the inhabitants were
engaged in revelry. The account given by
the Babylonian priest, Berosus, who lived
about the time of Alexander the Great, is as
follows: "In the 17th year of Nabonidus,
Cyrus came out of Persia with a great army,
and, having conquered all the rest of Asia,
came hastily to Babylonia. When Nabonidus
perceived that he was advancing to attack
him, he assembled his forces and opposed
him; but he was defeated and fled with a
few of his attendants and shut himself in
the city of Borsippa [the twin of Babylon].
Whereupon Cyrus took Babylon; and he
gave orders that the outer walls should be
demolished, because the city had proved very
troublesome to him and difficult to take. He
then marched to Borsippa to besiege Nabonidus: but as Nabonidus delivered himself
into his hands without holding out the place,
he was at first kindly treated by Cyrus, who
sent him out of Babylonia but gave him a
habitation in Carmania, where he spent the
remainder of his life and died" (contra Apion.
i. 20).

D

Dab'a-reh. See DABERATH.

Dab'be-sheth, in A. V. **Dabbasheth** [hump
of a camel].
A town on the boundary line of Zebulun
(Josh. xix. 11). Conder locates it at Dabsheh,
13 miles N. E. of Acre. Improbable.

Dab'e-rath, in A. V. once **Dabareh** erroneously (Josh. xxi. 28) [probably pasture land].
A city within the territory of Issachar,
given with its suburbs to the Gershonites
(Josh. xix. 12; xxi. 28; 1 Chron. vi. 72; War ii.
21, 3; Life 62). It has been identified as the
village of Deburieh at the base of mount
Tabor, on the northwestern side of the hill.

Da'gon [the name probably has no refer-
ence to either fish or grain].
The national god of the Philistines. At
Gaza, at Beth-dagon, and especially at Ash-
dod, he had a temple (Judg. xvi. 21, 23; 1
Sam. v. 1–7; 1 Chron. x. 10). Jonathan
Maccabæus, after defeating the Philistines,
drove them into the temple of Dagon in
Ashdod, and set fire both to the city and the
temple (1 Mac. x. 84; xi. 4). Dagon was

worshiped to some extent in Phœnicia and also in Assyria. The idol is considered to have had the head, arms, and upper parts of human form (1 Sam. v. 4), while the lower parts tapered away into the tail of a fish. Diodorus Siculus (ii. 4) mentions an idol, called Dercetus, of similar form, as having existed at Ashkelon, another Philistine town. It is questionable whether the image of a man with the extremities of a fish, which was found at Khorsabad, represents Dagon.

Da-la′iah. See DELAIAH.

Da′leth.

The fourth letter of the Hebrew alphabet. The English letter D has the same origin, and represents it in anglicized Hebrew names. It stands at the head of the fourth section of Ps. cxix., in which section each verse of the Hebrew begins with this letter.

The two Hebrew letters, daleth and resh (r), are somewhat similar now, and at certain stages of their development were distinguishable only when carefully written and on close scrutiny. In the Siloam inscription, for example, they are written Δ *and* Λ and on Hebrew coins ꟼ *and* ꟼ. This similarity caused constant difficulty to readers and copyists, and frequently misled them as to the true spelling of words, especially of obscure names where no guide to the original form existed.

Dal-ma-nu′tha.

A place situated probably on the western shore of the sea of Galilee in the vicinity of Magdala (Mark viii. 10; cp. Mat. xv. 39).

Dal-ma′ti-a.

A region on the eastern shore of the Adriatic Sea, with the small but numerous adjacent islands. It is traversed by the Julian continued as the Dinaric Alps, a part of the giant range separating Italy from France, Switzerland, and Germany. The mountain tribes were subdued in A. D. 9 by the Romans under Augustus Cæsar and Tiberius, the future emperor, and the province of Dalmatia was erected. It was regarded as part of Illyricum, which constituted the limit of Paul's missionary journeys in that direction (Rom. xv. 19). His associate Titus, after being for a time with Paul in the Italian capital, departed to Dalmatia, perhaps to plant the gospel among its wild inhabitants (2 Tim. iv. 10).

Dal′phon.

A son of Haman (Esth. ix. 7).

Dam′a-ris.

A woman converted through Paul's preaching at Athens (Acts xvii. 34).

Dam-a-scene′.

A native or inhabitant of Damascus (2 Cor. xi. 32).

Da-mas′cus.

A city of Syria, on a plateau watered by the rivers Abana and Pharpar (2 Kin. v. 12).

The tableland is about 2200 feet above the level of the sea, at the eastern foot of the Antilibanus chain of mountains, and contains about 500 square miles. Where watered by channels from the rivers, it is exceedingly fertile, so that the city is embosomed in gardens and orchards, in refreshing contrast to the neighboring desert. Three great trade routes center at Damascus; one leads southwestward to the Mediterranean seacoast and Egypt, another runs south to Arabia, and the third crosses the desert to Bagdad. The city is very ancient. It is mentioned as early as the time of Abraham (Gen. xiv. 15). In the days of David, Damascus was one of several petty states of southern Syria. It was captured and garrisoned by David (2 Sam. viii. 5, 6; 1 Chron. xviii. 5, 6). After he smote the Syrian kingdom of Zobah, a man called Rezon, a former subject of the king of Zobah, collected a band of men, seized Damascus, and founded the Syrian kingdom, which henceforth was so often in conflict with Israel (1 Kin. xi. 23, 24). Damascus was the capital of Hezion, Tabrimmon, and the Ben-hadads (1 Kin. xv. 18, 20; xx. 34; 2 Kin. viii. 7), of Hazael (1 Kin. xix. 17; 2 Kin. viii. 8–15), and of Rezin (xvi. 5). Tabrimmon and the first Ben-hadad were in league with the king of Judah (1 Kin. xv. 18; 2 Chron. xvi. 2). Ahab agreed to a covenant, obtaining the right to establish streets of bazaars in Damascus (1 Kin. xx. 34). At this period Damascus took a leading part among the western nations in resistance to Assyria. In alliance with kings of the seacoast and Ahab of Israel it met Shalmaneser at Karkar in 854 B. C., and, though defeated, checked the Assyrian advance. But in 842 Shalmaneser defeated Hazael, king of Damascus, at mount Hermon and forced him to pay tribute. When, in 734, Rezin of Damascus and Pekah of Israel planned to assault Jerusalem, Ahaz of Judah called in Tiglath-pileser, king of Assyria, who captured Damascus, carried the inhabitants captive to Kir, and killed Rezin (2 Kin. xvi. 5–9; Is. vii. 1–viii. 6: x. 9). This destruction is referred to by Amos (i. 3–5). But Damascus soon regained its prosperity (Ezek. xxvii. 18). From the Assyrians Damascus passed to the Babylonians, from them to the Persians, and then to the Macedonian Greeks. It was one of the ten cities originally forming the Decapolis. It was taken by the Roman general Metellus, and in the year 63 B. C. became a Roman province. Many Jews dwelt in Damascus, and supported several synagogues (Acts ix. 2; War ii. 20, 2). Near Damascus Saul of Tarsus, when on his way to persecute the Christians of the city, was smitten to the earth and heard the heavenly voice (Acts ix. 2, 3, 10; xxii. 6, 10, 11, 12; xxvi. 12); and from the walls he was let down, now himself a Christian, to escape the fury of the Jews (Acts ix. 24, 25; cp. xxvi. 20; Gal. i. 17). The traditional street called Straight is about two miles long, and runs

Entrance to the house of Ananias in Damascus.

from northeast to southwest, almost through the center of the city. It is a poor street now, but in the time of Paul it was a magnificent thoroughfare, flanked with Corinthian columns. At its eastern end is the east gate of the city. The large gateway, 38 feet high and 20 feet wide, and the two smaller side gates were built by the Romans, probably as early as the time of Paul. Of these the central and southern archways have long been built up with masonry, leaving only the small northern side gate open. In Paul's time the city was in the hands of Aretas, king of Arabia Petræa, but it soon reverted to the Romans (2 Cor. xi. 32). In A. D. 634 Damascus was invested and in 635 captured by the Arabs under Omar. In 1300 it was plundered by the Tartars, and in 1400 by Timur the Tartar. Since 1516 it has been held by the Turks. In July, 1860, 6000 oriental Christians were massacred by a Mohammedan mob composed of Druses and Bedouin, assisted by Turkish soldiers.

Dan [a judge].

1. A son of Jacob by Bilhah (Gen. xxx. 5. 6). He had one son, Hushim (Gen. xlvi. 23) or Shuham (Num. xxvi. 42). The future destiny of his descendants was thus predicted by Jacob: "Dan shall judge his people, as one of the tribes of Israel. Dan shall be a serpent in the way, an adder in the path, that biteth the horse's heels, so that his rider falleth backward" (Gen. xlix. 16, 17, R. V.); meaning that his tribe would contend with the foes of Israel as earnestly and craftily as would any of the tribes. Speaking on the same subject Moses compared Dan to a lion's whelp that leapeth forth from Bashan (Deut. xxxiii. 22).

2. The tribe to which Dan gave origin, and the territory in Canaan which it obtained by allotment (Num. i. 12, 38, 39). Its assigned territory contained, among other towns, Zorah, Ajalon, Ekron, Eltekeh, and ended opposite Japho—*i. e.* Joppa (Josh. xix. 40–46; xxi. 5, 23; cp. Judg. v. 17). The Danites, however, did not possess themselves of all this region, but were restricted by the Amorites to the hill country (Judg. i. 34, 35). Cramped for room, they sent spies to the extreme north of Palestine to look for a new location, who found what they desired in the town of Laish, occupied by foreigners. The Danites sent an expedition, seized the place, slew its inhabitants, and rebuilt it under the new name of Dan (Josh. xix. 47; Judg. xviii. 1–31). Aholiab and Samson were Danites (Ex. xxxi. 6; Judg. xiii. 2, 24).

3. A town in the extreme north of Palestine, the phrase "from Dan to Beersheba" or "from Beersheba to Dan" denoting the land in its entire extent from north to south (Judg. xx. 1; 1 Chron. xxi. 2). The town was originally called Laish, lion, or Leshem, perhaps place of lions (Lesham from *layish*, as Etam from *'ayiṭ*). The name Dan was given to it after its capture by the Danites (Josh. xix. 47; Judg. xviii.). Abraham pursued Chedorlaomer as far as Dan (Gen. xiv. 14); thought by some to be Dan-jaan (q. v.). But Dan-jaan may be Laish, that is Dan; if so, the familiar name Dan has supplanted the older

Along the "Street called Straight" in Damascus.

designation in Genesis (cp. Deut. xxxiv. 1)
At Dan Jeroboam fixed one of his golden
calves (1 Kin. xii. 29, 30; 2 Kin. x. 29; Amos
viii. 14). Benhadad destroyed the town with
other places in its vicinity (1 Kin. xv. 20; 2
Chron. xvi. 4); but it was rebuilt (Ezek.
xxvii. 19). Dan was in a fertile valley by
Beth-rehob (Judg. xviii. 9, 28), near Lebanon,
at the sources of the lesser Jordan (Antiq. v.
3, 1; viii. 8, 4), near the marshes of the
waters of Merom (War iv. 1, 1), and four
Roman miles west of Paneas (Onom). These
statements indicate Tell el-Kâdi, which signifies mound of the judge, and thus preserves, though perhaps accidentally, the sense
of the old name Dan. At the base of this
mound are two springs, whose waters presently unite and form the river Leddan, the
shortest but most abundant in water of the
three streams which flow together a few miles
below and form the Jordan.

Dance.

On joyous occasions of a secular or semisecular character dancing, accompanied by
music, was practiced among the Hebrews by
women, either singly or in groups, especially
in welcoming a victor home (Judg. xi. 34; 1
Sam. xviii. 6, 7; xxix. 5; cp. Jer. xxxi. 4, 13).
Children, apparently of both sexes, took part
in dances (Job xxi. 11; Mat. xi. 17; Luke vii.
32). Men probably engaged in dances among
themselves, as they did in Egypt (Ps. xxx.
11; Lam. v. 15; Ecc. iii. 4; Luke xv. 25).
Only on one occasion do we find a Jewish
princess dancing publicly in an assembly of
men after the Roman manner; acting a mythological story with the face masked, but with
the body clothed so as to exhibit the beauty
of the figure (Mat. xiv. 6; Mark vi. 22).
Dancing as part of a religious ceremony or
as an act of worship seems to have been common among the Hebrews. It was practiced
chiefly by women (Ex. xv. 20; Judg. xxi. 21,
23), but occasionally by men, as in the well-
known instance of David's dancing before the
ark (2 Sam. vi. 14–23; 1 Chron. xv. 29; Ps.
cxlix. 3; cl. 4). Dancing before images was
common among idolaters (Ex. xxxii. 19; 1
Kin. xviii, 26).

Dan'iel [God is my judge].

1. Son of David and Abigail, born at Hebron (1 Chron. iii. 1). He is called Chileab
in 2 Sam. iii. 3.

2. A priest who, doubtless in behalf of a
father's house, signed the covenant in the
days of Nehemiah (Ezra viii. 2; Neh. x. 6).
Chronologically he is the third of the name
mentioned in the Old Testament.

3. The celebrated Jewish prophet at the
Babylonian court. He sprang from princely
family of the tribe of Judah (Dan. i. 3–7).
When a youth, he was carried off with other
captives by Nebuchadnezzar after his first
siege of Jerusalem, in the third or, reckoning accession year as first year, the fourth
of Jehoiakim, 605 B. C. (i. 1; Jer. xxv. 1).

At Babylon the boy was selected with other
young captives of good birth and parts to be
trained for the state service. He and three
companions obtained leave from the master of
the eunuchs, under whose charge they were,
to substitute simple food for the viands assigned them by the king and which were
liable to be contrary to the Mosaic law and
defiled by heathen rites (Dan. i. 8). The four
young exiles all became proficient in Babylonian learning, while the grace of God enabled them to manifest uncompromising principle, even when it brought them face to
face with death. The period of tutelage
ended in the third year (5), when they were
given service at court; and Daniel continued
in it with varying prominence until 538 B. C.,
the first year of Cyrus (21). In Nebuchadnezzar's second year, 603 B. C., doubtless towards its close (cp. 5 and 18), Daniel interpreted the king's dream of the great image
(ii. 1–46). This success led to the prophet's
being made ruler over the province of Babylon, and head over its wise men (46–49). He
afterwards interpreted the vision which revealed the approaching madness of Nebuchadnezzar (iv.). About this time Ezekiel
cited Daniel as a notable example of righteousness and wisdom (Ezek. xiv. 14; xxviii.
3). In the first year of Belshazzar Daniel
himself had a vision and saw, under the
figure of animals, four successive empires
reaching to the time when the ancient of
days should sit, and one like a son of man
come with the clouds of heaven to set up a
spiritual kingdom which should endure eternally (vii.). The scene of the vision of the
third year of Belshazzar was at Shushan
(viii. 2), the Elamite capital, and residence
of the already renowned Cyrus, king of Persia (viii. 20; and see CYRUS). The prophet
himself was probably at Babylon (cp. Ezek.
viii. 1–3). In this vision he saw a ram trampled by a goat, and from the head of the latter, when its power was in turn broken, four
horns appearing, from one of which a little
horn sprang and wrought proudly, especially
toward the glorious land and its sanctuary;
whereby were symbolized the Medo-Persian
and Macedonian empires, the division of the
latter into four kingdoms, the rise of a fierce
king and his desecration of the sanctuary
(viii.). On the fall of the Babylonian empire,
Darius, in behalf of the conqueror, appointed
120 satraps over the new kingdom, with three
presidents over them, Daniel being one of
the three (vi. 1, 2; see CYRUS). Jealousy of
Daniel on account of his ability and eminence led to a plot against him, and he was
cast into the den of lions (3–23; 1 Mac. ii. 60).
In the first year of Darius, Daniel concluded
from the statements of Jeremiah (xxv. 11, 12;
xxix. 10) that the captivity was approaching
its close (Dan. ix. 1, 2). He humbled himself, confessed the sins of the nation and
prayed. In consequence there was revealed
to him the prophecy of the seventy weeks

(ix. 24). In the third year of Cyrus, king of Persia, he had a vision of the final conflict between the powers of the world and the kingdom of God (x.–xii.). As Daniel prophesied at the beginning of the dynasty of Nebuchadnezzar, and at its end, and in the reigns of Darius the Mede and Cyrus the Persian (vi. 28), he must have lived to an advanced age. The time and manner of his death are unknown. Daniel is referred to in Ezek. xiv. 14; xxviii. 3; 2 Esdras xii. 11; 1 Mac. ii. 60; Mat. xxiv. 15; Mark xiii. 14; Heb. xi. 33.

The book of Daniel is a book of the O. T. which in the Septuagint and English versions follows Ezekiel, but in the Hebrew canon is placed in the third division. It was not put with the prophets because its writer, although called a prophet (Mat. xxiv. 15; Antiq. x. 15, 4 and 6), and one of the greatest of them (Antiq. x. 11, 7), and although he was marvelously gifted by the Spirit of prophecy, was not regarded as officially a prophet. He had the *donum propheticum*, but not the *munus propheticum;* the prophetic gift, not the prophetic vocation. He was officially a statesman, and his life was passed in the business of the state. He does not use the common prophetic declaration, "Thus saith the Lord," and he does not exhort his contemporaries, as it was the function of the prophets to do. The greater part of the book is in Hebrew; but a portion which relates almost entirely to the life of the Jews in a foreign land and to the deeds of foreign kings and to prophecies concerning foreign empires, beginning with the middle of verse 4, chap. ii., and extending to chap. vii., verse 28, is in Aramaic, the commercial and diplomatic language of the time (cp. similar phenomenon in Ezra). The book may be divided into three sections: 1. Introduction, the preparation of Daniel and his three companions for their work (i.). 2. Witness borne by God through the four, at a foreign court and largely to foreigners, of his omnipotent and omniscient control of the powers of the world in their development and in their relation to the kingdom of God (ii.–vii.). This section is written in Aramaic. It includes Nebuchadnezzar's dream of the image made of four metals and its destruction (ii.); the attempt against Daniel's three companions and their deliverance from the fiery furnace (iii.); Nebuchadnezzar's dream of the tree hewn down (iv.); the writing on the wall at Belshazzar's feast (v.); the plot to destroy Daniel, and his deliverance from the lions' den (vi.); Daniel's vision of the four beasts and the being like unto a son of man (vii.). This last is placed out of chronological order that it may form the transition to 3. 3. Supplementary visions of Daniel, having the fortunes of God's people specially in view (viii.–xii.), comprising three visions: (1) Concerning the cessation of sacrifice, desolation of the sanctuary, opposition to the prince of princes (viii.; cp. 13,

25). (2) In view of the near completion of the predicted seventy years of exile, Daniel prepared for the great event by confessing national sins and supplicating forgiveness. From prophecies gone before, it might be supposed that the kingdom of Messiah would be established immediately at the expiration of the captivity; but in a vision Daniel is informed that 70 weeks must elapse after the decree to rebuild Jerusalem is issued before reconciliation is made and everlasting righteousness brought in (Dan. ix.). (3) He is further informed by a vision in the third year of the founder of the Persian empire in regard to the overthrow of that empire, the persecution of God's people that shall ensue, and the final relief of the saints and the resurrection to glory (x.–xii.).

The prophecy of the image, composed of four metals, broken by the stone (ii. 31–45), and that of the four beasts replaced by a being like unto a son of man (vii.), depict four worldly powers yielding place to the kingdom of God. The fourth empire is clearly the Roman; for 1. The second empire, the Medo-Persian, cannot be divided into two, since the Median kingdom in its separate existence was never an empire of world-wide sway. Historically, Media and Persia were one empire in the days of Median supremacy. There was a change of dynasty, a Persian prince obtained the throne of Media, and then the Medo-Persian career of universal conquest began. 2. Daniel speaks of the Medo-Persian empire as one (v. 28; vi. 8; viii. 20). 3. To divide the Medo-Persian empire into two empires requires the identification of the leopard with Persia instead of Greece. But the leopard has four heads (vii. 6). Persia was not broken into four parts, but the Macedonian empire was (viii. 21, 22; xi. 2–4). 4. The Roman empire was already within the prophet's view. On the common interpretation, the Romans are referred to in xi. 30; and Antiochus the Great in xi. 10^b–20, who was overwhelmingly defeated by the Romans at Magnesia in 190 B. C. (see ANTIOCHUS). It may be added that in the visions a horn represents a king and a kingdom (vii. 7, 24), be it Media, Persia, or Macedonia (viii. 20–22); and a little horn signifies the rise of a new king or power, it may be among the successors of Alexander (viii. 9, 23) or in the midst of the Roman empire (vii. 8, 24). A horn does not always represent one and the same king, and no more does a little horn stand for the same individual.

The prophecy of the seventy weeks also concerns the sufferings of the kingdom of God (ix. 24–27). The prophetic era from which the weeks are reckoned is a decree, either of God or of an earthly king, for restoring and building Jerusalem (25). The anointed one, the prince (25), and the anointed one (26) are interpreted, with more or less soundness of reasoning, as referring to one person or two persons, and as being Cyrus or a high priest or the line of high priests or Christ. The seven weeks and sixty-two weeks and one week, amounting in all to seventy weeks (24–27), are variously distributed. They are taken successively, so as to measure a period of 490 years; or the sixty-two is held to include the seven, so that a period of 434 years only is covered; or the numbers are taken in the reverse order from their mention in verse 25, and a significant period of seven weeks is made to follow the periods of sixty-two weeks and one week. The theories which regard the decree as an edict of God are mainly two. They make the era either the beginning of the exile, 605 B. C. (cp. Jer. xxv. 11), or the destruction of Jerusalem, 587 B. C. (cp. xxix. 10, written soon after the beginning of Jehoiachin's captivity, verse 2; xxx. 18; xxxi. 38). Need it be added that the year 450 B. C. has also been sought, on the theory that the seventy years of punishment were doubled (Jer. xvi. 18; but see Is. xl. 2), and a divine decree of favor to Zion is implied at their close? The theories which date the era from the decree of an earthly monarch are four: 1. The edict of Cyrus, 538 B. C. (Ezra i. 2–4; vi. 3–5; cp. Is. xliv. 28; xlv. 1, 13), under the provisions of which the rebuilding of the temple was begun (Ezra vi. 14, 15; Hag. i. 14, 15). 2. The edict of Darius (Ezra vi. 6–12). 3. The edict of the seventh year of Artaxerxes, 457 B. C. (vii. 7, 11–26); which granted to the Jews absolute authority in civil and religious matters (25, 26), and under which they proceeded to build the city walls (iv. 12). The work was temporarily interrupted by a new decree (iv. 21). 4. The edict of the twentieth year of Artaxerxes, 444 B. C., which included permission to restore and fortify the city (Neh. ii. 3, 5, 8, 17, 18). The problem thus has three factors, to each of which several interpretations are given: the decree, the anointed one, and the weeks; and these factors are susceptible of various combinations. Of all these combinations, using any one of the decrees as a starting-point, and reckoning forward either sixty-two or sixty-nine weeks of seven years each, and expecting either the time of Antiochus Epiphanes or that of Christ to be reached by this measurement, only one combination yields a result. All others require an invention of history or involve an unusual chronological artifice or end in an unsolved mystery or assume a gross miscalculation of the interval by the author. The one combination which coincides with known history throughout starts with the decree of Artaxerxes in his seventh year, 457 B. C. A period of seven weeks or forty-nine years came to a close about 408 B. C., and the reformation under Ezra and Nehemiah was conducted during this period and characterized this period as a whole. When this reform ceased to be the dominating feature of God's kingdom is unknown,

but Nehemiah's successor, who was a Persian and naturally not a maintainer of the exclusiveness of Jehovah's religion, was in office in 411 B. C., before the close of the seventh week. Then follow sixty-two weeks or 434 years, coming down through A. D. 26 to the time when Jesus began his public ministry, A. D. 27, probably early in that year. After these threescore and two weeks an anointed one was cut off (Dan. ix. 26), making, it may well be, the reconciliation for iniquity and bringing in the everlasting righteousness, spoken of in verse 24; and in the midst of this last week one caused the sacrifice and oblation to cease, not by forbidding them, but by the one sacrifice on Calvary that rendered all others henceforth unnecessary. Nevertheless, notwithstanding the coincidence of the prophecy with the known events in the history of God's kingdom, and the significance of this correspondence, yet quite probably the seventy, and the seven separated from it at the beginning, and the one week marked off from it at the end, are all symbolical, and measure symbolically, not mathematically, a vast period in the history of God's kingdom on earth. Other numbers are so used in the book of Daniel. The symbolism of four and ten, for example, even when the number corresponds with persons or events of history, probably often determined the particular number of historical instances to be cited, and was doubtless felt by the prophet as he recalled the dream and beheld the visions.

The largeness of the outlook and the comprehensiveness of the prophecies of Daniel are realized in the light of the use made of this book by the men of the Bible. 1. Our Lord chose the title "son of man," by which he referred to himself more often than by any other title, from Dan. vii. 13, 14; and thus placed that aspect of his mission and kingdom, which this title denotes, in the forefront. See SON OF MAN. 2. Christ warned men that the abomination of desolation, spoken of by Daniel the prophet, should yet stand in the holy place (Mat. xxiv. 15; Mark xiii. 14; Dan. xi. 31; xii. 11; and ix. 27, noting Greek text; cp. 2 Thes. ii. 1–12). Evidently, on Christ's explanation, the content of the prophecies was not exhausted when the idolatrous altar was erected on Jehovah's altar by Antiochus Epiphanes (1 Mac. i. 54). Either in some, if not all, instances the prophecy relates to a different event, or else the abomination of desolation is a conception embodying an idea which will come to manifestation in concrete form whenever the idea itself is present as' a potent principle in history. Likewise the apostles understood that the little horn of the fourth beast (Dan. vii. 24), and the king that speaketh marvelous things against God (xi. 36), belong to the future and are yet to be revealed (2 Thes. ii. 4; Rev. xiii. 5, 6). Characteristic features of the conflict between the world and God's kingdom undoubtedly belonged to the bitter struggle in the time of Antiochus Epiphanes, but not to that time only; and Christ and the apostles saw in these prophecies of Daniel an apocalypse of the future. These revelations were not exhausted by the events of the reign of Antiochus; they are big with meaning for the latter days of God's kingdom. 3. The beast which John saw coming up out of the sea (Rev. xiii. 1) is a composite picture of the four beasts which Daniel saw emerging from the sea (Dan. vii. 3–7). Daniel saw a lion with eagle's wings [and one head], a bear [with one head], a leopard with four wings and four heads, and finally a beast with ten horns [and one head]. On combining these four beasts as one animal, the beast that John saw is produced: like a leopard, but with the feet of a bear and the mouth of a lion, having ten horns and seven heads. Daniel describes four kingdoms of this world which rise successively, and are as fierce and terrible as wild beasts in their antagonism to the kingdom of God. John does not view the kingdoms individually, but all the kingdoms of this world collectively. He gazes upon them as one, notwithstanding external differences. And John sees the dragon, the tempter-serpent of Eden (Rev. xii. 3, 9), conformed in appearance to the beast, because the dragon is the animating and moulding spirit in the kingdom of the world. To neither Daniel nor John are the world powers presented in their political aspect, but solely as representatives of the world in its antagonism to the kingdom of God. It is not the fortunes of the nations, but their relation to God's kingdom, that is the prime object of the prophecy. This fact is important, and furnishes a clue to the revelation in chapters xi. and xii. of the book of Daniel. It suggests that in these chapters also the aim is not to unfold political history, but is mainly to sketch apocalyptically great movements of the world in relation to the kingdom of God. The enemies of Zion came, and had always come, from the north and south. Developing that historical circumstance apocalyptically, the vision pictures a struggle between the contending world-powers, a war of varying fortunes; the gradual overthrow of the king of the south and the ultimate triumph of the king of the north, and his final mortal conflict with the kingdom of God. The picture is a companion piece to Ezek. xxxviii. and xxxix. 4. Daniel speaks of the time of the end, that is the final time. It is the latter time of the indignation [of God] (Dan. viii. 19: cp. xi. 36), when judgment is being executed upon the kingdoms of the world and the eternal kingdom of God is being established (cp. x. 14), to be followed by the consummation (xii. 1c–3). It is the final period of the conflict between the powers of the world and the kingdom of God, ending in the complete

victory of the kingdom (xi. 40–xii. 4). The apostles also speak of this period, calling it the last hour, the last time, or the last days; and they allude to it as already begun in their day and not ended, and destined to witness a manifestation of antichrist (2 Thes. ii. 2–4; 2 Tim. iii. 1; 1 John ii. 18; Jude 18). These men of the New Testament clearly saw the scope and meaning of Daniel's prophecies concerning the final time, and they had a sense of living in that predicted period.

The unity of the book of Daniel is rarely questioned. The theory has, indeed, been advanced, and has its advocates at present, that the Aramaic section, so much at least as is comprised in chaps. ii.–vi., is an independent composition, penned in Aramaic, and written one, two, or three centuries before the time of the Maccabees. But generally the essential integrity of the book is conceded; it was written by one man. In the first seven chapters Daniel is spoken of in the third person and sometimes in commendatory terms (i. 19, 20; ii. 14; v. 11, 12; vi. 3; cp. Paul of himself, 2 Cor. ii. 15; x. 8; xi. 5, 23 seq.); and in the subsequent chapters he speaks in the first person. Many critics deny that the book was composed by Daniel; and their denial extends to those parts in which the first person is used as well as to that part where the third person is employed. They generally date its publication about 168 or 167 B. C., at the time of the Maccabees, and contend that it was written to support the faith of the Jews under the dreadful persecution then raging under Antiochus Epiphanes. The chief arguments against the genuineness of the book are: (1) Daniel is not mentioned among the worthies by the son of Sirach in the book of Ecclesiasticus (xlix.), about 200 B. C., although he mentions Ezekiel, Nehemiah, and the minor prophets. (2) The writer's use of Greek words, which indicate that he lived in the Grecian period. (3) Historical inaccuracies, which show that he was not an eyewitness of the events which he describes, but lived at a remote period from them. (4) The prophecies give details of history until the death of Antiochus Epiphanes only.

These arguments are answered as follows:
(1) The son of Sirach neglects to mention Daniel, it is true; but he also fails to mention Ezra and other notable men, like Gideon, Samson, and Jehoshaphat.
(2) The Greek words are confined to the names of musical instruments and are all found in one verse, iii. 5. The Greek origin of at least two of these names is freely granted: peˢanteˢrin for the Greek, psaltērion, and sumponeˢya for sumphonia. But does this fact militate against the composition of the book by Daniel in Babylon about 530 B. C.? By no means; for instruments such as those described were in use in the Tigris and Euphrates valleys in Daniel's day. Moreover, there is no question that at that time and in

that region music was a feature in triumphal processions and court life. Captives from distant lands were employed to play on their own instruments of music. Ashurbanipal so used Elamites. Sennacherib carried off from Judah singing men and singing women. Of the captive Jews the songs of Zion and the music of the harp were demanded (Ps. cxxxvii. 1-3). There was sufficient intercourse also between the empires on the Tigris and the western peoples to have led to the introduction both of the Greek instruments and their names. Assyrian kings from Sargon, 722 B. C. onward, not to speak of earlier monarchs, had led off prisoners and received tribute from Cyprus, Ionia, Lydia, and Cilicia, which were Greek lands. Nebuchadnezzar warred against the cities on the Mediterranean. It would be in accordance with custom for these conquerors to introduce Greek instruments and Greek-speaking musicians to their courts. Finally, the language of the passage in question is Aramaic, not Babylonian. The Aramæans had for centuries been in contact with the west. Their language was the international language of diplomacy (cp. 2 Kin. xviii. 26), and they were the intermediaries of trade, who handled the goods of Orient and Occident. Their language acquired an admixture of foreign words from these sources. The writer of the Book of Daniel is using Aramaic, and doubtless employs the names which were current among the Aramæans for instruments of this kind. It is for those who base an argument on these words against the genuineness of the Book of Daniel, to show that they were not current Aramaic before the sixth century B. C.

(3) The asserted historical inaccuracies are not statements which are disproved by history, but only statements which have seemed difficult to harmonize with the meager accounts of secular historians. No contradiction between Daniel's record and established history has been proven. The asserted historical inaccuracies have, moreover, been steadily diminishing before the increasing knowledge of the times of Cyrus. The existence of king Belshazzar was scouted : but now the records contemporary with the capture of Babylon have made him a well-known historical character ; explained why he raised Daniel to the third place of power in the kingdom instead of the second, for his father and he already occupied the two higher places of authority ; and have made clear why he and not Nabonidus is mentioned as king at Babylon on the night of the capture of the city (see BELSHAZZAR). They do not yet clear up the reference to Darius the Mede receiving the kingdom, but they show that the appointment of a regent for Babylonia by Cyrus was in accord with his policy. The allusions to Belshazzar as a descendant of Nebuchadnezzar agree with a custom of the time (see BELSHAZZAR). In view of the

revelations of the cuneiform inscriptions, it is bold to assert that there are historical inaccuracies in the book of Daniel.

(4) The prophecies do, indeed, give historical details until the death of Antiochus Epiphanes (viii.). But are the prophecies not definite for the times after Antiochus? The fourth kingdom described in chap. ii. and vii. can be none other than the Roman empire (see above), which succeeded to universal empire at a time subsequent to Antiochus, and in its later development is accurately described in the book of Daniel (cp. Antiq. x. 11, 7 ; 2 Esdras xii. 11).

The Aramaic of the book of Daniel has been proven, by recently discovered documents, to be an Aramaic current as early as the beginning of the fifth century B. C., at least in the west.

The prophecy of Daniel is quoted by Christ as genuine and certain of fulfilment (Mat. xxiv. 15). Josephus believed that the prophecies of Daniel were in existence before the time of Alexander the Great, 330 B. C. (Antiq. xi. 8, 5), yea, before the days of Artaxerxes (contra Apion. i. 8). The deliverance of Shadrach, Meshach, and Abednego from the fiery furnace and of Daniel from the lions' den are cited in 1 Mac. ii. 59, 60 ; cp. also i. 54 with Dan. ix. 27 ; xi. 31.

Dan-ja'an.

A place between Gilead (or even between the land of the Hittites toward Kadesh) and Zidon (2 Sam. xxiv. 6). The ruin Dâniân, on the coast midway between Acre and Tyre, can scarcely be its site, for the takers of the census who left Dan-jaan did not reach Tyre until they had passed Zidon. It may be identical with Dan, the conventional extreme north of the country (cp. the connection of each with Zidon, Judg. xviii. 28). The ancient versions indicate that Dan-jaan is a corruption for Dan-jaar, and that Dan is described as being in the forest.

Dan'nah [a low place, low ground].

A village in the hill country of Judah (Josh. xv. 49). The situation of the other towns of this group suggests a place much farther south than Idhna, 8 miles west by north of Hebron.

Da'ra. See DARDA.

Dar'da [perhaps, pearl of wisdom].

A son of Mahol, family of Zerah, tribe of Judah, who was celebrated for wisdom (1 Kin. iv. 31). In 1 Chron. ii. 6 the name appears as Dara.

Dar'ic.

A gold coin current in Persia, worth about five dollars, which had on one side a king with a bow and a javelin, while on the other was a somewhat square figure ; see MONEY. The chronicler reckons the value of the gold contributed by the princes in David's reign for the temple in darics (1 Chron. xxix. 7), not because darics circulated in Israel as early as David's reign, but because at the time of writing the daric was familiar to his readers and a common standard. The daric was current in the Persian period (Ezra ii. 69; viii. 27; Neh. vii. 70, 71, 72; in A. V. dram). The first issue was wont to be attributed to Darius Hystaspis (cp. Herod. iv. 166); but Prof. Sayce argues that daric really comes from the Babylonian *dariku*, a weight or measure which, like the English pound, commencing as a weight became afterwards a coin. Dariku figures in a contract in the 12th year of Nabonidus, five years before Cyrus' conquest of Babylon, and long before Darius was elected to the throne (Sayce, *Ezra*, etc., p. 38). Silver darics were also coined, which were worth about a shekel.

Da-ri'us [from Zend *dara*, king].

1. A king described as Darius the Mede, son of Ahasuerus (Dan. v. 31; ix. 1). When about 62 years old he was made king over the realm of the Chaldeans after the capture of Babylon by the army of Cyrus, and he reigned a part of one year at least (v. 31; xi. 1) before Cyrus (vi. 28). He set 120 satraps over the kingdom (vi. 1). The satraps were subject to three presidents, of whom Daniel was one (2). Presidents and satraps were at the court of Darius (6), and he had authority to write unto all peoples, nations, and languages that dwell in all the earth or land (25). He was inveigled into issuing the foolish decree, for violating which Daniel was cast into the lion's den (vi. 1-27). In his first year Daniel saw the vision of the seventy weeks (ix. 1-27). He has not been identified with certainty, but was probably sovereign of the Babylonian empire *ad interim* until Cyrus, who was pressing his conquests, was ready to assume the duties of king of Babylon. Josephus says that he was son of Astyages, and was known to the Greeks by another name (Antiq. x. 11, 4). Perhaps, then, he was Cyaxeres, son and successor of Astyages and father-in-law and uncle of Cyrus (Xenophon, Cyropaed. i. 5; viii. 7); or possibly Ugbaru, governor of Gutium, apparently a province in western Media or on its borders, who led the detachment of Cyrus' army which captured Babylon, held the city for at least four months until Cyrus arrived, and is spoken of in this connection in a cuneiform inscription as Cyrus' governor.

2. A king of Persia who in point of time followed after Cyrus (Ezra iv. 5). When he came to the throne, the building of the temple had been suspended owing to complaints from the jealous neighboring tribes; but Darius, on being applied to, caused a search to be made at Achmetha, the Median capital, where the edict of Cyrus permitting the work to be undertaken was found (Ezra vi. 1-12). The erection of the sacred edifice accordingly recommenced in his second year, sixth month, and twenty-fourth day (Ezra iv. 24; Hag. i. 15; ii. 18), and on the third day of the twelfth month of his sixth regnal year was completed (Ezra vi. 15). The proph-

ets Haggai and Zechariah prophesied during the reign of this monarch (Hag. i. 1; ii. 1, 10, 18; Zech. i. 1, 7; vii. 1), who was without doubt the Darius Hystaspis of the classical writers, the Dara Gustasp of Zend writings. He was son of Hystaspes, which Latin writers denoted by using the genitive case Hystaspis. Through his father he belonged to the family of the Achæmenides, which was already represented on the throne by Cyrus and Cambyses; but he was not in the line of succession. The leading events of his life are detailed in an inscription of Darius' own on a rock at Behistun, about 60 miles southwest of Hamadan. It is in three languages, Persian, Babylonian, and Amardian or Elamite. According to it, eight of his ancestors were kings. Cambyses, Cyrus' son, put his brother Bardes, called by Herodotus Smerdis, to death, and some time afterwards committed suicide. Then a Magian Gomates or Gaumata started up, pretending to be Bardes, who he alleged had not really been slain. According to Herodotus (iii. 67-79), with whose narrative the less detailed record on the stone essentially agrees, evidence of the fraud was discovered and a conspiracy formed against Gomates by seven men of rank, one of whom was Darius Hystaspis. In 521 B. C. they slew the Magian and saluted Darius king. Elam rose against the new monarch, but was temporarily subdued. Babylon followed under a leader called Nidintabel and stood a siege of two years (520-519 B. C.). When it became known that Darius was detained at Babylon, in conducting the siege, a general revolt of the provinces constituting the empire took place; in fact, the empire fell to pieces. Darius says: "While I was in Babylon these provinces rebelled against me: Persia, Susiana, Media, Assyria, Armenia, Parthia, Margiana, Sattagydia, and the Sacians." But he and his lieutenants subdued them all, generally ending by impaling the rebel leader. Babylon, in 514 B. C., revolted anew under Araḫu or Aracus, an Armenian; but the rebellion was put down, its leader and his chief adherents being impaled. The walls of the city were this time thrown down, and a great step taken to that utter destruction which the prophets foresaw. Darius now ruled over an empire extending eastward into India and westward to the Grecian Archipelago. He administered it, on the whole, wisely and well. After an unsuccessful campaign against the Scythians near the river Don, in what is now Russia, and a quarrel with the Greeks, in which his generals Datis and Artaphernes were defeated at 490 B. C. at Marathon, Darius died at the age of 73 (Ctesias) in 486 B. C., after a reign of 36 years.

3. The last king of Persia, who reigned from 336 to 330 B. C. His true name was Codomannus. He was defeated by Alexander the Great (1 Mac. i. 1; Antiq. xi. 8, 3), first at Issus in 333, when he fled into Persia, and

again at Arbela in 331. He died about four months later at the hands of his servants, with Alexander in hot pursuit of him.

Dar'kon [scattering].

Founder of a family, part of the children of Solomon's servants (Ezra ii. 56; Neh. vii. 58).

Date.

The fruit of the date palm or *Phœnix dactylifera* (2 Chron. xxxi. 5, A. V., margin), from which honey was made (War iv. 8, 3). The text and the R. V., like the Hebrew original, use the general name honey, without specifying the kind.

Da'than.

A son of Eliab, a Reubenite, who with Abiram, his brother, and On, a man of the same tribe, were prominent leaders in the rebellion of Korah the Levite. Their grievance was different from his. They thought that the leadership of Israel should have gone to the tribe to which they belonged, for Reuben was Jacob's eldest son. Then, again, they complained that Moses had taken them from a country where there was plenty, under the promise of leading them into a land flowing with milk and honey, while in fact all that he had done was to march them up and down amid naked rocks and barren sands (Num. xvi. 1–35, cp. 13, 14; xxvi. 7–11; Deut. xi. 6; Ps. cvi. 17).

Dath'e-ma.

A fortress in Gilead, into which the faithful Israelites fled for safety in the time of Judas Maccabæus (1 Mac. v. 9). They were relieved by Judas and his brother Jonathan. It cannot be identified with certainty.

Daugh'ter.

Besides corresponding to the several senses in which son is used, especially for child or remoter female descendant or as an expression of tender sympathy for a woman (Gen. xxx. 21; Ex. ii. 1; Luke xiii. 16; Mat. ix. 22), daughter denotes a female inhabitant of a country or town (Gen. xxiv. 3; Judg. xxi. 21), a female worshiper of a god (Mal. ii. 11; Is. xliii. 6), the suburb of a city (Num. xxi. 25, margin), the collective body of the citizens of a town or country (Ps. ix. 14; cxxxvii. 8; Lam. iv. 21; Zech. ii. 10). See HEIR, MARRIAGE, SLAVE.

Da'vid [beloved].

Son of Jesse and second king of Israel. His life falls into several distinct periods.

I. His youth, which was passed at Bethlehem of Judah. He was the youngest of eight brothers (1 Sam. xvi. 10, 11; xvii. 12–14). In the registry of the tribe of Judah (1 Chron. ii. 13–15) only seven of these sons of Jesse are named, probably because one died without issue. David's mother was tenderly remembered for her godliness (Ps. lxxxvi. 16; cxvi. 16). His ancestral history was picturesque, inspiring, and generally praiseworthy, but yet at times tainted by sin (Gen. xxxvii. 26, 27; xxxviii. 13–29; xliii. 8, 9; xliv. 18–34; Num.

i. 7; Josh. ii. 1–21; Ruth. iv. 17–22). In person he was ruddy and beautiful to look upon (1 Sam. xvi. 12). As youngest son, he was charged with the care of his father's sheep, and he displayed his fidelity and courage in this occupation by slaying both a lion and a bear which attacked the flock (11; xvii. 34–36). He possessed musical gifts of high order, at this period playing skillfully on the harp and later composing psalms. When king Saul had been rejected by God, the prophet Samuel was sent to Bethlehem and directed to anoint David as Saul's successor. There was no public proclamation of David, lest the hostility of Saul should be aroused. At most, the act was performed in the presence of the elders of the town, and, so far as appears, no word concerning the purpose of the anointing was spoken to the audience (xvi. 4, 5, 13), though Jesse and David were doubtless informed. It was a crisis in David's history. The Spirit of the Lord came mightily upon him. Still he did not despise his humble, daily work.

II. His service under Saul. Saul, forsaken by God, distressed by an evil spirit, and subject to melancholy and insanity, was advised by his attendants to attach a harper to his person to soothe him by music when disturbed; and one recommended David as a cunning musician, a man of valor and ready for war by reason of age, skill, and courage, even though perhaps not as yet experienced in battle, discreet, comely, pious (xvi. 14–18). Saul summoned him, was benefited by his music and pleased with his character, asked Jesse that he might remain, and appointed him one of his armorbearers (19–23; cp. 2 Sam. xviii. 15). The service thus begun proved a school for David. He learned war and government, had intercourse with able men, and saw the dark and bright side of court life. David did not, however, as yet remain continuously with Saul. The king's condition evidently improved, and David returned frequently to Bethlehem to have an oversight over his father's sheep (1 Sam. xvii. 15). While he was on a visit home the Philistines invaded Judah and encamped about 15 miles west of Bethlehem. Saul led forth the army of Israel to meet them. The three eldest brothers of David were with the army, and after they had been absent from home about six weeks, their father sent David to inquire about their welfare. Goliath's challenge stirred his spirit. He felt certain that God through him would remove the reproach from Israel, and he asked who the Philistine was that defied the armies of the living God. His words were reported to Saul, who perceiving the spirit by which the young man was animated intrusted the single combat to him. David put off the armor with which Saul had armed him, urging that he had not proved it. He showed true genius. Goliath was rendered slow of motion by weight of armor; the kind of weapon he carried obliged him to fight at close quarters; and he was vulnerable only in the face, which under the circumstances was out of reach. David approached him, unhampered in movement by any armor, with a sling, in the use of which he was proficient, with five stones that could be hurled from a distance, with the consciousness of the righteousness of his cause and with implicit confidence in God. The taunts between the two champions are characteristic of ancient battle. Goliath fell, struck by a stone from David's sling. After the combat David, on his way to Gibeah of Benjamin where Saul held court or to the tabernacle at Nob, displayed the head of the giant at Jerusalem, apparently in defiance to the Jebusites, who held the stronghold, and put the armor in the tent which he thenceforth occupied (xvii. 54). The sword was deposited in the tabernacle (xxi. 9). When David had gone forth to meet Goliath Saul, amazed at his spirit, asked Abner whose son such a youth could be; and when David returned triumphant the king put the same question to him, only to receive the simple answer, "I am the son of thy servant Jesse the Bethlehemite." This reply formed the sum and substance of the interview (xvii. 55–xviii. 1); David's ancestors were not notable for heroic achievement. The question of the king had also reference to the rank and material condition of the family, for Saul had promised to accept the victor as son-in-law and to free his father's family from taxation (xvii. 25; xviii. 18). He found that he had no occasion to be ashamed of the birth of his son-in-law. The victory over Goliath was a second crisis in David's life. The valor, modesty, and piety, which he displayed won for him the disinterested and enduring love of Jonathan (xviii. 1). He was no longer permitted to repair periodically to his father's house, but he remained continuously at court (2). The ovation which he received aroused the jealousy of Saul, who thenceforth was David's enemy (6–9). Saul saw that Samuel's prediction of the transfer of the kingdom from him to one better than he (xv. 17–29) approached fulfillment in David, and he attempted to prevent it. He endeavored to slay David with his spear (xviii. 10, 11). Failing in this, he reduced David in military rank and power (13). He gave his daughter, whom he had promised to David for a wife, to another (17–19). He endeavored to entrap him to death through his love for Michal (20–27). As David grew in favor (29, 30) Saul's fear increased, and he no longer concealed his purpose to slay David (xix. 1). This purpose was never after allowed by Saul's adherents to be abandoned, but was fostered by a party at court (xxiv. 9; Ps. vii. title). Appeased for a time, his jealousy soon revived, and he again attempted to smite David with his spear (1 Sam. xix. 4–9). Then he would have arrested David, who, however, escaped through Michal's deceit (10–17). David wrote Ps. lix.

at this time. He fled to Samuel at Ramah, whither Saul sent to seize him (18–24); fled next to Jonathan, who inquired and informed him that there was no longer safety for him at court (xx.).

III. The fugitive hero. Without confidence in God and sunk in despair David fled from Saul. Stopping at Nob, without faith, he told a lie (xxi. 1–9); then hurried to Gath and sought protection of Saul's enemy Achish. The lords of the Philistines, however, refused to harbor him who had formerly humiliated them, and they seized David (14; Ps. lvi. title). He feigned madness and made himself despicable, and Achish drove him away (Ps. xxxiv. title). He regained his faith in Jehovah (Ps. xxxiv.), returned to Judah, and abode in the cave of Adullam (1 Sam. xxii. 1), but placed his parents in Moab (3, 4). A motley company, mostly of unemployed and desperate men, numbering 400 at first, increasing eventually to 600, began to join him. Among these were Abiathar, the surviving priest of Nob, who brought an ephod with him, and the prophet Gad, whom David had probably met at Ramah (5, 20; xxiii. 6). David thus had religious aid and companionship. From Adullam he went to the relief of Keilah and delivered the town out of the hands of the Philistines (xxiii. 1–5). On Saul's preparing to attack him there, he fled to the wilderness of Judah (14; Ps. lxiii.), whither Saul, at the instigation of the Ziphites, pursued him until compelled to desist by an incursion of the Philistines (1 Sam. xxiii. 14–29). That trouble being settled, Saul sought David in the wilderness near Engedi, but was for the time conquered by the kindness of David, who had the king in his power in the cave, but spared his life (xxiv.; Ps. lvii.; cxlii.). David and his band of armed followers protected the exposed property of the Israelites from thieving marauders (1 Sam. xxiii. 1; xxv. 16, 21; xxvii. 8), and naturally enough expected some return in gifts of food. He did not levy tax or demand regular contributions of provisions. Nabal's scornful rejection of his request incensed him, and he was only saved from shedding blood in his fury by the wisdom and address of Nabal's wife (xxv.), whom David married after the death of her husband. David again came into the neighborhood of Ziph, and the Ziphites again informed Saul, who marched against David. David showed his magnanimity by not slaying the sleeping king, but merely carrying away from his side his spear and cruse of water (xxvi.). Despairing of always escaping Saul, David left Judah and obtained permission from Achish to occupy Ziklag, a frontier town toward the southern desert. Here he remained a year and four months, protecting the Philistines by warring with the desert tribes, yet sometimes wasting a remote village even of Philistia (xxvii.). When the Philistines went to Gilboa to war with Saul,

David was prevented from accompanying them by the lords of the Philistines (xxviii. 1, 2; xxix.). Returning, he found Ziklag in ruins. He pursued the retreating invaders and recovered the spoil (xxx.). When he heard the result of the battle of Gilboa, he mourned the fate of Saul and Jonathan in an elegy (2 Sam. i.).

IV. King of Judah. On the death of Saul the tribe of Judah, to which David belonged, elected him king, and he began to reign in Hebron (ii. 1–10), being then about thirty years old (v. 4). The rest of the tribes, under the leadership of Abner, one of the ablest men of the time, set up Ish-bosheth, Saul's son, at Mahanaim, and for the next two years civil war raged between his partisans and those of David. It ended by the assassination, sorely against David's will, both of Abner and of Ish-bosheth (ii. 12–iv. 12). David's reign at Hebron continued for seven years and six months. He had already several wives, and among the sons born to him at Hebron were Amnon, Absalom, and Adonijah (ii. 11; iii. 1–5; v. 5).

V. King of all Israel. On the death of Ish-bosheth, David was elected king over all the tribes, and he at once set to work to establish the kingdom (v. 1–5). Various towns in the territory of Israel were garrisoned by the Philistines, and others were held by the Canaanites. David began a siege of the Jebusite stronghold at Jerusalem. It was deemed impregnable by its inhabitants, but David took it by storm. He wisely made it his capital, and erected a palace there by the skill of Tyrian artificers. The new capital stood on the border of Judah and Israel. Its situation tended to allay the jealousy between north and south. Its deliverance from the hands of the Canaanites opened the highway between Judah and the north, facilitated intercourse, and tended to further cement the kingdom. The Philistines twice invaded the land, and twice suffered defeat near Jerusalem (v. 17–25; 1 Chron. xiv. 8–17). The king followed up the second victory by invading the country of the Philistines, took Gath, and by this conquest and by brief campaigns later (2 Sam. xxi. 15–22) so completely subjugated the Philistines that these hereditary enemies ceased to trouble Israel for centuries. The kingdom being established, David turned his attention to religious affairs. He brought the ark, with ceremony, sacrifices, and rejoicing, from Kirjath-jearim (Josh. xv. 9; 2 Chron. i. 4), and placed it within a tabernacle which he had pitched for it in the city of David (2 Sam. vi. 1–23; 1 Chron. xiii. 1–14; xv. 1–3). Next he organized the worship on a magnificent scale (1 Chron. xv.; xvi.), and planned a splendid temple (2 Sam. vii. 1–29; 1 Chron. xvii. 1–27; xxii. 7–10). Through the divine favor he now became very prosperous. To insure the safety of the nation, to keep it from idolatrous contamination, and to avenge insult offered to it, he waged war with surrounding nations, and subdued the Moabites, the Aramæans of Zobah and Damascus, the Ammonites, the Edomites, and the Amalekites (2 Sam. viii. 1–18; x. 1–19; xii. 26–31), thus extending his kingdom to the limits long before promised to Abraham (Gen. xv. 18). It was during the Ammonite war that David committed his great sin in the matter of Uriah the Hittite, for which God rebuked him through Nathan the prophet, and imposed the penalty that the sword should never depart from his house (2 Sam. xi. 1–xii. 23). David sincerely repented (Ps. li.). The chastisement was partly direct and partly the natural fruit of his example and transmitted character. The child died (2 Sam. xii. 19). Lawless lust and lawless vengeance were manifested in his own family (xiii.). Lawless and unfilial ambition triumphed for a time in his family and led to civil war (xiv.–xix.). The spirit of dissatisfaction and tribal jealousy fomented by Absalom showed itself after the suppression of Absalom's rebellion once more in the revolt of Sheba (xx.). David solemnly satisfied justice, according to the ideas of that age, in avenging Saul's bloody violation of the treaty rights of the Gibeonites (xxi.). He committed a sin of pride in numbering the people, and was punished by a pestilence (xxiv.; 1 Chron. xxi.). David was much occupied during his reign with the organization of internal affairs and with the preparation of material for the erection of the temple. He closed his reign by securing the succession to Solomon (1 Kin. i.), and by providing that the guilt of some who had escaped justice in his day should not go unpunished (ii. 1–11). He died in his seventy-first year, after having reigned forty (or, more precisely, forty and a half) years, seven and a half at Hebron and thirty-three at Jerusalem (2 Sam. ii. 11; v. 4, 5; 1 Chron. xxix. 27).

David early received the distinguished designation of the sweet singer of Israel (2 Sam. xxiii. 1). Ancient Hebrew tradition, much of which was unquestionably current about David's own time and shortly after, ascribed the composition of psalms to him both directly and indirectly. His fondness for music is recorded in the historical books; he played skillfully on the harp (1 Sam. xvi. 18–23; 2 Sam. vi. 5), and he arranged the service of praise for the sanctuary (1 Chron. vi. 31; xvi. 7, 41, 42; xxv. 1). He composed a lament over Saul and Jonathan, and over Abner, and a song of deliverance and last words (2 Sam. i. 17–27; iii. 33, 34; xxii. 1–51; xxiii. 1–7). His musical activity is referred to by Amos (vi. 5), Ezra (iii. 10), Nehemiah (xii. 24, 36, 45, 46), and the son of Sirach (Ecclus. xlvii. 8, 9). Such work on the part of David accorded with the times, for poetry and music had long been cultivated by the Hebrews as well as by the Egyptians and Babylonians (Num. xxi. 14; Judg. v.). Seventy-three psalms are designated David's in their Hebrew titles ; and as in many cases the intention is to indicate that he is the author (cp. iii., vii., xxxiv., li., etc.), it is possibly always the intention. Lix. and perhaps vii. are assigned to the time of his sojourn at Saul's court; xxxiv., lii., liv., lvi., lvii., lxiii., and cxlii., to the period of distress when he was a fugitive; and iii., xviii., xxx., li., and lx., to the years of varied experiences when he was king.

Though at times David committed deep-dyed sins, for which the early and comparatively dark period of the church's history in which he lived and his own deep penitence are his only defense, yet his general fidelity to Jehovah was such that he was called the man after God's own heart (1 Sam. xiii. 14). Speaking generally, he did that which was right in the eyes of the Lord, save in the matter of Uriah the Hittite (1 Kin. xv. 5). He served his generation by the will of God, and then fell on sleep (Acts xiii. 36). His influence on mankind can scarcely be overestimated. He, rather than his predecessor Saul, was the founder of the Jewish monarchy. His psalms, sung throughout Christendom century after century, revive his spiritual influence. He was an important link in the chain of ancestry of Him who was at once David's son and David's Lord (Mat. xxii. 41–45).

Da'vid, Cit'y of.
1. The Jebusite stronghold of Zion captured by David's men, and called by him the city of David, because he made it his royal residence (2 Sam. v. 6–9; 1 Chron. xi. 5, 7). It stood on the ridge, south of the later site of the temple. It was early settled, and was a walled town in the third millennium B. C. The ark was taken thither by David, and stayed there until the temple was built (2 Sam. vi. 12, 16; 1 Kin. viii. 1; 1 Chron. xv. 1–29; 2 Chron. v. 2). David was buried there (1 Kin. ii. 10). Solomon's queen, Pharaoh's daughter, dwelt there for a time (1 Kin. iii. 1), though he afterwards erected a palace for himself and her (vii. 1; ix. 24; 2 Chron. viii. 11). He was buried in the city of David (1 Kin. xi. 43; 2 Chron. ix. 31), as were Rehoboam (1 Kin. xiv. 31; 2 Chron. xii. 16) and many other kings (1 Kin. xv. 8, 24; xxii. 50; 2 Kin. viii. 24; ix. 28; xii. 21; xiv. 20; xv. 7, 38; xvi. 20; 2 Chron. xiv. 1; xvi. 14; xxi. 1, 20; xxiv. 16, 25; xxvii. 9). Jehoiada, the high priest, was also interred there (2 Chron. xxiv. 16). Hezekiah brought the upper watercourse of Gihon to the west side of the city of David (2 Chron. xxxii. 30; cp. xxxiii. 14). Millo was apparently within its limits (2 Chron. xxxii. 5). In Nehemiah's time there was a descent from the city of David by means of stairs (Neh. iii. 15, 16; xii. 37). It was fortified and garrisoned by the Syrians and Greeks during the Maccabee wars (1 Mac. i. 33; ii. 31; vii. 32; xiv. 36, 37). See JERUSALEM.
2. Bethlehem, the birthplace or at least the home of David (Luke ii. 4).

Day.
1. An interval of time comprising the period between two successive risings of the sun (Gen. vii. 24; Job iii. 6). The Hebrews reckoned it from evening to evening (Lev. xxiii. 32; Ex. xii. 18; War iv. 9, 12). This custom was probably due to the use of lunar months, which began with the appearance of the new moon. The exact designation of the civil day accordingly was evening-morning or night-day (Dan. viii. 14, margin; 2 Cor. xi. 25). But although the evening properly introduced a new day, it was often reckoned in connection with the natural day which, strictly speaking, it followed—e. g. the evening which began the fifteenth of Nisan is designated by the expression " the fourteenth day at even " (Ex. xii. 18; cp. 2 Chron. xxxv. 1; see also Lev. xxiii. 32). The days of the week were numbered, not named. The only exception was the seventh day, which was also called Sabbath.
2. The interval between dawn and darkness (Gen. i. 5; viii. 22). It was divided into morning, noon, and evening (Ps. lv. 17; cp. Dan. vi. 10); or its time was indicated by reference to sunrise, heat of the day, cool of the day, sunset, and the like. After the exile the use of hours became common, and the day from sunrise to sunset was divided into twelve hours (Mat. xx. 1–12; John xi. 9); the sixth hour being noon (John iv. 6; Acts x. 9), the ninth the hour of prayer (iii. 1; Antiq. xiv. 4, 3).
3. Any period of action or state of being (Zech. xii. 3 seq.); as day of trouble (Ps. xx. 1), day of his wrath (Job xx. 28), day of the Lord (Is. ii. 12; xiii. 6, 9; in the N. T. specially of the second advent of Christ, 1 Cor. v. 5; 1 Thes. v. 2; 2 Pet. iii. 10). So also in the phrase "in the day that," which is equivalent to "when" (Gen. ii. 4, 17; Lev. xiv. 2–20), and is often rendered so in the English versions (Lev. xiv. 57; Num. vi. 13; 1 Sam. xx. 19; Ps. xx. 9).

Days'man.
One who has set a day for hearing a cause; a mediator or an arbitrator (Job ix. 33).

Day'star. See LUCIFER.

Dea'con [Greek diakonos; in classical writers a servant, a waiting man, a messenger. It is used in this sense in Mat. xx. 26, where it is translated minister, and is distinguished from doulos, bond-servant or slave, occurring in the next verse; cp. also Mat. xxiii. 11; Mark ix. 35; x. 43; John ii. 5, 9].

A Christian officer, whose spiritual and moral qualifications are laid down in 1 Tim. iii. 8. It is justly assumed that the seven men chosen to relieve the apostles of the secular care of the widows and other poor people in the early church were deacons (Acts vi. 1–6; cp. the words ministration, diakonia, and serve, diakoneō, in vs. 1 and 2). Their charge of the needy did not debar them from the privilege of speaking publicly for Christ, for Stephen and Philip labored also as preachers and evangelists. They did so, however, in the exercise of a personal gift rather than of an official duty. A plurality of deacons existed in the church at Philippi, and shared with the bishops the duties of the church (Phil. i. 1).

Dea'con-ess.

A female deacon; like Phœbe, servant or *diakonos* of the church at Cenchreæ (Rom. xvi. 1; see margin of R. V.). Deaconesses are probably referred to in 1 Tim. iii. 11. They existed in the churches of Bithynia as early as A. D. 100, for Pliny, in his celebrated letter to the emperor Trajan regarding the Christians, reports having examined "two old women" of the Christian community "who were called ministers" (*ministræ*).

Dead Sea.

The name now given to the sheet of water called in the Bible the salt sea (Gen. xiv. 3; Num. xxxiv. 12; Deut. iii. 17; Josh. iii. 16), the sea of the Arabah or Plain (Deut. iii. 17; Josh. iii. 16), and the east or eastern sea (Ezek. xlvii. 18; Joel ii. 20; and R. V. of Zech. xiv. 8). Josephus calls it Asphaltitis (Antiq. i. 9, 1). It was named the Dead Sea by the Greeks as early as the latter half of the second century of the Christian era (Pausanias). It is situated in the deep volcanic rent or fissure which runs through Palestine from north to south; and is fed chiefly by the river Jordan, which empties into it on an average six million tons of water every twenty-four hours. Its surface was ascertained by the officers of the ordnance survey to be 1292 feet lower than the ocean level. The sea is like a long rectangle with the angles beveled off; but its regularity of form is interrupted by a projection into its southeastern side of a great promontory or peninsula called Lisan, or the Tongue. The length of the sea from north to south is on an average about 47 English miles, but it varies, a large portion of the southern shore being sometimes dry and sometimes covered with water. The breadth a little north of En-gedi is 9½ miles, and it is nearly as much everywhere north of the Lisan. Ancient watermarks indicate that the area, especially the length, was formerly much larger (War iv. 8, 4). The Lisan is about 9 miles long from north to south. Its banks are from 40 to 60 feet high; while, according to Tristram, its highest point is about 300 feet above the water. Lieut. Lynch, who in 1848 led an expedition for the exploration of the Jordan and the Dead Sea, found the maximum depth of the latter, as ascertained by sounding, to be 1278 feet; this was at a point near the mouth of the Arnon. Soundings farther north yield 1300 feet. South of the Lisan, on the contrary, the sea is quite shallow. Except on the north side, where the Jordan enters, the Dead Sea is nearly

surrounded by a rampart of cliffs, which in some places leave a narrow beach between them and the water, while in others they themselves constitute the coast line. These rise in successive terraces, which also exist along the lower part of the Jordan valley. On the western side, at En-gedi, the height from the seashore to the top of the cliffs is 1950 feet; a little farther north, at Râs esh Shufk, the top is 2519 feet above the Dead Sea, *i. e.* 1227 above the Mediterranean. Farther northward the elevation gradually decreases till it reaches 1400 feet above the Dead Sea. These western cliffs contain deposits of bitumen in both liquid and solid state. On the eastern side the precipitous mountains of Moab rise from 2500 to 3000 feet above the shore.

The Dead Sea is one of the most remarkable sheets of water on the face of the earth. No other one is known to occupy so deep a hollow on the surface of the globe. Its waters are much salter than those of the ocean, for while in the latter 100 lbs. of water contain 6 lbs. of salt, in the former 100 lbs. of water contain from 20 to 27.8 lbs. of salt. In consequence of this, eggs will float on its surface. A bather, too, finds himself buoyant, and when he comes ashore there is a greasy deposit of salt upon his skin, which tortures him if there happens to be a scratch on his body. The saltness of the water is due to the nature of the soil, which abounds in the chlorides of sodium, magnesium, and calcium. These substances are carried into the sea by the river and the brooks; and there being no outlet, the salt remains and accumulates year by year, while the water with which it comes goes off to a large extent in vapor, evaporation being immense, since the air comes dry and thirsty from the desert.

The Scripture name, Salt Sea, has been superseded by the name Dead Sea. The old belief, however, that there is a total absence of life in and around the sea is erroneous. Organic life scarcely exists in its waters; neither shellfish nor corals are found. But vegetation flourishes on its shores at the mouth of wadies and by springs of fresh water; and birds frequent its strand or fly over its surface. According to Lartet, fish are found in small numbers south of the Lisan. As a symbol of life in the new kingdom of God, Ezekiel pictures the healing of the waters of the Dead Sea, and the multiplication of fish till the species rival in number those of the Mediterranean (Ezek. xlvii. 6–12).

Dearth. See FAMINE.

De'bir.

1. A king of Eglon, ally of Adoni-zedek; defeated, captured, and executed by Joshua (Josh. x. 3, 27).

2. A city in the hill country of Judah, yet in the Negeb or south land. It was also

alled Kirjath-sepher, which may mean city
of books and indicate a literary people; and
Kirjath-sannah, city of a palm tree or perhaps peak (Josh. xv. 15, 19, 48, 49). In the
time of Joshua it was inhabited by Anakim,
had a king, and was head of other towns.
Joshua captured it and slew its inhabitants
(Josh. x. 38, 39; xi. 21; xii. 13); but it was
reoccupied by returned fugitives, and had to
be recaptured by Othniel (Josh. xv. 15–17;
Judg. i. 11, 12). It was assigned to the
priests (Josh. xxi. 13, 15; 1 Chron. vi. 57,
58). The most probable site proposed (better
perhaps than Dilbeh, 4½ miles southwest of
Hebron) is Dhâherîyeh, nearly 12 miles
southwest of Hebron, on a flat ridge, with
open, rocky ground all around. It is west
of the sites of Socoh, Anab, and Eshtemoh
(Josh. xv. 48–50). It is supplied from cisterns. The springs mentioned in Judg. i. 15
are not distinctly connected with Debir and
may be nearer Hebron.

3. A town on the boundary of the tribe of
Judah, near the valley of Achor (Josh. xv.
7). The name is perhaps preserved in ed-
Debr, a grotto near ed-Dumm, i. e. Adum-
mim, on the road between Jerusalem and
Jericho.

4. A place east of the Jordan, near Mahanaim (Josh. xiii. 26). The margin of R. V.
has Lidebir. Perhaps Lodebar (q. v.).

Deb'o-rah [a bee].

1. Rebekah's nurse, who accompanied her
from Mesopotamia and lived until Jacob's return from Paddan-aram. She had perhaps
returned to her kindred in Haran after the
death of Rebekah and accompanied Jacob
back to Canaan, or she had gone to him when
he was sojourning at Shechem. At any rate
she was with him at Bethel. There she died
at the age of about 155 years, for she could
not have been much younger than Isaac. She
was buried at the foot of the hill on which
the town stood and under an oak, called in
consequence Allon-bacuth, oak of weeping
(Gen. xxiv. 59; xxxv. 8).

2. A prophetess, the wife of Lappidoth.
She dwelt under a palm tree, called after her
name, between Ramah and Bethel, in mount
Ephraim, and there judged the Israelites.
She summoned Barak to undertake the contest with Sisera, and accompanied him to the
rendezvous of his army (Judg. iv. 4–14).
Afterwards she composed a song of triumph
for the victory (v. 1–31; cp. 7).

Debt'or.

One who owes another money. To foster
the spirit of brotherhood and mutual help-
fulness, the Mosaic law ordained that the
creditor release his brother Israelite from all
obligations at the year of release, which re-
curred every seven years (Deut. xv. 1–4). In
the intervening years custom permitted the
seizure and enslavement of a debtor, his
wife, and his children (2 Kin. iv. 1; Neh. v.
5, 8; Is. l. 1; Mat. xviii. 25). In the time

of Jesus, in accordance with Roman law, imprisonment was sometimes inflicted on a
debtor (Mat. v. 25; xviii. 30; Luke xii. 58).

De-cap'o-lis [an association of ten cities].
A district, beginning where the plain of
Esdraelon opens into the Jordan valley and
expanding eastward, which was dominated
by ten associated Greek cities. The Greek
population had come in the wake of Alexander's conquest. The ten cities originally
included in the association were Scythopolis,
i. e. Bethshean, Hippos, Damascus; Gadara,
Raphana, Kanatha; Pella, Dion, Gerasa, and
Philadelphia, i. e. Rabbath Ammon (Pliny,
His. nat. v. 16). Other towns were afterwards
added. Ptolemy enumerates eighteen. Three
roads connect Esdraelon with the commercial
highway which runs between Damascus and
Arabia along the margin of the desert. The
ten towns stood on these three roads and
on the highway. The district is called De-
capolita regio by Pliny (v. 15). Multitudes
from Decapolis followed Jesus at an early
period of his ministry (Mat. iv. 25). The
Gadarene demoniac, when the evil spirit was
expelled, published his deliverance in Decapolis (Mark v. 20). Jesus traveled through
its midst on his way from Tyre and Sidon to
the sea of Galilee, approaching the lake from
the eastern side (vii. 31).

Ruins of the Forum at Jeresh, ancient Gerasa,
one of the cities of the Decapolis.

Gerasa (Jeresh) is the best preserved example of a small colonial town in the Near East. The earliest settlement there goes back to the Early Iron Age when it was an Ammonite village. Largely a pagan city, it flourished under the Romans and was rebuilt in A.D. 65. Excavations began there in the 1920s. The most magnificent building was the Temple to Artemis, the patron goddess of the city, The Street of the Columns with more than one hundred columns transversed the town from north to south.

Opposite: Roman ruins lead into the modern village of Jeresh.
Top: Entrance to the Street of the Columns.
Lower left: Detail from the propylea to the Temple of Artemis.
Lower right: Niche for light to illumine the Street of the Columns. These were placed at street level and evenly spaced along the sides of the street.

De′dan.

A Cushite people (Gen. x. 7), but also related to Abraham through Keturah (xxv. 3). They were an important commercial people (Ezek. xxvii. 15, 20; xxxviii. 13) of Arabia (Is. xxi. 13), in the neighborhood of Edom (Jer. xxv. 23; xlix. 8; Ezek. xxv. 13), where caravan routes from southern, eastern, and central Arabia converged. The name probably lingers in Daidan, to the west of Taima and southeast of Aila. Formerly two distinct tribes of Dedanites were assumed: one Semitic, living near Edom; the other Cushitic, dwelling near Raamah (Gen. x. 7), which was thought to have been situated on the coast of the Persian Gulf. Raamah, however, is better located in southwestern Arabia; and then Dedan was one people, centered near Taima, and neighbor alike to the Edomites and the inhabitants of Raamah.

Ded-i-ca′tion, Feast of.

An annual festival instituted by Judas Maccabæus in 165 B. C. to celebrate the purification and renewal of the temple, exactly three years after it had been desecrated by the introduction of Greek idolatry and other pollutions by order of Antiochus Epiphanes (1 Mac. iv. 52–59; cp. i. 54, 59). The festival, called also lights (Antiq. xii. 7, 7), and celebrated much after the manner of the festival of tabernacles (2 Mac. x. 6, 7), lasted eight days, beginning on the 25th of Chislev (approximately December), and falling consequently in winter. Jesus was present at least once at Jerusalem during the festival, and delivered a discourse to the assembled multitude (John x. 22). The Jews still keep the festival.

Deer.

The English name of the genus *Cervus*, or of the family *Cervidæ*. The word occurs only in A. V. in the name fallow deer, but the hart is frequently mentioned. Tristram enumerates two species of the genus *Cervus* as still occurring in Palestine, the roebuck (*Cervus capreolus*) and the fallow deer (*Cervus dama*); whilst the teeth and bones of three others, the red deer (*Cervus elaphus*), the reindeer (*Cervus tarandus*), and the elk (*Cervus alces*), are found in bone breccia in caves in the Lebanon mountains.

De-grees′.

A word occurring in the titles of fifteen Psalms, cxx.–cxxxiv. inclusive, which are called Songs of Degrees. It is the rendering of the Hebrew *Ma‘aloth*, ascents or goings up (Ezra vii. 9), steps (Ex. xx. 26; 1 Kin. x. 19). A Jewish tradition tells that the fifteen Songs of Degrees were sung as an ascent was made by fifteen steps from the court of the women to that of the men, a view not now generally entertained. Gesenius and Delitzsch held that they were so called because there is in their composition a certain progression, the concluding words of one sentence being often the commencement of the next, as—

I will lift up mine eyes unto the hills
  From whence *cometh my help;*
My help cometh from the Lord,
  Who made heaven and earth.

But the repetition is the exception rather than the rule in these psalms. The common opinion is that they were sung by the pilgrims during the ascent to Jerusalem. Such a custom is, however, nowhere mentioned.

De-ha′ites, in A. V. **De-ha′vites.**

One of the tribes brought over to Samaria from the Assyrian empire to replace the ten tribes carried captive (Ezra iv. 9). Rawlinson believes that they were Dai or Dahi, a nomad tribe of Aryan descent mentioned by Herodotus (i. 125).

De′ker, in A. V. **Dekar** [perforation].

The father of Solomon's purveyor, Ben-deker (1 Kin. iv. 9, R. V.).

De-la′iah, in A. V. once **Dalaiah** (1 Chron. iii. 24) [Jehovah hath drawn out, *i. e.* delivered].

1. A descendant of Aaron. His family, grown to a father's house by the time of David, was made the twenty-third course of the priests (1 Chron. xxiv. 18).

2. A prince, son of Shemaiah, and one of those who urged king Jehoiakim not to burn the roll containing the prophecies of Jeremiah (Jer. xxxvi. 12, 25). Perhaps it is he or his grandson who is incidentally mentioned later (Neh. vi. 10).

3. One of the Nethinim, and founder of a family (Ezra ii. 60; Neh. vii. 62).

4. A son of Elioenai (1 Chron. iii. 24).

De-li′lah [delicate, wasted with longing or desire].

The Philistine woman from the valley of Sorek who lured Samson to his ruin (Judg. xvi. 4–18).

De′los, in A. V. **Delus.**

A small island in the Ægean, celebrated as the birthplace of Apollo and Diana. The Roman consul Lucius wrote to Delos concerning a pact of friendship established between the Romans and the Jews (1 Mac. xv. 23). It was at that time the center of an extensive commerce.

Del′uge. See FLOOD.

De′mas.

A fellow laborer of Paul, who sent salutations from Rome to the Colossians and to Philemon (Col. iv. 14; Philemon 24). Afterwards he deserted the apostle from unwillingness to suffer, and went to Thessalonica (2 Tim. iv. 10).

De-me′tri-us [belonging to Demeter, or Ceres, the goddess of agriculture and rural life].

1. Demetrius I., surnamed Soter, king of Syria 162–150 B. C., nephew of Antiochus Epiphanes. He had been kept as a hostage at Rome; but on hearing of his uncle's death he made his escape, and arriving safely in

Antioch made himself master of the kingdom, and put to death Lysias and the young Eupator (1 Mac. vii. 1-4). In war with him Judas Maccabæus lost his life (ix. 1-19). In 152 B. C. Alexander Balas, with the consent of the Roman senate, claimed the throne. The rivals met in a decisive battle in 150 B. C., and Demetrius was defeated and slain (x. 48-50; Antiq. xiii. 2, 4).

2. Demetrius II., surnamed Nicator, son of Demetrius I. In 148-7 B. C. he raised the standard of revolt against Alexander Balas, and with the aid of Ptolemy VI. defeated him. Alexander fled into Arabia, where he was murdered, and Demetrius became king of Syria (1 Mac. xi. 15-19). But Alexander's general Tryphon almost immediately proclaimed Alexander's young son Antiochus king (39, 40). The struggle lasted until 138 B. C., when Demetrius, during a plundering expedition in Persia, was taken prisoner by king Arsaces and kept in bonds for ten years. Before his departure on this expedition he gave the Jews their independence. Although they fell under the power of the Syrians again, this event was of national importance, and they dated their independence from it (1 Mac. xiii. 36-42; Antiq. xiii. 4, 9). Demetrius regained liberty and the throne in 128 B. C. An Egyptian pretender, supported by Ptolemy VII., took the field against him. Demetrius was defeated near Damascus, fled to Ptolemais, and took ship to Tyre, where he was murdered when about to land (Antiq. xiii. 9, 3).

3. A silversmith at Ephesus, who made for sale silver models of the celebrated temple of Diana. Believing his craft to be in danger from Christianity, he excited his fellow workmen against Paul, and stirred up the riot in which the mob cried for two hours, "Great is Diana of the Ephesians" (Acts xix. 24-41).

4. An approved Christian, commended by John also (3 John 12).

De′mon [among the Greeks, (1) a god or deity in general; (2) one's genius; (3) one's fortune; (4) the soul of some man belonging to the golden age, now acting as a tutelary divinity; a god of inferior rank].

An evil spirit (Luke viii. 29; x. 17-20). The designation is applied especially to the gods of the heathen (Deut. xxxii. 17; Ps. cvi. 37; and margin of 1 Cor. x. 20, and cp. Rev. ix. 20; all R. V.), and to inferior evil spirits, subject to the devil (Mat. xii. 24-27; Luke iv. 33; Jas. ii. 19; Rev. xvi. 14; all margin of R. V.); see DEMONIAC.

The Jews held various notions on the subject; such as, the demons were the spirits of the wicked dead (War vii. 6, 3), and could be exorcised by means of roots and the name of Solomon (Antiq. viii. 2, 5), or driven away by fumes from the roasting heart and liver of a fish (Tob. vi. 7, 16, 17).

De-mo′ni-ac [possessed by a demon].

A person possessed and ruled by a demon

(Mat. iv. 24, R. V. margin). The inhabitation of such a being in some cases affected the person physically, and produced certain ordinary diseases. Thus one possessed boy is described as having a deaf and dumb spirit and as being affected at intervals with morbid symptoms resembling those of epilepsy (Mark ix. 14-29; cp. Mat. xvii. 15, 18; Luke ix. 37-42). Hence the opinion of many is that possession was simply a Jewish hypothesis to account for bodily and mental diseases and for the visible effects on body and will of enslavement to sin. But this view takes no note of the fact that the demons speak (Mark i. 23, 24; iii. 11, 12; v. 7); that they possessed at times knowledge beyond that of men; as, for example, of the divinity of Christ (Mark i. 24); that they recognized their own distinct individuality independent of Jesus and independent of the person possessed (Mat. viii. 31); that the distant herd of swine became frenzied when the demons were cast out of the demoniac of Gadara and allowed to enter into them (Mat. viii. 30); that Jesus apparently recognized them as actually existing beings, and instructed his disciples, saying: "This kind can come out by nothing, save by prayer" (Mark ix. 29, R. V.); and that later, when the disciples reported that even the demons were subject unto them in his name, Jesus replied: "I beheld Satan as lightning fall from heaven. . . . Notwithstanding in this rejoice not, that the spirits are subject unto you; but rather rejoice, that your names are written in heaven" (Luke x. 17-20). Man was himself responsible for his hideous visitor. Probably not until a person was degraded and weakened by sin, personal or inherited, might he be taken captive by a demon (1 Sam. xvi. 14; with xiii. 8-14; xv. 10-31).

Dep′u-ty.

One empowered to act for another, generally of higher rank than himself; as a regent ruling in place of a king (1 Kin. xxii. 47); an official invested with the powers and rank of a Roman consul (Acts xiii. 7; xviii. 12; xix. 38, A. V.); see PROCONSUL.

Der′be.

A city in the southeastern part of Lycaonia, in Asia Minor. Paul was stoned and left for dead at Lystra, on his first missionary journey. On reviving, he went to Derbe (Acts xiv. 6, 20). On his second journey he again passed through it, and either there or at Lystra made the acquaintance of Timothy (xvi. 1). Gaius was a native of Derbe (xx. 4). The ruins of a town on lake Ak Gûl near Divle have been supposed to mark the site of Derbe; but Prof. Ramsey believes with Prof. Sterrett that the site is Zosta, 47 miles southsoutheast of Iconium, on the road which ran from Cilicia Tracheia through Laranda to Iconium.

Des′ert.

1. A rendering of the Hebrew *Midbar* and

the Greek *Eremos,* an unenclosed, uncultivated plain, where wild beasts roam at will
(Job xxiv. 5); often terrible in its solitude
and desolateness (Deut. xxxii. 10; and A. V.
of Is. xxi. 1), yet also capable of affording
pasturage (Ex. iii. 1, A. V.). The words are
usually rendered wilderness (Gen. xvi. 7;
xxi. 20; 1 Sam. xvii. 28; xxv. 21; Mat. iii.
1; Mark i. 13; Luke xv. 4).

2. A rendering of the Hebrew *ʿarabah,* arid
region (Is. xxxv. 1, 6; li. 3). With the definite article the word specially denotes the
plain of the Jordan and Dead Sea (Ezek.
xlvii. 8; 2 Sam. ii. 29), and is rendered in
the R. V. as a proper name, Arabah.

3. A rendering of the Hebrew *Yeshimon,* a
waste, a desolation (Ps. lxxviii. 40; cvi. 14;
Is. xliii. 19, 20). When the definite article
is prefixed as a proper name, Jeshimon
Jeshimon (Num. xxi. 20, A. V. and margin
of R. V.).

4. A rendering of the Hebrew *Haraboth,*
waste, desolate places (Is. xlviii. 21). In Ps.
cii. 6; Ezek. xiii. 4 the R. V. translates
it waste places.

De-u′el [invocation of God].

A Gadite, the father of Eliasaph (Num. i.
14; vii. 42; x. 20). Called in ii. 14 Reuel,
which means "friend of God." It is uncertain which of these two forms is correct.
The Samaritan text has Deuel everywhere,
whereas the Septuagint and the Syriac translators read Reuel; see DALETH.

Deu-ter-on′o-my [repetition of the law].

The name, derived from the Septuagint, of
the fifth book of the Pentateuch. The Greek
word, of which Deuteronomy is the English
form, is used in the Septuagint to translate
the expression "copy of this law" in chapter
xvii. 18. But this book is not merely the
repetition or copy of laws already given. It
is a rehearsal under peculiar circumstances
and for a special purpose. In Exodus, Leviticus, and Numbers, the legislation is represented as in process of enactment, the occasion
or the time when the successive installments
were received is commonly stated, and each
body of statutes is severally declared to proceed from God. In Deuteronomy, on the
other hand, the law is represented, not as
being enacted, but as being rehearsed and
expounded. Thirty and eight years have
elapsed since the greater part of the old legislation was given. The new generation, on
the eve of taking possession of Canaan, is
summoned to hear the law of the nation, to
be instructed in the application of its principles to the new circumstances which
await them, to have their apprehension of
its spirituality quickened, and then to renew
intelligently the covenant made with their
fathers. Instead of the Lord speaking unto
Moses, it is now Moses at the command of
God speaking to the people (i. 1-4; v. 1;
xxix. 1). The book consists first and mainly
of an address delivered in three installments,

committed to writing, and solemnly ratified
as a covenant (i.-xxx.). *First Address,* i. 6-
iv. 40; with supplementary statement, 41-49:
Rehearsal of the history of the people since
the covenant was made with the preceding
generation at Sinai as a motive for obedience
to Jehovah's laws. The speaker is declared
to be Moses (i. 1, 3, 5, 9, 15, 16, 19, etc.): the
date is the 40th year, 11th month, 1st day;
after the smiting of Sihon and Og, and after
the sin in the matter of Peor (i. 3, 4; iv. 3):
the place is beyond Jordan in the land of
Moab (i. 5. cp. Num. xxxiii. 48; xxxv. 1), in
the wilderness, in the Arabah (i. 1, cp. Num.
xxiii. 28; xxiv. 1). The phrase "beyond
Jordan" or "other side of Jordan" was
ambiguous and required precise definition.
To Abraham and the Canaanites it meant the
country east of the river; and as an established geographical term it meant the same
to Abraham's descendants. They had arrived
there; but they still called the place where
they were by the old inherited designation
"the other side of Jordan," just as they
called the neighboring bluffs Abarim or
"mountains of the other side." And the
people felt, too, that they were on the other
side of Jordan, outside of the promised land.
But with the river in front of them the
phrase was ambiguous, hence its repeated
elucidation by some expression like "in the
land of Moab." *Second Address,* v.-xxvi.:
Rehearsal of statutes which concerned the
people, with emphasis on the spirituality of
the laws and urgent insistence upon their
observance. These statutes are generally
either substantive laws, that is, rights and
duties (the procedure not being rehearsed),
or else laws which natural depravity might
lead men to ignore and where the appeal
must be to religious motives: such as, asylum
for the unintentional murderer, banishment
of idolatry, and consideration for the weaker
members and dependent classes of the community. The speaker is Moses (v. 1, 5, 22);
the date is at the end of the forty years, on
the eve of crossing the Jordan, after Balaam's
prophecy (viii. 2; ix. 1; xi. 31; xxiii. 4).
Third Address, xxvii., xxviii.: Conclusion of
the preceding, (1) Provision for writing the
law on plastered stones on mount Ebal, (2)
Blessings and curses annexed to obedience
and disobedience respectively. This great
address is closely followed by a brief address
(xxix., xxx.) at the ratification of the covenant as thus proclaimed (xxix. 1; xxx. 1).
This covenant, like the words of the former
one made at Horeb, was recorded in a book
(xxix. 20, 21, 27; xxx. 10; cp. Ex. xxiv. 4-8).
The place and date are alluded to in Deut.
xxix. 1, 5, 7, 8.

After delivering the address which forms
the body of the book of Deuteronomy, Moses
publicly appointed Joshua to be his successor
and gave a formal charge to him (xxxi. 1-8).
Moses delivered the written law to the priests
with a charge regarding its public reading

(9-13). He repaired with Joshua to the tabernacle that Joshua might be charged by Jehovah, and was there instructed to prepare a song for the people (14-23). He prepared and wrote the song (22), charged the Levites who bore the ark to put the completed book, which contained law and song, beside the ark for a witness (24-29), ordered an assembly called to hear and learn the song (28), and repeated it publicly (30-xxxii. 47). Moses' farewell (48-xxxiii. 29) and death (xxxiv.).

The distinctive feature of Deuteronomy is the evident preparation for the settlement in Canaan. 1. It affects the language. For example, the people are about to live a settled life; hence the camp which figures so largely, though of course not exclusively, in the former legislation disappears from Deuteronomy, except where reference is made to future war or to the encampment at Shittim where they then are. The speaker mentions houses, towns, city gates. 2. It leads to minor modifications of existing laws to adapt them to the new mode of life. For example, the law which required animals that were slain for food to be brought to the door of the tabernacle is changed to permit the people to slay for food in the town where they reside xii. 15, 21; Lev. xvii. 3, 4); and for the same reason the firstling of animals need no longer be offered to God on the eighth day, but the sacrifice may be postponed until the owner comes up from his distant home to the sanctuary at the annual feasts (Deut. xv. 20 with Ex. xxii. 30); and in the case of the Hebrew bondman who wishes to remain attached to the household of his master, rather than claim his legal freedom, the ceremony at the door-post suffices, and there is no longer insistence upon appearance before God (Deut. xv. 17 with Ex. xxi. 6). 3. It leads to the attempt to safeguard the interests of the dependent classes, the Levites, widows, orphans, strangers, and to protect them from the evils which evidently threatened to befall them in the future, in view of the spirit of self-seeking and indifference to others that had been manifested by the people time and again during the sojourn in the wilderness. 4. It leads to insistence upon one altar for the nation in the place where Jehovah shall record his name. The unity of the altar was intended to counteract the tendency to lapse into idolatry, by preventing the people from worshiping at the numerous local sanctuaries of the Canaanites; to render the worship of Jehovah a grander spectacle and of greater pomp than the rites of the idols of the Canaanites by uniting the numbers and the wealth of the Hebrews; and to give strength to the communal feeling and aid in binding the nation together. The spirit of jealousy between individuals and between tribes, the popular proneness to idolatry, and the willingness of large sections of the people to separate from their brethren and settle in attractive pastoral regions had already become manifest. The old law of the one altar is emphatically insisted upon at this crisis. It was essential to the unity of the nation and continuance of the theocracy. See ALTAR.

It has been urged that no distinction is made in Deuteronomy between priests and Levites such as appears in the legislation of Leviticus and Numbers. The priests are frequently called "the priests the Levites," and the passage xviii. 1-8, if it be isolated, may be interpreted to mean that any Levite might become a priest. But—1. The tribe of Levi is indeed assigned priestly functions (x. 6; xviii. 1-8; xxxiii. 8, 9). But that is correct, for the tribe as a whole was called to holy service, especially to priestly service. Even when the distinction between the priests and the lower order of the Levites was firmly established, the tribe as a whole is spoken of as priestly (1 Kin. xii. 31; Mal. ii. 1-4; iii. 3; cp. Heb. vii. 13). 2. The title "the priests the Levites" occurs in writings which were composed after the legislation of Leviticus was, as everybody admits, in full force. It is used by Ezekiel (xliii. 19; xliv. 15) and by the Chronicler (2 Chron. xxiii. 18; xxx. 27). It should also be remembered that Jeremiah uses the expression (xxxiii. 18, 21). 3. Deuteronomy is based on previous priestly legislation, for it presupposes the technical laws of the ritual. The speaker explicitly refers to former laws on the subject of which he is speaking, and these laws are known only from the books of Leviticus and Numbers (Deut. xviii. 1, 2 with Num. xviii. 20; Deut. xxiv. 8, 9 with Lev. xiii., xiv.; Num. xii.), or he makes allusions which imply these laws (Deut. xii. 15 with Lev. xvii. 3 seq.). 4. The passage Deut. xviii. 1-8 may be readily interpreted on the assumption that the laws of Leviticus were in force. Levi was to have no inheritance with Israel, but was to enjoy certain perquisites (Lev. vi. 17, 18; Num. xviii. 20, 21, 24, 26). The speaker presses this law with earnestness. The priests the Levites, the whole tribe of Levi have no inheritance; they shall eat the offerings (ver. 1). The dues of the priests, without the epithet "the Levites," are next spoken of. It is an urgent matter. The people must not defraud the priests of their income (3, 4 with Ex. xxix. 27, 28; Lev. vii. 34; Num. xviii. 11, 12, where slight changes are introduced). Finally, the rights of the Levites at the sanctuary are dwelt upon. If a Levite—not necessarily a Levite of lower rank—come from any part of the country to the sanctuary, he shall minister in the name of the Lord as all his brethren the Levites do, which stand before the Lord, and he shall fare as they do (6-8). The kind of service which he shall perform is not the matter at issue. The language covers both priestly service and the labors rendered by the lower order of the Levites (5, xvii. 12; and 1 Sam. ii. 11, 18; iii. 1; 2 Chron. xxiii. 6; xxix. 4, 5, 11).

The point insisted upon is that all Levites shall receive full recognition at the sanctuary and be accorded their prerogatives. It goes without saying that if the Levite be a priest, he shall serve and fare like his brethren the priests; if he be not a priest, he shall enjoy the privileges that belong to his brethren who are Levites but not priests. Those in power shall not deprive him of his prerogatives because he is obscure and from a distant part of the country. See PRIEST.

Dev'il [Greek *diabolos*, a slanderer].

1. An evil spirit (Mark i. 34; Luke iv. 33; viii. 29). A. V. and, in its text, R. V. do not observe the distinction made in the Greek original between a demon and the devil. Demons take possession of wicked men and are subject to the devil (Mat. iv. 24; xii. 24); see DEMONIAC.

2. The evil one, Satan, the greatest of all the fallen spirits (Rev. xii. 9; Mat. iv. 8–11; xiii. 38, 39; xxv. 41; cp. Jude 6). The general opinion is that the sin into which he fell was pride (1 Tim. iii. 6). He is the great enemy of God and man (1 Pet. v. 8; 1 John iii. 8), who tempted Christ and incites men to sin (Mat. iv. 1; John xiii. 2; Eph. iv. 27). He is "that old serpent" who tempted Eve (Wisdom ii. 23, 24; 2 Cor. xi. 3; Rev. xii. 9; xx. 2). Perhaps with reference to this transaction he is called a murderer from the beginning, and a liar, and the father of lies (John viii. 44; cp. 1 John iii. 8). When the good seed of truth is sown the devil either steals it away (Luke viii. 12) or sows tares (Mat. xiii. 38). He is continually going about like a roaring lion seeking whom he may devour (1 Pet. v. 8). He lays snares or practices wiles to injure the children of God (Eph. vi. 11; 2 Tim. ii. 26), and seduces them by his subtilty (2 Cor. xi. 3); but the tempted one is not to yield to him, but to resist him, and he will flee (Eph. iv. 27; James iv. 7). He had power to produce demoniacal possession (Acts x. 38), and he instigated the imprisonment of martyrs (Rev. ii. 10). He is finally to be cast into a lake of everlasting fire prepared for the devil and his angels (Mat. xxv. 41; cp. Jude 6). Preëminently sinful, unrighteous men, also those imbued with the spirit of lying and murder, are figuratively called children of the devil (John viii. 44; 1 John iii. 8, 10). Judas was even called by Jesus a devil (John vi. 70). His works Christ came to destroy (1 John iii. 8). Jude alludes to a dispute of the devil with Michael for the body of Moses (9; cp. Rev. xii. 7). Whence the apostle drew this illustration is unknown. He has been thought to quote an authoritative teaching of the Jewish church, or a familiar interpretation of Zech. iii., according to which the high priest represents Mosaism, or else to cite a moral tale current among the Jews.

Dew.

Moisture condensed from the atmosphere upon cold bodies. Used in Scripture figuratively for whatever comes noiselessly and even invisibly, but proves a refreshment and a blessing, as dew does to vegetation (Deut. xxxii. 2; Ps. cx. 3; Prov. xix. 12; Mic. v. 7).

Di'a-dem [a band or fillet, as being bound round].

1. The rendering of the Hebrew words *Ṣaniph, Ṣanoph,* and *Ṣanuph,* something bound round. It was a head dress for man and woman (Job xxix. 14, margin of R. V. turban; Is. iii. 23, in A. V. hoods, R. V. turbans). A royal diadem of this type was worn by kings (Is. lxii. 3), and is once mentioned as worn by the high priest (Zech. iii. 5), where it is translated miter, but on the margin of R. V. turban or diadem.

2. A rendering of the Hebrew word *Misnepheth,* a name applied specially to the miter of the Jewish high priest (Ezek. xxi. 26 in A. V.), and regularly translated so.

3. The rendering of the Hebrew word *Ṣᵉphirah,* circlet, crown (Is. xxviii. 5).

Di'al.

An instrument consisting of a surface which is graduated into hour lines, and furnished with a projecting gnomon to cast a shadow as the sun advances in his daily course, and thus point out the hours. The dial of Ahaz (2 Kin. xx. 11; Is. xxxviii. 8) may have been such an instrument, with either flat or concave dial and with graduated lines called steps or degrees, which Ahaz had introduced from Babylonia, where the sun dial was in use before the time of Herodotus (Herod. ii. 109), and at least as early as the eighth century B. C. Less likely it was a flight of steps at the palace of Ahaz, so designed and arranged that the shadow of an obelisk near by passed over the steps and thus indicated the time of day. The recession of the shadow on the dial of Ahaz has been variously explained as caused by a miraculous reversion of the earth's motion, or by a backward movement of the sun, or by refraction of the sun's rays, or by a solar eclipse. Unquestionably the recorded effect could have been produced by either of the two latter as well as by the former causes.

Di'a-mond.

A mineral of unequaled hardness and luster, transparent or translucent, and capable of taking a splendid polish. It is simply carbon, crystallized by the chemistry of nature, which that of art has not yet been able to imitate. Diamonds have long been known to exist in India and the island of Borneo.

Diamond is the rendering of—

1. The Hebrew *Yahᵃlom,* a precious stone (Ezek. xxviii. 13), one of those in the breastplate of the high priest (Ex. xxviii. 18, in R. V. margin sardonyx; xxxix. 11).

2. The Hebrew *Shamir,* a hard stone used to point graving instruments (Jer. xvii. 1); elsewhere rendered adamant (Ezek. iii. 9; Zech. vii. 12).

Diana of Ephesus.

Di-a′na.

The Roman goddess of the moon, and of field and woods, and of all forms of life and activity which were supposed to be influenced by the moon. She corresponded to the Greek Artemis, who was twin sister of Apollo, favorite child of Zeus, and huntress of the sky. She was the ideal of chastity and virginity, and is generally represented as a tall and beautiful maiden, with a quiver on her shoulder and a bow or a javelin in her right hand, and as engaged in hunting deer. The Asiatic Artemis, Diana of Ephesus, was a union of the Greek Artemis with the lusty Semitic moon-goddess, Ashtoreth. Her image was supposed to have fallen from heaven (Acts xix. 35), and it may have been originally a meteoric stone. Ancient authorities, however, state that it was of wood, though they differ as to the kind. Its form is known from ancient coins as the rude figure of a woman with crowned head, many breasts, and extended arms supported by props. Her primitive shrine near the sea, at the mouth of the Cayster, became eventually an imposing temple (see EPHESUS). Demetrius the silversmith and his fellow-craftsmen made silver models of it (Acts xix. 24).

Dib′lah, in A. V. **Diblath** [a rounded mass, cake].

A place in Palestine in the vicinity of a wilderness (Ezek. vi. 14 ; cp. Num. xxxiii. 46 ; Jer. xlviii. 22). Grave objections lie against the proposed emendation of the text to Riblah.

Dib′la-im [twin balls or cakes].

A parent in law to Hosea, if the transaction was real and not typical (Hos. i. 3).

Dib′lath. See DIBLAH.

Di′bon [a wasting away, a consumption].

1. A town north of the Arnon, wrested from Moab by the Amorites, taken by the Israelites (Num. xxi. 30 ; xxxii. 3), rebuilt by the Gadites (xxxii. 34), and hence called Dibon-gad (xxxiii. 45, 46), afterwards given over to the tribe of Reuben (Josh. xiii. 9, 17). It reverted to the Moabites (Moabite Stone 21, 28 ; Is. xv. 2 ; Jer. xlviii. 18, 22). It still exists, as a heap of ruins, retaining its old name Dhîbân, 3 miles north of the Arnon, slightly eastward from the Roman road. Tristram describes it as a twin city covering the tops and slopes of two adjacent knolls, and surrounded by a wall. There are caverns, cisterns, vaulted underground storehouses, rude semi-circular arches, and cyclopean buildings of basalt like those of Bashan. It was among the ruins of Dibon that Mr. Klein, in 1868, found the Moabite Stone (q. v.).

2. A village in the territory of Judah (Neh. xi. 25). Probably the same as Dimonah (q. v.).

Di′bon-gad. See DIBON.

Dib′ri.

A Danite, ancestor of him who was stoned to death in the days of Moses for blaspheming the Name (Lev. xxiv. 11–14).

Did′y-mus [a twin] : see THOMAS.

Dik′lah [a palm tree].

A people descended from Joktan (Gen. x. 27 : 1 Chron. i. 21), and who doubtless dwelt in Arabia and, as the name suggests, in a region abounding in palm trees.

Dil′e-an, in E. R. V. **Dilan** [cucumber field].

A town in the lowland of Judah (Josh. xv. 38). Exact site unknown.

Dill. See ANISE.

Dim′nah. See RIMMON.

Di′mon [probably a variant of Dibon].

A place in Moab (Is. xv. 9) ; apparently Dibon, by a common permutation of the labials. Jerome states that in his day both names were common for the town. The form with m is chosen by the prophet for its assonance with *dam*, blood, used in the same verse. The waters of Dibon are best regarded as the Arnon, as the waters of Megiddo are the Kishon (Judg. v. 19).

Di-mo′nah.

A town in the southern part of Judah, near Edom (Josh. xv. 22), probably the same as Dibon (Neh. xi. 25).

Di′nah [judgment or, perhaps, judged].

A daughter of Jacob by his wife Leah (Gen. xxx. 21). Going out apparently unprotected to see the Canaanite daughters of the land, she was either led astray or outraged by Shechem, the son of Hamor the Hivite. The young prince afterwards wished to take her in honorable marriage, and her brothers apparently consented, on condition that the Hivites should be circumcised. These acquiesced in the stipulation, and carried it out; but an attack on their town was suddenly made by Simeon and Levi, two of Dinah's full brothers, who slew all the males in the place, Hamor and Shechem among the rest (xxxiv. 1-29). Jacob took no part in the treacherous and cruel deed, regarded it as inexpedient (30), and denounced it with horror on his deathbed (xlix. 5-7). By this act of his sons, however, the conquered district fell to him as head of the tribe, and he bequeathed it, not to those who were answerable for the abhorred deed, but to Joseph (xlviii. 22).

Di′na-ites.

One of the foreign tribes brought over to Samaria to replace the ten tribes carried into captivity (Ezra iv. 9). Probably the Armenian people who were known to the Assyrians as Dayani.

Din′ha-bah.

The city of Bela, king of Edom (Gen. xxxvi. 32; 1 Chron. i. 43). Several towns of this name are known, but none in Edom. Jerome identified it with Dannaia, a town existing in his day in Moab, a little south of the Arnon.

Dinner. See MEALS.

Di-o-ny′si-us [belonging to Dionusos or Bacchus, the god of wine].

A member of the Athenian supreme court of Areopagus, who was converted through the preaching of Paul on Mars Hill, where the court held its sittings (Acts xvii. 34).

Di-ot′re-phes [nurtured by Zeus].

A member of the church of which Gaius, to whom John sent his third epistle, was a member. He loved to have the preeminence in the church to which he belonged, refused to receive the apostle John or the brethren who went forth for the sake of the Name, and excommunicated those who entertained them (3 John 9, 10).

Di′phath. See RIPHATH.

Dis-ci′ple.

A pupil or scholar (Mat. x. 24); especially the follower of a public teacher, like John the Baptist (ix. 14). A person taught of God (Is. viii. 16). It is used of all of whatever age who in faith received the divine Master's instructions (Mat. x. 42; Luke xiv. 26, 27, 33; John iv. 1; vi. 66), and especially of the twelve apostles (Mat. v. 1; viii. 25; x. 1; xii. 1, etc.).

Dis-eas′es.

Disease arises from the violation of physical or mental laws. The observance of these laws is often a moral act, and their transgression is sin (Prov. ii. 17-22; xxiii. 29-32); so that disease is in certain cases the punishment imposed by the Creator for sin. God, moreover, sometimes smites a sinner with disease where no natural cause can be traced (Ex. ix. 8 seq.; Num. xi. 33; xii. 9-11;

Deut. xxviii. 21, 22, 35, 60; 2 Sam. xxi. 1; xxiv. 15; 2 Kin. v. 27). From the connection between sin and various diseases, the latter are sometimes attributed to Satan, who seduced the race to its fall into sin and who is still the great tempter to sin (Luke xiii. 16); but the inference is not legitimate that every sick person is a sinner or that Satan is the immediate cause of our maladies (Job iii.-xlii.; John ix. 1-3). The chief forms of human disease are mentioned, such as fever (Deut. xxviii. 22; Mat. viii. 14; John iv. 52; Antiq. xiii. 15, 5), cutaneous disease (Lev. xiii. 6-8, 30, 39), dysentery (2 Chron. xxi. 15, 18; Acts xxviii. 8, R. V.), ophthalmia (Rev. iii. 18; Tobit ii. 10; vi. 8; xi. 13), boils (Ex. ix. 9; 1 Sam. v. 6), paralysis (1 Mac. ix. 55; Mat. viii. 6; ix. 2; Acts ix. 33).

Di′shan [probably pygarg].

A Horite tribe (Gen. xxxvi. 21, 28) under a chief (30).

Di′shon [pygarg, antelope].

A Horite tribe (Gen. xxxvi. 21, 26; 1 Chron. i. 38), organized under a chief (Gen. xxxvi. 30), and descended through Anah from Zibeon (24, 25). Many interpreters, however, discover two persons of this name: one in vs. 20, 26 30, the other in 25.

Dis-per′sion.

The body of Israelites scattered abroad in other lands than their own, the diaspora (Jer. xxv. 34, A. V. and margin of R. V.; John vii. 35; Jas. i. 1). Dispersion was threatened as a penalty if the people departed from the Mosaic law (Lev. xxvi. 33-37; Deut. iv. 27, 28; xxviii. 64-68). The captivity of the ten tribes and that of the two largely helped to fulfill these prophecies; for the mass of the ten tribes were never restored to their own land, and of the two a very large number chose to remain in the region to which they had been taken rather than return to their own country. A very considerable immigration of Jews took place into the cities and towns of Alexander the Great's empire, and into the kingdoms of Egypt, Syria, etc., into which it was afterwards divided; and later when the Roman empire established its sway over these and other regions, colonies of Jews sought a settlement in all the important places. Agrippa, in a letter to Caligula preserved by Philo, says: "Jerusalem is the capital not alone of Judæa but, by means of colonies, of most other lands also. These colonies have been sent out at fitting opportunities into the neighboring countries of Egypt, Phœnicia, Syria, Cœle-syria, and the farther removed Pamphylia, Cilicia, the greater part of Asia as far as Bithynia and the most remote corners of Pontus. In the same manner also into Europe: Thessaly, Bœotia, Macedon, Ætolia, Attica, Argos, Corinth, and the most and finest parts of the Peloponnesus. And not only is the mainland full of Israelitish communities, but also the most important islands: Eubœa, Cyprus, Crete. And I say nothing of the countries beyond the Euphrates, for all of them, with unimportant exceptions ,Babylon and the satraples that include the fertile districts lying around it, have Jewish inhabitants.'' Thus the Dispersion, with synagogue and doctrine, was found in all parts of the known world (Acts ii. 5–11; 1 Pet. i. 1; War ii. 16, 4; vii. 3, 3).

Div-i-na'tion.

The attempt to read the future and utter soothsaying either by a kind of inspiration or divine afflatus (Acts xvi. 16), or else by means of signs. In the latter sense, it includes augury or foretelling the future by means of natural signs, such as the flight of birds, the disposition of the entrails (Ezek. xxi. 21); hydromancy or foretelling from the

Because the liver is a bloody organ, ancient peoples believed it was probably the source of life itself. Therefore it was thought to be a reliable instrument to determine the will of the gods. This clay model, inscribed with cuneiform writing, was used by Babylonian diviners about 1600 B.C.

appearance of water poured into a vessel or of objects dropped into the water (Gen. xliv. 5); sorcery, in its original sense of foretelling by casting lots (Ezek. xxi. 21); and also astrology or the determination of the supposed influence of the stars on the destiny of a person (cp. Is. xlvii. 13). The Hebrews also included in divination necromancy or foretelling the future by calling up the spirits of the dead and conversing with them (1 Sam. xxviii. 8). The diviner sometimes pronounced blessing or cursing (Num. xxii. 6): not, however, as the magical spells of a sorcerer, but as prophecy revealed by the divine afflatus or familiar spirit or the sign (12, 13).

Di-vin'er.

A soothsayer; a practicer of divination. They were numerous among heathen nations (Deut. xviii. 9–12; 1 Sam. vi. 2; Is. xix. 3; Ezek. xxi. 21; Dan. ii. 2; Acts xvi. 16), and also at various times among the Israelites, who were informed of the diviner's imposture, warned against placing reliance in him, and threatened with punishment for the sin of consulting him (Lev. xix. 31; xx. 6, 27; Deut. xviii. 10; 1 Sam. xxviii. 8; Is. ii. 6; iii. 2, R. V.; Jer. xxvii. 9; xxix. 8; Ezek. xiii. 23; xxii. 28; Mic. iii. 6, 7, 11; Zech. x. 2).

He practiced his art for hire (Num. xxii. 7, 17, 18; Acts xvi. 16).

Di-vorce', Di-vorce'ment.

Annulment of the bonds of matrimony. Under the law of Moses a man could divorce his wife if he found some unseemly thing in her. She might then be married to another man. If her second husband also divorced her, the first one was not allowed to take her again. The process of divorce, when once resolved upon, was easy. All the husband had to do was to give his partner a bill of divorcement, and send her away (Deut. xxiv. 1–4; cp. Is. l. 1; Jer. iii. 8). Our Lord explained that this enactment was framed only on account of the Israelites' hardness of heart. He added that the original and just law, that of nature, is that a man cleave to his wife and they twain become one flesh, marriage being a permanent compact; and that a wife should not be divorced except for fornication, including what is now technically called adultery. If a man puts away his wife on other grounds and marries another, he commits adultery. If anyone marries a divorced woman, he also has committed the same sin (Mat. v. 31, 32; xix. 3–9; Mark x. 2–12; Luke xvi. 18; cp. 1 Cor. vii. 10–17). Protestants almost universally teach that willful, final desertion annuls the marriage bond (cp. 1 Cor. vii. 15) and a second marriage may be contracted by the deserted one.

Di'-za-hab, in A. V. Diz'a-hab [abounding in gold].

A place cited to indicate the locality and circumstances connected with the delivery of the farewell addresses of Moses (Deut. i. 1). Dhahab on the western shore of the gulf of Akaba, 75 miles south of Ezion-geber, has similarity of name in its favor, but that is all. It lies remote from the route of the Israelites. Perhaps Di-zahab was a district in Edom identical with Me-zahab (Gen. xxxvi. 39; cp. Septuagint of Num. xxi. 14, which has Zahab instead of Vaheb of R. V.).

Do'dai. See Dodo 2.

Dod'a-nim [a plural word, Dodanites].

A tribe related to Javan (Gen. x. 4). Against identifying them with the Dardanians or Trojans is the difference in the name; while the situation of Dodona, a place in Epirus, in Greece, the seat of a celebrated oracle, is against locating them there. The Septuagint and the Samaritan version in Gen. x. 4, and the common Hebrew text itself in 1 Chron. i. 7, have Rodanim (q. v.).

Dod-a-va'hu, in A. V. Dod'a-vah [perhaps love of Jehovah].

A man from Mareshah, father of that Eliezer who prophesied the destruction of Jehoshaphat's ships (2 Chron. xx. 37).

Do'do [loving].

1. A man of Issachar, ancestor of the judge Tola (Judg. x. 1).

2. An Ahohite, and the father of Eleazar, one of David's three mighty men of the first rank (2 Sam. xxiii. 9, in R. V., following the present Hebrew text, Dodai; 1 Chron. xi. 12). David appointed Dodai [or probably his son] as military commander over the course of the second month (1 Chron. xxvii. 4).

3. A man of Bethlehem, father of Elhanan, one of David's mighty men (2 Sam. xxiii. 24; 1 Chron. xi. 26).

Doe.

A female deer or antelope. In Prov. v. 19, R. V., it is the female ibex or wild goat of Sinai (*Capra beden*), in Hebrew *Ya'ᵃlah;* see WILD GOAT.

Do'eg [timid].

An Edomite, the chief of Saul's herdmen. He was at Nob at the tabernacle, detained before the Lord on account of a vow or uncleanness or signs of leprosy (Lev. xiv. 4, 11, 21), or was perhaps in sanctuary for some crime (cp. 1 Kin. i. 50), when David, a fugitive from Saul's court, arrived at Nob and obtained food and a sword from Ahimelech, who did not know that he was fleeing from the king (1 Sam. xxi. 7; Ps. lii. title). Doeg subsequently told Saul what had occurred, which so excited the king that he summoned Ahimelech and fellow priests and demanded an explanation. Not considering it satisfactory, he ordered the guard to kill the priests. They would not. The king then bade Doeg do the deed. He did so, slaying eighty-five men. He subsequently fell upon the village, massacred the women and children, and destroyed even the cattle (1 Sam. xxii. 7–23).

Dog.

The dog of Palestine is the same variety as the pariah or ownerless dog of India. During the earlier period of Bible history it is described as prowling about the streets and suburbs of cities (Ps. lix. 6, 14), feeding on what was thrown out to it (Ex. xxii. 31), licking up blood when it was shed (1 Kin. xxii. 38; Ps. lxviii. 23), or devouring dead bodies (1 Kin. xiv. 11; xvi. 4; 2 Kin. ix. 35, 36); nay, even sometimes congregating in packs, to surround and attack human beings (Ps. xxii. 16, 20). It was early trained sufficiently to aid the shepherd in protecting the flock against beasts of prey and thieves (Job xxx. 1). It was at length sometimes domesticated, accompanied its master from place to place (Tobit v. 16; xi. 4), and was in the house with him and picked up the crumbs from under his table (Mark vii. 28). Moreover, they licked the sores of beggars at the rich man's gate (Luke xvi. 21). The dog was also widely used by the ancients for hunting. But the great mass of dogs ran wild. On account of their food and habits, they were deemed unclean; and to call one a dog was a gross insult (1 Sam. xvii. 43; 2 Kin. viii. 13). The term dog is applied in a figurative sense to those who are incapable of appreciating what is high or holy (Mat.

vii. 6), who introduce false doctrines with cynical effrontery (Phil. iii. 2), who, like a dog returning to its vomit, go back to sins which nominally they had renounced forever (2 Pet. ii. 22; cp. Prov. xxvi. 11), or who are so vile as to submit to lust like dogs (Deut. xxiii. 18). The later Jews were accustomed to call the heathen dogs because ceremonially unclean; and even Jesus once employed the term in order vividly to express his doctrine of grace (Mat. xv. 26; Mark vii. 27).

Dok, in A. V. **Do'cus** [watchtower].

A little stronghold near Jericho, built by Ptolemy (1 Mac. xvi. 15), son-in-law of Simon Maccabæus (11, 12). Into this castle he received Simon and two of his sons, and then treacherously slew them (16). The murder was avenged by John Hyrcanus, a third son of Simon. He besieged Dok, and after a time Ptolemy fled beyond Jordan (Antiq. xiii. 7, 4; 8, 1). The name seems to remain in 'Ain Duk, a copious spring about four miles northwest of Jericho. A road leads by it from the Jordan valley into the hill country. Above the spring are traces of ancient fortifications.

Doph'kah.

A station of the Israelites on the route to Sinai between the Red Sea and Rephidim (Num. xxxiii. 12, 13). Site uncertain.

Dor [habitation].

A town of the Canaanites on the Mediterranean sea (Josh. xi. 2; 1 Mac. xv. 11), nine Roman miles north of Cæsarea (Onomast). Joshua defeated its king (Josh. xii. 23). It lay in the territory of Asher; but was given to the tribe of Manasseh (xvii. 11, cp. xix. 26), which, however, did not expel the Canaanites (Judg. i. 27). In the reign of Ramses III tribes from the northwest, including Philistines, raided this coast land, and later secured permanent settlement. One of these tribes, known as Zakala, or Thekel, gained possession of Dor, and was inhabiting it in the time of Ramses XII. The region about Dor was one of Solomon's tax districts (1 Kin. iv. 11). In the latter half of the 4th century B. C. Sidon obtained Dor and Joppa (Esmunazar Ins.). In 217 B. C. Antiochus the Great besieged it (Polybius 566); and about 138 B. C. Antiochus VII invested it by land and sea (1 Mac. xv. 11–14; Antiq. xiii. 7, 2). In the days of Alexander Jannæus it was held for a time by the tyrant Zoilus (xiii. 12, 2 and 4). In 64 B. C. Pompey granted it autonomy (xiv. 4, 4). In 56 B. C. it was rebuilt by Gabinius (5, 3). Remains of it exist near Khurbet Tantûra, on a low ridge by the coast, about 7½ miles north of Cæsarea.

Dor'cas [gazelle, the Greek rendering of the Aramaic *ṭᵉbitha*, gazelle].

Tabitha, a Christian woman of Joppa, a friend and helper of the poor. When she died, Peter was sent for, who, after prayer, bade her arise, and her life returned. The

Archaeologists uncovering ruins at Dothan.

fame thereof spread, and many believed on the Lord (Acts ix. 36–43). Dorcas societies are sewing circles for the poor, named from her.

Do'than [possibly wells].

A town not far from Shechem and Samaria, hard by a caravan route (Gen. xxxvii. 14, 17, 25 ; 2 Kin. vi. 13), near the plain of Esdraelon and a pass into the hill country of Judah (Judith iii. 10 ; iv. 6, 7). Joseph was cast into a pit in the vicinity, whence he was taken out and sold to the Midianites (Gen. xxxvii. 17–28). Elisha was once besieged in the town by the Syrians ; but the soldiers of the beleaguering army were miraculously struck with blindness, led to Samaria, had their vision restored, and were finally sent home without molestation (2 Kin. vi. 8–23). Its site is the ruin Tell Dôthân, near a well 9½ miles north, slightly east, of Samaria.

Dove.

A bird (Ps. lv. 6) having fine eyes (Song i. 15 ; v. 12), a plaintive voice (Is. xxxviii. 14), a gentle, affectionate disposition (Song ii. 14 ; v. 2 ; vi. 9), but not much sagacity (Hos. vii. 11). It is timid, and when frightened trembles (Hos. vii. 11). When wild it sometimes frequents valleys (Ezek. vii. 16), making its nest in the side of holes or fissures (Jer. xlviii. 28). When domesticated it flies when alarmed to windows or cotes (Is. lx. 8 ; cp. Gen. viii. 8–12). Jesus refers to it as proverbially harmless (Mat. x. 16). It was bought and sold within the temple courts (Mat. xxi. 12 ; Mark xi. 15 ; John ii. 14), for it was used in sacrifice (Luke ii. 24). The dove is a symbol of the Holy Spirit (Luke iii. 22).

Dove is but another name for pigeon, though in popular usage it is usually restricted to the smaller species. It is frequently translated pigeon in the English versions (Gen. xv. 9 ; Lev. i. 14 ; v. 7, 11 ; xii. 6, 8 ; xiv. 22, 30 ; xv. 14, 29 ; Num. vi. 10).

The doves constitute a family of birds (*Columbidæ*), of which Tristram enumerates four species as occurring in Palestine: the ringdove or wood pigeon (*Columba palumbus*), the stockdove (*Columba œnas*), the rock dove (*Columba livia*), and the ash-rumped rock dove (*Columba schimperi*). The ringdove visits Palestine in immense flocks in spring and autumn during its annual migrations; individuals also remain all the winter. The stockdove is found chiefly east of the Jordan, or in the valley of that river. The rock dove is abundant on the coast and in the highlands west of the Jordan. The ash-rumped rock dove is exceedingly abundant in the interior of the country and in the Jordan valley, taking refuge in caves and fissures. It is the species described in Jer. xlviii. 28.

Dove's Dung.

A substance which rose to famine prices during the siege of Samaria by Benhadad (2 Kin. vi. 25). Dung was also eaten during the siege of Jerusalem (War v. 13, 7). Pos-

sibly, however, dove's dung was the name of some herb, as the Arabs call a species of soap plant sparrow's dung.

Dow'ry.

Among the Israelites and neighboring nations a bridegroom or his father paid a dowry to the bride's father to induce him to give her in marriage (Gen. xxix. 15–20 ; xxxiv. 12 ; Ex. xxii. 17 ; 1 Sam. xviii. 25). The lowest legal amount seems to have been fifty shekels (Deut. xxii. 29 ; Ex. xxii. 15, 16). Occasionally the bride's father gave his daughter a wedding present (Josh. xv. 19 ; 1 Kin. ix. 16).

Drag'on [from Greek *drakōn*, a serpent, a dragon].

In the Old Testament the word dragon is often used to translate *Tannin*, a long animal. The word *tannin* denotes a land serpent (Ex. vii. 9 ; cp. iv. 3, 4 ; Ps. xci. 13 ; and doubtless Deut. xxxii. 33), great sea animals (plural, Gen. i. 21, in A. V. whales, in R. V. sea monsters ; Ps. lxxiv. 13 ; cxlviii. 7), and the crocodile of the rivers of Egypt (Ezek. xxix. 3). The last is described as having jaws, and scales to which fish could stick (4), and feet with which it disturbed the waters (xxxii. 2), as lying in the sea and in the branches of the Nile (xxix. 3 ; xxxii. 2), as swimming (6), and as taken with great hooks (xxix. 4 ; Herod. ii. 70) and with nets (xxxii. 3). It is used as a symbol for Egypt (Is. li. 9 ; and probably xxvii. 1).

The R. V. recognizes that the word *Tan*, rendered dragon in A. V. of Job xxx. 29 ; Ps. xliv. 19 ; Is. xiii. 22 ; xxxiv. 13 ; xxxv. 7 ; xliii. 20 ; Jer. ix. 11 ; x. 22 ; xiv. 6 ; xlix. 33 ; li. 37 ; Mic. i. 3, 8, and sea monster in Lam. iv. 3, should be translated jackal ; and, on the other hand, that the Hebrew text of Ezek. xxix. 3 ; xxxii. 2 should be emended to read dragon, where A. V. has once properly dragon and once whale.

The dragon of New Testament imagery is the old serpent, the devil (Rev. xii. 9 ; xx. 2), who is symbolically portrayed as in color red and having seven heads, ten horns, an enormous tail, and a huge mouth, from which he was able to cast forth water like a river after those whom he would destroy (xii. 3, 4, 15 ; xvi. 13). He was hurled from the heavens to the earth, where he persecuted the church, but was finally chained and imprisoned in the abyss (xii. 7–17 ; xx. 2, 3). In certain features the dragon bears resemblance to the beast of chap. xiii. This beast is a combination of Daniel's four beasts, and represents the combined powers of earth in opposition to the kingdom of God (Dan. vii.). The picture of the dragon was conformed to that of the beast, because the dragon, that old serpent, is the animating and moulding spirit in the kingdom of this world, and when he was portrayed in chap. xii., features of the world-power familiarized by Daniel were combined with the distinguishing feature furnished by the serpent of Genesis iii.

Drag'on's Well, in A. V. **Dragon Well**.

A well at Jerusalem, apparently between the Valley Gate and Dung Gate (Neh. ii. 13; cp. iii. 13, 14); called Jackal's Well in A. R. V.

Dream.

Ideas present to the mind during sleep. They may be classified as—1. Vain dreams (Job xx. 8; Ps. lxxiii. 20; Is. xxix. 8). 2. Dreams employed by God for the purposes of his kingdom. In producing them God works according to the laws of mind, and perhaps always employs secondary causes. They are (a) Intended to affect the spiritual life of individuals. That to the Midianite discouraged the enemy, and encouraged Gideon, who providentially heard it (Judg. vii. 13). Perhaps such was the dream of Pilate's wife (Mat. xxvii. 19). Many such providential dreams have been sent in modern times. John Newton, concerned about his soul's salvation, had a dream which made the way of salvation clear to him. (b) Directive and prophetic dreams, used when revelation was incomplete. They seem to have carried with them credentials of their divine origin. Divine communications were made in dreams to Abimelech (Gen. xx. 3), to Jacob (xxviii. 12; xxxi. 10), to Laban (xxxi. 24), to Joseph (xxxvii. 5, 9, 10, 20), to Pharaoh's butler and baker (xl. 5), to Pharaoh (xli. 7, 15, 25, 26), to Solomon (1 Kin. iii. 5), to Nebuchadnezzar (Dan. ii. 1, 4, 36; iv. 1 seq.), to Daniel (vii. 1 seq.), to Joseph the betrothed husband of Mary (Mat. i. 20), to the Magi (ii. 12). The power of accurately interpreting prophetic dreams was granted to certain favored people, as to Joseph (Gen. xli. 16) and to Daniel (Dan. ii. 25–28, 47). Dreams offered as revelations to the church were subjected to tests to determine their character. If they inculcated immoral conduct, they were by that very fact proclaimed false; and any man who sought by their means to lead Israel from the worship of Jehovah was to be put to death (Deut. xiii. 1–5; cp. Jer. xxiii. 25–32; xxix. 8; Zech. x. 2). See VISIONS.

Dress. See CLOTHING.

Drink.

The usual beverage of the Hebrews was water (Gen. xxi. 14; Ex. xxiii. 25; 1 Sam. xxv. 11; 1 Kin. xiii. 8; 2 Kin. vi. 22), though they also frequently used milk (Judg. v. 25), sour wine (Num. vi. 3; Ruth ii. 14), ordinary wine (Gen. xiv. 18; xxvii. 25; Josh. ix. 4; Judg. xix. 19; Neh. v. 15), and more rarely strong drink (Lev. x. 9).

Drink Of'fer-ing. See OFFERINGS.

Drom'e-da-ry [from Latin *dromedarius*, running camel].

1. The rendering of the Hebrew *Rekesh*, quickly running thing, in the A. V. of 1 Kin. iv. 28; but in Mic. i. 13, swift beast, and in Esth. viii. 10, a mule. The R. V. everywhere translates it swift steed.

2. The rendering of the Hebrew *Rammak*

(Esth. viii. 10) in the text of the A. V., and on the margin of the R. V. The text of the R. V. translates it steed. Gesenius understands it to mean a mare.

3. The rendering of the Hebrew *Beker*, a sort of camel, swift and capable of carrying merchandise (Is. lx. 6; Jer. ii. 23). In Arabic the word denotes a young camel of an age suitable for riding and bearing burdens. The R. V. accordingly renders it in the margin young camels.

The dromedary is a variety of the Arabian or one-humped camel (*Camelus dromedarius*), bred for speed and endurance. It can travel about 125 miles a day. The two-humped Bactrian camel (*C. bactrianus*) can also be improved into a dromedary.

Drop'sy.

A disease marked by an unnatural accumulation of watery liquid in any cavity of the body or in the tissues (Luke xiv. 2).

Dru-sil'la.

The youngest daughter of Herod Agrippa I., by his wife Cypros. Before the death of her father in A. D. 44, and when not yet six years old, she was promised in marriage to a certain Epiphanes, son of Antiochus (not, of course, the persecuting king of that name). The bridegroom promised to accept Judaism; but, on further reflection, he refused, and the proposed alliance fell through. Azizus, king of Emesa, was next applied to, the condition offered being the same as in the former case. He had no scruples, and Drusilla became his wife. She was possessed of great beauty, and was in consequence somewhat persecuted by her eldest sister Bernice, who was plain in appearance. Felix, procurator of Judæa, conceived a sinful passion for Drusilla, to which she responded all the more readily that Bernice's petty tyranny over her made her unhappy. In defiance of Jewish law, she left her legitimate husband, and married Felix, a foreigner and an idolater. They had a son called Agrippa, who grew up to manhood and married, but who perished, however, in an eruption of mount Vesuvius (Antiq. xviii. 5, 4; xx. 7, 1 and 2). One can well understand that when Paul, then a prisoner, reasoned before Felix and Drusilla of righteousness, temperance, and judgment to come, Felix trembled (Acts xxiv. 24, 25).

Dul'ci-mer.

The rendering of Aramaic *Sumphoneyah*, *Sumphoneya'*, or to follow the best attested traditional pronunciation, *Sumpon°yah* or *Sumpon'ya'* (Dan. iii. 5, 10, 15), probably meaning bagpipe, as the margin of the R. V. makes it. The real dulcimer is quite a different instrument. In its earliest and simplest form it consisted of a flat piece of wood, on which were fastened two converging strips of the same material, which were crossed by strings played by small hammers. Afterwards pegs for regulating the tension of the strings were superadded, and the flat piece of wood gave place to a resonance box.

Du'mah [silence].

1. A tribe descended from Ishmael (Gen. xxv. 14; 1 Chron. i. 30). Its territory was probably the region called Doumaitha by Ptolemy, and Domata by Pliny, on the confines of the Syrian and Arabian deserts. The town is now called Doomat el-jendel, meaning Dumah of the stones, and is situated in the district el-Jauf, in the northwestern part of the Arabian peninsula.

2. A symbolic designation of Edom, chosen on account of its assonance with Edom and in allusion to the desolation in store (Is. xxi. 11).

3. A town in the hill country of Judah (Josh. xv. 52). Its site is the ruin Dômeh, 10 miles southwest of Hebron.

Dung.

Dung was used for manuring plants (Luke xiii. 8; Ps. lxxxiii. 10). A dunghill, with straw trodden in it by the cattle, is referred to (Is. xxv. 10). In the East dried cowdung is constantly used for fuel (Ezek. iv. 12, 15). Beggars often lay on dunghills and ash heaps (1 Sam. ii. 8; Lam. iv. 5). As a punishment, the house of a man was sometimes made a dunghill (Dan. ii. 5), that is, probably, was converted into a privy (2 Kin. x. 27). Dung, as refuse, was swept away (1 Kin. xiv. 10; Phil. iii. 8).

Dung Gate. See Jerusalem II. 3.

Du'ra.

A plain in the province of Babylon where Nebuchadnezzar's golden image was set up (Dan. iii. 1). Several localities in Babylon were called Duru, which means a wall or fortification.

Dys'en-ter-y.

A disease characterized by inflammation and ulceration of the lower part of the intestines, with hemorrhage from the bowels. It is so constantly attended by fever that it is often called fever and dysentery. Publius, chief man of the island of Melita while Paul was there, suffered from this complaint, but was miraculously cured by the apostle (Acts xxviii. 7, 8, R. V.; in A. V. bloody flux).

E

Ea'gle.

A bird of prey (Job ix. 26; xxxix. 30; Hab. i. 8), large (Ezek. xvii. 3, 7), swift of flight (2 Sam. i. 23), seeing at a great distance, and which builds its nest on lofty rocks (Job xxxix. 27–29; Jer. xlix. 16). It was currently believed to bestow great care upon its young while training them to act for themselves, stirring up the nest and forcing them out, hovering over them and under them when they made their first weak attempts to fly (Deut. xxxii. 11; Ex. xix. 4, 5). Sir Humphrey Davy relates witnessing a pair of golden eagles similarly engaged above the crags of Ben Nevis. There is also probably an allusion to an ancient popular belief that the eagle, at the end of a certain period, moults and renews its youth (Ps. ciii. 5). The story was that the eagle, on reaching old age flew upward toward the sun until its feathers were singed and it fell into the sea. Thence it emerged in the strength of youth. The allusion may, however, be to the great age to which the eagle lives and retains the vigor of youth. As a carnivorous bird, feeding on reptiles and occasionally on carrion, it was unclean (Lev. xi. 13). The Hebrews, like the Arabs, applied the name which they used for eagle to birds that eat carrion, probably, like the Greek and Roman naturalists Aristotle and Pliny, including certain larger varieties of the vulture among the eagles (Mat. xxiv. 28; cp. Prov. xxx. 17). In alluding to the baldness of the eagle (Mic. i. 16), the prophet, if he does not refer to moulting, which is an inconspicuous process in the eagle, has some vulture in mind, whose head is bald and neck but scantily feathered.

Tristram enumerates eight species of the eagle subfamily as occurring in Palestine. Seven are of the typical genus *Aquila*, viz.: *Aquila chrysaëtus*, the golden eagle; *A. heliaca*, the imperial eagle; *A. clanga*, the greater spotted eagle; *A. rapax*, the tawny eagle; *A. pennata*, the booted eagle; *A. nipalensis*, the steppe eagle; *A. Bonelli*, Bonelli's eagle, and *Circaëtus gallicus*, the short-toed eagle. With the exception of the booted eagle, the others are not uncommon. By far the most abundant of all is the short-toed eagle. It feeds on reptiles. It is numerous in summer and autumn. In winter it occurs more sparingly, many apparently migrating southward.

Ear'nest.

Part payment in advance of a wage, a sum of money, or anything else promised, this being intended as a pledge or guarantee to the recipient that the bargain, contract, or promise will in due time be carried out. Blackstone says that the prepayment of a penny in England will legally bind a contract, and the handing over the smallest quantity of goods ordered will bind the engagement for the remainder. The earnest, as a rule, is the same in kind as the ultimate payment, of which it is the pledge. The Spirit in the hearts of Christians is the earnest of their inheritance (2 Cor. i. 22: v. 5; Eph. i. 13, 14).

Ear'ring.

Earrings were worn by the Israelites, men, women, and children (Ex. xxxii. 2), especially by the women (Ezek. xvi. 12; Judith x. 4). They were also worn by the Midianites (Num. xxxi. 50), Assyrians, Egyptians, and other peoples. The custom was innocent in itself. But the earring sometimes served as an amulet (cp. Is. iii. 20; in R. V. amulet). As used in idolatrous worship, they were worn by the men and women of Jacob's household, until he ordered the strange gods to be put away (Gen. xxxv. 4). They were made of gold (Ex. xxxii. 2; cp. Prov. xxv. 12) or other precious metal. It is often not clear from the narrative whether earrings or nose-rings are intended (Gen. xxiv. 22, 30; Ex. xxxv. 22).

Earth.

1. The world in which we dwell as distinguished from the heavens overhead (Gen. i. 1).

2. The dry land, as distinguished from the sea (Gen. i. 10); the habitable world (Gen. i. 28; x. 25; xviii. 18). It is frequently described in poetry. Hannah spoke of the earth standing on pillars, on which it had been placed by God (1 Sam. ii. 8; Job. ix. 6; Ps. lxxv. 3). The psalmist speaks of the inhabited earth as founded upon the seas and established on the floods (xxiv. 2; cxxxvi. 6; cp. Ex. xx. 4). Others speak literally or figuratively of the foundations of the earth (Ps. cii. 25; civ. 5–9; Prov. iii. 19; viii. 29; Is. xlviii. 13).

3. Vegetable soil (Gen. xxvii. 28; Ex. xx. 24; Ps. civ. 14).

4. The inhabitants of the world or of any region in it (Gen. xi. 1; Ps. xcviii. 9).

Earth'quake.

The quaking of the earth; a vibratory or undulatory movement extending superficially over a wide area, and downward, it is believed, from a mile or two to more than thirty miles. The vibrations are, perhaps, produced by contractions of portions of the earth's crust. Earthquakes and volcanoes are connected, and are confined to particular regions constituting continuous lines. One of these lines passes from the Taurus mountains to the gulf of Akaba, along the valleys of the Orontes and the Jordan. In severe earthquakes, at the point where the force is greatest, the hills move to and fro (Jer. iv. 24) and the foundations of the mountains, as it were, tremble (Ps. xviii. 7); clefts appear in the earth's crust (Zech. xiv. 4, 5) and chasms, into which men may fall, open and close (Num. xvi. 31–33); buildings are shaken down and their inhabitants often buried in the ruins; and if the sea is near, it may leave its bed for a few minutes nearly dry, and then bring in a wave upon the land which will sweep over it with destructive effect. Judæa was visited by a severe earthquake in the days of Uzziah and Jeroboam II. (Amos i. 1; Zech. xiv. 5; Antiq. ix. 10, 4). Another notable earthquake occurred in the seventh year of Herod the Great, which destroyed much cattle and upwards of 10,000 lives (Antiq. xv. 5, 2). An earthquake, accompanied with darkness, signalized the death of Christ (Mat. xxvii. 45, 51–54), and another heralded his resurrection (xxviii. 2). One occurred in Macedonia when Paul and Silas were in the jail at Philippi (Acts xvi. 26).

East.

The direction toward the sunrise (as is denoted by the Hebrew and Greek words employed in Josh. xi. 3; xii. 3, etc.; Mat. ii. 1). The Hebrews faced the point of the rising sun when they determined direction; hence the east was the front (as is denoted by the Hebrew word in Gen. ii. 8).

East, Children of the, or Men of, or People of.

A general designation of the tribes occupying the east country, who inhabited the region bordering on Ammon and Moab (Ezek. xxv. 4, 10), dwelt as far north as a district where people of Haran pastured their flocks (Gen. xxix. 1, 4), and extended far southward into Arabia.

East Country.

The region lying east of Palestine (Zech. viii. 7), especially the Arabian and Syrian deserts (Gen. xxv. 1–7).

East Sea or Eastern Sea. See DEAD SEA.

East Wind.

A wind blowing, broadly speaking, from the east. In Egypt it blasts the ears of corn (Gen. xli. 23, 27), and in Palestine the vines and vegetation generally (Ezek. xvii. 7–10; xix. 10–12). The east wind in these lands is hot and sultry, and deleterious to vegetation, because it has been blowing over the Arabian or Syro-Arabian desert (Hos. xiii. 15). Doubtless this same wind is meant in Jon. iv. 8, although the Ninevites themselves would not have called it an east wind.

East'er.

Originally the spring festival in honor of Eastra or Ostara, the Teutonic goddess of light and spring. As early as the eighth century the name was transferred by the Anglo-Saxons to the Christian festival designed to celebrate the resurrection of Christ. In the A. V. it occurs once, viz., in Acts xii. 4, but is a mistranslation. The original is *pascha*, the ordinary Greek word for passover. The R. V. properly employs the word passover.

E'bal.

1. A son of Shobal, and a descendant of Seir the Horite (Gen. xxxvi. 23; 1 Chron. i. 40).

2. The same as Obal (1 Chron. i. 22 with Gen. x. 28).

3. A mountain separated only by a narrow valley from mount Gerizim (Deut. xxvii. 12–14), west of the western highway and near the oaks of Moreh (xi. 30, R. V.), which were near Shechem (Gen. xii. 6, R. V.; xxxv. 4). When the Israelites passed the Jordan they were to set up great stones plastered, on which the words of the law were to be written. An altar also was to be built (Deut. xxvii. 1–8). Representatives of six tribes, those of Reuben, Gad, Asher, Zebulun, Dan, and Naphtali, were to stand on mount Ebal and pronounce curses on those who were guilty of certain heinous sins. The representatives of the remaining six tribes standing on mount Gerizim were to pronounce blessings (Deut. xi. 29; xxvii. 9–26). These directions were car-

ried out by Joshua (Josh. viii. 30–35). Mount Ebal lies on the northern side of Nablus, the ancient Shechem, whilst mount Gerizim lies on its southern side (Antiq. iv. 8, 44). Both are west of the road from the south to the north, and the branch road to Samaria and En-gannim passes between them. Ebal rises 3077 feet above the sea, and is steep, rocky, and barren. In some places a few stunted olive trees may be discovered on its lower part, and prickly pear above, in others it is destitute of vegetation. It is now called Jebel Eslâmîyeh.

E'bed [servant].

1. Father of Gaal (Judg. ix. 28, 30).
2. A chief of the father's house of Adin, who returned from Babylon with fifty males under the leadership of Ezra (Ezra viii. 6).

E'bed-me'lech [slave of the king].

An Ethiopian, a eunuch of the palace, who heard that Jeremiah had been cast into a dungeon where he would probably have soon died of hunger, and, having obtained the king's permission, drew him out by cords let down, and rags to protect the prophet's armpits against their sharpness (Jer. xxxviii. 7–13). Jeremiah was subsequently commissioned to inform him that, on account of the service he had rendered, he should be preserved when Jerusalem was taken (xxxix. 15–18).

Eb-en-e'zer [stone of help].

A commemorative stone set up by Samuel, seemingly near Mizpah, between Mizpah and Shen, where the Lord discomfited the Philistines (1 Sam. vii. 10, 12). Twenty years previously the Israelites themselves had been defeated at this place by the Philistines and had lost the ark (iv. 1; where the place is mentioned by its later name).

E'ber, in A. V. thrice **Heber** (1 Chron. v. 13; viii. 22; Luke iii. 35) [other side, region beyond].

1. A descendant of Shem through Arpachshad (Gen. x. 22, 24); and progenitor of a group of peoples (x. 21), embracing the Hebrews (xi. 16–26), the Joktanide Arabs (x. 25–30), and certain Aramæan tribes descended from Nahor (xi. 29; xxii. 20–24). The name is put for these peoples collectively (Num. xxiv. 24). Originally Eber belonged to the region beyond or east of the Euphrates, perhaps also of the Tigris, with respect to the later Hebrews (cp. Josh. xxiv. 2, 3, 14, 15), and to the Joktanide Arabs, and not unlikely with respect to his descendants, the ancestors of Abraham and Nahor, in Ur (Gen. xi. 28).

2. A priest, head of the father's house of Amok in the days of the high priest Joiakim (Neh. xii. 20).

3. A Gadite, head of a father's house in Gilead in Bashan (1 Chron. v. 13).

4 and 5. Two Benjamites, a son of Elpaal and a son of Shashak (1 Chron. viii. 12 and 22, 25).

E'bez. See ABEZ.

E-bi'a-saph. See ABIASAPH.

Eb'on-y.

Wood of various species of the genus *Diospyros*, which constitutes the type of the *Ebenaceæ* (Ebenads). The inner wood is black, very hard, and heavy. Ebony is used for inlaying and ornamental turnery. The men of Dedan traded with it in the markets of Tyre, having obtained it apparently from India or Ceylon (Ezek. xxvii. 15). The Greeks recognized two kinds of ebony, one variegated, from India, and the other black, from Ethiopia.

E'bron, in A. V. Hebron.

A town on the boundary line of Asher (Josh. xix. 28). Perhaps identical with Abdon.

E-bro'nah. See ABRONAH.

Ec-bat'a-na. See ACHMETHA.

Ec-cle-si-as'tes [Greek *ekklesiastēs*, one who sits and speaks in an assembly or church, a preacher].

The name borrowed from the Septuagint and applied to the O. T. book called in Hebrew *Koheleth*. The meaning of *Koheleth* is disputed. It is etymologically related to the word which means congregation. The English versions follow the Greek and Latin versions in rendering it "the preacher" (i. 1). The preacher is distinctly represented as Solomon, "son of David, king at Jerusalem" (i. 1), excelling all his predecessors in Jerusalem in wisdom and wealth (i. 16; ii. 7, 9). The book may be regarded either as a writing of Solomon himself in his old age or as words which, though not actually uttered by Solomon, accurately sum up his completed experience, are spoken from the standpoint of his finished course, teach the great lesson of his life as he himself learned it, and express the sentiments which he might rightly be supposed to entertain as he looked at life in the retrospect. The meaning of i. 12, 13 is, according to Hebrew grammar, either: "As for me, during my reign [which still continues] I have applied my heart to seek wisdom and have discovered that all is vanity," or "When I was king [as I am not now] I applied my heart to seek wisdom and discovered that all is vanity." The latter explanation is doubtless the correct one; for the language smacks everywhere of the vocabulary and grammar of the later postexilic Hebrew scriptures and of the Aramaic portions of Daniel and Ezra. The book recounts the feelings, experiences, and observations which would be unavoidable to the wise man situated as was Solomon.

The message concerns solely the present life on earth. The question is raised whether any real profit accrues to man from toil (i. 3). The method of investigation is that of the sage (i. 13). By observation and experience the preacher finds that man's one source of satisfaction lies in himself, in the normal and healthy exercise of his powers of mind and body in harmony with the physical and moral laws of the universe in which he is placed (ii. 24; iii. 12, 13, 22; v. 18; ix. 7–10). Vain are wisdom (i. 12–18) and pleasure (ii. 1–11). Still they have value; hence the preacher compares wisdom and folly (ii. 12–23). He concludes that the homely rewards of labor excel (24; cp. v. 12). The conclusion is strengthened by the fact that man's activities are bound to the stages of his growth. There is a time fixed and unalterable for the exercise of each power of mind and body, and everything is beautiful in its season (iii. 1–11). And other joy is often rendered impossible by injustice and oppression (16–iv. 3). Formalism and dishonesty are unwise; and wealth is often injurious, and is less desirable than health (v. 1–vi. 9). The preacher speaks of the value of a good name and the means of obtaining it (vii. 1–10); and of the value of wisdom as a safeguard (11–22), and in dealing with kings (viii. 1–9); and he insists on the general truth that godliness is the best policy (10–15). Death comes alike to all; let man find pleasure, then, in the common, humble joys of life. They are his portion (ix. 2–10). After sundry other shrewd observations, the preacher is led again to his main theme; exhorts young men to rejoice in their powers, but to use them mindful of being under moral government, makes his great appeal to youth to remember God, and sums up the matter in the pithy sentence: Fear God, and keep his commandments; for this is the whole duty of man. For God will bring every work into judgment [even now, whatever the Judge may do in the world to come] (xi. 9–xii. 14).

In his argument the writer appeals to man's relation to God in so far only as God is known in nature and experience. His references to God are thus in accordance with the methods of that philosophical school to which he belonged (see WISDOM), and are indispensable in a complete discussion of the means of adjusting oneself to the conditions which one learns by experience to be imposed upon him and under which he lives.

The startling character of some statements in Ecclesiastes led certain Jews to question its right to its place among inspired books. At last, however, its right to remain in the canon was universally accorded. There is no direct quotation from it or unequivocal allusion to it in the N. T.

Ed [a witness].

A word inserted in the A. V. and the R. V. of Josh. xxii. 34. It or a similar word was doubtless originally in the Hebrew. It is found in some manuscripts and versions, though it may be an insertion in them as it is in the English version. It is needful to the full meaning of the passage, which tells how the two and a half tribes east of the Jordan reared an altar as a witness that they were of common descent and religion with those west of the river. These latter, taking the altar to be the commencement of apostasy from Jehovah, were preparing to make war upon those who had erected it, when explanations were given and accepted as satisfactory (Josh. xxii. 1–34).

E'dar. See EDER.

E'den [pleasantness or, perhaps, plain].

1. A country in which God caused trees to grow from the ground and in this manner planted for Adam a garden, called from its situation the garden of Eden. A river went out of the country of Eden to water the garden, and being thence parted, became four heads, called Pishon, Gihon, Hiddekel, and Euphrates. Of these four rivers, the Euphrates is well known. Hiddekel is unquestionably the Tigris; the other two are doubtful. The Pishon surrounded or meandered through the land of Havilah, where there is gold; and the Gihon surrounded the land of Cush.

The main theories as to the site of the garden may be classed in two groups: I. Those which, while proposing to identify the four streams with still existing rivers, fail to find a geographical counterpart of the one stream divided into four. The site is by many sought in Armenia. The sources of the Tigris and Euphrates are in this region. The Pishon is supposed to be either the Phasis, in modern Persian Fas, or the Kur, the large tributary of the Araxes. The Gihon is identified with the Araxes, in Arabic known as *Gaihun er-Ras*. Objections to this theory are, (a) the difficulty in explaining the one river; (b) the absence of proof that the land of Cush ever extended to this region; (c) Havilah, as located by the biblical writers, did not lie in Armenia. By others the garden is thought of as situated between the Nile and India or between India and the Oxus. Havilah is identified with a portion of India, where gold was obtained; and Cush with either Ethiopia, which is called Cush in the Scriptures, or the plateau of central Asia which was inhabited by Cossæans. The Gihon, the river of Cush, is hence either the Nile, called by the Ethiopians *Gewon* or *Geyon*, or the Oxus. The same objections, *mutatis mutandis*, lie against the second theory as against the first. It may be added that the identification of the Gihon with the Nile is traceable as far back as Josephus. In his case it probably rests on a misconception. The only land of Cush in the geographical knowledge of the later Israelites was Ethiopia; and accordingly Josephus understood the Nile by the Gihon, because it is the great river of the land of Cush. II. Theories which seek an exact geographical counterpart to the biblical description and identify not only the four rivers, but also the one. Calvin observed that the Tigris and Euphrates are actually united for a short distance as one stream, which then divides and enters into the Persian gulf by two mouths; and he concluded that the district watered by the united streams was the site of the garden. There is reason to believe that this particular spot was formerly the bed of the Persian Gulf. But the general locality indicated has much in favor of its being the site of the garden. Friedrich Delitzsch thinks that the river of Eden is the Euphrates. Its channel being higher than the Tigris, its superabundant waters on entering the alluvial plain north of Babylon flowed from its banks and found their way across the plain to the Tigris. The district thus watered was extremely fertile. It was even known to the ancient Babylonians as the garden of the god Duniash. Here the garden of Eden is to be sought. The word *edinu* in Assyrian means plain; and the two river bottoms of southern Mesopotamia and the alluvial lowland form a plain, and were spoken of as an *edinu*. A descendant of Cush reigned in the Babylonian plain (Gen. x. 8–10); and Kashites, that is Cushites, who were related to the Elamites, early descended upon Babylonia and for a time held the political power. Hence the land of Cush may be satisfactorily regarded as having designated at one period Babylonia or its southern portion. Havilah was situated northwest of the Persian Gulf, according to Scripture notices, and may be assumed to have extended to the Euphrates and bordered on Babylonia. Under these circumstances, the Pishon may reasonably be identified with the Pallakopas canal, which was probably a natural channel originally; and the Gihon with a great Babylonian canal which branched from the Euphrates eastward at Babylon, and on which two of Nimrod's cities, Babylon and Erech, stood. It may be the canal near Babylon whose name was Kaḥana or Guḥana, corresponding to Gihon. This scholarly theory still lacks proof. Its weakness at present lies in its numerous assumptions, in the difficulty of showing that the bounds of Havilah ever extended to the banks of the Euphrates, and were not separated from the river by the land of Mesha, and of establishing the conjecture that the country near Babylon to the east was designated the land of Cush. Glaser offers a natural explanation of the language employed in the description. He regards the four heads, which are immediately afterwards called rivers, as the heads or tributaries of the river of Eden. These four affluents united somewhere below the garden or, to modify his theory, at the garden itself. The name Pishon he finds still lingering in the Middle Ages in the wady Faishan in northern central Arabia, which drains the rainfall toward the Persian Gulf. This region produced gold and corresponds to the location of Havilah as indicated by the biblical writers. He also believed that he found the name Gihon applied to the wady er-Rumma, which drains the country

about Jebel Shamar toward the Euphrates, and he concluded that the Cushites occupied this region during their migration from the east to Africa, and caused it to be known for a long time as the land of Cush. He erred, however, in his belief that he had found the wady er-Rumma called Gihon. The Arabian poet whom he quotes is speaking of a river of Cilicia.

The site of the garden of Eden is most probably to be sought about the head of the Persian Gulf. The locality is east of Palestine, as Gen. ii. 8 may mean. The Tigris and Euphrates rivers are there. Havilah was a district of northern central Arabia. A land of Cush corresponded approximately to Elam, where the names Kashshu and Cossæan long lingered. The plain of Babylonia could be and evidently was called an *edinu*, as Delitzsch has shown. Possibly the fact that the Persian Gulf was called a river may also have some bearing on the solution of the problem. The garden of Eden is referred to in Isa. li. 3; Ezek. xxviii. 13; xxxi. 9, 16–18; xxxvi. 35; Joel ii. 3; cp. Gen. xiii. 10.

2. A region in Mesopotamia; mentioned in connection with Gozan, Haran, Reseph, Telassar (2 Kin. xix. 12; Is. xxxvii. 12), and with Haran and Canneh (Ezek. xxvii. 23, 24). Apparently the locality in Amos i. 5, on the margin called Beth-eden. The region is mentioned in Assyrian documents by the name Bît-Adini, situated on both sides of the Euphrates north of the Belik river.

3. A Gershonite Levite, a son of Joah (2 Chron. xxix. 12; xxxi. 15).

E'der, in A. V. once **Edar** (Gen. xxxv. 21) and once **Ader** (1 Chron. viii. 15) [a flock].

1. A tower, beyond which Jacob on one occasion spread his tent (Gen. xxxv. 21). Exact situation unknown.

2. A town in the extreme south of Judah (Josh. xv. 21). Exact situation unknown.

3. A Benjamite, son of Elpaal (1 Chron. viii. 15).

4. A Levite, son of Mushi, of the family of Merari (1 Chron. xxiii. 23; xxiv. 30).

E'dom; in A. V. of O. T. four times **Idumea** [red].

1. A name of Esau, given in memory of his having sold his birthright for red pottage (Gen. xxv. 30; xxxvi. 1, 8, 19).

2. The Edomites collectively (Num. xx. 18, 20, 21; Amos i. 6, 11; ix. 12; Mal. i. 4).

3. The region occupied by the descendants of Edom, *i. e.* Esau. It was originally called mount Seir (Gen. xxxii. 3; xxxvi. 20, 21, 30; Num. xxiv. 18). At the time of the sixteenth or seventeenth dynasty, and probably as early as the twelfth dynasty (for these dates, see Adventures of Sinuhit), it was known to the Egyptians as Edimâ. In the mind of the Israelites Edom as the name of the country was doubtless associated with the settlement of their kinsman Edom in that region. It is a mountainous and extremely rugged country,

about 100 miles long, extending southward from Moab on both sides of the Arabah, or great depression connecting the southern part of the Dead Sea with the gulf of Akaba (Gen. xiv. 6; Deut. ii. 1, 12; Josh. xv. 1; Judg. xi. 17, 18; 1 Kin. ix. 26). The summit of mount Seir is believed to rise about 3500 feet above the adjacent Arabah. The lower part of the chain is of red Nubian sandstone, with dykes of red granite and porphyry; the summit is of a chalky limestone, probably of cretaceous age. Edom is not nearly so fertile as Palestine (cp. Mal. i. 2-4); but in the time of Moses it had fields, vineyards, wells, and a highway (Num. xx. 17, 19). The Edomite capital in the times of the Hebrew monarchy was Sela, believed to be the place afterwards called Petra. Other important towns were Bozrah and Teman. In the Greek period the name was modified into Idumæa (q. v.).

The wilderness of Edom was the Arabah at the southern extremity of the Dead Sea (2 Kin. iii. 8, 20).

E'dom-ites.

The descendants of Edom, i. e. Esau (Gen. xxxvi. 1-19), and others incorporated with them. As early as the return of Jacob from Mesopotamia Esau had occupied the land of Edom (Gen. xxxii. 3; xxxvi. 6-8; Deut. ii. 4, 5; Josh. xxiv. 4), having driven out the aboriginal Horites (cp. Gen. xiv. 6; xxxvi. 20-30; Deut. ii. 12, 22). The Edomites appear to have been first ruled by tribal chiefs called dukes, who were probably like Arab sheiks (Gen. xxxvi. 15-19, 40-43; 1 Chron. i. 51-54); but before the rise of the Hebrew monarchy they were governed by kings (Gen. xxxvi. 31-39; 1 Chron. i. 43-51). When the Israelites were approaching Canaan, they sought permission from the king of Edom to pass through his territory, giving assurance that the privilege would not be abused. He refused the request, and was prepared to fight if the Israelites had persisted in moving forward. But because the Edomites were descended from Abraham, the Israelites were forbidden to make war upon them and commanded to pass around their land (Num. xx. 14-21). Notwithstanding this hostility, an Edomite was regarded in the Mosaic law as a brother of the Israelites, and the posterity of the former were allowed in the third generation to become incorporated with the Hebrew people (Deut. xxiii. 7, 8), while it was not till the tenth generation that the descendants of a Moabite or an Ammonite could obtain the same privilege (3-6). Saul fought against the Edomites (1 Sam. xiv. 47); and David put garrisons in Edom after conquering the country (1 Chron. xviii. 13; Ps. lx., title; and 2 Sam. viii. 13, 14, where the word Syrians is doubtless the error of a copyist who misread daleth as resh). This conquest had been predicted by Balaam (Num. xxiv. 18). Joab, David's commander-in-chief, remained in Edom for six months, cutting off every male (1 Kin. xi. 15, 16); but Hadad,

one of the royal family, escaped with some others of his countrymen to Egypt, and became an active enemy of Solomon (14-22). After the death of Ahab of Israel, and during the reign of Jehoshaphat of Judah, Edomites, Ammonites, and Moabites invaded Judah (2 Chron. xx. 1; see MEUNIM), but perished in internecine strife caused by Jehovah (22, 23). About this time, and perhaps during years previously, a deputy or appointee was "king" in Edom (1 Kin. xxii. 47), perhaps the person called king in 2 Kin. iii. 9. Edomites aided Israel and Judah in the contest with Mesha, king of Moab (4-27); but in the reign of Jehoshaphat's son Joram they revolted. Joram vanquished them in the field, but could not reduce them to subjection (2 Kin. viii. 20-22; 2 Chron. xxi. 8-10). Amaziah was more successful. He slew 10,000 Edomites in the valley of Salt, took Sela, the capital, and put 10,000 Edomites to death by flinging them from the top of the rock (2 Kin. xiv. 7; 2 Chron. xxv. 11, 12). In the reign of Ahaz, when Judah was attacked by Pekah and Rezin, the Edomites invaded Judah, and carried off captives (2 Chron. xxviii. 17); and they rejoiced when Nebuchadnezzar destroyed Jerusalem (Ps. cxxxvii. 7). The prophets foretold the calamities that should befall Edom for its inveterate enmity towards Israel (Ezek. xxxv. 5, 6), but announced its ultimate incorporation into the kingdom of God (Jer. xlix. 7-22; Lam. iv. 21, 22; Ezek. xxv. 12-14; xxxv. 15; Joel iii. 19; Amos ix. 12; Obad. 1-21). When the captivity of the two tribes rendered the territory of Judah somewhat destitute of inhabitants, the Edomites seized on it as far as Hebron, and were themselves supplanted in mount Seir by the Nabathæan Arabs. See NABAIOTH. Judas Maccabæus retook Hebron and the other towns which the Edomites had occupied (1 Mac. v. 65; Antiq. xii. 8, 6). John Hyrcanus compelled the Edomites to submit to the rite of circumcision, and incorporated them with the Jewish people (Antiq. xiii. 9, 1). The Herods were Idumæans, i. e. Edomites. Many of the Zealots who took part in the defense of Jerusalem against the Romans, and were almost as dangerous to their fellow citizens as to the enemy, were also Idumæans. After this the tribe is little heard of again in history.

Ed're-i [strong].

1. The capital city of Bashan (Deut. iii. 10; Josh. xii. 4; xiii. 12, 31). There the Israelites fought the great battle with Og, which deprived him of his dominions and his life (Nu xxi. 33-35; Deut. i. 4; iii. 1, 10). Edrei has been identified with the modern village of Der'at, about 27 miles east of Gadara.

2. A fenced city of Naphtali (Josh. xix. 37).

Eg'lah [a calf].

One of David's wives, and mother of Ithream (2 Sam. iii. 5; 1 Chron. iii. 3).

Eg'la-im [two ponds].

A Moabite town (Is. xv. 8). Eusebius mentions a village Aigaleim, 8 Roman miles to the south of Areopolis; cp. also the town Agalla (Antiq. xiv. 1, 4) It is not the same as En-eglaim.

Eg'lath-sñe-li'shi-yah [third Eglath]. A place in Moab (Is. xv. 5 and Jer. xlviii. 34, R. V.). Compare the dual Eglaim.

Eg'lon [perhaps vituline].
1. A king of Moab, who captured Jericho, held it for eighteen years, and exacted tribute from Israel. He was assassinated by Ehud, the bearer of the tribute, who obtained a private interview with him on the pretext of bringing secret tidings (Judg. iii. 12–30).
2. A town in the lowland and assigned to Judah (Josh. xv. 39). Its king was one of the five allies who made war on Gibeon, but were defeated, captured, and executed, by Joshua (Josh. x. 3–23, 34–37; xii. 12). Its site is 'Ajlân, 16 miles northeast of Gaza.

E'gypt.
For the sake of convenience, the facts regarding Egypt are grouped under three heads: the country, the people, and the sojourn of the Israelites.

I. *The Country.*—1. *Its names.* The country was designated Aiguptos by the Greeks as early as the time of Homer. The ancient Egyptians themselves, however, commonly called their native land Kam-t, black, naming it from the color of the soil. To the Canaanites it was known as Misru, which probably means the fortified land, or closed land, so called on account of the fortifications along its Asiatic frontier at the isthmus of Suez, or it may denote simply the territory. This latter name the Hebrews employed almost exclusively, though they used it in the dual form Miṣraim, the two Egypts, viz., upper or southern and lower or northern; like the Egyptians themselves, considering the country double.

I. 2. *The territory and its divisions.* In ancient times Egypt was the country watered by the Nile from the Mediterranean Sea as far as the first cataract. In addition it included a series of oases in the western desert, and also the country between the eastern mouth of the Nile and the wady el-'Arish, the river of Egypt. The country is divided by nature into two tracts—a narrow valley, running from south to north, sunken in the midst of a desert; and the prolongation of the valley into a delta. These geographical divisions formed political boundaries also; Upper Egypt was coincident with the valley, ¯d Lower Egypt with the delta. The length of the Nile country from the sea to the first cataract is 550 miles, and its breadth from the head of the delta to the cataract varies from 14 to 32 miles. The area of this tract is about 11,342 square miles, of which at the time of the French occupation 6921 square miles were cultivable. Ancient Egypt was a small country, scarcely one-half again as large as New Jersey; but, at the same time,

in proportion to its width, it is the longest country in the world. It may be compared to New Jersey with its area increased by one half, elongated so as to extend from New York to Cincinnati, or from New York to Wilmington, N. C. It is nearly twice as far from Memphis to the cataract (about 460 miles) as from Memphis to Jerusalem (about 260), and the distance is greater from Memphis to the cataract than from Memphis to Damascus (about 410 miles). This long, narrow valley of the Nile, as far as the first cataract, was originally an estuary of the sea. Herodotus came to this conclusion (ii. 10), and his theory has been confirmed by geology. "The Nile mud," says Fraas, "rests on a bed of sea sand. The whole country between the first cataract and the Mediterranean was formerly a narrow estuary." In the strictest sense, Egypt, as the ancient Greeks said, is "the gift of the Nile." See NILE.

I. 3. *The adjacent region.* Ancient Egypt was bounded on either side by desert land. The waste country gradually rises from the Sahara in the west toward the east, and terminates in a chain of mountains which skirt the Red Sea. The desert region on the east of the river, extending to the Red Sea, and containing nearly 50,000 square miles, about equal in extent to Pennsylvania, was considered as forming geographically part of Arabia (Herod. ii. 8, 19), perhaps because like the Arabian peninsula in character, although it was separated from Arabia by the Red Sea and was politically no man's land, virtually uninhabited, whose scanty resources were worked by the Egyptians. The mountains rise to a height of 6600 feet. They form a broad and massive range of crystalline rock, running parallel with the coast of the Red Sea and sending forth numerous ramifications into the interior of the country. It was in these mountains, at Ḥammâmât on the caravan route between Ḳosêr and Thebes, that the ancient Egyptians quarried the hard, dark-colored stone which they used for sarcophagi and sphinxes; and at Jebel Dukha, nearly opposite the extremity of the Sinaitic peninsula, they mined copper and emerald. Extensive masses of limestone stretch from the mountains to the Nile, yielding the alabaster with which the ancient Egyptians embellished their buildings. The desert on the west of the Nile was assigned to Libya. It presents an entirely different aspect from the region east of the river. It consists of an immense, monotonous and stony tableland, 650 to 1000 feet above the level of the Nile, without mountains or valleys or even isolated hills of any considerable height, and without trace of crystalline or volcanic formations. The whole of this stony and absolutely unwatered plain consists of limestone with a few sand hills scattered here and there over it, and a barrier of sandstone penetrating into it not far from the Ethiopian border. The utter desolation of this region is relieved at five points only within the Egyptian territory by oases, mere specks in the desert, distant by a journey of from three to five days from each other, and by a journey of from three to sixteen days from the Nile. They owe their fertility to subterranean supplies of water, which are believed to be connected with the Nubian Nile or possibly with the Soudan. The combined population is about 35,000.

Ancient Egypt was thus an isolated country—sea on the north, desert and sea on the east, desert cleft only for nearly 1000 miles by the narrowest and least productive part of the Nile valley on the south, and the silent, illimitable desert on the west.

II. *The People.*—1. *Their origin.*—According to the Bible, Miṣraim was the son of Ham and the brother of Canaan, Put, and the Ethiopian Cush (Gen. x. 6). This description indicates an Asiatic origin for the Egyptians, but whether they were descended from Ham or incorporated with him is not determined. Their own traditions point to their immigration from southern Arabia. The type of the ancient Egyptian is Caucasian; but at the same time anatomy, character, and language

Ruins of the Great Temple of Amun at Karnak.

differentiate him from the Indo-European and Semitic peoples. On the other hand, many of the domestic utensils employed by the ancient Egyptians, as well as many of their customs, are said to be similar to those of the dwellers on the banks of the Zambesi and Niger, but totally different from those seen on the banks of the Indus and Euphrates. Not improbably Hamitic immigrants from Asia conquered an aboriginal race already settled on the banks of the Nile.

II. 2. *Their appearance.* The Egyptian was short of stature and slender of build. The head was large in proportion, and covered with black or brown hair—smooth, not woolly. The forehead was square, but receding, the eyes large, the cheeks full, the mouth wide, the lips tolerably thick. In color the Egyptian was dark, but not black. The women, not being exposed to the sun, had a lighter complexion.

II. 3. *Their language.* The Egyptian language is difficult to classify. Its vocabulary connects it with the Turanian tongues, and its grammar with the Semitic languages. Its modern descendant is the Coptic, which continued to be spoken in Lower Egypt until the seventeenth century. Though now dead, it is known by translations into it of the O. T. and N. T. Originally a kind of picture writing, which has been named hieroglyphic or sacred writing, was used. It consisted chiefly of representations of objects which occur in nature and art, such as birds, beasts, plants, and implements, together with mathematical symbols. These delineations are partly ideographs—that is, the picture is the word or idea, and they partly represent sounds which when combined yield a word. Hieroglyphic writing was used down to the latest times; but after a time the scribes began to dispense with the details of the pictures in order to write more rapidly, and thus arose the hieratic or priestly writing. It was employed wherever ornamentation was not an object. About the eighth century B. C. the demotic or popular writing came into vogue. It was used in social and commercial intercourse for writing the dialect which had developed among the people, and was a cursive form of the old hieroglyphs. When the attention of the modern world was directed to the ancient Egyptian writings, they could not be read, and for a long time no key could be found. But when Alexandria surrendered to the British in 1801 there fell into their hands a slab of black basalt, called the Rosetta stone, from its having been found by the French near the Rosetta branch of the Nile. It is now in the British Museum. On this stone is cut a decree by Ptolemy V., about 193 B. C. It is repeated in three languages and in three forms of writing—demotic, hieroglyphic, and Greek. A bilingual inscription, Greek and hieroglyphic, was found on an obelisk on the island of Philæ near the first cataract. The Greek of these texts was,

of course, easily read, being a known language, and the hieroglyphs were deciphered by comparison with it.

II. 4. *Their numbers.* The population of Egypt was greater in ancient than in modern times. Diodorus Siculus, contemporary of Julius Cæsar and Augustus, states, on the authority of the ancient Egyptian records, that the land contained in the time of the Pharaohs more than 18,000 cities and villages; and he gives the ancient population of the country as 7,000,000. In the days of Nero, on the basis of the revenue derived from the poll tax, it was estimated at 7,500,000, exclusive of the inhabitants of Alexandria (War ii. 16, 4). This number is quite reasonable in itself, for the country could support from 8,000,000 to 9,000,000 people. According to the census of 1882, the present population of Egypt proper is 6,811,448, or about 600 per square mile, and is therefore denser than that of most European states.

II. 5. *Their history.* When Egypt passed from the prehistoric to the historic age it seems to have existed as a number of small kingdoms. These were afterwards combined into an empire by Menes, the first historical king. Students of Egyptian chronology assign different dates to the commencement of Menes' reign. These vary from about 5700 B. C. to 2700 B. C. Manetho, a priest of Sebennytos in the reign of Ptolemy Philadelphus, reckons thirty dynasties from the accession of Menes to the Persian conquest of Egypt in 345 B. C. These are now generally grouped into three periods: those of the Old, the Middle, and the New Empires. To the Old Empire are assigned the first seven or ten dynasties. Its great feature was pyramid building, which reached its height under the fourth dynasty. That of the Middle Empire was the conquest of at least Lower Egypt by the Hyksos, or Shepherd Kings, from the northeast. They are generally supposed to have belonged to the Semitic race, but may have been Hittites. It is believed that it was during their domination that Abraham visited Egypt and that Joseph was prime minister. At this period a great economic change took place in Egypt. In the Old Empire the nobility and governors of the nomes had possessed large landed estates; but in the New Empire royal officials are in the place of the old aristocracy, and the crown and the great temples own the landed property. The New Empire began with the eighteenth dynasty. The first notable event in it was the expulsion of the Hyksos, when they had ruled by one account 511, by another 625 years. Afterwards, under native rulers, Egypt attained to high prosperity, and began a career of conquest and domination in western Asia, Thothmes III. being its greatest warrior, and Rameses II. not much inferior. The latter was probably the Pharaoh who oppressed the Israelites, and his son Meneptah the Pharaoh of the exodus. Other Pha-

Among the many mouments built by Ramses II (1290-1233 B.C.) is the giant cliff temple at Abu Simbel in Nubia. Four colossi represent Ramses II. Carved in a mountainside, the work is 210 feet in depth.

The Book of the Dead is the name given to hundreds of funerary texts discovered in Egyptian tombs. The texts have a general theme of judgment after death. This panel shows the heart of the deceased being weighed in a balance scale with truth. If the scales balance the deceased is entitled to a future life of happiness. The deceased will be devoured by the waiting monster should the scales not balance.

A relief from Medinet Habu showing two Philistine captives led by an Egyptian officer.

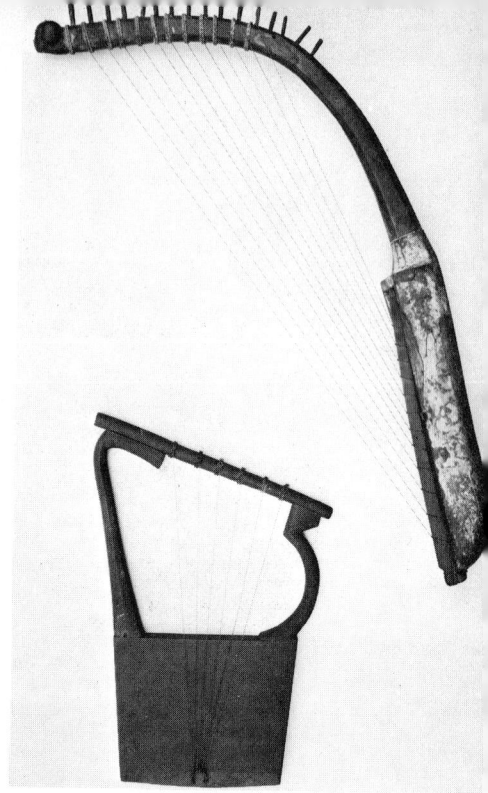

Egyptian musical instruments. The wooden lyre (top) from Thebes dates from the Eighteenth Dynasty. The wooden harp is from approximately the same period.

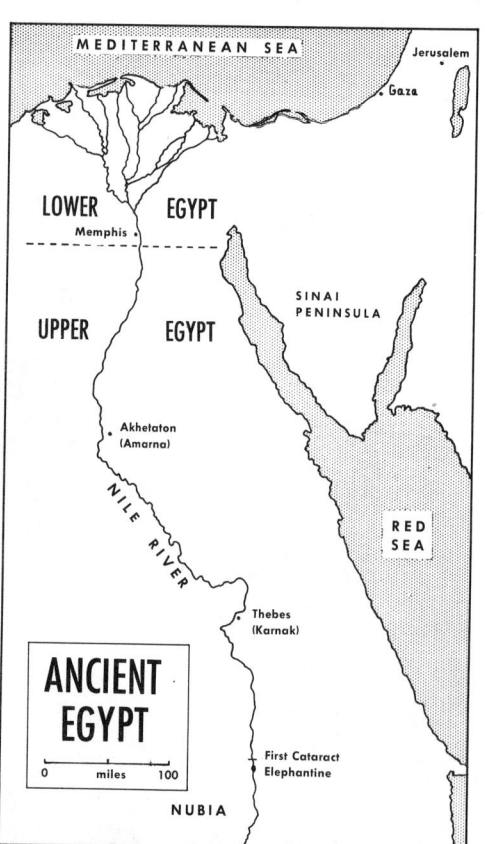

MEDITERRANEAN SEA

Jerusalem

Gaza

LOWER   EGYPT

Memphis

UPPER   EGYPT

SINAI
PENINSULA

Akhetaton
(Amarna)

NILE RIVER

RED
SEA

Thebes
(Karnak)

ANCIENT
EGYPT

0   miles   100

First Cataract
Elephantine

NUBIA

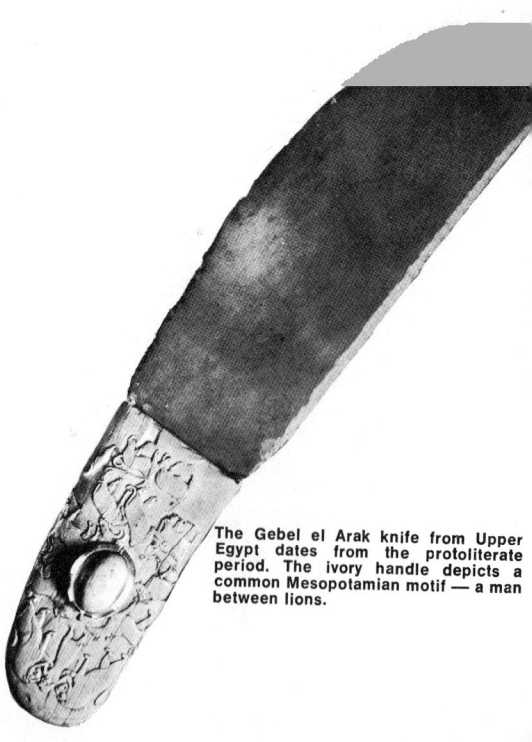

The Gebel el Arak knife from Upper Egypt dates from the protoliterate period. The ivory handle depicts a common Mesopotamian motif — a man between lions.

An Egyptian canopic jar..

The throne chair of Tutankhamon, the famed "King Tut." His name appears as Tutankhanton in the inlay, but in the gold work where it could more easily be altered it has been changed to Tutankhamon. The back of the throne depicts the king and his wife under the sun disk (Aton). Tutankhamon later renounced the Aton faith and turned to the worship of Amon.

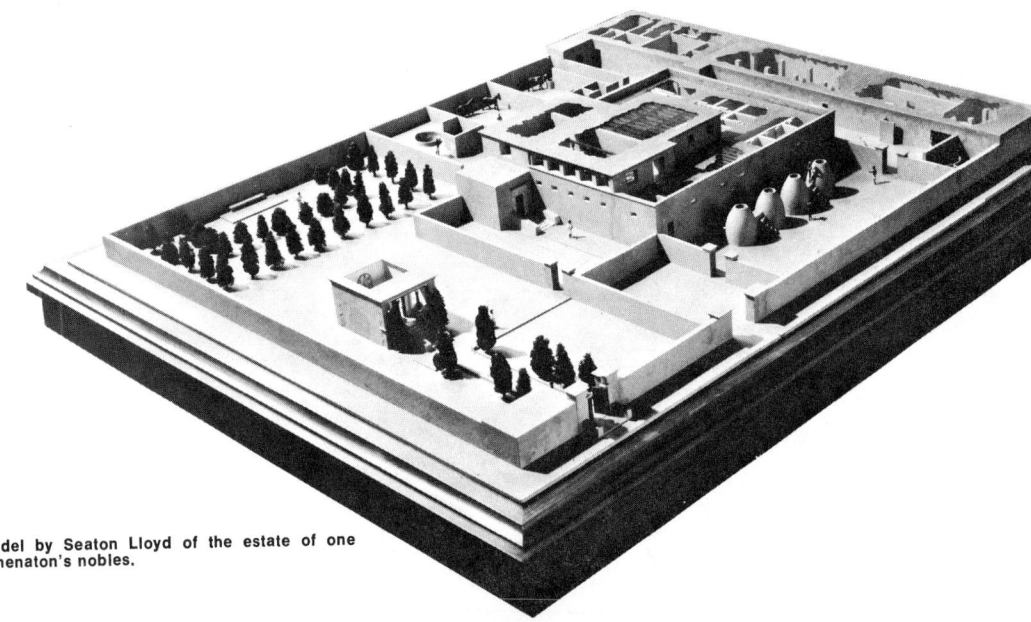

A model by Seaton Lloyd of the estate of one of Akhenaton's nobles.

Left: a relief, dating back to the Eighteenth Dynasty, showing Hapi, the god of the Nile. The relief is from the throne of the pharaoh Ay.
Below: From Tell el-Amarna comes this relief of Akhenaton, his wife, and one of their daughters worshiping Aton. With raised hands they present offerings to the Sun-god. Rays from the sun disk end in hands, two of which hold the Egyptian sign of life before the faces of Akhenaton and Nefertiti.

A granite statue of Horemhab, the commander of Tutankhamon's armies, later a pharaoh in his own right.

raohs are mentioned in the O. T.—Shishak,
So, Tirhakah, Necho, Hophra; see PHARAOH.
Tirhakah assisted in checking the advance
of Sennacherib, king of Assyria, toward
Egypt; but he was overthrown by Sennacherib's successor Esarhaddon. The Assyrians divided Egypt into twenty districts, and
appointed a governor over each. Tirhakah
stirred up revolt, and Egypt was reconquered
by Ashurbanipal, who plundered and destroyed Thebes in 664 B. C. (Nah. iii. 8–10).
Psammeticus, one of the petty rulers, rose in
revolt, and, aided by the Asiatic Greeks, restored Egypt to independence, founding the
twenty-sixth dynasty. In 525 B. C. Egypt
was conquered by Cambyses and became a
Persian satrapy. About a century and a quarter later Nephrites succeeded in completely
throwing off the Persian yoke, and became
the founder of the twenty-ninth dynasty;
but in 345 B. C. Egypt surrendered to Artaxerxes, and again became a Persian satrapy.
In 332 B. C. it welcomed the Macedonians and
Greeks, led by Alexander the Great; for it
saw in him a deliverer from the Persian yoke.
After his death it was ruled by the Ptolemies.
In 30 B. C. it became a province of the Roman
empire, and was governed by prefects until
A. D. 362. Joseph, Mary, and the infant
Jesus, took refuge there during the time that
Archelaus ruled Judæa. In A. D. 619 Egypt
was conquered by Chosroes II. of Persia, who
lost it again permanently in 628. Between
638 and 640 it passed to the Saracens, and
between 1163 and 1196 to the Turks.

II. 6. *Their religion.* The religion of the
Egyptians was a spiritualized nature worship, centering about veneration of the sun
and of the river Nile, two sources of life. A
vast number of deities were adored. They
represented the forces and phenomena of
nature. Ptah, whose name occurs in Meneptah, was chief. He represented the organizing and motive power developed from
moisture. The names of several others are
found in the O. T.—Ra, the sun god, illumi-
nator of the world and awakener of life (in
Ramses); Thum, the evening sun, the possessor of creative power and the dispenser of
the welcome evening breezes (in Pithom);

Bast, personification of sexual passion (in
Pi-beseth), and Amon, a god who animates
nature. Each nome or district had its special local deity or deities, to whom it paid
peculiar honors. Some among the people
were henotheists or worshipers of one god
as far exalted above the others and worthy
of all adoration, and perhaps some were even
monotheists. A remarkably clear knowledge
of ethical and religious truths was possessed
from very early times—truth in regard to
human conduct, sin, justification, immortality, and with all their nature worship even
in regard to God.

III. *The Sojourn of the Israelites in Egypt.*
1. *The descent into Egypt.* A grievous famine
prevailed throughout the whole known world,
or at least throughout that large part of it
about the eastern and southeastern shores of
the Mediterranean Sea, where dwelt a complex of nations cut off socially and, so far as
obtaining sufficient supplies for the necessities of life, economically from the mountains of Asia Minor and the rich valleys of
the Euphrates and Tigris (Gen. xli. 54; xlvii.
13). On occasion of this distress Joseph, who
had risen to authority at the court of Pharaoh
second only to that of the king, urged his
father and brethren to leave Canaan and
settle temporarily in Egypt (xlv. 9–11; xlvii.
4, 29, 30; xlviii. 21; l. 24). Accordingly Jacob
migrated with his tribe. It consisted of the
patriarch himself, his six sons and one daughter by Leah with twenty-five sons; his two sons
by Leah's maid with thirteen sons and one
daughter; his two sons by Rachel with twelve
sons, of which number three were already in
Egypt; and his two sons by Rachel's maid
with five sons (xlvi. 8–25). All the souls
which came with Jacob into Egypt, which
came out of his loins (even though perhaps
some were yet unborn, cp. Heb. vii. 9, 10),
were sixty-six souls (Gen. xlvi. 26). All the
souls of the house of Jacob which came into
Egypt first and last, including the head of
the house and Joseph with his two sons who
were born in Egypt, were seventy souls (ver.
27). This is also the enumeration of Ex. i. 5
(as in Gen. xlvi. 15, apparently exclusive of
Jacob, but in reality inclusive of him) and

Paintings from the Tomb of Khnemhotep about 1890 B.C., showing the migration of Asiatics into Egypt.

Deut. x. 22. The Septuagint, however, and Stephen who follows the Greek version (Acts vii. 14) reckon seventy-five. This result is due to the addition in Gen. xlvi. 20 of three grandsons and two great-grandsons of Joseph, whose names are obtained from Num. xxvi. 29 and 35 seq. The numerical correspondences of the register, a total of seventy, and the descendants of each maid precisely half those of her mistress (Leah 32, Zilpah 16, Rachel 14, Bilhah 7), suggest design, and can scarcely be altogether accidental. A comparison with Num. xxvi. leads to the belief that regard was had to the subsequent national organization in constructing this table, and that its design was to include those descendants of Jacob from whom permanent tribal divisions sprang, even if in a few instances they were still in the loins of the patriarch when he led his tribe into Egypt. The tribe of Israel settled in Goshen, and remained in and about this fertile region until the exodus (Gen. xlvii. 6, 11; Ex. viii. 22; ix. 26; xii. 37).

III. 2. *The sojourn as embedded in the national consciousness.* The descent of Jacob and his family into Egypt, their subsequent increase and enslavement, their sufferings and their exodus in a body, were recorded in their earliest historical document (Gen. xlvi. 4, 28–34; xlvii. 27; Ex. i. 9, 11, 15–22; ii. 11; xii. 31–37; xiii. 21). The feast of the passover, and to a less degree that of the tabernacles, bore testimony to the events, and kept the knowledge of them alive among the people. Psalmists pitched their songs of redemption and their hymns in celebration of Jehovah's might to its key, and from it prophets drew lessons. The standing types of the grievous oppression of the church and of God's redemptive power and love are Israel's bondage of old in Egypt and deliverance from that furnace of affliction. The tradition is not peculiar to one tribe, as though but a portion of the Hebrew folk had endured Egyptian slavery; it is not exclusively Judæan, but it is Ephraimite as well. The prophets of both kingdoms voice it—Isaiah, Micah, and Jeremiah, among the hills of Judah (Is. xi. 16; Mic. vi. 4; vii. 15; Jer. ii. 6; vii. 22), and Hosea and Amos in the kingdom of Samaria (Hos. ii. 15; viii. 13; ix. 3; xi. 1; xii. 9, 13; Amos ii. 10; iii. 1; ix. 7). The tradition is the common property of all Israel. The people as a whole had suffered Egyptian bondage.

III. 3. *The duration of the sojourn.* The biblical data are stated in the following terms: "He said unto Abraham, 'Thy seed shall be a stranger in a land that is not theirs, and shall serve them; and they shall afflict them 400 years . . . but in the fourth generation they shall come hither again'" (Gen. xv. 13–16). "The sojourning of the children of Israel, which they sojourned in Egypt, was 430 years" (Ex. xii. 40, R. V.); according to the Septuagint and Samaritan Pentateuch in this passage, the sojourning "in Egypt and in the land of Canaan was 430 years." God spake to Abraham "that his seed should sojourn in a strange land; and that they should bring them into bondage, and entreat them evil 400 years" (Acts vii. 6). "The law came 430 years after" the covenant (Gal. iii. 17).

These statements are interpreted to mean: (1) The children of Israel dwelt in Egypt 215 years. For the Seventy, either to remove an ambiguity or because their Hebrew manuscripts differed from the present Hebrew text, add the words "and in the land of Canaan" to the statement in Ex. xii. 40. Now from the date of the covenant with Abram, shortly after his arrival in Canaan, to the migration of his descendants into Egypt was about 215 years (Gen. xii. 4; with xxi. 5; xxv. 26; xlvii. 9), leaving 215 years for the sojourn of the children of Israel in Egypt. This statement is also made by Josephus, who says, "The Hebrews left Egypt 430 years after our forefather Abraham came into Canaan, but 215 years only after Jacob removed into Egypt" (Antiq. ii. 15, 2). In this statement he is following the Septuagint, but he nullifies his statement by saying elsewhere, "400 years did they spend under these labors" (Antiq. ii. 9, 1; War v. 9, 4; manifestly incorrect, for the Israelites were not *oppressed* for 400 years). But however Josephus may vacillate, Paul dates the law at Sinai 430 years after the covenant with Abram, and the genealogies give four generations between Jacob and the exodus, which may cover 215 years, but scarcely 400 years (Ex. vi. 16–20).

The biblical data are explained to mean (2) The children of Israel dwelt 430 years in Egypt. (1) The natural interpretation of Gen. xv. 13–16 requires this. (*a*) The statement is not that the Israelites should be afflicted 400 years, but that the entire sojourn as strangers in a land not theirs, where they shall be eventually brought into bondage, is 400 years. (*b*) The event is not to take place until after Abraham's death (ver. 15). (*c*) The four generations are equivalent to the aforementioned 400 years. In this passage, generation does not mean each succession of persons from a common ancestor, as it does in Ex. xx. 5; Job xlii. 16, but the age or period of a body of contemporaries, and this not in our modern sense of the average lifetime of all who pass the age of infancy, but the average period of the activity of any generation, and this is determined by the normal span of life. The generation lasts while any of its members survive (Ex. i. 6; Num. xxxii. 13; Judg. ii. 10; Ecc. i. 4). The period of a generation's activity may be judged from the length of the life of Isaac, 180 years; of Jacob, 147 years; of Levi, 137; of Kohath, 133; of Amram, 137; of Aaron, 123; of Moses, 120 (Gen. xxxv. 28; xlvii. 28; Ex. vi. 16, 18, 20; Num. xxxiii. 39; Deut. xxxiv. 7). Or the period of a generation's activity may be estimated from the record of three generations between the birth of Abraham and the descent into Egypt, when Jacob was still active, a period of 290 years. A generation was about 100 years. But are not just four generations registered—namely, Levi and Kohath, who came into Egypt with Jacob, Amram, Moses, and Moses' sons? A consecutive genealogy in Levi, Kohath, and Amram is admitted; but was Moses the son of Amram and Jochebed (Ex. vi. 20; 1 Chron. vi. 1-3)? A difficulty arises if the passage be so interpreted. (a) Amram and his brothers gave rise to the Amramites, Izharites, Hebronites, and Uzzielites; and these one year after the exodus amounted to 8600 males; that is, the grandfather of Moses had 8600 male descendants in the days of Moses, of whom 2750 were between the ages of 30 and 50 (Num. iii. 27; iv. 36). (b) In the parallel genealogy of the contemporaries of Moses Bezalel is seventh from Jacob and Joshua apparently eleventh (1 Chron. ii. 18-20; vii. 23-27). The language of Ex. vi. 20 does not necessarily, nor even evidently, mean that Amram and Jochebed were the immediate parents of Moses and Aaron. In Gen. xlvi. 18, great-grandsons of Zilpah are mentioned with others as sons who bore to Jacob. In Mat. i. 8 Joram is said to beget his great-great-grandson Uzziah. According to Gen. x. 15-18 Canaan begat nations. Where the birth of Moses is narrated in detail, he is not said to be the child of Amram and Jochebed (Ex. ii.). The reason for registering only four names in the genealogy of Moses and others (Ex. vi. 16-22) is that the first three names are official and give the tribe, family, and father's house to which Moses and Aaron belonged. The three names properly and at once classify Moses and Aaron. (2) 430 years for the sojourn is also the record of Ex. xii. 40. The statement does not include the sojourn of the patriarchs in Canaan, for (a) Abraham and Isaac were not sons of Israel, and (b) the verse in the Hebrew, Chaldee, etc., except Septuagint and Samaritan, makes no reference to Canaan. (3) A sojourn of 430 years best accounts for the number of the children of Israel at the exodus. (4) On the interpretation of the data as meaning that the sojourn lasted 430 years Paul's statement in Galatians can be accounted for. It is not his object to measure the exact time between the covenant and the law. His argument only requires him to prove that the law was given long after the covenant, and hence cannot disannul it. He proves it by citing the well-known period of the sojourn which intervened between the two events; the largest and most familiar single sum of years in the interval. He does not state that the law came exactly 430 years after the covenant; but he rather says that the law came, as we all know, 430 years after the covenant. It is indifferent whether he has the Hebrew or the Greek text in mind, and whether his Galatian readers refer to the Hebrew or to the Greek edition.

III. 4. *The multiplication of the Israelites during the sojourn.* (1) It has been pointed out (Keil) that if from the seventy souls who went down into Egypt there be deducted the patriarch Jacob, his twelve sons, Dinah, and Serah daughter of Asher, and also the three sons of Levi, the four grandsons of Judah and Asher, and those grandsons of Jacob who probably died without male offspring, inasmuch as their descendants are not named among the families of Israel (see Num. xxvi.), there will remain forty-one grandsons of Jacob (besides the Levites) who founded families; and if, furthermore, there be allowed but ten generations for the 430 years; nevertheless the forty-one men would increase to 478,224 males if each family averaged three sons and three daughters during the first six generations, and two sons and two daughters during the last four generations. These with the survivors of the ninth generation would amount to more than 600,000 men above twenty years of age. (2) It is a mistake to overlook the fact that the household of the patriarch included numerous servants (Gen. xxx. 43; xxxii. 5; xlv. 10), who were circumcised (Gen. xvii. 12, 13) and enjoyed full religious privileges (Ex. xii. 44, 48, 49, etc.), and with whom intermarriage was no degradation (Gen. xvi. 1, 2; xxx. 4, 9; Num. xii. 1; 1 Chron. ii. 34, 35).

III. 5. *The change of occupation during the sojourn.* When the Israelites settled in Goshen they were a comparatively small tribe, independent, and herdsmen. But after Joseph and the men of that generation died, a new king arose who knew not Joseph (Ex. i. 6-8). He saw the increasing numbers of the Israelites, and, fearing that they might ally themselves with the enemies of Egypt, took measures to render them a subject people and to check their increase. Taskmasters were placed over them, and rigorous service was exacted from them in the form of agriculture, brickmaking, and building (Ex. i. 11, 14; v. 6-8), while they still provided some at least of their own support by herding (ix. 4, 6; x. 9, 24; xii. 38).

III. 6. *The miracles wrought by Moses at the end of the sojourn.* The oppression of the Israelites lasted eighty years or more (Ex. vii. 7; cp. ii. 2 seq.). At length their cry came up unto God, and he sent Moses to deliver them (ii. 23 seq.). The humble ambassador of heaven was provided with miracles as his credentials. They were miracles; that is, in Scripture parlance, signs, wonders, and powers (Ps. lxxviii. 12, 43). They were wonderful, unusual, and intended to enforce attention. They were signs accrediting Moses as the messenger of God to the Israelites (Ex. iv. 8, 9, 30, 31; vi. 7) and to Pharaoh (iii. 20; iv. 21; vii. 3-5; viii. 22, 23). They were powers, not natural phenomena; for (1) design is apparent in them, and not the blindness of nature.

They form an orderly series; the one is in logical but not causal relation to its successor; they increase in severity, affording Pharaoh sufficient evidence at the outset of the divine authority of Moses, without inflicting unnecessary suffering upon the Egyptians; and when he refuses to let the Hebrews go, they become more intense. and bring ever-increasing pressure upon his obdurate heart until he finally yields. (2) A distinction was made, which nature does not make, between

ral in itself and as appears from the narrative, they retained their organization despite their enslavement. They did not amalgamate with the master race, but remained a distinct people and preserved the twelve great family divisions. By the end of the 430 years the families of the twelve sons had become twelve tribes, and the sons' sons, and in a few instances the sons' remoter descendants, had grown into large family connections. Accordingly, at the time of the exodus there was a people, Israel, divided into twelve tribes; and each tribe was subdivided into families or connections, which derived their names for the most part from the grandsons of Jacob (Ex. vi. 14 with Gen. xlvi. 9, and Num. xxvi. with Gen. xlvi.), and at the time of the second census numbered 57, without Levi; and each family connection into fathers' houses (Num. i. 2, 18, 20). Authority of various kinds was vested in (1) Princes by birth (Ex. xvi. 22), heads of the tribes or family connections (Num. i. 4, 16). (2) Elders, who were probably heads of tribes and families, and aged (Ex. iv. 29; xii. 21; xvii. 5-6). (3) Apparently also in priests (Ex. xix. 22, 24; perhaps cp. Ex. xxiv. 5). They were probably men out of the various tribes who were performing priestly functions for the Israelites; as Abraham, Isaac, and Jacob, as head of the family, had offered sacrifice. (4) The Egyptians had imposed further organization on the Israelites by setting officers (Ex. v. 6, 10, 19) over them; Hebrews (Ex. v. 15, 16), who had undoubtedly been appointed on the ground of their ability to direct. Through these various representatives Pharaoh and Moses communicated their will to all the people with dispatch. The children of Israel, grouped in tribes, families, and fathers' houses, officered and accustomed to obedience, were not an unwieldy horde, but a multitude with the organization of an army. They are fittingly called

Symbols of Upper Egypt (papyrus, left) and Lower Egypt (lotus) are featured on these columns.

the people of God and the Egyptians (viii. 22, 23; ix. 4, 25, 26; x. 22, 23; xi. 5-7; and cp. ix. 11; x. 6). (3) A pestilence might have slain a great number of the Egyptians in one night, but the tenth plague is a pestilence with a method. It is not a promiscuous death, the firstborn in every family of the Egyptians dies.

These signs, wonders, and powers belong to the first group of miracles recorded in Scripture. See MIRACLES.

III. 7. *The organization of the Israelites at the end of the sojourn.* The forefathers of the children of Israel had descended into Egypt as a family of twelve households, and had settled together in Goshen. As is quite natu-

the hosts or armies of the Lord, and it is significantly said that they went out of Egypt by their hosts (Ex. xii. 41).

III. 8. *The Pharaohs of the oppression and exodus*: Ramses II. is commonly regarded as the Pharaoh of the oppression, and Meneptah as the Pharaoh of the exodus.* This opin-

* In view of various references in the tablets of Tell el-Amarna to the Ḫabiri making war with the inhabitants of western Palestine in the days of Amenophis IV., and the similarity of this name to the word Hebrew, and the essential agreement of this date with the date of the exodus which Usher obtained from a study of the biblical data, certain recent writers are inclined

ion is based on the following considerations: (1) The Israelites had not obtained possession of Palestine in the days of Amenophis III. and IV.; for the country, whose condition at that time has been revealed by the tablets found at Tell el-Amarna, was broken up into petty governments, and under Egyptian suzerainty. Ramses II., moreover, and Ramses III., both of whom warred in Palestine, make no mention of the Israelites as being in the land; and the Hebrew records are silent as to an invasion of the country by these Egyptian monarchs. (2) In Ex. i. 11 it is noted that the children of Israel built for Pharaoh store cities, Pithom and Ramses. The site of

Model of an early Egyptian (Middle Kingdom) bakery.

Pithom has been identified and the ancient granaries uncovered. No remains have been found there of earlier date than the reign of Ramses II., and his name is inscribed on some of the stones. Apparently Pithom was built in the reign of Ramses II. It was Ramses II. also who erected a new town, with temples and shrines, adjacent to the ancient fortress at Zoan, and on this account the place was called Pa-Ramses, the city of Ramses. These correspondences with the Hebrew records indicate that Ramses II. was the Pharaoh of the oppression. (3) Meneptah, a son and successor of Ramses II., in an inscription in which he records his repulse of the Libyan invasion of his fifth year, closes with describing certain consequences of this victory. He mentions the ravaging of Pa-Kanana in southern Palestine, the capture of Ashkelon and Gezer in Philistia, the reduction of a town near Tyre, the spoiling of the people of Israel, and the widowhood of Khar, i. e. south-

to believe that Amen-hetep II., or Thothmes IV., was the Pharaoh of the exodus. The weighty objections to this theory are—1. Habiri is not the natural transliteration of 'Ibri, Hebrew, a word which begins with unpointed ain and short i. This objection, however, cannot be pressed; for a few words which begin with unpointed ain in Hebrew have initial guttural h in the tablets of Tell el-Amarna. 2. Ramses is a geographical designation (Ex. i. 11; xii. 37), and the theory in question is unable to explain how it could have been so in the days of Amen-hetep II. or Thothmes IV., years before the first Ramses ascended the throne of Egypt.

ern Palestine. The reference to the people of Israel has been plausibly explained as noting an attack on the children of Israel during their sojourn in the wilderness on the borders of southern Palestine. See PHARAOH. As already stated, Ramses III., who succeeded Meneptah after an interval, warred in Palestine, but does not mention the Israelites as being in the country. It is reasonable to believe that the Israelites left Egypt at the beginning of Meneptah's reign, but had not spent their forty years in the wilderness and arrived in Canaan by the reign of Ramses III. For the date of the exodus, see CHRONOLOGY.

E′hi. See AHIRAM.

E′hud [union].

1. A Benjamite, descended through Jediael (1 Chron. vii. 10).

2. A left - handed Benjamite, descended through Gera. He assassinated Eglon, king of Moab, then the oppressor of Israel, at Jericho. Fleeing to the hill country of Ephraim, he summoned the Israelites by sound of trumpet, put himself at their head, descended to the valley of the Jordan, seized the ford of the river, and slew 10,000 Moabites as they attempted to cross. He judged Israel for the remainder of his life, and kept the people true to Jehovah (Judg. iii. 15–iv. 1).

E′ker [one transplanted, a man of foreign descent settled in a place].

A man of Judah, a son of Ram, of the house of Jerahmeel (1 Chron. ii. 27).

Ek′ron [eradication].

The most northerly of the five chief Philistine cities (Josh. xiii. 3; 1 Sam. vi. 16, 17). It was assigned to Judah (Josh. xv. 45, 46), and afterwards to Dan (xix. 43); but the boundary line of Judah ran past it (xv. 11), and it was taken and possessed by the men of that tribe (Judg. i. 18). After a time it was recovered by the Philistines. When the people first of Ashdod and then of Gath became afraid to retain the ark of God, they sent it to Ekron, whence it was returned to Israel (1 Sam. v. 10). Samuel recovered Israel's border as far as Ekron (vii. 14); and the Philistines, fleeing when Goliath fell, were pursued to its gates (xvii. 52). Baal-zebub was worshiped there, a god Ahaziah king of northern Israel sought to consult (2 Kin. i. 2–16). Judgment was denounced against it and the other Philistine cities by the prophets (Jer. xxv. 20; Amos i. 8; Zeph. ii. 4; Zech. ix. 5, 7). In 701 B. C. it closed its gates against Sennacherib, but in vain. Alexander Balas, king of Syria, gave Ekron to Jonathan Maccabæus (1 Mac. x. 89). It still existed at the time of the Crusades. It is believed to be represented by the village of 'Akir, situated among fine gardens, 6 miles west of Gezer and 12 northeast from Azotus. Marks of antiquity are lacking, and the present village may be a short distance from the ancient site.

E'la, in A. V. Elah [terebinth or like tree]. The father of one of Solomon's purveyors (1 Kin. iv. 18).

El'a-dah, in R. V. Eleadah [God hath adorned].

A descendant of Ephraim (1 Chron. vii. 20).

E'lah [a large evergreen tree, like the ilex or terebinth].

1. A valley near Socoh in which Saul and the Israelites pitched, confronting the Philistines, just before the combat between David and Goliath (1 Sam. xvii. 2, 19; xxi. 9). Probably the wady es-Sunt, which is formed by the junction of three other valleys, and is about 14 or 15 miles west by south from Bethlehem. It is fertile and traversed by a stream. Wady es-Sunt means the valley of the acacia (*Acacia vera*), of which various trees exist in the valley.

2. A duke of Edom, named from his habitation (Gen. xxxvi. 41; 1 Chron. i. 52). See ELATH.

3. A son of Caleb, the son of Jephunneh (1 Chron. iv. 15).

4. A Benjamite, son of Uzzi (1 Chron. ix. 8).

5. The father of one of Solomon's purveyors. See ELA.

6. The son and successor of Baasha in the kingdom of Israel. He reigned part of two years. As he was drinking himself drunk in the house of his steward, in Tirzah, his capital, he was assassinated, with all his house, by Zimri, who commanded half his chariots. This fulfilled the prophecy made by Jehu, the son of Hanani, to Baasha. That it did so in no way justified the murderous deed (1 Kin. xvi. 6, 8–10).

7. The father of Hoshea, king of Israel (2 Kin. xv. 30; xvii. 1; xviii. 1).

E'lam [high].

1. A son of Shem or the inhabitants of Elam, as being Semites or becoming incorporated with the Semites by conquest (Gen. x. 22; 1 Chron. i. 17). Elam was a region beyond the Tigris, east of Babylonia. It was bounded on the north by Assyria and Media, on the south by the Persian Gulf, on the east and southeast by Persia. The name is preserved in the Greek *Elumais*, the Latin *Elymais*. Its capital was Shushan or Susa, which gave rise to the name Susiana, though sometimes Elymais and Susiana are made the names of adjacent instead of identical regions. Elam was the seat of an ancient empire. In the time of Abraham, Chedorlaomer, king of Elam, was recognized as sovereign by Babylonian states, and laid even the country on the Jordan under tribute (Gen. xiv. 1–11). In the eighth and seventh centuries B. C., in Assyria was the dominant power in western Asia, Elam was its doughty opponent; but was subjugated after repeated campaigns of the Assyrians under Sargon, Sennacherib, and Ashurbanipal. Shushan was at length taken about 645 B. C. Elamites rendered military service to the Assyrians in the invasion

of Judah (cp. Is. xxii. 6). But before the close of the century, Elam was relieved of the Assyrian yoke through the capture of Nineveh by the Babylonians and the fall of the Assyrian empire. When Ezekiel prophesied the invasion of Egypt by Nebuchadnezzar, he mentioned a prior slaughter of the Elamites, perhaps by Nebuchadnezzar (Ezek. xxxii. 24). But Elam, joining with Media, was ultimately to capture Babylon (Isa. xxi. 2; cp. 9). To this conquest and restoration the following prophecies regarding Elam seem to refer (Jer. xlix. 34–39; Ezek. xxxii. 24, 25). Elam was a province and Shushan a capital of the Persian empire (Dan. viii. 2; Herodotus iii. 91; iv. 83; v. 49). On the return of the Jews from Babylon, Elamites, who had long before been forcibly settled in Samaria, joined with others in attempting to prevent the rebuilding of the temple and city of Jerusalem (Ezra iv. 9). Elamites were present on that day of Pentecost which was notable for the descent of the Holy Spirit (Acts ii. 9). Elam or Susiana, now Khuzistan, is a province of modern Persia.

2. The fifth son of Meshelemiah, a Korahite Levite, in the reign of David (1 Chron. xxvi. 3).

3. A Benjamite, a son of Shashak (1 Chron. viii. 24).

4. The head of a family of which 1254 individuals returned from Babylon with Zerubbabel (Ezra ii. 7; Neh. vii. 12), and 71 more with Ezra (Ezra viii. 7). Its representative signed the covenant in Nehemiah's time (Neh. x. 14).

5. The other Elam, of whom just as many descendants returned as of No. 4 (Ezra ii. 31; Neh. vii. 34).

6. A priest who took part in the dedication of the wall of Jerusalem (Neh. xii. 42).

El'a-sa, in A. V. Eleasa.

A place at which Judas Maccabæus once camped (1 Mac. ix. 5); probably the ruins Il'asa, which lie midway between the two Beth-horons.

El'a-sah [God hath made]. The Hebrew name is sometimes anglicized as Eleasah.

1. A son of Shaphan. He and Gemariah carried a letter from Jeremiah in Jerusalem to the exiles in Babylon (Jer. xxix. 3).

2. A son of Pashur, induced by Ezra to put away his foreign wife (Ezra x. 22).

E'lath and Eloth, the singular or plural being used indifferently; also Elah and El, other forms of the singular [terebinth or other large tree].

A town on the gulf of Akaba (Deut. ii. 8; 1 Kin. ix. 26), on the eastern border of the wilderness of Paran (Gen. xiv. 6). The caravan routes between southern Arabia and Egypt and Phœnicia passed its gates, making its possession valuable to an exactor of tribute. It was taken by Chedorlaomer from the Horites (Gen. xiv. 6). In it dwelt a duke of Edom (xxxvi. 41), and it constituted the southern limit of the Edomites (Deut. ii. 8). It doubtless fell into the hands of David (2 Sam. viii. 14; cp. 1 Kin. ix. 26; 2 Chron. viii. 17). After a time it reverted to the Edomites. Uzziah rebuilt it and restored it to Judah (2 Kin. xiv. 22; 2 Chron. xxvi. 2). It was afterwards captured by the Syrians and long remained in their power (2 Kin. xvi. 6). Elath, called in the Greek and Roman period Aila and Ælana, gave the name Ælanitic to the gulf of Akaba, at the northeastern corner of which it was situated. It was long the station of a Roman legion. It was once the seat of a Christian bishopric. It was taken and retaken during the Crusades. It is now called Ailah and 'Akaba, and consists merely of extensive mounds of rubbish.

El-be'rith. See BAAI-BERITH.

El-beth'-el [God of Bethel].
The name given by Jacob to an altar which he reared at Bethel, after his return from Mesopotamia. It commemorated the appearance of God to him there in a dream when he was fleeing to escape the consequences of his brother's wrath (Gen. xxxv. 7; cp. xxviii. 10 seq.). The sanctuary was named after the God to whom it was dedicated. Cp. EL-EL-OHE-ISRAEL.

El'da-ah [God hath called].
A son or tribe descended from Midian and related to Abraham (Gen. xxv. 4; 1 Chron. i. 33).

El'dad [God hath loved].
An elder and officer of the Israelites who was summoned with sixty-nine others to assist Moses in bearing the burden of government. Eldad and Medad for some reason failed to present themselves with the others at the tabernacle; nevertheless they, too, although absent in the camp, were filled like the others with the divine Spirit, who worketh when and where he will. Joshua was jealous for Moses' honor, which he feared would suffer because they had received the gift without the intervention of Moses; but Moses rejoiced, and only wished that the Lord would put his Spirit upon all his people (Num. xi. 26–29).

El'der.
An official who, so far as can be judged, had by virtue of his right as firstborn succeeded to the headship of a father's house, of a tribal family, or of the tribe itself (1 Kin. viii. 1–3; Judg. viii. 14, 16). When he was the head and representative of a tribe or of the larger tribal families the elder was an important prince. In the ordinary course of nature, only men of mature age came into these positions, hence the designation elder. Other peoples which were organized on the tribal system had elders, as the Midianites and Moabites (Num. xxii. 4, 7). The title designates high officials generally in Gen. l. 7. They exercised authority over the people (Deut. xxvii. 1; Ezra x. 8), and rep-

resented the nation in affairs of state (Ex iii. 18; Judg. xi. 5–11; 1 Sam. viii. 4), in extending honor to a distinguished guest (Ex. xviii. 12), in concluding covenants (2 Sam. v. 3), and in religious acts (Lev. iv. 13–15; Josh. vii. 6). A body of seventy elders assisted Moses in the government of the Israelites (Num. xi. 16, 24). Each town had its elders, who were probably the heads of the several family connections in the place and who administered its civil and religious affairs (Deut. xix. 12; xxi. 2; Ruth iv. 2–11; 1 Sam. xi. 3; Ezra x. 14). These functions were still performed by the elders at the time of the Roman government of Judæa (Mat. xv. 2; xxi. 23; xxvi. 3, 47). See SYNAGOGUE and SANHEDRIN.

In the churches founded by the apostles elder or presbyter and bishop were interchangeable designations (Acts xx. 17 with 28, R. V.; Titus i. 5, 7), though not strictly synonymous. The former had primary reference to the dignity of the office, the latter to its duties. The distinction between elder or presbyter and bishop, as two separate orders of ministers, dates from the second century. The origin of the office of elder is not recorded, but elders existed practically from the beginning. In A. D. 44 they already existed in the church at Jerusalem (Acts xi. 30); Paul on his first missionary journey appointed elders in every church (xiv. 23), and they held office in churches not founded by Paul (Jas. v. 14; 1 Pet. v. 1). The office of elder in the Christian church was evidently suggested by the office of elder among the Jews, and was invested with similar authority. Elders were associated with the apostles in the government of the church (Acts xv. 2, 4, 6, 22, 23; xvi. 4; cp. xxi. 18). They were the bishops or overseers of the local churches (xx. 17, 28; Tit. i. 5), having the spiritual care of the congregation, exercising rule and giving instruction (1 Tim. iii. 5; v. 17; Tit. i. 9; Jas. v. 14; 1 Pet. v. 1–4; cp. Heb. xiii. 17), and ordaining to office (1 Tim. iv. 14). There were several bishops (Phil. i. 1) or elders (Acts xi. 30) in a local church. There is no intimation of any division of labor among them. As in the synagogue, so in the Christian church of apostolic times, preaching was not the peculiar function of the elders, nor was it restricted to them. They were, indeed, the regular pastors and teachers. Aptness to teach was an essential qualification for the office (1 Tim. iii. 2; Tit. i. 9). But any man who possessed the gift of prophecy or teaching exhorted (1 Cor. xii. 28–30: xiv. 24, 31).

In the government of Reformed churches the teaching elder is the minister, and the ruling elder is a layman who is an elder. The arrangement is convenient, but its existence in apostolic times is not universally admitted. Calvin interpreted 1 Tim. v. 17 as teaching two kinds of elders: first, those who both teach and rule, and second, those who rule only. But there is a wide dissent from this interpretation. It is urged that the apostle is speaking of two functions of the same office, the primitive elder having been, it is contended, both teacher and ruler. In the Apocalypse the elders are twenty-four in number, possibly with reference back to the twelve founders of tribes under the Jewish economy, and the twelve apostles under the Christian church (Rev. iv. 4, 10; v. 5, 6, 8, 14; vii. 11-13; xi. 16; xix. 4).

E'le-ad [God continueth].

A descendant, perhaps son, of Ephraim. He and his brother were killed by the people of Gath when attempting to carry away the cattle belonging to that Philistine town. Ephraim, who was alive at the time, greatly mourned his loss (1 Chron. vii. 20-22).

E-le-a'dah. See ELADAH.

E-le-a'leh.

A town rebuilt by the Reubenites (Num. xxxii. 3, 37). Later it fell into the hands of the Moabites (Is. xv. 4; xvi. 9; Jer. xlviii. 34). The ruins, now called el-'Al, are on top of a hill on the Roman road, scarcely 2 miles north of Heshbon. Tristram describes them as consisting of stone heaps with a single standing column.

E-le'a-sa. See ELASA.

E-le-a'sah [God hath made]. In Hebrew it is the same word as Elasah.

1. A descendant of Judah through Jerahmeel, but with Egyptian blood in his veins (1 Chron. ii. 39).

2. A descendant of Saul and Jonathan (1 Chron. viii. 37; ix. 43).

E-le-a'zar [God hath helped]. Grecized as Lazaros, in Latin Lazarus.

1. The third son of Aaron (Ex. vi. 23; Num. iii. 2) and father of Phinehas (Ex. vi. 25). With his brothers and his father he was consecrated a priest, and afterwards acted as such (Ex. xxviii. 1; Num. iii. 4; xvi. 37-40; xix. 3). He was not allowed to mourn when his elder brothers, Nadab and Abihu, were killed for offering strange fire (Lev. x. 6-20). He then became chief of the Levites, and second only to Aaron in priestly authority (Num. iii. 32). Before Aaron died on mount Hor, Eleazar, who had been directed to ascend the mountain with him, was invested with his sacred garments, and succeeded him in the high-priesthood (xx. 25-28; Deut. x. 6). He held this office during the remainder of Moses' life and the leadership of Joshua. He took a prominent part in distributing Canaan by lot among the several tribes (Josh. xiv. 1). He was buried in a hill belonging to his son Phinehas in mount Ephraim (xxiv. 33), and was succeeded by Phinehas (Judg. xx. 28; 1 Chron. vi. 4, 50).

2. A Levite, family of Merari, house of Mahli. Dying without sons, his daughters were taken to wife by their cousins (1 Chron. xxiii. 21, 22; xxiv. 28; cp. Num. xxxvi. 6-9).

3. A son of Abinadab. He was consecrated by the men of Kirjath-jearim to keep the ark when they nobly received it from Beth-shemesh after its restoration by the Philistines (1 Sam. vii. 1).

4. One of David's mighty men, a son of Dodo, the Ahohite (2 Sam. xxiii. 9; 1 Chron. xi. 12; cp. xxvii. 4 perhaps).

5. A priest, son of Phinehas. He assisted the high priest in the time of Ezra (Ezra viii. 33).

6. A son of Parosh, who was induced by Ezra to put away his foreign wife (Ezra x. 25).

7. A priest, one of those who acted as musicians at the dedication of the wall of Jerusalem in the time of Nehemiah (Neh. xii. 42).

8. Surnamed Avaran, of priestly descent, a son of Mattathias and brother of Judas the Maccabee (1 Mac. ii. 5). In the battle between Judas and the Syrians at Beth-zacharias, he boldly ran into the ranks of the enemy, crept under an elephant whose trappings indicated that it carried a royal rider, and thrust it in the belly. The beast in its fall crushed Eleazar to death (vi. 43-46).

9. An ancestor, perhaps great-grandfather, of Joseph, the husband of Mary (Mat. i. 15).

El-e-lo'he-Is'ra-el [God, the God of Israel]. The name given by Jacob to an altar which he erected near Shechem (Gen. xxxiii. 20).

E'leph [an ox].

A village of Benjamin (Josh. xviii. 28). Site unknown.

El'e-phant.

The English name for a genus of animals containing two recent species—*Elephas indicus*, the Indian, and *Elephas africanus*, the African elephant, with several others now extinct. Their tusks furnish ivory (1 Kin. x. 22, A. V. margin). The elephant was used in war (1 Mac. i. 17; iii. 34), each beast being in charge of an Indian driver, and bearing on its back a tower from which two, three, or four soldiers fought (1 Mac. vi. 37, where thirty-two is an obvious error; Livy xxxvii. 40). The entire body of elephants was under a master (2 Mac. xiv. 12). Before entering battle, it was customary to inflame them by the sight and even taste of wine (1 Mac. vi. 34; 3 Mac. v. 2).

E-leu'the-rus [free].

A river (1 Mac. xi. 7; Antiq. xiii. 4, 5) which flows from Lebanon and empties into the Mediterranean sea north of Tripoli (Pliny, Hist. nat. v. 17), and which formed the boundary between Palestine and Syria (1 Mac. xii. 30; Antiq. xv. 4, 1; Strabo xvi. 2, 12). It is now called Nahr el-Kebir.

El-ha'nan [God hath been gracious].

1. A son of Jair and perhaps a Bethlehemite, who slew [the brother of] Goliath of Gath (cp. 2 Sam. xxi. 19 with 1 Chron. xx. 5). The text of at least one passage, perhaps of both,

has become corrupt. The letters of "Bethlehemite Goliath," with the particle '*eth* between them, which stand together in the Hebrew text of Samuel, closely resemble those of "Lahmi the brother of Goliath."

2. A Bethlehemite, a son of Dodo, and one of David's thirty heroes of the second rank (2 Sam. xxiii. 24; 1 Chron. xi. 26).

E'li, I. [my God].

A word occurring in the utterance of Jesus on the cross, spoken in Aramaic, '*Eli*, '*Eli, lammah sh*e*baktani,* "My God, my God, why hast thou forsaken me?" (Mat. xxvii. 46; cp. Ps. xxii. 1). In Mark xv. 34, Eloi, an Aramaic synonym of Eli containing a different word for God, is used.

E'li, II. [probably elevation, height].

A high priest of the family of Ithamar (1 Sam. i. 9; 1 Kin. ii. 27 with 1 Chron. xxiv. 3, 6). He is said to have been the first of Ithamar's line to receive the office (Antiq. v. 11, 5; viii. 1, 3), but it is uncertain which priest of the other line he succeeded. Eli was also active as a judge of Israel. Being deeply pious, he had an essential qualification for his exalted offices. But there was one serious defect in his conduct: he did not deal firmly with his two sons, Hophni and Phinehas, when their behavior in the priestly office was scandalous (1 Sam. ii. 23–25, 29; iii. 13). Divine judgment was therefore denounced against him and his house by a prophet. Eli should see evil befall the sanctuary, his descendants should die in the flower of their age, his two sons should perish in one day, and a faithful priest should supersede Eli's descendants, from whom they should seek for subordinate priestly appointments that they might be fed (ii. 27–36). The message was confirmed by a similar revelation to young Samuel, which Eli received with resignation (iii. 11–18). Soon afterwards Hophni and Phinehas, as custodians of the ark, carried it to the field of battle, to aid the Israelites against the Philistines. Eli, now 98 years old and blind, being anxious for the ark, took his seat by the wayside to watch. A runner arrived from the scene of strife with the news of Israel's defeat, the death of Hophni and Phinehas, and the capture of the ark of God. On hearing that the ark of God had been taken by the enemy Eli fell backward from the seat and, being stout, broke his neck and expired (iv. 1–18). He had judged Israel forty years. Ahitub succeeded to the rank of high priest (xiv. 3); but with the death of Eli the office lost for a long time its importance, for the ark was in captivity and seclusion, and the tabernacle was no longer the place of Jehovah's gracious presence. Samuel the prophet was the religious leader of the people. The judgment against Eli's posterity was executed when Solomon deposed Eli's descendant Abiathar from the high priesthood, substituting Zadok in his room (1 Kin. ii. 35).

E-li'ab [God is a father].

1. The son of Helon, and the head of the tribe of Zebulun in the wilderness (Num. i. 9; ii. 7; vii. 24, 29; x. 16).

2. A Reubenite, son of Pallu and father of Dathan and Abiram (Num. xvi. 1, 12; xxvi. 8, 9).

3. A Levite, an ancestor of Samuel (1 Chron. vi. 27, 28). See ELIHU.

4. David's eldest brother. He was so tall and had so kingly a countenance that on seeing him Samuel exclaimed, "Surely the Lord's anointed is before him." But judged by the heart he was not worthy of the kingdom (1 Sam. xvi. 6, 7; xvii. 13). One defect which he had was his inability to appreciate the larger soul of David, his youngest brother (28, 29). His daughter Abihail married a son of David (2 Chron. xi. 18, R. V.).

5. A Gadite, of the heroic type who joined David at Ziklag (1 Chron. xii. 9).

6. A Levite, musician at the sanctuary in David's reign (1 Chron. xv. 20).

E-li'a-da, in A. V. once **Eliadah** (1 Kin. xi. 23) [God has known—*i. e.* kindly regarded].

1. A son of David, born at Jerusalem (2 Sam. v. 16; 1 Chron. iii. 8). Called also Beeliada (q. v.).

2. Father of Rezon of Zobah (1 Kin. xi. 23).

3. A Benjamite, one of Jehoshaphat's chief captains (2 Chron. xvii. 17).

E-li'ah. See ELIJAH 2 and 4.

E-li'ah-ba [God doth hide].

A Shaalbonite, one of David's mighty men (2 Sam. xxiii. 32; 1 Chron. xi. 33).

E-li'a-kim [God doth establish].

1. An ancestor of Christ. He lived before the captivity, and was descended from David through Nathan (Luke iii. 30, 31).

2. Son of Hilkiah. He was over king Hezekiah's household; and when Jerusalem had closed its gates against the Assyrians, he was one of three representatives of the king who were sent to confer with the rabshakeh of Sennacherib (2 Kin. xviii. 18, 26, 37; Is. xxxvi. 3, 11, 22). Next they were dispatched to lay the answer of the rabshakeh before Isaiah, and desire him to obtain divine direction in the great crisis which had arisen (2 Kin. xix. 2; Is. xxxvii. 2). The prophet so highly commended Eliakim, and made him such promises from God, as to suggest that he must be regarded as a type of the Messiah (Is. xxii. 20-25).

3. One of Josiah's sons, made king by Pharaoh-necho, who changed his name to Jehoiakim (2 Kin. xxiii. 34; 2 Chron. xxxvi. 4).

4. One of the priests who officiated at the dedication of the wall of Jerusalem (Neh. xii. 41).

5. A descendant of Zerubbabel and an ancestor of Christ (Mat. i. 13).

E-li′am [God is one of the family].

Father of Bath-sheba (2 Sam. xi. 3); by transposition of the constituent parts of the name called Ammiel (1 Chron. iii. 5). Perhaps he was David's mighty man of this name, the son of Ahithophel (2 Sam. xxiii. 34).

E-li′as. See ELIJAH.

E-li′a-saph [God hath added].

1. The head of the tribe of Gad in the wilderness (Num. i. 14; ii. 14; vii. 42).

2. A Levite, the son of Lael, and prince of the Gershonites during the wilderness wandering (Num. iii. 24).

E-li′a-shib [God hath restored].

1. The ancestor from whom the eleventh priestly course took its name (1 Chron. xxiv. 12).

2. A Levite and singer whom Ezra induced to put away his foreign wife (Ezra x. 24).

3 and 4. Two men, a son of Zattu and a son of Bani, similarly persuaded by Ezra (Ezra x. 27, 36).

5. The high priest, the second in succession from Jeshua (Neh. xii. 10). He lived in the time of Nehemiah, and with the priests rebuilt the sheepgate of Jerusalem (iii. 1, 20, 21). As high priest he could assign chambers in the temple to whomsoever he pleased (Ezra x. 6). He was allied by marriage with Tobiah the Ammonite, and his grandson was son-in-law of Sanballat (Neh. xiii. 4, 28). Not being strict in regard to the separation of Jew and gentile, he even assigned a chamber of the temple to Tobiah (5).

6. A son of Elioenai, a descendant of Zerubbabel (1 Chron. iii. 24).

E-li′a-thah [God hath come].

A son of Heman, and a musician in the reign of David (1 Chron. xxv. 4, 27).

E-li′dad [God hath loved].

A prince of the tribe of Benjamin at the time when the Israelites were encamped at Shittim on the eve of entering the promised land. He was appointed a member of the commission to divide the land among the tribes (Num. xxxiv. 21).

E-li′e-ho-e′nai, in A. V. **Elihoenai** [to Jehovah are my eyes]. See also ELIOENAI.

1. A Korhite porter, the son of Meshelemiah (1 Chron. xxvi. 3). A. V. has substituted the variant form Elioenai.

2. A son of Zerahiah. He with 200 followers accompanied Ezra from Babylon (Ezra viii. 4).

E-li′el [God is God].

1. A Levite, family of Kohath, and an ancestor of Samuel the prophet (1 Chron. vi. 34). See ELIHU.

2. A Mahavite, one of David's mighty men (1 Chron. xi. 46).

3. Another of David's heroes (ver. 47).

4. One of the Gadites who came to David at Ziklag (1 Chron. xii. 11).

5. A Levite, a son of Hebron. He lived in David's time (1 Chron. xv. 9, 11).

6. A Benjamite, a son of Shimhi (1 Chron. viii. 20).

7. Another Benjamite, a son of Shashak (1 Chron. viii. 22).

8. A chief man of the half-tribe of Manasseh east of the Jordan (1 Chron. v. 24).

9. An overseer of the tithes and offerings in the reign of Hezekiah (2 Chron. xxxi. 13).

E-li-e′nai [probably, to Jehovah are my eyes]. Probably a contraction of Elihoenai.

A Benjamite, a son of Shimhi (1 Chron. viii. 20).

E-li-e′zer [God is a helper].

1. A man of Damascus, the steward of Abraham (Gen. xv. 2; cp. xxiv. 2).

2. The younger son of Moses (Ex. xviii. 4; 1 Chron. xxiii. 15, 17).

3. A Benjamite, family of Becher (1 Chron. vii. 8).

4. A son of Zichri. He was a captain over the Reubenites in David's reign (1 Chron. xxvii. 16).

5. A priest who blew the trumpet before the ark in David's reign (1 Chron. xv. 24).

6. A prophet, son of Dodavah of Mareshah. He predicted the shipwreck of Jehoshaphat's vessels because he had joined with Ahaziah, of Ahab's family (2 Chron. xx. 37).

7. One of those whom Ezra sent for Levites, when it was found that there were few of them among the returning exiles (Ezra viii. 16).

8, 9, and 10. Three men, one a priest, one a Levite, and one a son of Harim, whom Ezra induced to put away their foreign wives (Ezra x. 18, 23, 31).

11. An ancestor of Christ who lived between the time of David and the captivity (Luke iii. 29).

E-li-ho-e′nai. See ELIEHOENAI.

E-li-ho′reph [God is a reward].

One of Solomon's scribes (1 Kin. iv. 3).

E-li′hu [he is God].

1. An Ephraimite, son of Tohu and an ancestor of Samuel the prophet (1 Sam. i. 1), apparently called also Eliab and Eliel (1 Chron. vi. 27, 34).

2. David's eldest brother, called also Eliab (cp. 1 Sam. xvi. 6 with 1 Chron. xxvii. 18). See JESSE.

3. A Manassite captain who with others joined David on his way to Ziklag (1 Chron. xii. 20).

4. A doorkeeper during David's reign, of the family of Obed-edom (1 Chron. xxvi. 7).

5. One of Job's friends, a Buzite, the son of Barachel (Job xxxii.–xxxvii.).

E-li′jah; in A. V. twice **Eliah** (1 Chron. viii. 27; Ezra x. 26); in A. V. of N. T. **Elias,** which is the Hebrew word transliterated into Greek and provided with a Greek termination [my God is Jehovah].

1. One of the greatest of the prophets. He was a Tishbite, having been born perhaps at

Tishbeh in Galilee; but he dwelt in Gilead (1 Kin. xvii. 1); see TISHBITE. He wore a garment of skin or of coarse camel-hair, which was girt about his loins with a leather girdle (2 Kin. i. 8; 1 Kin. xix. 13). When Ahab, influenced by his wife Jezebel of Tyre, had given himself to the worship of the Tyrian god Baal, Elijah suddenly appeared upon the scene. He presented himself before the erring king, and predicted a drought of indefinite duration as a penalty for the rejection of Jehovah. On account of the famine he retired first to the brook Cherith, where he was providentially fed by ravens; see RAVEN. When the brook became dry he went to Zarephath on the coast of the Mediterranean north of Tyre. A widow trusted God and shared her last cake with Elijah. God saw to it that her jar of meal and cruse of oil did not fail until the famine was ended; and when her son died he was restored to life at the prayer of the prophet (1 Kin. xvii. 1-24; Luke iv. 24-26). After many days, in the third year (1 Kin. xviii. 1; Luke iv. 25; Jas. v. 17), Elijah was directed to show himself to Ahab. Then followed the scene at mount Carmel. The priests of Baal endeavored to secure evidence of Baal's divinity, but failed. Then Elijah gathered the people about an ancient altar of the Lord, which had probably been erected by pious Israelites of the north whom the defection of the ten tribes prevented from worshiping at Jerusalem. It had been thrown down. Elijah repaired it, taking twelve stones for the purpose, thus silently testifying that the division of the twelve tribes into two kingdoms was at variance with the divine will. To obviate every possibility of fraud, he made the people drench the sacrifice and the altar with water. Then he cried to the Lord. Fire fell, and consumed the sacrifice and destroyed the altar. Jehovah had attested his existence and his power. Baal's prophets, proven to be impostors, were taken down to the brook Kishon, at the foot of the mountain, and slain at Elijah's bidding (1 Kin. xviii. 1-40; cp. Deut. xvii. 2-5; xiii. 13-16). The people had acknowledged Jehovah and obeyed Jehovah's prophet, and the token of God's returning favor was seen in the gathering clouds of rain; and the prophet, to do honor to the king as ruler of a realm now professedly the kingdom of God, girded up his loins and ran before the chariot of Ahab to the gate of Jezreel (41–46); see FORERUNNER. But Jezebel, furious at the destruction of her prophets, vowed the death of Elijah, who fled to mount Horeb. There, like Moses, he was divinely sustained for forty days and nights (Ex. xxiv. 18; xxxiv. 28; Deut. ix. 9, 18; 1 Kin. xix. 8), a foreshadowing of the similar incident in the life of Jesus (Mat. iv. 2; Luke iv. 2). Elijah was rebuked, sent back to duty, and told to anoint Hazael to be king of Syria and Jehu to be king of Israel, that they might be the scourge of God to idolatrous Israel, and Elisha to be prophet to chastise by words. Elijah cast his mantle upon Elisha, calling him to the work, and entrusted to him the further execution of the commission (1 Kin. xix. 1–21). When Jezebel had Naboth judicially murdered in order to obtain his vineyard for Ahab, Elijah met the king in the coveted plot of ground and denounced Jehovah's vengeance for the crime (xxi. 1–29). The death of Ahab at the battle of Ramoth-gilead was the beginning of the judgment which Elijah had uttered against the royal house (xxii. 1–40). When Ahab's son and successor Ahaziah, injured by a fall from a window, sent messengers to the idol temple at Ekron to ask whether he should recover from his hurt, Elijah stopped them and turned them back; and twice when a captain with fifty men was sent apparently to arrest him, he called fire from the sky which consumed them. The third captain begged for his life, and Elijah went with him to the king (2 Kin. i. 1–16). Finally the prophet obtained the honor, bestowed before only on Enoch (Gen. v. 24), of being translated to heaven without dying. A chariot and horses of fire appeared to him when he had gone with his attendant Elisha to the east of the Jordan, and, parting them asunder, took Elijah up in a whirlwind to heaven (2 Kin. ii. 1–12). The event seems to have occurred just before Jehoram of Israel ascended the throne (2 Kin. ii. with i. 18 and iii. 1) and during the reign of Jehoshaphat of Judah (iii. 11); yet Elijah wrote a document in which he addressed Jehoram of Judah, who indeed was a co-regent with Jehoshaphat, and threatened him with divine judgment, not only for sins committed during the lifetime of Jehoshaphat, but for murder which he committed after Jehoshaphat's death (2 Chron. xxi. 12; cp. 13 with 4). If Elijah was translated at the time indicated, he prophesied during his lifetime concerning future deeds of Jehoram, just as he foretold future acts of Hazael and Jehu (1 Kin. xix. 15–17). Less in accordance with the 'language of iii. 11 is the explanation that the account of Elijah's translation is inserted where it is in 2 Kings simply to complete the narrative of his public activity, and that Elijah was still alive when Elisha was with the army of Jehoshaphat in southern Judah, and was living when Jehoram became sole king. The last two verses of the O. T. predict that God will send Elijah before the coming of the great and dreadful day of the Lord (Mal. iv. 5, 6). The N. T. explains that the reference is to John the Baptist, who was like the Tishbite in humble dress and appearance (Mat. iii. 4; Mark i. 6), in fidelity and in work (Mat. xi. 11–14; xvii. 10–12; Mark ix. 11–13; Luke i. 17). There are those, however, who contend that while John appeared in the spirit and power of Elijah, the O. T. prophet is yet to come, in person, before the second advent of Christ. Elijah appeared on the mount of Transfiguration as the representative of the O. T. prophecy to do honor to Jesus, its theme (Mat. xvii. 4; Mark ix. 4; Luke ix. 30); and his ascension, to which there was nothing analogous in the history of John the Baptist, doubtless foreshadowed that of our risen Lord.

The miracles which were wrought during the ministry of Elijah belong to the second of the four miracle periods of redemptive history, the period of the life and death struggle between the religion of Jehovah and Baal worship, when the adherence of the people of northern Israel to the faith of their fathers was at issue, and all other questions regarding religious observances sank to minor importance. See MIRACLE.

2. A Benjamite, a son of Jeroham, resident at Jerusalem (1 Chron. viii. 27, R. V.).

3. A priest, a son of Harim. He married a gentile wife (Ezra x. 21).

4. An Israelite induced by Ezra to put away his foreign wife (Ezra x. 26, R. V.).

E-li'ka.

A Harodite, one of David's mighty men (2 Sam. xxiii. 25).

E'lim [strong evergreen trees; such as oaks, terebinths, palms].

The second encampment of the Israelites after the passage of the Red Sea. It was between Marah and the desert of Sin, and had twelve springs of water and seventy palm trees (Ex. xv. 27; xvi. 1; Num. xxxiii. 9, 10). Two valleys, wady Ghurundel and wady Useit, or Waseit, are rivals for the honor of representing the ancient Elim. The former has more water, and is commonly regarded as the site. Both are fringed with trees and shrubs, though the adjacent parts of the desert are bare. The vegetation consists of palm trees, tamarisks, and acacias.

E-lim'e-lech [God is king].

A man of Bethlehem of Judah, the husband of Naomi (Ruth i. 1, 5).

E-li-o-e'nai [my eyes (are turned) toward Jehovah]. The Hebrew form is a legitimate variant of Eliehoenai.

1. A descendant of Simeon (1 Chron. iv. 36).

2. A Benjamite, family of Becher (1 Chron. vii. 8).

3. A Levite (1 Chron. xxvi. 3, A. V.). See ELIEHOENAI.

4 and 5. Two Hebrews, each of whom was induced by Ezra to put away his foreign wife (Ezra x. 22, 27).

6. A man of Judah, descended from Shecaniah (1 Chron. iii. 23, 24).

E-li'phal [God has judged].

One of David's mighty men, a son of Ur (1 Chron. xi. 35). Apparently called Eliphelet, the son of Ahasbai (2 Sam. xxiii. 34). See UR.

E-liph'a-let. See ELIPHELET.

E-li'phaz [God is strong].

1. A son of Esau, by Adah, one of his wives (Gen. xxxvi. 4).

2. A Temanite, one of Job's friends (Job ii. 11; iv. 1; xv. 1; xxii. 1; xlii. 7, 9). Probably a descendant of No. 1, who had a son Teman (Gen. xxxvi. 11).

E-liph'e-leh, in R. V. **E-liph'e-le-hu** [God is distinguished (as excellent)].

A Levite, a singer and a harper, who acted also as a porter when David brought up the ark from the house of Obed-edom (1 Chron. xv. 18, 21).

E-liph'e-let, in A. V. twice **Eliphalet** [God is deliverance].

1. A son born to David in Jerusalem (1 Chron. iii. 6). A correct Hebrew alternate form is Elpalet (1 Chron. xiv. 5).

2. Another son of David's, born also at Jerusalem, probably after the death of the former (2 Sam. v. 16; 1 Chron. iii. 8; xiv. 7).

3. A son of Ahasbai, and one of David's mighty men (2 Sam. xxiii. 34). Apparently called Eliphal in 1 Chron. xi. 35.

4. A descendant of Jonathan and of Saul (1 Chron. viii. 39).

5. A son of Adonikam. He returned with Ezra from Babylon (Ezra viii. 13).

6. A son of Hashum. Ezra induced him to put away his foreign wife (Ezra x. 33).

E-lis'a-beth [God is an oath, i. e., a covenant maker].

A godly woman, a daughter of the house of Aaron, and bearing the name of Aaron's wife (Ex. vi. 23, Elisheba). She became the wife of the priest Zacharias and the mother of John the Baptist. She bore him when she was of advanced years, his birth and mission having been communicated beforehand by an angel to her husband. Though of different tribes, she and Mary of Nazareth were kinswomen, and Mary visited Elisabeth at a village (probably Juttah) in the hill country of Judæa. Elisabeth, inspired by the Holy Ghost, welcomed Mary as the mother of the Lord (Luke i. 5–45).

E-li'sha, in A. V. of N. T. **El-i-se'us** which is an imitation of the Greek modification of the name [God is salvation].

One of the two great prophets of the older period of Israelite history who labored in the northern kingdom. He was the son of Shaphat, dwelt at Abel-meholah in the Jordan valley, and belonged to a family of means; twelve yoke of oxen plowed his father's fields. God appointed him to succeed Elijah (1 Kin. xix. 16, 19). Elijah found him plowing and cast his mantle over him. Elisha understood the significance of the act; went home, gave a farewell feast to the people, and returned to be the follower and assistant of Elijah (19–21). When Elijah went beyond the Jordan to be translated to heaven, Elisha kept by him; and when told to ask a parting gift, had the wisdom to petition for a double portion of Elijah's spirit. He saw the fiery chariot bear his master away, and taking the mantle which had fallen from Elijah, struck the Jordan with it, which divided and permitted him to cross to its western side (2 Kin. ii. 1-18). His subsequent life was marked by a series of miracles, some of knowledge, others of power, expressly wrought in the name of the Lord. They belong to the second group of miracles in redemptive history. They occurred at a time when the religion of Jehovah was engaged in a desperate struggle for existence against Baal worship, and, like the miracles wrought by Elijah, were intended to accredit the prophet and to attest Jehovah to be the living God. The miraculous power was so much under Elisha's control that apparently he could exercise it at discretion; and he used it largely, as did Christ, in simple deeds of kindness. In the name of the Lord he healed with salt the waters of the spring at Jericho (19-22). He pronounced Jehovah's curse on lads who mocked in him the prophet of the Lord, and two bears presently tore forty-two of them (23-25). He foretold the success of the expedition against Moab (iii. 11-27), secured the increase of a widow's oil (iv. 1-7), predicted to a Shunammite woman the birth of a son, and at his prayer that son was restored to life when he had died (8-37). He named an antidote to a poisonous plant in the pot in which food was being cooked for the prophets (38-41). As prophet of the Lord he fed a hundred men with twenty barley loaves and a few ears of corn (42-44), told Naaman to wash in the Jordan and he would be healed of his leprosy (v. 1-19), and foretold its transference to Gehazi as a punishment of lying and covetousness (20-27). He made an iron ax head, that had fallen into the river, float to the surface (vi. 1-7). He informed the king of Israel of the movements and intentions of his Syrian rival (8-12). At his prayer, the Lord revealed to the prophet's servant horses and chariots of fire surrounding them for their protection (13-17), and caused blindness to fall on the Syrian emissaries sent to arrest them (17-23). He intimated, without being told it, that a messenger from the king of Israel was at the door to take his life (vi. 32, 33). He predicted great plenty and consequent cheapness of food in Samaria, while it was at famine prices during a siege; adding, however, that an unbelieving lord who discredited the prediction should not participate in the boon, and he did not, for he was trampled to death in a crowd (vii. 1-20). He informed Ben-hadad, king of Syria, of his approaching death (viii. 7-15). He declared the destruction of Ahab and his whole house, and sent a young prophet to anoint Jehu to execute the threatened judgment (ix. 1-x. 28). He predicted three victories over the Syrians (xiii. 14-19). Finally, after his death, a man hastily cast into the same sepulcher was at once restored to life on touching the prophet's bones (20, 21).

E-li'shah.
The descendants of Javan collectively, who inhabited the country of Elishah (Gen. x. 4). This country was maritime, and exported blue and purple dye stuffs (Ezek. xxvii. 7). It has been variously explained as Hellas, Elis, Æolis, Italy, and Carthage. Philological objections weigh against the first four; and there is no proof that Carthage was ever called Elissa, and this town was besides in Africa. Alishiya, whose king exchanged correspondence with the Pharaohs of the eighteenth Egyptian dynasty, has been suggested; a country hard by Cilicia. This identification commends itself.

E-lish'a-ma [God hath heard].
1. Son of Ammihud, and prince of the Ephraimites at the beginning of the sojourn in the wilderness (Num. i. 10; ii. 18), and ancestor of Joshua (1 Chron. vii. 26).
2. A man of Judah, descended through Jerahmeel and Sheshan (1 Chron. ii. 34, 41).
3. A son of David, born at Jerusalem (1 Chron. iii. 6). See ELISHUA.
4. Another son of David (2 Sam. v. 16; 1 Chron. iii. 8).
5. A priest, one of those sent by Jehoshaphat to teach in the cities of Judah (2 Chron. xvii. 8).
6. A prince and scribe in the reign of king Jehoiakim (Jer. xxxvi. 12, 20, 21), and probably identical with the grandfather of Ishmael of the seed royal who murdered Gedaliah, the governor of Judæa under the Babylonians (2 Kin. xxv. 25; Jer. xli. 1).

E-lish'a-phat [God hath judged].
One of the captains of hundreds who supported Jehoiada in the revolt against Athaliah (2 Chron. xxiii. 1).

E-lish'e-ba [God is an oath].
Daughter of Amminadab, and sister of Nahshon. She became the wife of Aaron, and the mother of Nadab, Abihu, Eleazar, and Ithamar (Ex. vi. 23).

E-lish'u-a [God is salvation].
A son of David, born at Jerusalem (2 Sam. v. 15; 1 Chron. xiv. 5). In the corresponding position in the third list of David's sons (1 Chron. iii. 6) the name Elishama appears. In view of the reading of the other catalogues, and since the name Elishama was borne by another of David's sons, mentioned farther on in all three lists, it is reasonable to believe that Elishama in 1 Chron. iii. 6 is a misreading of Elishua, as it is a quite intelligible one.

E-li'ud [perhaps from Hebrew *'eliy'hud*, God of Judah or of the Jews, a name which does not occur in the O. T.]
Son of Achim, and father of Eleazar, in the ancestry of Christ (Mat. i. 14, 15).

E-liz'a-phan or **Elzaphan**, the forms being interchangeable in Hebrew [God hath concealed].
1. Son of Uzziel, and chief of the Koha-

thites in the wilderness (Ex. vi. 18, 22; Num. iii. 30). He assisted in removing the bodies of Nadab and Abihu from the camp (Lev. x. 4). A new father's house was derived from him (1 Chron. xv. 8; 2 Chron. xxix. 13).

2. Son of Parnach, and prince of the tribe of Zebulun in the wilderness (Num. xxxiv. 25).

E-li'zur [God is a rock].

The prince of the Reubenites in the wilderness (Num. i. 5; ii. 10).

El'ka-nah [God hath created].

1. A Levite, family of Kohath, house of Izhar, division of Korah. He was brother of Assir and Abiasaph (Ex. vi. 24; 1 Chron. vi. 23 and perhaps 25).

2, 3, and 4. Three Levites, links in one genealogy, one the son of Joel, the second the son of Mahath, and the third the son of Jeroham. Like the preceding, they were of the family of Kohath, house of Izhar, Korhite division; but they were descended from Abiasaph (1 Chron. vi. 36, son of Joel; 26, 35, of Mahath; 27, 34, and 1 Sam. i. 1, of Jeroham). The last of the three belonged to the hill country of Ephraim, lived at Ramathaim of the Zophites, was the husband of Hannah and Peninnah, and the father of Samuel (1 Sam. i. 1; ii. 11, 20).

5. Another Korhite who had dwelt in Benjamin, perhaps because the Korhites were doorkeepers of the tabernacle which was pitched in Benjamin (1 Chron. ix. 19), and who joined David at Ziklag (1 Chron. xii. 6).

6. A doorkeeper for the ark during the reign of David (1 Chron. xv. 23).

7. A high dignitary at the court of Ahaz, second only to the king (2 Chron. xxviii. 7).

8. A Levite who dwelt in a village of the Netophathites (1 Chron. ix. 16).

El'kosh-ite.

A citizen of Elkosh (Nah. i. 1). The tradition that Alkush, two days' journey north of Nineveh, was the birth and burial place of Nahum is late, being unknown to early Arabian and Syrian writers; and the contents of the book of Nahum are against it. A credible, but unproven, identification is with the town Elcesi or Helcesæi in Galilee, which was pointed out to Jerome. According to another tradition, preserved by Epiphanius, Elkosh lay to the south of Begabar, in Syriac Bêt Gabrê, that is, Beit Jibrin in the lowland of Judah.

El'la-sar.

A place in or near Babylonia (Gen. xiv. 1, 9). See ARIOCH.

Elm.

An erroneous rendering of the Hebrew word 'Elah in Hos. iv. 13, A. V. The word is properly translated "oak" in Gen. xxxv. 4 and Judg. vi. 11, 19, with terebinth on the margin of R. V.

El-ma'dam, in A. V. **Elmodam.**

An ancestor of Christ, who lived before the ᵻxile (Luke iii. 28).

El'na-am [God is pleasantness].

The father of certain valiant men in David's army (1 Chron. xi. 46).

El'na-than [God hath given].

1. The father of Nehushta, mother of king Jehoiachin (2 Kin. xxiv. 8). He dwelt at Jerusalem, and was probably the prince Elnathan, son of Achbor (Jer. xxvi. 22; xxxvi. 12, 25).

2, 3, and 4. Three Levites, the first two chief men, and the third a man of understanding, sent for by Ezra to the brook Ahava (Ezra viii. 16).

E-lo'i [Aramaic, my God]. See ELI, I.

E'lon [an oak or terebinth].

1. A Hittite, whose daughter Esau married (Gen. xxvi. 34; xxxvi. 2).

2. A son of Zebulun, and founder of a tribal family (Gen. xlvi. 14; Num. xxvi. 26).

3. A Zebulonite who judged Israel for ten years, and was buried at Aijalon, in Zebulun (Judg. xii. 11, 12).

4. A village of Dan (Josh. xix. 43). Not identified; for Beit Ello, 8 miles northwest by west from Bethel, is not in the limits of the ancient territory of Dan.

E'lon-beth-ha'nan [Elon of Beth-hanan].

A town in Dan, to judge from its associates (1 Kin. iv. 9), perhaps identical with Elon. Its site is not Beit 'Anân, 8½ miles northwest of Jerusalem. This place is in Benjamin, a different tax district (18), and the name is differently spelled.

E'loth. See ELATH.

El'pa-al [God is a reward].

A man of Benjamin, son of Shaharaim, and head of a father's house (1 Chron. viii. 11, 12, 18).

El'pa-let, in R. V. **Elpelet.** See ELIPHELET.

El-pa'ran. See ELATH.

El'te-keh [perhaps, God is a dread].

A town of Dan assigned to the Levites (Josh. xix. 44; xxi. 23). and mentioned in the records of Sennacherib likewise in connection with Timnah and Ekron. In 701 B. C. Sennacherib destroyed the town, and in its vicinity the decisive battle between the Assyrians and Egyptians was fought. Not identified; certainly not Beit Likia, 2 miles south of the Nether Beth-horon.

El'te-kon [God is firmness].

A village in the hill country of Judah (Josh. xv. 59). Exact site unknown.

El'to-lad [birth, race].

A town in the extreme south of Judah (Josh. xv. 30), assigned to the Simeonites (xix. 4). Called in 1 Chron. iv. 29 simply Tolad, with omission of what is either the word for God or the Arabic article. Exact site unknown.

E'lul.

The sixth month of the year (Neh. vi. 15; 1 Mac. xiv. 27), approximately September.

E-lu'zai [perhaps, God is my strength].
One of the valiant men who came to David
to Ziklag (1 Chron. xii. 5).

El-y-ma'is. See ELAM.

El'y-mas [apparently from Arabic *'alim*,
learned].
A Jewish impostor, Bar-jesus by name,
which means son of Jesus or Joshua, who
pretended to learn the future through sorcery. Paul encountered him in Paphos, a
town of Cyprus, during his first missionary
journey. He sought to turn from the faith
Sergius Paulus, the Roman deputy or proconsul of the island, who seemed disposed to
accept the doctrine of Paul and seek for baptism. The apostle, therefore, severely rebuked the sorcerer and struck him with temporary blindness, the miracle removing the
last doubt which the proconsul had as to the
claims of Christian truth on his acceptance
(Acts xiii. 6–12).

El'za-bad [God hath bestowed].
1. One of the valiant Gadites who came to
David (1 Chron. xii. 12).
2. A Levite of the family of Obed-edom,
and a doorkeeper at the house of the Lord
(1 Chron. xxvi. 7).

El'za-phan. See ELIZAPHAN.

Em-balm'.
To attempt to preserve a dead body from
decay by the use of sweet spices. The Hebrews seldom embalmed their dead (Gen. l.
2, 26; cp. 2 Chron. xvi. 14; John xix. 39), but
the art of embalming was practiced by the
Egyptians from very early times. The em-
balmers were a numerous guild, who dwelt
at the cemeteries. They were divided into
three classes—the first made the incision in
the body, the second handled the spices, and
the third conducted the religious ceremonies
when the body was placed in the tomb. By
the time of the eighteenth dynasty, shortly
before the time of Moses, they had brought
their art to great perfection. The brain was
drawn through the nose with an iron hook
and replaced with spices. The entrails were
removed, and the abdominal cavity was
washed out by the injection of palm wine,

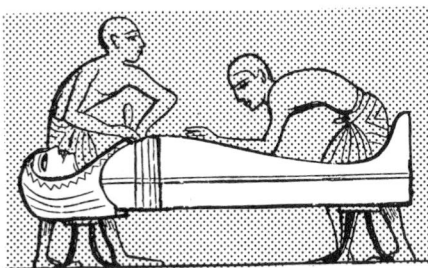

Egyptian embalming.

and then filled with bruised myrrh, cassia,
cinnamon, and other spices. Next the whole

body was plunged in natron or, more exactly,
subcarbonate of soda, and left in it for
seventy days. Then it was rolled in linen
bandages only three or four inches wide, but
of the extraordinary length of 700 or even
1000 yards. Gum Arabic was used to keep
the bandages in their place, and finally the
corpse, now mummified, was placed in a
case of wood or cartonnage, made in the shape
of a man, and carved and painted to represent the deceased person. It was often enclosed in a second or outer case of wood
or in a stone sarcophagus. A less expensive
method required no incision; the intestines
were dissolved by an injection of oil of cedar.
In the case of the poor, the abdomen was
merely purged and steeped in natron (Herod.
ii. 85–88, fully confirmed by Egyptian records
and mummies). According to the Sicilian
historian Diodorus, the interment of a rich
man cost the relatives the equivalent of about
$1200. A second-rate embalmment cost about
$400, and there was a much cheaper kind
for the common people. Embalming ceased
about A. D. 700. Many mummies are in the
British and other museums. Occasionally
one is unrolled, but it tends to fall to pieces
when exposed to the air.

Em-broid'ery.
Ornamentation by raised figures of needle-
work, executed with colored silks, gold or
silver thread, or any similar material differing from that of the original cloth. Bezaleel
and Aholiab were able to practice, among
other arts, that of embroidering in blue,
purple, scarlet, and fine linen (Ex. xxxv. 35;
xxxviii. 23). The screens for the door of the
tabernacle and the gate of the court (Ex.
xxvi. 36; xxvii. 16) and the girdle of the
high priest (xxviii. 39, R. V.; xxxix. 29) were
embroidered. The wealthy often wore embroidered garments (Judg. v. 30; Ps. xlv. 14).

E'mek-ke'ziz, in A. V. valley of **Keziz** [a
vale cut off or vale of fissure].
A town of Benjamin, evidently in a valley
and apparently near Jericho and Beth-hoglah
(Josh. xviii. 21). Scarcely to be connected
with wady el-Kaziz, a branch of the Kidron,
which seems to lie too far west and south.

Em'er-ald [Greek *smaragdos*].
1. The rendering of the Hebrew *Nophek*.
It was the first stone in the second row of
those on the Jewish high priest's breastplate
(Ex. xxviii. 18; xxxix. 11). The Syrians
imported precious stones of this kind into
Tyre (Ezek. xxvii. 16), and the Tyrians used
them for ornaments (xxviii. 13). The exact
stone intended is doubtful. It may be the
carbuncle (R. V. margin; cp. Septuagint).
2. The rendering of the Greek *Smaragdos*,
meaning a precious stone of a light green
color. The name was perhaps applied to any
green crystallized mineral. It was used for
signets (Ecclus. xxxii. 6); a rainbow is likened
to it (Rev. iv. 3); it was to be the fourth
foundation in the New Jerusalem (xxi. 19;

cp. Tobit xiii. 16). The emerald is a variety of beryl, distinguished by its color, which is bright green, from typical beryl, which is pale green, passing into light blue, yellow, or white. While the beryl is colored by iron, the emerald is colored by chromium. Anciently it was found in Cyprus, in Egypt, and in the mountains of Ethiopia.

Em'e-rods [a corrupted form of hemorrhoids].

Piles; external or internal tumors in the anal region, formed of dilated blood vessels (Deut. xxviii. 27). They were inflicted on the Philistines of Ashdod and Ekron, to compel them to send back the ark which they had captured (1 Sam. v. 6; vi. 11).

E'mim, in A. V. **Emims,** a double plural.

The ancient inhabitants of territory afterwards occupied by the Moabites. They were tall as the Anakim, and were once a numerous and powerful people (Deut. ii. 9–11). Chedorlaomer smote them in the plain of Kiriathaim (Gen. xiv. 5).

Em-man'u-el. See IMMANUEL.

Em'ma-us.

1. A village 60 furlongs from Jerusalem, a distance which could be traversed on foot between the hour for supper and the time of an evening meeting (Luke xxiv. 13, 29, 33; cp. Mark xvi. 14: John xx. 19). Vespasian located 800 veterans at " Emmaus distant sixty [according to another reading, thirty] furlongs from Jerusalem" (War vii. 6, 6). The Talmud states that Moza is Colonia. Kubeibeh, meaning the little dome, 7 miles northwest of Jerusalem on the Roman road, was pointed out to the Crusaders as the site of Emmaus. In the vicinity was the town of Mozah (Josh. xviii. 26). Three miles to the south of Kubeibeh is Kulonieh, that is colony, whose distance from Jerusalem is 4 miles or more according to the road followed. Probably, therefore, the site of Emmaus is to be found either at Kubiebeh or Kulonieh, or in the intervening country. The distance and tradition since the time of the Crusaders point to Kubeibeh; the Roman colony to which Emmaus was assigned may have left its name attached to a village in the southern part of its possessions. Conder's suggestion of the ruin Khamaseh, 8 miles southwest of Jerusalem, is not happy. The distance suits, but the name does not readily; for only rarely does the smooth breathing, which appears in the Greek form of Emmaus, represent the strong guttural ḥ, in Arabic ḫ, *i. e.* kh (cp. Huldah and Hermon).

2. A walled town of some note 18 miles, or 160 stades, westward from Jerusalem by a circuitous Roman road (1 Mac. iii. 40; ix. 50; War ii. 20, 4). Now 'Amwas.

Em'mor. See HAMOR.

E'na-im [two springs].

A town on the road from Adullam to Timnath [Gen. xxxviii. 14, 21, in A. V. open).

E'nam [place of fountains].

A village in the lowland of Judah (Josh. xv. 34); probably identical with Enaim.

E'nan [having eyes, seeing].

The father of the prince of the tribe of Naphtali in the days of Moses (Num. i. 15)

En-camp'ment. See CAMP.

En-chant'er.

One who practices any form of enchantment. In R. V. of Daniel (ii. 2) it is the rendering of the Aramaic *'Ashshaphim*, and denotes conjurers and exorcists who used incantations and pronounced spells for the purpose of securing the aid of evil spirits or of freeing the supposed victims of evil spirits from their torments.

En-chant'ment.

The practice of magical arts or the utterance of certain words whereby the aid of evil spirits is invoked, in order to produce supernatural effects over human beings, dangerous animals, or nature generally. Enchantment is not always distinguished from divination in the English versions (Num. xxiii. 23; xxiv. 1; and 2 Kin. xvii. 17, where enchantment is rather omen; and A. V. of Jer. xxvii. 9). Under enchantment are properly included magic (Ex. vii. 11), conjuration, exorcism (Dan. ii. 2, in A. V. astrologer), sorcery (Acts viii. 9, 11; xiii. 8, 10). The practicing of enchantments was forbidden by the Mosaic law (Deut. xviii. 10). Enchantments practiced to prevent a venomous snake from biting (Eccles. x. 11; cp. Ps. lviii. 5; Jer. viii. 17) belong, of course, to a different category. They require neither trickery nor the invocation of the powers of evil.

En'-dor. [fountain of habitation].

A town belonging to the tribe of Manasseh (Josh. xvii. 11; reference to En-dor wanting in Septuagint). Fugitives from Sisera's defeated army, fleeing home to the north, perished in its vicinity (Ps. lxxxiii. 10). Here dwelt the woman with a familiar spirit, whom king Saul consulted (1 Sam. xxviii. 7). It has been identified as the village of Endûr, on the northern shoulder of Little Hermon, 6 miles S. E. of Nazareth. See SAUL.

En-eg'la-im [fountain of two calves].

A place on the Dead Sea (Ezek. xlvii. 10).

En-gan'nim [fountain of gardens].

1. A village in the lowland of Judah (Josh. xv. 34). Site unknown.

2. A town on the boundary line of Issachar (Josh. xix. 21), assigned to the Gershonite Levites (xxi. 29). It seems to be the Ginæa of Josephus (Antiq. xx. 6, 1; War iii. 3, 4). It is the modern Jenin, a village of about 3000 inhabitants, on the southern margin of the plain of Jezreel, 5 miles northeast of Dothan and about 7 southwest from mount Gilboa.

En-ge'di [fountain of a kid].

A fountain and town originally called Hazazon-tamar, meaning pruning of a palm

(2 Chron. xx. 2), in the wilderness on the western shore of the Dead Sea, in the tribe of Judah (Josh. xv. 62). A difficult caravan route, crowded between mountain and sea, passed the spot. In the time of Abraham it was occupied by Amorites, who were smitten at the spot by Chedorlaomer (Gen. xiv. 7). David took refuge in the strongholds of the vicinity (1 Sam. xxiii. 29). In one of the caves where he was hiding he cut off the skirt of Saul's robe (xxiv. 1-22). The fountain, which still bears the name of 'Ain Jidy, is a copious hot spring of fresh water, bursting forth about 300 or 400 feet above the base of a vast cliff, midway between the mouth of the Jordan and the southern point of the sea (cp. Ezek. xlvii. 10). The hot water created an oasis, rich with semi-tropical vegetation and celebrated for palms, vineyards, and balsam (Song i. 14 ; Antiq. ix. 1, 2).

En-had'dah [fountain of vehemence].
A frontier village of Issachar (Josh. xix. 21). Not identified, though conjecturally near En-gannim.

En-hak'ko-re [fountain of him that called].
A spring in Lehi which burst forth when Samson cried to the Lord (Judg. xv. 18, 19). It was long pointed out.

En-ha'zor [fountain of the village].
A fenced city of Naphtali (Josh. xix. 37), mentioned in the list between Kadesh and Iron. Its site has not been positively identified.

En-mish'pat [fountain of judgment].
The same as Kadesh-barnea (Gen. xiv. 7).

E'noch, in A. V. once **Henoch** (1 Chron. i. 3) [initiated, dedicated]. The same name, borne by others, is rendered Henoch and Hanoch.
1 and 2. A son of Cain, and the city which Cain built and named after him (Gen. iv. 17, 18).
3. A descendant of Jared, and progenitor of Methuselah. He lived 365 years, and walked with God. He is the only one of the line of whom it is not said that he died. He was not ; for God took him (Gen. v. 18-24). He was translated, and did not see death (Ecclus. xliv. 16 ; xlix. 14 ; Heb. xi. 5). In Jude 14, 15 there is a prophecy of Enoch's in which he declares God's just judgment of the unrighteous. The words of this prophecy are found in the pseudepigraphical Book of Enoch, which is an extravagant production, amplifying the antediluvian history, and even rendering it incredible. Jude has either made a citation from this book or else both he and the author of the book quoted an old tradition. The N. T. writers have several times quoted uninspired, and even heathen, authors.

E'nosh, in A. V. **Enos,** except in 1 Chron. i. 1 [man].
The son of Seth (Gen. iv. 26 ; v. 6-11 ; 1 Chron. i. 1 ; Luke iii. 38).

En-rim'mon [fountain of Rimmon or of the pomegranate].
A town of Judah, inhabited after the captivity (Neh. xi. 29), and apparently consisting of the neighboring villages of Ain and Rimmon (see each).

En-ro'gel [perhaps, spy's or fuller's spring].
A fountain just outside Jerusalem (2 Sam. xvii. 17), near the valley of Hinnom and on the boundary line between Judah and Benjamin (Josh. xv. 7 ; xviii. 16). According to Josephus, it was in the king's garden (Antiq. vii. 14, 4). During Absalom's rebellion Jonathan and Ahimaaz took up their abode there, to be able to collect and send news to David (2 Sam. xvii. 17). Near by was the stone Zoheleth, where Adonijah instituted festivities when he conspired to seize the kingdom (1 Kin. i. 9). The traditional situation of the fountain, almost universally accepted, is Bir Eyub, the well of Job, just below the junction of the valleys of Hinnom and the Kidron, south of Jerusalem. This is a well, 125 feet deep, walled half way down and sunk the rest of the distance into the solid rock. That it is a well and not a fountain is scarcely a serious objection to the traditional identification (cp. Gen. xvi. 7 with 14). The well was doubtless suggested by the copious streams which at certain seasons are liable to gush from the ground at this spot. The identification of En-rogel with the Fountain of the Virgin in the side of Ophel has a few advocates, especially Grove and Conder.

En-she'mesh [fountain of the sun].
A fountain and town on the boundary line between Judah and Benjamin (Josh. xv. 7 ; xviii. 17). It is commonly identified with 'Ain Haud, a little east of Bethany, on the road between Jerusalem and Jericho, and the last spring until the Jordan valley is reached.

En-tap'pu-ah. See TAPPUAH 2.

E-pæn'e-tus [praiseworthy].
A convert belonging to Achaia, and the firstfruits of that region to Christ. Paul called him beloved (Rom. xvi. 5).

Ep'a-phras.
A Christian who, coming to Paul whilst he was a prisoner at Rome, gave a highly favorable account of the Colossian church, with which he was connected, perhaps as its minister. He joined the apostle in sending it salutations (Col. i. 7, 8 ; iv. 12). He remained in Rome, and was in some sense Paul's fellow-prisoner in Christ (Philem. 23). See EPAPHRODITUS.

E-paph-ro-di'tus [lovely, charming].
A Christian whom the church at Philippi sent with a present to the apostle Paul, then a prisoner at Rome. Soon afterwards he became seriously ill. It grieved him that the news of this sickness reached Philippi, and created anxiety among his friends there.

View of the theatre ruins at Ephesus. The seating capacity was about 25,000. This is where the riot occurred (Acts 19) and the crowd cried "Great is Diana of the Ephesians."

On this account Paul sent him back to Philippi as soon as his health permitted (Phil ii. 25–30; iv. 18), making him the **bearer of the Epistle to the Philippians.** Perhaps Epaphroditus and Epaphras were one and the same person, but there is a difficulty in accepting this view, for the former seems clearly connected with the church at Philippi, and the latter with that at Colossæ.

E′phah, I. [darkness].

1. A branch of the Midianites (Gen. xxv. 4; 1 Chron. i. 33), rich in camels and dromedaries (Is. lx. 6). They lived in northeastern Arabia.

2. A concubine of Caleb (1 Chron. ii. 46).

3. A man of Judah, a son of Jahdai (1 Chron. ii. 47).

E′phah, II. [perhaps from Egyptian *oiphi*, an old measure].

A measure of capacity containing ten omers (Ex. xvi. 36), and used for such articles as flour (Judg. vi. 19) or barley (Ruth ii. 17). It was equivalent to a bath or one-tenth of a cor (Ezek. xlv. 11, 14), and contained one Attic metretes or seventy-two sextaries (Antiq. viii. 2, 9; ix. 4, 5; and xv. 9, 2, where read metretes for medimnoi), and, if reckoned at 1952.17 cubic inches, contained a trifle more than 3 pecks, 5 quarts, American measure. Dishonest traders sometimes had an ephah of insufficient capacity and used it for fraud (Amos viii. 5).

E′phai [fatigued].

A Netophathite whose sons came with others to the Babylonian governor of Judæa after the fall of Jerusalem, and was promised protection (Jer. xl. 8). All were subsequently massacred by Ishmael (xli. 3).

E′pher [a calf or mule].

1. A branch of the Midianites (Gen. xxv. 4; 1 Chron. i. 33). Their exact location has not been determined.

2. A man of Judah descended from Ezrah (1 Chron. iv. 17).

3. A chief man in the half-tribe of Manasseh, east of the Jordan (1 Chron. v. 24).

E-phes-dam′mim [end or coast of Dammim].

A place within the territory of Judah, between Socoh and Azekah (1 Sam. xvii. 1). Called Pas-dammim in 1 Chron. xi. 13, a form perhaps due to corruption of the text. Commonly identified with the ruins Damun, about 4 miles to the northeast of Socoh.

E-phe′si-ans, E-pis′tle to the.

This epistle was written by the apostle Paul when he was a prisoner (iii. 1; iv. 1; vi. 20), probably at Rome A. D. 62, though some assign it to the Cæsarean imprisonment (Acts xxiv. 27). It is addressed to the saints which are at Ephesus and the faithful in Christ Jesus. R. V. notes, however, that some very ancient authorities omit the words "at Ephesus." The two chief N. T. manuscripts (Sinaitic and Vatican) omit them, and from very early times a difference of opinion appears as to its intended readers, though the tradition of the church called it "to the Ephesians." The most probable explanation is that it was a circular letter intended for all the churches of the province of Asia, and that, since Ephesus was the chief of these, the epistle naturally came to be considered as addressed to it. Perhaps the address was blank, and copies left in each city with the blank filled. Its circular character seems to be confirmed by the absence from it of local allusions and discussions. It is a doctrinal and ethical treatise in the form of an epistle. Like that to the Colossians, it was sent by Tychicus (vi. 21), and the similarity of language and thought shows that the two were written at the same time. Compare for example

Eph. i. 1, 2 with Col. i. 1, 2
" i. 3, 20; ii. 6; iii. 10; vi. 12 with Col. i. 5; iii. 1-3
" i. 6 with Col. i. 14
" i. 7 " " i. 14
" i. 8 " " ii. 23
" i. 9; iii. 9; vi. 19 with Col. i. 26; ii. 2; iv. 3
" i. 10 with Col. i. 20, 25
" i. 11 " " i. 12
" i. 17 " " i. 10
" i. 19, 20 " " ii. 12
" i. 20 " " iii. 1
" i. 22 " " i. 18
" i. 23 " " ii. 9

These are but examples, to which even the reader of the English Bible can add many more. The two epistles were evidently the product of the apostle's mind acting under the same circumstances. And Ephesians seems to have been written just after Colossians. In it the thought is carried further. The theme of Colossians is the preëminence of Christ's person and work. That of Ephesians is the establishment of the church, considered as the entire number of the redeemed. The Ephesians, in fact, may be said to sum up all Paul's previous teaching for the purpose of stating the purpose of God in the mission of his Son, which was the redemption of his chosen people to manifest to all the universe the riches of his grace. Hence, assuming salvation through faith, the divinity and finished work of Jesus and the calling of the gentiles, it advances to a complete theodicy. In chap. i. we have what may be called the divine side of the church's history, which originated in God's sovereign and eternal purpose (3-6), was effected by Christ's work (7-12), and is certified by the sealing of the Spirit (13, 14). He prays that they may understand the hope of Christ's calling, of which the risen and exalted Saviour is the first fruit and pledge (15-23). In chap. ii. we have the human side of the history, being taught that the elect are delivered out of sin and condemnation by unmerited grace (1-10), and are united, Jew and gentile, through Christ into one spiritual temple (11-22). In chap. iii. the apostle states his own position as the minister to the church of this divine mystery (1-13), and prays that they may realize

and enjoy what God has prepared for them (14-21). Chapters iv.-vi. are an extended exhortation to walk worthily of their high calling in all the relations of the present life. The Epistle to the Romans, addressed from the East to the West, was Paul's complete statement of the way of salvation. The Epistle to the Ephesians, addressed from the West to the East, was his complete statement of the whole purpose of God in human history. It may be said to mark the climax of his theological instruction. G. T. P.

Before the Epistle to the Ephesians was written, Paul had seen a new spiritual community arise in the world, composed of persons of different races; he had been teaching that this community, the church, is the body of Christ (Rom. xii. 5; 1 Cor. xii. 27; Col. i. 18; ii. 19); and he had been emphasizing the importance of harmony among its members (Rom. xii. 4-8; 1 Cor xii. 12-30). In writing at this time to the churches in the province of Asia, whose membership was composed of the most diverse racial elements and among whom speculative theories were rife which tended to subordinate Christ, it was natural for the apostle to give prominence to the conception of Christ as the head of the body, the church (Eph. i. 22, 23), from whom the whole body fitly framed and knit together through that which every joint supplieth, according to the working in due measure of each several part, maketh the increase of the body unto the building up of itself in love (iv. 16, R. V.; cp. ii. 11-22). And not only was the prominence of this thought natural at this time in a letter from Paul to Christians in the province of Asia; but such an expression of his mature thought about Christ was to be expected under these conditions from one whose deep interest in the subject is witnessed by his earlier epistles. J. D. D.

Eph'e-sus [according to tradition, permission].

A city of Lydia on the western coast of Asia Minor, at the mouth of the river Cayster, nearly midway between Miletus on the south and Smyrna on the north. Situated at the junction of natural trade routes, and near a far-famed shrine of an Asiatic nature goddess, whom the Greeks identified with Artemis, its growth was assured. In the eleventh century B. C. the town was seized by the Ionians, a section of the Greek race. Ephesus became one of the twelve cities belonging to their confederation, and itself the capital of Ionia. About 555 B. C. the city submitted to Crœsus, king of Lydia, whose capital was at Sardis, but it soon fell under the Persian domination. When the victories of Alexander the Great overthrew the Persian empire, Ephesus came under Macedonian-Greek rule. Hitherto it had been confined to a low, alluvial plain liable to be flooded. About 286 B. C., however, Lysimachus ex-

The marble street in Ephesus stands as a reminder of bygone days of splendor. Monuments, fountains, and marble benches once lined the street. The Apostle Paul ministered in Ephesus for two years and three months.

tended it to an adjacent eminence which the water could not reach. By this change of location the temple of Artemis was left outside the city walls. In 190 B. C. the Romans, after defeating Antiochus the Great at Magnesia, took Ephesus from him, and gave it to Eumenes II., king of Pergamos. On the death of Attalus III. of Pergamos in 133 B. C. it reverted to them, and eventually became the capital of the Roman province of Asia. In A. D. 29 the city was much damaged by an earthquake, but was rebuilt by the emperor Tiberius. Many Jews with Roman citizenship resided at Ephesus, and maintained a synagogue (Antiq. xiv. 10, 11 and 13; Acts xviii. 19; xix. 17); and Paul, on his way to Jerusalem, toward the end of his second missionary journey, paid a short visit to the place, preached in the synagogue, and left Aquila and Priscilla there, who continued the work (Acts xviii. 19-21). On his third journey he labored at Ephesus at least two years and three months, leaving the city after the riot which was stirred up by Demetrius, a maker of small silver models of the temple, who found his craft endangered by the preaching of the apostle (xix. 1-41; cp. 1 Cor. xv. 32; xvi. 8; 2 Tim. i. 18). Paul left Timothy behind to prevent the church from being corrupted by false doctrine (1 Tim. i. 3). Subsequently, returning from Europe and unable to revisit Ephesus, he summoned the elders of the church to him at Miletus (Acts xx. 16, 17). Tychicus was afterwards sent to Ephesus with the Epistle to the Ephesians (Eph. i. 1; vi. 21; 2 Tim. iv. 12). The church at Ephesus was one of the seven churches of Asia addressed in the book of Revelation (Rev. i. 11; ii. 1-7), and according to tradition the apostle John spent the last years of his life in the city. The third general council of the church was held at Ephesus, A. D. 431, and defined the doctrine of the person of Christ so far as affirming that Christ has two natures and one person; and in 449 a synod was convened, the so-called Robber Council, which restored Eutychus. The silting up of the harbor by mud brought down by the Cayster led to the decay of the city. Among its remains are the ruins of the wall and a gate, the stadium, a fine theater, Roman baths, and a library. The site of the great temple is a swamp.

An earlier Ionic temple was set on fire by Herostratos in 356 B. C. and destroyed; but it was rebuilt within a few years. The new structure was a magnificent work of Ionic architecture, four times as large as the Parthenon at Athens, and ranked as one of the seven wonders of the world. It stood on a platform about 425 feet in length and 239½ feet in width, measured from the lowest step. A flight of ten steps led to the pavement of the platform, and three more steps to the pavement of the temple. The temple itself was 342½ feet in length and 164 feet in width. It consisted of two rows of eight columns each in front and rear, and two rows of twenty columns each on either side of the sanctuary. These with two columns at each entrance of the sanctuary made one hundred in all. Each was a monolith of marble 55 feet in height, and the eighteen at each end were sculptured. The roof was covered with large white marble tiles. The cella or inner sanctuary, which these columns surrounded, was 70 feet wide and 105 long. Its internal ornamentation was of surpassing splendor, adorned with works of art by Phidias and Praxiteles, Scopas, Parrhasius, and Apelles. See illustration under DIANA. It was destroyed by the Goths about A. D. 260.

The theater was one of the largest known of all that have remained to modern times. The auditorium was semicircular, 495 feet in diameter, and the orchestra was 110. The stage was 22 feet wide. The theater contained 66 rows of seats, and afforded room for an audience of 24,500 persons.

Eph'lal [judicious].
A man of Judah of the family of Jerahmeel (1 Chron. ii. 37).

Eph'od [a covering].
1. An upper garment worn by the Jewish high priest. It was one of six sacred vestments which he was required to put on when about to conduct the worship of God (Ex. xxviii. 4), and was of gold, blue, purple, scarlet, and fine twined linen. It consisted of two shoulder pieces joined by the two edges (6, 7), and falling over the front and back part of the body. There was a hole in the top, doubtless for the head, with a woven border of the same materials around, to render the cloth less liable to tear (8, cp. 32). On it, so as to stand upon the shoulders of the priest when the ephod was worn, were two onyx stones, each having engraved upon it the names of six tribes (xxviii. 9; xxxix. 6, 7). In front, to rings attached underneath close to the coupling, the breastplate was bound with a lace of blue, so that the breastplate itself might be supported (xxviii. 25, 27, 28; xxxix. 19-21). David, desiring to ask counsel of God in the presence of the high priest, had the ephod brought near (1 Sam. xxiii. 9-12; xxx. 7, 8), for with it were the Urim and Thummim (Ex. xxviii. 30). An ephod might thus readily become an object of adoration or be used in the worship of an idol (Judg. viii. 27; xvii. 5). The robe of the ephod was a garment distinct from the ephod, was blue, and was sleeveless, fringed at the bottom with alternate bells of gold and pomegranates of blue, purple, and scarlet (Ex. xxviii. 31-35; xxix. 5; xxxix. 22-26).

A more simple ephod of linen, probably without the ornamentation, was worn by ordinary priests. The eighty-five whom Doeg slew all wore the linen ephod (1 Sam. xxii. 18). Samuel, also, wore an ephod while he was a child in charge of Eli, the high priest (1 Sam. ii. 18). David wore one when officiating before the ark as king (2 Sam. vi. 14).
2. The father of Hanniel, prince of Manasseh in the time of Moses (Num. xxxiv. 23).

Eph'pha-tha.
An Aramaic imperative signifying "be opened" (Mark vii. 34).

E'phra-im [double fruitfulness].
1. The younger son of Joseph and Asenath, daughter of Potipherah, priest of On. He was born while Joseph was prime minister of Egypt (Gen. xli. 45-52). When the two sons were brought to Jacob on his sickbed, to receive their grandfather's blessing, Jacob intentionally laid his right hand (the hand of greater honor) on the head of Ephraim, the younger grandson, and his left on that of Manasseh, the elder. Being remonstrated with by Joseph, he explained that both should become a people, but Ephraim should be the greater and should be the ancestor of a multitude of peoples or tribal families (Gen. xlviii. 8-20). Ephraim and Manasseh, though only grandchildren of Jacob, were treated as if they were his children, and their descendants were consequently regarded as two tribes instead of one. Ephraim had the sorrow of losing two of his sons, who were slain while making a raid on the cattle of the Philistines (1 Chron. vii. 20-22).
2. The tribe of which Ephraim was the progenitor (Josh. xvi. 4, 10; Judg. v. 14). The growth of the tribe was for a time retarded by the death of several of his sons in a fray against the Philistines (1 Chron. vii. 21-23). At the first census in the wilderness the Ephraimites numbered 40,500, being the lowest in number of the tribes excepting only Manasseh and Benjamin (Num. i. 33). They fell off during the wanderings, and at the second census numbered only 32,500, being now the lowest of all the tribes except Simeon (xxvi. 37); still the double tribe of Joseph was the largest of the tribes, and numbered 85,200 men, besides women and children (34, 37; cp. Deut. xxxiii. 17). When Joshua was the leader of Israel, the tribe rose rapidly in reputation, for he was himself an Ephraimite (Josh. xix. 50; xxiv. 30). The tribe was allotted territory west of the Jordan. Its southern boundary line ran from the Jordan at Jericho to Beth-el, Luz, Ataroth-addar, Upper Beth-horon. Lower Beth-horon, Gezer and the sea (Josh. xvi. 1-3, 5). The northern line ran through Michmethath, near Shechem, eastward to Taanath-shiloh, Janoah, Ataroth, and Naarah, reached Jericho and the Jordan (6, 7), and passed westward from Michmethath to En-tappuah, the river Kanah and the Mediterranean (8; cp. xvii. 7). It had the territory of the half-tribe of Manasseh, west of the Jordan, on the north, and Benjamin on the south; it reached the Mediterranean on the west and to the Jordan on the east. Shechem was within the territory of Ephraim (Josh. xxi. 20, 21; 1 Kin. xii. 25; 1 Chron. vi. 67). The Ephraimites failed to expel the Canaanites from Gezer, which was within the lot of Ephraim; but, either alone or in conjunction with their kindred the Manassites, they captured Beth-el (Judg. i. 22-26, 29). They acted patriotically in the fight celebrated in song by Deborah (v. 14). They quarreled with Gideon, who was a Manas-

site, for not having called them to aid him in expelling the Midianites from Canaan (viii. 1–3). They resolutely encountered in battle Jephthah, the deliverer of Israel, for not having summoned them to assist him in the Ammonite war, 42,000 of the tribe falling in the struggle (xii. 1–6). Micah, of graven image notoriety, resided in mount Ephraim (xvii. 1) ; and the Levite, the ill-treatment of whose concubine led to the hostilities against Benjamin, sojourned there (xix. 1). Jeroboam was a man of Ephraim, and after he had become king over the revolted ten tribes, he rebuilt Shechem in mount Ephraim to be his capital (1 Kin. xii. 25).

The hill country of Ephraim, or mount Ephraim, as it is sometimes called, was so much of the central range of Palestine as was occupied by the tribe of Ephraim. It did not include the towns of Taanach, Megiddo, Beth-shean, and Abel-meholah, on the north and east (1 Kin. iv. 8, 12), nor Kiriath-jearim, Gibeah, or the territory of Benjamin on the south (Judg. xviii. 12, 13 ; xix. 16 ; 1 Sam. ix. 4 ; 1 Kin. iv. 8, 18 ; 2 Chron. xv. 8). If it included territory north of Shechem (1 Chron. vi. 66, 68, with 1 Kin. iv. 12), it was thus bounded on three sides by the southern border of the plain of Esdraelon, the Jordan valley, and the territory of Benjamin. The term did not properly designate any part of the district occupied by Benjamin. Even Judg. iv. 5 and 2 Sam. xx. 1, 21 do not necessarily imply any broader use of the term. But after the establishment of the northern kingdom with its shifting southern frontier, the southern limits of the hill country of Ephraim were no longer clearly defined.

The wood of Ephraim, in which the battle took place between the forces of David and those of the rebel Absalom (2 Sam. xviii. 6 ; cp. xvii. 22, 24, 26, 27), was evidently east of the Jordan, and near Mahanaim, but its exact situation is unknown. It probably took its name either from the defeat of the Ephraimites in the time of Jephthah (Judg. xii. 1 seq.), or because it was opposite to the territory and mountain of Ephraim.

For the gate of Ephraim, see JERUSALEM II., 3.

3. The ten tribes of which Ephraim became the head. Used in this sense especially by the prophets (Is. vii. 2, 5, 9, 17 ; ix. 9 ; xvii. 3 ; xxviii. 3 ; Hos. iv. 17 ; v. 3 ; ix. 3–17).

4. A city to which Baal-hazor was adjacent (2 Sam. xiii. 23), probably the same place as Ephraim near to the wilderness (John xi. 54), and Aphærema, which at one time belonged to Samaria (1 Mac. xi. 34). The Roman general Vespasian took Ephraim and Bethel during his advance on Jerusalem (War iv. 9, 9). Robinson identifies it with Ophrah of Benjamin, and locates it at the modern village of Taiyibeh, on a conical hill standing on high land 4 miles east-northeast of Beth-el. The identification has met general acceptance.

E'phra-im-ite.

A member of the tribe of Ephraim (Judg. xii. 5). More frequently Ephrathite, as in the original.

E'phra-in. See EPHRON 2.

Eph'ra-thah, in A. V. **Ephratah** [fruitfulness, fruitful land]. A shorter form, occasionally used in the Hebrew text and preserved in the versions, is Ephrath.

1. The original name of Bethlehem in Judæa (Gen. xxxv. 19 ; xlviii. 7 ; Ruth iv. 11). It is sometimes called Bethlehem-ephratah (Mic. v. 2).

2. A wife of Caleb, son of Hezron. She was the mother of Hur (1 Chron. ii. 19, 50 ; iv. 4).

3. The territory of Ephraim (Ps. cxxxii. 6 ; see EPHRATHITE 2) ; or better, Kiriath-jearim, which belonged to Caleb-ephrathah (1 Chron. ii. 50, 51), and where the ark had been kept for a long time.

Eph'rath-ite.

1. A native or inhabitant of Ephrath, i. e. Bethlehem (1 Sam. xvii. 12 ; Ruth i. 2).

2. An Ephraimite, one belonging to the tribe of Ephraim (1 Sam. i. 1 ; 1 Kin. xi. 26).

E'phron [vituline].

1. A Hittite, resident at Hebron, and owner of the cave of Machpelah, which he sold to Abraham (Gen. xxiii. 8 ; xxv. 9).

2. A city which was taken from Jeroboam by Abijah (2 Chron. xiii. 19). Abandoning the Hebrew text for the traditional pronunciation of the synagogue, A. V. and the margin of the R. V. have Ephrain [two calves or fawns], an Aramaic dual. Commonly identified with the town of Ephraim.

3. A city east of the Jordan in the territory of Manasseh, in a pass near the road between Karnaim and Beth-shean. It was captured by Judas Maccabæus (1 Mac. v. 46–52 ; 2 Mac. xii. 27, 29 ; Antiq. xii. 8, 5).

4. A mountain ridge between Nephtoah and Kiriath-jearim, on the boundary between Judah and Benjamin (Josh. xv. 9).

Ep-i-cu-re'ans.

One of the leading philosophic sects of Greece and Rome. It derived its name and its existence from the great philosopher Epicurus. He was born 341 B. C. in the island of Samos, but was of Athenian descent, and made Athens the scene of his lifework. In 306 B. C. he founded a school or college with a garden attached, in which he taught for the next thirty-six years, till his death in 270 B. C. He is said to have written about three hundred philosophic books, nearly all of which are lost. In physics he, like Democritus, attributes all nature to changes among atoms in themselves eternal. He does not recognize a Creator ; but, with curious inconsistency, finds a place in his system for a multitude of gods, who, however, supremely happy in themselves, take no part in human affairs. With regard to his ethics, a popular misconception prevails. He desires that pleasure shall be pursued and pain avoided; but the notion that by pleasure he meant only sensual gratification is erroneous. He included under the term the pleasure derived from the exercise of the intellect and the moral faculty. Personally he was so pure that some thought he was destitute of passions. The Epicureans were mostly men of soft temperament, the very opposite of the Stoics, who were cast in an iron mould. Both philosophic sects rejected Paul's doctrine at Athens, but both showed their tolerance by taking the apostle to the court of Areopagus to have his teaching examined, in place of exciting a riot against him, as had been done at various places where he had preached (Acts xvii. 18-20).

Ep-i-lep'tic.

A person affected with the falling sickness, a disease which in its severe form is characterized by recurrent attacks of loss of consciousness with spasms (Mat. xvii. 15, in A. V. lunatic; Mark ix. 18). In this case the disease was occasioned by demoniacal possession.

E-pis'tles.

The name given to twenty-one books of the N. T. The earliest of them antedate the gospels, Paul having written his epistles to the Thessalonians about A. D. 52. They are letters which were written by the apostles, or which received apostolic sanction; and they are addressed to particular churches, and deal with doctrinal and practical questions, or to individuals, yet contain matter of wide import, or to Christians generally, and not to any one person or church. With the exception of the Epistle to the Hebrews and 1 John, they open, according to the custom of the time, with the name or title of the writer and that of the person or church addressed, and then follow words of greeting.

The epistles are classed in three groups, but the groups are neither exhaustive nor mutually exclusive. 1. Pauline; for the first thirteen begin with the statement that the letter was sent by Paul or by him in conjunction with other Christian workers, as Sosthenes (1 Cor. i. 1), Timothy (2 Cor. i. 1; Phil. i. 1; Col. i. 1; Philem. 1), or Silvanus and Timothy together (1 Thes. i. 1; 2 Thes. i. 1). Paul, as a rule, employed an amanuensis to write from his dictation (Rom. xvi. 22), the apostle adding the salutation in his own hand, which he says was the token in every epistle (1 Cor. xvi. 21; Col. iv. 18; 2 Thes. iii. 17). In the case of the Epistle to the Galatians, however, he departed from his rule, and wrote the whole letter with his own hand (Gal. vi. 11). 2. Within the group of Pauline epistles are three known as the pastoral epistles, namely, 1 and 2 Timothy and Titus. They are addressed to the persons whose names they bear, and contain directions for the training and governing of churches and the proper treatment of individual members. 3. Five epistles are called general in the titles prefixed to them in the A. V.: James, 1 and 2 Peter, 1 John, and Jude. In the early church, however, seven were classed as catholic; 2 and 3 John being included (Eusebius, Hist. Eccles. ii. 23), although these two are simple personal letters addressed to individuals. The word catholic was probably used in its sense of general, to denote an encyclical letter to the church at large; and the elect lady and Gaius, to whom 2 and 3 John respectively are addressed, were probably understood to represent the church universal.

The epistolary form was not a mere literary device, chosen for a doctrinal treatise. Usually at least the epistles were written in the way of ordinary correspondence. They were prompted by personal motives and were due to the writer's own initiative (Philemon, 2 John); or they were penned in reply to letters, or were based on information otherwise obtained, concerning matters requiring attention in any particular church (1 Cor. i. 11; 2 Cor. vii. 5-7; 1 Thes. iii. 5, 6). But they are adapted to all persons in like circumstances; Paul requested that certain of his epistles be read by others than by those only to whom they were addressed (Col. iv. 16). The apostles claimed that these epistles are the word of God (1 Thes. ii. 13; 1 Pet. i. 12), and from the beginning they ranked with the other Scriptures. Peter in A. D. 68 spoke of Paul's epistles as part of the Scriptures (2 Pet. iii. 15, 16), and Polycarp in A. D. 115 quoted the Psalms and Ephesians side by side as equally Scripture. See CANON.

The titles of the epistles were not part of the original composition, but were prefixed afterwards. They are lacking in early manuscripts, and are no part of Scripture. Most of them are founded on the first verse of the epistle; but that prefixed to the Epistle to the Hebrews is not derived from the letter itself, and is of doubtful accuracy. The notices appended to the epistles in the A. V. regarding the place where the letter was penned were likewise no part of the original composition.

Er [awake, on the watch].

1. A son of Judah who died in Canaan by a judgment of God for his wickedness (Gen. xxxviii. 1-7; xlvi. 12; 1 Chron. ii. 3).

2. A descendant of Judah, of the family of Shelah (1 Chron. iv. 21).

3. An ancestor of Christ, about midway between David and Zerubbabel (Luke iii. 28).

E'ran [watchful].

A descendant of Ephraim through Shuthelah, and founder of a tribal family (Num. xxvi. 36).

E-ras'tus [beloved].

A Christian, one of those who ministered to Paul. He was sent with Timothy from Ephesus into Macedonia just before the riot at the former place (Acts xix. 22). He is probably the person mentioned in 2 Tim. iv.

20 as having abode at Corinth, who was doubtless the Christian in high official position, chamberlain of the city of Corinth, who joined with Paul in sending salutations to the Roman converts (Rom. xvi. 23).

E'rech [Assyrian *Uruk* and *Arku*].

A city of Shinar or Lower Babylonia, one of those constituting part of Nimrod's kingdom (Gen. x. 10). It is now represented by the mounds of Warka, a considerable distance south of Babylon, on a marshy region, east of the Euphrates. The extreme antiquity of the city has been established by the Babylonian inscriptions. Archevites were settled in Samaria by Asnapper (Ezra iv. 9).

E'ri [watching].

A son of Gad and founder of a tribal family (Gen. xlvi. 16; Num. xxvi. 16).

E-sa'ias. See ISAIAH.

E-sar-had'don [Ashur hath given brothers].

The favorite, though not the eldest, son of Sennacherib, king of Assyria. The partiality so annoyed two other brothers, Adrammelech and Nergalsharezer, that they assassinated their father, escaping afterwards into Armenia (2 Kin. xix. 36, 37; 2 Chron. xxxii. 21; Is. xxxvii. 37, 38). When this base murder was perpetrated, Esar-haddon was himself conducting a campaign in the northwest, probably in Armenia. On receiving news of the event, he at once started with his army for Nineveh, but was met on the way by the rebel forces. The confederates were, however, defeated, and Esar-haddon was able to ascend the throne of Assyria on the 8th of Nisan, 680 B. C. The partiality of the father had not been misplaced. Esar-haddon was equally eminent as a military general and a political ruler. In his first year he defeated the son of Merodach-baladan in southern Babylonia. Later he commenced the restoration of the city of Babylon which Sennacherib, provoked by its continual revolts against the Assyrian domination, had given up to plunder. Esar-haddon also waged war against the Cimmerian barbarians who had descended upon the more civilized south from beyond the Caucasus; against the mountaineers of Cilicia, and against the children of Eden who were in Telassar (cp. Is. xxxvii. 12). In his fourth year he captured and pillaged Sidon, deported its inhabitants, razed the city to the ground, and erected a new town on the old site. Its king had escaped by sea, but he was pursued, taken, and beheaded. The same fate befell his two royal allies. Afterwards twelve tribes on the mainland and ten in Cyprus submitted to the Assyrian dominion. Among others were Manasseh, king of Judah, and the kings of Edom, Moab, Ammon, Gaza, Ashkelon, Ekron, and Ashdod. Esar-haddon successfully accomplished two most difficult military enterprises, the penetration of the Arabian desert and of far off Media. He turned his attention to a yet greater undertaking,

the conquest of Egypt, but he was for a time diverted from his purpose, being compelled in his eighth year to war with a tribe at the head of the Persian Gulf and near Ur. At length in his tenth year he made his great expedition against Egypt. Marching past Tyre, he left the city under siege. He entered Egypt, captured Memphis, and laid the entire country and its petty kings at his feet. He divided the valley of the Nile from Thebes to the Mediterranean into twenty satrapies. Over the less important in a spirit of conciliation he set governors of native descent, but over the more important he placed Assyrian governors. .He died 669 or 668 B. C., leaving his eldest son, Ashurbanipal, who for a short time previously had been associated with him in the government, to ascend the throne.

F'sau [hairy].

Son of Isaac and Rebekah, and elder twin brother of Jacob. Esau was so named because he was all over like a hairy garment (Gen. xxv. 21–26). As he grew up he became a skillful hunter, and was accustomed to bring home venison, doubtless the flesh of various antelopes, to his father Isaac. On one occasion he returned from the chase famishing, and asked for some red pottage which Jacob had just made ready. Jacob asked from him the surrender of his birthright as payment; and Esau, esteeming the higher blessings lightly, and caring more for present gratification, sold his birthright rather than wait for the preparation of food. From the red pottage, which was its price, Esau obtained a second name, Edom, *i. e.* Red (27–34; Heb. xii. 16, 17). When he was 40 years old he married two wives, Judith or Oholibamah and Basemath or Adah, both Hittites (Gen. xxvi. 34, 35; xxxvi. 1, 2). Afterwards he wedded Mahalath, called also Basemath, the daughter of Ishmael (xxviii. 9; xxxvi. 3). When Isaac was old and nearly blind, he designed to confer the covenanted blessing on Esau, who was his favorite son. But Jacob was Rebekah's favorite, and she induced him to personate Esau and fraudulently obtain the blessing. Esau resolved to kill his selfish brother, but did not like to carry out the murder while his father was living (xxvii. 1–41). To give time for this anger to cool, Jacob fled to Mesopotamia, and for twenty years was an exile (xxvii. 42–xxxi. 55). On his return he took means to appease his justly offended brother; and Esau, who was of a generous nature, dismissed his vindictive feeling, and gave Jacob a fraternal reception (xxxii. 3–xxxiii. 15). Prior to this Esau had taken up his abode in mount Seir, to which he at once returned (16). The reconciliation between the brothers was permanent, and both met to bury their father (xxxv. 29). Esau's descendants increased and ultimately dispossessed the original inhabitants of mount Seir and became the Edomite people (Deut.

ii. 4, 12, 22). Mount Seir could, accordingly, be called the mount of Esau (Obad. 8, 9, 19, 21). For the election of Jacob to be the child of promise and the rejection of Esau, see Gen. xxv. 23 ; Mal. i. 2, 3 ; Rom. ix. 12, 13.

Es'dras.

The Greek form of Ezra. It is used in the Septuagint and the Apocrypha, but does not occur in the canonical Scriptures. See APOC-RYPHA.

E'sek [contention].

A well dug by Isaac in the valley of Gerar, which the Philistine herdmen claimed (Gen. xxvi. 20).

E'shan, in A. V. **Eshean** [support].

A village in the mountains of Judah, grouped with Dumah and Hebron (Josh. xv. 52). Septuagint has Soma ; hence it may be identical with the ruin es-Simia, near Dumah, and about 8½ miles southwest by south of Hebron.

Esh'ba-al. See ISHBOSHETH.

Esh'ban [reason, intelligence].

A son of Dishon, descended from Seir the Horite (Gen. xxxvi. 26 ; 1 Chron. i. 41).

Esh'col [a cluster ; specially of grapes].

1. One of three Amorite brothers, residing near Hebron and confederate with Abram (Gen. xiv. 13, 24).

2. A valley near, probably north of, Hebron (Num. xiii. 22, 23 ; Deut. i. 24). The region round about Hebron is celebrated for its large clusters of luscious grapes. It is uncertain whether the valley bore this name before the time of Moses or not. At any rate the name henceforth suggested to the Israelites the spot where the spies, whom Moses had sent to spy out the land, cut the famous cluster which two of them carried suspended on a pole between them to save from being dashed and broken (Num. xiii. 24).

E'she-an. See ESHAN.

E'shek [violence, oppression].

A Benjamite, a descendant of Saul (1 Chron. viii. 39).

Esh'ka-lon-ite. See ASHKELONITE.

Esh'ta-ol [perhaps petition].

A town in the lowland of Judah (Josh. xv. 33), eventually allotted to the Danites (xix. 41). It is commonly mentioned in connection with Zorah (Judg. xiii. 25 ; xvi. 31 ; xviii. 2, 8, 11 ; 1 Chron. ii. 53). It has been identified as the village of Eshû'a, about 1½ miles east by north from Zorah, and 13 miles west, slightly north from Jerusalem.

Esh'ta-ul-ite, in R. V. **Eshtaolite.**

An inhabitant of Eshtaol (1 Chron. ii. 53).

Esh-te-mo'a, once **Eshtemoh** (Josh. xv. 50) [obedience].

1. A town in the hill country of Judah, given with its suburbs to the priests (Josh. xv. 50 ; xxi. 14 ; 1 Chron. vi. 57). David sent it some of the spoils obtained on the recap-

ture of Ziklag (1 Sam. xxx. 28). The site has been found at Semû'a, 9 miles south of Hebron, a considerable village with the foundation of ancient walls designed for a large town.

2. A Maacathite, son of Hodiah (1 Chron. iv. 19, R. V.).

Esh'ton [possibly uxorious].

A descendant of Chelub, reckoned in the genealogy of Judah (1 Chron. iv. 12).

Es'li [perhaps from Hebrew *'eṣli*, at my side (is God)].

An ancestor of Christ who lived after the captivity (Luke iii. 25).

Es'rom. See HEZRON.

Es-senes'.

An order of men among the Jews in the time of Christ, who numbered about 4000, and devoted themselves to a more or less ascetic life. Hoping by isolation to escape ceremonial defilement, they formed colonies by themselves. The wilderness of Judæa near En-gedi was a favorite place for their settlements, but there were colonies in various towns of Judæa also. Each colony had its own synagogue, a common hall for meals and assemblies, and provision for daily bathing in running water. Whoever became a member of the order gave up all that he possessed to it. They read the law of Moses daily and nightly, and endeavored to regulate their lives in every detail according to it. Their habits were simple. Their food and clothing were plain. They passed the day in husbandry and other useful industry. Money was almost unnecessary, as they supplied their needs by their own labor ; and when they traveled, they found lodging and food free of cost among their brethren. They had no slaves, as they recognized no distinction between men save that of clean and unclean. They did not deny the fitness of marriage ; but they abstained from wedlock, except one party among them. Their morality was lofty. They promised " to honor God, to be righteous toward man, to injure no one, either at the bidding of another or of their own accord, to hate evil, to promote good, to be faithful to every one, especially those in authority, to love the truth, to unmask liars, and to keep the hand from theft and the conscience from unrighteous gain " (Antiq. xviii. 1, 5 ; War ii. 8, 2–13).

Es'ther [from Persian *sitareh*, star].

A beautiful maiden, daughter of Abihail, and probably of the tribe of Benjamin (Esth. ii. 15 ; and cp. 5 with 7). Her Hebrew name was H^adassah, myrtle. Early left an orphan, she was brought up at Susa, the Persian metropolis, by Mordecai, her cousin, who adopted her. Ahasuerus, king of Persia, who by common consent is identified with Xerxes, when in wine, ordered Vashti the queen to be brought into the banquet hall and displayed in royal regalia to the revelers. Angered by her refusal to submit to such indignity, he followed the advice of his obsequious courtiers, and decreed her permanent seclusion and had his realm searched for a fair maiden to take her place. Eventually, in the seventh year of the king, Esther was selected and installed in the palace as queen. It was not known at the time that she was a Jewess. She came to the throne at a critical time. The royal favorite was Haman. Five years after Esther's elevation (Esth. ii. 16; iii. 7), Haman, annoyed by Mordecai's refusal to do him obeisance, wished to revenge himself by the massacre, not simply of Mordecai, but of all the large Jewish population scattered throughout the empire. He secured the king's consent by the offer of a heavy bribe and by allusion to the stubborn adherence of the Jews to their own laws and customs; and he sought to get the aid of the rabble in the work of slaughter by an appeal to their greed (Esth. ii. 5–iii. 15). Mordecai urged Esther to interfere for the protection of her race. She was afraid; but, on being solemnly addressed by her guardian, she, after fasting and prayer, risked her life by coming unbidden into the king's presence. With great prudence and tact she made a favorable opportunity for bringing to the king's attention the fact that Haman's plot invaded the palace and included her; and, since the edict of destruction could not be recalled, she gained permission for the Jews to defend themselves, and even to take the offensive against their foes. The time and manner of Esther's death are unknown. If Ahasuerus is Xerxes, as is universally believed, Esther was one of Xerxes' wives (cp. the wives of Xerxes' father, Herod. iii. 88; vii. 2; and also 2 Sam. iii. 2–5; xi. 26, 27; 1 Kin. i. 11; vii. 8; xi. 3; Dan. v. 2, 10), of whom one was Amestris, the daughter or granddaughter of Otanes, first definitely reported as already Xerxes' wife in 479 B. C., his seventh or eighth regnal year (Herod. ix. 109; cp. vii. 61; Ctesias, Exc. Pers. 20). Vashti was the reigning wife in Xerxes' third year (Esth. i. 3, 9), the year in which he convoked a great assembly to consult about a war with the Greeks (Herod. vii. 7, 8), and Esther was put into her place in the tenth month of the seventh year (Esth. ii. 16, 17), and was queen in the twelfth year also (iii. 7; v. 3).

The book of Esther is the last of the historical books of the O. T. In the Hebrew canon it stands among the Hagiographa; formerly, according to the Talmud, between Daniel and Ezra, but now just after Ecclesiastes and immediately before Daniel. This latter position is due to its being grouped with four other rolls which were used on five solemn anniversaries. The last of these anniversaries is Purim, hence Esther has been placed last among the Five Rolls. Long after the completion of the canon, the right of Esther to its place in that canon was called in question by the Jews, probably, however,

not seriously, but to afford opportunity for intellectual display in its defense. The Jews now regard it with special honor. Christians have been more divided on the subject of its merits. Melito of Sardis and Gregory of Nazianzus omitted it from their lists of canonical books; Athanasius classed it with non-canonical books, and Luther denounced it. Opposition to it was based mainly on the fact that the name of God does not occur in it even once. But iv. 14 implies the existence of Providence; iv. 16 recognizes fasting as a religious practice, and ix. 31 not merely fasting, but a cry or prayer. The great lesson of the book is, in fact, the overruling power of Providence.

Investigators who seek for a possible mythological or legendary origin for the narratives of the Old Testament argue that the book of Esther springs from such a source. The theory of a Babylonian origin is most in vogue. In its principal form at present it rests its claim for acceptance mainly on the evidence that Esther is a late form of the name of the Babylonian goddess Ishtar; and that Esther's other name Hadassah is the Babylonian word ḥadashatu, bride, originally myrtle, and is used as a title ·of goddesses. Mordecai is the same as Marduk, the patron deity of Babylon. He is the cousin of Esther, and it is possible thus to relate Marduk to Ishtar. Haman, the adversary of Mordecai, represents Humman or Hamman, a chief god of the Elamites, in whose capital Susa the scene is laid; and Zeresh, the wife of Haman, may be the same as Kirisha, an Elamite goddess, presumably the consort of Humman. Vashti is also an Elamite deity, presumably a goddess. The successful resistance of Mordecai and Esther to Haman, Zeresh, and Vashti is the conflict of the gods of Babylonia with the gods of Elam, in other words, it is the struggle between Babylonia and Elam for supremacy, which lasted for a thousand years and ended in the victory of Babylonia (Jensen, Wiener Zeitschrift f. d. Kunde des Morgenlandes, vi. 47 ff, 209 ff; Gunkel, Schöpfung und Chaos, 310–314, who admits that the basis is lacking so long as the word Pur remains unexplained, 314). If this theory were established, it might show that the Jews of the dispersion, feeding their hopes on the prophecies of deliverance, instituted a joyous feast and made use of the contest of Marduk and Ishtar with Humba and Washti to illustrate or typify the certain victory of the Jews over all their foes.

Before this theory is adopted, however, its foundations must be critically examined:

I. Regarding the Elamite deities. 1. The identification of Haman, the archenemy of the Jews, with the chief god of the Elamites. (1) The name of this deity was ordinarily written by the Assyrians Humba, but in certain phonetic connections it was reproduced by them as Umman, with a final nun, and this form could be represented in Hebrew by Human or Haman. So far good; but (2) the book of Esther tells more about Haman than his name. It knows him as the son of Hammedatha, and an Agagite (iii. 1, 10; viii. 5; ix. 24); and gives the names of ten sons of his (ix. 7–10). The Elamite theory does not account for these names, and fails to explain this descent. 2. Regarding Haman's wife Zeresh, whom the theory would identify with an Elamite goddess, there should be noted (1) the argument for the goddess Kirisha, thus: The deity Kirisha is apparently identical with the deity Kiririsha, who may have been a goddess. A temple was dedicated to Humba and Kiririsha, and hence Kiririsha or Kirisha may have been the wife of Humba (WZKM. vi. 63). The argument lacks cogency. (2) Some texts of Josephus give the initial letter in the name of Haman's wife as G (Antiq. xi. 6, 10; see Niese's edition); and reading Geresh instead of Zeresh, the sound approximates that of Kirisha, the Elamite deity, perhaps a goddess. But other copies of Josephus agree with the great manuscripts of the Septuagint (A, B, and Lucian). These typical texts support the Hebrew form of the name in this essential point and attest in various ways the sibilant zain, Z and not G, as the first letter in the name of Haman's wife. They allow scant resemblance to the name Kirisha. 3. The name of the Elamite deity Mashti (not Bar-ti, as Professor Sayce, using the alternative sound of the first sign, writes the name) may, for phonetic reasons, be pronounced Washti, and thus correspond to Vashti, the queen in the opening chapters of the book of Esther. Washti was "probably a goddess" (WZKM. vi. 51). Evidently much that is essential to the theory remains to be proven. Even if the assumption regarding the sex of this deity were established as a fact, it would be necessary to inquire whether Vashti was not the abbreviation of a compound name containing the name of this deity (cp. Ben-hadad). But, after all, Vashti may be a good Persian name, as befits the queen of Ahasuerus (see VASHTI).

II. Regarding the Hebrews who figure in the narrative: 1. Possibly the parents of Esther named their daughter, or friends of later years called the handsome maiden, after the bright and beautiful star of evening and morning (Is. xiv. 12; Rev. xxii. 16; cp. Lebana). But (1) there are obstinate etymological facts against identifying the name of Esther with that of the star-goddess Ishtar. The initial letter of Esther is aleph, whereas of Ishtar it is ain. All the Semitic dialects, east and west, in which the name of the goddess occurs, without exception preserved this distinction and maintained it until centuries after the book of Esther had been written and the celebration of Purim had become universal among the Jews throughout the world. It is reported, indeed, that the plural of Ishtar is written with aleph, not ain, in some Jewish incantations on sherds found in

Babylonia. The date of these sherds is not stated. But whether they are as early as the book of Esther or much later, this form of Ishtar is abnormal and sadly degenerate. The citation of it is irrelevant, for the vocabulary of the book of Esther is not degenerate. There is, however, no need to think of Ishtar at all; since Esther, as a Persian word, is the good name Stella, a star. (2) The evidence that *hadashatu* denotes a bride is valid. But there is no evidence whatsoever that it signified myrtle, and none that it was used as a characteristic epithet of goddesses. The comparison of it with Esther's own Hebrew name Hadassah is peculiarly unfortunate from the standpoint of etymology; for the Assyrian counterpart of Hadassah would be *'adassatu*, not *hadashatu*. (3) Finally, Esther is known in the book that bears her name as the daughter of Abihail and a queen of Ahasuerus; and the theory utterly fails to explain these relationships. 2. Mordecai means either belonging to Marduk or is a diminutive or hypocoristic form of Marduk. Now (1) the name Marduk and its diminutive Marduka were quite frequently borne by men in Babylon. (2) The form of the name in the book of Esther points to a man, not to a god. (3) Such names were not wanting among godly Hebrews: compare Apollos, Henadad, Shenazzar. The name Mordecai itself was borne by another Jew of the exile besides the cousin of Esther (Ezra ii. 2). (4) The narrative takes Mordecai's lineage back through several ancestors to the tribe of Benjamin (Esth. ii. 5).

Thus, on removing the mere surmises from the mass of evidence offered in support of the theory, the name Esther may perchance be, but yet scarcely is, a form of Ishtar in this narrative; Mordecai is certainly derived from Marduk; and Haman and Vashti may represent Elamite deities. But granting all this in favor of the theory, nevertheless: 1. No substantial ground has been found for regarding the personages who bear these names in the narrative as deities rather than people; and, moreover, the hypothesis fails to account for the ancestry of the chief actors in the events described. And why does king Ahasuerus appear? 2. Against the theory of a heathen origin is the acceptance of the event as historical, and the universal celebration of the festival in the first century by the Jews throughout the world (Antiq. xi. 6, 13; Septuagint; 2 Mac. xv. 36). 3. The principal events of the narrative are expressly claimed to be recorded in the state chronicles of Persia (Esth. ii. 23; vi. 1, 2; x. 2). 4. Finally, so far as any form of the theory assumes a heathen festival as the origin of Purim, the grand objection is that no heathen celebration has yet been discovered for the fourteenth and fifteenth days of Adar, the twelfth month of the year. See other articles such as MORDECAI, PROVINCE, VASHTI.

The language of the book of Esther is Hebrew, like that of Ezra and Nehemiah, but with more Persian words. From x. 2 it would seem that Xerxes was dead when it was penned. Its date is generally fixed about 425 B. C., forty years after his assassination, or at least in the reign of Artaxerxes, 465–425; and there is no valid reason to date it later. The book is not quoted in the N. T., nor alluded to. Certain additions to it appear in the Septuagint. Jerome separated them and put them at the end of the book, and they now find place in the Apocrypha.

E′tam [place of beasts of prey].

1. A village on the border of the south country and the lowland, transferred from Judah to Simeon (1 Chron. iv. 32; cp. Josh. xv. 32 and 42). In the cleft of a rock near by Samson dwelt for a time (Judg. xv. 8, 11), having gone down thither from Timnah. Perhaps the site is ‘Aitun, about 11 miles W. S. W. of Hebron. But the rock of Etam may have been nearer Samson's home. Chiefly for this reason Conder locates the cleft at Beit ‘Atab, 5 miles S. E. by E. of Zorah; Schick at Arak Isma‘in, in wady Isma‘in, 2½ miles E. S. E. of Zorah.

2. A town in the neighborhood of Bethlehem, fortified by Rehoboam for the defense of Judah after the secession of the ten tribes (1 Chron. iv. 3; 2 Chron. xi. 6; and Josh. xv. 60 in Septuagint). According to the Talmud, the temple at Jerusalem was supplied with water conducted from the spring of Etam, and an ancient aqueduct extends for 7 miles from the temple hill, past Bethlehem, to three pools, the lowest of which is fed by a neighboring spring, situated on the south, called ‘Ain ‘Atan. Josephus relates that Solomon was fond of driving out in the early morning to Etan (written also Etam), distant 2 schoinoi or 7 miles from Jerusalem, where there was a delightful prospect of gardens and rivulets (Antiq. viii. 7, 3; cp. Song vi. 11, 12; Eccl. ii. 5, 6). Here, then, at ‘Ain ‘Atan, near the village of Urtas and about 2 miles southwest of Bethlehem, was the site of Etam. The three reservoirs were discovered by pilgrims at quite a late date and named the pools of Solomon. The aqueduct is ancient, antedating the Christian era and the Roman period. Pontius Pilate probably used it as the last section of the great conduit which he undertook to build for the purpose of bringing water to Jerusalem from a distance of 200 stadia or 23 miles (Antiq. xviii. 3, 2; or 400 stadia, War ii. 9, 4). Another section extends from the three pools to the wady el-‘Arrub near Hebron, and a third reaches a few miles southward from the pools to the wady el-Biar.

E′tham [perhaps boundary].

The first encampment of the Israelites after leaving Succoth, as they were departing from Egypt. It was on the edge of the wilderness (Ex. xiii. 20; Num. xxxiii. 6). It apparently did not lie on the direct road from Egypt to the Philistine country (Ex. xiii. 17). The name was extended to a portion of the wilderness of Shur, requiring at least three days to cross it, and apparently reaching to or even including Marah (Num. xxxiii. 8; cp. Ex. xv. 22). Identifications have been proposed, but are all conjectural.

E′than [firmness, perpetuity].

1. A descendant of Judah, belonging to the tribal family of Zerah (1 Chron. ii. 6). He seems to have been the person of this name who was celebrated for his wisdom (1 Kin. iv. 31; Ps. lxxxix., title).

2. A Levite, of the family of Gershom, house of Libni (1 Chron. vi. 42, 43; cp. 20 and Num. xxvi. 58).

3. A Levite, of the family of Merari, house of Mushi. He was a son of Kishi or Kushaiah, and was appointed a singer in the time of David (1 Chron. vi. 44, 47; xv. 17, 19). His name, it appears, was changed to Jeduthun, praising one, after his appointment to service in the tabernacle at Gibeon (1 Chron. xvi. 38–41; cp. xv. 17, 19 with xxv. 1).

Eth′a-nim [incessant rains].

The seventh month (1 Kin. viii. 2), called also Tishri. It was approximately October. Within it fell the feast of trumpets, the great day of atonement, and the feast of tabernacles. See YEAR.

Eth′ba-al [with Baal, or, to judge from the Greek form, with him is Baal].

A king of the Tyrians and Sidonians, and father of Jezebel (1 Kin. xvi. 31; Antiq. viii. 13, 1 and 2; ix. 6, 6). He was priest of Ashtoreth, but slew his brother and seized the throne (contra Apion. i. 18).

E′ther [abundance].

A village in the lowland of Judah (Josh. xv. 42), but allotted to the tribe of Simeon (xix. 7). It is called Tochen in 1 Chron. iv. 32. The best suggestion as to its site is the ruined village of ‘Atr, about a mile northwest by north of Beit Jibrin.

E-thi-o′pi-a [Greek *Aithiopia*, sunburnt. Possibly, however, this may have been substituted for the Egyptian *Ethaush*, Ethiopia, with which it nearly agrees in sound].

1. A country called in the Hebrew language Cush, which is continually mentioned in connection with Egypt (Ps. lxviii. 31; Is. xx. 3–5; Ezek. xx. 4, 5; Dan. xi. 43; Nah. iii. 9) and sometimes with Libya or the Libyans (2 Chron. xvi. 8; Ezek. xxx. 5; xxxviii. 5; Dan. xi. 43; Nah. iii. 9), and must certainly have been in eastern Africa. It ran southward from Syene, the southern point of Egypt (Ezek. xxix. 10, R. V. margin; cp. Judith i. 10). It was manifestly the upper region of the Nile, the Soudan, Nubia with Kordofan, Sennaar, and northern Abyssinia, a region in large measure desert, though in places fertile. This general region was known to the Egyptians

as Kes. The rivers of Ethiopia (Is. xviii. 1; Zeph. iii. 10) were probably the White and Blue Niles, with the Atbara or Tacazze. The topazes of Ethiopia were celebrated (Job xxviii. 19). Its inhabitants were tall (Is. xlv. 14). They were colored men, probably black (Jer. xiii. 23). They engaged in mercantile transactions, selling the productions of their country in foreign lands (Is. xlv. 14), and as a consequence became wealthy (xliii. 3). When the Ethiopians, led by Zerah, invaded Judah, they were signally defeated by king Asa (2 Chron. xiv. 9-15; xvi. 8). An Ethiopian dynasty, the twenty-fifth, established itself in Egypt; to it belonged that Tirhakah who met Sennacherib in battle at Eltekeh (2 Kin. xix. 9; Is. xxxvii. 9). Isaiah (xx. 1-6) and Zephaniah (ii. 12) prophesied against the Ethiopians, while the psalmist predicted that Ethiopia would haste to stretch out her hands unto God (Ps. lxviii. 31; cp. lxxxvii. 4). The prophecy obtained fulfillment in the conversion of the Ethiopian eunuch (Acts viii. 26-40) and the introduction of the gospel into Abyssinia, which still remains a Christian kingdom.

2. There was an Asiatic as well as an African Cush. See CUSH 1 and 2.

Eth-ka′zin, in A. V. **It-tah-ka′zin**, with the case-ending.

A place on the boundary line of Zebulun (Josh. xix. 13).

Eth′nan [gift, hire].

A man of Judah, family of Hezron (1 Chron. iv. 7; cp. 5 and ii. 24).

Eth′ni [bountiful, munificent].

A Gershonite Levite (1 Chron. vi. 41). In ver. 21 he is called Jeatherai. The main difference is found in the last consonant. A scribe seems to have confounded the Hebrew letters nun and resh.

Eu-bu′lus [well advised, prudent].

A Roman Christian (2 Tim. iv. 21).

Eu′me-nes [well disposed].

King of Pergamos, 197-159 B. C. When the Romans defeated Antiochus the Great at Magnesia in 190 B. C., they assigned the greater part of the defeated king's realm north of the Taurus mountains to Eumenes in return for the services which he had rendered them (1 Mac. viii. 6-8; Livy xxxvii. 44). They bestowed Lycia and Caria on the Rhodians. The report, which Judas Maccabæus heard, that the Romans had taken India and Media also was not true.

Eu-ni′ce [blessed with victory].

A pious Jewess, mother of Timothy (Acts xvi. 1; 2 Tim. i. 5).

Eu′nuch [having the couch].

Properly a chamberlain; but in the East persons who had been rendered impotent were employed for this office, hence an impotent man (Is. lvi. 3; Mat. xix. 12). There is scarcely a doubt that the word is used in this sense throughout Scripture, even when it is rendered into English by some other term. There have been, and still are, married eunuchs (Gen. xxxix. 1, rendered officer, and 7). Eunuchs often obtained high position and great authority. The captain of the guard of Pharaoh and his chief butler and his chief baker were eunuchs (Gen. xxxvii. 36; xl. 2, 7, translated officer). Eunuchs ministered at the court of Babylon (Dan. i. 3). They served in the presence of the Persian king, and acted as doorkeepers of his palace (Esth. i. 10; ii. 21); a eunuch was over his harem (ii. 3, 14), and a eunuch was deputed to attend his queen (iv. 5). They served also at the court of Ahab and his son Jehoram, and they waited upon Jezebel (1 Kin. xxii. 9; 2 Kin. viii. 6; ix. 32). Even in Judah, although eunuchs were legally excluded from the congregation of the Lord (Deut. xxiii. 1), they were employed at David's court (1 Chron. xxviii. 1), and, in the last days of the monarchy, at the degenerate court of the successors of Josiah (2 Kin. xxiv. 15 with Jer. xxix. 2; 2 Kin. xxv. 19). The eunuchs in Judah were probably in most, if not in all, cases foreigners (Jer. xxxviii. 7). The cupbearer of Herod the Great was a eunuch, as were also the official who brought him his food and the one who assisted him to bed; and his favorite wife Mariamne was served by a eunuch (Antiq. xv. 7, 4; xvi. 8, 1). A eunuch was over the treasure of queen Candace of Ethiopia, and he was admitted to baptism (Acts viii. 27, 37; cp. Is. lvi. 3).

Eu-o′di-a, in A. V. **Euodias** [fragrance].

A Christian woman at Philippi blemished by bickering with Syntyche (Phil. iv. 2).

Eu-phra′tes [Greek modification of the Hebrew *Perath*, which is variously explained as meaning sweet or broad or with good fords].

One of the great rivers of western Asia and the world. It is formed by the junction of two streams: the Murad, rising in Armenia, between lake Van and mount Ararat, being the more easterly; and the Frat or Kara, rising about 40 miles northeast of Erzeroum, the more westerly. Sometimes the name Frat, cognate with the Hebrew *Perath*, is applied to both of these streams. They run in a westerly direction to about latitude 39° N., and longitude 39° E., after which the combined waters turn southward, break through the southern chain of the Taurus mountains, and at various places are not more than 50 miles from the Mediterranean. Then the river bends southeastward, constituting the western boundary of Mesopotamia. About latitude 31° N., longitude 47° E., the Tigris unites with the Euphrates, to constitute what is now called the Shat el-Arab, which, after a course of about 90 miles more, falls into the Persian Gulf. The whole length of the Euphrates is about 1800 miles. It was one of the rivers of Paradise (Gen. ii. 14). It was familiarly known to the Hebrews as "the great river" or simply "the river." It formed the limit in the northeasterly direction of the Hebrew dominion when its extension was at the greatest (xv. 18; cp. 2 Sam. viii. 3; 1 Chron. xviii. 3; 1 Kin. iv. 21, 24). It was a boundary between east and west, between Egypt and Assyria-Babylonia, each power desiring to possess the country between the brook of Egypt and the Euphrates. In the Persian period also it separated east from west (Ezra iv. 10, 11; v. 3; vi. 6; Neh. ii. 7). It was a boundary of the Seleucidan kingdom (1 Mac. iii. 32; vii. 8), and it was regarded as the eastern limit of the Roman empire. The greatest city on its banks was Babylon. Another important place was the old Hittite capital Carchemish, the scene of various battles, especially of one between the Babylonians and the Egyptians, the latter led by Pharaoh-necho (Jer. xlvi. 2). In the book of Revelation certain angels are described as being "bound in the great river Euphrates" (Rev. ix. 14), and the sixth vial was poured out upon the Euphrates itself (xvi. 12).

Eu-pol′e-mus [good at war].

Son of that John who obtained special privileges for the Jews from Antiochus the Great (1 Mac. viii. 17; 2 Mac. iv. 11). Eupolemus was one of two ambassadors sent by Judas Maccabæus to Rome to make a treaty with the Romans. Some think that he is the Jewish historical writer Eupolemus whom Alexander Polyhistor quotes so frequently.

Eu-ra′qui-lo [from Greek *eurakulōn*, the northeast wind].

A tempestuous northeast wind which blows over the Mediterranean (Acts xxvii. 14; in A. V. Euroclydon). The wind from that quarter, now called Gregali, blows generally in early spring, and is the most violent wind on the Mediterranean. It is sometimes termed a Levanter.

Eu-roc′ly-don [from Greek *eurokludōn*, perhaps a wind from the southeast or east].

A tempestuous wind which blows from the southeast or the east. It brought the vessel in which Paul was sailing toward Rome first into danger, and then to shipwreck (Acts xxvii. 14, A. V.). But the revisers prefer the reading *Eurakulōn*, which is in some manuscripts, and render Euraquilo.

Eu′ty-chus [fortunate].

A young man of Troas, who, falling asleep while Paul was preaching there, fell from the third loft or floor. He was taken up dead, but was miraculously restored to life by the apostle (Acts xx. 9, 10).

E-van′gel-ist [from Greek *euaggelistēs*, a messenger of good tidings].

An order of men in the primitive church distinct from apostles, prophets, pastors, and teachers (Eph. iv. 11). Their name implied that their special function was to announce the glad tidings of the gospel to those before ignorant of them, and as they were not pastors of particular churches, they were able to go from place to place preaching to those who as yet were without the Christian pale. Philip, who was the means of converting and baptizing the Ethiopian eunuch, was an evangelist (Acts xxi. 8), and we find him successively at Jerusalem (vi. 5), in Samaria (viii. 5), on the road between Jerusalem and Gaza (26), in the cities north of Ashdod (40), and finally at Cæsarea (40; xxi. 8). Timothy was also commanded by Paul to do the work of an evangelist (2 Tim. iv. 5). At a later date the name was given to the writers of the four gospels.

Eve [life].

The name given by Adam to the first woman because she was the mother of all living (Gen. iii. 20). Soon after his creation, she was brought into being to be a help meet for him (21, 22). The narrative has been variously interpreted as meaning that—1. Woman was formed from the rib of man, Adam being in a trance and beholding the operation, but feeling nothing; 2. Woman was not actually formed from man's rib, but Adam had a vision by which he was taught his oneness of nature with woman and her rights and privileges; 3. Woman's relation to man is set forth in allegory. From a literary point of view the third explanation is unlikely; for it is improbable that the writer intended to insert an allegory in the midst of historical narrative which includes the creation of the universe, the creation of man, and the flood. The two human beings were placed in the garden of Eden; and in order to test their obedience, they were forbidden to touch or taste the fruit of one particular tree. But the serpent under Satanic influence led Eve to question the goodness of God, and then to eat the forbidden fruit. She afterwards persuaded Adam to eat, who thus shared her guilt. The result was the fall of man (iii. 1-24; 2 Cor. xi. 3; 1 Tim. ii. 13). After the expulsion of the guilty pair from the garden, Eve successively became the mother of Cain, Abel, Seth, with other sons and also daughters (Gen. iv. 1, 2, 25, 26; v. 1-5).

E′vi.

One of the five kings of Midian, allies or vassals of Sihon, slain in the war waged by Moses against the Midianites because they seduced the Israelites to licentious idolatry (Num. xxxi. 8; Josh. xiii. 21).

E′vil.

The origin of evil is a problem which has perplexed speculative minds in all ages and countries. God is not the author of sin, but he permits it. He has permitted it, because the revelation of his infinite perfection is the highest conceivable good and the ultimate end of all his works, and there could be no manifestation of certain of his attributes if sin were not permitted. Were there no misery, there could be no mercy shown by

God; and there could be no revelation of his grace and justice, if there were no sin (Rom. ix. 22, 23). Sin is permitted that God's justice may be known in its punishment, and his mercy in its forgiveness. Holiness and sin may be nearly balanced on earth; but in the universe, sin is very limited in comparison with holiness, and the number of lost men and angels is doubtless small compared with the whole number of the rational creatures of God.

E-vil-mer'o-dach [in Babylonian, *Avil-marduk*, man of god Merodach].

Son and successor of Nebuchadnezzar. He ascended the throne as early as the seventh month of 562 B. C., and reigned only two years. In the first of these two he took Jehoiachin, the captive king of Judah, from his prison, and placed him above all the other rulers whom he had in thrall, giving him a daily allowance of food during the remainder of his life (2 Kin. xxv. 27–30; Jer. lii. 31–34). A conspiracy was formed against Evil-merodach, his own brother-in-law, Neriglissar or Nergalsharuṣur, being at its head. The king was accused of lawlessness and intemperance, and was put to death in 560 B. C. Neriglissar, the chief conspirator, then ascended the throne (Antiq. x. 11, 2; contra Apion. i. 20).

E'vil Spir'it. See DEMON.

Ex-e-cu'tion-er. See GUARD.

Ex'ile. See CAPTIVITY and DISPERSION.

Ex'o-dus [a going out, a way out].

1. The departure of the Israelites from Egypt, after they had been divinely emancipated from bondage in that land. There is considerable difficulty in settling the exact route of the Exodus. The miracles by the hand of Moses were wrought at Zoan, that is Tanis (Ps. lxxviii. 12), and Ramses was a suburb of that capital. Thence the Israelites journeyed to Succoth (Ex. xii. 37), the site of which is marked by Tell el-Maskhutah in the wady Tumilat, 32 miles south-southeast of Tanis and 11 miles west of Isma'iliya. They did not take the shortest route to Palestine, which lay through the land of the Philistines, but they went by the way of the wilderness by the Red Sea (xiii. 17, 18). Their first encampment after leaving Succoth was Etham. The site has not been identified; but it was on the edge of the wilderness (20). Thence they turned back and encamped before Pi-hahiroth, between Migdol and the sea, before Baal-zephon (xiv. 2; Num. xxxiii. 7). This camp has not been definitely located. It was, however, west of the Red Sea. From this place they marched through the Red Sea into the wilderness of Shur (Ex. xv. 4, 22; Num. xxxiii. 8), and thence along the coast of the Red Sea toward mount Sinai (Ex. xvi. 1; Num. xxxiii. 10, 15). For the date of the exodus, see CHRONOLOGY.

2. The book of Exodus, the second book of the Pentateuch. In the Hebrew Scriptures the title consists of the opening words, "And these the names." The name Exodus was appropriately given to the book by the Greek translators, because it narrates the departure from Egypt which was a turning point in Israel's history.

The book is a continuous narrative, and may be divided into three sections: 1. In Egypt (i.–xii. 36). The period of several centuries immediately following the descent of Jacob into Egypt is passed over with a single remark about the increase of the people after the death of Joseph (i. 7). Oppression of the Israelites (8 seq.). Birth, earlier life, and call of Moses (ii.–iv.). Struggle with Pharoah and infliction of the plagues; in connection with the last plague, institution of the passover (v.–xii. 36). 2. From Egypt to Sinai (xii. 37–xix. 2). Departure from Ramses (xii. 37–42). Supplementary regulation respecting the passover, stating the condition upon which foreigners could partake of it (43–51). Sanctification of the firstborn enjoined upon Moses (xiii. 1, 2); announcement to the people of a seven days' festival to be observed henceforth in connection with the passover, and of God's command to sanctify the firstborn (3–16). Passage of the Red Sea (xiv.), song of deliverance (xv. 1–19), bitter water at Marah, manna and quails (20–xvi.). At Rephidim: water from rock in Horeb, victory over Amalek, and visit of Jethro (xvii., xviii.). 3. At Sinai (xix. 3–xl. 38 and uninterruptedly to Num. x. 10). Establishment of the theocracy: theocratic covenant proposed by God on condition of obedience (xix. 3–6), approval of the terms by the elders of the people (7, 8), the ten commandments and subsidiary laws enacted and written in the book of the covenant (xx.–xxiii.; xxiv. 4; for analysis and form of these laws, see THEOCRACY, AMRAPHEL). Ratification of the covenant by the nation (xxiv. 1–8), and the covenant meal of the contracting parties (9–11). Moses in the mount; architectural specifications for the tabernacle and its furniture, tables of stone (12–xxxi.; for analysis, see TABERNACLE). The golden calf (xxxii., xxxiii.). Moses' second sojourn in the mount, with summarizing urgent repetition of covenant laws (xxxiv.). Construction and erection of the tabernacle (xxxv.–xl.). See PENTATEUCH.

Ex'or-cist [in Greek, administrator of an oath; expeller by adjuration].

One who professes by using words and ceremonies to eject evil spirits, and deliver from their malign influence. Certain impostors of this sort, vagabond Jews, were encountered by Paul at Ephesus (Acts xix. 13–19).

E'zar. See EZER, II.

Ez'bai.

Father of one of David's mighty men (1 Chron. xi. 37, possibly merely a variant reading of 2 Sam. xxiii. 35).

Ez'bon.

1. A son of Gad (Gen. xlvi. 16). See OZNI.
2. The head of a father's house, family of Bela, tribe of Benjamin (1 Chron. vii. 7).

Ez-e-ki'as. See HEZEKIAH.

E-ze'ki-el [God doth strengthen; or, perhaps, God is strong].

One of the greater Jewish prophets, a son of Buzi, and of priestly family (Ezek. i. 3). He grew up, until beyond the years of childhood, in the home-land; near Jerusalem, since he was of priestly descent; during the ministry of the prophet Jeremiah. He was carried captive from Judah with Jehoiachin, eight years after Daniel's deportation (xxxiii. 21; xl. 1; cp. 2 Kin. xxiv. 11–16). Josephus says that he was a youth at the time (Antiq. x. 6, 3). He was not a child, but was under the age when Levites assumed their duties and were reckoned in the census as men. He lived with the Jewish exiles on the river Chebar in Babylonia, probably at Tel-abib (Ezek. i. 1, 3; iii. 15); married probably as early as the sixth, at least by the ninth, year of the captivity, and had a house (viii. 1; xxiv. 1, 18).

His prophetic ministry began in the fifth year of Jehoiachin's captivity, seven years before the destruction of the temple at Jerusalem, while he was dwelling on the Chebar (i. 1, 2). He was then in his thirtieth year (i. 1), the age at which Levites entered upon service (Num. iv. 3). The theory that the thirtieth year does not refer to Ezekiel's age, but is a date reckoned either from the accession of Nabopolassar, Nebuchadnezzar's father, or from the reforms of Josiah, fails in view of Jer. xxv. 1, 3; 2 Kin. xxiii. 36; xxv. 2–6; Ezek. i. 2. Though an exile in a foreign land, Ezekiel had freedom to utter his prophecies, and was resorted to for advice by the elders of the people (viii. 1; xiv. 1; xx. 1); but his words were not followed faithfully (xxxiii. 30–33). It is evident from the affinities of thought and language, that he was quite familiar with Jeremiah's teaching. Perhaps as a frequenter of the sanctuary he had heard Jeremiah preaching at the temple or listened to the public reading of Jeremiah's prophecies there (Jer. vii. 2; xix. 14; xxvi. 2; xxviii. 5; xxxvi. 8); or later, while an exile in Babylonia, he may have had a collection of these discourses in written form (xxix. 1, 31; xxxvi. 32; Dan. ix. 2). At any rate he takes up brief doctrinal remarks, or suggestive allegories, or short speeches of Jeremiah, and develops and expands them, and often gives to them a literary finish: as the caldron (Jer. i. 13–15; Ezek. xi. 2–11; xxiv. 3–14), the two sisters (Jer. iii. 6–11; Ezek. xxiii. 1–49), forgiveness for the condemned, when penitent (a nation, Jer. xviii. 5–12, an individual, Ezek. xviii. 21–32); the evil shepherds replaced by the Davidic king (Jer. xxiii. 1–6; Ezek. xxxiv. 1–24), individual responsibility in view of

the proverb about the fathers eating sour grapes (Jer. xxxi. 29, 30; Ezek. xviii. 2–31). the new spiritual nature (Jer. xxxi. 33, 34; Ezek. xi. 19, 20; xxxvi. 25–29), the exiles, not the Jews in Jerusalem, the hope of the future (Jer. xxiv. 1–10; Ezek. xi. 15–21; xxxvii. 1–14). Ezekiel's prophetic activity extended over a period of at least twenty-two years (i. 2 with xxix. 17). The time and manner of his death are unknown. The late tradition that he was slain by a prince of the people because he denounced idolatry is worthless.

The book of the Prophet Ezekiel stands in the English Bible between Lamentations and Daniel. As these two books are placed among the Hagiographa in the Hebrew canon, Ezekiel's place in the Hebrew Scriptures is between Jeremiah and Hosea. The prophecies are arranged nearly, though not quite, in chronological order, and they are dated according to the years of Jehoiachin's captivity in which they were delivered. The book falls into three divisions:

I. Prophecies delivered before the capture of Jerusalem, foretelling its overthrow for its sins. In the fifth year the priest is called to the prophetic office and prepared for his work by a vision (i.–iii. 21), and then is directed to prophesy, by symbolical actions and their interpretation, the destruction of the city (iii. 22–vii.). In the sixth year, are denunciations of Judah for idolatry (viii.); symbolical departure of Jehovah from the temple because of its profanation (ix.–xi. 13); comfort, the exiles are still God's people, he will be a sanctuary to them (16), restore them to the land of Israel (17), give those that reform their lives a new heart (18–21). Unbelief and adherence to false prophets are the reasons for Jehovah's forsaking his city (xii.–xiv.); the event is certain (xv.–xvii.), but the repentant shall enjoy's God's favor (xviii.). Lamentation for the princes of Israel (xix.). In the seventh year, it is prophesied that, because Jehovah's name has been profaned in the sight of the heathen, he will punish the people, but will afterwards restore them for his name's sake (xx. 1–44); the doom is certain, the transgressions are come to remembrance before God (xx. 45–xxiii.). In the ninth year, the siege of Jerusalem and the dispersion of the people are symbolized by a caldron (xxiv.).

II. Prophecies of judgment against the nations: in the ninth year, against Ammon, Moab, Edom, and Philistia (xxv.); in the eleventh year, against Tyre and Sidon (xxvi.–xxviii.); and in the tenth, twenty-seventh, and eleventh years, against Egypt (xxix.–xxxii.).

III. Prophecies concerning the restoration, delivered after the capture and destruction of Jerusalem by Nebuchadnezzar. In the twelfth year, the evening before the news of the fall of the city reached the prophet, he received a second formal call to the prophetic work (xxxiii. 1–22). He is further taught that, after the judgment, the people shall recognize that Jehovah is God, and that a true prophet has been among them (23–33); a good shepherd, even David, shall be raised up (xxxiv.), their present foes punished (xxxv.), the people sanctified and restored to their land (xxxvi.), revived as from the dead, their twelve tribes reunited (xxxvii.), and their foes finally overthrown (xxxviii.–xxxix.). In the twenty-fifth year, the reëstablishment of God's church is disclosed, being symbolically exhibited in the vision of the temple enlarged and holy throughout, and the people cleansed and accepted by Jehovah (xl.–xliii.), its holy services (xliv.–xlvi.), the river of life issuing from it and making the desert to rejoice (xlvii.), and the distribution of the land among the tribes, and their common city known as the place where Jehovah is (xlviii.).

In this vision the temple that Ezekiel had known so well in his younger days is quite changed in appearance. Instead of the little hill of Zion, he beholds a high mountain, crowned by the buildings of a new and grander sanctuary. An angel, with a measuring rod and line, is standing at the gate. The new temple is modeled, indeed, after the old in its general arrangements, but it is so located with reference to the habitations of men, and its courts and chambers are so disposed, as to safeguard the holiness of Jehovah, who is soon to dwell there, and impress upon the worshipers Jehovah's separateness from both moral and ceremonial impurity. Many years earlier Ezekiel had seen in vision Jehovah leaving the old, desecrated temple (x. 18, 19; xi. 22–24); now the prophet beholds Jehovah returning by the same gate into the temple and the glory of Jehovah filling the house, and he hears a voice from within saying, "This is the place of my throne, ... where I will dwell in the midst of the children of Israel for ever; and the house of Israel shall no more defile my holy name" (xliii. 1–7). In the inner court, before the holy house, Ezekiel sees the altar of atonement provided for the new Israel and hears the declaration, "And I will accept you, saith the Lord Jehovah" (13–27). The worship of accepted Israel is now described by the prophet. In the new theocracy the reality will correspond to the divine ideal. The uncircumcised in heart or flesh will not enter into the sanctuary. The Levitical families who proved unfaithful of old will not be allowed to officiate at the altar; yet they will be given a place, albeit a humble one, in the temple. The priests, the sons of Zadok, whose very name means righteous, that had remained faithful, will alone fill the high office of priest before Jehovah (xliv.). An oblation unto Jehovah will be made of a portion of the land for the support of the services and ministry of the sanctuary (xlv. 1–6). For the prince also suitable pro-

vision will be made from the oblation-land, enabling him to maintain the public services in the name of the people, and he shall not abuse his power by oppressing the people or encroaching on the prerogatives of the priests (7–12; xlvi. 2, 16–18). The people likewise shall assemble in their own appointed place in the temple, when they worship (9). All members of the theocracy, official and lay, know and perform the duties in reference to atonement which belong to them in their several places and relations. Ezekiel is next shown a river issuing from the temple, swelling into a mighty stream, and bringing life and health to the regions of barrenness and death (xlvii. 1–12). The bounds of the land to be occupied by the restored community are described (xlvii. 13–20), and the location of the tribes (21–xlviii. 29); the oblation-land being divided between priests, Levites, the crown, and the city (xlviii. 8–22). The city belongs to all Israel in common (15–20, 30–34; cp. 19 and xlv. 6), and its name is Jehovah-shammah, Jehovah is there (xlviii. 35), symbolizing the central thought of the entire prophecy.

What was Ezekiel's contribution to Israel's thought? Critics of the school of Wellhausen regard Ezekiel as the father of the later formal Judaism. They assert that the description of the new Jerusalem in chaps. xl.–xlviii. is a program, and gave rise to the characteristic priestly regulations contained in Leviticus and Numbers. This theory is rejected by critics of the school of Ewald, however, and by all scholars who take the biblical view of the origin of Israel's institutions; and they cite evidence both that the characteristic legislation of Leviticus antedates Ezekiel, and also that the prophet did not intend these chapters as a program. Further the picture that is unfolded in those chapters is not an ideal which the prophet expected would be realized literally, but is purely symbolical; for in no other way is it possible to understand the high mountain of the new Zion, and the measurements, and the allotments of the land which are geometrical and not geographical, and the healing waters that issue from the sanctuary and presently become a mighty river, and the trees whose fruit is produced every month and whose leaves are for healing. Ezekiel's enrichment of Israel's thought, through these chapters and his other prophecies, is found in the spiritual teaching. Among other things he contributed: 1. To the thought of God. While others speak of Jehovah shepherding his people (Gen. xlviii. 15; Ps. xxiii.), gathering the scattered flock of Israel (Jer. xxiii. 3; xxxi. 10), and tenderly caring for them (Is. xl. 11), Ezekiel represents God as seeking his lost sheep (xxxiv. 11–16; cp. Mat. xviii. 12–14; Luke xix. 10). 2. To the vision of the new Jerusalem: the high mountain (Ezek. xl. 2; Rev. xxi. 10), the holy city, God's tabernacle among men (Ezek. xxxvii. 27; Rev. xxi. 3), the glory of God in it (Ezek. xliii. 2–5; Rev. xxi. 11), the city foursquare (Ezek. xlviii. 16, 30; Rev. xxi. 16), having twelve gates (Ezek. xlviii. 30–34; Rev. xxi. 12, 13), the river of life (Ezek. xlvii. 1; Rev. xxii. 1), and the trees on either side of the river, whose leaves are for healing (Ezek. xlvii. 7, 12; Rev. xxii, 2). As in Ezekiel, so in John the vision is symbolical. 3. But above all Ezekiel contributed to the spiritual conception of the Jerusalem of the future. Ezekiel depicts, indeed, as his predecessors had done, the fertility of the land in the new age (Ezek. xxxvi. 29, 30); but this aspect does not call forth his enthusiasm. Taking up a germinal teaching of Jeremiah's, he lays the emphasis on the renewed nature of the people and the holiness of the kingdom as the crowning glory of the coming time (xi. 19, 20; xxxvi. 24–29). The spiritually regenerate Zion is henceforth definitely before the minds of God's people as a noble idea and the great hope.

E'zel [separation, departure].
The place where David hid until Jonathan could inform him of Saul's disposition toward him (1 Sam. xx. 19).

E'zem, in A. V. twice **Azem** [a bone].
A village near the border of Edom in that part of the territory allotted to the tribe of Judah, which was afterwards assigned to Simeon (Josh. xv. 29; xix. 3; 1 Chron. iv. 29). Exact site unknown.

E'zer, I., in A. V. once **Ezar**, an error not found in the original edition of 1611 [enclosure, treasure].
A Horite tribe and its chieftain (Gen. xxxvi. 21, 30; 1 Chron. i. 38).

E'zer, II. [help].
1. A descendant, probably son, of Ephraim, killed in a raid against the Philistines (1 Chron. vii. 21).
2. A man of Judah, descended from Hur (1 Chron. iv. 4).
3. A Gadite who joined David at Ziklag (1 Chron. xii. 9).
4. A son of Jeshua. He was ruler of Mizpah, and repaired part of the wall of Jerusalem (Neh. iii. 19).
5. A priest who took part in the ceremony at the dedication of the rebuilt wall of Jerusalem (xii. 42).

E'zi-on-ge'ber, in A. V. often **Ezion-gaber** [backbone of a man].
A town on the Red Sea, at the northern end of the gulf of Akaba, near Elath, on the confines of Edom (Deut. ii. 8; 1 Kin. ix. 26; xxii. 48, 2 Chron. viii. 17). The Israelites encamped by the town as they journeyed in the wilderness (Num. xxxiii. 35). As Robinson suggested, the name may linger in el-Ghudyân, a small valley with brackish water opening into the Arabah from the western mountain some distance north of the fortress of 'Akaba, the approximate site of ancient

Elath. The respective letters correspond in Hebrew and Arabic.

Ez'nita. See ADINO.

Ez'ra, in R. V. once **Ezrah** (1 Chron. iv. 17), the pure Hebrew orthography [help].
1. A man who is registered with Judah (1 Chron. iv. 17).
2. One of the chief priests who returned from Babylon with Zerubbabel (Neh. xii. _, 7). A father's house bore his name in the next generation (ver. 13).
3. A priest descended from Zadok and from Phinehas (Ezra vii. 1–6). He was a ready scribe in the law of Moses, making the written law, which was in his hand (14), the subject of study and teaching (10, 11). In the seventh year of Artaxerxes Longimanus, king of Persia from 465 to 425 B. C., he was commissioned by the king to go to Jerusalem to inquire into the civil and religious condition of the Jewish community and conform it to the teaching of God's law (14). He was given orders on the authorities in the province Beyond-the-river for money and goods for the temple and for the exemption of the temple officials from taxation (21, 24). He was authorized to lead a fresh company of Jewish exiles to Palestine, in addition to those who had accompanied Zerubbabel and the high priest, Jeshua, eighty years before. On gathering together those who proposed to return, and mustering them, he found no Levites of the lower order; but on sending word to their chief, a few were persuaded to join him. After fasting and seeking God's guidance for the journey, the party, numbering over 1700 men, set forth on the twelfth day of the first month, in the seventh year of Artaxerxes, 458–457 B. C. (viii. 1–23, 31). On reaching Jerusalem four months later, on the first day of the fifth month (vii. 8), Ezra gave over the vessels he had received for the temple, offered sacrifice, and presented the king's orders to the neighboring governors (viii. 33–36). He was grieved to discover that Jews of Palestine, including even some of the priests, contrary to the law of Moses, had married heathen wives; but he succeeded in inducing most of them to divorce these foreign women (ix., x.). Thirteen years later, after Nehemiah had come to Jerusalem and repaired its walls, Ezra took the leading part in reading the law of Moses to the people of the colony (Neh. viii.). He died, according to Josephus, about the time of Eliashib's succession to the highpriesthood (Antiq. xi. 5, 5). He was certainly for a while contemporary with Eliashib (Neh. iii. 1; viii. 9). Ezra marks the transition from the prophets to the scribes. For his relation to the law and to the O. T. books, see CANON.
The book of Ezra consists of two parts: 1. A narrative of the return of the Jews from Babylonia under Zerubbabel in the year 538 B. C., the restoration of divine service, and the erection of the temple in the face of

Samaritan opposition (i.–vi.). 2. An account of the return of a second body of exiles under Ezra in the year 458–457, and of Ezra's energetic and successful measures to put a stop to the marriage of Israelites with foreigners (vii.–x.). The book is largely composed of copies of public records and official documents. The provincial documents and history are written in Aramaic (iv. 8–vi. 18; vii. 12–26); namely, copies of the letters sent to the Persian kings by officials of the province Beyond-the-river (iv. 8–16; v. 7–17; vi. 6–12), the royal replies and decrees imposing commands on these officials (iv. 17–22; vi. 3–5; and vii. 12–26, cp. 21, 24), and the brief connecting history referring primarily to provincial affairs (iv. 23–v. 5; vi. 1, 2, 13–18). Aramaic had been for several centuries the language of international commerce and diplomacy. The remainder of the book records the proper domestic history of Judah, and is written in Hebrew. It includes the royal edict issued in behalf of the Jews (i. 2–4), copies of Jewish archives (ii. 1–67; viii.; x. 18–44), and the connecting history. It has been supposed that the Aramaic narrative was written by a contemporary of Zerubbabel and eyewitness of the events described (cp. v. 4, where the pronoun we is used); but, since documents of the time of Artaxerxes are inserted (iv. 9–16; 17–22), the written narrative cannot date earlier than Ezra's time, and the pronoun we was employed in speaking of a past generation because the writer felt his identity with the Jewish people, past and present, as in ix. 6–15 and Neh. ix. 29, 33. Some would date the narrative even later; but see below.

At least a section of the book was written by Ezra, beginning with vii. 27, for it is expressed in the first person. Ezra, therefore, wrote history, and he may have compiled the book which bears his name, for the narrative closes during his lifetime. But why, it may be asked, if Ezra compiled the book which bears his name, are two passages in which Ezra is prominent, namely the ten opening verses of chapter vii. and the last chapter of the book, which is inseparable from the preceding ninth chapter, not expressed in the first person? The ten introductory verses are primarily genealogical. The use of the third person is natural. As the introduction was begun in the third person, it is with propriety concluded in the third person. Parallel changes of person occur in the book of Daniel, which is regarded as the work of one author. As to the last chapter of the book, it would seem that Ezra's record stopped at the ninth chapter and the narrative was concluded by another person, though not unlikely he was a contemporary of Ezra and acted under Ezra's authority, and was the scribe who drew up the protocol of the proceedings and wrote down the official list of the men who gave pledge (x. 18–44).

Some have supposed that those sections in which the pronoun I is not used were inserted in Ezra's narrative by another editor, whose hand is thought to be discernible in Nehemiah and Chronicles also, and many modern critics place the date of the supposititious editor after 330 B. C. The argument rests ultimately upon the fact that the books of Ezra and Nehemiah were reckoned as one book in the Hebrew canon, and upon the belief that the genealogies in the book of Nehemiah are carried down until the time of Alexander the Great; hence Ezra and Nehemiah must have been edited in the Grecian period. Now it is a credible, but not a necessary, supposition that the books of Ezra and Nehemiah were combined and supplemented by an editor. But apart from the possible implication of the genealogies (see NEHEMIAH), there is no reason to suppose that this hypothetical editor belonged to a younger generation than Ezra and Nehemiah. His supposed additions concern events in which Ezra and Nehemiah were participants, and the history is related as by an eyewitness (cp. above and see NEHEMIAH). And assuming that the books were not edited, and are entirely distinct from each other in authorship throughout, as they are confessedly in large part, there was reason for reckoning them as one. This reason is scarcely found in the purpose to conform the number of books to the number of letters in the Hebrew alphabet, twenty-two, or, by peculiar computation, twenty-four; but the reason is found rather in the fact that the books of Ezra and Nehemiah form a continuous narrative of postexilic Jewish history, and are concerned with the interrelated work of the contemporary rulers of the community, Ezra the priest and Nehemiah the civil governor. The two books were known to be of diverse authorship (Neh. i. 1), but were reckoned as one, just as the twelve minor prophets were counted as one book, although it was recognized that the twelve writings were by twelve different prophets.

Ez′rah. See EZRA 1.

Ez′ra-hite [alternate form of Zarhite].
A descendant of Zerah, belonging to the tribe of Judah, as Ethan (1 Kin. iv. 31; Ps. lxxxix., title; cp. 1 Chron. ii. 6) and Heman (Ps. lxxxviii., title: cp. 1 Chron. ii. 6).

Ez′ri [probably, (God is) a help].
Overseer of the laborers who tilled David's fields (1 Chron. xxvii. 26).

F

Fair Ha′vens.
A harbor in Crete, near the city of Lasea, where Paul's ship touched (Acts xxvii. 8). Mr. Smith of Jordanhill located it about 5 miles east of Cape Matala, a promontory on the southern shore of Candia, just west of which the coastline turns northward.

Faith.

As far as a difference exists between belief and faith, belief is assent to testimony, and faith is assent to testimony, united with trust. Faith is an active principle; it is an act both of the understanding and the will. The distinction between belief and faith is that between "believe me" and "believe on me." The verb believe thus does service for the two nouns faith and belief. In the Bible faith or belief is confidence in the absolute truthfulness of every statement which comes from God (Gen. xv. 6; Deut. xxxii. 20; Mark xi. 22; Rom. iv. 3–5). In this faith the heroes of Scripture acted (Heb. xi.). In a special sense, faith is reliance on God's testimony regarding the mission and atoning death of his Son, the Lord Jesus Christ (John v. 24), and on the testimony of Jesus regarding himself (cp. John iii. 18; Acts iii. 16; xx. 21; Rom. iii. 25). Faith in the Redeemer, whereby a sinner rests upon him alone for salvation, is essential to salvation (John iii. 15, 16, 18; Eph. ii. 8, etc.). Belief in his historical existence and in the truth of his claims may be produced by evidence, but faith in him, reliance upon him for salvation, cannot be. It is the gift of God (Eph. ii. 8); the Spirit applies the truth to the soul. Human means should be used, in coöperation with his Spirit, for its production (Rom. x. 17). It may exist in larger or in smaller measure (Rom. iv. 19, 20; xiv. 1). The apostles when they deplored the weakness of their faith prayed to Jesus for its increase (Luke xvii. 5). It works by love (Gal. v. 6), and overcomes the world (1 John v. 4). But with all its importance it is not the greatest of the three primary Christian graces, that position being occupied by love (1 Cor. xiii. 13).

The system of doctrine given by revelation of God is termed the faith (Acts vi. 7; xxiv. 24; Rom. i. 5, etc.).

Fal'con.

A diurnal bird of prey other than a vulture. The family includes among its genera falcons strictly so-called, hawks, kites, eagles. The word is used in R. V. to render the Hebrew *'Ayyah* (Job xxviii. 7; in A. V. vulture), an unclean bird (Lev. xi. 14; Deut. xiv. 13; in A. V. kite). Several varieties are mentioned by Tristram as occurring in Palestine: the hobby hawk (*Falco subbuteo*), the red-legged hobby (*F. vespertinus*), the Eleanora falcon (*F. eleanoræ*).

Fal'low Deer [deer of fallow or yellowish hue].

The rendering of the Hebrew *Yaḥmur* in A. V. of Deut. xiv. 5; 1 Kin. iv. 23. R. V. has roebuck (q. v.). The genuine fallow deer (*Dama vulgaris*) has horns, with their upper part palmated. The hair in summer is yellowish-brown all over, with spots; in winter the tints are less bright. The male is about three feet high at the shoulder. Its native country seems to be the Mediterranean region.

It occurs sparingly in Galilee and mount Lebanon.

Fa-mil'iar Spir'it.

The spirit of a dead person which professed mediums claimed to summon to consultation (Deut. xviii. 11), and which appeared to speak from the earth (Is. xxix. 4), or to dwell in the controlling medium (Lev. xx. 27, in Hebrew). The medium was called the possessor or lord of a spirit (1 Sam. xxviii. 7, in Hebrew). It revealed the future (Is. viii. 19). It was either a special spirit which was believed to always respond to the summons of the medium, as the English rendering would lead one to suppose, and who might raise other ghosts; or it was any spirit whom the medium desired. 1 Sam. xxviii. 8 is capable of either interpretation, "Divine by the ghost" in you or "whom I shall name." To consult familiar spirits was apostasy from Jehovah (Lev. xix. 31; Is. viii. 19). Under the Mosaic law a person pretending to possess the power of consulting a familiar spirit was to be put to death (Lev. xix. 31; xx. 6, 27; Deut. xviii. 11). Saul carried out this enactment, but when sorely troubled about his fate, he sought out a woman of Endor who had a familiar spirit, asked her to bring back Samuel to the world, and believed her statement that she had succeeded (1 Sam. xxviii. 3, 5–25). Manasseh favored them that professed to have familiar spirits (2 Kin. xxi. 6; 2 Chron. xxxiii. 6). His grandson Josiah carried out the Mosaic law against them (2 Kin. xxiii. 24). They probably included ventriloquists, and the voice of the spirit, which appeared to come in a whisper from the ground, emanated from the human pretender himself.

Fam'ine.

Deficiency of food, generally produced either by failure of rain leading to the withering of the crops, or by the prevention of the entrance of food into a beleaguered city. Famine compelled Abraham to leave Canaan and sojourn in Egypt (Gen. xii. 10). It was the first of a series of famines connected with the history of the patriarch and his descendants, and which led the Hebrews to temporarily withdraw from Palestine (xxvi. 1; xli. 27–56; xlvii. 13). Other famines occurred in the days of the judges which made Elimelech remove to Moab (Ruth i. 1), in David's reign (2 Sam. xxi. 1), in the time of Elijah (1 Kin. xvii. 1–xviii. 46), in Elisha's time (2 Kin. iv. 38; viii. 1), and in the reign of Claudius, A. D. 41–54, when severe local famines swept in succession from Judæa in his fourth year to Greece in his ninth year and Italy in his eleventh year (Acts xi. 28; Antiq. xx. 2, 5; 5, 2; Tacitus, Annals xii. 43). The chief famines produced in besieged cities by the foe outside preventing provisions from entering them are those during the siege of Samaria by Benhadad (2 Kin. vi. 24–vii. 20) and during the sieges of Jerusalem by Nebuchadnezzar (xxv. 1–3; Jer. lii. 1–6) and by Titus (War v. 10, 2 and 3).

Fan.

The winnowing fan, in Hebrew *Mizreh*, still called *midhra* by the Arabs, was a fork with six prongs, with which grain, after it had been threshed, was thrown up against the air to clear it of the chaff (Is. xxx. 24; Jer. xv. 7). A shovel was also used for the same purpose. See THRESHING.

Far'thing.

1. A Roman *Quadrans*, a small brass coin equal to the fourth part of an *as*. The Greeks used the Roman name, calling the coin *kodrantes*. In the time of Christ its value was about one-half of an English farthing, or one-quarter of a cent (Mat. v. 26; Mark xii. 42).

2. An *Assarion*, diminutive of the Latin *as*, a copper coin equal to about one cent (Mat. x. 29).

Fast.

Abstinence from food, or the period during which it takes place.

1. *Involuntary*, arising from the fact that nothing to eat is procurable. Of this type were apparently the forty days' fast of Moses on mount Sinai (Ex. xxxiv. 28; Deut. ix. 9), of Elijah on his journey to Horeb (1 Kin. xix. 8), and of our Lord during his temptation in the wilderness (Mat. iv. 2; Mark i. 13; Luke iv. 2); also of Paul (2 Cor. vi. 5).

2. *Voluntary*, from religious motives. In this sense it is often used regarding prescribed periods of abstinence. There do not appear to be any injunctions regarding fasting in the Mosaic law, and neither the verb "to fast," nor the nouns " fast " and " fasting," occur in the Pentateuch. If fasts are prescribed at all, it is in the ambiguous language " Ye shall afflict your souls " (Lev. xvi. 29; xxiii. 27; Num. xxix. 7). The first mention of voluntary fasting is in connection with king David, who refused food when he supplicated God for the life of the child borne to him in sin by the wife of Uriah (2 Sam. xii. 22). Many instances of the same unprescribed fasting are found in the later books of the O. T. (Ezra viii. 21; Neh. ix. 1; Esth. iv. 3; Ps. xxxv. 13; lxix. 10; cix. 24; Dan. vi. 18; ix. 3). Sometimes fasts were proclaimed at periods of calamity (Jer. xxxvi. 9; Joel i. 14), the object being to chasten the soul (Ps. xxxv. 13; lxix. 10) and make the voice heard in heaven (Is. lviii. 3, 4). The public fast signified that a load of guilt was resting on the people, for which they humbled themselves before God (1 Sam. vii. 6; 1 Kin. xxi. 9, 12). True fasting must not be confined to externals, but involves abstinence from iniquity and illicit pleasures (Is. lviii.). In Zechariah's days there were stated fasts in the fourth, fifth, seventh, and tenth months (Zech. viii. 19), to commemorate the commencement of the siege of Jerusalem in the tenth month (2 Kin. xxv. 1), its capture in the fourth month (3; Jer. lii. 6, 7), the destruction of the temple in the fifth month (2 Kin. xxv. 8, 9), and the murder of Gedaliah and the Jews that were with him in the seventh month (25). Anna served God with fasting (Luke ii. 37). The Pharisee did so twice in the week (Luke xviii. 12). When religious formalists fasted, they sometimes ostentatiously put on a sad countenance. This practice was denounced in the Sermon on the Mount (Mat. vi. 16, 17). The disciples of John the Baptist fasted; those of our Lord did not, at least while he was among them (Mat. ix, 14, 15; Mark ii. 18, 19; Luke v. 33–35), but afterwards in certain circumstances they did so (Acts xiii. 3; xiv. 23).

There are no injunctions laid upon Christians to fast; and the revisers, on the ground of textual criticism, have removed the word from Mat. xvii. 21; Mark ix. 29; Acts x. 30; 1 Cor. vii. 5.

Fat.

1. Abel offered the fat of the firstlings of his flock to Jehovah (Gen. iv. 4; cp. Num. xviii. 17). The principle was laid down in the Mosaic law that to the Lord belongs all the fat of sacrificial animals (Lev. iii. 16; vii. 23, 25). Neither it nor the blood was eaten (iii. 17), but was burned as an offering to Jehovah (Ex. xxix. 13, 22; Lev. iii. 3–5; iv. 8–10); for a sweet savor unto Jehovah (iv. 31). In view of the settlement in Canaan and the remoteness of the majority of the people from the altar, this provision was apparently abolished with respect to animals slain solely for food (Deut. xii. 15, 16, 21–24), the animals of the flock and herd being eaten as were non-sacrificial animals.

2. A wine vat (Joel ii. 24; Is. lxiii. 2, A. V.).

Fa'ther.

1. The immediate progenitor of a person (Gen. xlii. 13), or grandfather (xxviii. 13), or more remote ancestor (xvii. 4). See PARENTS.

2. The founder of a trade (Gen. iv. 20) or of anything. The ancestor or head, or one of the heads, of the inhabitants of a town (1 Chron. ii. 51; iv. 14, 18).

3. One who acts toward another with paternal kindness and wisdom (Gen. xlv. 8, Judg xvii. 10; xviii. 19). A title of respect and honor bestowed upon an authorized teacher, especially when aged (1 Sam. x. 12; 2 Kin. ii. 12), and upon royal advisers and prime ministers (Gen. xlv. 8).

4. God, either as the Creator of the human race (Mal. ii. 10; Antiq. iv. 8, 24; cp. Acts xvii. 28), or as the begetter and loving guardian of his spiritual children (Rom. viii. 15; Gal. iv. 6), or as standing in a more mysterious relation to Jesus (Mat. xi. 26; Mark xiv. 36; Luke xxii. 42). See GOD.

Fath'om.

A measure much used in reckoning depth of water (Acts xxvii. 28). It is the rendering of the Greek *Orguia*, which denotes the length of the outstretched arms, and was estimated at 4 cubits or 24 palms (Herod. ii. 149). The English fathom is 6 feet.

Feast.

1. A sumptuous meal attended by mirth and joyfulness (Dan. v. 1).

2. A time set apart by the canons of some religions for sacred joy. Besides the appointed seasons, called feasts or set feasts in the English versions (Lev. xxiii. 2, R. V. margin), which included the weekly Sabbath, the memorial of trumpet-blowing on the first day of the seventh month, and the day of atonement (3, 24, 27), the Mosaic law enjoined three annual celebrations expressly called feasts or rather festivals. They were the passover on the evening of the fourteenth day of the first month, with the accompanying feast of unleavened bread commencing on the fifteenth and lasting seven days (5–8) ; the feast of weeks, called also feast of harvest and day of first fruits (Ex. xxiii. 16 ; xxxiv. 22 ; Num. xxviii. 26), and in later times, because celebrated on the fiftieth day after the passover, Pentecost (Acts ii. 1) ; and the feast of tabernacles or ingathering, which commenced on the fifteenth day of the seventh month and continued for seven or eight days (Lev. xxiii. 34–44). These three annual festivals were deemed so important, that when they came every adult male not incapacitated by disease or infirmity was required to appear before the Lord at the sanctuary (Ex. xxiii. 17 ; Deut. xvi. 16). For further description of these feasts, see the appropriate articles. As Jesus desired to fulfill all righteousness, it may be assumed that he was customarily present at Jerusalem three times a year, on occasion of the three festivals (John ii. 23 ; vii. 2–37, etc. ; Mat. xxvi. 17 ; Mark xiv. 12 ; Luke xxii. 8 ; John xiii. 1). In addition to the festivals prescribed by the law, a festival called Purim was instituted to commemorate annually, on the fourteenth and fifteenth of Adar, the deliverance of the Jews from the plot of Haman (Esth. ix. 21–28). Later still the festival of dedication was appointed, which was instituted by Judas Maccabæus, to be celebrated annually for eight days, from the twenty-fifth day of Chislev, in commemoration of the rededication of the temple after its pollution by the agents of Antiochus Epiphanes (1 Mac. iv. 41–59 ; John x. 22). The Lord's Supper, instituted by Christ, or more broadly the Christian's life of faith, is also a feast (1 Cor. v. 8).

Fe'lix [happy].

A freedman of the emperor Claudius, who was appointed procurator of Judæa. The date of his appointment to office in Palestine is disputed. Cumanus succeeded the procurator Tiberius Alexander in A. D. 48 (Antiq. xx. 5, 2). According to Tacitus, Cumanus governed Galilee, and Felix ruled part of Samaria until, on the deposition of Cumanus, he was appointed procurator of the whole province by Quadratus, governor of Syria.

Josephus, who was a boy in Jerusalem in A. D. 48, and became historian of the Jews, represents Cumanus as procurator of Judæa, and states that Felix was sent as successor of Cumanus by the emperor Claudius to administer the affairs of Judæa in 52 (Antiq. xx. 7, 1 : War ii. 12, 8). Probably Cumanus and Felix exercised a joint procuratorship, with Cumanus higher in authority. In this article A. D. 52 is assumed as the date of his sole procuratorship in Judæa. He seems to have obtained this appointment partly through the influence of his brother Pallas, who was a great man at the court of Claudius. Nero, the successor of Claudius, transferred four Galilæan cities from Felix to Agrippa. Felix was cruel and tyrannical, and in the exercise of power showed the disposition of a slave (Tacitus, Hist. v. 9 ; Annals xii. 54). Jonathan, the high priest, had supported the appointment of Felix to the procuratorship, but displeased Felix by the fidelity with which he counseled him regarding his government of the Jews. Jonathan was murdered by the robbers, the so-called Assassins, encouraged, Josephus says, by Felix. The impunity with which this gross crime was committed emboldened the robbers. They became the terror of Judæa. Felix undertook to suppress them. He captured many of them, and crucified the ordinary sort, but sent their leader, Eleazar, to Rome (Antiq. xx. 8, 5 ; War ii. 13, 2). Next false prophets arose and led people in multitudes into the wilderness, where they were told God would show them the signals of liberty. Felix, believing these gatherings in the wilderness to be the commencement of revolt, attacked the people present and slew them in large numbers (War ii. 13, 4). An Egyptian soon afterwards made his appearance as a prophet and led out a great mob to the mount of Olives, under the pretense that they would see the walls of Jerusalem fall down, allowing them to enter the city. Felix attacked them with troops, slew about 400 and took about 200 prisoners. The Egyptian escaped. His insurrection was in A. D. 55 ; and when about five years later the riot about Paul arose, the Roman commandant at Jerusalem suspected that the apostle was the Egyptian back again to excite fresh troubles (Acts xxi. 38 ; Antiq. xx. 8, 6). Paul, arrested on the false charge of profaning the temple, was sent for protection from Jewish violence to Cæsarea, the seat of the Roman government for Judæa (Acts xxiii. 26), and the trial took place before Felix (xxiv. 1–23). Felix' wife Drusilla, a Jewess, whom he had seduced from her lawful husband (Antiq. xx. 7, 1, 2), was present at an interview when Paul reasoned of righteousness, temperance, and judgment to come, with such power that Felix trembled. He did not repent, however. Nor did he set Paul free, for he hoped that his prisoner would buy freedom (Acts xxiv. 24–26). On going out of office he left the apostle bound in order to please the Jews (27). This favor did not, however, prevent them from complaining of him after he had ceased to be procurator and returned to Rome, about A. D. 60. They represented that he had not acted well in the recent riots between Jews and Syrians at Cæsarea, and he would have been punished by Nero had not the powerful intercession of his brother Pallas, who was a favorite with the reigning emperor, been exerted in his favor (Antiq. xx. 8 9; cp. 8, 7; War ii. 13, 7). He was succeeded in the procuratorship by Porcius Festus.

Fenced Cit'ies.
Towns fortified by walls, towers, gates, and bars (Deut. iii. 5; 2 Chron. viii. 5; Neh. iii. 1–32). Such were the cities of the Canaanites and the Amorites when the Israelites warred against them (Num. xiii. 28; Deut. iii. 5; Josh. xiv. 12). After the Israelites had occupied Canaan, they, like their predecessors, had fenced cities (Deut. xxviii. 52; 2 Sam. xx. 6; 2 Kin. xiv. 13; 2 Chron. xii. 4; Jer. v. 17; Hos. viii. 14; Zeph. i. 16). For illustration and description of the walls, see JERUSALEM and LACHISH.

Fer'ret.
The rendering of the Hebrew *'ǎnaḳah*, a ceremonially unclean animal, classed by the Hebrews with reptiles (Lev. xi. 30; in R. V. gecko).

Fes'tus [festal, joyful].
Porcius Festus, who succeeded Felix as procurator of Judæa in the reign of Nero, while Pallas was still the emperor's favorite and Burrus was still alive (Antiq. xx. 8, 9). Pallas was put to death in A. D. 62, and Burrus died not later than February of the same year. Two years before the arrival of Festus, Paul could say that Felix had been for many years a judge unto the nation (Acts xxiv. 10, 27). If the procuratorship of Felix be reckoned from A. D. 48 (see FELIX), he would have been many years in office in Palestine in A. D. 54 or 55, and Festus may have succeeded him in 55 or 56, the second and third years of Nero respectively. This date is adopted by some authorities, with the result of putting the dates of important events in Paul's life, among others his imprisonment, four or five years earlier than the date generally accepted by leading investigators who date Felix' accession in 52 and Festus' appointment in 60. Festus fell on troublous times. The Assassins were murdering and pillaging. An impostor led a crowd of adherents into the wilderness, where the forces of Festus routed them with great slaughter. King Agrippa built a dining-room at the royal palace of Jerusalem, and its windows overlooked the courts of the temple. The Jews were annoyed, and built a wall to block the view. But the wall prevented the Roman guards also from seeing the inner courts, and Festus ordered its demolition.

On appeal to Nero, however, it was allowed to remain (Antiq. xx. 8, 11). The character of Festus contrasts favorably with that of Felix (War ii. 14, 1). He reinvestigated Paul's case, and was satisfied of his innocence; but, in attempting to please the Jews, he suggested that the apostle be tried at Jerusalem. It was against this injudicious proposal that Paul appealed to Cæsar (Acts xxv. 1–xxvi. 32). Festus died at his post, and was succeeded, about A. D. 62, by Albinus, who is not mentioned in the Scripture narrative (Antiq. xx, 9, 1).

Fe'ver.
A disease, or rather a genus of diseases, attended by dryness and heat of the body, with consequent thirst, a high pulse, and other symptoms. Fevers are of three leading types, intermittent, remittent, and continued. Fevers of all the types now named doubtless existed in ancient Palestine, though it is not possible in all cases to identify them with certainty. Fever is the rendering of the Hebrew *Ḳaddaḥath*, burning (Lev. xxvi. 16, in A. V. burning ague; Deut. xxviii. 22). In the latter passage it is associated with inflammation and fiery heat, both febrile symptoms. Fever is likewise the correct rendering of the Greek *Puretos*, from *Pur*, fire (Mat. viii. 15; Luke iv. 38; John iv. 52; Acts xxviii. 8). Galen and the Greek physicians divided fevers into greater and lesser. Luke in the passage quoted does so also, as might be expected from one who was himself a medical man. Fever so uniformly attends certain diseases that the two are mentioned together, as in the designation "fever and dysentery." When the sword, the famine, and the pestilence, are mentioned in this order of succession the pestilence was probably typhus fever.

Field.
In biblical usage, unenclosed ground, whether pasture or tillage (Gen. xxxvii. 7, 14–16), of whatever extent, from a small area to the territory of a people (xiv. 7, margin of R. V.; xxiii. 9; Ruth i. 6, rendered country; Mat. vi. 28; xiii. 24). It might be wooded (1 Sam. xiv. 25, rendered ground). Boundaries, when artificially marked, were indicated by stones (cp. Deut. xix. 14).

Fig.
A tree producing good fruit (Judg. ix. 10) and the fruit itself (Num. xiii. 23), both called *Tᵉenah* in Hebrew, while in Greek the tree is *Suke* and the fruit *Sukon*. The tree is native in western Asia. The young tree does not bear fruit unless the ground is cultivated (Luke xiii. 6–9), and old trees speedily degenerate and fail when neglected (Prov. xxvii. 18). The young fruit, or rather blossom, appears in spring before the leaves open, on branches of the last year's growth. It is the green fig (Song ii. 13). If blown from the tree (Rev. vi. 13), it is eaten, though immature. If green fruit is not on the tree when the leaves have opened, no figs will

be borne. The first ripe fruit is ready in June, in favored localities earlier (Is. xxviii. 4; War iii. 10, 8). The late figs grow on the new wood, keep appearing during the season, and are ripe from August onward. They are dried for preservation, pressed into cakes, and form a staple article of food (1 Sam. xxv. 18; xxx. 12). The tree was highly prized, and is often mentioned along with the vine (Deut. viii. 8; Ps. cv. 33; Jer. v. 17; Joel i. 12), and to sit under one's vine and one's fig tree was the symbol of prosperity and security (1 Kin. iv. 25; Mic. iv. 4; Zech. iii. 10). The barren fig tree of our Lord's parable meant the Jewish nation. Figs were used in medicine, and there is mention of their employment as a poultice (2 Kin. xx. 7).

The fig, the *Ficus carica* of cultivation, is a tree 20 to 30 feet high. The leaves, which come forth late in spring and are shed at the approach of winter, are often 8 or 10 inches across. They are heart shaped with three or four lobes. The fruit is of so anomalous a construction that botanists have had to give it a distinct name and place among fruits. It is a hollow receptacle, with minute flowers on its inner side, which later produce the true fruit. The tree is wild in southern Europe and the north of Africa. It is indigenous in Palestine, where it grows wild in fissures of rocks and on walls, besides being everywhere cultivated (Deut. viii. 8).

Fir and Fir Tree.

The rendering of the Hebrew Bᵉ*rosh*, Aramaic Bᵉ*roth* (2 Sam. vi. 5; Song i. 17). The R. V. places cypress on the margin. The tree grew with the cedar in Lebanon (1 Kin. v. 8, 10; Is. xiv. 8; xxxvii. 24; lx. 13; Zech. xi. 2). It was used for the woodwork of Solomon's temple along with cedar (1 Kin. v. 8, 10; vi. 15, 34; 2 Chron. ii. 8; iii. 5), for the planks of ships (Ezek. xxvii. 5), for spears (Nah. ii. 3, R. V.), and for musical instruments (2 Sam. vi. 5). The stork made its nest within its branches (Ps. civ. 17). The Vulgate translates the Hebrew word once by cypress (Song i. 17), but elsewhere by *abies*, fir, except 2 Sam. vi. 5; 2 Chron. ii. 8; Nah. ii. 3. The Septuagint commonly renders it by cypress, but also by pine and juniper. All of these trees belong to the *Coniferæ* or pine family. The only true fir of the region is *Abies cilica*. It grows on the higher parts of Lebanon and in the mountains northward, attaining a height of from 30 to 75 feet. The cypress (*Cupressus sempervirens*) is a tall tree, from 20 to 60 or 75 feet. The wood is reddish yellow, pleasant to the smell, and durable. It was much used for cabinet work. It is extensively planted in burial grounds in the East, for which its slender pyramidal form and gracefulness render it well adapted. See CYPRESS. The Syrian or Aleppo pine (*Pinus halepensis*) is found in the mountains of western Palestine, and is one of the characteristic trees of the lower Lebanon. It is inferior in size to the fir and the cypress. The stone pine (*Pinus*

maritima) grows on the coast and in sandy plains, but is not common. In Gilead there are extensive forests of *Pinus carica* on the highest mountains above the line where the evergreen oaks cease. A tall, fragrant juniper (*Juniperus excelsa*) grows abundantly on Lebanon. For Is. xliv. 14, see ASH.

Fire.

Fire was found to be indispensable (Ecclus. xxxix. 26). It was used in the arts (Gen. iv. 22), in the preparation of food (Ex. xvi. 23; Is. xliv. 16), and for warmth (Jer. xxxvi. 22; John xviii. 18; Acts xxviii. 2). Offerings were made to Jehovah by fire (Gen. viii. 20). The fire carried, as it were, the sacrifice to God, who took delight in the offering, or, to speak figuratively, smelled a sweet savor (21). The offerer kindled the fire himself (xxii. 6). Moses offered burnt offerings on the great altar, newly erected (Ex. xl. 29), but at the conclusion of the consecration of Aaron and his sons to the priesthood, fire came forth from the presence of the Lord and consumed the sacrifice (Lev. ix. 24). God accepted and appropriated the offering. This fire was not allowed to go out (vi. 9–13). Likewise at the dedication of the temple and the new altar, fire came from heaven and consumed the sacrifice (2 Chron. vii. 1). On other occasions also God indicated his acceptance of a sacrifice by causing it to kindle (Judg. vi. 21; 1 Kin. xviii. 23, 24; 1 Chron. xxi. 26; as to this matter, cp. Gen. xix. 24; Ex. ix. 23; 2 Kin. i. 12). Among the heathen there were fire worshipers (Wisd. xiii. 2). The worshipers of Moloch and some other idolaters burnt their children in the fire as an act of piety (2 Kin. xvi. 3; xxi. 6; Jer. vii. 31; Ezek. xvi. 20, 21).

Fire'pan.

A pan made of brass, gold, or silver (Ex. xxvii. 3; 1 Kin. vii. 50; 2 Kin. xxv. 15), and used for carrying fire (Lev. xvi. 12, where it is rendered censer).

Fir'kin.

A measure of capacity (John ii. 6). It is the rendering of the Greek *Metrētēs*, which, reckoned at 1952.17 cubic inches, held nearly 8 gallons, 3½ pints, wine measure, American standard.

Fir'ma-ment [Latin *firmamentum*, a support, a firm foundation].

The sky or heaven (Gen. i. 8), an expanse beaten out as it were, if we employ the figure embodied in the Hebrew word (cp. Ezek. i. 22), which divided the primeval watery mass (Gen. i. 6), so that part of the waters were above it and others were below it (i. 7; Ps. cxlviii. 4). The stars and planets were placed in it, where they move unimpeded (Gen. i. 14, 17). Birds fly in front of it (20, R. V. margin). The heavens, and presumably the firmament, are compared to a tent spread above the earth (Ps. civ. 2; Is. xl. 22), are likened in strength to a molten mirror (Job xxxvii. 18), and are spoken of as though having doors and windows, through which the rain pours and God's blessings descend (Gen. vii. 11; 2 Kin. vii. 2; Ps. lxxviii. 23; civ. 13). This conception was current in ancient Semitic thought. The doctrine of the division of the primeval fluid chaos is not unacceptable to modern thought; other features are regarded as naive. They are not taught in the Scriptures as facts. They lingered in Hebrew speech and imagery as an inheritance, and were used in both poetic and prose writings even when, for example, the agency of the clouds in bringing rain was understood (Gen. ix. 14; Job xxvi. 8; xxxvi. 27–29; xxxvii. 11; xxxviii. 34; Ps. lxxvii. 17; cxxxv. 7; Is. v. 6; Jer. x. 13).

First'born or **First'ling**, the former being used chiefly of men, the latter always of beasts.

To the firstborn offspring of men and animals God the giver has the first claim (cp. Gen. iv. 4). Among the Israelites an additional reason existed in the fact that Jehovah had purchased the people from Egyptian bondage. The tenth and last plague of Egypt had slain the firstborn of the Egyptians, and the firstborn of the Israelites had been preserved only by sprinkling blood on the lintels and door posts of the houses within which they resided (Ex. xii. 12, 13, 23, 29). Saved in this manner, they became consecrated to Jehovah. Every firstborn male of man and beast was holy to the Lord (xiii. 2; xxxiv. 19), and could not be used by man (Lev. xxvii. 26), but belonged to the sanctuary for sacrifice; but the firstborn of man

was redeemed (Ex. xiii. 13, 15; xxxiv. 20; cp. Lev. xxvii. 6). On this occasion he was brought to the sanctuary and presented to the Lord (Luke ii. 22; cp. Num. xviii. 15). The Levites were afterwards substituted for the Israelite firstborn (Num. iii. 12, 41, 46; viii. 13–19; cp. Ex. xxxii. 26–29; Deut. xxxiii. 9), and served at the sanctuary. Those of animals also, against which the tenth plague was partly directed, became similarly consecrated to Jehovah, but there were distinctions among them. The firstling of clean animals was sacrificed. Unclean animals, of which the ass is named as representative, either had the neck broken or were replaced by a lamb (Ex. xiii. 13, 15; xxii. 30; xxxiv. 20). On the establishment of the priesthood at Sinai, the disposition of these animals was specified. The fat of the clean animal was burned and the flesh was given to the priest. The unclean animal was redeemed or sold (Lev. xxvii. 27; Num. xviii. 15–18). Later, in view of the new circumstances in which it was foreseen that the people would be placed in Palestine, and the inconvenience and expense of the journey to the sanctuary, a delay was authorized in presenting the firstling at the house of God. The firstling might be kept beyond the eight days originally prescribed until the time of an annual festival; and the flesh, instead of falling as a perquisite to the priest, was given to the pilgrim who brought the animal, and to his family, to eat at the sanctuary (Deut. xv. 19, 20). But defective animals were eaten at home without religious ceremony (21–23).

For the legal privileges of the firstborn son, see BIRTHRIGHT.

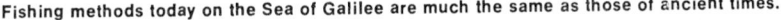

Fishing methods today on the Sea of Galilee are much the same as those of ancient times.

First'fruits.

The fruits first ripe, the plucking of which was an earnest of the coming harvest. First-fruits were to be given as an offering to Jehovah : on behalf of the nation, a sheaf at the feast of unleavened bread and two loaves at the feast of weeks (Lev. xxiii. 10, 17) ; and by individuals (Ex. xxiii. 19 ; Deut. xxvi. 1–11). The term is used figuratively in Rom. viii. 23 ; xi. 16 ; xvi. 5 : 1 Cor. xv. 20, 23 ; xvi. 15 ; Jas. i. 18 ; Rev. xiv. 4. See FIRSTBORN.

Fish'ing.

Fishing went on largely in Egypt in the main channel of the Nile and in the several branches into which it separates before reaching the Mediterranean (Is. xix. 8), and the Israelites when in bondage in Egypt did eat fish freely (Num. xi. 5). The fishing along the Mediterranean coast of Palestine was largely in the hands of the Tyrians and Sidonians in the north (Neh. xiii. 16) and the Philistines in the south. To the Israelites belonged the sea of Galilee, which was their chief fishing ground. Tristram enumerates twenty-two species of fish in its waters, many of which pass down the Jordan also ; but any that reach the Dead Sea die in its briny water. In certain places there were artificial fish ponds (Song vii. 4). Fish were on sale in Jerusalem (2 Chron. xxxiii. 14 ; Neh. xiii. 16). For fishing, lines, hooks, and spears were used (Job xli. 1, 7 ; Is. xix. 8 ; Amos iv. 2 ; Mat. xvii. 27), and nets were cast from boats (Luke v. 4–7).

Fitch [obsolete form of English *vetch*].

A tare (*Vicia*), an herb much cultivated as a forage plant (Is. xxviii. 25, 27, Hebrew *Ķeṣaḥ*). The plant so designated was sown broadcast ; and when its fruits were ripe, they were beaten out with a staff to separate the seeds. R. V., following Septuagint, Vulgate, and the Rabbins, places black cummin (*Nigella sativa*) on the margin, and considers the plant to have been what is now called, from its fennel-like leaves, fennel flower. It is of the crowfoot or buttercup order (*Ranunculaceæ*). It is a foot and a half high, with yellow or, more rarely, blue petals, many stamens, and several seed vessels, with numerous black acrid and aromatic seeds, which are used in the East for seasoning dishes and as a carminative. It grows wild in the Mediterranean lands, and is cultivated in Palestine for its seeds.

The Hebrew *Kussemeth* is likewise translated fitch in Ezek. iv. 9, A. V. ; but elsewhere in A. V. it is rendered rye, and everywhere in R. V. it is translated spelt.

Flag.

1. The rendering of the Hebrew *'Aḥu* in Job viii. 11. On the margin of R. V. it is translated reed grass, and also in the text of Gen. xli. 2, R. V., where A. V. renders it meadow. It was a water plant ; and grew, among other places, on the edge of the Nile. It is not likely that it was the flag, which is an iris, with three brightly colored petals. It seems to have been the Egyptian designation for the crowded mass of water plants, rushes, reeds, sedges found along the margin of the Nile.

2. The rendering of *Suph* (Ex. ii. 3, 5 ; Is. xix. 6), a plant growing by the brink of the Nile. It also grew in salt water (Jon. ii. 5, where it is rendered weeds). The Red Sea in Hebrew is called the sea of Suph. It is evident that the plant meant is not the flag, which does not grow in salt water. The word denotes aquatic vegetation, whether seaweeds or fresh water reeds and sedges.

Flag'on.

1. A vessel for holding liquids (Is. xxii. 24, in Hebrew *Nebel*).

2. The rendering in A. V. of the Hebrew word *'ăshishah*, something pressed closely together (2 Sam. vi. 19 ; 1 Chron. xvi. 3 ; Song ii. 5 ; Hos. iii. 1). The R. V. correctly translates it cake of raisins.

Flax.

The rendering of the Hebrew words *Pishteh* and *Pishtah* and of the Greek *Linon* (Is. xlii. 3 with Mat. xii. 20). It was a plant cultivated in Egypt and elsewhere (Ex. ix. 31). It had stalks, which were spread on flat roofs of houses and dried by exposure to the heat of the sun (Josh. ii. 6). Its fibers were fine (Is. xix. 9), and were woven like wool (Prov. xxxi. 13 ; cp. Hos. ii. 5). It is undoubtedly the flax plant (*Linum usitatissimum*), the type of the botanical order *Linaceæ*, or flaxworts. It is a small plant, with solitary erect stems, five sepals, five fugitive petals, with five perfect and as many rudimentary stamens. It is now found only in a state of cultivation. The woody fiber of the bark furnishes the flax fiber of which linen is woven, and the seeds constitute the linseed of commerce, valued on account of its oil.

Flea.

An insect, called in Hebrew *Par‘osh*, leaper (1 Sam. xxiv. 14 ; xxvi. 20). The species is very common in Palestine ; so much so that it has become a popular saying that the king of the fleas has his court at Tiberias.

Flesh.

1. The muscles of the animal body, whether of man, beast, bird, or fish ; or, less precisely, all its softer parts (Gen. xl. 19 ; Ex. xii. 8 ; xvi. 8 ; Lev. xxi. 5 ; Job x. 11 ; Luke xxiv. 39 ; 1 Cor. xv. 39). It is distinct from the spirit (Job xiv. 22 ; Is. x. 18, Hebrew ; xxxi. 3 ; Mat. xxvi. 41 ; Col. ii. 5).

2. All beings possessed of flesh, man and the inferior animals, especially man (Gen. vi. 13, 19 ; viii. 17 ; Acts ii. 17 ; Rom. iii. 20 ; 1 Cor. i. 29) ; often in contrast with God who is spirit (Ps. lvi. 4 ; Is. xxxi. 3 ; xl. 6–8 ; Joel ii. 28 ; Mat. xvi. 17).

3. Human nature deprived of the Spirit of God, dominated by the appetites and

obeyed by the mind (Rom. vii. 5; viii. 5–7; 2 Cor. vii. 1; Gal. v. 16–20; 2 Pet. ii. 10), thus including the whole unregenerated and unsanctified nature of man (Rom. viii. 8, 9; cp. John iii. 6).

Flint.

In Scripture, any hard or intractable rock (Deut. viii. 15; xxxii. 13; Ps. cxiv. 8); and hence figuratively, uncompromising firmness in the discharge of duty (Is. l. 7; Ezek. iii. 9). In it the miner sinks his shaft in quest of gold (Job xxviii. 9, R. V.). Broken fragments were used as rude knives (Ex. iv. 25; Josh. v. 2, R. V., where in Hebrew the generic word for rock is used).

Flood.

A stream, especially a great stream (Job xiv. 11; xxviii. 11 in A. V.), as the Nile in its inundations (Jer. xlvi. 7; Amos viii. 8 in A. V.), the Euphrates (Josh. xxiv. 2, A. V.), the Jordan (Ps. lxvi. 6, A. V.). An inundation (Dan. ix. 26; Nah. i. 8; Mat. vii. 25, 27; Luke vi. 48). A great restless mass of water; the sea and its currents (Ps. xxiv. 2; Jon. ii. 3).

Specially, the deluge in the time of Noah. It was sent as a divine judgment on the antediluvians for their wickedness (Gen. vi. 5–13). Secondary causes were employed to bring on the catastrophe. Two are mentioned: the fountains of the great deep were broken up, and the windows of heaven were opened. Thus part of the water was that of the ocean, the rest was produced by a downpour of rain continuing forty days and nights (vii. 11, 12). All the high mountains under the whole heaven were covered, fifteen cubits upward

the waters prevailed, and all flesh died that moved on the earth, man, bird, beast, and creeping thing. Noah only was left and they that were with him in the ark (vii. 19–23); see ARK. The waters prevailed 150 days, until at length the ark rested on the mountains of Ararat. Two and a half months later the tops of the mountains were seen (viii. 3–5). Three months later, after investigating the state of the water by means of birds which he sent forth, on New Year's day Noah removed the covering from the ark and saw that the face of the ground was dried; but eight weeks more elapsed before God gave command to go forth from the ark (viii. 13–15).

The months are reckoned at thirty days each, and the number of days which measure an interval is the difference between the dates obtained by simple subtraction (vii. 11 with viii. 3, 4). On this mode of reckoning, and dating from the day of entrance into the ark as first day, it is interesting to note the days and weeks. The first day which dawned fair and beautiful after the forty days and nights of rain was the forty-second, a recurring seventh day, fit reminder of divine rest and favor. Land was seen on a recurring first day, the new world wherein dwelt righteousness began like the old on a first day. Noah released the birds, at intervals of a week, either on successive sixth days, in expectancy of the morrow, or on seventh days. Noah removed the covering on New Year's day, old reckoning; but it was also a recurring seventh day. And eight weeks later, on the recurring seventh day, God released Noah from the ark.

vii. 4, 10.	COMMAND TO BEGIN EMBARKING THE ANIMALS,	2 mo. 10th day.
vii. 11.	ENTRANCE OF NOAH INTO THE ARK, and in the evening, as related by the Babylonian tradition, bursting of the storm.	2 mo. 17th day.
vii. 12.	Rain 40 days and 40 nights, so that	
	RAIN CEASED toward evening,	3 mo. 27th day.
vii. 24.	The waters prevailed on the earth	
viii. 3.	150 days, so that the	
viii. 4.	ARK STRANDED	7 mo. 17th day.
	The waters decreased continually until	
viii. 5.	TOPS OF THE MOUNTAINS VISIBLE,	10 mo. 1st day.
viii. 6.	After seeing the mountain tops, Noah waited 40 days; expecting that, as the rain had fallen 40 days, the waters would perhaps abate from the ground in 40 days; and then (or on the following day) the	
	RAVEN RELEASED, which returned not, After 7 days (cp. "yet other," v. 10) a	11 mo. 11th (or 12th) day.
viii. 8.	DOVE RELEASED, which returned, After yet other 7 days, the	11 mo. 18th (or 19th) day.
viii. 10.	DOVE RELEASED, which returned with olive leaf. So Noah knew that the waters were abated from off the earth. After yet other 7 days, a third time the	11 mo. 25th (or 26th) day
viii. 12.	DOVE RELEASED, which did not return, since food and shelter were now found outside the ark,	12 mo. 2d (or 3d) day.
	Notwithstanding these favorable indications, Noah did not leave the ark, but waited for God's command. After nearly a month, on New Year's day	
viii. 13.	NOAH REMOVED THE COVERING OF THE ARK, and saw that the waters were dried up and the face of the ground was dried,	1 mo. 1st day.
	But Noah still awaited God's bidding, and eight weeks later, the earth being dry, God gave the	
viii. 14, 15.	COMMAND TO GO FORTH FROM THE ARK,	2 mo. 27th day.

As is now generally known, the account of the flood was handed down by tradition. The description originated with eyewitnesses. Its language must be understood in the sense which it bore to the authors and promulgators of the narrative centuries before the days of Moses. The extent of the flood cannot be determined from the account of it which has been transmitted. The deluge may have been universal and covered the globe, or it may have been confined to a locality of greater or less extent. All the mountains under the whole heaven, that is within the horizon of the inmates of the ark as they drifted on the waters, were covered (compare the employment of similar language in Col. i. 23). The purpose of the flood was to destroy the corrupt race of man (Gen. vi. 7, 13, 17; vii. 4), and with man all animals dependent upon the existence of dry land were involved in destruction. This was also the result as discerned by those who were saved in the ark (vii. 21–23), and as confirmed by their descendants when they migrated in the earth. They met no survivors. They found the world uninhabited. Noah had been instructed to take the male and female of every kind of animal, and to gather food for them (vi. 20, 21). The language of the command was intended to be understood in its usual sense, as any man of that age would understand it. Noah doubtless took specimens of every animal of which he had knowledge and food suitable for them (cp. Dan. vi. 25); but there is no evidence that he believed himself to be commanded to seek for species as yet unknown, or if under supernatural impulse the animals unsought came to him (as some would unnecessarily interpret vii. 8, 9), to gather peculiar food and provide peculiar shelter for strange animals of different kinds and from different climes.

The tradition of the flood was current among the people from whom the Hebrews sprang. In the ancestral home of Abraham the flood was remembered as a great crisis in human history. An Assyrian scribe, recording the names of ancient kings, remarks concerning certain of them, that they "were after the flood." Ashurbanipal refers to inscriptions "of the time before the flood." The Babylonian priest Berosus devoted the second volume of his history to the ten antediluvian kings of the Chaldeans, considering that the flood marked the close of the first period of human history. The tradition of the deluge which was current in Babylonia and Assyria differed in some details from the Hebrew account. The Hebrews, Assyrians, and Babylonians once dwelt together in Babylonia, and were one people with one tradition, but in course of transmission from age to age this tradition underwent slight changes and received unessential additions. When the Semites of Babylonia became three nations, dwelling apart and diverse in religion, the tradition of the flood which each preserved bore the impress of the national peculiarities. The Hebrew account was monotheistic, the Assyrian and Babylonian narrative is polytheistic. It is further observable

to the attentive reader that the Hebrew account not only as a whole, but in minute particulars, is credible, and reflects the conditions of a primitive age, which cannot be said of the Assyrian and Babylonian.

The Assyrians and Babylonians themselves had slightly divergent traditions. The story, as current in Babylonia in the time of Alexander the Great, was recorded by Berosus (Antiq. i. 3, 6; con. Apion. i. 19), and is quoted in full by the church historian Eusebius. A form which is much older, which in fact is the oldest known and the best preserved, though even variations of it were current, is embodied in the epic that celebrates the deeds of Izdubar or Gilgamesh, king of Erech. Izdubar had been smitten with disease, and he determined to seek help from his ancestor Sitnapishtim, who had been translated to the gods, was dwelling "at the mouth of the rivers," and had knowledge of life and death. After a long journey, in which he encountered many difficulties and dangers, Izdubar found Sitnapishtim. He belonged to a generation long past, but still enjoyed the freshness and vigor of youth. Astonished, Izdubar exclaimed: "How camest thou, Sitnapishtim, to see life amid the gods?"

"I will open to you, Izdubar," replied Sitnapishtim, "the concealed story, and also the oracle of the gods [with reference to the cure of your disease] will I declare. You know the city of Surippak, which stands on the Euphrates. That city was old when the gods who dwelt therein were moved at heart to bring about a flood-storm. God Anu was there among others, and Bel and Ninib. The god Ea, however, deliberated with them, and he revealed unto me their purpose [by means of a dream (l. 177)]. 'Man of Surippak, son of Ubaratutu,' said he, 'tear down the house, build a ship, despise property, and save life. Bring into the ship seed of life of every kind.' I paid attention, and said to god Ea, 'O my lord, what thou hast commanded I will respect by carrying out.'

"On the morrow [preparations were begun]. On the fifth day I laid the framework—140 cubits its height, 140 cubits its extent above. I divided its interior, I provided a rudder. Over the outside I poured three measures [sars] of bitumen and likewise over the inside. When the ship was completed I filled it with all that I possessed—with silver, gold, and seed of life of every kind. I took on board all my men-servants and maid-servants, the cattle and the beast of the field, and the artisans.

"The sun-god set a time. 'When the sender of violent rain causes a heavy rain to pour down in the evening, enter into the ship and shut the door.' The set time came. He who sends violent rain caused a heavy rain to fall in the evening. The dawning of the day I feared, I trembled to behold the morning. I entered the ship, closed the door to shut it in, and committed the immense structure with its cargo to Puzur-bel, the pilot.

"As soon as the dawn appeared, a dark cloud ascended on the horizon. In the midst of it the storm-god rolled the thunder. The gods Nebo and Marduk marched on before, went as guides over hill and dale; the mighty pest-god tore loose the ship, the god Ninib caused the streams to overflow their banks. The Anunnaki, spirits

THE UNCHANGING LAND OF THE BIBLE

a FORTUNATE few can travel to the Holy Land and walk where Jesus walked. It is indeed a thrill to stand where the Apostles preached. To retrace the steps of Jesus is an experience never to be forgotten. For those who have always desired to travel to the Holy Land, and gaze on the part of the world that was the cradle of Christianity, the actual photographs which follow will afford the opportunity.

Two photographers have trudged the length and breadth of the unchanging land of the Bible, to bring to the reader, through pictures, the story of God's redemptive plan. Although the pictures are recent, the story is ancient. Strangely, however, the story of the land of the Bible, though old, is ever new.

From Bethlehem to Golgotha, the steps of Jesus have been followed. His triumphal entry into Jerusalem stirred the same sands which now lie under the Golden Gate. Gethsemane remains unchanged. The upper room, now silent, once echoed the song of Jesus and His disciples, before they went out to face the madness of a mob.

If one picture is really worth a thousand words, volumes are written in the following pages. And pictures are only necessary, because the frailty of human speech cannot adequately describe what the heart knows to be true.

Hear the unchanging truths uttered by Jesus as He stood by the Sea of Galilee! Know that this land was chosen by God, to give birth to this Christ, who remains as unchanging as the land of His birth!

THE SEA OF GALILEE. Matthew 8:24 ▶

GOLGOTHA, THE PLACE OF THE SKULL. THE SITE OF CHRIST'S CRUCIFIXION. *John 19:16-19*
WAILING WALL OF JERUSALEM'S TEMPLE. *(Destroyed 70 A.D. by Titus) Luke 21:20-24*
THE TOMB OF CHRIST. *John 19:41, 42* ➡

THE MOSQUE OF OMAR, SITE OF ISRAEL'S TEMPLE. *John 2:19-22, Matthew 24:1*

TEMPLE OF ARTEMIS AT JERASH, *of ancient Rome*

SAMARITAN HIGH PRIEST *with a scroll of the Law*

MT. TABOR, THE MOUNT OF THE TRANSFIGURATION, PLAIN OF ESDRAELON. *Matthew 17:1, 2*

THE GOLDEN GATE OF CHRIST'S TRIUMPHAL ENTRY.
Matthew 21:5

of the subterranean regions, lifted torches and made the land flicker by the light. The storm-god raised billows which reached to heaven. All light was turned to darkness. Man saw not his fellow, human beings were not discerned by those in heaven.

"The gods also were terrified at the flood-storm, sought refuge, ascended to heaven, and crouched at the wall like a dog in his lair. Then the goddess Ishtar, like a woman in travail, cried out—she of beautiful voice called: 'Mankind which was is become mud, the very evil which I foretold in the presence of the gods and just as I foretold it to them. A storm for the annihilation of my people I declared it would be. I brought forth men, but to what purpose? Like fry of fish they fill the sea.' The gods over the spirits of the subterranean regions wept with her, sitting bowed in tears, their lips covered.

"Six days and six nights * wind, flood-storm, and rain prevailed; on the seventh day the rain abated; the flood, the storm which had writhed like a woman in travail, rested; the sea withdrew to its bed, and the violent wind and the flood-storm ceased.

"I looked on the sea, at the same time shouting; but all men were become mud. I opened a window; and, as the light fell upon my face, I shrank back and sat down weeping; over my cheeks the tears coursed. I had looked on every side—a wide expanse, sea.

"A bit of land, however, rose to the height of twelve measures. To the country of Niṣir the ship took its course. A mountain of that land stranded the vessel and kept it from moving farther. On the first day and on the second day mount Niṣir held the ship, on the third day and on the fourth day likewise, on the fifth and sixth days likewise. When the seventh day came I released a dove. The dove flew hither and thither; there was no resting place, so it returned. Next I sent forth a swallow. The swallow also flew hither and thither, and, as there was no resting place, returned. Then I sent forth a raven. The raven flew away, and, when it saw that the waters had fallen, it approached, alighting but not returning.†

"I then sent forth [all the animals] to the four winds. I poured out a libation, I made an offering on the summit of the mountain. I set vessels by sevens, and underneath them spread sweet cane, cedar, and herbs. The gods smelled the savor and like flies gathered about the offerer.

"When the goddess Ishtar arrived, she raised aloft the great ornament which the god of the sky had made at her request. 'By the ornament of my neck, never will I forget; I will think of these days, and to eternity not forget them. Let all the gods come to the offering except Bel, for he inconsiderately caused the deluge and consigned my people to the judgment.' But Bel came also; and, when he saw the ship, was filled with wrath against the gods of the heavenly spirits. 'What soul has escaped?' he cried; 'not a man shall survive the judgment.' Then god Ninib opened his mouth and spake to the valorous Bel: 'Who else than god Ea has done this thing? Ea knows surely every exorcism.' Ea

* Mentioning the nights as well as the days, as does the Hebrew narrative at the same point. Delitzsch reads "six days and seven nights." His text thus contains a formula often found elsewhere, e.·g., l. 188. The majority of Assyriologists who have examined the tablet discern the marks for six days and six nights, not for seven nights.

† Or, the raven flew away and saw the abatement of the waters; [thereupon] he eats, alights carefully, but does not return.

also opened his mouth, and said to the valorous Bel: 'Thou, valorous chieftain of the gods, so utterly without reflection hast thou acted and caused the flood. On the sinner lay his sin, on the evil doer his evil deeds. Desist [from wrath] that he be not cut off: be gracious also. Instead of causing a flood-storm, send the lion and the hyena, famine and pestilence, and let them diminish men. And as for me, I did not reveal the purpose of the great gods; I sent Atraḥasis * a dream and he perceived the purpose of the gods.'

"Then Bel became reasonable, and went up into the ship, grasped my hand and led me up. He led up my wife also, and made her kneel at my side. Then turning to us he placed himself between us and blessed us, saying: 'Heretofore Sitnapishtim was a [mere] man; now let him and his wife be exalted to equality with the gods, and let him dwell afar off at the mouth of the rivers.' Thereupon he took me away and placed me afar off at the mouth of the rivers."†

The account of the flood existed in this form among the Assyrians and Babylonians before the seventh century B. C., for the colophon affixed to the tablet on which it is recorded states that the document is the property of Ashurbanipal, who reigned over Assyria from 668 to about 626 B. C., and that the words were copied from an older tablet. It existed in the same form centuries earlier, for fragments of it have been found which were written in the time of Ammizaduga, the fourth successor of Hammurabi, king of Babylon, who is believed on good evidence to have been Abraham's contemporary Amraphel.

A coin bearing a picture of the flood was struck at Apamea in Phrygia in the reign of

Coin of Apamea depicting Noah and ark.

the Roman emperor Septimius Severus, 193–211 A. D. A boat, inscribed with the letters NΩE, the Greek spelling of Noah, floats on the waves. A man and a woman are in it. A bird perches on it; and another bird flies toward the ves-

* In the account which Berosus wrote in Greek, this name is written Xisuthrus, the constituent parts being transposed. It is another name of Sitnapishtim.

† Such is essentially the cuneiform story. As here reproduced, it is slightly abridged; chiefly, however, by the omission of mutilated lines and of sentences whose translation is still uncertain.

sel, bearing a branch between its feet. Before the ark the former inmates are seen, having quitted it and got on dry land. Apamea was formerly called Kibotos, the Ark. The coins of towns frequently exhibited some prominent event in their history or local traditions.

Flute.

A musical instrument used in Babylon (Dan. iii. 5); in Aramaic *Mashroḳitha'*, whistle, pipe. Pipes consisting of one, two, or more reeds were in use. According to the Septuagint, it was Pan's pipe, which consisted of several reeds, joined side by side in a series, and gradually diminishing in length.

A flute or pipe, in Greek *Aulos*, was played in the house of mourning (Mat. ix. 23) and on occasions of joy (Rev. xviii. 22). See PIPE.

Flux. See DYSENTERY.

Fly.

1. A flying insect; a two-winged insect, one of the order *Diptera*, specially the domestic fly (*Musca domestica*). So troublesome are flies of various kinds in hot countries (Is. vii. 18; Ecc. x. 1) that the Ekronites worshiped a god Baal-zebub, lord of flies, who was supposed to be able to keep the annoyance within bounds (2 Kin. i. 2).

2. The rendering of the Hebrew *'Arob,* a voracious, biting insect of Egypt (Ex. viii. 21; Ps. cv. 31). It devoured (Ps. lxxviii. 45) and destroyed (Ex. viii. 24, margin). According to the Septuagint, the dog fly.

Fol'ly.

The absence of wisdom, disregard of the true nature of things in their relation to man and God. Hence injudicious action or conduct (Prov. xv. 21; Ecc. i. 17; x. 1; 2 Cor. xi. 1), and wickedness (Gen. xxxiv. 7; Deut. xxii. 21; Josh. vii. 15; Judg. xix. 23; xx. 6).

Food.

The food of the Hebrews, when they lived a simple nomadic life, consisted largely of bread and the products of the herd, such as milk, curds, and occasionally meat (Gen. xviii. 7, 8; Judg. v. 25). Wild honey was also eaten (Judg. xiv. 8, 9). When they adopted a settled life in Palestine, the products of garden, vineyard, and olive yard were added, such as lentils, cucumbers, beans (2 Sam. xvii. 28), pomegranates, figs, grapes (Num. xiii. 23; xx. 5; Mat. vii. 16). Sweet and sour wine were important articles of food. Fish were eaten, locusts also, and fowl and eggs (1 Kin. iv. 23; Neh. xiii. 16; Mat. iv. 18; Luke xi. 12). A simple repast consisted of bread and lentils (Gen. xxv. 34) or other pottage (2 Kin. iv. 38), or bread and wine (Gen. xiv. 18), or roasted grain and sour wine (Ruth ii. 14). Abraham honored his unexpected guests with a more pretentious meal, consisting of butter and milk, cakes made of fine flour, and the flesh of a calf (Gen. xviii. 3–8). A greater variety of foods came on the tables of the rich and great (1 Kin. iv. 22, 23; Neh. v. 18). See MEALS.

Fool.

One destitute of understanding or wisdom (2 Cor. xi. 16); especially a wicked man, the doctrine taught being that nothing shows a greater want of understanding than for a man to commit wickedness. The greater the talents, the greater the responsibility, and consequently the folly of misusing them for evil ends (1 Sam. xxvi. 21; 2 Sam. iii. 33; xiii. 13; Ps. xiv. 1; cp. 2, 3, etc.; Prov. xxvi. 10; Mat. v. 22). See FOLLY, PHILOSOPHY, and WISDOM.

Fool'ish-ness.

The same as folly (2 Sam. xv. 31; Prov. xxii. 15).

Foot'man.

1. A soldier who marches and fights on foot, in contradistinction to one on horseback (Num. xi. 21; 2 Kin. xiii. 7; 1 Chron. xviii. 4).

2. A runner (1 Sam. xxii. 17, A. V.), one of the king's bodyguard. See RUNNERS.

For'eign-er, in A. V. usually STRANGER.

A gentile; a person belonging to another people than Israel and owning other allegiance than to Israel and Israel's God (Deut. xxix. 22, 24), as the Egyptians (Ex. ii. 22); Jebusites (Judg. xix. 12), Philistines (2 Sam. xv. 19), Moabites, Ammonites, Edomites, Sidonians, Hittites (1 Kin. xi. 1). As a technical term foreigner does not include: 1. Slaves bought with money and captives taken in war; for they were in the power of their masters and subject to the laws of Israel (Gen. xvii. 12; Ex. xxi. 20, 21). 2. Proselytes to the religion of Israel (Gen. xxxiv. 14–17; Is. lvi. 6–8 Acts ii. 10). 3. The so-called sojourners or strangers. (See STRANGER.)

Israel was Jehovah's peculiar people (Deut. xiv. 1, 2); therefore idolatrous Canaanites specifically were not to be received into covenant relations of any sort (Ex. xxiii. 32), and all foreigners were debarred from eating the passover (Ex. xii. 43), entering the sanctuary (Ezek. xliv. 9; Acts xxi. 28; cp. Deut. xxiii. 3, 7, 8), and ascending the throne as king (Deut. xvii. 15). Intermarriage with them on equal terms was forbidden (Ex. xxxiv. 16; Deut. vii. 3; Josh. xxiii. 12, specifically Canaanites; cp. Gen. xxiv. 3, 4; xxvi. 34, 35; xxviii. 1; xxxiv. 14–17; Judg. xiv. 3; Ezra x. 2; Neh. xiii. 26, 27; Tob. vi. 12). The flesh of animals that died, which the Israelites were not allowed to eat, might be sold to foreigners (Deut. xiv. 21); money might be lent to them on interest (xxiii. 20; cp. Ex. xxii. 25); and debts could be collected from them even in the year of release, when they were remitted to Israelites (Deut. xv. 3). In later times strict Jews abstained from even eating and drinking with gentiles (Acts xi. 3; Gal. ii. 12). Yet access into Judaism was always open to the gentiles (Gen. xvii. 27; xxxiv. 14–17; Matt. xxiii. 15); and their ultimate engrafting into the kingdom was Israel's expectation.

Fore'run-ner.

A precursor; as 1. A runner who immediately precedes the horse or chariot of high officials in order to clear the way or make proclamation (see the verbs in Gen. xli. 43; 1 Sam. viii. 11; 2 Sam. xv. 1; 1 Kin. i. 5; xviii. 46; Esth. vi. 9). 2. Descriptive of a herald (Herod. i. 60). 3. The advance guard of an army (Wisdom xii. 8; Herod. iv. 121, 124; cp. ix. 14). 4. First fruits (Num. xiii. 20, Septuagint).

As a forerunner Christ has entered on our behalf into heaven, the holy of holies, into the immediate presence of God (Heb. vi. 20).

For'est.

An extensive wood (Is. xliv. 14). One grew on Lebanon, famed for its cedars and firs (1 Kin. vii. 2); another stretched from the Mediterranean Sea well into the hill country of Ephraim (Josh. xvii. 15, 18); a third was in Judah (1 Sam. xxii. 5); and a fourth existed beyond Jordan near Mahanaim (2 Sam. xviii. 6-9).

For-tu-nat'us [fortunate].

One of three messengers, apparently from Corinth, who reached Paul, and supplied what was lacking on the part of the church in that city (1 Cor. xvi. 17).

Foun'tain.

A spring arising from under a rock or a bank, or welling up from the ground (Deut. viii. 7). In the geography of Palestine it requires to be carefully distinguished from mere

Ruins of the Nymphaeum, the spouting fountains at Jeresh. The basin caught the overflow from the fountains.

wells, pools, and cisterns. Strong fountains are numerous in Palestine. They are the permanent source of rivers, and give life and fertility to the soil. Many towns are named from them, as En-dor and the other compounds of En. Figuratively, fountain symbolizes the permanent and inexhaustible source of spiritual blessings (Ps. xxxvi. 9; Jer. ii. 13; Rev. vii. 17; xxi. 6). Children are also described as a fountain proceeding from the parents (Deut. xxxiii. 28; Ps. lxviii. 26).

Foun'tain Gate. See JERUSALEM II. 3.

Fowl.

Any bird (Gen. i. 26; Lev. xi. 13–19).

Fowl'er.

One who catches birds by a net or other snare (Ps. cxxiv. 7; Prov. vi. 5); hence figuratively one who ensnares the innocent or unwary, and takes their life, or lures them to moral and spiritual ruin (Ps. xci. 3; cxxiv. 7; Hos. ix. 8).

Fox.

An animal which dwells in holes (Mat. viii. 20), especially among solitary ruins (Lam. v. 18), and is sly and careful for its own safety (Luke xiii. 32; Ezek. xiii. 4). Tristram enumerates two species as occurring in Palestine, the Egyptian fox (*Vulpes nilotica*), and the tawny fox (*Vulpes flavescens*). The former is abundant in central and southern Palestine, as well as east of the Jordan, and the latter, which is somewhat larger, and may perhaps be only a variety of the common fox (*Vulpes vulgaris*), in the wooded parts of the country.

Under the general name of fox, *Shu'al*, the Hebrews, like the modern inhabitants of Palestine, appear to have comprehended the jackal, which belongs to the dog family, although they had a special name for the jackal. The jackal is perhaps intended in Judg. xv. 4 (cp. R. V. margin); for it abounds in the lowland of Philistia, goes about by night in bands, and spends the day as a pack in some cave. It is thus easily caught; whereas the fox is a solitary animal and difficult to capture. The jackal also devours carrion (Ps. lxiii. 10), which the fox is loath to do. The jackal eats fruit as well as flesh, and may be intended in Song ii. 15, yet the fox tramples and destroys vineyards.

Frank'in-cense.

A fragrant gum of a tree (Ecclus. l. 8; Song iii. 6). It is white in color, as its Hebrew name L^ebonah denotes. It was an ingredient in the holy anointing oil with which priests were consecrated to their sacred functions (Ex. xxx. 34). It was added with oil to the meal offerings (Lev. ii. 1, 2, 15, 16, R. V.), and ultimately burned (vi. 15). No frankincense was added to sin offerings (Lev. v. 11) and offerings of jealousy (Num. v. 15). Pure frankincense was poured upon the twelve loaves of showbread (Lev. xxiv. 7; cp. also 1 Chron. ix. 29; Neh. xiii. 5). The dromedaries of Midian, Ephah, and Sheba, brought it to Palestine from Arabia (Is. lx. 6; Jer. vi. 20). The hill of frankincense (Song iv. 6) was probably a retired spot in the palace gardens, among exotic frankincense trees (cp. Ecc. ii. 5; Antiq. viii. 6, 6; ix. 1, 2). The frankincense of antiquity, the olibanum of European commerce, comes from *Boswellia floribunda,* one of the *Amyridaceæ* (Amyrids), growing in India, or from other species of the genus, especially *B. Carteri, B. Frereana* and *B. serrata,* of which there are two varieties, *B. serrata* proper, the *B. thurifera* of Roxburgh, and the variety *B. glabra.* The first and fourth species are Indian; the second and third occur on the Somali coast of Africa and on the south coast of Arabia. The frankincense itself is gum resin, which is dry, consists of tears often an inch long, with a balsamic odor, especially when burnt. A poor quality, reddish in color, is obtained in the spring; the best is gotten later, and is white.

Friend of the King.

A high court-official (Gen. xxvi. 26; 1 Kin. iv. 5), probably the king's confidential adviser. Under the Syro-Macedonian kings there was a specially privileged class known as the king's friends (1 Mac. ii. 18; iii. 38, vi. 10). See PRIEST.

Frog.

An amphibious animal (Ex. viii. 3; Rev. xvi. 13); in the Old Testament probably *Rana punctata,* the dotted frog of Egypt.

Front'let.

A band for the forehead; then, figuratively, the constant public exhibition of a trait or obedience to a command (Ex. xiii. 16; Deut. vi. 8, 9; xi. 18; cp. Prov. iii. 3). The injunction was interpreted literally by the later Jews. See PHYLACTERY.

Full'er.

One who cleanses undressed cloth from oil and grease, and renders it thick or compact by the application of pressure, or else one who thoroughly cleanses soiled garments (Mark ix. 3). The clothing was steeped in soap and water (Mal. iii. 2) and trodden, as the Hebrew name denotes. A fuller's field lay outside of Jerusalem. It had a highway and the conduit of the upper pool (Is. vii. 3; xxxvi. 2), and was so near the city that the Assyrian ambassadors, standing in the field and speaking, were heard and understood by the people on the city wall (2 Kin. xviii. 17). The conduit is commonly regarded as the channel which conducts the water from the Birket Mamilla, in the upper Hinnom valley northwest of Jerusalem, into the city. If, however, the conduit referred to is the tunnel connecting the fountain of the Virgin with the pool of Siloam, the fuller's field was in the valley of the Kidron.

Fur'long.

The rendering of the Greek noun *Stadion* (Luke xxiv. 13; John vi. 19; xi. 18; Rev. xiv.

20). The Greek *stadion* was 600 Greek and 606⅔ English feet, or about ⅛ of a Roman mile. It is a little less than an English furlong, which is 660 English feet, or ⅛ of an English mile. See MEASURE.

Fur'nace.

1. An oven for smelting iron from the ore (Deut. iv. 20; 1 Kin. viii. 51). See IRON.

2. A crucible for refining gold and silver, and for melting gold, silver, brass, tin, and lead (Prov. xvii. 3; Ezek. xxii. 20). See SMITH.

3. A bake oven; so in Neh. iii. 11; Is. xxxi. 9. See BREAD.

G

Ga'al [loathing].

A son of Ebed. With a band of followers he came to the city of Shechem, and, having gained the confidence of its inhabitants, began to vilify Abimelech, their absent king, and to assume authority. Zebul, the governor, sent word to Abimelech of what was going on, and advised him to lie in wait by night and advance against the town at dawn. He did so. Gaal went forth and gave him battle, but was put to flight (Judg. ix. 26–41).

Ga'ash [trembling, earthquake].

A hill in the hill country of Ephraim, south of Timnath-serah (Josh. xxiv. 30; Judg. ii. 9; 2 Sam. xxiii. 30; 1 Chron. xi. 32). Exact situation unknown.

Ga'ba. See GEBA.

Gab'bai [tax gatherer].

A Benjamite who consented to live in Jerusalem after the captivity (Neh. xi. 8).

Gab'ba-tha [an elevated place].

The equivalent in Aramaic of the Greek word *Lithostrōton,* a pavement of tessellated work (John xix. 13). On it stood the public tribunal on which Pontius Pilate sat to decide cases. Probably it was an open space in front of Herod's palace (cp. War ii. 14, 8). There is no reason to believe that Pilate, like Cæsar on his campaigns, carried a transportable pavement about with him, which he laid wherever he wished to erect his tribunal.

Ga'bri-el [man of God].

An angel of high rank sent to interpret a vision to the prophet Daniel (Dan. viii. 16–27). He was commissioned again to visit the prophet to give him skill and understanding, and reveal to him the prophecy of the seventy weeks (ix. 16–27). At a long subsequent period he was dispatched to Jerusalem to announce to Zacharias the birth of John the Baptist (Luke i. 11–22), and to Nazareth to hail the Virgin Mary as chosen to the high privilege of being mother of the Messiah (26–31). Gabriel described himself as habitually standing in the presence of God (19). Thence, doubtless, he departed at longer or shorter intervals to carry the divine messages to and from this earth or other worlds.

Gad [good fortune].

1. A son of Jacob by Zilpah, Leah's handmaid. At his birth Leah said, "Fortunate!" and she called his name Gad (Gen. xxx. 10, 11; cp. 13, R. V.). Jewish tradition adopted a different reading from the text, and made Leah say, "A troop or fortune cometh." Jacob prophesied: "Gad, a troop shall press upon him: but he shall press upon their heel" (Gen. xlix. 19, R. V.). Moses blessed God who enlarged Gad, and praised the valor of the tribe and its fidelity to duty (Deut. xxxiii. 20, 21). Gad had seven sons (Gen. xlvi. 16), each of whom, with the possible exception of Ezbon, founded a tribal family (Num. xxvi. 15–18).

2. The tribe of which Gad was the progenitor, the Gadites (Num. i. 14; Deut. xxvii. 13; Ezek. xlviii. 27, 28, 34). At the first census in the wilderness the Gadites capable of bearing arms were 45,650 (Num. i. 24, 25); at the second there were 40,500 (xxvi. 15–18). Valiant Gadites joined David at Ziklag (1 Chron. xii. 8). The territory occupied by the tribe was east of the Jordan, and was assigned them by Moses, but with the proviso that, before finally settling down in it, the warriors of the tribe should cross the river with their brethren, and give assistance in the conquest of Canaan (Num. xxxii. 21–32). The territory of the Gadites was situated between that of Reuben on the south and the half tribe of Manasseh on the north. It included the southern part of mount Gilead from the Jabbok southward to Heshbon, and from the vicinity of Rabbath-ammon on the east westward to the Jordan valley. In the valley it took in the entire eastern bank from Beth-nimrah, near the northern end of the Dead Sea, to the lake of Gennesaret (Josh. xiii. 24–28; Deut. iii. 12, 16, 17). The country was adapted to pasturage (Num. xxxii. 1–4). Ramoth in Gilead was in the territory of Gad, and was appointed a city of refuge (Josh. xx. 8). 2 Sam. xxiv. 5 probably means that the enumerators passed from the Arnon toward Gad and unto Jazer.

3. A prophet, David's seer, who, when David was in the cave of Adullam, advised him to quit that place of refuge and seek safety elsewhere (1 Sam. xxii. 5), and who later gave the king the option from God of three kinds of punishment for his having numbered the people (2 Sam. xxiv. 11–14). He aided in arranging the musical service of the sanctuary (2 Chron. xxix. 25), and wrote an account of David's reign (1 Chron. xxix. 29).

4. Perhaps a heathen deity was known by the name of Gad, for Isaiah represents the Israelites as engaging in idolatrous worship, and setting a table for Fortune [Hebrew Gad] and filling up mingled wine unto Fate [Hebrew Meni] (Is. lxv. 11, R. V.).

Gad-a-renes'.
Natives or inhabitants of Gadara, which Josephus calls the metropolis of Peræa and a place of strength, adding that it had wealthy inhabitants (War iv. 7, 3). He also describes it as a Greek city (Antiq. xvii. 11, 4). Eusebius places it east of the Jordan, nearly opposite to Tiberias and Scythopolis. It has been identified as Umm Keis, on a bold headland about 5½ English miles southeast from the southern side of the sea of Galilee, with the sea in full view and the river Yarmûk between. The most imposing ruins are the remains of two theaters. The hot springs belonging to Gadara are north of the Yarmûk, while Umm Keis lies to the south of that river. Gadarenes is the reading approved by textual criticism in Mat. viii. 28 (cp. Mark v. 1; Luke viii. 26, 37, A. V.). See GERGESENES.

Gadaritis was the designation of a political district east of the Jordan (War iii. 10, 10), having Gadara as its capital and extending to the southeastern shore of the sea of Galilee. But perhaps Matthew, in mentioning the country of the Gadarenes, speaks more broadly, since Gadara was a great city and its mention sufficiently indicated the general locality.

Gad'di [fortunate].
The spy from the tribe of Manasseh in the exploration of Canaan (Num. xiii. 11).

Gad'di-el [God hath given fortune].
The spy representing Zebulun in the exploration of Canaan (Num. xiii. 10).

Ga'di [a Gadite].
Father of king Menahem (2 Kin. xv. 14).

Ga'ham [flaming, burnt].
A son of Nahor and Reumah (Gen. xxii. 24).

Ga'har [hiding place].
Head of a family of Nethinim who returned from captivity (Ezra ii. 47; Neh. vii. 49).

Gai [valley].
A locality near Ekron, probably Gath (1 Sam. xvii. 52, R. V.; context and margin).

Ga'ius [a common Roman name, sometimes written *Caius*].
1. A Macedonian, one of Paul's companions who was dragged into the amphitheater during the riot at Ephesus (Acts xix. 29).
2. A man of Derbe, who accompanied Paul on his last journey to Asia (Acts xx. 4).
3. A Christian of Corinth, baptized by Paul, noted for hospitality to his fellow Christians (Rom. xvi. 23; 1 Cor. i. 14). Perhaps he was the person to whom John addressed his third epistle (3 John 1).

Gal'a-ad. See GILEAD.

Ga'lal [a rolling, as *e. g.*, the rolling of one's way on the Lord].
1. A Levite (1 Chron. ix. 15).
2. Another Levite, the son of Jeduthun (1 Chron. ix. 16; Neh. xi. 17).

Ga-la'tia.
A district of central Asia Minor, bounded on the north by Bithynia, Paphlagonia, and Pontus, on the east by Pontus and Cappadocia, on the south by Cappadocia and Ly-

caonia, on the west by Phrygia and Bithynia. Its name was derived from the fact that certain Gallic tribes, after having about 280 B. C. invaded Macedonia and Greece, migrated to Asia Minor and received this territory from Nicomedes, king of Bithynia, in return for services rendered him in war. Other Gallic tribes passed onward through central Europe, finally settling in Gaul, i. e. France. The Gauls were commonly called *Galatai* by the Greeks. The chief cities of Galatia were Pessinus, Ancyra, and Tavium. The territory, however, varied in size at different times according to the fortunes of war. In 189 B. C. the Galatians were subdued by the Romans, but retained their self-government, and were favored by their conquerors, since they were valuable allies. Hence under their last king, Amyntas, their territory was much extended to the south, so as to include part of Phrygia, Pisidia, Lycaonia, and Isauria; and, after the death of Amyntas (25 B. C.), this enlarged region became the Roman province of Galatia. In 7 B. C. Paphlagonia and part of Pontus were added on the north, and after A. D. 63 other territorial changes were frequently made. During the travels of Paul therefore the term Galatia was applicable both to the original Galatic territory and to the large Roman province. In which sense it is used in Acts xvi. 6 (where the A. V. has "when they had gone throughout Phrygia and the region of Galatia," and the R. V. "they went through the region of Phrygia and Galatia," but which Prof. Ramsay translates "they went through the Phrygo-Galatic region"), and in Acts xviii. 23 (which translation is open to similar differences of opinion), and in Paul's epistle to the "churches of Galatia," is disputed. If Galatia meant the Roman province, then Paul evangelized it on his first missionary journey (Acts xiii., xiv.) in company with Barnabas. If it meant the old territory of Galatia, then he evangelized it on his second journey (Acts xvi. 6). The churches of Galatia are also mentioned in 1 Cor. xvi. 1. In 2 Tim. iv. 10 we read that Crescens had gone to Galatia, which, however, many think meant Gaul (now France). 1 Peter is addressed to the Christians of Galatia among others (i. 1), and there Galatia clearly means the Roman province. There are, however, serious difficulties in so understanding it in The Acts and in the Epistle to the Galatians.　　　　G. T. P.

Ga-la'tians, E-pis'tle to the.

A letter addressed to the churches of Galatia (i. 2), showing that there were a number of them in different parts of the territory. What churches are thus described depends on the meaning we attach to the term Galatia (q. v.). The date of the epistle also turns on this point. If Galatia be the Roman province, and the churches of Galatia those founded on Paul's first journey (Acts xiii., xiv.),

then the epistle was probably written toward the latter part, or at the close, of Paul's second journey, since Gal. iv. 13 ("the first time," R. V.) implies that he had visited them twice, and since it seems necessary to date the epistle later than those to the Thessalonians, for the letters to the Thessalonians contain no allusion to the Judaistic attacks. If, however, Galatia means Galatia proper, and if it was evangelized on the second journey (Acts xvi. 6), then the epistle could not have been written before the apostle's sojourn in Ephesus, since Acts xviii. 23 mentions his second visit, on this interpretation, to Galatia. In conformity with this latter view are the facts, first, that the apostle appeals to his readers as if. he alone had been their spiritual father (Gal. iv. 13-20; v. 1), whereas on his first missionary journey Barnabas was associated with him; and, secondly, that Paul's description of his reception as an angel of God (iv. 14) hardly comports with any known experience of his on his first journey. Most scholars take this latter view, conclude that Galatia proper was evangelized on the second journey, and date the epistle in A. D. 55 or 56. Others, however, put it still later, thinking that its resemblance to Romans shows that it was written shortly before that epistle, say in the winter of 57-58. Whatever its readers and date, it was occasioned by the operations of certain Judaizing teachers among the Galatians, who assailed Paul's authority, and taught the necessity of observing the Mosaic laws. They declared that Paul, not being one of the original apostles, was dependent on others for his knowledge of the gospel. They seem also to have charged him with being himself inconsistent in his preaching of gentile freedom from the law. They also attacked his doctrine, and persuaded his converts to adopt Jewish observances. The very gospel being thus at stake, Paul wrote this epistle with great intensity of feeling and vigorous argument.

This epistle is the *magna charta* of Christian liberty. After the introduction (i. 1-10), in which the apostle opens the subject of their error in listening to false teachers, and vehemently asserts the divineness of the gospel which he had preached, he defends his apostolic authority (i. 11-ii. 21) as given directly by Christ and not dependent on man. He also shows that the Jerusalem church and the original apostles agreed with his position (ii. 1-10), and that (ii. 11-21) he had never changed his teaching, even when Peter at Antioch had seemed by his conduct to oppose it. In chap. iii. he defends his doctrine of justification by faith alone, appealing in proof to their own experience of salvation through faith (iii. 1-5), to the teaching of Scripture regarding the original Abrahamic way of salvation (iii. 6-9) and to certain facts, fully taught in Scripture, concerning the law, namely, that the law, since it requires perfect obedience as the condition of salvation, brings only a curse or penalty (iii. 10–12); that Christ has redeemed us from the curse, having become a curse for us (iii. 13, 14); that God ratified his covenant of salvation by faith with Abraham and his seed, and hence the law, which came later, cannot disannul the original compact (iii. 15–18), but was intended as a temporary discipline to make men realize that sin is a transgression of God's commandments (iii. 19, 20), that the law was therefore a tutor to bring sinners to Christ (iii. 21–24). In chap. iv. the apostle advances three more reasons for their fidelity to his gospel, namely, the analogy of sonship and its rights under the civil law (iv. 1–11), their personal affection for himself (iv. 12–20), and the illustration which the narrative of Genesis provided in the account of Hagar and Sarah and their sons (iv. 21–31). In v.–vi. 10 he applies the doctrine of freedom from the law, bidding them to maintain, yet not to abuse, their liberty, and to exercise it with meekness and a sense of responsibility. The closing verses, vi. 11–18, form the conclusion, probably in the apostle's own handwriting (see ver. 11 in R. V.), in which he summarizes the substance of his instruction.

The Epistle to the Galatians is of immense value. 1. It is important for the details it gives about the apostle's life. Its harmony with the account in The Acts of Paul's life, and of his relation to the church, has been much contested, but may be completely proved (see PAUL and the remarks, made at the proper chronological point in the article, concerning Paul's first visit to Jerusalem after his conversion, Gal. i. 18, 19; Acts ix. 26–29, and concerning the council at Jerusalem, Gal. ii. 2–10 and Acts xv.). 2. The epistle proves also that the older apostles were in accord with Paul, though to him was allotted the work among the gentiles. 3. It gives in briefer outline, and with special application, the same scheme of salvation and the same view of the Hebrew dispensation which is more elaborately and calmly presented in the Epistle to the Romans. All men being under law, and condemned as sinners by the law, salvation is impossible by the works of the law. Christ alone can save, since he has by his death met the claims of the law against those who believe. The law was never intended to save, but to be a schoolmaster (i. e. a slave who led children to school) to bring us to Christ. By faith Abraham was saved, and by faith alone do we become children of Abraham, partakers of the blessing and heirs of the promise. Judaism, as a method of salvation, was therefore a misinterpretation even of the Old Testament itself, and the distinction between Jew and gentile has been done away. The declaration of these truths made Christianity a world religion instead of a Jewish sect.

The Epistle to the Galatians was much used by early Christian writers: certainly by Polycarp, and in the Epistle to Diognetus, and by Justin Martyr, during the first half of the second century, and by Melito in the third quarter; and in the last quarter it is quoted by name, according to their custom in citing, by Irenæus, Clement of Alexandria, and Tertullian. It is contained in the Old Latin version, and is listed in the Muratorian fragment.   G. T. P. (supplemented).

Gal'ba-num.

A fragrant spice (Ex. xxx. 34; Ecclus. xxiv. 15), in Hebrew *Helb'nah*, in Greek *Chalbanē*. The Greek and Roman *Galbanum* was a gum brought from Persia. It is generally supposed to have come from two umbelliferous plants, *Ferula galbaniflua* and *F. rubricaulis*. The Levant galbanum of European commerce is a different plant. The umbelliferous plant from which it comes is imperfectly known.

Gal'e-ed [heap of witness].

A cairn erected by Jacob in mount Gilead, north of the Jabbok. The exact situation is unknown. It was between the respective homes of Laban and Jacob, and was intended as a memorial of the covenant concluded between them there, that neither would pass that place to do the other injury (Gen. xxxi. 45–54); see MIZPAH. The two names Gilead and Galeed are never confused in Hebrew. Their pronunciation is different; and the former is a common noun rather than a proper name, and took the definite article.

Gal'ga-la, in R. V. Gilgal.

A place (1 Mac. ix. 2), presumably one of the towns known as Gilgal.

Gal-i-læ'an.

A native or inhabitant of Galilee (Mark xiv. 70; Luke xiii. 1).

Gal'i-lee [Hebrew *galil*, circle, region, district].

Originally a district in the hill country of Naphtali (2 Kin. xv. 29; 1 Chron. vi. 76), Kedesh being one of its cities (Josh. xx. 7; xxi. 32). The twenty unimportant towns given by Solomon to Hiram were in the land of Galilee (1 Kin. ix. 11). In this region many of the Canaanites remained (Judg. i. 30–33; iv. 2), and the expression "Galilee of the nations" or "gentiles" implies that the district or region so called was inhabited chiefly by a non-Jewish population (Is. ix. 1; cp. 1 Mac. v. 15 and Mat. iv. 15). The name Galilee gradually extended until it included the country as far south as the plain of Esdraelon (1 Mac. v. 55; x. 30; xii. 47, 49). Many of its inhabitants had been carried away, especially during the Assyrian wars (2 Kin. xv. 29; 1 Kin. xv. 20), and the few Jews who settled in Galilee after the return were taken to Judæa by Simon Maccabæus about 164 B. C. (1 Mac. v. 23); but Galilee soon after became thoroughly Jewish. It formed part of the kingdom of Herod the Great, and on his death passed under the authority of Herod the tetrarch. It was the most northerly of the three provinces west of the Jordan into which (if Phœnicia be ignored) Palestine was divided in the times of the Romans. At the period of the Jewish war, A. D. 70, it was divided into Upper and Lower Galilee; and was bounded on the north by Tyrian territory, on the south by the northern boundary line of Samaria and Scythopolis to the Jordan, on the east by Hippene, Gadaris, Gaulonitis, and the kingdom of Agrippa, that is, by the Jordan and its lakes, and on the west by Phœnicia. Lower Galilee lay to the south of Upper Galilee, and extended from Tiberias to near Ptolemais, now Acre, on the Mediterranean Sea (War iii. 3, 1; Life 13, 14, 37; cp. also Judith i. 8). It was at that time densely populated. It furnished an army of 100,000 men (War ii. 20, 6). There were 240 cities and villages within the limits of the two Galilees (Life 45). The smallest of them, it is incorrectly stated elsewhere, had 15,000 inhabitants (War iii. 3, 2). The largest city was Sepphoris, and the largest village Japha (Life 45). The mixture of races tended to produce a distinct accent or even dialect (Mark xiv. 70; Luke xxii. 59; cp. Acts ii. 7). The people also was supposed to be one which never would produce a prophet (John vii. 41, 52). Nevertheless, nearly all the apostles of Jesus were natives of Galilee, and he himself was brought up in it and made it the chief scene of his ministry, laboring on its eastern limits by the sea of Galilee, and within its area at Chorazin, Bethsaida, Capernaum, Nain, Cana, and Nazareth.

Galilee is about 60 miles long by 25 broad. It is generally mountainous, with fertile valleys between. Its scenery is picturesque. Lower Galilee is divided from Upper Galilee on a line running almost due west from the northern end of the lake to Acre. It is a grain-growing region, with a less elevation above the sea level than Upper Galilee, its mountains being all under 1850 feet high. Upper Galilee has summits of 2000, 3000, and 4000 feet altitude. It is characterized by olive groves.

A view of the area where the Jordan River flows into the Sea of Galilee.

Ruins of an aqueduct which furnished water for a Roman flour mill. The mill was located on the shore of the Sea of Galilee near Magdala (Mejdel).

Gal'i-lee, Sea of.

A fresh-water lake, fed by the river Jordan. It was called originally sea of Chinnereth (Num. xxxiv. 11), later lake of Gennesaret (Luke v. 1; Antiq. xviii. 2, 1; cp. xiii. 5, 7; 1 Mac. xi. 67), and sea of Galilee or Tiberias (John vi. 1; xxi. 1). The latter name is preserved in the Arabic form Bahr Tabariya.

It is enclosed by hills, save where the Jordan enters and leaves. The hills on the eastern side rise to the height of 1000 feet and more; those on the western side toward the southern end of the lake are of like character, but toward the northwest they are lower and less steep. It is designated a sea, from its considerable extent, though its water is fresh. Its length from the entrance to the exit of the Jordan is 12¾ miles; its greatest breadth, which is opposite to Magdala, is 7½ miles. Its eastern side is destitute of conspicuous indentations, while on the western side there is a swelling bay extending from Tell Hum on the north to Tiberias on the south. The depression of the surface of the lake below that of the Mediterranean is 682.5 feet. Lying so low, it has a semitropical climate, and ice-crowned Hermon being at no great distance, sudden and violent storms at times rush down the mountain slope and terminate on the lake. The water abounds in fish. Tristram enumerates twenty-two species; two of *Blenniidæ*, seven of *Chromidæ*, one of *Siluridæ*, and twelve of *Cyprinidæ*. Some are called after biblical personages, viz., *Chromis Andreæ*, *C. Simonis*, and *C. Magdalenæ*. The best fish for the table of all now in the lake are the sheatfish (*Clarias macracanthus*) and the barbel (*Barbus longiceps*). The sheatfish, called by Josephus *Coracinus* (War iii. 10, 8), belongs to the same family as the American catfish, and attains a length of three feet. The most abundant fish is *Chromis tiberiadis*. Tristram saw them in shoals of over an acre in extent, so closely packed that it seemed impossible for them to move. Their dorsal fins, rising above the water, gave it at a distance an appearance as if a heavy shower were pattering on one spot of the glassy lake. The fish are taken in nets both from boats and from the shore.

The plain of Tabgha at the north end of the Sea of Galilee. This is the traditional spot where Christ fed the five thousand.

Of course, the same kinds of fish are found in the Jordan and its tributaries also.

Gall [remotely from Greek *cholē*, bile].
1. The bitter secretion of the liver, bile (Job xvi. 13: xx. 25). In Hebrew *M^ererah* and *M^erorah*, as being fluid or bitter. The poison of asps was anciently believed to come from their bile (xx. 14). Venomous, malignant feeling against what is good was called the gall of bitterness (Acts viii. 23).
2. A poisonous, bitter herb (Deut. xxix. 18; xxxii. 32, 33; Ps. lxix. 21), called in Hebrew *Rosh*, in Greek *Cholē*. It grew up spontaneously in the furrows of fields (Hos. x. 4, where the English versions translate it hemlock, though in all other passages they call it gall). It was associated in rhetorical language with wormwood (Deut. xxix. 18). A sore punishment was likened to a drink of gall water (Jer. viii. 14; ix. 15; xxiii. 15). A stupefying drink, made of wine mingled with gall, was mercifully offered to Jesus at the place of crucifixion (Mat. xxvii. 34). The characteristics do not well agree with hemlock, which is not bitter, nor with the poppy. They suit the colocynth, which, however, is called in the Bible the wild gourd.

Gal'ler-y.
A long room or corridor, or a partial story in a building (Ezek. xli. 15, 16; xlii. 3, 5). A different Hebrew word, rendered galleries in A. V. of Song vii. 5, doubtless means tresses, as it is translated in R. V.

Gal'ley,
A low flat-built vessel with one or more banks, *i. e.* rows of oars (Is. xxxiii. 21; 2 Mac. iv. 20).

Gal'lim [heaps].
1. A village near Gibeah of Saul and Anathoth (Is. x. 29, 30), apparently not a great distance from Bahurim (1 Sam. xxv. 44; 2 Sam. iii. 13–16).
2. A town of Judah called Gallim, mentioned by the Septuagint in a group with Tekoa, Bethlehem, Etam, and especially in

connection with towns southwest of Jerusalem (Josh. xv. between 59 and 60).

Gal′li-o.

Roman proconsul of Achaia at the time of Paul's first visit to Corinth. His original name was Marcus Annæus Novatus; but he was adopted into the family of Lucius Junius Gallio, and took the name Junius Annæus Gallio. He was the brother of the Roman philosopher Seneca, and, like him, was put to death by the emperor Nero. When the Jews, maddened by the success of Paul at Corinth, dragged him before the proconsul's tribunal, Gallio refused to take notice of religious questions, and summarily dismissed the case. He remained equally indifferent when the crowd took Sosthenes, the ruler of the synagogue, and beat him before the judgment seat (Acts xviii. 12-17). See SOSTHENES.

Gal′lows.

Haman had a gallows made fifty cubits high, on which to hang Mordecai (Esth. v. 14, R. V. margin, tree). Hanging by a rope about the throat was not a Persian method of punishment. Haman no doubt intended to impale Mordecai (cp. ii. 23; Herod. iii. 159).

Ga-ma′li-el [God's reward].

1. Son of Pedahzur and head of the tribe of Manasseh in the wilderness (Num. i. 10; ii. 20; vii. 54, 59).

2. A member of the Jewish sanhedrin, of the Pharisee sect, and a doctor of the law, held in high reputation by the Jewish people. He advised against persecuting the apostles, on the ground that if their work were simply man's, it would eventually fail; while if it were from God, opposition to it was wicked and vain (Acts v. 34-39). Gamaliel had Paul for one of his pupils in the law (xxii. 3). According to the Talmud, Gamaliel was the grandson of the celebrated rabbi Hillel. Its further statement that Gamaliel long presided over the sanhedrin is improbable, for at this time the presidency was held by the high priests. He died about A. D. 50.

Games.

In the N. T. there are numerous allusions, more or less clear, to the games of ancient Greece. The most important of these were four in number: the Olympic games, at Olympia, in the district of Elis, in the Peloponnesus; the Pythian games, at Delphi, in Phocis; the Nemean games, at Argos, in Argolis, in the Peloponnesus; and the Isthmian games, on the isthmus of Corinth. The contests carried on were chariot, horse, and foot racing, quoiting, boxing, wrestling, hurling the spear. The intending competitors went through a long course of severe training. Immense multitudes were spectators of their skill, and though the direct rewards of the victors were but slight, the honor given to them by their fellow citizens and countrymen was beyond measure great. Similar games were introduced into Judæa by hellenizing Jews in the reign of Antiochus Epiphanes, and were fostered by Herod the Great (1 Mac. i. 10, 14; Antiq. xv. 8, 1); see GYMNASIUM. As the Isthmian games were held in the vicinity of

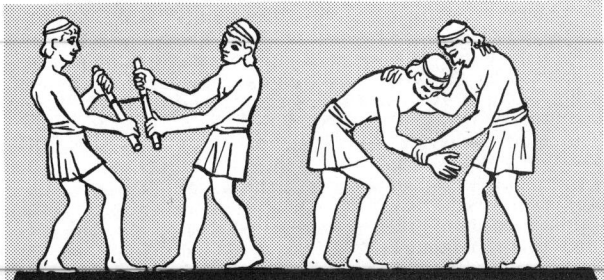

Grecian games of pulling and wrestling.

Corinth, and the other three at no great distance, it is natural for Paul's two epistles to the Corinthians to contain metaphors or comparisons borrowed from the games. In 1 Cor. ix. 24-27 there is allusion to the training of a competitor in the games, to running, and to fighting, the object in view being to gain a prize. There are scattered allusions of a similar kind through other epistles (Gal. ii. 2; v. 7; Phil. ii. 16; iii. 14; 2 Tim. ii. 5). In Hebrews there is a notable passage (xii. 1, 2). The vast multitude of men and women who have borne testimony to their faith in God is likened to the immense concourse of spectators at a foot race. The competitor lays aside every weight to make himself lighter, and the long, flowing garment, which else would beset him and perhaps throw him down. He requires patience to go forward perseveringly, but obtains it by looking at the umpire seated at the end of the course, ready to confer the prize if it be fairly won. Every one of these details had a distinct spiritual reference, which would come home with great power to every reader of the epistle who had seen any of the Grecian games.

Gam′ma-dim, in A. V. improperly Gammadims [valorous men].

Brave people who manned the towers of Tyre (Ezek. xxvii. 11, A. V. and E. R. V.).

Ga′mul [recompensed].

A descendant of Aaron whose family in David's reign was made the twenty-second course of the priests (1 Chron. xxiv. 17).

Gar′den.

The first garden or park mentioned in Scripture was that of Eden, which God

caused to grow for man in his state of innocence (Gen. ii. 8–iii. 24; Ezek. xxviii. 13;
xxxi. 8, 9). Gardens were watered by the
foot in Egypt (Deut. xi. 10) with water
raised from the Nile by sweep and bucket,
or by wheel from wells, and poured into the
irrigation ditch. By opening or closing this
furrow by the foot the water was led to the
spot desired. Irrigation was practiced in
Palestine also (Ecc. ii. 6; Is. lviii. 11; Jer.
xxxi. 12). Herbs were cultivated in gardens (1 Kin. xxi. 2); so also were lilies and
other flowers (Song v. 1; vi. 2), and fruit
trees (Jer. xxix. 5, 28; Amos ix. 14). The
garden of Gethsemane seems, from its name,
to have been an olive grove, and to have
had a press in it wherewith to express the
oil from the fruit. There was a royal garden at Jerusalem (2 Kin. xxv. 4), another at
Etam near Bethlehem (Antiq. viii. 7, 3; cp.
Song vi. 11; Ecc. ii. 5), another in the palace
at Shushan (Esth. i. 5). To protect gardens
against depredators they were enclosed with
a wall or hedge (Song iv. 12; Is. v. 2, 5), and
occasionally a lodge was placed within them,
attended by a watcher (Is. i. 8). In the
seclusion and coolness of gardens people
walked (Hist. of Susanna i. 7), sometimes
bathed (15), spread repasts (Esth. i. 5), engaged in devotion (Mat. xxvi. 36), practiced
idolatrous rites (Is. i. 29; lxv. 3; lxvi. 17;
cp. 2 Kin. xvi. 4), and occasionally buried
their dead (John xix. 41).

Ga′reb [rough, scabby].
1. An Ithrite, one of David's mighty men
(2 Sam. xxiii. 38; 1 Chron. xi. 40).
2. A hill near Jerusalem on the west (Jer.
xxxi. 39; cp. 38, 40). Exact situation unknown.

Gar′lic.
A bulbous plant resembling the onion, and
in Hebrew called from its odor *Shom.* It was
much eaten in Egypt (Herod. ii. 125), and
the Israelites when there used it for food
(Num. xi. 5). It is *Allium sativum*, of the
same genus as the onion, but with more taste
and scent than that esculent. It is a native
of central Asia, is grown largely in the Mediterranean region, and is eaten by the common people as a relish to their bread.

Gar′ment. See CLOTHING.

Gar′mite [pertaining to Gerem, or bony].
An appellation of probably the father of
Keilah (1 Chron. iv. 19).

Gar′ner.
A place for storing grain, a granary (Ps.
cxliv. 13; Joel i. 17; Mat. iii. 12).

Gar′nish.
To adorn, to decorate with ornamental additions (2 Chron. iii. 6; Job xxvi. 13; Mat. xii.
44; xxiii. 29; Luke xi. 25; Rev. xxi. 19).

Gar′ri-son.
A military post; a body of troops stationed
in a fort (1 Sam. xiv. 1, 15; 2 Sam. xxiii. 14–
16; 2 Cor. xi. 32). A different Hebrew word

from that used in the foregoing passages from
the O. T. is also rendered garrison by the Vulgate and English versions in 1 Sam. x. 5; xiii.
3. But this word certainly means a pillar in
Gen. xix. 26, and an officer stationed at a
place in 1 Kin. iv. 19. What does it mean in
1 Sam. x. 5; xiii. 3? There is no authority
for rendering it by garrison except that that
meaning yields good sense in these and some
other passages. The author of the Books of
Samuel, however, uses a different word for
garrison. Pillar is suitable in the first of
these passages. If this is the true meaning,
then the Philistines had erected memorial
columns in the land of Israel as monuments
of their victory or dominion, such as the Hebrews set up at Mizpah (1 Sam. vii. 12). It
was quite customary for conquerors to erect
memorials in the conquered country. Egyptian and Assyrian kings carved records of
their conquests on the cliff at the Nahr el-
Kelb near Beirut, which were never effaced,
not even when the Phœnicians regained their
independence, but exist to this day. Driver
believes that the word means pillar in xiii. 3
also, and cites Amos ix. 1 in proof that Jonathan could be said to have smitten a pillar.
But as the word means officer in 1 Kin. iv.
19, as this attested meaning yields good sense,
not only in 1 Sam. x. 5 and xiii. 3, but also
in 2 Sam. viii. 6, 14, and as a different word is
evidently used to denote a garrison, it is better
to believe that the author of the double Book
of Samuel always uses it in the sense of officer.
The smiting of a Philistine officer by Jonathan was an act of rebellion and a just cause
of war. It was so regarded by the Philistines. His overthrow of a pillar would have
been a mere act of wanton violence, unless
there was a body of Philistines posted in its
vicinity to protect it from desecration; and
it was not customary to guard such monuments.

Gash′mu. See GESHEM.

Ga′tam [puny].
A descendant of Eliphaz (Gen. xxxvi. 11;
1 Chron. i. 36), and chief of a tribe of the
sons of Esau (Gen. xxxvi. 16).

Gate.
In walled cities or palaces a gate was essential for the egress and ingress of the inhabitants, and for defense against the entrance of an enemy. It was often protected
by a strong tower (2 Chron. xxvi. 9), indeed
the gateway frequently led through the
tower. There were bars to place across the
gates, and render them stronger against assault (Deut. iii. 5; 1 Kin. iv. 13; 2 Chron.
viii. 5; xiv. 7). The gate was a place of public concourse where business was carried on
(1 Kin. xxii. 10; 2 Kin. vii. 1; Ezek. xi. 1);
legal transactions conducted and witnessed
(Gen. xxiii. 10, 18; Ruth iv. 1–11); cases tried
and judgment pronounced (Deut. xxi. 19;
xxii. 15; xxv. 7–9; Job xxxi. 21; Amos v.
15). There were gates in the enclosures

connected with the mansions of the aristocracy (Luke xvi. 20), where love of magnificence and display found expression (Prov.
xvii. 19).

Gath [wine press].

One of the five great Philistine cities (Josh.
xiii. 3; Judg. iii. 3; 1 Sam. vi. 17; vii. 14; xvii.
52). It was noted as the residence of a remnant
of the Anakim, men of great stature (Josh. xi.
22; cp. Num. xiii. 33; Deut. ii. 10, 11). To
this race, Goliath and the other gigantic warriors probably belonged (1 Sam. xvii. 4; 2
Sam. xxi. 15–22; 1 Chron. xx. 4–8). The town
was captured by David (1 Chron. xviii. 1).
During Solomon's reign, it had a king of its
own who was probably subject to the king at
Jerusalem (1 Kin. ii. 39, 42). It was fortified
by Rehoboam (2 Chron. xi. 8), but soon again
reverted to the Philistines. It was captured
by Hazael (2 Kin. xii. 17). Uzziah broke
down its wall (2 Chron. xxvi. 6); and henceforth it drops out of history. Micah, indeed,
names it, but he uses an ancient form of
speech (i. 10; cp. 2 Sam. i. 20). When afterwards the Philistine cities are mentioned,
Gath is missing (Jer. xxv. 20; Zeph. ii. 4;
Zech. ix. 5); and it is not referred to in Maccabees, nor by Josephus, when he relates
events subsequent to the year 750 B. C. Numerous theories have been offered as to its
site. It has been located—1. Near the sea;
at Yebnah (so the Crusaders); 2. In or on the
border of the Shephelah, at Beit Jibrin: or
Deir Dubban, 4½ miles north of Beit Jibrin;
or Kefr Dikkerin, 4 miles to the northwest
of Beit Jibrin; or, following the same highway 4 miles farther, at Tell es-Sâfiyeh on the
vale of Elah, at the junction of the Shephelah with the maritime plain; or Tell Zakariya, 5 miles east up the valley; or Tell el-
Menshiyeh, 6½ miles west of Beit Jibrin. All
that is known is that Gath lay inland, on the
borders of the Hebrew territory, and in a
sense between Ashdod and Ekron (1 Sam. v.
6–10; vii. 14; xvii. 52).

Gath-he'pher, in A. V. once through mis-
apprehension **Git-tah-he'pher** [wine press
of the well].

A town on the boundary line of Zebulun
(Josh. xix. 13). It was the birthplace of the
prophet Jonah (2 Kin. xiv. 25). In Jerome's
day it existed as a small village, 2 Roman
miles east of Sepphoris. This location corresponds with the village of el-Meshhed or
Meshhad, 3 miles northeast of Nazareth.
Here one of Jonah's tombs exists, its chief
rival being at the site of ancient Nineveh.

Gath-rim'mon [pomegranate press].

1. A town of the tribe of Dan (Josh. xix.
45), assigned to the Kohathite Levites (xxi.
42; 1 Chron. vi. 69). Exact site unknown.

2. A town in Manasseh west of the Jordan,
assigned to the Kohathite Levites (Josh. xxi.
25); probably an erroneous transcription of
Ibleam or Bileam (q. v.).

Gauls. See GALATIA.

Ga'za, thrice **Azzah** in A. V. and once in
R. V. (1 Chron. vii. 28), according as one or
other Greek modification of the Hebrew
word 'Azzah is imitated [strong].

1. The most southerly of the five Philistine
cities (Josh. xiii. 3; 1 Sam. vi. 17; Jer. xxv.
20), and very ancient (Gen. x. 19; el-Amarna
letters, 15th century B. C.). It stood on the
main road, between Mesopotamia and Egypt,
at the edge of the desert and at the junction
of a trade route from southern Arabia. Assigned to Judah (Josh. xv. 47), it was captured by the men of that tribe (Judg. i. 18),
but reverted to the Philistines (cp. Judg. vi.
4). Samson carried off the doors of the city
gate (Judg. xvi. 1–3). In prison and blinded
he ground grain there (20, 21). The tutelary
god of Gaza, as of Ashdod, was Dagon. The
last act of Samson's life was to bow with his
strength against the two middle pillars of
the temple of Dagon and throw them from
their place (23–31). Gaza was the limit of
Solomon's dominion toward the southwest
(1 Kin. iv. 24). Hezekiah smote the Philistines as far as Gaza's gate (2 Kin. xviii. 8).
The city was taken by Sargon in 720 B. C.
Pharaoh took the city (Jer. xlvii. 1), probably Pharaoh-necho or Pharaoh-hophra, i. e.
Apries (Herod. ii. 159, 161). Judgment was
denounced against it and the other Philistine cities by the prophets (Jer. xxv. 20;
xlvii. 1, 5; Zeph. ii. 4; Zech. ix. 5). One
sin specified was its sale of captured Hebrews
to the Edomites (Amos i. 6). It held out
against Alexander the Great for five months,
and when it fell its inhabitants were massacred. Jonathan Maccabeus was shut out of
Gaza, and burnt its suburbs; but he eventually made peace without storming the place
(1 Mac. xi. 61, 62). It was afterwards captured by his brother Simon (xiii. 43–48;
Antiq. xiii. 5, 5). About 96 B. C., after a year's
siege, it was devastated by Alexander Jannæus (Antiq. xiii. 13, 3). In 62 B. C. Pompey
placed it under the jurisdiction of Syria (xiv.
4, 4). Gabinius, the Roman governor of Syria,
built it in 57 B. C., probably on a new site,
and the old town perhaps became known as
Desert Gaza (xiv. 5, 3; Strabo xvi. 2, 30; cp.
Acts viii. 26). About A. D. 65 the Jews destroyed Gaza; but it rose again, and coins
are extant belonging to it which were struck
in honor of Titus and Hadrian. Later it became the seat of a Christian bishopric. In
A. D. 634 it was taken by the Arabs and, except during the brief intervals when it was
held by the Crusaders, has remained in Mohammedan hands. It is called Ghuzzeh by
the Arabs; is about 2½ miles from the Mediterranean, from which it is separated by a
waste of sand; and is situated on a low,
round hill, about 50 or 60 feet above the
plain, but extends from the hill across the
plain to the east and north. On the north
there are immense olive groves, the finest in
Palestine; and the great staple of the city is
soap, manufactured from the olive oil. Ghuz-

zeh is not fortified; but there are indications of the course of the ancient walls.

2. A town of Ephraim (1 Chron. vii. 28, R. V.), possibly represented by 'Azzun, twelve miles west by south of Shechem.

Ga-za'ra. See GEZER.

Ga'zath-ite. See GAZITE.

Ga-zelle'.

A small antelope, called in Hebrew *Ṣᵉbi*. Where A. V. renders this word by roebuck, R. V. substitutes gazelle; and where A. V. renders it by roe, R. V. generally places gazelle on the margin. There is no doubt that the gazelle (*Gazella dorcas*) is intended. It was ceremonially clean (Deut. xii. 22; xiv. 5), was hunted (Prov. vi. 5; Is. xiii. 14), and was swift-footed (2 Sam. ii. 18; 1 Chron. xii. 8). Its beauty and grace rendered it a term of endearing comparison (Song ii. 9, 17; viii. 14). It is about 3 feet 6 inches long by 1 foot 9 inches high. The horns are larger in the male than in the female; the limbs and whole form in both sexes graceful; the fur mostly fawn colored about the head, more fulvous on the other parts. It is found in Syria, Egypt, and Arabia, mostly in small groups or nearly solitary. It is timid, and flees from a pursuer rapidly and with great bounds. Tristram found a second species of gazelle (*Gazella arabica*), larger than the common one, east of the Jordan.

Ga'zer and **Ga-ze'ra.** See GEZER.

Ga'zez [shearer].

A son and perhaps also a grandson of the elder Caleb (1 Chron. ii. 46).

Ga'zite, in A. V. once **Gazathite.**

A native or inhabitant of Gaza (Josh. xiii. 3; Judg. xvi. 2).

Gaz'zam [devourer].

Founder of a family of Nethinim who returned with Zerubbabel (Ezra ii. 48).

Ge'ba, in A. V. thrice **Gaba** [a hill].

A city of Benjamin (Josh. xviii. 24), allotted to the priests (xxi. 17). It must be distinguished from Gibeah of Saul (Is. x. 29). Geba was the northern extreme of the kingdom of Judah (2 Kin. xxiii. 8; Zech. xiv. 10). A village, bearing the old name, marks the site, 6 miles N. N. E. of Jerusalem and 2 miles S. W. of Michmash.

Ge'bal [mountain].

1. A city on the Mediterranean Sea (Josh. xiii. 5; 1 Kin. v. 18, R. V.; Ezek. xxvii. 9), 42 miles north of Sidon. It was a dependency of Egypt in the 15th century B. C., but was independent and under its own king at the end of the 12th century. It frequently paid tribute to the kings of Assyria.

2. The northern portion of the mountains of Edom (Antiq. ii. 1, 2; ix. 9, 1; Ps. lxxxiii. 7); known also as Teman.

Ge'ber [a man, a hero].

Solomon's purveyor for the territory of southern Gilead (1 Kin. iv. 19), and probably father of the purveyor for northern Gilead and Argob (13).

Ge'bim [cisterns, locusts].

A village north of Jerusalem (Is. x. 31). Exact site unknown.

Geck'o.

The rendering of the Hebrew *'ᵃnaḳah*, a ceremonially unclean animal which the Hebrews classed with creeping things (Lev. xi. 30, R. V.). The gecko is a wall lizard. It has white spots on its back; and it emits a plaintive wail, whence the Hebrew name. The common gecko or fan-foot (*Ptyodactylus gecko*) is very common in Palestine. It frequents houses, running over the walls and ceiling. It is able to do this by reason of the peculiar construction of its toes, which are provided with plates under which a vacuum is created when the animal walks, thus causing it to adhere.

Ged-a-li'ah [Jehovah is great].

1. A harper, son of Jeduthun (1 Chron. xxv. 3), and head of the second of the twenty-four companies of twelve musicians each which David appointed for the service of the sanctuary (9).

2. An ancestor of the prophet Zephaniah (Zeph. i. 1).

3. A son of Pashhur in Jeremiah's time (Jer. xxxviii. 1).

4. A man of Judah of high birth, son of Ahikam, son of Shaphan. He was appointed by Nebuchadnezzar governor of Judah after the capture of Jerusalem. He fixed his residence at Mizpah, where he was treacherously assassinated by Ishmael of the seed royal (2 Kin. xxv. 22–26; Jer. xxxix. 14; xl. 5–xli. 18).

5. A priest whom Ezra induced to divorce his foreign wife (Ezra x. 18).

Ged'e-on. See GIDEON.

Ge'der [a wall].

A town, apparently in the extreme south of Judah (Josh. xii. 13). Exact site unknown. It may be the same as Beth-gader or Gedor 3.

Ge-de'rah [wall, enclosure, sheepfold].

1. A town in the lowland of Judah (Josh. xv. 36). Conder locates it at Jedireh, a ruin 4 miles and 4½ miles respectively to the northwest of Zorah and Eshtaol (33). See GEDE-ROTH.

2. A village of Benjamin (cp. 1 Chron. xii. 4). Conder suggests Jedireh, a ruin about 6 miles north by west of Jerusalem.

Ge'der-ite.

A man of Geder or Gederah (1 Chron. xxvii. 28; cp. Josh. xv. 36).

Ge-de'roth [enclosures, sheepfolds].

A town in or near the lowland of Judah (Josh. xv. 41). In Ahaz' reign it was taken by the Philistines (2 Chron. xxviii. 18). Its site, or that of Gederah, is commonly fixed at Katrah, called in 1 Mac. xv. 39 Kidron, in the maritime plain about 4 miles southwest by south of Ekron.

Ged′e-ro-tha′im [two enclosures, two sheep-folds].

A town within the territory of Judah (Josh. xv. 36), otherwise unknown. The Septuagint regards it as a common noun, and translates it "its cattle-enclosures." It is in favor of this rendering that, while the towns are reckoned up as but fourteen, fifteen names are given, including this one. Still this word must not be summarily rejected.

Ge′dor [wall, fortress, walled enclosure].

1. A son of Jehiel, and a brother of Ner, the ancestor of Saul (1 Chron. viii. 30, 31; ix. 35–37).

2. A town in the hill country of Judah (Josh. xv. 58; 1 Chron. iv. 4, 18). Its site is marked by the ruins Jedur, 7½ miles N. by W. of Hebron.

3. A town, apparently in the territory of Simeon, not far from the southwestern boundary of Palestine (1 Chron. iv. 39); see GEDER. The Septuagint, however, reads Gerar.

4. A village, apparently in Benjamin (1 Chron. xii. 7; cp. 1).

Ge-har′a-shim. See CHARASHIM.

Ge-ha′zi [valley of vision].

Elisha's servant. He told the prophet of their hostess' desire for a son, but when the lad that was given her died and the mother cast herself at Elisha's feet, Gehazi would have thrust her away (2 Kin. iv. 14, 27). To teach that it is not magic, but faith and prayer which avail, Elisha sent Gehazi to lay the prophet's staff on the dead child. He did so, but without effect (29–37). When Naaman the Syrian followed the directions of Elisha, and was cured of leprosy, he wished to make the prophet a present. The man of God refused; but Gehazi, regretting that the Syrian had been spared, ran after him, and told him that Elisha asked a talent of silver and two changes of raiment for needy friends. As penalty for his avarice and lying, and for bringing the prophetic office into contempt, the leprosy of Naaman cleaved to him (2 Kin. v. 20–27). More sayings and doings of Elisha's servant are subsequently reported, but the person referred to was probably Gehazi's successor.

Ge-hen′na. See HELL 2.

Gel′i-loth [circles, regions].

Apparently the same place as Gilgal, opposite the ascent of Adummim (cp. Josh. xv. 7 and xviii. 17).

Ge-mal′li [probably, possessor or rider of a camel].

Father of the spy Ammiel (Num. xiii. 12).

Gem-a-ri′ah [Jehovah hath completed or perfected].

1. A son of Hilkiah. He was one of two messengers sent by Zedekiah to Nebuchadnezzar. Jeremiah took advantage of the opportunity to send by them a letter to the captives in Babylon (Jer. xxix. 3).

2. A prince, son of Shaphan the scribe, and brother of Ahikam. He occupied a chamber in the temple. He joined in requesting Jehoiakim not to burn Jeremiah's writings (Jer. xxxvi. 10, 11, 12, 25).

Gen-e-al′o-gy.

The tracing backward or forward of the line of ancestry of an individual or a family. The regulations of the commonwealth of Israel necessitated this being done to a large extent. Succession to the royal sovereignty, the high-priesthood, the headship of tribe, tribal family, and father's house, depended upon lineage. There was general knowledge on the subject from the earliest period. Genealogy was revealed of itself by reason of the constitution of tribes, which were divided on the lines of growth into great families, and these in turn into smaller families and so-called houses. Birth in a household declared one's relation to the several divisions of the tribe as distinctly as the native place determined one's classification according to the geographical divisions and subdivisions of a kingdom. Definite genealogical records are traceable from the beginning of the Hebrew nation (Num. i. 2, 18; 1 Chron. v. 7, 17). Claimants in the days of Ezra sought their register among those that were reckoned by genealogy, but could not find it, on which account they, as polluted, were expelled from the priesthood (Ezra ii. 61, 62; Neh. vii. 63, 64). The endless genealogies against which Timothy and Titus were warned seemed to have been Gnostic genealogies of æons and other imaginary beings (1 Tim. i. 4; Tit. iii. 9).

Two genealogies of Christ are given; one by Matthew in the direct, and one by Luke in the reverse, order of descent (Mat. i. 1–16 and Luke iii. 23–38). Matthew's purpose is to show Christ's legal title to the throne of David and to the covenant with Abraham (Mat. i. 1). Luke begins with the second Adam, the eternally begotten Son of God, and ascends to the first Adam, the son of God by creation (Luke iii. 38). Apparently to help the memory, either Matthew or the official record from which he quoted made $3 \times 14 = 42$ generations for the period between Abraham and Jesus; viz., fourteen generations between Abraham and David, fourteen between David and the Babylonian captivity, and fourteen more between the Babylonian captivity and Jesus Christ. To carry out this artificial division Ahaziah, Joash, and Amaziah are omitted in the second fourteen. There may be similar omissions in the last fourteen. In Luke there are forty-one names in the line of descent from David to Jesus, against twenty-eight, or, with the omitted three, thirty-one in Matthew. If the Shealtiel and Zerubbabel of Matthew are the same as those of Luke, as can scarcely be questioned, the difficulty arises that in Matthew Shealtiel is the son of Jechoniah, but in Luke the son of Neri; indeed, the two lines of descent from David to Jesus are different in the two evangelists. They diverge from David; one line passes through Solomon and the other through his brother Nathan. Putting both in the direct order of descent, they stand thus:

From Matthew's genealogy.	From Luke's genealogy.
David.	David.
Solomon.	Nathan.
	Mattatha.
Rehoboam.	Menna.
Abijah.	Melea.
Asa.	Eliakim.
	Jonam.
Jehoshaphat.	Joseph.
Joram.	Judas.
	Symeon.
	Levi.
	Matthat.
Uzziah.	Jorim.
Jotham.	Eliezer.
Ahaz.	Jesus.
Hezekiah.	Er.
Manasseh.	Elmadam.
Amon.	Cosam.
Josiah.	Addi.
Jechoniah.	Melchi.
	Neri.
Shealtiel (Salathiel).	Shealtiel (Salathiel).
Zerubbabel.	Zerubbabel.
	Rhesa.
	Joanan.
Abiud.	Joda.
	Josech.
	Semein.
Eliakim.	Mattathias.
	Maath.
Azor.	Naggai.
	Esli.
Sadoc.	Nahum.
	Amos.
Achim.	Mattathias.
	Joseph.
Eliud.	Jannai.
	Melchi.
Eleazar.	Levi.
Matthan.	Matthat.
Jacob.	Heli.
Joseph, the husband of Mary.	Joseph, the husband of Mary.

Two explanations of these divergent genealogies are possible.

I. The early church generally explained both tables as recording the genealogy of Joseph. Julius Africanus (A. D. 220), the first known investigator of the question, adopted the theory that Joseph's grandfathers in the two genealogies, Melchi [Africanus has a corrupt text] and Matthan, had married successively the same woman, and that consequently Heli and Jacob were half-brothers, having the same mother but different fathers. Heli married and died childless; and Jacob, according to the law of Levirate marriage (Deut. xxv. 6), took the widow to wife, and raised up seed to his brother Heli by begetting a son Joseph. Hence Matthew can say, "Matthan begat Jacob, and Jacob begat Joseph;" and Luke can say, "Joseph the son of Heli, the son of Matthat."

A readier solution of the problem on the lines of this theory is that the table in Matthew contains the legal successors to the throne of David, while that in Luke gives the paternal ancestors of Joseph. The line of Solomon became extinct in Jechoniah, otherwise known as Jehoiachin; and the succession passed over to the collateral line of David which sprang from David's son Nathan. The representative of this line was Shealtiel. For a brief space the royal line and the natural lineage of Joseph were identical; but after Zerubbabel the two lines separated. The family of the elder son, in whom the title to the throne inhered, at length became extinct, and the descendants of the younger son succeeded to the title. Matthat of this line (by some identified with Matthan) became heir apparent. He is supposed to have had two sons, Jacob and Heli. The elder Jacob had no son, but probably a daughter, the Virgin Mary. The younger Heli had a son Joseph; and Joseph, since his uncle Jacob had no male descendant, became heir to his uncle and to the throne. Broad genealogical terminology enables Matthew to say "Jacob begat Joseph," and Luke to say "Joseph, the son of Heli."

II. Since the Reformation a different conception of the two genealogies has won favor, and is probably correct. According to this opinion, the table in Matthew gives the genealogy of Joseph, and exhibits him as heir to the throne of David, while the table in Luke gives the genealogy of Mary, and shows Jesus to be the actual son of David. With the clear declaration of Luke that Jesus had no human father, with the customary Hebrew usage of the word son for descendant however remote, and on the basis of the approved Greek text, the advocates of this view render Luke iii. 23, "Jesus, being son (as was supposed of Joseph) of Heli, etc." Jesus, according to Luke, is grandson of Heli, Mary's father, and thus a lineal descendant of David. A difficulty, not however peculiar to this theory, but lying equally against the first-mentioned hypothesis, is Matthew's record that Shealtiel was begotten by king Jechoniah, whereas Luke makes Shealtiel the son of Neri. Perhaps the simplest solution is the following: Jechoniah, who spent years in captivity, appears to have been the surviving nominal king of Judah in the year 562, twenty-five years after the fall of Jerusalem (2 Kin. xxv. 27). He apparently had no sons when carried off captive in 598 B. C. He was comparatively young, and children are not mentioned in the enumeration of his family (2 Kin. xxiv. 8, 12, 15). Jeremiah prophesied that no son of his should occupy the throne (Jer. xxii. 30; cp. what is said of his father, xxxvi. 30). In the genealogy as given in Mat. i. appears the entry, "After the carrying away to Babylon, Jechoniah begat Shealtiel." All Scripture references are in harmony, and the two genealogies are intelligible, if this notice in Matthew be understood as a broad declaration in genealogical form denoting legal succession to the throne. The title passed from Jechoniah on his death to Shealtiel, a lineal descendant of David. There may of course have been close kinship between Jechoniah and Shealtiel. If Jechoniah had no son surviving him, but only a daughter, the inheritance passed to her children according to the law (Num. xxvii. 8-11). The phraseology of the genealogies is therefore explained on the assumption that Neri married the daughter of Jechoniah and begat Shealtiel by her. Shealtiel's lineage was reckoned as usual through his father back to Nathan and David, but his title to the throne was reckoned through his maternal grandfather Jechoniah to Solomon and David.

In 1 Chron. iii. 17 is the record : "The sons of Jeconiah ; Assir [not to be rendered "the captive," for the definite article is not used], Shealtiel his son, and Malchiram, etc." The epithet "his son" is peculiar to Shealtiel, peculiar also in that it is deemed necessary to apply it to one of a group already designated as sons of Jeconiah. It marks Shealtiel as the king's successor. He could be called his son, if his daughter's son, just as Abiezer, son of the sister of Gilead, son of Manasseh, is reckoned among the sons of Manasseh, and apparently even among the sons of Gilead (1 Chron. vii. 14, 18 ; Num. xxvi. 30).

Hebrew genealogical tables are apt to differ in the principles of construction from modern registers of pedigree. 1. Symmetry is often preferred to the exhibition of the unbroken descent from father to son. Hence links were freely omitted, and the enumeration was otherwise left incomplete. Ten in the genealogy from Adam to Noah, and ten from Shem to Abraham. Seventy sons of Noah's sons, and seventy souls of the house of Jacob (Gen. xlvi. 27; see further EGYPT III. 1). 2. The genealogy may be tribal, rather than personal ; and son may denote the inhabitants of a country (Gen. x. 2-4, 6, 7, 22), a people or tribe (4, 13, 16-18, the words ending in "im" being gentile adjectives in the plural), a town (15), rarely an individual (8-10). Similar phenomena are found elsewhere (Gen. xxv. 2-4; 1 Chron. ii. 50-55; see SON). 3. The words bear and beget and father are used with a corresponding breadth of meaning ; as bear or beget a grandchild (Gen. xlvi. 12 with 15, 18, 25), or great-grandchild (12, and probably 21, 22), or grandchild's grandchild (Mat. i. 9), or country (Gen. xxv. 2, 3).

Gen-er-a'tion.

1. A begetting or producing, or the person or thing produced (Gen. ii. 4; v. 1) ; in Hebrew only plural *Toledoth*.

2. Each succession of persons from a common ancestor (Gen. l. 23; Ex. xx. 5; Deut. xxiii. 2) ; in Hebrew expressed by a modification of the proper numeral or by *Dor* with an ordinal number.

3. The age or period of a body of contemporaries, not in the modern sense of the average lifetime of all who survive infancy, but the average period of the activity of any body of contemporaries as determined by the normal span of life. The generation lasts as long as any of the members survive (Ex. i. 6 ; Num. xxxii. 13 ; Judg. ii. 10; Ecc. i. 4) ; in Hebrew *Dor*.

Gen'e-sis [Greek *genesis*, origin (of the world)].

The name, borrowed from the Septuagint, of the first O. T. book, called by the Hebrews from its initial word B^ereshith, "In the beginning." It naturally divides itself into three sections : first, the history of the universe, showing God's relation to it, and introducing human history (i.-ii. 3) ; second, a sketch of human history before Abraham, showing God's relation to the human race, and introducing the history of the chosen people (ii. 4-xi. 26) ; and third, the history of the covenant people down to the descent into Egypt (xi. 27-l.). The second section includes the creation of man and his original condition (ii. 4-25), the fall (iii.), the progress of sin (iv. 1-15), the worldly race (16-24), the godly line (25-v. 32), the increase of wickedness (vi. 1-8), the flood (vi. 9-ix. 17), the repeopling of the earth (ix. 18-x. 32), the building of the tower of Babel (xi. 1-9), and the Semitic race in its earliest germs (xi. 10-26). The third section includes the early history of Abraham, his call, and his sojourn in Canaan (xi. 27-xxv. 10), the life of Isaac from his father's death to the departure of Jacob for Mesopotamia (xxv. 11-xxvii. 40), the life of Jacob from his departure for Mesopotamia to the death of Isaac (xxvii. 41-xxxv. 29), the descendants of Esau (xxxvi.), the early history of Joseph to the time when he was sold into Egypt (xxxvii.), Judah's sin and shame (xxxviii.), Joseph in Egypt (xxxix.-xlv.), Jacob and his whole household with Joseph in Egypt (xlvi.-xlix.), and the death of Jacob and Joseph (l.).

The writer of the book has embraced his narrative after the introduction in ten successive sections, each under a caption beginning with the formula, "These are the generations of" (ii. 4; v. 1; vi. 9; x. 1; xi. 10; xi. 27; xxv. 12, 19; xxxvi. 1; xxxvii. 2). For unity and authorship, see PENTATEUCH.

Gen-nes'a-ret; in A. V. of 1 Mac. **Gennesar**, in R. V. of same **Gennesareth** [perhaps, garden of Hazor].

A land adjacent to the lake of Gennesaret, on its western shore (Mat. xiv. 34 ; Mark vi. 53) ; described by Josephus as a fertile plain, 30 stades in length by 20 in breadth, watered by a fountain called Capharnaum, and producing walnuts, palms, fig trees, olives, and grapes (War iii. 10, 8). It is almost certainly identical with the plain called el-Ghuweir, formed by a recession of the hills from the shore just north of Magdala.

The lake of Gennesaret (Luke v. 1 ; Antiq. v. 1, 22 ; xviii. 2, 1 and 3) or Gennesar (War. ii. 20, 6), or the water of Gennesareth or

The southern end of Lake Genessaret (also known as Lake Tiberias or Sea of Galilee) where the Jordan River leaves the lake. The mountains in the background are in Syria.

Gennesar (1 Mac. xi. 67; Antiq. xiii. 5, 7), was a common name for the sea of Galilee.

Gen'tiles.

All nations of the world other than the Jews (Is. xlix. 6; Rom. ii. 14; iii. 29). The Jews were the chosen people of God; their religion was sublime, and its truth stood in strong and favorable contrast to the untruths of the gentile religions; and strict laws were enacted to prevent the corruption of manners and of the true religion through contact with idolaters. These things led the Jews, though unjustly, to feel contempt for the gentiles. The Israelites had been chosen for a purpose. They were to be a light to the gentiles (Is. xlix. 1-6). The gentiles were embraced in the promises (Is. ii. 2-4; Amos ix. 12; Zech. ix. 7). The attitude of the Jews recalls that of the Indian Brahmins, who will not eat with their countrymen of inferior caste, and much less with those of no caste at all, or with strangers of another nation. When Peter, taught by the vision at Joppa, broke through caste restriction, visiting and eating with the gentile Cornelius, it gave offense to even Christian Jews (Acts x. 28; xi. 3); and when Paul, speaking from the steps of the castle of Antonia, declared that God had commissioned him to preach to the gentiles, the audience of Jews in the temple court cried out for his death (xxii. 21, 22). The early churches consisted largely of gentiles, and the first Council of Jerusalem declined to impose on the former the burden of the Mosaic law (xv. 1-29).

Ge-nu'bath [theft, robbery].

The son of the Edomite prince Hadad and the Egyptian queen's sister (1 Kin. xi. 20).

Ge'ra [a grain].

1. A son of Bela and grandson of Benjamin (Gen. xlvi. 21; 1 Chron. viii. 3).

2. Another descendant of Bela, perhaps remoter than son (1 Chron. viii. 3, and probably 7).

3. A Benjamite, father of Ehud (Judg. iii. 15).

4. A Benjamite, father of that Shimei who cursed David (2 Sam. xvi. 5).

Perhaps 3 and 4 denote the founder of the family to which Ehud and Shimei belonged, and are identical with the grandson of Benjamin.

Ge'rah. See WEIGHTS.

Ge'rar [water pot or a course or dry].

An ancient city on the southern border of Palestine near Gaza (Gen. x. 19; 2 Chron. xiv. 13), and early occupied by Philistines (Gen. xxvi. 1). The country subject to it extended toward Kadesh and Shur (xx. 1, 9 with xxvi. 6, 17, 18). It is commonly identified with the ruins Umm Jerrar, 6 miles south of Gaza on the wady Ghuzzeh. A location about 50 miles south, in the immediate vicinity of Kadesh, has been less plausibly urged, namely, the wady Jerur, a branch of the wady esh-Sheraif which drains into wady el-'Arish. Possibly this indicates the considerable extent of the region dominated by Gerar.

Ger-a-senes'.

The people of Gerasa (R. V. of Mark v. 1 and Luke viii. 26, 37 ; manuscripts vary between Gerasenes, Gadarenes, Gergesenes) ; Gerasa is probably still echoed by Kersa, the name of a ruin on the eastern shore of the sea of Galilee, opposite Magdala, 5 miles from the entrance of the Jordan into the lake. A short distance south of the site is the only place on this coast where the steep hills come down close to the water (viii. 32). The city of the Decapolis, known as Gersa, now Jerash, does not meet the conditions of the narrative, being 37 miles southeast of the sea of Galilee and 32 miles southeast of Gadara.

Ger-ge-senes'.

The people of Gergesa (Mat. viii. 28, A. V., but in R. V. Gadarenes). The introduction of the name Gergesenes into the text is ascribed to Origen, who is said to have felt that Gadara was too far from the lake, and was told by people acquainted with the region that an old town named Gergesa existed, and near it was the declivity down which the swine rushed. The ruin Kersa is probably this old town. See GERASENES.

Ger'i-zim [plural of *Gerizzi*, Gerizites ; cp. Girzite].

A steep rocky mountain forming the southern boundary of the valley in which Nablus, the ancient Shechem, lies, and facing the more elevated mount Ebal, on the northern side of the valley. Mount Gerizim rises 2849 feet above the level of the Mediterranean, and 700 feet above the town. When the Israelites conquered central Palestine Joshua carried out the direction given to Moses, and placed half of the tribes in front of mount Gerizim to pronounce blessings, and the other half over against mount Ebal to pronounce curses (Deut. xi. 29 ; xxvii. 12, 13 ; Josh. viii. 33-35). Jotham, the son of Gideon, standing on mount Gerizim, proclaimed his parable to the men of Shechem (Judg. ix. 7). Josephus (Antiq. xi. 8, 2, 7) says that Manasseh, brother of Jaddua, the high priest in the time of Alexander the Great, had married the daughter of a foreigner, Sanballat. The elders at Jerusalem commanded him either to divorce her, or no longer to approach the altar. Manasseh thought of divorcing her, though she was still dear to him ; but her father, Sanballat, deprecating this step, promised to build for his son-in-law, if he retained his wife, a rival temple to that of Jerusalem. He kept his word, erecting one on mount Gerizim. This was the origin of the Samaritan temple on that mountain, and must be dated before 330 B. C. If Sanballat was the Samaritan of that name who was an opponent of the Jews in the time of Nehemiah, about 445 B. C. (Neh. iv. 1 ; xiii. 28), and not an official sent by Darius Codomanus (Antiq. xi. 7, 2 ; xii. 5, 5), the temple was built considerably before 330, perhaps about 380 B. C. It was destroyed by

John Hyrcanus, 129 B. C. The erection of the edifice made Gerizim the Samaritan sacred mountain. It was to it that the woman of Samaria and Jesus referred as " this mountain " (John iv. 20, 21 ; cp. Antiq. xii. 1) ; and Jacob's well, at which they were conversing, was at the foot of mount Gerizim. Gerizim, now called Jebel et-Tôr, is a high table-land stretching far toward the east and southeast of Nablus. From the days of Benjamin of Tudela, a Jewish rabbi who traveled in Palestine about A. D. 1160, to recent times, the view was held that Gerizim, the mountain of blessings, was fertile, and Ebal, that of curses, barren. But with the exception of a small ravine coming down from Gerizim near Nablus, both mountains are equally barren.

Ger'shom [often interpreted as meaning " stranger there ;" but the vocalization and the variant form Gershon with its patronymic show that the Hebrews did not regard the word as having that meaning. It rather signifies "banishment." In Ex. ii. 22, the author, according to custom, plays upon the general sound].

1. Gershon, the son of Levi (1 Chron. vi. 16, 17, 20, 43, 62, 71). See GERSHON.

2. The elder son of Moses, born to him in Midian (Ex. ii. 22 ; xviii. 3). He gave rise to a father's house which was reckoned among the Levites, not among the priests (1 Chron. xxiii. 14-16).

3. A descendant of Phinehas the priest, and head of a father's house in that line in the time of Ezra (Ezra viii. 2).

Ger'shon [banishment].

A son of Levi, and founder of the Gershonite family (Gen. xlvi. 11 ; Ex. vi. 16 ; Num. iii. 17). He is sometimes called Gershom, which is formed by a different affix, but has the same meaning. His two sons, Libni and Shimei, gave rise to two subdivisions of the greater tribal family (Ex. vi. 17 ; Num. iii. 18 ; 1 Chron. vi. 17).

Ger'shon-ites.

The children and descendants of Gershon, constituting one of the three great divisions of the Levitical body. In the wilderness they encamped on the western side of the tabernacle, and had charge of the tabernacle itself, the tent with its hangings, and those of the courtyard (Num. iii. 23-26 ; iv. 21-28). To aid them in moving the tabernacle there were assigned them two wagons and four oxen (vii. 7). They consisted of two families, those of the Libnites and those of the Shimeites, and at the first census in the wilderness numbered 7500 males (iii. 21, 22). Of the thirteen cities assigned to them, two were in the half-tribe of Manasseh beyond the Jordan, four were in Issachar, four in Asher, and three in Naphtali (Josh. xxi. 27-33). They were reorganized by David (1 Chron. xxiii. 7-11).

Ge′ruth Chim′ham [the lodging-place of Chimham].

Probably a khan (Jer. xli. 17, R. V.). See CHIMHAM.

Ger′zites. See GIRZITE.

Ge′shan, in A. V. Gesham, an error which crept into the later editions, the original of 1611 having Geshan.

A man of Judah, a son of Jahdai (1 Chron. ii. 47).

Ge′shem and Gashmu, the latter being the Arabic form, of which Geshem is the regular Hebrew modification [rain, body].

An Arabian, a great opponent of the Jews after their return from captivity. He ridiculed the proposal of Nehemiah to rebuild the wall of Jerusalem, as if this were tantamount to rebellion (Neh. ii. 19). Not succeeding in deterring the Jew by this means, he joined with others in plotting violence, if not even actual murder, against him. Failing in this purpose also, he allowed the report to be circulated far and wide on his authority that Nehemiah was fortifying the city preparatory to rebelling against Persia and proclaiming himself king (vi. 1 seq.).

Ge′shur [a bridge].

A district lying between Hermon and Bashan and marching on Argob (Deut. iii. 14; Josh. xii. 5; xiii. 11, 13; 1 Chron. ii. 23). Evidently it was situated to the eastward of Maacah, for Maacah bordered on Naphtali. It constituted an Aramæan kingdom (2 Sam. xiii. 37; xv. 8). Here David obtained a wife, and hither his son Absalom fled after the murder of Amnon (2 Sam. iii. 3; xiii. 37).

Gesh′u-rites, in A. V. twice Geshuri, the Hebrew instead of the English term being employed.

1. The people of Geshur (Deut. iii. 14; Josh. xii. 5; xiii. 11, 13).

2. A people who dwelt in ancient times in the country south of Philistia in the direction of Egypt (Josh. xiii. 2; 1 Sam. xxvii. 8).

Ge′ther.

A family of the Aramæans (Gen. x. 23; 1 Chron. i. 17). Their locality has not been determined.

Geth-sem′a-ne [an oil press].

A garden, presumably of olives and furnished with a press to squeeze oil from the fruit. It was east of Jerusalem, a little beyond the brook Kidron, and at or near the foot of the mount of Olives (Mat. xxvi. 30 with 36; Mark xiv. 26 with 32; John xviii. 1). It was a favorite spot with our Lord, who often resorted to it for retirement (Luke xxii. 39; John xviii. 2), and it is now forever sacred as having been the scene of his agony and of his betrayal and arrest (Mat. xxvi. 36-56; Mark xiv. 32-52; Luke xxii. 39-53; John xviii. 1-12). The traditional site of Gethsemane lies a little east of the bridge by which the road from St. Stephen's gate of Jerusalem crosses the Kidron. The garden is situated at the angle made by the division of the road into two branches, one, the most northerly, leading directly up the face of the mount of Olives, while the more southerly one winds gently around the southern brow of the hill. The garden is nearly square, and the Latins have recently enclosed

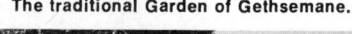

The traditional Garden of Gethsemane.

it with a wall, its northern side 150 feet and its western one 160 feet. Eight venerable olive trees are within, on which it is said the tax levy can be traced back to the occupation of Jerusalem by the Arabs in the seventh century; and many equally old are outside on the slope of the mount. These trees, however, did not witness our Lord's agony, for all the trees around Jerusalem were cut down during the siege of the city by Titus (War v. 12, 4). Robinson thinks that the spot is the same as that described by Eusebius as at the mount of Olives, and afterwards more definitely by Jerome as at the foot of the mount; but he is doubtful if it is the genuine Gethsemane. Thomson regards the position as too near the city, and too close to the great thoroughfare eastward to have served as a place for retirement on that dangerous and dismal night. He believes Gethsemane to have been in a secluded vale several hundred yards northeast of the traditional site. Barclay thinks it evident that the present enclosure, from its narrow dimensions, can occupy only in part the site of the ancient garden, and finds a better position higher up in the valley. The Greeks have recently enclosed an adjacent piece of ground to the east, on the slope of the mountain, as being the garden.

Ge-u'el [majesty of God].
The spy who represented the tribe of Gad in the exploration of Canaan (Num. xiii. 15).

Ge'zer, in A. V. twice **Gazer** [a place cut off]. In A. V. of 1 Mac. the Greek forms Gazera and Gazara are used.
An ancient Canaanite town (el-Amarna letters, 15th century B. C.), not far from Lachish and the lower Bethhoron (Josh. x. 33). It was on the boundary line of Ephraim (xvi. 3; cp. 1 Chron. vii. 28), and with its suburbs was assigned to the Kohathite Levites (Josh. xxi. 21; 1 Chron. vi. 67). The Ephraimites failed to expel the Canaanite inhabitants, and occupied the city with them at least for a time (Josh. xvi. 10; Judg. i. 29). More than one battle in David's reign was fought at or near Gezer (2 Sam. v. 25; 1 Chron. xiv. 16; xx. 4). One of the Pharaohs captured Gezer from the Canaanites, who seem again to have possessed it in every part. After burning it, he gave the ruins over to Solomon as a dowry with his daughter when she was married to the Hebrew king. The city was at once rebuilt. It was an important place in the wars of the Maccabees. Bacchides strengthened its fortifications (1 Mac. ix. 52). It was besieged and taken by Simon, and made stronger than before (xiii. 43, R. V. 48, 53; xiv. 34). M. Clermont Ganneau identified the site by inscriptions; one of which, perhaps as old as the Herods, marked the limits of Gezer, and gave in Hebrew letters the actual name. It is now called Tell Jezar and is situated about 18 miles west-northwest of Jerusalem, and 5⅔ east of Ekron.

Gez'rite. See GIRZITE.

Gi'ah [breaking forth, as of a spring].
A village somewhere between Gibeon in Benjamin and the ford of the Jordan near the Jabbok (2 Sam. ii. 24, cp. 16, 29).

Gi'ant.
A man of abnormally tall stature; like Og, king of Bashan, whose bedstead or sarcophagus was nine cubits long by four broad (Deut. iii. 11), Goliath of Gath, whose height was six cubits and a span (1 Sam. xvii. 4), and the man whom Benaiah slew, whose height was five cubits (1 Chron. xi. 23). A stalwart race of men like the Anakim and other early nations of Canaan and the country east of the Jordan (Deut. i. 28; ii. 10, 11, 20, 21; ix. 2). When Hebron was captured by the Hebrews, the Anakim who escaped destruction took refuge in the Philistine towns. Goliath of Gath, Ishbi-benob, and other huge Philistines were probably of this expelled race of the Anakim (1 Sam. xvii. 4; 2 Sam. xxi. 15-22). The valley of the Rephaim or giants near Jerusalem was a perpetual reminder, by its name, of the early stalwart race which long inhabited it (Josh. xv. 8; xviii. 16). The exact meaning of *nᵉphilim*, the word rendered giants in Gen. vi. 4; Num. xiii. 33, A. V., is uncertain, and accordingly it is left untranslated in R. V. It may refer to largeness of stature or fierceness of disposition or debased character or illegitimacy of birth. In the latter passage the word describes the Anakim. In the former passage the Nephilim, as the name is transliterated in R. V., are described as mighty men, men of renown. The description is the same as that given of David's most noted warriors (1 Chron. xi. 10, 24).

Gib'bar [mighty man, hero].
A man whose children, or a place of whose former inhabitants some descendants, returned from captivity with Zerubbabel (Ezra ii. 20). In the parallel passage in Neh. vii. 25 Gibeon stands in place of Gibbar.

Gib'be-thon [perhaps, conical height].
A town of Dan (Josh. xix. 44) assigned to the Levites of the family of Kohath (xxi. 20-23). The Philistines gained possession of it. Nadab was assassinated there while laying siege to the place (1 Kin. xv. 27). Omri before he ascended the throne also besieged the town (xvi. 15, 17).

Gib'e-a [a hill].
Probably a village (1 Chron. ii. 49); cp. GIBEAH 1.

Gib'e-ah [a hill].
1. A village in the hill country of Judah (Josh. xv. 57); probably south or southeast of Hebron. Jeb'ah (Jeb'a), on an isolated hill eight miles west by south from Bethlehem, lies outside the group included in verses 55-57.
2. A town of Benjamin near Ramah (Judg. xix. 13, 14); called also Geba, the masculine form of the same name (xx. 10, R. V. margin,

Gibeon, looking north.

with 4). It is designated Gibeah of Benjamin (ibid.; cp. 1 Sam. xiii. 2), and Gibeah of the children of Benjamin (2 Sam. xxiii. 29); and appears to be identical with Gibeah of Saul (1 Sam. xi. 4; 2 Sam. xxi. 6; Is. x. 29). Its inhabitants by their misbehavior brought down punishment, not merely on themselves, but on the whole tribe of Benjamin (Judg. xix., xx.). Gibeah was Saul's place of residence when he was called to be king (1 Sam. x. 26), and it remained his home and served as the political capital of his kingdom (xv. 34; xxii. 6; xxiii. 19). It existed in the days of Isaiah and of Hosea (Is. x. 29, distinguished from Geba; Hos. ix. 9; x. 9). The town was situated on the highway from Jerusalem to the north, about midway between Jerusalem and Ramah (Judg. xix. 13; Antiq. v. 2, 8, cp. viii. 12, 3; War v. 2, 1). Its site is doubtless Tell el-Fûl, 2½ miles north of Jerusalem. The archæological evidence indicates a settlement dating from at least the early Israelite period.

3. A hill or town in the hill country of Ephraim, belonging to Phinehas: where Eleazar the high priest, the son of Aaron, was buried (Josh. xxiv. 33; Antiq. v. 1, 29). Perhaps Jîbia with ancient ruins, 8½ miles west-southwest of Seilun (Shiloh), and 3½ miles east by south of Tibneh (Timnath). The tradition of the Samaritans, which locates the grave at 'Awertah, 4½ miles south of Shechem, is late.

4. Gibeah or hill of God (1 Sam. x. 5). Probably essentially the same as Gibeah of Saul, for it appears to have been Saul's home (11, 14). For the reason of the name, see ver. 5. Its identity with Ram Allah, height of

God, 4 miles northwest by north of Ramah, has been proposed. The determination depends largely upon the identification of Rachel's sepulcher and Zuph (cp. ver. 2–5 with xiii. 3).

Gib'e-ath [a hill].

A town of Benjamin, mentioned in immediate connection with Jerusalem (Josh. xviii. 28). The name is a mere variant of Gibeah.

Gib'e-ath-ite.

A native or inhabitant of Gibeah (1 Chron. xii. 3).

Gib'e-on [pertaining to a hill].

The chief city of the Hivites, a people of Canaan (Josh. xi. 19), included in the general designation Amorite (2 Sam. xxi. 2). They possessed also Chephirah, Beeroth, and Kiriath-jearim (Josh. ix. 17). They obtained a treaty with Joshua by false pretenses. The deceit was discovered, and they were made slaves of the Israelites (ix. 1–27). But the treaty was respected: the Gibeonites were aided against their enemies (x.); and several centuries later, when Saul violated its provisions by a massacre of Gibeonites, the sense of justice was satisfied by the execution of seven of Saul's sons (2 Sam. xxi. 1–9). Gibeon was within the territory assigned to the Benjamites (Josh. xviii. 25); and was given, with its suburbs, to the family of Aaron (xxi. 17). Saul's ancestors dwelt for a time in the town, and were men of influence (1 Chron. viii. 29; ix. 35). In the contest between Ish-bosheth and David, a battle took place here (2 Sam. ii. 8–17, 24; iii. 30). Here David gained a victory over the Philistines (1 Chron. xiv. 16; in 2 Sam. v. 25 Geba). In its vicinity Joab murdered Amasa (2 Sam. xx. 8). There also, in David's reign and in the early part of Solomon's reign, before the temple was built, stood the tabernacle and the brazen altar; and there Solomon sacrificed and in a dream received a message from God (1 Kin. iii. 4-15; 1 Chron. xvi. 39, 40; xxi. 29; 2 Chron. i. 3, 6, 13). Gibeonites returned from the exile (Neh. vii. 25), and aided in rebuilding the wall of Jerusalem (iii. 7). According to Josephus, Gibeon was 40 or 50 stadia (about 4½ to 6 miles) from Jerusalem (Antiq. vii. 11, 7; War ii. 19, 1). Its site is found at the modern village of el-Jib, 5½ miles northwest by north of Jerusalem. An oblong or oval hill stands in the midst of a basin consisting of broad valleys in a high state of cultivation. The hill is steep of ascent, being composed of horizontal layers of limestone rock that form great steps from the plain upward. The village is built on a broad summit at the northern end. The houses number forty or fifty, and are almost all, in whole or in part, ancient.

Southeast of the village, and quite a distance down the hill, is a fine fountain of water, which flows into a subterranean reservoir artificially cut. Not far from it, among olive trees, is an open reservoir 59 feet long by 36 feet broad; it was doubtless intended to receive the superfluous waters of the cavern. On the west is a tank, 11 by 7 feet in size, cut in the rock, and called el-Birkeh, the pool. In the plain a little lake, 6 to 8 acres in extent, is formed during the winter. One or other of these was doubtless the pool or great waters of Gibeon (2 Sam. ii. 13; Jer. xli. 12).

The wilderness of Gibeon was perhaps simply the uncultivated plateau between Gibeon and Ramah. If a desert is meant, it was at considerable distance east from the city (2 Sam. ii. 24).

Gib′e-on-ites.

The inhabitants of Gibeon or of that city with its three dependent towns (2 Sam. xxi. 1-4; cp. Josh. ix. 3, 7, 17).

Gib′lites, in R. V. **Gebalites.**

The people of the town and kingdom of Gebal (Josh. xiii. 5; 1 Kin. v. 18; in text of A. V. stonesquarers).

Gid-dal′ti [I have magnified].

A singer, a son of Heman (1 Chron. xxv. 4), and head of the twenty-second of the twenty-four companies of twelve musicians each which were appointed in David's reign for the service of the sanctuary (29).

Beginning with Hananiah the names in verse 4, read in their present sequence, but variously divided and conjoined and changed in vocalization, form a prayer. The sequence, however, is not preserved in verses 23-31.

Gid′del [he hath magnified].

1. Head of a family of Nethinim (Ezra ii. 47; Neh. vii. 49).

2. Head of a family of Solomon's servants (Ezra ii. 56; Neh. vii. 58).

Gid′e-on, in A. V. of N. T. **Gedeon** in imitation of the Greek pronunciation [a cutting off, a hewing down].

A son of Joash, family of Abiezer, tribe of Manasseh, who dwelt at Ophrah (Judg. vi. 11). While threshing wheat in the wine press at Ophrah, to hide it from the Midianite pillagers, he was called by the angel of Jehovah to deliver his people (12-24). At once he offered sacrifice (cp. Ex. xx. 24). That night he threw down his father's altar of Baal and built an altar of Jehovah (Judg. vi. 25-27). The townspeople demanded his death, but his father urged that Baal be allowed to contend for himself. Gideon thus acquired the name Jerubbaal, "Let Baal contend," and later, when the word Baal was shunned as abominable, Jerubbeseth, "Let the shameful thing contend" (28-32; 2 Sam. xi. 21; cp. Ish-bosheth). Having summoned the men of Manasseh, Asher, Zebulun, and Naphtali (Judg. vi. 35), he yet hesitated until his call had been confirmed by the miracle of the fleece (36-40). With his followers intentionally reduced to 300, that the glory of the victory might be not with man but with Jehovah, he made a night attack on the Midianite camp, which was pitched in the valley of Jezreel (33), by the hill of Moreh (vii. 1). The Midianites were thrown into confusion, fought each other and fled. The flight was to the Jordan and their own country beyond. Ephraimites, summoned by couriers from Gideon, seized the fords of the river to intercept fugitives, and captured and slew two princes of Midian and took their heads to Gideon, already across the river (24–viii. 3). Continuing the pursuit he and his band drove the Midianites to the confines of the desert, and brought back the two kings of Midian captive and put them to death (4-21). This victory was the celebrated day of Midian (Is. ix. 4; x. 26; Ps. lxxxiii. 11). A movement now set in to make him and his house royal, but he refused the crown because Jehovah was their king (Judg. viii. 22-28). However he had the earrings of the Midianites made into an ephod. If it was patterned after the ephod of the high priest, it was costly, for it was wrought with gold thread and bore precious stones set in gold. Gideon put it in his own city, where the angel of Jehovah had appeared unto him, and where he had been commanded to build an altar to Jehovah and offer sacrifice (vi. 12, 26). These high privileges had evidently led him to consider the priestly office open to him, with the priestly function of consulting Jehovah in behalf of the people by means of an ephod. His act was unwise as the event proved, and the ephod became a snare to Gideon and his family and a means of seduction to Israel (Judg. viii. 24–

27; cp. Lev. xx. 6). Gideon had many wives, and seventy sons, besides a son Abimelech, a concubine's child, who made himself king on the death of his father. Gideon died in a good old age (vi.–viii.; Heb. xi. 32).

Gid-e-o'ni [a cutting off].
Father of the prince of the tribe of Benjamin in the time of Moses (Num. i. 11).

Gi'dom [a cutting off].
A village apparently in Benjamin, between Gibeah and the rock of Rimmon (Judg. xx. 45).

Gier' Ea'gle.
1. The rendering in the A. V. of the Hebrew *Raham*, so named from its affection for its young. In R. V. the word is translated vulture, which is the meaning of gier. It was ceremonially unclean (Lev. xi. 18; Deut. xiv. 17). Undoubtedly the Egyptian vulture, Pharaoh's hen or chicken (*Neophron percnopterus*), is meant, which the Arabs still call *raham*. Its general color is white, but the primary feathers of the wings are black. The young are brown. The length of the adult is a little over two feet. It ranges in summer from the south of France, by southern Europe and northern Africa, to the west of India, where it is replaced by a closely allied species. The Egyptian vulture is a funereal-looking bird, generally seen acting as a scavenger in Eastern cities, camps, and outside hospitals. It is common in Palestine during its northern migration, and breeds in that country.
2. The rendering in the R. V. of the Hebrew *Peres* (Lev. xi. 13; Deut. xiv. 12). See OSSIFRAGE.

Gifts.
Gifts were given by fathers to sons (Gen. xxv. 6), or as dowry to daughters on their marriage (xxxiv. 12), or by people present by invitation at a wedding (Ps. xlv. 12). They were bestowed upon fellow men out of good will (Esth. ix. 22) or to secure favor (Prov. xviii. 16). It was forbidden to offer them to judges for the purpose of bribery (Ex. xxiii. 8; Deut. xvi. 19; Prov. xxix. 4). Monarchs bestowed them as a reward for service (Dan. ii. 48), or as a gracious favor to cause public rejoicings (Esth. ii. 18). They were brought by subjects as tribute (2 Sam. viii. 2, 6; 2 Chron. xxvi. 8; Ps. xlv. 12; lxxii. 10; Mat. ii. 11). Gifts were required for the expenses of religious worship (Mat. v. 23. 24; viii. 4; Luke xxi. 5). Essentially the same customs as to gifts still prevail throughout the East.
The gift of God is eternal life through Jesus Christ (John iv. 10; Rom. vi. 23). Christ received gifts for men (Eph. iv. 8). He not only opened up a way for them to God, and enables them to stand before the just and holy One, but he has obtained for them the gift of the Holy Ghost (John xiv. 16; xvi. 7; Acts ii. 38), and all the manifestations of the Spirit in the hearts and lives of believers, repentance (Acts v. 31), faith (Eph.

ii. 8), love (Rom. v. 5), joy, peace, long suffering, gentleness, goodness, meekness, temperance (Gal. v. 22). All Christian virtues are graces, that is gifts. God bestows various gifts upon men, qualifying them severally as he will for different forms of work in the kingdom (Rom. xii. 6; 1 Cor. vii. 7; xii. 4, 9; Eph. iv. 7–16). See MIRACLE, TONGUE.

Gi'hon [bursting forth, as a fountain or stream; a stream, river].
1. One of the four rivers of Paradise (Gen. ii. 13). See EDEN.
2. A spring in a valley outside the walls of Jerusalem from which the city obtained part of its water supply (2 Chron. xxxii. 30; xxxiii. 14; Antiq. vii. 14, 5). It was not in sight of the stone of Zoheleth, near En-rogel; but the sound of the trumpet and the noise of the shouting at Gihon were heard at En-rogel (1 Kin. i. 40–45). There was an upper and presumably a lower Gihon, as early as the time of Hezekiah at least (2 Chron. xxxii. 30). Upper Gihon is commonly identified with Birket Mamilla, and lower Gihon with Birket es-Sultan. The former of these pools is less than half a mile west, the latter not the third of a mile south, of the Jaffa gate. These pools, however, are not now fed by living springs. Largely on this account the question has been raised in recent years whether Gihon should not be identified with the fountain of the Virgin, on the eastern slope of Ophel, and distant some 400 yards from the pool of Siloam. with which it is connected by an ancient tunnel.

Gil'a-lai [perhaps weighty].
A Levite, a musician who took part in the dedication of the wall of Jerusalem when rebuilt under Nehemiah (Neh. xii. 36).

Gil-bo'a [a bubbling fountain].
The mountain on which Saul sustained defeat by the Philistines and met his death (1 Sam. xxviii. 4; xxxi. 1, 8; 2 Sam. i. 6, 21; xxi. 12; 1 Chron. x. 1, 8). It is the northeastern spur of mount Ephraim, and forms the watershed between the Kishon basin and the Jordan valley. The ridge lies west-northwest and east-southeast, being about 8 miles long and 3 to 5 miles in breadth; and is divided by ravines into several plateaus. The highest point, which is at Jebel Abu Madwar, is 1648 feet above sea level, and about 1200 feet higher than the plain of Esdraelon at its foot. The western slopes of the range are gradual, but those facing north are steep and rugged, with precipices in many places. The eastern slopes over the Jordan valley are also steep, in places precipitous, especially toward the south. On the table-lands and gentle western slopes pasture land is found, wheat and barley grow, and olives and figs are cultivated. The rest of the ridge is naked rock, or is covered with wild grass and brushwood. A village, Jelbon, preserves the memory of the name Gilboa.

Gil'e-ad, in A. V. of Maccabees **Galaad** [hard, rugged, rough].

1. The son of Machir and grandson of Manasseh. He founded a tribal family (Num. xxvi. 29, 30; Josh. xvii. 1).

2. Father of Jephthah (Judg. xi. 1).

3. A Gadite (1 Chron. v. 14).

4. The mountainous country east of the Jordan, extending from the table land of Moab northward to the Yarmuk at least (Deut. iii. 16, 17; 1 Sam. xxxi. 11), and perhaps further, since the ruggedness of the land continues unchanged north of that river. It is divided by the Jabbok into two parts (Josh. xii. 2). The southern half was assigned to the tribe of Gad, and the northern half was included in the territory of half Manasseh (Deut. iii. 12, 13; Josh. xiii. 24-31). The name is still connected with a mountain south of the Jabbok in its designation Jebel Jil'ad. The last interview between Laban and Jacob took place in mount Gilead (Gen. xxxi. 21). It was a place well suited for cattle (1 Chron. v. 9, 10; Song iv.); and the sight of Gilead and the land of Jazer (cp. 1 Chron. xxvi. 31) suggested to the Reubenites and the Gadites, who had large flocks and herds, the expediency of applying to Moses for permission, which was conditionally granted them, of settling permanently on the eastern side of the Jordan (Num. xxxii. 1-42: Josh. xiii. 8-11). Within the limits of Gilead grew the celebrated balm (Jer. viii. 22; cp. Gen. xxxvii. 25). In an extended sense the term Gilead includes the whole region east of the Jordan (Deut. xxxiv. 1; Josh. xxii. 9; Judg. xx. 1; 2 Sam. ii. 9; 1 Mac. v. 17, 24-27, 36; Antiq. xii. 8, 3; in ix. 8, 1, Gilead and Bashan are distinguished).

5. A mountain abutting on the valley of Jezreel (Judg. vii. 3; cp. ver. 1 and vi. 33). While Gilead in this passage may be a misreading for Gilboa, it must be remembered that the spring which best corresponds in position with that at which Gideon's men drank, and the mountain from which it issues, and the river down which the discomfited Midianites fled, are called respectively the spring, mountain, and river Jalud, which is Arabic for Goliath. To spring, mountain, and river, are thus attached a name which possibly perpetuates Gilead in a corrupt form. There is perhaps better evidence than the present name. Gilead was part of Naphtali (2 Kin. xv. 29). It may be that Naphtali extended across the Jordan to the east, but it is quite possible that Gilead denoted a rugged district of Naphtali west of the Jordan; and if so, the correctness of the text of Judg. vii. 3 is confirmed.

6. A city in the region of Gilead (Hos. vi. 8; cp. xii. 11).

Gil'gal [act of rolling, wheel, a circle].

1. The first encampment of the Israelites after crossing the Jordan, and their headquarters during the conquest of Canaan (Josh. iv. 19-24). The special association which they had with the name was the rolling away of their reproach by their circumcision after long neglect of the ordinance in the wilderness (Josh. v. 7-9). The camp was pitched between the Jordan and Jericho. On its site arose a town, which was on the northern border of Judah (xv. 7). There were quarries in its vicinity (Judg. iii. 19). These last two references are, however, believed by some authorities to indicate the existence of another Gilgal at the foot of the mountains. It is uncertain whether this town or another place of the name was on Samuel's circuit (1 Sam. vii. 16), and where, it may be judged, Saul, the opposition to him having ceased, was made king and the kingdom renewed (xi. 15). At any rate, it was at Gilgal in the Jordan valley where a muster of the people took place to form an army which should encounter the Philistines then oppressing the land, when Saul, finding it difficult to hold the people together until Samuel should come and offer sacrifice, himself offered burnt offerings (xiii. 4, 7, 8; cp. 12, 15). By this disobedience he forfeited the privilege of founding a dynasty (13, 14). There, too, for his obstinacy in sparing Agag he was rejected from being king and God's spirit withdrew from him (xv. 20-23; xvi. 14). To Gilgal the representatives of the tribe of Judah went to welcome David back after the death of Absalom (2 Sam. xix. 15, 40). Like other holy places, it became a focus of idolatry under the kings who succeeded Jeroboam, and it was in consequence denounced by the prophets (Hos. iv. 15; ix. 15; xii. 11; Amos iv. 4; v. 5). It is probably the house of Gilgal or Bethgilgal mentioned after the captivity (Neh. xii. 29). Its site is Jiljûlieh, a ruin 2 miles east of Jericho.

2. A village from which Elijah and Elisha went down to Bethel (Deut. xi. 30; 2 Kin. ii. 1-4; iv. 38 (?)). It was probably the present village of Jiljilia, on the top of a high hill, 7 miles north by west of Bethel; though when the levels are taken, its site is actually lower than that of Bethel.

3. A town associated with Dor and Tirzah (Josh. xii. 23); probably Jiljûlieh. a little north of the brook Kânah, and 5 miles northeast by north of Antipatris.

Gi'loh [exile].

A village in the hill country of Judah (Josh. xv. 51); enumerated with towns lying to the south of Hebron.

Gi'lo-nite.

A native or inhabitant of Giloh, as Ahithophel (2 Sam. xv. 12; xxiii. 34).

Gi'mel.

The third letter of the Hebrew alphabet. The Greek letter gamma, and consequently the English C have the same origin; but in the spelling of Hebrew and Greek names in the English versions, gimel and gamma (though not these letters only) are represented by G, their approximate equivalent in sound and a form fabricated out of C.

Gimel stands at the head of the third section of Ps. cxix. in several versions, since each verse of the section begins with this letter in the original.

Gim'zo [abounding in sycomores].

A town with dependent villages situated in Judah. It was taken by the Philistines during the reign of Ahaz (2 Chron. xxviii. 18). Robinson identified it with Jimzu, on an eminence about 3 miles east-southeast of Lydda.

Gin.

A noose or trap, laid on the ground, in which birds, beasts, and even men are caught (Job xviii. 9; Amos iii. 5). The two words *Mokesh* and *Pah*, of which it is the translation, are usually rendered by snare.

Gi'nath.

Father of Tibni (1 Kin. xvi. 22).

Gin'ne-thoi, in A. V. **Ginnetho** [gardener].

A chief of the priests who returned with Zerubbabel from Babylon (Neh. xii. 4, 7). In the next generation, a father's house among the priests, which occupies the same position in the corresponding catalogue, bore the name Ginnethon (ver. 16). The difference is merely that between a jod and a final nun. Probably Ginnethon stood originally in ver. 4.

Gin'ne-thon [gardener].

1. A father's house among the priests in the days of the high priest Joiakim (Neh. xii. 16); see GINNETHOI.

2. A priest who, doubtless in behalf of a father's house, sealed a covenant to worship Jehovah (Neh. x. 6).

Gird'le. See CLOTHING and HIGH PRIEST.

Gir'ga-shites, in A. V. once **Girgasites** [perhaps, dwellers on clayey soil].

A tribe of Canaan (Gen. x. 15, 16; xv. 21; Deut. vii. 1; Josh. iii. 10; xxiv. 11; Neh. ix. 8). It is not known what part of the country they inhabited. They must not be confounded with the Gergesenes.

Gir'zite, in A. V. **Gezrite**; in margin **Gizrites** and **Gerzites** respectively, following a Hebrew tradition.

A people living south of the Philistine country and mentioned with the Amalekites and Geshurites (1 Sam. xxvii. 8).

Gish'pa, in A. V. **Gispa** [blandishment].

An overseer of the Nethinim in Nehemiah's time (Neh. xi. 21).

Git'tah-he'pher. See GATH-HEPHER.

Git'ta-im [two wine presses].

A village of Benjamin (Neh. xi. 31, 33), to which the Beerothites fled probably at the time of Saul's cruelty (2 Sam. iv. 3; cp. xxi. 1, 2). Exact site unknown.

Git'tite [of Gath].

A native or inhabitant of Gath (2 Sam. vi. 10, 11; xv. 18, 19, 22).

Git'tith [Gittite].

A musical term (Ps. viii., lxxxi., lxxxiv., titles). It is the feminine form of the Hebrew adjective for Gittite, and it denotes either a musical instrument in use in Gath, or a vintage song to the tune of which the psalm should be sung, or a march of the Gittite guard (2 Sam. xv. 18).

Gi'zo-nite.

The designation of Hashem, one of David's mighty men (1 Chron. xi. 34), pointing either to his paternity or to his birthplace. But neither man nor place with a name like Gizoh is found in the Bible; and perhaps Gizonite is a corruption of Gunite (Septuagint, Lucian's text; cp. Num. xxvi. 48).

Giz'rite. See GIRZITE.

Glass.

1. A mirror (Ex. xxxviii. 8; Job xxxvii. 18; 1 Cor. xiii. 12, all A. V.); see MIRROR.

2. The rendering of Hebrew *Z⁰kukith* (Job xxviii. 17, R. V., where A. V. has crystal) and of Greek *'Ualos* and its adjective (Rev. iv. 6; xv. 2; xxi. 18, 21). It is probably real glass. Glass was known to the Greeks as early as the time of Herodotus, and to the Egyptians long before the exodus.

Glean'ing.

Gathering the grain which the reapers have failed to remove, or the grapes which remain after the vintage (Judg. viii. 2; Ruth ii. 2, 7, 9, 16; Is. xvii. 6). For the benefit of the poor, the fatherless, the widow, and the stranger, the owner was instructed by the law not to glean his harvest field or vineyard, nor return for a forgotten sheaf, nor gather fallen fruit (Lev. xix. 9, 10; xxiii. 22; Deut. xxiv. 19).

Glede [the glider].

The common kite (Deut. xiv. 13). The word is used to render the Hebrew *Ra'ah*; which, however, is a copyist's error for *Da'ah*; see DALETH. A later scribe seems to have written *Dayyah* on the margin as a correction, which afterwards crept into the text (for it is not mentioned in the corresponding list in Lev. xi.), and is rendered kite in R. V., vulture in A. V.

Gnat.

The rendering of the Greek *Kōnōps*, a small insect (Mat. xxiii. 24), abounding in marshes and vexatious by reason of its bite, from which the Egyptians protected themselves at night by sleeping under nets (Herod. ii. 95). It is evidently some species of *Culex*, a genus known by its hairy antennæ, plumed in the males, its proboscis, its slender body, its two gauzy wings, its long legs, and its blood-sucking propensities. "To strain *at*" in the A. V. is a misprint in the original edition of 1611 for "strain *out*." The earlier English versions have "out," and the R. V. corrects the error of A. V., and translates "to strain out the gnat, and swallow the camel." To anxiously strain out any small insect which has accidentally fallen into the water one is about to drink, but unconcernedly to swallow a camel, is to be particular about minute points of ceremony or of duty, while practicing gross violations of the moral law.

Goad.

A long pole sharpened at the point or iron-tipped, used to urge cattle forward (1 Sam. xiii. 21). With one Shamgar slew 600 Philistines (Judg. iii. 31). " It is hard for thee to kick against the pricks " (Acts ix. 5, A. V.) is the metaphor of a recalcitrant animal injuring itself against the ox goad. The words of the wise are compared to goads (Eccles. xii. 11).

Go'ah, in A. V. Goath [lowing].

A place near Jerusalem to the west or south (Jer. xxxi. 39).

Goat.

The rendering of quite a number of Hebrew words in the Old Testament, and of more than one Greek word in the New: *'Attud*, he goat, probably as leader of the flock ; *Tayish*, he goat, perhaps as butting ; *Saphir*, he goat, as the leaper ; *'Ez* she goat, also a goat without regard to sex ; *Sa'ir*, he goat, and *Se'irah*, she goat, as shaggy ; and the Greek words *Tragos*, he goat ; *'Aix*, goat, as the springer ; *'Eriphos* and *'Eriphion*, a young goat, kid. Goats were tended with the sheep by the same shepherd (Gen. xxvii. 9 ; xxx. 32), but in separate companies (Mat. xxv. 32). Their hair was woven into cloth (Ex. xxv. 4 ; xxxv. 26), the flesh and milk were used for food (Lev. vii. 23 ; Deut. xiv. 4 ; Prov. xxvii. 27), and in extremity their hairy skin served as clothing (Heb. xi. 37). They were an important item of a cattle owner's wealth (Gen. xxx. 33, 43 ; xxxi. 1 ; 1 Sam. xxv. 2 ; 2 Chron. xvii. 11). The goat was a sacrificial animal, used for burnt offering and sin offering (Gen. xv. 9 ; Ex. xii. 5 ; Lev. i. 10 ; iv. 24 ; Num. vii. 17 ; xv. 27 ; Ps. lxvi. 15 ; Is. i. 11 ; Ezra vi. 17 ; viii. 35 ; Heb. ix. 12). The domestic goat (*Capra hircus*) belongs to the great family of *Bovidæ*, or hollow-horned ruminants. The closest affinity is believed to be to the sheep, and there is a series of connecting links between the two animals. One of the few points of difference is that in the goat the horns are simply curved backward. Their habits are different. In Palestine the sheep may be seen grazing the tender herbage and grass, while the goats browse tender twigs and leaves. Every flock of goats has its own stately leader (cp. Jer. l. 8). The goat was very abundant in ancient Palestine, as was to be expected in a hilly and somewhat dry country. It is now more numerous than the sheep, and constitutes the chief wealth of the country. The ordinary goat of Syria is black in color, and has pendant ears a foot long hanging down below the recurved horns. It is Linnæus' *Capra mambrica*. His *Capra hircus*, variety *angorensis*, the Mohair goat,

is also occasionally bred in the north of Palestine.

Goat, Wild.

An animal, in Hebrew *Ya'el*, eminent. Its refuge is among the high hills (Ps. civ. 18) and rocks (Job xxxix. 1), En-gedi being its special haunt in Palestine (1 Sam. xxiv. 2). It is a species of ibex (*Capra beden*), called by the Arabs *beden*. It is of a much lighter color than the European ibex. Its horns are more slender and narrower, wrinkled, and knotted on the front face only. It is found in Egypt, Arabia, Persia, Moab, and in the wilderness of Judæa near the Dead Sea. Tristram met with it twice at its favorite spot, En-gedi, and found its teeth fossil in cave breccia on Lebanon, where it does not now occur. Wild goat is also the rendering of the Hebrew *'Akko*, perhaps meaning graceful neck (Deut. xiv. 5). It may be the same species.

Go'ath. See GOAH.

Gob [small pit, cistern, or locust].

A place at which war was waged with the Philistines twice in the reign of David (2 Sam. xxi. 18, 19). Site unknown. The text is uncertain. In 1 Chron. xx. 4 the seat of war is Gezer.

God.

The English word God is derived from a root meaning to call, and indicates simply the object of worship, one whom men call upon or invoke. The Greek word which it translates in the pages of the N. T., however, describes this object of worship as Spirit ; and the O. T. Hebrew word, which this word in turn represents, conveys, as its primary meaning, the idea of power. On Christian lips, therefore, the word God designates fundamentally the almighty Spirit who is worshiped and whose aid is invoked by men. This primary idea of God, in which is summed up what is known as theism, is the product of that general revelation which God makes of himself to all men, on the plane of nature. The truths involved in it are continually reiterated, enriched, and deepened in the Scriptures ; but they are not so much revealed by them as presupposed at the foundation of the special revelation with which the Scriptures busy themselves—the great revelation of the grace of God to sinners. On the plane of nature men can learn only what God necessarily is, and what, by virtue of his essential attributes, he must do ; a special communication from him is requisite to assure us what, in his infinite love, he will do for the recovery of sinners from their guilt and misery to the bliss of communion with him. And for the full revelation of this, his grace in the redemption of sinners, there was requisite an even more profound unveiling of the mode of his existence, by which he has been ultimately disclosed as including in the unity of his being a distinction of persons, by virtue of which it is the same God from whom, through whom, and by whom are all things, who is at once the Father who provides, the Son who accomplishes, and the Spirit who applies, redemption. Only in the uncovering of this supernal mystery of the Trinity is the revelation of what God is completed. That there is no hint of the Trinity in the general revelation made on the plane of nature is due to the fact that nature has nothing to say of redemption, in the process of which alone are the depths of the divine nature made known. That it is explicitly revealed only in the N. T. is due to the fact that not until the N. T. stage of revelation was reached was the redemption, which was being prepared throughout the whole O. T. economy, actually accomplished. That so ineffable a mystery was placed before the darkened mind of man at all is due to the necessities of the plan of redemption itself, which is rooted in the trinal distinction in the Godhead, and can be apprehended only on the basis of the Trinity in Unity.

The nature of God has been made known to men, therefore, in three stages, corresponding to the three planes of revelation, and we will naturally come to know him, first, as the infinite Spirit or the God of nature; then, as the Redeemer of sinners, or the God of grace; and lastly as the Father, Son, and Holy Ghost, or the Triune God.

1. *God, the Infinite Spirit.*—The conviction of the existence of God bears the marks of an intuitive truth in so far as it is the universal and unavoidable belief of men, and is given in the very same act with the idea of self, which is known at once as dependent and responsible and thus implies one on whom it depends and to whom it is responsible. This immediate perception of God is confirmed and the contents of the idea developed by a series of arguments known as the "theistic proofs." These are derived from the necessity we are under of believing in the real existence of the infinitely perfect Being, of a sufficient cause for the contingent universe, of an intelligent author of the order and of the manifold contrivances observable in nature, and of a lawgiver and judge for dependent moral beings, endowed with the sense of duty and an ineradicable feeling of responsibility, conscious of the moral contradictions of the world and craving a solution for them, and living under an intuitive perception of right which they do not see realized. The cogency of these proofs is currently recognized in the Scriptures, while they add to them the supernatural manifestations of God in a redemptive process, accompanied at every stage by miraculous attestation. From the theistic proofs, however, we learn not only that a God exists, but also necessarily, on the principle of a sufficient cause, very much of the nature of the God which they prove to exist. The idea is still further developed, on the principle of interpreting by the highest category within

our reach, by our instinctive attribution to him, in an eminent degree, of all that is the source of dignity and excellence in ourselves. Thus we come to know God as a personal Spirit, infinite, eternal, and illimitable alike in his being and in the intelligence, sensibility, and will which belong to him as personal spirit. The attributes which are thus ascribed to him, including self-existence, independence, unity, uniqueness, unchangeableness, omnipresence, infinite knowledge and wisdom, infinite freedom and power, infinite truth, righteousness, holiness and goodness, are not only recognized but richly illustrated in Scripture, which thus puts the seal of its special revelation upon all the details of the natural idea of God.

2. *God, the Redeemer of Sinners.*—While reiterating the teaching of nature as to the existence and character of the personal Creator and Lord of all, the Scriptures lay their stress upon the grace or the undeserved love of God, as exhibited in his dealings with his sinful and wrath-deserving creatures. So little, however, is the consummate divine attribute of love advanced, in the scriptural revelation, at the expense of the other moral attributes of God, that it is thrown into prominence only upon a background of the strongest assertion and fullest manifestation of its companion attributes, especially of the divine righteousness and holiness, and is exhibited as acting only along with and in entire harmony with them. God is not represented in the Scriptures as forgiving sin because he really cares very little about sin; nor yet because he is so exclusively or predominatingly the God of love, that all other attributes shrink into desuetude in the presence of his illimitable benevolence. He is rather represented as moved to deliver sinful man from his guilt and pollution because he pities the creatures of his hand, immeshed in sin, with an intensity which is born of the vehemence of his holy abhorrence of sin and his righteous determination to visit it with intolerable retribution; and by a mode which brings as complete satisfaction to his infinite justice and holiness as to his unbounded love itself. The biblical presentation of the God of grace includes thus the richest development of all his moral attributes, and the God of the Bible is consequently set forth, in the completeness of that idea, as above everything else the ethical God. And that is as much as to say that there is ascribed to him a moral sense so sensitive and true that it estimates with unfailing accuracy the exact moral character of every person or deed presented for its contemplation, and responds to it with the precisely appropriate degree of satisfaction or reprobation. The infinitude of his love is exhibited to us precisely in that while we were yet sinners he loved us, though with all the force of his infinite nature he reacted against our sin with illimitable abhorrence

and indignation. The mystery of grace resides just in the impulse of a sin-hating God to show mercy to such guilty wretches; and the supreme revelation of God as the God of holy love is made in the disclosure of the mode of his procedure in redemption, by which alone he might remain just while justifying the ungodly. For in this procedure there was involved the mighty paradox of the infinitely just Judge himself becoming the sinner's substitute before his own law and the infinitely blessed God receiving in his own person the penalty of sin.

3. *God, the Father, Son, and Holy Ghost.*— The elements of the plan of salvation are rooted in the mysterious nature of the Godhead, in which there coexists a trinal distinction of persons with absolute unity of essence; and the revelation of the Trinity was accordingly incidental to the execution of this plan of salvation, in which the Father sent the Son to be the propitiation for sin, and the Son, when he returned to the glory which he had with the Father before the world was, sent the Spirit to apply his redemption to men. The disclosure of this fundamental fact of the divine nature, therefore, lagged until the time had arrived for the actual working out of the long-promised redemption; and it was accomplished first of all in fact rather than in word, by the actual appearance of God the Son on earth and the subsequent manifestations of the Spirit, who was sent forth to act as his representative in his absence. At the very beginning of Christ's ministry the three persons are dramatically exhibited to our sight in the act of his baptism. And though there is no single passage in Scripture in which all the details of this great mystery are gathered up and expounded, there do not lack passages in which the three persons are brought together in a manner which exhibits at once their unity and distinctness. The most prominent of these are perhaps the formula of baptism in the triune name, put into the mouths of his followers by the resurrected Lord (Mat. xxviii. 19), and the apostolic benediction in which a divine blessing is invoked from each person in turn (2 Cor. xiii. 14). The essential elements which enter into and together make up this great revelation of the Triune God are, however, most commonly separately insisted upon. The chief of these are the three constitutive facts: (1) that there is but one God (Deut. vi. 4; Is. xliv. 6; 1 Cor. viii. 4; James ii. 19); (2) that the Father is God (Mat. xi. 25; John vi. 27; viii. 41; Rom. xv. 6; 1 Cor. viii. 6; Gal. i. 1, 3, 4; Eph. iv. 6; vi. 23; 1 Thes. i. 1; Jas. i. 27; iii. 9; 1 Pet. i. 2; Jude 1); the Son is God (John i. 1, 18; xx. 28; Acts xx. 28; Rom. ix. 5; Heb. i. 8; Col. ii. 9; Phil. ii. 6; 2 Pet. i. 1); and the Spirit is God (Acts v. 3, 4; 1 Cor. ii. 10, 11; Eph. ii. 22), and (3) that the Father, Son, and Holy Ghost are personally distinct from one another, distinguished by personal pronouns,

able to send and be sent by one another, to love and honor each the other, and the like (John xv. 26; xvi. 13, 14; xvii. 8, 18, 23; xvi. 14; xvii. 1). The doctrine of the Trinity is but the synthesis of these facts, and, adding nothing to them, simply recognizes in the unity of the Godhead such a Trinity of persons as is involved in the working out of the plan of redemption. In the prosecution of this work there is implicated a certain relative subordination in the modes of operation of the several persons, by which it is the Father that sends the Son and the Son who sends the Spirit; but the three persons are uniformly represented in Scripture as in their essential nature each alike God over all, blessed forever (Rom. ix. 5); and we are therefore to conceive the subordination as rather economical, *i. e.* relative to the function of each in the work of redemption, than essential, *i. e.* involving a difference in nature.

B. B. W.

Gog.

1. A Reubenite (1 Chron. v. 4).

2. The prince of Rosh, Meshech, and Tubal (Ezek. xxxviii. 2, R. V.), who is prophetically described as invading the land of Israel in the last times, and being defeated on the mountains with immense slaughter (Ezek. xxxviii., xxxix.). He and his people and his allies serve the prophet as a type of heathenism contending against the kingdom of God. The name was probably borrowed from Gyges, the chief of a Lydian princely family called the Mermnadæ. He belonged to the royal bodyguard, and was the confidant of the king. About 700 B. C. he murdered his sovereign, of the rival house of the Heraclidæ, and took possession of the throne of Lydia. He had great wealth, and made notable gifts to the temple of Apollo at Delphi. But he warred against the Greek cities in Asia Minor (Herod. i. 7–14). In his old age his country was invaded by the Cimmerians. He defeated them in battle and captured several of their chiefs. But fearing renewed invasion, he sent presents to Ashurbanipal, the Assyrian king. For a long time no one could be found among the Assyrians who understood the Lydian language spoken by the ambassadors. At length a man was obtained who comprehended what they said, and the friendship of Gyges was accepted. In a short time, however, Gyges aided Egypt in its revolt against Assyria. In retaliation the Assyrian king stirred up the Cimmerians to a fresh invasion of Lydia, in which, about 662 B. C., Gyges was killed, leaving his son Ardys to ascend the throne. See GOMER, MAGOG.

3. A mystic personage, akin in character to the Gog of Ezekiel, to appear immediately before the close of the present dispensation (Rev. xx. 8–15).

Goi'im. See TIDAL.

Go'lan [exile, emigration].

A city of Bashan, within the territory of

the half-tribe of Manasseh east of the Jordan. It was assigned, with its suburbs, to the Gershonite Levites (Josh. xxi. 27; 1 Chron. vi. 71), and was one of the cities of refuge (Deut. iv. 43; Josh. xx. 8; xxi. 27). Alexander Jannæus sustained a severe defeat near this place, and on a later campaign demolished the town (War. i. 4, 4 and 8). The town gave name to the small province of Gaulanitis, or Gaulonitis, as the name was also pronounced (Antiq. viii. 2, 3, various Greek texts). This region was situated between Hermon and the Yarmuk, and extended from the neighborhood of the Jordan eastward. The eastern border has not been determined. The district is divisible into a southern and more arable, and a northern and more rocky half. It was surveyed by Schumacher, who with other authorities considers that the site of the town was at Saḥem ej-Jaulân, about 17 miles east of the sea of Galilee, where there are extensive ruins. Gaulonitis is now known as Jaulân. It is a table-land watered by streams from Hermon and by numerous springs, and with pastures which are among the richest in Syria; yet it lies desolate.

Gold.
A precious metal anciently obtained in Havilah (Gen. ii. 11, 12); Sheba (1 Kin. x. 2; Ps. lxxii. 15), and Ophir (1 Kin. xxii. 48; 2 Chron. viii. 18; Job xxii. 24; Ps. xlv. 9). It was lavishly used for overlaying the furniture of the tabernacle and the temple, and ornamenting the latter edifice itself (Ex. xxv. 18; 1 Kin. vi. 22, 28). It was made into idols (Ex. xx. 23; xxxii. 31; Ps. cxv. 4; Is. xl. 19; Acts xvii. 29), crowns (Ps. xxi. 3), chains (Gen. xli. 42), rings (Song v. 14), earrings (Judg. viii. 26). It was used for coinage at a comparatively early date (Ezra ii. 69, R. V.; cp. Acts iii. 6; xx. 33). It serves as a symbol for a thing of genuine worth and great value (Lam. iv. 2; Rev. iii. 18).

Gol'go-tha [Greek from Aramaic *gulgalta'*, Hebrew *gulgoleth*, a skull]. See CALVARY.

Go-li'ath [exile, or an exile].
The giant from the Philistine city of Gath who was slain by David (1 Sam. xvii. 1–58; xxi. 9, 10; xxii. 10; cp. Josh. xi. 22; Num. xiii. 33); probably one of the Anakim. Perhaps another giant of Gath, besides the one slain by David, bore the name of Goliath (2 Sam. xxi. 19), just as two heroes of the time were called Elhanan; but see ELHANAN.

Go'mer, I. [perfection].
Daughter of Diblaim, and wife of Hosea the prophet (Hos. i. 3).

Go'mer, II.
A people descended from Japheth, and inhabiting the north (Gen. x. 2, 3; 1 Chron. i. 5, 6; Ezek. xxxviii. 6). They were probably the Cimmerians of classical history. They are mentioned by Homer as people of the far north (Odys. xi. 14). They came into Asia from the regions beyond the Caucasus (Herod. iv. 11, 12), settled in Cappadocia, and threatened

the Assyrian empire, but were defeated by Esarhaddon. Turning westward, they overran part of Asia Minor, fighting more than one battle with Gyges, king of Lydia, whose name is probably preserved in the Scripture Gog. Him they killed. They were afterwards driven out of Asia (Lydia) by Alyattes (Herod. i. 16). They are generally considered to have been identical with the Cimbri of Roman times, and the Cymry of Wales. Cambria and even Cumberland still preserve the memory of their name.

Go-mor'rah, in A. V. of N. T. Gomorrha [accumulation or, perhaps, submersion].
A city in the plain of the Jordan (Gen. x. 19; xiii. 10). Like Sodom its king was defeated by Chedorlaomer and the city plundered (xiv. 8–11). Soon afterward it was destroyed by fire from heaven on account of wickedness (xviii. 20; xix. 24–28; Deut. xxix. 23; Is. i. 9; Amos iv. 11; Jer. xxiii. 14; xlix. 18; Zeph. ii. 9; Mat. x. 15). Conder points out that there is a great bluff called Tubk 'Amriyeh, and near it a wady called Wady 'Amriyeh, about 10 miles north-northwest of En-gedi. The consonants are the same as in Gomorrah, and the modern name perhaps echoes the ancient name, although the original site of the town may be 35 or 40 miles farther south.

For the vine of the fields of Gomorrah (Deut. xxxii. 32), see VINE.

Go'pher Wood.
The wood of which the ark was made (Gen. vi. 14). Gesenius suggested that the Hebrew *gopher* is an altered form of *kopher*, pitch, and refers to trees of the pine family, and specially, perhaps, to the cypress, the three first consonants of the Greek *kuparissos* being nearly those of the word gopher.

Gor'gi-as.
A Syrian general under Antiochus IV. In 166 B. C. he led a detachment of troops from Emmaus, in the Philistine plain, where the main army was encamped, to make a night attack on Judas Maccabæus; but Judas, having learned of the plan, withdrew his forces and led them to a successful attack on Gorgias' own camp. When Gorgias returned, his followers saw their camp in flames and fled (1 Mac. iii. 38–iv. 25). A little more than a year later Gorgias was commanding at Jamnia, and he met and defeated Joseph and Azarias, who in the absence of Judas had charge of the troops in Judæa, and were advancing to attack the town (v. 55–62).

Gor-ty'na.
An important city in the southern part of Crete (1 Mac. xv. 23).

Go'shen.
1. A district of Egypt, adapted for flocks and herds, situated in the delta, a few miles to the northeast of On. It belonged to the nome called Arabia (Gen. xlvi. 34, Septuagint), and formed part of the land of Ramses (xlvi. 28; xlvii. 11, 27, Septuagint). Thither

Joseph went up in his chariot to meet his father who was coming from Canaan (xlvi. 28, 29). The Hebrews were allowed to settle there (xlvii. 6), and the mass of the people were still there at the time of their oppression (Ex. viii. 22; ix. 6).

2. A region in the south of Judah (Josh. x. 41; xi. 16). Exact situation unknown.

3. A town in the hill country of Judah (Josh. xv. 51). Exact site unknown.

Gos'pel.

The English word gospel is derived from the Anglo-Saxon gōdspel, which meant good tidings. This etymology is found in the *Ormulum*, Introduction, line 157. Later it became gŏdspel, which meant God-story, *i. e.* the story about God, *i. e.* Christ. The word, as now used, describes both the message which Christianity announces and the books in which the story of Christ's life and teaching is contained. A similar transition in meaning was experienced by the Greek word *euaggelion* (whence the Latin *evangelium* and our evangel) which gospel was and is used to translate. In the N. T. it never means a book, but the message which Christ and his apostles announced. It is called the gospel of God (Rom. i. 1; 1 Thes. ii. 2, 9; 1 Tim. i. 11); the gospel of Christ (Mark i. 1; Rom. i. 16; xv. 19; 1 Cor. ix. 12, 18; Gal. i. 7); the gospel of the grace of God (Acts xx. 24); the gospel of peace (Eph. vi. 15); the gospel of your salvation (Eph. i. 13); and the glorious gospel (2 Cor. iv. 4). It was preached by our Lord (Mat. iv. 23; xi. 5; Mark i. 14; Luke iv. 18; vii. 22); by the apostles (Acts xvi. 10; Rom. i. 15; ii. 16; 1 Cor. ix. 16, etc.), and by evangelists (Acts viii. 25). But in the post-apostolic age the term was also applied to the writings in which the apostolic testimony to Jesus was contained. Each one of them was called a gospel and the four together were called the gospel. Our present English usage, therefore, exactly corresponds with that of the early Christians of the age immediately succeeding the apostolic.

The Four Gospels.—Historical evidence shows that our four gospels have been attributed from the earliest times to Matthew, Mark, Luke, and John, respectively, and that from the very beginning of the post-apostolic age they were received by the church as authoritative documents and as containing the apostolic testimony to the life and teachings of Christ. In the second century they were quoted, commented upon, and described; so that there need be no doubt of their authenticity. An examination of the N. T. epistles also shows that our gospels describe Jesus as the same kind of person, doing the same kind of works, and having the same history to which the epistles allude. They may, therefore, be confidently accepted as trustworthy reports. The first three have much in common and, in general, present the

life of the Lord from the same point of view. They are called the synoptic gospels (from the Greek *sunopsis*, a seeing together), and in particular are quite different from John's. The synoptics take for their chief theme Christ's ministry in Galilee; the Fourth Gospel gives prominence to his labors in Judæa: though his betrayal, arrest, trial, crucifixion, and resurrection are so important that they are narrated by all. The only prior incident recorded by all the evangelists is the feeding of the five thousand. The synoptics also say comparatively little of the divinity of Christ, while John especially records the Lord's self-testimony to it. They present mainly Christ's teaching about the kingdom of God, his parables, his instruction of the common people: while John records his teaching about himself and this usually in the form of extended discourses. At the same time the Fourth Gospel assumes and implies the other three, and they in turn are often made intelligible only by the facts which John records. Thus John i. 15 implies the fact recorded in Mat. iii. 11, etc.; John iii. 24 the fact given in Mat. iv. 12; John vi. 2, 15, the whole synoptic story of the Galilæan ministry, etc. So in turn Christ's reception in Galilee and the willingness of Peter, Andrew, James, and John to leave all and follow him are only explicable by such events as are recorded in John i. and ii.; and the sudden rise of the Sabbath controversy in the synoptics (see Mark ii. 23, etc.) is likewise to be explained by the events of John v. Moreover, while the synoptics have the same general point of view, each of them has its individual characteristics, determined by the writer's purpose and the readers whom he had in mind. Matthew, writing from the Jewish point of view, sets Jesus forth as the royal Messiah. He constantly cites in proof O. T. prophecies, and is interested to give Christ's teaching concerning the true kingdom of God in contrast to the false views of current Judaism. Mark, writing evidently for gentiles, and possibly for the Romans in particular, represents mainly Christ's power to save as shown in his miracles. Luke, long the companion of Paul, sets the Lord forth as the gracious Saviour, and is fond of exhibiting his favor to the fallen, the outcast, and the poor. So John has his special purpose, which is to represent Jesus as the incarnate, divine Word, revealing the Father to those who would receive him. None of the gospels, however, aims at being a complete biography of our Lord. They are collections of his acts and words, made for the purpose of practical and doctrinal instruction. The student must construct his conception of the history of Jesus out of the materials furnished by the gospels. They themselves were prepared with other objects in view.

The question has often been asked from what sources the four evangelists derived their information. Matthew and John were apostles and therefore possessed personal knowledge of the events they record or were in a position to obtain it from those who had it. But Mark also was a companion of Paul and Peter, and is said, by very early tradition, to have embodied in his Gospel the preaching of Peter about Jesus. Luke himself assures us (i. 1–4) that his knowledge was obtained from "eyewitnesses .... of the word" and that he had made himself well acquainted with the facts. Thus the gospels give us the testimony of the apostles. The many coincidences of language in the synoptics confirm this. If any itinerant speaker or preacher, such as a foreign missionary home on furlough, relates at different places incidents of his experience abroad, he gradually settles into a fixed narrative through his very desire to be accurate, repeating the same stories in the same form, though now and then adding particulars which he had omitted elsewhere. It is probable that the apostles and early evangelists acted in much the same way; so that their recital became largely stereotyped. After a while parts of this narrative were put into writing for use in the newly founded churches. Thus a gospel narrative became current which, while doubtless differing in extent in different places, had much of its matter, even to the very words, in common. The verbal coincidences, therefore, of our synoptic gospels attest that they give us the common apostolic testimony to Jesus. The Fourth Gospel, on the other hand, contains material which at first was not so widely called for, but which John finally wrote, out of his own knowledge, when the needs of the church seemed to demand it. The coincidences between the synoptics have raised, however, the further question whether any of them have directly copied from the others. This question is often called the synoptic problem. The facts which enter into its solution are very many and complex. While the three have much in common, Matthew and Luke have much that is not in Mark, and each of them has much that is not in the others. Even Mark has some material peculiar to himself. Moreover, even in the sections which are in common the language of one evangelist often differs as remarkably as in other points it agrees with that of his colleagues. In the ancient church it was thought that Mark abbreviated Matthew and Luke. Many modern writers think, on the other hand, that Matthew and Luke drew from Mark his historical narrative [making its language fundamental to their own account, arranging its material to conform to their own purposes in writing, and adding matter from other sources oral and written. And it is quite customary to combine with this explanation the theory that a collection of the sayings of Jesus, written possibly by the apostle Matthew, early existed, from which also the two evangelists Matthew and

Luke drew. (J. D. D.).] But it seems to be more probable that all three were independent, but used largely the language of the gospel narrative which had become current; while at the same time they felt free also to use their own words because they were conscious of being fully acquainted with the facts. In attempting to trace the literary history of the synoptics we should not forget also the promise made by Christ to the apostles, and meant doubtless for others who might be employed in the proclamation of the gospel, "But the Comforter, even the Holy Spirit, whom the Father will send in my name, he shall teach you all things, and bring to your remembrance all that I said unto you" (John xiv. 26, R. V.).

To obtain a clear idea of the life of Christ it is necessary to construct a harmony of the gospels. This, of course, should be done with fidelity to the chronological indications, few though they are, which the gospels contain. But it should also be remembered that the indications of time and relation are not only few, but also often doubtful, and that, therefore, a harmony must be regarded in many points as merely approximate. Matthew's method is mainly topical, and, therefore, he seldom provides a basis for a harmony. Mark appears to be much more chronological, and his order may generally be followed; but there is much that he does not give at all. Luke follows in the first half of his work nearly the order of Mark, though with important differences, and he, too, is often topical in his method. But John's Gospel by noting successive feasts which Jesus attended provides the general framework into which the other material should be fitted. It is on this basis that the following outline and harmony have been prepared: We believe that the feast of John v. 1 was a passover; that therefore Christ's ministry included four passovers (John ii. 13; v. 1; vi. 4; xiii. 1), at the last of which he died. The ministry was thus about three years and a quarter in length, since John i. shows that Christ was baptized a few months before his first passover. Others however, denying that John v. 1 was a passover, make the ministry two and a quarter years in length. On this, as on many similar points, absolute demonstration is impossible. In the following table, moreover, the dates assigned to some of the events must likewise be regarded as open to question. It appears clear to most students that Herod the Great died about April 1, 4 B. C. If so, Christ was probably born in December, 5 B. C., or January, 4 B. C. We assume the date to be December 25, 5 B. C., without, however, meaning to affirm that there is any evidence for the exact day of the month. If then, when he was baptized, he was about thirty (Luke iii. 23), his baptism is probably to be assigned to the latter part of A. D. 26 or the beginning of A. D. 27. We assume for it January A. D. 27. If his ministry included four passovers, he died at the pass-over of A. D. 30. Many complex calculations tend to confirm these dates, though they are not capable of perfect demonstration. Our view assumes that "the fifteenth year of Tiberius Cæsar" (Luke iii. 1) is to be dated from the time when Tiberius became co-regent with Augustus in the empire (A. D. 11–12). At that time he became in the provinces the practical ruler. It is well known that our common Christian calendar dates the birth of Christ too late. The following harmony nearly agrees with Robinson's; but some changes in his arrangement have been introduced.

HARMONY OF THE FOUR GOSPELS.

Incidents.	Time.	Place.	Matthew.	Mark.	Luke.	John.
1. Introductory verses.	. . .	. . . .	. . .	. . .	i. 1–4	
2. Prologue to the Fourth Gospel.	. . .	. . . .	. . .	. . .	. . .	i. 1–18
3. The genealogy of Christ	. . .	. . . .	i. 1–17	. . .	iii. 23b–38	
4. Annunciation to Zacharias of John the Baptist's birth.	B. C. 6	The temple.	. . .	. . .	i. 5–25	
5. Annunciation to Mary of Christ's birth.	" 5	Nazareth.			26–38	
6. Mary's visit to Elisabeth.	" "	A city of Judah.		. . .	39–56	
7. Birth of John the Baptist.	" "	" "	. . .	. . .	57, 58	
8. Circumcision and naming of John.	" "	" "	. . .	. . .	59–79	
9. Annunciation to Joseph of Christ's birth.	" "	Nazareth.	18–23			
10 The birth of Jesus.	" "	Bethlehem.	24, 25	. . .	ii. 1–7	
11. Annunciation to the shepherds.	" "	Near Bethlehem.	. . .	. . .	8–14	
12. Visit of the shepherds to adore Christ.	" "	Bethlehem.			15–20	
13. Circumcision of Jesus.	" 4	"	. . .	. . .	21	
14. Presentation in the temple; prophecies of Simeon and Anna.	" "	Jerusalem.	. . .	. . .	22–38	
15. Visit of the Magi.	" "	Bethlehem.	ii. 1–12			
16. Flight into Egypt.	" "	Bethlehem to Egypt.	13–15			
17. Slaughter of the children by Herod.	" "	Bethlehem.	16–18			
18. Return from Egypt to Nazareth.	" "	Egypt to Nazareth.	19–23	. . .	39	
19. Life of Jesus at Nazareth for thirty years, but with one recorded visit to Jerusalem at the feast of the passover when 12 years of age: John in retirement in the desert.	B. C. 4–A. D. 26 A. D. 9	Nazareth.	. . .	. . .	ii. 40–52 i. 80	
20. The public ministry of John the Baptist.	A. D. 26	At the Jordan.	iii. 1–12	i. 1–8	iii. 1–18	19–28
21. Jesus baptized and witnessed by John.	" 27	" "	13–17	9–11	21–23a	29–34
22. The temptation of Jesus.	" "	Wilderness of Judæa (?).	iv. 1–11	12, 13	iv. 1–13	
23. John, Andrew, and Peter, meet Jesus.	" "	Near the Jordan.	. . .	. . .	. . .	35–42
24. Philip and Nathanael called.	" "	On the way to Galilee.	. . .	. . .	. . .	43–51
25. The first miracle; water changed to wine.	" "	Cana of Galilee.	. . .	. . .	. . .	ii. 1–11
26. Christ goes to Capernaum.	" "	Capernaum.	. . .	. . .	. . .	12

Early Judæan Ministry.

27. **The first passover**; money changers driven from the temple.	Apr. A. D. 27	Jerusalem.	. . .	. . .	. . .	ii. 13–25
28. Instruction of Nicodemus.	" "	"	. . .	. . .	. . .	iii. 1–21
29. Jesus preaches in Judæa.	" "	Judæa.	. . .	. . .	. . .	22

HARMONY OF THE FOUR GOSPELS.—*Continued.*

Incidents.	Time.	Place.	Matthew.	Mark.	Luke.	John.
30. Renewed testimony of John to Jesus.	A. D. 27	Judæa.	. . .	. . .	. . .	iii. 23-36
31. Jesus departs for Gal'e.	" "	Judæa to Galilee.	. . .	. . .	. . .	iv. 1-3
32. Interview with woman of Samaria.	" "	Near Sychar.	. . .	. . .	. . .	4-42
33. Cure of nobleman's son	" 27 or 28	Cana.	. . .	. . .	. . .	43-54
34. Imprisonment of John the Baptist.	. .	Fortress of Machærus.	xiv. 3-5	vi. 17-20	iii. 19, 20	

Early Galilæan Ministry.

Incidents.	Time.	Place.	Matthew.	Mark.	Luke.	John.
35. Commencement of Christ's public work in Galilee.	A. D. 28	Galilee.	iv. 12-17	i. 14, 15	iv. 14, 15	
36. First rejection at Nazareth.	" "	Nazareth.	. . .	. . .	16-30	
37. Call of Simon, Andrew, James, and John.	" "	Near Capernaum.	18-22	16-20	v. 1-11	
38. Cure of demoniac in the synagogue.	" "	Capernaum.	. . .	21-28	iv. 31-37	
39. Cure of Peter's wife's mother.	" "	"	viii. 14, 15	29-31	38, 39	
40. Cure of many on the same evening.	" "	"	16, 17	32-34	40, 41	
41. Circuit through Galilee	" "	Galilee.	iv. 23-25	35-39	42-44	
42. Cure of a leper.	" "	A city of Galilee.	viii. 2-4	40-45	v. 12-16	
43. Healing of paralytic.	" "	Capernaum.	ix. 1-8	ii. 1-12	17-26	
44. Call of Matthew (Levi); his feast.	" "	"	9-13	13-17	27-32	
45. **The second passover**; healing of impotent man at pool of Bethesda, and discussion with the Jews.	Apr. "	" Jerusalem.	. . .	. . .	. . .	v 1-47
46. Plucking ears of corn leads to discussion of the Sabbath question.	" "	On way to Galilee (?).	xii. 1-8	23-28	vi. 1-5	
47. Cure on Sabbath of man with withered hand.	" "	Capernaum.	9-13	iii. 1-6	6-11	
48. Plots against Jesus; extraordinary enthusiasm of the people; many follow him from all the land.	" "	Near Capernaum.	14-21	7-12	17-19	
49. Selection of the twelve apostles.	" "	" "	x. 2-4	13-19	12-16	
50. Sermon on the mount.	" "	" "	v. 1-viii. 1	. . .	20-49	
51. Healing of centurion's servant.	" "	Capernaum.	viii. 5-13	. . .	vii. 1-10	
52. Circuit through Galilee	" "	Galilee.	xi. 1			
53. Raising of widow's son	" "	Nain.	. . .	. . .	vii. 11-17	
54. Inquiry of John the Baptist about Jesus, and the latter's reply, etc.	" "	Galilee.	xi. 2-19	. . .	18-35	
55. Jesus anointed by a sinful woman.	" "	"	. . .	. . .	36-50	
56. A further circuit through Galilee with his disciples.	" "	"	. . .	. . .	viii. 1-3	
57. Beginning of the day of parables (see 63); cure of a demoniac; blasphemy of Pharisees reproved.	" "	Capernaum.	xii. 22-37	iii. 20-30	xi. 14, 15, 17-23	
58. Pharisees' desire for a sign commented on.	" "	"	38-45	. . .	16, 24-26, 29-36	
59. Christ's mother and brethren desire to see him.	" "	"	46-50	31-35	27, 28; viii. 19-21	
60. Woes against Pharisees	" "	"	. . .	. . .	xi. 37-54	
61. Discourses to the people on trust in God, against worldliness, etc.	" "	"	. . .	. . .	xii. 1-59	

HARMONY OF THE FOUR GOSPELS.—*Continued.*

Incidents.	Time.	Place.	Matthew.	Mark.	Luke.	John.
62. Remarks on the slaughter of the Galilæans.	A. D. 28.	Capernaum.	. . .	. . .	xiii. 1-5	
63. Parables of the sower, the tares, the seed growing secretly, the mustard seed, the leaven, the hid treasure, the pearl, the dragnet, and other sayings.	" "	"	xiii. 1-53	iv. 1-34	viii. 4-18; xiii. 18-21	
64. The three inquirers.	" "	Near sea of Galilee.	viii. 18-22	. . .	ix. 57-62	
65. The tempest stilled.	" "	Sea of Galilee.	23-27	35-41	viii. 22-25	
66. The demoniacs of Gadara (or Gerasa).	" "	East shore of sea of Galilee.	28-34	v. 1-20	26-40	
67. Inquiry of John's disciples and the Pharisees about fasting.	" "	Capernaum.	ix. 14-17	ii. 18-22	v. 33-39	
68. Raising of Jairus' daughter, and cure of woman with bloody issue.	" "	"	18-26	v. 21-43	viii. 41-56	
69. Cure of two blind men.	" "	"	27-31			
70. Cure of a dumb demoniac.	" "	"	32-34			
71. Second rejection at Nazareth.	" "	Nazareth.	xiii. 54-58	vi. 1-6a		
72. The **twelve** sent out.	" "	Galilee.	ix. 35-x.1, x. 5-xi. 1	6b-13	ix. 1-6	
73. Herod's inquiry about Jesus, with which is connected the account of the recent murder of John the Baptist.	A. D. 29 (?)	"	xiv. 1, 2, 6-12	14-16, 21-29	7-9	
74. The twelve return; Jesus retires with them across the sea; 5000 fed.	" "	Northeast coast of sea of Galilee.	13-21	30-44	10-17	vi. 1-14
75. Jesus walks on the water.	" "	Sea of Galilee.	22-33	45-52	. . .	15-21
76. Triumphal march through Gennesaret.	" "	Gennesaret.	34-36	53-56		22-71
77. Discourse on the Bread of Life at the time of the **third passover.**	Apr. A. D. 29	Capernaum.	. . .	. . .	. . .	
78. Reproof of Pharisaic traditions.	" "	"	xv. 1-20	vii. 1-23		

Later Galilæan Ministry.

Incidents.	Time.	Place.	Matthew.	Mark.	Luke.	John.
79. Daughter of Syrophœnician healed.	A. D. 29	Region of Tyre and Sidon.	xv. 21-28	vii. 24-30		
80. Deaf and dumb man healed and others.	" "	The Decapolis.	29-31	31-37	. . .	vii. 1
81. The 4000 fed.	" "	" "	32-38	viii. 1-9		
82. The Pharisees and Sadducees again require a sign.	" "	Near Magadan [A. V. Mat. Magdala]; in Mark, the parts of Dalmanutha.	39-xvi. 4	10-12		
83. Disciples warned against the leaven of the Pharisees, etc.	" "	Sea of Galilee.	5-12	13-21		
84. Blind man healed.	" "	Bethsaida.	. . .	22-26		
85. Peter's confession.	" "	Region of Cæsarea Philippi.	13-20	27-30	18-21	
86. Christ foretells his death and resurrection.	" "	" "	21-28	31-ix. 1	22-27	
87. The transfiguration.	" "	" "	xvii.1-13	2-13	28-36	
88. Healing of the demoniac boy.	" "	" "	14-21	14-29	37-43a	
89. Christ again foretells his death and resurrection.	" "	Galilee.	22, 23	30-32	43b-45	
90. The tribute money.	" "	Capernaum.	24-27			
91. Instructions to disciples on humility, etc.	" "	"	xviii.1-35	33-50	46-50	

HARMONY OF THE FOUR GOSPELS.—*Continued.*

The Last Journeys to Jerusalem.

Incidents.	Time.	Place.	Matthew.	Mark.	Luke.	John.
92. Final departure from Galilee; rejected in Samaria.	A. D. 29	From Galilee to Judæa.	xix. 1ᵃ	x. 1ᵃ	ix. 51–56	
93. The seventy instructed and sent out.	" "	" "	xi. 20–24	. . .	x. 1–16	
94. Christ attends the **feast of tabernacles.**	Oct. " "	Jerusalem.	. . .	. . .	. . .	vii. 2–52
95. [The woman taken in adultery] *bracketed in R. V.*	" " "	"	. . .	. . .	. . .	[53–viii. 11]
96. Discussion with the Jews during the feast.	" " "	"	. . .	. . .	. . .	viii. 12–59
97. Jesus apparently retires from Jerusalem and the seventy return to him.	" "	Judæa.	25–30	. . .	17–24	
98. A lawyer instructed; parable of the good Samaritan.	" "	"	. . .	. . .	25–37	
99. Jesus at the house of Martha and Mary.	" "	Bethany.	. . .	. . .	38–42	
100. The disciples taught how to pray.	" "	Judæa.	. . .	. . .	xi. 1–13	
101. **The feast of dedication;** blind man healed; parable of the shepherd; conflict with the Jews; Jesus retires to Peræa, beyond Jordan.	Dec." "	Jerusalem.	. . .	. . .	. . .	ix. 1–x. 39
102. Ministry in Peræa.	" 30	Peræa.	xix. 1ᵇ, 2	x. 1ᵇ	. . .	39–41
103. Parable of the barren fig tree.	" "	"	. . .	. . .	xiii. 6–9	
104. Healing infirm woman on the Sabbath.	" "	"	. . .	. . .	10–17	
105. Teaching and journeying toward Jerusalem; warned against Herod.	" "	"	. . .	. . .	22–35	
106. Dines with a Pharisee; healing of man with dropsy; parable of the great supper.	" "	"	. . .	. . .	xiv. 1–24	
107. Requirements of true disciples.	" "	"	. . .	. . .	25–35	
108. Parables of the lost sheep and coin and the prodigal.	" "	"	. . .	. . .	xv. 1–32	
109. Parable of the unjust steward.	" "	"	. . .	. . .	xvi. 1–13	
110. Pharisees reproved; parable of the rich man and Lazarus.	" "	"	. . .	. . .	14–31	
111. Instructs disciples in forbearance, faith, and humility.	" "	"	. . .	. . .	xvii.1–10	
112. The ten lepers.	" "	Between Samaria and Galilee (R. V. margin).	. . .	. . .	11–19	
113. The suddenness of his advent.	" "	Peræa.	. . .	. . .	20–37	
114. Parable of the importunate widow.	" "	"	. . .	. . .	xviii. 1–8	
115. Parable of the Pharisee and the publican	" "	"	. . .	. . .	9–14	
116. **The raising of Lazarus.**	" "	Bethany.	. . .	. . .	. . .	xi. 1–46
117. Counsel of Caiaphas; Jesus again retires.	" "	Jerusalem. Ephraim.	. . .	. . .	. . .	47–54
118. Precepts concerning divorce.	" "	Peræa (?).	xix. 3–12	x. 2–12		

HARMONY OF THE FOUR GOSPELS.—*Continued.*

Incidents.	Time.	Place.	Matthew.	Mark.	Luke.	John.
119. Christ blesses little children.	A. D. 30	Peræa.	xix. 13–15	x. 13–16	xviii. 15–17	
120. The rich young ruler, etc.	" "	"	16–30	17–31	18–30	
121. Parable of the laborers in the vineyard.	" "	"	xx. 1–16			
122. Third prediction of his death and resurrection.	" "	"	17–19	32–34	31–34	
123. **Ascent to Jerusalem;** request of James and John.	" "	"	20–28	35–45		
124. Two blind men healed near Jericho.	" "	Jericho.	29–34	46–52	35–43	
125. Conversion of Zacchæus.	" "	"	. . .	. . .	xix. 1–10	
126. Parable of the pounds	" "	"	. . .	. . .	11–28	
127. Arrival at Bethany six days before the passover.	" "	Bethany.	. . .	. . .	. . .	xi. 55–xii. 1

The Last Week.

Incidents.	Time.	Place.	Matthew.	Mark.	Luke.	John.
128. Supper at Bethany; anointed by Mary; hostility of rulers.	Saturday, Apr. 1, A. D. 30	Bethany.	xxvi. 6–13	xiv. 3–9	. . .	2–11
129. Triumphal entry into Jerusalem; spends night at Bethany.	Sunday, Apr. 2	Mount of Olives, Jerusalem, and Bethany.	xxi. 1–11	xi. 1–11	xix. 29–44	12–19
130. Cursing of barren fig tree; cleansing of temple; praises of the children; miracles.	Monday, Apr. 3	Near and in Jerusalem.	12–19	12–19	45–48; xxi. 37, 38	
131. Lesson of the fig tree.	Tuesday, Apr. 4	On the way to Jerusalem.	20–22	20–25[26]		
132. The sanhedrin demand Christ's authority; his reply and parables of the two sons, the wicked husbandmen, and the marriage of the king's son.	" "	Jerusalem.	23–32, 33–46; xxii. 1–14	27–33; xii. 1–12	xx. 1–8, 9–19	
133. Question of the Pharisees (tribute to Cæsar); of the Sadducees (the resurrection); of the lawyer (the great commandment); Christ's question (David's Lord).	" "	"	15–22, 23–33, 34–40, 41–46	13–17, 18–27, 28–34, 35–37	20–26, 27–40, 41–44	
134. Warnings against scribes and Pharisees.	" "	"	xxiii. 1–39	38–40	45–47	
135. The widow's mite.	" "	"	. . .	41–44	xxi. 1–4	
136. Visit of the Greeks; last teachings.	" "	"	. . .	. . .	. . .	xii. 20–50
137. Christ's prediction of the fall of Jerusalem, the future of the church, and the second advent.	Tuesday evening, Apr. 4	Mount of Olives.	xxiv. 1–31	xiii. 1–27	xxi. 5–28	
138. Instructions to watch; parables of ten virgins and talents; the last judgment.	" "	" "	32–xxv. 46	28–37	29–36	
139. Conspiracy of the rulers; treachery of Judas.	Tuesday evening Apr. 4, or Wednesday, Apr. 5	Jerusalem.	xxvi. 1–5, 14–16	xiv. 1, 2, 10, 11	xxii. 1–6	
140. Preparations for the passover.	Thursday, Apr. 6	Bethany and Jerusalem.	17–19	12–16	7–13	

HARMONY OF THE FOUR GOSPELS.—*Continued.*

Incidents.	Time.	Place.	Matthew.	Mark.	Luke.	John.
141. **The last passover;** strife of the disciples.	Thursday evening, Apr. 6	The upper room in Jerusalem.	xxvi. 20	xiv. 17	xxii. 14–18, 24–30	
142. The feet washing.	" "	" "				xiii. 1-20
143. The traitor announced; Judas withdraws.	" "	" "	21-25	18-21	21-23	21-35
144. The Lord's Supper.	" "	" "	26-29	22-25	19, 20	
145. Prediction of Peter's fall, and other warnings.	" "	" "	. . .	. . .	31-38	36-38
146. Last discourses with the disciples and prayer.	" "	" "	. . .	. . .	. . .	xiv. 1-xvii. 26
147. Renewed prediction of Peter's fall and of the scattering of the disciples.	" "	On the way to Gethsemane.	30-35	26-31		
148. The agony in the garden.	" "	Gethsemane.	36-46	32-42	39-46	xviii. 1
149. The arrest of Christ; dispersion of the disciples.	Thursday night, Apr. 6-7	"	47-56	43-52	47-53	2-12
150. Preliminary examination before Annas.	" "	High-priest's palace in Jerusalem.	. . .	. . .	. . .	13, 14, 19-24
151. Examination before sanhedrin; mockery of Jesus.	" "	" "	57, 59-68	53, 55-65	63-65	
152. Peter's denials.	" "	" "	58, 69-75	54, 66-72	54-62	15-18, 25-27
153. Final condemnation of Jesus by the sanhedrin.	Early Friday morning, Apr. 7	" "	xxvii. 1	xv. 1ᵃ	66-71	
154. Jesus led to Pilate, who seeks to secure his release.	" "	The governor's residence in Jerusalem.	2, 11-14	1ᵇ-5	xxiii. 1-5	28-38
155. Jesus before Herod.	Friday, Apr. 7	Jerusalem.	. . .	. . .	6-12	
156. Pilate further seeks to release Jesus; the Jews demand Barabbas.	" "	Governor's residence	15-26ᵃ	6-15ᵃ	13-25	39, 40
157. Pilate delivers Jesus to death; scourging.	" "	" "	26ᵇ-30	15ᵇ-19	. . .	xix. 1-3
158. Pilate again seeks to release Jesus.	" "	" "	. . .	. . .	. . .	4-16ᵃ
159. Judas' remorse and suicide.	" "	Jerusalem.	3-10			
160. Jesus led to crucifixion.	" "	"	31-34	20-23	26-33ᵃ	16ᵇ, 17
161. The crucifixion.	" "	Near Jerusalem.	35-38	24-28	33ᵇ, 34, 38	18-24
162. Incidents at the cross.	" "	" "	39-49	29-36	35-37, 39-45ᵃ	25-29
163. The death of Jesus.	Friday, 3. P. M., Apr. 7	" "	50	37	46	30
164. Incidents following his death.	Friday, Apr. 7	Jerusalem and vicinity.	51-56	38-41	45ᵇ, 47-49	
165. Taking down from the cross; burial.	" "	Near Jerusalem.	57-61	42-47	50-56	31-42
166. The watch at the sepulcher.	. . .	" "	62-66			

The Resurrection.

Incidents.	Time.	Place.	Matthew.	Mark.	Luke.	John.
167. Visit of the women.	Sunday, Apr. 9	Jerusalem and vicinity.	xxviii. 1-10	xvi. 1-8	xxiv.1-11	
168. Visit of John and Peter; return of Mary Magdalene to sepulcher and Christ's appearance to her.	" "	" "	. . .	[xvi. 9-11]*	12	xx. 1-18
169. Report of the watch.	" "	" "	11 15			
170. Interview with two disciples on the way to Emmaus.	" "	" "		[12, 13]*	13-35	

HARMONY OF THE FOUR GOSPELS.—*Continued.*

Incidents.	Time.	Place.	Matthew.	Mark.	Luke.	John.
171. Christ appears to the eleven Thomas being absent.	Sunday, Apr. 9	Jerusalem.	. . .	[xvi. 14]*	xxiv. 36–49	xx. 19–24
172. Christ, a week later, again appears to them, Thomas being present.	Apr. 16	"	. . .	. . .	. . .	25-29
173. Appearance to seven disciples; Peter's restoration, etc.	A. D. 30	Sea of Galilee.	. . .	. . .	. . .	xxi. 1–23
174. The great commission. See 1 Cor. xv. 6.	" "	Mountain in Galilee.	xxviii. 16–20	[15–18]*		
175. The ascension. See Acts. i. 1–11.	May 18, A. D. 30	Mount of Olives toward Bethany.	. . .	[19, 20]*	50–53	
176. St. John's closing words.	. . .	. . . . . .	. . .	. . .	. . .	xx. 30, 31; xxi. 24, 25

* The last twelve verses of Mark are in R. V. spaced from the preceding because of doubt whether they originally formed part of Mark's Gospel.

                                             G. T. P.

INDEX FOR FINDING ANY PASSAGE IN THE HARMONY.

Matthew.

Chapter and Verse.		Section.	Chapter and Verse.		Section.	Chapter and Verse.		Section.
i.	1–17	3	xii.	14–21	48	xxi.	20–22	131
	18–23	9		22–37	57		23–xxii. 14	132
	24–25	10		38–45	58	xxii.	15–46	133
ii.	1–12	15		46–50	59	xxiii.	1–39	134
	13–15	16	xiii.	1–53	63	xxiv.	1–31	137
	16–18	17		54–58	71		32–xxv. 46	138
	19–23	18	xiv.	1, 2	73	xxvi.	1–5	139
iii.	1–12	20		3–5	34		6–13	128
	13–17	21		6–12	73		14–16	139
iv.	1–11	22		13–21	74		17–19	140
	12–17	35		22–33	75		20	141
	18–22	37		34–36	76		21–25	143
	23–25	41	xv.	1–20	78		26–29	144
v.	1–viii. 1	50		21–28	79		30–35	147
viii.	2–4	42		29–31	80		36–46	148
	5–13	51		32–38	81		47–56	149
	14, 15	39		39–xvi. 4	82		57	151
	16, 17	40	xvi.	5–12	83		58	152
	18–22	64		13–20	85		59–68	151
	23–27	65		21–28	86		69–75	152
	28–34	66	xvii.	1–13	87	xxvii.	1	153
ix.	1–8	43		14–21	88		2	154
	9–13	44		22, 23	89		3–10	159
	14–17	67		24–27	90		11–14	154
	18–26	68	xviii.	1–35	91		15–26ᵃ	156
	27–31	69	xix.	1ᵃ	92		26ᵇ–30	157
	32–34	70		1ᵇ, 2	102		31–34	160
	35–x. 1	72		3–12	118		35–38	161
x.	2–4	49		13–15	119		39–49	162
	5–xi. 1	72		16–30	120		50	163
xi.	1	52	xx.	1–16	121		51–56	164
	2–19	54		17–19	122		57–61	165
	20–24	93		20–28	123		62–66	166
	25–30	97		29–34	124	xxviii.	1–10	167
xii.	1–8	46	xxi.	1–11	129		11–15	169
	9–13	47		12–19	130		16–20	174

Mark.

Chapter and Verse.		Section.	Chapter and Verse.		Section.	Chapter and Verse.		Section.
i.	1–8	20	i.	29–31	39	ii.	18–22	67
	9–11	21		32–34	40		23–28	46
	12, 13	22		35–39	41	iii.	1–6	47
	14, 15	35		40–45	42		7–12	48
	16–20	37	ii.	1–12	43		13–19	49
	21–28	38		13–17	44		20–30	57

INDEX FOR FINDING ANY PASSAGE IN THE HARMONY.—*Continued.*

Chapter and Verse.		Section.	Chapter and Verse.		Section.	Chapter and Verse.		Section.
iii.	31–35	59	ix.	33–50	91	xiv.	22–25	144
iv.	1–34	63	x.	1ᵃ	92		26–31	147
	35–41	65		1ᵇ	102		32–42	148
v.	1–20	66		2–12	118		43–52	149
	21–43	68		13–16	119		53	151
vi.	1–6ᵃ	71		17–31	120		54	152
	6ᵇ–13	72		32–34	122		55–65	151
	14–16	73		35–45	123		66–72	152
	17–20	34		46–52	124	xv.	1ᵃ	153
	21–29	73	xi.	1–11	129		1ᵇ–5	154
	30–44	74		12–19	130		6–15ᵃ	156
	45–52	75		20–25[26]	131		15ᵇ–19	157
	53–56	76		27–xii. 12	132		20–23	160
vii.	1–23	78	xii.	13–37	133		24–28	161
	24–30	79		38–40	134		29–36	162
	31–37	80		41–44	135		37	163
viii.	1–9	81	xiii.	1–27	137		38–41	164
	10–12	82		28–37	138		42–47	165
	13–21	83	xiv.	1, 2	139	xvi.	1–8	167
	22–26	84		3–9	128		9–11	168
	27–30	85		10, 11	139		12, 13	170
	31–ix. 1	86		12–16	140		14	171
ix.	2–13	87		17	141		15–18	174
	14–29	88		18–21	143		19, 20	175
	30–32	89						

Luke.

Chapter and Verse.		Section.	Chapter and Verse.		Section.	Chapter and Verse.		Section.
i.	1–4	1	viii.	26–40	66	xviii.	31–34	122
	5–25	4		41–56	68		35–43	124
	26–38	5	ix.	1–6	72	xix.	1–10	125
	39–56	6		7–9	73		11–28	126
	57, 58	7		10–17	74		29–44	129
	59–79	8		18–21	85		45–48	130
	80	19		22–27	86	xx.	1–19	132
ii.	1–7	10		28–36	87		20–44	133
	8–14	11		37–43ᵃ	88		45–47	134
	15–20	12		43ᵇ–45	89	xxi.	1–4	135
	21	13		46–50	91		5–28	137
	22–38	14		51–56	92		29–36	138
	39	18		57–62	64		37, 38	130
	40–52	19	x.	1–16	93	xxii.	1–6	139
iii.	1–18	20		17–24	97		7–13	140
	19, 20	34		25–37	98		14–18	141
	21–23ᵃ	21		38–42	99		19, 20	144
	23ᵇ–38	3	xi.	1–13	100		21–23	143
iv.	1–13	22		14, 15	57		24–30	141
	14, 15	35		16	58		31–38	145
	16–30	36		17–23	57		39–46	148
	31–37	38		24–26	58		47–53	149
	38, 39	39		27, 28	59		54–62	152
	40, 41	40		29–36	58		63–65	151
	42–44	41		37–54	60		66–71	153
v.	1–11	37	xii.	1–59	61	xxiii.	1–5	154
	12–16	42	xiii.	1–5	62		6–12	155
	17–26	43		6–9	103		13–25	156
	27–32	44		10–17	104		26–33ᵃ	160
	33–39	67		18–21	63		33ᵇ–34	161
vi.	1–5	46		22–35	105		35–37	162
	6–11	47	xiv.	1–24	106		38	161
	12–16	49		25–35	107		39–45ᵃ	162
	17–19	48	xv.	1–32	108		45ᵇ	164
	20–49	50	xvi.	1–13	109		46	163
vii.	1–10	51		14–31	110		47–49	164
	11–17	53	xvii.	1–10	111		50–56	165
	18–35	54		11–19	112	xxiv.	1–11	167
	36–50	55		20–37	113		12	168
viii.	1–3	56	xviii.	1–8	114		13–35	170
	4–18	63		9–14	115		36–49	171
	19–21	59		15–17	119		50–53	175
	22–25	65		18–30	120			

INDEX FOR FINDING ANY PASSAGE IN THE HARMONY.—*Continued.*

John.

Chapter and Verse.		Section.	Chapter and Verse.		Section.	Chapter and Verse.		Section.
i.	1–18	2	vii.	2–52	94	xviii.	15–18	152
	19–28	20		53–viii. 11	95		19–24	150
	29–34	21	viii.	12–59	96		25–27	152
	35–42	23	ix.	1–x. 38	101		28–38	154
	43–51	24	x.	39–42	102		39, 40	156
ii.	1–11	25	xi.	1–46	116	xix.	1–3	157
	12	26		47–54	117		4–16ᵃ	158
	13–25	27		55–xii. 1	127		16ᵇ, 17	160
iii.	1–21	28	xii.	2–11	128		18–24	161
	22	29		12–19	129		25–29	162
	23–36	30		20–50	136		30	163
iv.	1–3	31	xiii.	1–20	142		31–42	165
	4–42	32		21–35	143	xx.	1–18	168
	43–54	33		36–38	145		19–24	171
v.	1–47	45	xiv.	1–xvii. 26	146		25–29	172
vi.	1–14	74	xviii.	1	148		30, 31	176
	15–21	75		2–12	149	xxi.	1–23	173
	22–71	77		13, 14	150		24–25	176
vii.	1	80						

Gourd.

The rendering of the Hebrew *Ḳiḳayon* in Jonah iv. 6, 7. 9, 10, the margin of the R. V. substituting Palma Christi. The plant so designated grew up in a night, sheltering the prophet Jonah from the fierce heat of the Ninevite sun; but its decay was as rapid as its growth. The Septuagint translates the Hebrew word by the Greek *kolokunthē*, meaning the pumpkin (*Cucurbita pepo*), which may be considered the type of the gourd family (*Cucurbitaceæ*). A native of Astrakhan, along the northwestern coast of the Caspian Sea, it may well have been introduced into the Ninevite region before the time of Jonah. It is in favor of the identification that it is a plant of rapid growth. But the Hebrew *kikayon* is very like the Græco-Egyptian *kiki*, which means the castor-oil plant (*Ricinus communis*). This is sometimes called Palma Christi (Christ's palm). It is not, however, a palm, but a euphorbiaceous plant, like the little milky weeds called spurges. It is a native of India, but was cultivated in southern Asia and Egypt (Herod. ii. 94). It attains a height of from 8 to 10 feet, growing to a considerable height in a few days. The stem is purplish-red and covered with a pearl-blue bloom, the leaves are peltate and palmate, the flowers are in racemes, the seed vessel has three two-valved cells, each one-seeded. If this was the plant which shaded Jonah, its rapid growth was miraculous.

Gourd, Wild.

The rendering of the Hebrew word *Paḳku'oth*, splitters, bursters (2 Kin. iv. 39). It is the fruit of a wild vine growing in Palestine, which flourishes when other vegetation is dead or dying through excessive drought. A son of the prophets gathered a lapful of the fruit near Jericho, and put them into a pot to be cooked, but the moment the pottage of which they constituted the chief ingredient was put to the mouth the taste betrayed that there was death in the pot; in other words, that the fruits gathered were poisonous (38–41). The plant was pretty clearly one or other of two species of the gourd order, the colocynth, or the squirting cucumber, probably the former. The colocynth (*Citrullus colocynthis*) is a prostrate gourd-like plant with tendrils, growing in southern Spain, in northern, eastern, and southern Africa, in Arabia, India, etc. In Palestine it is wild on the maritime plain and in the Jordan valley, in the latter of which places the prophet found his wild gourd or wild vine. It may be seen of a lovely emerald green when all vegetation near has withered under the fiery hot wind of summer. If the traveler pluck the smooth gourd-like fruits and cut them across with his penknife, he will find that they both look and smell like the cucumber. If then he put them to his lips, he will feel as if he had touched fire. The colocynth is a valuable but dangerous medicine. The other claimant, the squirting cucumber (*Ecballium agreste*, formerly *Momordica elaterium*), also a gourd-like plant with tendrils, has prickly fruits, which, when it is ripe and the stalk is loosened, burst and squirt forth their poisonous pulp, a phenomenon which would quite agree with the etymology of the word. The squirting cucumber grows in waste places and by the roadside throughout Palestine, and its unfitness for food would probably be known to the young companion of Elisha.

Gov′ern-or.

One who governs a land by authority of a supreme ruler to whom he is subordinate. Joseph when prime minister of Egypt was called its governor (Gen. xlii. 6; xlv. 26). When Nebuchadnezzar, after capturing Jerusalem, departed, he left a governor, Gedaliah, behind, to rule the conquered people (Jer. xl. 5: xli. 2, etc.). After the captivity, the Israelites were ruled by Persian governors; Zerubbabel, Nehemiah, and others, though

Top, right: Ivory mirror handle from Cyprus. A hero is shown slaying a crested griffin. This piece dates from the twelfth century B.C.

Top, left: Ruins at ancient Corinth. The archaic temple of Apollo can be seen on the horizon.

Opposite: A punched electrum dump from Lydia. Dating back to the seventh century B.C., this is a fine example of one of the earliest coins.

Bottom, left: Black-figure ware vase from Athens. Theseus is depicted cutting off the head of the minotaur.

Bottom, right: This thirteenth century B.C. composition of an old woman, a young woman, and a little boy has been called "the finest Mycenaean carved ivory yet found at any site."

THE GOLDEN AGE OF GREECE

Top, left: This golden cup was uncovered from Mycenae, a city about fourteen miles southwest of Corinth.

Top, right: The Areopagus (Mars Hill) served as a meeting place of the court and council of Athens. Sixteen steps lead to the top. To the right of these affixed to the rock at ground level is a bronze plate bearing the Greek text of Paul's speech to the Areopagus.

Opposite: Ruins of the Parthenon at Athens. Bottom, left. Bronze statue of Poseidon (Zeus) dating back to 460 B.C.

Bottom, right: Ruins of the grand temple of Apollo at Delphi.

Jews by birth, being Persian officials (Neh. v. 14, 18; Hag. i. 14). Pontius Pilate was governor of Judæa when our Lord was crucified, and is so called (Mat. xxviii. 14), though his specific Roman title was procurator (q.v.).

For governor of a feast, see RULER.

Go'zan.

A town and district in Mesopotamia on the river Habor (2 Kin. xvii. 6; xviii. 11; xix. 12; 1 Chron. v. 26; Is. xxxvii. 12). In an Assyrian inscription the town Gozan is associated with Nisibis. Gozan is probably the Gauzanitis of Ptolemy, a province of Mesopotamia, on the upper reaches of the Khabour river, and along the southern slopes of mount Masius. It is unnecessary to follow Ewald, who, governed by 1 Chron. v. 26, thought that the river of Gozan was distinguished from the Habor, and found it in the Ozan, which empties into the Caspian Sea near Resht, and is supposed to have formed the northern boundary of Media. Ptolemy mentions a town of Media called Gauzania in its vicinity.

Grape. See VINE.

Grass.

A plant belonging to the endogenous order *Graminaceæ*, of which the ordinary grasses growing in fields, or the cultivated cereals, may be considered as typical representatives. Popularly, the term grass is extended to many other endogenous plants, and even to various exogens, especially those possessing linear leaves. This does not materially differ from the meaning of the word grass in the book of Genesis. In chap. i. 11, 12 the vegetable kingdom is divided into three great classes: grass, herbs, and trees. The word grass is used in a more limited sense when man's brief life on earth is compared to grass, which in the morning flourishes and in the evening is cut down and withers (Ps. ciii. 15; cp. also xxxvii. 2; xc. 5; xcii. 7; cii. 11; Is. xl. 6, 7; Mat. vi. 30; Luke xii. 28).

Grass'hop-per.

1. The rendering of the Hebrew *'Arbeh*, the numerous or gregarious, in A. V. of Judg. vi. 5; vii. 12; Job xxxix. 20; Jer. xlvi. 23. It is undoubtedly the migratory locust, as the R. V. makes it, and as even the A. V. has it in Ex. x. 4; Joel i. 4. See LOCUST.

2. The rendering of the Hebrew *Ḥagab* in Lev. xi. 22; Num. xiii. 33; Ecc. xii. 5; Is. xl. 22. It is very small (Num. xiii. 33) and voracious (2 Chron. vii. 13, where it is rendered locust). It perhaps derived its name from its covering the ground or hiding the sun. On the margin of Lev. xi. 22, R. V., it is admitted that it is unknown whether the animal was a grasshopper or a locust. The grasshopper family, now called *Acridiidæ*, consists of leaping orthopterous insects, with four-jointed tarsi, wing cases in repose placed like the two sloping sides of a roof, and long, tapering antennæ. The type is the great English grasshopper (*Locusta viridissima*).

3. The rendering of the Hebrew *Gob* and *Gobay*, creeper from the earth (Nah. iii. 17). It devours the grass (Amos vii. 1, where R. V. renders locust). It was probably an insect of the locust family; but of which species is unknown.

Grave.

The cavity in the ground in which a body is interred. The Jews were sometimes buried in graves dug in the earth (Tobit viii. 9, 18), but more commonly in caves scooped out in rocks or naturally existing (Gen. xxiii. 9; Mat. xxvii. 60; John xi. 38). See SEPULCHER.

Grav-en Im'age.

An image of wood, stone, or metal fashioned by means of a sharp cutting instrument as distinguished from one cast in a mould (Is. xxx. 22; xliv. 16, 17; xlv. 20; cp. Hab. ii. 18, 19). Sometimes, however, the image was first cast and then finished by the graver (Is. xl. 19; xliv. 10). Graven images were in use among the Canaanites before the Israelites entered the country (Deut. vii. 5; xii. 3). They were also used in Babylon and elsewhere (Jer. l. 38; li. 47, 52). The second commandment expressly forbade the people of God to make them (Ex. xx. 4; Deut. v. 8; cp. also Lev. xxvi. 1; Deut. xxvii. 15; Is. xliv. 9; Jer. x. 14; li. 17).

Greaves. See ARMOR.

Gre'cians.

1. The people of Greece (Joel iii. 6).

2. Jews who spoke Greek as distinguished from those who used Aramaic, which in N. T. times was popularly called by the Jews Hebrew (Acts vi. 1 and ix. 29, in R. V. Grecian Jews, and xi. 20, A. V. and margin of R. V.). See HELLENIST.

Greece, in A. V. of Daniel Gre'ci-a [from *Graikoi*, an old name of a tribe in Epirus, and of the Greeks generally. It fell into disuse, Hellenes taking its place, but it was revived by Sophocles].

A small but highly celebrated country in the southeast of Europe. Its northern limit was never perfectly defined; it may, however, be placed at the Olympian chain of mountains. On the south it was bounded by the Mediterranean; on the east by the Ægean Sea, now the Archipelago; and on the west by the Ionian Sea, now regarded as part of the Mediterranean; and the Adriatic Sea, now the gulf of Venice. Its position during the time when the Mediterranean was the highway of civilization gave it unequaled advantages, which it was not slow to seize.

The authentic history of Greece with its first written records dates from the first Olympiad, 776 B. C. Previous to that time, and including the period known as the heroic age, history is so mingled with legend that it is difficult to separate truth from myth. It seems certain, however, that the Greeks were descended from four tribes, which in turn claimed descent from a common ancestor, Hellen. Of these tribes, the Æolians and the Achæans played a prominent part during the heroic age, Homer sometimes speaking of the whole Greek people as Achæans. The other two tribes, the Dorians and the Ionians, became more important in historic times, the Athenians and the Spartans being descended from them respectively. The early historic period, from 776 B. C. to 500 B. C., may be regarded as a period of individual growth by the different states comprising the nation. These states were theoretically independent of each other, but were united by a common language and literature, by national games, and a general national development. There were also frequent though changing political alliances. During this period the foundations of Grecian architecture, art, literature, and philosophy were laid. Greece was early within the geographical knowledge of the Hebrews, who called it Javan, that is Ionia (Gen. x. 4) ; but it was known merely as a country at the ends of the earth (Is. lxvi. 19 ; Ezek. xxvii. 13 ; Joel iii. 6). About the year 500 B. C. Greece came into prominent notice on account of her struggle with Persia, at that time the great world-power. As early as 546 Cyrus captured Sardis, the capital of Lydia. The fall of this city was followed by the subjection of the Greek cities of Asia to the Persian yoke. The Hellespont was crossed by the Persians in the reign of Darius, and Macedonia submitted in 510. But the Greek cities of Asia rose and maintained determined revolt against their conquerors during the years 500 to 495 ; and the Greeks of Europe defeated the Persians at Marathon in 490, and, after suffering reverses at Thermopylæ, inflicted crushing defeats upon them at Salamis in 480, and at Platæa and Mycale in 479. The struggle with Persia resulted in drawing the entire nation together under the leadership of one state. The first state to attain this supremacy was Athens. She held the leadership for 70 years, but during the last 28 years of that time the energies of the nation were used in carrying on the Peloponnesian war. This war, which began in a quarrel between Corinth and her colonies, finally drew into the struggle the whole naval and military strength of the nation, led on one side by Sparta and on the other by Athens. The war resulted in the downfall of the Athenian power. Then followed the period of the Spartan supremacy, followed in turn by the Theban supremacy, which lasted until 338 B. C., when all Greece fell under the power of Philip of Macedon, and became thenceforth a part of the Macedonian empire. It is under the rule of Alexander the Great that Greece comes into direct contact for the first time with Judæa. On his march to Persia Alexander passed through Judæa, which fell into his hands without a struggle. See ALEXANDER. From this time Grecian influence spread rapidly and took firm hold in the countries situated around the eastern end of the Mediterranean Sea. Even after the Roman conquest the influence of the Greek language, culture, and philosophy remained paramount, and even influenced the Jewish religion itself. In the time of Christ the Greek language was spoken throughout the civilized world. After the death of Alexander, his empire fell into the hands of his generals, who parceled it out among themselves. At first Greece proper was held in the name of his infant son, but soon he, as well as all members of Alexander's family, were put to death, and the country became the prey of anyone strong enough to take it, until it finally fell under the dominion of Rome. The last struggle against Rome resulted in the battle of Leucopatra, 146 B. C., and shortly after Greece was declared a Roman province. The division of the Roman power into the Eastern and Western empires revived Greek influence for a time. The Eastern empire survived long after the Western empire fell, but finally it came to an end in the capture of Constantinople by the Turks in 1453. Some of the apostle Paul's most earnest labors took place in Greece, notably in Athens and Corinth, besides his general travels through Achaia, the name at that time for ancient Greece.

Greek.

1. A native of Greece, or one of the Greek race (Acts xvi. 1 ; xvii. 4). When Jew and Greek are contrasted in the N. T., the term Greek is used for a foreigner in general, the Greek being looked on as the highest type of gentile (Rom. i. 14, 16 ; x. 12).

2. After the Macedonian conquest of the East and the establishment of the kingdoms of Syria and Egypt, the name Greek was applied, especially by Orientals, to all who spoke the Greek language in ordinary life and enjoyed the privileges of Greek settlers in the kingdoms ruled by Alexander's successors. The Greeks who wished to see Jesus (John xii. 20) were foreigners, but it is not certain that they were of Greek race.

3. The language of the ancient Greeks. It belongs to the Aryan family of tongues, having affinities with the Sanscrit, with Latin, and nearly all the languages of western Europe. It excels in power of full and precise expression. Jews who spoke Greek (Acts xxi. 37 ; Rev. ix. 11) used the common idiom employed by the nations of their day. The O. T. was translated into Greek before the advent of Christ (see SEPTUAGINT) ; the N. T. (Matthew possibly excepted) was composed in Greek from the first.

Grey'hound.

The rendering of the Hebrew *Zarzir*, well girt or well knit in the loins, in Prov. xxx. 31. The greyhound is figured on the Assyrian monuments. The word may, however, denote the war horse (R. V. margin) as ornamented with girths and buckles about the loins; or the starling, as the corresponding word in Arabic, Syriac, and post-biblical Hebrew, denotes.

Grind'ing. See MILL.

Grove.

A group or clump of trees. In the A. V. it is uniformly a mistranslation of:—

1. The Hebrew word *'Eshel* (Gen. xxi. 33; cp. 1 Sam. xxii. 6). The R. V. renders this a tamarisk tree. See TAMARISK.

2. The Hebrew word *'asherah*, with its two plurals *'asherim* and *'asheroth* (Ex. xxxiv. 13, and elsewhere except Gen. xxi. 33). See ASHERAH.

Guard.

In Oriental countries, where the king, as a rule, is despotic, measures which give offense excite hostility against him personally. This necessitates that he should be continually defended by a bodyguard; and such a military organization is more than useless unless complete dependence can be placed on its fidelity. Hence, service in the bodyguard is considered specially honorable, and its captain is a high officer. Such an appointment was filled by Potiphar (Gen. xxxvii. 36; xli. 12), by Benaiah (2 Sam. xxiii. 22, 23; 1 Chron. xviii. 17), by Nebuzaradan (2 Kin. xxv. 8; Jer. xxxix. 9, 10), by Arioch (Dan. ii. 14), and others. The captain of the guard and his men were often employed to inflict capital punishment on political or other offenders. In Mark vi. 27, the Greek word is *spekoulatōr*, spy. Such spies constituted a division in each Roman legion, and under the empire acted as the bodyguard of a general and were employed as messengers and to seek out persons proscribed or sentenced to death.

Gud'go-dah. See HOR-HAGGIDGAD.

Guest.

One temporarily entertained in the house of another, even though it be for a few hours only at a feast (1 Kin. i. 41; Zeph. i. 7; Mat. xxii. 10, 11). Complete strangers were received as guests and shown great consideration (Gen. xviii. 1–8; xix. 3; Ex. ii. 20; Judg. xiii. 15; xix. 20–24; Job xxxi. 32). Important houses had a guest-chamber (Mark xiv. 14; Luke xxii. 11; cp. also 2 Kin. iv. 10), and at Jerusalem these rooms were freely placed at the disposal of Jews visiting the city at the annual festivals (Aboth, 34). Hospitality is enjoined in the N. T. (Heb. xiii. 2; cp. Mat. xxv. 43). Ordinary morality dictates that one should not be guest in the house of a notorious sinner; but prominent Pharisees went so far as to apply this principle indiscriminately to the acceptance of hospitality from people of the publican class (Luke v. 27–32; xix. 7).

Guilt' Of'fer-ing. See OFFERINGS.

Gu'ni [painted with colors].

1. A son of Naphtali, and founder of a tribal family (Gen. xlvi. 24; Num. xxvi. 48; 1 Chron. vii. 13).

2. A Gadite (1 Chron. v. 15).

Gur [lion's whelp or other young animal].

An ascent near Ibleam, where Ahaziah, king of Judah, was smitten by order of Jehu and mortally wounded (2 Kin. ix. 27). Exact situation unknown.

Gur-ba'al [sojourn of Baal].

A place inhabited by Arabs (2 Chron. xxvi. 7); probably in the desert to the southeast of Judah.

Gym-na'si-um, in A. V. **Place of Exercise.**

A public place in Jerusalem for athletic exercise and exhibitions, below the western cloister of the temple (War iv. 9, 12; vi. 3, 2; 6, 2), below the palace of the Asmonæans (Antiq. xx. 8, 11; War ii. 16, 3), below the citadel or acropolis (2 Mac. iv. 12, 27; not the Syrian fortress called the Acra, which was erected later, 1 Mac. i. 33). It was situated near the council house, by the first or innermost wall, and at the end of the bridge which led from the temple across the Tyropœon valley (War v. 4, 2; cp. vi. 6, 2). It was erected by hellenizing Jews, under the leadership of Jason, by permission of Antiochus Epiphanes (1 Mac. i. 10, 14; 2 Mac. iv. 7 seq.). The essential features of a gymnasium were: 1. An open court for boxing, wrestling, pitching quoits, and throwing the javelin (2 Mac. iv. 14, palæstra, discus); 2. A stadium or course for the foot race; 3. A colonnade for a place of recreation and for athletic exercises in winter (Antiq. and War, passim xystos); 4. A bathroom. The gymnasium at Jerusalem was condemned by strict Jews because it introduced heathen customs; led Jewish youth to wear the hat of Hermes, to exercise stark naked in public, and to be ashamed of the mark of their religion; and infected even the priests and caused them to neglect their official duties (1 Mac. i. 14, 15; 2 Mac. iv. 13–17). It existed until the overthrow of the city by Titus; and was not only resorted to for athletic sports, but was also occasionally used for popular assemblies (War ii. 16, 3).

H

Ha-a-hash'ta-ri [the Ahashtarite].

A Hezronite, son of Ashhur (1 Chron. iv. 6; cp. ii. 24).

Ha-ba'iah, and **Hobaiah** [Jehovah hath hidden]. The difference between the two forms of the name is merely one of traditional pronunciation.

Father of certain Jews claiming sacerdotal descent. Their names not being found in the register, they were put out of the priesthood (Ezra ii. 61; Neh. vii. 63; cp. R. V.).

Ha-bak'kuk [embrace, or perhaps the name of a garden plant].

A prophet of Judah. It is inferred from his psalm (chap. iii.) and from the directions to the chief musician (19) that he was of the tribe of Levi and one of the temple singers; but the evidence proves nothing (cp. the titles of Pss. iii. and lii.).

The book of Habakkuk is the eighth of the minor prophets. It consists of 1. A first complaint: his cry to God against violence and wickedness is unheeded (i. 2–4); iniquity is triumphant. The Lord's response: God is raising up the Chaldeans (5–10), but as guilty the Chaldeans shall be punished (11). 2. A second complaint: God's kingdom indeed shall not perish, and the Chaldeans shall be visited with judgment (12); but yet a moral problem remains: God allows the Chaldeans to waste and destroy those who are more righteous than they. Shall this go on (13–17)? The Lord's response: the Chaldeans are puffed up and unrighteous [that fact to the eye of faith, is sufficient; it dooms them (cp. i. 11; Is. x. 12–16), and dooms all like them]; but the just shall live by his faith (Hab. ii. 1–4). That truth, rightly understood, solves the problem. Moreover, faith in the certainty that God will punish wickedness enables the prophet to pronounce five woes against the great world-power for five forms of wickedness (5–20). 3. A prayer of praise (iii. 1–19), in which after an invocation and a petition that God in wrath remember mercy (2), the prophet describes God's appearance in majesty and the ensuing consternation of his enemies (3–15), and expresses the quiet confidence of faith in God (16–19).

The book is not dated, but was evidently a production of the Chaldean period. 1. The temple is still standing (ii. 20), and musical service is conducted (iii. 19). 2. The rise of the Chaldeans to a formidable power among the nations occurs during that generation (i. 5, 6), and the slaying of the nations by the Chaldeans had already begun (6, 17).

The Chaldeans had been long known to the Hebrews. They attracted renewed attention by their successful revolt from the Assyrians in 625 B. C.; and they began their great career of subjugation and attained to the leading place among the powers of the world on the fall of Nineveh in 612 or 606 B. C., and by their victory over the Egyptians at Carchemish in 605. Most critics accordingly date the prophecy in the early part of Jehoiakim's reign, about the time of the battle of Carchemish. It may, however, antedate the fall of Nineveh by some years; for not only had the Chaldeans bestirred themselves in 625 B. C. but military events before the collapse of Nineveh indicated the Chaldeans as the coming world-power; their subjugation of Judah had long been predicted by the Hebrew prophets (Mic. iv. 10; Is. xi. 11; xxxix. 6, 7); and their fierce, warlike character, their habitual cruelty and rapacity in war, and their method of battle, were known to all nations. There was thus, even before their victory at Carchemish, full justification for the declarations made in i. 5–10.

If the prophecy was uttered before the Chaldean success at Carchemish, Habakkuk in i. 2–4 is lamenting the carnival of wickedness which he witnessed in Israel or in the world at large.

Hab-az-zi-ni′ah, in A. V. **Habaziniah**.
A Rechabite who lived long before Jeremiah (Jer. xxxv. 3).

Ha-ber′ge-on [a small hauberk].
A coat of mail to defend the breast and neck (2 Chron. xxvi. 14; Neh. iv. 16; in R. V. coat of mail). In Job xli. 26, R. V. on good grounds substitutes pointed shaft in the text, and places coat of mail in the margin. Habergeon, or coat of mail. is also used to translate a different Hebrew word of uncertain meaning in Ex. xxviii. 32; xxxix. 23.

Ha′bor [joining to].
A river of Mesopotamia to which captives from the ten tribes were carried (2 Kin. xvii. 6; xviii. 11; 1 Chron. v. 26). It has been identified as the Khabour, which, flowing southward through Mesopotamia, after a course of 190 miles, falls into the eastern side of the Euphrates at Kerkisiyeh, the ancient Circesium. Those who regard Gozan as a river identify the Habor with that eastern branch of the Tigris above Nineveh which bears the same name.

Hac-a-li′ah, in A. V. **Hachaliah** [Jehovah is dark (from displeasure)].
The father of Nehemiah (Neh. i. 1).

Hach′i-lah [dark, gloomy].
A hill in the wilderness of Ziph (1 Sam. xxvi. 1–3), southeast of Hebron, and on the south of the desert, not far from Maon (xxiii. 19, 24–26). David concealed himself there whilst fleeing from Saul, and there Saul afterwards encamped when engaged in his pursuit.

Hach′mo-ni [wise].
The founder of the Hachmonite family, the members of which are called sons of Hachmoni (1 Chron. xi. 11; xxvii. 32), or simply Hachmonites (cp. 2 Sam. xxiii. 8).

Ha′dad, I. [sharpness, fierceness].
A son of Ishmael (Gen. xxv. 15, in A. V., following present Hebrew text, Hadar; 1 Chron. i. 30).

Ha′dad, II.
1. A deity worshiped by the Aramæans. It occurs in proper names, as in Benhadad, Hadadezer. The Assyrian scribes identified Hadad with their own weather-god Ramman, i. e., Rimmon.
2. A king of Edom, son of Bedad, and of the city of Avith. He smote Midian in the field of Moab (Gen. xxxvi. 35, 36; 1 Chron. i. 46, 47).
3. A king of Edom, whose city was Pau or Pai (1 Chron. i. 50). In Gen. xxxvi. 39 he is called Hadar. See DALETH.
4. An Edomite prince, who escaped from his country when Joab, at the head of the Israelite army, was engaged for six months

in the cruel task of cutting off every male in Edom. Hadad was then a little child, and was taken by his guardians to Egypt. The king of Egypt received him with much kindness, assigned him a house and land, provided him with food, and gave him an Egyptian princess, sister of the queen, to wife. But after the death of David and Joab, the great foes of his race, he returned to Edom and became an adversary to Solomon (1 Kin. xi. 14-22).

Ha-dad-e'zer [Hadad is a help].
Son of Rehob and king of Zobah, in Syria (2 Sam. viii. 3). He is frequently called Hadarezer, the latter form being doubtless an early misreading of daleth; see DALETH. When going to recover his border at the river Euphrates, he was met and defeated by king David. The Syrians of Damascus, who afterwards arrived to assist him, shared his fate. From Betah and Berothai, cities of Hadadezer, David took much brass or copper. Toi, king of Hamath, probably a Hittite by race, had formerly been at war with Hadadezer, and he congratulated David on his victory (2 Sam. viii. 3-13; 1 Chron. xviii. 3-10). Hadadezer renewed the war with David, became confederate with the Ammonites, and sent his army, led by his general, Shobach, to try another engagement with their common foe. David was victorious, and Shobach was among the slain. The dependent kings who had served Hadadezer now made peace with David, and Hadadezer is heard of no more (2 Sam. x. 6-19; 1 Chron. xix. 16-19).

Ha-dad-rim'mon [Hadad and Rimmon, two Syrian divinities]. Rimmon means also a pomegranate.
A city in the plain of Jezreel, near Megiddo (Zech. xii. 11). Jerome says that it was the place in his day called Maximianopolis. This is now called Rummâneh, and is about a mile northwest by west of Taanach.

Ha'dar. See HADAD, I. and II.

Ha-dar-e'zer. See HADADEZER.

Had'a-shah [new].
A village in or near the lowland of Judah (Josh. xv. 37). It has not been identified.

Ha-das'sah [a myrtle].
The original Jewish name of queen Esther (Esth. ii. 7). The name has a certain similarity in sound to that of Atossa, who was the mother of Xerxes (Herod. vii. 2). But the women were different. Esther was his queen.

Ha-dat'tah. See HAZOR-HADATTAH.

Ha'des. See HELL, 1.

Ha'did [sharp, pointed; a point].
A town of Benjamin, mentioned in connection with Lod, i. e. Lydda (Ezra ii. 33; Neh. xi. 34); perhaps Huditi, referred to by Thothmes III. (Karnak list). It is commonly identified with Adida, a town built upon a hill of the Shephelah and overlooking the plain (1 Mac. xii. 38; xiii. 13; Antiq. xiii.

6, 5). Its site is located at Hadîtheh, 3 miles east of Lydda.

Had'lai [frail].
A man of Ephraim (2 Chron. xxviii. 12).

Ha-do'ram.
1. An Arabian tribe descended from Joktan (Gen. x. 27; 1 Chron. i. 21).
2. A son of the king of Hamath (1 Chron. xviii. 10). See JORAM 1.
3. An officer over Rehoboam's levy (2 Chron. x. 18). See ADONIRAM.

Ha'drach.
A country mentioned in connection with Damascus and Hamath (Zech. ix. 1), and, in Assyrian inscriptions, with Zobah also. It lay on the Orontes, south of Hamath.

Ha'gab [a locust].
Founder of a family of Nethinim (Ezra ii. 46).

Hag'a-bah or **Hagaba** [a locust].
Founder of a family of Nethinim, distinct from that of Hagab (Ezra ii. 45; Neh. vii. 48).

Ha'gar, in A. V. of N. T. both times **Agar,** in imitation of the Greek [if Hebrew, flight].
An Egyptian bondwoman of Sarah, probably obtained during Abraham's sojourn in Egypt (Gen. xvi. 1; cp. xii. 10). After Abraham had been ten years in Canaan, and the promised son had not been born to him. Sarah, now 76 years old, despaired of sharing in the promise, and proposed earthly means to secure a son to Abraham and obtain the name of mother. In accordance with a custom of the times, she gave her maid to Abraham. When Hagar perceived herself to be with child she despised her mistress; and, being treated by her harshly, fled into the wilderness. There the angel of the Lord found her at a fountain between Shur and Bered, revealed to her the future of the child she was to bear, and bade her return to her mistress. Hagar called the name of the place "the well of the living one who seeth me" (Gen. xvi. 1-16). She then returned to her mistress, and in due time gave birth to Ishmael. Some fifteen years later the youth Ishmael mocked at the child Isaac. For this offense Hagar, with a skin of water on her shoulder, and Ishmael (for form of expression cp. xliii. 15) were expelled with God's approval from the family of Abraham. They wandered in the wilderness of Beer-sheba until the water was spent. The exhausted boy whom she had been supporting she cast, as one would a sick person (Mat. xv. 30), under the shade of a bush, and sat down a bow-shot off that she might not see him die. Again the angel of the Lord intervened, directing her to a well in the vicinity, and reminding her of the promise concerning the boy. The last we hear of Hagar is her taking a wife for her son out of the land of Egypt, whence she herself had originally come (xxi. 1-21). For Gal. iv. 21-31, see ISHMAEL.

Ha-gar-ene′, Ha′gar-ite, and **Ha′ger-ite.** See HAGRITE.

Hag′ga-i [festal, perhaps as born on a festival day].

A prophet, contemporary with Zechariah Hag. i. 1 with Zech. i. 1). He prophesied after the return from Babylon. The work on the temple had ceased for 15 years, and Haggai was largely instrumental in arousing the people to proceed with the building (Ezra v. 1, 2 : vi. 14).

The book of Haggai is the tenth of the minor prophets. It consists of four prophecies delivered within the space of four months in the second year of Darius Hystaspis, 520 B. C.

1. On the first day of the 6th month the prophet reproaches those who left the temple in ruins, and built ceiled houses for themselves, and he points out that God's blessing is withholden from their ordinary labor. In consequence of this exhortation, work on the temple was resumed on the twenty-fourth day of the same month (i.).

2. In the 7th month, 21st day, he encourages those who mourn over the humble character of the new building as compared with the splendor of the old edifice. He predicts that the latter glory of the house shall be greater than the former glory, for God will shake the nations and the desirable things of all nations, their silver and gold, shall come and fill the house with glory, and God will give peace in that place (ii. 1–9 ; Heb. xii. 26–28).

3. In the 9th month, 24th day, he adds a sequel to the first prophecy. As the touch of the unclean pollutes the clean, so their former neglect of God polluted their labor and God did not bestow his blessing. But their revived zeal for God will be accompanied by fruitful seasons from the Lord (ii. 10–19).

4. On the same day he adds a sequel to the second prophecy. When the Lord shakes the nations, he will establish Zerubbabel, who represents the royal line of David (ii. 20–23).

Hag′ge-ri. See HAGRI.

Hag′gi [festal or festival of (Jehovah)].

A son of Gad, and founder of a tribal family (Gen. xlvi. 16 ; Num. xxvi. 15).

Hag-gi′ah [a festival of Jehovah].

A Levite, a descendant of Merari (1 Chron. vi. 30).

Hag′gith [festal].

One of David's wives, the mother of Adonijah (2 Sam. iii. 4 ; 1 Kin. i. 5).

Ha′gri, in A. V. **Haggeri.**

Rather an adjective than a proper name (1 Chron. xi. 38) ; see MIBHAR.

Ha′grite; in A. V. **Hagarite,** and once **Hagerite,** and once, in Ps. lxxxiii. 6, **Hagarenes,** in which passage R. V. in its text follows A. V.

A nomad people who dwelt throughout all the land east of Gilead, and were rich in camels, sheep, and asses. During the reign of Saul they were vanquished, and in a large measure destroyed, by the Israelite tribes east of the Jordan (1 Chron. v. 10, 18–22). A Hagrite had charge of David's flocks (1 Chron. xxvii. 31). They are the Agraoi of the Greek geographers. It is questionable whether their name is at all connected with the town Hejer or Hejera, in the Arabian desert near the Persian Gulf.

Ha′i. See AI.

Hail.

Small globules of ice formed of raindrops which have been carried into a cold stratum of the atmosphere. Hail falls not merely in cold and temperate climates, but in hot, nay, even in tropical latitudes, where snow and ice are not to be found, except at great elevations. When it falls in the warmer regions, it tends to be larger than in temperate countries, as raindrops also are larger. In all places two or more hailstones can unite so as to make an irregularly shaped mass of ice, which, when large, becomes formidable by the momentum with which it descends. Hail occasionally falls in Egypt (Ex. ix. 22–25) between December and April. It is more frequent in Palestine (Josh. x. 11 ; Hag. ii. 17). The area affected by a hailstorm is generally a long, narrow line, so that of two places near each other, one may be in and the other out of the storm. Thus Goshen might escape it, whilst the adjacent district of Egypt to the westward might be in its track and suffer severely (Ex. ix. 26) ; and a pursuing army might be untouched by the storm, and yet see their fleeing foes beaten down by the falling stones (Josh. x. 11).

Hair.

The natural covering and ornament of the head. In Egypt men ordinarily shaved the head, but when mourning let the hair grow (Herod. ii. 36 ; iii. 12). The Assyrians wore it long (i. 195), falling to the shoulders. The Israelites also wore it tolerably long ; but cut it to prevent its reaching an extreme length (cp. Num. vi. 5 ; 2 Sam. xiv. 26 ; Antiq. xiv. 9, 4), and the services of the barber were sometimes employed (Ezek. v. 1) ; but they were forbidden to cut off the edge of the hair from about the temples, so as to round it (Lev. xix. 27), for that was a significant heathen custom (Herod. iii. 8). Hebrew women wore the hair long (Song. vii. 5 ; Rev. ix. 8 ; cp. 1 Cor. xi. 15), binding it up or braiding it (Judith x. 3 ; xvi. 8 ; 1 Tim. ii. 9 ; 1 Pet. iii. 3). Oil was used for the hair by both men and women (Ps. xxiii. 5 ; Mat. vi. 17). Herod the Great, in order to conceal his age, dyed his hair black (Antiq. xvi. 8, 1). The priests were forbidden to make any baldness upon the head (Lev. xxi. 5), and none of the Israelites was allowed to make a baldness between the eyes for the dead (Deut. xiv. 1) ; for it was a disfigurement of the body which God had created. The captive woman who was chosen by a Hebrew for his wife, and the leper in the day of his cleansing were required to shave the head for purposes of purification (Lev. xiv. 8, 9; Deut. xxi. 12). The Nazirite also, when the time of his service was ended, shaved his head as a sign of the fulfillment of his vow (Num. vi. 18). See BEARD.

Hak′ka-tan [the small or the younger].
Father of a certain Johanan (Ezra viii. 12).

Hak′koz, in A. V. sometimes **Koz**, once **Coz**, the first syllable being omitted since it is the definite article [the thorn].

1. A descendant of Aaron. His family had grown to a father's house in the time of David and was made the seventh of the twenty-four courses into which David distributed the priests (1 Chron. xxiv. 1, 6, 10). Perhaps it was members of this family who returned from Babylon with Zerubbabel, but, failing to find their register and establish their genealogy, were put from the priesthood (Ezra ii. 61, 62; Neh. vii. 63, 64). They appear to have eventually succeeded, however, in establishing their right to the office (Neh. iii. 21; cp. Ezra viii. 33).

2. A man of Judah (1 Chron. iv. 8).

Ha-ku′pha [bent, bowed, curved].
Founder of a family of Nethinim (Ezra ii. 51; Neh. vii. 53).

Ha′lah.
A district of the Assyrian empire, to which captives from the ten tribes were carried (2 Kin. xvii. 6; xviii. 11; 1 Chron. v. 26). Probably the district known later as Chalkitis, in Mesopotamia, near Gozan, in the basin of the Habor and the Saokoras (Ptolem. v. 18, 4). Those who identify the Habor with the eastern tributary of the Tigris bearing that name are apt, however, to identify Halah with the province of Kalachene (Strabo xi. 8, 4; Ptolem. vi. 1), on the eastern side of the Tigris near Adiabene, north of Nineveh on the borders of Armenia.

Ha′lak [smooth, bare].
A mountain in the south of Palestine on the way to mount Seir (Josh. xi. 17; xii. 7). Its identity has not been established.

Half′shek-el. See MONEY, TRIBUTE.

Hal′hul [perhaps, opening].
A village in the hill country of Judah (Josh. xv. 58). The Arabs still call the village Hulhûl or Halhûl. It is 3½ miles north of Hebron. It is a place of pilgrimage, being regarded as the birthplace of the prophet Gad.

Ha′li [necklace, collar].
A village on the boundary line of Asher (Josh. xix. 25). Guérin suggests Khurbet ʼAlia, 13 miles northeast of Acre.

Hal-i-car-nas′sus.
A city of Caria, renowned as being the birthplace of Herodotus and as containing the mausoleum erected by Artemisia, which was reckoned one of the seven wonders of the world. Alexander captured and almost totally destroyed the city in 334 B. C. It continued to exist, but did not thrive. It contained a colony of Jews (1 Mac. xv. 23; Antiq. xiv. 10, 23).

Hall.
A building, or large room in a building, devoted to public use. In A. V. it denotes

1. The court of the high priest's palace (Luke xxii. 55; in the R. V. court).

2. The official residence of the provincial governor, with its court where he sat in judgment. It was called the prætorium (Mark xv. 16; also Mat. xxvii. 27; John xviii. 28, 33; xix. 9; Acts xxiii. 35, where R. V. has palace or prætorium). See PRÆTORIUM.

Hal-le-lu′jah, in A. V. of N. T. **Alleluia**, in imitation of the Greek modification [praise ye Jehovah].

A compound word used by the writers of various psalms to invite all to join them in praising Jehovah (R. V. margin of Ps. civ. 35; cv. 45; cvi. 1, 48; cxi. 1; cxii. 1; cxiii. 1, 9; cxv. 18; cxvi. 19; cxvii. 2; cxxxv. 1, 21; first and last vers. of cxlvi.–cl.; cp. A. V. margin also). From these psalms John borrowed the term Alleluia (Rev. xix. 1, 3, 4, 6).

Hal-lo′hesh, in A. V. once **Halohesh** [the enchanter, the wizard].
Father of a certain Shallum (Neh. iii. 12). With Nehemiah he or the representative of his family sealed the covenant to worship Jehovah (x. 24).

Ham, I. [meaning uncertain; if Semitic, possibly dark-skinned, or, perhaps better, hot].
The youngest son of Noah, born after the latter's five hundredth year (Gen. v. 32; vi. 10; xi. 24); cp. CHRONOLOGY I. 3. At the time of the deluge he was married, but apparently had no children (Gen. vii. 7; 1 Pet. iii. 20). On occasion of his father's drunkenness he behaved undutifully and incurred a curse to descend upon such of his posterity as exhibited like degraded character (Gen ix. 22–27). The peoples of southern Arabia, Ethiopia, Egypt, and Canaan were largely descended from Ham, and in part were made his sons by conquest and annexation (Gen. x. 6–14).

Ham, II. [Egyptian *kam*, black, so called from the color of the alluvial mud of the Nile].
Egypt. Used in the Bible only in poetry (Ps. lxxviii. 51; cv. 23, 27; cvi. 22).

Ham, III. [meaning unknown. The initial Hebrew letter is different from that in I. and II.].
A place between Ashteroth-karnaim in Bashan and the Moabite country, where Chedorlaomer defeated the Zuzim (Gen. xiv. 5; cp. Deut. ii. 10). The order of enumeration makes it probable that Ham was north of Kiriathaim and the Arnon; but Schwartz, followed by Tristram, would identify it with the ruin called Hammat, ʼAnimah or Hamei·

tât, on the east side of the Roman road, 3 miles north of Rabbath Moab.

Ha'man [old Persian *umana*, well-disposed; or name of the deity Humba, Humman (see ESTHER)].

Son of Hammedatha (Esth. iii. 1). His father bore a Persian name, but Haman was none the less an Agagite (iii. 1; ix. 24), which, if it is not a local or obscure family name, may mean that he was of Amalekite descent and of the royal family of that Arabian tribe. Exalted by the Persian king to the highest official position, he received ostentatious reverence from time-servers. But on account of his unprincipled character, perhaps also for other reasons, the Jew Mordecai deliberately withheld from him the customary signs of respect. Haman planned revenge; in his hate plotting the destruction, not of Mordecai only, but of all Jews in the empire. His plan was frustrated by Esther, prompted by Mordecai; and Haman and his sons perished (vii. 10; ix. 7–10). See ESTHER.

Ha'math, in A. V. once **Hemath** (Amos vi. 14) and once **Amathis** (1 Mac. xii. 25), [fortification, citadel].

1. A city on the Orontes, north of Hermon (Josh. xiii. 5), about 120 miles north of Damascus. It was an early settlement of the Canaanites (Gen. x. 18). Toi, its king, congratulated David on his victory over Hadadezer, their common enemy (2 Sam. viii. 9, 10; 1 Chron. xviii. 3, 9, 10). Solomon took Hamath and built store cities in the region (2 Chron. viii. 3, 4). It soon, however, reverted to its old inhabitants, but they were often harassed by the Assyrians. Jeroboam II, king of Israel, captured Damascus and Hamath, which had formerly belonged to Judah, and kept them for the ten tribes (2 Kin. xiv. 28). About this time Amos (vi. 2) called the city Hamath the great. It was again for a short time free, and relying upon Judah for aid; but it was conquered by the Assyrians (2 Kin. xviii. 34; xix. 13). After the capture of Samaria by the Assyrians, it joined with the remnant of the inhabitants of that city in revolt, 720 B. C. But the uprising was quickly suppressed by Sargon. Colonists from Hamath, who brought with them Ashima, their god, were placed by the Assyrians in Samaria (2 Kin. xvii. 24, 30), while some of the exiles of Israel seem to have been located in Hamath (Is. xi. 11). Afterwards its history becomes merged in that of Syria, and it seems to have become subordinate to Damascus (Jer. xlix. 23). Ezekiel prophesied that the restored land of Israel should still extend northward to Hamath (Ezek. xlvii. 16, 17, 20; xlviii. 1). Hamath was known as Epiphania during the period of Grecian supremacy (Antiq. i. 6, 2), but is now called Hama or Hamah.

2. The district ruled by the city (1 Mac. xii. 25). One of its towns was Riblah (2 Kin. xxiii. 33).

The entering in of Hamath, that is, to judge from the similar phrase elsewhere (Gen. xiii. 10), the neighborhood of Hamath, was regarded as the northern border of Israel (Num. xiii. 21; xxxiv. 8; 1 Kin. viii. 65). To people on the south the term may have had special meaning, and denoted the long valley of Cœlesyria, between Lebanon and Anti-Lebanon, through which the road to Hamath lay. Porter considers that it was the pass between Lebanon and the Nusairiyeh mountains, about 60 miles north of Beirut, connecting the inland region of Syria with the coast of the Mediterranean.

Ha'math-ites.

The people of Hamath (Gen. x. 18).

Ha-math-zo'bah.

The neighbor kingdoms of Hamath and Zobah, or some small place called Hamath, belonging to the Syrian kingdom Zobah. It was captured by Solomon (2 Chron. viii. 3).

Ham'math, in A. V. once **Hemath** (1 Chron. ii. 55) [warmth, hot springs].

1. A fenced city of Naphtali (Josh. xix. 35). Probably one with Hammoth-dor and Hammon, which was assigned to the Levites (xxi. 32; 1 Chron. vi. 76), and to be identified with Emmaus, a village with warm baths at a little distance from Tiberias (Antiq. xviii. 2, 3; War iv. 1, 3). It is now called Hummâm Ibrahim Basha, and is on the western shore of the sea of Galilee, about 1½ miles south of Tiberias. The water is sulphurous and medicinal.

2. The founder of the house of Rechab, a family of the Kenites (1 Chron. ii. 55). The A. V. has here Hemath.

Ham-med'a-tha.

An Agagite, father of Haman (Esth. iii. 1).

Ham'me-lech [the king].

Father of Jerahmeel (Jer. xxxvi. 26, A. V. and margin of R. V.). The word suggests, however, that Jerahmeel was of royal blood, son of the king (R. V.).

Ham'mer.

A tool, called in Hebrew *Paṭṭish*, and used for smoothing metals and for breaking rocks (Is. xli. 7; Jer. xxiii. 29). It serves as a figure for any crushing power. Babylon was the hammer of the whole earth (Jer. l. 23). God's word is like a hammer that breaketh the rock in pieces (xxiii. 29). Other names for an implement of the same class are *makkabah* and *makkebeth*, used for driving the tent pin (Judg. iv. 21), in building operations (1 Kin. vi. 7), in the manufacture of idols (Is. xliv. 12; Jer. x. 4).

Ham-miph'kad. See MIPHKAD.

Ham-mol'e-cheth, in A. V. **Hammoleketh** [the queen].

A sister of Gilead (1 Chron. vii. 18). Several tribal families of Manasseh sprang from her.

Ham'mon [warm, sunny].

1. A frontier village of Asher (Josh. xix

28). Perhaps 10 miles south of Tyre and about a mile from the beach, at 'Ain Hamûl, ¾ of a mile from Umm el-'Amûd, where, as Renan has shown, Baal Hammon was worshiped.

2. A town of Naphtali. See HAMMATH.

Ham'moth-dor [warm springs of Dor]. See HAMMATH.

Ham-mu'el, in A. V. **Hamuel** [warmth of God].

A Simeonite, son of Mishma, probably of the family of Shaul (1 Chron. iv. 26).

Ham-o'nah [abundance, multitude].

Symbolical name of the city near which Gog is to be defeated (Ezek. xxxix. 16).

Ha'mon-gog [multitude of Gog].

A name to be given to a certain valley where the hosts which Gog brings with him shall be slain and buried (Ezek. xxxix. 11, 15). Situation unknown.

Ha'mor, in A. V. of N. T. **Emmor**, an imitation of the Greek [an ass].

The prince of Shechem (Gen. xxxiv. 20; Josh. xxiv. 32; Judg. ix. 28); a Hivite, a branch of the Amorites, and a prince of that tribe, at least, in central Palestine (Gen. xxxiv. 2; xlviii. 22). His son Shechem ruined Dinah, and both father and son fell victims to the vindictiveness of her brothers Simeon and Levi (xxxiv. 1–31).

Ham'ran. See HEMDAN.

Ha-mu'el. See HAMMUEL.

Ha'mul [pitied, spared].

Younger son of Perez, and founder of a tribal family of Judah (Gen. xlvi. 12; Num. xxvi. 21; 1 Chron. ii. 5).

Ha-mu'tal [akin to dew, refreshing like dew].

Daughter of Jeremiah of Libnah, wife of king Josiah, and mother of the kings Jehoahaz and Zedekiah (2 Kin. xxiii. 31; xxiv. 18; Jer. lii. 1).

Han'a-mel, in A. V. **Ha-nam'e-el** [perhaps, God hath pitied].

Son of Shallum, and cousin of the prophet Jeremiah (Jer. xxxii. 7–15).

Ha'nan [gracious, merciful].

1. One of David's mighty men (1 Chron. xi. 43).

2. A Benjamite, son of Shashak (1 Chron. viii. 23).

3. A son of Azel, a descendant of Jonathan (1 Chron. viii. 38; ix. 44).

4. A prophet, son of Igdaliah. His sons had a chamber in the temple (Jer. xxxv. 4).

5. Founder of a family of Nethinim, members of which returned from Babylon with Zerubbabel (Ezra ii. 46; Neh. vii. 49).

6. A man, probably a Levite, whom Ezra employed with others to make the people understand the law (Neh. viii. 7). He seems to have sealed the covenant (x. 10).

7 and 8. Two chiefs of the people, who also sealed the covenant (22, 26).

9. A son of Zaccur, appointed assistant treasurer by Nehemiah (Neh. xiii. 13).

Han'a-nel, in A. V. **Ha-nan'e-el** [God hath been gracious].

A tower at Jerusalem (Jer. xxxi. 38; Zech. xiv. 10), near the sheep-gate and the tower of Meah (Neh. iii. 1; xii. 39); see JERUSALEM, II. 3.

Ha-na'ni [gracious].

1. A son of Heman and head of the eighteenth of the twenty-four courses of musicians appointed by David for the sanctuary (1 Chron. xxv. 4, 25).

2. Father of the prophet Jehu (1 Kin. xvi. 1) and himself a seer. He rebuked king Asa, and was by his orders committed to prison (2 Chron. xvi 7).

3. A brother of Nehemiah who brought him news regarding Jerusalem (Neh. i. 2). He and the governor of the castle were afterwards given charge of the city (vii. 2).

4. A priest, son of Immer, induced by Ezra to put away his foreign wife (Ezra x. 20).

5. A Levite who played an instrument at the dedication of the wall of Jerusalem by Nehemiah (Neh. xii. 36).

Han-a-ni'ah [Jehovah hath been gracious].

1. A Benjamite, son of Shashak (1 Chron. viii. 24).

2. A son of Heman and head of the sixteenth of the twenty-four courses of musicians formed by David for the sanctuary (1 Chron. xxv. 4, 23).

3. One of king Uzziah's captains (2 Chron. xxvi. 11).

4. Father of Jeremiah's contemporary, the prince Zedekiah (Jer. xxxvi. 12).

5. Son of Azzur of Gibeon. In the fourth year of Zedekiah's reign he prophesied a return of the captives after two years' captivity. Jeremiah had given forth a different prediction. As a penalty, the false prophet was doomed to death, his decease occurring two months later (Jer. xxviii. 1–17).

6. Grandfather, or remoter ancestor, of Irijah, the captain of the watch who arrested Jeremiah on the charge of intending to desert to the Chaldeans (Jer. xxxvii. 13–15).

7. The Hebrew name of the captive called by the Chaldeans Shadrach (Dan. i. 6, 7; 1 Mac. ii. 59).

8. A son of Zerubbabel, and father of Pelatiah and Jeshaiah (1 Chron. iii. 19, 21); perhaps the ancestor of Christ called, by transposition of the constituent parts of the name, Joanan (Luke iii. 27, R. V.).

9. A son of Bebai, induced by Ezra to put away his foreign wife (Ezra x. 28).

10. An apothecary who helped to rebuild the wall of Jerusalem (Neh. iii. 8).

11. A priest who blew a trumpet at the dedication of the wall (Neh. xii. 41).

12. A chief of the people, who with Nehemiah sealed the covenant (Neh. x. 23).

13. The governor of the castle and joint ruler with Hanani, Nehemiah's brother, over Jerusalem (Neh. vii. 2 .

14. A priest, head of the father's house of Jeremiah, in the days of the high priest Joiakim, a generation after the exile (Neh. xii. 12).

Hand'breadth.

The breadth of the hand, a palm (Ex. **xxv.** 25) ; see CUBIT. It is used by the psalmist figuratively of human life, especially when life closes prematurely (Ps. xxxix. 5).

Hand'broad.

Measuring a handbreadth (Ezek. **xl.** 43 ; in R. V. handbreadth).

Hand'ker-chief.

A small cloth used by the Romans for wiping the hands and face. The Jews adopted it in the Roman period. They bound it about the head of their dead (John xi. 44 ; **xx.** 7 ; in English version, napkin). Once in Ephesus handkerchiefs were carried from the body of the apostle Paul unto the sick, and their diseases departed (Acts xix. 12). The man who received one pound from his lord hid it in such a cloth (Luke xix. 20 ; in English version, napkin).

Ha'nes [hieroglyphic, *Su-Chenen* or *Chenensu ;* Coptic, *Hnes*].

A city of Egypt (Is. xxx. 4) about 50 miles south of Memphis, and still known as Ahnas. In the Græco-Roman period it was known as Heracleopolis magna. It must not be confounded with Tahpanhes.

Hang'ing.

A form of punishment in which, after the criminal was put to death, his body was suspended from a tree or post. It was in vogue in Egypt (Gen. xl. 19, 22), among the Israelites (Deut. xxi. 22 ; Josh. x. 26 ; 2 Sam. iv. 12), and the Persians (Herod. iii. 125 ; ix. 78). The hanging intensified the disgrace. Among the Israelites, the elevation of the body on the tree was a call to God to witness that the guilty one had paid just and sufficient penalty, and was a testimony of God's abhorrence of sin. But while it remained exposed, it proclaimed that sin had been committed in Israel. The body was therefore buried out of sight at nightfall (Deut. xxi. 23 ; Josh. viii. 29 ; cp. Gal. iii. 13). Suicide was sometimes committed by hanging which caused strangulation (2 Sam. xvii. 23 ; Mat. xxvii. 5). See GALLOWS.

Han'i-el. See HANNIEL.

Han'nah [grace, compassion].

One of the two wives of Elkanah. She was her husband's favorite, and was in consequence subjected to petty annoyances by the rival wife. She vowed that if she gave birth to a man-child, she would devote him to the service of Jehovah. Her wish was gratified ; she became the mother of the prophet Samuel, and carried out her vow (1 Sam. i. 1–28). Her song of triumph is highly poetic, and was probably in the mind of the Virgin Mary when she expressed her gratitude in similar poetic strains on learning that she was to give birth to the Son of God (ii. 1–10 ; Luke i. 26–55).

Han'na-thon [regarded with favor].

A frontier town of Zebulun (Josh. **xix.** 14), on a road from Megiddo to Acco (El-Amarna letters), and hence adjacent to the territory of Asher.

Han'ni-el, in A. V. **Haniel** in 1 Chron. vii. 39 [favor or grace of God].

1. Prince of the Manassites who, when the Israelites were about to enter Canaan, was appointed on the committee to divide the land (Num. xxxiv. 23).

2. An Asherite, son of Ulla (1 Chron. vii. 39).

Ha'noch, in A. V. once **Henoch** (1 Chron. i. 33) [initiated, dedicated]. Exactly the same Hebrew word as that rendered Enoch.

1. A son of Midian, and a descendant of Abraham by Keturah (Gen. xxv. 4 ; 1 Chron. i. 33). The name is perhaps preserved in Hanâkuya, a place three days' journey to the north of Medina.

2. A son of Reuben, and founder of a tribal family (Gen. xlvi. 9 ; Ex. vi. 14 ; Num. xxvi. 5 ; 1 Chron. v. 3).

Ha'nun [enjoying favor].

1. A king of the Ammonites, son and successor of David's friend Nahash. The Hebrew king therefore sent to condole with him on his father's death, and congratulate him on his own accession. Evil counselors suggested that the real object of the embassy was to spy out the Ammonite capital, with the view of afterwards attempting its capture. Hanun, therefore, grossly ill-treated the ambassadors, shaving off half their beards and cutting off their garments in the middle. Knowing that the outrage would be resented, he prepared for war. He obtained the Syrians as his allies, but was defeated (2 Sam. x. 1–xi. 1 ; 1 Chron. xix. 1–xx. 3).

2 and 3. Two Jews who repaired portions of the wall of Jerusalem under Nehemiah (Neh. iii. 13, 30).

Haph-a-ra'im, in A. V. **Haph'ra-im,** an error from which the original edition of A. V. was free [two pits].

A frontier town of Issachar (Josh. xix. 19). Jerome identified it with Afarea, 6 Roman miles to the north of Legio. At this distance northwest of Lejjun is the ruined site of Farrîyeh ; while about 7 Roman miles east northeast of Lejjun lies the village el-'Afûle.

Hap-piz'zez, in A. V. **Aphses** [the dispersion].

A descendant of Aaron. His family became the eighteenth of the twenty-four courses into which David divided the priests (1 Chron. xxiv. 15).

Ha'ra [mountainous region].

A place in Assyria to which captives from the ten tribes were carried (1 Chron. v. 26).

Situation unknown. Some believe it to be a designation of Media, namely the mountain, or a corruption of "mountains" of Media.

Har'a-dah [terror].

An encampment of the Israelites in the wilderness, after being turned back from Rithmah (Num. xxxiii. 24). Palmer and Drake identified it with the present Jebel 'Aradeh, in the peninsula of Sinai, about 40 miles southwest of Elath. Both etymology and situation are against the identification.

Ha'ran, I. [meaning unknown].

1. A son of Terah, and brother of Abraham. He died early. in his native place, Ur of the Chaldees; but left a son, Lot, and two daughters, Milcah and Iscah (Gen. xi. 29).

2. A Gershonite Levite, son of Shimei (1 Chron. xxiii. 9).

Ha'ran, II., in A. V. of N. T., **Charran** [road, business].

1. A city of Mesopotamia, about 240 miles west by north from Nineveh and 280 northeast of Damascus. It was a commercial center; and, like Ur of the Chaldees, had the moon-god for its patron deity. Terah and Abraham sojourned in it for a time, and Terah died there (Gen. xi. 31, 32; xii. 4, 5). The family of Nahor settled there, and Jacob for a time resided there (xxiv. 24; xxviii. 10; xxix. 5). The Assyrians hunted in its vicinity as early as 1100 B. C.; and they long held sway over it. A capture of the city by them is mentioned (2 Kin. xix. 12). The Greeks called it Karrhai, and the Romans Carræ. In 53 B. C. the Roman triumvir Crassus, the colleague of Pompey and of Julius Cæsar, allowed himself to be outmaneuvered and defeated near Haran by the Parthian general Surena, by whose representatives he was soon afterwards barbarously slain. It is now a small Arab village, still retaining the name of Harrân, situated in upper Mesopotamia, on the Belik, a tributary of the Euphrates, about 240 miles west by north from Nineveh and 82 east from the gulf of Scanderoon.

2. Son of Caleb and Ephah, of the family of Hezron (1 Chron. ii. 46).

Ha'ra-rite [inhabitant of a mountain].

Possibly it means a mountaineer, one from the hill country of Judah or Ephraim (Simonis, Gesenius, Siegfried-Stade). But this designation seems too general. Probably, to judge from the context of 2 Sam. xxiii. 33, it means an inhabitant of a hamlet called Harar, mountain, from its location on some peak, like Gibeah, hill, and its inhabitants Gibeathites (2 Sam. xxiii. 11; 1 Chron. xi. 34, 35).

Har-bo'na and **Harbonah** [Persian, perhaps ass-driver].

A chamberlain of Ahasuerus (Esth. i. 10; vii. 9).

Hare.

An animal, in Hebrew *'Arnebeth*, said to

chew the cud, but not to part the hoof, and therefore unclean (Lev. xi. 6; Deut. xiv. 7). The opinion of the Hebrews that the animal chewed the cud was founded on a peculiar movement of its mouth. Physiologically, however, it is not a ruminating animal, but a rodent, and is so arranged by modern naturalists. The common hare of Palestine (*Lepus syriacus*) is two inches shorter than the European hare (*L. europæus*), and has slightly shorter ears. It frequents wooded and cultivated places. The common hare of southern Judæa and the Jordan valley (*L. judeæ* of Gray) has very long ears and light tawny fur. Tristram enumerates three other species of the southern frontier: *L. ægyptiacus*, the Egyptian hare, in the southeastern part of Judæa; *L. isabillinus*, in the sandy deserts of southeastern Palestine; and *L. sinaiticus*, with fur of a reddish hue.

Ha'rel [the mount of God].

A portion of the altar described by Ezekiel (xliii. 15). In the text of the A. V. it is rendered altar, and in that of the R. V. upper altar.

Ha'reph [picking, plucking off].

A son of Caleb, and ancestor of the inhabitants of Beth-gader (1 Chron. ii. 51).

Ha'reth. See HERETH.

Har-ha'iah.

Father of the goldsmith Uzziel (Neh. iii. 8).

Har'has.

An ancestor of Shallum, husband of Huldah the prophetess (2 Kin. xxii. 14). Called Hasrah in 2 Chron. xxxiv. 22. The two names differ in Hebrew in the second H, and not merely in transposition of letters.

Har'hur [inflammation, fever].

The founder of a family of Nethinim, some of whom returned from Babylon with Zerubbabel (Ezra ii. 51; Neh. vii. 53).

Ha'rim [flat-nosed, snub-nosed, or consecrated].

1. A descendant of Aaron. His family had grown to a father's house in the time of David and constituted the third course when David distributed the priests into divisions (1 Chron. xxiv. 1, 6, 8). Probably they were members of this family who returned from Babylon (Ezra ii. 39; Neh. vii. 42). A father's house among the priests in the next generation after the exile bore this name (Neh. xii. 15); see REHUM. At a later period some of this family were among those who had married foreign wives (Ezra x. 21). And later still a priest of this name, doubtless head of a father's house, signed the covenant to observe the law of God and to endeavor to prevent intermarriages with foreigners (Neh. x. 5).

2. Founder of a non-priestly family, members of which returned from Babylon with Zerubbabel (Ezra ii. 32; x. 31; Neh. iii. 11; vii. 35).

Ha'riph [autumnal rain].

Founder of a family, members of which

returned from Babylon with Zerubbabel (Neh. vii. 24). A prince of this name sealed the covenant, doubtless as representative of the family (x. 19). The same as Jorah (Ezra ii. 18), which also means autumnal rain.

Har′lot.
A prostitute (Gen. xxxviii. 15; Lev. xxi. 7; Deut. xxiii. 18; Josh. ii. 1; Judg. xvi. 1). To play the harlot or to go a whoring after, often means, in scriptural usage, to go with or after a paramour; in a figurative sense, to depart from Jehovah and give the affections and worship to other gods (Jer. ii. 20; iii. 1; Ezek. xvi. 15, 16; xxiii. 5).

Har-Mag′e-don. See ARMAGEDDON.

Har′ne-pher [perhaps, panting].
An Asherite, son of Zophah (1 Chron. vii. 36).

Ha′rod [fear, terror].
A well near which Gideon pitched while his adversaries, the Midianites, were by the hill of Moreh, in the valley (Judg. vii. 1). It is commonly, but without certainty, identified with the fountain of Jalûd, on the northwestern side of mount Gilboa, about a mile east by south of Jezreel. A village appears to have stood in the vicinity (2 Sam. xxiii. 25).

Ha′rod-ite.
An inhabitant of the town of Harod (2 Sam. xxiii. 25).

Har′o-eh. See REAIAH.

Ha′ro-rite.
Rather Harodite (q. v.), as there is reason to read this word (1 Chron. xi. 27; cp. 2 Sam. xxiii. 25).

Ha-ro′sheth [carving, artificers' work in wood or stone].
A town more fully called Harosheth of the gentiles or nations. Sisera had his residence there (Judg. iv. 2, 13, 16). Formerly the site was sought somewhere west of the waters of Merom, and not far from the northern Hazor. Now it is more commonly located at el-Harathîyeh, a small village on the northern bank of the Kishon, at the point where the stream, hidden among oleander bushes, passes through a narrow gorge to enter the plain of Acre.

Harp.
Rendering of the Hebrew word *Kinnor*, emitter of a tremulous sound; and in the N. T. of the Greek word *Kithara*, lyre, lute. It was a stringed musical instrument of the harp kind, small enough to be carried about (Is. xxiii. 16), and was played with the fingers (1 Sam. xvi. 23) or with a plectrum (Antiq. vii. 12, 3). It was played by Jubal, an antediluvian, of the race of Cain (Gen. iv. 21), was known to Laban (xxxi. 27), was the instrument with which David soothed Saul during his fits of melancholy madness (1 Sam. xvi. 16). The prophets and others used it for sacred purposes (1 Sam. x. 5; Ps. xliii. 4;

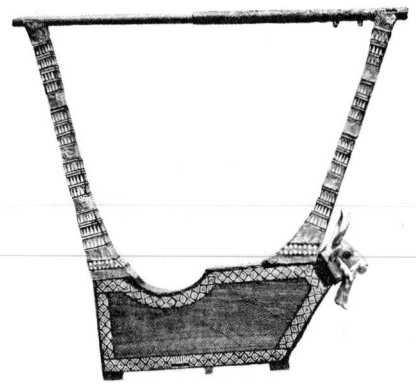

Ancient gold and mosaic harp.

xlix. 4), and it was played in the temple orchestra (1 Chron. xxv. 1, 3); see MUSIC. It was employed also in festive entertainments (Job xxi. 12). Even harlots sometimes carried it about with them (Is. xxiii. 15, 16). It was the instrument which the captive Jews hung on the Babylonian willows (Ps. cxxxvii. 2). Two kinds were in use in Egypt; a larger, of the height of a man, and a smaller, which was easily carried. The Hebrews were acquainted with the harp, but it is not certain that the word *kinnor* really means harp. The Seventy regarded it rather as a lyre or lute, than a harp, for they render the Hebrew word by *kithara*.

Har′row.
An implement of agriculture, consisting of a wooden frame armed with teeth of wood or iron (2 Sam. xii. 31). It is drawn over plowed land to level it and break the clods preparatory to sowing the seed, and to cover the seed when sown. It cannot be shown, however, that the Hebrew word in 2 Sam. xii. 31 denotes such an instrument. The Israelites broke the clods in some manner (Job xxxix. 10; Is. xxviii. 24; Hos. x. 11), but it is doubtful whether they used a harrow. The modern inhabitants of Palestine sometimes turn in the cattle for this purpose.

Har′sha [artificer's work, enchantment].
Founder of a family of Nethinim, some of whom returned from Babylon with Zerubbabel (Ezra ii. 52; Neh. vii. 54).

Hart.
A stag, or male deer, five years old, and which has developed its sur-royal or crown antler. It is the rendering of the Hebrew *′Ayyal*, deer, a wild, clean animal (Deut. xii. 15; xiv. 5; 1 Kin. iv. 23; Ps. xlii. 1; Song viii. 14). See DEER.

Ha′rum [exalted, high].
A man of Judah, father of Aharbel (1 Chron. iv. 8).

Ha-ru′maph [flat of nose].

Father of a certain Jedaiah (Neh. iii. 10).

Har′u-phite.

The designation of Shephatiah, a Benjamite, who joined David at Ziklag (1 Chron. xii. 5). The Hebrew traditional reading is Hariphite, a member of the family of Hariph (cp. Neh. vii. 24–32, where Hariph is enumerated with Benjamites).

Ha′ruz [sedulous, industrious].

Father-in-law of king Manasseh (2 Kin. xxi. 19).

Har′vest.

The period of harvest in ancient Palestine may be divided into two portions: that of barley and that of wheat harvest, the former preceding the latter by about a fortnight (Ruth ii. 23). Its beginning was consecrated by the bringing of the sheaf of firstfruits (Lev. xxiii. 10). It began in the lowlands before the crops were ripe on the hills. In the hot Jordan valley barley harvest commenced in April, when the Jordan was full (Josh. iii. 15; cp. v. 10), at the close of the rainy season (1 Sam. xii. 17, 18; Prov. xxvi. 1). Wheat harvest lingered in the uplands to the month of June. It was a hot time of the year (Prov. xxv. 13; Is. xviii. 4). When the harvest was completed, and the produce gathered in, there were great rejoicings (Is. ix. 3). The feasts of unleavened bread, of weeks or harvest, and of ingathering, had all a relation to the season of reaping. See YEAR.

Has-a-di′ah [Jehovah hath shown kindness].

A son of Zerubbabel (1 Chron. iii. 20).

Has-e-nu′ah. See HASSENUAH.

Hash-a-bi′ah [Jehovah hath imputed or devised].

1. A Merarite Levite, descended through Amaziah, and an ancestor of Jeduthun (1 Chron. vi. 45). Perhaps he is the descendant of Bunni mentioned as ancestor of Shemaiah (ix. 14; Neh. xi. 15).

2. A Merarite Levite, son of Jeduthun and head of the twelfth company of musicians appointed by David for the sanctuary (1 Chron. xxv. 3, 19).

3. A Kohathite Levite of the family of

Hebron, and inspector for the country west of Jordan (1 Chron. xxvi. 30; cp. xxiii. 12).

4. A Levite, son of Kemuel, prince of the tribe of Levi in David's reign (1 Chron. xxvii. 17).

5. A chief of the Levites during the reign of Josiah (2 Chron. xxxv. 9).

6. A Merarite Levite, who joined Ezra at the river of Ahava, and was apparently one of the twelve who were entrusted with the treasure which was being conveyed to Jerusalem (Ezra viii. 19, 24). Probably it was he who sealed the covenant (Neh. x. 11), and who was a chief Levite and one of the temple musicians (Neh. xii. 24).

7. The ruler, in Nehemiah's time, of half Keilah. He repaired part of the wall of Jerusalem (Neh. iii. 17).

8. A Levite, descended from Asaph (Neh. xi. 22).

9. A priest, head of the father's house of Hilkiah, in the time of Joiakim the high priest (Neh. xii. 21).

Ha-shab′nah.

One of those who with Nehemiah sealed the covenant (Neh. x. 25).

Hash-ab-ne′iah, in A. V. Hash-ab-ni′ah.

1. Father of a certain Hattush (Neh. iii. 10).

2. One of those Levites who by their exhortations prepared the returned exiles for sealing the covenant with Jehovah (Neh. ix. 5).

Hash-bad′da-na, in A. V. Hash-bad′a-na.

One of those who stood beside Ezra when he addressed the returned exiles (Neh. viii. 4).

Ha′shem [make astonished! lay waste!].

A Gizonite, mentioned in the catalogue of David's mighty men (1 Chron. xi. 34). See JASHEN.

Hash-mo′nah [place of fertility].

A camping ground of the Israelites in the wilderness (Num. xxxiii. 29, 30). Exact situation unknown.

Ha′shub. See HASSHUB.

Ha-shu′bah [esteemed, purposed].

A son of Zerubbabel (1 Chron. iii. 20).

Ha′shum [rich, wealthy].

Founder of a family, members of which re-

Harvesting on the Plain of Rephaim.

turned from Babylon with Zerubbabel (Ezra
ii. 19; x. 33; Neh. vii. 22). The representative of the family, or a person of this name,
supported Ezra while the latter addressed the
people (Neh. viii. 4), and then sealed the covenant (x. 18).

Ha-shu'pha. See HASUPHA.

Ha-si-dæ'ans, in A. V. **Asideans** and **Assi-
deans** [Greek '*Asidaioi*, from Hebrew *H^asidim*,
the pious].

A party among the Jews who held strenuously to the old faith (1 Mac. ii. 42). They
joined Mattathias, and later coöperated with
Judas Maccabæus in most of his plans (ii.
42; 2 Mac. xiv. 6), although contrary to his
judgment they sought peace from the Syrians
(1 Mac. vii. 13).

Has-mo-næ'an. See ASMONÆAN.

Has'rah [perhaps, want]. See HARHAS.

Has-se-na'ah, and without the definite
article **Senaah** [perhaps, thorny].

The sons of Hassenaah rebuilt the fish-
gate of Jerusalem (Neh. iii. 3). Of the children of Senaah, some three thousand returned from Babylon with Zerubbabel (Ezra ii.
35; Neh. vii. 38). Whether Senaah is a man
or a town is uncertain.

Has-se-nu'ah, in A. V. **Hasenuah**, and,
without the article, **Senuah** [perhaps, thorny].

1. A Benjamite, father of Hodaviah (1
Chron. ix. 7).

2. Parent of a certain Judah (Neh. xi. 9).

Has'shub, in A. V. of Nehemiah **Hashub**
[thoughtful].

1. A son of Pahath-moab. He repaired
part of the wall of Jerusalem (Neh. iii. 11).

2. A Jew who repaired part of the wall of
Jerusalem opposite to his house (Neh. iii. 23).
It was probably either he or No. 1 who signed
the covenant (x. 23).

3. A Merarite Levite, father of Shemaiah
(1 Chron. ix. 14; Neh. xi. 15).

Has-soph'e-reth. See SOPHERETH.

Ha-su'pha, in A. V. once **Hashupha** [made
bare].

Founder of a family of Nethinim, members of which returned from captivity with
Zerubbabel (Ezra ii. 43; Neh. vii. 46).

Hat.

The rendering of the Aramaic word *Kar-
bel*, binding, wrap (Dan. iii. 21; in R. V.
mantle). See CLOTHING.

Ha'thach, in A. V. **Hatach.**

A chamberlain of king Ahasuerus, who was
appointed to attend Esther (Esth. iv. 5, 10).

Ha'thath [terror].

A son of Othniel (1 Chron. iv. 13).

Hat'i-pha [captive].

One who founded a family of Nethinim,
members of which returned from Babylon
with Zerubbabel (Ezra ii. 54; Neh. vii. 56).

Hat'i-ta [engraving, exploration].

A porter who founded a family, members

of which returned from Babylon with Zerub-
babei (Ezra ii. 42; Neh. vii. 45).

Hat'til [tottering, vacillating].

One of Solomon's servants, who founded a
family, the members of which returned from
Babylon with Zerubbabel (Ezra ii. 57; Neh.
vii. 59).

Hat'tush [congregated, gathered together]

1. A man of Judah, son of Shemaiah, and
family of Shecaniah (1 Chron. iii. 22).

2. A chief of the priests, who returned
with Zerubbabel from Babylon (Neh. xii.
2, 7).

3. Head of a father's house, of the sons of
David, who returned with Ezra to Jerusalem
(Ezra viii. 2).

4. A son of Hashabneiah. He repaired part
of the wall of Jerusalem (Neh. iii. 10).

5. A priest who with Nehemiah sealed the
covenant (Neh. x. 4).

Hau'ran [hollow land, so called because a
depression or because of the multitude of its
caverns].

A region south of Damascus and bordering
on Gilead (Ezek. xlvii. 16, 18). In the
Greco-Roman period it designated a smaller
district. It was then known as Auranitis,
and was one of four provinces, having Trachonitis on the north and Gaulonitis and apparently Batanea toward the northwest (Antiq. xvii. 11, 4; xviii. 4, 6; War i. 20, 4; ii.
6, 3; 17, 4; iii. 3, 5). It thus probably consisted of the plain lying between Gaulonitis
and the present Jebel Hauran, and perhaps
included the latter. About the year 23 B. C.
Auranitis with Trachonitis and Batanea was
bestowed on Herod the Great by Augustus.
When Herod's kingdom was divided, these
districts constituted the major part of Philip's
tetrarchy (Luke iii. 1; Antiq. xvii. 11, 4). The
surface is flat, broken only by a few volcanic
mounds. The soil is so fertile that the Hauran is the granary for the whole region round.
Many towns and villages, mostly deserted,
exist within its limits, some of them "the
giant cities of Bashan," as they have been
called, built of basalt, with doors of the same
material.

Hav'i-lah [perhaps, sandy].

A district of Arabia, peopled in part by a
body of Cushites and in part by a body of
Joktanites, a Semitic people (Gen. x. 7, 29; 1
Chron. i. 9, 23). The association of Havilah
with Hazarmaveth and other places points to
a locality in central or southern Arabia. To
Havilah belonged the river Pishon; and the
region was rich in gold, aromatic gum, and
precious stones (Gen. ii. 11, 12). These productions strongly indicate the mountainous
district to the north of Yemama; and in this
neighborhood Havilah is best sought. How
far beyond these mountains the boundaries
of Havilah extended is not clear. From the
record of Saul's warfare with the Amalekites
it may be inferred that the Arabian desert
for several hundred miles north of the moun-

tains bore the name Havilah (1 Sam. xv. 7; cp. Gen. xxv. 18). Migrations of the people would also carry the name to distant localities, as perhaps to the coast of Africa near the straits of Bab el-Mandeb, where a gulf, Aualites, and a people, Abalitai, are traceable.

Hav-voth-ja'ir, in A. V. **Havoth-jair** [Jair's circuit of villages or of nomad encampments].

Unwalled towns in the northwestern part of Bashan, in the region of the Argob, where this tract approaches the country of the Geshurites and Maacathites, and where the boundaries between the rugged land, Gilead, and the open, sandy land, Bashan, insensibly merge into each other (Deut. iii. 4, 14). They were captured by Jair, a Manassite. Their number was liable to fluctuation, because they lay in a debatable land, and for other reasons (1 Chron. ii. 23). They are to be carefully distinguished from the sixty walled cities in the heart of Bashan, and likewise in the Argob (Deut. iii. 4, 5; 1 Kin. iv. 13). Since the boundary between Gilead and Bashan was not clearly defined by nature, it never was conventionally, and places on this undefined border are referred to as in Gilead or in Bashan, according to the momentary point of view of the narrator. The conquest of Bashan by the Israelites included the capture of the unwalled towns in the Argob on this invisible border; and when their capture by Jair is related in connection with the conquest of Og's kingdom, which was carried on from Edrei in Bashan as the center, the Havvoth-jair are described as in Bashan (Deut. iii. 14; Josh. xiii. 30). When, however, the eastern country is before the mind of a sojourner in the valley of the Jordan or in Canaan west of the river, he naturally speaks first of Gilead, and sometimes even uses that designation broadly for the entire highland east of the river, or he may speak of a conquest of Gilead which was not narrowly confined to the distinctively rugged land. From this point of view, he is apt to refer to the towns on the undefined border of Gilead and Bashan as in Gilead (1 Chron. ii. 21–23; indefinitely, Num. xxxii. 40 seq.; 1 Kin. iv. 13). The Havvoth-jair were scattered over this indefinite tract in the Argob; and hence, according to the shifting point of view, even of one and the same narrator, are mentioned as in Gilead or in Bashan. Some of them were doubtless more evidently in the open land, while others were more clearly in the rugged land.

Hawk.
The rendering of the Hebrew *Neṣ*, flyer (Job xxxix. 26). It was ceremonially unclean (Lev. xi. 16; Deut. xiv. 15), and included more than one species of the smaller predatory birds (ibid.). It comprehended the sparrow hawk (*Accipiter nisus*) and the kestrel (*Falco tinnunculus*). The former abounds in Lebanon and the hilly parts of Galilee in summer, and in Judæa and the Arabah in

winter; the latter, which is properly a falcon instead of a genuine hawk, is abundant in every part of Palestine throughout the year.

Haz'a-el [God hath seen].
A Syrian courtier whom Elijah was directed by Jehovah to anoint king over Syria (1 Kin. xix. 15, 17). Some years later, between 845 and 843 B. C., Ben-hadad, who then reigned over that country, with Damascus for his capital, hearing that Elisha was in the city, sent Hazael to ask the prophet whether he should recover of a serious illness from which he then suffered. Elisha told Hazael that his master would not recover, and that he himself would be king of Syria, and would perpetrate great cruelties on the people of Israel. He replied, "But what is thy servant, who is but a dog, that he should do this great thing?" Then, returning to his master, he falsely told him that the prophet foretold his recovery, and next day assassinated him and reigned in his stead (2 Kin. viii. 7–15, R. V.). In 842 the Assyrian king Shalmaneser warred against Hazael and exacted tribute. In 839 Shalmaneser again warred with him. Toward the close of Jehu's reign over Israel, about 820, Hazael smote the country of the Hebrews east of the Jordan (x. 32); and in the succeeding reign, crossing the river, he mightily oppressed the Israelites (xiii. 4–7), invaded the country of the Philistines, took Gath, and was only deterred from attacking Jerusalem by a rich present consisting of the dedicated treasures of the temple (xii. 17, 18). He died shortly after. The house of Hazael (Amos i. 4) is Damascus.

Ha-za'iah [Jehovah hath seen].
A man of Judah, family of Shelah (Neh. xi. 5).

Ha-zar-ad'dar. See ADDAR.

Ha-zar-e'nan and **Hazar-enon** [village of fountains].
A village on the northern boundary of Palestine, near Damascus (Num. xxxiv. 9; Ezek. xlvii. 17; xlviii. 1). Exact site unknown.

Ha-zar-gad'dah [village of good fortune].
A town in the extreme south of Judah (Josh. xv. 27). Exact site unknown.

Ha-zar-hat'ti-con. See HAZER-HATTICON.

Ha-zar-ma'veth [village of death].
A body of Joktanites who peopled a district in Arabia (Gen. x. 26; 1 Chron. i. 20). A region in Arabia Felix, in the south of the peninsula, is still called by the Arabs Hadramâut, which corresponds etymologically to Hazarmaveth. The place is mentioned in the inscriptions of the ancient Sabæans, the people of Sheba.

Ha-zar-shu'al [fox village].
A town in the extreme south of Judah, assigned to the Simeonites (Josh. xv. 28; xix. 3; 1 Chron. iv. 28). It was occupied after

the captivity (Neh. xi. 27). Perhaps the ruin eth-Tha'li, a word equivalent to Shual.

Ha-zar-su'sah, in plural **Hazar-susim** [village of a mare or mares].

A village belonging to the Simeonites (Josh. xix. 5; 1 Chron. iv. 31). Tristram places it at the ruin Susîn, 10 miles south of Gaza, on the caravan route to Egypt. Perhaps it is Sûsîyeh. 2 miles east by north of Semua.

Haz-a-zon-ta'mar, in A. V. once **Hazezon-tamar** (Gen. xiv. 7). See EN-GEDI.

Ha'zel.

The rendering in Gen. xxx. 37, A. V. of the Hebrew *Luz*, which is almost certainly, as the R. V. makes it, the almond tree.

Haz-e-lel-po'ni. See HAZZELELPONI.

Ha-zer-hat'ti-con, in A. V. **Hazar-hatti-con** [the middle Hazer or village].

A town on the border of the Hauran (Ezek. xlvii. 16). Exact site unknown.

Ha-ze'rim [villages].

Habitations of the Avvim (Deut. ii. 23); in the R. V. properly translated by villages.

Ha-ze'roth [encampments].

An encamping ground of the Israelites in the wilderness beyond Kibroth-hattaavah (Num. xi. 35) and on this side of Paran (xii. 16; xxxiii. 17; Deut. i. 1). It was there that Miriam and Aaron murmured against Moses (Num. xi. 35–xii. 16). 'Ain el-Hudera, about 36 miles northeast of mount Sinai, was suggested by Burckhardt, and adopted by Robinson and others, as the site. The identification rests, however, solely on the similarity of the name, and is uncertain. Palmer found at the spot many stone circles, which evidently marked the site of an encampment formed by a pastoral people.

Haz-e-zon-ta'mar. See HAZAZON-TAMAR.

Ha'zi-el [vision of God].

A Gershonite Levite, son of Shimei (1 Chron. xxiii. 9).

Ha'zo [perhaps, vision].

A son of Nahor and Milcah (Gen. xxii. 22). The name is probably preserved in the hilly region Hazû, which Esarhaddon traversed, not remote from the Hauran.

Ha'zor [an enclosure].

1. The capital of the Canaanite kingdom in the north of Palestine, ruled over in Joshua's time by Jabin. According to Josephus, it was situated above the waters of Merom (Antiq. v. 5, 1). The town was taken by Joshua and burnt (Josh. xi. 1–13; xii. 19). It was rebuilt, and was assigned to the tribe of Naphtali (Josh. xix. 36). In the days of Deborah and Barak it was ruled by another king Jabin. On the defeat of his general, Sisera, he attempted to continue the war against the Israelites, but was ultimately overcome and slain (Judg. iv. 1–24; 1 Sam. xii. 9). It is doubtful whether this or some other Hazor was the town fortified by Solomon (1 Kin. ix. 15), but it was certainly the

place so named whose inhabitants were carried into captivity to Assyria by Tiglath-pileser (2 Kin. xv. 29). In the neighboring plain Jonathan defeated Demetrius (1 Mac. xi. 67; in A. V. Nasor; Antiq. xiii. 5, 7). Robinson's identification of Hazor with Tell Khureibeh, 3½ miles west of the waters of Merom, is the most probable yet proposed. Conder locates it at Jebel Hadîreh, about 2 miles farther west.

2. A town in the extreme south of Judah, called also Kerioth-hezron (Josh. xv. 25, R.V.). Exact site unknown. Robinson located it at Kureitein, 12 miles south of Hebron. Hazor, a town of Judah near Kedesh, is mentioned in ver. 23; see HEZRON.

3. A village of Benjamin (Neh. xi. 33). Conder identifies it with the ruin Hazzur, 4 miles north-northwest of Jerusalem, and directly west of Beit Hanîna, perhaps Ananiah of ver. 32.

4. A region in the Arabian desert, eastward of Palestine. Jeremiah prophesied its plundering by Nebuchadnezzar (xlix. 28–33). Berosus states that Nebuchadnezzar conquered Arabia (con. Apion. i. 19). The name is probably a collective and refers to the settled village life of the community in contrast to the nomads. Exact situation unknown.

Ha-zor-ha-dat'tah, in A. V. punctuated as two places, **Hazor, Hadattah** [if the second word is Aramaic, the name means new village].

A town in the extreme south of Judah, apparently near Hazor 2. Exact site unknown (Josh. xv. 25).

Haz'ze-lel-po'ni, in A. V. **Hazelelponi** [give shade, thou who turnest toward me].

A woman of Judah, daughter of the ancestor of the men of Etam (1 Chron. iv. 3).

He.

The fifth letter of the Hebrew alphabet. The English letter E has the same origin, but is a vowel. Where he preserves its power as a consonant in Hebrew names, and properly at other times, it is represented by h in the English form; as in Abraham.

It stands at the head of the fifth section of Ps. cxix., since each verse in the section begins with this letter in the original.

Through some similarity of form combined with careless writing and slight effacement of the text, it was sometimes misread as aleph on the one hand and tau on the other.

Head'band.

The rendering of the Hebrew *Kishshur*, encircle, band (Is. iii. 20, in R. V. a sash; Jer. ii. 32, in E. V. attire). It is an article of female attire.

Heath.

The rendering of the Hebrew words '*Ar'ar* (Jer. xvii. 6; but R. V. margin, following the Septuagint, has tamarisk), in Arabic, juniper, *J. Oxycedrus* (Post), and '*aro'er* (Jer. xlviii. 6); both of which involve the idea of nakedness. Heath is a shrub, with minute, narrow, rigid leaves. The species *Erica verticillata*, a low shrub with racemed, pink, sweet-scented flowers, grows on the western slopes of Lebanon (Post). Most interpreters, however, regard the word, at least in Jer. xlviii. 6, as meaning a destitute person, since *'aro'er* has that sense in Ps. cii. 17.

Hea'then [dweller in the heath]. The word suggests the fact that the gospel first rooted itself in towns, the inhabitants of which became Christians, while the dwellers on heaths remained worshipers of false divinities. The word Pagan, from Latin *Paganus*, belonging to a village, rustic, has a somewhat similar reference.

One of a people who do not worship the God of the Bible, especially if they are addicted to idolatry. It is a frequent rendering of the Hebrew *Goy* and Greek *Ethnos*, each of which means nation or people. R.V. employs the word heathen only in O. T. and then only when the character of the gentile nations is clearly referred to; as in speaking of the abominations of the heathen (2 Kin. xvi. 3; Ezek. xxiii. 30), their filthiness (Ezra vi. 21), their ignorance of the truth, opposition to the true religion, barbarous trampling upon it and upon the people of God, and consequent exposure to the righteous indignation of Jehovah (Ps. lxxix. 1, 6, 10, but not cxv. 2; also in Jer. x. 25; Lam. i. 3, 10; Ezek. xxxiv. 28, 29; xxxvi. 6, 7, 15).

Heav'en, often **The Heavens** [probably originally, covering].

1. The sky, the expanse around the earth. It embraces all that is apart from the earth (Gen. ii. 1); hence heaven and earth comprehend the universe (Gen. i. 1; xiv. 19; xxiv. 3; Jer. xxiii. 24; Mat. v. 18). Beyond the visible firmament was the primeval watery mass (Gen. i. 7; Ps. cxlviii. 4); which is not further referred to in the account of creation, but out of which it is reasonable to believe the heavenly bodies were formed. These upper waters remained in Hebrew thought along with other conceptions. In the visible heavens are the stars and planets (Gen. i, 14, 15, 17; Ezek. xxxii. 7, 8). In the part of it next the earth is the atmosphere, in which clouds float, through which birds fly, and from which rain descends (Gen. i. 20; vii. 11; viii. 2; xxvii. 28; 2 Sam. xxi. 10; Ps. cxlvii. 8; Lam. iv. 19); see FIRMAMENT. The Hebrews, by a familiar idiom, spoke of the heaven of heavens (Deut. x. 14; 1 Kin. viii. 27; Ps. cxv. 16), meaning the heavens in their widest extent. The later Jews were fond of dividing the heavens into seven different strata. No fixed, definite conception of these several regions prevailed; but fancy was allowed fullest freedom. The highest was regarded as God's dwelling place. Paul describes Christ as ascending far above all the heavens (Eph. iv. 10); and he relates an experience, whether in vision or reality

he knew not, in which he was caught up into the third heaven and into Paradise (2 Cor. xii. 1–4).

2. The place where God's immediate presence is manifested (Gen. xxviii. 17; Ps. lxxx. 14; Is. lxvi. 1; Mat. v. 12, 16, 45, 48; xxiii. 9), where the angels are (Mat. xxiv. 36; xxviii. 2; Mark xiii. 32; Luke xxii. 43), and where the redeemed shall ultimately be (Mat. v. 12; vi. 20; xviii. 10; Eph. iii. 15; 1 Pet. i. 4; Rev. xix. 1, 4). Christ descended from heaven (John iii. 13), and ascended thither again (Acts i. 11), where he maketh intercession for the saints and whence he shall come to judge the quick and the dead (Rom. viii. 33, 34; Heb. vi. 20; ix. 24; Mat. xxiv. 30; 1 Thes. iv. 16).

3. The inhabitants of heaven (Luke xv. 18; Rev. xviii. 20).

Heave Of'fer-ing.

Every hallowed thing which the Israelites heaved, *i. e.* levied, took up, took away, from a larger mass and set apart for Jehovah (Lev. xxii. 12; Num. v. 9; xviii. 8; xxxi. 28, 29). In general it comprehended 1. From the most holy things, the portions of the meal offerings, sin offerings, and guilt offerings which were not required to be burned on the altar. These parts were perquisites of the priests, and were eaten by them in the precincts of the sanctuary (Num. xviii. 9, 10; cp. Lev. vi. 16). 2. From the holy gifts, Num. xviii. 11–19, (a) The heave offering of all wave offerings. It was assigned to the priest's family, for use as food by all the members, male and female, provided they were ceremonially clean (11). (b) The first fruits of the oil, wine, and grain (Num. xviii. 12; cp. 24, 30; Deut. xviii. 4; Neh. x. 39). A basketful of these first fruits was presented to Jehovah by the offerer and then spread as a feast for the offerer and his family as the guests of the Lord (Deut. xxvi. 2, 10, 11; cp. xii. 6, 7, 11, 12). Except this basketful the whole of the first fruits belonged to the priestly families, but could be eaten by those members only of the household who were ceremonially clean (Num. xviii. 13; Deut. xviii. 4). (c) Every devoted thing (Num. xviii. 14). (d) The flesh of every unredeemed firstling (15–18). 3. The tithe (21–24), which was assigned as a perquisite to the Levites.

Particular heave offerings were 1. From peace offerings the right thigh and three cakes, one out of each oblation (Lev. vii. 14, 32–34). 2. From the ram of consecration, used at the induction of the priests into office, the right thigh (Ex. xxix. 27). It belonged to a peace offering, and accordingly was given to the priests (28); but at the induction of Aaron, the first of the priestly line, it was burnt (22–25; Lev. viii. 25–28). 3. From the first dough, made from the new meal of the year, a cake (Num. xv. 20, 21).

He′ber [union, society, fellowship].

1. A son of Beriah, grandson of Asher, and founder of a tribal family (Gen. xlvi. 17; Num. xxvi. 45).

2. A Kenite, descendant of Moses' brother-in-law or father-in-law Hobab, and the husband of Jael, who slew Sisera (Judg. iv. 11–24).

3. A man registered with Judah, descended from Ezra, and ancestor of the men of Socoh (1 Chron. iv. 18).

4. A Benjamite, descended from Shaharaim through Elpaal (1 Chron. viii. 17).

For two others bearing this name in A. V., see EBER.

He′brew [pertaining to the other side or to Eber].

1. According to biblical history, the Hebrews were men from the other side of the Euphrates (Gen. xiv. 13 with xii. 5; Josh. xxiv. 2, 3; and see EUPHRATES). The name may have denoted this, or it may have been originally a patronymic formed from Eber, and have designated all his descendants, including the Israelites (Gen. x. 21), until the increasing prominence of the Israelites led to restricting its use to them; see EBER. Hebrews in the plural was applied to the Israelites (Gen. xl. 15; 1 Sam. iv. 6; xiii. 3; 2 Cor. xi. 22). In N. T. times it was used specially of those Jews who spoke Hebrew or rather Aramaic in distinction from the Hellenists, their fellow-countrymen who spoke Greek (Acts vi. 1). An Hebrew of the Hebrews was a thorough Hebrew; as, for example, a person of Hebrew parentage both on the father's and the mother's side (Phil. iii. 5).

2. The language spoken by the Hebrews (2 Kin. xviii. 26, 28; Is. xxxvi. 11, 13), and called, poetically, the language of Canaan (Is. xix. 18). There is reason to believe that Abraham found it in Canaan, instead of bringing it with him from Chaldea; and the tablets from Tell el-Amarna and the Moabite stone have shown that at least the Canaanites and the Moabites, if not even the adjacent tribes, spoke a language not very different from Hebrew. It belongs to the Semitic group of languages. Like the most of them, it is read from right to left, not, like English, from left to right. Its alphabet consists of twenty-two consonants. Their names are found in Ps. cxix., which is divided into groups of eight verses. In each of these groups a several letter of the alphabet dominates, beginning each verse. Originally the language was written without vowel-points, these not being introduced earlier than the sixth century A. D., or perhaps even a little later. They were the work of certain Jewish doctors called Masorites, whose headquarters were at Tiberias. With the exception of portions of the books of Daniel and Ezra and a few verses elsewhere in Aramaic, the whole of the O. T. was written originally in Hebrew.

Languages have their periods of growth, comparative perfection, and then decay. Two stages are traceable in Hebrew; these are generally called its golden and its silver age. The first extended from the commencement of the Hebrew nation to the Babylonian captivity, the second from the captivity till the language ceased to be spoken. During the golden age, while the Jews were generally independent, their language remained comparatively pure. During the silver age it was corrupted by a continually increasing influx of Aramaic, till the latter tongue superseded it altogether. The Aramaic in the time of our Lord had taken the place of the genuine Hebrew as the colloquial language (Mark v. 41), and had usurped its name; and Aramaic is intended by the Hebrew language, or the Hebrew tongue, or the Hebrew, or simply Hebrew, in John v. 2; xix. 13, 17, 20; Acts xxi. 40; xxii. 2; xxvi. 14; Rev. ix. 11.

He′brews, E-pis′tle to the.

The fourteenth of the N. T. epistles as they are arranged in the English Bible. That it was addressed to Jewish Christians is clearly shown by its contents. To no others would its arguments be so appropriate. They were in danger of returning to Judaism through the pressure of outward trial and opposition (ii. 1; iii. 12; iv. 1, 11; v. 12; vi. 6; x. 23–25, 29). They had been early converts (v. 12) and had received the gospel from its first preachers (ii. 3). They had long ago been persecuted (x. 32–34) and had often ministered to the saints (vi. 10; x. 34). There is no reference to gentile members in their churches, and their danger lay in a return not so much to the law as to the ritual. These allusions best suit the Hebrew Christians of Palestine, and to them doubtless, with perhaps other Jewish believers of the East, the epistle was addressed.

Its authorship has always been disputed. Even n the ancient church opinion was divided, though the canonicity and authority of the book were recognized. The early eastern church received it as Pauline, though it was felt to be unlike the rest of Paul's epistles, and theories were advanced to explain the difference. Clement of Alexandria, e. g., thought that perhaps Luke translated it from a Hebrew original. In the early western churches its Pauline authorship was doubted and denied, and Tertullian attributed it to Barnabas. For a while indeed in the western churches its history becomes obscure, so far as our information goes; but finally the eastern opinion became the universally accepted one. The book is anonymous. Chap. ii. 3, however, seems to imply that the author was not an apostle. It certainly implies that he was not one of the original apostles, and it is unlike Paul to represent himself as receiving the gospel from others (cp. Gal. i. 11-24). From xiii. 18, 19 we learn that the writer was well known to his readers and was unhappily separated from them. In xiii. 23 the reference to Timothy is not sufficient to indicate the author, nor does the expression "they of Italy" (xiii. 24) prove his locality, though the natural inference is that he was in Italy. The evidence of the contents and style also impresses different minds in different ways. It certainly is not a translation of a Hebrew original. Its doctrine has much in common with Paul, though the truth is put in a slightly different way. Its language has a large classic element in it, and its style has seemed to most critics unlike the apostle's, being smoother, often more elegant, and less impetuous. The omission of any address also is unlike Paul's usage elsewhere ; and the author seems to have used exclusively the Greek translation of the O. T., while Paul constantly shows his familiarity with the Hebrew as well. There is still room, therefore, for difference of opinion as to the author. Various suggestions have been made by those who deny that Paul wrote it. Luther guessed Apollos. The most plausible view, if Paul be not the author, is that which attributes it to Barnabas, who has at least some ancient testimony in his favor, and who in The Acts appears as the mediator between the Jewish Christians and Paul, much as this epistle seeks to establish its Hebrew readers in a doctrine which is thoroughly Pauline. The following analysis will exhibit the thought of the epistle :

(1) The author begins by stating the superiority of Christianity to all previous and possible revelation because of the superior dignity of Christ to all previous and possible organs of revelation (i.), a fact which should warn us not to forsake the gospel (ii. 1-4). Nor should the humiliation of Christ appear a difficulty, since just by it he becomes our Saviour and high priest (ii.). Christ, therefore, is of superior dignity even to Moses (iii. 1-6), and the warnings against unbelief in the older revelation which were addressed to Israel, are doubly applicable against unbelief in the final revelation of the gospel (iii. 7-iv. 13).

(2) The epistle then unfolds the value of Christ's high-priestly office (iv. 14-16) ; explaining its nature and showing that Christ did, and that it was predicted he would, exercise it (v.) ; and, after gently, yet vigorously, rebuking them for their failure to grasp the full truth of the gospel (vi.), unfolding the superiority of Christ's priesthood, as typified in Melchizedek, to the levitical, the consequent abrogation of the latter with its ritual, and the all-sufficiency of Christ's (vii.).

(3) Then the epistle shows that Christ's priesthood must now be necessarily exercised in heaven, so that his invisibility should be no difficulty to them. In this heavenly ministry Christ fulfills the types, realizes the promises and remedies the imperfections of the earthly ritual (viii. 1-x. 18).

(4) The fourth section (x. 19-xii. 29) urges them to live up to these truths by an enduring faith. The writer exhorts to renewed confidence in Christ and to the maintenance of their Christian associations (x. 19-25) ; depicts the hopelessness which would follow apostasy (x. 26-31) ; incites them by recalling their former zeal (x. 32-39), the examples of the Hebrew heroes of faith (xi.) and of Christ himself (xii. 1-3) ; and bids them consider their trials as but the chastening of the Lord preparatory to a glorious salvation (xii. 4-29).

(5) In ch. xiii. are added some specific exhortations.

This epistle is the only one in which the title of priest is applied to Christ, though of course the substance of the doctrine is elsewhere taught : it represents Christianity as the completion and goal of the old dispensation ; the clear announcement of that way of salvation previously taught by type and ritual. It gives the argument, therefore, most likely to establish Hebrews in the faith, and without it the N. T. teaching would be obviously incomplete.

The epistle was apparently written in Italy outside of Rome, such being a plausible inference from xiii. 24 ; was known to Clement of Rome, A. D. 96; and was probably written A. D. 65-68, while the temple was still standing (xiii. 10-14).   G. T. P.

He'bron [union].

1. A Levite, son of Kohath and founder of a tribal family (Ex. vi. 18 ; 1 Chron. vi. 2) ; see HEBRONITES.

2. A town in the hill country of Judah (Josh. xv. 48, 54), called originally Kirjath-arba, meaning either city of four, because consisting of four separate hamlets, or city of the croucher (Gen. xxiii. 2 ; Josh. xx. 7) ; see ARBA. It was built seven years before Zoan, in Egypt (Num. xiii. 22), and existed at least as early as the days of Abraham, who for a time resided in its vicinity, under the oaks or terebinths of Mamre (Gen. xiii. 18 ; xxxv. 27). Sarah died there, and Abraham bought the cave of Machpelah for a sepulcher. He purchased it from the Hittites who then occupied the town (xxiii. 2-20 . Isaac and Jacob for a time sojourned at Hebron (Gen. xxxv. 27 ; xxxvii. 14). It was visited by the spies, who found Anakim among its inhabitants (Num. xiii. 22). Its king, Hoham, was one of the four kings who allied themselves with Adoni-zedek against Joshua, but who were defeated, captured, and slain (Josh. x. 1-27). Hebron itself was afterwards taken, and its inhabitants destroyed (36-39). This account is supplemented by xi. 21, 22, where it is recorded that at that time Joshua cut off the Anakim from Hebron, Debir, Anab, and all the hill country, and utterly destroyed their cities. After this

first general campaign, however, the survivors of the old population gradually returned from their hiding places and retreats, and in the course of a few years rebuilt many of the ruined towns. Among those who thus returned were remnants of the three families of Anakim who had dwelt at Hebron. Here they were found reëstablished after the conquest of Canaan (xiv. 10, 12). Caleb claimed that district as his own; and when the tribe of Judah took possession of its allotted territory after the death of Joshua, Caleb retook Hebron (Judg. i. 10–15; and, apparently by anticipation, Josh. xv. 13–19). Hebron had dependent villages (Josh. xv. 54). was assigned to the priests, and was one of the cities of refuge (Josh. xx. 7; xxi. 10–13; 1 Chron. vi. 54–57). David sent thither part of the recaptured spoil of Ziklag (1 Sam. xxx. 31), and afterwards reigned in it for seven and a half years (2 Sam. ii. 1–3, 11, 32; v. 1–5, 13; 1 Kin. ii. 11; 1 Chron. xxix. 27), several of his sons being born there (2 Sam. iii. 2–5; 1 Chron. iii. 1–4; xi. 1–3; xii. 23–38). Abner was buried there (2 Sam. iii. 32), and the head of Ish-bosheth was placed in the same grave (iv. 1–12). It was at Hebron that Absalom raised the standard of rebellion (xv. 7–10). It was fortified by Rehoboam (2 Chron. xi. 10). When, during the captivity,

the Edomites occupied the south of Judah, Hebron, among other places, fell into their hands. It was recaptured from them by Judas Maccabæus, having then a fortress with towers and being the head of other towns (1 Mac. v. 65). It is not mentioned in the N. T. Hebron is now called el-Khulil er-Rahman. It is one of the oldest towns in the world which is still inhabited, instead of being simply a ruin. Hebron is situated in a valley and on an adjacent slope, 3040 feet above the level of the ocean. It is 19 miles south-southwest of Jerusalem, and 13½ south-southwest of Bethlehem. It has no walls at present, but possesses gates. The houses, which are of stone, are well built, with flat roofs, domed in the middle. It was formerly divided into three quarters, but has so increased since 1875 as to have required six more. The population is believed to be about 10,000, most of them Mussulmans, the remainder chiefly Jews. In the center and lowest part of the town are two large pools, which collect the rain water from the adjacent hills (2 Sam. iv. 12). There is a famous mosque, the precincts of which are called el-Haram (the enclosure). Within the enclosure is a cave, believed to be that of Machpelah (see MACHPELAH). The oak or terebinth of Abraham has been shown at two places; that

The old and the new blend into one in Hebron today.

which now exists is a genuine oak (*Quercus pseudococcifera*) (see MAMRE). There are twenty-five springs of water and ten large wells near Hebron, with vineyards and olive-groves.

3. A town of Asher (Josh. xix. 28, A. V.), but its Hebrew name is different from that of Hebron in Judah; see EBRON.

He'bron-ites.

The descendants of Hebron the Kohath-ite (Num. iii. 27; 1 Chron. xxvi. 30, 31).

He'gai and **He'ge.**

One of the chamberlains of king Ahasue-rus. He was the keeper of the women (Esth. ii. 3, 8, 15).

Heif'er.

A young cow (Gen. xv. 9; Deut. xxi. 3; 1 Sam. xvi. 2); see COW and PURIFICATION.

Heir.

Inheritance early became a custom. Abraham was acquainted with it (Gen. xv. 3, 4). Only sons of a legal wife, not those of a concubine, had the right of inheritance. Ishmael, son of the bondwoman, might not inherit with the son of the free woman (xxi. 10); and Abraham dismissed with presents the sons whom he had begotten by concubines (xxv. 5, 6). Still all of Jacob's sons were accorded equal rights. Daughters sometimes inherited like sons (Job xlii. 15). By the Mosaic law a man's property was divided on his death among his sons, the eldest obtaining double the portion assigned to his younger brothers (Deut. xxi. 15–17). When there were no sons, the property went to the daughters (Num. xxvii. 1–8), who, however, were required to abstain from marrying out of their own tribal family (Num. xxxvi. 1–12; Tob. vi. 10–12). If circumstances demanded that a man of other family marry a sole heiress, the children of such a marriage appear to have taken the name of the mother's father (1 Chron. ii. 34–41; Ezra ii. 61). Failing both sons and daughters, the inheritance went to the father's brother, and after him to the nearest of kin (Num. xxvii. 9–11). Greek and Roman rule introduced new customs, and made testaments and testators familiar to the Jews (Heb. ix. 16, 17). In a figurative sense, believers are heirs of God and joint heirs with Christ (Rom. viii. 17).

He'lah [scum, rust, verdigris].

One of the two wives of Ashhur, the ancestor of the men of Tekoa (1 Chron. iv. 5, 7).

He'lam.

A place east of Jordan, where David defeated Hadarezer, king of Syria (2 Sam. x. 16–19). Ewald and others doubtfully identify it with Alamatha, a town mentioned by Ptolemy as west of the Euphrates, near Nicephorium.

Hel'bah [fatness, a fertile region].

A city within the territory of Asher, from which the Canaanites were not driven out (Judg. i. 31). Site unknown.

Hel'bon [fat, fertile].

A city of Syria, celebrated for its wines (Ezek. xxvii. 18). It is commonly identified with Helbun, 13 miles north of Damascus. The village is situated in a narrow valley shut in by steep, bare cliffs and long, shelving banks 2000 to 3000 feet high. The bottom of the glen is occupied by orchards, and far up the mountain slopes are terraced vineyards. Along the terraces and in the valley below are extensive ruins. The wine was celebrated in Assyria, Babylonia, and Persia (Strabo xv. 735; Nebuchadnezzar 1 R. 65, 32).

Hel'dai [durable, transitoriness].

1. A Netophathite, descended from Othniel. He was David's captain for the twelfth month (1 Chron. xxvii. 15). Doubtless the person called Heled in xi. 30.

2. An exile who returned from Babylon (Zech. vi. 10), called also Helem (ver. 14).

He'leb [fatness].

The name given to Heled in 2 Sam. xxiii. 29. It may possibly be the original name, but probably arose from the mistake of an early copyist, which is quite intelligible and common.

He'led [endurance, transitory life].

The son of Baanah, a Netophathite, and one of David's mighty men (1 Chron. xi. 30). See HELEB and HELDAI.

He'lek [smoothness, portion, lot].

A son of Gilead, and founder of a tribal family of Manasseh (Num. xxvi. 30; Josh. xvii. 2).

He'lem, I. [blow, stroke].

An Asherite, brother of Shamer (1 Chron. vii. 35), and probably the person called Hotham in ver. 32.

He'lem, II. [dream, or, perhaps, manly vigor].

The same as Heldai 2 (Zech. vi. 10 with 14).

He'leph [permutation, change, exchange].

A frontier town of Naphtali (Josh. xix. 33). Van de Velde identified it with Beit Lif, in the mountains of Galilee, midway between Kadesh and Ras el-Abiad.

He'lez [perhaps, alertness].

1. A Paltite or Pelonite, David's captain for the seventh month (1 Chron. xxvii. 10).

2. A man of Judah, descended from Hezron (1 Chron. ii. 39).

He'li [Greek form of Eli, probably elevation].

The father of Mary, the mother of Jesus. This belief is founded on the Greek text, which represents Jesus as "being son (as was supposed of Joseph) of Heli" (Luke iii. 23).

Hel'kai [smooth].

A priest, head of the father's house Meraioth (Neh. xii. 15).

Hel'kath [smoothness, a part (of a field), a field].

A town on the boundary line of Asher

(Josh. xix. 25), assigned, with its suburbs, to the Gershonite Levites (xxi. 31). Called in 1 Chron. vi. 75 Hukok, which is probably a corruption of the text. Van de Velde and Robinson doubtfully identify it with Yerka, 8½ miles east by north of Acre.

Hel-kath-haz'zu-rim [field of the sharp knives].

A name given to the scene of the combat, at the pool of Gibeon, between twelve Benjamites of Ish-bosheth's party and the same number of David's men (2 Sam. ii. 16).

Hell.

1. The place of the dead. It is one rendering of the Hebrew word *Sh^e'ol* and the Greek '*Aidēs* (Ps. xvi. 10 with Acts ii. 27). R. V. of O. T. places Sheol either in the text or on the margin; in the prophetical books, on the margin with hell generally in the text, and in Deut. xxxii. 22; Ps. lv. 15; lxxxvi. 13, on the margin, with pit in the text. In N. T. it puts Hades in the text. The two words are also rendered grave (Gen. xxxvii. 35; Is. xxxviii. 10, 18; Hos. xiii. 14; and A. V. of 1 Cor. xv. 55, in R. V. death). The etymology of the words is in doubt. Sheol may mean the insatiable (cp. Prov. xxvii. 20, R. V.; xxx. 15, 16). Hades, when pronounced without the aspiration, means the unseen. Both words denote the place of the dead. The evidence is not all in, but it may be safely affirmed that for centuries the Hebrews shared the common Semitic conception of Sheol. This conception was vague and undefined. There was consequently room for the imagination to play, and fancy was fond of supplying all manner of details; and care must be taken not to confound fancies with faith. The ancient Hebrews, like other Semites, thought of Sheol as beneath the earth (Num. xvi. 30, 33; Ezek. xxxi. 17; Amos ix. 2). They pictured it as entered through gates (Is. xxxviii. 10), a dark, gloomy region, where the inhabitants pass a conscious, but dull, inactive existence (2 Sam. xxii. 6; Ps. vi. 5; Ecc. ix. 10). They regarded it as the place whither the souls of all men without distinction go (Gen. xxxvii. 35; Ps. xxxi. 17; Is. xxxviii. 10), where punishments may be suffered and rewards enjoyed, and from which a return to earth was not an impossibility (1 Sam. xxviii. 8-19; Heb. xi. 19). It is important to note, however, that in authoritative Hebrew doctrine Sheol was open and naked to God (Job xxvi. 6; Prov. xv. 11), that God was even there (Ps. cxxxix. 8), and that the spirits of his people, and their condition in that abode, were ever under his watchful eye. This doctrine of God's knowledge of his people after death, presence with them, and unceasing love for them, involved the blessedness of the righteous and the woe of the wicked after death, and two places of abode for them, the righteous being with the Lord and the wicked being banished from his presence. This doctrine lay also at the basis

of the related teaching of the eventual resurrection of the body, and the life everlasting. The doctrine of future glory, and even of the resurrection of the body, was cherished in O. T. times (Job xix. 25-27; Ps. xvi. 8-11; xvii. 15; xlix. 14, 15; lxxiii. 24; Dan. xii. 2, 3). A foundation for it was early afforded by the translation of Enoch and Elijah, and it was fostered by centuries of intimate association with the Egyptians, who had congruous teaching regarding the future life and the relation of morality in the present life to happiness beyond the grave. But it remained for Christ to bring immortality to full light, and, by revealing the bliss of the saved soul even out of the body in his presence, to dispel all gloom from the future abode of his saints (Luke xxiii. 43; John xiv. 1-3; 2 Cor. v. 6-8; Phil. i. 23). See PARADISE.

2. The place of woe. In this sense it is the rendering of the Greek *Gehenna* in Mat. v. 22, 29, 30; x. 28; xviii. 9; xxiii. 15, 33; Mark ix. 47; Luke xii. 5, and Jas. iii. 6. This word is the Greek form of the Hebrew *Gehinnom*, valley of Hinnom, where children were burnt to Molech. From the horrible sins practiced in it, its pollution by Josiah, and perhaps also because offal was burnt in it, the valley of Hinnom became a type of sin and woe, and the name passed into use as a designation for the place of eternal punishment (Mat. xviii. 8, 9; Mark ix. 43). From the scenes witnessed in the valley imagery was borrowed to describe the Gehenna of the lost (Mat. v. 22; cp. xiii. 42; Mark ix. 48). In 2 Pet. ii. 4, "to cast down to hell" is the rendering of the verb *tartaroō*, meaning "to cast down to Tartarus." The *Tartarus* of the Romans, the *Tartaros* of the Greeks, was their place of woe, situated as far below Hades as Hades was below heaven. Though the etymologies are different, Gehenna and Tartarus are essentially the same in meaning. Each is the place of punishment for the lost.

Hel'len-ist.

One, not of the Greek nation, who spoke Greek. The term is used specially of Jews, in whatever part of the world they lived, who had adopted the Greek tongue, and with it often Greek practices and opinions (R. V., margin of Acts vi. 1 and ix. 29). The text calls them Grecian Jews; the A. V. simply Grecians.

Hel'met. See ARMOR.

He'lon [perhaps, strong].

Father of Eliab, prince of Zebulun (Num. i. 9; ii. 7; vii. 24, 29; x. 16).

Hem.

The edge, border, or margin of a garment (Ex. xxviii. 33, 34; xxxix. 24, 25, 26, in the R. V. skirts; and Mat. ix. 20; xiv. 36, in the R. V. borders). The Jews attached a certain sacredness to the hem, fringe, or border of their garments.

He'mam. See HOMAM.

He'man [faithful].

1. A sage whose reputation for wisdom was high in Solomon's reign (1 Kin. iv. 31). He belonged to the tribe of Judah (1 Chron. ii. 6). He composed a meditative psalm (Ps. lxxxviii., according to its second and doubtless original title).

2. A singer in David's reign, a son of Joel, a grandson of the prophet Samuel, of the Levite family of Korah (1 Chron. vi. 33; xv. 17). He was also appointed to sound a brazen cymbal (19). He rose to prominence among David's musicians (xvi. 41, 42).

He'math. See HAMATH for Amos vi. 14, A. V., and HAMMATH for 1 Chron. ii. 55, A. V.

Hem'dan [pleasant, desirable].

A Horite, the eldest son of Dishon (Gen. xxxvi. 26). In the parallel passage, 1 Chron. i. 41, the Hebrew text and R. V. have Hamran, which A. V. erroneously represents by Amram. The two Hebrew words differ only in the third consonant. The difference is undoubtedly due to a scribe who confounded resh and daleth (q. v.). Whether Hemdan or Hamran was the original form cannot be determined at present.

Hem'lock. See GALL 2 and WORMWOOD.

Hen, I. See COCK.

Hen, II. [grace, favor, kindness].

A son of Zephaniah (Zech. vi. 14). But on the margin of R. V. Hen is translated, the passage reading thus, "for the kindness of the son of Zephaniah," in which case that son's name disappears.

He'na.

A city captured by the Assyrians (2 Kin. xviii. 34; xix. 13; Is. xxxvii. 13). It is mentioned with Sepharvaim and Ivvah, and is commonly identified with the ancient town of Ana, at a ford of the Euphrates, 160 miles northwest of Sepharvaim. But the two names are radically different. Or possibly Hena, was on an island of the Euphrates, where Assyrian inscriptions locate a certain Anat. The Targum translates Hena and Ivvah as verbs, not as names of towns; but Ivvah, if the same as Avva (2 Kin. xvii. 24), was a town. See AVVA.

Hen'a-dad [probably, favor of Hadad].

Founder of a Levitical family, whose sons supported Zerubbabel at the time the foundations of the temple were being laid (Ezra iii. 9), and assisted in rebuilding the wall of Jerusalem (Neh. iii. 18).

Hen'na [Persian *henna*, Arabic *ḥanna*].

The rendering of the Hebrew *Kopher*, covering, in the Septuagint and in R. V. of Song i. 14 and iv. 13. It is translated in the A. V. camphire. Henna is a plant of the *Lythrarieæ* or loosestrife order (*Lawsonia alba* or *inermis*), with opposite entire leaves, and fragrant, yellow and white flowers in corymbs or clusters (Song i. 14). The Greeks called it *kupros*, from the island of Cyprus, where it grew. In Palestine its special seat was the virtually

tropical region of En-gedi (Song i. 14) and Jericho (War iv. 8, 3). The leaves and young twigs are made into a fine powder, converted into paste with hot water, and used by oriental women and wealthy men to dye the finger and toe nails and the soles of the feet a reddish orange color. Some Egyptian mummies are found with these parts dyed in the same manner.

He'noch. See ENOCH for 1 Chron. i. 3, A. V., and HANOCH for 1 Chron. i. 33, A. V.

He'pher [pit, well].

1. A town west of the Jordan (Josh. xii. 17). The name belonged to a district also, probably near Socoh (1 Kin. iv. 10).

2. A son of Gilead, founder of a tribal family of Manasseh (Num. xxvi. 32; xxvii. 1; Josh. xvii. 2).

3. A man of Judah, son of Ashhur of Tekoa (1 Chron. iv. 6).

4. A Mecherathite, and one of David's worthies (1 Chron. xi. 36). See, however, remarks under UR, II.

Heph'zi-bah [my delight is in her].

1. Mother of king Manasseh (2 Kin. xxi. 1).

2. A symbolical name to be given to Zion (Is. lxii. 4).

He'res [sun].

1. An eminence in the district of Aijalon (Judg. i. 35). The meaning and a comparison with Josh. xix. 41, 42 render the opinion probable that mount Heres is essentially identical with the town Ir-shemesh, that is Beth-shemesh.

2. A pass east of the Jordan (Judg. viii. 13, R. V.).

3. An Egyptian city. See ON.

He'resh [artificial work, artifice, silence].

A Levite (1 Chron. ix. 15).

Her'e-sy [Greek *'airesis*, taking (especially of a town); a sect (Acts v. 17; xv. 5)].

1. A party, sect, or faction; strong party spirit, even when this is not produced on one side or the other by departure from sound doctrine (1 Cor. xi. 19, on margin of R.V. sects, factions; Gal. v. 20, on margin of R. V. parties).

2. A doctrine or a sect consequent upon departure from sound doctrine (2 Pet. ii. 1, margin of R. V. sects of perdition).

He'reth, in A. V. **Hareth,** the Hebrew pausal form.

A forest in Judah, in which David for a time lurked while his life was being sought by Saul (1 Sam. xxii. 5).

Her'mas.

A Christian at Rome to whom Paul sent his salutations (Rom. xvi. 14).

Her'mes.

1. The Greek god corresponding to the Roman Mercury (Acts xiv. 12, R. V. margin). See MERCURY.

2. A Christian (not the same as Hermas) at Rome, to whom Paul sent his salutations (Rom. xvi. 14).

Her-mog′e-nes [sprung from Hermes].

An inhabitant of the Roman province of Asia, who finally, with many others, turned away from the apostle Paul (2 Tim. i. 15).

Her′mon [mountain peak or sacred mountain].

A mountain called by the Sidonians Sirion, a coat of mail, and by the Amorites Senir or Shenir (Deut. iii. 8, 9). The last name belonged especially to a part of the mountain. Another name for it was Sion, elevated (iv. 48). It constituted the northeastern limit of the Israelite conquests under Moses and Joshua (Deut. iii. 8, 9; Josh. xi. 3, 17; xii. 1, 5; xiii. 5, 11; 1 Chron. v. 23). It figures in Hebrew poetry, being coupled with Tabor (Ps. lxxxix. 12), Zion (cxxxiii. 3), and Lebanon (Song iv. 8), really, however, overtopping them all. It constitutes the southern end of the Anti-Lebanon chain, and rises to the elevation of 9166 feet above the sea. It may be seen from many parts of Palestine. From the plain of Tyre, the north peak seems higher than the southern one, and the center more depressed than either. Having these peaks it is described as the Hermons (Ps. xlii. 6,

R. V.); or perhaps the word in this passage is a common noun and means peaks of Palestine. The summit of the mountain is covered with snow all the year round, wavy white furrows descending from the crest in the lines of the several valleys. The proper source of the Jordan is in Hermon. Some one of its solitary recesses rather than the summit of Tabor was probably the scene of our Lord's transfiguration. Hermon is now called Jebel esh-Sheik.

Her′mon-ites.

Natives or inhabitants of mount Hermon (Ps. xlii. 6, A. V.; in R. V., the Hermons).

Her′od.

The name of several rulers over Palestine and the adjacent regions or portions of them. Three are mentioned in the N. T. by the name of Herod and one by the name of Agrippa.

1. HEROD THE GREAT.—He was the second son of the Idumæan Antipas, or Antipater, by his wife Cyprus, who was of the same race (Antiq. xiv. 1, 3: 7, 3). Thus, neither by the father's nor by the mother's side was Herod a real Jew,

The Sea of Galilee with Mount Hermon in the distance.

though the Idumæans, who had been conquered 125 B. C. by John Hyrcanus, and compelled to be circumcised and adopt Judaism, had now become nominally Jews.

Antipater was made procurator of Judæa by Cæsar in 47 B. C. (Antiq. xiv. 8, 3 and 5). He had five children, Phasaelus, Herod, Joseph, Pheroras, and a daughter Salome (7, 3).* Phasaelus, the eldest son, was made governor of Jerusalem and vicinity by his father, and Galilee was committed to Herod, who was then 25 years old (9, 2). After the murder of Antipater, 43 B. C., Marc Antony visited Syria and appointed the two brothers tetrarchs, committing the public affairs of the Jews to them (13, 1). They were afterwards sorely pressed by Antigonus, last king of the Maccabæan family, and the Parthians. Phasaelus fell into their hands and committed suicide to avoid being put to death by them (13, 10). The Romans were now induced by Antony to espouse the cause of Herod; and war ensued with Antigonus and the Parthians, in the course of which Herod's brother Joseph was slain in battle (15, 10), Jerusalem was captured and Herod became king of Judæa in 37 B. C.

The surviving children of Antipater were now Herod, Pheroras, and Salome. Salome married her uncle Joseph (Antiq. xv. 3, 5; War i. 22, 4). After he had been put to death for adultery, 34 B. C., she married Costobarus, an Idumæan of good family whom Herod made governor of Idumæa and Gaza (Antiq. xv. 7, 9; War i. 24, 6). She divorced him (Antiq. xv. 7, 10), and against her will was married to Alexas, a friend of Herod's (War i. 28, 6). During the whole of Herod's reign, she engaged in intrigues against members of his family; but she was faithful to him, and he bequeathed to her Jamnia, Ashdod, and Phasaelis near Jericho (Antiq. xvii. 6, 1; 8, 1: 11, 5). She accompanied Herod's son Archelaus to Rome, when he went thither to obtain imperial sanction to ascend the throne. Her ostensible purpose was to assist him in prosecuting his claim, but her real object was to thwart him (War

ii. 2, 1-4). She died about A. D. 10, when Marcus Ambivius was procurator (Antiq. xviii. 2, 2). Pheroras, the youngest of the four sons of Antipater (Antiq. xiv. 15, 4), lived nearly as long as Herod. He was partner in the kingdom, had the title of tetrarch, and enjoyed the revenue accruing from the country east of the Jordan (War i. 24, 5). He was more than once accused of plotting the death of Herod, and matters came to a crisis shortly before the latter's death; but Pheroras died without being brought to trial (Antiq. xvii. 3, 3).

Herod the Great had ten wives from first to last (Antiq. xvii. 1, 3; War i. xxviii. 4). His first wife was Doris, a woman of an obscure family in Jerusalem. She bore him one son, Antipater, who took an active part in the events of Herod's reign, plotting against his younger half-brothers to secure the kingdom for himself. Herod, just before the capture of Jerusalem, by which he became king, married his second wife, the beautiful and chaste Mariamne, granddaughter of Hyrcanus. She bore him three sons, Alexander, Aristobulus, and the youngest son who died childless, and two daughters, Cyprus and Salampsio. Mariamne was put to death in 29 B. C. (Antiq. xv. 7, 4). About 24 B. C. he married Mariamne, daughter of Simon, whom he raised to the high-priesthood (xv. 9, 3; xviii. 5, 4). Herod also took to wife his two nieces, whose names are not given and who died childless, Malthace a Samaritan, Cleopatra of Jerusalem, Pallas, Phædra, and Elpis. With the two unnamed nieces and last three of known name history is not specially concerned. The descendants of the others are more important. Of Mariamne, Simon's daughter, Herod was born; Malthace became mother of Archelaus, Herod Antipas, and a daughter Olympias; and Cleopatra bore Herod and Philip.

The domestic troubles of Herod began early in his reign in the hatred which he incited in the beloved Mariamne toward himself; and they culminated in the last decade of his reign, when his sons had reached

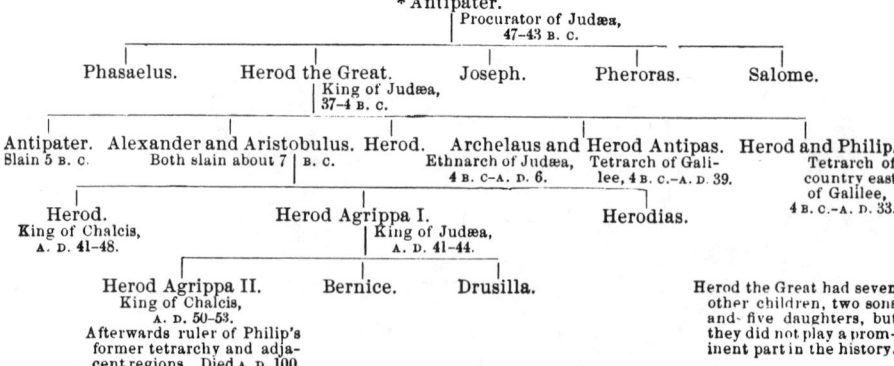

* Antipater.
Procurator of Judæa, 47-43 B. C.

| Phasaelus. | Herod the Great. King of Judæa, 37-4 B. C. | Joseph. | Pheroras. | Salome. |

| Antipater. Slain 5 B. C. | Alexander and Aristobulus. Both slain about 7 B. C. | Herod. | Archelaus and Herod Antipas. Ethnarch of Judæa, 4 B. C.–A. D. 6. Tetrarch of Galilee, 4 B. C.–A. D. 39. | Herod and Philip. Tetrarch of country east of Galilee, 4 B. C.–A. D. 33. |

| Herod. King of Chalcis, A. D. 41-48. | Herod Agrippa I. King of Judæa, A. D. 41-44. | Herodias. |

| Herod Agrippa II. King of Chalcis, A. D. 50-53. Afterwards ruler of Philip's former tetrarchy and adjacent regions. Died A. D. 100. | Bernice. | Drusilla. | Herod the Great had seven other children, two sons and five daughters, but they did not play a prominent part in the history. |

manhood. The domestic history eventually revolves about the eight young men, Antipater, son of Doris; Alexander and Aristobulus, sons of Mariamne; Herod, son of Mariamne, Simon's daughter; Archelaus and Antipas, sons of Malthace; and Herod and Philip, sons of Cleopatra. Alexander married Glyphyra, daughter of Archelaus, king of Cappadocia. Two sons were born to them whose history is not important (Antiq. xvi. 1, 2; War i. 24, 2). Aristobulus married his first cousin, Bernice, daughter of Herod's sister, Salome, and became the father of five children, several of whom played an important part later in the history. Of these two young men, sons of the beloved Mariamne, Antipater, the firstborn of Herod, was jealous. His jealousy was aroused against his half-brothers by the evident intention of his father to overlook his right as firstborn in their favor (War i. 22, 1), and he and his clique at court poisoned the mind of Herod against them. At length, about 7 or 6 B. C., Herod had them put to death, named Antipater his heir and appointed Herod, son of Mariamne, Simon's daughter, next in succession (Antiq. xvi. 11, 7; xvii. 3, 2; War i. 29, 2). This order conformed to birth, his sons Archelaus and Antipas, Herod and Philip, being doubtless younger than Herod, son of Mariamne. Antipater next accused Herod's sister, Salome, and his sons, Archelaus and Philip, who were in Rome being educated, of plotting the murder of Herod; but the crime charged against Salome was brought home to himself. He and his uncle Pheroras, Herod's brother, were accused of seeking the king's life. Pheroras died, but Antipater was cast into prison. Herod's suspicions were thereby aroused that Antipater had falsely accused Alexander and Aristobulus, who had already been executed, and he altered his will, appointing Antipas to be his successor, and passed over Archelaus, the elder brother, and Philip, as he still held them in suspicion (War i. 32, 7). Soon afterwards he ordered Antipater to be slain and altered his will again, giving the kingdom to Archelaus, making Antipas tetrarch of Galilee and Peræa, and Philip tetrarch of Batanea, Trachonitis, and Auranitis, and bestowing several cities on his sister Salome (Antiq. xvii. 8, 1; War i, 33, 7). Herod's disposition of his affairs was observed at his death, except that Archelaus was finally confirmed by the emperor Augustus not as king but as ethnarch of Judæa (Antiq. xvii. 11, 4 and 5).

Herod, son of Simon's daughter, Mariamne, married, or had married, Herodias, daughter of his half-brother, the dead Aristobulus. She, however, left him and married another half-brother of his, Herod the tetrarch, and her former husband disappears from history. So does Herod, son of Cleopatra and brother of Philip, the tetrarch. See HERODIAS and PHILIP. Aristobulus, as already mentioned,

had married his cousin, Bernice, daughter of Salome, and had begotten five children (War i. 28, 1). They were Herod, Agrippa, Aristobulus, Herodias, and Mariamne. Herod married Mariamne, daughter of Olympias, daughter of Herod the Great and the Samaritan Malthace; Agrippa married Cyprus, daughter of Salampsio and Phasaelus the younger, son of Herod the Great's brother, Phasaelus; Aristobulus married Jotape, daughter of a king of Emesa; Herodias married two uncles in succession, as already noted; and Mariamne married Antipater, son of Doris (Antiq. xviii. 5, 4; War i. 28, 5; cp. 4). Three of these children of Aristobulus are persons of note—namely, Herod, Agrippa, and Herodias. Herodias was the woman who crowned her infamies by telling her daughter to demand the head of John the Baptist in a charger. Herod was made king of Chalcis, and after his wife's death took his niece, Bernice, Agrippa's daughter, to wife. Agrippa became king Agrippa I. He married, had one son and three daughters. Three of these children are mentioned in Scripture, Agrippa II. and the two notorious women, Bernice and Drusilla.

Besides this domestic history of the rise of the family to power and the intrigues among its members, there is the political history of Herod's reign. Soon after he had been made ruler in Galilee, which was in 47 or 46 B. C., he came in contact with the sanhedrin through his summary execution of some robbers without the sanhedrin's formal permission. He was summoned for trial and appeared with an armed body guard, intimidating the council. He was acquitted for lack of evidence. Herod sought to be, for his own interest, on good terms with the successive representatives of the warring factions into which the Roman people were then divided. He obtained a generalship from Sextus Cæsar, president of Syria, a relative of the great Julius Cæsar; and then, after a time, gained the favor of Cassius, the most malignant of the great dictator's assassins. Then he cast in his lot with Marc Antony, one of the murdered man's chief avengers; nor was even this his last change of sides. About 41 B. C. Herod was made tetrarch of Galilee by Antony, and having, after fresh vicissitudes, gone to Rome in 40 B. C., as a fugitive rather than a visitor, his patron induced the Roman senate to appoint him king of the Jews. It was not, however, till 37 B. C. that, with the assistance of Sosius, a general of Antony's, he succeeded in taking Jerusalem, and commencing his actual reign. By his marriage at this time with Mariamne, granddaughter of Hyrcanus and daughter of Alexander, son of Aristobulus, he became allied with the royal Asmonæan family. He now endeavored to further strengthen his position by the removal of possible rivals. The principal members of the party of Antigonus, forty-five in number, were sought out and put to death. Soon afterwards Mariamne's brother, Aristobulus, a boy of seventeen, whom Herod had just raised to the high-priesthood, was drowned in a bath by Herod's orders, within a year after his elevation to the pontificate; and about 31 B. C. her grandfather, although eighty years old, was put to death (Antiq. xv. 1, 2; 3, 3; 6, 2). Herod's attention was called from these atrocities by the new crisis which had arisen. His patron Antony was totally defeated by Octavius in the sea fight at Actium on September 2, 31 B. C. The position of Herod was now critical, but he made a manly and judicious speech to the victorious Octavius, and was forgiven for his partisanship toward Antony. He was given the friendship of the man he had offended, and retained it through most of his life, besides having his dominions increased (xv. 6, 5-7; 10, 3). The murder of a wife's brother and her grandfather did not tend to increase her attachment to her husband, and by and by variance arose between Herod and Mariamne. It increased, till it culminated at length in the queen's being falsely accused and executed. Remorse followed in due course, and almost, if not altogether, deprived the king of reason (Antiq. xv. 7, 7; xvii. 6, 5; War i. 22, 5; 33, 5). Partly to divert his mind from gloomy remembrances, partly to please Octavius, now the emperor Augustus, he built theaters and exhibited games, both of these acts being inconsistent with Judaism. He also rebuilt, enlarged, and beautified a place named Strato's Tower, calling it, after his imperial patron, Cæsarea. It ultimately became the Roman capital of Palestine (Antiq. xv. 8, 5; 9, 6; cp. Acts xxiii. 23, 24). Then, to conciliate the Jews, he, between 19 and 11 or 9 B. C., rebuilt and beautified the temple. The birth of Jesus Christ took place at the close of Herod's life, after he had removed his rivals from other families by violent deaths, and when his domestic troubles were at their height. He had slain his sons Alexander and Aristobulus, and more recently Antipater, for plotting against his life; and now he was told that a child of David's line had just been born to be king of the Jews. The slaughter of the infants who came into the world about the same time and place was such a method of meeting the difficulty as would suggest itself to one with Herod's propensity to bloodshed (Mat. ii. 1-19). It was one of the last acts of his life. Seized at length with loathsome and mortal disease, he repaired to Callirhoe, the hot sulphur springs of the Zerka, the water from which runs into the eastern part of the Dead Sea. They came to be called, in consequence, by many, the baths of Herod; but they did not do the king much good (Antiq. xvii. 6, 5). He felt that he was dying, and that there would be rejoicing when he passed away. He therefore told his sister Salome and her husband Alexas to shut up the principal

Jews in the circus at Jericho, and put them to death whenever he expired, that there might be mourning at, though, of course, not for, his death. Then, about 4 B. C., he passed away, in the seventieth year of his age and the thirty-fourth of his reign, counting from the time when he actually obtained the kingdom. When news of his demise arrived, the circus prisoners were set free, and the death of the tyrant was welcomed as a relief instead of being attended by mourning, lamentation, and woe (Antiq. xvii. 6, 5; 8, 2).

2. HEROD THE TETRARCH.—A son of Herod the Great by his Samaritan wife called Malthace. He was, therefore, half Idumæan and half Samaritan, perhaps without a single drop of Jewish blood in his veins. He was called indifferently Antipas and Herod (Antiq. xvii. 1, 3; xviii. 5, 1: 6, 2; War ii. 9, 1), and it is customary to distinguish him from the other Herods of the family as Herod Antipas. He was the full brother of Archelaus, and was younger than Archelaus (Antiq. xvii. 6, 1; War i. 32, 7; 33, 7). He was educated with him and his half-brother Philip at Rome (Antiq. xvii. 1, 3). By the second testament of his father, the kingdom was bequeathed to him (6, 1); but by his father's final will he was appointed tetrarch of Galilee and the kingdom was given to Archelaus (8, 1). On his father's death he competed with his brother for the kingdom, but received only the tetrarchy of Galilee and Peræa (Antiq. xvii. 11, 4; Luke iii. 1). He erected a wall around Sepphoris, and made it his metropolis. Betharamphtha in Peræa he walled, and built a palace there. It was named Livias and Julias, after Augustus' daughter (Antiq. xviii. 2, 1); see BETH-HARAN. He also built Tiberias (3). He married a daughter of Aretas, king of the Nabathæan Arabs, whose capital was Petra; but afterwards, while lodging at Rome with Herod Philip, his half-brother, he indulged a guilty passion for his entertainer's wife, Herodias, and arranged to divorce his lawful consort and take Herodias instead. This immoral transaction was carried into effect. Herodias was a masculine woman, Herod a weak man; she was his evil genius, and made a tool of him, as Jezebel had done of Ahab. Aretas resented the injury inflicted upon his daughter, and he commenced a war against Herod and waged it successfully (5, 1). Herodias was the prime mover in the murder of John the Baptist (Mat. xiv. 1-13; Antiq. xviii. 5, 2). Because of his cunning, the tetrarch was described by our Lord as that fox (Luke xiii. 31, 32). But the tetrarch had a following, for mention is made of the leaven of Herod (Mark viii. 15); see HERODIANS. When the fame of Jesus began to spread abroad, the uneasy conscience of Herod made him fear that John had risen from the dead (Mat. xiv. 1, 2). He was present at Jerusalem at the time of the crucifixion, and Jesus was sent to him by Pilate. He thought that now he

would have the opportunity of seeing a miracle performed, but he was disappointed, and with his men of war set Jesus at naught. The same day he was reconciled to Pilate, whereas they had before been at variance (Luke xxiii. 7-12, 15; Acts iv. 27). The advancement of Herodias' brother Agrippa to be king, while her husband remained only tetrarch, aroused the envy of this proud woman, and she prevailed upon Herod to go with her to Rome and ask for a crown. Agrippa, however, sent letters after them to the emperor Caligula, accusing Herod of being secretly in league with the Parthians, and Herod was in consequence banished to Lyons in Gaul, A. D. 39, where he died (Antiq. xviii. 7, 1, 2; War ii. 9, 6, Greek text).

3. HEROD THE KING.—Josephus calls him simply Agrippa. Both names are generally combined, and he is designated Herod Agrippa I., to distinguish him from Herod Agrippa II., before whom Paul was tried. Agrippa I. was the son of Aristobulus, son of Herod the Great and Mariamne, granddaughter of Hyrcanus. He was educated in Rome with Drusus, son of the emperor Tiberius, and Claudius (Antiq. xviii. 6, 1 and 4); but the death of Drusus and lack of funds led to his return to Judæa (2). In A. D. 37 he made another journey to Rome to bring accusations against Herod the tetrarch (Antiq. xviii. 5, 3; War ii. 9, 5). He did not return when his business was transacted, but remained in the metropolis, cultivating the acquaintance of people who might be of use to him in the future. Among others, he ingratiated himself with Caius, son of Germanicus, who shortly became the emperor Caligula (Antiq. xviii. 6, 4; War ii. 9, 5). For rash words spoken in favor of Caius, Tiberius cast him into chains; but six months later Caius became emperor, and appointed Agrippa to be king of the tetrarchy which his late uncle Philip had governed, and also of the tetrarchy of Lysanias (Antiq. xviii. 6, 10). In A. D. 39 the emperor banished Herod the tetrarch, and added his tetrarchy, which was Galilee, to the kingdom of Agrippa (7, 2). Agrippa left his kingdom for a time, and resided at Rome (8, 7). During this sojourn at the capital he prevailed upon the emperor to desist from his determination to erect his statue in the temple at Jerusalem (8, 7 and 8). When Caligula was assassinated, and Claudius, against his own will, chosen in his room, Agrippa, who was then at Rome, acted as negotiator between the senate and the new emperor, whom he persuaded to take office. As a reward, Agrippa had Judæa and Samaria added to his dominions, which now equaled those of Herod the Great (Antiq. xix. 3-5; War ii. 11, 1-5). He commenced to build a wall about the northern suburb of Jerusalem, so as to include it in the city, but was ordered to abandon the work (Antiq. xix. 7, 2). He slew James, the brother of John, with the sword (Acts xii. 1, 2), imprisoned

Peter (3-19), and at Cæsarea, immediately after he had accepted divine honor, was miserably eaten up of worms (20-23; Antiq. xix. 8, 2). He died A. D. 44, in the fifty-fourth year of his age, leaving four children, of whom three are mentioned in Scripture, Agrippa, Bernice, and Drusilla (War ii. 11. 6).

4. AGRIPPA, commonly known as Herod Agrippa II. He was son of Herod Agrippa I., and consequently great-grandson of Herod the Great, and was the brother of the notorious women Bernice and Drusilla (War ii. 11, 6). At the time of his father's death, A. D. 44, he was 17 years old, and residing at Rome, where he was being brought up in the imperial household (Antiq. xix. 9, 1 and 2). The emperor Claudius was dissuaded from appointing him to the throne of his father on account of his youth, and Judæa was placed under a procurator. Agrippa remained in Rome. He successfully seconded the efforts of the Jewish ambassadors to obtain the imperial permission to retain the official robes of the high priest under their own control (xx. 1, 1). When his uncle Herod, king of Chalcis, died about A. D. 48, Claudius presently bestowed his small realm on the western slope of Anti-Lebanon on Agrippa (5, 2; War ii. 12, 1; 14, 4; cp. i. 9. 2), so that he became king Agrippa. He espoused the cause of the Jewish commissioners who had come to Rome to appear against the procurator Cumanus and the Samaritans, and he prevailed upon the emperor to grant them an audience (Antiq. xx. 6, 3; War ii. 12, 7). In A. D. 52 Claudius transferred him from the kingdom of Chalcis to a larger realm formed of the tetrarchy of Philip, which contained Batanea, Trachonitis, and Gaulonitis, the tetrarchy of Lysanias, and the province of Abilene (Antiq. xx. 7, 1; War ii. 12, 8). His constant companionship with his sister Bernice about this time began to create scandal (Antiq. xx. 7, 3). In A. D. 54 or 55 Nero added the cities of Tiberias and Taricheæ in Galilee and Julias in Peræa with its dependent towns to his dominion (8, 4). When Felix had been succeeded by Festus as procurator of Judæa, Agrippa went to Cæsarea to salute him, accompanied by Bernice. Paul was then in confinement. Festus laid his case before the king, and on the morrow the apostle was permitted to plead his cause before the procurator, the king, and Bernice. He was entirely successful in clearing himself (Acts xxv. 13-xxvi. 32). Soon afterwards Agrippa built an addition to the palace of the Asmonæans at Jerusalem (Antiq. xx. 8, 11). Later still he enlarged and beautified Cæsarea Philippi, and established theatrical exhibitions at Berytus (9, 4). When the troubles which culminated in the Jewish war began, Agrippa endeavored to dissuade the Jews from making armed resistance to Fadus the procurator and the Romans (War ii. 16, 2-5; 17, 4; 18, 9; 19, 3). When the war broke in its fury, he fought by the side of Vespasian

and was wounded at the siege of Gamala (iii. 9, 7 and 8; 10, 10; iv. 1, 3). After the capture of Jerusalem he removed with Bernice to Rome, where he was invested with the dignity of prætor. He died A. D. 100.

Her'od, Pal'ace of.

A palace-fortress erected by Herod the Great about the year 24 or 23 B. C. (Antiq. xv. 9, 1 and 3). It stood at the northwest corner of the upper city, adjoined the towers of Hippicus, Phasaelus, and Mariamne on their south, and formed with them a stronghold which excited the admiration of even the Romans (War v. 4, 4; 5, 8; vi. 8, 1; 9, 1). Its site is the modern citadel by the Jaffa gate. The three towers were built of white stone. Hippicus was square, with sides 25 cubits in length. To the height of 30 cubits it consisted of solid masonry; over this was a reservoir, 20 cubits deep; and over this again a two-story house, 25 cubits in height, surmounted by battlements 2 cubits high with turrets 3 cubits higher. The entire altitude of the tower was 80 cubits. Phasaelus was larger. Its stock was a cube of solid masonry measuring 40 cubits in each direction, surmounted by a cloister, and that in turn by a palatial tower. Its entire height was about 90 cubits. It was completed about the year 10 B. C. (Antiq. xvi. 5, 2). Mariamne had half the dimensions of Phasaelus, save that it was 50 cubits high. It was magnificently adorned by Herod as befitted a tower named in honor of his wife. The palace proper on the south of these towers was entirely walled about to the height of 30 cubits, and was further protected by turrets which surmounted the wall and stood at equal distances from each other. Within were open courts with groves of trees, and numerous apartments, among which two were conspicuous for size and beauty, and were called Cæsareum and Agrippium, after Herod's friends (Antiq. xv. 9, 3; 10, 3; War i. 21, 1; v. 4, 4). The palace was occupied by Sabinus, the procurator of Syria (Antiq. xvii. 10, 2 and 3; War ii. 3, 2 and 3). In it Pilate erected golden shields in honor of the emperor Tiberius; and it is expressly called the house of the procurators (Philo, de legat. ad Caium, xxxviii. and xxxix.). The procurator Florus took up his quarters in this building, erected his tribunal before it, and sentenced men to scourging and crucifixion (War ii. 14, 8 and 9). It was burned by the seditious Jews at the beginning of the war with the Romans. The three mighty towers, however, withstood the flames, and were allowed by the conqueror to stand as a witness to the kind of city the Romans had overthrown (War ii. 17, 8; vii. 1, 1).

He-ro'di-ans.

A Jewish party in the time of our Lord, who were evidently partisans of the Herod family. The Herods were not of proper Jewish descent, and they had supplanted a royal family not merely Jewish, but of priestly blood and rank. They also supported their authority by trying to please their Roman patrons. If the Herodians took the part of the Herods in these two respects, then they were in direct antagonism to the Pharisees, with whom, however, they combined at Jerusalem to entangle our Lord by the ensnaring question about paying tribute to Cæsar (Mat. xxii. 16; Mark xii. 13); and earlier in Galilee had joined in plotting against his life (Mark iii. 6; cp. Mark viii. 15). Another view is that, condoning the Herods' Idumæan descent, the Herodians supported them merely as the representatives of national against foreign rule, in which case their union with the Pharisees would be quite natural.

He-ro'di-as.

Daughter of Aristobulus, and half-sister of Herod Agrippa I. She was married to Herod, the son of Herod the Great by Mariamne, the high priest Simon's daughter. This husband is called Philip in the N. T., but is not entitled a tetrarch (Mat. xiv. 3; Mark vi. 17). He was a different person from Philip the tetrarch. It is customary to speak of him as Herod Philip, which was probably his full name. See PHILIP 4. His half-brother, Herod the tetrarch, indulged a guilty passion for her, and divorcing his wife, a daughter of king Aretas of Arabia, married Herodias while her first husband was still alive (Antiq. xviii. 5, 1, 4; 6, 2; 7, 2; War ii. 9, 6). John the Baptist reproved the guilty pair, on which Herodias plotted his death, and when her daughter Salome had gained Herod's favor by dancing before him at a gathering of the dignitaries of his tetrarchy, extorted from him a promise to give her the head of John the Baptist. The king was sorry, but, for his oath's sake, complied with her wishes (Mat. xiv. 3–12; Mark vi. 17–29; Luke iii. 19, 20; cp. Prov. vi. 26). On the banishment of the tetrarch, Herodias went with him into exile (Antiq. xviii. 7, 2; War ii. 9, 6).

Herodias' daughter Salome married Philip the tetrarch, son of Herod the Great. After his death she married her first cousin, Aristobulus, son of king Agrippa's brother Herod and great-great-grandson of Herod the Great (Antiq. xviii. 5, 4).

He-ro'di-on.

A Christian at Rome whom Paul called his kinsman, and to whom he sent a salutation (Rom. xvi. 11).

Her'on.

The rendering of the Hebrew *'ănaphah* (Lev. xi. 19, on margin of R. V. ibis; Deut. xiv. 18). The bird so designated was held to be typical of a family, for it is followed by the words "after its kind." The heron family (*Ardeidæ*), is placed under the *Grallatores* or Waders. The birds which it includes are generally of large size. They have a long bill, long bare legs adapted for wading, a large hind toe, and large wings, their flight, however, being comparatively slow. Their food is principally fish and reptiles. The family contains the herons, the egrets, etc. The buff-backed heron (*Ardea bubulcus*), often called the white ibis, is the most abundant. These birds live and breed in vast numbers in the swamps of lake Huleh, and they associate with cattle in the pastures, where several purple ibises may usually be seen with them. The common heron (*Ardea cinerea*) occurs on the Jordan and its lakes, on the Kishon, and on the seacoast of Palestine. With it are found also the purple heron (*Ardea purpurea*) and several egrets.

He′sed [pity, mercy].
Father of one of Solomon's purveyors (1 Kin. iv. 10).

Hesh′bon [reason, intelligence].
The city of Sihon, the Amorite king, but apparently taken originally from the Moabites (Num. xxi. 25-30, 34). It was assigned by Moses to the Reubenites, and after the conquest was rebuilt by the men of that tribe (xxxii. 37; Josh. xiii. 17). But it stood on the boundary line between Reuben and Gad (Josh. xiii. 26), came to be possessed by the latter, and was assigned as a town of Gad to the Levites (Josh. xxi. 39: 1 Chron. vi. 81). The Moabites held it in Isaiah's and Jeremiah's times (Is. xv. 4; xvi. 8, 9; Jer. xlviii. 2, 33, 34). Later still it was in the possession of Alexander Jannæus and Herod the Great (Antiq. xiii. 15, 4; xv. 8. 5). It is still known as Hesbân, a ruined city standing on an isolated hill, with the remains of a wall, an archway, and a temple. The sides of the valley which commences just west of the hill are honeycombed with caves and sepulchers. A great reservoir, a little eastward from the ruins of Heshbon, is probably one of the pools which were outside the town walls (Song vii. 4).

Hesh′mon [fatness, fertile soil].
A town in the extreme south of Judah (Josh. xv. 27).

Heth. See CHETH and HITTITES.

Heth′lon [perhaps, a hiding place].
A place on the northern boundary of Palestine, as prophesied by Ezekiel, near the entering in of Hamath (Ezek. xlvii. 15; xlviii. 1; cp. Num. xxxiv. 8). Not identified.

Hez′e-ki. See HIZKI.

Hez-e-ki′ah, in A. V. once **Hizkiah** (Zeph. i. 1), once **Hizkijah** (Neh. x. 17), in A. V. of N. T. **Ezekias**, the Greek form [strength or a strong support is Jehovah; or, in the longer Hebrew form in 2 Chron. xxviii. 27; Hos. i. 1, etc., Jehovah doth strengthen].
1. Son of Ahaz, king of Judah. He was associated with his father in the government in 728 B. C. From the fact that Ahaz was not buried in the royal sepulcher, Neteler has argued that he had been smitten with some disease which was regarded as a divine judgment on his sin. Being incapacitated for ac-

tive participation in the affairs of state, Hezekiah was made active ruler. Hezekiah is said to have begun to reign at the age of 25, but the number seems to be corrupt. He was a devoted servant of Jehovah, and commenced his reign by repairing and cleansing the temple, reorganizing its religious services and its officers, and celebrating a great passover, to which he invited not merely the two tribes, but the ten (2 Chron. xxix. 1-xxx. 13). He removed the high places, cast down the images, and broke in pieces the brazen serpent which Moses had made, but which had become an object of idolatrous worship. He gained a victory over the Philistines, and in other ways became great and prosperous. In his fourth regnal year, 724 B. C., Shalmaneser commenced, and in 722 B. C. Sargon completed, the siege of Samaria, carrying the ten tribes into captivity (2 Kin. xviii. 9, 10). In 714 B. C., according to the method of reckoning already employed by the Hebrew annalist, began the series of Assyrian invasions which formed a marked feature of Hezekiah's reign and terminated disastrously for Assyria. The biblical account of these events is presented as a connected narrative. It falls into three sections: the beginning of the invasions about 714 (2 Kin. xviii. 13; Is. xxxvi. 1; probably 2 Chron. xxxii. 1-8; cp. invasion of Philistia in 711, Is. xx. 1); the main campaign of 701, in its first stage (2 Kin. xviii. 14-16), and in its final stage (17-xix. 35; 2 Chron. xxxii. 9-21; Is. xxxvi. 2-xxxvii. 36); and the end of the troubler in 681 (2 Kin. xix. 36, 37; Is. xxxvii. 37, 38). Sargon was still on the throne of Assyria in 714; but he had placed his son Sennacherib in high military position before that date, and Sennacherib may have led the troops of his father which in 720 or 715 and the beginning of 714, probably at the latter date, "subjugated Judah" according to the Assyrian account, when the main army of Assyria was waging war to the north and east of Assyria. Apparently immediately after the beginning of these invasions, in 714, Hezekiah was sick, probably from a carbuncle, and nigh unto death; but was granted a new lease of life for fifteen years (2 Kin. xx. 1-11; Is. xxxviii.). To inquire into the sign which Hezekiah received at this time was the ostensible object of an embassy from Merodach-baladan, king of Babylon. The real object was to persuade Judah's king to join the great confederacy which was being secretly formed against the Assyrian power. Hezekiah was quite elated by the coming of the Babylonian ambassadors, and displayed to them his financial resources; but the prophet Isaiah warned him that the people of Judah would be carried captive to that same place from which the ambassadors had come (2 Kin. xx. 12-19; 2 Chron. xxxii. 31; Is. xxxix. 1-8). Hezekiah joined the confederacy. Sargon, who was an able general, broke in upon the allies before their plans were matured. His expedition against

Ashdod, conducted by his tartan (Is. xx. 1), took place in 711, and was occasioned by the refusal of Philistia, Judah, Edom, and Moab to pay tribute. In 710 he dethroned Merodach-baladan and made himself king of Babylonia. In 705 Sargon was murdered, and his son Sennacherib ascended the Assyrian throne. This change of rulers was the signal for new uprisings. To quell revolt in the west, Sennacherib advanced as far as the country of the Philistines in 701, conquering Phœnicia on the way and receiving envoys from Ashdod, Ammon, Moab, and Edom suing for peace. Many towns still held out, and Sennacherib proceeded against Joppa, Bethdagon, Ashkelon, and other places. Turning eastward, he captured Lachish, pitching his camp there, and receiving tribute from the terrified Hezekiah. This tribute consisted of thirty talents of gold, three hundred, or, according to the Assyrian scribe who perhaps computes by a lighter standard, eight hundred talents of silver. Besides this, according to the Assyrian report, were precious stones, costly woods, articles of ivory, daughters of Hezekiah, women of the palace, and others. To obtain the precious metals, Hezekiah stripped the doors and pillars of the temple of their plating. News, however, reached Sennacherib while still at Lachish of an alliance between the Philistine towns and Egypt and Ethiopia (2 Kin. xviii. 21, 24), and, unwilling to have so strong a fortress as Jerusalem in his rear, he sent a detachment from his army to garrison the city. Hezekiah had heard of the advance of the southern army, and of the sturdy resistance of Ekron to the Assyrians. His faith in Jehovah also revived under the exhortations of Isaiah, and he refused to admit the Assyrian troops into the city. In the meantime the Assyrian king had broken camp at Lachish and fallen back on Libnah (2 Kin. xix. 8). Hearing of Hezekiah's new attitude of defiance, he dispatched messengers with threatening letters to him, vowing future vengeance; and, not daring to meet the Egyptians and Ethiopians while Ekron and Jerusalem were in his rear, he retreated to Eltekeh. There the battle took place. The Egyptians were repulsed, but the spoils of victory were inconsiderable. Sennacherib now turned his attention to the hostile towns in the vicinity. His devastation and his advance toward Jerusalem were only terminated by the sudden plague which smote his army, whereby in one night 185,000 of his warriors perished (2 Kin. xix. 35, 36). See SENNACHERIB. Besides Isaiah, Hosea and Micah were contemporaries of Hezekiah (Hos. i. 1; Mic. i. 1). The king died about 698, leaving his son Manasseh to ascend the throne (2 Kin. xx. 21; 2 Chron. xxxii. 33).

2. An ancestor of the prophet Zephaniah (Zeph. i. 1; in A. V. Hizkiah).

3. A son of Neariah, akin to the royal family of Judah (1 Chron. iii. 23).

4. A man of whose descendants through Ater some returned with Zerubbabel (Ezra ii. 16; Neh. vii. 21). Probably it was the representative of his family who signed the covenant under Nehemiah's rule (Neh. x. 17; in A. V. Hizkijah).

He′zi-on [vision].
Father of Tabrimmon and grandfather of Benhadad, king of Syria (1 Kin. xv. 18).

He′zir [a swine, a pig].
1. A descendant of Aaron. His family had grown to a father's house in the time of David and became the seventeenth course of the priests (1 Chron. xxiv. 15).
2. A chief of the people who with Nehemiah sealed the covenant (Neh. x. 20).

Hez′rai [enclosed].
A Carmelite, one of David's mighty men (2 Sam. xxiii. 35). In 1 Chron. xi. 37 called Hezro, a difference doubtless due to an ancient scribe's confusion of jod and vau. See VAU.

Hez′ro. See HEZRAI.

Hez′ron, in A. V. of N. T. **Esrom** (Mat. i. 3), in imitation of the Greek modification of the name [shut in, surrounded].
1. A place on the southern boundary line of Judah, not far from Zin and Kadesh-barnea (Josh. xv. 3); perhaps the town Hazor (ver. 23). It was near enough Addar to be coupled with it in the form Hazar-addar (Num. xxxiv. 4). For Kerioth-hezron (Josh. xv. 25, R. V.), see HAZOR 2.
2. A son of Reuben, and founder of the Hezronite family (Gen. xlvi. 9; Ex. vi. 14; Num. xxvi. 6; 1 Chron. v. 3).
3. Son of Perez, of the tribe of Judah, and founder of a tribal family (Gen. xlvi. 12; Num. xxvi. 21; Ruth iv. 18; 1 Chron. ii. 5).

Hid′dai [joyful].
A man from the brooks of Gaash. He was one of David's heroes (2 Sam. xxiii. 30). Called in 1 Chron. xi. 32, Hurai.

Hid′de-kel [Hebrew; in Assyrian *idiklat*, Old Persian *tigra*, Greek *tigris*].
The river Tigris, which goeth in front of Assyria (Gen. ii. 14, R. V.; Dan. x. 4). It is still called Hiddekel by a large portion of the people living near its banks. Its principal sources in central Armenia spring from the southern slope of Anti-Taurus. The western flows by Diarbekr, winding for above 150 miles. The two eastern, known as Bitlis Chai and Bohtan Chai, rise south of lake Van, and are about 100 miles long. After the junction of these streams the river proceeds nearly east-south-east, through the Kurdistan mountains, gradually increased by various affluents, especially the greater and lesser Zab and the Diyalah from the eastern, with smaller feeders from the western side, finally joining the Euphrates. In antiquity, it emptied through its own mouth into the Persian Gulf. In its course it passes the ruins of Nineveh, which

lie on the left or eastern bank, nearly opposite Mosul on its right side. Lower down it separates Bagdad into two portions; and afterwards passes the ruins, first of Ctesiphon, the Parthian capital, and then those of Seleucia, which, under the Greek dynasty, became the rival of Babylon. The whole course of the Tigris to the junction with the Euphrates is 1146 miles, only a little more than half the length of the sister stream.

Hi'el [probably, God liveth].

A native of Bethel, who, in Ahab's reign, fortified Jericho, bringing down on himself the fulfillment of Joshua's imprecation. His eldest son died, perhaps was sacrificed, when the foundation of the city was laid, and his youngest son when the gates were set up (1 Kin. xvi. 34 with Josh. vi. 26).

Hi-e-rap'o-lis [sacred city].

A city in Asia Minor, in the valley of the Lycos near the confluence with the Meander. Not far distant were Colossæ and Laodicea (Col. iv. 13). It was a seat of worship of the Syrian goddess Atargatis, and was celebrated for its warm baths. It is now called Pambûk-Kalah-si.

Hig-ga'ion [a deep sound; meditation].

A musical term occurring in Ps. ix. 16. The word is used elsewhere in the sense of solemn sound, meditation (Ps. xix. 14; xcii. 3; Lam. iii. 63).

High' Pla-ces.

Localities selected as shrines for the worship of God or of false divinities, or the shrines themselves. They were established on lofty heights (Num. xxii. 41; 1 Kin. xi. 7; xiv. 23), within or near towns (2 Kin. xvii. 9; xxiii. 5, 8), and even in valleys (Jer. vii. 31; cp. Ezek. vi. 3). The Canaanites possessed them, and the Israelites were strictly enjoined to destroy them when they entered Canaan (Num. xxxiii. 52; Deut. xxxiii. 29; cp. ancient high places excavated at Gezer, Tell es-Sâfiyeh, Taanach). The Moabites also had high places (Num. xxi. 28; xxii. 41; Josh. xiii. 17, see the name Bamoth-baal; Is. xv. 2; Jer. xlviii. 35). Immorality was common on the way to those shrines (Jer. iii. 2; cp. 2 Chron. xxi. 11).

A suitable area, of a size determined by circumstances, was prepared by leveling the ground. On it stood an altar (1 Kin. xii. 32), which, as at Petra, might be a part of the living rock left standing, with steps to approach it, when the spot was leveled. Near the altar was a wooden Asherah; and not far off was a pillar or a row of pillars, consisting of unhewn stones, six feet or more in length, set on end, as at Gezer and Petra (1 Kin. xiv. 23; Jer. xvii. 2; see ASHERAH and PILLAR). Houses were often connected with these sanctuaries (1 Kin. xii. 31; 2 Kin. xxiii. 19), for sheltering the idol (2 Kin. xvii. 29, 32), and presumably for other purposes also. Benches around the sides of the area or a chamber

afforded a place for the worshipers to sit and partake of the sacrificial feast (1 Sam. ix. 12, 13, 22). Priests were attached to the high place (1 Kin. xii. 32; 2 Kin. xvii. 32), who burnt incense and offered sacrifice (1 Kin. xiii. 2; cp. iii. 3; xi. 8).

At times the worship of Jehovah was conducted by the Israelites on high places; but this was forbidden by law, which insisted upon one altar for all Israel. The purpose of this law was to foster the national spirit and guard against schism, to prevent the people from worshiping at idolatrous shrines, and losing or corrupting the religion of Jehovah, and to secure the support of a national sanctuary which would enable the worship of Jehovah to be conducted on a scale of magnificence commensurate with his glory, and equal, if not superior, to the pomp displayed at the heathen temples. The worship of Jehovah at other altars was legitimate only during the time that the national sanctuary had temporarily ceased, during the period when Jehovah had forsaken Shiloh and the temple was not yet erected (Ps. lxxviii. 60, 61, 67–69; 1 Kin. iii. 2, 4; 2 Chron. i. 3). Altars and sacrifices elsewhere than at Jerusalem were also legitimate in the northern kingdom when the pious were precluded from attendance at Jerusalem, and could not worship Jehovah at all, unless according to the primitive law (1 Kin. xviii. 30–32); see ALTAR. Solomon, sinfully complying with the wishes of his heathen wives, erected high places in the mount of Corruption for Ashtoreth, Chemosh, and Milcom or Molech (2 Kin. xxiii. 13). Jeroboam, to counteract the influence of the national sanctuary at Jerusalem, made a house of high places at Bethel and ordained priests (1 Kin. xii. 31, 32; xiii. 33), purposing the adoration of Jehovah, but by idolatrous symbols (xii. 28–33; xiii. 2). These places were denounced by the prophets (xiii. 1, 2; Hos. x. 8). Not merely at Bethel, but at other cities in Samaria, did schismatic high places exist (1 Kin. xiii. 32; 2 Kin. xvii. 32; 2 Chron. xxxiv. 3). The action of Asa and Jehoshaphat in the kingdom of Judah with regard to high places was ineffective (1 Kin. xv. 14 with 2 Chron. xiv. 3; xv. 17; 1 Kin. xxii. 43 with 2 Chron. xvii. 6). Jehoram, Jehoshaphat's son, made high places in the mountains of Judah (2 Chron. xxi. 11). So did Ahaz, and that too for the worship of false divinities, where he sacrificed and burnt incense (xxviii. 4, 25). Hezekiah broke them down (2 Kin. xviii. 4, 22), but they were re-erected by Manasseh (xxi. 3; 2 Chron. xxxiii. 3), and again removed by Josiah (2 Kin. xxiii. 5, 8, 13). The high places were denounced by the prophets (Ezek. vi. 3), and emphasis was laid on the fact that Zion was Jehovah's dwelling-place, his sanctuary and holy mountain (Is. ii. 2, 3; viii. 18; xviii. 7; xxxiii. 20; Joel ii. 1; iii. 17, 21; Amos i. 2; Mic. iv 1, 2).

High' Priest.

The supreme pontiff and the representative of the nation before Jehovah. Aaron was appointed to this office after the establishment of the covenant at Sinai and after the erection of the tabernacle had been authorized (Ex. xxvii. 21; xxviii.). The reference in Ex. xvi. 33, 34, where Moses bids Aaron lay up a pot of manna before the Lord, is not an anticipation of this call; for the command was probably issued by Moses at a later time, at least it was obeyed by Aaron at a later time, and is recorded here because the entire story of the manna is related here (31–35). The first hint that it was important for the sons of Aaron to be admitted to the privilege enjoyed by the elders of Israel was given after the covenant had been proclaimed (Ex. xxiv. 1, 9). The distinction accorded them, however, did not suggest the national priesthood to them. Aaron was not the priest of the nation at this time. He was the prophet of Moses. The addition of his sons to the commission appointed to witness a manifestation of God's glory might suggest that Aaron's present office was to be inherited by his sons. At any rate it foreshadowed their call to future work. The legal head of the house of Aaron held the office of high priest; and the succession was probably determined by primogeniture, unless legal disabilities interfered (Lev. xxi. 16–23). Political considerations, also, not infrequently played a part in his selection (1 Kin. ii. 26, 27, 35). His age when he might assume office was twenty, according to tradition. Aristobulus, however, officiated when he was seventeen (Antiq. xv. 3, 3). He must govern his conduct by special laws (Lev. xxi. 1–15). His duties were the oversight of the sanctuary, its service, and its treasure (2 Kin. xii. 7 seq.; xxii. 4); the performance of the service on the day of atonement, when he was obliged to enter the holy of holies, and the consultation of God by Urim and Thummim. Besides these distinguishing duties, he was qualified to discharge any priestly function; and it was customary for him to offer the sacrifices on Sabbaths, new moons, and annual festivals (War v. 5, 7). He presided also over the sanhedrin when religious questions were before that body (Mat. xxvi. 57; Acts v. 21). His official garments, besides the raiment of white linen which he wore in common with other priests (q. v.) were—1. Breastplate: square, made of gold, and blue, purple, scarlet, and fine twisted linen, set with four rows of precious stones, three in a row, each inscribed with the name of a tribe. Within the breastplate were the Urim and Thummim (q. v.). 2. Ephod: an embroidered vestment of the same rich materials as the breastplate. It was intended for the front and back of the body, and was made in two parts clasped together at the shoulder by onyx stones. Each stone bore the names of six tribes. The ephod carried on its front the breastplate, and was bound about the waist by a girdle of gold, blue, purple, scarlet, and fine twisted linen. 3. Robe of the ephod: which was longer than the ephod, and worn

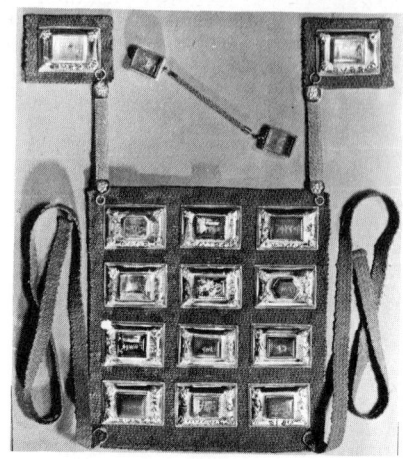

Replica of Aaron's breastplate (Exod. 28:15-21; 39:8-21). Each stone represents one of the twelve tribes of Israel and has the name of the tribe engraved on it.

underneath it, entirely blue, sleeveless, and adorned below with a fringe of alternate pomegranates and golden bells; see BELL. 4. Miter: a cap or turban, made of linen and surmounted, in later times at least, by another of blue, and this in turn by a triple crown of gold. A gold plate, bearing the inscription Holiness to Jehovah, was fastened to the front by a blue ribbon (Ex. xxviii.; Ecclus. xlv. 8–13; Antiq. iii. 7, 1–6; cp. 1 Mac. x. 20). The high priest wore this official garb when discharging his peculiar duties, except that on the day of atonement he laid it aside while he entered the holy of holies to make atonement for the priesthood and the sanctuary. The mode of consecration is described in Ex. xxix. Among other ceremonies the sacred oil was poured upon his head (7; Lev. viii. 12; Ps. cxxxiii. 2), and hence by way of distinction he is designated the anointed priest (Lev. iv. 3, 5, 16; xxi. 10; Num. xxxv. 25). The common priests seem to have been consecrated by having the oil sprinkled on their garments only (Ex. xxix. 21; Lev. viii. 30); but rabbinical tradition makes the difference consist in the quantity of oil used. It was poured abundantly on the head of the high priest and sparingly upon the heads of the ordinary priests. At first the high-priesthood was for life, but Herod, and afterwards the Romans, jealous of the power which a life tenure of the office gave to the high priest, made and unmade the pontiffs at will. Jesus is the High Priest of our profession, of whom the Jewish dignitary of the same designation was only the type (Heb. iii. 1–3; viii. 1–6; ix. 24–28). For the chief priests of the N. T., see PRIESTS, end of the article.

THE LINE OF THE HIGH PRIESTS.

I. *From the Establishment of the Aaronic Priesthood to the Exile.*—The biblical catalogues are two (1 Chron. vi. 1-15; Ezra vii. 1-5), each of which omits links of the genealogy, as is quite usual in Hebrew genealogical tables.

Levi.

Gershon. Kohath. Merari.

Amram. Izhar. Hebron. Uzziel.

Aaron. Moses (1 Chron. xxiii. 13). Miriam.

Nadab. Abihu. Eleazar. Ithamar.

Phinehas.

Abishua.

Bukki. Eli, succeeded Abishua or Uzzi (Antiq. viii. 1, 3; v. 11, 5).

Uzzi. Hophni. Phinehas, officiated during the lifetime of his father, who by reason of age resigned the office to him (Antiq. v. 11. 2).

Zerahiah. Ark in the country of the Philistines seven months (1 Sam. vi. 1); then in Kirjath-jearim twenty years (1 Sam. vii. 2), until the second battle of Ebenezer, and for years afterwards, until David removed it. Ahitub. Ichabod.

Meraioth.

Ahijah, in Shiloh wearing ephod (1 Sam. xiv. 3, 18). Ark or ephod (LXX.; cp. ver. 19) taken temporarily to Gibeah. Ahimelech (1 Sam. xxii. 9, 11, 12). Priest at Nob, showbread and ephod mentioned (1 Sam. xxi. 1, 2, 4, 6, 9). Slain with 85 others (1 Sam. xxii. 11-18). Nob put to the sword (1 Sam. xxii. 19).

Amariah.

Ahitub. In default of a son of Ahimelech in Saul's reign to take charge of the tabernacle, the duty devolved upon the head of the other priestly line.

Zadok, perhaps 1 Chron. xii. 27, 28. Abiathar, escaped and fled to David (1 Sam. xxii. 20); with an ephod (xxiii. 6, 9; xxx. 7).

Ark removed from Kirjath-jearim and deposited in the house of Obed-edom (2 Sam. vi. 1-11; 1 Chron xiii. 13, 14). Transferred to the city of David (2 Sam. vi. 12 seq.). Zadok and Abiathar the priests assist (1 Chron xv. 11, 12). Ark placed in a tent and an altar erected (2 Sam. vi. 12, 17; cp. vii. 2). Zadok and Ahimelech, son of Abiathar, are named as the priests during a certain period of David's reign (2 Sam. viii. 17; 1 Chron. xviii. 16). The date is uncertain; it is not improbably after Absalom's revolt.

and Abiathar follow David

Zadok, and the Levites bearing the ark, in his flight (2 Sam. xv. 24 seq.). Zadok and Abiathar are called the priests (2 Sam. xv. 35; xvii. 15; xix. 11; xx. 25). Their sons who serve as messengers are Ahimaaz and Jonathan respectively (2 Sam. xv. 27, 36). In the attempt to debar Solomon from the succession and advance Adonijah,

Abiathar favors Adonijah (1 Kin. i. 7).

Zadok is loyal to David (1 Kin. i. 8). Zadok and Ahimelech, son of Abiathar, superintend the division of the priests into courses (1 Chron. xxiv. 3, 6, 31). They do this as the active heads of their respective fathers' houses. In consequence of a second conspiracy in favor of Adonijah, made after Solomon had ascended the throne,

Zadok is put into the room of Abiathar (1 Kin. ii. 26, 35).

By the deposition of Abiathar, the house
of Eli falls (1 Kin. ii. 27), and

Zadok is sole high priest.
Ahimaaz.
Azariah.

Amariah, chief priest in the reign of Jehoshaphat, about 853 B. C. (2 Chron. xix. 11).
Jehoiada, in the reigns of Athaliah and Joash, dying in the reign of Joash at the age of 130 years (2 Kin. xi. 4–19; xii. 2; 2 Chron. xxii. 10 seq.; xxiv. 15).
Zechariah, son of Jehoiada, perhaps high priest, slain by Joash between 819 and 805 B. C. (2 Chron xxiv. 20, 22).
Johanan.
Azariah, who officiated in the temple at Jerusalem about 750 B. C., in the reign of Uzziah (1 Chron. vi. 10, 2 Chron. xxvi. 17).
Urijah, about 732 B. C., in the reign of Ahaz (2 Kin. xvi. 10).
Azariah, about 727 B. C., in the reign of Hezekiah (2 Chron. xxxi. 10, 13).
Amariah.
Ahitub.
Meraioth (1 Chron. ix. 11; Neh. xi. 11).
Zadok.
Shallum or **Meshullam** (1 Chron. vi. 12; ix. 11).
Hilkiah, in the eighteenth year of the reign of Josiah, 622 B. C. (1 Chron. ix. 11; 2 Chron. xxxiv. 8, 9).
Azariah.
Seraiah.
Jehozadak, who was carried captive to Babylonia by Nebuchadnezzar in 587 B. C. (1 Chron. vi. 15).
Interval of fifty years during the exile.

II. *From the Exile to the Maccabæan Priests.*
Jeshua, son of Jehozadak, who returned from captivity with Zerubbabel, and was high priest from at least 538 to 520 B. C. (Ezra ii. 2; iii. 2; Neh. xii. 10; Zech. i. 7; iii. 1; vi. 11).
Joiakim (Neh. xii. 10, 12), in the days of [Arta]xerxes (Antiq. xi. 5, 1).
Eliashib, in the twentieth year of Artaxerxes, 446 B. C., and still in office after 433 B. C. (Neh. iii. 20; xii. 10; xiii. 4, 6).
Joiada.
Jonathan (Neh. xii. 11), or rather Johanan (22, 23). in Greek John, high priest, as early as 411 B. C. (Elephantine papyri) and in the reign of Artaxerxes [Mnemon] (Antiq. xi. 7, 1; cp. 5, 4), who occupied the throne from 405 to 362 B. C.
Jaddua, high priest when Alexander the Great visited Jerusalem, 332 B. C., and died about the same time as Alexander, 323 B. C. (Neh. xii. 11; Antiq. xi. 8, 4 and 5 and 7).
Onias, in Hebrew perhaps Coniah, contemporary of Arius, who was king of Sparta from about 309 to 265 B. C. (1 Mac. xii. 7, 20; Antiq. xi. 8, 7).
Simon the Just, son of Onias.
Eleazar, son of Onias and brother of Simon, in the time of Ptolemy Philadelphus, who reigned from 285 to 247 (Antiq. xii. 2, 5).
Manasseh, uncle of Eleazar (Antiq. xii. 4, 1).
Onias II., son of Simon the Just, in the time of Ptolemy Euergetes, who reigned from 247 to 222 (Antiq. xii. 4, 1).
Simon II., son of Onias II. (Antiq. xii. 4, 10).
Onias III., son of Simon II., in the time of Seleucus IV., called Philopator, who reigned from 187 to 175 B. C (2 Mac. iii.; Antiq. xii. 4, 10).
Joshua, in Greek **Jesus,** son of Simon II., who assumed the name **Jason,** induced Antiochus Epiphanes, who reigned from 175 to 164 B. C., to depose Onias (2 Mac. iv. 7, 26–35). After holding office about three years, Jason was supplanted, about 171 B. C., by
Menelaus, called also **Onias,** son of Simon II. (Antiq. xii. 5. 1; xv. 3, 1). According to 2 Mac. iv. 23, he was the brother of Simon the Benjamite. Menelaus held office ten years (Antiq. xii. 9, 7), and was put to death in the time of Judas Maccabæus (2 Mac. xiii. 3–8).
Jakim, with the Greek name of **Alcimus,** who was not of the high-priestly line, although of the stock of Aaron, put in office by Demetrius, 161 B. C., and retained office three years (1 Mac. vii. 5–9, 12–25; ix. 1, 54–56; Antiq. xii. 9, 7; xx. 10, 1).
Vacancy of seven years (Antiq. xx. 10, 1).

III. *The Maccabæan Priest-kings.*
Jonathan, of the priestly family of Joarib (1 Mac. iii. 1; 1 Chron. xxiv. 7), made high priest in 152 B. C. by Alexander Balas, who was contending for the Syrian throne (1 Mac. x. 18–21), and held office for seven years in round numbers (Antiq. xx. 10, 1).
Simon, his brother, for eight years.
John Hyrcanus, son of Simon, for thirty years.
Aristobulus, son of Hyrcanus, for one year.
Alexander Jannæus, son of Hyrcanus, for twenty-seven years.
Hyrcanus, son of Alexander, for nine years.
Aristobulus, son of Alexander, for three years three months.
Hyrcanus, a second time, for twenty-four years, from 63 B. C.
Antigonus, son of Aristobulus, for three years, three months, until Herod the Great took possession of Jerusalem in 37 B. C. (Antiq. xiv. 16, 4; xx. 10, 1).

IV. *From the Accession of Herod the Great until Jerusalem was taken by Titus.*—During this period there were twenty-eight high priests (Antiq. xx. 10, 1), one being generally removed to make way for his successor.
Appointed by Herod the Great, king from 37 to 4 B. C.:
Hananel, in Latinized Greek **Ananelus** (Antiq. xv. 2, 4).
Aristobulus, grandson of Hyrcanus, for one year, about 35 B. C. (Antiq. xv. 3, 1 and 3).
Hananel, a second time (Antiq. xv. 3, 3).
Jesus, son of Phabes (Antiq. xv. 9, 3).

Simon, son of Boethus (Antiq. xv. 9, 3), from about 24 to 5 B. C.
Matthias, son of Theophilus and son-in-law of Boethus (Antiq. xvii. 4, 2).
Joazar, son of Boethus (Antiq xvii. 6, 4; 13, 1).
Appointed by Archelaus, who ruled from 4 B. C. to A. D. 6:
    Eleazar, son of Boethus, who did not abide long in office (Antiq. xvii. 13, 1).
    Jesus, son of Sie (Antiq. xvii. 13, 1).
Appointed by Quirinius, president of Syria:
    Annas, or **Ananus,** son of Seth, who obtained the office in A. D. 6 or 7, Joazar, whom the multi-
    tude had made high priest, being put down (Antiq. xviii. 2, 1; cp. 1, 1).
Appointed by Valerius Gratus, procurator of Judæa A. D. 14–25:
    Ismael, son of Phabi, who held office but a short time (Antiq. xviii. 2, 2).
    Eleazar, son of Annas, for one year (Antiq. xviii. 2, 2).
    Simon, son of Camithus, for one year (Antiq. xviii. 2, 2).
    Joseph Caiaphas, son-in-law of Annas, from about A. D. 18 to 36 (John xviii. 13; Antiq. xviii. 4, 3).
Appointed by Vitellius, president of Syria:
    Jonathan, son of Annas, in A. D. 36 (Antiq. xviii. 4, 2 and 3; cp. xix. 6, 4; xx. 8, 5).
    Theophilus, son of Annas, in A. D. 37 (Antiq. xviii. 5, 3).
Appointed by king Herod Agrippa I., who reigned from A. D. 41 to 44:
    Simon Cantheras, son of Boethus (Antiq. xix. 6, 2).
    Matthias, son of Annas (Antiq. xix. 6, 4).
    Elionæus, son of Cantheras (Antiq. xix. 8, 1).
Appointed by Herod, king of Chalcis, who died in A. D. 48:
    Joseph, son of Camydus (Antiq. xx. 1, 3).
    Ananias, son of Nedebæus (Antiq. xx, 5, 2), sent in bonds to Rome during the procuratorship of
    Cumanus, but acquitted and still in office in A. D. 57, two years before Felix was suc-
    ceeded by Festus (Acts xxiii. 2; xxiv. 1, 27).
Appointed by king Agrippa II.:
    Ismael, son of Phabi (Antiq. xx. 8, 8), about A. D. 59, who went to Rome and was detained there as
    hostage (xx. 8, 11).
    Joseph, called **Cabi,** son of the former high priest Simon (Antiq. xx. 8, 11).
    Annas, son of Annas, for three months in A. D. 62 (Antiq. xx. 9, 1).
    Jesus, son of Damnæus (Antiq. xx. 9, 1).
    Jesus, son of Gamaliel (Antiq. xx. 9, 4; cp. War iv. 5, 2).
    Matthias, son of Theophilus, appointed about A. D. 64 (Antiq. xx. 9, 7).
Made high priest by the people during the war:
    Phanas, or **Phannias,** son of Samuel (Antiq. xx. 10; War iv. 3, 8).

Hi′len. See HOLON 1.

Hil-ki′ah [portion of Jehovah (cp. Job xxxi. 2), or Jehovah is the portion (cp. Ps. xvi. 5)].

1. A Levite, son of Amzi, descended from Merari (1 Chron. vi. 45. 46).

2. Another Merarite Levite, son of Hosah (1 Chron. xxvi. 11).

3. Father of Eliakim, who was over the household in Hezekiah's reign (2 Kin. xviii. 18, 26; Is. xxii. 20; xxxvi. 3).

4. A priest, father of Jeremiah (Jer. i. 1).

5. Father of Jeremiah's contemporary Gemariah (Jer. xxix. 3).

6. The high priest contemporary with Josiah, who aided the king in his reformation of religion, and found the book of the law (2 Kin. xxii. 4–14; xxiii. 4; 1 Chron. vi. 13; 2 Chron. xxxiv. 9–22). See JOSIAH.

7. A chief of the priests who returned from Babylon with Zerubbabel (Neh. xii. 7). In the next generation a father's house bore this name (ver. 21).

8. One of those who stood by Ezra when he read the law to the people (Neh. viii. 4).

Hill.

A conspicuous natural elevation of land. The name is generally applied to a natural eminence smaller than a mountain and larger than a mound; but the terms are relative, the same height being sometimes known by both names (Is. xxxi. 4), or called a mountain in one locality and a hill in another (Rev. xvii. 9). Hill is chiefly the rendering of the Hebrew *Gib′ah* and the Greek *Bounos.* Not infrequently it is also employed in the

A. V., and much less frequently in the R. V. (Ps. ii. 6; iii. 4; xv. 1; xxiv. 3; xlii. 6; Mat. v. 14; Luke iv. 29), to translate Hebrew *Har* and Greek *'Oros,* which are usually rendered mountain.

Hil′lel [he hath praised].
Father of Abdon the judge (Judg. xii. 13, 15).

Hin.
A Hebrew liquid measure, containing about one gallon and three pints, U. S. wine measure (Ex. xxix. 40; Antiq. iii. 8, 3). See MEASURE.

Hind.
A female stag, in Hebrew *'Ayyalah* (Gen. xlix. 21; Job xxxix. 1; Ps. xviii. 33; Prov. v. 19; Song ii. 7; Jer. xiv. 5). See HART.

Hinge.
In ancient times in the East heavy doors turned on pivots, which were constructed on the upper and lower corners of one side and inserted in sockets. The socket is probably more especially referred to in 1 Kin. vii. 50. See also Prov. xxvi. 14.

Hin′nom, Val′ley of; known also as the valley of the son of Hinnom or of the children of Hinnom.
A valley at Jerusalem, near the gate of potsherds (Jer. xix. 2; not east gate as in A. V.). The boundary between Judah and Benjamin passed from En-rogel by the valley of the son of Hinnom to the southern side of Jerusalem, and thence to the top of the mountain which faces the valley of Hinnom from the west, and is at the outermost

part of the vale of Rephaim (Josh. xv. 8; xviii. 16). If the term "shoulder of the Jebusite (the same is Jerusalem)" includes the hill on the west of the Tyropœon valley, and not merely the temple hill; in other words, if the term denotes the plateau which juts out southward between the great encircling wadies, and which was not only crowned by the citadel of the Jebusites, but also occupied by their dwellings without the walls and by their fields, then the description in the Book of Joshua identifies the valley of Hinnom with at least the lower part of the valley which bounds Jerusalem on the south, and is now known as the wady er-Rababeh, near its junction with the ravine of the Kidron. At the high place of Tophet, in the valley of Hinnom, parents made their children pass through the fire to Molech. Ahaz and Manasseh were guilty of this abomination (2 Chron. xxviii. 3; xxxiii. 6). Jeremiah foretold that God would visit this awful wickedness with sore judgment, and would cause such a destruction of the people that the valley would become known as the valley of slaughter (vii. 31–34; xix. 2, 6; xxxii. 35). Josiah defiled the high place to render it unfit for even idolatrous rites, and thus to stop the sacrifices (2 Kin. xxiii. 10). From the horrors of its fires, and from its pollution by Josiah, perhaps also because offal was burnt there, the valley became a type of sin and woe, and the name Ge-hinnom, corrupted into Gehenna, passed into use as a designation for the place of eternal punishment.

Hip-po-pot'a-mus [Greek *'ippopotamos*, river horse]. See BEHEMOTH.

Hi'rah [nobility].
An Adullamite, a friend of Judah (Gen. xxxviii. 1, 12).

Hi'ram; in Chronicles **Hu'ram**, except in the Hebrew text of 2 Chron. iv. 11ᵇ; ix. 10 [probably consecration]. In Hebrew the name is also written Hirom (1 Kin. v. 10, 18; vii. 40, R. V. margin).

1. A king of Tyre. According to the citation which Josephus makes from the Phœnician historian Dios. and from the Tyrian annals which Menander translated, Hiram succeeded his father Abibaal, reigned thirty-four years, and died at the age of 53 (Antiq. viii. 5, 3; con. Apion. i. 17, 18). He enlarged the city of Tyre by constructing an embankment on the eastern side, built a causeway to connect the city with the island on which the temple of Jupiter or Baal-samem stood, dedicated a golden pillar in this temple, rebuilt old sanctuaries, roofing them with cedars cut on Lebanon, and erected temples to Hercules and Astarte. He was a friend of both David and Solomon (1 Kin. v. 1; 2 Chron. ii. 3). Some time after David had captured the stronghold of Zion, Hiram sent an embassy to him; and, when David desired a palace, Hiram furnished the cedar timber and the masons and carpenters (2 Sam. v. 11). This

was evidently before the birth of Solomon (2 Sam. vii. 2, 12; xi. 2). When Solomon ascended the throne, Hiram sent congratulations. For a consideration he furnished cedar and fir for building the temple, and skilled workmen to assist in preparing the timber and stone (1 Kin. v. 1–12; 2 Chron. ii. 3–16). He also advanced 120 talents of gold (1 Kin. ix. 14), and joined Solomon in sending to Ophir for the precious metal (1 Kin. ix. 26–28; 2 Chron. ix. 21). In partial payment for his contributions, he was offered twenty towns in Galilee, which however he refused (1 Kin. ix. 10–12; 2 Chron. viii. 1, 2); see CABUL. The chronological statements of Josephus and the Bible have never been reconciled. Josephus' statement that the temple was begun in Hiram's eleventh year (Antiq. viii. 3, 1) or twelfth (con. Apion. i. 18) need not receive serious consideration; for it is probably a calculation of his own, and not a citation from the archives. Either the thirty-four years assigned as the duration of Hiram's reign or the text of 1 Kin. ix. 9–12 may be corrupt. The passage in Kings is parallel to 2 Chron. viii. 1, and this latter passage does not require the assumption that Hiram lived to the end of the twenty years wherein the temple and the royal palace were built.

2. An artificer, whose father was a Tyrian and his mother a widow of Naphtali (1 Kin. vii. 13, 14), but by birth a woman of Dan (2 Chron. ii. 14). He executed the bronze or copper work in connection with Solomon's temple, as the pillars, the laver, the basins, the shovels (1 Kin. vii. 13–46; 2 Chron. ii. 13, 14). The title father (2 Chron. ii. 13; iv. 16) probably denotes a master workman or a counselor.

History.
Biblical history is the record of that series of events which form the basis for the religion of the Bible (cp. Mark x. 2-9; Rom. xv. 4; 1 Cor. x. 11). It may be divided into four periods: 1. An account of the creation of the universe, showing God's relation to the world, and introducing human history. 2. A sketch of human history, showing God's relation to the human race, and introducing the history of the chosen people. 3. The history of the chosen people, showing God's dealing with them and the preparation for the advent of Christ. 4. The history of the establishment of the Christian church, which is to reach all nations. Inter-biblical history falls between sections 3 and 4.

1. AN ACCOUNT OF THE CREATION OF THE UNIVERSE, showing God's relation to the world, and introducing human history (Gen. i. 1–ii. 3). See CREATION and SABBATH. The great doctrine is that God is the creator and lord of all things. It denies materialism and atheism. In implying that God is personal and omnipotent, it makes reasonable his supernatural manifestation in human history.

2. A SKETCH OF HUMAN HISTORY, show-

ing God's relation to the human race and introducing the history of the chosen people (Gen. ii. 4–xi. 26). The events of this period fell almost entirely under human observation, and were capable of transmission by human testimony. The period is divided into two parts by the flood. The narrative is symmetrical; ten generations before the flood, from Adam to Noah inclusive, and ten generations after the flood, from Shem to Abraham inclusive (v.; xi. 10–26). The postdiluvian period is divided into two parts at Peleg, in whose days the earth was divided. From Shem to Peleg inclusive are five generations, and from Reu to Abraham inclusive are five. In the antediluvian period are detailed the covenant with Adam, its failure through man's disobedience, the downward course of man in sin, his punishment by a flood, and the deliverance of Noah. In the postdiluvian period are related the new and unconditioned covenant with Noah, the new command laid upon man, the increasing population, the growing independence of men from God, their punishment by confusion of speech and dispersion. The genealogy of the Sethitic-Semitic line to Abraham is recorded, and at the same time its common origin with the other families of the earth is made plain. The locality where the recorded events occurred was the basin of the Tigris and Euphrates rivers; at least, every definite geographical reference is to this region (ii. 14; viii. 4; x. 10; xi. 2, 28). From this center the people spread on all sides, especially toward the west and southwest, where the course of migration was not blocked by great mountains (x.). By the close of the period the inhabited world, so far as it was within the sphere of history, extended from the Caspian Sea, the mountains of Elam and the Persian Gulf on the east, westward to the isles of Greece and the opposite shore of Africa, and from the neighborhood of the Black Sea on the north to the Arabian Sea on the south. The length of the period from Adam to Abraham was at the lowest calculation 1946 years, but it may have been much longer; see CHRONOLOGY. This period, longer than the time that has elapsed since the birth of Christ, was remarkably barren in miracles, in the scriptural meaning of that word; see MIRACLE. With the personal history of man began those theophanies, rare indeed though they were (Gen. iii. 8 seq.), which are important in the history of revelation. During this period man made progress in civilization. He had been created with capacity, and was commanded to subdue nature. He advanced from the unclothed state, passing beyond rude garments of leaves and afterwards of skins (ii. 25; iii. 7, 21) to woven clothing; from a food of fruits that grew of itself to food obtained by agriculture and herding (i. 29; iv. 2); from uncertain abodes to movable tents, settled habitations (iv. 17, 20), and large cities built of brick (xi. 3, 4);

from the family to the tribe and the kingdom (x. 10); from no implements to tools of metal and instruments of music (iv. 21, 22). In this period also simple speech became diversified dialects and languages (x. 5; xi. 1, 6, 9). Man recognized the duty of walking before God in holiness of life (iii. 2, 3, 10; iv. 7; v. 22; vi. 9); distinguished between clean and unclean animals (vii. 2; viii. 20); erected altars and worshiped God by bloody and bloodless offerings (iv. 3, 4; viii. 20); and prayed to God in his character of Jehovah (iv. 26). Religion, however, suffered decadence (vi. 2, 5), and idolatry became widespread (Josh. xxiv. 2). See especially GENESIS, EDEN, ADAM, SATAN, SERPENT, ABEL, CAIN, ENOCH, FLOOD, NOAH, BABEL.

3. THE HISTORY OF THE CHOSEN PEOPLE, showing God's dealing with them, and the preparation for the advent of Christ. This period differs from the preceding in the shifting of the central locality from the valley of the Tigris and Euphrates to Palestine. Canaan becomes the center of the history. The duration of the period, regarded as having begun with Abraham's birth, was reckoned by Usher at 1996 years, and so stands on the margin of many editions of the English version. There are certainly errors in this calculation; but whether they equalize themselves, or whether the total length should be several centuries more or less, cannot be determined as yet from the biblical and other data. At the beginning of this period, and on several occasions later, besides the ordinary ways in which God reveals himself to man and to the prophets, he appeared in theophanies. This period also embraces three of the four great miracle epochs; namely, at the deliverance of the people from Egypt and their establishment in Canaan under Moses and Joshua, during the mortal struggle between the worship of Jehovah and Baal worship in the time of Elijah and Elisha, and during the Babylonian captivity. These miracle epochs were separated from each other by centuries during which there were, with extremely rare exceptions, no miracles. This period may conveniently be divided into sections according to the progressive stages in the outward development of the people of God.

I. *An independent tribe in Canaan under Abraham, Isaac, and Jacob.* The patriarch was the priest and responsible ruler of the tribe. The history is reviewed in the articles on ABRAHAM, DREAMS, VISIONS, THEOPHANY, MELCHIZEDEK, ISAAC, JACOB.

II. *A folk of twelve tribes for a long time in Egyptian bondage.* See EGYPT, JOSEPH, PHARAOH, MIRACLE, EXODUS, MARAH, MANNA, QUAIL, REPHIDIM.

III. *A nation, constituted at Sinai, and independent.* Led to Sinai the people became a nation by accepting the covenant which God proposed, and which was contained in ten commandments, and formed the constitution of the nation. Jehovah is king, who henceforth dwells in the tabernacle in the midst of his people, reveals his will to prophet and priest, and exercises the legislative, judicial, and executive offices through laws which he reveals, judgments which he pronounces, and officials whom he raises up. The nation was

III. 1. *A brotherhood of twelve tribes under a religious constitution, and with a common sanctuary* (Ex. xix.-1 Sam. vii.). The high priest was the chief representative, and was aided by prophets and occasional leaders, like Moses. See SINAI, THEOCRACY, TENT OF MEETING, TABERNACLE, LEVITES, LEVITICUS, CAMP.

Leaving Sinai the Israelites journeyed to Kadesh. On account of their lack of faith, they were turned back into the wilderness, where they sojourned thirty-eight years; see NUMBERS, WILDERNESS OF THE WANDERING, KORAH. At length they encompassed the land of Edom, and found a crossing at the head of the Arnon valley. The conquest of the country east of the Jordan followed; see SIHON, OG. The camp was then pitched in the Jordan valley; see SHITTIM, BALAAM, BAAL-PEOR, MIDIAN, DEUTERONOMY. On the death of Moses, the Jordan was crossed and Canaan conquered and possessed; see JOSHUA, CANAAN, SHILOH. After the settlement of the Israelites in Canaan, Joshua died, and was succeeded at intervals by other persons of ability and influence, fifteen in number, who led the people against their enemies and exercised governmental functions; see JUDGES, SAMUEL. Unifying forces were at work during the times of the judges, and a national feeling existed and sometimes manifested its strength; but still the people too often allowed natural barriers and petty jealousies and local interests to separate them. There are bright examples of godliness and filial piety, but along with these is the spectacle of a people easily seduced to idolatry; see JUDGES. During this entire period the weaknesses and defects of the human parties to the covenant were disclosed. At the very beginning of the period lack of faith in God was shown at Kadesh, the existence of tribal jealousy was manifested in the rebellion of Korah and his company against the high-priesthood of Aaron and the political supremacy of Moses, and the readiness of the people to lapse into idolatry became apparent in the affair of the golden calf, and in their ensnarement by the seductions of Baal-peor. The great political blunders of the period were the league made by Joshua with the Gibeonites, and the failure of Israel to occupy Jerusalem. These defects and blunders were of far-reaching consequence in the history of Israel.

III. 2. *A monarchy of twelve tribes.* The people had failed to foster the centralizing influences which their religion designedly provided, allowed senseless tribal jealousies to sunder them, and accustomed themselves to turn from God to idols. The threatening attitude of neighboring nations made them realize the need of organization, a strong government, and a military leader. Samuel was old. They turned away from the good provision which God had made, but which they had neglected, and demanded an earthly king. By the side of the high priest and the prophet there was now a permanent earthly ruler, with supreme political power, instead of the judges whom God was wont to raise up. Saul was the first king, but on account of his overestimate of his position, his failure to recognize the superior functions of the high priest and prophet, he was denied the privilege of founding a dynasty; and finally his willful transgression of God's explicit command led to the rejection of him from being king, to the withdrawal of God and God's prophet from him, and the choice of David; see SAMUEL. BOOKS OF, SAUL, DAVID. Under David the twelve tribes were reunited after seven years of civil war, Jerusalem was taken from the Jebusites and made the political and religious capital, the borders of the kingdom were extended by conquest far to the northeast of Damascus, and the acquired country was laid under tribute. Deputies were placed in Edom also. See JERUSALEM. David was succeeded by Solomon, under whom the temple was erected, Jerusalem greatly embellished and its fortifications extended, and the fame of Israel enhanced. But his exactions made the people discontented, and on his death the failure of his son to discern the gravity of the situation incited ten tribes to revolt from the house of David. See SOLOMON, REHOBOAM, ISRAEL.

III. 3. *A monarchy consisting chiefly of the tribe of Judah*, ten tribes having revolted and formed a rival schismatic apostate kingdom. The causes which led to this revolt were long standing and many; see ISRAEL. The kingdom of Judah possessed the greater strength. It had material strength; the stronger natural position, the capital, the organized government, and the worship to which the people were accustomed. It had moral strength; the consciousness of adhering to the legitimate line of kings, which has ever been a mighty force in history, the true religion with its elevating influence, the sense of loyalty to Jehovah, and a line of godlier kings. It had the providential care of God, who was preserving the knowledge and worship of himself among men, and was preparing the way for his Messiah. The religious history of Judah during this period was marked by a decline in the days of Rehoboam (1 Kin. xiv. 22), and again in the days of his son Abijam (xv. 3), and yet again in the days of Jehoram and Ahaziah (2 Kin. viii. 27). The cause of this religious declension was the corruption introduced by Solomon and intermarriage with idolaters. Rehoboam's mother was an Ammonitess, for whom Solomon had built a high place to Milcom, and who had sacrificed to this abomination of her people. Jehoram was son-in-law of Ahab and Jezebel. Each of these periods of religious decay was followed by reformation, the first under king Asa and the second under Jehoash, but Jehoash himself afterwards turned away from the Lord, and another religious revival became necessary, only to be followed by the dominance of idolatry later under the pernicious influence of Ahaz. The encroachments of the Assyrians on the Hebrew people began in this period. The divided nation, largely degenerate in religion, was not in condition to offer effective resistance ; and by slow but steady advance, which began in the days of Ahab, the Assyrians pushed their conquest until they had overthrown the northern kingdom. See ISRAEL, SAMARIA, SARGON.

III. 4. *The monarchy of Judah sole survivor.* The southern kingdom was now exposed to the attacks of the Assyrians, and later of their successors, the Babylonians ; see HEZEKIAH, SENNACHERIB, MANASSEH, NEBUCHADNEZZAR. The religious condition also of the people was not good, although great prophets, like Isaiah, Jeremiah, and Micah were laboring to advance the truth. Its kings, with the exception of Hezekiah and Josiah, did not render true and steadfast allegiance to Jehovah, and the people were like-minded. There was an idolatrous party in the state which had been triumphant in the reign of Ahaz. Idolatry was deep-rooted among the people, and the reforms of any king affected the nation only superficially. Foreign idolaters were also in the land. The nation drifted to destruction. The army of Nebuchadnezzar visited Jerusalem at brief intervals during the course of two decades, several deportations of Jews to Babylonia took place, and the city was taken and burned in 587 B. C. The Hebrew people had failed to conserve the elements of national strength, and to abide under the shadow of the Almighty, and they fell. See JUDAH.

IV. *A subject people.*—1. *Judah in the Babylonian exile.* See CAPTIVITY.

IV. 2. *Judah in Palestine.* In the first year of his reign over Babylon, 538 B. C., Cyrus issued an edict which permitted the Jews to return to Palestine and rebuild the temple. Forty-three thousand embraced the opportunity and returned under Zerubbabel. This colony was

(a) *A province of the Persian empire, subordinated to the province Beyond-the-river.* It remained such for two hundred years. Twice it enjoyed local governors of its own, appointed by the Persian monarch ; see ZERUBBABEL and NEHEMIAH. But for the greater part of the time its civil affairs were subject to the jurisdiction of the Persian satrap beyond the river. He had authority to appoint a deputy for Judah, and to call on the Jews for men or money. But the local administration was left to the high priest, and he gradually came to be regarded as the political as well as the religious head of the

nation. Immediately on the return of the exiles from Babylon the foundations of the temple were laid. The work was pushed on under the exhortations of the prophets Haggai and Zechariah despite interruptions and opposition, and the building was completed in 515 B. C. The walls were erected under the supervision of Nehemiah by authority of Artaxerxes in 445 B. C. ; see JERUSALEM. At this time also Ezra the priest was in the city, zealous for the law of God, and successfully laboring for the purity of religion ; see EZRA and CANON. About 365 B. C. there was a dispute between two brothers about the high-priesthood, which ended by one killing the other within the precincts of the temple. In connection with this affair Bagoses, general of the army of Artaxerxes Mnemon, entered the temple (Antiq. xi. 7, 1). In March or April, 334 B. C. Alexander of Macedon crossed the Hellespont, defeated the Persian satraps, then marched on, and the next year gained a victory over the Persian monarch Darius Codomannus at Issus, a defile near the northeastern angle of the Mediterranean Sea, laid Syria at his feet, and entered Jerusalem. After an almost uninterrupted career of conquest, extending eastward as far as the Punjab, Alexander died at Babylon in June, 323 B. C. See ALEXANDER.

(b) *Judæa subject to Egypt.* Ptolemy Soter wrested Palestine from Syria, to which it had fallen after Alexander's death, in 320 B. C., and the Ptolemies retained it, except for occasional brief periods, until 198 B. C., when the cruelty of Ptolemy Philopator drove the Jews to seek the protection of Antiochus the Great ; see PTOLEMY. During these 122 years the Jews were governed by their high priest subject to the king of Egypt. At this time the Hebrew Scriptures were translated into Greek at Alexandria in Egypt. See VERSIONS.

(c) *Judæa subject to Syria.* Antiochus the Great wrested Palestine from Egypt in 198 B. C. by his victory over Ptolemy Philopator at Paneas. The Syrians not only supported the Grecian party among the Jews which attempted to hellenize the nation, but they also endeavored by force to impose idolatry upon the Jews. The sacrilegious tyranny of the Syrians became intolerable to the pious portion of the nation, and led to the Maccabæan revolt in 166 B. C. See GYMNASIUM, JASON, ANTIOCHUS.

A period of independence under the Maccabæan priest-kings followed ; see MACCABEES. It lasted from 166 B. C. until Pompey took Jerusalem in 63 B. C.; but the Maccabees were allowed to hold the throne until 40 B. C., when Herod the Great was appointed king of Judæa by the Roman senate. He began his actual reign by the capture of Jerusalem in 37 B. C. During this period the Pharisees and Sadducees became recognized parties, exerting great political and religious influence. See PHARISEES, SADDUCEES, COUNCIL.

(d) *Under the Romans.* During this period

the affairs of Judæa were administered by appointees of the Romans ; first by Herod the Great, then by Archelaus, and afterwards by procurators, except from A. D. 41–44, when Herod Agrippa I. reigned as king ; see JUDÆA, HEROD, PROCURATOR. The maladministration of these officials exasperated the people and drove them to revolt. Obstinate war raged from A. D. 66 until the fall of Jerusalem in A. D. 70. The remnant of the Jewish people who remained in Palestine were denied access to their capital, and had no longer national existence. While the Jews still constituted a nation under the Romans, in the days of Herod the king, Jesus of Nazareth was born and a new period of biblical history began.

4. THE HISTORY OF THE ESTABLISHMENT OF THE CHRISTIAN CHURCH, which is to reach all nations.—I. *Christ's preparation for the establishment of his Church*, by example, teaching, and redemption. See JESUS, GOSPEL, APOSTLES.

II. *The Church among the Jews.* The church was founded by the risen Christ. Ten days later, at Pentecost, the promised Spirit was given, and the church's work was initiated by Peter's sermon, increase of believers, and baptism ; see PENTECOST, HOLY SPIRIT, TONGUES, BAPTISM, CHURCH. During the next few years, six perhaps, the church experienced the difficulties incident to the imperfections of believers and to persecution ; but it grew steadily in purity and numbers. See ANANIAS, DEACONS, STEPHEN. The persecution which arose on the death of Stephen scattered the brethren abroad, and the evangelization of the Jews in Palestine and Syria began. The gospel was carried to Samaria and to the cities on the seacoast from Gaza to Cæsarea. See PHILIP. For the purpose of persecuting the believers who were now found in the Jewish colony in Damascus, Saul went thither, and was converted, and was told that he was to be a teacher of the gentiles. The vision of Peter at Joppa, and its complement in the conversion of Cornelius and his baptism with the Holy Spirit, opened the eyes of the church to the truth, already theoretically known, that the Holy Spirit is for all believers, Jew and gentile. See CORNELIUS. At Antioch Jewish believers from the West, who had been driven from Jerusalem by the persecution which had arisen on the death of Stephen, began to preach Jesus to the Greeks also (Acts xi. 20, R. V.), and now the followers of Jesus began to be called Christians, no longer being identified with the Jews. The church was now ready to undertake the evangelization of the gentiles ; the truth of the equality of all believers was known, a man had been raised up to work among the gentiles, and the first beginnings had been made.

III. *The Church among Jews and gentiles.* Paul and Barnabas, called by the Holy Ghost, began the evangelization of Jews and gentiles in Asia Minor. The question about the obligations of gentile converts arose. The council at Jerusalem took a firm stand for Christian liberty, refused to impose circumcision and the observance of the Mosaic law upon gentile converts, and only insisted upon certain moral duties and certain matters of expediency which it was necessary to emphasize on account of the state of public opinion. The rights of gentile Christians were now secure. On a second missionary journey, Paul, under the direction of the Spirit, came to Troas, and was called by a vision to extend his labors to Europe, and the evangelization of Europe from Philippi to Rome ensued. See PAUL, JOHN, PETER.

Hit'tites.

A people, known also as children of Heth, and connected by blood or conquest with Canaan (Gen. x. 15 ; xxiii. 3). For centuries they occupied the region extending from northern Palestine to the Euphrates, and numbered Kadesh on the Orontes, Hamath and Carchemish among their important cities (Josh. i. 4 ; 1 Kin. x. 29). As early as the time of Abraham, bodies of them had taken up their abode in Canaan proper, and apparently had adopted the language of Canaan. Abraham met with them at Hebron, and it was from a Hittite that he purchased the cave of Machpelah (Gen. xxiii. 1–20 ; xxv. 9). Esau married two Hittite wives (xxvi. 34, 35 ; xxxvi. 2). The spies sent out by Moses found the Hittites occupying the mountains (Num. xiii. 29). They took part in the war against the invading Hebrews under Joshua (Josh. ix. 1, 2). They were also among the tribes which aided Jabin, king of Hazor, in the great battle in which he was so signally defeated by Joshua at the waters of Merom (xi. 3). The man who betrayed Luz, or Bethel, built a second Luz in the land of the Hittites (Judg. i. 26). After the conquest of Canaan by Joshua, Hittites still remained in the country, intermarriages taking place between them and the Israelites (iii. 5, 6). One of David's followers was Ahimelech the Hittite (1 Sam. xxvi. 6). Uriah, against whom David sinned so deeply, was of the same race (2 Sam. xi. 3, 17, 21). In the reign of Solomon the Hittites and other tribes who remained in the land had levied on them a tribute of bond-service (1 Kin. ix. 20, 21 ; 2 Chron. viii. 7, 8). Hittite women were in Solomon's harem (1 Kin. xi. 1). The Hittites were the Kheta, or Khita, of the Egyptian monuments, the Hatti of the Assyrian inscriptions, and the Kēteioi of Homer (Odyssey xi. 521). From Egyptian and Assyrian sources and Hittite remains we learn that when the power of the Hittites was at its height, their sway or their influence was paramount from the Archipelago to the Euphrates, their northern or northeastern capital being Carchemish, on that river, and their southern or southwestern one Kadesh, on the Orontes. For five hundred years they carried on a struggle, with intervals of peace, with the Egyptians, fighting great battles with Thothmes III., in the sixteenth century B. C., and with Seti I. and Ramses II. The siege of Kadesh by the latter Egyptian monarch was celebrated in an epic by the poet Pentaur. For four hundred years, beginning 1100 B. C., they carried on a contest with the Assyrians, generally holding their own against that great power, till, in 717 B. C., Sargon, the Assyrian king, captured Carchemish, and terminated their empire. Sculptures, doubtless Hittite, with hieroglyphics not yet satisfactorily read, have been found at Carchemish, at Hamath, and throughout a great part of Asia Minor. The Hittites were a sturdy race of men. They are generally represented as beardless. They wore pointed hats and loose tunics. Their shoes were tilted up at the tips, and fastened by a large bandage round the foot and ankle. They are like the shoes still worn by the peasantry of Asia Minor, and are the best preservative for the feet when the country is covered with snow. The Hittites also wore long gloves, covering the forearm, with one compartment for the thumb and another for the four fingers. These are believed to be a survival of the time when the Hittites lived among the snowclad range of Taurus and the Armenian mountains.

Hi'vites.

One of the races of Canaan before the conquest of the country by the Hebrews (Gen. x. 17; Ex. iii. 17; Josh. ix. 1). They scattered into several communities. A body of them dwelt at Shechem in the time of Jacob (Gen. xxxiii. 18 with xxxiv. 2), and their descendants still had influence in the city several generations after the conquest (Judg. ix. 28). A body of them also dwelt in Gibeon and its vicinity. They obtained a treaty of peace from Joshua by stratagem, but on their deceit being discovered, they were made hewers of wood and drawers of water (Josh. ix.). They had also an extensive settlement, probably their principal one, at the foot of Lebanon, from mount Hermon to the entering in at Hamath (Josh. xi. 3; Judg. iii. 3). In these northern mountain regions they had villages of their own as late as the time of David (2 Sam. xxiv. 7). Those of Palestine proper were, with the other Canaanites who remained in the land, required to render bond-service to Solomon in connection with his extensive building operations (1 Kin. ix. 20-22).

Hiz'ki, in A. V. Hezeki [my strength, or a strong support is (God)].

A Benjamite, son of Elpaal (1 Chron. viii. 17).

Hiz-ki'ah. See HEZEKIAH 2.

Hiz-ki'jah. See HEZEKIAH 4.

Ho'bab [lover].

The father-in-law of Moses, according to the traditional vowel points of the Hebrew text (Judg. iv. 11). But the father-in-law of Moses was Reuel, or, to call him by what appears to have been his honorary title, Jethro, his excellency. Hobab is definitely stated to have been the son of Reuel (Num. x. 29 , and if the traditional vocalization is ignored, and regard paid to the Hebrew text only, the Hebrew words may equally well be translated " Hobab the brother-in-law of Moses" (Judg. i. 16; iv. 11, R. V.). Moses' father-in-law Reuel, or Jethro, visited Moses in the camp at Rephidim and returned to his own land (Ex. xviii. 1, 5, 27). A year later, when the Israelites were about to advance from Sinai, Moses urged Hobab, the son of Reuel, to accompany them and aid them with his knowledge of the desert. Hobab finally consented (Num. x. 29; Judg. i. 16; iv. 11). After the conquest of Canaan, his family settled in Judah, south of Arad, and were still there in the time of Saul and David (Judg. i. 16; 1 Sam. xv. 6; xxvii. 10; xxx. 29). Hobab belonged to the Kenites (Judg. i. 16; iv. 11), a family of the Midianites.

Ho'bah.

A town on the left, that is to the north, of Damascus. Hobah was the extreme limit to which Abraham pursued the defeated eastern kings (Gen. xiv. 15). Wetzstein mentions a place of this name between Tadmor and Homs.

Hod [majesty].

An Asherite, son of Zophah (1 Chron. vii. 37).

Hod-a-vi'ah, in A. V. once Ho-da'iah (1 Chron. iii. 24) [Jehovah is his praise, or he hath praised Jehovah].

1. A son of Elioenai, descended through Shecaniah from David (1 Chron. iii. 24).

2. One of the heads of the half-tribe of Manasseh east of the Jordan (1 Chron. v. 24).

3. A Benjamite (1 Chron. ix. 7).

4. A Levite, founder of a family, some members of which returned from Babylon (Ezra ii. 40). He is called Judah (iii. 9), virtually a synonymous name, and through a slight corruption of the Hebrew text, Hodevah, or, as traditionally read, Hodeiah (Neh. vii. 43 and R. V. margin).

Ho-de'iah. See HODAVIAH 4.

Ho'desh [new moon].

A wife of Shaharaim (1 Chron. viii. 9).

Ho-de'vah. See HODAVIAH 4.

Ho-di'ah, in A. V. of Nehemiah Ho-di'jah [splendor of Jehovah].

1. A man who was reckoned as belonging to the tribe of Judah, perhaps because of his marriage with the sister of Naham (1 Chron. iv. 19, R. V.). A. V. does not give a correct rendering of the Hebrew text.

2. One of the Levites employed by Ezra to explain the law to the people (Neh. viii. 7), and to assist on the day of penitence and prayer (ix. 5). He was probably one of the two Levite Hodiahs who sealed the covenant (x. 10 or 13).

Hog'lah [a partridge].

A daughter of Zelophehad (Num. xxvi. 33).

Ho'ham.

A king of Hebron, who entered into a league against Joshua, and was defeated, captured, and executed (Josh. x. 1-27).

Holm Tree.

The evergreen oak (*Quercus ilex*), the rendering of the Hebrew *Tirzah*, hard tree, in the only passage where it occurs (Is. xliv. 14; in A. V. cypress). The two Greek translators, Aquila and Theodotion, render it by wild oak, and the Vulgate by *ilex*.

Ho'lon [probably sandy].

1. A town in the hill country of Judah (Josh. xv. 51), given, with its suburbs, to the priests (xxi. 15). Called also Hilen (1 Chron. vi. 58). Not identified.

2. A Moabite town (Jer. xlviii. 21), perhaps Horon.

Ho'ly.

The ordinary Hebrew word for holy is *Kadosh*, separated. It is represented in the N. T. by the Greek word '*Agios*. It is used for what is set apart from a common to a sacred use, as the utensils and ministers of the sanctuary, and certain days (Ex. xx. 8; xxx. 31; xxxi. 10; Lev. xxi. 7; Num. v. 17; Neh. viii. 9; Zech. xiv. 21); for what is separated from ceremonial defilement (Ex. xxii. 31; Lev. xx. 26) or immorality (2 Cor. vii. 1; 1 Thes. iv. 7), including false worship and heathen practices (Lev. xx. 6, 7; xxi. 6). In a larger sense God is holy, for he is separated from all other beings by his infinite perfections, by his being, wisdom, power, holiness, justice, goodness, and truth, the glory of which fills the earth (Is. vi. 3). Even holy angels ascribe holiness to him (Is. vi. 3; Rev. iv. 8; xvi. 5).

Ho-ly Ghost'.

The Spirit of God, the Holy Spirit. The word spirit now more correctly expresses the idea than does the term ghost, which has narrowed its meaning, and commonly denotes a disembodied spirit wandering on earth. The name Holy Spirit is used three times only in the O. T. (Ps. li. 11; Is. lxiii. 10, 11), but there are numerous references to his work. The Spirit of God is the divine principle of activity everywhere at work in the world, executing the will of God. The Spirit is sent forth by God (Ps. civ. 29, 30) and given by God (Num. xi. 29; Is. xlii. 1, 5). The Spirit brooded over chaotic matter in the beginning and is everywhere present (Gen. i. 2; Ps. cxxxix. 7), and is thus immanent and the energy in cosmical processes (Job. xxvi. 13; Is. lix. 19); is the source of physical, intellectual, and moral life (Gen. vi. 3; Job xxxii. 8; xxxiii. 4; xxxiv. 14; Ps. xxvii. 3; civ. 30; cp. Is. xlii. 5); is able to produce supernatural effects (1 Kin. xviii. 12; 2 Kin. ii. 16). He abides with the people of God (Is. lxiii. 11; Hag. ii. 5), and bestows varied powers for the work of the kingdom, strength (Judg. iii. 10;

vi. 34; xi. 29; xiii. 25; xiv. 6, 19; xv. 14; 1 Sam. xi. 6; xvi. 13; 1 Chron. xii. 18), skil' (Ex. xxxi. 3), wisdom (Num. xi. 17, 25; xxvii. 18), in short, everything needful for the work of the kingdom (Is. xi. 2; Zech. iv. 6). He instructed the people of God (Neh. ix. 20) by inspiring the prophets (Num. xxiv. 2; 1 Sam. x. 6; Hos. ix. 7; Mic. iii. 8; Zech. vii. 12). He works upon the heart of the individual child of God. It was foretold that this work would be especially powerful and widespread in the Messianic period, when the Spirit shall be poured out on the people of God (Is. xliv. 3), will give to them a new heart and a new spirit (Ezek. xxxvi. 26), produce sorrow for sin (Zech. xii. 10); yea, be poured out on all flesh (Joel ii. 28). The Spirit is grieved when men resist his holy work (Is. lxiii. 10; cp. Ps. cvi. 33). Jesus promised that on his departure the Spirit should come and dwell with every believer, clothe with power, guide and teach the church, bear witness of Christ and glorify him, convict the world of sin, righteousness, and judgment (Luke xxiv. 49; John vii. 37-39; xiv. 25, 26; xv. 26; xvi. 7-14; Acts i. 8).

The N. T. treats of Messianic times and the dispensation of the Spirit, and consequently the Spirit is mentioned much oftener in the N. T. than in the O. T. All the attributes of the Spirit revealed in the O. T. are disclosed in the N. T. in exercise. The doctrine of the Spirit advances beyond the teaching of the O. T. chiefly in becoming more definite in respect to his personality. Though the word spirit is neuter in Greek and feminine in Hebrew, yet the Spirit is sometimes called who, not which, the masculine form of the pronoun being used (Eph. i. 13, 14; cp. cautiously John xvi. 13). The Spirit further speaks in the first person, using the pronouns I and me (Acts x. 19, 20; xiii. 2); is associated with the Father and the Son in the baptismal formula and the apostolic benediction (Mat. xxviii. 19; 2 Cor. xiii. 14); can be grieved (Eph. iv. 30; cp. Rom. viii. 26).

Memorable acts of the Spirit at the beginning of the Christian dispensation are the miraculous conception of Jesus by the Holy Ghost (Mat. i. 18-20); the descent of the Spirit upon Jesus at his baptism, in the form of a dove visible to him and to John the Baptist (Mat. iii. 16; Mark i. 10; John i. 32), and the effusion of the Holy Ghost in the likeness of tongues of fire on the day of Pentecost, and the accompanying gift of languages (Acts ii. 4). See GOD, INSPIRATION, PENTECOST.

Ho'ly Place. See TABERNACLE, TEMPLE.

Ho-ly Spir'it. See HOLY GHOST.

Ho'mam [possibly destroyer].

Son of Lotan, and grandson of Seir (1 Chron. i. 39). The name appears in Gen. xxxvi. 22 as Hemam. The difference in Hebrew is trifling, and is doubtless due to a misreading. The latter name has jod where the former has vau (q. v.).

Ho'mer [a heap].

A measure for dry substances and liquids. It contained ten baths or ephahs (Ezek. xlv. 11, 14) and one hundred omers (Ex. xvi. 36). It held about thirty-six pecks, U. S. measure. See EPHAH, MEASURE.

Hon'ey.

A sweet, thick fluid collected by bees from flowers and fruit and deposited in the cells of a comb (Judg. xiv. 8; Ps. xix. 10); much esteemed as an article of food (Gen. xliii. 11; 2 Sam. xvii. 29), and eaten as found in the comb or as prepared in various ways (Ex. xvi. 31; 1 Sam. xiv. 26). Wild honey was deposited by bees in rocks, trees, and other places (Deut. xxxii. 13; Judg. xiv. 8; 1 Sam. xiv. 25; Mat. iii. 4). Because it acts like a leaven, producing fermentation, honey might not be used in offerings made by fire unto the Lord (Lev. ii. 11). An artificial honey or syrup was prepared from dates (War iv. 8, 3).

Canaan was described as flowing with milk and honey (Ex. iii. 8, 17).

Hook.

The Hebrews and contemporary peoples used hooks of various kinds:

1. Curtains were hung by means of hooks, those employed about the tabernacle being made of gold and silver (Ex. xxvi. 32, 37; xxvii. 10).

2. By means of flesh hooks meat was lifted from the pot (Ex. xxvii. 3: 1 Sam. ii. 13, 14), and on firmly fixed hooks slain animals were hung up (Ezek. xl. 43, but the meaning of the word rendered hook in this passage is disputed).

3. Hooks resembling thorns, and sometimes called so in Hebrew (Amos iv. 2), were used in fishing (Job xli. 1; Hab. i. 15). See FISHING.

4. A large hook was thrust through the mouth of a fish or other aquatic animal, and attached by a cord to a stake, when it was desired to keep it alive (Job xli. 2; Ezek. xxix. 4). A similar hook was used for leading about lions and other beasts (2 Kin. xix. 28; Ezek. xix. 4, in A. V. chains; cp. xxxviii. 4), and for a like purpose were inserted in the lips of captives (2 Chron. xxxiii. 11, R. V. margin).

5. Pruning hooks were used by vinedressers (Is. ii. 4; xviii. 5).

Hoph'ni [pertaining to the fist].

A son of Eli. He and his brother Phinehas discharged the priest's office in the old age of Eli, but showed themselves unworthy of the sacred office by scandalous behavior. Eli mildly remonstrated when summary proceedings were required; and, in consequence, the divine judgment was pronounced against him and his house. When it was resolved that the ark of God should be taken to the battlefield, Hophni and Phinehas, who as officiating priests were its custodians, accompanied it, and were both slain in the disastrous battle which followed (1 Sam. ii. 22–iv. 22).

Hor [mountain].

1. A mountain on the border of the Edomite country, where Aaron died and was buried (Num. xx. 22–29; xxxiii. 37–39, 41; Deut. xxxii. 50). Josephus says that it was one of the mountains surrounding Petra (Antiq. iv. 4, 7). Tradition has settled on Jebel Hârûn, meaning Aaron's mountain, a great two-topped eminence of sandstone, about 4800 feet high, on the eastern side of the Arabah, nearly midway between the southern extrem-

Mount Hor, the traditional burying place of Aaron.

ity of the Dead Sea and the northern end of the gulf of Akaba. It is the highest and wildest of the whole Edomite range. Petra is close by, to the west; but the ruined city is not visible from the summit. On its summit stands a tomb, nominally that of Aaron; but the upper part of it, at least, is only a modern Mohammedan mosque. The tradition, however, is open to serious question. It appears to rest on the false identification of Kadesh with Petra. Jebel Hârûn is in the midst of Edom, and not on its border, as was Hor. If Edom extended to the gulf of Akaba (Deut. ii. 8), the Israelites could not reach the traditional mountain without crossing Edom, which they were forbidden to do. Jebel Madara, about 15 miles northeast of Kadesh, has been suggested, and satisfies the conditions. Still, if Madara is really written in Arabic with the letter dal (Seetzen), it is doubtful whether the name echoes Moserah (Num. xxxiii. 37 with Deut. x. 6).

2. A mountain on the northern boundary of Palestine, between the Mediterranean Sea and the entering in of Hamath (Num. xxxiv. 7, 8). It was probably a prominent peak of Lebanon.

Ho'ram [elevation].

A king of Gezer, defeated and slain by Joshua (Josh. x. 33).

Ho'reb [dry, desert].

The mount of God in the peninsula of Sinai (Ex. iii. 1; xviii. 5), where the law was given to Israel (Deut. iv. 10–15; v. 2; 1 Kin. viii. 9; xix. 8). The names Horeb and Sinai are used almost interchangeably (for example, Horeb in Ex. xvii. 6; Deut. i. 6; 1 Kin. viii. 9; xix. 8; 2 Chron. v. 10; but Sinai in Ex. xix. 11; xxiv. 16; xxxi. 18; Lev. vii. 38; xxv. 1; Deut. xxxiii. 2; Judg. v. 5). This phenomenon has been variously explained. It has been held that the two terms did not denote exactly the same thing. Horeb has been regarded as the name of the range, and Sinai as a prominent peak (Hengstenberg, Robinson); or Horeb is thought of as a lower part or peak of mount Sinai (Gesenius); or Horeb was the northern and lower portion of the range, while Sinai was the southern portion, especially its highest point. On the other hand, the two terms have been held to denote the same object; and Ewald believed Sinai to be the older name of the mountain afterwards called Horeb (cp. Judg. v. 5). On this theory the choice between the names would depend on individual preference, on the date of the records used, or upon the writer's mood (study Ex. xix. 1, 2ᵃ in the context xviii. 13–xix. 6; and xix. 11ᵇ in the context 9–13).

Ho'rem [enclosed, sacred].

A fenced city of Naphtali (Josh. xix. 38). Not identified. There is no reason to think of Hura or Kurah, 3½ miles west by north of Yarun, nor of Harah, 6½ miles north by east of Yarun.

Ho'resh [a dense wood or thicket].

A locality, probably at the time overgrown with bush, where David lurked (1 Sam. xxiii. 16, R. V. margin). In the text the word is rendered wood.

Hor-hag-gid'gad, in A. V. **Hor-hagidgad** [mountain or cavern of Gidgad, i. e. perhaps, thunder].

An encampment of the Israelites in the wilderness (Num. xxxiii. 32). The same as Gudgodah (Deut. x. 6, 7; cp. Num. xxxiii. 31–33). Site unknown. It must not be identified with wady Ghudaghid, for the names are entirely different in etymology.

Ho'ri [cave-dweller or man of Khar].

1. A Horite tribe descended from Lotan, and called by the general name of the stock to which it belonged (Gen. xxxvi. 22).

2. Father of Shaphat the spy (Num. xiii. 5).

Ho'rite, in A. V. of Deut. **Ho'rims**.

Cave-dwellers, the aborigines of mount Seir, and hence called the children of Seir (Gen. xxxvi. 20). They were defeated by Chedorlaomer and his allies (Gen. xiv. 6). They were governed by chieftains (xxxvi. 29, 30). They were subsequently destroyed by the posterity of Esau (Deut. ii. 12, 22).

Hor'mah [a devoted place, destruction].

1. A region to the south of Canaan, in Seir, north of both Kadesh and mount Hor. When the Israelites after their loss of faith presumed to advance from Kadesh toward Canaan, the Amalekites and Canaanites came down, smote them, and drove them as far as " the desolation," as the district was called from its devastation some thirty-eight years later (Num. xiv. 45; Deut. i. 44). On the second departure of the Israelites from Kadesh, after the lapse of these thirty-eight years, while they were encamped at mount Hor, the Canaanites under the king of Arad again attacked them and made some captives. Israel vowed their destruction if Jehovah would aid, devastated their cities, and called the wasted region Hormah, desolation (Num. xxi. 1–3).

2. The town Zephath, called Hormah after its devotion. It was situated in the south country, toward the border of Edom, near Ziklag, and was allotted to Judah, but was afterwards transferred to Simeon (Josh. xv. 30; xix. 4). After the death of Joshua, Judah assisted Simeon to take the town. It was inhabited by Canaanites; and had either escaped destruction when the region was first devastated in fulfillment of the vow (Num. xxi. 2), or it had been rebuilt by fugitives who returned. At any rate, it was still included in the old vow; and it was now devoted to destruction, man and beast were slain, and the town was henceforth called Hormah (Judg. i. 17). Joshua had already defeated its king (called proleptically king of Hormah), who, it may be judged, was absent from his city, assisting men of his own race at Hebron at the time of his defeat, as the king of Jerusalem and the king of Gezer

were away from their cities when Joshua smote them (Josh. xii. 14; cp. x. 10, 33). After the town had been devoted, it was inhabited by Simeonites (1 Chron. iv. 30). It was hospitable to David when he lived as an outcast, and to his friends there David sent of the spoils of Ziklag (1 Sam. xxx. 30).

Horn.
Part of Palestine, especially its southern portion, being a pastoral country, the Israelites were exceedingly familiar with the horns of animals. In early times they converted them into trumpets (Josh. vi. 13), or into flasks for such substances as oil (1 Sam. xvi. 1, 13; 1 Kin. i. 39). When God exalts the horn of an individual, the meaning is that he confers great power and prosperity (1 Sam. ii. 10: Ps. lxxxix. 24); but when one exalts or lifts up the horn, it means that he indulges in arrogance and insolence (Ps. lxxv. 4, 5). Horn denotes political power, the image being drawn from bulls which push with their horns (Ps. cxxxii. 17; Jer. xlviii. 25), and in prophetic language signifies a kingdom (Dan. vii. 8, 11, 21; Zech. i. 18, 19) or kings (Rev. xvii. 12, 16).

Horns of the altar were projections resembling horns placed at the corners of the altar of burnt offering (War v. 5, 6). They were smeared with the blood of the sacrifice (Ex. xxix. 12; Lev. iv. 7), and the bodies of the victims offered in sacrifice appear to have been bound to them (Ps. cxviii. 27), and offenders clung to them for safety from punishment (1 Kin. ii. 28).

Horn was also used to denote a peak (Is. v. 1, R. V. margin). The horns of Hattin are the traditional mount of Beatitudes.

Hor'net.
The rendering of the Hebrew word Ṣir'aḥ, according to the ancient versions. The hornet (*Vespa crabro*) is of the same genus as the wasp, but larger and more formidable. Either the common hornet or a closely allied species is common in Palestine. Hornets were to be sent to drive out the Canaanite nations before the Israelites (Ex. xxiii. 28; Deut. vii. 20; Josh. xxiv. 12; Wisd. xii. 8). It is doubtful whether hornet is here used in a literal or a figurative sense. In favor of the former it may be alleged that Ælian relates that the Phaselites were driven from their territory by hornets, and in favor of the latter that we have no detailed account of the Canaanites being thus expelled. If used figuratively, the sting of the hornet would stand for the terror produced in Canaanite minds by the approach of the irresistible Israelite armies.

Hor-o-na'im [two caverns or ravines].
A Moabite city at the foot of a declivity, and apparently not far from Zoar (Is. xv. 5; Jer. xlviii. 3, 5, 34; Moabite Stone 31). Doubtless the town Oronæ which Alexander Jannæus took from the Arabians, and his son Hyrcanus restored to Aretas (Antiq. xiii. 15, 4; xiv. 1, 4). Situation unknown.

Hor'o-nite.
A native or inhabitant of Horonaim or, more probably, of Beth-horon (Neh. ii. 10, 19).

Horse.
The horse was early subdued by man. Mention is made of its rider in the time of Jacob (Gen. xlix. 17). Mountainous Palestine was not well adapted for its use, and in early times it was principally employed in the maritime plain and in the valley of Jezreel. There were many horses in Egypt (xlvii. 17; Ex. ix. 3; Egyptian records from 18th dynasty onward). When the exodus took place Pharaoh's pursuing army was equipped with chariots and horses (xiv. 9; xv. 19). They existed also in the force of the northern Canaanites led by Sisera, Jabin's commander-in-chief (Judg. iv. 15; v. 22). In Deut. xvii. 16, the king who was to be elected when monarchy was established among the Israelites was forbidden to multiply horses, notwithstanding which prohibition Solomon imported them in great numbers from Egypt, paying for each animal 150 shekels of silver (a little more than $97). He afterwards exported them to the kings of the Hittites and those of the Syrians (1 Kin. x. 28, 29; 2 Chron. i. 16, 17; ix. 28). Horses afterwards became common in Israel and Judah (2 Kin. ix. 18; Is. ii. 7), and were used in battle (1 Kin. xxii. 4; 2 Kin. iii. 7; ix. 33). Foreign kings rode on horseback (Esth. vi. 8), while it was considered lowly in a sovereign to sit upon an ass (Zech. ix. 9), and accorded with the simple manners of the early Hebrew patriarchs, judges, and kings (Gen. xxii. 3; Judg. x. 4; xii. 14; 1 Kin. i. 33). Horses were sometimes dedicated to the sun (2 Kin. xxiii. 11). They are frequently mentioned in the prophecies of Zechariah (Zech. i. 8; vi. 2, 3; x. 5; xiv. 20), and in the book of Revelation (Rev. vi. 2, 4, 5, 8; xix. 11, etc.).

Horse'leech.
A large leech (*Hæmopsis sanguisuga*), common in Palestine. The leech was known to the Hebrews by the name 'ᵃluḳah, to the Aramæans 'ᵃluḳa, to the Arabs 'alaḳat, from its adhering to the flesh (Prov. xxx. 15). It is noted for its insatiable appetite for blood. In the proverb it is used figuratively. Its two insatiable daughters are perhaps named in the first line of ver. 16. The margin of the R. V. substitutes vampire. The blood-sucking vampires (*Desmodidæ*), which are confined to the warmer parts of South America, are not meant; but certain female specters, which are superstitiously believed to haunt graves and suck human blood. The ground for this interpretation is that in Arabic 'aulaḳ is the name of a demon, and 'aluk is equivalent to ghoul.

Ho'sah [fleeing for refuge].
1. A porter in the time of David (1 Chron. xvi. 38; xxvi. 10).

2. A village, probably mentioned by Thothmes III, on the frontier of Asher, and appar-

ently south of Tyre (Josh. xix. 29). Conder
suggests the ruin 'Ezzîyat el-Fôka, about 7
miles south by east of Tyre, and 2½ inland
from the Mediterranean. The names, however, are quite dissimilar.

Ho-san'na [save, we pray].

A short prayer to Jehovah for deliverance,
taken from Ps. cxviii. 25. It was an acclama-
tion of the people when they marched around
the altar at the feast of tabernacles, and most
of the prayers used at that festival began with
it. It was taken up by the multitude of the
disciples at the triumphal entry of Jesus into
Jerusalem, when they hailed him as the son
of David (cp. Mat. xxi. 9, 15 with Ps. cxviii.
25, 26).

Ho-se'a, in A. V. of N. T. **Osee**, in imitation of the Greek form [save]. Identically
the same word as Oshea or Hoshea (Num.
xiii. 8, 16), the first name of Joshua, and as
Hoshea, king of Israel (2 Kin. xv. 30).

A prophet, son of Beeri, whose predictions were uttered in the reigns of Uzziah,
Jotham, Ahaz, and Hezekiah, kings of Judah, and Jeroboam II., king of Israel (Hos.
i. 1). Assuming that Hosea prophesied during
as many as twelve or thirteen years of Jeroboam's reign, and that he lived to see the
overthrow of Samaria in 722 B. C., his ministry extended over a period of forty years.
Hosea was doubtless a citizen of the northern
kingdom, for he speaks of "our king" and
"the land," meaning northern Israel, without feeling the need of a restrictive adjective (i. 2; vii. 5); and he prophesied to the
people of that kingdom. He was a contemporary of Isaiah, who labored in Judah (i. 1
with Is. i. 1); he began his prophetic activity in the reign of the second Jeroboam,
when Jeroboam and Uzziah were contemporaries, that is, before 749 B. C., doubtless some
years before Isaiah appeared, and he ceased
much earlier than did Isaiah. Hosea was
also a contemporary of Amos in the northern
kingdom, and of Micah who prophesied in
Judah.

The book of Hosea is the first of the minor
prophets, not only in the order of their arrangement, but probably also in the order
of time. It consists of two portions, chapters
i.-iii. and iv.-xiv. The first part belongs to
the earlier period of the prophet's ministry;
for the first chapter at least dates from the
reign of the second Jeroboam, or within six
months after its close, before the destruction
of the house of Jehu (i. 2-4). These first
three chapters furnish the key to the whole
book, in which the unfaithfulness of Israel
to Jehovah during the entire national history is pressed home on the conscience (iv.
1-v. 7; vi. 4-vii. 16; viii.-xi.), the necessity
of chastisement is shown, and the unquenchable love of Jehovah for his erring people is
earnestly taught (vi. 1-3; xii.-xiv.). In
chapters i.-iii. the unfaithfulness of Israel
and the Lord's patience and forbearance are

set forth under the analogy of an adulterous
wife. Regarding the account of the prophet's
marriage interpreters have been divided in
opinion from ancient times. Is the story of
the unfaithful wife an allegory or a fact? It
is argued that it was allegorical and not real,
because—1. It is impossible that God would
have commanded a prophet to enter such a
revolting alliance, and one which was apt to
lessen his influence with the better part of
the people, as a marriage with a woman of
impure life would do. 2. The law of Moses
forbade a priest to marry an unchaste woman
(Lev. xxi. 7); and as the prophets were also
a sacred class, although not bound by the
strict priestly laws, God would scarcely direct
them to enter into wedlock with the unclean.
3. The action of the first chapter, if real,
would require years for its performance, involving not only the prophet's marriage, but
also the birth of several children; and the
symbolic lesson would be lost. On the other
hand, the narrative is held to be the story
of domestic tragedy in real life and the
command which is recorded in chap. i. 2,
directing the prophet to take "a wife of
whoredom," is regarded as meaning not a
woman already steeped in sin, but one who
was as yet innocent in act. After her marriage with Hosea, she revealed a deeply
seated propensity to impurity, proved unfaithful to her marriage vows, and was divorced (ii. 2). The "children of whoredom"
are understood to be either the prophet's
own sons and daughters who inherited the
mother's evil tendencies, or else the offspring
of an adulterous union whom the prophet
acknowledged for his own. Eventually by
God's direction the prophet took the woman
back from her life of shame and restored her
to her former position of wife (iii. 1); and thus
typified God's readiness to restore apostate,
idolatrous, sinful Israel to favor. Several
objections lie against this theory. 1. The
words she "bare him a son" (i. 3) are incompatible with the interpretation that the
prophet acknowledged a bastard child. 2.
The words of chap. ii. 2 are spoken by
Jehovah to the Israelites, as appears further
on; and not spoken by the prophet to his
children. 3. Not the woman, but a woman,
is alluded to in chap. iii. 1; whereas the expression should properly be definite, if it referred to a woman who had already been mentioned in chap. i. All difficulties, exegetical
or moral, disappear on the theory that the
account is an allegory. Such allegorical recitals or acted stories were common in prophetic teaching (Jer. xxv. 15-29; Zech. xi.
4-17). But whether allegorical or actual,
the adulterous woman and her equally adulterous children symbolize Israel and its
tribes in their unfaithfulness to Jehovah, attachment to other gods, and alliances with
the nations (cp. Is. xlvii. 8, 9; Luke xix. 44).

The second part of the book of Hosea, consisting of chapters iv.-xiv., is not a series of

discourses, nor even one continuous sermon, but is a summary of his prophetic teaching, prepared by him towards the close of his ministry. The prophecy thus contains the gist of his public addresses. He may have used notes, but they were scarcely needed. His memory sufficed. The sharp, pithy sayings with which he had barbed his arrows, and the striking similes by which he showed up the true character of the sins of his day, were not apt to be forgotten by him; and frequent speech upon the same themes gave a stereotyped form to the material as it lay in the prophet's mind, and preserved the rhythm and fervor of impassioned public address to living men. At the end of his life he set down in writing bits from his sermons, such descriptions and warnings and exhortations as were universal and eternal in their application.

The prophecies of chapters iv.–xiv. were for the most part uttered originally when Assyria was filling the heart of Israel with a great dread. Not a few striking and significant public events occurred during the years of Hosea's prophetic activity to which he makes no reference at all in the written summary of his teaching, or only the vaguest and most general allusions; such as the glory of Jeroboam's reign and the extension of Israel's borders (2 Kin. xiv. 25, 28), the murder of Zechariah by Shallum and the latter's assassination by Menahem (xv. 10, 14), the invasions of Galilee by Tiglath-pileser (xv. 19, 29). Still there are occasional indications of date for particular passages. If, for instance, Tiglath-pileser completely denuded the country of its inhabitants, when he deported the two tribes and a half from the region east of the Jordan (1 Chron. v. 26), then the words of the prophet concerning Gilead, as a city of them that work iniquity, were first spoken before the year 733 B. C. (Hos. vi. 8; and xii. 11, but this latter passage may refer to the past). The butchery of the inhabitants of Beth-arbel (x. 14) has been often, and quite appropriately, regarded as an event of Shalmaneser's reign, 727–722 B. C. If it does belong to the history of Shalmaneser the words of the prophet were uttered about 725 B. C. The frequent references of the prophet to the dallying of the government, now with Assyria and now with Egypt, comport best with the course that marked Israel's politics at the time of Pekah and Hoshea (v. 13; vii. 11; viii. 9; xiv. 3; particularly xii. 1 with 2 Kin. xvii. 3, 4); and accordingly it is probable that the rebuke of Israel for its foreign policy was uttered during the reigns of its last two kings.

The paragraphs into which chapters iv.–xiv. are divided in the R. V. form units of thought complete in themselves. They are grouped together in suitable, though often subtle, logical connection with each other; but they do not flow in smooth, continuous discourse.

1. Chapter iv. 1–vi. 3. The thought that binds the various utterances together is sin and the need of repentance. The people are arraigned for gross iniquity (iv. 1–19), and the princes and priests as being the leaders in sin (v. 1–15). The arraignment is followed by a beautiful exhortation to repentance and the promise of God's return in favor (vi. 1–3).

2. Chapter vi. 4 – x. 15. The unifying thought is the grievous punishment that must come for heinous sin. Fitful repentance does not satisfy God (vi. 4–11). The immoral life and shameless excess of the mighty is manifest to God (vii. 1–7) Israel's stupidity and folly in seeking aid from the powers of the world. For its foolishness it shall be chastised (8–16). The invader is near because of Israel's idolatry and schism (viii. 1–7). Israel has drawn judgment upon itself by dallying with Assyria, by religious abuses, and by trusting in human means (8–14). Israel's infidelity (ix. 1–9), and consequent punishment (10–17). Israel, flourishing like a vigorous vine, only increases its idolatry; but judgment shall spring up as abundant and as destructive as the noxious weed (x. 1–8). Israel's sin compared to that of Gibeah (9–11). As one sows, so shall one reap (12–15).

3. Chapter xi. 1–xiii. 16, a passage characterized by yearning and expostulation. Jehovah's love for Israel is the unquenchable love of a father for his child, even for a wayward child (xi. 1–11). Jacob relied upon his own strength and shrewdness at first, but finally importuned God and prevailed; therefore turn from earthly alliances to thy God (xi. 12–xii. 6 [Heb. xii. 1–7]). Ephraim, a dishonest tradesman, and, having become rich, excuses himself of sin; but Jehovah will cast him out of his home, he who saved Israel from Egypt will now punish (xii. 7–14). Ephraim's idolatry condemned (xiii. 1–8), and its consequence declared (9–16).

4. Chapter xiv. 1–9. Exhortation to repentance, confession, and humble supplication, and the promise of Jehovah's gracious acceptance of the penitent and bestowal of richest blessings.

Genuineness has been denied to the references in the book of Hosea to Judah (particularly i. 7; iv. 15; v. 10–14; vi. 11; xi. 12 [Heb. xii. 1]), to the restoration of Israel to God's favor and their return to their native land (e. g., i. 10–ii. 1 [Heb. ii. 1–3]), and to the sole legitimacy of the Davidic monarchy (i. 4; iii. 5; viii. 4; xiii. 10, 11). The genuineness of these passages is, in general, denied on the ground of a lack of sequence with the preceding context or a variation of the meter. It must not be forgotten, however, that sudden transitions characterize the style of Hosea, that rhythm, not meter, is, as a rule, the mark of exalted prophetic utterance, and that an author may choose variation of literary form rather than monotony

Then, too, the book of Hosea is a mosaic made up of bits from many discourses. Concerning the three classes of passages to which exception has been taken, 1. The references to Judah. "An occasional side glance at Judah, a people so intimately connected with his own, must not be denied to the prophet" (Harper, on chap. v. 5); especially since he saw the moral conditions in Judah becoming assimilated to those of Ephraim (Oman, Presb. and Refd. Rev. x. 468–470). 2. The references to a restoration of Israel to God's favor and their return to their own country. (1). A reference to restoration to God's favor is demanded by the symmetry, since each section of chaps. i.–iii. (i. 10–ii. 1; ii. 14–23; iii. 5), and greater sections of the book as a whole, end with promises. (2). It is the custom of prophecy not to close with the threatening of doom and leave the people to despair, but to let the light of hope break through the dark clouds and irradiate the great future. (3). Continuing the picture of the destruction of Israel in battle for its sins, the verses of hope (i. 10–ii. 1) represent the victory of united Israel and Judah over their foes. (4). Thought was turned to the possibility of a return both by the prospect of imminent exile for the nation, and also presently by the knowledge that many Israelitish captives were in Assyria (2 Kin. xv. 29; 1 Chron. v. 26; Is. ix. 1). 3. The references to the legitimacy of the Davidic monarchy and the illegitimacy of northern Israel's kings. (1). It is necessary to reject the genuineness not only of these prophecies in Hosea, but also of the prediction of the universal dominion of the Davidic king which was uttered in northern Israel by a contemporary prophet of Judæan birth (Amos ix. 11). (2). To the believer in the moral government of the universe the failure and fall of one dynasty after another in the north, during the preceding two centuries, was conclusive evidence of their rejection by God; and the continuance of the Davidic monarchy confirmed the prophetic words, spoken in the southern kingdom concerning that line, and was itself independent proof that God had chosen the house of David.

Ho-sha′iah [Jehovah hath saved].

1. Father of Jezaniah and Azariah (Jer. xlii. 1; xliii. 2).

2. A man, doubtless a prince of Judah, who walked immediately behind the chorus of those who gave thanks in the procession at the dedication of the second temple (Neh. xii. 32).

Hosh′a-ma [probably, Jehovah hath heard].

One of the family or descendants of king Jeconiah (1 Chron. iii. 18).

Ho-she′a, in A. V. of Num. xiii. 8, 16 **Oshea** [save].

1. The earlier name of Joshua, the son of Nun, which was changed by Moses into Joshua (Num. xiii. 8, 16).

2. Son of Azaziah and prince of Ephraim in David's reign (1 Chron. xxvii. 20).

3. A son of Elah. With the connivance of Tiglath-pileser, king of Assyria, he conspired against Pekah, king of Israel, slew him, and ascended the throne (2 Kin. xv. 30). His reign lasted about nine years, from about 730 to 722 B. C. He did evil in the sight of Jehovah, but still was better than the average of the preceding kings. Shalmaneser, king of Assyria, made an expedition against him. Not being able to repel the invader, Hoshea paid tribute (xvii. 3); but knowing that the powerful kingdom of Egypt looked with jealousy on the approach of the Assyrians to its frontiers, he soon sought assistance from Egypt. Trusting that aid would be forthcoming, he withheld the annual tribute from Assyria (4). Shalmaneser again invaded the Israelite territory, took Hoshea captive, and laid siege to Samaria. See SHALMANESER. The city was reduced to great straits, but it held out three years. At the end of the three years Shalmaneser was killed or died, and was succeeded by Sargon, who claims the honor of capturing the city. He carried the leading inhabitants into captivity, and placed them in Halah and in Habor, by the river of Gozan, and in the cities of the Medes (5, 6). This event is known as the captivity of the ten tribes. It was not any special wickedness on the part of Hoshea that brought it on. The cup of Israel's iniquity had been filling for centuries, and Hoshea's iniquities only added the last drop which made the cup full to overflowing (7–23). See SAMARIA, SARGON, ISRAEL.

4. One of those who sealed the covenant (Neh. x. 23).

5. The Hebrew name of the prophet Hosea. See HOSEA.

Host.

A multitude, especially when organized; an army (Gen. xxi. 22; Judg. iv. 2) or the division of an army (Ex. vii. 4, in A. V. armies; xii. 41; Num. ii. 3, in A. V. armies; 1 Kin. ii. 5); the angels, constituting a heavenly host (1 Kin. xxii. 19; Ps. cxlviii. 2; Luke ii. 13); and the stars (Deut. iv. 19; 2 Kin. xxiii. 5). The Semites comprehended heaven and all its forces and beings, heaven and all that is therein, in the phrase host of heaven; and in the phrase host of the earth, they included the earth and all that is therein, the forces of nature like wind, lightning, heat and cold, and things animate and inanimate (Gen. ii. 1; Ps. xxxiii. 6; and see Anshar and Kishar in CREATION).

The title Lord of hosts has sometimes been explained as meaning that Jehovah is the God of the armies of Israel. In proof David's words to Goliath are cited: "Thou comest to me with a sword and with a spear, but I come to thee in the name of the Lord of hosts, the God of the armies of Israel" (1 Sam. xvii. 45). The prophet Isaiah is also quoted, who says: "The Lord of hosts shall come down to fight upon mount Zion" (Is. xxxi. 4). But this is too narrow a generalization. Jehovah did fight for his people; he was indeed "the Lord strong and mighty, the Lord mighty in battle." But the Lord of hosts was more than the war God of Israel. The Greek translators grasped the true meaning of the title, and rendered it *Pantokratōr*, the Almighty. The word hosts which is used in the title refers to the armies of the universe. The designation pictures the universe, in its spiritual and material aspects, as forming a vast army, in numerous divisions, of various kinds of troops, in orderly array under the command of Jehovah. One division consists of the angels. It was the Lord, the God of hosts, who appeared to Jacob at Bethel when he beheld the ladder and the angels of God ascending and descending (Gen. xxviii. 12, 13; Hos. xii. 4, 5). "Who in the skies can be compared unto the Lord? Who among the sons of the mighty is like unto the Lord, a God very terrible in the council of the holy ones, and to be feared above all them that are round about him? O Lord God of hosts, who is a mighty one like unto thee, O Jehovah?" (Ps. lxxxix. 6-8; cp. R. V.). Another host consists of the stars, in their beautiful order and wonderful array. Jehovah is their commander. Isaiah bids those who would know God to go forth, and lift up their eyes on high and see. "Who hath created these?" he asks. He who bringeth out [into the field like a general] their host by number, he who calleth them all by name, and upon them layeth commands (Is. xl. 26; xlv. 12). Yet another host consists of all the forces of nature; they stand at the bidding of Jehovah, worshiping and serving him (Neh. ix. 6; Ps. ciii. 21). The Lord of hosts sendeth sword, famine, and pestilence (Jer. xxix. 17). "The Lord, which giveth the sun for a light by day and the ordinances of the moon and of the stars for a light by night, which stirreth up the sea that the waves thereof roar, the Lord of hosts is his name" (Jer. xxxi. 35, R. V.). The Greeks, looking at the heavens above them, and at the earth around them, called what they saw cosmos, the beauty of harmony. The Romans, discovering the same harmonious relations and movements, named the entirety of creation a universe, combined as one. To the poetic imagination of the Hebrews, with their knowledge of the omnipotent reigning God, the regularity and order everywhere apparent suggested an army in vast, numerous, and varied divisions, acting under the command of one will. The Lord of hosts, he is the king who alone commands.

Ho'tham [seal, signet ring].

1. An Asherite, son of Heber, family of Beriah (1 Chron. vii. 32).

2. An Aroerite, two of whose sons were among David's mighty men (1 Chron. xi. 44). The misprint of Hothan for Hotham in A. V. has been corrected in R. V.

Ho'than. See HOTHAM 2.

Ho'thir.

A son of Heman, David's seer and singer (1 Chron. xxv. 4).

Hour. See DAY and NIGHT.

House.

In Palestine and other parts of the East the houses of the common people, constituting more than three-fourths of the whole, have only one story and sometimes only one room. The interior is frequently divided

Foundation lines of a dwelling unearthed in excavations at Shechem exemplify a type of house that studies at several sites indicate was a common Israelite architectural style between the tenth and eighth centuries B.C. This home was probably destroyed by the Assyrians about 724 B.C.

into two portions, one several feet higher than the other. The door from the outside leads into the lower portion, which is occupied by the cattle. Troughs for their feed are arranged along the side of the platform where the family dwell. This higher floor is reached by a short flight of steps. Sometimes there is a loft above the stable for guests. These several apartments are not walled off from each other. The walls of the house are often of mud or sun-dried brick, even when, as in Palestine, stone is procurable (cp. Job xxiv. 16; Ezek. xiii. 10-16). The roofs are made of branches of trees, canes, palm leaves, etc., covered with a thick stratum of earth. Materials so flimsy cannot long resist the heavy rains which at certain seasons fall in warm countries. There would be no difficulty in temporarily creating an aperture in the flimsy roof, and letting down a man on a bed, as was done at Capernaum in the case of the paralytic healed by our Lord (Mark ii. 1-12; Luke v. 18-26); only a shower of dust would descend.

The houses of the better class are generally built, as of old, in a quadrangle, around a central courtyard, which in certain cases may contain a fountain, or even a well (2 Sam. xvii. 18). The upper chamber is an important room in the second story, sometimes constituting all there is of a second story, being built above the general level of

Top: Flat-roofed houses cling to the hillside in the village of Endor.
Left: Two styles of houses are seen near the ancient site of Succoth in central Jordan. In the foreground are the flat-roofed houses whose prototype goes back into far antiquity. In the distance are the conical-roofed houses developed in Syria and most commonly seen there.

Opposite: These houses in the village of Gadara are contemporary yet meet all the archaeological evidence for houses in the Old Testament period.

Top: Domed-roof houses dot the landscape at Anathoth, the home of Jeremiah the prophet.
Middle: Tents are home and the desert floor is a playground for these Arab children. This encampment is in the Valley of Achor near Jericho.
Bottom: Up the steps to home — in the ruins at Bethany.

the roof (Judg. iii. 20, R. V. margin ; 1 Kin. xvii. 19 ; 2 Kin. iv. 10 ; Mark xiv. 15 ; Acts i. 13 ; ix. 37). The roofs of all houses are flat. They are generally, and should always be, surrounded by battlements (Deut. xxii. 8). They are well adapted for storing and drying agricultural produce (Josh. ii. 6), for walking to and fro (2 Sam. xi. 2), for conversation (1 Sam. ix. 25, 26), for idolatrous worship (2 Kin. xxiii. 12), or for religious meditation and prayer (Acts x. 9). There is a staircase outside the house, by which the roof can be reached without entering the building (cp. Mat. xxiv.

Hu'kok. See HELKATH.

Hul [circle, circuit].

The second son of Aram (Gen. x. 23 ; 1 Chron. i. 17). Huleh, the region immediately north of the waters of Merom, may possibly preserve the name.

Hul'dah [weasel].

A prophetess, who lived in the second quarter of Jerusalem (2 Kin. xxii. 14, R. V.). She was the wife of Shallum, keeper of the wardrobe, and was held in the highest esteem. She lived during the reign of Josiah,

In modern Jericho stands this mud-brick house with thatch roof, typical of the valley structures in ancient Palestine.

17; Mark xiii. 15). The windows are generally narrow, and mostly open into the courtyard instead of facing the street.

The Arabs call the lower story the winter house or simply the house, and the upper one the summer house. Or if both are on the same floor, the summer house is the outer and the winter house the inner room or rooms (Jer. xxxvi. 22 ; Amos. iii. 15).

Ho'zai [perhaps, (Jehovah) is seeing].

Writer of a history which treated of king Manasseh (2 Chron. xxxiii. 19, R. V.). In A. V., following the Septuagint, the Hebrew word *Hozay* has been translated as though it were a common noun, and the book cited appears as a collection of sayings by the seers (cp. 18). This translation involves the assumption that the Hebrew word has lost both its initial and its final letter, or at least the final one.

Huk'kok [hewn in, decreed].

A town on the boundary line of Naphtali (Josh. xix. 34). Yakûk, about 6 miles west by north of Tell Hum, has in its name the corresponding Arabic root.

and prophesied the destruction of Jerusalem, but added that on account of his piety toward Jehovah, the king should die before the coming of the catastrophe (2 Kin. xxii. 12-20 ; 2 Chron. xxxiv. 20-28).

Hum'tah [place of lizards or, perhaps, fortress].

A town in the hill country of Judah (Josh. xv. 54). Site unkown.

Hunt'er and **Hunt'ing.**

Hunting was a favorite pastime of ancient kings (Gen. x. 9). The Babylonian and Assyrian monarchs delighted in it, and were proud of their achievements, recording their success in inscriptions, and depicting their deeds in sculpture to adorn the walls of their palaces. In Palestine game existed during the entire biblical period in certain localities, as in the wilderness of Judah, the thickets of the Jordan, the more notable forests, and the south country (Gen. xxv. 27; Antiq. xvi. 10, 3). Many of the animals recognized as clean and fit for food were wild, and could only be obtained by hunting. When the animal was slain, its blood was poured out upon the earth and not eaten (Deut. xii. 15, 16, 22). Hunting was practiced in order to exterminate noxious beasts (Ex. xxiii. 29; 1 Kin. xiii. 24), to secure food (Gen. xxvii. 3; Ecclus. xxxvi. 19), and as sport (War i. 21, 13). People hunted alone or in companies (Jer. xvi. 16), on foot or on horseback (War i. 21, 13), and on the great plains in chariots. The hunter used bow and arrows (Is. vii. 24) and the spear (Antiq. xvi. 10, 3). Decoys were employed (Jer. v. 26, 27), and nets and traps (Job xviii. 10; Ecclus. xxvii. 20) and pits (2 Sam. xxiii. 20; Ezek. xix. 4, 8). Babylonians, Assyrians, and Persians kept dogs trained for the chase.

Hu'pham.

A son or remoter descendant of Benjamin, and founder of a tribal family (Num. xxvi. 39). Called Huppim (Gen. xlvi. 21; cp. 1 Chron. vii. 12, 15), and perhaps Huram (1 Chron. viii. 5). Huram would seem to be descended from Bela or Gera. Huppim is not registered with either Bela, Becher, or Jediael in 1 Chron. vii. 12, unless he is descended from Bela through Ir or Iri (ver. 7).

Hup'pah [a covering].

A descendant of Aaron. His family became the thirteenth course of the priests (1 Chron. xxiv. 13).

Hup'pim. See HUPHAM.

Hur [whiteness, splendor].

1. A man of Judah, family of Hezron, house of Caleb (1 Chron. ii. 18, 19). He was the grandfather of Bezaleel (20; Ex. xxxi. 1, 2). With Aaron, he supported the arms of Moses during the fight with the Amalekites (Ex. xvii. 10-12). He was associated with Aaron in the government of the Israelites while Moses was absent in mount Sinai (xxiv. 14). Josephus, writing many centuries after the event, calls Hur the husband of Miriam, Moses' sister (Antiq. iii. 2, 4). The O. T. is silent on the subject.

2. One of five kings of Midian slain by Moses (Num. xxxi. 8; Josh. xiii. 21).

3. Father of Solomon's purveyor in mount Ephraim (1 Kin. iv. 8).

4. Father of a certain Rephaiah (Neh. iii. 9).

Hu'rai [perhaps, a linen weaver].

One of David's mighty men from the brooks of Gaash (1 Chron. xi. 32). Called Hiddai in 2 Sam. xxiii. 30.

Hu'ram [noble, ingenuous].

1. A king of Tyre (2 Chron. ii. 3). See HIRAM.

2. A Tyrian artificer (2 Chron. iv. 11, 16). See HIRAM.

3. A Benjamite, perhaps a son of Bela (1 Chron. viii. 5). See HUPHAM.

Hu'ri [perhaps, a linen weaver].

A Gadite (1 Chron. v. 14).

Hu'shah [haste, emotion].

A town of Judah, to judge from 1 Chron. iv. 4, and xxvii. 11.

Hu'shai [hasty, hastening].

An Archite, one of David's two leading counselors. He remained faithful to his sovereign during Absalom's rebellion, and effectually defeated the counsel of Ahithophel (2 Sam. xv. 32-37; xvii. 5-16). See AHITHOPHEL and BAANA 2.

Hu'sham [haste, passion].

A man of the land of the Temanites, who succeeded Jobab as king of Edom (Gen. xxxvi. 34, 35; 1 Chron. i. 45, 46).

Hu'shath-ite.

An inhabitant of Hushah (2 Sam. xxi. 18; xxiii. 27).

Hu'shim [not impossibly, opulent, rich in children].

1. The son of Dan (Gen. xlvi. 23). Called in Num. xxvi. 42 Shuham. The difference is due to a transposition of the consonants.

2. A Benjamite family, sons of Aher (1 Chron. vii. 12).

3. One of the three wives of the Benjamite Shaharaim (1 Chron. viii. 8, 11).

Husk.

A kind of food eaten by swine, and which the prodigal son, when in poverty and deserted by his fair-weather friends, was glad to share (Luke xv. 16). It is the pod of the carob tree (*Ceratonia siliqua*), and is also called locust bean and St. John's bread. The tree is a handsome evergreen, attaining a height of 30 feet, thornless, and with leaves like the ash. The legumes are borne in great profusion, and are often a foot long. When green they are used for cattle and swine and in times of great famine are eaten by people. A syrup is made of the pulp of the pods.

Huz. See Uz.

Huz'zab.

Apparently a poetic term for Nineveh (Nah. ii. 7). The Targum understands it to mean the queen. But in the margin of the A. V. it is rendered "that which was established" or "there was a stand made," and in that of the R. V. "and it is decreed." Both of these renderings make Huzzab simply a part of the Hebrew verb *yaṣab*, to place or establish.

Hy'a-cinth, or in modified form **Ja'cinth.**

1. The name of a color (Rev. ix. 17).

2. A precious stone, constituting the eleventh foundation of the New Jerusalem (Rev. xxi. 20; R. V. margin, sapphire) and one of the twelve jewels in the high priest's breastplate (Ex. xxviii. 19, R. V.; on the margin, amber). In modern usage the name is given to the mineral zircon.

Hy-e'na.

An animal which feeds on offal, but is often driven from it by the dogs (Ecclus. xiii. 18). The striped hyena (*Hyæna striata*) is common in every part of Palestine, living in caves and tombs, coming forth after dark to rifle graves or otherwise seek after prey.

The valley of Zeboim in 1 Sam. xiii. 18 means the valley of hyenas.

Hy-me-næ'us [pertaining to Hymen, the god of marriage].

One who made shipwreck of his faith, blasphemed, and was excommunicated by Paul (1 Tim. i. 20). He declared that the resurrection was already past. Philetus was associated with him in this error (2 Tim. ii. 17, 18).

Hymn.

A spiritual meditation designed, or at least suitable, for singing or chanting in the worship of God. The Book of Psalms is the earliest hymn book in existence. Other magnificent Hebrew religious odes are the songs of Moses (Ex. xv. 1-19; Deut. xxxii. 1-43), Deborah (Judg. v.), Hannah (1 Sam. ii. 1-10), Mary (Luke i. 46-55), and Zacharias (68-79). The last two are known as the Magnificat and the Benedictus respectively, from the first word of the Latin translation. The Hebrew psalms were often sung to the accompaniment of music (2 Chron. xxix. 27, 28; cp. R. V. of 1 Chron. xvi. 42). In the N. T. three terms are used for Christian songs : psalms, hymns, and spiritual songs or odes (Eph. v. 19; Col. iii. 16). Josephus uses two of these words. namely hymns and odes, in reference to the psalms of David (Antiq. vii. 12, 3). The hymn which Christ and his disciples sang after supper on the night of the betrayal (Mat. xxvi. 30) was doubtless part of Ps. cxv.–cxviii., which were sung by the Jews on the night of the passover after supper. The early Christians sang hymns in public worship and privately as a means of worshiping God and of edification and comfort (Acts xvi. 25 ; 1 Cor. xiv. 26 ; Eph. v. 19; Col. iii. 16). Fragments of early Christian hymns, known as such from the meter in the Greek text, are preserved in 1 Tim. iii. 16 ; Eph. v. 14; cp. Rev. xv. 3, 4. At the beginning of the second century, in the reign of Trajan, the Christians of Bithynia were reported by Pliny as singing songs to Christ as God (Epis. x. 96).

Hys'sop.

A plant of Egypt and Palestine (Ex. xii. 22), in Hebrew *'Ezob*, in Greek *'Ussōpos*, which springs out of walls, and was of so small a size that it stood at one end of the scale of magnitude which had the cedar of Lebanon at the other (1 Kin. iv. 33). It was aromatic, and was largely used, under the law, often in bunches, with cedar wood and wool, for ceremonial purification (Lev. xiv. 4, 6, 49, 51, 52; Num. xix. 6, 18; Ps. li. 7; Heb. ix. 19). A sponge filled with vinegar was put upon hyssop and raised to the lips of Jesus when he was on the cross (John xix. 29). The common hyssop (*Hyssopus officinalis*) is a sweet-smelling plant, belonging to the order *Labiatæ*, or Mints. It is a small bushy herb which grows to a height of 12 or 18 inches, and has small, hairy, lanceolate leaves. But Tristram states that its area is the south of Europe, the Danubian province. and Siberia. Moreover, the statement of two of the evangelists (Mat. xxvii. 48 ; Mark xv. 36) that the sponge of vinegar offered to Jesus was put upon *kalamos*, a reed which the common hyssop does not produce, has led some interpreters to think that a different plant from the common hyssop is intended, perhaps the caper plant (*Capparis spinosa*), sometimes called by the Arabs *'aṣuf*. It is common in Palestine and the adjacent regions, grows out of walls, and could furnish a reedy stem three or four feet long, to which a sponge might be affixed. Rabbinical tradition identifies the Hebrew *'ezob* with the Arabic *ṣa'ṭar*, commonly held to be *Origanum*. marjory. This plant is common in Palestine, growing on walls and rocks. Its thick, hairy leaves and hairy branches can be made into a bunch, and would hold liquids for sprinkling. It is a small herb, however, and could not furnish a rod ; but the bunch of hyssop used in sprinkling was attached, it is argued, to a rod of cedar, and such a sprinkler was seized as the most available means at hand of reaching the sponge to the lips of the crucified Jesus.

I

Ib'har [(God) doth choose].

One of king David's sons born at Jerusalem (2 Sam. v. 15 ; 1 Chron. xiv. 5).

I'bis.

A bird (Lev. xi. 19, R. V. margin), allied to the herons and storks. It was formerly venerated by the Egyptians. See HERON.

Ib'le-am [the people faileth].

An ancient city (Thothmes' list), in the territory of Issachar, given to the tribe of Manasseh ; but the Canaanite population was not expelled (Josh. xvii. 11, 12 ; Judg. i. 27). Near it Ahaziah, king of Judah, was mortally wounded by the followers of Jehu (2 Kin. ix. 27). Zechariah, king of Israel, was slain there (xv. 10, text of Lucian). It is generally identified with Bileam, a town of Manasseh given to the Levites (1 Chron. vi. 70); perhaps Bel'ameh, a ruin one mile south of Jenin (cp. Judith iv. 4 ; vii. 3).

Ib-ne'iah [Jehovah doth build].

A Benjamite, son of Jeroham and head of a father's house (1 Chron. ix. 8).

Ib-ni'jah [Jehovah doth build].

A Benjamite, father of Reuel (1 Chron. ix. 8).

Ib'ri [a Hebrew].

A son of Jaaziah (1 Chron. xxiv. 27).

Ib'sam, in A. V. **Jibsam** [fragrant].

A man of Issachar, family of Tola (1 Chron. vii. 2).

Ib'zan [active].

A judge who ruled over Israel, or part of it, for seven years. He was a native of Bethlehem, apparently that in Zebulun, was buried in his native place, and was succeeded by a Zebulunite. He had thirty sons and thirty daughters, doubtless by a plurality of wives (Judg. xii. 8–10).

Ich'a-bod [the glory is not].

Son of Phinehas and grandson of Eli. The name commemorated the fact that the glory had departed from Israel, for the ark of God was taken (1 Sam. iv. 19–22).

I-co'ni-um.

A city of Asia Minor, which is described by Xenophon as the last city in Phrygia to one traveling eastward (Anabasis i. 2, 19). Under the Roman and the Greek empires Iconium

A stone idol of Baal discovered in the ruins at Baalbek, Lebanon.

was considered the capital of Lycaonia. It was situated in a fertile spot in the high, waterless plain of Lycaonia. Barnabas and Paul visited it on the first missionary journey both going and returning (Acts xiii. 51, 52; xiv. 1–6, 19–22; cp. xvi. 2; 2 Tim. iii. 11). It has had an unbroken history and the same name until the present time, being now known as Koniah. It is the capital of the pashalic of Karaman; and is a large city surrounded by a wall built of the materials derived from older structures.

Id'a-lah.

A border town of Zebulun (Josh. xix. 15). Site unknown.

Id'bash [perhaps honey-sweet].

A man of Judah (1 Chron. iv. 3).

Id'do, I. [hap, happy].

The chief at Casiphia through whom Ezra, when conducting a company of exiles from Babylonia to Jerusalem, obtained the contingent, which was lacking, of Levites and Nethinim for the service of the temple (Ezra viii. 17–20).

Id'do, II. [loving, affectionate].

1. Son of Zechariah, and a chief in David's reign of the half-tribe of Manasseh east of the Jordan (1 Chron. xxvii. 21).

2. A man induced by Ezra to put away his foreign wife (Ezra x. 43). In A. V. the name is written Jadau, a mongrel word arising from the translators' pronouncing the consonants of the text with the vowels of the margin. The real alternative to Iddo is Jaddai, as in the margin of R. V.

Id'do, III. [decked, adorned].

1. A Levite, a descendant of Gershom (1 Chron. vi. 21). Apparently called Adaiah synonymously (41).

2. Father of Ahinadab, Solomon's purveyor at Mahanaim (1 Kin. iv. 14).

3. A seer who wrote a book of visions concerning Jeroboam and in which events of Solomon's reign were related (2 Chron. ix. 29), a book on genealogies, in which deeds of Rehoboam were recorded (xii. 15), and a history which treated of king Abijah's acts (xiii. 22).

4. Grandfather of the prophet Zechariah (Zech. i. 1, 7; cp. Ezra v. 1; vi. 14). He is not unreasonably believed to be identical with Iddo, a chief of the priests who returned with Zerubbabel to Jerusalem and whose name is that of a father's house in the next generation. The head of this house at the time mentioned is a priest named Zechariah (Neh. xii. 4, 16). The difference in spelling the name Iddo in these two verses of Nehemiah in the Hebrew is merely the difference between jod and vau (q. v.).

I'dol [a mental or material image].

An image, a sculpture, or other representation of any person or being, intended as an object of worship, or as the embodiment and efficient presence of a deity (Ex. xx. 4, 5, 23; Judg. xvii. 3; 1 Sam. v. 3, 4; Rom. i.

23). They were made of silver, of gold (Ps. cxv. 4 ; cxxxv. 15), of wood, or other material (Is. xliv. 13–17). When metallic, they were fashioned by running melted metal into a mold, in which case they were called molten images ; or they consisted of plates of metal over a wooden frame or over a molten body, and were termed graven images. When of wood or stone, they were made by graving tools or other instruments, and were also called graven images. The process of manufacture is described in Isaiah and Jeremiah (Is. xl. 19, 20 ; xliv. 9–20 ; Jer. x. 9). Some were small, especially those designed as household gods or teraphim (Gen. xxxi. 34 ; xxxv. 1–4) ; some were as large as a human being (1 Sam. xix. 16) ; some, such as that erected by Nebuchadnezzar in the plain of Dura, were colossal (Dan. iii. 1). Various epithets are applied to idols, which express the commingled loathing and contempt with which they were regarded by the enlightened servant of Jehovah. One of the most notable is vanity.

I-dol'a-try.

Idolatry was practiced at a comparatively early period of man's history. The immediate ancestors of Abraham worshiped other gods (Josh. xxiv. 2), in addition to Jehovah, it may be believed, and doubtless by means of idols. Laban had images, which Rachel was too justly accused of stealing (Gen. xxxi. 30, 32–35). The Egyptians made figures of the gods to serve as objects of worship, and in the innermost sanctuary of their temples lay the symbol of a god and a sacred animal (Herod. ii. 63, 138). The Canaanite nations had idols, which the Israelites, on succeeding to the land, were ordered to destroy (Ex. xxiii. 24); xxxiv. 13 ; Lev. xix. 4 ; Num. xxxiii. 52; Deut. vii. 5 ; xxix. 17). The second commandment was directed against idolatry (Ex. xx. 4, 5 ; Deut. v. 8, 9), forbidding man to bow down to images, sculptures, statues, and pictures. And the teachers of Israel followed up this injunction by pointing out and ridiculing the impotency of idols (Ps. cxv. ; Is. ii. 8, 18, 20, 21 ; xl. 19, 20 ; xliv. 9–20 ; Jer. x. 3–5). Their helplessness was discovered when the ark of the Lord was in the temple of Dagon (1 Sam. v. 3–5). The apocryphal book of Bel and the Dragon treats of the deceitful practices of the priests in the idol temples. Of the nations with whom the Israelites were brought into contact during Scripture times, all but the Persians were idolaters ; and the divinities whom their images represented were other gods than Jehovah. When the Israelites borrowed idolatrous practices from the neighboring nations, two well-marked stages were traceable in the progress of error. At first they attempted to worship Jehovah by means of images ; see JEROBOAM. Then they entirely departed from Jehovah, and the idols they made were designed to represent other divinities ; see

BAAL. In N. T. times church members who lived in heathen communities were required to take precautions to avoid compromising themselves with idolatry. The council of Jerusalem enjoined that they should abstain from the flesh of animals that had been sacrificed to idols (Acts xv. 29). Paul gave the same injunction, but explained that in the case of those who had no faith in idols, abstinence was designed to avoid casting a stumbling-block in the path of the weaker brethren (1 Cor. viii. 4–13). If receiving hospitality at any house, and meat which might possibly have been offered to an idol was set on the table, the Christian guest was not required to ask any questions for conscience' sake ; but if he was expressly told that the food had been offered to an idol, then he was to abstain. The same rule was to be carried out with regard to food purchased for the household in the ordinary market (x. 18–33). About A. D. 300 images were introduced into some Christian churches for instruction and ornament only. In 736 the eastern emperor Leo issued edicts against them. In 780 the empress Irene introduced image worship into the eastern church, and in 787 the second council of Nice gave them ecclesiastical sanction.

Id-u-mæ'a, in A. V. of O. T. and Apocrypha **Idumea** [pertaining to Edom].

The name used by Greeks and Romans in slightly different spelling, for the country of Edom (Mark iii. 8 ; and in A. V. only, Is. xxxiv. 5, 6 ; Ezek. xxxv. 15 ; xxxvi. 5). After the fall of Jerusalem, in 587 B. C., the Edomites began to press northward (Ezek. xxxvi. 5). They themselves were driven from Petra westward by the Nabathæans about 300 B. C., and before the middle of the second century B. C. they were occupying, not only southern Judah, but also Hebron and the country to its north as far as Bethzur (1 Mac. iv. 29 ; v. 65). Judas Maccabæus warred against them successfully ; and John Hyrcanus, about 126 B. C., completely subjugated them and placed them under a Jewish governor (Antiq. xiii. 9, 1).

I-e'zer. See ABIEZER.

I-e'zer-ite. See ABIEZERITE.

I'gal, in A. V. once **Igeal** (1 Chron. iii. 22) [he will vindicate].

1. The spy sent forth by the tribe of Issachar to search out the land of Canaan (Num. xiii. 7).

2. One of David's mighty men, the son of Nathan (2 Sam. xxiii. 36). He occupies the same position in the catalogue as does Joel in 1 Chron. xi. 38, and it is natural to identify the two. But the relation of the two lists at this point is difficult to determine ; and as Igal and Joel are differently described, they may be different persons, nephew and uncle.

3. A son of Shemaiah, a descendant of king Jeconiah (1 Chron. iii. 22).

Ig-da-li′ah [great is Jehovah].

Father of the prophet Hanan (Jer. xxxv. 4).

I′ge-al. See IGAL.

I′im [ruins].

1. A town east of the Jordan (Num. xxxiii. 45). See IYE-ABARIM.

2. A town in the extreme south of Judah (Josh. xv. 29). Site unknown.

I-je-ab′a-rim. See IYE-ABARIM.

I′jon [a ruin].

A fortified city of Naphtali, one of those captured by Benhadad, king of Syria, at the instigation of Asa (1 Kin. xv. 20; 2 Chron. xvi. 4). Its inhabitants were subsequently carried into captivity by Tiglath-pileser (2 Kin. xv. 29). Robinson located it, probably correctly, on Tell Dibbin, a hill 110 feet high, on the eastern border of Merj ʻAyûn, meadow of springs, which seems to preserve a trace of the old name. The site is about 8 miles north-northwest of Banias.

Ik′kesh [perverse].

Father of David's captain and mighty man Ira (2 Sam. xxiii. 26; 1 Chron. xi. 28).

I′lai [supreme].

One of David's mighty men (1 Chron. xi. 29), called Zalmon in 2 Sam. xxiii. 28.

Il-lyr′i-cum.

A country bounded on the north by Pannonia, on the south by Epirus, on the east by Macedonia, and, when it included Dalmatia, on the west by the Adriatic Sea. It is traversed from northwest to southeast by the Noric, Carnic, and Julian Alps, constituting the most easterly portion of the great Alpine chain. Along the coast are excellent harbors and numerous islands. The Illyrian race inhabiting the region were wild mountaineers, who were a thorn in the side of their neighbors, the Macedonians; and, when they descended to the seacoast, they so practiced piracy as to bring them into collision with the Romans, who, in 229 B. C., began to conquer them, and finally made Illyricum, or Illyria, a province of the empire. The apostle Paul preached the gospel from Jerusalem and round about even to Illyricum (Rom. xv. 19). In the later years of the Roman empire the name Illyricum gained a much wider meaning. A great part of Illyricum in the more limited sense constitutes Bosnia, Herzegovina, and Montenegro.

Im′age. See IDOL.

Im′la or **Imlah** [he, *i. e.* God, doth fill].

Father of the prophet Micaiah (1 Kin. xxii. 8, 9; 2 Chron. xviii. 7, 8).

Im-man′u-el, in A. V. of N. T. **Emmanuel**, the Greek pronunciation [God with us].

A son whom "the maiden" should bear (Is. vii. 14, R. V. margin). Before the son is born, or at the time of his birth, historical events will justify naming him "God with us"; before he attains to years of moral determination, the land of northern Israel and Damascus will be forsaken, and unexampled punishment will be inflicted on Judah (ver. 16, 17); and hence during the years of his moral maturity, he shall eat the products of a land that has been wasted by the nations (ver. 15, 18 seq.). Isaiah had in mind that worthy Son of David about whom prophecy had begun to cluster: for 1. He foretells the birth of a son, not simply of a child. 2. He utters this prophecy to the house of David in view of God's rejection of the faithless successor of David who then occupied the throne. 3. On the natural interpretation of viii. 8, which observes the previous use of Immanuel as the name of the son, does justice to the pronoun of the second person in the clause preceding Immanuel, and affords an easy transition to the succeeding verse, Immanuel is a person; and if so, he is a native of Judah, and sufficiently great to be singled out as a representative, for Judah is spoken of as the land of Immanuel; and he is a powerful personage, for because of him the rage of the nations is vain (ver. 9 seq.). 4. The Messiah is definitely before the prophet's mind in ix. 6, 7 and xi. 1; and violence is required to separate these prophecies from that of chap. vii. The Messianic hope was awake at this period of history. 5. The use of the article with maiden is adequately explained. Isaiah uses it to designate the young woman, unknown by name, yet definite, who is to be the mother of Messiah (cp. Mic. v. 3). 6. Looking back, this meaning seems to have been the mind of the Spirit (Mat. i. 22, 23).

The prophet is, therefore, thinking of David's son, who might appear at any time. But he is not predicting the birth of Hezekiah and expecting him to be the Messiah; for 1. Hezekiah was already born. This prophecy was delivered in 734 B. C., and Hezekiah was on the throne, a vigorous ruler in 727 B. C. 2. After the lapse of a year and when Hezekiah was a youth, the prophet still continues to look forward to the future for the going forth of the shoot out of the root of Jesse. 3. Hezekiah did not eat curds and honey; the processes which issued in the spoliation and subjection of the land had only begun in Hezekiah's time. If ver. 18–25 of Is. vii. are included in the prophecy, the fly of Egypt did not come upon Judah in Hezekiah's day. Even ver. 17 presents a picture which belongs to the remoter future; days such as had not been were not brought upon Ahaz and his people, only the beginning of the process which resulted in the predicted calamity was seen.

Immanuel was a sign. But Ahaz did not live until any child born that year reached the age of moral self-determination, for Ahaz died before the fall of Samaria in 722. He did not live to see the land forsaken (16). Immanuel was not a sign to compel faith in Ahaz, but one that called for faith. Like many other signs of the O. T., it called for present faith and occurred only when the prophecy was fulfilled (Ex. iii. 12).

The birth, infancy, and youth of Messiah are described as actually passing before the prophet's sight; but the prophet himself did not understand that the Messiah was necessarily to be born immediately, for when the Messiah did not appear within a year, Isaiah shows no signs of disappointment, loses no faith in the prophetic revelation, continues his activity, makes still greater disclosures regarding Immanuel, and enjoys the continued confidence of his fellow countrymen. Isaiah would inquire what and what manner of time the Spirit which was in him did signify.

The promise of immediate deliverance from the advancing enemy (Is. vii. 3–11) is confirmed by an appeal to an event which might occur sooner or later. But whether occurring at once or long subsequently, it is confirmatory, because it implies the deliverance promised to Ahaz. The assurance, already given by God (2 Sam. vii. 11–17), that the Messiah should be born of the royal family of David was a sign to the house of David, including Ahaz, that the purpose of Rezin and Pekah to destroy the kingdom and place a new king over the people should not stand (Is. vii. 13, 14). And the remoter the sign, that is the remoter the birth of Messiah, the stronger was the guarantee of the long continuance of the royal family of Judah.

The birth and infancy of Immanuel measure the progress of the predicted events. "I see his birth, who is God's guarantee of the continued existence and deliverance of Judah, as though it is already at hand. I do not know the times and the seasons, but it is revealed to me as a sign to you, and as though about to occur. As such it contains a measure of time for the immediate future. Before the child comes to the years when one chooses between right and wrong, the northern land shall be forsaken. At the time of life when one's moral faculties have matured, he, the scion of the royal house of Judah, will dwell in a wasted land." Any child would serve for measuring the time; but the child chosen is Messiah because the prophecy of deliverance rested upon the promises which centered in the Messiah.

Now let us measure the period. 1. Before Christ attained the age when man's moral faculties are mature the northern kingdom was desolate. In fact before a child, born in the year of this meeting between Isaiah and Ahaz, could have reached moral maturity the land of the north was desolate. The meeting is known to have taken place in 734 B. C. By 722 Damascus and the district governed by it had been ravaged by the Assyrians, the two and a half tribes of Israel east of the Jordan had been carried off, Samaria had fallen and a large body of its inhabitants had been deported. Ahaz saw the beginning of this, but died before its accomplishment. The house of David saw the complete fulfillment. The process thus begun continued. In 65 years Ephraim had ceased to be a people. At Christ's appearance, this was still true. The ten tribes no longer existed as a nation, and no longer occupied the land of their fathers. 2. At a time when a child's moral faculties would be mature, Ahaz himself had gone to Damascus, had done homage to the Assyrian king, and had acknowledged that Judah was a tributary state to Assyria. The land itself was not actually devastated, but it had bowed itself down to the foreign yoke. From this time onward, with the exception of short intervals, it was in a sense subject to the dominant world-power, and it was looked upon by the great empire of each period as a dependency, and whenever Judah claimed independence it was visited sooner or later by the imperial power which claimed sovereignty and was punished and wasted. Its nationality was not blotted out and the royal family was not destroyed nor overlooked; but Judah was, generally speaking, a dependency. When Christ actually appeared, Judah was still acknowledging a foreign sovereign. In other words, all the processes foretold by Isaiah began in the lifetime of Ahaz, and their results were in full force when the Messiah actually appeared.

Im′mer [talkative].

1. A descendant of Aaron. His family had become a father's house in the time of David, and was made the sixteenth course of priests (1 Chron. xxiv. 1, 6, 14). The ruler of the house of God in the days of Jeremiah, and an antagonist of the prophet, apparently belonged to this house (Jer. xx. 1), and doubtless they were members of this family who returned from Babylon with Zerubbabel (Ezra ii. 37; Neh. xi. 13). Two priests of this house were among those who about a century after the return were guilty of marrying foreign wives (Ezra x. 20). A little later another son of Immer took part in the honorable work of rebuilding the walls of Jerusalem (Neh. iii. 29).

2. A person or a place in Babylonia whence exiles returned. He or they failed, however, to prove their genealogy (Ezra ii. 59; Neh. vii. 61).

Im′na [he, i. e. probably God, doth restrain].

An Asherite, a son of Helem (1 Chron. vii. 35).

Im′nah, in A. V. once **Jimna** and once **Jimnah** (Gen. xlvi. 17; Num. xxvi. 44) [he allotteth].

1. Son of Asher and founder of a tribal family (Num. xxvi. 44; 1 Chron. vii. 30; Gen. xlvi. 17).

2. A Levite, father of Kore, in Hezekiah's reign (2 Chron. xxxi. 14).

Im′rah [stubborn, refractory].

An Asherite, son of Zophah (1 Chron. vii. 36).

Im′ri [eloquent].

1. A man of Judah, son of Bani, and a descendant of Perez (1 Chron. ix. 4).

2. Father of that Żaccur, who rebuilt part of the wall of Jerusalem after the captivity (Neh. iii. 2).

In'cense.

Fragrant substances designed to be burnt, especially in religious worship. Sweet incense was largely used as an element in the Israelite ritual (Ex. xxv. 6; xxxv. 8, 28; xxxvii. 29). The ingredients were stacte or opobalsamum, onycha, galbanum, and pure frankincense in equal proportions, tempered with salt. It was not allowed to be made for ordinary purposes (Ex. xxx. 34–38; Lev. x. 1–7). An altar of incense was fashioned of acacia wood overlaid with pure gold. It belonged to the oracle (1 Kin. vi. 22), but was placed in the holy place, just outside the veil which concealed the holy of holies; and each morning, when the high priest dressed the lamps, he burned incense on it (Ex. xxx. 1–9; Luke i. 10); see ALTAR. Once a year on the great day of atonement, he brought the incense within the veil, and, burning it on a fire in a censer in the most holy place, enveloped the mercy seat in a cloud of the odoriferous smoke which it sent forth (Lev. xvi. 12, 13). When the altar was dedicated, each of the princes brought a gift of incense carried in a spoon (Num. vii. 14, 20, etc.). Where so many animal sacrifices were offered as there were in the courts, both of the tabernacle and the temple, the smell of blood must have polluted the atmosphere, and the burning of incense exerted a good sanitary influence. But it had also a symbolic reference. It availed to make atonement (Num. xvi. 46, 47), for it was typical of the intercession of the appointed high priest. The psalmist requested that his prayer might be set forth before Jehovah as incense (Ps. cxli. 2); the worshipers prayed outside the temple while Zacharias offered incense within its walls (Luke i. 10); and in an apocalyptic vision an angel burnt incense on the golden altar, the smoke ascending with the prayers of saints (Rev. viii. 3–5). The worshipers of false divinities, no less than those who adored the true God, burnt incense (2 Chron. xxxiv. 25; Jer. xlviii. 35).

In'di-a [in Hebrew *Hodû*, through Persian *Hidhu*, from Hindu, the river Indus].

A district on the lower Indus, conquered by Darius the Great and incorporated with the Persian empire (Herod. iii. 94; iv. 44; Persepolis inscription). It formed the eastern limit of the Persian empire (Esth. i. 1; viii. 9; cp. Herod. iv. 40). Alexander the Great crossed the Indus on his career of conquest. The occurrence of the name in 1 Mac. viii. 8 is suspicious. Luther substituted Ionia. At any rate Judas Maccabæus was misinformed if he was told that the Romans had taken India from Antiochus.

In'gath-er-ing, Feast of. See TABERNACLES, FEAST OF.

In-her'it-ance. See HEIR.

Ink'horn.

A horn or anything similar for holding ink. It was carried at the side (Ezek. ix. 2). The inkhorn is still in use in the East. It consists of a case of wood, horn, or metal, with a head at one end for holding the ink, and a long shaft in which the reeds for writing are kept. The case is worn stuck in the girdle.

Inn.

An oriental inn bears little resemblance to an occidental hotel. The inn was not so necessary in primitive times. Travelers readily found reception in the houses of the hospitable (Ex. ii. 20; Judg. xix. 15–21; 2 Kin. iv. 8; Acts xxviii. 7; Heb. xiii. 2). The public inn was a mere place of shelter for man and beast. Like the modern khans, it was probably a large, quadrangular court, with a well in the center and around the sides rooms for travelers, chambers for goods, and stalls for cattle. The rooms were destitute of furniture. The traveler spread his mat on the floor, if he had one to spread; if not, then his shawl-like mantle sufficed for mattress and covering. He also provided food for himself and fodder for his cattle. Free lodging places of this sort were erected by liberal wealthy men for the benefit of wayfarers (cp. Jer. xli. 17). Rarely was there a host from whom food could be purchased (Luke x. 34, 35).

In-spi-ra'tion.

The terms inspiration and inspired are used in English with great latitude of meaning, and this latitude is reflected to some extent in their usage in the English Bible. They occur, however, only twice in the English Bible, and in both cases in a religious sense (Job xxxii. 8; 2 Tim. iii. 16). In the former passage the word is used loosely to give expression to the broad fact that men are not independent of God as intellectual beings, but that for small and great, old and young alike, it is "the breath [or inspiration] of the Almighty [that] giveth them understanding." In the latter passage the word inspired is used in its more proper and specific sense as a direct predicate of the written Scriptures, affirming that quality of divinity in them by virtue of which they are "profitable" for the great ends for which they are given. The Scriptures which the apostle had particularly in mind in this passage were the sacred books of the Jews, what we call the O. T.; but the affirmation he makes will naturally hold good of all writings which rightly share the high title of Scripture with them. The quality which he thus makes the fundamental characteristic of Scripture is expressed in the original Greek, not by the simple word inspired, but by a compound word, God-inspired, possibly of his own coinage, by which the divine source of the inspiration is emphasized. He adduces this fundamental quality of Scripture as the ground on which the unique value of the Scriptures rests: "All scripture," he says, "is given by inspiration of God, and is [therefore] profitable, etc." (A. V.), or, "Every Scripture, [seeing that it is] inspired of God, is also profitable, etc." (R. V.). Inspiration, according to the apostle, is, therefore, the fundamental quality of the written Scriptures, by virtue of which they are the word of God, and are clothed with all the characteristics which properly belong to the word of God. In accordance with the teaching of this classical passage, Scripture is uniformly recognized, throughout the N. T., as the very word of God, and is treated as possessing all the qualities which would naturally flow from its divine origin. Thus it is currently cited by the exclusive titles Scripture, the Scriptures, the Oracles of God (Rom. iii. 2) or the Living Oracles (Acts vii. 38, R. V.), and its words are ordinarily adduced by the authoritative formula, "It is written." Its divine character is explicitly expressed in the constant ascription of the words cursorily quoted from it to God as their author (Acts xiii. 34 ; 1 Cor. vi. 16 ; Mat. i. 22 ; ii. 15 ; Rom. i. 2), or more specifically to the Holy Spirit (Heb. iii. 7 ; ix. 8 ; x. 15 ; Acts i. 16 ; iv. 25, R. V. ; xxviii. 25) ; and that, even when they are not ascribed to God in the original passages, but are spoken of or even addressed to him, and can be thought his only because they are part of the Scripture text (Acts iv. 24, 25 ; xiii. 34, 35 ; Mat. xix. 6, 7, 8, 10 ; iv. 4, 7 ; vii. 21 ; x. 30). While on the other hand the human writers of Scripture are said to have spoken "in" the Holy Spirit (Mark xii. 36 ; Mat. xxii. 43, both R. V.), and are treated as merely the media through whom God the Holy Ghost speaks (Mat. i. 22 ; ii. 15 ; Acts i. 16 ; iv. 25 ; xxviii. 25 ; Rom. i. 2). Accordingly, the very words of Scripture are accounted authoritative and "not to be broken" (Mat. xxii. 43 ; John x. 34, 35 ; Gal. iii. 16) ; its prophecies sure (2 Pet. i. 20 ; John xix. 36, 37 ; xx. 9 ; Acts i. 16 ; cp. Ezra i. 1 ; Dan. ix. 2) ; and its whole contents, historical as well as doctrinal and ethical, not only entirely trustworthy, but designedly framed for the spiritual profit of all ages (2 Tim. iii. 16 ; Rom. xv. 4 ; 1 Cor. x. 11 ; Rom. iv. 23 ; ix. 17 ; 1 Cor. ix. 10 ; Gal. iii. 8, 22 ; iv. 30 ; 1 Pet. ii. 6 ; cp. 2 Chron. xvii. 9 ; Neh. viii. 1). That the books of the N. T. are given to the church as equally Scripture with those of the O. T., and share with them in all their divine qualities, is shown by the equal claim to authority which is made for them (1 Cor. vii. 40 ; xiv. 37 ; 2 Thes. iii. 4, 14 ; Gal. i. 8) ; the similar representation of their authors as the organs of God (1 Thes. ii. 13 ; iv. 2 ; 1 Cor. ii. 13, 16 ; vii. 40) ; and the inclusion of N. T. books along with those of the O. T. under the common sacred title of Scripture (2 Pet. iii. 16 ; 1 Tim. v. 18).

B. B. W.

In'stant and **In'stant-ly.**
As an adjective or adverb, in the obsolete sense of earnest or steadfast (Luke vii. 4 ; Acts xxvi. 7 ; Rom. xii. 12, A. V. ; 2 Tim. iv. 2.)

I'ob, in A. V. **Job.** See Jashub.

Iph-de'iah, in A. V. **Iph-e-de'iah** [Jehovah doth deliver].
A Benjamite, son of Shashak (1 Chron. viii. 25).

Iph'tah. in A. V. **Jiphtah** [he openeth or setteth free].
A town of Judah (Josh. xv. 43). Site unknown.

Iph'tah-el, in A. V. **Jiphthah-el** [God doth open or set free].
A valley on the boundary line between Zebulun and Asher (Josh. xix. 14, 27). The name is perhaps found in Jotopata, the modern Tell Jefât, 9 miles north by west of Nazareth.

Ir. See Iri.

I'ra [watchful].
1. Priest or chief minister to David ; a Jairite (2 Sam. xx. 26) or a man of Jattir (Syriac text and Lucian's).
2. One of David's mighty men, a Tekoite, son of Ikkesh (2 Sam. xxiii. 26 ; 1 Chron. xi. 28).
3. An Ithrite, one of David's mighty men (2 Sam. xxiii. 38 ; 1 Chron. xi. 40).

I'rad.
A descendant of Cain (Gen. iv. 18).

I'ram [perhaps, pertaining to a city, or watchful].
A chieftain of Edom (Gen. xxxvi. 43 ; 1 Chron. i. 54).

I'ri and probably **Ir** [pertaining to a city, or watchful].
A Benjamite, family of Bela (1 Chron. vii. 7, 12).

I-ri'jah [Jehovah doth see or provide].
A captain of the guard. During the temporary departure of the Chaldeans from the siege of Jerusalem, he arrested Jeremiah, who was going out at the gate of Benjamin, on the charge of attempting to fall away to the enemy (Jer. xxxvii. 13).

Ir-na'hash [city of Nahash or of a serpent].
A town listed with the tribe of Judah (1 Chron. iv. 12). The margin renders city of Nahash. The chronicler may intend the town of Abigail's father (2 Sam. xvii. 25).

I'ron, I.
A metal, in Hebrew *Barzel*, in Greek *Sideros*. Tubal-cain, of the race of Cain, worked in brass and iron (Gen. iv. 22). As early as the Mosaic period, there were axes and other instruments of iron (Num. xxxv. 16 ; Deut. xix. 5, margin). If Og's couch was a bed, it was made of iron (iii. 11). In the time of Joshua, vessels were made of the metal (Josh. vi. 19, 24) ; and chariots of iron

for war purposes were in use (Josh. xvii. 16), continuing through the period of the judges, and on to later times (Judg. i. 19; iv. 3, 13). Of iron were made armor and weapons, as spearheads and breastplates (1 Sam. xvii. 7; Rev. ix. 9); agricultural implements, as harrows and threshing instruments (2 Sam. xii. 31; Amos i. 3); builder's tools and nails (1 Kin. vi. 7; 1 Chron. xxii. 3); graving tools (Job xix. 24; Jer. xvii. 1); barbed irons for fishing (Job xli. 7); gates, bars, fetters (Ps. cv. 18; cvii. 10, 16; cxlix. 8; Is. xlv. 2; Acts xii. 10); idols (Dan. v. 4). Iron was imported from Tarshish, Greece, and the north, doubtless from the vicinity of the Black Sea (Jer. xv. 12; Ezek. xxvii. 12, 19). It was obtainable in Palestine (Deut. viii. 9), being abundant on the Lebanon· mountains. The ore was reduced in furnaces (Deut. iv. 20; 1 Kin. viii. 51) which, to judge from those in use in Lebanon, were built of stone, about ten feet in height and three in diameter. Charcoal was used in them, and the fire was blown by bellows (Ezek. xxii. 20; cp. Jer. vi. 29). The process was laborious and involved enormous waste. See SMITH.

I'ron, II. [timidity, reverence, or rather, possessing a view, conspicuous].

A fortified city of Naphtali (Josh. xix. 38); probably the present village of Yârûn, 10 miles west from the waters of Merom.

Ir'pe-el [God healeth].

A town of Benjamin (Josh. xviii. 27). Conder thinks it probably the village Râfât, 6½ miles north by west of Jerusalem, the ancient and modern names having the same meaning.

Ir-she'mesh [city of the sun].

A town of Dan (Josh. xix. 41), probably the same as Beth-shemesh.

I'ru [pertaining to a city, or watchful].

A son of the celebrated Caleb (1 Chron. iv. 15).

I'saac [he laugheth, or laughing one].

The son of Abraham and Sarah, born in the south country, doubtless at Beer-sheba (Gen. xxi. 14, 31), when his father was 100 years old and his mother about 90 (xvii. 17; xxi. 5). When the promise was made that Sarah should bear him a son, Abraham laughed questioningly (xvii. 17-19). Later when Sarah heard the promise from the mouth of the stranger stopping at the camp, she laughed incredulously (xviii. 9-15); and when the child was born she joyfully confessed that God had prepared laughter for her and her friends (xxi. 6). To commemorate these events and the faithfulness of God, Abraham called the boy's name Isaac, one laugheth (3). He was circumcised on the eighth day (4); and being the child of promise and legal heir he had higher privileges than Ishmael had, Abraham's son by the handmaid (xvii. 19-21; xxi. 12; xxv. 5, 6). To exhibit and develop Abraham's faith, God commanded him

to offer Isaac as a burnt offering. Isaac was then a youth (xxii. 6), perhaps 25 years old, as Josephus says; but he filially acquiesced in the purpose of his father. When Abraham had laid him upon the altar, and thus shown his readiness to give all that he possessed to God, the angel of the Lord forbade the sacrifice and accepted a ram instead, thus testifying against child-sacrifices, practised by the Canaanites and many other idolatrous peoples, and teaching to all men that human sacrifices are an abomination to the Lord (xxii. 1-18).

Isaac dwelt in the south country, at Beer-lahai-roi (xxiv. 62). In disposition he was retiring and contemplative; affectionate also, and felt his mother's death deeply (63, 67). He married at the age of 40 years, but his two sons were not born until he was 60 (xxv. 20, 26). Because of a famine he moved fifty miles north, to Gerar (xxvi. 1, 6). There Jehovah appeared to him, telling him not to go to Egypt and re-affirming the Abrahamic covenant (2-5). It had been the settled policy of Abraham, whenever he was in foreign parts (xx. 13), to represent Sarah as his sister; and Isaac, in similar peril at Gerar, likewise tried to pass off Rebekah as his sister, but without success (xxvi. 6-11, same document as xii. 10-20). Leaving Gerar, he pitched his camp in the valley of Gerar (xxvi. 17), and opened again the wells that his father had dug. Thence he removed to Beer-sheba, which long remained his headquarters (23; xxviii. 10). Jehovah appeared to him during the night, and encouraged him; and he erected an altar, as his father had done (xxvi. 24, 25). Abimelech, the king of Gerar, visited him and entered into a treaty with him (26-31). This sworn agreement, sheba‘, gave a new occasion for linking the memory of an oath with the name of the place (33; cp. xxi. 31).

Esau, the elder of Isaac's two sons, was his favorite, although God had declared that the elder should serve the younger. Jacob was Rebekah's favorite (xxv. 28) When Isaac was much over 100 years old (xxvii. 1 with xxv. 26; xxvi. 34), Rebekah and Jacob took advantage of his age and of the blindness and the bluntness of feeling which it produced; and deceived as to the person, Isaac transferred the Abrahamic blessing to the younger son. Soon after, at the instigation of Rebekah, who wished to save Jacob from the murderous wrath of Esau, but feigned a different reason, Isaac sent Jacob to Laban in Paddan-aram to get a wife (xxvii. 46-xxviii. 5).

Some twenty years later Isaac was residing near Hebron, where he had sojourned in his father's later life (xxxv. 27; cp. xxiii. 2). There he died at the age of 180 years (xxxv. 28), and was buried by his two sons beside his parents and his wife in the cave of Machpelah (xlix. 30, 31). The N. T. alludes to Isaac as a child of promise (Gal. iv. 22, 23), and instances his tent life and his blessing

Esau and Jacob as evidences of his faith (Heb. xi. 9, 20).

I-sa′iah, in A. V. of N. T. **Esaias,** the Greek modification [Jehovah hath saved].

A prophet of Judah in the reigns of Uzziah, Jotham, Ahaz, and Hezekiah, kings of Judah (Is. i. 1; cp. vi. 1; vii. 3; xiv. 28; xx. 1, 2; xxxvi.-xxxix.). He was the son of Amoz, who must not be confounded with the prophet Amos. He lived in Jerusalem, and prophesied concerning Judah and Jerusalem; his prophecies concerning Samaria, Damascus, Philistia and other nations being subordinate to those which directly concerned Jerusalem, and being introduced because of their relation to Zion and the people of God. It is disputed whether the vision which he saw in the year that king Uzziah died (vi.) marked his call to the prophetic office, or was intended to deepen his spirituality. Other prophets experienced similar renewed quickening. Ezekiel's inaugural call was by a vision; and long afterwards, when he was a distinguished prophet, his call to the prophetic office was confirmed, and he was warned, like Isaiah, of the indifference with which the people would receive his message (Ezek. xxxiii. 21-33). Peter, after several years of service as a disciple of Christ and in the apostolic office, had his insight into Christ's teaching deepened and was introduced into a wider work by a vision (Acts x.). Paul, long after he had been called to labor among the gentiles, was summoned by a vision to work in a new field, Europe (Acts xvi. 9, 10). So God may have purposed an increase and a deepening of the spiritual life of Isaiah, in sending him this vision. By the year 734 B. C. Isaiah was a married man (Is. viii. 3), with a son named Shear-jashub, which means a remnant shall return (vii. 3). A second son was afterwards born to him, whom by divine direction he called Maher-shalal-hash-baz, which means spoil speedeth, prey hasteneth. The names of both sons enshrine prophecies. Isaiah's wife is called a prophetess (viii. 3), probably merely because she was the wife of a prophet.

Isaiah spoke much on the relations of Israel, both as a church and as a body politic, to the world. In regard to political relations he urged king and people to put trust in Jehovah and avoid entangling alliances with earthly powers (viii. 12-14; etc.). In 734 B. C., when Syria and Israel joined forces in order to capture Jerusalem, and put a creature of their own upon the throne, he declared Jehovah's purpose that the attempt should fail, and he vainly endeavored to persuade Ahaz to rely on Jehovah and not put confidence in heathen princes (vii.). Ahaz unwisely rejected this advice, called in Tiglath-pileser, king of Assyria, and became his vassal (2 Kin. xvi. 7, 8, 10); see TIGLATH-PILESER. Under Hezekiah the prophet's

counsel was treated with more respect. The Assyrians invaded Judah in Hezekiah's fourteenth year, about 714 B. C. (2 Kin. xviii. 13; Is. xxxvi. 1). Shortly afterwards, in the same year, Hezekiah fell dangerously sick, and Isaiah foretold his recovery (2 Kin. xx. 1-11). Then followed the embassy of Merodach-baladan, 712 or 711 B. C. (Is. xxxix.), the conquest of Ashdod by Sargon's army, 711 B. C. (xx.), and the expeditions sent against Jerusalem by Sennacherib, 701 B. C. (2 Kin. xviii. 14). During the last-named crisis, Isaiah's prophecies and encouraging words nerved the government to refuse the Assyrian demands.

The time and manner of Isaiah's death are not known with certainty. Hezekiah died in 698 or 697 B. C. The murder of Sennacherib and accession of Esarhaddon, which occured in 681 and 680, are recorded (Is. xxxvii. 38). Doubtful Jewish tradition affirms that Isaiah was martyred by Manasseh, having been sawn asunder, and some have supposed that Heb. xi. 37 alludes to the manner of his death. The date involved is not impossible, for Isaiah may have begun his ministry after 740 B. C., prophesied in the reigns of the four kings, Uzziah, Jotham, Ahaz, and Hezekiah, survived Hezekiah, and written his acts first and last (2 Chron. xxxii. 32), heard of the murder of Sennacherib, and have suffered martyrdom in or after the eighteenth year of Manasseh, at the age of not more than 80 years. At any rate, in writing his history of Uzziah's reign (2 Chron. xxvi. 22), Isaiah used probably records and other authoritative sources for the earlier part of the reign.

The book of the Prophet Isaiah is divisible as follows: I. Introduction (i.). II. A prophecy against Jerusalem (ii.-iv.), with a continuation or closely related prophecy (v.). The denunciation culminates in iv. with the effect of the judgment and a picture of the glory of Messianic times. This prophecy may have been delivered during the prosperous times of the joint reign of Uzziah and Jotham. III. The vision of chap. vi., which, as every one admits, stands in close relation to the Book of Immanuel (vii.-xii.). IV. Ten burdens for the nations (xiii.-xxiii.), divided by chap. xx., which is of international import, into two series of five burdens each, and culminating in judgment upon the whole world (xxiv.), and followed by Judah's triumph and blessedness (xxv.-xxvii.). V. A group of prophecies dealing exclusively with Judah and Samaria and pronouncing woe and weal (xxviii.-xxxiii.), culminating as before in judgment on all nations and Zion's happy future (xxxiv., xxxv.). VI. A historical section (xxxvi.-xxxix.), describing the initiatory operations of the Assyro-Babylonian power in Judah, and serving as an introduction to the Book of Consolation, which was offered in view of the sore judgment upon Judah (xl.-lxvi.). This Book of Consolation

A scroll of the Book of Isaiah, opened to chapter forty. Discovered in one of the caves near the Dead Sea, this scroll is made of seventeen sheets of parchment sewn together and is almost twenty-four feet long. The darkened portions in the center are the result of many hands holding the scroll at these points.

treats of the relation of the church of Israel to Jehovah (xl.-xlviii.), the relation of the church to the nations (xlix.-lvii.), the abrogation of national distinctions, and the glorious future of the church (lviii.-lxvi.). The prominent figure in these chapters is the servant of the Lord (see SERVANT OF JEHOVAH).

The genuineness of chapter l. was called in question by Koppe in 1797. Soon afterwards Döderlein assigned the composition of the last twenty-seven chapters to the time of the exile. This theory, enlarged to include xiii.-xiv. 23; xxi. 1-10; xxiv.-xxvii.; xxxiv.; xxxv., has found numerous advocates. Still other passages have been added as the need of adjustment has appeared, such as xi. 10-xii. 6; but there is not the same unanimity in rejecting them among the adherents of the theory. The arguments advanced in support of the main theory are all comprehended in three. 1. The language is late and the style is peculiar. 2. The allusions to the condition of Jews and gentiles reveal the time of the exile. 3. The statements concerning the condition of the people agree with the historical facts, but those which relate to the future have fallen short of fulfillment.

To these arguments the answer, which must unfortunately be stated summarily, is rendered: 1. There has not been shown a single word of known late date, nor a single foreign element which there is any reason to believe was not current in Jerusalem in the days of Isaiah. Every word, phrase, and form is found in earlier Hebrew literature or may be explained by the history of the times. As to the style being peculiar, change of style is consistent with unity of authorship. The style of Shakespere changed. His literary activity lasted but twenty-five years, yet four distinct periods are discernible in his plays, marked by differences of style. The literary activity of Isaiah was continued through at least forty years and perhaps sixty. And is the style so peculiar after all? Those who deny the Isaianic authorship find it incumbent upon them to explain the similarity of style. Augusti accounts for the ascription of these chapters to Isaiah in the first instance by the fact that "they were composed so entirely in the spirit and manner of Isaiah." Gesenius and De Wette ascribe the similarity of style to imitation or the work of a conforming hand. Umbreit calls the unknown author of the chapters in dispute, "Isaiah risen again" as from the dead. 2. To the argument that the allusions, which are made in these chapters to the condition of Jews and gentiles, reveal the time of the exile, it is replied: *a.* The prophets frequently transport themselves to the future and describe what they are predicting as already past; for instance, although Zebulun and Naphtali had been ravaged and their inhabitants carried into captivity, the acknowl-

edged Isaiah says of them: "The people that walked in darkness *have* seen a great light" (ix. 2). *b.* The explicit references to Babylon, the exile, and the restoration are few. *c.* The acknowledged Isaiah and his contemporary prophets were already living in anticipation of the Babylonian exile. There is scarcely an event connected with the exile, to which the author refers, but was known to the Israelites in the time of Isaiah. The prophets of the time predicted the destruction of Jerusalem and the temple (Amos ii. 5; Micah iii. 12; Is. iii. 8; vi. 11), the desolation of the land of Judah (Hos. viii. 14; Amos ix. 11, 14; Is. iii. 25, 26; vi. 11, 12; xxxii. 13), the captivity of the people of Judah (Is. xi. 12; Mic. i. 14-16). This captivity was to be in Babylon (Is. xxxix. 6, 7; cp. xi. 11; Mic. iv. 10). There should be a return from exile (Joel iii. 1; Is. xi. 11). Jerusalem and the temple should be rebuilt (Mic. iv. 2; although the destruction of Jerusalem had been foretold, iii. 12; cp. Joel iii. 16, 17, 20), and many people would come to Jerusalem to worship (Is. ii. 2-4; xi. 10; xviii. 7; Mic. iv. 1-3). *d.* The spiritual condition of the people, as exhibited in these chapters, is that of the time of Isaiah; idolatry under every green tree (lvii. 5 and i. 29; 2 Kin. xvi. 4) and among the oaks (lvii. 5 and i. 29; Hos. iv. 13) and in gardens (lxv. 3; lxvi. 17 and i. 29); the slaying of children in the valleys (lvii. 5 and 2 Chron. xxviii. 3; xxxiii. 6; 2 Kin. xxiii. 10); ascending a high mountain to offer sacrifice (lvii. 7 and 2 Chron. xxviii. 4; Hos. iv. 13; cp. Ezek. vi. 13); hypocrisy (lviii. 2-4 and xxix. 13); Sabbath-breaking (lviii. 13 and Amos viii. 5; Jer. xvii. 19-27); bloodshed and violence (lix. 3, 7 and i. 15; Mic. vii. 2); falsehood, injustice, and oppression (lix. 3, 4, 6, 7, 9 and v. 7, 23; x. 1, 2; Mic. ii. 1, 2; vii. 3); neglect of the temple worship (xliii. 23, 24 and 2 Chron. xxviii. 24; xxix. 27; 2 Kin. xv. 4; 2 Chron. xxvii. 2; 2 Kin. xv. 35; 2 Chron. xxxiii. 10). Burning incense upon bricks (lxv. 3) was appropriate to a worship derived from either Egypt, Assyria, or Babylonia, and was practiced in Jerusalem before the exile (2 Kin. xxiii. 12; Jer. xix. 13). Swine's flesh was offered and eaten (lxv. 4) by the Egyptians on the festival of Selene and Dionysus (Herod. ii. 47, 48) and commonly enough by the Babylonians. 3. To the argument that the statements concerning the condition of the people agree with the historical facts, whereas those which relate to the future have fallen far short of fulfillment, it is replied that the assertion applies with equal force to the acknowledged writings of the prophet Isaiah. He foretold the destruction of the cities, the utter desolation of the land, and the removal of the inhabitants far hence (vi. 11, 12). This was fulfilled to the letter. But he prophesied also the flocking of the gentiles to the standard of Jesse's son, the return of the captive people of God from all parts of the world, the drying up of rivers which were obstacles in the course of the march, a highway from Assyria for the remnant of the people, the wolf dwelling in peace with the lamb (xi. 6-8, 10-12, 15, 16; see also Amos ix. 11-15; Mic. v. 4; vii. 12). These are the same predictions as those which in the latter portion of the book are pointed to as the extravagant utterances of an enthusiast and as having fallen short of fulfillment. Unless these numerous passages be exscinded, the acknowledged Isaiah, and often his contemporaries also, living two centuries before the fall of Babylon and the hopes which that event are supposed to have awakened, wrote in precisely the same manner as the author of the last section.

A special ground on which the denial of the genuineness of the last twenty-seven chapters rests is the mention of Cyrus by name (xliv. 28; xlv. 1). So also Josiah was foretold by name (1 Kin. xiii. 2). If predictive prophecy is possible, if it was ever uttered by holy men taught by the Holy Spirit, then the name of Cyrus could have been penned by Isaiah. Otherwise the words, as they stand, were not uttered until nearly two hundred years after Isaiah. The church has always believed in predictive prophecy and in the inspiration of Isaiah.

Is'cah [perhaps, discerning or expectant].

A daughter of Haran and sister of Milcah (Gen. xi. 29), and consequently sister of Lot (27). Iscah has been regarded as another name of Sarai (Antiq. i. 6, 5; Targum Jonathan); but in that case Sarai would have been Abraham's niece and not his half-sister (Gen. xx. 12).

Is-car'i-ot [probably, man of Kerioth].

A designation of Judas the traitor (Mat. x. 4; Luke vi. 16), which belonged to his father Simon before him (John vi. 71, R. V.). It was used to distinguish him from the other apostle called Judas (Luke vi. 16; Acts i. 13, 16). It seems to mean that Judas was a native of Kerioth in the south of Judah (Josh. xv. 25); or perhaps of Koreæ, on the northeastern border of Judæa (Antiq. xiv. 3, 4; War i. 6, 5). In the codex Bezæ the word is written *apo Karuōtou* everywhere in the Fourth Gospel, and is so written in John vi. 71 in the codex Sinaiticus. Accordingly Judas was probably a Judæan; and perhaps he was the only apostle from Judæa, and the rest were Galilæans.

Ish'bah [he praises or praising one].

A man of Judah, ancestor or head of the inhabitants of Eshtemoa (1 Chron. iv. 17).

Ish'bak [perhaps, he leaveth or relinquishing one].

An Arab tribe descended from Abraham through Keturah (Gen. xxv. 2).

Ish-bi-be'nob [my dwelling place is on a height].

A Philistine giant who was on the point of killing David, but was himself slain by Abishai (2 Sam. xxi. 16, 17).

Ish-bo'sheth [man of shame].

One of Saul's younger sons, originally called Eshbaal, the Lord's man, which was changed to Ish-bosheth, man of shame, either during his lifetime when the glory of his house departed, or in later times when the name Baal fell into disrepute through its idolatrous associations (2 Sam. ii. 8 with 1 Chron. viii. 33; ix. 39). He was not present at the battle of Gilboa; or, if present, he escaped the slaughter on that disastrous day. On the death of Saul, David obtained the sovereignty over Judah, but the other tribes refused him allegiance and proclaimed Ishbosheth king as successor to his father Saul. Ish-bosheth was then aged about 40, and reigned two troubled years (2 Sam. ii. 8-10). His capital was at Mahanaim, east of the Jordan (ii. 8, 12). He was unsuccessful in the war which he waged with David to secure the undisputed sway over the twelve tribes (ii. 12-iii. 1). He brought a serious charge against his main supporter, Abner, who thereupon offered his services to David, and, on David's making demand on Ish-bosheth, conducted David's wife Michal back to him (6-21). When Abner was murdered at Hebron, Ishbosheth lost heart (27; iv. 1). He was soon afterwards assassinated, and his head carried in triumph to David. But by David's order the severed head was honorably interred in the tomb of Abner at Hebron, and the assassins were put to death for their crime (iv. 5-12). With the death of Ish-bosheth the dynasty of Saul came to an end, although a grandson of Saul's remained (iv. 4).

Ish'hod, in A. V. **Ishod** [man of splendor].

A Manassite whose mother was Hammoleketh (1 Chron. vii. 18).

Ish'i, I. [my husband].

A name by which the Israelites call Jehovah, when they return to their allegiance. It supersedes the synonymous one Baali, my master, because the word Baal had come into ill repute through its association with idolatry (Hos. ii. 16, 17).

Ish'i, II. [saving, salutary].

1. A man of Judah, son of Appaim, house of Jerahmeel (1 Chron. ii. 31).

2. A man of Judah, father of Zoheth (1 Chron. iv. 20).

3. A Simeonite whose sons led a band which overcame the Amalekites of mount Seir, and seized on their settlements (1 Chron. iv. 42).

4. Head of a father's house of the half-tribe of Manasseh east of the Jordan (1 Chron. v. 24).

I-shi'ah. See ISSHIAH.

I-shi'jah. See ISSHIJAH.

Ish'ma [desolation or, perhaps, distinction].

A man of Judah, descended from Hur (1 Chron. iv. 3, 4).

Ish′ma-el [God heareth].

1. The son of Abraham by Hagar the Egyptian maid; born when Abraham was eighty-six years old, after he had been ten full years in Canaan (Gen. xvi. 3, 15; cp. xii. 4). He was the child of worldly wisdom, not of faith; he was born of parents who, in the face of God's promise, were blinded by seeming impossibilities, and sought by earthly means to enable God to fulfill his engagements. When the rite of circumcision was instituted for the family of Abraham, Ishmael, then thirteen years of age, was circumcised (xvii. 25). The next year Isaac was born, when his mother was past age, the child of promise, a rebuke to unbelief (xxi. 5). At his weaning, the customary feast was made, when Ishmael was seen to be mocking. This was the first occasion in the family of Abraham that those born after the flesh in doubt of God's way mocked at the heirs of promise; and Paul seizes upon the allegory in the incident (Gal. iv. 22–31). This misbehavior of Ishmael led to the expulsion of him and his mother. They wandered in the wilderness of Beer-sheba till both were nearly perishing with thirst. The angel of the Lord directed Hagar to some water among the shrubs, and the life of herself and her son was preserved. Ishmael grew up in the wilderness of Paran, south of Canaan, where he lived by his bow. Eventually he married a wife from Egypt, his mother's ancestral home (Gen. xxi. 3–21). In fulfillment of a promise made by God to Abraham, Ishmael became the progenitor of twelve princes (xvii. 20; xxv. 12–16); see ISHMAELITES. He had also a daughter, who was married to Esau (xxviii. 9; xxxvi. 10). Ishmael took part with Isaac in burying their father Abraham (xxv. 9). He himself died at the age of 137 (xxv. 17).

2. A descendant of Jonathan (1 Chron. viii. 38; ix. 44).

3. A man of Judah, father of the high judicial functionary Zebadiah (2 Chron. xix. 11).

4. A son of Jehohanan. He took part in the successful conspiracy against Athaliah (2 Chron. xxiii. 1).

5. A son of Nethaniah, who belonged to the seed royal of Judah. When Nebuchadnezzar departed from Palestine, after the capture of Jerusalem, he left behind him as governor of Judah a certain Jew called Gedaliah, who promised protection to any of the conquered people who placed themselves under his rule. Among others Ishmael came, but with hostile intent. Instigated by the king of the Ammonites, he assassinated Gedaliah, massacred at the same time the people with him. After further murders he carried off captives, including the king's daughters, and finally attempted to make his way to the Ammonite country. Johanan, son of Kareah, and others went forth to fight with him. They found him at Gibeon. His captives turned to Johanan, but he himself succeeded in escaping with eight men to the king of

Ammon, who had instigated his crimes (2 Kin. xxv. 25; Jer. xl. 7–16; xli. 1–18).

6. A son of Pashhur, who was induced by Ezra to put away his foreign wife (Ezra x. 22).

Ish′ma-el-ite, in A. V. often **Ishmeelite**, an orthography true to the Hebrew word, but English literature has adopted the former spelling.

A descendant of Ishmael. The Ishmaelites had Egyptian blood, as well as the blood of Abraham, in their veins. Twelve princes sprang from Ishmael (Gen. xvii. 20; xxv. 12–16). He may have had more sons, and possibly some of those enumerated were grandsons. Twelve was an approved number. Twelve was carefully preserved as the number of the tribes of Israel, and twelve was the recognized number of the kings of the Hittites in their confederacy. The Ishmaelites in their twelvefold division dwelt in settlements and in movable camps in the desert of northern Arabia, in the region included between Havilah, Egypt, and the Euphrates (xxv. 18; Antiq. i. 12, 4). Occasionally one of their tribes acquired permanent residence and civilization, as the Nabathæans; but they mostly possessed the character of their ancestor and dwelt like the untamable ass of the desert (Gen. xvi. 12). Like Ishmael, too, they were celebrated for their skill with the bow (Is. xxi. 17). To Ishmaelites traveling as carriers between Gilead and Egypt, or, more definitely, to "certain Midianites, merchants," in the caravan, Joseph was sold by his brethren (Gen. xxxvii. 25–28). In Ps. lxxxiii. 6 they are mentioned with Edomites, Moabites, and Hagarenes.

In a wider sense, the nomadic tribes of northern Arabia generally; either because the Ishmaelites were the chief people of the desert, and their name came to be used as a synonym for any nomad of the region, or because an Ishmaelite confederacy had been formed which included tribes of other blood (Judg. viii. 24; cp. vii. 25; viii. 22, 26; Judith ii. 23). All the Arabs, after the example of Mohammed, claim descent from Ishmael.

Ish-ma′iah, in A. V. once **Ismaiah** (1 Chron. xii. 4) [Jehovah heareth].

1. A Gibeonite who joined David at Ziklag (1 Chron. xii. 4).

2. Son of Obadiah and head in David's reign of the Zebulunites (1 Chron. xxvii. 19).

Ish′me-el-ite. See ISHMAELITE.

Ish′me-rai [probably, Jehovah keepeth]. A Benjamite, son of Elpaal (1 Chron. viii. 18).

I′shod. See ISHHOD.

Ish′pah, in A. V. **Ispah** [perhaps, bald]. A Benjamite, son of Beriah (1 Chron. viii. 16).

Ish′pan.
A Benjamite, son of Shashak (1 Chron. viii. 22).

Ish′tob [men of Tob]. See TOB.

Ish′u-ah. See ISHVAH.

Ish'u-ai and **Ishui**. See Ishvi.

Ish'vah, in A. V. **Ishuah** and **Isuah** [perhaps, equality].

The second son of Asher (Gen. xlvi. 17; 1 Chron. vii. 30). He probably died childless; or, if he had descendants, they did not constitute a tribal family or perpetuate his name (cp. Num. xxvi. 44).

Ish'vi, in A. V. **Ishuai**, **Ishui**, **Isui**, and **Jesui** [perhaps, equal].

1. The third son of Asher, and founder of a tribal family (Gen. xlvi. 17; Num. xxvi. 44; 1 Chron. vii. 30).

2. A son of Saul (1 Sam. xiv. 49).

Isle, Is'land.

The rendering of the Hebrew '*I*, meaning 1. Habitable land, as opposed to water (Is. xlii. 15). 2. An island in the ordinary sense of the word (Jer. xlvii. 4). 3. A maritime country, even when constituting part of a continent; the coast land of Palestine and Phœnicia (Is. xx. 6, in R. V. coast land; cp. xxiii. 2, 6), and the coasts and islands of Asia Minor and Greece (Gen. x. 5). 4. The remotest regions of the earth and their inhabitants (Is. xli. 5; Zeph. ii. 11). This employment of the term may have arisen: (*a*) By synecdoche, the isles of the Mediterranean being remote and scarcely known. (*b*) From the current belief that the world was surrounded with water, so that the most distant region was the coast land of the world-ocean.

Is-ma-chi'ah [Jehovah supporteth].

An overseer connected with the temple in Hezekiah's reign (2 Chron. xxxi. 13).

Is-ma'iah. See Ishmaiah.

Is'pah. See Ishpah.

Is'ra-el [he striveth with God, or God striveth].

1. The name given to Jacob when he was returning from Mesopotamia and just about to cross the brook Jabbok, where he expected to meet Esau (Gen. xxxii. 22–32); see Jacob.

2. The whole body of the descendants of Jacob at any one time. This use of the word began in his own lifetime (Gen. xxxiv. 7). It was common during the wilderness wanderings (Ex. xxxii. 4; Deut. iv. 1; xxvii. 9), though the designation children of Israel was yet more frequent both during this and the former period. Down to the death of Saul, Israel and the children of Israel, when used as a national designation, comprehended the Hebrews generally, without distinction of tribes. There were, however, geographical and other causes already at work which tended to separate Judah from the rest of Israel; and the distinction had come to be recognized before the actual division of the people into two kingdoms took place (1 Sam. xi. 8; xvii. 52; xviii. 16); see Judah. It was used also under the united monarchy (1 Kin. xi. 42). In the parallelism of Hebrew poetry it often corresponds in the second line of the couplet to Jacob in the first (Num. xxiii. 7,

10, 21; xxiv. 5; Ps. xiv. 7). After the exile the reference is frequently to the people of the various tribes who returned to Jerusalem (Ezra ix. 1; x. 5; Neh. ix. 2; xi. 3).

3. The tribes which acted independently of Judah. The split of the Hebrew people into two kingdoms occurred on the death of Saul. The northern and eastern tribes recognized Saul's son Ish-bosheth as king, and the tribe of Judah followed David. From this time onward Israel is frequently used to denote the ten tribes. Ish-bosheth reigned two years and was assassinated, but seven years elapsed before the breach was healed and David was anointed king of all Israel (2 Sam. ii. 10, 11). The jealousies, however, remained, and on the death of Solomon the rupture became final. Ten tribes followed Jeroboam and one clave to the house of David. The ten tribes which were rent from the house of David were Reuben, Gad, and half Manasseh east of the Jordan, and west of the river half Manasseh, Ephraim, Issachar, Zebulun, Naphtali, Asher, Dan, and lastly Benjamin, which belonged in part to the northern kingdom, Bethel, Gilgal, and Jericho, chief places in the tribe of Benjamin, being within the bounds of the northern kingdom.

The causes which led to the schism were: 1. The isolation of Judah caused by nature and augmented by Joshua's blunder. 2. The ancient jealousy between the two powerful tribes of Ephraim and Judah. It had caused a temporary disruption of the kingdom after Saul's death; it broke out again after the defeat of Absalom because Judah was the first to welcome the king back (2 Sam. xix. 15, 40–43). It had been freshly provoked by Solomon's lavish adornment of Jerusalem on the borders of Judah, and at his death resulted in permanent separation. 3. Discontent caused by the excessive luxury of the throne. The people were groaning under oppressive burdens. Solomon's love of splendor had led to taxation to support his enormous household and maintain his display, and to enforcement of labor to carry out his great works (1 Kin. iv. 22, 23, 26; v. 13–16). The reasonable request of the people for relief was perversely refused by Rehoboam. 4. Idolatry, fostered by foreign marriages (1 Kin. xi. 1–11). A subtle corruption spread through all ranks owing to the encouragement given to false religions, attachment to the worship of Jehovah was weakened, and one great unifying force was destroyed. 5. The folly of Rehoboam in refusing the request of the people for relief intensified the disintegrating forces and precipitated the catastrophe (1 Kin. xii. 3–5, 12–16).

As compared with Judah in respect to strength the northern kingdom had ten tribes, twice the population, and nearly three times the extent of territory. But it was more exposed to war and less easy of defense than Judah. It was the apostate nation, and defection from God is weakness and inevitably undermines the stability of a state. It had an inferior religion with its lower moral tone, and many of its best spirits forsook it; the priests and Levites migrated into Judah (2 Chron. xi. 13, 14).

The capital of the northern kingdom was at Shechem at first. It was soon removed to Tirzah, and then Omri founded Samaria and transferred the seat of government to the new city (1 Kin. xii. 25; xiv. 17; xv. 21; xvi. 23, 24).

Jeroboam, the first king, was afraid that if his people visited Jerusalem for worship, they would be won over to their old allegiance; he therefore established two shrines, one at Dan in the extreme north, and the other at Bethel, in the south of the kingdom. At each of these places he erected a golden calf, which he designed as an aid to the worship of Jehovah ; see CALF. Judgment was threatened against him and his race for this partial apostasy, and after his son, Nadab, had reigned two years, the dynasty was swept away. Nineteen kings in all sat upon the throne. See CHRONOLOGY. Their united reigns covered a period of about 210 years ; seven of them reigned but two years or less ; eight were slain or committed suicide and the throne was transferred to another family, and in only two instances was the royal power held by as many as four members of the same family in succession. None of the kings removed the calves from Bethel and Dan ; indeed, under Ahab, who was influenced by his wicked heathen wife, Jezebel, the apostasy was rendered complete by the introduction of the worship of Baal instead of Jehovah. But God raised up prophets who contended steadfastly for the worship of Jehovah, at whatever risk to themselves. The most notable were Elijah and Elisha (q.v.). After the suppression of Baal worship, other prophets, especially Hosea and Amos, labored for the reformation of the moral life of the nation.

The northern Israelites were frequently at war with Judah. Indeed, the two kingdoms were in hearty alliance only while the house of Omri held the throne of Israel, when the royal families of Israel and Judah were united by intermarriage. When the Syrian kingdom of Damascus rose to power it necessarily affected the politics of the adjacent kingdom of Israel. Often the two were at war. They united, however, in making common cause against the Assyrians in the days of Ahab ; and 120 years later they were again in alliance, their common object being the capture of Jerusalem. It was this danger that led Ahaz, king of Judah, terrified for his throne and life, and having no faith in Jehovah, to act contrary to the exhortations of Isaiah and to call in Tiglath-pileser, king of Assyria, at the price of independence. Judah became tributary to Assyria, and its king did homage to the Assyrian monarch at Damascus (2 Kin. xvi. 8-10). Tiglath-pileser

relieved Judah of the invaders, ravaged northern Israel, struck a blow at the Philistines, besieged and ultimately captured Damascus and slew Rezin, deported the Israelites from the country east of the Jordan, connived at the death of Pekah or actually ordered it, and placed Hoshea on the throne about 730 B. C. Hoshea rebelled against Assyria after Tiglath-pileser's death. The Assyrian armies returned, in 722 Samaria fell and a large number of the inhabitants were carried off to Assyria. See CAPTIVITY and SARGON. The place of the deported Israelites was supplied by colonists from five districts in the Assyrian empire, who, mingling with the remaining Israelite population of central Palestine, laid the foundations of what afterwards became the Samaritan nation.

The captivity of Israel was a punishment because the people had sinned against the Lord their God and had feared other gods, walking in the statutes of the nations and of the kings of Israel (2 Kin. xvii. 7, 8). They were apostate. They had broken the covenant (15; cp. Ex. xx.–xxii. ; Hos. vi. 7 ; viii. 1), rejecting the statutes of the Lord. Their apostasy had manifested itself in two directions : they walked in the statutes of the nations whom the Lord cast out (2 Kin. xvii. 8, 15, 17; cp. Hos. ii. 13 ; iv. 2, 11, 15 ; Amos ii. 6–9), and they walked in the statutes of the kings of Israel, especially in the matter of the calf worship and its attendant ceremonies and ordinances, and in the general idolatry that followed in its train (2 Kin. xvii. 8, 16 ; Hos. viii. 4–6 ; x. 5, 8 ; xiii. 2–4). They had sinned despite the fact that the Lord had testified unto them by prophets and by providences (2 Kin. xvii. 13 ; Hos. xii. 10 ; Amos ii. 9–11 ; iv. 6–13). Their sin issued in separation and degradation and paved the way for punishment. They separated from Judah, and thus weakened were overthrown. Their idolatry, drunkenness, and licentiousness weakened the manhood of the nation, deprived it of sturdiness, and made its soldiery no better in character and moral purpose than the warriors of Egypt, Assyria, and Babylonia.

Is'ra-el-ite.

A descendant of Israel, i. e., of Jacob (Ex. ix. 7) ; and consequently, by implication, the possessor of true religious knowledge, a faithful servant of Jehovah, and an heir of the promises (John i. 47; Rom. ix. 4 ; xi. 1 ; 2 Cor. xi. 22).

Is'sa-char [there is hire].

1. The ninth son of Jacob, the fifth by Leah (Gen. xxx. 17, 18 ; xxxv. 23). His sons were Tola, Phuvah or Pua, Job or Jashub, and Shimron (xlvi. 13 ; Num. xxvi. 23, 24 ; 1 Chron. vii. 1). With them he went down with Jacob into Egypt (Gen. xlvi. 13 ; Ex. i. 3). Jacob, shortly before death, with keen and prophetic insight into character, described Issachar and his children as a strong

ass, couching down between the sheep folds, who submits to the burdens imposed by foreign masters, provided they permit him to remain in his pleasant land (Gen. xlix. 14, 15).

The descendants of Issachar formed a tribe, consisting of five great tribal families, the posterity of his five sons (Num. xxvi. 23, 24). Its prince in the early period of the wanderings was Nethaneel, son of Zuar (Num. i. 8; ii. 5; vii. 18; x. 15), and at a later period Paltiel, son of Azzan (xxxiv. 26). At the first census in the wilderness it numbered 54,400 fighting men (i. 28, 29); at the second 64,300 (xxvi. 25); while in David's reign it reached 87,000 (1 Chron. vii. 5). Igal, son of Joseph, was the spy from the tribe (Num. xiii. 7). The men of Issachar were among those who stood on mount Gerizim to bless the people (Deut. xxvii. 12). Moses, in predicting the future of the tribes, foretold Issachar's joyous and quiet life (xxxiii. 18). One of the judges, Tola, belonged to the tribe of Issachar (Judg. x. 1); so did king Baasha (1 Kin. xv. 27). The princes of Issachar had the political insight to discern the fit moment for turning from Saul's family and accepting David as the king of all Israel (1 Chron. xii. 32). About that time Omri, son of Michael, was head of the tribe (xxvii. 18). Many men of Issachar, although they belonged to the northern kingdom, attended Hezekiah's passover (2 Chron. xxx. 18). In the apocalyptic vision 12,000 of the tribe of Issachar were sealed (Rev. vii. 7), this being the normal number.

When the land of Canaan was distributed by lot, the fourth lot taken after the ark was removed to Shiloh came forth for the tribe of Issachar. Its territory was bounded on the north by Zebulun and Naphtali, on the east by the Jordan, on the south and west by Manasseh and probably Asher. Jezreel and Shunem lay within its limits, while Chesulloth and mount Tabor were on its northern border, and En-gannim near the southern line (Josh. xix. 17–23); but towns within it were held by Manasseh (xvii. 10, 11) and others by the Gershonite Levites (xxi. 6, 28, 29; 1 Chron. vi. 62–72). The tribe of Issachar occupied the greater part of the plain of Jezreel, or Esdraelon, constituting the low, level, and fertile plain of the Kishon. The character of their territory combined with the tribal traits explains why the people of Issachar, in accordance with Jacob's prophecy, were so ready to submit to servitude. They had much to lose, and lived on ground well adapted for the action of the war chariots of their enemies, while the tribes located among the mountains could not so readily be attacked in this manner. That the people of Issachar were not exceptionally cowardly is plain from their conduct in the battle with Sisera, which elicited the commendation of Deborah (Judg. v. 15).

2. A Levite, appointed doorkeeper in David's reign (1 Chron. xxvi. 5).

Is-shi′ah, in A. V. once **Ishiah** (1 Chron. vii. 3) and twice **Jesiah** (1 Chron xii. 6; xxiii. 20) [Jehovah lendeth or Jehovah forgetteth (cp. Jer. xxiii. 39)].

1. A man of Issachar, family of Tola (1 Chron. vii. 3).

2. One of those who came to David at Ziklag (1 Chron. xii. 6).

3. A Levite, descended from Moses, and head of the house of Rehabiah (1 Chron. xxiv. 21; cp. xxiii. 14–17).

4. A Levite, family of Kohath, house of Uzziel (1 Chron. xxiii. 20; xxiv. 25).

Is-shi′jah, in A. V. **Ishijah** [Jehovah lendeth or forgetteth].

A son of Harim, induced by Ezra to put away his foreign wife (Ezra x. 31).

Is′sue.

A man's disease, probably blennorrhea or perhaps gonorrhea (Lev. xv. 2–15; cp. War v. 5, 6; vi. 9, 3). An issue of blood is a female complaint (Lev. xv. 25–30; Mat. ix. 20).

Is′u-ah. See ISHVAH.

Is′u-i. See ISHVI.

It′a-ly.

A geographical name which, in the fifth century B. C., meant only a small district in the extreme south of what is now called Italy; but which gradually extended its signification, till in the first century of the Christian era it began to be used in the same sense that we now attach to the word. In the days of the apostles Italy, and, indeed, the greater part of the civilized world, was ruled from Rome (q. v.). A cohort called the Italian was stationed in Syria (Acts x. 1). Aquila and Priscilla, who were of Jewish descent, resided for a time in Italy (xviii. 2). Paul's appeal to Cæsar involved his sailing into Italy (xxvii. 1, 6), and his ship coasted along Italy from Rhegium to Puteoli (xxviii. 13–16). The salutation in the Epistle to the Hebrews, "They of Italy salute you" (Heb. xiii. 24), indicates the presence of Christians, not only in Rome, but in other parts of the country (cp. Acts xxviii. 14). During the Roman imperial period, the state of the country in comparison with the capital was wretched.

I′thai. See ITTAI.

Ith′a-mar [palm-coast].

The youngest son of Aaron (Ex. vi. 23; 1 Chron. vi. 3; xxiv. 1). With his father and his three elder brothers he was consecrated to the priestly office (Ex. xxviii. 1; 1 Chron. xxiv. 2). Upon him devolved the duty of enumerating the materials gathered for the tabernacle (Ex. xxxviii. 21). The Gershonites and the Merarites acted under his superintendence (Num. iv. 21–33). He founded a priestly family (1 Chron. xxiv. 4, 5, 6), which continued after the captivity (Ezra viii. 2). To this family belonged Eli and his descendants, who held the office of high priest for several generations. See HIGH PRIEST.

Ith′i-el [God is with me, or, possibly, there is a God].

1. One of the two persons to whom Agur addressed his prophecy (Prov. xxx. 1); but see R. V. margin for another possibility.

2. A Benjamite, son of Jesaiah (Neh. xi. 7).

Ith′lah, in A. V. **Jethlah** [a hanging or lofty place].

A town of Dan (Josh. xix. 42). Site unknown.

Ith′mah [bereavement].

A Moabite, one of the valiant men of David's army (1 Chron. xi. 46).

Ith′nan [perhaps, perennial].

A town in the extreme south of Judah (Josh. xv. 23). Situation unknown.

Ith′ra [abundance, excellence].

An Israelite, or rather Ishmaelite, who married Abigail, David's sister, and became the father of Amasa (2 Sam. xvii. 25; 1 Kin. ii. 5, 32; 1 Chron. ii. 17). In the last three passages he is called Jether, which is the Hebrew form of the name.

Ith′ran [abundance, excellence].

1. A Horite, son of Dishon (Gen. xxxvi. 26; 1 Chron. i. 41).

2. An Asherite, son of Zophah (1 Chron. vii. 37); apparently the same as Jether (38).

Ith′re-am [abundance of people].

The sixth son born to David at Hebron. His mother was Eglah (2 Sam. iii. 5; 1 Chron. iii. 3).

Ith′rite.

A family who dwelt at Kirjath-jearim (1 Chron. ii. 53). Two of David's mighty men were Ithrites (2 Sam. xxiii. 38; 1 Chron. xi. 40). The word is derivable from Jether or, if the customary vocalization is neglected, from Jattir.

It-tah-ka′zin. See ETH-KAZIN.

It′tai [perhaps, plowman].

1. A son of Ribai, from Gibeah of Benjamin. He was one of David's mighty men (2 Sam. xxiii. 29). Called in 1 Chron. xi. 31, Ithai.

2. An inhabitant of Gath, the commander of 600 men, who followed David from that Philistine city. He was faithful to the king through all vicissitudes, and led a third part of the royal army in the battle which resulted in the death of Absalom (2 Sam. xv. 18-22; xviii. 2, 5).

It-u-ræ′a [pertaining to Jetur].

A region occupied by a people called Jetur, who were descended from Ishmael (Gen. xxv. 15; 1 Chron. i. 31). The tribe of Jetur was at war with the Israelitish tribes east of the Jordan (v. 19). In Asmonæan times Aristobulus conquered a portion of Ituræa, and annexing it to Judæa, compelled the vanquished inhabitants to adopt the rite of circumcision (Antiq. xiii. 11, 3). It was a mountainous country, including part of Anti-Lebanon. Its prince, Ptolemy, son of Mennæus, had territory in Cœlesyria, with Chalcis as stronghold, and proved a bad neighbor to Damascus (Strabo xvi. 2, 18, 20; Antiq. xiii. 16, 3). In 66 B. C. he purchased immunity from Pompey (xiv. 3, 2). His son Lysanias was put to death by Antony (xv. 4, 1), and the country was farmed to Zenodorus (xv. 10, 1; for Zenodorus' domain cp. also 2 and 3). Part of Ituræa and Trachonitis constituted the tetrarchy of Philip (Luke iii. 1). Josephus enumerates the constituent parts of Philip's tetrarchy differently, and he is not careful always to enumerate in one and the same way (Antiq. xvii. 8, 1; 11, 4, where part of the house of Zenodorus is included; xviii. 4, 6; War ii. 6, 3). The name Ituræa or Jetur is radically different from Jedur, the present designation of a district southwest of Damascus.

I′vah. See IVVAH.

I′vo-ry.

A substance derived from the tusk of the elephant, hippopotamus, walrus, and other animals. In Hebrew it is called *Shen*, tooth, or *Shenhabbim*, a compound word in which *habbim* probably denotes some animal. It is first mentioned in the Bible as having been brought from abroad by Solomon's ships (1 Kin. x. 22; 2 Chron. ix. 21). It seems to have come from India, and was made into a throne for the king (1 Kin. x. 18). Afterwards, when luxury had established itself to a larger extent in Jerusalem, beds (Amos vi. 4), and even houses were made or overlaid with the precious material (1 Kin. xxii. 39; Amos iii. 15; Ps. xlv. 8). The Tyrians inlaid benches for rowers with it (Ezek. xxvii. 6). Ethiopia also supplied ivory to the ancient world (Herod. iii. 97, 114).

Iv′vah, in A. V. **Ivah.**

A city which the representative of Sennacherib could boast that the Assyrians had captured (2 Kin. xviii. 34; xix. 13; Is. xxxvii. 13). It is doubtless the same as Avva (q. v.).

I-ye-ab′a-rim, in A. V. **Ije-abarim** [ruins of the district of Abarim].

A halting place of the Israelites in the wilderness, on the border of Moab (Num. xxi. 11; xxxiii. 44). In ver. 45 the place is called simply Iyim, in A. V. Iim; because the context sufficiently defined the locality to be in Abarim.

I′yim. See preceding article.

Iz′har, I., in A. V. once **Iz′e-har** (Num. iii. 19) [bright, oil, especially olive oil].

A Levite, son of Kohath, and founder of a tribal family (Ex. vi. 18, 19; Num. iii. 19, 27; 1 Chron. vi. 18, 38). From him descended the rebel Korah (Num. xvi. 1).

Iz′har, II., in A. V. **Jezoar** [whiteness].

A man of Judah, family of Hezron, son of Ashhur (1 Chron. iv. 5-7). Another reading is Zohar.

Iz-li′ah, in A. V. **Jezliah** [perhaps, deliverance].

A Benjamite, son of Elpaal and descended from Shaharaim (1 Chron. viii. 18).

Iz-ra-hi′ah [Jehovah doth arise (cp. Is. lx. 2)].

A man of Issachar, family of Tola, and son of Uzzi (1 Chron. vii. 3).

Iz′ra-hite.

A member of the family, or an inhabitant of the town, of Izrah (1 Chron. xxvii. 8), perhaps the same as Ezrahite.

Iz′ri [fashioning, creative].

A Levite, son of Jeduthun, and head of the fourth course for the musical service of the sanctuary (1 Chron. xxv. 11). Called in ver. 3 Zeri (q. v.).

Iz-zi′ah, in A. V. **Jeziah** [perhaps, Jehovah exulteth].

A son of Parosh. He was induced by Ezra to put away his foreign wife (Ezra x. 25).

J

Ja′a-kan, in A. V. of 1 Chron. i. 42 **Jakan**. Written **Akan** in Gen. xxxvi. 27 [Horite name of uncertain meaning].

A descendant or prominent branch of the Horites of mount Seir, who were eventually dispossessed by the Edomites (Gen. xxxvi. 20, 21, 27; 1 Chron. i. 38, 42; Deut. ii. 12). At the time of the exodus sons of Jaakan constituted a tribe which occupied a district on the borders of Edom near mount Hor, where Aaron died. The Israelites encamped at certain of their wells (Deut. x. 6; Num. xx. 21–23; xxxiii. 31).

Ja-a-ko′bah [supplanting].

A Simeonite prince (1 Chron. iv. 36).

Ja′a-lah, or **Jaala** [doe, female ibex].

The founder of a family, ranked among the children of Solomon's servants (Ezra ii. 56; Neh. vii. 58).

Ja′a-lam. See JALAM.

Ja′a-nai, in R. V. **Janai** [perhaps, voracious or, possibly, Jehovah answers].

A Gadite chief (1 Chron. v. 12).

Ja′ar [a forest].

A proper name occurring in the margin of Psalm cxxxii. 6, R. V. It is believed to be the same as Kirjath-jearim.

Ja-a-re-or′e-gim. See JAIR II.

Ja-ar-e-shi′ah, in A. V. **Jaresiah** [Jehovah doth nourish or plant].

A Benjamite, son of Jeroham (1 Chron. viii. 27).

Ja′a-sai and **Ja′a-sau.** See JAASU.

Ja-a′si-el, in A. V. once **Jasiel** (1 Chron. xi. 47) [God maketh].

1. A Mesobaite, one of David's mighty men (1 Chron. xi. 47).

2. A son of Abner (1 Chron. xxvii. 21).

Ja′a-su, in A. V. **Jaasau**, in R. V. margin **Jaasai** [possibly, Jehovah maketh].

A son of Bani. He was induced by Ezra to put away his foreign wife (Ezra x. 37).

Ja-az-a-ni′ah [Jehovah doth hearken].

1. Son of a Maacathite (2 Kin. xxv. 23). See JEZANIAH.

2. A Rechabite, son of a certain Jeremiah, not the prophet of that name (Jer. xxxv. 3).

3. A son of Shaphan. He was a leader of idolatry in Ezekiel's time (Ezek. viii. 11).

4. A son of Azzur and prince of Judah, who was seen by Ezekiel in vision (Ezek. xi. 1; cp. viii. 1, 3; xi. 24).

Ja′a-zer. See JAZER.

Ja-a-zi′ah [Jehovah consoleth].

A Levite, registered as head of a father's house with the family of Merari (1 Chron. xxiv. 26, 27), and perhaps called his son or descendant (Beno). No hint is elsewhere given of Merari having a third son. Can Jaaziah represent the house of the dead Eleazar (28; cp. xxiii. 22), or is the passage 26ᵇ, 27 an interpolation?

Ja-a′zi-el or **Aziel** [God consoleth].

A Levite of the second rank, one of the musicians who played on the psaltery at the removal of the ark from the house of Obed-edom, and afterwards as a regular duty in the tent at Jerusalem (1 Chron. xv. 18, 20; and probably xvi. 5). In the last passage the form Jeiel is probably a copyist's error.

Ja′bal [in Hebrew a stream, a river].

Son of the Cainite Lamech, by his wife Adah. He was the father of such as dwell in tents and have cattle (Gen. iv. 20).

Jab′bok [effusion].

An eastern tributary of the Jordan. Jacob forded it on his way back from Mesopotamia (Gen. xxxii. 22). Rising near Rabbath Ammon, it flows for 12 miles from that town toward the northeast and then sweeps around toward the northwest. After holding this course for about 15 miles it turns westward, and for 17 miles flows through a valley which cleaves mount Gilead in twain. On emerging into the valley of the Jordan it bends toward the southwest and enters the Jordan at a point about 43 miles south of the sea of Galilee and 23 miles north of the Dead Sea. It is now known as the nahr ez-Zerka or blue river; and the gorge through which it flows is called the wady ez-Zerka. The Jabbok was a recognized frontier. It formed the western boundary of the Ammonites, and separated them from the Amorite kingdom of Sihon and later from the tribe of Gad. It divided mount Gilead into two parts, of which the southern was held by Sihon before the Israelite conquest, and afterwards was assigned to Gad, while the northern was possessed by

The Brook Jabbok at its confluence with the Jordan River.

Og and passed from him to the half tribe of Manasseh (Num. xxi. 24; Deut. ii. 36, 37; iii. 12, 13, 16; Josh. xii. 2-6).

Ja′besh [dry].
1. A town. See JABESH-GILEAD.
2. Father of king Shallum (2 Kin. xv. 10).

Ja-besh-gil′e-ad [Jabesh of Gilead].
A town of Gilead. It is believed to have stood at or near ed-Deir, 9½ miles southeast and in full view of Beth-shean on the other side of the river. Ed-Deir is in the wady el-Yabis, which seems to preserve the old name Jabesh. In the war waged against Benjamin in the days of the judges on account of the matter of the Levite and his concubine, none of the men of Jabesh-gilead took part. For this indifference to a national sin, they were condemned to utter destruction. Only 400 unmarried girls were saved alive and given for wives to 400 of the remaining men of Benjamin (Judg. xxi. 8-15). The place was soon reoccupied. Shortly after Saul had been chosen king, Nahash, king of the Ammonites, besieged Jabesh-gilead. The town was sore pressed; and the Ammonite king doomed every man to the loss of the right eye on the surrender of the town. This was intended as an insult to the whole Israelite nation. Saul raised the siege by defeating the besieging army (1 Sam. xi. 1-11). The men of the town remembered their deliverer with gratitude, and when, after the battle of Gilboa, his headless body, with those of his sons, was fastened to the wall of Beth-shean, they crossed the Jordan, carried off the corpses, burnt them and buried the bones in the vicinity of Jabesh-gilead (xxxi. 11-13; 1 Chron. x. 11, 12) from which they were ultimately removed to the sepulcher of Kish (2 Sam. xxi. 12-14). David

sent the men of Jabesh his personal thanks for what they had done (ii. 4-7).

Ja′bez [he makes sorrow].
1. A man of Judah, whose mother gave him the name Jabez, because she bore him in sorrow. He was more honorable than his brethren. He prayed that God would enlarge the boundary of his possessions, besides keeping him from evil. God granted his request (1 Chron. iv. 9, 10).
2. A place, doubtless in Judah, where families of scribes dwelt (1 Chron. ii. 55).

Ja′bin [he discerneth, intelligent].
1. A Canaanite, king of Hazor in Galilee and its dependent towns and the head of the confederacy of northern and central kings whom Joshua defeated at the waters of Merom. After the battle the Israelites took and burned Hazor and slew its king (Josh. xi. 1-14).
2. Another king of Canaan who reigned at Hazor, probably a lineal descendant of the first (Judg. iv. 2). He, too, had kings fighting under him (v. 19). He oppressed the Israelites twenty years; but at length his commander-in-chief Sisera was defeated by Barak at the river Kishon and afterwards murdered. Jabin continued the war, but was ultimately destroyed (iv. 2-24).

Jab′ne-el [God doth cause to be built].
1. A town on the northern border of Judah (Josh. xv. 5, 11). It is the same place as the Philistine city of Jabneh, the wall of which was broken down by Uzziah (2 Chron. xxvi. 6); and it was known later as Jamnia (1 Mac. iv. 15; v. 58; 2 Mac. xii. 8, 9). It is represented by the village of Yebnah, about 4 miles inland from the Mediterranean, and 9 northeast by north of Ashdod.
2. A frontier town of Naphtali (Josh. xix. 33). Conder identifies it with the ruin Yemma, about 7 miles south by west of Tiberias. More commonly it is identified with Jamnia or Jamnith, a village of upper Galilee, built on a rocky height and fortified by Josephus (Life 37; War. ii. 20, 6); and whose site is sought in the neighborhood of the plain of Huleh and Banias (War ii. 6, 3; but text is uncertain).

Jab′neh [he causes to be built]. See JABNEEL.

Ja′can, in A. V. **Jachan** [troublous].
A Gadite, probably head of a father's house (1 Chron. v. 13).

Ja′chin [he doth establish].
1. A son of Simeon, and founder of a tribal family (Gen. xlvi. 10; Ex. vi. 15; Num. xxvi. 12). Called Jarib in 1 Chron. iv. 24, which is doubtless due to an erroneous reading of the text by a copyist.
2. A descendant of Aaron. In the time of David, his family was made the twenty-first of the courses into which the sacerdotal body was divided (1 Chron. xxiv. 17). It dwelt at

Jerusalem, according to the probable meaning of ix. 10; but it is not at all certain that the priest Jachin, who was resident at Jerusalem after the captivity, was of this family (Neh. xi. 10).

3. The right-hand pillar of two set up in the porch of Solomon's temple (1 Kin. vii. 15–22), probably as a symbol of firmness. See BOAZ.

Ja′cinth. See HYACINTH and LIGURE.

Jack′al.

The rendering in the R. V. of the Hebrew plurals *Tannim* and *Tannoth*, which in the A. V. are regularly translated by dragon (q. v.). The creature intended is a mammal (Lam. iv. 3, in A. V. sea monsters) and dwells in the wilderness (Is. xxxv. 7; xliii. 20) and in deserted places (xxxiv. 13, 14; Jer. xlix. 33; li. 37).

The jackal (*Canis aureus*) is, it will be seen, placed in the dog genus *Canis*. It differs from the dog in its long and pointed muzzle. The name *aureus*, golden, refers to the color of the under fur, which is brownish yellow, mottled with black, gray, and brown hairs. Its length is about thirty inches, and its height at the shoulder seventeen. It hunts in packs, and feeds chiefly on carrion, though it carries off and devours children when opportunity arises. It has been called the lion's provider, the opinion being entertained that when its voice is heard, the lion, following on, tries to claim his share of the prey. It raises the most unearthly yell of all of its compeers. It is found throughout Palestine, especially frequenting ruins. See also FOX; and for the jackal's well, see DRAGON'S WELL.

Ja′cob [he supplanteth, supplanter].

A son of Isaac and Rebekah, a twin with Esau, but born a short time after him, and therefore considered the younger brother (Gen. xxv. 21–26). He was born when his father was sixty years old (26). As he grew he became a quiet, inoffensive man, dwelling in tents (27). He was his mother's favorite, while the father preferred Esau (28). As Esau came in from hunting, faint with hunger, Jacob chanced to have pottage of lentils ready boiled, but selfishly forbore to relieve his brother's necessities till he had compelled him first to surrender the privilege of his birthright (29–34). Positive fraud followed. When Isaac was about 137 years old and nearly blind, Rebekah induced Jacob to dress himself in Esau's raiment, make his neck and hands artificially hairy, and passing himself off as Esau, obtain from Isaac, who thought himself near death, the blessing belonging to the birthright. Esau recalled the first wrong when this second one was perpetrated, and resolved that when his father died, he would kill his brother (xxvii. 1–41). Rebekah heard the threat, and to give time for Esau's wrath to cool, sent Jacob away to her relatives in Haran, on the pretext of seeking a wife. While on this journey he had the night vision in which a ladder connected earth and heaven, angels ascended and descended, and God standing above assured him of the covenant blessing (xxvii. 42–46; xxviii. 1–22). Jacob sojourned in Paddan-aram at least twenty years, while he was in Laban's employ, serving him fourteen years for his two daughters, Leah and Rachel, and six for a payment in cattle. During this period in Haran there were born to him eleven sons: by Leah six, Reuben, Simeon, Levi, Judah, Issachar, and Zebulun, besides a daughter, Dinah; by Bilhah, Rachel's maid, two, Dan and Naphtali; by Zilpah, Leah's maid, two, Gad and Asher; and by Rachel one, Joseph (xxix., xxx.). The last was born when Jacob was ninety or ninety-one years of age (cp. xlvii. 9 with xli. 46, 47, 54; xlv. 11). Six years later, perceiving that Laban and his sons, envying his prosperity, were turning against him, he became alarmed. While pasturing his flocks, probably three days from Haran (xxx. 36; xxxi. 22) on the Euphrates, he sent for his wives (xxxi. 4), crossed the river, and fled with his family and possessions toward Canaan (21). Three days later Laban was informed of Jacob's flight. He was busy shearing his sheep; but he presently gathered his male relatives, started in pursuit of the fugitives, and after a week's journey by forced marches overtook them on mount Gilead, apparently between the Yarmuk and the Jabbok, scant 300 miles from the Euphrates, at least ten days after Jacob's departure and probably longer, for Laban was busy shearing sheep when he received information of the flight and was unprepared for the journey. God shielded Jacob from injury, and a reconciliation and a treaty of amity between the alienated parties took place. A heap of stones was erected and a covenant meal eaten to establish the agreement that neither party should pass that point to attack the other (xxxi.). Jacob had manifestations of the divine favor at Mahanaim and on the Jabbok, where a man wrestled with him until break of day, showed his superiority to Jacob by disabling him by a touch, and before departing blessed him, saying: "Thy name shall be called no more Jacob, but Israel; for thou hast striven with God and with men, and hast prevailed." And Jacob called the name of that place Peniel, face of God, for he said: "I have seen God face to face, and my life is preserved" (xxxii. 22–32; cp. the name xxxiii. 20; Hosea xii. 4). This event proved a crisis in the life of Jacob. Heretofore he had been trusting to his own strength and shrewdness for success. He now learns that his own strength is of no avail in wrestling with God and that he must resort to prayer for the blessing which he cannot do without. Henceforth the record of his worshiping becomes frequent. Before he crossed the Jordan, he met Esau, and obtained forgiveness for the wrongs which had so long made him an exile. Then the brothers parted, Esau returning to mount Seir and Jacob going to Canaan (xxxiii. 1–18). Jacob sojourned in Canaan at Shechem, where he bought a parcel of ground from the chief of Shechem, on which he pitched his camp and erected an altar (xxxiii. 18–20). While here his daughter Dinah was illtreated by the chief's son. The deed was avenged by two of Jacob's sons, Simeon and Levi, and the other sons joined in spoiling the town. Jacob feared the consequences of this act; but since his sons had captured the place, slain the males, appropriated the wealth, and made captive the women and children, he recognized the conquest of the town and the consequent ownership of it by his tribe (xlviii. 22; cp. xxxvii. 12). From Shechem Jacob removed to Beth-el. There Deborah died and was buried (xxxv. 6–8); see DEBORAH. There also, at the place where God had appeared to him as he went to Paddan-aram, God appeared to him again when he came back from Paddan-aram (xxxv. 9; xxviii. 10–22), emphasized the change of his name to Israel (without, of course, finding it necessary to tell again why the new name had been given at the Jabbok) and confirmed the blessing of the Abrahamic covenant to him. As he drew near to Bethlehem on his way to Hebron, his twelfth and last son, Benjamin, was born, and his beloved Rachel died (9–20). At length Jacob came to his father Isaac at Mamre (27). Isaac died about twenty-three years later, and was buried by Esau and Jacob (28, 29). Jacob seems to have dwelt at Mamre during the next thirty-three years; for he was at Hebron about ten years after his return (xxxvii. 14; cp. 2), and he was evidently still there when he was summoned to go down to Egypt (xlvi. 1). Jacob was 130 years old when he went to Egypt (xlvii. 9), and he lived there seventeen years. He gave a special blessing, first to Joseph's children and then to his own, after which he died at the age of 147 (xlvii. 28; xlviii.: xlix.). His body was embalmed, taken to Canaan with much pomp, and interred in the cave of Machpelah (l. 1–14). Jacob had glaring faults of character. For his sins he suffered severely, and in his old age he was sorely chastened by the loss of Joseph. In his later life he acknowledged, at least tacitly, the sinfulness of his earlier career and his failure to walk before God, and he spoke only of God's grace (xlviii. 15, 16). He was animated also in his latter days by unwavering faith in God (21; Heb. xi. 21).

The Hebrew nation, as descended from Jacob, is often called in Scripture the children of Israel (Ex. xiv. 16, 29; xv. 1, etc.). The prophets often use Jacob and Israel as parallel names in their poetic couplets (Deut. xxxiii. 10; Is. xliii. 1, 22; xliv. 1). See ISRAEL.

Jacob's well, beside or on the edge of which Jesus sat when conversing with the woman of Samaria, was at Sychar, near to the parcel of ground that Jacob gave to his son Joseph. "Jacob," the woman of Samaria said, "drank

Jacob's well, near Sychar.

Entrances to Jacob's well seen through an opening in the unfinished church built at the site.

thereof himself, and his sons, and his cattle" (John iv. 5, 6, 12; cp. Gen. xxxiii. 18–20; xxxvii. 12). A tradition, going back as far as the time of the Bordeaux pilgrim, A. D. 333, and accepted by Jews, Samaritans, Christians, and Mohammedans, identifies Jacob's well with the Bîr Ya'kûb. It is situated at the eastern mouth of the valley between mount Ebal on the north and mount Gerizim on the south, about 2 miles eastsoutheast from Nablus, the modern Shechem, and half a mile southsouthwest of 'Askar, believed by many to be Sychar. Maundrell, generally very accurate, made its diameter 9 feet and its depth 105. Dr. John Wilson, measuring a line with which a boy was let down into it with a light in 1843, determined it to be 75 feet deep. Conder reported its depth in 1875 as 75 feet. It is less deep now than formerly, because somewhat choked with rubbish. The water is good, but is not easy to reach (John iv. 11). The shaft is lined with masonry in the upper part. The lower part is cut through soft limestone. A low subterranean vault, 20 feet long from east to west and 10 broad, the crypt of an ancient Christian church, is built over the well, the mouth of which is contracted and covered with one or more large stones. There is a fine fountain a little to the west, and many others in the valley. The well, however, was dug, perhaps, because the fountains were appropriated. It is in the vicinity of what from the fourth century has been popularly considered to be Joseph's tomb.

For Jacob-el and Joseph-el, see JOSEPH.

Ja'da [wise].

A son of Onam, a man of Judah, family of Hezron, house of Jerahmeel (1 Chron. ii.28,32)

Ja'dau. See IDDO II.

Jad-du'a [known].

1. One of the chiefs of the people who, with Nehemiah, sealed the covenant (Neh. x. 21).

2. A high priest, son of Jonathan and the fifth in descent from the high priest Jeshua, who returned with Zerubbabel from Babylon (Neh. xii. 11, 22). He was probably a youth in the reign of Darius Nothus, and survived Darius Codomannus, the Persian sovereign defeated by Alexander the Great at Arbela in 331 B. C. See HIGH PRIEST.

Ja'don [he ruleth, judgeth, or abideth].

A Meronothite, who repaired part of the wall of Jerusalem after the captivity (Neh. iii. 7)

Ja'el [wild goat, ibex].

The wife of Heber the Kenite (Judg. iv. 17). Sisera, Jabin's general, trusting to the peace subsisting between his royal master and Heber, fled to her tent after he was defeated by Barak. On his approach Jael went out, invited him to enter, and gave him milk to relieve his thirst. But as he lay sleeping in the tent, she took a hammer and drove a tent pin through his temples, fixing his

head to the ground. When the victorious Barak passed, she called him in to see what she had done (Judg. iv. 11–22). Deborah highly commended the deed of Jael (v. 24–27), though it was cruel and treacherous. It reveals a rudeness of manners and a hardness of character which found frequent exemplification in those early times.

In v. 6 a judge named Jael may be referred to, who is not elsewhere mentioned. A simpler explanation is that Deborah means that although the heroic woman Jael was then living, yet no one ventured to undertake the deliverance of Israel until Deborah arose.

Ja'gur [a lodging, an inn].

A town in the extreme south of Judah (Josh. xv. 21). Site unknown.

Jah.

A form of Jehovah occurring in poetry (Ps. lxviii. 4; R. V. of lxxxix. 8). In various other places Jah, or, rather, Yah in Hebrew is rendered Lord in the A. V. and R. V. In the Hebrew sometimes Jah and Jehovah stand together, Jah first (Is. xii. 2 and xxvi. 4, margin of R. V.).

Ja'hath [perhaps, grasping; cp. Mahath].

1. A man of Judah, family of Hezron, descended through Shobal (1 Chron. iv. 2; cp. ii. 19, 50).

2. A son of Libni, a Levite, family of Gershom (1 Chron. vi. 20, and perhaps 43). The reference in ver. 43 may belong to the succeeding.

3. A Levite, family of Gershom and head of a subdivision of the house of Shimei (1 Chron. xxiii. 10).

4. A Levite, family of Kohath, house of Izhar (1 Chron. xxiv. 22).

5. A Merarite Levite, an overseer of the workmen engaged in repairing the temple during Josiah's reign (2 Chron. xxxiv. 12).

Ja'haz and **Jahzah**, in A. V. once **Jahaza** (Josh. xiii. 18), and twice **Jahazah** (Josh. xxi. 36; Jer. xlviii. 21) [a place trodden under foot, an open space].

A place in the plain of Moab (Jer. xlviii. 21) where Sihon, king of the Amorites, was defeated by the Israelites (Num. xxi. 23; Deut. ii. 32; Judg. xi. 20). It was assigned to the Reubenites (Josh. xiii. 18), and set apart for the Merarite Levites (Josh. xxi. 36; 1 Chron. vi. 78). It was taken from Israel by Mesha, king of Moab (Moabite Stone, 18–20), and it was held by Moab in the time of Isaiah and Jeremiah (Is. xv. 4; Jer. xlviii. 21, 34). Its site is unknown.

Ja-ha-zi'ah. See JAHZEIAH.

Ja-ha'zi-el [God seeth].

1. A Levite, family of Kohath, house of Hebron (1 Chron. xxiii. 19).

2. One of the Benjamite warriors who joined David at Ziklag (1 Chron. xii. 4).

3. A priest in David's reign who was employed to sound a trumpet in the sanctuary (1 Chron. xvi. 6).

4. A Levite, son of Zechariah of the Asaph family, who prophesied in the time of Jehoshaphat (2 Chron. xx. 14).

5. Father of a chief of the people who returned from Babylon (Ezra viii. 5).

Jah'dai [perhaps, he directeth or directive].

A man of Judah, enrolled with Caleb's posterity (1 Chron ii. 47).

Jah'di-el [God maketh glad].

A leading man in the half tribe of Manasseh east of the Jordan (1 Chron. v. 24).

Jah'do [union].

A Gadite, son of Buz (1 Chron. v. 14).

Jah'le-el [God doth grievously afflict].

A son of Zebulun, and founder of a tribal family (Gen. xlvi. 14; Num. xxvi. 26).

Jah'mai [perhaps, lusty].

A prince of Issachar, of the family of Tola (1 Chron. vii. 2).

Jah'zah. See JAHAZ.

Jah'ze-el and **Jahziel** [God distributeth].

A son of Naphtali, and founder of a tribal family (Gen. xlvi. 24; Num. xxvi. 48; 1 Chron. vii. 13).

Jah-ze'iah, in A. V. **Jahaziah** [Jehovah seeth].

A son of Tikvah who opposed the proposition that the Jews put away their foreign wives (Ezra x. 15, R. V.); but see margin.

Jah'ze-rah [may he lead back].

A priest descended from Immer (1 Chron. ix. 12).

Jah'zi-el. See JAHZEEL.

Ja'ir, I. [he enlighteneth].

1. A son of Segub and grandson of Hezron, of the tribe of Judah, and his wife, who was of the family of Machir, of the tribe of Manasseh (1 Chron. ii. 21, 22). He was reckoned with the tribe of Manasseh (v. 23; Num. xxxii. 41; Deut. iii. 14). At the time of the conquest by the Israelites under Moses of the country east of the Jordan, he took villages in the Argob, on the border of Bashan and Gilead, and called them Havvoth-jair (q. v.).

2. A Gileadite who judged Israel twenty-two years, succeeding or surviving Tola in office. Each of his thirty sons had an ass for riding purposes, which in that age was an indication of standing in the community. They also had thirty cities, called Havvoth-jair. He may have belonged to the family of the earlier Jair (cp. perhaps JAIRITE), and have inherited prerogatives connected with the Havvoth-jair, or have used his influence to place his sons over these encampments (Judg. x. 3–5).

3. A Benjamite, Mordecai's father or remoter ancestor (Esth. ii. 5).

Ja'ir, II. [he arouseth].

Father of Elhanan (1 Chron. xx. 5); called in 2 Sam. xxi. 19, Jaare-oregim, where oregim has gotten into the text by error from the line below.

Ja'ir-ite.

A descendant of some Jair or other, whose name was written as is that of Jair, I. (2 Sam. xx. 26).

Ja-i'rus [Greek form of Jair].

A ruler of the synagogue (Mark v. 22; Luke viii. 41), probably at Capernaum. His young daughter lay at the point of death; and he went to Jesus, beseeching him to heal her. On the way to the house word reached them that the child was dead (Mark v. 23, 24, 35; Luke viii. 42, 49); but the father, with confidence in Jesus' power, still entreated (Mat. ix. 18), and Jesus told him to put away all fear and to trust him (Mark v. 36; Luke viii. 50). Entering the house with Peter, James, and John (Mark v. 37; Luke viii. 51; cp. Mat. ix. 19) he found it full of noisy professional mourners, and rebuked them and said: "The damsel is not dead, but sleepeth" (Mat. ix. 24; Mark v. 39; Luke viii. 52). He used the word sleep as he did afterwards in the case of Lazarus (John xi. 11–14). Taking the three disciples and the parents (Mark v. 40), he went into the chamber where the dead child lay (40; Mat. ix. 25), took her by the hand, and said in the language of the people *T*elitha' kumi, Maid, arise (Mark v. 41; cp. Mat. ix. 25; Luke viii. 54). She obeyed. He bade the parents not to tell what had taken place (Mark v. 43; Luke viii. 56). But such a miracle could not be kept from public knowledge (Mat. ix. 26).

Ja'kan. See JAAKAN.

Ja'keh [pious].

The father of that Agur whose words are recorded in Prov. xxx. In the Hebrew Bible his name is followed by the words *Hammassa'*, translated in the A. V. the prophecy, and in the R. V. the oracle. The margin of the R. V. translates the title Jakeh of Massa, and refers to Gen. xxv. 14, where Massa figures as a son of Ishmael.

Ja'kim [he raises up].

1. A descendant of Aaron. His family grew to a father's house and was made the twelfth of the twenty-four courses into which David divided the priests (1 Chron. xxiv. 12).

2. A Benjamite (1 Chron. viii. 19).

Ja'lam, in A. V. **Jaalam** [perhaps, hidden or pertaining to a wild goat].

A son of Esau by his wife Oholibamah. He became a chieftain of Edom (Gen. xxxvi. 5, 18; 1 Chron. i. 35).

Ja'lon [perhaps, obstinate].

A son of Ezrah, registered with the tribe of Judah (1 Chron. iv. 17).

Jam'bres [perhaps, opposer].

One of two Egyptian magicians who attempted to counterwork Moses (2 Tim. iii. 8). See JANNES.

Jam'bri.

Founder of a family which dwelt at Medeba

(1 Mac. ix. 36, 37; Antiq. xiii. 1, 2). The orthography is uncertain. It may represent the Hebrew name Omri or Imri; and even Amorite has been conjectured.

James [a form of the name Jacob].

1. James the son of Zebedee (Mat. iv. 21; x. 2; Mark i. 19; iii. 17), and brother of the apostle John (Mat. xvii. 1; Mark iii. 17; v. 37; Acts xii. 2), one of the earliest disciples (Mat. iv. 21; Mark i. 19, 29; cp. John i. 40, 41) and most trusted apostles (Mat. xvii. 1; Mark v. 37; ix. 2; xiii. 3; xiv. 33; Luke viii. 51; ix. 28) of our Lord. Of his birthplace or early home we are told nothing. His occupation as a fisherman on the sea of Galilee, in partnership with Peter and Andrew (Luke v. 10), might seem to suggest a contiguous locality. But the fishery of the sea of Galilee was expressly kept free for every Israelite, and a social difference between the sons of Zebedee and the sons of Jonas may be implied in the facts that the former kept hired servants (Mark i. 20), and that John at least was known to the high priest (John xviii. 16) and may have had a house in Jerusalem (xix. 27). His father, Zebedee, appears only once in the pages of the gospels (Mat. iv. 21; Mark i. 19), where he raises no obstacle to his sons' following Jesus. From Mat. xxvii. 56, compared with Mark xv. 40; xvi. 1 and with John xix. 25, it seems reasonable to infer that his mother was named Salome and was sister to the mother of Jesus: in which case James would be a near kinsman of Jesus, and like him of Davidic descent. His name occurs only in the synoptic gospels and the book of The Acts, although he is alluded to twice in the Gospel of John (i. 40 41; xxi. 2). It never occurs apart from that of John, which it ordinarily precedes (Mat. iv. 21; x. 2; xvii. 1; Mark i. 19, 29; iii. 17; v. 37; ix. 2; x. 35, 41; xiii. 3; xiv. 33; Luke v. 10; vi. 14; ix. 54), while John is designated as the brother of James (Mat. iv. 21; x. 2: xvii. 1; Mark i. 19; iii. 17; v. 37). From this it has been inferred that he was the older brother; while the occasional reverse usage in Luke (viii. 51, R. V.; ix. 28) and Acts (i. 13, R. V.; xii. 2 only) is supposed to arise from John's greater prominence in the apostolical circle. Along with John, he received from Christ the surname Boanerges or son of thunder (Mark iii. 17), and along with him earned his Master's rebuke for the fierceness of his anger against the Samaritan village which would not receive Jesus (Luke ix. 55), and the indignation of his fellow apostles for his ambitious self-seeking (Mark x. 41). After the crucifixion we find him with the other apostles in Galilee (John xxi. 2), and in Jerusalem (Acts i. 13), and his record closes with his death by the sword at the hands of Herod Agrippa I., probably A. D. 44 (xii. 2). He was the first of the apostolic band to seal his testimony with his blood.

2. James the son of Alphæus and one of the apostles of our Lord (Mat. x. 3; Mark iii. 18; Luke vi. 15; Acts i. 13). Nothing further is certainly known of him. It is natural, however, as it has been usual, to assume that the James of Mat. xxvii. 56; Mark xv. 40; xvi. 1; Luke xxiv. 10 is this James: in which case we may learn that he bore the surname of "the little" (E. V., "the less"), possibly with reference to his stature (Mark xv. 40); that his mother was called Mary, and was one of the women who accompanied Christ; and that he had a brother named Joses. Levi, or Matthew, who, according to Mark ii. 14, was son of Alphæus, may be another brother: and it is possible to fill in the ellipsis of Luke vi. 16; Acts i. 13 so as to make the apostle Judas another brother. It is possible further to identify the Mary of Clopas of John xix. 25 with Mary the mother of James; and it is then possible, though scarcely natural, to read John xix. 25 as declaring that Mary of Clopas was Jesus' mother's sister. By this combination, James, the son of Alphæus, would be made out to be the cousin-german of our Lord. It is common, on this assumption, to take still another step, and, on the ground of the similarity between the names of the Lord's brethren and those of the sons of Alphæus, so obtained, to suppose that this near relative of our Lord's is intended by "James the Lord's brother." The whole construction is, however, very insecure, and does not seem to satisfy the biblical facts.

3. James, the Lord's brother (Mat. xiii. 55; Mark vi. 3; Gal. i. 19), and the head of the church at Jerusalem in the apostolic age (Acts xii. 17; xv. 13; xxi. 18; Gal. i. 19; ii. 9, 12). This James is mentioned by name only twice in the gospels (Mat. xiii. 55; Mark vi. 3), but the outlines of his life may be traced by means of the notices of the "brethren of the Lord," who constituted a distinct class, both during our Lord's life, when they did not believe on him (John vii. 5), and after his resurrection, when they are found among his followers (Acts i. 14). The exact relationship which these "brethren" bore to our Lord has always been a matter of dispute. Some, identifying them with the sons of Alphæus, represent them as his cousins. Others think of them as his half-brothers, children of Joseph by a former marriage. As they always appear with Mary, living and journeying with her and holding just such relations with her as would naturally be borne by her children (Mat. xii. 46, 47; Luke viii. 19; John ii. 12), there is no reason to question the natural implication that they were Jesus' own brothers. As James' name stands first in the lists (Mat. xiii. 55; Mark vi. 3), it is probable that he was the oldest of our Lord's brothers. He doubtless shared their unbelief (John vii. 5), and doubtless also their natural anxieties in his behalf (Mark iii. 31, seq.). When or how the change was wrought in him by which he became a servant of

Christ (Acts i. 14; Jas. i. 1) we are not told: possibly, as in the case of Paul, his conversion was due to a special appearance of the risen Lord (1 Cor. xv. 7). From the very first organization of the church in Jerusalem, James appears as its head (Acts xii. 17; xv. 13; xxi. 18; Gal. i. 19; ii. 9, 12). As early as A. D. 40, when Paul first visited Jerusalem after his conversion, James' position was such that Paul felt it necessary to name him along with Peter as having been seen by him (Gal. i. 19). The reference of Acts xii. 17 (A. D. 44), where James is clearly the official head of "the brethren," as well as that of xxi. 18 (A. D. 58), where he seems to stand at the head of the elders of the church (cp. xv. 6), enable us to estimate wherein his preëminence consisted. As he was not an apostle (the R. V. margin gives the correct translation of Gal. i. 19), we cannot be far wrong in assuming that he was the head of the board of elders of the church at Jerusalem; that is, what we should call the "pastor" of that church. See ELDER. As such, his name stands for the church of Jerusalem (Gal. ii. 12), of which he was the natural representative (Acts xii. 17; xv. 13; xxi. 18); and visitors to the church made themselves known in the first instance to him and laid their errand before him (xii. 17; xxi. 18; Gal. i. 19; ii. 9). In his position, James' life-work was naturally to smooth the passage of Jews over to Christianity. That he stood on the same platform of faith with Paul is apparent not only from Paul's assertion in Gal. ii. 9, but also from James' remarks recorded in Acts xv. 13; xxi. 20. But on both occasions he speaks also in behalf of the Jewish-Christian conscience, and it is equally apparent that, as Paul became as all men to all men because he was sent to all, James became as a Jew to Jews because he was sent to Jews. The use of his name by intense Judaizers (Gal. ii. 12, and the later Clementine literature) is thus explicable, as also the admiration which is said to have been conceived for him by the Jews themselves, who are reported to have given him the surname of "the just" (Eusebius, H. E. ii. 23). After Acts xxi. 18 (A. D. 58) we meet no further reference to James in the N. T. Secular history tells us, however, that he was martyred in a popular outbreak of the Jews in the interregnum between the death of the procurator Festus and the appointment of his successor, i. e., A. D. 62 (Antiq. xx. 9, 1; Eusebius, H. E. ii. 23).

4. James, the father or brother of the apostle Judas (Luke vi. 16; Acts i. 13). Nothing further is known of him.   B. B. W.

James, E-pis'tle of.

This letter does not announce itself as the production of an apostle, but describes its author simply as James, a bond-servant of God and of the Lord Jesus Christ (i. 1, R. V. margin). It is most natural to think of

James, the Lord's brother, as meant, and all the characteristics of the letter agree with this attribution. The letter bears a distinct flavor of primitiveness: the Christian place of worship is still spoken of as a synagogue (ii. 2); Christians are not sharply discriminated from Jews (i. 1); the sins rebuked and errors corrected are such as would naturally spring up in a Jewish soil; while there is not a trace of the controversies which already in the sixth decade of the first Christian century were distracting the whole church. It is, therefore, usually dated about A. D. 45, and considered the earliest of the N. T. writings. It is addressed to the twelve tribes which are of the Dispersion (i. 1. R. V.), that is, not to the dispersed Jews, nor yet to the whole Christian church, considered as the spiritual Israel, but, probably, to the Christians (ii. 1, 5, 7; v. 7) among the Jewish Dispersion, as the Jews dwelling outside the Holy Land were technically called (John vii. 35; cp. 2 Mac. i. 27). The object of its writing was to reform and correct those sins and errors to which its lately Christianized Jewish readers continued to be liable, and to encourage them in the sore trials to which they were exposed.

After the address (i. 1), James first consoles his readers in their trials and exhorts them to steadfastness, pointing out at the same time the source of the temptation to apostasy (i. 2–21). He proceeds then to warn them against mere word-service, explaining what is meant by true faith (i. 22–27), what will be the effect of true faith on the prevalent sin of respect of persons (ii. 1–13), and how a true faith evinces itself (ii. 14–26). Exhortations against hasty assumption and misuse of the functions of religious teachers and exposure of their root in a jealous heart follow (iii. 1–18); and then reproofs of contentiousness (iv. 1–12) and self-sufficiency (iv. 13–v. 6). The epistle closes with exhortations to patience in suffering (v. 7–12) and to prayer as the sufficient resource of the Christian in every need (13–18), along with a final declaration of the joy of Christian propagandism (19–20).

The linguistic and rhetorical character of the epistle is very high. It is written in Greek which is surpassed in purity by that of no N. T. writings except those of Luke, and in a strikingly elevated and picturesque style resembling that of the Hebrew prophets. It contains more imagery drawn from nature than all the epistles of Paul, in this recalling the manner of our Lord's synoptic speeches, to which it presents numerous parallels. The tone and matter of its teaching are appropriate to its early date and the recent emergence of its readers from Judaism. The section on faith and works (ii. 14–26) has often been misapprehended as a polemic against Paul's doctrine of justification by faith, or at least as a corrective of perversions of that doctrine. It is really a rebuke of a prevalent Jewish notion—that mere intellectual assent to divine teaching is all that is necessary for salvation. James pointedly as Paul makes faith the instrument of salvation (ii. 22, 23), and Paul as firmly as James insists that the only saving faith is the faith that works (Gal. v. 6).

There is clear evidence of the use of this epistle by the church from the very earliest times. Origen, however, writing early in the third century, is the first writer to quote it explicitly by name; and there was a period during which the Latin writers seem to have used it little. Luther, not fully seeing its harmony with Paul, permitted himself to speak unguardedly about it. It is historically indicated as an integral portion of the sacred canon.   B. B. W.

Ja'min [the right hand, prosperity].
1. A son of Simeon and founder of a tribal family (Gen. xlvi. 10; Ex. vi. 15; Num. xxvi. 12).
2. A man of Judah, family of Jerahmeel (1 Chron. ii. 27).
3. One of the Levites who, under the direction of Ezra, read the law of God to the people and caused them to understand it (Neh. viii. 7, 8).

Jam'lech [let him constitute a king].
A Simeonite prince (1 Chron. iv. 34).

Jam'ni-a. See JABNEEL.

Ja'nai. See JAANAI.

Ja'nim, in A. V. **Janum** [sleep].
A village in the hill country of Judah [Josh. xv. 53].; doubtless to the west or southwest of Hebron.

Jan'nai, in A. V. **Janna.**
The father of Melchi in the ancestry of Christ (Luke iii. 24).

Jan'nes.
One of two Egyptian magicians who attempted to counterwork Moses, Jambres being the other (2 Tim. iii. 8). The reference is to the occurrences described in Ex. vii. 11, 12, 22; viii. 7, 18, 19; and ix. 11, where, however, the names of the magicians are not given nor their number. They were known to late Jewish tradition, being found in the Targum of the pseudo-Jonathan. The Talmud mentions Johana and Mamre. Jambres is believed to be the Greek form of Jamreh, opposer. Mamre, from the same root, is used in the Talmud for one who resists the decisions of the sanhedrin. Jannes is perhaps a corruption of Johanan (cp. Jannæus), but in sound suggests the Hebrew Yani', he hinders or dissuades.

Ja-no'ah, and **Ja-no'hah** in A. V. of Joshua [rest, quiet].
1. A town of Naphtali, captured by Tiglath-pileser (2 Kin. xv. 29). Not identified. Yânûh, 6½ miles east by south of Tyre, is not in the district described.
2. A town on the boundary line of Ephraim

(Josh. xvi. 6, 7). It has been fixed at Yânûn, 7 miles S. E. of Shechem.

Ja'num. See JANIM.

Ja'pheth [beauty, or let him enlarge].
A son of Noah, and doubtless one of the two elder sons (Gen. x. 21; cp. ix. 24), born about Noah's five hundredth year (v. 32; vi. 10); see NOAH. At the time of the deluge he was married, but had no children with him in the ark (vii. 7; 1 Pet. iii. 20). On the occasion of Noah's drunkenness, Japheth acted to him in a dutiful manner, and in consequence received a blessing, the essential part of which was that he should receive large territory and enjoy free action and that he should occupy the tents of Shem, not in the sense of conquering the Semites, but of dwelling with them in peace and sharing their privileges (Gen. ix. 20–27). "The language of the N. T. is the speech of Japheth entered into the tents of Shem, the gospel is the proclamation of salvation translated out of Semitic into Japhetic, and the converted heathen are for the most part Japhetic people dwelling in the tents of Shem" (Delitzsch). Japheth was the progenitor of the people who inhabited, or perhaps in some cases conquered and annexed, Gomer, Magog, Madai, Javan, Tubal, Meshech, and Tiras (Gen. x. 2), extending from the high plateau south of the Caspian Sea westward through the mountain region south of the Black Sea to the islands and northern shores of the eastern Mediterranean, with settlements farther west.

Ja-phi'a [shining, gleaming].
1. A king of Lachish, defeated, captured, and executed by Joshua (Josh. x. 3–27).
2. A son of David, born at Jerusalem (2 Sam. v. 15).
3. A border town of Zebulun (Josh. xix. 12). It is by many identified with Yâfa, a little less than 2 miles southwest of Nazareth.

Japh'let [may he deliver].
An Asherite, family of Heber (1 Chron. vii. 32).

Japh'le-tite, in A. V. **Japhleti.**
The descendants of a certain Japhlet, apparently not the same as the Asherite of that name. Their location was on the border of Ephraim, near Beth-horon (Josh. xvi. 3).

Ja'pho. See JOPPA.

Jar.
A vessel of earthenware, but occasionally of other material (John ii. 6; cp. Odyssey xiii. 105), used for either dry articles or liquids. An earthen jar, generally having one or two handles, was used for drawing water and for bearing it home from the well or fountain (Ecc. xii. 6). Ordinarily women fetched the water for the household, carrying the jar on the head or the shoulder (Gen. xxiv. 13, 15, 16; John iv. 28), but men sometimes brought it (Mark xiv. 13). Wine was stored in earthern jars (Herod. iii. 6; Anabasis vi. 1, 15; cp. Odyssey ii 290), which

were often of great size (Odyssey ii. 340, *pithos*). Oil also was kept in them; and

Waterpots produced by the potters at Hebron.

they were used in the house for holding meal (1 Kin. xvii. 12, in A. V. barrel).

Ja'rah [honey].

A descendant of king Saul (1 Chron. ix. 42). Called Jehoaddah in viii. 36.

Ja'reb [contentious or let him contend].

A king of Assyria whose name has not been identified (Hos. v. 13; x. 6), or else Jareb is not a proper name at all, but a descriptive term, and the Hebrew is to be rendered, as on the margin of R. V., a king that should contend.

Ja'red, in A. V. once **Jered** (1 Chron. i. 2) [perhaps descent].

Son of Mahalaleel and father of Enoch (Gen. v. 16–20; 1 Chron. i. 2; Luke iii. 37). See CHRONOLOGY.

Jar-e-si'ah. See JAARESHIAH.

Jar'ha.

An Egyptian servant of a man of Judah called Sheshan. The master gave his daughter in marriage to Jarha (1 Chron. ii. 34, 35).

Ja'rib [an adversary, or he doth contend].

1. A son of Simeon (1 Chron. iv. 24); see JACHIN.

2. A chief man who was with Ezra the priest at the river of Ahava (Ezra viii. 16).

3. A priest who was induced to put away his foreign wife (Ezra x. 18).

Jar'muth [a height].

1. A town in the lowland, whose king was defeated, captured, and slain by Joshua (Josh. x. 3–27; xii. 11). It was assigned to Judah (xv. 35), and was inhabited after the captivity

(Neh. xi. 29). Eusebius identified it with a village known in his day as Jermochôs, in Latin Jermucha, 10 Roman miles from Eleutheropolis on the road to Jerusalem. The site is marked by the ruined village of Yarmûk.

2. A town of Issachar, assigned to the Gershonite Levites (Josh. xxi. 28, 29). It is called Ramoth (1 Chron. vi. 73) and Remeth (Josh. xix. 21), synonyms of Jarmuth. Not identified. The village of er-Râmeh, 5½ miles north by west of the city of Samaria, does not lie within the bounds of Issachar. Nothing but altitude recommends el-Mezar or Wezar, on one of the highest points of mount Gilboa.

Ja-ro'ah.

A Gadite, descended through Buz (1 Chron. v. 14).

Ja'shar, in A. V. **Jasher** [righteous, upright].

The Book of Jashar is quoted in Josh. x. 13; 2 Sam. i. 18; and in Septuagint of 1 Kin. viii. 53. From these citations, the book was evidently a collection of poems which were apparently accompanied by introductory, and perhaps also concluding, explanatory remarks in prose. It resembled in this respect the psalms with prose introductions, such as Ps. xviii. and li., or the book of Job with its prose introduction (i.–iii. 1) and conclusion (xlii. 7–17). In 1751 there appeared a volume which professed to be an English translation of the Book of Jashar, alleged to have been found, but the production was an impudent forgery.

Ja'shen [sleeping].

A name in the catalogue of David's mighty men (2 Sam. xxiii. 32) occupying the place of Hashem in 1 Chron. xi. 34. Perhaps the preceding letters Bni, rendered "sons of" in the English versions, form part of the name; or they may have been repeated from the preceding word, Shaalbonite, which terminates with them.

Ja'sher. See JASHAR.

Ja-sho'be-am [let the people return (to God)].

1. A man of the family of Hachmoni and chief of David's mighty men (1 Chron. xi. 11). He is reasonably identified with the son of Zabdiel, of the children of Perez, and consequently of the tribe of Judah, who was made military captain over the course for the first month (1 Chron. xxvii. 2, 3). Called in 2 Sam. xxiii. 8 Josheb-basshebeth (q. v.).

2. A Benjamite who joined David at Ziklag. He belonged to the family of the Korahites, probably the Levitical family of that name who kept the doors of the tabernacle (1 Chron. xii. 1, 2, 6).

Ja'shub [he returns].

1. A son of Issachar, and founder of a tribal family (Num. xxvi. 24; 1 Chron. vii. 1). Called Job in Gen. xlvi. 13, probably through a copyist's omission of the Hebrew letter sh.

2. A son of Bani whom Ezra induced to put away his foreign wife (Ezra x. 29).

Jash-u-bi-le'hem [perhaps, bread returns].

Probably a man, and not a locality; a member of the family of Shelah, tribe of Judah (1 Chron. iv. 22).

Ja'si-ẹl. See JAASIEL.

Ja'son [healing].

1. One of the two envoys sent by Judas Maccabæus to Rome to invoke aid against the Syrians (1 Mac. viii. 17). It was perhaps his son who was sent to renew this alliance (xii. 16).

2. A high priest, son of Simon II., who held office from about 174–171 B. C., and used his influence to hellenize the Jews (2 Mac. iv. 7–26); see HIGH PRIEST.

3. A man of Cyrene and author of a history of the Jewish war for freedom, 175–160 B. C. (2 Mac. ii. 23); see APOCRYPHA 14.

4. A Christian, a relative of Paul (Rom. xvi. 21). He was probably the Jason who resided at Thessalonica, gave lodging to Paul and Silas in his home during their visit to the city, and was dragged by the Jews and their abettors before the rulers for this act of hospitality to objectionable men and only released on giving bail (Acts xvii. 5–9).

Jas'per.

The rendering of the Hebrew *Yashᵉpheh* (cp. Arabic *Yasb*) and the Greek *Iaspis*, a precious stone (Ex. xxviii. 20; Ezek. xxviii. 13; Rev. iv. 3). Jasper is a variety of quartz, of a red, brown, yellow, green, or gray color, and opaque. Among the ancients the term was of broader meaning. It included, according to Pliny, a transparent or translucent green variety (cp. Rev. xxi. 11), and hence denoted a kind of chalcedony or agate. The Septuagint renders the Hebrew word by onyx.

Jath'ni-el [God bestoweth gifts].

A Korhite doorkeeper, son of Meshelemiah (1 Chron. xxvi. 2).

Jat'tir [excellence].

A town in the hill country of Judah assigned to the priests (Josh. xv. 48; xxi. 14; 1 Sam. xxx. 27; 1 Chron. vi. 57). Robinson identified it with the ruin of 'Attîr, on a hill about 13 miles south-southwest of Hebron. The two names are, however, radically different.

Ja'van.

1. A region settled by descendants of Japheth (Gen. x. 2). The name corresponds etymologically with Ionia, and denotes the Greeks; see GREECE. Javan was synonymous with the farthest west, where Jehovah's fame had not been heard (Is. lxvi. 19). From early days the country had commercial

relations with Phœnicia (Ezek. xxvii. 13·; Joel iii. 6, in English version Grecians).

2. A town or people of Yemen in Arabia, whence cassia and calamus were exported (Ezek. xxvii. 19).

Jave'lin.

A smaller kind of spear, which was intended to be thrown (Job xli. 29), was borne suspended between the shoulders (1 Sam. xvii. 6), and could be stretched out in the hand (Josh. viii. 18). The Hebrew name for it was *kidon*. The A. V. never translates this word by javelin, but renders it by spear in Josh. viii. 18, 26; Job xli. 29; Jer. vi. 23; by lance in Jer. l. 42; and by shield or target in 1 Sam. xvii. 6, 45; Job xxxix. 23. Wherever javelin occurs in A. V. the Revisers have properly substituted spear.

Ja'zer, in A. V. twice **Jaazer** [helpful].

A city east of the Jordan in Gilead (2 Sam. xxiv. 5; 1 Chron. xxvi. 31). The Israelites captured it and drove out the Amorite inhabitants (Num. xxi. 32). It stood in a region well fitted for pasturage (xxxii. 1, 3). It was assigned to the tribe of Gad (Josh. xiii. 25), who rebuilt the city (Num. xxxii. 34, 35; 2 Sam. xxiv. 5); and it was appointed to the Merarite Levites for residence (Josh. xxi. 39; 1 Chron. vi. 81). It passed into Moabite hands (Is. xvi. 8, 9; Jer. xlviii. 32); was taken by Judas Maccabæus from the Ammonites (1 Mac. v. 8). According to Eusebius, Jazer was situated 10 Roman miles to the west of Rabbath Ammon, and 15 from Heshbon; and a considerable tributary of the Jordan took its rise near the town. Jerome mentions a village called Azor, 8 Roman miles to the west of Rabbath Ammon. These various places are commonly identified with wady Sir, an upper branch of wady Kefren, and the ruins Sir and Sar, on opposite sides of the valley. The distance from Rabbath Ammon approximately corresponds, but the names are radically different from Jazer and Azor. Beit Zer'ah, about 11 miles south by west of Rabbath Ammon, is preferred by Conder, but has no claims.

Ja'ziz [he moves about].

A Hagrite, the overseer of David's flocks (1 Chron. xxvii. 30).

Je'a-rim [forests].

A mountain crossed by the boundary line of Judah (Josh. xv. 10), and which, to judge from its connection with Chesalon (q. v.), was at that point about 8 miles to the northeast of Beth-shemesh.

Je-ath'e-rai, in A. V. **Jeaterai.** See ETHNI.

Je-ber'e-chi'ah [Jehovah doth bless].

Father of Isaiah's contemporary Zechariah (Is. viii. 2).

Je'bus [a place trodden under foot (as a threshing-floor)].

The name borne by Jerusalem while the

city was in the possession of the Jebusites (Josh. xv. 63; Judg. xix. 10; 1 Chron. xi. 4). The area included within Jebus was, of course, small compared with the dimensions of Jerusalem in the time of Solomon. Its citadel was the stronghold of Zion (2 Sam. v. 7; 1 Chron, xi. 5).

Jeb'u-site, in A. V. twice **Jebusi** (Josh. xviii. 16, 28), the Hebrew word being transliterated instead of being translated.

A tribe of Canaan before the conquest of the country by the Hebrews (Gen. x. 16; xv. 21; Ex. iii. 8). At the date of the exodus they were one of the mountain tribes (Num. xiii. 29; Josh. xi. 3). They are known only as dwelling at Jebus, *i. e.* Jerusalem. Their king was slain by Joshua (x. 23-26), their territory was assigned to Benjamin (xviii. 28), and later their city was taken by the men of Judah, on the border of which tribe it stood, and set on fire (Judg. i. 8; Josh. xv. 8); but the Jebusites either never lost the citadel (Antiq. v. 2, 2), or recovered the city in whole or in part. They dwelt with the children of Judah and Benjamin as strangers (Josh. xv. 63; Judg. i. 21; xix. 11). They still held the stronghold of Zion at the beginning of David's reign (2 Sam. v. 6, 7); and even after he had captured it the old inhabitants were not wholly expelled, for Araunah, who had a threshing-floor on the site afterwards occupied by Solomon's temple, was a Jebusite by birth (2 Sam. xxiv. 16, 18; 2 Chron. iii. 1). Solomon subjected the remnant of the Jebusites to bond service (1 Kin. ix. 20).

Jec-a-mi'ah. See JEKAMIAH.

Jech-i-li'ah and **Jech-o-li'ah.** See JECOLIAH.

Jech-o-ni'ah and **Jech-o-ni'as.** See JECONIAH.

Jec-o-li'ah and **Jechiliah**, in A. V. once **Jecholiah** (2 Kin. xv. 2) [Jehovah has prevailed].

The mother of king Uzziah (2 Kin. xv. 2; 2 Chron. xxvi. 3).

Jec-o-ni'ah, in R. V. of N. T. **Jechoniah**, in A. V. of N. T. **Jechonias** [Jehovah doth establish].

An unessential variant of the name of Jehoiachin, king of Judah, a cognate root being used and the constituent parts transposed (1 Chron. iii. 16, etc.).

Je-da'iah, I. [Jehovah has cast or shown].
1. A Simeonite (1 Chron. iv. 37).
2. A son of Harumaph, who repaired part of the wall of Jerusalem opposite to his house (Neh. iii. 10).

Je-da'iah, II. [Jehovah knoweth].
1. A descendant of Aaron. His family had grown to a father's house in the time of David, and was numbered the second course when David distributed the priests into divisions (1 Chron. xxiv. 1, 6, 7). Members of the family returned from Babylon

(Ezra ii. 36; Neh. vii. 39); cp. the two following.
2. A chief of the priests who returned from Babylon with Zerubbabel (Neh. xii. 6, 7). In the next generation a father's house bore this name (ver. 19).
3. Another chief priest with the same history (Neh. xii. 7, 21).
4. One of those who came from the captivity bringing gifts for the temple in the days of the high priest Joshua (Zech. vi. 10, 14).

Je-di'a-el [known of God].
1. A son of Benjamin, and founder of a family (1 Chron. vii. 6, 10, 11). The older interpreters regarded Jediael as another name of Ashbel (Num. xxvi. 38). Perhaps he was a later chief.
2. A Manassite who joined David at Ziklag (1 Chron. xii. 20).
3. One of David's mighty men, a son of Shimri (1 Chron. xi. 45).
4. A Korahite doorkeeper in the reign of David (1 Chron. xxvi. 1, 2).

Je-di'dah [beloved].
Wife of Amon and mother of king Josiah (2 Kin. xxii. 1).

Jed-i-di'ah [beloved of Jehovah].
A name which Nathan the prophet, by divine direction, gave to Solomon (2 Sam. xii. 25).

Je-du'thun [praising, praise].
1. A Levite, one of the three chief singers or rather musicians appointed in the time of David, and founder of an official musical family (1 Chron. xvi. 41; xxv. 1, 6; 2 Chron. v. 12; xxxv. 15; Neh. xi. 17). He or his family is mentioned in the title of three psalms (xxxix., lxii., lxxvii.). He was evidently known earlier as Ethan; see ETHAN 3.
2. Father of Obed-edom the doorkeeper and apparently of the family of Korah, a division of the Kohathites (1 Chron. xvi. 38; cp. xxvi. 1, 4, and also 8, 12, 15). Some interpreters, however, hold him to be Jeduthun, the singer, of the family of Merari.

Je-e'zer. See ABIEZER.

Je-e'zer-ite. See ABIEZRITE.

Je-gar-sa-ha-du'tha [Aramaic, heap of witness].
Laban's designation of the cairn Galeed (Gen. xxxi. 47); see GALEED.

Je-hal'le-lel, in A. V. **Je-ha-le'le-el** and **Jehalelel** [he praiseth God].
1. A man registered with the tribe of Judah and founder of a family (1 Chron. iv. 16).
2. A Merarite Levite (2 Chron. xxix. 12).

Jeh-de'iah [Jehovah inspires with joy].
1. A Levite, family of Kohath, house of Amram (1 Chron. xxiv. 20).
2. A Meronothite who had charge of David's asses (1 Chron. xxvii. 30).

Je-hez'kel, in A. V. **Je-hez'e-kel** [God doth strengthen].

A descendant of Aaron whose family was made the twentieth course of the priests (1 Chron. xxiv. 16).

Je-hi'ah [Jehovah liveth].

A doorkeeper for the ark in David's reign (1 Chron. xv. 24).

Je-hi'el [God liveth].

1. A Levite of the second degree, who played a psaltery at the removal of the ark to Jerusalem and afterwards as a regular duty in its tent (1 Chron. xv. 18, 20; xvi. 5).

2. A Levite, family of Gershon and chief of the house of Laadan in David's reign (1 Chron. xxiii. 8). He gave rise to the father's house named from him Jehieli (xxvi. 21, 22).

3. A son of Hachmoni in David's reign (1 Chron. xxvii. 32).

4. A son of Jehoshaphat, placed by his father over one of the fenced cities of Judah, but slain with others of his brothers by Jehoram (2 Chron. xxi. 2-4).

5. A Levite, family of Kohath and house of Heman the singer (2 Chron. xxix. 14, in R. V. Jehuel). He aided Hezekiah in his religious reformation, and is perhaps the assistant overseer of the temple revenues who served during the same reign (2 Chron. xxxi. 13).

6. A ruler of the temple at the time of Josiah's religious reformation (2 Chron. xxxv. 8).

7. Father of Ezra's contemporary Obadiah (Ezra viii. 9).

8. A son of Elam and father of Ezra's contemporary Shechaniah (Ezra x. 2). He may be the person of this name whom Ezra induced to put away his foreign wife (x. 26).

9. A priest, of the course of Harim, induced by Ezra to put away his foreign wife (x. 21).

For others whose name is thus spelled in A. V. see JEIEL.

Je-hi'e-li. See JEHIEL 2.

Je-hiz-ki'ah [Jehovah doth strengthen].

A son of Shallum, and one of the heads of the Ephraimite tribe in the reign of Pekah. He assisted in securing the release of the captives from Judah (2 Chron. xxviii. 12).

Je-ho-ad'dah, in A. V. **Je-ho'a-dah** [Jehovah hath adorned].

A son of Ahaz, and a descendant of Jonathan, Saul's son (1 Chron. viii. 36). Called in ix. 42 Jarah.

Je-ho-ad'dan, in R. V. of Kings **Jehoaddin** [perhaps, Jehovah hath made pleasant].

Mother of king Amaziah. She was from Jerusalem (2 Kin. xiv. 2; 2 Chron. xxv. 1).

Je-ho'a-haz and, contracted, **Joahaz** [Jehovah hath laid hold].

1. A variant form of the name of Ahaziah, youngest son of Jehoram, king of Judah (2 Chron. xxi. 17; cp. xxii. 1), the constituent parts of the name being transposed.

2. The son and successor of Jehu in the kingdom of Israel. He began to reign in 821 B. C., apparently as associate of his father, and reigned seventeen years (2 Kin. x. 35; xiii. 1). He continued the calf worship established by Jeroboam. As a penalty for this apostasy, the Syrians, first under Hazael and then under Ben-hadad, were permitted to carry on successful hostilities against him, capturing city after city, till at length he had no force left but 50 horsemen, 10 chariots, and 10,000 footmen. In distress he called on Jehovah, who gave Israel a saviour. This saviour of Israel appeared after the death of Jehoahaz, in the persons of his two successors Jehoash and Jeroboam. The former recovered the cities which the Syrians had taken from his father, and the latter restored the ancient boundaries of Israel. Probably Jehoash received unintended assistance from the king of Assyria, who, attacking the Syrians in the rear, compelled them to desist from the invasion of the Israelite kingdom, and return to defend their own country. Jehoahaz was succeeded by his son Jehoash (2 Kin. xiii. 2-9, 22-25).

3. A younger son of Josiah, who, on the death of Josiah, was placed by the people of Judah on his father's throne. He was then twenty-three, and reigned only three months, during which time his tendencies were evil rather than good. He was deposed and taken in chains to Riblah by Pharaoh-necho, king of Egypt, and afterwards carried down into Egypt. Necho, as victor over Josiah, decided to dispose of the throne of Judah, and gave it to Jehoiakim, Jehoahaz' elder brother (2 Kin. xxiii. 30-34; 2 Chron. xxxvi. 1-4). Jehoahaz was also called Shallum (1 Chron. iii. 15; Jer. xxii. 10-12), and he is the first of the lion's whelps (Ezek. xix. 1-9). Although the third of Josiah's sons in point of age and the first to occupy the throne, he is enumerated fourth in 1 Chron. iii. 15, perhaps by way of intentional degradation.

Je-ho'ash. See JOASH I.

Je-ho-ha'nan [Jehovah is gracious].

1. A Korahite Levite, who had the sixth course of the doorkeepers in David's reign (1 Chron. xxvi. 3).

2. The second in honor of Jehoshaphat's captains. He had under him 280,000 men (2 Chron. xvii. 15).

3. Father of Jehoiada's supporter, Ishmael, in the revolt against Athaliah (2 Chron. xxiii. 1).

4. A priest, head of the father's house of Amariah. He lived in the days of the high priest Joiakim (Neh. xii. 13).

5. A son of Eliashib (Ezra x. 6, R. V.) See JOHANAN 9.

6. A son of Bebai, induced by Ezra to put away his foreign wife (Ezra x. 28).

7. A son of Tobiah the Ammonite (Neh. vi. 18, R. V.). JOHANAN 10.

8. A priest who officiated at the dedication

of the wall of Jerusalem by Nehemiah (Neh. xii. 42).

Je-hoi'a-chin [Jehovah doth establish].

The son and successor of Jehoiakim in the kingdom of Judah. He came to the throne in the year 598 or 597 B. C. According to 2 Kin. xxiv. 8, he was then eighteen years old; according to 2 Chron. xxxvi. 9, his age was eight. The discrepancy exists in the Septuagint Greek as well as in the Hebrew text. One or other of the numbers is corrupt, which of the two is doubtful. He did that which was evil in the sight of the Lord, according to all that his father had done. But his reign continued only three months and ten days. During this short period Nebuchadnezzar, king of Babylon, sent his generals to besiege Jerusalem, which surrendered after the eighth year of Nebuchadnezzar had begun (cp. 2 Kin. xxiv. 12; cp. Jer. lii. 28); see CHRONOLOGY. Jehoiachin, his wives, his mother, the palace servants, every dignitary in the city and the country, with all the skillful artisans, were carried into captivity (2 Kin. xxiv. 8–16; 2 Chron. xxxvi. 9, 10). For a long period he seems to have been in actual confinement; but in the thirty-seventh year of his exile, 562 B. C., Evil-merodach ascended the throne of Babylon, released him from prison, and assigned him a daily allowance of, or for, food while he lived (2 Kin. xxv. 27–30; Jer. lii. 31–34). Jeremiah, who prophesied during, and after, the brief reign of Jehoiachin, frequently mentions him under the name Jechoniah or Coniah. On these modifications of the name, see JECONIAH.

Je-hoi'a-da [Jehovah hath known].

1. The father of that Benaiah who held high military office in the latter part of David's and in Solomon's reign (2 Sam. xxiii. 22; 1 Kin. iv. 4). Jehoiada was probably the priest (1 Chron. xxvii. 5, text; but not as in A. V. chief priest), and the leader of the Aaronites who brought 3700 men to David at Ziklag (xii. 27).

2. A son of Benaiah, second to Ahithophel in David's counsels (1 Chron. xxvii. 34). Most commentators believe that some copyist accidentally wrote Jehoiada son of Benaiah for Benaiah son of Jehoiada. There is no reason, however, why a grandson of Jehoiada, bearing the same name, should not be occupying a position of influence at this time.

3. A high priest during the usurpation of Athaliah. His wife concealed in the temple the young prince Joash, the only surviving direct representative of the royal line of David, and Jehoiada planned and successfully carried out the revolt which led to the slaughter of Athaliah and the proclamation of Joash as king. Jehoiada's wife was the daughter of king Joram and the sister of Ahaziah; the high priest was, therefore, the uncle of the young monarch whom he befriended and placed on the throne. So long as he lived he was instrumental in keeping the king true to the worship of Jehovah (2 Kin. xi. 1–xii. 16; 2 Chron. xxii. 10–xxiv. 14). He died at the age of 130, and, in recognition of his eminent services to church and state, he was buried in the city of David among the kings (15, 16). After his death Joash turned from the Lord and ungratefully put Jehoiada's son to death for rebuking the sins of the people (17–22).

4. A priest who was succeeded in Jeremiah's time by Zephaniah in the office of second priest and overseer of the temple (Jer. xxix. 26; cp. lii. 24).

5. A son of Paseah, who repaired a gate of Jerusalem (Neh. iii. 6; in R. V. Joiada).

Je-hoi'a-kim [Jehovah doth establish].

A son of king Josiah by his wife Zebidah (2 Kin. xxiii. 34, 36). He was called originally Eliakim, God doth establish. On the death of Josiah the people placed Jehoahaz, third son of Josiah in age, on the throne; but three months afterwards Pharaoh-necho put him in chains and carried him to Egypt, and made his elder brother Eliakim king in his stead, changing his name to Jehoiakim. He began to reign about 608 B. C., at the age of twenty-five years. He was obliged to collect heavy tribute from the people for Pharaoh. He departed from Jehovah, whom his father had so faithfully served, and went back to idolatry. Jeremiah wrote a roll threatening the divine judgment unless repentance took place; but Jehoiakim treated the matter with contempt, and after listening to three or four leaves of the roll cut it up and committed it to the flames (Jer. xxxvi.). Babylon was now the dominant Asiatic power. In the fourth year of Jehoiakim's reign, Nebuchadnezzar, son of the Babylonian king, defeated Pharaoh-necho at Carchemish and advanced, probably afterwards, against Jerusalem, and Jehoiakim became his servant (2 Kin. xxiv. 1; Jer. xlvi. 2; Dan. i. 1, 2; see CHRONOLOGY). Three years later he rashly rebelled against Nebuchadnezzar. There were other troubles afflicting the kingdom. Syrians, Moabites, and Ammonites made predatory incursions into its territories, as did bands of Chaldeans, whom Nebuchadnezzar probably dispatched on learning of the revolt (2 Kin. xxiv. 2). The Babylonian king himself, or his army, eventually entered Jerusalem and bound the Jewish rebel with chains to carry him to Babylon (2 Chron. xxxvi. 6). He was carried in a cage with hooks into the presence of the king of Babylon, who was in the camp at Jerusalem or perhaps at Riblah (Ezek. xix. 5–9); but perhaps the specific reference in ver. 9 is to his son Jehoiachin. The purpose of carrying him to Babylon was, however, abandoned. He died or was murdered, and his body had the burial of an ass, being drawn and cast forth beyond the gates of Jerusalem (Jer. xxii. 19; xxxvi. 30; Antiq. x. 6, 3). He reigned eleven years and was succeeded by his son Jehoiachin (2 Kin. xxiii. 36; xxiv. 6).

Je-hoi'a-rib [Jehovah doth contend].

A descendant of Aaron. His family had grown to a father's house in the time of David and was numbered the first course when David distributed the priests into divisions (1 Chron. xxiv. 1, 6, 7), and it dwelt at Jerusalem (ix. 10).

For other persons of the name, see JOIARIB.

Je-hon'a-dab. See JONADAB.

Je-hon'a-than, variant form of **Jonathan**, with which it freely interchanges in Hebrew [Jehovah hath given].

1. Son of Uzziah, and an official appointed by king David. He was charged with the oversight of the royal treasures which were in various places outside of Jerusalem (1 Chron. xxvii. 25, in R. V. Jonathan).

2. One of the Levites sent by Jehoshaphat to teach in the cities of Judah (2 Chron. xvii. 8).

3. A priest, head of the father's house of Shemaiah in the days of the high priest Joiakim (Neh. xii. 18).

Je-ho'ram [Jehovah is high].

1. Son of Ahab and king of Israel (2 Kin. iii. 1); see JORAM 3.

2. A priest, one of those sent by Jehoshaphat to instruct the people (2 Chron. xvii. 8).

3. Son of Jehoshaphat and king of Judah (2 Kin. viii. 16); see JORAM 5.

Je-ho-shab'e-ath. See JEHOSHEBA.

Je-hosh'a-phat, in A. V. of N. T. **Josaphat** [Jehovah hath judged].

1. Son of Ahilud and recorder under David and Solomon (2 Sam. viii. 16; xx. 24; 1 Kin. iv. 3).

2. One of the priests appointed to blow a trumpet before the ark when it was being brought up from the house of Obed-edom to the city of David (1 Chron. xv. 24, in R. V. Joshaphat).

3. Son of Paruah and Solomon's purveyor in the territory of Issachar (1 Kin. iv. 17).

4. Son and successor of king Asa on the throne of Judah. He appears to have been associated with his father in the latter's 37th regnal year, the 11th of Omri (1 Kin. xvi. 28, 29, Septuagint), and to have become sole king on the death of his father five years later, about 871 B. C. (xxii. 41, 42). He reigned twenty-five years, including the time that he was associated with Asa. He was thirty-five years old at his accession. His mother was Azubah, daughter of Shilhi (1 Kin. xxii. 41, 42; 2 Chron. xvii. 1). He was a good king. He worshiped Jehovah, and sought not unto the Baalim (1 Kin. xxii. 43; 2 Chron. xvii. 3), although the people still sacrificed on high places (1 Kin. xxii. 43). Therefore the Lord greatly prospered him. In the third year of his reign, he took measures for instructing his people,

sending princes and Levites, with the book of the law in their hands, to teach in the cities of Judah (2 Chron. xvii. 7-9). The fear of the Lord fell upon the neighboring kingdoms. Philistines and Arabians paid tribute (10, 11). He garrisoned the fenced cities of his realm (12-19). He terminated the desultory warfare which had gone on between Israel and Judah since the time of Rehoboam. He made peace with Israel and took Athaliah, daughter of Ahab, as a wife for his son (1 Kin. xxii. 44; 2 Kin. viii. 18, 26). When he found that Jehovah was thus blessing him, he was encouraged to remove the high places and the Asherim out of Judah (2 Chron. xvii. 5, 6). He put away also the remnant of the sodomites out of the land (1 Kin. xxii. 46).

About 853 B. C. he went on a visit to king Ahab, and was persuaded to join him, with the army of Judah, in the attempt to re-take Ramoth-gilead from the Syrians. Dressed in the royal robes of Ahab, he went into battle. Ahab was mortally wounded; Jehoshaphat, notwithstanding his exposure, survived (1 Kin. xxii. 1-38; 2 Chron. xviii. 1-34). On his return home he was reproved by the prophet Jehu, son of Hanani, for having fraternized with such a king as Ahab (2 Chron. xix. 1, 2). He resumed his work of reformation in church and state, promoting the worship of Jehovah, and appointing judges in the walled towns of Judah, with a supreme court, consisting of Levites, priests, and laymen of high position, in Jerusalem (4-11). After this reform had begun a great confederacy of Ammonites, Moabites, and Edomites invaded Judah from the southeast, making their headquarters at En-gedi on the western side of the Dead Sea. Jehoshaphat claimed the promise of deliverance which Solomon had asked (2 Chron. vi. 24-30 with xx. 9). Jahaziel prophesied deliverance, and Jehoshaphat went forth with thanksgiving and placed singers before the army to praise the Lord. Success was achieved without fighting. Hostilities broke out in the confederate army, the Ammonites and Moabites attacked and destroyed the Edomites, and then quarreling among themselves, turned their weapons against each other (xx. 1-30). After this event, perhaps in late autumn during the time of peace, Jehoshaphat, who had been building ships at Ezion-geber, asked Ahaziah, king of Israel, to take part in a mercantile voyage. The prophet Eliezer rebuked him for joining himself with Ahaziah, and the ships were wrecked. Ahaziah desired to share in a new venture, but Jehoshaphat refused (2 Chron. xx. 35-37; 1 Kin. xxii. 48, 49). In 852 B. C. or later, Jehoram, king of Israel, desired to render Moab again tributary to Israel, and sounded Jehoshaphat on his willingness to aid. Jehoram had exhibited signs of godliness by a considerable reformation (2 Kin. iii. 2), and Jehoshaphat consented to join him. The expedition

enjoyed partial success (2 Kin. iii. 4-27).
Jehoshaphat died at the age of sixty, about
the year 850 B. C., and was buried in the city
of David, leaving his son Jehoram to ascend
the throne (1 Kin. xxii. 50).

5. Son of Nimshi and father of Jehu, king
of Israel (2 Kin. ix. 2, 14).

Je-hosh'a-phat, Val'ley of.

A valley where all nations shall be gathered by Jehovah for judgment (Joel iii. 2, 12).
At least as early as the time of Eusebius, in the
fourth century A. D., the valley of Jehoshaphat
was identified with the valley of the Kidron,
so that now Jews, Roman Catholics, and Mohammedans fix the scene of the last judgment here. This identification is only a conjecture, based on the cited passages and
Zech. xiv. So far as evidence goes, no valley
actually bore this name. Joel doubtless
chose this designation, which means "Jehovah hath judged," as symbolic of the event.

Je-hosh'e-ba and **Jehoshabeath**, interchangeable forms in Hebrew [Jehovah is an
oath].

Daughter of Jehoram and sister of Ahaziah,
kings of Judah, and wife of the high priest
Jehoiada. On the murder of Ahaziah and
the slaughter of the seed royal, Jehosheba
rescued his infant son Joash and hid him in
the temple until he could be safely proclaimed king (2 Kin. xi. 2 ; 2 Chron. xxii. 11).

Je-hosh'u-a and **Jehoshuah.** See JOSHUA.

Je-ho'vah.

The common European pronunciation of
the Hebrew tetragram *Yhvh*, one of the names
of God (Ex. xvii. 15). The original name was
occasionally used even by so late a writer as
Nehemiah (i. 5 ; v. 13 ; viii. 1), in fact a form
of it constitutes the latter part of his name.
But it was not the favorite name of God with
him ; and it had ceased to be pronounced
when the Greek version was made, for the
translators substituted Lord. The custom
had grown up among the Hebrews in reading to pronounce the word *'adonay*, Lord, in
its stead or, when it follows *'adonay*, to pronounce *'elohim*, God (Gen. xv. 2), as in English we say namely instead of viz. When the
vowel points were added to the Hebrew con-
sonantal text, the vowels of *'adonay* and
'elohim were given to the tetragram. This
pointing gave rise to the European pronunciation, Jehovah, current since the days of
Petrus Galatinus, confessor of Leo X., A. D.
1518. The substitution of the word Lord by
the later Hebrews and by the translators of
the Septuagint led to the like substitution in
the English version (Gen. ii. 4). In such instances Lord is printed in small capitals. The
tetragram is generally believed to have been
pronounced Jahweh, *Yahweh*, because the
divine name Jah (Ps. lxxxix. 8, R. V.) and the
forms *Yeho*, *Ye* and *Yah*, *Yahu*, which occur
constantly in proper names, as in the Hebrew
of Jehoshaphat, Joshaphat, Shephatiah, can
all be derived from *Yahweh* in accordance

with the laws of philology. *Yahweh* is an
archaic form. It probably represents the
Qal imperfect of the verb *hawah*, later *hayah*,
to be or become. If this is so, it means " He
who in the absolute sense exists and who
manifests his existence and his character "
(Ex. iii. 13, 15). The creator, upholder, and
moral governor of the universe is *'elohim*,
God ; the covenant God of Abraham, Isaac,
and Jacob, the God in whom lay their
present strength and their hope for their future existence, is *'El shadday*, God almighty ;
but the God of revelation and grace, dwelling with his people, guiding and delivering
them, and receiving their worship is Jehovah.

Whether the name was known to other
peoples before it attained to celebrity through
the Hebrews is still a question. Men began
to call upon the name of Jehovah in the
days of Enosh, the third from Adam (Gen.
iv. 26). It must not be inferred, however,
that they necessarily used the name Jehovah.
They worshiped the God of revelation and
grace, whatever name they may have employed to denote the idea. Its first occurrence in recorded proper names is in Jochebed, an ancestress of Moses (see also 1 Chron.
ii. 8, 24). It can scarcely be sought in
Moriah. Evidence of its use in proper names
is thus found earlier than are traces of the
employment of *Shadday* for like purpose
(Num. i. 6, 12). In the generation after the
exodus, it appears in Joshua (Num. xiii. 16).
It then becomes frequent (1 Chron. vi. 6, 7, 36).

To know that God is Jehovah and to know
the name of Jehovah do not denote a mere
external acquaintance with the word Jehovah, but an experience of God manifesting
himself to his people in grace and love (1
Kin. viii. 43 ; Ps. xi. 10 ; xci. 14 ; Is. lii. 6 ;
Jer. xvi. 21). In Ex. vi. 2–8 God promises
that the children of Israel shall be delivered
from bondage and have an experience of his
gracious intervention and love such as their
forefathers had not known. See PENTATEUCH.

Je-ho-vah-ji'reh [Jehovah will see or pro-
vide].

The name given by Abraham to the place
where God provided a ram to be offered in
sacrifice, instead of Isaac (Gen. xxii. 14). Exact site unknown.

Je-ho-vah-nis'si [Jehovah is my banner].

The name given by Moses to an altar built
by him at Rephidim as a memorial of Israel's
victory over Amalek (Ex. xvii. 15, 16).

Je-ho-vah-sha'lom [Jehovah is peace].

An altar built by Gideon in Ophrah to
commemorate the visit of Jehovah's angel,
who summoned him to deliver Israel, and,
when Gideon expected to die because he had
seen the heavenly one, said to him : " Peace
be unto thee ; . . . thou shalt not die " (Judg.
vi. 23, 24).

Je-hoz'a-bad [Jehovah hath endowed].

1. A Korahite porter, son of Obed-edom (1
Chron. xxvi. 4).

2. Son of a Moabitess, and a servant of Joash and one of his assassins (2 Kin. xii. 21 ; 2 Chron. xxiv. 26). He was put to death for the deed (2 Chron. xxv. 3).

3. A Benjamite, a high military captain under king Jehoshaphat (2 Chron. xvii. 18).

Je-hoz'a-dak. See JOZADAK.

Je'hu [probably, Jehovah is He].
1. A Benjamite of Anathoth, who joined David at Ziklag (1 Chron. xii. 3).
2. A prophet, son of Hanani. He denounced judgment against Baasha and his house for continuing in the sin of Jeroboam I. (1 Kin. xvi. 1-4, 7). He reproved Jehoshaphat for helping ungodly Ahab (2 Chron. xix. 2), and wrote a book in which the acts of Jehoshaphat were narrated (xx. 34).
3. The founder of the fourth dynasty of rulers in the kingdom of Israel. He was a son of Jehoshaphat and grandson of Nimshi. For brevity's sake he was often called the son of Nimshi (1 Kin. xix. 16 ; 2 Kin. ix. 2). Somewhat earlier than 854 B. C., he was a soldier in the service of Ahab (2 Kin. ix. 25). Ahab and Jezebel were rejected for their crimes, and Elijah received a command from God to anoint Jehu king over Israel (1 Kin. xix. 16, 17). The commission was executed by Elijah's successor, Elisha, who for that purpose sent a young prophet to Ramoth-gilead, where Jehu was with the army. The prophet anointed Jehu king over Israel and commissioned him to destroy the house of Ahab. On learning the purpose of the prophet's visit, Jehu's fellow officers resolved to support him. They went to Jezreel, where the reigning king, Jehoram, Ahab's son, was at the time. The watchman on the tower in Jezreel descried the party in the distance, and presently identified Jehu by his furious driving. Ahaziah, king of Judah, was visiting Jehoram ; and the two kings, each in his chariot, went out to meet the advancing company. They met at the vineyard which Ahab had wrongfully gotten through the judicial murder of Naboth. The parley was short, and Jehoram was killed by an arrow sent with great force from Jehu's bow, and his body was cast into the plot of ground which had been Naboth's. Ahaziah also, whose mother was Ahab's daughter, was smitten by Jehu's order. By his command also, Jezebel, the queen-mother, Ahab's heathen queen and evil genius, was flung from a window and killed (2 Kin. ix. 1-37). Then he induced their guardians to slay the seventy princes of the royal house ; and the heads were piled in two heaps at the gate of Jezreel. Jehu had been ordered to smite the house of Ahab (ix. 7) ; hence his deeds thus far, apart from their needless brutality, were acts of obedience. As such they are commended (x. 30). But they were not wrought in singleness of heart, from a sense of duty and for the honor of Jehovah (31) ; and the prophet Hosea condemns the motive (Hos. i. 4). Next Ahab's

great men and his familiars were slain, and then Ahaziah's forty-two brothers. Finally the priests and worshipers of Baal were summoned to a festival of the god, and all who managed to get into Baal's temple were massacred (2 Kin. x. 12-28). But Jehu himself took no heed to walk in the law of God, and did not depart from the schismatic calf worship (2 Kin. x. 29, 31). He ascended the throne about 842 B. C. In that year, according to Assyrian records, he paid tribute to Shalmaneser, king of Assyria, who came into the neighborhood to wage war against Hazael. He reigned twenty-eight years (36). About 821 B. C., on account of advancing age and the loss of his energy and military skill, his son Jehoahaz was probably associated with him. But the change did not prevent his reign from closing in disaster. Hazael cut Israel short (2 Kin. x. 32) ; see CHRONOLOGY. A promise had been given that the dynasty of Jehu should continue for four generations ; and it did so, the line of descent being Jehoahaz, Jehoash or Joash, Jeroboam II., and Zechariah (2 Kin. x. 30 ; xv. 8-12).

4. A man of Judah, family of Jerahmeel (1 Chron. ii. 38)

5. A Simeonite (1 Chron. iv. 35).

Je-hub'bah [hidden].
An Asherite, family of Beriah (1 Chron. vii. 34).

Je-hu'cal and **Jucal**, interchangeable Hebrew forms [he is able].
A son of Shelemiah and prince of Judah. King Zedekiah sent him and others to ask the prayers of Jeremiah, when the Babylonian siege of Jerusalem was imminent (Jer. xxxvii. 3). Afterwards he wished the prophet to be put to death on the ground that his prediction of the capture of Jerusalem by the Babylonians discouraged its defenders (xxxviii. 1-6).

Je'hud [praise].
A town in the original territory of Dan (Josh. xix. 45). Robinson identified it with the village of el-Yehudiyeh, 8 miles east by south of Jaffa. His view has been generally accepted.

Je-hu'di [a man of Judah, a Jew].
A messenger sent by king Jehoiakim to ask Baruch for the roll written by Jeremiah. He was afterwards employed to read it, which he did, till the king, enraged at its contents, cut it in pieces and cast it into the fire (Jer. xxxvi. 14, 21, 23).

Je-hu-di'jah [Jewess].
One of the two wives of Mered, the other being Bithiah, an Egyptian princess (1 Chron. iv. 18, A. V.). Jehudijah is, however, not a proper name, but an adjective meaning Jewess ; and it has the definite article. She was called the Jewess to distinguish her from the Egyptian.

Je'hush. See JEUSH.

Je-i'el, in A. V. twice **Jehiel** (1 Chron. ix. 35; xi. 44) [perhaps, treasure of God].

1. Father of the inhabitants of Gibeon and an ancestor of king Saul (1 Chron. ix. 35, 36, 39); see KISH 2.

2. A son of Hotham, an Aroerite, in the reign of David (1 Chron. xi. 44). Perhaps he was the Reubenite chief (v. 7, 8).

3. A Levite musician (1 Chron. xvi. 5, first half); see JAAZIEL.

4. A Levite of the second degree, who was a doorkeeper and played the harp at the removal of the ark to Jerusalem and afterwards as a regular duty in the tent at Jerusalem (1 Chron. xv. 18, 21; xvi. 5).

5. A Levite of the sons of Asaph (2 Chron. xx. 14).

6. A scribe who recorded the number of soldiers in Uzziah's army (2 Chron. xxvi. 11).

7. A Hebrew who was induced by Ezra to put away his foreign wife (Ezra x. 43).

For others whose name is thus spelled in A. V., see JEUEL. Jehiel in R. V. is a different name.

Je-kab'ze-el. See KABZEEL.

Jek-a-me'am [he doth assemble the people].
A Levite, family of Kohath, house of Hebron (1 Chron. xxiii. 19; xxiv. 23).

Jek-a-mi'ah, in A. V. once **Jecamiah** (1 Chron. iii. 18) [Jehovah doth gather].
1. A man of Judah, descended through Sheshan from Jerahmeel (1 Chron. ii. 41).
2. A son or descendant of Jeconiah (1 Chron. iii. 18).

Je-ku'thi-el [reverence for God].
A man of Judah, father of the inhabitants of Zanoah (1 Chron. iv. 18).

Je-mi'mah, in A. V. **Jemima** [a pigeon, a dove].
The first of the three daughters born to Job after his great trial (Job xlii. 14).

Jem'u-el [perhaps, warmth or desire of God].
A son of Simeon (Gen. xlvi. 10; Ex. vi. 15). In Num. xxvi. 12; 1 Chron. iv. 24 he is called Nemuel. He founded a tribal family.

Jeph'thah, in A. V. of N. T. **Jeph'tha-e** [he doth open or set free].
A Gileadite, in the twofold sense of having a certain man called Gilead for his father and the country of Gilead for his early home. He was an illegitimate child, and his brothers born in wedlock expelled him from the paternal abode. He saw injustice in the treatment which he received, and years later he charged the elders of Gilead, among whom were probably his brothers, with being party to the iniquity and animated by hatred. He fled to the land of Tob, probably in the Hauran, where life was free and where with trusty weapon abundant food was to be had. There he made a name for himself by his prowess, and attracted a band of the unemployed around him as their chief. He must

not be thought of as a lawless freebooter, however, for he was a man with a conscience. He sought sufficient justification before undertaking an enterprise, he feared God and taught his daughter the fear of God, and he won her entire confidence and religious respect. About the time of Jephthah's expulsion, the Ammonites invaded the Israelitish territory east of the Jordan and held it in subjection eighteen years. In this extremity the elders of Gilead, who had driven Jephthah away, were compelled as a last resort to urge the fugitive to return and become their chief and deliverer. On assuming headship over the Gileadites, Jephthah informed the neighboring tribe of Ephraim of the distress of Gilead, but he exhorted them in vain to come to the help of their brethren. He also demanded of the king of the Ammonites the ground of his hostility, and in reply justified Israel for taking up arms. While yet the issue of the war was doubtful, Jephthah had vowed that if he were permitted to achieve victory, he would offer to God as a burnt offering whatever first came to him out of his house. On his return from the defeat of the Ammonites what first came was his only daughter, and who, moreover, was his only child. He was greatly troubled when he saw her, but felt compelled to do with her according to his vow. Probably he sacrificed her (cp. 2 Kin. iii. 27), though many have thought that he may have redeemed her with money (Lev. xxvii. 1–8) and doomed her to perpetual celibacy. The Israelite women were accustomed four times a year to mourn her sad fate. Hostilities breaking out between him and the Ephraimites, who complained that he had slighted them in making arrangements for his Ammonite campaign, he answered their false accusation and defeated them in battle. Jephthah judged Israel six years (Judg. x. 6–xii. 7). Samuel cited him as one proof of Jehovah's faithfulness to his promise to raise up a deliverer for Israel in time of need (1 Sam. xii. 11), and he is cited in the Epistle to the Hebrews as a man of faith (Heb. xi. 32).

Je-phun'neh [it will be prepared].
1. Father of Caleb, the representative spy from the tribe of Judah (Num. xiii. 6).
2. An Asherite (1 Chron. vii. 38).

Je'rah [moon, month].
An Arabian tribe descended from Joktan (Gen. x. 26; 1 Chron. i. 20).

Je-rah'me-el [God hath compassion].
1. A descendant of Judah through Perez and Hezron (1 Chron. ii. 9; cp. 4, 5). Two wives are mentioned and a numerous progeny is registered (25–41).
2. Son of a Levite called Kish, not Saul's father (1 Chron. xxiv. 29).
3. One of the officers sent by king Jehoiakim to arrest Baruch (Jer. xxxvi. 26). He was probably of royal blood (R. V.). See HAMMELECH.

Je're͏d [descent].

1. Son of Mahalaleel (1 Chron. i. 2, A. V.); see JARED.

2. A man of Judah and father of the inhabitants of Gedor (1 Chron. iv. 18).

Jer'e-mai [high].

A Hebrew who was induced by Ezra to put away his foreign wife (Ezra x. 33).

Jer-e-mi'ah, in A. V. of N. T. **Jeremy** and **Jeremias** (Mat. ii. 17; xvi. 14) [Jehovah doth establish].

1–3. A Benjamite and two Gadites who joined David at Ziklag (1 Chron. xii. 4, 10, 13).

4. Head of a father's house in eastern Manasseh (1 Chron. v. 24).

5. A native of Libnah and the father of Hamutal, wife of king Josiah and mother of Jehoahaz (2 Kin. xxiii. 30, 31).

6. Son of Habaziniah and father of Jaazaniah, a Rechabite (Jer. xxxv. 3).

7. The great prophet, a son of Hilkiah, a priest of Anathoth, in the territory of Benjamin (Jer. i. 1). He was called to the prophetic office by a vision. He was young at the time, and felt his immaturity and inexperience and inability to speak to men; but Jehovah reached out a hand and touched Jeremiah's mouth, putting into it words, and setting him over nations and kingdoms, on the one hand to root out, overthrow, and destroy, and on the other to plant and to build. He was told, further, that he would meet with violent opposition from princes, priests and people, but that they should not prevail (i. 4–10). He began to prophesy in the thirteenth year of the reign of Josiah, and continued his work till the capture of Jerusalem, in the fifth month of the eleventh year of Zedekiah's reign (2, 3). Thus his public life extended through the last eighteen years of Josiah's reign, the three months during which Jehoahaz ruled, the eleven years of Jehoiakim, the three months of Jehoiachin, and the eleven years and five months of Zedekiah, in all about forty-one years. Nor did he, even then, cease from his prophetic functions (xlii.–xliv.). The men of Anathoth, his paternal home, were among the first to oppose him, and threatened to kill him if he did not desist from prophesying. He persevered in his mission despite the persecution, but he keenly felt this opposition to the work of God from his countrymen, the chosen people of God, and he cried to God for judgment (Jer. xi. 18–21; xii. 3). The hostility to the prophet, which began at Anathoth, after a time became general, and again evoked a cry for judgment upon his opponents (xviii. 18–23; cp. also xx. 12). But he remained faithful to his duty in spite of obloquy and persecution. In the fourth year of Jehoiakim's reign Jeremiah dictated the prophecies which he had been uttering during the preceding twenty years, and the scribe Baruch wrote them in the roll of a

book. Knowing that he himself was hindered, for some reason not stated, and would doubtless still be hindered for a long time, from going to the house of God, the prophet told Baruch to take the roll to the sanctuary and read it before the people who would be coming to the temple on occasion of a fast. The roll finally reached the king, who, after hearing a few leaves or columns read, cut the roll in pieces and flung it into the fire (xxxvi. 1–26). By divine direction the prophet at once prepared a second roll like the first, but with additions (27–32). A foe of his, the priest Pashhur, chief governor of the temple, put him in the stocks; but he was released the next day (xx. 1–3). During the siege of Jerusalem the Jewish authorities looked at Jeremiah's prophecies of the success of the Chaldeans and the subsequent captivity of Judah from the political or military, instead of from the religious, point of view; and they claimed that his unfavorable predictions discouraged the defenders of Jerusalem. And when the Chaldeans temporarily raised the siege to meet the Egyptians, and Jeremiah was about to take advantage of their absence to go to Anathoth on business, the charge was made against him that he was deserting to the Chaldeans, and he was thrown into prison (xxxvii. 1–15). After many days king Zedekiah released him from his cell and committed him to the court of the guard (16–21); but the princes soon had him cast into the dungeon to die (xxxviii. 1–6). An Ethiopian eunuch, however, took compassion on him, and obtained the king's leave to take him from the miry pit and put him back in the court of the guard. The prophet was there when Jerusalem was taken (7–28). The Chaldeans looked upon him as one who had suffered much for them, and Nebuchadnezzar gave express orders for his kind treatment. Accordingly, Nebuzaradan, the Chaldean official, sent and had Jeremiah taken out of the court of the guard and brought to him with the other captives to Ramah, set him free, and granted him leave to go to Babylon or stay in the home land. On his choosing the latter, Nebuzaradan gave him victuals and a present, and sent him to the protection of Gedaliah, whom Nebuchadnezzar had made governor of Judah (xxxix. 11–14; xl. 1–6). On the murder of Gedaliah, he strongly urged the Jews not to flee to Egypt. It was in vain; they not merely went thither themselves, but they compelled the prophet to accompany them on their journey (xli. 1–xliii. 7). He delivered his last predictions at Tahpanhes, in Egypt (xliii. 8–xliv. 30). The time and manner of his death are unknown. Besides the prophecies to which his name is attached, and his Lamentations, he may have written some of the psalms, which resemble his compositions in style.

Beyond most prophecies the book of Jeremiah reveals the spiritual life of its author.

His was a message of doom to his native land, and a message that brought the hatred of his fellow-countrymen upon him; and the burden of it forced from him the bitter lament that he had ever been born (xv. 10; xx. 14–18). But he remained true to duty. He was a lone man, misunderstood, maligned, persecuted, his efforts for the moral welfare of his countrymen foredoomed to failure, without the solace of domestic life and social joys (xvi. 1–9), often kept in ward, forced to turn for consolation and sympathy and companionship to God only. Being thus thrown much upon God, he came to realize the sense of individual responsibility to God (xvii. 9; xxxi. 29, 30). And so it comes to pass that in Jeremiah is notably exhibited the possibility and reality of communion between the individual soul and God.

Religion in the heart and in the life is a dominant note in Jeremiah's preaching. He was called to the prophetic office five years before the eventful discovery of the book of the law in the temple, during repairs to the edifice; and he was in the midst of his work when king Josiah, under the profound impression made upon him by the words of the book, led the crusade against idolatry and inaugurated a revival in the national worship. Jeremiah, too, exhorted the people to hearken to the words of the covenant entered into at mount Sinai; and he pointed out that God had visited them with the evils threatened therein for disobedience, and that to obey is the first requirement of the covenant (Jer. xi. 1–8). Jeremiah would guard the people from limiting reform to things external. He would carry it into the inner life. In the spirit of the older prophets of the familiar proverb, and of the covenant itself (1 Sam. xv. 22; Is. i. 11–17; Amos v. 21–24; Mic. vi. 6–8; Prov. xv. 8; Deut. x. 12), and using the rhetorical negation, frequently employed for emphatic antithesis (e. g. Deut. v. 3), he denied that God commanded sacrifice, and insisted that the one requirement is obedience. God commanded sacrifice indeed (Ex. xx. 24; xxiii. 14–19; Deut. xii. 6), but did not speak of sacrifice. Sacrifice was not the theme, God spoke of moral conduct (Jer. vii. 21–28; cp. vi. 20; xiv. 12). The sacrifices of the obedient are pleasing to God (xvii. 24–26; xxvii. 19–22; xxxiii. 10, 11, 18; the latter verse in a section lacking in the Greek version); but the fasts and sacrifices of those who love to wander from him are not acceptable (xiv. 10–12). Trust in the presence of Jehovah in the midst of Israel, in being Jehovah's temple, is also vain; and equally vain is the mere possession of the law of Jehovah. Obedience alone avails (vii. 4–7; viii. 7–9). Eventually even the ark will be no more remembered (iii. 16). God looks at the heart (xi. 20; xvii. 10; xx. 12). To serve God man must remove carnal lust from it (iv. 4; cp. Deut. x. 16), wash it of wickedness (iv. 14),

and return to God with the whole heart and not feignedly (iii. 10; xvii. 5). In due time Jeremiah foretold the new covenant when the people shall have a new heart and God's law written in it (xxiv. 7; xxxi. 33; xxxii. 39, 40). His vision descried the true glory of the kingdom of the future. Henceforth this truth holds a chief place in the mind of God's people.

Jeremiah committed some of his prophecies to writing in the reign of Jehoiakim, but the roll was destroyed by the king (xxxvi. 1, 23). They were soon rewritten, however, with large additions (32). The present book is a further enlargement, including the later prophecies; and is a rearrangement, prepared at the close of his ministry; for prophecies of different periods are placed together and those of the same period are often dispersed. The book consists of an introduction narrating the prophet's call (i.), three sections of prophecy, often recorded in connection with the event that called forth the prophetic utterance (ii.–li.), and a historical appendix, added probably by a later writer (lii.; cp. li. 64). The three prophetic sections are: I. Prediction of the approaching judgment of Judah and the promise of restoration from exile (ii.–xxxiii.). It includes a general denunciation of Judah (ii.–xx.), denunciation of the civil and religious rulers (xxi.–xxiii.), an unfolding of the design and duration of the judgment (xxiv.–xxix.), and prophecy of the blessings which will follow the judgment (xxx.–xxxiii.). II. History of the infliction of the judgment (xxxiv.–xliv.), including denunciations of the corruption which prevailed immediately before the destruction of the city (xxxiv.–xxxviii.), an account of the destruction of the city (xxxix.), and of the wretched conditions of the remnant, and the prophecies spoken to them (xl.–xliv.). III. Predictions respecting foreign nations (xlvi.–li.), introduced by an address to Baruch (xlv.).

The Messiah is spoken of in xxiii. 5–8; xxx. 4–11; xxxiii. 14–26; and Jehovah's sure covenant with Israel is dwelt upon in xxxi. 31–40; xxxii. 36–44; xxxiii.

The text of the Septuagint differs considerably from the Hebrew: chapters xlvi.–li. are not only arranged in a different order among themselves, but the entire section has been inserted after xxv. 13; chapters xxix. 16–20, and xxxiii. 14–26, and xxxix. 4–13, and lii. 28–30 are wanting in the Greek; and in many other places the Greek version presents a shorter text than the Hebrew (e. g. ii. 1, 2; vii. 1–3). This shorter text is often due to the absence of unimportant words; such as the customary lack of "the prophet" when Jeremiah is named (e.g. xxviii. 5,11,15), "the king," when the proper name is given (xxxvi. 32; xxxvii. 17) and *vice versâ* (e. g. xxvi. 22, 23; xxxvii. 18, 21), "of hosts" after Jehovah (e. g. vi. 6, 9), "of hosts, the God of Israel," the sufficient title Lord being used instead (e. g. vii. 21; xix. 15), and "saith the Lord," where the expression is parenthetic (e. g. ii. 9; iii. 10; vii. 13).

In chronological order the prophecies and narratives, so far as they bear explicit dates, stand thus:

In Josiah's reign of thirty-one years:
In the 13th year . . . Chap. i.
Between the 13th { ii.-vi. (cp. iii. 6), and probaby vii.-xii., and
and 31st years.   { xiv.-xx.
In Jehoahaz's reign of three months:
                          None.
In Jehoiakim's reign of eleven years:
In the beginning . . . xxvi., and probably xxii. 1-19 (cp. 10, 18, 19).
In the 4th year. . . . xxv.; xxxvi.; xlv.; xlvi. 1-12.
After the 4th year . . xxxv. (cp. 1, 11).
In Jehoiachin's reign of three months:
                          Probably xxii. 20-30, and perhaps xiii. (cp. 18 with xxii. 26 and 2 Kin. xxiv. 12).
In Zedekiah's reign of eleven years:
In the beginning . . . xxiv.; xlix. 34-39.
In his 4th year . . . . xxvii. (cp. 3, 12, xxviii. 1); xxviii.; li. 59-64.
In unnoted years . . . xxi.; xxix.
During the earlier } xxxiv.
part of the siege, }
while Jeremiah }
was yet free. }
During the interrup- } xxxvii. (cp. 4, 5).
tion of the siege. }
After the resumption { xxxii. (in the 10th year);
of the siege, while { xxxiii.; xxxviii.;
Jeremiah was in { xxxix. 15-18.
ward. {
In Judah after the fall of Jerusalem:
                          xxxix. 1-14; xl. 1-xliii. 7.
In Egypt . . . . xliii. 8-13; xliv.
Undated. but not al- { xxiii.; xxx.; xxxi; xlv.;
ways without indi- { xlvi. 13-xlviii.; xlix.-
cations of time. { li. 58.
Appendix . . . . . . lii.

8. A chief of the priests, who returned with Zerubbabel from Babylon (Neh. xii. 1, 7). A father's house bore his name in the next generation (12).

9. A priest, doubtless head of a father's house, who set his seal to the covenant to keep separate from the foreigners and observe the law of God (Neh. x. 2).

Jer'e-moth and **Jerimoth** [probably heights].

1. A Benjamite, family of Becher (1 Chron. vii. 8).

2. A Benjamite (1 Chron. viii. 14), perhaps the person called Jeroham (27).

3. A Levite, family of Merari, house of Mushi (1 Chron. xxiii. 23; xxiv. 30).

4. A descendant of Heman and head of the fifteenth course among the musicians in David's reign (1 Chron. xxv. 4, 22).

5. A son of Azriel and prince of Naphtali in David's reign (1 Chron. xxvii. 19).

6-8. Two descendants of Elam (Ezra x. 26, 27) and a son of Bani (x. 29, in A. V., according to another reading, Ramoth), who consented to put away their foreign wives.

For persons who bear the name Jerimoth only, see JERIMOTH.

Jer'e-my. See JEREMIAH.

Je-ri'ah, once **Jerijah** [probably, founded by Jehovah].

A Levite, family of Kohath, house of Hebron (1 Chron. xxiii. 19; xxiv. 23; xxvi. 31).

Jer'i-bai [contentious].

A son of Elnaam, and one of David's mighty men (1 Chron. xi. 46).

Jer'i-cho [place of fragrance].

An important city situated in the valley of the Jordan (Deut. xxxiv. 1, 3), west of the river, near the Dead Sea, and at the foot of the ascent to the mountainous table-land of Judah. It was known as the city of palm trees (ibid.; Judg. iii. 13). It is first mentioned in Scripture when the Israelites encamped at Shittim on the other side of the Jordan (Num. xxii. 1; xxvi. 3). As it was strongly fortified and commanded the valley of the lower Jordan and the passes into the western mountains, its conquest by the Israelites was essential to their advance. Joshua accordingly sent spies to examine it (Josh. ii. 1-24), led the Israelites across the river, and pitched camp near the city. By divine command the men of war went round the city once a day for six consecutive days, with the ark of the covenant in their midst and seven priests blowing on trumpets in front of the ark. On the seventh day they compassed the city seven times; and on the seventh circuit, when the signal was given by a long blast with the horn, the host shouted, the walls fell, and the Israelites entered. The place had been put under the ban. Except Rahab, who had protected the spies, and her father's family, all living creatures were slain. The silver and the gold, with other valuables, were put into the treasury of the house of the Lord. Finally, Joshua foretold that if any one ever fortified the town he should lose his elder son when the foundations were being laid, and the younger one when the gates were being set up (Josh. v. 13-vi. 26). The place was assigned to Benjamin, and stood on the boundary between the tribes of Ephraim and Benjamin (xvi. 1, 7; xviii. 12, 21). It was occupied as a royal residence by Eglon, king of Moab, when he oppressed the Israelites (Judg. iii. 13). David's ambassadors, returning from the Ammonite king by whom they had been insulted, stopped at Jericho until their beards grew (2 Sam. x. 5; 1 Chron. xix. 5). In Ahab's reign Hiel the Bethelite fortified the city, but lost or sacrificed his two sons as predicted by Joshua (1 Kin. xvi. 34). During Elijah's lifetime there was a community of the prophets at the place (2 Kin. ii. 5). Elijah, when about to be translated to heaven, passed through it with Elisha, and Elisha returned to it after finally parting with Elijah (4, 15, 18). The captives of Judah, taken by the Israelite army under Pekah, were set free at Jericho (2 Chron. xxviii. 15). In its vicinity Zedekiah was captured by his Babylonian pursuers (2 Kin. xxv. 5; Jer. xxxix. 5; lii. 8). Three hundred and forty-five of its former inhabitants and their descendants returned from captivity with Zerubbabel (Ezra ii. 34; Neh. vii. 36). Some of its new populace helped to rebuild the wall of Jerusalem (iii. 2). Bacchides, the Syrian general, repaired the fortifications of Jericho during the Maccabæan period (1 Mac. ix. 50). In the early years of Herod the Great the Romans plundered Jericho (Antiq. xiv. 15, 3). Subsequently Herod beautified it, established a royal palace, and on the hill behind the town built a citadel which he named Cyprus (xvi. 5, 2; xvii. 13, 1; War i. 21, 4 and 9). There was also a hippodrome there at the time of Herod's death (Antiq. xvii. 6, 5; War i. 33, 6 and 8). The road from Jerusalem to Jericho was the scene of the action in the parable of the good Samaritan (Luke x. 30). At Jericho itself Jesus restored sight to blind Bartimæus and his companion (Mat. xx. 29; Luke xviii. 35). There also he brought salvation to Zacchæus, whose home was in Jericho (xix. 1, 2).

Jericho, lying 825 feet below the level of the Mediterranean, had a tropical climate. Palms, balsams, sycomores, and henna flourished (Song i. 14; Luke xix. 2, 4; War iv. 8, 3). The rose plant of Jericho was proverbially fine (Ecclus. xxiv. 14). Ancient Jericho stood close by the copious spring 'Ain es-Sultan, apparently the fountain healed by Elisha (War iv. 8, 3). The early Amorite town apparently was destroyed before Israelite influence had affected its life. The ancient walls were seriously damaged, but were replaced by others equally powerful. The modern village of 'Erîha (the Hebrew Yᵉrîḥo a little altered) is 4¾ miles west of the Jordan, and 1½ southeast of the fountain.

Je′ri-el [probably, founded by God].
A descendant of Tola, of the tribe of Issachar (1 Chron. vii. 2).

Je-ri′jah. See JERIAH.

Jer′i-moth [probably, heights].
1. A Benjamite, family of Bela (1 Chron. vii. 7).
2. A Benjamite who joined David at Ziklag (1 Chron. xii. 5).
3. A son of David, and father of Mahalath, a wife of Rehoboam (2 Chron. xi. 18).
4. A Levite, an overseer in connection with the temple in Hezekiah's reign (2 Chron. xxxi. 13).

For others whose name sometimes appears as Jeremoth, see JEREMOTH.

Je′ri-oth [curtains].
One of Caleb's wives (1 Chron. ii. 18).

Jer-o-bo′am [the people become numerous].
1. An Ephraimite, who founded the kingdom of the ten tribes. His father was an official under Solomon, named Nebat, of the village of Zeredah in the Jordan valley; his mother's name was Zeruah, who was a widow at the time of his birth (1 Kin. xi. 26). As a young man he showed industry and ability; and Solomon, who was engaged in building operations at Jerusalem, made him overseer of the heavy work assigned to the house of Joseph (27, 28). One day as Jeroboam was walking outside of Jerusalem he was met by a prophet, Ahijah of Shiloh, clad in a new garment, who rent the cloth in twelve pieces, and gave ten to Jeroboam as a pledge that Jehovah destined him to be king over ten out of the twelve tribes. News of the transaction reached Solomon, who sought to kill Jeroboam, but he escaped to Egypt, and was kindly received by Shishak, its king (29–40). When the refugee was notified that Solomon was dead and that an assembly of the tribes was to take place at Shechem to make Solomon's son Rehoboam king, he returned to attend the meeting. He put himself forward as spokesman of the people, and urged the alleviation of their burdens. Rehoboam denied the petition, returning a foolish and exasperating answer. Ten tribes thereupon revolted from the house of David and elected Jeroboam king. The prophecy of Ahijah had come true; yet Jeroboam resolved to depart from the counsel by which it had been accompanied. The prophet had exhorted him to remain true to Jehovah, in which case the crown should descend permanently in his family (37, 38). But he was afraid that if the people went up statedly to Jerusalem to worship they would be won back to the house of David and would reject and slay him. He therefore established a center of worship at each of the two extremities of his kingdom, Dan in the north and Beth-el in the south. In defiance of the commandment which forbids the adoration of God by means of images, he set up a golden calf in each of the two places (xii. 26–30; 2 Chron. xiii. 8), and recommended the worship as not altogether new by using the familiar words of Aaron (Ex. xxxii. 4). It would seem that he still desired to worship Jehovah under the image of the calf. He not only thus established houses of high places which lacked the ark and the shekinah, but he made Israelites who were not of the tribe of Levi priests, doubtless because few or none of the lawful priests and other Levites consented to serve in the idolatrous and schismatic worship (1 Kin. xii. 31; 2 Chron. xi. 13–15; xiii. 9). He further decreed that the harvest festival, which was celebrated in Judah on the fifteenth day of the seventh month, should be observed in the northern kingdom on the fifteenth day of the eighth month (1 Kin. xii. 32, 33). The mass of the people conformed. Thus Jeroboam made Israel to sin. This abhorrent worship continued until the fall of the kingdom. The successive kings, with the possible exception of Hoshea, supported it and are accordingly described as walking in the way of Jeroboam, the son of Nebat, who made Israel to sin (1 Kin.

xv. 26, 34; xvi. 19, 31; xxii. 52; 2 Kin. iii. 3; x. 29; xiii. 2, 11; xiv. 24; xv. 9, 18, 24, 28). The idolatry established by Jeroboam was one cause which led to the carrying of the ten tribes into captivity to Assyria (2 Kin. xvii. 16); for it kept the Hebrew nation divided in twain and made two inferior kingdoms where there had been one strong united people; and, as it was a degradation of the lofty spiritual worship of Jehovah, it resulted in lowering the spiritual tone of the northern Israelites. Jeroboam was rebuked for his apostasy, first by an unnamed prophet from Judah, and then by Ahijah, the Shilonite, who had promised him the kingdom; but he continued to the end unrepentant (1 Kin. xiii. 1–xiv. 18). He fortified Shechem and Penuel, both sacred places. The former he made his residence, but seems to have taken up his abode later at beautiful Tirzah (1 Kin. xii. 25; xiv. 17; Song vi. 4). There was a desultory warfare between Jeroboam and Rehoboam (1 Kin. xv. 6), and a great battle was fought between Jeroboam and Rehoboam's son and successor, Abijam, in which the army of Israel was defeated with enormous slaughter, and Beth-el, which was only 10 miles from Jerusalem, temporarily lost to Israel (7; 2 Chron. xiii. 1–20); see ABIJAM. Jeroboam was made king about 931 B. C., and reigned twenty-two years (1 Kin. xiv. 20). One son of his had died in infancy (1–17); another, Nadab, ascended the throne (20).

2. The son of Joash, king of Israel, and his successor on the throne of the ten tribes. He was of the dynasty of Jehu, and the third in descent from that ruler. He became king in Samaria about the year 790 B. C., and reigned forty-one years. He found the kingdom in a low state, but raised it again to prosperity, capturing Damascus, the capital of Syria, and Hamath in the valley of the Orontes, and restoring to Israel the country from the entrance of Hamath to the Dead Sea. These successes had been predicted by Jonah (2 Kin. xiv. 23–28; cp. Deut. iii. 17). Amos prophesied in Jereboam's reign (Amos i. 1), drawing a dark picture of the moral and religious state of Israel at the time (ii. 6–v. 27; viii. 4–6, etc.), and predicted judgment from God (vii. 1–9; viii. 7–10). For these prophecies of doom the priest at Beth-el made a complaint against him to Jeroboam, but it does not seem to have brought any penalty on the prophet (vii. 10–17). Hosea also began his prophetic work in the northern kingdom during the lifetime of Jeroboam. The first three chapters pertain to that period. On the death of Jeroboam, his son Zechariah ascended the throne (2 Kin. xiv. 29).

Je-ro'ham [he findeth mercy].

1. A Levite, an ancestor of the prophet Samuel (1 Sam. i. 1; 1 Chron. vi. 27, 34).

2. A Benjamite, whose sons were chief men and dwelt at Jerusalem (1 Chron. viii. 27).

See JEREMOTH 2. He may be identical with the following.

3. A Benjamite. father of Ibneiah who dwelt at Jerusalem (1 Chron. ix. 8).

4. A priest of the house of Malchijah (1 Chron. ix. 12; Neh. xi. 12).

5. A Benjamite of Gedor. whose sons joined David at Ziklag (1 Chron. xii. 7).

6. Father of the chief of the tribe of Dan in the reign of David (1 Chron. xxvii. 22).

7. Father of one of the captains who aided Jehoiada in putting Joash on the throne of Judah (2 Chron. xxiii. 1).

Je-rub'ba-al and **Je-rub'be-sheth.** See GIDEON.

Jer'u-el [probably, founded by God].

A wilderness in Judah, adjacent to the cliff of Ziz, and therefore in the vicinity of En-gedi (2 Chron. xx. 16). Exact situation unknown.

Je-ru'sa-lem [to the Hebrews it meant foundation of peace, secure habitation].

The sacred city and well-known capital of Judah, of Judæa, of Palestine, and of the Jews throughout the world. For the sake of convenient reference and clearness, the subject is presented under certain heads: I. Name. II. The city in itself: 1. Site; 2. Water supply; 3. Artificial defenses; 4. Notable buildings in the time of Christ. III. The history of the city: 1. The Canaanite city; 2. The city of the Hebrews; 3. The city since Titus. IV. Modern excavation.

I. *The name.* The earliest known name is *Urusalim, i. e.,* Jerusalem. It was in use at the dawn of the 15th century B. C., before the conquest of Canaan by the Israelites under Joshua, for it is found in letters from its subject prince to Amenophis IV., king of Egypt, his lord. Salem, of which Melchizedek was king, is a natural abbreviation of Jerusalem and not unlikely denoted this city. The place is mentioned as Jerusalem in the account of the conquest of Canaan, but in that narrative it is also referred to as Jebus; in fact, this latter name is frequent after the conquest during the occupation of the city by the Jebusites; but when David captured the city and made it his capital, the old name of Jerusalem, or abbreviated Salem (Ps. lxxvi. 2), became once more the sole designation. The pronunciation of the final syllable has been modified by the later Jews, so that it resembles a dual and quite appropriately suggests a double city.

II. 1. *The site.* Jerusalem is situated on a table-land on the crest of the central ridge of Palestine and at one of its highest points. It has the same latitude as the northern end of the Dead Sea. The portion of the table-land occupied by the city is isolated from the rest of the plateau, except on the north. On the other sides it is encompassed by deep ravines. This jutting promontory is itself cut by another valley which, followed upward from its mouth at the southeastern

Jerusalem, from the southern slope of the Mount of Olives, looking across the Kidron Valley toward the temple area. The city walls date from the Middle Ages.

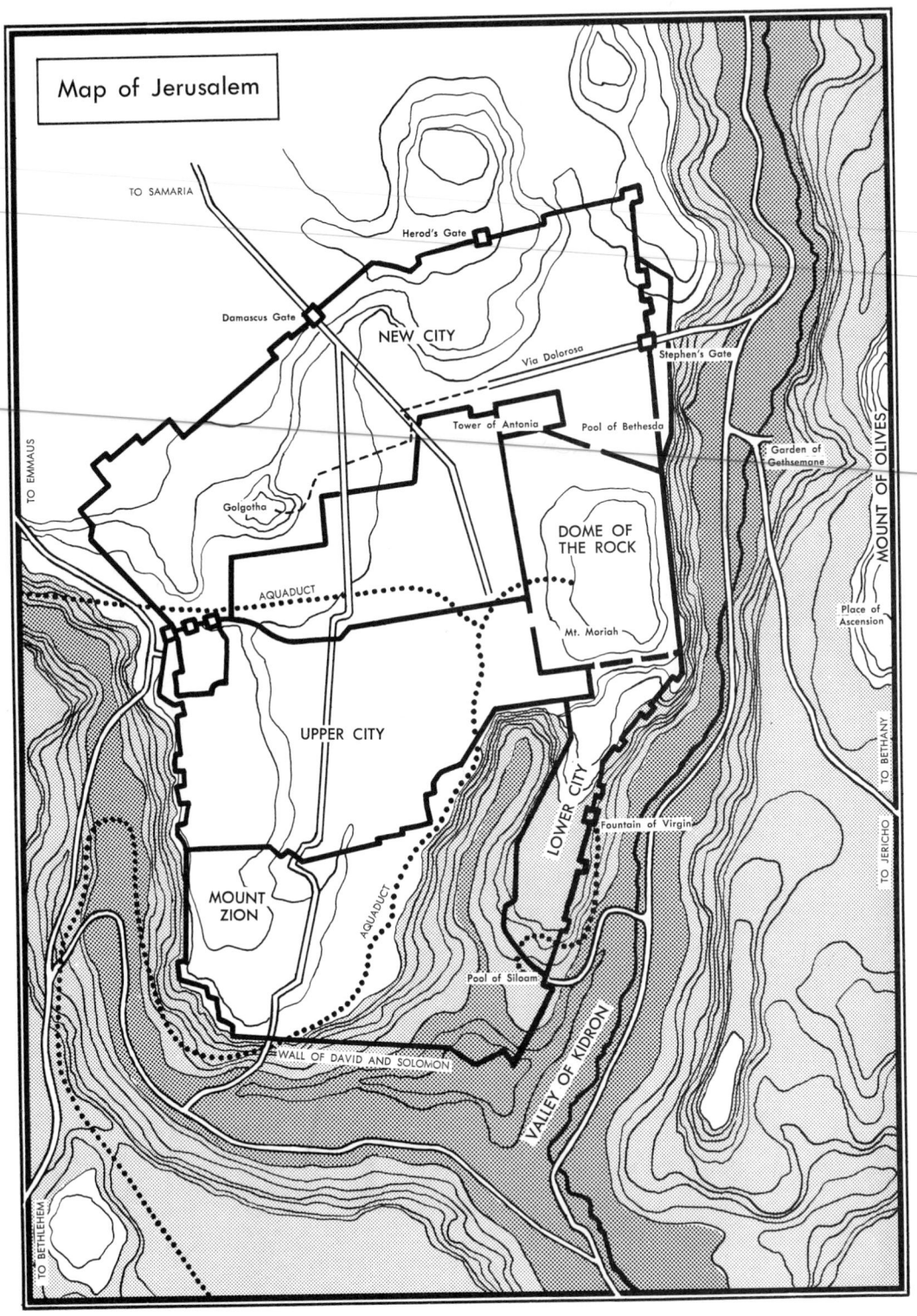

Map of Jerusalem

TO SAMARIA

Herod's Gate

Damascus Gate

NEW CITY

Via Dolorosa

Stephen's Gate

Tower of Antonia

Pool of Bethesda

Garden of Gethsemane

TO EMMAUS

Golgotha

DOME OF THE ROCK

Place of Ascension

AQUADUCT

Mt. Moriah

MOUNT OF OLIVES

UPPER CITY

LOWER CITY

Fountain of Virgin

TO JERICHO

TO BETHANY

MOUNT ZION

AQUADUCT

Pool of Siloam

VALLEY OF KIDRON

WALL OF DAVID AND SOLOMON

TO BETHLEHEM

corner of the promontory at the junction of
the southern and eastern ravines, trends like
the arc of a circle for nearly a mile northward, midway sending a branch from its
concave side due west. Such at least was
the original configuration of the city's site;
but in the course of centuries, through municipal improvements and the devastation of
war, heights have been lowered and valleys
filled. As a result of these ramifications,
there are three principal hills,
an eastern, a southwestern,
and a northwestern. The eastern hill is a ridge extending
for somewhat more than half
a mile from north to south,
which rises to a height of
from 200 to 300 feet above its
encompassing valleys, tapers
to a blunt point at its southern extremity, and at its
northern end is almost separated (the reference is to the
ancient topography) from the
table-land, of which it is a
part, by a branch of the eastern ravine. This ridge attains
a general altitude of 2400 feet
above sea level. There is some
evidence that a slight depression or valley, about 100 feet
wide and in places 40 feet
deep, lay athwart it toward
the southern end from the so-
called fountain of the Virgin
northwesterly to the Tyropœon valley. The southwestern hill is much the largest of
the three. In form it is oblong, with a spur thrown out
on the northeastern corner
toward the eastern ridge. It
rises abruptly from the encircling valleys. Its broad summit begins at an altitude of
about 2400 feet above the level of the sea and
swells 150 feet higher, with its greatest elevation on the west. The third hill is rather
a projection of the plateau than an isolated
mound. It lies north of the one just described. The present elevation of that part
included in the ante-Christian city is about
2450 feet. This triad of hills, with the
protecting ravines, afforded a strong position for a city, although it is encircled beyond the ravines by hills which tower above
it. The mountains are round about Jerusalem.

The eastern ravine is the valley of the
Kidron. The hill to the east, which faces
and overlooks the hills of the city, is the
mount of Olives. The long ridge which runs
north and south is the temple hill, called at
least in that portion of its extent where the
sanctuary stood, mount Moriah. Its southern
tapering extremity was known as Ophel.
The pool in the valley at its extreme southern

point is Siloam, and a pool just north of the
temple area is Bethesda.

Which height was mount Zion? This question has received three principal answers: 1.
Mount Zion was the southwestern hill. This
view has prevailed since the fourth century.
(1) Zion was the city of David (2 Sam. v.
7–9), and Josephus says that the upper city,
unquestionably the southwestern hill, was
called the citadel by David (War v. 4, 1).

**Pool of Siloam in the Kidron Valley. It is connected to the
Virgin's Fountain by the Siloam Tunnel which was built during the time of Hezekiah.**

Strangely enough, however. Josephus does
not explicitly call it Zion. (2) Micah distinguishes Zion from the temple hill (iv. 2). (3)
Too much building is spoken of in Neh.
iii. for Zion to be part of the temple hill.
(4) The sanctity of Zion is accounted for by
the fact that it was for many years the abiding place of the ark, and was celebrated as
such by David (2 Sam. vi. 12–18; 1 Kin. viii.
1–4; Ps. ii. 6). The name Zion thus became
the title for Jerusalem as a whole in its
quality as a holy city (Ps. xlviii.; lxxxvii.;
cxxxiii.3). 2. Mount Zion was the northwestern hill (Warren). This hill is identified with
that quarter of the city called by Josephus
the Acra, which in Greek means hilltop or
citadel. It is, indeed, styled by him the
lower city, for so it was in his day; but
originally it was much higher, and was cut
down by Simon Maccabæus because it commanded the temple (Antiq. xiii. 6, 7). It
was originally a suitable site for the Jebusite

fortress. 3. Mount Zion was a portion of the temple hill. The main arguments for this view are (1) The temple hill is best adapted by nature for a stronghold. (2) The temple could be reached by going from the fountain gate, up the stairs of the city of David, and past the water gate (Neh. xii. 37), steps which may be those that have been discovered ascending the ridge from the pool at the southern end. (3) Zion is spoken of as holy in terms such as are never applied to Jerusalem, but are intelligible if Zion was the hill on which the temple stood. Zion is called the hill of the Lord, the holy hill, the dwelling place of Jehovah (Ps. ii. 6; ix. 11; xxiv. 3; cxxxii. 13). (4) In the First Book of the Maccabees Zion is the temple hill (i. 33-38). The invariable distinction of the city of David from mount Zion and the sanctuary shows that the terms had undergone a change of meaning since 2 Sam. v. 7. The simplest explanation is that mount Zion was part of the temple hill, and by synecdoche often used for the whole of it, whereas the designation city of David, which denoted the municipality of Jerusalem (2 Sam. v. 7; Antiq. vii. 3, 2), was extended, with the growth of population, beyond the bounds of mount Zion and embraced the new suburbs on the neighboring hills, around which the protecting walls of the city were cast. The term

city of David might then on occasion include the sanctuary or exclude it. The Syrians erected a fortress in the city of David, but Judas Maccabæus came and took possession of the sanctuary on mount Zion (1 Mac. i. 33 seq.; iv. 36 seq.).

A section of Nehemiah's wall on the Hill of Ophel.

The third opinion is correct, proved so by excavation. Zion, the stronghold of the Jebusites, occupied the southern end of the eastern ridge, south of the temple, south also of the transverse ravine. Parts of the old walled town have been explored, traceable even into the third millennium B. C.

II. 2. *Water supply.* Although Jerusalem was often long and closely besieged and suffered grievous famine from having its supplies of food cut off, there is no record of the inhabitants having ever lacked water. In fact, it was the besiegers who were apt to want water, not the besieged. There is no spring north of the city, and none is known at present east, west, or south which was not commanded by the walls, except En-rogel. A living fountain to supply the Mamilla pool and the pool of the Sultan on the west has not been discovered. The southwestern hill is likewise without springs, so far as known, although the dragon's well may have been such (Neh. ii. 13). But the temple hill is well supplied (Tacitus, Hist. v. 12). The known living sources and their reservoirs are the fountain of the Virgin on the eastern side, with abundant water which was conducted by a subterranean channel to the pool of Siloam (see GIHON); the fountain of Siloam at the southern end of the hill, where also are to be sought, though their identification is difficult, the king's pool, the pool that was made, and Solomon's pool (Neh. ii. 14;

The Church of St. Anne dates back to Crusader times. To the right are excavations of the Pool of Bethesda.

iii. 16; War v. 4, 2); on the western side of the ridge, directly west of the temple, the so-called healing baths, Hammam esh-Shifa; and just north of the ridge, Bethesda.

The springs were supplemented by cisterns. The towers, which were upon the city walls, contained immense reservoirs for rain water (War v. 4, 3); and numerous cisterns, of which not a few still exist, were found in all parts of the city (Tacitus, Hist. v. 12).

Besides the supply afforded by the springs and cisterns of the city, water was brought from a distance. The Mamilla pool west of the city, regarded by many as the upper pool in the fuller's field, may be, as the name denotes, the serpent's pool (Is. vii. 3; xxxvi. 2; War v. 3, 2). An aqueduct brought the water from it to the pool of the patriarch east of the Jaffa gate. This is known to tradition as the pool of Hezekiah, and is probably the pool Amygdalon—i. e. pool of the almond or tower, mentioned by Josephus (War v. 11, 4). From it a subterranean conduit passes eastward. A reservoir was also constructed at a late period north of the temple area, in ground made where the small valley diverged westward from the Kidron. It was fed from the west. It is now known as the pool of Israel, and is probably identical with the pool Strouthios (pool of the sparrow or of soapwort, which was used for cleansing wool), which existed when Jerusalem was besieged by Titus, and lay in front of the tower of Antonia (War v. 11, 4). But the most extensive aqueduct was that which brought water to Jerusalem from beyond Bethlehem; see ETAM. It is believed to considerably antedate the Christian era.

II. 3. *Artificial defenses.* Immediately after capturing Jerusalem, David took measures to enclose the city with a wall. The old Jebusite stronghold, henceforth called the city of David, already existed. David, in addition, fortified the city round about, from Millo even round about (2 Sam. v. 9; 1 Chron. xi. 8). Solomon built Millo and the wall of Jerusalem, closing up the gap in the city of David (1 Kin. ix. 15, 24; xi. 27). Succeeding kings made repairs and additions, until eventually at least the wall passed near the present Jaffa gate on the west (2 Chron. xxvi. 9), approached the valley of Hinnom on the south (Jer. xix. 2), ran near the pool of Siloam (2 Kin. xxv. 4), included Ophel (2 Chron. xxvii. 3; xxxiii. 14), and on the north enclosed the suburb which grew up on the northwestern hill (2 Kin. xiv. 13; 2 Chron. xxxiii. 14; Jer. xxxi. 38). This wall was razed to the ground by Nebuchadnezzar (2 Kin. xxv. 10).

Nehemiah rebuilt the wall out of the old material (Neh. ii. 13-15; iv. 2, 7; vi. 15). It began, so to speak, at the sheep gate (iii. 1), which was near the pool of Bethesda (John v. 2). This pool has been discovered near to the church of St. Anne, about 100 yards from the gate now called St. Stephen's, and on what was originally the northern side of that branch of the Kidron valley which was interposed between the temple hill and the main plateau. The sheep gate stood, therefore, in this branch valley or on the slope of the plateau to the north or northwest. Near the sheep gate, in the direction away from the temple, were the towers of Meah and Hananeel (Neh. iii. 1; xii. 39). Then came the fish gate, in the new or second quarter of the city (iii. 3; Zeph. i. 10), and next the old gate (Neh. iii. 6; xii. 39). Some distance on from the latter point was the broad wall (iii. 8; xii. 38), and farther on the tower of the furnaces (iii. 11; xii. 38). To this there succeeded the valley gate, the technical designation of the valley on the west of the city being used (iii. 13; cp. ii. 13-15), then the dung gate (iii. 14), then the gate of the fountain, the wall of the pool of Siloam by the king's garden, at the southeastern corner of the city, and the stairs that go down from the city of David (15); to the east of this point was the water gate [of the temple?], with a large open place before it (viii. 1-3; xii. 37). The wall next went past the sepulchers of David, the pool that was made, and the house of the mighty (iii. 16); the going up to the armory, at the turning of the wall (19); the house of the high priest, Eliashib (20); then various points indicated by other houses unto the turning of the wall, the corner (24); the turning of the wall and the tower which standeth out from the king's upper house, that was by the court of the guard (25). Now the Nethinim dwelt here in Ophel from over against the water gate [of the temple?] toward the east and this tower that standeth out (26; cp. xi. 21). Then a piece of wall from this tower to the wall of Ophel (iii. 27). The horse gate came next, above which the priests resided (28). It was on the eastern side of the city, overlooking the Kidron valley (Jer. xxxi. 40). Then a portion of the wall over against the house of [the priest] Zadok, then a section repaired by the keeper of the east gate [of the temple, probably] (Neh. iii. 29). Presently the house of the Nethinim; then a section from over against the gate of the Miphkad [which was probably a gate of the temple at the place where the sin offering was burned, called the Miphkad, cp. Ezek. xliii. 21] to the upper chamber of the tower (iii. 31); and, finally, the sheep gate, which was the starting point of the description (32).

Two important gates of the former wall are not mentioned, though one at least existed at this time, the corner gate (2 Kin. xiv. 13; 2 Chron. xxvi. 9; cp. Zech. xiv. 10) and the gate of Ephraim (Neh. viii. 16; xii. 39). The corner gate appears to have been the extreme northwestern point of the city (Jer. xxxi. 38), and it was distant 400 cubits from the gate of Ephraim (2 Kin. xiv. 13). Through this latter gate the road to Ephraim passed; presumably, therefore, it was in the

The Tower of Antonia, the northwest corner of the temple area. It is believed that after the Roman soldiers rescued Paul from the mob, he addressed the crowd from these stairs.

northern wall of the city, and if so, then east of the corner gate. It was certainly west of the old gate (Neh. xii. 39). Beginning with the sheep gate and following the northern wall westward, the order of gates and towers is sheep gate, towers of Meah and Hananeel, fish gate, old gate, gate of Ephraim, corner gate. Whether the broad wall and tower of furnaces were beyond the corner gate is difficult to determine. It is to be observed that the gates of the corner and Ephraim occur in that part of the wall where it is recorded that "they left Jerusalem" (iii. 8, R. V. margin), as though the wall required no repairs at this point.

There was also a gate of Benjamin, through which the road to Benjamin passed (Jer. xxxviii. 7; Zech. xiv. 10). This may have been but another name for the gate of Ephraim. After the fall of Samaria and the virtual disappearance of Ephraim from geographical parlance, the gate of Ephraim would naturally come to be known as the gate of Benjamin, and when the walls of the city were rebuilt, after the exile, to be called indifferently the gate of Benjamin or of Ephraim or, eventually, of Damascus.

During the interval between Nehemiah and Christ the fortifications of Jerusalem suffered many vicissitudes. About 150 years after the building of Nehemiah's wall, the high priest, Simon the Just, found it necessary to fortify the temple and the city so that they might be able to stand a siege (Ecclus. l. 1-4; for need, cp. Antiq. xii. 1, 1). In 168 B. C. Antiochus Epiphanes had the walls of Jerusalem thrown down and a fortress with a great and strong wall and mighty towers erected in the city of David, perhaps a broad designation meaning the city as distinct from the temple (1 Mac. i. 31, 33, 39; 2 Mac. v. 24-26). This fortress became celebrated as the Acra. It overlooked the temple (Antiq. xiii. 6, 7), and for twenty-five years was a menace to the Jews. About two years after the demolition of the city walls, Judas Maccabæus partly restored them, strengthening the outer wall of the temple; but only to have his work undone (1 Mac. iv. 60; vi. 18-27, 62). His brother and successor, Jonathan, however, renewed the work, proposing additional fortifications and rebuilding and repairing the walls, particularly around the temple hill (1 Mac. x. 10; xii. 36, 37; Antiq. xiii. 5, 11). His brother Simon carried the work to completion (1 Mac. xiii. 10; xiv. 37; Antiq. xiii. 6, 4). Under this great priest-king, not only were the walls of the city built, but the foreign garrison was forced in the year 142 B. C. to evacuate the Acra (1 Mac. xiii. 49-51). After a time the fortress was demolished and the hill on which it had stood was graded down so as to be lower than the level of the temple (1 Mac. xiv. 36; xv. 28; Antiq. xiii. 6, 7). Simon appears also to have taken up his residence in the fortress Baris, which

The Damascus Gate, the main entry into the Old City.

The old Jewish cemetery on the slopes of the Mount of Olives. Absalom's tomb is on the lower left and Zechariah's tomb is on the right.

A section of the Old City.

protected the temple on the north (1 Mac. xiii. 52; cp. Neh. ii. 8). In the reign of John Hyrcanus a portion of the fortifications of the city was dismantled by Antiochus Sidetes, but the ruin seems to have been repaired by John (Antiq. xiii. 8, 3; 1 Mac. xvi. 23). John also remodeled and strengthened the fortress Baris (Antiq. xviii. 4, 3; cp. xv. 11, 4). Pompey found the defenses of Jerusalem strong. On finally capturing the city in 63 B. C., he demolished the walls (Tacitus, Hist. v. 9; and next two references). Cæsar allowed them to be rebuilt (Antiq. xiv. 8, 5; War i. 10, 3 and 4). On the north they consisted of two walls which Herod and his Roman allies took in the year 37 B. C., but did not destroy (Antiq. xiv. 16, 2 and 4; cp. xv. 1, 2).

At the time of Christ, Jerusalem had the two walls aforementioned on the north, and shortly afterwards three. Josephus identifies the first and innermost wall as the work of David, Solomon, and succeeding kings. He describes it by reference to landmarks of his day as extending from the tower of Hippicus, which stood immediately south of the modern Jaffa gate at the northwest corner of the old city wall, eastward to the west cloister of the temple; and from the tower of Hippicus south and east by the pool of Siloam and Ophel to the eastern cloister of the temple (War v. 4, 2). It enclosed the southwestern and eastern hills. The second wall encompassed the northern and principal business quarter of the city (War v. 4, 2; for bazaars in this section, 8, 1; i. 13, 2; Antiq. xiv. 13, 3). It began at the gate Gennath, that is, by interpretation, the garden gate, which belonged to the first wall and stood not far east of the tower of Hippicus (War v. 4, 2; 3, 2 for gardens); and terminated at

the tower of Antonia, formerly called Baris, north of the temple (War v. 4, 2). Herod Agrippa I., who reigned over Judæa from A. D. 41 to 44, undertook a third wall in order to include within the city limits the unprotected suburb of Bezetha, which had grown up outside of the fortifications. After laying the foundations, however, he relinquished the work at the command of the emperor Claudius. It was finally completed by the Jews themselves. It began at the tower of Hippicus, extended northward to the tower of Psephinus, at the northwest corner of the city (War v. 3, 5; 4, 3); turned eastward and passed on to the women's towers, which stood west of the northern highway and near the monuments of Helena, queen of Adiabene (v. 4, 2; Antiq. xx. 4, 3); included the traditional site of the camp of the Assyrians (War v. 7, 3); passed the caves of the kings; bent southward at the corner tower, near the monument of the fuller; and joined the old wall at the valley of the Kidron (v. 4, 2). The circumference of the walls was 33 stadia, a little less than 4 miles (v. 4, 3). The defenses of the city were augmented by the fortress of Antonia at the temple, and by the palace of Herod with its adjacent towers on the western wall. All these fortifications Titus razed to the ground on his capture of the city in A. D. 70. He left only the group of three towers, Hippicus, Phasaelus, and Mariamne, and so much of the wall as enclosed the city on the west side. He spared this portion of the wall in order that it might afford protection to his garrison, and the towers that posterity might see what kind of a city it was which Roman valor had taken (War vii. 1, 1).

II. 4. *Notable buildings in the time of Christ.* Besides the walls which have been already

Air view of Jerusalem and environs. The Kidron Valley is on the right, the Hinnom Valley on the left.

View of the Kidron Valley, looking northeast from Jerusalem. Visible are the Garden of Gethsemane, the Church of All Nations, the Russian Church, and the Mount of Olives.

described, there were many structures to awaken conflicting emotions in the pious and patriotic Israelite. Foremost was the temple. Adjoining it on the north, within its area and controlling it, was the fortress of Antonia occupied by a Roman garrison; west of it stood the council house, probably the place where the council of the nation or sanhedrin met; a little more to the westward, at the farther end of the bridge which sprang from the western cloister of the temple and spanned the Tyropœon valley, lay the gymnasium or xystos, an object of abhorrence on account of its demoralizing and heathenizing influence; above it, looking down into it and peering across the valley into the sanctuary, rose the palace of the Asmonæans, recalling the heroic achievements of the Maccabees. Or taking a wider circuit, to the north of the temple beyond the fortress of Antonia was the pool of Bethesda with its healing waters; away to the west, at the opposite side of the city from the temple, stood the magnificent palace of Herod with its impregnable towers, the residence of the procurators when in Jerusalem; around toward the south was the pool of Siloam, and not too far from it were the sepulchers of the kings (see the several articles). In this neighborhood may best be sought the very large amphitheater erected by Herod the Great in the plain (Antiq. xv. 8, 1). It was, perhaps, the same as the hippodrome, which lay south from the temple (War ii. 3, 1), for chariot races as well as wild beast fights and gladiatorial combats seem to have taken place in it (Antiq. xv. 8,

1), and in the hippodrome men were confined (xvii. 9, 5; War i. 33, 6). Other buildings were the house of the high priest (Mat. xxvi. 3; Luke xxii. 54; War ii. 17, 6); the house of records, near the temple (War ii. 17, 6; vi. 6, 3); the palace of the proselyte queen of Adiabene, Helena (ibid.).

III. 1. *The city of the Canaanites.* If the Salem of Melchizedek be Jerusalem, as is probable, the city first emerges in history in the days of Abraham, when it already had a king of the Semitic race, who was at the same time priest of the Most High God (Gen. xiv. 18). Manetho, an Egyptian priest and historian of the third century before Christ, transmits a tradition, which may contain considerable truth and which chronologically belongs here, to the effect that the nation of the shepherd kings to the number of 240,000 were driven out of Egypt by Thoummosis [or Amosis, *i. e.* Aahmes (Eusebius, Chron. 15–17)], and fled toward Syria; but fearing the Assyrians, who had dominion over Asia, they built a city in the country now called Judæa of sufficient size to contain the multitude and named it Jerusalem (con. Apion. i. 14, 15). This expulsion of the shepherds took place, according to Manetho, several centuries before the exodus of the children of Israel, and must not be confounded with the later event (i. 26 seq.). It occurred somewhere about 1600 B. C. The earliest mention of Jerusalem in a document of which the original is extant is about 1500 B. C., when it still has a Semite as its governor, but is subject to Amenophis IV., king of Egypt.

The Pool of the Sultan, just outside the walls of the Old City of Jerusalem. Animals are traded and sold here on Fridays. In the background is the modern church of St. Andrew.

This was before the exodus. When the Israelites entered Canaan, Jerusalem was ruled by a king, still a Semite, and occupied by Amorites, or more definitely by Jebusites. Joshua defeated its king and his allies at Gibeon, drove them down the pass of Beth-horon, and slew them in the lowland (Josh. x.). But no attempt was made to enter the city. The Jebusites still dwelt in it. It was allotted to the tribe of Benjamin ; but as it stood on the border of Judah, its castle commanded a portion of the territory of two tribes (Josh. xv. 8 ; xviii. 28). In the war which was waged by the several tribes against the Canaanites within their own bounds after the death of Joshua, Judah fought against Jerusalem, took it, and set it on fire (Judg. i. 8). But apparently Judah did not capture the citadel. Neither did Benjamin (21). Hence, when the city was rebuilt, it was still under the shadow of the Jebusite stronghold and its inhabitants were Jebusites. It was a city of foreigners and a reproach in the midst of the land (Josh. xv. 63 ; Judg. i. 21 ; xix. 11, 12). Such was the state of affairs when David began his career. When he had slain Goliath, he returned from the field of battle by way of Jerusalem and brought the head of the Philistine thither. Possibly he erected it on a spear in view of the city; at any rate he displayed it before the eyes of the Jebusites (1 Sam. xvii. 54). It was a prophecy to this stronghold of mocking foreigners of what awaited them. And when he became king of all Israel, and found a united and enthusiastic nation obedient to him, and the jealousy between Judah and Benjamin allayed, he at once led his troops against the border town, and in face of the derision of the inhabitants, who believed their walls to be impregnable, gained possession (2 Sam. v. 6 seq.). Henceforth for many centuries Jerusalem was a city of the Hebrews.

III. 2. *The city of the Hebrews.* David made Jerusalem the capital of his kingdom, and took measures to make it the religious center also. The ark, which had had no dwelling place of its own since Jehovah forsook Shiloh, he brought to Jerusalem and pitched a suitable tent for it, and he began the collection of materials for a temple. The city shared in the prosperity of Solomon's reign. The walls were enlarged, the temple was erected on a scale of great magnificence, and surrounded by a wall which gave it the appearance of a fortress, and a royal palace was built not inferior to the temple in splendor. In the next reign, however, the army of Shishak, king of Egypt, entered the city and robbed the temple and the palace of their treasures (1 Kin. xiv. 25 seq.), and about eighty years later bands of Philistines and Arabs gained brief admission to the city and carried off plunder (2 Chron. xxi. 17). The population was in the meanwhile increasing, quarters of the city began to be distinguished

(2 Kin. xx. 4 ; xxii. 14), and before the beginning of the eighth century a suburb on the northwestern hill was enclosed by an addition to the city wall. This part of the city was the mercantile district, and continued to be such after the exile and until the destruction of the city by Titus (War v. 8, 1). Here were the sheep and the fish gates, and the quarter was skirted by the valley of the cheesemongers. In the reign of Amaziah a portion of the city wall was broken down, and temple and palace were despoiled of treasure by the northern Israelites (2 Kin. xiv. 13, 14). Uzziah and Jotham repaired the ruin, strengthened the walls, and erected new towers for defense (2 Chron. xxvi. 9 ; xxvii. 3). But they had perhaps other ruins to care for than those wrought by war, for in Uzziah's reign the city was visited by a memorable earthquake (Amos i. 1 ; Zech. xiv. 5; Antiq. ix. 10, 4). Under Ahaz the city was besieged, but not taken, by the northern Israelites in alliance with the Syrians (2 Kin. xvi. 5), and shortly afterwards, by reason of the king's inclination to heathenism, the lamps of the temple were allowed to go out, the offering in the holy place ceased, and the temple was closed (2 Kin. xvi. 14 seq. ; 2 Chron. xxviii. 24 ; xxix. 7). Hezekiah reopened the temple and restored the service, but he was obliged to empty the royal and the sacred treasuries and to strip the plates of gold from the temple doors in order to raise a sum sufficient to purchase exemption from a threatened raid by the Assyrians ; and even this relief was but temporary, for eventually Assyrian troops stood before the walls (2 Chron. xxix. 3 ; 2 Kin. xviii. 15 seq.). The city was, however, delivered by the providential outbreak of pestilence in the camp of the enemy (2 Kin. xix. 35). When Manasseh returned from captivity he built walls for the city and strengthened the fortifications (2 Chron. xxxiii. 14). During the reigns of the sons and grandson of Josiah the city experienced its overwhelming calamities. Nebuchadnezzar besieged it in the days of Jehoiakim, entered it, bound but eventually released the king, and carried off costly vessels from the temple and a number of noble youth (2 Kin. xxiv. 1 ; 2 Chron. xxxvi. 6 ; Dan. i. 1). Again he came, emptied the royal and the sacred treasuries, seized the remaining vessels of gold and silver belonging to the temple, carried king Jehoiachin a prisoner to Babylon, and deported the best and most useful citizens (2 Kin. xxiv. 10 seq.). Nine years later, in the reign of Zedekiah, he laid siege to the city for the third time. The investment lasted two years. The misery within the walls was extreme. Finally a breach was made, the city was taken, the temple and the palaces were burnt, the wall was broken down, and the remnant of the population, save the poorest, was deported (2 Kin. xxv.). The city lay waste for fifty years. Zerub-

babel and 50,000 followers returned to Jerusalem in 538 B. C., and at the beginning of the next year laid the foundation of the temple (Ezra ii. 64, 65; iii. 8). The walls of the city were rebuilt under Nehemiah about 445 B. C. The supreme power was then in the hands of the Persians, from whom it passed, under Alexander the Great, to the Macedonian Greeks. The city was taken by Antiochus the Great 203 B. C., retaken by the Egyptians in 199, and opened its gates again to Antiochus coming as a friend in 198. In 170 B. C. Antiochus Epiphanes took Jerusalem, subsequently desecrating the temple; see HISTORY. But the Maccabees arose; and in 165 B. C. Judas retook the city and purified the temple. The kings of the Asmonæan race built near the temple a citadel called Baris or the tower; see ANTONIA, TOWER OF. Pompey captured Jerusalem 63 B. C., breaking down part of the wall; Crassus despoiled the temple in 54 B. C. and the Parthians plundered the city in 40 B. C. Jerusalem was taken again in 37 B. C. by Herod the Great, who repaired the walls, adorned the city with various edifices, and rebuilt the temple on a scale of magnificence which markedly contrasted with the comparatively humble character of Zerubbabel's temple. The work began 20-19 B. C., and was not quite completed when our Lord was on earth. Herod also strengthened the citadel and called it Antonia (q. v.). When he passed away there were two walls, in whole or in part encompassing Jerusalem, against one in Solomon's time. A third wall was begun by Herod Agrippa (about A. D. 42 or 43) a dozen years after the crucifixion. In A. D. 70 the Romans, under Titus, took Jerusalem, the temple and nearly all

III. 3. *The city since Titus.* Under the emperor Hadrian the Romans commenced to refortify Jerusalem as a gentile city, and hold it against its former inhabitants. This seems to have been one main cause of the Jewish revolt under Bar-cocheba (about A. D. 132 to 135). On its suppression, the rebuilding of the city was resumed and completed. The old name Jerusalem was discarded. It was called Colonia Ælia Capitolina: Colonia to denote that it was a Roman colony, Ælia in honor of Hadrian, whose prænomen was Ælius, and Capitolina because it was dedicated to Jupiter Capitolinus. To this heathen deity a temple was dedicated on the spot where those of Solomon, Zerubbabel, and Herod had stood. The Jews were forbidden, on pain of death, to enter within its walls. The Christians were, perhaps, by this time sufficiently distinguished from the Jews not to come under the prohibition. The name Ælia continued for many centuries. The emperor Constantine first partially, and then completely, removed the prohibition against the Jews entering the Holy City. In 326 Helena, his mother, caused two churches to be built at Bethlehem and on the mount of Olives, and in 336 the emperor himself erected the first church of the Holy Sepulcher; see CALVARY. In June, 613, Jerusalem was taken by storm by the Persians under Chosroes II., thousands of the inhabitants were massacred and other thousands were carried off prisoners to Persia, and the church of the Holy Sepulcher was burnt down. In 628, on the death of Chosroes, Jerusalem was retaken by the Roman emperor, Heraclius. In 637 it surrendered on conditions to the Arabs under Omar. Soon

Sketch of a Roman medal commemorating the capture of Jerusalem.

the city having been burnt or otherwise destroyed during the siege. He broke down all the walls, with the exception of part of the western one and three towers, Hippicus, Phasaelus, and Mariamne, which he left to show posterity the nature of the defenses he had succeeded in capturing (War vii. 1, 1).

afterwards the conqueror built the Dome of the Rock, which Europeans call the mosque of Omar, upon, or very near, the site of temple of Solomon. During the period that Jerusalem was ruled by the Saracens, the treatment of the Christian pilgrims who visited the sacred shrines varied. Once the church of the Holy Sepulcher was set on fire under a Fatimite ruler, but on the whole there was toleration. It was different when the Saracens were displaced by the Turks in A. D. 1077. The insults and oppression practiced by the semi-savages who had now gained power, threw all middle and central Europe into a ferment, and brought on the crusades. In the first of these religious expeditions Jerusalem was taken by storm on July 15, 1099, and a Christian kingdom established, which continued eighty-eight years. During the Christian occupation the buildings connected with the Holy Sepulcher were enlarged and made more splendid, and other edifices erected in the city. In 1187 it had to be surrendered to Saladin, sultan of Egypt and Syria; and with the exception of two short periods, when the Christians again possessed the city, it remained under Mohammedan rule until Dec. 1, 1917, when it surrendered to the English.

The population of the city in 1863 was estimated at 5000 Mohammedans, 3606 Christians, and 7100 Jews, total 15,706 (Keith Johnston). In 1892 Dr. Selah Merrill, United States consul at Jerusalem, reported to his government that the Jews alone amounted to 25,322. In this year also a railway was completed from Jaffa to Jerusalem. Ten years later the Jews had increased in number to 40,000.

IV. *Modern excavation.* "An inscription in Arabic over the Yâfa [*i. e.* the Jaffa] gate," says Prof. Robinson, "as well as others in various places, records that the present walls of Jerusalem were rebuilt by order of sultan Suleiman in A. H. [the year of the Hegira] 948, corresponding to A. D. 1542. They appear to occupy very nearly the site of the former walls of the middle ages, which were several times thrown down and rebuilt during the crusades, a slight deviation only being visible around the northwest corner, on both the northern and western sides. The materials were probably those of the former walls; and are in great part apparently ancient" (*Bib. Res.* i. 384). The foundations are in some places built of very large stones, which may have formed part of the ancient walls. It may be asked also, May not fragments of the old first, second, and third walls have escaped destruction, even in places where they did not coincide in direction with the present city walls? The answer must be in the affirmative. Prof. Robinson, in 1838, found near the Damascus gate large ancient beveled stones, which had apparently never been disturbed since they were first put in position. He regarded them as probably belonging to the guardhouse defending a gate which existed prior to the days of Herod (*Bib. Res.* i. 463). Robinson also believed that he and Mr. Whiting found traces of the northwestern part of the foundations of Agrippa's wall (465), the observation having been confirmed by Hanauer before the remains were covered with buildings (*Palestine Explor. Fund Quarterly Statement,*

Oct., 1892, p. 295). Sir Charles Warren, under the auspices of the Palestine Exploration Fund, made extensive excavations in Jerusalem from Feb., 1867, till April, 1870, sinking shafts through the *débris*, which at one place was 125 feet deep, covering the ancient city. He found and traced for a considerable distance the wall of Ophel (Wilson and Warren, *Recovery of Jerusalem*, 286–289). Since then Mr. Henry Maudsley, C. E., traced the course of the first wall by relics of it still remaining on mount Zion (*Twenty-one Years*, 59). When, in 1885, an excavation was made for the foundation of the Grand New Hotel, a little north of Hippicus, a portion of the second wall was traced for about 120 feet. Excavation was continued by the Exploration Fund, with Dr. F. J. Bliss as director, and ancient walls along the valley of Hinnom were discovered. For Jebusite walls, see Section II, 1, end.

Je-ru'sha and **Jerushah** [possession].
Wife of Uzziah, king of Judah, and mother of his successor, Jotham (2 Kin. xv. 33; 2 Chron. xxvii. 1).

Je-sha'iah, in A. V. twice **Jesaiah** (1 Chron. iii. 21; Neh. xi. 7) [Jehovah is opulent, or Jehovah hath saved].
1. A son of Jeduthun, and a musician in the reign of David (1 Chron. xxv. 3).
2. A Levite, son of Rehabiah; he also was in David's reign (1 Chron. xxvi. 25).
3. A son of Hananiah, and a descendant of Zerubbabel (1 Chron iii. 21).
4. A son of Athaliah and head of the father's house of Elam, who, with seventy males, returned from Babylon with Ezra (Ezra viii. 7).
5. A Merarite Levite who returned in the same company (Ezra viii. 19).
6. A Benjamite, the father of Ithiel (Neh. xi. 7).

Jesh'a-nah [old].
A city in the hill country of Ephraim, wrested by Abijah from the northern kingdom (2 Chron. xiii. 19; cp. xv. 8). It is believed to be the village called Isanas, where Herod the Great defeated the general of Antigonus (Antiq. xiv. 15, 12). Ruins of an Israelite town by Burj el-Isâneh, 4 miles north of Beth-el, half a mile east of the highway, may mark the site. See SHEN.

Jesh-a-re'lah. See ASHARELAH.

Je-sheb'e-ab [father's dwelling].
A descendant of Aaron. His family became the fourteenth course of the priesthood (1 Chron. xxiv. 13).

Je'sher [probity, uprightness].
A son of Caleb (1 Chron. ii. 18).

Jesh'i-mon [a waste, a desert].
1. A wilderness at the northeastern end of the Dead Sea, not far from Pisgah and Peor (Num. xxi. 20; xxiii. 28). Beth-jeshimoth was situated in it; see BETH-JESHIMOTH.
2. A wilderness to the north of the hill Hachilah and of Maon (1 Sam. xxiii. 19, 24; xxvi. 1, 3).

It is probable that Jeshimon in these passages is not a proper name, but should be rendered desert, as in R. V.

Je-shi'shai [pertaining to an old man].

A Gadite, descended from Buz (1 Chron. v. 14).

Jesh-o-ha'iah [perhaps, Jehovah doth humble].

A Simeonite prince (1 Chron. iv. 36).

Jesh'u-a, in A. V. once **Jeshuah** (1 Chron. xxiv. 11), an inconsistency not found in the original edition of A. V. [a late form of Joshua, Jehovah is salvation].

1. Joshua, the military leader in the wars of Canaan (Neh. viii. 17).

2. A descendant of Aaron. His family had grown to a father's house in the time of David and was made the ninth of the twenty-four courses into which David divided the priests (1 Chron. xxiv. 1, 6, 11).

3. One of the Levites in Hezekiah's reign who had to do with the receipt and distribution of the freewill offerings in the temple (2 Chron. xxxi. 15).

4. A high priest who returned with Zerubbabel from Babylon (Ezra ii. 2; Neh. vii. 7). He was the son of Jozadak. He built the altar of burnt offering, and encouraged the workmen and the people generally to rebuild the temple (Ezra iii. 2-9). In Zechariah's prophecies he is called Joshua, and stands as the priestly representative of the returned exiles to whom divine support is given (Zech. iii. 1-10; vi. 11-13).

5. A man of the house of Pahath-moab, some of whose children returned with Zerubbabel and others from captivity (Ezra ii. 6; Neh. vii. 11).

6. A Levite, head of a Levitical family, who, with members of the family, returned from captivity with Zerubbabel (Ezra ii. 40; Neh. vii. 43; xii. 8). He actively assisted Jeshua, the high priest, in stimulating the workmen and people to rebuild the temple (Ezra iii. 9). The representative of the house bearing his name affixed his seal to the covenant (Neh. x. 9). From the last passage, it appears that Jeshua was the son of Azaniah (9). In Neh. xii. 24 the word *ben*, the son of, after Jeshua is probably a corruption; perhaps a corruption of Bani (cp. ix. 4, 5). Not unlikely it was this Levite Jeshua who was the father of the ruler of Mizpah, Ezer, who repaired a portion of the wall (iii. 19).

7. A Levite, probably of the aforementioned family, who aided Ezra in explaining the law to the people (Neh. viii. 7), and in preparing them for a more heartfelt worship of Jehovah (ix. 4, 5).

8. A village of southern Judah (Neh. xi. 26).

Jesh'u-run, in A. V. once **Jesurun** (Is. xliv. 2) [righteous one].

A name of endearment used in poetry for the nation of Israel with reference to the moral character which they were created to exhibit (Deut. xxxii. 15; xxxiii. 5, 26; Is. xliv. 2).

Je-si'ah. See ISSHIAH.

Je-sim'i-el [God setteth up].

A prince of the tribe of Simeon (1 Chron. iv. 36).

Jes'se.

Son of Obed, family of Perez. He was descended from Nahshon, chief of the tribe of Judah in the days of Moses, and from Ruth the Moabitess (Ruth iv. 18-22). He was father of eight sons, the youngest of whom was David (1 Sam. xvii. 12-14). To judge from 1 Chron. ii. 15, one of them died without leaving posterity: unless, as is less probable, Elihu (xxvii. 18) has been lost from the register. Jesse had two daughters, but by a different wife from David's mother (ii. 16; cp. 2 Sam. xvii. 25). Jesse lived at Bethlehem, to which Samuel was sent to anoint a king from among his sons. After seven of them had been passed before him in the order of their birth, David was called from the flock which he was tending, and on his arrival was anointed king (1 Sam. xvi. 1-13). After Saul had become jealous of David he usually called him the son of Jesse (xx. 31; xxii. 7; xxv. 10), in order to emphasize David's humble origin. Saul ignored the fact that his own father was no more a king than was David's father. In the cave of Adullam David was joined by his father, his mother, and his brothers. He allowed his brothers to share the dangers of his wanderings, but placed his parents under the protection of the king of Moab, the native land of his ancestress Ruth, till he knew what God had in store for him in the future (xxii. 1-4). It is uncertain when Jesse died. Although of good ancestry and himself an able man, yet his station in life was lowly. This humble position of the family is alluded to by the prophets (Is. xi. 1, 10; cp. Mic. v. 2; Rom. xv. 12), and was recalled by all who refused the rule of the house of David (2 Sam. xx. 1; 1 Kin. xii. 16; 2 Chron. x. 16).

Jes'u-i. See ISHVI.

Jes'u-run. See JESHURUN.

Je'sus, an imitation of the Greek form of Jeshua, which in turn is a late form of Jehoshua or Joshua [Jehovah is salvation].

1. Joshua, the military leader in the wars of Canaan (A. V. of Acts vii. 45; Heb. iv. 8); see JOSHUA.

2. An ancestor of Christ, who lived about four hundred years after David (Luke iii. 29). The A. V., following a different Greek text, calls him Jose.

3. In the Septuagint the name occurs several times in the Apocrypha. It was borne by the author of Ecclesiasticus, and twelve persons with this name are mentioned by Josephus outside of his references to Joshua and to Christ. It was a common name among the Jews of the Greek-speaking period.

4. A Jewish Christian, also called Justus, associated with Paul (Col. iv. 11).

5. The name of our Lord. See JESUS CHRIST.

Je'sus Christ.

Our Lord was named Jesus in accordance with the directions of the angel to Joseph (Mat. i. 21) and Mary (Luke i. 31). When given to ordinary children it merely expressed, if anything, the parent's faith in God as the saviour of his people, or their faith in the coming salvation of Israel. When given to Mary's child it was designed to express the special office he would fulfill: "Thou shalt call his name Jesus, for he shall save his people from their sins" (Mat. i. 21). Christ is from the Greek *Christos*, anointed, corresponding to the Hebrew *Mashiah*, anointed, Messiah. Jesus therefore was our Lord's personal name and Christ was his title (the Christ); though the latter was early used also as a proper name, as it is by us, either alone or with Jesus.

It is the object of the following article to sketch the progress of our Lord's life on earth, so as to place its principal events in their probable order and relation.

Chronology. The exact dates of the birth, baptism, and death of Jesus cannot be absolutely demonstrated; but most scholars now agree within narrow limits. Our ordinary Christian calendar originated with Dionysius Exiguus, a Roman abbot who died A. D. 556. He first selected the year of the incarnation as that before and after which dates should be reckoned. He fixed, however, on the year of Rome, 754, as that in which Christ was born, and that year consequently equals A. D. 1. But the statements of Josephus make it clear that Herod the Great, who died shortly after Jesus was born (Mat. ii. 19–22), died several years before the year of Rome, 754. His death occurred thirty-seven years after he had been declared king by the Romans, which was in A. U. C. 714. This might be 751 or 750, according to whether Josephus counted fractions of a year as whole years or not. The year 750 is, however, made the more probable from the further statement of Josephus that shortly before Herod's death he put to death two Jewish rabbis, and that on the night of their execution there occurred an eclipse of the moon. Astronomical calculations show that in 750 there was a partial lunar eclipse on the night of March 12 or 13; but in 751 there was no eclipse. Josephus also narrates that Herod died shortly before the passover, which began in 750 on April 12. We may, therefore, with considerable confidence date Herod's death about April 1, in the year of Rome 750, which was 4 B. C. Before that date, therefore, we must place the events given in the gospels which occurred between the birth of Jesus and the death of Herod, for which a period of two or three months is probably required. Christ's birth, therefore, is to be placed at the close of 5 B. C. or beginning of 4 B. C. The observance of December 25th did not arise

until the fourth century, so that it has no authority. It may, however, be accepted as an approximation to the truth, and then Christ's birth would be assigned to December 25, 5 B. C. This puts it five years earlier than in the calendar of Dionysius, who assigned it to December 25, A. D. 1. The date of the opening of our Lord's public ministry is to be obtained principally from Luke iii. 23, where it is said that at his baptism he was about thirty years of age. The expression is obviously indefinite; but, assuming that he was born December 25, 5 B. C., he would be thirty on December 25, A. D. 26. The traditional date of the baptism is January 6, and if we suppose at any rate that it occurred early in A. D. 27, Luke's expression, "about thirty years of age," would be correct. This date also is somewhat confirmed by the statement of the Jews (John ii. 20), made shortly after his baptism, "forty and six years was this temple in building." The rebuilding of the temple by Herod was begun, as might be shown, in 20–19 B. C.; so that the forty-six years, supposing them to have elapsed when the remark was made, would bring us again to A. D. 27. If, finally, "the fifteenth year of the reign of Tiberius" (Luke iii. 1), when John the Baptist began his ministry, be reckoned, as it properly may be, from the time when Tiberius was associated with Augustus in the empire (A. D. 11 to 12), it coincides with A. D. 26 and further agrees with our other calculations. It is true that all these items of evidence contain in them points on which opinions may not unreasonably differ; yet the dates we have given appear to be the most probable and to support one another. The length of Christ's ministry and consequently the year of his death are to be fixed by the number of passovers which John notes in his Gospel. If we had only the synoptic gospels (see GOSPEL), we might infer that his ministry was only a year in length, and this was in ancient times a not uncommon opinion. But John's Gospel speaks of at least three passovers (ii. 13; vi. 4; xiii. 1), and it is highly probable that the feast referred to in John v. 1 was also a passover. If so, Christ's ministry included four passovers, at the last of which he died; and, if he was baptized early in A. D. 27, his first passover was in April of that year, and he died in A. D. 30, when the passover festival began on April 7. Those who think that John v. 1 does not refer to a passover date Christ's death in A. D. 29. We thus obtain as the probable leading dates in Christ's life: birth, December 25 (?), 5 B. C.; baptism and beginning of his ministry, January (?), A. D. 27; death, April 7, A. D. 30.

Political condition of the Jews. When Jesus was born Herod the Great, an able but cruel man, was king of the Jews. His kingdom included Samaria and Galilee as well as Judæa. He was an Idumæan by descent, though professing the Jewish religion. His father, Antipater, had been made governor of Judæa by Julius Cæsar, and, after several changes of fortune, Herod had been declared king of the Jews by the Romans in 40 B. C. But, while an independent king in many ways, Herod ruled by the favor of and in dependence on the Romans, who had become the practical rulers of the world. On his death, 4 B. C., his kingdom was divided among his sons. Archelaus received Judæa and Samaria. Herod Antipas received Galilee and Peræa. Herod Philip received the territory northeast of the sea of Galilee (Luke iii. 1). But in the tenth year of his reign Archelaus was deposed by Augustus, and from that date Judæa and Samaria were ruled by Roman governors, styled procurators, until the destruction of Jerusalem, with the exception of the years A. D. 41–44, when Herod Agrippa I. was invested with the royal power (Acts xii. 1). During the ministry of Christ, therefore, Galilee and Peræa, where he spent most of his time, were under the rule of Herod Antipas (Mat. xiv. 3; Mark vi. 14; Luke iii. 1, 19; ix. 7; xiii. 31; xxiii. 8–12), while Samaria and Judæa were ruled directly by the Romans through their governor, who at that time was Pontius Pilate. The rule of the Romans, whether direct or indirect, irritated the Jews exceedingly, and, during Christ's life, the land was in an almost constant state of political ferment. While the Romans sought to give the nation as much self-government as possible, so that their sanhedrin, or chief court, exercised jurisdiction in a very large number of cases; and while the conquerors granted many privileges to the Jews, especially in respect to their religious observances, yet the nation fretted under a foreign domination, which was very positive, when it wished to be so, and which did not intend ever to grant them their old liberty. The Jewish aristocracy, however, including most of the Sadducees, were not unfriendly to the Romans. The Pharisees, who comprised the strictest religionists, were disposed to devote themselves to the conservation of Judaism, while generally avoiding political complications. We read also of Herodians, who doubtless favored the claims of the Herodian family to the Jewish throne, while from Josephus we learn of political patriots who successively arose in the vain endeavor to throw off the Roman yoke. In such a condition of things, one who claimed to be Messiah would easily be involved in political difficulties. We shall see that Jesus carefully and successfully avoided these in order that he might proclaim the true, spiritual kingdom of God.

Religious condition of the Jews. As already implied, this was largely affected by the state of political affairs. So far as the official classes were concerned, the purely religious hopes of the Old Testament had been almost forgotten, and even among the people the idea of an earthly kingdom had nearly dis-placed that of a spiritual one. We meet in the gospels with two leading sects, the Pharisees and the Sadducees. The former were religious and had the greater influence among the people; but they had substituted theological and ceremonial tradition, as well as casuistic subtleties, for the word of God, and in their hands the religion of Moses and the prophets had become a narrow, barren, and unspiritual form. The Pharisees naturally opposed the spiritual and unconventional religion which Jesus taught, and especially his appeal from tradition to Scripture. The Sadducees, on the other hand, were the aristocrats. They included the high-priestly families. They were infected by gentile culture, rejected the Pharisaic traditions, and were more interested in politics than in religion. They were led finally to oppose Jesus, because they thought that his success would disturb the existing political relations (John xi. 48). Meanwhile the ceremonies of God's worship were carried on with much magnificence in the temple at Jerusalem, the people attended with fidelity and in great numbers the religious festivals, and the zeal of the nation for their religious privileges and traditions was never greater, while every now and then some outbreak of mingled patriotism and fanaticism fanned the embers of popular hope into a flame. Yet there were some who still preserved the spirit and faith of a pure religion. They were found mainly, though not wholly, among the humble classes. In them the expectation of a saviour from sin had not died out, and from the bosom of one of these pious circles did Jesus himself come. The Jewish people, therefore, in Christ's lifetime were still a religious people. They knew the Old Testament, which was read in their synagogues and taught to their children. The nation was in a state of religious interest as well as of political unrest. These facts explain to us the popular excitement caused by the preaching of John the Baptist and of Jesus, the opposition of the ruling classes to them both, and the success of the method which Jesus pursued in preaching his gospel, as well as the fate which he himself saw from the beginning to be, even humanly speaking, inevitable.

Life of Jesus. The circumstances of the birth of Jesus, as recorded in the gospels, were in accord with his dignity and the predictions of Messiah, yet such also as to harmonize with the lowly appearance which the Saviour was to make on earth. As Malachi (iii. 1: also iv. 5, 6) had prophesied that a herald, in the spirit and power of Elijah, should precede the Lord when he should come to his temple, so Luke tells us first of the birth of John the Baptist, the herald of the Christ. A certain pious priest, named Zacharias, who had no child and was far advanced in years, was discharging his duties at the temple. He was chosen by lot, as the custom was, to offer the incense, representing the prayers of Israel, on the altar in the holy place. To him the angel Gabriel appeared and announced that he was to be the father of the promised forerunner of Messiah. This was probably in October, 6 B. C. After his term of service in the temple was over, he and his wife, Elisabeth, returned to their home in a city in the hill country of Judah (Luke i. 39), and awaited the fulfillment of the promise. Six months later the angel appeared to Mary, a maiden probably of Davidic descent, who lived in Nazareth and was betrothed to Joseph, who was certainly descended from the great king of Israel (Mat. i. 1–16; Luke i. 27); see GENEALOGY. Joseph was a carpenter by trade, a man of humble station though of high descent, and a devout Israelite. To Mary the angel announced that she was to become the mother of Messiah (Luke i. 28–38) by the power of the Holy Spirit working in her, and that the child, who was to be called Jesus, should have the throne of his father David. For her comfort also she was told of the pregnancy of Elisabeth, who was her kinswoman. When the angel left her, Mary hastened for protection and sympathy to the house of Zacharias. At their meeting, the spirit of prophecy came on these two women. While Elisabeth greeted Mary as the mother of her Lord, Mary, like Hannah of old (1 Sam. ii. 1–10), broke forth in a song of praise for the salvation of Israel that was coming and for the honor which had been conferred on her. It is evident that these strange events were regarded by them both in the spirit of strong faith and holy exaltation, the perfect expression of the historic hope of Israel. When the time drew near for Elisabeth to be delivered of the child which she had conceived, Mary returned to Nazareth. Her further protection against reproach was, however, secured by God himself. Joseph, seeing her condition, was disposed quietly to put her away without public accusation, but even this gentle treatment was forestalled. An angel revealed to him in a dream the cause of Mary's condition; told him that he was to have Messiah for his child; and that, as Isaiah had foretold, the latter was to be born of a virgin. With faith, equal to Mary's, Joseph believed the message and made Mary his legal wife. It was thus secured that Mary's child was born of a virgin, and at the same time that he had a legal human father and his mother was protected by the love and respectability of a husband. There can be little doubt that these facts were made known by Mary herself at a later time. The fact that neither Christ nor his apostles appeal to his miraculous conception in proof of his Messiahship occasions no reason for doubting the narrative. The event was not one which could be used as public proof. But the narrative of Christ's birth beautifully harmonizes with what we now know of his dignity and his mission upon

earth. The Messiah was to be the perfect flower of Israel's spiritual life; and so Jesus was born in the bosom of this pious family circle where the pure religion of the O. T. was believed and cherished. The Messiah was to appear in lowliness; and so Jesus came from the home of the Nazarene carpenter. The Messiah was to be the son of David, and so Joseph, his legal father, and probably Mary, his actual mother, were descended from David. The Messiah was to be the incarnation of God, a divine person uniting to himself a human nature, and so Jesus was born of a woman but miraculously conceived by the power of the Holy Ghost. After relating the birth of John and the prophetic song which burst from the long-sealed lips of his father Zacharias (Luke i. 57–79), over the advent of Messiah's forerunner, the evangelist Luke explains how Jesus came to be born in Bethlehem. The emperor Augustus had ordered an enrollment of all the subjects of the empire, and although Palestine was under Herod, its inhabitants also were included in the decree. The enrollment of the Jews, however, evidently took place after the Jewish method, by which each father of a household was registered, not at his dwelling place, but at the place where his family belonged in view of its ancestry. Hence Joseph had to go to Bethlehem, the original home of David. Mary accompanied him. The lodging place, or khan, where strangers were permitted to sojourn, was already fully occupied when they arrived, and they only found shelter in a stable, which may have been, as early tradition affirms, in a cave near the town. Such caves were often used about Bethlehem for stables. We are not told that any cattle were occupying the stable. It may have been unused at the time. Nor would a stable in that country and among that people have seemed as offensive a lodging place as it might with us; but it was a lowly abode for the birthplace of Messiah. Yet such it was destined to be, for there Mary's child was born, and she laid him in a manger (Luke ii. 7). But though born so humbly, he was not to be without attestation. That night shepherds in a field near Bethlehem were visited by angels, who told them of Messiah's birth and where he lay, and sang in the hearing of the shepherds: "Glory to God in the highest, and on earth peace among men in whom he is well pleased" (Luke ii. 14, R. V.). The shepherds hastened to Bethlehem and saw the child. They related what they had seen and heard, and then returned again to their flocks. All this was again in striking harmony with the mission of Messiah. Yet we should remember that the event occurred in a circle of humble peasants, and that it made no noise in the busy world. For a while Joseph and Mary lingered in Bethlehem. On the eighth day the child was circumcised (Luke ii. 21) and the appointed name, Jesus, was given to him. Forty days after his birth (Lev. xii.) his parents took him, as the law directed, to the temple and Mary offered her gifts of purification and presented her child unto the Lord. The firstborn male child of the Hebrew mother was to be redeemed by the payment of five shekels (Num. xviii. 16), and this is meant when it is said that they brought him " to present him to the Lord." The mother was also to offer her thanksgiving, and it is specially noted by Luke that Mary gave the offering of the poor, " a pair of turtle doves, or two young pigeons." The modest circumstances of the family are thus further attested. Yet the lowly Messiah was not to leave his Father's house without recognition. An aged saint, Simeon by name, came into the temple and the spirit of inspiration fell upon him at sight of the child. He had been promised by God that he should not die till he had seen Messiah. Taking the infant in his arms, Simeon gave thanks and predicted the glory and sorrow of his life (Luke ii. 25-35). Anna also, a prophetess of great age, who continually dwelt in the temple, bore witness to the advent of the Christ (Luke ii. 36-38). But a more remarkable attestation was soon to follow. Shortly after Joseph and Mary had returned to Bethlehem, certain magi from the east appeared in Jerusalem and declared that they had seen Messiah's star in the heavens and were come to worship him. They had doubtless learned from the Jews scattered throughout the east of the expectation of a coming king in Judæa who would be man's great deliverer. They were doubtless also students of the stars, and God used their superstitious notions to make them witnesses of the gentile world, waiting in the half-light of natural religion for the coming of the Saviour, of whom they felt the need, but whose real character they did not understand. In the east they had seen a star which for some reason they considered to portend the birth of the Jewish king. Coming to Jerusalem, they inquired for him. Their message troubled the equally superstitious Herod, and summoning the scribes, he demanded where Messiah was to be born. When told that he was to be born in Bethlehem, Herod sent the magi there, but bade them promise to inform him if they found the child. On the way the magi saw the star again over Bethlehem, and, having found Jesus, offered him rare gifts of frankincense, gold, and myrrh. We can imagine with what renewed awe Joseph and Mary must have received these unexpected and strange visitors. They were another sign of the high destiny of the child. The magi, however, were warned of God not to return to Herod, for that wicked man only intended to use them to destroy the newly born king. They departed home, therefore, by another way. Joseph also was warned by an angel of the impending danger and instructed to take Mary and the babe to Egypt, well out of Herod's reach. It was none too soon, for presently the cruel king, whose readiness to murder even his own sons is related by Josephus, sent soldiers to slay all the male children in Bethlehem who were less than three years old. He hoped thus to accomplish the object in which he had been foiled by the departure of the magi without informing him concerning the child they had sought. Bethlehem was a small place and the number of children slain may not have been large ; but the act was cruel enough at the best. Jesus, however, had escaped. How long he was kept in Egypt we do not know. Probably it was a couple of months. There were many Jews there, so that Joseph could easily find a refuge. But in due time the angel informed him of Herod's death and directed him to return. It was apparently his first purpose to rear the child in Bethlehem, David's city. But his fear of Archelaus, Herod's son, made him hesitate. Again God gave him instructions, and in accordance with them Joseph and Mary sought once more their old home in Nazareth. In consequence of this, Jesus appeared among the people, when his public life began, as the prophet of Nazareth, the Nazarene. Such are the few incidents preserved in the gospels of the birth and infancy of Jesus. Wonderful as they appear to us, they attracted no attention at the time on the part of the world. The few persons concerned in them either forgot them or kept them to themselves. But when the church was founded we may suppose that Mary told them to the disciples. Matthew and Luke have related them to us quite independently of each other, the former to illustrate the royal Messiahship of Jesus and his fulfillment of prophecy ; the latter to explain the origin of Jesus and the historical beginnings of his life.

After the return to Nazareth, nothing is told us of Jesus' life, except the one incident of his visit with his parents to the temple when he had become twelve years of age (Luke ii. 41-51). That incident, however, is instructive. It shows the continued piety of Joseph and Mary and the devout training which they sought to give the child. It shows also the early, spiritual development of Jesus, for he was already mainly interested in those religious questions on which the Jewish rabbis gave instruction to their pupils. We are not to imagine the boy of twelve as instructing the doctors, but as a pupil in one of their temple schools, and yet as showing by his questions a spiritual insight which amazed them. The incident also illustrates the natural, human life which Jesus led. He grew, we are told, " in wisdom and stature [or age], and in favor with God and men " (Luke ii. 52). The wonders of his infancy were doubtless kept a secret by Joseph and Mary, and Jesus appeared to his companions and the family in no wise a supernatural being, but only remarkable for his mental force and moral purity. Putting together, however, other facts incidentally mentioned in the gospels, we can form some idea of the circumstances in which the childhood and young manhood of Jesus were passed. He was a member of a family. He had four brothers and some sisters (Mark vi. 3, etc.). Some have supposed that these were the children of Joseph by a former marriage; others that they were Christ's cousins. It seems to us most natural and scriptural to believe that they were the children of Joseph and Mary, born after Jesus. But at any rate, Jesus grew up in a family, experiencing the pleasures and the discipline of family life. He became, like Joseph, a carpenter (3), so that he was accustomed to manual labor. But mental discipline also was not wanting. Jewish children were well instructed in the Scriptures, and our Lord's familiarity with them is evident from his teaching. His parables also reveal a mind sensitive to the teaching of nature, and which must have delighted always to ponder the evidence of God's mind in the works of his hand. Nazareth, though somewhat secluded, was on the edge of the busiest part of the Jewish world and not far from some of the most famous scenes of Israel's history. From the cliff back of the town the eye could contemplate many places associated with great events. Not far off was the sea of Galilee, around which was gathered the varied life of the world in miniature. It was a period also, as has been said, of much political excitement, and Jewish homes were often agitated with the report of stirring events. There is no reason to suppose that Jesus grew up in isolation. We should rather imagine him keenly alive to the progress of events in Palestine. While the language commonly spoken by him seems to have been the Aramaic, which had displaced the older Hebrew among the later Jews, he must often have heard Greek used and may have been familiar with it. All this period of his life, however, the evangelists pass over. Their books were written not to give biographies of Jesus, but to report his public ministry. We can see enough, however, to prove the naturalness of our Saviour's human life, the fitness of his surroundings to prepare him for his future work, the beauty of his character, and thus the gradual unfolding of his humanity in expectation of the hour when he was to offer himself as God's Messiah to his people. That hour drew nigh when, perhaps in the summer of A. D. 26, John, the son of Zacharias, who had hitherto led a life of ascetic devotion in the desert (Luke i. 80), received from God his commission to summon the nation to repentance for their sins in preparation for Messiah's coming. John moved from place to place along the Jordan valley, and administered the rite of baptism to those who believed his message. He called both the nation and individuals to repentance for sin, spoke in the tone of the older prophets, especially of Elijah, and announced that Messiah was at hand, that he would purify Israel with judgments, and make expiation for the world's sin (Mat. iii.; Mark i. 1–8; Luke iii. 1–18; John i. 19–36). The effect of his ministry was widespread and profound. Even from Galilee the people flocked to his preaching. The sanhedrin sent a deputation to inquire his authority (John i. 19–28). While the ruling classes were unmoved by his appeal (Mat. xxi. 25), popular wonder and excitement were aroused, and the purely religious character of his message led the truly pious to believe that the long-deferred hope of Israel was at last to be fulfilled. After John's ministry had continued for some time, perhaps for six months or more, Jesus appeared amid the multitude and asked the prophet to baptize him. The inspired insight of the Baptist recognized in him one who had no need of repentance; saw in him, in fact, no less than the Messiah himself. "I have need," he said, "to be baptized of thee, and comest thou to me?" (Mat. iii. 14). We are not to suppose that Jesus did not already know himself perfectly well to be the Christ. His reply rather shows the contrary: "Suffer it now: for thus it becometh us to fulfill all righteousness." The baptism meant for him, partly, self-dedication to the work which John had announced, and also the conscious taking upon himself of the sin of the people whom he had come to save. As he came from the baptism (Mark i. 10), John (John i. 33, 34) saw the heavens opened and the Spirit of God, in the form of a dove, descending and remaining on him, and a voice came from above: "This is my beloved Son, in whom I am well pleased" (Mat. iii. 17). This was the full endowment of our Lord's human nature with spiritual power for his ministry. How truly human, as well as divine, he was through it all is shown by the temptation which immediately followed. He was not to enter on his work without adequate mental preparation. Realizing his vocation, he was led by the Spirit into the wilderness, doubtless for meditation. There the great tempter met him, and sought to pervert his purpose to selfish and worldly ends. Jesus must have himself related this experience to his disciples. While we are not to doubt the outward reality of the tempter and the physical features of the scene as described to us (Mat. iv. 1–11; Luke iv. 1–13), we should not forget that the power of the temptation lay in the subtlety with which the world was presented to Jesus as more attractive than the life of stern obedience to God, with its probably fatal close. For forty days the temptation lasted, and Jesus returned from it to the Jordan fully dedicated to the lowly, suffering lot which he knew to be God's will for his Messiah. Forthwith he began to call disciples. Yet with no loud proclamation of his advent did he inaugurate his work. The Baptist pointed him out to some of his own disciples as the Lamb of God (John i. 29, 36). Two, John and Andrew, followed the new teacher. Simon was soon added to the number (35–42). The next day Philip and Nathanael were invited (43–51). With his little band Jesus quietly returned to Galilee, and at Cana performed his first miracle, in which the disciples saw the first signs of his coming glory (ii. 1–11). We must be impressed with the absence of any attempt to make a public display. The new movement began with the faith of a few obscure Galilæans. But St. John's account makes it clear that Jesus was fully sensible of who he was and what he had come to do. He was only waiting for the favorable moment to offer himself to Israel as her Messiah. That moment was naturally found in the approaching passover (April, A. D. 27). From Capernaum, whither he and his family and disciples had gone (12), he ascended to Jerusalem, and there proceeded to cleanse the temple of the traders who profaned it. It was an act worthy of a prophet to reform the flagrant abuses of God's service; but Christ's words, "Make not my Father's house a house of merchandise," indicate that he claimed to be more than a prophet (16). It was, in fact, a public summons of Israel to follow him in the work of religious reformation, for only when the Jews had rejected him would he proceed to organize the new church of the future; but he himself did not expect them to follow him. This is proved by his veiled prediction of his death at their hands (19), while in the conversation with Nicodemus he clearly brought out the necessity of a new birth and of his own suffering (iii. 1–21), in order that any might enter the kingdom which God's love had sent him to establish. For our knowledge of this early Judæan ministry of Jesus we are indebted to St. John (ii. 13–iv. 3). It lasted apparently about nine months. After the passover Jesus retired from the city to the Judæan country, and having found the nation unwilling to follow him, he began to preach, as the Baptist was still doing, the necessity of repentance. For a while the two worked side by side. Not till John's providential mission was plainly over would Jesus begin an independent one of his own. Both labored together for the spiritual quickening of the nation. Jesus began finally to attract more disciples than John did. This led him to terminate his Judæan ministry, for neither would he appear as a rival of his coworker (John iv. 1–3). He turned once more toward Galilee. On the way through Samaria occurred his memorable interview with the woman at Jacob's well (4–42). But he hastened northward. Arriving in Galilee, he found that his fame had preceded him (43–45). A nobleman from Ca-

pernaum sought him out, even in Cana, where he was stopping, and secured from him the cure of his son (46–54). It was clear that Galilee was the place where he should labor and that the fields were white to harvest (35). Then, it would seem, an event occurred which indicated that the hour for him to begin his proper work had indeed providentially arrived. The news came that John the Baptist had been cast into prison by Herod Antipas. The work of the herald was over. The old Jewish church had been sufficiently called to repentance and reformation, and she had refused to listen. Jesus began forthwith in Galilee to preach the kingdom of God, to announce the germinal principles of the new dispensation, and to gather the nucleus of the future church.

The great Galilæan ministry of Jesus lasted about sixteen months. He took for his center the busy mart of trade, Capernaum. In Galilee he was in the midst of a population prevailingly Jewish, yet in a region removed from interference by the religious authorities of the nation. His evident purpose was to set forth the true, spiritual kingdom of God, and by mighty works to convince men of his own authority and of the character of the kingdom. He asked for faith in himself. He unveiled the real character of God and his requirements of men. He did not apply to himself the name Messiah, for it would have been too easily misunderstood by carnal minds. He generally called himself the Son of man. He did not at first speak of his death. They were not ready to hear of that. He taught the principles of true religion, with himself as its authoritative expounder. His mighty works roused the greatest enthusiasm. He was thus enabled to attract wide attention, till the whole land was eager to see and hear him. But, as he foresaw, the final result was the disappointment of the people with his unworldly ideas. Only a little band faithfully clave to him. Yet by his teaching he laid down truths which that band of disciples were to carry, after his death, throughout the world. For the order of events in the lower or early Galilæan ministry we refer to the harmony in the article GOSPEL. We can here only note the leading phases of the history. The first was that of the opening of the work. This was marked by startling miracles, by the summons to believe the gospel, and by the awakening of enthusiastic interest in Jesus on the part of the Galilæans. It included the events in the harmony, beginning with the first rejection at Nazareth and ending with Levi's feast. The close of this phase of his work, which lasted perhaps four months, found Jesus the center of universal interest in Galilee, and gathered about him a little company of devoted followers. We are not told much about his teaching as yet; but from what we are told and from the significant miracles he performed—such as the cure of the demoniac (Mark i. 23–27), the healing of the leper (40–45), the cure of the paralytic (ii. 1–12), the miraculous draught of fish (Luke v. 1–12)—it is clear that the burden of his message was substantially that which he announced in Nazareth (iv. 18–21), "The Spirit of the Lord is upon me, because he hath anointed me to preach the gospel to the poor; he hath sent me to heal the brokenhearted, to preach deliverance to the captives, and recovering of sight to the blind, to set at liberty them that are bruised, to preach the acceptable year of the Lord." The aspect of affairs, however, soon began to change, for opposition arose on the part of the Pharisees. This is the second phase of the Galilæan ministry. Jesus visited Jerusalem (John v. 1) and there healed the impotent man on the Sabbath. At once conflict with the rulers and rabbis broke out. Yet the conflict seems to have been purposely provoked by Jesus, in order that through it the difference between the spirit of his teaching and that of current Judaism might appear. We see in him now the spiritual interpreter of the Old Testament, bringing out its real meaning, and doing so (v.) with express appeal to his own authority as the Son of God and the divinely appointed teacher of men. This phase included, besides John v., the incidents of plucking the ears of corn and the healing of the man with the withered hand; see Gospel. The conflict with the Pharisees and the continued advance of popular interest led next to the organization of his disciples, which constituted the third phase of this part of his ministry. He now appointed his twelve apostles, and, on one famous day, gave in the sermon on the mount a description of the character and life of the true members of God's kingdom. It is a sublime exhibition of a genuinely religious life, in joyful unison with its heavenly Father, and consecrated to his service in the salvation of the world, the real fulfillment of the old law, though utterly opposed to the formality and superficiality of Pharisaism, the ideal of trust and communion of man in relation to God. The sermon on the mount was not meant by Jesus to teach the way of salvation, nor did it constitute by any means his whole gospel. He, like the apostles, taught salvation through faith in himself. But in this sermon, over against Pharisaism and popular ignorance, he set forth that spiritual life which is the manifestation of the divine kingdom and to entrance into which faith in Jesus leads. The outlines of the new organization having thus been enunciated, we read, as the fourth phase, of a succession of miracles and tours through lower Galilee—Jesus being accompanied by his apostles—for the purpose of extending his influence. This phase extends in the harmony from the close of the sermon on the mount to the time when Herod inquired

concerning the new teacher. During these months the popular interest in Jesus steadily increased, but the opposition of the Pharisees increased equally. The most notable point in the history just here is the great day of parables. The parable was a form of instruction in which Jesus was unrivaled. It was intended to convey truth to receptive minds, and yet to avoid such open expression of it as would give his enemies a plea for interfering with him. The appearance of parables in his teaching just at this period shows the increasing gravity of the situation, necessitating a certain reserve on Christ's part. We must, at the same time, admire the incomparable skill with which he embodied in these simple stories the profoundest truths concerning the origin and progress and perils and destiny of the spiritual kingdom which he was establishing in the world. At length, however, the work in Galilee came to a crisis. Herod Antipas began to inquire concerning Jesus, and the fact was a warning that complications, such as had already led to John's imprisonment, and still more recently to his murder, might ensue. A sufficient opportunity had, moreover, been given to the people to test their relation to the truth. Just then an event occurred which decided the matter. Jesus had sought temporary retirement with the twelve; but the multitudes had followed him to a desert place on the northeastern shore of the sea of Galilee, and, in compassion for their needs, he had miraculously fed them, five thousand in number, from five loaves and two fishes. The enthusiastic Galilæans wished to take him by force and make him a king (John vi. 15); but that very fact proved that they had wholly misunderstood his mission. It was time to bring his work to a close. From the beginning he had intimated that he had come to die, and that only by dying could he be their Saviour (iii. 14, 15). It was now time to prepare for the sacrifice. On the next day after the feeding of the five thousand Jesus delivered in Capernaum the discourse, recorded in vi. 22–71, upon himself as the bread of life and on the necessity of eating his flesh and drinking his blood. Then, after some parting denunciation of the Pharisaic misrepresentations of religion (Mark vii. 1–23), he brought his public ministry in Galilee to a close by retiring with his disciples from the region in which he had hitherto been working.

The next great period in Christ's life is called the later Galilæan ministry; see harmony, in article Gospel. It lasted about six months. In it Jesus went, for the only time in his life, into gentile territory, viz., the regions of Tyre and Sidon. Then, having apparently passed southward along the eastern side of the upper Jordan and the sea of Galilee, we find him in the region of Decapolis. Again he went far into the northern part of Galilee, and finally returned again to

Capernaum. The period was mainly devoted to the preparation of his disciples for his death and for the extension of his gospel to all peoples. He preached little, and then mainly to gentiles or to the half-heathen people on the south and east of the sea of Galilee. Finally, near Cæsarea Philippi, at the base of mount Hermon, he elicited from Peter and the rest the full confession of his Messiahship, and, in connection therewith, he plainly told them of his coming death and resurrection, and of the necessity that every follower of his should be willing also to bear the cross. Shortly after occurred the transfiguration, in which three of his apostles beheld his glory, and in which, it would seem, he devoted himself finally, with sublime exaltation of spirit, to the sacrifice to which law and prophecy, as he was reminded by Moses and Elias, had looked forward. Afterwards he repeated the prediction of his death, and, having returned to Capernaum, further instructed his disciples (Mat. xviii.) in that conception of God's service as one of humility, self-sacrifice, and love, of which his own great act of self-devotion was to be the permanent example.

It was now probably the early autumn of A. D. 29, and leaving Capernaum for the last time Jesus "steadfastly set his face to go to Jerusalem" (Luke ix. 51). The next period of his ministry is called the last journeys to Jerusalem. It is impossible to follow in exact order our Lord's movements, for St. Luke, on whom we are mainly dependent for the record of this period, does not follow a precise chronological method of narration. But the main features of the period are clear enough. Jesus now sought to attract the public attention of the whole land, including Judæa. He sent out the seventy to announce his coming. He visited Jerusalem at the feast of tabernacles (John vii.), and again at the feast of dedication (x. 22), and on both occasions offered himself repeatedly to the people. He called himself the light of the world and the good shepherd of God's flock, and boldly contended with the rulers who opposed his pretensions. He also moved back and forth through Judæa and Peræa, and explained in popular discourse and with more beauty of illustration than ever before the true religious life and the true idea of God and of his service. Here belong the parables of the good Samaritan, the wedding-feast, the lost sheep, the lost coin, the prodigal son, the unjust steward, the rich man and Lazarus, the importunate widow, the Pharisee and the publican. Thus the announcement of the gospel became more complete, while the fierceness of the opposition of the rulers became more intense, until an event occurred which brought matters to a climax. Word was brought to Jesus of the sickness of his friend Lazarus in Bethany. Going to him, he found him already four days dead, and forthwith he eclipsed all his previous

miracles by raising the dead man to life (xi. 1–46). The miracle was so stupendous and performed so near Jerusalem that it had a profound effect on the people of the capital; and the sanhedrin, under the lead of Caiaphas, the high priest, decided that the influence of Jesus could be destroyed only by his death (47–53). Forthwith Jesus retired from the vicinity (54), evidently determined that he should not die until the passover. As that drew near he began to approach the city through Peræa (Mat. xix.; xx.; Mark x.; Luke xviii. 15-xix. 28), teaching as he went, but again predicting his death and resurrection, until he reached Bethany once more, six days before the feast (John xii. 1). At Bethany, Mary, the sister of Lazarus, anointed his head and feet while he was at supper, an event in which Jesus saw a silent prophecy of his coming burial. But the next day he made the triumphal entry on an ass's colt into Jerusalem. By that he invited the anger of the rulers, offered himself publicly as Messiah, and illustrated the peaceful character of the kingdom he had come to found. The next day he returned again to the capital, on his way cursing the barren, though blooming, fig tree, which was so apt an emblem of the barren, though pretentious, Jewish church. Then, as three years before, he cleansed the temple of the traders who profaned its courts, thus once more calling the nation to follow him in a purification of Israel. But though the pilgrims to the festival crowded about him and had hailed him at the triumphal entry as the Messiah, the rulers maintained their resolute enmity. On the next day (Tuesday) he again visited the city. Arrived at the temple, he was met by a deputation from the sanhedrin, which demanded his authority for his acts. This he refused to give, knowing that they were already resolved to destroy him, while, by the parables of the two sons, the wicked husbandmen, and the marriage of the king's son, he described their disobedience to God, the infidelity of Israel to her high trust, and the certain desolation of the faithless church and city. Forthwith he was questioned by a succession of parties who sought to find accusation against him or to weaken his reputation. The Pharisees and Herodians asked about the lawfulness of giving tribute to Cæsar; the Sadducees about the resurrection; a lawyer about the great commandment; and he, having silenced each in turn, discomfited them by his question concerning David's address to Messiah as Lord, for the psalmist's language clearly implied that his own claim to be the Son of God and equal with God was not blasphemous. It was a day of bitter conflict. Jesus vehemently denounced the unworthy leaders of the people (Mat. xxiii. 1–38). When certain Greeks desired to see him he saw in their coming a presage of the Jews' rejection of him, and that the gentiles were to be his followers, and realized that the end was at hand (John xii. 20-50). As he left the temple he sadly remarked to his disciples that soon the splendid building would be in ruins, and later on the same evening he gave to four of them his prediction of the destruction of Jerusalem, the spread of the gospel, the sufferings of his followers, and his own second advent, a prediction which shows to us that amid the lowering storm of Jewish hostility the vision of Jesus was clear, and that he moved on to his fate knowing it to be the appointed path to ultimate success. It is probable that on that very night the plot was formed to destroy him. Judas, one of the twelve, had, we may believe, long been alienated from the spiritual ideas of the Master. He was grieved also at Christ's refusal to seek a worldly kingdom ; for Judas was, John tells us, an avaricious man. At the supper at Bethany he had become finally and fully conscious of his entire want of sympathy with Jesus, and as the disappointment which he felt over the failure of his hopes grew keener he resolved to wreak his anger on the Lord by betraying him to the rulers. His offer changed their plans. They had purposed to wait until the festival was over and the crowds had departed. But in the absence of any real charge against Jesus they were only too glad to avail themselves of the traitor's proposal. The next day (Wednesday) seems to have been spent by Jesus in retirement. He probably remained in Bethany. On Thursday afternoon the paschal lambs were to be slain, and after sunset the paschal supper, with which the seven-day feast of unleavened bread began, was to be eaten by all pious Israelites. On that day Jesus sent Peter and John into the city to prepare the passover for him and the twelve. He sent them, no doubt, to the house of a disciple or friend (Mat. xxvi. 18) ; but by the device of telling them to follow when they entered the city a man whom they would meet bearing a pitcher of water, he kept the place of assembly secret from the rest of the disciples, for the purpose no doubt of preventing Judas from betraying it to the rulers, and thus possibly interfering with the last precious interview with the apostles. When evening came he observed with them the passover supper. For the order of events during the evening, see again the harmony. The view of some that according to John's Gospel (xiii. 1, 29 ; xviii. 28 ; xix. 31) Jesus was crucified on Nisan 14th, the day on which the paschal lamb was slain, and therefore that he did not eat the passover supper at the regular time, but anticipated it by a day, appears to be quite inconsistent with the language reported by Matthew (xxvi. 17-19), Mark (xiv. 12-16), and Luke (xxii. 7-13, 15), and the expressions appealed to in John may be explained on the hypothesis which we are following.* It should be noted that in all

* John xiii. 1 does not mean that all that is

probability Judas withdrew before the establishment of the eucharist, and that Jesus twice predicted the fall of Peter, once in the upper room and again while on the way to Gethsemane. John's Gospel does not relate the establishment of the eucharist, but it gives the Lord's last discourses with the apostles, in which he comforted them in view of his departure from them by revealing the unchangeable spiritual union between himself and them, and the mission of the Spirit which would bring to fruition their relation to him. It records also his sublime high-priestly prayer (xvii.). On the way to Gethsemane Jesus further warned the disciples that they would soon be scattered, and appointed a meeting with him, after his resurrection, in Galilee. The agony in the garden was his final and complete surrender of himself to the last great act of sacrifice. It was interrupted by the coming of Judas with a company of soldiers, obtained doubtless from the garrison near the temple on the ground that a seditious person was to be arrested (John xviii. 3, 12), together with some of the Levitical guard and servants of the chief priests. Judas knew that Jesus was wont to resort to Gethsemane. Some suppose, however, that he had first gone to the upper room and, finding that Jesus had departed, followed to Olivet, at the base of which the garden lay. Jesus, after a brief expostulation, submitted to arrest ; whereupon his disciples fled. The captors took him first to Annas (13), the father-in-law of Caiaphas, where he had a preliminary examination while the sanhedrin was being convened (13, 14, 19-24). It is not improbable that Annas and Caiaphas lived in the same palace, for Peter's denials are said to have occurred in the court of the palace, both while this examination before Annas and the later one before the sanhedrin were taking place. At the first examination Jesus refused to answer the inquiries, and demanded that evidence against him be produced. He was sent bound, however, to the apartments of Caiaphas, where the sanhedrin had hastily assembled. No harmonious evidence of blasphemy, which was the crime they sought to prove against him, could be found ; so that the high priest was forced to solemnly adjure him to say if he were Messiah. Thereupon Jesus made the claim in the most explicit manner, and the angry court condemned him as worthy of death for blas-

recorded in ch. xiii. was "before the feast of the passover," but is an introductory remark describing the loving spirit in which the fatal passover was entered upon by Jesus; xiii. 29, "buy those things that we have need of against the feast," may refer to things necessary for the next day, on which the freewill offerings of the people were presented; xviii. 28, "that they might eat the passover," may mean simply "keep the paschal festival;" xix. 31, "the preparation," was not the preparation for the passover, but for the Sabbath.

phemy. The unjust spirit of his judges appeared in the ribald mockery to which he was subjected. It was, however, the law that the decisions of the sanhedrin must be made in the daytime. Hence very early in the morning the court convened again and the same formalities were gone through (Luke xxii. 66–71), and then, since permission of the governor was required for the execution of a criminal, they hastened with Jesus to Pilate. The indecent haste of the whole proceeding shows their fear that the people might prevent his destruction. Pilate probably resided in Herod's palace on the hill of Zion. But the distance from the high priest's house was not great, and it was still very early when the governor was summoned forth to hear their request. They wished him at first to grant permission for the execution without inquiring into the charges, but this he refused to do (John xviii. 29–32). Then they accused Jesus of "perverting the nation, and forbidding to give tribute to Cæsar, saying that he himself is Christ a king" (Luke xxiii. 2). After Jesus had acknowledged to the governor that he was a king (3), Pilate examined him privately (John xviii. 33–38), and discovered the wholly non-political and harmless character of his claims. He forthwith declared that he found no fault in him and that he would let him go. But the governor was in reality afraid to thwart the will of his dangerous subjects, and when they fiercely demanded the crucifixion of Jesus he fell back on various weak expedients to shift the responsibility. Having learned that Jesus was from Galilee, Pilate sent him to Herod Antipas (Luke xxiii. 7–11), who also was then in Jerusalem; but Herod refused to exercise jurisdiction. Meanwhile the crowd had increased, and the governor appealed to them to say what prisoner he should release, as his custom was, at the passover. He evidently hoped that the popularity of Jesus would rescue him from the chief priests. But the latter persuaded the rabble to ask for Barabbas. The message of his wife further increased Pilate's anxiety to release Jesus; but though he several times appealed to the multitude in his behalf, they were implacable and bloodthirsty. The governor was afraid to act on his own convictions and weakly gave permission for the execution. Yet while the scourging which always preceded crucifixion was in progress in the hall of his palace he could not rest. Again he sought to satisfy the Jews by the spectacle of Jesus bleeding and thorn-crowned, but they, made bold with success, cried out that he ought to die because he made himself the Son of God (John xix. 1–7). This, however, increased Pilate's superstitions, so that again he examined Jesus privately and again sought to release him (8–12); but the Jews finally appealed to his political ambition and practically accused him of disloyalty to Cæsar in abetting a rival

king. This decided the matter. Pilate had the grim satisfaction of hearing the Jews proclaim their supreme allegiance to the emperor (13–15), and therewith he handed Jesus over for execution. Jesus thus died for no crime and without any real legal process. His death was literally a judicial murder. The execution was carried out by four soldiers (John xix. 23) under charge of a centurion. With him also two common robbers were led to death. The victims usually carried their crosses, either the whole of them or the transverse portion. Jesus seems to have carried the whole, since he fainted under it. The place of crucifixion was a short distance outside the city; see GOLGOTHA. The victim was usually nailed to the cross on the ground and then the cross was placed upright in the hole prepared for it. The crime of the offender was written on a tablet and placed over his head. In Jesus' case the accusation was written in Hebrew, Greek, and Latin. Its longest form is given by John (xix. 19), "Jesus of Nazareth, the king of the Jews." Mark tells us that it was "about the third hour" (i. e. 9 A. M.) when the crucifixion was completed. If we remember that the proceedings began "as soon as it was day" (Luke xxii. 66), their completion about nine o'clock will not seem incredible. It is moreover in accord with the haste which had characterized the action of the Jews from the beginning.

Into the incidents which the gospels have preserved as occurring during the crucifixion we cannot go here. Such sufferers often remained alive for several days; but the already exhausted frame of Jesus did not endure the agony so long. At the ninth hour he expired with a great cry. The words spoken from the cross, however, indicate that he retained his consciousness to the end, and that he fully realized the significance of all that happened. When he died there seem to have been but few present. The crowd which followed him at first had returned to the city. The mocking priests also had left him. A few disciples and the soldiers are all that we know to have been present at the end. The rulers were, therefore, not aware that he had died. Unwilling to have the bodies hanging on the cross over the Sabbath, they went to Pilate and asked that their legs might be broken; but, when the soldiers came to Jesus for this purpose, they found him already dead. One, however, pierced his side to make sure, and John, who was near, saw blood and water issue from the wound (xix. 34). Jesus seems to have died literally of a broken heart. Meanwhile Joseph of Arimathæa, a secret disciple of Jesus, though a rich man and a member of the sanhedrin—who, however, had not consented to his Master's condemnation (Luke xxiii. 51)—knowing that death had come, had begged for the body of Jesus. By him and a few others it was laid in a garden of Joseph's, in a new tomb hewn out of a rock.

Now it is clear that the disciples were wholly disconcerted and overwhelmed by the sudden arrest and death of their Lord. Though he had on three recorded occasions forewarned them of his death and of his resurrection on the third day, they were too distressed to have any hope. Though he had told them to go to Galilee to meet him, they lingered in Jerusalem. Their conduct will not seem incredible nor the narrative doubtful to those who know the prostration which often accompanies bitter disappointment and sorrow. Hence Jesus appeared to them in Jerusalem and its vicinity. The resurrection narratives in the gospels are not intended, however, to be complete accounts of the events. They do not pretend to marshal the evidence for the reality of the resurrection. That consisted in the testimony of apostles to whom he repeatedly appeared (1 Cor. xv. 3-8). In the gospels we have a number of incidents preserved either because of their intrinsic interest or for the sake of the spiritual instruction which they provided to believers. The order of events seems to have been nearly the following: Early in the morning of the first day of the week two companies of pious Galilæan women proceeded to the sepulcher to anoint the body of Jesus for permanent burial. The one company consisted of Mary Magdalene, Mary the mother of James, and Salome (Mark xvi. 1). Joanna and other unnamed women were probably in the second party (Luke xxiv. 10, which is a general statement, including the report of all the women). The first party saw the stone rolled away from the tomb, and Mary Magdalene, supposing that the body had been stolen, returned to Peter and John with the news (John xx. 1, 2). Her companions went on, and entering the tomb heard from the angel the news of the resurrection and the message to the disciples (Mat. xxviii. 1-7; Mark xvi. 1-7). As they hastened away, we may suppose that they met the other company of women, and that all returned again to the tomb, but only to receive from two angels a more emphatic assurance and direction (Luke xxiv. 1-8). The women then hastened toward the city with the news and on the way Jesus met them (Mat. xxviii. 9, 10). Meanwhile Mary Magdalene had reported to Peter and John that the tomb was empty, and they had run thither and found it even so (John xx. 3-10). She had followed them and, when they departed from the garden, she remained, and to her also did Jesus appear (11-18). All the women finally returned to the disciples and reported the wonderful news. It was not, however, on the testimony of these women that faith in the resurrection of Jesus was to rest. During the day he appeared to Peter (Luke xxiv. 34; 1 Cor. xv. 5), later to two disciples journeying to Emmaus (Luke xxiv. 13-35), and in the evening to all the eleven except Thomas (36-43; John

xx. 19-23). At that time he ate before them, proving the reality of his physical resurrection. Since, however, Thomas even yet would not believe, the disciples still lingered in Jerusalem, and on the following Sunday Jesus again appeared to them, and proved to the doubting apostle that he had indeed risen (John xx. 24-29). Then, it would appear, the apostles returned to Galilee. We next read of seven of them fishing in the sea of Galilee and of the Lord's appearance to them (John xxi.). By appointment also he met them on a mountain of Galilee and gave to them "the great commission," with the assurance of his power and presence (Mat. xxviii. 16-20). This may very probably have been the occasion when five hundred disciples were present (1 Cor. xv. 6). Soon after he appeared also to James (7), but where we know not. Finally he brought the apostles again to Jerusalem, and leading them out to the mount of Olives to a place where Bethany was in sight (Luke xxiv. 50, 51) he was taken up into heaven and a cloud received him out of their sight (Acts i. 9-12). We have thus ten appearances of the risen Saviour recorded in the New Testament, while Paul properly adds the appearance to him on the way to Damascus (1 Cor. xv. 8). There were doubtless, however, other appearances not recorded. Luke says (Acts i. 3) that "he showed himself alive after his passion by many proofs, appearing unto them by the space of forty days" (R. V.). Yet he did not continue with them in constant intercourse as he had done before. He rather manifested himself to them (John xxi. 1, R. V.). The forty days between his resurrection and ascension formed evidently a transitional period, intended to train the disciples for their future work. It was necessary to give ample, repeated, and varied proof of the resurrection, and this was done as we have seen. It was necessary to give them instruction concerning the necessity of his death and the character of the kingdom which through their labors he was to establish. It was requisite to point out to them the fulfillment of Scripture by his death and resurrection, for thus alone would they see the continuity of the new dispensation with the old. For this instruction they had not been ready before his death, but it is repeatedly referred to as having been given during these forty days (Luke xxiv. 44-48; John xx. 21-23; xxi. 15-22; Acts i. 3-8). And finally the experiences of the forty days trained the disciples to think of their Master as absent and yet living; as invisible and yet near them; as risen to a new life and yet retaining the old nature and even the old, though now glorified, body, which they had loved; as exalted but still the same, so that they were prepared to go forth and proclaim him as the glorified Son of God and crowned king of Israel. yet also the Man of Nazareth and the Lamb of God who takes away the sin of the world. Meanwhile the Jews affirmed that his disciples had stolen his body. Fearing this, they had on the day of his death requested from Pilate a military watch to guard the tomb. When the resurrection occurred, accompanied, as we are told, by the descent of an angel who rolled the stone from the tomb, the soldiers were overcome with fright and afterwards fled. Superstitious pagans as they were, they doubtless were little more affected by what they had seen than ignorant men usually are by what they consider ghostly appearances. But the rulers, who may possibly have accounted for the soldiers' report by supposing a trick on the part of the disciples, gave the men money to keep the matter quiet, and thus the report was given out that the body had been stolen while the soldiers slept (Mat. xxviii. 11–15). When, however, the apostles began, on the day of Pentecost, to give their testimony to the resurrection, and the number of believers in it grew rapidly (Acts ii., etc.), it was by attempts at force, not by proofs, that the chief priests tried to silence their witness and subdue the growing sect (Acts iv.).

We have not sought in this article to exhibit the teaching of Jesus, but the outward framework and historic movement of his life. In the latter there appears, as we gather it from the gospels, a gradual, progressive revelation of himself and of his message, which constitutes one of the strongest evidences of the truthfulness of the accounts on which our knowledge is based. The reality of the humanity of Christ made it possible for him thus to appear as a real character of human history, related to a particular environment, and to present in his life a career which moved naturally, yet steadily, forward to a definite goal. His was a genuinely human life and, therefore, capable of historical treatment. At the same time Jesus knew and declared himself to be more than man (e. g. Mat. xi. 27; John v. 17–38; x. 30; xvii. 5, etc.). As his self-revelation advanced his disciples realized his divine dignity (Mat. xvi. 16; John xx. 28). Then later reflection and experience, under the illumination of the Spirit, made his divinity still more evident to them, until the last surviving apostle was led to become the fourth evangelist and to present in his Lord's earthly career the incarnation of the personal divine Word. Yet St. John never forgot nor obscured the real humanity of Jesus. He gives us the full truth concerning the person of the great Master. "In the beginning was the Word, and the Word was with God, and the Word was God" (John i. 1), and "the Word was made flesh, and dwelt among us, (and we beheld his glory, the glory as of the only begotten of the Father,) full of grace and truth" (14). "These [things] are written," he concludes, "that ye might believe that Jesus is the Christ, the Son of God; and that

believing ye might have life through his name" (xx. 31).   G. T. P.

Je′ther [abundance, eminence, excellence].

1. A descendant of Judah through Jerahmeel. He died childless (1 Chron. ii. 32; cp. 26, 28).

2. A man registered among the descendants of Judah, but the lineage is not traced beyond his father, Ezra (1 Chron. iv. 17).

3. An Asherite, apparently the same as Ithran, son of Zophah (1 Chron. vii. 37 with 38).

4. A form of Jethro, Moses' father-in-law (Ex. iv. 18, R. V. margin).

5. The firstborn son of Gideon. His father bade him fall upon the captives, Zebah and Zalmunna, and slay them; but the youth shrank from the deed, and they escaped the disgrace of dying at the hands of a boy (Judg. viii. 20, 21).

6. The father of Amasa, Absalom's commander-in-chief (1 Kin. ii. 5). See ITHRA.

Je′theth.

A chieftain of Edom (Gen. xxxvi. 40; 1 Chron. i. 51).

Jeth′lah. See ITHLAH.

Je′thro [his preëminence, his excellence].

A priest of Midian and Moses' father-in-law (Ex. iii. 1). He is called Reuel (ii. 18; Antiq. ii. 12, 1). Reuel, which means friend of God, seems to have been his personal name, and Jethro, his excellence, to have been his honorary title. His seven daughters tended his flocks; and Moses, who had fled from Egypt, rendered them a service which led to his introduction to Jethro's family and marriage with Zipporah, one of the daughters. Moses kept his father-in-law's flocks for about forty years (Ex. iii. 1, 2; Acts vii. 30). When called by God to return to Egypt and achieve the emancipation of the Hebrews, Moses obtained Jethro's permission to depart, and took with him his wife Zipporah and his two sons (Ex. iv. 18–20); but he afterwards sent her and her two sons temporarily back to her father's house (24–26; xviii. 2); see ZIPPORAH. After the passage of the Red Sea, which conducted the Israelites into the vicinity of Jethro's country, the Midianite priest brought his daughter and her two sons back to Moses (xviii. 1–7). He rejoiced in the deliverance of the Israelites, offered sacrifices to Jehovah, and suggested the appointment of judges when he saw that the Hebrew leader was wearing himself out by deciding even trivial cases personally (8–27). See HOBAB.

Je′tur [possibly, nomad or nomadic camp].

A people descended from Ishmael (Gen. xxv. 15; 1 Chron. i. 31; v. 19). See ITURÆA.

Je′u-el [perhaps, treasure of God].

1. A man of Judah, family of Zerah. At one period he, with 690 of his clan, lived at Jerusalem (1 Chron. ix. 6).

2. A Levite, a descendant of Elizaphan.

He took part in the reformation under Heze-kiah (2 Chron. xxix. 13, in A. V. Jeiel).

3. A contemporary of Ezra who with members of his family returned from Babylonia with the scribe (Ezra viii. 13, in A. V. Jeiel).

Je'ush, in A. V. once **Jehush** (1 Chron. viii. 39) [perhaps, hastening].

1. A son of Esau by his wife Oholibamah (Gen. xxxvi. 5). He became a chieftain in Edom (18).

2. A Benjamite, son of Bilhan (1 Chron. vii. 10).

3. A Levite, family of Gershon and a son of Shimei (1 Chron. xxiii. 10, 11).

4. A descendant of Jonathan (1 Chron. viii. 39).

5. A son of Rehoboam (2 Chron. xi. 19).

Je'uz [counseling].

A Benjamite, son of Shaharaim by his wife Hodesh (1 Chron. viii. 10).

Jew [from Latin *Iudæus*, Greek *Ioudaios*, Hebrew *Y°hudi*].

One belonging to the tribe or to the kingdom of Judah (2 Kin. xvi. 6; xxv. 25). Then the meaning was extended, and the word was applied to any one of the Hebrew race who returned from the captivity; and finally it comprehended any one of that race throughout the world (Esther ii. 5; Mat. ii. 2). Their language (2 Kin. xviii. 26; Neh. xiii. 24) was Hebrew. For their history while they were in Palestine, see HISTORY. Dispersion among the nations, to the ends of the earth, was foretold as the doom of the people of the kingdom of God in case they forsook God and obeyed not his law (Lev. xxvi. 33, 39; Deut. iv. 27; xxviii. 25, 36, 37, 64–68; Is. vi. 12; xi. 11, 12).

Jew'ess.

A woman of the tribe of Judah (1 Chron. iv. 18, R. V.) or of the Hebrew race (Acts xvi. 1; xxiv. 24).

Jew'ry. See JUDÆA.

Jez-a-ni'ah; in full **Jaazaniah** (2 Kin. xxv. 23) [Jehovah doth hearken].

A captain of the forces, son of Hoshaiah, a Maacathite (2 Kin. xxv. 23; Jer. xl. 7, 8; xlii. 1). He came with his men to pay his respects to Gedaliah, whom Nebuchadnezzar had appointed governor of Judah after the capture of Jerusalem. Jezaniah had no complicity in the subsequent murder of Gedaliah, and seems to have taken a prominent part in attempting to bring the perpetrators to justice. He joined in appealing to Jeremiah, the prophet, to ask advice of God concerning the purpose of the remnant of the Israelites to migrate to Egypt (xlii.). He was a brother of Azariah, or more probably Azariah is a corruption of Jezaniah (xliii. 2).

Jez'e-bel [unmarried, chaste].

1. Daughter of Ethbaal, king of the Zidonians and former priest of Astarte (1 Kin. xvi. 31; con. Apion. i. 18). She became the wife of Ahab, king of Israel. She was a woman of masculine temperament and swayed her husband at will. She was a devoted worshiper of Baal, and intolerant of other faiths To please her, Ahab reared a temple and an altar to Baal in Samaria, and set up an Asherah (1 Kin. xvi. 32, 33). Though legally only the king's consort, and not the ruler of the country, yet she slew all the prophets of Jehovah on whom she could lay hands (xviii. 4–13). When she planned the death of Elijah (xix. 1, 2), and afterwards effected the judicial murder of Naboth, she similarly ignored the king's authority, though he condoned the deed (xxi. 16–22). On account of these murders and other violations of the moral law, the divine sentence was pronounced against her that the dogs should eat Jezebel by the wall of Jezreel (23). The prophecy was fulfilled. When, eleven years after Ahab's death, Jehu executed pitiless vengeance on the royal household, Jezebel painted her face, tired her head, and, looking out at a window, called to him as he approached : " Had Zimri peace, who slew his master ? " Jehu looked up at the window and said : " Who is on my side ? who ? " Two or three eunuchs looked out. " Throw her down," he cried, and they unhesitatingly obeyed. She fell in front of his chariot, which he intentionally drove over her, and her blood bespattered the horses and the wall. About an hour later, recalling that the dead woman was a king's daughter, he gave directions to bury her; but it was found that dogs, the scavengers of oriental cities, had anticipated him, and had left of her nothing but the skull, and the feet, and the palms of the hands (2 Kin. ix. 7, 30–37).

2. A woman at Thyatira who called herself a prophetess, and seduced some members of the Christian church there to commit fornication and eat things sacrificed to idols. It is probable that Jezebel is a symbolic name. If so, it was given because of a resemblance between her and Ahab's idolatrous and wicked queen (Rev. ii. 20, 23).

Je'zer [formation].

A son of Naphtali, and founder of a tribal family (Gen. xlvi. 24; Num. xxvi. 49; 1 Chron. vii. 13).

Je-zi'ah. See IZZIAH.

Je'zi-el [assembly of God].

A Benjamite, son of Azmaveth, who joined David at Ziklag (1 Chron. xii. 3).

Jez-li'ah. See IZLIAH.

Je-zo'ar. See IZHAR.

Jez-ra-hi'ah [Jehovah shineth forth].

An overseer of singers in Nehemiah's time (Neh. xii. 42).

Jez're-el [God soweth].

1. A fortified town (1 Kin. xxi. 23. wall; 2 Kin. ix. 17, tower; x. 7, 8, gate), in the territory of Issachar (Josh. xix. 17, 18), not far from mount Gilboa (1 Sam. xxxi. 1–5 with xxix. 1 and 2 Sam. iv. 4). The Israelites encamped

at a fountain in its vicinity just before the battle of Gilboa (1 Sam. xxix. 1 ; cp. 2 Sam. iv. 4), the Philistines following them to the same locality (1 Sam. xxix. 11). Ish-bosheth ruled over Jezreel among other places (2 Sam. ii. 9); and it was one of the capitals of Ahab (1 Kin. xviii. 45), and also of his son (2 Kin. viii. 29). Naboth was a Jezreelite, his vineyard was in close proximity to Ahab's palace, and he was stoned outside the city (1 Kin. xxi. 1, 13). Jezebel met her violent death in Jezreel (23; 2 Kin. ix. 10, 30–35). The heads of Ahab's seventy sons were piled at the gate of Jezreel by order of Jehu (x. 1–11). The bloodshed in these sanguinary transactions is called by Hosea "the blood of Jezreel," and he prophesied that it should be avenged (Hos. i. 4). The crusaders correctly identified Jezreel with the Parvum Gerinum, now the village Zer'in. The discovery lapsed into oblivion, and was not revived till 1814. The identification is now universally ac-

Today a little boy threshes grain at Jezreel, the traditional site of the palace where Queen Jezebel met her death.

cepted. Though in a plain, the site was an admirable one for a fortified city, standing as it does upon the brow of a very steep, rocky

The road winds from Nazareth through the valley to the city of Jezreel.

descent, of 100 feet or more, toward the north-east, with a splendid view all the way to the Jordan. The fountain of Jezreel, which is below the village, is copious and good. It is called 'Ain el-Meiyiteh. Another and yet more copious one, 'Ain Jâlûd, is at no great distance. The ancient vineyards seem to have been to the east of the city, where rock-cut wine presses now exist.

The valley of Jezreel is either the great plain intersecting Palestine immediately north of Carmel, or, better, that part of it which, adjacent to Jezreel, descends from Jezreel eastward to the Jordan (Josh. xvii. 16; Hosea i. 5). In Gideon's days the Midi-anites and Amalekites pitched within its limits (Judg. vi. 33). The whole central plain is now called the plain of Esdra-elon, a slight modification of Jezreel (cp. Judith i. 8; iv. 6; vii. 3). Through all by-gone time it has been a battlefield of nations.

2. A town in the hill country of Judah (Josh. xv. 56). It seems to have been from this place that David obtained his wife Ahinoam the Jezreelitess (1 Sam. xxv. 43; xxvii. 3). Exact situation unknown.

3. A man of Judah. descended from Hur (1 Chron. iv. 3).

4. A son of the prophet Hosea. So named because Jehovah had declared that he would avenge the blood of Jezreel on the house of Jehu (Hos. i. 4, 5).

Jib'sam. See IBSAM.

Jid'laph [he weepeth].

A son of Nahor and Milcah (Gen. xxii. 22). It is not known where he settled.

Jim'na and **Jimnah.** See IMNAH.

Jiph'tah. See IPHTAH.

Jiph'thah-el. See IPHTAH-EL.

Jo'ab [Jehovah is father].

1. Son of Seraiah and descendant of Kenaz, who was reckoned with the tribe of Judah. He was the father of the inhabitants of the valley of craftsmen (1 Chron. iv. 13, 14).

2. A son of Zeruiah (2 Sam. viii. 16), David's half sister (1 Chron. ii. 16; cp. 2 Sam. xvii. 25). Joab was, therefore, David's nephew. He was the second of three broth-ers, Abishai, Joab, and Asahel, all men of heroic type. He first appears in public life at the head of David's soldiers in the war with Ish-bosheth. He commanded at the battle which followed the tournament at Gibeon, and was victorious (2 Sam. ii. 12–32). Abner, Ish-bosheth's commander-in-chief, after a quarrel with his royal master, had an interview with David. Joab reproved the king for allowing Abner to depart in peace, denounced Abner as a spy, recalled him, and, with the connivance of Abishai (iii. 30, 39; cp. ii. 24), assassinated him at a nom-inally friendly interview. Joab committed the murder in vengeance for the death of his younger brother Asahel at the hands of Abner at the battle of Gibeon (iii. 30);

where, however, Abner had acted reluctantly and strictly in self-defense. Probably, also, a second reason was the apprehension of Joab and Abishai that Abner might be given the command of the army. David felt him-self politically too weak to bring them to justice, yet he never condoned the crime (2 Sam. iii. 6–39). In the assault on the Jebusite stronghold on mount Zion Joab was the first to enter the fortress, and as a reward was made the commander of the armies of all Israel (2 Sam. iv. 8, with 1 Chron. xi. 6). He soon afterwards repaired a portion of the city (8). After David's conquest of the Edomites (2 Sam. viii. 13, 14; 1 Chron. xviii. 12), Joab remained in Edom with the army for six months, cutting off every male (1 Kin. xi. 14–17). He commanded in the war with the confederate Syrians and Ammonites (2 Sam. x. 1–14; 1 Chron. xix. 1–19), and he pressed the siege of Rabbah so successfully that he could have taken the town by storm; but instead of doing so he sent for David that the king might have the credit of the victory (2 Sam. xi. 1; xii. 26–29; cp. 1 Chron. xx. 1–3). He obeyed David's order to put Uriah in the forefront of the battle that he might be slain (2 Sam. xi. 6–27). It was Joab who sent to David the wise woman of Tekoa to induce him to forgive Absalom (xiv. 1–27); but he did not interfere further in the case until his barley field had been set on fire by the prince (28–33). When Absalom rebelled Joab remained loyal to David, and led one of the three divisions of the royal forces which defeated the rebels (xviii. 1, 2). Then, in defiance of the king's command, he thrust three darts through the heart of the revolting prince, terminating his life (9–17), and afterwards he spoke some plain though not unwise words to the king on his extrav-agant grief at the death of a rebellious son (xix. 1–8). David shortly afterwards ap-pointed Amasa to be captain of the host in the room of Joab (13), and when Sheba re-belled Amasa was employed to lead the forces sent to crush the revolt. Joab was overcome by jealous hate, and at an avowedly friendly interview, stabbed him dead just as he had killed Abner in similar circumstances; but this time there was no pretense of a blood feud between the parties. Then Joab and Abishai put down the rebellion (xx. 1–22). Joab thus again became commander-in-chief (23; cp. also 1 Kin. ii. 34, 35) He was op-posed to David's numbering the people, and intentionally did the work imperfectly (2 Sam. xxiv. 1–9; 1 Chron. xxi. 1–6). When Adonijah set himself up for king Joab went with him (1 Kin. i. 7), but, with his other supporters, deserted him on hearing that Solomon had been proclaimed king (28–49). David on his deathbed indicated his wish that Joab should be brought to justice for the murders of Abner and of Amasa. Solo-mon carried out the sentence. Joab, cling-ing to the horns of the altar in the court of the tabernacle, fell by the hand of Benaiah, chief of the bodyguard, and was buried in his own house in the wilderness (ii. 5, 6, 28–34).

3. Founder of a family, members of which returned from captivity (Ezra ii. 6; viii. 9; Neh. vii. 11).

For 1 Chron. ii. 54. A. V., see ATAROTH 4.

Jo′ah [Jehovah is brother].

1. A son of Obed-edom (1 Chron. xxvi. 4).

2. A Levite, son of Zimmah and a descendant of Gershom (1 Chron. vi. 21). Perhaps he was the Levite, son of Zimmah and descendant of Gershon who assisted at the religious reformation under king Hezekiah (2 Chron. xxix. 12).

3. A son of Asaph. He was the recorder under king Hezekiah (2 Kin. xviii. 18, 26; Is. xxxvi. 3, 11, 22).

4. A son of Joahaz. He was recorder under king Josiah (2 Chron. xxxiv. 8).

Jo′a-haz [Jehovah hath laid hold of].

Father of king Josiah's recorder Joah (2 Chron. xxxiv. 8). For others, see JEHOAHAZ.

Jo-a′nan, in A. V. **Joanna** [Greek form of *Yoḥanan*, Jehovah hath been gracious].

An ancestor of Christ, who lived about 500 B. C. (Luke iii. 27).

Jo-an′na [a Greek form of *Yoḥanan*, Jehovah hath been gracious].

The wife of Chuza, steward of Herod the tetrarch. She was one of those women who ministered to Jesus of their substance (Luke viii. 3), and one of the party who accompanied Mary Magdalene to the sepulcher of our Lord (xxiv. 10).

For the man called Joanna in A. V., see JOANAN.

Jo-an′nan. See JOHN 2.

Jo′a-rib. See JOIARIB 2.

Jo′ash, I., and **Jehoash** [Jehovah is strong]. The longer form is used in 2 Kin. only, but the shorter form also occurs there frequently.

1. A man of Judah, family of Shelah (1 Chron. iv. 22).

2. A man of Manasseh, family of Abiezer and father of Gideon (Judg. vi. 11, 15). He lived at Ophrah, and was apparently a man of substance. He had reared an altar to Baal and an Asherah. These Gideon was directed to throw down, and he did so. The idolaters demanded that Joash should surrender his son to be put to death for the sacrilege, but Joash shrewdly said: "If Baal is a god, let him plead for himself" (Judg. vi. 11–32).

3. A Benjamite of Gibeah who came to David at Ziklag (1 Chron. xii. 3).

4. A son of Ahab (1 Kin. xxii. 26; 2 Chron. xviii. 25).

5. Son of Ahaziah, king of Judah. When Athaliah, the mother of Ahaziah, heard that her son had been slain, she massacred all the seed royal except Joash, and ascended the

throne. Joash, then only an infant, escaped by the artifice of the late king's sister Jehosheba, wife of the high priest. He was hidden with his nurse for six years in the temple. In the seventh year, Jehoiada, the high priest, summoned five captains of the royal bodyguard, put them under oath, and showed them the king. Five companies of armed men were arranged for (2 Kin. xi. 5–7), probably consisting of three companies of the guard and two courses of Levites with spears from the temple arsenal; and on a Sabbath day these five bodies were drawn up across the court of the temple in front of the altar, representative men of the nation assembled by appointment, and the king was brought into their midst, crowned, and greeted with loud acclaim. Athaliah, hearing the noise, hurried into the temple; but, by the high priest's orders, she was at once ejected and slain, leaving Joash now without a rival. Then Jehoiada framed two covenants: the one that the youthful ruler and his people should serve Jehovah, and the other that they should discharge their mutual duties as king and subjects. Then they proceeded to the house of Baal, and broke it down, destroying the images and killing the officiating priest (2 Kin. xi. 1–20; 2 Chron. xxiii. 10–21). Joash ascended the throne 835 B. C., but was the only legitimate king since 842, and his reign was apparently dated from this year, with 841 as his first regnal year. So in England, the Commonwealth was ignored and the first year of Charles II.'s actual reign was called the twelfth: king *de jure* on the death of Charles I., January 30th, 1648–49, king *de facto* at the Restoration, May 29th, 1660. Joash was seven years old at his coronation and he reigned forty years. While a child, the character of his rule depended wholly on his advisers. Happily, he was under the direction of the high priest, Jehoiada, and as long as that wise and pious counselor lived, Joash did well, one notable measure of his being the repair of the temple, though the people still continued generally to worship at the high places (2 Kin. xii. 1–16). But on the death of Jehoiada both the king and his people apostatized from Jehovah, and began to set up Asherim and other idols. Zechariah, the son of Jehoiada, denounced judgment upon the evil doers, on which Joash gave orders for his murder; and the multitude, breaking out into riot, stoned him to death (2 Chron. xxiv. 15–22; Mat. xxiii. 35). Soon afterwards Hazael, king of Syria, having captured the Philistine city of Gath, threatened Jerusalem, and had to be bought off with the contents of the temple treasury. When the invaders departed, Joash was suffering from sore diseases. Amaziah, his son, conducted the government; and in the course of three years, as it would appear, the servants of Joash slew him in his bed in revenge for the murder of Zechariah (2 Kin

xii. 20 ; 2 Chron. xxiv. 25) ; see Chronology. He was buried in the city of David, but not in one of the proper sepulchers of the kings. Joash was an infant in 842 B. C. and was seven years old in 835 (2 Kin. xi. 21), and his son Amaziah was twenty-five years old in 804 (xiv. 2). The son was accordingly born in 828, in Joash's fourteenth or fifteenth year. In oriental life this is physically possible and is readily paralleled. The early marriage of Joash was desirable and was doubtless urged by the high priest Jehoiada, since Joash was the sole survivor of his family and in his offspring lay the only hope that so great a calamity would be averted as the extinction of the direct line of David.

6. Son of Jehoahaz, king of Israel. He began to reign about 805 B. C., and reigned sixteen years. He continued the worship of the two calves at Bethel and Dan. Nevertheless he felt veneration for Elisha, and sorrowed when the great prophet lay dying. Elisha told him to open the window eastward and shoot out an arrow. He did so. The prophet then bade him take arrows and smite upon the ground. He did so, smiting the ground thrice. The arrows symbolized victories which he was to gain over the Syrians; and had he struck six times instead of three, the number of victories would have been doubled (2 Kin. xiii. 14–25). Afterwards he furnished 100,000 mercenaries to Amaziah, king of Judah, for an Edomite expedition. A prophet directed them to be sent home. Though they had been paid in advance for the services which they were not allowed to render. yet they departed in a rage, and plundered the territory of Judah as they went along (2 Chron. xxv. 6–10, 13). Perhaps on this account, Amaziah sent Joash a challenge to fight. Joash remonstrated, but Amaziah would not forbear. A battle took place at Beth-shemesh, in which Joash was victorious; and he followed up his success by breaking down a part of the wall surrounding Jerusalem, and carrying off the treasures of the temple and the palace, with hostages as guarantees against further disturbance of the peace. On the death of Joash, his son, Jeroboam II., ascended the throne (2 Kin. xiv. 8–16 ; 2 Chron. xxv. 17–24).

Jo′ash, II. [perhaps, Jehovah hath hastened (to help)].

1. A Benjamite, family of Becher (1 Chron. vii. 8).

2. An officer who had charge of David's oil cellars (1 Chron. xxvii. 28).

Jo′a-tham. See Jotham 2.

Job, I. (Gen. xlvi. 13, A. V.). See Jashub.

Job, II. [one ever returning to God (Ewald). If derived from *'ayeb*, it denotes not one persecuted (Gesenius), but rather one characterized by hostility].

An O. T. saint who dwelt in the land of Uz (Job i. 1). He is mentioned for the first time elsewhere by Ezekiel (xiv. 14, 16, 20).

He lived under patriarchal conditions, in some district to the east of Palestine and near the desert, at a time when the Chaldeans made raids in the west (i. 17). There is no reason to doubt that he is an historical personage and that he passed through the remarkable experiences which are described, albeit with poetic license, in the book which bears his name. These experiences brought the question to the forefront, Why does God permit the righteous to suffer? and afforded the material for a magnificent philosophical poem.

The book of Job is a poetic book of the O. T. which gives an account of the sufferings of Job, of the argument carried on between himself and his friends concerning the reasons for his sufferings, and of the solution of the problem. It is not known whether the poem was written during the lifetime of Job or later. The prologue (i.–iii. 2), the introductions to the various speeches and especially to Elihu's speech (xxxii. 1–5), and the epilogue narrating the prosperity of Job in his latter days under Jehovah's blessing (xlii. 7–17), are in prose.

In the opening of the book, Job is represented as being very prosperous, possessing many flocks and herds, a large number of servants, and a numerous family. Satan is permitted to try Job's faith in God, first by causing him to be despoiled of his possessions, and to be bereaved of his family ; when this means fails, Satan is further permitted to cause Job much suffering in body. Job's faith triumphs over all difficulties, and he is finally restored to more than his former prosperity.

The book between the introduction and conclusion may be divided into three main parts, each of which may be again divided into three minor parts. The introduction describes Job's prosperity and happy condition. In part first, first subhead, we find Job's first affliction described, the loss of his property and family ; under the second head comes the second stage of the affliction, the attack on Job's person, and under the third head, the coming of his three friends to condole with him. Part second contains the argument between Job and his three friends, this being threefold, each friend speaking three times (except the third, who speaks twice), and Job replying to each. This forms the principal part of the book. The three friends argue on the basis that affliction is always and necessarily a result of sin, and as Job accepts this general principle, but denies its application to himself, misunderstandings result, and the speakers are as far from a solution of the situation in the end as in the beginning. Firstly, Eliphaz begins the argument by expressing in general the sinfulness of man and hinting at, rather than boldly asserting, Job's special sinfulness. Job answers, declaring his innocence. Secondly, Bildad continues in the same strain, insisting that the Lord cannot be unjust, therefore man must be at fault. Job answers as before that he is innocent, appealing to God to lighten his burden of affliction. Thirdly, Zophar follows with the same argument, implying more directly that Job must be a sinner. The second series of speeches (xii.–xx.) now begins. The same arguments are gone over by the speakers in the same order, the friends becoming more vehement and impatient of what they consider Job's obstinacy. In the third series (xxi.–xxxi.) Eliphaz openly accuses Job of secret sin. After Job's earnest denial, Bildad falls back on the first position, and Zophar remains silent.

During the whole course of this argument Job has been profoundly conscious of his own uprightness, yet he cannot understand God's apparent harshness to him. His inward struggle becomes more intense as his outward situation appears more hopeless, but he remains firm in his determination that whatever befall him still will he trust in God. Then the thought bursts upon him that some time, in God's own pleasure, he will be justified. It may not be in this life, but it will certainly come. That carries with it a conviction of immortality, and with the statement, "I know that my redeemer liveth, and that he shall stand up at the last upon the earth : and after my skin hath been thus destroyed, yet from my flesh shall I see God," Job reaches a foundation from which nothing can afterwards move him (xix. 25, 26).

In the third part of the book, Elihu, who until this time has been a silent listener, proposes to argue out the matter upon a different basis. Instead of regarding the afflictions of men as a punishment for sin, he declares that they are often sent as a means of strengthening and purifying the children of God. They are not, then, the expression of an angry and implacable God, but the chastening of a loving father. In this Elihu appears as the messenger of the Lord, preparing the way for his coming, and offering an argument which Job could dispute or accept. Job accepts this view (xxxii.–xxxvii). Then Jehovah speaks and shows to Job that man knows far too little to justify him in attempts fully to explain the mysteries of God's rule ; and Job humbles himself before the Lord (xxxviii. 1–xlii. 6). Finally, Job is restored to double his former prosperity, and his family is restored to the same number as before (xlii. 7–17).

The consistent progress of the argument is strong evidence for the literary unity of the book. The assumption of interpolations or supplements is needless so far as the dramatic development is concerned. But whether the poem has been supplemented by the addition of chapters xxxii.–xxxvii. and xxxviii.–xlii., as many students of it contend, or not, these chapters are the work of a master mind and gifted poet, to whom God had spoken, and who with clear insight removed the errors of the popular doctrine that distorted the view of the moral question, and to the primary truths which Job had discovered added a fuller disclosure of the truth, though not the final one (xxxii.–xxxvii.), and directed attention to the humble position which it behooves ignorant and impotent man to take before God and the mysteries of the divine government (xxxviii.–xli.). Behind the seen is the unseen (as shown to the reader in the two opening chapters, i. 6–12 ; ii. 1–6), and the disputants had argued in total ignorance of the reasons for God's action and of the compensation for the sufferer which God had in store (as made known to the reader in the closing chapter, xlii.). In fact this outcome of the argument (chap. xxxviii. 1–xlii. 6) would seem to have been in the author's thought when he wrote the opening passage to his poem, for it accounts for his introduction of Satan into the plot and his intimation thereby that reasons may exist for God's procedure which lie beyond the ken of man.

Jo′bab [shouting, trumpet call, howling, a desert].

1. An Arabian tribe descended from Joktan (Gen. x. 29 ; 1 Chron. i. 23). It is not known what district they occupied.

2. A king of Edom. He was the son of Zerah of Bozrah (Gen. xxxvi. 33 ; 1 Chron. i. 44, 45).

3. A king of Madon, who entered into the northern confederacy against Joshua, but, with his allies, was totally defeated at the waters of Merom (Josh. xi. 1 ; xii. 19).

4 and 5. Two Benjamites, a son of Shaharaim and a remoter descendant (1 Chron. viii. 9, 18).

Joch′e-bed [Jehovah is glorious, or Jehovah is the great one].

A daughter of Levi, who married her nephew Amram and became the ancestress of Miriam, Aaron, and Moses (Ex. vi. 20 ; Num. xxvi. 59) ; see EGYPT iii. 3.

Jod, in A. R. V. Yodh.

The tenth letter of the Hebrew alphabet. English I and its modification J come from the same source, and both are used to represent it in anglicizing Hebrew names, as in Jechoniah. It stands at the head of the tenth section of Ps. cxix. in several versions, in which section each verse begins with this letter. It was often confused by readers with vau (q. v.).

Jo′da.

An ancestor of Christ, who lived near the time of the exile (Luke iii. 26). A. V., following a different reading, has Juda—i. e., Judah.

Jo′ed [Jehovah is witness].

A Benjamite, descended from Jeshaiah (Neh. xi. 7).

Jo′el [Jehovah is God].

1. A Levite, family of Kohath, and an an-

cestor of Samuel the prophet (1 Chron. vi. 36 with 34, 38). Probably he is not identical with Shaul (24), but belongs to the collateral line descended through Zephaniah from Tahath.

2. The elder son of Samuel the prophet and father of Heman the singer (1 Sam. viii. 2; 1 Chron. vi. 33; xv. 17). Called once in the Hebrew text and A. V. Vashni (vi. 28). This name the R. V. relegates to the margin, placing Joel in italics in the text.

3. A Gershonite Levite, who with 130 of his brethren, of whom he was the head, aided in bringing up the ark from the house of Obed-edom to the city of David (1 Chron. xv. 7, 11, 12). He seems to have been the son of Ladan (1 Chron. xxiii. 8), and guardian of the treasures dedicated to God (xxvi. 21, 22).

4. A man of Issachar, and a chief of that tribe. He was descended through Uzzi (1 Chron. vii. 3).

5. One of David's valiant men, a brother of Nathan (1 Chron. xi. 38); see IGAL.

6. Son of Pedaiah and ruler of western Manasseh in David's reign (1 Chron. xxvii. 20).

7. A chief of the Gadites in Bashan prior to the reigns of Jotham king of Judah and Jeroboam II. king of Israel (1 Chron. v. 12; cp. 17).

8. A Reubenite (1 Chron. v. 4), probably he whose family had much cattle in Gilead (8, 9).

9. A Kohathite Levite, son of Azariah, who aided in cleansing the temple during Hezekiah's reign (2 Chron. xxix. 12).

10. One of the Simeonite princes who seized pasture land at Gedor (1 Chron. iv. 35–43).

11. A son of Nebo, induced by Ezra to put away his foreign wife (Ezra x. 43).

12. A Benjamite, son of Zichri, overseer at Jerusalem during the government of Nehemiah (Neh. xi. 9).

13. Son of Pethuel, and the author of the second among the minor prophetic books (Joel i. 1). His history is unknown.

The book opens with a description of dire distress caused by a plague of locusts and apparently aggravated by drought (i. 4–12, 17–20; cp. Amos. vii. 1, 2, 4). Locusts are a natural figure for an invading army (Rev. ix. 3–11); and the oldest interpreters of the prophecy regard them in it merely as symbols of Israel's foes. An actual devastation by these insects may, however, be intended in chap. i.; and probably in chap. ii. also, where they are likened to an army, for swarms of locusts occasionally come into Palestine from the northeast, and they quite frequently perish in the sea (cp. ii. 20). If locusts were actually wasting the country, the event served the prophet as a type of the dreadful day of the Lord and as an occasion for his message.

The book consists of a sublime address, comprising, first, a twice repeated tale of judgment, followed in each instance by a call to repentance and prayer (i. 2–ii. 17), and, secondly, an announcement of the blessings, near and remote, material and spiritual, that follow upon repentance (ii. 18–iii. 21 [Hebrew text, iv. 21]). The prophecy thus falls into four parts:

1. The prophet depicts the distress that has occurred or is impending, and calls upon the inhabitants to mourn (i. 2–12) and to repent and cry unto Jehovah (13, 14).

2. The prophet explains the event. The day of Jehovah is at hand, and shall come as destruction from the Almighty (15). A day of affliction: a people great and strong, like an irresistible army, executing the will of Jehovah (ii. 1–11). But even now repentance may avail (12–17).

3. The result of repentance. Jehovah, jealous for his land, promises to destroy the spoilers, to give seasons of plenty which shall make good the first suffering and loss, and not to allow that his people be again put to shame (18–27).

4. This deliverance is the herald of deliverance "afterward." Having poured out the rain to make the earth bring forth abundantly, Jehovah will pour out his spirit upon all flesh. The sun shall, indeed, be darkened, symbolical of the wrath of God, before the terrible day of Jehovah cometh (as described in iii. 14–17); and whosoever calleth on the name of Jehovah shall be saved, for in mount Zion shall be those that escape (ii. 28–32). In those days, when Jehovah shall bring back the captivity of Judah, all enemies of the kingdom shall be brought to judgment. In one picture Joel exhibits God's successive judgments of the nations, and the final, universal judgment, culminating in the establishment of Zion forever (iii. 1–21 [Hebrew text, iv. 1–21]).

What is the date of the prophecy?

1. Joel cites earlier prophecy (ii. 32). Part of the declaration is found verbally in Obadiah (Ob. 17), and Joel may have quoted from that book. He may, however, be alluding to a previous announcement of his own; or he may have had Is. iv. 2, 3 in mind, where the thought and the several words occur.

2. The book mentions the scattering of Israel among the nations (iii. 2), but the reference is not to the ten tribes specifically, but to the children of Abraham, Isaac, and Jacob, God's people and heritage, and is moreover a prophecy. So, too, the captivity of Judah and Jerusalem is mentioned (iii. 1), but likewise prophetically in the spirit of Deuteronomy (xxviii.) or Hosea (vi. 11) or of Micah (iii. 12; iv. 10). For the prophet and people are in Judah, Zion exists (Joel ii. 1, 15), the temple is standing (i. 14; ii. 17), and the service is regularly conducted, although the meal and drink offerings have been cut off by reason of the destruction of vegetation (i. 9–13; cp. ii. 14).

3. The reference to past events begins with

the last clause of iii. 2 [Hebrew text, iv. 2], as the grammatical construction seems to indicate. Hostile nations had parted Jehovah's land among them, cast lots for the captives, plundered the temple of its silver and gold, sold children of Judah to the Greeks, and shed innocent blood (2–6, 19). The allusions are not to the period after the exile, nor to the time between the first deportation of the Jews and the fall of the city, nor to the earlier period when the Assyrians were invading the land, for (a) Judgment is not pronounced against Assyria or Babylon or later enemies, but only against Judah's foes, Tyre and Sidon, Philistia, Edom, and Egypt (iii. 4, 19). Tyre and Sidon had forgotten the brotherly covenant (4; Amos i. 9, and had purchased Jewish captives from the Philistines and sold them to the remote Greeks. Philistia and Edom had done violence to Judah (Joel iii. 4, 19; 2 Chron. xxi. 16, 17; xxviii, 17, "again").

(b) There is no reference to Syria, from which Judah scarcely suffered before the reign of Ahaz (2 Kin. xii. 17). During and after the reign of Ahaz, the prophets of Judah frequently refer to Syria as a hostile power (Is. vii. 8; viii. 4; xvii.; Jer. xlix. 23–27; Zech. ix. 1).

(c) Nor is any mention made of the Assyrians, who did not come into conflict with Judah until after the time of Ahaz, and who for a half century preceding Ahaz's reign had not been active in western Asia.

(d) There is reference to the Greeks, not as present in Palestine or as hostile to Judah, but simply as a nation afar off to whom the Phœnicians and Philistines had sold captive children of Judah, and as contrasted with the men of Sheba, a nation at another extremity of the earth, to whom Judah shall sell captives taken from Philistia and Phœnicia (Joel iii. 1–8). Accordingly the opinion has found a general, though not a universal acceptance, with commentators, that the prophecy was uttered before the time of Ahaz. The position of the book as second among the minor prophets indicates that the belief was current at the time of forming the canon that Joel began to prophesy after Hosea had commenced his prophetic labors and before Amos had entered upon his, that is, during the reign of Uzziah, king of Judah, and while Jeroboam was on the throne of Israel (Hos. i. 1; Amos i. 1; vii. 10).

Jo-e′lah [possibly, let him help].
A son of Jeroham of Gedor. He joined David at Ziklag (1 Chron. xii. 7).

Jo′e-zer [Jehovah is help].
A Korahite who joined David at Ziklag (1 Chron. xii. 6).

Jog′be-hah [lofty].
A town of Gad (Num. xxxii. 35; Judg. viii. 11). Its name still lives in Jubeihah, a village, 6 miles northwest of Rabbath Ammon on the road from es-Salt and the Jordan.

Jog′li [led into exile].
Father of Bukki, of the tribe of Dan (Num. xxxiv. 22).

Jo′ha.
1. A Benjamite, son of Beriah (1 Chron. viii. 16).
2. A Tizite, son of Shimri and one of David's mighty men (1 Chron. xi. 45).

Jo-ha′nan [Jehovah is gracious].
1. A Benjamite who joined David at Ziklag (1 Chron. xii. 4).
2. The eighth of the Gadites who did so. He was made a captain in David's army (1 Chron. xii. 12, 14).
3. A member of the high-priestly line, who lived about 800 B. C. (1 Chron. vi. 10).
4. An Ephraimite (2 Chron. xxviii. 12).
5. The eldest son of king Josiah (1 Chron. iii. 15). He seems to have died young.
6. A captain, son of Kareah. He and his men made their submission to Gedaliah, whom Nebuchadnezzar set as governor over Judah (2 Kin. xxv. 22, 23; Jer. xl. 8, 9). He warned Gedaliah of the plot to murder him (13, 14); and when the governor, neglecting the warning, was assassinated, he led the force which went to avenge his death (xli. 11–15). He afterwards counseled and carried out a removal of the Jewish remnant to Egypt, against the advice of Jeremiah (16–xliii. 13).
7. A son of Elioenai (1 Chron. iii. 24).
8. A son of Hakkatan, of the clan of Azgad. With 110 males, he accompanied Ezra from Babylon (Ezra viii. 12).
9. Son of Eliashib, but scarcely of the high priest Eliashib. Ezra went to Johanan's chamber, and, refusing to eat or drink, mourned over the sin of those who had contracted foreign marriages (Ezra x. 6, in R. V. Jehohanan).
10. Son of Tobiah, the Ammonite, who married a Jewess in the days of Nehemiah (Neh. vi. 18, in R. V. Jehohanan).
11. A high priest (Neh. xii. 22), grandson of Eliashib (23; cp. 11). In ver. 11, the name appears as Jonathan, doubtless through corruption of the text. The Jews at Elephantine opposite Syene in Egypt, whose temple was destroyed in 411 B. C. by the command of a local official at the instigation of the Egyptian priests, at once sent word of the outrage to Johanan in the hope that he might be able to secure them redress (Elephantine Papyri). Josephus, who correctly calls him John, says that he killed his brother Jesus in the temple, believing that he was about to supersede him in the high priesthood. This murder was committed in the reign of Artaxerxes Mnemon, 405–362 B. C. (Antiq. xi. 7, 1; cp. 5, 4).

John [Greek 'Ιōannēs, from Hebrew Yoḥanan, Jehovah hath been gracious].
1. Father of Mattathias, the instigator of the Maccabæan revolt (1 Mac. ii. 1).
2. Eldest son of Mattathias (1 Mac. ii. 2, in

A. V. Joannan). He was surnamed Gaddis (in A. V. Caddis), a word of unknown meaning. He was slain by the children of Jambri, about 160 B. C. (ix. 36, 38, 42; and 2 Mac. viii. 22, where he is erroneously called Joseph).

3. A man who obtained special privileges for the Jews from Antiochus the Great (2 Mac. iv. 1 '. He was son of Accos and father of Eupoiemus (1 Mac. viii. 17).

4. Son of Simon, the Maccabee (1 Mac. xiii. 53; xvi. 1). He became known as John Hyrcanus. About 142 B. C. he was appointed by his father commander-in-chief of the army (xiii. 53). He met and defeated Cendebæus in battle near Jamnia (xvi. 1–10). When his father and two brothers were murdered in 135 B. C., and he himself was marked for destruction, he took the offensive against his adversary and drove him from Judæa (Antiq. xiii. 8, 1). He exercised the office of high priest and civil governor from 135 to 105 B. c. Antiochus Sidetes, king of Syria, invaded Judæa, and in the fall of 134 B. C. laid siege to Jerusalem. After a year, the Syrians took the city and dismantled its fortifications (xiii. 8, 2 and 3). The death of Antiochus afforded John an opportunity to enlarge his domains, and he conquered Samaria and Idumæa. He also renewed the alliance with the Romans and thereby secured the restoration of Joppa and other towns to Jewish authority. He also repaired the walls of Jerusalem (1 Mac. xvi. 23). The civil war which broke out in Syria in 125 B. C. and a succession of Syrian kings from whom, for one reason or another, he had nothing to fear, enabled John to maintain his independence without difficulty. He favored the Pharisees at the first, but when they unreasonably clamored for his resignation of the high-priesthood, he went over to the Sadducees. With his death in 105 B. C. the power of the Maccabees and, with it, of Israel rapidly waned. See MACCA'BEES.

5. John the Baptist. The immediate forerunner of Jesus, whose way he was sent to prepare. John was born of godly parents, and was of full priestly descent, both his father Zacharias and his mother Elisabeth being descendants of Aaron (Luke i. 5). At the same time Elisabeth, the Levite, was cousin to the Virgin Mary, who belonged to the tribe of Judah (36). The residence of John's parents was at a town in the hill country of Judæa (39), perhaps Juttah or the priestly city of Hebron. When Zacharias, in the performance of his priestly duties, was burning incense in the temple at Jerusalem, the angel Gabriel appeared to him, promised that he should become the father of a son, directed that the child should be named John, and be brought up as a Nazirite, like Samson and Samuel, and foretold that he should be filled with the Holy Spirit from birth and prepare the people for the Lord (Luke i. 8–17). John was born

in the year 5 B. C. He spent his early years in seclusion in the wilderness near his home, west of the Dead Sea (80). In A. D. 26 he appeared as a preacher in the wilderness adjoining the Jordan. His ministry is believed to have been exercised during a Sabbatic year (iii. 1, 2), in which the people were relieved of labor in the fields and had leisure to attend John's preaching. He came to announce a new dispensation, proclaiming the advent of the kingdom of God and the baptism of the Holy Spirit (Mat. iii. 2, 11), to prepare the people in intellect and heart for the reception of Christ (3, 8), to point out the Christ in the person of Jesus (John i. 15), and to show the union of the two dispensations in the Christ, as the Lamb of God (29, 36). He addressed himself with great earnestness and plainness of speech to the immense multitudes who repaired to him from all quarters. He urged the necessity of immediate and sincere repentance, the special reason assigned being that the kingdom of heaven was at hand. The penitents, after confessing their sins, were baptized by John in the Jordan; and he became distinguished from others of the name by being called the Baptist. The baptism by water which he administered typified cleansing from sin. He did not regard it as enough, but directed his hearers to One who should come after him, whose shoe-latchet he was not worthy to unloose, and who would baptize them with the Holy Ghost and fire (Mat. iii. 5–12). Notwithstanding this confession of inferiority to Jesus, our Lord sought baptism at his hands. John remonstrated, which shows that he knew Jesus to be the Messiah; but he obeyed, for he recognized his own subordinate position (13–17). He knew Jesus from the teaching of his parents, and the correctness of this information was confirmed to him by the visible descent of the Holy Spirit upon Jesus at his baptism. By this sign he was authorized to declare Jesus to be the Christ (John i. 32, 33). Malachi had foretold the appearance of Elijah, the prophet, before the great and terrible day of the Lord, to turn the heart of the fathers to the children and the heart of the children to their fathers. John denied that he was Elijah in person (John i. 21); he defined his own mission and characteristics by simply quoting Is. xl. 3. But John came in the spirit and power of Elijah (Mal. iv. 5, 6, with Luke i. 17), he was the messenger sent to prepare the way before Christ (Mal. iii. 1, with Mark i. 2), and Jesus applied these predictions to John (Mat. xi. 10, 14; xvii. 12, 13). There was a resemblance between the two men also in their cheap and coarse attire, which they wore to symbolize the renouncement of ease and luxury, and in their blunt manners, which rendered them fitter for the wilderness than for kings' courts (2 Kin. i. 8, and Mat. iii. 4; xi. 8; Mark i. 6). John had said of Jesus, "He must increase, but I must decrease;" and without jealousy he saw the fulfilment of his prediction (John iii. 25-30). His public ministry was short, but his popular success was immense. At length, toward the close of A. D. 27 or in the early part of 28, having with his usual fidelity reproved Herod the tetrarch for living in sin with his brother Philip's wife, he was committed to prison (Luke iii. 19, 20). While there, perplexed and impatient at Christ's method of developing his work, and perhaps feeling that he was forgotten while others were helped, he sent two of his disciples to ask if Jesus were the promised Messiah. In reply Jesus pointed to his works. When the two disciples departed, Jesus took the opportunity of passing a high panegyric on John (Mat. xi. 2-15). John was the greatest of the prophets in that he was privileged to prepare the people for the Christ's appearance and to point out the Christ to them. The vindictiveness of the adulteress Herodias caused John's death. She persuaded her daughter, who had pleased Herod by her dancing, to ask the head of the Baptist. It was given her, and the headless body was soon afterwards removed by John's disciples and buried. Finding their master gone, they remembered his testimony to the Lamb of God, and became disciples of Jesus (Mat. xiv. 3-12; Mark vi. 16-29; Luke iii. 19, 20). Josephus attributes the death of John the Baptist to Herod's jealousy of his great influence with the people. He says also that the destruction of Herod's army in the war with Aretas, which soon after occurred, was generally considered a divine judgment on the tetrarch for the murder of John. The historian makes the place of the Baptist's imprisonment and death the fort of Machærus (Antiq. xviii. 5, 2). Machærus, now called Mekaur, is situated in the mountains on the eastern side of the Dead Sea, about 5 miles north of the Arnon, and on the top of a conical hill 3800 feet above the Dead Sea. The wall of circumvallation of the old stronghold still remains clearly traceable, while inside are a deep well and two dungeons. One of the latter may have been the prison in which John was confined.

6. Father of the apostle Peter (John i. 42; xxi. 15-17, both R. V.). He is called Jonah in Mat. xvi. 17. See JONAH.

7. John the apostle. A son of Zebedee, and brother of that James who suffered martyrdom under Herod Agrippa I. (Mat. iv. 21; Acts xii. 1, 2). It is reasonably inferred that he was younger than James, and that his mother was named Salome and was sister to the mother of Jesus; see JAMES. His father was a master fisherman on the sea of Galilee, and his two sons aided him in his occupation (Mark i. 19, 20). John had attended the preaching of the Baptist at the Jordan, and was evidently the unnamed disciple to whom and Andrew John the Baptist pointed out Jesus as the Lamb of God (John i. 35-40). He

doubtless accompanied Jesus back to Galilee, and attended the wedding at Cana (ii. 1-11). But he had not been summoned yet to permanent fellowship with Jesus, and he resumed his work on the lake, sometimes together with his brother in partnership with Peter (Luke v. 10). From their business Jesus called James and John to follow him (Mat. iv. 21, 22; Mark i. 19, 20). Later they were appointed apostles (Mat. x. 2). Jesus named them Boanerges, sons of thunder (Mark iii. 17), evidently because of their vehemence. The impetuosity of their natural temperament, not yet fully chastened by grace, was shown when John rebuked one who cast out demons in Christ's name, but did not follow Christ in the company of the disciples (Luke ix. 49); and when, finding their Master rejected in a Samaritan village, they wished to call down fire from heaven on the inhabitants (52-56). They showed selfishness once in joining with their mother to ask for the places of honor beside Jesus in his future kingdom; but at the same time their zeal was manifested, for they declared themselves ready to face death for him (Mat. xx. 20-24; Mark x. 35-41). But the natural defects of their character were overcome, and their very vehemence, chastened by grace, became an element of strength and a glory. John was a man of deep spiritual insight and loving disposition, and in consequence he was the disciple whom Jesus peculiarly loved. He was one of the three apostles whom Jesus chose to be with him at the raising of Jairus' daughter (Mark v. 37; Luke viii. 51), at the transfiguration (Mat. xvii. 1; Mark ix. 2; Luke ix. 28), and at the agony in the garden (Mat. xxvi. 37; Mark xiv. 33). At the last supper he occupied the place next to Jesus at the table (John xiii. 23). He followed Jesus from Gethsemane into the palace of the high priest, to whom he was known, and to the place of crucifixion; and on the cross Jesus commended his mother Mary to John's loving care, and he accepted the trust (xviii. 15; xix. 27). When the tomb of Christ was reported to him to be empty, he ran with Peter to the sepulcher to investigate, and learned by what he saw that Christ had risen (xx. 1-10). With the other disciples he saw the risen Christ the same evening and again a week later (Luke xxiv. 33-43; John xx. 19-30; 1 Cor. xv. 5), and like them John went to Galilee, as Jesus had directed, and again saw the Lord (Mat. xxvi. 32; xxviii. 10, 16; John xxi. 1-7). While there, through a misunderstanding of an utterance of Jesus, the idea got abroad among the brethren that John was not to die (John xxi. 22). After the ascension, he abode for some time with the ten other apostles in an upper room at Jerusalem (Acts i. 13), and after Pentecost he became Peter's colleague in active missionary work (iii. 1). Both were imprisoned by the Jewish authorities, and witnessed ι good confession (iv. 19). Both were sent by their fellow-apostles to Samaria to aid in the work begun by Philip (viii. 14). John was one of the apostles who remained in Jerusalem during the persecutions that soon assailed the infant church, and he was still there, a pillar of strength, when Paul visited the city after his first missionary journey (xv. 6; Gal. ii. 9). Five books of the N. T. are ascribed to him—the Fourth Gospel, three epistles, and the book of Revelation. In the title of the last-named work the author is called St. John the Divine. Tradition fixes on Ephesus as the scene of his later ministrations, and it is probable that the seven churches of Asia enjoyed his care (Rev. i. 11). When he penned the Revelation, probably in A. D. 95, he was in the island of Patmos, an exile for the word of God and the testimony of Jesus (Rev. i. 9). The accession of Nerva is said to have freed him from danger and enabled him to return to Ephesus. Polycarp, Papias, and Ignatius were his pupils. Polycarp's disciple Irenæus states that he continued to reside at Ephesus until his death in the reign of Trajan.

8. John Mark. Mark the evangelist. Mark, however, was only the surname; John was the proper, and probably the earlier, name (Acts xii. 12, 25). See MARK.

9. A Jewish dignitary who took part with Annas, Caiaphas, Alexander, and as many as were of the kindred of the high priest, which perhaps he was himself, in calling the apostles Peter and John to account for their preaching (Acts iv. 6).

John, E-pis'tles of.

The First Epistle of John is evidently by the author of the Fourth Gospel. The same characteristic phraseology is found in both works and the same way of constructing sentences. The epistle moreover plainly supposes the readers' acquaintance with the gospel. Both were evidently sent primarily to the same churches, and in the opinion of many the epistle was an accompaniment of the gospel. The opening words of the epistle suggest at once the gospel's prologue, and parallels between the two books may be found in nearly every verse of the epistle. The epistle, moreover, has in view the world as the antagonist of the church and the field of its operations (ii. 2, 15–17; iv. 3–5; v. 4, 5, 19), and warns against heresies which struck at the integrity of Christ's person (ii. 18–26; iv. 1–3; v. 6–10). These features harmonize with the date and purpose of the gospel. The two works therefore clearly came from the same hand and at about the same time. The epistle seeks to apply to Christian life the truth whose historical revelation is recorded in the gospel. It, no less than the gospel, claims to be by an apostle. The writer was one of those who had lived in personal contact with Christ (i. 1–3, 5; iv. 14) and writes in an authoritative manner as became an apostle (i. 4; ii. 1; iv. 6, 14). How deeply he had absorbed the teaching of his Lord is proved by the similarity of phraseology and thought between the epistle and Christ's discourses in the gospel. The Johannean authorship of the epistle is vouched for by Irenæus and the Muratori Fragment; while earlier quotations by Polycarp, Papias, etc., prove its use in the church from the beginning of the second century. Its train of thought may be outlined as follows: After the introduction (i. 1–4), in which John declares the purpose of his ministry to be the declaration to men of the manifestation of the life-giving, divine Word, in order that they may have joyful fellowship in him with the original apostles, he teaches that the character of God, as learned from Christ, must determine the character of the Christian's inward and outward life (i. 5–ii. 6); hence he urges to love of the brethren, warns against love of the world and heretical teaching (ii. 7–27). He next insists (ii. 28–iii. 24) on the necessity of doing righteousness, and so of abiding in God, in view of the coming second advent of Christ; since at it our divine sonship will be fully manifested and that sonship is distinguished by obedience and love. Then he reminds his readers (iv.) that the test of having the Spirit of God is to be found in the true confession of Christ as the incarnate Son of God, in adherence to apostolic teaching, and in love; and that right faith in Jesus is the condition of the whole spiritual life of love (v. 1–12). In the conclusion (v. 13–21) he tersely summarizes the purpose of the epistle as intended to confirm them in faith and communion with God, and solemnly recites the historical and spiritual facts on which their eternal life steadfastly reposes.

The Second Epistle of John. Quite in accord with the reserve shown by the apostle John, the author of the second epistle calls himself "the elder," a designation used by Peter of himself (1 Pet. v. 1) and given by Papias to all the apostles. The author writes to "the elect lady and her children," expressing his joy at the Christian life of her children and warning her against heretical teachers. The brevity of the epistle easily explains the paucity of references to it in the earliest writers. In fact, the external evidence is larger than would be expected. The most ancient historical testimony ascribes the epistle to the apostle John. Clement of Alexandria was acquainted with at least one shorter epistle by the apostle, and Irenæus quotes 2 John 10, 11, as coming from John the disciple of the Lord. Moreover, the Johannean authorship is abundantly proved by the remarkable coincidences of language and thought with 1 John and no motive can be imagined for its forgery. Some have supposed that by the elect lady was meant a church; others suppose her an individual named Kuria (the Greek for lady). It is probably best to leave the name indefinite.

The Third Epistle of John. Another brief letter addressed by the elder to Gaius the well-beloved, expressing joy at the hospitality to the brethren which Gaius had shown, and urging his friend to continue to imitate that which is good. Reference is also made to a certain Diotrephes who had opposed the writer; and on the other hand to a Demetrius who is praised. It is impossible to identify this Gaius with any of that name mentioned in the N. T.; see GAIUS 3. He appears to have been a prominent man in one of the churches of Asia, but not an officer of the church. This epistle is remarkably like the first and second in style and thought: so that there is no reason to doubt that the three were by the same writer.

All John's epistles, with those of James, Peter, and Jude, are frequently included in the number of the so-called "catholic" or "general" epistles, i. e. those addressed not to particular churches or persons, but to large or many communities. 1 John was no doubt sent to the churches of Asia, among which the Fourth Gospel was first issued. To 2 and 3 John, however, this title does not apply, nor are they styled "general" in A. V. or R. V. They were probably placed among the "general" epistles simply because, being brief, they were attached to 1 John.

G. T. P. (supplemented).

John the Divine, The Revelation of St.

See REVELATION.

John, Gos'pel according to St.

The title prefixed to the Fourth Gospel, in accordance with the universal belief of the early church that the book was written by the apostle John. Like the other gospels it does not mention the writer's name, but both internal and external considerations support the traditional belief.

I. *Internal evidence.* (1) The writer was one of the apostles. This appears from his use of the first person plural (i. 14 and perhaps xxi. 24) and from many items of minute description, especially concerning the impression made on the disciples by events in Christ's life, etc. (i. 37; ii. 11, 17; iv. 27, 54; ix. 2; xi. 8-16; xii. 4-6, 21, 22; xiii. 23-26; xviii. 15; xix. 26, 27, 35; xx. 8), and from the explicit statement in xxi. 24. (2) He mentions a "disciple whom Jesus loved" (xiii. 23; xix. 26; xx. 2; xxi. 7, 20, 21). who, in xxi. 24, is said to be the author. All the apostles, however, are mentioned by name in the book except Matthew, James the son of Alphæus, Simon Zelotes, and the sons of Zebedee. The three former did not belong to the narrower circle of intimate disciples, to one of whom this title would alone be applicable, and James the son of Zebedee died early (Acts xii. 2). John, therefore, alone remains. (3) That the writer was a Jew is proved incontestably by the strongly Hebraistic character of his style in writing Greek. (4) He shows intimate acquaintance

with the geography, history, and customs of the Jews during Christ's ministry (e. g. i. 21, 28, 46; ii. 6; iii. 23; iv. 5, 27, R. V.; v. 2, 3; vii. 40-52; ix. 7; x. 22, 23; xi. 18; xviii. 28; xix. 31), and his book gives more personal details than any of the gospels. The internal evidence thus harmonizes strikingly with the Johannean authorship. Nothing stronger could be asked, short of an explicit statement. The latter, in fact, is almost given in xxi. 24, for, according to the unanimous testimony of early Christian history, John was the only apostle who lived long enough to give rise to the belief that he would survive till the second advent. Chap. xxi. is evidently an addition by the author to his work, which was originally intended to close with chap. xx. It amounts substantially to an affirmation that St. John was the author of the whole treatise.

II. *External evidence.* The testimony of Irenæus (born about A. D. 115-125 and bishop of Lyons in the last part of the second century), who was a disciple of Polycarp, who was a disciple of St. John, is explicit that John wrote this Gospel in Ephesus after the other gospels had been issued. This is of itself sufficient evidence. It is confirmed, however, by a line of testimonies from the very close of the apostolic age. The First Epistle was plainly written by the author of the Gospel, and its apostolic authority is attested by its use by Polycarp (A. D. 110) and Papias (A. D. 130-140). The Ignatian epistles (A. D. 100) show that the Gospel was familiar and authoritative to the churches of Asia Minor at the beginning of the second century. Justin (A. D. 150) used it freely, and quotes from it, evidently considering it one of "the memoirs of the apostles," which he says were called gospels, and were written by the apostles and their companions. In the Teaching of the Apostles the use of the Fourth Gospel is thought by many to be implied; and, while that is perhaps doubtful, the more recently recovered apocryphal Gospel of Peter shows that the Fourth Gospel formed with the other three the narrative upon the basis of which the pseudo-Peter wrote. Tatian's Diatessaron was a harmony of the gospels used in the churches, and is a combination of our four. The MS. of Syriac gospels, recently found by Mrs. Lewis, proves that in the second century our four gospels were the accepted ones in the Syrian church. Finally, it is certain that even the earliest heretics (Gnostic) of the second century accepted the Fourth Gospel as apostolic. Thus external evidence amply confirms the belief that the Fourth Gospel was written by St. John, and, as such, was received as authoritative by the church from the very beginning of the post-apostolic age. The evidence also points to its composition in Asia Minor (tradition says Ephesus) in the last quarter of the first century. The opponents of Jesus are called simply the Jews (i. 19; ii. 18;

v. 10; vii. 15, etc.), explanations are given about the Jewish feasts (vi. 4; vii. 2; xi. 55; xix. 31), the sea of Galilee is explained by its gentile name, sea of Tiberias (vi. 1), and the designation in the prologue of Christ as the Word of God points to a period when Christianity was confronted with such philosophical tendencies as we know existed in Asia Minor. This explains also the apparent purpose of the book. It was to give Christ's testimony to himself as the incarnate Son of God and Saviour of the world (xx. 30, 31). It assumes acquaintance with the other gospels and intends to supplement them; see GOSPEL. They had not given those great discourses of the Lord, in which he had replied to the attacks of the Jews upon his divine claims or had unfolded to his disciples the mysteries of his being and their spiritual relations to himself. This self-testimony of Jesus John determined to set down, especially since heresies had risen which denied some aspects of the person of Christ. With this he combined also, as was natural, many items of personal reminiscence. The result was to provide the church with a complete portrayal of her divine-human Lord.

John's Gospel begins with a prologue (i. 1–18), in which the apostle summarizes the great truth about to be shown in the life of Christ, viz. the existence of a second divine person whose office it is to reveal God and who is, therefore, called the Word, who, besides being the universal source of life and light to creation, became incarnate as Jesus Christ, and thus to those who believed, revealed God and imparted salvation. He then relates; 1. The opening testimonies to Jesus given by John the Baptist and by Jesus himself to his first disciples (i. 19–ii. 11). 2. Christ's revelation of himself in a series of acts and, still more, of discourses addressed to inquirers or to his adversaries (ii. 12–xii. 50). This includes (a) his testimony at his first passover (ii. 12–25), and the discourse with Nicodemus (iii. 1–21), together with the renewed testimony of the Baptist (22–36); (b) the conversation with the woman of Samaria (iv. 1–42); (c) the second miracle in Galilee (43–54); (d) Christ's defense to the Jews of his divine dignity and authority (v.); (e) his presentation of himself as the bread of life (vi.); (f) his renewed defense of his authority and dignity at the feast of tabernacles (vii., viii.); (g) the healing of the blind man and parable of the good shepherd (ix. 1–x. 21); (h) Christ's final testimony to the Jews (22–42); (j) the raising of Lazarus and its consequences (xi.); (k) the testimony given at Bethany, in the triumphal entry, and at the visit of the Greeks (xii.). 3. Christ's revelation of himself in connection with his death and resurrection (xiii. 1–xxi. 25). This includes (a) his last discourses with his disciples (xiii.–xvii.); (b) his arrest, trial, and crucifixion, in which he bore witness, particularly before Pilate, to

his person and work (xviii., xix.); (c) his resurrection and certain testimonies connected with it (xx., xxi.). The result is to show that in the human Jesus there was the eternal Son of God, who by his person, teaching, and redeeming work has revealed God and secured eternal life to those who receive him. St. John thus represents the mission of Jesus as the climax of God's self-revelation and as the procurement for believers of that light which consists in knowledge of the highest truth and of that life which consists in spiritual union with God, which together constitute the perfect good and the everlasting salvation. "These [things]" he says, "are written, that ye might believe that Jesus is the Christ, the Son of God; and that believing ye might have life through his name" (xx. 31).

G. T. P.

Joi'a-da [Jehovah hath known].

1. A son of Paseah, who repaired a gate of Jerusalem (Neh. iii. 6; in A. V. Jehoiada).

2. A high priest, great grandson of Jeshua (Neh. xii. 10). One of his sons married a daughter of Sanballat, the governor of Samaria, and for thus defiling the priesthood was expelled, probably from Jerusalem, by Nehemiah (xiii. 28).

Jo'a-kim [Jehovah doth establish].

A high priest, son of Jeshua (Neh. xii. 10, 12, 21–26), in the reign of [Arta]xerxes (Antiq. xi. 5, 1).

Joi'a-rib or **Jehoiarib**, the two forms freely interchanging in Hebrew [Jehovah defends].

1. A descendant of Aaron. See JEHOIARIB.

2. A chief of the priests who returned from Babylon with Zerubbabel (Neh. xii. 6, 7). In the next generation a father's house bore this name (19; cp. 1 Mac. ii. 1, Joarib being the Greek form).

3. A man of understanding who was returning from Babylon with Ezra and was sent with others from the encampment on the river of Ahava to secure Levites and Nethinim for the service of the temple (Ezra viii. 16, 17).

4. A man of Judah, descended from a certain Zechariah (Neh. xi. 5).

Jok'de-am [perhaps, possessed by people].

A town in the mountains of Judah (Josh. xv. 56). Site unknown.

Jo'kim.

A man of Judah, family of Shelah (1 Chron. iv. 22).

Jok'me-am [the people is brought together].

A town of Ephraim (1 Chron. vi. 68), apparently near Abel-meholah (1 Kin. iv. 12, where A. V., contrary to the Hebrew text, calls it Jokneam). The Kohathite Levites were given residence in it (1 Chron. vi. 66, 68). Instead of this town, Kibzaim is given in Josh. xxi. 22, and is commonly believed to be another name of the same place.

Jok'ne-am [the people is permitted to possess, or it is allowed to possess people].

1. A town on or near mount Carmel (Josh. xii. 22). The boundary line of the tribe of Zebulun extended to the river that is before Jokneam (xix. 11). It was given with its suburbs to the Merarite Levites (xxi. 34). The identification proposed by Eli Smith and Robinson is generally accepted, namely Tell Keimûn, probably the Cyamon of Judith vii. 3, on the southern margin of the plain of Esdraelon, on the slopes of Carmel, a little south of the Kishon, and about 15 miles northwest by west of Jezreel. It commands the main pass from the western portion of Esdraelon to the more southern plain.

2. A place mentioned in A. V. of 1 Kin. iv. 12 ; but see JOKMEAM.

Jok'shan [perhaps, a fowler].

A tribe and its progenitor descended from Abraham by Keturah (Gen. xxv. 1, 2). From Jokshan sprang Sheba and Dedan (3). Exact place of settlement unknown.

Jok'tan [Hebrew Yoktan, little, small].

A person or rather tribe descended from Shem through Eber and from whom thirteen tribes of Arabia sprang (Gen. x. 25, 29 ; 1 Chron. i. 19–23). The Mussulmans correctly or incorrectly call Joktan Kahtân.

Jok'the-el [probably, subjection to God or it is made to serve God].

1. A village in the lowland of Judah (Josh. xv. 33, 38). The identification with the ruin Kutlâneh, about four miles east by south of Ekron and 4 west-southwest of Gezer, is groundless.

2. A name given by Amaziah, king of Judah, to Sela, now Petra, when he had taken it in war (2 Kin. xiv. 7, R. V.).

Jo'na. See JONAH 2.

Jon'a-dab and **Jehonadab** [Jehovah is bounteous].

1. Son of David's brother Shimeah (2 Sam. xiii. 3).

2. A son of Rechab, the Kenite (Jer. xxxv. 6 ; cp. 1 Chron. ii. 55). He became head of the tribe and gave character to it by his rule requiring his people to dwell in tents, refrain from agriculture, and abstain from wine (Jer. xxxv. 6, 7) in order to preserve primitive simplicity of manners. Jehu, finding that Jonadab sympathized with his work of suppressing Baal worship, took him to Samaria, where he aided Jehu in putting out of Baal's temple all who were not priests of that god, in preparation for the massacre which was to ensue (2 Kin. x. 15, 23).

Jo'nah, in A. V. of N. T. **Jonas,** twice **Jona,** the Greek genitive case (Mat. xvi. 17 ; John i. 42) [a dove].

1. A prophet of Israel, a son of Amittai, and citizen of Gath-hepher in Galilee, who before the close of the reign of Jeroboam II. foretold Israel's recovery of its borders from the entering of Hamath to the sea of the plain (2 Kin. xiv. 25 ; Jon. i. 1).

The book of Jonah is the fifth in order of the minor prophetic books in the Hebrew original and in the English version. In the Septuagint it is the sixth ; not, however, in all editions. It may be divided into three sections :—

I. Jonah's disobedience (i.). He was bidden to go to Nineveh and cry against it. But he desired the destruction of the city, probably because its punishment would humble an enemy of Israel ; and he feared lest it should repent at his message and be spared to the destruction of his nation. Accordingly he took ship at Joppa to flee to Tarshish. A great storm arose. The ship was in danger. At length the sailors cast lots to ascertain on whose account the storm had been sent. The lot fell upon Jonah. He told them that he was a worshiper of the God of heaven who had made the sea and the dry land ; and that, if they would cast him overboard, the sea would become calm. They reluctantly obeyed. The sea became quiet ; and the prophet, who had disappeared in the depths, was swallowed by a great fish which the Lord had prepared. II. Jonah's prayer (ii.). Surprised at finding himself alive in the midst of the sea, the prophet gave thanks to God for his present escape from death and gratefully expressed the hope of ultimate deliverance. The fish at length vomited him upon the dry land. III. Jonah's message and its results (iii., iv.). Bidden a second time to go to Nineveh, he obeyed and delivered his message. The Ninevites publicly repented and God spared the city. At this Jonah was displeased ; not that his prophecy had been nullified by the repentance of the people, for he and his hearers expected that it would be (iii. 9; iv. 2), but probably because he felt that the doom of his own country was sealed. But by the withering of a gourd the Lord taught him the lesson of divine compassion on man and beast generally, irrespective of man's relation to the church.

The motive that led Jonah to flee was probably a narrow and mistaken patriotism. He feared that Nineveh would repent and that God in his mercy would spare the city. Jonah wished Nineveh to perish (iv. 2, 4, 11) ; for it was a powerful foe of Israel and, if it were not destroyed, the doom of Israel was sealed.

The purpose of the book is primarily to teach that God's purposes of grace are not limited to the children of Abraham, but the gentiles can receive mercy while still outside the pale of Israel's law. But besides this great lesson the book of Jonah affords illustrations of truth, which from their nature may perhaps even be regarded as types teaching truth.

1. Nineveh repented at the preaching of one prophet ; whereas Israel repented not, although many prophets were sent to it (cp. Mat. xii. 41). This seems to be a type, to be related to and look forward to a general

truth, that the gentiles yield a readier acquiescence to the doctrines of God than Israel had done : acquiescing not more readily to the moral law indeed, but to the revelation of God as a whole ; for example, to his method of salvation as outlined in Hosea xiv. (cp. Is. ii. 2-4 with 5).

2. Jonah, an Israelite and God's servant sent to preach to the gentiles, is an evidence of God's will that the people of God's kingdom shall lead the gentiles to repentance and to God. Jonah was not the only Israelite in whom this truth was exemplified : Elijah was sent to a woman of Zarephath (1 Kin. xvii.), Elisha cured Naaman the Syrian (2 Kin. v.), Christ talked to a woman of Samaria about the things of God and healed the daughter of a Syrophœnician woman (Mark vii. ; John iv.).

3. Jonah, an Israelite and God's servant fleeing from duty, is cast into the sea, but is delivered in order that he may fulfil his mission. This illustrates the prophetic doctrine that the children of Israel, untrue to their assigned task, shall be cast forth from their native land ; but a remnant, chiefly of the southern kingdom, shall be saved to fulfil Israel's mission to the world (Is. xlii. 1-4; xlix. 1-13; cp. ii. 2-4; xi. 10).

4. Jonah, an Israelite and God's servant cast into the depths of Sheol and yet brought up alive out of the pit (Jon. ii. 2, 6), illustrates and probably portended the death for sins not his own, and the burial and the resurrection of the Messiah, the representative Israelite and perfect servant of the Lord (Mat. xii. 40).

It has been urged that the book of Jonah nowhere claims to have been written by that prophet. But the title (i. 1) is like the title of Hosea, Joel, Micah, Zephaniah, Haggai, and Zechariah, books of which the authorship is not disputed. It is urged further that the book was written long after Jonah's time, because 1. In the prayer ascribed to him are some quotations from late psalms (ii. 3 with Ps. xlii. 7 ; 5 with Ps. lxix. 1 ; 9 with Ps. l. 14). But the psalms may equally well contain quotations from Jonah. 2. The language contains Aramaic elements and grammatical constructions which are found in the latest books. But they are found in early books too. Jonah belonged to the northern kingdom, and the linguistic features of the book resemble those in early literature of the north ; for example, the song of Deborah, the narratives of Elijah and Elisha, and the prophecies of Hosea. The word *ṭaʿam*, classed as Aramaic in meaning, is the Assyrian word for a royal command, and is so used in the book of Jonah in the mouth of the Assyrian king. 3. The failure to give the name of the Assyrian king indicates that it was unknown to the author. But the reference is merely to the ruler as such ; and the king of Nineveh is spoken of just as are the king of the children of Ammon (Judg. xi. 12, 13), the king of

Moab (1 Sam. xxii. 3), the king of Edom (2 Kin. iii. 9, 12), the king of Assyria (xxiii. 29; 2 Chron. xxxiii. 11), the king of Damascus (2 Chron. xxiv. 23, though fully known, cp. 2 Kin. xii. 17, 18), whose personal names did not require mention. Ordinarily the Hebrews spoke of the king who ruled at Nineveh as the king of Assyria, but here he is called the king of Nineveh. So they spoke of Sihon as the king of the Amorites (Num. xxi. 21, 29; Deut. i. 4 ; iii. 2 ; iv. 46), but also as the king of Heshbon (Deut. ii. 26 ; Josh. xii. 5; xiii. 27), where he resided ; and Benhadad they called the king of Syria (1 Kin. xx. 1), but also the king of Damascus (2 Chron. xxiv. 23) ; and Ahab they entitled the king of Israel, but also the king of Samaria (1 Kin. xxi. 1, R. V.). 4. Against an early date is urged late doctrine in the book. However, before Jonah's day Elijah and Elisha had been sent by the God of Israel on missions to foreigners. And in Jonah's day the universality of Jehovah's moral government (Gen. vi.–viii.; xviii. 25), and the conditional character of his predictions (Ex. xxxii. 14; Is. v. 1-7 ; vi. 10 ; xxxviii. 1, 5) were understood in Israel.

The prophecy may be dated before or soon after the close of the reign of Jeroboam II (2 Kin. xiv. 25). It perhaps belongs chronologically after Amos (Amos i. 1) and probably before the vigorous reign of Tiglath-pileser over Assyria, which began in 745 B. C.

The narrative has been variously regarded as myth, legend, parable, history. The chief interpretations are—1. The allegorical or parabolical. This conception of the prophecy is much in vogue, for it avoids the miracle or, if no miracle was involved in the escape of Jonah, the extraordinary nature of the event. It interprets Jonah as a type of Israel fleeing from the duty imposed on the nation to bear witness to the world for God. The sea typifies, as frequently, the raging nations; the sleep of Jonah represents Israel's sloth to fulfil its mission to the gentiles, for which it is delivered into captivity to the world, but yet is preserved alive ; having been disciplined, it is ready to engage in its appointed mission, but it is still narrow and needs to be taught the wideness of God's mercy. In support of this view it is pointed out that Jeremiah speaks of Nebuchadnezzar under the figure of a dragon swallowing up Israel, but compelled to disgorge his prey (li. 34), and Hosea represents the exile of Israel as lasting three days (vi. 2). If, however, there was any borrowing at all, Jeremiah is as likely to have borrowed from Jonah as *vice versâ*. Hosea was a contemporary prophet with Jonah in the northern kingdom, and might draw a lesson from Jonah's experience, if there is any interdependence of Hos. vi. 2 and Jon. i. 17. 2. The historical. The miraculous element is magnified or minimized according to individual judgment and knowledge. The conception of the narrative as historical has these supports: (1) The form of the book is historical and has left this impression on its readers. (2) Jonah himself was unquestionably a historical personage. (3) While it is conceivable that the words of Christ regarding Jonah in the belly of the fish and at Nineveh do not imply his belief in the events, it is highly probable that they do, especially since Jonah was a real person (Mat. xii. 39, 40; Luke xi. 29, 30). (4) The narrative was regarded by the Jews as historical (Antiq. ix. 10, 2). (5) The repentance of the Ninevites is credible. They were given to superstition; national distress and a low state of the empire would dispose them to listen to a warning from the gods; the arrival from a foreign country of a strange prophet, of whose peculiar history they may have heard, was calculated to affect them; the Spirit of God worketh when and where he will. It is urged, indeed, against the historical character of the book that (a) permanent conversion of the Ninevites did not take place. Certainly it did not, and it is nowhere asserted that it did. The statement merely is that the men of that generation repented under the lead of their king. So the men of Judah in Hezekiah's and Josiah's reigns sanctified themselves under the leadership of those kings. (b) Against the historical character of the book is also urged the size ascribed to Nineveh (iii. 3; iv. 11). But see NINEVEH. (c) Also the rapid growth of the gourd or ricinus has been regarded with suspicion (iv. 10). But was this growth miraculous or extraordinary? Verse 10 is rendered by the Targum, "which this night was, and in another night perished." Probably the words describe merely the ephemeral character of the plant. From the narrative itself, verses 6–8, it does not appear that the growth was supernaturally rapid (cp. Ps. xc. 6; Mat. vi. 30). (d) It is further urged that the book was scarcely regarded as a historical narrative when the Hebrew canon was arranged, or it would have been placed among the historical, and not among the prophetical, books. But the recorded events are typical and prophetic, like the events narrated in Zech. vi. 9–15. And, what is more, the Hebrew canon does not make the distinction between historical and prophetical books. The prose writings of official prophets are grouped by themselves. Omitting Ruth, the books from Joshua to 2 Kings inclusive are classed as prophetic. This collection forms continuous history, and it is immediately followed by a second group denominated prophetic, and containing all the remaining books which bear the name of an official prophet. Here Jonah rightly belongs, and here the book has been placed. See CANON.

2. Father of Simon Peter (Mat. xvi. 17; John i. 42; xxi. 15). In R. V. of John Simon's father is called John on the authority of manuscripts. See BAR-JONAH.

Jo′nam, in A. V. **Jonan**, the reading of variant texts [perhaps a modification of the Hebrew Yoḥanan, Jehovah hath been gracious].

An ancestor of Christ, who lived about two hundred years after David (Luke iii. 30).

Jo′nas. See JONAH.

Jon′a-than [Jehovah has given].

1. A Levite, son or remoter descendant of Gershom, son of Moses (Judg. xviii. 30, R. V.). He was doubtless the Levite who had sojourned at Bethlehem-judah, but had left that town to seek another residence, and, when passing through Ephraim, was hired by Micah to officiate as priest before an image of Jehovah (xvii. 7–13). But Danites, on their way to found a settlement on the upper Jordan, seized Micah's idol and persuaded the mercenary priest to go with them, promising that he should be the priest, not of a single household, but of a tribe. Thus Jonathan became the first of a line of priests who officiated at the shrine of the stolen idol all the time that the tabernacle was in Shiloh, till the captivity of the land or district (xviii. 3–6, 14–31). Jonathan had dishonored his descent from Moses, and accordingly the letter nun was inserted in the Hebrew word for Moses, changing it to Manasseh, "a causer to forget" (30 A. V.). The inserted letter was not incorporated into the text, but was suspended above the line.

2. Eldest son of king Saul (1 Sam. xiv. 49; cp. xx. 31). His father gathered an army of 3000 men, and placed 1000 of them at Geba under the command of Jonathan, who presently smote the Philistine garrison or deputy at Geba and thus provoked war (xiii. 3). During its course, attended only by his armor-bearer, he climbed the steep side of the gorge of Michmash to an outpost of the Philistines on its northern brink, and falling boldly upon them slew twenty men. The tumult at the outpost started a panic in the camp; and when Saul came to attack he found Philistines confusedly fighting each other. A rout ensued. Saul pronounced a curse on any who should eat food during the pursuit. Ignorant of the oath, Jonathan, seeing wild honey, ate a little; and for this act his father would have given him up to death. But the people intervened (xiv.). At the time of Goliath's defiance of Israel Jonathan discerned the nobility of David's soul, and loved him forthwith and remained steadfast in friendship for him, even when Saul suggested that David would some day be king in their stead. He kept David informed of the king's moods and purposes, till at length Saul, angered by what he considered Jonathan's unfilial conduct, threw a javelin at him, as he had more than once done at David (xviii.–xx). On this occasion Jonathan was seeking to discover whether a reconciliation of Saul with David was possible. David was lying in concealment in the fields waiting

for word. The two friends anticipated the difficulty Jonathan might have in conveying this information to David, especially if Saul should show himself of evil mind toward the son of Jesse, for Saul and the party opposed to David would watch Jonathan to prevent him from communicating with David and again frustrating their plans. Accordingly, to disarm suspicion, Jonathan arranged to go out with company, and as though to hunt, and by means of arrows to give a sign to David. He did so, and then, finding that suspicion had been allayed and that he was no longer observed, he sent the boy back to the town with the bow and arrows, and remained for a final interview with David. The two friends met once after this in the wood of Ziph (1 Sam. xxiii. 16–18). Jonathan was killed, with two of his brothers and their father, at the battle of Gilboa, and his bones, like theirs, were affixed to the wall of Beth-shean, till the men of Jabesh-gilead removed them and gave them honorable burial (xxxi. 1, 11–13; 1 Chron. x. 2, 8–12). David deeply lamented his death (2 Sam. i. 17–27). Jonathan left one son, called Mephibosheth and Merib-baal, who was lame (2 Sam. iv. 4). David showed him kindness for Jonathan's sake, and the line of his descendants is traceable for several generations in increasing numbers, as if all danger of its extinction had passed away (2 Sam. ix. 1–13; 1 Chron. viii. 33–40; ix. 39–44).

3. Uncle of king David. He was a counselor, a man of understanding, and a scribe (1 Chron. xxvii. 32). Some expositors believe that in this passage the Hebrew word for uncle is used in a general sense for relation, and they identify this counselor with David's nephew Jonathan (R. V., margin).

4. Son of the high priest Abiathar. He was one of two young men who concealed themselves at En-rogel, near Jerusalem, during Absalom's rebellion, and sent David information of everything passing in the city (2 Sam. xv. 36; xvii. 15–22). When Adonijah attempted to usurp the throne and was celebrating a feast, Jonathan brought the news that Solomon had been proclaimed king, a piece of intelligence which led to the breaking up of the assemblage (1 Kin. i. 41–49).

5. A son of David's brother Shimeah, and distinguished as the slayer of one of the gigantic men of Gath (2 Sam. xxi. 21, 22).

6. One of David's mighty men, son of Shage or, rather, Shammah the Hararite (1 Chron. xi. 34; cp. 2 Sam. xxiii. 11). The text of 2 Sam. xxiii. 32, 33 is to be emended by comparison with Chronicles.

7. An official under David (1 Chron. xxvii. 25). See JEHONATHAN.

8. A son of Kareah. After the capture of Jerusalem by Nebuchadnezzar, he placed himself under the protection of Gedaliah (Jer. xl. 8). The name is not found in the corresponding passage (2 Kin. xxv. 23). Perhaps it accidentally dropped out of Kings

or erroneously crept into the text of Jeremiah.

9. A scribe, in whose house Jeremiah was imprisoned (Jer. xxxvii. 15, 20).

10. A son of Jada (1 Chron. ii. 32).

11. A descendant of Adin (Ezra viii. 6).

12. An opponent of Ezra's proposal that foreign wives should be put away (Ezra x. 15, R. V.).

13. A Levite of the lineage of Asaph (Neh. xii. 35; cp. xi. 15, 17).

14. A priest, head of a father's house in the days of the high priest Joiakim (Neh. xii. 14).

15. A high priest, son of Joiada (Neh. xii. 11). See JOHANAN 11.

16. Youngest son of the priest Mattathias (1 Mac. ii. 5). When his brother Judas Maccabæus was slain in battle in 160 B. C., Jonathan was chosen his successor (ix. 23–31). The forces at his disposal were, however, too few for offensive operations against the Syrians, and he withdrew into the wilderness of Tekoa (33). He was surnamed Apphus (ii. 5), which is thought to mean Dissembler, and to have been given him on account of his first exploit, in which he laid an ambush for the children of Jambri and slew them because they had killed his brother John (ix. 37–41). On a Sabbath day in 157 B. C. he repulsed an attack of the Syrians under Bacchides on the Jordan, probably on the eastern bank; but after the victory he and his followers leaped into the river and swam to the other side (ix. 43–48), where they remained (58). outwitting the attempts which were made to assassinate their leader (60, 61). Jonathan and Simon afterwards fortified themselves at Bethbasi in the wilderness, probably of Tekoa; and when Bacchides besieged the fortress, Jonathan left Simon to defend the place, while he himself ravaged the surrounding country (62, 66). Bacchides was so straitened that he made peace with Jonathan and withdrew from Judæa (67–72). Jonathan took up his residence at Michmash, and began to judge the people (73). When Alexander Balas revolted against Demetrius, king of Syria, the latter hastened to secure Jonathan as an ally, and gave him authority to gather troops. The Syrians who were still in the strongholds of Judæa fled, and Jonathan entered Jerusalem in 152 B. C. (x. 1–14). Alexander, equally desirous to have the support of Jonathan, appointed him high priest of the Jews and king's friend, and Jonathan put on the pontifical robes at the feast of tabernacles in 152 B. C. (15–21). Upon hearing of this event, Demetrius hastened to make further concessions to the Jews (22–45). Jonathan, however, gave no credence to the words of Demetrius; and Alexander, when he secured the throne of Syria in 150 B. C. appointed him governor of Judæa (46, 59–66). In 148–7 B. C. Demetrius II. raised the standard of revolt against Alexander. Demetrius was assisted by Apollonius, who

sent a threatening message to Jonathan. Jonathan seized Joppa and defeated Apollonius in the neighboring plain (67–87). When Alexander's father-in-law, Ptolemy, intervened in the war, Jonathan showed his friendship and accompanied him to the borders of Syria (xi. 1–7). Ptolemy proved treacherous to Alexander and placed Demetrius on the throne. Jonathan was able to secure the friendship of the new king, and rendered him great service by a contingent of 3000 Jewish soldiers, who quelled an insurrection against Demetrius in Antioch. Demetrius proved false, and Jonathan sided with the young Antiochus and fought successfully with the troops of Demetrius near Kedesh in Galilee. Jonathan now sought the aid of the Romans and Spartans (xii. 1, 2); he also undertook aggressive operations against Demetrius, and defeated his troops and allies in the vicinity of Hamath (24–35). But Tryphon, who had championed the cause of the young Antiochus, now lifted up his hand against his master and sought to destroy Jonathan also. He persuaded the Jewish leader to come with but a small bodyguard to Ptolemais. When Jonathan entered, the gates of the city were closed, Jonathan's escort was put to the sword, he himself was seized and kept for a time a prisoner and finally slain in Gilead in 143 B. C. (39–48; xiii. 12–23). The bones of Jonathan were recovered and buried in the family sepulcher at Modin (25–27).

17. A general who, at the command of Simon Maccabæus, took possession of Joppa. He was a son of Absalom (1 Mac. xiii. 11).

Jo′nath e′lem re-ho′kim, in A. V. **Jonath-elem-rechokim** [the silent dove of them that are afar off or, by changing the pronunciation of the middle word, the dove of the distant terebinths].

Probably the air to which Ps. lvi. was to be set (Ps. lvi. title).

Jop′pa, in A. V. once **Japho** (Josh. xix. 46), and so twice on margin of R. V. of O. T., this being the Hebrew form, while Joppa is derived from the Greek [beauty].

An ancient town (Thothmes' list), walled (el-Amarna letters), assigned to Dan (Josh. xix. 46); the seaport of Jerusalem to which timber cut on Lebanon for the building of Solomon's temple was floated from Tyre (2 Chron. ii. 16). Jonah embarked at Joppa in a ship about to sail to Tarshish, when he sought to flee from Jehovah (Jon. i. 3). When the temple was being rebuilt, after the return of the Jews from Babylon, rafts of cedar trees were again floated from Tyre to Joppa (Ezra iii. 7, R. V.). In Maccabæan times Joppa was garrisoned by the Syrians (1 Mac. x. 75). The Jews of the town were induced to go aboard ships, and 200 of them were treacherously drowned. In retribution Judas set fire by night to the docks and boats in the harbor and slew the fugitives (2 Mac. xii. 3–6).

Eventually Simon captured the town, garrisoned it, completed the harbor, and restored the fortifications (1 Mac. xii. 33, 34; xiv. 5, 34). The disciple Tabitha, a woman full of good deeds, lived at Joppa. Having died, she was raised to life at the prayer and word of Peter. As a result many believed (Acts ix. 36–42). Peter remained at Joppa for some time, lodging with Simon a tanner (43); and thither the servants of Cornelius came to invite Peter to Cæsarea (x. 5–48). Joppa, now called Jaffa, is built by the sea, on a rocky hill. A small harbor is formed by a ledge of rocks lying parallel to the shore, but entrance to it from the south is barred by rocks. The northern end is open, but shallow; and the one passage through the reef is but ten feet wide. The orchards of Joppa were already famous in ancient Egypt. They contain orange, lemon, apricot, quince, and other fruit trees, and are watered by means of Persian water wheels. Soap is made at Joppa, and there are tanneries on the shore. It is a gate of entrance into Palestine for pilgrims, and a railroad runs thence to Jerusalem.

Jo′rah. See HARIPH.

Jo′rai.

A Gadite (1 Chron. v. 13).

Jo′ram and **Jehoram**, the forms being interchangeable in Hebrew [Jehovah is high].

1. A son of Toi, king of Hamath, who was sent by his father to congratulate David on his victory over Hadadezer (2 Sam. viii. 10). Called in 1 Chron. xviii. 10 Hadoram, which in this case probably means "the god Addu or Hadad is exalted."

2. A Levite, descended from Moses' son Eliezer (1 Chron. xxvi. 25; cp. xxiii. 15, 17).

3. Son of Ahab, king of Israel. On the death of his elder brother, Ahaziah, he succeeded to the throne 853 B. C., and reigned till 842 B. C. He put away the image of Baal which his father had made, but adhered to the calf worship instituted by Jeroboam. On the death of Ahab, Mesha, king of Moab, had rebelled and withheld tribute. To recover his dominion over Moab, Joram obtained the assistance of king Jehoshaphat of Judah, and of the Edomite ruler. As the confederates were marching around the southern portion of the Dead Sea, they were nearly perishing with thirst, but Elisha bade them dig trenches, and on the following morning water came rushing down the wady and filled the trenches. Not only did the water supply the needs of the Israelites, but, looking ruddy under the rays of the morning sun, was mistaken by the Moabites for blood; and, supposing that the Israelites had fallen out among themselves, they rushed to the spoil. Joram and his allies rose against them when they were thus off their guard, and put them to flight, and then overran Moab, but without being able permanently to reduce it to subjection (2 Kin. iii. 1–27); see MOABITE

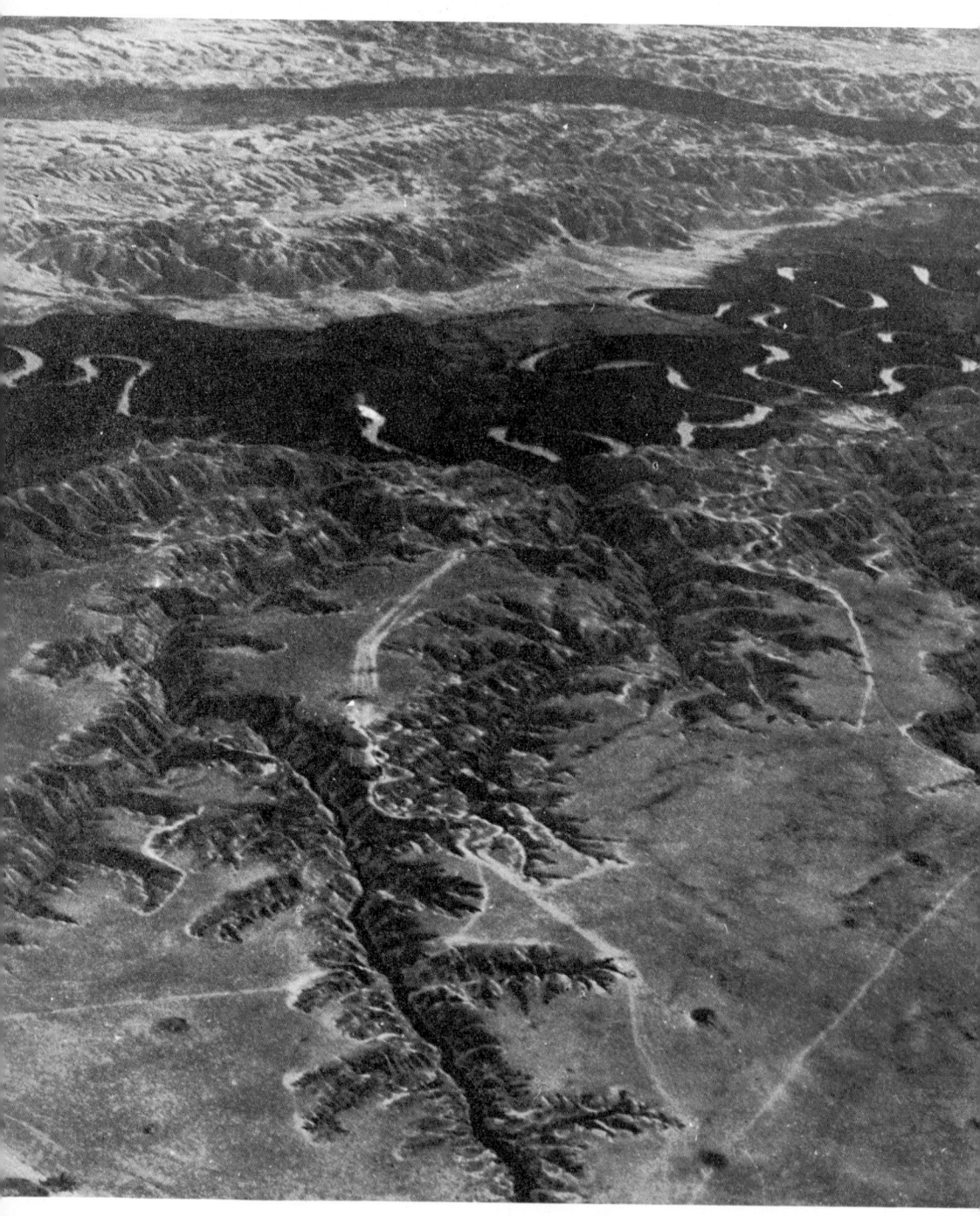

A view of the Jordan River valley.

STONE. Joram was without doubt the king to whom the king of Syria sent Naaman to be cured of his leprosy (v. 1–27) ; and to whom Elisha made known every movement of the Syrian invaders, and who had them in his power at Samaria, and by Elisha's advice sent them home unmolested (vi. 8–23) ; and who, during the famine, when Ben-hadad was besieging Samaria, vowed vengeance against Elisha for the distress (24–31 ; called in verse 32 the son of a murderer). His end was tragic. He was at Jezreel, seeking cure from wounds received at Ramoth-gilead, when a watchman announced the approach of Jehu. Mounting his chariot and accompanied by his nephew, the king of Judah, in another chariot, the two kings drove forth to meet Jehu. They came up to him at the field which Joram's mother had gotten for his father by having its owner, Naboth, slain. Jehu shot Joram through the heart with an arrow and, recalling a prophecy to mind, had the body thrown from the chariot into the field of Naboth (ix. 14–26). With Joram the dynasty of Omri ceased, and that of Jehu began.

4. One of the priests sent by Jehoshaphat to instruct the people (2 Chron. xvii. 8).

5. Son of Jehoshaphat. From about 854 B. C. he was associated with his father in the government, and in 849 B. C., in the fifth year of Jehoram, king of Israel, the reins of government were transferred entirely to his hands (2 Kin. viii. 16 ; cp. i. 17 ; iii. 1). No sooner did he feel himself secure on his throne than he murdered all his brothers and some other princes of Judah (2 Chron. xxi. 1–4). He had for his wife a daughter of Ahab, who led him into gross forms of heathenism, as Jezebel had seduced Ahab (2 Kin. viii. 18 ; 2 Chron. xxi. 6, 11). As in other cases, his departure from Jehovah brought with it adversity. The Edomites rose in rebellion, and though he gained a victory over them, yet this did not prevent their achieving their independence. Libnah also revolted, and successfully (2 Kin. viii. 20–22 ; 2 Chron. xxi. 8–10). Philistine and Arab marauders entered Judah and plundered the palace, carrying off the king's wives and children, with the single exception of Jehoahaz, or Ahaziah, the youngest boy (2 Chron. xxi. 16, 17 ; xxii. 1). A writing from the prophet Elijah was handed to the king, denouncing his apostasy and his wickedness, and threatening him with painful disease and death ; see ELIJAH. He was soon afterwards seized with dysentery, which became chronic and continued for two years (2 Chron. xxi. 18, 19). During this sickness Ahaziah acted as regent (2 Kin. ix. 29 with viii. 25, 26). There was no pretense at lamentation when his death occurred. His sole reign, beginning in the fifth year of Jehoram of Israel, was eight years. He died in 842 B. C., leaving his one surviving son Ahaziah to ascend the throne (2 Kin. viii. 24 ; 2 Chron. xxi. 12–xxii. 1).

Jor'dan [descender].

The most important river in Palestine. It rises from various sources. The eastern source is at Banias, the ancient Cæsarea Philippi, where a copious stream, the Banias, issues from a cave in a lofty cliff. The central and largest source is at Tell el-Kâdi, probably the ancient Dan, where from two great springs the abundant Leddan takes its rise. The third source, the most northern and highest perennial one, is the fountain, below Hasbeiya, from which the river Hasbâny flows. Thomson says that the Hasbâny is the longest by 40 miles. the Leddan much the largest, and the Banias the most beautiful. From the source of the river at Banias to the lake of the Huleh the distance is 12 miles ; the junction of the Banias and the Leddan taking place about midway between these points, and the confluence with the Hasbâny a fraction of a mile lower. The lake itself is 4 miles long. The Jordan, emerging from it at its southern side, next makes its way 10½ miles more to the sea of Galilee, which is 12½ miles long. After passing through this lake, it pursues a tortuous course, till it enters the Dead Sea, at a point 65 miles in a straight line from the southern part of the sea of Galilee. Including the two lakes, and taking no note of the windings, the river from Banias to the Dead Sea is 104 miles long. As far as is known, it stands absolutely alone among the rivers of the world in the fact that throughout the greater part of its course it runs below the level of the ocean. When it issues from the cave at Banias it is 1000 feet above the level of the Mediterranean. By the time it enters the lake of the Huleh it has fallen to within seven feet of sea level. At the sea of Galilee it is 682 feet below the sea level, and when entering the Dead Sea 1292 feet. It was appropriately named Jordan, the descender. The stream is tortuous also. Lieut. Lynch, of the American navy, who in 1848 led an expedition from the United States, sailed from the sea of Galilee to the Dead Sea. Lieut. Lynch wrote : "In a space of 60 miles of latitude and 4 miles of longitude the Jordan traverses at least 200 miles. . . . We have plunged down twenty-seven threatening rapids, besides a great many of lesser magnitude."

The biblical associations with the river proper attach mainly to the stretch from the sea of Galilee to the Dead Sea. The river was fringed, as it is now, with a thicket of trees and shrubs, principally tamarisks, oleanders, and willows, among which lions lurked (Jer. xlix. 19 ; Zech. xi. 3). The valley in its southern part, where the depression below sea level is greatest, is virtually a tropical country, and under irrigation produced crops of tropical luxuriance (War iv. 8, 3). On account of its fertility Lot, forgetful of moral considerations, chose it as the place of his residence (Gen. xiii. 8–13). The river was not bridged until Roman

The Jordan River.

times, but was forded. The fords are frequent and easy in the upper stream and as far down as the mouth of the Jabbok, where Jacob crossed (xxxii. 10; xxxiii. 18). Below that point the river is rarely fordable, and then only at certain seasons of the year. The current of the river is so rapid near Jericho that the numerous pilgrims who go thither to bathe are always in danger, and not infrequently are swept away. For the Israelites to cross the Jordan at any time, and above all when the river was in flood, required the miracle or extraordinary providence of the checked waters (Josh. iii. 1–17; iv. 1–24; Ps. cxiv. 3, 5). The fulness of the Jordan, with the overflow of its water over the banks immediate to its channel, during the time of harvest (March or April in that warm valley) is produced by the melting of the snow on mount Hermon (Josh. iii. 15). The fleeing Midianites, pursued by Gideon, crossed by the fords at and above the mouth of the Jabbok (Judg. vii. 24; viii. 4, 5). David, when fleeing from Absalom and on returning to his kingdom, crossed twice somewhere between Jericho and the Jabbok (2 Sam. xvii. 22, 24; xix. 15–18). Elijah and Elisha, amidst the wonderful events at the close of Elijah's career, crossed at Jericho (2 Kin. ii. 5–8; 13–15). Naaman the Syrian, as directed by the prophet, washed seven times in the Jordan, somewhere in its upper reaches, either north or south of the sea of Galilee, and was cured of his leprosy (2 Kin. v. 14). John the Baptist administered the special rite which gave him his designation. in the Jordan, and it was there that our Lord was baptized (Mat. iii. 6, 13–17).

Jo'rim.
An ancestor of Christ, who lived about 350 years after David (Luke iii. 29).

Jor'ke-am, in A. V. **Jorkoam** [perhaps, pallor or fear of the people, or possibly, stability, expansion].
A place peopled by members of the family of Hezron and house of Caleb (1 Chron. ii. 44).

Jos'a-bad. See JOZABAD.

Jos'a-phat. See JEHOSHAPHAT.

Jo'se. See JESUS 2.

Jo'sech.
An ancestor of Christ, who probably lived after the exile (Luke iii. 26). The A. V., following a different reading, calls him Joseph.

Jos'e-dech. See JOZADAK.

Jo'seph [may he add]. The name has also the sound of a verb of different etymology, meaning "he taketh away;" and the Hebrew writer in Gen. xxx. 23, 24, following custom, plays upon the sound and upon both etymologies when he explains, not what the root of the word is, but the reason for bestowing the name.
1. The eleventh of Jacob's twelve sons, and the elder son of Rachel, who, when she

gave him birth, said, "The Lord add to me another son," and therefore called his name Joseph (Gen. xxx. 22–24). He was born in Paddan-aram, about six years before the return of Jacob to Canaan (25; cp. xxxi. 41), when Jacob was 90 or 91 years old. He was his father's favorite child, because he was the son of his old age and Rachel's child; and he made him a coat such as was worn by young people of the better class (xxxvii. 3). The father's favoritism aroused the envy of the elder brethren; and their ill-will was increased by two dreams which Joseph had, and which foreshadowed the time when his father, his mother, and his brethren should bow down and do him obeisance. When Joseph was seventeen years old (xxxvii. 2), Jacob sent him to Shechem, where his brothers were feeding their flocks, to ask after their welfare. On reaching Shechem, he found that they had gone on to Dothan, and he followed them thither. As he was seen approaching, the brothers proposed to slay him and report to his father that a wild beast had devoured him. Reuben, however, prevailed upon them not to take Joseph's life, but to cast him alive into a pit, intending eventually to take the youth out and restore him to his father. In Reuben's absence a caravan of Ishmaelites, traveling on the great highway that led down into Egypt, drew near. To Midianite merchantmen of the company Joseph was sold. A kid of the goats being killed, his coat was dipped in the blood and the besmeared garment was sent to Jacob, who concluded that his son had been torn to pieces by some wild beast (Gen. xxxvii. 1–35). Meanwhile the slave dealers took Joseph down into Egypt, and sold him to Potiphar, the captain of Pharaoh's guard. The young slave's ability was soon discovered, and Potiphar gave him charge of all his house. But on false accusations he was committed to prison, where he was confined for years. There he so gained the confidence of the jailer that all the prisoners were committed to his charge. God enabled him to interpret prophetic dreams of the chief butler and the chief baker of Pharaoh, who were confined with him in prison, and his interpretation in each instance was found correct. Two years later Pharaoh dreamed two prophetic dreams, which no one could interpret, and the chief butler, who had been restored to his royal master's favor, remembered Joseph and told of the occurrences in the prison. Joseph was immediately sent for, and interpreted the dreams, both of which had the same meaning. Seven years of great plenty were to be succeeded by seven years of grievous famine. He ventured to recommend that some one should be appointed to collect the surplus produce during the seven years of plenty, and store it against the years of famine. Pharaoh approved the plan; and, having had evidence of the wisdom of Joseph (xli. 9–13, 25–36), he appointed him superintendent of the royal granaries and as such the head of a department of the state and one of the officials next in rank to the king (xli. 39–44). Joseph was now thirty years of age (xli. 46). He had been chastened and humbled by the sufferings of thirteen years. Pharaoh gave him Asenath, daughter of a priestly family at On, to wife; and before the famine began two sons were born to him, Manasseh and Ephraim (xli. 50–52). The famine came as predicted (see NILE), and affected all the known world, especially the western part of it around the Mediterranean (xli. 54, 56, 57; see WORLD). In Egypt, however, there was a store of food, and Joseph's brothers went thither to buy grain. They did not recognize Joseph, but he knew them; and as they did obeisance to him, he saw that the dreams which brought him into such trouble had come to be verified. After testing their character in various ways, on their second visit he revealed himself to them, forgave them the wrong they had done him, and persuaded them and their father to settle in Egypt. Pharaoh warmly welcomed them. The king who acted thus kindly has long been believed to have been Apepi II. or Apophis (Eusebius). At any rate, he was doubtless of the Hyksos or Shepherd dynasty, and being himself a Semite, was the more ready to welcome men of a race identical with his own. Joseph died at the age of 110 years, and his body was embalmed and put in a coffin in Egypt; but he had left strict injunctions that when the exodus took place his remains should be removed to Canaan (Gen. xlii.–l.; Heb. xi. 22). His wishes were carried out; and his remains were ultimately buried near Shechem, in the very center of the promised land (Ex. xiii. 19; Josh. xxiv. 32).

The particulars of Joseph's life, which involve Egyptian customs, are borne out by the monuments and the papyri. It is known, for instance, from the Rosetta stone that it was the habit of the king to release prisoners at his birthday feast and on other great occasions. References to magicians and soothsayers are frequent, and great stress is laid on dreams as messages from the gods. When Joseph was sent for in the prison, although there is express mention of haste, yet he stayed to shave himself and put on clean raiment (Gen. xli. 14). Shaving was particularly practiced and among the priests was a religious rite. The term "Lord over the whole land" has been found but once (on a monument in the museum of Turin), but the investiture of an official of high rank is frequently depicted and agrees with the description in Genesis, the signet ring, the linen vesture, and the chain about the neck being prominent. The phrase, also, "According unto thy word [mouth] shall all my people be ruled" is emphasized by the fact that the hieroglyph for ruler is a mouth. An economic change, whereby the land came to be owned entirely by the king and the priests,

took place some time before the rise of the New Empire; see EGYPT II. 5.

There is reference to Egyptian conceptions of propriety in the separate setting of bread for Joseph, for his brethren, and for the Egyptians present (Gen. xliii. 32). Joseph ate by himself, because he was a man of highest rank and a member of the priestly class, which kept apart from the laity. The Egyptians ate by themselves, for Egyptians held aloof from foreigners; the priests ate and drank nothing that was imported (Porphery iv. 7), and the people generally considered it an abomination to use the eating utensils of the Greeks (Herod. ii. 41), and ostracized shepherds, swineherds, and cowherds, even when native Egyptians, because the occupation of tending cattle was incompatible with the refinement and cleanliness demanded by Egyptian standards (Gen. xlvi. 34; Herod. ii. 47; cp. 164). This objection to herdsmen was probably the cause of Joseph's settling his kindred in the land of Goshen, where they would not come in contact with the natives of the land.

Jacob-el and Joseph-el are names of places in Palestine conquered by Thothmes III., the Egyptian warrior-king, long after the descent of Jacob and his sons into Egypt and a century or two before the exodus. It is doubtful whether they stand in any relation to the patriarch Jacob and his son Joseph. They are names like Jiphthah-el or Iphtah-el, a valley in the territory of Zebulun (Josh. xix. 14), may mean God doth supplant and God doth take away, and they were in use in Babylonia as personal names.

An Egyptian story, known as the Tale of the Two Brothers, recounts the temptation of a young man in the home of his elder brother, similar to the experience of Joseph in the house of Potiphar (Gen. xxxix.). The younger brother is saved from the wrath of the elder by the interposition of the sungod, who makes a river full of crocodiles to flow as a barrier between the two. The further adventures of the twain, at length reconciled to each other, are equally fabulous. The story was transcribed in the reign of Seti II., of the nineteenth dynasty, centuries after the time of Joseph; but when the tale was composed is not known. Such incidents were not uncommon, and were introduced into story (Homer, Iliad vi. 155 seq.).

The two tribes of Manasseh and Ephraim descended from Joseph's two sons. The blessings pronounced on Joseph by the dying Jacob were designed for these tribes as well as for Joseph himself (Gen. xlviii. 8–22; xlix. 22–26). In Ps. lxxx. 1 Joseph is a poetic designation of the tribes of Manasseh and Ephraim.

2. Father of the spy from the tribe of Issachar (Num. xiii. 7).

3. A son of Asaph and head of a course of musicians in the reign of David (1 Chron. xxv. 2, 9).

4. An ancestor of Christ, who lived between the time of David and the exile (Luke iii. 30).

5. A son of Bani, induced by Ezra to put away his foreign wife (Ezra x. 42).

6. A priest, head of the family of Sheba-niah in the days of the high priest Joiakim (Neh. xii. 14).

7. An ancestor of Christ who lived after the exile (Luke iii. 26, in R. V. Josech).

8. Son of Mattathias, in the ancestry of Christ (Luke iii. 24, 25).

9. Son of Zacharias. When Judas Macca-bæus sent Simon to aid the Jews in Galilee and himself went to fight in Gilead, he left Joseph and Azarias in charge of the forces in Judæa. They engaged in battle, contrary to their orders, and were defeated (1 Mac. v. 18, 55–62).

10. The husband of Mary, the mother of Jesus (Mat. i. 16; Luke iii. 23). For his an-cestry see GENEALOGY. When Mary was found with child before marriage, Joseph was minded to put her away without public exposure, for he was a just man. But an angel informed him in a dream that the child to be born had been miraculously conceived by the Holy Spirit. Now he had no hesita-tion in carrying out his contract with her, and he made her his wife (Mat. i. 18–25). Being a descendant of David, he had to go to Bethlehem, the early home of his ances-tors, for enrollment, according to the decree of the emperor Augustus, and was there with Mary when Jesus was born (Luke ii. 4, 16). He was with Mary when, at the presentation of Jesus in the temple, Simeon and Anna gave forth their prophetic utterances (33). Warned by an angel in a dream that Herod plotted the murder of the child, Joseph con-ducted the flight into Egypt (Mat. ii. 13, 19). He returned to Nazareth when Herod was dead (22, 23). He was accustomed to go with Mary annually to the passover at Jerusalem, and he took Jesus also to the feast when our Lord was twelve years old (Luke ii. 43), and he also safely reached Nazareth on the return journey (51). He was a car-penter (Mat. xiii. 55), and was assisted in his work by the young man Jesus (Mark vi. 3). Apparently Joseph was alive when Jesus' min-istry had well begun (Mat. xiii. 55); but as we do not hear of him in connection with the crucifixion, it may be inferred that he died previously to that event. This was the reason why Jesus, when on the cross, com-mended Mary to the kindness of the apostle John, which he would scarcely have done had her natural guardian still been alive (John xix. 26, 27).

11. The same as Joses 1 (Mat. xiii. 55, R. V.). See BRETHREN OF THE LORD.

12. A Jew of Arimathæa, a member of the sanhedrin, a councilor of honorable estate, who looked for the kingdom of God (Mark xv. 43). He had not consented to the resolu-tion of the sanhedrin to put Jesus to death,

for he was a disciple of Jesus, although se-cretly, for, like Nicodemus, the only other member of the governing body who believed on our Lord, he was fearful of publicly com-mitting himself. Both became more cour-ageous when they saw the crucifixion. Joseph went boldly to Pilate, begged the body of Jesus, and laid it in his own new tomb, which he had hewn out in a rock (Mat. xxvii. 57–60; Luke xxiii. 50–53; John xix. 38).

13. A Christian called Barsabbas or son of Sabbas, and Justus. He had companied with Jesus and the disciples from the time of Jesus' baptism, and was one of two who were considered worthy to fill the vacancy among the apostolic twelve produced by the apostasy of Judas; but the lot fell upon Matthias (Acts i. 21, 26). He was probably a brother of Judas, called Barsabbas (Acts xv. 22).

14. The personal name of Barnabas (Acts iv. 36, in A. V. Joses).

Jo'ses [a Greek form of Joseph].

1. One of the brethren of the Lord (Mark vi. 3). In Mat. xiii. 55, R. V. prefers the manuscripts which gave the name as Joseph.

2. The personal name of Barnabas, for a time the missionary colleague of Paul (Acts iv. 36, in R. V. Joseph).

Jo'shah [perhaps, uprightness].

A Simeonite, son of Amaziah (1 Chron. iv. 34).

Josh'a-phat [Jehovah hath judged].

1. A Mithnite, one of David's mighty men (1 Chron. xi. 43).

2. A priest, one of the trumpeters before the ark during its removal to Jerusalem (1 Chron. xv. 24, in A. V. Jehoshaphat).

Josh-a-vi'ah [perhaps, Jehovah setteth upright].

One of David's mighty men (1 Chron. xi. 46).

Josh-be-ka'shah [possibly, seat of hard-ness].

A singer, son of Heman (1 Chron. xxv. 4), and head of the seventeenth course of singers (24).

Josh-eb-bas'she-beth, in A. V. margin **Josheb-bassebet.**

A textual corruption in 2 Sam. xxiii. 8 for, apparently, Ish-baal, there is a Lord. Baal was altered, as was often done after it had acquired idolatrous associations, to *bosheth*, shame; and instead of bosheth, *i. e.* b-sh-th, the word *b-sh-b-th* which ends the preceding verse was seen by a copyist. His identity with Jashobeam is fairly established by com-parison of this verse with 1 Chron. xi. 11 and verses 8 and 9 with 1 Chron. xxvii. 2, 4. This latter form is perhaps another mode of avoiding the name Baal.

Josh-i-bi'ah, in A. V. **Josibiah** [Jehovah gives an abode].

A Simeonite, family of Asiel (1 Chron. iv. 35).

Josh'u-a, in A. V. once Jehoshua (Num. xiii. 16), and once Jehoshuah (1 Chron. vii. 27), the latter an inconsistency not found in A.V. in the original edition of 1611. Jehoshua developed into Jeshua (Nev. viii. 17), and this form was Grecianized and appears as Jesus (Acts vii. 45) [Jehovah is salvation].

1. An Ephraimite, the son of Nun (Num. xiii. 8, 16). He commanded the Israelites in their successful conflict with the Amalekites at Rephidim (Ex. xvii. 8-16). A personal attendant on Moses, he was with him on mount Sinai when the golden calf was made, and mistook the noise of idolatrous revelry in the camp for the shouting of hostile combatants (xxiv. 13; xxxii. 17, 18). He had charge of the first tent of meeting (xxxiii. 11). As prince of Ephraim, he was a member of the commission of twelve sent to report on the land of Canaan and its assailability; and he joined Caleb in seeking to persuade the people to go and possess the land (Num. xiii. 8; xiv. 6-9). For this the two narrowly escaped being stoned to death (10), but God rewarded them for their fidelity and trust in Jehovah by keeping them alive to enter the promised land (30, 38). At the end of the forty years' sojourn in the wilderness, by divine direction Moses placed Joshua before the high priest and the congregation in Shittim and publicly ordained him to be his successor (Num. xxvii. 18-23; Deut. i. 38); and just before death, the lawgiver took Joshua to the tabernacle to receive his charge from the Lord (xxxi. 14, 23). On the death of Moses, Joshua began immediate preparations for crossing the Jordan. The people were allowed three days in which to prepare victuals (Josh. i. 10, 11), the two and a half tribes were reminded of their obligation to render their brethren armed assistance (12-18), and spies were dispatched to search out Jericho (ii. 1). The camp was then moved to the river and the people carefully instructed as to the order of march (iii. 1-6). He showed his military skill in the plan of campaign which he adopted for the conquest of Canaan: a central camp, advantageously situated; the capture of the towns which commanded the approaches to his camp; great campaigns following up victories; see CANAAN. He blundered, however, in making a treaty with the Gibeonites and in not garrisoning the citadel of the Jebusites. By these two mistakes Judah was to a degree isolated from the northern tribes. He carried out the injunction to assemble the people on Ebal and Gerizim to hear the blessings and the cursings (viii. 30-35). His campaigns had broken the power of the Canaanites, but not exterminated them (see CANAAN). But although the prospect of further fighting remained, the time had come to plan for the settlement of the country. Aided by the high priest and a commission, he superintended the allotment of the conquered country, begin-

ning the distribution while the camp was at Gilgal (xiv. 6-xvii.), and completing it and assigning cities of refuge and the Levitical towns after he had removed the tabernacle to Shiloh (xviii.-xxi.). For himself he asked and obtained a town, Timnath-serah, in mount Ephraim (xix. 50). When old, he convoked an assembly of the people at Shechem, because it was the place of Abraham's first altar on entering Canaan and the locality where the tribes had invoked blessings and cursings upon themselves. There he made them a powerful address, urging them not to forsake Jehovah (xxiv. 1-28). Soon afterwards he died, at the age of 110, and was buried at the place of his choice, Timnath-serah (29, 30).

The Book of Joshua properly follows Deuteronomy in the Hebrew Scriptures and in the English Bible; for it continues the history from the death of Moses, which was the last event recorded in Deuteronomy. It is more intimately connected with the Pentateuch than with the books which follow it: for the spirit of the Mosaic times was still active in the history which it recounts; and it is the sequel of Genesis in that it records the possession of the promised land for which Abraham waited, as related in Genesis. But since it was not written by Moses, it was kept distinct from the five books of Moses in the Hebrew Scriptures. In these Scriptures it is the first of "the prophets;" and begins that division of them called the "former prophets," which embraces all the books of the English Bible betwee Joshua and 2 Kings inclusive, except Ruth; see CANON. The book may be divided into three sections: I. The conquest of Canaan (i.-xii.); including the preparation for crossing the Jordan and the passage of the river (i.-iv. 18), the establishment of the camp and celebration of the passover (iv. 19-v. 12), the capture of Jericho and Ai, the confirmation of the covenant on Ebal, and the treaty with the Gibeonites (v. 13-ix.), the southern and northern campaigns (x., xi.), and the summary (xii.). II. The distribution of Canaan (xiii.-xxii.); including a description of the land which remained to be divided (xiii.), its allotment, with the assignment of cities of refuge and the allotment of towns to the tribe of Levi (xiv.-xxi.), and the temporary misunderstanding about the altar on the Jordan, as though it were intended to divide the nation (xxii.). III. Joshua's farewell address and death (xxiii., xxiv.).

It is expressly stated that Joshua wrote "these words," including at least the account of the proceedings at Shechem (xxiii.-xxiv. 25) in the book of the law of God (xxiv. 26). The concluding verses of the book (xxiv. 29-33) were written after the death of Joshua, Eleazar, and the men of that generation. The simplest theory is that the conquest of Hebron, Debir, and Anab by Caleb took place after the death of Joshua and is recorded proleptically in xv. 13–20 (see HEBRON), that Zephath is called Hormah by anticipation in xii. 14, and that this verse reflects an event which occurred after the death of Joshua (Judg. i. 17 ; see HORMAH) ; and that xix. 47 records the migration of the Danites in the days of the judges. It is reasonable to conclude from the general character of the documents and casual statements in them that large portions of the book were in writing in the time of Joshua. At any rate, they received final form while the town of Ai was still in ruins (viii. 28), before the reign of Solomon, while the Canaanites still dwelt in Gezer (xvi. 10 with 1 Kin. ix. 16), and before the reign of David, at a time when the Jebusites still occupied the stronghold of Jerusalem (xv. 63). In general, see PENTATEUCH.

2. A native of Beth-shemesh, the owner of a field to which the kine drawing the cart which carried the ark from the Philistine country made their way (1 Sam. vi. 14).

3. The governor of Jerusalem during the reign of Josiah (2 Kin. xxiii. 8).

4. The high priest while Zerubbabel was governor of Judah (Hag. i. 1, 12, 14 ; ii. 2–4 : Zech. iii. 1–9). Called in Ezra and Nehemiah Jeshua (q. v.).

Jo-si'ah, in A. V. of N. T. **Josias** [Jehovah healeth].

1. Son and successor of Amon as king of Judah. He came to the throne about the year 639 B. C., when eight years old. In his youth his adviser seems to have been the high priest Hilkiah, and Josiah hearkened to him. In the eighth year of his reign he began the attempt to conform his own conduct as king, and the life of the court, to the laws of God. In his twelfth regnal year he commenced to suppress idolatry and other unlawful worship; a work which he prosecuted for years not only in Judah and Jerusalem, but after his eighteenth year in Israel also (2 Kin. xxii. 1, 2 ; 2 Chron. xxxiv. 1–7, 33). In his eighteenth year he took energetic steps to repair and adorn the temple ; and the workmen, entering with enthusiasm into his plans, acted with exemplary fidelity in using the money entrusted to them for the purpose. While the repairs of the temple were being executed, Hilkiah, the high priest, found the book of the law in the house of the Lord, and handed it over to Shaphan, the scribe, who read it to the king. Josiah was deeply impressed by the prophecy that if the people departed from Jehovah dreadful consequences would ensue. He rent his clothes and humbled himself before God, who was pleased to give him the gracious assurance that the threatened calamity should not come in his time (2 Kin. xxii. 8–20 ; 2 Chron. xxxiv. 15–28). The prophecy which so affected Josiah was Deut. xxviii.–xxx., especially xxix. 25–28. The book found by Hilkiah must thus have contained Deuteronomy at

least, and it may have been a copy of the entire Pentateuch. The sacred books had, doubtless, been generally destroyed and lost sight of during the apostasy and persecution in the long reign of Manasseh (2 Kin. xxi. 16 ; 2 Chron. xxxiii. 9 ; and the book found by Hilkiah was probably the temple copy of the law, which had been hidden or thrown aside during the profanation of the sanctuary (Deut. xxxi. 9, 26) ; or possibly it was a law book that had been placed in the wall, according to an ancient custom, when the temple was first built. That Deuteronomy was an old book at the time may be argued from the fact that it reflects the condition of Israel in early times and not in the reign of Josiah. It enjoins upon the people the extermination of the Canaanites and Amalekites (xx. 16–18 ; xxv. 17–19), but in Josiah's day there was no occasion for such a law. It contemplates foreign conquest on the part of the Israelites (xx. 10–15) ; but in Josiah's day and for nearly a century previously the question was not of conquest, but whether Judah could maintain its existence at all. It vests the supreme authority under Jehovah in a judge and the priesthood, but makes provision for a time when the Israelites should desire a king (xvii. 8–20 ; xix. 17) ; but in Josiah's day the Israelites had been ruled by kings for centuries. It discriminates against Ammon and Moab in favor of Edom (xxiii. 3–8) ; but in Josiah's day and for a long time previously Egypt was the representative of the people of God (Is. lxiii. 6 ; Joel iii. 19 ; Obad.), and Jeremiah promises future restoration to Moab and Ammon, but denies it to Edom (xlviii. 47 ; xlix. 6, 17, 18). The legislation of Deuteronomy was in force long before the time of Josiah : it was observed at the coronation of Joash in 835 B. C. (2 Kin. xi. 12), and was followed by Joash's son and successor, Amaziah (xiv. 6 ; cp. Deut. xxiv. 16). The reading of the book to the people affected them as it had the king. So deep was the impression produced that a second assault upon idolatry was begun, more sweeping than the first. After the king and his subjects had together covenanted to worship Jehovah only, they proceeded to take the vessels of Baal, of the Asherim, and of the heavenly bodies, burn them, and cast the ashes into the brook Kidron. The Asherah in the house of the Lord was similarly burnt, the residences of the sodomites were broken down, and the high places were destroyed, not merely through the kingdom of Judah, but through the former territory of the northern tribes, now largely empty of its Israelitish inhabitants. The valley of Hinnom and the shrine of Topheth, in which children had been made to pass through the fire to Molech, were defiled, and other sweeping reforms effected. When at Bethel, Josiah took the bones of the idolatrous priests from their graves, and burnt them on the altar, thus fulfilling the prophecy of a man of God in Jeroboam's time (1 Kin. xiii. 2). Nor did he scruple to slay the living idolatrous priests themselves on the altars on which they had been accustomed to sacrifice. Then he concluded by holding a passover, so well attended and so solemn that nothing like it had been celebrated since the time of Samuel (2 Kin. xxiii. 1-25; 2 Chron. xxxiv. 29-xxxv. 19). Thirteen years afterwards Pharaoh-necho, king of Egypt, marched an army along the maritime portion of Palestine on his way to the Euphrates, where he designed to try his strength against the great Assyrian power. Situated as the small and comparatively feeble kingdom of Judah was between the Assyrian and Egyptian empires, then in mutual hostility, it was difficult for it to maintain neutrality; indeed, Josiah seems to have looked on himself as a vassal of the Assyrian king, legally and morally bound to give him military aid in war; and he gave battle to Pharaoh-necho at Megiddo in the plain of Jezreel, and in the fight was mortally wounded by an arrow. His attendants removed him from his war chariot to a second conveyance, which brought him to Jerusalem. He had, however, only reached that capital when he died. Great lamentations were made for him by Jeremiah, the singing men and the singing women, and the people generally. His loss to his country was irreparable. The religious reforms which he had commenced were assailed, and the parsial independence which his country had enjoyed under his rule passed away. He had reigned thirty-one years, but was only thirty-nine when he died, about 608 B. C. (2 Kin. xxii. 1; xxiii. 29, 30; 2 Chron. xxxv. 20-27; cp. Zech. xii. 11). Jeremiah and Zephaniah prophesied during the latter part of his reign (Jer. i. 2; iii. 6; Zeph. i. 1).

2. A son of Zephaniah, in Zechariah's days (Zech. vi. 10). Perhaps the same as Hen of ver. 14; but see HEN.

Jos-i-bi′ah. See JOSHIBIAH.

Jos-i-phi′ah [Jehovah will increase].

Head of the house of Shelomith, who returned from exile with Ezra (Ezra viii. 10).

Jot. A transliteration of the Greek word *iota* (Mat. v. 18), the name of the letter of the Greek alphabet which corresponds to the Hebrew jod and is its equivalent etymologically. The discourse, of which Mat. v. 18 forms a part, was probably spoken in the vernacular Hebrew; and the allusion to the law is a reference to Hebrew literature. The word jot, therefore, doubtless stands for the Hebrew jod. At the beginning of the first century A. D. this letter did not always differ in size from the other letters of the Hebrew alphabet (see examples on coins, article MONEY), although as sometimes written it was one of the smaller ones (see VAU); perhaps, therefore, the point of the comparison does not lie in the smallness of the letter. But in many Hebrew words the use of the jod is a matter of comparative indifference, and in such cases the letter may be employed or dispensed with at the pleasure of the writer; hence figuratively jod signifies a matter that seems to be of small moment.

Jot′bah [pleasantness, goodness].

The town of king Amon's grandfather (2 Kin. xxi. 19).

Jot′ba-thah, in A. V. once **Jotbath** (Deut. x. 7) [goodness, pleasantness].

A station of the Israelites in the wilderness, apparently near Ezion-geber (Num. xxxiii. 33). The place abounded in brooks of water (Deut. x. 7). Situation unknown.

Jo′tham, in A. V. once **Joatham** (Mat. i. 9), in imitation of the Greek form [Jehovah is upright].

1. Youngest son of Gideon. He escaped when his seventy brothers (the offspring of polygamy, of course) were massacred by their half-brother Abimelech; and afterwards, in contempt of the usurpation, standing on mount Gerizim, he uttered the parable, audible to the Shechemites in the valley below, of the trees anointing a king (Judg. ix. 1-21).

2. A king of Judah, who reigned as regent of his father, Uzziah, while the latter was a leper (2 Kin. xv. 5). His regency began while Jeroboam II. was still king of Israel (1 Chron. v. 17). Further evidence of the partial contemporaneousness of the regency of Jotham and the reign of Jeroboam exists, if the earthquake took place while Uzziah and Jeroboam were reigning (Amos i. 1; Zech. xiv. 5) and occurred coincidently with or shortly after Uzziah's invasion of the priest's office (Antiq. ix. 10, 4). Jotham became sole ruler when his father died, about 734 B. C. He followed Jehovah, but did not interfere with the high places at which the people worshiped other gods. He built the high gate of the temple and worked on the wall on the hill of Ophel, south of the holy house. He erected cities in the uplands of Judah and castles and towers in the forests. He gained a victory over the Ammonites and made them tributary. During his reign of sixteen years Isaiah and Hosea continued to prophesy (Is. i. 1; Hos. i. 1). At the close of his reign the allied Israelites and Syrians began their invasion of Judah. He died at the age of forty-one; surviving his father scarcely a year, it seems. He left his son Ahaz to ascend the throne (2 Kin. xv. 32-38; 2 Chron. xxvii. 1-9). With Jotham, Hoshea is connected by a strange synchronism: "Hoshea reigned in the twentieth year of Jotham" (2 Kin. xv. 30). This reference has been explained as meaning the twentieth year since Jotham began to reign, his accession having been recorded (ver. 5), but his reign and death not having been yet described by the author of Kings. Whatever be the true explanation, this strange synchronism goes far to bring the data of

MT. GERIZIM, ANCIENT SHECHEM AND MT. EBAL. *Joshua 8:33*

LIVESTOCK ON THE SEA OF GALILEE ▶

THE BURNING BUSH. *Exodus 3:2-5*

NAZARETH, SITE OF GABRIEL'S VISIT TO MARY; AND THE LOCALE OF CHRIST'S BOYHOOD.
Matthew 2:23

CHURCH OF THE VISITATION, AIN KARIM, WHERE MARY VISITED ELIZABETH. *Luke 1:39-42*

AIN KARIM, JUDAH, ST. JOHN'S CHURCH, SITE OF JOHN'S BIRTHPLACE. *Luke 1:39, 57*

BETHLEHEM, THE BIRTHPLACE OF JESUS. *Matthew 2:1*

THE RIVER JORDAN, SITE OF CHRIST'S BAPTISM. Matthew 3:13-17

GREEK ORTHODOX MONASTARY OF ST. GEORGE, WILDERNESS OF JUDAH, SITE OF THE TEMPTATION OF CHRIST. Matthew 4:1-11

JERICHO EXCAVATIONS, BEYOND THE MOUNTAIN OF THE THIRD TEMPTATION. Matthew 4:1-1.

THE MT. OF OLIVES THROUGH THE TEMPLE ARCADE. *Mark 13:3*

EXCAVATIONS NEAR THE TOMB OF ABRAHAM. *Genesis 25:8-10*

the Hebrew record into harmony with the Assyrian chronology.

3. A son of Jahdai (1 Chron. ii. 47).

Jour'neys of the Is'ra-el-ites. See WILDERNESS OF THE WANDERING.

Joz'a-bad, in A. V. once **Josabad** (1 Chron. xii. 4) [Jehovah has bestowed].

1. A Gederathite who joined David at Ziklag (1 Chron. xii. 4).

2 and 3. Two Manassites who assisted David to pursue the Amalekites after their capture of Ziklag (1 Chron. xii. 20).

4. A Levite, one of the overseers of the tithes in Hezekiah's reign (2 Chron. xxxi 13).

5. A chief of the Levites in the time of Josiah (2 Chron. xxxv. 9).

6. A Levite, son of Jeshua (Ezra viii. 33). Perhaps he was the Jozabad who by order of Ezra took part in teaching the people the law (Neh. viii. 7), and was the Levitical chief who had the oversight of the outward business of the house of God (Neh. xi. 16); he may have been the Levite of the name, who was induced by Ezra to put away his foreign wife (x. 23).

7. A priest, a son of Pashhur, induced by Ezra to put away his foreign wife (Ezra x. 22).

Joz'a-car, in A. V. **Jozachar** [Jehovah has remembered].

Son of an Ammonitess and one of the two assassins of Joash, king of Judah (2 Kin. xii. 21). Called erroneously Zabad in 2 Chron. xxiv. 26; see BETH and DALETH.

Joz'a-dak and **Jehozadak**, in A.V. **Josedech** in Haggai and Zechariah [Jehovah is just].

Father of Jeshua, the high priest (Ezra iii. 2, 8). He was carried captive to Babylonia by Nebuchadnezzar (1 Chron. vi. 15).

Ju'bal [a stream, a moist region; perhaps also music].

The younger son of Lamech, by his wife Adah. Jubal was the father of all such as handle the harp and pipe (Gen. iv. 21).

Ju'bi-le, in A. R. V. and some editions of A. V. **Jubilee** [joyful shout, sound of the trumpet].

The fiftieth year occurring after seven times seven years had been counted from the institution of the festival or from the last jubilee (Lev. xxv. 8-10); cp. the calculation of Pentecost. It derived its name from the custom of proclaiming it by a blast on the trumpet. As every seventh year was a Sabbatic year, the jubilee followed immediately after one of this character. In the tenth day of the seventh month (the great day of atonement), in the fiftieth year, the trumpet of the jubilee was sounded. It proclaimed liberty to all Israelites who were in bondage to any of their countrymen, and the return to their ancestral possessions of any who had been compelled through poverty to sell them. Even the ground for that year was allowed to remain fallow, though it had been

so in the previous Sabbatic year. To prevent injustice to one who having purchased land could retain it only to the first jubilee, the practice (thoroughly in conformity with the principles of political economy) was to give for the purchased possession only the worth of the temporary occupation till the jubilee year. But one purchasing from another a house in a walled city retained it permanently; it did not revert to the original owner at the jubilee, since city lots were apparently not bound up with the several portions of Canaan as originally allotted to families. Those of the unwalled villages were regarded as belonging to the field and did so return; so also did the houses of Levites wheresoever situated (Lev. xxv. 8-55; xxvii. 17, 18; Num. xxxvi. 4). There appears to be an allusion to the jubilee in Is. lxi. 1-3 and Ezek. xlvi. 17; cp. also Neh. v. 1-13.

Ju'cal. See JEHUCAL.

Ju'da. See JUDAH, JUDAS, JODA.

Ju-dæ'a, in A. V. in canonical books once **Judea** (Ezra. v. 8), and thrice **Jewry** (Dan. v. 13; Luke xxiii. 5; John vii. 1) [Latin from Greek *Ioudaia*, Jewish land, and that in turn from Hebrew *Yᵉhudah*].

A geographical term first introduced in the Bible in Ezra v. 8, A. V., to designate a province of the Persian empire. It is there the rendering of the Aramaic *Yᵉhud*. The R. V. translates it "the province of Judah." The land of Judæa is mentioned in 1 Esdras i. 39, and the kings of Judæa in verse 33. The land of Judæa is also spoken of in Maccabee times after the Persian had given place to the Macedonian-Greek dominion (1 Mac. v. 45; vii. 10, A. V.). On the banishment of Archelaus Judæa was annexed to the Roman province of Syria; but it was governed by procurators appointed by the Roman emperor. The succession of procurators was interrupted for a brief period by the reign of Herod Agrippa I., A. D. 41-44. The procurator resided at Cæsarea. His immediate superior was the proconsul, or president, of Syria, ruling from Antioch (Luke iii. 1; Antiq. xvii. 13, 5; xviii. 1, 1). This arrangement obtained when our Lord carried out his ministry on earth, and Judæa is often mentioned in the N. T. (Luke xxiii. 5-7; John iv. 3; vii. 3; Acts i. 8). Its northern boundary may be considered as extending from Joppa on the Mediterranean to a point on the Jordan about 10 miles north of the Dead Sea. Its southern boundary may be drawn from the wady Ghuzzeh, about 7 miles southwest of Gaza, through Beer-sheba, to the southern portion of the Dead Sea. The length from north to south is about 55 English miles, and that from east to west the same. See HISTORY.

Ju'dah, Grecianized **Judas,** genitive **Juda,** and once anglicized **Jude** (Jude i.) [object of praise].

1. The fourth son of Jacob, the fourth also

of Leah. He was not associated with his brothers Simeon and Levi, when by treachery and murder they avenged the wrong done to Dinah, who was the full sister of all three (Gen. xxxiv.). He married a Canaanite, a daughter of Shua of Adullam, and had two sons, Er and Onan, who were slain by divine judgment for their sins (xxxviii. 1–10). Prior to this he had had a third son, Shelah (5). Afterwards, by Tamar, the deceased Er's widow, Judah became the father of twin sons, Perez and Zerah (11–30; xlvi. 12; Num. xxvi. 19). It was through Perez that Judah became the ancestor of David (Ruth iv. 18–22), and when the fullness of time was come, of our Lord (Mat. i. 3–16). Judah saved Joseph's life by proposing that he should be sold instead of murdered (Gen. xxxvii. 26–28). When Joseph, whose relationship to his brother was not suspected, proposed to detain Benjamin in Egypt, Judah deprecated the step' in a speech marked by great natural eloquence, and ended by offering himself to remain a prisoner provided Benjamin was set free (xliv. 33, 34). The result of this splendid advocacy was that Joseph, with no further delay, revealed himself to his brethren (xlv. 1). When Jacob was on his way to Egypt he chose Judah, though not the eldest son, to go before him to Joseph, to show the way before him unto Goshen (xlvi. 28). On account of the sins of Reuben, Simeon, and Levi, they were passed over, and the blessing of the birthright was bestowed by Jacob on Judah (xlix. 3–10). See SHILOH.

2. A tribe sprung from Judah. It was divided into five tribal families which proceeded from his three sons and two grandsons (Num. xxvi. 19–21; 1 Chron. ii. 3–6). The prince of the tribe of Judah in the early period of the wanderings was Nahshon, the son of Amminadab (Num. i. 7; ii. 3; vii. 12–17; x. 14). Another prince was Caleb, son of Jephunneh (xiii. 6; xxxiv. 19). At the first census in the wilderness it numbered 74,600 (i. 26, 27); and at the second census, taken at Shittim on the eve of entering Canaan, 76,500 (xxvi. 22). It was one of the tribes which stood on mount Gerizim to bless the people (Deut. xxvii. 12). Achan, who brought trouble upon all Israel by his greed, belonged to the tribe of Judah (Josh. vii. 1, 17, 18). After the death of Joshua, this tribe was the first one sent to take possession of its allotted territory; and its fighting men, with the aid of the Simeonites, captured such towns as were found occupied by the Canaanites, and drove out the inhabitants of the hill country (Judg. i. 1–20); see CANAAN 2.

The tribe of Judah occupied the greater part of southern Palestine. The boundary drawn for it by Joshua commenced at the extreme southern point of the Dead Sea, passed thence, probably by wady-el-Fikreh, south of the ascent of Akrabbim, to the wilderness of Zin, thence by the south of Kadesh-barnea and the brook of Egypt to the Mediterranean Sea. The eastern border was the Dead Sea. The northern boundary started from the northern end of the sea, at the mouth of the Jordan, and passing by Beth-hoglah and near Jericho, went up by the ascent of Adummim, by En-shemesh, to En-rogel and the valley of the son of Hinnom, south of Jerusalem, passed on to Kirjath-jearim, and thence by Beth-shemesh and Timnah, north of Ekron, to Jabneel, and on to the Mediterranean. That sea itself constituted the western boundary, but a portion of the area was almost always in the hands of the Philistines (Josh. xv. 1–12; cp. also 13–63; xviii. 11–20). The length of the territory of the tribe of Judah from north to south was about 50 miles where most thickly inhabited, but about 95 miles from Jerusalem to Kadesh-barnea; and its breadth from the Jordan to the Philistine plain was about 45 miles. As to its physical features, it is naturally divided into three regions: the hill country of Judah (Josh. xv. 48; Luke i. 39); the lowland or Shephelah (Josh. xv. 33), and the plain near the Mediterranean Sea. The country about Beer-sheba was known as the Negeb or south. A great part of Judah is rocky and barren, but it is admirably adapted for the culture of the vine and for pasture (cp. Gen. xlix. 11, 12). The artificially-terraced hills (now neglected) were once the scene of extensive cultivation. Parts of the territory were regarded as a wilderness, especially the region south of Arad (Judg. i. 16) and that immediately west of the Dead Sea (Ps. lxiii. title). The city of Judah (2 Chron. xxv. 28) is the city of David (2 Kin. xiv. 20). The text is probably corrupt.

Soon after their conquest of Canaan the Israelites were oppressed by the king of Mesopotamia, but Othniel of the tribe of Judah delivered the nation from the foreign domination (Judg. iii. 8–11). In the troublous times which now came upon the Israelites, due to their neglect of God, to tribal jealousies, and to failure to dispossess all the heathen, Judah, Dan, and Simeon became a group by themselves, separated from the other tribes to the north by a strip of country several miles broad which was traversed with inconvenience, in part by reason of its Canaanite inhabitants, Amorites, Gibeonites, and Jebusites, and in part on account of its natural roughness and wildness, being cleft by deep transverse valleys between Jerusalem and Jericho. It was also separated from Gad and Reuben by the chasm of the Jordan and the Dead Sea. The tribe had its own difficulties to contend with, being beset by the Philistines (Judg. iii. 31; x. 7; xiii. 1), and took little part in the wars of the other tribes against oppressors. Boaz and Ruth lived in Bethlehem at this time. Judah, however, united with the other tribes to punish Benjamin (xx. 1, 18). In the time of Eli and Samuel, when the Philistines oppressed both Judah and Benjamin, intercourse with the northern tribes became closer; and Judah was included in the kingdom of Saul. After the death of Saul, the men of Judah supported the claims of their tribesman David to the throne, and for seven years warred in his behalf. When his cause triumphed, Jerusalem on the border of Judah and Benjamin was made the capital of all Israel. The promise had been given to David that his posterity should forever occupy his throne (2 Sam. vii. 13–16; 1 Chron. xvii. 12, 14, 23), though chastisement would be inflicted if there were a departure from Jehovah. The promise was not intended to do away with the necessity for wisdom in the king, and when Rehoboam manifested his unacquaintance with the first principles of government, ten tribes were lost to the house of David. See ISRAEL.

Judah and a large part of Benjamin remained loyal to David's line, and constituted the main elements of the kingdom of Judah. This kingdom lasted from about 931 B. C. until the fall of Jerusalem in 587 B. C. During this time nineteen kings of David's line, exclusive of the usurping queen Athaliah, occupied the throne; see CHRONOLOGY. Its territory was nearly coincident with that of the tribes of Judah and Benjamin, save that the northern boundary fluctuated, Bethel being sometimes held by Judah, especially after the fall of Samaria. An event which exercised the most powerful influence on the history and ultimate fate of the rival kingdoms was the construction of the two golden calves by Jeroboam, that the people of his kingdom might have local sanctuaries, and not have to visit Jerusalem for worship, and perhaps be there won over to their old allegiance. One effect this had was to make all who were faithful to Jehovah emigrate to the kingdom of Judah, bringing it no mean accession of spiritual and even of political strength (1 Kin. xii. 26–33; xiii. 33; 2 Chron. x. 16, 17). The first relations of the two rival kingdoms were naturally those of mutual hostility. This, doubtless, emboldened the neighboring nations to intermeddle in Jewish affairs, and in the fifth year of Rehoboam's reign Shishak, king of Egypt, plundered Jerusalem (1 Kin. xiv. 25–28; 2 Chron. xii. 1–12). War between Judah and Israel went on in a languid way during the first sixty years of their separate existence (1 Kin. xiv. 30; xv. 7, 16; 2 Chron. xii. 15; xiii. 2–20); after which, under Ahab and Jehoshaphat, not merely peace, but a political and family alliance took place between the two reigning houses. In consequence, the worship of Baal was introduced into Judah, and at last became a potent factor in the destruction of the kingdom. Two great parties were formed, the one attached to the worship of Jehovah, the other in favor of Baal and other foreign divinities. During the subsequent period of the kingdom of Judah these parties were in continual conflict with each other, first one

and then the other becoming temporarily dominant, according as the reigning monarch was its friend or its opponent. As at other periods of the theocracy, fidelity to Jehovah brought temporal as well as spiritual prosperity, while apostasy from him was attended by disaster. Among the good kings were Asa, Jehoshaphat, Hezekiah, and Josiah, while Ahaz, Manasseh, and some others were conspicuously the reverse. The foreign relations of the kingdom were important. Egypt was Judah's neighbor on the southwest, and was frequently involved in the affairs of Judah. The Egyptian kings Shishak and Zerah and, after a long interval, Necho warred with Judah. On the other hand, Egypt was regarded as a valuable ally against the great empires on the Tigris and Euphrates; and the blow inflicted upon the Assyrians by Tirhakah in the reign of Hezekiah contributed to the deliverance of Judah, and later the advance of the Egyptians compelled the army of Nebuchadnezzar to raise the siege of Jerusalem temporarily. See PHARAOH. On the capture of Jerusalem by the Babylonians, a large body of Jews found refuge in the country of the Nile. During all these years the varied influences of Egyptian culture and religion were exerted upon the people of Judah. In respect to the powerful nations on the Tigris and Euphrates, there were, of course, an Assyrian and a Babylonian period. The Assyrian period began in 734 B. C., when Ahaz invoked the aid of Tiglath-pileser against the allied kings of Israel and Syria, and afterwards did homage to him at Damascus. After the Assyrian conquest of the northern kingdom a decade later, Judah was exposed for nearly a century and a quarter to the greed and fury of the Assyrians, until Nineveh was overthrown by the Babylonians. Sargon, Sennacherib, Esarhaddon, and Ashurbanipal, four successors on the Assyrian throne, mention more or less extensive conquests of Judah. Three of these four kings are mentioned in the Hebrew records (Is. xx. 1; xxxvi. 1; xxxvii. 38), and perhaps the fourth also (see ASNAPPAR). The Babylonian period began in 605, when Jehoiakim was subjugated by Nebuchadnezzar. In less than a score of years Jerusalem was in ruins and the people of Judah were deported to Babylonia. The divine promise to David did not preclude the temporary loss of the throne by his descendants.

The causes which led to the fall of Jerusalem and the exile were: 1. Those causes which issued in the disruption of the kingdom and the fall of Samaria, which left Judah solitary. See ISRAEL. 2. The neglect of God's command to exterminate the Canaanites. When the Israelites could not, that is, would not, utterly destroy the Canaanites, they preserved the leaven of corruption in their midst. 3. Social and political alliances with idolatrous peoples. 4. The loss of moral strength by apostasy and the loss of enthusiasm for a great cause on earth, the establishment of God's kingdom. 5. Refusal to repent at the call of the prophets. 6. When these agencies had wrought ruin to the state and to manhood, when it was time to yield, the persistent resistance to the dominant empire made with the help of petty alliances was a short-sighted policy, and a mistaken estimate of the coming imperial power. Little Judah should not have been submissive to Assyria, but should have yielded to Babylon toward the last. Such was the exhortation of Jeremiah. From the very beginning of their national existence the Hebrew people needed to husband all their resources, physical and political, moral and spiritual, if their kingdom was to stand amidst the empires of the world. On the return from exile, Zerubbabel, a descendant of David, was the civil ruler ; but he was only a local governor under the Persians. He was followed after a time by Nehemiah, also of the tribe of Judah. Except during the administration of these two men, the governor of the Persian province Beyond-the-river, of which Judah formed a part, was the responsible head. After the conquest of Alexander the Great, Judæa belonged to Egypt and Syria in turn. The successful revolt of the Maccabees against the Syrians led to the establishment of a dynasty of priest-kings, who sprang from the tribe of Levi, but occupied the throne of David. See MACCABEES. They were succeeded by an Idumæan dynasty, beginning with Herod the Great, ruling under the authority of the Romans. See HEROD, HISTORY, JERUSALEM. When the scepter reverted to the house of David the kingdom was no longer temporal but spiritual, and the sovereign no earthly potentate, but the Son of God.

To judge from the context, by Judah the tribal territory is meant in Josh. xix. 34. The passage has not been satisfactorily explained, the word Judah is not found in the Septuagint; perhaps the text is corrupt.

3. A Levite, among whose descendants was Kadmiel (Ezra iii. 9). See HODAVIAH.

4. A Levite who returned from Babylon with Zerubbabel (Neh. xii. 8).

5. A Levite, induced by Ezra to put away his foreign wife (Ezra x. 23).

6. A Benjamite, son of Hassenuah, and second in command over the city of Jerusalem (Neh. xi. 9).

7. One who took part in the dedication of the wall, probably a prince of Judah (Neh. xii. 34).

Ju'das, genitive **Juda** ; the Greek form of the Hebrew proper name Judah.

1. Judah, son of Jacob (Mat. i. 2, 3, A. V.).

2. An ancestor of Jesus, who lived before the exile (Luke iii. 30 ; in A. V. Juda).

3. Judas Maccabæus, third of the five sons of the priest Mattathias (1 Mac. ii. 1-5). His father, driven to desperation by the determination of Antiochus Epiphanes to force idolatry upon the Jews, began the struggle for religious liberty. On the death of Mattathias, in 166 B. C., Judas, in compliance with his father's wish, assumed the military leadership of the faithful Jews (ii. 66 ; iii. 1). He entered immediately upon a career of victory. A combined Syrian and Samaritan army, under the command of Apollonius, advanced against him. He routed it, slew Apollonius, and took his sword (10, 11). Judas fought with this sword during the remainder of his life (12). He defeated another Syrian army under Seron near Beth-horon (13-24), and, probably still in 166 B. C., won a decisive battle with Gorgias near Emmaus (27-iv. 25). In the following year Antiochus sent a large army into Judæa under the command of Lysias, but it was defeated by Judas at Beth-zur (iv. 26-34). In consequence of these successes, the Jews recovered control of the temple, purified it, and consecrated it anew (36-53). This event was celebrated by the annual feast of dedication (John x. 22). This Syrian war was followed by offensive operations under Judas and his brother Simon against hostile neighboring nations (1 Mac. v. 9-54). Antiochus Eupator succeeded his father Antiochus Epiphanes on the throne of Syria, and reigned from 164 to 162 B. C. Under the guidance of Lysias he renewed the war with the Jews. Lysias defeated Judas at Beth-zacharias (vi. 28-47), and laid siege to Jerusalem (48-54), but was compelled by complications at home to conclude a peace with Judas and return to Antioch. The Jews acknowledged the suzerainty of Syria, but were promised the free exercise of their religion (55-61). Demetrius Soter, who reigned from 162 to 150 B. C., again favored the Grecian party among the Jews, and put the hellenizer Alcimus into the high-priesthood (vii. 1-20). Judas resisted the efforts of this high priest (23, 24), and Demetrius sent an army under Nicanor to support Alcimus; but Nicanor was defeated at Capharsalama and again at Adasa near Beth-horon (26-50). During the brief peace which ensued Judas began negotiations with the Romans, and obtained from them assurances of friendship and assistance (viii.) ; but probably before the answer of the senate was returned, Demetrius sent another army under Bacchides into Judæa in 160 B. C. Judas offered valiant resistance to the invaders at Elasa, but his troops were worsted and he himself was slain (ix. 1-18). His body was recovered by his brothers, and buried in the family sepulcher at Modin (19). It was some time before the patriotic party recovered from the demoralization caused by their defeat and the death of their leader, but at length they offered the command to Judas' brother Jonathan (23-31).

4. Son of Chalphi and one of the two captains who stood by Jonathan Maccabæus at Hazor when all the rest had fled, and enabled him to retrieve the day (1 Mac. xi. 70).

5. A son of Simon Maccabæus (1 Mac. **xvi.** 2). His father devolved the command of the army upon him and his brother John, and sent them against Cendebæus. The two brothers gained a great victory over the Syrian general near Kidron, not far from Ashdod (2–10). Judas was wounded in the battle (9). In 135 B. C., about three years later, he and his brother Mattathias were treacherously murdered in the castle of Dok by a kinsman by marriage, either at a feast at the same time that their father Simon was assassinated (14–17) or a little later (Antiq. xiii. 8, 1).

6. Judas of Galilee, who, in the days of the enrollment, raised a revolt; but he perished, and all, as many as obeyed him, were scattered abroad (Acts v. 37; cp. Luke ii. 2). Josephus calls him several times a Galilæan, but once a Gaulonite, of the city of Gamala, implying that he was from Gaulonitis, east of the Jordan. It appears that, with the support of a Pharisee called Sadduc, Judas imbued his countrymen with the belief that the enrollment under Quirinius was the commencement of their reduction to a state of servitude. He founded a philosophic sect whose chief tenet was that their only ruler and lord was God (Antiq. xviii. 1, 1 and 6; War ii. 8, 1). Josephus states that Judas succeeded in making some of the Jews revolt, and implies, but does not directly mention, that he lost his life. He expressly states, however, that his sons were slain (Antiq. xx. 5, 2). The indirect consequence of this attempt was the rise of the party of zealots, who largely contributed to the disturbances which provoked the Jewish war of A. D. 66–70.

7. Judas Iscariot, son of Simon Iscariot (John vi. 71, R. V.), and the apostle who betrayed his divine Lord, and that by a kiss. By being surnamed Iscariot he is distinguished from another of the twelve who was named Judas (Luke vi. 16; John xiv. 22). The surname probably meant that he came originally from Kerioth (see ISCARIOT), and may thus indicate that he was not a Galilæan. Judged by his character, he followed Jesus probably because he expected to derive earthly advantage from the establishment of Christ's kingdom. Jesus, without naming any person, early referred to the future act of treason which one of the twelve would commit (John vi. 70). Judas was appointed to keep the bag, but he yielded to dishonesty, and appropriated part of the money to himself. When Mary of Bethany in her affection for Jesus broke the alabaster box of precious ointment and anointed him, Judas was the spokesman of himself and others in denouncing what he considered extravagance; not that he cared for the poor, but that he wished the price of the ointment to be put into the bag, whence he could help himself as he had done before (John xii. 5, 6). Jesus mildly

reproved him; but the rebuke aroused his resentment, and he went to the chief priests and offered to betray Jesus unto them for a price. They agreed with him on thirty pieces of silver, about $19.50, an ordinary price for a slave. From that time Judas sought an opportunity to deliver Jesus unto them (Mat. xxvi. 14–16; Mark xiv. 10, 11; Ex. xxi. 32; Zech. xi. 12, 13). At the passover supper Jesus, in order to carry out his design of being crucified at the feast, pointed out the traitor. The devil had already put into the heart of Judas to betray his Master (John xiii. 2). When Jesus solemnly said, "One of you shall betray me," each disciple asked, "Lord, is it I?" Peter beckoned to John to ask Christ who it was. Jesus replied enigmatically that it was one of those that were dipping with him in the dish (Mat. xxvi. 23; Mark xiv. 20), one to whom he would give the sop (John xiii. 26, R. V.): in other words, his own familiar friend, one who ate bread with him (18; Ps. xli. 9). Jesus and Judas, it would seem, were dipping together in the dish; and Jesus dipped the sop that he then held in his hand, and gave it to Judas (John xiii. 26). After the sop Satan entered into Judas (27). He also asked: "Is it I, Rabbi?" Jesus answered: "Thou hast said," which was the equivalent of "Yes" (Mat. xxvi. 21–25 R. V.). Even yet the disciples did not know just what Jesus meant, and when he added, "That thou doest, do quickly," they supposed that this was a direction to the treasurer to lose no time in buying some articles of which they had need. The traitor went at once to the chief priests. It is probable that Judas was not at the institution of the sacrament. He was present at the supper, and partook of it with the twelve (Mat. xxvi. 20); but he went out immediately after receiving the sop (John xiii. 30), and the eucharist was after the supper (Mat. xxvi. 26–29; Mark xiv. 22–25; Luke xxii. 19, 20). Luke in narrating the events of the supper, changes the actual order that he may place the spirit of Christ and the spirit of the disciples in contrast (xxii. 15–20 and 21–24). After the departure of Judas the tone of Jesus' conversation changes. When supper was ended he led the eleven to the garden of Gethsemane. Thither Judas came, accompanied by a great multitude with swords and staves, from the chief priests and elders. In accordance with a sign which had been agreed upon, in order to point out Jesus to the soldiers, Judas advanced and saluted Jesus with a kiss, and Jesus was seized (Mat. xxvi. 47–50). The next morning, when Judas, now in calmer mood, saw that Jesus was condemned, and was likely to be put to death, he awoke to the enormity of his guilt, and went to the chief priests with the confession, "I have sinned in that I have betrayed the innocent blood," and offered to return the money. His conscience was not so seared as the consciences of the chief priests, who, having seduced the erring apostle into his great sin, then turned round on him and said, "What is that to us? see thou to that." On which he cast down the silver pieces in the temple, and went and hanged himself (Mat. xxvii. 3–5), and falling headlong he burst asunder in the midst, and all his bowels gushed out (Acts i. 18). The 109th Psalm, directed primarily against some contemporary of the writer, found fulfillment in Judas (Ps. cix. 8; Acts i. 20). But no heavenly coercion compelled the son of perdition (John xvii. 12) to fulfill his destiny. Nor was he, a suppliant, refused mercy; he did not ask it.

8. One of the twelve apostles, carefully distinguished from Judas Iscariot (John xiv. 22). He was son or perhaps brother of James (Luke vi. 16; Acts i. 13; see R. V. text and margin). He was also called Thaddæus, for this name is found in other lists in the place corresponding to his (Mat. x. 3; Mark iii. 18). The received text of Mat. x. 3 has "Lebbæus, whose surname was Thaddæus." These two surnames are believed to mean the same thing: the former coming from Hebrew and Aramaic *leb*, heart, and the latter from Aramaic *thad*, a mother's breast, and both signifying a beloved child.

9. One of the four brethren of the Lord (Mat. xiii. 55; Mark vi. 3, in A. V. Juda), and probably the author of the Epistle of Jude. See BRETHREN OF THE LORD, JUDE.

10. A man who lived at Damascus, in the street called Straight, and with whom Paul lodged just after his conversion (Acts ix. 11).

11. Judas, surnamed Barsabbas. He was a leading man in the church at Jerusalem, and was chosen with Silas to accompany Barnabas and Paul to Antioch, bearing the letter from the council at Jerusalem to the churches of Syria and Cilicia. He had prophetic gifts. His subsequent history is unknown (Acts xv. 22, 27, 32). He bears the same surname as the disciple Joseph, who was proposed for the apostleship, and was prob bly his brother (i. 23).

Jude, in E. R. V. of Jude 1 **Judas.**

An English form of the name Judas, given in the A. V. to the writer of the Epistle of Jude (ver. 1). He describes himself simply as "brother of James," by whom the author of the Epistle of James and leader of the church in Jerusalem seems to be meant. In this case Jude should be a brother of the Lord, and not an apostle; and these inferences seem borne out by the presence of a Judas in the lists of our Lord's brethren (Mat. xiii. 55; Mark vi. 3), and by the apparent implication of verse 17 of his epistle, that its writer was not an apostle. Those who identify the brothers of the Lord with the sons of Alphæus, nevertheless, identify Jude with the apostle Judas. Except his bare name, nothing is recorded of him beyond what we may infer from the facts that the brethren of the Lord did not believe in him during his life on earth (John vii. 5) and that after his resurrection they were his followers (Acts i. 14). An interesting story told of his grandchildren by the church writer, Hegesippus, and preserved by Eusebius (H. E. iii. 20), confirms the possible inference from 1 Cor. ix. 5 that he was married, and implies that he was dead before A. D. 80.

The General Epistle of Jude is a brief epistle. It names its author as Judas, a bond servant of Jesus Christ and brother of James (ver. 1, R. V. margin); that is probably Judas, the brother of the Lord (Mat. xiii. 55; Mark vi. 3). Its address is quite general: "to them that are called, beloved in God the Father, and kept for Jesus Christ" (ver. 1, R. V.). Nevertheless, it is probable from the character of the epistle, which seems intended for a special occasion and is full of allusions which would be likely to be intelligible only to Jews, that some particular body of Christians was intended, which, from the circumstances of sending the letter, did not need to be specified in the address. It is most natural to think of it as intended for the Jewish Christians dwelling in Palestine. The letter has been largely used by 2 Pet. ii., [verses 4–18 with the exceptions of verses 14 and 15 being represented in 2 Pet. ii.–iii. 3]; and must have been written before it, probably not much before: it seems most natural to date it about A. D. 66. [Those students who hold the genuineness of 2 Peter, but contend for its priority to Jude, are apt to date the Epistle of Jude between the death of Peter about A. D. 68 and the accession of the Roman emperor Domitian in A. D. 81. The reason for fixing upon A. D. 81 as the limit is found in an ancient tradition, quoted by Eusebius from Hegesippus, who wrote as early as A. D. 170, from which it appears that Jude, the Lord's brother, had died before or at latest early in the reign of Domitian.] It was called out by the outbreak among Jude's readers of an alarming heresy with immoral tendencies, probably something like the incipient gnosticism rebuked in the pastoral epistles and the Apocalypse (ver. 3, 4, 10, 15, 16, 18), and was designed to save the churches addressed from its inroads. After the address (ver. 1, 2), it assigns the reason for its writing (ver. 3, 4) and then first announces the condemnation in store for the false teachers (ver. 5–16), and afterwards divulges the duty of true Christians in the circumstances (ver. 17–23), concluding with a rich and appropriate doxology (ver. 24, 25). Owing doubtless to its brevity, there are no very clear traces of the use of Jude in the very earliest fathers of the church. In the latter part of the second century, however, it is found in full use in the Greek and Latin churches alike [being included in the Old Latin version, listed in the Muratorian fragment, quoted and referred to as Jude's by

Clement of Alexandria and Tertullian and later by Origen]; and was clearly from the beginning a part of the Christian canon.

B. B. W. (supplemented).

Judge.

1. A civil magistrate (Ex. xxi. 22; Deut. xvi. 18). On the advice of his father-in-law, and in order to relieve himself of overwork, Moses organized the judiciary of Israel, acting henceforth himself in matters of great importance only and for the adjudication of cases of less moment assigning a judge to each thousand, to each hundred, to each fifty, and to each ten (Ex. xviii. 13–26). For all the tribal subdivision heads already existed, known as princes and elders, who possessed civil and religious authority; and in the judicial system which he organized Moses included these officials and they retained under the new regulations their hereditary function of judging (Deut. i. 15–17; cp. xxi. 2, and see THOUSAND). Before his death Moses gave directions that the Israelites, on settling in Canaan, appoint judges and officers in all their towns, with instructions to refer matters too difficult for these magistrates to the priests (xvi. 18–20; xvii. 2–13; xix. 15–20; cp. Josh. viii. 33; xxiii. 2; xxiv. 1; 1 Sam. viii. 1). With the establishment of the kingdom the king became supreme judge in civil matters (2 Sam. xv. 2; 1 Kin. iii. 9, 28; vii. 7; cp. 1 Sam. viii. 5). David assigned Levites to the judicial office, and appointed six thousand as officers and judges (1 Chron. xxiii. 4; xxvi. 29). Jehoshaphat organized the judiciary in Judah still further, setting judges in the fortified cities, with a supreme court at Jerusalem, consisting of Levites, priests, and the heads of fathers' houses under the presidency of the high priest in religious matters and of the prince of Judah in civil matters (2 Chron. xix. 5–8).

2. A man whom God raised up to lead a revolt against foreign oppressors and who, having freed the nation and shown thereby his call of God, was looked to by the people to maintain their rights. The judges were saviors like unto Moses. They numbered twelve, not including Abimelech, who was a petty king and not called of God (ix.). They were Othniel of Judah, deliverer of Israel from the king of Mesopotamia; Ehud, who expelled the Moabites and Ammonites; Shamgar, smiter of six hundred Philistines and saviour of Israel; Deborah, associated with Barak, who led Naphtali and Zebulun to victory against the northern Canaanites; Gideon, who drove the Midianites from the territory of Israel; Tola and Jair; Jephthah, subduer of the Ammonites; Ibzan, Elon, Abdon, and Samson, the troubler of the Philistines. Eli and Samuel also judged Israel (1 Sam. iv. 18; vii. 15), but the former acted in his official capacity as high priest and the latter as a prophet of Jehovah. These judges did not form an unbroken succession of rulers, but appeared sporadically.

They were often local, discharging their duties in restricted districts. They apparently exercised only such authority as was spontaneously accorded to them. They could not order the various tribes to war. Some of the oppressions and not a few of the judges were evidently contemporaneous and overlapped. Shamgar, for example, was contemporary with Ehud, for the account of his exploit is inserted in the midst of the narrative of Ehud's work (iii. 31); and a Philistine oppression of Judah was coeval with the Ammonite domination east of Jordan and attack on Judah, Benjamin and Ephraim (x. 7). See CHRONOLOGY III.

These facts throw light on the distracted state of the nation during the period of the judges. The political districts, moreover, are found to be those that were separated by the Jordan and by the heathen barrier between Judah and the north. The song of Deborah and the history of Jephthah show the laxity of the bonds which united the tribes, and make known what tribes were able and willing to join forces and fortunes. The isolation of Judah is remarkable; see JUDAH. But there were centralizing influences at work. National feeling existed, for the war of extermination waged against Benjamin shows the sense of national guilt and national responsibility. There was one ark for all the tribes in the national tabernacle at Shiloh (Josh. xviii. 1; Judg. xxi. 19; cp. Ex. xxiii. 14–17). It was carried to Bethel, where the tribes had gathered for battle and would worship the Lord and ask counsel of him (Judg. xx. 18–29). Great oppressions united the people in common misery and called for united action; great deliverers united the hearts of the people in loyalty and pride about one head; and great deliverances, obtained by united action, bound tribes together in common glory.

The period of the judges has been called Israel's iron age. The people frequently lapsed into idolatry, and worship at the sanctuary was rendered difficult by the distracted state of the country. Rudeness of manners was displayed in Jael's murder of Sisera, in Jephthah's sacrifice of his daughter, in Gideon's treatment of the men of Succoth, in the sin of the men of Gibeah. Against these shadows, however, there stand out brightly the trust and filial piety of Jephthah's daughter, the fidelity of Ruth to Naomi, and the kindly and upright character of Boaz.

Judg'es, Book of.

A historical book of the O. T. placed after the book of Joshua. It continues the narrative from his death, and consists of three parts. 1. Introduction: departure of the tribes to occupy the districts allotted to them (see Josh. xv.–xxi.), and a list of the towns left by them in the possession of the Canaanite idolaters (Judg. i.–ii. 5). Joshua's wars of conquest had not depopulated the country (see

CANAAN). II. History of the judges as saviors of Israel, from the death of Joshua to that of Samson (ii. 6–xvi. 31). This section has its own introduction in prophetic style, summarizing the events of the period and pointing out the religious lesson (ii. 6–iii. 6), followed by more or less detailed accounts of six judges and brief mention of other six. The assumption of kingship by Abimelech, son of Gideon, is recorded as an integral part of the history, although he was a petty king rather than a judge, and was not a saviour of Israel. III. Two appendices, namely, an account of Micah's image worship and its establishment among the Danites of the north (xvii., xviii.), and of the sin of the men of Gibeah and the consequent war for its punishment (xix.–xxi.).

The date of the composition of the Book of Judges is difficult to determine. At any rate, the following facts must be satisfied. All schools of criticism at present acknowledge the great antiquity of the song of Deborah, and that it is practically contemporary with the event which it celebrates. This section, the second and main portion of the book, could not have been written until after the death of Samson (xvi. 30, 31). In the appendices, the recurring expression, "in those days there was no king in Israel," points to the composition of these chapters at least after the establishment of the kingdom. The tabernacle was no longer at Shiloh (xviii. 31) when they were written. The mention of the "captivity of the land" (xviii. 30) has been interpreted as a reference to the ravages of Tiglath-pileser in the north (2 Kin. xv. 29), or to the deportation of the ten tribes after the fall of Samaria. But this explanation conflicts with the parallel statement, "all the time that the house of God was in Shiloh" (Judg. xviii. 31). Moreover, historical circumstances in the reigns of David, Solomon, and Jeroboam (1 Kin. v.–vii.; xii. 28–31) make it highly improbable that this image worship continued to be practiced until the time of Tiglath-pileser or the Assyrian exile. Hence from the time of David Kimchi many interpreters have understood the captivity of the land to refer to the capture of the ark by the Philistines, when Jehovah forsook Shiloh. Several expositors have adopted the conjecture of Houbigant that the last letter in the phrase "captivity of the land" has become corrupt, and that the Hebrew text originally had nun instead of tzade, which would then read "captivity of the ark." Keil thinks that the reference is to a conquest of the land of the northern Danites and enslavement of its population by the neighboring Syrians of Damascus. Any of these suppositions is beset by fewer difficulties than the assumption that Micah's image worship continued until the fall of Samaria. The expression "from Dan even to Beersheba" (xx. 1) was, of course, appropriate in the times of the judges, for it

doubtless originated then. For x. 11–13; cp. i. 31, 32, 34; iii. 13, 31; vi. 3, 9, 10, 33. The indications of time, which are found in the appendices, thus point to the period before David's reign over all Israel. The general introduction to the book was written while the Jebusites still occupied the stronghold at Jerusalem (i. 21). All these indications of time strongly favor the inference that the book as a whole was written in the time of Samuel, if not actually by that prophet himself, as the Jews of old believed. Critics who deny the Mosaic authorship of Deuteronomy assume that a late reviser worked over the material, because the book reflects the same religious conception as does Deuteronomy.

As the analysis of the work shows, these histories were gathered and placed in their present framework in order to exhibit their religious teaching and serve as an admonition to subsequent ages. This religious significance of the events, which the compiler desired to exhibit, was not concealed from the actors themselves. The song of Deborah and the national uprising to punish the perpetrators and abetters of the crime of Gibeah reveal the consciousness of the participants that they were engaged in sacred warfare and that the history which was being enacted was full of religious instruction.

Judg'ment Hall. See PRÆTORIUM.

Ju'dith [object of praise, praiseworthy; also feminine of Yᵉhudi, a Jew, and meaning a Jewess].

1. A wife of Esau and daughter of Beeri, the Hittite (Gen. xxvi. 34). She was also called Oholibamah (xxxvi. 2; cp. ANAH).

2. Heroine of the book of Judith; see APOCRYPHA.

Ju'li-a [feminine form of Latin *Julius*].

A Christian woman at Rome (Rom. xvi. 15), not unlikely the wife of Philologus.

Ju'li-us.

A centurion of the Augustan band, employed to conduct Paul and other prisoners to Rome (Acts xxvii. 1). He showed courtesy to the apostle, allowing him to visit his friends at Sidon (3). At Crete he did not believe Paul's prediction of the coming storm (11); but after the tempest broke he heeded Paul's advice and kept the sailors from forsaking the ship (31). When the vessel was wrecked, the guard wanted to kill the prisoners lest any should escape; but he forbade the butchery, desiring to save Paul (42, 43).

Ju'ni-as, in A. V. **Junia**.

A Jewish Christian at Rome, a kinsman and fellow-prisoner of Paul, and in Christ before him (Rom. xvi. 7).

Ju'ni-per.

Not the coniferous tree of the genus *Juniperus*, of which several species occur in Lebanon, Galilee, and Bashan; but a leguminous plant (*Retama rætam*), an almost leaf less broom (1 Kin. xix. 4, 5 ; Job xxx. 4 ; Ps. cxx. 4) ; see BROOM.

Ju'pi-ter.

The supreme god of the Romans. He corresponded to the Zeus of the Greeks, and in the only part of the N. T. in which the name is introduced (Acts xiv. 12, 13) the Greek text has Zeus. Zeus had a noted temple at Olympia in Elis (Herod. ii. 7), from which he derived his designation of Olympius. Antiochus Epiphanes erected a temple to him under that title at Athens, dedicated the temple at Jerusalem to Jupiter Olympius, and at the request of the Samaritans, Josephus says, called the sanctuary on Gerizim by the name of Jupiter, the protector of strangers (2 Mac. vi. 2; Antiq. xii. 5, 5). The worship of Jupiter, which Paul and Barnabas met with at Lystra, existed at the time over the whole Greek and Roman world. He had temples and a priesthood ; garlands were presented to him, as were also offerings of other kinds, and oxen and sheep were sacrificed to propitiate his favor.

Ju-shab-he'sed [loving-kindness is returned].

A son of Zerubbabel (1 Chron. iii. 20).

Jus'tus [just, righteous].

1. A surname of Joseph, the unsuccessful candidate for the apostleship rendered vacant by the fall of the unworthy Judas (Acts i. 23).

2. A godly man of Corinth, whose house adjoined the synagogue, and with whom Paul lodged (Acts xviii. 7). His fuller name was Titus Justus (R. V.).

3. The surname of a Jew called Jesus, who joined Paul in sending salutations to the Colossians (Col. iv. 11).

Ju'tah and **Jut'tah** [extended, inclined].

A town in the hill country of Judah, mentioned with Maon, Carmel, and Ziph, and doubtless in their vicinity (Josh. xv. 55). With its suburbs it was assigned to the priests (xxi. 16). It is now called Yuttah, and stands on a low eminence, about 5½ miles S. by W. of Hebron. The supposition is credible that Jutah was the city of Judah in the hill country to which Mary went to visit Elisabeth (Luke i. 39), and that Judah ('Iouda) has been substituted for Jutah ('Iouta). The more common view, however, is that Hebron was the city of Elisabeth.

K

Kab, in A. V. **Cab.**

A Hebrew dry measure (2 Kin. vi. 25) ; containing, according to rabbinical tradition, one sixth of a seah or one one hundred and eightieth of a homer. See MEASURE.

Kab'ze-el and once **Jekabzeel** (Neh. xi. 25) [God brings together].

A city in the extreme south of Judah

(Josh. xv. 21). It was the home of David's heroic supporter, Benaiah (2 Sam. xxiii. 20 ; 1 Chron. xi. 22). The town was inhabited after the exile (Neh. xi. 25 ; where it is called by the synonymous name of Jekabzeel). Exact situation unknown.

Ka'desh, including **Ka - desh - bar'ne-a** [consecrated]. The meaning of Barnea is unknown.

1. A fountain, city or town, and wilderness on the southern frontier of Judah and of Palestine (Num. xx. 16 ; xxxiv. 4 ; Josh. xv. 3 ; Ps. xxix. 8 ; Ezek. xlvii. 19 ; xlviii. 28) ; distinguished as Kadesh-barnea from other places bearing the name Kadesh (Num. xiii. 26 with xxxii. 8 ; Deut. i. 19 with 46). At an early period it was called En-mishpat or Fountain of Judgment (Gen. xiv. 7). It was in the wilderness of Paran (Num. xiii. 3, 26), in the wilderness of Zin (Num. xx. 1 ; xxvii. 14), eleven days' journey from Sinai by way of mount Seir (Deut. i. 2), in the uttermost of the border of Edom (Num. xx. 16). It appears to have been not a great distance from the highway between Palestine and Egypt, for Hagar's well was situated between Kadesh and Bered, and on the road to Egypt (Gen. xvi. 7, 14 ; cp. xx. 1). The place was overrun by Chedorlaomer (xiv. 7). Into the region adjacent Hagar fled (xvi. 7, 14), and Abraham sojourned there for a time (xx. 1). The Israelites, during their wanderings, twice encamped at Kadesh. They arrived in the neighborhood in the second year about the fifth month (Num. xiii. 20 ; cp. x. 11), sent thence the spies into Canaan, received the discouraging report there about the difficulties of conquest (xiii. 26), refused to advance, and were condemned to remain in the wilderness, and abode at Kadesh many days (Deut. i. 46). They returned to Kadesh in the first month (Num. xx. 1) of the fortieth year (xxxiii. 36, 38 ; cp. Deut. ii. 7, 14). Here Miriam died and was buried (Num. xx. 1) ; and here Moses smote the rock that water might gush out, as, in similar circumstances, it had done at Rephidim (xx. 1-13) ; see MERIBAH. But he and Aaron sinned in acting in their own name. From Kadesh ambassadors were sent to the king of Edom to ask permission for the Israelites to pass through his territory (xx. 14, 16, 22 ; Judg. xi. 16, 17). In 1842, the Rev. J. Rowlands discovered a fountain called by the Arabs Kades or Kudes, on the east of Jebel Helal. In 1878, the Rev. T. W. Holland, and in 1881 the Rev. Dr. H. Clay Trumbull, visited the spot and revived the identification. The name remains in wady Kadîs, Jebel Kadîs, and 'Ain Kadîs ; the site answers to the biblical description in every respect ; and confirmation is afforded by the name of the adjacent wady, Abu Retemât. On the ground that the Israelites encamped twice at Kadesh (Num. xiii. 26 ; xx. 1, 22 ; xxxiii. 36), many interpreters had long been of the opinion

⁢

Ain Gederiat in the Sinai Desert, possibly the Kadesh-barnea of Numbers 33:36.

that Rithmah was practically identical with Kadesh (xii. 16 with xxxiii. 18); and now it appears that the wady nearest and parallel to that of Kadîs bears the name corresponding to Rithmah, wady Abu Retemât. 'Ain Kadîs is about 77 miles to the south of Hebron and 51 miles south of Beersheba. The spring, which is of sweet water, issues from under a rugged spur of rock belonging to the north-eastern mountain range west of the Arabah. The stream is copious, and is intercepted in its course by two or three wells built round with masonry. Then after traversing the oasis which it has created, it is finally lost in the desert beyond. This identification has been generally accepted as probably correct. Numerous other sites had previously been suggested, especially 'Ain el-Weibeh, on the western side of the Arabah, northwest of Petra. Robinson had failed to discover any spring called Kadîs, and settled on the spring el-Weibeh because of its copiousness and its proximity to the borders of Edom. Wetzstein identified Kadesh with Kadus, north of Jebel Madara; but see KEDESH 1.

2. The name is perhaps contained in "the land of Tahtim-hodshi" (2 Sam. xxiv. 6), corrected by means of Lucian's text to "the land of the Hittites, toward Kadesh."

Kad′mi-el [God is of old].

A Levite, head of a tribal house, who returned from Babylon with Zerubbabel (Ezra ii. 40; Neh. vii. 43; xii. 8). He helped to oversee the workmen engaged in rebuilding the temple (Ezra iii. 9). The representative of the house sealed the covenant (Neh. x. 9), perhaps being the same person who had previously assisted in the public confession (ix. 4, 5).

Kad′mon-ites [people of the east].

A tribe dwelling somewhere between Egypt and the Euphrates (Gen. xv. 19), probably in the Syrian desert.

Kain [possession, creature, smith].

1. The tribal name from which the more familiar gentile adjective Kenite is derived (R. V. of Num. xxiv. 22; Judg. iv. 11, margin). See KENITE.

2. A village in Judah, in A. V. spelled Cain (Josh. xv. 57); perhaps it was an old settlement of the Kenites. See CAIN 3.

Kal′lai [swift].

A priest, head of the father's house of Sallai in the time of Joiakim, the high priest (Neh. xii. 20).

Ka′mon; in A. V. **Camon**.

The place where the judge Jair the Gileadite was buried (Judg. x. 5). The site is unknown. Eusebius and Jerome locate it in the plain of Esdraelon, between Megiddo and Acre; but presumably it was in Gilead, as Josephus states (Antiq. v. 7, 6). Polybius mentions a town Kamoun which was taken by Antiochus in his war with Ptolemy Philopator, immediately after he had captured Scythopolis and at the same time that he took Pella, Abila, Gadara and other places in Gilead (Hist. v. 70, 12).

Ka′nah [place of reeds].

1. A brook which formed part of the boundary line between Ephraim and Manasseh (Josh. xvi. 8; xvii. 9). Robinson identified it with the wady Kânah, which rises south of Shechem, and joins the 'Aujah, the combined streams falling into the Mediterranean 4 miles north of Joppa. This seems too far south, but the identity of the ancient and modern names is in its favor.

2. A town on the boundary of Asher (Josh. xix. 28). It was plausibly identified by Robinson with the modern Kânâ, about 7½ miles southeast of Tyre. It is a village with no marks of antiquity, but lower down the ravine which comes from it are old sculptures on the face of the southern cliffs.

Kaph. See CAPH.

Ka-re'ah. in A. V. once **Careah** [bald].
Father of the captains Johanan and Jonathan, who came to Gedaliah, the Babylonian governor of Judah (2 Kin. xxv. 23; Jer. xl. 8).

Kar'ka, in A. V. **Kar'ka-a,** retaining the final syllable which denotes direction [rent, ravine].
A place on the southern boundary of Judah (Josh. xv. 3). The name has the definite article, and may be a common noun meaning simply the ravine (Wetzstein).

Kar'kor [foundation].
A place east of the Jordan, where Zebah and Zalmunna encamped with their army (Judg. viii. 10). Site unidentified.

Kar'tah [city].
A town of Zebulun given to the Merarite Levites (Josh. xxi. 34). Not identified.

Kar'tan [perhaps an old dual, twin towns].
A town of Naphtali, given to the Gershonite Levites (Josh. xxi. 32). Called in 1 Chron. vi. 76 Kiriathaim, A. V. Kirjathaim. Site unidentified.

Kat'tath.
A town of Zebulun (Josh. xix. 15); identified sometimes with Kitron of Judg. i. 30, and sometimes with Kartah.

Ke'dar [probably, mighty]. To the Hebrews the name was also suggestive of the black tents.
A tribe descended from Ishmael (Gen. xxv. 13), children of the east, dwelling in black tents, possessing flocks and camels (Song i. 5; Is. lx. 7; Jer. xlix. 28, 29), and having villages also in the wilderness (Is. xlii. 11). They were an Arabian tribe (Is. xxi. 13, 16; Ezek. xxvii. 21). They were ruled by princes (ibid.), and were skillful in archery (Is. xxi. 16, 17). They dwelt between Arabia Petræa and Babylonia. The people of Kedar were Pliny's Cedrai, and from their tribe Mohammed ultimately arose.

Ked'e-mah [toward the east].
A tribe descended from Ishmael (Gen. xxv. 15; 1 Chron. i. 31). Not mentioned elsewhere.

Ked'e-moth [ancient places or beginnings].
A city east of the Jordan, near the wilderness (Deut. ii. 26), allotted to the Reubenites (Josh. xiii. 18) and assigned to the Merarite Levites for residence (xxi. 37; 1 Chron. vi. 79). Site unidentified.

Ke'desh [sacred place, sanctuary].
1. A town in the extreme south of Judah (Josh. xv. 23), probably different from Kadesh-barnea (ver. 3). Its site is perhaps

Kadus, about 6 miles north of Jebel Madara near wady el-Yemen.
2. A town of the Canaanites taken by Thothmes III, later by Joshua after the defeat of its king (Josh. xi. 12; xii. 22), allotted to the tribe of Naphtali (xix. 37) and, to distinguish it from other towns of the name, called Kedesh-naphtali (Judg. iv. 6; Tob. i. 2) and Kedesh in Galilee (Josh. xx. 7), given to the Gershonite Levites for their residence, and made a city of refuge (7; xxi. 32). It was the residence of Barak (Judg. iv. 6). Its inhabitants were removed to Assyria by Tiglath-pileser (2 Kin. xv. 29). Jonathan defeated the army of Demetrius there (1 Mac. xi. 63, 73; Antiq. xiii. 5, 6). Robinson identified it with the village of Kades in Upper Galilee, about 4½ miles northwest of the waters of Merom.
3. A city of Issachar given to the Gershonite Levites (1 Chron. vi. 72; in Josh. xxi. 28 Kishion, A. V. Kishon). See KISHION.

Ke-hel'a-thah [an assembly].
A station of the Israelites in the wilderness (Num. xxxiii. 22, 23). Not identified.

Kei'lah.
A town in the lowland of Judah (Josh. xv. 44; 1 Chron. iv. 19). The Philistines fought against it, but David attacked them and delivered the town. Nevertheless he did not remain in the town when Saul approached, lest the men of Keilah should surrender him to Saul (1 Sam. xxiii. 1–13). The town was inhabited after the captivity (Neh. iii. 17, 18). The identification with Kila, a ruined village 8½ miles northwest of Hebron, is scarcely tenable; for Kila is in the mountains and Keilah was situated in the lowland.

Ke-la'iah [perhaps, contempt]. See KELITA.

Kel'i-ta [dwarf].
A Levite, called also Kelaiah, who was induced by Ezra to put away his foreign wife (Ezra x. 23). He was employed with others by him to read and interpret the law to the people (Neh. viii. 7), and with Nehemiah sealed the covenant (x. 10).

Kem'u-el [perhaps, congregation of God].
1. Son of Nahor and Milcah, and head of a younger branch of the Aramæans (Gen. xxii. 21).
2. A prince of the tribe of Ephraim and a commissioner for the allotment of Canaan (Num. xxxiv. 24).
3. A Levite, father of Hashabiah (1 Chron. xxvii. 17).

Ke'nan. See CAINAN.

Ke'nath [possession].
A town on the western slope of the Jebel Hauran, on the extreme northeastern border of Israelitish territory. It was the most easterly of the ten cities of the Decapolis (Pliny, Hist. Nat., 5, 16), and was near Bostra (Jerome, Onom.). Imposing ruins of it still remain, which bear the name Kanawat.

It was taken by Nobah, probably a Manassite, who called it after his own name (Num. xxxii. 42). The new name, however, did not permanently supplant the old one. The town passed again into gentile hands (1 Chron. ii. 23). Herod the Great was defeated here by the Arabians (War i. 19, 2).

Ke′naz [perhaps, hunting].

1. A descendant of Esau through Eliphaz (Gen. xxxvi. 11). He became a chieftain in mount Seir (15), probably taking his title from the clan which he ruled (40–43). The reference in Josh. xv. 17; 1 Chron. iv. 13 is probably likewise to the tribe. See KENIZZITE.

2. A descendant of Caleb, son of Jephunneh (1 Chron. iv. 15). A name has evidently dropped out of the text before it.

Ke′nez-ite. See KENIZZITE.

Ke′nite.

A tribe of which a branch dwelt in Canaan or vicinity in the time of Abraham (Gen. xv. 19), while another portion of the same people settled in Midian, and by the time of Moses had become incorporated with the Midianites (Judg. i. 16; iv. 11; cp. Num. x. 29). The Midianite Kenites may, however, have been merely a tribal family descended from a man of Midian named Cain, and have had nothing in common with the Kenites who dwelt in Canaan. The latter occupied rocky fastnesses near to Amalek (Num. xxiv. 20–22). It may perhaps be gathered from this that before the conquest of Canaan the Kenites dwelt in the rugged, rocky country northeast of the Amalekites and to the east and southeast of Hebron. Hobab the Midianite, of the family of the Kenites, accompanied the Israelites on their march from mount Sinai to Canaan to aid them with his knowledge of the country (Num. x. 29–32). When the Israelites crossed the Jordan, encamped at Gilgal, and took Jericho, Hobab's family pitched their tents at Jericho; but after the conquest of Canaan they cast in their lot with the tribe of Judah, and settled in the wilderness of Judah, south of Arad and southeast of Hebron (Judg. i. 16). This choice perhaps indicates that they were indeed a branch of the old Kenite tribe of Canaan and sought the home of their forefathers. One Kenite, however, did not care to dwell with his brethren in the south, but took up his abode near Kedesh in Naphtali (Judg. iv. 11). The Kenites who settled in the south of Judah were still there in friendly relations with the Israelites in the time of Saul and David (1 Sam. xv. 6; xxvii. 10; xxx. 29). They had their registry with Judah (1 Chron. ii. 55).

Ken′iz-zite, in A. V. Kenezite, save once (Gen. xv. 19).

One of the tribes in or near Canaan in the time of Abraham (Gen. xv. 19). Found settled in mount Seir, it became subject to the victorious descendants of Esau, when they took

possession of the country (Deut. ii. 12), amalgamated with the conquerors, and looked to one of Esau's descendants as its head. This chieftain was known as Kenaz from the tribe which he ruled (Gen. xxxvi. 11, 15, 40–42). Individuals of the tribe, on the other hand, united with the sons of Jacob, Jephunneh the Kenizzite apparently taking to wife a woman of the tribe of Judah, and Othniel the Kenizzite becoming the first judge of Israel after the conquest. See CALEB 2.

Ker-en-hap′puch [the horn of paint].

The youngest of Job's three daughters born after his great trial (Job xlii. 14).

Ke′ri-oth, in A. V. once **Kirioth** (Amos ii. 2) [cities].

1. A town in the extreme south of Judah, properly Kerioth-hezron (Josh. xv. 25). The same as Hazor 2 (q. v.). Possibly it was the birthplace of Judas Iscariot, as the latter half of the name means man of Kerioth.

2. A town of Moab (Moabite Stone 13; Jer. xlviii. 24), apparently fortified (41). It possessed palaces (Amos ii. 2). It is supposed to be a synonym of Ar, the ancient capital of Moab, because it seems to be referred to as the capital (ibid.), and because in enumerations of the towns of Moab when Kerioth is cited Ar is omitted (Jer. xlviii.; Moabite Stone) and vice versa (Is. xv., xvi.; cp. Josh. xiii. 16–21). Unidentified; not Kureiyât, for which see KIRIATHAIM.

Ke-ri-oth-hez′ron. See KERIOTH 1 and HAZOR 2.

Ke′ros [the reed of a weaver's loom].

Founder of a family of Nethinim, members of which returned from captivity (Ezra ii. 44; Neh. vii. 47).

Ket′tle. See POT.

Ke-tu′rah [incense].

One of Abraham's wives (Gen. xxv. 1; cp. xvi. 3). The narrative is found at the close of the history of Abraham. It owes this position to literary considerations, which obtain throughout the book of Genesis, and not to chronological ones. The writer is in the habit of giving a brief account of the subordinate line of descendants, and forthwith dismissing them from his pages in order to proceed with the main history. From all that appears Abraham may have taken Keturah to wife long before the death of Sarah. She became the ancestress of the tribes of Zimran, Jokshan, Medan, Midian, Ishbak, and Shuah (Gen. xxv. 1, 2; 1 Chron. i. 32). Her sons were not regarded as on the same level with Isaac, and their father gave them gifts and sent them away during his lifetime to the east country (Gen. xxv. 6). A tribe *Keṭúra* is mentioned in late Arabian genealogies as dwelling near Mecca.

Key.

An instrument for turning bolts (Judg. iii. 25). An oriental key consists of a piece of wood with pegs fastened on it corresponding

to small holes in a wooden bolt within. See
LOCK. It is generally carried in the girdle,
but occasionally it is fastened to something
else and borne over the shoulder (cp. Is. xxii.
22). The key is the symbol of authority
(ibid.; Mat. xvi. 19; Rev. i. 18; iii. 7; ix.
1; xx. 1). It is also the symbol of access to
that from which one would otherwise be shut
out (Luke xi. 52).

Ke-zi'ah, in A. V. **Kezia** [cassia].
The second of Job's daughters born after
his great trial (Job xlii. 14).

Ke'ziz. See EMEK-KEZIZ.

Kib'roth-hat-ta'a-vah [the graves of lust].
A place in the Sinaitic peninsula, between
mount Sinai and Hazeroth, where the Israelites were buried who were slain by a plague
for lusting after the flesh pots of Egypt
(Num. xi. 33–35; xxxiii. 16, 17; Deut. ix.
22). In 1870 Palmer and Drake believed
that they had found the site at Erweis el-
Ebeirig, a day's journey from 'Ain el-Ḥuḍera.
It is an elevated table-land well adapted for
the encampment of a great multitude, and
with traces for many miles round of having
been so employed. Tradition says that it
was the camp of a great Hajj caravan, which
in the distant past sojourned here and was
never heard of again.

Kib'za-im [two heaps]. See JOKMEAM.

Kid.
A young goat. It was highly esteemed as
an article of food (Luke xv. 29). The flesh
was boiled and eaten (Judg. vi. 19), being
sometimes cooked in milk (Ex. xxiii. 19).
The law probably did not prohibit the use
of a sucking kid for food, but forbade that it
be cooked in its own mother's milk. The
relation between even a lower animal and
its offspring was sacred and should not be
disregarded by man. A kid might be used
as a burnt offering (Judg. xiii. 15, 19). The
Hebrew words, *Sa'ir* and *S^e'irah*, rendered
kid of the goats in A. V., are translated by
goat and he goat in R. V. (Gen. xxxvii. 31;
and wherever kid occurs in Lev., Num., and
Ezek.). See GOAT.

Kid'ron, in A. V. of 1 Mac. and N. T.
Cedron [dark, turbid].
1. A ravine which begins about half an
hour's walk to the northwest of Jerusalem
near the so-called tombs of the judges,
trends for a mile and a half toward the
southeast, turns sharply to the south and
continues in this direction past the city as
far as the valley of Hinnom and En-rogel.
Here it bends again to the southeast and
pursues a tortuous course to the Dead Sea.
No stream flows in it except during continuous heavy rains in winter, and there is no
evidence that its bed was ever occupied by a

The Kidron Valley. The village of Silwan is on the left in this view southeast from the Old City wall
at Jerusalem.

perennial brook Indeed, the word brook, which is connected with it in the English version, represents a Hebrew word which commonly either means a ravine occupied by the channel of a torrent dry during the hot season or denotes the winter torrent itself. By writers who use Greek, the Kidron is expressly called winter brook (John xviii. 1; 1 Mac. xii. 37). The name may be derived from the turbid water of the winter torrents or from the gloominess of the valley, especially in its lower part. To speakers of the Greek language, the Greek form of the name suggested the word for cedar and the rivulet came to be frequently called the brook of the cedars (John xviii. 1, R. V. margin ; 2 Sam. xv. 23, codex Vat.). The Kidron separates Jerusalem from the mount of Olives and had to be crossed by those going from the city to Bethany or Jericho (2 Sam. xv. 23). It was regarded as the eastern boundary of the city (1 Kin. ii. 37 ; Jer. xxxi. 40). The portion of the valley lying near the southern part of the city was early used as a common burying ground (2 Kin. xxiii. 6) ; and godly kings, who from time to time found it necessary to cleanse the temple of idolatrous symbols, made the Kidron valley the dumping place for the ashes of these abominations (1 Kin. xv. 13; 2 Chron. xxix. 16; xxx. 14; 2 Kin. xxiii. 4). Athaliah is reported to have been led away to the Kidron for execution that the temple might not be defiled by her blood (Antiq. ix. 7, 3).

2. A town near Jamnia and Ashdod (1 Mac. xv. 39; xvi. 9, 10), fortified by Cendebæus and occupied by a detachment of his Syrian army because it commanded several roads into Judæa (xv. 41). See GEDEROTH.

Ki'nah [song of mourning, lamentation].
A village in the extreme south of Judah (Josh. xv. 22). Situation unknown.

Kine. See Cow.

King.
The head of that form of state which is specifically called a kingdom. The title formerly implied autocratic power. Nimrod ruled over a kingdom in Babylonia containing several cities (Gen. x. 10). Chedorlaomer was king of Elam and head of a confederacy of kings (xiv. 1, 5). Pharaoh held sway over the princes of Egypt (xii. 15). Nebuchadnezzar of Babylon and Artaxerxes the Persian were each a king over kings (Ezra vii. 12; Dan. ii. 37, cp. 2 Kin. xxiv. 17). In Canaan in the time of Abraham the rule of a king was often over one town only (Gen. xiv. 2, 18; xx. 2). Some centuries later Joshua enumerated thirty-one kings whom he had conquered within the bounds of Canaan (Josh. xii. 7–24). It was not until centuries after the tribes and nations adjacent to Palestine had been ruled by kings, that the Israelites demanded a visible monarch. Although the demand when made was prompted by unbelief and in so far was rebellion against

Jehovah, yet it was not in itself at variance with the theocracy and the invisible, but efficient, rule of Jehovah ; for the theocracy in its very institution contemplated the administration of the several offices of government by human agents; see THEOCRACY. Moses foresaw the need that would arise for a visible king and he provided for the event, just as provision was made for prophets and priests to make known the will or legislation of Jehovah and for judges to represent the unseen Judge (Deut. xvii. 14–20). When the king was chosen the theocracy was not abolished. The nominally uncontrolled sovereign was required to be the vicegerent of Jehovah ; and when Saul, mistaking his position, sought to act independently, another was chosen to supersede him and his posterity on the throne. The same rule obtained with all Saul's successors ; when they gave up fidelity to Jehovah, they forfeited their title to the kingdom (1 Kin. xi. 31-36). For the succession of kings who ruled in Judah and Israel, see CHRONOLOGY.

A man became king of a nation through appointment to the office by one higher in authority (1 Sam. ix. 16 ; xvi. 1, 13 ; 2 Kin. xxiii. 33, 34 ; xxiv. 17), by the choice of the people (1 Sam. xviii. 8 ; 2 Sam. v. 1-3 ; 1 Kin. xii. 20; 2 Kin. xxiii. 30), or by usurping a throne (1 Kin. xv. 27, 28), or by inheritance (xi. 36). The ceremony of coronation among the Israelites consisted regularly in placing on the throne, putting the crown upon the head, anointing with oil, and proclamation (2 Kin. xi. 12; cp. 1 Sam. x. 24; 2 Sam. ii. 4; v. 3; 1 Kin. i. 34; 2 Kin. xxiii. 30). It was doubtless regularly accompanied by sacrifice, and sometimes also by a solemn procession (1 Sam. xvi. 2, 5; 1 Kin. i. 25, 43–46). The king often led the army to battle in person (Gen. xiv. 5; Num. xxi. 23; 1 Sam. viii. 20; xiv. 20), made treaties in behalf of himself and his people (Gen. xxi. 22–32; 1 Kin. xv. 19), enacted laws and executed them (Esth. iii. 12, 13; viii. 7–12; Dan. iii. 4–6, 29; vi. 6–9), exercised judicial functions (2 Sam. xv. 2; Is. xxxiii. 22), and had the power of life and death (2 Sam. xiv. 1–11; 1 Kin. i. 51, 52; ii. 24–34; Esth. iv. 11; vii. 9, 10). The restraints upon the king were the fear of God and man. The popular will might not always be ignored (1 Sam. xiv. 45; xv. 24). The endurance of the people might not be overtaxed with impunity (1 Kin. xii. 4). There were officers of religion, both priests and prophets, who in religious matters were independent of the king and did not hesitate to rebuke misdemeanors (1 Sam. xiii. 10–14; xv. 10–31; 2 Sam. xii. 1–15; 1 Kin. xviii. 17, 18; xxi. 17–22; 2 Chron. xxvi. 16–21). But a despotic king sometimes broke through these restraints (1 Sam. xiii. 17–19; 1 Kin. xii. 13–16; Jer. xxvi. 20–23. In view of the royal duties and prerogatives, the king required physical, mental, and moral qualities of a high order to rule well.

Physical superiority is appreciated the moment it becomes visible. Thus, when Saul was presented to his future subjects, and they saw him tower head and shoulders above all the multitude present, they raised the shout, "God save the king" (1 Sam. x. 23, 24; cp. also xvi. 7). In order to be an able judge the king must be a man of penetration, able to disentangle truth from falsehood, and punish, not the innocent, but the guilty. This is the reason why there was such emotion among the Israelites when Solomon, trying his first case, that of the two women and the child, so signally detected where the truth and where the falsehood lay (1 Kin. iii. 23; cp. Is. xi. 1–9). But penetration was not enough; the moral element was requisite to make the sovereign give, without fear or favor, the verdict which he considered just. For the protection of his person and assistance in the discharge of his duties the king had a bodyguard, the captain of which generally acted as executioner (2 Sam. xv. 18; xx. 23 with 1 Kin. ii. 25, 29); see GUARD. Wealthy kings had magnificent palaces, surrounded themselves with luxury, and lived in state (1 Kin. x). See also SEPULCHER.

God is compared to a king possessed of unlimited power, and using it under the influence of supreme beneficence (Ps. v. 2; x. 16). He is the King of kings (1 Tim. vi. 15). Christ is a king. He called himself so, but explained that his kingdom is not of this world (John xviii. 33–38). He also is the King of kings (Rev. xix. 16).

King'dom.

1. The territory or the people ruled over by a king (2 Kin. xv. 19).

2. The sovereign rule of God over the universe (1 Chron. xxix. 11; Ps. xxii. 28; cxlv. 13; Mat. vi. 13).

3. A sovereignty which Daniel predicted God would establish on earth, and which, when once set up, should remain forever. In distinction from the kingdoms of this world, which are exhibited under the figure of beasts, the kingdom of God has for its representative a person like unto a son of man (Dan. vii. 13, 14, R. V.). John the Baptist and our Lord declared that it was at hand (Mat. iii. 2; iv. 17). Jesus taught his disciples to pray for its coming (vi. 10), instructed his apostles on their first mission to say that it was at hand (x. 7), spoke of it afterwards as having come (xii. 28, and illustrated its nature by parables. It is called the kingdom of heaven and the kingdom of God. Matthew prefers the former and Mark and Luke the latter designation (cp. Mat. xiii. 24, 31, 33, 44, 45 with Mark iv. 11, 26, 30; Luke xiv. 15; xvii. 20, etc.). The kingdom is spiritual in character, and no carnal weapons may be used in its establishment (John xviii. 33–37). Commenced on earth with the royal ministry of Christ, it shall be consummated amid the bliss of the eternal world (Mat. xxv. 31–46; Luke xxiii. 42, 43). The kingdom of God is thus the "invisible church." It is the whole spiritual commonwealth of God's children, the true company of all faithful people. It is represented by the organized or visible church, but is more comprehensive and greater than the visible church in any age or all ages.

Kings, Books of the.

The two Books of the Kings were originally one book, but were divided in the Septuagint into two. They are placed among "the prophets" in the Hebrew canon, in that group of Scriptures which, because standing first among the prophets, were known as "former prophets." The writings of the former prophets form a continuous narrative which begins at the death of Moses and ends with the exile. Joshua is the first book in the series and the Books of the Kings are the last. These latter were written to point out the religious teaching of the national history during the period of the kingdom from the accession of Solomon. The author shows the growth and decay of the kingdom, indicates the causes which worked to effect these results, and draws attention to the large part played by forces of a moral and religious character (cp. 2 Kin. xvii.). His narrative covers a period of more than four hundred years, and he is consequently dependent upon former historians for his facts. He draws chiefly from the "book of the chronicles of the kings of Israel" (1 Kin. xiv. 19), down to the death of Pekah, and the "book of the chronicles of the kings of Judah" (29), down to the death of Jehoiakim. It is generally believed that these chronicles were originally, as the titles suggest, two separate works. Probably they were ultimately united into one and constituted the work quoted by the chronicler as the "book of the kings of Judah and Israel" (2 Chron. xvi. 11). These two chronicles contained more than the present Books of the Kings, for the writer of Kings refers his readers to them for further details (1 Kin. xiv. 19, 29), and the chronicler quotes portions which the writer of Kings does not (2 Chron. xxvii. 7; xxxiii. 18). It is commonly held that these two chronicles were not the public annals, but a compilation from several documents. This opinion is based on the fact that writings of various prophets are mentioned as having been inserted in the book of the kings of Israel (2 Chron. xx. 34; cp. xxxii. 32), which could not have been done if the book were the state annals added to from day to day by the royal scribe. The double chronicles were written before the fall of Jerusalem; for the phrase "unto this day" refers, so far as can be determined, invariably to the time when the city and temple were in existence (1 Kin. viii. 8); and if it does not prove that the writer of the present books of the Kings lived before the exile, it at least shows that the writer of the book from which he quotes did. Whether the writer of the present Books of the Kings began the work before the destruction of Jerusalem or not, he did not complete it until after the middle years of the Babylonians exile (2 Kin. xxv. 27). He perhaps finished it before the close of the exile, since the work contains no allusion to the deliverance of the people from Babylon.

The author is chiefly concerned with the history of the Davidic monarchy. Like the author of Genesis, he disposes of subsidiary matters before treating his main theme. In following this method, he records events relating to Israel before giving the contemporaneous history of Judah. This leads him to sometimes narrate the same event in connection with both the northern and the southern kingdoms (1 Kin. xv. 16 with 32 ; 2 Kin. xvii. 5, 6 with xviii. 9).

The work is divided into three parts. I. The reign of Solomon (1 Kin. i.–xi.). II. A synchronistic account of the kingdoms of Judah and Israel until the captivity of Israel (xii.–2 Kin. xvii.). III. The kingdom of Judah until the Babylonian exile.

Kir [wall, fortified town].

1. The place from which the Aramæans migrated to Syria (Amos ix. 7), and to which those of them living in Damascus were carried back again on being conquered by the Assyrians (2 Kin. xvi. 9 ; Amos i. 5). Its inhabitants are represented as arrayed with Elam against Judah (Is. xxii. 6). Not identified. Gesenius' doubtful identification of it with a region called Kur, between the Black and the Caspian seas, is groundless. Nor is Schrader's identification of it with Media probable (cp. Is. xxi. 2 with xxii. 6), for there is no reason for believing that the Aramæans came from Media. Furrer's identification with the district Cyrrhestica, northwest of Antioch, lacks proof.

Kir of Mo'ab.

A fortified city of southern Moab (Is. xv. 1), thought to be Kir-haresheth and Kir-heres (xvi. 7, 11 ; Jer. xlviii. 31, 36 ; in A. V. sometimes Kir-haraseth and Kir-haresh). It was strong enough to resist the combined forces of Israel, Judah, and Edom (2 Kin. iii. 25). Its modern name, traceable back to the Targum, is Kerak. It is 11 miles east from the southern bay of the Dead Sea, south of the Lisan or tongue, and 18 south of the Arnon river. It stands on a triangular hill, at an elevation of 3323 feet above the Mediterranean, on a rocky platform which rises at its southeastern extremity to 3720 feet. Except at one or two spots, the hill is isolated from the neighboring hills by precipices falling sheer down to the deep valleys below. Its weak point for military purposes is that it is commanded by adjacent hills 4050 feet high. Kerak constitutes a triangle from 2400 to 3000 feet on each side. It is entered by two arched tunnels, probably

of Roman age. There are remains of Roman crusading, and Mohammedan times. There is a great castle which was built by king Fulco about A. D. 1131, and which from 1183 to 1188 defied the efforts of Saladin to effect its capture. Kerak was also found impregnable by Ibrahim Pasha in 1841. Its present population is believed to be about 8000, of whom 1600 are Christians.

Kir-har'a-seth, Kir-har'e-seth, Kir-ha'-resh, Kir-he'res [city of bricks or city of pottery]. See KIR OF MOAB.

Kir'i-ath, in A. V. **Kirjath** [city].

A town of Benjamin (Josh. xviii. 28), sometimes identified with Kirjath-jearim.

Kir-i-a-tha'im, in A. V. sometimes **Kirja-tha'im** [twin cities].

1. An ancient city of the Emim (Gen. xiv. 5), rebuilt by the Reubenites (Num. xxxii. 37 ; Josh. xiii. 19), which afterwards fell into the hands of the Moabites (Moabite Stone 10 ; Jer. xlviii. 1, 23 ; Ezek. xxv. 9). It is believed that its site was at Kureiyât, north of the Arnon, and $2\frac{1}{2}$ miles south by east of Ataroth. The ruins are on two hills.

2. The same as Kartan (q. v.) (1 Chron. vi. 76).

Kir-i-ath-ar'ba, in A. V. **Kirjath-arba** [city of Arba, or perhaps, city of the croucher].

An old name for the city of Hebron, pointing to the fact that it was the city of Arba, or the Arba, father of Anak. Perhaps he was its founder (Gen. xxiii. 2 ; Josh. xiv. 15 : xv. 13, 54 ; xx. 7 ; xxi. 11 ; Judg. i. 10). The old name was not obsolete even in the time of Nehemiah (Neh. xi. 25). See HEBRON.

Kir-i-ath-a'rim, in A. V. **Kirjath-arim**. See KIRIATH-JEARIM.

Kir-i-ath-ba'al, in A. V. **Kirjath-baal** [city of Baal]. See KIRIATH-JEARIM.

Kir-i-ath-hu'zoth, in A. V. **Kirjath-huzoth** [city of streets].

A Moabite town near Bamoth-baal (Num. xxii. 39, 41). It may have been the same as Kiriathaim.

Kir-i-ath-je'a-rim, in A. V. **Kirjath-jearim** [city of woods or forests].

A town belonging originally to the Gibeonites (Josh. ix. 17). It was on the western part of the boundary line between the tribes of Judah and Benjamin (Josh. xv. 9 ; xviii. 14, 15), but pertained to Judah, being considered a town belonging to the hill country of the latter tribe (xv. 48, 60 ; Judg. xviii. 12). After the ark had been returned to the Israelites by the Philistines, it remained in safe custody in Kiriath-jearim for the next twenty years, until the second battle of Ebenezer, and longer (1 Sam. vi. 19–vii. 2). Some of its population returned from captivity (Neh. vii. 29 ; in Ezra ii. 25 the name appears as Kiriath-arim). It was called also Kiriath-baal (Josh. xv. 60 ; xviii. 14), Baalah (xv. 9, 11), or Baale (2 Sam. vi. 2 ; cp. 1 Chron. xiii. 6).

Eusebius states that it was situated 9 or 10 Roman miles from Jerusalem on the road to Diospolis, *i. e.* Lydda, and accordingly it is commonly identified with Kuriet el-'Enab, 7 miles west by north of Jerusalem. Conder argues for the ruins 'Erma, 11 miles west by south of Jerusalem, and 2¼ south by west of Kesla. But contrary to his opinion, Josh xv. 10 is surely against the location proposed by him. 'Erma and Jearim are also radically different, and the site is too remote from the other Gibeonite settlements.

Kir-i-ath-san'nah, in A. V. **Kirjath-sannah.** See DEBIR.

Kir-i-ath-se'pher, in A. V. **Kirjath-sepher.** See DEBIR.

Kir'i-oth. See KERIOTH.

Kir'jath. See KIRIATH.

Kir-jath-ar'ba, etc. See KIRIATH-ARBA, etc.

Kish, in A. V. of N. T. Cis, in imitation of the Greek.

1. A Benjamite, son of Jeiel (1 Chron. viii. 30; ix. 35, 36).

2. A Benjamite, father of king Saul and son of Abiel (1 Sam. ix. 1), but also registered as a son of Ner and a descendant of Jeiel of Gibeon (1 Chron. viii. 33; ix. 36, 39). This latter genealogy may indeed merely register the fact that Kish was a descendant of Ner, without implying that he was his immediate son; and allow of the insertion of Abiel and others between Kish and Ner.

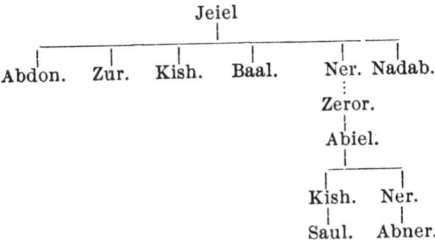

Jeiel

Abdon. Zur. Kish. Baal. Ner. Nadab.

Zeror.

Abiel.

Kish. Ner.

Saul. Abner.

But perhaps only one Kish and one Ner descended from Jeiel. If so, the explanation of the genealogy is that Ner's descendants became two tribal houses, those of Kish and Ner. The former, the important royal family of Saul, looked to Ner's son Kish as its founder; but it was merely a younger branch of the older, but less distinguished, line of Ner. Both houses belonged to the family of Jeiel, and hence Kish as well as Ner is registered, according to the familiar principle, among Jeiel's sons (ix. 36). Saul's father, Kish, and Abner's father, Ner, are mentioned as sons of Abiel also (1 Sam. ix. 1; xiv. 51), and either Ner or Abner is stated to have been Saul's uncle (xiv. 50). Abiel may be, as some expositors suppose, or may not be, another name or the uncorrupted form of Jeiel.

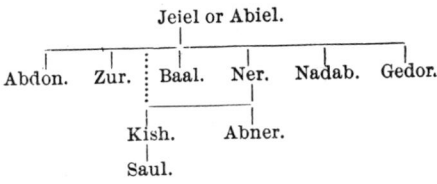

Jeiel or Abiel.

Abdon. Zur. Baal. Ner. Nadab. Gedor.

Kish. Abner.

Saul.

3. A Levite, in David's time, of the family of Merari, house of Mahli (1 Chron. xxiii. 21, 22; xxiv. 29).

4. A Levite, family of Merari and son of Abdi, who aided in the revival under Hezekiah (2 Chron. xxix. 12).

5. A Benjamite, an ancestor of Mordecai (Esth. ii. 5).

Kish'i. See KUSHAIAH.

Kish'i-on, in A. V. once **Kishon** (Josh. xxi. 28) [hardness].

A border town of Issachar (Josh. xix. 20), given to the Gershonite Levites (xxi. 28). In 1 Chron. vi. 72 Kedesh appears in its stead, probably by a copyist's error. Site unknown.

Ki'shon, in A. V. once **Kison** (Ps. lxxxiii. 9) [bending, curving, tortuous].

1. The most important river of Palestine next to the Jordan. "That ancient river, the river Kishon" swept away the soldiers of Sisera's beaten army when they fled northward from Taanach and attempted to cross the stream (Judg. v. 19-21; Ps. lxxxiii. 9). The priests of Baal who had the contest with Elijah were slain on its southern bank (1 Kin. xviii. 40). It is now called the Nahr el-Mukutta'. Conder and Kitchener state that its real source is near Khurbet el-Mezrah and the springs called el-Mujahiyah, the place of bursting forth of water. From this spot, which is only a little west of Beth-shean, a series of pools extends, and then a continuous stream. As the name Kishon implies, the river is tortuous, making great curves as it proceeds in a generally northwesterly direction through the plain of Esdraelon. It looks an insignificant stream, of 15 or 18 feet across, but has treacherous banks, and a muddy bottom, so much so that when the Turks and Arabs were defeated by the French in the battle of mount Tabor, on April 16, 1799, the fate of the vanquished host was the same as that of Sisera's army. Toward Harosheth of the gentiles, Jabin's city, the Kishon runs through a narrow gorge under the cliffs which constitute the northern side of mount Carmel, the water at one place being nearly hidden by oleander bushes. Then the stream enters the plain of Acre. Sand dunes, dotted with palm trees, interfere with it in the latter part of its course; and it is only when full of water that it can overcome the obstacle, and make a proper entrance into the Mediterranean.

2. A town, so spelled in A. V. See KISHION.

Kiss.

A salutation, common in the Orient from

patriarchal times onward, between persons of the same sex and to a limited extent between individuals of different sexes. Fathers and mothers kissed their children and descendants (Gen. xxxi. 28, 55; xlviii. 10; 2 Sam. xiv. 33, etc.), and children their parents (Gen. xxvii. 26, 27; l. 1; 1 Kin. xix. 20). Brother and sister kissed each other (Song viii. 1), and brother kissed brother (Gen. xlv. 15; Ex. iv. 27). So did other relatives and kinsfolk (Gen. xxix. 11; Ex. xviii. 7; Ruth i. 9). Comrades kissed each other; so did friends (1 Sam. xx. 41; 2 Sam. xix. 39; xx. 9; Acts xx. 37). In the time of our Lord, a guest invited to a house expected on entering to be kissed by his entertainer (Luke vii. 45). It was in these circumstances that Christians were enjoined to salute each other with a holy kiss (Rom. xvi. 16; 1 Cor. xvi. 20; 2 Cor. xiii. 12; 1 Thes. v. 26), or with a kiss of love (1 Pet. v. 14), symbolical of Christian brotherhood. As kissing between friends, guests, and entertainers lapsed, the salutation enjoined by the apostle fell also into desuetude. In all the foregoing cases a kiss was, or at least professed to be, an expression of love. It therefore added to the baseness of Judas' treachery that he had not merely betrayed his Lord, but did so by means of a kiss (Mat. xxvi. 48, 49; Luke xxii. 47, 48; cp. Prov. xxvii. 6). In all love there is a greater or less amount of respect. The feet of kings were kissed in token of great respect and to tender allegiance (Ps. ii. 12), and the same idea was involved in the kiss given to idols (1 Kin. xix. 18; Hos. xiii. 2). A kiss was sometimes thrown by the hand to the idol (Job xxxi. 27). When women kissed the feet of our Lord, it indicated the unbounded respect and affection which they felt for his character and work (Luke vii. 38, 45).

Kite.

A bird of prey of the falcon family, with long, pointed wings and usually long, forked tail. The word is used in R. V. to render the Hebrew *Da'ah* and *Dayyah* (Lev. xi. 14; Deut. xiv. 13; Is. xxxiv. 15; in A. V. vulture) and twice in A. V. to render *'Ayyah* (Lev. xi. 14; Deut. xiv. 13; in R. V. falcon). Both birds were ceremonially unclean (Lev. xi. 14). The Hebrew name of the former corresponds to the Arabic *hadayyeh*, vernacular for the kite. It is of various kinds (Deut. xiv. 13). The black kite (*Milvus nigrans*) is found in central and southern Europe, northern Africa, and western Asia. It appears in Palestine in March, gliding noiselessly in the air, looking down for its food, which consists of offal, for, being a somewhat cowardly bird, it does not molest poultry. It breeds in trees, ornamenting its nest with rags of different colors. The black-winged kite (*Elanus cæruleus*) also occurs in Palestine, but is rare.

Kith'lish, in R. V. Chithlish.

A village in the lowland of Judah (Josh. xv. 40). Not identified.

Kit'ron.

A town in the territory of Zebulun, but from which the Canaanites were not driven out (Judg. i. 30). Compare KATTATH.

Kit'tim or Chittim, the latter being the more consistent, and in A. V. more frequent spelling [origin and meaning unknown].

Descendants of Javan, who inhabited Cyprus and other islands and coasts of the eastern Mediterranean (Gen. x. 4; 1 Chron. i. 7; Is. xxiii. 1, 12; Jer. ii. 10; Ezek. xxvii. 6; and Dan. xi. 30, where the language of Num. xxiv. 24 is used; Antiq. i. 6, 1). The name is connected definitely with Cyprus, chiefly through Kition, an ancient town on the southern coast of the island, and through the Kiti, whom Thothmes III. mentions as possessing the island. The name was eventually greatly extended. In 1 Mac. i. 1 Alexander the Great is said to have come out of the land of Chittim, and in viii. 5 Perseus is called king of Chittim, meaning Macedonia.

Knead'ing Trough.

A shallow vessel, usually of wood and

Bronze implements, weapon blades, and knife blades excavated from Megiddo.

portable, in which dough is worked into a well-mixed mass preparatory to baking (Ex. xii. 34). The Egyptians kneaded the dough with their feet (Herod. ii. 36) or with their hands.

Knife.

The Hebrews used a knife which they called *ma'akeleth*, eating instrument, for slaughtering animals for food or sacrifice, and for cutting up the carcass (Gen. xxii. 6; Judg. xix. 29; cp. Lev. viii. 20; ix. 13). Another word, *hereb*, which commonly signifies a sword, denotes a knife made of flint (Josh. v. 2), and perhaps a knife for shaving (Ezek. v. 1; in R. V. sword); see FLINT. The Egyptians also, when embalming a corpse, used a sharp stone knife for making an incision in the body (Herod ii. 86). The Hebrew scribes sharpened the stylus with a small knife (Jer. xxxvi. 23). Herod the Great was accustomed to use a knife for paring fruit, and attempted to kill himself with it (Antiq. xvii. 7, 1).

Knop.

1. The rendering of the Hebrew *Kaphtor* in Ex. xxv. 33–36; xxxvii. 17–22, where it constitutes a part of the candlestick used in the tabernacle. In other passages the Hebrew word apparently denotes the capital of a column (Amos ix. 1; Zeph. ii. 14, both R. V.). It seems to have been some projecting support for the branches of the candlestick, and for the corollas of the ornamental flowers; but its precise nature is unknown. Josephus perhaps states that it represented a pomegranate (Antiq. iii. 6, 7), but his words are not clear.

2. The rendering of the Hebrew *P'ka'im* (1 Kin. vi. 18; vii. 24), an ornament cut in cedar, and associated with open flowers in the woodwork of Solomon's temple. Since the feminine form of the word denotes wild gourds, the R. V. places gourds on the margin of the first passage, as if the ornament was shaped like a gourd.

Ko'a.

A people named between Babylonians and Assyrians (Ezek. xxiii. 23), located by Friedrich Delitzsch east of the Tigris, south of the lower Zab.

Ko'hath [perhaps, assembly].

A son of Levi and founder of the great Kohathite family (Gen. xlvi. 11; Ex. vi. 16, 18).

Ko'hath-ite.

A member of the great Levite family founded by Kohath. This was subdivided into the families or houses of the Amramites, the Izharites, the Hebronites, and the Uzzielites (Ex. vi. 18; Num. iii. 27). Moses and Aaron were of the Kohathite family (Ex. vi. 20). The Kohathites pitched on the south side of the tabernacle in the wilderness (Num. iii. 29). When the priests had covered the sanctuary and its vessels, the Kohathites carried them, but were not to touch

any holy thing, lest they should die (iv. 15, 17–20; 2 Chron. xxxiv. 12). At the first census in the wilderness, the Kohathite males from a month old and upward were 8600 (Num. iii. 28), and those from thirty to fifty years old 2750 (iv. 34–37). In the subsequent allotment of cities to the family, the priests, the descendants of Aaron, had shares with the other Kohathites, the former obtaining thirteen cities out of the tribes of Judah, Simeon, and Benjamin, and the latter ten cities out of the tribes of Ephraim, Dan, and Manasseh (Josh. xxi. 4, 5; 1 Chron. vi. 61, 66–70).

Ko-la'iah [voice of Jehovah].

1. Father of the false prophet Ahab (Jer. xxix. 21).

2. A Benjamite (Neh. xi. 7).

Koph, in A. R. V. **Qoph.**

The nineteenth letter of the Hebrew alphabet. English Q comes from the same source; but in anglicized Hebrew names c or k represents it, as in Cain and Korah. It heads the nineteenth section of Ps. cxix., in which section each verse of the original begins with this letter.

Ko'rah, in A. V. once **Kore** (1 Chron. xxvi. 19) and once **Core** (Jude 11) [ice, baldness].

1. A son of Esau by his wife Oholibamah, born in Canaan (Gen. xxxvi. 5, 14), who founded a tribe which dwelt in Edom and was ruled by a chieftain (18).

2. A son of Eliphaz and grandson of Esau (Gen. xxxvi. 16). But the name has crept into the text erroneously, not being found in ver. 11, 12 or 1 Chron. i. 36.

3. A son of Hebron (1 Chron. ii. 43). See MARESHAH 2.

4. A Levite, family of Kohath, house of Izhar (Num. xvi. 1). In conjunction with the Reubenites Dathan, Abiram, and On he rebelled against Moses and Aaron. He was jealous that Aaron, a Levite of the same family as he and only his equal in rank, should have the office of priest for all Israel. The Reubenites were discontented because the leadership in Israel, which belonged to Reuben as the firstborn of Jacob, was possessed by the tribe of Levi, represented by Moses and Aaron. At length Korah and his company, sons of Levi (7), who formed a large portion of the conspirators, but not all of them, for at least Dathan and Abiram were absent (12), assembled against Moses and Aaron, publicly charged them with usurping the supremacy over the tribes, and claimed that all the congregation was holy and that any one might officiate as a priest (3). Moses replied that God would himself decide the matter, and he bade Korah and his company provide themselves with censers and be ready to offer incense on the morrow (6–11). Moses sent word to Dathan and Abiram to appear likewise on the morrow, but they refused on the ground that Moses had no right to summon

them (12–15). Moses then turned to Korah, saying: " Be thou and all thy company present with censers, two hundred and fifty censers besides those of yourself and Aaron " (16–17). They did so, assembling at the tabernacle (18). Korah gathered also the whole congregation of Israel there and incited them against Moses and Aaron (19). God directed Moses and Aaron to separate themselves from the multitude that it might be destroyed, but Moses interceded for the people (20–22). Moses was then directed to bid the congregation remove from the district in the camp occupied by Korah, Dathan, and Abiram (24). It will be remembered that the division of the Levites to which Korah belonged were accustomed to pitch on the south of the tabernacle in immediate proximity to the tribe of Reuben ; see CAMP. Accordingly, followed by the elders of Israel, and certainly also by Korah, Moses went to the locality where the tents of Korah, Dathan, and Abiram were pitched and warned the congregation to leave the district (25, 26). The people obeyed. Dathan and Abiram, together with their families, appeared at the door of their tents (27). The earth opened and swallowed them up with their households and Korah with his servants (32, 33 ; xxvi. 10). The sons of Korah, however, were not destroyed (11). After the earthquake fire devoured the two hundred and fifty men that offered incense (xvi. 35 ; cp. 40). See KORHITE.

Ko'rah-ite and **Ko'rath-ite.** See KORHITE.

Ko're [a partridge].

1. The rebellious Levite, founder of a house (1 Chron. xxvi. 19) ; see KORAH 4.

2. A Levite of the house of Korah (1 Chron. ix. 19 ; xxvi. 1).

3. A Levite, son of Imnah, appointed over the freewill offerings during the reign of Hezekiah (2 Chron. xxxi. 14).

Kor'hite, in R. V. everywhere and in A. V. twice **Korahite,** and in A. V. once **Korathite.**

A descendant of that Korah who was swallowed up in the wilderness as a punishment for his rebellion. The Korhites constituted a father's house among the Kohathites. Heman the singer and Samuel the prophet were Korhites (1 Chron. vi. 33–38). The descendants of Heman were organized by David as singers (xv. 17 ; xvi. 41, 42 ; xxv. 4, 5). Psalms xlii. (which probably once included xliii.), xliv.–xlix., lxxxiv., lxxxv., lxxxvii., lxxxviii., bear the name of the family in the title. Korhites were gatekeepers (1 Chron. ix. 19 ; xxvi. 19) and bakers for the sanctuary, preparing the showbread and sacrificial cakes (ix. 31, 32).

Koz. See HAKKOZ.

Ku-sha'iah.

A Levite of the family of Merari, house of Mushi (1 Chron. xv. 17), in vi. 44 called Kishi.

L

La'a-dah [order].

A man of Judah, family of Shelah. He was the father of the inhabitants of Mareshah (1 Chron. iv. 21).

La'a-dan. See LADAN.

La'ban [white].

1. Son of Bethuel, and grandson of Nahor Abraham's brother. He lived at Haran in Paddan-aram (Gen. xxiv. 10, 15 ; xxviii. 5, 10 ; also xxix. 5 ; xxxi. 53). He was the brother of Rebekah. When he saw the valuable presents which Abraham's servant had given Rebekah, he readily allowed her to go to Canaan to become Isaac's wife (Gen. xxiv. 1–67). When Jacob fled from the vengeance of Esau he went to Laban his uncle. He found him the head of a household, father of several sons (xxx. 35 ; xxxi. 1) and at least two daughters (xxix. 16), owner of slaves (24, 29), and the possessor of a flock of sheep and goats (9, xxx. 30 ; xxxi. 38). Jacob remained with him at least twenty years, serving him seven for his daughter Rachel, and then, having Leah handed over to him in a fraudulent way, a second seven to obtain the daughter for whom he really cared, and then six more for cattle. At the end of the twenty years, Jacob, perceiving that his prosperity had excited the enmity of Laban and his sons, fled with his wives, his children, and his cattle, in the direction of Canaan. He was overtaken by Laban in mount Gilead ; but the pursuer, warned by God not to molest Jacob, made a covenant with him, and the two parted to meet no more (Gen. xxix.–xxxi.). Laban worshiped the God of his fathers, the God of Nahor (xxxi. 53), Jehovah (xxiv. 50 ; xxx. 27) ; but he combined idolatry with his worship, making use of household gods called teraphim (xxxi. 30 ; cp. xxxv. 4) and practicing divination (xxx. 27, R. V.).

2. An unidentified place in the Sinaitic peninsula (Deut. i. 1). It is mentioned with Hazeroth ; hence some have thought that it may have been the same as Libnah, the second station from Hazeroth (Num. xxxiii. 20).

La'chish [perhaps, tenacious, difficult to capture].

A fortified city in the lowland of Judah (Josh. xv. 33, 39). At the time of the conquest of Palestine, its king was defeated and slain by Joshua (x. 3–35 ; xii. 11). Rehoboam strengthened its defenses (2 Chron. xi. 9). Amaziah, king of Judah, having fled thither from conspirators at Jerusalem, was pursued and slain in the town (2 Kin. xiv. 19 ; 2 Chron. xxv. 27). Lachish was besieged by Sennacherib, king of Assyria ; and it was from the camp in front of it that the rabshakeh was dispatched to demand the surrender of Jerusalem (2 Kin. xviii. 14, 17 ; cp. xix. 2, and 2 Chron. xxxii. 9 ; Is. xxxvi. 2 ; xxxvii. 8). Lachish is charged with being the beginning

Modern Tell el Duweir, the fortified city of Lachish.

of sin to the daughter of Zion, for the transgressions of Israel were found in her (Mic. i. 13). Nebuchadnezzar again besieged Lachish, with other fenced cities of Judah (Jer. xxxiv. 7). It was inhabited after the captivity (Neh. xi. 30). The site is found at Tell el-Hesy, 16 miles east by north of Gaza and 11 miles west-southwest of Beit Jibrin. Excavation has laid bare the wall of the ancient city, as well as later constructions believed to belong to the times of Rehoboam, Asa, Jehoshaphat, Uzziah, Jotham, and Manasseh. Ten towns seem to have occupied the place in succession. The lowest is called Amorite, and is reported to be about a quarter of a mile square. It was built on a bluff, about 60 feet above the stream which flowed on the east, and 40 feet above the level country on the north. A ravine protected it on the south, and another on the west. The northern wall of the town stood on the edge of the bluff. It was about 8 feet thick, with a great tower at the northeastern corner, 56 by 28 feet, with rooms about 10 feet square, enclosed by a wall 9 or 10 feet thick. Other later walls, at least twice as thick, were erected before the conquest of Canaan by the Hebrews. Flint, copper, bronze, and iron implements, with bronze weapons and large quantities of pottery have been unearthed. There were also two inscriptions found, one in old Hebrew characters, the other in cuneiform. The latter dates from about the fifteenth century B. C., and conveys the information that the king then ruling at Lachish was called Zimrida.

La'dan, in A. V. **Laadan** [well ordered].
1. An Ephraimite in the ancestry of Joshua (1 Chron. vii. 26).
2. A Gershonite in whom several fathers' houses had their origin (1 Chron. xxiii. 7–9; xxvi. 21).

La'el [devoted to God].
A Gershonite, father of Eliasaph (Num. iii. 24).

La'had [oppressed, oppression].
A son of Jahath, a man of Judah (1 Chron. iv. 2).

La-hai'-roi. See BEER-LAHAI-ROI.

Lah'mam, in R. V. margin, **Lahmas**.
A village in the lowland of Judah (Josh. xv. 40), thought to be possibly marked by the ruined village of el-Lahm, 2½ miles south of Beit Jibrin.

Lah'mi.
The brother of Goliath the Gittite. He was slain by Elhanan the son of Jair (1 Chron. xx. 5). The word Lahmi, however, corresponds to the last part of the Hebrew word for Bethlehemite in 2 Sam. xxi. 19. One or other text is corrupt. See ELHANAN.

La'ish [a lion].
1. A man of Gallim, father of Palti (1 Sam. xxv. 44).
2. A Canaanite city in the extreme north of Palestine, "in the valley that lieth by Beth-rehob." The Danites captured the city, and rebuilt it, altering the name to Dan (Judg. xviii. 7–29). See DAN 3.
3. A village (Is. x. 30). See LAISHAH.

La'i-shah, in A. V. **Laish** [a lion].
A village in Benjamin between Gallim and Anathoth (Is. x. 30).

Lak'kum, in A. V. **La'kum** [obstruction].
A town of Naphtali (Josh. xix. 33). Site unknown.

Lamb.
The flesh of lambs was early used as food (Lev. iii. 7 with vii. 15 ; 2 Sam. xii. 4 ; Amos vi. 4) ; and lambs and kids were largely offered in sacrifice even before the promulga-

tion of the Mosaic law (Gen. iv. 4; xxii. 7). When the passover was instituted in Egypt, a lamb or a kid of the first year was sacrificed and eaten (Ex. xii. 3, 5). Under the Mosaic law a male lamb of the first year was offered for a burnt offering every morning and another every evening, while on the Sabbath there were two (Ex. xxix. 39–41; Num. xxviii. 4). On the first day of each month (Num. xxviii. 11), during the seven days of the passover (16, 19), at the feast of weeks (26, 27), on the day of blowing of trumpets (xxix. 1, 2), and on the day of atonement (7, 8), seven male lambs of the first year formed part of the special burnt offering; while at the feast of tabernacles the lambs numbered fourteen during each of the first seven days and seven on the eighth day (13–36). For all the principal sacrifices of ordinary occasions a lamb might be used; as a male lamb for a burnt offering (Lev. ix. 3; xxiii. 12, 18; Num. vi. 14; vii. 15), a ewe lamb for a sin offering for others than the nation or rulers (Lev. iv. 27, 32; Num. vi. 14), and a male or female lamb for a guilt offering (Lev. v. 6; xiv. 12, 21; Num. vi. 12) or for a peace offering (Lev. iii. 6, 7; xxiii. 19; Num. vii. 17). In every case the lamb must be without blemish. All this points to our Lord. He resembled a lamb in his spotless purity (1 Pet. i. 19). He was like a lamb also in his gentleness and in his submission to unmerited suffering without murmur or complaint (Is. liii. 7 with Luke xxiii. 25; Acts viii. 32; 1 Pet. ii. 21–23). Finally, he, like a lamb, was sacrificed for guilt not his own. Hence he is called the Lamb of God, which taketh away the sin of the world (John i. 29, 36), the Lamb slain from the foundation of the world (Rev. xiii. 8), or simply the Lamb (Rev. v. 6, 8, 12; vii. 14, 17; xiv. 1, 4). Both in the O. T. and in the N. T. the term lamb is at times used figuratively for child (Is. xl. 11; John xxi. 15).

La′mech [possibly, a strong young man].
1. A son of Methusael, of the race of Cain. He had two wives, Adah and Zillah. By Adah he was the father of Jabal and Jubal, and by Zillah he had a son, Tubal-cain, and a daughter, Naamah. His address to his wives, in its Hebrew reproduction, is a fine specimen of Hebrew poetry. There are two principal interpretations of Gen. iv. 23. 1. Lamech declares himself a murderer, saying: "I have slain a man." Stung by remorse, he confesses the rebuke of conscience. He had slain another to his own wounding and hurt. Or else he excuses himself for a murder committed in self-defense, having slain a man for wounding him. 2. Lamech utters a threat: "I will slay any man who wounds me," his words being a song of exultation on the invention of the sword by his son Tubal-cain, sung in anticipation of the advantage he would have in avenging wrongs done to him. The attempt has been made to

explain the poem as simply an expression of Lamech's determination to put the new weapon to its lawful use; but expositors quite generally agree that Lamech is vaunting himself. If Cain, who slew a man, is under God's protection and shall be avenged sevenfold should one dare to slay him, surely Lamech with the new weapon, a visible and surer defense, shall be avenged seventy and sevenfold (Gen. iv. 18–24).
2. An antediluvian patriarch of the race of Seth. He was son of Methuselah and father of Noah. He feared the Lord, rested in God's promise for the removal of the curse of sin, and on the birth of his son Noah gave expression to the hope that this child would lead men to a better and a happier life under God's blessing, saying: "This same shall comfort us for our work and for the toil of our hands, because of the ground which the Lord hath cursed" (Gen. v. 25, 28–31).

La′med, in A. R. V. **Lamedh.**
The twelfth letter of the Hebrew alphabet. English L comes from the same source, and represents it in anglicized Hebrew names. It stands at the head of the twelfth section of Ps. cxix., in which section each verse of the original begins with this letter.

Lam-en-ta′tions.
Mournful speeches or compositions, elegies such as the lament of David over Saul and Jonathan (2 Sam. i 17–27).
The Lamentations of Jeremiah are an O. T. book placed in the English Bible between Jeremiah and Ezekiel, but in the Hebrew Scriptures among the Hagiographa or Sacred Writings, between Ruth and Ecclesiastes. Let the English reader take note of the fact that of the five chapters of Lamentations. i., ii., iv., and v. have each twenty-two verses, and iii. $22 \times 3 = 66$. There are twenty-two distinct letters in the Hebrew alphabet, and in chapters i., ii., and iv. the verses are arranged alphabetically, verse 1 beginning with aleph, verse 2 with beth, verse 3 with gimel, and verse 4 with daleth, and so on to the end. In chap. iii. the first three verses begin with aleph, the second three with beth, and so on to the end. However, in chapters ii.–iv. the order of the letters ain and pe is not the same as in chap. i. and Ps. cxix., but is reversed, pe preceding ain. The fifth chapter has not an alphabetical arrangement. The theme of the whole five elegies or lamentations is the capture and destruction of the Jewish capital, with dreadful suffering to its defenders by famine, the sword, and outrage of every kind. The catastrophe, it is admitted, was brought on by the sins of the people, not omitting even the prophets and the priests. In various places the Jewish state is personified as a man, and bemoans its hard fate (i. 9, 11, 12–22; ii. 18–22), or the prophet, as representing the nation, speaks in the first person (ii. 11; iii. 1–51, and also

52-66). Notwithstanding that this book is anonymous, in the Hebrew being named only by its first word " How," notwithstanding also that it is arranged among the Hagiographa, critics, even of rationalistic tendencies, attribute the first four chapters to Jeremiah ; the fifth or non-alphabetical chapter may, they think, possibly have come from another author. In the Septuagint the following statement is prefixed to the book : " And it came to pass after Israel was led into captivity and Jerusalem laid waste, that Jeremiah sat weeping and lamented this lamentation over Jerusalem, and said." The ascription of the book to the prophet is thus ancient ; and it has been commonly, though not without exception, assigned to him by both ancient and modern scholars, the admission being general that the elegies must have been written in or near the times of Jeremiah. The prophet lamented for Josiah (2 Chron. xxxv. 25). If his elegies on the subject were committed to writing, they have been lost, and are not our present book of Lamentations.

Lamp.

A vessel designed to contain an inflammable liquid, which it is proposed to burn for illuminating purposes, and a wick to lift the liquid by capillary attraction to feed the flame (Herod. ii. 62). The seven lamps of the golden candlestick of the tabernacle and temple were made of gold (Ex. xxxvii. 23; 1 Kin. vii. 49) and burned olive oil (Ex. xxvii. 20). Tongs were used to trim the wick, and dishes to receive the snuff (xxv. 38). The ordinary lamp for domestic use was made of earthenware. It might have a cover which

Ancient lamps used in the Near East.

was either removable or made of one piece with the rest of the lamp. Near the center of the cover or top was a hole for in-

troducing the oil. There was another opening at the margin of the cover, or else a sprout, for the wick.

The Hebrew word regularly rendered lamp is *Ner*. It is translated light in 2 Sam. xxi. 17, A. V., and candle in Jer. xxv. 10 and Zeph. i. 12. In the latter passage, R. V. places lamp on the margin ; and everywhere else in both O. and N. T., except in these two passages, R. V. substitutes the word lamp in the text where A. V. has candle. The Hebrew word *Lappid* is also often rendered lamp in O. T. ; for example, Judg. vii. 16, 20, A. V. ,and Is. lxii. 1 ; Dan. x. 6. But it is of more general meaning. It is translated firebrand in Judg. xv. 4 ; and torch in Nah. ii. 4 ; Zech. xii. 6 ; and in R. V. of Gen. xv. 17 ; Judg. vii. 16, 20 ; and lightning in Ex. xx. 18. The Greek word rendered lamp in Mat. xxv. 1 and Rev. iv. 5 is translated lights in Acts xx. 8, and torches in John xviii. 3 and margin of R. V. of Mat. xxv. 1.

The extinction of the lamp of anyone means figuratively the destruction of his family (Prov. xiii. 9). At Gezer a lamp enclosed in a double bowl takes the place of the infant in a jar so frequently buried under the high place during the Amorite period as a sacrifice.

Lan'cet. See SPEAR.

Lan'guage. See TONGUE.

Lan'tern.

Lanterns were carried by the band of Roman soldiers who were sent with Judas to arrest Jesus (John xviii. 3). The Romans made the sides of lanterns out of bladder or plates of translucent horn.

La-od-i-ce'a [pertaining to Laodice].

A city called originally Diospolis, city of Zeus, which was enlarged and improved by Antiochus II., and named by him Laodicea, after his wife Laodice. It was the chief city of Phrygia Pacatiana, in Asia Minor, and was situated a little south of Colossæ and Hierapolis, on the river Lycos, a tributary of the Meander. It manufactured cloth and garments from the black wool produced by a breed of sheep in its vicinity ; and it was the seat of a medical school, whose physicians prepared the Phrygian powder for the cure of ophthalmia. It numbered many Jews among its inhabitants (Antiq. xiv. 10, 20). Epaphras labored there (Col. iv. 12, 13), and is regarded as the founder of its Christian church. Paul felt greatly desirous of spiritually benefiting the Laodiceans (ii. 1). He sent them salutations; and he wrote a letter, of which perhaps a copy only was left at Laodicea (iv. 15, 16). It is believed to be the letter known as the Epistle to the Ephesians. Laodicea was one of the seven churches in Asia addressed in the book of Revelation. It is sharply rebuked (Rev. i. 11; iii. 14–22), and the words in which the rebuke is couched contain allusions to the products and the wealth for which the city was noted. About the year 65 of the Christian era, Laodicea, Colossæ, and Hierapolis were destroyed by an earthquake. The citizens rebuilt Laodicea out of their own resources, without the customary aid from Rome. Its ruins still exist at a place called Eski Hissar, near Denizlu, about 56 miles east-southeast of Smyrna.

Lap'pi-doth, in A. V. **Lapidoth** [torches]. Husband of Deborah the prophetess (Judg. iv. 4).

Lap'wing.

The rendering of the Hebrew *Dukiphath* in A. V. of Lev. xi. 19; Deut. xiv. 18. The lapwing (*Vanellus cristatus*), a member of the sub-family *Charadriinæ*, or true plovers, is found in flocks in winter in Palestine. R. V., following the Septuagint and Vulgate, substitutes the hoopoe (*Upupa epops*), the type of the *Upupidæ*, a family of fissirostral birds (birds with deeply cleft bills). The hoopoe is a bird about a foot long, grayish-brown above, with the wings and shoulders black, barred with white, and a large crest of feathers upon the head. It is found in central and southern Europe, in Asia, and in northern and central Africa. Tristram says that it appears in Palestine in March, spreading in small parties over the whole country. On the approach of winter it makes a short migration to Egypt and the Sahara.

La-se'a.

A seaport of Crete, near the Fair Havens, passed by the vessel which carried Paul (Acts xxvii. 8). In 1856 the Rev. G. Brown discovered ruins which mark the supposed site on the southern coast about 5 miles east of the Fair Havens.

La'sha [a fissure].

A place mentioned with the cities of the plain (Gen. x. 19). Jerome says it was at Callirrhoe, a ravine east of the Dead Sea, notable for its hot springs, which were visited by Herod the Great during his last illness. The gorge in which they rise is so narrow that it may quite appropriately be called a fissure. There is not room enough in it for a village of ordinary size. The stream from Callirrhoe, now called the Zerka Ma'in, enters the Dead Sea at the eastern side, about 11 miles in a direct line from the mouth of the Jordan. The springs are about 3 miles up the stream.

Las-sha'ron, in A. V. **Lasharon** [probably, to Sharon].

A town whose king was one of those slain by Joshua (Josh. xii. 18). The Hebrew text may, however, be read king over Sharon. The indications of the Septuagint are that the original text of the verse was "the king of Aphek [which belongs] to Sharon."

Las'the-nes [probably, very strong].

A Cretan who raised an army of mercenary soldiers for Demetrius II., by which the latter effected a landing in Cilicia and set up the standard of revolt against Alexander Balas (Antiq. xiii. 4, 3). He was rewarded with high office, perhaps the governorship of Cœlesyria. Demetrius calls him kinsman and father (1 Mac. xi. 31, in A. V. cousin; 32). The latter title implies that he was a man of considerable age; the former means either that he was related to Demetrius, or that he held a high position at court. He was notified by letter of the terms of peace agreed upon between Demetrius and Jonathan Maccabæus, and of the concessions made to the Jews (32–37).

Latch'et.

The thong with which the sandal was bound to the foot (Is. v. 27; Mark i. 7; cp. Gen. xiv. 23).

Lat'in.

The language spoken by the Romans. Though from the first century B. C. on for some hundred years the supreme power in Palestine was in the hands of the Romans, whose vernacular language was Latin, yet it did not root itself in that country. A few words only were adopted, as *prætorium* and *centurio*, which are written in Greek letters in Mark xv. 16, 39, 45. But since Latin was the language of the Roman officials, the inscription over the cross of Christ was written in Latin as well as in Greek and Aramaic (John xix. 20).

Lat'tice.

A network formed of crossed laths and covering a window (Judg. v. 28; Prov. vii. 6, in A. V. casement; 2 Kin. i. 2; Song ii. 9.)

La'ver.

A basin or trough in which to wash. A laver of brass or copper was used in connec-

Laver.

tion with the tabernacle services. It stood upon a base of brass in the court between the altar and the door of the tabernacle. Both laver and base were made of the mirrors given by the women who assembled to minister at the door of the tent of meeting (Ex. xxxviii. 8 ; cp. xxxiii. 7). Women served at the door of the tabernacle (1 Sam. ii. 22, R. V.), as did the Levites (Num. iv. 23 ; viii. 24). They probably came at stated intervals, as did the Levites and priests (Deut. xviii. 6 ; Luke i. 8, 23), to render various kinds of service, such as the performance of sacred dances and instrumental and vocal music (Ex. xv. 20 ; Judg. xxi. 21 ; Ps. lxviii. 25). The priests washed their hands and their feet in the laver before ministering at the altar or entering the sanctuary (Ex. xxx. 17–21 ; Lev. viii. 11). This ceremony symbolized the holiness that is required in the service of God. In Solomon's temple there were a molten sea and ten lavers instead of one (1 Kin. vii. 23–26, 38–40, 43). Some of the arrangements were afterwards altered by Ahaz (2 Kin. xvi. 17).

Law.

Of the several meanings which the word law possesses, two are employed in Scripture.

1. A uniformly acting force which determines the regular sequence of events ; any uniformly acting influence or motive which controls the will (Rom. vii. 23).

2. A rule of conduct enjoined by a competent authority and, if need be, enforced by penalties. This is the principal meaning of the word in Scripture. Many laws have commenced as customs, which, arising naturally in the intercourse between members of the same society, ultimately gained such acceptance that the community finally resolved to enforce them as laws. But a law may be imposed by a ruler, human or divine, without any reference to previous custom or legislation. In the English version law is mainly the rendering of Hebrew *Torah*, instruction, Aramaic *Dath*, perhaps meaning established, and Greek *Nomos*, custom, law ; and it denotes, except as noted under 1, an authoritative rule of conduct whether revealed from within or from without. It may be imposed by the constituted authorities of the state, which are ordained of God (Ezra vii. 26 ; Esth. i. 19 ; Dan. vi. 8), or proceed immediately from God, being revealed in a supernatural manner audibly as at Sinai or through the Spirit to prophets (Zech. vii. 12) or made known in the constitution of our nature (Rom. ii. 14, 15). They who fear God and keep his commandments are wise ; and the godly wisdom which they have acquired from the study of the written law, from observation of the human heart, and from a life of holiness, when given forth in instruction is the law of the wise which is a fountain of life (Prov. xiii. 14), and when taught by parents to children is the law of father and mother which to them that obey is

a chaplet of grace about the head (Prov. i. 8, 9).

The term "the law" with the definite article, but without any other qualifying word, occasionally refers to the whole O. T. in general (John xii. 34 ; 1 Cor. xiv. 21 ; cp. John x. 34 ; xv. 25), but it is employed much more frequently as the title of the Pentateuch (Josh. i. 8 ; Neh. viii. 2, 3, 14 ; Mat. v. 17 ; vii. 12 ; Luke xvi. 16 ; John i. 17). The law of Moses was given by God through Moses (Ex. xx. 19–22 ; Mat. xv. 4 ; John i. 17). It is the law of God (Josh. xxiv. 26 ; 2 Chron. xxxi. 3). It was written in a book (Josh. i. 7, 8), included the legislation contained in Exodus, Leviticus, Numbers, and Deuteronomy (Mark xii. 26 with Ex. iii. 6 ; Mark vii. 10 with Ex. xx. 12 ; xxi. 17 ; Luke ii. 22 and John vii. 22, 23 with Lev. xii. 2, 3 ; Mat. viii. 4 with Lev. xiv. 3 ; Mat. xix. 8 and xxii. 24 with Deut. xxiv. 1 and xxv. 5), and was the title of the Pentateuch, constituting the first division of the canon (Luke xxiv. 44) ; see PENTATEUCH. The legal portion consists of the ten commandments, which form the fundamental law of the theocracy, and statutes based on them. It was given at Sinai. The fundamental law was uttered audibly in the hearing of the whole congregation. The body of statutes controlled the general form of worship, protected human rights, regulated personal conduct, and prescribed sacred seasons and sacrifice. It was given at the same time as the ten commandments, but through Moses. See THEOCRACY. When the tabernacle was erected, the legislation was enacted which in detail regulated approach to God. See LEVITICUS. Thirty and eight years later Moses rehearsed the law publicly before the new generation, placed the emphasis where the experience of a third of a century had taught him to be advisable, and introduced modifications which the prospective change in the circumstances of the people rendered necessary. See DEUTERONOMY. It is generally held that when all that is local and temporary is put away the remaining portion of the commandments, constituting the essential part, was designed for the Christian as well as the Jewish dispensation, and will not become obsolete at any future time (cp. Ex. xx. 12 or Deut. v. 16 with Eph. vi. 2, 3). The ten commandments, being the fundamental law and a summary of the whole moral code, endure. They are founded in the immutable nature of God and in the permanent relations of men on earth. Of the fourth commandment Christ said : "The Sabbath was made for man," hence its principles remain in force while man continues on earth. Regarding the fifth commandment, the apostle Paul evidently considers both the precept and the essential part of the promise still in force, though the local or temporary portion, "the land" of Canaan, disappears, and "the earth" takes its place (Eph. vi. 2, 3). The ceremonial law apparently referred to in Heb.

viii. 7 as the first covenant, is there described as decaying and waxing old, and being ready to vanish away (13 ; cp. also chapters viii. –x.). Hence the apostles declined to impose it on the gentile converts (Acts xv. 23–29, etc.). Its function has been to point, by means of its priesthood, its sacrifices, its ceremonies, and its symbols to Christ, our great High Priest, and his atoning sacrifice for sin. When the antitype came, the types were no longer needful, though the memory of what they had been rendered them objects of interest, and will do so through all future ages. The enactments constituting the civil and criminal code of the Israelites were admirably adapted to the state of civilization which the people had then reached ; but these laws were freely modified as the circumstances contemplated by them changed. Moses himself was the first to introduce modifications, and David and others made additions.

Law'yer.

One versed in the law of Moses, of which he was the professional interpreter, a scribe (Mat. xxii. 35 with Mark xii. 28) ; see SCRIBE. In Luke xi. 44 the words " scribes and Pharisees " are omitted in R. V., and there is no contrast between scribes and lawyers (45). The lawyers joined the Pharisees in rejecting the preaching of John the Baptist (Luke vii. 30). They considered themselves above the need of instruction from Jesus ; and when one of them did condescend to hold communication with him, it was to try to puzzle him by means of a difficult question (Mat. xxii. 35 ; Luke x. 25 ; cp. Luke xiv. 3). Jesus denounced them at last in severe language for laying heavy burdens on the people, and keeping back from them the key of knowledge (Luke xi. 45–52).

Lay'ing on of Hands.

An act symbolizing dedication to a special purpose. The Israelites placed their hands on the heads of the Levites, dedicating them to the service of the Lord at the tabernacle in the stead of the firstborn of all the tribes. They pressed down their hands upon the heads of the Levites, doubtless with the intention of signifying thereby that, with God's permission and by his authority, they transferred their own obligation to service to the Levites (Num. viii. 5–20). The Israelite, who brought an animal to the sacrificial altar, placed his hands upon the victim's head, thereby dedicating it to God and making it his own representative and substitute (Lev. i. 4 ; xvi. 21). The aged Jacob laid his hands on the heads of Joseph's sons, giving them a place among his own sons, and bestowing upon them the covenant blessing, transferring it from himself as its past possessor to them (Gen. xlviii. 5–20). The hands of presbytery were laid upon the head of Timothy. The young man was thereby set apart to official service and grace was bestowed (1 Tim.

iv. 14). Imposition of the hands of presbytery denoted not only commission, but also the bestowal, by those divinely authorized, of official spiritual grace ; or at least it signified the authoritative recommendation of the candidate to God as a recipient of grace.

Laz'a-rus [from Hebrew 'El'azar, God hath helped].

1. The name of the beggar in the parable of the rich man and Lazarus. He was laid at the gate of the rich man desiring to be fed with the crumbs which fell from the sumptuously furnished table. He was also afflicted with ulcers. Yea, even the dogs licked his sores. Nothing is said of his and nothing of the rich man's character ; but when they died Lazarus was carried by angels into Abraham's bosom, while the rich man went to the place of woe. At first sight it might appear that the one was rewarded simply for being poor, and the other punished for being rich ; but the hint that the rich man's brothers, who evidently lived exactly as he had done, did not believe Moses and the prophets, and as to their life needed repentance, shows that a moral element entered into the case, and that conduct, not position, decided their ultimate destiny (Luke xvi. 19–31).

2. A member of the family of Bethany, and brother of Martha and Mary. He was an object of deep affection not only to his sisters, but to Jesus, which speaks well for his character. He was chosen for the signal honor of being raised from the dead, and when he fell sick with a grievous disease the sisters sent word to Jesus, who was beyond the Jordan, but he did not respond at once. Two days later, when Lazarus was dead, Jesus went to Bethany. Being met by Martha outside the village, he had an important conversation with her in which he called forth an expression of her faith in the resurrection and in his power to do all things, and declared himself to be the resurrection and the life. When Mary had come, Jesus went with the sisters and their friends to the sepulcher, which was of the usual kind then in use among the Jews, namely, a cave either natural or artificial in the face of a rock. After the stone had been rolled away, Jesus prayed to the Father. He did this for the sake of the people that stood by, that in the miracle they might discern proof that the Father had sent him. Then he said in the hearing of all present : " Lazarus, come forth !" and the dead awoke to life and came forth (John xi. 1–44). The effect of this miracle was profound. It was the cause of the enthusiastic reception of Jesus at Jerusalem. It also brought the sanhedrin to their decision to put him to death ; for the people were hailing him as king, and if they should accept him and his undisguised doctrine of the spiritual nature of Christ's kingdom, all hope of their rising against the Romans and endeavoring to restore the theocracy

would vanish. The rulers decided that it was better for one man to perish, whether he were guilty or not, rather than for the whole nation to be lost (xi. 45–53 ; xii. 9–19). Lazarus was present at a supper given in honor of his great benefactor by Simon the leper at Bethany six days before the passover (xii. 1, 2). The extent to which his restoration to life tended to bring new followers to Jesus so irritated the Jewish authorities that they plotted to put him also to death (10, 11). This is the last mention of Lazarus in Scripture. The plot to take his life does not seem to have been carried out, and in due time he doubtless died a second death, the time, the place, and the circumstances of which are all unknown.

Lead.
One of the metals known to the ancients, in Hebrew '*Ophereth*. It was taken as spoil from the Moabites (Num. xxxi. 22), was used by the Egyptians (con. Apion. i. 34), was obtained in large quantities in the peninsula of Sinai, was found in Egypt, and was imported from Tarshish (Ezek. xxvii. 12). It was used for weights (Zech. v. 7), for sinkers on fish lines (Iliad xxiv. 80), and for tablets on which inscriptions were written (Tacitus, Annal. ii. 69; Pliny, Hist. Nat. xiii. 21 ; Pausanias ix. 31, 4). Job xix. 24 has been understood to refer to such tablets ; but the words probably mean that, since a book (23) is liable to perish, Job desires the letters to be cut in the rock and then, to render them more distinct and durable, to be filled with molten lead. It is questionable whether it was consciously employed for cupellation (Ezek. xxii. 20).

Leaf.
1. Foliage of a tree (Gen. iii. 7 ; viii. 11).
2. Part of the wing of a folding door, when each of the two wings was divided either lengthwise or crosswise (1 Kin. vi. 34; Ezek. xli. 24). The leaf as well as the entire door is called *deleth*, because it turns on hinges or pivots. In the former passage, the door of the holy place in Solomon's temple is referred to. It was the fourth part of the wall (1 Kin. vi. 33); and was probably oblong like the wall itself, and measured 5 cubits in width by 7½ in height (cp. 2). The measurement presumably includes the two doorposts and the lintel, leaving an opening at least 4 cubits wide by 7 high. This was closed by two doors, each of which was divided perpendicularly or horizontally into halves. If divided horizontally through the middle, the leaf measured 2 by 3½ cubits, or 3 by 5¼ feet, and was quite ample to afford ingress and egress to the priests in their daily ministrations, without requiring the entire door to be opened.
3. The page or column of a roll (Jer. xxxvi. 23; cp. 2).

Le'ah [wild cow].
The elder daughter of Laban. She was less attractive than her younger sister, Rachel, one chief defect being that her eyes were tender. By a trick she was passed off on Jacob as his bride, when he had served seven years for Rachel. Leah became the mother of Reuben, Simeon, Levi, Judah, Issachar, Zebulun, and their sister Dinah (Gen. xxix. 16–35 ; xxx. 17–21).

Leas'ing.
Lying, falsehood (Ps. iv. 2; v. 6, A. V.). As the word is now obsolete. R, V. substitutes falsehood and lies.

Leath'er.
The art of tanning and dying skins was understood by the Hebrews (Ex. xxv. 5; Acts ix. 43). Leather was used by them and other nations of antiquity for numerous purposes: for articles of clothing (Lev. xiii. 48; Num. xxxi. 20), coverings of tents (Ex. xxvi. 14), bottles (Judith x. 5), shields. The leather of the shield was oiled to keep it soft and shining (2 Sam. i. 21; Is. xxi. 5). Seal or porpoise skin was used for making a superior kind of sandal (Ezek. xvi. 10; in A. V. badgers' skin). Elijah and John the Baptist wore leathern girdles (2 Kin. i. 8; Mat. iii. 4).

Leav'en.
A substance used to produce fermentation in dough and make it rise (Ex. xii. 15, 19; xiii. 7). In Scripture times leaven generally consisted of a little old dough in a high state of fermentation. Its disadvantages were that the bread thus produced had a disagreeably sour taste and smell. To obviate these defects yeast or barm is now employed as leaven. The use of leaven was forbidden in all offerings made by fire to the Lord (Lev. ii. 11). But when the offering was to be consumed by man, leaven might be used (vii. 13; xxiii. 17). The principal reason for the prohibition was that fermentation is incipient corruption, and was emblematic of corruption. It is used for corrupt doctrine (Mat. xvi. 11; Mark viii. 15) and for wickedness in the heart (1 Cor. v. 6–8); and it symbolized moral influence generally, whether good or bad, as when the kingdom of heaven is compared to leaven which a woman hid in three measures of meal till the whole was leavened (Mat. xiii. 33). The Israelites were forbidden to eat leavened bread or to have any leaven in their houses during the passover festival. The absence of leaven symbolized the incorruptness of life which God's service requires, reminded them of the haste in which they had fled out of Egypt, their dough in their troughs, and suggested the affliction of Egypt by the insipidity of the bread (Ex. xii. 39; Deut. xvi. 3; 1 Cor. v. 7, 8).

Leb'an-a and Lebanah [white (this being a poetic designation for the moon)].
Founder of a family, members of which returned from captivity (Ezra ii. 45; Neh. vii. 48).

Leb'a-non [white].
A snow-clad mountain range (Jer. xviii.

14), with hills of less elevation running from it in every direction (Hos. xiv. 5). Its streams rendered the rich soil of the valleys extremely productive. The lower zone was covered with vines (6, 7), but the mountains were most noted for their forests of gigantic cedars. Fir trees or cypresses also abounded [1 Kin. v. 6–10 ; 2 Kin. xix. 23 ; Is. xl. 16 ; lx. 13 ; Zech. xi. 1). Lions and leopards roamed in the woods (2 Kin. xiv. 9 ; Song iv. 8). The trees were felled, and the timber was used not only in the construction of palaces and temples, but also by the Phœnicians for the masts of ships (Ezra iii. 7 ; Ezek. xxvii. 5). Lebanon was the northwestern boundary of the promised land (Deut. i. 7 ; xi. 24 ; Josh. i. 4 ; xi. 17 ; xii. 7 ; xiii. 5). It is of limestone formation. The mountains consist of two ranges, running north and south, separated by the valley of the Litany and the Orontes. In the Grecian period the name Lebanon became restricted to the western range, while the eastern received the name Anti-Lebanon. This distinction still exists. The intervening valley is called Cœlesyria, that is hollow Syria, or the Bekaa. The chain may be considered to commence about 15 miles southeast of Sidon, and to run to

about 12 miles northeast by north of Tripoli, a distance of about 100 miles. The greatest elevation of Lebanon is at its northern end ; of Anti-Lebanon, at its southern end in mount Hermon. "For 10 miles the northern end of this ridge [of Lebanon] is over 10,000 feet above the sea. For another 10 miles it is between 7500 and 8000 feet. Then for 20 miles it sinks to an average of from 6500 to 7000 feet. Then it rises in the grand truncated cone of Jebel Sunnîn to over 8500 feet. Again it sinks to the plateau between Sunnîn and Kenîseh, to about 6000 feet. The highest peak of Kenîseh rises again to nearly 7000 feet. Then comes the pass of the Damascus road at Khan Muzhir, 5022 feet. Then the ridge of Jebel Barûk and Jebel Nîha, over 40 miles long, about 6500 feet, the latter ending in the picturesque Twins (Tomât Nîha). Finally, Jebel Rihân, which sinks gradually to the level of the plateau of Merj 'Ayûn. Jebel Kenîseh, and Jebel Sunnîn, at the center of the chain, although not the highest, are from their isolation far the most imposing peaks " (Post, *Quar. State. Exp. Fund*, 1892). The highest peaks are Jebel Makmal and Kurnat es-Sauda, each about 10,200 feet. The present population

These Lebanese village women draw water from an ancient well dug by the Crusaders.

of Lebanon is estimated by Dr. Post at 200,-
000. The people live mostly in villages ro-
mantically situated on rocky platforms or
on the mountain slopes.

Leb'a-oth [lionesses].
A town in the extreme south of Judah
(Josh. xv. 32). See BETH-LEBAOTH.

Leb-bæ'us. See JUDAS 8.

Leb'ka-mai.
An artificial name (Jer. li. 1. A. R. V.),
which, when the consonants are exchanged
according to the system called Athbash,
yields KSDIM, that is, Chaldeans. The
method is explained, and another instance
is cited, in the article SHESHACH.

Le-bo'nah [incense, frankincense].
A town north of Shiloh (Judg. xxi. 19).
It has long been identified with Lubban, on
the road between Shechem and Jerusalem, 3
miles west by north of Shiloh.

Le'cah [perhaps, going, a journey]
A village of Judah (1 Chron. iv. 21), to
judge from the context. Site unknown.

Leek.
The rendering in Num. xi. 5, of the
Hebrew *Ḥaṣir*, which commonly denotes
grass. The leek (*Allium porrum*) is probably
intended in this passage: for it is mentioned,
along with onions and garlic, as eaten in
Egypt; the word is so rendered by the
Targum of Onkelos, Septuagint, Vulgate, and
Syriac; and *ḥªṣir* is used in Aramaic for the
leek.

Lees.
Dregs or sediment deposited from wine or
other liquor (Is. xxv. 6). The liquor was
allowed to stand on the lees that its color
and body might be better preserved (Is.
xxv. 6).
To settle on their lees is to settle down in
contentment with one's character and circumstances (Jer. xlviii. 11; Zeph. i. 12). To
drink the lees of the cup of wrath means to
drain the cup, enduring the punishment to
the utmost (Ps. lxxv. 8, rendered dregs).

Le'gion.
The chief subdivision of the Roman army
(War iii. 4, 2). It originally contained 3000
foot soldiers with a contingent of cavalry.
From 100 B. C. to the fall of the empire the
number varied from 5000 to 6200, while from
Augustus to Hadrian or during the N. T.
period 6000 seems to have been the regular
complement and the cavalry was not considered as forming a constituent part of the
legion. At this time the legion consisted of
ten cohorts, each cohort of three maniples,
and each maniple of two centuries (cp. Mat.
xxvii. 27, R. V. margin); and was officered
by tribunes and centurions (War iii. 5, 3;
Acts xxi. 31, 32, R. V. margin; xxiii. 23),
numbering ten and sixty respectively. In
Scripture legion is used to denote any large
host (Mat. xxvi. 53; Mark v. 9).

The military standard of the Romans was
at first a bunch of straw attached to a pole.
Later an eagle and four other animals formed
the standards of a legion, but after 104 B. C.
the eagle alone was employed (Pliny, Hist.
Nat. x. 4). It was committed to the custody of
the chief centurion. In addition to the eagle,
the standard also commonly bore a small image of the emperor, and the introduction of
these images into Jerusalem by Pontius Pilate
caused an insurrection of the Jews (Antiq.
xviii. 3, 1; War ii. 9, 2). But while the great
standard of the whole legion was the eagle,
each cohort and century had its own standard,
and these minor ensigns assumed a variety
of forms.

Le'ha-bim.
A tribe sprung from or incorporated with
the Egyptians (Gen. x. 13; 1 Chron. i. 11),
probably the same as the Lubim (q. v.).

Le'hi [cheek, jawbone].
A place in Judah (Judg. xv. 9), elevated
(11, 13), where the Philistines spread themselves when they advanced into Judah to
seize Samson. It may have been a ridge.
It received its name either from a series of
jagged crags resembling a jawbone, or from
Samson's exploit with the jawbone of an ass.
At any rate, that part of it where Samson
beat down the Philistines, who seem to have
been fleeing, and cast aside the jawbone which
had served him as a weapon, was remembered,
and it was pointed out as Ramath-lehi, height
of the jawbone (17). Guérin locates Lehi at
'Ain el-Lehi, northwest of Bethlehem, about
2 miles west-southwest of Mâlhah, and hence
not far from Etam (cp. 11), on the high
plateau. But the existence of 'Ain el-Lehi
appears doubtful. The survey map does not
indicate it. Moreover, Lehi is best sought
near some other Etam, for Samson went from
Timnah down, not up, to the rock at Etam.

Lem'u-el [devoted to God].
The royal author of Prov. xxxi., who reproduces what was taught him by his mother
(ver. 1).

Len'til.
A plant (2 Sam. xxiii. 11), boiled as pottage
(Gen. xxv. 29, 34) and in times of scarcity
made into bread (Ezek. iv. 9). The modern
Arabic name is identical with its Hebrew
designation *ªdashim*. The lentil (*Ervum
lens*) is a papilionaceous plant, allied to the
vetches. It has compound leaves, with five
to six pairs of oblong leaflets, white flowers
striped with violet, and small broad legumes.
Pottage made from it is red. It was this which
was given to Esau when he was famishing, and
it was from it that his second name Edom was
derived. The plant is wild in Moab, and is
cultivated in all parts of Palestine. The seeds
when boiled are thoroughly wholesome. It
is from them that *Revalenta arabica* is made,
and they are of late quite familiar at most
vegetarian restaurants and in many households.

Leop'ard.

A wild animal ; in Hebrew *Namer*, spotted beast, in Greek *Pardalis*. It was, as its name implied, a spotted animal (Jer. xiii. 23). It was very swift (Hab. i. 8). Its appropriate food was the kid (Is. xi. 6), but it sometimes attacked man (Hos. xiii. 7, 8) ; lurking for the purpose in the vicinity of cities or villages (Jer. v. 6), though its ordinary habitation was among the mountains (Song iv. 8). The leopard (*Felis pardus* or *Leopardus*) was believed by the ancients and some moderns to be a hybrid between the lion and the panther ; hence its name, which is compounded of *leo* and *pardus*, lion and panther. Now it is generally held that these are merely varieties of the same species. The appropriate habitat of the leopard or panther is Africa and southern Asia. In Palestine it now occurs chiefly in the region east of the Jordan ; but it was evidently more common in Scripture times than at present, in the country west of the river.

In Dan. vii. 6 it symbolizes a fierce nation and its king, doubtless Greece (viii. 21) ; and in Rev. xiii. 2 the composite creature, which combines the four beasts of Daniel and typifies the united powers of this world, has the body of a leopard.

Lep'er.

A person affected with the disease of leprosy (2 Kin. vii. 8 ; Mat. x. 8). The leper was excluded from intercourse with his fellowmen and from the sanctuary, was required to exhibit the usual signs of mourning and to give the warning cry to all that approached, " Unclean! unclean!" (Lev. xiii. 45; Luke xvii. 12, 13), and he was regarded as a dead man (Num. xii. 12). Strangely enough, if the leprosy was spreading, the sufferer was unclean ; but if it overspread the whole man, he was adjudged clean (Lev. xiii. 6, 12, 13). Some expositors understand this to mean that, while the disease manifested activity, the law imputed pollution ; but when it might be regarded as having run its course, it lost its character as a curse from God. Others understand the meaning to be that only when the leper was acknowledged to be defiled in every part by this disease, which typified sin, could he be admitted to the privileges of atonement. Yet other interpreters believe that the rapid eruption over the whole body was a sign that the crisis had been passed and recovery had set in. See PURIFICATION.

Lep'ro-sy.

1. A dreadful disease, in Hebrew *Ṣara'ath*, scourge. The symptoms are described in Lev. xiii. 1–46. There were skin diseases from which it required to be carefully distinguished. It , was not a superficial, but was a deep-seated malady. It often began as a rising, or a scab, or a bright spot, which tended to spread, turning white the hair covering the parts affected (xiii. 2, 3,

7, 8, 10, 24, 25, 27, 35, 36). Raw flesh tended to appear (10, 14–16, 24). Among the parts of the body specially liable to attack were the scalp of the head, the beard, the top of the head, or the forehead, after these had become bald ; also any spot which had been accidentally injured by fire (24, 29, 30, 42). A leper was to be excluded from the camp ; was required to let the hair of his head go loose and his clothes be rent ; while he was to cover his upper lip, and cry, " Unclean ! unclean !" (45, 46). He had to appear repeatedly before the priest, who was to pronounce on the character of the disease (1–44) ; and in the event of the malady departing, he was to go through an elaborate process of cleansing and sacrifice (xiv. 1–32). In the description of the disease given in Lev. xiii. there is no mention of the leper's hue changing to a snowy white, as was the case with Miriam (Num. xii. 10) and Gehazi (2 Kin. v. 27), and momentarily with Moses (Ex. iv. 6). Not even those whose circumstances were comfortable were exempt from this disease. Thus, it affected Naaman, when commander-in-chief of the army of Syria (2 Kin. v. 1–14), and Uzziah during the later years of his reign over Judah (xv. 5 ; 2 Chron. xxvi. 21) The regulations about excluding the leper from society were carried out among the Hebrews (Num. v. 1–4 ; xii. 10, 15 ; 2 Kin. vii. 3, 8, 10 ; xv. 5 ; 2 Chron. xxvi. 21 ; cp. also Luke xvii. 12) ; but the fact that the king of Syria seems to have leaned on Naaman's hand, even when he was a leper, and that Naaman dwelt with his family and was accompanied by servants, shows that leprosy, though loathsome, was not actually contagious (2 Kin. v. 18). The disease to which the English word leprosy is now confined is a formidable malady, technically called *Elephantiasis Græcorum*, elephant disease of the Greeks. It appears under two forms. The tuberculated or black leprosy is at present the more common, and the name is restricted to it by some authorities. It affects primarily the skin and mucous membranes. The anæsthetic or white leprosy affects the nerves principally, and produces numbness. The symptoms of the two forms are often united, and one form frequently passes into the other. The coming of the disease is preceded by lassitude for months or years. Then circular spots or blotches of irregular form and varying extent appear on the forehead, the limbs, and the body. After a time, the central portion of the spots and blotches becomes white, and the parts affected contract a certain numbness. In the worst cases the joints of the fingers and toes fall off one by one, and injuries to the other parts produce mutilation and deformity. Thomson says: " The 'scab' comes on by degrees in different parts of the body ; the hair falls from the head and eyebrows; the nails loosen, decay, and drop off; joint after joint of the fingers and toes shrink up and slowly fall away. The gums are absorbed, and the teeth disappear. The nose, the eyes, the tongue, and the palate are slowly consumed." Again, he says, that when approaching the Jaffa gate of Jerusalem he was startled by the sudden apparition of a crowd of beggars, without eyes, nose, or hair. They held up handless arms, and unearthly sounds gurgled through throats without palates. This loathsome and fatal disease is popularly believed to be identical with that of Leviticus and the other books of the Bible (cp. Num. xii. 12). But the disease mentioned in Scripture seems to have been curable (Lev. xiv. 3), whereas *Elephantiasis Græcorum* is not, except in the early stages. If not elephantiasis, what was it? Sir Risdon Bennett (*Diseases of the Bible*, 15-52) and others believe probably *Lepra vulgaris*, now merged in the genus *Psoriasis*, and called *Psoriasis vulgaris*, the dry tetter. It is a non-contagious, scaly disease, generally commencing about the elbows and knees, as small circular patches of silvery-white scales, which spread till they become the size of a quarter or a half dollar, by which time the scales have fallen from the central portion of the circle, leaving it red ; other circles arising coalesce. Afterwards the abdomen, the chest, and the back become affected, and in rare cases the disease extends at last also to the head, face, and hands. The constitutional disturbance is trifling, and the disease is curable, though it is liable to recur. It is simply a skin disease, in no way endangering life. Or the white leprosy of the O. T. may have been *Psoriasis guttata*, in which the scattered patches are said to give an appearance to the skin as if it had been splashed with mortar. Perhaps the Hebrew term ṣara'ath was a generic one, and the elephantiasis and the psoriasis two of its species; and it is quite possible that different varieties have prevailed at different times. If the leprosy of the Old and that of the New Testament were identical, then confirmation is given to the opinion that the former was psoriasis, for Luke (v. 12, 13), himself a physician, employs the Greek word *lepra*, which was technically used of psoriasis. With this Josephus' description of leprosy agrees, for (Antiq. iii. 11, 4) he defines a leper to be a man who has a misfortune in the color of his skin, and makes no allusion to graver symptoms. He mentions also that among the gentiles lepers were not excluded from society, but were competent to discharge important functions in the body politic.

2. The same word ṣara'ath was applied to a greenish or reddish appearance in a garment and to hollow greenish or reddish strakes in the wall of a house (Lev. xiii. 47-59; xiv. 33-37). It may be some minute cryptogamous plant, an algal or a fungal, which has grown upon the garment or wall after it has become wet in the rainy season.

Le'shem. See DAN 3.

Le-tu'shim.

A tribe descended from Dedan (Gen. xxv. 3). They doubtless settled in Arabia.

Le-um'mim [peoples, nations].

A tribe descended from Dedan (Gen. xxv. 3). They doubtless settled in Arabia.

Le'vi [adhesion, associate].

1. Third son of Jacob and Leah (Gen. xxix. 34). He took part with Simeon, Leah's second son, in massacring Hamor, Shechem, and the men of their city, in revenge for the injury done by Shechem to their sister Dinah (xxxiv. 25-31). Jacob on his deathbed remembered with fresh abhorrence this deed of blood, and, referring to Simeon and Levi, said, " Cursed be their anger, for it was fierce ; and their wrath, for it was cruel : I will divide them in Jacob, and scatter them in Israel " (xlix. 7). Levi had three sons : Gershon or Gershom, Kohath, and Merari (Gen. xlvi. 11), and died in Egypt at the age of 137 (Ex. vi. 16). See LEVITES.

2 and 3. Two ancestors of Christ, one the son of Symeon, and the other a son of Melchi (Luke iii. 24, 29, 30).

4. Another name for the apostle Matthew (cp. Mat. ix. 9-13 ; Mark ii. 14-17 ; Luke v. 27-32).

Le-vi'a-than [one spirally wound].

A great aquatic animal mentioned only in poetic passages. He was formed by God to play in the sea (Ps. civ. 26). He has limbs, head, neck, eyes, nose, jaw, mouth, teeth, and tongue (Job xli. 1, 2, 7, 12, 14, 18, 19, 22), and is covered with scales and an impenetrable hide (7, 15-17, 26-29). He lieth upon the mire or maketh the sea to boil like a pot (30, 31). He is too large to be taken by fish hook or harpoon (1, 26), is terrible of aspect (9), and mighty in strength, but comely of proportion (12). He is poetically described as breathing fire and smoke (19-21), as is God in Ps. xviii. 8 and as are the horses in Rev. ix. 17. When God worked salvation by dividing the sea, he destroyed the sea monsters which inhabited it, broke the heads of leviathan and left his carcass to be eaten by the people of the desert (Ps. lxxiv. 14). As the sea is the type of the restless, surging nations of the earth, so leviathan which dwells therein, leviathan the flying serpent, leviathan the swift serpent, leviathan the crooked serpent, and the dragon symbolize the fierce and terrible powers of the world which have afflicted the people of God, but whom God will ultimately destroy (Is. xxvii. 1). Leviathan is commonly regarded as the crocodile (Job xli. 1, R. V. margin). As such the imagery is apt. Egypt, its habitat, is the typical oppressor of the kingdom of God, and Egypt's power was broken and its king thwarted when God divided the Red Sea for the deliverance of his people. Leviathan may, however, be merely a creation of the popular fancy, an imaginary sea monster; the inspired poets and prophets of Israel subsidizing fable to serve in the illustration of truth. In Job iii. 8 leviathan may be a fabulous dragon which caused eclipses by swallowing sun and moon, and the cursers of the day may be conjurers who claimed the power to produce eclipses by his aid. Or in this passage leviathan may be the untamable, terrible crocodile which only conjurers of highest skill claimed ability to summon to their aid.

Le'vites.

1. The descendants of Levi, the son of Jacob. He had three sons : Gershon or Gershom, Kohath, and Merari, each of whom founded a tribal family (Gen. xlvi. 11 ; Ex. vi. 16 ; Num. iii. 17 ; 1 Chron. vi. 16–48). Moses and Aaron were Levites of the house of Amram and family of Kohath (Ex. vi. 16, 18, 20, 26).

2. The men of the tribe of Levi charged with the care of the sanctuary. Aaron and his sons were set apart for the priesthood and the office was made hereditary. But the tabernacle and its service had been projected on a noble scale. The care and transportation of the costly sanctuary and the preparation of materials for the elaborate service entailed labors which no one man and no one family was equal to. Helpers were needed. The charge of the tabernacle was an honorable work. Who should undertake it ? The firstborn belonged to God. This conviction was deepened by the circumstances connected with the deliverance from Egypt. When the firstborn of the Egyptians were slain, blood on the lintel and side door posts was needed to protect the Israelite firstborn males from a similar fate. They had then become the special property of Jehovah, and henceforth were consecrated to him as a memorial (Ex. xiii. 11–16). But instead of the firstborn of all the tribes, the Levites were chosen for service in connection with the sanctuary ; and the choice was made because, when the people had broken the covenant with Jehovah by making the golden calf, the Levites alone had voluntarily returned to their allegiance and shown zeal for God's honor (xxxii. 26–29; Num. iii. 9, 11–13, 40, 41, 45 seq.; viii. 16–18). The firstborn males of Israel, exclusive of the Levites, numbered 22,273 in the census taken at Sinai (Num. iii. 43, 46). There were 22,000 Levites (39); but the items given in verses 22, 28, and 34 foot up 22,300. Either an error has occurred somewhere in the transcription, or else 300 of these Levites were themselves firstborn and therefore could not serve as substitutes for the firstborn of the other tribes. The 22,000 were substituted. The remaining 273 firstborn of Israel were redeemed by the payment of five shekels apiece (46–51).

It was the duty of the Levites to transport the tabernacle and its furniture when the camp moved ; and when the camp rested to erect the tent, have care of it, and assist the priests in their varied work (Num. i. 50-53 ; iii. 6–9, 25–37 ; iv. 1–33 ; 1 Sam. vi. 15, 2 Sam. xv. 24). As the sons of Aaron were Levites as well as priests, they are frequently included under the designation Levite (Deut. xxxiii. 8–10 ; Josh. xiv. 3 ; xxi. 1, 4 ; Mal. iii. 3) ; and also, either as higher officials or as Levites, they might, if they saw fit, discharge any service that pertained to the Levites.

The age at which the obligation of service began was thirty years (Num. iv. 3 ; 1 Chron. xxiii. 3–5), and twenty-five years (Num. viii. 24), and twenty years (1 Chron. xxiii. 24, 27). The divergent practice at different periods of the history explains the peculiarity in part. It is even conceivable that a reduction in the age for entrance and a lengthening of the term of service was made by Moses himself some time during the course of forty years, and such a change is expressly stated to have been made by David. But it is noticeable that both in the book of Numbers and in the book of Chronicles the age of thirty years is forthwith followed by an earlier age. Also in Numbers iv. the service of the Levites who were thirty years old is defined by an explanatory clause : " every one that entered in to do the work of service, and [even] the work of bearing burdens " (47, 49) ; and, in fact, the particular service is defined by the specifications of the entire chapter. It is, therefore, not at all improbable that at thirty years of age the Levites became eligible to full service of every sort that pertained to Levites at the sanctuary, including the high and honorable offices of bearing the tabernacle and its sacred furniture in public procession and, at a later period, of serving in positions that brought distinction and called for wisdom and discretion (Num. iv. 1–33 ; 1 Chron. xxiii. 3–5) ; but the Levites began general service at first at twenty-five years of age, and performed the various duties belonging to their calling with the exceptions that have been noted ; at least the higher duties are not mentioned in connection with the more youthful age (Num. viii. 24–26 ; 1 Chron. xxiii. 25–32). David, however, saw fit to make a further reduction in the age at which the simpler duties should be undertaken, and he directed that the Levites should enter upon service at the same time of life as that at which the other Israelites became liable to military service, namely, at twenty years (1 Chron. xxiii. 24, 27), seeing that the need of transporting the ark no longer existed (25, 26) and the service of the sanctuary had become a routine, and a sort of apprenticeship was a useful preparation for the regular ecclesiastical duties. Twenty years was henceforth the legal age for the Levites to enter upon service (2 Chron. xxxi. 17 ; Ezra iii. 8). At this age they commenced as assistants to the priests and chief Levites (1 Chron. xxiii. 28–31 ; cp. 2 Chron. xxix.

34; xxxv. 11), but probably not until they reached thirty years were they regarded as experts, or eligible for the higher offices of doorkeeper or member of the temple orchestra or administrator or judge (1 Chron. xxiii. 3-5). They retired from active service at fifty, but were free to render assistance to the Levites who succeeded them in the work at the sanctuary (Num. viii. 25, 26).

An official dress was not prescribed for the Levites, but on great occasions they drew on festal raiment (1 Chron. xv. 27; 2 Chron. v. 12). It was an innovation when the Levitical singers in the first century A. D. obtained permission from king Agrippa, with the sanction of the sanhedrin to wear linen garments as constantly as did the priests (Antiq. xx. 9, 6). They were not required to devote their entire time to the sanctuary nor to dwell continually near it; but on the allotment of Canaan they were distributed to various towns (Josh. xxi. 20-40). Exclusive of the towns allotted to the Levites who were priests, all of which were in Judah, Simeon and Benjamin, the Levitical towns numbered thirty-five and were situated among the remaining tribes on the north and east (Josh. xxi. 5-7). Since the Levites as a tribe were "wholly given unto the Lord in behalf of the children of Israel," and were appointed to service at the tabernacle, it was natural that in the northern districts, where no Levitical priests dwelt, the lower order of the Levites should be drawn upon by the idolater Micah and after him by the idolatrous migrating Danites to furnish a man for priestly services (Judg. xvii. 8-13; xviii. 18-20, 30, 31). In David's reign the Levites were divided into four classes: 1. Assistants to the priests in the work of the sanctuary; 2. Judges and scribes; 3. Gate keepers; 4. Musicians. Each of these classes, with the possible exception of the second, was subdivided into twenty-four courses or families to serve in rotation (1 Chron. xxiv.-xxvi.; cp. xv. 16-24; 2 Chron. xix. 8-11; xxx. 16, 17; Ezra vi. 18; Neh. xiii. 5). On the disruption of the monarchy, many Levites and priests (out of Benjamin) quitted the northern kingdom and came to Judah and Jerusalem (2 Chron. xi. 13-15).

Le-vit'i-cus [relating to the Levites].

The third book of the Pentateuch. When the tabernacle had been erected and a priest appointed to minister at the altar, the next step was to regulate access to God. This is the object of the ordinances contained in Leviticus. In approach to Jehovah sacrifices and a priesthood were needed, and intercourse with God requires the attainment and maintenance of purity, both ceremonial and moral. To exercise a proper control over these matters several manuals were prepared, which were placed together and form the book of Leviticus. 1. A directory of procedure to be followed by the worshiper and the priest at the offering of the various kinds of sacrifice (Lev. i. 1-vi. 7), and a book on the disposal of the sacrifice (vi. 8-vii. 36). The directory of procedure was drawn up at Sinai after the tabernacle had been erected, and the book on the disposal of the sacrifice was written at the same general time, when "he commanded the children of Israel to offer their oblations unto Jehovah" (i. 1; and cp. vii. 38 with i. 2). 2. A record of the consecration of Aaron and his sons to the priestly office (viii.-ix.), an official act prescribed during Moses' first sojourn in Sinai (Ex. xxix.), which established the priesthood and was the precedent for future ordinations. To this record an account of the punishment of Nadab and Abihu for illegal approach was appended, together with legislation which was enacted to meet deficiencies revealed in the laws on this occasion (Lev. x.). 3. A directory of ceremonial purity (xi.-xvi.), containing laws concerning foods that defile, diseases or natural functions that render unclean, and the ceremonial national purification (already prescribed, Ex. xxx. 10). This directory is ascribed to Moses as the representative of Jehovah (Lev. xi. 1, etc.), when Israel was in the wilderness (xiv. 34; xvi. 1). 4. The law of holiness (xvii.-xxvi.), statutes concerning holiness of life, given by Moses (xvii. 1, etc.), at Sinai (xxv. 1; xxvi. 46; cp. xxiv. 10). These several collections are followed by an appendix on vows, tithes, and things devoted (xxvii.). Occasionally a law is repeated in a new connection and for a different purpose. At times also the legislation is interrupted by the narrative of events that led to enactments (x. 1-7, 12-20; xxi. 24; xxiv. 10-23). Possibly some laws, but certainly not all, that were framed after the departure from Sinai were inserted for the sake of convenience in their proper place among the laws relating to the same subject.

Throughout the book but one sanctuary (xix. 21 et passim) and one altar for all Israel are recognized (i. 3; viii. 3; xvii. 8, 9), and the sons of Aaron are the sole priests (i. 5). The Levites are only incidentally mentioned (xxv. 32, 33). Variations in the laws or their statement as found in Leviticus and Deuteronomy are intelligible when it is remembered that 1. Leviticus is a manual for the priests, to guide them through the technicalities of the ritual; while Deuteronomy is primarily not a law book at all, but a popular address to instruct the people in their own duties and to exhort them to fidelity. Deuteronomy omits matters of detail which concern priests only. 2. The laws of Leviticus are dated at Sinai an entire generation before the addresses contained in Deuteronomy were delivered at Shittim. Accordingly the legislation of Leviticus is presupposed in Deuteronomy. This is the standpoint of the Bible.

The essentials of the legislation of Leviticus are reflected in the history in the early recognition of the Aaronic priesthood. So far as the evidence reaches, the priests were sons of Aaron exclusively (Deut. x. 6; Josh. xiv. 1; xxi. 4 and 18 with 1 Kin. ii. 26; Judg. xx. 27, 28; 1 Sam. i. 3; ii. 27, 28; xiv. 3; xxi. 6 with 1 Chron. xxiv. 3; 1 Sam. xxii. 10, 11, 20; xxiii. 6; and 2 Sam. viii. 17 with Ezra vii. 3 and 1 Chron. xxiv. 3). The Levites are sojourners and subordinate (Judg. xvii. 7-9; xix. 1; 1 Sam. vi. 15; 2 Sam. xv. 24). Compare also the one house of the Lord (Judg. xviii. 31; xix. 18; 1 Sam. i. 7, 24; iii. 3; iv. 3), and the feast of the Lord, at the tabernacle visited by all Israel (Judg. xxi. 19; 1 Sam. i. 3; ii. 14, 22, 29); see further the articles PRIEST, HIGH PRIEST, LEVITES, ALTAR, DEUTERONOMY.

Lib′er-tines [freedmen].

A section of the Jewish community who had a synagogue at Jerusalem, and were among the foes of the first martyr, Stephen (Acts vi. 9). They were probably Jews, who, having been taken prisoners in battle by Pompey and other Roman generals, had been bondsmen at Rome, but were afterwards restored to liberty.

Lib′nah [whiteness, pellucidness].

1. An encampment of the Israelites in the wilderness (Num. xxxiii. 20). Situation unknown.

2. A city in the lowland between Makkedah and Lachish (Josh. x. 29-31), captured by Joshua (30, 39; xii. 15). It was situated in the territory allotted to Judah (xv. 42), and was subsequently assigned to the descendants of Aaron (xxi. 13; 1 Chron. vi. 57). When Jehoram, son of Jehoshaphat, was king, Libnah revolted against Judah (2 Kin. viii. 22; 2 Chron. xxi. 10). Sennacherib, king of Assyria, warred against it (2 Kin. xix. 8; Is. xxxvii. 8). The father of Hamutal, the mother of Jehoahaz and Zedekiah, was from this place (2 Kin. xxiii. 31; xxiv. 18; Jer. lii. 1). Exact situation is unknown.

Lib′ni [white, pure].

1. Son of Gershon, and grandson of Levi. He was founder of a minor tribal family or father's house (Ex. vi. 17; Num. iii. 18, 21; xxvi. 58).

2. A Levite, family of Merari, house of Mahli (1 Chron. vi. 29).

Lib′y-a and **Libyans**.

A rendering of *Put* (Jer. xlvi. 9; Ezek. xxx. 5; xxxviii. 5 in A. V.) and *Lubim* (Dan. xi. 43). A country and its inhabitants in the western part of Lower Egypt or on its borders. The people are said to be distinguished by the Egyptians as *Tehenu*; later *Pit*, *Phaiait*, probably equivalent to the Hebrew *Put*; and *Rebu* or *Lebu*, that is in Hebrew *Lubim*, and others. The Libya of the Romans was an immense and vaguely defined tract extending from the Nile delta and valley westward

across the entire African continent. It comprised all north Africa west of Egypt, except the small Greek settlements of Cyrene and Barca, and the Phœnician colonies of Carthage, Utica, and Hippo. It was nearly all a sandy desert, studded here and there with oases, on which palms grew. Its tribes were brave, but were not very formidable, owing to their being scattered and unable to unite. The Romans divided the African region bordering the Mediterranean as far west as the Syrtis Major, or the country between Egypt and the province of Africa, into Libya Marmarica in the east and Libya Cyrenaica or Pentapolis in the west. The latter was formed with Crete into a province in 67 B. C. Its capital was Cyrene, and it was from this western province that representatives were present at Jerusalem on Pentecost (Acts ii. 10; cp. Antiq. xvi. 6, 1).

Lice.

The rendering of the Hebrew *Kinnam* or *Kinnim* (Ex. viii. 16-18; Ps. cv. 31), referring to some small insect noxious to man. Josephus understood the word to mean lice (Antiq. ii. 14, 3). The Septuagint renders it by *sknips*, an aphis or other small insect that sucks or gnaws. R. V. margin translates it sandflies or fleas.

Lic′tor. See PRAETOR.

Lieu-ten′ant. See SATRAP.

Lign-al′oes [wood or tree aloes]. See ALOES.

Lig′ure.

The rendering of the Hebrew *Leshem*, a gem, the first stone in the third row of the high priest's breastplate (Ex. xxviii. 19). This translation is derived from the Septuagint, Vulgate and Josephus (War v. 5, 7); but it is impossible to identify the ligurium of the ancients with any known gem. The R. V. renders the Hebrew word by jacinth or amber.

Lik′hi [characterized by knowledge].

A Manassite, family of Shemida (1 Chron. vii. 19).

Lil′y.

1. The rendering of the Hebrew words *Shoshan*, *Shoshannah*, and *Shushan*. The plant so designated is found in pastures where sheep and gazelles feed (Song ii. 16; iv. 5; vi. 3), and among thorns (ii. 2), besides being cultivated in gardens (vi. 2). It was so much at home in valleys that it was designated the lily of the valleys (Song ii. 1). It was a sweet-scented plant, dropping a myrrh-like perfume (v. 13). The Hebrew word was rendered *krinon* by the Greek translators. The *krinon* is a plant which grows beside the water (Ecclus. l. 8) and among the grass of the field (Mat. vi. 28). It is often mentioned in connection with frankincense and the rose (Ecclus. xxxix. 13, 14). It is the type of a life of beautiful deeds. The high priest, coming forth from the sanctuary is compared with

it (l. 8). It excels Solomon in his glorious array (Mat. vi. 29).

The words *shushan* and *krinon* were not always used with reference to the lily in its modern scientific sense; but included with

Scarlet Turk's Cap.

the true lily various plants that resemble the lily. The lotus was known to the ancient Egyptians by the name of *seshnin*, and is called by Herodotus *krinon* (ii. 92). The ordinary word for a lily in Arabic is still *súsan;* but it is used generically rather than

Red Anemone.

specifically, including the tulip and even the anemone and ranunculus. What varieties of lily were anciently cultivated in the gardens of Palestine is not known. In the fields the scarlet Turk's cap (*Lilium chalcedonicum*) grows sparingly. Besides the true lily, other genera of the order *Liliaceæ*, as

hyacinths and tulips, grow in profusion in the spring. A fine, dark violet flower, known as *súsan*, is found far and wide in the Hauran. Thomson describes a splendid iris, which he calls the Huleh lily, growing among the oak woods around the northern base of Tabor and on the hills of Nazareth. The flower is dark purple and white. He believes that it is the lily referred to by Jesus. Red anemones are so marked a feature of the valleys of Palestine in the spring that various travelers, Tristram included, have suggested that *Anemone coronaria,* the red variety of which is very common, was probably the lily of the N. T., while others would identify the anemone with the rose of Sharon. See ROSE.

Lime.

A material prepared by burning limestone, shells, and other calcareous substances (Is. xxxiii. 12; Amos ii. 1), and used for making mortar and plaster, and for whitewashing walls (Deut. xxvii. 2, in E. V. plaister; Mat. xxiii. 27; Acts xxiii. 3). See MORTAR.

Lin'en.

1. Fine linen is the rendering of the Hebrew word *Shesh*, white, applied to a stuff of which vestments were made. It was in it that Joseph was arrayed by Pharaoh's order (Gen. xli. 42). Of this material also were made the curtains, vail, and door hangings of the tabernacle (Ex. xxvi. 1, 31, 36), and the hangings for the gate of the court and for the court itself (xxvii. 9, 16, 18). The distinguishing attire of the high priest consisted of the ephod, breastplate, robe of blue, and the gold plate on the miter; and of these the ephod and breastplate contained fine linen (Ex. xxviii. 6, 15). Other official garments were common to the high priest and the ordinary priest, the tunic, girdle, breeches, and headdress (Ex. xxviii. 40-42; xxxix. 27-29; cp. Lev. xvi. 4). The headdress, however, of the high priest was a miter or turban, while a simple cap appears to have been worn by the ordinary priest. Of these four articles of priestly dress, the girdle was embroidered, consisting largely of linen (Ex. xxxix. 29). The three other garments were made of fine white linen exclusively (xxviii. 39; xxxix. 27, 28). On the margin of Gen. xli. 42 and of Ex. xxv. 4 the R. V. substitutes cotton. On the margin of Ex. xxviii. 39 the R. V., referring to the coat and miter of the high priest, substitutes silk. The same Hebrew word is translated marble in Esth. i. 6 and Song v. 15 (where the reference is to pillars), and silk in Prov. xxxi. 22.

2. The Hebrew word *Bad* is a synonym for *shesh*, but is more general in its meaning, hence it is rendered merely linen (Ex. xxviii. 42 with xxxix. 28). It sufficiently described the material of the priest's raiment, when there was no need to explicitly state the quality of the stuff (ibid.; Lev. vi. 10; xvi.

4). Of it was made the plain ephod worn by the boy Samuel, by the priests at Nob, and by David on the occasion of removing the ark (1 Sam. ii. 18; xxii. 18; 2 Sam. vi. 14). In it the man with the inkstand in Ezekiel's vision, and Daniel's heavenly comforter were clothed (Ezek. ix. 2; Dan. x. 5).

3. The rendering of the Hebrew *Pishteh*, flax, the material of which the goods are made being thought of (Jer. xiii. 1). It is used in contrast to woolen clothing (Lev. xiii. 47; Deut. xxii. 11). It describes the material of the priestly garments, the headtires, breeches, and girdles (Ezek. xliv. 17, 18).

4. The rendering of the Hebrew *Buṣ*, which occurs only in the later books, and of the Greek *Bussos*. Of this material were made the robe, not the ephod, which David wore at the removal of the ark (1 Chron. xv. 27), the vail of the temple in part, the other stuffs employed being blue, purple, and crimson (2 Chron. iii. 14), the clothing of the Levites who were musicians at the dedication of the temple (v. 12), the cords which fastened the hangings in Ahasuerus' palace (Esth. i. 6), the state dress of Mordecai (viii. 15), the garments of the rich man at whose gate Lazarus sat (Luke xvi. 19), and of the luxurious city of Babylon (Rev. xviii. 16), and the bright and pure raiment of the Lamb's wife (xix. 8).

Shesh is originally an Egyptian word, in old Egyptian *shenti*; *bus* is the Aramaic equivalent (cp. Targ. Onk. Gen. xli. 42), and *bussos* is etymologically the same word as *bus*. It is interesting to note that Ezekiel uses *shesh* for goods imported from Egypt, and *buṣ* for stuffs that came from Syria. Whether the words denote linen or fine cotton cloth, or comprehend both, is much debated. Linen and cotton were employed in Egypt from the earliest times for mummy cloths.

5. The rendering of the Hebrew word *'Eṭun*, from *'aṭan*, to bind (Prov. vii. 16; in R.V. yarn). It was imported from Egypt, where the most skillful manufacturers of linen lived.

6. Linen yarn is the rendering of the Hebrew word *Mikveh* in A. V. of 1 Kin. x. 28; 2 Chron. i. 16. R. V. renders it a drove. Septuagint and Vulgate regarded the Hebrew word as composite, and rendered it "and out of Koe," which was a place near Egypt, according to Eusebius.

7, 8. The rendering of the Greek word *Sindon*, a fine Indian cloth, muslin, later linen. A tunic or perhaps a sheet might be made of it (Mark xiv. 51), and in this material the body of Jesus was wrapped for burial (Mat. xxvii. 59). It is a synonym of *othonioi*, though more special in meaning (Luke xxiii. 53 with xxiv. 12; John xix. 40; xx. 5, 7). In classical Greek the latter word means either genuine linen or sail cloth.

9. The rendering of the Greek *Linon*, linen (Rev. xv. 6, A. V. and margin of R. V.). The text of R. V. has precious stones, from another reading *lithon*.

Lin'tel.

The transverse piece of wood or other material constituting the upper part of a doorway or casement (Ex. xii. 22), called in Hebrew *Mashḳoph*.

1. Lintel is also the rendering of the Hebrew *'Ayil*, a ram, in 1 Kin. vi. 31. It may denote a projecting lintel or post. The Hebrew word occurs eighteen times in an architectural sense in Ezek. xl. and xli., where it is rendered post (ver. 9, etc.), with jamb on the margin of R. V.

2. The rendering of the Hebrew *Kaphtor*, in A. V. of Amos ix. 1 and Zeph. ii. 14, which is translated chapiter in R. V. In Ex. xxv. and xxxvii., where it occurs sixteen times, it is rendered knop in both versions.

Li'nus.

A Christian at Rome who joined Paul in sending salutations to Timothy (2 Tim. iv. 21). According to Irenæus and Eusebius, he was the first bishop of Rome. See BISHOP. No lofty preeminence was attached to the office, for he is mentioned without distinction between two other members of the church at Rome.

Li'on.

The *Felis leo* of naturalists. The lion is diffused over the whole of Africa and portions of southern Asia, as far east as the province of Guzerat in India. It was formerly found in Greece, but does not now occur wild in that country or anywhere in Europe. In Scripture times it was common in Palestine. The Hebrews had no fewer than six words to designate it in different states or at successive stages of growth. The ordinary words were *'aryeh* and *'ari*, which occur eighty times in the O. T. Allusion is made to the lion's strength (2 Sam. i. 23; Prov. xxx. 30) and courage (2 Sam. xvii. 10; Prov. xxviii. 1), to his teeth (Joel i. 6), to his tendency to crouch before springing on his victim (Gen. xlix. 9), to his tendency to prey on sheep, calves, and other beasts (1 Sam. xvii. 34; Is. xi. 6, 7), or upon man (1 Kin. xiii. 24; Jer. ii. 30), and to his roaring (Job iv. 10; Prov. xx. 2; 1 Pet. v. 8). He is represented as lurking in thickets (Jer. iv. 7), forests (v. 6), or other coverts (xxv. 38). A special haunt of his appears to have been among the trees and bushes fringing the Jordan (xlix. 19). Of the living creatures seen by Ezekiel in vision one had the face of a lion (Ezek. i. 10; x. 14). The first of the four living creatures seen by John was like a lion (Rev. iv. 7). Our Lord is called the Lion of the tribe of Judah (v. 5; cp. Gen. xlix. 9).

Liz'ard.

Any small lacertilian reptile. It was called *lᵉta'ah* by the Hebrews, and was regarded as unclean (Lev. xi. 30). The R. V. understands the four animals associated with it to be the gecko, the land crocodile, the sand lizard, and the chameleon; but states on the margin that the words are of uncertain meaning, but probably denote four kinds of lizards. Lizards abound in Palestine and the adjacent countries. The number of species is very great. In the woods and on cultivated ground the green lizards are the most beautiful, especially *Lacerta viridis* and *L. lævis*. Of the same family (*Lacertidæ*), but of a different genus (*Zootica*), are the wall lizards, which appear in warm weather in multitudes, crawling over walls, rocks, and stony ground. Other families of eriglossate lacertilians are represented in Palestine, as the *Scincidæ*, *Zonuridæ*, *Agamidæ*, and *Monitoridæ*. The first of these contains the skinks or sand lizards (Lev. xi. 30; in A. V. snail). They chiefly inhabit desert districts, are generally small and of the yellowish color of the desert, are as common as the true lizard, but unlike it do not climb, and hide themselves under stones or by burrowing rapidly in the ground. The family of *Zonuridæ* is represented by the glass snake (*Pseudopus pallasi*). Its hind legs are rudimentary, so that it looks much like a snake. It is black, and attains a length of two or two and a half feet, of which the tail forms two-thirds. Closely related to this family are the *Agamidæ*, containing *Uromastix spinipes*. This reptile inhabits the sandy deserts of Africa and Arabia, and is common in the wilderness of Judæa. It attains a length of two feet. Its body is green in color, spotted with brown. It has a powerful tail, encircled with rows of strong spines, which it uses as a weapon of defense. The Hebrew name was *ṣab*, rendered great lizard (Lev. xi. 29; in A. V. tortoise). The Arabs still call it *dabb*. The family of *Monitoridæ* or *Varanidæ* contains the monitors, of which the land crocodile of the ancients (Lev. xi. 30; in A. V. chameleon), commonly known as the land monitor, the *waran el-'ard* of the Arabs (*Psammosaurus scincus*), is common in southern Judæa, the peninsula of Sinai, and the sandy parts of Egypt. It attains a length of four or five feet, and has a long snout, sharp, pointed teeth, and a long, tapering tail. The water monitor, *waran el-bahr* (*Hydrosaurus niloticus*), is slightly larger than its congener of the land, and is readily distinguished from it by the high keel along the whole length of its tail. Both reptiles are extremely rapid in their movements, and are strong, fully justifying their supposed Hebrew name *koaḥ*, strength. They feed on small lizards and jerboas, and devour the eggs and young of the crocodile with avidity. They are eaten by the natives.

Loaf.

A mass of bread. It was made of the flour of barley (2 Kin. iv. 42; John vi. 9) or wheat (Lev. xxiii. 17 with Ex. xxxiv. 22), round in shape (Ex. xxix. 23; Judg. viii. 5, in Hebrew *kikkar*, disc), and of a size convenient for baking and carrying with one (1 Sam. x. 3; Mat. xiv. 17; John vi. 9). See BREAD and SHOWBREAD.

Lo-am'mi [not my people].

The symbolic name of the prophet Hosea's second son by his wife Gomer (Hos. i. 8, 9).

Loan.

Anything, especially money, that is lent. In the early ages of the Hebrew nation loans were not sought for the purpose of obtaining capital, but for the necessaries of life. The Israelites were commanded to open their heart to their brother, who had fallen into poverty, and to lend him sufficient for his need (Deut. xv. 7-11). They were forbidden to charge interest for any loan to a poor Israelite (Ex. xxii. 25; Lev. xxv. 35-37). But unto a foreigner they might lend on interest (Deut. xxiii. 20), and the poor Israelite might sell himself as a servant (Lev. xxv. 39; 2 Kin. iv. 1). If a pledge was asked from a poor Israelite for a loan, the creditor was not to go into the debtor's house to obtain it, but to remain outside and allow it to be brought out to him. If the pledge was a garment, it was to be returned to the owner before the evening, as probably it might be part of his sleeping attire (Ex. xxii. 26, 27). No one was to take the upper or nether millstone as a pledge, thus preventing the debtor and his family from grinding corn for their daily food (Deut. xxiv. 6). Nor could anyone take a widow's garment (17). Finally, when the seventh year, called the year of release, came, the debt was to be forgiven (xv. 1-11). The practice of suretyship, however, unfortunately grew up (Prov. vi. 1), and in later times interest was sometimes exacted for loans, although the practice was condemned by the prophets (Jer. xv. 10; Ezek. xviii. 13). The beneficent regulations of the law were systematically ignored after the exile, and Nehemiah took vigorous measures to terminate the abuse (Neh. v. 1-13). The Roman law was a marked contrast in its severity to that of Moses. By a law of the twelve tables a creditor could put his insolvent debtor in fetters and cords. Doubtless with allusion to the ordinary procedure Jesus describes the lord of a debtor as commanding that he, his wife, his children, and all that he had, be sold in liquidation of the debt (Mat. xviii. 25), and, when he had abused leniency which was shown him on his appeal for mercy, be delivered to the torturers till he should pay all that was due (34). In the time of Christ banking was a regular institution (Mat. xxv. 27; Luke xix. 23). A public building was provided in Jerusalem, where documents relating to loans, whether interest-bearing or not, might be deposited (War ii. 17, 6). See BANK.

Lock.

A fastening for a door (Judg. iii. 23), evidently as ancient as in modern times, consisting of a short bolt of wood, which slides through a groove in an upright piece attached to the door and enters a socket in the doorpost. Above the groove in the upright are holes containing small iron or wooden pins. When the bolt is thrust into the socket, these pins drop into corresponding holes in the bolt and hold it in place. The key is furnished with a like number of projections, and, when introduced into a hollow in the bolt underneath the pins, raises them and allows the bolt to be shoved back. When the lock is inside, a hole through the door admits the hand with the key, and even the hollow in the bolt is often large enough to admit the hand (Song v. 5).

Lo'cust.

The rendering of the Hebrew word *'Arbeh* and the Greek *Akris*. The insect referred to is evidently the migratory locust (*Œdipoda migratoria*), or in some cases possibly an allied insect, *Œdipoda cinerescens, Acridium peregrinum*, or other species. The locust is two inches or more in length. It is a winged, creeping thing. Like other insects of the order *Orthoptera*, it has four wings. Those of the anterior pair are narrow, while those of the posterior pair are broader, folded up when not in use, and transparent. It has six legs, on four of which it walks, while the hindmost pair, which are much longer than the others and equal to the body in length, it uses

Locust.

for springing (Lev. xi. 21, 22). The mouth is furnished with cutting jaws, by means of which it nips off leaves and blades of grass. They were clean insects (ibid.), and John the Baptist ate them, as many Orientals did before him and still do (Mat. iii. 4). They are prepared by being slightly roasted, dried in the sun, and salted. When used the head, wings, legs, and intestines are commonly removed, and only the fleshy portion is eaten. The locust is exceedingly destructive to vegetation, and locusts blown into the valley of the Nile by the east wind, constituted the eighth Egyptian plague (Ex. x. 4, 5, 12, 15, 19). In some passages, as Judg. vii. 12 and Jer. xlvi. 23, the A. V. renders *'arbeh* grasshopper; the R. V. uniformly translates it locust. The locust is distinguished from the grasshopper by the shortness of its antennæ. It must not be confounded with the harvest fly, which is commonly called locust in the United States.

Many other words refer to different species of locusts difficult to identify, or some of them may mean the migratory locust in different stages of development (Lev. xi. 22; Joel i. 4). The eggs of the various species of locust are deposited in April or May, in a cylindrical hole excavated in the ground by the female. They are hatched in June. The young insect emerges from the egg a wingless larva. It enters the pupa state, when it has rudimentary wings enclosed in cases. It is more voracious in this stage of its development than at any other period. In another month it casts the pupa or nymph skin, and has become the imago or perfect insect.

Lod [perhaps, strife, contest].

A town of Benjamin, built by the sons of Elpaal, a man of Benjamin (1 Chron. viii. 12), and generally mentioned in connection with Ono (Neh. xi. 35). It was inhabited after the Babylonian captivity (Ezra ii. 33; Neh. vii. 37), and is believed to have been the Lydda of the Greek period (1 Mac. xi. 34); see LYDDA. It still exists as Ludd, about 11 miles southeast of Joppa. In it are the remains of the church of St. George, the Christian martyr of Nicomedia and adopted in the fourteenth century as the patron saint of England, who was said to have been a native of the place.

Lo-de'bar [perhaps, without pasture].

A place in Gilead (2 Sam. ix. 4, 5; xvii. 27), probably the same as Lidebir (Josh. xiii. 26, R. V. margin). See DEBIR 4.

Lodge.

A shelter erected for the watchman of a garden for occupation during the time of ripe fruit (Is. i. 8; in xxiv. 20, A. V. cottage, R. V. hut). Not improbably the structure intended is the kind built among the branches of a tree or, where trees are lacking, upon posts, and consisting of a rude floor, a roof of mats or branches, and sides of branches.

Log [depth].

A Jewish measure of capacity used specially for oil (Lev. xiv. 10, 12, 15, 21, 24). The rabbins believe it to have contained twelve hins, so that it equaled the 720th part of an homer or about three gills.

Lo'is.

Timothy's grandmother, a woman of unfeigned faith (2 Tim. i. 5).

Look'ing-glass. See MIRROR.

Lord.

When used of God and printed in small letters with only the initial a capital, it is usually the rendering of the Hebrew *'Adon*, master (Ex. xxiii. 17; Ps. cxiv. 7), much more frequently of *'adonay*, properly my master (Ex. iv. 10; Is. xl. 10), or of the Greek *Kurios*, master, sir (Mat. i. 20). When printed in small capitals, it represents the Hebrew YHVH, Jehovah, the most sacred and incommunicable name of God, used of himself alone (Gen. ii. 4) See JEHOVAH.

Lord of Hosts. See HOST.

Lord's Day.

The day specially associated with the Lord Jesus Christ. The expression occurs but once in the N. T., where John says, "I was in the Spirit on the Lord's day" (Rev. i. 10). Various interpretations have been offered. 1,

John, it is said, is speaking of the Sabbath or seventh day of the week, which God himself has called "My holy day" (Is. lviii. 13). But if he intended the seventh day, it is strange that he did not use the customary designation. 2. It is held to be the day of Christ's birth. But that day is unknown, and it was not known or observed by the primitive church. 3. It is contended that the expression Lord's day is the same as the day of the Lord in 2 Pet. iii. 10, where it undoubtedly means the day of the second advent, and John would state that he was rapt, in vision, to the day of judgment. But John is apparently dating his vision. In the preceding sentence he mentions the place where he was at the time he received the revelation, the isle of Patmos; and declares the cause of his being on that island. In this sentence he states the day when he had the vision. It is also to be noticed that he does not speak of the day of the Lord, which is the constant designation of the day of the second advent, but uses the adjective *kuriakē*; a distinction which was observed ever afterwards between the day of the second advent and the first day of the week when Christ rose from the dead. 4. It has been thought possible that John means the anniversary of the resurrection. But none of the early fathers can be quoted either for this interpretation or for this use of the designation Lord's day. 5. Friday or crucifixion day, which, however, seems to have had no special honor from the apostles, this being reserved for 6. Sunday or resurrection day. On the resurrection day itself our Lord appeared to his disciples (Luke xxiv. 13–49; John xx. 1–25). After eight days, which in ordinary usage meant a week, Jesus a second time honored the first day of the week (John xx. 26). Since Pentecost occurred fifty days after the second day of unleavened bread (Lev. xxiii. 11, 15; see WEEKS, FEAST OF), it probably fell on the first day of the week in the year of Christ's crucifixion; and so the effusion of the Holy Spirit took place on the first day of the week (Acts ii. 1). The Christians at Troas in Paul's time seem to have regarded that day as the stated one on which they were accustomed to assemble to break bread (Acts xx. 7). On the same day of the week the Christians were to lay by them in store the money which they designed to give in charity (1 Cor. xvi. 2). These passages, aided by reasonings on more general principles, have led the great majority of Christians to consider the Lord's day a day set apart by the example of our Lord and his apostles for sacred purposes, and standing in a certain relation to the Sabbath of the ten commandments; see SABBATH. It may be added that some members of the primitive church made no distinction between days, including Jewish festivals and Sabbaths and possibly the first day, rightly or wrongly esteeming every day alike. They were not to be harshly judged, they were acting out of the fear of God (Rom. xiv. 5). Some of the Jewish converts continued to keep the seventh day and the Jewish festivals. It was a matter of liberty (Col. ii. 16), so long as the convert did not regard the observance as necessary to salvation (Gal. iv. 10).

Lord's Sup'per.

The name given by Paul to the commemorative ordinance instituted by our Lord on the evening preceding his crucifixion (1 Cor. xi. 20). Paul's account is the earliest record of the institution of the supper by at least two or three years. It was written probably early in A. D 57, just twenty-seven years after the supper was instituted. The apostle had introduced it five years earlier, when he organized the Corinthian church and "delivered unto them" the ordinance (23). He pledges his own truthfulness and authority for the correctness of his account by saying, "I received and I delivered"; and he refers to the source of his information: he had not been an eyewitness of the event, he had not been present at the institution of the supper, but he had received from the Lord what he had delivered unto them. These words are capable of two interpretations: either Paul had been granted a special communication direct from the risen Lord, or else he had received the account from the Lord through the Lord's apostles, participants in the first supper. Matthew an eyewitness and Mark, the companion of Peter who was present at the institution of the supper, also record the circumstances; and so does Paul's companion, Luke. Wishing to fulfill all righteousness and to honor the ceremonial law whilst yet it continued, Jesus made arrangements to eat the passover with his disciples (Mat. xxvi. 17–19). As the paschal lamb was killed in the evening, and its flesh eaten the same evening, the paschal feast necessarily took place in the evening (Mat. xxvi. 20). Wine mixed with water had come into use on such occasions, because that was regarded as the best way of using the best wine (cp. 2 Mac. xv. 39). When, therefore, our Lord was about to follow up the supper by the communion, there was wine mixed with water on the table. So also was there unleavened bread. He and his disciples were sitting (Mat. xxvi. 20), by which is meant that, after the custom of that time, they half sat, half reclined on couches (Mark xiv. 18, R. V. margin). When the paschal feast was finished, Jesus took bread and blessed it, at the same time rendering thanks for it, and, giving it to the disciples, said: "This is my body which is given for you: this do in remembrance of me." And the cup in like manner after supper, saying: "This cup is the new covenant in my blood, even that which is poured out for you" (Luke xxii. 19, 20, R. V.), "which is shed for many unto remission of sins" (Mat. xxvi. 28, R. V.). The object for which the Lord's Supper was instituted was to keep him in remembrance (Luke xxii. 19). It was to show forth the Lord's death till he come (1 Cor. xi. 25, 26). The feast was not confined to the apostles nor to the Jewish Christians, but was celebrated in the churches of the gentiles also, for instance at Corinth (1 Cor. x. 15–21). It was understood to be the privilege of the church for all time. The table on which the bread was placed was known as the Lord's table (x. 21); the cup of wine retained the old name which it bore at the Jewish passover, cup of blessing (x. 16), and was also called the cup of the Lord (21; xi. 27).

Lo-ru′ha-mah [not having obtained mercy].

The symbolic name of the prophet Hosea's daughter by his wife Gomer (Hos. i. 6, 8).

Lot, I.

The use of the lot to determine doubtful questions was much in vogue among the nations of antiquity (Esth. iii. 7; Jon. i. 7; Mat. xxvii. 35). Stones or inscribed tablets or the like were put into a vessel and, having been shaken, were drawn out or cast forth. The act was commonly preceded by prayer, and was an appeal to God to decide the matter (Acts i. 23–26; Iliad iii. 316–325; vii. 174–181). In the early history of the Jewish people God was pleased to use the lot as a method of making known his will, so that the weighty statement was made in Prov. xvi. 33, "The lot is cast into the lap; but the whole disposing thereof is of the Lord." The land of Canaan was divided among the twelve tribes by lot (Josh. xiv. 2; xviii. 6); for the method, see CANAAN. On one occasion Saul and Jonathan stood on one side and Jonathan cast lots against the people. The king and his son being thus singled out, they cast lots with each other, Jonathan being finally pointed out by this method of inquiry (1 Sam. xiv. 40–45). The courses of the priests, etc., were settled by lot (1 Chron. xxiv. 5, seq.). By casting lots after prayer the question was decided whether Joseph Barsabbas or Matthias should be Judas Iscariot's successor in the apostleship (Acts i. 15–26). This method of selection was not repeated by the apostles after the descent of the Holy Spirit.

Lot, II. [covering, or myrrh].

Son of Haran, Abraham's brother, and consequently nephew to the patriarch himself, whom he accompanied from Mesopotamia to Canaan (Gen. xi. 31; xii. 5), and to and from Egypt (xiii. 1). Like his uncle, he acquired much cattle; and his herdsmen and those of Abraham quarreled over the pasturage. Abraham proposed that he and Lot separate, and generously invited Lot to choose first. Lot, seeing that the hills were less fertile than the valley of the Jordan,

chose the latter, and became a resident in Sodom. He did not take into account the character of the people among whom he was going to settle, and the probable effect of their evil example on his family, though he maintained his own integrity among them and was distressed from day to day by the sight and the story of lawless deeds (2 Pet. ii. 8). During the invasion of Chedorlaomer and his confederate kings, Lot was made prisoner, and owed his release to the courage and skill of Abraham (Gen. xiii. 2–xiv. 16). When two angels were sent to Sodom to warn him of its approaching destruction, the conduct of the mob toward these strangers showed how ripe the city was for destruction. Lot was saved from its overthrow; but his wife, looking back, was killed, being overwhelmed by a shower of falling salt. His sons-in-law, probably prospective ones (xix. 14, R. V. margin; cp. 8), remained behind, and perished (xix. 1–29; Wisd. x. 6–9). Soon afterwards, under the influence of wine, Lot unconsciously became a participant in abhorrent deeds. The Moabites and Ammonites were his descendants (30–38).

Lo′tan.

A tribe of Horites, dwelling in mount Seir (Gen. xxxvi. 20) and governed by a chieftain (29).

Love′ Feasts.

The rendering of the Greek *Agapai* in 2 Pet. ii. 13, R. V. (on margin and in A. V. deceivings). In Jude 12 the rendering is feasts of charity. They were entertainments held in churches in connection with the Lord's Supper. Chrysostom states that after the early community of goods had ceased, the wealthier members brought contributions of food and drink to the church, of which, at the conclusion of the services and after the celebration of the Lord's Supper, all partook, the poorest not excepted, by this means helping to promote the principle of love among Christians. As the purity of the church declined and ceremony increased, scandals arose in connection with these feasts. The council of Laodicea, A. D. 320, and that of Carthage, A. D. 397, forbade them to be held in churches; so did the council of Orleans, A. D. 541, that of Trullo A. D. 692, and that of Aix-la-chapelle A. D. 816; but all these councils together did not quite succeed in extinguishing the love feasts' excessive tenacity of life in the western church, while in the Greek church they still continue to exist. Of more modern religious denominations, love feasts were revived by the Moravians. John Wesley introduced them into the great organization which he founded. They exist also among the Sandemanians.

Low′land or Sheph′e-lah; variously rendered in A. V. by the vale, the valley, the low country, the plain.

The region of low hills between the plain

of Philistia and the high central range of Palestine. It is described by Eusebius (in his *Onomasticon* under *Sephela*) as "all the low country about Eleutheropolis [the modern Beit Jibrin] toward the north and west;" but in O. T. times the term comprehended the low, hilly country lying to the east and south as well. The hills rise to a height of from 500 to 800 feet, with a few higher summits. On their slopes the olive flourishes. The district is separated from the central Judæan range by a series of valleys which run north and south from Aijalon to near Beer-sheba; and it is itself cut by several wide, fertile valleys which lead from the Judæan ridge to the sea. It was assigned, as part of their inheritance, to the tribe of Judah; and when they found that they had too much territory, a small portion of it in the north was allotted to Dan (Josh. xv. 33 seq.; xix. 40 seq.). It included such notable places as Adullam, Beth-shemesh, Gezer, Eglon, Lachish, and part of the valleys of Aijalon, Sorek, and Elah (33 seq.; 1 Sam. xvii. 1, 2; 2 Chron. xxviii. 18).

Lu'bim.
An African people from whom Shishak, king of Egypt, drew part of his army for the invasion of Palestine (2 Chron. xii. 3; xvi. 8; cp. Dan. xi. 43; Nah. iii. 9), doubtless the primitive Libyans.

Lu'cas. See LUKE.

Lu'ci-fer [the light bearer or bringer].
The planet Venus, as the morning star. With the exception of the sun and moon, Venus is the brightest object in the sky. It appears as a morning or an evening star according as it is west or east of the sun, returning to the same position about every nineteen months. As the former, Venus is the harbinger of daylight. The prophet likened the splendor of the king of Babylon to Lucifer, son of the morning (Is. xiv. 12; in R. V. day-star), and Jesus calls himself the bright, the morning star (Rev. xxii. 16; cp. 2 Pet. i. 19). The application of the name Lucifer to Satan, the rebel angel hurled from heaven, has existed since the third century, especially among poets. It is based on the erroneous supposition that Luke x. 18 is an explanation of Is. xiv. 12.

Lu'ci-us.
1. A Roman official who in the year 174 of the Seleucidan era, 139-8 B. C., issued letters in favor of the Jews to various kings subject to Rome (1 Mac. xv. 16). He is entitled a consul, which identifies him with Lucius Calpurnius Piso, one of the consuls for the year 139 B. C. It is possible, however, that he was the prætor Lucius Valerius who conducted the proceedings in the Roman senate which led to their making a league of friendship with the Jews, to the issuance of the aforementioned letters, and in the days of Hyrcanus II. to action favorable to the Jews (Antiq. xiv. 8, 5).

2. A Christian from Cyrene, who was a teacher in the church at Antioch (Acts xiii. 1). He is commonly supposed to have been the kinsman of Paul, who at Corinth joined with the apostle in sending salutations to the brethren at Rome (Rom. xvi. 21).

Lud.
1. A people classed among the Semites (Gen. x. 22); believed to be the Lydians (Antiq. i. 6, 4; compare order of enumeration in Gen.), occupying, however, a wider territory than Lydia in western Asia Minor. It is not clear in what manner the Lydians were related to the Semites, whether by blood or by conquest. According to Herodotus (i. 7), their first king was a son of Ninus and grandson of Belus, that is, he was descended from the Assyrians.
2. A people related to the Egyptians (Gen. x. 13), also the country which they inhabited. They are mentioned as bowmen in the armies of Egypt and Tyre (Jer. xlvi. 9; Ezek. xxvii. 10; xxx. 5). Libyans is too broad a translation (Jer. xlvi. 9, A. V.); though the Ludim are doubtless to be sought in northern Africa, west of the Nile.

Lu'dim [plural of Lud]; see LUD 2.

Lu'hith [perhaps, made of planks].
A Moabite town approached by an ascent (Is. xv. 5; Jer. xlviii. 5); according to Eusebius and Jerome, Loueitha, between Areopolis, that is Rabbath, Moab, and Zoar.

Luke, in A. V. once **Lucas** (Philem. 24) [N. T. Greek *Loukas*, probably an abbreviation of Latin *Lucanus* or perhaps *Lucilius*].
A friend and companion of St. Paul, who joined him in sending from Rome salutations to the Colossian church (Col. iv. 14) and to Philemon (Philem. 24). In the former place he is described as "the beloved physician" and in the latter place as one of the apostle's fellow-laborers. He was also with Paul in Rome at a later time when 2 Timothy was written (2 Tim. iv. 11), and then the apostle gives a touching tribute to his friend's fidelity in the words "Only Luke is with me." These are all the notices of Luke by name in the N. T., for he must not be identified with the Lucius of Acts xiii. 1 nor with the one mentioned in Rom. xvi. 21; see LUCIUS. We find, however, in the second century the tradition already established that Luke was the author of the Third Gospel and of The Acts, both of which were certainly written by the same hand (Acts i. 1). Accordingly we may learn more of him from The Acts, in which he intimates his presence with Paul during certain portions of the latter's missionary journeys by the use of "we" or "us" in the narrative (Acts xvi. 10–17; xx. 5–xxi. 18; xxvii. 1–xxviii. 16). From these passages it appears that Luke joined Paul on the second missionary journey at Troas and went with him to Philippi. Again on the third journey Luke rejoined the apostle at Philippi and went

with him to Jerusalem. He appears to have remained in Palestine during the two years in which Paul was imprisoned at Cæsarea, for he sailed with the apostle from Cæsarea to Rome; see ACTS. In Col. iv. 14 Luke is plainly distinguished from Paul's Jewish companions (cp. ver. 11). He was therefore a gentile. Early tradition made him a native of Antioch in Syria, and this is quite probable. At any rate, his interest in and familiarity with the church of Antioch is evident (Acts vi. 5; xi. 19-27; xiii. 1-3; xiv. 26-28; xv. 1, 2, 30-40; xviii. 22, 23). Ramsay, however, considers him a Philippian (*St. Paul the Traveler*, p. 202). The time and manner of his death are unknown.

The Gospel according to St. Luke is the Third Gospel according to the order of the books of the N. T. as usually arranged. It is addressed to a certain Theophilus, probably a gentile Christian; claims to be based upon careful investigation of the apostolic testimony; and was intended to furnish Theophilus, as well as other readers, with assured knowledge of the truth in which he had been instructed. Its material is doubtless derived both from earlier documents and from information obtained by Luke personally from the actors in the history. The narrative may be divided as follows: 1. Introductory verses (i. 1-4). 2. The immediate preparation for the appearance of Jesus, consisting of the annunciations and births of John the Baptist and Jesus, with some significant events from the latter's infancy and boyhood (i. 5-ii. 52). 3. The inauguration of Christ's ministry, including (*a*) the ministry of John the Baptist, (*b*) the baptism of Jesus, to which is appended his genealogy, and (*c*) the temptation of Jesus (iii. 1-iv. 13). 4. The Lord's ministry in Galilee (iv. 14-ix. 50). In this part of his Gospel Luke often follows the same order as Mark, but not always. He also introduces more of the teaching of Jesus than Mark does, in this often corresponding with Matthew. He is, however, independent of both Mark and Matthew even where he covers the same ground. [Many students of this Gospel, while agreeing that he made no use of Matthew's Gospel, but that each of these evangelists drew independently from a common source for the teachings of Jesus, yet believe that he used Mark's Gospel, or a narrative underlying Mark's Gospel and recounting the events of Jesus' ministry, and made its order of incidents his standard, although occasionally seeing fit to depart from it (J. D. D.).] Luke, moreover, has some material peculiar to himself in these chapters. The following analysis will bring out the progress of this portion of his narrative: (*a*) Introductory description (iv. 14, 15). (*b*) Opening of the Galilæan work, including the first visit to Nazareth, miracles in Capernaum and tour through Galilee, the call of four disciples and the healing of the leper (iv. 16-v. 16).

(*c*) Rise of opposition, in the face of which Christ vindicated his teaching, including the cure of the paralytic, Levi's call and feast, discourse about fasting, and the Sabbath controversy (v. 17-vi. 12). (*d*) Organization of the disciples, including the appointment of the twelve and Christ's discourse on the characteristics of true discipleship (sermon on the mount) (vi. 13-49). (*e*) Incidents illustrative of the gracious ministry of Jesus, including the healing of the centurion's servant, the raising of the widow of Nain's son, the inquiry of John the Baptist, and Christ's reply and discourse concerning John, the anointing of Jesus by a sinful woman (vii. 1-50). (*f*) The extension of Christ's work, including his tours through Galilee with a company of disciples; his teaching by parables; the visit of his mother and brethren; the four great miracles of stilling the tempest, healing the Gadarene demoniac, and the woman with the issue of blood, and raising Jairus' daughter; the sending out of the apostles; Herod's desire to see Jesus and the latter's subsequent retirement, followed by the feeding of the 5000 (viii. 1-ix. 17). (*g*) Christ's instructions to his disciples in view of the close of the Galilæan ministry and his coming death, including Peter's confession, Christ's prediction of his death and resurrection, the transfiguration and the cure of the demoniac boy, warnings against pride (ix. 18-50). 5. The journeyings of Jesus to Jerusalem (ix. 51-xix. 48). This part of Luke contains a large amount of material peculiar to him. It is probably not arranged in exact chronological order, but rather in accordance with certain topics. Some of the material given here really belongs in the Galilæan ministry (ix. 57-60; xiii. 18-21; probably xi. 14-xiii. 5). But the section describes in the main a series of journeys toward Jerusalem, ending in the final ascent, with discourses appropriate to the situation. It may be subdivided as follows: (*a*) The departure from Galilee and instructions concerning the true spirit of disciples, including Christ's rejection by a Samaritan village, his replies to three inquirers, the mission of the seventy, and their return, the lawyer's question and the parable of the good Samaritan, Christ in the house of Martha and Mary, instructions about prayer (ix. 51-xi. 13). (*b*) Denunciation of the Pharisees and instructions concerning the duty of confessing him, against covetousness, and concerning watchfulness, etc. (xi. 14-xiii. 5). (*c*) Discourses illustrative of the true Israel and of the true service; the former including the parable of the barren fig tree, the woman with the spirit of infirmity, the parables of the mustard seed and leaven, the warning against self-deception and the lamentation over Jerusalem; the latter including the healing of the dropsical man, and the beautiful parables of the wedding feast, the great supper, the lost sheep, the lost coin, the lost son, the unjust steward, the rich man and Lazarus, the importunate widow, interspersed with incidents and teachings on the same general subject (xiii. 6-xviii. 30). (d) The final ascent to Jerusalem, including a renewed prediction of death and resurrection, the healing of Bartimæus, the conversion of Zacchæus, the parable of the pounds, and the triumphal entry (xviii. 31-xix. 48). 6. The last week in Jerusalem, including the final teachings of Jesus in the temple and to his disciples, his arrest, trials, crucifixion, and burial (xx.-xxiii. 56). 7. Appearances of Jesus after his resurrection, his last directions to his disciples to preach his gospel, and his final departure (ascension) from them (xxiv.).

St. Luke states (i. 3) that his narrative is written "in order." This use of this phrase elsewhere (Acts xi. 4; xviii. 23; and Greek text of Luke viii. 1 and Acts iii. 24) shows that he does not necessarily mean exact chronological order. While chronological in general outline, his arrangement is often topical. The book, however, is, like The Acts, a careful and systematic presentation of the life of the Founder of Christianity. Luke also expressly disclaims personal acquaintance with Jesus, and bases his work on the testimony of eyewitnesses (apostles) whose reports he had accurately studied. His Gospel shows a truly historical spirit. This appears e. g. in the personal account of the origin of John the Baptist and of Jesus, in his dating by secular events the birth of Jesus and the public appearance of John (ii. 1, 2; iii. 1, 2), and his presentation of the ministry of Christ in such a manner as to bring out its leading religious ideas, its triumph over opposition, and the historical foundation which it laid for Christianity (see the analysis above). It shows also the evangelist's fondness for those aspects of the Lord's teaching and work, whereby he revealed himself as the divine-human Saviour of men. Christ's gospel is here described as universal in its mission (ii. 32; iii. 6; iv. 24-27; xxiv. 47, etc.), a gospel for the lost and the lowly (vii. 36-50; xv.; xix. 1-9, etc.), a message of salvation to the poor and distressed (vi. 20-26; vii. 11-18; ix. 56; xii. 32, etc.). It delineates the graciousness of Christ's personal character—his piety, compassion, charity, prayerfulness, holiness, tenderness. In recording the Lord's utterances about the rich, Luke uses more unqualified language than the other evangelists do (i. 52, 53; vi. 24, 25; xvi. 25, etc.), though he also makes it clear that he did not understand Christ to denounce rich men as such, but only so far as they put trust in riches and were not rich toward God (xii. 21). In what he reports about Samaritans also (x. 33; xvii. 16) he doubtless wished to illustrate the destruction of national prejudices by the gospel. In short this Gospel presents Christ as establishing a religion which seeks to uplift and save suffering and sinful humanity. The writer's

medical vocabulary also occasionally appears and confirms the belief that he was Luke. See iv. 35, "when the devil had *thrown* him;" iv. 38, "holden with a *great* fever;" v. 18, "*taken with* a palsy;" vi. 19, "*healed* them;" viii. 44, "the issue of her blood *stanched;*" x. 34, "*bound up* his wounds, *pouring in* oil and wine" (see Hobart, *Medical Language of St. Luke*).

The date of the composition of this Gospel depends on that of The Acts. 1 Tim. v. 18, however, seems to contain a quotation from it. If so, it was certainly written before A. D. 66. At any rate, Luke's report of Christ's prediction of the fall of Jerusalem is not, as some hold, a sufficient ground for dating this Gospel after that event; since Luke's language is only an interpretation of Christ's words, designed to make their meaning plain to gentile readers (Luke xxi. 20; cp. Mat. xxiv. 15; Mark xiii. 14), and since the Christians, on the basis of Christ's prophecy, were looking forward to the destruction of the city, as is proven by Mark's report and other evidence. It may have been composed during the two years (58-60) during which Luke was in Palestine while Paul was imprisoned in Cæsarea. Or the materials may then have been gathered and the book written afterwards in Rome. It is best to assign it, somewhat vaguely, to the years 58-65. The author apparently intended it to be the first of a series of works on the origin of Christianity, for the preface evidently contemplated the work of the apostles as well as the life of Christ (i. 1, 2), and the brevity of the report of Christ's parting instructions in the last chapter was probably due to the author's intention to resume the subject as he does in the first chapter of The Acts. There is abundant evidence for its use in the churches of the second century as an authoritative gospel; see GOSPEL. It was mutilated and then used by the Gnostic Marcion, in the second quarter of the second century, as the only true gospel, which at least shows its authority before that time. The first formal mention of Luke as its author, so far as our extant literature shows, occurs about A. D. 170 (in the Muratorian Fragment), but there is no reason to doubt that the tradition had been long established and rested on good grounds.

G. T. P. (edited).

Lu'na-tic [insane, with lucid intervals]. The Greek word is derived from *selēnē*, moon, as the English word is from the Latin *luna*, moon, for it was believed that the disease is affected by the light or by the periodic changes of the moon. Lunacy is distinguished from demoniacal possession (Mat. iv. 24), for it was often due to other causes. Yet possession by a demon might give rise to lunacy (Mat. xvii. 15 with Mark ix. 17). A comparison of these two passages has led to the opinion that the Greek word denotes epilepsy. Hence R. V. uses epileptic instead of lunatic

Lute. See PSALTERY.

Luz [almond tree].

1. A Canaanite town, afterwards Bethel (Gen. xxviii. 19; xxxv. 6; xlviii. 3; Josh. xviii. 13; Judg. i. 23). In Josh. xvi. 2 it is distinguished from Bethel and located to the west. See BETHEL.

2. A town in the Hittite country, built by an inhabitant of Luz in mount Ephraim, who betrayed that town to the Israelites and was allowed by them to depart with his family uninjured (Judg. i. 22–26). Site unknown. About 12 miles southeast by east of Sidon is the town Luezeh, and 4½ miles west by north of Banias is the ruin Luweizîyeh.

Lyc-a-o'ni-a [popularly interpreted as pertaining to king Lycaon or abounding in were-wolves].

An elevated, rugged, inland district of Asia Minor, bounded on the north by Galatia, on the south by Cilicia and Isauria, on the east by Cappadocia, and on the west by Phrygia. It was mainly suitable for pasturage only. Its peculiar dialect, probably mingled Greek and Syriac, was still spoken when Paul visited the district and preached in three of its cities, Iconium, Derbe, and Lystra (Acts xiii. 51–xiv. 23, especially 11).

Ly'ci-a [explained as pertaining to Lycus, son of Pandion (Herod i. 173)].

A province of Asia Minor, jutting southward into the Mediterranean Sea, and bounded on the north by Caria, Phrygia, Pisidia, and Pamphylia. Paul on his last voyage to Jerusalem passed Rhodes, an island off its western coast, and landed at Patara, within its limits, where he took ship for Phœnicia (Acts xxi. 1, 2). On his voyage to Rome he landed at Myra, another city of Lycia, whence he sailed in an Alexandrian vessel bound for Italy (xxvii. 5, 6).

Lyd'da.

A village of considerable size near Joppa (Acts ix. 38; Antiq. xx. 6, 2), probably the town called Lod in the O. T. The gospel early took root in it (Acts ix. 32). Shortly before 153 B. C. the town with the district about it formed a distinct government in connection with Samaria, but in 145 B. C. it was transferred to Judæa (1 Mac. xi. 34; cp. 28; x. 30, 38). Peter visited it, and his cure of Æneas through the name of Jesus resulted in a large increase of disciples (Acts ix. 33–35). It was burnt by Cestius in the time of Nero, but was soon rebuilt (War ii. 19, 1). See LOD.

Lyd'i-a [nominally from Ludos, its reputed founder (Herod i. 7)].

1. A region on the western coast of Asia Minor, with Sardis for its capital. Thyatira and Philadelphia were within its limits. It was very fertile and had a mild climate, and consequently it was densely populated. The customs of its inhabitants were Semitic in character, and their religion was apparently a mingling of Syrian and Phrygian worship (Duncker). The state rose to power about 689 B. C., under Gyges, when the Greeks on the coast and the tribes of Asia Minor were subdued. In 549 B. C. Crœsus, the last king, was defeated by Cyrus, and Lydia became a Persian province. It never regained independence. Antiochus III., of Syria, forced to cede it to the Romans (cp. 1 Mac. viii. 8). Many Jews dwelt there (Antiq. xii. 3, 4), and Christian churches were founded (Rev. i. 11).

2. A woman of Thyatira, a town of Lydia, though it is not known whether this was the origin of her name. Thyatira was noted for its dyeing, and Lydia made her living in Philippi, to which she had removed, by selling purple dyes or dyed goods. She was a worshiper of God before Paul arrived at Philippi. She received the gospel of Christ gladly, and, though by birth an Asiatic, became Paul's first convert in Macedonia and Europe. At her urgent invitation Paul and his missionary associates took up their abode with her; and when Paul and Silas were released from prison, to which they had been consigned after a riot of which they were the innocent cause, they returned to her house (Acts xvi. 14, 15, 40).

Ly-sa'ni-as [ending sadness].

A tetrarch of Abilene in the fifteenth year of Tiberius (Luke iii. 1). Some critics have thought that Lysanias, son of Ptolemy, who ruled Chalcis in Cœlesyria during the years 40 to 34 B. C. (Antiq. xiv. 13, 3; xv. 4, 1), gave name to this tetrarchy, and that Luke is in error. But the highest authorities explain the facts in a very different manner. Lysanias who ruled Chalcis is never called tetrarch, and Abila nowhere appears in his dominions. From Antiq. xv. 10, 1–3, it appears that the house or territory of Lysanias was hired by Zenodorus about 25 B. C., became known as the country of Zenodorus, lay between Trachonitis and Galilee, chiefly about Paneas and Ulatha, and hence apparently did not include Chalcis in Cœlesyria, and strictly speaking was distinct from Batanea, Trachonitis, and Auranitis. These districts were bestowed on Herod the Great and passed to his son Philip the tetrarch, Augustus confirming to him Batanea, Trachonitis, Auranitis, and part of the house of Zenodorus (xvii. 11, 4) which included Paneas (8, 1). In A. D. 37 the emperor Caligula made Herod Agrippa king of the tetrarchy of Philip and added the tetrarchy of Lysanias (xviii. 6, 10). This latter tetrarchy had its capital at Abila, some eighteen miles northwest of Damascus, and was distinct from the kingdom of Chalcis (xix. 5, 1; xx. 7, 1; War ii. 11, 5). In the reign of the emperor Tiberius the region about Abila was ruled by a tetrarch named Lysanias (see ABILENE), in exact agreement with Luke's statement. Although far north, it may have been the remaining part of the country of Zenodorus, which after his death and the division of his land, as before mentioned, had been formed into a tetrarchy or kingdom under a younger Lysanias, perhaps of the same line as the former ruler of Chalcis.

Ly'si-as.

1. A general of the army of Syria during the reigns of Antiochus Epiphanes and Antiochus Eupator. When Antiochus Epiphanes went to Persia about 165 B. C., he appointed Lysias, who was of royal blood, viceroy during his absence, with the duty of quelling the Jewish insurrection under the Maccabees (1 Mac. iii. 32–37). After operating through others, Lysias found it necessary to take the field himself; but he was defeated by Judas with great loss (38–40 ; iv. 1–22, 28–35). When the news of Antiochus' death arrived in 163 B. C., Lysias seized the reins of government and ruled in the name of the young Antiochus, although the late king had named Philip for regent during the minority of the heir to the throne (vi. 14–17). In this capacity Lysias undertook another campaign against the Jews. He gained a victory over Judas and laid siege to Jerusalem ; but the news that Philip was on his way from Persia to claim the regency, compelled him to make terms of peace with the Jews and return to Antioch (vi. 28–63). He maintained himself successfully against Philip, but was put to death in 162 B. C. by Demetrius I. (vii. 1–4).

2. Roman commandant at Jerusalem, who rescued Paul from the mob of Jews (Acts xxii. 24). See CLAUDIUS LYSIAS.

Lys'tra.

A city of Lycaonia and a Roman colony, where Paul cured a man crippled from birth, and would have been worshiped as a god had he not refused. It was there also that he was stoned and left for dead (Acts xiv. 6–21 ; 2 Tim. iii. 11). Either at Lystra or Derbe he first met Timothy (Acts xvi. 1, 2). The site is Zoldera, one mile north of Khatyn Serai and twenty-two miles south-southwest of Iconium.

M

Ma'a-cah, in A. V. often **Maachah**, and in R. V. of Josh. xiii. 13 **Maacath**, the archaic (Canaanite) spelling [compression, oppression].

1. A place in Syria (2 Sam. x. 6, 8), sometimes called Aram-maacah or Syria-maachah (1 Chron. xix. 6, 7) ; see ARAM 2 (4). Its inhabitants were descended from Nahor (Gen. xxii. 24).

2. Wife of Machir, the son of Manasseh (1 Chron. vii. 15, 16).

3. A concubine of Caleb, the son of Hezron (1 Chron. ii. 48).

4. Wife of Jehiel and ancestress of king Saul (1 Chron. viii. 29 ; ix. 35).

5. Daughter of Talmai, king of Geshur. She became one of David's wives and mother of Absalom (2 Sam. iii. 3).

6. Father of Hanan, one of David's mighty men (1 Chron. xi. 43).

7. Father of the ruler of the Simeonites in David's reign (1 Chron. xxvii. 16).

8. Father of Solomon's royal contemporary Achish of Gath (1 Kin. ii. 39) ; see ACHISH.

9. Wife of Rehoboam, and daughter, or in view of 2 Chron. xiii. 2 perhaps, the granddaughter, of Absalom (1 Kin. xv. 2 ; 2 Chron. xi. 20–22), and mother of king Abijah. After the death of the latter, she remained queenmother (g'birah) ; but her grandson Asa took this position from her because she had made an abominable image for an Asherah (2 Chron. xv. 16 R. V.). She is called Michaiah in 2 Chron. xiii. 2 ; but this is probably a textual corruption, for in the seven other places where her name occurs it is Maacah.

Ma-ac'a-thite in A. V. **Maachathite**, but in Deut. iii. 14 **Maachathi**, the Hebrew form instead of the English.

A descendant of a person named Maacah, or a native or inhabitant of the Syrian kingdom of Maacah or of the town of Beth-maacah in Naphtali (Josh. xii. 5 ; 2 Sam. xxiii. 34).

Ma'a-chah. See MAACAH.

Ma-ach'a-thi. See MAACATHITE.

Ma'a-dai [perhaps, wavering].

A son of Bani, induced by Ezra to put away his foreign wife (Ezra x. 34).

Ma-a-di'ah [ornament of Jehovah].

A chief of the priests who returned from the Babylonian captivity (Neh. xii. 5, 7). In the next generation, a father's house among the priests, which occupies the same position in the corresponding catalogue, bears the name Moadiah (ver. 17). The reason for this traditional variation is not yet clear. Perhaps the name should always be pronounced Moadiah.

Ma'ai.

A priest who blew a trumpet at the dedication of the second temple (Neh. xii. 36).

Ma'a-leh-a-crab'bim. See AKRABBIM.

Ma'a-rath [a place bare of trees].

A town in the hill country of Judah (Josh. xv. 59), doubtless north of Hebron and near Halhul.

Ma'a-reh-ge'ba [place destitute of trees at Geba].

A place adjacent to Geba (Judg. xx. 33, R. V.). On the margin it is translated the meadow of Geba or Gibeah ; in the text of A. V., the meadows of Gibeah.

Ma'a-sai, in A. V. **Ma-as'i-ai** [perhaps, work of Jehovah].

A priest of the family of Immer (1 Chron. ix. 12). The name may be an abbreviation of Maaseiah by curtailment or possibly another form of that word ; or perhaps it is an accidental transposition of the letters of Amasai.

Ma-a-se′iah [work of Jehovah].

1. A Levite of the second degree, who acted as porter in the reign of David (1 Chron. xv. 18), and played a psaltery (ver. 20).

2. One of the captains of hundreds, who coöperated with the high priest Jehoiada in overthrowing Athaliah and placing Joash on the throne of Judah (2 Chron. xxiii. 1).

3. An officer who seems to have acted with Jeiel the Levite in keeping a list of the military men in Uzziah's reign (2 Chron. xxvi. 11).

4. A prince of the royal house, a son of Jotham more probably than of Ahaz, since the latter was too young to have adult children. He was slain during Pekah's invasion of Judah (2 Chron. xxviii. 7).

5. The governor of Jerusalem in Josiah's reign (2 Chron. xxxiv. 8).

6. Ancestor of Seraiah and Baruch (Jer. xxxii. 12; li. 59, A. V.). The name is radically different from that which is elsewhere represented by Maaseiah. See MAHSEIAH.

7. Father of the false prophet Zedekiah (Jer. xxix. 21).

8. A priest, father of the temple official Zephaniah (Jer. xxi. 1 ; xxix. 25).

9. Son of Shallum and doorkeeper of the temple (Jer. xxxv. 4). He was doubtless a Levite (1 Chron. xxvi. 1). See SHALLUM.

10. A man of Judah, family of Shelah. He lived at Jerusalem after the captivity (Neh. xi. 5).

11. A Benjamite, whose descendants lived at Jerusalem after the captivity (Neh. xi. 7).

12-15. A man of the house of Pahath-moab and three priests, one a member of the house of the high priest Jeshua, one of the house of Harim, and the third of the house of Pashhur, each of whom put away his foreign wife (Ezra x. 18, 21, 22, 30).

16. Father of that Azariah who repaired the wall of Jerusalem beside his house (Neh. iii. 23).

17. A chief of the people who signed the covenant with Nehemiah (Neh. x. 25).

18. A priest who marched in the procession at the dedication of the wall of Jerusalem (Neh. xii. 41), perhaps one of the six who stood by Ezra when he read the law to the people (viii. 4).

19. A Levite, probably, who marched in the procession at the dedication of the wall (Neh. xii. 42), perhaps one of the thirteen who expounded the law as it was read to the people (viii. 7).

Ma-as′i-ai. See MAASAI.

Ma′ath.

An ancestor of Christ, who lived after the time of Zerubbabel (Luke iii. 26).

Ma′az [anger].

A descendant of Judah through Jerahmeel (1 Chron. ii. 27).

Ma-a-zi′ah [consolation of Jehovah].

1. A descendant of Aaron. His family had grown to a father's house by the time of David and was made the last of the twenty-four courses into which the priests were divided (1 Chron. xxiv. 1, 6, 18).

2. A priest who, doubtless in behalf of a father's house, sealed the covenant in the days of Nehemiah (Neh. x. 8).

Mac′ca-bee.*

A family, also called Asmonæan from one of its ancestors, which ruled Judæa from 166 B. C. to 37 B. C.; see ASMONÆAN. The title Maccabæus, in A. V. Maccabeus, was first given to Judas, third son of Mattathias (1 Mac. ii. 4), but at an early date it was transferred to the entire family and to others who had a part in the same events. The origin and meaning of the term have eluded research. It is usually derived from *makkabah*, a hammer, either in allusion to the crushing blows inflicted by Judas and his successors upon their enemies, or perhaps

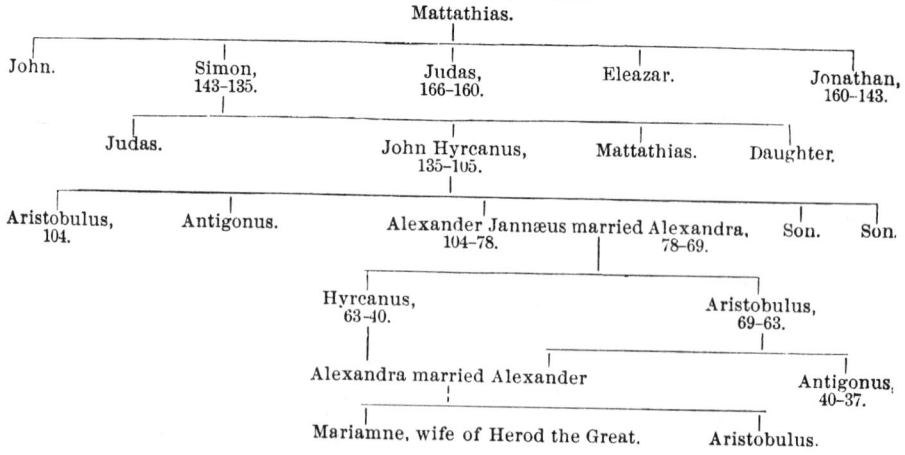

*THE MACCABÆAN FAMILY.

Mattathias.

| John. | Simon, 143-135. | Judas, 166-160. | Eleazar. | Jonathan, 160-143. |

| Judas. | John Hyrcanus, 135-105. | Mattathias. | Daughter. |

| Aristobulus, 104. | Antigonus. | Alexander Jannæus married Alexandra, 104-78. / 78-69. | Son. | Son. |

| Hyrcanus, 63-40. | Aristobulus, 69-63. |

| Alexandra married Alexander | Antigonus, 40-37. |

| Mariamne, wife of Herod the Great. | Aristobulus. |

because a cap worn by Judas was shaped like a hammer at its top point. It has also been explained as composed of the initials of the Hebrew words in the sentence, "Who is like to thee among the gods, Jehovah?", or in the sentence, "What is like my father?", or as being the Hebrew word *makbi*, extinguisher. None of these interpretations is, however, more than a conjecture. The first of the family mentioned is Mattathias, an aged priest, who, driven to desperation by the outrages of Antiochus Epiphanes, raised a revolt against him and fled to the mountains, followed by those who were zealous for the faith of Israel. Mattathias died about two years afterwards, but the revolt was carried on by his five sons. Judas, the third son, was the first military leader, 166 B. C. By avoiding pitched battles, and harassing the Syrians by vigorous and persistent guerilla warfare, he and his devoted band defeated and routed every detachment of the Syrian army sent against them. He retook Jerusalem, purified the temple, and restored the daily sacrifice. A feast to celebrate this restoration was instituted and was kept annually thereafter. This was the winter feast of dedication alluded to in John x. 22. Judas fell in battle 160 B. C., whereupon his younger brother Jonathan, who was already high priest, assumed command of the army. About this time John the eldest brother was captured and killed by the children of Jambri (1 Mac. xi. 36) ; and shortly before this another brother, Eleazar, had been crushed to death underneath an elephant which he had wounded in battle. During the leadership of Jonathan the Syrians were occupied with civil war, so that not only was Judæa left in peace, but the favor of the Jews was sued for, and Jonathan was able to strengthen his position. He made a treaty with the Romans and also with the Spartans. He was treacherously slain by Tryphon, a Syrian general, in 143 B. C. On his death the leadership fell to Simon, the last remaining son of Mattathias. The most important event that fell under his rule was the granting of Jewish independence by the Syrian king Demetrius II. Coins were struck bearing the name of Simon, and contracts were dated "in the first year of Simon high priest and governor." Simon and two of his sons were treacherously slain by his son-in-law Ptolemy, in Dok near Jericho 135 B. C. The one son who escaped, John, assumed the power and was known as John Hyrcanus. He was a shrewd and vigorous ruler and enlarged his province. He conquered the Edomites and merged them in the Jewish people. After a long and prosperous reign he died a natural death, and was succeeded by his son Aristobulus, a cruel and unprincipled man who killed his mother and brother. He changed the theocracy into a kingdom, calling himself king, but retained at the same time the high-priesthood. After a reign of one year he was succeeded by a brother, Alexander Jannæus, during whose reign the country was torn by the dissensions of the Sadducees and Pharisees. He had a troubled reign of 27 years, and was followed by his widow Alexandra, who reigned for 9 years. She left two sons, Hyrcanus and Aristobulus, who quarreled about the succession. Hyrcanus was established as high priest while Aristobulus seized the civil authority. Civil war broke out. The Romans interfered, and at first upheld Aristobulus, but later deposed him and carried him to Rome. Hyrcanus was nominally king, but the real ruler was Antipas, or Antipater, an Idumæan, who had been appointed procurator of Judæa under Hyrcanus by the Romans. A period of quarrels and dissensions among the members of the reigning family followed, during which time Antipater steadily grew in influence and power with the Romans, until, the Maccabæans falling into disfavor, the crown of Judæa was given to Antipater's son, Herod. For 1, 2, 3, and 4 Maccabees, see APOCRYPHA.

Mac-e-do′ni-a.

A country lying immediately to the north of Greece. Little is known of it prior to 560 B. C., and for more than 200 years afterwards it possessed no special interest. But under Philip of Macedon (359–336 B. C.) and his yet more celebrated son Alexander the Great (336–323 B. C.), it rose to world-wide power and imperial importance ; see PHILIP 1 and ALEXANDER 1. Under his successors the empire was divided, and the country declined, till in 168 B. C. it was conquered by the Romans, and in 142 B. C. became a Roman province. Macedonia is not mentioned by name in the O. T. ; but the Macedonian empire is referred to in Dan. ii. 39 ; vii. 6 ; viii. 5, 8. In 1 Mac. i. 1 Chittim is Macedonia. Paul, summoned in a vision by a man of Macedonia, on his second journey, passed from Asia into Europe, and preached the gospel in that continent first on Macedonian soil. At this time he passed through the Macedonian towns of Neapolis, Philippi, Amphipolis, Apollonia, Thessalonica, and Berœa (Acts xvi. 9–xvii. 14). When Paul departed, Silas and Timothy continued the work (xvii. 14, 15 ; xviii. 5). Paul revisited the region (xix. 21, 22 ; xx. 1–3 ; cp. 2 Cor. ii. 13 ; vii. 5 ; 1 Tim. i. 3). Gaius and Aristarchus, Macedonians, were Paul's companions in travel, and were in danger on his account during the riot at Ephesus (Acts xix. 29). Secundus, also a Macedonian, was one of those who waited for him at Troas, when for the last time he was to leave Philippi on his way to Jerusalem (xx. 4). Paul's converts in Macedonia made a collection for the poor Christians of the Jewish capital (Rom. xv. 26). They also ministered to the wants of the apostle himself (2 Cor. viii. 1–5), the Philippians being the most prominent in the work of charity (Phil. iv. 15).

Mach-ban′nai, in A. V. **Mach′ba-nai** [perhaps, clothed with a cloak].

One of the Gadite heroes who joined David at Ziklag (1 Chron. xii. 13).

Mach′be-na, in A. V. **Machbenah** [a bond or cloak].

A town of Judah, to judge from the context (1 Chron. ii. 49). See CABBON.

Ma′chi.

Father of the spy from the tribe of Gad (Num. xiii. 15).

Ma′chir [sold].

1. The firstborn and only son of Manasseh (Gen. l. 23; Josh. xvii. 1). His mother was an Aramitess (1 Chron. vii. 14). He was the founder of the family of the Machirites, which would have been the sole family of Manasseh. But as posterity increased, new families were set apart from the main line through the firstborn; and thus Machir became one among the families of Manasseh (Num. xxvi. 29). The family, called collectively Machir, was a man of war, and subjugated Gilead. This district was accordingly assigned to the family for its inheritance (Num. xxxii. 39, 40; Josh. xvii. 1). and was given by Moses. The name of Machir was once used poetically for the whole tribe of Manasseh, west as well as east of the Jordan (Judg. v. 14).

2. A son of Ammiel, in Lo-debar, east of the Jordan (2 Sam. ix. 4, 5), who brought provisions to David during the rebellion of Absalom (xvii. 27).

Mach′mas. See MICHMASH.

Mach-na-de′bai.

A son of Bani, induced by Ezra to put away his foreign wife (Ezra x. 40).

Mach-pe′lah [duplication, doubling].

A place before Mamre, where was a field with trees and a cave belonging to Ephron, a Hittite (Gen. xxiii. 9, 17, 19). The place was purchased by Abraham for 400 shekels of silver in order to use the cave as a sepulcher for Sarah, his wife. He himself was buried there by his sons, Isaac and Ishmael (xxv. 9, 10). There also Isaac and Rebekah were buried, so likewise were Leah and Jacob (xxxv. 29; xlvii. 28–31; xlix. 29–33; l. 12, 13), and perhaps others of whom we have no record. There were monuments to the patriarchs at Hebron in the time of Christ (War iv. 9, 7). The cave is probably correctly identified as the one which undoubtedly lies beneath the great mosque at Hebron. Christians have all along been excluded from the mosque and the cavern beneath; but the Prince of Wales on April 7th, 1862, the Crown Prince of Prussia in November, 1869, and the two sons of the Prince of Wales, one of whom is now King George, on April 5th, 1882, were permitted to make an imperfect examination. On the slope of the hill looking towards the west stands the Haram, a sacred enclosure, in form an oblong lying northwest and southeast, surrounded by walls of similar masonry to those of early date around the temple area at Jerusalem, and measuring externally about 197 feet in length and 111 feet in breadth. The ancient Christian church, which completely filled the southeastern end of the enclosure, has been converted into a mosque. In the mosque, close to its northwestern wall and about ten feet southwest of the main entrance, is a round opening, about a foot in diameter, through the stone flooring. Through this hole a glimpse is had into a shaft about twelve feet square and fifteen feet deep, with a door in the southeastern wall. This chamber is supposed to be an anteroom to the double cave situated immediately to the southeast under the floor of the mosque. Two entrances to the cave are marked in the flagging of the mosque, but they cannot be

Mosque of Abraham at Hebron, built over the reputed Cave of Machpelah. Abraham, Sarah, Isaac, Rebekah, Leah, and Jacob were buried in this cave.

opened without tearing up the pavement. Their position would indicate that they afforded access to the cave through its roof of rock. The floor of the mosque and the courtyard in front are fifteen feet higher than the street which skirts the Haram on the long southwestern side. In the northwestern corner of the enclosure is a shrine sacred to Joseph, but he was buried at Shechem (Josh. xxiv. 32).

Ma'dai.
A people descended from Japheth (Gen. x. 2; 1 Chron. i. 5), doubtless the inhabitants of Media.

Ma'di-an. See MIDIAN.

Mad-man'nah [dunghill].
A town in the extreme south of Judah (Josh. xv. 31; 1 Chron. ii. 49); perhaps identical with Beth-marcaboth (q. v.).

Mad'men [dunghill].
A town in Moab (Jer. xlviii. 2).

Mad-me'nah [dunghill].
A town near Jerusalem and on the north (Is. x. 31). Not identified.

Mad'ness.
1. Weakness or disorder of the intellect, rendering a person void of right reason (Deut. xxviii. 28). David, when feigning to be mad, made marks on the doors of the gate and let the spittle fall down upon his beard (1 Sam. xxi. 13, 14, where the two principal Hebrew synonyms are used). It may manifest itself in hallucinations (Acts xii. 15), or in wild raving (1 Cor. xiv. 23), or even in violence, such as hurling about firebrands and arrows (Prov. xxvi. 18). Its symptoms are temporarily produced by drink (Jer. xxv. 16; li. 7).
2. A state of uncontrollable emotion, as infatuation (Jer..l. 38) or fury (Ps. cii. 8; Luke vi. 11; Acts xxvi. 11).

Ma'don [contention, strife].
A town of northern Canaan, whose king was in confederacy with the king of Hazor (Josh. xi. 1–12; xii. 19). Site unknown. On the survey map it stands with a query at Madîn, 5 miles west by north of Tiberias.

Mag'a-dan.
A locality into the borders of which Jesus went after crossing the sea of Galilee (Mat. xv. 39, in A. V. Magdala). It seems to have been on the western shore of the lake and may have included Magdala (cp. Mark viii. 10).

Mag'bish [congregating].
A person or town, it is uncertain which (Ezra ii. 30). If a place, its site is unknown.

Mag'da-la [probably, a tower].
A town which, according to the Talmud, stood on the western shore of the sea of Galilee, near Tiberias and Hammath, and within less than a Sabbath day's journey of the water. It exists in the wretched village el-Mejdel, scarcely 3 miles north of Tiberias. In Mat. xv. 39 the R. V., following the best

manuscripts, substitutes Magadan (q. v.). See also MAGDALENE.

Mag-da-le'ne [of Magdala]. Mag-da-le'ne is the Greek pronunciation, like Abilene; Mag'da-lene is the English pronunciation, like Damascene, Gadarene, Nazarene.
A designation of one of the Marys, implying that she came from some Magdala, probably from the village now called el-Mejdel, on the western shore of the sea of Galilee, about 3 miles north-northwest of Tiberias. The word Magdalene makes no such imputation on the moral character of Mary as is now conveyed by the term Magdalen.

Mag'di-el [honor of God].
A duke descended from Esau (Gen. xxxvi. 43; 1 Chron. i. 54).

Ma'gi [Greek *Magoi*, the plural of *Magos*; in Behistun inscription *Magushu*].
The religious caste to which the wise men belonged, as their title indicates, who came from the east to worship the infant Jesus (Mat. ii. 1, R. V. margin). The Magi were a priestly caste, numerous enough to be regarded as one of the six tribes of Media (Herod. i. 101). When the Persians conquered the Medes, the Magi retained their influence in the new empire. An attempt on their part to seize the crown led to a dreadful slaughter of them, notwithstanding which their power soon revived (iii. 79). They worshiped the elements, fire, air, earth, and water, especially the first. The only temples they had were fire temples, generally on house tops, where they kept the sacred element burning night and day. What to do with the dead was a question which, with their views, involved much perplexity. The corpse could not be burned, buried, cast into water, or left to decay in the air without defiling an element. It was therefore exposed to be devoured by carrion-loving birds or beasts (Herod. i. 140, who probably errs in speaking of its after-burial; Strabo xv. 3, 20). To do this in the least offensive manner they erected towers called towers of silence, with transverse bars at the top, on which vultures and ravens might stand while they did their melancholy work. The Magi wore as sacerdotal vestments a white robe, with a headdress consisting of a tall felt cap, with lappets at the side which concealed the jaws. They claimed to be mediators between God and man, intervening in all sacrifices (Herod. i. 132; vii. 43). They interpreted dreams and omens and claimed the gift of prophecy (i. 107, 120; vii. 19, 37, 113). They were diligent in killing such animals as were regarded as belonging to the bad creation (i. 140). The foreigner was apt to observe the religious doctrine and priestly functions of the Magi less attentively than their incantations; and in process of time the Greeks bestowed the epithet Magos on any sorcerer who employed the methods and enchantments of the East. The Jew Bar-jesus was

a Magus (Acts xiii. 6, Greek text and R. V. margin), and so was Simon, often called Magus, of Samaria (viii. 9).

Ma-gi′cian [remotely from Greek *Magoi*, Magi].

A man who pretends to have preternatural powers, which he has obtained by the study of an occult science or the practice of a black art in connivance with evil spirits, and which he calls magic (cp. Acts xix. 19); see SORCERER. In the Bible magician is the rendering of *ḥartom*, one of the class of sacred scribes, who were skilled in writing and acquired vast information (Dan. i. 20), and who often claimed occult knowledge, practiced magic (Ex. vii. 11), and undertook to interpret dreams (Gen. xli. 8; Dan. ii. 10). The Egyptian magicians who withstood Moses were two in number, and their names were Jannes and Jambres (2 Tim. iii. 8).

Ma′gog.

A people descended from Japheth (Gen. x. 2), at one period inhabiting a northern land (Ezek. xxxviii. 2, 15). Josephus identified them with the Scythians (Antiq. i. 6, 1), and his identification is commonly accepted. The final struggle of heathenism with the kingdom of God is prophetically portrayed by Ezekiel under the figure of an invasion of the land of Israel by the hordes of the king of Magog and their overthrow. Ezekiel's description is referred to and its imagery is borrowed by John (Rev. xx. 8, 9). See GOG.

Ma-gor-mis′sa-bib [fear round about].

A prophetic name given to Pashhur, a priest and governor of the temple who illtreated the prophet Jeremiah (Jer. xx. 3).

Mag′pi-ash [apparently moth slayer].

One of the chiefs of the people who with Nehemiah sealed the covenant (Neh. x. 20).

Ma′ha-lah. See MAHLAH 2.

Ma-ha′la-lel, in A. V. and in N. T. of R. V. **Ma-ha-la′le-el,** in A. V. of N. T. **Ma-le′-le-el** [praise of God].

1. An antediluvian patriarch in the line of Seth (Gen. v. 12–17; Luke iii. 37).

2. One of the tribe of Judah, family of Perez, who lived in Jerusalem after the captivity (Neh. xi. 4).

Ma′ha-lath [sickness, anxiety, grief].

1. A musical term (Ps. liii.; lxxxviii. titles); which, judged by Hebrew etymology, refers to sadness. The words *al maḥ⁺lath l⁺annoth* (Ps. lxxxviii. title) then mean "mournfully to chant."

2. Daughter of Ishmael and a wife of Esau (Gen. xxviii. 9). Called also Bashemath (q. v.).

3. Daughter of Jerimoth and one of Rehoboam's wives (2 Chron. xi. 18).

Ma′ha-li. See MAHLI.

Ma-ha-na′im [two camps].

The name given by Jacob to a place east of Jordan where the angels of God met him,

apparently in two detachments, just after he had finally parted from Laban and before he crossed the Jabbok (Gen. xxxii. 2). It was on the boundary line between the tribes of Gad and Manasseh (Josh. xiii. 26, 30). It was afterwards assigned to the Merarite Levites (xxi. 38; 1 Chron. vi. 80). Commencing as a sacred spot, it ultimately became a fortified city. It was Ish-bosheth's capital (2 Sam. ii. 8, 12, 29). David retired thither while his rebellious son Absalom was in possession of Jerusalem (xvii. 24, 27; xviii. 24, 33; xix. 32; 1 Kin. ii. 8). Ahinadab the son of Iddo was Solomon's purveyor in the region (iv. 14). The site has not been identified. Robinson and long before him the Jewish traveler Moses hap-Parchi, about 1315, suggested Mahneh, about 4 miles east of ed-Deir. Tristram prefers Birket Mahneh, which he locates about 21 miles southeast of Gadara and 22 southwest of Edrei.

Ma′ha-neh-dan [camp of Dan].

A place behind, that is west of, Kirjath-jearim (Judg. xviii. 12), between Zorah and Eshtaol (xiii. 25), so named when the Danite spies encamped at the spot.

Ma′ha-rai [impetuous].

A Netophathite, one of David's mighty men (2 Sam. xxiii. 28; 1 Chron. xi. 30). He was David's captain for the tenth month (xxvii. 13).

Ma′hath [seizing or instrument of seizing].

1. A Kohathite Levite, descended by the line of Zephaniah, Tahath, and Abiasaph (1 Chron. vi. 35). He was an ancestor of Samuel (33).

2. Another Levite, one of the overseers who looked after the tithes and freewill offerings in Hezekiah's reign (2 Chron. xxxi. 13). Probably he was the son of Amasai, a descendant of Kohath (xxix. 12).

Ma′ha-vite.

A designation of unknown meaning appended to the name of Eliel, one of David's mighty men (1 Chron. xi. 46). The passage is probably corrupt, for the word is plural and yet joined to the singular.

Ma-ha′zi-oth [perhaps, vision of significance].

A Levite, a descendant of Heman (1 Chron. xxv. 4). He obtained the twenty-third lot among the singers (30).

Ma′her-shal′al-hash′baz [spoil speedeth, prey hasteth].

The words which Isaiah was directed to display on a public tablet and have duly witnessed, and a year later was told to give as a name to his second son. They predicted the speedy conquest of Damascus and Samaria by the king of Assyria (Is. viii. 1–4). The preliminary formality drew public attention to the enigmatical words and attested that God was preparing and revealing the event a year before its occurrence.

Mah'lah, in A. V. once **Mahalah** (1 Chron. vii. 18) [disease].

1. Daughter of Zelophehad (Num. xxvi. 33; xxvii. 1).

2. Another Manassite, whose mother was Hammoleketh (1 Chron. vii. 18).

Mah'li, in A. V. once **Mahali** (Ex. vi. 19) [sick, weak].

1. A Levite, son of Merari and brother of Mushi. He founded a tribal family or house (Ex. vi. 19; Num. iii. 20, 33; xxvi. 58). His grandsons married their cousins (1 Chron. xxiii. 22).

2. A Levite, family of Merari, house of Mushi (1 Chron. vi. 47; xxiii. 23; xxiv. 30).

Mah'lon [sickly].

Elder son of Elimelech and Naomi, and the first husband of Ruth (Ruth i. 2; iv. 10).

Ma'hol [dancing, joy].

Father of Heman, Chalcol, and Darda, three noted wise men (1 Kin. iv. 31).

Mah-se'iah, in A. V. **Maaseiah** [Jehovah is a refuge].

An ancestor of Jeremiah's friend, Baruch, and of the chief chamberlain, Seraiah (Jer. xxxii. 12; li. 59).

Ma'kaz [an end].

A town whence one of Solomon's purveyors drew supplies (1 Kin. iv. 9). Site unknown.

Ma'ked, in A. V. once **Maged.**

A town of Gilead, in which Jews were shut up by the heathen (1 Mac. v. 26). It was captured by Judas Maccabæus, and the Jews were released (36). Hitzig identifies it with Maḳad, a town which he locates on the border of the Hauran, near Edrei.

Mak-he'loth [assemblies, especially for the worship of God].

An encampment of the Israelites in the wilderness (Num. xxxiii. 25, 26). Site unknown.

Mak-ke'dah [perhaps, a place of shepherds].

A Canaanite town in the lowland, taken by Joshua (Josh. xv. 41). Near it was a cave (x. 16). The site has not been identified. Eusebius located it 8 Roman miles east of Eleutheropolis. But as this location would be in the mountains, his statement, if correct, must be interpreted as meaning northeast or southeast.

Mak'tesh [a mortar, a trough, a hollow].

A locality at Jerusalem (Zeph. i. 11). The Targum identifies it with the Kidron valley; another supposition is that it was the valley separating the temple from the city.

Mal'a-chi [my messenger, or messenger (of Jehovah)].

A prophet, the writer of the last book of the O. T. (Mal. i. 1). Nothing is known of his history except what may be learned from his book. As the name means my messen-

ger (so in iii. 1), some have supposed it to be, not the proper name, but the title of a prophet, perhaps of Ezra. But as each of the eleven preceding minor prophecies has its author's name prefixed, there is a strong presumption that it is so in the present case also, and that Malachi was the actual name of the prophet who penned the book. It may be divided into the following sections: 1. God's special love for Israel, shown in his choice of Jacob instead of Esau (i. 2–5), was not requited: *a*. The priests and people (6,14) dishonored God by presenting blemished offerings (6–14); punishment threatened for this departure from the norm established by God for the priesthood and once realized (ii. 1–9); *b*. The people dealt treacherously against their brethren, intermarrying with the heathen (11) and putting away their own wives (14, 16) and doing deeds of violence (ii. 10–17). 2. Judgment imminent. God's messenger is about to prepare the way, the Lord himself will suddenly come to his temple, the messenger of the covenant shall come as judge and purify Levi from dross and visit evil doers (iii. 1–6; cp. Ex. xxiii. 20–23; Mat. xi. 10). 3. Call to repentance; for then the Lord will come in blessing and judgment, putting to nought the complaint that he makes no distinction between the good and the evil. Those who have turned from sin to God will be his peculiar treasure, but the wicked shall be burned as stubble (iii. 7–iv. 3). Exhortation to remember the law of Moses, and announcement of the mission of Elijah to prepare for the terrible day of the Lord (iv. 4–6; Mat. xvii. 10–13; Luke i. 17).

When the prophecy was delivered the Jewish people were not under a king, but under a governor (Mal. i. 8), doubtless one appointed by the Persian emperor (Neh. v. 14). Zerubbabel's temple was standing, as was the altar, and sacrifices were being offered as in the olden time (i. 7–10); hence Malachi is later than Haggai and Zechariah. But the outburst of religious life which had immediately followed the return from Babylon, and had resulted in the rebuilding first of the sanctuary and then of the fortifications of Jerusalem, had had time to expend its force. Priests and people were corrupt. This condition suits the time of Nehemiah (Neh. xiii.). The generally accepted date, which originated with Vitringa, is 420 B. C. Davidson prefers 460 to 450 B. C.

Mal'cam, in A. V. **Malcham** [regnant, rule].

1. A Benjamite, son of Shaharaim and Hodesh (1 Chron. viii. 9).

2. The chief deity of the Ammonites (Jer. xlix. 1, 3. in A. V. their king; Zeph. i. 5; perhaps Amos i. 15, where it is rendered their king). See MOLECH.

Mal-chi'ah, in A. V. once **Melchiah** (Jer. xxi. 1) [Jehovah is king].

A royal prince, into whose dungeon the prophet Jeremiah was cast (Jer. xxxviii. 6). It is natural to identify him with the father of the official Pashhur mentioned in ver. 1 and xxi. 1.

For others, see MALCHIJAH.

Mal'chi-el [God is king].

A son of Beriah and grandson of Asher, and founder of a tribal family (Gen. xlvi. 17; Num. xxvi. 45).

Mal-chi'jah, in A. V. often **Malchiah** [Jehovah is king].

1. A Levite, family of Gershom, house of Shimei (1 Chron. vi. 40).

2. A descendant of Aaron. His family had grown to a father's house in the time of David, and became the fifth course when David distributed the priests into divisions (1 Chron. xxiv. 1, 6, 9). Apparently members of a subdivision of his family, viz., the house of Pashhur, returned with Zerubbabel from Babylon (Ezra ii. 38). He is also probably referred to in 1 Chron. ix. 12 and Neh. xi. 12, where a priestly line is traced back through Pashhur to one of this name. The royal prince Malchiah of Jeremiah xxxviii. 6 (and hence probably of ver. 1) is a different person.

3. A royal prince (Jer. xxxviii, 6). See MALCHIAH.

4, 5. Two sons of Parosh, both induced by Ezra to put away their foreign wives (Ezra x. 25).

6. A son of Harim, induced by Ezra to put away his foreign wife (Ezra x. 31). He joined with another Hebrew in repairing part of the wall of Jerusalem and the tower of the furnaces (Neh. iii. 11).

7. A son of Rechab. He also repaired part of the wall of Jerusalem (Neh. iii. 14).

8. A goldsmith who repaired part of the wall of Jerusalem (Neh. iii. 31).

9. A priest who with others officiated at the dedication of the wall of Jerusalem (Neh. xii. 42); perhaps, one of those who assisted Ezra when the law was explained to the people (Neh. viii. 4).

10. A priest who, doubtless in behalf of a father's house, signed the covenant (Neh. x. 3).

Mal-chi'ram [the king, i. e. God, is exalted].

A son of king Jehoiachin (1 Chron. iii. 18).

Mal-chi-shu'a, in A. V. **Melchi-shua** in 1 Samuel [the king, i. e. God, is salvation].

A son of king Saul (1 Sam. xiv. 49; 1 Chron. viii. 33; ix. 39). He was killed at the battle of Gilboa (1 Sam. xxxi. 2).

Mal'chus [Greek of Semitic *malku*, king].

The high priest's servant whose ear Peter cut off (John xviii. 10).

Ma-le'le-el. See MAHALALEL.

Mal'lo-thi.

A son of Heman (1 Chron. xxv. 4). He obtained by lot the leadership of the nineteenth course of singers (26).

Mal'lows.

The rendering of the Hebrew *Malluah*, salt plant (Job xxx. 4, A. V.). Since genuine mallows are mucilaginous and not saline, the R. V. alters the name of the plant to salt-wort; see SALTWORT.

Mal'luch [reigning or counselor].

1. A Levite, family of Merari, house of Mushi (1 Chron. vi. 44).

2. A chief of the priests, who returned from Babylon with Zerubbabel (Neh. xii. 2, 7). A father's house bore his name in the next generation (ver. 14, R. V.). In the latter passage the form Malluchi, in itself an unessential variation, is probably due to dittography. The final letter of Malluchi is the initial letter of the following word, and moreover is not found in the Septuagint. The consonants of Malluchi are written in the Hebrew text, but were read Melicu (A. V. and margin of R. V.).

3, 4. A son of Bani and a son of Harim, each of whom was induced by Ezra to put away his foreign wife (Ezra x. 29, 32).

5, 6. A priest and a chief of the people who signed the covenant (Neh. x. 4, 27).

Mal'lu-chi. See MALLUCH 2.

Mam'mon [Greek from Aramaic *mamon, mamona'*, wealth, riches].

A personification of wealth (Matt. vi. 24; Luke xvi. 9, 11, 13).

Mam're [fatness, strength].

1. The town or more probably district of Hebron (Gen. xxiii. 19; xxxv. 27), to the west of Machpelah (xxiii. 17). A grove was there, near Hebron, where Abraham several times resided (xiii. 18; xiv. 13; xviii. 1, etc.). In Josephus' time an aged terebinth was pointed out as Abraham's tree, 6 stades or ⅔ of a mile from Hebron (War iv. 9, 7); in the fourth century, one at Ramet el-Khulil, 2 Roman miles north of Hebron, which Constantine enclosed within the walls of a basilica. The remains of this building are called the house of Abraham. The tree which now claims the honor of being Abraham's oak, and which was already celebrated as such in the sixteenth century, is a genuine oak (*Quercus pseudococcifera*). Its trunk has a girth of 26 feet at the ground, and its branches extend over an area of 93 feet in diameter (Thomson). It stands a little more than a mile northwest of Hebron, near the head of the wady Sebta.

2. An Amorite chieftain who dwelt at Mamre and who with his brothers, Eshcol and Aner, helped Abraham to retake the captives and the spoil carried off by Chedorlaomer (Gen. xiv. 13, 24). He was probably designated by the name of the district over which he ruled.

Man. See ADAM.

Man'a-en [Greek form of Menahem, consoler, comforter]. Manahem is another Greek form of the Hebrew name.

A Christian prophet or teacher in the church at Antioch. He had been brought up with Herod the tetrarch as his companion (Acts xiii. 1, A. V.), or was his foster brother, brought up at the same mother's breast (R. V.). He may have been a descendant, or at least a relative of Manahem, the Essene, who predicted to Herod the Great, when yet a schoolboy, that he would obtain the kingdom. When the prophecy was fulfilled, Herod held him and his sect in high esteem (Antiq. xv. 10, 5).

Man'a-hath [rest].

1. A son of the Horite, Shobal (Gen. xxxvi. 23) ; perhaps even a place inhabited by a branch of the tribe of Shobal (1 Chron. i. 40).

2. A place to which Benjamites of Geba were carried captive by their fellow-tribesmen (1 Chron. viii. 6). Descendants of Salma, of the family of Caleb, tribe of Judah, probably formed half the population of it or of another place of the name (ii. 54) ; see MANAHATHITES.

Ma-na'hath-ites, in A. V. **Manahethites.**

The inhabitants of a place or the descendants of a man Manahath (1 Chron. ii. 54). To judge by the context, a place is intended. For Manahethites in ver. 52, A.V., see MENUHOTH.

Ma-nas'seh, in A. V. of N. T. **Manasses,** the Greek form [making to forget].

1. The elder son of Joseph. He was born in Egypt, his mother being Asenath, daughter of Poti-phera, priest of On. In race, therefore, he, like his brother Ephraim, was half Hebrew, half Egyptian (Gen. xli. 50, 51). When Jacob desired to bless the two boys, Joseph took Ephraim in his right hand, toward Jacob's left, and Manasseh in his left, toward Jacob's right ; but the dying patriarch crossed his arms, so as to lay his right hand on Ephraim's head and his left on that of Manasseh, intimating prophetically that while both sons should become ancestors of great peoples, Ephraim should excel (xlviii. 8-21).

2. The tribe which descended from Manasseh. It consisted of seven tribal families, of which one was founded by his son Machir and the remaining six sprang from his grandson Gilead (Gen. l. 23 ; Num. xxvi. 28-34 ; Josh. xvii. 1, 2). At the first census in the wilderness the tribe numbered 32,200 fighting men (Num. i. 34, 35) ; at the second, which was taken thirty-eight years later, 52,700 (xxvi. 34). After Moses had defeated Sihon king of Heshbon, and Og king of Bashan, one-half the tribe of Manasseh joined with the tribes of Reuben and Gad in requesting permission to settle east of the Jordan, and obtained the leave they sought, on condition of going armed before their brethren, who had not yet obtained settlements, and aiding in the war west of the Jordan (xxxii. 33-42 ; cp. 1-32 ; xxxiv. 14, 15 ; Deut. iii. 12, 13 ; xxix. 8 ; Josh. xii. 4-6 ; xviii. 7). They observed the conditions laid down (Josh. i. 12-18 ; iv. 12) ; and when the war had been successfully fought out, were honorably dismissed to the territory they had chosen. A temporary mis-

understanding about the building of an altar at one time threatened unpleasant consequences ; but on explanation being given, matters were amicably arranged (xxii. 1-34). The region given to the half-tribe of Manasseh east of the Jordan comprehended part of Gilead and all Bashan (Deut. iii. 13-15), Mahanaim in one direction being on its boundary line (Josh. xiii. 29-33). It is between 65 and 70 miles from east to west, by 40 or more from north to south. It is mostly a table-land of 2500 feet elevation, one of the richest parts of Palestine, and to this day the granary of a large part of Syria. It is studded with ruined towns. The other half of the tribe crossed the Jordan and had their inheritance in central Palestine, west of the river. It was bounded on the south by Ephraim, on the northwest by Asher, and on the northeast by Issachar. Its southern boundary ran by Janoah and Taanath-shiloh, near Shechem, and along the northern bank of the brook Kanah to its entrance into the Mediterranean (Josh. xvii. 5-10). But the children of Ephraim had cities in the midst of the inheritance of the children of Manasseh (xvi. 9), and, on the other hand, Manasseh had various towns, viz., Beth-shean, Ibleam, Dor, En-dor, Taanach, and Megiddo, within the territories of Issachar and Asher (xvii. 11 ; cp. 1 Chron. vii. 29). The Manassites, however, failed to expel the Canaanite inhabitants of the cities just named, but eventually put them to tribute (Josh. xvii. 12, 13 ; Judg. i. 27, 28). Levitical cities were allotted from Manasseh as from the other tribes, including Golan in Bashan in the region east of the Jordan, one of the six cities of refuge (Josh. xx. 8 ; xxi. 27). The hero and judge Gideon was a Manassite, and the most eminent man the tribe produced (Judg. vi. 15 ; cp. 35 ; vii. 23). Some Manassites joined David at Ziklag (1 Chron. xii. 19, 20). No fewer than 18,000 offered him their services during his reign at Hebron (31 ; cp. 37). The eastern Manassites, in conjunction with the two tribes east of the Jordan, waged war with the Hagarites and took possession of their country. They were themselves carried into exile by Tiglath-pileser (v. 18-26). Some Manassites came to Asa when they saw that the Lord was with him (2 Chron. xv. 9) ; men of the same tribe also attended the great passover in Hezekiah's reign and also in Josiah's reign (xxx. 1, 10, 11, 18 ; xxxi. 1 ; xxxiv. 6, 9).

3. An intentional modification of the name Moses (Judg. xviii. 30, A. V.) ; see JONATHAN 1.

4. Son and successor of good king Hezekiah. He ascended the throne about the year 698 B. C., when he was only twelve years of age. He undid the work of reformation which had been carried out in the former reign. He established the high places, built an altar to Baal, and reared an Asherah ; made altars for the worship of the host of heaven within the two courts of the temple,

and caused one of his sons to pass through the fire. Prophets warned him, but he paid no attention to their threatenings. Instead of listening, he shed much innocent blood throughout every part of Jerusalem. The victims were doubtless chiefly those who, retaining their fidelity to Jehovah, opposed Manasseh's reactionary religious measures (2 Kin. xxi. 1–16). Tradition makes Isaiah one of these, which is possible but doubtful. As a penalty for his wickedness, God left him to his enemies. Two kings of Assyria, Esarhaddon and Ashurbanipal, report receiving tribute from him. The Assyrian king by whom he was carried captive to Babylon (2 Chron. xxxiii. 11) was probably Ashurbanipal, who crushed his rebellious brother Shamash-shumukin, king of Babylon, about 647 B. C. and placed the forfeited crown on his own head. Manasseh repented, and was after a time restored to his kingdom. He put away the idols which had been his ruin, and restored the worship of Jehovah. He also added to the fortifications of Jerusalem (2 Chron. xxxiii. 12–19). After a reign of fifty-five years, a longer one than any other king of Judah had enjoyed, he died about the year 642 B. C., leaving his son Amon to ascend the throne (2 Kin. xxi. 17, 18; 2 Chron. xxxiii. 20). For the Prayer of Manasseh, see APOC-RYPHA 12.

5 and 6. A son of Pahath-moab and a son of Hashum, each of whom was induced by Ezra to put away his foreign wife (Ezra x. 30, 33).

Man'drake.

The rendering of the Hebrew *Duda'im,* amatory plants. They were supposed to act as a love philter (Gen. xxx. 14–16; on margin of R. V. love apples). They are odoriferous (Song vii. 13). The mandrake (*Mandragora officinalis*) is a handsome plant of the Solanaceous (night shade) order. It has wavy leaves and pale violet, white, or deep blue flowers. Its fruit is small and yellow. The forked root bears a slight resemblance to the human body. It is found in the Jordan valley and along the rivers running into it, in the plains of Moab and Gilead, and in Galilee.

Ma'neh. See WEIGHTS.

Man'ger.

A feeding place for cattle, a crib or trough, in Greek *Phatnē* (Luke ii. 7, 12; in xiii. 15 rendered stall; cp. Is. i. 3). Mangers are ancient (Iliad x. 568; xxiv. 280; Herod. ix. 70). In Palestine the stable is usually in the owner's house, a portion of the interior being set apart for the cattle and furnished with mangers built of small stones and mortar in the shape of a box.

Man'na [what is it? or rather, it is manna, since an article called *mannu* was already known to the Egyptians and was imported from the peninsula of Sinai].

A food on which the Israelites mainly subsisted during the forty years' sojourn in the wilderness. It was first bestowed in the wilderness of Sin, in the second half of the second month, when the people murmured, owing to the deficiency of food. The descent of manna was described as a raining of bread from heaven (Ex. xvi. 1–4, 12; Ps. lxxviii. 24; cv. 40). In the morning, when the dew was gone up, there lay upon the face of the wilderness a small round flake, small as the hoarfrost on the ground. When the children of Israel saw it for the first time they said one to another: "It is manna," for they wist not what it really was. And Moses said unto them: "It is the bread which the Lord hath given" (Ex. xvi. 13–15; Num. xi. 9). It was white like coriander seed, with a yellowish tinge and resinous appearance like bdellium, and tasted like wafers made with honey or like fresh oil (Ex. xvi. 31; Num. xi. 8). It was ground in mills, beaten in mortars, boiled in pots, and made into cakes (Num. xi. 8). The people were directed to gather an omer a day (about 5.8 pints) for each member of their households, and not to attempt to keep any till the morrow. Some of the people disobeyed this injunction, but the hoarded manna decayed and stank. On the sixth day two omers were gathered for each person, as none descended on the Sabbath (Ex. xvi. 22–30). An omerful, which evidently was preserved from decay, was kept by Aaron and his successors to show future generations the nature of the food on which the Israelites had subsisted in the wilderness (32–34); see HIGH PRIEST. A year after it was first given, at the same season, the

Manger.

people are mentioned as having it, and again toward the end of the forty years. It is referred to because the people were murmuring against the food (Num. xi. 4–9; xxi. 5), but the boon which they failed to appreciate was not withdrawn. It was continued during the whole of the forty years' desert wanderings (Ex. xvi. 35; Deut. viii. 3, 16; Neh. ix. 20; Ps. lxxviii. 24), and did not cease till the day after the Israelites had crossed the Jordan, encamped at Gilgal, and begun to eat of the produce of Canaan (Josh. v. 10–12). The question has been mooted, Was manna a substance for the first time created in the wilderness, or was it a natural product miraculously multiplied? Various plants exude a manna-like substance, either emanating spontaneously from the plant itself or produced by the puncture of an insect. The *Tamarix mannifera*, a variety of the *Tamarix gallica*, does so, and grows in the peninsula of Sinai. The exudation is dirty yellow in color, but white when it falls on stones. It melts in the heat of the sun. It is produced during a period of from six to ten weeks, the height of the season being June. *Alhagi maurorum* and *A. desertorum*, two species of camel's thorn, also exude a manna-like substance, and there are other manna-bearing plants. The Arabs use plant manna of different kinds as butter and honey. But the present yield of the entire peninsula is less than half a ton in the best years. It is never made into bread. Moreover, if taken in more than the most limited quantities it is purgative. So that even if it were produced abundantly, there would be great difficulty in identifying it with the manna of Scripture.

Ma-no'ah [rest, quiet].
A Danite belonging to the village of Zorah, and father of Samson (Judg. xiii. 1–25).

Man'slay-er. See MURDER.

Man'tle.
The large, sleeveless, outer garment or, as a rendering of the Hebrew M^e*'il*, an occasional garment worn between the tunic and the outer garment. See CLOTHING.

Ma'och [oppression].
Father of Achish, king of Gath (1 Sam. xxvii. 2). See ACHISH.

Ma'on [dwelling, habitation, abode].
1. A town in the hill country of Judah (Josh. xv. 55), the residence of Nabal (1 Sam. xxv. 2), now Ma'in, about a mile and a half south from Carmel of Judah, and 8½ south of Hebron. In the wilderness in the vicinity of Maon David and his men for a time took refuge (1 Sam. xxiii. 24, 25).
2. Son of Shammai, of the tribe of Judah, and ancestor of the inhabitants of Beth-zur (1 Chron. ii. 45). Maon may indeed in this passage possibly be used collectively for the inhabitants of the town of this name (cp. Bethlehem, ver. 54), and that Maon is immedi-

ately called the father of Beth-zur may be paralleled by 1 Chron. i. 8, 9, 11, 13.
3. A people that oppressed Israel (Judg. x. 12). The English versions translate Maonites. See MEUNIM.

Ma'o-nites. See MAON 3 and MEUNIM.

Ma'ra [bitter, sad of spirit].
The name chosen by Naomi to express her bereavements (Ruth i. 20).

Ma'rah [bitter, bitterness].
A fountain of bitter water in the wilderness of Shur on the route to Sinai, at which the Israelites halted when three days or a little more had elapsed after their passage of the Red Sea. The badness of the water, and perhaps its scantiness, opened their eyes to the hardships which they might expect; and they murmured. Moses was directed by God to cast a certain tree into the waters, whereby they were rendered palatable, either miraculously or through the chemical and medicinal properties of the tree (Exod. xv. 23–26; Num. xxxiii. 8, 9). Since the days of Burckhardt, Marah has been generally located at 'Ain Hawarah, about 47 miles from Suez, and a few miles inland from the Red Sea, from which it is separated by a range of hills. The well measures about 20 feet across, but is much wider at the bottom. Its depth is perhaps 25 feet. The soil of the region abounds in soda, and the water of the well is consequently salty and bitter. The principal rival claimant to Hawarah has been wady Ghurundel, which, however, is generally regarded as Elim. The recent identification of the site of Pithom with Tell el-Maskhuta leads to the inference that Marah may be 'Ayun Musa, the wells of Moses, a group of springs 7½ miles south-southeast of Suez and 52 south-southeast of Pithom. The water of some of these springs is drinkable, but of others very bitter and nauseous. The Arabs do not like their camels to partake of it.

Mar'a-lah [trembling, reeling].
A frontier village of Zebulun toward the sea (Josh. xix. 11). Not identified.

Mar-an ath'a, in A. V. **Maran-atha.** See ANATHEMA MARAN-ATHA.

Mar'ble.
Limestone, especially in a crystalline condition, which is capable of taking polish. It was called in Hebrew *shayish* and *shesh*, from its brightness, and in Greek *marmaros*. It was used for columns and costly pavements (Esth. i. 6; Song v. 15), and was employed in Solomon's temple (1 Chron. xxix. 2). Josephus, in describing the walls of this edifice, mentions that they were built of white stone, but does not specify the kind of stone (Antiq. viii. 3, 2). White, yellow, and red marble is obtained in Lebanon, but a choicer variety came from Arabia. Red and white marble was employed in the Greco-Roman period for palatial buildings in

Palestine, both east and west of the Jordan. In Herod's temple the pillars of the cloisters were monoliths of white marble, twenty-five cubits high (War v. 5, 2).

Mar′cus. See MARK.

Ma-re′shah [at the head].

1. A town in the lowland of Judah (Josh. xv. 44; cp. 1 Chron. iv. 21). Rehoboam strengthened its fortifications (2 Chron. xi. 8). The great battle between king Asa and Zerah the Ethiopian was fought in its vicinity (xiv. 9, 10). In the Grecian period it was an important town, inhabited by Edomites, and known as Marissa (Antiq. xiii. 9, 1; xiv. 1, 3, 9). It was plundered by Judas Maccabæus (1 Mac. v. 66; 2 Mac. xii. 35; Antiq. xii. 8, 6). John Hyrcanus planted a Jewish colony there (Antiq. xiii. 9, 1; 10, 2); but Pompey made the town free in 63 (xiv. 4, 4). Gabinius fortified it (xiv. 5, 3). It was finally destroyed by the Parthians in 40 B. C. (xiv. 13, 9). According to Eusebius, its ruins existed 2 Roman miles from Eleutheropolis; and Bliss has located it at Tell Sandahannah, one mile south by east of Beit Jibrin.

2. The father of Hebron (1 Chron. ii. 42). The form of expression, in the light of its context, suggests that Mareshah was the progenitor of the inhabitants of Hebron; but the mention of Hebron's sons in the following verse makes it probable that Hebron was a man. If so, he is not mentioned elsewhere.

Mark, in A. V. of N. T. thrice **Marcus** (Col. iv. 10; Philem. 24; 1 Pet. v. 13) [Latin *marcus*, a large hammer].

The evangelist to whom is traditionally assigned the Second Gospel. Mark was his surname (Acts xii. 12, 25; xv. 37); his first name was John, by which alone he is designated in Acts xiii. 5, 13. His mother, Mary, was in comfortable circumstances, and her house in Jerusalem was one of the meeting places of the Christians (Acts xii. 12-17); see MARY. There are several instances in the N. T. of Jews with Latin surnames (Acts i. 23; xiii. 9), so that the addition of Marcus to John does not imply a mixed Jewish and gentile descent. Mark was also the cousin of Barnabas (Col. iv. 10, R. V., in A. V. sister's son). He accompanied Barnabas and Paul from Jerusalem to Antioch of Syria (Acts xii. 25) and afterwards on their missionary journey (xiii. 5); but, for some unstated reason, he left them at Perga (13) and returned to Jerusalem. Whatever was the reason of Mark's conduct on that occasion, Paul disapproved of it so much that he refused to take him with them when a second journey was proposed (xv. 38). This caused a contention between the two missionaries, so that they separated and Barnabas, with Mark, sailed to Cyprus to resume his evangelistic work. After this Mark disappears from the history for about ten years. We next find him in Rome with

Paul and joining with the apostle in sending salutations (Col. iv. 10; Philem. 24). It thus appears that the former cause of variance between the two men had been removed; and, at a still later period, Paul speaks of Mark in highly commendatory terms: "Take Mark, and bring him with thee: for he is useful to me for ministering" (2 Tim. iv. 11, R. V.). This last reference further implies that Mark had been in the east, certainly in Asia Minor and perhaps still further east. With this corresponds 1 Pet. v. 13, according to which he was with Peter in Babylon, provided that Babylon is there to be understood literally. Peter calls Mark his son, which, if not a mere term of endearment, may mean that Mark had been one of Peter's converts. The fact that Peter, when released by the angel from prison, went to the house of Mark's mother (Acts xii. 12) may indicate his intimacy with the family. Tradition varies on the point whether Mark had been an immediate follower of Jesus. Many think, however, that the young man who was present at the time of Christ's arrest (Mark xiv. 51, 52) was Mark himself. The incident is mentioned by no other evangelist, and there would seem to be no motive for recording it except the wish to give a personal reminiscence. The time and place of Mark's death are unknown. Early tradition represents him as the interpreter of Peter. Among others, Papias of Hierapolis, who wrote about A. D. 140, quoting "the elder" as his authority, says: "Mark, having become Peter's interpreter, wrote down accurately, though not in order, as many as he remembered of the things said or done by the Lord. For he neither heard the Lord nor followed him, but at a later time, as I said, [he followed] Peter, who delivered his instructions according to the needs [of the occasion], but not with a view to giving a systematic account of the Lord's sayings. So that Mark made no mistake, thus writing down such things as he remembered; for of one thing he took forethought, [namely] not to leave out any one of the things he had heard or to state falsely anything in them" (Eusebius, hist. eccles. iii. 39). This reference to Mark as the interpreter of Peter may either mean that he accompanied Peter, in the later years of the apostle's life, on his missionary journeys and acted as his spokesman when addressing gentile audiences; or the phrase may merely describe Mark's work in writing down the preaching of Peter in the Gospel which goes by his name. There can be little doubt that Mark was in Rome with both Paul and Peter. Tradition also made him the founder of the church in Alexandria, but the value of the tradition is uncertain. The main point to be observed is that Mark's early history and his later association with the chief apostles fitted him to become the writer of a gospel.

The Gospel according to St. Mark is the second of our four gospels, though not necessarily the second in order of composition. It is the shortest of the four, but this brevity is not usually due to condensation of the material. What Mark does give he generally describes with much detail. The story moves forward rapidly, with pictorial power; and consists of a succession of descriptive scenes. These proceed in a more chronological order than in Matthew or Luke. Especial stress is laid on the deeds of Christ rather than on his formal instruction by word of mouth; only four parables being related as compared with eighteen miracles, and but one of Christ's longer discourses being given at any length (xiii.). Christ is depicted as the mighty Son of God (i. 11; v. 7; ix. 7; xiv. 61; also viii. 38; xii. 1–11; xiii. 32; xiv. 36), the conquering Saviour. The narrative deals mainly with two themes: the ministry in Galilee (i. 14–ix. 50), and the last week at Jerusalem (xi. 1–xvi. 8). These sections are connected by a somewhat brief survey of the intervening period (x. 1–52). In its entirety, it may be divided as follows: 1. Beginning of the gospel of Jesus Christ, including the ministry of John the Baptist and the baptism and temptation of Jesus (i. 1–13). 2. The opening of the Galilæan ministry; giving the place and the message, the call of the first four apostles, miracles in Capernaum and Galilee (i. 14–45). 3. Christ's triumph over rising opposition, including the curing of the paralytic, Levi's feast and the discourse on fasting, and the Sabbath controversy (ii. 1–iii. 6). 4. Extension of Christ's work amid increasing opposition, including the description of the multitudes who followed him; the appointment of the twelve; replies to the Pharisees; the visit of his mother and brethren; the parables of the sower, the seed growing secretly, and the mustard seed, with remarks; the great miracles of stilling the waves, the Gadarene demoniacs, the woman with a bloody issue, and the raising of Jairus' daughter; the (second) rejection at Nazareth; the sending out of the twelve; Herod's inquiry about Jesus together with an account of the death of John the Baptist; the feeding of the 5000; the walking on the sea; and Christ's denunciation of Pharasaic traditionalism (iii. 7–vii. 23). 5. A period of comparative retirement, embracing the later Galilæan ministry (see GOSPEL): including the healing of the Syrophœnician's daughter in the borders of Tyre and Sidon and of a deaf-mute in Decapolis; the feeding of the 4000; the refusal to give the Pharisees a sign and the warning of the disciples against them; healing of a blind man near Bethsaida, followed by incidents near Cæsarea Philippi, including the prediction by Christ of his death, Peter's confession, etc., the transfiguration, the cure of the demoniac boy, a renewed prediction of Christ's death and, on return-

ing to Capernaum, special instructions to the disciples (vii. 24–ix. 50). This period is specially complete in Mark. 6. Christ's closing ministry in Peræa: including the question of the Pharisees about divorce; the blessing of the children; the rich young ruler; and explanations to the disciples; the ascent to Jerusalem, including a third prediction of his death, the request of James and John, the healing of Bartimæus (x.). 7. The last week, including the triumphal entry; the blasting of the barren fig tree; the (second) cleansing of the temple; the visit of the deputation from the sanhedrin; the parable of the wicked husbandmen; the questions of the Pharisees and Herodians, of the Sadducees, and of the scribe (lawyer); Christ's question about the son of David: a brief report of his denunciations of the Pharisees and scribes (cp. Mat. xxiii); the widow's gift; the discourse on the mount of Olives; Judas' treachery and, in connection with it, the supper at Bethany; a brief account of the last evening with the disciples and the institution of the Lord's Supper; the agony in Gethsemane; the arrest; the trial of Jesus at night before the sanhedrin; Peter's denials; the trial before Pilate, and the crucifixion; the burial; the announcement of Christ's resurrection to certain women by an angel seated in his empty tomb (xi. 1–xvi. 8).

The last twelve verses of Mark's Gospel, as found in A. V., are believed by most scholars not to have formed the original close of the book. Hence in R. V. they are separated by a space from the preceding verses. They were certainly added at a very early time, perhaps at the beginning of the second century. They seem to have been formed in part out of the other gospels and they truthfully describe the beliefs of the apostolic churches on the subjects with which they deal. Chap. xvi. 8, however, is too abrupt an ending. The original close must have been lost at a very early time, soon after the book was finished. Some have supposed that Mark was prevented from finishing. The last twelve verses of our Mark, when regarded as an ancient addition to and completion of the book, are powerful evidence for the existence and circulation of the other gospels as well as for the reception of Mark's own narrative.

This Gospel was in general circulation among the Christians as early as the middle of the second century, and was included by Tatian in his Diatessaron, or Harmony of the Four Gospels. Irenæus, writing in the last quarter of the second century, repeatedly quotes it, and quotes it as Mark's; and, as others before him (such as Papias), declares Mark to have been Peter's disciple and interpreter. Thus ancient and trustworthy tradition represents the Gospel of Mark as in some degree connected with Peter's preaching about Christ. This relation to Peter is confirmed by the many vivid particulars which it contains, which seem to be due to the reminiscences of an eyewitness (e. g. i. 40; ii. 1-4; iii. 5; v. 4-6; vi. 39, 40; vii. 34; viii. 33; x. 21; xi. 20); by its superiority to the other Gospels in those sections where Peter alone was an eyewitness or competent to give a full account (cp. the account of Peter's denials); and, as Eusebius noticed, by its silence regarding matters which reflect the credit on Peter (Mat. xvi. 17-19; Luke v. 3-10). This reported dependence on Peter must not be pressed, however, to the exclusion of other sources of information; for Mark had abundant opportunities to learn from other eyewitnesses besides Peter, and from other members of the primitive Christian community, such as his kinsman Barnabas and Paul and the disciples who frequented his mother's house (Acts xii. 12, 17). In the ancient church Mark was supposed by some, as, for example, Augustine, to have abbreviated Matthew; but this is impossible, since he adds many details which are not in Matthew. Others believe that Matthew and Luke drew from Mark. However that may be, the opinion now generally held is that Mark itself is quite independent of the other gospels. The most probable view is that all three of the synoptic gospels were independent of one another. The verbal agreement between them rarely extends to an entire verse, and these agreements are to be explained by the writers all using very largely the language in which the apostolic reports of Christ's words and deeds were circulated among the churches. Tradition states that Mark wrote his Gospel at Rome either shortly before or shortly after Peter's death. If so, it must be dated A. D. 65-68. On other grounds also scholars now generally assign it to about that period, shortly before the fall of Jerusalem.

Mark's Gospel was evidently written primarily for gentiles. This appears, e. g., in his explanations of places and customs and terms (i. 9; iii. 17; v. 41; vii. 3, 4, 11, 34; xii. 42; xiv. 12; xv. 22, 42, etc.). He uses also a good many Latin words in Greek form, which may indicate that his book was originally published, as tradition states, at Rome. Unlike Matthew, he says nothing of Christ's relation to the Mosaic law, but few allusions to the fulfillment of prophecy are noted, and there is an almost total absence of quotation from the Old Testament.
G. T. P. (edited).

Mar'ket of Ap'pi-us. See APPII FORUM.

Ma'roth [bitterness, bitter fountains].

A town of Judah (Mic. i. 12). Site unknown.

Mar'riage.
Marriage is a divine institution, constituted at the beginning before the origin of human society. The Creator made man male and female, and ordained marriage as the indispensable condition of the continuance of the race (Gen. i. 27, 28). He implanted social affections and desires in man's nature. He made marriage an ennobling influence, powerfully contributing to the development of a complete life in man and woman. He declared it to be not good for man to be alone and provided a help meet for him (Gen. ii. 18). Abstinence from marriage is commendable at the call of duty (Mat. xix. 12; 1 Cor. vii. 8, 26), but its ascetic prohibition is a sign of departure from the faith (1 Tim. iv. 3).

Monogamy is the divine ideal. The Creator constituted marriage as a union between one man and one woman (Gen. ii. 18-24; Mat. xix. 5; 1 Cor. vi. 16). He preserves the number of males practically equal to the number of females in a nation.

Marriage is a permanent relation (Mat. xix. 6). The Creator has indicated the permanence of the relation by making the growth of affection between husband and wife, as the years pass, to be a natural process, invariable under normal conditions. Moral ends require that the relation be permanent: the disciplining of husband and wife in obedience to the obligations which spring from their relations to each other, and the adequate training of children to obedience and virtue. It cannot be dissolved by any legitimate act of man. It is dissolved by death (Rom. vii. 2, 3). It may be dissolved on account of adultery (Mat. xix. 3-9). Protestants, following Paul, teach that it may be dissolved by willful, deliberate, final desertion (1 Cor. vii. 15). It is probable, however, that in those times desertion was accompanied by adulterous or marital consorting with another person. The marriage of persons divorced on improper grounds is forbidden (Mat. v. 32; xix. 9; 1 Cor. vii. 10, 11). In the sight of God, a civil tribunal cannot annul a marriage; it declares whether the marriage has been sinfully annulled by one or both of the persons concerned.

Among the antediluvians, Adam, Cain, Noah, and his three sons appear each as the husband of one wife. But polygamy was already practiced, Lamech having two wives (Gen. iv. 19); and the purity of marriage was impaired by men allowing themselves to be governed by low motives in the choice of wives (vi. 2). Polygamy was unwisely adopted by Abraham, when he thought that he must needs help God to fulfill his promise (Gen. xvi. 4). Isaac had one wife. Jacob took two wives and their maids. Moses, who was correcting abuses, not suddenly abolishing them, permitted the Israelites, on account of their dullness of spiritual perception and their enslavement to the customs of the age, to put away their wives for a less fault than the gravest breach of marital fidelity; and he did not forbid polygamy, but discouraged it. He regulated what he found; but the record of the primitive period showed that the state of things among the Israelites was not the ordination of the Creator. Moses' service to the cause of matrimony consisted in setting a higher ideal by establishing the degrees of consanguinity and affinity within which marriage is proper (Lev. xviii.), discouraging polygamy (Lev. xviii. 18; Deut. xvii. 17), securing the rights of inferior wives (Ex. xxi. 2-11; Deut. xxi. 10-17), restricting divorce (Deut. xxii. 19, 29; xxiv. 1), and requiring purity in the married life (Ex. xx. 14, 17; Lev. xx. 10; Deut. xxii. 22). Polygamy continued to be practiced more or less by wealthy individuals after the time of Moses, as by Gideon, Elkanah, Saul, David, Solomon, Rehoboam, and others (Judg. viii. 30; 1 Sam. i. 2; 2 Sam. v. 13; xii. 8; xxi. 8; 1 Kin. xi. 3). The evils of polygamy are exhibited in Scripture by the record of the jealousies of the wives of Abraham and Elkanah (Gen. xvi. 6; 1 Sam. i. 6), and beautiful pictures are presented of the felicity of marriage between one man and one woman (Ps. cxxviii. 3; Prov. v. 18; xxxi. 10-29; Ecc. ix. 9; cp. Ecclus. xxvi. 1-27).

In the family to which Abraham belonged marriage was permitted with a half-sister and with two sisters (Gen. xx. 12; xxix. 26). Marriage with a full sister was not rare in Egypt, and was allowed in Persia (Herod. iii. 31). Marriage with a half-sister by the same father was permitted at Athens, and with a half-sister by the same mother at Sparta. The Mosaic law prohibited alliance with persons so closely related by blood as these and with others less near of kin (Lev. xviii. 6-18); but in case a man died childless, his brother took the widow (Deut. xxv. 5). Such marriage was ordained, but it was not compulsory. The Roman law was not unlike the Hebrew. It declared marriages to be incestuous, " when the parties were too nearly related by consanguinity—that is, by being of the same blood, as brother and sister; or by affinity—that is, by being connected through marriage, as father-in-law and daughter-in-law."

The selection of a wife for a young man devolved on his relations, especially on his father (Gen. xxi. 21; xxiv.; xxxviii. 6; 2 Esd. ix. 47), though sometimes the son made known his preference and the father merely conducted the negotiations (Gen. xxxiv. 4, 8; Judg. xiv. 1-10). Only under extraordinary circumstances did the young man make the arrangements (Gen. xxix. 18). Likewise it was the consent of the maid's father and eldest brother that was sought, it not being necessary to consult her (Gen. xxiv. 51; xxxiv. 11). Occasionally a parent looked out an eligible husband for a daughter or offered her to a suitable person in marriage (Ex. ii. 21; Josh. xv. 17; Ruth iii. 1, 2; 1 Sam. xviii. 27). Presents were given to the parents, and sometimes to the maiden (Gen. xxiv. 22, 53; xxix. 18, 27; xxxiv. 12; 1 Sam. xviii. 25). Between betrothal and marriage

all communication between the affianced parties was carried on through a friend deputed for the purpose and termed the friend of the bridegroom (John iii. 29).

The marriage itself was a purely domestic affair, without definite religious services, though probably the espousal was ratified by an oath (Prov. ii. 17; Ezek. xvi. 8; Mal. ii. 14). After the exile it became customary to draw up and seal a written contract (Tob. vii. 14). When the day appointed for the wedding arrived, the bride bathed (cp. Judith x. 3; Eph. v. 26, 27), put on white robes, often richly embroidered (Rev. xix. 8; Ps. xlv. 13, 14), decked herself with jewels (Is. lxi. 10; Rev. xxi. 2), fastened the indispensable bridal girdle about her waist (Is. iii. 24; xlix. 18; Jer. ii. 32), covered herself with a veil (Gen. xxiv. 65), and placed a garland on her head. The bridegroom, arrayed in his best attire, with a handsome headdress and a garland on his head (Song iii. 11; Is. lxi. 10), set out from his home for the house of the bride's parents, attended by his friends (Judg xiv. 11; Mat. ix. 15), accompanied by musicians and singers and, if the procession moved at night, by persons bearing torches (1 Mac. ix. 39; Mat. xxv. 7; cp. Gen. xxxi. 27; Jer. vii. 34). Having received his bride, deeply veiled, from her parents with their blessing and the good wishes of friends (Gen. xxiv. 59; Ruth iv. 11; Tob. vii. 13), he conducted the whole party back to his own or his father's house with song, music, and dancing (Ps. xlv. 15; Song iii. 6-11; 1 Mac. ix. 37). On the way back they were joined by maidens, friends of the bride and groom (Mat. xxv. 6). A feast was served at the house of the groom or of his parents (Mat. xxii. 1-10; John ii. 1, 9); but if he lived at a great distance the feast was spread in the house of the bride's parents (Mat. xxv. 1), either at their expense or the groom's (Gen. xxix. 22; Judg. xiv. 10; Tob. viii. 19). The groom now associated with his bride for the first time (John iii. 29). In the evening the bride was escorted to the nuptial chamber by her parents (Gen. xxix. 23; Judg. xv. 1; Tob. vii. 16, 17), and the groom by his companions or the bride's parents (Tob. viii. 1). On the morrow the festivities were resumed, and continued for one or two weeks (Gen. xxix. 27; Judg. xiv. 12; Tob. viii. 19, 20).

The spiritual relation between Jehovah and his people is figuratively spoken of as a marriage or betrothal (Is. lxii. 4, 5; Hos. ii. 19). The apostasy of God's people through idolatry or other form of sin is accordingly likened to infidelity on the part of a wife (Is. i. 21; Jer. iii. 1-20; Ezek. xvi.; xxiii.; Hos. ii.), and leads to divorce (Ps. lxxiii. 27; Jer. ii. 20; Hos. iv. 12). The figure is continued in the N. T.; Christ is the bridegroom (Mat. ix. 15; John iii. 29), and the church is the bride (2 Cor. xi. 2; Rev. xix. 7; xxi. 2, 9; xxii. 17). The love of Christ for the church, his solicitude for her perfection, and his headship are held up as the standard for imitation by husbands and wives (Eph. v. 23–32).

Mar'se-na.

One of the seven princes of Persia who were permitted to see the king's face (Esth. i. 14). He was perhaps the celebrated Mardonius, the cousin of Xerxes and one of his chief advisers in the early part of his reign (Herod. vii. 5, 9). The third consonant in the Hebrew fo.m of his name is samech, which represents a sound not always distinguished from a dental. See PRINCE.

Mars' Hill. See AREOPAGUS.

Mar'tha [lady, mistress].

Sister of Mary and Lazarus of Bethany (John xi. 1, 2). The three were tenderly attached to Jesus. Martha loved him and desired to make him comfortable and show him respect in her house. Mary gave evidence of a deeper appreciation by her hunger for the words of truth that fell from his lips; and when Martha would have him rebuke Mary for not assisting her to attend to his external wants, Jesus taught that he himself regarded the inward craving of his followers for spiritual fellowship with him as more essential than their concern for his external honor (Luke x. 38–42). Both sisters were sincere believers (John xi. 21–32). The house where Jesus was received is called Martha's (Luke x. 38); and the supper which was given to him at Bethany, at which Lazarus was present and Martha again served, where Mary anointed his feet (John xii. 1–3) was at the house of Simon the leper (Mat. xxvi. 6; Mark xiv. 3). From these facts it has been inferred that Martha was probably the wife or widow of Simon.

Ma'ry [N. T. Greek *Maria* and *Mariam*, from Hebrew *Miryam*, Miriam. Also Latin *Maria*].

Six women of the name mentioned in the New Testament.

1. Mary the (wife) of Clopas or Cleophas, a Mary so designated in John xix. 25. "Wife," according to a method of Greek speech, is not found in the original Greek, but is properly supplied both by A. V. and R. V. Clopas of the R. V., Cleophas of the A. V., is apparently to be identified with Alphæus (Mat. x. 3; Mark iii. 18; Luke vi. 15), the two names being variant forms of the same Aramaic original. He and Mary were thus the parents of the apostle James the Less, who had also a brother Joses (Mat. xxvii. 56; Mark xv. 40; Luke xxiv. 10). Those who understand the Lord's "brethren" to have been his cousins on his mother's side, suppose that this Mary was a sister of the Virgin, and that John (xix. 25) mentions only three women at the cross. But it is unlikely that two sisters should have had the same name, and other considerations make the cousin theory improbable; see BRETHREN OF THE LORD. In that case John mentions four women at

the cross. One of them was Mary the wife of Clopas; but, beyond the fact that her husband and sons were, like herself, disciples of Jesus and that probably one of her sons was an apostle, we know nothing more of her. Besides being at the cross, Mary was one of the women who followed the body of Jesus to the tomb (Mat. xxvii. 61), and on the third day took spices to the sepulcher, and to whom the risen Saviour appeared (Mat. xxviii. 1; Mark xv. 47; xvi. 1; Luke xxiv. 10). See No. 2 of this article; also ALPHÆUS, JAMES.

2. Mary the Virgin; the Virgin Mary. All the authentic information about her comes from Scripture. We are told that, in the sixth month after the conception of John the Baptist, the angel Gabriel was sent from God to Nazareth, a city or village of Galilee, to a virgin named Mary, who was residing there and who was betrothed to a carpenter named Joseph (Luke i. 26, 27). Joseph is explicitly declared to have been a descendant of David. Mary is not so described; but many believe that she too was of Davidic lineage, because she was told that her child should receive "the throne of his father David," also because our Lord is said to have been of "the seed of David according to the flesh" (Rom. i. 3; 2 Tim. ii. 8; cp. Acts ii. 30), and again because, in the opinion of many scholars, the genealogy of Christ given by Luke (iii. 23–38) is through his mother, in which case Mary's father is supposed to have been Heli. However this may be, Gabriel hailed Mary as a highly favored one, and announced to her that she should have a son whose name she should call Jesus. "He," said the angel, "shall be great, and shall be called the Son of the Most High: and the Lord God shall give unto him the throne of his father David: and he shall reign over the house of Jacob forever; and of his kingdom there shall be no end" (Luke i. 32, 33, R. V.). When Mary asked how this could be, since she was a virgin, she was told that it would be wrought by the power of the Holy Ghost, "wherefore also that which is to be born shall be called holy, the Son of God" (Luke i. 35, R. V.). These expressions revealed to Mary that she was chosen to be the mother of Messiah, and with humble piety she accepted the honor which God was mysteriously to confer upon her. For her comfort she was informed by the angel that her kinswoman Elisabeth was also to become a mother, whereupon Mary hastened to the village of Judah where Zacharias and Elisabeth lived. At her coming Elisabeth was made aware of the honor intended for Mary, and broke out into an inspired song of praise. Thereupon Mary also gave voice to a hymn of thanksgiving ("The Magnificat," Luke i. 46–55). We learn from all this the profound piety and solemn joy with which these holy women contemplated the power and grace of God which was through their offspring to

fulfill the ancient promises to Israel and bring salvation to the world. Mary remained under the protection of Elisabeth until just before the birth of John, when she returned to Nazareth. Soon after the cause of her condition was revealed in a dream to Joseph, who at first had thought of quietly putting her away from him (Mat. i. 18–21). He was directed to marry her and to call the name of the child Jesus, "for it is he that shall save his people from their sins." It was pointed out also to him that Isaiah had predicted that Messiah would be born of a virgin. Joseph reverently obeyed. He "took unto him his wife; and knew her not till she had brought forth a son: and he called his name Jesus" (Mat. i. 24, 25, R. V.). By this marriage Mary was protected, her mysterious secret was guarded, and her child was born as the legal son of Joseph, and therefore through him heir of David. The birth, however, took place at Bethlehem. A decree of Augustus that all the world should be enrolled was being carried out in Palestine, and compelled Joseph, being of Davidic descent, to repair to David's city to be enrolled. Mary accompanied him. Finding no room in the inn, or khan, they were compelled to lodge in a stable, perhaps, however, one that was then not being used by cattle. There Jesus was born, and his mother "wrapped him in swaddling clothes, and laid him in a manger" (Luke ii. 7). With reverent, trustful awe Mary heard the shepherds relate the vision of angels which they had seen and the song of peace which they had heard heralding the Saviour's birth. Of course, she did not know that her child was God made flesh. She only knew that he was to be Messiah, and with true piety she waited for God to make his mission clear. On the fortieth day after the birth Mary went, with Joseph and Jesus, to Jerusalem to present the child to the Lord and to offer in the temple the offering required by the law (Lev. xi. 2, 6, 8) from women after childbirth. The fact that her offering is said to have been that required of poor people—a pair of turtle doves or two young pigeons—indicates the humble circumstances of the family. When, however, the parents brought in the child, they were met by the aged Simeon who rejoiced over the birth of Messiah, but foretold to Mary that she should have great sorrow because of what would happen to him (Luke ii. 35). After this Joseph and Mary appear to have returned to Bethlehem and to have lived in a house (Mat. ii. 11). There Mary received the wise men from the east who came to worship Jesus (Mat. ii. 1–11). Soon after she fled with Joseph and the child to Egypt, and afterwards by divine direction they returned to Nazareth. There she must have devoted herself especially to the rearing of the child of promise who had been committed to her care and of whose future she must have thought continually. One glimpse of Mary's

character is given us when Jesus was twelve years old. She was in the habit piously of attending with Joseph the yearly passover (Luke ii. 41), though this was not specifically required of Jewish women (Ex. xxiii. 17). With like piety Joseph and Mary took Jesus with them, as soon as he reached the age when it was customary for children to attend, and his delay in the temple and his words when his parents found him with the doctors, were the occasion of increased awe to his parents. "His mother kept all these sayings in her heart" (Luke ii. 51). Mary did not understand how great her child really was nor how he was to fulfill his mission. It was hers reverently and trustfully to rear him for God's service, and this she did so long as he was under her. If the "brethren of the Lord" (see BRETHREN OF THE LORD) were, as is probable, the children of Joseph and Mary, born after Jesus, Mary was the mother of a large family. We read also of Christ's sisters (Mark vi. 3). But nothing further is recorded of Mary until the beginning of Christ's public ministry. She then appears at the marriage in Cana (John ii. 1–10). She evidently rejoiced in her son's assumption of Messianic office and fully believed in him. But she ventured improperly to direct his actions, and thus elicited from him a respectful but firm rebuke. Mary must understand that in his work she could share only as a follower. While as her son he gave her reverence, as the Messiah and Saviour he could only regard her as a disciple, needing as much as others the salvation he came to bring. A similar truth was brought out on the next occasion on which she appears (Mat. xii. 46–50; Mark iii. 31–35; Luke viii. 19–21). While Jesus was teaching on the great day of parables, Mary with his brethren desired to see him. Perhaps they wished to restrain him from a course which seemed to be bringing upon him opposition and peril. His reply again declared that the spiritual bond between him and his disciples was more important than any human tie. "For whosoever shall do the will of my Father which is in heaven, he is my brother, and sister, and mother" (Mat. xii. 50, R. V.). While Christ pursued his ministry, Mary and his brethren appear to have still lived in Nazareth. As no mention is made of Joseph, it is natural to suppose that he had died. But at the crucifixion Mary appears with other women at the cross. Unlike his brethren (John vii. 5) she had always believed in her son's Messiahship, and therefore it is not strange to find that she followed him on the last fatal journey to Jerusalem. With a mother's love, as well as with a disciple's sorrow, she beheld his crucifixion, and to her Jesus spoke in the hour of his suffering. He gave her to the care of his beloved disciple John, and "from that hour that disciple took her unto his own home" (John xix. 25–27). After the ascension she was with the apostles in the upper room in Jerusalem (Acts i. 14), and this is the last notice of her in Scripture. We do not know the time or manner of her death. The tomb of the Virgin is shown in the valley of the Kidron, but there is no reason to believe in its genuineness. Later legends were busy with her name, but none contain trustworthy information. As presented in Scripture, she is simply a beautiful example of a devoted and pious mother.

3. Mary Magdalene. The designation given to this Mary (Mat. xxvii. 56, 61 ; xxviii. 1 ; Mark xv. 40, 47 ; xvi. 1, 9 ; Luke viii. 2 ; xxiv. 10 ; John xix. 25 ; xx. 1, 18) doubtless indicates that she was a resident of Magdala, on the southwestern coast of the sea of Galilee. Out of her Jesus had cast seven devils (Mark xvi. 9 ; Luke viii. 2), and she became one of his most devoted disciples. The old belief that she had been a woman of bad character, from which the current use of the word Magdalen has arisen, rests merely on the fact that the first mention of her (Luke viii. 2) follows closely upon the account of the sinful woman who anointed the Saviour's feet in a city of Galilee (Luke vii. 36–50). This, however, is hardly sufficient proof. What form her terrible malady had taken we do not know. She became a disciple during the early Galilæan ministry, and was one of those who joined the little company of Christ's immediate followers, and ministered to him of her substance (Luke viii. 1–3). She was one of the women at the cross (Mat. xxvii. 56 ; Mark xv. 40 ; John xix. 25) and observed the Lord's burial (Mat. xxvii. 61). Early on the third day she, with Mary the wife of Clopas and Salome, went to the sepulcher to anoint the body of Jesus (Mark xvi. 1). Finding the stone rolled away she quickly returned to the city and told Peter and John that the body of Jesus had been taken away (John xx. 1, 2). Then, following the apostles, she returned again to the garden and lingered there after they had gone. To her first Jesus appeared (Mark xvi. 9 ; John xx. 11–17), and she reported his resurrection to the other disciples (xx. 18). Nothing further is known of her history.

4. Mary of Bethany. A woman who, with her sister Martha, lived in "a certain village" (Luke x. 38) which John reveals to have been Bethany (John xi. 1 ; xii. 1), about a mile east of the summit of the mount of Olives. On the first occasion when Jesus is recorded to have visited their house (Luke x. 38–42), Mary appears as eager to receive his instruction. Martha requested Jesus to bid Mary help her in serving the entertainment, but he replied : "But one thing is needful : for Mary hath chosen the good part, which shall not be taken away from her" (Luke x. 42, R. V.). John (xi.) further relates that Mary had a brother named Lazarus whom the Lord raised from the dead. When Jesus reached the house, after Lazarus

had been four days dead, Mary at first "still sat in the house" (John xi. 20, R. V.), but afterwards was summoned by Martha to meet the Lord who had called for her (ver. 28). As Martha had done, Mary exclaimed, "Lord, if thou hadst been here, my brother had not died," and the grief of the sisters deeply moved the sympathetic Saviour. Afterwards, six days before his last passover (John xii. 1), Jesus came to Bethany, and a supper was made in his honor in the house of Simon the leper (Mark xiv. 3). While it was in progress Mary brought an alabaster box of pure ointment, very costly, and, breaking the box, poured the ointment on the head of Jesus (ibid.), and anointed his feet, wiping them with her hair (John xii. 3). It was an act of rare devotion, testifying both to her gratitude and to her sense of the high dignity of him whom she honored. Judas, and some other of the disciples, were disposed to find fault with the waste ; but Jesus commended the act and declared that "wheresoever the gospel shall be preached throughout the whole world, that also which this woman hath done shall be spoken of for a memorial of her" (Mat. xxvi. 6–13 ; Mark xiv. 3–9). He looked upon her act also as a loving, though doubtless unintentional, consecration of him to his approaching sacrifice (John xii. 7, 8).

5. Mary the mother of Mark. The Christian woman in whose house the disciples had met to pray for the release of Peter, when he was imprisoned by Herod Agrippa, and to which Peter at once went when delivered by the angel (Acts xii. 12). Her son was the author of our Second Gospel ; see MARK. She was evidently in comfortable circumstances (13), and her house is supposed to have been one of the principal meeting places of the early Jerusalem Christians. According to A. V. in Col. iv. 10 she was the sister of Barnabas ; but R. V. correctly translates "cousin" instead of "sister's son," and it does not appear whether Mark's relationship to Barnabas was on his father's or his mother's side. Nothing is told us of Mary's husband.

6. Mary of Rome. A Christian woman at Rome to whom Paul sent his salutation (Rom. xvi. 6). The A. V. reads "who bestowed much labor on us," implying that Mary at one time had greatly assisted the apostle. The R. V., however, properly reads "who bestowed much labor on you." Mary had thus been an active worker in the Christian cause at Rome. Beyond this reference we know nothing of her.

G. T. P.

Mas'a-loth. See MESALOTH.

Mas'chil [attentive, intelligent, or rendering intelligent].

A Hebrew word occurring in the titles of Ps. xxxii., xlii., xliv., xlv., lii., liii., liv., lv., lxxiv., lxxviii,, lxxxviii., lxxxix., and cxlii. It doubtless means either a didactic poem (cp. Ps. xxxii. 8, "I will instruct," same word radically), or else a reflective poem.

Mash.
A branch of the Aramæans (Gen. x. 23). Called in 1 Chron. i. 17 Meshech, and essentially so in the Septuagint of Gen. x. 23. This is due to its confusion by copyists with the more familiar name; or else, if the original text, it points to an intermingling of Japhetic and Semitic people in Meshech.

Ma'shal. See MISHAL.

Ma'son.
A workman skilled to hew and saw stones into shape for building purposes and erect walls (2 Sam. v. 11; 1 Kin. vii. 9; 1 Chron. xxii. 2; 2 Chron. xxiv. 12). The art made great progress among the ancient Egyptians; as the pyramids, built under the fourth

Reproduction of a tomb painting from Thebes, about 1450 B.C., showing masons at work. This painting is from the tomb of Rekh-mi-Re, governor of the town, Vizier of Upper Egypt.

dynasty, and numerous temples show. The Hebrews served in brick and mortar while they were in bondage in Egypt (Ex. i. 11, 14); but there is no mention of their being employed in shaping and laying stones. In Solomon's time the Phœnicians had more skill in the art than the Hebrews, who as yet had not had occasion to erect great structures of stone, and Phœnician masons were accordingly hired to build the temple and Solomon's palace. They managed blocks of stone 12 and 15 feet in length and even longer, and proportionately broad and high (1 Kin. vii. 10). But they were doubtless Hebrew workmen who afterwards erected walls and fortresses, built aqueducts and reservoirs, arches and bridges, and fashioned columns (2 Chron. xxxiii. 14; Ezra iii. 10; Song v. 15; Antiq. xv. 11, 2). They also understood the use of the plummet (Amos vii. 7; Zech. iv. 10; Is. xxviii. 17).

Mas'o-retes and **Masorites.** See OLD TESTAMENT.

Mas'pha. See MIZPEH 2 and 5.

Mas're-kah [a vineyard].
An Edomite city (Gen. xxxvi. 36; 1 Chron. i. 47). Exact site unknown.

Mas'sa [carrying, a load, a burden].
A tribe descended from Ishmael (Gen. xxv. 14; 1 Chron. i. 30; cp. Prov. xxx. 1 and xxxi. 1, R. V. margin); generally identified with the Masani, a tribe of the Arabian desert near the Persian Gulf (Ptol. v. 19, 2), northeast of Dumah. The Assyrian inscriptions mention Mas'u, as the name may be read, with Tem'u and Niba'âtu, cp. Gen. xxv. 13, 15.

Mas'sah [testing, temptation].
A name given by Moses to the place at Horeb where the smitten rock yielded water, because the Israelites there in unbelief put Jehovah to a test (Ex. xvii. 7; Ps. xcv. 8, 9, R. V,; and also Deut. xxxiii. 8, where the thought is expressed that Jehovah tested the fidelity of the Levites in the person of Moses). In Ex. xvii. 7 the place is called Meribah also; possibly so in the two other passages already cited, where, however, two distinct events and places may be in the writer's mind. The name Massah alone is used in Deut. vi. 16; ix. 22; and used of this event, it would seem, since Israel's rebelliousness against Jehovah soon after leaving Egypt (ix. 7), and apparently before reaching Horeb (8), is dwelt upon, and the event at Massah is mentioned in the same breath with similar events that occurred in the immediate vicinity of Horeb (22). See MERIBAH.

Ma-thu'sa-la. See METHUSELAH.

Ma'tred [driving forward].
The mother-in-law of Hadar, king of Edom (Gen. xxxvi. 39; 1 Chron. i. 50).

Ma'tri [rainy].
A Benjamite family, from which sprang Kish and his son king Saul (1 Sam. x. 21).

Mat'tan [a gift].
1. A priest of Baal slain before the altar of that god during the revolution which led to the death of Athaliah and the elevation of Joash to the throne of Judah (2 Kin. xi. 18; 2 Chron. xxiii. 17).
2. Father of Shephatiah (Jer. xxxviii. 1).

Mat'ta-nah [a gift].
One of the stations of the Israelites in or near the Moabite territory (Num. xxi. 18, 19). The Greek texts differ variously from the Hebrew; hence possibly the word Mattanah was not in ver. 19 originally, and in ver. 18 is a common noun and part of the last line of the song, thus: And from a wilderness a gift.

Mat-ta-ni'ah [gift of Jehovah].
1. A singer, son of Heman, in David's time (1 Chron. xxv. 4, 16).
2. A Levite, of the sons of Asaph, and founder of a branch of the family (2 Chron. xx. 14). Probably he himself is mentioned in 1 Chron. ix. 15, and Neh. xiii. 13; and the

representative of the house in Neh. xii. 8; cp. Ezra ii. 41; Neh. xi. 17, 22; xii. 25.

3. A Levite descended from Asaph. He was one of those who aided king Hezekiah in his work of religious reformation (2 Chron. xxix. 13).

4. A son of king Josiah. He was placed on the throne and his name was altered to Zedekiah by Nebuchadnezzar (2 Kin. xxiv. 17); see ZEDEKIAH.

5–8. Four Hebrews, a son of Elam, a son of Zattu, a son of Pahath-moab, and a son of Bani, who were induced by Ezra to put away their foreign wives (Ezra x. 26, 27, 30, 37).

Mat′ta-tha [gift].

A son of Nathan and grandson of king David (Luke iii. 31).

Mat′ta-thah. See MATTATTAH.

Mat-ta-thi′as [Greek form of Mattithiah, gift of Jehovah (see Septuagint, 1 Chron. ix. 31; xxv. 3)].

1 and 2. A name borne by two ancestors of Christ, separated from each other by five generations, who lived after the time of Zerubbabel (Luke iii. 25, 26).

3. A priest, founder of the Maccabee family (1 Mac. ii. 1–70). See MACCABEE.

4. Son of Absalom, and a captain in the army of Jonathan Maccabæus. He distinguished himself at the battle of Hazor by remaining at the side of Jonathan when all the other captains save one had fled (1 Mac. xi. 70). He was perhaps a brother of Jonathan, son of Absalom (xiii. 11).

5. Son of Simon Maccabæus. His father, his brother, and he were treacherously murdered by his brother-in-law in the castle of Dok (1 Mac. xvi. 14). See JUDAS.

Mat-tat′tah, in A. V. **Mat′ta-thah** [gift].

A son of Hashum, induced by Ezra to put away his foreign wife (Ezra x. 33).

Mat′te-nai [bestowment].

1. A priest, head of the father's house Joiarib in the time of Joiakim (Neh. xii. 19).

2 and 3. Two Hebrews, a son of Hashum and a son of Bani, each of whom was induced to put away his foreign wife (Ezra x. 33, 37).

Mat′than [gift].

A near ancestor of Joseph, and in law of Christ (Mat. i. 15).

Mat′that [gift].

Two ancestors of Christ; the one near, the other quite remote (Luke iii. 24, 29).

Mat′thew [N. T. Greek *Maththaios* or *Matthaios*, from Hebrew *Mattithyah*, gift of Jehovah].

A publican or taxgatherer, in the service either of the Roman or Herodian government, stationed at Capernaum. While sitting at "the place of toll" (R. V.) he was called by Jesus to become his follower and, leaving his business, he immediately obeyed (Mat. ix. 9; Mark ii. 14; Luke v. 27). He was afterwards appointed one of the twelve apos-

tles (Mat. x. 3; Mark iii. 18; Luke vi. 15) Mark and Luke give his name as Levi and state that his father was named Alphæus. Either he had originally two names, as was not uncommon among the Jews, or he received the name Matthew when he became a Christian, as Simon did that of Peter. He is always called Matthew in the lists of apostles and as the author of our First Gospel. The acceptance by Jesus of a publican as a disciple evidently led others of the outcast classes to follow him and increased the opposition of the Pharisees. This appears at the feast which Matthew gave to Jesus soon after his conversion, when many "publicans and sinners" were present, and when, in answer to the criticism of the Pharisees, the Lord made the famous reply, "I am not come to call the righteous but sinners to repentance" (Mat. ix. 10–13; Mark ii. 15–17; Luke v. 29–32). Matthew himself does not say that the feast was in his house (Mat. ix. 10), but Mark (ii. 15) and Luke (v. 29) do, and Luke adds that it was a great feast. Some have identified Matthew's father Alphæus with the father of James the less; but Matthew and James are not joined together in the lists of apostles as other pairs of brothers are. The identification is therefore to be rejected. Matthew finally appears among the apostles after Christ's resurrection (Acts i. 13), but the N. T. gives no further information about him. Tradition states that he first preached among the Jews, and from the character of his Gospel, this is not improbable.

The Gospel according to St. Matthew is the first of our four gospels. It was from the beginning of the post-apostolic age universally ascribed to this apostle. Its contents may be arranged as follows:

1. The descent, birth, and infancy of the royal Messiah (i. and ii.). The special object of this section is to set forth Jesus as the son of David and the Christ of prophecy.

2. Introduction to the public ministry of Christ (iii. 1–iv. 17), relating the preparatory work of the Baptist, the baptism and temptation of Jesus, and the latter's settlement in Capernaum in accordance with prophecy.

3. The Galilæan ministry of Christ (iv. 18–ix. 35). This important section begins with Christ's call of the four leading disciples (iv. 18–22), and a summary description of his teaching and healing, and of his fame throughout Palestine (iv. 19–25). Then follows, as an example of his teaching, the sermon on the mount (v.–vii.), to which is appended a collection of incidents, mostly miracles, which illustrated his teaching (viii. 1–ix. 34).

4. The mission of the apostles (ix. 36–x. 42); beginning with an account of Christ's compassion on the shepherdless people, his appointment of the twelve, and his instructions to them.

5. Christ in conflict with increasing opposition (xi. 1–xv. 20), comprising the inquiry

of the Baptist and Christ's discourse concerning John, together with other remarks occasioned by popular unbelief; the opposition of the Pharisees, beginning with the Sabbath controversy and culminating in the charge that Jesus was in league with Beelzebub, together with Christ's reply and his refusal to give them a sign; the visit of his mother and brethren; a collection of the parables of Jesus spoken at this time; his (second) rejection at Nazareth; Herod's inquiry and the death of the Baptist; the feeding of the 5000 and walking on the water; Christ's final rupture with the Pharisees in Galilee and his denunciation of their formalism.

6. Christ's retirement from Capernaum and instruction of his disciples (xv. 21–xviii. 35); comprising the healing of the daughter of the woman of Canaan the feeding of 4000, refusal of a sign and warning against the leaven of the Pharisees and Sadducees, the confession and rebuke of Peter, Christ's first prediction of his death, the transfiguration and the cure of the demoniac boy; the return to Capernaum, the provision of tribute money, and instruction of the disciples concerning the humble, self-denying, loving, and forgiving spirit of true discipleship.

7. The closing ministry of Christ in Peræa and Judæa (xix., xx.); comprising instructions about divorce, blessing the children, the rich young ruler, the parable of the laborers in the vineyard, the ascent to Jerusalem, with another prediction of his death, the request of James and John, and the healing of Bartimæus at Jericho.

8. The last week of Christ's ministry (xxi.–xxviii.), comprising the triumphal entry and the cleansing of the temple; the withering of the barren fig tree; the deputation from the sanhedrin; the parables of the two sons, the wicked husbandmen, and the marriage of the king's son; the questions of the Pharisees, Sadducees, and a lawyer, with Christ's question in reply concerning the son of David; woes against the scribes and Pharisees; the eschatological discourse on Olivet, followed by the parables of the virgins and of the talents and a description of the last judgment. Then follow the treachery of Judas, the last passover, the agony in Gethsemane, the arrest and trial of Jesus before the sanhedrin, Peter's denials, the remorse of Judas, the trial before Pilate, and the crucifixion and burial. The last chapter relates the appearance of Jesus to the women, the report of the Roman watch, and the gathering of Christ with his disciples on a mountain in Galilee, when he gave them the commission to preach his gospel to the world and promised to be always with them.

The arrangement of this Gospel is chronological only in general outline. In the second half, indeed, beginning with xiv. 6, it follows with seldom a deviation what is probably the true order of events, but this is because that order naturally agreed with the evangelist's object. His primary motive was to arrange his matter topically. He wished especially to present the teaching of Christ concerning the nature of the kingdom of heaven and the character of its disciples, the miracles by which he illustrated his teaching and revealed his authority, and the fruitless opposition to him of the Pharisees, representing current Judaism. Hence the large place which he gives to the teaching of Jesus. Hence, too, his habit of grouping together both instructions upon certain subjects and incidents which illustrated the teaching; thus the sermon on the mount (v. 1–vii. 29) is followed by the record of works of healing which were wrought at different times and places (viii. 1–ix. 34), the parables of chap. xiii. are followed presently by a series of mighty deeds (xiv. 1–36), and the discourse rebuking Pharisaic traditions (xv. 1–20) is followed by a tour of mercy through a gentile region (21–39). He sets forth Jesus as the royal Messiah, who brought about the fulfillment of law and prophecy, and established in the church, by his redeeming work and spiritual teaching, the true kingdom of God, which is meant to embrace all nations. The fulfillment of prophecy is frequently noted (i. 22, 23; ii. 5, 6, 15, 17, 18, 23; iii. 3; iv. 14–16; viii. 17; xi. 10; xii. 17–21; xiii. 14, 15, 35; xxi. 4, 5; xxvi. 24, 31, 56; xxvii. 9, 35), and there are about a hundred quotations, more or less formal, from the O. T. While Matthew wrote from the Hebrew point of view, he brings out the destination of the gospel for the gentiles (e. g. viii. 10–12; x. 18; xxi. 43; xxii. 9; xxiv. 14; xxviii. 19), represents the opposition to Christ of current Judaism (e. g. v. 20–48; vi. 5–18; ix. 10–17; xii. 1–13, 34; xv. 1–20; xvi. 1–12; xix. 3–9; xxi. 12–16; xxiii., etc.), and shows by his explanations of terms (i. 23; xxvii. 33), places (ii. 23; iv. 13), Jewish beliefs (xxii. 23) and customs (xxvii. 15; see also xxviii. 15), that he wrote not merely for Jews, but for all believers.

That the author of this Gospel was really the apostle Matthew is attested by the unanimous tradition of the ancient church. The tradition is confirmed (1) by the conclusive evidence, furnished by the contents, that the writer of this Gospel was a Jewish Christian emancipated from Judaism; (2) by the improbability that so important a book would have been attributed to so obscure an apostle without good reason; (3) by the likelihood that a publican would keep records; (4) by the modest way in which the writer speaks of the feast given by Matthew to Jesus (ix. 10; cp. Luke v. 29).

Ancient tradition also affirmed that Matthew wrote his Gospel originally in Hebrew. Papias, bishop of Hierapolis in Phrygia, writing about A. D. 140, says: "Matthew composed the *logia* in the Hebrew dialect, and each one interpreted them as he was able" (Eusebius, hist. eccl. iii. 39, 16).

Papias probably means that in former days, before his time, each one interpreted these Aramaic logia in his private reading as best he could. It may be fairly inferred also from Papias' words that he had the Gospel of Matthew in Greek; and there is no evidence that he had ever seen a copy of Matthew in Aramaic. Some scholars reject the tradition of an original Hebrew; others suppose that the Greek is a translation, or that Matthew issued two gospels, one edition in Hebrew or Aramaic, the other in Greek. Many modern scholars think that Matthew wrote in Hebrew merely a collection of the sayings of Jesus, which are incorporated in our Greek Gospel together with historical matter taken from Mark. On this theory the Gospel of Matthew, by whomsoever the narrative and the discourses were combined, is history of the first rank, since it comprises a report of Jesus' sayings by one who heard them and a record of Jesus' acts as they were narrated by an eyewitness. The theory is, however, confronted (1) by the testimony of antiquity that our Greek Gospel is by Matthew; (2) by the use made of the term *logia* in the New Testament, by Philo, and by the early fathers (Acts vii. 38; 1 Pet. iv. 11, R. V.), and its constant application to inspired books, either in whole or in their parts (Rom. iii. 2; Heb. v. 12); (3) by the fact that the dependence of our Matthew on Mark is an unproven hypothesis (see MARK and GOSPEL); and (4) by the utter improbability that an original gospel contained discourses only, and not other historical matter, words of Jesus and no acts, and especially that it did not contain an account of the passion of Christ. Whatever, therefore, may be thought of the tradition that Matthew wrote in Hebrew, our Gospel in Greek must certainly be attributed to him. He was quite competent to write it as it is, since most of the recorded words and deeds fell under his own observation.

The date of composition is probably to be assigned to A. D. 60-70. The baptismal formula (Mat. xxviii. 19), which has been regarded as evidence of a late date, is matched by a similar formula in a benediction (2 Cor. xiii. 14); and the word church for an organized body (Mat. xviii. 17) was early used, being so employed by Stephen, Paul, and James (Acts vii. 38; xx. 28; Jas. v. 14). The fall of Jerusalem seems not to have occurred (Matt. v. 35; xxiv. 16). The most ancient tradition, that of Irenæus (about A. D. 175), assigns it to the period when Peter and Paul were preaching the gospel in Rome (Hær. iii. 1, 1). The place of its composition is unknown. The acquaintance with it shown by post-apostolic writers in widely scattered localities proves that it obtained, as soon as it was published, general circulation.   G. T. P. (supplemented).

Mat-thi′as [probably a variant form of Mattathias, gift of Jehovah (see Septuagint, 1 Chron. xxv. 21, A)].

One of those disciples who companied with the followers of Christ from the time of Christ's baptism and was a witness of the resurrection. He accordingly had qualifications for the apostleship. The question whether he or another disciple with similar qualifications should fill the place in the number of the Twelve made vacant by the treachery of Judas was submitted to God by prayer; and when lots were given, Matthias was chosen, and he was at once numbered with the apostles (Acts i. 21-26). Nothing more is known of his history.

Mat-ti-thi′ah [gift of Jehovah].

1. A Levite, son of the singer Jeduthun (1 Chron. xxv. 3), and himself one of the musicians of the sanctuary who played the harp (xv. 18, 21). He was afterwards made head of the fourteenth of the courses into which the musicians were divided by David (xxv. 21).

2. A Levite of the sons of Korah, family of Kohath. He was the eldest son of Shallum, and was placed in charge over the things that were baked in pans (1 Chron. ix. 31).

3. A son of Nebo, induced by Ezra to put away his foreign wife (Ezra x. 43).

4. A priest or Levite who supported Ezra when he addressed the returned exiles regarding the law (Neh. viii. 4).

Mat′tock.

An instrument for loosening the soil, shaped like a pickaxe or hoe with two blades in different planes, the cutting edge of one resembling that of an axe, and the other that of an adze. It is used specially for grubbing up the roots of trees. In the O. T. mattock is the rendering of: 1. The Hebrew *Maḥⁿreshah*, cutting instrument, in 1 Sam. xiii. 20, 21. *Maḥⁿresheth*, a similar word from the same root, occurs in ver. 20, and is believed to denote the plowshare. Both of these implements were made of metal. 2. The Hebrew *Ma'der*, dressing instrument. It was used in digging and dressing vineyards (Is. vii. 25).

In 2 Chron. xxxiv. 6 the Hebrew is believed to be corrupt, and for mattock of the A. V., the R. V. substitutes ruins.

Maul.

The rendering of the Hebrew *Mephis*, breaker. a weapon of war (Prov. xxv. 18).

Maz′za-roth.

A feature of the starry heavens (Job xxxviii. 32). The margin of both English versions interprets it as the signs of the zodiac, equivalent to the Hebrew *Mazzaloth* (2 Kin. xxiii. 5, margin). The parallel passage, Job ix. 9, suggests that the *Mazzaroth* are a constellation of the southern sky, a cluster among the stars that are chambered in the south. Other interpretations have also been proposed.

Mead'ow.

1. The rendering of the Egyptian word *Aḥu*, in A. V. of Gen. xli. 2, 18. The word denotes reed-grass or, as it is rendered in Job viii. 11, flags.

2. The rendering of the Hebrew *Ma'areh* (Judg. xx. 33, A. V.) ; see MAAREH-GEBA.

Me'ah [a hundred].

A tower at Jerusalem not far from that of Hananeel and the sheep gate (Neh. iii. 1; xii. 39) ; see JERUSALEM II. 3.

Meal Of'fer-ing. See OFFERINGS.

Meals.

The Israelites ate in the morning and in the evening (Ex. xvi. 12; 1 Kin. xvii. 6; John xxi. 4, 12). This custom did not forbid a morsel at other hours. Laborers partook of a light repast at noon (Ruth ii. 14). Later the ascetic Essenes did with two meals, the first at the fifth hour or eleven o'clock in the morning, and the other in the evening (War ii. 8, 5). Among the stricter Jews of the time of Christ, the fast of the night was not broken by a meal on an ordinary day before nine o'clock, which was the hour of prayer (Acts ii. 15) ; and on the Sabbath food was not served before twelve o'clock, when the service in the synagogue was over (Life 54). The chief meal of the day took place in the evening (War i. 17, 4; Life 44; cp. Gen. xix. 1-3; Ex. xii. 18; Ruth iii. 7). Feasts were sometimes spread at noon by the Egyptians and Syrians (Gen. xliii. 16; 1 Kin. xx. 16).

As to the posture at meals, the ancient Hebrews, like the ancient Egyptians and Greeks (Iliad x. 578; Anab. vi. 1, 3) and modern Arabs, were in the habit of sitting, probably on mats spread on the floor or ground (Gen. xxvii. 19; Judg. xix. 6; 1 Sam. xx. 5, 24; 1 Kin. xiii. 20). Reclining on couches came into use later (Esth. i. 6; vii. 8; Ezek. xxiii. 41; John xxi. 20), and probably prevailed in the Greco-Roman period (Mark vii. 4; in A. V. tables). Three couches were ordinarily placed about a table, being arranged so as to form three sides of a square and leave the fourth side open for the admittance of serv-ants with the dishes. The couches were designated highest, middle, and lowest re-spectively, the highest being to the right of the servants as they approached the table. Generally, only three persons occupied a couch, but occasionally four or five. The body lay diagonally on the couch, the head being near the table and the feet stretched out toward the back of the couch. The left elbow rested on a cushion and supported the upper part of the body. The right arm re-mained free. The head of the person re-clining in front of another rested on or near the breast of him who lay behind (John xiii. 23; xxi. 20). The three positions on each couch were also termed highest, middle, and lowest, the highest person being the one who had nobody at his back. The position of honor (Mat. xxiii. 6, R. V.) was the highest place on the highest couch. Women took their meals with men, occasionally at least (Ruth ii. 14; 1 Sam. i. 4; Job i. 4).

The Hebrews and Greeks, like the modern Arabs, washed their hands before eating (Mat. xxvi. 23; Iliad x. 577; Odys. i. 136), since generally there was a common dish into which the hand of each was dipped. This cleanly custom became a ritual observance with the Pharisees, and as such was con-demned by Christ (Mark vii. 1-13). A bless-ing was asked before the meal by Samuel (1 Sam. ix. 13), by Christ (Mat. xiv. 19; xv. 36; xxvi. 26), and by the early Christians (Acts xxvii. 35). It was also customary among the Jews in the time of Christ (cp. War ii. 8, 5). A piece of bread served as a spoon and was dipped into the bowl of grease or meat, or the thick soup or pottage was ladled with the hollow hand into a dish. Occasionally separate portions were served in the same manner to each (Ruth ii. 14; 1 Sam. i. 4; John xiii. 26). Prayer after meals developed out of Deut. viii. 10 (War ii. 8, 5).

At pretentious meals on festive occasions, when a large company of guests gathered about the table, greater ceremony was ob-served. It was courteous to receive the guest with a kiss (Luke vii. 45), and indispensable to provide water for him to wash his feet and hands with (Gen. xviii. 4; xix. 2; Luke vii.

Several dozen different dishes are often set before the guest in a modern Arab home.

44; John ii 3) He came in his best attire,
of course, and often with the hair, beard, feet,
and sometimes clothes, perfumed (Amos vi.
6; Wisd. ii. 7). Occasionally he was anointed
at the house of the host (Luke vii. 38; John
xii. 3). The participants at the feast sometimes wore a wreath on the head (Is. xxviii.
1; Wisd. ii. 7, 8; Antiq. xix. 9, 1). They
were arranged according to rank (1 Sam. ix.
22; Luke xiv. 8; and so in Egypt, Gen. xliii.
33). Portions of food were placed before
each (1 Sam. i. 4), and the guest of honor received a larger or choicer share (5; ix. 24;
so in Egypt, Gen. xliii. 34). A ruler was
sometimes appointed to preside at the feast,
taste the viands. and direct the proceedings
(Ecclus. xxxii. 1, 2; John ii. 9, 10). The
banquet was rendered merrier by music (Is.

v. 12; Ecclus. xxxii. 5, 6), singing (2 Sam
xix. 35; Amos vi. 4-6), dancing (Mat. xiv. 6;
Luke xv. 25), and riddles (Judg. xiv. 12)
These customs receive illustration from the
manner of feasts among the Greeks. The
guests were apt to be placed according to
rank, and the guest of honor received the
choicest food (Herod. vi. 57; Iliad vii. 321).
At the conclusion of the meal garlands and
various kinds of perfumes were given to the
guests, and wine was served. Ordinarily a
governor, chosen from among the company
(Anab. vi. 1, 30), presided. His command
was law. He tasted the food and drink before they were placed on the table, directed
the servants, fixed the proportion in which
the wine and water were mixed, and determined the quantity which each of the company should drink. He also proposed the
amusements. The pleasure was heightened
by songs, and by the spectacle of dancing
(Plato, Sympos. ii., Legg. 671; Anab. vi. 1,
3–13).

A gruesome custom existed among the
Egyptians, according to Herodotus (ii. 78).
At the banquets of the wealthy the image of
a dead body in a coffin was carried round
and shown to each of the company with the
remark: "Look upon this, then drink and
enjoy yourself; for when dead you will be
like this."

Me-a′rah [a cave].

A place near Sidon (Josh. xiii. 4); commonly, but without certainty, identified with
a district of caves, on the top of Lebanon,
east of Sidon, known as Mughar Jezzim or
caves of Jezzim. Conder suggests Moghei-
rîyeh, 6 miles northeast of Sidon.

Meas′ure.

Top: Ancient table of measures of surface and
length and weights. Below: Measure of capacity.
These measures are from Nippur, Babylon,
founded about 4,000 B.C. and one of the earliest
centers of Mesopotamian culture.

I. MEASURES OF LENGTH.

The unit was the cubit, 18 inches or more;
see CUBIT.

> 4 fingers = 1 handbreadth;
> 3 handbreadths = 1 span;
> 2 spans = 1 cubit.

The finger, accordingly, was ¾ inch.

In the Greco-Roman period distance was
measured by miles and stades. 5000 Roman
feet = 1 Roman mile = 1478.7 meters =
4851.43 English feet. Eight *stadia* (Luke
xxiv. 13, rendered furlong) were loosely reckoned to the mile; although theoretically the
stadion was 600 Greek feet or 625 Roman
feet, the length of the race course at Olympia.

II. MEASURE OF AREA.

Acre is the rendering of the Hebrew *Ṣemed*,
yoke, and *Ma‘anah*, furrow (1 Sam. xiv. 14;
Is. v. 10). The Roman *actus*, furrow, was 120
Roman feet in length, and the *jugerum*, yoke,
was a piece of land two *actus* long by one
actus broad or less than ⅔ of an acre. Probably the Hebrew acre was not very different.

III. MEASURES OF CAPACITY.

The unit was the ephah for dry substances and the bath for liquids, the ephah and the bath being of equal capacity (Ezek. xlv. 11), and containing a trifle more than 3 pecks, 5 quarts, U. S. dry measure, or 8 gallons, 1 quart, 1⅓ pints, U. S. wine measure. See EPHAH.

Liquid Measure.

12 logs = 1 hin ;
6 hins = 1 bath ;
10 baths = 1 homer, or cor (Ezek. xlv. 14).

The log, accordingly, contained a trifle over .9 pint or about 3⅔ gills, and the hin about 5 quarts, 1⅓ pints. A third part, Hebrew *shalish* (Ps. lxxx. 5; Is. xl. 12, rendered measure) was probably the third of a bath, and hence corresponded to a seah. The Greek measure *metrētēs* (John ii. 6, rendered firkin) contained in Athens 39.39 liters or 41.61 U. S. liquid quarts.

Dry Measure.

6 kabs = 1 seah
3 seahs or measures ⎫   1 ephah (Ex. xvi.
      or   ⎬ =   36; Num. xv. 4,
10 omers or tenth parts ⎭   Septuagint).
10 ephahs = 1 homer (Ezek. xlv. 11).

The kab was equivalent to about 3⅗ pints, and the seah to 9⅗ quarts. The Greek *choinix* (Rev. vi. 6, rendered measure) is estimated at 1.094 liters or .99301 quart. The Roman *modius* (Mat. v. 15, rendered bushel) contained .948 imperial peck, or 7.82 U. S. dry quarts.

Meat Of'fer-ing. See OFFERINGS.

Me-bun'nai [built].
A Hushathite, one of David's mighty men (2 Sam. xxiii. 27). The name is probably to be read Sibbecai, in accordance with xxi. 18 and 1 Chron. xi. 29; xxvii. 11.

Me-che'rath-ite.
A person related by birth or residence to Mecherah (1 Chron. xi. 36). No person or place called Mecherah is known. The passage in Chronicles must be compared with 2 Sam. xxiii. 34.

Me-co'nah, in A. V. **Mekonah** [foundation, place].
A town in the territory of Judah (Neh. xi. 28), named in connection with Ziklag and other towns of the extreme south. Not identified.

Me'dad [love].
A man who, though not present at the tabernacle when the Spirit was imparted to the elders, yet received the gift (Num. xi. 26–29). See ELDAD.

Me'dan.
A tribe descended from Abraham and Keturah and mentioned in connection with Midian (Gen. xxv. 2; 1 Chron. i. 32). Wetzstein observes that the Arabian geographer Yakut mentions a wady Medân near the ruined town of Dedân (cp. Gen. xxv. 3).

Mede, in A. V. once **Median** (Dan. v. 31).
A person belonging to the Median nationality; a native or an inhabitant of Media (2 Kin. xvii. 6; Esth. i. 19; Is. xiii. 17; Dan. v. 28, 31).

Med'e-ba, in 1 Mac. **Medaba** [water of quietness].
An old Moabite town mentioned with Heshbon and Dibon in Num. xxi. 30. It was allotted to the tribe of Reuben (Josh. xiii. 9, 16). In the war of Ammon with Israel, in the reign of David, an Aramæan army hired by the Ammonites, marched hither (1 Chron. xix. 7); see RABBAH. The town reverted to Moab (Moabite Stone 30; Is. xv. 2). John Maccabæus was seized and slain here by sons of Jambri or Ambri, a powerful family of the town. The act was revenged by his brothers Jonathan and Simon (1 Mac. ix. 36–42; Antiq. xiii. 1, 2 and 4). John Hyrcanus took the town after a siege lasting nearly six months (9, 1). The ruins are still called Mâdeba, and are situated about 16 miles east by south of the mouth of the Jordan, and 6 to the south of Heshbon. They are on an eminence, from which the city extended eastward into the plain. There are remains of a city wall, and of temples and other buildings, with Greek, Roman, and Phœnician inscriptions. At the southeast angle of the city is a fine tank or reservoir 120 yards square, and in the vicinity are many caves which have been used as cisterns.

Me'di-a.
A country in Asia lying east of the Zagros mountains, south of the Caspian Sea, west of Parthia, and north of Elam. Its length was about 600 miles, its breadth about 250, and its area about 150,000 square miles. But when the empire was at the greatest it extended beyond these limits, especially in the northwest. A great part of Media proper was a table-land 3000 feet high. The rest consisted of seven parallel mountain chains running from the northwest to the southeast, with fertile and well-watered valleys between. The pasturage was excellent, and the country was noted for its horses. The early inhabitants were in all probability a non-Aryan and non-Semitic race, who were conquered by Aryans, the Madai of Gen. x. 2 (cp. Herod. 7, 62). The history of Media begins to be known in the ninth century B. C. Berosus the Babylonian, it is true, makes the Medes, about 2458 B. C., capture Babylon and establish there a Median kingdom, which lasted 224 years; but it is not known on what authority his statement rests. About 835 the country was probably invaded by Shalmaneser, king of Assyria, and later by Shamshi-Ramman his son, who reigned from

823–810, and by Rammannirari, who was king from 810–781, with the result that the Medes became tributaries of Assyria. Tiglath-pileser conquered and annexed districts of Media. When Sargon captured Samaria, 722 B. C., he placed Israelites in the cities of the Medes (2 Kin. xvii. 6 ; xviii. 11). About 710 the Medes themselves were more thoroughly conquered by Sargon, who exacted from them a tribute of the fine horses for which Media was celebrated. Sennacherib also boasts of tribute received from Media, and Esarhaddon placed governors in the country. In all this there is no trace of the Medes forming a united nation under one king (contrary to Herod. i. 96, seq.). Under Phraortes, 655–633 B. C., Media became a formidable power. About 625 his son Cyaxares allied himself with Nabopolassar of Babylon, besieged and captured Nineveh, and thus terminated the great Assyrian empire (cp. Antiq. x 5, 1). The victors divided the spoil between them, the share of Cyaxares being Assyria proper and the countries dependent on it toward the north and northwest. The marriage of Nebuchadnezzar, son of Nabopolassar, with Amyites or Amytis, daughter of Cyaxares, cemented the alliance between Babylonia and Media, and greatly strengthened both monarchies. When Cyaxares died, in 593, his son Astyages became king. In his old age, about 550 the Persians, whose country lay south and southeast of Media, successfully rebelled, and Cyrus their leader became king of Media and Persia. The conquerors and the conquered were both of the fine Aryan race, and they became a dual nation, Medo-Persia. In 330 B. C. Media became a part of Alexander's empire. After this conqueror's death it was united to Syria (1 Mac. vi. 56), and later it formed a part of the Parthian empire.

In the Hebrew Scriptures the Medes are introduced as at least one of the nationalities which should take part in the capture of Babylon (Is. xiii. 17, 18 ; cp. also Jer. li. 11. 28) ; and Elam and Media are named as the two countries from which the conquerors of Babylon should come (Is. xxi. 2, 9). On the capture of the great city by the Medo-Persians under Cyrus in 539, Darius the Mede took the kingdom of Babylon (Dan. v. 31 ; cp. 28). The Medo-Persian empire is the second kingdom (Dan. ii. 39), the bear (vii. 5), and the two-horned ram (viii, 3–7, 20). One horn was higher than the other, and the higher came up last (ver. 3) ; in other words, the Median power came first, but the Persian, which followed, surpassed it in strength.

Me'di-an. See MEDE.

Med'i-cine.

Egypt was early renowned for medical knowledge and skill. Cyrus of Persia sent to Egypt for an oculist, and Darius had Egyptian physicians at Susa (Herod. iii. 1,

129). For each disease there was a practitioner (Herod. ii. 84). They embalmed (Gen. l. 2) ; they treated diseases of the eye and feet (Herod. iii. 1, 129) ; women practiced midwifery (Ex. i. 15). They had many medicines (Jer. xlvi. 11). Even the word chemistry is perhaps derived from *Kam-t*, the ancient name of Egypt. In Greece the physicians of Crotona enjoyed the highest reputation, while those of Cyrene in Africa stood next (Herod. iii. 131).

The physician and his coadjutor the apothecary are mentioned in the writings of the Hebrews, beginning as early as the exodus from Egypt (Ex. xv. 26 ; 2 Chron. xvi. 12 ; Jer. viii. 22 ; Mat. ix. 12 ; Mark v. 26 ; War ii. 8, 6 ; and Ex. x. x. 35 ; Neh. iii. 8 ; Ecc. x. 1 ; Ecclus. xxxviii. 8). The means and medicines which they employed for effecting cures were bandages (Is. i. 6), applications of oil and of oil mingled with wine, and baths of oil (Is. i. 6 ; Luke x. 34; Jas. v. 14 ; War i. 33, 5), salves and poultices (2 Kin. xx. 7 ; Jer. viii. 22), roots and leaves (Ezek. xlvii. 12 ; War ii. 8, 6), and wine (1 Tim. v. 23). "The Lord created medicines out of the earth ; and a prudent man will have no disgust at them " (Ecclus. xxxviii. 4).

Med-i-ter-ra'ne-an Sea [midland sea].

The sea which lies between Europe and Africa. In Scripture it is referred to simply as the sea, since it was the chief one in the current thought of the Hebrews (Num. xiii. 29; Acts x. 6) ; or it is called the great sea (Num. xxxiv. 6 : Josh. xv. 47), or the hinder or western sea (Deut. xi. 24 ; Joel ii. 20 ; in A. V. utmost and uttermost), or the sea of the Philistines (Ex. xxiii. 31). The Greeks and Romans usually spoke of it as the sea or our sea ; after the O. T. period they termed it the sea on this side of the pillars of Hercules (Aristotle), or the internal sea (Pliny). The designation Mediterranean is late. Its length is 2000 miles, and its narrowest part is between Sicily and the African coast, where it is only 79 miles in width. In O. T. times the Phœnician navigators were acquainted with it in its entire extent from Syria to the straits of Gibraltar or, using the Greek designation, to the pillars of Hercules.

Me-gid'do, once Megiddon (Zech. xii. 11) [place of troops].

An important town in Palestine, mentioned as Mejedi among the towns captured by Thothmes III. of Egypt in the twenty-second year of his reign. When the Israelites entered Canaan, Megiddo had a native king, who was slain by Joshua (Josh. xii. 21). It was within the limits of the tribe of Issachar ; but was assigned to the Manassites, who, however, failed to drive out the Canaanite inhabitants (xvii. 11 ; Judg. i. 27 ; 1 Chron. vii. 29). It had waters, doubtless some stream, in its vicinity (Judg. v. 19), and was not far from Taanach and Beth-shean (i. 27 ; 1 Kin. iv. 12). Solomon strengthened its fortifications (ix. 15). Ahaziah, king of Judah, wounded by the partisans of Jehu, fled to Megiddo, and died there (2 Kin. ix. 27). In the plain near the city the battle was fought between Pharaoh-necho and Josiah, in which the latter was killed (xxiii. 29 ; 2 Chron. xxxv. 22 ; 1 Esdras i. 29). A great mourning for the death of the good king took place (2 Chron. xxxv. 25 ; Zech. xii. 11). The name Megiddo enters into the composition of Armageddon (q. v.). Robinson, and 500 years before him Moses hap-Parchi, considered Megiddo to have been at el-Lejjûn, on the chief tributary of the Kishon, about 9 miles west slightly north of Jezreel. Thomson, however, located the site at Tell el-Mutasellim, less than a mile north of el-Lejjûn. Recent excavation has shown that the citadel crowned the height marked by Tell el-Mutasellim ; while the camp of the legion, which the Romans stationed at Megiddo, stood five minutes' walk distant at the hamlet known as el-Lejjûn, which perpetuates the Latin name and where bricks have been found bearing the stamp of the sixth legion. The place had great strategic importance, since it commanded the pass through the mountains between the plains of Sharon and Esdraelon.

Me-het'a-bel, in A. V. once **Mehetabeel** (Neh. vi. 10) |God blesses].
1. The wife of Hadar, king of Edom (Gen. xxxvi. 39 ; 1 Chron. i. 50).
2. Father of a certain Delaiah (Neh. vi. 10).

Me-hi'da [conjunction, union].
Founder of a family of Nethinim, members of which returned from captivity (Ezra ii. 43, 52).

Me'hir [price].
A man of Judah (1 Chron. iv. 11).

Me-ho'lath-ite.
A native or inhabitant of a place called Meholah (1 Sam. xviii. 19) ; perhaps Abel-meholah, Elisha's native village.

Me-hu'ja-el.
Son of Irad, and father of Methusael, of the race of Cain (Gen. iv. 18).

Me-hu'man [faithful, a eunuch; if the name is related to Aramaic, $m^e haiman$].
One of the seven chamberlains who served in the presence of king Ahasuerus (Esth. i. 10). See article ABAGTHA.

Me-hu'nim, Mehunims. See MEUNIM.

Me-jar'kon [waters of the yellow color, yellow waters].
A spot in the territory of Dan near Joppa (Josh. xix. 46). A place on the river 'Aujah has been suggested (Kiepert, Conder). The river flows from a swamp, through canes, willows, rushes, and grass, and then in a deeply-hollowed channel, whence it carries away vegetable soil enough to render the water yellow. Thus the name suits. The stream is never dry, and in winter is unford-

able. It falls into the Mediterranean, 3¾ miles north of Joppa.

Me-ko'nah. See MECONAH.

Mel-a-ti'ah [Jehovah hath set free].
A Gibeonite who helped to rebuild part of the wall around Jerusalem (Neh. iii. 7).

Mel'chi [probably by contraction for Hebrew *Malkiyyah*, Jehovah is king].
A name borne by two ancestors of Christ who lived, the one before, the other after, the time of Zerubbabel (Luke iii. 24, 28).

Mel-chi'ah. See MALCHIAH.

Mel-chis'e-dec. See MELCHIZEDEK.

Mel-chi-shu'a. See MALCHI-SHUA.

Mel-chiz'e-dek, in A. V. of N. T. **Melchisedec** [king of righteousness or justice].
King of Salem and priest of the most high God (Gen. xiv. 18 seq.). By Salem, Jerusalem is probably meant ; for 1. The city was in existence, bore the name of Jerusalem, and was under a king before the conquest of Canaan by the Israelites. 2. The name Jerusalem means city or, to the Hebrew ear, foundation of peace or safety, so that Salem is an appropriate abbreviation. 3. Salem is used as the name of Jerusalem in Ps. lxxvi. 2. 4. The comparison of David's Lord with Melchizedek in Ps. cx. 4 appears most apt if Melchizedek was king of the same city as David. 5. Jerusalem is on the route from Hobah and Damascus to Hebron, whither Abraham was going.

Melchizedek, as described in Hebrews v. 10 ; vi. 20 ; vii., was without father, without mother, without genealogy. This statement means that his pedigree is not recorded (cp. Ezra ii. 59, 62). This mode of expression was familiar to the Assyrian scribes, was used by the Jewish rabbis, and is known to Greek and Latin writers. He is further described as having neither beginning of days nor end of life, of whom it is testified that he lives. He suddenly emerges from the unknown and as suddenly disappears ; it is not known whence he came or whither he went, neither birth nor death is assigned to him, he is a type of undying priesthood.

Melchizedek was priest of God Most High. *El 'elyon* appears late among the Phœnicians as a title of Saturn, the begetter of heaven and earth (Sanchoniathon quoted by Eusebius, Praep. i. 10). If *El 'elyon* is not in Melchizedek's conception the absolutely only God, he is the highest, the God of the gods ; a lofty idea, even though not a pure monotheism. Melchizedek came forth from his royal city to welcome the returning benefactor of the peoples of Canaan ; and Abraham recognized him as a priest of the true God and publicly testified to sharing the same or a kindred faith by paying tithes to him who was representative of God Most High, to the priest who had ascribed the victory to the Creator of heaven and earth (cp. Acts x. 35).

The author of the Epistle to the Hebrews

shows how great a personage Melchizedek was, to whom even Abraham, and through him virtually Levi, paid tithes, thus admitting their inferiority. When thus our Lord was made a high priest after the order of Melchizedek, he held a higher office than the Aaronic priesthood.

Me'le-a.
An ancestor of Christ, who lived shortly after David (Luke iii. 31).

Me'lech [a king].
A son of Micah, a descendant of Saul and Jonathan (1 Chron. viii. 35; ix. 41).

Mel'i-cu. See MALLUCHI.

Mel'i-ta.
The island where Paul was shipwrecked (Acts xxviii. 1). Two islands bore this name in ancient times. One, now called Melida, lies in the Adriatic Sea off the coast of Dalmatia, the other is now known as Malta. The latter is now probably universally believed to be the island where the ship of Paul was wrecked. This opinion is strongly confirmed by the fact that Mr. Smith, of Jordanhill, who was accustomed to sail in a yacht on the Mediterranean, investigated first the direction from which the wind Euroclydon or Euraquilo blew, then the course in which the ship would drift, and her probable rate of progress while she lay-to under storm sails. The result was that he found she would reach Malta just about the time which the narrative in The Acts requires. The vessel had been driven to and fro in the (sea of) Adria (xxvii. 27); see ADRIA. The traditional site of the shipwreck is St. Paul's Bay, on the northeast coast of the island. In The Acts the inhabitants of the island are called barbarians because they were neither Greeks nor Romans.

Mel'on.
A succulent plant and its edible fruit, in Hebrew *'abaṭṭiaḥ*, which the Hebrews ate when in Egypt (Num. xi. 5). Melons of all sorts were cultivated in Egypt, and the watermelon (*Cucumis citrullus*) is still called *baṭṭiḥ* by the Egyptians, and is grown in immense quantities.

Mel'zar [probably from a Persian word meaning steward].
A man whom the chief of the eunuchs set over Daniel and his companions (Dan. i. 11, 16, A. V.). But in Hebrew it has the article before it; the R. V. and the margin of the A. V. therefore translate it steward.

Mem.
The thirteenth letter of the Hebrew alphabet. English M comes from the same source, and represents it in anglicized Hebrew names. It stands at the head of the thirteenth section of Ps. cxix., in which section each verse of the original begins with this letter.
For Hebrew letters, whose similarity of form to mem has caused difficulty to copyists, see *e. g.* BETH.

Mem'phis [Egyptian *Men-nefer*, place of good, or, as it was interpreted to Plutarch, haven of good].
An important Egyptian city, said by Herodotus to have been built by Menes, the first historical king of Egypt, on land reclaimed by him from the Nile. It stood in the plain on the western side of the Nile, about 10 miles above the apex of the delta. It became the metropolis and capital of Lower Egypt, and the third, the fourth, the fifth, the seventh, and the eighth dynasties were considered Memphite by Manetho. The deity specially worshiped in the city was Ptah. Memphis remained a flourishing city even after the capital was transferred to Thebes, and did not lose its importance until Alexandria was founded. To the Hebrews Memphis was known as Noph, from the demotic *Men-nofi*, and Moph, from *Menf* (Is. xix. 13; text of Hos. ix. 6; cp. Assyrian *Minpi*). After the fall of Jerusalem and murder of Gedaliah, the Jews left in the land fled to Egypt, and some of them settled at Memphis (Jer. xliv. 1). Judgment was threatened against the city by Jeremiah and Ezekiel (xlvi. 19; cp. also ii. 16 and xlvi. 14; Ezek. xxx. 13, 16; cp. also Is. xix. 13; Hos. ix. 6). A considerable part of Memphis existed in the middle ages, but materials from it were continually carried away to be used for building purposes in Cairo. Now it is all but gone, two Arab villages occupying its site. But twenty pyramids, which constituted its necropolis, and the celebrated sphinx present the most impressive memorials of its former greatness.

Me-mu'can.
One of the seven princes of Persia and Media at the court of Ahasuerus who saw the king's face. Memucan's counsel was adverse to Vashti (Esth. i. 14, 15, 21).

Men'a-hem [comforter].
A son of Gadi who, when the news reached Tirzah that Shallum had murdered king Zechariah, went to Samaria, slew Shallum, and reigned in his stead (2 Kin. xv. 14). The town of Tiphsah refused to admit him within its gates, so he captured it, and perpetrated cruelties on the inhabitants (ver. 16). His throne was unsteady; and when Pul, better known as Tiglath-pileser, king of Assyria, invaded the land, Menahem purchased exemption from devastation for his realm and support for his own tottering throne by the payment of 1000 talents of silver, nearly two million dollars, which represented a much greater purchasing value then than now. The money was raised by a tax on the wealthiest men in Israel, who had to pay 50 shekels, about $32.50, each. There must, therefore, have been more than 60,000 Israelites able to contribute this amount under compulsion. Tiglath-pileser, as recorded in the Assyrian sculptures, claims Minihimmu (Menahem) of Samaria as one of his tributaries. In religion the Israelite king ad-

hered to the calf worship of Jeroboam I.
He reigned ten years, from about 747 to 738
B. C. inclusive, and was succeeded on the
throne of Israel by his son Pekahiah (2 Kin.
xv. 17, 22).

Me′nan. See MENNA.

Me′ne.

The first word of the inscription written
by a hand on the wall at Belshazzar's feast:
MENE, MENE, TEKEL, UPHARSIN (Dan. v.
25). These mysterious words are Aramaic.
They are rendered on the margin of R. V.
"Numbered, numbered, weighed, and divisions;" Pharsin being the plural of the noun
p‘res, Mene being the regular passive participle of its verb in the Peal species, and
Tekel being regarded as likewise a passive
participle, with the vocalization which is traditionally given to it changed from *t‘kil* to
t‘kel to conform to the sound of *m‘ne′*. These
letters were not vocalized as written on the
wall, and might have been pronounced in a
variety of ways. Even if the correct pronunciation had occurred to one of the wise
men as among several possibilities, he had
no means of establishing the correctness of
his reading or of interpreting the words.
Daniel solved the enigma (25–28). How
difficult it was to determine the true pronunciation is illustrated by the proposal which
has been made by scholars to regard Mene as
the absolute state of the noun *manya′*, maneh,
and to read the words "A maneh, a maneh,
a shekel and half manehs," or "Numbered
have been a maneh, a shekel, and half manehs." The words as thus read have been
sometimes understood as symbolizing under
the figure of weights that a worthy person
(Nebuchadnezzar, the virtual founder of the
empire) had been succeeded by an inferior
ruler (Belshazzar), and that the empire was
about to be divided into halves.

Me′ni [fate, destiny].

The name of the god of destiny, whom
idolatrous Hebrews worshiped (Is. lxv. 11,
margin). In the text the English versions
prefer the alternative interpretation of the
word, regarding it as a common noun and
not a proper name.

Men′na, in A. V. **Menan.**

An ancestor of Christ, who lived shortly
after the time of David (Luke iii. 31).

Me - nu′hoth [apparently, the resting
places].

A place, if the present Hebrew text is correct, of which half the inhabitants were
descended through Shobal from Caleb of the
tribe of Judah (1 Chron. ii. 52, R. V.). The
name, if vocalized as in the present Hebrew
text, would not give rise to the gentile adjective of ver. 54, which is rendered Manahathites. Perhaps, therefore, Menuhoth
should be read Manahath (q. v.).

Me-on′e-nim [augurs].

The augurs' oak or terebinth stood near

Shechem (Judg. ix. 37; not plain, as in A.
V.). See remarks under MOREH.

Me-on′o-thai [my habitations].

A man of Judah, the father of the inhabitants of Ophrah (1 Chron. iv. 14).

Meph′a-ath [beauty].

A town of the Reubenites (Josh. xiii. 18),
given to the Merarite Levites (xxi. 37; 1
Chron. vi. 79). In Jeremiah's time it was in
the hands of the Moabites (Jer. xlviii. 21).
Site unknown.

Me-phib′o-sheth [destroying shame].

1. Son of king Saul by Rizpah, the daughter
of Aiah. He was executed at the instance
of the Gibeonites (2 Sam. xxi. 8, 9).

2. The son of Jonathan. He was five
years old when the tidings came of his
father's and his grandfather's death at Gilboa. Under the influence of panic, the
nurse took him up in her arms and fled with
him; but in her flight she let him fall, so
that he became lame in both his feet (2 Sam.
iv. 4). For a long time he lived at Lo-debar,
east of the Jordan, whence David called him
to court to show him kindness for his father
Jonathan's sake, restoring to him the estates
of Saul and appointing him a place at the
royal table (ix. 1–13). During the rebellion
of Absalom he remained at Jerusalem, and
was accused by his servant Ziba of disloyalty. David believed the accusation and
transferred Mephibosheth's estates to Ziba.
After the return of David, Mephibosheth attempted to clear himself of the charge, and
David restored half the estates to him; but
he declared that he did not wish the property, since he had his desire in the restoration of the king (xvi. 1–4; xix. 24–30). He
had a son Micha (ix. 12), through whom the
race of Jonathan was perpetuated. In 1
Chron. viii. 34; ix. 40 Mephibosheth is called
Merib-baal, a striver is the Lord or perhaps,
striver against Baal. This was probably his
original name, *bosheth*, shame, being substituted for *baal*, lord, by later writers when the
word Baal had become distasteful through association with idolatry.

Me′rab [increase].

Saul's elder daughter (1 Sam. xiv. 49).
Her father promised her in marriage to
David, and then, breaking faith, gave her
as a wife to Adriel the Meholathite (xviii.
17–19). Their five sons were given up by
David to the Gibeonites to be put to death
for the sin of Saul (2 Sam. xxi. 8, margin;
cp. Greek of Lucian, Peshito).

Me-ra′iah [contumacy, stubbornness].

A priest, head of the father's house Seraiah
in the days of Joiakim, a generation after
the exile (Neh. xii. 12).

Me-ra′ioth [rebellions].

1. A priest, son of Zerahiah (1 Chron. vi.
6, 7, 52). He lived while the house of Eli
had charge of the tabernacle

2. A priest, son of Ahitub and father of

the younger Zadok of the high-priestly line (1 Chron. ix. 11; Neh. xi. 11). He seems to have lived about half a century before the exile.

3. A father's house among the priests in the days of Joiakim (Neh. xii. 15). See MEREMOTH.

Me-ra'ri [bitter, unhappy].

Son of Levi, and founder of one of the three Levitical families (Gen. xlvi. 11; Ex. vi. 16; Num. xxvi. 57).

Me-ra'rites.

One of the three great families of the tribe of Levi. They were descended from Merari. In the wilderness they encamped on the north side of the tabernacle (Num. iii. 35), had under their charge its boards, bars, pillars, sockets, and vessels (36; iv. 29–33), and were under the direction of Ithamar, the youngest son of Aaron (iv. 23). To enable them to carry these materials there were assigned to them four wagons and eight oxen (vii. 8). They were subdivided into the Mahlites and the Mushites (iii. 20, 33); and at the first census in the wilderness numbered 6200 males from a month old and upward (33, 34), being fewer in total number than the other families of Levi. Of these, 3200 were from 30 to 60 years old (iv. 42–45), a larger proportion than in the other families. The cities assigned to them numbered twelve, of which four were in the tribe of Zebulun, four in that of Reuben, and four in that of Gad; one of them, Ramoth-gilead, being a city of refuge (Josh. xxi. 34–40; 1 Chron. vi. 63, 77–81). They were reorganized by David (1 Chron. xxiii. 6, 21–23). They had a due part with their fellow Levites in the musical service of the sanctuary, holding six of the twenty-four offices (1 Chron. vi. 31, 44; xxv. 3). Members of the family are mentioned among those who aided in cleansing the temple in Hezekiah's reign (2 Chron. xxix. 12), and a small, but notable, company of them returned with Ezra to Jerusalem after the exile (Ezra viii. 18, 19).

Mer-a-tha'im [twofold rebellion].

A symbolical name for Babylon (Jer. l. 21).

Mer'cu-ry, in A. V. **Mer-cu'ri-us.**

A deity worshiped by the Romans and, under the name of Hermes, by the Greeks also. He was the herald of the gods, and specially attended upon Jupiter. He was quick in his movements, was a good speaker, and was credited with having been the inventor of letters, of music, and of other arts. Paul and Barnabas were looked upon as gods by the people of Lystra, when the cripple was healed at the apostle's word; and as Paul was the chief speaker, they took him for Mercury and Barnabas, whom he accompanied, for Jupiter (Acts xiv. 12).

Mer'cy Seat.

The covering of the ark; called in Hebrew *Kapporeth*, covering (especially if not exclu-

sively in the sense of atonement), and in Greek '*Ilastêrion*, propitiatory (Ex. xxvi. 34; Heb. ix. 5). Its name did not suggest a mere lid, but brought to mind the act and place of atonement and the accomplished atonement. The rendering mercy seat is therefore a happy one, adopted by Tyndale from Luther. It was made of pure gold; its length was two and a half cubits, and its breadth a cubit and a half. On each side of it and wrought as one piece with it stood a cherub, with its face toward the other cherub, but bent downward toward the mercy seat, and with outstretched wings, so that a wing of each extended over the mercy seat and met that of the other cherub. Between these cherubim Jehovah's glory was manifested, and there Jehovah communed with his people (Ex. xxv. 17–22; xxx. 6; Num. vii. 89). There was a similar arrangement in Solomon's temple (1 Kin. vi. 23–28; viii. 6–11; 1 Chron. xxviii. 11). Once a year, on the great day of atonement, the high priest, after he had offered a sin offering for himself, entered the most holy place and burnt incense, symbol of accepted worship, in the presence of Jehovah, which rose and enveloped the mercy seat in a cloud. He then sprinkled the blood of the sacrificed bullock on and before the mercy seat. Having sacrificed the goat that was the sin offering for the nation, he carried its blood also beyond the veil, into the most holy place, and sprinkled it upon and before the mercy seat. He made atonement for the sins of himself and the nation in the presence of the covenant law, which was written on the tables of stone and was lying in the ark, and of Jehovah, who dwelt between the cherubim (Lev. xvi. 2, 13–17).

Me'red [rebellion].

Son of Ezrah, who was reckoned as belonging to the tribe of Judah. He had a daughter of Pharaoh to wife and probably also a Jewess (1 Chron. iv. 17, 18, R. V.).

Mer'e-moth [elevations].

1. A chief of the priests, who returned from Babylon with Zerubbabel (Neh. xii. 3, 7). In the next generation a father's house among the priests, enumerated in the corresponding position in the catalogue, bears the name Meraioth (ver. 15). One of the two names is probably a misreading of mem or jod.

2. A priest, son of Uriah. He was employed to weigh the silver and gold brought by Ezra from Babylon (Ezra viii. 33). He repaired part of the wall of Jerusalem (Neh. iii. 4, 21), and is probably the person of the name who sealed the covenant (x. 5).

3. A son of Bani, induced by Ezra to put away his foreign wife (Ezra x. 36).

Me'res.

One of the seven princes of Persia and Media who saw the king's face in the reign of Ahasuerus (Esther i. 14).

Mer'i-bah [contention, strife].

1. A common noun used once, perhaps oftener, in addition to Massah to designate the place at Horeb, near Rephidim, where the people strove with Moses (Ex. 17) for water; and God gave them drink from the rock (1–7). The word is not found in this passage in the Vulgate, but is attested by other ancient versions.

2. A second locality, namely, Kadesh-barnea in the wilderness of Zin, where also the people strove with Moses and with Jehovah and water was miraculously brought from the rock (Num. xx. 3, 13, 24; xxvii. 14; Deut. xxxii. 51). The waters of this Meribah are the waters of strife, which are mentioned in the A. V. of Ps. cvi. 32 and Ezek. xlvii. 19; xlviii. 28. For strife the R. V. in its text of the first passage substitutes Meribah, in the second Meriboth-kadesh, and in the third Meribath-kadesh. This event may well be referred to in Ps. lxxxi. 7, where it is God who proves Israel; and in Deut. xxxiii. 8, where God proves Levi and where Meribah is mentioned with Massah; and in Ps. xcv. 8, R. V., where also Meribah is mentioned with Massah (see MASSAH). It is to be noted that there is nothing surprising, under the circumstances, in the outbreak of discontent at the scarcity of water, which was experienced more than twice or thrice. The localities are different and quite far apart. The time is different. The conduct of Moses is very different on the two occasions.

Mer-ib-ba'al. See MEPHIBOSHETH.

Mer-i-bath-ka'desh [contention at Kadesh] and **Meriboth-kadesh** [contentions at Kadesh].

A station of the Israelites in the wilderness (Ezek. xlvii. 19; xlviii. 28, R. V.). See MERIBAH 2.

Mer'o-dach [Assyrian and Babylonian *Marduk*].

The patron deity of Babylon (Jer. l. 2). See BEL.

Mer'o-dach-bal'a-dan, in 2 Kin. xx. 12 **Berodach-baladan** [Merodach has given a son]. Berodach may be a copyist's misspelling for Merodach, or represent the approximation of sound between m and b in Babylonian.

A king of Babylon, son of Baladan (2 Kin. xx. 12), of the dynasty of Bit-Yakin. He was a man of great ability, courage, and enterprise. The dynasty had its capital at Bit-Yakin, in the marshes near the mouth of the Euphrates, a district which was the ancestral home of the Chaldean tribe. Merodach-baladan succeeded to this petty throne. About 731 B. C. he did homage to Tiglath-pileser, king of Assyria; but when, in 722, the Assyrian army was absent carrying on the siege of Samaria, and news reached Babylonia that the king of Assyria had died or been murdered, Merodach-baladan took the opportunity of becoming king of Baby-

lon. Sargon, king of Assyria, recognized him in 721. He reigned eleven years. In 712, or thereabouts, Merodach-baladan sent the embassy to Hezekiah, which, traveling with the ostensible object of congratulating Hezekiah on his recovery (2 Kin. xx. 12–19; 2 Chron. xxxii. 31; Is. xxxix. 1–8), was really designed to invite him to join in a confederacy with the rulers of Babylon, Susiana, Phœnicia, Moab, Edom, Philistia, and Egypt for a grand attack on the Assyrian empire. Sargon suspected what was going on, attacked his enemies individually before they had time to unite, and vanquished them one by one. In 710 Sargon took Babylon, and in 709 Bit-Yakin, capturing Merodach-baladan at the latter place. Some time after Sargon's death Merodach-baladan was again free, and in 704 or 703 he reëntered Babylon, and slew the Assyrian viceroy, who was then its ruler. But his second reign lasted only from six to nine months. He was defeated and driven from Babylon to Bit-Yakin by Sennacherib, Sargon's son and successor. In 700, in connection with the revolt of a Chaldean called Nergal-ushezib or Shuzub, Merodach-baladan raised his head again. Sennacherib took the road to Bit-Yakin, but Merodach-baladan avoided battle and fled to a town in the midst of the sea. Sennacherib again prevailed, quelling the revolt in 698. In 697 he attacked the last refuge of Merodach-baladan, which was a fragment of territory given him by the Elamites. The Assyrian king employed Phœnician ships for the purpose. Merodach's small settlement, which he had abandoned, was captured and burnt, and he was not able to raise his head again. Though he may have ultimately failed in his enterprises, yet he had not lived in vain. The Chaldeans, whose chief he was, and who seem to have been a Semitic race, became from his days the dominant caste in Babylon.

Me'rom [a height, a high place].

By the waters of Merom Joshua defeated the kings of northern Canaan and their allies (Josh. xi. 5, 7), who according to tradition had pitched their camp near Beroth (the wells, or have Beroth and Merom become confused? see BETH) in upper Galilee, not far from Kedesh (Antiq. v. 1, 17). These waters are usually identified with a lake on the Jordan, 11 miles north of the sea of Galilee, or with the streams that flow through its basin. This lake is 4 miles long by 3½ broad, its surface lies 689 feet above the sea of Galilee, and it is almost certainly the body of water called by Josephus the lake Semechonitis (Antiq. v. 5, 1; War iv. 1, 1). It occupies the southern portion of a very marshy basin about 15 miles long by 5 broad. The basin is now called the Huleh and the lake Baheiret el-Huleh or lake of the Huleh. Huleh, an Arabic name given also to the plain south of Hamath, perhaps echoes the name

A man-made pond in the north end of the Huleh Valley. In ancient times this basin was known as the waters of Merom.

of the district Ulatha, between Trachonitis and Galilee (Antiq. xv. 10, 3).

Me-ron′o-thite.

An inhabitant of Meronoth (1 Chron. xxvii. 30; Neh. iii. 7). Meronoth has not been identified.

Me′roz [probably, a place of refuge].

A town which gave no assistance in the fight with Sisera (Judg. v. 23). Its site is unknown, though el-Murussus, a ruin about 4½ miles northwest of Beth-shean, has been suggested, or Kefr Misr, on the southern slope of mount Tabor, 6½ miles northwest of el-Murussus.

Mes′a-loth, in A. V. **Masaloth** [perhaps, from Hebrew *mᵉsilloth*, ascents, stairs].

A place in the district of Arbela (1 Mac. ix. 2). Josephus understood it to be the region of fortified caves at Arbela in Galilee, which were only to be reached by steps (Antiq. xii. 11, 1).

Me′sech. See MESHECH.

Me′sha, I.

The limit in one direction of the region occupied by the descendants of Joktan (Gen. x. 30). Not identified. Mouza, on the eastern coast of the Red Sea, about 100 miles from the straits of Bab el-Mandeb, Bischa in northern Yemen, the district Mesene at the northwestern end of the Persian Gulf, and Massa′ (cp. Septuagint and Gen. xxv. 14) have been suggested.

Me′sha, II. [perhaps, retreat, withdrawal].

A Benjamite, a son of Shaharaim by his wife Hodesh (1 Chron. viii. 8, 9).

Me′sha, III. [salvation].

1. A man of Judah, family of Hezron, house of Caleb. He was ancestor of the inhabitants of Ziph (1 Chron. ii. 42).

2. A king of Moab, son of Chemosh-melech. He rendered to king Ahab the tribute of 100,000 lambs and as many rams, namely their wool (2 Kin. iii. 4). Ahab was slain at the battle of Ramoth-gilead about 853 B. C., which probably took place in the early spring, "the time when kings go forth to war," and Ahaziah thereby became sole king. The discomfiture of Israel and Judah at Ramoth-gilead and the death of Ahab were the signal to Mesha to refuse the tribute of this year, the second of Ahaziah (Antiq. ix. 2, 1), to Israel (2 Kin. i. 1). Jehoshaphat, king of Judah, returned from Ramoth-gilead to Jerusalem, say in May, and undertook a religious reformation of the nation (2 Chron. xix.). After this work of reform had begun (xx. 1), the Ammonites and Moabites, in alliance with the Edomites, who had been persuaded to revolt, invaded Judah. Jehoshaphat defeated the allies and reduced Edom to its former subjection, and a time of peace ensued (30). Ahaziah died at the end of this year, perhaps in December or January or later, and Jehoram his brother succeeded him (2 Kin. i. 17). The next year, 852 B. C., or later, Jehoram, desiring to render Moab again tributary, asked aid of Jehoshaphat (iii. 7). The latter probably wished to chastise the Moabites still further for their invasion of Judah, and, therefore, although he had been rebuked for allying himself with ungodly Ahab and Ahaziah,

consented, for Jehoram had exhibited signs of godliness by a considerable reformation (2). Jehoram advanced with his confederates, Jehoshaphat and an unnamed Edomite king, round the southern end of the Dead Sea. The allied armies almost perished with thirst, but Elisha bade them dig trenches, predicting that water would come. It flowed into the valley early in the morning; and as the ruddy light of the sun shone on it, the Moabite king, doubtless Mesha, thinking it was blood and inferring that the three invading armies had quarreled and turned their swords against each other, carelessly advanced with his forces to take the prey. He was routed, and the Israelites entered his land and beat down his cities (24, 25). At Kir-hareseth, seeing that the battle was too sore for him and failing in a desperate attempt to break through the lines of the enemy, he took his eldest son and heir apparent and offered him as a burnt offering to Chemosh on the city wall. The besiegers apparently felt that they were in part responsible for occasioning this human sacrifice and that they had incurred the wrath of God, and they raised the siege and returned to the land of Israel without resubjugating Moab (25–27). The Moabite stone was erected partly for the purpose of commemorating this revolt and its successful issue ; see MOABITE STONE.

Me'shach.
The name given by the prince of the eunuchs at Babylon to Mishael, one of the three faithful Jews afterwards saved from the fiery furnace (Dan. i. 7; ii. 49; iii. 13–30).

Me'shech, in A. V. once **Mesech** (Ps. cxx. 5).
A people descended from Japheth (Gen. x. 2). They traded in the Tyrian markets in slaves and vessels of brass (Ezek. xxvii. 13). They were allies of Tubal, and allies or subjects of Gog, the prince of Rosh, Meshech, and Tubal (Ezek. xxxii. 26; xxxviii. 2, 3; xxxix. 1, R. V.). Meshech and Tubal are associated together in the Assyrian inscriptions as they are in the Bible. In the days of Tiglath-pileser, about 1120 B. C., and Shalmaneser, 859–825, the land of Musku, that is Meshech, lay in the mountains to the north of Assyria and bordered on Tabal, that is Tubal, in the west. They were gradually driven northward to near the Black Sea. Herodotus calls the two races the Moschoi and Tibarenoi, and locates them in the mountains southeast of the Black Sea (Herod. iii. 94; vii. 78). The Moschoi dwelt between the source of the Phasis and Cyrus rivers (Pliny vi. 4).

Me-shel-e-mi'ah [Jehovah recompenses].
A Levite, family of Kohath, house of Izhar and Korah. He and his sons were doorkeepers of the sanctuary (1 Chron. ix. 21; xxvi. 1). In xxvi. 14 he is called Shelemiah.

Me-shez'a-bel, in A. V. **Meshezabeel** [God sets free].

1. Father of a certain Berechiah (Neh. iii. 4).
2. One of those who sealed the covenant (Neh. x. 21).
3. A man of Judah, family of Zerah (Neh. xi. 24).

Me-shil'le-mith [recompense, retribution].
See MESHILLEMOTH 2.

Me-shil'le-moth [recompenses].
1. An Ephraimite, father of that Berechiah who urged the release of the captives brought from Judah by Pekah's army (2 Chron. xxviii. 12).
2. A priest descended from Immer (Neh. xi. 13), called Meshillemith in 1 Chron. ix. 12.

Me-sho'bab [restored].
One of the Simeonite princes who seized upon the pasture lands near Gedor (1 Chron. iv. 34–41).

Me-shul'lam [a friend].
1. A Benjamite, descended from Shaharaim through Elpaal (1 Chron. viii. 17).
2. A leading man among the Gadites in the reign of Jotham (1 Chron. v. 13).
3. An ancestor of Shaphan the scribe (2 Kin. xxii. 3).
4. A priest, son of Zadok, and father of the high priest Hilkiah who lived in Josiah's reign (1 Chron. ix. 11; Neh. xi. 11). See SHALLUM 7.
5. A Kohathite Levite who with others helped faithfully to superintend the workmen who repaired the temple in Josiah's reign (2 Chron. xxxiv. 12).
6. A priest, son of Meshillemith of the house of Immer (1 Chron. ix. 12).
7. A son of Zerubbabel (1 Chron. iii. 19).
8. A Benjamite, father of Sallu (1 Chron. ix. 7; Neh. xi. 7).
9. Another Benjamite, son of Shephatiah (1 Chron. ix. 8).
10. A chief man whom, with others, Ezra sent from the river of Ahava to secure Levites to go to Jerusalem (Ezra viii. 16).
11. One of those who busied themselves, probably adversely, in the matter of inducing the Jews who had married foreign wives to put them away (Ezra x. 15).
12. A son of Bani, induced by Ezra to put away his foreign wife (Ezra x. 29).
13. A son of Berechiah. He helped to repair two portions of the wall of Jerusalem, at the second of which he had a chamber (Neh. iii. 4, 30). Johanan, son of Tobiah the Ammonite, married his daughter (vi. 18).
14. Son of Besodeiah. He with another returned exile repaired the old gate of the wall of Jerusalem (Neh. iii. 6).
15. One of those who stood on Ezra's left hand while he read and explained the law to the people (Neh. viii. 4).
16. A priest who, doubtless in behalf of a father's house, sealed the covenant (Neh. x. 7).
17. A chief of the people who did so (Neh. x. 20).

18. One of the princes of Judah who marched in the procession at the dedication of the wall of Jerusalem (Neh. xii. 33).

19. A priest, head of the father's house Ezra in the days of the high priest Joiakim (Neh. xii. 13).

20. Another priest at the same date, head of the father's house Ginnethon (Neh. xii. 16).

21. A porter who lived at the same date (Neh. xii. 25).

Me-shul'le-meth [a female friend].

Wife of king Manasseh, and mother of king Amon (2 Kin. xxi. 19).

Me-so'ba-ite. See Mezobaite.

Mes-o-po-ta'mi-a [land between rivers].

The rendering, borrowed from the Septuagint, for the Hebrew Aram-naharaim; see Aram 2, (1). It is a Greek name which appears after the time of Alexander the Great. The Greek and Roman geographers used the term for the whole country between the Euphrates and Tigris rivers, excluding the mountainous region where the rivers take their rise and ordinarily also the low-lying plain of Babylonia in the other direction. Thus limited, its upper portion is hilly and fertile and its lower part, especially toward the Tigris, is a salt desert. Mesopotamia is now called by the Arabs Jezireh or the island.

Some of its inhabitants were present on that day of Pentecost on which the Holy Spirit descended (Acts ii. 9). Stephen includes Ur of the Chaldees in Mesopotamia (vii. 2).

Mes-si'ah, in A. V. of N. T. **Messias** (John i. 41; iv. 25), the Greek form [anointed one].

A Hebrew word, to which the Greek word *Christos* answers. It was applicable to any person anointed with the holy oil; as the high priest (Lev. iv. 3, 5, 16; 1 Sam. xii. 3, 5, Hebrew) or the king (2 Sam. i. 14, 16). The title is given to the patriarchs Abraham and Isaac and to the Persian king Cyrus, as chosen ones to administer the kingdom of God (Ps. cv. 15; Is. xlv. 1). When God promised David that the throne and scepter should remain in his family forever (2 Sam. vii. 13), the title acquired a special reference and denoted the representative of the royal line of David (Ps. ii. 2; xviii. 50; lxxxix. 9; lxxxix. 38, 51; cxxxii. 10, 17; Lam. iv. 20; Hab. iii. 13). And when prophecy began to tell of a king who should appear in this line and be the great deliverer of his people (Jer. xxiii. 5, 6), whose goings forth are from of old, from everlasting (Mic. v. 2–5), and who should uphold the throne and kingdom of David forever (Is. ix. 6, 7), the title of the Messiah, *par excellence*, naturally became attached to him (Dan. ix. 25, 26; Targum Onkelos, Num. xxiv. 17–19), and ultimately became a customary designation of him, being as common as the title son of David (John i. 41; iv. 25; and in the form Christ, Mat. i. 1 et passim).

The term Messianic prophecy denotes all prophecy which treats of the person, work, or kingdom of Christ, whether it does so with express mention of Christ or speaks of the future salvation, glory, and consummation of God's kingdom without mention of the mediator. The term Messianic times does not refer exclusively to the period when Christ lived on earth. It generally comprehends the dispensation which Christ inaugurated and conducts as mediatorial king, whether viewed in its entirety or in some of its aspects.

Met'als.

The metals used in ancient times were gold, silver, iron, copper, lead, and tin (Num. xxxi. 22); see the several articles. Perhaps antimony was employed for coloring the eyelids and eyebrows. See Paint.

Me-theg-am'mah [probably, bridle of the mother city, *i. e.* jurisdiction of the metropolis].

A town taken by David from the Philistines (2 Sam. viii. 1). The reference is doubtless to Gath and its suburbs (1 Chron. xviii. 1).

Me-thu'sa-el. See Methushael.

Me-thu'se-lah, in A. V. of N. T. **Mathusala** [perhaps, man of a weapon].

Son of Enoch and father of the Sethite Lamech (Gen. v. 21–27). If the number of years which are assigned to him refer to his own individual life, he is notable for having lived to a greater age than any other man recorded in history. See Chronology.

Me-thu'sha-el, in A. V. **Me-thu'sael** [man of God].

Son of Mehujael, and father of Lamech, of the race of Cain (Gen. iv. 18).

Me-u'nim, in A. V. also **Mehunim** and **Mehunims** [plural of the gentile adjective from Maon, denoting the people of Maon].

A people whose capital was probably the city of Ma'ân, 12 miles southeast of Petra. They inhabited mount Seir (2 Chron. xx. 1, emended text, with 10; cp. Septuagint). A body of them were smitten by the Simeonites near Gedor, where they dwelt as strangers (1 Chron. iv. 39–41). They are mentioned in connection with Philistines and Arabians (2 Chron. xxvi. 7). Some of them, probably captives of war and their descendants, served at the temple in Jerusalem as Nethinim (Ezra ii. 50; Neh. vii. 52). They are mentioned in Judg. x. 12, according to the Hebrew text, where the Septuagint has Midian. The Meunim are identified by the Septuagint with the Minæans. If the identification be correct, they are only a northern settlement of that people.

Mez'a-hab [waters of gold].

An ancestress of the wife of Hadar, king of Edom (Gen. xxxvi. 39; 1 Chron. i. 50); or perhaps a district, of which Matred was a native. The R. V. hyphenates the name.

Me-zo'ba-ite, in A. V. **Mesobaite**.

Apparently a gentile adjective, as in the English and Greek versions (1 Chron. xi. 47); but the Hebrew text is evidently corrupt.

Mi'a-min. See MIJAMIN.

Mib'har [choice].

One of David's mighty men, son of Hagri or better a Hagrite (1 Chron. xi. 38); see remarks about the text under Bani.

Mib'sam [sweet odor].

1. A tribe descended from Ishmael (Gen. xxv. 13; 1 Chron. i. 29).

2. A Simeonite (1 Chron. iv. 25).

Mib'zar [a fortification, a stronghold].

An Edomite chieftain (Gen. xxxvi. 42; 1 Chron. i. 53).

Mi'ca, in A. V. **Micha** once **Micah** (1 Chron. ix. 15) [evidently, like Micah, an abbreviation of Micaiah, who is like Jehovah? (cp. Mic. i. 1 with Jer. xxvi. 18 R. V., and 2 Chron. xxxiv. 20 with 2 Kin. xxii. 12)]. A variant Hebrew spelling yields the English form Micah, cp. 2 Sam. ix. 12 with 1 Chron. viii. 34.

1. A son of Mephibosheth (2 Sam. ix. 12). The interchangeable form of the name, Micah, is given him in 1 Chron. viii. 34, 35; ix. 40, 41.

2. A Levite who sealed the covenant (Neh. x. 11).

3. A Levite descended from Asaph (1 Chron. ix. 15; Neh. xi. 17, 22; and xii. 35, where the form Micaiah is used).

Mi'cah, in A. V. thrice **Michah** (1 Chron. xxiv. 24, 25) [who is like Jehovah?]. See MICA.

1. A Levite, family of Kohath, house of Uzziel (1 Chron. xxiii. 20; xxiv. 24, 25).

2. An Ephraimite who stole from his mother 1100 shekels of silver, about 725 dollars, but afterwards gave them back again. His mother dedicated 200 of them to the Lord for images. A graven and a molten image were made of them and placed in the house of Micah, and Micah consecrated his son to be priest. A Levite chanced to pass that way, and Micah embraced the opportunity to secure an accredited minister at the sanctuary. A Levite, though not a priest, was better than the layman, Micah's son. The Levite consented for hire to minister before Jehovah in a house of images, contrary to the second commandment. Sometime afterwards, migrating Danites passed that way, allured the Levite to go with them, and carried off Micah's images, despite his protestations (Judg. xvii., xviii.).

3. A son of Merib-baal (1 Chron. viii. 34, 35; ix. 40, 41); see MICA 1.

4. A Reubenite who lived several generations before 730 B. C. (1 Chron. v. 5).

5. Father of Abdon. He was born before Josiah's reign (2 Chron. xxxiv. 20; 2 Kin. xxii. 12, where the form Micaiah is used); cp. ACHBOR 2.

6. A descendant of Asaph (1 Chron. ix. 15, A. V.); see MICA 3.

7. A Morashtite, a native apparently of Moresheth-gath (Mic. i. 14), a town believed to have been in Judah, not far from Gath and for a time a dependency of the Philistine city. He prophesied in the reigns of Jotham, Ahaz, and Hezekiah (Mic. i. 1; and Jer. xxvi. 18, where the form Micaiah is used). He therefore began his career a little later than his contemporaries Hosea and Isaiah (cp. i. 1 with Is. i. 1 and Hos. i. 1). He spoke upon the same great themes as Isaiah and so similarly that, as Calvin has said, Micah was, as it were, Isaiah's colleague.

Micah's style is simple; not rugged, but elegant. He is plain-spoken in the rebuke of sin (i. 5; ii. 1, 2; vi. 10-12). His transitions of thought are often abrupt, but a logical connection is seldom difficult to discern. He is fond of the interrogation (i. 5; ii. 7; iv. 9; vi. 3, 6, 7, 10, 11), uses irony (ii. 11), introduces a metaphor, and retains it and carries it forward (i. 6; iii. 2, 3, 6; iv. 6-8, 13; vi. 10, 11, 14, 15), and delights in paronomasia or play upon words, employing it largely in the first chapter and perhaps allowing it to determine the form of the concluding paragraph of the book. That paragraph is spoken in praise of Jehovah, and is based on the rhetorical question, "Who is a God like unto thee?" the prophet closing his prophecy by publishing the claim with its ground which his own name makes.

Micah drew confidence and strength from the character of God, as revealed in the ten commandments, in his dealing with Israel, and in individual experience (ii. 7; vi. 3-5; vii. 15). God himself does justice and loves mercy, and he requires these traits in his people. The promises of God were also a source of strength and sweet encouragement to the prophet. He knew that Israel's security lay in God's purpose to save his people according to the promise made to Abraham (vii. 20) and centered in the son of David (v. 2-6; cp. Luke i. 72-75). The foes of the kingdom cannot prevail. Chapter v. is based on the same truth as Ps. ii.; and, like the sweet message of forgiveness and restoration (vii. 8-20), rests upon God's word.

The book of Micah is the sixth of the minor prophets. Its author prophesied in the reigns of Jotham, Ahaz, and Hezekiah (i. 1). Its contents also show that it was written after the reigns of Omri and Ahab (vi. 16), at the time when Assyria was the power which the Israelites dreaded (v. 5, 6), and in part at least while Samaria and the northern kingdom were still in existence (i. 6, 14); but how long before the fall of Samaria the words of i. 5-7 were uttered cannot be determined, for from the time of Uzziah and Jotham the prophets were foretelling the approaching doom of Samaria (Hos. i. 6; iii. 4; v. 9; Amos ii. 6; iii. 12; v. 1-3, 27;

vi. 1, 7–11, 14; Is. vii. 8, 9; viii. 4) and the desolation of Judah (Hos. v. 10; Amos ii. 4; Is. vi. 1, 11–13; vii. 17–25). The allusion to the desolation of Bashan and Gilead may indicate a period later than 733–732 B. C., when Tiglath-pileser ravaged that territory and deported its inhabitants (Mic. vii. 14, where the days of old refer to the occupation of the region by Israel from the time of the conquest onward, cp. 14 with 20). The prophecy of iii. 12 was spoken during the reign of Hezekiah (Jer. xxvi. 18), though Micah may have discoursed on this theme before.

The prophecies of Micah, although they refer especially to Judah and were spoken to the people of the southern kingdom, yet concern all Israel (Mic. i. 1, 5–7, 9–16). The abrupt transitions indicate that the book is rather a summary of the prophet's teaching than a series of distinct discourses. The expression "Hear ye," repeated three times, serves to mark the beginning of three divisions, each of which likewise ends with a message of hope. I. Judgment upon Samaria for its incurable disposition toward idolatry (i. 2–8), and upon Judah as involved in like guilt (9–16). Woe upon the oppressors of the people and prophecy of the ruin and captivity of the nation (ii. 4, 5) as a punishment for the unrighteousness and injustice of its representative men (1–11). Yet a remnant shall be restored (12, 13). II. Denunciations passing into prophecies of salvation. Rebuke of the civil and religious authorities for heartless indifference to truth and right and for the mercenary character of their doctrine and government (iii. 1–11); the consequent abandonment of Zion by Jehovah to the power of its foes (12); but the ultimate exaltation of Jehovah's kingdom in moral influence among men and in peace, prosperity, and power (iv. 1–8). But at present dismay, helplessness, captivity (9, 10), followed by the overthrow of its enemies for their sinful opposition to Jehovah (11–13). But at present discomfiture for Zion (v. 1), until he shall come forth unto God that is to be ruler in Israel, whose goings forth are from of old, from everlasting (2–4). This foreordination of God regarding the Messiah assures and secures the deliverance of Zion from the Assyrians (5, 6; cp. Is. vii. 4–16), and is the pledge and potency that guarantees the survival of God's people throughout the ages and their ultimate triumph over all foes and attainment of conformity to God's ideal (Mic. v. 7–15). III. Jehovah's controversy with the people as a whole, not with the wealthy and the official classes only (vi. 1–5), explaining the requirements of true religion (6–8; see also Is. i. 11–17), lamenting its absence and the presence of its very opposite (Mic. vi. 9–vii. 6), and closing with the prophet's own confidence in a glorious future due to the forgiving grace of Jehovah and his faithfulness to his covenant with Abraham (7–20).

Chap. iv. 1–3 is almost identical with Is. ii.

2–4, but is more closely connected than in the corresponding passage in Isaiah with the verses which immediately follow. Joel expresses a similar thought (Joel iii. 10). Isaiah certainly quoted his words, as the introduction, "And it shall come to pass," shows; and he may have cited them from Micah. But the verbal variations between Isaiah and Micah, and between these prophets and Joel, may be explained by supposing that each adopted a traditional prediction current in his day. At any rate God's people of old had authoritative prophecy upon which they relied, and favorite passages which they quoted, just as Christians of to-day have.

The integrity of the text of Micah has been impugned. The evidence urged as proof of interpolation consists mainly in the following facts, frequently reinforced by a denial that the style is Micah's: I. Exile is presupposed (ii. 12, 13; vii. 7–20; Wellhausen). But surely Micah might look forward to an exile of the people, for 1. On the theory of the Mosaic origin of the addresses in Deuteronomy, it was natural for Micah to look forward to the exile of the people. As foreseen and foretold, sin meant national weakness and ruin; and this condition in that age of the world had for its ordinary result subjugation by the great world powers and deportation into slavery (Deut. xxviii. 31–37, 47–53; cp. Is. i. 19, 20). 2. The exile of Judah, or at least of the upper classes, is taught in admittedly genuine passages of Micah, and an exile undoubtedly of the nation as a whole is clearly announced by Isaiah (Mic. i. 15, 16; ii. 3–5, 10; Is. v. 13; vi. 11–13; vii. 3; a remnant shall return, x. 21). A forward look to the exile is therefore quite in place in the prophecy of Micah. Critics of this trend, who regard the context as genuine, reject the clause in iv. 10 where Babylon is mentioned as a place of exile. It is called a gloss; and it may certainly be omitted without injury to the sense. But (1) so may many clauses admittedly genuine be omitted without destroying the connection. And (2) Isaiah speaks of Babylon as a place of exile, in a prophecy which Micah may have had in mind (Is. xxxix. 6, 7). Once again Isaiah, having before his mind's eye the children of Israel scattered throughout the inhabited world, mentions Shinar, *i. e.*, Babylon, as one of the lands of the exile (xi. 11). This portion of the chapter, like the clause in Micah, is exscinded, primarily because of this reference to Babylonian exile. II. Messianic elements: the reassembling of Israel and their triumphant breaking forth under the leadership of their king (Mic. ii. 13); the peace and prosperity of Zion in the Messianic period, and the accession of the gentiles (iv. 1–8); and the person of the Messiah (v. 2–8). But these thoughts were unquestionably contemporary with Micah (Hos. xi. 8–11, not to refer to disputed passages in Hosea; Is. ii. 2–4; iv. 2–6, ix. 1–7

[Heb. viii. 23–ix. 6] ; x. 20–22 ; xi. 1–10 ; see also Amos ix. 11–15, and the remarks on its genuineness). III. The universalism which finds expression in Jehovah's relation to the gentile world. The answer to this objection is : 1. The presuppositions are not wanting in Micah's own thought, as reflected in passages admittedly genuine (i. 2). 2. A universalistic conception appears in Amos' denunciation of Jehovah's punishment upon the nations for their hostility to the kingdom of God (Amos, chaps. i. and ii.) ; in the attitude of Jehovah to Damascus, Egypt, and Assyria, proclaimed by Isaiah ; and in the writings ascribed to J. and E., contemporary with Micah, in which mention is made of God's moral government of the world (Gen. ii.–xi. ; xviii. 25, etc.). IV. The eschatological ideas of a world attack upon Zion and its failure, in contrast with the prophecy of the overthrow of Zion by its enemies (Mic. iv. 11–13 with iii. 12). The two ideas are, however, not inconsistent. The conflict of the world power with Judah is viewed by Micah, as by other prophets of his own time and later, from two points : Jehovah gives up his people to the sword and to captivity because of their sins ; but in so far as the hostility of the world is directed against Zion in its religious significance, it is a struggle against Jehovah and must issue in the destruction of the opposing nations (Is. i. 19, 20 ; viii. 5–8 and 9, 10 ; x. 5–7 and 12–16 ; comp. Is. iii. 8, 24–26 ; v. 13, 26–30). No sword formed against her shall prosper. The progress of the Assyrian advance into Judah under Sennacherib in the days of Isaiah and perhaps of Micah, and its failure, offered a striking illustration of the twofold principle here proclaimed as a truth valid for all time (2 Kin. xviii. 13–xix. 37 ; cp. xviii. 11, 12 and xix. 4–7 ; Vos, Presb., and Ref'd Rev. x. 305). V. Condemnation of the pillars and the Asherim, which were used in the popular worship, but were not condemned until the high places were made an object of attack by the prophets, that is, after the Deuteronomic reform. But 1. Notice the implication that the addresses in the book of Deuteronomy are not Mosaic in their origin. 2. The attitude of Micah is that of his predecessor Hosea. The very building of pillars is condemned by Hosea (Hos. x. 1, 2). And Hosea condemns all idols and must, therefore, have opposed the images of the goddess Asherah (cp. ii. 5, 13 ; iv. 12, 17 ; viii. 4–6 ; and Mic. i. 7). 3. The entire passage Mic. v. 9–14 is similar to Is. ii. 6–8. VI. The transitions from threatening to promise (Mic. ii. 12, 13 ; iv. 1–8 ; vii. 7–20). This sequence is, however, customary among the prophets. It is their uniform habit after denouncing doom to illumine the darkness with a ray of promise, and thus encourage the godly to stand fast and strive and hope. It is, however, the habit of those critics who bring forward the objection mentioned to exscind these passages of promise, or many of them, and thus trim the prophecies to suit a theory.

Several remarks that bear on the genuineness of chapters vi. and vii. may be thrown loosely together. The thought of the exiles scattered far and wide (Mic. vii. 12) is not surprising in a contemporary of Isaiah ; and the hope that the walls of Jerusalem will be rebuilt (vii. 11) is natural after one has pictured the enemy treading down Zion as the mire of the streets (10). Over against Ewald's assignment of chapters vi. and vii. to the time of Manasseh (a date, it will be observed, which need not fall outside of Micah's lifetime) may be placed Cornill's opinion that everything in these chapters applies well to the time of Ahaz. The anticipation of exile (vii. 7–20), and the ravaging of the kingdom by its foes, yet their submission (vi. 13–16 ; vii. 16, 17), and the transition from threatening to promise, characterize chapters i.–v. equally with vi. and vii. Chapters vi. and vii. form a natural advance from the denunciation of the official representatives of the nation (i.–iii., to Jehovah's controversy with the people as a whole (vi., vii.). The figure of Jehovah in controversy with Israel was familiar to the prophets of this period (Hos. iv. 1 ; xii. 2 ; cp. Is. i. 2–24) ; and to refer to events of Israel's early history, as in vi. 4, 5 ; vii. 15, 20, was a common practice with Micah (i. 15 ; v. 6), Hosea, and Isaiah. As the prophecies of chapters i.–v. resemble Isaiah's utterances, so chapter vi. resembles Is. i.

Mi-ca′iah, in A. V. **Michaiah** except in 1 Kin. xxii. 8–28 ; 2 Chron. xviii. 6–27 [who is like Jehovah ?].

1. Daughter of Uriel of Gibeah, wife of Rehoboam, and mother of king Abijah (2 Chron. xiii. 2). According to xi. 20, Abijah's mother was Maacah, daughter of Absalom. Micaiah is probably a corruption of Maacah, for so Abijah's mother is always called elsewhere, and she was probably granddaughter of Absalom and daughter of Uriel by his wife Tamar, Absalom's daughter. See MAACAH 9.

2. A prophet, son of Imlah. Being desired by Ahab to concur in the favorable prediction given by the prophets of Baal regarding Ahab's expedition against Ramoth-gilead, he did what was required of him, but with such transparent insincerity that he was adjured to speak the truth, on which, in the name of Jehovah, he predicted the death of Ahab in the coming fight. The order was given to make him a prisoner till the event should prove his unfavorable vaticination to be untrue (1 Kin. xxii. 8–28 ; 2 Chron. xviii. 6–27).

3. One of Jehoshaphat's princes sent by him to teach in the cities of Judah (2 Chron. xvii. 7).

4. The prophet, better known as Micah (Jer. xxvi. 18, E. R. V. ; see A. R. V. margin).

5. Father of Achbor. He lived before Josiah's reign (2 Kin. xxii. 12); see MICAH 5.

6. A son of Gemariah, who reported to the Jewish princes in the reign of Jehoiakim the contents of Jeremiah's book as read by Baruch (Jer. xxxvi. 11–13).

7. A descendant of Asaph (Neh. xii. 35); see MICA 3.

8. A priest, one of those who blew trumpets when the wall of Jerusalem was dedicated by Nehemiah (Neh. xii. 41).

Mi'cha. See MICA.

Mi'cha-el [who is like God?].

1. A man of Asher, father of the representative from that tribe on the commission to spy out Canaan (Num. xiii. 13).

2. A Gadite, descended from Buz and head of a father's house in Gilead (1 Chron. v. 13; cp. 11, 14, 16).

3. Another Gadite, ancestor of the preceding (1 Chron. v. 14).

4. A Levite, family of Gershom and ancestor of Asaph (1 Chron. vi. 40).

5. A chief man of the tribe of Issachar, family of Tola, house of Uzzi (1 Chron. vii. 3).

6. A Benjamite, family of Beriah (1 Chron. viii. 16).

7. A Manassite captain who joined David at Ziklag (1 Chron. xii. 20).

8. Father of Omri, who ruled the people of Issachar in David's reign (1 Chron. xxvii. 18).

9. A son of king Jehoshaphat (2 Chron. xxi. 2).

10. Father of Zebadiah, of the sons of Shephatiah (Ezra viii. 8).

11. An archangel (Jude 9), one of the chief angelic princes who helped the man clothed in linen against the spiritual being behind the Persian empire, called the prince of the kingdom of Persia (Dan. x. 13), who contended for Israel (21; xii. 1), and who with his angels wars victoriously against the enemies of the people of God (Rev. xii. 7). When the doctrine of angels was wrought out by the Jews after .he exile, Michael was made one of seven a. .hangels (Tob. xii. 15), Gabriel being, of course, included in the number (Dan. viii. 16; ix. 21), and five others being added to make up seven, namely; Raphael (Tob. iii. 17), Uriel (2 Esd. iv. 1), Chamuel, Jophiel, and Zadkiel. The common belief that Michael disputed with Satan about the body of Moses, to which Jude refers and upon which he bases a lesson (Jude 9; cp. 2 Pet. ii. 11) is reflected in the Targum of Jonathan on Deut. xxxiv. 6, which ascribes the burial of Moses to Michael and other angels. The form of expression in Zech. iii. 1, 2 and Jude 9 may have been derived from the current account; but more probably the words of the prophet Zechariah determined the phraseology of the common belief.

Mi'chah. See MICAH.

Mi-cha'iah. See MICAIAH.

Mi'chal [perhaps, a brook].

The younger daughter of king Saul (1 Sam. xiv. 49). After Saul had failed to fulfill his promise to give his elder daughter Merab to David, he learned that Michal was in love with the young hero, and he gladly embraced the opportunity which this affection afforded him to expose David to the risk of death. He offered Michal to David on condition that he should slay a hundred Philistines. David accomplished the assigned task and received Michal to wife (1 Sam. xviii. 27, 28). She aided David in escaping from her father's machinations, but after the former became a fugitive Saul married her to another man, regardless of the obligations she was under to David (xxv. 44). When Abner, Ish-bosheth's general, sought to make up matters with David, the king required that his wife Michal should be restored to him, which was done (2 Sam. iii. 15). But when David was bringing the ark to Jerusalem and, in the intensity of his religious zeal, danced before the Lord, Michal thought the hero and king was acting in an undignified manner, and she despised him in her heart, and rebuked him with scornful and untrue words. But David replied that he had humbled himself before the Lord and would continue to do so, but that he would be held in honor by those in whose sight she falsely insinuated he had acted in a lewd manner. After a time Michal died childless (2 Sam. vi. 14–23).

Mich'mash, and twice **Michmas** (Ezra ii. 27; Neh. vii. 31), and so in A. V. of 1 Mac. ix. 73 [something hidden away].

A town near the mount of Bethel (1 Sam. xiii. 2), east of Beth-aven (5), and north of Geba (xiv. 5, in A. V. Gibeah; Is. x. 28, 29). The Philistines encamped at Michmash to war with Saul; but through the valor of Jonathan and his armor bearer at the craggy pass near by a slaughter was begun among them and they were routed by the army of Israel (1 Sam. xiii. 5–7, 15 seq.; xiv. 1–23). Exiles from Michmash returned from the captivity (Ezra ii. 27; Neh. vii. 31). They were Benjamites (xi. 31). Jonathan Maccabæus took up his residence at Michmash and exercised judgeship (1 Mac. ix. 73, in A. V. Machmas; Antiq. xiii. 1, 6). The pass of Michmash, still retaining the name of Mukhmâs, is 7½ miles north by east of Jerusalem, 2 northeast of Geba, and 3 south by east of Bethel. The village of Mukhmâs is one of an humble character; the pass is probably, as Robinson thought, the wady es-Suweinit, and the two rocks of Bozez and Seneh which flanked the pass (1 Sam. xiv. 4) are described by him as two conical, or rather spherical, hills, with rocky sides.

Mich'me-thath, in A. V. **Michmethah.**

A town on the boundary line between Ephraim and Manasseh. It lay "before Shechem" (Josh. xvi. 6; xvii. 7). Site doubtful.

Mich'ri [valuable].

A Benjamite (1 Chron. ix. 8).

Mich'tam [engraving, inscription].

A word occurring in the titles of Psalms xvi.; lvi.–lx. It has been understood as meaning: 1. Concealed, secret, hence a mystery or a hitherto unknown composition. 2. Golden psalm. 3. Epigram, a poem intended, like an inscription, to record memorable thoughts, and often indulging in refrains. The last opinion has most support.

Mid'din [extensions].

A village in the wilderness of Judah (Josh. xv. 61). Site unknown.

Mid'i-an, in A. V. of N. T. **Madian** [strife, contention].

1. A son of Abraham by Keturah, sent away with gifts into the wilderness, and in whom the Midianites were linked with Abraham. The person and tribe form one conception (Gen. xxv. 1–6).

2. A region in the Arabian desert near the Ælanitic gulf, occupied by the Midianites (Gen. xxv. 6). It was bordered by Edom on the northwest. Its boundaries were never demarked, and doubtless shifted considerably at different periods; but all the region referred to in the O. T. as dominated by the Midianites is found within an area which measures about 175 miles from north to south. About the time of the exodus Midian controlled the pasture lands east of Horeb in the peninsula of Sinai (Ex. iii. 1). A district adjacent to Moab and near the Amorite kingdom, whose capital was Heshbon, was occupied by Midianites, who had been settled there for some time (Gen. xxxvi. 35; Num. xxii. 4; xxv. 1, 6; Josh. xiii. 21). The intervening region east of Edom to the Red Sea doubtless belonged to Midian. The Midianites who were routed in the valley of Jezreel fled in this direction, and Gideon in pursuing them passed Succoth and the Gadite town of Jogbehah (Judg. viii. 5, 10, 11; cp. Gen. xxxvii. 25. 28). In David's time a royal refugee from Edom found temporary asylum in Midian, probably southeast of Edom, before he went into Egypt (1 Kin. xi. 17, 18). The center of population was east and southeast of the Ælanitic gulf of the Red Sea, where the name has lived from age to age and is still preserved in the ruins called Madyan.

Mid'i-an-ites.

A people of the desert (Gen. xxv. 2, 6; Num. x. 29–31; Is. lx. 6; Hab. iii. 7; Judith ii. 26). Five families of them sprang from Midian (Gen. xxv. 4). Of these five, the name of Ephah has been identified with much probability with a name on the Assyrian inscriptions of the 8th century before Christ, which denotes a tribe of northern Arabia. Midianite merchants, who were with the caravan of Ishmaelites coming from Gilead, bought Joseph and carried him to Egypt (Gen. xxxvii. 25, 28). The father-in-law of Moses was a Midianite (Ex. iii. 1). Midianites joined with Moabites in hiring Balaam to curse the Israelites and afterwards seduced the people to idolatry and licentiousness (Num. xxii. 4, 6; xxv.). The Israelites were consequently directed to make war on them. They did so, killing the five kings of Midian with all the male population of the district and the married women (xxxi.). These kings were allies or vassals of Sihon, king of the Amorites (Josh. xiii. 21). In the period of the judges, Midianites, in conjunction with the Amalekites and the children of the east, entered Canaan, with their cattle and their tents, like locusts for multitude, everywhere appropriating the crops, and reducing to the greatest distress those who had sown them. After the oppression had lasted for seven years, God raised up Jerubbaal, or Gideon, to deliver the now repentant people. The decisive battle was fought in the plain of Jezreel. It resulted in the complete defeat of the foreign oppressors. Their two princes, Oreb and Zeeb, were taken and put to death; and later their two kings, Zebah and Zalmunna, shared the same fate. The land had rest, then, for the normal period of forty years (Judg. vi.–viii.; ix. 17; Psalm lxxxiii. 9–12; Is. ix. 4; x. 26).

Mig'dal-el [tower of God].

A fortified city of Naphtali (Josh. xix. 38). Its identification with el-Mejdel, that is Magdala, on the sea of Galilee, is contrary to the order of enumeration. Its site is probably Mujeidil, 12½ miles northwest of Kades, i. e. Kedesh, and 11 miles north-northwest of Yarun, i. e. Iron.

Mig'dal-gad [tower of Gad or fortune].

A town at or near the lowland of Judah (Josh. xv. 37). El-Mejdel has been suggested, inland 2½ miles east, slightly north, from Ashkelon. This location would be in the country of the Philistines.

Mig'dol [tower; in Egyptian *makthal*, tower].

An encampment of the Israelites while they were leaving Egypt. It was near the sea (the Red Sea according to Ex. xv. 4, 22; Deut. xi. 4); was before Pi-hahiroth and before Baal-zephon (Ex. xiv. 2; Num. xxxiii. 7). After the capture of Jerusalem by Nebuchadnezzar, Jews fled to Egypt and took up their abode in a place called Migdol (Jer. xliv. 1; xlvi. 14). If the marginal reading of Ezek. xxix. 10; xxx. 6 is correct, Migdol was in the extreme north of Egypt. Ancient authors mention a Migdol or Magdolon 12 miles distant from Pelusium, on the northeastern frontier of Egypt, and the Makthal most frequently mentioned on the Egyptian monuments was situated near the Mediterranean Sea (Ebers). Brugsch identifies this place with Tell es-Samût, and regards it as the site of the encampment of the Israelites. But this situation does not harmonize with the location of the camp on the Red Sea, as the term Red Sea is understood. Other fortresses on the frontier, however, went by the name of Migdol (Ebers). Naville has expressed the opinion that Migdol was at the present station of the Serapeum, midway between lake Timsah and the Bitter Lakes; while Ebers locates it at the southern end of the Bitter Lakes, near the Persian monument. Here the gulf of Suez at the time of the exodus was narrow and probably shallow. It was also liable to be driven back by an east wind, so as temporarily to leave a dry way at a particular spot.

Mig'ron [possibly, a precipice].

A village of Benjamin, south of Aiath and north of Michmash (Is. x. 28). The site may be marked by the ruins Makrun. Saul once camped in its vicinity, in the outermost part of Gibeah (1 Sam. xiv. 2). If the site of Gibeah is Tell el-Fûl, as is commonly believed, or perhaps even if Geba is intended, and if the text of 1 Sam. xiv. 2 is pure, there would seem to have been two Migrons, one north and the other considerably south of Michmash.

Mij'a-min, in A. V. sometimes **Miamin** [from or on the right hand].

1. A descendant of Aaron. His family had grown to a father's house by the time of David, and became the sixth of the twenty-four courses into which David distributed the priests (1 Chron. xxiv. 1, 6, 9).

2. A chief of the priests who returned with Zerubbabel from Babylon (Neh. xii. 5, 7). In the next generation a father's house among the priests bore the name Miniamin (ver. 17). The difference between these names is unessential, being wholly external; in one form the letter nun is assimilated, in the other it is not.

3. A son of Parosh, induced by Ezra to put away his foreign wife (Ezra x. 25).

4. A priest who, doubtless in behalf of a father's house (cp. number 2), sealed the covenant in the time of Nehemiah (Neh. x. 7). Perhaps it was he who was one of the trumpeters at the dedication of the wall (xii. 41); see MINIAMIN 3, and for form of the name see under 2 of this article.

Mik'loth [rods].

1. A military captain in David's reign, who was on duty with another captain in the second month (1 Chron. xxvii. 4).

2. A Benjamite, of the family of Jeiel of Gibeon (1 Chron. viii. 32; ix. 37, 38).

Mik-ne'iah [possession of Jehovah].

A Levite of the second degree, a gate keeper of the ark, who played the harp in David's reign (1 Chron. xv. 18, 21).

Mil'a-lai [eloquent].

A Levite who played a musical instrument at the dedication of the wall of Jerusalem (Neh. xii. 36).

Mil'cah [counsel or counselor].

1. A daughter of Haran and sister of Lot. She became the wife of Nahor and the mother of Huz, Buz, Kemuel, Chesed, Hazo, Pildash, Jidlaph, and Bethuel (Gen. xi. 29; xxii. 20–23). She was the grandmother of Rebekah (xxii. 23; xxiv. 15, 24).

2. A daughter of Zelophehad (Num. xxvi. 33).

Mil'com. See MOLECH.

Mile [thousand (paces)].

In the only passage of the Bible in which the word occurs (Mat. v. 41) the Roman mile is intended, containing 1000 paces of 5 Roman feet each, and equivalent to 4851.43 English feet, or about $\frac{12}{13}$ of an English mile.

Mi-le'tus, in A. V. once **Miletum.**

A seaport to which Paul came a day after he had been at Trogyllium (Acts xx. 15). Thither he summoned the elders of the church at Ephesus, to give them exhortations and bid them farewell (17–38). At Miletus Trophimus was once left when he was sick (2 Tim. iv. 20, in A. V. Miletum). The city was on the seacoast of Ionia, about 36 miles south of Ephesus, and near the boundary line between that region and Caria. It had a celebrated temple of Apollo, and was the birthplace of the philosophers Thales and Anaximander, and perhaps of Democritus. Scarcely any relics of the city now remain.

Milk.

An important article of diet, especially in the East. The milk of cows (2 Sam. xvii. 29; Is. vii. 22), sheep (Deut. xxxii. 14), goats (Prov. xxvii. 27), and camels (cp. Gen. xxxii. 15) was and is still used. The milk of the camel is excellent, being rich and strong, but not very sweet. Milk was used in its natural state and as curds and as cheese (Deut. xxxii. 14; Judg. v. 25; 2 Sam. xvii. 29). It was kept in skin bottles, and served in dishes (Judg. iv. 19; v. 25).

Mill.

In Palestine and neighboring lands the mill was a simple machine, consisting of two round millstones (Deut. xxiv. 6). In the mill in use among the people to-day, the stones are generally made of basalt, about a foot and a half in diameter and from two to four inches thick. The nether stone is slightly convex on the top. It has a peg in the center, about which the upper stone revolves. This upper stone is slightly concave on the under side in order to fit on the nether stone, and is pierced by a hole in the center which receives the peg and into which the grain is dropped by hand. It is turned by means of an upright handle near the circumference. The meal falls over the edge of the nether stone into a cloth spread underneath or into a platter. The work of grinding is laborious and menial. It was performed by the women (Ecc. xii. 3, R. V. margin; Mat. xxiv. 41), slave women (Ex. xi. 5; Is. xlvii. 2), and prisoners (Judg. xvi. 21). In ordinary Jewish house-

Millstone and base, excavated near Capernaum.

holds, however, it was not regarded as at all degrading for the female portion of the family to grind meal every morning for a day's consumption, rising up for the purpose, at least in winter, long before daybreak. If the millstone was taken away, the family was left without ground grain till it was returned, on which account it was forbidden by the Mosaic law to take the mill or the upper millstone to pledge, for he taketh (a man's) life to pledge (Deut. xxiv. 6). The cessation of the sound of grinding betokens utter desolation (Jer. xxv. 10; Rev. xviii. 22).

A larger mill, constructed on the same principle, but turned by an ass, was also in use (Mat. xviii. 6, R. V. margin).

Mil'let.

A cereal (*Panicum miliaceum*), in Hebrew *dohan*, in Arabic *duhn*. Ezekiel was bidden to use it as an ingredient of the bread which he was ordered to prepare (Ezek. iv. 9). It is extensively used in western and southern Asia, northern Africa, and southern Europe. The stalks make an excellent fodder for cattle, while the grain is fed to poultry, and affords a nutritious and palatable food for man. It is possible that under the Hebrew *dohan* other allied species of cereals may be included, and especially *Sorghum vulgare*, the Indian millet, a taller grass much cultivated in India and southwestern Asia, and known to the natives as *doura*.

Mil'lo [filling, terrace].

1. A house, *i. e.* probably a fortress, at Shechem (Judg. ix. 6, 20).

2. A bastion at Jerusalem, in existence in the time of David, rebuilt by Solomon, and strengthened by Hezekiah as a precaution against the expected siege by the Assyrians (2 Sam. v. 9; 1 Kin. ix. 15, 24; xi. 27; 2 Chron. xxxii. 5). Its site is unknown. It was in or at the city of David, apparently intended to cover the old Jebusite stronghold (2 Chron. xxxii. 5). General considerations lead to the conjecture that it may have stood on the southwestern hill, on the northeastern corner, on the spur that overlooked the Tyropœon valley and faced the temple.

Mine.

The operation of mining, by which gold, silver, iron, copper, and precious stones were obtained, is graphically described in Job xxviii. 1–11. The Egyptians carried on mining operations from an early period. As early as the fourth dynasty they discovered copper in wady Maghârah, in the peninsula of Sinai, and commenced mining and smelting operations, which continued for many years. Work was suspended during the domination of the Hyksos, but was resumed under Thothmes III., and was carried on under Ramses II., who is commonly believed to have been the Pharaoh of the oppression. The miners were criminals, prisoners of war, and slaves, working under the whip of the taskmaster and often in fetters. The mines had broad, low openings. The shaft penetrated to a considerable depth. The roof was supported by pillars of stone which the miners left and by timber of acacia wood. The gold and silver mines of Spain were celebrated (1 Mac. viii. 3). Canaan was described to the expectant Israelites as a land whose stones are iron, and out of whose hills thou mayest dig brass (Deut. viii. 9); but there is no account of their having carried on mining operations in Palestine. That the Hebrews understood how to drive shafts is shown by the tunnel which they cut from the fountain of the Virgin to the pool of Siloam. Iron mines now exist on Lebanon.

Min'i-a-min [from or on the right hand].

1. One of those who, under the direction of a Levite, Kore, took charge of the freewill offerings in the temple and distributed them to the Levites during Hezekiah's reign (2 Chron. xxxi. 15).

2. A father's house among the priests in the days of the high priest Joiakim (Neh. xii. 17); see MIJAMIN 2.

3. A priest, one of those who blew trumpets at the dedication of the wall of Jerusalem (Neh. xii. 41); see MIJAMIN 4.

Min'is-ter.

1. A personal attendant and helper, not a menial, in Hebrew *mᵉshareth*, in Greek *'upēretēs*. Joseph, the slave, when raised to a position of honor and trust in his master's household, ministered unto him (Gen. xxxix. 4). Abishag was given honorable and influential place by David, and she ministered unto him (1 Kin. i. 4, 15). Joshua attended Moses, took charge of the first tent of meeting, and succeeded Moses in office (Ex. xxiv. 13; xxxiii. 11; Josh. i. 1). Elisha attended Elijah, poured water on his hands, and succeeded him (1 Kin. xix. 21; 2 Kin. iii. 11). The attendant of the synagogue aided the officiating teacher in the service (Luke iv. 20). The disciples attended Jesus and were eyewitnesses (i. 2; Acts xxvi. 16). John Mark attended Paul and Barnabas during a part of the first missionary journey (xiii. 5).

2. A public functionary in the service of

the state or of God, in Hebrew *m^eshareth*, in Greek *leitourgos;* as the priests and Levites in the performance of the duties of the sanctuary (Ex. xxviii. 43; Num. iii. 31; Deut. xviii. 5; Is. lxi. 6; cp. Septuagint; Luke i. 23; Heb. ix. 21), Christ as high priest in the heavenly sanctuary (Heb. viii. 2), Paul in administering the gospel unto the gentiles (Rom. xv. 16). The epithet is applied to the civil magistrate as a public official (xiii. 6). It designates an *attaché* of the royal court (1 Kin. x. 5), often a person of high rank (2 Chron. xxii. 8; Esth. i. 10); and it is used of the angels (Ps. ciii. 21; civ. 4).

3. One engaged in the service of another, and regarded primarily as the master's own representative and servant, and not as acting in behalf of others, in Greek *diakonos;* for example, a magistrate as the representative of God, an avenger for wrath to him that doeth evil (Rom. xiii. 4). It is used especially for God's minister in the gospel; as Timothy (1 Thes. iii. 2), Paul and Apollos (1 Cor. iii. 5), Tychicus (Eph. vi. 21), Epaphras (Col. i. 7). The term *diakonos* was also used in a restricted sense for deacon, a church officer with specified duties distinguishing him from a bishop.

Min'ni.

A people of Armenia (Antiq. i. 3, 6) inhabiting the district near lake Van, probably between that and lake Urumiah, and adjacent to the kingdom of Ararat on the Araxes. In 830 B. C. Shalmaneser, king of Assyria, pillaged the country of the Minni. In 716 B. C. and again in 715 the king of Minni revolted against Assyria, but in 714 he was anew subdued. The Minni continued to give trouble at intervals, especially during the reign of the Assyrian king Ashurbanipal (668-626); till at length about 606 B. C. they took part with the Medes, Cimmerians, and other nationalities in capturing Nineveh and ending the Assyrian empire. In Jer. li. 27 (R. V.) the kingdoms of Ararat, Minni, and Ashkenaz are described as uniting for the destruction of Babylon.

Min'nith.

A town of the Ammonite country (Judg. xi. 33). It exported wheat to Tyre (Ezek. xxvii. 17). According to Eusebius, there was a village called Manith 4 Roman miles from Heshbon in the direction of Philadelphia.

Min'strel.

A musician (Rev. xviii. 22, in A. V. musician); especially one who sings to the accompaniment of an instrument.

1. The Hebrew word *M^enaggen*, which is rendered minstrel in 2 Kin. iii. 15, signifies a player on a stringed instrument, as harp or lyre. Music was employed by the Hebrews to still excitement; and when Saul was troubled by an evil spirit, David was summoned to the court to act as minstrel (1 Sam. xvi. 14-23). Music, sometimes at least,

formed part of the religious exercises of the prophets (1 Sam. x. 5-10); and Elisha summoned a minstrel to play before him while he waited for God to speak to him (2 Kin. iii. 15). The music calmed the prophet's mind, recalled his thoughts from the outside world, and gladdened his spirit. "Prophecy," says Maimonides, "dwelleth not in the midst of melancholy nor in the midst of apathy, but in the midst of joy."

2. The minstrels hired by Jairus (Mat. ix. 23, A. V.) were flute players (R. V.), who with singers and wailing women were employed as professional mourners (2 Chron. xxxv. 25; Jer. ix. 17-20; xlviii. 31 with 36).

Mint.

An herb of the genus *Mentha*, of which there are several species. It is called in Greek *'ēduosmon*, sweet smelling (Mat. xxiii. 23). Horsemint (*Mentha sylvestris*) is the most common species in Syria, and grows wild on all the hills. It is not known certainly which sort the ancient Israelites cultivated.

Miph'kad, in R. V. **Hammiphkad**, incorporating the Hebrew article [appointed place].

A gate at Jerusalem, probably of the temple (Neh. iii. 31): see JERUSALEM II. 3.

Mir'a-cle.

Miracles are wonders, signs, types, powers, works of God (Deut. xi. 3; xxix. 3; Ps. lxxviii. 7, 11, 12, 43; xcv. 9; Mark ix. 39; Luke xxiii. 8; John ii. 11, 23; ix. 3; Acts ii. 22; vi. 8; viii. 13; see R. V.). They are not merely wonderful events; but are also signs, types, powers, works of God. They are not merely supernatural events, like the creation of the world; for God is not represented as bringing the universe into existence as a sign of attestation. Nor are they merely extraordinary providences, which men sometimes term miracles of providence, and which are brought about by secondary means and are not signs; such as the storm which dispersed the Spanish Armada. The locusts which were blown into Egypt by the strong east wind and blown away again by the west wind (Ex. x. 13, 19), and the arrival of quails, which migrate in the spring and supplied the camp of Israel with meat for an evening (xvi. 13) were extraordinary providences, but with additional elements. They were foretold and were intended as signs. The plague of locusts was one of the signs and wonders wrought at Zoan (Ps. lxxviii. 42, 46), and the quails were sent that Israel might know that Jehovah is God and their God (Ex. xvi. 12). In the narrowest biblical sense, miracles are events in the external world, wrought by the immediate power of God and intended as a sign or attestation. They are possible because God sustains, controls, and guides all things, and is personal and omnipotent. Perhaps the manner of working these deeds in the realm of the physical universe is illustrated by the power of the human will. Man wills, and muscular force is exerted which controls or counteracts nature's laws; as when one hurls a stone into the air against the law of gravitation. Miracles are not to be credulously received, but their genuineness must be tested. The tests are: 1. They exhibit the character of God and teach truths concerning God. 2. They are in harmony with the established truths of religion (Deut. xiii. 1–3). If a wonder is worked which contradicts the doctrines of the Bible, it is a lying wonder (2 Thes. ii. 9; Rev. xvi. 14). 3. There is an adequate occasion for them. God does not work them except for great cause and for a religious purpose. They belong to the history of redemption; and there is no genuine miracle without an adequate occasion for it in God's redemptive revelation of himself. 4. They are established, not by the number of witnesses, but by the character and qualifications of the witnesses. The miracles of the Bible are confined almost exclusively to four periods, separated from each other by centuries; the time of 1. The redemption of God's people from Egypt and their establishment in Canaan under Moses and Joshua. 2. The life and death struggle of the true religion with heathenism under Elijah and Elisha. 3. The exile, when Jehovah afforded proof of his power and supremacy over the gods of the heathen, although his people were in captivity (Daniel and his companions). 4. The introduction of Christianity, when miracles attested the person of Christ and his doctrine. Outside of these periods miracles are rare indeed (Gen. v. 24). They were almost totally unknown during the many centuries from the creation to the exodus.

The working of miracles in the apostolic age, although not confined to the apostles (Acts vi. 8; viii. 5–7), were the signs of an apostle (2 Cor. xii. 12; Heb. ii. 4; cp. Acts ii. 43; Gal. iii. 5).

Mir′i-am [obstinacy, rebellion].

1. Sister of Aaron and of Moses (Ex. xv. 20; Num. xxvi. 59). It was probably she who watched over the ark which contained the infant Moses (Ex. ii. 4–8). After the passage of the Red Sea, she took a timbrel and led the Israelite women with timbrels and with dances, saying: "Sing ye to the Lord, for he hath triumphed gloriously; the horse and his rider hath he thrown into the sea" (xv. 20, 21). She was a prophetess (ibid.), and she and her brothers were chosen by God to be leaders of the Hebrew people (iv. 15, 29, 30; Mic. vi. 4); but she instigated Aaron, and they made Moses' marriage with a Cushite woman the occasion of murmuring against his superior position and influence. They claimed that God had spoken by them as well as by Moses. For this insubordination to the will of God, she was

made a leper as white as snow, but owing to the intercession of Moses was speedily healed (Num. xii. 1–16; Deut. xxiv. 9). She died, and was buried in Kadesh (Num. xx. 1).

2. A man of Judah, descended from Ezrah (1 Chron. iv. 17).

Mir′mah, in A. V. **Mirma** [deceit].

A Benjamite, son of Shaharaim by his wife Hodesh (1 Chron. viii. 10).

Mir′ror.

A polished surface intended to reflect objects, especially the face (Wisdom vii. 26; 2 Cor. iii. 18; Jas. i. 23). Ancient mirrors were made of molten brass or other alloy of copper (Ex. xxxviii. 8; Job xxxvii. 18), and were round, oval, and square, and often provided with a handle. If they acquired rust spots, they were polished anew (Ecclus. xii. 11). They lacked the perfection of the modern

Egyptian bronze mirror with sculptured handle. This is probably the type of mirror the Israelite women took with them on the exodus.

glass, and the image in them was less clear and true (1 Cor. xiii. 12). As the material was metal, R. V. substitutes mirror for glass, the rendering of A. V. Opinion is divided as to whether mirrors or transparent garments are referred to in Is. iii. 23.

Later, in the West, mirrors were sometimes made of tin. Praxiteles, in the time of Pompey, is said to have been the first to make them of silver. They were even made of gold.

Mis′gab [high place, the high fort].

An unidentified Moabite city (Jer. xlviii. 1).

Mish′a-el [who is God?].

1. A Levite, family of Kohath, house of Uzziel (Ex. vi. 22; Lev. x. 4).

2. One of Daniel's three companions, called by the Babylonians Meshach (Dan. i. 6, 7, 11, 19; ii. 17; 1 Mac. ii. 59).

3. One of those who stood by Ezra when he preached to the people (Neh. viii. 4).

Mi′shal, in A. V. once **Misheal** (Josh. xix. 26) [prayer].

A village of Asher (Josh. xix. 26), given with its suburbs to the Levites of the Gershonite family (xxi. 30). It is called in 1 Chron. vi. 74 Mashal. Not identified.

Mi'sham [swiftness].

A Benjamite, a son of Elpaal, who with his brothers built Ono and Lod (1 Chron. viii. 12).

Mi'she-al. See MISHAL.

Mish'ma [hearing].

1. A tribe descended from Ishmael (Gen. xxv. 14; 1 Chron. i. 30). The name perhaps lingers either in Jebel Misma', midway between Damascus and Jauf, or in the other Jebel Misma', about 150 miles due east of Taima.

2. A descendant of Simeon (1 Chron. iv. 25).

Mish-man'nah [fatness].

One of the Gadites who came to David at Ziklag (1 Chron. xii. 10).

Mish'ra-ites.

A family which was connected with Kirjath-jearim (1 Chron. ii. 53).

Mis'par, in A. V. **Mizpar**; but the original edition of A. V. had the correct spelling, Mispar [a narrative, a number].

One of those who returned with Zerubbabel from captivity (Ezra ii. 2). In Neh. vii. 7 the feminine form is used, Mispereth.

Mis'pe-reth. See MISPAR.

Mis-re-photh-ma'im [burnings or elevations at the waters].

A place to which Joshua pursued the kings defeated at the waters of Merom (Josh. xi. 8), on the frontier of the country of the Zidonians (xiii. 6). It is now commonly, and probably correctly, identified with the ruins and the fountain el-Musheirifeh, 11 miles north of Acre, and ½ mile from the sea, at the foot of Ras en-Nakurah.

Mite.

A small coin, worth about ⅛ cent (Mark xii. 42). See MONEY.

Mi'ter.

The headdress or turban, called in Hebrew *misnepheth*, which was worn by the high priest. It was made of fine linen. Its distinguishing characteristic was a golden plate inscribed with the words Holiness to the Lord, and affixed in front by a blue-colored lace (Ex. xxviii. 4, 36–39; Lev. xvi. 4; Ezek. xxi. 26, in A. V. diadem); see HIGH PRIEST, and for Zech. iii. 5 see DIADEM.

Mith'kah, in A. V. **Mithcah** [sweetness].

An encampment of the Israelites in the wilderness (Num. xxxiii. 28, 29).

Mith'nite.

Probably an inhabitant of a town called Methen (1 Chron. xi. 43).

Mith're-dath [given by Mithra, the animating spirit of fire].

1. Treasurer under Cyrus, king of Persia, through whom the sacred vessels were restored to the Jews (Ezra i. 8).

2. One of those who in the reign of Artaxerxes Longimanus complained that the Jews were rebuilding the walls of Jerusalem (Ezra iv. 7).

Mit-y-le'ne.

A city between Assos and Chios visited by Paul (Acts xx. 13–15). It was the capital of the island of Lesbos in the Grecian Archipelago, and was noted for being the birthplace of the poet Alcæus, the statesman Pittacus, and the poetess Sappho. It is still called Mitylen.

Mi'zar [smallness].

A hill on the eastern side of the Jordan, probably within sight of the peaks of Hermon (Ps. xlii. 6). Exact situation unknown.

Miz'pah and **Mizpeh** [watchtower].

1. The name given to the cairn north of the Jabbok, called Galeed or heap of witness, to indicate the special thing to which it bore witness, namely, that God is the watcher between the covenanting parties (Gen. xxxi. 44–49); see GALEED.

2. A town in Gilead, east of the Jordan (Judg. x. 17; xi. 11); probably identical with Mizpeh of Gilead (xi. 29) and with Ramath-mizpeh or height of Mizpeh (Josh. xiii. 26), otherwise known as Ramoth in Gilead or Ramoth-gilead (Deut. iv. 43; 1 Kin. iv. 13) and Ramah (2 Kin. viii. 28, 29). It was situated in the territory of Gad, on the boundary (Josh. xiii. 26), assigned to the Levites (xxi. 38), and appointed a city of refuge (Deut. iv. 43; Josh. xx. 8). Jephthah dwelt here (Judg. xi. 34), and it was the residence of the taxgatherer for one of the twelve districts into which Solomon divided the country (1 Kin. iv. 13). To gain and hold possession of it battles were fought between Israel and the Syrians (1 Kin. xxii. 3 seq.; 2 Kin. viii. 28). It was taken and burned by Judas Maccabæus (1 Mac. v. 35, in A. V. Maspha). According to Eusebius, it lay 15 Roman miles west of Philadelphia, on the Jabbok. It is commonly identified with es-Salt, about 10 miles east of the mouth of the Jabbok and the crossing of the Jordan at Damieh; but the ruined town of Jal'ud, about 6 miles north of es-Salt, has strong claim to be the site.

3. A place at the foot of mount Hermon (Josh. xi. 3), not identified. The land of Mizpah is probably the same as the valley of Mizpeh (8).

4. A village in or near the lowland of Judah (Josh. xv. 38), commonly identified with Tell es-Safi, 7½ miles north-northwest of Beit Jibrin. Eusebius located it north of Eleutheropolis, that is, Beit Jibrin, in the direction of Jerusalem.

5. A town of Benjamin (Josh. xviii. 26), not far from Ramah (25; 1 Kin. xv. 22) and over against Jerusalem (1 Mac. iii. 46, in A. V. Maspha). The tribes were summoned to it at times for conferences (1 Sam. vii. 5–17; x. 17; Judg. xx. 1–3; xxi. 1, 5, 8). It was fortified by Asa as a defense against the northern tribes (1 Kin. xv. 22; 2 Chron. xvi. 6). After the destruction of Jerusalem, the Babylonian governor fixed his residence

here (2 Kin. xxv. 23-25; Jer. xl, 6-16; xli.
1-16). It was inhabited after the captivity
(Neh. iii. 7, 15, 19). Robinson believed its
site to have been either at Neby Samwil,
which means prophet Samuel, or at Tell el-
Fûl, conspicuous eminences north of Jerusalem; but he decides in favor of the former.
This identification has received cordial acceptance. The place is 2935 feet above the
sea level, and about 4 miles north-northwest
of Jerusalem, from which it is distinctly
seen.

6. An unidentified place in Moab (1 Sam.
xxii. 3).

Miz′par. See MISPAR.

Miz′peh. See MIZPAH.

Miz′ra-im [dual form of *miṣru*, probably,
defense, defensed land].

Egypt, the dual form pointing to the two
countries of Upper and Lower Egypt, settled
by descendants of Ham (Gen. x. 6); see
EGYPT.

Miz′zah [possibly, fear].

The chief of a tribe in the land of Edom,
a descendant of Esau, and also of Ishmael
(Gen. xxxvi. 3, 4, 13, 17; 1 Chron. i. 37).

Mna′son.

An early disciple from Cyprus, who accompanied Paul on his last journey from Cæsarea
to Jerusalem, and with whom the apostle
was to lodge (Acts xxi. 16).

Mo′ab [scarcely, water of a father; probably, desire].

1. Son of Lot by an incestuous union with
his elder daughter (Gen. xix. 37).

2. The descendants of Moab, Lot's son,
closely related to the Ammonites (Gen. xix.
37, 38). They were conquered by Ramses II.
(inscription on base of statue at Luxor).
They had become numerous before the time
that the Israelites crossed the Red Sea (Ex.
xv. 15); had taken possession of the country
from the plain of Heshbon unto the wady
Kurahi, which emerges at the southern end
of the Dead Sea, and formed the boundary
of Moab toward Edom; and with their kindred the Ammonites had absorbed and destroyed the remnants of the stalwart race
which had previously occupied the country
east of the Jordan (Deut. ii. 10, 11, 19-21;
cp. Gen. xiv. 5). Shortly before the arrival
of the Israelites, Sihon, king of the Amorites,
had wrested from them the pasture land
north of the Arnon, though the country was
still remembered as the land of Moab, con-
fining Moab for a time to the country south
of the Arnon (Num. xxi. 13-15, 26-30). The
Moabites showed a commercial friendliness to
the migrating Israelites (Deut. ii. 28, 29), but
refused them permission to pass through their
land (Judg. xi. 17; cp. Deut. xxiii. 4). Because, doubtless, of the kinship between the
Moabites and Israelites, Moses was forbidden
to attack them (Deut. ii. 9; cp. 19). Nevertheless, the king of Moab, alarmed when the
Israelites encamped in his vicinity, sent for
Balaam to curse them (Num. xxii.–xxiv.;
Josh. xxiv. 9). For this hostile attitude the
Israelites were commanded to exclude them
from the congregation to the tenth generation, and to maintain a coldness and indifference toward them forever (Deut. xxiii. 3-6;
Neh. xiii. 1). The last encampment of the
Israelites before they crossed the Jordan was
at Shittim in the plains that lay within the
old bounds of Moab (Num. xxii. 1-Josh. iii. 1),
While they were there, Moabite and Midianite women seduced them to licentious idolatry (Num. xxv.; Hos. ix. 10). Early in the
time of the judges Eglon, king of Moab, invaded Canaan, established his seat of government at Jericho, and oppressed the Israelites of the adjacent hill country 18 years
until he was assassinated by Ehud (Judg. iii.
12-30; 1 Sam. xii. 9). Elimelech sojourned
in Moab, and thence came his two daughters-
in-law, Orpah and Ruth. Ruth married Boaz
and became the ancestress of David (Ruth i.
22; iv. 3, 5, 10, 13-17; Mat. i. 5-16). Saul
warred with the Moabites (1 Sam. xiv. 47),
and David, when a fugitive from Saul, put
his father and mother in charge of the
king of Moab (xxii. 3, 4). After David became king, he overcame the Moabites, laid
them under tribute, and doomed a large proportion of them to death (2 Sam. viii. 2, 12;
1 Chron. xviii. 2, 11). The Moabites were
subject to Omri and his son; but on the
death of Ahab they rebelled, and neither of
Omri's grandsons, Ahaziah, who was incapacitated for the attempt by a fall, nor Jehoram was able to subdue them (2 Kin. i. 1;
iii. 4-27; Moabite Stone). Jehoshaphat was
king of Judah at that time, and the Moabites
formed a confederacy with the Ammonites,
Edomites, and others for the invasion of
Judah, but the allies turned their weapons
against each other, and Judah did not need
to strike a blow (2 Chron. xx. 1-30; cp. Ps.
lx. 8; lxxxiii. 6; cviii. 9). The year that
Elisha died, bands of Moabites invaded the
kingdom of Israel (2 Kin. xiii. 20). They
paid tribute to Tiglath-pileser and Sennacherib, kings of Assyria. They entered
Judah in the reign of Jehoiakim (2 Kin.
xxiv. 2). Many of the towns north of the
Arnon had reverted to Moab (cp. Is. xv.).
The prophets denounced the Moabites often
as types of the enemies of the kingdom of God
(Is. xv.; xvi.; xxv. 10; Jer. ix. 26; xxv. 21;
xxvii. 3; xlviii.; Ezek. xxv. 8-11; Amos ii. 1,
2; Zeph. ii. 8-11). Some of the Jews, who fled
from Jerusalem when Nebuchadnezzar invaded Judah, took refuge in Moab, but returned when Gedaliah was appointed governor (Jer. xl. 11). Nebuchadnezzar subjugated the Moabites (Antiq. x. 9, 7). They
disappear henceforth from history as a nation,
though still existing as a race (Ezra ix. 1;
Neh. xiii. 1, 23; Antiq. i. 11, 5). Alexander
Jannæus placed them under tribute (Antiq.
xiii. 13, 5).

3. The country occupied by the Moabites. It was bounded on the west by the Dead Sea. It was separated from Edom on the south by the wady Kurahi, known in its upper course as the wady el-'Ahsy. This fact is learned from the towns which are mentioned as situated in Moabite territory. On the east lay the desert (Num. xxi. 11). The northern boundary which the Amorites and Israelites recognized was the Arnon (Num. xxi. 13; Deut. ii. 36; iii. 12; Josh. xii. 1; Judg. xi. 18), but the Moabites at an early date possessed (Num. xxi. 26), and always regarded as theirs and frequently occupied, a considerable district north of the river (Is. xv.; Moabite Stone 8–30). Moab is chiefly a rolling plateau, about 3200 feet above the level of the sea, and is well adapted for pasturage. The western edge descends abruptly to the Dead Sea, and the face of the bluff is cut by deep valleys. The shore of the Dead Sea is comparatively fertile from the great abundance of springs.

The field of Moab was the territory of Moab (Gen. xxxvi. 35; Num. xxi. 20, R. V.). The plains of Moab were those parts of the Arabah or level valley of the Jordan which at one time were included within the bounds of Moab. They lay on the east of the river, opposite Jericho, and along the eastern shore of the Dead Sea (Num. xxii. 1; xxxiii. 48, 49).

The Moabite Stone.

Mo'ab-ite Stone.

An inscribed stone found within the territory of Moab, and recording Moabite history. On the 19th of August, 1868, the Rev. F. Klein, a German in the employ of the Church Missionary Society, was en-

camped at Dhîbân, the ruins of the ancient Moabite town of Dibon, when he was informed by a sheik that within ten minutes' walk from his tent there lay an inscribed stone. Proceeding to the spot, he found lying on its back a slab of black basalt, three feet ten inches high, two feet broad, and a foot and two and a half inches thick, rounded at the top and the bottom to nearly a semicircle. The inscription consisted of thirty-four lines of writing in an unknown character, running across the stone, about an inch and a quarter apart. He at once set on foot negotiations for its transfer to the Berlin Museum. Unhappily, M. Clermont-Ganneau, of the French Consulate, also attempted to obtain it for the Paris Museum. This ran it up to a nearly prohibitory price. Then the Arabs fell to fighting over the expected money. The dispute settled nothing, so kindling a fire under the stone, and pouring water on it when it was hot, they broke it into fragments, which they distributed among the several granaries, to act as blessings to the grain. Prior to the destruction, a messenger from M. Clermont-Ganneau had obtained a squeeze of the inscription; but having to escape precipitately on horseback and crumpling up the paper while it was still wet, it broke into seven pieces, and was not of much use. Better squeezes of the two larger portions of the broken stone were afterwards obtained by a messenger from Sir Charles Warren and by another from M. Clermont-Ganneau; and finally a number of fragments of the stone itself reached Jerusalem, and are now some in Paris and others in London. With the aid of the squeezes the pieces were put together. It was found that of about 1100 letters, 669 in all, or less than two-thirds, had been recovered, and that the language was akin to Hebrew. The inscription is as follows:

1. I am Mesha, son of Chemoshmelech, king of Moab, the D-
2. ibonite. My father reigned over Moab for thirty years, and reign did
3. I after my father. And I have made this high place for Chemosh in Ḳrḥh on account of the deliverance of Me-
4. sha, because he saved me from all the kings and because he let me see my pleasure on all that hated me. Omr-
5. i was king of Israel, and he afflicted Moab many days, because Chemosh was angry with his la-
6. nd. And his son succeeded him; and he also said: "I will afflict Moab." In my days he spake thus.
7. But I saw my pleasure on him and on his house, and Israel perished with everlasting destruction. Now Omri had taken possession of all the [la-]
8. nd of Medeba, and dwelt in it during his days and half the days of his sons [or his son], forty years; but resto-
9. re it did Chemosh in my days. And I built Baalmeon and I made in it the reservoir (?) and I built
10. Kiriathen. And the men of Gad had dwelt in the land of Ataroth from of old, and built for himself had the king of I-

11. srael Ataroth. And I fought against the city and took it and slew all the [people of]
12. the city, a sight unto Chemosh and to Moab. And I brought back from there the altar hearth of Daudoh (?) and drag-
13. ged it before Chemosh in Kerioth. And I settled the men of Srn in it and the men of
14. Mhrth. And Chemosh said to me: "Go, take Nebo against Israel." And I
15. went by night and fought against it from break of dawn until noon, and to-
16. ok it and slew all of them, seven thousand men and boys and women and gir-
17. ls and maidservants; for I had devoted it to Ashtor-Chemosh. And I took thence the altar-hear-
18 ths of Jehovah and dragged them before Chemosh. Now the king of Israel had built
19. Jahaz; and he abode in it while he fought against me. But Chemosh drove him out from before me. And
20. I took two hundred men of Moab, all its chiefs; and led them against Jahaz and took it
21. to add to Dibon. I built Ḳrḥh, the wall of the woods and the wall of
22. the mound. And I built its gates and I built its towers. And
23. I built the king's palace, and made the enclosures of the [. . . . . . for the wat] ers in the midst of
24. the city. And there was no cistern in the midst of the city, in Ḳrḥh. And I said to all the people: "Make for
25. yourselves, every one a cistern in his house." And I cut out the cutting for Ḳrḥh with the help of prisoner-
26. s of Israel. I built Aroer and made the highway on the Arnon.
27. I built Beth-bamoth, for it was pulled down. I built Bezer, for ruins
28. . . . . Dibon fifty, for all Dibon was obedient. And I reigned
29. over one hundred in the cities which I added to the land. And I built
30. Medeba and Beth-diblathen and Beth-baal-meon, and took thither the [herdsmen]
31. . . . . the sheep of the land. And as for Horonen, there dwelt in it the so[n] of De[d]an. And De[dan] said
32. . . . . Chemosh said to me: "Go down, fight against Horonen;" and I went down and . . . .
33. . . . . and Chemosh [resto]red it in my days. And I . . . . . thence ten (?)
34. . . . .

To judge from Mesha's own words, the stele was a memorial commemorative not merely of his recovery of independence for Moab from Israel, but of his glorious and successful reign as a whole (l. 4, 31); erected late in his reign, after the death of Ahab, after the humiliation of that house also, and not improbably after the extinction of the line of Omri by Jehu, and the entrance of Israel into its period of dire distress (l. 7).

The Hebrew records date the revolt of Moab after the death of Ahab (2 Kin. i. 1; iii. 5): a date which conflicts with a usual understanding of the inscription, to the effect that the revolt occurred in the middle of Ahab's reign. But the statements of the stone may be readily interpreted in harmony with the Hebrew account, and that in one of two ways:

1. The two accounts may be combined. The capture of the frontier town of Medeba was effected by Mesha about the middle of Ahab's reign (l. 8); but the Moabite king did not attempt actually to throw off the Israelitish yoke until after Ahab's death.

2. Or, better, in accordance with the well-known custom of the times, whereby the royal descendants of Omri, as of other founders of dynasties, were designated simply as his sons; in view of the ascription of round forty years to the occupation of Medeba by the Israelites; in view of Moabite grammar, whereby the collocation beth nun he in line 8 may be properly rendered his sons; and in view of the probability which arises from Mesha's own words that he was acquainted with the final overthrow of Omri's sons; lines 7 and 8 of the inscription may be translated: "Now Omri had taken possession of all the land of Medeba, and [Israel] dwelt therein during his days and half the days of his sons, forty years." This is the same story as told by the Hebrew writers. The revolt of Moab did actually occur midway in the reign of Omri's sons, as it were dividing their reign in twain, and lending in Moabitish eyes an aspect to the latter half of their rule far different from the former. See OMRI and MESHA.

Mo-a-di'ah [perhaps, host of Jehovah].
A father's house among the priests in the time of the high priest Joiakim (Neh. xii. 17); see MAADIAH.

Mo'din [informers or prognosticators, prognostication (cp. Is. xlvii. 13)].
The native town of the Maccabees (1 Mac. ii. 1), with the family tomb where Mattathias and two of his sons, Judas and Jonathan, were buried (ii. 70; ix. 19; xiii. 25). It stood on the edge of the plain of Philistia (xvi. 4, 5), and the tomb was visible from the sea (xiii. 29). The town was still in existence in the time of Eusebius and Jerome, in the vicinity of Diospolis, that is Lydda. The Talmud states its distance from Jerusalem at 15 Roman miles. The site is disputed. Hitzig located it at el-Burj, 2½ miles south of Midieh; and Robinson, following mediæval pilgrims, at Latrun. The more recent suggestion of Forner has been favorably received, that the site is Midieh, hard by the road to Jerusalem via Beth-horon, about 6 miles from Lydda and 18 from Jerusalem. One half mile north of the ruined village of Midieh, and about the same distance west of the modern village rises a hill, from the summit of which vessels on the sea are visible and where the foundations of a stately tomb have been found.

Mol'a-dah [birth, origin].
A town in the extreme south of Judah (Josh. xv. 26), assigned to the Simeonites (xix. 2; 1 Chron. iv. 28). It was inhabited after the captivity (Neh. xi. 26). It is doubtless the town known in the Greek period

as Malatha, in Idumæa, to which Herod Agrippa I., during the earlier and less prosperous period of his life, retired in debt and in depression of spirits (Antiq. xviii. 6, 2). The Onomasticon locates Malatha 4 Roman miles from Arad and on the road from Hebron to Aila, that is Elath. Robinson is commonly followed in his identification of it with Milh, on the Roman road 7½ miles southwest of Arad, where there are vestiges of an extensive town with important wells. It is about 14 miles east by south from Beersheba, and 22 south by west from Hebron.

Mole.

1. The rendering of the Hebrew *Tinshemeth* (Lev. xi. 30, A. V.). See CHAMELEON.
2. The rendering of the Hebrew words *Ḥᵃphor peroth*, digging of holes or digging of rats (Is. ii. 20). The two words are better regarded as one, *Ḥᵃpharparoth*, diggers. These may be rats or moles. It is believed that no species of *Talpa*, the genus to which the common mole (*T. europæa*) belongs, exists in Palestine, its place being taken by the mole rat (*Spalax typhlus*), which is probably the animal intended by Isaiah. This animal is very common in the Holy Land, living underground in small societies. It resembles the mole in appearance, but is not of the same order, being a rodent feeding on vegetables, chiefly bulbs, whereas the mole is insectivorous. It is larger than the mole, being eight or more inches long. It is silvery gray in color, is tailless, and has only minute or rudimentary eyes.

Mo'lech, in A. V. twice **Moloch**, a spelling introduced into the English version through the Greek text of Amos v. 26 and its quotation by Stephen in Acts vii. 43. The Hebrew text and R. V. have "your king" in place of Moloch [reigning one, king].

A deity worshiped by the children of Ammon (1 Kin. xi. 7). The article is prefixed to his name where it occurs in the Hebrew, indicating that the word is not a proper name, but an appellative preserving its meaning of reigning one. He was known also as Milcom (1 Kin. xi. 5, 33) and Malcam (Jer. xlix. 1, 3, R. V.; Zeph. i. 5; and R. V. margin 2 Sam. xii. 30; 1 Chron. xx. 2), proper names formed by the familiar terminations om and am. He was an aspect of Baal (Jer. xxxii. 35), whose name is a common noun likewise and signifies lord. Baal was worshiped with human sacrifices at Tyre under the name of Melcarth, king of the city; and an exceedingly detestable feature of Molech's worship was the burning of children to him in the fire. The practice was in vogue early; and when the Israelites were at Sinai and expected soon to be neighbors of the Ammonites, the law was enacted that if any man made or permitted his children to "pass through the fire to Molech" he was to be put to death (Lev. xviii. 21; xx. 1–5). Nevertheless Solomon in his old age erected

an altar to Milcom, being led into this idolatry by the Ammonite wives whom he loved; and in the following centuries children were burnt to Molech in the valley of Hinnom at the high place of Topheth (Ps. cvi. 38; Jer. vii. 31; xix. 4, 5; Ezek. xvi. 21; xxiii. 37, 39; cp. Is. xxx. 33). Ahaz burnt children of his there (2 Chron. xxviii. 3), and Manasseh made at least one of his sons to pass through the fire (2 Kin. xxi. 6). The northern Israelites were also guilty of this hideous rite (2 Kin. xvii. 17; Ezek. xxiii. 37). Josiah destroyed the altars which Solomon built on the mount of Corruption to this false divinity and other heathen gods, and defiled the high place of Topheth (2 Kin. xxiii. 10, 13).

Mo'lid [begetter].

A man of Judah, family of Hezron, house of Jerahmeel (1 Chron. ii. 29).

Mo'loch. See MOLECH.

Mol'ten Sea or **Bra'zen Sea.**

A great basin made by Solomon of brass which David had taken as booty (1 Chron. xviii. 8). It stood in the inner court of the temple between the altar of burnt offering and the sanctuary, somewhat toward the south; and was intended for the priests to wash their hands and feet in before entering the sanctuary or approaching the altar (1 Kin. vii. 39; 2 Chron. iv. 6; Antiq. viii. 3, 6; cp. Ex. xxx. 18–21). It was round, 10 cubits in diameter and 5 in height, and held 2000 baths (1 Kin. vii. 23, 26; in 2 Chron. iv. 5 incorrectly 3000). The brim curved outward like a cup, and the sides were ornamented with two rows of knops underneath the brim (1 Kin. vii. 24, 26). It was not an exact hemisphere, but its sides bulged out like a tulip, as appears from the statement of its capacity and from the comparison of it to a lily. It stood upon twelve brazen oxen, in four groups of three each, facing the four quarters. Ahaz took it down from the oxen (2 Kin. xvi. 17); and finally, when Nebuchadnezzar captured Jerusalem, he broke the basin in pieces (xxv. 13, 16; Jer. xxvii. 19–22).

Mon'ey.

Money was early coined by the Greeks and the peoples of Asia Minor within the sphere of Greek influence. Staters, made of an alloy of gold with silver called electron, were struck in Lydia in Asia Minor and silver coins at Ægina as early as 700 to 650 B. C. In the rest of western Asia and in Egypt people were content to use gold and silver in bars, rings, and other forms, probably stamped with the value, but not issued by authority (Josh. vii. 21; and cp. name of talent, *kikkar*, circle). In business transactions reliance was not placed on the stamp, but the quantity was determined by weighing (Gen. xxiii. 16; xliii. 21); cp. WEIGHTS. Counting was rarely resorted to (2 Kin. xii. 11), and then only to form a general estimate. Shekel in the early period does not mean a coin bearing an authoritative stamp, but a certain weight (*shekel*) of silver. The weights formed a series in the denomination of talent, maneh, shekel, gerah, and beka or half shekel; see WEIGHTS. Darius Hystaspis, 521–486 B. C., is credited with the introduction of coinage into Persia (Herod. iv. 166), whereby the Jews became acquainted with

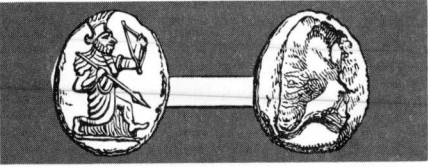

Gold daric.

coins. The ordinary daric (Ezra ii. 69 ; in A. V. dram) was a thick gold coin, showing on one side the king, kneeling and holding a bow and a javelin. On the reverse was an irregular square, doubtless the mark of the punch with which the lump of metal was driven into the die. It was worth about five dollars ; see DARIC. After the fall of the Persian empire, the Greek system came into vogue in Palestine, and money was reckoned by talents and drachmas (1 Mac. xi. 28 ; 2 Mac. iv. 19).

Silver half shekel of Year 1.

In the year 141–140 B. C., Simon Maccabæus obtained the right to coin money for his nation with his own stamp (1 Mac. xv. 6), and issued silver shekels and half shekels and perhaps

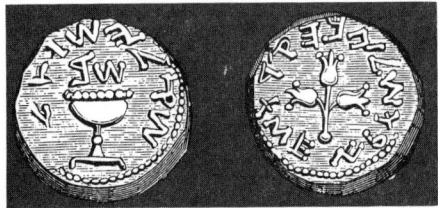

Shekel of Year 2.

copper half, quarter, and sixth shekels. The silver coins show a vase on the obverse with the date above and the legend "shekel (or half shekel) of Israel ; " and on the reverse a branch bearing flowers encircled by the words "Jerusalem the holy." The small copper coin of John Hyrcanus, which is represented in the accompanying cut, bears on the obverse within a wreath of olive the inscription, "Jehohanan the high priest, head

and friend of the Jews." The reverse has a Greek symbol, the united cornucopias, between which is a pomegranate. Herod the

Copper coin of John Hyrcanus.

Great and his successors down to Herod Agrippa II. issued copper coins, but only with Greek legends.

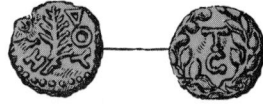

Copper coin of Herod Antipas, Tetrarch of Galilee.

The money of the Greeks, however, continued to circulate along with the Jewish coinage. The coins consisted of drachmas and tetradrachmas. The silver drachma (Luke xv. 8, R. V. margin) in the time of the Herods and the procurators was equivalent to the Roman denarius and worth about 16 cents ; the silver stater or tetradrachma (Mat. xvii. 27, margin), struck by the Greek cities of Syria and Phœnicia, was worth about 66 cents, but soon afterwards became much debased. The lepton was a small copper coin (Luke xii. 59 ; xxi. 2, rendered mite), not the lepton of the Greek system, but the smallest copper coin in circulation, worth about $\frac{1}{8}$ cent and equal to half the quadrans (Mark xii. 42). The name denotes small. It was a Jewish coin, for only Jewish money was allowed to be offered in the temple ; and it was probably a copper coin issued by John Hyrcanus or other Maccabæan prince. The didrachma, which corresponded to the half shekel (Mat. xvii. 24, margin), was probably not in circulation or but little used in Palestine. The talent employed in Palestine (1 Mac. xi. 28 ; Mat. xviii. 24) was the Attic talent, which Alexander had made the lawful standard throughout his empire and which afterwards maintained its supremacy. It was not a coin, but money of account ; was divided into minas (1 Mac. xiv. 24 ; Luke xix. 13–25, rendered pound) ; and it consisted of 60 minas or 6000 drachmas. It suffered great depreciation, the drachma falling off from about 67.5 grains to about 55 grains or 16 cents under the early Cæsars.

With the advent of the Romans in Palestine, the money of the Romans had also come into circulation. The denarius (Mat. xviii. 28 ; rendered penny) was a silver coin. In the time of the empire its obverse almost invariably bore the head of the reigning sovereign or of some member of the imperial family. From the time of Augustus to that of Nero, its standard weight was 60 grains, equivalent to about 17 cents. It was the tribute money payable by the Jews to the

Denarius with image and superscription of Tiberius Caesar.

imperial treasury (Mat. xxii. 19). The assarion (x. 29; Luke xii. 6, rendered farthing), the Greek name of the Roman as, was a small copper coin, the value of which was reduced in 217 B. C. to $\frac{1}{16}$ of a denarius or to about 1 cent. The quadrans (Mat. v. 26; Mark xii. 42; rendered farthing) was the

Procurator's copper coin.

fourth part of an as, or $\frac{1}{4}$ cent. The procurators of Judæa were also accustomed to coin money. They issued copper pieces in the name of the imperial family and with the legend in Greek letters. The coin which is represented in the accompanying cut bears the name of Ti. Claudius Cæsar Germanicus written in Greek on the margin, and in the center two palm branches laid crosswise with the date, "year 14," between them. The reverse contains the name of the emperor's wife, Julia Agrippina. It was struck in A. D. 54, during the procuratorship of Felix.

The gold coin which was current in Palestine during the N. T. period was the Roman denarius aureus, generally termed simply aureus (Antiq. xiv. 8, 5, rendered pieces of gold), which passed for 25 silver denarii.

The national coinage of Israel was revived

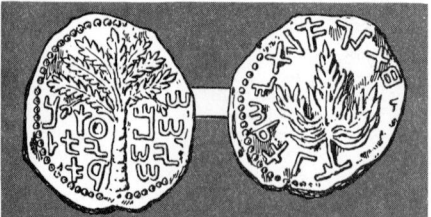

Shekel of Simon, Prince of Israel.

by Eleazar, the priest, and Simon, the prince, during the first revolt, A. D. 66-70. Silver

shekels and quarter shekels and copper coins with various devices and old Hebrew inscriptions were issued. The shekel of Simon, of which a copy is here given, shows on the obverse a palm tree and the legend "Simon, prince of Israel," and on the reverse a vine and "Year one of the redemption of Israel." On the suppression of this revolt and the capture of Jerusalem, coins were struck in Rome with the image and name of the emperor Vespasian on the obverse, and a female

Silver coin of Vespasian, commemorating the capture of Jerusalem.

captive under a palm tree, with the inscription "Judæa subdued" or "Judæa captive" on the reverse; cp. medal, article JERUSALEM. Herod Agrippa II., king of part of Galilee and the region to the east, continued to issue

Copper coin of Herod Agrippa II.

copper coins after the fall of Jerusalem. The one depicted dates from the reign of Titus. It bears the head of the emperor, his name and titles, on the obverse; and on the reverse a winged victory holding a wreath and a palm branch, and the date, "year 26 of king Agrippa." During the second revolt, which was headed by Bar-cocheba, A. D. 132-135, shekels and quarter shekels of silver and also of copper, with old Hebrew inscrip-

Shekel of Bar-cocheba.

tions, were again coined. The shekel shows a tetrastyle temple on the obverse, probably a conventional representation of the beautiful gate of the temple at Jerusalem. At the sides of it appears the word Simon, perhaps the personal name of the leader of the revolt; while above it a star is introduced, doubtless in allusion to the surname of the leader, Bar-cocheba, son of a star. To obtain quarter shekels the Roman denarius was restruck, which at this time so nearly equaled the quarter shekel in value that it could be substituted for it without inconvenience.

Mon'ey Chan-gers.

When a census was taken every Israelite, whether rich or poor, who had reached the age of twenty years, was required to pay half a shekel into the treasury of the Lord as an offering to make atonement (Ex. xxx. 13-15). Later it was customary, according to Maimonides, to pay this poll tax annually. Besides this tax, pious Israelites made freewill offerings, which they cast into chests placed in the court of the women (Mark xii. 41). This money must be in native coin; and as several currencies circulated in Palestine in the time of Christ, and as multitudes of Jews from foreign lands visited Jerusalem at the passover, bringing the coin of their country with them, need arose of facilities for exchanging foreign for native money. The business of the money changer sprang up. They had stalls in the city; and as the feast approached they were admitted to the precincts of the temple and placed their tables in the court of the gentiles. The premium paid for half a shekel was, according to the Talmud, a *kollubos*, equal to twelve grains of silver and worth about three cents. From this premium the money changer was called a *kollubistēs* (Mat. xxi. 12), and from the table at which he sat a *trapezitēs* (Mat. xxv. 27). On two different occasions Jesus overturned the tables of the money changers and drove the cattle dealers from the court, because their presence and too often their dishonesty and avarice were incompatible with the sanctity of the place and with the quiet which is necessary for worship (John ii. 14-16; Mat. xxi. 12, 13).

Month.

In Egypt the Israelites were acquainted with a year of twelve months of thirty days each, with five additional days to produce conformity with the solar year of 365 days (Herod. ii. 4), and in the account of the flood the months are reckoned at thirty days each (Gen. vii. 11, 24; viii. 3, 4). Afterwards, however, the Hebrews appear to have used a lunar month. This may be gathered (1) from the two words for month which denote respectively new moon and lunation and indicate the original measurement; (2) from passages like Gen. i. 14; Ps. civ. 19; Ecclus. xliii. 6-8; (3) from the observance of the day of the new moon by special offerings to Jehovah (Num. x. 10; xxviii. 11-14; 2 Chron. ii. 4); and (4) from the coincidence between the passover, which was always celebrated on the evening of the fourteenth day

of the month, and the full moon (Ps. lxxxi. 3-5); see further Antiq. iii. 10, 3 and 5; iv. 4, 6, and article YEAR. A lunation requires a little more than twenty-nine days and a half. The months would accordingly average twenty-nine and thirty days alternately. When, however, a month is spoken of generally, thirty days are meant (cp. Num. xx. 29; Deut. xxxiv. 8 with xxi. 13). The months were commonly distinguished by number. The names of only four Hebrew months are found in Bible narratives relating to the period before the captivity. They are the first month, Abib (Ex. xiii. 4, etc.); the second month, Zif (1 Kin. vi. 37); the seventh, Ethanim (viii. 2); and the eighth, Bul (vi. 38). After the captivity the names in common use among the Babylonians and other Semites were employed. See YEAR.

Moon.

The principal luminary of the night (Gen. i. 16; Ps. cxxxvi. 9), relied upon to measure time, marking off moons or months, and regulating the day of the passover, and thus aiding in regulating the feasts of the year (Gen. i. 14; Ps. civ. 19; Ecclus. xliii. 6, 7; Antiq. iii. 10, 5). Almost all the nations with which the ancient Hebrews came into contact worshiped the moon. Ur of the Chaldees, from which Abraham emigrated, and Haran, where he settled for a time and where Jacob dwelt for twenty years, were noted seats of the moon's worship. When Abraham removed to Canaan, he had neighbors who worshiped the moon (cp. with caution ASHTORETH and SINAI). The Egyptians sacrificed the pig to the moon, when the disk was at its full (Herod. ii. 47). In the time of the Assyrian and Babylonian invasions of Palestine, the Hebrews came again into contact with people who regarded the moon as one of the great gods. At this time the worship of the moon and other heavenly bodies made serious inroads on the religion of Jehovah (2 Kin. xxi. 3; xxiii. 4, 5; Jer. vii. 18; viii. 2). The moon was adored by a kiss of the hand (Job xxxi. 26, 27), with the burning of incense (2 Kin. xxiii. 5). In heathen temples the moon was often represented by the crescent as a symbol and by an image in the form of a human being. This heathenism had its check in the sublime doctrine of Jehovah. The sun and moon were made by the God of Israel, were created for the useful purpose of giving light, and were serviceable to man in affording a convenient measurement of time.

Different from the worship of the moon was the childish conception that the varying appearance of the moon from night to night at its rising, during its course across the sky, and at its setting, which are due to atmospheric and astronomic conditions, presaged political occurrences. The aspect of the moon may indicate weather probabilities; but the folly of basing predictions of national events on such phenomena was pointed out by the prophets (Is. xlvii. 13). The Hebrews seem to have shared in the widespread belief, apparently justified by the statements of travelers in equatorial regions, that the moon may affect the health and under circumstances produce evil consequences to muscles and nerves. But the child of God can safely intrust himself to the watchful care of Jehovah (Ps. cxxi. 6).

As the months were lunar, the new moon marked the beginning of the month; and the day of the new moon, being the commencement of a natural division of time, was observed as a holy day. No set convocation seems to have been prescribed; but additional sacrifices were offered (Num. xxviii. 11–14), trumpets were blown (Num. x. 10; Ps. lxxxi. 3), ordinary labor was suspended (Amos viii. 5), and the day offered favorable opportunity for religious instruction (2 Kin. iv. 23; Ezek. xlvi. 1, 3). It was kept with joy and feasting (1 Sam. xx. 5; Judith viii. 6). The new moon of the seventh month marked the beginning of the seventh recurrence of a fixed portion of time, and consequently fell under the Sabbath law, and was observed as such in addition to the usual worship on the day of the new moon (Lev. xxiii. 24, 25; Num. xxix. 1–6). After the exile this celebration assumed the character of a new year's festival.

The advent of the new moon was calculated at an early period (1 Sam. xx. 5, 18). The Babylonian astrologers watched for it on the evening when it was expected to be seen, in order to take note of its appearance. According to the Talmud, the sanhedrin assembled seven times a year early in the morning of the thirtieth day of the month. Watchmen were stationed on the heights about Jerusalem to watch for the new moon and report it as soon as seen. When the evidence of its appearance was deemed sufficient, the sanhedrin pronounced the word M⁾kuddash, it is consecrated, and the day became the first of the new month, leaving twenty-nine days for the preceding month. If fogs or clouds prevented the moon from being discerned, the day was reckoned as the thirtieth and the new month began on the morrow. The announcement of the new moon was made to the country at large by lighting a beacon fire on the mount of Olives, which was repeated by similar signals from other mountain tops. The Samaritans are said to have thwarted this plan by kindling fires prematurely. In consequence the signals were discontinued, and the announcement of the new moon was made by messengers.

Moph. See MEMPHIS.

Mo′rash-tite, in A. V. **Morasthite.**

A native or inhabitant of Moresheth, as was the prophet Micah (i. 1; Jer. xxvi. 18); see MORESHETH-GATH.

Mor′de-cai [perhaps, Persian, signifying little man, or the common Babylonian name, a diminutive or hypocoristic form of Merodach (see ESTHER).]

1. A Benjamite, son or descendant of Jair, son of Shimei, son of Kish (Esth. ii. 5). The relative clause which as verse 6 follows this genealogy may refer to the last name of the series (cp. 2 Chron. xxii. 9), and state that Kish, a Benjamite, was carried into exile with king Jeconiah in 598 B. C.; or the clause may relate to an earlier name in the list, for example, to Jair (cp. Gen. xxiv. 47), in which case Mordecai was a descendant of Jair, a Benjamite, who was carried away to Babylonia with Jeconiah. He brought up Hadassah or Esther, his uncle's daughter, adopting her as his own after her father and mother had died. She acted under his direction in the series of events which ended by making her queen of Persia as wife of Ahasuerus (Esth. ii. 7–20). This king was Xerxes, who reigned from 486 to 466 B. C. Through Esther Mordecai informed the king of a plot against his life, and the two conspirators were executed (21–23). When Haman was the king's favorite, Mordecai declined to prostrate himself before him, refusing to pay the customary civility because of Haman's unprincipled character or perhaps because Haman was an Agagite. The insulted dignitary determined to wreak vengeance not on Mordecai alone, but on the entire Jewish people, and the king granted him leave (iii. 5–11). One night Ahasuerus could not sleep, and to relieve the tedium of his waking hours, he desired that the book recording the chronicles of the kingdom should be read to him by his attendants. The conspiracy came up in the part read, and the king remembered that he had done nothing for his deliverer. When morning dawned he requested Haman, who had come to ask permission to hang Mordecai, to take that faithful subject, array him in royal apparel, and conduct him through the streets of the city (Susa) mounted on a horse belonging to the sovereign, and to proclaim before him as he went along: "Thus shall it be done to the man whom the king delighteth to honor." This was the commencement of Haman's fall, and of a series of events which resulted in the death of Haman and his sons, and the promotion of Mordecai to be the second man in the empire (Esth. vi.–x.). Some interpreters would identify Mordecai with the eunuch Matacas or Natacas, who, according to Ctesias, was the chief favorite of Xerxes.

2. A Jew who returned from Babylon with Zerubbabel (Ezra ii. 2; Neh. vii. 7).

Mo′reh [archer, or the first rain, or teacher].

1. A terebinth or oak tree and grove near Shechem (Gen. xii. 6; Deut. xi. 29, 30), which most probably took its name from an archer or teacher who at one time or other

dwelt there. Abraham encamped by it when he arrived in Canaan from Mesopotamia, and erected an altar there to Jehovah who appeared unto him. It was probably the tree under which Jacob buried the amulets and idols that his family had brought with them from Haran, and where Joshua erected a stone to commemorate the covenant which the people renewed there, and whither the men of Shechem went to make Abimelech king (Gen. xxxv. 4; Josh. xxiv. 26, though slightly different words are used for terebinth in these two passages from that employed in Gen. xii. 6; Judg. ix. 6). The identity of the tree with the oak or terebinth of the augurs near Shechem is not so obvious (Judg. ix. 37).

2. A hill in the valley of Jezreel to the north of the spring of Harod (Judg. vii. 1). Not positively identified. Jebel Duhy, or Little Hermon, about 8 miles northwest of mount Gilboa and 1 mile south of Nain, has been suggested.

Mor'esh-eth-gath [possession of Gath or of a wine press].

A town mentioned in connection with places in Judah, and therefore evidently situated in the same region (Micah i. 14). Jerome located it in the vicinity of Eleutheropolis. Gath in the name is generally supposed to denote the Philistine city and to indicate that Moresheth was near it. Perhaps the town was the home of the prophet Micah (i. 1).

Mo-ri'ah [the meaning is unknown. The definite article prefixed to the word shows that it is not a proper name and that it does not contain the divine name Jehovah; and the orthography further shows that the word does not mean "appearance or provision of Jehovah"].

1. A district of country, on one of whose hills Abraham prepared to sacrifice Isaac; probably the region lying round about the hill of the same name on which the temple was afterwards built, and taking its name from that hill or from some circumstance common to both it and the hill (Gen. xxii. 2; Antiq. i. 13, 1 and 2). The Samaritans, and after them a few modern scholars like Bleek, Tuch, Stanley, identify Moreh near Shechem with Moriah (see Samaritan text) and Gerizim with the scene of Abraham's sacrifice. The Samaritan identification doubtless rests on the fact that Abraham did build an altar at Moreh (Gen. xii. 6, 7), and the identification was encouraged by the desire to enhance the religious glory of their country. But the etymology of Moreh and Moriah is different.

2. The hill on which was the threshing floor of Ornan the Jebusite. David purchased the floor and erected an altar on it, and Solomon made it the site of the temple (2 Sam. xxiv. 18 seq.; 2 Chron. iii. 1). The original hill has been much altered artificially and part of its slopes are hidden

beneath accumulated rubbish and embankments, but its general contour has been determined. Mount Moriah stood between the Kidron and Tyropœon valleys, and lifted its summit directly opposite the mouth of that ravine which forms the western branch of the latter valley. On the north a slight depression separated it from the narrow neck of land which connected it with the main plateau. It is difficult to state exact dimensions; to call its original area 600 feet from north to south by 300 from east to west may be not far from the truth. Its highest point is now, according to Warren, 2448 feet above the ocean. Other platforms are 2430 and 2420 feet, from which the east and west slopes very rapidly fall.

Mor'tar I.

A vessel in which grain and spices are pounded with a pestle (Num. xi. 8; Prov. xxvii. 22). The Arabs of the present day use stone mortars in which to pound wheat for making *kibby*, their national food, and the sound of braying the grain with the pestle may be heard at all hours in the towns.

Mor'tar II.

A substance used to bind bricks or stones together in a wall. Various materials were used. 1. Mud or clay without lime (Nah. iii. 14), frequently employed by peasants in Palestine. 2. Mortar properly so called, consisting of sand and lime mixed with water, which was employed in building the better class of houses (cp. Ezek. xiii. 10). Palestine is a limestone country, and lime is easily obtained (Is. xxxiii. 12). 3. Bitumen in regions like Babylonia where clay and lime are scarce (Gen. xi. 3, R. V. margin). The walls of houses were (Lev. xiv. 42) and still are daubed or plastered with mud or mortar, often mixed with straw and pebbles, to protect them against the weather. The mortar used for this purpose in Egypt consists of one half clay, one quarter lime, and the rest ashes and straw.

Mo-se'rah, in A. V. **Mosera** [bond, fetter].

An encampment of the Israelites in the wilderness near Bene-jaakan (Deut. x. 6). In Num. xxxiii. 30, the plural form Moseroth is used as the name of the place. The site is unknown; but it was near mount Hor, by the border of Edom (Num. xx. 23; xxxiii. 37; with Deut. x. 6), in the country of the Horites (cp. Gen. xxxvi. 20, 27 with 1 Chron. i. 42). Jebel Madara sounds much like Mosera; but is not the exact equivalent, if the Arabic spelling has been correctly reported by travelers. See HOR.

Mo-se'roth. See preceding article.

Mo'ses [from the Egyptian *mes* or *mesu*, extraction, a son].

The great Hebrew leader and legislator. He was a Levite, family of Kohath, house of Amram (Ex. vi. 18, 20). Jochebed is called the mother of Moses (ver. 20); but this expression is doubtless to be understood in the sense of ancestress, Amram and Jochebed being founders of the tribal house into which Moses was born; see EGYPT. The edict requiring the Hebrew male children to be cast into the Nile brought Moses into imminent peril of his life. But his mother saw that he was a goodly child, or, as Stephen words it, exceeding fair (Acts vii. 20); and she hid him three months in her house. When she could hide him no longer, she placed him within an ark of bulrushes, which had been daubed with bitumen and pitch to render it water-tight; put it among the flags on the river's bank; and posted Miriam, then a young girl, to watch the result. By and by Pharaoh's daughter, attended by her maidens, came to the river to bathe. Her name was Thermuthis, according to Josephus (Antiq. ii. 9, 5). Eusebius calls her Merris, which sounds like Meri, one of the younger daughters of Ramses II. The rabbins identify her with Bithiah (1 Chron. iv. 18). She espied the ark, and had it opened. She saw by the features and color of the infant that he was a Hebrew. He wept and she was touched with pity. At this critical moment Miriam stepped forward, and with admirable tact asked: "Shall I go and call thee a nurse of the Hebrew women, that she may nurse the child for thee?" The princess bade her go, and the child's mother was called and the infant committed to her care. When he was weaned he was taken to Pharaoh's daughter, who adopted him and called him Moses. The name was doubly fitting, the child having been drawn from the water and being adopted as a son (Ex. ii. 1–10). The adopted son of a princess required a princely education, and Moses became instructed in all the wisdom of the Egyptians (Acts vii. 22), who were then unsurpassed in civilization by any people in the world. This was designed to fit him for high office under the government, if not even for the Egyptian throne. But in God's intention it was to prepare him for the leadership of the Hebrews. He was possessed of great natural ability, and the training which he received schooled him for the great work for which he was destined. He became familiar with court life and intercourse with princes, with the grandeur and pomp of religious worship and with ritualistic conventionalities and symbolism, with letters and the literary ideas of the time. He witnessed the administration of justice, and he acquired a general acquaintance with the arts which were practiced in civilized life. He remembered, however, his origin, believed the promises which had been made to the Hebrew people, and before the close of his sojourn in Egypt he had discovered the call of God to him to be the judge and the deliverer of the Israelites. Going out to observe the state of his countrymen, he saw

one of them struck by an Egyptian. Moses killed the oppressor, and hid his body in the sand. Another day he tried to reconcile two Hebrews who were striving together, on which the one who was in the wrong insolently asked: "Who made thee a prince and a judge over us? intendest thou to kill me, as thou killedst the Egyptian?" Moses was alarmed to find that his deed of the previous day had become known, and on learning that it had reached the ears of Pharaoh, who said that he would kill him for it, fled from Egypt to the land of Midian. He had refused to be called the son of Pharaoh's daughter, had cast in his lot with the people of God, and had assumed the position of deliverer and judge (Ex. ii. 11–15; Acts vii. 24–28; Heb. xi. 24, 25). He was now forty years old (Acts vii. 23). On arriving in Midian, Moses aided the daughters of Jethro to water their flocks. This act introduced him to Jethro, who was a priest. Jethro showed him hospitality, furnished him with employment, and gave him one of his daughters to wife. She bore Moses two sons, Gershom and Eliezer (Ex. ii. 22; iv. 20; xviii. 3, 4). He remained in Midian forty years (Acts vii. 30), intimately associated with a people who were descended from Abraham and perhaps worshiped the God of Abraham (cp. Ex. xviii. 10–12). This period was likewise a time of preparation. He enjoyed close fellowship with a leading man of the Midianites, a man of sound judgment (Ex. xviii.) and a priest. Here Moses widened his acquaintance with religious thought and forms of worship. He learned the roads of the wilderness, its resources, climate, and mode of life of its inhabitants. Amid its solemn grandeur and in its deep solitude he had opportunity for reflection. At the close of this period he was astonished to see a bush burning and yet remaining unconsumed. As he turned aside to look more narrowly at a sight so unique, he received an authenticated call from Jehovah, and the objections were overcome which he raised on the ground of insufficiency for the work (Ex. iii. 11), inability to tell the people in what character God would manifest himself for their deliverance (13), lack of credentials to secure the recognition of the people (iv. 1), and lack of eloquence to persuade (10). These difficulties were removed; and Moses acquiesced, but unwillingly. God was displeased, but promised that Aaron should help Moses (14). Moses took his wife Zipporah and his sons to return to Egypt (20). Two sons had been born to him. One of them, doubtless the younger, he had not circumcised, because Zipporah regarded the rite as bloody. In yielding to her in this matter Moses had shown himself unfaithful in his own household and unfit for his high commission. God was displeased with this neglect of the sign of the covenant; and now, as Moses was returning to Egypt with his family, God brought him nigh unto death at the inn. But Zipporah discerned the cause and, desirous of saving her husband's life, at once took a knife and performed the operation, saying, "A bridegroom of blood art thou to me" (Ex. iv. 24–26). Arriving in Egypt, Moses repeatedly, in conjunction with Aaron, conveyed to Pharaoh the divine commands, the rejection of which brought on the obstinate king and his people the succession of judgments known as the ten plagues (v.–xiii. 16). When the departure from Egypt took place, it was Moses who, under divine guidance, led the people. At Sinai he was admitted to intimate relations with God. God allowed all the people to hear his voice in articulate words; but he permitted Moses to see him manifested and he spake unto Moses face to face, as a man speaketh unto his friend (Ex. xxiv. 9–11; xxxiii. 11, 17–23; xxxiv. 5–29), and he revealed his will to Moses from time to time for the instruction of his people, as he did afterwards to the successive prophets. In communion with God Moses obtained the statutes based on the ten commandments (see THEOCRACY). Immediately afterwards, during a sojourn of forty days on the mount, he was made acquainted with the form, dimensions, and materials of the tabernacle and its furniture (see TABERNACLE), and received from God the two tables of stone; but on finding that in his absence the people had taken to worshiping a golden calf, he dashed the tablets to the ground as he neared the camp and broke them in his righteous indignation and in token of the fact that the covenant, of which they were the fundamental law, had been annulled by the sin of the people. He then inflicted punishment upon the people; and all who had not held aloof from the place of idolatrous worship, or had not retired when reminded of their sin by the act of Moses, in their obstinacy were exposed to death at the hands of the Levites who offered themselves as executioners. Having acted symbolically and judicially, Moses now acted mediatorially and interceded for the people, and God promised that his angel should accompany the host. Moses was again called into the mountain, and the portions of the covenant respecting the service of God, which had been grossly violated in a fundamental principle, were singled out and emphasized, and he received two other tables inscribed like the first (xix., xx.; xxxii.–xxxiv.). On each of these occasions he fasted forty days and nights (Ex. xxiv. 18; xxxiv. 28; Deut. ix. 9, 18), as Elijah afterwards did (1 Kin. xix. 8), both in this respect foreshadowing the similar fast of our Lord (Mat. iv. 2). The name of Moses is forever associated with the laws given at Sinai and during the subsequent desert wanderings (see LEVITICUS and NUMBERS).

When Moses came down from mount **Sinai**,

after the second sojourn of forty days, with the tables of the law in his hand, the skin of his face shone, sending forth beams (Hebrew, horns), and the people were afraid to come nigh him (Ex. xxxiv. 29, R. V. margin). Moses called to them, and they returned to him; and he spake with them and gave to them all that the Lord had spoken with him. "And *till* Moses had done speaking with them, he put a veil on his face. But when Moses went in before the Lord to speak with him, he took the veil off, until he came out" (33, 34, A. V.). The R. V., following the Septuagint and Vulgate and correctly rendering the Hebrew, says just the contrary: "And when Moses had done speaking with them, he put a veil on his face." He did not wear the veil while speaking either with the people or with the Lord. He wore the veil, not to hide the splendor (A. V.), but to conceal the vanishing away of the splendor (R. V.); and he wore it until he returned to the presence of the Lord, where the light of his countenance was rekindled. Moses "put a veil upon his face, that the children of Israel should not look steadfastly on the end of that which was passing away" (2 Cor. iii. 13, R. V., cp. 7).

In the second year of the sojourn of the Israelites in the wilderness, Moses is mentioned as having married a Cushite woman (Num. xii. 1). Zipporah may have died during the preceding year, although her death is not recorded (cp. Ex. xviii. 2). Among the later Jews the story ran that the Cushite woman was an Ethiopian princess named Tharbis, who had fallen in love with Moses on the occasion of his leading an Egyptian army into Ethiopia, while he was still a member of Pharaoh's household (Antiq. ii. 10, 2). The tale is evidently a fabrication. The marriage took place in the wilderness, when Miriam and Aaron were jealous of Moses' superiority in public affairs. They were leaders of the host, directors of the national life, and prophets as well as Moses; and on this ground they claimed that their opposition to Moses' marriage with the foreigner should have been heeded by him. The Cushite woman was probably one of the mixed multitude which accompanied the Israelites in the flight from Egypt (Ex. xii. 38).

Shortly after leaving Kadesh, Korah and other princes rebelled against the authority of Moses and Aaron, but were signally punished by God (Num. xvi.); see KORAH. At the second encampment at Kadesh, Moses and Aaron grievously sinned (Num. xx.). When bidden by God to speak unto the rock that it give forth its water, Moses said to the assembled people: "Hear now, ye rebels; shall we bring you forth water out of this rock?" The brothers failed to observe their subordinate position. They claimed to be the leaders and providers of the people, whereas it was God who had led the Israelites from Egypt and had fed them for forty years in the wilderness. They took to themselves the honor which belonged to God alone. When called upon to act for God, they acted in their own name, and used for their own glory the power delegated unto them. For this sin of treason they were denied the privilege of conducting the people into the promised land. It was a sore chastisement to Moses, but it made no change in the fidelity of this great servant of the Lord. After the condemnation he was faithful, as he had been before. He started the people once more on their march to Canaan. He led Aaron up mount Hor, stripped him of his official robes, and transferred his office to Eleazar, thus himself aiding in carrying out the death sentence. When the people were bitten by the fiery serpents, he interceded with God for them, and at God's bidding erected the brazen serpent and bade his dying countrymen look and live. He led the armies of Israel into the territory of Sihon and Og, and conquered it for Israel. When the camp was pitched in a valley in the mountains of Abarim, and glimpses of the land of Abraham, Isaac. and Jacob were obtained, the pent-up emotions of Moses' soul again, as on other unrecorded occasions since his transgression found relief in prayer: "O Lord God, thou hast begun to show thy servant thy greatness, and thy strong hand : . . . . Let me go over, I pray thee, and see the good land that is beyond **Jordan**, that goodly mountain, and Lebanon.' But the answer came : "Let it suffice thee ; speak no more unto me of this matter . . . . for thou shalt not go over Jordan" (Deut. iii. 24–27). The camp was moved and pitched at Shittim in the valley, and Moses put his house in order that he might die. He delivered a parting address to the people ; see DEUTERONOMY. He led Joshua, whom God had appointed to succeed him, before the high priest in the presence of the congregation, placed his hands upon him, and, giving him a charge, transferred to him the office which he himself had so honorably and efficiently filled for forty years. He afterwards led Joshua to the door of the tabernacle to receive a charge from God. Then he taught the people a song that they might have words of religious wisdom in their memory and on their tongues, bestowed his farewell blessing on the several tribes, ascended mount Nebo and viewed the promised land from its summit, and died. He was 120 years old, yet was his eye not dim nor his natural force abated. God buried him near by (Deut. xxxiv.).

It was during the forty years in the wilderness that the principal literary work of Moses was done. He kept a record of the encampments (Num. xxxiii.), made a note of events, such as the battle with Amalek (Ex. **xvii.** 14), committed the statutes founded on **the** covenant law to writing (xxiv. 4-7), pre**served** a copy of his farewell address (Deut.

xxxi. 24). He had also the richness, vividness, and depth of thought requisite for writing Hebrew poetry, which is very simple in its structure and a ready vehicle for fervid utterance. The most spontaneous of his poems, written under the intense feeling of the moment, was the song which he uttered when Pharaoh was overthrown in the Red Sea (Ex. xv. 1–18). Moses ascribes the glory to Jehovah (1–3), describes the event (4–12), anticipates its effect upon the enemies of Israel (13–15), and discerns in it a guarantee that Jehovah will bring Israel into the promised land (16–18). The song may have been composed in a few moments. Ps. xc. is the product of a quieter mood and of reflection. His didactic song, embodying the religious lessons of the preceding forty years, was prepared with the design of its being committed to memory by the people (Deut. xxxii. ; cp. xxxi. 19, 22). His farewell blessing of the tribes, like the farewell words of Jacob to his sons, was also cast in poetic form (Deut. xxxiii.). Moses had literary ability ; in these several forms of literature he had predecessors among the Egyptians ; and especially did he have also the stimulus afforded by their literary ideas and the example of their histories, and the incentive of the awakened national life of the Hebrews, and the stirring events amid which he lived to lead him to write a connected history of his people, such as is found in the Pentateuch. For his authorship of that work see PENTATEUCH.

As the organizer of a nation Moses under the guidance of God provided Israel with civil and religious institutions. These institutions were timely in the sense that both kinds were regarded by the peoples of that day as normal and essential to a state, their character corresponded to the ideals of the age, and they represented the highest moral and religious truth possessed by men. The laws were not as a whole novel. The constitution consisted of ten commandments. It had long been known to Israel that idolatry, proscribed by the second commandment, was abhorrent to Jehovah (Gen. xxxv. 2). There is evidence that the Sabbath day was instituted long before the fourth commandment was promulgated at Sinai. Long also before Israel heard the law at Sinai, murder, adultery, theft, and false witness-bearing were universally held to be crimes punishable by man. The significance of Israel's constitution lay in the fact that recognized moral obligations were made the fundamental law of the kingdom, and that the tenth commandment probed back of the outward act into the inner nature of man and located the source of sin in the evil desires of the heart. The main portion of the Book of the Covenant consists of statutes based on the covenant law of the Decalogue (Ex. xxi. 1–xxiii. 19). In certain cases **at least** old laws were reaffirmed and ancient customs were made laws of the kingdom. The codex of Hammurabi (see AMRAPHEL) enables the student to trace more of the ordinances back into the period before Moses than he had previously been able to do; and it shows also that the idea of codification, which is so marked a feature of the Book of the Covenant, had dawned upon man centuries before the time of Moses. The ecclesiastical legislation of Moses was also timely; providing a sanctuary with the ground plan of the prevalent type of Egyptian temple, as an edifice stable, symmetrical in its proportions, and employing the approved symbolism of the day in its appointments and ritual, with a priesthood and priestly organization and priestly functions in general like those of contemporary nations. It was a sacred house and a worship that embodied the good in the religious thought and practice of the civilized world, that were intelligible alike to Israelite and gentile, and were distinguished by monotheism and spirituality, and by the exhibition of the way in which the sinner may approach the holy God. Moses was inspired, but a body of laws and a form of worship entirely hidden from the foundation of the world were not revealed to him. Moses was a prophet, and was inspired as other prophets were inspired. Under the influence of the Holy Spirit he was made an infallible communicator to his fellow-men of the mind and will of God. He spent days in personal communion with God, who enlightened his mind concerning God and the nature of the kingdom, led him infallibly to discern the laws appropriate to the condition of the people and adapted to discipline them in the spirit of the kingdom, and prompted and controlled and enabled him to frame legislation and found institutions, more or less out of old materials and on old models indeed, yet distinguished from all analogies among contemporary peoples by the exhibition of the spiritual nature and holiness of God, by the extrication of man's conduct from civil relations merely and bringing it into relation to God also, and by the power to lift the secular life into the true service of God.

Moses had the wisdom of a statesman. He observed the opposition to him which was manifested in his own family (Num. xii.), the jealousy of other tribes and his own to the pre-eminence of himself and Aaron (xvi.), the worldly considerations by which the people were actuated (xxxii.), their lack of faith in Jehovah at critical moments, and their readiness to lapse into idolatry. He meditated on these weaknesses which threatened the national existence; and when he came to prepare his farewell address he insisted upon the law of the one altar and upon the spirituality of religion as the great means under God of overcoming these defects by deepening the moral life on the one hand, and on the other hand by preserving purity of worship and doctrine, binding the

people together as one nation, and making their own religion a grander spectacle than the ceremonies at heathen shrines; see ALTAR and DEUTERONOMY. After his death the greatness of Moses was universally recognized (Jer. xv. 1; Heb. iii. 2). He had, moreover, the distinguished honor of being permitted to reappear as the representative of O. T. law, with Elijah, the representative of O. T. prophecy, to hold converse with Jesus on the mount of transfiguration (Mat. xvii. 3, 4). See MICHAEL 11.

Moth.

An insect proverbial for its destruction of clothing (Job xiii. 28; Mat. vi. 19; Jas. v. 2). Its larva feeds upon wool (Is. li. 8), and out of the same substance builds itself a house or case, in which it lives (Job xxvii. 18), protruding its head while eating. The clothes moth (*Tinea*) is intended, of which several species, as *T. pellionella* and *vestianella*, feed on fur and wool.

Mount.

1. A mountain. The word is now used almost exclusively in poetry or as part of a compound name, as mount Carmel, mount Tabor, mount Zion, mount of Olives (1 Kin. xviii. 19: Ps. xlviii. 2; Zech. xiv. 4); see CARMEL, ZION, etc.

2. A mound, especially one raised against the wall of a besieged city by the assailing army (Jer. vi. 6; Dan. xi. 15; and R. V. of 2 Sam. xx. 15; 2 Kin. xix. 32), and on which the battering ram was placed (Ezek. xxvi. 8, 9); see illustration under LACHISH. In Is. xxix. 3 a different Hebrew word is used, which R. V. renders fort.

Moun'tain.

Of the mountains in or near Palestine the loftiest was mount Hermon. Then followed the Lebanon range. Compared with those towering elevations such hills as mount Zion, mount Moriah, mount Carmel, mount Tabor, etc., were very inferior eminences (Deut. iii. 25). Mountain is a natural image for eternal continuance (Deut. xxxiii. 15; Hab. iii. 6), for stability (Is. liv. 10), for difficult, dangerous, wearisome paths in life (Jer. xiii. 16), for insurmountable obstacles (Zech. iv. 7; Mat. xxi. 21).

Mount of Con-gre-ga'tion.

A mountain in the farthest north (Is. xiv. 13); the reference probably being to a conception common in ancient mythology and current among the Babylonians, that the gods assembled on a mountain of the north. That the Babylonians located the mountain in the north may at least be inferred by analogy, but the evidence is confined as yet to this passage, where the king of Babylon is the speaker.

Mourn'ing.

The mourning of the oriental was and is ostentatious. Public expression was given to grief principally by removing ornaments and neglecting the person (Ex. xxxiii. 4; 2 Sam.

xiv. 2; xix. 24; Mat. vi. 16–18), rending the clothes by slitting the tunic at the throat or tearing the coat or the outer mantle (Lev. x. 6; 2 Sam.. xiii. 31; Joel ii. 13), shaving the head or plucking out the hair (Ezra ix. 3; Jer. vii. 29), putting on sackcloth (Joel i. 8), sprinkling ashes or dust on the head (2 Sam. xv. 32), fasting (Ps. xxxv. 13), weeping and lamenting (Joel i. 8, 13). Several of these modes were usually combined (Gen. xxxvii. 34; 2 Sam. iii. 31, 32; xiii. 19; xv. 32; Ezra ix. 3, 5; Job i. 20; Jer. xli. 5). Friends came to the house of mourning, and flute players and professional mourners, chiefly women, were also employed, who made loud lamentations (Jer. ix 17, 18; Mat. ix. 23; Acts ix. 39); see MINSTREL. As at the present day, funeral feasts were given to the crowds that assembled at the funeral (Jer. xvi. 7; Baruch vi. 32). After the funeral women came forth very early in the morning to visit the grave, as they are still accustomed to do, and to pray, weep and sob or chant hymns or beat their breasts (Mark xvi. 1, 2). Many of them are professionals; but others are sincere mourners, relatives of the deceased and their sympathizing friends (John xi. 31). Customs, in general similar, prevailed in Egypt, Persia, and Scythia (Herod. ii. 66, 85; iv. 71; viii. 99; ix. 24).

The period of mourning varied. It was thirty days for Aaron and Moses (Num. xx. 29; Deut. xxxiv. 8), and seven days for Saul (1 Sam. xxxi. 13). The Egyptians observed seventy days for Jacob, and seven more days were devoted to public mourning for him at the threshing floor of Atad (Gen. l. 3, 10).

Mouse.

A small rodent quadruped, *Mus musculus* and other allied species of the family *Muridæ*. It was an unclean animal (Lev. xi. 29), but was eaten by Israelites in Isaiah's time, who gave themselves up to heathenism and paid no attention to the Mosaic law (Is. lxvi. 17). The field mouse (*Arvicola arvalis*) was destructive to crops (1 Sam. vi. 5). The Hebrew word for mouse, *'akbar*, is a comprehensive one, including not merely the genus *Mus*, but most of the family *Muridæ*, with many animals from other families having either an affinity or an analogy to the typical mice. The Arabs include the jerboa under the designation *'akbar*, and they eat it, and various other mouse-like animals, such as sand rats, which belong to the subfamily *Gerbillinæ*, and dormice, of the related family *Myoxidæ*.

Mo'za [a going forth, issue].

1. A man of Judah, family of Hezron, house of Caleb (1 Chron. ii. 46).
2. A descendant of Jonathan (1 Chron. viii. 36, 37).

Mo'zah.

A town of Benjamin (Josh. xviii. 26). Not identified. The name is etymologically dif-

ferent from Beit Mizza, a ruined village, about 5 miles west-northwest of Jerusalem.

Mul'ber-ry Tree.

A tree of the same order as the fig. It is cultivated in Syria for the sake of its leaves, on which the silkworm feeds. A cooling drink is made from its berries, the juice being expressed, sweetened with honey, and flavored with spices. The juice of the berries was shown to elephants to prepare them for battle (1 Mac. vi. 34; cp. 3 Mac. v. 2). A mulberry is mentioned in N. T. under the name of sycamine.

Mulberry is the rendering of the Hebrew *Baka'*, weeping, distilling; a tree which grew near Jerusalem and of which the leaves rustled in the wind (2 Sam. v. 23, 24; 1 Chron. xiv. 14, 15). In these passages and in Ps. lxxxiv. 6 the margin of R. V. has balsam tree. Royle suggested that the tree intended is that called *bak* by the Arabs, or rather *shajrat al-bak*, the gnat tree, which he identifies with the poplar. Two species of poplar are common along the banks of streams and in moist soil in Palestine, the white poplar and the Euphrates poplar; but there is no etymological connection between *bak* and *baka'*.

A bough of the mulberry tree.

Mule.

A graminivorous animal, called in Hebrew *pered* (1 Kin. xviii. 5). The mule is a hybrid between the horse and the ass. It is often mentioned with horses (Ps. xxxii. 9), and was much used for riding and for carrying burdens (2 Sam. xiii. 29; 2 Kin. v. 17; 1 Chron. xii. 40). It is not mentioned before the time of David, but was in common use from his days onward. The Tyrians obtained mules in Armenia (Ezek. xxvii. 14).

In A. V. of Gen. xxxvi. 24 the Hebrew

plural *yemim* is translated mules; but it should rather be rendered hot springs, as it is in the Vulgate and in R. V. In A. V. of Esth. viii. 10, 14 *rekesh* is rendered mule, in 1 Kin. iv. 28 dromedary. R. V. substitutes swift steed.

Mup'pim.

A son of Benjamin (Gen. xlvi. 21); see SHEPHUPHAM.

Mur'der.

Just after the deluge it was enacted that whoso sheddeth man's blood, by man shall his blood be shed: for in the image of God made he man (Gen. ix. 6). The avenger of blood had the right to put the murderer to death (Num. xxxv. 19); but if the manslayer reached a city of refuge he was temporarily safe. The cities of refuge were not instituted for the benefit of the deliberate murderer; they were designed for the man who had accidentally committed manslaughter (Num. xxxv.). Even if the deliberate murderer had fled for asylum to the altar, and probably taken hold of its horns, he was to be taken from it and put to death (Ex. xxi. 14; cp. 1 Kin. ii. 28-34). At the city of refuge the manslayer was given a trial. The concurrent testimony of at least two witnesses was required to convict him of murder (Num. xxxv. 30; Deut. xvii. 6). If guilty of deliberate murder, no ransom was accepted (Num. xxxv. 31), he was delivered to the avenger of blood to be slain (19; Deut. xix. 12). If acquitted, he was granted asylum in the city. See CITY OF REFUGE.

Mu'shi.

A Levite, son of Merari, and the founder of a tribal family or house (Ex. vi. 19; Num. iii. 20; xxvi. 58; 1 Chron. vi. 19, 47; xxiii. 21, 23; xxiv. 26, 30).

Mu'sic.

Music is ancient (Gen. iv. 21). Among the Hebrews, Miriam and her companions took timbrels and danced and sang praises to the Lord for his deliverance of the Israelites at the Red Sea (Ex. xv. 20). The people danced and sang in idolatrous worship about the golden calf (Ex. xxxii. 6, 18). In family feasts and religious festivals they sang, played on musical instruments, and danced (Jer. xxv. 10; 1 Mac. ix. 39; Luke xv. 25). Marriage processions, as they passed through the streets, were accompanied with music and song (Jer. vii. 34). Women and maidens welcomed the victorious warrior on his return home with music, song, and dance (Judg. xi. 34; 1 Sam. xviii. 6). Kings had their court musicians (2 Chron. xxxv. 25; Ecc. ii. 8). The accession of a king and his marriage and his feasts were made joyous with music (2 Sam. xix. 35; 1 Kin. i. 40; Ps. xlv. 8, R. V.). The shepherd might have his harp (1 Sam. xvi. 18). The mind might be quieted and refreshed by music (1 Sam. x. 5; xvi. 16; 2 Kin. iii. 15). Psalms might be sung to the accompaniment of the harp (Ps. xcii. 1-3; cxxxvii. 2; cp. Amos vi. 5).

The musical instruments of the Hebrews were of three classes: stringed instruments, wind instruments, and instruments of percussion. Stringed instruments consisted of a body of wood with strings of gut, and were played with the fingers of one or both hands or were struck with a plectrum of wood, ivory, or metal. They were chiefly the harp and psaltery. The harp was in general use among the people both for worldly and sacred music; the psaltery was commonly though not exclusively, reserved for religious purposes. The psaltery was tuned to the soprano register, the harp an octave lower (1 Chron. xv. 20, 21). The wind instruments were chiefly flutes or pipes and horns. The pipe was often played with other instruments (1 Sam. x. 5; 1 Kin. i. 40; Is. v. 12; xxx. 29; Ecclus. xl. 21), was employed to lead dancing (Mat. xi. 17), and was played at weddings (1 Mac. iii. 45; Rev. xviii. 22). It was specially the instrument of lamentation (Jer. xlviii. 36; Mat. ix. 23, R.V.; War iii. 9, 5). The Bible does not mention its use in the temple service, not even in 1 Mac. iv. 54; but it was used in sacred music (1 Sam. x. 5) and was heard in processions of worshipers marching to the house of God (Is. xxx. 29), and in the later temple it had an assigned place, especially at the passover and feast of tabernacles. The ram's horn, or an imitation of it, was sometimes used to increase the noise

An Egyptian orchestra reproduced from a fifteenth century B.C. Thebes tomb painting. The girls are playing a harp, lute, double pipe, and seven-stringed lyre.

of other instruments (1 Chron. xv. 28; 2 Chron. xv. 14; Ps. xcviii. 6, rendered trumpet), but was generally blown by itself. Its principal employment was not in music, but for military purposes and to make proclamations. Straight, narrow, silver trumpets, about a cubit in length, and called ḥăṣōṣᵉrah, were used by the priests to announce festivals, to call the congregation, and on advancing to battle (Num. x. 1–10). They were rarely blown by laymen (Hos. v. 8; perhaps, 2 Kin. xi. 14 and 2 Chron. xxiii. 13). Of the instruments of percussion the timbrel or tabret was the popular instrument; it was usually played by women and was employed on festive occasions, especially to beat time at the dances and for singers (Gen. xxx² 27; Ex. xv. 20; Judg. xi. 34, Ps. lxxxi. 2). Cymbals of brass were used in the temple service (1 Chron. xv. 19).

Music was cultivated by the companies which gathered about the prophets (1 Sam.

288 were trained musicians, who were depended upon to lead the less skilled body of assistants (1 Chron. xxv. 7, 8). They were divided into twenty-four courses, containing twelve trained musicians each. Of these courses four belonged to the family of Asaph, six to that of Jeduthun, and fourteen to that of Heman. The orchestra which accompanied the singing consisted of stringed instruments, but cymbals were also used, being probably struck by the chief musician to beat time (1 Chron. xv. 19–21). It appears from this passage that the proportion of psalteries to harps was eight to six. In Herod's temple there were ordinarily two psalteries, nine harps, and one cymbal, and on certain days pipes were added. The participation of priests with trumpets in the orchestra of stringed instruments was exceptional (2 Chron. v. 12, 13; vii. 6). In the second temple the trumpets, when blown in connection with the regular orchestra, were

This relief sculpture of three captive lyre players, possibly Jews from Lachish, under the watchful eye of an Assyrian guard is from a wall of Sennacherib's palace at Nineveh, seventh century B.C.

x. 5), various instruments being employed as an orchestra. It is not mentioned as belonging to the service of the tabernacle in the early period. David introduced it into the worship at the sanctuary, and Solomon promoted it (2 Sam. vi. 5, 14; 1 Kin. x. 12; 1 Chron. xv., xvi.). Hezekiah and Josiah paid special attention to its restoration (2 Chron. xxix. 25; xxxv. 15). David was assisted in his work by Asaph, Heman, and Ethan or Jeduthun, three masters of music. A choir of singers and musicians, with Asaph at its head, was formed of Levites, and stationed before the ark at the tabernacle on Zion, while Heman and Jeduthun, with their choirs, were assigned to the old tabernacle at Gibeon (1 Chron. xvi. 4–6, 39–42). These three choirs were afterwards united in the temple. In David's reign they numbered 4000 members (1 Chron. xxiii. 5), of whom

heard only in the pauses or as responsive music (Ezra iii. 10, 11). The musicians stood on the east of the great altar (2 Chron. v. 12). In Herod's temple they occupied a broad staircase, which led from the court of Israel to the court of the priests. In this later temple a choir of boys, standing at the foot of the stairs, lent their higher voices to the song of the Levites.

Little is known of the character of the music. The Hebrews had a scale of eight tones. Their sacred choirs probably sang in unison the same simple melody, divided into two parts, the one an octave higher than the other, and representing the male and female voices, and were accompanied by the instruments in the same tones (1 Chron. xv. 20, 21). Melodies are probably named in the titles of Ps. ix., xxii., xlv., lvi., lvii., and others. Antiphonal and responsive singing was practiced (Ex. xv. 21 ; Neh. xii. 31–43) and was often heard in the temple service (Ezra iii. 10, 11 ; Jer. xxxiii. 11) ; several psalms were arranged for this purpose, e. g., xxiv. 7–10 ; cxxxvi. The congregation seldom, if ever, joined in the singing in the first temple, but at its close they united in saying amen (1 Chron. xvi. 7, 36). In the Herodian temple the people sometimes participated by singing responses.

Mus'tard.
A garden herb (Luke xiii. 19), which in comparison with other herbs becomes a great tree (Mat. xiii. 32 ; Mark iv. 32), on whose branches the birds rest for the sake of obtaining its seeds. Its seeds are, hyperbolically speaking, less than all seeds (Mat. xiii. 32). The largeness of the plant grown from seeds so small illustrates the increase of the kingdom of heaven from a very small beginning. The mustard seed was employed proverbially by the Jews, just as it was by Jesus (Mat. xvii. 20 ; Luke xvii. 6), to denote anything very minute. The common mustard of Palestine is *Sinapis nigra* or black mustard. It grows wild, attaining the height of a horse and rider, as travelers have noticed. It is also cultivated in gardens for its seed, which is used as a condiment. Those who seek another identification generally consider the mustard of Scripture to have been *Salvadora persica*, the type of the natural order *Salvadoraceæ* or Salvadorads. Royle, who supported this view, says that it has a succulent fruit, tasting like garden cress. It is, however, small, and apparently confined to the low valley of the Jordan ; and it is not an herb.

Muth-lab'ben [die for the son].
An expression of doubtful meaning in the title of Ps. ix. It probably indicates a familiar melody.

Myn'dos, in A. V. Myndus.
A small town of Caria, situated on the seacoast (Herod. v. 33). It was not far from Halicarnassus, for Alexander led a detachment of troops across the intervening country in one night. In the time of Simon Maccabæus it was subject to Rome (1 Mac. xv. 23). Its site is probably marked by the small sheltered port of Gumishlu.

My'ra.
A city of Lycia, where Paul, when a prisoner on his way to Rome, changed ships (Acts xxvii. 5, 6). Myra was one of the principal cities of Lycia. It stood some two miles from the sea, and was built on and about a cliff, at the mouth of the gorge leading into the interior mountain region. It is now called Dembra.

Myrrh.
1. A fragrant substance, called in Hebrew *mor*, in Greek *smurna*. It was an ingredient in the oil with which Aaron and his succes-

sors were anointed (Ex. xxx. 23). Beds and garments were perfumed with it (Ps. xlv. 8 ; Prov. vii. 17 ; Song iii. 6), and an oil of myrrh was used in the purification of women (Esth. ii. 12). The magi brought it from the east to present to the infant Jesus (Mat. ii. 11). At the crucifixion it was offered to him in wine, probably to deaden pain (Mark xv. 23), and was an ingredient in the spices designed for anointing his body (John xix. 39). It was used for embalming the dead (Herod. ii. 86). The tree which produced it grew in Arabia (iii. 107 ; Pliny xii. 16). The plant which produced it was probably *Balsamodendron myrrha*. It is a small tree, with odoriferous wood and bark, short spiny branches, trifoliolate leaves, and plum-like fruit. It grows in Arabia Felix, and furnishes the myrrh of commerce.

2. The rendering of the Hebrew *Lot* (Gen. xxxvii. 25 ; xliii. 11). Myrrh is not a happy translation ; it should have been ladanum (R. V. margin), called by the Greeks *lēdon* and *ladanon*, and by the Arabs *lâdan* ; is cognate with the Hebrew *lot*. It is a highly fragrant resin, containing a volatile oil, and is produced by *Cistus creticus* and various other species of rock rose. It grows in parts of Syria.

Myr'tle.
A tree, called in Hebrew *h*ᵃ*das*. It grew in the mountains near Jerusalem, and booths were made of its branches at the feast of tabernacles (Neh. viii. 15). It is mentioned also in Is. xli. 19 ; lv. 13 ; Zech. i. 8, 10, 11. The tree is undoubtedly the common myrtle (*Myrtus communis*), which grows in Palestine.

My'si-a.
A province in the extreme northwest of Asia Minor ; bounded on the north by the Propontis, now sea of Marmora, on the south by Lydia, on the east by Bithynia, and on the west by the Hellespont. The Troad lay within its limits. Paul and Silas passed through it to Troas, one of its cities (Acts xvi. 7, 8). Assos, to which Paul sailed to meet his associates, was another (xx. 13). A third was Pergamos, one of the seven churches in Asia (Rev. i. 11 ; ii. 12–17).

Mys'ter-y.
A word borrowed from the heathen religion, in which a mystery was a secret and peculiar doctrine, which distinguished one religion from another, and found expression in rites, ceremonies, and purifications to which only initiated persons were admitted. The word does not imply that the doctrine is incomprehensible. In the N. T. it denotes a secret hidden from the world till the appointed time (Rom. xvi. 25), or until man has been prepared by the Spirit of God to receive and appreciate it (Mark iv. 11), which forms a characteristic and essential doctrine and finds expression in the life (1 Tim. iii. 16).

N

Na'am [sweetness, pleasantness].

A son of the celebrated Caleb (1 Chron. iv. 15).

Na'a-mah [sweet, pleasant].

1. Daughter of Lamech, and sister of Tubal-cain (Gen. iv. 22).

2. An Ammonitess, a wife of Solomon and the mother of king Rehoboam (1 Kin. xiv. 21, 31; 2 Chron. xii. 13).

3. A town in the lowland of Judah (Josh. xv. 41). Not identified.

Na'a-man [pleasantness, delight].

1. A grandson of Benjamin, a son of Bela and founder of a family (Gen. xlvi. 21; Num. xxvi. 40).

2. Commander of the army of Ben-hadad, king of Damascus. He was an able general, and had won deliverance for the Syrians, but he was a leper. In Syria leprosy did not exclude from human society, as it did in Israel, though it was a loathsome disease. In one of the Syrian raids into the Israelite territory, the soldiers had brought away a little maid, who became a slave to Naaman's wife. This girl expressed to her mistress the wish that Naaman were with Elisha in Samaria, as the prophet would heal him of his leprosy. The speech of the maiden was reported to her master, who resolved to seek a cure from Elisha. His sovereign, the king of Syria, wrote a letter of introduction for him, and sent him to the king of Israel to be cured. When the Israelite ruler received it he thought that the real intention of his correspondent was to pick a quarrel and declare war. Elisha reassured the king, and desired that Naaman should be sent to him, when he would learn that there was a prophet in Israel. When he came with his horses and chariot to Elisha's door, the prophet in order to humble his pride and teach him that he owed his cure not to man, but solely to the power of God, did not appear but sent out a message that he should dip seven times in the Jordan. Naaman, feeling affronted, and despising the means, started for home in a passion, saying, "Are not Abana and Pharpar, rivers of Damascus, better than all the waters of Israel? may I not wash in them and be clean?" But his servants soothed his temper, and urged him to dip in the Jordan. He did so, and was cured. Filled with gratitude, he wished to reward Elisha. The prophet desired to impress upon the Syrian the freeness of God's blessings, and refused all recompense; but Gehazi, his servant, acted in a very different spirit. Naaman renounced idolatry, and became a worshiper of Jehovah; and he carried home two mules' burden of earth to build an altar to Jehovah. He lived, however, in a heathen community and could not altogether escape outward participation in heathen customs. His king was an idolater, a worshiper of Rimmon; and it was Naaman's official duty to support him when he entered the temple and bowed before the god. The prophet of Jehovah permitted Naaman to fulfill his secular duties, even though to do so involved his assisting his king to perform heathen worship (2 Kin. v.).

Na'a-ma-thite.

A native or inhabitant of Naamah; as Zophar, Job's friend (Job. ii. 11; xi. 1; xx. 1; xlii. 9). The place was probably in Arabia.

Na'a-rah [a girl].

1. A wife of Ashhur, the ancestor of the inhabitants of Tekoa (1 Chron. iv. 5, 6).

2. A town on the boundary line of Ephraim, east of Bethel, and not far from Jericho (Josh xvi. 7). In A. V. the name is written Naarath. The final th is archaic, and is probably due in the text to the presence of the local ending. The town is doubtless one with Naaran (1 Chron. vii. 28). Archelaus diverted half the water supply of Neara to irrigate the palms of his palace at Jericho (Antiq. xvii. 13, 1). Eusebius mentions a village Noorath, 5 Roman miles from Jericho. A plausible conjecture for the site is on the Nahr el-'Aujah, with its plentiful water; perhaps at the ruin el-'Aujah.

Na'a-rai.

One of David's valiant men (1 Chron. xi. 37; apparently a diverse reading, perhaps the correction, of Paarai, 2 Sam. xxiii. 35).

Na'a-ran. See NAARAH 2.

Na'a-rath. See NAARAH 2.

Na'a-shon. See NAHSHON.

Na-as'son. See NAHSHON.

Na'bal [foolish, wicked].

A sheepmaster, resident in Maon, who pastured his flocks around the village Carmel in Judah, on the confines of the wilderness. His wife's name was Abigail. David and his followers had dwelt for some time in the neighborhood, and had used their might to protect the property of the people from marauding bands of robbers. When Nabal was shearing his sheep, David sent ten young men to solicit assistance for himself and his followers. Nabal sent back a churlish refusal, which so irritated David that he put his men in motion with the intention of cutting off Nabal and every other male belonging to the household. Abigail, who was a clever and judicious woman, made ready a present for David, and, starting promptly, apologized for her husband's conduct, allayed the resentment which it had caused, and prevented the gathering storm from breaking on her home. Returning to her abode, she found a great feast in progress, and her lord completely intoxicated. Next morning, when he was sober, she told him how narrowly he had escaped destruction. He was profoundly affected by the intelligence, and never recovered from the shock which it caused, but died in ten days. After a time, Abigail became one of David's wives (1 Sam. xxv. 1-42).

Nab-a-thæ′ans, in A. V. **Na′bath-ites.**
See NEBAIOTH.

Na′both.

An inhabitant of Jezreel, who had a vineyard at that town near one of Ahab's palaces. The king wished to buy it, but its owner would not sell it because it had descended to him from his ancestors. At the instance of Jezebel, Naboth's life was sworn away by suborned witnesses, he and his sons (2 Kin. ix. 26), to whom the vineyard would have descended, were stoned to death, their bodies were left to be devoured by the dogs, and the vineyard was seized by Ahab. This act of violence called down the judgment of God on the guilty king and his yet guiltier wife (1 Kin. xxi. 1-24; xxii. 34-38; 2 Kin. ix. 30-37).

Na′chon. See NACON.

Na′chor. See NAHOR.

Na′con, in A. V. **Nachon** [prepared, ready].
The designation of a threshing floor at which Uzzah was struck dead for touching the ark (2 Sam. vi. 6), and hence called Perez-uzzah, i. e. breach of Uzzah (8). It is not certain that Nacon is the original spelling of the name; see CHIDON.

Na′dab [of one's freewill, liberal].
1. The eldest of Aaron's four sons (Ex. vi. 23; Num. iii. 2; xxvi. 60; 1 Chron. vi. 3; xxiv. 1). With his brother Abihu, he was granted the privilege of a near approach to Jehovah at Sinai (Ex. xxiv. 1), and was subsequently appointed to the priesthood (xxviii. 1), but both of them afterwards offered strange fire to God, and as a penalty were consumed by fire (Lev. x. 1-7; Num. xxvi. 61). From the fact that a command was immediately thereafter given to Aaron not to drink wine or strong drink when he entered the tabernacle, it may be inferred that Nadab and Abihu had done so, and were under the influence of liquor when they committed the sin which cost them their lives (Lev. x. 9). They both died childless (Num. iii. 4; 1 Chron. xxiv. 2).
2. A man of Judah, family of Hezron, house of Jerahmeel (1 Chron. ii. 28, 30).
3. A Benjamite, a son of Gibeon and Maachah (1 Chron. viii. 30; ix. 36).
4. Son of Jeroboam I., and his successor on the throne of Israel. He began to reign about 910 B. C. He followed the evil example of his father with respect to calf worship. He led the forces of his kingdom to besiege Gibbethon, but was murdered with his relatives by Baasha, who then mounted the vacant throne. This massacre fulfilled the threatenings of Jehovah against Jeroboam and his house. Nadab reigned less than two full years (1 Kin. xiv. 10, 11, 20; xv. 25, 30).

Nad′a-bath, in A. V. **Na-dab′a-tha.**
A place, probably a village, in or near Moab (1 Mac. ix. 37; in Antiq. xiii. 1, 4 Gabatha).

Nag′gai, in A. V. **Nagge.**
An ancestor of Christ (Luke iii. 25).

Na′ha-lal and **Nahalol** (Judg. i. 30), in A. V. once **Nahallal** (Josh. xix. 15) [pasture].
A village of Zebulun (Josh. xix. 15), from which, however, that tribe failed to drive out the Canaanite inhabitants (Judg. i. 30). It was assigned to the Merarite Levites (Josh. xxi. 35). The Jerusalem Talmud says that it was afterwards called Mahlul. Schwarz and Van de Velde identify this with the village of Ma′lûl, 3½ miles west of Nazareth.

Na-ha′li-el [valley and brook of God].
An encampment of the Israelites, between Beer, in the desert east of Moab, and Bamoth, which lay between Dibon and Baal-meon (Num. xxi. 19), and hence probably on one of the northern tributaries of the Arnon. Not identified; although the name is possibly preserved in Encheileh, the valley of the Arnon from the Balua eastward to the mouth of the Seil Sa′ideh, a distance of about 2 miles.

Na-hal′lal. See NAHALAL.

Na′ha-lol. See NAHALAL.

Na′ham [solace, consolation].
Brother of Hodiah's wife (1 Chron. iv. 19, R. V.). The translation of A. V. is impossible.

Na-ham′a-ni [compassionate].
One of those who returned with Zerubbabel from Babylon (Neh. vii. 7).

Na′ha-rai, in A. V. once **Nahari** (2 Sam. xxiii. 37), a misspelling of late editions from which the original edition of 1611 was free [snoring, snorting].
A Beerothite, Joab's armorbearer (2 Sam. xxiii. 37; 1 Chron. xi. 39).

Na′hash [serpent].
1. Father of Abigail and Zeruiah, David's sisters (2 Sam. xvii. 25; cp. 1 Chron. ii. 16). Probably his widow, the mother of Abigail and Zeruiah, married Jesse and became the mother of David. This explanation is better than the assumption that Nahash was the name of Jesse's wife; or, as the later Jews interpreted the passage, that Nahash was another name of Jesse.
2. An Ammonite king who besieged Jabesh-gilead, and when its inhabitants offered to surrender and become tributary, would not accept the proposal unless every man in the place consented to lose the right eye. He determined to put a reproach upon Israel. A week's time was given in which to seek help. Before it expired, Saul, just before elected king, appeared with a relieving army, totally defeated the Ammonites, and saved Jabesh-gilead and its defenders (1 Sam. xi. 1-11). Either this Nahash or a son of his

bearing the same name treated David kindly, perhaps because he was at variance with Saul (2 Sam. x. 2).

3. A man who lived in Rabbah of the Ammonites (2 Sam. xvii. 27). He may have been the king aforementioned, or an Israelite who had settled in Rabbah after its capture by David (2 Sam. xii. 29).

Na'hath [descent or quiet].

1. A descendant of Esau and also of Ishmael. He became a chieftain of Edom (Gen. xxxvi. 3, 4, 13, 17 ; 1 Chron. i. 37).

2. A Kohathite Levite (1 Chron. vi. 26) ; probably the person elsewhere called Tohu and Toah (1 Sam. i. 1 ; 1 Chron. vi. 34).

3. A Levite, one of those who had charge of the tithes and offerings under Hezekiah (2 Chron. xxxi. 13).

Nah'bi [concealed].

The representative spy from the tribe of Naphtali (Num. xiii. 14).

Na'hor, in A. V. twice **Nachor** (Josh. xxiv. 2; Luke iii. 34) [breathing hard, snorting].

1. A son of Serug, and grandfather of Abraham (Gen. xi. 24, 25).

2. A son of Terah, and brother of Abraham (Gen. xi. 27). He married his niece Milcah, daughter of Haran and sister of Lot (29). He is not mentioned as emigrating from Ur with Terah, Abraham, and Lot ; but later he is found in Mesopotamia at Haran (xxiv. 10 ; xxvii. 43). Eight sons were born to him by Milcah, from whom sprang Aramæan tribes. Four others traced their descent from his concubine (xxii. 21-24). One of his sons by Milcah was Bethuel, who became the father of Rebekah and Laban (xxiv. 15, 29).

Nah'shon, A. V. has once **Naashon** (Ex. vi. 23), and in N. T. **Naasson** [enchanting, ominous].

A prince of the tribe of Judah in the early period of the wilderness wanderings (Num. i. 7; ii. 3; vii. 12, 17; x. 14). His sister was married to Aaron, who was of the tribe of Levi (Exod. vi. 23). Nahshon was the grandfather or remoter ancestor of Boaz, Ruth's husband, and the fifth backward in the genealogy of David (Ruth iv. 20-22; 1 Chron. ii. 10-12). This placed him in the ancestry of our Lord (Mat. i. 4 ; Luke iii. 32, 33).

Na'hum [compassionate].

A prophet born at Elkosh, doubtless a village of Palestine. He prophesied to Judah (i. 15), not to the ten tribes in captivity. The position of the book among the minor prophets, after Micah and before Habakkuk and Zephaniah, is evidence that it was written between the commencement of Hezekiah's and the close of Josiah's reign (Mic. i. 1; Zeph. i. 1); and that the prophet cites the destruction of No-amon in Egypt (iii. 8-10), which was overthrown by the Assyrians in 664 B. C., and predicts the fall of Nineveh (7), which occurred about 606 B. C., narrows

the limits within which the composition of the book must be sought to the fifty-eight years intervening between these events. It was a time when the people of Judah were despondent by reason of the persistent invasions of the Assyrians and the captivity of their king.

The theme of the prophecy is the burden of Nineveh (i. 1). The prophet insists on the familiar truth that Jehovah is a jealous God, whose vengeance is certain to fall on his adversaries, but who is a stronghold to those that trust in him (2-8), urges the people to turn a deaf ear to the counsel of those who were speaking against Jehovah's tardiness and advising the abandonment of his service (9-11), declares the unalterable purpose of the Lord to deliver his people (12-14), and exhorts them to unswerving loyalty to their God and the faithful observance of his worship (15). On the basis of this truth, the prophet proceeds to describe the overthrow of the worldly power which was then oppressing the kingdom of God. He pictures the siege of the city (ii. 1-10), and takes occasion to taunt the city which had been as a den of lions (11-13). Returning to the description of the siege, he attributes the judgment which befalls the city to its whoredoms (iii. 1-4). This allusion leads to a change of the figure, and he depicts the punishment as the punishment of a harlot (5-7). He draws attention to the fact that Nineveh is not better than No-amon, which went into captivity (8-10), and he predicts that like No-amon Nineveh shall be destroyed (11-19).

The prophecy opens with an address poetic in character and alphabetic in form (i. 2-15; in Heb. i. 2-ii. 1). But it is not an alphabetic psalm of the ordinary kind, in which the verses begin with the letters of the alphabet in their conventional sequence (cp. Ps. cxix.). The prophet has done more. He has allowed the consecutive sounds to introduce topics rather than verses and to follow each other singly or in groups throughout the stately oration. He teaches the ear to listen for certain sounds and to hear them with satisfaction. I. The prophet enunciates a doctrine of Jehovah, God of Israel (sounding aleph in the very first word *'el*, God), the doctrine that forms the basal truth of his prophecy, namely, that Jehovah, though slow to anger, yet taketh vengeance on his adversaries (2, 3; aleph beginning important words). Then the prophet describes the majesty and might of Jehovah in nature: he is in the whirlwind and in the storm, and the clouds are the dust of his feet (beth being heard thrice in this part of verse 3); he rebukes the waters that they dry up and vegetation languishes (4, which begins with gimel); the mountains and hills tremble before him (5; he being heard four times in prominent words, and the conjunction vav being used four times also, if that is intentional); the fierceness of his indignation none can withstand (6 ; the significant words beginning once with zayin and twice with hheth in proper order). The truth that has been set forth involves on the one hand the goodness of Jehovah to his people and his knowledge of them (7 ; facts stated in words beginning with teth and yodh), and on the other hand, the overthrow of evil (8 ; the principal word being *kalah*, yielding the two sounds kaph and lamedh and followed twice by that of mem in the word "place"). The climax of doctrine has been reached. II. A new section of the exalted discourse opens, in which the prophet bases prediction on the truth that has been set forth. He reiterates the impotence of opposition to Jehovah : first in the form of a question (9 ; which in its main part begins with another mem and ends with nun): next as a declaration, repeating the conclusion of the doctrinal section (the consecution of sounds being allowed to recur, kaph being heard once and lamedh twice in the two words that dominate the thought, *kalah* and *lo'*, and immediately afterwards mem thrice). Then the prophet foretells the destruction of God's foes (10-13; samekh beginning four consecutive words and fairly hissing through verse 10, while ayin snarls four times in consecutive words in verse 11 and four times in the second half of verse 12 and in the first word of verse 13 . The prediction of the deliverance of God's people proceeds (14 ; tsadhe beginning the verse, and qoph being the initial letter of two words at its close). Finally, in view of the truth that has been presented, the prophet exhorts God's people to continue steadfast and undismayed in his service and worship (15; resh and sin and shin being prominent tones, repeatedly heard in the first half of the verse; and tav being the last letter of the verse and the concluding sound of the prophecy which began with aleph). This last verse, both by its thought and rhythm, forms the transition to chap. ii.

Daleth and pe are missed from this enumeration : but when the story of the sounds is fully told, these letters are found. The ear is satisfied. It hears that which it awaits. The prophet's exalted utterance begins with aleph in verse 2 and presently beth is heard, while at the end of the verse aleph and beth are sounded together; aleph is twice heard at the beginning of verse 3, followed by gimel and daleth together; then beth is twice heard, followed by daleth; then aleph and beth are taken up again in the characteristic word of the closing statement, followed by a word containing gimel; verse 4 begins with gimel, allows beth to be repeatedly heard, and sounds aleph at the beginning and end of the last clause. In these verses aleph has been heard ten times as a radical letter, beth seven times as such, gimel and daleth each twice; whereas tau has not been heard at all in the first two verses, and sin is not sounded until verse 3. The group

of letters from he to yodh is used with more restraint; he indeed begins and ends verse 5, and is often repeated in the verse, and vav is heard at the beginning or end of almost every word ; the thought of verse 6 is embodied in a word beginning with zayin and is twice repeated in synonyms beginning with hheth ; teth is heard at the beginning of verse 7, and the emphatic word that introduces the last clause begins with yodh. The first part of the poem issues in the exultant conclusion that wickedness will be overthrown, and the second part opens with the reiteration of this truth as the basis of prediction and exhortation (verses 8 and 9). Between the two and introductory to the second is a question suggestive of the folly of striving against Jehovah. In each passage the poet plays with the consecutive sounds kaph, lamedh, and mem, while the gist of the question begins with mem and ends with nun. In verses 9-12 the sounds of mem, nun, samekh, ayin, and tsadhe abound, indeed, are dominant notes. Pe is also heard, but quite subordinately and perhaps without intention on the prophet's part, although its occurrence gratifies the expectant ear. In verses 13 and 14 qoph, resh, shin, and tav are allowed prominence ; tav, shin, and resh at the end of consecutive syllables (beginning of verse 13), and shin, qoph, resh, qoph, tav at the beginning of syllables in the last four words of verse 14. Verse 15 shows resh in three consecutive words, followed by sin and shin in three consecutive words, and ending with the radical tau.

2. An ancestor of Christ, born scarcely three centuries earlier (Luke iii. 25). A. V. uses the Greek form of the name, Naum.

Nail.

1. The horny scale at the end of the finger (Deut. xxi. 12 ; Dan. iv. 33).

2. A tent pin (Judg. iv. 21), which was of large size and commonly made of wood. Those used to fasten the curtains of the tabernacle were of brass (Ex. xxvii. 19).

3. A pin, commonly of metal, used for driving into wood or other material to hold separate pieces together, or left projecting for hanging things on. It might be made of iron (1 Chron. xxii. 3), or of gold, or be gilded (2 Chron. iii. 9). It was sometimes driven between the stones of a wall (Ecclus. xxvii. 2). Idols were fastened securely in place by nails (Is. xli. 7 ; Jer. x. 4), and victims were often affixed to the cross by means of a nail driven through each hand and the feet (John xx. 25).

Na'in.

A town where our Lord raised to life the only son of a widow woman (Luke vii. 11-17). It is still called Nain, and is in the northwest corner of the eminence called Jebel Duhy, or Little Hermon, 2 miles west-southwest of En-dor, and 5 miles south-southeast of Nazareth. It is a small hamlet, little more

than a cluster of ruins; with ancient sepul-
chral caverns chiefly on the east of the village.

Na'ioth [habitations].

The quarter in Ramah where the prophets,
who gathered about Samuel to work under
his direction, dwelt as a community (1 Sam.
xix. 18–xx. 1).

The word occurs in this passage only. It
was not understood by the ancient translators, and was slightly altered by the Massoretes; hence the versions show confusion.
But in the Hebrew text itself there is no
wavering. The word is used six times, and
without variation. It has the nature of a
proper name, being without the article (xix.
23; xx. 1). It is either a feminine singular, of
archaic form like Ephrath and Zarephath (so
Septuagent in Vatican text and Lucian) or a
rarer formation like the noun *gazith ;* or else
it is a feminine plural, written defectively
because of the previous occurrence of vav,
and of the same type as *g^eviyyāh* or *r^evāyāh.*
It may be related to *nāveh,* habitation (2 Sam.
xv. 25; Job v. 3), or *nāvāh,* habitation (Job
viii. 6), as *r^evāyāh* is related to *rāveh* and
rāvāh ; or the relation may be that of *sāday,*
field, to *sādeh.* Accordingly, it is well to adhere to the common interpretation habitation or habitations; see PROPHETIC ASSO-
CIATIONS.

Name.

English names, such as James, Robert,
Anne, have a meaning, but it is known only
to those who have studied the etymology.
In biblical times it was different. The names
of persons were not only significant, but as a
rule everybody knew the meaning as soon
as the name was heard. Sarah, Jacob, Miriam,
Jehoshaphat, Martha, Rhoda, Dorcas were
intelligible to all.

The name was probably given by the
Hebrews on the eighth day after birth (Gen.
xvii. 12; xxi. 3, 4; Luke i. 59; ii. 21). The
child might be given the name of a natural
object; as Terah, wild goat, Leah, wild cow,
Jonah, dove, Tamar, palm tree, Tabitha,
gazelle. It might receive a name expressive
of its physical condition; for example,
Shiphrah, beauty; or of the parents' hope
regarding it, as Noah, rest (Gen. v. 29).
Some names were given prophetically, as
that of Jesus because he should be a saviour
(Mat. i. 21). Many names testified to the
piety or gratitude of the parents, as Simeon,
hearing (Gen. xxix. 33), or Nethaniah, Jehovah hath given, or Elizur, God is a rock. Others
were commemorative of national events, as
Ichabod (1 Sam. iv. 21); yet others were
family names (Luke i. 59–61; cp. iii. 23–38).
When character had developed, a new name
was sometimes given as expressive of it; as
Israel and Cephas. In the later period,
when several languages were spoken in Palestine, a name was often translated and the
person was known by two names, as Cephas
after the Aramaic and Peter after the Greek,

Thomas and Didymus, both names meaning
twin, Messiah and Christ, both meaning
anointed. At this time also names were
transformed, the Hebrew Jehohanan became
in Greek Joannes, and Joseph became Joses.

Surnames were lacking among the Hebrews; persons were designated by adding
to the personal name the name of their city,
as Jesus of Nazareth, Joseph of Arimathæa,
Mary Magdalene, Nahum the Elkoshite; or
by a statement of their descent, as Simon
son of Jonah; by their disposition, trade, or
other characteristic, as Simon Peter, Nathan
the prophet, Joseph the carpenter, Matthew
the publican, Simon the zealot, and Dionysius
the Areopagite. Every Roman had three
names; a *prænomen,* which was his personal
name and stood first, a *nomen,* which was that
of his *gens* or house and stood second, and a
cognomen or surname which was that of his
family and came last. Thus M. Antonius
Felix, the procurator, was Marcus of the
clan Antonia and the family called **Felix.**
Frequently only the nomen and cognomen
were given, the personal name being omitted; as Julius Cæsar, Pontius Pilate, Claudius
Lysias.

Name is often used in Hebrew in the sense
of revealed character and essence. God
swears by his great name to carry out his
purpose (Jer. xliv. 26), that is, he swears by
his attested power to accomplish his word.
The name of God which is excellent in all
the earth (Ps. viii. 1), is that expression of
his being which is exhibited in creation and
redemption. The name of the God of Jacob
which sets the king on high (Ps. xx. 1) is the
manifested power of Israel's God. The name
of God was in the angel which led Israel
through the wilderness (Ex. xxiii. 21), because in him the revealed might and majesty
of God himself dwelt. The name of God
dwelt in his sanctuary (2 Sam. vii. 13), the
place where he manifested himself. To
know the name of God is to witness the
manifestation of those attributes and apprehend that character which the name denotes
(Ex. vi. 3, with 7; 1 Kin. viii. 43; Ps. xci.
14; Is. lii. 6; lxiv. 2; Jer. xvi. 21).

Na-o'mi [pleasant].

Wife of Elimelech, Elimelech went with her
and his two sons to sojourn in Moab, because
famine prevailed in Judah. The sons married
Moabite women. Elimelech and his sons
died, and Naomi accompanied by her daughter-in-law Ruth returned to Bethlehem of
Judah (Ruth i.–iv.).

Na'phish, in A. V. once **Nephish** (1 Chron.
v. 19) [respiration].

Son of Ishmael (Gen. xxv. 15; 1 Chron. i.
31), and founder of a clan with which the
Israelite tribes east of the Jordan were at
one time in conflict (1 Chron. v. 18–22).

Naph'ta-li, in A. V. twice **Nephthalim**
(Mat. iv. 13, 15), once **Nepthalim** (Rev. vii.
6) [obtained by wrestling].

1. Sixth son of Jacob, and second by Bilhah, Rachel's maidservant. Rachel gave him this name because she had wrestled in prayer for God's favor and blessing (Gen. xxx. 8).

2. The tribe descended from Naphtali. It was subdivided into four great families which sprang from the four sons of Naphtali (Gen. xlvi. 24; Num. xxvi. 48, 49). The prince of the Naphtalite tribe early in the wilderness wanderings was Ahira, son of Enan (Num. i. 15; ii. 29; vii. 78, 83; x. 27): at a later period it was Pedahel, son of Ammihud (xxxiv. 28); its representative spy was Nahbi, son of Vophsi (xiii. 14). At the first census in the wilderness its fighting men were 53,400 (ii. 29, 30); at the second they were 45,400 (xxvi. 50). The tribe of Naphtali pitched on the north side of the tabernacle, beside those of Dan and Asher (ii. 29). Arrived in Canaan, they were one of the six tribes which stood upon mount Ebal to pronounce curses on transgressors of the law (Deut. xxvii. 13; cp. Josh. viii. 33). The territory allotted to them was in northern Palestine. It was bounded on the east by the upper Jordan and the sea of Galilee, on the south by Issachar and Zebulun, and on the west by Zebulun and Asher (Josh. xix. 34). It was a long, narrow strip of land, about 50 miles from north to south, and varying from about 10 to 15 from east to west. It is mostly mountainous (Josh. xx. 7), and is quite fertile. Its boundary ran by mount Tabor (xix. 34), and it numbered Ramah, Hazor, Kedesh, Iron, and Beth-anath among its fortified cities (36–38). The Gershonite Levites had three cities allotted them within its limits; they were Kedesh, Hammoth-dor, and Kartan. The first of them was a city of refuge (Josh. xx. 7; xxi. 6, 32; 1 Chron. vi. 62, 76). Up to the early period of the judges the Naphtalites had not succeeded in expelling the Canaanites from Beth-shemesh and Beth-anath; they had, however, made them tributary. The Naphtalites took a large share in the fighting under Deborah and Barak, being mentioned with Zebulun as having jeopardized their lives unto death in the high places of the field (Judg. iv. 6, 10; v. 18). They also responded to the summons to arms issued by Gideon (vi. 35; vii. 23). A thousand captains, with 37,000 fighting men, came to David at Hebron, to aid him in the contest with Ish-bosheth (1 Chron. xii. 34; cp. 40). Their ruler some time afterwards was Jerimoth, son of Azriel (xxvii. 19; cp. Ps. lxviii. 27). Ahimaaz was Solomon's purveyor in Naphtali (1 Kin. iv. 15). Hiram, not the Tyrian king, but the skillful worker in metal, was a widow's son of the tribe of Naphtali (vii. 14). The land of Naphtali was ravaged by Benhadad, king of Syria (1 Kin. xv. 20; 2 Chron. xvi. 4), and many of its inhabitants were subsequently carried into captivity by Tiglath-pileser, king of Assyria (2 Kin. xv. 29). To these calamities Isaiah alludes, and comforts the afflicted people by intimating in the name of the Lord that the territory now ravaged should one day receive special privilege, so that they who walked in darkness should see a great light (Is. ix. 1–7). This prophecy was fulfilled when our Lord made the region on which the invasion had fallen the special seat of his ministry (Mat. iv. 12–16). Chorazin, Capernaum, and Tiberias were within the limits of what had been Naphtali.

Naph'tu-him [plural of *naphtuḥi*].

A tribe of Egyptian descent, mentioned between the Libyans of Lower and the Pathrusim of Upper Egypt (Gen. x. 13; 1 Chron. i. 11). Ebers derives the name from *na-ptah*, the [people] of Ptah, or inhabitants of Middle Egypt, in the district about Memphis, the seat of Ptah's worship. Napata, an ancient capital of Ethiopia, on the Nile near the fourth cataract, has also been suggested.

Nap'kin. See HANDKERCHIEF.

Nar-cis'sus [the narcissus or daffodil].

A Roman, whose household was in the Lord and was greeted by Paul in his letter to the church (Rom. xvi. 11).

Nard. See SPIKENARD.

Na'sor. See HAZOR.

Na'than [he has given].

1. Son of Attai, and father of Zabad, belonging to the house of Jerahmeel, family of Hezron, tribe of Judah (1 Chron. ii. 36).

2. A distinguished prophet in the reign of David and Solomon. The proposal to build the temple was submitted to him by David. At first he was favorable to the project, but afterwards received a message from the Lord directing that not David, but his successor was to have the honor of building the holy house (2 Sam. vii. 1–17; 1 Chron. xvii. 1–15). Nathan was afterwards sent to David to bring him to a sense of his great sin in the matter of Uriah the Hittite. This the prophet did by the parable of the ewe lamb (2 Sam. xii. 1–15; cp. Ps. li. title). In his official capacity as prophet of the Lord he named the young Solomon Jedidiah (2 Sam. xii. 25). With his and Gad's concurrence, or possibly at their instigation, David arranged the musical service for the sanctuary (2 Chron. xxix. 25). When Adonijah aspired to the throne in lieu of Solomon, he sent no intimation of his intention to Nathan, believing probably that the prophet was too loyal to David to be seduced from his allegiance (1 Kin. i. 8–10). Nathan advised Bathsheba to go at once and tell David what had occurred, arranging that he would come in and confirm her words. The plan was carried out, and David gave orders to Zadok the priest, Nathan the prophet, and Benaiah, chief of the bodyguard, to proclaim Solomon (11–45). Nathan wrote a history in which he described the reign of David and part at least of that of Solomon (1 Chron. xxix. 29; 2 Chron. ix. 29).

3. The father of one and brother of another of David's mighty men (2 Sam. xxiii.
36 ; 1 Chron. xi. 38) ; see IGAL.

4. The third of those children of David
who were born in Jerusalem (2 Sam. v. 14).
He, or possibly the prophet, was father of
Solomon's officials, Azariah and Zabud (1
Kin. iv. 5). His family is mentioned in Zech.
xii. 12. Through him David and Jesus Christ
are connected by natural lineage (Luke iii.
31) ; while it is through Solomon that Joseph,
the husband of Mary, is connected with
David (Mat. i. 6).

5. A chief man with Ezra at the brook of
Ahava (Ezra viii. 16).

6. A son of Bani, induced by Ezra to put
away his foreign wife (Ezra x. 39).

Na-than'a-el [God hath given].

A native of Cana in Galilee, whom Jesus
declared to be an Israelite indeed in whom
was no guile. His attention was directed by
Philip to Jesus as the Messiah of O. T. prophecy. But as Nazareth is not mentioned in
O. T. prophecy and besides had a questionable reputation, he felt difficulty in accepting the Messianic claims of one who had
been brought up in that town; but he at
once yielded to the evidence which the superhuman knowledge of Jesus furnished
(John i. 45–51). He was in the boat with
Simon Peter when the miraculous draught
of fishes was brought in (xxi. 2). The name
does not occur in the lists of the apostles given
in the first three gospels, but he was probably the same person as Bartholomew.

Other persons of the name are mentioned
in O. T., but there the original Hebrew form
is used. See NETHANEL.

Na-than-me'lech [the king hath given].

A chamberlain who lived in Josiah's time
within the precincts of the temple (2 Kin.
xxiii. 11).

Na'um. See NAHUM 2.

Naz-a-rene' [belonging to Nazareth].

1. One born or resident in Nazareth (Mat.
ii. 23 ; R. V. of xxvi. 71 ; Mark xvi. 6). In
Is. xi. 1 the Messiah is called *neṣer* or shoot
out of the roots of Jesse ; an offspring of the
royal family indeed, but of that family shorn
of its glory and reduced to its original humble condition. He is frequently called the
Branch also (Jer. xxiii. 5 ; xxxiii. 15 ; Zech.
iii. 8 ; vi. 12). On the most probable interpretation of Mat. ii. 23, the evangelist sees a
fulfillment of Isaiah's prophecy in the providence which led the parents of Jesus to take
up their residence in Nazareth again and resulted in Jesus being a Nazarene. If Nazareth means protectress or guardian, Matthew
finds the fulfillment merely in the similarity
of sound and in the low esteem in which the
town and its inhabitants were held ; but if
the name is derived from the same root as
neṣer (see NAZARETH), then Matthew finds
the fulfillment in the meaning chiefly (Mat.
xxvi. 71, R. V. ; Mark xvi. 6, R. V.).

2. An adherent of the religion founded by
Jesus ; a Christian. It is used contemptuously (Acts xxiv. 5).

Naz'a-reth [verdant, offshoot; or perhaps
protectress (see below)].

A town of Galilee (Mat. ii. 23), where
Joseph and Mary lived (Luke ii. 39), and
where Jesus was brought up (iv. 16) and
spent the greater part of thirty years (iii. 23
with Mark i. 9). He was accordingly known
as Jesus of Nazareth (Mat. xxi. 11 ; Mark i.
24). He was held in favor there (Luke ii.
52 ; iv. 16) ; but after he entered on his mission, he was twice rejected by his fellow
townsmen (iv. 28–31 ; cp. Mat. iv. 13 ; and
xiii. 54–58 ; Mark vi. 1–6). Nazareth stood
upon a hill (Luke iv. 29). The town was
either small and unimportant or of recent
origin ; for it is not mentioned in the O. T.
or in the Apocrypha or by Josephus. It is
still called en-Nâṣirah. It lies in a secluded
valley in Lower Galilee, a little north of the
great plain of Esdraelon, and is about 15
miles west-southwest of Tiberias, 20 southwest of Tell Hum, the reputed site of Capernaum, and 19 southeast of Acre. The valley is
about a mile from east to west and, on an
average, a quarter of a mile from north to
south. The hill on the northwest rises about
500 feet above the valley, and is cut into
ravines on its eastern slope. On that eastern
declivity stands the village of Nazareth.
The houses are better than those in many
other villages in Palestine, being made of
the white limestone which is conspicuously
displayed along all the higher parts of the
investing hills. They are prettily situated
among fig trees, olive trees, and some cypresses, while down below in the valley are
gardens surrounded by hedges of prickly
pear. In the midst of the gardens is the
fountain of the Virgin, from which Nazareth
derives its water, and whither doubtless
Mary frequently went to obtain water for
her household. Nazareth now contains 4000
or more inhabitants. A considerable majority of them belong to the Greek church ; a
smaller proportion are Roman Catholics ;
about one-fifth of all the inhabitants are
Mohammedans, and there are also a number
of Protestants. There is a fine Franciscan
convent. The monks point out many sacred
sites in Nazareth, but only the fountain of
the Virgin rests on good evidence. The site
of the attempted precipitation was probably
near the Maronite church, where there are
two or three bare scarps, 20, 30, 40, or 50
feet high.

The name Nazareth is written in several
forms in the manuscripts of the N. T. Nazareth and Nazaret are the best attested, but
the Alexandrian text has Nazarath, and in
Mat. iv. 13 and Luke iv. 16 the Sinaitic and
Vatican texts have Nazara. The different
forms probably represent popular variations
of the name in Palestine itself; the town

View of the town of Nazareth.

The traditional site of Mary's Well in Nazareth. The well itself is located inside the adjacent Greek Orthodox Church of the Annunciation.

having been called in Aramaic Nâs^{e}ra', or with the feminine ending t (th) retained, as was frequently the case in the names of towns (Zarephath, Daberath, Bozkath, Timnath), and pronounced under Hebrew influence, Nâsereth (cp. Aramaic *'igg^{e}ra'* and *'iggereth*, a letter). As thus explained, the word is a feminine participle. It is rare for the Semitic sound ṣ to be represented by z in Greek, as this explanation of Nazareth requires; but it is not unparalleled (cp. Zilpah, Hebrew *Ṣilpah*, Greek *Zelpha*). The Syriac preserves ṣ, using the form *Nâṣ^{e}rath*. The Arabs who conquered the country heard the emphatic sibilant and perpetuated the name in the form en-Nâṣirah. The Arabic name signifies helper or victor. The derivation of the original name is frequently sought in the Hebrew root *naṣar*, watch, protect, guard, so that Nazareth means protectress or guardian. But this root in Aramaic, including Syriac, is *n^{e}ṭar*. Probably, therefore, the name Nazareth is derived from the root which appears in Hebrew *neṣer* and Aramaic *niṣra'*, sprout (Targum, Job xxxi. 8), Nazareth accordingly signifying verdant place or offshoot.

Naz′i-rite, in A. V. **Nazarite** [separated, consecrated (to God)].

A person, male or female, who was specially consecrated to God. Nazirites probably existed of old among the Hebrews, but their mode of life was brought under the regulations of the law at Sinai. The Nazirite vowed to separate himself unto the Lord for a certain specified period. He did not, however, become a hermit; he continued to live in human society. Nor was he necessarily an ascetic. By the law he must not drink wine or strong drink nor eat any product of the vine during the days of his separation; for from the time of the nomadic patriarchs the vine was the symbol of a settled life and culture, which were quite right in themselves, but were removed from the ancient simplicity of life and manners. See JONADAB. Nor must the Nazirite shave his head. The long hair was the visible sign of his consecration to God; the hair was the glory of the head and the product of the body he had devoted to God; and the cutting of the hair, which God made grow, was popularly regarded as rendering the head in a measure common (cp. Ex. xx. 25; Num. xix. 2; Deut. xv. 19). Finally, the Nazirite must not render himself ceremonially unclean by touching a dead body, even if the corpse should be that of a near relative. When the time approached for his vow to expire, he appeared before the priest, made certain prescribed offerings, shaved off his hair and burned it, after which he might again drink wine (Num. vi. 1–21). One might be a Nazirite for life instead of for a limited period, and might be dedicated to that mode of existence at or even before his birth. This was the case

with Samson (Judg. xiii. 4, 5) and with Samuel (1 Sam. i. 11, 28). Samson, however, permitted deviations from not only the law of the Nazirite, but at the same time from other laws and ancient customs and the dictates of refinement. In the time of Amos profane people tempted the Nazirites to break their vow of total abstinence from wine, even offering it to them to drink (Amos ii. 11, 12). After the exile Nazirites became comparatively numerous (1 Mac. iii. 49; War ii. 15, 1). John the Baptist was consecrated a Nazirite from his birth (Luke i. 15). The prophetess Anna was not unlikely a Nazirite (ii. 36, 37). It seems to have been the Nazirite vow that Paul was induced to take to allay the storm which his friends saw to be gathering against him on his last visit to Jerusalem (Acts xxi. 20–26). Wealthy persons often bore the legal expenses of poor Nazirites (Antiq. xix. 6, 1).

Ne′ah [emotion].

A place on the boundry line of Zebulun (Josh. xix. 13). Site unknown.

Ne-ap′o-lis [new city].

The seaport of Philippi, and the first place in Europe at which Paul touched (Acts xvi. 11; implied also in xx. 6). It was situated on the Strymonian Gulf, 10 miles east-southeast of Philippi. It is now called Kavalla, and is a Turkish city with Greek and Roman ruins in its vicinity.

Ne-a-ri′ah [perhaps, Jehovah hath shaken out (cp. Neh. v. 13; Ex. xiv. 27)].

1. A Simeonite captain, who took part in a successful war against the Amalekites near mount Seir during the reign of Hezekiah (1 Chron. iv. 42).

2. A descendant of Shecaniah (1 Chron. iii. 22, 23).

Ne′bai. See NOBAI.

Ne-ba′ioth, in A. V. of Genesis **Nebajoth** [to the Hebrew ear probably high places].

A tribe descended from Ishmael (Gen. xxv. 13, 16; xxviii. 9; xxxvi. 3; 1 Chron. i. 29) and rich in flocks (Is. lx. 7). In the seventh century before Christ the Assyrians report the tribe in Arabia, and mention it, as does the Old Testament, in connection with Kedar. The letters th (=tau) make doubtful its identity with the Nabataeans (t=teth), who, as early as the fourth century before Christ, took possession of mount Seir, and spread thence northeastward into the country east of the Jordan (1 Mac. v. 25; ix. 35) as far as the Hauran and Damascus (Antiq. xiii. 15, 2). The entire country from the Euphrates to the Ælanitic gulf of the Red Sea became known as Nabatene (Antiq. i. 12, 4). They were conquered by Pompey in 62 B.C., and in A.D. 105 Trajan converted their kingdom into a Roman province. Their capital was Petra, the ancient Sela. One of their kings, Aretas, is mentioned in 2 Cor. xi. 32.

Ne-bal'lat.

A town of Benjamin inhabited after the captivity (Neh. xi. 34), now Beit Nebâla, about 4 miles northeast of Lydda and 1½ north of el-Haditheh, *i. e.* Hadid, and west by north of Bethel.

Ne'bat [look, aspect].

Father of Jeroboam I. (1 Kin. xi. 26).

Ne'bo [as name of a deity, is Semitic Babylonian *Nabû*, announcer ; as a geographical name it may indicate that the place was a seat of Nebo's worship, or correspond to Arabic *naba'*, and denote elevation].

1. A Babylonian god (Is. xlvi. 1), who presided over knowledge and literature. The special seat of his worship was at Borsippa, near Babylon. In Isaiah's time images of Nebo were used as objects of worship (Is. xlvi. 1).

2. A peak of the Abarim mountains over against Jericho (Num. xxxiii. 47 ; Deut. xxxii. 49), and the summit, apparently, of Pisgah (Deut. xxxiv. 1). Its probable site is Jebel Neba, 8 miles east of the mouth of the river Jordan. From its summit, especially from the elevation called Ras Siaghah, there are visible in the clear atmosphere of spring Hermon, at the foot of which lay Dan ; and the mountains of Naphtali ; and the hill country of Ephraim and Judah, which are bounded, and at Carmel washed by, the hinder sea ; and the depression which marks the south country ; and the Dead Sea and the Jordan valley.

3. A Moabite town near or on mount Nebo (Num. xxxii. 3). It was rebuilt by the Reubenites (xxxii. 37, 38 ; xxxiii. 47 ; cp. 1 Chron. v. 8), but came again into Moabite hands (Moabite Stone, 14 ; Is. xv. 2 ; Jer. xlviii. 1, 22). The site is generally believed to be marked by the ruins which are called Nebbeh, and are situated 6 miles southwest of Heshbon.

4. A town mentioned just after Bethel and Ai (Ezra ii. 29 ; Neh. vii. 33). Not identified. Neither Beit Nûba, 13 miles westsouthwest of Bethel, nor Nûba, about 7 miles northwest by north of Hebron, is etymologically identical with it.

Neb-u-chad-rez'zar and **Nebuchadnezzar** [*Nabu-kudurri-uṣur*, Nebo, defend the boundary]. The two forms represent different Hebrew methods of reproducing the name.

Son of Nabopolassar and king of Babylon. His father headed a successful revolt of the Babylonians against Assyria and founded the Babylonian empire in 625 B. C. Pharaoh-necho, who ascended the throne of Egypt in 610 B. C., finding the power of Assyria weakened, led an army to the Euphrates in order to protect Egyptian interests (2 Kin. xxiii. 29 ; 2 Chron. xxxv. 20). But Nineveh, the capital of Assyria, was taken by wild Manda, the allies of Nabopolassar, 612 or 606 B. C., and the Egyptians had to reckon with the new claimants of the Assyrian dependencies.

Nabopolassar sent his son Nebuchadnezzar to meet them. The prince defeated them in 605 B. C. with great slaughter at the battle of Carchemish, drove them back to their own land, and subjugated the intervening regions (2 Kin. xxiv. 7 ; Jer. xlvi. 2). But news arrived that his father was dead. Committing affairs in the west to his generals, he hastened back to Babylon and ascended the throne in 605 B. C. (con. Apion. i. 19). Information regarding his reign is derived chiefly from the Jewish sacred writers, including Nebuchadnezzar's contemporaries Jeremiah, Ezekiel, and Daniel, supplemented by notices on inscribed bricks, and the statements of the Babylonian historian Berosus, who lived about 250 years after Nebuchadnezzar. After its subjection, Judah rendered tribute to him for three years and then revolted (2 Kin. xxiv. 1). Nebuchadnezzar returned to Palestine after a while, suppressed the revolt, threw one king in fetters, presently ordered the new king to be carried captive to Babylon, and placed yet another king on the throne (2 Chron. xxxvi. 6, 10) ; see JEHOIAKIM, JEHOIACHIN, ZEDEKIAH. Zedekiah remained professedly loyal for about eight years ; in the ninth year he struck for independence, being assisted by the advance of an Egyptian army (Jer. xxxvii. 5). The ultimate result was that Jerusalem was besieged and taken, 587 B. C., the temple burnt, and the leading inhabitants of the capital and the country carried into captivity (2 Kin. xxiv. ; xxv. ; 2 Chron. xxxvi. 5–21 ; Jer. xxxix. : lii.). About this time, probably in the seventh year of the Tyrian king Ithobalos and not of Nebuchadnezzar, Nebuchadnezzar began the siege of Tyre, which lasted thirteen years (Ezek. xxix. 18 ; con. Apion. i. 21 ; Antiq. x. 11, 1). In his twenty-third year, 582 B. C., he warred against Cœlesyria, Moab, and Ammon, and deported several hundred Jews (Jer. lii. 30 ; Antiq. x. 9, 7). Afterwards he chastised Egypt for the part it had taken in the Jewish war. About 572 B. C. he invaded Egypt (cp. Ezek. xxix. 19), and in his thirty-seventh year, 569 or 568 B. C., he again led his army against the Egyptians. It is probable that Nebuchadnezzar carried on other military campaigns, though the record of them is lost. He acted on the policy of transporting the inhabitants of conquered countries to other parts of the empire, and had thus at command much servile labor, which enabled him to carry out important works. He built the great wall of Babylon, erected a magnificent palace for himself, and repaired the great temple of Merodach at Babylon, the temple of Nebo at Borsippa, and many other sanctuaries. He is said to have built hanging gardens to remind his wife Amuhia of her native Median hills (con. Apion. i. 19 ; Antiq. x. 11, 1), and to have constructed near Sippara a huge reservoir for irrigation, reputed to have been 140 miles in circumference and 180 feet in depth, besides canals across the land, and quays and breakwaters on the Persian Gulf. The form of madness from which he suffered when pride overthrew his reason was that called lycanthropy, in which the patient fancies himself one of the inferior animals, and acts as such. Nebuchadnezzar imagined that he had become an ox, and went forth to eat grass like other cattle (Dan. iv.). He reigned more than forty-three years and died after a brief illness in the year 562 B. C., leaving his son Evil-merodach to ascend the throne.

Neb-u-shaz'ban, in A. V. **Nebushasban** [*Nabu-shizibanni*, Nebo, save me].

A Babylonian prince who held the office of rab-saris under Nebuchadnezzar (Jer. xxxix. 13).

Neb-u-zar-a'dan [*Nabu-zir-iddina*, Nebo hath given offspring].

The captain of the guard in the army of Nebuchadnezzar, which captured Jerusalem. He was chief in command of the troops which completed the destruction of the city and burnt the temple (2 Kin. xxv. 8-11, 18-21; Jer. xxxix. 9, 10; lii. 12-30; cp. xli. 10; xliii. 6). To the prophet Jeremiah, who had recommended his countrymen to submit to the Babylonians, he, by express orders from the victorious sovereign, showed all kindness (Jer. xxxix. 11-14; xl. 1-5). Five years later he deported a body of Jews (lii. 30).

Ne'co and **Necoh**, in A. V. **Necho** and **Nechoh** [Egyptian *Neku, Nekau, Nekhao*]. See PHARAOH.

Nec'ro-man-cy. See FAMILIAR SPIRIT and WIZARD.

Ned-a-bi'ah [Jehovah hath impelled or is bountiful].

A son of king Jeconiah (1 Chron. iii. 18).

Nee'dle.

A sharp instrument required for embroidering and sewing (cp. Ex. xxxv. 35; Ecc. iii. 7; Mark ii. 21). The eye was called simply the hole (Mat. xix. 24, Greek). Fancy a camel trying to go through the eye of a needle! Yet this extreme suggestion aptly illustrates the difficulty, or rather impossibility, for them that trust in riches to enter into the kingdom of God (Mark x. 24-26).

Ne'geb, The [dry].

The grazing region lying a few miles south of Hebron (Gen. xviii. 1 with xx. 1; Num. xiii. 22); called in R. V. the South (Gen. xii. 9, R. V. margin). As a physical division of the country, it contrasted with the hill country, the lowland, and the Arabah (Josh. x. 40; xii. 8). The northern part of it was allotted to the tribes of Judah and Simeon (xv. 21-32; xix. 1-9). Notable places in it were Kadesh-barnea (Gen. xx. 1), Beer-lahai-roi (xxiv. 62), Beer-sheba (Josh. xv. 28), Ziklag (xv. 31), and Arad (Num. xxi. 1).

Neg'i-nah and plural **Neginoth** [playing on a stringed instrument; a stringed instrument].

A musical term occurring in the title of many psalms, where it denotes a stringed instrument, and is so rendered in R. V. (Ps. lxi.). Elsewhere the word often means song music.

Ne-hel'a-mite.

The designation of the false prophet Shemaiah (Jer. xxix. 24). It may be derived from his native place or from an ancestor, it is uncertain which. On the margin of the A. V. it is rendered dreamer.

Ne-he-mi'ah [Jehovah hath consoled].

1. One of the chief men who returned with Zerubbabel from Babylon (Ezra ii. 2; Neh. vii. 7).

2. Son of Azbuk and ruler of half the district of Beth-zur. He repaired part of the wall of Jerusalem (Neh. iii. 16).

3. A Jew of the captivity, son of Hachaliah (Neh. i. i). He was discharging his duty of cupbearer to Artaxerxes Longimanus, king of Persia, when the king observed that he looked sad, and questioned him as to the cause of his sorrow. Nehemiah frankly told him it was the state of ruin in which the city of his fathers' sepulchers, Jerusalem, was lying. He therefore begged permission to go and build again the wall of the city. The king accorded him an escort of cavalry for the journey, gave him letters commending him to the different Persian governors by the way, and appointed him governor of Judah, as Zerubbabel had been (Neh. i. 1-ii. 9; v. 14). He arrived at Jerusalem in the twentieth year of Artaxerxes' reign, 445 B. C. Ezra the priest was then at the Jewish capital, having come from Babylonia thirteen years previously. Nehemiah, on reaching the capital, made a journey by night around the city and viewed the ruined walls. He now intimated to the people his intention of rebuilding the walls, and solicited their active aid. They gave it with good will, each notable man undertaking a part of the wall (Neh. iii.). The neighboring gentile tribes did not like to hear that Jerusalem was being rebuilt, and three of their representatives, Sanballat, the Horonite, Tobiah, an Ammonite, and Geshem, an Arab, put forth active efforts to stop the building. But they could neither circumvent nor intimidate Nehemiah, who resolutely held on his course. The builders also guarded against sudden attack by working with one hand while with the other they carried a weapon (ii. 10; iv.-vi.; Ecclus. xlix. 13). The wall was rebuilt in fifty-two days (vi. 15), in the year 445 B. C., 70 years after the temple had been completed. Attention was next turned to the instruction of the people (viii.), and a religious revival followed, which led to all the leading men, both of priests and people, sealing with Nehemiah a covenant to worship Jehovah (ix., x.). After governing Judah for twelve years, Nehemiah, in 433 B. C., returned to Susa. He

asked for further leave of absence (xiii. 6), and, returning to Jerusalem, seems to have governed it for the remainder of his life, trying to enforce the law of Moses against all who in any way departed from its provisions (xiii. 8–31). Josephus states that he died at a great age (Antiq. xi. 5, 8). A successor, Bagohi by name, was in office in 411 B. C. (Elephantine papyri). For his connection with the formation of the canon, see CANON.

The Book of Nehemiah stands in the Hagiographa, or third division of the Hebrew Scriptures, immediately after Ezra and before Chronicles. In counting the books of Scripture, the Jews reckoned Ezra and Nehemiah as one book; see EZRA.

Nehemiah, informed of the wretched condition of Jerusalem (i), obtains permission of the Persian king Artaxerxes to visit Jerusalem temporarily as a royal commissioner (ii.; cp. 6). He incites the people to rebuild the walls (17). The names of the builders (iii.). He finds it necessary to arm the builders because of the opposition of the Samaritans (iv.). While the wall is in process of construction he corrects abuses among the people (v.). The wall is finished notwithstanding all attempts of Sanballat and Tobiah to terrify Nehemiah, and the secret aid furnished these foreigners by nobles of Judah (vi.). The city being large, but the population scanty, Nehemiah desires to increase the number of the inhabitants (vii. 4). To this end he gathers together the nobles, the rulers, and the people with the view first of reckoning them by genealogy and then of drafting some to dwell in Jerusalem. The register of them that came up at the first with Zerubbabel (vii. 6–73). It is the register of Ezra ii. 1–70. Before the registration was accomplished, the seventh month arrived, which brought the populace to Jerusalem to the feast. The people ask that the law of Moses be read. The reading results in, first, their building booths in which to dwell during the feast (viii.), and, second, in repentance of their sins and of their guilt in intermarriage with foreigners (ix.). They subscribe or seal a covenant to obey God's law and to abstain from intermarriage with the heathen. A list of those who sealed (x.). These religious acts having been performed, the original intention of making a registration of the people and securing additional inhabitants for the city is carried out. Lots are cast to draft one in ten from the country people to dwell in Jerusalem in addition to those already inhabiting the city (xi. 1, 2). A list of the families who dwelt at Jerusalem (3–24). A list of the priests and Levites who returned at the first with Zerubbabel (xii. 1–9). List of high priests from Jeshua to Jaddua (10, 11). A list of the heads of the priestly houses in the generation after the return (12–21). A list of the heads of the Levites at the same time and shortly after

(22–26). The dedication of the wall (27 seq.) In the interval during which Nehemiah was absent at the Persian court abuses had grown up: the Levites had been illy provided for (xiii. 10), the law of the Sabbath was observed with laxity (15), and intermarriages with foreigners had not entirely ceased (23). These abuses Nehemiah corrected.

Not only does the title assign the authorship of the book to Nehemiah (i. 1), but throughout the book Nehemiah speaks in the first person, except (1) when state documents and their dockets are inserted (x. 1; xii. 26); (2) incidentally in the midst of the account of Ezra's religious work, where the presence of Nehemiah as civil governor lending his official sanction; with other persons of authority, is briefly recorded (viii. 9; and (3) after an allusion to the days of David and Asaph and to the days of Zerubbabel, the days of Nehemiah are mentioned (xii. 47). In this last-mentioned passage the third person was in better taste in this connection than the first person would have been; and besides, the passage is a retrospect, taken after Nehemiah's return from the Persian court, and refers to what took place during the twelve years of his former administration.

It is universally admitted that Nehemiah wrote the main portion of the book. And the prayer of ix. 6–38, which in the Septuagint is introduced by the words, "and Ezra said," and which in fact bears traces of being an utterance of Ezra (cp. 10 with Ezra ix. 7, 15; 30 with Ezra ix. 1, 2, 11; and 8, 36 with Ezra ix. 9, 15), would be properly inserted without change of phraseology by Nehemiah in his historical work. But the narrative in viii. 9 and x. 1 gives to Nehemiah the title of Tirshatha. Tirshatha is doubtless the Persian equivalent of *peḥah*, governor (Ezra ii. 63 with Hag. i. 1). The use of the third person in these and other passages is compatible with the theory of Nehemiah's authorship; but the title of Tirshatha given him is not so readily explained on the supposition that Nehemiah wrote the passages, for he elsewhere styles himself, and is referred to as, the *peḥah* (v. 14, 18; xii. 26). Most modern critics believe that traces of another hand are discernible. Still the use of the first person plural in x. 30, 32, 34, a part of the section viii.–x., suggests an eyewitness of the events. If another than Nehemiah had a hand in compiling the book, the question whether this writer was contemporary with Nehemiah or later depends chiefly upon whether the genealogies (xii. 10, 11, 22) are brought down to the reign of Darius Codomannus, king of Persia from 336 to 330 B. C., and to the high-priesthood of Jaddua, who was officiating when Alexander the Great visited Jerusalem (Antiq. xi. 8, 4). If they are brought down to this date, neither Nehemiah nor a contemporary could have penned the words; but if the references to Jaddua merely name him as a youth, and include him because he was the heir to the office of high priest, the passages easily fall within the lifetime of Nehemiah and the reign of Darius Nothus, king of Persia from 424 to 405 B. C. It will be observed that the enumeration of families is assigned to the time of Joiakim, son of Jeshua and great-great-grandfather of Jaddua (xii. 12, 26,, and the latest recorded events occurred in the generation before the high-priesthood of Jaddua (xii. 23; xiii. 28). The book was originally reckoned one with Ezra; see EZRA.

Ne'hi-loth [wind instruments] (Ps. v. title).

Ne'hum [consolation].
One of those who returned from the Babylonian captivity (Neh. vii. 7). Called in Ezra ii. 2 Rehum (cp. 3 Esdras v. 8), for which Nehum may be a copyist's error.

Ne-hush'ta [bronze].
Daughter of Elnathan of Jerusalem. She became the wife of Jehoiakim and mother of Jehoiachin (2 Kin. xxiv. 8).

Ne-hush'tan [piece of brass]. See BRAZEN SERPENT.

Ne-i'el.
A frontier village of Asher (Josh. xix. 27). Not identified. Perhaps the same as Neah (13).

Ne'keb [a hollow, perhaps a pass or a cavern].
A frontier village of Naphtali (Josh. xix. 33). The R. V. joins the name with the preceding word, calling the place Adami-nekeb. The Jerusalem Talmud calls Nekeb Siadatha. This name Conder finds lingering, in a corrupted form, in Seiyâdeh, a ruin 3½ miles west by north of the exit of the Jordan from the sea of Galilee. But see ADAMI-NEKEB.

Ne-ko'da [perhaps, distinguished, a herdman].
Founder of a family of Nethinim (Ezra ii. 48, 60).

Nem'u-el.
1. A Reubenite, brother of Dathan and Abiram (Num. xxvi. 9).
2. A son of Simeon (Num. xxvi. 12); see JEMUEL.

Ne'pheg [a sprout, an offshoot].
1. A Levite, family of Kohath, house of Izhar (Ex. vi. 21).
2. One of the sons born to David in Jerusalem (2 Sam. v. 15; 1 Chron. iii. 7; xiv. 6).

Neph'i-lim. See GIANT.

Ne'phish. See NAPHISH.

Neph'i-sim, or **Ne-phu'sim**; while in **Nephishesim** or **Nephushesim**, two spellings, one with sh, the other with s, are apparently combined in the same word [expanded ones].
A family of Nethinim (Ezra ii. 50; Neh. vii. 52), perhaps originally captives taken from the tribe Naphish (q. v.).

Neph'tha-lim. See NAPHTALI.

Neph'to-ah [an opening].
The fountain of the waters of Nephtoah (or by a slight change of the Hebrew text, fountain of Meneptah) was west of Jerusalem, on the boundary between Judah and Benjamin (Josh. xv. 9; xviii. 15). Name and location favor 'Ain Lifta, 2 miles N. W. of Jerusalem. Porter prefers 'Ain Yalo, 3 miles S. W. of Jerusalem. The Jerusalem Talmud identifies it with En Etam, and Conder suggests 'Ain 'Atan, 2½ miles S. W. of Bethlehem.

Ne-phu'she-sim and **Ne-phu'sim.** See NEPHISIM.

Nep'tha-lim. See NAPHTALI.

Ner [a lamp].
1. A Benjamite, son of Abiel and father of Abner (1 Sam. xiv. 51). He or Abner was Saul's uncle (50). If Abner was Saul's uncle, Ner was Saul's grandfather and identical with the following.
2. A Benjamite, son of Jeiel and father or remoter ancestor of Saul's father, Kish (1 Chron. viii. 33; ix. 35, 36). See KISH 2.

Ne're-us [a sea god who, under Poseidon or Neptune, ruled the Mediterranean Sea].
A Roman Christian to whom Paul sent a salutation (Rom. xvi. 15), not improbably the son of Philologus.

Ner'gal.
A heathen deity worshiped by the Babylonians (2 Kin. xvii. 30). The chief seat of his worship was Cuthah. He was ruler of the nether world, and god of war and pestilence; and was represented under the form of a colossal winged lion with a human face.

Ner-gal-sha-re'zer [Babylonian *Nergal-sharuṣur*, Nergal, protect the king].
One of Nebuchadnezzar's princes, who held the office of rab-mag (Jer. xxxix. 3, 13). He is supposed to be Nergalsharuṣur, known to the Greeks as Neriglissar or Nerigasolasar, who married a daughter of Nebuchadnezzar, murdered his brother-in-law Evil-merodach, and ascended the throne as the latter's successor (con. Apion. i. 20), reigning from 559 to 556 B. C.

Ne'ri.
An ancestor of Christ and somehow genealogically the father of Shealtiel (Luke iii. 27).

Ne-ri'ah [lamp of Jehovah].
Son of Maaseiah, and father of Baruch and Seraiah (Jer. xxxii. 12; xxxvi. 4; li. 59).

Net.
The net was used by the Hebrews in fowling (Prov. i. 17). Doubtless, as in Egypt, the clap net was used, a familiar form of which consisted of two half hoops or frames covered with netting and attached to a common axis. The trap was spread open flat, and the bait placed in the center. The motion of the bird at the bait released a spring, the two sides closed suddenly, and the bird was caught.
The net was also used in hunting (Is. li. 20). It was cast about the game (Job xix. 6)

or over it (Ezek. xii. 13; xix. 8), or laid to catch the feet (Ps. ix. 15; xxv. 15; lvii. 6; Lam. i. 13). Throughout the ancient world, as sculpture and narrative reveal, it was usual to extend nets on stakes so as to inclose a large space as by a fence, a single opening being left as an entrance. Through this gateway various kinds of game were driven, such as hares, boars, deer; and once within the inclosure, they were under control and easily dispatched. Small nets were used to close gaps between bushes or to bar a path. Purse nets were laid, that animals might run into them as into a tunnel and find no exit.

In fishing both drag nets (Hab. i. 15; Mat. xiii. 47, 48) and casting nets (iv. 18; John xxi. 6; Herod. i. 141) were used. The Hebrews were acquainted with the common drag net of Egypt (Is. xix. 8). It was quite large, its cords were made of flax, the lower edge was weighted with lead and sunk to the bottom of the river or sea, and the upper edge was floated by pieces of wood; see illustration, article FISHING. This form of net was widely used throughout the world (Homer, Odyssey xxii. 384–387; Pliny, Hist. Nat. xvi. 8, 13).

Ne'ta-im [plantings].

A place in Judah with royal plantations (1 Chron. iv. 23, R. V.).

Neth'a-nel, in A. V. **Ne-than'e-el** [God hath given]. The Greek form is Nathanael.

1. Prince of the tribe of Issachar at an early period of the wilderness wanderings (Num. i. 8; ii. 5; vii. 18, 23; x. 15).

2. Jesse's fourth son, and David's brother (1 Chron. ii. 14).

3. One of the priests who blew trumpets when the ark was brought up to the city of David (1 Chron. xv. 24).

4. A Levite, father of Shemaiah (1 Chron. xxiv. 6).

5. A son of Obed-edom in David's reign (1 Chron. xxvi. 4).

6. One of the princes whom Jehoshaphat sent to teach in the cities of Judah (2 Chron. xvii. 7).

7. A chief of the Levites in Josiah's reign (2 Chron. xxxv. 9).

8. A son of Pashhur, induced by Ezra to put away his foreign wife (Ezra x. 22).

9. A priest, head of the father's house of Jedaiah in the days of the high priest Joiakim (Neh. xii. 21).

10. A priest's son who blew a trumpet at the dedication of the wall of Jerusalem (Neh. xii. 36).

Neth-a-ni'ah [Jehovah has given].

1. A son of Asaph (1 Chron. xxv. 2), the head of the fifth course of singers (12).

2. A Levite sent with others by Jehoshaphat to teach in the cities of Judah (2 Chron. xvii. 8).

3. Father of Jehudi (Jer. xxxvi. 14).

4. Father of that Ishmael who assassinated Gedaliah (2 Kin. xxv. 23, 25).

Neth'i-nim, in A. V. **Nethinims** [given].

Temple servants or slaves given by David and the princes for the service of the Levites (Ezra viii. 20). Prior to their appointment, similar functions seem to have been discharged by the Midianites, whom Moses gave over to the Levites (Num. xxxi. 47), and at a subsequent period by the Gibeonites, whom Joshua assigned as hewers of wood and drawers of water for the house of God (Josh. ix. 23). Even after the Nethinim were associated with them or superseded them, the number of the Nethinim may have been too small for the elaborate temple services instituted by David's son and successor, and been increased; for we find in the books of Ezra (ii. 55–58) and Nehemiah (vii. 57–60) the children of Solomon's servants, i. e. slaves, mentioned after and numbered with the Nethinim. Although they were organized by David, it was probably under a different name; for the word Nethinim occurs only in the books of Ezra and Nehemiah, with a solitary passage in 1 Chronicles (ix. 2). They discharged the more menial duties required by the temple worship. Of the Nethinim and the children of Solomon's servants, 392 returned from captivity with Zerubbabel (Ezra ii. 58; Neh. vii. 60), and 220 more with Ezra (Ezra viii. 17–20). The Nethinim seem to have been naturalized foreigners rather than people of true Israelite descent (1 Chron. ix. 2; Ezra ii. 59; Neh. vii. 61), and several of the names on the list of their leading men have a foreign aspect (Ezra ii. 43–54; Neh. vii. 46–56). They were probably descendants of the Midianites and Gibeonites, who have been already mentioned, and of various bands of captives taken in war; they continued to be designated by the name of the prince or tribe from whom they were taken, as the children of Sisera, of Rezin, of Meunim, and of Nephisim (Ezra ii. 48, 50, 53; with 1 Chron. v. 19–21; 2 Chron. xxvi. 7). The children of Tabbaoth and Keros, and of Solomon's servants the children of the Sophereth (Ezra ii. 43, 44, 55), which mean the children of the rings, of the weaver's comb, and of the scribal office, apparently denote the official duties in the temple which the men of these classes discharged. Other names are those of progenitors; and yet others seem to be the names of the native places of the captives, as perhaps Nekoda, Harhur, Harsha (ver. 48, 51, 52). Some of them lived on Ophel, a southern prolongation of the temple hill (Neh. iii. 26, 31; xi. 3, 21), others in the villages round about Jerusalem (Ezra ii. 70; Neh. vii. 73). Holding an official position at the temple, although the office was menial, they were exempt from imperial taxation (Ezra vii. 24). They seem to have adopted with some cordiality the covenant made at the instance of Nehemiah to worship Jehovah. (Neh. x. 28, 29).

Ne-to'phah [dropping, falling in drops].

A town of Judah, evidently near Bethlehem (1 Chron. ii. 54); Ezra ii. 21, 22; Neh. vii. 26). It was the home of two of David's mighty men (2 Sam. xxiii. 28, 29). Netophathites with Seraiah at their head were among the men who assembled loyally about Gedaliah, whom Nebuchadnezzar had made governor of Judah on the fall of Jerusalem (2 Kin. xxv. 23; Jer. xl. 8 seq.). Fifty-six of the town's people returned after the exile (Ezra ii. 22). It was not originally assigned to the Levites, but after the return its dependent villages were occupied by certain of them, including singers (1 Chron. ix. 16; Neh. xii. 28). On the survey map it is located, with a query, at the ruin Umm Tôba, the Om Tûba of Tobler, and the Antûbeh of Van de Velde, 2 miles northeast of Bethlehem. Beit Nettíf has also been suggested. It stands on a rocky crest, 12 miles west of Bethlehem. The distance seems rather great. Neither Umm Tôba nor Beit Nettíf is the true counterpart etymologically of Netophah.

Ne-to′pha-thite, in A.V. of Neh. xii. 28 **Netophathi**, the Hebrew form being preserved. An inhabitant of Netophah (2 Sam. xxiii. 28).

Net′tle.

1. The rendering of the Hebrew *Ḥarul*, burning plant, one that inflames. Men driven by want take refuge under it (Job xxx. 7). Along with the stinging nettle, Hebrew *kimm⁶shon*, it overspreads the sluggard's unweeded garden (Prov. xxiv. 31). In fact it springs up everywhere when cultivation of the land is neglected (Zeph. ii. 9). The plant cannot be identified R. V. places wild vetches on the margin.

2. The rendering of the Hebrew *Ḳimmosh* in Is. xxxiv. 13 and Hos. ix. 6. The rabbinical idea that the plant is a nettle has been generally adopted. The Roman or pill nettle (*Urtica pilulifera*) is found everywhere in Palestine. The Hebrew word itself is probably more general in signification and comprehends a large class of weeds. A modification of the word is *ḳimm⁶shon* (Prov. xxiv. 31), which the English versions render thorns.

New Moon. See MOON.

New Tes′ta-ment.

The second of the two portions into which the Bible is naturally divided. Testament represents the Latin word *testamentum*, which is used to translate the Greek word *diathēkē*, covenant (2 Cor. iii. 14). The N. T. embodies the new covenant of which Jesus was the Mediator (Heb. ix. 15; cp. x. 16, 17 and Jer. xxxi. 31–34). The first covenant was dedicated with blood (Heb. ix. 19, 20), but was in no sense a testament: the second, while primarily a covenant was also a testament; that is, it was not merely dedicated with blood, but it required the death of the testator to give it force. It would not have had proper efficacy had not Jesus its Mediator died an atoning death.

With the possible exception of Matthew's Gospel, the books of the N. T. were written in Greek. This language had taken deep root in Palestine during the more than three centuries which had elapsed since the conquest of the Holy Land by Alexander the Great; and the merits of the language itself and that of the literature which it enshrined, had given it the widest currency among educated men throughout the Roman empire, though Greece had now for a considerable time lost its political independence.

The original manuscripts of the books of the N. T. and the copies made during the first three centuries have disappeared. Papyrus, which was commonly used for letters (2 John 12), soon wore out, and in the time of Diocletian, A. D. 303, it was customary for the persecutors of Christians to seek for copies of the Scriptures and destroy them. The art of printing was unknown, but transcribers laboriously multiplied copies. The four gospels were most frequently transcribed, and after them the epistles of Paul. The Revelation was copied least often. No fewer than 3791 ancient manuscript copies of the N. T. in whole or in part exist, their abundance markedly contrasting with the small number of the classical writers which have come down to our own day.

Corruptions of the text soon crept in. Copyists were fallible, careless, and often imperfectly acquainted with Greek. Men of the patristic age and later were not governed by the modern demand for scientific exactness, and they handled the text with considerable license. They attempted to improve the grammar and the style, to correct supposed errors in history and geography, to adjust the quotations from the O. T. to the Greek of the Septuagint, and to harmonize the gospels. They incorporated marginal notes, and they added to the gospel narratives incidents obtained from authentic sources, as John vii. 53–viii. 1 and Mark xvi. 9–20. The various readings which thus originated are very numerous. They number 150,000. Nineteen-twentieths of these are, however, of no authority, being evidently not genuine, and only the merest fraction of the remainder are of any consequence as affecting the sense. The very number of these readings, and the fact that they were made originally in different parts of the world, and from a variety of manuscripts, enables biblical students to detect and eliminate the errors, and approximate to the original text more closely than if the various readings were fewer. This tedious but necessary work has been carried out with untiring energy by textual critics. It is possible indirectly to gain access to the readings in manuscripts which have perished, for there were early versions of the N. T. in different languages, such as the Syriac and Latin, and quotations from the N. T. are found in the writings of the early Christians, especially in Clement of Alexandria and Origen. In most cases these versions and citations were made from manuscripts not now existing, but the translation shows what the original must have been.

The N. T. manuscripts fall into two divisions: Uncials, in Greek capitals; at first without breathings or accents and with no separation between the different words, except occasionally to indicate the beginning of a new paragraph, and very little even between the different lines; and Cursives, in small running hand, and with divisions of words and lines. The change between the two kinds of Greek writing took place about the tenth century. Only five manuscripts of the N. T. approaching to completeness are more ancient than this dividing date. The first, designated by biblical critics A, is the Alexandrian manuscript. Though taken to England by Cyril Lucar, patriarch of Constantinople, as a present to Charles I., it is believed that it was written, not in that capital, but in Alexandria, whence its title. Its date is believed to be the middle of the fifth century. In addition to a large portion of the O. T. and the First Epistle of Clement and part of the Second, it contains the whole of the N. T. except Mat. i.–xxv. 5; John vi. 50–viii. 52; 2 Cor. iv. 13–xii. 6. The page is divided into two columns, and the text is marked off into chapters, Mark containing forty-eight. The second, known as B, is the Vatican manuscript. It has been in the Vatican library at Rome from 1475 or an earlier period, but not till 1857 was an edition of it published, and that one, by Cardinal Mai, when issued, was uncritical and of little value. But in 1889–90 a facsimile of it came forth, so that now it is fully accessible to scholars. The Vatican manuscript dates from the middle of the fourth century, if not even from an earlier period. Besides most of the O. T., it contains all the N. T. except Heb. ix. 14, xiii. 25, 1 and 2 Tim., Titus, Philem., and Rev. It has three columns to the page, and is divided into short chapters, Matthew having 170. The third, C, or the Ephraem manuscript, is a palimpsest. In the twelfth century the original writing was washed out to make room for the text of several ascetic treatises of Ephraem the Syrian. Traces of the older writing were, however, discernible, and in 1834 the original text was revived by an application of prussiate of potash. It is believed that it belongs to the fifth century, and perhaps a slightly earlier period of it than the manuscript A. It contains portions of the O. T. and five-eighths of the N. T. The lines run across the page. The fourth, D, is the manuscript of Beza, to whom it belonged after it was taken from the abbey of St. Irenæus in Lyons at the sack of the city in 1562. It is commonly dated in the sixth century. It contains the greater part of the Greek text of the gospels and The Acts, together with a Latin translation. It

is for the most part the only witness among Greek manuscripts to a type of text which was widely current as early as the second century, and of which the other principal representatives are the Old Latin and the Old Syriac versions. It is written stichometrically, i. e., in single lines containing as many words as could be read at a breath, consistently with the sense. The fifth, called א (the Hebrew first letter, aleph), is the Sinaitic manuscript, obtained in 1844 and 1859 by Tischendorf from the monks belonging to the convent of St. Catherine on mount Sinai. Besides the major part of the O. T., it contains the whole N. T. without a break, together with the epistle of Barnabas and a large part of the Shepherd of Hermas. The last twelve verses of Mark are lacking, but it is suspicious that the page where they occur seems to be a cancel. It was made in the fourth century. It has four columns to the page.

The cursive manuscripts, though numerous, are of too late date to stand on the same level for critical purposes as the uncials.

The first printed edition of the Greek N. T. actually published was that of Erasmus, who issued it in 1516. It was reprinted in 1518, a second and more correct edition followed in 1519, a third in 1522, a fourth in 1527. Cardinal Ximenes, the Roman Catholic primate of Spain, had been engaged for some years in preparing an edition of the Greek N. T., but various causes of delay kept it back from the world till 1521 or 1522. From being made at Alcala, called by the Romans Complutum, it is known as the Complutensian edition. Among other editions of the Greek N. T. which followed, none were more celebrated than those of Robert Stephens of Paris. They appeared in 1546, 1549, 1550, and 1551. Then Beza the reformer came upon the scene, and issued several editions of the Greek N. T. between 1565 and 1604, based on Stephens' third edition (1550), which in turn had been founded mainly on Erasmus' fourth or fifth edition. Stephens' edition of 1550 is the *textus receptus* in England, but on the continent of Europe this designation and authority are generally given to the first Elzevir edition, printed at Leyden in 1624. This Elzevir text is mainly that of Stephens' edition of 1550, from which it differs in 278 places, including merely orthographic variations. It was mainly from Beza's edition of 1598 that the A. V. of the English Bible was made.

The division of the O. and N. T. into our present chapters has been generally ascribed to Cardinal Hugo, who died in 1263, a Dominican monk, who used it for his concordance to the Vulgate. Its application in this concordance certainly brought this division into repute, and established the practice of citing by chapters instead of referring to the book merely or to some prominent narrative in the book (cp. Mark ii. 26; xii. 26; Rom. xi. 2); but there is reason to believe that the present division antedates Hugo, and was due to Stephen Langton, archbishop of Canterbury, who died in 1228. The division of the N. T. into our present verses was made by Robert Stephens in the Greek N. T. which he published in 1551. The first English N. T. to be so divided was Whittingham's translation, Geneva, 1557, and the first English Bible so divided was the Geneva version of 1560.

Ne-zi'ah [bright, pure, illustrious].

Founder of a family of Nethinim, members of which returned with Zerubbabel from the Babylonian captivity (Ezra ii. 54; Neh. vii. 56).

Ne'zib [statue, idol, military station].

A town in the lowland of Judah (Josh. xv. 43). Beit Nusib, about 9 miles west-north-west of Hebron, is scarcely the site; for it is in the hill country.

Nib'haz.

An idol, one of two worshiped by the Avvites, a tribe brought with others from the Assyrian empire to colonize Samaria after the captivity of the ten tribes (2 Kin. xvii. 31). The Jewish rabbins derived the name from the Semitic root *nabah*, to bark, and considered that Nibhaz had the figure of a dog; but there is no reason to think that they were correct.

Nib'shan [soft, level soil].

A town in the wilderness of Judah (Josh. xv. 62). Site unknown.

Ni-ca'nor [victorious].

1. Son of Patroclus and one of the king's friends whom Lysias, regent in western Syria during the absence of Antiochus Epiphanes, in 166 B. C. selected to lead the army to suppress the Judæan revolt (1 Mac. iii. 38; 2 Mac. viii. 9). The Syrians were defeated. Nicanor stood high in the favor of Demetrius I. also, and was appointed governor of Judæa by him (1 Mac. vii. 26; 2 Mac. xiv. 12). He professed friendship for Judas Maccabæus, but the Jew was not deceived. Nicanor engaged in battle with Judas at Capharsalama, and was slain in battle with him near Beth-horon, 160 B. C. (1 Mac. vii. 27–49; 2 Mac. xv. 1–36).

2. One of the seven men who were chosen in the church at Jerusalem to look after the Greek-speaking widows, and apparently the poor in general (Acts vi. 5).

Nic-o-de'mus [victor over the people].

A Pharisee and a member of the sanhedrin. Convinced by the miracles which Jesus wrought that the teacher of Nazareth had come from God, he sought an interview with him; but by night, to escape observation or because the hour was convenient. Jesus explained to him the nature of the new birth, and the love of God for the world which prompted him to give his only begotten Son

that whosoever accepted him in faith might have eternal life (John iii. 1–21). At a meeting of the sanhedrin, when the members began to denounce Jesus as an impostor, Nicodemus pointedly asked whether the law condemned a man unheard (vii. 50–52). After the death of Christ Nicodemus took about a hundred pounds' weight of myrrh and aloes, and aided in preparing the body for burial (xix. 39).

Nic-o-la'i-tans.

A party or sect in the churches of Ephesus and Pergamos whose practice and doctrine are severely censured. Following the doctrine of Balaam, they taught that Christians were free to eat things offered to idols and to commit the excesses of heathenism (Rev. ii. 6, 14, 15), contrary to the command issued by the apostolic council held at Jerusalem A. D. 50 (Acts xv. 29). Presumably the Nicolaitans were the followers of some heresiarch called Nicolaus. But that he was the deacon of that name in the church at Jerusalem lacks proof. The earliest trace of the theory that the sect originated in the teaching of the deacon is found in the writings of Irenæus, about A. D. 175 (adv. haeres. i. 26, 3). A sect of Nicolaitans existed among the Gnostics of the third century. They, too, taught the freedom of the flesh; and they may have grown out of these corrupt Christians of the apostolic age.

Nic-o-la'us, in A. V. and E. R. V. **Nic'o-las** [victor over the people].

A proselyte of Antioch, who was one of the seven elected at the instance of the apostles to look after the interests of the Greek-speaking widows and apparently the Christian poor in general (Acts vi. 5).

Ni-cop'o-lis [city of victory].

A place at which Paul, when he wrote the Epistle to Titus, hoped to winter (Titus iii. 12). The note appended to the epistle makes it sent from Nicopolis of Macedonia, but it is of no authority. The place referred to in this postscript was situated on both sides of the river Nestus, which was the boundary line between Thrace and Macedonia. It is now called Nikopi. But the probability is that the Nicopolis at which Paul meant to winter was the town in Epirus, 4 miles from Actium, which Augustus founded in 30 B. C. to commemorate his victory. Herod the Great built a number of its public edifices (Antiq. xvi. 5, 3). Its ruins remain at Prevesa.

Ni'ger [black].

A Latin surname of Simeon, a prophet and teacher in the church of Antioch (Acts xiii. 1).

Night.

The period of darkness (Gen. i. 5). It was divided into three watches: sunset to midnight, midnight to cock-crow, cock-crow to sunrise (Lam. ii. 19; Judg. vii. 19; Ex. xiv. 24). The Greek and Roman division into four watches was in use in N. T. times (Luke

xii. 38; Mark vi. 48). At this period the night, from sunset to sunrise, was divided into twelve hours (cp. Acts xxiii. 23).

Night Hawk.

The rendering of the Hebrew *Tamush*, violent one; an unclean bird mentioned in Lev. xi. 16; Deut. xiv. 15. It is doubtful what bird is meant. The English versions make it the night hawk, which is another name for the night jar, better known as the goatsucker (*Caprimulgus europæus*), or some species akin to it. The Septuagint and Vulgate identify it with the owl.

Night Mon'ster.

The rendering of the Hebrew *Lilith* (Is. xxxiv. 14, R. V. Margin; in A. V. screech owl). .The word in Hebrew means simply nocturnal, and may denote any female nocturnal bird or beast. In Assyrian, it was applied to a nocturnal demon. See under SATYR.

Nile.

The great river of Egypt (Is. xxiii. 3, in A. V. Sihor; Jer. ii. 18, margin of R. V.); in Hebrew *Shihor*, dark, turbid, and *Y'or*, stream. Its waters covered so vast an expanse, especially during the inundation, that it is sometimes called a sea (Nah. iii. 8). The ultimate sources of the river are the streams which feed the Victoria Nyanza in equatorial Africa. But the Nile in a narrower sense, as it presents those peculiarities which have made it famous, is formed by the confluence of the White and the Blue Nile at the town of Khartum; from which point to its principal mouths at Damietta and Rosetta, a distance of upwards of 1800 miles, it traverses an absolutely barren country and receives one tributary only, the Atbara, on the east side, about 180 miles below Khartum. The banks rise several hundred feet and at places to upwards of 1000 feet, resembling two large canal embankments, and wall the valley all the way to Cairo, where they diverge abruptly toward the east and northwest and face the protruded delta. A short distance above Assuan, the ancient Syene, a ridge of granite, extending for 180 miles from east to west, lies athwart the river's course. The stream breaks through this barrier, plunges down the rocks of the last or, on ascending the river, first cataract, and enters the bounds of ancient Egypt. All above that cataract was Ethiopia; all below was Egypt. The granite of this transverse ridge is colored; it is the well-known light-brown stone of which so many of the polished statues of the Pharaohs are made. Below Cairo the river divides and seeks the sea by several great channels. These mouths are now two, the Damietta and the Rosetta; but formerly they numbered seven, of which the most important were the eastern or Pelusiac, the western or Canopic, and the middle or Sebennytic (Herod. ii. 17).

As the river pursues its tortuous course through thirsty land, much of its water is consumed by evaporation and infiltration and still more by the extensive system of irrigating canals. The loss at the time of the inundation within Egypt proper is about one-third of the total volume.

This annual overflow is the famous feature of the Nile. Its occurrence in a rainless region was mysterious to the ancients (Herod. ii. 19–25). It is explained by the fact that all the sources of the Nile lie within the region of abundant periodical rains. These fall copiously on the sources of the White Nile about the time of the equinoxes, and in Abyssinia a little later. The Abyssinian rains, being nearer the mouth, cause a first rise, which reaches Egypt about the middle of June. This is followed in the course of a month by a sudden increase, due to the influx of the rising waters of the White Nile, when the river begins to swell steadily in volume with a resulting inundation which commences in the latter part of August. Toward the end of September the water ceases to rise, remaining at about the same height for a fortnight or more; but during the first half of October it rises again and attains its highest level. During a good inundation it reaches a height of 40 feet at Assuan and of 23 to 27 at Cairo. About the end of November most of the fields are left dry and covered with a fresh layer of rich brown slime; this is the time when the lands are put under culture. Occasionally inundation does not take place. Tradition was current and found record in an inscription on the rocks at Sahel, an island of the first cataract, that in the reign of Toser or Toser-Sa, a Pharaoh of the third dynasty, the inundation failed for seven years and a sore famine resulted. It failed for seven years in the time of Joseph (Gen. xli. 54); and it failed likewise for seven years in the reign of the caliph el-Mustansir, the resulting famine reaching its height A. D. 1070.

In the time of the Pharaohs the Egyptian agricultural year was divided into three equal parts; the period of the inundation (from the end of June to the end of October), that of the growing of the crops (from the end of October to the end of February), and that of the harvest (from the end of February to the end of June).

Nim'rah [limpid and wholesome water].

An abbreviation of Beth-nimrah (cp. Num. xxxii. 3 with 36); see BETH-NIMRAH.

Nim'rim [perhaps, a plural of Nimrah, limpid waters, or an abnormal plural for leopards].

A locality in Moab, noted for its waters (Is. xv. 6; Jer. xlviii. 34). Opinion as to its identification is divided between Beth-nimrah in the Jordan valley and the wady Nemeirah, near the southern end of the Dead Sea, where the ruins of a town Nemeirah, the leopard, exist. Tristram locates the site higher up the valley, where it is said there is an old Moabite city with the name Springs of Nemeirah. It has many well-watered gardens still in cultivation.

Nim'rod.

A Cushite, a mighty hunter and a potent monarch, the beginning of whose original kingdom embraced Babel, Erech, Accad, and Calneh, cities in the land of Shinar (Gen. x. 8-10; Mic. v. 6). The only ancient king of Babylonia known, who fits this description, and was at the same time celebrated in tradition and song, was Izdubar or, as there is reason to pronounce his name, Gilgamesh. He freed Babylonia from the oppressive rule of the Elamites and became king of Erech. He was a slayer of wild beasts, and his encounters with animals, not less than his exploits in war, were embodied in a poem, and formed a favorite subject for engraver and sculptor. His life became embellished with legend, and he was occasionally addressed in prayer by men of after ages; but through all the attributes which accumulated about him the fact remained clearly discerned that he was a mortal man. There is, however, no proof that Nimrod and Gilgamesh are identical, and the attempt to establish a relationship between their names has thus far proved fruitless.

Nim'shi [perhaps, drawn out, or active, lively].

An ancestor of Jehu (1 Kin. xix. 16; 2 Kin. ix. 2), who was generally designated the son of Nimshi.

Nin'e-veh.

The capital of the Assyrian empire. The Hebrews embraced the entire population which was collected about the capital, and occupied the district at the confluence of the Tigris and the Upper Zab under the designation of Nineveh the great city (Gen. x. 11, 12; Jon. i. 2; iii. 3; Judith i. 1). Nineveh in the narrower sense stood on the eastern bank of the Tigris, at the mouth of a small tributary which is now known as the Khosr, about 27 miles above the confluence of the Zab with the main stream. It was built by a people of Babylonian origin (Gen. x. 11). Its tutelary deity was the goddess Ishtar, to whom from a very early period a temple had existed in the place. This sanctuary engaged the attention of Shamshiramman about 1800 B. C., and after falling into decay, was rebuilt with splendor by Ashuruballit about 1400 B. C. Asshur, 60 miles south of Nineveh and on the opposite bank of the river, was the ancient seat of government; but Shalmaneser erected a palace at Nineveh about 1300 B. C., and made it his capital, and from that period it was looked upon as the chief city of Assyria. Ashurnaṣirpal and his successor Shalmaneser, whose united reigns extended from about 885 to 825, had palaces in both Nineveh and Calah, and resided sometimes in one place, sometimes in the other. Their successors

dwelt in Nineveh in the broad sense; but the palace was not always in Nineveh proper, but was often erected in one of the suburbs, as Calah or Dur-sharrukin or Tarbisu. The Assyrians were great warriors, and the spoils of the conquered cities and nations were brought to the capital and used to embellish it. It was also the center of some literary activity. About 650 B. C. Ashurbanipal gathered a great library, consisting of documents inscribed on clay tablets, which related to history, ritual, incantation, astronomy, mathematics. It was composed for the most part of copies of older works, which had been brought from Babylonia. The prophet Nahum calls Nineveh the bloody city (iii. 1), both because of the wars which it had waged for centuries with the surrounding nations, and because of the cruelty which was practiced by the victors. Ashurnaṣirpal, for example, was accustomed after his victories to cut off the hands and feet, and the noses and ears, and put out the eyes of his captives, and to raise mounds of human heads. In 625 B. C., when the Assyrian empire began to decline in vigor, Nabopolassar, governor of Babylon, declared himself independent,

Relief sculpture from Ashurbanipal's palace at Nineveh. On the second register is a military band with drums, cymbals, and lyre.

and in 612 or 606 B. C. the Umman-manda, fierce nomadic peoples of far northeastern lands, acting in confederation with Nabopolassar, descended upon the plain and by their own might captured and destroyed Nineveh. They were greatly aided by a sudden rise of the Tigris, which carried away a great part of the city wall and rendered the place indefensible. So complete was the desolation that in classic times the departed Nineveh became like a myth. Yet all the while part of the city lay buried under mounds of apparent rubbish. Rich, English resident at Bagdad, inspected the mound called Kouyunjik, on the eastern bank of the Tigris, in 1820, and became convinced that it concealed the ruins of Nineveh. In 1843 Botta, French consul at Mosul, on the western bank of the Tigris, began to make excavations. He was soon diverted to Khorsabad, 10 miles off, the site of Dur-sharrukin. Between 1845 and 1850 Layard commenced operations at Nimroud, 18 miles south of Kouyunjik; then he made excavations at the latter place itself, which proved to be the site of Nineveh. George Smith conducted further excavations at the place from 1873 to 1876, and after his death the work was taken up and extended to other mounds by Rassam. The walls of Nineveh have been traced, and indicate a city 3 miles in length by less than a mile and a half in breadth, containing an area of about 1800 English acres. But, as already said, the Hebrews and perhaps other foreigners were accustomed to include under the name of Nineveh the complex of cities which included besides Nineveh Calah, 18 miles south, Resen between Calah and Nineveh, and Rehoboth-Ir, broad places or suburb of the city, which is perhaps identical with Rebit Nina, suburb of Nineveh, which lay to the northeast of the city. These are the four places which are enumerated in Gen. x. 11, 12 as composing the great city. But they were not the only towns which sprang up in the environs of Nineveh. Yarimja, on the river directly south of Nineveh, marks an ancient site, and near the Tigris, 3 miles above Nineveh, was Tarbisu, with a royal palace, beginning the imposing line of habitations and walled towns which extended along the river southward to Calah. Back from the river, northeast of Nineveh and beyond Rebit Nina, at the foot of the eastern mountains, was Dur-sharrukin or Sargon's burg, a town about as large as Calah, built about 707 B. C., and containing a great palace. Seven miles southeast, and also at the foot of the eastern mountain, was another town scarcely inferior in size to Calah. Its ancient name is unknown, but it is situated hard by Baasheihah. It was one of a series of towns which extended to Calah. Birtelleh, 6 miles south, probably marks the site of an ancient town, and Keremlis, 3 miles farther on, is known to do so. Imgurbel, with its palace and temple which Ashurnasirpal adorned, was 6 miles south of the latter place, and was 9 miles from Calah. Other towns and villages dotted the plain within the bounds which have been thus defined. It may be that Diodorus Siculus, of the first century B. C., is citing an authentic tradition when he states that Nineveh formed a quadrangle measuring 150 stadia by 90, or 480 in circuit, about 60 miles. Strabo, a few years later, says that it was much larger than Babylon.

Ni'san [Assyrian *Nisannu*, probably opening, beginning].

The name given after the captivity to Abib, the first month of the year (Neh. ii. 1; Esth. iii. 7). It nearly corresponds to March. See YEAR.

Nis'roch.

A god worshiped by Sennacherib. It was in the temple of Nisroch at Nineveh that he was assassinated (2 Kin. xix. 37; Is. xxxvii. 38). Nisroch is the Hebrew pronunciation of the name. Perhaps it represents the Assyrian god Nusku, or is composite and contains the name of the god Ashur.

Ni'ter.

Saltpeter, potassium nitrate; but among the ancients sodium carbonate and potassium carbonate. It is an alkali (Prov. xxv. 20), and in solution was used in washing clothes (Jer. ii. 22).

No and in R. V. once **No-amon** (Nah. iii. 8) [Egyptian *nu-āa*, the large city, or *nu-amen*, Amon's city].

The Egyptian city of Thebes, often called by this name on the monuments. Herodotus found its distance from On to be a voyage of nine days up the river (ii. 9). After the expulsion of the Hyksos from Egypt, Aahmes I., the founder of the eighteenth dynasty, turned his attention to the reorganization and improvement of the kingdom, and among other works embellished Thebes. The city at once rose to chief importance as the capital of the new empire, and became large, splendid, and populous. Homer speaks of its hundred gates (Iliad ix. 381). Its tutelary divinity was Amon, and the high priest of Amon was second only to the king. It remained the center of Egyptian civilization and power until, first, Esarhaddon, king of Assyria, conquered Egypt, in 672 B. C., and, afterwards, Ashurbanipal, his son and successor, subjugated the country and plundered the city in 664 B. C. (Nah. iii. 8). But even after that disaster, Thebes long remained a place of importance (Jer. xlvi. 25; Ezek. xxx. 14-16; Herod. ii. 3; iii. 10). It was finally destroyed utterly by the Roman prefect, Cornelius Gallus, for its participation in the revolt of Upper Egypt in 30-29 B. C. against oppressive Roman taxation. Splendid remains of the city, consisting of temples, obelisks, sphinxes, etc., still exist at Luxor and Karnak, on the eastern, and Kurna and Medinet-Habu, on the western side of the river. West of what was the site of the city there is a gorge cut into the lower limestone which contains the tombs of the ancient Theban kings.

No-a-di'ah [Jehovah hath met].

1. Son of Binnui. He was one of those who took charge of the gold and silver vessels brought by Ezra and the returned captives from Babylon (Ezra viii. 33).

2. A prophetess whose evil vaticinations were intended to frighten Nehemiah (Neh. vi. 14).

No'ah I., in A. V. of Matthew and Luke **Noe** [rest].

Son of Lamech of the posterity of Seth (Gen. v. 28, 29). The reason for bestowing the name Noah is stated in words which bear some resemblance to the name in sound. He called him Noah, saying: "This same shall comfort us ($y^e nah^a menu$) for our work and for the toil of our hands, because of the ground which the Lord hath cursed." This method is one of several which are employed by the Hebrew writers. The references to the years of Noah's life are capable of several explanations, in accordance with ancient methods of statement and of constructing genealogical registers. Several methods are mentioned in the article on CHRONOLOGY. The application of the first two of these to the data referring to Noah is simple and needs no explanation. The third method is more intricate, but is also applicable. According to it, in the family of Lamech, 182 years after it succeeded to the position of prominence among the children of Seth and became the family through which the church descended, a son was born whom his father called Noah, saying: "This one shall comfort us." Long afterwards, among the descendants of this child of hope, who are collectively called Noah, just as the descendants of Israel were frequently called Israel, appeared one in whom the hopes were realized, who proved a comforter, whose conduct and worship were rewarded by God's promise not to curse the ground again for wicked man's sake nor to smite any more everything living, who built the ark and who was the family's head and representative. He is referred to by the tribal name. His eldest son was about 100 years old when the flood came. This event occurred in the six hundredth year of Noah, that is, 600 years after the family which was spoken of as Noah had attained to leadership. If the third method is the true one, such is its application to the record concerning Noah.

Noah was a just man and, like Enoch, walked with God (Gen. vi. 9). But it was a time of almost universal apostasy. It was an age of religious indifference, when even the sons of God had become worldly and in contracting marriage chose by the outward appearance rather than by the disposition of the heart (vi. 2), and when men generally were living for the present moment, eating and drinking, marrying and giving in marriage (Mat. xxiv. 38). It was also an age that was defiant of God: there was secret hostility of the heart; men formed their plans without regard to God, every imagination and device of man's heart was evil (Gen. vi. 5); there was open defiance also; the earth was filled with violence, the strong oppressed the weak (11). The age was so corrupt that God purposed to destroy mankind; but a respite apparently of 120 years was given (3). By his exemplary life at least, Noah was a preacher of righteousness (2 Pet. ii. 5). To him God, the creator and judge of all, revealed his purpose to destroy man, and commanded him to build an ark to save himself and his family and keep alive the various kinds of animals, for a flood of waters was to overwhelm the land. Noah did so. When the ark was finished, Jehovah, God of redemption, bade Noah enter the ark with his family and provide for their use the clean animals which they needed for food and sacrifice; and he who had created the beasts and the birds had them also go by pairs into the vessel for the preservation of their species. The same God of redemption shut Noah in. Then the flood broke in all its violence. See FLOOD. When at length the judgment purposed by the creator and governor of the universe was accomplished he remembered Noah and made the waters to assuage. After catching the first glimpse of the mountain tops, Noah waited the same length of time as the storm had raged, and then sent forth birds to discover whether the waters were abated from the surface of the earth. When he learned that they were, he tarried yet in the ark, waiting until God should bid him disembark. On New Year's day he removed the covering and saw that the ground was dry, but it was eight weeks longer before God bade him go forth. Then he built an altar and offered burnt offerings to the God of his redemption, who accepted the worship and purposed in his heart not to curse the ground again and smite every living thing on account of man's wickedness. God proceeded to reveal this purpose. As he had blessed Adam when he created him and had commanded that he be fruitful and multiply, so now at the beginning of a new world he blessed Noah and bade him be fruitful. He also laid injunctions on the head of the new race; but of the seven precepts of Noah, as they are called, which were regarded by the Jews as antecedent to the law and the observance of which was required of all proselytes, three only are expressly mentioned here: the abstinence from blood, the prohibition of murder, and the recognition of the civil authority (Gen. ix. 4-6). The remaining four, the prohibition of idolatry, blasphemy, incest, and theft, rested on the general sense of mankind. God further, in revealing his purpose not to curse the ground again for man's sake, pledged himself not to cut off all flesh again by the waters of a flood and adopted the rainbow as the sign of the engagement by which he had bound himself (8-17).

Noah naturally devoted himself to agriculture. Among other works he planted a vineyard, and he drank himself drunk on the wine. His son Ham mocked at his disgrace, but the other sons sought to protect their father. When Noah recovered, and learned what had occurred, with insight into character, and with that knowledge which he had derived before the flood of God's ordination that the evil propensities of parents descend to children and that God blessed the righteous in their generations (Ex. xx. 5, 6), he foretold degradation among the posterity of Ham, for some reason singling out one only of Ham's sons, predicted the subjection of this branch of the tribe to the descendants of the high-minded and godly brothers, pronounced the divine blessing on the families of Shem and Japheth, and announced especially their united service of Jehovah, God of Shem (Gen. ix. 20–27); see CANAAN, JAPHETH, and SHEM.

Noah lived, or the family which he represented continued its leadership, for 350 years after the flood (Gen. ix. 28). Then the Semites, as distinguished from the other descendants of Noah, became the leading family and the line in which the church descended. The flood seems to be referred to in Ps. xxix. 10, where *mabbul*, the special word for the flood, is used. Isaiah (liv. 9) and Ezekiel (xiv. 14) both allude to Noah. Our Lord compares the days of Noah to those which should precede his own second coming (Mat. xxiv. 37); the patriarch's faith is commended in Heb. xi. 7, and Peter twice alludes to the eight saved from the deluge when it overwhelmed the ungodly (1 Pet. iii. 20; 2 Pet. ii. 5). The Greeks and Romans had a story about a flood from which only two people were saved, Deucalion and his wife Pyrrha; and this Deucalion may be Noah under a different name. However this may be, the Babylonians at any rate preserved a tradition of the same flood of which the Hebrews had knowledge. They called the hero of it Ṣitnapishtim and Atraḥasis. See FLOOD.

No'ah II. [a moving, wandering].
A daughter of Zelophehad (Num. xxvi. 33, xxvii. 1; xxxvi. 11; Josh. xvii. 3).

No-a'mon. See No.

Nob [elevation].
A town of the priests (1 Sam. xxii. 19), in the territory of Benjamin (Neh. xi. 32), on the north and apparently within sight of Jerusalem (Is. x. 32). After the capture of the ark, the tabernacle was for a time pitched at Nob, with Ahimelech as high priest. He was ignorant of the variance between Saul and David, and when the latter came to Nob, Ahimelech allowed him and his men to eat the showbread and gave him the sword of Goliath. This act was reported to Saul, who summoned the priests and had them slain, and smote Nob, men, women, and children with the sword. Abiathar, however, escaped and told David (1 Sam. xxi., xxii.). The place was inhabited after the exile (Neh. xi. 32), but its site has not been identified.

Robinson contents himself with locating it "somewhere upon the ridge of the mount of Olives northeast of the city."

No'bah [barking].
1. A Manassite, presumably, who captured the town of Kenath, on the western slope of the Jebel Hauran, and gave it his own name (Num. xxxii. 42). The old name was probably ere long restored. See KENATH.
2. A town mentioned in connection with the Gadite town of Jogbehah. A road leading to the country of the nomads passed on the east (Judg. viii. 11). The site of Nobah is accordingly to be sought near the boundary between Gad and the Arabian desert.

No'bai, in A. V. and margin of R. V. **Nebai,** which is the traditional pronunciation.
One of the chiefs of the people who with Nehemiah sealed the covenant (Neh. x. 19).

Nod [in Hebrew, wandering, exile].
A district on the east of Eden to which Cain went and there abode (Gen. iv. 16). Not identified.

No'dab [nobility].
An Arab tribe of the Syrian desert, to judge from their allies (1 Chron. v. 19).

No'e. See NOAH.

No'gah [brilliance].
A son of David (1 Chron. iii. 7; xiv. 6).

No'hah [rest].
The fourth son of Benjamin (1 Chron. viii. 2), who, however, did not give rise to a tribal family. He is not mentioned among those who accompanied Jacob into Egypt, probably because he was born after the migration into Egypt. Keil offers a different explanation. He supposes that Nohah either is another name for Shephupham (Num. xxvi. 39, R. V.), or else was a celebrated chief who was descended from Shephupham and whose name supplanted Shephupham as the designation of the family.

Non. See NUN.

Noph. See MEMPHIS.

No'phah [possibly, a breeze].
A Moabite town (Num. xxi. 30), not elsewhere mentioned. The text is open to question.

Nose Jew'el.
A jewel inserted, generally by means of a ring, into the side of the nostril for ornament (Is. iii. 21, R. V.).

Nose Ring.
A ring worn as an ornament, especially by women (R. V. of Gen. xxiv. 47; Ezek. xvi. 12). It was inserted through the partition between the nostrils or in the side of the nose.

Num'ber and **Nu'mer-al.**
There is no evidence that the ancient Hebrews used figures to denote numbers. The numerals which occur in the present text of the Hebrew Scriptures, in the Siloam inscription,

and on the Moabite stone, are spelled in full. The Hebrews employed the letters of the alphabet to represent numerals as early as Maccabæan times, using aleph for one, beth for two. This practice is exhibited on the coins of Simon; see MONEY. In the Nabathæan inscriptions of the first century the numerals are generally spelled, but they are occasionally represented by signs, upright strokes for the smaller units, a figure like 5 without the upper horizontal arm for five, and other marks. In the Aramaic inscriptions of the same period at Palmyra signs are also used. On the lion weights, which were used by Aramæan traders in Nineveh in the eighth century B. C., the weight is indicated by upright strokes for the units and a horizontal stroke for ten. In yet earlier centuries the Assyrians and Babylonians used cuneiform signs to indicate number.

Numbers were used symbolically and conventionally. Three had apparently no symbolism ; but emphasis was conventionally expressed by it ; as "The temple of the Lord, the temple of the Lord, the temple of the Lord, are these" (Jer. vii. 4), "O earth, earth, earth" (xxii. 29), "I will overturn, overturn, overturn it" (Ezek. xxi. 27), "Holy, holy, holy" (Is. vi. 3), and the triple blessing (Num. vi. 24-26). The threefold character of the baptismal formula and the apostolic benediction resulted from the doctrine of the Trinity (Mat. xxviii. 19 ; 2 Cor. xiii. 14). Four does not play an important part. Four corners or quarters of the earth were recognized, north, south, east, and west (Is. xi. 12), and hence four winds (Dan. vii. 2), and four chariots (Zech. vi. 1, 5). Seven was early a sacred number among the Semites (Gen. ii. 2 ; iv. 24 ; xxi. 28). It did not derive its character from the fact that it was equal to three plus four. Not arithmetical, but religious considerations were involved ; see SABBATH. Ten was recognized as a complete number, and was constantly used as such ; there were ten commandments (Ex. xxxiv. 28), ten antediluvian and ten postdiluvian patriarchs (see CHRONOLOGY), and a tenfold division of the book of Genesis. Twelve was the basis of the duodecimal system of the Babylonians, and as a result found employment in common life. Something of it was probably inherited by the Hebrews, and was enhanced by the fact that the tribes of Israel were twelve. Forty was a round number much in vogue (Ex. xxiv. 18 ; 1 Kin. xix. 8 ; Jonah iii. 4 ; Mat. iv. 2 ; and CHRONOLOGY III.

Num'bers.

The fourth book of the Pentateuch. In the Hebrew Scriptures it is named "In the wilderness" (see Num. i. 1). Its modern designation originated with the Greek translators, and was chosen on account of the two enumerations of the people which the book relates ; the first at Sinai in the second year of the exodus, the second on the Jordan in the fortieth year.

It may be divided into three main sections : 1. In the wilderness at Sinai (i. 1-x. 11). Census of the people, exclusive of the Levites, with assignment of a place for each tribe in the encampment (i., ii.) ; census of the Levites, their location in the camp, and specific duties (iii., iv.) The unclean removed from the camp (v. 1-4). Law that the restitution for a trespass go to the priest in case the person wronged, to whom it ordinarily went, has died and is without heirs (5-10). Laws about jealousy and Nazirites, and form of the priest's blessing (v. 11-vi.). Offering of the princes at the dedication of the tabernacle (vii.). The place of the seven lamps (viii. 1-4). Consecration of the Levites (5-22), and the age of entering service (23-26) ; see LEVITES. Observance of the passover and law of the supplementary celebration (ix. 1-14). The guiding pillar of cloud (15-23) and silver signal trumpets (x. 1-10). 2. On the way from Sinai to the Jordan (x. 11-xxi. 35). Order of march (x. 11-28). Hobab invited to go with Israel (29-32). A stage of the journey (33, 34). Words used when the ark set forward and when it rested (35, 36). Murmurs against the manna, seventy elders to aid Moses, descent of quails (xi.). Miriam's leprosy (xii.). At Kadesh : the spies and their report, the people faithless and condemned to die in the wilderness (xiii., xiv.). Supplementary legal specifications (xv.). Rebellion of Korah, Dathan, and Abiram ; and related events (xvi., xvii.) ; in consequence, duties and privileges of the priests and Levites affirmed (xviii.). Law for purification of those defiled by contact with a dead body (xix.). Return to Kadesh : death of Miriam, sin of Moses and Aaron, embassy to Edom (xx. 1-21). Death of Aaron, journey from mount Hor around Edom to plains of Moab, fiery serpents, conquest of the country east of the Jordan (xx. 22-xxi. 35). 3. At Shittim opposite Jericho (xxii. 1 xxxvi. 13). Balaam (xxii.-xxiv.). Sin of Baal-peor (xxv.). Census of the new generation (xxvi.). Laws regarding inheritance by daughters (xxvii. 1-11). Public announcement of Joshua as Moses' successor (12-23). Further regulation of the daily offerings and of vows (xxviii.-xxx.). War with Midian (xxxi.). Assignment of the conquered country east of Jordan to the Reubenites, Gadites, and half-tribe of Manasseh (xxxii.). Itinerary from Egypt to Shittim (xxxiii.). Boundaries of the land and a commission on allotment (xxxiv.). Laws of the cities of refuge (xxxv.). Supplementary law concerning inheritance by daughters (xxxvi.).

The book of Numbers is recognized by all schools of criticism to reflect the same social conditions and laws as Leviticus.

Nu-me'ni-us [pertaining to the new moon].

A Jew, son of Antiochus and a member of

the senate (Antiq. xiii. 5, 8), sent as ambassador to Rome and Sparta in 144 B. C. by Jonathan Maccabæus, and dispatched a second time to Rome by Simon in 140 B. C. (1 Mac. xii. 16; xiv. 24; xv. 15).

Nun, in A. V. and Hebrew text once **Non** (1 Chron. vii. 27) [fish].

1. Father of Joshua, the military leader (Ex. xxxiii. 11; Josh. i. 1), descended through Tahan and perhaps Beriah from Ephraim (1 Chron. vii. 27).

2. The fourteenth letter of the Hebrew alphabet. English N has the same origin and represents it in anglicized Hebrew names. It heads the fourteenth section of Ps. cxix., in which section each verse of the original begins with this letter.

Nurse.

1. A wet nurse, *meneḵeth*, employed to suckle an infant (Ex. ii. 7-9; 2 Kin. xi. 2). Deborah, who had nursed Rebekah, remained an honored servant in the family (Gen. xxiv. 59; xxxv. 8), as was frequently the case (Odyssey xix. 15, 251).

2. A male or female attendant, *'omen*, who acted as nurse, *i. e.*, had the care of small children, either when infants (Num. xi. 12; Ruth iv. 16) or when older but still helpless (2 Sam. iv. 4).

Nuts.

1. The rendering of the Hebrew *Boṭnim*, pistachio nuts (Gen. xliii. 11, R. V. margin). The true pistachio tree (*Pistacia vera*) belongs to the order *Anacardiaceæ* (anacards or terebinths). Its leaves have, as a rule, three or four leaflets. Its fruit, which is a little less than an inch in diameter, consists of a bony shell surrounded by a dry covering and enclosing a sweet, somewhat oily kernel. The nuts are eaten like almonds or used for making confectionery. It is a native of western Asia, from which it has been introduced into southern Europe. It is not now common in Palestine. Jacob sent some of its fruit, with other vegetable produce, as a present to the Egyptian prime minister (Gen. xliii. 11).

2. The rendering of the Hebrew word *'egoz*, walnut (Song vi. 11). The walnut tree (*Juglans regia*), in America distinguished as the English walnut, is native from the Caucasus to the mountains of northern India. It is cultivated in Galilee and along the slopes of Lebanon and of Hermon.

Nym'phas [sacred to the muses].

A Christian at Laodicea or Colossæ, to whom Paul sent salutation (Col. iv. 15).

O

Oak.

1. A rendering of the Hebrew word *'Elah*, a strong tree. The Hebrew word occurs in fifteen passages of the O. T. In three of these it serves as a geographical designation and is treated as a proper name, valley of

Elah (1 Sam. xvii. 2, 19; xxi. 9; R. V. margin, terebinth . In two passages, where it is associated with another word, *'allon*, which is rendered oak, it is translated terebinth in R. V., but teil tree and elms in A. V. (Is. vi. 13; Hos. iv. 13). In the remaining ten passages it is rendered oak, with terebinth on the margin of R. V.

2. The rendering of the Hebrew *'Elon*, strong one, in the text of nine passages of the R. V., terebinth being placed on the margin. The A. V., following the Targums and Vulgate, uniformly renders *'elon*, by plain, but on the margin of Judg. ix. 6 it substitutes oak. There were the oak of Moreh (Gen. xii. 6; Deut. xi. 30), the oak of Mamre (Gen. xiii. 18; xiv. 13; xviii. 1), the oak in Zaanannim (Judg. iv. 11), the oak of the pillar that was in Shechem (ix. 6), the oak of the augurs (ix. 37, R. V. margin), and the oak of Tabor (1 Sam. x. 3).

3. The rendering of the Hebrew word *'El*, strong tree, in Is. i. 29.

4. The uniform and doubtless correct rendering of the Hebrew word *'Allon*. It occurs in eight passages, and was a species of oak associated with Bashan (Is. ii. 13; Ezek. xxvii. 6; Zech. xi. 2). Under a tree of this species near Bethel Deborah, Rebekah's nurse, was buried (Gen. xxxv. 8). It was probably the prickly oak (*Quercus coccifera*) ; see illustration, article ABRAHAM.

5. The rendering, probably correct, of the Hebrew word *'Allah* (Josh. xxiv. 26).

Oak is the meaning of *'allon*, for it was a characteristic tree of Bashan. *'Elah* differed from it (Is. vi. 13; Hos. iv. 13), and hence is probably the terebinth ; and the three related words, *'elah*, *'el*, and *'elon*, may denote three kinds of terebinth. They may, however, designate any large tree, and not specify the terebinth in particular. Several species of oak grow in Palestine. *Quercus sessiliflora* grows high up on Lebanon and in the Hauran. Four varieties of the prickly evergreen oak (*Q. coccifera*) occur : one is *Q. pseudococcifera*, and is found on Carmel, in Gilead, and in Bashan, often being of magnificent growth; another is *Q. calliprinos*, which is found in Lebanon, on Tabor, and in Gilead. Valonia oak (*Q. ægilops*) is deciduous. It is common in Galilee and Gilead.

Oath.

An appeal to God in attestation of the truth of a statement or of the binding character of a promise (Gen. xxi. 23; xxxi. 53; Gal. i. 20; Heb. vi. 16). Its violation was an offense against God (2 Chron. xxxvi. 13; Ezek. xvii. 13, 18). Sometimes the appeal was to the sovereign or other sacred object (Gen. xlii. 15; 2 Sam. xi. 11; Mat. v. 33, xxiii. 16-22). Jehovah condescended to confirm his promise to the patriarch by an oath, swearing by himself (Gen. xxii. 16; Heb. vi. 13-20). An oath was commonly made by lifting the hand unto God (Gen. xiv. 22;

Ezek. xx. 5, 6; Rev. x. 5; Homer, Iliad xix. 254), but it was sometimes made by placing the hand under the thigh of the person to whom the promise was made (Gen. xxiv. 2; xlvii. 29), probably as an invocation of the posterity, which should proceed from the loins, to guard the oath and avenge its violation. The oath was occasionally taken before the altar (1 Kin. viii. 31). Abraham gave Abimelech seven ewe lambs as witness of the oath (Gen. xxi. 27–31). An oath was sometimes intensified by slaying an animal, dividing it into two parts, and passing between the pieces (xv. 8–18). Each party to the oath invoked upon himself the fate of the victim if he broke the covenant. By the Mosaic law, in certain judicial investigations, a man to clear himself was required to swear an oath of the Lord (Ex. xxii. 11; Num. v. 19–22). Any man swearing an oath or making a vow to God was required to carry out his promise, as was a woman, if being a virgin her father did not disallow her oath when she uttered it, or being married her husband did not interfere. If she was a widow, or had been divorced, her oath stood (Num. xxx.). If anyone swore falsely by the name of the true God, he profaned the divine name (Lev. vi. 3; xix. 12; cp. Is. xlviii. 1; Jer. xii. 16; Mal. iii. 5); and no one was under any circumstances to swear by a false god (Josh. xxiii. 7). The man is commended in Ps. xv. 4 who does not change, although he has sworn to his hurt. Our Lord condemned the use of oaths, even when taken with the best intention, declaring that whatever went beyond "yea, yea, or nay, nay," was of the evil one (Mat. v. 33–37). He was delivering the sermon on the mount and correcting various perversions of the law which the scribes had introduced; and among other evils, he condemned swearing in ordinary communications between man and man. But the judicial oath is lawful; for it was enjoined by God (Ex. xxii. 11), and Christ himself did not hesitate to answer when he was put upon his oath by the high priest (Mat. xxvi. 63). The oath was recognized as lawful by the apostles also, for they called on God to witness to the truth of what they said (2 Cor. xi. 31; Gal. i. 20). The mischief which may arise from a rash oath was well illustrated in that of Herod the tetrarch, which made him against his will the murderer of John the Baptist (Mat. xiv. 3–12).

O-ba-di'ah [worshiper of Jehovah].

1. A man of Issachar, family of Tola, house of Uzzi (1 Chron. vii. 3).

2. A Gadite hero who joined David at Ziklag (1 Chron. xii. 9).

3. Father of the chief of the Zebulunites in David's reign (1 Chron. xxvii. 19).

4. A descendant of Jonathan (1 Chron. viii. 38; ix. 44).

5. The governor of Ahab's palace, who during the persecution of Jehovah's prophets by queen Jezebel, hid a hundred prophets, in two companies of fifty, in a cave (1 Kin. xviii. 3, 4). He was sent by his royal master to look for grass for the horses and mules during the great drought, and while so engaged fell in with Elijah, who persuaded him to announce to the king the presence of the prophet (5–16). Elijah's interview with the king led to the contest at Carmel, which was followed by the slaughter of Baal's prophets.

6. One of the princes sent by Jehoshaphat to teach in the cities of Judah (2 Chron. xvii. 7).

7. A prophet of Judah (Obad. 1). Josephus believed that he was the God-fearing Obadiah of Ahab's palace, but the prophet probably lived at least a century after Ahab.

The book of Obadiah is the fourth of the minor prophets. It consists of a solitary chapter, and foretells the destruction of Edom (1–9) and the reason of it, namely, Edom's unbrotherly attitude toward the children of Jacob (10, 11), warns Edom accordingly not to exult over the children of Judah in their distress (12–16), and predicts the deliverance and enlargement of Israel (17–21). The entire prophecy derives its incentive and strength from the great truth, clearly discerned by other holy men of God as well as by Obadiah, that the day of Jehovah is coming upon all nations (15) to the destruction of every foe, native and foreign, of God's rule on earth; and the kingdom shall be Jehovah's (21; cp. Is. ii. 12, 17, 20, 21; x. 12–19; Joel iii. 12–21; Amos v. 18; ix. 8–15; Micah iv. 11–13).

Much uncertainty exists as to the date of the prophecy. I. It is very generally ascribed to the Chaldean period, when Jerusalem was alternately subject to the king of Egypt and the king of Babylon, and was finally captured by Nebuchadnezzar in 587 B. C., razed to the ground, and its inhabitants carried into captivity. This view is based on the description of Judah's calamity (10–16), and the fact is appealed to that Edom gave its sympathy to Babylon at this crisis (Ps. cxxxvii. 7) and prophets of the time severely denounced Edom (Jer. xlix. 7–22; Ezek. xxv. 12–14; xxxv.). II. The prophecy may, however, be much earlier, for 1. No allusion is made to the striking features of the fall of Jerusalem, the burning of the temple, the razing of the walls, and annihilation of the city. 2. The relation of verses 1–9 to Jer. xlix. 7–22. It is generally conceded that the unity and movement of Obadiah's thought and the general nature of the resemblance between the two passages indicate Jeremiah's dependence on Obadiah. 3. The hostile attitude of Edom was of long standing (Ezek. xxxv. 5), and the feeling against Edom expressed by Obadiah was voiced by Amos more than a century before the Chaldean invasion (Amos i. 6, 9, especially 11, 12; ix. 12; cp. Joel iii. 19). 4. Particular historical conditions, which are presupposed by the prophet, existed as early as the reign of Amaziah. Jerusalem had been plundered by Egyptians in the time of Rehoboam (1 Kin. xiv. 25, 26), by Arabians and Philistines in the reign of Jehoram (2 Chron. xxi. 16, 17; cp. Amos i. 6); and in the reign of Amaziah, who slaughtered the Edomites the king of Israel entered Jerusalem, broke down the northern wall of the city, plundered the temple and palace, and carried off hostages (2 Kin. xiv. 14, 17; 2 Chron. xxv. 11, 12, 23, 24). These events may well have called forth those manifestations of Edom's unbrotherly spirit, which Obadiah rebukes. In that case the prophecy would date from about 791 B. c., and antedate Joel cp. Obad. 17; Joel ii. 32; see JOEL); but if it does, its position after Joel is a marked departure from the prevailing chronological order of the minor prophets. III. The book may, however, be approximately in its proper chronological place, and accordingly date from the time of Ahaz. For calamities befell Judah in the reign of Ahaz: the king of Damascus wrested Edom from Judah, the king of Israel ravaged to the gates of Jerusalem, the Philistines took the cities of the lowland, and Ahaz stripped the temple of its treasures to buy aid from the king of Assyria, did homage to this foreigner, and made Judah a vassal state, Israelites also were carried into captivity (Obad. 20; Amos i 6, 9; cp. 1 Chron. v. 26); then the Edomite did violence to his brother Jacob, refrained from extending aid, and became as one of Judah's enemies (2 Chron. xxviii. 17; 2 Kin. xvi. 6, R. V margin; Obad. 10, 11). The year 731 B. c. or slightly earlier, in the reign of Ahaz when Judah was so deeply humiliated, was an appropriate time for Obadiah to take up his prophecy against the Edomites, rebuke them for their indifference to Judah's woes and for their open hostility in the past and present, and warn them not to exult over Judah s present distress, for their own time of punishment is coming

8. A Levite, one of the overseers over the workmen who repaired the temple in the reign of Josiah (2 Chron. xxxiv. 12).

9 Founder of family, presumably of the lineage of David (1 Chron. iii. 21).

10. A descendant of Joab. He came from Babylon with Ezra (Ezra viii. 9).

11. A priest who, doubtless in behalf of a father's house, sealed the covenant made in the time of Nehemiah (Neh. x. 5).

12. A Levite, apparently founder of a family of porters (Neh. xii 25). He seems to have been the Levite Obadiah, son of Shemaiah (1 Chron. ix. 16), called Abda in Neh. xi. 17.

O'bal [corpulence].

A people descended from Joktan (Gen. x. 28). 'Abil is the name of one of the oldest tribes of Arabia (Delitzsch) and of a district in Yemen (Halévy). Bochart suggests Pliny's Avalitæ on the African coast, near the straits of Bab el-Mandeb. In 1 Chron. i. 22 the name is written Ebal, jod being used instead of vau. These letters were often confused by copyists.

O'bed [server, worshiper].

1. Son of Ephlal, of the house of Jerahmeel, tribe of Judah (1 Chron. ii. 37).

2. Son of Boaz and Ruth, and grandfather of David (Ruth iv. 17, 21, 22).

3. One of David's mighty men (1 Chron. xi. 47).

4. A Levite, one of the doorkeepers, son of Shemaiah, house of Obed-edom (1 Chron. xxvi. 7).

5. The father of a certain Azariah, in the time of Athaliah (2 Chron. xxiii. 1).

O-bed-e'dom [serving Edom, or Edom is serving].

1. A Gittite, that is a native either of the Philistine Gath, and, if so, probably a member of David's bodyguard, or else of the Levitical city of Gath-rimmon in Dan. He lived between Kirjath-jearim and Jerusalem, near the spot where Uzzah was struck dead for touching the ark. The ark was therefore taken to his house by David's order, where it remained three months, blessings attending him and his family for giving it accommodation (2 Sam. vi. 10-12; 1 Chron. xiii. 13, 14; xv. 25). If a Levite, he is doubtless identical with Obed-edom the Korahite (see number 3). The Korahites were a division of the Kohathite family to which Gath-rimmon was assigned, and the statement that God blessed him (1 Chron. xxvi. 5) seems to refer to 1 Chron. xiii. 14 and 2 Sam. vi. 11.

2. A Levite of the second degree, who with others acted as doorkeeper for the ark, and was moreover a musician who played the harp at the removal of the ark to Jerusalem, and afterwards as a regular duty in the tent erected for the ark (1 Chron. xv. 18, 21; xvi. 5).

3. A Levite, who as doorkeeper marched in front of the ark at its removal to Jerusalem (1 Chron. xv. 24). He is probably one with Obed-edom, son of Jeduthun, a doorkeeper for the ark in the tent at Jerusalem (xvi. 38), and who is generally, though on uncertain grounds, held to be the person mentioned in the preceding clause of the verse. He appears to be Obed-edom the Korahite (xxvi. 1, 4; cp. also 10 with xvi. 38), whose sons and grandsons, with their brethren, sixty-two in number, were among the ninety-three, of whom the courses were formed in David's reign (xxvi. 8). Their station was at the southern gate (15). The family was still on duty in the reign of Amaziah (2 Chron. xxv. 24).

O'bil [a camel keeper].

An Ishmaelite who had charge of David's camels (1 Chron. xxvii. 30).

Ob-la'tion. See OFFERING.

O'both [water skins].

A station of the Israelites before their arrival in the desert east of Moab (Num. xxi. 10, 11; xxxiii. 43, 44). Situation unknown.

Och'ran, in A. V. **Ocran** [troubled].

An Asherite, father of Pagiel (Num. i. 13).

O'ded [he hath restored].

1. Father of the prophet Azariah (2 Chron. xv. 1). In ver. 8 the text is evidently corrupt.

2. An Israelite prophet in the reign of Pekah. Meeting the army of the northern kingdom returning from battle with many captives of Judah, the prophet remonstrated with them on their unbrotherly conduct, and in the name of Jehovah called on them to send the captives home. His words produced a great effect. Some of the leading men in Samaria, persuaded by him as to the path of duty, refused to allow the army to bring the prisoners inside the city. They then clothed the naked, fed the hungry, and, mounting the feeble on asses, took them to Jericho, and handed them over to their countrymen (2 Chron. xxviii. 9–15).

Od-o-me'ra, in A. V. **Od-o-nar'kes.**

Chief of a nomad tribe, or possibly an officer under Bacchides, whom Jonathan Maccabæus smote (1 Mac. ix. 66).

Of'fer-ings.

Offerings to God of various kinds can be traced from the dawn of human history. In the O. T. alone there are mentioned among others of early times the vegetable offering (Gen. iv. 3), the sacrifice of the firstling of the flock (iv. 4), the burnt offering (viii. 20; Ex. x. 25), the sacrificial meal (Gen. xxxi. 54), and the drink offering (xxxv. 14). An elaborate ritual of sacrifice existed among the great nations of antiquity, notably in Babylonia and Egypt, long before the days of Moses.

Offerings of many kinds to God constituted a marked feature of the Israelitish worship. Extended information on the subject is found in Lev. i.–vii., but not there exclusively. Offerings were of two classes, public and private, according as they were offered at the expense of the nation or of an individual, and they were of three kinds: drink offerings, vegetable or meal offerings, and animal offerings or sacrifices. The shedding of blood was a necessary accompaniment of every offering made in accordance with the religion of Jehovah. Without it there is no remission of sins; and hence a bloodless offering could not be accepted from man, for man by nature and practice is a sinner and has no right to approach God. It is true that in certain cases, such as extreme poverty, a bloodless offering was permitted; but it was made and accepted only in connection with the blood of the great public altar (Lev. ii. 2, 8; v 11–13).

The drink offering was not independent under the law. It was made only in connection with the meal offering which accompanied all burnt offerings, except perhaps that of Lev. xii. 6, and all peace offerings which were Nazirite, votive or freewill (Num. vi. 17; xv. 1–12). It was excluded from sin and trespass offerings.

The vegetable offering, called meat offering in A. V. and meal offering in R. V., consisted of white meal, or of unleavened bread, cakes, wafers, or of ears of grain roasted, always with salt and, except in the sin offering, with olive oil (Lev. ii. 1, 4, 13, 14; v. 11). It might form an independent offering: and part might be placed on the altar and the rest belong to the priest, as in private voluntary offerings (ii.), and when accepted as a sin offering from the very poor in lieu of an animal (v. 11–13); or else the whole might be consumed on the altar. In this latter case it corresponded to the burnt offering; and was made at the consecration of the high priest and at the cleansing of the leper (vi. 19–23; xiv. 10, 20). Or the vegetable offering might be subordinate, an accompaniment of a sacrifice. It was thus the invariable concomitant of the burnt offering, except perhaps that of Lev. xii.; and of peace offerings, except those obligatory at the feast of weeks. In these cases, according to tradition, it was entirely consumed on the altar. In other cases, part was placed on the altar and the rest went to the priest; namely, the wafers at the consecration of priests (viii. 26–28), in the thank offering (vii. 12–15), and at the release of the Nazirite (Num. vi. 13–20).

Animal offerings or sacrifices called for cattle, sheep and goats of both sexes, rarely for doves. The animal was required to be free from blemish and at least eight days old. Sacrifices were of three kinds, in each of which the blood made atonement (Lev. i. 4; xvii. 11). 1. The burnt offering, for which a male lamb, ram, goat, or bullock was prescribed. The case in 1 Sam. vi. 14 was extraordinary. The blood was sprinkled round about upon the altar, and the entire animal was consumed on the altar. It was expressive of the entire self-dedication of the offerer to Jehovah. 2. The sin offering and the trespass or guilt offering; for the former of which a bullock, a male or female goat, a female lamb, a dove, or a pigeon was used (Lev. iv. 4, 23, 28, 32; v. 7), while for the latter a ram was prescribed or, in the case of the leper and the Nazirite, a male lamb (vi. 6; xiv. 12, 21; Num. vi. 12). The blood was symbolically displayed, but in different ways. In the sin offering a portion of the blood was sprinkled before the Lord and smeared on the horns of the altar of incense, and the rest was poured out at the base of the altar of burnt offering, when the sin had been committed by the high priest or the nation; but in the case of other sinners, a part was put on the altar of burnt offering, and the rest was poured out as before (Lev. iv. 6, 7, 17, 18, 25, 30, 34). In the trespass offering all the blood was scattered over the altar. The fat only was burnt on the altar. The flesh of those sin offerings of which the blood was taken into the sanctuary was burnt without the camp, whereas the flesh of other sin offerings and of trespass offerings belonged to the priests (Lev. vi. 26, 30; vii. 6, 7; cp. Ex. xxix. 14; Lev. iv. 3, 12, 13, 21; xvi. 27; Heb. xiii. 11, 12). No part of these offerings was eaten by the offerer, as in the peace offerings; for the sacrificer came as one unworthy of communion with God, and these offerings were for purposes of expiation. The sin offering was made for sins of which the effect terminates primarily on the sinner; the trespass offering for sins of which the effects terminate primarily on another, and for which, in addition to the sacrifice, restitution was made through the hands of the priest to the person injured or, in case of his death without heirs, to the priest (Lev. v. 16; vi. 5; Num. v. 7, 8). But sins committed deliberately and for which the penalty was death could not be expiated (Num. xv. 30, 31). Atonement could be made for unintentional sins; for non-capital sins, like theft, for which punishment had been endured and restitution made; and for sins which the guilty one voluntarily confessed and for which he made compensation when possible. 3. The peace offering. Three kinds are distinguished: the thank offering in recognition of unmerited and unexpected blessings; the votive offering, in payment of a vow; and the freewill offering, probably not in gratitude for a special favor, but as an expression of irrepressible love for God (Lev. iii.). Peace offerings might also be prompted by the felt need of renewing peaceful communion with God (Judg. xx. 26; xxi. 4; 2 Sam. xxiv. 25). Any animal authorized for sacrifice, of either sex, might be used, but no bird. The blood was sprinkled; the fat was consumed on the altar; and, when the offering was private, the breast and shoulder went to the priests, and the rest of the flesh was eaten by the offerer and his friends before the Lord at the place of the sanctuary (Lev. iii., vii. 11–21; cp. 22–27; Ex. xxix. 20–28; Deut. xii. 7, 18; 1 Sam. ii. 15–17); see WAVE OFFERING. The meal before Jehovah was a eucharistic feast. It signified that Jehovah was present as a guest.

The sacrificial acts were five: 1. Presentation of the sacrifice at the door of the sanctuary by the offerer himself as his personal act. 2. Laying on of hands. The offerer placed his hands on the victim's head, thereby dedicating it to God and making it his own representative and substitute (cp. Lev. xvi. 21); see LAYING ON OF HANDS. 3. Slaying the animal by the offerer himself, who thus symbolically accepted the punishment due for his sin. In later times the priests slew the animal. 4. Symbolic application of the blood.

The priest sprinkled or smeared it on the altar and poured it out at the base. In specified cases a part was put on the offerer, or it was sprinkled before the veil of the sanctuary (Lev. iv. 6), or carried into the holy place (vi. 30), or even into the holy of holies (xvi. 14). 5. Burning the sacrifice, the whole of it or its fat only, on the altar of burnt offering, whereby its essence and flavor ascended to God.

Og.

A king of the Amorites of Bashan (Deut. iii. 1, 8), whose rule extended from the Jabbok to mount Hermon (8, 10 with Num. xxi. 23, 24). He had residences at both Ashtaroth and Edrei (Josh. xii. 4, 5; xiii. 12). He was huge of stature, the last of the Rephaim; and had an iron bedstead or sarcophagus of ironstone, 9 cubits long by 4 broad, of course longer and wider than its occupant. This relic was preserved in Rabbath Ammon (Deut. iii. 11). After the Israelites had conquered Sihon, they left their families and their cattle at the secure camp at Pisgah, and marched against Og. They defeated and slew him at Edrei and took possession of his country (Num. xxi. 20, 32–35; Deut. iii. 14). This territory was given to the half-tribe of Manasseh (Deut. iii. 13).

O'had.

A son of Simeon (Gen. xlvi. 10; Ex. vi. 15). He did not found a tribal family.

O'hel [a tent].

A son of Zerubbabel (1 Chron. iii. 20).

O-ho'lah, in A. V. **Aholah** [her tent].

Samaria and the kingdom of Israel personified as a woman of bad character (Ezek. xxiii. 1–49). Her name typified her infidelity to Jehovah.

O-ho'li-ab, in A. V. **Aholiab** [father's tent].

An artificer of the tribe of Dan, who assisted Bezalel in making furniture for the tabernacle (Ex. xxxi. 6; xxxv. 34, 35).

O-hol'i-bah, in A. V. **Aholibah** [my tent is in her].

Jerusalem and the kingdom of Judah personified as a woman of bad character (Ezek. xxiii. 1–49), although possessing Jehovah's tent.

O-hol-i-ba'mah, in A. V. **Aholibamah** [my tent is a high place].

A wife of Esau, daughter of Anah the Hivite (Gen. xxxvi. 2). She gave name to an Edomite family, organized under a chief (41). She was also called Judith, the praiseworthy (xxvi. 34; cp. ANAH).

Oil.

The oil used by the ancient Hebrews was chiefly olive oil. The fruit of the olive ripens in the autumn. It was, and is still, obtained by shaking the tree or beating it (Deut. xxiv. 20; and Is. xvii. 6; xxiv. 13, R. V. text and margin). The oil was expressed from the berries by treading them with the foot (Deut. xxxiii. 24; Mic. vi. 15), often in a shallow cavity hewn in the native rock, or by crushing them in a basin or circular trough under a wheel, collecting the outflowing oil, and then, in order to secure every drop that the berries contained, squeezing the pulp in a press constructed for the purpose. The expressed oil was collected in a rock-hewn vat or in a jar, and the impurities were allowed to settle. The fresh oil was specifically known to the Hebrews as *yiṣhar* (cp. Joel ii. 24, Hebrew text). Pure beaten olive oil (Ex. xxvii. 20; xxix. 40) was the finest in quality. Leaves, twigs, and dirt having been removed, the olives were beaten to pieces and crushed, and put into a basket, and the oil was allowed to flow out of itself. It was, as it were, a sort of first fruit, obtained before the pulp was placed under the press.

Oil was so important a product of Palestine that oil and wine are frequently mentioned, with or even without grain, as the chief harvest gain (Num. xviii. 12; Deut. vii. 13; Neh. x. 39; xiii. 5, etc.). Oil was used for illuminating purposes, being burned in lamps (Ex. xxv. 6; Mat. xxv. 3). Pure beaten olive oil was prescribed for the continual light in the sanctuary (Ex. xxvii. 20). Oil was used for food (1 Chron. xii. 40; Ezek. xvi. 13). It was mixed with meal and made into bread (1 Kin. xvii. 12); and cakes of fine flour mingled with oil, or with oil poured upon them, were part of the meal offering (Lev. ii. 1, 4–7), the oil being prescribed probably on account of its common use in food. Oil was used in medicine for mollifying wounds (Is. i. 6; Mark vi. 13). Sometimes wine was added to the oil, as was done by the good Samaritan in the case of the wounded Israelite (Luke x. 34). Herod was put in a bath of warm oil in the hope of alleviating his disease (War i. 33, 5). Oil was used as a cosmetic for anointing the body, especially after a bath, and for rendering the hair smooth (Ps. xxiii. 5; civ. 15; 2 Sam. xiv. 2). Olive oil was used for anointing kings (1 Sam. x. 1; xvi. 1, 13; 1 Kin. i. 39; 2 Kin. ix. 1, 6); and was called holy because employed in behalf of God (Ps. lxxxix. 20). A holy oil of composite and expensive character was used for the anointing of high priests. The tabernacle, the ark, the table, the candlestick, the altar, the laver and its foot were also anointed with the same precious compound (Ex. xxx. 22–33).

Oil Tree.

The literal rendering of the Hebrew words *'Eṣ shemen*, tree of oil, in Is. xli. 19. The words are translated olive wood (1 Kin. vi. 23; in A. V. olive tree) and wild olive (Neh. viii. 15; in A. V. pine branch). From its wood the two cherubim in the oracle of Solomon's temple were made, each of which was ten cubits high (1 Kin. vi. 23, 26), and also the doors of the oracle and the door posts for the entrance of the temple (31–33). It is generally believed to be the oleaster (*Elæagnus hortensis*), sometimes called the wild olive, but which, though it has a certain superficial resemblance to the true olive, is not really akin to it. The oleaster is a shrub or tree. It yields an oil, but much inferior to that of the olive. It is abundant in Palestine, especially near Hebron, Samaria, and mount Tabor. Other investigators identify the oil tree with *Balanites ægyptiaca*, which is called *zakkum* by the Arabs, and from which they extract an oil. But it now grows around the Dead Sea, and not on the mount of Olives (Neh. viii. 15).

Oint'ment.

Fragrant ointments were highly prized among the Hebrews (Eccl. vii. 1). They were used in dressing the hair and in purifying and perfuming the skin (Esth. ii. 12; Eccl. ix. 8), and Jesus was several times anointed with ointment brought by women who regarded him with adoration (Mat. xxvi. 6–13; Luke vii. 36–50). Ointments, with other spices, were employed on the dead body and in embalming (Luke xxiii. 56). Balm of Gilead and eye salve were used in medicine (Jer. viii. 22; Rev. iii. 18). In the ritual an ointment or holy oil was used, composed of myrrh, cassia, cinnamon, calamus, and olive oil (Ex. xxx. 25). In Palestine the usual ointment consisted of perfumed olive oil. The Hebrew word for oil is sometimes rendered ointment in A. V. (2 Kin. xx. 13), and this rendering is allowed to stand in E. R. V. in Prov. xxvii. 9; Ecc. vii. 1; ix. 8; x. 1; Song i. 3; iv. 10; Is. lvii. 9; Amos vi. 6. See Perfumery.

Old Tes'ta-ment.

The first of the two portions into which the Bible is naturally divided. The title was borrowed from the apostle Paul, who in 2 Cor. iii. 14, says: "For until this day remaineth the same veil untaken away, in the reading of the O. T." [in R. V. covenant]. The O. T. consists of thirty-nine books which, in the order in which they stand in the English Bible, naturally divide into three classes: seventeen historical books (Genesis to Esther), five poetical books (Job to Song of Solomon), and seventeen prophetical books. Poems and fragments of poems occur in the historical books (Gen. iv. 23, 24; ix. 25–27; xlix. 2–27; Ex. xv. 1–18; Judg. v.); prophecy also is found in the historical books (Gen. iii. 15; ix. 11–16; 2 Sam. vii.) and history in the prophetical books (Is. vii.; Jer. xxvi.; xxxvii. 11–xxxix. 14; xl. 7–xliii. 8); and poetry abounds in the prophetical books. The Hebrew Bible contains all these books and no more; but there is a difference in the arrangement and in the classification. See Canon. The English Bible has adopted the arrangement of the old versions.

The whole of the O. T. was originally written in Hebrew, excepting only Ezra iv. 8–vi. 18; vii. 12–26; Jer. x. 11; Dan. ii. 4–vii. 28, which are in Aramaic. The letters of the Hebrew and Aramaic alphabets were similar. A primitive form of them was in use in Phœnicia as far back as 1500 B. C. An early form is seen on the Moabite stone, in the Siloam inscription, and on Maccabæan coins. They passed through various changes of form until they ultimately became the familiar square character of the extant Hebrew manuscripts and printed editions of the Hebrew Bible. The books of the O. T. were written in the older script; but in the course of their multiplication by manuscript copies, the older characters were gradually transliterated into the square.

In writing the Hebrews made use of consonants only, leaving the vowels to be supplied by the reader. But between the seventh and the tenth centuries of the Christian era Jewish scholars, resident chiefly at Tiberias in Palestine, supplied vowel points which indicated the proper vocalization and followed the traditional pronunciation. These vowel signs gave greater fixity to the meaning of the texts. These men are called Masoretes or Massoretes, from *mâsorah* or better *massorah*, tradition; and the text, as supplied with vowels and otherwise improved, is known as the Masoretic text. They also added a system of accents to indicate the proper accentuation of the words and the manner in which they are to be conjoined or disjoined. In the Jewish schools of Babylonia a different method of indicating the vowels, but yielding substantially the same pronunciation, was in vogue. The Babylonian punctuation was written above the lines of the text.

At an early period the words were often separated by a dot or spacing (cp. the dot, Moabite Stone; Siloam Inscription; the spacing, Carpentras Stele, probably 4th century B. C.); and hence Hebrew manuscripts not improbably existed which were spaced in a similar manner. The Talmudic rules for copying manuscripts directed that a space equal to the width of a letter be left after each word.

The Jews have divided the Hebrew text of the books of Moses into fifty-four sections or pericopes, for reading on the Sabbaths of the year. For example, the first section extends from Gen. i. 1 to vi. 8; and the second from vi. 9 to xi. 32. These larger sections are broken into smaller ones, of two kinds, main divisions and subdivisions, technically called open and closed, and indicated by the letters pe and samech respectively. Thus in the second pericope one open section contains the narrative of the flood (vi. 9–ix. 17), which is subdivided into the four closed sections, vi. 9–12, introduction; vi. 13–viii. 14, the ark and the flood; viii. 15–ix. 7, Noah leaves the ark, sacrifices, and receives God's blessings and commands; ix. 8–17, the covenant of the rainbow. Another open section contains the generations of Shem and Terah (xi. 10–32). Its closed sections are closely followed by the R. V. in paragraphing the English text. The verses were first numbered in the Hebrew Bible in Bomberg's edition of 1547,

in which the number was noted on the margin opposite every fifth verse by the appropriate letter of the Hebrew alphabet used numerically. Arias Montanus, in his Hebrew Bible with interlinear Latin translation, published at Antwerp in 1571, was the first actually to break up the Hebrew text into chapters. To number the verses, he added the Arabic numerals in the margin. See BIBLE.

The Hebrew text of the O. T. has come down practically unchanged since at least the second century of the Christian era. From this form all existing manuscripts are derived. The preservation of this standard text, in its integrity and with freedom from errors, during its transmission through two thousand years has been due to the existence of professional scribes to whom its copying, pronunciation, and interpretation were entrusted and to the elaborate rules adopted for their guidance which rendered mistakes in copying unlikely to occur and made the detection of a chance error almost certain. Aaron ben Moses ben Asher, who flourished in the earlier half of the tenth century, prepared an edition conformed to the original according to the minute tradition of the scribes. This work of ben Asher was highly prized for its accuracy, and from it all western manuscripts are descended.

But duplicate passages, such as Gen. x. 4 and 1 Chron. i. 7 or 2 Kin. viii. 26 and 2 Chron. xxii. 2, reveal the existence of occasional errors that got into the standard text before the second Christian century. They occur more in numbers and in proper names than in narratives, and they are chiefly due to transcribers mistaking one Hebrew character for another that closely resembled it (see BETH, DALETH), improperly uniting two words into one or separating one word into two (see MOLE 2), attaching an initial letter to the preceding word, or accidentally repeating or omitting letters or words. Not all differences, however, are errors. Some, as in Ps. xiv. and liii., are the result of a revision undertaken by the author himself or by others in order to adapt the work to a new purpose; or like Is. ii. 2–4 and Mic. iv. 1–3, are due to freedom of quotation. As in the case of the N. T., three aids exist for biblical critics who attempt to eliminate copyists' errors and restore the text to its primitive purity. They are, first, the collation of Hebrew manuscripts, which has been carried on with perseverance, portions of from 1500 to 2000 manuscripts having been used in the comparison; second, the examination of early versions made from the Hebrew into other languages before the Masoretic text was established; and third, the study of passages quoted or alluded to in the Apocrypha, the N. T., or other writings.

It is believed that the original manuscripts of the O. T. books were written on skins; see BOOK. That many of them were, is certain (Ps. xl. 7; Jer. xxxvi. 14, 23). The existing manuscripts are usually of parchment or, in the East, of leather. They are not old. In the British Museum is a manuscript of the Law, written on vellum, which is believed to have been penned before A. D. 850; and in the Karaite synagogue at Cairo is a codex of the former and latter prophets, without vowels, which was written A. D. 895, if it is correctly dated. The oldest extant manuscript of which the date can be affirmed with certainty is a manuscript of the latter prophets (Major and Minor), punctuated after the Babylonian system. It was brought from the Crimea, is dated A. D. 916, and is now kept in the imperial library at St. Petersburg. The oldest manuscript of the entire O. T. is dated A. D. 1010. It too is at St. Petersburg. The scarcity of ancient Hebrew manuscripts is to a large extent due to the practice of the Jews, which is alluded to in the Talmud, of burying all sacred manuscripts which became defective through wear or otherwise faulty.

After the invention of printing, the book of Psalms was put in type and published in 1477. Eleven years later, in 1488, the whole printed Hebrew Bible was issued in folio from a press at Soncino in the duchy of Milan. A printed manual edition was first issued by Bomberg in 1517. The great rabbinic Bible of Jacob ben Hayyim, published by Daniel Bomberg at Venice in 1524-25 in four volumes, is based upon a careful collation of manuscripts and faithfully reproduces the standard text of the scribes at Tiberias. Van der Hooght's edition of the Hebrew text was first published at Amsterdam in 1705. It has held its ground on account of its accuracy, being reprinted with minor corrections by Aug. Hahn in 1831 and by C. G. G. Theile in 1849. It has about 1000 marginal readings, most of them of considerable antiquity. Yet more important is the edition of the Masoretic text, with critical and Masoretic appendices, prepared by S. Baer and Franz Delitzsch. Genesis appeared in 1869, and other books have followed at intervals. This edition and that of Ginsburg, issued at London in 1894, are revisions of the text of Jacob ben Hayyim, designed to conform it more closely to the teachings of the Massora. Kittel's edition, printed at Leipzig, 1906, reproduces the text of Jacob ben Hayyim, and gives in footnotes the more important variants of the manuscripts and versions.

Ol'ive.

A tree largely cultivated in Palestine in olive yards (Ex. xxiii. 11; Josh. xxiv. 13; Judg. xv. 5; 1 Sam. viii. 14). It grew also in Assyria (2 Kin. xviii. 32). Strabo mentions it among the trees of Armenia, and it is supposed to be indigenous in northern India and other temperate regions of Asia. The wood was used for timber (1 Kin. vi. 23, 31, 32, 33). A valuable oil was obtained from the berries, and had extensive use; see OIL.

Plants grown from the drupe or from slips

cut from below the grafted branches, and the shoots which spring up around the trunk, are of the wild variety and require grafting. And a good, fruitful olive tree, if its cultivation is neglected, deteriorates and becomes wild. The wild olive is a shrub or low tree; and any berries which it may produce are small and of no value. The process of grafting a cutting from the wild olive tree into one of the cultivated kind is alluded to in Rom. xi. 17, 24 to illustrate the grafting of the gentile converts on what hitherto had been the Jewish church. In gardening the process was different; it was the grafting of a cutting from the cultivated tree into a stock of the wild olive to alter and improve its nature.

From an olive tree the dove plucked the leaf when the flood was subsiding (Gen. viii. 11). An olive branch is now an emblem of peace. The olive was also a symbol of prosperity and divine blessing, of beauty and strength (Ps. lii. 8; Jer. xi. 16; Hos. xiv. 6). The aged olive tree is often surrounded by young and thrifty shoots (Ps. cxxviii. 3). Women sometimes adorned themselves with garlands of olives on festal occasions (Judith xv. 13), and at the Olympic games in Greece the victor's crown was composed of olive leaves.

The olive tree of Palestine is the common *Olea europæa*. It has lanceolate, entire, leathery, evergreen leaves of a dusty color, and small whitish, monopetalous flowers. The nearest approach to it of familiar garden plants is the privet. The olive is still cultivated through nearly every part of Palestine.

Ol'ives, Mount of, and Ol'i-vet, the latter word being a Latin form, borrowed from the Vulgate, and meaning a place where many olive trees grow.

A hill which is before Jerusalem on the east (Zech. xiv. 4), separated from it by the valley of the Kidron (2 Sam. xv. 14, 23, 30). Its summit with the farther slope was reckoned as a Sabbath-day's journey from the city (Acts i. 12), or, according to Josephus, at 5 or 6 stades (Antiq. xx. 8, 6; War v. 2, 3). David, barefoot and with covered head, went up its ascent when he fled from Absalom. On its summit God was wont to be worshiped (2 Sam. xv. 32). The glory of the Lord appeared there to Ezekiel in a vision (Ezek. xi. 23), and Zechariah prophetically portrayed Jehovah standing on the mountain to interpose in behalf of his people (Zech. xiv. 4). Jesus went often to the mount of Olives (Luke xxi. 37; xxii. 39; John viii. 1). He was descending its slope when the multitude welcomed him to the city with hosannas (Luke xix. 37, 38). He had crossed its summit when Jerusalem burst into full view, and he wept over the fate which he knew awaited the city (41-44). He was sitting on the mount with his disciples gazing across the valley at the splendid temple and the city, when he prophesied the destruction of both (Mat. xxiv. 3; Mark xiii. 3). After

An exact counterpart of an olive crushing machine used in antiquity is still giving good service in Bethlehem today.

Olive trees in a garden in Emmaus.

The Mount of Olives viewed from the northeast corner of the Old City, Jerusalem.

his last passover he retired to the mount of Olives (Mat. xxvi. 30; Mark. xiv. 26). The garden of Gethsemane was to the west of it, either at its base or some small distance up its ascent. Bethany and Bethphage were on the eastern side (Mat. xxi. 1; Mark xi. 1; Luke xix. 29). It was near the former of these villages that our Lord's ascension took place (xxiv. 50). The mount of Olives is unquestionably the eminence now called by the Arabs Jebel et-Tôr, east of Jerusalem. Properly speaking, it is a chain of hills rising into three or, as some reckon, four summits, and with two lateral spurs. One spur runs westward, starting at the bend of the Kidron, about a mile north of Jerusalem, and attains an elevation of 2737 feet above the sea. This northern spur is generally identified with Josephus' hill of Scopus, or the watchman (War ii. 19, 4). The other spur is separated from the main ridge by the Kidron. It also runs westward, and faces the city on the south. It has been designated the hill of Evil Counsel, from the late and worthless tradition that Caiaphas had a country place on its summit and in his house the chief priests met and consulted about putting Jesus to death (John xi. 47-53). Its altitude is 2549 feet.

Of the four peaks into which the range of Olivet rises, the most northerly one, called Karem es-Seiyad, is the highest, being 2723 feet above sea level. It was formerly called Galilee, either because Galilæans encamped there when they came to Jerusalem to the festivals, or because in the fourteenth century it was believed to be the place of the ascension where the angels addressed the disciples as men of Galilee. The second peak is called the Ascension. As early as A. D. 315 it was regarded as the spot whence Jesus ascended to heaven, and Constantine crowned it with a rotunda and a basilica. The latter has been replaced by a succession of churches of the Ascension. This is the mount of Olives proper. It stands directly opposite to the eastern gate of Jerusalem, and rises to 2643 feet above the level of the ocean, 371 above the bed of the Kidron, and 208 over the temple plateau. The third hill is called the Prophets', from what are called the prophets' tombs on its side. The fourth hill is named the mount of Offense, from the belief that Solomon there built the idolatrous shrines for his heathen wives. The Ascension hill and the hill of the Prophets are so slightly dissevered that some reduce the four summits to three.

At the foot of the mount of Olives proper, at the traditional site of Gethsemane, the road forks, including the garden in its crotch. One branch runs south, rises by a gradual ascent, winds round the southern shoulder of the mountain, and continues on to Bethany and Jericho. It was built in the seventh century A. D. by the calif Abd-el-Melek. The northern fork runs east, and at

the distance of about fifty yards divides into three. The middle one, steep and rugged, leads up the face of the mountain, crosses it near the summit, and goes on past the so-called stone of Bethphage to Bethany. As early as the fourth century the Christians of Jerusalem, when celebrating the triumphal entry of Jesus into the city, used to come in procession over this road. The two branches on either side of this steep middle road also reach the top of the mountain, but they follow a more gradual ascent. Farther up the Kidron valley a Roman road to the Jordan climbed the western slope of the ridge near 'Ain eṣ-Ṣuwan, crossed the crest about half a mile north of the top of Olivet, in the depression north of Karem es-Seiyad, descended into the wady and crossed it near the ruin Bukei'dan and, keeping the wady Rûâbeh hard by on the north, continued on to the Jordan.

Chapel of the Ascension on the Mount of Olives. Crusader architecture is below the Islamic dome.

Ol'i-vet. See OLIVES, MOUNT of.

O-lym'pas.

A Roman Christian to whom Paul sent his salutation (Rom. xvi. 15).

O'mar.

A descendant of Esau through Eliphaz (Gen. xxxvi. 11), and chieftain of a tribe of the name (15).

O-me'ga.

The last letter of the Greek alphabet, hence used figuratively for the last or for the end (Rev. i. 8, 11; xxi. 6; xxii. 13).

O'mer.

A measure for dry articles. It contained a tenth part of an ephah (Ex. xvi. 36), and was one hundredth of a homer (Ezek. xlv. 11). The omer contained nearly 6 pints. See MEASURE.

Om'ri [untaught or impetuous or like a sheaf].

1. A man of Benjamin, family of Becher (1 Chron. vii. 8).

2. A man of Judah, family of Perez (1 Chron. ix. 4).

3. Son of Michael and prince of the tribe of Issachar in David's reign (1 Chron. xxvii. 18).

4. A king of Israel. Before gaining the throne he was commander of the Israelite army in the reign of Elah and not unlikely in that of Baasha also; and he may have subjugated Moab at this time (Moabite Stone 7, 8). He was conducting the siege of Gibbethon, which belonged to the Philistines, when news arrived that Zimri had murdered Elah, and usurped the throne. The army at once proclaimed Omri king of Israel. He accepted the honor, and led his troops against the town of Tirzah, the national capital, where Zimri was. The latter, despairing of his ability to hold the throne, committed suicide (1 Kin. xvi. 15-20). But the nation was divided. One half adhered to Omri and the other half supported the claims of Tibni; and it was not until the death of Tibni five years later that Omri became the undisputed sovereign of all Israel (21-23). The statement of ver. 23, "in the thirty-first year of Asa began Omri to reign over Israel" (in Hebrew simply "Omri reigned"), refers, not to the time of his proclamation by the soldiery and his assumption of the royal title (although the twelve years of his reign are counted from this event), but to his attainment of the sole authority in the kingdom (cp. ver. 15, 29). He transferred the seat of government from Tirzah to Samaria, which he built for the purpose (24). He followed the idolatries of Jeroboam and acted in other respects more wickedly than any of his predecessors on the throne of the ten tribes (26; Mic. vi. 16). He died about 874 B. C., and was buried in Samaria. His son Ahab succeeded him on the throne (1 Kin. xvi. 28). Omri made an impression on history outside of Israel. Not only did the Moabites remember his name; but after his death and the annihilation of his family the Assyrians for a time still attached his name, which they wrote Ḥumri, to the reigning monarch and land of Israel.

On, I. [strength].
A Reubenite chief who took part in the rebellion of Korah (Num. xvi. 1); see KORAH.

On, II. [Egyptian *An*, light].
An old and renowned city of Lower Egypt, on the east of the Nile, in the delta, several miles from the river and 19 miles north of Memphis. It was the principal seat of the worship of the sun; hence called Heliopolis by the Greeks (cp. Ex. i. 11, Septuagint) and Beth-shemesh by Jeremiah (xliii. 13). Apparently Isaiah had this city in mind; and by a slight change in the first letter of the name turned city of the sun into city of destruction, to denote the overthrow of idolatry (Is. xix. 18; cp. margin).

With the temple of the sun were connected a training school for priests and a medical school, and these institutions were visited by all the Greek philosophers who went to Egypt to study. In Herodotus' day the priests of On were esteemed the most learned in history of all the Egyptians (ii. 3). It was the daughter of a priest of On whom Pharaoh gave to Joseph to wife (Gen. xli. 45, 50; xlvi. 20).

O'nam [strong, wealthy].
1. A Horite (Gen. xxxvi. 23; 1 Chron. i. 40).
2. A man of Judah, house of Jerahmeel (1 Chron. ii. 26, 28).

O'nan [strong].
A son of Judah by a Canaanitess. That his brother might have no heir, he sinned; but he himself died without male issue (Gen. xxxviii. 4-10; xlvi. 12).

O-nes'i-mus [useful, profitable].
A slave of Philemon, whom Paul was the means of converting at Rome, and whom he sent back to his Christian master requesting that he might be received, not as a servant, but as a brother beloved (Philem. 10-19). He was a man of Colossæ, and with Tychicus carried from Rome to that city the epistles to the Colossians and to Philemon (Col. iv. 7-9).

On-e-siph'o-rus [bringing advantage].
A Christian whose home was probably at Ephesus (2 Tim. i. 18). When he was at Rome he sought out the apostle Paul, then a prisoner, and showed him great kindness (16). The members of his household were with Timothy, and Paul sent them his salutations (iv. 19).

O-ni'as, in A. V. once **O-ni'a-res** (1 Mac. xii. 19) [Greek for perhaps Coniah]. The form Oniares is an old corruption, in which the two names Onias Arius are blended (cp. Antiq. xii. 4, 10).
A high priest of the Jews, who held office from about 323 to 300 B. C. He was a contemporary of Arius, king of Sparta, who reigned from 309 to 265 B. C. (1 Mac. xii. 7, in A. V. Darius, a corruption of Arius; 19, 20). Onias succeeded Jaddua, and was the father and predecessor of Simon the Just (Antiq. xi. 8, 7; xii. 2, 5). He is probably referred to in Ecclus. l. 1. Josephus errs in regarding Onias III., a later pontiff, as the recipient of the letter from Arius.
For others of the name, see HIGH PRIEST.

On'ion.
A plant, the bulbous root of which was much used in Egypt as an article of food (Num. xi. 5; Herod. ii. 125). It is *Allium cepa*, called in Hebrew beṣel, in Arabic baṣal. It has been cultivated from an early period in Egypt and other parts of the east.

O'no [strong].
A town of Benjamin (Neh. xi. 35), in a plain of considerable size (vi. 2), built or rather rebuilt by a Benjamite called Shamed

(1 Chron. viii. 12). Some of its inhabitants returned from the Babylonian captivity (Ezra ii. 33 ; Neh. vii. 37). It is considered to have been at Kefr 'Ana, about 7 miles inland east by south from Joppa.

On'y-cha.

The rendering of the Hebrew *Sh^eheleth* (Ex. xxx. 34). It was one of the ingredients in a perfume made for the service of the tabernacle. It is believed to have been the operculum (lid) of a shell mollusc called stromb or wing-shell, which being burnt gave out a certain perfume.

O'nyx [a finger nail, an onyx].

The rendering of the Hebrew *Shoham*. The Hebrew word denotes a precious stone (Job xxviii. 16, R. V. margin beryl ; Ezek. xxviii. 13). It was found in the land of Havilah (Gen. ii. 12). Two of these stones, each graven with the names of six Israelite tribes, were put on the shoulder pieces of the high priest's ephod (Ex. xxviii. 9. 12), and another was the second stone in the fourth row on his breastplate (xxviii. 20). David gathered such stones for the service of the future temple (1 Chron. xxix. 2). The onyx is a cryptocrystalline variety or subvariety of quartz. It is in layers of different colors, which alternate with each other and bear some resemblance to the white and flesh-colored bands of the finger nail.

O'phel [a swelling, a bulge].

The southern part of the eastern hill at Jerusalem, enclosed by the city wall ; perhaps originally a massive circular tower or projection in the fortifications at this point. The general locality is indicated by the proximity of the pool of Shelah, *i. e.*, doubtless Siloam, the court of the guard, the water gate, and the horse gate (Neh. iii. 15–27 ; see JERUSALEM, paragraph on the walls) ; the pool of Siloam, the eastern court of the temple, and the Kidron valley (War v. 4, 1 and 2 ; 6, 1). Jotham built much on its walls, and Manasseh increased their height (2 Chron. xxvii. 3 ; xxxiii. 14). After the exile, if not before, the Nethinim had their residence in this quarter, because of its convenience to the temple (Neh. iii. 26 ; xi. 21). At the ophel, or bulge, in Samaria Gehazi deposited the goods gotten by deceit from Naaman (2 Kin. v. 24, R. V. margin) ; and in a city of Moab Mesha built the wall of the ophel (Moabite Stone 22).

O'phir.

A tribe descended from Joktan (Gen. x. 29 ; 1 Chron. i. 23), and the country which they inhabited. This region was celebrated for its gold (xxix. 4 ; Job xxii. 24 ; xxviii. 16 ; Ps. xlv. 9 ; Is. xiii. 12), to obtain which, Hiram, in conjunction with Solomon, sent a navy from Ezion-geber (1 Kin. ix. 28). The ships brought back algum or almug trees as well as gold (x. 11), and probably also silver, ivory, apes, and peacocks (22 ; cp. xxii. 48). Jehoshaphat attempted to imitate

the enterprise, but his ships were wrecked at Ezion-geber (xxii. 48). As this port was on the gulf of Akaba, the route to Ophir was by the Red Sea and not by the Mediterranean. The voyage out and back in the ships of that day, with the peculiar winds of the Red Sea, and including the lying in port, lasted, it may be judged, three years (x. 22 ; cp. xxii. 48) ; see RED SEA. Three opinions exist as to its situation : 1. Ophir was at Sofala, on the eastern coast of Africa, opposite the island of Madagascar. In favor of this view is the fact that it was formerly an emporium for gold. But when it is noted that the algum or almug tree is apparently the sandalwood, which is a native of India, and is not believed to occur either in Arabia or Africa, and that other products of Ophir brought by the seamen had also Indian names, it is probable that Ophir was in India, or else was a mart of exchange for Indian goods. 2. Josephus says that it was the Golden Land in India (Antiq. viii. 6, 4), perhaps on the river Cophen (i. 6, 4) ; and hence it has been conjecturally located at Abhira, at the mouth of the Indus. 3. Ophir was in southern or southeastern Arabia. This opinion is probably correct ; for the majority of the Joktanites, perhaps all of them, settled in Arabia. Moreover, Ophir is mentioned between Sheba and Havilah.

Oph'ni [perhaps, the musty or the Ophnite]. The Hebrew uses the definite article.

A village of Benjamin (Josh. xviii. 24). Robinson suggests its identity with Gophna, on the highway from Samaria to Jerusalem, a day's march north of Gibeah (War v. 2, 1) ; the modern Jufna, 3 miles northwest by north of Bethel. This identification assumes that the boundary of Benjamin turned northward near Bethel, for Bethel was on the northern boundary.

Oph'rah [hind].

1. A son of Menothai, of the tribe of Judah (1 Chron. iv. 14).

2. A town of Benjamin (Josh. xviii. 23), evidently north of Michmash (1 Sam. xiii. 17). According to the Onomastikon, of the fourth century A. D., it was a village then called Ephraim, five miles to the east of Beth-el. Robinson doubtfully identified it with et-Taiyibeh, on a conical hill 4 miles northeast by east of Beth-el, with a splendid view from its summit, which he felt could not have been left unoccupied in ancient times. His opinion has been widely accepted, although the place seems far north for a town of Benjamin.

3. A village west of the Jordan, occupied by the Abiezrites, a family of Manasseh (Judg. vi. 11, 15 ; cp. Josh. xvii. 1, 2). It was the home of Gideon, where he was called to his mission and built an altar, where he made an ephod to the ensnaring of Israel, and where he was buried (Judg. vi.–viii.). Conder, pointing out that according to the

Samaritan Chronicle, Ophrah was the ancient name of Fer'ata, 6 miles west by south of Shechem, suggests this village as its site. Fer'ata is, however, commonly regarded as Pirathon (q. v.).

Or'a-tor.
1. The rendering of the Hebrew *Laḥash,* an incantation, preceded by *nᵉbon,* skillful in enchantment (Is. iii. 3). The R. V. accurately translates the phrase by skillful enchanter.
2. The rendering of the Greek *Rhètōr,* public speaker, pleader, in Acts xxiv. 1, applied to Tertullus. He was a professional advocate engaged by Paul's Jewish enemies to prosecute the apostle before the Roman procurator.

Or'chard. See GARDEN.

O'reb [a raven].
1. One of two Midianite princes defeated, captured, and put to death by Gideon. He was slain at a rock, which came to be called in consequence the rock of Oreb (Judg. vii. 25; viii. 3; Ps. lxxxiii. 11; Is. x. 26).
2. A rock on which the Midianite prince Oreb was killed by Gideon (Judg. vii. 25; Is. x. 26). Exact situation unknown; but doubtless it was west of the Jordan near the river (Judg. vii. 25; viii. 4).

O'ren [a species of pine tree].
A man of Judah, house of Jerahmeel (1 Chron. ii. 25).

Or'gan. See PIPE.

O-ri'on.
A constellation (Job ix. 9; xxxviii. 31; Amos v. 8), in Hebrew *Kᵉsil,* a man without understanding, an irreligious person, a fool. The ancient versions unite in this identification. The Targums and the Syriac version render the word by giant, and the Septuagint and Vulgate employ the name Orion. In the classic mythology Orion is represented as a man of great strength, celebrated as a worker in iron and as a hunter. Being killed by the goddess Diana, he was transferred to the heavens and bound to the sky (cp. Job xxxviii. 31), and became the constellation Orion.

The constellation is visible in all latitudes. It disputes with the Great Bear the distinction of being the finest constellation of the sky. Two of its stars—Betelgeuse at the upper part of his right arm as he faces the spectator, and Rigel at his uplifted left foot—are of the first magnitude. About 100 stars in the constellation are visible to the naked eye, and 2000 or more may be seen under the telescope.

Or'na-ments.
Orientals adorn themselves with ornaments to an extent deemed excessive by occidental taste. It has ever been so. Hebrews, Egyptians, Midianites. Syrians, both men and women, were fond of wearing ornaments (Gen. xxiv. 22; Ex. iii. 22; xi. 2; xxxii.

2; Num. xxxi. 50). Women wore beads and pearls, and articles of gold, silver and brass (Song i. 10, 11; 1 Tim. ii. 9); earrings, nose rings, pendants, necklaces, chains, brazen mirrors, armlets, bracelets, finger rings, anklets (Gen. xxiv. 22, 47; xxxv. 4; Ex. xxxv. 22; Num. xxxi. 50; Is. iii. 18–23). Men of all classes except the poorest wore seal rings (Gen. xxxviii. 18), which were useful in business as well as ornamental. Nor did they regard rings for the arms as effeminate. Saul, like the kings of Assyria, wore a ring about the arm or wrist (2 Sam. i. 10). It was a national custom with the Ishmaelites for the men to wear earrings (Judg. viii. 25, 26), and men among the Hebrews sometimes did so (Ex. xxxii. 2). Men of high rank wore a gold chain as badge of office (Gen. xli. 42; Dan. v. 29).

Ornaments were laid aside in time of mourning (Ex. xxxiii. 4–6).

Or'nan [perhaps, piny]. See ARAUNAH.

Or'pah [neck, mane].
The wife of Chilion, and the sister-in-law of Ruth. She consented to remain in her native country, Moab, when Ruth, drawn by affection to her mother-in-law, Naomi, insisted on accompanying her to Palestine (Ruth i. 4, 14, 15; cp. iv. 10).

Or-tho-si'a, in A. V. **Orthosias.**
A city on the coast of Phœnicia, between Tripoli and the river Eleutherus (1 Mac. xv. 37; Pliny, Hist. Nat. v. 17).

Os-nap'per. See ASNAPPER.

Os'pray, obsolete form of **Osprey.**
The rendering of the Hebrew *'Ozniyyah* (Lev. xi. 13; Deut. xiv. 12), an unclean bird. It is either a species of eagle or more vaguely the eagle genus. The Septuagint translates it *'aliaietos,* that is, *Pandion haliaëtus.* It is a dark brown eagle widely distributed throughout the world, frequenting seacoasts, and living on fish. In Palestine it occurs along the Mediterranean, especially in the lagoons at the mouth of the Kishon.

Os'si-frage [bone breaker].
The rendering in A. V. of the Hebrew *Peres,* breaker. It was an unclean bird (Lev. xi. 13; and Deut. xiv. 12). The R. V. translates it gier eagle. It is believed to be the lammergeyer, or bearded eagle (*Gypaëtus barbatus*). The English name ossifrage and the Hebrew *peres* both refer to the fact that the bird delights in bones, snakes, and tortoises, which it breaks. This it sometimes does by taking them up to a great height in the air and dropping them on a stone. The ossifrage is 3½ feet high; the expansion of its wings is about 9 feet. Its claws are not adapted for carrying off living prey, and its disposition is cowardly. In Palestine the ossifrage is rare and tending to extinction, its chief haunts being the ravines of the Arnon, east of the Dead Sea.

Os'trich.

1. The rendering of the Hebrew Ya'en, feminine Ya'anah, probably the voracious bird. It was ceremonially unclean (Lev. xi. 16; Deut. xiv. 15), makes a mournful sound (Mic. i. 8), inhabits the wilderness (Is. xiii. 21; xxxiv. 13), and was believed to forsake its eggs (Lam. iv. 3). The A. V. translates the masculine form by ostrich, the feminine form by owl.

2. The rendering of the Hebrew, Ranan, utterer of tremulous sounds (Job xxxix. 13, in A. V. peacock). The female deposits her eggs on the ground to be warmed in the dust; and it was commonly supposed that she abandoned them to their fate, forgetting that the foot might crush them or that the wild beast might trample them (14, 15). The speed of the ostrich is such that it distances a man on horseback (18).

3. The A. V. inaccurately renders Nosah by ostrich in Job xxxix. 13. It means a feather, as in Ezek. xvii. 3, 7.

The ostrich (Struthio camelus) belongs to the aberrant subclass or division called Ratitae, or struthious birds. They are among the largest in size of the class, but are not able to fly, the deprivation being compensated by great power of running. The common ostrich is 6 or 8 feet high. The ostrich feathers which are used for ladies' hats are the

A bread oven in Eastern Cyprus. The design is the same as those used in antiquity.

quill feathers of the wings and tail. The bird prepares a nest by rolling in the sand and scooping out a hole about 6 feet in diameter. An egg is laid every other day, until the eggs number ten, twelve, or more. Each egg is about three pounds in weight. They appear to be hatched partly by the heat of the sun, but mainly by incubation, the male bird sitting on them for about twenty hours to the hen's four. The male takes charge of the young brood. At night the bird utters a hoarse, complaining cry, alluded to in Mic. i. 8. The ostrich is diffused over the greater part of Africa. It still occurs in Arabia, but its area there seems to have been diminished since O. T. times.

Oth'ni [probably, lion of (God)].

A porter, the son of Shemaiah (1 Chron. xxvi. 7).

Oth'ni-el [lion of God, powerful one of God].

A son of Kenaz and brother or half brother of Caleb, son of Jephunneh the Kenizzite (Josh. xv. 17; 1 Chron. iv. 13); see CALEB. Caleb promised to give his daughter Achsah in marriage to any hero who took the town of Debir or Kirjath-sepher. Othniel effected its capture and received Achsah (Josh. xv. 15-17; Judg. i. 11-13). He subsequently delivered the Israelites from the tyranny of Cushan-rishathaim, king of Mesopotamia, and became judge, and the land had rest forty years (iii. 8-11).

Ov'en. See BREAD.

Owl.

1. The rendering of the Hebrew Bath hayya'anah (Lev. xi. 16, A. V.). See OSTRICH 1.

2. The rendering of the Hebrew Kos, a cup, an owl. It was ceremonially unclean (Lev. xi. 17; Deut. xiv. 16, little owl), and frequented waste places (Ps. cii. 6). Probably the southern little owl (Athene glaux) is intended, which is universally distributed through Palestine, occurring in olive yards, rocks, thickets, and among ruins and tombs.

3. The rendering of the Hebrew Yanshuph. It was ceremonially unclean (Lev. xi. 17; Deut. xiv. 16, great owl) and frequented waste places (Is. xxxiv. 11; R. V. margin, bittern). It is rendered ibis in the Septuagint and Vulgate, and owl in the Targums and the Syriac version. Tristram believes that the species was the Egyptian eagle owl (Bubo ascalaphus). It lives in caves and among ruins, and is common about Petra and Beer-sheba.

4. The rendering of the Hebrew Tin-

shemeth (Lev. xi. 18; in A. V. swan). The Septuagint renders it heron, and the Vulgate swan.

5. The rendering of the Hebrew Lilith, nocturnal specter (Is. xxxiv. 14; in A. V. screech owl, in R. V. night monster). The screech or barn owl (Strix flammea) is found in Palestine frequenting ruins.

6. The rendering of the Hebrew Kippoz (Is. xxxiv. 15; in R. V. arrow snake). The corresponding word in Arabic, kiffâza, denotes the arrow snake.

Ox.
The male of the species Bos taurus, though ox frequently signifies any animal of the kind, without respect to sex (Ex. xx. 17), and the plural oxen is often synonymous with cattle (Gen. xii. 16). The ox was early domesticated. Abraham had sheep and oxen (Gen. xii. 16; xxi. 27); so had his contemporary Abimelech (xx. 14), and the Egyptians at the time of the ten plagues (Ex. ix. 3). The ox was used for plowing (1 Kin. xix. 19), for drag-

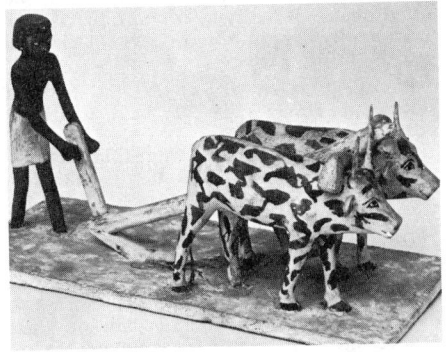

Model of an Egyptian plowing with yoked oxen.

ging carts or wagons (Num. vii. 3; 2 Sam. vi. 6, etc.), and for treading out grain (Deut. xxv. 4). They were eaten (1 Kin. i. 25; cp. Mat. xxii. 4), and were largely sacrificed, especially in connection with the burnt offerings (Num. vii. 87, 88; 2 Sam. xxiv. 22; 2 Chron. v. 6; vii. 5, etc.). A yoke of oxen was two oxen designed to be yoked together for the plow, for a cart, or for anything similar. Tristram says that the common cattle of southern and central Palestine are small in size, those of northern Palestine are larger. The largest herds are now beyond the Jordan.

The word t'o, rendered wild ox (Deut. xiv. 5, A. V.) and wild bull (Is. li. 20, A. V.), is translated in R. V. by antelope (q. v.). See UNICORN.

Ox'goad. See GOAD.

O'zem.
1. A son of Jesse (1 Chron. ii. 15).
2. A son of Jerahmeel (1 Chron. ii. 25).

O-zi'as. See UZZIAH.

Oz'ni [eared, attentive].
A son of Gad, and founder of a tribal family (Num. xxvi. 16). He was either called also Ezbon (Gen. xlvi. 16), or else on Ezbon's death he took his place and founded a tribal family, as did Hezron and Hamul in Judah (Num. xxvi. 19-21).

P

Pa'a-rai.
One of David's mighty men (2 Sam. xxiii. 35, most probably a diverse reading of 1 Chron. xi. 37).

Pad'dan and **Pad-dan-a'ram**, in A. V. **Pa'dan** and **Pa-dan-a'ram** [plain, plain of Aram, i. e., Syria]; see ARAM 2 (1).

Pa'don [freedom, redemption].
Founder of a family of Nethinim, members of which returned from captivity (Ezra ii. 44; Neh. vii. 47).

Pa'gi-el [a meeting with God].
Head of the tribe of Asher in the wilderness (Num. i. 13; ii. 27; vii. 72, 77; x. 26).

Pa-hath-mo'ab [governor of Moab].
Founder of a family, members of which returned from the Babylonian captivity (Ezra ii. 6; vii. 4; Neh. vii. 11). Some of them married heathen wives, from whom Ezra persuaded them to separate (Ezra x. 30). The representative of the family signed the covenant (Neh. x. 14), and Hashub, a member of the family, rebuilt or replaced part of the wall of Jerusalem (iii. 11).

Pa'i. See PAU.

Paint.
In ancient Egypt and Assyria the custom of painting a black rim around the eyes prevailed among the women. The Hebrews seem to have regarded the practice as a meretricious art, unworthy of a woman of high character (2 Kin. ix. 30; Jer. iv. 30; Ezek. xxiii. 40; War iv. 9, 10). The eyeball under the lids and edge of the lids, and sometimes the eyebrows, were blackened. Doubt-

less various dye stuffs were used for the purpose. Antimony, burnt to blackness and pulverized, was employed (Septuagint). Probably lead also was used, as it is in Persia. The ordinary *kohl*, which is used by women in Egypt at the present day, is a powder obtained from almond shells or by burning a fragrant resin. The powder was kept in small, covered jars; and was applied, both dry and moistened with oil, by means of a probe made of wood, silver, or ivory, and blunt at the end.

For cosmetics applied to other parts of the body, see HENNA; and for pigments used to color walls and other objects, see COLORS.

Pal′ace.

David occupied a royal residence at Jerusalem (2 Sam. v. 9; vii. 1, 2), but Solomon's commodious and magnificent abode was the first in Jerusalem to be constructed on a grand scale (1 Kin. vii. 1–12). It was thirteen years in course of erection, whereas the temple was completed in seven years (vi. 38; vii. 1). It contained the house of the forest of Lebanon (2–5), which took its name from its numerous cedar pillars. This house was 100 cubits or 150 feet long, 50 cubits wide, and 30 cubits high. Its walls were of solid masonry. Within were four rows of cedar pillars. Probably one row ran parallel with each wall, and the four rows formed the four sides of a rectangular court, about 30 by 80 cubits in dimension: or else the pillars were disposed in two double rows parallel to the long sides of the building and left a court in the center. Beams extended from the pillars to the walls and supported three tiers of chambers. These chambers looked down into the court. This building was at once armory and treasure house (x. 17, 21; Is. xxii. 8), and may have served other purposes as well. A hall of pillars was the reception and waiting room of the palace (1 Kin. vii. 6). It was 50 cubits in length and 30 cubits in breadth, and had a portico in front of its portal. This portico was not unlikely the main entrance to the palace. Next came the hall of judgment (ver. 7), open in front, but probably closed on the other three sides by solid walls pierced by doors only. It was the throne room. The great ivory throne overlaid with gold stood there (x. 18-20). These three buildings probably opened on a rectangular court, the sides of which were the portal in the central part of the inner long wall of the house of the forest of Lebanon, the inner doors and wall of the hall of pillars, and the open front of the throne room. Behind the throne room was the inner court where the king dwelt. The principal entrance to it was probably through the throne room, so that the king pronounced judgment and granted audiences in the gate of his palace. This court was, of course, adorned with flowers and fountains, and surrounded by cloisters. The palace of Pharaoh's daughter (vii. 8) was next to the throne room, according to Josephus (Antiq. viii. 5, 2). Solomon's palace was constructed on the general model which prevailed in western Asia, and which is now familiar from the remains of the royal abodes unearthed in Assyria, Babylonia, and Persia. Some conception of its elegance and beauty may be formed from casual references in the Book of Esther to the palace of the Persian king at Shushan (Esth. i. 5, 6, 9; ii. 3, 14; v. 1, 2; vii. 7). See HOUSE; ASMONÆANS, PALACE OF THE; HEROD'S PALACE; and PRÆTORIUM.

Pa′lal [a judge, or he hath judged].

A son of Uzai. He helped to rebuild the wall of Jerusalem (Neh. iii. 25).

Pal-an-quin′.

A covered conveyance, arranged both for sitting and reclining, and carried by means of poles on the shoulders of two, four, or six men or borne as a litter between two camels, horses, or mules. The royal palanquin, provided by Solomon for his bride, consisted of a frame made of cedar, with small ornamental pillars of silver, a bottom of gold, costly coverings of purple for the seat, and perhaps embroideries lovingly made by the daughters of Jerusalem (Song iii. 9, in A. V. chariot; by Ewald and Delitzsch rendered bed of state).

Pal′es-tine (Joel iii. 4) and **Pal-es-ti′na** (Ex. xv. 14; Is. xiv. 29, 31), in R. V. always **Philistia.**

In the O. T. the name denotes the country of the Philistines (cp. Herod. vii. 89). The name now designates a country in the southwest corner of Asia, constituting the southern portion of Syria, and which for a long time was in the possession of the Hebrews. That portion of this territory which lies west of the Jordan the ancient Hebrews called Canaan as distinguished from the land of Gilead on the east of the river. After the conquest the entire country became known as the land of Israel (1 Sam. xiii. 19; 1 Chron. xxii. 2; Mat. ii. 20), but after the division of the kingdom this name was often given to the northern realm. In the epistle to the Hebrews (xi. 9) it is called the land of promise. Soon after the beginning of the Christian era Greek and Latin writers denominate it Palæstina. In the Middle Ages it became known as the Holy Land (cp. Zech. ii. 12; 2 Mac. i. 7).

1. *Boundaries and Extent of Palestine.* The Hebrews occupied the region from Kadesh-barnea and the wady el-ʻArish on the south to mount Hermon on the north, and from the Mediterranean Sea on the west to the desert on the east, except the plain of the Philistines and the country of Moab. In prosperous reigns powerful kings extended their sway beyond these limits and held dominion over Hamath and Damascus and beyond, as far as the river Euphrates, and over Ammon, Moab, and Edom. The Hebrews themselves were accustomed to say that their country

extended from Dan to Beer-sheba, a distance of 150 miles. The southern boundary was then the wady el-Fikreh and the river Arnon. These limits included the thickly populated portion of the land. Taking the smaller limits, which exclude most of the territory occupied by the tribe of Simeon and part of that occupied by Naphtali, the boundaries form a parallelogram, the altitude of which, measured by the latitudes of Dan and the southern extremity of the Dead Sea, is 145 miles, and the base 70 miles. The area is 10,150 square miles. This includes the Philistine country, which, at its utmost extent from Carmel to Beer-sheba, had an area of 1765 square miles, leaving 8385 square miles as the territory occupied by the Hebrews. The survey assigns to eastern Palestine, from Hermon to the Arnon, about 3800 square miles; and to western Palestine, as far south as Beer-sheba and including Philistia, 6040 square miles.

2. *Population of Palestine.* The Hebrews at the time of the conquest numbered 600,-000 men, or else 600 clans (see THOUSAND). If the men alone numbered 600,000, the population was 2,000,000, in a territory of 8300 square miles. Massachusetts, with an area of 8315 square miles, had a population of 2,238,943 in 1890, and New Jersey, with an area of 7815 square miles, had a population of 1,444,933. David took the census of a much larger region. The present population is estimated at 600,000. That it was formerly much larger is evident from the statements of the Bible and Josephus, and from the numerous ruins of former towns. Scarcely a hilltop of the multitude always in sight but is crowned with a city or village, inhabited or in ruins.

3. *The Geology of Palestine.* A band of Nubian or Petra sandstone extends along the eastern coast of the Dead Sea and along part of the wall of rock flanking the Jordan valley on the east, and appears on the western slopes of Lebanon and Anti-Lebanon. It is generally of a dark red or blackish color. Above this lies the most important geological formation in Palestine, the cretaceous limestone which constitutes the main part of the table-land of the country both east and west of the Jordan. At Jerusalem there are two beds of the limestone, an upper or harder layer, called by the inhabitants *misseh*, and an inferior soft one, denominated *melekeh*. The reservoirs, sepulchers, and cellars under and around the city have been excavated in the soft *melekeh*, while the foundations of the buildings are on the hard *misseh*. The large quarries near the Damascus gate are in the *melekeh*. From them came the stone of which the temple walls were constructed. These beds of cretaceous limestone underlie a newer series which, commencing at mount Carmel, runs nearly south to Beer-sheba, from which it then curves in a southwesterly direction parallel to the Mediterranean. Out-

liers of it exist also northeast, east, and southwest of Jerusalem and around Shechem. From the abundance in them of the little *foraminifera* called nummulites, the beds are named the nummulitic limestone. They belong to the Eocene Tertiary, and probably to the Middle Eocene. This rock is so connected with the cretaceous limestone that the two are generally held to constitute but a single formation, called the cretaceo-nummulitic series. Flanking the nummulitic limestone on the west a long continuous band of calcareous sandstone extends through the Philistine country and appears in scattered patches farther north, to near mount Carmel. As a rule, it is porous and soft, and as it easily weathers away, it exposes the harder limestone of the table-land which dips beneath it, and makes the descent from the uplands to the lowlands of Judæa and Samaria more abrupt than it otherwise would be. Between this sandstone and the Mediterranean lie raised beaches belonging to the upper Pliocene, or to recent times. All these are sedimentary beds. A few igneous rocks, however, exist in the land. A minute patch of very old igneous rocks, an outlier of the great mass of granite, porphyry, diorite, and felsite, which occurs farther south in the Arabah and especially at Sinai, is combined with the carboniferous rocks. On the eastern side of the Jordan, nearly all the way from the roots of mount Hermon to south of the sea of Galilee, and east and southeast to the Hauran, beyond the limits of Palestine, the country is overspread by an immense mass of volcanic material, basalt, dolerite, felsite, none of it older, and some of it apparently more recent, than the Pliocene Tertiary. There are detached portions of the same volcanic rocks in western Palestine, west and northwest of the sea of Galilee, with fragments in other quarters. Along the Mediterranean coast of Palestine, wherever the ground is low and level, there is a row of sand dunes, some rising 200 feet in height. Those on the southwest of the country may have been at least partly formed by the blowing of sand from the Egyptian and Sinaitic deserts. Those farther north obtained the sand from the weathering of the calcareous sandstone of Philistia. They tend to encroach upon the cultivated parts adjacent, the wind continually blowing particles from them inland. Palestine lies in one of the lines in which earthquake action is potent; and both in ancient times and more recently portions of the country have been seriously convulsed. To recapitulate, the geological structure of Palestine consists of a layer of red sandstone over the primitive rocks; then comes the chalky limestone which forms the mass of the country, overlaid with nummulite limestone and alluvial soil; and lastly in the northeast appear colossal erupted masses of volcanic rock.

4. *The Physical Geography of Palestine.*
The physical divisions of Palestine are five:
the maritime plain, the low country or
Shephelah, the central mountain range, the
Jordan valley, and the eastern table-land.
These form parallel zones, and with certain
modifications extend through the entire
length of the country from north to south.
They are broken only by the plain of
Esdraelon, which lies athwart the mountain
range and connects the seacoast with the
Jordan valley. 1. The maritime plain lies
along the coast of the Mediterranean Sea for
the entire length of the country, being
broken only by mount Carmel. North of
Carmel it is quite narrow, but south of that
mountain it is 6 miles wide and increases in
width southward. It is an undulating plain
100 to 200 feet above sea level, and very
fertile. Between Carmel and the 'Aujah,
which empties into the sea north of Joppa,
it was called Sharon, south of Joppa it was
occupied by the Philistines. 2. The low
country or Shephelah is a region of low hills
situated between the maritime plain south
of Carmel and the high central range. It
forms a terrace with an elevation of about
500 feet above the sea level. The name is
applied almost exclusively to that part of the
low hilly country which extends from the
latitude of Joppa southward to Beer-sheba,
and which is sharply separated from the
central range by a series of valleys running
north and south. 3. The central mountain
range is a continuation of the Lebanon
mountains. South of the river Leontes the
lofty ridge drops to a high plateau which
reaches southward as far as the northern end
of the sea of Galilee and Acre. This is
Upper Galilee. It contains a number of hills
between 2000 and 3000 feet in elevation;
while several rise considerably above that
height, like Jebel Jermuk which is 3934 feet.
Lower Galilee is triangular, having the sea

of the sea of Galilee. Southwest of the sea is
mount Tabor, 1843 feet high; and farther south
mount Gilboa, with one peak 1698 feet and
another 1648 feet. The southern part of
Lower Galilee descends into the plain of
Esdraelon, most of the places in which do not
exceed 200 or 300 feet in height. South of the
plain of Esdraelon the range is broken by
many wadies, mountains are scattered into
groups, and its inner recesses are accessible
from the maritime plain, Esdraelon, and the
Jordon valley. Carmel is thrust out as a
spur toward the northwest. The average
watershed is 2000 feet high. But mount Ebal
rises 3077 feet and its companion Gerizim
2849. This was Samaria. From Bethel to
Hebron and almost to Beer-sheba, a distance
of about 45 miles, the range forms one compact mass with precipitous sides on the east
and west and with an average height of 2200
feet. Bethel, however, has an elevation of
2930 feet above sea level, the highest part of
Jerusalem 2598, Bethlehem 2550, and Hebron
3040. About 15 miles south of Hebron it
slopes down to the desert of the wandering.
The summit of the range is the narrow
table-land which was occupied by the tribes
of Benjamin and Judah. 4. The Jordan
valley is a remarkable chasm which begins

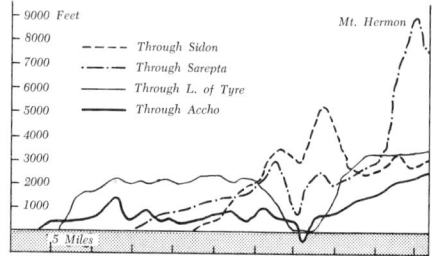

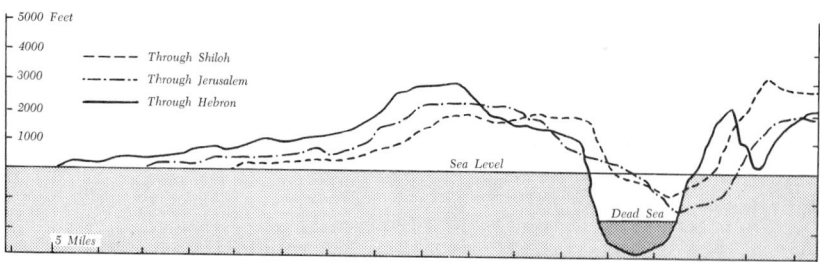

Cross sections of Palestine on the parallels of Hebron, Jerusalem, and Shiloh.

of Galilee and the Jordan as far as Beth-
shean on its eastern side and the plain of
Esdraelon on the southwestern side. It consists of a series of low ridges running east
and west. Its elevation is considerably less
than that of Upper Galilee, many of its hills
being only 400, 500, or 600 feet high, though
there are a few loftier peaks immediately west

at the foot of mount Hermon, 1700 feet
above sea level, but with lofty mountains on
each side, and grows rapidly deeper as it goes
southward until at the surface of the Dead
Sea it is 1290 feet lower than sea level; see
DEAD SEA and JORDAN. Though not an
impassable barrier, it prevented free intercourse between the peoples who dwelt east

of it south of the Jabbok as far as Edom, and the tribes of Judah and Benjamin on the west. 5. The eastern table-land is a great fertile plain, much of it more than 3000 feet in elevation, stretching from the bluffs which overlook the Jordan valley to the Syrian desert. It is cut in twain by the gorge of the Jabbok and the northern portion is further cleft by the Yarmuk, immediately south of the sea of Galilee.

5. *The Principal Roads of Palestine.* The physical structure determined the course of travel. The great commercial and military highway between Egypt and the empires of the east passed through Palestine. It crossed the wady el-'Arish near its mouth, followed the seacoast to Gaza, where it was met by a road from Elath and Arabia, and continued through the plain of the Philistines to Ashdod. Beyond Ashdod it forked. One branch followed the coast by Joppa and Dor, and avoided mount Carmel by keeping to the seashore at the base of the headland; but the way is only 600 feet wide under the headland, and is broken by rocks. The other branch, and the main line of travel, continued from Ashdod through Ekron and Lod and crossed the mountains to the plain of Esdraelon by one of three passes. The western road emerged by Tell Keimun and led to Acre, Tyre, Sidon, and the north. The central road crossed to el-Lejjun (Megiddo), traversed the plain of Esdraelon and Lower Galilee to the plain of Gennesaret, followed the Jordan northward, and by one branch entered the valley of the river Litany between Lebanon and Anti-Lebanon, and led to Hamath and the north. The other branch crossed the Jordan between the waters of Merom and the sea of Galilee, and went northeastward to Damascus. The third and most frequented route from the maritime plain passed through the plain of Dothan to En-gannim, where it divided, one branch joining the aforementioned road across Lower Galilee, and the other leading to Beth-shean, and, dividing again, continuing to Gilead or to Damascus. By any of the northern routes Carchemish on the Euphrates might be reached. There was another road from the plain of Esdraelon to Egypt. It traversed the hill country, passing by Samaria, Shechem, Bethel, Jerusalem, Bethlehem, Hebron, and Beer-sheba. At this point the road branched, and there was a choice of routes; the highway along the seacoast might be gained by diverging to the west, or the journey might be continued by way of Rehoboth and 'Ain Muweileh, and thence across the desert to Egypt. A route from Beth-shean to Edom, which was also used by travelers to Jerusalem, passed down the Jordan valley to Jericho, where persons going to Jerusalem took the steep road up the mountains to the capital. From Jericho the road continued along the western shore of the Dead Sea to En-gedi, where it was joined by a road

from Jerusalem and Bethlehem, and thence continued to Edom and Elath at the head of the Red Sea, where it joined the caravan routes from Egypt and Gaza to southern Arabia. East of the Jordan a caravan route led from Damascus along the edge of the desert southward to Arabia; see DECAPOLIS. It was joined by roads running from Beth-shean across Gilead; by a road from Shechem down the wady Far'ah to the ford of the Jordan below the mouth of the Jabbok, and thence across Gilead to Rabbath Ammon; and by another from the ford at Jericho by way of Heshbon. West of the Jordan Galilee was crossed by a road running almost due east from Acre, which joined the road to Damascus near the point where it crossed the Jordan, midway between the waters of Merom and the sea of Galilee. The high table-land occupied by the tribes of Benjamin and Judah was not easy of access from the maritime plain. A way, however, led from the plain of Sharon and the Nahr el-'Aujah at Ras el-'Ain (Antipatris) southeastwardly into the hill country, and joined the road from Samaria to Jerusalem at a point two miles southwest of Bethel. From the seaport of Joppa a road led to Jerusalem by the valley of Aijalon and Beth-horon. From Ashdod the capital was most readily reached by wady es-Surar and Beth-shemesh; but a route to Jerusalem and also to Bethlehem was afforded by the wady es-Sunt past Socoh. Access to the hill country in the vicinity of Hebron was had through the wady el-'Afranj by Beit Jibrin, and by the wady el-Hesy by Lachish.

6. *The Meteorology of Palestine.* The great contrasts in physical features have given Palestine a remarkable range of climate, from the perpetual snow on mount Hermon to the tropical heat of the Jordan valley at Jericho and En-gedi. The average temperature at Jerusalem in January, which is the coldest month, is about 49.4° F., and the greatest cold 28°. In August the average is 79.3°, and the greatest heat is 92° in the shade. See also YEAR.

7. *The Botany of Palestine.* In consequence of the great diversity of surface and climate, the flora is extensive and plants of many latitudes flourish. Tristram showed that of 3002 flowering plants and ferns known to exist in Palestine, a large number for so small a country, 2563 are Palæarctic, and most of them belong to its Mediterranean section; 161 are Ethiopian, 27 Indian, and 251 peculiar. In the region which lies between the Taurus mountains and the southern point of the peninsula of Sinai, and between the Mediterranean Sea and the Syrian desert, Dr. Post has found 850 genera and about 3500 species.

8. *The Zoology of Palestine.* The distribution of the several species of animals essentially agrees with that of the Palestinian plants. Of 113 mammalia known to occur in Pales-

tine, Tristram found 55 to belong to the
Palæarctic region, the same to which our
European species belong ; 34 were Ethiopian,
16 Indian, and 13 peculiar to the land. The
same species sometimes belongs to two regions.
Of 348 species of birds, 271 were Palæarctic, 40
Ethiopian, 7 Indian, and 30 peculiar. Of the
91 reptiles and amphibians, 49 were Palæarctic, 27 Ethiopian, 4 Indian, and 11 peculiar. Of 43 fresh-water fishes, 8 were Palæarctic, 2 Ethiopian, 7 Indian, and 26 peculiar. In the case of both plants and animals,
the African and Indian types come chiefly
from the low-lying region around the Dead
Sea, and to a less extent from the low valley
of the Jordan.

9. *The Ethnology of Palestine.* The aboriginal inhabitants of Palestine were a tall, stalwart race, consisting of Anakim (Josh. xi.
21, 22), Rephaim (Gen. xiv. 5), Emim, Zamzummim, and Horites (Deut. ii. 10-23). Traces
of the primitive population continued to exist as late as the time of the monarchy
(2 Sam. xxi. 16-22). When Abraham arrived,
the country was occupied chiefly by the
Amorites and other smaller tribes of Canaanites, but Philistines and Phœnicians were settled on the seacoast and Hittites dwelt on the
northern border and at Hebron. The Hittites are regarded as a Turanian people from
the Taurus mountains. The Philistines came
from the west. The Canaanites, including
the Phœnicians, either belonged to the Hamitic race by blood or became incorporated
with it (Gen. x. 6, 15-20). They early spoke
a Semitic language. These various peoples
were conquered, but not utterly exterminated, by the Hebrews under the leadership
of Moses and Joshua. The occasional introduction of Edomites, Ammonites, and Moabites by conquest and immigration did not
bring a new strain into the blood, for these
peoples were Semitic and like the Hebrews
descended from Abraham. The conquest of
Aramæan tribes, so far as it resulted in adding foreigners to the commonwealth of Israel,
added Semites. After the fall of Samaria,
the Assyrians deported the northern and
eastern tribes of the Israelites and introduced colonists from Hamath, Babylonia,
and Elam (2 Kin. xvii. 24 ; Ezra iv. 9). They
were largely Semites and Aryans. A large
immigration of Greeks followed in the wake
of the conquest of Alexander the Great,
colonized Ptolemais, built the Greek towns
of the Decapolis, and introduced the Greek
language, customs, and culture. Later, Roman
officials and a Roman army of occupation
were in the country, and ultimately Roman
colonists came. In the second quarter of the
seventh century of the Christian era the
country was subjugated by the Mohammedans, and in many of the towns and villages
Arabian military colonies were planted. The
Turks made their appearance as conquerors
in western Asia A. D. 1086, and except for
short periods Palestine has ever since been
under their rule ; but people of Turkish
descent are very few in the country.

10. *The History of Palestine.* The early
history of Palestine, before the arrival of
Abraham, is involved in obscurity. The
succession of races who inhabited the country may be gathered from the Hebrew records,
as already pointed out. The kings of Babylonia early began their invasions of the west,
and the campaign of Chedorlaomer in eastern
Palestine in the time of Abraham is described
in Gen. xiv. The Babylonians impressed
their culture, including their complicated
script and their language as a medium of
international communication, upon the inhabitants. After the expulsion of the shepherd kings from the country of the Nile, the
great Pharaohs of the eighteenth dynasty
extended their sway far into Asia. Thothmes
III. conquered Canaan and exacted tribute
from the nations dwelling as far as the
Euphrates. During the reigns of Amenophis III. and IV., who succeeded him after
an interval, Canaan was garrisoned by Egyptian troops and governed by Egyptian officials. But in the latter reign the grasp of
Egypt was evidently weakening. The Hittites were threatening the northern frontier,
lawlessness prevailed in various parts of the
land, travel was insecure, individual states
were in a foment of discontent or in rebellion,
and various tribes were extending their territory at the expense of Egypt. Under the
succeeding dynasty Seti I. passed through
Palestine and waged war with the Hittites
on the Orontes ; Ramses II. invaded Palestine and penetrated beyond ; and Meneptah's
armies ravaged southern Palestine and the
coast of Philistia, and wasted the crops of the
Israelites, who were perhaps in the wilderness of the wandering near Kadesh-barnea ;
see EGYPT and PHARAOH. Ramses III., of
the twentieth dynasty, overran Palestine
while the Israelites were still in the desert.
When the power of the country had been reduced by these wars, the Hebrews appeared
on the scene. Under the leadership of Moses,
they conquered the region east of the Jordan ;
and in the following year, under Joshua,
they crossed the river, and after repeated
campaigns took possession of Canaan. From
this time onward, until the fall of Jerusalem
in the first century of the Christian era, the
history of Palestine is largely the history of
the Hebrew people. See HISTORY.

11. *The Topography of Palestine.* As nearly
as can be estimated, 622 towns west of the Jordan are mentioned in the Bible and the Apocrypha. Other early documents refer to many
of these towns by name. In 1874 Mariette Bey
published geographical lists taken from tablets round the necks of the figures of captives represented on the great gateway of the
temple at Karnak. They belong to the reign
of Thothmes III. There are 118 names, of
which no fewer than one-third throw light
on the topography of Palestine and the Book

of Joshua. References to towns of Palestine in the time of Amenophis III. and IV. occur in the letters which were discovered at Tell el-Amarna. Later references are found in contemporary records of Assyria, especially in documents which relate to campaigns conducted in Palestine. Eusebius, bishop of Cæsarea in the first half of the fourth century of the Christian era, wrote a tract concerning the names of places in the sacred Scriptures. It was translated and enlarged by Jerome, resident at Bethlehem a century later. The work is commonly known as the Onomasticon of Eusebius and Jerome. The notices regarding the situation of ancient places in Palestine, according to the information possessed by the learned authors, are often valuable, sometimes absurd. The information gathered by Reland and published by him in 1714, ar d the travels of Seetzen and Burckhardt, especially east of the Jordan, in the beginning of the present century, prepared the way for the systematic, scientific investigation conducted by Dr. Robinson. He visited Palestine in 1838, accompanied by a former pupil of his, Rev. Dr. Eli Smith, American missionary at Beirût, who greatly aided the inquiry by his knowledge of Arabic. They found by asking the natives what certain ruins or yet inhabited villages were called, that they often bore the old Hebrew names still, a little modified as pronounced by Arab lips. Their discoveries in the topography of Palestine were very important, and were given to the world by Prof. Robinson in 1841 in three octavo volumes. Returning from America, Dr. Robinson resumed his researches in Palestine in 1852, accompanied again by Rev. Dr. Eli Smith and others. He made fresh discoveries, embodied in his *Later Biblical Researches*, 1856. Dr. Robinson brought to bear on his inquiry not merely keen observation and a sound judgment, but great learning; and his conclusions, many of them disputed at the time, are now much more largely accepted. On June 22, 1865, a society named The Palestine Exploration Fund, was formed in England to prosecute in a scientific spirit all branches of inquiry regarding the Holy Land. Since then it has conducted an ordnance survey of a great part of Palestine, and constructed a superb map of the country in twenty-six sheets. This result is a permanent and splendid achievement. The society has also carried on excavations, especially at Jerusalem and Lachish. As a result of all past investigations, about one-half of the biblical sites have been identified with certainty or great probability.

Pal'lu, in A. V. once **Phallu** (Gen. xlvi. 9) [distinguished].

A son of Reuben, and founder of a tribal family (Gen. xlvi. 9; Ex. vi. 14; Num. xxvi. 5).

Palm.

A tree, called in Hebrew *tamar, timmorah,*

and *tomer,* and in Greek *phoinix.* It is a tall tree (Song vii. 7, 8), straight and upright (Jer. x. 5). It is a fruit tree (Joel i. 12), and sufficiently ornamental to have been carved in various parts of Solomon's temple and other sanc-

Date Palm.

tuaries (1 Kin. vi. 29, 32, 35; Herod. ii. 169). Its great leaves were used as tokens of victory and peace (1 Mac. xiii. 51; 2 Mac. x. 7; John xii. 13; Rev. vii. 9; imitated in 2 Esdr. ii. 43–47). These leaves are often popularly called branches; and this designation is employed in the English versions (Lev. xxiii. 40; Neh. viii. 15; John xii. 13), but is not botanically correct. Scarcely any palms have branches at all; and the date palm, the species grown in parts of Palestine, is not one of the few exceptions to the rule. The leaves are large and feathery, from 4 to 6 feet in length; they are quite accessible, as there are generally a number of young plants around the foot of the parent stem. Palm trees flourished on the banks of the Nile. They grew at Elim, in the wilderness near the Red Sea (Ex. xv. 27), and in Edom (Virgil, Georg. iii. 12). They grew in various parts of Judæa also (Pliny Hist. Nat. v. 14); as in the valley of the Jordan, at Jericho, and En-gedi, and on the coast of the sea of Galilee (Gen. xiv. 7, in the proper name; Deut. xxxiv. 3; Ecclus. xxiv. 14; Antiq. ix. 1, 2; War i. 6, 6; iii. 10, 8); in the south of Judah (Josh. xv. 31, 49, in the names Sansannah and Kirjath-sannah), in mount Ephraim near Bethel (Judg. iv. 5; xx. 33), near Jerusalem (Neh. viii. 15; John

xii. 13). They grew also in the desert east of Damascus, at the town named from them, Tadmor, Tamar, and Palmyra. They flourished also in the lower valleys of the Tigris and Euphrates (Herod. i. 193). The tree was regarded by the Greeks and Romans as peculiarly characteristic of Palestine and the neighboring regions. Phœnicia took its name in Greek from the date palm; and the coin struck at Rome to commemorate the capture of Jerusalem represented a woman, emblem of the country, sitting disconsolate under a date palm; see JERUSALEM and MONEY. The tree which was once so common has almost disappeared from Palestine, except in the maritime plain of Philistia and in the neighborhood of Beirût, but it is being cultivated anew near Jericho. The palm tree in Scripture almost always means the date palm (*Phœnix dactylifera*), which grows about 60 or 80 feet high, having a single upright stem of uniform thickness through its entire length and marked by the scars of fallen leaves. The stem terminates above in a circle of great feathery leaves, perennially green. It is believed to attain a great age, from a hundred to two hundred years. The domestic uses of the palm are numerous. The leaves are employed for covering the roofs and sides of houses, for fences, mats, and baskets. When the tender part of the spatha is pierced, a sweet juice exudes, from which sugar is obtained by evaporation, and a strong drink called arrack by fermentation or distillation (War iv. 8, 3; Herod. i. 193). The fruit, which it produces annually in numerous clusters and great abundance, constitutes its chief value, being largely used as an article of food. Even the stony seeds are ground, and yield nourishment to the camel of the desert. Another palm tree may have been known to many Israelites: the Palmyra, which grows at Tadmor in the wilderness. It is *Borassus flabelliformis*, the specific name implying that it has fan-shaped leaves.

Palm'er-worm.
The rendering of the Hebrew *Gazam*, devourer, an insect which devoured vines, fig trees, olive trees, and the produce of the gardens and fields generally (Joel i. 4; ii. 25; Amos iv. 9). Probably a kind of locust, or a locust in a certain stage of its growth (R. V. margin). When the A. V. was made, palmer-worm denoted a sort of hairy caterpillar which has no fixed abode, but wanders like a palmer or pilgrim from place to place.

Pal'sy.
A partial or total loss of sensibility, voluntary motion, or both, in one or more parts of the body (Mark ii. 3, 9–12; Acts ix. 33–35). It is produced by disease of the brain, the spinal cord, or particular nerves. Under this term the ancients included a variety of diseases affecting the muscles.

Pal'ti, in A. V. once **Phalti** (1 Sam. xxv. 44) [abbreviation of Paltiel, deliverance by God].

1. The representative spy from the tribe of Benjamin (Num. xiii. 9).
2. The man to whom Saul married Michal, David's wife, and from whom she was later wrested away and restored to David (1 Sam. xxv. 44; 2 Sam. iii. 15, where the unabbreviated form is used).

Pal'ti-el, in A. V. once **Phaltiel** (2 Sam. iii. 15) [deliverance by God].
1. Prince of the tribe of Issachar and a contemporary of Moses (Num. xxxiv. 26).
2. The same as Palti 2 (2 Sam. iii. 15).

Pal'tite.
A member of the family, or an inhabitant of the town, of Pelet or Palti. To judge from 2 Sam xxiii. 26 compared with 1 Chron. xxvii. 10, the Paltites were reckoned to Ephraim.

Pam-phyl'i-a [popularly interpreted by the Greeks as meaning an assemblage of mingled tribes].
A stretch of coast land in Asia Minor. It was bounded on the north by Pisidia; on the south by a gulf of the Mediterranean, called the sea of Pamphylia, across which Paul sailed (Acts xxvii. 5); on the east by Cilicia; and on the west by Lycia and part of Phrygia. Pamphylia contained Jewish communities (ii. 10). Its towns, Perga and Attalia, were visited by Paul on his first missionary journey (xiii. 13; xiv. 24, 25; xv. 38).

Pan'nag.
A product of Palestine which the Tyrians purchased (Ezek. xxvii. 17). The R. V., following the Jewish Targum, suggests that perhaps it was a kind of confection.

Pa'per. See PAPYRUS.

Pa'per Reed.
Papyrus; the rendering in the A. V. of the Hebrew '*Arah*, nakedness (Is. xix. 7); see PAPYRUS. The corresponding word in Arabic means an open place; and R. V. renders the Hebrew word by meadow.

Pa'phos.
A town at the southwestern extremity of Cyprus, near cape Zephyrion. It was called Old Paphos to distinguish it from the newer mercantile town some miles to the northwest. It was the capital of the Roman province of Cyprus, and the residence of the proconsul. In its vicinity was a celebrated temple of the Cyprian Venus (Homer, Odyssey viii. 362). The town was visited by Paul (Acts xiii. 6–13). It is now called Kuklia.

Pa-py'rus.
The rendering of the Hebrew word *Gome'*; a plant which grows in mire (Job viii. 11, R. V. margin; in Is. xxxv. 7 rendered rush), and of which the tiny ark of Moses (Ex. ii. 3, R. V. margin; in text, bulrushes), and also larger boats (Is. xviii. 2, R. V.) were made. The plant referred to is the paper reed (*Papyrus antiquorum*). But the papyrus is not a grass, as the word reed might suggest; nor is it a rush. It is a giant sedge, with a triangu-

lar stock 8 or 10 feet high, terminating in a tuft of flowers. It grows in the plain of Sharon, near the sea of Galilee, and in the waters of the Huleh, commonly thought of as Merom; and it formerly flourished on the

Papyrus growing along the shore line of the Hula Reservation.

Nile, though now extinct upon that river. Its use was widespread (2 Esdr. xv. 2; 3 Mac, iv. 20). The Egyptians made shoes, baskets. boats, and other articles of it; and used sheets, formed of strips of the pith, as writing paper. On such material, called in Greek *chartēs*, the apostle John wrote his Second Epistle (2 John 12).

Par'a·ble.

A method of speech in which moral or religious truth is illustrated from the analogy of common experience. The comparison may be expressed, as by the word like, or be implied. The limits between the parable and simile and metaphor are not well defined. Often there is scarcely any difference, except that the simile and metaphor are short and the parable comparatively long. "Ye are the light of the world" is a metaphor; "like a lamb dumb before his shearer" is a simile; but "the kingdom of heaven is like unto leaven, which a woman took, and hid in three measures of meal, till it was all leavened," is a parable (Mat. xiii. 33). The parable has certain advantages. One is, that this means of conveying truth makes it adhere to the memory much more than a plain didactic statement would do. For instance, no didactic statement as to the

willingness of our Lord to receive penitent sinners would have had an effect at all equal to that produced by the parable of the prodigal son (Luke xv. 11-32). A second advantage in a parable is that when it is needful for a prophet or a preacher to censure a powerful personage, who will not allow himself to be directly found fault with, it is possible by a skillfully framed parable to make him not merely listen patiently, but condemn himself before he discovers that it is himself he is condemning. This was done with much skill by the prophet Nathan when he went to reprove David for his great sin in the matter of Uriah the Hittite.

The following are the chief parables in the O. T.: the trees anointing a king (Judg. ix. 8-20), the ewe lamb (2 Sam. xii. 1-14), the widow, one of whose two sons slew the other (2 Sam. xiv. 4-20), the soldier who let his captive escape (1 Kin. xx. 35-42), the thistle which asked for the cedar's daughter as a wife for his son (2 Kin. xiv. 9-11), the vineyard (Is. v. 1-7), the two eagles and a vine (Ezek. xvii. 1-10), the lion's whelps (xix. 1-9), Oholah and Oholibah (xxiii. 1-49), the boiling pot (xxiv. 1-14).

An important part of our Lord's teaching was by means of parables; and when Scripture parables are spoken of, generally those of Jesus are meant. Christ used the parabolic form of teaching at every period of his public ministry (Mark iii. 23; Luke vi. 39; vii. 40-50), but there came a time when a distinct change took place and he gave a larger place to parables in his public instruction (Mat. xiii. 3; Mark iv. 2). Two reasons are assigned why he adopted to such an extent this method of teaching. One given by Matthew is that it was prophesied (Mat. xiii. 34, 35; cp. Ps. xlix. 4; lxxviii. 2, 3). The other, emanating from our Lord, explains the former. He used parables because it was not given unto his auditors to know the mysteries of the kingdom of heaven, since seeing they saw not and hearing they did not understand (Mat. xiii. 10-16). This statement of Jesus has been interpreted to mean that he clothed the truths of the kingdom in images in order to make them more intelligible to his hearers and to impress them indelibly on their memory. But this was true of a certain class of hearers only and in many cases, even in respect to them, only after the parable had been explained. Jesus rather meant that his auditors generally were unprepared to hear and heartily believe the spiritual truths of the kingdom; and while the time had come to teach these doctrines to his followers who were to carry on his work after his departure (Mark iv. 33, 34), the truth was henceforth hidden from those who had heard without repentance, was cautiously uttered in the hearing of obdurate enemies who were watching to seize upon his words and employ them against him, and was veiled from the fickle multitude who would refuse to listen to his words if they perceived the full import of them (Mark iv. 11, 12).

With perhaps only one exception (Mat. xviii. 23–35), the recorded parables, which were spoken after this form of instruction became prominent in Jesus' public teaching, fall into three groups: I. Eight illustrating the nature of the kingdom of heaven (Mat. xiii. 1–50; Mark iv. 26–29), followed by one by way of application (Mat. xiii. 51, 52). These were spoken during one day on the shore of the sea of Galilee (xiii. 1, 53). They contain five fundamental truths: 1. Sower and seed: the varied reception of the gospel by different classes of hearers. 2. Tares and wheat: evil springs up among the good. 3. Seed growing secretly, mustard seed, and leaven: growth of the church imperceptibly, externally, internally. 4. Hid treasure, and pearl of great price: value of the kingdom, necessity of sacrifice to obtain it. 5. Net gathering all kinds of fish: mixed condition of the visible church until the end of the world. II. Nineteen, or thereabout, illustrating the kingdom of heaven in the individual life (Luke x. 25–xix., except xiii. 18–21). Most of them, if not all, were delivered after Christ's departure from Galilee, in the interval of six months between the feast of tabernacles and his last passover. They include the parables of the good Samaritan, the friend at midnight, the rich man and his barns, the waiting servants, the shut door, the chief seat, the supper and excuses for not attending it, the lost sheep, the lost money, the prodigal son, the unjust steward, the rich man and Lazarus, the servant's duty, the importunate widow, the Pharisee and the publican, and the pounds. III. Five or, with Mat. xxiv. 32–35, six, which were delivered during the last week at Jerusalem, and point to judgment and the consummation of the kingdom. The attitude of those called is illustrated by the parables of the two sons and the wicked husbandmen (Mat. xxi. 28–46), and the need of the wedding garment, of watchfulness, and of fidelity is shown by the parables of the marriage of the king's son, the ten virgins, and the five talents (Mat. xxii. 1–14; xxv. 1–30).

In interpreting the parables, rigid inquiry should be made into the circumstances in which each was delivered at first, and the doctrine or argument which it was intended primarily to convey. This done, it is at once seen that the teaching of the parable is of universal application, suited for all analogous circumstances and for all succeeding time.

Par'a-clete [Greek *paraklētos*, a legal assistant, advocate, or intercessor].

The word occurs in R. V. on the margins of John xiv. 16, 26; xv. 26; xvi. 7, where helper or advocate is given as the English equivalent. In the text of these passages the translation is comforter, but in 1 John ii. 1 it is advocate. It is applied to:

1. The Lord Jesus Christ. He was the advocate, by implication in John xiv. 16, who guided, counseled, and strengthened the disciples while he was present with them, and he is now the Christian's advocate with the Father, and pleads the believer's cause with God (1 John ii. 1) as he did while on earth (Luke xxii. 31, 32; John xvii.).

2. The Holy Spirit, who is Christ's advocate with the believer, glorifying Christ and declaring him (John xv. 26; xvi. 14), vindicating him from man's unworthy thoughts, showing him to be chief among ten thousand and altogether lovely, and exhibiting him as man's great need; and he is the Spirit of truth, who teaches the believer and guides him into the truth (xv. 26; xvi. 13, 14), convicting of sin, righteousness, and judgment (ver. 8), who teaches to pray and makes intercession with groanings that cannot be uttered (Rom. viii. 26, 27).

Par'a-dise.

A pleasure ground, orchard, or park, in Hebrew *pardes* (Ecc. ii. 5; Song iv. 13, R. V. margin; in Neh. ii. 8 rendered forest). Solomon's gardens at Etham and the hanging gardens at Babylon are called paradises in the Greek text of Josephus (Antiq. viii. 7, 3; con. Apion. i. 20), and the garden of Eden is called the paradise (*paradeisos*) of Eden in the Septuagint (Gen. ii. 8).

Paradise was the region of bliss which man had lost, and it naturally came to be a designation for the place of the righteous dead. The later Jews distinguished between a supernal and an infernal paradise, the former being a part of heaven, the latter a division of hades assigned to the souls of the just.

In the N. T. paradise means heaven in two instances (2 Cor. xii. 4; cp. 2; Rev. ii. 7; cp. xxii. 2); see HEAVEN. Accordingly it naturally denotes heaven in the remaining instance (Luke xxiii. 43).

Pa'rah [heifer, young cow].

A village of Benjamin (Josh. xviii. 23), commonly identified with the ruins Fârah in the wady Fârah, 5½ miles northeast of Jerusalem.

Pa'ran [perhaps, a region abounding in caverns].

A wilderness between mount Sinai, or more exactly between Hazeroth, several days' march from Sinai, and Canaan (Num. x. 12; xii. 16). It was on the south of Judah (1 Sam. xxv. 1–5). In it Kadesh was situated (Num. xiii. 26), and apparently also Elath on the Red Sea (Gen. xiv. 6; see EL-PARAN). It lay east of the wildernesses of Beer-sheba and Shur (Gen. xxi. 14, 21; cp. xxv. 9, 12–18; xxviii. 9). It included the wilderness of Zin, or insensibly merged itself in it without a sharply defined boundary (Num. xiii. 26 with xx. 1). These data indicate the plateau or mountain land (Deut. xxxiii. 2; Hab. iii. 3), lying south of Canaan, and bounded on the other sides by the wilderness of Shur, the curved range of mountains known as Jebel et-Tih or mountain of the wandering, and the Arabah. It is the wilderness where the Israelites wandered thirty and eight years. Most of it is from 2000 to 2500 feet above sea level. There is a wady, or valley, in the Sinaitic Peninsula, called wady Feiran, which looks very much like Paran altered. Niebuhr thought that they might be identified; but it is so difficult to harmonize the Scripture location of the place with this view, that Robinson, Stanley, and most inquirers, decline to ac:ept the identification. The wady Feiran is between mount Sinai and the Red Sea. Paran is not reached till after the departure from Sinai in the opposite direction.

Par'bar [probably, colonnade].

A precinct on the western side of the outer court of the temple (1 Chron. xxvi. 18). It contained chambers for officials and stalls for cattle (2 Kin. xxiii. 11, where the plural is rendered suburbs and precincts).

Parch'ed Corn.

Roasted grain used as food (Lev. xxiii. 14; Ruth ii. 14; 1 Sam. xvii. 17). Thomson describes the method of preparing it at present in vogue. A number of the best ears of grain, not too ripe, are plucked, with the stalks attached. After being tied in small parcels, a blazing fire of dry grass and thorn bushes is kindled under them, which burns off the chaff and roasts the grain.

Parch'ment.

The skin of sheep or goats prepared for use as a writing material or for other purposes. The skin is first soaked in lime to remove the hair, and is then shaved, washed, dried, stretched, and smoothed. Herodotus relates that the ancient Ionians used the skins of goats and sheep, because of the scarcity of papyrus (Herod. v. 58). In Herodotus' own time papyrus was the common writing material. Parchment was first obtained at Pergamos; and when Ptolemy forbade the export of papyrus, Eumenes II., king of Pergamos, adopted parchment for the books of his great library, and such skins became known as *chartæ pergamenæ*, whence the word parchment is derived. In the time of Josephus and earlier, parchment was used by the Jews for the manuscripts of their sacred writings (Antiq. xii. 2, 11); and it was a provision of the Talmud that the law should be written on the skins of clean animals, tame or wild, and even of clean birds. Papyrus was a common writing material (2 John 12, in E. V. paper), but Paul refers to parchments of his, about which he is especially solicitous (2 Tim. iv. 13).

Par'ents.

The fifth commandment inculcates upon children the duty of reverencing their parents and attaches a promise to its fulfillment (Ex. xx. 12; Deut. v. 16; Ephes. vi. 1, 2). Upon the parents rests the obligation of bringing up the children in the fear of the Lord, and not provoking them to wrath (Gen. xviii. 19; Deut. vi. 7; Ephes. vi. 4). According to the Mosaic law, a son that smote father or mother, or cursed them, was punished with death (Ex. xxi. 15, 17; Lev. xx. 9; Deut. xxvii. 16); and as an extreme measure, parents were enjoined to bring a stubborn and rebellious son before the elders for trial and execution (Deut. xxi. 18–21). The Mosaic law thus regulated the power of parents. According to Roman law, as set forth in the twelve tables, the life and liberty of children were in the father's hands. In Hebrew law the right of life and death did not rest with the parents, but was vested in the judicial body. Custom permitted an impoverished parent to sell a daughter to be a maidservant, but the Mosaic law carefully guarded her rights (Ex. xxi. 7–11). Israelitish custom further permitted a creditor to seize a bankrupt debtor and enslave his wife and children (2 Kin. iv. 1; Neh. v. 5; Is. l. 1; Mat. xviii. 25); and in cases of grave sin the entire family was involved in the extermination of the offender (Josh. vii. 24).

Par'lor.

Eglon's summer parlor was an upper chamber exposed to the cool breezes (Judg. iii. 20, cp. R. V. margin). See HOUSE.

Par-mash'ta [probably, a Persian name, very great, superior].

A son of Haman (Esth. ix. 9).

Par'me-nas [probably, faithful].

One of the seven men elected to look after the Greek-speaking widows and, apparently, the poor and financial affairs generally in the apostolic church (Acts vi. 5).

Par'nach.

A Zebulunite (Num. xxxiv. 25).

Pa'rosh, in A. V. once **Pharosh** (Ezra viii. 3) [a flea].

Founder of a family, members of which returned from the Babylonian captivity (Ezra ii. 3; viii. 3). One of the clan was called Pedaiah (Neh. iii. 25). Other members of it married foreign wives, whom Ezra induced them to put away (Ezra x. 25).

Par-shan'da-tha [a Persian name, given to Persia].

A son of Haman (Esth. ix. 7).

Par'thi-ans.

A people who, when first heard of, occupied a region nearly corresponding to the modern Persian province of Khorasan, a considerable distance southeast of the Caspian Sea. The length of Parthia proper was about 300 miles, its breadth from 100 to 120, its area about 33,000 square miles, or slightly more than that of Scotland and nearly that of Indiana. The first mention of the Parthians is in the inscriptions of Darius Hystaspis. They revolted against the Persians, 521 B. C., but were soon subdued again. From the Persians, they passed to Alexander the Great, and then to his eastern successors, the Seleucidæ. About 256 B. c. Bactria successfully revolted against Seleucidan domination, and Parthia, under Arsaces I., immediately followed the example. His successors are generally known as the Arsacidæ. Mithridates I., who reigned thirty-eight years, from 174 to 136 B. c., raised the kingdom founded by Arsaces into an empire, extending 1500 miles from east to west, with a varying breadth from north to south of 100, 300, or 400 miles. The western boundary was the Euphrates. The chief city was Ctesiphon on the Tigris, opposite Seleucia. After ridding themselves of the Macedonian-Greek domination, the Parthians came into frequent collision with the Romans, one standing bone of contention between them being the possession of Armenia. From 64 B. C. to A. D. 225 they set limits to the Roman empire in the East. In 40-37 B. c. their armies overran Asia Minor and Syria, took and plundered Jerusalem, and placed Antigonus, the last of the Asmonæans, on the throne (Antiq. xiv. 13, 3; War i. 13, 1). Jews from Parthia were present at Jerusalem on the day of Pentecost (Acts ii. 9), and may have carried the gospel to Parthia when they returned home. After wielding power for nearly 500 years, the Parthians became enervated by luxury, and the Persians about A. D. 224, rose in revolt, and under the leadership of Ardashir, family of Sassan, terminated the Parthian dominion, substituting the second Persian or Sassanian empire in its room.

Par'tridge.
A wild bird, called in Hebrew ḳore', the crier or caller, in Greek perdix, which was

Greek Partridge.

hunted on the mountains of Palestine (1 Sam. xxvi. 20). The caged partridge was used as a decoy bird (Ecclus. xi. 30). Jeremiah compares the amasser of ill-gotten wealth to the partridge which, according to

the belief of the Israelites of his time, gathers young which it has not brought forth (Jer. xvii. 11, R. V.), or sitteth on eggs which it has not laid (R. V. margin). Two species are found in Palestine, the desert or Hey's sand partridge (Ammoperdix heyi), which is the only species at En-gedi, in the wilderness of which David was when he compared himself to a hunted partridge; and the chukar partridge (Caccabis chukar), which is abundant in all the hilly parts of Palestine. It has richly barred feathers on the flanks, deep red legs and bill, and deep black gorget. It is a large and fine bird, a variety of the Greek partridge (Caccabis saxatilis), but larger, and it exceeds the chukar partridge of India in size.

Pa-ru'ah [flourishing].
The father of Solomon's purveyor in Issachar (1 Kin. iv. 17).

Par'va-im.
A designation of gold used for the ornamentation of Solomon's temple (2 Chron. iii. 6). Gesenius derived it from Sanscrit pûrva, in front, eastward, and gave it the sense of eastern or oriental gold; but most investigators believe that it denotes a locality in Ophir.

Pa'sach [perhaps, a divider].
An Asherite, of the family of Beriah (1 Chron. vii. 33).

Pas-dam'mim. See EPHES-DAMMIM.

Pa-se'ah, in A. V. once **Phaseah** (Neh. vii. 51) [lame].
1. A man of Judah, descended from Chelub (1 Chron. iv. 12).
2. The father of a certain Jehoiada, who repaired the old gate of Jerusalem (Neh. iii. 6). He was the founder of a family of Nethinim, members of which returned from captivity (Ezra ii. 49; Neh. vii. 51).

Pash'hur, in A. V. **Pashur.**
1. Son of Malchiah, and one of several officials who had influence with king Zedekiah and bitterly opposed the prophet Jeremiah (Jer. xxi. 1; xxxviii. 1, 4; cp. xxi. 9 with xxxviii. 2). It is natural to suppose that his father is the Malchiah mentioned in xxxviii. 6, a royal prince into whose dungeon the prophet was cast. His identity with the priest Pashhur, the son of Malchijah (1 Chron. ix. 12), is doubtful; especially as to his companion, but not to him, is given the priestly title (Jer. xxi. 1).
2. A son of Immer, a priest. He put Jeremiah in the stocks on account of his discouraging predictions (Jer. xx. 1-6).
3. The father of an opponent of Jeremiah named Gedaliah (Jer. xxxviii. 1).
4. The founder of a priestly family, members of which returned from the Babylonian captivity (Ezra ii. 38; Neh. vii. 41, and perhaps 1 Chron. ix. 12). Some of his descendants married foreign wives, whom Ezra induced them to put away (Ezra x. 22).

5. A priest, doubtless head of a father's house, who, with others, sealed the covenant, made in the days of Nehemiah, by which it was agreed to forbid the intermarriage of their children with foreigners and to keep the law of God (Neh. x. 3).

Pas'sa-ges, The. See ABARIM.

Pass'o-ver [passing over (Ex. xii. 23; Antiq. ii. 14, 6)].

1. The first of the three annual festivals at which all the men were required to appear at the sanctuary (Ex. xii. 43; Deut. xvi. 1), known also as the feast of unleavened bread Ex. xxiii. 15; Deut. xvi. 16). It was instituted in Egypt to commemorate the culminating event in the redemption of the Israelites (Ex. xii. 1, 14, 42; xxiii. 15; Deut. xvi. 1, 3). That night was to be much observed unto the Lord, when he smote all the firstborn in the land of Egypt, but passed over the houses of the Israelites where the blood had been sprinkled and the inmates were standing, staff in hand, awaiting the deliverance promised by the Lord. The festival began on the fourteenth of Abib at evening, that is in the beginning of the fifteenth day, with the sacrificial meal (Lev. xxiii. 5). A lamb or kid was slain between the evenings, that is towards sunset (Ex. xii. 6; Deut. xvi. 6), between the ninth and eleventh hours (War vi. 9, 3). It was roasted whole, and was eaten with unleavened bread and bitter herbs (Ex. xii. 8). The shed blood denoted expiation, the bitter herbs symbolized the bitterness of Egyptian bondage, the unleavened bread was an emblem of purity (cp. Lev. ii. 11; 1 Cor. v. 7, 8). The Israelites pleading the blood, mindful of the afflictions from which they awaited deliverance, and putting away wickedness, were the people of the Lord in holy, glad communion before him. The supper was partaken of by the members of every household. If the family was small, neighbors joined until the company was large enough to consume the entire lamb (Ex. xii. 4). The head of the household recited the history of the redemption. At the first institution the participants stood, in later times they reclined. Other minor features were introduced: four successive cups of wine mixed with water, to which there is no reference in the law; singing of Psalms cxiii.–cxviii. (cp. Is. xxx. 29; Ps. xlii. 4); a dish of fruits reduced with vinegar to the consistency of lime as a reminder of the mortar used during the Egyptian bondage. The paschal supper was the introductory ceremony and chief feature of the festival, which lasted until the twenty-first day of the month (Ex. xii. 18; Lev. xxiii. 5, 6; Deut. xvi. 6, 7). That the event was to be commemorated by a festival of seven days' duration (Ex. xii. 14–20) was not communicated to the people until the day of the flight (xiii. 3–10). They were directed regarding one evening only (xii. 21–23), and informed that the service was

to be kept perpetually (24, 25). The attendance of the pilgrims was required at the supper only. They were at liberty to depart on the morrow (Deut. xvi. 7). The first day, that is the fifteenth, was kept as Sabbath and likewise the seventh; no work was done and there was a holy convocation (Ex. xii. 16; Lev. xxiii. 7: Num. xxviii. 18, 25; of which only the last is emphasized in Ex. xiii. 6; Deut. xvi. 8). On the morrow after the Sabbath, that is on the second day of the festival, a sheat of the first ripe barley was waved by the priest before the Lord to consecrate the opening harvest (Lev. xxiii. 10–14, cp. Josh. v. 10–12, R. V. margin; Septuagint of Lev. xxiii. 7, 11; Antiq. iii. 10, 5); see WEEKS, FEAST OF. This was an incidental feature: the act consecrated the opening harvest, but it held a subordinate place; the second day, when it was performed, was not observed as a Sabbath; and altogether the relation of the passover to the agricultural year was less marked than in the festivals of weeks and tabernacles. During the passover day by day continually, in addition to the regular sacrifices of the sanctuary, two bullocks, one ram, and seven lambs were offered as a burnt offering, and a he goat as a sin offering (Lev xxiii. 8; Num. xxviii. 19–25). During the seven days also unleavened bread was eaten. They had no leaven in their houses on the night of the passover, and consequently the dough which they seized in their hurried flight was unleavened (Ex. xii. 8, 34, 39). It was baked thus. Henceforth unleavened bread was associated in their minds, not only with the thought of sincerity and truth, which was the essential idea, but also with that of the hurried flight from Egypt (Deut. xvi. 3). Celebrations of the passover are recorded at Sinai (Num. ix. 1–14), on entering Canaan (Josh. v. 11), under Hezekiah (2 Chron. xxx. 1–27; with reference to Solomon, 5, 26), under Josiah (2 Kin. xxiii. 21–23; 2 Chron. xxxv. 1–19), in the days of Ezra (Ezra vi. 19–22). See also Mat. xxvi. 17 seq.; Mark xiv. 12 seq.; Luke xxii. 7 seq.; John xviii. 28; Antiq. xvii. 9, 3; xx. 5, 3; War vi. 9, 3).

2. The lamb or kid killed at the festival of the passover (Ex. xii. 21; Deut. xvi. 2; 2 Chron. xxx. 17). Christ is our passover (1 Cor. v. 7). Like the paschal lamb, he was without blemish (Ex. xii. 5 with 1 Pet. i. 18, 19), not a bone was broken (Ex. xii. 46 with John xix. 36), his blood was a token before God (Ex. xii. 13), and the feast was eaten with unleavened bread (18 and 1 Cor. v. 8).

Pat'a-ra.

A maritime city on the southwest of Lycia. Paul took ship there for Phoenicia on his last voyage to Palestine (Acts xxi. 1). It possessed a famous oracle of Apollo. It still exists as a ruin under its old name, though gradually becoming overwhelmed by moving sand dunes.

A young son is receiving some expert instruction in the observance of the Seder, the Passover meal. Special dishes are used for the Passover. On the Seder plate is a roasted bone, a roasted egg, bitter herbs, parsley, charoses (a mixture of apples, nuts, wine, sugar, cinnamon to serve as a reminder of the mortar used during the Egyptian bondage), and three pieces of matso (unleavened bread). The wine cup will be filled four times. Instructions for observing the Seder as well as the story of the Passover are in the Haggedah. Each member of the family

Path'ros [land of the south (Gesenius, Brugsch), house of the goddess Hathor in the south (Ebers)].

The country of southern or Upper Egypt. It is mentioned between Egypt and Cush (Is. xi. 11); and is known in Egyptian texts as Pa-to-ris, with Thebe as its capital. It was the original seat of the Egyptians themselves (Ezek. xxix. 14); and the first historical king of Egypt, Menes, is reported to have resided in Upper Egypt, in whose time all the lower country north of lake Mœris was a swamp (Herod. ii. 4, 15, 99). Isaiah foretold the dispersion of Israel to the remotest regions and their eventual return, among other places from Pathros (Is. xi. 11; cp. vii. 18). After the capture of Jerusalem by Nebuchadnezzar, Jews, probably refugees, were dwellers in Pathros (Jer. xliv. 1, 2, 15).

Path-ru'sim.

One of seven peoples proceeding from Mizraim. They are the inhabitants of Pathros (Gen. x. 14; 1 Chron. i. 12).

Pat'mos.

An island to which the apostle John was banished for the word of God, and for the testimony of Jesus Christ, and where he saw the visions recorded in the book of Revelation (Rev. i. 9). It is a small, rocky island, one of the Sporades, in the Grecian Archi-

Hebrew race and nation. It is applied to Abraham (Heb. vii. 4), to the twelve sons of Jacob (Acts vii. 8, 9), and to king David (ii. 29). The title is commonly given to the godly men and heads of families, whose lives are recorded in the O. T. previous to the time of Moses, as the antediluvian patriarchs whose lineage is given in Gen. v. In the patriarchal system the government of a clan is regarded as the paternal right. It resides in the first instance in the progenitor of the tribe, and descends from him to the firstborn son or eldest lineal male descendant. The head of each several family, into which the increasing tribe expands, exercises a similar government within his own limited sphere.

The patriarchal dispensation was the period before the establishment of the theocracy at Sinai, when each patriarchal head of a family was the priest of his own household, and God communed with him as such.

Pat'ro-bas.

A Christian at Rome, to whom Paul sent salutations (Rom. xvi. 14).

Pa'u [bleating (of sheep)].

A town of Edom, the city of king Hadar (Gen. xxxvi. 39). Site unknown. Called in 1 Chron. i. 50 Pai, vau and jod being interchanged; see VAU.

The isle of Patmos.

pelago, and is now called Patino. It lies off the southwestern coast of Asia Minor, about 30 miles south of Samos; and is about 15 miles in circumference, and generally barren.

Pa'tri-arch.

The father or chief of a race; a name given in the N. T. to the founders of the

Paul (Greek *Paulos*, from Latin *Paulus*, little).

The great apostle to the gentiles. His Jewish name was Saul (Hebrew *Sha'ul*, Greek *Saulos*). He is so called in The Acts until after the account of the conversion of Sergius Paulus, proconsul of Cyprus, from which point in the narrative (Acts xiii. 9) the name Paul alone is given him. In his epistles the apostle always calls himself Paul. It is not strange that some have supposed that he took the name Paul from the proconsul. But this is in reality quite improbable in itself, and fails to observe the delicacy with which Luke introduces the apostle's gentile name when his work among the gentiles, by whom he was known as Paul, began. It is more probable that, like many Jews (Acts i. 23; xii. 12; Col. iv. 11), and especially in the dispersion, the apostle had from the beginning both names. He was born in Tarsus, the chief city of Cilicia (Acts ix. 11; xxi. 39; xxii. 3), and was of the tribe of Benjamin (Phil. iii. 5). It is not known how the family came to reside in Tarsus, though one ancient tradition represents it as having removed there from Gischala in Galilee after the latter place had been captured by the Romans. It is possible, however, that the family had at an earlier time formed part of a colony settled in Tarsus by one of the Syrian kings (Ramsay, *St. Paul the Traveler*, p. 31), or they may have voluntarily migrated, as so many Jews did, for commercial purposes. Paul seems, however, to have had a large and even influential family connection. In Rom. xvi. 7, 11 he salutes three persons as his kinsmen, two of whom, Andronicus and Junias (R. V.), are said to have been "of note among the apostles," and to have become Christians before Paul did. From Acts xxiii. 16 we learn that his "sister's son," who seems to have resided, perhaps with his mother, in Jerusalem, gave information to the chief captain of the plot to kill Paul, from which it may be inferred that the young man was connected with some of the leading families. This is also confirmed by the prominence of Paul, though himself a young man, at the time of Stephen's death. He was apparently already a member of the council (Acts xxvi. 10), and soon afterwards the high priest intrusted to him the work of persecuting the Christians (ix. 1, 2; xxii. 5). His language in Phil. iii. 4-7 further implies that he occupied originally a position of large influence, and that opportunities of honor and gain had been open to him. His family connections, therefore, cannot have been obscure. Though he was brought up in the strict observance of the Hebrew faith and traditions, his father having been a Pharisee (Acts xxiii. 6), he was born a free Roman citizen. We do not know by what means his ancestor obtained citizenship. It may have been for service to the state or possibly by purchase. Its possession may have had some connection with the apostle's Roman name Paulus. But, however acquired, his Roman citizenship became of great importance in the prosecution of his Christian work and more than once saved his life. Tarsus was one of the intellectual centers of the East, and the seat of a famous

school of learning in which Stoicism was the dominant philosophy. It is scarcely probable, however, that Paul came under these influences when a boy, for his parents were strict Jews, and he was early sent to Jerusalem to be educated. Like other Jewish boys he was taught a trade, which in his case was the manufacture of tents, such as were used by travelers (xviii. 3). But, as he himself says (xxii. 3), he was brought up in Jerusalem. He must, therefore, have been sent there when quite young. And his education in Jerusalem tended to deepen the hold upon him of his inherited Pharisaic traditions. He was instructed "according to the perfect manner of the law of the fathers" (ibid.). He had for his teacher one of the most learned and distinguished rabbis of the day. This was Gamaliel, the grandson of the yet more famous Hillel. It was this Gamaliel whose speech, recorded in Acts v. 34-39, prevented the sanhedrin from attempting to slay the apostles. Gamaliel, indeed, had some leaning, strangely for a Pharisee, toward Greek culture, and his speech in The Acts shows the reverse of a bitter, persecuting spirit. But he was famous for rabbinical learning, and at his feet the young man from Tarsus became versed not only in the teaching of the O. T., but in the subtleties of rabbinical interpretation, while it is plain also that his zeal for the traditions of the fathers and his narrow Pharisaism burned with the fiery intensity of youth. Thus the future apostle grew up an ardent Pharisee, trained in the religious and intellectual ideas of his people, and from his personal qualities, his course of education, and probably his family connections prepared to take a high position among his countrymen.

He first appears in Christian history as the man at whose feet the witnesses who stoned Stephen laid their clothes (Acts vii. 58). He is described as being then a young man. The position he is here said to have occupied was not an official one. It seems to imply, however, especially when taken with the statement (viii. 1) that he "was consenting unto his death," that Paul was active in the persecution of the first Christian martyr. He was doubtless one of the Hellenists, or Greek-speaking Jews, mentioned in Acts vi. 9 as the original instigators of the charge against Stephen. We cannot be wrong in supposing that Paul's hatred of the new sect had already been aroused; that he not only despised their crucified Messiah, but regarded them as being both politically and religiously dangerous; and that he was already prepared, with bitter but conscientious fanaticism, to oppose them to the death. So we find him, immediately after Stephen's death, taking a leading part in the persecution of the Christians which followed (Acts viii. 3; xxii. 4; xxvi. 10, 11; 1 Cor. xv. 9; Gal. i. 13; Phil. iii. 6; 1 Tim. i. 13). He did this with the fierceness of a misguided conscience. He was the type of the religious inquisitor. Not content with waging the persecution in Jerusalem, he asked of the high priest letters to the synagogues in Damascus that he might bring from thence any Christian Jews whom he might find (Acts ix. 1, 2). Large powers of internal administration were granted to the Jews even by the Romans, and in Damascus, which was under the control of Aretas, king of the Nabathæans, the governor was particularly favorable to them (ix. 23, 24 ; 2 Cor. xi. 32), so that Paul's persecution of the Christians is not in the least incredible. The important thing to observe, however, is that according to the express testimony of Luke and of Paul himself, he was filled with fury against them up to the very moment of his conversion, and believed that in persecuting them he was rendering the highest service to God. He did not have a doubt as to the righteousness of his course, nor did his heart fail him in its execution.

It was on the way to Damascus that his sudden conversion occurred. Paul and his companions, probably on horseback, had been following the usual road across the desert from Galilee to the ancient city. Damascus had been nearly reached. It was the hour of noon and the sun was blazing in the zenith (Acts xxvi. 13). Suddenly a light from heaven, brighter than the sun, streamed round about them, and, overcome by its blinding brilliance, Paul fell upon the ground. His companions, too, fell to the ground (14), though they appear to have afterwards arisen, while he remained prostrate (ix. 7). Out of the light he heard a voice, saying in the Hebrew language: "Saul, Saul, why persecutest thou me? it is hard for thee to kick against the goad" (xxvi. 14 R. V.). He replied: "Who art thou, Lord?" He heard in answer: "I am Jesus whom thou persecutest" (15). "Arise, and go into the city, and it shall be told thee what thou must do" (ix. 6 ; xxii. 10). His companions heard the sound of the voice (ix. 7), but did not understand what was said (xxii. 9). Paul, however, was found to be blinded by the light, so they led him by the hand into Damascus, where he lodged in the house of a certain Judas (ix. 11). For three days he remained blind and fasting, praying (9, 11) and meditating on the revelation which had been made to him. On the third day the Lord commanded a certain Jewish Christian, named Ananias, to go to Paul and lay his hands on him that he might receive his sight. The Lord assured Ananias, who was afraid of the persecutor, that the latter had already seen him in a vision coming to him. Thereupon Ananias obeyed. Paul confessed his faith in Jesus, received his sight, accepted baptism, and forthwith, with his characteristic energy and to the astonishment of the Jews, began to preach in the synagogues that Jesus was the Christ, the Son of God (ix. 10–22).

Such is the narrative of the conversion of Saul of Tarsus. Three recitals of it are given in The Acts ; one by Luke (ix. 3–22) ; one by Paul himself before the Jews (xxii. 1–16) ; again by Paul before Festus and Agrippa (xxvi. 1–20). The three accounts entirely agree, though in each of them particulars are dwelt on which are not found in the others. The story in each case is told with special regard to the purpose of the narrator. Paul in his epistles also frequently alludes to his conversion, attributing it to the grace and power of God, though he does not describe it in detail (1 Cor ix. 1, 16 ; xv. 8–10 ; Gal. i. 12–16 ; Eph. iii. 1–8 ; Phil. iii. 5–7 ; 1 Tim. i. 12–16 ; 2 Tim. i. 9–11). The fact, therefore, is supported by the strongest possible testimony. It is certain also that Jesus not only spoke to Paul, but visibly appeared to him (Acts ix. 17, 27 ; xxii. 14 ; xxvi. 16 ; 1 Cor. ix. 1). While the form in which he appeared is not described, we may be sure that it was a glorious one ; so that Paul realized at once that the crucified Jesus was the exalted Son of God. He himself describes it as "the heavenly vision" (Acts xxvi. 19), or spectacle. a word elsewhere used only in Luke i. 22 and xxiv. 23 to describe the manifestation of angelic beings. There is no ground therefore for the allegation that it was an illusion of any kind. At the same time the mere appearance of Christ did not convert Paul. This was the work of the Spirit in his heart, enabling him to apprehend and accept the truth which had been revealed to him (see especially Gal. i. 15). Ananias also was evidently made use of in order to connect Paul's new life with the already existing church. The various rationalistic attempts which have been made to explain Paul's conversion without acknowledgment of the objective and supernatural interposition of the Lord are wrecked upon the testimony of Paul himself that he had thought up to the time of his conversion that it was his religious duty to persecute Christianity, and that his change was due to the sovereign exercise of God's power and grace. The expression, "It is hard for thee to kick against the goad," does not imply that he had been an unwilling persecutor or that he already believed that Christianity might be true, but describes the folly of any resistance to the purpose of God with him. At the same time his previous history had been an unconscious preparation for his future work. His Roman citizenship, his rabbinical training, as well as his natural qualities of mind fitted him for his life task. There is reason to believe also that with all his zeal he had not found spiritual peace in Judaism (Rom. vii. 7–25). If so, the manner of his conversion must have made him vividly realize that salvation is alone through the grace of God in Christ. His religious experience therefore was also part of his preparation to become the great expounder of the gospel as providing justification for the sinner on the ground of Christ's merits received through faith alone. As soon as he was converted Paul began evangelistic work. This was partly due to his natural energy, but also to the fact that it had been revealed to him that God's purpose in calling him was to make him a missionary and apostle (Acts ix. 15; xxvi. 16–20; Gal. i. 15, 16). He began work in the synagogues of Damascus and pursued it with success. This raised against him persecution from the Damascene Jews, who were aided by the governor of the city (2 Cor. xi. 32); so that he was compelled to flee secretly, being let down by his disciples in a basket from a window in the city's wall (Acts ix. 23–25; 2 Cor. xi. 33). Instead of returning to Jerusalem, however, he went to Arabia and afterwards returned to Damascus (Gal. i. 17). We do not know where he went in Arabia, nor how long he stayed, nor what he did there. It is not improbable that the time was mainly spent in meditation upon the great change which had come over his life and the truth as it had now been revealed to him. But three years after his conversion he determined to leave Damascus and visit Jerusalem again. He tells us (Gal. i. 18, 19) that his main purpose was to visit Peter; that he remained in Jerusalem only fifteen days; and that of the apostles he saw Peter only, though he mentions that he also saw James, the Lord's brother. Luke, however (Acts ix. 26–29), gives further particulars. It appears that the Christians in Jerusalem were afraid of him because of his former reputation and did not believe he was really a disciple; but that Barnabas, with that generosity of mind which was ever characteristic of him, took Paul to the apostles and related the story of his conversion and subsequent changed life. We are also told that Paul preached as fearlessly in Jerusalem as he had done at Damascus and directed his efforts especially toward his old friends, the Greek-speaking Jews (ix. 28, 29). These, too, plotted at once against his life. The threatening danger caused the brethren to send him away, so they took him to Cæsarea and sent him from there to Tarsus (29, 30; Gal. i. 21). He departed the more willingly because in the temple the Lord had appeared to him in a vision bidding him go and telling him distinctly that his mission was to the gentiles (Acts xxii. 17–21). The two accounts in The Acts and Galatians of this visit to Jerusalem have sometimes been thought inconsistent, but they may be naturally harmonized. It is highly probable that Paul would want to visit Peter in order that his work might proceed in unison with that of the original apostles, of whom Peter was the most prominent. It is equally natural that the Jerusalem Christians should be at first afraid of him; and the conduct of Barnabas, who was, like Paul, a Hellenistic Jew, is in keeping with his action through-

out the whole history. Fifteen days, moreover, are not too short a time for the events described in The Acts. It is, in fact, confirmed by the Lord's command to Paul to depart quickly (xxii. 18). Nor is Luke's statement that Barnabas brought Paul "to the apostles" inconsistent with Paul's statement that he saw Peter only, together with James. The reception of the new convert even by Peter alone, not to speak of James, who occupied almost an apostolic position (see Gal. ii. 9), was equivalent to apostolic recognition of him, and this is all that Luke's expression was meant to describe. It is further worthy of remark that it was now realized fully, both by Paul and the leaders in Jerusalem, that the new convert was a chosen apostle of Christ, and that his mission was to the gentiles. At the same time the question does not appear to have been raised of what would be the relation of gentile converts to the Mosaic law. Neither did any foresee how important Paul's mission was to become. His commission, however, was admitted, and he was sent forth to Tarsus to engage in such work as might open before him.

Paul's stay in Tarsus is nearly a blank to us. It probably lasted six or seven years; see below on the chronology of Paul's life. No doubt he engaged in missionary work, and probably founded the churches of Cilicia, which are mentioned incidentally in Acts xv. 41. If at any time he felt the intellectual influences of Tarsus, this must have been the period. As already remarked, Tarsus was one of the centers of the Stoic philosophy, and Paul's appreciation of Stoicism plainly appears in his speech at Athens. But we must be content with the little information that has been given us. While doubtless not inactive, Paul was waiting for the Lord by his providence to make plain the way in which his chosen ambassador was to go.

At length, however, the purpose of God began to appear. Some of the Greek-speaking Jewish Christians who had been driven from Jerusalem by the persecution which followed Stephen's death came to the great city of Antioch in Syria. It was situated on the Orontes, north of the Lebanon range, had been the capital of the Syrian kingdom, and was then the residence of the Roman governor of the province. It was rated as one of the chief cities of the empire. Its mixed population and its extensive commerce made it a center of wide influence. Lying just outside of Palestine and at the entrance to Asia Minor, connected also by traffic and politics with the whole empire, it formed a natural base of operations from which the new faith, if it was to be separated from Judaism, could go forth to the conquest of the world. In Antioch the Christian refugees began, we are told (Acts xi. 20), to preach to the gentiles (A. V. Grecians; R. V. Greeks). There is a difficult question of the text in the original; but the context leaves no room for doubt that the work was among gentiles. Many were converted, so that a distinctively gentile church sprang up in the metropolis of Syria. When the fact was reported at Jerusalem, Barnabas was sent to investigate. With noble breadth of view, he saw the Lord's hand in the new development in spite of the fact that the converts were uncircumcised. He also seems to have realized that this was the divine opening for Paul; for he went to Tarsus to seek him and brought him to Antioch. Together they labored for a year in Antioch. Many more gentiles were converted, and the non-Jewish character of the church was signalized by the fact that to the disciples in Antioch was the name Christians first given, evidently by their heathen neighbors. Thus began Paul's connection with Antioch. Thus also arose on the page of church history the first gentile Christian organization. It was to be the starting point for Paul's mission to the pagan world.

While Paul was at Antioch, a prophet from Jerusalem, named Agabus, predicted in the Christian assembly that a famine was soon to occur. This was seized upon by the brethren at Antioch as an occasion for evincing their love to and fraternity with the Christians of Judæa. The fact is a remarkable proof of the sense of obligation which these gentiles had to those from whom they had received their new faith, as well as of the extent to which the gospel broke down at once the barriers which had existed between races and classes. Contributions for the relief of the Judæan Christians were made at Antioch, and the same were sent to the elders at Jerusalem by the hands of Barnabas and Saul (Acts xi. 29, 30). This visit of Paul to Jerusalem probably occurred in A. D. 44, or shortly after. It is not mentioned by Paul in Galatians, no doubt because he did not see any of the apostles. Some writers indeed have tried to identify it with the visit recorded in Gal. ii. 1–10; but that plainly occurred after the dispute concerning the circumcision of gentiles had sprung up, and Luke distinctly assigns the rise of that controversy to a later date (Acts xv. 1). The purpose of Paul in Galatians was to recount the opportunities he had had of obtaining his gospel from the older apostles; and if on this occasion, as Luke intimates (xi. 30), he met only the elders of the church, and if the brief visit was purely on a matter of charity, his argument in Galatians did not require him to mention the journey. Barnabas and Paul soon returned to Antioch, taking with them John Mark (xii. 25).

The time had at length arrived when Paul's historic missionary work to the gentiles was to begin. It was indicated by the Spirit to the prophets belonging to the church in Antioch (Acts xiii. 1–3). They were directed to set apart two of their number, Barnabas and Paul, for the work to which God had called them. Thus by divine direction and under the auspices of the church at Antioch, the apostle's first missionary journey began. Its exact date is uncertain. We can only assign it to the years between A. D. 45–50; perhaps, 46–48. Neither is there any clear indication how long a time it occupied. Barnabas, who was the older, is mentioned as the leader; but Paul speedily took the chief place through his ability in speaking. John Mark also went as their helper. The party went from Antioch to Seleucia, at the mouth of the Orontes, and thence sailed to Cyprus, the original home of Barnabas. Landing at Salamis, on the east coast of Cyprus, they began work, as was natural, in the Jewish synagogues. Then they moved through the island from place to place until they reached Paphos on the southwest coast. Here they attracted the notice of Sergius Paulus, the Roman proconsul, and were violently opposed by a Jewish sorcerer, Bar-jesus, who called himself Elymas, learned one, and who had previously won the patronage of the proconsul (Acts xiii. 6, 7). Paul, with much indignation, rebuked the sorcerer and smote him with blindness; and the effect of the miracle and of the missionaries' teaching was the conversion of Sergius (8–12). Then leaving Cyprus, the party, of whom Paul was now the recognized head (13), sailed north toward Asia Minor and came to Perga in Pamphylia. There John Mark, for some unexplained reason, left them and returned to Jerusalem. Nor do Paul and Barnabas appear to have remained in Perga, but journeyed northward into Phrygia until they reached Antioch, called Pisidian because it lay toward Pisidia. This was the chief city of the Roman province of Galatia. There they entered the Jewish synagogue and, on invitation of the rulers of the synagogue, Paul made the great address recorded in Acts xiii. 16–41, the first recorded specimen of his preaching. After rehearsing the divine leading of Israel with a view to the coming Messiah, he related the testimony of the Baptist and the rejection of Jesus by the Jewish rulers, but declared that God had raised him from the dead, that in him the ancient promises to Israel were being fulfilled, and that only through faith in him could men be justified. He also warned the Jews not to repeat the crime of their rulers in Jerusalem. The speech aroused the enmity of the leading Jews; but it made an impression on some others, and yet more on those gentiles who were already under the influence of the synagogue and who ever formed the connecting link for Paul between the synagogue and the pagan world. The next Sabbath the break took place between the missionaries and the synagogue, and the former began to address their work directly to the gentiles. The chief people of the city, however, were excited by the Jews against the Christians, and Paul and

Barnabas were expelled (Acts xiii. 50). From Antioch they went to Iconium, another city of Phrygia, where many converts, both Jewish and gentile, were made (51). But the Jews again succeeded in raising persecution, and the missionaries passed on to Lystra and Derbe, important cities of Lycaonia (xiv. 1-6). At Lystra the miraculous cure of a lame man by Paul led to an attempt on the part of the heathen populace to offer worship to the missionaries, calling them Jupiter and Mercury; and this occasioned the second recorded speech of Paul (15-18), in which he reasoned against the folly of idolatry. At Lystra Timothy was probably converted (see Acts xvi. 1; 2 Tim. i. 2; iii. 11). The brief popularity of the apostle was, however, soon followed by renewed persecution under Jewish instigation (Acts xiv. 19), so that he was stoned, dragged out of the city, and left for dead. When he revived he departed with Barnabas to Derbe, which was probably at the southeastern limit of the province of Galatia (20). It would have been possible for the missionaries to cross the mountains into Cilicia, and so go directly by way of Tarsus, back to Syrian Antioch. Their route had followed a rough circle. But they would not return until they had placed the new churches on a firm basis. Hence they returned from Derbe to Lystra, from Lystra to Iconium, from Iconium to Pisidian Antioch, and from Antioch to Perga, in each place organizing the church and encouraging the disciples. At Perga they preached, as they had seemingly not done at the former visit; then, going to its seaport, Attalia, they returned to Antioch in Syria (Acts xiv. 21-26). Thus the first missionary tour of the apostle was completed. It covered the regions next toward the west of those already occupied by the gospel. His method was to offer the gospel first to the Jews and then to the gentiles. He found a large number of the latter already influenced by Judaism, and therefore somewhat prepared to receive Christianity. His method was to found churches in the principal cities, and his journeys were facilitated by the fine roads which the Roman government had made between her military posts. The Greek language also was everywhere understood. Providence had thus prepared the way for the prepared herald of the gospel to the world. [On the missionary journeys of Paul, the student should consult Conybeare and Howson's *Life and Epistles of St. Paul;* and, especially for the first journey, the first part of Ramsay's *Church in the Roman Empire.*]

The success of Paul's work among the gentiles led, however, to controversy within the church. Certain strict Jewish Christians from Jerusalem went to Antioch and declared that unless the converted gentiles were circumcised, they could not be saved (Acts xv. 1). Some years before this time God

had revealed to the church through Peter that gentiles were to be received without observance of the Mosaic law (x. 1-xi. 18). But the strict Jewish party, made up mostly of converted Pharisees (xv. 5), would not abide by this teaching; and the announcement of their doctrines in Antioch so disturbed the church there that the brethren determined to send Paul and Barnabas, with others, to Jerusalem to consult with the apostles and elders about this question. This is the visit described in Acts xv. and Gal. ii. 1-10. Both accounts are entirely harmonious, though written from different points of view. Paul tells us that a revelation from God directed him to go (Gal. ii. 2). It was a great crisis. The whole future of the new religion was depending on the issue. But the result was a triumph of Christian loyalty and charity. Paul and Barnabas proclaimed to the mother church what God had done through them. When the strict Jewish Christians opposed them, a council was held of the apostles and elders (Acts xv. 6-29). Peter reminded the church of God's will as shown in the case of Cornelius; Paul and Barnabas related the mighty attestations which God had given to their mission; James, the Lord's brother, pointed out that prophecy had foretold the calling of the gentiles. It was resolved to heartily recognize the uncircumcised converts as brethren, but to direct them to avoid certain practices which were specially offensive to the Jews. Paul tells us in Galatians that the church in Jerusalem stood by him against the "false brethren;" and also that James, Peter, and John gave him the right hand of fellowship, he to go to the gentiles, they to the Jews. Thus Paul retained fellowship with the other apostles while at liberty to go on his own divinely appointed mission. How bitter the controversy was on the part of the Judaizers is shown by their subsequent hatred and hostility to Paul. But he had gained his point. The unity of the church was preserved. The liberty of the gentiles was preserved. A practical adjustment was made by which reasonable Jewish prejudice was conciliated, while the way was open for the carrying of the gospel to all peoples, unencumbered by Jewish ceremonialism. A brief reminder of the controversy occurred indeed soon after in Antioch which ought to be mentioned (Gal. ii. 11-21). Peter had gone there and, being in entire agreement with Paul, had lived in free association with the gentiles. But when Jews from Jerusalem came to Antioch, Peter and even Barnabas withdrew from this association. This led Paul publicly to rebuke Peter, and in his rebuke he outlined the doctrinal ground on which he rested the rights of the gentiles in the church. Salvation is by faith alone, he said, because the believer has died with Christ to the law; *i. e.* Christ by dying has met all the obligations of the law for his people, and therefore nothing more than faith in Christ can be made the condition of any one's becoming a Christian. We thus see that the rights of the gentiles in the church involved for Paul much more than a question of church unity. He saw that it involved the essential principle of the gospel. By his defense of this principle, as well as by his missionary work, Paul was the chief agent in the establishment of universal Christianity.

The council at Jerusalem was probably held in A. D. 50 ; see the chronology below. Not long after it Paul proposed to Barnabas a second missionary journey (Acts xv. 36). He was unwilling, however, that John Mark should again go with them, and this led to the final separation of the two great missionaries. Paul thereupon took with him Silas; see SILAS. They first visited the churches of Syria and Cilicia, and then passed northward, through the Taurus mountains, to the churches which had been founded on Paul's first journey. They thus came first to Derbe, then to Lystra. At the latter place Paul determined to take Timothy with him, and circumcised him to prevent giving offense to the Jews, for Timothy's mother was a Jewess. Paul thus showed willingness to conciliate Jewish prejudice ; though he would not yield an inch when the principles of the gospel were at stake. From Lystra they appear to have gone to Iconium and Pisidian Antioch. Their movements here, however, are much disputed by scholars. Ramsay and others, who believe that the churches of the first journey were the "churches of Galatia" to which the epistle with that name was afterwards written (see GALATIA, GALATIANS, EPISTLE TO THE), hold that Paul went directly north from Pisidian Antioch through the Roman province of Asia, but without preaching, since he was "forbidden by the Holy Ghost to preach the word in Asia" (Acts xvi. 6) ; that when they came "over against Mysia" (7, R. V.) they attempted to go into Bithynia, but were again forbidden ; then passing by (or, as the original may mean, neglecting) Mysia they turned westward through or alongside of Mysia to Troas. The commoner view is that from Pisidian Antioch the travelers moved northeastward into Galatia proper ; that on the way Paul was for a while disabled by sickness, and that this led him to improve the opportunity, sick though he was, of preaching in Galatia and so of founding the "churches of Galatia" (Gal. iv. 13-15) ; that this movement to the northeast from Pisidian Antioch was due to the command not to preach in Asia ; that when his work in Galatia proper was done, he attempted to enter Bithynia, but was again forbidden ; and so, as on the former theory, he turned west through or alongside of Mysia to Troas. This whole period is very briefly described by Luke. The Spirit was directing the missionaries to Europe, and Luke's narrative likewise hastens forward.

At Troas there appeared the vision of the man of Macedonia (Acts xvi. 9) ; in response to whose call the missionaries, now joined by Luke himself, took ship for Europe, and landing at Neapolis, went forward to the important city of Philippi. Here a church was founded (xvi. 11-40), which ever remained specially dear to the apostle's heart (see Phil. i. 4-7 ; iv. 1, 15). Here, too, Paul first came into conflict with Roman magistrates and found that his citizenship was a protection for his work (Acts xvi. 20-24 ; 37-39). From Philippi, where Luke remained. Paul, Silas, and Timothy went on to Thessalonica. The brief account in Acts xvii. 1-9 of the work done there is supplemented by the allusions made to it in his two epistles to that church. He had much success among the gentiles ; he laid with great care the foundations of the church ; and he gave the example of industry and sobriety by supporting himself by his trade while preaching the gospel (1 Thes. ii., etc.). But persecution arose, instigated by the Jews, so the brethren sent Paul to Berœa, and from there, after marked success even in the synagogue, to Athens. His sojourn at Athens was rather disappointing, and is memorable chiefly for the address before the philosophers on Mars' hill (Acts xvii. 22-31), in which Paul showed his appreciation of the truths which the gospel had in common with Stoicism, while he yet faithfully proclaimed to a critical audience their duty to God and what God required them to believe. At Corinth, on the contrary, to which he next went, he remained eighteen months, and his work was most successful. Here he made the acquaintance of Aquila and Priscilla and abode with them (xviii. 1-3). At first he preached in the synagogue, but afterwards, because of the opposition of the Jews, in the house of a gentile, Titus Justus, who lived next to the synagogue (5-7, R. V.). In both The Acts (xviii. 9, 10) and 1 Cor. (ii. 1-5) there are allusions to the great anxiety of mind with which the apostle prosecuted his mission in Corinth, and to his earnest determination to proclaim in Greece as elsewhere the simple gospel of the Crucified ; while 1 Cor. amply testifies both to his success and to the many temptations to which the Christians of Corinth were exposed, and which from the beginning occasioned the apostle special solicitude. The needs of other churches also pressed upon him, so that from Corinth he wrote the two epistles to the Thessalonians for the purpose of warning against certain doctrinal and practical perils by which that church was threatened. The hostility of the Jews also did not cease, and, on the coming to Corinth of the new proconsul, Gallio, they accused Paul of violation of the law. But the proconsul properly decided that the matter pertained to the synagogue itself and that the apostle had broken no law of which the gov-

Top, left: The Taurus mountain range dominates this section of present day Turkey. The churches at Derbe, Lystra, and Iconium were located in this general area.

Top, right: Ruins at Philippi, chief city of Macedonia. Paul established a Christian colony there.

Opposite: This is the reputed section of the city wall in Damascus where Paul was let down by basket.

Below: Ruins of a Roman aqueduct in Antioch of Pisidia. Paul probably preached in this area during his first missionary journey.

Top, left: St. Paul's Bay in Malta where Paul suffered shipwreck. In ancient times this island was known as Melita. On the large islet, left is a statue of Paul to commemorate the event of Acts 27.

Top, right: Ruins of the bema, Corinth. Paul was brought before the tribunal (bema) by Corinthian Jews (Acts 18: 12-27).

Opposite: View of Athens from the Acropolis. While in Athens Paul delivered his famous address, now inscribed at the top of the Areopagus.

Below: Ruins of the Forum in Salamis, Cyprus. The Forum existed in Paul's and Barnabas' time. Cyprus was the first preaching stop on Paul's first missionary journey.

ernment could take cognizance. The empire thus at this period protected the Christians from Jewish violence by identifying them with the Jews, and Paul was permitted to continue his work unmolested. His mission to Corinth was one of the most fruitful in the history of the early Christian church. At length, however, Paul turned his face again to the east. From Corinth he sailed to Ephesus. He did not remain there, however, but, promising to return, sailed to Cæsarea, made apparently a hasty journey to Jerusalem, and, having saluted the church there, returned to Antioch, whence he had originally started (Acts xviii. 22). Thus was completed his second missionary journey. Its result had been the establishment of Christianity in Europe. Macedonia and Achaia had been evangelized. The gospel had thereby taken a long step forward toward the conquest of the empire. After remaining some time at Antioch, Paul, probably in A. D. 54 began his third journey. He first traversed "the region of Galatia and Phrygia in order, stablishing all the disciples" (23), and then settled in Ephesus. It thus appears that the previous divine prohibition to preach in the province of Asia had been removed. Ephesus was the capital of Asia and one of the most influential cities of the East. Hence the apostle for 3 years made it his center of operations (xix. 8, 9; xx. 31). For 3 months he taught in the synagogue (xviii. 8), and then for 2 years in the school or lecture hall of a certain Tyrannus (9). His work in Ephesus was marked by great thoroughness of instruction (xx. 18–31); by the exercise of astonishing miraculous power (xix. 11, 12); by great success, so that "all they which dwelt in Asia heard the word of the Lord" (10), and even some of the chief officers of Asia became Paul's friends (31); yet also by constant and fierce opposition (23–41; 1 Cor. iv. 9–13; xv. 32); and finally, by the care of all the churches (2 Cor. xi. 28). This period of the apostle's life is especially rich in incidents. Much occurred of which The Acts tells nothing. Here Paul heard of attacks made on him and his doctrine by Judaizing teachers in Galatia; and in reply he wrote the famous Epistle to the Galatians, in which he defends his apostolic authority, and gives the first formal statement and proof of the doctrines of grace. The condition of the Corinthians also occasioned him much anxiety. In reply to inquiries from Corinth he wrote a letter, now lost, concerning the relations of believers to the pagan society about them (1 Cor. v. 9). But later reports showed that more serious troubles had arisen. Hence our 1 Cor. was written, an epistle which finely exhibits the apostle's practical wisdom in the instruction and discipline of the infant churches. Even so, however, the seditious elements in the Corinthian church would not yield. Many think that Paul, after writing 1 Cor., himself made a hurried visit to Corinth for disciplinary purposes (cp. 2 Cor. xii. 14; xiii. 1). At any rate, before leaving Ephesus he sent Titus to Corinth, probably with a letter, to secure the discipline of a refractory member of the church. Titus was to rejoin him in Troas. When he failed to do so, Paul passed on in much anxiety to Macedonia, whither Timothy and Erastus had preceded him (Acts xix. 22). At length, however, Titus rejoined him (2 Cor. ii. 12–14; vii. 5–16), with the good news that the Corinthian church had obeyed the apostle and were loyal in their love for him. Whereupon Paul wrote our 2 Cor., the most biographical of all his epistles, in which he rejoices in their obedience, gives directions concerning the collection he was making for the Judæan saints, and once more defends his authority as an apostle of Christ. From Macedonia he himself went to Corinth and passed the winter of A. D. 57–58 there. No doubt he completed the discipline and organization of the Corinthian church; but the visit is most memorable because he then wrote the Epistle to the Romans. In it he states most completely the doctrine of the way of salvation. He evidently regarded Rome as the place where his labors should culminate. He could not, however, go there at once, because he felt it necessary to return to Jerusalem with the gifts of the gentiles to the mother church. Christian work had already been begun at Rome, and was being carried on mainly by Paul's own friends and disciples (cp. Rom. xvi.). Hence, he sent the epistle from Corinth that the Christians of the capital might possess complete instruction in the gospel which Paul was proclaiming to the world.

Paul now set out on his last journey to Jerusalem. He was accompanied by friends who represented various gentile churches (Acts xx. 4). The apostle's work among the gentiles had been much opposed by Judaizers, and even the ordinary Jewish Christians often regarded him and it with distrust. Hence arose his scheme of proving the loyalty of the gentile churches by inducing them to send a liberal offering to the poor Christians of Judæa. It was to carry this offering that he and his friends left Corinth for Jerusalem. His plan had first been to sail direct to Syria, but a plot of the Jews led him to change his route and to return by way of Macedonia (xx. 3). He lingered at Philippi while his companions went on to Troas, but he was rejoined at that place by Luke (5). After the passover he and Luke went on to Troas, where the others were waiting for them and where all remained seven days (6). A church had grown up at Troas, and an interesting account is given by Luke of the events of the apostle's interview with it on the day and night before he left it (7–12). From Troas Paul went by foot about twenty miles to Assos, whither his companions had already gone by boat (13). Thence they sailed to Mitylene, on the eastern shore of the island of Lesbos, and then, coasting southward they passed between the mainland and the island of Chios, touched the next day at the island of Samos, and the day following reached Miletus (14, 15). The A. V. states (Acts xx. 15) that they "tarried at Trogyllium" after leaving Samos; see TRO-GYLLIUM. The R. V. with the best manuscripts omits this clause. Miletus was about 36 miles from Ephesus, and as Paul was in haste, he determined not to go to Ephesus, but to send for the elders of the church. At Miletus he took leave of them in the affectionate address recorded in Acts xx. 18–35. No words could more strongly exhibit the apostle's devotion to his work, and his love for his converts, and his realization of the spiritual perils to which they would be exposed. Leaving Miletus, the ship went with a straight course to Cos (Acts xxi. 1, in A. V., Coos), an island about 40 miles to the south; then, the next day, Rhodes, an island and city about 50 miles southeast of Cos, was reached; and from Rhodes the course lay eastward to Patara, on the coast of Lycia (Acts xxi. 1). At Patara a ship for Phœnicia (Syria) was found and the party went on board (2), and, passing west of Cyprus, reached Tyre (3). There they remained a week, and the disciples of Tyre urged Paul not to go to Jerusalem (4); but after an affectionate farewell he sailed (5, 6) to Ptolemais, the modern Acre, and came the next day to Cæsarea (7, 8). At Cæsarea the company abode with Philip the evangelist. There too the prophet Agabus, who at an earlier time had foretold the famine (xi. 28), bound his own hands and feet with Paul's girdle, and predicted that so would the Jews bind Paul and deliver him to the gentiles. But in spite of this warning and the lamentation of the brethren, Paul insisted on going forward (xxi. 11–14). So, in company with a number of the disciples, he went on to Jerusalem, thus completing what is known as his third missionary journey.

The prediction of Agabus was soon fulfilled. Paul was at first indeed well received by the brethren in Jerusalem, and on the day following his arrival went in to James, the Lord's brother, and the elders of the church. When he had related his work among the gentiles, they glorified God. At the same time they reminded him that many of the Jewish Christians had heard evil reports about him and doubted his fidelity to Moses. It was proposed, therefore, that he should give an ocular proof that he still held the Jewish customs in honor. He was to join with four men, who at that time were performing a Nazirite vow in the temple. To this Paul assented, for he was ever anxious not to give needless offense to the Jews, and the observance proposed was probably little more than what he had done of his own will at Corinth (xviii. 18). While Paul insisted

that no gentile should observe the Mosaic law, and while he maintained that no Christian Jew was bound to observe it, he found no fault with Jews who chose to observe it, and held himself at liberty to observe its regulations or not as circumstances might seem to make expedient. His assent to this proposal, therefore, was not inconsistent with his action on other occasions. But the expedient proved unavailing for the purpose for which it was intended. Certain Jews from Asia saw him in the temple and raised a tumult. They falsely charged him with having brought gentiles into the temple, and declared to the populace that he had everywhere taught men to dishonor both the temple and the law (xxi. 27-29). A riot speedily ensued in which Paul would probably have been slain, had not the commander of the Roman garrison, Claudius Lysias, hastened with soldiers to quell the uproar. He was leading Paul, bound with two chains, into the castle for examination and the Jews were following with many outcries, when the apostle desired liberty to speak. The commander was surprised that the prisoner could use Greek, for he had taken him to be an Egyptian insurrectionist who had recently given trouble to the government (38). When Paul explained that he was a Tarsian Jew, Lysias allowed him to address the multitude. He did so in the Hebrew tongue (xxii. 2). He related his early life and the story of his conversion. They heard him till he uttered the word "gentiles," when the uproar was renewed, and Lysias withdrew him into the castle for safety and further examination. The examination would have been by scourging, had not Paul remarked to the centurion that he was a Roman citizen (25). When this was reported to Lysias, he unbound Paul and, feeling that the matter was a serious one, directed the priests to convoke the sanhedrin on the following day that the prisoner might be tried.

The appearance of Paul before the council led, however, to another tumult (Acts xxiii. 1-10). The apostle was now fighting for his life. He had no hope of justice, and should the council condemn him, Lysias might give him over to execution. With much shrewdness he succeeded in dividing his enemies. He claimed to be a Pharisee, and to be on trial for teaching the doctrine of the resurrection of the dead. This was true, as far as it went, and it served Paul's purpose. The hatred of the Pharisees and Sadducees for each other was greater than their hostility to Paul, and the two sects quickly arrayed themselves on opposite sides. The commander feared that Paul would be pulled to pieces between his defenders and his opponents, and so by his orders the soldiers removed the prisoner again to the castle.

That night the Lord appeared to Paul in a vision and bade him be of good cheer, since he was certainly to bear his testimony at Rome (Acts xxiii. 11). This consummation was to be effected, however, in an unexpected way. Some of the Jews formed a plot to kill Paul and, to accomplish this, it was determined to request the commander to bring the prisoner once more before the council. But Paul's nephew heard of the plot and managed to inform his uncle and the commander (12–22). Thereupon Lysias sent Paul under a strong guard to Cæsarea with a letter to Felix, the procurator, referring the case to him. When Felix learned that the accused was from Cilicia, he declared that he would wait until the accusers came, and meanwhile placed Paul for safe keeping in Herod's palace, which was used as the prætorium or residence of the procurator. Then followed two years of imprisonment in Cæsarea. When the Jews appeared before Felix, they made a general accusation against Paul of sedition and especially of profanation of the temple, complaining of the violence with which Lysias had taken their prisoner out of their hands (Acts xxiv. 1–9). To this Paul replied by an explicit denial and a demand that witnesses should be produced against him (10–21). Felix appears to have been sufficiently acquainted with the matters in dispute to perceive that Paul had not committed any crime worthy of punishment. He dismissed the accusers on the plea that he must learn further particulars from Lysias, and directed that Paul should be kept in confinement, but that his friends should be allowed to visit him freely. Felix and his wife Drusilla were also much impressed by what Paul had said and "heard him concerning the faith in Christ" (24). In fact, the apostle seems to have exercised a strange fascination over the procurator, who trembled before his solemn preaching and promised to send for him again. He hoped also that Paul would pay for his liberty (25, 26). But the apostle would not bribe the procurator, and the latter deferred decision of the case, so that when, after two years, Porcius Festus succeeded Felix, Paul was still a prisoner (27).

The Jews hoped that the new governor would prove more favorable to their desires than Felix had been. But Festus refused to send Paul to Jerusalem for trial, and required his accusers to confront him again in Cæsarea (Acts xxv. 1–6). Again, however, they were unable to prove any crime against him, while he persistently maintained his innocence (7, 8). Festus, however, willing to please the Jews, asked Paul if he would go to Jerusalem to be tried. Paul knew that such a course would probably prove fatal to him. He availed himself, therefore, of his right as a Roman citizen and appealed unto Cæsar (9–11). This took the case out of the procurator's hands and necessitated the prisoner's transmission to Rome. Before he could be sent, however, Agrippa II. and his sister Bernice came to visit Festus, doubtless to congratulate him on his accession to office; and the procurator, who was not well versed in Jewish disputes and yet was bound to send to the emperor a full account of the case, related the matter to Agrippa, who expressed his desire to hear what the prisoner had to say. Forthwith it was arranged that Paul should state his cause before the assembled company. Agrippa's familiarity with Jewish affairs would be of service to the procurator in preparing his report to the emperor (12–27).

Paul's defense before Agrippa forms one of his most notable speeches. In it he displayed the courtesy of a gentleman, the eloquence of an orator, and the fearlessness of a Christian. He reviewed his life in order to show that he had been governed only by the wish to obey the God of Israel, and maintained that his course as a Christian had not only been determined by God's direction, but had been the fulfillment of the Hebrew prophecies themselves (Acts xxvi. 1–23). When Festus interrupted him with the exclamation that he was mad, Paul appealed earnestly to Agrippa. But the king was not disposed to be more than an observer and critic of what he deemed a new fanaticism. He replied with some contempt: "With but little persuasion thou wouldest fain make me a Christian" (28, R. V.). Nevertheless he admitted that Paul had done no crime, and might have been set at liberty if he had not appealed unto Cæsar (31, 32). In the autumn of the same year, A. D. 60 (see chronology below), Paul was sent to Rome. He was committed, with other prisoners, to the care of a centurion, Julius, of the Augustan band or cohort. He was accompanied by Luke and Aristarchus, a Thessalonian (xxvii. 1, 2). The account of the voyage is related by Luke with singular detail and accuracy (see James Smith, *The Voyage and Shipwreck of St. Paul*). The apostle was treated also with notable courtesy by the centurion. Leaving Cæsarea in a coasting ship of Adramyttium, they touched at Sidon and then sailed to Myra in Lycia. There they were transferred to an Alexandrian merchant ship bound for Italy. The wind, however, was not favorable. They were compelled at first to keep coasting northwestward until over against Cnidus on the coast of Caria. Then putting southward, they rounded with difficulty cape Salmone, on the eastern extremity of Crete, and managed to reach Fair Havens, a port on the southern shore of the same island (Acts xxvii. 3–8). It was now after the Fast, *i. e.* the 10th of Tishri or day of atonement (9), when the season of navigation was drawing to a close. The weather also continued threatening. Paul counseled against sailing further, but the centurion followed the advice of the master and the owner of the ship, who wished to go on to Phœnix, further west on the coast of Crete, where there was a better harbor (9–12). But when they had left Fair Havens, a fierce northeast wind came down upon them and drove them to the south. Passing south of Cauda (or Clauda A. V., the modern Gozzo), and having lightened the ship, they were driven for fourteen days before the gale in a westerly direction. Paul alone maintained his courage and that of the rest, for an angel of the Lord assured him that no life would be lost (13-26). On the fourteenth night the sounding lead told of their approach to land ; and, casting four anchors, they waited for the day. When daylight came, they perceived in the unknown land a small bay with a beach; so cutting off their anchors, they hoisted the foresail to the wind and made for the beach (27-40, R. V.). The ship, however, grounded, and soon began to break up under the violence of the waves. Thereupon the whole company cast themselves overboard and, as Paul had predicted, all reached land in safety (41-44). In this thrilling adventure, which Luke relates with so much detail, the conduct of Paul beautifully illustrates the courage of the Christian and the influence over others which a man of faith can exercise in times of peril.

The land on which they had been cast was the island of Melita, the modern Malta, which lies 58 miles south of Sicily. The inhabitants kindly received the shipwrecked company, and Paul by his works gained special honor among them (Acts xxviii. 1-10). After three months, however, they were put on board another Alexandrian ship, which had wintered in the island, and, after touching at Syracuse and Rhegium, arrived at Puteoli, a harbor of southwestern Italy. There Paul found Christian brethren with whom he tarried seven days (11-14). Meanwhile word of his arrival had reached the Christians in Rome, so that some of them went to meet him at the Market of Appius and the Three Taverns, two places distant from Rome about 43 and 33 miles respectively (15, R. V.). According to the A. V. (16) the centurion delivered his prisoners to the captain of the guard, and this has been usually understood to mean the prefect of the prætorian guard, who at this time, A. D. 61, was the celebrated Burrus. The R. V., however, with the best manuscripts, omits this statement. Mommsen, followed by Ramsay, thinks that the prisoners were delivered to the captain of another corps, to which Julius the centurion himself belonged, and whose duty it was to superintend the transportation of grain to the capital and to perform police duty. We really cannot tell to whose custody Paul was delivered. We only know that he was held in military confinement, chained to a soldier (xxviii. 16 : Phil. i. 7, 13), but allowed to lodge by himself. Appeals to Cæsar were slow processes. Paul soon hired a dwelling and continued in it for two years (Acts xxviii. 30).

So began Paul's first imprisonment in Rome. The Acts closes with an account of how after three days he summoned the chief of the Jews, related the reason of his presence in the capital, and on an appointed day expounded to them the gospel ; but that when they, like their countrymen elsewhere, disbelieved, Paul again declared that he would turn to the gentiles. His imprisonment, therefore, did not prevent his missionary activity. The last verses of The Acts relate that for two whole years he received all who came to him and preached the kingdom of God and the things concerning the Lord Jesus Christ without hindrance from the authorities (xxviii. 17-31). But still more light is thrown on this period of Paul's life by the epistles which he wrote during it. They are those to the Colossians, to Philemon, to the Ephesians, and to the Philippians. The first three were probably written in the earlier part of the period and that to the Philippians toward its close. These epistles show that the apostle in Rome had many faithful friends working with him. Among these were Timothy (Col. i. 1 ; Phil. i. 1 ; ii. 19 ; Philem. i.), Tychicus (Eph. vi. 21 ; Col. iv. 7), Aristarchus (Col. iv. 10 ; Philem. 24), John Mark (Col. iv. 10 ; Philem. 24), and Luke (Col. iv. 14 ; Philem. 24). His friends had unhindered access to him ; they acted as his messengers to the churches and also as his co-workers in Rome ; and they made the imprisoned apostle the center and head of the gentile Christian work throughout the empire. The epistles further show the personal activity of the apostle's life. With great zeal and success, in spite of his bonds, did he preach the gospel. He was an ambassador in bonds (Eph. vi. 20). He desired his friends to pray that God would open for him a door of utterance (Col. iv. 3). In Onesimus, the runaway slave, we see an example of the fruit of his labors (Philem. 10). As time went on the success of his work increased. He wrote to the Philippians (i. 12, 13, R. V.) that the things which had happened unto him had fallen out unto the progress of the gospel, so that his bonds were manifest in Christ throughout the whole prætorian guard and to all the rest. He sent greetings also (iv. 22) from them of Cæsar's household. At the same time he was opposed even by some of the Christians, probably of the Jewish Christian type (i. 15-18). But he regarded their opposition with equanimity, and was confident that he would be finally released (Phil. i. 25 ; ii. 17, 24 ; Philem. 22). His imprisonment was only God's way of enabling his ambassador to fulfill to the uttermost his chosen mission. Finally, the epistles testify to the apostle's continued superintendence of the churches throughout the empire. New heresies had arisen in Asia. In the epistles of the imprisonment Paul gave his ripest instructions concerning the person of Christ and the eternal purpose of God revealed in the gospel, while the practical directions which they contain disclose the breadth of his grasp on Christian duty and the fervor of his own Christian life.

Although the book of The Acts leaves Paul a prisoner at Rome, there is abundant reason to believe that he was released after two years' confinement and resumed his missionary journeys. The evidence for this may be summarized as follows : (1) The closing verse of The Acts accords better with this view than with the supposition that the imprisonment which has been described ended in the apostle's condemnation and death. Luke emphasizes the fact that no one hindered his work, thus certainly giving the impression that the end of his activity was not near. Moreover (2) Paul fully expected to be released (Phil. i. 25 ; ii. 17, 24 ; Philem. 22), and this expectation was fully justified by the treatment which he had always received at the hands of Roman officials. It should be remembered that Nero's persecution of the Christians had not yet begun ; that it was a sudden outbreak, preceded by no official illtreatment of them : and that in the view of Roman law, the Christians were as yet only a sect of the Jews, whose liberty to maintain their religion was fully recognized. It is, therefore, altogether probable that, when Paul's case came before the imperial tribunal, he was acquitted of any crime of which Roman law could take cognizance. No doubt also the report of Festus was a favorable one (see Acts xxvi. 31), nor do the Jews appear to have sent any accusers to Rome to appear against him (xxviii. 21). (3) The tradition that he was released and resumed his journeys, and was again arrested dates from an early period. Clement of Rome, A. D. 96, seems clearly to imply that Paul went to Spain, for he says that in his journeys "he reached the limit of the west." His journey to Spain is also mentioned in the so-called Muratori Fragment, A. D. 170. With this agrees the history of Eusebius, A. D. 324, which reports, as the common tradition, that "after he [Paul] had made his defense, the apostle was sent again on the ministry of preaching, and a second time having come to the same city [Rome], he suffered martyrdom." It must be admitted that this traditional evidence is not sufficiently strong to be absolutely demonstrative ; but it is early and strong enough to confirm the rest of the evidence, and no sufficient counter-evidence can be adduced. (4) The epistles to Timothy and Titus may be proved to be Pauline by abundant external and internal evidence. No place for them, however, can be found in the history of Paul related in The Acts. They must, therefore, have been written later, and that fact compels us to accept the tradition given by Eusebius.

We must, therefore, believe that Paul's appeal from Festus to Cæsar resulted in his release. His subsequent movements can only be inferred from the allusions contained in the epistles to Timothy and Titus and from tradition. We may suppose that after his release he went, as he had intended (Phil. ii. 24 ; Philem. 22), to Asia and Macedonia. From 1 Tim. i. 3 we learn that he had left Timothy in charge of the churches about Ephesus when he himself went to Macedonia. Where he was when he wrote 1 Tim. is not clear, but he hoped soon to be able to return to Ephesus (1 Tim. iii. 14). From Titus 'we learn that he had left Titus in charge of the churches of Crete, and expected to winter in Nicopolis (Titus iii. 12). There were, however, three cities by that name to which this reference may apply, one in Thrace, near Macedonia, another in Cilicia, and a third in Epirus ; so that the name does not help us much to fix the apostle's locality. It is probable, however, that Nicopolis in Epirus was the one referred to. If we accept the early tradition that Paul went to Spain (see above), we may suppose that he did so after having been in Asia and Macedonia ; that after that, on his return from Spain, he stopped at Crete and left Titus on that island ; then that he returned to Asia, from which place he doubtless wrote the Epistle to Titus. We learn from 2 Tim. iv. 20 that he had passed through Corinth and Miletum, the one in Greece, the other in Asia. There is nothing to show whether he carried out his intention of wintering in Nicopolis. Many suppose, however, that he did go to Nicopolis in Epirus, and was there rearrested and sent to Rome. But while the apostle's movements during this closing period of his life are somewhat uncertain, the epistles then written show that he occupied himself, in addition to evangelizing new regions, with the perfecting of the organization of the already existing churches. He evidently felt that his career must soon close, and that the churches would be exposed to new dangers, from both without and within. Hence the pastoral epistles, as they are called, round out the apostle's instruction of the churches by solidifying their organization and practically equipping them for their future work.

The release of Paul from his first Roman imprisonment probably occurred in A. D. 63, and his subsequent activity lasted about four years. According to Eusebius, his death took place in A. D. 67 ; according to Jerome, in A. D. 68. How he came to be rearrested we do not know. There are a few slight hints furnished, however, by the Second Epistle to Timothy, which was written from Rome shortly before his death. We should remember, moreover, that in A. D. 64 Nero's persecution of the Christians in Rome broke out ; and it was doubtless followed by sporadic outbreaks against them in the provinces (1 Pet. iv. 13–19). It may be, as some have supposed, that Paul was informed against as a leader of the now proscribed sect by the Alexander mentioned in 2 Tim. iv. 14. At any rate, and wherever he was arrested, he was sent to Rome for trial, either because, as before, he appealed to Cæsar, or because he was charged with a crime committed in Italy, perhaps with complicity in the burning of Rome, or because the provincials wished to gratify Nero by sending so notable a prisoner to the capital. Only Luke, of his former friends, was with him when 2 Tim. was written (2 Tim. iv. 11). Some had even deserted him (i. 15; iv. 10, 16), while others had gone away on various errands (10, 12). Yet when arraigned before the tribunal he was at first not condemned (17), though he continued to be held on some other charge. Possibly he was able to disprove a charge of criminal conduct, but was retained in custody because he was a Christian. He speaks of himself as a prisoner (i. 8) in bonds (16), as if an evil-doer (ii. 9), and regards his fate as sealed (iv. 6–8). No doubt he was finally condemned to death simply because he was a Christian, in accordance with the policy begun by Nero in A. D. 64. Tradition relates that the apostle was beheaded, as became a Roman citizen, on the Ostian Way.

In giving this outline of the life of the apostle Paul, we have necessarily followed the express testimony of The Acts and epistles. But it should not be forgotten that many other events occurred in his active and checkered career. To some of these allusions are made in his epistles (Rom. xv. 18, 19; 2 Cor. xi. 24–33). Yet the well-known events of his life, taken with his epistles, make plain the character of the man and the supreme value of his work. It is difficult to gather into one picture the many features of his versatile character. He was by nature intensely religious and his religion controlled his whole being. This was true of him even as a Jew, much after his conversion. Keenly intellectual, he grasped truth at its full value and logically wrought out its implications. Yet truth possessed his heart equally with his intellect, and his emotions were as fervid as his logical processes were vigorous. At the same time the practical aspects of truth were seen by him no less than its theoretical side. If on the one hand he fully wrought out dialectically the content of his doctrinal ideas, on the other hand he applied Christianity to life with the wisdom and completeness of a practical man of affairs. He was intense in his affections, at times ecstatic in his religious experiences, ever progressive in his statements of truth, capable of soaring to the loftiest heights of religious thought, and of embodying in action the truth for which he stood. This versatility, intensity, purity, breadth of mental and spiritual life, when used by the all-controlling Spirit of God, fitted Paul for the work for which the providence of God intended him.

And that work consisted in authoritatively interpreting to the gentile world, in action and in written statement, the mission and message of Christ. How Paul did this in action is narrated in the book of The Acts. Through his agency the universalism of Christianity, its independence of the Jewish ritual, its adaptation to all mankind, was historically established. Other men also contributed to the result. But it was Paul's divinely given task to bear the burden of this achievement, and to him, as to no other man, Christianity owes its possession of a worldwide destiny. All this was done, of course, in accordance with the purpose of Christ and under his direction. But the student of Christian history must recognize in Paul the principal agent used to accomplish the result. On the other hand, the epistles of Paul disclose in written statement the doctrinal and ethical interpretation of Christ's word and work, which accompanied Paul's missionary activity and made it profound and permanent. It is, therefore, to Paul as a theologian that we rightly look with the greatest admiration. His theology took shape from the peculiar experience of his own conversion. By that sudden transition he was made to realize the impossibility of man's saving himself, the dependence of the sinner on the sovereign grace of God, and the completeness of the redeeming work which Jesus, the Son of God, had done through death and resurrection. It followed that only by union with Christ through faith can any man be saved. Salvation consists in justification of the sinner by God on the ground of Christ's obedience, and when thus justified the sinner, being united to Christ, is made to partake of all the spiritual benefits, external and internal, in heaven and on earth, which Christ has purchased for him. The Spirit inspired Paul to set forth on this foundation the truth of Christ's whole work and person. In the epistles to the Galatians and Romans the way of salvation itself is most fully elaborated, while in the epistles of the imprisonment the exalted dignity of Christ, and the whole breadth and end of God's eternal purpose of grace in Christ and his church find their full expression. Besides these principal themes, almost every phase of Christian truth and duty is touched upon in his epistles. His is emphatically the theology of grace. He sounded the depths of this truth. He interpreted the Hebrew Messiah to the gentile world. He was raised up to explain to the world the Saviour in whom it was invited to believe and the work which the Saviour had done. Paul was preëminently the theologian of the apostles as well as the most aggressive missionary. It is not possible to understand Christianity, unless we unite with the teaching and work of Jesus Christ the interpretation thereof furnished by his apostle Paul.

Chronology of Paul's life. While the order of events in Paul's life and the relative dates of his epistles are in the main quite clear, there is some dispute concerning the precise years to which both events and epistles are to be assigned. In the book of The Acts two dates may be regarded as certain, viz., the ascension of Christ in A. D. 30 (though some scholars assign this to A. D. 29) and the death of Herod Agrippa (Acts xii. 23), which all admit to have taken place in A. D. 44. Neither of these dates, however, is of much assistance in determining the absolute chronology of Paul's life. That depends mainly on the date assigned to the accession of Festus as procurator of Judæa. According to the common and most probable opinion Festus became governor (xxiv. 27) in A. D. 60. Josephus assigns nearly all the events during the governorship of Felix to the reign of Nero, which began in October, A. D. 54, and Paul (10) speaks of Felix as having been "of many years a judge unto this nation." It is hardly possible, therefore, to assign Paul's arrest when he appeared before Felix to a date earlier than A. D. 58. Then Paul was kept two years in confinement in Cæsarea, which would make the accession of Festus, who then succeeded Felix, to have taken place in A. D. 60. It can hardly have been later, since Festus was succeeded by Albinus in A. D. 62, and the events recorded of him imply that he was governor for more than a year. But if Festus became governor in A. D. 60, Paul was sent to Rome in the autumn of that year, and arrived at Rome in the spring of A. D. 61, having spent the winter on the way. Then the close of The Acts, and probably the apostle's release from his first Roman imprisonment, are to be dated in A. D. 63 (xxviii. 30).

For the earlier events of Paul's life, we date back from the accession of Festus. Assuming the latter to have been in A. D. 60, then Paul's arrest, which occurred two years before (Acts xxiv. 27), was in A. D. 58. This was at the close of his third journey. The winter preceding his arrest he had spent in Corinth (xx. 3), the preceding autumn in Macedonia (2), and before that, for three years, he had been in Ephesus (31), to which he had gone from Antioch after a rapid tour through Galatia and Phrygia (xviii. 23). Hence four years must be allowed for the third journey. If he was arrested in Jerusalem in the spring of A. D. 58, he must have begun this journey in the spring of A. D. 54. The third journey followed the second by a moderate interval (23), and for the latter at least two years and a half must be allowed, since eighteen months were spent in Corinth (11), and the preceding events of the tour may fairly be supposed to have occupied a year more (xv. 36-xvii. 34). If, therefore, the second journey closed in the autumn of A. D. 53, it probably began in the spring of A. D. 51. The second journey in turn began some days (xv. 36) after the council of Jerusalem. This latter epoch-making event may, therefore, be assigned to the year A. D. 50. The first missionary journey can only be roughly located between A. D. 44, the date

of Herod's death (xii.), and A. D. 50, the date of the council (xv.). We may probably assign it to the years A. D. 46–48, though it is not possible to say how long a time it consumed.

For the date of Paul's conversion, we must combine the results given above with his statements in the Epistle to the Galatians. In Gal. ii. 1 he says: "Then fourteen years after I went up again to Jerusalem with Barnabas." This visit is undoubtedly the one to the council which we have located in A. D. 50. But from what event are these fourteen years to be counted? According to some commentators, they are to be reckoned from his conversion mentioned in Gal. i. 15. If so, his conversion was in A. D. 36 or 37, according as we count the fourteen years exclusively or inclusively of the first one of them. But in Gal. i. 18 Paul notes that he first visited Jerusalem three years after his conversion. Hence it is more natural to date the fourteen years of Gal. ii. 1 from the close of the previously mentioned three years. In that case, according as we reckon exclusively or inclusively, his conversion was in A. D. 33 or 35. It is most in accordance with Hebrew custom to reckon inclusively. Hence we may assign his conversion to A. D. 35, his subsequent visit to Jerusalem (Gal. i. 18) to A. D. 37, and the fourteen years after (ii. 1) to A. D. 50. As already remarked, all of these dates are disputed. Some assign the accession of Festus to A. D. 55, and therefore push back all the other dates five years earlier than those given above. Other critics vary on special points. Some assign Paul's death to A. D. 64, supposing that he died in the first year of Nero's persecution. But the dates given above appear to be by far the most probable. They yield, with some other details, the following table:

Death, resurrection, and ascension of Christ	A. D.	30
Conversion of Paul	"	35 (?)
First subsequent visit to Jerusalem (Gal. i. 18)	"	37
Paul at Tarsus	"	37–43
Visit to Jerusalem with the gifts from Antioch (Acts xi. 30)	"	44
First missionary journey	"	46–48 (?)
Council at Jerusalem	"	50
Second missionary journey	"	51–53
1 and 2 Thessalonians	"	52
Third missionary journey	"	54–58
Galatians	"	55
1 Corinthians	"	56 or 57
2 "	"	57
Romans	"	57–58
Arrest	"	58
Imprisonment in Cæsarea	"	58–60
Accession of Festus	"	60
Paul arrives at Rome	"	61
Colossians, Philemon, Ephesians	"	61 or 62
Philippians	"	62 or 63
Release from first Roman imprisonment	"	63
1 Timothy	"	64 or 65
Titus	"	65 or 66
Hebrews, if by Paul	"	66 or 67
2 Timothy	"	67
Death of Paul	"	67

G. T. P.

Pave'ment. See GABBATHA.

Pe.
The seventeenth letter of the Hebrew alphabet. It comes from the same source as English P, but was pronounced like p or ph, according to its position. It is accordingly represented in anglicized Hebrew names, though too often arbitrarily, by either p or ph. It heads the seventeenth section of Ps. cxix., in which section each verse of the original begins with this letter.
Copyists sometimes experienced difficulty in distinguishing pe from beth (q. v.).

Peace Of'fer-ing. See OFFERINGS.

Pea'cock.
1. The rendering of the Hebrew word *Tukki*. The rendering is doubtless correct, for, along with ivory and apes, *tukkiyyim* were imported by Solomon in ships of Tarshish (1 Kin. x. 22; 2 Chron. ix. 21). Now the words for ivory and ape are of Indian origin, and *tukki* also finds a satisfactory origin in Malabar *togei*, Old Tamil *tokei*, *togei*, a peacock. The peacock (*Pavo cristatus*) is a native of India, where it may be found in the jungles, generally running pretty rapidly away when disturbed. As the natives do not allow it to be molested, it often makes its way into the villages.
2. See OSTRICH 2.

Pearl.
A precious article of commerce (Mat. xiii. 45, 46; Rev. xxi. 21; also Job xxviii. 18, in R. V. crystal), used as an ornament by women (1 Tim. ii. 9; Rev. xvii. 4). Pearls are found inside the shells of several species of *Mollusca*. They consist of carbonate of lime interstratified with animal membrane, and are formed by the deposit of the nacreous substance around some foreign body within the mantle lobes, such as a grain of sand, which acts as an irritant and serves as a nucleus. This substance is the same as the mother of pearl, which forms the lustrous inner lining of the shell. Pearls of large size and fine quality are yielded by the pearl oyster (*Meleagrina margaritifera*), which abounds in the Indian seas, especially in the Persian Gulf and near Ceylon. It sometimes attains a length of 10 or 12 inches.

Ped'a-hel [God hath saved].
A prince of the tribe of Naphtali in the wilderness (Num. xxxiv. 28).

Pe-dah'zur [a rock, i. e., God, hath saved].
Father of the prince of Manasseh in the wilderness (Num. i. 10; ii. 20).

Pe-da'iah [Jehovah hath saved].
1. The father of Joel, prince of Manasseh (1 Chron. xxvii. 20).
2. A citizen of Rumah and maternal grandfather of king Jehoiakim (2 Kin. xxiii. 36).
3. A brother of Shealtiel or possibly, though not probably, his son (1 Chron. iii. 18, 19). See ZERUBBABEL.
4. A descendant of Parosh. He rebuilt

and repaired part of the wall of Jerusalem (Neh. iii. 25).
5. One of those, probably priests, who stood on Ezra's left hand when he addressed the people (Neh. viii. 4).
6. A Benjamite of the family of Jeshaiah (Neh. xi. 7).
7. A Levite; one of those appointed by Nehemiah over the treasures (Neh. xiii. 13).

Pe'kah [an opening (of the eyes), deliverance].
Son of Remaliah. He was a captain under Pekahiah; but he conspired against his king, slew him, and reigned in his stead. He adhered to the calf worship of Jeroboam I. (2 Kin. xv. 25-28). When Jotham's reign was drawing to a close, Pekah entered into an alliance with Rezin, king of Syria, against Judah. They purposed to dethrone the king, and place the crown on a creature of their own. The allied kings began their great invasion of Judah just as the reins of government passed from Jotham into the hands of Ahaz. The Syrians advanced through the country east of the Jordan to Elath, intending to rendezvous at Jerusalem. Pekah led his army directly toward the capital of Judah, burning and pillaging as he went. The inhabitants of Jerusalem were greatly alarmed. Isaiah, however, was directed to encourage the king and the people with the assurance that the plan of the enemy would fail, and to exhort them to put their trust in Jehovah. Ahaz spurned the advice, preferring to trust to the king of Assyria, and purchased the aid of Tiglath-pileser. The advance of the Assyrian army through Galilee (2 Kin. xv. 29) to Philistia, in 734 B. C., compelled the allied kings to withdraw their troops from Judah in order to protect their own dominions. Pekah carried off a multitude of captives as he departed; but on the remonstrance of the prophet Oded, he clothed and fed them and sent them home (2 Kin. xvi. 5-9; 2 Chron. xxviii. 5-15; Is. vii. 1-13). During the next two years Tiglath-pileser was at Damascus, doubtless leading his army across the territory of Israel as he marched from Philistia. From Damascus detachments of the Assyrian army were sent forth, which overran the country east of the Jordan and carried off many Israelites captive (1 Chron. v. 26). In 730 B. C. Hoshea murdered Pekah and ascended the throne in his stead (2 Kin. xv. 30). This deed was accomplished with the connivance of Tiglath-pileser, as the Assyrian records relate. The present Hebrew text assigns twenty years to the reign of Pekah (2 Kin. xv. 27). It is impossible that he occupied the throne of Samaria during all these years, for Menahem, a predecessor of his, was on the throne about 738 B. C., in the reign of Tiglath-pileser (2 Kin. xv. 19). Critics of all schools accordingly admit that twenty years are much too long. There is a bare possibility, however, that the Hebrew writer,

when he summarizes the reign of Pekah, and states that "in the fifty-second year of Uzziah Pekah reigned over Israel in Samaria —twenty years," does not mean that Pekah reigned all of these twenty years in Samaria. Pekah was associated with Gileadites (2 Kin. xv. 25). It is just possible that he set up his authority in northern Gilead and Galilee in 749 B. C., during the confusion which accompanied the death of Jeroboam II., and maintained his power during the greater part of Menahem's reign, being the cause of Menahem's feeling of insecurity until Tiglathpileser invaded the north and established Menahem's sway over the whole country (2 Kin. xv. 19). Then Pekah, like Abner before him, abandoned opposition, professed loyalty, and was given a high military position in the service of the king to whom he had hitherto refused obedience. After Menahem's death and in the absence of Tiglathpileser, and perhaps backed by Rezin, he seized the throne in the fifty-second year of Uzziah and again reigned. See CHRONOLOGY.

Pek-a-hi'ah [Jehovah hath given sight or delivered].

Son and successor of Menahem in the kingdom of Israel. He came to the throne about 737 B. C., and reigned two years, adhering to the calf worship of Jeroboam I. He was assassinated in his palace at Samaria by Pekah, a captain of his, who then usurped the throne (2 Kin. xv. 23–26).

Pe'kod.

A locality in Babylonia and its inhabitants (Jer. l. 21; Ezek. xxiii. 23); doubtless the Pukudu, a Babylonian people.

Pe-la'iah [Jehovah hath made illustrious].

1. One of the Levites who with Ezra caused the people to understand the law (Neh. viii. 7) and sealed the covenant (x. 10).

2. A man of Judah, descended from Shecaniah (1 Chron. iii. 24).

Pel-a-li'ah [Jehovah hath judged].

A priest descended from Malchijah (Neh. xi. 12).

Pel-a-ti'ah [Jehovah hath set free].

1. One of the Simeonite captains in the successful war between that tribe and the Amalekites (1 Chron. iv. 42).

2. A prince of Israel, and son of Benaiah. He misled the people. In vision Ezekiel saw him, and he prophesied against him, and Pelatiah suddenly died (Ezek. xi. 1–13; cp. viii. 1, 3; xi. 24).

3. A son of Hananiah, and a grandson of Zerubbabel (1 Chron. iii. 21). Perhaps he was the person of this name who was a chief of the people and with Nehemiah sealed the covenant (Neh. x. 22).

Pe'leg, in A. V. of N. T. **Phalec** [division].

A son or descendant of Eber (Gen. x. 25; xi. 16). He takes his name from the fact that in his days the earth was divided. The division alluded to may be the separation of the descendants of Arpachshad from the Joktanide Arabs (x. 24–29); or it may refer to the scattering of the descendants of Noah in consequence of the confusion of tongues at Babel.

Pe'let [liberation].

1. A son of Jahdai, of the tribe of Judah (1 Chron. ii. 47).

2. A Benjamite who joined David while he was at Ziklag (1 Chron. xii. 3).

Pe'leth [swiftness].

1. A Reubenite, father of that On who joined in Korah's rebellion (Num. xvi. 1).

2. A man of Judah, family of Hezron, house of Jerahmeel (1 Chron. ii. 33).

Pel'e-thites.

Certain members of David's bodyguard. Apparently they were from the Philistine country, as were the Cherethites and the men of Gath, who were their comrades in arms. They were faithful to David during the calamities of his later years, and took a prominent part in the war in which Absalom lost his cause and his life (2 Sam. xv. 18–22). They also helped in the fight with Sheba (xx. 7). The name which they bear is doubtless a gentile adjective, like those with which it is connected; but it is not a contraction of *Pelishti*, Philistine, as some scholars have supposed.

Pel'i-can.

The rendering of the Hebrew word *Ḳa'ath*, probably meaning the vomiter. The word is twice translated cormorant in the text of A. V. (Is. xxxiv. 11; Zeph. ii. 14); but elsewhere pelican, as everywhere in R. V. The bird was ceremonially unclean (Lev. xi. 18; Deut. xiv. 17), lived in the wilderness (Ps. cii. 6), and frequented ruins (Isa. xxxiv. 11; Zeph. ii. 14). It is probably the common or roseate pelican (*Pelecanus onocrotalus*), though rivers and lakes, rather than ruined cities, unless the ruins are interspersed with marshes, are its appropriate place of abode. Its four toes, being all connected by large webs, adapt it for aquatic life. It sometimes, however, perches on trees. Its bill is large and furrowed, and has under it a large pouch in which the bird carries the fish on which its young feed. Its height is from 5 to 6 feet; the expansion of its wings 12 or 13. A few individuals are found on the sea of Galilee; a much larger number on the shallow lakes of Egypt and on the Nile.

Pel'o-nite.

A word corresponding in 1 Chron. xi. 27; xxvii. 10 to Paltite in 2 Sam. xxiii, 26, and in 1 Chron. xi. 36 apparently to Gilonite in 2 Sam. xv. 12; xxiii. 34. In 1 Chron. xxvii. 10 the person who is designated by this epithet is further said to be of the children of Ephraim. No person or place is known from which this adjective could be derived; certainly not from Pallu, who was a Reubenite and whose descendants were called Palluites

(Num. xxvi. 5). In view of these circumstances, Pelonite is not unreasonably believed to be either a corruption of the text or else to mean "such and such a one," as it does in other connection (e. g. 1 Sam. xxi. 2), and to have been inserted in the passages mentioned by a scribe who could not read the original word in the text which he was copying.

Pen and inkwells used by ancient Egyptian scribe.

Pen.

1. A stylus or graving tool made of iron and used by writers for cutting letters on stone (Job xix. 24; Ps. xlv. 1; Jer. viii. 8; xvii. 1). In Hebrew it is called *'et* and once *heret* (Is. viii. 1).

2. A reed pen used for writing with ink on papyrus (3 John 13; cp. 2 John 12). The mention of a penknife or knife of a writer in Jeremiah xxxvi. 23, and of a roll in which the prophet's words were written, imply that reed pens had been introduced among the Israelites by the time of Jehoiakim.

The Hebrew words rendered pen of the writer in Judg. v. 14, A. V. mean literally staff of a marshal or scribe (R. V.).

Pe-ni′el. See PENUEL 2.

Pe-nin′nah [ruby or coral].

One of Elkanah's two wives, the other being Hannah (1 Sam. i. 2-6).

Pen′ny.

The rendering of the Greek *Denarion*. It was the denarius, a silver coin of the Romans (Mat. xxii. 19-21), worth about 17 cents in the time of Christ (xviii. 28, R. V. margin). See MONEY. It was the ordinary pay of an agricultural laborer for a day (Mat. xx. 2, 9, 13). Two were given to the innkeeper by the good Samaritan for looking after the wounded Jew, though he promised to supplement this sum if the expense should exceed it (Luke x. 35). The apostles calculated that 200 would be needed to buy sufficient bread to feed 5000 people (Mark vi. 37). This would be one denarius for each twenty-

five, or two thirds of a cent to each person. The prices in Rev. vi. 6 were those asked during a dearth.

Pen′ta-teuch [Greek *pentateuchos*, consisting of five books].

The first five books of the O. T., viz., Genesis, Exodus, Leviticus, Numbers, and Deuteronomy. The word nowhere occurs in Scripture, the Israelites calling these books collectively the law (Josh. i. 7; Mat. v. 17), the law of Moses (1 Kin. ii. 3; Ezra vii. 6; Luke ii. 22), the law of the Lord (2 Chron. xxxi. 3; Luke ii. 23), the book of the law (Josh. i. 8), the book of Moses (2 Chron. xxv. 3, 4), the book of the law of Moses (Josh. viii. 31), the book of the law of God (Josh. xxiv. 26), the book of the law of the Lord (2 Chron. xvii. 9). This fact suggests that the five books were considered as one; and they still are so in Hebrew manuscripts, though severally cited by their opening words. The division into five distinct books is mentioned by Josephus (con. Apion. i. 8). It may have originated with the Greek translators or been ancient. But whether or not the Septuagint translators adopted or originated this five-fold division, from them at least emanated the modern names Genesis, Exodus, Leviticus, Numbers, and Deuteronomy.*

* The division of the law of Moses into five books furnished the model, it is thought, for the similar division of the Psalter. If it did, it is ancient; for the Psalter was early divided into five books. Proof that it did is sought in the alleged discovery that the contents of each book are so arranged that the opening psalm shall correspond to the respective book of the Pentateuch. Ps. i., with its comparison of the righteous to a tree planted by the rivers of water, is a reminder of the garden of Eden in the first book of the Pentateuch. Ps. xlii., with which the second book of the Psalter opens, is the cry of a man in distress, oppressed by the enemy, and thinking himself forgotten by God, but anticipating deliverance out of all his trouble. It recalls the affliction of Israel in Egypt and their deliverance, as related in Exodus. In Ps. lxxiii., with which the third book begins, the doubts of the psalmist regarding the justice of God's dealing with men vanish when he considers the end of the wicked. The psalm is supposed to reflect gratitude for God's goodness in giving the law of Leviticus, which was an abiding mercy. Ps. xc., a prayer of Moses, in which God is besought to teach us to number our days, corresponds to Numbers. Ps. cvii., which begins the fifth book, speaks of the goodness of the Lord in the days of trouble, and is thus like Deuteronomy, which recapitulates the instances of God's loving kindness to Israel. It must be confessed that the correspondence is rather fanciful; and if an editor set about securing correspondence, it is strange that he did not adopt a more appropriate arrangement. Ps. viii., with its reference to the heavens, the work of God's fingers, to the moon and stars which he ordained, and to man whom he made and to whom he gave dominion over all creatures, would have better corresponded with Gen. i. Ps. lxvi. of the second book, which tells of the works of God, how he turned the sea into dry land for the people to pass through, and how he tried the Israelites, laid sore burdens on them

The events recorded in the first book of the Pentateuch were transmitted to the time of Moses, as is now known, by tradition oral and written; the subsequent occurrences fell under his own observation, and he was himself an actor in the most stirring events. Writing was practiced long before the time of Moses. It was common in Egypt, where he was educated; in Arabia, through a portion of which he passed; and in Canaan, where his ancestors had sojourned and whither he was leading the people. And the various forms of literature represented in the Pentateuch were familiar literary conceptions of Moses' time (see MOSES). Though the five books themselves are not attributed as a whole to Moses in any verse which they contain, yet the Pentateuch testifies expressly to the Mosaic authorship of its contents. Two passages of the narrative portion are attributed to his pen; the account of the victory over Amalek (Ex. xvii. 14), and the itinerary of the march of the Israelites from Egypt to the plains of Moab opposite Jericho (Num. xxxiii. 2). A didactic song, reciting the dealing of the Most High with Israel, is declared to have been written and uttered by Moses (Deut. xxxi. 19, 22, 30; xxxii. 44); and a hymn of praise, evoked by the deliverance from Pharoah at the Red Sea, is recorded as sung by Moses (Ex. xv. 1-18; cp. 21). The legal portion consists of three distinct bodies of law. The first is entitled the book of the covenant, and comprises the ten commandments which formed the fundamental law of the nation, and specific regulations based on them (Ex. xx.-xxiii.). This book Moses is expressly said to have written (Ex. xxiv. 4). The second body of laws pertains to the sanctuary and service (Ex. xxv.-xxxi., xxxv.-xl., Leviticus, and major legal part of Numbers). This legislation is constantly declared to have been revealed by the Lord to Moses (Ex. xxv. 1, etc.). The third body of legislation expressly and repeatedly claims to be the address of Moses to the new generation of people on the eve of their entrance into Canaan. It contains a brief rehearsal of the way which God has led them and then repeats sundry portions of the law with the special object of exhibiting its spirituality, emphasizing the features which are of vital religious importance in the new circumstances in which the people will soon be placed, and modifying details to adapt the laws to the new requirements of the settled life in Canaan. Moses wrote this address and delivered it into the custody of the Levites (Deut. xxxi. 9, 24-26). These are the explicit claims, scattered throughout the

and caused men to ride over their heads, and then brought them out into a wealthy place, should have opened the book. It has an obvious reference to the events recorded in Exodus, whereas Ps. xlii. has not. Ps. lxxvi. or lxxviii. should form the opening of the third book in order to correspond appropriately to Leviticus.

Pentateuch itself, to its Mosaic authorship. The remainder of the O. T. refers to the law as the work of Moses and written in a book (Josh. i. 7, 8; Ezra vi. 18; Neh. viii. 1, 18); and abounds in explicit references to the law of Moses (Josh. i. 7, 8; viii. 31-35; Judg. iii. 4; 1 Kin. ii. 3; 2 Kin. xviii. 6, 12; cp. Deut. xxiv. 16; 2 Kin. xxi. 7, 8; Dan. ix. 11, 13; Ezra iii. 2; vi. 18; vii. 6; Neh. viii. 1, 18; Mal. iv. 4). One feature of this law, namely, the law of the one altar, was in abeyance during the captivity and seclusion of the ark after the Lord had forsaken Shiloh (1 Sam. iv. 11, 21, 22; vi. 1; vii. 2; Ps. lxxviii. 60; Jer. vii. 12-15; xxvi. 6). During this period the people under the leadership of Samuel sacrificed where they could (1 Kin. iii. 2-4), as their fathers had done in the olden time before the covenant had been entered into between Jehovah and the Israelites, of which the law and the ark were the sign and pledge. Once again this specific law was in abeyance. The pious Israelites of the northern kingdom were prevented from going up to Jerusalem to worship. They had to choose between refraining from sacrifice altogether or worshiping God as did Abraham, Isaac, and Jacob. They properly chose the latter alternative. All other cases of sacrifice offered elsewhere than at the central sanctuary were strictly in accord with the law which expressly provided that wherever Jehovah manifested his name, there sacrifice was fitting (Ex. xx. 24; see Judg. ii. 1, 5; vi. 19-24; xiii. 15-22; and ALTAR). The law of Moses was known and its authority acknowledged even in the northern kingdom. The prophets Hosea and Amos, who labored among the ten tribes, although they do not mention the name of Moses, constantly refer to the laws recorded in the Pentateuch and use its very language. At a still later time the temple copy of the book of the law was unused and cast aside during the half century of Manasseh's reign when the religion of Jehovah was neglected; but when the temple was being repaired, preparatory to the restoration of Jehovah's worship, this book was found, or so much of it at least as contained Deuteronomy (2 Kin. xxii. 8; xxiii. 25); or, less likely, the book which the high priest found was a copy of the law of God which had been embedded in the wall of the temple as a record at the time of building the sanctuary. Daniel, Ezra, and Nehemiah allude to the written law of Moses. That Moses was the author of the Pentateuch was the opinion of the Jews of Christ's time (Mark xii. 19; John viii. 5; Antiq. preface 4; con. Apion. i. 8). Christ and the evangelists call the Pentateuch Moses and the book of Moses (Mark xii. 26; Luke xvi. 29; xxiv. 27, 44), and speak of its having been given by Moses and committed to writing by Moses (Mark x. 5; xii. 19; John i. 17; v. 46, 47; vii. 19).

The Mosaic authorship of the Pentateuch

is impugned. The principal objections formerly urged against it were several verses in which reference has been found to times subsequent to the death of Moses. 1. In Gen. xii. 6 we read: "And the Canaanite was then in the land" (cp. xiii. 7). The meaning assigned to these words is that the Canaanites had ceased to be there when the writer lived. The words, however, actually state only that the Canaanites were in the country when Abraham was there, and were occupying the land promised to him. 2. In Gen. xiv. 14 we read that Abraham pursued the defeated confederates to Dan. In the patriarch's time, however, the place was called Laish, the name Dan not having been given it till the time of the judges (Judg. xviii. 29). The question is, however, whether Dan in Genesis is the place mentioned in the Book of Judges. If it is, the more familiar name may have been substituted in the place of Laish in the course of repeated transcription. The Hebrew text has not been preserved in absolute purity. 3. In Gen. xxxvi. 31 the words occur: "Before there reigned any king over the children of Israel," as if the Hebrew monarchy under Saul had already been established when the author wrote. But the kings of Edom who are mentioned in ver. 32-43 reigned before Moses; and Moses notes that the descendants of Esau already had kings, although the Israelites, to whom the promise had been given that kings should arise among them (Gen. xvii. 6, 16; xxxv. 11), as yet had none. 4. Moses is said to be beyond Jordan, meaning east of the river, as though the writer himself were in Canaan (Deut. i. 1). The expression, however, does not imply this. Abraham, Isaac, and Jacob spoke of that region as "beyond Jordan," and the designation became a fixed geographical term. Moreover that country was not Canaan, not the promised land. Moses was still beyond Jordan. No matter on which side of the river the people were, they designated the mountains east of the Dead Sea Abarim, those beyond, and in later times they called the country between the Jabbok and the Arnon Peræa, region beyond. 5. It is universally admitted that Deut. xxxiv. 5-12, in which the death of Moses is recorded and comparison made between him and prophets subsequently raised up (5, 10, etc.), cannot have been from his pen. But an addition of this sort does not militate against the Mosaic authorship of the Pentateuch as a whole.

The orthodox theologian and commentator Vitringa expressed the opinion in 1707, in the interest of the credibility of Genesis, that Moses edited and supplemented records left by the fathers and preserved among the Israelites. In 1753, Jean Astruc, a French physician of ability, but profligate, attempted to discriminate two leading authors in Genesis, whose writings Moses used and who are distinguished by their employment respectively of the words Elohim, that is God, and

Jehovah. Besides the writings of these two, he thought he could detect ten minor documents relating chiefly to foreign nations and in which no name of God is found. This hypothesis was adopted by Eichhorn, and elaborated with learning and ingenuity. He steadfastly insisted that Moses compiled Genesis, and was the author of the rest of the Pentateuch. It was soon discovered, however, that the principles which govern the partition of Genesis were capable of being applied with similar results to the entire Pentateuch; and if so, the original documents covered the history of Moses' own time, and were scarcely put together by Moses to form the present Pentateuch. The grounds on which the partition is made are chiefly four: 1. The alternate use of the divine names God and Jehovah in successive paragraphs or sections. 2. The continuity of each so-called document when taken separately. 3. The diversity of style, diction, and ideas in the different documents. 4. Repetitions or parallel passages, often contradictory, indicative of distinct documents. Starting in simple form, the hypothesis underwent constant modification under careful criticism in order to remove the difficulties which beset it. The form which it now assumes is that four principal original documents were used by an editor or redactor in compiling the Pentateuch: an Elohistic, in which the divine title is Elohim, and which supplies about one-half the matter; a Jehovistic and another Elohistic, which have many mutual likenesses and are closely united; and finally the document of the Deuteronomist. The second and third documents, referred to as J E, are regarded as the oldest and dated about 1000–800 B. C. The greater part of Deuteronomy or D is assigned to the year 621 B. C. or half a century earlier (2 Kin. xxii. 8). And the first mentioned, usually denominated P to indicate that its author was a priest, is commonly dated at the close of the exile. To each of these main divisions there is a code of law; to J E, Ex. xx.–xxiii.; to D, Deut. xii.–xxvi.; and to P the priestly and other legislation of Exodus, Leviticus, and Numbers. It will be observed that there are two distinct matters involved in the modern theory: first, the existence of documents out of which the Pentateuch was constructed, and, second, the date of these documents. Wellhausen dates them as above, holding that the legislation of Leviticus is later than that of Deuteronomy. But 1. This theory involves the denial of the truth of the historical narrative in the O. T., not the assertion of occasional or minute inaccuracies, but the rejection of the credibility of the O. T. narrative almost as a whole. Wellhausen makes no concealment of the fact. 2. Furthermore, to date the so-called documents so late is forbidden by the fact of the development of doctrine. In the Pentateuch, the conceptions entertained and the doctrine taught concerning the future state, divine retribution, the spiritual character of true worship, angels, and the Messiah are rudimentary. They appear in developed form in late books, in Job, the Psalms, and the prophets; a strong argument that the writer of the Pentateuch lived at an earlier age and in a different intellectual environment. Dillmann, while accepting the existence of documents, opposed Wellhausen's arrangement, insisting that history required the existence of the Levitical legislation before that of Deuteronomy, and so far he is more in accord with the teaching of Scripture. 3. The early existence of the laws and institutions of the Pentateuch is attested by the traces of them in the writings of the early prophets. A short time since, it was customary to admit the genuineness of the passages where these traces are found, but to deny that they were derived from Deuteronomic or priestly documents. Now it is universally conceded that these laws and institutions were in full force when the passages were written; but the logical result of this concession, namely that the Pentateuchal law and organization were in existence in the eighth century B. C., is avoided by declaring that these references are late interpolations in the genuine writings of the prophets. As a rule no proof for this declaration is offered. The decision is magisterial. It is pronounced without appeal from the master's mere assertion. Believers in the Mosaic authorship of the Levitical and Deuteronomic law point with confidence to the evident indissolubleness of these references from the context and their inseparable connection with the original argument, which show that they are not interpolations, but an essential part of the discourse of the prophets of the eighth century. 4. The theory of the late origin of Israel's institutions asserts, as a fundamental postulate, that the law and the elaborate ritual of Israel were the result of a gradual development. As in nature, so in art, law, and ritual, the simple ever precedes the complex, and the rude the refined. The thesis, as a general principle, is demonstrable and is universally accepted; and it is true also in the case of the civil law and the worship of Israel. But there is another truth, to speak of but one, namely, that Israel was the heir of the ages. Development in law and in the ritual of divine worship had been going on for centuries. The Israelites did not begin with nothing, any more than do the founders of a modern state or the framers of a modern constitution. They did not create *ex nihilo*. Under Moses they appropriated the mature fruits of man's labor and man's experience. Among the nations with whom they were in close touch in the Mosaic era, among the Babylonians from the midst of whom their forefathers had emigrated and the Egyptians with whom they had sojourned, the development of the forms of worship had reached

maturity in an elaborate refinement; and the legal sense of the Semites had developed so far as to discern a unity underlying manifold laws and to adopt the principle of codification. The statutes organized as a body of law and incorporated in the book of the covenant, the sanctuary as described in Exodus, and the ritual that is outlined in Leviticus were not strange novelties to the people assembled at Sinai, but were familiar conceptions and already full of significance, appealing to the sense of justice and appreciation for the rights of the lowly and helpless which the Semites possessed long before the days of Moses, representing types of sacred architecture and ritual approved by the most refined contemporary peoples, embodying lofty ideals possessed in common with the ethnic religions of the day, employing a symbolism that was, as it were, the universal religious speech among the men of that age, and giving expression to the common innate sense of propriety in the worship of God. The whole was molded and dominated by the truth of one God only, holy, gracious, and spiritual. The civil law of Israel and the sanctuary, priesthood, and ritual, rich, refined, elaborate, are not things new under the sun; but Moses, a statesman and religious leader, in long and intimate communion with God and under direct divine teaching and control, selected suitable materials from the legal and ritualistic wealth of the age and organized them into a vehicle that was a perfect expression of God's will for quickening, fostering, disciplining, and guiding the moral and religious consciousness of Israel and giving a proper and intelligible display of those great truths concerning God which Israel held and for which Israel was to bear witness among men. The law and worship of Israel as exhibited in the legislation at Sinai, however long the period of development may have been that preceded them, were timely, in entire harmony with the conceptions of the Mosaic age. See MOSES, ALTAR, AMRAPHEL, PRIEST, TABERNACLE, THEOCRACY.

Turning to the literary aspect of the question, what are the objections to the theory of documents? 1. The impossibility of separating the documents from each other in strict adherence to the principle that certain words are characteristic of the several writers. To take an example from the use of different divine names, which is the starting point of the hypothesis and the phenomenon most evident to English readers, the name Jehovah, which in A. V. is generally translated LORD, betokens J, and should not occur, according to the theory, in the book of Genesis in the documents E and P. But, in fact, it does occur there in these documents, in v. 29; vii. 16; xiv. 22; xv. 1, 2; xvii. 1; xx. 18; xxi. 1 b, 33; xxii. 11, 14, 15, 16; xxviii. 21. Nor should the name of God appear in the document J; yet it does in iii. 1-5; iv. 25; vi. 2, 4; vii. 9;

ix. 26, 27 ; xxxiii. 5, 11 ; xliii. 14, etc. Here are more than a score of instances in Genesis alone and in respect to but two characteristic words, where the critical principle fails. When obstinate facts like these oppose the critical theory, they are exscinded. The compiler is said to have introduced the awkward words arbitrarily or from another document. In some cases J is said to have used the name God discriminatingly, which is a virtual abandonment of the theory. If the writer used the divine name discriminatingly in some cases, he may have done so in all, as the defenders of the Mosaic authorship maintain. On the theory of the Mosaic authorship, these words are in place ; and it is ordinarily apparent that they are discriminatingly employed. God denotes the divine being in his relation to the universe at large as creator, preserver, and governor of all his creatures and all their actions. Jehovah denotes God as he reveals himself to man, especially in grace. 2. The asserted continuity of the documents when taken separately is fictitious. J's narrative ending in iv. 25, 26 is continued in v. 28 b, 29 ; vi. (1–4) 5–8. These passages do not relate unbroken history, they are disconnected fragments, there is no continuity. J's narrative in vi. 5–8 is continued in vii. 1–5. The account is fragmentary again, not continuous. Whence came the ark into which Noah was commanded to enter? J's narrative embraces x. 21, 25–30 ; xi. (1–9), 28–30 ; xii. 1–4 a. Who was Terah, and who were Haran and Abram? Where is the smoothness of continuous narrative? P narrated i. 1–ii. 4 a, concluding with the emphatic declaration that God saw everything that he had made ; and behold, it was very good. The after listing the genealogy of Adam (v. 1–28 a, 30–32), he suddenly said: "And the earth was corrupt before God" (vi. 9–22). How did that become corrupt which God had pronounced very good? Again, P's uncouth narrative of the early history of Abraham is cut out of J's account, thus: xi. 27, 31, 32 ; xii. 4 b, ; 5 xiii. 6 a, 11 b, 12 a. It is continued in xvi. 1 a, 3, 15, 16 ; xvii. Over against this uncouthness in the hypothetical documents, believers in the Mosaic authorship are able to show unity of theme, unbroken continuity of thought, balanced treatment of the parts, and progressive narrative. See GENESIS. 3. The theory that there are parallel accounts marked by difference of style fails as a trustworthy principle in the only case where it can be tested by external evidence. It is asserted that in the narrative of the flood the storm which produced the deluge is described twice in three successive verses: "The same day were all the fountains of the great deep broken up, and the windows of heaven were opened" (vii. 11, P), and "It came to pass after the seven days that the waters of the flood were upon the earth, and the rain was upon the earth forty days and forty nights" (10, 12, J). It is urged

also that there are two literary styles apparent here : the former exuberant, vivid, poetic, the latter a bald statement of the facts in simple prose. But the account of the flood was also handed down by the Babylonians and Assyrians ; and when the Assyro-Babylonian narrative is compared with the Hebrew record, it is found to show the same repetitions which occurring in Genesis are called parallel narratives, and to exhibit like differences of style in the corresponding places. The narrator depicts the breaking and raging of the storm with equal picturesqueness and even greater exuberance than the Hebrew writer ; but when he comes to state how long the storm lasted, he naturally expresses himself simply. He says : "Six days and nights wind, storm and rain prevailed ; on the seventh day the rain abated, the storm which had struggled like a woman in travail, rested ; the sea withdrew to its bed, the violent wind and the flood-storm ceased ;" see the Assyrian account in article FLOOD. On the theory of Mosaic authorship, there is no difficulty in accounting for difference of style. Different themes require different statement. Dates, genealogies, and the like do not call the imagination into exercise. Vivid and picturesque description belongs to the narration of lively and vivid incidents. 4. The critical theory that there are parallel accounts of the same event which are marked by contradictions likewise fails to stand the test of external evidence. It is contended that according to P God forewarns Noah of an impending destructive flood of waters, but does not reveal to him whether it will be caused by melting snows or continuous rains or tidal wave ; and thus P contradicts J, who states that the Lord bade Noah enter into the ark, because in yet seven days he would cause it to rain upon the earth. But again the Assyrian account shows that the Hebrew narrative does not embody two divergent accounts, but is the record of successive progressive events. For according to it, as in Genesis, man was first warned of coming destruction and bidden build a boat. The ruin was, accordingly, to be wrought by a flood of water, but whether the deluge would be due to rain, or a freshet, or the inflowing sea was not disclosed. When the appointed time approached, however, the prophecy became definite and foretold rain. The Hebrew account, with its present material and the present arrangement of that material, is essentially the ancient account handed down from the fathers. And the criticism which distributes the narrative among different writers on the ground of differences of style or alleged contradictions is demonstrably invalid. [For full discussion of the subject, see William Henry Green, *The Higher Criticism of the Pentateuch* and *The Unity of the Book of Genesis*].

Pen′te-cost. See WEEKS, FEAST OF.

Pe-nu'el and once **Peniel** (Gen. xxxii. 31) [face of God].

1. Originally an encampment east of the Jordan, first named by Jacob because he had there seen God face to face, yet his life had been preserved (Gen. xxxii. 30, 31). In the time of the judges there was a tower there, which Gideon broke down, and a city, the inhabitants of which he slew (Judg. viii. 8, 9, 17). It was fortified by Jeroboam I. (1 Kin. xii. 25).

2. A man of Judah, and the ancestor of the inhabitants of Gedor (1 Chron. iv. 4).

3. A Benjamite, family of Shashak (1 Chron. viii. 25).

Pe'or [an opening, a cleft].

1. A mountain in Moab looking toward the desert, or Jeshimon (Num. xxiii. 28). From it the camp of Israel at Shittim was in full view (xxiv. 2). A mountain still bore the name in the time of Eusebius and Jerome. It stood opposite Jericho, on the road to Heshbon, above or to the east of Livias, now Tell er-Rameh. Accordingly Peor was a peak of the Abarim range near wady Hesbán.

2. A Moabite divinity worshiped in mount Peor, and often called Baal-peor. See BAAL-PEOR.

Pe-ræ'a or **Perea** [the land beyond].

The region between the Jabbok and the Arnon, beyond Jordan (War iii. 3, 3); cp. signification and location of Abarim. The name was, however, used in a wider sense; for Josephus calls Gadara, on the banks of the Yarmuk, the capital of Peræa (War iv. 7, 3).

Per'a-zim. See BAAL-PERAZIM.

Pe-re'a. See PERÆA.

Pe'res. See MENE.

Pe'resh [distinction, separation, dung]. A man of Manasseh (1 Chron. vii. 16).

Pe'rez, in A. V. of O. T. **Pharez** except thrice (1 Chron. xxvii. 3; Neh. xi. 4, 6); in A. V. of N. T. **Phares** [a breach].

A son of Judah, one of twins whom Tamar bore (Gen. xxxviii. 24–30). He became the founder of a tribal family which took its name from him, and of two other tribal families which sprang from his sons and were named from them (Num. xxvi. 20, 21; 1 Chron. ii. 4, 5). He was an ancestor of David and consequently of Christ (Ruth iv. 12–18; Mat. i. 3).

Pe-rez-uz'za and **Perez-uzzah** [breach of Uzza].

The name given by David to the place where Uzza was struck dead for touching the ark (2 Sam. vi. 8; 1 Chron. xiii. 11). Exact situation unknown.

Per-fum'er-y.

Spices of various kinds, such as aloes, cassia, cinnamon, myrrh, frankincense, spikenard, which were raised in the Jordan valley or imported from Arabia and elsewhere, formed the basis of perfumery (Ecclus. xxiv. 15). The spice was compelled to yield its fragrance by at least four different methods. It was tied in a bundle or enclosed in a bag (Song i. 13); it was reduced to powder and burned as incense (iii. 6); its aromatic matter was separated by boiling, and the extract was carried as scent in smelling-bottles suspended from the girdle, or was mixed with oil and used as an ointment (i. 3; Is. iii. 20; John xii. 3). Frequently several spices were compounded (Ex. xxx. 23, 24; John xix. 39). Perfumery was applied to the person and garments and furniture (Ps. xlv. 8; Prov. vii. 17; Song iv. 11). It was used in the temple service both as incense and as ointment (Ex. xxx. 22–38).

Per'ga [doubtless citadel, burg].

A town in Pamphylia, and under the Romans the capital of the province, on the right bank of the river Kestros, 60 stades from the mouth. Paul and Barnabas visited the town on the first missionary journey, both going and returning (Acts xiii. 13, 14; xiv. 25). In the vicinity was a celebrated temple of the goddess Artemis of the Asiatic type (cp. Diana of Ephesus), who was known as the queen of Perga.

Per'ga-mum, in A. V. **Pergamos** [citadel, burg]. Both forms of the name were used by the ancients.

The most important city of Mysia, situated on the north bank of the river Caicus, about 20 miles from the sea. It was once the capital of a wealthy kingdom ruled over by a dynasty of kings, several of them called Attalus. The first of these kings, Attalus I., came to the throne in the year 241 B. C. He defeated the Gauls and settled them in the district henceforth known as Galatia. His son Eumenes, who succeeded him, 197 B. C., adorned the city and founded a celebrated library, which ultimately was second only to that of Alexandria. Attalus III., who died in the year 133 B. C., bequeathed to the Romans his movable property. They misinterpreted the bequest to mean the kingdom, appropriated it, erected it into the province of Asia, and made Pergamum the capital. In 6 B. C., however, the residence of the proconsul, who in imperial times acted as governor of the province, was transferred to Ephesus. Marc Antony promised the library (which did not belong to him) to Cleopatra and had it removed to Egypt, where it was added to the renowned Alexandrian library. The acropolis of Pergamum crowned a steep hill that rose 1000 feet above the plain. Near the summit stood an immense altar to Zeus, erected by Eumenes II. to commemorate the victory won by his father over the Gauls; and at a short distance from this altar there was an elegant temple of Athene. In the Roman period a temple to the divine Augustus was also built on the acropolis. Outside of the city there was a famous shrine of

Æsculapius, god of medicine, to which people from all quarters flocked for healing. Parchment, called in Latin *pergamena*, and in Greek *pergaménē*, was so named because it was first obtained at Pergamum. The third of the seven churches of Asia addressed in the book of Revelation was that at Pergamum. It is said that Satan's seat was there, and that a faithful martyr, Antipas, had been put to death in the place. It must, therefore, have been a stronghold of antichristian idolatry (Rev. i. 11; ii. 12-17). It is now called Bergama or Bergma, and still exists as a town of mean-looking wooden houses interspersed with the more splendid relics of antiquity.

Pe-ri'da. See PERUDA.

Per'iz-zites [dwellers in unwalled villages].

An important section of the Canaanites, often enumerated as one of the tribes of Palestine (Gen. xv. 20; Ex. iii. 8; Josh. ix. 1), and perhaps, like the Rephaim, an aboriginal people who were of different race from the Canaanites and in the land before them (cp. Gen. xiii. 7; Josh. xvii. 15; and the omission of them in Gen. x. 15 seq.). They were in the country as early as the days of Abraham and Lot (Gen. xiii. 7). In Joshua's time they inhabited the mountain region (Josh. xi. 3), dwelling in the territory afterwards given over to the tribes of Ephraim, Manasseh (xvii. 15), and Judah (Judg. i. 4, 5). They were not extirpated, but, contrary to the law of Moses (Deut. vii. 3), allowed to enter into marriage alliances with their conquerors, seducing them into idolatry (Judg. iii. 5, 6). Solomon imposed upon these Perizzites a yoke of bondservice (1 Kin. ix. 20, 21; 2 Chron. viii. 7).

Per'se-us.

Son and successor of Philip III., and last king of Macedon. In 171 B. C. he resumed the war with the Romans which his father had waged; but, after three years of desultory fighting and occasional success, he was completely defeated (1 Mac. viii. 5) by L. Æmilius Paulus in the battle of Pydna, which ended the Macedonian monarchy. He fled, but was captured and taken to Rome, where he graced the triumph of his conqueror.

Per'si-a.

Persia proper, the seat of the Persians when they first became known to the Western nations as a settled people, lay southeast of Elam and nearly corresponded to the province of modern Persia called Fars, or Farsistan, a modification of the original native name Pârça. Persia, in this limited sense, was bounded on the north by Great Media (Media Magna), on the southwest by the Persian Gulf, on the east by Carmania (now called Kerman), and on the northwest by Susiana. Its length was at most about 250 miles; its average breadth about 200; its area considerably less than 50,000 square miles. In looser usage, the term Persia denoted the plateau of Iran, the region bounded by the Persian Gulf, the valleys of the Tigris and the Cyrus, the Caspian Sea, the rivers Oxus, Jaxartes, and Indus (1 Mac. vi. 1; 2 Mac. i. 19). But when the Persian empire was at the height of its power, it stretched from the empire of India on the east to the Grecian Archipelago on the west; and from the Danube, the Black Sea, mount Caucasus, and the Caspian Sea on the north, to the Arabian and Nubian deserts on the south (Esth. i. 1; x. 1); and it was nearly 3000 miles long, with a varying breadth of 500 to 1500 miles. It had an area of 2,000,000 square miles, half that of Europe. The race inhabiting Persia proper was Aryan, and closely related to the Median race.

The Persians are not mentioned in the table of nations (Gen. x.). They did not attain to prominence until many centuries after Moses. About 700 B. C. the country of Parsu, *i. e.* Persia, was one of the allies of Elam. But soon Teispes, a chief of the tribe and a member of the family of the Achæmenidæ, conquered Elam and established himself as king in the district of Ansan or Anzan, as the name is also written. His descendants branched into two lines, one reigning in Ansan and the other remaining in Persia. His great-grandson, Cyrus II., king of Ansan, united the divided power, conquered Media about 550 B. C., Lydia in Asia Minor a little later, and Babylonia in 539. He allowed the Hebrew exiles to return to their own land; see CYRUS. Dying in 529 B. C., he was succeeded by his son Cambyses, but reserved a small portion of his vast dominions for his younger son, Smerdis. The arrangement worked badly. Cambyses became jealous of Smerdis, and had him privately put to death. In 525 the king conquered Egypt. As he was returning to Persia, the news reached him that Smerdis, whom he believed to be dead, was really alive (which was not true), and had assumed the sovereignty, the Persian army supporting his claim. Troubled by the tidings, the monarch drew a short sword from its sheath and gave himself a wound which in a few days proved fatal. He died 522 B. C. The so-called Smerdis, who was really one of the Magi, now ascended the throne. When it was discovered that he was not the true Smerdis, a conspiracy was formed against him, and he was slain. Darius, son of Hystaspes, one of the leaders of the plot and apparently the next heir to the throne when the family of Cyrus became extinct, began to reign, 521 B. C., being then about twenty-eight years of age. The accession of the new king was the signal for a general revolt of the provinces, but the insurrection was suppressed, and Darius organized a new empire which extended from India to the Grecian Archipelago and the Danube. It was under him that the temple at Jerusalem was rebuilt. He died 486 B. C.; see DARIUS 2. His son and successor was Xerxes, the Ahasuerus of the Book of Esther and probably of Ezra iv. 6. He reconquered the Egyptians; and he attempted an invasion of Greece, but was repulsed with great loss to the Persians; see AHASUERUS 2. After a reign of twenty years, he was assassinated in 465 B. C. His son and successor, a much more respectable character, but still fickle and feeble, was Artaxerxes Longimanus. He was not unfriendly to the Jews. He allowed Ezra to lead a large number of them back to Jerusalem, and he permitted Nehemiah to rebuild the walls of the city; see ARTAXERXES. He reigned forty years, dying in 425 B. C. His successors were Xerxes II., 425; Sogdianus, 425; Darius Nothus, the Illegitimate, 424; Artaxerxes Mnemon, of good memory, 404; Artaxerxes Ochus, 359; Arses 338: and Darius Codomannus, 336. The last king was conquered by Alexander the Great in 331 B. C., and with him the first Persian empire passed away. See DARIUS 3.

The royal residences were Persepolis (2 Mac. ix. 2), Shushan (Neh. i. 1; Esth. i. 2), Ecbatana, that is Achmetha (Ezra vi. 2; Antiq. x. 11, 7), and to an extent Babylon (Ezra vi. 1).

When Cyrus the Great allowed the Jews to return to their own land 538 B. C., he did not grant them their independence. They were placed under governors appointed by the Persian emperor (Neh. iii. 7), and formed part of the satrapy beyond the river (Ezra viii. 36) which consisted of Syria, Palestine, Phœnicia, and Cyprus (Herod. iii. 91). They were subjects of Persia for 207 years, from 539, the year in which Cyrus entered Babylon, to 332, that in which Alexander the Great completed the conquest of Palestine.

The faith of their imperial lords was Zoroastrianism, but no effort was made to enforce it on the subject peoples. It was a spiritual religion, recognizing the distinction between God and nature, between spirit and matter, and consequently being averse to images of God. Its fundamental ethical principle was the essential contradiction between good and evil, light and darkness. It conceived of two realms of spirits: one with a hierarchy of angels and archangels, where Ahuramazda or Ormazd, as the name is written in modern Persian, the all-wise lord, God in the fullest sense, presides over the seven holy spirits, who are his ministers and the expression of his attributes, and over thousands of worthy ones; and another realm of evil spirits ruled over by Ahriman, the spiritual enemy. It was deeply tainted with dualism, and Ahriman was probably regarded as self-existent. It taught the duty of man to eradicate evil and cultivate good, and to strive after holiness in thought, word, and deed, which will be rewarded by immortality and heaven. It paid homage to fire, air, earth, and water as the creation of Ahuramazda. See MAGI. Later Judaism shows traces of the Persian supremacy.

What once had been Persia passed first to the Macedonian Greeks and their successors of the same race. Then it became part of the Parthian empire. In A. D. 211 or 212 Ardashir laid the foundations of a new Persian sovereignty, ruled by a dynasty called after his family Sassanian. In 224 he defeated and slew the last Parthian king. The Sassanian dynasty became powerful, met the Roman armies on equal terms, and set limits to the extension of their sway in the east. In A. D. 636 and 641, Yazdejard, or Yezdejerd III., the last of the dynasty, was defeated by the Saracens, and Persia came under Mohammedan rule, which has continued till now. Some of the bolder spirits refused to submit to Mohammedan domination, and fled to the deserts and the mountains. Finally, a number of Persian refugees landed in Guzerat about A. D. 717, seeking and obtaining an asylum in India. Their successors constitute a limited but important section of the Indian community. They are called Parsees. They have become prosperous, and are loyal to the English throne.

Per'sis [Persian].
A Christian at Rome who labored diligently in the Lord, and to whom Paul sent his salutation (Rom. xvi. 12).

Pe-ru'da and **Perida** [scattered, a kernel].
A subdivision of the children of Solomon's servants who returned from captivity (Ezra ii. 55; Neh. vii. 57).

Pes'ti-lence.
An infectious or contagious disease, a plague. While the sending of pestilence is frequently mentioned as from God (Ex. ix. 15; Lev. xxvi. 25; Deut. xxviii. 21), he very often, if not in all cases, uses secondary causes for its production. The punishment which is threatened is often described as the sword, the famine, and the pestilence, and these words tend to stand in this order (Ezek. vi. 11). There is reason for this order. War breaks out. The people of the invaded country cannot cultivate their fields, or, if they do, they find their crops reaped and destroyed by the enemy. Besiegers invest the cities and intentionally cut off the supplies with the object of forcing a surrender. Famine ensues in country and town. The starvation, the carnage, and the unsanitary condition of the cities crowded during the siege bring a pestilence.

Pe'ter.
The Greek form of the Aramaic surname Cephas (John i. 42; 1 Cor. i. 12; iii. 22; ix. 5; xv. 5; Gal. i. 18; ii. 9, 11, 14), meaning a rock, which Christ bestowed upon Simon or,

more properly, Symeon (Acts xv. 14; 2 Pet. i. 1, R. V. margin) on his first appearance before him (John i. 42), and afterwards explained more fully in its prophetic import (Mat. xvi. 18 seq.; Mark iii. 16). Simon was the son of a certain John (John i. 42, R. V.; xxi. 15, 16, 17, R. V.) or Jona (Mat. xvi. 17, probably a syncope of John), who, with his sons, Andrew and Peter, prosecuted the trade of a fisherman on the sea of Galilee in partnership with Zebedee and his sons (Mat. iv. 18; Mark i. 16; Luke v. 3 seq.). He was a native of Bethsaida (John i. 44), and subsequently dwelt with his family at Capernaum (Mat. viii. 14; Luke iv. 38).

Peter was probably a disciple of John the Baptist, and was in the first instance brought to Jesus by his brother Andrew (John i. 41, 42), who was one of the favored two disciples of John whom he pointed to Jesus immediately after his return from the temptation in the wilderness (John i. 35 seq.). With prophetic insight into his character, Jesus at once conferred upon him the surname of Cephas, or Peter, that is, "Rock" (John i. 42). In common with the earliest followers of Jesus, Peter received three separate calls from his Master: first, to become his disciple (John i. 40 seq.; cp. ii. 2); secondly, to become his constant companion (Mat. iv. 19; Mark i. 17; Luke v. 10); and, thirdly, to be his apostle (Mat. x. 2; Mark iii. 14, 16; Luke vi. 13, 14). Peter's ardor, earnestness, courage, vigor, and impetuosity of disposition marked him from the first as the leader of the disciples of Jesus. He is always named first in the lists of the apostles (Mat. x. 2; Mark iii. 16; Luke vi. 14; Acts i. 13). In the more intimate circle of the most favored three disciples, he is likewise always named first (Mat. xvii. 1; Mark v. 37; ix. 2; xiii. 3; xiv. 33; Luke viii. 51; ix. 28). He was the natural spokesman of the apostolical band. He was the first to confess Jesus as the Christ of God (Mat. xvi. 16; Mark viii. 29), but was equally forward to dissuade him from his chosen path of suffering (Mat. xvi. 22; Mark viii. 33), receiving from Christ the appropriate praise and blame.

Peter's life exhibits three well-marked stages. First, there is the period of training, as exhibited in the gospel narrative. During these years of personal association with Christ, he learned to know both Christ and himself. And though he brought them to an end in a threefold denial of the Master whom he had boasted that he at least would never forsake (Mat. xxvi. 69 seq.; Mark xiv. 66 seq.; Luke xxii. 54 seq.; John xviii. 15 seq.), Jesus closed them with a loving probing of his heart and restoration of his peace and confidence (John xxi. 15 seq.). Secondly, the period of leadership in the church, as exhibited in the earlier chapters of The Acts. During these years Peter justified his surname, and fulfilled the proph-

ecy that on him should the edifice of the church be raised. It was by his bold and strong hand that the church was led in every step. It was he who moved the disciples to fill up the broken ranks of the apostolate (Acts i. 15); it was he who proclaimed to the assembled multitudes the meaning of the pentecostal effusion (ii. 14); he was the leader in the public healing of the lame man and in the subsequent sermon and defense (iii. 4, 12; iv. 8); it was by his voice that Ananias and Sapphira were rebuked (v. 3, 8). Above all, it was by his hand that the door of salvation was opened alike to the Jews in the great sermon at Pentecost (ii. 10, 38), and to the gentiles in the case of Cornelius (x.). Thirdly, the period of humble work in the kingdom of Christ, exhibited in the epistles of the N. T. When the foundations of the church had been laid, Peter takes a subordinate place, and in humble labors to spread the boundaries of the kingdom, disappears from the page of history. In the church at Jerusalem James takes henceforth the leading place (xii. 17; xv. 13; xxi. 18; Gal. ii. 9, 12). The door had been opened to the gentiles, and Paul now becomes the apostle to the gentiles (Gal. ii. 7). As the apostle to the circumcision (8), Peter prosecuted henceforth his less brilliant work, wherever Jews could be found, and contentedly left Jerusalem to James and the civilized world to Paul. The book of The Acts closes its account of him at the meeting at Jerusalem (Acts xv.), when his policy of breaking down the barriers for the gentiles met with universal acceptance. We hear of him afterwards at Antioch (Gal. ii. 11), possibly at Corinth (1 Cor. i. 12), certainly in the far east at Babylon (1 Pet. v. 13), and certainly as prosecuting his work through missionary journeys, taking his wife with him (1 Cor. ix. 5). Finally, we know that he glorified God by a martyr's death (John xxi. 19). Beyond this, Scripture tells us nothing of his fortunes, labors, sufferings, or successes, except what can be learned from his two Epistles. In them he stands before us in a singularly beautiful humility, not pressing the recognition of personal claims to leadership upon the Christian community, but following up the teaching of Paul or of Jude with his own, and exhorting his readers to hold fast to the common faith.

No character in Scripture history, we may even say in all literature, is drawn for us more clearly or strongly than Peter's. In the gospels, in The Acts, and in the epistles it is the same man that stands out before us in dramatic distinctness. Always eager, ardent, impulsive, he is preeminently the man of action in the apostolic circle, and exhibits the defects of his qualities as well as their excellences throughout life (Mat. xvi. 22; xxvi. 69-75; Gal. ii. 11). His virtues and faults had their common root in his enthusiastic disposition; it is to his praise that along with the weed of rash haste, there grew more strongly into his life the fair plant of burning love and ready reception of truth. He was treated with distinguished honor by his Lord: he was made the recipient of no less than three miracles in those early days of the gospels; he was granted a special appearance after the resurrection (1 Cor. xv. 5); Jesus could find time in his own passion and while saving the world to cast on him a reminding glance and to bind up his broken heart. Accordingly the life of Peter is peculiarily rich in instruction, warning, and comfort for the Christian, and his writings touch the very depths of Christian experience and soar to the utmost heights of Christian hope.

Authentic history adds but little to our knowledge of Peter's life beyond what we glean from the N. T. Conformably to the notice of his martyrdom in John xxi. 19, we are credibly told that he died by crucifixion about the same time with Paul's death by the sword, that is about A. D. 68. The place of his death is not incredibly witnessed to be Rome. Legend was early busy with his life; the Roman legend of a twenty-five years' episcopate in Rome has its roots in early apocryphal stories originating among the heretical Ebionites, and is discredited not less by its origin and manifest internal inconsistencies than by all authentic history.

The First Epistle General of Peter. The author of this epistle announces himself as the apostle Peter (i. 1); and the whole internal character of the letter as well as exceptionally copious historical attestation bears out the assertion. It is addressed "to the elect who are sojourners of the Dispersion in Pontus, Galatia, Cappadocia, Asia, and Bithynia" (i. 1), which is evidently a somewhat metaphorical description of the whole body of Christians inhabiting the region comprised in modern Asia Minor. That the readers in the mind of the author were largely of gentile origin is clear from such passages as i. 14; ii. 9, 10; iii. 6; iv. 3. These were churches founded and nurtured in large part by the apostle Paul, and to them Paul had written his letters to the Galatians, Ephesians, and Colossians; Peter writes to them as those who owed their conversion to others than himself (i. 12, 25), and in order to testify that the gospel they had received was "the true grace of God" and to exhort them to "stand fast therein" (v. 12). Thus he publishes his hearty agreement with the apostle Paul and at the same time pens what is preeminently the epistle of hope. The order in which the countries to which it was sent are enumerated (i. 1), names them from east to west, and suggests that the letter was written in the east. This is borne out by the salutation sent from the Babylonian church (v. 13). Its date is set by its pretty copious use of the Epistle to the Ephesians on the one side, and the death

of Peter on the other, as between A. D. 63 and A. D. 67: it is most probable that it was written about 64 or 65. Allusion is made to the epistle as being Peter's in 2 Pet. iii. 1 (cp. i. 1); it is unmistakably quoted by Polycarp, a disciple of the apostle John; it is definitely quoted also as the writing of the apostle Peter by Irenæus and Tertullian in the closing decades of the second century; and from the very beginning it has always held a secure place in the Christian Bible in every part of the world, and has always been in the fullest use by Christians of every land.

The style in which the letter is written is at once simple, striking, and forcible, abounding in sudden and abrupt transitions and admirably reflecting the character of the writer. The whole mode of presentation of its matter is special and characteristic, though the doctrine presented is distinctly the same as that of the epistles of Paul, set forth here with prevailing reference to the grace of God and the future hope. The epistle is filled to a remarkable degree with reminiscences of earlier Christian writings, particularly of the epistles to the Romans and Ephesians and James (cp. 1 Pet. i. 6, 8 with Rom. ix. 32, 33; 1 Pet. ii. 5; iii. 8, 9; iv. 7–11 with Rom. xii. 1, and 16, 17, and 3, 6; 1 Pet. ii. 18 and iii. 1–7 with Eph. vi. 5 and v. 22, 23; 1 Pet. i. 1, 6, 7, 23 and v. 6 with Jas. i. 1, 2, 3, 18 and 1 Pet. iv. 10), thus revealing a characteristic of Peter's. It is remarkable for the combined depth and beauty of its Christian teaching. After the greeting (i. 1, 2) there follows an introductory section (i. 3–12) in which God is praised for the blessings of salvation. The body of the letter (i. 13–v. 11) consists of (1) a series of exhortations to a diligent Christian walk, correspondent to the teaching its readers had received (i. 13–ii. 10); (2) a number of particular directions for the special relationships of life (ii. 11–iv. 6); and (3) some closing instructions for the present needs of the readers (iv. 7–v. 11). It ends with salutations and announcements (v. 12–14).

The Second Epistle General of Peter. The author of this epistle describes himself as "Symeon Peter, a bond servant and apostle of Jesus Christ" (i. 1, R. V. margin), and represents himself as having been present at Christ's transfiguration (i. 16), and as having received from him a prediction as to his death (i. 14; cp. John xxi. 19), and also as standing on an equality with the apostle Paul (iii. 15). A lack of simplicity in the style and of ease in expression contrast with the simplicity of style exhibited by Peter in the First Epistle; and this difference was made as early as Jerome's time an argument for diversity of authorship. Jerome himself thought that such difference as appears was due to Peter's use of different interpreters. Perhaps so (cp. MARK). At any rate, the distinct claim of the author to be the apostle

Peter is borne out by the character of the letter itself; for it does not lack traits characteristic of Peter's manner or points of likeness to his speeches recorded in The Acts, and it shows peculiarities to Peter's discourse in its employment of a number of unusual words which are common to it and the First Epistle, and in the habit, observable in the first letter also, of giving both the negative and positive aspect of a thought (for example, 1 Pet. i. 12, 14, 15, 18, 19 and 2 Pet. i. 16, 21; ii. 4, 5; iii. 9, 17). Traces of the use of this epistle in the very earliest days of the church are not numerous or very clear; but Origen at the opening of the third century speaks of it in a manner which shows that it was used in the church of his day; and although doubts were cherished in some quarters concerning its authorship, these are overborne by the weighty historical evidence.

The form of its address is quite general: "to them that have obtained a like precious faith with us" (i. 1); but iii. 1 shows that the same readers, or some one territorial group among them, are in view to whom 1 Peter had been sent. The place from which it was written cannot be confidently ascertained; if the allusion in i. 14 implies that Peter was on the verge of his martyrdom, we may think of Rome. In that case the letter should be dated in A. D. 68; and the nature of the errors rebuked in it, and its use of the Epistle of Jude (or vice versa) as well as its allusion to 1 Peter will accord with this date.

Its object, as is declared in iii. 1, 17, 18, was to stir up the minds of its readers to remember what had been taught them, to the end that they might be saved from the errors now becoming prevalent and might grow in grace and the knowledge of the Lord and Saviour Jesus Christ. It was written, in other words, to rebuke the nascent gnosticism creeping into the churches, and to build up Christians in true knowledge and purity. The contents of the letter are in full accord with its object. After the usual apostolical greeting (i. 1, 2), it passes insensibly into an earnest exhortation to growth in grace and knowledge (3–11), and thence into a reminder of the grounds on which this knowledge, itself the basis of piety, rests (12–21), and a denunciation of the false teachers (ii. 1–22). The readers are then reminded of the nature and surety of the teaching given them as to the second advent and the end of the world (iii. 1–13); and the letter closes with an exhortation to them to make their calling and election sure, including a commendation of Paul's letters, and concludes with a doxology (14–18).   B. B. W. (supplemented).

Peth-a-hi′ah [Jehovah hath set free].

1. A descendant of Aaron whose family became the nineteenth course of priests (1 Chron. xxiv. 16).

2. A Levite who was induced by Ezra to put away his foreign wife (Ezra x. 23). He was probably the Levite of the name who assisted Ezra in his religious work (Neh. ix. 5).

3. A man of Judah, family of Zerah, and an official of the Persian king for all matters concerning the people (Neh. xi. 24).

Pe′thor [cleft, opening].

A town near the Euphrates (Num. xxii. 5), by the mountains of Aram or Mesopotamia (Num. xxiii. 7; Deut. xxiii. 4). While the Israelites were in Egypt, the town was captured by the Hittites, and they retained it until the ninth century B. C., when it was wrested from them by Shalmaneser II., king of Assyria, and converted into a colony of the conquerors. It was situated far north of Palestine, on the western bank of the Euphrates, near the river Sagura, now Sajur, a few miles south of the Hittite capital Carchemish.

Pe-thu′el [probably, noblemindedness of God].

Father of the prophet Joel (Joel i. 1).

Pe′tra. See SELA.

Pe-ul′le-thai, in A. V. **Pe-ul′thai** [perhaps, full of work, laborious].

A Levite, a doorkeeper, son of Obed-edom (1 Chron. xxvi. 5).

Pha′lec. See PELEG.

Phal′lu. See PALLU.

Phal′ti. See PALTI.

Phal′ti-el. See PALTIEL.

Pha-nu′el [face or presence of God].

An Asherite, the father of Anna (Luke ii. 36).

Pha′raoh [Egyptian *per-āa*, great house].

A title used as the general designation of the sovereign of Egypt, both with and without the personal name attached.

Of the Pharaohs mentioned in the Bible, several, among whom are the Pharaohs of Abraham and Joseph, cannot be identified with any degree of certainty. Of those that are better known there are:

1. THE PHARAOH OF THE OPPRESSION. It is quite generally, though not universally, believed that this was Ramses II., third king of the nineteenth dynasty and son of Seti I. See EGYPT III. 8. Both belonged to the New Empire. Ramses while yet a mere child was made coregent by Seti, and reigned sixty-seven years, from 1348 to 1281 B. C. according to Dr. Mahler's calculation. He was a great warrior and penetrated farther into Asia than even Thothmes III. had done, advancing as far as Asia Minor and to the vicinity of the Tigris. The Libyans, the inhabitants of Asia Minor, and islanders of the Mediterranean made war against Egypt, but Ramses defeated them. His great expeditions were directed against the Hittites and their allies, and occupied many campaigns. His most notable exploit was during an ex-

pedition to Kadesh, on the Orontes, the southern Hittite capital, in which he was led by treacherous Bedouin Arab guides into

A limestone plaque from the city of Akhenaton (Tell el Amarna) depicts the pharaoh Akhenaton and his beautiful wife Nofretete.

an ambuscade, from which he extricated himself by great personal prowess; but he failed to take the city or inflict on the Hittites such a defeat as would terminate the war. He entered into a treaty of peace and amity, sealed by his marrying the daughter of the Hittite king. The peace which ensued allowed Ramses to devote his attention to building operations, to founding and enriching libraries, and to establishing schools. Especially in the delta did he erect buildings, among which were Pa-Ramses and in part at least Pithom. His mummy is now in the museum at Bulak.

2. THE PHARAOH OF THE EXODUS. He is believed to have been Meneptah II., the thirteenth son of Ramses II. On his accession to the throne he maintained the treaty of peace which his father had entered into with the Hittites. In the fifth year of his reign Lower Egypt was invaded by the Libyans and their allies. The mercenaries of the Egyptian king, rather than himself, ultimately gained a complete victory over their invaders. A hymn was composed to celebrate this success and other victories. The translation is doubtful in minor points, but is essentially as follows:

The chiefs bow down, making their
  salutations of peace,
Not one of the peoples of the bow [i. e.
  hostile foreigners] lifts up its
  head:
The land of the Libyans is vanquished,
The land of the Hittites is tranquilized,
Ravaged is the place Pa-Kanana [in Southern
  Palestine] with all violence,

Carried away is the place Ashkelon,
Overpowered is the place Gezer,
The place Innuam [near Tyre] is brought to
  naught,
The people Isiraalu are spoiled, they have no
  seed,
The place Khar [i. e. southern Palestine] has be-
  come like the widows of Egypt.
All the world is at peace,
Every one that was rebellious is subdued by the
  king Meneptah.

Isiraalu is mentioned in close connection with places in Philistia, Phœnicia, and Palestine. It cannot be rendered Jezreel, for the orthography of the word and the use of the determinative which signifies people are both against it. It alone is without the determinative for land or city. It accordingly is a nomadic tribe or else a people dwelling in a country not their own. Leaving no seed to a spoiled and harried people was a common mode which the Egyptians had of recording the destruction of the crops or supply of grain. The natural meaning of the inscription accordingly is that troops, who were acting under Meneptah and waging war against the peoples of Palestine and vicinity, ravaged the Israelites and destroyed their fields or storehouses of grain. All available evidence indicates that the Israelites had not conquered Canaan and settled in Palestine as

Some scholars believe Amenhotep II was the pharaoh of the exodus. On this limestone relief he is portrayed standing in his chariot and shooting arrows at a copper target.

yet. The Habiri, who were warring in Palestine in the reign of Amenophis IV., six or seven generations before Meneptah, if Hebrews, were such in the wide racial sense, and perhaps included no Israelites at all. The inscription of Meneptah and the biblical record agree, if the inscription means, as has been inferred by Dr. W. W. Moore, that within two or three years after the exodus Egyptian or Canaanitish subjects of Meneptah attacked the Israelites near Kadesh-barnea. The Hebrews had feared to advance from Kadesh and had begun their dreary life of forty years in the wilderness. Here they pastured their flocks and herds, and doubtless, like Isaac when in the same quarter (Gen. xxvi. 12), sowed seed and raised what crops a scantily watered soil permitted. Their grain was destroyed by the enemy; and the event may possibly be referred to in Num. xiv. 45; Deut. i. 44-46, for their sojourn at Kadesh had been long enough to permit the young crop to be growing, but not the grain to be ripe. On this interpretation the Pharaoh of the exodus was not drowned in the Red Sea. The biblical record does not necessarily mean that he was. It is not necessary to believe that he did in person everything which is charged to him. What is done in Pharaoh's name and by Pharaoh's servants can be described as done by him; and what his emissaries suffer he can be said to suffer.

3. SHISHAK. Called by the monuments Sheshenk and by Manetho Sesonchis, the first ruler of the twenty-second dynasty. According to an inscription found in Abydos, Shishak was the son of an Assyrian conqueror named Nemret. The names of his successors are also more Assyrian than Egyptian in origin. An account of his expedition into Palestine (1 Kin. xiv. 25, 26; 2 Chron. xii. 2-9), with the usual embellishments and exaggerations, is found on the south wall of the temple at Karnak. In the list given there of cities conquered in that expedition occurs the name Judha-malek, which may possibly mean royal city of Judah. He was probably an able statesman, as he was able to avoid a rupture with Solomon while keeping Solomon's enemy as a guest (1 Kin. xi. 40). He shrewdly took advantage of the unsettled state of affairs in Palestine after the division of the kingdom, to make his invasion at that time when resistance to an enemy was necessarily weakened by dissensions at home. He also created a balance of power for himself in Egypt by reëlevating to a position of power the priests of Apis at Memphis, rivals of the priests of Thebes. Jeroboam took refuge at his court some time after the twenty-fifth year of Solomon (1 Kin. vi. 38; vii. 1; ix. 10, 24; xi. 27), and the invasion of Judah took place in the fifth year of Rehoboam; accordingly, the longest time required by the biblical data for the reign of Shishak is 21 years, though a shorter time would suffice. This demand is met by the Egyptian monuments, for they mention the thirty-ninth year of his reign.

4. ZERAH the Cushite, who undertook an expedition against Judah in the reign of Asa, leading an army composed of Ethiopians and Libyans, doubtless in addition to the Egyptian troops. His forces were routed at Mareshah (2 Chron. xiv. 9-15; xvi. 8). The monuments do not mention this military expedition, as it is their custom to pass over in silence their own defeats. Zerah is commonly identified with Osorkon I. or II., successors of Shishak in the twenty-second or Bubastite dynasty. He may have been called Cushite by the biblical writer either because he was crown prince when he led the expedition against Judah, in which case he bore the title Prince of Cush; or because he was by birth an Ethiopian, Osorkon II. being the son-in-law, not the son, of the preceding monarch.

5. So, contemporary of Hoshea, king of Israel (2 Kin. xvii. 4); see So.

6. TIRHAKAH, third and last king of the twenty-fifth dynasty, which is known also as the Ethiopian dynasty. As a youth of twenty he went north from Napata, the capital of Ethiopia, with a king, probably his uncle Shabaka, when the latter invaded Egypt. A decade later this nephew was in command of the Egyptian and Ethiopian forces which were marching against the Assyrians. Sennacherib, king of Assyria, advancing through Philistia in the direction of Egypt in 701 B. C., heard a report that Tirhakah, king of Ethiopia, was coming against him (2 Kin. xix. 9). In his own account of the affair Sennacherib, without mentioning their personal names, says that the kings of Egypt and the archers, chariots and horses of the king of Ethiopia met him in battle at Eltekeh (Cylinder ii. 73-81). About 690 B. C. Tirhakah became the Pharaoh. In 671 B. C. Sennacherib's son, Esarhaddon, king of Assyria, penetrated into the midst of the country, defeated Tirhakah, whom he calls king of Ethiopia, took Memphis, made Tirhakah's son a captive, and assumed the title of king of Egypt, Pathros, and Ethiopia. Tirhakah found refuge in Ethiopia, and on Esarhaddon's death, in 669 or 668 B. C., returned to Egypt. Ashurbanipal sent an army against him, styling him king of Egypt and Ethiopia, and defeated his troops at Karbanit, near the mouth of the Canopic branch of the Nile. Tirhakah retired to Thebes. He still had the support of several minor kings of Egypt, among whom was Necho. Ashurbanipal afterwards pursued him thither and took Thebes. The Assyrian king presently records the death of Tirhakah. This event occurred about 664 B. C. The Egyptian records attest the fact that he reigned at least 26 years, so that his possession of the royal title can be traced back as far as 690 B. c. at least.

7. NECHO, son of Psammetick I. He was the second ruler of the twenty-sixth dynasty and reigned 16 years, from 610 to 594 B. C He attempted to complete a canal connecting the Red Sea with the Nile, and sent a suc-

cessful expedition to circumnavigate Africa (Herod. ii. 158; iv. 42). He slew king Josiah at Megiddo as the latter unwisely opposed his march toward Assyria. Herodotus says that Necho defeated the Syrians at Magdolus (Megiddo), and afterwards took Cadytus, one of the large cities of Syria (ii. 159). This has been identified with Gaza, but better with Kadesh, the Hittite city on the Orontes. On Josiah's death, the people set up his son Jehoahaz, but Pharaoh dethroned and carried him off to Egypt, setting up in his stead his elder brother, Jehoiakim (2 Kin. xxiii. 29-34; 2 Chron. xxxv. 20-xxxvi. 4). Necho seems to have left his army at Carchemish and gone back to Egypt. In 605 B. C. he returned to his army, the object being to protect the interests of Egypt west of the Euphrates. But he came too late and found himself opposed to Nebuchadnezzar, the Babylonian conqueror of Assyria, was utterly routed by him, and lost all of Egypt's Asiatic possessions (2 Kin. xxiv. 7).

8. PHARAOH-HOPHRA, the Uah-ab-ra of the Egyptian monuments, the Ouaphris of Manetho, and the Apries of Herodotus. He was the second successor of Necho, separated from him by the short reign of Psammetick II. He reigned 19 years, from 589 to 570 B. C. He was on the throne while Jeremiah and his fellow-fugitives from Palestine still lived. The prophet intimated that Pharaoh-hophra should be given into the hands of his enemies, as Zedekiah, the last king of Judah, had been (Jer. xliv. 30). He was a warrior, and appears to have conquered the combined fleets of Cyprus and Sidon in a sea fight. He failed at last in an attack on the Greek colony of Cyrene. His army, in consequence, revolted: he was captured, confined, and ultimately put to death.

Phar'a-thon. See PIRATHON.

Pha'res and **Pha'rez.** See PEREZ.

Phar'i-sees [probably, separated].

One of the three chief Jewish sects, the others being the Sadducees and the Essenes. It was the straitest sect (Acts xxvi. 5). In all probability the Pharisees originated in the period before the Maccabæan war, in a reaction against the hellenizing spirit which appeared among the Jews and manifested itself in the readiness of a part of the people to adopt Grecian customs. Those who regarded these practices with abhorrence and their spread with alarm were incited to strict and open conformity to the Mosaic law. They were drawn yet more closely together as a party by the fierce persecution which Antiochus Epiphanes, 175-164 B. C., set on foot against the faithful Israelites who would not abandon Judaism and accept the Greek faith, when he attempted to destroy the holy Scriptures, and commanded that whosoever was found with any book of the covenant or consented to the law, should be put to death (1 Mac. i. 56, 57). The Hasidæans, who

were mighty men of Israel, even all such as were voluntarily devoted unto the law (ii. 42; cp. i. 62, 63), participated in the Maccabæan revolt as a distinct party. They were probably the Pharisees, they certainly corresponded to that sect. When the war ceased to be a struggle for religious liberty, and became a contest for political supremacy, they ceased to take an active interest in it. They are not mentioned during the time that Jonathan and Simon were the Jewish leaders, 160-135 B. C. The Pharisees appear under their own name in the time of John Hyrcanus, 135-105 B. C. He was a disciple of theirs, but left them and joined the Sadducees (Antiq. xiii. 10, 5 and 6); and his son and successor, Alexander Jannæus, endeavored to exterminate them by the sword. But his wife, Alexandra, who succeeded him in 78 B. C., recognizing that physical force is powerless against religious conviction, favored the Pharisees (15, 5; 16, 1). Thenceforth their influence was paramount in the religious life of the Jewish people.

The Pharisees held the doctrine of foreordination, and considered it consistent with the freewill of man. They believed in the immortality of the soul, in the resurrection of the body, and in the existence of spirits; that men are rewarded or punished in the future life, according as they have lived virtuously or viciously in this life; that the souls of the wicked shall be detained forever in prison under the earth, while those of the virtuous rise and live again, removing into other bodies (Acts xxiii. 8; Antiq. xviii. 1, 3; War ii. 8, 14). These doctrines distinguished them from the Sadducees, but did not constitute the essence of Pharisaism. Pharisaism is the final and necessary result of that conception of religion which makes religion consist in conformity to the law, and promises God's grace only to the doers of the law. Religion becomes external. The disposition of the heart is less vital than the outward act. The interpretation of the law and its application to the details of ordinary life accordingly became a matter of grave consequence, lawyers acquired increased importance, and expositions of the law by recognized authorities grew to a body of precepts of binding force. Josephus, who was himself a Pharisee, describes them as not merely accepting the law of Moses, and interpreting it more skillfully than others, but adds that they had delivered to the people a great many observances by succession from the fathers which are not written in the law of Moses (Antiq. xiii. 10, 6), these being the traditional interpretations of the elders, which our Lord pronounced to be of no binding authority (Mat. xv. 2, 3, 6).

At first, when one incurred great danger in joining the party, the Pharisees were men of strong religious character. They were the best people in the nation. Subsequently Pharisaism became an inherited belief and the profession of it was popular, and men of character very inferior to that of the original members of the sect joined its ranks. With the lapse of time also the essentially vicious element in the system developed and laid the Pharisees, as commonly represented by the members of the sect, open to scathing rebuke. John the Baptist called them and the Sadducees a generation of vipers; and it is well known how severely our Lord denounced them for their self-righteousness, their hypocrisy, their inattention to the weightier matters of the law, while being very particular as to minute points, with other faults (Mat. v. 20; xvi. 6, 11, 12; xxiii. 1–39). They became an intriguing body of men (Antiq. xvii. 2, 4). They took a prominent part in plotting the death of Christ (Mark iii. 6; John xi. 47–57). Yet they always numbered in their ranks men of perfect sincerity and the highest character. Paul in his early life was a Pharisee, and was accustomed to bring forward the fact when he was reasoning with his countrymen (Acts xxiii. 6; xxvi. 5–7; Phil. iii. 5). His teacher, Gamaliel, was of the same sect (Acts v. 34).

Pha'rosh. See PAROSH.

Phar'par [swift].
Presumably the less important of the two rivers of Damascus, for Naaman mentions it only second (2 Kin. v. 12). According to the local tradition, which can be traced back to the middle of the sixteenth century, the Pharpar is the Taura, one of seven canals which are drawn off from the Barada as it nears Damascus. It is more common, however, outside of Damascus, to identify the Pharpar with the A'waj, the only independent stream except the Barada within the territory of Damascus, but distant a ride of three hours from the city. It is formed by the confluence of several streams which take their rise in mount Hermon. It pursues a tortuous course through the plain to the south of the city and finally enters the most southerly of three inland lakes. In dry weather its waters are sometimes absorbed before they even enter the lake.

Pha·se'ah. See PASEAH.

Pha·se'lis.
A city of Lycia, on the gulf of Pamphylia, with three excellent harbors. It enjoyed considerable commerce in early times (Herod. ii. 178). It was independent (1 Mac. xv. 23) until the war of 78–75 B. C., when the Romans destroyed it because it had become a center of organized piracy. It was rebuilt, but did not rise to importance again. Its ruins exist near Tekrova.

Phas'i-ron.
Probably a Bedouin chief (1 Mac. ix. 66).

Phe'be. See PHŒBE.

Phe-ni'ce. See PHŒNICIA and PHŒNIX.

Phe-ni'ci-a. See PHŒNICIA.

Phi'col, in A. V. **Phichol** [possibly, mouth of all, *i. e.* commanding all].
The captain of the army of Abimelech, king of Gerar; present when treaty was made between Abimelech and Abraham, and between Abimelech or his successor with like title and Isaac (Gen. xxi. 22; xxvi. 26). There is no need to assume that he was older than Isaac.

Phil-a-del'phia [brotherly love].
1. A city of Lydia, in Asia Minor, about 27 miles southeast of Sardis, in the plain of the Hermus. It was built by Attalus Philadelphus, on a part of mount Tmolus. In A. D. 17 it was destroyed by an earthquake, but was soon rebuilt. It was the seat of one of the seven churches of Asia addressed in

Ruins of a Roman theatre in Amman, Jordan. In ancient times Amman was known as Rabbath-Ammon, chief town of the Ammonites. Later it was rebuilt and renamed Philadelphia by Ptolemy Philadelphus (245-246 B.C.).

the book of Revelation (i. 11; iii. 7–13). Unlike most of the seven, it receives commendation and encouragement, unmixed with censure. It is now called Allah Shehr, and continues to be inhabited. The walls of the ancient city, which are still standing, enclose several hills, with the remains of a temple and other buildings.
2. A later name of Rabbah of the Ammonites. See RABBAH.

Phi-le'mon [Greek, loving or affectionate (cp. *philēma*, a kiss)].
A convert of the apostle Paul's (Philem. 19), who resided in the same city with Archippus and from which Onesimus had come, viz. Colossæ (cp. Philem. 2 with Col. iv. 17; and Philem. 10 with Col. iv. 9). There was a church in his house (Philem. 2). Paul calls him a fellow-laborer (1) and speaks of his kindness to the saints (5–7). As Paul had never been in Colossæ (cp. Col. ii. 1), we may suppose that Philemon was converted in Ephesus during the apostle's ministry there (cp. Acts xix. 10). It is not improbable that Archippus was Philemon's son and Apphia his wife (Philem. 2).

The Epistle of Paul to Philemon is the brief letter sent by Paul, in conjunction with Timothy, to Philemon. The latter's slave, Onesimus, had run away, perhaps taking with him some of Philemon's money (18, 19); and, having made his way to Rome, had there been converted through the instrumentality of the apostle (10). Paul would gladly have retained him as a free attendant, but did not feel at liberty to do so without Philemon's consent (13, 14). He doubtless felt too that Onesimus, as a Christian, ought to seek the forgiveness of his master; and he was equally anxious that Philemon should both forgive and receive the converted wrongdoer. So he sent Onesimus back to Philemon, urging the latter to receive him as a brother beloved (16), telling of the love he himself bore toward the convert (10, 12), and offering to repay Philemon for whatever loss Onesimus had caused him (18, 19). The letter is an exquisite production. It reveals the delicacy of Paul's feeling and the graciousness of his relations with his friends. It also illustrates the effect of Christianity on social relationships generally, the spirit of love and justice which were destined to reorganize society. When Onesimus carried this letter to Philemon, he accompanied Tychicus, who also bore the Epistle to the Colossians (Col. iv. 7–9) and that to the Ephesians (Eph. vi. 21, 22). All three epistles were written at the same time, probably A. D. 61 or 62, and from Rome. The genuineness of the Epistle to Philemon, though it is so brief a letter, is well attested, being contained in the Syriac and Old Latin versions, named in the Muratorian fragment, accepted by Marcion, quoted by Origen and expressly as Paul's, and included by Eusebius among the undisputed books. It thus strongly supports the genuineness of the other epistles with which it is associated.

G. T. P. (supplemented).

Phi-le′tus [worthy of love].

One who joined with Hymenæus in propagating the error that the resurrection is already past (2 Tim. ii. 17, 18).

Phil′ip [fond of horses].

1. Father of Alexander the Great (1 Mac. i. 1). He was a son of Amyntas II. of Macedon. He took charge of the government about 360 B. C., as guardian of the royal infant, and by skillful negotiations and successful war delivered the country from the danger which beset it by reason of the hostility of the Pæonians, Illyrians, and Athenians. He then ascended the throne, perhaps by usurpation. He captured Amphipolis and annexed it to his dominions in 358, and crossing the river Strymon, he took possession of Thracian territory and founded Philippi in 356. These achievements marked only the beginning of his unchecked career of conquest in Greece, by which he raised Macedonia from an obscure state to be the domi-

nant power in Grecian affairs. He was assassinated in 336 B. C., and was succeeded by Alexander.

2. Another king of Macedon, and third of the name. He entered into an alliance with Hannibal against the Romans in 215 B. C., but they held him in check with the coöperation of the Ætolians. After seven years he was glad to make a separate peace. In 200 B. C. the Romans invaded his kingdom. He successfully resisted them for two years, but in 197 he was completely defeated (1 Mac. viii. 5) by the Roman general Flaminius at Cynocephalæ in Thessaly, and forced to conclude a humiliating peace. He died in 179 B. C.

3. Foster brother of Antiochus Epiphanes (2 Mac. ix. 29), and one of his privileged friends (1 Mac. vi. 14). When Antiochus was in Persia, nigh unto death, he appointed Philip regent during the minority of the young Antiochus (15). Lysias, however, who was in Syria, usurped the position (17). Philip returned in haste, and obtained temporary possession of Antioch, the capital (55, 63). But Lysias succeeded in capturing the city. According to Josephus, Philip was executed (Antiq. xii. 9, 7), but perhaps he escaped and fled to Egypt before the city fell (2 Mac. ix. 29).

It has been conjectured, on insufficient grounds, that he is identical with Philip, the Phrygian who was made governor of Judæa by Antiochus (2 Mac. v. 22), and that he was the master of the elephants at the battle of Magnesia (Livy xxxvii. 41).

4. A son of Herod the Great, and the first husband of Herodias and brother or half-brother of Herod Antipas (Mat. xiv. 3; Luke iii. 19). He is not called the tetrarch, and there is reason to believe that he was a different person from Philip the tetrarch, half-brother of Herod Antipas. In giving the genealogy of a portion of Herod the Great's family, Josephus states that Herodias married Herod, son of Herod the Great by Mariamne, daughter of the high priest Simon; that she left him to live with Antipas his half-brother; and that her daughter Salome married Philip the tetrarch, son of Herod the Great by Cleopatra of Jerusalem, and after Philip's death took another husband (Antiq. xviii. 5, 4). Thus, according to Josephus, the first husband of Herodias was a different person from Philip the tetrarch. The writers of the N. T. agree with Josephus in that they make Herodias' first husband a brother of Herod Antipas the tetrarch, and do not identify him with Philip the tetrarch, whom they also know (Luke iii. 1). They differ as to his name. It is commonly believed that both authorities are right, and accordingly the first husband of Herodias is often designated Herod Philip. For among the children of Herod the Great two sons, born of different mothers, were named after Herod's father Antipas or Antipater. Three

of his sons, born of three different mothers, were called Herod; one of whom, however, had a second name Antipas, and was spoken of indifferently either as Herod or Antipas (Antiq. xvii. 1, 3; xviii. 5, 1; 6, 2). One of the sons whom his wife Cleopatra of Jerusalem bore was called Philip; and it is probable that Mariamne's son, who is called Herod by Josephus, had the name of Philip also. Herod Philip, after the execution of his half-brothers Alexander and Aristobulus, was next in order of birth to Antipater, Herod the Great's firstborn, and for a time he was recognized as next in succession to the throne (Antiq. xvii. 3, 2); but he was passed over in Herod's later wills.

5. Philip the Tetrarch. One of the two sons of Herod the Great and Cleopatra of Jerusalem. He was brought up at Rome with his half-brothers Archelaus and Antipas (Antiq. xvii. 1, 3; War i. 28, 4). In A. D. 4 he advocated the claims of Archelaus to succeed their common father, and was himself appointed by the emperor Augustus to be over Batanea, Trachonitis, Auranitis, and certain parts of Zeno's house about Jamnia (War ii. 6, 1–3; cp. Antiq. xvii. 11, 4). He was still tetrarch of the region of Ituræa and Trachonitis in the fifteenth year of Tiberius Cæsar when John the Baptist began his public life (Luke iii. 1). He married Salome, the daughter of Herod, Mariamne's son, and Herodias (Antiq. xviii. 5, 4). He enlarged the town of Paneas, at the source of the Jordan, and named it Cæsarea. It was afterwards often spoken of as Cæsarea Philippi (Mat. xvi. 13), to distinguish it from Cæsarea on the sea. He also raised the village of Bethsaida to the dignity of a city and called it Julias, in honor of Julia, daughter of Augustus and wife of Tiberius (Antiq. xviii. 2, 1; War ii. 9, 1). He reigned thirty-seven years, from 4 B. C. to A. D. 33, dying in the twentieth year of Tiberius Cæsar. His character was excellent, and his rule was mild and just (Antiq. xviii. 4, 6). His dominions were annexed to the province of Syria, but in A. D. 37 were assigned to Herod Agrippa I. Coins of his have been found inscribed with his title, *Tetrarchos*.

6. Philip the Apostle. One of the twelve apostles (Mat. x. 3). His home was in Bethsaida, on the sea of Galilee, and he was a fellow-townsman of Andrew and Peter. Jesus met him at Bethany beyond the Jordan, where John was baptizing, won his faith, and called him to be a disciple. He found Nathanael and brought him to Jesus, in the conviction that an interview with the Master would convince Nathanael that Jesus was the Messiah. His confidence was justified (John i. 43–48). A year later Jesus chose him to be an apostle. When our Lord was about to perform the miracle of feeding the five thousand, he first proved Philip, and awoke a conception of the magnitude of the miracle by asking Philip: "Whence

are we to buy bread, that these may eat?" (John vi. 5, 6). On the day of the triumphal entry into Jerusalem, certain Greeks desired to see Jesus, and applied to Philip, who put them in communication with Jesus (xii. 20–23). In making the acquaintance of Christ, the disciples had been making acquaintance with the Father; but when Christ spoke to them about their having known and seen the Father, Philip appeared not to understand and said: "Show us the Father, and it sufficeth us" (xiv. 8–12). He is named after the resurrection as one of the apostles who met in the upper chamber (Acts i. 13). This is the last authentic notice we have of him, ecclesiastical traditions regarding his future life being confused and contradictory.

7. Philip the Evangelist. He was one of the seven men of good report, full of the Spirit and of wisdom, chosen to be deacons to look after the interests of the Greek-speaking widows and probably the poor generally in the church at Jerusalem, and is mentioned next in order to the martyr Stephen (Acts vi. 5). Persecution followed the death of Stephen, and the Christians were scattered abroad. Philip became an evangelist. He visited Samaria, preached the gospel, wrought miracles, and made many converts (viii. 4–8; xxi. 8). Among them was Simon the sorcerer, popularly known as Simon Magus (viii. 9–25). Afterwards, by direction of an angel, Philip went along the road from Jerusalem to Gaza, on which, after a time, he met, preached to, and baptized the Ethiopian eunuch (26–39). He afterwards visited Azotus (Ashdod), and then went on preaching till he reached Cæsarea (40). He was still in that city years afterwards when Paul passed through it on his last journey to Jerusalem; and the fact is noted that Philip had four virgin daughters who had the gift of prophecy (xxi. 8, 9).

Phi-lip'pi [pertaining to Philip].
A Macedonian city, called originally Krenides or place of small fountains. It was within the limits of ancient Thrace, but in 356 B. C. Philip II. of Macedon annexed the country as far as the river Nestus and thus took in the town, which he enlarged and strengthened and called after his own name. In its vicinity were rich gold and silver mines, the produce of which greatly aided Philip in carrying out his ambitious projects. In 168 B. C. the Roman consul Paulus Æmilius inflicted a decisive and very sanguinary defeat on Perseus, the last of the Macedonian kings; and Philippi, with the rest of the territory, fell into the hands of the victors. In 42 B. C. two decisive battles took place in the neighborhood between Brutus and Cassius, two of Cæsar's leading assassins, and Octavian and Antony, his chief avengers. After Octavian had become Augustus Cæsar he took an interest in

the place where he had gained the victory, and sent a Roman colony to Philippi. Not merely does Luke mention that it was a colony (Acts xvi. 12), but coins exist with the inscription, *Colonia Augusta, Jul. Philippensis.* It was the first city of the district; not the capital, which was Amphipolis, but either the place of first importance or the first city reached by a traveler from the sea, Neapolis belonging to Thrace and not being attached to the Roman province of Macedonia until the time of Vespasian. About A. D. 52 Paul visited the city, making various converts, of whom the chief were Lydia of Thyatira, the damsel possessed with the spirit of divination, and the Philippian jailer (Acts xvi. 12-40). The second of these successes had brought on persecution and imprisonment of the evangelists or they would not have had access to the jailer to do him spiritual good (1 Thess. ii. 2). Paul had to leave the place abruptly on this occasion, but he visited it again at a future period, sailing thence to Syria (Acts xx. 6). Philippi lies inland about 10 miles northwest of its seaport Neapolis, the two being separated by a mountain range, the pass over which is about 1600 feet above the sea level. At first Philippi was confined to a small hill rising from the midst of a plain; in the Roman period it extended to the plain. The riverside was the bank of the Gangites, now called Angista, along the shore of which the walls of the Roman city ran. The ruins, consisting of a theater, columns, etc., are extensive, the most interesting being a gateway, supposed to be that by which the apostle went out to the riverside. No one now lives on the spot, but there is a Turkish village, named Bereketli, in the immediate vicinity.

Phi-lip'pi-ans.

The natives or inhabitants of Philippi (Phil. iv. 15).

The Epistle of Paul to the Philippians is the sixth of the epistles as they are arranged in our N. T. It was written by Paul, associating also Timothy with him, to all the saints in Christ Jesus which are at Philippi, with the bishops and deacons (i. 1); a Christian community of which Paul himself had gathered the nucleus, and the first one of the churches which he had founded in Europe. When Paul wrote the epistle, he was a prisoner (i. 7, 13, 14, 16). But where, in Cæsarea or in Rome? He was apparently in the custody of the prætorian guard (i. 13, R. V.), and he sends salutations from the saints that are of Cæsar's household (iv. 22). Many about him were actively engaged in propagating Christianity (i. 14-18). These references, as well as the whole tone of the letter, make it clear that the epistle was written from Rome during the apostle's first Roman imprisonment; see PAUL. It is also most probably to be dated toward the close

of that period, in A. D. 62 or 63. This follows from several facts. 1. He had been for some time in Rome (i. 12). 2. He was expecting his release (i. 25; ii. 23, 24). 3. The Philippians had sent him a gift (iv. 10) by the hands of Epaphroditus (ii. 25); Epaphroditus, however, had been taken sick in Rome, the Philippians had heard of it, and Epaphroditus had learned of their sorrow over his illness (ii. 26). A considerable time, therefore, had elapsed since Paul had reached the capital.

The epistle was written primarily to acknowledge the gift which the Philippians had sent to Paul. Contrary to his custom, he had more than once received such gifts from them (iv. 15). But the apostle also seized the opportunity to tell them about himself and to warn them against error. It is the letter of a pastor to his flock. It was not called forth, like many of his epistles, by any crisis in the church. It abounds in spiritual advice for the Christian life. At the same time it is valuable for the light it throws on Paul's situation in Rome. It was sent by the hand of Epaphroditus (ii. 25, 30) who, having recovered from his illness, was about to return to Philippi. It may be divided into the following sections: 1. Introduction (i. 1, 2). 2. Gratitude for their fidelity; expression of his love for them; prayer for their sanctification (i. 3-11). 3. Account of how God had used him, though a prisoner, to extend the gospel; of the opposition to him on the part of some, but of his own contentment; of his wish at times to die, but of his devotion to them and confidence that he would be spared to them; and of his earnest desire that they might stand firm (i. 12-30). 4. Appeal to them for spiritual unity, through self-forgetfulness and love, after the example of Christ, that they may perfect the work of service which he had ever set before them (ii. 1-18). 5. Promise to send to them Timothy and, if possible, to go himself shortly; meanwhile he will send Epaphroditus (ii. 19-30). 6. Exhortation to joyfully pursue the Christian life, based on his own joy in self-surrender to Christ and in the eager pursuit of the reward which Christ offers; to which he adds a warning against those who misuse the freedom of the gospel that they may indulge their fleshly appetites (iii.). 7. Concluding exhortations to individuals and to all, the keynotes of which are joy, contentment, holiness (iv. 1-9). 8. Final acknowledgment of the gift they had sent him and of his joy in their love, with a few parting salutations (10-23). G. T. P. (edited).

The unity of the epistle has been questioned. Polycarp, who was a disciple of the apostle John, in a letter to the Philippians, written between A. D. 110 and 115, casually alludes to Paul as having written letters to them (Polycarp iii. 2, "who also wrote you letters"); and accordingly the attempt has been made to establish the existence of two letters joined together in the epistle as it now exists, united for example at iii. 1, the second and earlier letter consisting of iii. 2-iv. 23. The genuineness of each of the two hypothetical letters is, of course, a part of the theory. The words of Polycarp are, however, misunderstood; for he apparently knew the epistle in its present form only, and the plural letters was a common usage instead of the less vivid singular. Moreover, the efforts that have been made to partition the epistle, either at iii. 1 or elsewhere, have not been regarded as successful by the jury of scholars. The epistle as it stands yields a satisfactory analysis. Abrupt transitions from personal to general matters, or the introduction of a new thought when the writer seemed about to close, as at the beginning of chapter iii., are common in letters of personal correspondence, such as this epistle is (cp. EPISTLE).

Phi-lis'ti-a [land of foreigners or immigrants].

A word occurring in poetical passages of the O. T. (Ps. lx. 8; lxxxvii. 4; and R. V. of Is. xiv. 29), and meaning the land of the Philistines. It was mainly that part of the maritime plain of Canaan which lies between Joppa and Gaza, approximately fifty miles in length and fifteen in breadth. The greater portion is very fertile, bearing heavy crops of grain, as well as oranges, figs, olives, and other fruits. The coast line has a row of sand dunes, and the sand continually encroaches on the cultivated districts. Of the five dominant towns (Josh. xiii. 3; 1 Sam. vi. 17) three, Gaza, Ashkelon, and Ashdod, were on the coast, Ekron about six miles inland, and Gath was situated among the hills of the lowland. All were walled.

Phi-lis'tines.

A people mentioned in Gen. x. 14, and tabulated with descendants of Mizraim; in other words, as belonging to Egypt. They went forth from the Casluhim, and were a remnant of the isle or seacoast of Caphtor (Jer. xlvii. 4; Amos ix. 7); see CAPHTOR. Probably they were Cretans. The country near Gaza was inhabited first by the Avvim, but settlers from Caphtor destroyed these aborigines and dwelt in their room (Deut. ii. 23). Philistines were in the region about Gerar and Beer-sheba as early as the time of Abraham (Gen. xxi. 32, 34; xxvi. 1, unless the name is here used proleptically). In the 15th century B. C. tribesmen from the northern coast of the Mediterranean were found in Canaan, e. g., the Sherdanu and Danunu (el-Amarna tablets); and later from the same region a great migration of clans, including the Purasati, i. e. Philistines, took place, moving eastward and southward by land and sea to the very borders of Egypt, where it was stopped by the army of Ramses III, in the third year of his reign, about 1192 B. C.;

but settlements of these people remained along the coast (see DOR). For travelers leaving Egypt the shortest way into Canaan was along the coast; but after the desert was passed the road was flanked by the fortified towns of Gaza, Ashkelon, Ashdod, and Ekron. At the exodus from Egypt the tribes of Israel, migrating with their women, children, and cattle, were ill prepared for war and might well hesitate to fight their way; and they were directed to go by another route (Ex. xiii. 17, 18). A generation later Joshua, with an army under his command, did not attack the cities on the coast or Gath in the lowland (Josh. xiii. 2, 3; Judg. iii. 3). But the tribe of Judah, when it settled in its allotted territory, took Gaza, Ashkelon, and Ekron (i. 18). Shamgar slew 600 Philistines with an oxgoad (iii. 31). Not long after this Israel, on account of its idolatries, was sold into the hands of the Philistines (x. 6, 7). They were delivered (11), but sinning again came under the same domination for forty years. From this they were delivered by Samson, but the Philistines ultimately proved his ruin (xiv.-xvi.). Early in Samuel's public life they defeated the Israelites, slaying, among others, Hophni and Phinehas, Eli's sons, and capturing the ark of God (1 Sam. iv.-vi.). Twenty years later Samuel defeated them in battle at the same place, which he called Ebenezer, the stone of help, because Jehovah had helped him there (vii. 3-12). It was an overwhelming defeat. The Philistines were permanently humbled, and came no more within the border of Israel. Their army often crossed that border, and intrenched itself in strong positions, and a Philistine invasion was a constant menace. But the Israelites had recovered their border from Ekron to Gath, regaining possession of the Shephelah or lowland, and the Philistines did not again dispossess them (vii. 13, 14). The power of the Philistines was formidable during the reign of Saul (x. 5; xii. 9; xiv. 52), but he and his son Jonathan smote them at Geba and Michmash (xiii. 1-xiv. 31). They soon appeared again within the territory of Judah, near Socoh; but fled when their champion Goliath was slain (xvii. 1-58; xviii. 6; xix. 5; xxi. 9; xxii. 10). Saul and David had various encounters with them (xviii. 27, 30; xix. 8; xxiii. 1-5, 27, 28); but at length to escape Saul David twice sought refuge in their country (xxi. 10-15; xxvii.-xxix.; Ps. lvi. title). On the second occasion the king of Gath placed the town of Ziklag under David's authority (1 Sam. xxvii. 6). The Philistines had penetrated to the very heart of Canaan when they defeated the Israelites on mount Gilboa and slew Saul and his sons (xxviii. 4; xxix. 11; xxxi. 1-13; 1 Chron. x. 1-14). David, when king, repelled invasions of the Philistines and also fought against them in their own country (2 Sam. iii. 18; v. 17-25; viii. 1; xix. 9; xxi. 15-22; xxiii. 9-17; 1 Chron. xi. 13; xviii. 1; xx.

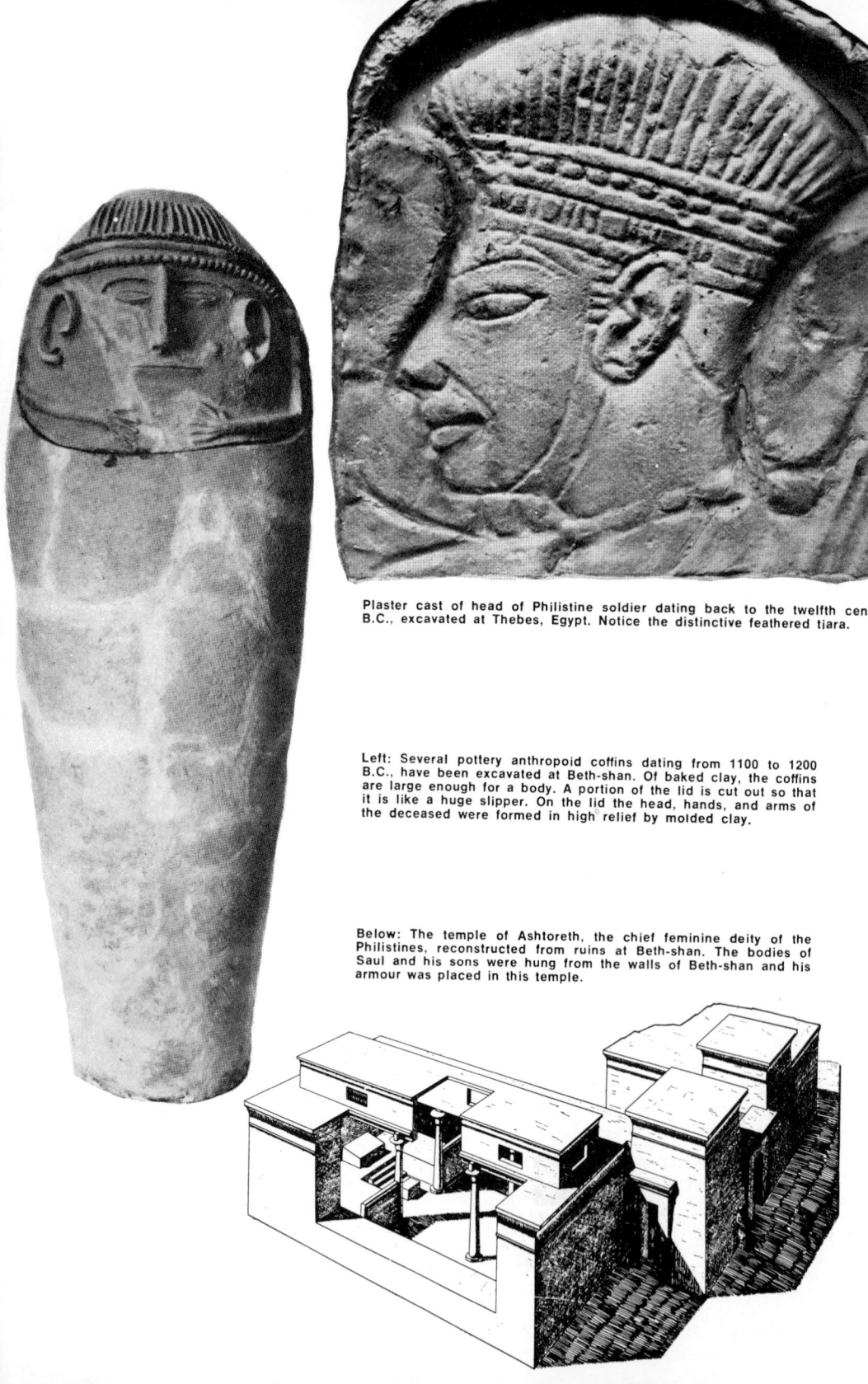

Plaster cast of head of Philistine soldier dating back to the twelfth century B.C., excavated at Thebes, Egypt. Notice the distinctive feathered tiara.

Left: Several pottery anthropoid coffins dating from 1100 to 1200 B.C., have been excavated at Beth-shan. Of baked clay, the coffins are large enough for a body. A portion of the lid is cut out so that it is like a huge slipper. On the lid the head, hands, and arms of the deceased were formed in high relief by molded clay.

Below: The temple of Ashtoreth, the chief feminine deity of the Philistines, reconstructed from ruins at Beth-shan. The bodies of Saul and his sons were hung from the walls of Beth-shan and his armour was placed in this temple.

Examples of Philistine pottery. Philistine pottery was usually
elaborately decorated with metopes enclosing stylized birds,
usually with a back-turned head. They also commonly have friezes
of spirals and groups of interlocking semi-circles. The large jug
has a strainer spout used to separate the barley husks from the
beer and to prevent the user from swallowing the barley husks.
The discovery of an extensive number of these jugs and similar
wine craters has led more than one archaeologist to conclude that
the Philistines were "mighty carousers."

The mound of Beth-shan has revealed very important remains of Philistine culture. The lowest
level reached by excavators dates from about the fourteenth century B.C. Beth-shan was held by
the Philistines during the time of Saul.

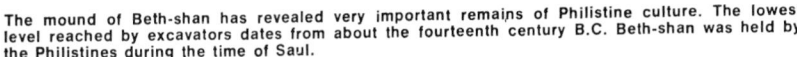

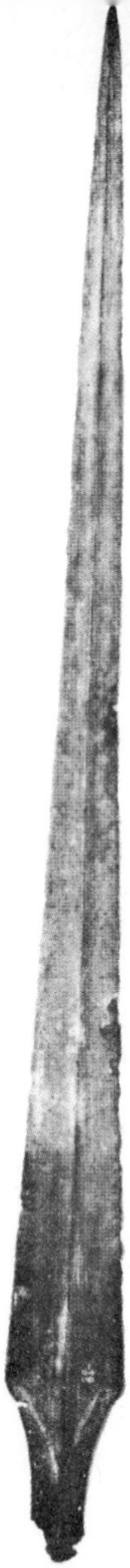

Map Labels

Eben-ezer

Tell Qasileh · Aphek

ISRAEL

Joppa · Azor

Baal-hazor

Bethel · Ophrah

Mizpah

Gibbethon Beth-horon · Michmash

Jabneel · Gibeon · Ramah

Gezer

Ekron Aijalon Gibeah · △ Geba

Timnah Eshtaol Kiriath-jearim · Nob

Zorah Jebus

Ashdod Beth-shemesh △ Beth-lehem

Azekah Beth-zur

Ashkelon Gath Sochoh · Tekoa

PHILISTINES Adullum

Libnah Keilah

· Lachish ⊙ Hebron En-gedi

Eglon **JUDAH** · Ziph

⊙ Gaza Debir · Carmel

Yurza Ziklag?

Gerar Masada

· Sharuhen

· Beer-sheba

Peculiar to the Philistines was
the use of huge broadswords.
This bronze shardana broad-
sword, length 1.07 m, was
recovered from Beit Dagin,
near Jaffa-Tel-Aviv.

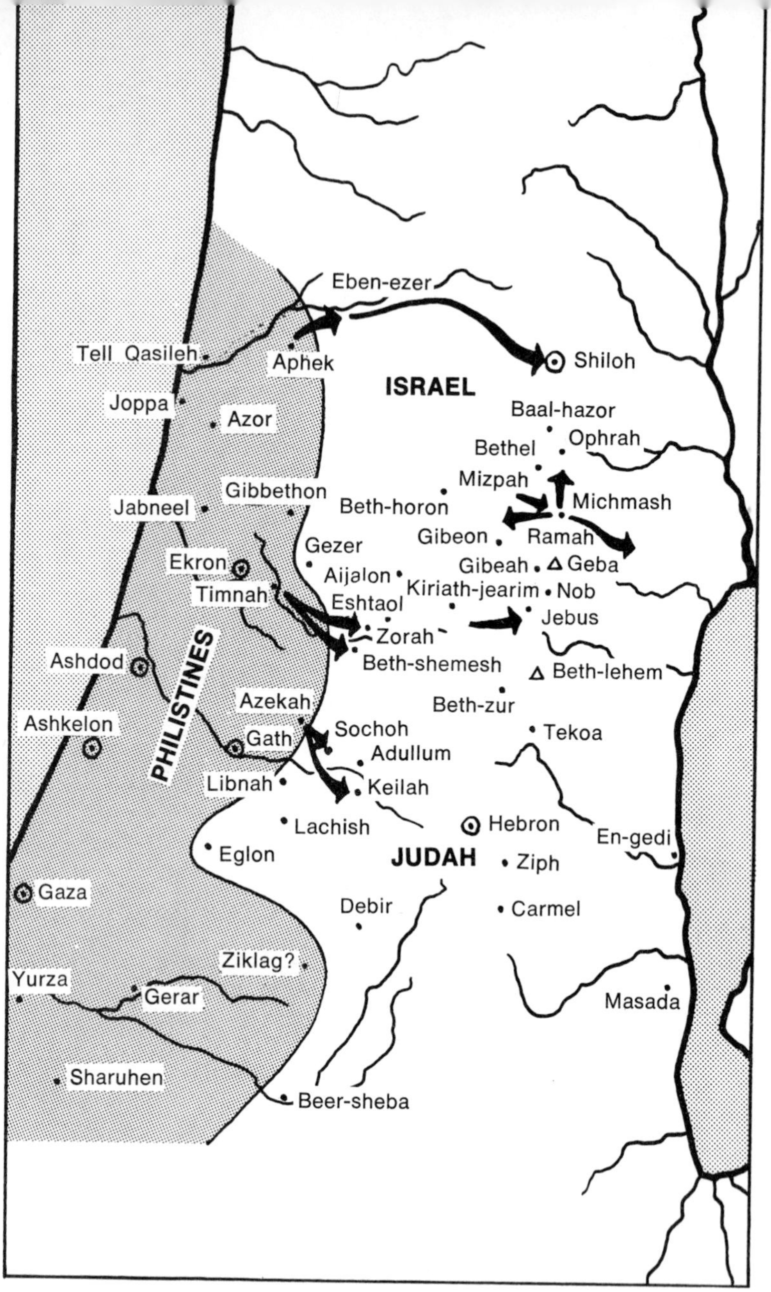

Philistine cities and areas of expansion.

Representation at Medinet Habu of Egyptians battling the invading "Peoples of the
Sea" or Philistines. Note the use of ox carts, broad swords, and round shields, typical
of Aegean peoples.

4, 5). After his death the Philistines are less frequently mentioned, as if their power was waning. Under Nadab, the son of Jeroboam I., and some other short-lived kings, the Israelites besieged Gibbethon, a Philistine city (1 Kin. xv. 27; xvi. 15). The Philistines sent presents to Jehoshaphat (2 Chron. xvii. 11); but they invaded Judah in the reign of his successor, Jehoram (xxi. 16), and also in that of Ahaz (xxviii. 18). Uzziah and Hezekiah successfully invaded Philistia (2 Kin. xviii. 8; 2 Chron. xxvi. 6, 7). Judgment against them is frequently threatened by the prophets (Is. xi. 14; Jer. xxv. 20; xlvii. 1–7; Ezek. xxv. 15–17; Amos i. 6–8; Obad. 19; Zeph. ii. 4, 5; Zech. ix. 5–7). Many Philistines accompanied Gorgias, the Syrian general of Antiochus Epiphanes, in his invasion of Judah (1 Mac. iii. 41). Judas Maccabæus afterwards captured Azotus (Ashdod) and other Philistine cities (v. 68). Jonathan Maccabæus burnt Azotus, with the temple of Dagon, and the city of Ashkelon (x. 83–89). He also burnt the suburbs of Gaza, but took no further hostile measures, as the city itself was surrendered on his demand (xi. 60, 61). The Philistines are not mentioned by name in the N. T., and seem ultimately to have merged in the Jewish nation.

The Mediterranean is once called the sea of the Philistines (Ex. xxiii. 31).

Phi-lol'o-gus [fond of words].

A Christian at Rome, apparently the head of a Christian household (Rom. xvi. 15).

Phi-los'o-phy [love of wisdom].

The spirit of pure philosophy, which seeks to penetrate to the essence of things in themselves, is foreign to the Eastern mind. The great distinction between Eastern and Western philosophy has been historically that oriental reasoning remained in the sphere of religion and was never divorced from religious axioms, while occidental investigation came to be conducted, even by profoundly religious minds, in a far wider sphere than religion and by the reason unassisted by the postulates of religion. Moral philosophy has characterized the East, metaphysics the West. For the biblical student the contrast between Greek and Hebrew thought, their separate development, their eventual contact, and their mutual influence are important. The Hebrew mind reflected on the view of the world which is presented by revelation. It drew wisdom from the experience of former generations, which was handed down by the ancients, from observation of human life and the results of conduct, and from the study of the adaptations of nature to an end. It thus gained true principles for the government of conduct, it sought to discover to what extent religious truth was approved by the test of human experience, and it wrestled with the paradoxes of the moral government of God, especially with the question of the

sufferings of the righteous and the prosperity of the wicked. From these varied sources and manifold investigations the Hebrew wise man was confirmed in the conviction that the fear of God is the beginning of wisdom. Hebrew philosophy, or wisdom as the Bible calls it, received a great impulse through the interest of Solomon, who both gathered the maxims of other men, and out of his own shrewd observation and varied experience gave utterance to new proverbs. The proverbs of Solomon largely concern conduct in relation to the individual and to God, such as chastity, temperance in meat and drink, self-control, honesty, suretyship, behavior in the presence of the mighty. From these things Hebrew thought proceeded to view morality in larger relations. From the consideration of apparent exceptions to its conclusions, it advanced to moral questions, and looked upon events not in their immediate personal results, but in the light of their effect upon posterity and of divine retribution in time to come. The Hebrew philosopher further studied nature, and saw that a divine purpose exists everywhere (Ps. civ. 24). Everywhere is the impress of thought. Intelligence is involved in the creation and preservation of the universe (Prov. iii. 19). He found wisdom to be an attribute of God, which is everywhere revealed in nature. It existed before God proceeded to create. He personified wisdom (Prov. i. 20–33; viii. 12), and represented it existing from everlasting, as brought forth before the creation of the world, present with God when he established heaven and earth, ordained to rule in the created universe (viii. 22–31; Job xxviii. 12–27). Wisdom was not itself a person, but it was looked upon as objective to God, as "the reflection of God's plan of the world," as the principle which God ordained for the world. By later writers the thought was developed and wisdom was still further distinguished from God (Wisd. vii. 22–viii. 5; ix. 4, 9); see WISDOM.

Greek philosophy is usually said to begin with Thales about 640 B. C. Three main periods are distinguished: 1. The pre-Socratic schools which arose among the Greek colonies of Asia Minor. The great subject of inquiry was the constitution of the universe. Is there one underlying element; such as moisture, or the subtle and all-pervading air, or one eternal, infinite, immovable, unchangeable Being, or the instantaneous balance of power? 2. The Socratic schools represented by Socrates, Plato, and Aristotle, 469–322 B. C. Athens was the center of philosophic thought, and inquiry was directed to ideas, form (or essence) of things. But it was not a barren metaphysics that was cultivated; a lofty morality was inculcated. Socrates used inductive reasoning by which he sought to discover the permanent element underlying the changing forms of appearances and opinions; and the truth which he thus discovered he attempted to fix by a general definition or statement. Aristotle allowed absolute authority to the reason alone, and accepted nothing which he could not prove by logic. 3. The post-Socratic schools. Philosophy had culminated in Aristotle, and discussion reverted to ethics founded on metaphysics. Epicurus, 342–270 B. C., declared that the character of actions is determined by their result, and that permanent pleasure is the highest good. Zeno the Stoic, about 308 B. C., taught that moral character resides in the act itself, independent of the result; and inculcated the obligation of absolute obedience to the commands of duty. The Skeptics taught that certainty is not attainable in human knowledge; and early members of the school held that when we are convinced that we can know nothing, we cease to care, and in this way attain happiness.

Alexander the Great died in 323 B. C., and Aristotle in 322. Thus when Greek philosophy had reached its climax, Greek culture began to be introduced into Palestine and among the Jews of the dispersion. Epicureanism and Stoicism were developed in Greece during the period of the first close contact of Greek and Hebrew, but they exercised little influence on Hebrew thought compared with the power exerted by Plato and Aristotle. The influence of the Socratic schools was seen in the Sadducees perhaps, who seem like Aristotle to have rejected everything which unaided reason did not teach, although they professed to be governed by a different principle. The influence of the Socratic schools was seen in the Alexandrian school of Jewish thinkers, whose prominent representative was Philo, a contemporary of Christ. They held to the teaching of Moses; but at the same time they took what they approved of in Greek philosophy, learning especially from divine Plato, and endeavored to show that it was already taught in the O. T. They combined the doctrines of the Greek sage and of Moses into a new system, and removed inconsistencies by arbitrarily allegorizing Scripture, even down to its geography. The influence of the Greek philosophy was seen in the improved methods and enlarged scope of debate. Paul advances a formal philosophic argument in his address in the midst of the Areopagus and in the beginning of his Epistle to the Romans (Acts xvii. 30; Rom. i. 19, 20). The influence of Greek philosophy was seen further in borrowed ideas, such as the preëxistence of the soul (Wisdom viii. 19, 20); in new words and new content of words, as in the use of the word form in the Aristotelian sense of essence or sum total of attributes (Phil. ii. 6); and in nice discrimination of thought and precision of definition. Gnostic speculations later came from the East; and the attempt to combine Gnosticism with Christianity led Paul to combat it by presenting the true relation of Christ to God and the world in the Epistle to the Colossians.

Phin'e-has, in A. V. of 1 Mac. **Phinees** [perhaps Egyptian, *pa-nehsi*, the negro (Petrie)]. A Hebrew etymology is not apparent.

1. Son of Eleazar, and grandson of Aaron (Ex. vi. 25). He ran a spear through an Israelite and a Midianite woman who had come into the camp at Shittim together, this summary punishment terminating a plague which was then raging as a judgment against the idolatries and impurities into which the Midianitish women were leading the Hebrews. An everlasting priesthood was therefore promised to him and his descendants (Num. xxv. 1-18; Ps. cvi. 30; 1 Mac. ii. 54). With a short interruption when the house of Eli, of the lineage of Ithamar, officiated as high priests, Phinehas and his sons held the office until sacrifice ceased with the destruction of Jerusalem and the temple by the Romans in A. D. 70. Phinehas went as priest with the army on the punitive expedition against the Midianites (Num. xxxi. 6), and was sent with ten princes to remonstrate with the tribes east of the Jordan on their erection of an altar, erroneously supposed to be for schismatic worship (Josh. xxii. 13). He received as his share of the promised land a hill in mount Ephraim (xxiv. 33). Through him the Israelites inquired of the Lord whether they should attack the Benjamites for condoning the sin of the inhabitants of Gibeah (Judg. xx. 28).

2. The younger of Eli's two degenerate sons. He was killed in the battle with the Philistines in which the ark of God was taken; and when the news of the catastrophe arrived, they so affected the feelings of his wife that the pains of premature childbirth came upon her, and she died (1 Sam. i. 3; ii. 34; iv. 11, 19-22).

3. Father of a certain Eleazar (Ezra viii. 33), evidently a priest.

Phle'gon [burning, scorching].

A Christian at Rome to whom Paul sent his salutation (Rom. xvi. 14).

Phœ'be, in A. V. **Phebe** [pure, bright, radiant].

A servant or deaconess of the church at Cenchreæ, the eastern port of Corinth. On her removing to Rome, Paul cordially commended her to the Christians there; for she had been a helper or patron of many, a term which may imply that she made it a duty to stand by foreigners in their civic helplessness (Rom. xvi. 1, 2). See DEACONESS.

Phœ-ni'ci-a, in A. V. once **Phenicia** (Acts xxi. 2), and twice **Phenice** (xi. 19; xv. 3) [Greek, land of the date palm, or of purple dyeing, or of dark skinned people].

A narrow strip of territory between the Mediterranean Sea on the west and on the east the crest of the Lebanon range and the detached hills running south from it. The northern limit may be regarded as Arvad. Southward, after the settlement of the He-

brews on the coast, Phœnicia practically
terminated at the Ladder of Tyre, about 14
miles south of Tyre, although Phœnicians
still dwelt in Achzib and Accho (Judg. i. 31).
In the time of Christ Phœnicia extended
southward as far as Dor, about 16 miles south
of Carmel. The distance from Arvad to the
Ladder of Tyre is about 125 miles. The
chief cities were Tyre and Sidon, of which
Sidon was the first to rise to celebrity. Phœnicia was called Canaan by the ancient Hebrews (Is. xxiii. 11), and its inhabitants were
reckoned as Canaanites and classed with the
Hamitic peoples (Gen. x. 15). This classification makes probable, but does not necessarily imply, that they were of Hamitic
blood. According to their own tradition,
they had migrated from the Erythræan Sea,
by way of Syria, to the coast of Canaan
(Herod. i. 1; vii. 89). According to Arabian
authors, the migration was across the northern Arabian desert. The Phœnicians thus
traced their origin to the neighborhood of
the Persian Gulf, an early abode of the Hamitic race. In course of time they adopted
the Semitic language. The territory which
the Phœnicians inhabited had good natural
harbors; mount Lebanon afforded them an
almost inexhaustible supply of timber, with
which ships were constructed, and they became the most skillful navigators known to
antiquity. They not merely traded with distant countries accessible by Mediterranean
routes, but they colonized spots favorable for
commerce, some of which afterwards rose
into importance. Their most celebrated
colony was Carthage, on the African coast,
near modern Tunis, which was long a rival
of Rome, by which it was at last destroyed.
Of the Carthaginian leaders who figured in
the Punic wars, some, if not all, had names
purely Phœnician, and almost Hebrew.
Thus, Hannibal means the grace of Baal,
and Hasdrubal, a help is Baal. When our
Lord visited the coasts of Tyre and Sidon, he
was within the Phœnician territory (Mat.
xv. 21; Mark vii. 24, 31). Various Christians
who were scattered abroad, owing to the persecution which followed the martyrdom of
Stephen, found their way to Phœnicia (Acts
xi. 19). Paul and Barnabas went through it
on their way from Antioch to Jerusalem (xv.
3). Paul, on his last voyage to Jerusalem,
sailed in a Phœnician vessel, which brought
him to Tyre (xxi. 2, 3). See TYRE, BAAL,
JEZEBEL, and HIRAM.

Phœ'nix, in A. V. **Phe-ni'ce** [date palm].
A haven in Crete (Acts xxvii. 12), safe
throughout the year because the entrance to
its harbor opens toward the northeast and
southeast (R. V., cp. text and margin). It is
now called Lutro, and is the only harbor on
the south of Crete which is safe at every
season of the year.

Phryg'i-a.
A large and important province of Asia

Minor, which, after its original boundaries
were curtailed by the disseverance from it
of Galatia, was bounded on the north by
Bithynia; on the south by Lycia, Pisidia,
and Isauria; on the east by Lycaonia and
Galatia; and on the west by Caria, Lydia,
and Mysia. The region is a high table-land between the chain of Taurus on the south, Olympus on the north, and Temnus on the west. Of
its towns, four are mentioned in the N. T.,
Laodicea, Colossæ, Hierapolis, and Antioch of
Pisidia, which is reckoned by Strabo to
Phrygia. At this period Phrygia had ceased
to be a province and was merely a local
name. Antiochus the Great settled 2000
Jewish families from Babylonia and Mesopotamia in Lydia and Phrygia (Antiq. xii. 3,
4), and Jews from Phrygia were present at
Jerusalem on that day of Pentecost signalized by the descent of the Holy Spirit (Acts
ii. 10). Phrygia was traversed by Paul on
his second and third missionary journeys
(Acts xvi. 6; xviii. 23).

Phu'rah. See PURAH.

Phut. See PUT.

Phu'vah. See PUVAH.

Phyg'e-lus, in A. V. **Phy-gel'lus**.
A Christian in the province of Asia who,
with others, deserted the apostle Paul in the
latter part of his life (2 Tim. i. 15).

Phy-lac'te-ry [a safeguard, an amulet].
A prayer band consisting of short extracts
from the law of Moses, and worn on the forehead or on the arm (Mat. xxiii. 5). The
phylactery eventually assumed the form of
a small case, made of parchment or black
sealskin. The one for the forehead contained four compartments, in each of which
was placed a strip of parchment inscribed
with a passage of Scripture. The four passages were Ex. xiii. 2-10, 11-17; Deut. vi.
4-9; xi. 13-21. It was fastened with straps
on the forehead, just above and between the
eyes. The other case, which was bound on
the left arm, contained but one compartment, in which a strip of parchment was
placed bearing the same four quotations from
the law. The first three of these were interpreted as enjoining the custom, but are
rather to be understood figuratively (see
FRONTLET). Phylacteries are worn by every
male Jew during the time of morning prayer,
except on the Sabbath and festivals, which
days are themselves signs and render phylacteries unnecessary (cp. Ex. xiii. 9).

Phy-si'cian. See MEDICINE.

Pi-be'seth [Egyptian, *Pa-bast*, abode of the
goddess Bast].
An Egyptian city (Ezek. xxx. 17), in Greek
form written Bubastos or Bubastis (Herod.
ii. 59, 137). It is now called Tell Basta, and
is on the delta near Zagazig, on the western
side of the Pelusiac branch of the Nile. It
is about 45 miles northeast by north of modern Cairo, and 30 southwest by south of an-

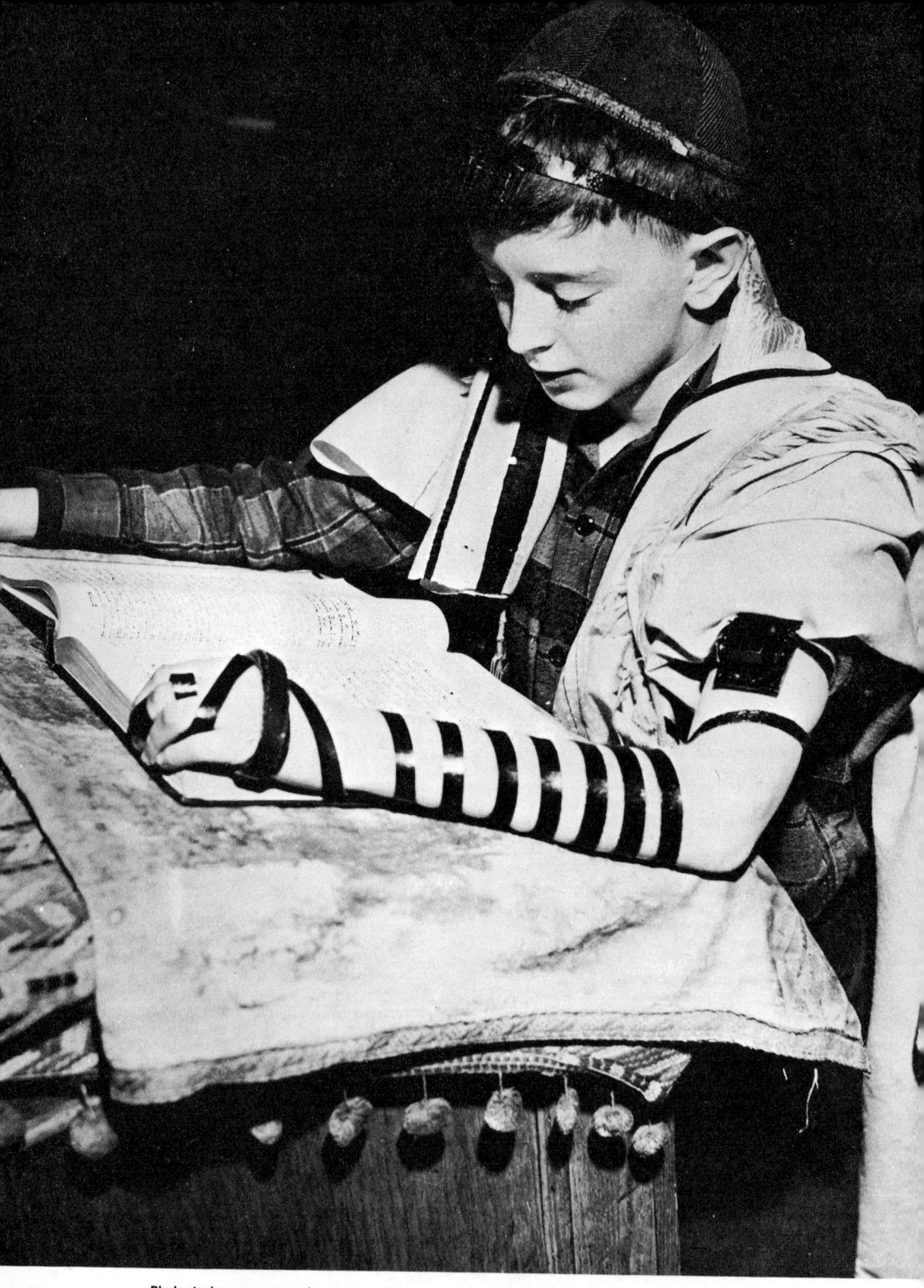

Phylacteries are worn by this thirteen-year-old diligently preparing for his Bar Mizvah.

cient Zoan. Among the ruins are the remains of a once splendid temple of red granite, dedicated to the goddess of the place.

Piece.

In O. T., when piece refers to money and
is not italicized, it denotes a certain amount
of precious metal, whether coined or uncoined (Gen. xxxiii. 19; 1 Sam. ii. 36) The
word piece was chosen by the translators because it is vague, and they did not know the
value of the money indicated by the several
Hebrew words. Piece is also employed by the
translators, where the unit of weight or the
coin is not expressly mentioned by the Hebrew writer, but where he ordinarily means
a shekel (Judg. xvii. 2 ; 2 Sam. xviii. 11, in
A. V. shekel ; cp. Deut. xxii. 19; 1 Kin. x.
29, where both versions have shekel). In N.
T. also a piece of silver commonly denotes
the shekel or its equivalent (Mat. xxvi. 15
with xxvii. 9 and Zech. xi. 12); but in Luke
xv. 8 it is a drachma, worth about 16 cents.

Pi'e-ty.

Filial piety, dutifulness in the family (1
Tim. v. 4).

Pi'geon. See DOVE.

Pi-ha-hi'roth [probably, house or place of
sedge].

The last station of the Israelites on leaving Egypt, near Baal-zephon and Migdol, and
on the sea (Ex. xiv. 2, 9; Num. xxxiii. 7, 8).
The site is disputed. Brugsch regards the
name as Hebrew, which then might mean
mouth of the caverns; and he identifies it
with the Serbonian bog, which the Greeks
called Barathra, and at the bottom of which
they represented the monster Typhon as
lying. But the name is doubtless Egyptian. Keil asserts that it has incontestably been preserved in 'Ajrud, on the
Pilgrim road, about 16 miles northwest of
Suez. But the two names have only one
letter in common. Naville identifies it with
Pikerehet, or Pikeheret, near Pithom (q. v.).
Not merely is there a similarity of sound,
but Pharaoh had a farm there; and the Septuagint, instead of "before Pi-hahiroth," inserts "before the farm." The city was an
important one, which disputed with Pithom
the honor of being the capital of the eighth
nome, or district, of Lower Egypt. Its special deity was Osiris. Naville believes that
it was the same place as Serapiu, or Serapeum,
the only known sanctuary of Osiris in that
region. Two roads ran from it: the one
to Clusma, 9 miles off. the other to Pelusium.

Pi'late [armed with a javelin, or wearing
the *pilus* or felt cap which was worn by a
manumitted slave as the emblem of liberty].

Pontius Pilate, fifth Roman procurator in
Judæa after the deposition of Archelaus in
A. D. 6. See PROCURATOR. Through the in-
fluence of Sejanus he was appointed by the
emperor Tiberius procurator of Judæa about
A. D. 26, in succession to Valerius Gratus.

He arrived in Judæa the same year. He was
accompanied by his wife (Mat. xxvii. 19).
For a long time it was illegal for a Roman
governor who was appointed to a dangerous
province to take his wife with him, but since
the time of Augustus it was permitted (Tacitus, Ann. iii. 33).

Pilate sent a detachment of troops into
Jerusalem by night, carrying with them
their ensigns, which had hitherto always been
left outside the city. On these ensigns were
silver eagles and small images of the emperor, and they gave great offense to the
Jews. Deputations went to Cæsarea, the
official residence of the procurators, to urge
the removal of the ensigns, and Pilate, after
in vain attempting to intimidate the petitioners, was obliged at last to comply with
their request (Antiq. xviii. 3, 1; War ii. 9,
2 and 3). Some time afterwards, taking
the sacred money called Corban, he began to expend it in making an aqueduct
to bring water into Jerusalem from the uplands south of the capital. The Jews considered that this was applying to secular uses
money which had been dedicated to God;
and on Pilate's visiting Jerusalem they beset
his tribunal with much clamor and tumult.
Having been told beforehand that such an
occurrence was likely to happen, he had
taken the precaution of mingling his soldiers
in disguise among the multitude, armed with
sticks, if not with concealed daggers. When
the tumult was at its height he gave them a
signal to attack the rioters with the sticks,
which they did so vigorously that some were
killed, and the rest, fleeing in panic, trampled many of their number to death. The
riot seems not to have been renewed, and
the aqueduct was made; but the affair increased the disfavor with which the people
regarded Pilate (Antiq. xviii. 3, 2; War ii. 9,
4). Pilate attempted to dedicate some gilt
shields in honor of the emperor Tiberius and
place them within Herod's palace at Jerusalem. They were inscribed with the imperial
name, but were without the imperial portrait.
Still they gave offense. The people appealed
to him in vain to forbear. Then the influential men of the city forwarded a petition
to the emperor, who ordered Pilate to take
the shields back again to Cæsarea (Philo,
Legat. ad Caium xxxviii.). In narrating this
event, Philo, or rather Agrippa I., in a letter
which Philo cites, describes Pilate as a man
of inflexible disposition, and merciless, as
well as obstinate. He also says that he feared
they might complain to the emperor about
Pilate in respect to his corruption and his
acts of violence, and his habit of insulting
people, and his cruelty, and his continual
execution of people untried and uncondemned, his never-ending and gratuitous
and most grievous inhumanity. Pilate was
in office when John the Baptist and our
Lord began their respective ministries (Luke
iii. 1). It was the custom of the procurators

to go up to Jerusalem when the immense gatherings took place at the leading Jewish festivals. On these occasions they took up their residence in the palace of Herod. It was probably at one of these that Pilate fell upon the Galilæans, and mingled their blood with their sacrifices (Luke xiii. 1, 2). The Galilæans were a turbulent class of men, prone to misbehave when they came up to the festivals (Antiq. xvii. 10, 2 and 9). There is no reason to believe that Pilate would have treated them as he did unless they had first broken out into riot. It is probable that Herod Antipas took offense at the summary way in which his subjects were slain by Pilate on this occasion; but whatever may have been the origin of the variance between the two, Herod's ill-will was appeased by Pilate's acknowledgment of the tetrarch's jurisdiction in Galilæan affairs (Luke xxiii. 6–12) on the day when our Lord was put to death.

The character of Pilate, which these various incidents of his official career reveal, is seen in his treatment of Jesus also. Pilate was a worldling willing enough to act justly if this could be done consistently with his interests, and to avoid criminal acts provided that this could be done at small cost; but if heavy payment were needed, Pilate was not the man to give it. His secret question to himself was not, What is my duty? but, What is my interest? He acquitted our Lord of evil, was desirous of releasing him, and was aware that justice required that this should be done; but he knew also that it would further increase his unpopularity; so to please the Jewish people, he gave orders to scourge him in whom he had just before declared that he had found no crime. He allowed the Roman soldiers, whom a single word from him would have restrained, to inflict new tortures on the already lacerated body of Jesus, and after many more insults and injuries to the uncomplaining sufferer, finally answered the Jewish clamors for the crucifixion of the Son of God by giving sentence that it should be as they required (Mat. xxvii.; Luke xxiii.).

Pilate's government ended abruptly. A Samaritan impostor promised his countrymen that, if they would go to the top of mount Gerizim, he would show them where Moses had hidden certain golden vessels of the tabernacle. Moses never was at mount Gerizim; he had not crossed the Jordan; yet a deluded multitude gathered at a village at the foot of the mountain in order to go up. Unfortunately they carried arms. Pilate, therefore, seized all the ways to Gerizim with horsemen and foot soldiers, attacked the mass of the professed treasure-seekers, slew many, and made prisoners of others and sent them to execution. The Samaritans forwarded a complaint against Pilate to his immediate superior, Vitellius, president of Syria. Vitellius appointed a new procurator,

and ordered Pilate to proceed to Rome to answer to the emperor for his conduct. Before Pilate arrived Tiberius had died, March 16th, A. D. 37 (Antiq. xviii. 4, 1 and 2). It is reported that Pilate was banished to Vienne, on the Rhone, in the south of France, and ultimately committed suicide.

Various *Acta Pilati*, Acts of Pilate, are extant, but no two of them agree, and all are considered to be spurious.

Pil'dash.
A son of Nahor and Milcah (Gen. xxii. 22).

Pil'ha, in A. V. **Pil'e-ha** [a slice, plowing].
One of those who with Nehemiah sealed the covenant (Neh. x. 24).

Pill.
To take the skin or rind off, to peel (Gen. xxx. 38, R. V. peel).

Pil'lar.
1. A stone erected as a sign of the holiness of a place (Gen. xxviii. 18), as a memorial of some person or event (xxxi. 45; Josh. iv. 5–9; 1 Sam. vii. 12; 2 Sam. xviii. 18; and see GARRISON), or as a representative of parties present (Ex. xxiv. 4). Isaiah prophesied that the time is coming when the converts to the true faith in Egypt shall erect an altar and a pillar to the Lord (Is. xix. 19), as Abraham and Jacob did of old in Canaan. The pillar was used by the heathen. The Canaanites erected pillars in connection with the worship of Baal. The Israelites were strictly enjoined, in the oldest legislation, to break them and overthrow the altars (Ex. xxiii. 24, R. V.), and they were forbidden to erect similar pillars beside the altar of the Lord (Deut. xvi. 22). Pillars, however, found favor among the degenerate Israelites of the northern kingdom (Hos. iii. 4; x. 1, 2), and even in Judah (Mic. v. 13, R. V.).
2. A support, much used in ancient architecture for upholding roofs and curtains (Ex. xxvi. 32; Judg. xvi. 26). The earth and the heavens were often spoken of poetically as supported by pillars (1 Sam. ii. 8; Job. ix. 6; xxvi. 11). Strong men and fundamental principles are figuratively called pillars (Gal. ii. 9; 1 Tim. iii. 15).

Pil'low. See BOLSTER.

Pil'tai [characterized by deliverance].
A priest, head of the father's house of Moadiah in the days of the high priest Joiakim (Neh. xii. 17).

Pine and **Pine Tree.**
1. The rendering of the Hebrew *Tidhar*, the name of a tree in Lebanon (Is. xli. 19; lx. 13; R. V. margin, plane). It has not been properly identified.
2. The rendering of *'Es shemen*, oil tree (Neh. viii. 15, in R. V. wild olive). See OIL TREE.

Pin'na-cle.
A part of the temple, the edge of which

was at a great height above the ground (Mat. iv. 5). Exact identification is impossible. The Greek word *pterugion*, like pinnacle which is used to translate it, literally means a little wing; and it denotes the fin of a fish, the border of a garment, or the end of the breastplate (Lev. xi. 9; Num. xv. 38; Ex. xxviii. 26, in Septuagint). It may be simply the edge of the roof or court. Lightfoot, influenced by the meaning of the Greek word, suggested the porch which projected on each side of the temple like wings (War v. 5, 4). Others have thought of the royal porch which adjoined the temple and towered 400 cubits above the valley of the Kidron (Antiq. xv. 11, 5; xx. 9, 7). The golden spikes which were erected on the roof of the temple to prevent birds from alighting, have been thought of also as most nearly resembling slender towers or pinnacles in the modern sense; but they were many, and the evangelists speak of the pinnacle as though there were but one (R. V.).

Pi'non.
A chieftain of Edom (Gen. xxxvi. 41; 1 Chron. i. 52), probably catalogued by the name of his town (Gen. xxxvi. 40); see PUNON.

Pipe.
1. A wind instrument, called in Hebrew *ḥalil*, pierced instrument, and in Greek *aulos*. It existed in a variety of forms. The single pipe or reed was held vertically and blown by a mouthpiece at the end. A different kind was held and blown like a flute. The double pipe consisted of right and left tubes, which were blown at the same time, and played each with the corresponding hand. The holes of a pipe numbered two, three, or four. It was used in orchestra or was played alone (1 Sam. x. 5; 1 Kin. i. 40), and it accompanied merry song, religious praise, and the funeral dirge (Is. v. 12; xxx. 29; Mat. ix. 23; xi. 17). See MUSIC.
2. A wind instrument of ancient origin, called *'ugab* (Gen. iv. 21), which was used in merrymaking (Job xxi. 12; xxx. 31), and was deemed worthy of employment in the praise of God (Ps. cl. 4). According to the Targums it was a pipe. The Vulgate and in Ps. cl. the Septuagint explain it as a wind instrument, the *organon*. The A. V. always translates it organ, doubtless in the sense of mouth organ or set of pipes. The R. V. uniformly renders it pipe.
It is uncertain whether *neḳeb* (Ezek. xxviii. 13) denotes a pierced instrument (E. V. pipe) or a perforated gem.

Pi'ram [like a wild ass, swift].
A Canaanite king of Jarmuth, one of those defeated by Joshua before Gibeon (Josh. x. 3).

Pir'a-thon, in R. V. of 1 Mac. ix. 50 **Pharathon** [nakedness, prominence]. In A. V. of 1 Mac. the adjective Pharathoni is used.
A town in the mount of the Amalekites,

in the Ephraimite territory. Abdon, the judge, and Benaiah, the military official, were Pirathonites (Judg. xii. 13–15; 2 Sam. xxiii. 30; 1 Chron. xxvii. 14). It was fortified by Bacchides (1 Mac. ix. 50; cp. Antiq. xiii. 1, 3). Robinson identified it plausibly with Fer'ata, on a hill about 6 miles west by south of Shechem. Conder suggests Fer'on, 14 miles west by north of Shechem; see OPHRAH.

Pis'gah [a part, piece, division].
That part of the Abarim range of mountains near the northeastern end of the Dead Sea (Deut. xxxiv. 1 with iii. 27 and xxxii. 49). The Dead Sea was under its slopes (Deut. iii. 17). Its top looked down upon the desert (Num. xxi. 20). The field of Zophim on its top was visited by Balaam and Balak (xxiii. 14). From its summit, called Nebo, a large part of Canaan west of the Jordan was visible, and from it Moses viewed the promised land (Deut. iii. 27; xxxiv. 1–4); see NEBO. It was on the southern border of the realm of Sihon, king of the Amorites (Josh. xii. 2, 3). As late as the time of Eusebius, the mountainous country adjacent to mount Peor was called Phasgo. But the name is no longer attached to the eastern mountains, but seems to linger in the rocky headland, Ras el-Feshkah, on the opposite side of the sea.

Pi'shón. See EDEN.

Pi-sid'i-a.
A district of Asia Minor, bounded on the north by Phrygia; on the south by Lycia and Pamphylia; on the east by Lycaonia; and on the west by Caria. It formed a part of the Roman province of Galatia. The mountain chain of Taurus runs through it, and its turbulent inhabitants were so brave that they were never entirely subdued either by the Persians or by the Romans. Its chief town was Antioch, visited by Paul (Acts xiii. 14).

Pi'son. See EDEN.

Pis'pah.
An Asherite, son of Jether (1 Chron. vii. 38).

Pit.
A large deep hole in the ground. It may be either natural or artificial (Gen. xiv. 10; xxxvii. 20, 24).
Figuratively it is used for the grave or death (Job xxxiii. 18, 24), and it is employed thrice to render *sheʾol* (Num. xvi. 30, 33; Job xvii. 16); see SHEOL and ABYSS.

Pitch.
1. The rendering of the Hebrew *Kopher*, covering. The ark of Noah was daubed over with it, to render the junction of wooden planks impervious to water (Gen. vi. 14). It was probably asphalt from Hit, in Babylonia. See BITUMEN.
2. The rendering of the Hebrew *Zepheth*,

liquid. The ark of Moses was covered over with it (Exod. ii. 3). The streams in the land of Edom were to become pitch of this character (Is. xxxiv. 9). The last passage suggests that it also was asphalt from some locality. See BITUMEN.

Pitch'er.
A water jar of earthenware (cp. Judg. vii. 19), in the East generally having one or two handles. See JAR, and the illustrations, JACOB and Fountain of the Virgin.

Pi'thom [Egyptian *pa-tum*, abode of Tum {*Tum* being the setting sun, worshiped by the Egyptians as a god)].
One of the two store cities which the Israelites built when in bondage in Egypt built for Pharaoh (Exod. i. 11). Excavations, made under the auspices of the Egyptian Exploration Fund, by Edouard Naville at Tell el-Maskhuta, showed this to be the ancient Pithom. It is on the south side of the sweet-water canal which runs from Cairo to Suez through the wady Tumilat. There seems to have been at the spot an ancient shrine dedicated to Tum; but inscriptions dug up indicate that the city and fortifications did not come into existence till the time of Ramses II., the Pharaoh, it is believed, of the oppression. No more ancient monuments than his have been found in the place. To the northeast of the temple of Tum are extensive subterranean buildings. The walls are 9 feet thick, built of crude bricks joined by thin layers of mortar. A most interesting observation was made that some bricks had been manufactured with and some without straw (cp. Exod. v. 10–12). The walls inclosed a number of rectangular chambers not communicating with each other, the only access to them being from above. Naville believes that they were storehouses or granaries, into which the Pharaohs gathered the provisions necessary for armies or even for caravans about to cross the desert into Syria. At the time of the Greek dynasty Pithom received the new name of Heroopolis, city of heroes, which the Romans abridged into Ero, as is proved by Latin inscriptions from the locality. Sayce compares Ero with Egyptian *ara*, a storehouse. It was in the land of Goshen: for the Septuagint substitutes Heroopolis for Goshen in Gen. xlvi. 28, and the Coptic version, translated from the Septuagint, reads near Pithom, in the land of Ramses. All around the sacred buildings of Pithom was the civil city of Thuku, believed to be the Succoth of Exod. xii. 37.

Pi'thon.
A descendant of Jonathan (1 Chron. viii. 35; ix. 41).

Plague.
An infliction sent by God as a punishment for sin. In most of the cases mentioned in the Bible the infliction is an epidemic or other disease, but it may be also a judgment of a different character. A disease to be a plague need not be miraculous. The particular disease which God has attached as a penalty for the violation of this or that physical or mental law may be properly called a plague, if the act has moral quality. And even a disease which arises from ignorance of sanitary laws and from a violation of nature in no wise criminal, and which in itself is without moral significance, may become in God's hands an instrument for the punishment of evil doers, God predetermining and arranging for the time and place of its outbreak with this end in view. What is called in English by way of emphasis the plague is a highly malignant form of typhus fever, due to neglect of sanitary precautions, which has frequently originated at Cairo, in Egypt, and spread to Syria, Asia Minor, and the adjacent regions. It is probable that it has been used in times past as a chastening rod.
The first plague mentioned in Scripture was that sent on Pharaoh, Abraham's contemporary, for the protection of Sarah, the patriarch's wife (Gen. xii. 17). The next plagues in point of time were the ten inflicted on Egypt. They were not phenomena with which the Egyptians were previously unacquainted; but in most cases, if not in all, they were distresses common to the country. Yet they were not mere natural phenomena in aggravated form; they exhibited unmistakably miraculous features; see EGYPT III. 6. The first consisted in the change of the river water into blood or something like it (Ex. vii. 14–25); the second, in the vast multiplication of frogs (viii. 1–15); the third, in lice, sand flies, or fleas, produced from the dust (16–19); the fourth, in swarms of flies (20–32); the fifth, in murrain on the cattle (ix. 1–7); the sixth, in boils and blains on man and beast (8–12); the seventh, in a destructive hailstorm (13–35); the eighth, in locusts brought by the east wind (x. 1–20); the ninth, in dense darkness (21–29); and the tenth, in the death of all the firstborn (xi. 1–xii. 30). A plague was sent upon the Israelites for making and worshiping the golden calf (Ex. xxxii. 35); and another for murmuring against the sustenance provided for them by God (Num. xi. 33, 34); another slew the spies who had brought up an evil report of the land (xiv. 37); another raged among the people for murmuring at the righteous punishment of the rebels Korah, Dathan, and Abiram. In this visitation 14,700 perished (xvi. 46–50). In another plague sent upon the people on account of the idolatries and impurities at Baal-peor 24,000 died (xxv. 9; Josh. xxii. 17; Ps. cvi. 29, 30). The infliction of the emerods, or piles, upon the Philistines is called a plague (1 Sam. vi. 4). A plague or pestilence, in which 70,000 perished, followed on David's numbering the people (2 Sam. xxiv. 13–25; 1 Chron. xxi.

12–30). A plague was threatened against Jehoram, king of Judah, and his people (2 Chron. xxi. 14, 15).

Sometimes the word plague is used of diseases which are not epidemic: it is applied, for instance, to an issue of blood (Mark v. 29, 34, literally scourge), to leprosy in individuals (Lev. xiii. 3, 5, 6), and even to the spreading of some inferior forms of vegetation on the walls of presumably damp houses (xiv. 35).

Plain.

In the A. V. seven different words are rendered plain. Three of these deserve special notice, sheᵉphelah, kikkar, and ʿᵃrabah. The term sheᵉphelah, or lowland, as R. V. renders it, was the technical designation for the districts of southern and in part of central Palestine, between the higher hills on the east and the low-lying plain along the Mediterranean on the west. In Josh. xv. 33–47 forty-two towns of Judah, with their villages, are enumerated as being within its bounds. Some of these were, however, generally in Philistine hands, and hence Obad. 19 mentions the lowland of the Philistines. See LOWLAND.

Kikkar, which means circle, circuit, was applied especially to the plain of the Jordan from at least Succoth on the north to Sodom and Gomorrah on the south (Gen. xiii. 10, 11, 12; xix. 17, 28; Deut. xxxiv. 3; 2 Sam. xviii. 23; 2 Chron. iv. 17). The valley as far north as the sea of Galilee was probably included in the designation (War iv. 8, 2).

The word ʿᵃrabah, which is rendered plain in A. V. of Deut. ii. 8; iii. 17, etc., is generally left untranslated in R. V. See ARABAH.

Plane.

The rendering of the Hebrew ʿArmon, naked one (Gen. xxx. 37; Ezek. xxxi. 8). So R. V. and the ancient versions, except that the Septuagint renders it pine in Ezekiel. The A. V., following the rabbinical interpretation, calls it chestnut. The oriental plane tree (Platanus orientalis) grows from 70 to 90 feet high. It has palmately lobed leaves, resembling those of the sycamore maple, which is the reason why the latter tree is sometimes called a plane, and has the specific name pseudo-platanus. The oriental plane is indigenous in southern Europe and western Asia. In Palestine it is wild by the side of mountain streams, besides being cultivated in many places.

Plas′ter. See MORTAR I.

Pledge. See LOAN.

Ple′ia-des [daughters of sailing, stars which indicate by their rising the time of safe navigation; or perhaps, the full or compact group].

The Hebrew word Kimah is the name of a brilliant star or constellation (Job ix. 9; xxxviii. 31; and Amos v. 8, in A. V. the seven stars), and in the opinion of the majority of ancient writers it denotes the Pleiades. An Arabic designation for the Pleiades is Thuriyyaʾ, which likewise signifies a compact group.

The Pleiades are a cluster of stars in the constellation Taurus (the Bull), in the shoulder of the animal. For some unknown reason they were anciently said to be seven; and since only six were usually seen, the notion arose of a lost Pleiad. Six stars are visible to the naked eye on ordinary nights, but more may be seen by persons of very good sight. With the aid of a telescope a hundred stars may be counted. Josephus uses the setting of the Pleiades as a note of time (Antiq. xiii. 8, 2).

Plow.

In Palestine the plow is of primitive character. It consists of a pole or the branch of a tree, to one end of which the yoke is attached, while from the other end a small branch projects or else through the end a beam is thrust which is sheathed in a thin plate of iron and forms the share (Is. ii. 4). It was dragged by oxen or cows, and was guided by the hand (Judg. xiv. 18; Job i. 14; Ecclus. xxxviii. 25, 26; Luke ix. 62). Such an implement can do little more than scratch the surface of the ground. Hence

Contemporary farmer plowing with the same type of implements used in Bible days. Note use of mule and ox, strictly forbidden by Scripture.

The ancient method of scattering seeds in sowing is used in parts of the Holy Land today.

the same land has to be plowed over and over again. When Elisha was plowing with twelve yoke of oxen there were probably twelve plows, each with its pair of bullocks and its man, Elisha being the last of the twelve (1 Kin. xix. 19, 20).

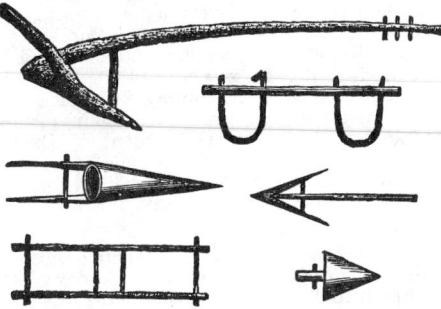

Plow, plowshares, and yokes still used in Asia Minor.

Poch'e-reth-haz-ze-ba'im [perhaps, capturing gazelles].

Name of a division of Solomon's servants' members of which returned from Babylon (Ezra ii. 57; Neh. vii. 59). The A. V. divides the name, makes the latter part a place, and calls the man Pochereth of Zebaim.

Po'et-ry.

Poetry is one of the earliest forms in which the literary taste of a people begins to express itself. It is rhythmical and regular in form, like the motions of the dancer which it so frequently accompanied in ancient times (Ex. xv. 20, 21). It is naturally born of the emotions, and is called forth by individual or national joy or sorrow or deep concern. The imagination also and the habit of expressing thought in vivid language borrowed from nature, which are vital elements in poetry, come to manifestation during the childhood of a people. The Hebrews formed no exception to the rule. The words of Sarah at the birth of her son have the poetic ring (Gen. xxi. 6, 7). The blessing which Jacob bestowed on his sons as the time of his death approached was couched in the sentious and picturesque form of Semitic poetry (xlix.). The song which sprang spontaneously from Moses' lips, when he beheld the overthrow of Pharaoh's host in the sea and discerned at once the moral effect which it would have on the nations of Canaan, was also an utterance born of strong feeling and cast into the simple form of Hebrew poetry.

Ancient Semitic poetry does not rhyme. Poems have been discovered which show a certain cæsural arrangement, but this feature is not essential. Assonance, alliteration, and rhyme, so common in occidental poetry, oc-

casionally occur in Hebrew poetry, but they also are not essential and they are extremely rare. Nor is there a regular recurrence of long and short syllables or feet; but the rhythmical tendency was strongly felt and unconsciously led to producing lines of nearly the same number of words or word-groups, or, to state the matter somewhat differently, the same number of main accents, including at times a secondary accent. The line, moreover, was made to end at a break in the sense except in extremely rare cases, such as Ps. xcvi. 12.

The essential formal characteristic of Hebrew poetry is parallelism. By this is meant that the sentiment of one line is echoed in the next.

The name was given to this feature by Bishop Lowth in 1753, who investigated the phenomenon and drew attention to synonymous, antithetic, and synthetic parallelism (de Sacr. Poesi. Hebr. xix.). Parallelism is of various kinds:

1. Synonymous, when the thought of the first line is repeated in other words in the second line, as in Gen. iv. 23:

> Adah and Zillah, hear my voice;
> Ye wives of Lamech, hearken unto my speech.

The couplet:

> For I have slain a man to my wounding [or, for wounding me],
> And a young man to my hurt [or, for bruising me],

likewise exhibits synonymous parallelism; and at the same time it shows the exegetical importance of an acquaintance with this principle, for Lamech must not be understood to speak of two murders. He mentions killing but one man. This principle also enables the expositor of Scripture to interpret ambiguous words; for example, in Ps. xxii. 20:

> Deliver my soul from the sword;
> My darling from the power of the dog,

the parallelism determines that the darling referred to is not a dear friend, but means the psalmist's soul or his life.

2. Progressive, in which the second line expresses a new idea more or less closely related to the first; as in Job iii. 17:

> There the wicked cease from troubling;
> And there the weary be at rest.

3. Synthetic or constructive, in which there is parallelism of structure only, while the thought of one line serves as the foundation upon which to build a new thought; as Ps. xxv. 12:

> What man is he that feareth the Lord?
> Him shall he instruct in the way that he shall choose:

or Prov. xxvi. 4:

> Answer not a fool according to his folly,
> Lest thou also be like unto him;

or Ps. xxiv. 9:

> Lift up your heads, O ye gates;
> Yea, lift them up, ye everlasting doors:
> And the King of glory shall come in.

4. Climactic, in which the characteristic words are repeated and form the ladder on which the thought climbs to completion or to emphatic reiteration; as in Ps. xxix. 5:

> The voice of the Lord breaketh the cedars;
> Yea, the Lord breaketh in pieces the cedars of Lebanon;

and in Ps. cxxi. 3, 4:

> He will not suffer thy foot to be moved:
> He that keepeth thee will not slumber;
> Behold, he that keepeth Israel
> Shall neither slumber nor sleep.

5. Antithetic, in which the thought is made more clear by contrast; as in Mat. viii. 20:

> The foxes have holes,
> And the birds of the air have nests;
> But the Son of man hath not where to lay his head.

6. Comparative, in which the thought is explained by comparison with something else that is familiar; as in Ps. xlii. 1:

> As the hart panteth after the water brooks,
> So panteth my soul after thee, O God.

The parallelism usually yields a distich, but tristichs are not uncommon, as may be seen from the examples already cited. Tetrastichs and pentastichs also occur (Ps. i. 3; xxvii. 4, 9; xxxvii. 7, 14, 20, 25, 28, 34, 40). The stanza is not essential to Hebrew poetry. It is used, however, in Ps. xlii. and xliii., which form one poem, divided into three equal parts by a recurring verse. Ps. xlvi. consists of three groups of three verses each, the conclusion of each group being marked by Selah, and the last two groups closing with a refrain. There are also alphabetical psalms, in which the principle is more or less fully observed of beginning the successive verses with the letters of the alphabet in consecutive order (Ps. xxv.; xxxiv.; xxxvii.). Ps. cxix. consists of twenty-two groups of eight verses each. The number of groups equals the number of letters in the Hebrew alphabet, and the initial letter of each verse in a group is in the original that letter of the alphabet which numerically corresponds to the group. The book of Lamentations is constructed on a similar alphabetical plan; see LAMENTATIONS.

Poetry is usually classified as epic, dramatic, lyric, and didactic. Neither the epic nor the drama is found in the Bible; but the Book of Job has a semi-dramatic form, for there is action, which forms the basis of drama, in the prologue and epilogue, and there is a regular alternation of speakers throughout. See also SONG OF SONGS. The lyrics are the most numerous poems. No period of Israelitish history after the exodus is without them. They consist of triumphal odes which celebrate the deliverance wrought by Jehovah, like the song of Moses at the Red Sea, and the song of Deborah; psalms of the penitent suing for mercy or expressing the joy of forgiveness (Ps. xxxii.; li.), and of the poor and needy crying out in distress, calm in faith, or praising God for succor (xxxviii.; and iii.; xxiii.; Hab. iii.; and 1 Sam. ii. 1-10; Is. xxxviii. 10-20; Luke i. 46-55); psalms of the coming Redeemer and his kingdom (Ps. ii.; xlv.; lxxii.): and plaintive elegies, as the lament of David over Saul and Jonathan, the songs of mourning for Judah, and the Lamentations (2 Sam. i. 17-27; Ps. xliv.; lx.; lxxiv.).

Poi′son.

Any substance, vegetable, animal, or mineral, which produces a morbid or deadly effect when introduced into the animal organism (2 Kin. iv. 39, 40; Rom. iii. 13). The venom of serpents is denoted in Hebrew either by ḥemah, heat (Deut. xxxii. 24, 33; Ps. lviii. 4), a general word which is also used for hot passion and the heat produced by wine, or by ro'sh (Deut. xxxii. 33; Job xx. 16), which also signifies a bitter herb; see GALL. The custom of anointing arrows with the poison of snakes is probably alluded to in Job vi. 4. It was a practice of great antiquity and considerable extent (Homer, Odyssey i. 261, 262; Pliny, Hist. Nat. xi. 115; xviii. 1). Vegetable poison was also employed for this purpose, as that obtained from the yew tree (Hist. Nat. xvi. 20). The Gauls used a poisonous herb called *limeum*, perhaps leopard's bane (xxvii. 76).

The suicide of Ptolemy Macron by poison, the alleged murder of Pheroras by poisoned food, and the fame of Arabian women for skill in preparing poisonous potions (2 Mac. x. 13; Antiq. xvii. 4, 1), serve to show that the crimes prevalent at that time in Rome were not left uncommitted in Judah and the East (cp. Mark xvi. 18); but the absence of direct mention of them in the Bible indicates that they were not common among the Jews.

Pol′lux. See CASTOR AND POLLUX.

Pome′gran-ate [apple, having many grains or seeds].

The pomegranate (*Punica granatum*), in Hebrew called *rimmon*, in Arabic *rummân*, is a tree from 12 to 15 feet high, having oblong-oblanceolate entire leaves, without dots. Here and there on the branches occasional thorns are found. The flowers have generally scarlet petals proceeding from a large leathery calyx. The fruit is about the size of an orange, and has a hard, red rind, filled with numerous seeds enveloped in bright red pulp; hence the English name, which means an apple with many seeds. The pulp is most refreshing to the taste. The pomegranate is wild in northern Africa and western Asia, and possibly so in Gilead.

It was largely cultivated in Palestine in Scripture times (Num. xiii. 23; xx. 5; Deut. viii. 8; 1 Sam. xiv. 2; Song iv. 3, 13; vi. 7, 11; viii. 2; Joel i. 12; Hag. ii. 19). The expressed juice of the fruit made a pleasant drink (Song viii. 2, R. V.). Pomegranates

Pomegranate.

of blue, purple, and scarlet stuff alternating with bells made of gold were put along the skirts of the robe connected with the high priest's ephod (Exod. xxviii. 33, 34; xxxix. 26). The chapiters of the two pillars at the porch of Solomon's temple had each around them a double row with a hundred pomegranates each (1 Kin. vii. 20; 2 Kin. xxv. 17; 2 Chron. iii. 16). The fruit is still much cultivated in Palestine.

Pom'mel.
Rounded portion or bowl of a chapiter (2 Chron. iv. 12, 13; in R. V. and in 1 Kin. vii. 41, 42, bowl).

Pon'ti-us. See PILATE.

Pon'tus [the sea].
The eastern half of the coast of Asia Minor on the Pontus Euxinus, or Black Sea, from the first word of which the name of the province was derived. It may be described as reaching from the valley of the Phasis in Colchis to the river Halys, and extending inland southward across the mountains to Cappadocia. About 400 B. C. an independent kingdom of this name was established. Six of its successive kings were called Mithridates. The last of them maintained, till his death in 63 B. C., a fierce struggle with the Romans, who reduced the kingdom to the position of a protected state, united it with Bithynia, and formed the province of Bithynia and Pontus. Jews resided in Pontus

(1 Pet. i. 1). Jews from Pontus were at Jerusalem during the pentecostal effusion of the Holy Spirit (Acts ii. 9). Aquila the Jew was born in the province (xviii. 2).

Pool.
A reservoir for water, supplied by rain or else by springs, like the pool of Siloam. From the pool the water was sometimes conducted in channels to town and garden (2 Kin. xx. 20; Ecc. ii. 6; Ecclus. xxiv. 30). The pools of Bethesda, Siloam, and Gihon were at Jerusalem, and water was also conducted to the city from the reservoirs at Etam; and there were pools at Hebron, Gibeon, Samaria, and Heshbon (2 Sam. ii 13; iv. 12; 1 Kin. xxii. 38; Song vii. 4).

Poor.
The unequal distribution of the blessings of life is not ideal in the sight of God. Now God gave Canaan to his people (Ex. vi. 4, 8). Accordingly the Mosaic law provided for a general participation of the people in the ownership of the land; and while it permitted freedom of sale, it secured a readjustment of property and a return to each family of its inheritance in Canaan every fifty years (Lev. xxv. 13, 23). But notwithstanding all that law and instruction can do, the poor are always present, sometimes through sins of their own or their ancestors, sometimes through the inscrutable but wise providence of God. The poverty which springs from indolence or personal crime was theoretically excluded from Israel, the kingdom of God; and its poor were regarded from the standpoint of the theocracy as the unfortunate and chastened but beloved children of God. All the poor, especially widows, orphans, and strangers, enjoyed the care of God and the godly, and all were specially favored by the law. Every hungry person had the right to pluck and eat for present need in the vineyard or grainfield of another (Deut. xxiii. 24, 25). Every poor person was authorized at harvest to glean after the reapers, to cut the grain that was left standing at the edge of the field, and to take any forgotten sheaf which remained in the field when the harvest was over. At the vintage and in fruit-picking time what was left hanging on the branches belonged to the poor (Lev. xix. 9, 10; xxiii. 22; Deut. xxiv. 19–21). In the seventh year and fiftieth year the land was not tilled, and what grew of itself was not harvested, but was free to all to eat (Lev. xxv. 4–7, 11, 12). The poor man in his extremity might sell his services to a master for a term of years, but regained his freedom in the year of release (38–42). If a loan were required by a poor man, it was to be bestowed, even though the near approach of the release of the seventh year would soon give him the legal right of not repaying the debt (Deut. xv. 7–10). The poll tax, which each man had to pay for the ransom of his soul or life on the taking of a census, was the same

in amount for both rich and poor, being half a shekel; but in offerings presented at the tabernacle or temple, a cheaper form of gift was sometimes prescribed for the poorer worshiper (Lev. xii. 8; xiv. 21; xxvii. 8). The prosperous were encouraged to invite the poor to the sacrificial feasts and to remember them on other joyous occasions (Deut. xvi. 11, 14). There are many beautiful examples of kindness shown to the needy (Job xxxi. 16–22). There were also warnings in the law against the oppression of the poor (Ex. xxii. 21–27). At the same time, justice must not be violated. A judge must not give a verdict in favor of a man because he was poor; the claims of justice were to be paramount over every other consideration (Ex. xxiii. 3; Lev. xix. 15). The kindly provisions of the law, however, were frequently ignored in times of religious declension, and the prophets have occasion to rebuke hard-heartedness and injustice toward the poor (Is. i. 23; x. 2; Ezek. xxii. 7, 29; Mal. iii. 5). There were also abuses of the good law itself. There were those who obeyed the letter, but not the spirit, who bestowed alms to be seen of men (Mat. vi. 1). Many gracious promises are made to the pious poor, and the divine procedure to them is shown to be that of loving care (1 Sam. ii. 6; Job v. 15; xxxiv. 28; xxxvi. 15; Ps. ix. 18; x. 14; xii. 5; xxxiv. 6; xxxv. 10). Blessings are also promised to the man who pities the poor (Ps. xli. 1; Prov. xiv. 21, 31; xxix. 7, etc.). Our Lord in the course of his ministry showed his great love for the poor (Mat. xix. 21; Luke xviii. 22; John xiii. 29, etc.), and it was a special characteristic of his ministry that to the poor the gospel was preached (Mat. xi. 5; Luke xiv. 21–23). The early church considered it one of its most sacred duties to look after its poor, and as far as its limited resources would allow, the poor also outside its communion (Acts ii. 45; iv. 32; vi. 1–6; xi. 27–30; xxiv. 17; 1 Cor. xvi. 1–3; Gal. ii. 10; 1 Thes. iii. 6).

The poor in spirit are the humble, whether rich or poor in this world's goods (Mat. v. 3).

Pop'lar.
The rendering of the Hebrew *Libneh*, white, applied to a tree (Gen. xxx. 37). It ranked with trees of which the shadow is good (Hos. iv. 13). If it is the poplar, the species is *Populus alba*, a tall tree with white wood, and the leaves white and cottony on the lower side. In the first passage the R. V., following the Septuagint, has storax on the margin, referring to *Styrax officinale*, sometimes called *libnah* in Arabic, a resinous shrub from 10 to 20 feet high, a native of the Levant; see STACTE. The Septuagint understands the white poplar to be meant in Hos. iv. 13.

Por'a-tha [probably, having many chariots].
One of Haman's sons (Esth. ix. 8).

Porch.
A walk protected by a roof supported by pillars; a colonnade; a portico. There were often porches of this character in royal or other mansions (1 Kin. vii. 6, 7), and there was a notable one on the eastern front of Solomon's temple (vi. 3; Ezek. viii. 16; Joel ii. 17). Sometimes there was a colonnade on an upper floor (Judg. iii. 23). The porches of the pool of Bethesda, and Solomon's porch connected with the second temple, were also colonnades (John v. 2; x. 23), called in Greek *stoa*. The porch where Peter's second denial took place was doubtless the passage from the street to the court of the house; and in the parallel passage it is styled the fore-court (Mat. xxvi. 71; Mark xiv. 68, R. V. margin).

Por'ci-us. See FESTUS.

Por'cu-pine [a spinous pig].
The rendering of the R. V. in Is. xiv. 23; xxxiv. 11; Zeph. ii. 14 of the Hebrew *Kippod*, the one rolling itself together. The corresponding word in other Semitic dialects denotes both the hedgehog and the porcupine. The European porcupine (*Hystrix cristata*) is common in Palestine, especially in the gorges leading down to the valley of the Jordan. A brush-tailed porcupine (*Atherura hirsutirostris*) has also been found in Judæa. The A. V. translates *kippod* by bittern.

Por'poise.
The rendering of *Tahash* in the R. V. on the margin of Ex. xxv. 5 and elsewhere where the text has seal and A. V. has badger. This marginal rendering follows Niebuhr's remark that the name *tuhas* is given to a species of porpoise by the Arabs near cape Mussendum.

Pos'ses-sion. See DEMONIAC.

Por'ter.
A gate keeper (1 Chron. ix. 22, 23; and xvi. 38, in R. V. doorkeeper). Keepers were stationed at the city gate (2 Sam. xviii. 26; 2 Kin. vii. 10), at the doors of the temple (1 Chron. ix. 22), at the entrance of private houses (Mark xiii. 34). When David organized the Levites for the service of the tabernacle, he assigned the duty of acting as doorkeepers to a large section of them, 4000 in number. They were not all needed at once, so he distributed them into courses, officiating in succession (1 Chron. xxiii. 5; xxvi. 1–19).

Post.
1. The upright timber at the side of a door (1 Kin. vi. 33). A stone pillar sometimes took the place of wood. A Hebrew slave who did not desire to embrace the opportunity of freedom afforded by the arrival of the seventh year, but preferred to remain permanently in the master's house, allowed an awl to be thrust through his ear into the door or doorpost (Ex. xxi. 6; Deut. xv. 17) as a sign of attachment to the house.
2. A courier (Esth. iii. 13; Job ix. 25).

Pot.

The most frequent word is the Hebrew
sir, a vessel made in various sizes, large and
small (2 Kin. iv. 38), and of different materials, earthenware and metal (Ex. xxxviii.
3), and used for manifold purposes, such as
for boiling flesh (xvi. 3 ; 2 Chron. xxxv. 13 ;
Job xli. 31 ; and Ezek. xxiv. 3–5, in R. V.
caldron), for washing (Ps. lx. 8), for refining
metals (Prov. xxvii. 21).   The term *dud*
might also designate a similar pot (Job xli. 20 ;
in 1 Sam. ii. 14 rendered kettle ; in 2 Chron.
xxxv. 13 rendered caldron) ; so also might
kallahath, which is rendered caldron (1 Sam.
ii. 14 ; Mic. iii. 3). In Job xli. 20 the word
translated caldron in A. V. should be rushes.
Water for domestic purposes was kept in
earthen pots (John. ii. 6) ; see WATERPOT.

Pot'i-phar [who is of the sun].

The captain of Pharaoh's guard and owner
of Joseph. His wife attempted to seduce the
young slave from the path of virtue, and
when she failed, she induced Potiphar to im-
prison him on a charge which she knew to be
false (Gen. xxxix. 1–20).

Pot-i-phe'ra, in A. V. **Poti-pherah** [Egyp-
tian *Pet-p-ra*, who is of the sun, belonging to
the sun].

A priest of On, or Heliopolis, the city of
the sun. He was the father of Asenath, who
was given in marriage to Joseph (Gen. xli. 45–
50 ; xlvi. 20).

Pot'ter.

One who makes earthenware pots and similar vessels. The clay was trodden by foot
of man to reduce it to a paste (Is. xli. 25 ;
Wisd. xv. 7). It was then placed on a horizontal wheel, before which the potter sat,
turning the wheel with his hand as he
shaped the vessel, or keeping the wheel
in motion with his foot, while he fashioned the revolving clay with his hand
and arm. The finished work was glazed and
baked in a furnace (Jer. xviii. 3, 4 ; Ecclus.
xxxviii. 29, 30). The ability of the potter to
mold the clay into any shape he desired is
used in Is. xlv. 9 ; Jer. xviii. 5–12 ; Rom. ix.
20–25 to illustrate God's sovereignty over
man. God, of course, in the exercise of sovereignty acts only in accordance with his infinite perfections of wisdom, justice, goodness, and truth.

Pot'ter's Field.   See AKELDAMA.

Pound.   See MONEY and WEIGHTS.

Pow'der.

The fine particles into which any substance
is crushed or ground (Ex. xxxii. 20). Pulverized spice of any kind, intended to be
burnt as incense (Song iii. 6).

Præ'tor.

One of the chief civil magistrates in a

The potter at his wheel.

Roman colony, in Greek commonly designated *stratēgos* (Acts xvi. 12, and 20, 35, R. V. margin). There were usually two, elected annually by the colonists; and occasionally styled consuls. Two lictors attended each prætor; cleared the way before him, saw that due respect was shown him by the public, and executed his orders (35, 38, R. V. margin).

Præ-to'ri-um [belonging to a prætor].

The tent of a general; the official residence of a provincial governor; a palace. In the N. T. it denotes:

1. The palace occupied by Pontius Pilate at Jerusalem and where his judgment seat was erected (Mark xv. 16; and margin of R. V. of Mat. xxvii. 27; John xviii. 28, 33; xix. 9, cp. 13). Some have understood the castle of Antonia; but Herod's palace was the building occupied by the procurators. See HEROD, PALACE OF.

2. Herod's palace at Cæsarea, in which Paul was confined (Acts xxiii. 35, R. V. margin; in text, palace; in A. V., judgment hall).

3. The prætorian guard at Rome, the duty of which was to guard the imperial palace and its occupant, the emperor (Phil. i. 13; in A. V., palace; on the margin, Cæsar's court).

Prayer.

Prayer is communion with God. It implies that God is a person, able and willing to hear us, who has created the universe and still preserves and governs all his creatures and all their actions. He is not the slave of his own laws. He can produce results by controlling the laws of nature or coöperating with them as readily as a man can; nay more readily, for he is God. He can influence the hearts and minds of men more readily than even a man can induce his fellow-men to action. God has foreordained both the prayer and its answer. He has had a plan from the beginning; and he accomplishes this plan both by the manner in which he established the universe and the laws which he set in operation, and also by his constant presence in the universe, upholding it and controlling it.

Prayer is instinctive with man. In his extremity of need he cries out to God. And God requires prayer of all men; but to pray to God implies a right relation to him. Acceptable prayer can be offered unto God by the righteous only. The prayer of the wicked is abomination unto him (Prov. xv. 29; xxviii. 9). Only those who have forsaken sin are authorized to draw nigh unto God in prayer. There is no propriety in rebels against the authority of God approaching him, except with renunciation of their rebellion and a petition for pardon. Prayer is the communion of the child of God with his Father in heaven. It consists of adoration, thanksgiving, confession, and petition

(Neh. i. 4-11; Dan. ix. 3-19; Phil. iv. 6). It has been engaged in by God's people from the beginning.

Prayer is thus the natural expression of the religious feelings, and further God's blessings are given in answer to prayer (1 Kin. ix. 3; Ezek. xxxvi. 37; Mat. vii. 7). God is attentive to every prayer that is rightly offered to him. He heareth the young ravens when they cry; and God's people have the promise that he will answer their prayers (Ps. lxv. 2). James, citing history, says that the supplication of a righteous man availeth much in its working (Jas. v. 16, R. V.). Christ speaking to his disciples said: "Whatsoever ye shall ask in my name, that will I do" (John xiv. 13). God's people present their petitions to God and leave to him to decide whether it is wise to grant the request or not. They know that God alone can tell whether the granting of the prayer would be for their own good or for the welfare of the kingdom of God or for God's glory. The apostle John, writing to believers, states the doctrine of prayer with its necessary condition when he says: "This is the boldness which we have toward him, that, if we ask anything according to his will, he heareth us" (1 John v. 14, R. V.). "The answer will be such as we, if duly enlightened, would ourselves desire." God often blesses his children best when he denies their requests. And when they pray they desire him to deny their requests if in his sight it is best to do so.

We must pray in the name of Christ, because sinful man cannot approach God. We must draw near, not claiming any inherent right of our own to come, but in the name of him who hath washed us from our sins in his blood and made us to be priests unto God.

Prayer is addressed to God in his fullness, as the triune God. Prayer to each of the three persons in the Godhead, Father, Son, and Holy Ghost, is involved in the apostolic benediction: "The grace of the Lord Jesus Christ, and the love of God, and the communion of the Holy Ghost, be with you all" (2 Cor. xiii. 14). Prayer was addressed to the risen Christ. Christians called upon his name (1 Cor. i. 2). Stephen petitioned him, Paul besought him and rendered thanks to him, the redeemed ascribe glory and dominion to him (Acts vii. 59, 60; 2 Cor. xii. 8, 9; 1 Thes. iii. 11; 1 Tim. i. 12; Rev. i. 5, 6).

Prep-a-ra'tion.

The day before the Sabbath (Mark xv. 42; John xix. 31; Antiq. xvi. 6, 2; cp. Judith viii. 6). The preparation for the Sabbath of the passover was the eve of a peculiarly high day (John xix. 14, 31).

Pres'by-ter-y.

The whole body of *presbuteroi*, elders in a church (1 Tim. iv. 14). See ELDER and LAYING ON OF HANDS.

Pres'ents. See GIFTS.

Priest [contracted from Latin *presbyter,* Greek *presbuteros,* elderly, an elder].

An authorized minister. It sometimes denotes a minister of state or responsible adviser of the king (2 Sam. viii. 18; see R. V. margin). In 2 Sam. xx. 26 the official is described as priest to David (see R. V. margin), and in 1 Chron. xviii. 17 as chief about the king. In 1 Kin. iv. 5 the title is qualified and explained by friend of the king (see FRIEND OF THE KING). Very frequently the ministers at the sanctuary are described as Levitical priests, as though the designation *kohen,* minister, priest, rather needed descriptive qualification.

An authorized minister of a deity who, on behalf of a community, officiates at the altar and in other rites. The essential idea of a priest is that of a mediator between man and God. The priests formed a distinct class in the nations of antiquity generally; as in Egypt, Midian, Philistia, Greece, Rome (Gen. xlvii. 22; Ex. ii. 16; 1 Sam. vi. 2; Acts xiv. 13).

In the absence of a regularly organized priesthood, priestly functions were exercised from time immemorial by private individuals, as Cain, Abel; and by patriarchs in behalf of a family or tribe, as Noah, Abraham, Isaac, Jacob, Job. The natural head of a body of people acted as priest. There were those among the Israelites at the time of the exodus who possessed this prerogative by natural right, and who had been influenced by the pressure of increasing priestly duties, arising from the growth of the Hebrew population, and by the spectacle of the Egyptian priesthood, to devote themselves professionally to priestly functions (Ex. xix. 22). Even after the organization of the Levitical priesthood priestly prerogatives existed outside of that order. When God himself dispensed with the mediation of the ordained priests and manifested himself immediately to a man, that man recognized his right to offer sacrifice at once without the intervention of the regularly constituted mediators (Judg. vi. 18, 24, 26; xiii. 16); and when for political reasons it became impossible for those who feared God in the northern kingdom to avail themselves of the offices of the Levitical priests, the primitive law was recalled and the father of the family or other person indicated by ancient custom erected the altar and offered sacrifices to Jehovah (1 Kin. xviii. 30).

When the Hebrew nation was organized at Sinai a national sanctuary and service were projected on a noble scale, such as became the essential dignity of Jehovah, and appeared to no disadvantage when brought into comparison with the purest worship of the most cultured nations of that age. Priests were needed for its altar. Aaron and his sons were appointed to that office, and the priesthood was made hereditary in the family and restricted to it (Ex. xxviii. 1; xl. 12-15;

Num. xvi. 40; xvii.; xviii. 1-8; and cp. Deut. x. 6; 1 Kin. viii. 4; Ezra ii. 36 seq.). All the sons of Aaron were priests unless debarred by legal disabilities (Lev. xxi. 16 seq.). Accordingly when they are referred to as a class, they are mentioned either simply as the priests or as the priests the sons of Aaron, in allusion to their descent as a family (i. 5; 2 Chron. xxvi. 18; xxix. 21; xxxv. 14; cp. Num. iii. 3; x. 8; Josh. xxi. 19; Neh. x. 38), or as the priests the Levites, in allusion to the tribe to which they belonged (Deut. xvii. 9, 18; xviii. 1; Josh. iii. 3; viii. 33; 2 Chron. xxiii. 18; xxx. 27; Jer. xxxiii. 18, 21; cp. Ex. xxxviii. 21), or later as the priests the Levites the sons of Zadok, as designation of a branch of the family (Ezek. xliv. 15; cp. xliii. 19). This method of designating the priests, as will be seen from the passages cited, was in vogue at a time when beyond all question the distinction between priest and Levite was firmly established. The distinction is recognized in the history: the ministers at the altar of the tabernacle and temple and the users of Urim and Thummim always belong to the family of Aaron.

The duties of the priests were mainly three: to minister at the sanctuary before the Lord, to teach the people the law of God, and to inquire for them the divine will by Urim and Thummim (Ex. xxviii. 30 and Ezra ii. 63; Num. xvi. 40; xviii. 5; 2 Chron. xv. 3; Jer. xviii. 18; Ezek. vii. 26; Mic. iii. 11). The priest was subject to special laws (Lev. x. 8 seq.); and in respect to marriage, he could only take to wife one of his own nation, a virgin or a widow who had not been divorced, and her genealogy in the ancient records must be as regular as that of the priest himself (xxi. 7; Ezra x. 18, 19; con. Apion. i. 7). His dress when on duty consisted of 1. Short breeches, reaching from the hips to the thighs. 2. A coat fitting close to the body, woven in one piece without seam, at least in later times extending to the ankles, and which was gathered about the loins with a symbolically ornamented girdle. 3. A cap shaped like a cup. These several articles were made of white linen (Ex. xxviii. 40-42; Antiq. iii. 7, 1-3). Priests and others officially connected with the solemn service often wore a linen ephod; but it was not prescribed and it was not made of varied and costly materials like the one worn by the high priest (1 Sam. ii. 18; xxii. 18; 2 Sam. vi. 14).

On the conquest of Canaan, in view of the present needs of the descendants of Aaron, who were then doubtless in the third generation, but more especially with a view to future demands, thirteen towns were designated where residence and lands for pasturing cattle were legally theirs (Josh. xxi. 10-19). In the course of centuries they increased to a numerous body. Accordingly David divided them into twenty-four courses. Except during the great festivals, when all the courses were employed, each course officiated for a week at a time, the change being made on the Sabbath before evening sacrifice (1 Chron. xxiv. 1–19 ; 2 Kin. xi. 5, 9 ; Antiq. vii. 14, 7). Four only of these courses appear to have returned from Babylon with Zerubbabel (Ezra ii. 36–38) ; but the old number was eventually reconstructed (cp. Luke i. 5, 9). There were distinctions in rank among the priests. The supreme pontiff was the high priest (q. v.). Next to him stood the second priest (2 Kin. xxv. 18), who was probably the same as the ruler of the house of God (2 Chron. xxxi. 13 ; Neh. xi. 11) and the captain of the temple (Acts iv. 1 ; v. 24). The chief priests who are mentioned in the N. T. were the officiating high priest, former high priests still alive, and members of their families. They were an anomaly of the times. The law which regulated the succession to the high-priesthood had come into abeyance through political confusion and foreign domination. High priests were made and unmade at the will of the rulers.

Prince.

A person of chief rank or authority in any official relation ; as the king of a nation (1 Kin. xiv. 7), satrap over a province (Dan. iii. 2, A. V.), head of a tribe (Num. i. 16) or of a tribal family (xxv. 14), a sheik (Gen. xxiii. 6), a chief officer over the servants of a king (Dan. i. 7). Prince is the rendering of various Hebrew and Greek words.

Seven princes of Media and Persia had access to the king's presence and held the highest official position after the throne (Esth. i. 14). Apparently they were the seven counselors of the king (Ezra vii. 14). In the year 521 B. C. an event occurred which perhaps explains the origin of these privileges. Seven men of the first rank in Persia (Herod. iii. 77), having slain the false Smerdis, entered into a compact with each other, as they were about to choose one of their number to be king, that each of the seven should have liberty to enter the palace without being announced, and that the king should not be allowed to marry outside of these seven families (84).

Pris'ca and Pris-cil'la [old woman and little old woman].

The wife of Aquila, who went with him in his wanderings, and showed at least equal zeal with her husband in advancing the Christian cause. Paul's estimate of her was high (Acts xviii. 1–3, 18, 26 ; Rom. xvi. 3 ; 2 Tim. iv. 19), and in three out of five verses she is named before her husband. See AQUILA.

Pris'on.

A special place was set apart in Egypt for the confinement of criminals. It was under the charge, and in the house, of a military officer, and the prisoners were often bound as well as kept in ward (Gen. xl. 3, 4 ; xlii. 16, 17). The prison was an institution among the Philistines also ; Samson was imprisoned,

blinded, bound with fetters, and compelled to labor (Judg. xvi. 21).

Among the Hebrews there was a prison in Samaria in the reign of Ahab, which was under the charge of the governor of the city (1 Kin. xxii. 27). Later there is notice of the detention of prisoners at Jerusalem in the court of the guard (Jer. xxxvii. 21), and in the dry cistern that was in the court (xxxviii. 6) ; but private houses were also used for the purpose (xxxvii. 15). The prison fare was bread and water (1 Kin. xxii. 27). In the Roman period the procurator's palace at Cæsarea on the sea, the castle of Antonia, and doubtless the palace of Herod at Jerusalem, had rooms where accused persons were confined (Acts xxiii. 10, 35). The prison at Jerusalem into which Herod Agrippa I. cast Peter was protected by iron gates, and important prisoners were bound with chains and guarded by soldiers in the cell, while other soldiers kept watch before the door (xii. 6, 10).

The Mamertine prison at Rome, where Jugertha was left to starve to death, and where according to tradition Peter was confined, is on the slope of the Capitoline hill toward the forum. It dates from the earliest ages of the city. It consists of two cells, one over the other. The lower one is 19 feet long, 10 wide, and 6½ high. It is entirely underground. It is vaulted, the walls gradually contracting. To judge by the slope of the walls, the chamber was originally about 10 feet in height, and was closed by a conical vault, arched in shape, but not constructionally an arch. Entrance to it was originally obtained only through a hole in the ceiling, through which criminals were let down. The floor is the native rock, from which a spring bursts, said in the legend to have been miraculously caused to flow by Peter in order to baptize his jailers.

Proch'o-rus [probably, leading in a choric dance].

One of the seven men elected to look after the Greek-speaking widows and probably the Christian poor at Jerusalem (Acts vi. 5).

Pro-con'sul [one acting for a consul].

The governor of a Roman province which was administered by the senate (Acts xiii. 7 ; xviii. 12 ; xix. 38, R. V.). He was appointed for one year, exercised in this province all the powers of a consul, and was attended by quæstors, who collected the revenues and paid them into the treasury managed by the senate.

Proc'u-ra-tor [steward, administrator].

The agent of the Roman emperor, who resided in imperial (as distinct from senatorial) provinces, received the revenues and paid them into the emperor's private exchequer. The military governor and chief magistrate was called proprætor or legate ; but in the smaller imperial provinces and sometimes in parts of larger ones the office of legate was dispensed with, and the entire government civil and military was intrusted to a procurator. Such was the case in Judæa. When Archelaus was deposed by the emperor Augustus in A. D. 6, Judæa, Samaria, and Idumæa were erected into a division of the prefecture of Syria, called the province of Judæa, and placed under procurators (Antiq. xvii. 11, 4; 13, 5; Tacitus, Annal. xii. 23; Hist. v. 9). They were successively Coponius (Antiq. xviii. 1, 1; 2, 2; War ii. 8, 1); Marcus Ambivius; Annius Rufus, in whose time the emperor Augustus died; Valerius Gratus, who held office eleven years (Antiq. xviii. 2, 2); Pontius Pilate, who was appointed by the emperor Tiberius, deposed after ten years, and arrived at Rome just after the death of Tiberius, which occurred in March 37 (Antiq. xviii. 2, 2; 4, 2; 6, 5; War ii. 9, 2; Tacitus, Annal. xv. 44; Luke iii. 1); Marullus, appointed by the emperor Caius (Antiq. xviii. 6, 11), and after an interval which concluded with the three-year reign of Herod Agrippa over Judæa (Acts xii. 1–23); Cuspius Fadus, who was appointed by the emperor Claudius; Tiberius Alexander (Antiq. xix. 9, 2; xx. 1, 2; 5, 2; War ii. 11, 6); Cumanus, appointed after the death of Herod, king of Chalcis and later recalled by the emperor Claudius (Antiq. xx. 5, 2; 6, 2 and 3; War ii. 12, 1 and 6); Felix, appointed by Claudius (Antiq. xx. 7, 1; War ii. 12, 8; Tacitus, Hist. v. 9; Annal. xii.); Porcius Festus, sent out by Nero (Antiq. xx. 8, 9; War ii. 14, 1; Acts xxiv. 27); and on the death of Festus, Albinus (Antiq. xx. 9, 1; War ii. 14, 1); and finally Gessius Florus, appointed by Nero shortly before the twelfth year of his reign (Antiq. xx. 11, 1; War ii. 14, 2 seq.; Tacitus, Hist. v. 10).

As appears from the cited passages and their context, these procurators were subject to the governor of Syria; but in Judæa itself their authority was supreme. The Roman garrison stationed in the province stood at their command; all important matters came before their judgment seat; they had the power of life and death (War ii. 8, 1); and their sentence was executed by the soldiers. They commonly resided at Cæsarea by the sea; but they were wont to go up to Jerusalem at the feasts and sometimes to winter there (Antiq. xviii. 3, 1), and they visited various cities of their dominion as occasion required. When in Jerusalem, they were accustomed to occupy the palace of Herod. See HEROD, PALACE OF.

Proph'et.

An authoritative and infallible teacher of God's will. Speaking of the order of prophets conceived of as a unity, God promised to raise them up from among the chosen people, qualify them by putting his words into their mouth, enable them to speak all that he commanded them, and maintain the authority of his word which they should speak (Deut.

xviii. 18, 19). Every prophet of God, and preëminently Christ, was like unto Moses (18; Acts iii. 22, 23), in similarity of endowment, of doctrine, of attitude toward the law, of didactic work. The same authoritative and representative character of the prophet is referred to by Zechariah. Words are given to the prophet by God; the words are sent by his Spirit to the prophets, are given to be taught to the people, and have been accredited in the past by their fulfillment (Zech. i. 6; vii. 12; also Neh. ix. 30). The same facts regarding the prophet are abundantly illustrated in individual instances. The prophets did not inherit the office nor receive it by human appointment, but were chosen, prepared, and called of God; and the call was often soul-searching (Ex. iii. 1–iv. 17; 1 Sam. iii. 1–20; Jer. i. 4–10; Ezek. i. 1–iii. 15). In various ways the word of the Lord came to them. They were commanded to proclaim it. They were accredited by signs, by the fulfillment of their predictions, and by the conformity of their teaching to the law. And God held man accountable for obedience to their word (Deut. xiii. 1–5; xviii. 18–20).

But there were also false prophets. Besides heathen prophets who spoke in the name of an idol (Deut. xviii. 20; 1 Kin. xviii. 19; Jer. ii. 8; xxiii. 13), there were false prophets who spoke in Jehovah's name (Jer. xxiii. 16–32). They were of two classes: first, conscious impostors, enticed to claim the gift by the consideration and influence which true prophets enjoyed; and courted on account of their smooth words (1 Kin. xxii. 5–28; Ezek. xiii. 17, 19; Mic. iii. 11; Zech. xiii. 4); and probably, secondly, sincere and even godly men, whose doctrine might be based on the law of God, but who were self-deceived in that they had not been called to the prophetic office by God and were not infallible religious guides. Tests were therefore established for distinguishing the true from the false. The true prophet was recognized— 1. By signs (Ex. iv. 8; Is. vii. 11, 14). But signs alone were not sufficient, for they might occasionally come to pass accidentally or be wrought by artifice (Deut. xiii. 1, 2; cp. Ex. vii. 11, 22; 2 Thes. ii. 9). 2. By the fulfillment of his predictions (Deut. xviii. 21, 22). This credential gains in evidencing power as time goes on and the historic events and developments take place which the prophets foretold of old. 3. By his teaching (Deut. xiii. 1–5; Is. viii. 20). If the doctrine taught by the claimant of a call from God led men away from the Ten Commandments, the speaker was manifestly not a man of God. The true prophet's teaching was found to agree with the doctrine of the law concerning God, his nature, character, and worship, and concerning the conduct of man. But there was more than mere servile agreement with the law of God. Planting themselves on the doctrines of the law, the prophets unfolded its principles in their application to human conduct and in their revelation of God. And among the sages of all history the prophets whom Israel accepted tower aloft and stand alone in the purity, value, and fitness of their teaching.

Prophecy included the prediction of future events (Is. v. 11–13; xxxviii. 5, 6; xxxix. 6, 7; Jer. xx. 6; xxv. 11; xxviii. 16; Amos i. 5; vii. 9, 17; Mic. iv. 10). Prediction was an important part of the prophet's work, and it furnished his credentials in part. But more important still, the prophet had to deal with the present and the past, and to instruct men in God's ways (Is. xli. 26; xlii. 9; xlvi. 9). The use of the English word prophet must not be permitted to emphasize unduly the predictive side of prophecy. The English word is derived from the Greek *prophētēs*, which means one who speaks for another, an interpreter or proclaimer, and one who speaks beforehand, a predictor. This twofold meaning is due to the two senses of the preposition *pro*, for and before.

The Hebrew word *nabi'*, which is translated prophet, means one who announces. It seems to have been a comprehensive general term at first. The active participle is used in another Semitic language, the Assyrian, for an announcer. In the Hebrew Scriptures Abraham is called a prophet (Gen. xx. 7). Between him and God there was direct personal intercourse, with him was the secret of the Lord, to him God revealed himself and his purposes (Gen. xv. 1–18; xviii. 17), he was able to teach his descendants the true knowledge of God (xviii. 19), and he had power of intercession with God (23–32). Miriam, who expressly claims that the Lord had spoken by her, was a prophet (Ex. xv. 20; Num. xii. 2, 6). Aaron as the spokesman of Moses is called his prophet (Ex. vii. 1; cp. iv. 16). The *nabi'*, or prophet, was a person qualified by God to be his spokesman to men. And this is the fundamental idea which underlies the term as used in Deut. xviii. 18. One of the qualifications was prophetic vision (1 Sam. iii. 1). Looked at in this aspect, the prophet was sometimes called a seer (1 Sam. ix. 9, in Hebrew *ro'eh*; Is. xxx. 10, in Hebrew *ḥozeh*). And when this was the main aspect in which he was regarded by the people, and this qualification was the one of highest value in popular estimation, seer was the designation in vogue among the people. This was the case for a considerable period in the early history of Israel. Samuel and Gad and Iddo were known by this title. But Samuel ceased to be merely a seer to whom the people resorted when they would inquire of the Lord, desiring to know God's will as to duty, or seeking direction in national affairs, or craving light upon private matters. Samuel went out among men as an authoritative teacher of the nation sent by God, and this public proclamation was the distinctive idea in prophecy (1 Sam. x. 10–13; xix.

20). The teaching function, as seen in Moses, became prominent again; and beginning with Samuel and his followers, and with renewed force several centuries later, the prophet became a constant presence in the national life, an ambassador of heaven to the kingdom of Israel, an authoritative preacher of righteousness, an interpreter of past and present history on its moral side, an admonisher of the consequences which God the judge has annexed to conduct, a forewarner of the certainty of the divine judgment on sin, and a fosterer of fidelity toward Jehovah. To foretell the future or make known the secret counsel of God, as did Nathan when he forbade David to build the temple and announced God's purpose to establish David's throne, forever remained functions of the prophet; but they became a comparatively small part of his work. Other features were more constantly in evidence, and as a result the restricted name of seer gave place again to the broader designation of prophet (1 Sam. ix. 9). Samuel was called a seer by his contemporaries, but his great successors, whom God raised up and inspired to teach the nation, were commonly designated prophets by the men of their generation. Seer was not banished from use, but the title of prophet, which had never been entirely disused (Judg. iv. 4; 1 Sam. x. 10–13; xix. 20), was raised again to its former prominence (iii. 20). Amos had prophetic vision (Amos i. 1; viii. 1; ix. 1) and was called a seer by the priest of Bethel (vii. 12); but he was also called to prophesy on the basis of this prophetic sight, and he did so (vii. 15).

Referring to the prophet's special endowment from on high, he was called a man of the Spirit (Hos. ix. 7). In common with other ministers of God, official or private, he is a man of God, a servant of God, a messenger of the Lord, a shepherd of God's people, a watchman, an interpreter.

That the prophet was to be raised up from the people of Israel alone did not prevent God, who worketh when and where he will, in caring for his kingdom to send a dream to a Philistine, an Egyptian, a Midianite, a Babylonian, a Roman (Gen. xx. 6; xli. 1; Judg. vii. 13; Dan. ii. 1; Mat. xxvii. 19). Even Balaam, who was a soothsayer, and as such was invited by the king of Moab to curse Israel, was temporarily used by God. These foreigners were in momentary contact with the kingdom of God. For its protection and advantage a glimpse of the future was given to them. They did not thereby become prophets, any more than did Hagar or Manoah and his wife, to whom the angel of the Lord appeared and afforded a glimpse of the future. They were not men of the Spirit, the intimates of God.

The prophets were taught of the Spirit of God (1 Kin. xxii. 24; 2 Chron. xv. 1; xxiv. 20; Neh. ix. 30; Ezek. xi. 5; Joel ii. 28; Mic. iii. 8; Zech. vii. 12; Mat. xxii. 43; 1 Pet.

i. 10, 11). In this God worked in accordance with the psychological nature of man. An audible voice or an angelic messenger occasionally came (Num. vii. 89; 1 Sam. iii. 4; Dan. ix. 21); but the instruction was ordinarily imparted by dreams, visions, and inward suggestions recognized by the prophets as not of themselves. They were not under the permanent influence of the Spirit. The word of the Lord came unto them. They waited for revelation (Lev. xxiv. 12). And their natural mental discernment is distinguished from the divine word which came to them. Samuel's private thought is distinguished from God's (1 Sam. xvi. 6, 7). Nathan at first approved of David's purpose to build a temple for the Lord, but afterwards told the king that God had forbidden its construction (2 Sam. vii. 3). The prophets did not exercise the prophetic power at all times, but when God told them to speak.

From the time of Samuel the office was regularly transmitted. Though the prophets who are mentioned by name are few, there were many anonymous ones (1 Kin. xviii. 4; 2 Kin. ii. 7-16). The office seems not to have ceased until the death of Malachi. At the approach and advent of Christ the tongue of prophecy was again loosed (Luke i. 67; ii. 26-38). In the church of the N. T. also there were prophets (1 Cor. xii. 28). They were not an order, like apostles and elders. They were men and women (Acts xxi. 9), and they were specially illumined expounders of God's revelation. They spake by the Spirit, occasionally foretold the future (xi. 27, 28; xxi. 10, 11), and taught and exhorted to great edification (1 Cor. xiv. 3, 4, 24). Paul ironically gives the title to a heathen writer, who so correctly described the immoral character of the Cretans that he had proven himself to that extent a mouthpiece of the truth (Tit. i. 12).

The call of the prophets came immediately from God himself (Amos vii. 15). The prophet was aware of a definite moment when the call came. Moses was called to his comprehensive work at the bush (Ex. iii. 1-iv. 17). Samuel had a special revelation in his youth (1 Sam. iii. 1-15), which was the beginning of his reception of revelation (iii. 19-iv. 1). Elisha knew when he was called to the office, and also when he was qualified for the work (1 Kin. xix. 19, 20; 2 Kin. ii. 13, 14). The vision seen by Isaiah in the year that Uzziah died (Is. vi.) has been supposed by many to have been his original call, but it may have been a later experience, designed to fit him for a new and greater work, like the vision that came to the apostle John long after his call (Rev. i. 10), to Peter at Joppa (Acts x.), to Paul in Jerusalem (Acts xxii. 17), and like the experience of Ezekiel (Ezek. xxxiii. 1-22) who had been called to the prophetic office by a vision many years before (i. 1, 4), and of Elijah, whose inaugural call is not men-

tioned, but who was afterwards commissioned at Horeb for a special work (1 Kin. xix.). Jeremiah knew when he was called, and interposed objections (Jer. i. 4-10). Hosea refers to the time when Jehovah spake at the first by him (Hos. i. 2). In the call of the prophets human instrumentality is mentioned but once, namely, in the case of Elisha (1 Kin. xix. 19. Evidence that the prophets were anointed with oil and inducted into office has been sought in Ps. cv. 15. But the psalmist is speaking of the patriarchs. He speaks in the name of God, and uses the language of his own time in alluding to them as prophets (Alexander, Wellhausen; anointed with the Spirit), or as priests, who were anointed ones, and prophets (Perowne), or as kings, who also were anointed, and prophets (Gen. xx. 7; xxiii. 6; Delitzsch; Baethgen; tribal chiefs equal in rank to anointed kings). Is. lxi. 1 has also been cited, but the anointing there spoken of is the unction of the Spirit. The case of Elisha has also been appealed to (1 Kin. xix. 16), where Elijah is told to anoint Elisha to be prophet in his room. But there is no evidence that even Elisha was ever anointed with oil. Elijah carried out the command by casting his cloak upon Elisha. Figuratively speaking, he anointed Elisha when he cast his mantle upon him (cp. 1 Kin. xix. 15 with 2 Kin. viii. 13, where the command to anoint is fulfilled by speaking a word). The prophet's cloak was the sign of the prophet's vocation (2 Kin. i. 8; ii. 9, 13-15), so that throwing it to him was a symbol of the call to the prophet's office.

To the prophets' mode of life there is only incidental allusion. Evidently in most respects it was like that of other men. As an appropriate dress for their work a garment of hair was frequently worn by them (2 Kin. i. 8; Zech. xiii. 4; cp. Mat. iii. 4); not as an ascetic's habit, but as a mourner's garb, symbolic of mourning for the sins of the people. Sackcloth also was worn for the same purpose (Is. xx. 2). The rough garment was not worn next to the skin, after the manner of ascetics; but was a mantle, cast about the shoulders over other raiment. For the subsistence of the prophets wild fruits were at their disposal (2 Kin. iv. 39; Mat. iii. 4). Contributions were made for their support (1 Sam. ix. 8; 1 Kin. xiv. 2, 3; 2 Kin. iv. 42). Hospitality was shown them (1 Kin. xvii. 9; xviii. 4; 2 Kin iv. 8, 10). Some were Levites, and shared in the Levitical revenues. Some had private means; as Elisha and Jeremiah (1 Kin. xix. 19, 21; Jer. xxxii. 8-10). Perhaps some were supported at court by royal bounty, like Gad, the king's seer, and others who bore the same title (2 Sam. xxiv. 11; 1 Chron. xxv. 5; 2 Chron. xxxv. 15). The prophets usually dwelt in houses like other men (1 Sam. vii. 17; 2 Sam. xii. 15; 1 Kin. xiv. 4; 2 Kin. iv. 1, 2; v. 9; xxii. 14; Ezek viii. 1). See also PROPHETIC ASSOCIATIONS.

Literary activities and duties devolved upon the prophets, as historians and writers of prophecy. The events of the reigns of David and Solomon were recorded in the histories of Samuel the seer, Nathan the prophet, and Gad the seer, and in the prophecy of Ahijah (1 Chron. xxix. 29; 2 Chron. ix. 29). Events of the reign of Rehoboam were written in the histories of Shemaiah the prophet and Iddo the seer (2 Chron. xii. 15), and of Jeroboam in the vision of Iddo the seer (ix. 29), of Abijah in the commentary of Iddo the prophet (xiii. 22), of Jehoshaphat in the history of Jehu, son of Hanani (xx. 34 with xix. 2), of Uzziah first and last and of Hezekiah in the writings of Isaiah (xxvi. 22; xxxii. 32). The four great historical works, the books of Joshua, Judges, Samuel, and Kings, were classed by the Jews as the Former Prophets in the canon, and were evidently written by prophets. In the time of Isaiah and Hosea the prophets entered upon their great careers as writers of prophecy. They committed their prophetic utterances in summary, or in considerable detail, or as isolated and individual prophecies, to writing.

Spiritually the prophets were prepared to receive divine communications. They were holy men, men who were surrendered to God's service and who lived in communion with God, men of habitual prayer (like Samuel, 1 Sam. vii. 5; viii. 6; xii. 23; xv. 11), who retired at times to their watch tower, that is, composed their minds and gave themselves up to quiet contemplation, in order to wait for revelation (Is. xxi. 8; Hab. ii. 1). Moses withdrew for forty days into the quiet and solitude of mount Sinai for communion with God, when the pattern of the tabernacle was to be shown him. Occasionally, in the early period, music was employed to stimulate devotion and awaken religious feeling (1 Sam. x. 5), or to soothe the mind and attune the heart for meditation, when the will of the Lord was sought (2 Kin. iii. 15). It was perhaps not accidental that the prophets were sometimes by a river's side and soothed by the steady flow or the placidness of the stream, when the communication came (Ezek. i. 3; Dan. x. 4), and that Samuel heard the Lord speak when night had fallen (1 Sam. iii. 2–10). By these various means the prophet's soul was kept or made ready for the operation of the Holy Spirit. God in holding communication with men worked in accordance with the laws of man's mind.

There were men who possessed and exercised the prophetic gift, who were not officially prophets. David was a prophet; he wrote of Christ; but he was not a prophet officially. He was king, and his writings were not assigned a place among the prophetic Scriptures. Daniel had the gift of prophecy in an eminent degree; but he did not devote his life to teaching the people; he

was officially a statesman and governor under Babylonian and Persian kings. His writings, like those of David, were placed among the Hagiographa or sacred writings, and not with the works of official prophets. See CANON. The Former Prophets and the Latter Prophets are designations in the Hebrew canon for the authors respectively of the historical books of Joshua, Judges, 1 and 2 Samuel, 1 and 2 Kings, and of the strictly prophetical books beginning with Isaiah. The authors were prophets; anonymous in the case of the Former Prophets, but named in the case of the strictly prophetical books. The reason was that prophecy, not history, required authentication. The designation does not refer to the time when the books were composed, but to the respective places of these two groups of books; Kings, for example, being written after Isaiah, but holding a place among the Former Prophets. There were great prophets, like Elijah and Elisha, who did not commit their discourses to writing. They are termed oral prophets by modern scholars. The literary productions of other prophets who recorded their prophecies are cited, excerpted from, and incorporated in the books of the Former Prophets and other Scripture.

Of the Latter Prophets, Hosea, Amos, and Jonah labored in the northern kingdom; the rest exercised their office among the people of Judah and Benjamin, either in Palestine or in the land of exile. Classed chronologically, and including Daniel, they are: 1. In the Assyrian period, from shortly before the accession of Tiglathpileser, 745 B.C., to the decay of the Assyrian power, about 625 B.C., Hosea, Amos, and Jonah in the north, and Joel, Obadiah, Isaiah, Micah, and Nahum in Judah. 2. During the Babylonian period in Judah, from 625 B.C. to the fall of Jerusalem, in 587 B.C., Jeremiah, Habakkuk, and Zephaniah. 3. During the exile in Babylonia, Ezekiel and Daniel. 4. During the period of the restoration, Haggai, Zechariah, and Malachi. See MUSIC, NAIOTH.

Proph′et-ess.

1. A woman called of God to the prophetic office. Miriam was a prophetess (Ex. xv. 20, 21; Num. xii. 2; Mic. vi. 4). So was Deborah (Judg. iv. 4). The Israelites resorted to her for judgment, and the Lord revealed his will through her to the nation (5, 6, 14). So was Huldah. She was consulted by the high priest at the command of the king in regard to the teaching of Deuteronomy, and she declared the counsel of the Lord (2 Kin. xxii. 12–20). Four virgin daughters of Philip the evangelist prophesied (Acts xxi. 9).

2. A prophet's wife, as is probably meant in Is. viii. 3.

Pro-phet′ic As-so-ci-a′tions.

The presence of a company of prophets at Gibeah of God, the home of Saul, is mentioned in 1 Sam. x. 5. Whether they were a wandering band of prophets, going from

town to town, or formed a community of
prophets resident at Gibeah, cannot be determined. The designation of the place as
the hill of God was probably derived, not
from the abode of these prophets, but from
the high place of worship that was upon it
(verse 5). The word rendered company in
A. V., band in R. V., is not the word translated company in 1 Sam. xix. 20; and the
phrase is not definite, but is merely a band
of prophets.

Samuel dwelt at Ramah (1 Sam. vii. 17;
xxviii. 3), where he was the head of a company of prophets (xix. 18-20). More definitely, he was at Naioth, in Ramah, a building or locality in the town of Ramah inhabited by this community of prophets (see
NAIOTH). Jewish tradition is represented
by the Targum of Jonathan, which renders
the word Naioth by house of instruction;
and this translation has given rise to the
phrase "school of the prophets," with its
misleading suggestions. The prophets who
gathered together naturally, indeed, employed their leisure in the study of things
pertaining to God: but there is no hint in
the narrative that they were at school or
were novitiates in training for the prophetic
office. The word and the narrative indicate
that there was at Ramah a community of
men already endowed with the prophetic
gift and with power, in co-operation with
God, spiritually to affect those who came in
contact with them (1 Sam. x. 10; xix. 20-
23); who dwelt together at or round about
Samuel's house; under his conduct engaged
in worship, giving utterance in praise and
exhortation to their exalted religious feelings
and apprehension of truth (cp. prophesying,
1 Sam. x. 5; 1 Chron. xxv. 1-3), and doubtless standing likewise under his direction in
whatever other religious duties devolved upon
them as prophets. The situation may be
conceived thus: Shiloh, the religious meeting place of Israel, had been forsaken of
God. The prophets gathered about God's
great representative and the chief spiritual
force of the time in order to cultivate their
own spiritual life in common worship, to
praise God together as the Spirit gave them
utterance (1 Sam. xix. 20), to engage in united
prayer in behalf of the nation (xii. 23; xv.
11 with 35; xvi. 1), and to go forth in companies for the revival and instruction of the
people (x. 5, 10). They sought on the one
hand to benefit themselves by religious fellowship, hold prolonged communion with
God amidst favorable surroundings, and
thereby not only to satisfy their spiritual
longings, but also to quicken their spiritual
apprehension and qualify themselves for
God's use of them as his spokesmen; and
they sought on the other hand to afford a
center of reformation in the midst of great
apostasy.

Two hundred years later, in the northern
kingdom, prophetic communities made their
appearance for a brief while. They were
probably founded by Elijah, on the model of
the earlier society under the presidency of
Samuel. The members were designated sons
of the prophets. The name denotes that
they belonged to the prophetic order; just
as a son of the apothecaries was one who followed the trade of an apothecary, a son of
the goldsmiths was a professional practitioner
of the goldsmiths' art, and sons of the singers
were members of the singers' guild (Neh. iii.
8, 31; xii. 28). The members of the prophetic order were called prophets and sons
of the prophets indifferently, and the word
of the Lord was revealed to them (1 Kin. xx.
35-38, 41; 2 Kin. ii. 3, 5; ix. 1). The associations which they formed were comparatively large (2 Kin. ii. 7, 16; iv. 42, 43), occupied a common building or compound (iv.
38; vi. 1-4), and were located at Gilgal,
Beth-el, and Jericho (ii. 3, 5; iv. 38). Beth-el
was a prominent seat of idolatrous worship,
and Jericho was hard by another such place;
and the establishment of an organized society
of prophets at them shows that the founder
intended the prophetic community to be a
counterpoise to apostate worship and a center
of reformation. Elijah, and after him Elisha,
stood at the head of these communities, visited them in turn (ii. 1, 2, 4; iv. 38), was
looked up to with respect and called master
(vi. 5). Elisha was regarded with peculiar
affection; they desired his presence with
them, sat before him as having him for their
president (and perhaps teacher), referred
their plans and their difficulties to him, and
were sent forth by him to perform prophetic
functions (iv. 38, 40; vi. 1-7; ix. 1). Though
not without revelation themselves they could
learn much of the will of God from the
greater prophet, as Miriam and Aaron did
from Moses (ii. 16-18; cp. sitting before a
prophet as equivalent to inquiring of God,
Ezek. viii. 1; xiv. 1-7; xx. 1). The spiritual
condition even of prophets could be promoted by the use of the means of grace, and
meditation on God's law could benefit even
inspired men of God.

There is no evidence that these societies
existed after the time of Elisha, neither in
Is. viii. 16 nor in Amos vii. 14. Huldah the
prophetess was not connected with such a
society; she did not dwell in the college, as
the A. V. renders, but in the second quarter
of the city (2 Kin. xxii. 14, R. V.).

Pros′e-lyte.

In the N. T., a convert to Judaism. The
Pharisees compassed sea and land to make
one proselyte (Mat. xxiii. 15). The Roman
poet Horace mentions the trait as characteristic of the Jews (Sat. i. 4, 142 and 143). Proselytes were present when the pentecostal
effusion took place (Acts ii. 10). One of the
men chosen to look after the poor in the
early Christian church was Nicolas, a proselyte of Antioch (vi. 5). They were quite

numerous in Antioch (War vii. 3, 3). At Damascus great numbers of women were converts to Judaism (ii. 20, 2). The chamberlain of queen Candace was evidently a convert (Acts viii. 27), and the royal family of Adiabene, east of the Euphrates, adopted the Jew's religion (Antiq. xx. 2–4). At Antioch, in Pisidia, many proselytes followed Paul and Barnabas (Acts xiii. 43). The rabbins recognized two orders of proselytes. One were proselytes of righteousness. They consented to be circumcised and baptized, and to offer sacrifice. They adopted Judaism in its entirety. The proselytes of the gate or of sojourning were much less advanced. They agreed to observe what were called the seven precepts of Noah (see NOAH), but declined to be circumcised or to embrace Judaism.

Prov′erbs, The.

A poetical book on practical piety. It follows the Book of Psalms in the Hebrew collection and also in the Greek, Latin, and English versions. The Hebrew word which has been rendered proverb embraces more than a maxim. It includes also the fable, the riddle, the satire, the parable (Num. xxiii. 7; Is. xiv. 4; Ezek. xvii. 2). The several parts of the book of Proverbs are: 1. Title, i. 1–6, descriptive of the entire book; declaring the purpose of the collection to be "to know wisdom and instruction; ... the words of the wise and their dark sayings," and designating it the proverbs of Solomon, son of David, king of Israel. This title, however, does not affirm that the book in all its parts is from Solomon (cp. Ps. lxxii. 20, although each psalm in the book is not thereby ascribed to David; see titles of Ps. xlii.–l.). 2. Main contents. I. Praise of wisdom, i. 7–ix. 18; a didactic poem in the form of addresses by a father to his son, and specially designed for young men. II. The proverbs of Solomon, x.–xxii. 16; maxims arranged in no precise order and consisting in each case mostly of two contrasted sentences. III. Without formal superscription, but which may be called from the opening verse, compared with xxiv. 23, the words of wise men, xxii. 17–xxiv. 22. Among these words is a poem on the drunkard's woes. Supplemented by the sayings of the wise, xxiv. 23-34, including an ode on the sluggard. IV. Proverbs of Solomon copied out by the men of Hezekiah, xxv.–xxix.; having all the characteristics of the popular proverb, and consisting of pithy sentences not only of two, but also of three, four, or five parallel clauses each. Three appendices: (1) The words of Agur, xxx.; enigmatical sayings in which numbers play a significant part. (2) The words of king Lemuel, xxxi. 1–9; maxims on practical life addressed to him by his mother. (3) Praise of the virtuous woman, xxxi. 10–31; a poem in which each of the twenty-two verses begins with a letter of the Hebrew alphabet in regular order.

The particular ascription of certain sections of the book to Solomon, and of other sections apparently to other authorship, indicates that Solomon was not the author of the entire work; and the title of the fourth section, "These also are proverbs of Solomon, which the men of Hezekiah king of Judah copied out," is valid evidence that the book of Proverbs did not receive its present shape before the reign of Hezekiah. The brief introduction (i. 1–6) fittingly describes the entire book, and the poem in praise of wisdom (7–ix. 18) is not ascribed to Solomon, and forms the preface to the proverbs of Solomon, which immediately follow, or more probably to all the maxims of wisdom which constitute the remainder of the book. The introduction and poem may, therefore, be safely attributed to the hand and brain of another literary man than Solomon, and dated not earlier than the reign of Hezekiah. The second and fourth sections, chap. x.–xxii. 16 and xxv.–xxix., or nearly two-thirds of the book, are ascribed to Solomon. The absence of a polemic against idolatry has been urged as evidence that the proverbs in these sections originated or were collected after the cessation of the great struggle which the prophets carried on with encroaching heathenism. It may with equal justice be advanced as proof that these sections antedate that struggle. If the absence of polemic proves anything, it affords evidence that these proverbs were collected either before the division of the kingdom and the encroachments of idolatry, or after the exile, when idolatry had lost its attractiveness. The language of these sections favors, though it does not establish, the ascription to Solomon, for it is pure Hebrew. It is free from foreign orthography and forms, such as are found in some books which were written immediately before the exile or subsequently to it. Furthermore proverbial literature is very ancient. It appeared early among the Hebrews also (1 Sam. xxiv. 13; 2 Sam. xii. 1; Judg. ix. 7). That Solomon composed and collected proverbs has early attestation (Prov. xxv. 1; 1 Kin. iv. 32; x. 1 seq.; Ecclus. xlvii. 13–17). The titles, therefore, which attribute the maxims in these two sections of the book of Proverbs, may safely be regarded as authentic.

Prov′ince.

The rendering of the Hebrew and Aramaic M⁽ᵉ⁾dinah, jurisdiction, and the Greek Eparchia, government.

The young men or servants of the princes of the provinces, who fought under Ahab against Benhadad (1 Kin. xx. 14), were not Israelites (15). They probably served the chieftains who ruled various districts in Gilead and the Hauran, and made common cause with Israel in resisting the encroachment of the Syrians upon the country south of Damascus.

The provinces of the Babylonian and Persian empires were divisions of the realm for administrative purposes (Dan. ii. 49 ; iii. 3). Darius the Great, who as king of Persia, had dominion from India to Ethiopia (Herod. iii. 90–94), divided this great empire into twenty governments called satrapies (i. 192 ; iii. 89); see SATRAP. These satrapies or large provinces were subdivided into smaller governmental districts, which the Jews designated likewise by the general term province (Ezra viii. 36 ; Neh. ii. 7, 9; Esth. iii. 12; viii. 9; cp. Herod. iii. 120, 128; vi. 42; with iii. 127 ; v. 11, 27, 30; see also DARIUS 2 . In the days of Ahasuerus these minor provinces numbered one hundred and twenty-seven (Esth. i. 1). During the Persian period Judah was at first under the jurisdiction of the governor beyond the river (Ezra v. 3, 6), but by royal decree it was made a separate province and granted a governor of its own (ii. 63; v. 8).

The provinces of the Roman empire were of two classes, imperial and senatorial. The imperial provinces were under the direct and sole control of the emperor; they comprehended all the frontier provinces which were supposed to need the presence of an army of occupation to hold them in subjection ; they were governed by a military officer called a legate, who was appointed by the emperor; their revenues were received by imperial agents termed procurators, and were paid into the private exchequer of the emperor. The smaller imperial provinces, and parts of larger ones like the subprovince of Judæa, were ruled by a procurator only, the presence of a legate not being deemed necessary. Cilicia (Acts xxiii. 34), Galatia, and Syria, of which Judæa was a part, were imperial provinces. The senatorial provinces were administered by the senate ; they did not require to be kept under control by military force ; their governor was styled a proconsul. He was attended by quæstors, who received the revenues and paid them into the public treasury, which was managed by the senate. Cyprus (Acts xiii. 4, 7), Macedonia (xvi. 12), Achaia (xviii. 12), and Asia (xix. 10) were senatorial provinces.

Psalms, Book of.

A collection of religious poems which were specially employed in the public worship of the God of Israel. In Hebrew it is called Book of Praises. The title in the English version is borrowed from the Greek translation (cp. Luke xx. 42). The general designation Psalms of David is derived from the number of psalms, seventy-three in all, expressly ascribed to David in the Hebrew titles (cp. Heb. iv. 7).

The psalms number 150. They are divided into five books; in imitation, it is thought, of the fivefold division of the Pentateuch ; see footnote, PENTATEUCH. This division is ancient. It is indicated in the Septuagint, and is marked by headings in the Hebrew

text. Its existence in the chronicler's day is, however, scarcely evidenced by 1 Chron. xvi. 35, 36, compared with Ps. cvi. 47, 48, as Delitzsch believes, for the passage in the psalm is as probably derived from the words in Chronicles as vice versa. These books begin respectively with Ps. i., xlii., lxxiii., xc., and cvii. Each book is arranged to close with a doxology. In the first book all the psalms are attributed to David except four (i., ii., x., xxxiii.). These are so-called orphan psalms; that is, they are anonymous. In the Septuagint all except i., which is introductory, and ii. are ascribed to David; x. being united to ix. and xxxiii. bearing the title "To David." The divine name Jehovah is generally employed in the psalms of this book. In the second book, of the thirty-one psalms the first eight are a collection of songs of the sons of Korah. Seven are expressly ascribed to them ; and xliii., whether written by them or not, was composed as the conclusion of xlii. This group is followed by a psalm of Asaph. Then comes a group of twenty psalms attributed to David with the exception of two (lxvi., lxvii.). Of the two exceptions, however, lxvii. is ascribed to David in the Septuagint. The book closes with an anonymous and a Solomonic psalm (lxxi., lxxii.). In this book the divine name is prevailingly Elohim, God ; and two psalms duplicate two of the first book, substituting the word God for Jehovah (liii. and lxx.; cp. xiv. and xl. 13-17). The third book contains seventeen psalms. The first eleven are attributed to Asaph, four to the sons of Korah, and one each to David and Ethan. This collection of psalms was gathered after the destruction of Jerusalem and burning of the temple (lxxiv. 3, 7, 8; lxxix. 1). The fourth book likewise contains seventeen psalms. The first is ascribed to Moses, two to David ; and the remaining fourteen are anonymous. The Septuagint gives eleven to David, leaving only five anonymous (xcii., c., cii., cv., cvi.). The fifth book has twenty-eight anonymous psalms, while fifteen are assigned to David and one to Solomon. The ascriptions differ considerably in the Septuagint. This collection was made late, for it includes psalms which refer to the exile (cxxvi., cxxxvii.). It will be seen that the composition of the psalms ranges over a long period of time. That David was the author of early psalms is supported by abundant early testimony, direct and indirect. See DAVID.

The titles of the psalms are ancient. They were not only in their place when the Greek version was made, but they were old at that time ; for musical and other terms which occur were not understood by the translators. As they stand, they are not infallible ; lxxxviii., for example, having two titles. The titles have been exposed, like the rest of the text of the Old Testament, to the ordinary vicissitudes of transmission ; and errors have doubtless crept in during the process of copying which must be discovered and removed by textual criticism. In the titles the Hebrew preposition *lamed* constantly occurs. It is translated "to" in the phrase "to the chief musician " (Ps. iv. title, in R. V. for), and "of" in such expressions as a "psalm of David" (Ps. iii), a "Michtam of David " (xvi.), "a psalm of the sons of Korah " (xlvii.), "a psalm of Asaph " (l.), "a song of David" (lxv.), "a prayer of Moses the man of God " (xc.), "a prayer of the afflicted " (cii.), and "*a psalm* of David " (xi.), "*a psalm* of the sons of Korah " (xliv.), "*a psalm* of Solomon " (lxxii.), and simply "of David " (cxxii.), "of Solomon " (cxxvii.); and "for" in "a song for the Sabbath day " (xcii.), "a psalm for the thank-offering " (c., R. V. margin). The force of this preposition in Hebrew speech was manifold. In the titles prefixed to poems four important meanings must be borne in mind by the interpreter. It may denote—1. Possession, belonging to (Ps. xxiv. 1, represented by the possessive case). 2. Authorship (Hab. iii. 1). 3. Dedication (Gen. xvi. 14, Beer-lahairoi, the well [consecrated] to the Living one who seeth me; Is. viii. 1). 4. Intended purpose. When the preposition is employed several times in a title, it may, of course, be used each time in a different sense (Ps. iv, rendered for, of, in A. V. to, of; xviii., for, of, of, unto; Is. v. 1, for or to, and touching). The simple phrases "of David" (Ps. xi.), " of Asaph" (lxxxi.), and the Hebrew order of the words "of David, a psalm " (Ps. xxiv.), " of the sons of Korah, a Maschil" (xliv.), " of the sons of Korah, a psalm" (xlvii.), suggest that the word psalm or Michtam or prayer (iv., xvi., xvii.) is an epithet descriptive of the poem, and in these and similar cases might be separated by a comma or other punctuation from the prepositional phrase that follows, thus "a psalm; of David," "a song; for the Sabbath day." Further, the preposition seems often to refer to a collection to which the particular psalm originally belonged, as in the phrase " of the sons of Korah." This clue leads to the belief that the similar phrase " of David " refers to a collection prepared by David.

The book of The Psalms, as at present constituted in the Old Testament, was the hymn book of the second temple. Its rich devotional songs were also sung in private gatherings for the worship of God (Mat. xxvi. 30 ; see PASSOVER . Like modern hymn books, it was composed of the hymns of the ages, and in many cases the source from which these psalms were derived is stated in the titles. From these it appears that there were collections in use before the present Psalter was compiled. 1. The collection of David. Seventy-three psalms of the completed Psalter belonged originally to this earlier book of praise, according to the notes in the Hebrew text (iii.–ix.. xi.–xxxii., xxxiv.–xli., li.–lxv., lxviii.–lxx., lxxxvi., ci., ciii., cviii.–cx., cxxii,.

cxxiv., cxxxi., cxxxiii., cxxxviii.-cxlv.). In the Greek version the note is not found with cxxii. and cxxiv., and occurs with xxxiii., xliii., lxvii., lxxi., xci.,, xciii.–xcix., civ., and cxxxvii., in addition to the psalms provided with it in the Hebrew text. In this collection a number of psalms were provided with a prose introduction stating the occasion ; and all that had this preface, or at least thirteen of them, were taken over into the completed book of The Psalms (iii., vii., xviii., xxxiv., li., lii., liv., lvi., lvii., lix., lx., lxiii., cxli.). No psalm of the completed Psalter has an introduction of this kind, except those that are marked "of David." To judge from the name, from the definite ascription of the authorship to David by means of a relative clause in the title of certain psalms thus marked (vii., xviii.), from David's known possession of poetic gifts, and from the ancient testimony to his interest in the musical service of the sanctuary (see DAVID), this collection was formed by David, and was the psalm book of the temple in pre-exilic times. Probably it contained both sacred poems of David's own composition and psalms selected by him from various sources ; and it would be quite in accordance with the history of hymnody if this collection of sacred songs, used by many generations in public and private worship, received additions of appropriate hymns as time went on, yet retained its original title of Prayers of David (Ps. lxxii. 20). Is not the present book of The Psalms, although it contains sacred poems written after the destruction of Jerusalem by the Babylonians, nevertheless often entitled the Psalms of David ? (see first paragraph). When the contents of this Davidic collection were combined with other collections each of its psalms was marked as taken from the book of David. Writings of prophets, priests, and poets who lived before the Babylonian exile survived that calamity, and it is not surprising that a body of religious songs should have outlived the catastrophe and been ultimately incorporated in the new hymnal. 2. A collection used by the sons of Korah, a family some of whom were officially connected with the sanctuary as singers (see KORHITE). Eleven psalms are attested as having belonged to this collection (xlii., xliv.–xlix., lxxxiv., lxxxv., lxxxvii., lxxxviii.). 3. A collection arranged by Asaph or members of his family, who were official musicians and singers at the sanctuary (see ASAPH). Twelve psalms are known to have belonged to this body of hymns, and in all the divine name kept prominent is God (l., lxxiii.–lxxxiii.). Besides these three collections there were many fugitive hymns which in course of time received the approval of the religious authorities for use in public worship. But the three primary collections supply two-thirds of the psalmody admitted into the completed Psalter.

After these collections had been formed three minor groupings of psalms came into existence. 1. By culling mainly from the three primary collections a group of psalms was assembled in which the prominent thought is God in the fulness of his attributes (xlii.-lxxxiii.). Because the word God, in Hebrew Elohim, predominates, these psalms are sometimes designated Elohistic. The group contained the collection of Asaph, perhaps the whole of it, consisting of twelve numbers, seven Korahite psalms, about a score from the psalter of David, and one from a book of Solomon's. It was made for the purpose of meeting a felt need in the worship; and it included, first, psalms that were written originally in adoring contemplation of God, in the fulness of the conception; and, secondly, psalms in which the divine name, if it was not originally God, was Jehovah, and was changed to God or Lord in order to adapt the psalm to the special use (cp. xiv. with liii., and cviii. 1-5 with lvii. 7-11; Jehovah being changed to God or Lord or vice versa). Scarcely an Elohistic psalm is found in the Psalter outside of this group (consider xc.). The group was given a place as a whole, and, so far as known, without diminution of number, in the completed Psalter; but the division of the Psalter into five books cut it in twain. 2. A collection of fifteen psalms formed from various sources, mostly from fugitive pieces, and entitled Songs of Ascents. It, too, was kept intact in the final arrangement of the Psalter. 3. Further, and mainly from the three primary collections, a selection was made by the chief musician. It contained fifty-five psalms which appear in the completed Psalter; namely, thirty-nine from the collection of David, nine from that of the sons of Korah, and five from that of Asaph, with one or two from anonymous sources (lxvi. and lxvii., unless the latter is Davidic, see Septuagint). To these fifty-five the Septuagint adds the xxxth, from David's collection. The prayer of Habakkuk was also included (Hab. iii. 19). All the psalms in the present Psalter that are provided with musical directions once belonged to this collection. Not all the psalms that once had a place in it, however, have musical notes. This latter fact, rather than the former, indicates a collection; since the musical notes might conceivably be mere instructions to the director of the temple music and account for the mention of him. The fact that a psalm had belonged to the chief musician's collection is noted in connection with it in the completed Psalter.

Internal evidence for the date of a psalm may come from several sources. 1. Diction and grammatical constructions. The inquiry along these lines demands caution in view of the limited amount and scope of the literature available for comparison, the draughts upon the common Semitic stock of words enforced on the poet by the insistent call for synonyms in the parallelism of Hebrew verse (cp. Ps. xix. 2-4), the vocabulary of poetry, which is characteristically rich in unusual words and constructions, and the dialects among the Hebrews in Palestine with their different content of words and forms (cp. Judg. v.; 1 Kin. xvii.-2 Kin. viii.; Hosea; Jonah). 2. Historical events and conditions reflected in the psalm. Unless an occurrence of known date is explicitly mentioned (Ps. cxxxvii.), the evidence is inconclusive; for a suitable occasion which is familiar to the modern interpreter (as for Ps. xlvi. the deliverance from Sennacherib) may not have been in the mind of the psalmist at all. The critical question must ever be: Are the terms of the description so specific as to determine the event with certainty and render negligible the consideration of other similar crises? 3. The stage of religious development which the psalm reveals. The argument from this source is apt to turn on theories regarding the date of the documents contained in the Pentateuch or of other Old Testament literature, or on opinions about the insight into spiritual things and the depth of religious experience possessed by earnest men in the early days of the monarchy. There are writings, however, which are acknowledged by all schools of criticism to be some of them earlier than David, others contemporary with him, and yet others not later than the eighth century. These writings afford a common, though limited, ground on which to discuss the extent of the religious knowledge and experience of individual men. 4. The fact that the speaker in the psalm, who uses the pronoun of the first person singular or plural, in many instances represents the community, and is not the psalmist voicing his own personal emotions. The individualization of the nation, however, was common from the earliest times to the latest in Israel. It is found in the Ten Commandments and their preface, and frequently in the prophets. Hence its employment in a psalm is practically no aid towards determining the date of composition (cp. first person singular, Deut. vii. 17; viii. 17; ix. 4; Is. xii. 1, 2; Jer. iii. 4; x. 19, 20; xxxi. 18, 19; Hos. viii. 2; xii. 8; xiii. 10; Mic. ii. 4. Moreover, these various criteria determine the date of those sections only to which they apply (Ps. xix. 7-14; li. 18, 19), and do not necessarily fix the date of the entire psalm. The cautious investigator discovers that in many cases a negative result only is attainable, namely, that sufficient reason does not exist for denying the authenticity of the title; or the outcome of the inquiry, stated positively, may be that the contents of the psalm are suitable to the occasion attested by the title.

Technical terms used are Neginah, a stringed instrument, and its plural Neginoth; and Nehiloth, wind instruments (iv., v., lxi.). Terms probably musical: Alamoth, maidens, perhaps maiden or treb'e voices (xlvi.; 1 Chron. xv. 20); Gittith, a cither of Gath, perhaps, or a march of the Gittite guard (viii., lxxxi., lxxxiv.); Selah, an orchestral interlude or a change from *piano* to *forte* (iii. 2); Sheminith, the eighth (vi.; xii.; 1 Chron. xv. 21). Terms indicative of the character of the psalm: Maschil, a didactic or reflective poem (xxxii., and twelve others); Michtam, perhaps epigrammatic (xvi., lvi.–lx.); Mizmor, a lyric poem, regularly translated psalm (iii., et passim); Shiggaion, probably a wild dithyrambic (vii.; Hab. iii. 1). Other terms are understood to indicate familiar melodies: Aijeleth hash-Shahar, hind of the dawn (xxii.); Jonath elem rehokim, the silent dove of them that are afar off, or, changing the pronunciation of the second word, the dove of the distant terebinths (lvi.); Mahalath, heaviness (liii., lxxxviii.); Muth-labben (ix.); Shoshannim and Shoshannim Eduth and Shushan Eduth, lilies the testimony (xlv., lx., lxxx.). The songs of ascents or degrees were probably designed for pilgrims going up to Jerusalem.

Psal'ter-y.

The usual rendering of the Hebrew *Nebel*, when a musical instrument is intended. In four passages it is translated viol (Is. v. 12, in R. V. lute; xiv. 11; Amos v. 23; vi. 5). *Nebel* is doubtless the Greek *nabla*, which was reputed to be of Sidonian origin; and it is usually translated by this Greek word in the Septuagint (1 Sam. x. 5; 2 Sam. vi. 5; 1 Chron. xiii. 8; xv. 16, 20). The body of the instrument was made of wood (2 Sam. vi. 5; 2 Chron. ix. 11), or, later, of metal (Antiq. viii. 3, 8). The strings were of gut (*minnim*), and their number in the common instrument is unknown, but in a special variety they were ten (Ps. xxxiii. 2; xcii. 3). It was tuned to the soprano register (1 Chron. xv. 20). It could be carried about while it was played (1 Sam. x. 5; 2 Sam. vi. 5). The name psaltery, which is occasionally given to this instrument in the Septuagint (Ps. xxxiii. 2; lvii. 8), has been thought to identify it with the *santir* of the Arabs; but the history of the *santir* and its name seems to be as follows: The Assyrians used a musical instrument consisting of a long, low, horizontal body over which strings were strung. It was played with a plectrum. See illustration under MUSIC. The Greeks adopted it as the twenty-stringed *magadis* and the forty-stringed *epigoneion*. Later the *magadis* received the name *psalterion*, and was apparently borrowed with its new name from the Greeks by the Aramæans (Dan. iii. 5, if *p'santerin* does not represent a different instrument here) and by the Arabs. By the latter it was called *santir*. In the light of this probable history of the *santir*, the identity of its name with psaltery is seen not to identify it with the Hebrew *nebel*. The tradition regarding the *nebel* indicates that

it was a kind of harp. Josephus says that the difference between the *kinura* [Hebrew *kinnor*, harp] and the *nabla* was that the former had ten strings and was played with the plectrum, while the latter had twelve notes and was played with the hand (Antiq. vii. 12, 3). According to Eusebius, the *psalterion* was called *nabla* by the Hebrews and had the metallic sounding-board above; and Augustine on Ps. xlii. describes it as having the sounding-board above the strings, and not below as in the cither, the strings of the psaltery being stretched between a curved arm and the drum or resonance box in which it terminates above. Isidorus and Cassiodorus describe the psaltery as triangular in shape, like the Greek letter delta. If they do not confound it with the *trigōnon*, which had a triangular frame, and if they correctly give the shape of the psaltery, it appears to have resembled the upright harp which Assyrian musicians carried while they played it. See illustration under MUSIC. The original form of the sounding-board and the arm probably bore resemblance to a skin bottle and its neck, and obtained for the musical instrument its name of *nebel*, bottle. It was one of the instruments which the company of prophets whom Saul met were playing when he came in their way (1 Sam. x. 5), and one of those used at David's removal of the ark to Jerusalem (2 Sam. vi. 5). When he permanently organized the instrumentalists into an orchestra for the sanctuary, some were appointed to perform on the psaltery (1 Chron. xv. 16, 20, 28; xvi. 5; xxv. 1, 6); and it was subsequently in continual use for divine worship (2 Chron. v. 12). It was played also at festive gatherings (Is. v. 12; Amos vi. 5). It was often combined with the harp (1 Sam. x. 5; 2 Sam. vi. 5; 2 Chron. ix. 11; Ps. lxxxi. 2; cviii. 2). For its use in the sanctuary, see MUSIC.

Ptol-e-ma'is. See ACCHO.

Ptol'e-my.

The name borne by all the male rulers of Egypt of the house of Lagus, which began with Ptolemy Soter, one of the generals of Alexander the Great, and lasted until the Roman conquest of Egypt and the death of Cleopatra. The early Ptolemies, especially the first three, were wise and efficient rulers and raised Egypt to a high position of power and influence. They held many foreign possessions, among which were Phœnicia, Cœle-syria, Cyprus, and Cyrenaica, and for a while Palestine. They patronized art, letters, and science, and raised Alexandria, their capital, to be the leading university center of Grecian culture. They were friendly to the Jews, encouraging them to settle in Alexandria, granting them special privileges and giving to many of them high civil and military positions.

The later rulers of this house were, however, weak and wicked. Wars with their neighbors were frequent, revolts on the part of their people at home became common, incest and the murder of relatives were well known in the palace, and the loss of all the foreign possessions heralded the loss of the throne itself.

Three of the rulers of this line and several men of humbler rank are mentioned in the Books of the Maccabees:

1. Ptolemy IV., called Philopator. He was suspected of causing the death of his father, and his first act on coming to the throne was the murder of his mother and younger brother. His whole reign was a series of debaucheries and crimes. Encouraged by the weakness and profligacy of Ptolemy, Antiochus III., king of Syria, made war on

This pottery juglet filled with thirty-five silver tetradrachmas probably was the private bank of a Shechem resident in the second century B.C. The coins cover a minimum of ninety years from at least 285-193 B.C.

him with a view to wresting Phœnicia from Egypt, but was utterly defeated by the Egyptian army at the battle of Raphia, 217 B. C. (3 Mac. i. 1–5). After this battle, Ptolemy sacrificed in Jerusalem, but being prevented from entering the holy of holies, attempted to assassinate all the Jews in Alexandria in revenge. A somewhat fanciful account of this is found in the Third Book of Maccabees. He died in 205 B. C.

2. Ptolemy VI., called Philometor, began to reign in 181 B. C., at the age of seven, under the regency of his mother, Cleopatra. He reigned for some years alone and for some years conjointly with his brother, Physcon, called Ptolemy VII. Later, the kingdom was divided between them, Physcon ruling over Cyrene and Libya, and Philometor over Egypt and Cyprus. His generals invaded Syria and so came into contact with Antiochus Epiphanes, by whom they were completely defeated at Pelusium 171 B. C. Cyprus also was taken by Antiochus, and Alexandria

would doubtless have fallen but for the interference of the Romans, who began at that time to exercise a quasi protectorate over Egypt. Philometor interfered frequently in the affairs of Syria, siding one time with the pretender Alexander Balas (1 Mac. x. 51–57) and afterwards with Alexander's rival, Demetrius Nicator (xi. 1–18). While engaged in battle in Syria, he fell from his horse, and died shortly afterwards from the effects of the injury, 145 B. C. Ptolemy showed special favor to the Jews. It was by his permission that Onias built a Jewish temple at Leontopolis copied after the temple at Jerusalem.

3. Ptolemy VII., Physcon, also called Euergetes, was first co-regent with his brother Philometor, 170–164 B. C., but after the death of the latter reigned alone, 145–117 B. C. He is sometimes reckoned as Ptolemy VIII., his nephew Eupator, son of Philometor, reigning for a few days after his father's death. The early part of his reign was a series of crimes against his own family and such debauchery as alienated and disgusted his subjects, who revolted several times. Like his predecessors, he interfered in the affairs of Syria, lending aid first to Zabinas, and then against him. He is mentioned (1 Mac. xv. 16) as in correspondence with Rome, and it is probably he who is meant in 1 Mac. i. 18.

4. Ptolemy, a general of Antiochus Epiphanes (2 Mac. iv. 45; vi. 8; viii. 8). He took part in the expedition which Lysias organized against Judas Maccabæus (1 Mac. iii. 38). It is possible that he is identical with Ptolemy Makron (2 Mac. x. 12), who, first served Ptolemy Philometor in Cyprus, then passed into the service of Antiochus Epiphanes and later into that of Antiochus Eupator. Falling into disfavor with the latter, he ended his life by taking poison, 164 B. C.

5. Ptolemy, son-in-law of the high priest Simon. He murdered his father-in-law and two of his brothers-in-law in the stronghold of Dok, near Jericho (1 Mac. xvi. 11 seq.).

Pu'a. See PUVAH.

Pu'ah.

One of the Hebrew midwives who disobeyed the command of the Egyptian king to kill the male children at their birth (Ex. i. 15).

For others called Puah in the English versions, but which is a different word in Hebrew, see PUVAH.

Pub'li·can.

A farmer of the Roman taxes and customs. In place of appointing revenue officers to raise fixed taxes from the community, the Romans and their deputy princes like the Herods were accustomed to put up to auction the privilege of farming the public revenues, or some specified part of them, in the several provinces, cities, towns, and districts. Those who bid at the auction were necessarily wealthy men or representatives of wealthy companies; for they undertook to pay a given sum into the treasury (*in publicum*), and they were obliged to give security to the government for the sums they promised to pay. In some cases they in turn sold the right of farming portions of the revenue to subcontractors, in others they engaged a number of subordinate agents to do the actual work of collecting the taxes. They themselves were generally Romans of equestrian rank, while their subordinates, of course, were of inferior dignity. The subordinates or actual collectors of the taxes and customs are called publicans in the English version of the N. T. It was understood that the farmers were to repay themselves for their labor and the risk they had undertaken by taking from the taxpayers a fraction more than they paid over to the government. No proper means were adopted to prevent that fraction from assuming great proportions. With a few honorable exceptions, the publicans, great and small, were extortioners (cp. Luke iii. 12, 13; xix. 8). They were unpopular among all classes in the provinces, except, perhaps, with the Roman governors, who often received part of the plunder for conniving at the oppressions practiced. Sometimes the subcontractors, and in most cases the subordinate tax-gatherer, in the conquered countries belonged to the native population. Thus Zacchæus, a Jew, seems to have been subcontractor for the revenues of Jericho (Luke xix. 1, 2), and Matthew, or Levi (also a Jew), apparently a tax collector paid by the farmer for the revenues of Capernaum (Mat. ix. 9; Mark ii. 14; Luke v. 27). It added to the unpopularity of the Jews who accepted office as the agents of the Roman publicans, or themselves became farmers of the revenue from particular towns, that they raised taxes for a foreign and heathen government. They were not admitted into society; nay, it was considered disreputable for anyone to be their friend and associate. It was one of the charges brought against our Lord that he ate with publicans and sinners (Mat. ix. 10–13) and that he was their friend (xi. 19). He honored them by choosing one of their number as an apostle (ix. 9; x. 3). Quite agreeing with popular opinion as to the low moral state of the average publican (v. 46, 47; xviii. 17), he still invited them as freely as he did others into the kingdom of God. His kindness touched their hearts, and not a few of them were baptized (xxi. 31, 32; Luke iii. 12; vii. 29; xv. 1; xviii. 13, 14). He introduced a penitent publican into his parable of the Pharisee and the publican (9–14).

There is no passage in the N. T. in which publican signifies the keeper of a public house.

Pub'li-us.
The chief man and a land owner on the island of Melita, when Paul was there. He entertained the apostle and his companions for three days. He was rewarded; for Paul by prayer and the laying on of hands cured the father of Publius of fever and dysentery (Acts xxviii. 7, 8). His name suggests that he was a Roman; and his title, which is also found in inscriptions relating to Malta, seems to mean that he was the highest Roman official on the island.

Pu'dens [bashful, modest].
A Christian at Rome who joined Paul in sending salutations to Timothy (2 Tim. iv. 21). In an inscription found in that capital, a man of the same name and perhaps the same as he is stated to have been a servant of Tiberius, or Claudius. The facts that in the letter to Timothy Pudens, Linus, and Claudia go together, and the poet Martial, who went to Rome about A. D. 66 and abode there many years, mentions three persons bearing the same names, have suggested that the poet may have referred to Paul's three friends. If so, Pudens was an Umbrian, who became a centurion and was sent on military duty to the remote north; and Claudia was the wife of Pudens and apparently of British origin, being probably the daughter of king Tiberius Claudius Cogidubnus, mentioned in a Latin inscription found at Chichester in A. D 1723. With the sanction of king Tiberius Claudius Cogidubnus, a man named Pudens gave the site at Chichester for the erection of a temple by a guild of carpenters.

Pu'hites. See PUTHITES.

Pul.
1. An African country and people. The latter are coupled with Tarshish and Lud, apparently all three being skillful in archery (Is. lxvi. 19). One opinion is that Pul is the island of Philæ on the Nile in Upper Egypt on the confines of Ethiopia. It is, however, more probably a copyist's error for Put (q. v.).
2. A king of Assyria; see TIGLATH-PILESER.

Pulse.
Leguminous plants or their seeds, specially peas and beans, which are eminently nourishing. On these Daniel and his companions desired to be fed (Dan. i. 12, 16, R. V. margin, herbs). Parched pulse is mentioned in 2 Sam. xvii. 28, but the word pulse is plausibly supplied by the translators; it is not in the original.

Pun'ish-ment.
The penalty due for sin inflicted for the satisfaction of justice. So Adam, Eve, and Cain were punished by God. Punishment is not inflicted for the good of the offender. The destruction of the men of Sodom for their wickedness was not intended to benefit them. The execution of the murderer does not aim at his reformation. Chastisement, not punishment, is intended to reform the of-

fender. Nor is punishment primarily inflicted with a view to the prevention of crime, although this is a great end. The civil authority enforces law by penalty for the protection of the state, since purely moral considerations, such as the inherent righteousness of an act or the sense of justice, fail to prevent men from violating the rights of others. Deterring the evil-disposed was an object in the infliction of punishment which the Mosaic law had in view, but it was not the principle on which the law was based (Deut. xiii. 11; xvii. 13; xix. 20; xxi. 21). If the prevention of sin were the main end, justice would be merged into benevolence toward the citizens of the state. Yet the chief end of punishment is not to restrain the criminal from further crime nor to deter others from doing similar acts of violence. Sin ought to be punished irrespective of the effect which the punishment may have in preventing others. The indignation which men feel toward the offender himself, when they witness a flagrant act of wrongdoing, such as murder, oppression, or cruelty, and the demand which they instinctively make for his punishment show that they discern guilt in the sinner, and that they do not think in the first instance of the need of deterring others from the commission of like crimes. The wrongdoer is punished because he deserves to be. So, under the Mosaic law, the state must execute justice and punish the offender, or be held guilty of participating in and condoning the crime (Lev. xx. 4, 5; Num. xxv. 4, 11; Deut. xxi. 8; Josh. vii. 11–15). The people must cleanse Jehovah's land from the blood of murder. The execution of the murderer was an expiation of the land (Num. xxxv. 33, 34; Deut. xxi. 8).

The majesty of the law is maintained only when the punishment bears an adequate proportion to the crime committed, neither too little nor too much. The penalty need not be, and seldom is, an exact equivalent. The penalty for theft is not the restitution of the stolen property nor its exact value in money. Enforced restitution does not clear the thief. Law has been violated, guilt incurred, and punishment is demanded.

The laws of the Hebrews were stern, but the punishments were not cruel. In rare cases the family of the criminal was extirpated by the immediate act of God or by his express command (Num. xvi. 32, 33; Josh. vii. 24, 25; 2 Kin. ix. 25, 26); but this extent of punishment was recognized as extraordinary; it was not appointed by the law as the prescribed penalty for any crime, and the law expressly forbade that fathers should be punished for the children (Deut. xxiv. 16). For a special case of impurity, the heinousness of which was aggravated by the relation of the party concerned to the sanctuary of God, and for incestuousness of peculiar abhorrence, the penalty was burning with fire (Lev. xx. 14; xxi. 9; cp. Gen. xxxviii. 24).

But there was no cruelty involved. The guilty ones were not burnt alive; they were first stoned to death, and then their bodies were consumed by fire (cp. Josh. vii. 15, 25; see also Deut. xxi. 22, 23). The hand of a woman who had used it in a shameless act to assist her husband in his struggle with an adversary was cut off (Deut. xxv. 11, 12). Was this undue severity? Retaliation for bodily injury, when inflicted willfully and not in a quarrel, eye for eye, tooth for tooth, was legalized. So it was by ancient Greek law and by the Roman laws of the twelve tables. In the later Jewish law (Antiq. iv. 8, 35), and perhaps in the earlier law as well, a ransom in lieu of the maiming might be accepted by the injured person. This exemption was based on Ex. xxi. 29, 30 on the principle that, since in so great a matter as the infliction of death by one's ox, a fine might take the place of the surrender of the owner's life, in all lesser cases of injury a fine might also be accepted. In its humanity the Hebrew administration of justice compares favorably with Roman methods. Unlike Roman law, the Hebrew penal code did not authorize the punishment of the parricide by scourging him to the effusion of blood and then sewing him up in a sack and drowning him; nor did it sanction the torture of witnesses, who were slaves, and of accused persons to extract testimony (Acts xxii. 24; see DEACONESS), the punishment of the condemned by stocks and cruel scourging (Mat. xxvii. 26; Acts xvi. 24; War ii. 14, 9), the mockery of those about to be executed (Mat. xxvii. 27–31), crucifixion (26, 32, 44; Antiq. xvii. 10, 10), condemnation of criminals to fight with each other as gladiators or with wild beasts (1 Cor. xv. 32; War vi. 9, 2; vii. 2, 1), scourging to death, starving to death (see PRISON), and burning to death, not infrequently by clothing the victim in a shirt steeped in pitch and setting it on fire.

The Hebrew law did not rudely abolish established usage, even when custom fell short of the standard erected by God (see SLAVE, CONCUBINE, DIVORCE); it recognized the people's hardness of heart (Mark x. 5); but it brought custom under law, checked excesses, reformed abuses; it took solemn account of man's conception of right and justice as prevalent in that age, guarded against vengeance and vindictiveness, satisfied the sense of justice, and thus maintained the august majesty of law; and it set higher standards before man and was a distinct advance toward perfection. The form of punitive justice was further determined by the essential idea of the theocracy, which required that not only crimes against the state and society, but also violations of religious ordinances should be punished. The relation of the Israelites to their divine King resulted in God's punishing sin when man failed to do so, and in God's reserving to himself the right to punish certain specified sins, e. g., to inflict childlessness (Lev. xx. 4–6, 20, 21). Furthermore, the administration of justice was a matter in which the entire community was concerned, and consequently the people participated in its execution. The people stoned the criminal condemned to death.

The offenses mentioned in the penal law were:

1. Violation of the religious duties of the covenant. There were (1) capital offenses, which the human tribunal punished with death. They were five: sacrifice to idols Ex. xxii. 20; Lev. xx. 2; Deut. xiii. 6–17; xvii. 2–7), sorcery, professed intercourse with a familiar spirit, soothsaying (Ex. xxii. 18; Lev. xx. 27), profanation of the Sabbath (Ex. xxxi. 14, 15; xxxv. 2), blasphemy (Lev. xxiv. 10–16), and false prophecy, whether uttered in behalf of heathen deities or in the name of Jehovah (Deut. xiii. 1–5; xviii. 20). The penalty was death by stoning. Instances of the infliction of the death penalty on persons charged with these offenses are recorded in the history; for sacrificing to idols (2 Kin. x. 18–25; xi. 18; xxiii. 5, 20), for exorcising the dead (1 Sam. xxviii. 3, 9), for profaning the Sabbath (Num. xv. 32–36), for blasphemy (1 Kin. xxi. 13), for uttering false prophecy (xviii. 40; xx. 27, 28). (2) Offenses punishable by cutting off the offender from his people. They endangered covenant institutions and the fundamental ordinances of worship. They were refusal to receive circumcision, the sign of the covenant (Gen. xvii. 14), neglect of the passover, the covenant sacrifice, and consumption of leavened bread during the feast of unleavened bread (Ex. xii. 15; Num. ix. 13), performance of work and refusal to fast on the day of atonement (Lev. xxiii. 29, 30), use of blood or fat for food, since they belonged to sacrifice and atonement (vii. 25–27; xvii. 14), offering elsewhere than at the sanctuary (xvii. 4), slaughtering sacrificial animals without making a peace offering, and eating the peace offering after the prescribed limit (vii. 18; xvii. 9; xix. 8), use of the holy anointing oil and the incense for common purposes (Ex. xxx. 33, 38), neglect to purify one's self from defilement, and eating sacrifice in an unclean condition (Lev. xxii. 3; Num. xix. 20). The punishment of cutting off is in some instances accompanied by the death penalty or by threat of divine judgment. When accompanied by the death penalty, the execution of the offender was committed to man. The threat of divine judgment reserved the infliction to God himself. The question whether the punishment of cutting off in all cases implied death, even when the death penalty was not expressly annexed, has given rise to much debate. The phrase has been interpreted to mean excommunication, as rabbinical writers understand; or loss of the rights belonging to the covenant; or death,

which in breaches of the ritual was intended to be commuted to banishment or deprivation of civil rights, or death in all cases, either invariable and without remission, or else voidable by repentance and use of the means of propitiation for ceremonial defilement. It probably means expulsion from the fellowship of Israel or, as is otherwise stated, the congregation of Israel (Ex. xii. 15, 19; Num. xvi. 9; xix. 13), and, whether specifically stated or not, includes divine intervention for the extermination of the evil-doer (Gen. xvii. 14 with Ex. iv. 24; Lev. xvii. 10; xx. 3, 5, 6; xxiii. 30). Accidental breach or mere neglect did not involve this dire punishment. Only when a person offended with high hand and showed bold contempt for the law was he cut off from his people (Num. xv. 30, 31).

2. Unchastity. (1) Abominations that defile the people and the land. The penalty was death. They were adultery and the seduction of a betrothed virgin, not a slave girl (Lev. xx. 10; Deut. xxii. 21–27), unnatural lust, both beastiality and sodomy (Ex. xxii. 19; Lev. xx. 13, 15, 16), incestuous relations with mother-in-law or daughter-in-law (11, 12, 14). Unchastity on the part of a priest's daughter, since it defiles at the same time the father who was set apart to holy service, was punished not only by death, but also by burning the body (xxi. 9). (2) Unclean, but less repugnant, conjugal relations were punished by cutting the offenders off from their people or by childlessness (Lev. xx. 17–21). (3) The hand of a woman, which was used in a shameless and unchaste act to distress the adversary of her husband, was to be cut off (Deut. xxv. 11, 12). (4) Unchastity which is neither adulterous, unnatural, nor incestuous. The seduction of a virgin entailed marriage, the payment of the usual price for a wife, and in certain cases a fine (Ex. xxii. 16, 17); and the ravisher was obliged to marry the maid and pay her father fifty shekels, and forfeited the right of divorce (Deut. xxii. 28, 29).

3. Insubordination to the constituted authorities. The penalty was death. (1) Impiety toward parents: striking or cursing father or mother (Ex. xxi. 15, 17; Lev. xx. 9), incorrigibility coupled with habitual drunkenness (Deut. xxi. 18–21). (2) Refusal to submit to the decree of the priest or judge (xvii. 12). (3) Treason, which is not treated in the law, but, according to the history, was punished by death and confiscation of property (1 Sam. xx. 31; xxii. 16; 2 Sam. xvi. 4; xix. 29; 1 Kin. ii. 8, 9; xxi. 13, 15).

4. Crimes against the person, life, character, and property of another. (1) Willful murder and man-stealing were punished by death (Ex. xxi. 12, 16; Deut. xxiv. 7); see MURDER. (2) Bodily injury, inflicted intentionally or through carelessness, was punished according to circumstances by compensation or retaliation, an eye for an eye, a tooth for a

tooth (Ex. xxi. 18–36). (3) A false witness incurred the penalty of the crime for which the accused was on trial (Deut. xix. 16, 19), and a false accusation against a young wife's honor was punished by chastisement, a fine of 100 shekels, and forfeiture of the right of divorce (xxii. 13–19). (4) For injury to property the law required, according to circumstances, either simple compensation or a fine paid to the owner and amounting to several times the value of the stolen goods (Ex. xxii. 1–15).

The punishments recognized by the Mosaic law were death, chiefly by stoning, and in extreme cases the burning or hanging of the body; chastisement, the stripes not to exceed forty (Deut. xxv. 3); retaliation, compensation, which is scarcely a punishment, and fine; forfeiture of rights; and in a special case the loss of a hand. Death was sometimes inflicted by the sword, spear, or arrow, but without the forms of Hebrew law and in extraordinary cases (Ex. xix. 13; xxxii. 27; Num. xxv. 7; 1 Kin. ii. 25). The sword of the magistrate did not symbolize Hebrew judicial authority. Imprisonment, chains, and stocks were used by the authority of priests and kings, but they were not an institution of the early days of the Hebrew nation (Ezra vii. 26; Jer. xx. 2; Acts v. 40).

Pu'non [perhaps, darkness or fog].

A station of the Israelites in the wilderness not long before their arrival in Moab (Num. xxxiii. 42, 43). Probably the small town called Phainon by Eusebius, in the desert east of mount Seir, between Petra and Zoar; cp. PINON.

Pu'rah, in A. V. **Phurah** [bough].

The servant, doubtless armor-bearer, of Gideon (Judg. vii. 10, 11).

Pu-ri-fi-ca'tion.

Under the Mosaic law these were of four kinds: 1. Purification from uncleanness contracted by contact with a corpse (Num. xix.; cp. v. 2, 3), not a carcase (Lev. v. 2). For this purpose the ashes of a heifer were required, a female animal as in the case of the sin offering for the common people. It was necessary for the heifer to be red, the color of blood in which the life resides; to be without blemish, and never to have been used in the service of man. It was slain without the camp, its blood was sprinkled toward the sanctuary, and the carcase was burned together with cedar, hyssop, and scarlet. The ashes were gathered and preserved without the camp. When needed, they were mingled with living water; and a clean person, with a bunch of hyssop, sprinkled them upon the unclean on the third and seventh day. It only remained for the defiled to wash his clothes and bathe, in order to be ceremonially clean. The defilement of a Nazirite, whose consecration had been interrupted by contact with a corpse, was of greater moment, for he was

specially dedicated to ceremonial purity. After a week's separation, on the seventh day he shaved off his hair, the sign of his vow. On the eighth day he brought the same offerings as a man who had been defiled by an issue or as a mother might after childbirth (Num. vi. 9–12). A guilt offering followed (ver. 12), preparatory to his reinstatement as a Nazirite; cp. the guilt offering of the leper.

2. Purification from uncleanness due to an issue (Lev. xv.; cp. Num. v. 2, 3). On the seventh day after recovery, the unclean person after bathing in living water and washing the raiment was clean; and on the eighth day he repaired to the sanctuary and offered two doves or young pigeons, one for a sin offering, the other for a burnt offering. Uncleanness due to contact with a person having an issue, or with anything rendered unclean by such a person, was in ordinary cases cleansed by a bath, the uncleanness remaining until evening (Lev. xv. 5–11).

3. Purification of a mother after childbirth. After the days of uncleanness, which were seven for a man child and fourteen for a female child, were over, those of purification followed, during which she touched no hallowed thing, lest she defile it, and for the same reason was forbidden access to the sanctuary. For a son these were to continue thirty-three, and for a daughter sixty-six days, after which she brought a lamb of the first year or, in case of poverty, two pigeons or two doves for a burnt offering and a young pigeon or dove for a sin offering (Lev. xii. 8; Luke ii. 21–24).

4. Purification of the leper (Lev. xiv.). The candidate for purification presented himself on the appointed day at the gate of the camp, later at that of the city. The priest killed a clean bird, holding it so that the blood flowed into an earthen vessel of living water. He made a sprinkler by binding a bunch of hyssop with a scarlet cord on a cedar handle, and dipped the sprinkler and a living bird into the bloody water, sprinkled the person undergoing purification, and released the bird; see AZAZEL. This much of the ritual was also performed in purifying a house of leprosy. The candidate was then pronounced clean; and having washed his clothes, shaved off all his hair, and bathed, he might enter camp or city, but must remain outside of his habitation seven days. On the seventh day he again washed his raiment, shaved and bathed, and was clean. On the eighth day he appeared at the sanctuary with two male lambs and a ewe lamb of the first year or, if his means were limited, with one lamb and two doves or pigeons, togther with a meal offering and a measure of oil. One he lamb was taken for a guilt offering. The priest put some of its blood on the candidate's right ear, right thumb, and right great toe. He did likewise with some of the oil, after sprinkling a little of it before the Lord, and poured

the rest on the candidate's head. The ceremony was completed by offering the remaining lambs or pigeons for a sin offering and a burnt offering.

Pu'rim [from Persian *pur*, a lot; or perhaps Babylonian *pur* or *bur*, a stone].

A Jewish festival, instituted to celebrate the deliverance of the exiles in Persia from the wholesale massacre of their race planned by Haman. He had cast *pur*, or a lot, to ascertain a favorable day for carrying out his scheme. The festival was kept on the fourteenth and fifteenth days of the month Adar, approximately February (Esth. ix. 20–28). In 2 Mac. xv. 36 it is called the day of Mordecai. Josephus mentions that in his time all the Jews of the inhabited world kept the festival (Antiq. xi. 6, 13). Some have thought that the feast of the Jews mentioned in John v. 1 was that of Purim; but the statement that Jesus went up to Jerusalem is opposed to this view, for Purim was celebrated throughout the land, and only at three great feasts was a visit to Jerusalem compulsory. Purim was not one of the three. From the time of its institution it has enjoyed great popularity among the Jews. The celebration has assumed a fixed form. The 13th of Adar they keep as a fast day. In the evening, which is the beginning of the 14th day, they assemble in their synagogues. After the evening service the reading of the book of Esther is begun. When the name of Haman is reached, the congregation cry out, "Let his name be blotted out," or "The name of the wicked shall rot," while the youthful worshipers spring rattles. The names of Haman's sons are all read in a breath, to indicate that they were hanged simultaneously. Next morning the people repair again to the synagogue, and finish the formal religious exercises of the festival and then devote the day to mirth and rejoicing before the Lord, the wealthy giving gifts to the poor. The keeping of the Purim festival on the 14th of Adar from age to age is a strong argument for the historic character of the incidents recorded in the book of Esther. See ESTHER.

Purple.

A color which in ancient and modern usage comprehends violet and all the hues intermediate between violet and crimson. In ancient times it included crimson and other reds (Pliny, Hist. Nat. ix. 61, 62; Mark xv. 17 with Mat. xxvii. 28). Purple raiment was costly, and consequently its use was the privilege of the rich exclusively. It was worn by persons of wealth and high official position (Esth. viii. 15; cp. Mordecai's elevation to office, 2; Prov. xxxi. 22; Dan. v. 7; 1 Mac. x. 20, 62, 64; 2 Mac. iv. 38; cp. 31; Luke xvi. 19; Rev. xvii. 4), and especially by kings, as by the kinglets of Midian (Judg. viii. 26). Indeed, it was a sign of royalty (1 Mac. viii. 14; Homer, Iliad, iv. 144), and was put on Jesus in mockery of his claims. Rich cloths of purple were used as coverings for the seats of princely palanquins (Song iii. 10), awnings for the decks of luxurious ships (Ezek. xxvii. 7), and drapery for idols (Jer. x. 9). It was largely employed in the hangings of the tabernacle (Ex. xxv. 4; xxvi. 1, 31, 36), and in the garments of the high priest (xxviii. 5, 6, 15, 33; xxxix. 29). The Jews interpreted the color symbolically (War v. 5, 4).

Purple dye was obtained from various kinds of shell fish (1 Mac. iv. 23; War v. 5, 4), and was yielded by a thin liquor, called the flower, secreted by a gland in the neck. The amount yielded by each fish was very small, much labor was required to collect it in quantity, and the price was correspondingly great. The larger purples were broken at the top to get at the gland without injuring it, but the smaller ones were pressed in mills (Pliny, Hist. Nat. ix. 60). Two species of *Murex* were used by the ancient Tyrians, *Murex trunculus* and *Murex brandaris*, and yielded crimson. The *Murex* is common throughout the Mediterranean Sea, but the shade of color varies with the coast.

Jewish children are active participants in the joyous Feast of Purim activities. In addition to the celebration in the synagogue, special costume parties, plays, and the colorful costume parade, the *Adloyada*, mark the day.

Purse.

A bag for carrying money (Luke x. 4; xii. 33; xxii. 35), which, however, was not a necessity, as money was often carried in the girdle (Mat. x. 9, R. V. margin). The purse or common treasury of the disciples was in charge of Judas (John xii. 6; xiii. 29, R. V margin), the same word was used to describe it as that which designated the chests for offerings at the temple. Before coins came into use, pieces of silver and gold of various sizes and shapes were tied in a bag or in the girdle, or rings of the precious metal were strung on a cord (Gen. xlii. 35; Prov. vii. 20), and weights and scales were carried for weighing out the desired quantity (Deut. xxv. 13; Mic. vi. 11).

Put, in A. V. **Phut** in Gen. x. 6; Ezek. xxvii. 10; xxxviii. 5, margin.

A people related to the Egyptians (Gen. x. 6), and the country inhabited by them. The prevalent opinion is that the name denotes Libya in whole or in part. It is mentioned in association with Egypt and other African countries, especially with Lubim (Nah. iii. 9) and Lud (Ezek. xxvii. 10; and Is. lxvi. 19 in Septuagint; between Cush and Lud, Jer. xlvi. 9; Ezek. xxx. 5); it is rendered Libyans by the Septuagint in Jeremiah and Ezekiel; it is also identified with Libya by Josephus (Antiq. i. 6, 2); and the western part of Lower Egypt is called in Coptic Phaiat. Another view is strenuously defended by Ebers and Brugsch, which connects Put with Punt. Punt lay south or southeast of Cush, and is commonly identified with the Somali country in Africa, east of the straits of Bab el-Mandeb, and on the adjacent coasts of Asia, near Aden, in Arabia.

Pu-te'o-li [little wells].

A seaport in Italy which Paul's vessel reached the day after it had been at Rhegium. The apostle found Christians there, and enjoyed their hospitality (Acts xxviii. 13). Founded in the sixth century B. C., it was originally called Dicæarchia, and was the ordinary landing place of travelers to Italy from Egypt and the East (Antiq. xvii. 12, 1; xviii. 7, 2; Life 3). It was on the northern shore of the bay of Naples, near the site where the modern city of that name now stands. Its old name of Puteoli still exists, little changed, as Pozzuoli. The whole region round is volcanic, and the crater of the Solfatara rises behind the town.

Puth'ites, in A. V. **Puhites.**

A family in Kirjath-jearim (1 Chron. ii. 53).

Pu'ti-el [probably, afflicted by God].

Father-in-law of Eleazar, Aaron's son (Ex. vi. 25).

Pu'vah and **Puah;** instead of first form A. V. has **Phuvah** (Gen. xlvi. 13), **Pua** (Num. xxvi. 23).

1. A son of Issachar and founder of a tribal family (Gen. xlvi. 13; Num. xxvi. 23; i Chron. vii. 1).

2. A man of Issachar, son of Dodo, and father of the judge Tola (Judg. x. 1).

Py'garg.

The rendering of the Hebrew *Dishon*, treader or leaper, the name of a clean animal (Deut. xiv. 5). The pygarg of the ancients was a white rumped antelope. It seems to have been the addax (*Antilope addax,* or *Addax nasomaculatus*). The horns, which exist in both sexes, are twisted and ringed. It has a white patch on the forehead, and the hinder parts are grayish-white. It is about the size of a large ass. It is a native of northeastern Africa (cp. Herod. iv. 192), but its range extends to the southeastern frontier of Palestine.

Pyr'rhus.

The father of Sopater (Acts xx. 4, R. V.).

Q

Qoph. See KOPH.

Quail.

A bird which the children of Israel twice during their journeying near Sinai providentially had for food in great abundance. In the wilderness of Sin the birds covered the camp on one evening (Ex. xvi. 12, 13); at the graves of lust they were driven by the southeast wind from the sea, and fell in vast quantities in and around the camp, lying in places three feet deep (Num. xi. 31–34; Ps. lxxviii. 26–31). Each time it was the spring of the year. The bird was called in Hebrew $s^e lav$, and the similarity between the Hebrew word and the Arabic *salwâ*, a quail, proves that to be the bird intended. It is the quail of Europe, not of America, is called *Coturnix dactylisonans*, or *communis*, and is placed in the *Tetraonidæ* or grouse family, and the *Perdicinæ*, or partridge subfamily. It is the smallest species of the partridge type, being only about $7\frac{1}{2}$ inches long. Its general color is brown, with buffy streaks above and buff below. It is migratory, arriving in Palestine from the south in immense numbers in March, and going southward again at the approach of winter. Quails fly rapidly and well, and take advantage of the wind; but if the wind changes its course, or the birds become exhausted from long flight the whole immense flock is apt to fall to the ground, where they lie stunned (cp. Antiq. iii. 1, 5). In this condition they are captured in great quantities on the coasts and islands of the Mediterranean Sea. The Israelites spread the quails, which they could not eat at once, round about the camp (Num. xi. 32) in order to dry them in the sun and

Writing tables and benches found in the Scriptorium in Qumran.

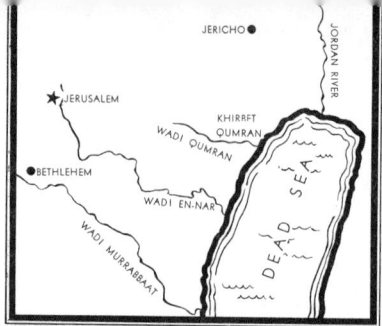

Map of the northern sector of the Dead Sea showing Qumran and its environs.

Many ancient manuscripts, among them scrolls of Old Testament books, commentaries on Old Testament books, apocryphal books, astronomical and cryptical writings, and other documents were discovered in the Qumran caves which border the Dead Sea. Except for the Book of Esther, scrolls of all the Old Testament books were found, and they were immediately recognized as the oldest manuscripts of these books now in existence. Other manuscripts, especially the Manual of Discipline, provided valuable insights into the life and beliefs of an important group of Jews which lived in the Qumran Community during the time of Christ. Since 1947, at least four hundred manuscripts have been found in eleven caves. The richest source was Cave 4 which contained over ninety Bible manuscripts and scores of other writings.

Many archaeologists and scholars agree that the members of the Qumran Community probably belonged to the marrying segment of the Essenes. This group separated itself from the normative Judaism of the day and practiced monastic rules of discipline. The Qumran Community made use of a body of literature in addition to the canonical Scriptures. The large number of apocryphal writings discovered indicates the high regard in which such writings were held by the Qumran Community. When it became apparent that the Community would be destroyed by the approaching Roman legion in A.D. 68, the precious manuscripts were placed in jars and hidden in caves.

The area of the Qumran caves in the Judean wilderness, about two miles from the Dead Sea. Cave 4, marked by a circle in the photograph, contained what seems to have been the bulk of the library of the Qumran Community.

Above: Ruins of the domestic section of the Qumran Community. A mill for grinding grain is in the foreground.

Right: Reconstructed scroll jar discovered at Qumran.

Below: This copper scroll, discovered in Cave 3, was sawed into strips at the University of Manchester, England, and published. It contained a puzzling report of hidden treasure, the authenticity of which is doubted by many scholars.

air, as the Egyptians did with fish (Herod. ii. 77).

Quar'tus [fourth].

A Corinthian Christian who joined with Paul in sending a salutation to the church of Rome (Rom. xvi. 23).

Qua-ter'ni-on.

Four united persons or things; a guard of four soldiers (Acts xii. 4). Four quaternions, *i. e.*, four companies, each of four soldiers, sixteen in all, were set to look after Peter when he was in prison at Jerusalem, each quaternion discharging the duty for one watch of three hours. During the night watches, two soldiers slept with the apostle in his cell, while the other two mounted guard before the door.

Queen.

The consort of a king, or a woman who reigns by her own right. Vashti and Esther were queen consorts (Esth. i. 9; ii. 22). Even after the death of the king her husband, the queen, especially if mother of the new monarch, retained respect and influence (2 Kin. x. 13); for the practice of polygamy made the position of even the chief wife precarious, and at any time the king might capriciously promote over her head some one of her rivals; but the queen mother, *i. e.*, the mother of the king, had an unalterable relation to the monarch, and was often the most potent female personage. Three queens regnant or women who occupied the throne are mentioned in Scripture: Athaliah, who, after perpetrating a massacre of the seed royal, usurped the throne of Judah; the queen of Sheba (1 Kin. x. 1–13; 2 Chron. ix. 1–12); and Candace, queen of the Ethiopians (Acts viii. 27). The last two, it is believed, came to their high dignity in a perfectly legitimate way.

The queen of heaven was a false divinity, in honor of whom the Jews in Jeremiah's time made cakes, burnt incense, and poured out drink offerings (Jer. vii. 18; xliv. 15–30). She was probably the Phœnician goddess Ashtoreth (q. v.), partly the moon and partly the planet Venus personified.

Quick'sand.

A sandbank which moves, quick being used in the nearly obsolete sense of living. The quicksands of which the sailors on board Paul's ships were afraid (Acts xxvii. 17), and which were the terror of ancient mariners, were two in number, the Greater and the Lesser Syrtis, the former constituting the southeastern, and the latter the southwestern part of that great indentation in the north African coast south of Sicily. The Greater Syrtis, now called the gulf of Sidra, curves inward on the African coast for about 126 miles, and measures 264 miles between the two promontories at its mouth. It is shallow, and full of quicksands. The Lesser Syrtis does not run so far inland. At its mouth it measures about 69 miles from the island of **Kerkenna** on the north to that of Jerba on the south. It is dangerous to navigate, owing to its winds and tides. It is now called the gulf of Cabes.

Qui-ri'ni-us, in A. V. **Cyrenius**; the former being the original Latin name, the latter the modification it underwent among the Greeks.

A Roman who became governor of Syria (Antiq. xviii. 1, 1). Under him an enrollment was made which led Joseph to go with Mary his espoused wife to Bethlehem. This visit to Bethlehem took place in the reign of Herod the Great, at the close of the year 5 or beginning of 4 B. C. The enrollment was not a local affair, but was made in pursuance of a decree of the Roman emperor Augustus that all the world should be taxed. This was the first enrollment made when Quirinius was governor of Syria (Luke ii. 1–5, R. V.). Quirinius was twice sent as *legatus Augusti*, i. e., governor, to Syria. His first administration fell somewhere between 7 and 2 B. C. During it he carried on the war with the Homonadenses of Cilicia, probably sharing the official duties and title with Varus, who was governor of Syria from 7–4 B. C. Thus Varus directed the civil business of the province while Quirinius conducted its military and foreign affairs (cp. the dual administration of Vespasian and Mucianus). Quirinius was proconsul of Asia in 3–2 B. C., if the Tivoli inscription is correctly interpreted by Ramsay; and he was *legatus Augusti* for Syria the second time A. D. 6–9. The first enrollment was conducted in the Jewish manner, by tribes and families. The second, made in A. D. 6–7 after Judæa had been incorporated into the Roman empire, was resented as a mark of servitude and occasioned disturbances, stirred up by Judas, a Galilæan (Acts v. 37; Antiq. xvii. 13, 5; War ii. 8, 1). Luke connects the first enrollment with Quirinius, without mentioning Varus, because it was commonly spoken of as the first enrollment under Quirinius in distinction from the notable enrollment under him which gave rise to the tumults.

A brief biography of Quirinius is furnished by Tacitus (Annal. iii. 48). He says: "About this time he [the emperor Tiberius] asked the senate that the death of Sulpicius Quirinius [which occurred in A. D. 21] might be celebrated by public obsequies. Quirinius was in no way related to the old and patrician family of the Sulpici, but was born at Lanuvium, a municipal town. As a reward for his military and administrative services, he obtained the office of consul under Augustus [in 12 B. C.], and soon afterwards the honors of a triumph for having taken the strongholds of the Homonadenses in Cilicia. While attending Caius Cæsar as rector, when the former obtained Armenia, he paid court to Tiberius, who was staying at Rhodes. Tiberius mentioned the fact in this letter.

praised him for his good offices, and accused Marcus Lollius of being the author of the depravity of Caius Cæsar and his animosity. But to other people the memory of Quirinius was by no means dear, because of his persistence in the trial of Lepida [his wife, whom he had convicted of adulteries, poisonings, and treasonable dealings, but who yet succeeded in gaining the compassion of the people], and also of his sordid avarice in his old age, although very powerful."

Quiv'er.

A case for containing arrows (Is. xlix. 2; Lam. iii. 13). The Assyrian archers on foot carried the quiver on the back, with the opening usually at the right shoulder, but archers who fought from chariots hung the quiver at the side of the vehicle; see illustration under Bow and RAM. The Egyptians also slung the quiver across the back, but they seem to have allowed it to hang horizontally and to have drawn out the arrows from beneath the left arm.

R

Ra'a-mah, in R. V. once **Raama** (1 Chron. i. 9), the Hebrew spelling in this instance [shaking, quivering, trembling].

Collective name for a Cushite people, associated with Sheba (Gen. x. 7; 1 Chron. i. 9). Men of the two tribes brought precious stones and gold to the markets of Tyre (Ezek. xxvii. 22). Raamah is mentioned in inscriptions of Sheba as a place near Ma'in, in southwestern Arabia.

Ra-a-mi'ah [trembling caused by Jehovah]. See REELAIAH.

Ra-am'ses. See RAMESES.

Rab'bah, in A. V. twice **Rabbath** (Deut. iii. 11; Ezek. xxi. 20), the Hebrew form when joined with a following word [great, i. e., the capital].

1. A city at the headwaters of the Jabbok, 23 miles east of the Jordan. It was the chief city of the Ammonites. When David was king, the Ammonites defied Israel, prepared for war, and hired auxiliaries from the Aramæans. The hired army marched to the town of Medeba (1 Chron. xix. 7; or perhaps "waters of Rabbah"). Joab and the Israelites were encamped before the gate of Rabbah, and presently the Aramæans pitched camp behind them in the open field. The Israelites were beset before and behind (2 Sam. x. 8, 9; 1 Chron. xix. 9). By dividing his forces Joab met and defeated both enemies (2 Sam. x. 13, 14). The next spring Joab besieged Rabbah again. During a sally from the gate, Uriah the Hittite was killed. That part of the city lying between the citadel and the river, and called the city of waters, fell into the hands of Joab, but the citadel held out. David was sent for to complete the conquest and associate it with his name.

He came, took the city, and condémned the inhabitants to forced labor (2 Sam. xi. 1; xii. 26-31; 1 Chron. xx. 1-3). In time the Ammonites recovered the city. Judgments were denounced against it by Jeremiah (xlix. 2-6) and Ezekiel (xxi. 20). It was embellished by Ptolemy Philadelphus (285-247 B. C.), and in his honor named Philadelphia. This city was the eastern limit of Peræa (War iii. 3, 3), and the southernmost of the ten cities of the Decapolis. The commercial highway between Damascus and Arabia which skirted the desert passed through it, and there was also a trade road from Philadelphia by way of Gerasa and Pella to Scythopolis. The modern name is 'Ammân, an echo of Ammon.

2. A city, with dependent villages, in the hill country of Judah (Josh. xv. 60). Perhaps its site is the ruin Rubba, about 14 miles west by south of Bethlehem.

Rab'bath. See RABBAH.

Rab'bi, and Rabboni.

A doctor, teacher, or master; a respectful term applied by the Jews to their spiritual instructors (Mat. xxiii. 7; John i. 38). The later Jewish schools are said to have had three grades of honor: rab (master), the lowest; rabbi (my master), the second; and rabboni (my lord, my master), the highest of all. When John wrote, the termination which denotes my had lost its especial significance as a possessive pronoun, for John explains rabbi and rabboni as meaning simply master (John i. 38; xx. 16).

Rab'bith [multitude].

A frontier village of Issachar (Josh. xix. 20). Conder doubtfully identifies it with the present village of Râba, among hills 8 miles south of mount Gilboa, and 7 southeast of Jenin.

Rab-bo'ni. See RABBI.

Rab'-mag.

A title of high office, borne by Nergal-sharezer, a chief officer in Nebuchadnezzar's army (Jer. xxxix. 3). Four explanations have been offered, none of which rests on a sure foundation. 1. It denotes the chief of the Magi. According to this view, the Median and Persian religious caste was influential in Babylonia in the reign of Nebuchadnezzar, who had a Median princess for his wife, and its head man accompanied the army. The Magi are, however, called in Greek *Magoi*, singular *Magos*, which appears in Semitic as *Magushu*, not as *mag*. 2. It is the Hebrew modification of *rubû îmga*, exalted prince, a title which Nabuna'id ascribes to his father and which Nebuchadnezzar assumes. The word *îmga* is not well understood, and its long initial vowel is a strong argument against its identity with *mag*. 3. It represents *rab mahhû*, chief prophet or soothsayer, who appears from this passage in Jeremiah to have accompanied the army, as did the augurs of Rome. 4. Since *mah* denotes a prince, as does *rab*, the combination prince-

prince is the title for a high military official. But such a title seems scarcely distinctive.

Rab'-sa-ris [*rab sha reshu*, chief who is head, the latter part being modified to suit the Hebrew ear into *saris*, eunuch].

An official title. A rab-saris accompanied the armies of Sennacherib and Nebuchadnezzar (2 Kin. xviii. 17; Jer. xxxix. 3). The officer at Nebuchadnezzar's court, who is called master of the eunuchs in the English version and whose title is given in Hebrew as *rab sarisim*, perhaps, held the same office (Dan. i. 3).

Rab'sha-keh [Assyrian *rab shak*, head officer, general].

Title of a military official, associated with the tartan and the rab-saris of Sennacherib in command of an expedition against Jerusalem (2 Kin. xviii. 17). On this occasion he conducted the parley with the officials of Hezekiah (19, 26, 27, 37), and was perhaps head of the expedition (xix. 8).

Ra'ca.

An Aramaic term *reka'*, worthless: an expression of contempt (Mat. v. 22).

Ra'cal, in A. V. **Rachal** [trade, commerce].

A place in Judah to which David sent some of the recovered spoil of Ziklag (1 Sam. xxx. 29). Site unknown.

Race. See GAMES.

Ra'chab. See RAHAB.

Ra'chal. See RACAL.

Ra'chel, in A. V. once **Rahel** (Jer. xxxi. 15) [ewe].

The younger daughter of Laban. She was possessed of much personal beauty, and Jacob fell in love with her at first sight, when he met her at the well near Haran, in Mesopotamia, where she was watering her flock. As he possessed no property and it was customary to pay the parents a price for the bride, he served her father seven years for her, and then, being cheated by the substitution of the elder sister, Leah, who was much less highly favored, served another seven for the younger maiden, the only one who had gained his affections. He married her also (Gen. xxix. 1-30), and she became the mother of Joseph (xxx. 22-25) and Benjamin, dying when the latter was born (xxxv. 16-18). She was buried a little to the north of Ephrath, better known as Bethlehem. The grave was situated at a place which a traveler from Bethel would reach before he came to Bethlehem. Jacob erected a pillar to mark the spot. This pillar long remained (19, 20). It was near Zelzah (1 Sam. x. 2). The reputed site was alluded to by Jerome and the Bordeaux pilgrim in the fourth century, and is accepted as correct by Jews, Christians, and Mohammedans. The erection called Kubbet Râhîl, tomb of Rachel, is a small building like a mosque, with a dome. It has an open apartment to-

Tomb of Rachel, near Bethlehem.

ward the east and a small enclosure toward the west. The present structure is of no great antiquity.

The prophet Jeremiah represents Rachel as weeping for her children, the descendants of her son Joseph, the people of Ephraim and Manasseh who were in captivity (Jer. xxxi. 15; cp. 9, 18). At Ramah was her voice heard : not because the prophet foresaw that the captives of Judah and Benjamin would be brought to Ramah after the fall of Jerusalem before being led into exile (xl. 1), for Rachel is not weeping over the Jews; but either because a town called Ramah was perhaps near Rachel's grave (cp. 1 Sam. x. 2; and RAMAH 2), or more probably because Ramah was a height in the territory of Rachel's remaining children, the descendants of Benjamin, and near the border of depopulated Ephraim, whence the desolation of the land was visible. This picture which the prophet drew of weeping Rachel found fulfillment in the slaughter of the innocents at Bethlehem in the land of Judah (Mat. ii. 18), although the descendants of Leah, not Rachel, wept. Rachel looking on the wasted land of Ephraim, and bewailing her slain and exiled children, was witness that the process had begun which terminated in the possession of the promised land by foreigners, the occupation of the throne by an Edomite, and the slaughter of Leah's children in the endeavor to slay the legitimate king and destined saviour of all Israel, Ephraim, Benjamin, and Judah alike. The picture of Rachel found more than a counterpart in the sorrow of the women of Bethlehem. It found completion, and it found renewed realization. Rachel wept again, this time with Leah. Rachel's hope for the return of her children to the Lord their God and David their king (Jer. xxx. 9) was bound up in Leah's yearning for that son of David in whose days Judah should be saved and Israel dwell in safety (xxiii. 6). Rachel's cry was the first wail of that lamentation which continued through the centuries and was heard at Bethlehem when a foreign king, in hostility to the son of David, legitimate king of the Jews, was able to send armed men to the city of David and slay the children. The process begun when Rachel first wept was being completed. The prophetic picture was finding final fulfillment.

Rad'dai [cutting under, subjugating].

A son of Jesse, and brother of David (1 Chron. ii. 14).

Ra'gau. See REU.

Ra-gu'el. See REUEL.

Ra'hab I. [ferocity, insolence, violence].

A poetical name for Egypt (Ps. lxxxvii. 4; lxxxix. 10; Is. xxx. 7, R. V.; li. 9). In Is. li. 9 it is parallel with dragon; see DRAGON. In Job. ix. 13; xxvi. 12, R. V., especially, some interpreters understand a sea monster, and some even discern an allusion to the Semitic myth of the sea monster Tiamat who attempted to reduce the ordered universe to chaos, but was subdued by the sun-god Marduk. This interpretation is not necessary, but it is possible. The inspired poets and prophets might, of course, borrow the creations of fancy to illustrate truth; cp. LEVIATHAN.

Ra'hab II., in A. V. of N. T. once **Rachab** (Mat. i. 5) [broad].

A harlot whose house was on the wall of Jericho. She harbored the spies sent by Joshua to explore the city, hid them when they were searched for, and, finally, let them down by a cord on the outer side of the wall, so that they escaped to the Israelite camp (Josh. ii. 1-24). When Jericho was taken, Rahab and her family were spared, and incorporated with the chosen people (vi. 22-25; Heb. xi. 31; James ii. 25). It was probably she who became the wife of Salmon and the mother of Boaz, and a link in the chain of ancestry both of king David and of our Lord (Mat. i. 5).

Ra'ham [affection, tenderness].

A man of Judah, family of Hezron, house of Caleb (1 Chron. ii. 44).

Ra'hel. See RACHEL.

Rain. See YEAR.

Rain'bow.

A bow appearing in the part of the heavens opposite to the sun, consisting of the prismatic colors, and formed by the refraction and reflection of the sun's rays from drops of rain or vapor. It is exceeding beautiful (Ecclus. xliii. 11, 12). After the flood God selected the rainbow, which had often before been seen in the sky, and appointed or consecrated it as the token of the promise that he would not again destroy the earth by a flood (Gen. ix. 12-17). It became the symbol of God's faithfulness and of his beneficence toward man (Rev. iv. 3).

Rai'sin. See VINE.

Ra'kem [variegated]. The Hebrew word is elsewhere rendered Rekem.

A Manassite (1 Chron. vii. 16).

Rak'kath [a shore].

A fenced city of Naphtali, and, from its etymology, presumably on the shore of the sea of Galilee (Josh. xix. 35). The rabbins place it where Tiberias now stands.

Rak'kon [thinness, or perhaps a shore].

A village of Dan (Josh. xix. 46). Conder suggests as its site Tell er-Rekkeit, 2½ miles north of the mouth of the 'Aujah, and 6 north of Joppa.

Ram, I.

1. The male of the sheep (Ezek. xxxiv. 17); see illustration under SHEEP. It was used as food (Gen. xxxi. 38), might be brought as a burnt offering or a peace offering (xxii. 13; Lev. i. 10; viii. 18; and iii. 6; ix. 4), and was appointed for a guilt or trespass offering (v. 15; vi. 6). Rams' skins dyed red were used, with other appliances, as coverings of the tabernacle (Ex. xxvi. 14), and rams' horns as war and apparently jubilee trumpets in the time of Joshua (Josh. vi. 4-6, 8, 13). The two-horned ram seen by Daniel in prophetic vision was the Medo-Persian power, the first or smaller horn that came up being the empire of the Medes, the second or greater horn which rose at a later period that of the Persians (Dan. viii. 3-7, 20).

2. The battering-ram was an instrument of war, used to beat down the gates and walls

Ram.

of a besieged city (Ezek. iv. 2; xxi. 22; War v. 6, 4). It consisted of a log of wood iron-pointed, swung by ropes from a support above and generally within a tower (War v. 11, 5). In attacking a fort or city, it was often necessary to throw up a mound of earth to serve as an inclined plane and enable the besiegers to bring the battering-ram and other military engines against the walls (Ezek. iv. 2), see also illustration under LACHISH.

Ram, II., in A.V. of N. T. **Aram**, in imitation of the Greek form [high]. The name assumes various Greek forms, as Aram, Arran, Arni.

1. A man of Judah, a son of Hezron, and brother of Jerahmeel (Ruth iv. 19; 1 Chron. ii. 9; Mat. i. 3; Luke iii. 33, R. V., text and margin).

2. A man of Judah, family of Hezron, house of Jerahmeel (1 Chron. ii. 25, 27).

3. A descendant of Buz, founder of a family of the Buzites, and an ancestor of Elihu (Job xxxii. 2). He has sometimes been identified with Aram of Gen. xxii. 21; but Aram was not descended from Buz (nor *vice versa*), and Aram and Ram are different names in Hebrew.

Ra'mah, in A. V. of N. T. **Rama**, in imitation of the Greek [a height].

1. A town in Benjamin (Josh. xviii. 25), not far from Gibeah, Geba, and Beth-el (Judg. iv. 5; xix. 13, 14; Is. x. 29). It was fortified by Baasha, king of Israel, to keep the people of Judah from making military excursions northward (1 Kin. xv. 17, 21, 22; 2 Chron. xvi. 1-6); hence apparently south of Beth-el. It seems to have been the place where the captives of Judah were massed together before their deportation to Babylon (Jer. xl. 1). The town was reoccupied after the captivity (Ezra ii. 26; Neh. xi. 33). According to Josephus, Ramah was distant 40 stades from Jerusalem (Antiq. viii. 12, 3). Robinson located it at er-Ram, on a height 5 miles north of Jerusalem. His views have been generally accepted. It is now a small Arab village, having, however, hewn stones and fragments of pillars, the remains of antiquity.

2. A town where the parents of Samuel lived (1 Sam. i. 19; ii. 11; cp. with i. 1), where he himself was born and had his residence (vii. 17; viii. 4; xv. 34; xvi. 13; xix. 18, 19, 22, 23; xx. 1), and where he was buried (xxv. 1; xxviii. 3). For the sake of distinction from other towns of similar name it was called Ramathaim-zophim (cp. i. 1 with 19, etc.). The town cannot be located with certainty. 1. It has been identified with Ramah of Benjamin. On this theory the place is rightly described, so it is contended, as situated in the hill country of Ephraim (1 Sam. i. 1), and it is different from the unnamed town in the land of Zuph where Saul first met Samuel (ix. 5 seq.). Robinson called this identification in question, and probably justly, although his opinion has not been followed by all authorities. 2. It lay south of Benjamin, for (a) The passage 1 Sam. i. 1 does not clearly locate Ramathaim in the hill country of Ephraim, but rather states that a certain man of the family of Zuph dwelt in Ramathaim, a city

of the Zophites, who were a branch of the Kohathite Levites, and were called Ephraimites because their assigned home was in the hill country of Ephraim, whence they had migrated (cp. Josh xxi. 5; 1 Chron. vi. 22-26, 35, 66 seq.). (b) If this be the true interpretation, then the unnamed city where Saul met Samuel is doubtless Ramathaim-zophim, for it is in the land of Zuph. This district lay outside the borders of Benjamin (1 Sam. ix 4-6), and south of Benjamin, i. e., in such a situation that a person going from a city in or quite near it to Gibeah of Benjamin came to Rachel's sepulcher on the borders of Benjamin (x. 2), between Beth-el and Bethlehem (Gen. xxxv. 16, 19). (c) It is now plain why Saul did not know the prophet Samuel by sight, which could scarcely have been the case had the prophet resided at Ramah of Benjamin, only 2½ miles from Saul's home (cp. also 1 Sam. viii. 1, 2). 3. Another location for Ramathaim may be sought in the territory of Ephraim (Antiq. v. 10, 2) where the Zophites dwelt; but not in Benjamin and not the nameless town of 1 Sam. ix. 5. Beit Rima, 13 miles northeast of Lydda, has been suggested. Compare with caution RAMATHAIM.

3. A town on the boundary line of Asher (Josh. xix. 29). If it is not the same town as Ramah of Naphtali (36), its site may be at Râmeh, about 13 miles S. E. by S. of Tyre.

4. A fenced city of Naphtali (Josh. xix. 36). It is believed to have been situated at er-Râmeh, about 5 miles southwest of Safed and 17 east of Acre.

5. Ramoth-gilead (cp. 2 Kin. viii. 28 with 29, and 2 Chron. xxii. 5 with 6).

6. A village in Simeon (Josh. xix. 8; in A. V. Ramath). It is doubtless the same as Ramoth of the South (1 Sam. xxx. 27); and was also known as Baalath-beer (q. v.).

Ra'math [height], the Hebrew form of Ramah when joined to a following word.

A village of Simeon (Josh. xix. 8, in R. V. Ramah), known also as Ramoth of the South (1 Sam. xxx. 27). See RAMAH 6.

Ra-math-a'im, in A. V. **Ram'a-them** [twin heights].

A town which gave name to one of three governmental districts which were detached from Samaria and added to Judæa (1 Mac. xi. 34; cp. x. 30, 38). Its location must be sought near the southern border of Ephraim.

Ra-math-a-im-zo'phim [the twin heights (of the) Zophites].

The residence of Samuel's father (1 Sam. i. 1); see RAMAH 2.

Ra'math-ite.

A native or inhabitant of any town called Ramah (1 Chron. xxvii. 27). Which of them is referred to in the passage is not known.

Ra-math-le'hi. See LEHI.

Ra-math-miz'peh. See MIZPAH 2.

Ram′e-ses [Egyptian, *Ra-mesu*, son of the sun].

A town of Egypt. It was in the most fertile district of the country (Gen. xlvii. 11), the land of Goshen (6), the region where Pharaoh bade Joseph locate his father and brothers. Ramses II built a town on the eastern frontier of Egypt, and gave it his own name. Perhaps it was the store city Raamses or Ramses, which the Israelites built for Pharaoh (Exod. i. 11); see EGYPT III. 8. At the exodus the Israelites marched from Rameses to Succoth (xii. 37).

Ra-mi′ah [exalted is Jehovah].

A son of Parosh, induced by Ezra to put away his foreign wife (Ezra x. 25).

Ra′moth [high places, height].

1. A son of Bani, induced by Ezra to put away his foreign wife (Ezra x. 29). The R. V. reads Jeremoth in the text, and relegates Ramoth to the margin.

2. A town of Issachar, assigned for residence to the Gershonite Levites (1 Chron. vi. 73); see JARMUTH.

3. A town in Gilead; see RAMOTH-GILEAD.

4. A town of the south (1 Sam. xxx. 27); see RAMAH 6.

Ra-moth-gil′e-ad [heights of Gilead]. See MIZPAH 2.

Ram′ses.

A method of anglicizing the Egyptian *Ramesu*. See PHARAOH and RAMESES.

Ra′phah and **Rapha** [he has healed].

1. A son of Benjamin (1 Chron. viii. 2); but he is not enumerated with those who accompanied Jacob into Egypt (Gen. xlvi. 21), and was probably born after the descent into Egypt. He did not found a tribal family; his descendants, if there were any, were included in other families of the Benjamites. Compare remarks under NOBAH.

2. A descendant of Jonathan (1 Chron. viii. 37). Called in ix. 43 Rephaiah, a synonymous name.

Ra′phon.

A town of Gilead, besieged by the Ammonites, but relieved by Judas Maccabæus (1 Mac. v. 37). It was apparently not far from Carnaim (43). It may be identical with Raphana, which was one of the original cities constituting the Decapolis, and was situated south of the sea of Galilee and east of the Jordan.

Ra′phu [healed, cured].

A Benjamite, father of Palti (Num. xiii. 9).

Ra′ven.

A bird, black in color (Song v. 11), omnivorous, feeding even on carrion (Prov. xxx. 17), and hence ceremonially unclean (Lev. xi. 15). Noah sent one forth from the ark. It did not return to him, finding, doubtless, floating carcases on which it was able to feed (Gen. viii. 7). It frequents valleys (Prov. xxx. 17), and makes its nest in solitary places (Is. xxxiv. 11). By divine providence ravens fed Elijah with bread and flesh morning and evening at the brook Cherith during the drought and famine (1 Kin. xvii. 2–7). The consonants of the words for ravens and Arabians are the same in Hebrew; and when the text is written without vowels, as originally, it is impossible to determine, if the context does not decide, whether Arabs or ravens are meant. It is generally admitted now that the Septuagint and Vulgate are right, and that the Hebrew writer intends to state that Elijah was fed by ravens. The bird referred to in Scripture is undoubtedly the common raven (*Corvus corax*), which is found in every part of Palestine. It is black, with steel-blue and purple iridescence, and is about 26 inches long. The name is broad enough, however, to include other *Corvidæ*. Another species (*Corvus umbrinus*) occurs in southern Palestine and in the valley of the Jordan.

Ra′zor.

A sharp instrument for removing the beard or hair (Is. vii. 20; Ezek. v. 1). See KNIFE, BEARD, HAIR.

Re-a′iah, in A. V. once **Reaia** (1 Chron. v. 5) [Jehovah has seen, or provided for].

1. A son of Shobal, and descended from Judah through Hezron (1 Chron. iv. 2), called in ii. 52 Haroeh, *i. e.*, the seeing One.

2. A Reubenite (1 Chron. v. 5).

3. Founder of a family of Nethinim, members of which returned from captivity (Ezra ii. 47; Neh. vii. 50).

Re′ba [perhaps, a fourth part or quarter].

One of the five Midianite kings, allies or vassals of Sihon, slain by the Israelites in the war waged by Moses against Midian, because they seduced Israel to licentious idolatry (Num. xxxi. 8; Josh. xiii. 21).

Re-bek′ah, in N. T. **Rebecca** (Rom. ix. 10) [a rope with a noose, *i. e.*, a young woman whose beauty ensnares men].

A daughter of Bethuel. When she came with her pitcher to a well near the city of Nahor, in Mesopotamia, the servant of Abraham, who had been sent to obtain a wife for Isaac, presented himself and asked permission to drink from her pitcher. She not only granted his request, but volunteered to draw water for his camels. He had asked God for this very sign; her conduct showed that she was of a generous disposition, he saw that she was beautiful; and he at once gave her expensive presents, as for a future bride. He did not at the time know her name, but asked what it was, and then added the inquiry whether he might lodge at her father's house. She was willing; and when her brother Laban's consent had been obtained, the delegate took up his temporary residence in their dwelling, and explained the object of his journey to Mesopotamia. He ended by petitioning that Rebekah should accompany him to Canaan and become the wife of Isaac. Laban gave his consent, and the maiden, adding hers, went with the servant, married Isaac, and became the mother of Esau and Jacob (Gen. xxiv. 1–67). She preferred Jacob to Esau; and although she had the prophecy that Jacob should have the preeminence, she did not leave the matter in God's hands, but suggested a deceit by which the younger obtained the blessing belonging by birth to the elder (xxv. 28, xxvii. 1–xxviii. 5). She died apparently while Jacob was in Mesopotamia, and was buried in the cave of Machpelah (xlix. 31).

Re′cah, in A. V. Rechah.

An unknown place in the tribe of Judah (1 Chron. iv. 12).

Re′chab [a horseman].

1. A son of Rimmon, a Beerothite. He was a captain of a band under Ish-bosheth and one of Ish-bosheth's murderers (2 Sam. iv. 2, 6).

2. A Kenite (1 Chron. ii. 55), father of that Jehonadab who was invited by Jehu to mount his chariot and see his zeal for the Lord (2 Kin. x. 15, 23), and who placed his tribe under a rule of life. See RECHABITES.

3. Father of Malchijah, the ruler of Beth-haccherem (Neh. iii. 14).

Re′chab-ites.

A Kenite tribe, which dwelt among the Israelites. Their chief Jonadab, son of Rechab, commanded them to abstain from wine and all intoxicating liquor, not to live in houses, or plant or possess vineyards, but to dwell in tents. The object of these regulations was the preservation of primitive simplicity of manners. When Jeremiah tested their obedience years later he found them faithful. A promise was therefore given them that they should never want a man to represent them in all succeeding time (Jer xxxv. 1–19). Professed descendants of the sect still exist in Mesopotamia and Yemen.

Re-cord′er.

An official of high rank in the Hebrew government from the time of David onward. He was called *mazkir*, one who brings to mind, and probably derived his title from his official duty of recording important events and advising the king respecting them. At any rate he held one of the highest offices of state. He was numbered among the chief officials of David and Solomon (2 Sam. viii. 16; 1 Kin. iv. 3). The prefect of the palace, the scribe, and the recorder represented Hezekiah in public business (2 Kin. xviii. 18, 37); and in the reign of Josiah the scribe, the governor of the city, and the recorder were placed in charge of the repairs of the temple (2 Chron. xxxiv. 8).

Red Sea.

The sea called by the Hebrews *Yam suph*, or sea of sedge. The Greek term, of which Red Sea is the literal translation, is *Eruthra Thalassa*, used by Herodotus (ii. 8), the Septuagint (Ex. xv. 4, 22), Josephus (Antiq. ii. 11, 1; 15, 1). The Greeks derived the name from Erythras, a fabulous king who reigned in the adjacent country (Strabo xvi.; Pliny, His. Nat. vi. 23). He possibly corresponds to Edom, or represents the red-skinned people, including Edomites, Himyarites, and original Phœnicians. Not unlikely the name denotes sea of the red land, contrasted with the black soil of Egypt (Ebers). "The Eocene and Cretaceous limestones assume by weathering a rich reddish-brown hue, and under the evening sun the eastern range glows with a ruddy radiance, which in the morning is equally seen on the western cliffs, while these colors contrast with the clear greenish-blue of the sea itself. Such an appearance would naturally suggest to early voyagers the name Red Sea " (Dawson, *Egypt and Syria*, 59).

Overlooking the city of Eilat on the Gulf of Aqaba, Red Sea.

By the Erythræan Sea, the ancients understood not merely the Red Sea as limited by modern geographers, but also the Indian Ocean, and ultimately the Persian Gulf. In the restricted sense in which the term is used in modern geography, the Red Sea is about 1490 miles long, with an average breadth of about 150 miles. At its northern part it terminates in two gulfs, Suez and Akaba, which enclose between them the Sinaitic Peninsula. The gulf of Akaba lies on the east, and is about 100 miles long by 15 broad. At its northern end stood the towns of Elath and Ezion-geber. The gulf of Suez, on the west of the peninsula, is about 180 miles long by 20 broad; but it formerly extended farther northward and included, in prehistoric times at least, lake Timseh and the Bitter Lakes. The shores of both lakes abound in reeds, and this feature sufficiently accounts for the Hebrew designation, sea of sedge. The Hebrew term *Yam suph* denotes the Red Sea of modern geography, or at least so much of it as embraces the peninsula of Sinai; for it lay to the east of Egypt (Ex. x. 19), on it was an encampment of the Israelites not far from Sinai (Num. xxxiii. 10, 11), by taking the way of the *Yam suph* the Israelites compassed the land of Edom (xxi. 4), and Ezion-geber in the land of Edom was on this sea (1 Kin. ix. 26). The *Yam suph* was crossed by the Israelites, and the pursuing Egyptian hosts sank into its depths (Ex. xv. 4, 22). Brugsch advocated the view that the sea crossed was not the Red Sea, but the weedy Serbonian bog, which is separated from the Mediterranean by a narrow isthmus. The general opinion, however, based on constant Scripture representation, is that the sea crossed by the Israelites was the gulf of Suez, probably at a point immediately north or just south of the Bitter Lakes.

The navigation of the sea is at all times somewhat perilous, from the sudden changes of the wind and the strength with which it often blows. The voyage from end to end was rendered slow by the prevalent wind in the northern part of the sea blowing toward the south during nine months of the year, and in the southern part blowing northward during the same period. Besides this, the mariner has to be on his guard against coral reefs and small islands, which in many places rise above the surface of the sea.

Reed.

1. Any tall, broad-leaved grass growing in a wet place. It is called *ḳaneh* in Hebrew, *ḳalamos* in Greek (Is. xlii. 3 with Mat. xii. 20). When an odorous variety is intended, it is translated calamus or cane. It grows or grew in the Nile and elsewhere in the water (1 Kin. xiv. 15; Is. xix. 6; xxxv. 7), and is so tall and in such abundance that it helps to furnish shelter and concealment even for the bulky hippopotamus (Job xl. 21). It is

easily shaken by the wind (1 Kin. xiv. 15), and so fragile that if one lean upon it, it will break with a ragged fracture, the projecting points entering and piercing the hand (2 Kin. xviii. 21; Is. xxxvi. 6; Ezek. xxix. 6, 7). In this last respect, it affords a lively picture of the treatment Egypt had given to the Israelites when they leaned upon that power in seasons of emergency. It was a reed which the persecutors of our Lord thrust into his hand for a scepter, and with which they afterwards struck him on the head; and it was to this or another stem of the same plant that the sponge was affixed which they dipped in vinegar and put to his lips (Mat. xxvii. 29, 30, 48). The plant referred to is probably *Arundo donax*, which grows in the Nile and is common throughout Palestine, is at least 10 feet high, and has leaves as long and as broad as those of a sword. It is cultivated in France, where its long, straight, and light stems are made into fishing rods, arrows, fences, poles for vines.

A reed stalk was used as a measuring rod, and came to denote a fixed length of six long cubits (Ezek. xl. 5; xli. 8). Likewise in Babylonia six cubits made a reed or *ḳanu*.

2. The rendering in Jer. li. 32 of the Hebrew *'agam*, a marsh. It does not seem to be a plant, and is translated marsh on the margin of the R. V.

Re-el-a'iah [trembling caused by Jehovah].

One of the leading men who accompanied Zerubbabel and Jeshua from Babylon (Ezra ii. 2). Called in Neh. vii. 7 by the synonymous name of Raamiah.

Re-fin'er.

One who refines the precious metals, as silver or gold, by causing them to pass repeatedly through the furnace till their dross is taken away (Zech. xiii. 9; cp. Ps. xii. 6). It is said that the refiner knows when the process is complete by seeing his image reflected in the precious metal purified. God is compared to a refiner of silver, by which is meant that he casts his people into the furnace of affliction, till they are refined and purified (Mal. iii. 2, 3). Then they clearly reflect his image in their souls.

Ref'uge. See CITY OF REFUGE.

Re'gem [friend].

A man of Judah, a son of Jahdai (1 Chron. ii. 47).

Re-gem-me'lech [friend of the king].

A man sent from Bethel with companions to put a question to the priests regarding fasting (Zech. vii. 2).

Re-ha-bi'ah [Jehovah is comprehensive].

Son of Eliezer, and grandson of Moses (1 Chron. xxiii. 17; xxiv. 21; xxvi. 25).

Re'hob [an open space, a broad street].

1. A place situated toward Hamath; see BETH-REHOB.

2. A town on the boundary line of the territory of Asher (Josh. xix. 28), perhaps the

same as Rehob, which belonged to Asher (30).
From Rehob the Canaanites were not expelled (Judg. i. 31). Rehob was assigned to
the Levites (Josh. xxi. 31; 1 Chron. vi. 75).
The site is unknown.

3. Father of Hadadezer, king of Zobah (2
Sam. viii. 3, 12).

4. A Levite who sealed the covenant (Neh.
x. 11).

Re-ho-bo'am, in A. V. of N. T. **Roboam**
[the people is enlarged].

Son of king Solomon by Naamah, an Ammonitess, one of his wives (1 Kin. xiv. 31).
Although son of a wise father, he was himself a man of small mind. On the death of
Solomon about 931 B. C., representatives of
all the twelve tribes promptly assembled at
the central city of Shechem to make Rehoboam, who was his lawful successor, king
Various causes more or less remote had led
to jealousy and a growing coldness between
Judah and the tribes to the north and east;
see HISTORY. Recently the people had suffered under grievous taxation levied to support Solomon's splendor, and opportunity
was taken to lay the grievances of the people
before the future ruler. The spokesman was
Jeroboam, an able man who had been an official under Solomon and had been told by
the prophet Ahijah that he should become
king of ten tribes. The popular demand was
that taxation might be lightened. Rehoboam asked three days for deliberation. He
consulted the old men who had till lately
been counselors of his father, who advised
him to accede to the request and speak good
words to the petitioners, and assured him
that the people would then be his servants
forever. He next consulted the young men
who had grown up with him, and they urged
him to say to the people: " My little finger
is thicker than my father's loins. And now
whereas my father did lade you with a
heavy yoke, I will add to your yoke; my
father chastised you with whips, but I will
chastise you with scorpions." It indicated
the mental caliber of Rehoboam that he rejected the counsel of the sages and uttered
the words of folly which his young companions had put into his mouth. The effect
was instantaneous. Ten out of the twelve
tribes renounced their allegiance to Rehoboam, departed to their homes, and were
forever lost to the house of David. The
king sent after them Adoram, who was over
the tribute, but they stoned him to death,
on which his master, fearing that the next
missiles would be directed against himself,
hastily mounted his chariot, and drove to
Jerusalem (1 Kin. xii. 1-20; 2 Chron. x. 1-
19). Judah and a large part of Benjamin,
together with the Simeonites, were left
him. He mustered the entire militia of
his kingdom to attempt the subjugation of
the revolted tribes, but the prophet Shemaiah
forbade the enterprise (1 Kin. xii. 21-24; 2

Chron. xi. 1-4). He therefore contented himself with fortifying a number of cities in Judah
and Benjamin and provisioning the garrisons
(5-12). The erection of the golden calves by
his rival at Bethel and Dan drove southward almost the whole body of the priests
and Levites, which greatly increased the
strength of the kingdom of Rehoboam; but
after three years he himself lapsed into idolatry (1 Kin. xiv. 21-24; 2 Chron. xi. 13-17;
xii. 1) In the fifth year of his reign, Shishak,
king of Egypt, invaded his kingdom, capturing some of the fenced cities, ultimately taking Jerusalem itself, and plundering the temple and the palace (1 Kin. xiv. 25-28; 2
Chron. xii. 2-12); see PHARAOH. Rehoboam
had eighteen wives and sixty concubines,
twenty-eight sons and sixty daughters (21).
Abijah his son claimed that at the time of
his great mistake he was young and tenderhearted; in reality, he was at that time forty-
one years old. He reigned seventeen years,
and died about 915 B. C., leaving his son,
Abijah, to ascend the throne (1 Kin. xiv. 21,
31; 2 Chron. xii. 13, 16).

Re-ho'both [broad places, streets; figuratively roominess, freedom].

1. A well dug by Isaac in the valley of
Gerar. Since the Philistine herdsmen did
not claim it, as they had its two predecessors,
he named it Rehoboth, meaning room (Gen.
xxvi. 22). Robinson identified the valley as
the wady Ruheibeh, a day's journey south
of Beer-sheba; but he could find no wells.
Stewart met with one, which was subsequently seen also by Rowlands. Palmer and
Drake fell in with a second one, which had
previously escaped notice from having been
covered by fallen masonry.

2. A suburb of Nineveh (Gen. x. 11); see
REHOBOTH-IR.

3. A town "by the river" (Gen. xxxvi.
37; 1 Chron. i. 48). "The river" commonly
denotes the Euphrates. Chesney suggested
as its site Rahabeh, 3 miles from the right
(the west) bank of the river, 8 miles below
the mouth of the Khabour. There is a castle
at the spot, with extensive ruins around.
Four or five miles lower down, and on the eastern bank, is a second Rahabeh, called Rahabeh Malik (Royal Rahabeh). One or other
is probably the proper site, but it is not possible to decide on their relative claims. Jewish tradition is in favor of the second.

Re-ho'both-ir [open spaces or markets of
the city].

A city which formed part of the great city
Nineveh or, as we would say, Greater Nineveh (Gen. x. 11; in A. V. the city Rehoboth).

Re'hum [beloved].

1. A chancellor of Persia in the country
beyond the river, who in the time of Artaxerxes complained against the Jews for rebuilding the temple (Ezra iv. 8, 9).

2. One of the principal men who returned
with Zerubbabel from Babylon (Ezra ii. 2)

Called in Neh. vii. 7, probably by a copyist's error, Nehum.

3. A chief of the priests, who returned with Zerubbabel from Babylon (Neh. xii. 3, 7). In the next generation a father's house, occupying the corresponding position in the enumeration, bears the name Harim (ver. 15). One of these names has probably been miswritten by transposing the Hebrew letters.

4. One of those who with Nehemiah sealed the covenant (Neh. x. 25).

5. A Levite, son of Bani. He repaired part of the wall of Jerusalem (Neh. iii. 17).

Re'i [friendly, sociable].
One who did not join in Adonijah's attempt to usurp the throne (1 Kin. i. 8).

Reins.
The kidneys. They were supposed by the ancient Hebrews and others to be the seat of longing and desire (Ps. vii. 9; xvi. 7; xxvi. 2; lxxiii. 21; Prov. xxiii. 16; Jer. xii. 2).

Re'kem [variegation].
1. One of the five kings of Midian, allies or vassals of Sihon, slain in the war waged by Moses against the Midianites because they had seduced Israelites to licentious idolatry (Num. xxxi. 8; Josh. xiii. 21).

2. A son of Hebron, a descendant of Caleb (1 Chron. ii. 43).

3. A city of the Benjamites (Josh. xviii. 27). Site unknown.

Rem-a-li'ah [Jehovah hath adorned].
Father of king Pekah (2 Kin. xv. 25).

Re'meth [probably, a high place].
A frontier town of Issachar (Josh. xix. 21). See JARMUTH.

Rem'mon and **Rem-mon-meth'o-ar.** See RIMMON 1 and 2.

Rem'nant.
The portion of the people that survives the judgment sent to remove the dross from the kingdom of God (Ezra ix. 8; Zech. xiv. 2). Because of Jehovah's love for his people, this godly remnant shall be gathered from the nations among which Israel has been scattered and form the nucleus of a new Israel, holy, living in accordance with Jehovah's law, loyal to him, and defended and blessed by him (Is. i. 26; iv. 2-6; vi. 13; x. 20-23; xi. 11-xii. 6; Jer. xxiii. 3; xxxii. 36-44; Amos ix. 8-15; Mic. iv. 6-8; v. 7, 8; Zeph. iii. 13; Zech. viii. 12; xiii. 9).

Rem'phan. See REPHAN.

Re'pha-el [God hath healed].
A Levite, son of Shemaiah, of the family of Obed-edom, and a doorkeeper of the sanctuary (1 Chron. xxvi. 7).

Re'phah [riches].
An ancestor of Joshua and probably son of Beriah (1 Chron. vii. 25).

Re-pha'iah [Jehovah hath healed].
1. A man of Issachar, family of Tola (1 Chron. vii. 2).
2. A descendant of Jonathan (1 Chron. ix.

43). Called in viii. 37 Rapha, a synonymous name, he hath healed.

3. One of four Simeonite captains who led an expedition into Edom, destroyed a community of Amalekites who were dwelling there, and took possession of their land (1 Chron. iv. 42, 43).

4. A son of Hur and ruler of half the district about Jerusalem, who aided in repairing the wall (Neh. iii. 9).

5. The founder of a family which is loosely registered with the royal descendants of David, and is presumably a collateral line sprung from David (1 Chron. iii. 21).

Reph'a-im, in A. V. twice **Rephaims** (Gen. xiv. 5; xv. 20) [probably, giants; but also explained as meaning extinct aborigines].
1. A people of large stature who in ancient times, even before the arrival of Abraham, dwelt in Palestine, east and west of the Jordan (Gen. xiv. 5; Deut. ii. 11, 20; iii. 11; and Gen. xv. 20; Josh. xvii. 15). A remnant of them appears to have taken refuge among the Philistines, when the Hebrews entered Canaan (2 Sam. xxi. 16, 18, 20, 21, R. V. margin).

2. A valley near Jerusalem and Bethlehem (Antiq. vii. 4, 1; 2 Sam. xxiii. 13, 14), southwest of Jerusalem and the valley of Hinnom (Josh. xv. 8; xviii. 16), and quite fertile (Is. xvii. 5); presumably once inhabited by the Rephaim. The Philistines were twice defeated there by David (2 Sam. v. 18-22; xxiii. 13; 1 Chron. xi. 15; xiv. 9). It is probably the broad valley, about three miles long, lying southwest of Jerusalem, beginning beyond the ravine that bounds the city on the south and west, and extending half way to Bethlehem. It declines rapidly toward the west; and is stony, but fertile.

Re'phan, in A. V. **Remphan.**
A god who has a star associated with him, and who was worshiped by the Israelites in the wilderness (Acts vii. 43). The passage is quoted from the O. T. The name represents *Raiphan*, a corrupt transliteration in the Septuagint of *Kaivan*, which was a name of Saturn among the Syrians, and was understood to be the god Chiun (Amos v. 26). In view of this extremely probable origin of the name Rephan, the proposed identification of it with an Egyptian god Renpu falls to the ground.

Reph'i-dim [expanses, stretches].
A camping ground of the Israelites in the wilderness between the wilderness of Sin and Sinai (Ex. xvii. 1; xix. 2; Num. xxxiii. 12, 15). There was no water obtainable, and the people murmured till Moses, accompanied by elders, went forward to Horeb by divine command and smote a rock, from which water at once issued (Ex. xvii. 5, 6). The water flowed down the wady to the camp of the Israelites and supplied them during their sojourn at mount Sinai also. Rephidim was the scene of the battle with Amalek, when

Moses with uplifted hand pointed to Jehovah as the ensign under which Israel fought (Ex. xvii. 8–16). The situation is not properly determined. Robinson, and after him, but independently, Wilson, fixed it at the spot where a wall of rocks called Wateiyah, running northeast and southwest, approaches the wady esh-Sheikh; while Burckhardt, Stanley and others locate it in the beautiful and comparatively well-watered wady Feiran. See MERIBAH.

Re'sen.
A city of Assyria, a suburb of Nineveh, and part of the complex of towns known as the great city. It was situated between Nineveh and Calah (Gen. x. 11, 12), and, therefore, it is not the town Resh-eni, north of Dur-sharrukin. Its exact situation is uncertain.

Resh.
The twentieth letter of the Hebrew alphabet. English R comes from the same source, and represents it in anglicized Hebrew names. It heads the twentieth section of Ps. cxix., in which section each verse of the original begins with this letter.
Copyists experienced some difficulty in distinguishing resh from daleth (q. v.).

Re'sheph [a flame].
A descendant of Ephraim and probably son of Beriah (1 Chron. vii. 25).

Re'u, in A. V. once **Ragau** (Luke iii. 35) [friend].
A descendant of Eber and an ancestor of Abraham (Gen. xi. 18–26).

Reu'ben [behold a son].
1. Jacob's eldest son, the first by his wife Leah (Gen. xxix. 31, 32; xxxv. 23; xlvi. 8; 1 Chron. ii. 1; v. 1). Reuben was guilty of gross misconduct (Gen. xxxv. 22); but when his brothers plotted to kill Joseph, Reuben came forward with the proposal to cast him into a pit, designing to restore him eventually to his father. He was not with them when Joseph was sold to the Midianite Ishmaelites, and was greatly moved when, visiting the pit, he found it empty (xxxvii. 21–29). When the brothers found themselves in trouble in Egypt twenty years later, Reuben was quick to remind his brothers that he had not concurred in their plot to take Joseph's life (xlii. 22–24). When Jacob was reluctant to send Benjamin to Egypt, Reuben offered two of his sons as pledge that he would bring Benjamin home again in safety (37). Reuben had four sons in all: Hanoch, Phallu, Hezron, and Carmi (Gen. xlvi. 8, 9; Ex. vi. 14; 1 Chron. v. 3). Jacob, when about to die, pronounced Reuben to be unstable as water and declared that he should not have excellence. By his heinous deed he had forfeited the birthright (Gen. xlix. 3, 4)
2. The tribe formed by descendants of Reuben, and the territory in which they

dwelt. The tribe was divided into four great tribal families, the posterity of Reuben's four sons (Num. xxvi. 5–11). Its prince at the beginning of the sojourn in the wilderness was Elizur (Num. i. 5; ii. 10; vii. 30–35; x. 18). At that time the tribe numbered 46,500 fighting men (i. 20, 21); at the second census thirty-eight years later, they had decreased to 43,730 (xxvi. 7). The Reubenite chief was head of the camp made up of the three tribes, Reuben, Simeon, and Gad, the aggregate military strength of which was 151,450 (Num. ii. 10, 16). The spy from the tribe was Shammua, son of Zaccur (xiii. 4). Dathan, Abiram, and On, who joined the Levite Korah in revolt against Moses and Aaron, were Reubenites (xvi. 1–50; xxvi. 9; Deut. xi. 6); see KORAH 4. After the battles with Sihon and Og, the Gadites and Reubenites, with whom half the tribe of Manasseh joined, being rich in cattle, petitioned Moses to be allowed to settle east of the Jordan, that region being well adapted for flocks and herds. Their request was granted on condition that they would send the greater number of their warriors across the Jordan to help their brethren in the war with the Canaanites (Num. xxxii. 1–42; Josh. xviii. 7). They did so, and took part in all of Joshua's wars in Canaan (Josh. iv. 12). Afterwards they returned with honor to their own territory; but the erection of a memorial altar by them and their Israelite brethren east of Jordan led to a temporary misunderstanding which nearly involved them in civil war (xxii. 1–34). The Reubenites took no part in the contest with Sisera, and were referred to reproachfully in Deborah's song (Judg. v. 15, 16). They joined in war with the Hagarites, in which they prevailed, the victors making a great slaughter of the enemy, and living in their territory to the time of the captivity (1 Chron. v. 18–22). Ezekiel allotted them a place in the reoccupied Canaan (Ezek. xlviii. 6, 7), and named a gate after them in the restored Jerusalem (31). When the book of Revelation records the sealing of the 144,000, it assigns Reuben a quota of 12,000 (Rev. vii. 5). The boundary of the territory of Reuben was on the east the country of the Ammonites, on the south the river Arnon (Num. xxi. 24), on the west the Dead Sea and the river Jordan (Josh. xiii. 23), while on the north the boundary line ran from the Jordan south of Bethnimrah to Heshbon (Josh. xiii. 17, 26; xxi. 37; and Num. xxxii. 36; Josh. xiii. 27). Included in these limits were Aroer, on the edge of the valley of Arnon, and the city in the middle of the valley, all the plain by Medeba, Heshbon and its subordinate towns, Dibon, Bamoth-baal, Beth-baal-meon, Jahaz, Kedemoth, Mephaath, Kiriathaim, Sibmah, Zereth-shahar, Beth-peor, the slopes of Pisgah, Beth-jeshimoth; in short, the southern part of the Ammonite kingdom which had been ruled over by Sihon (Josh.

xiii. 15–23). The four cities of Bezer, Jahaz, Kedemoth, and Mephaath, with their suburbs, were assigned to the Merarite Levites (Josh. xxi. 7, 36, 37; 1 Chron. vi. 63, 78, 79); the first of these, Bezer, was a city of refuge (Josh. xx. 8; 1 Chron. vi. 78). The Reubenites had an exposed position, the Moabites being in their immediate vicinity, while desert marauders could invade their territory both from the east and the south. If the list of Reubenite cities given in this section be compared with those in Moabite possession incidentally mentioned in Is. xv., xvi., Jer. xlviii., and on the Moabite stone, it will be seen that in the times of Mesha and these prophets Reuben had its limits greatly curtailed by Moabite conquest. The whole territory, which is a table-land quite capable of cultivation, is now deserted by its settled inhabitants, and is given up to the nomad and plundering tribes of the desert.

Reu'el, in A. V. once **Raguel** (Num. x. 29) in imitation of the Greek form [friend of God].

1. A descendant of Esau and also of Ishmael (Gen. xxxvi. 2–4).

2. Moses' father-in-law (Ex. ii. 18). See JETHRO.

3. A Benjamite, a son of Ibnijah (1 Chron. ix. 8).

4. A Gadite, father of Eliasaph (Num. ii. 14); see DEUEL.

Reu'mah [exalted].

A concubine of Nahor, Abraham's brother (Gen. xxii. 24).

Rev-e-la'tion [an unveiling]. It is derived from the Latin *revelatio*, unveiling; hence to reveal, to expose to sight, and, metaphorically, to disclose to the mind truth otherwise unknown. Greek *Apokalupsis;* whence English *Apocalypse.*

In the O. T. the noun revelation does not occur; but the verb reveal is used in the sense of making known secrets (e. g. Prov. xi. 13) and then of God's disclosure of his will to man (e. g. Deut. xxix. 29; Is. xxii. 14; Dan. ii. 19, 22, 28; Amos iii. 7). In the N. T. revelation is used for the disclosure by God or Christ or the Spirit of truth concerning divine things previously unknown (e. g. Rom. xvi. 25; 1 Cor. xiv. 6, 26; 2 Cor. xii. 1; Gal. i. 12; Rev. i. 1) or of duty specially required (Gal. ii. 2), and then for the manifestation or appearance of persons or events previously concealed from sight (e. g. Rom. ii. 5; 1 Pet. i. 13). In theology revelation means the communication of truth by God to man, and is usually applied to such communications as have been conveyed through supernatural agencies.

The Revelation of St. John the Divine is the last book of the N. T., also called, from the Greek, the Apocalypse. The name is given to it because, as its opening words state, it is a disclosure of the future, and, therefore, preëminently a revelation. Its author describes it as a communication concerning "things which must shortly come to pass," which God gave to Jesus Christ, and which Christ gave by his angel to his servant John, to be in turn communicated to the church (Rev. i. 1–3). The work is addressed to seven churches of the Roman province of Asia: Ephesus, Smyrna, Pergamum, Thyatira, Sardis, Philadelphia, and Laodicea (4, 11), the number seven being selected probably because, as the sacred number, it signified completeness, and thus indicated that the book was really addressed to the whole church. The author calls himself, after the manner of the Hebrew prophets (cp. Is. i. 1; Joel i. 1; Amos i. 1, etc.), simply John (Rev. i. 1, 4, 9; xxii. 8), and relates that the visions of the book were seen by him when confined in the island of Patmos "for the word of God and the testimony of Jesus" (i. 9). Patmos lies off the southwestern coast of Asia Minor, and John had been banished to it because he was a Christian. This points to a period of persecution by the Roman government. The opening vision was of the exalted Christ, who is represented in a symbolic portraiture as standing in the midst of seven golden candlesticks which represent the seven churches (10–20). Christ gives to the seer messages to the seven churches, and after that follows a succession of other visions. The revelation is said to have been given on the Lord's day (10), by which we are doubtless to understand the first day of the week. The visions described are of a highly symbolical character. Many of the figures and much of the language are taken from the O. T. prophets, especially from Daniel and Ezekiel, and the meaning cannot be understood without constant reference to them.

Examining the book more closely, we find that after the introduction (i. 1–3) and salutation (4–8), it consists of seven chief divisions, extending to xxii. 7, after which the book closes with an epilogue (8–21). These divisions constitute in fact seven visions, or series of visions, and are themselves subdivided usually into seven parts. Each series opens with a vision, which presents as a whole the idea of the series, and which is then followed in most instances by a sevenfold representation of its elements. These visions are probably not to be understood as representing events which were to follow one another in history in the order of time, but as symbolical portraitures of certain religious truths or principles which were to be realized in the experience of the church. The whole is intended for the church's comfort and warning amid the conflicts of time and in preparation for the second coming of her Lord (i. 7, 8. xxii. 7, 10, 17, 20). The seven series of visions, which show the analysis of the book, are the following:

1. The vision of the glorified Christ amid his church, followed by seven messages to

the seven churches of Asia (i. 9–iii. 22).
Here the main thought is of instruction,
warning, and encouragement for the church
in her present condition.

2. The vision of God, presiding over the
destinies of the universe and adored by all
creation, and of the exalted, but redeeming,
Lamb of God, who holds in his hand the
sealed book of the divine decrees (iv., v.), followed by the breaking of the seals in seven
visions, whereby is portrayed the sevenfold
purpose of God from the going forth of
Christ to conquer unto the last judgment
(vi. 1–viii. 1). Between the sixth and seventh
seals an episode is introduced, which shows
the safety of the people of God amid the
judgment which befalls the world (vii.).

3. The vision of the trumpets (viii. 2–xi.
19). It opens with the vision of an angel
offering the prayers of the saints to God
(viii. 2–6). Then each trumpet is followed
by a vision of destruction upon the sinful
world, ending again with the last judgment.
Between the sixth and seventh trumpets an
episode again is introduced, descriptive of
the preservation of the witnessing church
(x. 1–xi. 14). The main thought here appears
to be that in reply to the prayers of the
saints for God to vindicate his truth, they
are shown the desolations which befall the
sinful world amid which they are to bear
their testimony.

4. The vision of the church, under the
figure of a woman, bringing forth the Christ,
against whom the dragon, or Satan, wages
war (xii.), followed by visions of the beasts,
which Satan will use as his agents (xiii.), of
the militant church (xiv. 1–5), and of the
advancing stages of Christ's conquest (6–20).
This may be called the vision of conflict.

5. The vision of the vials, or bowls,
containing the last plagues, or judgments
of God (xv., xvi.). The opening vision (xv.)
depicts the triumph of the saints, while the
seven bowls represent the sevenfold judgment of God on a wicked world (xvi.).

6. The vision of the harlot city, Babylon
(xvii.), followed by the victory of Christ
over her, and over his enemies in league
with her, ending again in the last judgment
(xviii. 1–xx. 15). Between the sixth and seventh scenes of this triumph an episode is introduced (xx. 1–10), which is probably descriptive of the complete safety and spiritual deliverance of Christ's people throughout the
whole period of the age-long battle. Some
scholars, however, place the division between
the sixth and seventh series of visions at
xix. 11.

7. The vision of the ideal church, the
bride of Christ, or new Jerusalem (xxi. 1–8),
followed by a description of her glory (9–
xxii. 7).

General agreement prevails among both
critical and devotional students of the Revelation that the book as it stands has unity,
and a unity that is easily recognized. Struc-
tural unity is apparent in its having a framework consisting of seven groups of usually
seven episodes and in a general grammatical
and linguistic similarity.

The author of the book of the Revelation
was a Jewish Christian. with a noble universalistic outlook, thoroughly conversant with
the contents of the Old Testament and with
its literary forms, and able to mold characteristic prophecies of Daniel and Ezekiel into
his own picture of the church's conflict and
final glory (see DANIEL and EZEKIEL). His
name was John (Rev. i. 1, 4, 9; xxii. 8).
That he was John the apostle has been the
constant tradition of the church from the
earliest time. It is specifically so stated by
Justin Martyr in the middle of the second
century, by Melito also and Irenæus of the
same century. It is confirmed also by a
comparison of the book with the Gospel and
First Epistle of John, for all three books
have in common many doctrinal ideas and
many more peculiarities of language. The
Revelation, indeed, is less smoothly written
than the Gospel or Epistle; but that is partly
because of its subject, which led the author
to employ unusual expressions in his descriptions, and partly because he was bent on
repeating and combining the language of the
older prophets. Some scholars, indeed, both
in ancient and modern times (as Dionysius
of Alexandria, A. D. 247–265), have contended
that the Revelation and the Gospel could not
have been written by the same person. But
examination, as well as the steadfast tradition of the church, makes the division of
authorship both improbable and unnecessary.

An effort has been made to trace the source
of the Revelation, especially of chapters xii.
and xiii. and related passages, to Babylonian
mythology. Thus far the investigation—1.
Has ignored the plain meaning of these chapters, which unquestionably depict the church
opposed by Satan's spiritual power (Rev. xii.
3–17; see verse 9), by the powers of the
world united and subservient to Satan (xiii.
1–10), and by false prophecy, like Elijah
calling down fire from heaven, coming in
sheep's clothing, and perhaps impersonat-
ing the Lamb (xiii. 11–17). 2. Has overlooked
the inherent symbolism of nature, which
speaks to poets of all races independently of
each other. 3. Has assumed details for
Babylonian myths for which there is no
archæological evidence. 4. Has failed to see
that for the author the immediate and sufficient source of the imagery is Hebrew
Scripture as contained in Gen. iii. and Dan.
vii. (see DANIEL), while the imagery and
thought of Jer. li. 1–12 lend a further deep
coloring to chap. xvii.

Concerning the date of the Revelation, two
principal opinions have been held. One assigns it to the year or two immediately preceding the fall of Jerusalem in A. D. 70.
This was after the persecution of the Christians by Nero had broken out, and it is sup-

posed that the terrors of the fall of Jerusalem, combined with those of the Neronian persecution, provide many of the lurid figures used by the seer. Most rationalistic critics also accept approximately this date, and see in Revelation no inspired prophecy at all, but only a human vaticination suggested by the calamities of the age. But the traditional opinion, voiced by Irenæus as early as A. D. 175-200, has ever assigned Revelation to the close of the reign of Domitian, A. D. 96. The testimony is strong that John was imprisoned in Patmos by Domitian, and returned to Ephesus after that tyrant's death. It is unlikely that so specific and unanimous a tradition should be mistaken. The condition of the seven churches likewise suits the later date better than the earlier; the style does not require the Revelation to precede the Gospel, nor are most of the reasons advanced for the earlier date satisfactory to those who believe in the inspiration of the book.

The interpretations of Revelation have been innumerable. Four general classes of interpretation may, however, be distinguished. (1) The præterist interpretation, which regards the work as a description of what was taking place when the book was written. This view destroys its prophetic character, and is certainly to be rejected. (2) The futurist interpretation, which sees in the book predictions of events yet to be fulfilled. This view is met by the difficulty that all prophecy, and this one in particular, closely connects itself with the situation of the church and prophet, to whom it was given. (3) The historico-prophetical interpretation, which sees in the visions a successive portrayal of the events of Christian history. The difficulty with this view is that few expositors can agree on the details of the fulfillment, and that it disregards the contemporaneous character of the seven series of visions. (4) The spiritual, symbolic interpretation, which regards the visions as figurative portraitures of certain truths or principles, destined to find their place in the history of the church, and the contemplation of which in pictorial representation is intended to encourage and comfort Christ's people until he comes again in glory and to judgment. While no expositor can feel sure that he has understood the meaning of all the contents of the Revelation, the last method of interpretation has the advantage of directing the attention of readers to certain large and important truths, under the form of pictures, thus making this most mysterious book of Scripture practically helpful.   G. T. P. (supplemented).

Re-ven'ger. See AVENGER OF BLOOD.

Re'zeph [a hearthstone for cooking upon, a pavement].

A place which the rabshakeh boasted that the Assyrians had destroyed (2 Kin. xix. 12;

Is. xxxvii. 12), doubtless the town Rasappa, long residence of an Assyrian governor. Perhaps it is the modern Ruṣafa, some miles west of the Euphrates on the route to Palmyra.

Re-zi'a. See RIZIA.

Re'zin.

1. A king of Damascus. About 738 B. C. he paid tribute to Tiglath-pileser, king of Assyria. Four years later, in the time of Ahaz, he joined with Pekah, king of Israel, in an effort to capture Jerusalem and place a creature of their own upon the throne of David. They failed, after eliciting from Isaiah a celebrated prophecy (Is. vii. 1-ix. 12). On this campaign, before attempting to unite his troops with those of Pekah, Rezin marched to Elath on the gulf of Akaba and took the town from Judah (2 Kin. xvi. 6). The aid of Tiglath-pileser had been purchased by Ahaz; and the Assyrian king, after chastising the Philistines for their participation in the hostilities against Judah, marched against Damascus, besieged it during the years 733 and 732 B. C., ravaged the surrounding district, finally captured the city, and slew Rezin (7-9, and Assyrian inscriptions).

2. Founder of a family of Nethinim, members of which returned from the captivity (Ezra ii. 48; Neh. vii. 50).

Re'zon [importance, princeliness].

A son of Eliada, and a subject of Hadadezer, king of Zobah. When David captured Zobah, Rezon gathered a band of men, seized Damascus, and founded the Syrian kingdom, with which, while it lasted, the Israelites had continual relations, hostile or friendly (1 Kin. xi. 23-25).

Rhe'gi-um.

A city of Greek origin on the coast of Italy, opposite to Messina in Sicily. Paul's vessel touched at Rhegium after having made a circuit from Syracuse (Acts xxviii. 13). Rhegium is now called Reggio, and is the capital of Calabria. It is a town of considerable size, and exports oranges, lemons, wine, oil, etc.

Rhe'sa.

A descendant of Zerubbabel, and an ancestor of Christ (Luke iii. 27).

Rho'da [a rose bush].

A servant girl of Mary, the mother of Mark. When Peter, after having been miraculously released from prison, knocked at the door of the gate of Mary's house, Rhoda was sent to see who was there. On hearing Peter's voice, she was elated with joy, and, forgetting in her excitement to let him in, ran back to tell that it was Peter. The apostle had for some time to continue the knocking before he could gain admittance (Acts xii. 13-16).

Rhodes, in A. V. of 1 Mac. xv. 23 **Rhodus** [a rose bush].

An island off the coast of Caria, in the

southwest of Asia Minor. It is about 45 miles long by 20 broad, and is remarkable for its orange and citron groves. The island was at the junction of great commercial routes for coasting vessels, and became a commercial center which ranked with Alexandria and Carthage. Its capital, also called Rhodes, was famed for its Colossus, a great lighthouse, said to have been 70 cubits, or about 105 feet, high. It was erected between 300 and 288 B. C. The Rhodians were semi-independent under the Romans (1 Mac. xv. 23), except during nine years in the reign of Claudius, beginning A. D. 44, and again in the time of Vespasian. The vessel in which Paul sailed to Palestine from Assos touched at Rhodes (Acts xxi. 1) which was then a splendid city. As the Rhodians long remained unsubdued by the Romans, so, led by the knights of St. John, who in A. D. 1310 had possessed themselves of the island, they defied the power of the Turks till 1522, when they had to surrender on terms, the knights being allowed to transfer themselves to the isle of Malta. Since that time Rhodes has remained subject to the Turks.

Ri'bai [contentious].

A Benjamite of Gibeah, and the father of Ittai, one of David's mighty men (2 Sam. xxiii. 29; 1 Chron. xi. 31).

Rib'lah [fertility].

A town in the land of Hamath (2 Kin. xxiii. 33; xxv. 21). The Egyptians were encamped there when Jehoahaz was brought in as a prisoner (xxiii. 33). When Zedekiah was captured after his escape from Jerusalem, he was brought to Nebuchadnezzar, then encamped at Riblah, who put out his eyes, and had him bound to be carried to Babylon. His sons and the princes of Judah were also slain at Riblah (xxv. 6, 7, 21; Jer. xxxix. 5-7; lii. 9-11, 27). Buckingham, in 1816, met with ruins at a place called by him Rubla, but now more generally spelled Ribleh, on the right bank of the Orontes, about 36 miles north by east of Ba'al-bek, in the midst of the great plain of Cœlesyria, very suitable for the encampment of a great army, and with easy access southward or northward if commotion arose. The ruins consist of low mounds surrounded by the remains of old buildings. It is extremely doubtful whether it is identical with Riblah on the northern boundary of Palestine, east of Ain (Num. xxxiv. 11).

Rid'dle.

In biblical usage, any dark saying, of which the meaning is not at once clear and must be discovered by shrewd thought (Num. xii. 8, in E. V. dark speeches; Prov. i. 6, R. V. margin). It may be a parable (Ps. xlix. 4; lxxviii. 2; in E. V. dark saying), and be proposed merely in order to arouse attention and start inquiry, and make the truth more vivid and impressive, the

propounder intending to give an explanation immediately (Ezek. xvii. 2-24); or the riddle may be set forth for men to guess, as the riddle of Samson and those of Solomon and Hiram to which Josephus refers (Judg. xiv. 12-19; Antiq. viii. 5, 3). The riddle of Samson was proposed in verse. It was not properly a riddle at all, since the discovery of its meaning was not within the realm of possibility for the Philistines. It was not guessable, for they were not acquainted with the facts on which it was based.

The Greeks and Romans were fond of the riddle or enigma. One of the most celebrated was put into the mouth of the monster named the sphinx, which had been sent to ravage the territory of Thebes. She asked: "What animal goes on four feet in the morning, on two at noon, and on three in the evening?" After many had failed, Œdipus answered that it was man, who in infancy creeps on all fours, at maturity walks on two feet, and in old age uses a staff. Thereupon the sphinx flung herself to the ground and perished.

Rie, obsolete spelling of Rye. See SPELT.

Rim'mon I., in A. V. twice **Remmon** (Josh. xix. 7, 13); in R. V. once **Rimmono** (1 Chron. vi. 77) [a pomegranate].

1. A Benjamite, whose two sons were captains under Ish-bosheth, and became his murderers (2 Sam. iv. 2).

2. A town in the south of Judah near Ain (Josh. xv. 32; 1 Chron. iv. 32; Zech. xiv. 10), so near indeed as to form, apparently, one community with it (Neh. xi. 29). It was soon transferred with Ain and other towns to Simeon (Josh. xix. 7). It is identified with the ruin Umm er-Rumâmîn, about 10 miles northeast by north of Beer-sheba.

3. A border town of Zebulun, but assigned to the Levites (Josh. xix. 13; 1 Chron. vi. 77; and Josh. xxi. 35, where Dimnah is doubtless a misreading, resh being mistaken for daleth, q. v.). Methoar in A. V. of Josh. xix. 13 is improperly regarded as part of the name; whereas it describes the boundary as "stretching" to Neah. The name of the town is preserved in Rummâneh, a village 6 miles north, slightly east, of Nazareth.

3. A rock near Gibeah, where 600 vanquished Benjamites took refuge and remained four months (Judg. xx. 45-47; xxi. 13). It is probably the detached limestone eminence 3½ miles east, slightly north, of Bethel. It is separated from all approach on the south, the north, and the west by ravines, and has caverns, in which the refugees may have lived. The name still lingers in Rammun, a village on the summit.

Rim'mon II. [thunderer].

A Syrian god, who had a temple at Damascus, in which Naaman and his royal master were accustomed to bow themselves for worship (2 Kin. v. 18). In Assyria Rimmon, or Ramman as his name was pronounced there, was numbered among the twelve great deities. He was the god of rain and storm, lightning and thunder. Sometimes he was dreaded as the destroyer of crops and the scatterer of the harvest, and at others was adored as the lord of fecundity. He was identical with Hadad, the supreme god of the Syrians. The two names are combined in Hadad-Rimmon.

Rim′mo-no. See RIMMON.

Rim-mon-pe′rez, in A. V. **Rimmon-parez** [pomegranate of the breach or cleft].

A camping ground of the Israelites in the wilderness (Num. xxxiii. 19, 20). Situation unknown.

Ring. See ORNAMENT and SEAL.

Rin′nah [a wild cry, a shout].

A man of Judah, a son of Shimon (1 Chron. iv. 20).

Ri′phath.

A people descended from Gomer (Gen. x. 3; in 1 Chron. i. 6 Diphath; see DALETH). Josephus identifies them with the Paphlagonians (Antiq. i. 6, 1). The name is perhaps preserved in the Riphæan mountains, which were supposed by the ancients to skirt the northern shore of the world.

Ris′sah [a ruin, or dew, rain].

A camping ground of the Israelites in the wilderness (Num. xxxiii. 21, 22). Exact situation unknown.

Rith′mah [broom, plant].

A camping ground of the Israelites in the wilderness (Num. xxxiii. 18, 19); perhaps hard by Kadesh in the wady known as Abu Retemât, the equivalent of the ancient name; see KADESH 1.

Riv′er.

Of several words translated river, only three require mention here: 1. *Nahar*, a stream, in Greek *potamos*, applied to the largest rivers known to the Hebrews, as the Tigris and Euphrates (Gen. ii. 14; Rev. ix. 14), the Abana and Pharpar (2 Kin. v. 12), the Jordan (Mark i. 5), and the affluents of the Upper Nile (Zeph. iii. 10). The river or the great river usually denotes the Euphrates (Gen. xv. 18; xxxi. 21). 2. *Nahal*, sometimes a perennial stream like the Jabbok (Deut. ii. 37), but usually a winter torrent, the bed of which is dry in summer; a wady. See BROOK. 3. *Yᵉʾor*, a stream, used almost exclusively of the Nile and its mouths, and sounding much like the native Egyptian name of that river (Gen. xli. 1; 2 Kin. xix. 24; Ezek. xxix. 3). It once denotes the Tigris (Dan. xii. 5–7; cp. x. 4, R. V. margin).

Riv′er of E′gypt.

1. The Nile, and specifically its most eastern channel, the Pelusiac branch (Gen. xv. 18); see SHIHOR. In this passage the two great rivers, the Nile and the Euphrates, are named broadly as the boundaries of the promised land. 'The brook of Egypt or wady el-‘Arish was commonly regarded as the southwestern limit of Palestine; but the country between this wady and the eastern branch of the Nile was mainly desert, and the Nile was virtually on the boundary of Egypt. The passage means that the descendants of Abraham should possess the land as far as Egypt. The distinction between the Nile and the wady el-‘Arish is well established; for the former is a *nahar* and the latter a *nahal*.

2. A great wady or *nahal*, uniformly called in the R. V. the brook of Egypt. It was the southwestern border of Canaan (Num. xxxiv. 5; 1 Kin. viii. 65; 2 Kin. xxiv. 7), and the limit in the same direction of the tribe of Judah (Josh. xv. 4, 47). It was known to the Assyrians by the same name as to the Hebrews, and likewise as a boundary. It is the wady el-‘Arish, a watercourse nominally dry, but which after heavy rains runs northward from the desert, being fed by tributaries, one of which passes Kadesh-barnea. It falls into the Mediterranean, about 50 miles south of Gaza.

Farming in the delta region of "The River of Egypt."

Ri-zi′a, in A. V. **Rezia** [delight].

An Asherite, a son of Ulla (1 Chron. vii. 39).

Riz′pah [a hot stone].

A daughter of Aiah and concubine of Saul. On her account the quarrel arose between Ish-bosheth and Abner, which resulted in Abner's going over to David (2 Sam. iii. 6–8). Her children, Armoni and Mephibosheth, were put to death during the famine which arose in David's reign on account of Saul's treatment of the Gibeonites (2 Sam. xxi. 8–11).

Road.

An inroad, a raid, an incursion into an enemy's country (1 Sam. xxvii. 10, in R. V. raid). This sense is now obsolete in ordinary language. When a road in the modern sense is intended, the A. V. and R. V. generally use the term way, or sometimes path. See PALESTINE 5.

Rob′ber. See THIEF.

Ro-bo′am. See REHOBOAM.

Rock.

Rocks were found nearly everywhere in

the hilly and mountainous districts of Palestine. Some had definite names, as the rock of Oreb (Judg. vii. 25), the rock of Etam (xv. 8). See OREB, ETAM.

Rock-badg'er.

The rendering of the Hebrew *Shaphan*, on the margin of the R. V., where coney appears in the text. The animal intended by the Hebrew word is small and wary, dwells among the rocks (Ps. civ. 18; Prov. xxx. 24, 26), and chews the cud, but does not part the hoof (Lev. xi. 5; Deut. xiv. 7). The corresponding name in the dialect of southern Arabia denotes the *Hyrax syriacus*. the so-called rock-badger. The hyrax looks like a rabbit or badger, but has more affinity to the rhinoceros and the tapir; indeed, its structure is so anomalous that it has been given a whole order, *Hyracoidea*, to itself. It moves its jaws as if it were chewing the cud, but it does not really ruminate. The species *syriacus* is found in the peninsula of Sinai, northern Palestine, and the region round the Dead Sea. Its fur is tawny, with a yellow spot on the back. It lives in clefts of rocks, but does not scoop out a hole. Small parties meet together, with a sentinel on some eminence to give warning of danger. It is rarely seen except in the morning and evening, when it comes forth to feed.

Rod'a-nim [a plural form, Rodanites].

A people descended from Javan (Hebrew text of 1 Chron. i. 7; and Septuagint and Samaritan text of Gen. x. 4). If Rodanim is the correct reading, the people of Rhodes and of the neighboring islands of the Ægean Sea are probably intended. See DODANIM.

Roe.

A deer (*Capreolus capræa*, the *Cervus capreolus* of Linnæus) which is described under ROEBUCK 2 (2 Sam. ii. 18; 1 Chron. xii. 8, in Hebrew *s̟bi*; and Prov. v. 19, A. V., in Hebrew *ya'ălah*); see GAZELLE and DOE.

Roe'buck.

1. The rendering in A. V. of the Hebrew *S̟ebi* in Deut. xii. 15, 22; xiv. 5; xv. 22; 1 Kin. iv. 23. R. V. substitutes gazelle (q. v.).

2. The rendering in R. V. of the Hebrew *Yaḥmur*. The animal was ceremonially clean and used for food (Deut. xiv. 5; 1 Kin. iv. 23, in A. V. fallow deer). Etymology indicates that its color was reddish. According to Arabian authorities, it casts its horns every year, which is characteristic of deer. In northern Galilee the name *yaḥmur* is still given to the roebuck (*Capreolus capræa*, or *Cervus capreolus*). In Europe it is a small deer about two feet high at the shoulder, but in Asia it attains to a larger size. In summer it is dark reddish-brown, in winter yellowish-gray. It has a large patch of white on the rump. The antlers are about a foot long, with three points. It is wild over a great part of Europe and Asia. In Palestine it is found on mount Carmel and mount Lebanon.

By many, however, the *yaḥmur* is identified with the bubale, one of the bovine antelopes. It is about the size of a large stag, has a long head, a narrow forehead, and reddish or pale brown hair. Its flesh is most savory.

Ro'ge-lim [fullers, perhaps, or spies].

A town in Gilead where Barzillai lived (2 Sam. xvii. 27; xix. 31). Site unknown.

Roh'gah [clamor].

An Asherite, family of Beriah, house of Heber (1 Chron. vii. 34).

Roll.

The sheet of papyrus or the parchment on which documents were frequently written in ancient times was rolled up or wound around a stick, like a modern map, and thus constituted a roll (Jer. xxxvi. 2) or a volume in the original sense of the term (Ps. xl. 7, A. V.); see BOOK. The word rendered roll in Is. viii. 1, A. V., should be translated tablet.

Ro-mam-ti-e'zer [I have exalted help].

A singer, a son of Heman (1 Chron. xxv. 4). He obtained the twenty-fourth lot among the courses of the singers (31). See GIDDALTI.

Ro'mans.

1. Inhabitants of Rome (1 Mac. viii. 1; Acts ii. 10, "sojourners from Rome," R. V.).

2. Those who represent the Roman government (John xi. 48; Acts xxv. 16; xxviii. 17).

3. Those, wherever born or of whatever race, who possessed the rights of citizenship in the Roman empire (Acts xvi. 21, 37, 38; xxii. 25, 26, 27, 29). By the Porcian Law, which was so named because it was proposed and carried by P. Porcius Læca, a tribune of the people, 248 B. C., it was declared that no magistrate had the right to bind, scourge, or kill a Roman citizen. The life of one so privileged could not be taken away except by a decision of the whole people met in the *comitia centuriata*, a general assembly of the people, voting in divisions called centuries. If a magistrate or ruler of any kind gave orders to scourge one entitled to the protection of this law, the latter had only to utter the words, "I am a Roman citizen," and all procedure was stayed till the people had decided on his case. When the power formerly possessed by the people was transferred to the emperor, it was to him that the right of appeal lay. The privileges of Roman citizenship were first limited to residents in Rome itself; then they were extended to various Italian tribes and cities; then to the greater part of Italy; then to places beyond the Italian peninsula; and so on and on till, it is said, Caracalla (A. D. 211-217) conferred them on every inhabitant of the Roman empire. During the transition period individuals who had rendered service to Rome might be declared citizens, or the privilege might be purchased for money, even in towns or districts which were not as yet

enfranchised. Sometimes also manumitted slaves were granted citizenship. These explanations make it easy to understand how Paul, though of Jewish descent (Phil. iii. 5), could still be a Roman citizen; and how Claudius Lysias thought it worth his while to purchase the privilege for a great sum of money (Acts xxii. 28); and how, when he had given orders that Paul should be scourged, and was informed by the centurion that the apostle was a Roman citizen, procedure was immediately stopped (25–29). One can also understand the alarm of the authorities at Philippi when they had taken the responsibility of having Paul and Silas openly beaten, and, to make matters worse, uncondemned, without first taking means to ascertain whether or not they were Roman citizens (xvi. 36–38). It will appear also that Paul simply exercised his legal right when he took his appeal to Cæsar; that is, to the Roman emperor (xxv. 11).

Ro'mans, E-pis'tle to the.

The first of St. Paul's epistles according to the order in which they are placed in our N. T. In order of composition, however, it was the sixth, since it was written from Corinth, as appears from the salutations (cp. xvi. 23 with 1 Cor. i. 14 and 2 Tim. iv. 20), and from the fact that it was carried to Rome by Phœbe, a servant or deaconess of the church at Cenchreæ (Rom. xvi. 1), which was near Corinth (Acts xviii. 18); and, if so, it must have been written during the visit to Greece mentioned in Acts xx. 2, 3. That was in the winter of A. D. 57–58. The apostle had long wished to visit Rome (Rom. i. 10–12; xv. 23), and it was his purpose, his work in the east having been finished (xv. 23), to visit the capital on his way to Spain (28). Before doing so, however, he was determined to return to Jerusalem to present the gifts of the gentile churches (25, 26). Not knowing, however, what might be his fate on this dangerous journey (30–32; Acts xx. 22), he sent this letter to the Christians at Rome, where he had many friends (cp. Rom. xvi.), for, as the apostle of the gentiles, he considered the church at Rome to be under his care (xv. 15, 16), although he had never visited it. The theme of the epistle, which is one of the most elaborate ever written by him, was naturally determined by the controversies through which he had passed and by the need of stating, formally and completely, the gospel which he preached among the gentiles. It is a full presentation, therefore, of the way of salvation. Hence its supreme importance. That he addressed it to the Christians at Rome indicates, no doubt, his appreciation of the influence which the church of the world's metropolis would exert, and the consequent necessity of establishing it in the faith that it might resist the assaults of error.

Whereas the Epistle of Paul to the Gala-

tians is the *magna charta* of universal Christianity, the Epistle to the Romans is its constitution. The epistle may be analyzed as follows: After the salutation (1–7) and statement of his interest in them (8–15), he epitomizes the character of his gospel and. in doing so, gives the theme of the epistle: "The gospel is the power of God unto salvation to every one that believeth. For therein is the righteousness of God revealed from faith to faith" (16, 17).

He then proves the universal need of righteousness (i. 18–iii. 20). He first shows that the gentile world is in a state of sin and just condemnation (i. 18–32), and then that the Jewish world is no exception, but is likewise guilty before God (ii.). To the objection that this destroys the privileges of the Jew, he replies by showing that their privilege consisted in being the trustees of revelation, but that their own Scriptures declared them to be sinful (iii. 1–19), so that there is no exception to the universal guilt. In fact, the law only increases the consciousness of sin (20).

He then states the righteousness which God has provided for every believer through the redemptive and sacrificial work of Christ (iii. 21–30), and proves that this way of salvation is that taught in the O. T. (31–iv. 25), that it is the basis of Christian experience (v. 1–11), and that it proceeds upon the same principle of moral government, on which God acted when he dealt with mankind in the person of their first head and representative, Adam (12–21).

The apostle then refutes three objections which would be brought against his doctrine of salvation by the work of Christ for us received through faith alone. The first objection is that on this doctrine men may continue in sin and yet be saved, to which he replies no, because faith in Christ involves vital union with him, whereby the believer rises with Christ into a new moral life (vi. 1–14). The second objection is that Paul's doctrine of deliverance from the law released men from moral obligation, to which he replies no, because the believer accepts a new and higher obligation, whereby he devotes himself to the will of God (vi. 15–vii. 6). The third objection is that Paul's doctrine makes the law of God an evil thing, to which he replies no, for the reason that the law cannot save is not that the law is evil, but that man is sinful and cannot keep it (7–25).

Having refuted objections, he shows (viii.) that on the basis of Christ's redemptive work provision is made for the spiritual renewal, complete sanctification, and final glorification of those who are in Christ, and who, being chosen and called by God, will certainly enjoy the perfect fruition of God's love. Having thus stated the gospel way of salvation, the apostle proceeds to adjust it to the fact that Israel, the chosen people, had as a nation rejected it. He does this by teaching

Titus, the son of the Roman emperor Vespasian, after a long siege captured Jerusalem and erected the famed Arch of Titus adjacent to the Roman Forum to commemorate the event. One relief in the arch (detail in above photo) depicts Titus carrying off plunder from the Temple in Jerusalem: the seven-branched lampstand, the ark, and trumpets.

Now preserved in the Palestine Archaeological Museum, this Roman sarcophagus provides a classic example of Roman art.

Typical of Roman ruins scattered throughout the famed, once-flourishing Roman Empire are these — the Triumphal Arch in Jeresh built in honor of the Emperor Hadrian.

This Roman flour mill from Pompeii is a good example of mills used in Bible times.

A mourning Jew and Jewess flank a palm tree, the symbol of Judea on this bronze coin of Vespasian. Vespasian conquered all of Judea except Jerusalem. The coin was struck and inscribed *Judaea Capta* in honor of the victory.

that the saving promise of God had never been made to the Jews as a nation, but only to the "election," the true seed of Abraham, whom God had chosen (ix. 1–13), and he justifies from Scripture this doctrine of sovereign election (14–29); then, further, that the rejection of the Jews was due to their refusal of the very way of salvation taught by their own Scriptures (30–x. 21), yet that the rejection of Israel was not complete, for the promised remnant, the election, did believe (xi. 1–10), and, finally, that in the end the Jews will be converted, and with the gentiles trust in the promised Redeemer (11–36).

The rest of the epistle consists of an exhortation to Christian living (xii.), to the performance of civil and social duties (xiii.), and to Christian charity and unity (xiv. 1–xv. 13), ending with personal messages and salutations (14–xvi. 27).   G. T. P.

Did the epistle to the Romans in early days ever exist in a shorter form than at present? In view of certain phenomena two theories especially have attracted attention. They have literary interest, but no doctrinal importance. According to one theory, an abridgment of the epistle was prepared for general circulation; being shortened by the omission of local references, such as "in Rome" (i. 7) and chapters xv. and xvi., but retaining the entire doctrinal instruction and the essence of the practical appeal. Evidence for the existence of the epistle in this shorter form is sought in the presence of the doxology (xvi. 25–27) in some manuscripts at the end of chapter xiv. or both there and at the end of chapter xvi.; in the lack of quotation from chapters xv. and xvi. in the writings of Tertullian, Irenæus, and Cyprian; and in the apparent omission of these chapters by Marcion. The lack of citation from these chapters is without significance, however, in view of their character. They have never been much quoted. The salutations especially do not lend themselves to quotation. The theory of an abridged edition of the epistle must rest mainly on the occurrence of the doxology at the end of chapter xiv. in some manuscripts. This is a frail support; and it is especially weak in view of the fact that no extant manuscript is an abridgment, but all manuscripts of the epistle without exception contain chapters xv. and xvi.

The other theory, and one widely held, is that chapter xvi. did not form a part of the epistle originally, but constituted a brief note commending Phœbe to the church at Ephesus. For chapter xv. is not easily separated from chapter xiv., but follows it naturally, and simply develops the appeal that is made in chapter xiv. to the spirit of Christian self-sacrifice on the part of those who are strong in conscience. Moreover, chapter xv. closes, in verse 33, with a benediction such as occurs at the end of other letters written by Paul (2 Cor. xiii. 11; 1 Thes. v. 23; 2 Thes. iii. 16; Phil. iv. 9), and forms

the natural conclusion to the epistle to the Romans. Chapter xvi. would, therefore, seem to be appended. That the latter chapter was originally a letter commending Phœbe to the church at Ephesus, not to the Christians in Rome, may be gathered, it is argued, from the following considerations: 1. It is intended to accredit Phœbe (xvi. 1). 2. Aquila and Priscilla, to whom salutations are sent (xvi. 3), were certainly living in Ephesus about three years before the epistle to the Romans was written, and they were not in Rome when Paul wrote the second letter to Timothy (2 Tim. iv. 19). 3. The reference to Epænetus, "the firstfruits of Asia" (Rom. xvi. 5, R. V.), would be more natural in a letter to Ephesus than to Rome. 4. It is unlikely that Paul would have as many acquaintances in a church he had not visited as he salutes in chapter xvi. The objections to this theory that chapter xvi. is a brief note to the church at Ephesus are—1. Salutations were occasionally added, as here, after a doxology or a benediction, even when followed by Amen (Phil. iv. 20; 2 Thes. iii. 16; cp. 2 Tim. iv. 18). 2. The fact that chapter xvi. forms part of the epistle in all extant manuscripts. 3. Aquila and Priscilla migrated from place to place a great deal. They were residing in Rome when all Jews were notified to leave the city, they lived at Corinth for about a year and a half and accompanied Paul to Ephesus, where actively working for Christianity they remained at least until he returned from a trip to Jerusalem. It would not be strange if they went back to Rome, especially in connection with the apostle's plan to visit the city and introduce the Christian religion (Acts xix. 21). 4. That Epænetus, a convert of the province of Asia, found his way to Rome occasions no surprise; for Christians, Jews, and gentiles were constantly going to the imperial capital for various reasons from all parts of the world, for example, Epaphras of Colossæ and Aquila of Pontus and Herod the tetrarch. 5. The persons saluted in chapter xvi. bear names that are proven to have been current in Rome, and some of them were common among the early Christians of the city. 6. It is not necessary to assume that the people to whom he sends greetings were in every case personal acquaintances of the apostle; it is enough that they were known to him as earnest, active Christians through references to them in letters to him from Aquila, Priscilla, and others concerning affairs in Rome.

Rome.

The date 753 B.C. is accepted by the best authorities for the traditional founding of Rome by Romulus, who became its first king. The little kingdom grew in size and importance, absorbing its immediate neighbors through the reigns of seven kings, until the tyranny of Tarquinius Superbus drove the people to take the government into their own hands and establish a republic. In the beginning, the power was entirely in the hands of a few patrician families, the plebeians merely acquiescing in measures taken. The plebs, however, demanded and obtained privilege after privilege until every Roman citizen had a voice in the government. During the period of the republic, Rome extended her boundaries at first over all Italy, and finally over the whole known world.

Rome's first contact with Asia occurred 190 B. C., when the Roman army defeated Antiochus the Great, king of Syria, at the battle of Magnesia, and Rome assumed a protectorate over certain cities in Asia Minor (cp. 1 Mac. i. 10). Most of Rome's conquests after this were of a peaceful nature, other nations willingly acknowledging her superiority.

In 63 B. C. Judæa became formally subject to Rome, being taken by Pompey after he had reduced the Seleucidan kingdom to the level of a province. It was required to pay tribute, but was left for a time under native rulers.

Meantime, several parties jealous of each other had been growing up in the state. As the result of an internal political struggle, the triumvirate of Cæsar, Pompey, and Crassus was formed to rule, but by the death of Crassus, and the defeat of Pompey in a civil struggle, the power fell into the hands of Cæsar alone. This did not last long. Cæsar was murdered by his enemies in 44 B. C., civil war again broke out, a second triumvirate was formed by Antony, Octavian, and Lepidus, and, like the first, was soon reduced to one man, Octavian. Full of ambition, Octavian had himself proclaimed emperor with the title of Augustus, and the Roman empire began.

It was during the reign of Augustus that Christ was born; during that of his successor Tiberius, that the crucifixion took place. The martyrdom of James the brother of John took place in the reign of the emperor Claudius (Acts xi. 28; xii. 1, 2). It was to the emperor Nero that Paul appealed (xxv. 11). The destruction of Jerusalem prophesied by our Lord (Mat. xxiv.; Mark xiii.; Luke xix. 41–44; xxi. 5–36) was accomplished in the year A. D. 70 by Titus, who afterwards became emperor.

When the empire was at its greatest size it extended 3000 miles from east to west, and 2000 from north to south, and contained a population of about 120,000,000.

Weakened by excesses and corruption within, and attacked by enemies without, the empire began to fail, receiving its first serious check on the final separation of the eastern empire in 395, and coming finally to an end by the capture of Rome by the Goth Odoacer in 476.

During the decline of Rome's civil power the Christians there had been growing in power and influence. Although it had been the policy of Rome to tolerate the religions of her conquered peoples, the Christians were persecuted almost from the first. This was due mainly to two causes: their uncompromising attitude toward all heathen rites and religions, and their unceasing efforts to make converts. The persecutions were especially severe under Nero, who attempted to throw on the Christians the blame for some of his own nefarious deeds. Persecutions were also very severe under Domitian, but notwithstanding constant imprisonment and death the Christians continued to grow in numbers and influence until the church in Rome and the bishop of Rome became no inconsiderable factor in the general growth of Christianity. The Christian religion was officially adopted and declared the religion of the state by the emperor Constantine early in the fourth century.

Roof. See HOUSE.

Room.

1. A chamber or other apartment in a house (Acts i. 13). See HOUSE and PALACE.

2. In A. V. room is also used in the sense of place or position in society, a meaning which is now obsolete (Mat. xxiii. 6; Luke xiv. 7, 8; xx. 46). Uppermost or chief room is the translation of the Greek prōtoklisia, first place for reclining; see MEALS. The scribes and Pharisees were censured for seeking the place of honor at feasts, desiring to recline on the most important couch. R. V. substitutes place or seat for room, when used in this obsolete sense.

Rose.

The rendering of the Hebrew Ḥᵃbaẓẓeleth (Song ii. 1; Is. xxxv. 1), in the English versions and by several Jewish scholars of the Middle Ages. Modern interpreters are divided in opinion. The most important suggestions are the following: 1. Some expositors, including Tristram, following the Targum of Song ii. 1, and sometimes appealing to a doubtful etymology, understand the beautiful, white sweet-scented narcissus (Narcissus tazetta), common in spring in the plain of Sharon and in the hill country. 2. A Syriac word, seemingly kindred to the Hebrew name, denotes colchicum and the crocus, which are strikingly alike and which, when the rainy season sets in, carpet the fields with bright flowers. The prevalent opinion, perhaps represented by R. V. margin, is that meadow saffron (Colchicum autumnale) is meant, with its pale lilac flowers. 3. An Assyrian word still nearer to the Hebrew form, refers to marsh plants, so that the Hebrew has been understood by some interpreters of late to denote Cyperus syriacus, known also as Cyperus papyrus, which grows on the Nahr el-'Aujah in the plain of Sharon and in other marshy districts of Palestine. It flowers toward the end of autumn.

The true rose is a native of Media and Persia. It was early transplanted to the countries on the Mediterranean, and grows on the mountains of Palestine. The maid who recognized the voice of Peter at the gate, was named Rhoda, a rose (Acts xii. 13); and the true rose is probably intended in Wisd. ii. 8; Ecclus. xxiv. 14; xxxix. 13; l. 8, where the Greek word is used. Tristram, however, judges from its growing at Jericho and by the waters, that the oleander is meant in these passages.

Rosh [in Hebrew a head, a chief, a prince].
1. A son of Benjamin, who went down to Egypt with Jacob and his sons (Gen. xlvi. 21). He did not give rise to a tribal family (Num. xxvi. 38), because probably, like Er and Onan of Judah, he died without issue.
2. A northern people mentioned with Meshech and Tubal (Ezek. xxxviii. 2, 3; xxxix. 1, both R. V. text). Gesenius believes Rosh to be the Russians, though they are nowhere else mentioned by this or any similar name for centuries afterwards. The text of the A. V. and the margin of the R. V. render Rosh "chief prince," in which case Rosh as a proper name disappears.

Ru'by.
1. The plural, rubies, is the rendering of the Hebrew *P'ninim*, which occurs only in the plural. The margin of the R. V. has coral, red coral or pearls. The name may signify branches and thus aptly describe coral; but this signification is not established. It was ruddy in hue (Lam. iv. 7), and was precious (Job xxviii. 18; Prov. iii. 15). The color is a good reason for not regarding it as a pearl. The true or oriental ruby is, like the sapphire, a variety of corundum. It is a clear, bright gem, rich red in color. The spinel ruby is a deep red, and the balas ruby a rose-red, variety of spinel.
2. The marginal rendering of the Hebrew *'Odem*, red gem (Ex. xxviii. 17; Ezek. xxviii. 13). In the text it is translated sardius, which is the better rendering.

Rue.
A plant, in Greek *pēganon*, of which the Pharisees, careful about minute points, were scrupulously accurate in paying tithes (Luke xi. 42). It is *Ruta graveolens*, a half shrubby plant, two or three feet high, with pinnate bluish-green leaves, all dotted over with odoriferous glands and yellowish corymbose flowers, mostly with eight stamens. Its odor is very powerful. It is a native of the Mediterranean region. It was cultivated in Palestine as a medicine, and perhaps as a condiment for food. Had it been wild, it would not have been a tithable plant.

Ru'fus [red].
A son of that Simon of Cyrene who was compelled to bear the cross of Christ (Mark xv. 21). He may have been the same as the Rufus at Rome to whom Paul sent a salutation (Rom. xvi. 13).

Rue.

Ru-ha'mah [she hath obtained mercy].
One of the symbolical names with which the children of Judah and Israel shall eventually greet each other (Hos. ii. 1).

Rul'er.
In a general sense, any one who exercises authority. More particularly:
1. Officer of a synagogue (Luke viii. 41). See SYNAGOGUE.
2. Member of the sanhedrin, whether priest or layman (John iii. 1; vii. 26; Acts iv. 5 with 8 and 15; cp. xxiii. 5).
3. Archon or civil magistrate of a city (Acts xvi. 19). In Macedonia and regions under Macedonian influence such officials were technically called politarchs or rulers of the city (xvii. 6, 8).
4. The governor of a feast, who prepared it and had the direction of it, but was not the host (Ecclus. xxxii. 1; 2 Mac. ii. 27; and John ii. 8, but margin "steward").

Ru'mah [height, high place].
The home of a grandfather of Jehoiakim (2 Kin. xxiii. 36); perhaps Arumah near Shechem (cp. Antiq. x. 5, 2), or Rumah in Galilee (War iii. 7, 21), represented by the ruin Rumeh, 6 miles north of Nazareth.

Run'ners.
A class of soldiers who served as a bodyguard to the king (1 Sam. xxii. 17, in A. V. footmen, R. V. guard), were posted at the door of the royal palace at Jerusalem (1 Kin. xiv. 27; 2 Kin. xi. 19), had their own guard room (1 Kin. xiv. 28), escorted the king to the temple (28), and executed the king's commands (1 Sam. xxii. 17; 2 Kin. x. 25). In each instance, see R. V. margin. Perhaps

they ran before the royal chariot (see FORE-RUNNER).

Rush. See PAPYRUS.

Rust.

A corrosive or disfiguring accretion, in Greek *ios*, which denotes the rust of iron, the verdigris of brass, the tarnish on gold and silver (Jas. v. 3). The Greek word *brōsis*, eating, corrosion, is used in Mat. vi. 19, 20.

Ruth [possibly, sightly].

A Moabitess married first to Mahlon of Bethlehem, who was sojourning in Moab with his parents and brother because of a famine in Judah. The three men died. Ruth left her native land and accompanied her mother-in-law Naomi to Bethlehem. While gleaning in the field of Boaz, a kinsman of Naomi's deceased husband, she found favor in his eyes. Custom required a kinsman of Mahlon to marry Ruth ; and Boaz took her to wife, after one nearer of kin than he had refused. By this marriage Ruth became an ancestress of David. The transaction between Boaz and Ruth was not a levirate marriage (Deut. xxv. 7–10 ; cp. Ruth i. 11–13), for Boaz was not a brother of Ruth's deceased husband. Custom required that when the widow of a childless man desired to sell his estate if there was no brother, then the nearest of kin and heir to the deceased should buy or redeem it of the widow (iv. 3, 4, 9). The property was thereby retained in the family. Custom was also urgent that the kinsman voluntarily assume levirate duties or take the woman to wife, if he would not thereby endanger his own inheritance (iii. 9 ; iv. 5, 6). It was considered magnanimous to do so, and a mark of loyalty to the family. A son born of such union was legally the son of the deceased (iv. 5, 10, 14, 17) ; and doubtless ultimately received the firstborn's right in the estate.

In the Hebrew collection the Book of Ruth is placed among the rolls which were publicly read on specified anniversaries ; because, its scenery being the harvest field, it was read at Pentecost, the harvest festival. In the Septuagint and in Josephus' enumeration of the canonical books it stands immediately after Judges, as in the English version. The events recorded occurred in the days of the judges (i. 1), 60 years or more before David's birth (iv. 21, 22). The marriage of a pious Israelite with a Moabitess is recounted, and the issue of the marriage is an ancestor of David. After the exile such a marriage would have been regarded as discreditable, and would not have been invented. The narrative is, accordingly, historical. Its historical character receives confirmation from the appropriateness of the event to the period, for about that time friendly intercourse prevailed between Israel and Moab (1 Sam. xxii. 3, 4). The event is related without disapprobation and without explanation or apology ; an indication that it was committed to writing before the exile.

The language is also as pure as admittedly early writings, such as Judges v. The book did not receive its final literary form until a considerable time after the event ; for it explains the drawing off of the shoe in matters of attestation as a custom of former times (iv. 7), and it brings down the genealogy to David.

Rye. See SPELT.

S

Sab′a-oth [in Hebrew, hosts, armies].

The Lord of Sabaoth is the same as Lord of hosts, the second part of the title being left untranslated (Rom. ix. 29 with Is. i. 9 ; Jas. v. 4). See LORD.

Sa′bat. See SHEBAT.

Sab′bath [rest].

The divinely instituted day of rest, ordained for all men. God having completed the work of creation in six days ceased from creative work on the seventh day. And God blessed the seventh day, and hallowed it ; because that in it he rested from all his work which he had made in a creative manner (Gen. ii. 1–3) ; see CREATION. The next reference to a division of time into periods of seven days occurs in the account of the flood, when Noah was forewarned of the imminence of the storm a week before it broke in its fury, and again when he sent forth the birds at intervals of seven days to discover through them the stage of water (Gen. vii. 4 ; viii. 10, 12). But it is not only in this express mention of the week, but also in the entire chronology of the flood, when interpreted according to its own principles, that the hebdomadal division of time is found to have existed at that early date. The events are measured by intervals of the week both in the Hebrew narrative and in the Assyrian account ; see FLOOD. And what is more, there is repeated evidence that the seventh day was regarded as a season of divine benevolence toward man. According to both accounts, and reckoning from the day when the flood began, the divine power which caused the storm was restrained at the close of a sixth day, and the first day that dawned fair and beautiful was a seventh day ; and the day when the inmates of the ark were permitted to disembark, and when they offered sacrifices of thanksgiving, was likewise a seventh day. A glance at the chronology will show that not improbably Noah dispatched the birds in connection with the conventional seventh day because it was a day of divine favor.

From the days of Noah until the exodus there is no express mention in the Hebrew records of a sanctification of the seventh day by rest from labor and by religious worship. There is no reason why there should be.

There was no event specially to emphasize the day. And probably in that age the Sabbath was somewhat less sharply marked off from the other days of the week, even among the people of God, than it was later; for the nomad shepherds had certain labors which must be performed, and the Israelites in Egypt were not their own masters and could not rest on the seventh day : but when the nation was organized at Sinai a different mode of life was adopted, the people were able to frame their own laws, they formed an independent community, they led camp life in the wilderness and exchanged it for the settled life of agriculturists and traders, and as a natural result rest on the Sabbath made a greater outward difference than it had done before. Still, in both the Hebrew and Babylonian literature relating to the period before the exodus there are incidental references to a period of seven days (Gen. xxix. 27, 28). These are doubtless to be understood in the sense in which we use the term week, reckoning seven days from any date we please. At any rate time was frequently measured by periods of seven days. Several causes doubtless contributed to make this custom general, among others the phasing of the moon. But over and beyond the appropriateness of a lunar subdivision of the lunar month, there was the conception, traceable in the narrative of the flood, that the seventh day was one of divine rest and favor toward men.

It is disputed whether the name Sabbath was used for the recurring seventh day in Assyria and Babylonia. A day of propitiating the gods was called by a name which may be pronounced *shabattu*, Sabbath. But other pronunciations are equally possible, and yield a sense which satisfies the given description of the day. There is no evidence that it was a particular day of the week or a day when labor was suspended. Tablets, copied in the reign of Ashurbanipal, about 650 B. C., show that the seventh, fourteenth, nineteenth, twenty-first, and twenty-eighth days of each month were regarded as inauspicious for certain specified acts. These unlucky days, it will be observed, are not connected with the phasing of the moon; for it does not quarter on the nineteenth day, and in months of thirty days, as were those in question, it would only occasionally quarter on the seventh day. The unluckiness of the day was connected with the number seven. Not only was the recurring seventh day ill-fated, but also the nineteenth, that is the forty-ninth day, the seventh seventh day reckoned from the first day of the preceding month. These recurring seventh days were not days of national rest when the tablets were in force ; a few specified acts only were dangerous on those days. Business and toil proceeded as usual. The most that can at present be claimed is that if these tablets bear witness to the Sabbath at all, they testify to the degradation of the nobler conception of an earlier age. They do not perpetuate the thought which is discoverable in even the Assyrian narrative of the flood. They are not up to the standard of the fourth commandment as promulgated in Israel centuries before at Sinai, and familiar in all its loftiness to the Israelites of the time of Jeremiah, who was a younger contemporary of Ashurbanipal.

As in these tablets, so among the Hebrews, it was not the moon which determined the Sabbath ; for among the Hebrews it was not the seventh day only which was sacred, but the day which began and which consecrated the seventh month, and the entire seventh year, and the completion of the seventh seventh year. And these seasons were all associated with the idea of rest, of worship, of liberty, of good will to man, and of divine favor.

The first occurrence of the name Sabbath in the Hebrew records is in Ex. xvi. 23. The Israelites had not reached mount Sinai, nor had the ten commandments been spoken from its summit, but in the wilderness of Sin when manna began to be given a double amount fell on the sixth day ; and Moses said : "This is that which the Lord hath spoken, To-morrow is a solemn rest, a holy sabbath unto the Lord : bake that which ye will bake, ... and all that remaineth over lay up for you to be kept until the morning." None fell on the morrow, and Moses said in regard to what had been kept over : "Eat that to-day ; for to-day is a sabbath unto the Lord : to-day ye shall not find it in the field. Six days ye shall gather it ; but on the seventh day is the sabbath, in it there shall be none" (23–26 ; cp. 5).

Shortly afterwards the commandment requiring the Sabbath to be kept was promulgated with nine other laws by Jehovah at Sinai, and afterwards written by the finger of God on tables of stone (Ex. xxxi. 18 ; Deut. ix. 10). Like its companion laws, it was of perpetual obligation. It commences, "Remember the sabbath day to keep it holy," the word remember being appropriately used, since the people did not now for the first time learn that the Sabbath existed. In repeating the laws forty years later at Shittim, Moses recalls the fact that the Lord their God had commanded them to observe the day ; and then instead of stating the reason for the ordination of the Sabbath, he assigns Jehovah's deliverance of his people from bondage or labor in Egypt as the reason why Israel specially is under obligation to keep the day of rest instituted by God (Deut. v. 15). The Sabbath was to be kept by a holy convocation for the worship of the Lord (Lev. xxiii. 3 ; cp. Ezek. xlvi. 3), and should be a sign showing that God was their sanctifier (Ex. xxxi. 13). The doctrine clearly was that the day was ordained by God ; that it was established as a day of physical rest and refreshment for man; that the obligation to keep it arises from God's own example, his connecting a blessing with it, and his explicit command, and that his redemption of his people lays them under special obligation to set the day apart; that it is to be observed by God's people as a Sabbath unto him, and is to include a holy assemblage for worship. It was a reminder of God's complacency in the contemplation of his finished work, and of Jehovah's redemption of his people from Egyptian service. In the tabernacle and temple worship the preëminence of the Sabbath over the other days of the week was shown by the offering upon it of two lambs, while one was sacrificed on an ordinary week day (Num. xxviii. 9, 19). The twelve cakes of showbread were also to be presented on that day (Lev. xxiv. 5-8; 1 Chron. ix. 32). In enforcing the law, no fire was allowed to be lit by an Israelite in his habitation on the Sabbath day; anyone doing work on it was to be put to death; and one who gathered sticks on the Sabbath in the wilderness was in fact stoned to death (Ex. xxxv. 3; Num. xv. 32-36); see PUNISHMENT. Isaiah (lvi. 2-6; lviii. 13) and Jeremiah (xvii. 21-27) strongly counseled the keeping of the day. A psalm or song was composed for the Sabbath, in which delight is expressed in the worship of Jehovah and thought is directed to God's works of creation (Ps. xcii). Ezekiel complains that the Sabbaths had to a large extent been profaned or polluted (Ezek. xx. 12, 24; xxii. 8, 26; xxiii. 38). In Nehemiah's time, traders, especially those of Tyre, continually brought merchandise to Jerusalem for sale on the sacred day, till Nehemiah peremptorily forbade the practice to be continued, and took strong measures against those who attempted to disregard his directions (Neh. x. 31; xiii. 15-22). At the commencement of the war of independence under the Maccabee family, the Jews were of opinion that they had no right to defend themselves on the Sabbath if they were attacked by an enemy. The campaign therefore began with the slaughter of 1000 unresisting Jews, consisting of patriots and their families. The survivors resolved in future to defend themselves if they were directly attacked on the sacred day, but not to engage in offensive operations (1 Mac. ii. 31-41). Even then they were at a disadvantage with the gentiles, who labored under no such restriction. The latter pushed on siege and other operations on the Sabbath unmolested, provided they abstained from directly attacking the Jews. Pompey raised his banks and mounted his battering-rams against Jerusalem on the Sabbath without any interference from the inhabitants, but delayed the effort to breach the walls till the sacred day was over (Antiq. xiv. 4, 2 and 3). In the time of our Lord the Pharisees applied the law to the most trivial acts, and forbade many works of

necessity and mercy. They denounced Jesus because he healed sick people on the Sabbath, though if ox, or ass, or sheep fell, into a pit on that day, they did not consider it at all unlawful to take him out without delay. They also led forth the animals to be watered just as on ordinary week days (Mat. xii. 9-13; Luke xiii. 10-17). It was not merely to healing on the Sabbath that they objected. When the disciples of Jesus, passing on the Sabbath through the grain fields, plucked some of the ears, and, rubbing them in their hands, ate them, being hungry, the Pharisees denounced this as though it were in essence the same as reaping, threshing, and grinding. Our Lord made a notable reply: "The sabbath was made for man, and not man for the sabbath: so that the Son of man is Lord even of the sabbath" (Mark ii. 23-28). The Sabbath was instituted for the benefit of mankind, its obligation lasts as long as man has the same needs as at creation, the Son of man is not the slave of the Sabbath, but its lord.

The day for synagogue worship was the seventh day of the week, Saturday (Mat. xii. 9, 10; Acts xiii. 14). The apostolic Christian church from the beginning held assemblages for worship on the first day of the week, which was the day on which Christ rose from the dead for our justification (Acts ii. 1, probably; xx. 7). On that day the apostle Paul directed the Christians of Galatia and Corinth to make their weekly contribution to the charities of the church (1 Cor. xvi. 1, 2). It was designated the Lord's day (Rev. i. 10); see LORD'S DAY. This day, like the former appointment of the seventh day, sets apart one whole day in seven to be a Sabbath unto the Lord. It is equally a reminder of the Lord's redemption of his people. It is accompanied by the same evidence of divine favor in the form of physical and spiritual blessings.

The Sabbath of the land was a year in which the land of Canaan had a solemn rest. It came round once every seven years. In it the ground was not sown or reaped, nor the vineyard pruned, nor its fruits gathered in. The spontaneous growth of field and orchard was free to all. In the Sabbatic year also the creditor released the Hebrew debtor from his obligation and freed the Hebrew slave (Ex. xxiii. 10, 11; Lev. xxv. 3-7; Deut. xv. 1-18; Neh. x. 31). On the completion of seven such Sabbatic years, that is, at the end of forty-nine years, the trumpet was blown to proclaim liberty throughout the land, and the year of jubile was ushered in (Lev. xxv. 8-10); see JUBILE. Reliable historical notices of the observance of the Sabbatical year are the covenant of Nehemiah's time (Neh. x. 31), the 150th year of the Seleucidan era or 164-163 B. C. (1 Mac. vi. 49, 53; cp. Antiq. xii. 9, 5), the 178th Seleucidan year or 136-135 B. C. (Antiq. xiii. 8, 1; War i. 2, 4), the decree issued by Cæsar exempting the Jews from tribute during the Sabbatic year (Antiq. xiv. 10, 6 ; cp. Tacitus, Hist. v. 4), the year 38–37 B. C. (Antiq. xiv. 16, 2 ; xv. 1, 2), and the year before the fall of Jerusalem, A. D. 68–69 (Talmud). See also Antiq. xi. 8, 5. If the Israelites disobeyed God's laws, they were to be carried into captivity, the land lying desolate, having rest and being left to enjoy its Sabbaths, or the rest which the Israelites had not allowed it on their weekly and septennial Sabbaths (Lev. xxvi. 34–43). Jeremiah prophesied that the people should be punished for their idolatry by the desolation of their land and their bondage to the Babylonians for seventy years (Jer. xxv. 7–11). The chronicler also connects the captivity with the disobedience of the people and the pollution of the temple; and he adds that they were servants unto the Babylonians for seventy years, as Jeremiah had foretold they should be, until the land had enjoyed her Sabbaths ; for as long as she lay desolate she kept Sabbath, to fulfill three score and ten years (2 Chron. xxxvi. 14, 16, 20, 21). It must not be inferred from these words that the people had ignored the Sabbatic year exactly seventy times, or that the neglected Sabbatic years were continuous ; and it is not stated that the Sabbatic year was neglected. Doubtless it had been neglected sometimes, for an idolatrous and disobedient people would scarcely obey an injunction when obedience would apparently involve pecuniary loss.

Evidently any period of time which was kept as a Sabbath could be called a Sabbath. Not only were the seventh day and the seventh year Sabbaths, but also the day of atonement on the tenth day of the seventh month (Lev. xxiii. 32).

A Sabbath-day's journey was a journey of limited extent proper, in the estimation of the scribes, on a Sabbath day. The expression occurs in Acts i. 12, where this is stated to be the distance between mount Olivet and Jerusalem, or from Jerusalem to a place on the mountain from which Bethany was visible (Luke xxiv. 50). If the measurement be made from the eastern gate of Jerusalem (the Jewish method of reckoning) to the site of the church of the Ascension, crowning the mount of Olives, the distance, as the crow flies, will be about 2250 English feet; but in actual travel it will be considerably more. According to Josephus, the mount was distant 6 or 7 stades from the city (Antiq. xx. 8, 6 ; War v. 2, 3). The regulation of the Sabbath-day's journey had its origin in the injunction not to leave the camp on the Sabbath (Ex. xvi. 29). It was reckoned at 2000 cubits, partly on the erroneous interpretation of Num. xxxv. 5, according to which the district pertaining to a Levitical city extended 2000 cubits from the wall on every side, and partly on the belief, derived from Josh. iii. 4, that the camp of the Israelites

was 2000 cubits from the tabernacle, to which of course they might go on the Sabbath. A man might travel on the Sabbath within the city where he resided as far as its limits allowed, be the city never so large.

Sa-be′ans.

The people of Sheba (Is. xlv. 14), a nation far off (Joel iii. 8) ; also the people of Seba (Is. xlv. 14 ; cp. Ezek. xxiii. 42).

Sab′tah and Sabta.

A Cushite people (Gen. x. 7 ; 1 Chron. i. 9), probably of southern Arabia. The important city of Sabbatha or Sabota in the country of the Chatramotites (Hadramaut) is strongly advocated, but the identification is doubtful. Gesenius suggests Sabat, Saba, or Sabai, near the modern Arkiko, an Abyssinian town on a bay of the Red Sea.

Sab′te-ca, in A. V. Sabtecha and Sabtechah.

A Cushite people (Gen. x. 7 ; 1 Chron. i. 9), probably of southern Arabia. More precise geographical details cannot be given.

Sa′car [merchandise].

1. A Hararite, father of one of David's mighty men (1 Chron. xi. 35). In 2 Sam. xxiii. 33 Sharar.

2. A son of Obed-edom (1 Chron. xxvi. 4).

Sack′but.

A mediæval wind instrument, having a long bent tube of brass with a movable slide for changing the pitch of the tone, as in the trombone. The instrument referred to by this name in the English version of Dan. iii. 5, belonged to an entirely different class. It was a stringed instrument. It is called in Aramaic sabb′ka', which, if Semitic, probably describes the lacing of the strings. The name is evidently identical with the Greek sambukē, which was an instrument of music somewhat like the harp or lyre, but with only four strings. Strabo affirms that the Greek word is of barbarian, i. e. oriental, origin ; and Athenæus states that the instrument was invented by the Syrians.

Sack′cloth.

A coarse cloth, of a dark color, usually made of goat's hair (Rev. vi. 12). It was called in Hebrew sak, from which the English word is derived. It was worn customarily by mourners (2 Sam. iii. 31 ; 2 Kin. xix. 1, 2), often, if not habitually, by prophets (Is. xx. 2 ; Rev. xi. 3), and by captives (1 Kin. xx. 31 ; cp. Is. iii. 24). The garment of sackcloth probably resembled a sack, with openings made for the neck and arms, and slit down the front. It was cast about the loins (Gen. xxxvii. 34 ; 1 Kin. xx. 31), and girded on (2 Sam. iii. 31 ; Ezek. vii. 18 ; Joel i. 8) ; and was usually worn over other raiment (Jon. iii. 6 ; cp. 2 Sam. xxi. 10), but sometimes next to the skin (1 Kin. xxi. 27 ; 2 Kin. vi. 30 ; Job xvi. 15 ; Is. xxxii. 11).

The cloth was also used for making sacks, which were known by the same name as the material (Gen. xlii. 25 ; Josh. ix. 4).

Sac'ri-fice. See OFFERINGS.

Sad'du-cees.

A Jewish party, the opponents of the Pharisees (Antiq. xiii. 10, 6). They were comparatively few in number, but they were educated men, and mostly wealthy and of good position (ibid. ; xviii. 1, 4). The name, judged by the orthography, is derived from Zadok, which was often written Saddouk in Greek. The rabbins say that the party took its name from its founder Zadok, who lived about 300 B. C.; but since it appears that the members and adherents of the highest priestly aristocracy constituted the party, it is now generally believed that the name refers to the high priest Zadok, who officiated in David's reign, and in whose family the high-priesthood remained until the political confusion of the Maccabæan times, his descendants and partisans being Zadokites or Sadducees.

In opposition to the Pharisees, who laid great stress on the tradition of the elders, the Sadducees limited their creed to the doctrines which they found in the sacred text itself. They held that the word of the written law was alone binding (Antiq. xiii. 10, 6). They maintained the right of private interpretation (xviii. 1, 4). They held to the letter of Scripture, even when it led to severity in the administration of justice (xx. 9, 1). In distinction from the Pharisees, they denied : 1. The resurrection and future retribution in Sheol, asserting that the soul dies with the body (Mat. xxii. 23–33; Acts xxiii. 8; Antiq. xviii. 1, 4 ; War ii. 8, 14). 2. The existence of angels and spirits (Acts xxiii. 8). 3. Fatalism : contending for the freedom of the will, teaching that all our actions are in our own power, so that we are ourselves the causes of what is good and receive what is evil from our own folly, and affirming that God is not concerned in our doing good or not doing what is evil (Antiq. xiii. 5, 9; War ii. 8, 14). In denying immortality and the resurrection, they were relying on the absence of an explicit statement of these doctrines in the Mosaic law, and they failed to hold the faith of the patriarchs regarding Sheol, which, though it was undeveloped, yet contained the germs of the later biblical doctrine of the resurrection of the body and a future retribution. The patriarchs unquestionably believed in the continued existence of the soul after death. In affirming that there is neither angel nor spirit, the Sadducees were setting themselves against the elaborate angelology of the Judaism of their time; but they went to the other extreme, and again fell short of the teaching of the law (Ex. iii. 2; xiv, 19). They probably at first emphasized the truth that God directs affairs with respect to man's conduct, punishing or rewarding in this life according to man's deeds are good or evil. If they actually taught, as Josephus affirms they did,

that God is not concerned in our doing good or refraining from evil, they rejected the clear teaching of the Mosaic law which they professed to believe (Gen. iii. 17 ; iv. 7 ; vi. 5–7). It is probable that they began by denying what is not expressly tar ght in the letter of Scripture ; but as they y elded more fully to Greek influence, they adopted the principles of the Aristotelian philosophy, and refused to accept any doctrine which they could not prove by pure reason.

As to the origin and growth of the Sadducees, Schürer suggests that the priestly house of Zadok, which was at the head of affairs in the fourth and third centuries B. C. under the Persian and Grecian kings, began, unconsciously perhaps, to place political above religious considerations. In the time of Ezra and Nehemiah the family of the high priest was worldly and inclined to resist the strict separation of Jew from gentile. See ELIASHIB 5. In the time of Antiochus Epiphanes a large number of priests were friendly to Greek culture (2 Mac. iv. 14–16), and the high priests Jason, Menelaus, and Alcimus were pronounced Hellenizers. The people took a determined stand under the Maccabees for purity of Israel's religion ; and when this party triumphed and the Maccabees secured the high-priesthood, the Zadokites were forced into retirement and driven to politics, and they continued to be ready to neglect the customs and traditions of the elders and favor Greek culture and influence. John Hyrcanus, Aristobulus, and Alexander Jannæus (135–78 B. C.) favored the Sadducees, and the conduct of political affairs was largely in their hands under the Romans and the Herods, for the high priests of this period were Sadducees (Acts v. 17 ; Antiq. xx. 9, 1). The Sadducees, as well as the Pharisees, who visited John the Baptist in the wilderness, were addressed by him as a generation of vipers (Mat. iii. 7). They joined with the Pharisees in demanding from our Lord a sign from heaven (Mat. xvi. 1–4), and Jesus warned his disciples against both (6–12). The Sadducees attempted to embarrass him by putting to him an ensnaring question regarding the resurrection, but he refuted their arguments, and reduced them to silence (xxii. 23–33). They joined with the priests and the captain of the temple in persecuting Peter and John (Acts iv. 1–22). Both Pharisees and Sadducees were in the sanhedrin which tried Paul, and the apostle, taking note of the fact, cleverly set them at variance with each other (xxiii. 6–10).

Sa'doc [Hebrew Ṣadok, just, righteous].

An ancestor of Christ, who lived after the exile (Mat. i. 14).

Saf'fron.

A fragrant plant (Song iv. 14), called in Hebrew karkom, in Arabic karkam. It is the saffron crocus (Crocus sativus), a native, apparently, of northern Italy and of western Asia. From a remote period of antiquity it has been largely cultivated in southern Europe and Asia. The flowers are light violet in color, veined with red. The dried stigmas, pulverized or pressed, yield a yellow dye. Clothing and rooms were sprinkled with water scented with saffron, olive oil perfumed with it was used as an ointment, food was spiced with it, and it was employed in medicine.

Sa'la and **Salah.** See SHELAH.

Sal'a-mis.

A city on the east or southeast coast of Cyprus, traditionally reported to have been built by Teucer, from the island of Salamis, off the coast of Greece. It contained synagogues of the Jews, in which Paul on his first missionary journey preached (Acts xiii. 4, 5). The place was subsequently named Constantia, and is now called Famagusta.

Sa-la'thi-el. See SHEALTIEL.

Sal'e-cah, in A. V. **Sal'cah** and **Sal'chah** [perhaps, a road].

A city of Bashan, near Edrei (Deut. iii. 10; Josh. xii. 5; xiii. 11). It was on the boundary of Og's kingdom, and afterwards constituted the northern limit of the Gadites (1 Chron. v. 11). It is now known as Salkhad, a slight modification of the ancient name, 35 miles east of Edrei, and 66 east, very slightly north of the Jordan, opposite to Beth-shean, in Samaria.

Sa'lem [complete, peaceful, peace].

A natural abbreviation of the name Jerusalem, the city or foundation of peace (Ps. lxxvi. 2; and probably Gen. xiv. 18). See MELCHIZEDEK and SHALEM.

Sa'lim [perhaps, Aramaic *sh^elim*, completed].

A place near which were the waters of Ænon (John iii. 23); see ÆNON.

Sal'lai [perhaps, exalted].

1. A chief of a family of Benjamites who resided at Jerusalem (Neh. xi. 8).

2. A father's house among the priests after the captivity (Neh. xii. 20); see SALLU.

Sal'lu [elevation, exaltation].

1. A Benjamite, a son of Meshullam and a chief of a family resident at Jerusalem (1 Chron. ix. 7; Neh. xi. 7).

2. A chief of the priests who came from Babylon with Zerubbabel (Neh. xii. 7). In the next generation a father's house, which occupies the same position in the corresponding catalogue, bore the name Sallai (ver. 20). One of the two names has probably been misread, the difference being merely that between a jod and a vau (q. v.).

Sal'ma. See SALMON.

Sal'mai, in A. V. **Shalmai,** in R. V. of Ezra ii. 46 **Shamlai;** the forms being confused in the Hebrew text itself.

Founder of a family of Nethinim, mem-

bers of which returned from captivity with Zerubbabel (Ezra ii. 46; Neh. vii. 48).

Sal'mon or **Salmah** or **Salma.**

Father of Boaz. He was a man of Judah, descended through Perez, Hezron, and Ram (Ruth iv. 18–21; Mat. i. 4; Luke iii. 32). In the Hebrew text of Ruth. iv. 20, not 21, the form Salmah is used, of which Salma is the later orthography (1 Chron. ii. 11). He has sometimes been thought to have been the ancestor of the inhabitants of Bethlehem, mentioned in 1 Chron. ii. 51, 54. But the genealogy of Salma, ancestor of the Bethlehemites, is traced back by the line of Caleb, not of Ram. The different lineage probably indicates a different person; though, of course, genealogies may intertwine. For Salmon of Ps. lxviii. 14, see ZALMON.

Sal-mo'ne.

A promontory, constituting the most easterly portion of Crete (Acts xxvii. 7). It is called Salmonia in an inscription. It is now known as Cape Sidero.

Sa'lom. See SALU.

Sa-lo'me [probably, whole, perfect, integrity, peace].

The wife of Zebedee, and the mother of James and John (cp. Mat. xxvii. 56 with Mark xv. 40 and xvi. 1). She was one of the Christian women who from a distance saw the crucifixion (Mat. xxvii. 56), and who went to the sepulcher of our Lord on the resurrection morning with sweet spices to anoint his body (Mark xvi. 1).

Salt.

Salt of poor quality could be scraped up on the shore of the Dead Sea, when the salty water had evaporated, or be cut from the neighboring cliffs. It was used in Canaan and the adjacent regions as a condiment and preservative for animal food (Job vi. 6; Ecclus. xxxix. 26). Under the law, it was presented with offerings of all kinds (Lev. ii. 13; Ezek. xliii. 24; Antiq. iii. 9, 1). Salt land is unfruitful (Job xxxix. 6), and when a captured city was doomed to utter destruction the final step sometimes was to sow it with salt. Abimelech thus treated Shechem (Judg. ix. 45). Salt preserves from corruption and renders food palatable, and is therefore used figuratively for the true disciples of Jesus, who by their precepts and example raise the moral tone of society (Mat. v. 13; Mark ix. 50; Luke xiv. 34). Salt is also used for wholesome character and speech (Mark ix. 50; Col. iv. 6). The impure salt of Syria, when exposed to the rain and sun or stored in damp houses, is apt to lose its taste and become useless. It cannot be used like much other refuse as a fertilizer, for it is good for nothing (Mat. v. 13; Luke xiv. 35). During the convulsion in which the guilty cities of the plain were destroyed, Lot's wife, lingering in the doomed region, perished, and was transformed into a pillar of salt (Gen.

xix. 26; Wisd. x. 7; Antiq. i. 11, 4). She was probably overwhelmed by a shower of salt or incrusted with salt.

A covenant of salt was a covenant of permanent continuance and perpetual obligation (Lev. ii. 13; Num. xviii. 19; 2 Chron. xiii. 5).

Salt, Cit'y of.
A city in the wilderness of Judah. It is mentioned along with En-gedi on the shore of the Dead Sea, from which therefore, presumably, it was not far distant (Josh. xv. 62). Exact situation unknown.

Salt, Val'ley of.
A valley in which the army of David slew 18,000 men of Aram (2 Sam. viii. 13) or rather Edom (14; 1 Chron. xviii. 12; cp. 1 Kin. xi. 15–17; Ps. lx. title); see DALETH. Amaziah, king of Judah, slew 10,000 Edomites in the valley of Salt, and then took their capital, Sela (2 Kin. xiv. 7; 2 Chron. xxv. 11). The natural locality in which to look for the valley of Salt is at the southern end of the Dead Sea, where there is a range of hills 5 miles in length, consisting of layers of salt, and between this chain and the sea is a valley 6 or 8 miles long. It is against this identification, however, that the Hebrew word ge' applied to it is the appropriate one for a glen rather than a broad valley. It may have been a gorge descending from the Edomite hills, in the direction of the salt range.

Salt Sea.
The name given in the O. T. to what is now generally called the Dead Sea (Gen. xiv. 3; Num. xxxiv. 3, 12; Deut. iii. 17; Josh. xv. 2, 5). See DEAD SEA.

Salt'wort.
The rendering of the Hebrew Malluaḥ, saline plant (Job xxx. 4; in A. V. mallows). It was used as food by the very poor. Two genera of plants are commonly so designated, Salicornia and Salsola, but neither is suitable for food. The plant intended is probably some other chenopod, as spinach or better sea purslane (Atriplex halimus). This latter is a bush. It grows abundantly in salt marshes along the Mediterranean and on the shores of the Dead Sea. Its small, thick, sour leaves would, in extreme need, furnish a miserable food.

Sa'lu [elevated, exalted].
A Simeonite, father of Zimri whom Phinehas slew (Num. xxv. 14; in A. V. of 1 Mac. ii. 26 Salom).

Sal-u-ta'tion.
Among the Hebrews salutation on meeting consisted in the expression of good wishes or a solemn blessing. The forms most prevalent were: 1. "Blessed be thou of the Lord," or "God be gracious unto thee," or the equivalent (Gen. xliii. 29; Ruth iii. 10; 1 Sam. xv. 13). 2. "The Lord be with thee," to which the rejoinder was, "The Lord bless thee" (Ruth ii. 4). 3. "Peace be unto thee," or

"Peace be upon thee," peace meaning welfare (Luke xxiv. 36). This was the commonest of all salutations, and is still in use among the Jews. The reply is: "Upon thee be peace." If the occasion made the words appropriate, the form was: "Peace be unto thee, and to thine house" (1 Sam. xxv. 6; Luke x. 5). 4. "Hail!" a common salutation in the Greek period (Mat. xxvi. 49; xxvii. 29; xxviii. 9; Luke i. 28). 5. "Let the king live forever" was the salutation addressed by a subject to the Hebrew monarch (1 Kin. i. 31), and was employed in the Babylonian and Persian courts (Neh. ii. 3; Dan. ii. 4; iii. 9; v. 10; vi. 6, 21).

At parting a blessing was invoked (Gen. xxiv. 60; xxviii. 1; xlvii. 10; Josh. xxii. 6), which eventually assumed the conventional form, "Go in peace," or "Farewell" (1 Sam. i. 17; xx. 42; 2 Sam. xv. 9; Mark v. 34; Acts xvi. 36); and the rejoinder to a superior might be, "Let thy servant find grace in thy sight" (1 Sam. i. 18).

Abraham and Lot rose up to meet passing strangers, bowed before them to the earth, and pressed hospitality upon them (Gen. xviii. 2; xix. 1); Boaz exchanged greeting with his reapers (Ruth ii. 4); travelers on the road saluted workmen in the field (Ps. cxxix. 8); members of a family greeted each other in the morning and after long separation (Ex. iv. 27; Prov. xxvii. 14). The salutation was often withheld from men of a different religion (Mat. v. 47); and rightly so, when it was apt to lead to fellowship and to imply a wish for the success of a bad cause (2 John 11). Messengers might be charged to salute no man by the way (2 Kin. iv. 29; Luke x. 4), for the formality incident to offering a greeting and receiving a response involved delay. The bow was not a mere nod, but profound obeisance or prostration; and in deferential greeting a rider dismounted from his beast or left his chariot (1 Sam. xxv. 23; 2 Kin. v. 21).

Letters in Palestine, before the conquest of the country by the Hebrews, and in Egypt, always began with salutations. The greetings are all framed on the same model. A son begins a letter to his father thus: "To Dudu, my lord, my father, speaketh thus Aziru thy son, thy servant. At the feet of my father I prostrate myself. Unto the feet of my father may there be peace." A subject addresses his liege, the king of Egypt, after this manner: "To the king my lord, my god, my sun-god, speaketh thus Yapahi thy servant and the dust of thy feet. At the feet of the king my lord, my god, my sun-god, seven times seven times I prostrate myself." The governor of a district writes to his equals: "To the kings of Canaan, servants, my brothers, thus the king." And Pharaoh begins a letter to a neighboring monarch with the words: "To Kallima-Sin, king of Karduniyash, my brother, speaketh thus Nibnuariya [Amenophis iii.] the great king, king of Egypt, thy brother. To me is peace [welfare]. May peace be to thee and thy house, to thy children, magnates, horses, chariots, in thy land may there be abundant peace."

The usual epistolary salutation in the Greco-Roman period in Palestine was briefer, more direct, more businesslike, and in it the name of the writer commonly stands first. " King Alexander to his brother Jonathan, greeting " (1 Mac. x. 18). " King Demetrius unto the nation of the Jews, greeting " (25; and so Acts xv. 23; xxiii. 26; Jas. i. 1). The letter was frequently concluded with a salutation, derived from Latin usage, " Farewell " (Acts xv. 29; xxiii. 30). To the brief salutation after the Latin manner, the Hebrews, following their own customs, often added a prayer for peace (2 Mac. i. 1). Their salutation also was often elaborate (1–5), and the old order was frequently observed (ix. 19, 20). The salutations with which Paul begins his letters are equally manifold (Rom. i. 1–7). In the epistles to Timothy he wishes his true child in the faith, grace, mercy, and peace; but his usual greeting is, " Grace unto you and peace," and he was apt to close his letters with salutations from himself and others (1 Thes. i. 1; v. 26–28, his first letter).

Sa-ma′ri-a.

1. The capital of the ten tribes during the longest period of their history. It was built or commenced by Omri, king of Israel, on a hill purchased for two talents of silver or about $3800. The former owner's name was Shemer; and as it expressed the idea of watching, guarding, keeping, it suggested an appropriate designation for a city on a hill. Accordingly Omri called the city *Shom'ron*, place of watch (1 Kin. xvi. 24). The eminence which the city crowned was sometimes denominated the mountain of Samaria (Amos iv. 1; vi. 1). It stood in the midst of a fertile valley (Is. xxviii. 1). The site was so well chosen that the city continued to be the capital of the kingdom to the captivity of the ten tribes, the successive sovereigns reigning, and at their death being buried, there (1 Kin. xvi. 28, 29; xx. 43; xxii. 10, 37, 51, etc.). Scarcely was Samaria built before hostilities arose between Benhadad I., king of Syria, and Omri. The former, if his son spoke the truth, had the advantage, and, to please the victor, Omri had to make streets in Samaria for Syrian merchants (1 Kin. xx. 34). During the reign of Ahab, Omri's son and successor, the city was unsuccessfully besieged by Benhadad II. (1–21). In or near the capital was a pool, on the side of which the royal attendants washed the blood-stained chariot in which Ahab's body was brought home from Ramoth-gilead (xxii. 38). In the days of probably Joram it was unsuccessfully besieged by Benhadad II. (2 Kin. vi. 8–vii. 20). The elders of Samaria, afraid of displeasing Jehu, obeyed his order to murder Ahab's seventy sons (x. 1–10). All along from the commencement of the city it had been a place notorious for its idolatry. Ahab had led the way in this heathen worship by rearing a temple and an altar to Baal (1 Kin. xvi.

Samaritan high priests with Torah of the Pentateuch.

Samaritan camp for the Passover, on the top of Mount Gerizim.

Samaritan Passover in progress. Heating water for the ceremonies.

Samaritans today observe the Passover (Pesach) in almost the same way it was observed two to three thousand years ago. Samaritan families make a pilgrimage to Mount Gerizim and set up tents, one for each family. Late in the afternoon the preparations for the feast begin. All males, dressed in festive white garments, gather and stoke fires in two pits, one for roasting the sheep, the other for burning offal and remains of the feast.

Exactly at sunset several "lambs without blemish" are sacrificed. The slaughter is a signal for general rejoicing.

The second part of the ceremony, the roasting of animals, takes place at about ten o'clock following strict orders issued by the high priest. During the three-hour roasting period participants usually spend some time in prayer, talking, and resting.

At one o'clock in the morning the third part of the ceremony begins. The men have washed their hands and feet, put on white garments, girded their loins, and taken staves to the assembly area. Matsos and bitter herbs along with the roasted animals are portioned out by the high priest. After the blessing, the men eat hastily, using their hands to pull apart the meat, and then bring portions to the women and children who remain in the tents. In twenty minutes all that is left is a mound of bones. The bones, utensils, and any leftover matsos are burned. The Samaritans stay awake until dawn, reciting prayers.

Ruins of the city gate of Samaria. In II Kings 7:1, 16-20, Elisha promised that on the morrow at this gate a measure of fine flour would "be sold for a shekel and two measures of barley for a shekel."

The well at Sebaste on the hill of Samaria.

32), and as in his reign reference is made to 400 prophets of the Asherah who ate at Jezebel's table (xviii. 19), it is probable that the idol so named remained till Jehu's reign (2 Kin. xiii. 6). Attendant on this idolatry was great corruption of morals (Hos. vii. 1-8; xiii. 16; Amos iv. 1; viii. 14). Against these idolatrous practices Elijah worked (1 Kin. xviii.). Elisha made the city his headquarters (2 Kin. v. 3-9; vi. 32). And doubtless Hosea labored there. Samaria and the kingdom were threatened with judgment by many prophets (Is. vii. 9; viii. 4; Jer. xxxi. 5; Ezek. xvi. 46, 51, 53, 55; xxiii. 33; Hos. viii. 5, 6; xiii. 16; Amos iii. 12; Mic. i. 5-9). At length, the menaced infliction came. The siege was begun by the Assyrians under Shalmaneser, 724 B. C., and three years later, in 722, the city was captured by the king of Assyria (2 Kin. xvii. 3-6). The glory of the capture is claimed by Sargon, Shalmaneser's successor, who in that year ascended the throne; see SARGON. The conquerors repeopled the town with foreigners (24); see SAMARITAN. In 332 or 331 B. C. Alexander the Great took Samaria, and transferred its inhabitants to Shechem, placing Syro-Macedonians in their room. About the year 109 B. C. Samaria was besieged by John Hyrcanus, who drew around it a wall of circumvallation 80 stades or about 9 miles in extent. The city held out for a year, but was ultimately forced by famine to surrender. The victor demolished it, attempting to efface all proofs that a fortified city had ever stood on the hill (cp. Mic. i. 6; Antiq. xiii. 10, 2 and 3; War i 2, 7 and 8). It was again inhabited in the time of Alexander Jannæus. Pompey annexed it to the province of Syria. Gabinius fortified it anew (Antiq. xiii. 15, 4; xiv. 4, 4; 5, 3). It was rebuilt and refortified by Herod the Great, who called it Sebaste, a Greek word corresponding to Augustus, the title of his patron, the first Roman Emperor (xv. 8, 5). The evangelist Philip labored there with success; among others Simon Magus believed and was baptized (Acts viii. 5-13). To carry on this work Peter and John were sent from Jerusalem (14-25). The site of Samaria is the hill, 5½ miles northwest of Shechem, on which the village of es-Sebustieh stands. The sides are steep, the summit a table-land about a mile from east to west. The ancient city wall is traceable in nearly its entire extent; and there have been unearthed foundations, at the western end of the plateau, believed to be those of Omri's palace and Ahab's ivory house (1 Kin. xxii. 39), and on the western slope the remains of the great gateway and its massive flanking towers.

2. The territory occupied by the ten tribes, or the kingdom of Israel personified (1 Kin. xiii. 32; xxi. 1; 2 Kin. xvii. 24; Neh. iv. 2; Is. vii. 9; Jer. xxxi. 5; Ezek. xvi. 46; Amos iii. 9). See ISRAEL.

3. The district of Samaria, occupying central Palestine, between Galilee on the north and Judæa on the south (1 Mac. x. 30). Josephus' description of its limits (War iii. 3, 4, and 5) is not very intelligible, but he makes it plain that the northern limit passed through "a village that is in the great plain called Ginea." This is apparently En-gannim (Josh. xix. 21; xxi. 29), at the southern angle of the plain of Esdraelon. The southern limit was the toparchy Acrabattene, some

6 or 7 miles south of Shechem. Samaria extended to the Jordan on the east, but did not reach the Mediterranean on the west. Accho belonged to Judæa. The Talmud makes Antipatris the western limit. It comprehended the old territories of Manasseh west of the Jordan, and of Ephraim, with a portion of Issachar and Benjamin. Pompey, in 63 B. C., attached it to the province of Syria (Antiq. xiv. 4, 4). In A. D. 6 the emperor Augustus erected Judæa, Samaria and Idumæa into a division of the prefecture of Syria, called the province of Judæa, and placed it under procurators (xvii. 13, 5; cp. 11, 4), and this arrangement obtained in the time of our Lord.

Sa-mar'i-tan.

In the only passage in which the word is found in the O. T. (2 Kin. xvii. 29) it means an individual belonging to the old kingdom of northern Israel. In later Hebrew literature it signifies an inhabitant of the district of Samaria in central Palestine (Luke xvii. 11). How, then, did the Samaritan nationality or race arise? When Sargon captured Samaria, he carried into captivity, by his own account, 27,280 people. That he left many Israelites in the land is evident. Finding that the remaining Israelites were rebellious, he began a systematic course for their denationalization. He introduced colonists from Babylonia and Hamath (2 Kin. xvii. 24) and Arabia, who continued to practice idolatry in their new home. The population of the country had been thinned, and the cultivation of the soil interrupted, by these wars, so that opportunity was afforded for wild beasts to multiply, which God used as a scourge. Lions killed some of the idolaters. The newcomers concluded that they did not understand how to worship the particular god of the country, and they informed the king of Assyria. He sent them a priest from among the captive Israelites, who took up his residence at Bethel and began to instruct the people regarding Jehovah. He was unable to persuade them to abandon their ancestral idolatry. They erected images of their gods on the high places of the Israelites, and combined their idolatries with the worship of Jehovah (25–33). This dual worship they kept up until after the fall of Jerusalem (34–41). Esarhaddon continued the policy of his grandfather, Sargon (Ezra iv. 2), and the great and noble Asnapper, perhaps Ashurbanipal, completed the work by adding to the population people from Elam and elsewhere (9, 10).

The new province of the Assyrian empire was weak, and Josiah or his agents traversed its whole extent, everywhere destroying the high places with which it abounded (2 Chron. xxxiv. 6, 7). The idols were still on these high places, but it is probable that idolatry was decreasing under the influence of the Israelites who remained in the land and through the teaching of the priests. And this act of Josiah's was another blow to it. Several decades later some among the Samaritans were in the habit of visiting the temple at Jerusalem for worship (Jer. xli. 5). When Zerubbabel led back his band of exiles from Babylonia to Jerusalem, the Samaritans asked permission to participate in the erection of the temple on the ground that they had worshiped the God of Israel ever since the time of Esarhaddon (Ezra iv. 2).

There was early a repugnance on the part of most of the Jews to social and religious association with the Samaritans, and this feeling developed into intense antipathy as years rolled on (Ezra iv. 3; Ecclus. l. 25, 26; Luke ix. 52, 53; John iv. 9). The Samaritans were neither of pure Hebrew blood nor of uncontaminated worship. Josephus (Antiq. ix. 14, 3) says that when the Jews were in prosperity, the Samaritans claimed that they were allied to them in blood; but when they saw them in adversity, they declared that they had no relationship to them, but were descended from the Assyrian immigrants. When the offer of the Samaritans to assist in rebuilding the temple was rejected by Zerubbabel, Jeshua, and their associates, the Samaritans made no further efforts at conciliation, but did their best with other adversaries to prevent the completion of the work (Ezra iv. 1–10); they also opposed the rebuilding later on of the walls of Jerusalem by Nehemiah (Neh. iv. 1–23). Their leader on the latter occasion was Sanballat, the Horonite. It was he whose son-in-law was put out of the priesthood by Nehemiah; and the father-in-law probably founded the Samaritan temple on mount Gerizim, which he designed for the use of the expelled dignitary; see SANBALLAT. Henceforward fugitives from discipline at Jerusalem were accustomed to go to the rival edifice on mount Gerizim where they were sure of obtaining a warm welcome (Antiq. xi. 8, 7). During the persecution under Antiochus Epiphanes they declared that they were not of the same race as the Jews, and gratified the tyrant by expressing a desire that their temple on mount Gerizim might in future be dedicated to Jupiter, the defender of strangers (2 Mac. vi. 2). About 129 B. C. John Hyrcanus took Shechem and Gerizim, destroying the Samaritan temple (Antiq. xiii. 9, 1); but the worshipers continued to offer their adorations on the summit of the hill where the sacred edifice had stood. They did so when our Lord was on earth (John iv. 20, 21).

In the time of Christ their theological tenets did not essentially differ from those of the Jews, and especially of the Sadducean sect. They shared with them the expectation of a coming Messiah (John iv. 25). They, however, accepted no more of the O. T. than the Pentateuch. The main cause for the Samaritans' receiving the gospel so gladly when Philip preached to them was the miracles which he wrought (Acts viii. 5, 6); but another undoubtedly was that, unlike Judaism, Christianity followed the example and teaching of its founder and admitted Samaritans within its pale and to the same privileges as those possessed by the Jewish converts (Luke x. 29–37; xvii. 16–18; John iv. 1–42). About 150 Samaritans still exist at and around Nablus, the ancient Shechem.

Sa-mar'i-tan Pen'ta-teuch.

The Samaritans possessed the Pentateuch in Hebrew. It was quoted by Jerome, Eusebius, and other Christian fathers. In A. D. 1616 Pietro della Valle purchased a copy from the Samaritans of Damascus, which was placed in 1623 in the library of the Oratory in Paris. By the end of the eighteenth century fifteen other copies, more or less complete, had reached Europe, and the number has since been increased. Morin, or Morinus, who first studied it, considered the Samaritan text vastly superior to that of the Masoretes. Controversy on the subject went on, with occasional intervals, for nearly two centuries, till, in 1815, the great Hebrew scholar Gesenius, who had made a very careful examination of the Samaritan text, proved it to be far inferior to that of the Hebrew Masoretes, and of small critical value. Most of the Samaritan rolls, containing the whole or a part of the Pentateuch, are supposed not to be older than the tenth century of the Christian era; one or two in the custody of the Samaritans at Nablus, the ancient Shechem, are considered to be older. The several rolls are in the Samaritan character, that on the Maccabæan coins, which was also that of the Hebrews before they introduced the present square letters. The Samaritan text frequently differs from the Hebrew text of the Masoretes. In Deut. xxvii. 4 we read that Moses directed the people when they passed the Jordan to set up certain stones in mount Ebal, plaster them, and write on them the law. Here the Samaritans have substituted Gerizim for Ebal, to increase the veneration for their sacred mountain. There are various other less important variations; see CHRONOLOGY. Most of them are manifestly due to the haste of the scribes or to alterations which they deliberately made. In about 2000 places the text agrees with that of the Septuagint against the Hebrew readings, which indicates that the Greek translators used a Hebrew text much like that possessed by the Samaritans. An interesting inquiry is: At what date and how did the Samaritans obtain this Pentateuch? An old and still widely-received opinion is that they did so by transcribing copies of the sacred volume which had existed among them prior to the disruption of the monarchy, under Rehoboam 931 B. C. Another view is that the volume was circulated among them by the priest who was sent to instruct the heathen colonists brought from Assyria to repeople Samaria after its original inhabitants had been carried captive, about 722 B. C. A third opinion is that the Samaritan Pentateuch was carried from Jerusalem by a renegade priest about the time that the temple was built on mount Gerizim. The form of the letters and the alteration already mentioned of Ebal into Gerizim in the sacred text afford a certain slight support to the third hypothesis. At any rate the change was made after Gerizim had become the scene of temple worship.

The Samaritan Pentateuch must not be confounded with the Samaritan version of the Pentateuch, made into the dialect of the Samaritans early in the Christian era. They possess an Arabic translation also, made in the eleventh or twelfth century, a book of Joshua, founded on the canonical book of the same name and written about the thirteenth century A. D., and some other literature.

Sa'mech, in A. R. V. SAMEKH.

The fifteenth letter of the Hebrew alphabet. No letter of the English alphabet originally corresponds to it, and s is forced into service in anglicizing Hebrew names which contain it, as Joseph. It heads the fifteenth section of Ps. cxix., in which section each verse of the original begins with this letter.

Sam-gar-ne'bo [Shumgir-Nabu, be gracious, Nebo!]

One of Nebuchadnezzar's princes who entered Jerusalem (Jer. xxxix. 3).

Sam'lah [a garment].

A king of the Edomites, a native of Masrekah (Gen. xxxvi. 36, 37).

Sa'mos [a height by the seashore].

An island about 80 miles in circumference off the coast of Asia Minor, south by west of Ephesus, and nearly opposite to the promontory of Trogyllium. After the defeat of Antiochus the Great by the Romans at Magnesia, in 190 B. C., it was independent (1 Mac. xv. 23); but it was under the influence of Pergamos, and along with Pergamos it passed into the hands of the Romans in 133 B. C. At the time Paul reached it (Acts xx. 15), it still enjoyed the autonomy conferred upon it by the Romans in 19 B. C. Its inhabitants were noted for commercial enterprise. Many of their coins still exist.

Sam-o-thra'ce, in A. V. Sam-o-thra'ci-a [Samos of Thrace].

An island in the archipelago off the coast of Thrace and opposite the mouth of the Hebrus. It has an area of about 30 square miles, and has in it a mountain 5000 feet high. Paul's vessel made a straight course to the island from Troas, in Asia Minor (Acts xvi. 11).

Samp'sa-mes.

A country, rather than a king, which was friendly to Rome (1 Mac. xv. 23). Not identified.

Sam'son [sunny, little sun, perhaps, destroyer].

One of the most eminent of the Hebrew judges. He was the son of a Danite called Manoah, was born at Zorah, within the limits of the southern territory of Dan, and had his birth and his subsequent career announced beforehand to his parents by the angel of the Lord. He was a Nazirite from his birth, no razor coming upon his head, and no wine or strong drink entering into his mouth. As long as he submitted to these restrictions he was capable of heroic achievements against the Philistines (Judg. xiii. 1–24). Circumstances conspired at this time to separate Judah and Dan from the rest of the Hebrews and to compel these two tribes to act alone. They were at the mercy of the Philistines, who had promptly embraced the opportunity to oppress them. Isolated, Judah was able to do little more than harass the oppressors by bold deeds and stratagems. The Spirit of the Lord early moved Samson to commence his lifework in the camp of Dan (25); but almost from the outset he showed one conspicuous weakness in his character. He was the slave of passion. He was betrothed to a Philistine woman, a native of Timnath; but she married another man, and in revenge Samson, aided perhaps by his friends, caught 300 jackals or foxes, tied them together in pairs by the tails, with a burning torch between, and turned them loose amidst the ripened grain of the Philistines (xiv. 1–xv. 5). The Philistines invaded Judah and demanded that Samson be delivered unto them. He permitted his craven countrymen to bind him in whom they failed to perceive their deliverer. But when he was about to be surrendered to the uncircumcised Philistines the Spirit of the Lord came mightily upon him, and he snapped the ropes asunder. The Philistines, amazed at his display of strength, feared him. He seized the jawbone of an ass, and as the Philistines turned to flee, he pursued them and slew a thousand men in round numbers. They fell in several heaps. Samson acknowledged that the work was of God, and confessed his own need of help lest he die of thirst. God, in his providence caused a spring to give forth its water. The men of Judah now recognized him as their deliverer (6–20). Afterwards he fearlessly went to Gaza, and there he fell into sin. The Gazites thought that their opportunity had come to seize him, and they shut the city gates; but at midnight he came to the gate, and, finding it closed, laid hold of its doors and plucked them and the bar away and carried them to the top of a hill in the direction of Hebron. An entanglement with the woman Delilah, from the valley of Sorek, caused his ruin. By direction of her countrymen, she importuned him to tell her in what his great strength lay. At first he gave her deceitful answers, but at last he revealed the secret. If his head were shaved, he would

become weak as another man. The Philistines at once shaved his head, and found that his strength had departed. They therefore put out his eyes, and made him grind in the prison house at Gaza. They brought him out to exhibit him to the people on occasion of a great festival and public sacrifice to their god Dagon. His hair had by this time begun again to grow, and he was again fulfilling his Nazirite vow. The great temple was full of people, and some three thousand more were on the roof. Samson knew the structure of the building, for he had been in Gaza before when he possessed his sight. He asked the lad who attended him to let him rest himself against the two middle pillars on which the roof was supported, and grasping them he prayed to God for one more manifestation of favor and the gift of strength that he might be avenged on the Philistines. He then dragged the pillars from their position, brought down the roof and perished with a multitude of his foes (xvi. 1–31). Notwithstanding the defects in his character, the N. T. names him with those Hebrew heroes whose animating principle was faith (Heb. xi. 32).

Samson had the strength of a man in a preternatural degree. When the Spirit of the Lord impelled him from time to time, he accomplished his great deeds. His strength did not reside in his long hair. His unshorn locks were the external evidence of his relation to God, a public profession that he was acting as the servant of the Lord. When he allowed his hair to be cut, he broke his vow, and it is significantly said that the Lord abandoned him. His marvelous strength failed when God left him, and it returned when God granted his prayer. His preternatural strength was a sign, testifying to the men of Judah that this Nazirite was indeed called of God to deliver them from their enemies, and bearing witness among the Philistines to the superiority of the servant of Jehovah.

Various attempts have been made to group the deeds of Samson. Ewald, led by a favorite theory of his, thought he could discover a drama in five acts. In fact the narrative itself describes five groups of related deeds. 1. Those that resulted from his wooing of the woman of Timnath; namely, his rending the lion, slaughter of thirty Philistines at Ashkelon, release of the jackals bearing burning torches among the ripened grain of the Philistines, and a defeat of the Philistines who had burned the woman. 2. The events at the rock of Etam, when his fellow-countrymen asked permission to deliver him into the hands of the Philistines, and he broke his bonds of rope in the presence of the uncircumcised, slew a thousand of their number with the jawbone of an ass, and by prayer obtained water to quench his thirst. 3. The visit to Gaza, when he carried off the doors of the city gate. 4. His passion for the Philistine woman Delilah, when he broke the seven green withes wherewith she had bound him and then the nine cords with which she next bound him, and tore away the web with which she had woven his locks. 5. A blind slave at Gaza, when he pulled down the pillars on which the roof of Dagon's temple rested. The particular achievements in the five groups are twelve as enumerated. Samson's name may be interpreted as meaning sunny, and a strenuous effort has been made by Roskoff, Steinthal, and others like minded, to connect them with the twelve labors of Hercules or with the Babylonian Izdubar or otherwise with the sun-god Shamash. Hercules wandered in search of adventures, slew a lion, slept, was sold as a slave, immolated himself voluntarily. Izdubar overcame the lion, rejected the advances of Ishtar, the goddess of love. Hercules is a sun-myth. The story of Izdubar is the history of an ancient king of Erech embellished with legend and wrought out into an epic in twelve parts; see NIMROD. But with neither the sun-god nor the king of Erech is Samson to be identified; for—1. The ancient Hebrews themselves assigned Samson to a time well within their historical period, in the generation before Samuel and Saul. 2. The Hebrew account of Samson states definitely the place of his birth and his deeds, and gives the location of his grave. 3. The enumeration of twelve labors is a matter of some importance to those who would identify Samson with Hercules or Izdubar, but in itself the number is not of consequence. And the number twelve is not so readily made out. The cry of Samson to God for drink can scarcely be called a labor of Samson's. The narrative speaks of other deeds of Samson which it does not specify (Judg. xiii. 25), showing that the narrator did not think of twelve achievements only. 4. While the strength which Samson exercised was the gift of God and was not inherent in him as a man, while it failed when he was left to himself, yet it was preternatural in the sense that what he accomplished by it might have been a work of nature, but was not. In most of the examples afforded of it, it finds parallels in human annals. David without a weapon slew a lion and a bear; Jonathan and his armor-bearer, and Eleazar and Shammah and Abishai each single-handed performed prodigies of valor equal to Samson's (1 Sam. xiv. 1–17; 2 Sam. xxiii. 9–12, 18), and modern history proves other parallels. The nature of the feats performed in carrying off the doors of Gaza's gate and in dragging the two columns from their position cannot be determined until information is at hand regarding the structure of these particular doors and the architecture of Dagon's temple. The deeds may have been superhuman and miraculous.

Sam'u-el, in A. V. once **Shemuel** (1 Chron. vi. 33) [name of God].

The earliest of the great Hebrew prophets after Moses and the last of the judges. His father, Elkanah, was a Levite, family of Kohath, house of Izhar (see ELKANAH 4); he was a Zophite, because descended through Zophai or Zuph (1 Sam. i. 1; 1 Chron. vi. 26, 35); and he was a man of the hill country of Ephraim or an Ephraimite, because the family had been assigned residence in that tribe (Josh. xxi. 5; 1 Chron. vi. 66). Elkanah lived in Ramah or, as it was called to distinguish it from other towns of the name, Ramathaim of the Zophites (1 Sam. i. 1, 19; ii. 11). He had two wives, Peninnah and Hannah. Hannah had no child and prayed earnestly to God that she might give birth to a boy, vowing that if her prayer were answered the infant should be devoted for life to Jehovah, apparently as a Nazirite, for she added, "There shall no razor come upon his head" (cp. Num. vi. 1–5). Her petition was granted. She named the boy Samuel; and when he was weaned she brought him to the tabernacle at Shiloh, and put him in charge of the high priest, Eli, to train him for his sacred duties (1 Sam. i.; ii. 1–17). While yet a child he ministered before God, clad in the simple linen ephod which was worn by ordinary priests when engaged in the sanctuary and even by laymen (ii. 18). He lived at the tabernacle, sleeping in some chamber connected with it, opened the doors of the sanctuary in the morning, and otherwise assisted Eli in his ministrations (iii. 1, 3, 15). He had not advanced beyond early boyhood when Jehovah revealed to him the approaching doom of Eli's house for the foolish indulgence which the father had shown to his unworthy sons (iii. 1–18). Josephus says that Samuel was twelve years old at this time (Antiq. v. 10, 4). His statement is about right; but his authority for it is unknown. By the time that the child had reached manhood all Israel, from Dan even to Beer-sheba, knew that he was established to be a prophet of the Lord, for the Lord revealed himself to Samuel in Shiloh (1 Sam. iii. 20, 21). Soon afterwards the judgment threatened against Eli and his house began by the death of Eli's two sons in battle, the capture of the ark by the Philistines, and the death of Eli on hearing the fatal news (iv. 1–22). The ark was soon restored to the Israelites; but it was kept in seclusion and placed for safe keeping with a proper guardian at Kirjath-jearim until the people should be spiritually prepared to receive it. Samuel was an accredited prophet and, since the death of Eli, the chief religious authority in the land. He addressed himself to the work of reforming the people. Twenty years after the restoration of the ark he found the moral condition of the nation improved, and he convoked an assembly at Mizpah, near the place where the ark had been lost, to make confession of sin, to fast before the Lord and to beseech a return of his favor. The Philistines gathered their forces to battle when they heard of this assembly; but Samuel exhorted the people to pray for deliverance, and he himself besought the Lord for Israel. A thunderstorm discomfited the Philistines, the Israelites discerned the hand of God, embraced the opportunity, pursued the enemy, and gained such a victory over the Philistines as deterred those pertinacious foes from again invading the land while Samuel was at the head of affairs (1 Sam. vii. 3–14); see PHILISTINES and SAMUEL, BOOKS OF. This signal deliverance indicated that God had raised up Samuel to be judge, in the usual sense of defender and director. Like Deborah, and more fully like Moses, Samuel was accredited prophet and judge. In the discharge of his duties he went annually in circuit to Bethel, Gilgal, and Mizpah; but his residence was at Ramah, where a company of prophets gathered about him to be at his service in the work of reform (vii. 15–17; xix. 18–20). Here he built an altar to the Lord; for God had forsaken Shiloh, the ark was in necessary seclusion, the covenant was in abeyance because the Israelites had broken it by their idolatries and sacrilege, and he was Jehovah's representative; see ALTAR. During the years of his vigorous administration the land enjoyed freedom from foreign domination. When he was old he made his two sons judges at Beer-sheba. They proved themselves unworthy of their high trust, taking bribes and perverting justice. Their misconduct and the threatening attitude of the surrounding heathen nations produced the request on the part of the Israelite elders and people for the institution of kingly government; and Samuel was divinely commissioned to anoint first Saul, and when he was rejected, David; see the detailed account in SAMUEL, BOOKS OF. Samuel died while David was a fugitive from Saul in the wilderness of En-gedi. He was buried in his house at Ramah, all Israel lamenting his loss (xxv. 1). On the night before the battle of Gilboa, Saul desired the woman with the familiar spirit at En-dor to call up Samuel from Sheol (xxviii. 3–25); see SAUL. Heman, one of David's singers, was a grandson of Samuel (1 Chron. vi. 33, R. V.; cp. 28). Samuel is in the list of O. T. heroes whose animating principle was faith (Heb. xi. 32).

Sam'u-el, Books of.

Two books of the O. T. They were originally one, as appears from the Masoretic note to 1 Sam. xxviii. 24, which states that this verse is the middle of the book. They are treated as one by Josephus in his enumeration of the books of the O. T., and in Hebrew manuscripts. The division was introduced into the printed Hebrew Bible in 1517, and was derived from the Septuagint and Vulgate. As Samuel is the leading person during the first half of the period covered, as he was one of the greatest of the prophets that Israel ever had, the organizer of the kingdom, the agent in the selection of both Saul and David for the throne, and the coadjutor of Saul so long as the king remained faithful to his theocratic obligations, the book appropriately bears Samuel's name. As it contains the history of the first two kings, it is divided in the Septuagint into two books, and called First and Second of Kingdoms; and the two books which continue the history, and are known in the English version as First and Second Book of the Kings, are called Third and Fourth of Kingdoms in the Septuagint. Jerome substituted Book of Kings for Book of Kingdoms in his Latin version.

The work is divisible into three sections: 1. Samuel, the prophet and judge (i.–vii.), including his birth and early life, the causes which led to his call to the prophetic office (iii. 20), and which left him as prophet in possession of the sole authority and opened the way for his judicial administration (iv.), his reformatory work, and the attestation of his right to the judgeship, which was afforded by the deliverance of Israel from Philistine oppression by his hand (vii. 1–12). Summary of his administration (13–17). 2. Saul the king (viii.–xxxi.), including (a) The popular demand for a king in Samuel's old age and Samuel's promise to accede to it (viii.), the interview between Samuel and Saul and the anointing of Saul in private (ix. 1–x. 16), the public assembly called by Samuel at Mizpah, and the selection of Saul by lot (17–26), the dissatisfaction of a portion of the people (27), the occasion which won the people for their divinely appointed king and his induction into office (xi.), Samuel's farewell address (xii.). (b) Revolt against the Philistines, and Saul's failure to observe his theocratic obligations (xiii.), the feat of Jonathan, leading to the rout of the Philistines (xiv. 1–46), summary of Saul's wars (47, 48), his family (49–51), the particulars of one of these wars, that with Amalek, in which Saul again and in aggravated manner shows his contempt for his theocratic obligations (xv.). Then follows (c) An account of the latter years of Saul's reign, with special reference to the relations between the king and David (xvi.–xxxi.); Saul having been rejected by God, Samuel by divine direction anoints David (xvi. 1–13), Saul troubled by an evil spirit summons David as harpist to court (14–23), David slays Goliath and becomes a permanent *attaché* of Saul's court (xvii. 1–xviii. 5), jealousy of Saul and his attempts on David's life (6–xix. 17), flight of David from court and his wandering life (18–xxvii. 12), invasion of the Philistines and Saul's inquiry of the woman with the familiar spirit (xxviii.), David, expelled from the Philistine camp, pursues a marauding band of Amalekites (xxix., xxx.), battle of Gilboa and death of Saul (xxxi.). 3. David the king (2 Sam. i.–xxiv.). Announcement of Saul's death to David (i.), contest for the throne between David, supported by the men of Judah, and Ish-bosheth as head of the other tribes (ii.–iv.), David made king by all Israel (v. 1–3), his reign (4–xxiv.). See DAVID.

The author of the double book was a prophet, for it is placed among the prophets in the Hebrew canon. Samuel wrote a book and laid it up before the Lord (1 Sam. x. 25), and part of the double book may be derived from the History of Samuel the Seer (1 Chron. xxix. 29); but scarcely half of the book could have come from his pen, for he died before the end of Saul's reign (1 Sam. xxv. 1). It was written after David's death (2 Sam. v. 5). An allusion to the kings of Judah probably indicates that the book was not completed until after the division of the Israelites into the kingdoms of Judah and Israel (1 Sam. xxvii. 6), but the distinction between Israel and Judah existed in the time of David (xi. 8; xvii. 52; xviii. 6; 2 Sam. iii. 10; xxiv. 1). From Jer. xv. 1 it has been inferred that Jeremiah was acquainted with 1 Sam. xii. There is no reference to the captivity, and it is universally believed that the book was composed before the fall of Jerusalem.

There were several documents relating to the period treated in the book, such as the History of Samuel the Seer, the History of Nathan the Prophet, and the History of Gad the Seer (1 Chron. xxix. 29), but the author does not mention the sources whence he derived his information, as do the authors of Kings and Chronicles, and it is uncertain what records he used. Wellhausen presents an analysis of the books and their sources (*Prolegomena*[3]). 1. Samuel as a youth. He is in training for the priesthood, and he foretells the collapse of the government which existed before the kingdom was established (1 Sam. i.–iii.). The story was invented after Samuel's career had made him noted. Chap. ii. 1–10 is an addition of unknown origin, and verses 27–36 are a Deuteronomistic but preëxilic insertion (pp. 126, 281, 415; cp. Kittel ii. 29, Anm. 6). 2. Account of the fall of the house of Eli (iv.–vi.); but iv. 18[b] is an addition (p. 254). 3. Saul's elevation to the throne. There are two accounts of this. (a) According to one account, Saul was privately appointed king by Samuel, who is a seer, and uses his authority to arouse Saul to the help of Israel (ix. 1–x. 16); but ix. 9 is a gloss, and x. 8 is from a later hand. Samuel bade Saul to await the fitting opportunity to come forward (x. 7), and about a month later (ver. 27[b], R. V. margin) the opportunity is afforded by the investment of Jabesh-gilead by the Ammonites. Saul summons the people to arms, leads them against the foe, is victorious, is hailed as deliverer, and is taken to Gilgal and made king (xi.); but verses 12–14 are an interpolation by the author of viii. and x. 17 seq., intended to harmonize this account with his own. The Philistines in Israel and their defeat by Saul and Jonathan (xiii., xiv., except that xiii. 7–15, with x. 8, are from a later hand, but older than chap. vii.). (b) According to the other account, Samuel called the people to repentance (vii. 2–4). Then he summoned them to Mizpah, near Jerusalem, to pray for relief from the oppression of the Philistines. The Philistines fell upon the assembly, but were routed and driven from the borders (5–14). Samuel administered the government successfully until he became old (15–17). Samuel having grown old and his sons proving illfitted to rule, the elders of Israel ask for a king, desiring to cast off the rule of God and become like other nations (viii.). Saul was accordingly chosen king by lot at Mizpah (x. 17–27[a]), and Samuel delivered a farewell address (xii.). 4. Chap. xv. is a secondary production. It is the original from which xiii. 7–15 is copied, and it is closely related to xxviii. 3–25. 5. There are two complete documents about David, which supplement each other. The first is contained in 1 Sam. xvi.–2 Sam. viii. The second account embraces 2 Sam. ix.–1 Kin. ii. It is mutilated at the beginning, but is otherwise intact, except that 2 Sam. xxi.–xxiv. are additions. The first account embodies a history of David from his anointment by Samuel to his flight from Saul. It is connected with 1 Sam. xiv. 52 in xvi. 14. David, as a brave man, recommended by his skill in playing the harp, comes to Saul's court and is made his armorbearer (xvi. 14–23); but ver. 14 shows marks of the redactor. Something followed this originally, telling of wars with the Philistines, but quite different from the fight between David and Goliath, which now stands here. In the conflict with the Philistines David acquits himself with distinction, is promoted step by step, and is given the king's daughter to wife (xviii. 6–30); but the reflections on Saul are due to a late reviser. Chap. xviii. 29[a], Septuagint, is continued in the reference to the popular applause which is accorded David, and which arouses the jealousy of Saul, so that in a fit of madness he hurls a spear at David (xix. 9, 10). After discussing the matter with Jonathan, David fled. Saul slew the priests at Nob, because their chief had befriended David (xxi. 2–7, E. V. 1–6; xxii. 6–23). The fugitive gathered a band of desperate men about him and abode in the wilderness of Judah (xxii. 1–5). There are various additions to this continuous history of David. The anointing of David (xvi. 1–13), which depends on the legend of the battle of the shepherd boy with Goliath (xvii. 1–xviii. 5). Saul's purpose to slay David is urged by Jonathan as a reason why David should hide himself (xix. 1–7), which is a late addition, for it shows acquaintance with chap. xvii. After Saul had hurled his spear at David, the latter fled for the first time (xix. 8–10). But David is still at home, and with the aid of his wife escapes a second time, fleeing to Samuel in Ramah (xix. 11–24); but verses 18–24 are corrupt and were unknown to the author of xv. 35. Verse 18 seems to look back to xvi. 1–13. David is in Gibeah. The king misses him at the feast; and when the deadly hatred of Saul is proven, David finally flees for good (xx.); but this account is impossible in its present setting. David at Nob obtains the sword of Goliath from the high priest (xxi. 8–10, E. V. 7–9). For fear of Saul David flees that day to Achish, king of Gath (11–16, E. V. 10–15). The account of David's life in the wilderness, a fugitive from Saul (xxiii.–xxvii.), contains three additions to the early document, namely, xxvii. 7–12; xxvi. 1–25; and xxiii. 14–xxiv. 23, E. V. 22. The last two are parallel. Chapter xxvi. was placed before chapter xxvii. on account of xxvi. 19, and the passage xxiii. 14–xxiv. 23 was placed before xxv. to avoid juxtaposition with xxvi. Chapter xxviii. 1, 2 is the immediate continuation of chapter xxvii., and is itself continued in xxix.–xxxi. Verses 3–25, Saul's interview with the woman of En-dor, is closely related to xv., which is the original from which xiii. 7–15 is copied. Neither xv. nor xxviii. belongs to the fundamental tradition. Each is a prelude to the events that follow.

Biblical critics of all schools are agreed that the author of the Books of Samuel derived the material for his history from various sources, and all critics would rejoice to have these sources definitely determined. But all are not agreed that Wellhausen's analysis, which is essentially that of the divisive school, is successful nor that his method is legitimate. The analysis is based upon contradictions which are alleged to exist between certain parts of the narrative. To this allegation of contradictions and consequent evidence of diversity of document it is replied:

I. The author saw no contradictions between these separate parts.

II. The argument that contradictions exist in the account rests upon a special private exposition of the narrative, and upon a manipulation of the text, which combine to produce inconsistencies. Other interpretation is valid which, without effort, shows a consistent narrative throughout. 1 Sam. vii. 13, 14 is said to be irreconcilably contradictory to all else that has been transmitted. Subsequently we find the domination of the Philistines in no wise overthrown; they not only continue to press across the borders in Samuel's lifetime, but they are in possession of the Israelite land, one of their officials dwells at Gibeah of Benjamin (Wellhausen). Driver, with more caution, says: "The consequences of the victory at Eben-ezer are in vii. 13 generalized in terms hardly reconcil-

able with the subsequent history: contrast the picture of the Philistines' ascendancy immediately afterwards (x. 5; xiii. 3, 19), etc." The passage does not affirm, as Wellhausen assumes it does, that the Israelites captured Ekron and Gath. They may have done so; the passage states that Israel recovered possession of its ancient territory. The Philistines came no more as occupants within the border of Israel, but Israel delivered its border from Ekron to Gath out of the hand of the Philistines (vii. 13, 14; cp border, Jer. xxxi. 17). The hand of the Lord was against the Philistines all the days that Samuel ruled (ver. 13); all his days being equivalent, as the expression frequently is in Scripture, to his administration. The Philistines, however, repeatedly crossed the border of Israel afterwards. They did so before Samuel died. They even placed officers in towns of Judah for the collection of tribute, as David did in Damascus (2 Sam. viii. 6; in E. V., garrisons). But they did not settle in the country again, nor did they expel the Hebrews who inhabited it (as Judg. i. 34–36).

By the victory at Eben-ezer Samuel delivered the Israelites from the dominion of the Philistines and recovered the borders of Israel, and during his vigorous administration the dread of his name deterred the Philistines from renewing their invasions, and his presence inspired the Israelites with confidence; but when he grew old, and began to relinquish the reins of government to his inefficient sons, the people lost heart at the thought of their inveterate enemies. Samuel was too old to lead them to battle, his sons were despicable, the Ammonites and the Philistines were as mighty as ever and only biding their time. The senility of a ruler, or the accession of a new and untried king, was usually the opportunity for which a waiting foe watched. Nahash the Ammonite may have already begun to harass the Israelites across the Jordan (1 Sam. xii. 12), though this interpretation is not absolutely necessary. "Make us a king," the elders of Israel said to Samuel, "that he may go before us and fight our battles" (viii. 5–20). The claim of a foreign prince to suzerainty over a people might be ignored for years; but in time, when the former lord became strong enough, he himself visited the refractory with an army and punished them, or else trusting to the fear which his prowess had begun to inspire, on noting the weakness and helplessness of his former tributaries, he sent his officials to inquire why the tribute had been withheld, and to receive it anew. If the demand was acceded to, the domestic government of the subject people was not disturbed. This latter course the Philistines pursued. When the inability of Israel to offer resistance became evident, perhaps after the rejection of Samuel by the representatives of the people was known, the Philistines asserted their authority (ix. 16), sent officials into the country (x. 5), and ultimately, as a precautionary measure, perhaps not until Saul was proclaimed king at Gilgal, went so far as to forbid fires in the forges lest the Israelites should provide themselves with weapons (xiii. 19-22).

When the elders of Israel, dismayed by the strength of the hostile nations by which they were surrounded, demanded a king, the aged Samuel was hurt at the slight which was apparently put upon him; but he was divinely informed that the people were not rejecting him, but through lack of faith were repudiating the rule of the invisible King, and he was instructed to accede to the popular request. Accordingly he dismissed the elders with the promise that he would do as they desired (1 Sam. viii.).

Shortly after this God revealed to the prophet that a man of Benjamin should come to him, and that he should anoint this Benjamite to be king and the deliverer from the Philistines (1 Sam. ix. 16). When Saul arrived Samuel entertained him, and in the evening the two sat on the housetop and communed together. The subject of their conversation is not hard to divine. The prophet told Saul of his call to deliver Israel from the newly reimposed yoke of the Philistines, instructed him out of his experience how to meet the foe, and informed him upon what conditions he might have God's help in war. On the morrow, before Saul left, Samuel privately anointed him, gave him several signs by which he should know of a surety that God had called him to the work, and dismissed him with the charge to be governed by providential indications, "and," said the prophet, "go down to Gilgal and tarry seven days till I come and show thee what thou shalt do" (x. 7, 8). The meaning of this charge must be gathered from the housetop conference and from the event (ix. 16-25; xiii. 8). Saul was not to proclaim himself king nor to attempt to free the nation from Philistine domination until circumstances indicated the time, and then he was to make Gilgal the rendezvous and wait seven days for the prophet to come to offer sacrifice, to entreat the favor of the Lord on the undertaking, and to instruct him (x. 8; xiii. 12). The object of this delay at Gilgal was to declare publicly that the king was merely the vicegerent of heaven, to show the people that Saul recognized that his royal authority did not include the priestly office, that king and prophet must work together. It was clearly the idea of the two men that they should coöperate. Saul observed the principle that underlay this advice. For a time he exalted the prophet and ranked himself only as a colaborer (xi. 7), and he felt that he needed to know the will of the Lord through the prophet (xxviii. 15); and Samuel for his part, when Saul was established on the throne, purposed still to assist the people of God (xii. 23), and even after Saul's sin and God's rejection of him Samuel went up to Gibeah of Benjamin, where Saul held court, to assist him in the administration of the kingdom by instructing him as to God's will (xiii. 15), but the text of this verse is suspicious.

As directed by Samuel, Saul returned to his father's house. The signs occurred, and especially when he met a band of prophets, prophesying as they passed the station of the Philistine official, the Spirit of the Lord smote him there, and he, too, prophesied. His countrymen were worshiping God while their enemies triumphed over them. He discerned the anomaly and prophesied. The man was awakening to the religious aspect of his appointed work (1 Sam. x. 9-13).

Samuel now fulfilled his promise to the representatives of the nation. He did not use his authority to place Saul on the throne; the matter was too delicate and the issues too great. He summoned the people to Mizpah and the choice was left to God. The lot was cast before the Lord, and Saul was chosen, a man of fine appearance, fitted to call forth the admiration and win the confidence of the people; a man of the tribe of Benjamin, the border tribe between north and south, in order to avoid the ancient and growing dissension in the nation. The choice was publicly committed to God in order to secure the allegiance of the pious part of the people for the divinely appointed king. The people shouted "God save the king," and the kingdom was formally established (1 Sam. x. 24, 25). The precautions taken by Samuel were fully justified by the event. The selection, although made by God himself, did not approve itself to all the people; there were jealousies, and the dissatisfied asked in disdain, "How shall this fellow, out of one of the smallest families of a small tribe, save us?" (27). But Saul quietly retired to his father's house, accompanied by certain men of valor, to bide his time and await developments. He made no claim to the throne in the face of disaffection; he did not begin a civil war to secure the crown; but he let the matter drop until God should change the heart of the people and place him on the throne without shedding the blood of his brethren. He devoted himself to attending to his father's estate.

About a month elapsed in this manner (1 Sam. x. 27, E. R. V. margin). Nahash the Ammonite had pushed his invasion almost to the Jordan and was now besieging Jabesh in Gilead. The people of that town were in distress. Nahash imposed ignominious conditions of surrender, as a taunt to all Israel. The men of Jabesh, however, secured a week's respite in order to send messengers into all the coasts of Israel. Some of these messengers, or all of them, came to Gibeah and made known their distress. Saul was in the field, but when he returned and learned the extremity of his fellow-countrymen, and the reproach offered to Israel by their heathen foe, the Spirit of God came mightily upon

him, and he sent through all the borders of
Israel calling the people to follow him and
Samuel. They responded as one man. Saul
led them to victory, raised the siege of Jabesh, and put Nahash to flight (xi. 1–11).
The Philistines had no cause to forbid the
relief of Jabesh in Gilead ; on the contrary,
it was to their advantage that the country
tributary to them should be kept intact. The
same story of subject peoples being left by the
sovereign state to settle their own domestic disputes and fight out their quarrels with their
neighbors is familiar in the annals of Assyria
and Egypt. Flushed with victory and proud
of their leader, the people asked : " Who is he
that said, Shall Saul reign over us? bring
the men that we may put them to death."
Saul forbade slaughter, and at Samuel's suggestion the people went to Gilgal, which was
not far off, renewed the kingdom and made
Saul king, and this act being accomplished,
Samuel formally delivered the government
into Saul's hands (xi. 12–xii. 25).

Saul was now king, but the work which he
had been raised up to do was only begun.
The Ammonites were driven from the borders, but the Israelites still suffered the humiliation of subjection to the Philistines.
They managed indeed their own internal
affairs ; they had a king of their own with
a royal guard of three thousand men ; but
they paid tribute to the Philistines, must
tolerate Philistine officials in their borders,
and were compelled to keep their forges idle.
Saul was biding his time. Two years, according to the present questionable Hebrew text,
passed by, when the opportunity arrived.
Jonathan smote the Philistine official at Geba,
and the Philistines assembled their armies to
avenge the insult and quell the insurrection.
The time for action had come ; Saul blew the
trumpet for war, and the Israelites assembled
after him at Gilgal. This was what Samuel
had charged him to do (1 Sam. xiii. 1–7). Wellhausen excludes the interview between Samuel and Saul at Gilgal from the original narrative as being a late addition. He bases his
exclusion of it on the change of place between verses 4 and 16. Wellhausen identifies Gibeah of Benjamin with Geba of Benjamin (vers. 3, 4, 16). He may be right in so
doing, for the two names are confused also
in the text of Judges. But he does not accurately give the statements of the Hebrew
account. "At the beginning of the narrative," he says, "Saul is at Gibeah, and there
the Philistines seek for him, stopping before
the place because they meet with resistance
there. Suddenly it is silently assumed (xiii.
7) that Saul has remained at Gilgal since his
selection as king." In view of verse 4, this
is misrepresentation on the part of Wellhausen. What the passage plainly says is
quite different. Saul's troops were in Michmash and Bethel and Jonathan's in Gibeah
of Benjamin when Jonathan smote the Philistine official in Geba (2, 3). Then Saul blew

the trumpet and the people gathered together
after him to Gilgal (3, 4 ; cp. 7). According
to the analysis of Wellhausen, xiii. 1–6 is
continued in verse 16, " Now, as for Saul and
Jonathan and the people that were found
with them, they were dwelling in Geba of
Benjamin and the Philistines had encamped
in Michmash." This is straightforward and
consistent; but Wellhausen continues: " In
xiii. 16 the reader again has the impression
that Saul had been long at Gibeah with his
men, when the enemy pitched their camp
opposite. Only thus can the contrast between the circumstantial participle and the
inchoative perfect be understood." But the
statement of Wellhausen is again inaccurate.
The narrative had left the Philistines at
Michmash (ver. 5) and Saul at Gilgal according to Wellhausen's analysis (ver. 4), and
still at Gilgal, if verse 7 be included in the
narrative. Now it states that Saul and his
men were abiding at Geba of Benjamin,
but the Philistines had encamped in Michmash. The same difficulty, if difficulty
it be, lies against the narrative which Wellhausen calls original, as against the narrative
which appears in the present Hebrew text.
This simply means that the section which
Wellhausen omits, verses 7 to 15, is in place,
which tells of the events at Gilgal, and
concludes by saying that Samuel arose and
went up from Gilgal unto Gibeah of Benjamin ; and Saul after having numbered his
troops, was with Jonathan and these men at
Geba of Benjamin. The departure from
Gilgal is expressly stated with regard to
Samuel, and it is not necessary explicitly to
repeat it in regard to Saul and his men, it is
understood of itself. And the author used
the participle to indicate the continuing circumstance that Saul was abiding at Geba.

The passage is intelligible with the present
Hebrew text. The supposed difficulty likewise vanishes when the text is emended by
the aid of the Septuagint. The Greek translation has an additional clause, and Driver
conjectures that the original text read :
" And Samuel arose and gat him up from
Gilgal [and went on his way. And the rest
of the people went up after Saul to meet the
men of war ; and they came from Gilgal] to
Gibeah of Benjamin and Saul numbered,"
and so forth. "The omission in the Masoretic text is evidently due to the recurrence
of 'from Gilgal'" (*Text of Samuel*, p. 78). In
view of verse 16 this new text justifies Wellhausen's identification of Gibeah and Geba
in this chapter ; but it implies that verses 7
and 8b form an integral part of the original
narrative. And this result Driver accepts,
rejecting Wellhausen's exclusion of x. 8 and
xiii. 7–15, from the original narrative (*Introduction*[6], p. 176). Thus either with the
Masoretic text upon which the English version is based, or with the text as emended
by the aid of the Septuagint, the entire chapter is a unit.

But while 1 Sam. xiii. is a unit in itself, it is asserted to be distinct in authorship from chap. xv.; for in these two chapters there is a double and contradictory account of Saul's rejection by God. But the assertion cannot stand examination. Samuel indeed twice rebuked Saul at Gilgal, but he only once declared that God had rejected Saul from being king. When at the beginning of his reign, when about to undertake the special work to which he had been called, Saul failed to obey Samuel's charge to wait seven days until the prophet should come to implore God's aid by sacrifice, he was rebuked but he was not rejected : " Hadst thou been faithful to the theocratic requirements, thy kingdom would have been established forever; but now it shall not continue. God hath chosen a man after his own heart and appointed him to be prince over his people " (xiii. 13, 14). Saul is not declared unworthy to be king over God's people, Samuel does not abandon him, but goes to the capital, where he can still assist him. The prophet only declares that Saul's kingdom shall not continue forever; it shall eventually pass from Saul's family under the control of another. But after Saul's second flagrant violation of his theocratic obligations, when he disobeyed the command of God in the war with Amalek, he was rejected from being king (xv. 23); and Samuel abandoned him and came no more to see him until the day of his death (34, 35), a man of a different tribe was anointed (xvi. 1, 13), the spirit which qualified the theocratic king for his high office departed from Saul and came mightily upon David (13, 14), and not Saul, but David, became the deliverer of Israel (xvii.).

The account of Samuel's judgeship and of Saul's elevation to the throne, the earlier years of his reign, and his rejection by God, is thus found to be capable of consistent interpretation throughout. Examination of the history of David reveals its consistency likewise. See DAVID and JONATHAN. There is no ground, therefore, for the assumption that contradictory documents have been combined to form the First Book of Samuel.

III. It further appears that while the contents of the alleged documents into which the narrative has been distributed are consistent, they also imply each other. (1) The original narrative in 1 Sam. ix. 16, and x. 5, implies that the Philistines had renewed the exercise of sovereignty over Israel. The explanation is found in the preceding chapter, which is alleged to be a later narrative; for the threatening attitude of the Philistines and other ancient foes, when Samuel began to relax the reins of government, is implied in viii. 1, 5, 20. The original narrative thus requires chap. viii. as an integral part. The only escape is to magisterially declare that the Israelites had been subject to the Philistines ever since the ark was taken, that

Samuel never delivered Israel from the Philistine yoke, that the story of the second battle of Ebenezer is a pure fabrication (vii. 2–17). And this dogmatic assertion Wellhausen does not hesitate to make. He says that "there cannot be a word of truth in the entire narrative." Driver does not explicitly deny that the event occurred, but he admits that chaps. ix. and x. do not connect directly with vii. 1, and says that "it is probable that the original sequel of iv. 1ᵇ to vii. 1, has here been omitted to make room for vii. 2 ff." In other words, vii. 2–17 and viii. afford a consistent picture of the times, as has been already shown; and it is the theory of the divisive critics which fails to explain the existing phenomena. (2) The original narrative in xi. implies the public selection of Saul to be king which is related in the alleged later narrative (x. 17–27). If, as asserted, Saul had only been anointed in private (x. 1), what gave him such respect in the eyes of the people a month later that men from all the tribes sprang to arms at his summons and followed him to the relief of Jabesh in Gilead? Chapter xi. requires that some event preceded like that which is recorded in the alleged later narrative (x. 17–27). (3) The original narrative of David's career, it is said, first mentions him as an adult man, accustomed to arms, who is skillful in playing the harp and is accordingly summoned by Saul to court, to soothe him with music whenever he is suffering from his malady (xvi. 14–23), and it is continued in xviii. 6–30. But it is manifest that these two passages do not connect; xviii. 6 refers to the return of David from the slaughter of the Philistine (R. V. margin, Philistines). The account of the combat between David and Goliath, which is assigned to a different and later author, intervenes and supplies the missing link; but this has been eliminated from the original narrative by the divisive critics, largely on the allegation that in xvii. 33 David is represented as a youth, and in verses 55–58 Saul does not know David. On other equally valid interpretation these alleged inconsistencies with the original narrative do not exist. See DAVID. To make them out the divisive critics are obliged to discard xvii. 14. Saul is not asking who David is, but is inquiring who and what David's father is. That something is needed between xvi. 23, and xviii. 6, is admitted. Wellhausen says it was something quite different from what now stands there, because chap. xvii. tells of David's killing but one man, whereas xviii. 7 speaks of him as having slain his ten thousand. As though the slaying of their champion, and thereby putting the Philistines to flight, was not in the language of song the slaying of ten thousand ! The author of the Book of Samuel evidently understood it so. Thus the original narrative of David's career implies the existence of the alleged later story, and again the

only escape from this dilemma is to assert
that some part of the original narrative has
been replaced by something quite different.
The Book of Samuel does not make the difficulty. It is the theory which fails to explain the existing phenomena.

San-bal'lat [the moon-god Sin hath given
life].

An influential Samaritan (Neh. ii. 10). He
was a Horonite. This designation scarcely
means a native of Horonaim in Moab, else he
would probably be called a Moabite; but
rather describes him as a man of Beth-horon
(cp. iv. 2; vi. 2). He was opposed to the rebuilding of the wall of Jerusalem by Nehemiah and tried, unsuccessfully, to stop it (iv.
7, 8). Next he plotted with others to invite
Nehemiah to a conference, and assassinate
him (vi. 1-4). This new device failing, he
tried intimidation, but in vain (5-14).

Sanballat the Horonite was a contemporary
of the high priest Eliashib, great-grandfather
of Jaddua; was associated with Tobiah the
Ammonite; and opposed the rebuilding of
the wall of Jerusalem by Nehemiah in the
twentieth year of Artaxerxes (iii. 1; iv. 7).
He was governor of Samaria shortly before
408 B. C., the 17th year of Darius Nothus (Elephantine papyri). A son of the high priest
Joiada took Sanballat's daughter to wife, and
for this offense was expelled by Nehemiah
(xiii. 4, 28). Josephus mentions one Sanballat,
a Cuthean by birth, whom Darius, the last
king [of Persia, 336-330 B. C.] sent to Samaria
as governor (Antiq. xi. 7, 2; 8, 2), but who,
on the defeat of Darius, went over to Alexander the Great, 332 B. C. (8, 4). His daughter Nicaso was taken to wife by Manasseh,
brother of the high priest Jaddua. This foreign marriage offended the Jewish authorities, and they drove Manasseh from the altar
at Jerusalem; but Sanballat, with the appro-
bation of Alexander, built a temple on mount
Gerizim and made his son-in-law its priest
(7, 2; 8, 2 and 4). These statements of the Jewish historian do not accord with the facts of
Sanballat's history already recited. The older
commentators thought that Josephus speaks
of a later Sanballat. Josephus, however,
doubtless has in mind Sanballat the Horonite
and the marriage referred to in Neh. xiii. 28;
but he has probably lowered the date of Sanballat 100 years to conform the facts to his
belief that the son-in-law of Sanballat not
only founded or greatly promoted the Samaritan religion, but also built the temple on
Gerizim, and that this temple was erected
after Alexander's conquest of the country
(Antiq. xiii. 9, 1; 200 years before 128 B. C.
or thereabout), and that Alexander and the
high priest Jaddua were contemporaries (xi.
8, 5). Josephus assigns a false date here; as
he also does when he dates Nehemiah's commission in the twenty-fifth year of Xerxes,
who reigned but 21 years (Antiq. xi. 5, 7), instead of in the twentieth year of his successor, Artaxerxes (Neh. ii. 1), and when he

dates the arrival of Ezra in Jerusalem in the
seventh year of Xerxes (Antiq. xi. 5, 2), instead of 21 years later, in the seventh year
of Artaxerxes (Ezra vii. 1, 8), and when he
confounds Onias I. with Onias III., who lived
a century later (1 Mac. xii. 7, 20; Antiq. xii
4, 10).

San'dal. See CLOTHING, SHOE.

San'he-drin and **Sanhedrim** [Talmudic
Hebrew, from Greek *sunedrion*, a council].

The name generally given by writers on
Jewish antiquities and history to the highest
Jewish assembly for government in the time
of our Lord. The English version uses the
more familiar word council; see COUNCIL.

San-san'nah [a palm leaf].

A town in the extreme south of Judah
(Josh. xv. 31); perhaps the same as Hazar-
susah, which occupies the corresponding position in the list of cities assigned to the
Simeonites (cp. Josh. xix. 5).

Saph [a basin, foundation, threshold].

A Philistine giant, slain by Sibbechai in a
battle at Gob (2 Sam. xxi. 18). Called in 1
Chron. xx. 4 Sippai.

Sa'phir. See SHAPHIR.

Sap-phi'ra [beautiful, or, less probably, a
sapphire].

The wife of that Ananias who was struck
dead for having lied unto God. She shared
her husband's sin and its penalty (Acts v.
1-10).

Sap'phire.

A precious stone (Tobit xiii. 16), called in
Hebrew *sappir*, in Greek *sappheiros*. It was
the middle gem in the second row of the high
priest's breastplate (Ex. xxviii. 18), and
adorned the second foundation of the New
Jerusalem (Rev. xxi. 19). It was susceptible
of a fine polish (Lam. iv. 7), and was of great
value (Job xxviii. 16; cp. Song. v. 14; Is.
liv. 11). The sapphire is one of the three
varieties of corundum, the others being
corundum proper and emery. It is of a bluish color, and transparent or translucent (cp.
Ex. xxiv. 10). It is inferior in hardness only
to the diamond, and is still greatly prized
The ancients obtained it from India and
Ethiopia. Fine specimens are brought from
Ceylon.

Sa'rah, in A. V. of N. T. twice **Sara** (Heb.
xi. 11; 1 Pet. iii. 6) [a princess].

1. The wife of Abraham, ten years his
junior, married to him in Ur of the Chaldees (Gen. xi. 28-31; xvii. 17). She was also
his half-sister, being the daughter of his
father, but not of his mother (xx. 12). Her
name was originally Sarai, meaning perhaps
princely or contentious. When Abraham
departed from Haran to go to Canaan, Sarai
was about sixty-five years old (xii. 4). Evidently she was a well-preserved woman: for
she lived to be one hundred and twenty-seven
years old; and shortly after leaving Haran,
when about to enter Egypt, Abraham feared

lest her beauty should attract the Egyptians and lead to his murder, and he represented that she was his sister, keeping back the fact that she was his wife (10–20). Years later he did so again at the court of Abimelech, king of Gerar (xx. 1–18). Why he did so is not stated, nor is it said that Abimelech was influenced by her beauty. The king of Gerar may have thought of the desirability of an alliance with the powerful Hebrew chieftain, and, with this end in view, determined to take a woman of the immediate family of Abraham into his harem, as was frequently done by princes of that period when they concluded alliances. Sarai was childless; and when about seventy-five years old concluded that she was an obstacle to the promise made to Abraham of numerous posterity, and persuaded her husband to take Hagar, her handmaid, as secondary wife. He did so, and became the fatl er of Ishmael (xvi. 1–16). Afterwards Sarai, when about eighty-nine, received a promise from God that she should herself bear a son (cp. Heb. xi. 11, 12), and in the course of a year gave birth to Isaac the child of promise. It was when this promise was made to her that God changed her name to Sarah, meaning princess (Gen. xvii. 15–22; xviii. 9–15; xxi. 1–5). When Isaac was weaned, his parents made a great feast, at which Sarah saw Ishmael, Hagar's son, mocking. She insisted that both mother and son should be sent away (9–21). Sarah died at Kirjath-arba (Hebron) at the age of 127 (xxiii. 1, 2), and was buried in the cave of Machpelah, which Abraham purchased at that time for a family sepulcher.

2. For Sarah of Num. xxvi. 46, A. V., a different word in Hebrew, see SERAH.

Sa'rai. See SARAH 1.

Sar'a-mel. See ASARAMEL.

Sa'raph [burning, fiery].
A descendant of Shelah, the son of Judah. At one time he exercised dominion in Moab (1 Chron. iv. 22).

Sar'dine. See SARDIUS.

Sar'dis.
A city, first of the Mæonians and then of the Lydians, situated at the foot of mount Tmolus, on the eastern bank of the river Pactôlus, in the midst of a fertile region, about 50 miles east of Smyrna. The acropolis crowned a hill, 950 feet high, a spur of the mountain. The Lydian town lay at its foot on the west, between the acropolis and the river; but the Romans eventually built to the north of the acropolis. In 546 B. C. Cyrus the Great wrested the city from Crœsus, the rich Lydian king, and it became the seat of a Persian satrap. The Athenians burned it in 499 B. C., and thereby brought on the Persian invasions of Greece in the reigns of Darius and Xerxes. In 334 B. C. it surrendered to Alexander the Great, after his victory at the Granicus. In 214 B. C. it

was taken by Antiochus the Great, but he lost it on being defeated by the Romans at Magnesia in 190 B. C. The Romans annexed it to the kingdom of Pergamos; but when in 129 B. C. they erected the province of Asia, Sardis fell within its bounds. In A. D. 17, when it was destroyed by an earthquake, the emperor Tiberius remitted the taxes of the citizens and rebuilt the city. Jews dwelt in the city (Antiq. xiv. 10, 24), and a Christian community early grew up there (Rev. i. 11; iii. 1, 4). Sardis (now called Sert-Kalessi) is a miserable hamlet; but on the site of the Lydian town are the remains of a magnificent temple of Artemis, built in the 4th century B. C. to replace an older structure; and a temple of Zeus, said to stand above the foundations of Crœsus' palace. Immediately outside of the temple of Artemis, at the eastern end, the walls of a Christian church are still standing, which were erected before the 4th century, A. D.

Sar'di-us, in A. V. of Rev. iv. 3 **Sardine.**
A variety of chalcedony, which the Greeks called *sardios* and *sardion*. It was a precious stone (Rev. iv. 3), and constituted the sixth foundation of the wall about the New Jerusalem (xxi. 20). Two sorts, distinguished by their color, were known by the name of sardius: the transparent red being our carnelian and the brownish red being the variety of carnelian to which we restrict the name sardius. According to Pliny, it was found near Sardis, whence it derived its name, but the finest qualities were brought from Babylon. The best carnelians now come from India; some also occur in Arabia, whence the ancient Hebrews may have obtained them.

In the O. T. sardius is the rendering of the Hebrew *'Odem*, reddish gem. It was the first stone in the first row on the high priest's breastplate (Ex. xxviii. 17), and was one of the stones with which Tyre adorned itself (Ezek. xxviii. 13). The marginal reading is ruby, but the Septuagint renders *'odem* by *sardion*. So does Josephus in one place (War v. 5, 7), while in another he has sardonyx, which is but another variety of chalcedony (Antiq. iii. 7, 5).

Sar'do-nyx.
A variety of chalcedony, called by the Greeks *sardonux*, finger-nail onyx. It forms the fifth foundation of the wall surrounding the New Jerusalem (Rev. xxi. 20). It is like the onyx in structure, but includes layers of carnelian along with others of white, whitish-brown, or sometimes of black color. It was obtained chiefly in India and Arabia (Pliny, Hist. Nat. xxxvii. 23).

Sa-rep'ta. See ZAREPHATH.

Sar'gon [Assyrian *Sharrukinu*, the constituted king].
A king of Assyria, mentioned by name in Scripture in Is. xx. 1 only. He succeeded the last Shalmaneser. He was perhaps of

royal blood, as he claims ; but it is believed
that he usurped the throne, assuming the
name of Sargon, an ancient and celebrated
Babylonian king.   He either secured the
throne and then completed the siege of Samaria, which Shalmaneser had begun in 724
B. C., or else he ascended the throne immediately after the fall of Israel's capital, and,
perhaps as the general who had brought
these military operations to a successful termination, claimed the capture as an act of
his accession year.   The biblical record is
not clear (2 Kin. xvii. 1–6).   The Hebrew
writer relates that Shalmaneser came against
Hoshea, and proceeds by saying that the
king of Assyria found conspiracy in Hoshea
and cast him into prison, and that the king
of Assyria besieged Samaria three years, and
in the ninth year of Hoshea took the city.
Until the claim of Sargon to have captured
Samaria came to light, readers of the Hebrew
narrative inferred that Shalmaneser was the
conqueror of Samaria.   But the inference
was not warranted, for the writer continues
to speak of the king of Assyria, where it is
probable that he does not mean the conqueror
of Samaria (ver. 24, 26, 27).   He does not
specify the particular king, but uses the general title ; and when he recurs to the siege,
he names Shalmaneser as the besieger, but
continues by saying, "They took it" (xviii.
9, 10).   At any rate, Samaria fell in the closing months of 722 B. C., and Sargon ascended
the throne on the 12th of Tebet, the tenth
month, of that year.   Immediately after his
accession, the Babylonians, assisted by the
Elamites, revolted, and Sargon was for a
time unable to reduce them to subjection.
In 720 the remaining Israelites of Samaria
in alliance with the men of Hamath rebelled,
but Sargon subdued them, and placed captive
Hamathites as colonists in Samaria.   In the
same year he defeated the allied forces of
Hanun, king of Gaza and Sib'e, better known
to readers of the Bible as So, the tartan of
Egypt in a battle fought at Raphia.   Sargon
took Carchemish, the capital of the Hittites,
in 717, and with the capture of their capital
the empire of the Hittites fell.   In 716 his
armies waged war in Armenia, in 715 they
were still engaged in war in Armenia, and
were carrying on operations in Media.   In
this year also Arab tribes were planted as
colonists in Samaria by his orders, and he received tribute from Pharaoh of Egypt.   He
boasts of having subjugated Judah.   The
tablet on which this boast appears was inscribed before the close of 714, to judge from
its contents.   The combined Assyrian and
Hebrew data point to the end of 715 or the
beginning of 714 as the date when Hezekiah
acknowledged the suzerainty of Assyria by
beginning to pay tribute.   Merodach-baladan
incited the nations from Elam to the Mediterranean Sea to revolt from Assyria.   In 711,
therefore, Sargon dispatched troops against
Ashdod, and in 710 he captured Babylon and

assumed the title of king of Babylon.   He
began to erect a new palace and town 10
miles northeast of Nineveh in 712 and named
it Dur-sharrukin, Sargonsburg.   The ruins
are known as Khorsabad ; see NINEVEH.
He took up his residence there about 707.
He was murdered in 705 and was succeeded
by his son Sennacherib.

Sa′rid [survivor].
A village on the southern frontier of Zebulun (Josh. xix. 10, 12).   Conder, reading with
Septuagint and Syriac version d instead of
r, places it doubtfully at Tell Shadûd, on the
northern part of the plain of Esdraelon, 5
miles southwest of Nazareth.

Sa′ron.   See SHARON.

Sar′se-chim.
One of Nebuchadnezzar's princes who entered Jerusalem (Jer. xxxix. 3).

Sa′ruch.   See SERUG.

Sa′tan [Hebrew *saṭan*, an adversary].
The devil (Mat. iv. 1 with 10, 11 ; Mark i.
13) ; preëminently "the adversary" (Job i. 6 ;
Zech. iii. 1, margin), because animated by
a disposition hostile to all goodness and
the chief opponent of God and man (Job ii.
3 ; Luke xxii. 3 ; cp. 1 Chron. xxi. 1 and Ps.
cix. 6, but see R. V.), aiming to undo the
work of God (Mark iv. 15), seeking to persuade men to sin (Luke xxii. 3 ; Acts v. 3 ;
xxvi. 18), desirous of leading them to renounce God (Job ii. 5 ; Mat. iv. 9, 10), and
endeavoring to prevent their acceptance and
salvation by God (Zech. iii. 1, 2).   He is sometimes influential in bringing about physical
sickness, pecuniary loss, bereavement (Job i.
11–22 ; ii. 4–7 ; Luke xiii. 16).   He is, however, under the control of God.   Only by
God's permission can he pursue his malicious
designs (Job i. 12 ; ii. 5, 6 ; Luke xxii. 32).
When permission is granted him to carry
out his evil plots, it is only that he may become an instrument in furthering the divine
plan.   In Job's case, the vain efforts of Satan
to induce the patriarch to sin resulted in disciplining his character and maturing his faith
in God.   In the fully revealed doctrine of
Satan, which is seen in the N. T., he is the
god of this world who has access to the hearts
of men, deceives them, and receives their
witting or unwitting obedience (Luke xxii.
3 ; Acts v. 3 ; xxvi. 18 ; 2 Cor. iv. 4 ; 2 Thes.
ii. 9 ; Rev. xii. 9).   He is the ruler of a kingdom, having principalities, powers, and demons under him (Mat. xii. 24, 26 ; Luke xi.
18 ; Rev. xii. 7).
Satan was the seducer of Adam and Eve
(2 Cor. xi. 3 ; Rev. xii. 9).   This fact may
have become known to them.   If not, it was
discerned as soon as the existence of the
devil and his work became known, for the
temptation of Eve came from without through
the persuasions of an irrational creature.
The malignant spirit behind the serpent,
hostile to good, seeking to undo the work of

God, and supernaturally lending speech to the reptile, or communicating with the mind of the woman, so that she thought she heard articulate speech, was evidently Satan. This doctrine went hand in hand with the doctrine concerning the devil, and received the highest sanction (Wisd. ii. 24; John viii. 44; Rom. xvi. 20; 2 Cor. xi. 3; Rev. xii. 9); see SERPENT. Satan produced demoniacal possession (Mat. xii. 22-29; Mark iii. 22-27; Luke xi. 14-23). He approached Jesus with temptation (Mat. iv. 1-11). He steals the word from the heart of the ignorant or inattentive hearer (Mark iv. 15). He entered into the heart of Judas before the commission of the great crime (Luke xxii. 3; John xiii. 27). He had to do with Peter's fall (Luke xxii. 31). It was under temptation by Satan that Ananias and Sapphira lied to the Holy Ghost (Acts v. 3). He hindered Paul in his ministry (1 Thes. ii. 18), having previously sent a messenger to buffet him (2 Cor. xii. 7). Pergamos, where a faithful Christian, Antipas, suffered martyrdom, was a place where Satan dwelt (Rev. ii. 13). Men with hearts unchanged are under Satan's power (Acts xxvi. 18). An assembly of those who have grievously erred from the faith, and perhaps from morality, is the synagogue of Satan (Rev. ii. 9; iii. 9; cp. 1 Tim. v. 15). Those who are expelled from the church are said to be delivered to Satan; but this is designed to produce their reformation, and not their destruction (1 Cor. v. 5; 1 Tim. i. 20). There are depths in Satan which inexperienced Christians fail to fathom (Rev. ii. 24). He is, moreover, so plausible that he seems to be an angel of light (2 Cor. xi. 14). He sometimes gains advantages over Christians (ii. 11), but he shall ultimately be bruised under their feet (Rom. xvi. 20). He is the real agent in the operations carried on by the man of sin (2 Thes. ii. 1-12), but the day will come when, after a temporary triumph, Satan shall be expelled from the earth, and, being bound, shall be cast into the abyss (Rev. xii. 9; xx. 1, 2). See DEVIL.

Simon Peter was called Satan when he took it upon him to contradict Christ's prophecy of his death and resurrection, for he was a stumbling-block to Christ, opposed him, and minded not the things of God (Mat. xvi. 23; Mark viii. 33).

Sa'trap [from Persian *khshatrapâwan*, abbreviated *khshatrapâ*, protector of the land, in Hebrew *'ᵃhashdrapan*].

The official title of the viceroy, who, in behalf of the Persian monarch, exercised the civil and military authority in several small provinces combined in one government. Each of these provinces had its own governor (Ezra viii. 36 and Esth. iii. 12, in A. V. lieutenant). The title is used in Aramaic historical documents written after the Persian conquest, in referring to high officials of the Babylonian empire and of the kingdom ruled

by Darius the Mede (Dan. iii. 2 and vi. 1, in A. V. prince).

Sa'tyr.

A sylvan god of the Greeks and Romans, a companion of Bacchus. At first he was represented with long-pointed ears, snub nose, and goat's tail. At a later period goat's legs were added. He was supposed to possess a half brutal and lustful nature. Satyr is the rendering of the Hebrew *Sᵉ'ir*, he goat, and is applied to wild animals or demons which should dance among the ruins of Babylon (Is. xiii. 21) and of the Edomite cities (xxxiv. 14). The word commonly signifies a he goat. In two passages it denotes an object of idolatrous worship (Lev. xvii. 7; 2 Chron. xi. 15, both R. V.). In the latter place it is mentioned with calf idols, suggesting that it refers to idols having the likeness of goats. In Is. xiii. 21, 22 it is associated with wild animals, in xxxiv. 14 with a creature of the night also, which may be either some nocturnal animal (in A. V. the screech owl) or a nocturnal demon; see NIGHT MONSTER. In the adaptation of Isaiah's words in Revelation, the language is quoted from the Septuagint and the word demons is used (Rev. xviii. 2, R. V.). Accordingly, interpreters dispute whether the Hebrew prophet meant that wild goats, ostriches, wolves, jackals, and other beasts of the desert should wander among the forsaken ruins, or whether he introduced into the imagery of his poetic description a popular belief in demons which appeared in the form of goats and haunted desert places.

Saul [asked (of God)].

1. A king of Edom, from Rehoboth, on the Euphrates (Gen. xxxvi. 37, 38, in R. V. Shaul).

2. The first king of Israel, son of Kish, a Benjamite; see KISH. The prophet Samuel had grown old; his sons showed by their conduct that they did not possess his upright character and could not carry on his work; and the surrounding nations were evidently ready to harass and oppress Israel (1 Sam. viii. 1, 3, 20; xii. 12). The elders of Israel accordingly came to Samuel and demanded that the form of government be changed and that a visible king be set over them, so that they might be like the well-organized nations about them, and have one who could lead them to victory over their foes (viii. 4, 5, 19, 20). Although the ultimate organization of the Hebrews as a kingdom, with an earthly monarch as the representative of Jehovah, had long been contemplated (Gen. xvii. 6, 16; xxxv. 11; Deut. xvii. 14-20), yet the spirit of the people in demanding a king at this crisis was irreligious. They lacked abiding faith in God, without which the rule of Jehovah as theocratic king was impossible. They were turning from faith in the invisible God to put confidence in a visible king. By divine direction Samuel informed the elders what the people would have to en-

ure from a king, but on their persisting in their demand, he promised to do as they desired and dismissed them.

The elevation of Saul to the throne. About this time the asses of Kish, a Benjamite, went astray, and his son, Saul, was sent to seek them. Saul was at the time a young man, perhaps thirty-five years old; and he was head and shoulders taller than any of the people. Not finding the asses, after three days' search, he was about to give up the quest and return home. His servant, however, suggested one further effort. Persons of whom the servant made inquiry concerning the asses probably told him that there was a man of God in the neighboring city who might give the desired information, and he persuaded Saul to go to him. The man of God was Samuel, who had been told by God to expect a Benjamite and to anoint him prince over Israel. Saul and his family in Gibeah knew Samuel well by report (1 Sam. x. 14–16), but Saul seems not to have met the prophet before and not to have understood that Samuel was the man of God of whom the people spake. He refers to him as the man (ix. 7), and on meeting him at the city gate does not know him (18, 19). Samuel informed Saul that the asses had been recovered, intimated to him that he would be chosen king, and put him in the place of honor at the sacrificial feast which he was about to celebrate. Next morning, as the guest was leaving the town, the prophet took a vial of oil, poured it upon his head, and having kissed him, said, "Is it not that the Lord hath anointed thee to be prince over his inheritance?" and charged him not to disclose the secret, to go to Gilgal at the proper time and tarry there seven days, until he himself should come and offer sacrifice and give instruction (ix. 20–x. 16). Samuel soon summoned the people to Mizpah. The choice was left to God. The lot was cast, and Saul was chosen. But he had hidden himself. When he was brought from his hiding place and stood forth, towering above the multitude, he was received with enthusiasm. God had selected a man of fine appearance in order to win the admiration and confidence of all the Israelites, and a man of the tribe of Benjamin, which stood on the border between Ephraim and Judah, in order to satisfy both north and south. Samuel had committed the choice to God in order to secure the allegiance of the godly men for the king. A large company of men, obedient to God, escorted Saul home; but certain men of Belial were nevertheless dissatisfied, and Saul retired to private life until private jealousies should be overcome. He devoted himself to the cultivation of his father's fields. A month later (xi. 17, Septuagint) the town of Jabesh in Gilead was straitly besieged by the Ammonites. At the request of the citizens, the besiegers scornfully granted a truce of seven days in order that the townspeople might invoke the aid

of their fellow-countrymen. The messengers, or some of them, came to Gibeah with their mournful story. Saul heard it when he returned from the field. The Spirit of God stirred him. He sent summons to the tribes to follow him and Samuel to the rescue of their imperiled brethren. Jabesh was relieved. The people asked where were they who had refused to recognize Saul as king, and they carried Saul to Gilgal, the nearest place of customary sacrifice, where he was inducted into office and Samuel laid down his judgeship (xi. 1–xii. 25); see SAMUEL, BOOKS OF.

The reign of Saul. The age of Saul when he began to reign is unknown, as the Hebrew text of 1 Sam. xiii. 1 is defective, the numeral being omitted. The number thirty is derived from the Septuagint. He was at any rate old enough to have a son capable of holding a military command. Saul established a small standing army of 3000 men; 2000 of these were with him at Michmash and Bethel, and 1000 were stationed with Jonathan at Gibeah (xiii. 2). Jonathan smote a Philistine garrison, or rather deputy, at Geba (3); see GARRISON. The Philistines heard thereof, and held the Israelites in abomination. The Israelites, learning of their danger, responded to Saul's summons to assemble at Gilgal (3, 4), whither Samuel had promised to come in this emergency and entreat the favor of the Lord (8, 11, 12; x. 8). A Philistine army advanced into the land of Israel and pitched at Michmash. Great fear seized the Israelites, Samuel intentionally delayed to appear, the people began to scatter and leave the king, and a descent of the Philistines upon Saul and his decreasing forces seemed imminent (xiii. 8, 11, 12); and therefore Saul presumed to conduct the sacrifice. But Samuel came, rebuked the king for transgressing God's command (x. 8), and declared that Saul on account of his disobedience should not found a dynasty (xiii. 9–14). Samuel went to Gibeah, where he would be near the king (15; but see Septuagint). Saul and Jonathan took post at Geba of Benjamin, while the Philistines lay encamped at Michmash. By a feat of valor, Jonathan started a panic in the garrison of the Philistines, which spread to their camp and to their prowling bands. Saul took advantage of it, and secured a victory (xiii. 15–xiv. 46). Afterwards Samuel directed Saul to wage a war of extermination against the Amalekites. Saul undertook the war, but he spared the best of the cattle to sacrifice to the Lord at Gilgal, and also saved their king. For this second act of disobedience, by which he showed that he could not be trusted to act as God's instrument, but desired to assert his own will in God's kingdom, he was rejected from being king (xv. 1–35); see SAMUEL, BOOKS OF. Samuel, therefore, was sent to Bethlehem to anoint David king (xvi. 1–13). The Spirit of the Lord now departed from

Saul, and he began to be troubled by an evil spirit. A harper was required to charm away his melancholy madness, and David was selected to discharge the duty (14–23). The plaudits with which the youthful son of Jesse was welcomed on returning from his great victory over Goliath so excited Saul's jealousy that before long the hero was a fugitive, pursued with relentless fury by the now vindictive monarch (xvii.–xxx.) ; see DAVID. At last the end came. The Philistines, invading the Israelite territory, pitched in Shunem, near the valley of Jezreel. Saul, following to give them battle, established his headquarters on the slope of mount Gilboa. Sad forebodings of his fate troubling him, he made a night journey quite close to the Philistine camp, to En-dor, where lived a woman who was reputed to have the power of calling up even the dead, and he was there informed that he and his sons should perish on the morrow (xxviii. 1–25). The morrow came, and the battle began. The Philistine archers did great execution in the Israelite ranks. They slew three of Saul's sons, including the eldest, the unselfish and heroic Jonathan. They seriously wounded Saul himself, on which he called to his armor-bearer to thrust him through. The young man declined the responsibility, whereupon the erring monarch fell upon his sword, and died. The victorious Philistines, finding his corpse, severed the head from the body, and affixed the latter, with the bodies of his sons, to the wall of Beth-shean, whilst they sent his armor as a trophy to be kept in the temple of Ashtaroth. The men of Jabesh-gilead, whom Saul had saved in the early part of his reign, feeling gratitude for their deliverance, crossed the Jordan by night to Beth-shean, took down the bodies, and gave them honorable interment, while David mourned the fate of the Lord's anointed and the beloved Jonathan in plaintive poetry (xxxi. ; 2 Sam. i.). The length of Saul's reign is not stated in the O. T., but both Paul and Josephus are able to assign it forty years (Acts xiii. 21; Antiq. vi. 14, 9).

Saul and the woman of En-dor. The old man covered with a robe, who figures in the interview between the woman of En-dor and Saul (1 Sam. xxviii. 3–19), has been explained in three different ways. He was the woman's accomplice, and when he appeared she uttered a loud cry, and she pronounced the man who had come to seek her aid to be Saul. The loud cry was her customary trick. She knew that the king was in the neighborhood, and she had at once detected that her visitor was he, in his tall stature, in his bearing, in his words, and in the manner of his attendants. Or else the appearance was a spirit, quite unexpected by her, at which she uttered a loud cry, because she was really startled. If an unexpected appearance, it was either the devil, as Luther and Calvin believed, and as those understand who think that certain phenomena of ancient sorcery and modern spir-

itualism are due to Satanic agency (see DEVIL and DEMONIAC), or else Samuel, reappearing as did Moses and Elijah on the mount of Transfiguration (1 Chron. x. 13, Septuagint Ecclus. xlvi. 20), and so most of the evangelical interpreters since the Reformation. The basis for the opinion that Samuel appeared is that the narrator refers to the person as though he is Samuel (1 Sam. xxviii. 14, 15, 16, 20), and that the words spoken by him were fulfilled. The biblical recorder simply describes what occurred. It is to be noted that the woman was a lawbreaker, and was also condemned by the religion of Jehovah. Moreover, she alone saw the apparition, and she described the appearance in most vague terms—an old man rising from the earth and covered with a robe. This description would apply to any aged person, but Saul concluded that Samuel had really appeared. The words which were uttered by the robed figure boldly forecast the future as a fortune teller does or else predicted it with full knowledge. The words came true, but they were in part fulfilled by Saul's own deliberate act. If Samuel himself appeared, then this is the sole instance recorded in Scripture where the spirit of a departed saint has returned to earth and conversed with men, since the case of Moses and Elijah in converse with the transfigured Christ is not analogous. Moreover, it would be strange, indeed, if, after God had refused to answer Saul, either by dreams or by prophets, his servant Samuel should appear, and especially if he should appear at an interview strictly forbidden by God, and at the behest of a woman who was condemned alike by the law of the land and by the law of God (Ex. xxii. 18; Lev. xx. 27; Deut. xviii. 10–14; 1 Sam. xxviii. 3, 9; 1 Chron. x. 13).

3. The original name of the apostle Paul (Acts vii. 58; xiii. 9).

Sav'iour.

One who saves from any evil or danger (2 Kin. xiii. 5; Neh. ix. 27). In the O. T. it is specially used of God, Jehovah, viewed as the deliverer of his chosen people Israel (2 Sam. xxii. 3; Ps. cvi. 21; Is. xliii. 3, 11; xlv. 15, 21; xlix. 26; lxiii. 8; Jer. xiv. 8; Hos. xiii. 4). The Greek word *sōtēr*, preserver, deliverer (Herod. vii. 139), is used by the classical writers specially of their gods, though sometimes a king assumed the title, as did Ptolemy Soter and Demetrius I. In the N. T. it is used of God the Father (1 Tim. i. 1; iv. 10; Titus i. 3; iii. 4; Jude 25), but especially of Jesus Christ the Son, who saves his people from their sins (Mat. i. 21), delivering them out of their sinful condition and misery, from guilt, the wrath of God, the power of sin and the dominion of Satan, and bringing them into a state of salvation in blessed communion with God (Luke xix. 10; Acts v. 31; Rom. v. 8–11; Phil. iii. 20, 21; 1 Tim. i. 15; 2 Tim. i. 10; Tit. ii. 13, 14; Heb. vii. 25).

Saw.

A toothed tool for cutting wood and for snaping stone (1 Kin. vii. 9; Is. x. 15). Victims of persecuting rage were sometimes sawn asunder (Heb. xi. 37). If David cut the Ammonites of Rabbah, and other towns which fell into his hands, with saws, harrows, and axes (2 Sam. xii. 31; 1 Chron. xx. 3), it was an act of exceptional severity on his part, and foreign to all else that is known of his character. A change of resh to mem in the verb used in Chronicles, and of resh to daleth in the verb in Samuel, would make the record state that David exacted labor from the captives (2 Sam. xii. 31, R. V. margin).

The saws used by the ancient Egyptians had, so far as known, but one handle. The blade was usually of bronze, let into the handle or bound to it by thongs. The teeth commonly inclined toward the handle. The wood was placed perpendicularly in a frame, and was sawn downward. The Assyrians used a double-handled saw also, with a blade of iron.

Scape'goat. See AZAZEL.

Scar'let.

A bright, rich crimson, not the hue of recent origin known as scarlet. The coloring matter was obtained by the Israelites from an insect (*Coccus ilicis*), called *kermez* by the Arabs, whence the English word crimson is derived. The insect abounds in Palestine on the holm oak (*Quercus coccifera*). The female alone yields the coloring matter. She attains the form and size of an ordinary pea, is violet-black in color, covered with a whitish powder, and wingless. Filled with eggs containing red matter, she adheres to the leaves and twigs of the oak, and feeds on its juices. From the resemblance of the insect to a berry, the Greeks called it *kokkos*, berry. It is related to the cochineal insect of Mexico (*Coccus cacti*); but it yields a much less valuable dye, and has been supplanted commercially by its Mexican congener. The color was called by the Hebrews *shani*, brightness, crimson, *sh'ni tola'ath*, brightness of the worm, worm crimson, *tola'ath shani*, worm of brightness, crimson worm, *tola'*, worm, and in Greek *kokkinos*, pertaining to the coccus.

The color and the method of obtaining it were early known (Gen. xxxviii. 28). It was much used in the hangings of the tabernacle and in the high priest's vestments. It was employed in the ceremony attending the purification of the leper, and in the preparation of the water of separation (Lev. xiv. 4; Num. xix. 6; Heb. ix. 19).

Scep'ter.

A rod held in the hands of kings as a token of authority (Ps. xlv. 6; Amos i. 5; Wisd. x. 14; Heb. i. 8; War i. 33, 9). It has been used from time immemorial. The staff was not, however, a symbol of royal sovereignty exclusively. It might be carried by any leader (Judg. v. 14, R. V.; Baruch vi. 14), among the Greeks by kings, judges, heralds, and speakers given the floor by the herald (Iliad i. 238; ii. 100; vii. 277; xxiii. 568). Nor is the Hebrew name *shebet* a specific term, but it denotes any rod, such as the walking stick, which was often carried as a mark of dignity (Gen. xxxviii. 18), the shepherd's staff (Lev. xxvii. 32; Ps. xxiii. 4; Mic. vii. 14), or the rod used in threshing cummin (Is. xxviii. 27). The royal scepter was doubtless often of wood. The scepter of Ahasuerus was made of gold (Esth. iv. 11), and so too was the famed scepter of Agamemnon (Iliad ii. 100). A reed was placed in Christ's hand when he was mocked as king (Mat. xxvii. 29).

Sce'va.

A member of one of the Jewish families from which the high priests were ordinarily chosen. His seven sons were exorcists (Acts xix. 14).

School.

There were no schools for children in ancient Israel. But instruction was not lacking. Parents gave their children religious instruction (Gen. xviii. 19; Deut. vi. 7; Susanna 3; 2 Tim. iii. 15). The older people had opportunity for obtaining further knowledge from the priests and Levites, who could be found at the sanctuary and in the towns assigned to them throughout the land, and who occasionally itinerated for the purpose of publicly teaching the statutes of the law (Lev. x. 11; 2 Chron. xvii. 7-10; Hag. ii. 11). Every seven years, at the feast of tabernacles, the law was read publicly in the audience of assembled Israel (Deut. xxxi. 10-13). The great festivals themselves, and songs written for the purpose (19, 30; xxxii. 1-43), kept alive the knowledge of those events at the birth of the nation which obligated the Israelites as a people to serve Jehovah, their redeemer and bountiful benefactor. The prophets by their public preaching spread religious knowledge and quickened religious life. Business negotiations and legal processes were conducted in the open street, affording constant instruction to the public through eye and ear. Reading and writing were perhaps not uncommon among the young (Judg. viii. 14; Is. x. 19).

In the Greco-Roman period the education of the young was carefully attended to (con. Apion. i. 12; ii. 19). Elementary schools were established in connection with the synagogues, where the children were taught to read from the Scriptures, to write, and to cipher. About 75 B. C. attendance upon this primary instruction was made compulsory, and under Gamaliel the age for attendance was fixed at six years. Slaves and others were employed as tutors by the wealthy (Antiq. xvi. 8, 3). The scribes also imparted advanced instruction. The subject which they discussed was

727 — Schoolmaster/Scourge

the law. Chambers connected with the outer court of the temple, and outside of Jerusalem a room in the synagogue, were used as lecture rooms (Luke ii. 46). The instruction was nominally free, but it is said that in the time of Herod the Great the porter collected entrance money. Not only was instruction imparted directly to the pupils in these schools, but learned men held public disputations with each other there in the presence of the scholars.

School'mas-ter.

The rendering in Gal. iii. 24, 25, A. V., of the Greek *Paidagōgos*, one who leads a boy, a pedagogue. It is translated tutor in the R. V. of this passage and 1 Cor. iv. 15. The *paidagōgos*, or pedagogue, in a Greek household was a trusted slave, to whose care the children were committed (Life 76; Herod. viii. 75). He always accompanied them when they were out of doors. He was responsible for their personal safety, guarded them from physical evil and bad company, and led them to and from school. The law as a pedagogue led us to Christ. It prepared us to receive him as our Redeemer. It displayed the justice of God and convinced us that we were unrighteous; its threatenings pressed us to seek refuge from the wrath and curse of God; it made apparent the inability of man to obtain salvation by the works of the law; it exhibited the plan of salvation in types and ceremonies and excited to faith in the coming Redeemer (Gal. iii. 24; Rom. iii. 19–21; iv. 15; vii. 7–25).

Sci'ence.

The rendering of the Hebrew *Madda‘* and the Greek *Gnōsis* in Dan. i. 4 and A. V. of 1 Tim. vi. 20. The word is not used in its modern sense. It does not denote knowledge gained by observation of phenomena and systematized. The Hebrew and Greek words mean simply knowledge. The false knowledge spoken of by Paul is the teaching of Judaizing and mystic sects in the apostolic age, which they boastfully claimed to be certain (cp. Col. ii. 8), against which Paul urgently warns men (1 Cor. viii. 1, 7), and which counterfeits the true knowledge which he praised and in which he desired Christians to grow (xii. 8; xiii. 2; Phil. i. 9).

Scor'pi-on.

A small animal with a tail armed with a sting which inflicts great pain (Rev. ix. 5, 10). It was called ‘*aḳrab* by the Hebrews, and *skorpios* by the Greeks. It abounds in Palestine, and is common in the wilderness south of Judah (Deut. viii. 15); see AKRABBIM. Rehoboam threatened to chastise his subjects, not with whips, but with scorpions (1 Kin. xii. 11; 2 Chron. x. 14), which many 'nterpreters think mean whips armed with sharp points to make the lash more severe. The scorpion is a small invertebrate animal of the order *Arachnida*. It is closely akin to the higher spiders, having, like them, eight legs;

but it differs in shape, and in having the poison bag not in proximity to the jaws, but at the extremity of the tail. It has a pair of nippers like the lobster. The tail is long and jointed, and capable of being curled up over the back. The last joint is swollen, contains the venom gland, and is armed with a perforated sting by means of which the poison is discharged. The scorpion feeds principally on beetles and locusts, which it seizes with its nippers and stings to death. Some eight or more species exist in Palestine. The largest is about eight inches long, and black.

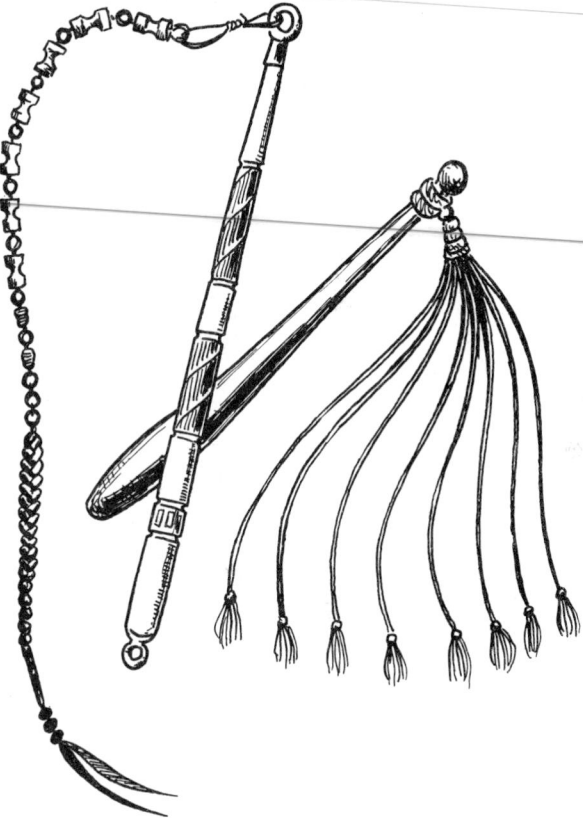

Roman scourges.

Scourge and Scourg'ing.

Scourging is severe punishment or torture by lashing. It was not imposed as a penalty by the Mosaic law, not even according to Lev. xix. 20 (see R. V. against A. V.). The law authorized beating, when the culprit lay down and was smitten on the back (Deut. xxv. 2, 3); but this was not scourging, and is distinguished from scourging (2 Cor. xi. 24, 25). Scourging is perhaps alluded to by Rehoboam as a known punishment (1 Kin. xii. 11, 14), and it was employed by Antiochus Epiphanes to drive the Jews by its tortures to eat swine's flesh (2 Mac. vi. 30; vii. 1). As a legal penalty it was recognized by the later Jewish law, which prescribed beating or scourging for ecclesiastical offenses; such as transgression of ceremonial ordinances for which the Mosaic law did not specify the punishment, disobedience of the orders of the sanhedrin, and heresy. Rods were used for beating (2 Cor. xi. 25); and for scourging a whip was employed, which consisted of three thongs, one of ox hide and two of ass's hide. The number of stripes ranged from a few blows up to thirty-nine, this limit being set in order to avoid all danger of exceeding the forty blows allowed by the Mosaic law in corporal punishment (Deut. xxv. 2, 3). When the punishment was inflicted in the synagogue (Mat. x. 17; xxiii. 34), it was administered by the ḥazzan or attendant; but culprits were also beaten before the sanhedrin (Acts v. 40).

The Romans used a scourge of cords or thongs, made more painful by various expedients which cruelty suggested. Pieces of lead or brass, or small, sharp-pointed bones, were attached to the lashes. The Romans employed scourging as a punishment or as torture to extract confession or testimony. After the Porcian law of 248 B. C. and the Sempronian law of 123 B. C., Roman citizens were exempted from scourging (Livy x. 9); but free persons not Roman citizens might be beaten, and slaves scourged, and lawless governors did not scruple to scourge free provincials and Roman citizens (War ii. 14, 9; Tacitus, Hist. iv. 27). Criminals condemned to crucifixion were ordinarily scourged before being executed (Livy xxxiii. 36); so Jesus, and many of the Jews before the revolt and after the siege of Jerusalem by the Romans (Mat. xxvii. 26; War ii. 14, 9; v. 11, 1). The victim was stripped to the waist, and bound in a stooping position, with the hands behind the back, to a post or pillar. The suffering under the lash was intense. The body was frightfully lacerated. The Christian martyrs at Smyrna about A. D. 155 were so torn with the scourges that their veins were laid bare, and the inner muscles and sinews, and even the bowels, were exposed (Eusebius, Hist. iv. 15).

Screech Owl.

The rendering of the Hebrew *Lilith*, a nocturnal being (Is. xxxiv. 14; in R. V. night monster). It frequents the ruins of cities. Tristram believes it to be the tawny owl (*Syrnium aluco*), which is found in Gilead, Bashan, Lebanon, and the valley of the Jordan, breaking in on the stillness of night with its hooting. See NIGHT MONSTER and SATYR.

Scribe.

1. A public writer (Ezek. ix. 2), who was employed as an amanuensis to write at dictation (Jer. xxxvi. 4. 18, 32), and to draw up legal documents (xxxii. 12, probably).

2. A secretary; a government or other clerk (2 Kin. xii. 10; Ezra iv. 8). Levites were employed as scribes for the business of repairing the temple (2 Chron. xxxiv. 13).

3. A copier of the law and other parts of the Scriptures (Jer. viii. 8). The most noted of these earlier scribes was the priest Ezra, who was a ready scribe in the law of Moses, and had set his heart to seek the law of the Lord and to do it, and to teach in Israel statutes and judgments (Ezra vii. 6, 10). In this latter respect he is the prototype of the scribes of later times, who were professional interpreters of the law. In the N. T. they are called *grammateis*, or more exactly *nomikoi*, rendered lawyers, and *nomodidaskaloi*, teachers of the law. They devoted themselves: 1. To the study and interpretation of the law, which it will be remembered was both civil and religious; and to determining its application to the details of daily life. The decisions of the great scribes became the oral law or tradition. 2. To the study of the Scriptures generally in regard to historical and doctrinal matters. 3. To teaching, each noted scribe having a company of disciples about him; see SCHOOL. The profession of scribe received a great impulse after the return of the Jews from exile, when prophecy had ceased and it only remained to study the completed Scriptures and make them the basis of the national life. The scribes were becoming numerous in the Maccabæan period (1 Mac. vii. 12), and at the time of Christ had attained paramount influence among the people. The sanhedrin counted many of them among its members (Mat. xvi. 21; xxvi. 3). Though there were candid men among them who believed in Christ's teaching (viii. 19), yet the mass of them were hopelessly prejudiced against him. They murmured at or found fault with much that he and his disciples said or did (xxi. 15), and they had a large share in the responsibility for his death. They were also associated with the rulers and elders in the persecution of Peter and John (Acts iv. 5, etc.), and in that which led to the martyrdom of Stephen (vi. 12); but the section of them which agreed with the Pharisees in opinion took Paul's part with respect to the resurrection (xxiii. 9).

Scrip.

A bag or wallet for carrying provisions or articles required on a journey (Mat. x. 10, in R. V. wallet). The scrip of modern Palestine is the skin of a kid stripped off whole from the carcass and tanned, and slung from the shoulder by straps. Every shepherd and farmer has such an article. David when a shepherd carried one (1 Sam. xvii. 40).

Scrip'ture.

A writing, a narrative or other matter committed to writing (Dan. x. 21, in R. V. writing); especially the sacred writings of the Hebrews, viewed either collectively or individually, or even a single passage or quo tation from them, as in Mark xii. 10; xv. 28; Luke iv. 21; John xix. 37. When this collection of sacred documents is thought of as forming one book, the word is singular, the Scripture (John vii. 42; x. 35; xvii. 12; xix. 28; Gal. iii. 22). More frequently the many documents from different authors which constitute the O. T. are in mind and the plural is used, the Scriptures (Mat. xxi. 42; Luke xxiv. 27; John v. 39; Rom. i. 2). The epistles of Paul at once took their place with the other Scriptures as authoritative (2 Pet. iii. 16). See CANON, INSPIRATION.

Scyth′i-an.

A native of Scythia. This name was applied originally to the region immediately north of the Black Sea, and east of the Carpathian mountains. When the conquests of Alexander the Great revealed the existence of men in Asia like the European Scythians in race, an Asiatic Scythia began to be recognized; and finally, all northeastern Europe and central and northern Asia were supposed to be traversed by the nomad Scythian race. They were far behind in civilization; so that at last the name Scythian was used as we now use Tartar, or the Greeks and Romans used the term Barbarian (2 Mac. iv. 47; Col. iii. 11); see BETH-SHEAN.

Sea.

1. The ocean or general gathering of the waters, as distinguished from the dry land of the globe (Gen. i. 10; Ps. viii. 8; Rev. vii. 1–3; xxi. 1).

2. A more or less detached portion of that ocean (Gen. xlix. 13; Acts x. 6), or a large inland lake of fresh or salt water (Num. xxxiv. 11, 12; Mat. iv. 18). The chief seas with which the Israelites had to do were the Mediterranean, the Red Sea, the Dead Sea, and the sea of Galilee. The Mediterranean was referred to as the sea, or was called the great sea, the sea of the Philistines, the hinder or western sea, in A. V. the utmost and uttermost sea; see MEDITERRANEAN SEA. The Dead Sea was variously known as the Salt Sea, the eastern sea, sea of the Arabah or the plain, and according to A. V. of Zech. xiv. 8, the former sea; see DEAD SEA. The sea of Galilee was also named the sea of Chinnereth, lake of Gennesaret, and sea of Tiberias; see GALILEE, SEA OF.

3. A large river with its network of branches, channels, and irrigating canals, as the Euphrates (Jer. li. 36, 42) and the Nile (Nah. iii. 8).

4. The large basin in Solomon's temple where the priests washed their hands and feet preparatory to ministering in the sanctuary or at the altar (1 Kin. vii. 39); see MOLTEN SEA.

Sea Mew.

The rendering in R. V. of Lev. xi. 16 and Deut. xiv. 15 of the Hebrew noun *Shaḥaph*, a bird ceremonially unclean. The A. V. makes it the cuckoo. The Septuagint and Vulgate regard it as a sea mew or gull. Sea mew is an indefinite term, broad enough to include gulls, terns, and petrels, all of which abound on the shore and lakes of Palestine. If any single species is meant, perhaps it is the *Sterna fluviatilis*, the common tern, or sea swallow. This bird looks lean, which the name *shaḥaph* may denote; and it might be included under the designation sea mew, for the *Sterninæ*, or terns, are a sub-family of the *Laridæ*, or gulls. It is plentiful along the shores of Palestine.

Sea Mon′ster.

Any great fish of the sea (Gen. i. 21; Job vii. 12; in A. V. whale). It is the rendering of the Hebrew *Tannin*. See DRAGON. In Lam. iv. 3, the Hebrew *tannin*, although it is singular number, stands in the Hebrew before a plural verb. It is doubtless a copyist's error for *tannim*, jackals. This reading is adopted by the R. V.

Seal.

1. The rendering of the Hebrew *Taḥash* in R. V., with porpoise on the margin (Ex. xxvi. 14; xxxv. 7; Num. iv. 25; Ezek. xvi. 10); in A. V. badger. Its skin was used for the outer covering of the tabernacle and for sandals. *Taḥash* corresponds to the Arabic *tuḥas*, which embraces seals and specially denotes the dugong (*Halicore hemprichii*). The latter belongs to the order *Sirenia*, of which the nearest allies are mammals of the whale order. It is generally ten to twelve feet long, with a round head, breasts for suckling its young, and a fish-like tail. The color is slaty above and white below. It is believed to be one of the animals, if not indeed the animal, which gave rise to the fabled mermaid, half woman, half fish. It is common among the coral banks of the Red Sea, whence it extends as far as the coasts of Australia.

2. A signet ring or cylinder, engraven with the owner's name or some design, or both (Ex. xxviii. 11: Esth. viii. 8). It was worn on the finger, if a ring, or was strung on a cord and hung around the neck (Gen. xxxviii. 18, R. V.; Jer. xxii. 24). Men affixed their seal as signature to letters or other documents (1 Kin. xxi. 8; Neh. ix. 38; Esth. viii. 8; Jer. xxxii. 10, 44; John iii. 33). These were usually written on clay, and the seal was pressed on the soft material and left its mark (Job xxxviii. 14). Chests, boxes, tombs, or anything which required to be guarded from being opened, were sealed with the signet of the person who had authority to prohibit intrusion (Job xiv. 17; xli. 15; Dan. vi. 17; Mat. xxvii. 66; Rev. v. 1).

Se′ba.

A Cushite people (Gen. x. 7), who probably dwelt originally in southern Arabia. Seba is associated with Sheba as a remote southern country (Ps. lxxii. 10); and with Egypt and Ethiopia as though in Africa, whither many Cushites migrated (Is. xliii. 3; xlv. 14).

Tombs at Petra near the Siq.

The city of Sela, or Petra, was located in a fertile basin at an elevation of 2700 feet, about fifty miles south of the Dead Sea. It was strategically situated on the important trade route linking the port of Ezion-geber with Ammon and Damascus. Surrounded by precipitous terrain, the area may be entered by a narrow twisting cleft known as the "Siq."

Excavations give evidence of habitation of this area in neolithic times. It was controlled by the Edomites in the thirteenth century B.C. The prophet Obadiah seems to refer to the Edomites dwelling in Petra (Obad. 1:3-4). The Edomites abandoned Petra sometime during the Persian period. In the fourth century B.C. the Nabatu, Red Sea shipping plunderers, established headquarters here. During the first century B.C. the Nabateans reached their peak of creativity. Beautiful monuments, altars, cisterns, and carved obelisks give evidence of their artistic ability.

In 106 A.D. the Roman emperor Trajan incorporated Petra into the Roman empire and the city was reduced in size. Crosses carved on doorways and walls testify to the presence of an active Christian community in Petra during the fifth century.

The Snake Monument on the western perimeter of Petra. There is a high place just opposite the snake monument where sacrifices were offered.

Opposite page:

Top: The Wadi Tubgha at Petra. The mountains of Edom are in the distance.
Bottom, left: The urn tomb, located in the southern part of the city.
Bottom, right: El-Khazneh, the treasury, near the entrance of the Siq to the basin of Petra.

The monastery at Petra.

Josephus identifies Seba with the isle of
Meroë (Antiq. ii. 10, 2). The region so named
is situated between the Nile and its affluent,
the Atbara. It is about 400 miles long by
200 broad. But this district is not called
Seba in Egyptian documents, and was known
to the Hebrews as Cush. Rather then is
Seba identical with the neighboring country
on the Red Sea, possessing the harbor Saba
and the town Sabai.

Se'bam, in A. V. **Shebam**. See SIBMAH.

Se'bat. See SHEBAT.

Sec'a-cah [hedge, inclosure].

A village in the wilderness of Judah (Josh.
xv. 61). Conder places it doubtfully at the
ruin called Sikkeh or Dikkeh, about 2 miles
east of Bethany.

Se'cu, in A. V. **Sechu** [hill, watchtower].

A village near Samuel's town of Ramah (1
Sam. xix. 22), probably in the direction of
Gibeah (9). Conder doubtfully suggests as
its site Shuweikeh, about 3 miles northwest
by north of er-Ram (Ramah 1).

Se-cun'dus [second, secondary; following,
favorable].

A man of Thessalonica who accompanied
Paul from Macedonia int. Asia Minor (Acts
xx. 4).

Seer. See PROPHET.

Se'gub [exalted].

1. The youngest or younger son of Hiel.
He died when his father set up the gates of
Jericho, which he was then fortifying (1
Kin. xvi. 34), completing the fulfillment of
the curse pronounced by Joshua (Josh. vi.
26).

2. Son of Hezron, by a daughter of Machir
(1 Chron. ii. 21, 22).

Se'ir [hairy, shaggy].

1. A land and its inhabitants. Seir was
the mountain range of Edom (Gen. xxxvi.
21; Num. xxiv. 18; Ezek. xxxv. 15). The
original inhabitants of these mountains were
Horites or cave dwellers (Gen. xiv. 6). In
Gen. xxxvi. 20 the original population is
personified as an individual and the tribes
descended from it are classed as children
(cp. Mizraim or Egypt, Gen. x. 6, 13). Seir
is elsewhere used collectively for the people
(Ezek. xxv. 8). Esau took up his abode in
mount Seir (Gen. xxxii. 3), and his descendants dispossessed the Horites (Deut. ii. 12;
Josh. xxiv. 4). A remnant of the Amalekites (1 Sam. xiv. 48; xv. 7; 2 Sam. viii. 12)
took refuge in these mountain fastnesses,
but were finally destroyed by the Simeonites
(1 Chron. iv. 42, 43).

2. A ridge on the border line of the territory of Judah west of Kirjath-jearim (Josh.
xv. 10). It is commonly supposed to be that
on which the village of Saris stands.

Se'i-rah, in A. V. **Se'i-rath** [a hairy animal, she goat]. Applied to a locality, it may
mean shaggy with trees.

A locality in mount Ephraim, probably in

the southeastern part, to which Ehud escaped
after murdering Eglon (Judg. iii. 26).

Se'la, in A. V. once **Selah** (2 Kin. xiv. 7)
[rock].

A place in Edom taken by Amaziah, king
of Judah, and named by him Joktheel (2
Kin. xiv. 7). It is scarcely referred to in
Judg. i. 36; but probably in 2 Chron. xxv.
12; Is. xlii. 11; Obad. 3; and perhaps in Is.
xvi. 1. The inhabitants dwelt high, among
clefts (Obad. 3). These indications point to
the ravine called by the Greeks Petra, which
is simply a translation of the Hebrew Sela.
About 300 B. C. Petra passed from the
Edomites to the Nabathæan Arabs. The
dynasty which now began to rule in Petra
contained several kings of the name of
Aretas, one of whom is mentioned in 2
Cor. xi. 32. The kingdom of the Nabathæans came to an end in A. D. 105 and Arabia
Petræa was made a province of the Roman
empire. See NEBAIOTH. The place was
rediscovered by Burckhardt in 1812, and
has since been visited by various travelers.
It lies in the nook of a deep chasm excavated
by water on the northeastern flank of mount
Hor. The valley, with branching side valleys, may be 4500 feet long by 740 to 1500
broad, and is surrounded on all sides by precipitous sandstone cliffs. The main gorge is
called wady Mûsa, the valley of Moses,
though probably he was never there. A
rivulet traverses it through its whole length.
The variegated colors of the rock—red,
brown, purple, yellow—add to the beauty of
the spot. There are tombs, remains of temples, an amphitheater, a triumphal arch, etc.,
most of them apparently of Roman times.
Besides these, there are tombs and dwelling
houses in the adjacent cliffs, some of which
may be of older date. On the height above,
overlooking the ancient city, is the great
high place; and yet other altars stand on
neighboring lofty sites.

Se'lah [elevation].

A word occurring seventy-one times in
the Psalms, as well as in Hab. iii. 3, 9, 13.
Stainer gives six distinct opinions as to its
meaning: (1) a pause; (2) a repetition, like
da capo; (3) the end of a strophe; (4) a
playing with full power (*fortissimo*); (5) a
bending of the body, an obeisance; and (6)
a short, recurring symphony (*ritornello*). It
probably means an orchestral interlude (cp.
opinion 6) or a change from *piano* to *forte*.

Se-la-ham-mah'le-koth [rock of division
or escapes].

A cliff in the wilderness of Maon. It was
so called because David on one side of the
eminence eluded Saul on the other (1 Sam.
xxiii. 28). Conder points out that about 8
miles east-northeast of Maon there is a
cliff at the wady el-Malâki, a narrow but
deep chasm, impassable except by making a
circuit of many miles. Saul might here have
come near enough to see David, and yet not

have been able to reach the place where David was, except by making a long detour.

Se'led [exultation].

A man of Judah, family of Jerahmeel (1 Chron. ii. 30).

Se-leu'ci-a [relating to Seleucus].

A city on the seacoast of Syria (1 Mac. xi. 8), north of the mouth of the Orontes. It was built on the site of an earlier town by Seleucus Nicator, founder of the Kingdom of Syria, and was the seaport of Antioch, which lay about 20 miles up the river. Pompey made the city free. Paul and Barnabas sailed thence for Cyprus (Acts xiii. 4). At es-Suweidiyeh, about 4 miles to the south, two piers of the harbor are called Paul and Barnabas.

Se-leu'cus.

A king of Syria (1 Mac. vii. 1; 2 Mac. iii. 3), called Philopator. He was son and successor of Antiochus the Great, and reigned from 187–175 B. C., when he was murdered by Heliodorus, one of his courtiers. He was followed on the throne by Antiochus Epiphanes; see ANTIOCHUS. During his father's

Seleucus Philopater.

reign he fought in the disastrous battle of Magnesia. During his own administration he sought to strengthen his kingdom, and was conciliatory toward the Jews; although it is said that he attempted to plunder the temple (2 Mac. iii. 4–40), possibly to help raise the enormous tribute which he was compelled to pay the Romans.

Sem. See SHEM.

Sem-a-chi'ah [Jehovah hath sustained].

A Levite, descendant of the doorkeeper Obed-edom (1 Chron. xxvi. 7).

Sem'e-in, in A. V. SEMEI [Greek from Hebrew Shim'i, Shimei].

An ancestor of Christ, who lived after the time of Zerubbabel (Luke iii. 26).

Sem-it'ic.

The languages which, speaking broadly, were or are vernacular to the descendants of Shem are called Shemitic or Semitic, the former being derived from the Hebrew Shem, and the latter ultimately from the Greek form Sem. The Semitic languages constitute one of the leading families of languages. As not all the descendants of Shem speak these tongues, and some do so who are descended from other

sons of Noah, it has been proposed to call them the Syro-Arabian languages, but the term Semitic holds its place. Doubtless there was at first but one Semitic language, but the separation of the tribes speaking it led ultimately to its divergence into several dialects. In each the roots of the words are nearly always triliteral, the three radical letters being three consonants. Many triliterals appear to be based on preëxisting biliterals; and it is even supposed by some that originally there were but two radical consonants. The various modifications of meaning were produced from these roots by the use of vowels, of which three only, a, i, and u, were originally employed: thus the three consonants ḳ, ṣ, r suggest the idea of cutting off, and kaṣar denotes he reaped, k°ṣor reap, ḳôṣer reaper, kaṣîr harvest, kaṣûr reaped. The meaning was also modified by laying stress on certain of the consonants and by means of affixes: thus gadal he became large, giddal he magnified, gaddel magnify, migdal a tower.

The Semitic family of languages falls into two great divisions, northern and southern. The northern division subdivides into an eastern group consisting of the Babylonian and Assyrian; a central group composed of the various dialects of the Aramaic language, embracing Syriac, Neo-Syriac, Mandaitic, and the dialect of the Babylonian Talmud in the east, and in the west Samaritan, the so-called Chaldee of the Bible, Targums, and Jerusalem Talmud, and the dialect of the Palmyrene and Nabathæan inscriptions; and a western group containing Hebrew, Moabite, and Phœnician. The southern division is subdivided into Arabic, Himyaritic or Sabæan of southern Arabia, and Ge'ez or Ethiopic and Amharic of Africa.

Semitic writing is in most of the dialects from right to left: that is, in the other direction from English. Hence the title-page in the Hebrew Bible is at what looks like the end of the volume. From this it reads backward, till it ends at what, if it were English, would be called the beginning of the book.

The intellectual ability of the Semitic race is shown by the place which the Jews take in every Christian country where they settle. Its prowess is also great; but in bygone history, whenever the Semites and the Aryans have encountered each other in war, the contest, however severe and protracted, has in the long run ended in favor of the Aryans. Thus the Aryan-Persian terminated the Semitic-Babylonian empire. Aryan Rome ultimately destroyed Semitic Carthage, and the Aryan warriors of Europe, after a time, set bounds to the Saracen Semites.

Se-na'ah. See HASSENAAH.

Se'neh [thorn bush, bramble].

A sharp rock, one of two which flanked a pass running east and west between Michmash and Gibeah. It was the more southerly of the cliffs, and nearer Gibeah than Michmash. It was between these two rocks that Jonathan and his armor-bearer passed when they were going to surprise the Philistine garrison (1 Sam. xiv. 4, 5). It overlooked the wady Suweinît, about 3½ miles southeast by south of Michmash.

Se′nir, in A. V. twice **Shenir** (Deut. iii. 9; Song iv. 8) [coat of mail].

The Amorite name of Hermon (Deut. iii. 9). In Song iv. 8 Senir and Hermon are distinguished, each probably being a distinct peak of the giant mountain. Fir timber was obtained on Senir (Ezek. xxvii. 5).

Sen-nach′e-rib [the moon-god Sin hath increased the brothers].

A son of Sargon, who succeeded to the Assyrian throne on the murder of his father, on the 12th of Ab, 705 B. C. Though a warrior, he was inferior to Sargon in ability. He was boastful, cruel, and not wise enough to perpetuate his conquests by conciliating those whom he had vanquished. On his accession Merodach-baladan of Babylon attempted to throw off the Assyrian yoke. Sennacherib defeated him and his ally, the king of Elam, placed Belibni on the Babylonian throne, and returned in triumph to Nineveh, laden with captives and spoil. Discontent and rebellion manifested themselves in the west also, among the peoples who had submitted to Sargon. To quell this revolt, Sennacherib in 701 appeared in Phœnicia, capturing Great and Little Zidon, Zarephath, Achzib, and Accho, but Tyre appears to have held out. Neighboring states hastened to announce their submission. Proceeding to the Philistine country, he took Ashkelon, Beth-dagon, and Joppa. Next he invested and captured Lachish, sent a detachment of his troops to Jerusalem, secured the release of the dethroned king of Ekron from Jerusalem, defeated the combined armies of Egypt and Ethiopia at the battle of Eltekeh, and added Ekron to his conquests. On this campaign he not only took Lachish and Eltekeh, cities of Judah, but by his own account took 46 fortified towns of Judah, carried away 200,150 people captive, and seized multitudes of horses, mules, asses, camels, and sheep. His career of conquest was cut short by the plague, which devastated his army and compelled him to return to Nineveh. No express mention is, of course, to be expected in the Assyrian inscriptions of his failure to possess himself of Jerusalem, but it is clearly implied; for he is unable to tell of the capture of the city, and he apparently covers up the inglorious conclusion of the campaign by placing at the close of his narrative the account of the tribute which he received from Hezekiah. Here is his own account of the matter: "Hezekiah himself I shut up like a bird in a cage in Jerusalem, his royal city. I erected fortifications against him and blocked the exits from the gate of his city. I severed his towns, which I plundered, from his dominions and gave them to Mitinti, king of Ashdod, Padi, king of Ekron, and Ṣilbel, king of Gaza. Thus I diminished his country. To the former contribution, their annual gift, I added the tribute of subjection to my sovereignty and imposed it on them. The fear of the glory of my sovereignty overwhelmed him, even Hezekiah; and he sent after me to Nineveh, my royal city, the Arabs and his loyal subjects, whom he had brought for the defense of Jerusalem, his royal city, and had furnished with pay, along with thirty talents of gold, 800 talents of pure silver, precious stones, couches of ivory, thrones of ivory, elephants' hides, ivory, rare woods of various kinds, a vast treasure, as well as his daughters, the women of his palace, and others; and he sent his ambassador to offer homage." A story was told the Greek historian Herodotus by the Egyptian priests that Sennacherib advanced

Baked clay prism, dating back to 686 B.C. inscribed with the annals of Sennacherib. The tablet gives his version of the siege of Jerusalem under King Hezekiah.

against Egypt, and had reached Pelusium, when immense numbers of field mice destroyed the bowstrings of the Assyrians, who next morning commenced their flight from the country. For the series of historic events in which Sennacherib and Hezekiah figure as antagonists, see HEZEKIAH. Sennacherib's failure against Jerusalem was in 701 B. C. In the meantime new troubles for Sennacherib arose in Babylonia; and in the third year of Belibni, in 700 B. C. the Assyrian king marched to the south, removed Belibni, and placed his own son Ashurnadinshum on the throne. Freed from concern for the south Sennacherib next turned his attention to the northwest and brought Cilicia under the Assyrian yoke. In 694 he made a novel expedition by ship and attempted to root out the followers of Merodach-baladan from their last refuge, at the mouth of the Ulai.

The campaign was in a measure successful; but the Elamites invaded Babylonia, seized Ashurnadinshum, and placed a Babylonian king on the throne, who held the country for a year and a half. But though Sennacherib took Erech, captured the Babylonian king, and devastated Elam, yet another Babylonian king ascended the throne, and the Assyrians did not succeed in finally chastising Babylonia until 689. Then Sennacherib advanced against Babylon, captured and plundered the city, massacred the inhabitants, fired the buildings, razed the walls and temples, and flooded the ruins with water from the Euphrates and its canals. The last eight years of his reign were mostly peaceful. He had some time before surrounded Nineveh with a wall, 8 miles in circumference. About 695 B. C. he finished a great palace which he had built for himself in the northwestern part of Nineveh. It was 1500 feet long and 700 broad, with great courts, halls, and chambers. He restored another palace, and constructed a system of canals by which he brought good drinking water to the city. After a reign of twenty-four years and five months, he was assassinated on the 20th of Tebet, which possibly fell at the close of 681, but more probably corresponds with January, 680. The deed was done by two of his sons, Adrammelech and Sharezer, who were excited against him because his favorite in the family was another brother, Esarhaddon (2 Kin. xix. 37; 2 Chron. xxxii. 21).

Se-nu'ah. See HASSENUAH.

Se-o'rim [barley].

A descendant of Aaron. His family had grown to a father's house in the time of David, and constituted the fourth course when David distributed the priests into divisions (1 Chron. xxiv. 1, 6, 8).

Se'phar [numbering].

A place which formed the limit in one direction of the territory settled by the descendants of Joktan (Gen. x. 30). It was probably in southern Arabia. Despite the first letter, it is commonly identified with Zafâr, which begins with the Arabic pointed za (teth). Two places bore this name. One was a seaport in Hadramaut, near the incense mountain; the other was in southern Yemen, and was the capital of the Himyarite kings.

Seph'a-rad.

This place of captivity of people of Jerusalem (Obad. 20) may be Sardis in Asia Minor.

S-p-r-d the city (Sardis inscription, 5th century B. C.) is Sardis; and Sparda, a district frequently mentioned in Persian inscriptions along with Ionia, Armenia, and Cappadocia, is doubtless identical with Sardis. The name occurs in Assyrian inscriptions as early as the time of Esarhaddon, 680–668 B. C. Perhaps happier is the identification with Shaparda, which Sargon, who transported Israelites to the cities of the Medes (2 Kin. xvii. 6), and boasts of having subjugated Judah, mentions as a district of southwestern Media.

Seph-ar-va'im [twin Sipparas].

A place from which the Assyrians brought colonists to inhabit Samaria (2 Kin. xvii. 24, 31). Not improbably the same town is referred to in xviii. 34 and xix. 13. On the eastern bank of the Euphrates, above Babylon and hard by the border of Mesopotamia stood the famous city of Sippar. It was a seat of the worship of the sun-god, and hence was known as Sippar of Shamash. But Anunit, wife of the god of the sky, was also specially worshiped there, apparently in a distinct section of the city. Hence there was also Sippar of Anunit. The duality of the town sufficiently explains the Hebrew name, which is dual in form and is equivalent to the twin cities of Sippara. It is now called Abu Habba.

Se'phar-vites.

Natives or inhabitants of Sepharvaim (2 Kin. xvii. 31).

Se-phe'la. See SHEPHELAH.

Sep'tu-a-gint. See VERSIONS.

Sep'ul-cher.

The Hebrews, as a rule, buried their dead in caverns, natural or artificial (Gen. xxiii. 9; Is. xxii. 16; Mat. xxvii. 60; John xi. 38), natural caves being often extended by exca-

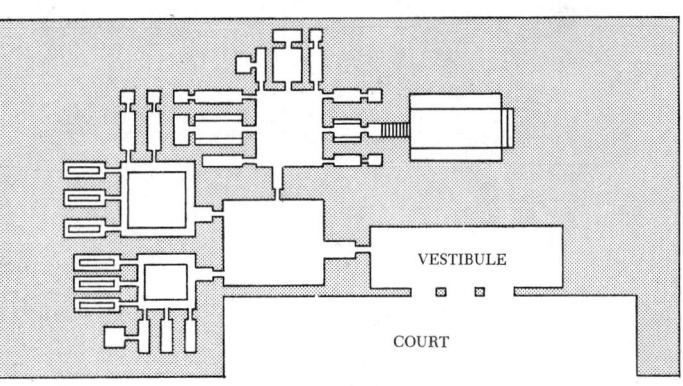

Plan of the Tombs of the Kings.

vation (Gen. l. 5). The cliffs near Jerusalem are full of such sepulchers. The entrance to the cavern or its chambers was closed by a stone (Mat. xxvii. 60) to exclude jackals and other beasts that prey upon dead bodies. It was desirable that the sepulchers should be at a distance from human habitations. They might be in gardens attached to dwellings (2 Kin. xxi. 18, 26), or within the city walls (1 Kin. ii. 10); but they were generally outside the town. Even then trees or gardens might surround them (John xix. 41). Often, however, they were excavated high up in the face of a precipitous cliff, with their entrance far above the ground. Frequently the tomb was whitewashed (Mat. xxiii. 27), not only for cleanliness and beauty, but also that it might be clearly seen and not touched, for the touch brought defilement. Inside the sepulcher the individual grave was sunk in the floor and covered by a slab of stone, or was cut as a niche in the wall, or driven as a shaft into the side of the cavern and closed by a flat stone or door, or a shelf for bodies was hewn around the chamber. Sometimes there were double tiers of niches or shafts. Coffins were not necessary; but occasionally among the wealthy the body was inclosed in a stone sarcophagus, and placed in the tomb. The entrance was sometimes richly ornamented. Sometimes a monument was erected. It might consist of a simple pillar (2 Kin. xxiii. 17, R. V.), or it might assume the form of a mauso-

leum (1 Mac. xiii. 27). The Hebrews and their neighbors were fond of family burial places, and the sepulcher with its chambers and niches was adapted to this purpose (Gen. xlix. 29-31; 2 Sam. ii. 32; 1 Kin. xiii. 22; 1 Mac. ix. 19; xiii. 25). Public burial places were used by the poor and were provided for strangers (2 Kin. xxiii. 6; Jer. xxvi. 23; Mat. xxvii. 7). When the Palestine explorers found a grave dug down in the ground and covered with earth, they assumed it to be a Christian tomb; but if they found one running horizontally into a cliff, they presumed it to be Jewish. See GRAVE.

Sep′ul-cher, Ho′ly. See CALVARY.

Sep′ul-chers of the Kings, or of Da′vid.

The royal burial place in the city of David, not far from the king's garden and the pool of Shelah (1 Kin. ii. 10; 2 Chron. xxi. 20; Neh. iii. 15, 16), and doubtless in the field of burial which belonged to the kings (2 Chron. xxvi. 23; cp. 2 Kin. xv. 7). Theodoret quotes Josephus as saying that the tomb is near Siloam, is in fashion like a cave, and reveals the royal lavishness (Quæst. 6 in iii. Reg.). It consisted of several chambers (Antiq. vii. 15, 3). It was robbed of large treasure by John Hyrcanus; and the report of the sum which that prince had obtained led Herod the Great to search it, in the hope of securing additional

Entrance to Tombs of the Kings, Jerusalem.

plunder; but he became frightened, abandoned the search, and erected a propitiatory monument of white stone at its mouth (ibid.; xiii. 8, 4; xvi. 7, 1; War i. 2, 5). It was extant in the time of Christ (Acts ii. 29). All the kings from David to Hezekiah inclusive were buried in the city of David. The common royal sepulcher was by implication ordinarily used; but Asa and probably Hezekiah had tombs of their own (2 Chron. xvi. 14; xxxii. 33, R. V.), and Jehoram, Joash, Uzziah, and Ahaz were not admitted to the royal sepulcher (xxi. 20; xxiv. 25; xxvi. 23; xxviii. 27). Manasseh, Amon, and Josiah were buried at Jerusalem in their own tombs (2 Kin. xxi. 18, 26; xxiii. 30 with 2 Chron. xxxv. 24). Jehoahaz died in Egypt, and Jehoiachin and Zedekiah doubtless in Babylonia. Jehoiakim was probably left unburied.

The caverns of the kings, which are referred to by Josephus (War v. 4, 2), may be what is now known as the grotto of Jeremiah.

Se'rah, in A. V. once **Sarah** (Num. xxvi. 46) [abundance].

A daughter of Asher (Gen. xlvi. 17; 1 Chron. vii. 30).

Se-ra'iah [soldier of Jehovah]

1. A son of Kenaz (1 Chron. iv. 13).

2. A scribe who had held office under David (2 Sam. viii. 17); see SHAVSHA.

3. A Simeonite, son of Asiel (1 Chron. iv. 35).

4. One of those sent to arrest Baruch the scribe and Jeremiah the prophet (Jer. xxxvi. 26).

5. The chief priest when Nebuchadnezzar captured Jerusalem. He was put to death by Nebuchadnezzar at Riblah (2 Kin. xxv. 18–21; Jer. lii. 24–27). He was the father of Jehozadak, who was carried into captivity; and the grandfather of Jeshua, who was high priest immediately after the exile; and he was also an ancestor of Ezra, the scribe (1 Chron. vi. 14, 15; Ezra iii. 2; vii. 1).

6. "A quiet prince," or "the chief chamberlain," or the "quartermaster," the son of Neriah. He was carried captive to Babylon (Jer. li. 59–64, A. V., R. V., and margin).

7. The son of Tanhumeth, a Netophathite (2 Kin. xxv. 23; Jer. xl. 8).

8. One of those who accompanied Zerubbabel from Babylon (Ezra ii. 2). Called in Neh. vii. 7 Azariah.

9. A chief of the priests who returned from Babylon with Zerubbabel (Neh. xii. 1, 7). A father's house bore his name in the next generation (ver. 12). Possibly the same as number 8.

10. A priest, doubtless head of a father's house and probably of the father's house just mentioned, who with Nehemiah signed the covenant to keep separate from the heathen and observe the law of God (Neh. x. 2). Probably also he is identical with the following.

11. A priest, son of Hilkiah and ruler of the house of God after the exile (Neh. xi. 11; cp. the preceding). The name Azariah occurs in the corresponding place in 1 Chron. ix. 11. Different persons are probably intended, of whom Azariah lived before and Seraiah after the exile. Possibly, however, different persons are intended, each of whom lived after the exile, Azariah being a predecessor of Seraiah. Or the text may be corrupt; in one of the passages the name may have been misread by a copyist; or as both names belong to the high-priestly genealogy and succeed each other there (1 Chron. vi. 12–15), something may have slipped from the text, as, for example: "Seraiah, son of" may have been lost before Azariah in Chronicles, or "son of Azariah" after Seraiah in Nehemiah.

Ser'a-phim.

Celestial beings who stood before the enthroned Lord when he appeared in vision to Isaiah. Each had six wings; with twain he covered his face, and with twain he covered his feet, and with twain he did fly. And one cried unto another, and said: "Holy, holy, holy, is the Lord of hosts: the whole earth is full of his glory" (Is. vi. 2, 3). The prophet having confessed his sinfulness, one of the seraphim flew unto him, having a live coal in his hand, which he had taken with the tongs from off the altar; and he touched the prophet's mouth with it, and said: "Lo, this hath touched thy lips; and thine iniquity is taken away, and thy sin purged."

Scripture affords no further information regarding the seraphim. They are mentioned in this one passage only. What were they? 1. Gesenius derives their name from the Arabic *sharafa*, high, noble. The Arabic root would regularly be *saraph* in Hebrew; but there is no evidence that it was ever used by the Hebrews. No other word in Hebrew is traceable to this root. Gesenius has sought his derivation outside of the Hebrew lexicon. These facts stamp his explanation as improbable. 2. Cheyne conjectures that the seraphim are the serpent-like lightning, referring to the fact that *saraph* and *s^eraphim* denote the fiery serpents in the wilderness (Num. xxi. 6, 8; Is. xiv. 29; xxx. 6). But even if the words seraphim and fiery serpent have the same form in the singular number, which is uncertain, and if they are from the same Semitic root, which is probable, they yet need not signify the same beings or similarly shaped beings. Shape is not denoted by the name. The common characteristic, which finds expression in the word, is burning, in the transitive sense; not ardent or glowing beings, but beings that burn things. Nor do the seraphim resemble serpents outwardly, for they have hands, feet, and wings. Cheyne admits that Isaiah did not regard them as animals in form. 3. The seraphim are identical with the Egyptian griffins, *serref* (Dillmann, quoting L. Stern), and were borrowed by the Israelites. If so, they were personifications of natural objects or phenomena; and in the vision of Isaiah they symbolically represent the powers of nature attendant upon nature's Lord (cp. Zech. vi. 1–8, R. V.). 4. They are an order of angels. So the Jews understood. The Targum inserts the word in Ezek. i. 8; Zech. iii. 7. They are consuming beings, who cry "Holy, holy, holy," who are most impressed with the attribute of holiness in God, worship him most fondly in that character, and execute his purposes of holiness in the world (Delitzsch, modified). The conclusive argument in favor of this theory against the third is that their adoration of holiness in God and their employment in the ministry of atonement indicate moral beings, and not physical powers personified.

Se'red [fear].

A son of Zebulun, and founder of a tribal family (Gen. xlvi. 14; Num. xxvi. 26).

Ser'gi-us Pau'lus [Paulus means small, little].

The proconsul of Cyprus, which constituted a senatorial province in Paul's time (Acts xiii. 5–12); see CYPRUS. The inscription on a coin found at ancient Soli, on the northern coast of the island, mentions "Paulus proconsul."

Se'ron [perhaps, a Greek form of Hiram (cp. Herod. vii. 98)].

Commander of the army of Syria (1 Mac. iii. 13) in the reign of Antiochus Epiphanes. He attempted to suppress the revolt of the Jews, but was defeated by Judas Maccabæus near Beth-horon in 166 B. C. (14–24). Josephus states that Seron lost his life in the battle (Antiq. xii. 7, 1).

Ser'pent.

1. An animal which creeps on its belly (Gen. iii. 1, 14); having head, tail, and body (15; Ex. iv. 4), but no limbs. It is generically called *naḥash* in Hebrew, *ophis* in Greek (Gen. iii. 13 with 2 Cor. xi. 3; Num. xxi. 9 with John iii. 14). As it wriggles along, its mouth is apt to come in contact with the dust, which it licks (Mic. vii. 17; cp. Gen. iii. 14; Is. lxv. 25). The bite of some species infuses fatal poison into the wound (Num. xxi. 6; Ps. lviii. 4; Prov. xxiii. 32). Some can be charmed (Ecc. x. 11). The serpent is found in the wilderness and in inhabited districts, by the road, in hedges, on rocks, in walls (Gen. xlix. 17; Num. xxi. 6; Prov. xxx. 19; Ecc. x. 8; Amos v. 19).

The fiery serpents which bit the children of Israel in the wilderness and caused death (Num. xxi. 6), were a kind of snake found in Arabia and elsewhere, whose bite produces the fiery burning of inflammation and thirst. See BRAZEN SERPENT.

The serpent of the temptation was an ordinary snake, one of the beasts of the field, comparable with them in subtlety and skill in securing prey, and, after it was involved in the temptation of man, cursed among them (Gen. iii. 1, 14). Perhaps Eve saw nothing more than a snake; but the devil was in this serpent, as afterwards the demons were in men and in the swine, controlling it, lending it supernatural subtlety, and using it as a means by which to approach Eve (Wisd. ii. 24; John viii. 44; Rom. xvi. 20; 2 Cor. xi. 3; Rev. xii. 9); see SATAN. It suffered in the punishment, as did other innocent animals when made the instruments of sin (Lev. xx. 15, 16). Its mode of locomotion was not new, it had doubtless always crept; but now this groveling on the earth and accidental swallowing of dust is made the memorial of its degradation. It does not suffer thereby, save as it is loathed and killed by man. But the more distinctly man recognizes that the evil spirit was the serpent's master, the more does man transfer his enmity to the archfiend.

2. A species of serpent, in Hebrew *pethen* (Ps. xci. 13, in E. V. adder). See ASP.

Se'rug, in A. V. of N. T. **Saruch** [shoot, branch].

Son of Reu, father of Nahor, and ancestor of Abraham (Gen. xi. 20, 23; 1 Chron. i. 26; Luke iii. 35).

Serv'ant.

One who serves, in Hebrew usually *'ebed*. It is a general term, including voluntary and involuntary service, and embracing all who are under obligation of any kind to render service to another, from the slave captured in war or purchased at a price, to the envied official of a king and the willing worshiper of God (Gen. xxxix. 1 with xli. 12; xl. 20; Ex. xxxii. 13; Acts xvi. 17). It is systematically employed by orientals when addressing a superior, whether man or God (Gen. xxxii. 4, 20; l. 18; Deut. iii. 24; 2 Sam. ix. 2; Luke ii. 29; Acts iv. 29); and is applied to conquered nations compelled to pay tribute to their conqueror (2 Sam. viii. 2). God also designates his worshipers servants (Gen. xxvi. 24; Num. xii. 7; 2 Sam. vii. 5). See MINISTER, SLAVE.

Ser'vant of Je-ho'vah.

One who acknowledges Jehovah as his God and, by implication of the term, faithfully performs his will; as Abraham (Ps. cv. 6), Moses (26), David (cxxxii. 10), Isaiah (Is. xx. 3).

The prominent figure in Is. xl.–lxvi. The view most widely entertained by modern commentators is that the servant of the Lord in these chapters is Israel, the eye of the prophet being fixed sometimes on the nation as a whole, sometimes on the godly portion, sometimes on that perfect representative of Israel, that Israelite indeed, Christ. Against other views there may be urged: 1. The servant of chapter liii. is interpreted by the Jewish Targums as Messiah. 2. The prophet Zechariah apparently identifies the Branch, a familiar designation of Messiah, with the servant whereby the iniquity of the land is taken away (Zech. iii. 8–10; cp. Jer. xxiii. 5–8). 3. The description of the suffering servant of chapter liii. actually finds its counterpart in Christ.

The interpreter of Is. liii. must be ever mindful of certain controlling facts: 1. When this chapter was penned, the Hebrews were fully acquainted with the sense of guilt (Gen. xxxix. 9; 2 Sam. xii. 5–13; Is. vi. 5–7; cp. Pss. xxxii. and li.). 2. The godly among the Israelites recognized themselves as sinful and as involved in the guilt of the nation, in its disobedience to God's law and in its failure to fulfil the purpose of its selection to be God's servant among men. Israel's best men felt this truth keenly (Neh. i. 6, 7; Dan. ix. 5–11, 20). Israel was a unit, a solidarity: the sin of a part of the people involved all in guilt (Deut. xxi. 1, 7, 8; Josh. vii. 1, 11, 13, 15, 25; Judg. xx. 6, 10, 13). 3. When this chapter, Is. liii., was written, the Israelites were familiar with the symbolism of atonement. Those critics who regard this prophecy as an utterance of Isaiah as a rule believe that the book of Leviticus had been in existence for centuries, while those who accept this chapter as a product of the exilic times hold it to be later than Ezekiel and written after the sacrificial system had long been in operation. The prophecy was uttered when the truths were well known that God might pardon after sufficient punishment had been inflicted (Is. xl. 2), yet the mere punishment of sin or compensation for an injury does not cleanse the sinner. Punishment and restitution and cleansing are required (Is. iv. 3, 4; vi. 6, 7; liii. 10; Lev. v. 14–16; Num. v. 5–8; Ps. li. 2, 7). 4. The doctrine of substitution was also known. It pervades the chapter (verses 5, 6, 11, 12). It was publicly illustrated on the annual day of atonement (Lev. xvi. 20–22). 5. To fulfil these conditions and satisfy the creed of Israel, the servant of Jehovah must be of sufficient worth to be substituted for Israel, must be identical with Israel in order that he may really represent Israel before God and that it may be said that Israel has actually met its obligations in him; and yet the servant must be distinct from Israel so as not to be involved in Israel's guilt and to have no obligation of service to discharge for himself. These doctrinal requirements point not obscurely to the need of divinity in him who fills the office assigned to the Lord's servant in Is. liii.

Seth, in A. V. once **Sheth** (1 Chron. i. 1) [appointed, substituted].

A son of Adam. He was born after the murder of Abel, for whom to a certain extent he became a substitute (Gen. iv. 25; v. 3). He became the father of Enos, and died at the age of 912 (Gen. v. 6–8; Luke iii. 38).

Se'thur [hidden].

The representative spy from the tribe of Asher (Num. xiii. 13).

Sev'en.

Seven is an ordinary numeral, and it was commonly used without religious significance; but it was also a sacred number among the Hebrews and other Semites, and also among the Aryans of Persia and even of Greece (Iliad xix. 243). Its sacredness is traceable to remote antiquity. It is seen in the seven pillars of wisdom's house (Prov. ix. 1), the seven locks into which Samson, who was consecrated to God, braided his hair (Judg. xvi. 13, 19), the seven victims to atone for the broken covenant (2 Sam. xxi. 6, 9), the seven stones of the ancient Arabs smeared with the blood of the covenanting parties (Herod. iii. 8), the seven lambs to attest the conclusion of a treaty (Gen. xxi. 28–30), the Hebrew words for oath and taking an oath, which incorporate the number seven, and the sacredness of the seventh portion of time. The idea that seven derived its sacred character from the fact that three plus four make seven, is pure fancy. It was sacred because men saw that God recognized the number. He placed seven luminaries in the sky, sun, moon, and five planets. He caused the moon to phase every seven days. These phenomena, however, were but confirmatory and served as reminders of a greater recognition. God had blessed the seventh day and hallowed it. Far more was needed than the signs of the sky to originate the sacredness of seven. Twelve did not become a sacred number, although God made the moon to mark off twelve months in the year, placed twelve starry signs in the zodiac, and made the sun to conform its course to the zodiac and to return in spring as nearly at the conclusion of twelve lunar months as the moon renews itself after four phasings. Man noted these phenomena in the earliest times, adopted them into his daily life and language, and celebrated certain of them with religious festivals. In Babylonia man even made twelve the basis of an arithmetical system, and in Assyria his pantheon contained twelve great gods. Notwithstanding all this, twelve did not become a sacred number; but seven did become a sacred number, and the seventh portion of time a sacred season; and not merely was the recurring seventh portion of time sacred, but it involved a benediction. It was cherished in hoary antiquity as a season of divine favor toward man, when the manifestation of God's good will was to be expected. See SABBATH.

Se-ve'neh, in A. V. **Sy-e'ne** [Egyptian *sun,* affording entrance].

A town constituting the extreme limit of Egypt in one direction. Which direction depends on the translation of Ezek. xxix. 10; xxx. 6. If, as is probable, the preferable rendering is that of the margin, "from Migdol to Syene," then the town of Seveneh is in the south of Egypt, on the borders of Ethiopia, and is the Roman Syene, the modern Assouan, on the Egyptian side of the first cataract, where a few remains of the ancient city exist. Here, or on the island hard by, the border garrison was stationed (Herod. ii. 30). On the island, as early as the time of the Persian conquest of Egypt, a Jewish colony maintained a temple to Jehovah (Elephantine papyri); see ALTAR.

Sha-al′bim, once **Sha-al-ab′bin** (Josh. xix. 42) [foxes].

An Amorite city within the territory of Dan (Josh. xix 42), which the Amorites did not yield (Judg. i. 35) until some time after the settlement of the Hebrews in the land (1 Kin. iv. 9). Not identified. Selbit, 3 miles northwest of Aijalon, has little in its favor.

Sha-al′bo-nite.

A native or inhabitant either of an unknown town called Shaalbon, or more probably of Shaalbim (2 Sam. xxiii. 32; 1 Chron. xi. 33).

Sha′a-lim, in A. V. **Sha′lim** [foxes].

A district apparently in Ephraim, through which Saul, on leaving the land of Shalishah, passed in quest of his father's asses (1 Sam. ix. 4). Situation unknown.

Sha′aph.

1. A son of Jahdai, included in the registry of Caleb (1 Chron. ii. 47).

2. A son of Caleb by his concubine Maachah. He was ancestor of the inhabitants of Madmannah (1 Chron. ii. 49).

Sha-a-ra′im, in A. V. once **Sharaim** [two gates].

1. A town in the lowland of Judah (Josh. xv. 36), apparently west of Socoh and Azekah (1 Sam. xvii. 52 with 1). Not identified. Sa'ireh among the hills, 5 miles northeast by north of Socoh, has not the proper location; and the tell and village of Zakariya, on either side of wady es-Sunt and about 2½ miles to the northwest of Socoh, have only one consonant in common with Shaaraim, and besides appear to be named after the prophet Zechariah, whose grave is shown there.

2. A town of Simeon (1 Chron. iv. 31); see SHARUHEN.

Sha-ash′gaz.

A chamberlain of king Ahasuerus (Esth. ii. 14).

Shab′be-thai [pertaining to the Sabbath].

A chief Levite, prominent in Ezra's time (Ezra x. 15; Neh. viii. 7; xi. 16).

Sha-chi′a.

A Benjamite, son of Shaharaim (1 Chron. viii. 10).

Sha′drach [probably Babylonian, *Shudur-aku*, decree of the moon-god].

The name given by the prince of the eunuchs at Babylon to Hananiah, one of the three faithful Hebrews afterwards miraculously saved from the fiery furnace (Dan. i. 7; iii. 12–30).

Sha′ge-e, in A. V. **Shage** [wandering].

A Hararite, the father of one of David's mighty men (1 Chron. xi. 34). Some expositors would read Agee instead of Shage, on the ground of 2 Sam. xxiii. 11. The more appropriate comparison with 2 Sam. xxiii. 32, 33, and the reading of Lucian's recension of the Septuagint render more probable the conjecture that the name is really Shammah; see SHAMMAH 4.

Sha-ha-ra′im [the double dawning].

A Benjamite, who had numerous descendants (1 Chron. viii. 8).

Sha-haz′u-mah, in A. V. **Sha-haz′i-mah**, as in Hebrew margin [not improbably, lofty places].

A town on the border of Issachar (Josh. xix. 22). Situation unknown.

Sha′lem [entire, safe].

A town near Shechem (Gen. xxxiii. 18), according to the Greek, Latin, and Syriac versions, followed by A. V. It is scarcely Salem (Gen. xiv. 18), for that town is probably Jerusalem; nor Salim, 4 miles east of Shechem, which is not mentioned in the O. T. The word is probably a common noun, to be rendered, with R. V., in peace or safety.

Sha′lim. See SHAALIM.

Shal′i-shah, in A. V. **Shalisha** [a third part].

A district apparently in the hill country of Ephraim, traversed by Saul in quest of his father's asses (1 Sam. ix. 4). Its situation is unknown. It does not seem to be the same as Baal-shalishah.

Shal′le-cheth [casting out].

A gate of Solomon's temple on the west (1 Chron. xxvi. 16).

Shal′lum [retribution].

1. A son of Naphtali (1 Chron. vii. 13); see SHILLEM.

2. A descendant of Simeon through Shaul (1 Chron. iv. 24, 25).

3. A descendant of Judah through Sisamai (1 Chron. ii. 40, 41).

4. The chief porter at the sanctuary (1 Chron. ix. 17, 18). If before the exile, as is probable, he is mentioned by Jeremiah (Jer. xxxv. 4). He was a son of Kore, a Korhite, and he and his family were keepers of the gates of the sanctuary (1 Chron. ix. 19). The name Shallum may be equivalent to Meshelemiah or Shelemiah (xxvi. 1, 14), whether the registry of chapter ix. be referred to the time before or after the exile. A comparison of ix. 21 with xxvi. 2 raises a strong presumption against the identification. If notwithstanding this, the registry be regarded as post-exilic and Shallum be identified with Shelemiah, then Shallum is not the name of a person, but of the family, in the registry.

5. A son of Jabesh, who murdered king Zechariah and reigned in his stead over the ten tribes, but in a month was himself assassinated by Menahem (2 Kin. xv. 8–15).

6. Father of a certain Jehizkiah (2 Chron. xxviii. 12).

7. A member of the high-priestly family of Zadok, and an ancestor of Ezra. He lived several generations before the capture of Jerusalem by Nebuchadnezzar (1 Chron. vi. 12–15; Ezra vii. 2). Called Meshullam in 1 Chron. ix. 11; see MESHULLAM 4.

8. A son of Tikvah, and the husband of Huldah, the prophetess, and in the reign of Josiah the officer who had charge either of the priests' garments which were kept in the temple or of the king's wardrobe (2 Kin. xxii. 14; 2 Chron. xxxiv. 22).

9. Uncle of Jeremiah, and the father of Hanameel (Jer. xxxii. 7, 8). He was not a member of the high-priestly family, as some have thought; for his son lived at Anathoth, a town where priests of Ithamar's line dwelt (1 Kin. ii. 26), and the high priests of this time belonged to the line of Eleazar.

10. Another name for Jehoahaz, son of Josiah, king of Judah (2 Kin. xxiii. 30–34); see JEHOAHAZ.

11 and 12. A porter of the temple, and a son of Bani, each of whom was induced by Ezra to put away his foreign wife (Ezra x. 24, 42).

13. A son of Hallohesh, ruler of half the district of Jerusalem. With his daughters, he repaired part of the wall of Jerusalem (Neh. iii. 12).

Shal′lun [perhaps, spoliation].

A ruler of part of Mizpah, who repaired the gate of the fountains at Jerusalem (Neh. iii. 15).

Shal′mai. See SALMAI.

Shal′man.

Tiglath-pileser mentions Salamanu of Moab among the various princes who were tributary to him (II. R. 67, 60), and Schrader believes that this person is Shalman, the destroyer of Beth-arbel, to whom Hosea refers (Hos. x. 14), and that Beth-arbel is the town of that name east of the Jordan, near Pella. These identifications may be correct, but they are unsupported. It is not known that Salamanu of Moab invaded the land of Israel, but it is known that Shalmaneser of Assyria did. In the light of present knowledge, it is more natural to regard Shalman as an abbreviation of Shulmanu-asharidu (shortened in 2 Kings to Shalmaneser), and to think of Beth-arbel as being the town of Galilee, from which Shalmaneser's army was certainly not far distant. See SHALMANESER 4.

Shal-ma-ne′ser [Assyrian *Shulmanu-asharidu*, god Shulman is chief].

The name of several Assyrian kings:

1. The builder, or rather rebuilder, and fortifier of the town of Calah (q. v.). He reigned about 1300 B. C.

2. The son of Ashurnaṣirpal. He reigned from about 860 to 825 B. C., and was the first Assyrian king who came into conflict with the Israelites. He was energetic and persistent in purpose. He crossed the Euphrates with hostile intent as early as his first year and wasted the Hittite country as far as the Mediterranean; and he repeatedly crossed the river later, besides waging war in the countries north, east, and south of Nineveh. To resist him in the west, the Syrian league was formed, which included Damascus, Hamath, and the twelve kings of the coast, and was at times reënforced by the soldiers of the neighboring nations. Thus, for instance, the army of Ahab of Israel was found fighting side by side with the men of Damascus against the common Assyrian foe at Karkar in 854 B. C.; see AHAB, BEN-HADAD. Shalmaneser claims to have won the battle of Karkar; but he gained nothing if he did, and at once led his army back to Nineveh. After three years he returned, but his onward course was again stopped by the allies. The following year, the eleventh of his reign, he crossed the Euphrates and plundered many towns of the kingdom of Hamath, but he was again checked. In his fourteenth year he returned and conquered. The power of the league was broken. In his eighteenth year, 842 B. C., he defeated Hazael of Damascus at mount Hermon. The kings of Tyre and Sidon, and Jehu of Israel, in dismay hastened to make submission by sending tribute.

3. King from 783 to 773 B. C. His reign does not touch Hebrew history.

4. Successor of Tiglath-pileser. Before his accession to the throne, and even afterwards, he was known by the name of Ululai, in Greek Iloulaios (Ptolemy's canon). He reigned from the 25th of Tebet, the tenth month, 727 B. C., to the 12th of Tebet, 722 B. C. In 725 he undertook an expedition to foreign parts. According to the Syrian annals cited by Josephus, Shalmaneser overran Phœnicia. On the approach of the Assyrians, Sidon, Acre, and Tyre on the mainland revolted from the dominion of island Tyre and acknowledged the suzerainty of the invader. The Assyrian king thereupon withdrew. He returned, however, to war against the island. His ships, manned by his Phœnician subjects, were scattered by the Tyrians in a naval engagement. After this defeat Shalmaneser marched away, leaving troops enough to maintain a siege of the city, which was sustained for five years (Antiq. ix. 14, 2), when Tyre submitted to Sargon. When Shalmaneser arrived in the west, Hoshea paid him tribute, as he had done to his predecessor, but he soon stopped his payments, relying upon So of Egypt to aid him in fighting the Assyrians, and perhaps encouraged by the stern resistance of Tyre. Shalmaneser promptly had him seized and imprisoned. It is quite probable that Hoshea had gone forth with his troops to oppose Shalmaneser and was defeated and captured; and that this battle took place at the strategic point and noted battleground, Arbela in Galilee. This con-

jecture, which identifies Shalman of Hos. x. 14 with Shalmaneser, is alluring; but it is only conjecture. After seizing the king, whether at Arbela or elsewhere, Shalmaneser laid siege to the capital. Samaria stood this siege for three years and then fell into the hands of the Assyrians (2 Kin. xvii. 1–6; xviii. 9, 10). Whether Shalmaneser was still on the throne or had just been succeeded by Sargon, is still a question; see SARGON.

Black obelisk of Shalmanezer III, a four-sided pillar of black limestone, six and one-half feet high, with twenty small panels in bas relief. In the top panel King Jehu or his representative kneels before Shalmanezer. Other panels portray representatives from different countries bringing tribute to the monarch.

Sha'ma [hearing, or he hath heard].
A son of Hotham, the Aroerite. He was one of David's mighty men (1 Chron. xi. 44).

Sham-a-ri'ah. See SHEMARIAH.

Sha'med. See SHEMED.

Sha'mer. See SHEMER.

Sham'gar.
A son of Anath (Judg. iii. 31). Shortly before the time of Deborah, for fear of the Philistines, travelers avoided the highways and crept along by-paths (v. 6). But Shamgar undertook single-handed a war with the oppressors. Their dead, slain from time to time by his oxgoad, at length amounted to six hundred. He thus saved Israel (iii. 31); but he is not called a judge, and no years are assigned him in the chronology.

Sham'huth [desolation].
An Izrahite, David's captain for the fifth

month (1 Chron. xxvii. 8). Perhaps identical with Shammah, one of David's mighty men. See SHAMMAH 4.

Sha'mir [a thorn].
1. A town in the hill country of Judah (Josh. xv. 48); probably represented by the ruin Sômerah, about 13 miles west-southwest of Hebron.
2. A town in mount Ephraim, which the judge Tola, though a man of Issachar, made his residence, and where he was buried (Judg. x. 1, 2). Site unknown.
3. A Levite, a son of Micah (1 Chron. xxiv. 24).

Sham'ma [desolation].
An Asherite, a son of Zophah (1 Chron. vii. 37).

Sham'mah [desolation].
1. A descendant of Esau and also of Ishmael (Gen. xxxvi. 3, 4, 13, 17). He became a duke of Edom (17).
2. Third son of Jesse, and brother of David (1 Sam. xvi. 9; xvii. 13). See SHIMEA 3.
3. One of David's first three mighty men, a son of Agee, a Hararite (2 Sam. xxiii. 11). Shammah the Hararite is named in ver. 33; and in view of 1 Chron. xi. 34 and textual considerations, is reasonably believed to be this person mentioned again as father of Jonathan. The words in Samuel and Chronicles are to be read: "Jonathan, son of Shammah the Hararite."
4. A Harodite, also one of David's mighty men (2 Sam. xxiii. 25). In 1 Chron. xi. 27 the plural form Shammoth is used. Shamhuth of 1 Chron. xxvii. 8 is perhaps another external and unessential variation of this man's name.

Sham'mai [waste].
1. A son of Onam, house of Jerahmeel, tribe of Judah (1 Chron. ii. 28).
2. A son of Rekem, house of Caleb, tribe of Judah (1 Chron. ii. 44).
3. A son of a certain Ezrah, registered with the tribe of Judah (1 Chron. iv. 17).

Sham'moth [desolations]. See SHAMMAH 4.

Sham-mu'a, in A. V. once **Shammuah** (2 Sam. v. 14) [something heard, fame].
1. The representative from the tribe of Reuben sent to spy the land of Canaan (Num. xiii. 4).
2. A son of David by Bath-sheba, born at Jerusalem (2 Sam. v. 14; 1 Chron. iii. 5); see BATH-SHUA. He bore an uncle's name (ii. 13). In 1 Chron. iii. 5 he is called Shimea; an unessential variant, having the same meaning as Shammua, differing only in the mode of formation.
3. A Levite descended from Jeduthun (Neh. xi. 17).
4. A priest in the days of the high priest Joiakim. He was head of the father's house of Bilgah (Neh. xii. 18).

Sham'she-rai.

A Benjamite, a son of Jeroham (1 Chron. viii. 26).

Sha'pham.

A Gadite dwelling in Bashan (1 Chron. v. 12).

Sha'phan [hyrax, rock badger].

A scribe in the reign of Josiah. When Hilkiah found the book of the law, he gave it to Shaphan, who read it at first privately, and then to the king. Afterwards he was one of those who went to Huldah, the prophetess, to consult her regarding the threatenings contained in the book (2 Kin. xxii. 8-14). He was the father of Ahikam (Jer. xxvi. 24; xxxix. 14), Gemariah (xxxvi. 10), and Jaazaniah (Ezek. viii. 11), and the grandfather of Gedaliah (2 Kin. xxv. 22).

Sha'phat [he hath judged].

1. The representative from the tribe of Simeon who was sent to spy the land of Canaan (Num. xiii. 5).

2. A Gadite in Bashan (1 Chron. v. 12).

3. Son of Adlai, and David's overseer of the herds that were in the valleys (1 Chron. xxvii. 29).

4. Father of the prophet Elisha (1 Kin. xix. 16).

5. A son of Shemaiah, registered with the descendants of David (1 Chron. iii. 22).

Sha'pher. See SHEPHER.

Sha'phir, in A. V. **Saphir** [beautiful].

A town in Judah (Mic. i. 11). Not identified. Robinson and others locate it at es-Suwâfîr, 5 miles southeast of Ashdod.

Sha'rai [perhaps, free].

A son of Bani, induced by Ezra to put away his foreign wife (Ezra x. 40).

Shar'a-im. See SHAARAIM.

Sha'rar [firm].

A Hararite, father of one of David's mighty men (2 Sam. xxiii. 33). Called in 1 Chron. xi. 35 Sacar.

Sha-re'zer, in A. V. **Sherezer** in Zech. vii. 2 [protect the king].

1. A son of Sennacherib. With one of his brothers he murdered his father (2 Kin. xix. 37; Is. xxxvii. 38).

2. A man sent from Bethel to the priests at Jerusalem to inquire whether the fasts should be kept, now that the cause for them no longer existed (Zech. vii. 2).

Shar'on, in A. V. of N. T. **Saron** (Acts ix. 35) [a plain].

1. The seacoast between Joppa and Carmel, and extending back to the hills of Samaria. It was a fertile region (Is. xxxv. 2), a pasture land for flocks (1 Chron. xxvii. 29; Is. lxv. 10); but like a desert when devastated (Is. xxxiii. 9). Among its flowers, lilies and anemones are prominent; see LILY, ROSE. Lydda was at its southern limit (cp. Acts ix. 35). Its length is about 50 miles, its breadth 9 or 10. It is not flat, but agreeably undulated, with here and there groves of oak, and with ex-

cellent pasturage, except that in places thorns and thistles too much abound.

2. A pasture region east of the Jordan (1 Chron. v. 16). Situation undetermined.

Sha-ru'hen.

A village in the territory of Simeon (Josh. xix. 6), apparently the place called Shaaraim (1 Chron. iv. 31) and Shilhim (Josh. xv. 32). The fortified town Sherohan or Sheruhan, on the road from Egypt to Gaza, a place mentioned in the records of Amosis I, Thothmes III, and later Pharaohs, is probably meant.

Sha'shai [whitish, pale].

A son of Bani, induced by Ezra to put away his foreign wife (Ezra x. 40).

Sha'shak.

A Benjamite, a son of Elpaal (1 Chron. viii. 14, 25).

Sha'ul [asked].

1. A king of Edom, from Rehoboth on the Euphrates (Gen. xxxvi. 37, in A. V. Saul; 1 Chron. i. 48).

2. A son of Simeon by a Canaanitish woman (Gen. xlvi. 10; Ex. vi. 15; 1 Chron. i. 48). He founded a tribal family (Num. xxvi. 13).

3. A Kohathite Levite, descended through Korah, Abiasaph, and Tahath (1 Chron. vi. 24).

Sha'veh [a plain].

A valley, afterwards called the king's dale, near Salem, in which the king of Sodom met Abraham after the defeat of Chedorlaomer (Gen. xiv. 17, 18). Absalom reared a memorial pillar for himself there (2 Sam. xviii. 18), which according to Josephus stood about a quarter of a mile from Jerusalem (Antiq. vii. 10, 3).

Sha'veh-kir-i-a-tha'im, in A. V. **Shaveh Kiriathaim** [plain of Kiriathaim].

A plain near the city of Kiriathaim, in the territory afterwards assigned to Reuben. It was at first inhabited by Emim (Gen. xiv. 5). Exact situation unknown.

Shav'sha and **Shisha** [original Hebrew orthography and meaning of name unknown].

A scribe of David and afterwards of Solomon (1 Chron. xviii. 16; 1 Kin. iv. 3). Probably identical with the scribe Seraiah (2 Sam. viii. 17) and doubtless with the scribe Sheva (2 Sam. xx. 25).

She'al [an asking].

A son of Bani induced by Ezra to put away his foreign wife (Ezra x. 29).

She-al'ti-el, in A. V. of 1 Chron. iii. 17 and of N. T. **Salathiel**, the Greek form [I have asked God].

A son of king Jeconiah (1 Chron. iii. 17; Mat. i. 12) and also of Neri (Luke iii. 27). He was the father of Zerubbabel (Ezra iii. 2, etc.), and yet apparently his uncle, or possibly, though not probably, his grandfather (1 Chron. iii. 17-19). The explanation probably is that, while neither the son of Jeconiah nor the father of Zerubbabel after the flesh, he was the legitimate successor of Jeconiah to the royal title, and on his own death the right to the throne passed to Zerubbabel. He is the link in the royal succession connecting Jeconiah with Zerubbabel. See ASSIR, ZE-RUBBABEL, and GENEALOGY II.

She-a-ri'ah [Jehovah hath esteemed].
A descendant of Jonathan (1 Chron. viii. 38).

Shear'ing House.
The place where Jehu slew the forty-two brethren of Ahaziah, king of Judah, who were going to Ahaziah at Samaria while he was on a visit to the wounded king of Israel (2 Kin. x. 12–14). It took its name either from the fact that shepherds there bound the sheep which they were about to shear, or because they were in the habit of meeting there (Targum; R. V. margin). The Hebrew name is *Beth 'eḳed haro'im*, in the Septuagint *Baithakath*. The name perhaps lingers in Beit Kâd, about 3 miles east by north of En-gannim, and about 16 northeast by north of Samaria.

She-ar-ja'shub [a remnant shall return].
A son of Isaiah. His name was designed to embody a prophecy (Is. vii. 3; cp. x. 21).

She'ba, I. [a man].
A Cushite people descended through Raamah and closely related to Dedan (Gen. x. 7), but also classed as a Semitic people descended through Joktan (28) and, like Dedan, from Abraham through Jokshan (xxv. 3). So far as connected with Abraham, they migrated eastward (xxv. 6; cp. Job i. 15; vi. 19). They dwelt in the south (Mat. xii. 42), and traded in gold, incense, and precious stones (1 Kin. x. 1 seq.; Ps. lxxii. 10; Is. lx. 6; Jer. vi. 20; Ezek. xxvii. 22; xxxviii. 13). Sheba was a country and people of southwestern Arabia, well known from its own records and classical geographers. Its capital was Saba, where is now the ruin of Meriaba. The Sabeans were a great commercial people. They traded not only in the products of their own land, but also in those of India and Ethiopia. Their language was Semitic. They spread widely, and have left traces of their name on the eastern coast of Arabia, and in the northern desert along with the Nabathæans. It is readily conceivable that in their dispersion they became mingled with other tribes by intermarriage or attached to them by political relations, and hence they might trace their descent by different lines and be classed variously in a genealogy.

She'ba, II. [seven, an oath].
1. A Simeonite town, mentioned after Beersheba (Josh. xix. 2). Three views are entertained regarding it. 1. Its site may be Tell es-Seb'a, 3 miles east of Beer-sheba. 2. It is a corruption of Shema (cp. Septuagint and xv. 26). 3. Since it is lacking in 1 Chron. iv. 28, and this agrees with the summation in

Josh. xix. 6, it is an abbreviated form of Beer-sheba (see R. V.) or accidentally introduced into the text by dittography.
2. A Benjamite, a son of Bichri. After the collapse of Absalom's rebellion and the concurrence of the ten tribes with Judah in restoring David to his throne, Sheba blew a trumpet, and summoned the ten tribes to renounce their allegiance. He was besieged in Abel of Beth-maacah and lost his life there, for the inhabitants cut off his head and threw it over the wall to Joab (2 Sam. xx. 1–22).
3. A Gadite dwelling in Gilead in Bashan (1 Chron. v. 13, 16).

She'bah. See SHIBAH.

She'bam. See SIBMAH.

Sheb-a-ni'ah [perhaps, Jehovah hath dealt tenderly].
1. A Levite who was a trumpeter in David's time (1 Chron. xv. 24).
2. A father's house among the priests in the generation after the exile (Neh. xii. 14); see SHECANIAH 3. Its representative set his seal to the covenant (x. 4).
3. A Levite who assisted at the feast of tabernacles in Ezra's time (Neh. ix. 4, 5), and in behalf of his house sealed the covenant (x. 10).
4. Another Levite who sealed the covenant (Neh. x. 12).

Sheb'a-rim [fractures, breaches, ruins; perhaps, quarries].
A locality near Ai (Josh. vii. 5). Site unknown.

She'bat. in A. V. **Sebaṭ**, and 1 Mac. xvi. 14, A. V. **Sabat**, R. V. **Sebat**.
The eleventh month of the year (Zech. i. 7); see YEAR.

She'ber [breaking, fracture].
A son of Caleb, by his concubine Maacah (1 Chron. ii. 48).

Sheb'na, in R. V. twice **Shebnah** (2 Kin. xviii. 18, 26) [tenderness].
The steward of the king's house under Hezekiah (Is. xxii. 15), a man of great influence, apparently a foreigner, and fond of display (16, 18). As was customary among the wealthy, he built himself a sepulcher in his lifetime (16). Isaiah rebuked him, calling him the shame of his lord's house; and predicted his fall and his retirement from Judah, and the elevation of Eliakim to his place (17–25). Probably later, in 701 B. C., Eliakim held the position of house steward, while Shebna was only Hezekiah's scribe or secretary (2 Kin. xviii. 18, 26, 37; xix. 2).

Sheb'u-el, in Septuagint and Lucian everywhere **Shu'ba-el** [return, O God].
1. A son of Gershom, and a grandson of Moses (1 Chron. xxiii. 16; xxvi. 24; in xxiv. 20 Shubael).
2. A son of Heman, in David's time (1 Chron. xxv. 4; in verse 20 Shubael).

Shec-a-ni′ah, in A. V. **Shechaniah** except 1 Chron. xxiv. 11 ; 2 Chron. xxxi. 15 [Jehovah hath dwelt].

1. A descendant of Aaron. His family had grown to a father's house in the time of David, and became the tenth of the twenty-four courses into which David divided the priests (1 Chron. xxiv. 1, 6, 11).

2. A Levite in king Hezekiah's reign (2 Chron. xxxi. 15).

3. A chief of the priests, who returned with Zerubbabel from Babylon (Neh. xii. 3, 7). In the next generation a father's house probably bore his name, although it is written Shebaniah (ver. 14) ; see remarks under BETH for the misreading of caph as beth. See SHEBANIAH 2.

4. Founder of a family, presumably a descendant of David, but not in the line of succession to the throne (1 Chron. iii. 21, 22), for he is loosely registered, his kinship with Zerubbabel not being given. Perhaps his was the family of which the representative returned from Babylon with Ezra (Ezra viii. 3). The name of this representative has probably fallen out of the Hebrew text between Shecaniah and the words " of the sons of Parosh." The parallel passage, 1 Esdr. viii. 29, R. V., has: "Of the sons of David, Attus the son of Sechenias." This agrees indeed with the fact that Hattush was a grandson of Shecaniah (1 Chron. iii. 22), but it is not supported by either the Septuagint or Hebrew of Ezra viii. 3.

5. A son of Jahaziel and descendant of Zattu, who returned from Babylon with Ezra (Ezra viii. 5, Septuagint ; 1 Esdr. viii. 32).

6. A son of Jehiel, one of the sons of Elam. He confessed the guilt of himself and his brethren who had married foreign wives, and proposed to Ezra that they should put them away (Ezra x. 2, 3).

7. Father of Shemaiah, the keeper of the east gate in Nehemiah's time, and probably a Levite (Neh. iii. 29), and not the man of Judah (1 Chron. iii. 22).

8. Father-in-law of Tobiah, the Ammonite. He was the son of Arah (Neh. vi. 18).

She′chem, in A. V. once **Sichem** (Gen. xii. 6), twice **Sychem** (Acts vii. 16), Greek forms [shoulder].

1. A walled town (Gen. xxxiv. 20), by mount Gerizim (Judg. ix. 7), in the hill-country of Ephraim (Josh. xx. 7). Abraham camped near it (Gen. xii. 6). He found Canaanites in the land, but was taught that this was the land promised him for his descendants ; and forthwith he built an altar to Jehovah (7). Jacob, coming back to the promised land, found a tribe of Hivites inhabiting Shechem (xxxiv. 2). He bought a parcel of ground from them (xxxiii. 18, 19), where Joseph's body was eventually buried (Josh. xxiv. 32; in Acts vii. 16 oddly confounded by Stephen with Abraham's purchase of Machpelah). On account of the mistreatment of their sister,

Simeon and Levi broke treaty and massacred the male inhabitants, and the sons of Jacob pillaged the town (Gen. xxxiv. 25–29 ; xlviii. 22). Jacob condemned the deed (xxxiv. 30, xlix. 5–7). Joseph's brothers for a time fed their flocks near Shechem (xxxvii. 12, 13). The town fell into the hands of the Habiru in the 15th century B. C. (El-Amarna letters). In the vale of Shechem the tribes assembled solemnly to assume obligation to the law of Jehovah (Josh. viii. 30). The boundary between the tribes of Ephraim and Manasseh passed near it (xvii. 7), and it was one of the cities of refuge and a Levitical city (xx. 7 ; xxi. 21). Joshua summoned the tribes thither to hear his farewell address (xxiv. 1). In the time of the judges, a temple of Baalberith was maintained in the town (Judg. viii. 33 ; ix. 4). Gideon's concubine lived there ; and her son, Abimelech, was for a time assisted in his political designs by its citizens (ix. 1, 3, 6), but they turned against him and he destroyed the town (23, 45). At Shechem the ten tribes rejected Rehoboam and made Jeroboam king (1 Kin. xii. 1–19). Jeroboam fortified the town, and occupied it for a time as his capital (25). It continued in existence after the fall of the northern kingdom (Jer. xli. 5) ; and became the chief city of the Samaritans (Ecclus. l. 26; Antiq. xi. 8, 6). It was captured by John Hyrcanus (xiii. 9, 1). Shechem, or Nablus, is about 31½ miles north of Jerusalem and 5½ southeast of Samaria. It lies in the upland valley bounded by mount Ebal on the north, and mount Gerizim on the south. The valley was known as Mabartha, the defile, being a pass from the seacoast to the Jordan ; and Vespasian, leading his army from Emmaus to Jericho, camped at Shechem for a night (War iv. 8, 1). After the war Shechem was rebuilt, and the new town was named Flavia Neapolis in honor of Flavius Vespasian, now Roman emperor. This name still persists in the form Nablus. The original settlement was probably at the eastern end of the valley ; at Tell Balâṭa, which hides walls of great strength and thickness. The town to-day stands at the western end of the pass, at the watershed, 1870 feet above sea level. It occupies the bottom of the valley, at its narrowest point, where the two mountains are only 100 yards apart; and climbs the slope of Gerizim to the foot of the cliffs. The town has gates, but is not walled. The streets are narrow and vaulted ; in rainy weather some of them become the beds of streams. The district is copiously watered by springs, and is fertile. The orchards produce mulberries, oranges, pomegranates, olives. The bulk of the inhabitants are Mohammedans, about 24,000 in number ; in addition to whom are a few hundred Greek Christians, a small Jewish population, and about 150 Samaritans.

2. The son of Hamor, the Hivite, who was prince of Shechem (Gen. xxxiv. 1–31).

The eastern side of the foundation of Shechem's gigantic fortress-temple, generally interpreted as "The House of El-berith" (Judg. 9:4, 46). The reconstructed forecourt is supported by a retaining wall erected by modern excavators to prevent further erosion.

3. A son of Gilead, and the founder of a tribal family (Num. xxvi. 31; Josh. xvii. 2).

4. A Manassite, a son of Shemidah (1 Chron. vii. 19).

Shed′e-ur [emission, light].

Father of Elizur, the Reubenite chief in the wilderness (Num. i. 5; ii. 10).

Sheep.

Sheep were early domesticated (Gen. iv. 2). They were herded by the Hebrew patriarchs (xii. 16), and by their descendants when sojourning in Egypt and when settled in Canaan (Ex. x. 9; xii. 32, 38; 1 Chron. xxvii. 31), even down to the latest times (Luke ii. 8). The wilderness of Judæa and the south country, and the plateau of Moab, were pasture lands (Num. xxxii. 1; Judg. v. 16; 1 Sam. xvi. 11; xxv. 2); and so was the country around Haran (Gen. xxix. 2), and the land of Midian (Ex. ii. 16), and of Uz and the Hagarenes (Job i. 3; 1 Chron. v. 20, 21), and of the tribes of Kedar and Nebaioth (Is. lx. 7; Ezek. xxvii. 21; cp. 1 Sam. xv. 7, 9). In these regions the sheep, owing to the heat and dryness of the climate, require water daily (Gen. xxix.

8, 10; Ex. ii. 16–19). The sheep was a clean
animal and used for food; its flesh was eaten
(1 Sam. xiv. 32; xxv. 18; 2 Sam. xvii. 29; I
Kin. iv. 23), and the rich milk of the ewes was
drunk (Deut. xxxii. 14; Is. vii. 21, 22; 1 Cor.
ix. 7). The skin served as rude clothing (Heb.
xi. 37; cp. Zech. xiii. 4; Mat. vii. 15), and it
was sometimes converted into leather (Ex.
xxvi. 14). From the wool, cloth was woven
(Lev. xiii. 47, 48; Job xxxi. 20; Prov. xxvii.
26; Ezek. xxxiv. 3); hence wool was a valuable commodity, and was rendered as tribute
(2 Kin. iii. 4; Is. xvi. 1). Sheep shearing
was made a time of feasting and frolic (Gen.
xxxviii. 12; 1 Sam. xxv. 4, 11, 36; 2 Sam. xiii.
23). The horns of rams served as flasks and
trumpets (Josh. vi. 4; 1 Sam. xvi. 1). As
the sheep was a clean animal, it was used in
sacrifice by the Hebrews and other peoples
(Ex. xx. 24; John ii. 14; Num. xxii. 40). An
animal of the flock might be taken for a
burnt offering (Lev. i. 10), a sin offering of
the common people (iv. 32), a guilt and a
trespass offering (v. 15; vi. 6), and a peace
offering (xxii. 21); see LAMB, RAM. The
sheep was known for its affection (2 Sam.
xii. 3), docility (John x. 3, 4), meekness and
submissiveness (Is. liii. 7; Jer. xi. 19), helplessness when left to itself (Mic. v. 8; Mat.
x. 16), and its need of guidance (Num. xxvii.
17; Ezek. xxxiv. 5; Mat. ix. 36; xxvi. 31).

The sheep of Palestine and the adjacent
regions are usually white (Ps. cxlvii. 16; Is.
i. 18; Ezek. xxvii. 18), but occasionally they
are black or brown, or piebald, either white
and tawny or white and black (Gen.
xxx. 32). Two breeds of sheep are
found in Palestine. In the northern districts a short-wooled variety
is raised, of which both the rams
and ewes are horned. But the
broad-tailed sheep (*Ovis laticaudata*)
is more general. It has been bred
since early ages in Arabia and Palestine (Herod. iii. 113; cp. Ex. xxix.
22; Lev. iii. 9; vii. 3; viii. 25).
The tails which are offered for sale
in the markets ordinarily weigh ten
or fifteen pounds; but when the
sheep is well fattened, the tail
grows to an enormous size. The
Arabs regard it as a delicacy, fry-
ing it in slices.

Sheep'fold and **Sheep'cote.**
An inclosure for sheep (Jer. xxiii.
3; Ezek. xxxiv. 14), whither the flock
was ordinarily driven for the night.
Many were permanent pens, surrounded by a stone wall (cp. Num.
xxxii. 16) and entered by a gate
(John x. 1). The wall was often surmounted with branches of thorny
shrubs. The sheep lay in the yard
under the open sky; but doubt-
less there were in former days, as there are
now, low, flat buildings on the sheltered side

of the area, in which the flocks were shut up
on cold nights. It was common for several
flocks to pass the night in one fold under the
care of an under-shepherd, who guarded the
door. The shepherds came in the morning,
and were admitted by the under-shepherd.
Each shepherd knew the sheep of his own
flock, and was known by them (John x. 3,
4). Less substantial inclosures were hastily
formed of tangled thorn branches for temporary use on pastures remote from home,
and caves and other natural shelters were
also taken advantage of for protecting the
sheep at night, the shepherds camping with
their flocks. On ranges exposed to the raids
of robbers or hostile tribes, towers were
erected, about which the flocks and herds
were pastured and at night folded (2 Kin.
xvii. 9; 2 Chron. xxvi. 10; Mic. iv. 8).

Sheep Gate. See JERUSALEM II. 3.

Sheep Mar'ket, in R. V. **Sheep Gate.** See
JERUSALEM II. 3.

She'e-rah, in A. V. **She'rah** [consan-
guinity, a female relative].
A daughter of Ephraim, or perhaps of
Beriah. She or rather her descendants built
upper and nether Beth-horon and Uzzen-
sheerah (1 Chron. vii. 24). She may have
married Becher and given rise to the tribal
family of the Becherites.

She-ha-ri'ah [Jehovah hath broken forth
as the dawn].
A Benjamite, son of Jeroham (1 Chron. viii.
26).

Sheep following their shepherd, near Bethlehem.

Shek'el [weight].
A weight used for metals (Gen. xxiv. 22

1 Sam. xvii. 5, 7); see WEIGHTS. At an early period this quantity of silver, uncoined, was a recognized standard in financial transactions (Gen. xxiii. 15, 16). Half a shekel was to be given by each man as a ransom for his life when a census was taken (Exod. xxx. 14, 15). The value of the shekel was about 65 cents; see WEIGHTS. In 141–140 B. C. the fourth year of Simon Maccabæus' priestly rule, Antiochus VII., not yet king of Syria, but having authority, allowed him to coin money in his own name, and silver shekels and half shekels commencing from about that period exist. See MONEY.

She-ki′nah. See THEOPHANY.

She′lah, I., in A. V. of Genesis **Salah,** of N. T. **Sala,** in imitation of the Greek form [a missile, a shoot, a sprout].

1. The son of Arphaxad (Gen. x. 24; xi. 12–15; 1 Chron. i. 18).

2. A pool at Jerusalem, near the king's garden, erroneously translated in the A. V. Siloah (Neh. iii. 15). Probably the same as Siloam (q. v.).

She′lah, II. [prayer].

The third son of Judah by a Canaanite woman. He was the founder of a tribal family (Gen. xxxviii. 2, 5, 11, 14, 26; Num. xxvi. 20).

Shel-e-mi′ah [Jehovah recompenses].

1. A doorkeeper of the sanctuary in David's time (1 Chron. xxvi. 14). See MESHELE-MIAH.

2. Son of Cushi (Jer. xxxvi. 14).

3. Son of Abdeel (Jer. xxxvi. 26).

4. Son of Hananiah (Jer. xxxvii. 13).

5. Father of Jucal (Jer. xxxviii. 1).

6, 7. Two men, descendants of Bani, each of whom was induced by Ezra to put away his foreign wife (Ezra x. 39, 41).

8. Father of that Hananiah who assisted to rebuild the wall of Jerusalem (Neh. iii. 30).

9. A priest whom Nehemiah appointed one of three treasurers of the tithes, which they were commissioned to distribute among the Levites (Neh. xiii. 13).

She′leph [extraction].

A Semitic people descended through Joktan (Gen. x. 26; 1 Chron. i. 20), and doubtless dwelling in southern Arabia. The name is a common one in Yemen.

She′lesh [triad].

An Asherite, son of Helem (1 Chron. vii. 35).

Shel′o-mi [peaceful].

Father of Ahihud, who was prince of Asher in the latter part of the wilderness wanderings (Num. xxxiv. 27).

Shel′o-mith [peaceful].

1. A Danite, a daughter of Dibri, and mother of the Israelite who was put to death in the wilderness for blasphemy (Lev. xxiv. 11).

2. A Levite, family of Kohath, house of Izhar (1 Chron. xxiii. 18). Called Shelomoth in xxiv. 22.

3. A descendant of Moses through Eliezer. He and his brethren were appointed by David over the dedicated treasures (1 Chron. xxvi. 25, 26, in R. V., following the Hebrew text, Shelomoth; cp. xxiii. 15–17).

4. A Gershonite Levite, son of Shimei (1 Chron. xxiii. 9, in R. V. Shelomoth). .

5. A son or daughter of Rehoboam (2 Chron. xi. 20).

6. Son of Josiphiah (Ezra viii. 10). The Hebrew text is faulty. The Septuagint shows that he was a member of the family of Bani: "Of the sons of Bani, Shelomoth, the son of Josiphiah."

7. A daughter of Zerubbabel (1 Chron. iii. 19).

Shel′o-moth. See SHELOMITH.

She-lu′mi-el [pacified, or a friend is God].

The prince of the tribe of Simeon early in the wilderness wanderings (Num. i. 6; ii. 12; vii. 36, 41; x. 19).

Shem, in A. V. of N. T. **Sem** [name].

One of the two elder sons of Noah (Gen. x. 1, 21; cp. ix. 24), and probably the firstborn (v. 32). For explanation of xi. 10, see CHRONOLOGY, section relating to the period from the creation to Abraham. With his descendants, he is mentioned last in the catalogue of Gen. x. in accordance with the author's custom of disposing of subordinate genealogies before presenting the main line of the people of God. He was born about the five hundredth year of Noah's life (see NOAH). At the time of the deluge he was married, but had no children (Gen. vii. 7; 1 Pet. iii. 20). After that catastrophe, he acted with filial respect to his father when the latter committed his great sin. Shem, in consequence, received a blessing, the wording of which implied that God would bless Shem and that the worship of the true God should continue in his family (Gen. ix. 23, 27). He was progenitor of the people who inhabited or perhaps in some cases held in subjection Elam, Asshur, Arphaxad, Lud, and Aram (x. 21, 22).

She′ma [rumor, fame].

1. A town in the extreme south of Judah (Josh. xv. 26); cp. SHEBA 2.

2. A son of Hebron, belonging to the tribe of Judah (1 Chron. ii. 43, 44); see MA-RESHAH 2.

3. A Reubenite, a son of Joel (1 Chron. v. 8; cp. 4).

4. A Benjamite, head of a father's house in Aijalon (1 Chron. viii. 13). Called in verse 21 Shimei, in A. V. Shimhi.

5. One of the men, probably priests, who assisted Ezra at the public reading of the law (Neh. viii. 4).

She-ma′ah [rumor, fame].

A Benjamite of Gibeah, who joined David at Ziklag (1 Chron. xii. 3).

She-ma′iah [Jehovah hath heard].

1. A Simeonite (1 Chron. iv. 37).

2. A Reubenite, a son of Joel (1 Chron. v. 4).

3. A Levite, chief of the sons of Elizaphan, who to the number of two hundred took part in the ceremonies attendant on the removal of the ark from the house of Obed-edom to mount Zion (1 Chron. xv. 8–11).

4. A Levite, a son of Nethanel. He was a scribe in the time of David, and noted down the twenty-four divisions then made of the priests (1 Chron. xxiv. 6).

5. Eldest son of Obed-edom (1 Chron. xxvi. 4). He was the father of various valiant sons who, with him, were doorkeepers of the tabernacle (1 Chron. xxvi. 6).

6. A prophet in the reign of Rehoboam, who forbade the king to attempt the conquest of the revolted ten tribes (1 Kin. xii. 22–24 ; 2 Chron. xi. 2–4). Five years later, when Shishak invaded the land, he declared that the invasion was permitted as a punishment for sin. Thereupon the princes humbled themselves, and the affliction was made lighter (xii. 5–8). Shemaiah wrote a history of Rehoboam's reign (15).

7. One of the Levites sent by Jehoshaphat to teach the people (2 Chron. xvii. 8).

8. A Levite, descendant of Jeduthun. He helped to cleanse the temple in Hezekiah's reign (2 Chron. xxix. 14, 15). He is, perhaps, the Levite mentioned in 1 Chron. ix. 16, and he may be the person called Shammua in Neh. xi. 17.

9. A Levite in Hezekiah's reign who, with others, had to distribute the firstlings, tithes and gifts to the Levites in the cities (2 Chron. xxxi. 15).

10. A chief Levite in Josiah's reign who, with others, was liberal in his donations of animals for the the passover services (2 Chron. xxxv. 9).

11. Father of Urijah, of Kirjath-jearim, who was put to death by king Jehoiakim for the true prophecies he had uttered (Jer. xxvi. 20–23).

12. Father of Delaiah, the latter being a prince in the reign of Jehoiakim (Jer. xxxvi. 12).

13. A Nehelamite, a false prophet among the exiles in Babylonia, who prophesied a speedy return from captivity. He wrote to the people of Jerusalem and the priest who had oversight of the temple, and complained that Jeremiah remained unpunished, who declared that the exile would be long. When Jeremiah heard the complaint, he foretold that Shemaiah should leave no posterity and not live to see the return (Jer. xxix. 24–32).

14. A chief of the priests who returned from Babylon with Zerubbabel (Neh. xii. 6, 7). In the next generation a father's house bore this name (ver. 18).

15. A son of Adonikam, and one of the chief men who accompanied Ezra from the land of the captivity to Canaan (Ezra viii. 13).

16. A chief man whom Ezra sent with others to Iddo to obtain Levites who were lacking in the party leaving the land of the captivity for Canaan (Ezra viii. 16).

17 and 18. Two men, one descended from the priest Harim, and the other from the layman Harim, each of whom was induced by Ezra to put away his foreign wife (Ezra x. 21, 31).

19. A son of Shecaniah (1 Chron. iii. 22) ; see SHECANIAH 4.

20. Keeper of the east gate, and probably a Levite. He repaired part of the wall of Jerusalem in Nehemiah's time (Neh. iii. 29); see SHECANIAH 7.

21. A Levite, descended from Bunni. He was an overseer of the business of the house of God in Nehemiah's time (Neh. xi. 15; cp. 1 Chron. ix. 14).

22. A false prophet, son of Delaiah, son of Mehetabel. He was hired by Tobiah and Sanballat to frighten Nehemiah into going with him into the temple and shutting the doors to avoid assassination (Neh. vi. 10–13). In carrying out his plan, he shut himself in his house and pretended to fear for his life.

23. A priest who, doubtless in behalf of a father's house, sealed the covenant in the days of Nehemiah (Neh. x. 8).

24. A prince of Judah who took part in the ceremonies at the dedication of the wall of Jerusalem (Neh. xii. 34).

25. A Levite of the lineage of Asaph (Neh. xii. 35).

26. One of the company of Levite musicians at the dedication of the wall of Jerusalem (Neh. xii. 36).

27. A priest who blew a trumpet on the same occasion (Neh. xii. 42).

Shem-a-ri'ah, in A. V. once **Shamariah** (2 Chron. xi. 19) [Jehovah hath kept].

1. A Benjamite who joined David at Ziklag (1 Chron. xii. 5).

2. A son of Rehoboam (2 Chron. xi. 19).

3 and 4. A son of Harim and a son of Bani, each of whom was induced by Ezra to put away his foreign wife (Ezra x. 32, 41).

Shem-e'ber [meaning unknown]. In Septuagint the form is Sumobor.

The king of Zeboiim, defeated, with the other kings ruling over the cities of the plain, by Chedorlaomer and his confederates (Gen. xiv. 2, 8, 10).

She'med, in A. V. **Shamed**, the pausal form [destruction]. These forms of the name are derived from the Vulgate ; but the present Hebrew text and the Septuagint, codex Vaticanus, have Shamer.

A Benjamite, descended from Shaharaim through Elpaal. He was a rebuilder of Ono and Lod, with their dependent villages (1 Chron. viii. 12).

She'mer, in A. V. of Chronicles **Shamer**, the pausal form [the lees, or crust of wine].

1. The man from whom Omri purchased the hill on which to build Samaria (1 Kin. xvi. 24).

2. A Merarite Levite, the son of Mahli (1 Chron. vi. 46).

3. An Asherite (1 Chron. vii. 34). The same as the Shomer of verse 32.

She-mi'da, in A. V. once **Shemidah** (1 Chron. vii. 19) [fame of wisdom].

A son of Gilead, and founder of a tribal family (Num. xxvi. 32; Josh. xvii. 2).

Shem'i-nith [eighth].

A musical term (1 Chron. xv. 21; and Ps. vi. and xii., titles). Stainer reviews three opinions which have been given regarding it: (1) The pitch of an octave; (2) the name of a scale or tune; and (3) the number of strings on the instrument used. Perhaps, in contrast with alamoth, it means an octave below (Gesenius, Delitzsch).

She-mir'a-moth [lofty name].

1. A Levite and singer in the reign of David (1 Chron. xv. 18, 20).

2. A Levite, one of those employed by Jehoshaphat to teach the people (2 Chron. xvii. 8).

She-mit'ic. See SEMITIC.

Shem'u-el [name of God]. The same Hebrew name as that commonly rendered Samuel.

1. A son of Ammihud. He was appointed as the representative for the tribe of Simeon on the commission to divide Canaan (Num. xxxiv. 20).

2. A man of Issachar, family of Tola, and head of a father's house (1 Chron. vii. 2).

3. The prophet Samuel (1 Chron. vi. 33, A. V.).

Shen [a tooth, a jagged rock].

A spot a little on one side of the place where Samuel set up the stone which he called Ebenezer (1 Sam. vii. 12). The text is suspicious. The Greek and Syriac versions indicate Jeshanah. See JESHANAH.

She-naz'zar, in A. V. **Shenazar** [apparently O moongod, protect].

A son or descendant of Jeconiah (1 Chron. iii. 18).

She'nir. See SENIR.

She'ol. See HELL.

She'pham.

A place on the northeastern border of Canaan, near Riblah (Num. xxxiv. 10, 11). Site unknown.

Sheph-a-ti'ah, in A. V. once erroneously **Shephathiah** (1 Chron. ix. 8) [Jehovah hath judged].

1. A Haruphite, one of the Benjamites who joined David at Ziklag (1 Chron. xii. 5).

2. A son born to David at Hebron by one of his wives, Abital (2 Sam. iii. 4; 1 Chron. iii. 3).

3. Son of Maacah and head of the Simeonite tribe in David's reign (1 Chron. xxvii. 16).

4. The father of a Benjamite who dwelt at Jerusalem (1 Chron. ix. 8).

5. A son of king Jehoshaphat (2 Chron. xxi. 2).

6. A prince, son of Mattan. He was one of those who advised Zedekiah to put the prophet Jeremiah to death, as his unfavorable prophecies were discouraging the defenders of Jerusalem during its siege by Nebuchadnezzar's army (Jer. xxxviii. 1).

7. Founder of a family, 372 members of which returned from captivity with Zerubbabel (Ezra ii. 4; Neh. vii. 9), and eighty-one more with Ezra (Ezra viii. 8).

8. A man of Judah, family of Perez. He evidently lived before the exile (Neh. xi. 4).

9. A man whose descendants, classified with Solomon's servants, came from Babylon with Zerubbabel (Ezra ii. 57; Neh. vii. 59).

Sheph'e-lah [low land].

A well known name in the geography of Palestine, used, however, in the English versions only in 1 Mac. xii. 38, A. V., and then in the form Sephela. See LOWLAND.

She'pher, in A. V. **Shapher** [beauty, elegance].

A mountain constituting an encampment of the Israelites in the wilderness (Num. xxxiii. 23, 24). Situation unknown.

Shep'herd.

One whose occupation it is to take charge of a flock of sheep. Abel was a keeper of sheep (Gen. iv. 2). The occupation of the patriarchs from Abraham to Jacob and his sons was pastoral (xiii. 1–6). There were nomad shepherds who owned flocks and herds, dwelt in tents, and moved from place to place to find pasture for their cattle and afford them protection, like Jabal, Abraham, and the Rechabites (iv. 20; xiii. 2, 3, 18 with xx. 1; Jer. xxxv. 6–10). There were also wealthy sheep owners who dwelt in towns while their flocks were driven from pasture to pasture by their servants (1 Sam. xxv. 2, 3, 7, 15, 16; cp. Gen. xxxvii. 12–17). Then there was the settled shepherd, who led the flock from the permanent fold to the pasture in the morning, and in the evening brought it home again (John x. 1–4); see SHEEPFOLD. The care of the flock was often committed to a son (Gen. xxxvii. 2; 1 Sam. xvi. 11, 19), or a daughter (Gen. xxix. 9; Ex. ii. 16, 17), or a hired servant (Gen. xxx. 32; Zech. xi. 12; John x. 12). The shepherd was ordinarily responsible to the owner for any loss of sheep (Gen. xxxi. 39). The Mosaic law relieved him of responsibility if he could prove that the loss was not due to his neglect (Ex. xxii. 10–13).

The shepherd went to the fold in the morning, where several flocks were lying, and called. His own sheep knew his voice and followed him. The sheep which belonged to other owners or were under the care of other keepers paid no attention to the strange voice (John x. 2–5). The shepherd led his own flock to pasture, spent the day with them there, and sometimes the night also (Gen. xxxi. 40; Song i. 7; Luke ii. 8); defended them from wild beasts and robbers (1 Sam. xvii. 34, 35; Is. xxxi. 4); kept the restless sheep from trespassing on cultivated ground, searched for the strayed sheep, and brought them back (Ezek. xxxiv. 12; Luke xv. 4); and tenderly cared for the delicate and the weak (Is. xl. 11; Ezek. xxxiv. 4, 16; Zech. xi. 9). The sheep which kept near the shepherd had each a name and answered to it, and were the recipients of many little kindnesses. Such is still the case in the Orient. Where the pastures are dried up or covered with snow, as in the late autumn and winter, the shepherd must provide food for the flock. He cuts down branches from the trees of the forest, and the sheep and goats feed upon the green leaves and tender twigs.

The shepherd carried a garment in which to wrap himself in inclement weather, a pouch for food, and some defensive weapon (1 Sam. xvii. 40; Jer. xliii. 12). A long rod, doubtless generally in ancient times as now with a crook at the upper end, was used to manage the flock, keep it together, guide it, defend it, and chastise the disobedient (Ps. xxiii. 4; Mic. vii. 14; Zech. xi. 7). The shepherd was aided by dogs (Job xxx. 1); not intelligent, faithful dogs, but lazy, mean brutes, which loitered behind the flock, but were of service; they gave warning of danger by their bark.

Jehovah was the Shepherd of Israel, and especially of the faithful section of the people (Gen. xlix. 24).

Christ is the good Shepherd, entering into the sheepfold by the door, calling out his own sheep by name, and so possessing their confidence and affection that they follow him, while they refuse to follow any other. He satisfactorily met the test of supreme devotion to his flock and to his duty by laying down his life for the sheep (John x. 1–18).

All who had responsible positions in the theocracy, prophets, priests, and kings, were looked on as pastors of the Israelitish people. They were under-shepherds, aiding Jehovah, and their unfaithfulness was frequently pointed out (Is. lvi. 11). And in the Christian church, the elders or bishops are pastors or shepherds, under Christ, the chief Shepherd, appointed to tend the flock of God (1 Pet. v. 1–4).

She'phi and **She'pho** [smoothness].

A son or tribe of Shobal, descended from Seir, the Horite (Gen. xxxvi. 23); for the two forms, cp. VAU.

She-phu'pham and **Shephuphan** [perhaps, horned sand snake]; see ADDER 1.

A son or remoter descendant of Benjamin, and founder of a tribal family (Num. xxvi. 39; in A. V. Shupham). In the same verse his name appears as Shupham (in Shupham-

ites). He is also called Muppim (Gen. xlvi. 21) and Shuppim (1 Chron. vii. 12, 15). The letters m and s or sh were very much alike in ancient Hebrew. He was perhaps known also as Shephuphan (1 Chron. viii. 5). In this passage Shephuphan is probably listed as a descendant of Bela, although it is not impossible that the enumeration of Bela's sons closes with Gera and that Shephuphan is registered as a son of Benjamin. In vii. 12 Shuppim is catalogued among the sons of Benjamin, but it is not clear whether he is enrolled as a son in the strict sense or as descended from Benjamin's son Bela through Ir or Iri (7). In the latter case he was born after the descent of Jacob's family into Egypt, but is enumerated with those who went down into Egypt, because he founded a tribal family. See EGYPT III. 1.

She'rah. See SHEERAH.

Sher-e-bi'ah [Jehovah hath made to tremble].

1. A Levite, head of a family, who came from Babylon with Zerubbabel (Neh. xii. 8). The representative of the family sealed the covenant (x. 12). It was a family of singers (xii. 24).

2. Head of a family of Levites who returned with Ezra from Babylon (Ezra viii. 18). He was perhaps the representative of a part of the aforementioned family which had remained behind when the exiles returned with Zerubbabel, and as representative he officially bore the family name. He is probably intended in ver. 24, although the present text describes him as a priest, and was one of the men to whose custody during the journey Ezra committed the gifts for the temple.

3. One of the Levites who assisted Ezra, reading the law to the people, and giving the sense, so that the listeners might understand what they heard (Neh. viii. 7). He took part in the public confession of sin after the feast of tabernacles (ix. 4).

She'resh [perhaps, root or sprout].

A man of Manasseh, family of Machir (1 Chron. vii. 16).

She-re'zer. See SHAREZER.

She'shach.

According to ancient tradition, a cypher for Babel (Jer. xxv. 26, R. V., margin; li. 41), constructed on the system known as Athbash. The letters of the alphabet were numbered both in their regular order of sequence and in the reverse order; and when the cypher of a name was desired, its consonants were replaced by those which have the same numbers in the reverse enumeration. B is the second letter of the Hebrew alphabet and s or sh is the second from the end, l is the twelfth letter from the beginning and k is the twelfth from the end; hence the cypher for Babel was Sheshak. Possibly, however, there is no cypher, and

Sheshach is the name of a quarter of the city, perhaps Shish-ku (Lauth, Delitzsch).

She'shai [whitish].

A son or family of Anak, resident at Hebron, and driven thence by Caleb (Num. xiii. 32, cp. 33; Josh. xv. 14).

She'shan.

A man of Judah, family of Hezron, house of Jerahmeel (1 Chron. ii. 31). He had no sons, but only daughters, one of whom he gave in marriage to an Egyptian slave (34, 35). See AHLAI.

Shesh-baz'zar.

A prince of Judah, whom Cyrus made governor, to whom he restored the sacred vessels which had been carried to Babylon by Nebuchadnezzar, and who returned to Jerusalem and laid the foundation of the temple (Ezra i. 8, 11; v. 14, 16). Sheshbazzar may have been the Babylonian name of Zerubbabel, as Belteshazzar was that of Daniel.

Sheth, I. [compensation].

A son of Adam (1 Chron. i. 1). See SETH.

Sheth, II. [tumult].

A designation of the Moabites as makers of war and tumult (Num. xxiv. 17, A. V.).

She'thar-boz'e-nai, in A. V. **Shethar-boznai.**

A Persian official who with others attempted to prevent the returned Jewish exiles from rebuilding the temple (Ezra v. 3, 6; vi. 6).

She'va [vanity].

1. A man of Judah, family of Hezron, house of Caleb. He was the ancestor of the inhabitants of Machbena and Gibea (1 Chron. ii. 49).

2. A scribe in David's reign (2 Sam. xx. 25). See SHAVSHA.

Shew'bread. See SHOWBREAD.

Shi'bah, in A. V. **Shebah** [seven, an oath]. Feminine form of Sheba.

A well at Beer-sheba which Isaac's servants redigged, and which Isaac named Shibah on account of the covenant he had just made with Abimelech (Gen. xxvi. 33).

Shib'bo-leth [an ear of grain, or a river or stream].

The local dialect of the Ephraimites was characterized by the absence of the palatal sibilant sh at the beginning of a word and the use of the lingual sibilant s in its stead. When Jephthah, at the head of the Gileadites, had vanquished the Ephraimites and seized the fords of the Jordan, many of the defeated tribe came to the river, desiring to pass. On being asked if they were Ephraimites, and denying the fact, they were required to pronounce the word Shibboleth, and if they called it Sibboleth, were slain without further ceremony (Judg. xii. 5, 6). The word has entered the English language, and is used to mean a test word or the watchword or pet phrase of a party or sect.

Shib'mah. See SEBMAH.

Shic'ron. See SHIKKERON.

Shield. See ARMOR.

Shig-ga'ion, and plural **Shigionoth** [wandering, irregular].

A musical term (Ps. vii. title; Hab. iii. 1). Probably a dithyrambic ode, erratic, wild, enthusiastic.

Shi'hon. See SHION.

Shi'hor, in A. V. **Sihor,** except 1 Chron. xiii. 5 [to the Hebrew ear, black, turbid].

The river Nile (Is. xxiii. 3; Jer. ii. 18, see R. V. margin). Its eastern or Pelusiac branch was on the boundary of Egypt toward Canaan (Josh. xiii. 3; 1 Chron. xiii. 5); see RIVER OF EGYPT 1. The R. V., however, and many commentators regard the Shihor in the last two passages as a title of the brook of Egypt, the wady el-'Arish (Josh. xiii. 3, R. V. margin). According to Brugsch, the name belonged in the first instance to a canal, Shihur, on the eastern boundary of Egypt, parallel to the course of the Pelusiac branch.

Shi-hor-lib'nath [turbid stream of Libnath].

A small river at the southwestern corner of Asher (Josh. xix. 26) and apparently near Carmel. It is now commonly believed to be the Zerka, 6 miles south of Dor, a town of Asher.

Shik'ke-ron, in A. V. **Shicron** [drunkenness].

A town on the northern border of the tribe of Judah (Josh. xv. 11). Site unknown.

Shil'hi [one armed with a dart].

Father of Azubah, Jehoshaphat's mother (1 Kin. xxii. 42).

Shil'him [missile weapons, sprouts].

A town in the extreme south of Judah (Josh. xv. 32); see SHARUHEN.

Shil'lem [retribution].

A son of Naphtali, and founder of a tribal family (Gen. xlvi. 24; Num. xxvi. 49). Called Shallum, a synonymous and more common name, in 1 Chron. vii. 13.

Shil'ling. See PENNY.

Shi-lo'ah [a sending of waters, an aqueduct]; see SILOAM.

Shi'loh [tranquillity, rest].

A town north of Bethel, south of Lebonah, and on the east side of the highway connecting Bethel with Shechem (Judg. xxi. 19), and hence within the territory of Ephraim. There the Israelites under Joshua set up the tabernacle (Josh. xviii. 1), and divided by lot the, as yet, unappropriated parts of Canaan (8–10; xix. 51; xxii. 9). When the western tribes were convened to call the tribes east of the Jordan to account for their building of an altar, it was at Shiloh that the gathering took place (12). In the times of the judges there was there an annual feast of Jehovah

(Judg. xxi. 19; 1 Sam. i. 3), at which the Benjamites on one occasion obtained wives by capture (Judg. xxi. 16–23). The tabernacle, with the ark, was still there in the time of Eli and during the early years of Samuel (Judg. xviii. 31; 1 Sam. i. 9, 24; ii. 14, 22; iii. 3, 21; iv. 3, 4; xiv. 3). The capture of the ark was understood to mean that God had forsaken Shiloh (Ps. lxxviii. 60; Jer. vii. 12, 14; xxvi. 6, 9). The covenant made at Sinai, of which the ark and the ritual were the outward sign and privilege, was suspended. When the ark was returned by the Philistines it was not taken again to Shiloh (1 Sam. vi. 21; vii. 1, 2; 2 Sam. vi. 2, 11, 17), but the work of reviving true religion, preparatory to the restoration of covenant privileges, was begun by Samuel. Ahijah the prophet, who told Jeroboam of his approaching greatness, lived at Shiloh, and it was thither that the king's consort repaired to inquire about the issue of their sick child's malady (1 Kin. xiv. 2, 4). It continued to be inhabited at least as late as the time of Jeremiah (Jer. xli. 5). Shiloh has been successfully identified by Robinson as Seilûn, about 10 miles north-northeast of Bethel. The ruins are in a valley surrounded by hills. In the sides of the narrow valley are many tombs. A fine spring of water is in the vicinity.

There are three main interpretations of Shiloh in the difficult passage Gen. xlix. 10, each of which receives recognition in R. V.: 1. Shiloh is a proper name, which designates the Messiah and refers to the peacefulness of his disposition and his reign. 2. Shiloh, place of tranquillity, is the town in central Palestine where the tabernacle was placed immediately after the conquest of Canaan by Joshua (Josh. xviii. 1). 3. Shiloh is not a proper name, nor is it a simple word. It is a compound, composed of the relative pronoun *she*, the preposition *l*, and the pronominal suffix of the third person masculine *oh*. The same form of the suffix occurs twice in the following verse. This phrase has been interpreted as meaning "that which is his," "whose it is," or "his own one." The second of these three meanings would happily correspond to Ezek. xxi. 27, but is not grammatically allowable; and the first regarded as objective, "he shall come to that which is his," is grammatically difficult, for an objective relative clause with indefinite antecedent is preceded by a preposition or the sign of the accusative. This conception of the word as a phrase is old, having been entertained by the translators of the ancient versions, namely, Septuagint, Targums of Onkelos and Jonathan, Syriac, and Jerome.

On the first interpretation and commonly on the third the Messiah is expressly referred to. In the second the reference is to the covenant blessing, which the prophets of a later age discerned to belong in its fullness to Messianic times. Reuben had forfeited his birthright by misconduct (Gen. xlix. 4; xxxv.

22), Simeon and Levi had incurred their father's just censure (xlix. 5–7; xxxiv. 30), and Judah was consequently assigned the place of the firstborn, and became the representative of the tribe and the peculiar possessor of the blessing covenanted to Abraham and his seed (xlix. 8). The promise of victory to the woman's seed (iii. 15), the blessing of God's favor centered in Shem (ix. 26, 27), the further centralization of the covenant blessing in the family of Abraham (xvii.), belonged henceforth preëminently to Judah, the possessor of the birthright. By him, according to the first and third interpretations, the prerogative shall be held until one who is his, one of his tribe, the man of peace comes, to whom shall be the obedience of the peoples, and in whom the covenant blessing shall be still further centered. This interpretation, with many modifications of detail, according as the scepter is thought of restrictedly as the emblem of royalty or is regarded as the symbol of leadership in general, is represented in the text of the English versions. And it is argued that this essentially must be the true interpretation, because the town of Shiloh does not fulfill the historical conditions, for neither is there any reason why Jacob, apart from special revelation, should think of Shiloh as the future place of worship, nor did Judah occupy preeminence among the tribes before the tabernacle was pitched in Shiloh, save somewhat in numbers and in being permitted to lead the van, while the people were marching to Canaan, and to pitch their tents in front of the tabernacle. The leadership was at first in the hands of Moses, of the tribe of Levi, which excited the jealousy of the princes of Reuben, and after Moses' death, and until the tabernacle was pitched at Shiloh, the authority was exercised by Joshua, of the tribe of Ephraim.

But it is more natural to regard Shiloh in this passage as the name of the town, for it is such everywhere else, and on this interpretation the words of Jacob are at once intelligible. This view is commonly entertained by those who deny that Jacob uttered the words, and who affirm that the address is a prophecy after the event. But the address is not the utterance of a late prophet, commenting on the past history of the twelve tribes and putting his reflections in the mouth of their common ancestor Jacob, for the descriptions do not fit the actual state of things at any period of the national history; see, for example, ver. 13 and ZEBULUN. Believers in the genuineness of the address hold that the town of Shiloh is meant, and they are able fairly to explain how Jacob came to use the name, and how Moses the Levite and Joshua the Ephraimite could lead the people while yet the scepter was acknowledged as belonging to Judah. The argument of Delitzsch may be amplified. Shiloh doubtless existed in the days of the patriarchs;

and Jacob, who looked for the ultimate return of his people to Canaan (Gen. xv. 13–16; xlvi. 3, 4; xlviii. 21), employs this name, place of tranquillity, as an omen of the future, playing upon it as Esau played upon the name Jacob and Micah upon the names of the towns of Judah. It made no difference that God raised up men from other tribes to meet special emergencies, the birthright and its accompanying privileges belonged to Judah. It was accorded to him by the position assigned him at the head of the marching host and in camp in front of the tabernacle. It was accredited to him by God's multiplication of his descendants, so that his tribe was much larger than any single tribe during the forty years in the wilderness. It was confirmed by the lot falling first to his tribe when the conquered land was distributed at Gilgal. The actual coming to the town of Shiloh was not contemplated as necessary by Jacob. The fulfillment of his words was more literal than his expectation. He had merely the peaceable possession of the promised land in view. The erection of the tabernacle at Shiloh, a town which Joshua may have been led to choose by having knowledge of Jacob's words, marked the first stage in the realization of the promise. A new period had been reached in Israel's history. The conquest was completed, the inheritance was theirs, possession had begun, rest had been won. Judah, the possessor of the birthright, had come to a place of tranquillity in Canaan, having obtained the obedience of the peoples, and being now ready to occupy and enjoy his conquered possession (xlix. 10–12). The words do not mean that when he should come to Shiloh the scepter should depart. They are to be understood as the similar language in Is. xlii. 4: "He shall not fail nor be discouraged, till he have set judgment in the earth." This does not mean that the servant will then fail and lose courage. So Jacob meant that the privilege conferred by the birthright, which centered in the Abrahamic covenant, should not be transferred until Judah had obtained the promised blessing, the possession of Canaan, when he would enter upon its enjoyment. A new period opens to him. He was still accorded by God the first position among the tribes, being called to go up first against the Canaanites still in the allotted land. He was called to go up first against the Benjamites in the war against that tribe to punish national sin. And the first and only deliverer of all Israel during the period of the judges proper sprang from Judah (Judg. iii. 7–11). Saul, a Benjamite, was raised up like the judges to deliver Israel (1 Sam. ix. 16; x. 6), and might have retained the throne in his family (xiii. 13, 14; xv. 23, 26, 28), but he lost the opportunity through sin, as Reuben had lost the birthright, and the permanent royal line was taken from Judah. The obedience of the Canaanites

was but the foretaste, and the possession of the land and enjoyment of its fertility were but a type, of the Messianic triumphs and peace involved in the covenanted mercies. As time went on, the fullness of meaning was revealed. The prophets dwelt with delight on the truth that in the latter days all nations shall flow unto the mountain of the Lord's house, the law shall go forth from Zion and the word of the Lord from Jerusalem, and he shall judge between the nations and reprove many peoples; and they shall beat their swords into plowshares and their spears into pruning hooks, nation shall not lift up sword against nation, neither shall they learn war any more. But they shall sit every man under his vine and under his fig tree, and none shall make them afraid; for the mouth of the Lord of hosts hath spoken it (Is. ii. 2–4; Mic. iv. 1–5; Joel iii. 9–21).

Shi-lo′ni [a Shilonite].

According to the A. V., a man of the tribe of Judah (Neh. xi. 5). But the word is preceded by the definite article in the Hebrew text, and hence is not a proper name. The R. V. correctly translates it the Shilonite, and Shiloni, as a man, disappears. See SHILONITE 2.

Shi′lo-nite.

1. A native or inhabitant of Shiloh (1 Kin. xi. 29).

2. A member of the tribal family of Shelah (Neh. xi. 5, in A. V. Shiloni).

Shil′shah [triad].

An Asherite, son of Zophah (1 Chron. vii. 37).

Shim′e-a, once **Shimeah** (2 Sam. xiii. 3); the two modes of spelling correctly representing the Hebrew text, where, except in the case noted, the Aramaic form is employed [something heard, fame].

1. A Levite, family of Merari, house of Mahli (1 Chron. vi. 30).

2. A Levite, family of Gershom (1 Chron. vi. 39, 44).

3. A brother of king David (2 Sam. xiii. 3; 1 Chron. xx. 7). In A. V. of 1 Chron. ii. 13 he is incorrectly called Shimma, the Hebrew having Shimea. In 1 Sam. xvi. 9; xvii. 13 his name appears as Shammah. Has one letter dropped out of the Hebrew text, or is Shimea, the later and nobler name, changed from "desolation" to "fame" after the nation's deliverance from the Philistines? Especially is this latter conjecture probable, if Shammah was a memorial name, like Ichabod.

4. A son of David; see SHAMMUA 2.

5. Another Shimeah, whose name in Hebrew is spelled differently from the foregoing (1 Chron. viii. 32); see SHIMEAM.

Shim′e-am.

A Benjamite, a son of Mikloth, resident in Jerusalem (1 Chron. ix. 38). In viii. 32 he is called Shimeah, a synonymous name. This name differs in its third radicle from the familiar name Shimea or Shimeah.

Shim'e-ath [rumor].
An Ammonitess, mother of one of king Joash's assassins (2 Kin. xii. 21).

Shim'e-ath-ites.
A Kenite family of scribes, descended through a certain Shimeah from the founder of the house of Rechab and resident at Jabez (1 Chron. ii. 55).

Shim'e-i, in A. V. once **Shimi** (Ex. vi. 17), once **Shimhi** (1 Chron. viii. 21) [famous].
1. A son of Gershon, and a grandson of Levi. He founded a subdivision of the tribal family of Gershon (Ex. vi. 17; Num. iii. 18, 21; 1 Chron. xxiii. 7, 10; Zech. xii. 13).
2. A Levite, family of Merari, house of Mahli (1 Chron. vi. 29).
3. A Simeonite, probably of the family of Shaul. He had sixteen sons and six daughters (1 Chron. iv. 24–27).
4. A Levite, son of Jahath, of the family of Gershom (1 Chron. vi. 42).
5. A Benjamite, head of a father's house in Aijalon (1 Chron. viii. 21, in A. V. Shimhi). Called Shema in ver. 13.
6. A Levite, family of Gershon, and head of one of the subdivisions of Ladan, which latter was apparently a division of the house of Libni (1 Chron. xxiii. 9).
7. A Levite, head of the tenth course of singers in David's reign, and evidently a son of Jeduthun, for his name is needed to make out the six spoken of in ver. 3 (1 Chron. xxv. 17).
8. A Ramathite, who was over David's vineyards (1 Chron. xxvii. 27).
9. A Benjamite, the son of Gera. He was of Saul's family, which had lost the throne. When he saw David, with his attendants, descending the eastern slope of the mount of Olives, while Absalom was in possession of Jerusalem, he thought it safe to insult the fallen potentate, which he did in gross language. He was forgiven by David, but was afterwards put to death by Solomon for disobeying a command of the king (1 Kin. ii. 44–46).
10. An adherent of David and Solomon during Adonijah's usurpation (1 Kin. i. 8). He was probably the son of Elah, who became Solomon's purveyor in the territory of Benjamin (iv. 18).
11. A Reubenite (1 Chron. v. 4).
12. A Levite, a son of Heman, who helped to purify the temple in Hezekiah's reign (2 Chron. xxix. 14–16). He may be identical with the following.
13. A Levite, brother of Conaniah, in Hezekiah's reign. He was one of those who looked after the tithes (2 Chron. xxxi. 12).
14. A Benjamite, son of Kish and an ancestor of Mordecai (Esth. ii. 5).
15. A man belonging to the royal family

of Judah, and a brother of Zerubbabel (1 Chron. iii. 19).
16, 17, 18. Three men, one a Levite, one a son of Hashum, and one a son of Bani, each of whom was induced by Ezra to put away his foreign wife (Ezra x. 23, 33, 38).

Shim'e-ites. See SHIMEI 1.

Shim'e-on [a hearkening, an answering (of prayer)].
A son of Harim, induced by Ezra to put away his foreign wife (Ezra x. 31).

Shim'hi. See SHIMEI 5.

Shim'i. See SHIMEI 1.

Shim'ma. See SHIMEA 3.

Shi'mon.
A man who had his registry with the tribe of Judah (1 Chron. iv. 20).

Shim'rath [watching, guarding].
A Benjamite, son of Shimei of Aijalon (1 Chron. viii. 21).

Shim'ri, in A. V. once **Simri** (1 Chron. xxvi. 10) [watchful].
1. A Simeonite, son of Shemaiah (1 Chron. iv. 37).
2. Father of one of David's mighty men (1 Chron. xi. 45).
3. A Merarite Levite, a son of Hosah (1 Chron. xxvi. 10).
4. A Levite, who lived in the reign of Hezekiah. He was a son of Elizaphan of the family of Kohath, house of Uzziel (2 Chron. xxix. 13).

Shim'rith [vigilant].
A Moabitess, mother of one of king Joash's assassins (2 Chron. xxiv. 26). Called in 2 Kin. xii. 21 Shomer.

Shim'ron, in A. V. once **Shimrom** (1 Chron. vii. 1), an error not in the original edition of 1611 [watching, a guard].
1. A son of Issachar, and founder of a tribal family (Gen. xlvi. 13; Num. xxvi. 24).
2. A border town of Zebulun (Josh. xi. 1; xix. 15). Not identified. Semûnieh, 5 miles west of Nazareth, has been conjectured among other places.

Shim-ron-me'ron.
A Canaanite town, whose king was vanquished and slain by Joshua (Josh. xii. 20). Probably the full name of Shimron.

Shim'shai [sunny].
A scribe, one of those who complained to Artaxerxes Longimanus that the Jews were rebuilding the temple (Ezra iv. 8).

Shin.
The twenty-first letter of the Hebrew alphabet. English S comes from the same source, and with sh represents it in anglicized Hebrew names; as in Simeon, Shimea, Ishmael. It heads the twenty-first section of Ps. cxix., in which section each verse of the original begins with this letter.

Shi'nab.
The king of Admah, who was defeated by Chedorlaomer (Gen. xiv. 2, 8, 10).

Shi′nar.

A country in which the cities of Babel, Erech, Accad, and Calneh were situated (Gen. x. 10; xi. 2; Dan. i. 2). Hence, in Hebrew usage, Shinar comprehended the alluvial plain of Babylonia. The same region, perhaps, was known to Semites of Mesopotamia as Shanhar, as appears from an inscription of Tell el-Amarna. In the days of Abraham, Amraphel was king of the whole or a large part of it (Gen. xiv. 1, 9). Some of the Jews were to be carried thither as captives (Is. xi. 11; Zech. v. 11).

Shi′on, in A. V. **Shihon** [destruction, ruin].

A town of Issachar (Josh. xix. 19). The site is perhaps at ʿAyûn esh-Shaʾîn, 3 miles west-northwest of mount Tabor.

Ship.

Little boats were used by dwellers on the upper Euphrates for descending the river to Babylon (Herod. i. 194). They were circular in form. The ribs were made of willow, over which hides were stretched as a covering. They were steered by two men who stood upright, each with a spar which they thrust alternately. The largest vessels carried 5000 talents. On the Nile boats built of acacia wood were used (ii. 96).

Boats were doubtless used on the sea of Galilee in O. T. times, but they are not mentioned. In the Roman period the sea was alive with small fishing vessels (Luke v. 2; John vi. 22, 23; War ii. 21, 8; iii. 10, 9; Life 33). They were propelled by oars; but some, at least, had both oars and sails (Mark iv. 38 with Luke viii. 23); they carried an anchor and a pilot (Life 33).

The Israelites were not a seafaring people; although shipbuilding was far advanced among the Egyptians and doubtless among the Phœnicians before the exodus, and the Hebrews had the spectacle of ships on the Mediterranean before their eyes during the whole period of their national history. Solomon conducted commercial enterprises, and Jehoshaphat attempted to imitate him; but these were transient efforts and were more or less dependent upon Phœnician sailors. The rafts of cedar and fir destined for Solomon's temple were floated to Joppa by Tyrians (1 Kin. v. 9; 2 Chron. ii. 16), and the timber for the second temple was likewise brought by sea to Joppa by Phœnicians (Ezra iii. 7). The crew of the vessel in which Jonah sailed from Joppa was also composed of foreigners (Jonah i. 5). In the Roman period, piratical expeditions by Jews are reported (Antiq. xiv. 3, 2; War iii. 9, 2 and 3).

Both merchant vessels and war ships were used on the Mediterranean (Num. xxiv. 24; Dan. xi. 30; Jonah i. 3; 1 Mac. xi. 1). In war, vessels were employed for transporting troops (xv. 3, 4; 2 Mac. xiv. 1) and for fighting at sea (1 Mac. viii. 23, 32; Antiq. ix. 14, 2; cp. War iii. 10, 1). Some of these sea-going vessels were propelled by sails alone; others by both sails and oars. A gallant merchantman of Tyre was built of planks and calked (Ezek. xxvii. 5, 9); had masts, linen sails, and tackling (7; Is. xxxiii. 23), benches of boxwood, and oaken oars (Ezek. xxvii. 6, R. V.). It was manned by sailors and guided by a pilot (8, 27). When luxuriously furnished, the sails were embroidered and a rich awning was spread (7). Such vessels made the voyage to Tarshish (Jonah i. 3, 5, 6, 13), and even navigated the Atlantic Ocean from Spain to England; see TIN. The ship of Alexandria, in which Paul was conveyed from Myra to Malta, was large enough to accommodate a crew and passengers numbering 276 persons, besides a cargo of wheat (Acts xxvii. 37, 38). The vessel in which Josephus was wrecked had 600 persons on board (Life 3). The Alexandrian wheat ship, described by Lucian as driven into the port of Athens by rough weather, was 120 cubits, or 180 feet, in length, doubtless including the projection at each end, and 45 feet in breadth. Its size attracted attention. Its measurement is supposed to have been about 1200 or 1300 tons. The exceptionally large war galley of Ptolemy Philopator measured, according to Athenæus, 420 feet in length and 57 feet in breadth. Paul's ship was in charge of a master and the owner (Acts xxvii. 11), and was managed by a crew (30). It was built of planks (44), carried a foresail, which could be raised and lowered (40, R. V.), and by implication a foremast and a mainmast, and was steered by rudders, doubtless two (40). Four anchors were stowed at the stern and several forward (29, 30), and a small boat was towed behind, which could be raised by ropes to the deck or davits (16, 17, 30, 32). Soundings were taken (28). It was customary for ships to have an eye painted or carved on each side of the stem. Paul's vessel was unable to face the gale, literally to keep the eye to the wind (15).

A fishing vessel on the Sea of Galilee. Note the use of both oars and sails.

A ship of Paul's time, depicted at Pompeii, shows a foremast inclined like a bowsprit, but intended to carry a square sail, and one large mast with one square sail fitted to a yard of great length. The yard was composed of two spars spliced together, and was placed with its center against the mast. The sail was strengthened by ropes sewed across it vertically and horizontally; and if torn, the rent was confined to the square in which it occurred. The sail was furled by being drawn up to the yard. The deck was protected by a rail. The stern post, and in many vessels the stem post also, rose in a curve. It was customary, as in this ship, for the stern post at least to terminate in the head of a water fowl. The sign of the ship (Acts xxviii. 11) was painted or carved on each side of the prow. The vessel was steered by two broad oars or paddles, one on each quarter and acting through a port hole. The anchors were similar to those in modern use, except that they had no flukes. To prevent the starting of the planks in a storm, cables or chains, called helps or undergirders (xxvii. 17), were passed around the vessel at right angles to its length and made tight.

Shi'phi [abounding, abundant].
A Simeonite, son of Allon (1 Chron. iv. 37).

Shiph'mite.
A native or inhabitant of probably Siphmoth (1 Chron. xxvii. 27).

Shiph'rah [splendor, beauty].
One of the Hebrew midwives in Egypt who declined to kill the male babes (Ex. i. 15).

Shiph'tan [judicial].
An Ephraimite, father of Kemuel (Num. xxxiv. 24).

Shi'sha. See SHAVSHA.

Shi'shak. See PHARAOH 3.

Shit'rai.
A Sharonite, who looked after David's herds on the plain of Sharon (1 Chron. xxvii. 29).

Shit'tah Tree and Shittim Wood.
A tree (Is. xli. 19). The R. V. renders the word by acacia tree or wood. It grew in the Jordan valley, from the sea of Galilee to the Dead Sea (see BETH-SHITTAH and SHITTIM). It was plentiful in the wilderness of Sinai, and its timber was largely used in the tabernacle, for the woodwork of the ark, the altars and their staves, the table, the boards, bars, and pillars (Ex. xxv. 5, 10, 13, 23; xxvi. 15, 26, 32; xxvii. 1, 6; xxx. 1, 5). The wood was used in Egypt in boat building (Herod. ii. 96), and Josephus speaks of its strength and durability (Antiq. iii. 6, 5). The Arabic name *sant* is the same word as the Hebrew *shittah*, and denotes the acacia. There are several species. *Acacia seyal* and *tortilis* are found in the valleys about the Dead Sea and southward, and *Acacia nilotica* grows in the southern part of the peninsula of Sinai and in Egypt. Other species are found in various parts of Palestine. The genuine acacias are

generally small trees, growing from 15 to 25 feet high, thorny, with bipinnate leaves, and pods with several seeds. The wood is hard and close-grained. Certain species yield the gum Arabic of commerce.

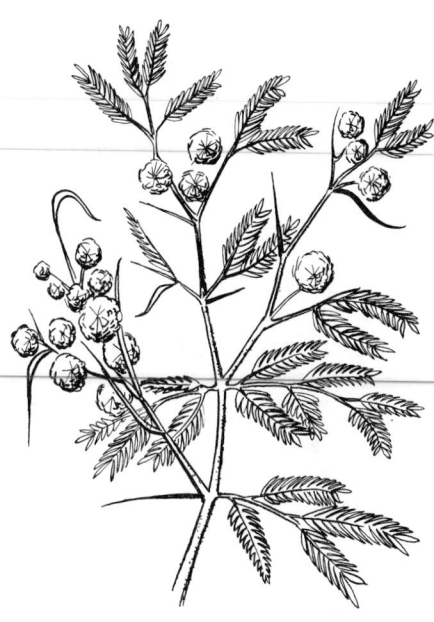

Shittah tree.

Shit'tim [acacias].
1. An important encampment of the Israelites in the plains of Moab, east of Jordan, opposite Jericho (Num. xxii. 1 with xxv. 1). The camp had been removed from Pisgah on the mountains of Abarim and pitched at Shittim after the conquest of Sihon and Og (xxi. 20; xxii. 1; xxxiii. 47, 48). It was located on a table-land, the topmost of the three terraces which at this point form the valley of the Jordan, and among the long groves of acacia trees. It extended from Beth-jeshimoth even unto Abel-shittim (xxxiii. 49; cp. xxiii. 28), a distance of 3 miles and more. It was arranged in an orderly manner, the Israelites dwelling according to their tribes (xxiv. 2, 5, 6); see CAMP. The sojourn at Shittim was eventful. While the Israelites were encamped there, Balaam attempted to curse them (xxii.–xxiv.), the people committed sin with the daughters of Moab and Midian at Baal-peor, and were plagued in consequence (xxv.), the second census was taken (xxvi.), occasion arose for enacting laws regarding the inheritance of daughters (xxvii. 1–11), Joshua was publicly proclaimed the successor to Moses (12–23), daily offerings and vows were further regulated (xxviii.–xxx.), war was waged with

the five Midianite tribes of the neighborhood on account of the deliberate attempt which they had recently made to seduce the Israelites into licentious idolatry at Baal-peor (xxxi.), Reuben and Gad, at their own request, received inheritance east of the Jordan (xxxii.), an itinerary of the journey from Egypt to the Jordan was drawn up by Moses (xxxiii.). Measures were also taken for the occupation of Canaan: in view of recent events, the expulsion of the Canaanites and the destruction of their altars and idols were urgently commanded anew; the boundaries of the land were defined, and a commission was appointed to superintend the allotment of territory to the tribes; and it was ordered that cities be assigned to the Levites, and that six cities of refuge be designated for the unintentional murderer (xxxiii. 50–xxxv.). The matter of the inheritance of daughters was further regulated (xxxvi.). Then Moses delivered his farewell address (see DEUTERONOMY), Joshua received a solemn charge, and Moses ascended Nebo and died. After the death of Moses, Joshua sent forth two spies from Shittim to examine and report on the defenses of Jericho (Josh. ii.). Then camp was broken at Shittim, and the people crossed the Jordan (iii.).

2. A valley, dry and comparatively unfruitful, where only the acacia or shittah tree grows (Joel iii. 18). If a particular valley is in the prophet's mind, it is the Arabah about the Dead Sea (cp. Ezek. xlvii. 1–12). The prophet names it from the encampment of the Israelites at Shittim, and he selects it as a type because the waters of its sea were practically lifeless, and its southern portion consisted of barren rocks and cliffs of salt. After Jehovah has judged all nations, the kingdom of God shall flourish and the kingdoms of the world become waste (Joel iii. 9–21). The mountains of Judah shall drop down new wine, its hills flow with milk, its wadies be brooks of water, and from the house of the Lord shall go forth waters that shall make glad the valley of acacias. In other words, the desert shall blossom as the rose; spiritual life shall proceed from the Lord God and shall supply the needs of his kingdom (cp. Rev. xxii. 1, 2).

Shi'za [vehement love].
A Reubenite, father of one of David's heroes (1 Chron. xi. 42).

Sho'a.
A country and its inhabitants, mentioned in connection with the Babylonians, Chaldeans, and Assyrians (Ezek. xxiii. 23); and doubtless the Shutu who are mentioned by the Babylonians and Assyrians as occupying a hilly country with steppes, adjacent to Babylonia on the northeast, and between the Tigris river and the mountains of Elam and Media (Delitzsch, *Paradies*, 334).

Sho'bab [restored, rescued].
1. A man of Judah, family of Hezron,

house of Caleb. His mother was Azubah (1 Chron. ii. 18).
2. A son of David, born to him at Jerusalem (2 Sam. v. 14).

Sho'bach [one who pours out].
Commander-in-chief under Hadarezer, king of Zobah (2 Sam. x. 16). Called in 1 Chron. xix. 16, 18, Shophach. The difference is doubtless due to a scribe's confusion of beth and pe, but even so the names are strictly synonymous.

Sho'bai [one who leads captive].
A Levite, founder of a family of doorkeepers, members of which returned with Zerubbabel from captivity (Ezra ii. 42).

Sho'bal [flowing, a stream, a twig, a traveler].
1. A tribe of Horites (Gen. xxxvi. 20), consisting of several families (23), and ruled by a chieftain (29).
2. A son of Hur, a man of Judah, family of Hezron, house of Caleb. He was ancestor of the inhabitants of Kirjath-jearim (1 Chron. ii. 50; iv. 1, 2, 4).

Sho'bek [one who forsakes].
One of the Jewish chiefs who with Nehemiah sealed the covenant (Neh. x. 24).

Sho'bi [one who leads captive].
Son of a resident in Rabbah of the Ammonites named Nahash (2 Sam. xvii. 27). Shobi brought food and other necessaries to David at Mahanaim.

Sho'cho, Shochoh, Shoco. See SOCO

Shoe.
Hebrew shoes were, as a rule, simply sandals affixed to the foot by straps known as

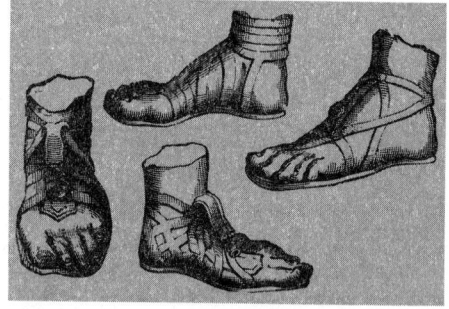

Sandals.

latchets; see CLOTHING. Shoes were not worn in the sitting room or at the table (cp. Luke vii. 38); and in well-appointed houses a servant stood ready to unloose the latchet and remove the shoe of the guest (cp. Mark i. 7). Shoes were also removed when one was about to tread holy ground (Ex. iii. 5; Josh. v. 15); and the absence of shoes in the description of the priest's garments is supposed to indicate that the priests performed their duties in the temple barefoot. To be without shoes and stript of superfluous raiment might betoken the captive's plight (Is. xx. 2), and was a customary sign of mourning (2 Sam. xv. 30); while to wear shoes in time of sorrow, and attire the head, was a concealment of grief (Ezek. xxiv. 17, 23). In the olden time in Israel, in matters of redemption and exchange, a man drew off his shoe and gave it to him with whom he had concluded the agreement, as confirmation of the transaction (Ruth iv. 7, 8); and the shoe of the man who refused to take his deceased brother's wife was loosed, with other insult (Deut. xxv. 9, 10). To cast the shoe upon a place symbolized the act of taking possession or, possibly, of treating it as a slave upon whom as a task the master flings his shoes in order that they may be carried or cleaned (Ps. lx. 8).

Sho'ham [a beryl or onyx].
A Levite, son of Jaaziah (1 Chron. xxiv. 27).

Sho'mer [keeper, watchman].
1. An Asherite, son of Heber (1 Chron. vii. 32). See SHEMER.
2. A Moabitess, mother of one of king Joash's assassins (2 Kin. xii. 21). See SHIMRITH.

Sho'phach. See SHOBACH.

Sho'phan. See ATROTH-SHOPHAN.

Sho-shan'nim [lilies].
A word occurring in the titles of Psalms xlv. and lxix. Three opinions exist as to its meaning: symbolical of the contents of the psalm, a musical instrument resembling a lily, a familiar melody. It doubtless indicates a popular air. This appears from the combinations Shoshannim Eduth, "Lilies a testimony" (Ps. lxxx. title), and Shushan Eduth, "Lily a testimony" (Ps. lx. title).

Show'bread.
Literally "bread of the presence." It consisted of twelve loaves of bread, laid in two rows and displayed on a table in the holy place before the Lord continually. The bread was changed every Sabbath, and the old loaves were eaten by the priests in the holy place (Ex. xxv. 30; Lev. xxiv. 5–9; 1 Sam. xxi. 6; Mat. xii. 4). The bread was also known as the continual bread (Num. iv. 7, where the name showbread is also used); and continual pile or arrangement (2 Chron. ii. 4, translated showbread) or the bread of the pile or arrangement (1 Chron. ix. 32, translated showbread), because arranged in rows or columns (Lev. xxiv. 6). Josephus says the bread was unleavened (Antiq. iii. 6, 6). Each loaf contained two-tenths of an ephah of fine flour, such as was used for honored guests and for the king's table (Gen. xviii. 6; 1 Kin. iv. 22), and was employed in various offerings (Lev. ii. 1; v. 11; etc.). The twelve loaves represented the twelve tribes of Israel (Lev. xxiv. 7 with Ex. xxviii. 10–12; also Ex. xxiv. 4; xxviii. 21). These twelve loaves set in the presence of Jehovah probably signified the constant communion of his people with him in those things which his bounty provided and they enjoyed in his presence and used in his service. The Kohathites had charge of the showbread (1 Chron. ix. 32).

The table of showbread was made of acacia wood overlaid with gold. It was bordered by a golden crown, and had a ring at each corner for the rods by which it was carried. It measured 2 cubits long, 1 broad, and 1½ high (Ex. xxv. 23–29; for its transportation, see Num. iv. 7, 8). It stood in the holy place, by the northern wall, that is, to the right of one entering the tabernacle (Ex. xl. 22). In Solomon's temple there were ten tables for showbread, corresponding to the ten candlesticks, although like the candlesticks apparently only one was in use at a time (1 Chron. xxviii. 16; 2 Chron. iv. 8, 19; xiii. 11; Antiq. viii. 3, 7); hence only one is mentioned in 1 Kin. vii. 48; 2 Chron. xxix. 18. The table which belonged to the second temple was carried off by Antiochus Epiphanes, but a new one was provided by Judas Maccabæus (1 Mac. i. 22; iv. 49). Titus carried it to Rome (War vii. 5, 5).

Shu'a, in A. V. twice **Shuah** (Gen. xxxviii. 2, 12) [wealth].
1. A Canaanite, whose daughter became Judah's wife or concubine, and the mother of his sons, Er, Onan, and Shelah (Gen. xxxviii. 2, 12; 1 Chron. ii. 3).
2. An Asherite, a daughter of Heber (1 Chron. vii. 32).

Shu'ah [depression].
A son of Abraham, by Keturah (Gen. xxv. 2), that is, an Arab tribe descended from them, doubtless the Shuhites who dwelt near the land of Uz (Job ii. 11). Their land is plausibly identified with a district of the same name, in Assyrian Suḫu, on the west of the Euphrates, near the mouth of the Belich and Khabour.
For others whose name is rendered Shuah in A. V., see SHUA and SHUHAH.

Shu'al [a fox or jackal].
1. An Asherite, son of Zophah (1 Chron. vii. 36).
2. A district near Ophrah, to the north of Michmash (1 Sam. xiii. 17). Exact situation unknown.

Shu'ba-el. See SHEBUEL.

Shu'hah, in A. V. **Shuah** [depression, a small pit].
A man of Judah (1 Chron. iv. 11).

Shu'ham [depression or, perhaps, a pitman].
The son of Dan, and founder of the tribal family (Num. xxvi. 42). Called in Gen. xlvi. 23 Hushim.

Shu'hite. See SHUAH.

The table of showbread. In the center of the table is the golden pan for baking the bread. The vessel that was filled with wine is beneath the table.

Shu'lam-mite, in A. V. **Shulamite.**

A young woman mentioned in the Song of Solomon (vi. 13). In all probability the name is derived from that of the town of Shunem. The Septuagint translates it by *Sounamitis, i. e.* Shunammite; and the town of Shunem was known in the time of Eusebius as Shulem, and to-day bears the name Sôlam. The form Shulammite may have been preferred to Shunammite because of its assonance with Solomon, in Hebrew *Sh⁰lomoh.*

Shu'math-ites [from *shumah*, garlic].

One of the leading families in Kiriath-jearim (1 Chron. ii. 53).

Shu'nam-mite.

A native or inhabitant of Shunem; as Abishag (1 Kin. i. 3), and she whose son Elisha restored to life (2 Kin. iv. 8, 12; viii. 1).

Shu'nem [possibly, two resting places].

A town of Canaan, taken by Thothmes III, in the territory of Issachar (Josh. xix. 18), opposite mount Gilboa (1 Sam. xxviii. 4). The Philistines encamped there before the battle with Saul. The site is at Sôlam, on the western slope of a hill 3½ miles north by east of Jezreel, 5 north of the western end of mount Gilboa, and about 16 miles from Carmel, whither the Shunammite woman went to find Elisha (2 Kin. iv. 25).

Shu'ni [possibly, calm, quiet].

A son of Gad, and founder of a tribal family (Gen. xlvi. 16; Num. xxvi. 15).

Shu'pham. See SHEPHUPHAM.

Shup'pim.

1. A Benjamite (1 Chron. vii. 12, 15); see SHEPHUPHAM.

2. A Levite, who served as a doorkeeper at the sanctuary (1 Chron. xxvi. 16). The Hebrew text is doubtless corrupt. Perhaps the name crept in from the preceding verse, which ends with a word very like Shuppim.

Shur [wall, fortification].

1. A locality in the wilderness, south of Palestine, or more exactly south of Beer-lahai-roi, and east of Egypt (Gen. xvi. 7; xxv. 18). It has not been identified, but was doubtless connected with the frontier fortresses of Egypt. It gave name to the wilderness through which the Israelites marched for three days immediately after crossing the Red Sea (Ex. xv. 22). This waste was also sometimes called the wilderness of Etham (Num. xxxiii. 8).

Shu'shan [to the Hebrews the name would suggest lily].

A city and royal residence in the Persian empire (Neh. i. 1; Esth. i. 2), in the province of Elam, on the river Ulai (Dan. viii. 2). It was also a royal treasure city (Herod. v. 49). The place referred to in these passages is Susa. Ashurbanipal captured the city about 660 B. C., and later it became subject to the Babylonian kings. The royal family to which Cyrus, who conquered Babylon, be-

longed ruled over Ansan, which appears to
have been a district of eastern Elam. When
Cyrus, by his military achievements, established the Persian empire, Susa was elevated
to the rank of a capital of the empire, sharing this distinction with Ecbatana and Babylon. When Alexander the Great entered
Susa, in 331 B. C., it had in it immense treasures, of which he took possession. In 315 B.
c. it was captured and plundered anew by
Antigonus. After this it began to decline,
but was still defensible when the Saracens
conquered Persia. The site of the city is at
Sus, in latitude 32° 10′ north, longitude 48°
26′′ east, between the river Eulæus (the Roman name for Daniel's Ulai) and the Shah-
pur, and about 100 miles from the Persian
Gulf. The chief ruins are found within an
area of about 6000 feet long by 4500 broad,
the circumference being about 3 miles; but
if scattered remains be taken in, the 3 miles
may become 6 or 7. They consist of a series
of mounds, in one of which the explorers
laid bare the ruins of a palace, doubtless that
begun by Darius, and in which Xerxes held
his court. It seems to have been there that
Esther's Ahasuerus held his feasts and his
banquets (Esth. i. 2, 3, 9; ii. 18, etc.).

Shu'shan-chites, in A. V. **Susanchites**
[from Elamite *Susinak*, Susian].

Natives or inhabitants of the Persian Susa,
the Shushan of the O. T. The Shushanchites
were brought, with others, to central Palestine to supply the place of the ten tribes carried into captivity (Ezra iv. 9).

Shu'shan E'duth. See SHOSHANNIM.

Shu'the-lah.

1. A son of Ephraim, and founder of a tribal family (Num. xxvi. 35, 36; 1 Chron.
vii. 20).

2. Another descendant of Ephraim in the
same line (1 Chron. vii. 21).

Si'a-ha and **Sia** [assembly].

A family of Nethinim, members of which
returned with Zerubbabel from the captivity
(Ezra ii. 44; Neh. vii. 47).

Sib'be-cai, in A. V. twice **Sibbechai** (2
Sam. xxi. 18; 1 Chron. xx. 4) [perhaps, en-
tangling].

A Hushathite, one of David's mighty men
(1 Chron. xi. 29). He won renown by slaying the Philistine Saph, one of the sons of
the giant (2 Sam. xxi. 18). He commanded
the division of the army for the eighth month
(1 Chron. xxvii. 11). He is called in 2 Sam.
xxiii. 27 Mebunnai (q. v.).

Sib'bo-leth. See SHIBBOLETH.

Sib'mah, in A. V. once **Shibmah** (Num.
xxxii. 38) [coolness].

A town assigned to Reuben (Num. xxxii.
38; Josh. xiii. 19), but which afterwards reverted to Moab. It was celebrated for its
vines (Is. xvi. 8, 9; Jer. xlviii. 32). The
masculine form of the name is Sebam (Num.

xxxii. 3; in A. V. Shebam). According to
Jerome, it was situated scarcely half a mile
from Heshbon. Not identified. Conder suggests Sûmia, 3 miles west by north of Heshbon.

Sib'ra-im [perhaps, hope].

An unidentified place on Ezekiel's northern
boundary of Canaan (Ezek. xlvii. 16).

Sic'cuth.

A word occurring in Amos v. 26, E. R. V.;
but in A. R. V. and A. V. translated tabernacle (cp. the word Succoth). Regarded as a
proper name, it corresponds to Sakkut, a
designation given by the Babylonians to the
planet Saturn. Another designation which
they had for the planet was Kaiman, or in
modified pronunciation Kaiwanu (cp. Chiun,
Amos v. 26, A. V. and E. R. V.).

Si'chem. See SHECHEM.

Si'cy-on.

A Dorian town in the Peloponnesus
(Herod. viii. 43), on the gulf of Corinth, 10
miles northwest of the city of Corinth. The
old town at the harbor was abandoned in 303
B. C., and the populace removed to the new
town, about 2 miles inland, which occupied
a strong natural position. The city became
a member of the Achæan league in 251 B.
C. Half a century later it began to show
friendliness to the Romans, and continued to
do so during the fifty years that followed;
and in 146 B. C., on the destruction of Corinth
by the Roman general, Mummius, it was rewarded with a large portion of the conquered
territory and with the management of the
Isthmian games. It held this distinction for
a century, until Corinth was founded again
and made a Roman colony. The Roman
senate addressed the letter to Sicyon mentioned in 1 Mac. xv. 23, about 139 B. C.

Sid'dim [plains].

A valley, full of bitumen pits, in the region
of the Salt or Dead Sea. There Chedorlaomer
defeated the king of Sodom and his allies
(Gen. xiv. 3, 8, 10).

Si'de.

A maritime town of eastern Pamphylia in
Asia Minor. It maintained close commercial
relations with Aradus in Phœnicia, gave the
title Sidetes to Antiochus VII., who was
brought up in the town, and was one of the
places to which the Roman senate sent letters
in favor of the Jews (1 Mac. xv. 23).

Si'don and **Zidon**; in A. V. usually, in R.
V. always, **Zidon** in O. T.; in A. V. and R.
V. always **Sidon** in N. T. [a fishery].

An ancient city of the Canaanites (Gen. x.
15), on the seacoast, 22 miles north of Tyre.
It was subject to Egypt in the 15th century
B. C. Its importance is attested by Homer,
who often mentions Sidon, but never Tyre,
and who uses Sidon and Sidonian as synonymous with Phœnicia and Phœnician. It
was the northern limit of the Canaanites, in
the narrow sense (Gen. x. 19). Its territory

was near Zebulun (xlix. 13) and the boundary of Asher reached it (Josh. xix. 28, where and in xi. 8 it is called Great Zidon). The tribe of Asher, however, failed to expel the Canaanite inhabitants (Judg. i. 31). In the period of the judges the Zidonians oppressed the Israelites (x. 12), and the latter people are accused of worshiping the gods of Zidon (6). Of these gods, Baal, symbolizing the sun, was doubtless the chief (1 Kin. xvi. 31); the principal object of worship, however, was Ashtoreth, a goddess of fertility (xi. 5, 33; 2 Kin. xxiii. 13). Ethbaal, a king of Zidon, was the father of Jezebel (1 Kin. xvi. 31). Isaiah predicted that it would be visited with judgment which would make its inhabitants pass to Kittim, that is, Cyprus (Is. xxiii. 12). It was for a time subject to the neighboring

B. C. it opened its gates to Alexander the Great. From his successors it passed, in 64 B. C., to the Romans. People from Sidon came to Galilee to attend on the preaching of Jesus and witness his miracles (Mark iii. 8; Luke vi. 17, etc.). He once visited the region, and probably the city (Mat. xv. 21; Mark vii. 24, 31). Herod Agrippa II. was highly displeased with the people of Tyre and Sidon, but they made peace with him "because their country was fed from the king's country" (Acts xii. 20). Paul touched at the port (xxvii. 3). Since N. T. times Sidon has seen many vicissitudes. The modern city, called Saida, lies on the northwestern slope of a small promontory jutting out into the sea. The ancient harbor was formed by a ridge of rocks parallel to the shore. It

Ruins of a Crusader castle on an island in Sidon harbor. The island is connected to the mainland by an arched bridge.

city of Tyre (Antiq. ix. 14, 2). In 701 B. C., it submitted to Sennacherib, king of Assyria. In 678 B. C. it was destroyed by Esarhaddon. Jeremiah predicted its subjugation by Nebuchadnezzar, king of Babylon (Jer. xxvii. 3, 6). Ezekiel denounced judgment against it because it had been "a pricking brier to the house of Israel" (Ezek. xxviii. 21, 22). Joel charges the Zidonians and others with having helped to plunder Jerusalem, carrying off silver and gold, and selling its inhabitants for slaves (Joel iii. 4-6). About 526 B. C. Zidon submitted to Cambyses, son of Cyrus, king of Persia. The Zidonians sold cedar timber to the Jews for the temple which Zerubbabel was building (Ezra iii. 7). It revolted against Artaxerxes Ochus, king of Persia, in 351 B. C., but was retaken and destroyed. To get rid of the Persians, in 333

was partly filled up with stones and earth by Fakhr ed-Din, the ruler of the Druses, in the seventeenth century. There is a wall protecting the land side of the city. The highest ground, which is crowned by the citadel, is on the southern side. The city is enveloped in gardens and orchards, but has not much commerce; that having been largely diverted from it to Beirut. Its population has been estimated at 5000 to 10,000. It has in and around it a few broken granite columns; and various sarcophagi, including the celebrated one of Esmunazar, were brought from tombs in its vicinity.

Si-do'ni-ans, in A. V. frequently **Zidonians**, in R. V. always so except once (Deut. iii. 9).

Siege. See WAR.

Sig'net. See SEAL 2.

Si'hon [sweeping out, a brush].

A king of the Amorites, whose capital was Heshbon. He drove the Moabites from the country between Heshbon and the Arnon and took possession of it (Num. xxi. 26–30). Five Midianite tribes were his vassals (Josh. xiii. 21). When the Israelites arrived in the wilderness on the southeast of the Arnon, Moses sent messengers to him to ask permission to cross his territory (Num. xxi. 21, 22 ; Deut. ii. 26). He refused. Thereupon the Israelites entered his domains under the necessity of fighting their way to the Jordan. Sihon gathered his army together at Jahaz and opposed the invaders, but he was defeated and his kingdom was taken possession of by the Israelites (Num. xxi. 21–32 ; Ps. cxxxv. 11). The country thus seized was included between the Jordan, the Jabbok, and the Arnon (Num. xxi. 24, 32 ; Deut. ii. 36 ; Judg. xi. 22). The camp of Israel was pitched at Pisgah, a secure position on the mountains of Abarim, nearly in the center of the conquered district, preparatory to the campaign against Bashan (Num. xxi. 20 ; cp. xxii. 1 ; xxxiii. 47). Sihon's kingdom was afterwards assigned to the tribes of Reuben and Gad, who desired it because it afforded good pasturage (Num. xxxii. 1–4, 33-38).

Si'hor. See SHIHOR.

Si'las, or uncontracted **Silvanus** [sylvan].

A distinguished member of the apostolic church at Jerusalem. He was sent with Paul to communicate the decision of the council held at that city to the Christians at Antioch (Acts xv. 22, 27, 32). When Paul declined to take John Mark with him on the second missionary journey, and parted with Barnabas, he chose Silas as his companion (40), and the two were imprisoned together at Philippi (xvi. 19, 25, 29). Silas was with Paul during the riot at Thessalonica (xvii. 4), and was sent away with him to Berœa, remaining there with Timothy after the apostle had been obliged to depart (14). The two were, however, soon directed to follow Paul to Athens (15). They started to join him, but do not seem to have come up with him till after his arrival at Corinth (xviii. 5). In this city Silas was an esteemed coworker of Paul's (2 Cor. i. 19). The same individual who in The Acts is familiarly named Silas is unvaryingly called by his full name Silvanus in the epistles. He was associated with Paul and Timothy in sending the two letters to the Thessalonians (1 Thes. i. 1 ; 2 Thes. i. 1). He is probably the Silvanus who carried to its destination the First Epistle of Peter (1 Pet. v. 12).

Silk.

A fine, soft thread produced by various species of caterpillars, and a fabric woven from the thread. Silk reached the markets of the west shortly after the conquest of Alexander the Great. It was known to the Greeks as *sērikon*, pertaining to the Sers, a people of India from whom it was obtained. It was a choice article of merchandise (Rev. xviii. 12), fit for the clothing of Roman emperors (War vii. 5, 4). As late as the reign of the emperor Aurelian, A. D. 270–275, unmixed silk goods were sold for their weight in gold. The fine raiment referred to in Ezek. xvi. 10, 13 by the term *meshi* was probably silk, as the rabbinical interpreters understood and as it is rendered in the E. V. Ezekiel doubtless saw the stuff in Babylonia. A rich cloth is meant by *dᵉmeshek* (Amos iii. 12), which is commonly regarded as damask (in R. V. rendered silken cushions).

Sil'la [twig, basket]. The meaning "way, street," assigned by Thenius, is obtained by altering the Hebrew text.

An unknown place near Millo (2 Kin. xii 20).

Si-lo'ah, an erroneous transliteration of Shelah in A. V. of Neh. iii. 15. See SILOAM.

Si-lo'am [sent ; specially, a sending of water through an aqueduct].

A pool at Jerusalem (John ix. 7) ; probably identical with Shiloah, the waters of which go softly (Is. viii. 6), and the pool of Shelah, which was by the king's garden (Neh. iii. 15). Josephus says that it was situated at the extremity of the valley of cheesemongers, near a bend of the old wall beneath Ophlas, *i. e.* Ophel (War v. 4, 1 and 2). The name is preserved in the Birket Silwân, which occupies the general site of the ancient pool. It is a rectangular reservoir, 58 feet long, 18 broad, and 19 deep, built of masonry, the western side of which has considerably broken down. The fountain is a small upper basin excavated in the rock. It is really the termination of the tunnel which was cut to conduct the water from the fountain of the Virgin. From the lower reservoir, the water flows in a small rill across the road and irrigates gardens in the Kidron valley.

In 1880 an inscription of six lines was discovered on the walls of this tunnel by a youth who had entered from the Siloam end. It proved to be written in pure Hebrew, and is supposed to date from the time of Ahaz or Hezekiah. A portion of the first three lines has been destroyed by the wearing away of the rock, and occasionally a letter cannot be made out with certainty. Still the sense is plain. It describes how the workmen, who had excavated toward each other from the two ends of the tunnel, met. It is as follows, as nearly as possible. "[Behold] the piercing through! And this was the manner of the piercing through. While yet [the miners were lifting up] the pick one toward another, and while there were yet three cubits to be [cut through, there was heard] the voice of each calling to the other ; for there was a fissure (?) in the rock on the right hand . . . . And on the day of the piercing through, the miners smote the one so as to meet the other, pick against pick. And the water flowed from the source to the pool, 1200 cubits ; and 100 cubits was the height of the rock over the head of the miners."

The tower in Siloam which fell (Luke xiii. 4) was probably one on the Ophel ridge, near Siloam. It was not in the neighboring village of Silwân, for this place dates from the Middle Ages.

Sil-va'nus. See SILAS.

Sil'ver.

A precious metal. Its ore was mined from the earth (Job xxviii. 1) and melted in a furnace, by which process the dross was separated from the richer metal (Ps. xii. 6 ; Prov. xvii. 3 ; xxv. 4 ; Ezek. xxii. 22). It was obtained in Arabia (2 Chron. ix. 14 ; cp. 1 Kin. x. 22, 27) and Tarshish (Jer. x. 9 ; Ezek. xxvii. 12), Spain being a large producer (1 Mac. viii. 3). It was used as a medium of exchange from remotest antiquity (Gen. xxiii. 16 ; xxxvii. 28). The amount required was weighed out (Job xxviii. 15 ; Is. xlvi. 6), for silver was not coined until late, among the Jews not until long after the exile (1 Mac. xv. 6) ; see MONEY. Personal ornaments (Gen. xxiv. 53 ; Ex. iii. 22 ; Song i. 11), crowns (Zech. vi. 11), musical instruments, as trumpets (Num. x. 2), and household utensils of the wealthy, like Joseph's drinking cup (Gen. xliv. 2) were made of silver. Large quantities of the metal were used in the tabernacle and temple for sockets (Ex. xxvi. 19), hooks, chapiters and fillets of the pillars (xxvii. 10 ; xxxviii. 19), platters and bowls (Num. vii. 13 ; 1 Chron. xxviii. 17 ; Ezra i. 9, 10), cups (2 Kin. xii. 13), candlesticks, and tables (1 Chron. xxviii. 15, 16). Idols and models of idol shrines were constructed of silver (Ps. cxv. 4 ; Acts xix. 24).

Sil'ver-ling.

The rendering of the Hebrew *Keseph*, silver, in Is. vii. 23, which is elsewhere translated by shekel or piece of silver.

Si-mal-cu'e, in R. V. **Imalcue.**

An Arabian who brought up the young Antiochus, son of Alexander Balas (1 Mac. xi. 39) ; in Antiq. xiii. 5, 1 called Malchus. The name doubtless contains the Arabic word *malik*, king.

Sim'e-on, in R. V. of N. T. **Symeon,** in imitation of a Greek form, when the persons are not mentioned in O. T. (Luke iii. 30 ; Acts xiii. 1 ; xv. 14) [hearing].

1. The second-born son of Jacob by Leah (Gen. xxix. 33). In conjunction with his brother Levi, he massacred the Hivite inhabitants of Shechem on account of the injury done by one of their number to Dinah (Gen. xxxiv. 24–31) ; see DINAH. When one of Jacob's sons was to be kept a prisoner in Egypt as security for return of the rest, Joseph took Simeon and bound him (xlii. 24). The prediction of Simeon's future by the dying Jacob returns to the subject of the massacre, and threatens Simeon as well as Levi that they will be scattered in Israel (xlix. 5–7).

2. The tribe of which Simeon, the son of Jacob, was the progenitor. He had six sons : Jemuel or Nemuel, Jamin, Ohad, Jachin or Jarib, Zohar or Zerah, and Shaul. With the exception of Ohad, all these founded tribal families (Gen. xlvi. 10 ; Num. xxvi. 12–14 ; 1 Chron. iv. 24). The prince of the tribe in the early times of the wilderness wanderings was Shelumiel, son of Zurishaddai (Num. i. 6 ; ii. 12 ; vii. 36, 41 ; x. 19), and at a later period Shemuel, son of Ammihud (xxxiv. 20). At the first census in the wilderness the tribe numbered 59,300 fighting men (i. 23 ; ii. 13), at the second 22,200 (xxvi. 12–14). Shaphat, son of Hori, was the spy from the tribe (xiii. 5). Moses, before his departure, blessed the tribes, but omitted to mention Simeon explicitly (Deut. xxxiii.). This omission is probably due to the artificial construction of the poem. Moses wanted twelve for the number of the tribes. He formed two groups, departing from the order of birth, and placing the children of Jacob's two wives in the first group and those of the two maids in the second.

Leah 3	Leah's maid 1
Rachel 3	Rachel's maid 2
Leah 2	Leah's maid 1

The first group contains eight, Simeon being omitted, and the second group contains just half as many. The first group is subdivided into three minor groups, beginning with three of the elder children of Leah and closing with Leah's youngest two, and having Rachel's three in the center. The second group is made to correspond to this arrangement. It begins with Leah's firstborn by her maid and closes with her second son by the same maid, and the two sons of Rachel by her maid are placed between. The blessings pronounced upon these tribes are framed within a benediction upon all Israel (2–5, 25–29). The tribe of Simeon could best be omitted from the particular enumeration, because it was to be scattered in Israel (Gen. xlix. 5–7). The same punishment also awaited Levi, but recent deeds had partly atoned for the past and given the tribe of Levi a position of honor among the people of God. After Moses' death the tribe of Simeon was not assigned a self-contained territory, but was granted possession in the midst of Judah. The Simeonites, however, although not explicitly mentioned, were not excluded from the blessing invoked on the tribes. They were included in the general benediction upon Israel as a whole, with which the poem opens and closes. The tribe of Simeon was one of those who stood at the foot of mount Gerizim to pronounce blessings (Deut. xxvii. 12).

When the land of Canaan was distributed

by lot, the second lot taken at Shiloh came forth for the tribe of Simeon, and land was assigned them in the extreme south of Canaan, in the midst of the inheritance of the children of Judah (Josh. xix. 1, 2, 9), and the two tribes made common cause against the Canaanites (Judg. i. 1, 3, 17). Among the Simeonite cities were Beer-sheba, Ziklag, and Hormah (Josh. xix. 2-9), in the southern part of Judah. In the reign of Hezekiah the Simeonites smote the people of Ham and the Meunim who dwelt in the valley of Gedor, 500 of them also slaughtered the Amalekites of mount Seir; in both cases occupying the territory of the vanquished tribes (1 Chron. iv. 24-43). It is believed that ultimately a great part of the tribe disappeared, but it was recognized by Ezekiel in his prophecies of the future Canaan (Ezek. xlviii. 24, 25, 33), and in the apocalyptic vision there were sealed 12,000 Simeonites (Rev. vii. 7).

3. An ancestor of Christ, who lived after David but before Zerubbabel (Luke iii. 30).

4. A priest of the family of Joarib, and an ancestor of the Maccabees (1 Mac. ii. 1).

5. A righteous and devout man, to whom it had been revealed by the Holy Spirit that he should not see death till he had seen the Lord's Christ. Coming into the temple when Joseph and Mary had just brought in the infant Jesus, Simeon recognized him as the promised Messiah, expressed his willingness now to depart in peace, and made a prophetic address to Mary with respect both to her and her child (Luke ii. 25-35).

6. Simon Peter (Acts xv. 14); see PETER.

7. A Christian prophet or teacher at Antioch. He was surnamed Niger, black, and may perhaps have been of African race (Acts xiii. 1).

Si′mon [hearing]. Simon and Symeon imitate Greek modes of representing the Hebrew name *Shim‘on*, Simeon.

1. Second son of the priest Mattathias. He was called Thassi, which may perhaps mean director or guide (1 Mac. ii. 3, in Syriac Tharsi). With his brothers he sympathized with his father in the revolt against the religious intolerance of the Syrians (14). Regarding him as the wisest of the sons, his father, when about to die, appointed him the adviser of the family, but gave the military authority to Judas, a younger brother (65, 66). He held a military command under Judas, and led a detachment of troops to the aid of the Jews in Galilee (v. 17, 20-23). After the death of Judas Jonathan was chosen leader. He made Simon commandant of the entire coast (xi. 59; xii. 33, 34). When Jonathan was seized and held prisoner by Tryphon, the conduct of the war devolved on Simon, as the last remaining brother of the Maccabee family (xiii. 1-9). He at once completed the fortifications of Jerusalem, and secured possession of Joppa (10, 11).

When Tryphon invaded Judæa, Simon dogged his army (20), and when Tryphon withdrew from the country, Simon rebuilt and provisioned the strongholds of Judæa (33). He also allied himself with Tryphon's rival, Demetrius II., and obtained from him the recognition of the independence of Judæa, 142 B. C. (34-42). Thereupon he besieged and captured Gezer (43-48, in A. V. Gaza). In the spring of 141 he reduced the Syrian citadel at Jerusalem (49-52). A season of peace followed, during which Simon devoted his energies to internal administration and the encouragement of commerce and agriculture (xiv. 4-15). He embellished the family tomb at Modin, in which he had placed the remains of his brother Jonathan (xiii. 25-30). The Spartans and Romans renewed the league with him (xiv. 16-24; xv. 15-24). He was acknowledged by the Jews as high priest and captain and leader (xiii. 42; xiv. 41, 42, 47; xv. 1, 2), and in 140 B. C. authorized to wear the purple (xiv. 43, 44). Antiochus Sidetes, when on the eve of coming to Syria to help defend the cause of the absent Demetrius against Tryphon, made concessions to Simon, and gave him authority to coin money (xv. 6), but afterwards became estranged from him, and demanded the surrender of Joppa, Gezer, and the citadel at Jerusalem (26-31). Simon refused, and war ensued, 138-7 B. C., but the Syrians were worsted. In the early spring of 135 B. C., while on a tour of visitation to the cities of his dominion, he was treacherously murdered in the castle of Dok, near Jericho, by his son-in-law (xvi. 14-16).

2. Father of Judas Iscariot (John vi. 71). He too bore the designation Iscariot (ibid. and xiii. 26, R. V.).

3. Simon Peter (Mat. x. 2); see PETER.

4. Simon the Zealot, one of the twelve apostles (Luke vi. 15; Acts i. 13); see CANANÆAN.

5. One of the Lord's brethren (Mat. xiii. 55; Mark vi. 3); see BRETHREN OF THE LORD.

6. A Pharisee, at whose house our Lord once ate, on which occasion a woman, who was a sinner, anointed his feet (Luke vii. 36-50).

7. A householder in Bethany. He had been a leper, and not improbably had been cured by Christ. When our Lord was at meat in his house Mary, the sister of Lazarus, anointed his feet with precious ointment (Mat. xxvi. 6-13; Mark xiv. 3-9; John xii. 1-8). Martha served, and Lazarus was one of those who ate. The presence of the brother and two sisters, and the active part taken by the sisters, as well as the fact that Simon's house was in the town of Lazarus and his sisters, makes it evident that Simon was a relative or intimate friend of theirs. But there is no reason to believe that he was their father or the husband of Mary. He may have been the husband of Martha; see MARTHA.

8. The Cyrenian who was compelled to bear the cross of Christ. He was the father of Alexande₁ and Rufus (Mat. xxvii. 32).

9. A sorcerer (now popularly called Simon Magus, *i. e.*, Simon the magician) who so amazed the people of Samaria with his arts that they said : "This man is that power of God which is called Great." He was apparently converted through the instrumentality of Philip the evangelist, by whom he was baptized. Having subsequently offered to buy with money the privilege of conferring the Holy Ghost on anyone he wished by the imposition of hands, he was sternly rebuked by Peter, who declared that his heart was not right with God, and that he was still in the gall of bitterness and in the bond of iniquity. He took the reproof meekly, and begged the apostle to pray for him that none of the evils threatened might be allowed to befall him (Acts viii. 9-24). He was afraid, but there is no evidence that he was penitent. Ecclesiastical tradition makes Simon recommence his sorceries, and become the persistent antagonist of the apostle Peter, following him about from place to place and seeking encounters with him, but only to be signally defeated. He is said to have helped to originate gnosticism. Contradictory accounts are given as to the manner of his death.

10. A tanner at Joppa, in whose house Peter lodged (Acts ix. 43 ; x. 6, 17, 32).

Sim'ri. See SHIMRI.

Sin, I.

"Any want of conformity unto, or transgression of any law of God, given as a rule to the reasonable creature" (Rom. iii. 23 ; 1 John iii. 4 ; Gal. iii. 10–12). A sin of omission is the neglect to do what the law of God commands ; a sin of commission is the doing of anything which it forbids. See EVIL.

Sin, II.

1. A wilderness through which the Israelites passed on their way from Elim and the Red Sea to Rephidim and mount Sinai (Ex. xvi. 1 ; xvii. 1 ; Num. xxxiii. 11, 12). The identification is disputed. The choice lies between Debbet er-Ramleh or plain of sand, in the interior of the peninsula at the foot of Jebel et-Tih, and the desert plain el-Markhah on the coast. If the latter, the Israelites on leaving it probably continued to journey along the coast and turned inland through the wady Feiran.

2. A city and stronghold of Egypt (Ezek. xxx. 15, 16). The Septuagint read Sais, which, however, was never an important fortress. The Vulgate renders it Pelusium, which was "the key of Egypt," strongly fortified, and necessary to be captured before an army could enter Egypt from the northeast. The name Sin suggests Sun, the Greek Syene and modern Assuan, at the first cataract ; and the order of enumeration of Egyptian cities, from south to north (16–18) lends confirmation to this identification.

Si'nai, in A. V. of N. T. twice **Sina** (Acts vii. 30, 38) [perhaps, pertaining to Sin, the moon-god].

A mountain, called also Horeb, at which the Israelites, traveling by way of Marah, Elim, and the Red Sea, arrived in the third month after their departure from Egypt (Ex. xix. 1). It was distant from Kadesh-barnea eleven days' journey by way of mount Seir (Deut. i. 2). A wilderness, sufficiently large for the camp of Israel, lay at its foot (Ex. xix. 2) ; so close that the mountain could be touched (12), and yet its upper part was visible from the camp (16, 18, 20). From this mountain the law of the ten commandments was given, and at its base the covenant was ratified which made the Israelites a nation with Jehovah as king (xx. 1–xxiv. 8). All the legislation contained in Ex. xx. to Num. x. was enacted on or at the foot of mount Sinai, according to repeated statement (Ex. xxiv. 12 ; xxxi. 18 ; xxxiv. 2 ; Lev. i. 1 ; xvi. 1 ; xxv. 1 ; xxvi. 46 ; xxvii. 34 ; Num. i. 1 ; ix. 1). The only later visit to the mount recorded in Scripture is that of Elijah when he was threatened by Jezebel (1 Kin. xix. 8).

A theory has found favor that mount Sinai stood within the borders of mount Seir, but the opinion prevails that Sinai is to be sought among the mountains in the interior of the Sinaitic peninsula. Tradition in favor of mount Serbâl, on the wady Feiran, is traceable as far back as the time of Eusebius, for Jebel Mûsa only to that of Justinian. But neither tradition is regarded as weighty. Serbâl is the more imposing of the two. It is a solitary, majestic mountain, 6712 feet high, visible from a great distance. But at its foot is no wilderness which could be called the wilderness of Sinai. Jebel Mûsa is part of a short ridge of granite formation, extending about 2 miles from northwest to southeast. The ridge has two peaks : Râs es-Sufsâfeh, or peak of willows, at the northern end with an altitude of 6540 feet ; and Jebel Mûsa, the traditional Sinai, at the southern end rising to a height of about 7363 feet. A plateau at the head of the wady es-Sadad and almost due east of Jebel Mûsa has been regarded by some scholars, including Tischendorf, as the site of the encampment of the Israelites, but its area is too limited to accommodate any considerable host. The base of Râs es-Sufsâfeh toward the northwest consists of a precipitous cliff. At the bottom of the cliff lies the plain of er-Râhah, about one square mile in extent, and, with the adjacent wadies esh-Sheikh and ed-Deir, entirely suitable for a camping ground. The biblical description makes it scarcely necessary, if not idle, to inquire whether the law was given from Jebel Mûsa or Râs es-Sufsâfeh, and whether one peak or the other was known as the mount of God in distinction from the rest of the clump.

The monastery of St. Catharine, a convent of Greek monks, is situated on the eastern slope of the mountain, at the foot of Jebel Mûsa, in the wady ed-Deir, 5014 feet above sea level. Surrounded by massive granite walls, it is as it were a fortress. Its founda-

of Jebel Katherîn, 2¼ miles southwest of Jebel Mûsa. Her head and one hand are said to be contained in a marble sarcophagus in the chapel of the monastery. The monastery has often been destroyed and rebuilt. The church of the Transfiguration is an early Christian basilica with mosaics of the seventh or eighth century. The oldest part of

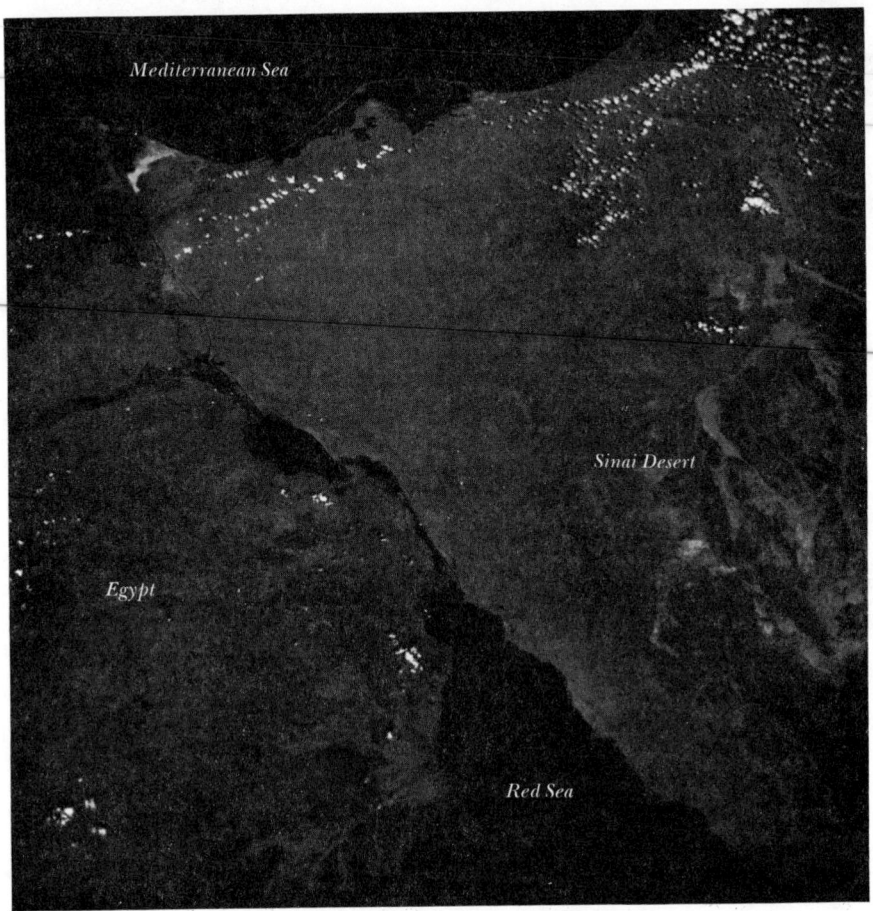

The Sinai Peninsula as viewed from outer space. This picture was taken on the Apollo 7 flight.

tion is ascribed to the emperor Justinian in A. D. 527, who is said to have built it around a tower erected long before by Helena, mother of Constantine; but this ascription is probably due to confusion with the fact, attested by his private secretary, that Justinian built a castle in 530 for the protection of the monks who dwelt in the region. The monastery is named after St. Catharine, who was tortured on the wheel and beheaded in Alexandria in A. D. 307, and whose body is said by the monks to have been carried by angels from Alexandria to the lofty summit

it is probably the chapel of the Burning Bush, at the back of the apse and on the reputed site of the event it commemorates. Formerly between 300 and 400 monks lived within the convent walls; but the number at present does not exceed 40. In the garden are fig, orange, olive, almond, apple, and apricot trees, grape vines, and a few lofty cypresses. The library is exceedingly valuable. It contains many manuscripts, predominantly Greek and Arabic, but also many others, including some written in Syriac and Ethiopic. Here, in 1844 and 1859, Tischen-

The monastery of St. Catherine, nestled on the eastern slope of Mount Sinai.

dorf found the codex Sinaiticus, which dates from about A. D. 400; see NEW TESTAMENT. Here also, in 1892, Mrs. Lewis discovered a manuscript which contains the text of the Old Syriac Gospels, and was probably written in the fifth century; see VERSIONS.

Si′nim, Land of.

A country cited to illustrate the promise that gentile converts or the scattered Israelites shall be gathered from the remotest regions of the earth. " Lo, these shall come from far: and, lo, these from the north and from the west; and these from the land of Sinim " (Is. xlix. 12). Since the west and north have been mentioned; the land of Sinim is not to be sought there, but in the south or east. Wherever the prophet was when he uttered these words, his words exclude the Sinim of Phœnicia (Gen. x. 17), for they were not a remote people. Besides this, they were an unimportant tribe. For the same reason, the people of Syene or Pelusium, or other Egyptian town (however the name Sin in Ezek. xxx. 15, 16 is understood) are excluded. They were almost in the heart of the inhabited world, separated from the remote bounds of the earth by Ethiopia and Libya at least. Moreover, the inhabitants of none of these towns constituted a distinct nation; nor could the land of Sinim on the Nile be spoken of, as it is by Isaiah, unless it meant Egypt, and none of these towns was important enough to be employed in a designation for all Egypt. The chief theories are: 1 The expression was chosen as a designation of the lands south of Palestine, because in that direction lay the town of Sin (Pelusium), the wilderness of Sin (Ex. xvi. 1), and mount Sinai. But this region was too near at hand to denote the remotest countries. Sheba and Cush, which are used to denote the utmost parts of the earth toward the south, lay far beyond. 2. The Sinim were the Shinas, who have dwelt from ancient times at the foot of the Hindu Kush mountains. 3. The most prevalent view is that the Chinese are meant. The prophet does not assert that Israelites were already living in China (if his words be restricted to a return of the exiles). They may have been; for the presence of Israelites in China is attested as early as the third century B. C., and it is not known how much earlier they emigrated. But the people were scattered far and wide, and yet wider dispersion was in prospect (Is. xi. 11). They should be recovered from the farthest bounds of earth where they are found. Does it seem strange that the name of the Chinese should be known in western Asia? It is historically certain from the Chinese records that Chinese merchants visited foreign lands as early as the twelfth century B. C., and that foreign merchants entered China as early as the tenth century. It is probable that direct commercial relations existed between China and India, and hence indirectly at least with the countries farther west. Porcelain ware with Chinese characters written upon it has been discovered at Thebes in Egypt. M. Pauthier reports the Chinese tradition to the effect that in 2353 B. C. an envoy arrived from a far country bringing as a present a divine tortoise one thousand years old, bearing on its back an inscription, written in strange characters like tadpoles, briefly recounting the world's history since creation. A second embassy of the people of the long-trailing robes arrived in 1110 B. C., and it took them a whole year to return to their own country from Siam by the seacoast. The characters resembling tadpoles suggest the Assyrian and Babylonian cuneiform script; and long-trailing robes, which were not worn in the hot countries south of China, would agree with the theory that the embassadors were Babylonians or Assyrians.

Si'nite.

A Canaanite tribe, mentioned between the Arkite and the Arvadite (Gen. x. 17). A place named Sin not far from Arka was known to Jerome, and Strabo mentions a fortress called Sinna on mount Lebanon.

Sin Of'fer-ing. See OFFERINGS.

Si'on [elevated].

A name for mount Hermon (Deut. iv. 48). For mount Sion at Jerusalem, a different word in Hebrew, see ZION.

Siph'moth [variantly read Shiphmoth].

A haunt of David during his wanderings, to which he sent part of the spoils of Ziklag (1 Sam. xxx. 28; cp. 1 Chron. xxvii. 27).

Sip'pai. See SAPH.

Si'rah [recession or effervescence].

A well or cistern 20 stades from Hebron (Antiq. vii. 1, 5) from which Abner was treacherously recalled to Hebron by Joab (2 Sam. iii. 26). It is probably 'Ain Sârah, 1½ miles northwest of Hebron.

Sir'i-on [cuirass, coat of mail].

The name given by the Sidonians to mount Hermon (Deut. iii. 9; Ps. xxix. 6).

Sis'a-mai. See SISMAI.

Sis'e-ra [battle array].

Commander of a Canaanite army which held northern Israel in subjection. Defeated on the Kishon and fleeing northward, probably on his way to the overlord of the Canaanite king. He sought refuge with Heber the Kenite, who was at peace with the Canaanites. Heber's wife saw him coming, went forth, and invited him into her tent, but killed him while he slept (Judg. iv., v.; 1 Sam. xii. 9; Ps. lxxxiii. 9); see JAEL. Probably those Nethinim who were known as the children of Sisera were descended from captives taken at this time (Ezra ii. 53; Neh. vii. 55).

Sis'mai, in A. V. **Sisamai.**

A man of Judah, family of Hezron, house of Jerahmeel (1 Chron. ii. 40).

Sis'ter.

A kinswoman; a full sister or a half-sister (Gen. xx. 12; Deut. xxvii. 22; 1 Chron. ii. 13–17 with 2 Sam. xvii. 25); or a wife (Song iv. 9; Tobit v. 20; vii. 16; viii. 4); or a woman of the same tribe (Num. xxv. 18) or the same religion (Rom. xvi. 1; Jas. ii. 15).

Sis'trum.

A musical instrument (2 Sam. vi. 5, R. V. margin), consisting of several metallic rods in an oval metallic frame. The rods were either loosely inserted or loose rings were hung on them, so that the instrument would jingle when shaken.

Sith'ri, in A. V. **Zithri** [a hiding place is (Jehovah)].

A Levite, family of Kohath, house of Uzziel (Ex. vi. 22). Zithri in A. V. of ver. 21 is a modern misprint of Zichri (q. v.). The error has been corrected in some recent editions.

Sit'nah [accusation, enmity (cp. Satan)].

A well dug by Isaac in the Philistine country, not far from Gerar; but the inhabitants of the district disputed his right to it (Gen. xxvi. 21). Palmer and Drake in 1870 found a small valley called wady Shutnet er-Ruheibeh. The first portion of the name corresponds to Sitnah, and Ruheibeh to Rehoboth, which was in the immediate vicinity of Sitnah (22).

Si'van.

The third month of the Babylonian and Jewish year (Esth. viii. 9), extending from the new moon of May to that of June. See YEAR.

Slave.

Slavery existed in remote antiquity. Slaves were acquired: 1. By capture, especially in war (Num. xxxi. 9; 2 Kin. v. 2; War iii. 4, 1; vi. 9, 2). 2. By purchase from slave owners (Gen. xvii. 27; xxxvii. 28, 36; Ezek. xxvii. 13; Joel iii. 6, 8). 3. By birth from slaves owned (Gen. xvii. 12). 4. In payment of debt; thieves unable to make restitution and, though contrary to the spirit of the Mosaic law, a debtor or his children being sold as slaves (Ex. xxii. 3; 2 Kin. iv. 1; Neh. v. 5, 8; Amos ii. 6; Mat. xviii. 25). 5. Among the Hebrews there was also the voluntary sale of one's self or one's daughter on account of poverty (Ex. xxi. 2, 7; Lev. xxv. 39, 47), and reduction to slavery on account of theft, as already mentioned.

The price of a slave varied of course according to circumstances. It was reckoned in Hebrew judicial cases as averaging 30 shekels (Ex. xxi. 32). The Jewish slaves in Alexandria in the third century B. C. brought about the same, 120 drachmas (Antiq. xii. 2, 5). Joseph at seventeen years of age was purchased for 20 shekels (Gen. xxxvii. 28).

Among the Hebrews the legal status of a Hebrew slave was very different from that of the slave who was not an Israelite. The Hebrew slave had manumission after six years of service, if he chose; might not be harshly treated, nor sent away empty on his release; and, if owned by a foreign sojourner in Israel, had the privilege of redemption at a price legally regulated, the moment he could secure the necessary money (Ex. xxi. 2–6; Lev. xxv. 43, 47–55; Jer. xxxiv. 8–16). The rights of the Hebrew maid were the subject of further special legislation (Ex. xxi. 7–11). All Hebrew slaves, both those who had elected to remain with their masters when the seventh year had come and those who had not served six years, were released at the year of jubilee (Lev. xxv. 40). This provision was necessitated when the law regarding the restoration of every man's

inheritance at the jubile was enacted. The return of the slave to his inheritance was involved, whether he chose to go back to his master's family afterwards or not. The slave also who was not an Israelite fared well among the Hebrews. The Mosaic law recognized that he possessed rights. He might be whipped or beaten, but not maimed or killed (Ex. xxi. 20, 21, 26, 27; Lev. xxiv. 17, 22). In case a captive slave girl was taken to wife, she acquired new rights (Deut. xxi. 10–14). All these non-Hebrew slaves were regarded as members of the commonwealth of Israel (Gen. xvii. 10–14); and they were equal before God, participating in the religious festivals and sacrifices (Ex. xii. 44; Lev. xxii. 11; Deut. xii. 12, 18; xvi. 11, 14), and enjoying the rest of the Sabbath day (Ex. xx. 10; xxiii. 12). Another humane feature of the Mosaic law made Canaan an asylum for slaves who escaped to it from a foreign country. They were not to be surrendered, but were allowed to dwell in the land wherever they chose (Deut. xxiii. 15, 16). It also forbade, on pain of death, the stealing of men and the selling or holding of them (Ex. xxi. 16; Deut. xxiv. 7); and there is no evidence that slave markets ever existed in Israel. The Mosaic law contrasts most favorably with the laws of contemporary heathen nations in its humanity toward slaves. The intercourse between master and slave was often cordial (Gen. xxiv.; Ruth ii. 4). The slave was regarded as entitled to justice (Job xxxi. 13–15); he sometimes inherited the property of his master (Gen. xv. 2, 3), and was sometimes admitted into the family as son-in-law (1 Chron. ii. 34, 35).

Christianity avoided a sudden reversal of established usages (1 Cor. vii. 21), urged the slave to obey his master (Eph. vi. 5–8; Col. iii. 22–25; 1 Tim. vi. 1, 2; 1 Pet. ii. 18–21), and sent the runaway slave voluntarily back to his Christian master (Philem. 10–16). But it also promulgated principles which improved the condition of slaves in the Roman empire. It recognized the equality of slave and master in God's sight (1 Cor. vii. 21, 22; Gal. iii. 28; Col. iii. 11). It exhorted the master to treat his slaves considerately, reminding him that they had rights which God will maintain (Eph. vi. 9; Col. iv. 1).

Slime. See BITUMEN.

Sling.

A simple weapon usually consisting of a piece of leather, with two strings attached to its opposite sides and a stone inserted. It was whirled once or twice round the head and one string let go, whereby the stone was projected with great force. On the field of battle the stones were either carried in a bag by the slinger, or piled at his feet (1 Sam. xvii. 40).

It seems to have been used in warfare by practically all the peoples of antiquity; by

An Arab shepherd boy with his sling.

the Egyptians, Syrians (1 Mac. vi. 51; ix. 11), Assyrians, Persians (Anab. iii. 3, 18), and in the far west by Sicilians (Herod. vii. 158) and mercenaries in the Roman army. Among the Hebrews the Benjamites in the times of the judges and in the reign of Saul were noted for their skill in its use, being able to sling stones with the left hand (Judg. xx. 16: 1 Chron. xii. 2). David slew Goliath with a stone from a sling (1 Sam. xvii. 48–50). Slingers served in the armies of Jehoram, Jehoshaphat, and Uzziah (2 Kin. iii. 25; 2 Chron. xxvi. 14), and were effective as late as the war with the Romans (War ii. 17, 5; iv. 1, 3).

Smith.

An artificer who forges iron and brass into tools and weapons, a blacksmith (1 Sam. xiii. 19; Is. xliv. 12; liv. 16), like Tubal-cain (Gen. iv. 22); or one who refines and shapes the precious metals, a goldsmith (Is. xl. 19). The blacksmith used a charcoal furnace, bellows, tongs, anvil, and hammer (Ecclus. xxxviii. 28). See BELLOWS.

Smyr′na [myrrh].

A city of great antiquity on the western coast of Asia Minor. It was possessed by the Æolian Greeks, and finally the Ionian Greeks admitted it into their confederacy. The Lydian king, Alyattes, destroyed it, and it lay waste for some 200 years, till the plan of rebuilding it was formed by Alexander the Great, and executed by his immediate successors, on a new site near by. It then became a large and flourishing commercial center, retaining its importance under the Romans. It became a part of the province of Asia, organized after 133 B. C. Its church was the second of the seven addressed by John in the book of Revelation. It escapes all censure. but it is exhorted to remain constant in the midst of persecution (Rev. i. 11; ii. 8–11). Its bishop Polycarp suffered martyrdom by fire, near the stadion, probably in A. D. 169. In A. D. 178 Smyrna was destroyed by an earthquake, but was speedily rebuilt. Lying as it does at the extremity

of a fine bay, in the track of trade, it is admirably adapted for commerce, and even under Turkish rule remains a highly flourishing city, the largest and most important in Asia Minor.

Snail.

1. The rendering of the Hebrew *Ḥomeṭ*, one prostrate on the ground (Lev. xi. 30; in R. V. sand lizard).

2. The rendering of the Hebrew *Shabbᵉlul*, moist, slimy one (Ps. lviii. 8), a genuine snail, especially of the shell-less family (*Limacidæ*).

Snow.

Snow occurs in the hilly country of Palestine, as at Sepphoris in Galilee, Nazareth, Jerusalem, Hebron (1 Mac. xiii. 22; War i. 16, 2; iv. 8, 3). It may be expected in January or February, although the winter often passes without it. It sometimes falls to the depth of a foot, but seldom lies longer than a day. On mount Lebanon it is found lingering on the heights and in the ravines late in the summer, and it crowns the summit of Hermon the year round. It is frequently referred to in Scripture as the standard of whiteness and the emblem of purity (Ps. li. 7; Is. i. 18; Lam. iv. 7; Mat. xxviii. 3). It is poetically described as stored by God in his treasury (Job xxxviii. 22), commanded by him to fall (xxxvii. 6; Ps. cxlvii. 16), and descending like wool or birds or a swarm of locusts (ibid.; Ecclus. xliii. 17). Its value as a source of moisture to the ground was recognized (Is. lv. 10). Men took advantage of it in summer to cool their beverages (cp. Prov. xxv. 13). Clean snow would yield pure water for washing purposes (Job ix. 30).

So.

King of Egypt, whose aid against Assyria Hoshea king of Israel endeavored to secure about 724 B. C. (2 Kin. xvii. 4). As the Hebrew consonants may be pronounced Seve′, he is commonly identified, and doubtless correctly, with Sib′e, tartan of Egypt, who in 720 B. C. in alliance with Hanun king of

It was used for washing the person (Job ix. 30, R. V. margin, lye), for washing clothes (Jer. ii. 22 ; Mal. iii. 2), and as a flux in smelting ores (Is. i. 25, R. V. margin, lye). The Greek translators regarded it as a plant or obtained from a plant, for they represented it by the Greek word *poa*, grass, grass-like plant. The root of the soapwort (*Saponaria officinalis*) is largely used in Palestine for washing linens, because it does not cause them to shrink. The employment of the alkali for smelting purposes indicates that it was in the form of ashes. It was doubtless obtained from such plants as the glasswort (*Salicornia fruticosa*) and the saltwort (*Salsola kali*), which are to this day reduced to ashes for the soda which they yield.

So'co and **Socoh**, according to the alternate Hebrew orthography ; in A. V. variously spelled **Socoh, Socho, Sochoh, Shocho, Shochoh, Shoco** [thorn, hedge of thorns].

1. A town in the Shephelah or lowland of Judah (Josh. xv. 35). It stood on the hilly border of the valley of Elah, in a strong position isolated from the rest of the ridge. The Philistines pitched between it and Azekah just before Goliath stood forth as their champion (1 Sam. xvii. 1). It was rebuilt or refortified by Rehoboam (2 Chron. xi. 7). It was captured, with the dependent villages, in the reign of Ahaz (xxviii. 18). Robinson successfully identified it with the ruins of Shuweikeh, 13 miles west by south of Bethlehem. The modern name perpetuates the ancient one.

2. A town in the hill country of Judah (Josh. xv. 48). Its site is found at another Shuweikeh, 10 miles south-southwest of Hebron.

It is doubtful which of the two towns is referred to in 1 Kin. iv. 10 and 1 Chron. iv. 18.

So'di [a familiar acquaintance].
Father of the spy from the tribe of Zebulun (Num. xiii. 10).

Sod'om, in A. V. of N. T. once **Sodoma** (Rom. ix. 29).

One of the five cities in the plain of the Jordan (Gen. xiii. 10). When Lot separated from Abraham, he chose it for his residence, though even then the place was notorious for its wickedness (11, 12). It was plundered by Chedorlaomer (xiv. 11), but the goods and captives were recovered by Abraham and restored (21-24). Subsequently it and at least three other cities of the plain were destroyed by God on account of their wickedness. God probably effected his purpose by causing an eruption of burning asphalt and sulphur. Lot and his two daughters were spared (xix. 1-29 ; Deut. xxix. 23 ; Is. i. 9, 10 ; iii. 9 ; xiii. 19 ; Jer. xlix. 18 ; l. 40 ; Lam. iv. 6 ; Ezek. xvi. 46-56 ; Amos iv. 11 ; Zeph. ii. 9 ; Mat. x. 15 ; xi. 24 ; Luke x. 12 ; xvii. 29 ; Rom. ix. 29 ; 2 Pet. ii. 6 ; Jude 7). In the Apocalypse the great city of sin is spiritually called Sodom and Egypt (Rev. xi. 8).

Signpost at Sodom.

Gaza, met Sargon king of Assyria in battle at Raphia on the Mediterranean, about 20 miles south of Gaza. The allies were routed, Sib'e fled, Hanun was captured, and presently Pharaoh paid tribute to Assyria. It is doubtful whether Sib'e was Shabako, king of Egypt. Etymology is against the identification. At this time at least he was tartan rather than Pharaoh.

Soap.
Not the composition familiar in modern domestic use. The Hebrew words *bor* and *borith*, that which cleanses, denote an alkali.

The exact site of Sodom is unknown. Two substantial arguments are advanced for the northern end. 1. From a point near Bethel, Abraham and Lot could see all the plain of Jordan (Gen. xiii. 3 with 10). Care must be exercised, however, in interpreting the word all. 2. Chedorlaomer, coming from the south, had smitten the Amorites of Hazezon-tamar, i. e., En-gedi, before he was opposed by the king of Sodom and his allies (xiv. 7, 8), a fact which seems to indicate that the meeting took place between En-gedi and the northern end of the sea. On the other hand, there are three weighty arguments for the southern end. 1. Asphalt is found in large quantities at the southern end of the sea only (cp. Gen. xiv. 10). 2. Assuming that the sea covers the site (cp. xiv. 3), the cities might have been situated at the southern end, where the water of the bay has a depth of from 2 to 20 feet, but could not have been in the northern part, where the sea is from 600 to 1000 feet deep. And geologically considered, only the southern end of the sea can be of origin at all recent. 3. Zoar, one of the cities (xiii. 10), lay at the southern end of the sea (War iv. 8, 4).

For the vine of Sodom, see VINE OF SODOM.

Sod'om-ite.

A person guilty of sodomy, the unnatural vice of Sodom (Gen. xix. 5). The word is employed in the E. V. to render the Hebrew *Kadesh*, one consecrated, a man dedicated to impure heathen worship (Deut. xxiii. 17; in Job xxxvi. 14, unclean). A woman thus dedicated practiced uncleanness as a priestess in the service of Ashtoreth or Asherah in Canaan, of Ishtar in Babylonia (Gen. xxxviii. 21, 22; Deut. xxiii. 17; Hos. iv. 14; in every case rendered harlot). Sodomy was forbidden by the Mosaic law (Deut. xxiii. 17); but sodomites were found in Judah during the reign of Rehoboam (1 Kin. xiv. 24); Asa and Jehoshaphat cut them off (xv. 12; xxii. 46); but others arose in their room, and Josiah, to rid the land of them, broke down their houses (2 Kin. xxiii. 7).

So'journ-er, in A. V. and sometimes in R. V. **Stranger.** See STRANGER.

Sol'o-mon [peaceable].

David's youngest son, at least by Bathsheba (2 Sam. xii. 24; 1 Chron. iii. 5; and cp. Antiq. vii. 14, 2). He was born at Jerusalem. David named him Solomon, peaceable, in anticipation of the peace and quietness of his reign in contrast with his own stormy life (1 Chron. xxii. 9); but through the prophet Nathan he was divinely honored with the name Jedidiah, beloved of Jehovah (2 Sam. xii. 25). When David was old and feeble, Adonijah, one of his sons born at Hebron, and probably the eldest now that Amnon and Absalom were dead, planned to rule independently of his father's sanction; but the design was thwarted by the prophet Nathan with the aid of Zadok the priest and Bena-

iah the military commander, supported by David's bodyguard. Solomon was proclaimed king (1 Kin. i. 5–40), and the party of Adonijah at once collapsed. David soon afterwards died, and Solomon began his sole reign about the year 970 B. C., being at the time probably about twenty years old. Obedient to the dying charge of his father, he dealt out justice to Abiathar and Shimei; and when Adonijah began anew to plot against the king, he put him to death and ordered the execution of Joab likewise, who was implicated in the conspiracy (ii. 1–46). The young king soon brought as his queen to Jerusalem Pharaoh's daughter (iii. 1). At that time the worship at the sanctuary, which had been broken up when the Lord forsook Shiloh, was still interrupted. The tabernacle was at Gibeon and the ark at Jerusalem. The people worshiped at high places. Solomon went to Gibeon to sacrifice. There God appeared to him in a dream by night and bade him ask for anything he chose. He asked for an understanding heart, that he might be able justly to judge the people of God, for it was part of a king's duty in those days to administer justice. His request was granted, as he soon afterwards showed by the skillful manner in which he disentangled truth from falsehood when he decided between the two women, each of whom claimed the living babe as her own (1 Kin. iii. 2–28; 2 Chron. i. 3–12). Twenty or more years later the Lord appeared to him again, conditionally promised to continue the throne in Solomon's own line, and gave him solemn warning (1 Kin. ix. 1–10; 2 Chron. vii. 12–22).

His father had subdued the neighboring nations. Against Hamath only is it recorded that Solomon went to war. He was obliged to control that city in order to secure the northeastern portion of his dominions. Hadad the Edomite and Rezon of Damascus were hostile to Solomon, but the Hebrew monarch probably gave himself but little concern about them. He fortified Hazor at the crossing of the upper Jordan, and built a tower in Lebanon, in order to hold Damascus in check; and saw to it that the road by Edom to Ezion-geber was open and safe. Otherwise Solomon's relations with neighboring kings were friendly, and he was able to devote himself to the organization of his kingdom and to the arts of peace.

David had amassed a great store of precious metals for the construction of a magnificent temple to Jehovah. Solomon took up the work, and with Tyrian help finished it in seven years (1 Kin. v., vi.; 2 Chron. ii.). Then, after furniture had been made for it, it was dedicated (1 Kin. vii. 13–viii. 64; 2 Chron. ii.–vii.). Next, the monarch erected a palace for himself, which took thirteen years in building (1 Kin. vii. 1–12); see PALACE. He also laid out gardens and vineyards in various parts of the country, as at Etam, perhaps, and at Baal-hamon (ix. 19,

R. V. ; 2 Chron. viii. 6, R. V. ; Ecc. ii. 5, 6 ; Song viii. 11).

Solomon showed sagacity in government. He surrounded himself with eminent officials, among whom the son of the high priest held the first place (1 Kin. iv. 2–6). He maintained the army at full strength. For administrative purposes, he divided the kingdom into twelve districts, entirely independent of the old tribal lines (7–19). Nor did he fail to take a prominent part in the religion of the state. He led the nation in prayer at the dedication of the temple, and invoked the divine blessing upon the assembled multitude.

Commerce flourished in his kingdom, and brought wealth (1 Kin. x. 14–21 ; 2 Chron. ix. 13, 14, 21, 27) ; and voyages were successfully made to Ophir, and traffic was conducted with India (1 Kin. x. 22, 23 ; 2 Chron. ix. 10–22). For the protection and fostering of trade, he built store cities, among others Palmyra, in the desert midway between Damascus and the Euphrates (1 Kin. ix. 18, 19).

Solomon was interested in literary pursuits : he was a naturalist, and wrote treatises on plants, from the cedar that groweth on Lebanon to the hyssop that springeth out of the wall. He spoke also of beasts, and of fowls, and of creeping things, and of fishes (1 Kin. iv. 33). He collected and composed many proverbs, some of which constitute part of the O. T. ; see PROVERBS. Two psalms (lxxii. and cxxvii.) are attributed to him by their titles. See also ECCLESIASTES and SONG OF SONGS.

The splendor of his court, the magnificence of his table, and his pomp when on excursions corresponded to his wealth and political power (1 Kin. x. 4, 5, 21 ; Song iii. 7–11). People came from all parts to hear his wisdom (1 Kin. iv. 34 ; x. 23–25). The report of his wisdom was carried even to southern Arabia, and the queen of Sheba journeyed to Jerusalem to test it and to see his magnificence (1–13).

Solomon erred in two respects. He established a harem, which included from first to last about one thousand members. Doubtless not a few of these were hostages, princesses given him as pledges of political amity. Now many of these women were foreigners by birth and idolatrous in their religion, and he allowed himself to be persuaded by them to erect idol shrines (1 Kin. xi. 1–8). For this apostasy Solomon was punished. The kingdom in its great extent and power was taken from the dynasty, and only a fragment of it left to the family (9–13). The example of Solomon's disloyalty to Jehovah had direct influence in producing this penal result. Also influential to this end was the announcement by the prophet Ahijah to Jeroboam that God would rend ten tribes from Solomon and give them to him (28–39). Jeroboam became a recognized opponent of the king ; but not until Solomon's son Rehoboam ascended the throne did Jeroboam secure a kingdom. A second, a less obvious, yet an important error was Solomon's luxury, which imposed a burden on his over-taxed subjects, shook their loyalty to the throne, and sowed the seeds of future rebellion. See REHOBOAM.

Solomon reigned forty years (1 Kin. xi. 42 ; 2 Chron. ix. 30, 31), dying about 931 B. C. The events of his life and reign were recorded in the Book of the Acts of Solomon (1 Kin. xi. 41), the History of Nathan the Prophet, the Prophecy of Ahijah the Shilonite, the Visions of Iddo the Seer (2 Chron. ix. 29).

Sol'o-mon's Porch.

A splendid colonnade, reputed to have been built by Solomon, on the east side of the temple area, on an artificial embankment built up from the valley of the Kidron (Antiq. xx. 9, 7 ; War v. 5, 1). It is once mentioned that Christ walked in it (John x. 23) ; and the apostles were not infrequently there (Acts iii. 11 ; v. 12).

Sol'o-mon's Serv'ants.

Certain persons whose descendants were associated with the Nethinim, 390 or 392 of the two classes combined returning with Zerubbabel from the captivity (Ezra ii. 55–58 ; Neh. vii. 57–60). Some of their names have a foreign aspect. They seem to have been the descendants of those Canaanites of various tribes from whom Solomon exacted bond service for the sake of the temple and other magnificent buildings (1 Kin. v. 13–18 ; ix. 21). See NETHINIM.

Sol'o-mon's Song. See SONG OF SONGS.

Sol'o-mon, Wis'dom of. See APOCRYPHA.

Son.

1. A male child ; an immediate male descendant (Gen. xxvii. 1). Other prominent significations are :

2. A remoter male descendant. For instance, Jehu, son of Nimshi, was really Nimshi's grandson, for he was the son of Jehoshaphat, the son of Nimshi (cp. 2 Kin. ix. 20 with 2). The Israelites were known as sons or children of Israel or Jacob centuries after the death of the patriarch (Mal. iii. 6 ; Luke i. 16).

3. A person received into filial relation by adoption or marriage (Ex. ii. 10 ; cp. Esth. ii. 7), or as member of a tribe by adoption or marriage into the tribe (Gen. xvii. 9–14) ; and probably a people as incorporated with another people by conquest.

4. A kindly form of address used by an elderly man to a younger friend (1 Sam. iii. 6, 16 ; iv. 16 ; 2 Sam. xviii. 22 ; cp. Josh. vii. 19).

5. Member of a guild or profession, as son of the apothecaries (Neh. iii. 8, in R. V. one), sons of the singers (xii. 28). Worshiper of a god, as the sons of Chemosh (Num. xxi. 29).

6. Inhabitant of a city or country, as sons of Zion (Lam. iv. 2), sons of Bethlehem (Ezra ii. 21, in E. V. children), sons of the province (1, in E. V. children), sons of Javan (Gen. x. 4).

7. Possessor of a quality, as son of Belial or worthlessness (1 Sam. xxv. 17), son of strength, *i. e.*, a valiant man (xiv. 52), son of peace (Luke x. 6).

Son of God.

A title of the Messiah (Ps. ii. 7; John i. 49; cp. 2 Sam. vii. 14); in its deepest sense expressive of the mysterious relation existing between the eternal Father and the eternal Son. In the Revised Version of the New Testament the designation Son of God is used about forty-five times, in about forty-four unequivocably denoting our Lord (Mat. iv. 3, 6; xvi. 16; xxvi. 63; xxvii. 43; Mark i. 1), and in the remaining one characterizing Adam (Luke iii. 38). In John iii. 18 Christ is called the only begotten Son of God. Two reasons are suggested for the appellation: his eternal generation (Heb. vii. 3), and his miraculous birth by the operation of the Holy Ghost (Luke i. 35). As son of God, Christ is God with all the infinite perfections of the divine essence (John i. 1–14; x. 30–38; Phil. ii. 6), and is equal with God (John v. 17–25). He is subordinate in mode of subsistence and operation; that is, he is of the Father, is sent by the Father, and the Father operates through him (John iii. 16, 17; viii. 42; Gal. iv. 4; Heb. i. 2). Accordingly, the word son is not a term of office, but of nature. He has the same nature, a fact which includes equality with God.

The claim was put forth by our Lord (Luke xxii. 70; John x. 36; xi. 4; xix. 7), and urged by the apostles (Acts ix. 20; Gal. ii. 20, etc.; 1 John iii. 8; v. 5, 10, 13, 20), and it was for maintaining it that he was condemned by the sanhedrin on a charge of blasphemy (Mat. xxvi. 63–66; Mark xiv. 61–64); but the justice of his claim had been acknowledged on the occasion of his baptism by the descent upon him of the Holy Ghost, accompanied by an audible utterance from his heavenly Father (Mat. iii. 16, 17; Mark i. 10, 11; Luke iii. 22; John i. 32–34). It was similarly acknowledged at the transfiguration (Mat. xvii. 5; Mark ix. 7; Luke ix. 35; 2 Pet. i. 17). It was sustained by his character and by his works (John i. 14; x. 36–38; Heb. i. 3). And he was declared to be the Son of God with power, according to the spirit of holiness by the resurrection of the dead (Rom. i. 4), and by his ascension (Heb. i. 3).

In one passage of the O. T. the expression Son of God appears (Dan. iii. 25, A. V.), but the R. V. alters this to a son of the gods. The speaker was a Babylonian heathen.

For the title sons of God applied to men, see SONS OF GOD.

Son of Man.

A person possessed of humanity in distinction from divinity and the brute nature; a human being, with the emphasis on human (Num. xxiii. 19; Job xxv. 6; Ps. viii. 4; Is. li. 12); see SON 7. When Daniel fell affrighted on his face before the heavenly messenger, Gabriel addressed him as son of man (Dan. viii. 17). When Ezekiel had seen the vision of Jehovah and fallen upon his face, a voice said: "Son of man, stand upon thy feet" (Ezek. ii. 1), and thenceforth the prophet is constantly addressed as son of man. It was foretold (Dan. vii. 13, 14, R. V.) that the hostile worldly power, represented by beasts, shall succumb before the Ancient of days, and one like to a son of man, coming with the clouds of heaven, shall receive dominion and a kingdom, that all the peoples, nations, and languages shall serve him; his dominion is an everlasting dominion which shall not pass away, and his kingdom that which shall not be destroyed. This figure seen in vision, a human being in contrast with the beasts that typified the kingdoms of the world, symbolized the saints of God in their corporate aspect, to whom universal and everlasting dominion shall be given (14 with 27).

The title was adopted by our Lord, evidently with reference to Dan. vii. 13, 14, 27 (cp. Mat. xxiv. 30; Mark xiv. 62). He is recorded in the gospels as having applied it to himself seventy-eight times. It is also used of him by Stephen (Acts vii. 56); see also Heb. ii. 6; and Rev. i. 13; xiv. 14, R. V. margin. Christ did not choose the title to assert that he had a fellow-feeling for man and was a brother to all men; nor did he employ it to denote that he was a mere man and not divine, for he constantly claimed divine attributes (Luke v. 24). He chose a title which, by reason of its several possible interpretations, until fully defined by Jesus himself, could not be used against him by his foes. By it—1. He identified himself with that human being in Daniel's vision who receives a universal and everlasting dominion (Dan. vii. 14; cp. Mat. xvi. 28; xxviii. 18). 2. He identified himself with the saints of the Most High, regarded collectively as a people, which the human figure in the vision symbolized; making himself their embodiment and their representative before God (Dan. vii. 13, 27; cp. Mat. xxv. 31, 40; Mark x. 45 "a ransom for many"; Luke xii. 8, 9). 3. He assumed for himself the sufferings and the glory that should follow which were predicted for that human kingdom in its efforts to establish itself and overcome the world (Dan. vii. 21, 22, 25; cp. Mat. xvii. 22, 23; Mark x. 45; Luke ix. 26; xviii. 31–33) 4. He implies that he comes with the clouds of heaven to receive the kingdom (Dan. vii 13; cp. Mat. xxiv. 30; xxvi. 64). 5. He emphasized the human and humane in contrast with the brutal and bestial (Dan. vii. 4–9,

13; cp. Mat. xxv. 31 with 35 and 36; Mark x. 45 "minister, and to give his life"; Luke xix. 10).

Son of man and Son of God are united in the same person. "Who do men say that the Son of man is? . . . . Simon Peter answered and said, Thou art the Christ, the Son of the living God. And Jesus answered and said unto him, Blessed art thou, Simon Bar-Jonah: for flesh and blood hath not revealed it unto thee, but my Father which is in heaven" (Mat. xvi. 13, 16, 17). "The high priest said unto him, I adjure thee by the living God, that thou tell us whether thou be the Christ, the Son of God. Jesus saith unto him, Thou hast said: nevertheless I say unto you, Henceforth ye shall see the Son of man sitting at the right hand of power, and coming on the clouds of heaven" (xxvi. 63, 64).

Song.

A poetical composition, generally brief, capable of being set to music and sung, whether or not it was intended for singing or was ever actually sung (Ex. xv. 1–18; Deut. xxxi. 30–xxxii. 44). It was often sung to the accompaniment of music (Ex. xv. 20, 21; Is. xxxviii. 20). It might be secular or religious (Gen. xxxi. 27; Num. xxi. 17, 18; and Ps. xcii., title; cxxxvii. 3, 4); in praise of men or of God (1 Sam. xviii. 6, 7; Ps. xxviii. 7); the expression of light-heartedness or deep emotion; the utterance of innocent mirth or the outcome of a bacchanalian revel (Ps. lxix. 12).

Song of Songs, The.

The last of the five poetical books of the O. T. in our present English Bible. This arrangement is derived from the Septuagint. In the Hebrew Scriptures the Song stands between Job and Ruth, in the third section of the canon, and is one of the five smaller rolls which formed a group by themselves because they had come to be read on the five great anniversaries. The Song was read on the eighth day of the passover festival, the book being allegorically interpreted with reference to the history of the exodus. The Song of Solomon is more fully called The Song of Songs, which is Solomon's (i. 1). The reduplication of the word song was not intended to denote that it is a collection of many songs, nor that it is the chief one of the many songs of Solomon; but it has superlative force, like servant of servants, holy of holies, Lord of lords, heaven of heavens, vanity of vanities (Gen. ix. 25; Ex. xxvi. 33; Deut. x. 17; 1 Kin. viii. 27; Ecc. i. 2), and intimates that the production is a song of the highest character. In the Vulgate the title is literally translated *Canticum Canticorum*, from which the name Canticles is derived.

Several speakers take part in the dialogue. The distinction between them is quite clear in the Hebrew original, because the grammatical forms indicate gender. The R. V. marks change of speaker by space between the verses or sections. How many prominent personages are there in the poem? Are there two, besides the daughters of Jerusalem, who resemble the chorus in a Greek play; or are there three, either actually speaking or introduced in the remarks of the Shulammite maid? According to the latter view in its general form, the three chief speakers are a country maid, her rustic lover, and Solomon. The maid is betrothed to her country swain; but she is noticed by Solomon and his companions during some journey to the north (vi. 10–13), brought to Jerusalem, and there, surrounded by the women of the palace, wooed by the king in the hope of gaining her affections. But the maid resists all enticements. When Solomon praises her, she responds by praising her rustic lover. She longs for him by day, and dreams of him by night. She sustains her devotion to him by recalling his speeches. She is true to him and to her vows. At length the parted lovers are reunited (viii. 5–7), and she is praised by her brothers for resisting all allurements. Throughout Solomon appears in an unfavorable light. He attempts to persuade the maid to forsake her proper allegiance (vii. 1–9), and he commits greater sin. The poem, according to this view, celebrates a pure affection, which holds out against the temptations of a court, and is strong enough to resist the seductive arts of a king.

This interpretation, which is known as the shepherd hypothesis, seeks support in expressions of the Shulammite, which are cited as passionate exclamations to her distant lover (i. 4, 7; ii. 16). But everything is much simpler in these passages themselves and throughout the poem, if the Shulammite's avowals of love are in all cases referred to king Solomon himself. The simple country maid has no adequate conception of royal life and occupations. She thinks of the king, the shepherd of the people (cp. Jer. xxiii. 4), under the figure of a rustic shepherd of her native hills, and she addresses him in language borrowed from the shepherd life familiar to her. And everywhere she naturally draws imagery from the pastoral and horticultural mountain life to which she was accustomed.

Instead of regarding the Shulammite as a country girl, some interpreters, especially in England, see in her the daughter of Pharaoh whom Solomon married. She is a stranger, dark of complexion, and a prince's daughter (i. 5; vii. 1). The blackness of skin, however, was due to sunburn (i. 6), and the title of prince's daughter probably does not indicate her birth, which was apparently lowly (ibid.; ii. 9), but her present high rank to which she has been raised (cp. vi. 12; 1 Sam. ii. 8), daughter meaning female or woman in general (cp. Song vi. 9; 1 Sam. i. 16), and the phrase signifying "O noble woman."

The Song has been regarded as a drama.

Few, however, have imagined that it was designed for presentation on the stage. It has been thought to consist of four acts (Ewald at first, Friedrich), or of five acts containing from thirteen to fifteen scenes (Ewald, Böttcher, and others), or of six acts with two scenes each (Delitzsch, Hahn). Bossuet discovered seven acts, each filling a day, concluding with the Sabbath, inasmuch as the bridegroom on this day does not, as usual, go forth to his rural employments. His several days are: i. 1–ii. 6; ii. 7–17; iii. 1–v. 1; v. 2–vi. 9; vi. 10–vii. 11; vii. 12–viii. 3; viii. 4–14. Delitzsch's scheme is as follows : Act 1. Mutual passion of the lovers (i. 2–ii. 7), concluding with, "I adjure you, O daughters of Jerusalem." The scene is laid in the palace of Solomon. Scene 1. Dialogue between the Shulammite maid and the court ladies, daughters of Jerusalem, at a meal (i. 2–8). Scene 2. Enter Solomon : dialogue between him and the maiden, who is not yet his bride (9–ii. 7). Act 2. Mutual seeking and finding (ii. 8–iii. 5), concluding with "I adjure you." The scene is the Shulammite's country home. Scene 1. She relates a rapturous meeting with Solomon (ii. 8–17). Scene 2. She relates a dream, in which she thought she had lost her beloved, but found him again (iii. 1–5). Act 3. Bringing the betrothed to the capital and the marriage (iii. 6–v. 1), with the introduction, "Who is this?" and the conclusion, "Eat, O friends; drink, yea, drink abundantly, O beloved." Scene 1. Procession to the palace (iii. 6–11). Scene 2. Dialogue between Solomon and his betrothed in the wedding chamber (iv. 1–16). The wedding must be supposed to follow; and then v. 1, Solomon's morning greeting to his bride, and afterwards his exhortation to the guests. Act 4. Love disdained, but regained (v. 2–vi. 9). Scene 1. Shadows fall on the married life. The Shulammite dreams of seeking her beloved, but finding him not (v. 2–vi. 3). Scene 2. She has found her beloved again (vi. 4–9). Act 5. The Shulammite the beautiful, but humble princess (vi. 10–viii. 4), with the introduction, "Who is she?" and the conclusion, "I adjure you." Scene 1. In the royal gardens; dialogue between the Shulammite and the daughters of Jerusalem (vi. 10–vii. 6). Scene 2. In the palace; Solomon and the Shulammite alone (vii. 7–viii. 4). Act 6. The confirmation of love's bond in the Shulammite's old home (viii. 5–14), beginning "Who is this?" Scene 1. Solomon and his bride appear in the presence of her kinsfolk (5–7). Scene 2. The Shulammite in her paternal home; dialogue between her and her brothers and the king (8–14).

But the opinion that the Song is a drama, although widely entertained in modern times and unobjectionable in itself, has not failed to meet with decided and well-founded opposition. The Song does not naturally conform to the rules of dramatic unity. A regular plot is not yielded by the poem itself. A

consecutive narrative can only be made out by supplying connecting links of which the poem knows nothing. Indeed, the several parts have been made to tell very different continuous tales, according as interpreters have supplied this or that connecting link. The Song as it stands is a continuous composition, with the love of Solomon and his bride for its one theme ; but the several scenes are grouped rather than linked, and the transitions are abrupt. The arrangement is not pleasing to the occidental mind, which loves order and logical sequence, but the structure of the poem is in entire harmony with oriental methods of literary composition.

Three leading methods of interpretation have been adopted, and all still find advocates : the allegorical, the literal, and the typical methods. The Jews, who have always greatly prized the Song of Songs, have generally regarded it as a spiritual allegory. Its sole intention was to teach God's love for ancient Israel. He is the Lover, and it the being beloved. The allegorical interpretation was introduced into the Christian church by Origen, a great allegorizer, early in the third century, but it underwent a modification. Christ became the Lover, and his church or the individual soul the beloved one. The details of this scheme may be learned from the headings of the several chapters in the A. V. On the literal interpretation the poem is an historical tale, a true story of Solomon's love for the Shulammite. The typical interpretation, to a certain extent, harmonizes the other two. The pure, spontaneous, mutual love of a great king and an humble maid was seen to exemplify the mutual affection between Jehovah and his people, and the story was told, not merely because it was beautiful, but chiefly because it was typical of this great religious truth. The Song of Songs is thus analogous to Messianic psalms, which are based on the personal experiences or official position of David or Solomon, and exhibit truths regarding the great king. The comparison of the mutual love between the church and its divine head to that of a bride and a bridegroom frequently occurs in the N. T. (Eph. v. 25–33; Rev. xix. 7–9; xxi. 9, etc.).

Regarding the date and authorship of the Song, it will be perceived at once that the shepherd theory disposes of the possibility that the poem proceeded from the pen of Solomon. The king had his faults, but there is no reason to believe that he was a monster of iniquity such as the poem, when interpreted on the shepherd hypothesis, depicts him. The shepherd hypothesis requires the assumption of another and a later author than Solomon. Turning to the marks of authorship and date found in the poem, the title first engages attention : "The Song of songs, which is Solomon's" (i. 1). The words are ambiguous, according to the Hebrew idiom ; they may mean either that Solomon was the author of the Song (cp. Hab. iii. 1, Hebrew), or that the Song is about Solomon (cp. Is. v. 1, Hebrew). The ambiguity is admitted, but the probabilities unquestionably favor the belief that the title attributes the poem to Solomon. The mind of the author as revealed in the Song admirably comports with all that is known of Solomon. The figurative language in the speeches of the king not merely reflects nature, but mirrors the gardens of exotics of which Solomon was fond. Extensive knowledge of all realms of nature, such as he possessed who spake of trees, from the cedar even unto the hyssop, and of beasts, fowl, creeping things, and fishes, is exhibited throughout the poem. And a minute and accurate picture of the time of Solomon is presented. Aramaisms are urged as indicating a later date than Solomon. But the orthography, apart from three words, is not Aramaic; and the syntactic peculiarity of the poem is confined to the use of a relative pronoun which occurs among other places in the song of Deborah and the history of Elisha, both of which are confessedly ancient Hebrew compositions, the former antedating the reign of Solomon by several centuries. Ewald and Hitzig believed that the poem was produced in the best period of the Hebrew language, and at a time of great national prosperity. They attributed it to a poet who lived in the generation after Solomon. The three Aramaic forms, *n*e*tar*, keep (i. 6; viii. 11, 12), *b*e*roth*, fir (i. 17), *s*e*thav*, winter (ii. 11), are regarded by these critics as an idiom in the dialect of northern Palestine, and they accordingly attribute the song to a poet of the northern kingdom. But, assuming that these words were characteristic of the north, Solomon himself in addressing the Shulammite maid, who was probably from Shunem, and in quoting her speeches, may have adopted these words in order to give to his poem the northern flavor. It is affirmed that *pardes*, orchard, park (iv. 13), and *'appiryon*, palanquin (iii. 9, R. V; in Sanscrit *paryâna*; others, Greek *phoreion*) are of Aryan origin, and accordingly betray the post-exilic date of the poem. But even if they are of Aryan origin, why should it be thought strange that a king who sent his ships to distant Ophir, traded with India, and brought to Palestine Indian goods and objects with Aryan names, such as apes, peacocks, algum wood, should also import the palanquin and retain its native name, and give the oriental designation to the gardens which he filled with oriental plants?

Sons of God.

Worshipers and beneficiaries of God; see SON 3. Such was its common Semitic meaning in early times. There is abundant reason to believe that this is its signification in the celebrated passage where it first appears in the Bible. "It came to pass, when men began to multiply on the face of the ground,

and daughters were born unto them, that the sons of God saw the daughters of men that they were fair; and they took them wives of all that they chose" (Gen. vi. 1, 2). Three interpretations have been proposed. The sons of God are: 1. The great and noble of the earth, and the daughters of men are women of inferior rank (Samaritan version; Greek translation of Symmachus; Targums of Onkelos and Jonathan). 2. Angels, who left their first estate and took wives from among the children of men (Book of Enoch, Philo, Josephus, Justin Martyr, Clement of Alexandria, Tertullian). 3. Pious men, worshipers of God, who were especially represented by the descendants of Seth. They were attracted by the beauty of women who did not belong to the godly line, married with them, and became secularized (Julius Africanus, Chrysostom, Cyril of Alexandria, Augustine, Jerome). The first interpretation has no longer any advocates. In favor of the second, it is asserted that the term denotes angels everywhere else in the O. T. (Job i. 6; ii. 1; xxxviii. 7; cp. a similar expression Ps. xxix. 1; lxxxix. 6; R. V. margin; but not Dan. iii. 25); that the designation describes angels according to their nature, whereas the ordinary word for angels, *mal' akim*, messengers, refers to their official employment; and that this interpretation is confirmed by Jude 6 and 2 Pet. ii. 4. But that the term relates to the nature of angels lacks proof; it is quite as natural that it should describe angels as worshipers of God. As to the passages in Jude and Peter, to cite them is begging the question, since exegetes point out other references, as Is. xxiv. 21–23; moreover in Jude the word "these" in verse 7 and elsewhere does not refer to angels that kept not their own principality (verse 6, R. V.), but to certain ungodly men (verse 4). And unless the title be restricted to the special form which it has in the passage under discussion, it is not true that the term denotes angels in all other places where it occurs in the O. T. The worshipers of the heathen deity Chemosh are called the people of Chemosh, and his sons and daughters (Num. xxi. 29; Jer. xlviii. 46). When the men of Judah, professed worshipers of Jehovah, took heathen women to wife, Judah was said to have married the daughter of a strange god (Mal. ii. 11). Moses was directed to say to Pharaoh: "Thus saith the LORD, Israel is my son. . . . . Let my son go" (Ex. iv. 22, 23). Other passages are: "Ye are the children [or sons] of the LORD your God" (Deut. xiv. 1). "They have dealt corruptly with him [Jehovah], they are not his children [or sons]." "Is not he [Jehovah] thy father?" "The LORD saw it, and abhorred them, because of the provocation of his sons and his daughters" (xxxii. 5, 6, 19). "Ye are the sons of the living God" (Hos. i. 10). "When Israel was a child . . . . I . . . .

called my son out of Egypt" (xi. 1). "Bring my sons from far, and my daughters from the end of the earth; every one that is called by my name, and whom I have created for my glory" (Is. xliii. 6, 7). The pious are the generation of God's children (Ps. lxxiii. 15), and Ephraim is his dear son (Jer. xxxi. 20). Taking a broader survey, and examining Semitic literature other than Hebrew, one observes the same fact. Many a Babylonian styled himself the son of the god whom he worshiped and upon whom he relied for protection and care.

Furthermore, the opinion that the title in Gen. vi. 2 means angels is not the earliest view, so far as the records go. The earliest attested interpretation, that of the Samaritan version, regarded the sons of God as men; and later when the angelic theory arose, it was the opinion of a particular school among the Jews, while the more influential party in religious matters still taught that the sons of God were men.

The theory that angels are meant contradicts the doctrine of Scripture concerning angels. Its writers nowhere countenance the idea that an angel could or would enter into marriage with a human being. They invariably represent the passions of angels, fallen and unfallen, as spiritual, not carnal. The notion is quite foreign to Scripture that woman's beauty could arouse animal love in an angel.

The interpretation that the sons of God in Gen. vi. 2 were pious people, the worshipers of the true God, more especially that they were the godly descendants of Adam through Seth, whose genealogy is given in Gen. v., is not only in accordance with Semitic, and particularly biblical, usage of the designation, as already shown, but it is consistent with the context. The sons of God are contrasted with the daughters of men, that is, of other men. So Jeremiah says, "God did set signs in Israel and among men;" and the English version supplies the word other before men, in order to bring out the sense (Jer. xxxii. 20). Likewise the psalmist says that the wicked "are not in trouble as men; neither are they plagued like men;" and again the English version supplies the word other (Ps. lxxiii. 5). After the same manner Gen. vi. 1, 2 may be read: "When mankind began to multiply on the face of the ground, and daughters were born unto them, the sons of God saw the daughters of other men that they were fair; and they took them wives of all that they chose." The meaning of the writer is that when men began to increase in number, the worshipers of God so far degenerated that in choosing wives for themselves they neglected character, and esteemed beauty of face and form above piety. The offspring of these marriages were perhaps stalwart and violent (4). Mixture of race in marriage often produces physical strength in the descendants, and lack of religion in the parents

is apt to be reproduced in the children. The intermarriage of the sons of God and the daughters of men was offensive in the sight of God. Sentence was pronounced against the wrongdoers (3). The penalty is not denounced on angels, who were not only implicated, but were the chief sinners, if the sons of God were angels. The punishment is pronounced against man only. Man, not angels, had offended.

Sons of God everywhere in Scripture, from the earliest to the latest times, means the worshipers and beneficiaries of God, both among mortal and immortal beings. But the content of this idea did not remain the same through the ages. It became larger with increasing knowledge of the riches of God. It enlarged, for example, at the time when the Israelites were delivered from Egypt. God said: "I have seen the affliction of my people" (Ex. iii. 7); and again: "Say unto Pharaoh, Israel is my son, my firstborn; who is as dear to me," so the following words imply, "as Pharaoh's firstborn is to him" (iv. 22 with 23); and again: "I will take you to me for a people, and I will be to you a God" (vi. 7). Heretofore the title had emphasized a filial relation of men to God, their dependence upon him for protection and care, and their duty of reverence and obedience. Now God formally accepts the obligations which implicitly devolve on him. The content of the title was further enlarged through the teaching of Jesus Christ. He took truths already known, shed light on them, and connected them with this designation. He exhibited the fact that God is an actual father and that his people are actual children of God. They are such by the new birth (John iii. 3, 5, 6, 8; cp. Rev. xi. 11), begotten of God (John i. 12, 13; v. 21; and so Eph. ii. 5; Jas. i. 18; 1 Pet. i. 23), made partakers of the divine nature through the mediation of the indwelling Spirit (John vi. 48–51; xv. 4, 5; and so 1 John iii. 9), and possessing a like character with God, resembling him in holiness, love, and elevation above the illusions of earth (1 John iii. 9; iv. 7; v. 4), although falling far short of the divine character in this life (i. 8, 10) They have been adopted as sons (Gal. iv. 5), are taught by the Spirit to say Abba, Father (6; Rom. viii. 15), and are led by the Spirit (14).

Sons of the Pro′phets. See PROPHETIC ASSOCIATIONS.

Sooth′say-er [sayer of truth].

A diviner (Josh. xiii. 22, with Num. xxii. 7), one who prognosticates future events (Jer. xxvii. 9, R. V., in Hebrew *on^enim*). As rendering of the Aramaic *Gaz^erin*, it denotes one who professed to be able to interpret dreams (Dan. iv. 7) and explain dark sentences (9; v. 11, 12), and to whom men in desperation resorted to obtain, if possible, the revelation of secrets (ii. 27).

Sop′a-ter [of good parentage].

A Christian of Berœa, and one of Paul's companions from Greece as far as the province of Asia, when the apostle was returning from his third missionary journey (Acts xx. 4). He was son of Pyrrhus (R. V.).

Soph′e-reth, in R. V. of Ezra **Hassophereth**, with the Hebrew article [secretariate].

The name, probably denoting an office, belonging to a certain class of Solomon's servants. Members of it returned from captivity with Zerubbabel (Ezra ii. 55; Neh. vii. 57).

Sor′cer-er.

One who practices sorcery, uses potions that derive a supposed efficacy from magical spells, and professes to possess supernatural power or knowledge, gained in any manner, especially through the connivance of evil spirits (Ex. vii. 11; Antiq. xvii. 4, 1; Life 31). Sorcerers were found in Egypt (Ex. vii. 11), Assyria (Nah. iii. 4), Babylonia (Is. xlvii. 9; Dan. ii. 2), and other heathen lands (Deut. xviii. 10); but were strictly forbidden in Israel (Ex. xxii. 18; Deut. xviii. 10), and warning was uttered against their deception (Jer. xxvii. 9), and their punishment was foretold (Mic. v. 12; Mal. iii. 5; Rev. xxi. 8). The Hebrew and Greek words for sorcerer and sorcery are sometimes rendered witch and witchcraft in the English versions. Simon, called Magus or magician, and Bar-jesus were prominent sorcerers in apostolic history (Acts viii. 9, 11; xiii. 6, 8). A sorceress, and likewise the sorcerer and the practicer of other forms of the black art, were not to be permitted to live (Ex. xxii. 18: Lev. xx. 27; Deut. xviii. 10–12). God's own attitude toward such persons and those who consulted them was also one of destruction (Lev. xx. 6, 23; Deut. xviii. 12; Wisd. xii. 4–6).

So′rek [a choice vine].

A valley in which Delilah lived (Judg. xvi. 4). It is doubtless the wady es-Surâr, which commences about 13 miles west, slightly south, of Jerusalem, and pursues a tortuous course in a northwesterly direction toward the Mediterranean Sea. It is traversed by a stream which falls into the sea about 8½ miles south of Joppa. The name Sûrîk is still borne by a ruin north of the valley, 2 miles from Zorah, Samson's birthplace.

So-sip′a-ter [saviour of a father].

A Christian who joined with Paul in sending salutations (Rom. xvi. 21).

Sos′the-nes [of sound strength].

A ruler of the Jewish synagogue at Corinth when Paul was there. In the outbreak which Paul's preaching excited, the crowd seized Sosthenes and beat him before the judgment seat of Gallio (Acts xviii. 17, R. V.). Perhaps he became a Christian, for one Sosthenes is associated with Paul as a brother Christian in the address to the Corinthians (1 Cor. i. 1).

So′tai [deviator].

One of the class known as **Solomon's servants**. He founded a family, members of which returned with Zerubbabel from captivity (Ezra ii. 55; Neh. vii. 57).

Soul.

In ordinary English usage, a spirit is an immaterial, incorporeal being, which may or may not be associated with a body, as "God is a Spirit," "My spirit hath rejoiced in God my Saviour" (John iv. 24; Luke i. 47); a soul is a spirit that is or at least has been embodied, as the souls of them that had been slain (Rev. vi. 9); and a ghost is a disembodied spirit.

Theologians entertain two main views as to the soul, and consequently as to the nature of man and irrational animals. One is embraced under the. doctrine of trichotomy. Trichotomists differ considerably among themselves; but according to the doctrine, in its general outlines, man consists of three parts or essential elements, body, soul and spirit (1 Thes. v. 23). The body is the material part of man's constitution. The soul, in Hebrew *nephesh*, in Greek *psuchē*, is the principle of animal life: man possesses it in common with the brutes; to it belong understanding, emotion, and sensibility, and it ceases to exist at death. The spirit, in Hebrew *ruaḥ*, in Greek *pneuma*, is the mind, the principle of man's rational and immortal life, the possessor of reason, will, and conscience. God created man by enlivening inorganic matter formed into a body, and then creating a rational spirit and infusing it (Gen. ii. 7), and at death the dust or body returns to the earth as it was, and the spirit returns unto God who gave it (Ecc. xii. 7). The soul of life, in Hebrew *nephesh ḥayyah*, in the instance of the animal (Gen. i. 21, 24) is only the animal soul, which is physical and material in its nature, and perishes with the body of which it is the vital principle; but the soul of life in the instance of man (ii. 7) is a higher principle, the rational soul, which was inbreathed by the Creator and made in his image. Usually the biblical writers do not distinguish the *psuchē* or animal soul, which is the lower side of the human soul, from the *pneuma* or rational soul, the higher side, since they constitute one soul, *psuchē*, in distinction from the body, and they are sometimes designated in their unity by *pneuma*, and sometimes by *psuchē*. Commonly the sacred writers speak of man as constituted of body and soul, or body and spirit, and not of body, soul, and spirit; but in 1 Cor. xv. 44, as in 1 Thes. v. 23 and Heb. iv. 12, Paul requires the distinction between the animal and the rational soul for the purposes of his discussion, and he accordingly makes it.

According to dichotomy, on the other hand, there are only two essential elements in the constitution of man: the body formed from the dust of the earth, and the soul or principle of life (Gen. ii. 7). The soul is the principle of the whole life of whatever subject is spoken of, whether man or beast. It is the principle of all life, physical, intellectual, moral, religious. There is not one substance, the soul, which feels and remembers, and another substance, the spirit, that has conscience and the knowledge of God. The soul of the brute is the living principle in the brute: it is conscious of the impressions which are made by external objects on the organs of sense belonging to the body; it is endowed with that measure of intelligence which experience shows the lower animals to possess, but it is irrational and mortal. Brutes perish because God does not will that the living principle in them should continue. The soul of man is the same in kind with that of the brute, but it differs in being of a higher order: in addition to the attributes of sensibility, memory, and instinct, it has the higher powers which pertain to the intellectual, moral, and religious life, and it has continued existence after the death of the body, not because of its inherent nature, but because God wills to preserve it. It is argued from the usage of words in Scripture in defense of this dualism that 1. Soul of life, nephesh ḥayyah, means simply animate existence, a being in which there is a living soul, and there is no authority to make it mean one thing in the case of a brute and quite another thing in the case of a man. 2. The Bible does not ascribe to beasts a psuchē only, and both a psuchē and pneuma to man. The living principle in brutes is called spirit, ruah, as well as soul, nephesh, psuchē. "Who knoweth the spirit of man whether it goeth upward, and the spirit of the beast whether it goeth downward to the earth?" (Ecc. iii. 21; cp. 19, R. V. margin; Gen. vii. 15). 3. No distinction is observed in the use of the words soul and spirit. The souls of them that were slain for the word of God are in heaven (Rev. vi. 9; xx. 4), and likewise the spirits of just men made perfect (Heb. xii. 23).

Trichotomists quote 1 Thes. v. 23: "The God of peace himself sanctify you wholly; and may your spirit and soul and body be preserved entire, without blame at the coming of our Lord Jesus Christ" (cp. Heb. iv. 12), as evidence that Paul distinguishes the animal soul from the rational spirit. But dichotomists reply that Paul's language is quite analogous to that employed in the command, "Thou shalt love the Lord thy God with all thy heart, and with all thy soul, and with all thy mind, and with all thy strength" (Mark xii. 30; cp. Luke i. 46, 47). The intention in the demand for love, and in the prayer for preservation, is simply to lay stress on the whole man, and the description is accordingly plethoric. As heart, soul, strength, and mind are not so many essential elements in man's constitution, so there is

no proof that body, soul, and spirit are. The main passage relied upon to support the trichotomist position is 1 Cor. xv. 44: "It is sown a natural body; it is raised a spiritual body. If there is a natural body, there is also a spiritual body." Trichotomists interpret the sōma psuchikon or natural body as one marked by the qualities of the psuchē or animal soul; namely, by physical appetites and passions, such as hunger, thirst, and sexual appetite. These are founded in "flesh and blood," or that material substance of which the present human body is composed. The resurrection, or spiritual body, on the other hand, will be marked by the qualities of the pneuma or rational soul. It will not be composed of flesh and blood, but of a substance which is more like the rational than the animal soul. There is, however, another interpretation, not only in harmony with the doctrine of the dual constitution of man, but in accord with the general usage of the words psuchikos and pneumatikos, natural and spiritual. The resurrection body of the redeemed will not be marked by the qualities of ordinary animal life, right and proper though that life is, but the resurrection body will be opposed to everything carnal, and will be characterized by the qualities which belong to the Spirit-led man. This appears from a study of the words. In established usage among the Greeks psuchē was the common word for the vital principle; which, however, might be thought of as a disembodied soul, the immortal part of man, and the organ of thought and judgment (Herod. ii. 123; v. 124; Plato, Tim. x., i. e., p. 30ᵇ), hence psuchikos referred primarily to the ordinary animal life, and is so used by Paul, James, and Jude (1 Cor. ii. 14; Jas. iii. 15; Jude 19). Pneumatikos, on the other hand, almost exclusively has reference in Scripture to the Pneuma 'agion, the Holy Spirit. It is opposed to carnal and fleshly, to human nature deprived of the Spirit of God; it refers to possession and control by the Holy Spirit as contrasted with the domination of the flesh (1 Cor. iii. 1); it denotes what is effected by the Spirit and pertains to the Spirit (Rom. i. 11; 1 Cor. ii. 13; xii. 1). Hence a spiritual body, contrasted with a natural body, is a body not only free from fleshly lusts, but elevated above the physical passions and appetites which are natural to man (Mat. xxii. 30), in vital union with the Spirit of God, and marked by the qualities which characterize the Spirit-led man.

South, The. See NEGEB.

South Ra'moth. See RAMAH 6.

Sow. See SWINE.

Sow'er and Sow'ing.
Sowing began with the rain of October; see YEAR. The seed was required to be ceremonially clean (Lev. xi. 37, 38). The

sower held the vessel containing the seed in the left hand, and scattered the seed with his right; see illustration, article PLOW. When the soil was favorable, he seems sometimes to have cast in front of the plow, which then served the purpose of a harrow to cover the seed. Wheat was best sown, it was thought, in rows (Is. xxviii. 25, R. V.). The sowing of mixed seed was forbidden (Lev. xix. 19; Deut. xxii. 9), as being contrary to nature as established by the Creator; but the planting of several kinds of seeds in different sections of the same field was permitted.

Spain.

The well-known country in the southwestern portion of Europe. Its mines yielded gold and silver (1 Mac. viii. 3). Paul desired to visit it (Rom. xv. 24, 28), and probably carried out his intention, for Clement of Rome, writing from Italy about A. D. 96, says that Paul "reached the bounds of the west," and the Muratorian fragment, written about A. D. 170, states explicitly that he went to Spain. This visit must have taken place after Paul's imprisonment at Rome which is recorded in The Acts. See TARSHISH.

Spar'row.

The rendering of the Hebrew *Sippor*, chirper, in Ps. lxxxiv. 3; cii. 7; and R. V. of Prov. xxvi. 2. The word is more frequently translated bird; in fact, it is often employed as a general term for bird or fowl (Ps. viii. 8; cxlviii. 10; Ezek. xvii. 23). It may be a bird of prey (Jer. xii. 9; Ezek. xxxix. 17), such as the raven and crow, which are passerine birds, although they feed on carrion; or it may be a bird ceremonially clean, and large enough to be eaten as food (Lev. xiv. 4; Neh. v. 18). It may live in the mountains or in the town (Ps. xi. 1; lxxxiv. 3), and may build its nest in trees or on the ground or about human habitations (Deut. xxii. 6; Ps. lxxxiv. 3). The term includes doves and pigeons (Gen. xv. 9, 10), and the etymology indicates that in the first instance it designates chirping birds, like the sparrow and the finch.

In the N. T. sparrow is the rendering of the Greek *Strouthion*, which denotes any small bird, especially one of the sparrow kind. It was sold and eaten (Mat. x. 29; Luke xii. 6, 7).

The house sparrow (*Passer domesticus*), familiarly known as the English sparrow, is found through Europe, northern Africa, and western Asia, and is common in the coast towns of Palestine. Two species of southern Europe, closely allied to it, the Italian sparrow (*Passer italiæ*) and the marsh sparrow (*Passer hispaniolensis*), also occur, the latter chiefly in the Jordan valley, where it breeds in vast numbers in the thorn trees. The tree sparrow (*Passer montanus*) is a near relative of the house sparrow, and perhaps in Palestine should not be separated from it; but the sparrows which frequent the sacred precincts on the temple hill and are common on the mount of Olives have sometimes been spoken of by writers of authority as tree sparrows. Another sparrow (*Passer moabiticus*) is found in the vicinity of the Dead Sea, but is rare. The rock or foolish sparrow (*Petronia stulta*) is common on the central ridge of Palestine. It never resorts to inhabited dwellings. Thomson says that a sparrow which has lost its mate is often seen sitting alone on the housetop, lamenting its fate (cp. Ps. cii. 7). Tristram is inclined to see in this passage a reference to the blue thrush (*Monticola cyanus*), a solitary bird which perches on the housetop, uttering meanwhile a monotonous and plaintive note.

Spar'tans.

Inhabitants of the celebrated city of Sparta in Greece. It was known also as Lacedæmon. Jonathan Maccabæus refers to an ancient friendship which existed between the Spartans and the Jews in the days of king Arius and the high priest Onias, about 300 B. C. (1 Mac. xii. 7, 19–23; in A. V. Lacedemonians); and he sent letters to them, when he sent an embassy to Rome, to renew the friendship with them (2, 5). Jonathan did not live to hear their answer, but Simon received cordial letters from them (xiv. 16, 20–23).

Spear.

The spear, called in Hebrew *hᵃnith*, consisted of a metallic head on a shaft (1 Sam. xiii. 19; xvii. 7; Is. ii. 4). It could be carried in the hand; stuck in the ground when not wanted; and though used for thrusting, could be hurled (1 Sam. xviii. 10, in A. V. javelin; xxvi. 7, 8; 2 Sam. ii. 23; John xix. 34).

A long spear, the Arab *rumḥ*, was used (Judg. v. 8; 1 Chron. xii. 8, 24; Neh. iv. 13; Jer. xlvi. 4). It was called *romaḥ* by the Hebrews, and was used for thrusting (Num. xxv. 7, 8, R. V.), not for throwing. In R. V., it is once rendered lance (1 Kin. xviii. 28), in A. V. of 1611 lancer, later corrupted into lancet.

Spear'men.

The rendering of the Greek *Dexiolabos* or, as in the Alexandrian manuscript, *Dexiobolos* in Acts xxiii. 23, a body of troops distinguished from the legionary soldiers and the cavalry. In the only other passage where the word occurs, which is late, they are distinguished from archers and targeteers. Evidently they were light-armed soldiers who carried a weapon in the right hand.

Spelt.

The revised rendering of the Hebrew *Kussemeth* (Ex. ix. 32 and Is. xxviii. 25, in A. V. rye; Ezek. iv. 9, in A. V. fitches). Spelt is an inferior kind of wheat, the chaff of which slightly adheres to the grain. It was sown in Egypt, springing up after the barley (Ex. ix. 32). The Egyptians made their bread of it (Herod. ii. 36, 77). Rye is a northern plant, and is not grown in Egypt and Palestine.

Spice.

1. The rendering of the Hebrew *Bosem* and its plural *B^esamim*, which are used generically for fragrant stuff, spice, spicery (Ex. xxv. 6 with xxx. 23, 24; 1 Kin. x. 10; Song iv. 10, 14). Spice is a vegetable substance possessing aromatic and pungent qualities (Song iv. 16). The chief spices were myrrh, cinnamon, calamus, and cassia or costus (Ex. xxx. 23, 24). Southern Arabia was the great, but not exclusive, producer of them (1 Kin. x. 2; Ezek. xxvii. 22). *Bosem* in Song v. 13; vi. 2, and *basam* in v. 1, are probably applied specifically to balsam or balm of Gilead (R. V. margin).

2. *N^eko'th* (Gen. xxxvii. 25; xliii. 11) is probably a specific term for tragacanth or storax (R. V. margin). A form of this word is perhaps used in 2 Kin. xx. 13; Is. xxxix. 2 for spices in general.

3. *Sammim*, fragrant odors, were aromatic substances used in the preparation of incense (Ex. xxx. 7). Three are specified: stacte or opobalsamum, onycha, and galbanum (34).

4. The rendering of the Greek *Arōma*, a generic term (Mark xvi. 1), including myrrh and aloes (John xix. 40).

Spice Mer'chant.

The rendering of the Hebrew *Rokel* in 1 Kin. x. 15. It means simply, as the R. V. makes it, a merchant; and A. V. renders it so elsewhere, *e. g.* Ezek. xxvii. 13.

Spi'der.

An animal of the class *Arachnida*, called in Hebrew *'akkabish*. It weaves a web (Job viii. 14; Is. lix. 5). The number of species in Palestine amounts to 600 or 700. In A. V. spider is the rendering of the Hebrew *S^emamith*, poisonous thing (Prov. xxx. 28, in R. V. lizard).

Spike'nard.

A fragrant plant, in Hebrew *nerd* (Song iv. 13, 14), from which an aromatic ointment was made, called *nardos* in Greek (Mark xiv. 3). It is believed to be *Nardostachys jatamansi*, a plant of the Valerian family, with fragrant roots, growing in the Himalaya Mountains at an elevation of 11,000 to 17,000 feet. It was used by the Hindus as a medicine and perfume from remote antiquity, and was early an article of commerce. The long distance which it had to be brought to Palestine rendered it on its arrival very precious. The alabaster cruse of it, which was poured over the head of Jesus, was worth 300 denarii (Mark xiv. 3, 5). According to Pliny, the ointment varied in price from 25 to 300 and even 400 denarii a pound, according to the quality (Hist. Nat. xii. 26; xiii. 2, 4). In Mark xiv. 3; John xii. 3 (see R. V. margin), the spikenard is described by the Greek adjective *pistikos*, a variant of *pistos*, genuine, or of *pistos*, liquid. Some interpreters, however, think that the adjective

denotes the place where this variety was obtained.

Spin'ning.

Spinning was the work of the women (Ex. xxxv. 25). The wheel was unknown, and spinning was done by hand. Distaff and spindle were used (Prov. xxxi. 19). The flax or wool was wound on the distaff, which was held under the arm or stuck upright in the ground, and the thread was drawn out by hand. To the end of this thread the spindle, with a circular rim to steady it when revolving, was attached and by rotating it the spinner twisted the thread.

Spir'it. See SOUL and HOLY GHOST.

Spring. See FOUNTAIN.

Sta'chys [an ear of grain].

A Christian at Rome to whom the apostle Paul sent a salutation (Rom. xvi. 9).

Stac'te.

The rendering of the Hebrew *Nataph*, a drop. It denotes a sweet spice, which was used for incense (Ex. xxx. 34; cp. Ecclus. xxiv. 15). The Septuagint interprets *nataph* by *staktē*, which likewise signifies a drop or exudation, and was employed for the oil which trickles from fresh myrrh or cinnamon. It is believed, however, that *nataph* is the gum of the storax tree, or else opobalsamum (R. V. margin).

The storax (*Styrax officinalis*) is a resinous shrub or small tree, from 10 to 20 feet high, with flowers resembling those of the orange in color, size, and fragrance, and mostly growing in spikes of four or five. The tree is very showy when in bloom. It is native in Asia Minor and Syria, and abounds in Galilee. The officinal storax is the inspissated juice of the bark; it is used medicinally as an expectorant, and also in perfumery. The liquid storax of commerce is the product of an entirely different plant.

Opobalsamum (R. V. margin) is a resinous juice, also called balm and balm of Gilead (q. v.).

Star.

The number of the stars and their grouping in constellations early attracted man's attention (Gen. xxii. 17; Is. xiii. 10). Orion, Pleiades, the Bear, the zodiac were pointed out (Job ix. 9; xxxviii. 31, 32), planets were known and named (2 Kin. xxiii. 5; see BABYLONIA, CHIUN, LUCIFER), perhaps meteors or comets are referred to (Jude 13), the position of certain stars served as dates (Antiq. xiii. 8, 2), and in Egypt the successive rising of thirty-six constellations marked off an equal number of ten-day periods in the year; see WEEK. The stars were recognized in Israel as the handiwork of God (Gen. i. 16; Ps. viii. 3), and as under his control (Is. xiii. 10; Jer. xxxi. 35).

But among the heathen and the degenerate Israelites the stars became objects of wor-

The method of spinning wool is much the same today as it was in Biblical days.

ship (Deut. iv. 19; 2 Kin. xvii. 16); altars were reared, and incense was burnt to them (xxi. 5; xxiii. 5). They were believed to exercise influence, not only in the ordinary economy of nature (cp. Job xxxviii. 31, A. V.), but also over the affairs of men. This belief was widespread among the heathen. Deborah may perhaps be subsidizing a phrase of current speech, in which a reminiscence of heathen notions lingers, when she poetically describes the stars from their courses fighting against Sisera (Judg. v. 20); but Bertheau is probably correct in understanding her to speak poetically of divine assistance (iv. 15), as if heaven or, to use her own words, as if the stars, forsaking their usual orbits, had fought against Sisera (cp. Ps. xviii. 9). A reference has also been seen in her words to a providential storm which discomfited the Canaanites; and ver. 21 and Josephus (Antiq. v. 5, 4) are cited in confirmation: but Josephus probably deduces this storm from the analogy of Josh. x. 10, 11 and 1 Sam. vii. 10. The stars were also supposed by the heathen to portend coming events, and they were observed with a view to prognostication (Is. xlvii. 13). See Astrologers. J. D. D.

Several stars mentioned in the N. T. require particular notice :

1. The day-star (2 Pet. i. 19) is probably a figurative description of the signs immediately preceding the second advent. Others understand it as the Spirit's illumination of the believer's heart.

2. The morning star (Rev. ii. 28): the bright, the morning star (xxii. 16, R. V.). Both these phrases are probably designations of Christ as the herald to his people of the eternal day. See Lucifer.

3. The star of the wise men; see Magi. The usual view has been that this was a purely supernatural phenomenon, a starlike object which appeared to the Magi in their eastern sky, and suggested to them, perhaps through their acquaintance with the prophecy of Balaam (Num. xxiv. 17) or other predictions, that the king of the Jews was born, and which afterwards reappeared, as they journeyed from Jerusalem to Bethlehem, and guided them on their way until it rested over the house in which Jesus was. Others, however, consider it a natural phenomenon providentially used to direct the Magi. In Dec., 1603, the astronomer Kepler noted a conjunction of Jupiter and Saturn, joined in March, 1604, by Mars, and in Oct., 1604, by a brilliant new star, which gradually faded and vanished in Feb., 1606. Kepler calculated that the planets were in conjunction in 7 and 6 B. C., and, supposing that the new or variable star had followed the conjunction then as it did in 1604, believed it to be the star of the Magi. Others have identified the Magi's star with the planetary conjunction itself, and the calculations of Kepler have been corrected by Ideler, Pritchard, and Encke, with the result that we know that in 7 B. C. there were three conjunctions of Jupiter and Saturn, in May, September, and December. Hence, it has been supposed that the Magi saw the heavenly spectacle in May :

connected it, through their astrology and knowledge of Hebrew prophecy and expectation, with the birth of a Jewish king; and, when going from Jerusalem to Bethlehem in December, saw again the conjunction overhead. But the word star can hardly mean a conjunction, and this view would place Christ's birth earlier than other considerations warrant. If we can believe that Kepler's variable star followed the conjunction, as he supposed, it would answer the conditions better than the conjunction itself. It is on some accounts more probable that the event was a natural rather than a supernatural phenomenon. The Magi were doubtless astrologers, and would attach special ideas to the positions and variations of the stars. The star did not go before them to Judæa, but only, after its reappearance, did it seem to lead them from Jerusalem to Bethlehem. On the other hand, many think that Mat. ii. 9 cannot fairly be understood of anything but a supernatural phenomenon; nor can the astronomical calculations above described safely be held to have identified the star, even if it be regarded as a natural object.   G. T. P.

Sta′ter. See MONEY.

Steel.

A modified form of iron, resulting in elasticity and hardness. The earliest known and simplest method of reducing iron from its ore was capable of yielding steel. The Chalybes in Pontus were celebrated for hardening iron, and their name was used by the Greeks for steel. Steel seems to have been used in ancient Egypt. Comparison with Syriac *palᵉda*, as well as the context, suggests that the Hebrew word *paldah* in Nah. ii. 3 means steel (R. V., in A. V. torches).

Where steel occurs in A. V., brass is correctly substituted in R. V.

Steph′a-nas [crowned].

A Christian convert at Corinth. His household was the first fruit of Paul's labors in the province of Achaia. The apostle himself baptized its members, and they set themselves to minister unto the saints. Stephanas also visited the apostle, bringing him aid, and was with him when the First Epistle to the Corinthians was penned (1 Cor. i. 16; xvi. 15, 17).

Ste′phen [a wreath or crown].

The first Christian martyr. He is first mentioned as first in the list of the seven men chosen by the Jerusalem Christians, at the suggestion of the apostles, to superintend the distribution of the church's alms (Acts vi. 5). Since the appointment of these seven men, usually regarded as the first deacons, arose from the complaints made by the Greek-speaking or Hellenistic Jewish Christians that their widows were neglected in the daily ministration, and since Stephen is itself a Greek name, and since the subsequent persecution of Stephen arose among the Greek-speaking Jews of Jerusalem, it is

probable that Stephen himself was a Hellenist, and perhaps had come from abroad. He was a notable man; full of faith and of the Holy Ghost (5), who, after his appointment, became more than ever conspicuous as a preacher and worker of miracles (8). His activity occasioned for the first time opposition to the church among the foreign Jews, who had synagogues in Jerusalem. The trouble originated particularly in the synagogue of the Libertines (or freedmen) and Cyrenians and Alexandrians, with whom united certain Jews from Cilicia and Asia (9). These charged Stephen with blaspheming Moses and God, and, more especially, with declaring that Jesus would destroy the temple and change the customs derived from Moses (11–14). Luke states that the witnesses produced against Stephen were suborned and false, as those against Christ had been; but Stephen must have said something which could be thus perverted. He was brought before the sanhedrin, and from his defense, reported in Acts vii. 2–53, we can understand his position. He first recited God's early choice and guidance of the patriarchs (2–22), apparently to bring out the fact that God from the beginning had been leading Israel to a definite goal; then, continuing the history, he showed that the Hebrews had repeatedly resisted God's purpose with them, both in the days of Moses and subsequently (23–43), and had failed to see the temporary and typical character of both tabernacle and temple (44–50). Then, suddenly stopping his argument, he bitterly charged them with resisting, as their fathers had done, the Holy Ghost, with having slain the Christ as their fathers had slain the prophets, and with failing to keep in reality their own law (51–53). At this point the listeners gnashed upon him with their teeth and prepared to rush upon him. A vision was given him of the Son of man standing (as though to receive him) at the right hand of God; and, when he declared it, they seized him, cast him out of the city, and stoned him. It was not lawful for them to put anyone to death without permission from the Romans, but the martyrdom was evidently the result of an uncontrollable outbreak. The speech and death of Stephen mark the transition of Christianity from its earliest Jewish form to its extension among the gentiles. Peter preached Christianity as the fulfillment of prophecy; Stephen preached it as the goal of Hebrew history. Yet while Stephen declared that Christianity could not be limited by Judaism, he did not set forth, like Paul afterwards, its gentile mission or its deliverance, by the doctrine of salvation by faith alone, from its Jewish environment. He marks, therefore, the transition from Jewish to gentile Christianity. Moreover, the persecution which followed his martyrdom led to the dispersion of the disciples, and so in fact to the carrying of the gospel to the Samaritans and then to the gentiles. Stephen's personal character also was very beautiful. As a man he was "full of faith and of the Holy Ghost" (vi. 5) ; as a preacher, "full of faith and power" (8) ; before the council, his enemies "saw his face as it had been the face of an angel" (15) ; and his last words were: " Lord, lay not this sin to their charge " (vii. 60).

The inspiration of Stephen, so far as his recorded speech is concerned, is a disputed question. He is said (vii. 55) to have been "full of the Holy Ghost," but some of his historical statements are thought by many not to harmonize with the O. T. Others hold that they can be harmonized, or at least might be, if we knew all the facts. Either view can be adjusted to the doctrine of inspiration, since the phrase "full of the Holy Ghost" need not mean "inspired" in the technical sense (see Acts vi. 3; Eph. v. 18), and since the inspiration of Luke merely guarantees the correctness of his report of what Stephen said, not the correctness of Stephen's utterances themselves.   G. T. P.

Stocks.

An instrument of punishment, called in Hebrew *sad*, consisting of a wooden frame, hence called *xulon* in Greek, in which the feet were put and firmly held (Job xiii. 27 ; xxxiii. 11 ; Acts xvi. 24). The prisoner sat meanwhile. A special form of the apparatus, apparently, was called in Hebrew *mahpeketh*, turning, torsion, because the body was forced into an unnatural position (2 Chron. xvi. 10, R. V. margin ; Jer. xx. 2). It included shackles or rather a collar; at least these could be used on the prisoner at the same time (xxix. 26, R. V.), so that his neck, arms, and legs could all be held fast together.

Sto'ics [Greek *stoikos*, pertaining to the porch].

A sect of philosophers, one of two which Paul encountered at Athens (Acts xvii. 18). Their founder was Zeno of Citium in Cyprus, who must not be confounded with an earlier philosopher, Zeno of Elea, in Italy. The Cyprian Zeno was born, it is believed, between 357 and 352 B. C., and died between 263 and 259, having lived little short of a century. Removing from his native place to Athens, he taught for about fifty-eight years in a *stoa*, or porch, on the public market place. His doctrine was essentially pantheistic. The Stoics distinguished matter and force as the ultimate principles in the universe ; and the force working everywhere they called reason, providence, God, and regarded it as conscious and thinking, yet dependent and impersonal, a breath or a fire which forms, permeates, and vivifies all things, and which in accordance with inexorable necessity calls beings and worlds into existence and destroys them again, so that at the end of a cosmical period the universe is resolved into fire in a general conflagration,

and the evolution of the world begins again, and so on without end. The human soul is a spark or emanation of this conscious but impersonal deity. It survives the body, but lives only for a cosmical period, and is reabsorbed at last into the source from which it came. The Stoics classed themselves among the followers of Socrates, and resembled him in their theory of life. They rigidly severed the morally good from the agreeable. They declared that an act is good or evil in itself, and that pleasure should never be made the end of an action. The highest good is virtue. Virtue is a life conformed to nature, or the agreement of human conduct with the law of the universe, and of the human with the divine will ; it is especially resignation in respect to fate. The cardinal virtues are practical wisdom as to what is good and evil, courage, prudence or self-restraint, and justice. Zeno encouraged his followers to hold their feelings in rigid control, so as to be as much as possible independent of all disturbing influences, whatever occurrences might take place. Stoicism made noble characters. It continued as a power for about 400 years, its most eminent professors being the slave Epictetus, the philosopher Seneca, and the emperor Marcus Aurelius.

Stom'a-cher.

A part of dress, once worn by women, covering the pit of the stomach and the breast, and often highly ornamented. It is the rendering adopted in Is. iii. 24 of the Hebrew *Pethigil*, applied to an article of female attire. The meaning of the Hebrew word is not definitely known. A. R. V. renders it robe ; Luther, wide mantle.

Stone.

Palestine is a stony country, and it was often necessary to clear a field of stones preparatory to its cultivation (Is. v. 2). An enemy's fields were marred by throwing stones on them, and his wells were choked with stones (2 Kin. iii. 19, 25).

Stones were put to various uses: 1. For moles, quays (War i, 21, 6), city walls (1 Kin. xv. 22 ; Neh. iv. 3) ; for dwellings (Lev. xiv. 45 ; Amos v. 11), palaces (1 Kin. vii. 1, 9), fortresses, temples (vi. 7) ; for the pavement of courtyards and for columns (Esth. i. 6), and in Herodian times at least for paving streets (see STREET) ; and for aqueducts, reservoirs, bridges ; dykes about vineyards (Prov. xxiv. 30, 31) ; altars (Ex. xx. 25). In building altars the Israelites used unhewn stones, likewise for an ordinary dyke, and when heaps of stones were made to commemorate an event (Gen. xxxi. 46) or to mark the grave of a notorious offender (Josh. vii. 26 ; viii. 29 ; 2 Sam. xviii. 17), a custom still in vogue in Syria and Arabia, but not restricted to the graves of evildoers. But for some purposes the stones were sawn and hewn (1 Kin. vii. 9, 11) ; and, where suitable, stones of enormous size were used, as in the walls of the temple (10) and the mole at Cæsarea (War i. 21, 6).

2. Single stones were used to close the mouth of cisterns and wells, and the entrance of tombs (Gen. xxix. 2; Mat. xxvii. 60; John xi. 38), to mark boundaries (Deut. xix. 14), and probably as way marks (Jer. xxxi. 21). In Roman times mile stones were erected along the chief public highways; as, for example, on the road between Tyre and Sidon and between Pella and Gerasa, where they are still to be seen. Stones were set up to commemorate persons and events (Gen. xxxi. 45; xxxv. 14, 20; 2 Sam. xviii. 18), and were sometimes inscribed with a record of deeds (Herod. ii. 106; see MOABITE STONE). Stones, both in their natural state and graven, served as idols (Lev. xxvi. 1; Deut. xxix. 17; 2 Kin. xix. 18; cp. Is. lvii. 6). Certain small stones, called in Greek *baituloi* and *baitulia*, which were often, if not always, meteorites and held sacred because they fell from heaven, played a part in gentile superstition. They were said to move, talk, and guard from evil. The Greek name, if it had a Semitic origin, as there is scarcely reason to doubt, is akin to *beth'el* and may indicate that the stone was regarded as the abode of a supernatural power, spirit, or god. The name was not used by the Semites to designate the rude stone pillars which they set up at places of worship (Deut. xii. 3; see HIGH PLACES). The Israelites sometimes consecrated a single stone as a memorial to God (Gen. xxviii. 18–22; xxxv. 14; 1 Sam. vii. 12; Is. xix. 19), and they might give a religious name to the place (Gen. xxviii. 19; xxxv. 7) or even to the stone (1 Sam. vii. 12), just as they sometimes called an altar by God's name (Gen. xxxiii. 20; Ex. xvii. 15; cp. Gen. xxxv. 7); but in the recorded cases they did not regard deity or power as resident in the stone or altar and did not pay 't divine honor. If they worshiped, they worshiped God apart from the memorial stone (Gen. xxxi. 54; xxxv. 1, 7; 1 Sam. vii. 9).

3. Stones were hurled by slings and catapults (Judg. xx. 16; 1 Sam. xvii. 40; 2 Chron. xxvi. 15; Wisd. v. 22; 1 Mac. vi. 51), and were a means of putting criminals to death (see STONING). Flints were used for striking fire (2 Mac. x. 3), and were shaped into rude form to serve as knives (Josh. v. 2). Weights for scales were often cut out of stone (Deut. xxv. 13; see WEIGHTS), and tablets of stone were employed for written documents (Ex. xxiv. 12). Vessels for holding water were hewn from stone (Ex. vii. 19; John ii. 6), tables also (Ezek. xl. 42). A rounded stone, of thirty pounds' weight or so, was rolled back and forth over grain to crush it to flour, or two stones were formed into a mill for grinding (Deut. xxiv. 6).

The white stone mentioned in Rev. ii. 17 has been variously interpreted. 1. One of the stone tablets, written with the name of a person, which were used in some methods of casting the lot. 2. The stone or bean, bearing the name of a candidate, which was cast at elections in Greece. 3. The pebble of acquittal used in Greek courts. 4. The ticket presented to the victor at the Olympic games. 5. The instructions which the Roman emperors caused to be thrown to victorious contestants in the arena. And best—6. A small stone, a common writing material, white to symbolize the heavenly character of the victorious believer, and marked with the name bestowed as sign and seal of his future glory.

Figuratively stone denotes hardness or insensibility (1 Sam. xxv. 37; Ezek. xxxvi. 26), firmness or strength (Job vi. 12; xli. 24). A living stone is a stone in its natural condition, sound and not disintegrating. The followers of Christ are living stones built into the spiritual temple, of which Christ himself is the chief corner stone (Eph. ii. 20–22; 1 Pet. ii. 4–8).

Stones, Pre'cious.

All the precious stones referred to in the canonical Scriptures, except three, are enumerated in R. V. of Ex. xxviii. 17–20 and Rev. xxi. 11, 19–21, text and margin. The three remaining ones are adamant (Ezek. iii. 9), and ligure and sardine (Ex. xxviii. 19; Rev. iv. 3, both A. V.), and of these at least two are merely other names for two of those already mentioned. The precious stones are adamant, agate, amber, amethyst, beryl, carbuncle, chalcedony, chrysolite, chrysoprase or chrysoprasus, crystal, diamond, emerald, jacinth or hyacinth, jasper, lapis lazuli, ligure, onyx, pearl, ruby, sapphire, sardius or sardine, sardonyx, and topaz.

Ston'ing.

The ordinary mode of capital punishment prescribed by Hebrew law (Lev. xx. 2); see PUNISHMENT. It was an ancient method; and it was not confined to the Hebrews, but was practiced by the Macedonians and Persians as well. The execution took place outside the city (Lev. xxiv. 14; 1 Kin. xxi. 10, 13; Acts vii. 58). The witnesses placed their hands on the head of the criminal in token that the guilt rested on him (Lev. xxiv. 14). They laid aside any clothing that might impede them in their solemn duty (Acts vii. 58). In cases of idolatry, and apparently in other cases also, the witnesses hurled the first stones (Deut. xiii. 9; xvii. 7; cp. John viii. 7; Acts vii. 58). The rabbins state that the culprit was stripped of all clothing except a cloth about the loins, and was thrown to the ground from a scaffold about 10 feet high by the first witness, the first stone was cast by the second witness, on the chest over the heart of the criminal, and if it failed to cause death, the bystanders completed the execution. Sometimes the body was afterwards suspended until sundown or burnt (Deut. xxi. 23; Josh. vii. 25; Antiq. iv. 8,

24), and according to late Jewish law was not buried in the family grave.

Stool, in R. V. Birth'stool.

A chair of peculiar form, upon which the patient sat during parturition. It was denominated '*obnayim*, double stones, by the Hebrews (Ex. i. 16), on account of its likeness to the potter's wheel. It is called *kursee el-wiladeh* by the modern Egyptians.

Stork.

A bird called in Hebrew $ h^asidah $, affectionate, on account of its love for its young. It was ceremonially unclean (Lev. xi. 19; Deut. xiv. 18), dwelt in fir trees (Ps. civ. 17), and was migratory (Jer. viii. 7). It is the *Ciconia alba*, a white heron-like bird, which spends its winter in central and southern Africa, but in spring visits continental Europe, Palestine, and northern Syria in large numbers. It is about 4 feet high, with long red bill and legs, white plumage, and glossy black wings. It feeds on frogs and small reptiles or, lacking these, on offal, and hence was ceremonially unclean. It is regarded as a sacred bird, and in most places is unmolested, so that it fearlessly visits the haunts of man. The black stork, *Ciconia nigra*, named from the color of its back and neck, is also found in Palestine, being common in the valley of the Dead Sea. It breeds in trees.

Stran'ger, in R. V. generally Sojourner.

A stranger in the Mosaic law, and in the O. T. generally, means one not of Israelitish descent dwelling with the Hebrews, as distinguished from a foreigner temporarily visiting the land (Ex. xx. 10; Lev. xvi. 29; xvii. 8; 2 Sam. i. 13; Ezek. xiv. 7). The stranger was not a full citizen, yet he had recognized rights and duties. He was under the protection of God, and the Israelites were charged to treat him kindly (Lev. xix. 33, 34; Deut. x. 18, 19). His rights were guarded by injunctions in the law (Ex. xxii. 21; xxiii. 9). When poor, he enjoyed the same privileges as the Hebrew poor (Deut. xxiv. 19, 20). The prohibitions that rested on an Israelite rested on him (Ex. xii. 19; xx. 10; Lev. xvi. 29; xvii. 10; xviii. 26; xx. 2; xxiv. 16; and xvii. 15, which was modified later by Deut. xiv. 21); but he was not obligated to all positive religious duties which devolved on the Israelite. He was exempt, if he chose to be and if he was a free man, from circumcision and participation in the passover (Ex. xii. 43–46). The Israelites were encouraged to invite him to the sacrificial meals (Deut. xvi. 11, 14). He was allowed to sacrifice to the Lord, he shared in the atonement made for the sin of the congregation on account of sin unwittingly committed, he had the privilege of a sin offering for aught done unwittingly by himself, and the city of refuge offered him asylum in case of need (Lev. xvii. 8; Num. xv. 14, 26, 29; xxxv. 15). In case he contracted uncleanness he was required to employ the rights of purifi-

cation (Lev. xvii. 15; Num. xix. 10). If he accepted circumcision for his household, he was admitted to the passover (Ex. xii. 48, 49). The chief disability under which he labored was that in case he became a bondman, the year of jubile did not bring him release, he could be bought and made an inheritance for the purchaser's children (Lev. xxv. 45, 46).

Ammonites and Moabites formed an exceptional class among the strangers. They were not allowed membership in Israel even by circumcision (Deut. xxiii. 3), but the son of an Israelite and a Moabitess might be admitted (cp. Jesse and Rehoboam). With the idolatrous Canaanites who were in the land at the time of the conquest intermarriage was strictly forbidden (vii. 3), but the remnant which was left after the conquest eventually became to a large extent proselytes. In Solomon's reign the census revealed 153,600 strangers in the realm (2 Chron. ii. 17).

In the N. T. the word stranger does not have this technical signification, but denotes one who is unknown (John x. 5), an alien (Luke xvii. 16, 18), a sojourner away from home (xxiv. 18, A. V.; Acts ii. 10, A. V.), an Israelite dwelling in the Dispersion (1 Pet. i. 1, A. V.).

Straw.

Wheat and barley straw, ground and cut to small pieces in the process of threshing, and doubtless often mixed with beans or barley, was used by the ancient Hebrews as fodder for their cattle, camels, asses, and horses (Gen. xxiv. 25, 32; Judg. xix. 19; 1 Kin. iv. 28; Is. xi. 7). The Egyptians, in making bricks, mixed it with clay to render them more compact and prevent their cracking. When Pharaoh withheld the chopped straw, the Hebrew slaves were compelled to go forth into the field and gather stubble, or rather stalks, for themselves, and chop their own straw (Ex. v. 7, 12, 16). Straw was probably not used by the ancient Hebrews as a litter in the stall. In Palestine to-day dried dung serves for this purpose.

Stream. See RIVER.

Street.

The streets of oriental towns were generally narrow, tortuous, and dirty (Antiq. xx. 5, 3; War ii. 14, 9; 15, 5). They were seldom wide enough to permit two laden camels to pass each other; but some were sufficiently broad for chariots to be driven through them (Jer. xvii. 25; Nah. ii. 4). Great cities were sometimes adorned by a grand avenue or even by several, as Alexandria and Babylon. In Damascus the street called Straight was a magnificent thoroughfare, 100 feet broad and divided into three avenues by rows of columns. Many streets were flanked by blank walls, seldom pierced except by doors, the windows of the houses opening on interior courts. The streets devoted to stores were lined by salesrooms with open fronts; and bazaar streets, each surrendered to one kind of business, were features of the ancient city (Jer. xxxvii. 21; War v. 8, 1). The intersections of the streets were centers of concourse and display (Prov. i. 21; Mat. vi. 5; Luke xiii. 26). At the gates were broad, open places where business was transacted. There is no evidence that the streets were paved in ancient times. But Josephus affirms that Solomon paved the roads leading to Jerusalem with black stones (Antiq. viii. 7, 4); and at the time of the Herods pavements were laid (xvi. 5, 3; xx. 9, 7), and efforts were in some instances made toward keeping the streets clean (xv. 9, 6).

Stripes. See SCOURGE.

Strong Drink.
Intoxicating liquor, in Hebrew *shekar* (1 Sam. i. 13–15; Prov. xx. 1; Is. xxix. 9). Wine and strong drink were forbidden to the priest, when about to enter the sanctuary (Lev. x. 9; cp. Ezek. xliv. 21), and kings and princes were warned against its use, lest it lead to perversion of judgment (Prov. xxxi. 4, 5); yet Isaiah was compelled to point to the sad spectacle of priests and prophets, even in Judah, scandalously failing in duty through wine and strong drink (Is. xxviii. 7). Wine, strong drink, vinegar, any liquor of grapes, and even fresh grapes were forbidden the Nazirite (Num. vi. 3; cp. Judg. xiii. 4; Luke i. 15); see NAZIRITE. Both wine and strong drink were allowed at the feast spread by the bringer of tithes (Deut. xiv. 26). On the basis of the exhortation, "Give strong drink unto him that is ready to perish" (Prov. xxxi. 6), kind-hearted women of Jerusalem provided stupefying draughts for criminals condemned to death (Mishna; cp. Mark xv. 23).

Stub'ble. See STRAW.

Su'ah [sweepings].
An Asherite, a son of Zophah (1 Chron. vii. 36).

Su'cath-ite, in A. V. Suchathite.
A native or an inhabitant of an unknown place called Sucah (1 Chron. ii. 55).

Suc'coth [booths or huts].
1. A place east of the Jordan (Judg. viii. 4, 5; and Jerome on Gen. xxxiii. 17), at which Jacob, on his return from Mesopotamia, after crossing the Jabbok (Gen. xxxii. 22), built himself a house, with booths for his cattle, giving the spot from the latter circumstance the name of Succoth (Gen. xxxiii. 17). He journeyed thence to Shechem (18). It was in the valley of the Jordan, near Zarethan (1 Kin. vii. 46; Ps. lx. 6; cviii. 7), and was assigned to the Gadites (Josh. xiii. 27). In the time of Gideon it was an important town, ruled by seventy-seven elders. They refused him assistance when he was pursuing Zebah and Zalmunna, and were in consequence punished by him when

he returned a victor (Judg. viii. 5–16). The site must be sought near the ford of Damieh, on the road between es-Salt and Nablus. Tell Deir 'Alla scarcely marks the place, although the Talmud states that the latter name of Succoth was Dar'alah; for the tell is on the northern side of the Jabbok, and the narrative almost certainly indicates that Succoth was on the southern side.
2. The first camping ground of the Israelites after leaving Rameses (Ex. xii. 37; xiii. 20; Num. xxxiii. 5, 6). Succoth is probably the Hebrew modification of Thuku, the Egyptian name of the civil city surrounding the sacred buildings of Pithom (q. v.).

Suc-coth-be'noth.
An idol which the Babylonian colonists set up in Samaria (2 Kin. xvii. 30). The tutelary deity of Babylon was Marduk, and his consort was Zarpanitum, although numerous other deities were worshiped in the city. The historian Rawlinson, followed by Schrader, proposed to identify Succoth-benoth with Zarpanitum, the latter part of the two names being essentially the same. Friedrich Delitzsch has a more plausible theory. He regards Succoth-benoth as a Hebraization of the Assyrian words *sakkut binûti*, supreme judge of the universe, and he considers it to have been in this instance a title of Marduk.

Su'chath-ite. See SUCATHITE.

Suk'ki-im, in A. V. Sukkiims [to the Hebrew ear, people living in huts, nomads].
One of the peoples furnishing soldiers to the army of Shishak, king of Egypt, when he invaded Palestine. They were evidently an African race (2 Chron. xii. 3).

Sun.
The luminary of the day, created by God (Gen. i. 16; Ps. lxxiv. 16; cxxxvi. 8), preserved by God (Jer. xxxi. 35; Mat. v. 45), and subject to God (Ps. civ. 19); influential in promoting vegetation (Deut. xxxiii. 14; 2 Sam. xxiii. 4), and also burning it with its heat (Jon. iv. 8). It is spoken of as rising and setting; is poetically described as occupying a tent in the heavens; its rising in the morning with vigor and joy is likened to a bridegroom coming forth from his chamber (Ps. xix. 4–6). Death in the meridian of one's days, and the sudden loss of prosperity, are likened to the setting of the sun at midday (Jer. xv. 9; Amos viii. 9; Mic. iii. 6). The sun was worshiped by the nations contemporary with the Hebrews, notably by the Phœnicians under the name of Baal, by the Assyrians under that of Shamash, and by the Egyptians under that of Ra; see ASSYRIA, BAAL, EGYPT II. 6, ON. The Hebrews were warned against all such heathenism, but sun worship nevertheless found entrance among them. Altars were erected to all the host of heaven (2 Kin. xxi. 5), incense was burned to the sun and horses were dedicated to it

(xxiii. 5, 11 ; cp. the Persian worship, Herod. i. 189 ; vii. 54), and kisses were thrown to it with the hand (Job xxxi. 26, 27).

Joshua commanded the sun to stand still. The older commentators referred the words of Hab. iii. 11 to this event, but the Hebrew construction and the context are against it. Sun and moon withdraw into their habitation. Dread before the presence of the Lord seizes all nature, and reveals itself in the trembling of the mountains, in the raging of the sea, and in the withdrawal of their light by sun and moon (10, 11). The first reference to the astronomical lengthening of the day at Beth-horon is found in Ecclesiasticus, and its author evidently believed that the sun and moon were checked in their courses. "Did not the sun go back by his hand ? And did not one day become as two" (Ecclus. xlvi. 4). Josephus also understood that the day was lengthened (Antiq. v. 1, 17). Unquestionably God could work this wonder, with all that it involved. The circumstances, however, scarcely afforded an adequate occasion for so stupendous a miracle. Another interpretation has much in its favor. It is certain that Josh. x. 12ᵇ and 13ᵃ are poetry. Verses 12–15 in all probability form a paragraph by themselves (cp. the repetition, 15 and 43), and are quoted from the Book of Jashar, a collection of poems with introductory and perhaps concluding remarks in prose (see JASHAR ; cp. Job with its prose introduction and conclusion ; cp. the position of the quoting clause in Josh. x. 13 and 2 Sam. i. 18). Joshua's words are the impassioned utterance of a general inspiring his army on the field of battle. Desirous that Israel may have time completely to overthrow the foe, he apostrophizes sun and moon. In fervent, imperious words, he demands time. "Sun, stand thou still upon Gibeon ; and thou, Moon, in the valley of Aijalon." God granted his wish. Before the light of day failed, the people had avenged themselves of their enemies. A hail-storm assisted the Israelites, and they drove the enemy to Azekah and Makkedah, and made a great slaughter. This event, it seems, was worked up poetically in the Book of Jashar; and must be interpreted as poetry, as one interprets the psalmist when telling of the gift of manna, he says: "He commanded the skies above, and opened the doors of heaven ; and he rained down manna upon them to eat, and gave them of the corn of heaven" (Ps. lxxviii. 23, 24) ; or as one understands the poet who, after relating the passage of the Red Sea and the Jordan, adds: "The mountains skipped like rams, and the little hills like lambs" (cxiv. 6) ; or as one understands the prophet Habakkuk when he pictures Jehovah as a warrior and says: "Thou didst ride upon thine horses, upon thy chariots of salvation" (Hab. iii. 8).

For the recession of the sun's shadow on the dial of Ahaz, see DIAL.

Suph [sedge].

A locality (Deut. i. 1, R. V.), situation unknown. The A. V., following the Vulgate and the Septuagint, assumes that the Hebrew word for sea has fallen out of the text. On this assumption the text originally was *yam suph*, Red Sea, and the reference was to that part of the sea known as the gulf of Akaba.

Su'phah [a rotatory storm, cultivable soil in the midst of dry land].

Probably a proper name, denoting the region in which Vaheb was situated (Num. xxi. 14, R. V.). Tristram connects it with the Sufieh, the name of an oasis southeast of the Dead Sea, but the sibilants do not correspond.

Sup'per. See MEAL.

Sure'ty.

A person who makes himself liable for the obligations of another (Prov. xxii. 26, 27). A surety was sometimes offered for a service to be rendered (Gen. xliv. 32) ; and, when commercial transactions were common, a surety was often required to be found before credit was given. The formalities consisted in giving the hand, in the presence of witnesses, to the person to whom the debt was due, and promising to discharge the obligation in case the debtor defaulted (Prov. vi. 1, 2 ; xvii. 18). The folly of becoming surety, especially in behalf of a stranger, was proverbial (xi. 15 ; xvii. 18 ; xx. 16) ; but it was regarded as proper under circumstances and for a moderate amount, and as a neighborly act (Ecclus. viii. 13 ; xxix. 14, 20), yet its grave dangers and its liability to abuse by a dishonest client were recognized (xxix. 16–18).

Su'san-chite. See SHUSHANCHITE.

Su-san'na [a lily].

One of the women who ministered to Jesus of their substance (Luke viii. 3).

Su'si [horseman].

Father of Gaddi, the spy from the tribe of Manasseh (Num. xiii. 11).

Swad'dling Band.

A cloth in which infants were wrapped (Job xxxviii. 9 ; Ezek. xvi. 4 ; Luke ii. 7, 12). The babe was laid diagonally on a square piece of cloth and two corners were turned over its body, one over its feet, and one under its head. The whole was then fastened by bands wound around the outside.

Swal'low.

1. A bird, in biblical and talmudic Hebrew *dᵉror*, shooting straight out or freedom. It frequented the sanctuary at Jerusalem, and nested there (Ps. lxxxiv. 3), and it was found in company with other small birds, like the sparrow (ibid. ; Prov. xxvi. 2, R. V.). The barn swallow of Great Britain (*Hirundo rustica*) is abundant in Palestine from March to the approach of winter. Several other species also occur, but are less common.

2. The rendering in the R. V. of the Hebrew *Sus* or *Sis*, a bird with a chattering note

(Is. xxxviii. 14), and migratory (Jer. viii. 7). Swallow is the rendering adopted by the Septuagint, Vulgate, and Syriac versions, but the A. V., following the rabbins, translates it crane Tristram believes that the common swift (*Cypselus apus*) is called *sis* in the vernacular Arabic. It visits Palestine in immense numbers in its migrations, remaining from April to November, and building in the interval. Two other species of the genus occur in Palestine, the white-bellied swift (*Cypselus melba*) and the white-rumped swift (*Cypselus affinis*).
3. The rendering in A. V. of the Hebrew '*Agur* (Is. xxxviii. 14; Jer. viii. 7). The R. V. in both passages renders it crane.

Swan.
The rendering of the Hebrew *Tinshemeth*, breathing, inflation, a name applied to an unclean bird (Lev. xi. 18; Deut. xiv. 16; text of A. V., margin of R. V.). The R. V. text makes it the horned owl. The same name belonged to a reptile classed with the lizards (Lev. xi. 30, in R. V. chameleon, in A. V. mole). Tristram thinks that the bird was probably either the purple gallinule (*Porphyrio cæruleus*) or the glossy ibis (*Ibis falcinellus*).

Swear'ing. See OATH.

Sweat.
It is a common occurrence for perspiration to break out suddenly over the body when the individual is under the influence of strong mental excitement. Well-authenticated cases have been recorded in which this perspiration has been colored with blood. The phenomenon is recognized in medical science, and is called *diapedesis*, or the oozing of the blood corpuscles through the walls of the blood vessels without rupture. During Christ's agony in Gethsemane his sweat became as it were great drops of blood falling down upon the ground (Luke xxii. 44).

Swine.
The swine was a ceremonially unclean animal (Lev. xi. 7; Deut. xiv. 8). It is dirty, does not refuse to eat offal and carrion, and the use of its flesh for food in hot countries is supposed to produce cutaneous diseases. It was not raised by the Arabs (Pliny, Hist. Nat. viii. 78), and was regarded as unclean by Phœnicians, Ethiopians, and Egyptians. In Egypt, however, a pig was sacrificed and eaten on the annual festival of the moon-god and Osiris (Bacchus); nevertheless, a man who accidentally touched a pig at once washed, a swineherd was not allowed to enter a temple, and was compelled to find a wife among the people of his own occupation, as no other man would give a daughter to him in marriage (Herod. ii. 47; con. Apion. ii. 14). To the Jews swine's flesh was abominable (Is. lxv. 4), the pig was the emblem of filth and coarseness (Prov. xi. 22; Mat. vii. 6; 2 Pet. ii. 22), and to feed swine was the lowest and most despicable occupation to which a Jew could be reduced (Luke

xv. 15). Yet pork found entrance to the idolatrous feasts of degenerate Hebrews (Is. lxv. 4; lxvi. 17). In the reign of Antiochus Epiphanes the command to a Jew to offer or to taste swine's flesh was used as a means of determining whether he was loyal to the religion of his fathers or was willing to accept the worship favored by his conquerors (1 Mac. i. 47, 50; 2 Mac. vi. 18, 21; vii. 1, 7). But many Jews affected Grecian manners, and John Hyrcanus some years later found it advisable to issue an edict that no one should keep swine. In the time of Christ one large herd of swine at least was pastured in the Decapolis (Mark v. 11–13), a region colonized by Greeks, among whom the swine was highly esteemed as an article of food. There is no reason to suppose that Jews owned either these swine or those in the far country fed by the prodigal son (Luke xv. 13). See BOAR.

Sword.
A weapon with which an adversary was cut by being struck or was thrust through (1 Sam. xvii. 51; xxxi. 4; 2 Sam. ii. 16; Mat. xxvi. 51). It had hilt and blade (Judg. iii. 22), was carried in a sheath (1 Sam. xvii. 51; Jer. xlvii. 6), and girded on the loins (Ex. xxxii. 27; 2 Sam. xx. 8), usually at the left side (Judg. iii. 16 with 15, 21). The hilt was often highly ornamented, at least among the Egyptians and Assyrians. The blade was commonly made of iron (Is. ii. 4), perhaps also of bronze, as not seldom in Egypt. It was straight or slightly curved, long or short (Judg. iii. 16, a cubit long), single or double edged (ibid.; Ps. cxlix. 6).
In the Roman period a short, slightly curved dagger was worn under the clothing by the Jewish *sicarii*, or assassins (Antiq. xx. 8, 10; War ii. 13, 3). Roman infantry wore the sword on the left side and the dagger on the right, but the cavalry wore the sword on the right (iii. 5, 5). This, however, was not an invariable rule.

Syc'a-mine Tree.
The mulberry tree, called in Greek *sukaminos* (Luke xvii. 6). The black mulberry (*Morus nigra*), a tree 20 or 30 feet high, is the species commonly cultivated for its leaves and fruit. The silk worm feeds on the leaves. The fruit is dark red or black, with an uneven surface. The tree has been planted extensively in Palestine.

Sy'char.
A town of Samaria, in the vicinity of the land given by Jacob to his son Joseph, near Jacob's well (John iv. 5; cp. Gen. xlviii. 22). Formerly it was supposed to be a Greek corruption of Shechem, or a nickname for the city after it became the abode of the Samaritans, either from Hebrew *sheḳer*, falsehood, or *shikkor*, drunkard; but it is now believed by many to be the village of 'Askar, on the eastern declivity of mount Ebal, a little north of Jacob's well.

Sy'chem. See SHECHEM

Syc′o-more.

A fig tree, called in Hebrew *shikmah*, in Greek *sukomorea*. It was abundant in the lowland of Judah (1 Kin. x. 27; 1 Chron. xxvii. 28; 2 Chron. i. 15; ix. 27), grew in the Jordan valley (Luke xix. 4), and was cultivated in Egypt (Ps. lxxviii. 47). Its timber was much used, although less durable than cedar (Is. ix. 10). The tree is the *Ficus sycomorus*, a fig tree, 25 to 50 feet high and 60

The large Jewish synagogue at Tel Aviv.

feet broad, with persistent, heart-shaped leaves downy beneath. It is often planted by the wayside on account of its grateful shade (cp. Luke xix. 4). The fruit grows in clusters on twigs which spring directly from the trunk and larger branches, but cannot be eaten until it has been punctured and the insect that infests it has been allowed to escape (cp. Amos vii. 14).

The sycomore must not be confounded with our sycamore (*Platanus occidentalis*), which is not mentioned in the Bible.

Sy-e′ne. See SEVENEH.

Sym′e-on. See SIMEON.

Syn′a-gogue [in Greek an assembly, a synagogue].

A Jewish place of worship. The building served also for local law court and school. Previous to the captivity, worship of the highest kind could be performed only at the temple at Jerusalem. Of course, the Scriptures could be publicly read elsewhere (Jer. xxxvi. 6, 10, 12–15), and the people could resort to the prophets anywhere for religious instruction (2 Kin. iv. 38). Worship at Jerusalem was impossible when the people were in captivity in Babylon, and it seems to have been then and there that synagogues first

arose. They were designed to be places, not of sacrifice, but of scriptural instruction and prayer. The English word synagogue occurs only once in the O. T. (Ps. lxxiv. 8). The margin of R. V. has "places of assembly" instead of synagogues, and the Septuagint renders by a word which means a feast, a festival, a holiday. It is not, therefore, certain that there is any reference to a synagogue in the O. T. In the first century they were found wherever Jews dwelt. Even small communities of Jews in the lesser cities outside of Palestine had their synagogues; as in Salamis in Cyprus (Acts xiii. 5), Antioch of Pisidia (14), Iconium (xiv. 1), Berœa (xvii. 10). In large cities synagogues were often numerous; as in Jerusalem (vi. 9) and Alexandria. These religious communities maintained an existence separate from the state, and managed their own religious and civil affairs, subordinate, of course, to the law of the land (Antiq. xix. 5, 3). A board of elders managed the affairs of the synagogue and of the religious community which it represented (Luke vii. 3–5). The special officers, who directed the worship, maintained order and looked after the temporalities, were: 1. The ruler of the synagogue (Acts xviii. 8). In some synagogues several rulers were in office (xiii.15; Mark v.22). The ruler presided at the service; appointed or permitted suitable members to pray, read the Scriptures, and exhort (Acts xiii. 15); and was responsible for the proprieties (Luke xiii. 14). The services were not conducted by permanent officers set apart for the duty, but by private members who had shown qualifications for it. Thus Jesus read the Scriptures in the synagogue at Nazareth (iv. 16), and he often taught in the synagogues (Mat. iv. 23). Paul and Barnabas were called on by the rulers of the synagogue at Antioch of Pisidia for words of exhortation (Acts xiii. 15). 2. One or more attendants for the humbler and menial duties. They brought the Scriptures to the reader and replaced the roll in its depository (Luke iv. 20), and they inflicted the corporal punishment to which the authorities sentenced a member. 3. Dispensers of alms (cp. Mat. vi. 2). 4. Wealthy men of leisure, if possible ten or more, who represented the congregation at every service. The congregation assembled every Sabbath for worship (Acts xv. 21), and on the second and fifth days of the week to hear a portion of the law read. The men and the women sat apart. At the Sabbath service prayer was offered by a member of the congregation. It consisted chiefly in reading Deut. vi. 4-9; xi. 13-21; Num. xv. 37-41; and offering some or all of the eighteen prayers and benedictions. The people were accustomed to stand during this prayer (Mat. vi. 5; Mark xi. 25), and united in saying Amen at its close. A lesson from the law was read (Acts xv. 21) by several members, each taking a short paragraph in turn. This reading was prefaced and concluded by thanksgiving. Then came a lesson from the prophets, read by the person who had opened the service with prayer. The reading was followed by an exposition and an exhortation given by the reader or some other person (Luke iv. 16-22; Acts xiii. 15). The service was concluded by a benediction, which was pronounced by a priest, if one were present, and the congregation said, Amen. The synagogue was called by the Jews in their own language assembly house. Ruins of these buildings still exist in Galilee at Tell Hum, which is perhaps the site of Capernaum, at Irbid, Kefr Bir'im, Nebartein, and some

Ruins of the synagogue at Capernaum.

other places. These were rectangular structures. All lay north and south, and had a large middle portal and two smaller side doors on the southern side. The interior was divided into five aisles by four rows of columns, and the two northern corners were formed by double-engaged columns. At Tell Hum there are Corinthian capitals; at Irbid a mixture of Corinthian and Ionic. The faces of the lintels over the gateways have as a frequent ornament the representation of a scroll of vine leaves with bunches of grapes. At Nebartein there is a figure of the seven-branched candlestick, with an inscription; at Kefr Bir'im what is intended apparently for the paschal lamb; while at Tell Hum,

there are both the lamb and the pot of manna. The assembly room was provided with a reading desk, a chest or closet for the Scriptures, and seats for at least the elders and richer members (Mat. xxiii. 6; Jas. ii. 2, 3). The more honorable seats were near the place where the Scriptures were kept. The congregation was divided; the men on one side, the women on the other. Punishment ordered by the authorities of the synagogue was inflicted in the building, possibly in some chamber (Mat. x. 17; Acts xxii. 19).

The great synagogue denotes a council, said to have been organized by Nehemiah about 410 B. C. It consisted of 120 members (Megilloth, 17, 18), Ezra was its president. To this body the prophets transmitted the law of Moses (Pirke aboth i. 1). Simon the Just, who died about 275 B. C., was one of the last of its members (ibid.). It was succeeded by the sanhedrin (x. 1). Its special work was to reorganize religious worship among the returned captives and gather together the canonical books. Such is the Jewish tradition. The existence of the great synagogue has been doubted, since there is no mention of any such body in the Apocrypha, in Josephus, or in Philo. Nor does the name appear anywhere in Scripture. But the tradition is not to be wholly rejected. The great synagogue was probably a council of scribes for the decision of theological questions; contained from first to last, during an existence of a little more than a century and a half, about 120 prominent members; and numbered among them all the leading scribes from Ezra to Simon the Just.

Syn'ty-che [fortunate].

A woman in the Philippian church whom Paul exhorted (Phil. iv. 2).

Syr'a-cuse.

A celebrated city on the east coast of Sicily, founded about 735 B. C. by a colony of Corinthians and Dorians, led by Archias of Corinth. It greatly flourished. About 413 B. C. its inhabitants defeated and destroyed an Athenian fleet of 200 vessels. In 212 B. C. it was taken by the Romans. Paul saw it on his voyage to Rome (Acts xxviii. 12). It was taken by the Saracens in A. D. 878. It still exists, but is now much reduced in size.

Syr'i-a.

A country along the eastern coast of the Mediterranean and extending far inland. It comprehended most of the regions known in O. T. times as Canaan and Aram. The name is sometimes used as a translation of Aram; but inaccurately, being much too broad a term. The word Syria is an abbreviated form of Assyria, and became current after the conquests of Alexander the Great. Syria formed the most important province, both commercially and from a military point of view, of the kingdom of the Seleucidæ, whose capital was at Babylon. It soon became apparent

Detail of carved stone architrave.

The main attraction of all the ancient ruins of Tell Hum (Capernaum) is the impressive remains of an early Jewish synagogue. The ruins date from the second or third century A.D. and it is possible that they rest on remains of the synagogue in which Jesus taught.

The richly ornamented synagogue was two stories high, a basilica-type structure of three aisles with a gallery for the women around all walls except the southern one.

Close-up view of the restored synagogue.

Detail of carved capital.

Inscription on a column of the synagogue. Two columns bear inscriptions honoring the people who made donations for the building. One inscription is in Greek. The other is in Aramaic and is of special interest because of the New Testament names mentioned, "Alphaeus, son of Zebedee, son of John, made this column; on him be blessing."

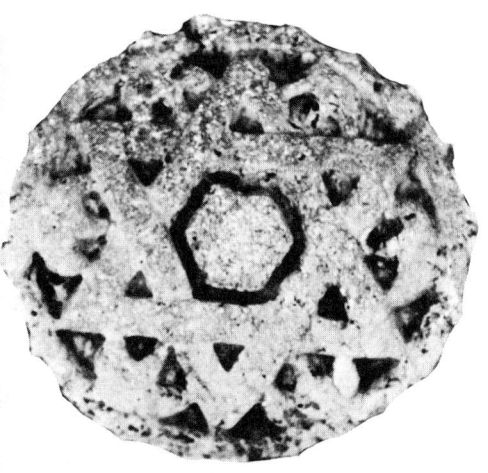

Stone carving of the six-pointed "Star of David" found at Capernaum.

that western Asia required a government of its own, more in the Greek spirit than was the system suitable for the far east. For this purpose Antioch was founded as a royal city about 300 B. C. (cp. 1 Mac. iii. 37 and 31, 32). The kingdom of the Seleucidæ was gradually reduced by the encroachment of its foes, until at the close of the second century B. C. only Syria was left. With the Roman conquest in 64 B. C., the kingdom was erected into the province of Syria, with a Roman governor resident in Antioch. The name Syria was limited to this province, which included the country west of the Euphrates from the Taurus mountains to the borders of Egypt. From the time of Augustus it was governed by a consular legate of the emperor. In A. D. 70 Judæa was separated from Syria and made a distinct province under an imperial legate.

Syr'i-ac Ver'sion. See VERSIONS.

Syr'i-an.

One of the Syrian race, or an inhabitant of Syria. In O. T. times the word Syria was not in use ; and where Syrian occurs in the E. V. of the O. T. it denotes a native of Aram, properly called an Aramæan (Gen. xxviii. 5) ; see ARAM, DAMASCUS, and for the period after the conquests of Alexander the Great, SYRIA.

Sy-ro-phœ-ni'ci-an, in A. V. **Syropheni-cian.**

A Phœnician of Syria in distinction from the Libyphœnicians of north Africa (Mark vii. 26 ; cp. Mat. xv. 22). A new distinction arose toward the end of the second century of the Christian era, when the province of Syria was divided into Syria Magna and Syria-Phœnice.

Syr'tis. See QUICKSAND.

T

Ta'a-nach, in A. V. once **Tanach** (Josh. xxi. 25).

A Canaanite city, mentioned about 1600 B. C. in connection with the advance of Thothmes III. against Megiddo. Its king was defeated and slain by Joshua (Josh. xii. 21). It lay within the limits of Issachar, but was nominally possessed by the Manassites (Josh. xvii. 11 ; 1 Chron. vii. 29). Residence in it was assigned to the Kohathite Levites (Josh. xxi. 25). The Manassites failed to expel the Canaanite inhabitants, but ultimately rendered them tributary (Judg. i. 27). The great battle between Barak and Sisera was fought near Taanach (v. 19). The place was important in Solomon's reign (1 Kin. iv. 12). The mound Ta'annak, the site of the ancient city, is situated among the low hills on the southern edge of the plain of Jezreel, 5 miles to the southeast of ancient Megiddo.

Ta-a-nath-shi'loh [approach to Shiloh].

A town on the border between Ephraim and Manasseh (Josh. xvi. 6). It is the ruin Ta'na, 7 miles southeast by east of Shechem.

Tab'ba-oth [rings].

A family of Nethinim, represented in Zerubbabel's colony (Ezra ii. 43 ; Neh. vii. 46).

Tab'bath.

A place near Abel-meholah (Judg. vii. 22). Site unknown.

Ta-be'al, in R. V. **Tabeel** [probably, goodnot ; a scornful modification of Tabeel (q. v.)].

A man whose son the allied kings, Rezin of Damascus and Pekah of Israel, attempted to place on the throne of David as their puppet king of Judah (Is. vii. 6).

Ta'be-el [Aramaic, God is good].

1. Probably the original pronunciation of Tabeal (q. v.).

2. A Persian petty governor, probably of Syrian descent, one of those who complained to Artaxerxes Longimanus that the wall of Jerusalem was being rebuilt (Ezra iv. 7).

Tab'e-rah [burning].

A place where the Israelites murmured, and the fire of the Lord burnt among them in the uttermost part of the camp (Num. xi. 1–3 ; Deut. ix. 22). The burning abated at the intercession of Moses. The event perhaps occurred at no formal encampment, or only in the uttermost part of the camp at Kibroth-hattaavah (Num. xi. 1, 35).

Ta'ber-ing.

Striking frequently, as on a tabor, tabret, tamborine, or timbrel (Nah. ii. 7).

Tab'er-na-cle [a tent].

1. A provisional tent where the Lord met his people (Ex. xxxiii. 7–10) ; see TENT OF MEETING.

2. The movable sanctuary in the form of a tent which God directed Moses at Sinai to make, that God might dwell as king among his people (Ex. xxv. 8, 9). Hence it was called "the dwelling" (9 ; xxvi. 1, margin of R. V.), and, as the place where Jehovah met his people, "the tent of meeting" (xl. 34, 35, in R. V.), and as the depository of the tables of the law or testimony, "the tent of the testimony" (xxxviii. 21 ; cp. xxv. 21, 22 ; Num. ix. 15). It was also known by the general designation house of Jehovah (Ex. xxxiv. 26 ; Josh. vi. 24). The materials for its construction were largely obtained in the vicinity : the acacia wood of the wilderness, hair and skins of the flocks, skin of the tachash, a porpoise or similar brute, from the Red Sea. Gold, silver, brass, and linen, or perhaps muslin, were liberally furnished by the people, who gave their ornaments for the work (Ex. xxxv. 21–29). The lavish expenditure of precious metals for this temporary structure and its furniture was justified, since none of this wealth would be lost when

Model of the tabernacle constructed by Dr. Conrad Shick.

the movable tent gave place to a permanent edifice. The sacred vessels might serve in a new sanctuary or be wrought into new forms, and the gold and silver that were used in construction and ornamentation were available in any future building.

The architectural specifications for the tabernacle are drawn up systematically; and begin with the ark, which was the central and essential feature of the appointed meeting-place between Jehovah and his people (Ex. xxv. 22). I. The essential and permanent features: the ark, table of showbread, and candelabrum (Ex. xxv. 10-40), which were symbols of heavenly things (Heb. ix. 23). Their housing (Ex. xxvi. 1-37). The altar of burnt offerings (xxvii. 1-8). The court (9-19). Continual testimony to be borne by the maintenance of light from pure beaten oil (20, 21). No such specifications for the showbread were required. The ordination of xxv. 30 sufficed, since the finest flour was always used in offerings. II. The means of approach. A priesthood; authorized and appointed (xxviii. 1), garments (2-43), and consecration (xxix. 1-36). After mediating priests have been provided, atonement of the altar is specified (37) and the continual sacrifice (38-42). III. When the way of approach has been opened, the specifications advance to the altar of incense (xxx. 1-10), symbolical of the adoration of God by his people cleansed of sin. Only here is the altar of incense mentioned apart from the other furniture in a description of the tabernacle. It is ordered in its logical place in the worship of God by his people. Elsewhere it is named with the other furniture in the unvarying order of ark, table, candlestick, altar of incense, altar of burnt offering; as in the account of the manufacture of the furniture (xxxvii. 25-28), in the enumeration of the completed furniture (xxxix. 38), in the directions for the erection of the tabernacle (xl. 5), and in the record of its erection (26). IV. Provision for the needs of the service: the half shekel atonement money (Ex. xxx. 11-16), the laver (17-21), the holy anointing

This portal consisted of a row of five pillars overlaid with gold, resting in sockets of brass, and supporting a curtain. The interior was divided into two apartments by four similar pillars sunk in sockets of silver and hung with a curtain (32, 37). These rooms were respectively the western, oil (22-33), and the incense (34-38).

The tabernacle formed a parallelogram, 30 cubits long by 10 broad, with the entrance at the eastern end. The rear end and the two sides were made of boards, 48 in number, 20 on each side and 8 in the rear, of which 2 formed the posts at the angles. Each plank was 10 cubits long by 1½ cubits broad, and was overlaid with gold. They were scarcely cut from the log in a single piece, but were probably framed of several pieces. They were set on end, and were held in place at the bottom by tenons sunk in sockets of silver, two to each plank, and they were bound together laterally by transverse bars of acacia wood, which were arranged five on a side externally and thrust through rings attached to each plank (xxvi. 15-30). The entire front was left as an entrance, called the holy of holies, measuring 10 cubits in every direction, and the sanctuary or holy place, which was 20 cubits long by 10 cubits in breadth and height (xxvi. 16 for height; 16, 18 for length; 16 with 22-24 for width; see Antiq. iii. 6, 4). The hangings were four: 1. The ceiling and apparently the walls were hung with a curtain of white twined linen, blue, purple, and scarlet, and figured with cherubim. This curtain was made in ten pieces, each 28 cubits by 4, sewed together in two sheets. These sheets were then looped together. One formed the ceiling and three sides of the holy of holies, and the other the ceiling and two sides of the sanctuary (1-6). 2. The main external covering was of goats' hair, and consisted of eleven narrow curtains, each 30 cubits by 4; that is, 2 cubits longer than the under curtain of linen (cp. 13). These strips were united into two great curtains, which were looped together. The smaller one, which was made of five strips, covered

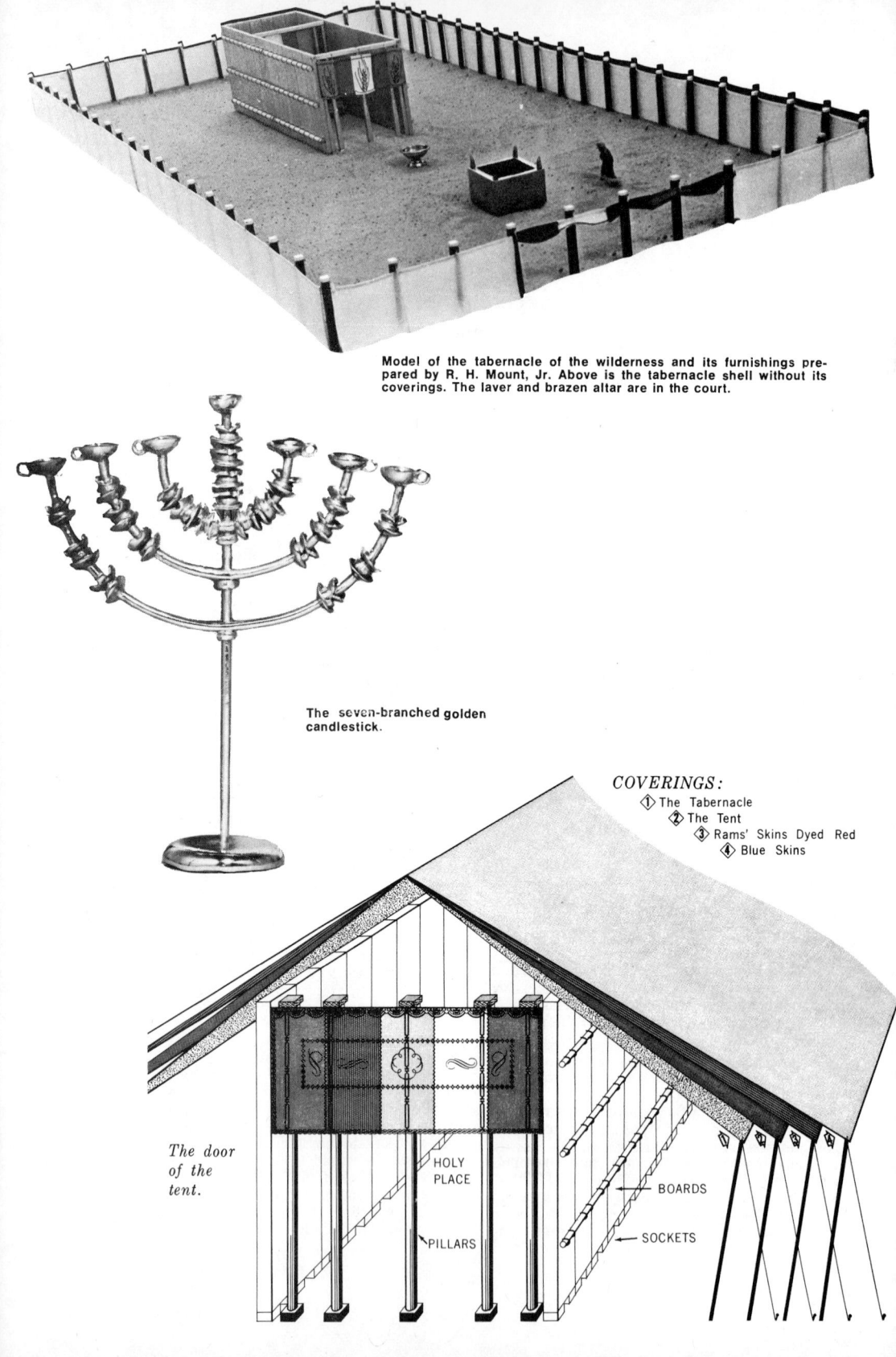

Model of the tabernacle of the wilderness and its furnishings prepared by R. H. Mount, Jr. Above is the tabernacle shell without its
coverings. The laver and brazen altar are in the court.

The seven-branched golden
candlestick.

COVERINGS:
① The Tabernacle
② The Tent
③ Rams' Skins Dyed Red
④ Blue Skins

The door
of the
tent.

HOLY
PLACE

BOARDS

PILLARS

SOCKETS

Ark of the covenant which contained a golden pot of manna, Aaron's rod which budded, and two tables of the law.

The table of showbread.

Altar of incense

Portion of a stamp from Israel showing the emblems of the twelve tribes grouped around the menorah of the second temple. The theme of the stamp is taken from Numbers 1:51, 52. ". . . And the children of Israel shall pitch their tents [around the tabernacle], every man by his own camp, and every man by his own standard, throughout their hosts." A portion of the text is inscribed on the lower half of the stamp (not shown).

the top and three sides of the holy of holies; the larger one covered the top and sides of the sanctuary, and had one breadth depending over the portal in front (7-13). 3. Over this covering of goats' hair a double roof of red-dyed rams' skins and tachash (perhaps porpoise) skins was thrown (14). 4. Two veils were hung, one at the entrance to the sanctuary and the other in front of the holy of holies. Each was wrought of blue, purple, scarlet, and fine twisted linen; but on the inner veil, which separated the holy of holies, were figures of cherubim, in token of the presence and unapproachableness of Jehovah, while the outer veil, which was passed by the priests when they entered the sanctuary to minister, lacked symbols to prevent man's ingress (31-37).

The tabernacle stood in a courtyard, like itself rectangular in form, its longer sides, running east and west, being 100 cubits, and the shorter two, running north and south, 50. The court was inclosed by a fence, 5 cubits high, formed of pillars filleted with silver, resting in sockets of brass, placed 5 cubits apart, and hung with fine twisted linen. The entrance was at the east. It was 20 cubits wide and was closed by a curtain of blue, purple, scarlet, and fine twisted linen, hung on four pillars (Ex. xxvii. 9-18). The tabernacle was pitched in the western half of this area, the laver and the altar of burnt offering being erected in the open eastern half. The ark was the central feature. It stood in the holy of holies. In the sanctuary, immediately in front of the veil that separated it from the holy of holies, stood the altar of incense, which however belonged to the oracle (1 Kin. vi. 22, R. V.; Heb. ix. 3, 4). In this apartment also were the table of showbread on the right hand and the golden candlestick on the left. In the court stood the laver and the altar of burnt offering. For the description of these objects and their symbolism, see the several articles.

The tabernacle was dedicated on the first day of the second year after the departure of the Israelites from Egypt. A cloud rested on it by day and a pillar of fire by night during all the period of the wandering. When the people broke camp, the Levites took the structure to pieces and put it together again at the new camping ground (Ex. xxvi.; xxvii. 9 19; xxxv. 4-xxxvi. 38; xl. 1-38). During the conquest of Canaan the ark remained in the camp at Gilgal. After the settlement of the Israelites, Joshua set up the tabernacle at Shiloh, where it remained during the period of the judges (Josh. xviii. 1). Apparently with the lapse of time chambers for the occupancy of the priests and for the storing of gifts came to cluster about it (1 Sam. iii. 3; cp. the encampment of the Levites about it, Num. iii. 23, 29, 35), and not unlikely the court was surrounded by a more substantial structure than hangings of linen. It was spoken of

as a tent (2 Sam. vii. 6), the tent of meeting (Josh. xix. 51; 1 Sam. ii. 22), Jehovah's dwelling (Josh. xxii. 19, 29, translated tabernacle), Jehovah's house (Judg. xix. 18; 1 Sam. i. 7, 24; iii. 15), and as the abode of Israel's king Jehovah's residence or palace (1 Sam. i. 9; iii. 3, translated temple). By the capture of the ark by the Philistines, the tabernacle lost its glory and its value (Ps. lxxviii. 60). In the reign of Saul it was at Nob (cp. 1 Sam. xxi. 1 with Mark ii. 26). During the greater part of David's reign, and in that of Solomon until the building of the temple, the tabernacle was at the high place of Gibeon (1 Chron. xvi. 39; xxi. 29). Afterwards Solomon laid it up in the temple (1 Kin. viii. 4; 2 Chron. v. 5), which was constructed on the same model, but in every part was of dimensions twice as great.

Tab'er-na-cles, Feast of.

The last of the three great annual festivals at which every man of Israel was required to appear before the Lord at the sanctuary, and the second of the harvest festivals (Deut. xvi. 16; 2 Chron. viii. 12, 13; cp. 1 Kin. ix. 25; xii. 32, 33; Zech. xiv. 16). It took its name from the custom of dwelling in booths during its celebration (Lev. xxiii. 40-42), which, after the establishment of the sanctuary at Jerusalem, were erected in the open places of the city, on the roofs and in the courts of the houses, in the precincts of the temple (Neh. viii. 16), and in the open country outside the walls. It was the culminating festival of the year; and while preëminently and essentially agricultural, it combined an historical association, the reverse in this respect of the passover (Lev. xxiii. 39, 43). It was kept in the seventh month, which by reason of the number was sacred, at the close of the agricultural season, when all the products of the year from grainfield, oliveyard, and vineyard were garnered. Hence the name feast of ingathering, under which it was instituted (Ex. xxiii. 16; xxxiv. 22; Lev. xxiii. 39; Deut. xvi. 13, 15). It began on the fifteenth day of the month, and was celebrated during seven days. The special burnt offering amounted to seventy bullocks, distributed on a decreasing scale over the week, together with two rams and fourteen lambs daily; and as a sin offering a he goat was daily sacrificed (Num. xxix. 12-34; cp. Lev. xxiii. 36; Ezra iii. 4). The booths made of the boughs of trees suggested the vintage life; but they were also made a reminder of the march from Egypt through the wilderness (Lev. xxiii. 43; cp. Hos. xii. 9). Every seven years the law of Moses was publicly read, the year of reading coinciding with the year of release, when there was no occasion to celebrate an ingathered harvest (Deut. xxxi. 9-13). The festival occurred almost immediately after the day of atonement. The people, purged ceremonially from their sinfulness, could keep the feast with a glad sense of their fitness to commune with the bountiful God. The needy were remembered (Deut. xvi. 14). An eighth day of solemn assembly was added to the festival. It was distinct from the festival; the requirement to dwell in booths did not extend to it, and its offerings stood in no relation to those of the festival proper (Lev. xxiii. 36, 39; Num. xxix. 35–38; Antiq. iii. 10, 4). It was not intended to conclude the feast of tabernacles, but only to bring the annual cycle of festivals to a fitting close. Later, however, the festival was spoken of as continuing for eight days (2 Mac. x. 6; Antiq. iii. 10, 4). It is disputed whether the seventh or the eighth day was the great day referred to in John vii. 37. Splendid ceremonies were subsequently added to those prescribed in the law for the festival. At the time of the morning sacrifice the people took branches of palm, myrtle, and willow intertwined and fruit in their hands, repaired to the temple, and marched around the altar of burnt offering once daily and seven times on the seventh day, after the manner of compassing Jericho (Antiq. iii. 10, 4; xiii. 13, 5; cp. 2 Mac. x. 6, 7). Another custom, possibly also in vogue in Christ's day, was that daily during the festival, at the time of the morning and evening oblation, a priest filled a golden vessel with water at the pool of Siloam and carried it to the temple, where it was received with trumpet blast and the words of Is. xii. 3: "With joy shall ye draw water out of the wells of salvation." It was mixed with the wine of the sacrifices and. while priests blew trumpets and Levites played on instruments and sang psalms, was poured out beside the altar, whence it was conducted by a sewer into the Kidron valley. It was also customary in the evening following the first day of the festival, and perhaps on the subsequent evenings, to illuminate the court of the women from two lofty stands, each supporting four immense lamps, which threw their light not only into the courts of the temple, but far and wide over the city. The wicks were made of the cast-off linen of the priests. Levites, stationed on the steps of the court, rendered instrumental music and sang psalms; and a dance was performed by prominent laymen and priests.

Jews who were unable to attend the celebration at Jerusalem on account of the distance of the city from their home, especially Jews dwelling in foreign countries, kept the festival at the synagogue of the town where they lived, but of course without the offering of sacrifices.

Tab'i-tha. See DORCAS.

Ta'bor.

1. A mountain on the boundary of the territory of Issachar (Antiq. v. 1, 22; perhaps Josh. xix. 22), situated inland among the mountains (Jer. xlvi. 18). It is a notable mountain (Ps. lxxxix. 12), though vastly inferior in size to Hermon. The forces of Issachar and Zebulun assembled there preparatory to fighting with Sisera (Judg. iv. 6, 12, 14). In 218 B. C., Antiochus the Great captured a town on its summit and fortified the

Mount Tabor.

place (Polybius v. 70, 6). Josephus encircled the top with a wall for defence (Life 37 ; War iv. 1, 8). Tabor, now called Jebel et-Tor, is a detached hill of limestone, rising 1843 feet above the level of the Mediterranean, in the northeastern part of the plain of Jezreel, about 12 miles north of mount Gilboa, 5½ east by south of Nazareth, and 12 west by south of the southern curve of the lake of Gennesaret. From the west-northwest it looks like a truncated cone, and from the southwest the segment of a sphere. The sides are steep. The northern side is covered with thickets of oak and terebinth. The top is flat and elliptical. In the second century the opinion was current that Tabor was the scene of the transfiguration, and ecclesiastical buildings in commemoration were erected from time to time on the summit. The theory is beset by the difficulty that there was a town on the summit in the days of Christ.

2. A town of Zebulun, given to the Merarite Levites (1 Chron. vi. 77), perhaps the place on the border of Issachar (Josh. xix. 22). The latter is scarcely identical with the border town Chisloth-tabor (12), which rather corresponds with Chesulloth (18).

3. The oak or terebinth of Tabor (1 Sam. x. 3; not plain, as in A. V.), apparently in the territory of Benjamin.

Tab′ret.
A musical instrument (1 Sam. x. 5), a timbrel (q. v.).

Tab-rim′mon, in A. V. **Tab′rim-on** [Aramaic, Rimmon is good].
A son of Hezion, and father of Benhadad I., king of Syria (1 Kin. xv. 18).

Tache.
A catch for taking hold or holding together. It was used about the tabernacle for coupling curtains together (Ex. xxvi. 6, 11, in R. V. clasp).

Tach′mo-nite, in R. V. **Tahchemonite.**
A word found in 2 Sam. xxiii. 8. It is doubtless a corruption, in the Hebrew text itself, of "the Hachmonite," a copyist having mistaken Hebrew h for t. See HACHMONI.

Tad′mor [formed from *tamar*, a palm tree].
A town in the desert (2 Chron. viii. 4). It was fortified by Solomon, doubtless to control the caravan route across it. In the parallel passage (1 Kin. ix. 18, R. V.) it is called Tamar in the wilderness, and described as being not only in the desert, but also in the land. This latter phrase is probably broad enough to denote the extensive kingdom of Solomon (19; iv. 21, 24). The suggestion has been made that the town may be identical with Tamar at the southeastern corner of the promised boundaries of the land (Ezek. xlvii. 19 ; xlviii. 28), probably on the road from Hebron to Elath ; see TAMAR 5. This identification is in itself suitable, and may include or correct Tadmor in 2 Chron.

viii. 4, which has been proposed in explanation of 1 Kin. ix. 18. But the text of Kings is suspicious : for the phrase "in the land" is superfluous, since all the towns mentioned were in the land, and the text departs from the parallel enumeration in Chronicles in failing to locate in Hamath the store cities of Solomon. Perhaps the original text was "Tamar in the wilderness, in the land of Hamath all the store cities." Tadmor eventually became subject to the Romans, who Latinized the name into Palmyra (Antiq. viii. 6, 1). Between A. D. 251 and 273 it was at first partially, and then for a time totally, independent. The place still retains the name of Tadmûr. It is in an oasis about 140 miles east-northeast of Damascus, and about 120 from the Euphrates. It is now a ruin, stretching more than a mile and a half. It has long rows of Corinthian columns and a few of the Ionic order, with a number of tower-like tombs. The inscriptions found in the place have been chiefly Greek and Semitic.

Ta′han [perhaps, inclination].
A descendant of Ephraim, and founder of a tribal family (Num. xxvi. 35). His descent was probably through Telah, Rephah, and Beriah to Ephraim (1 Chron. vii. 25).

Ta-hap′a-nes. See TAHPANHES.

Ta′hash, in A.V. **Thahash** [porpoise or similar fishlike animal].
A son of Nahor by his concubine Reumah (Gen. xxii. 24).

Ta′hath [that which is beneath].
1. A station of the Israelites in the wilderness (Num. xxxiii. 26, 27). Situation unknown.
2. A Levite, family of Kohath, house of Izhar, and of the line of Korah and Abiasaph (1 Chron. vi. 24, 37). From him two families branched, Uriel and Zephaniah.
3. An Ephraimite, son of Bered, family of Shuthelah (1 Chron. vii. 20).
4. A son of Eleadah, and a descendant of Tahath, son of Bered (1 Chron. vii. 20).

Tah-che′mo-nite. See TACHMONITE.

Tah′pan-hes, and once **Tehaphnehes** (Ezek. xxx. 18) ; in A. V. once also **Tahapanes** (Jer. ii. 16).
An Egyptian city (Ezek. xxx. 18), to which Jews fled to escape Babylonian vengeance after the murder of Gedaliah (Jer. xliii. 7–9). Jews seem to have become permanent residents there (xliv. 1 ; xlvi. 14). The Septuagint translators render the name Taphne or Taphnai, obviously the same as Daphne, a fortified city on the Pelusiac channel of the Nile (Herod. ii. 30, 107), probably marked by the ruins of Defenneh, 12 miles north of Pithom.

Tah′pe-nes.
A queen of Egypt in the time of Solomon (1 Kin. xi. 19, 20).

Tah're-a, and **Tarea** [perhaps, adroitness or cunning].

A descendant of king Saul through Jonathan (1 Chron. viii. 35 ; ix. 41).

Tah-tim-hod'shi.

A region visited by David's census takers in connection with Gilead, before they came to Dan-jaan and roundabout to Zidon (2 Sam. xxiv. 6). The name is elsewhere unknown, and perhaps stands for "the Hittites toward Kadesh ;" see KADESH 2.

Tal'ent.

A weight used both for ordinary commodities and for the precious metals, but of different standard in the respective cases ; see WEIGHTS. The value of the talent of gold was about $29,374.50; and that of silver about $1950. The talent of the Greco-Roman period was Attic, varying from $1180 to $960. From the parable of the talents, in which a master distributes talents among his servants, according to their several ability, to be put to profitable use (Mat. xxv. 14–30), the English figurative use of the word talents is probably derived in such expressions as that one uses his talents well.

Tal'i-tha cu'mi [Aramaic, maiden arise] (Mark v. 41).

Tal'mai [pertaining to furrows].

1. A son of Anak, and probably founder of a family of Anakim (Num. xiii. 22), driven from Hebron by Caleb (Josh. xv. 14; Judg. i. 10).

2. A king of Geshur, whose daughter Maacah was one of David's wives, and Absalom's mother (2 Sam. iii. 3 ; xiii. 37).

Tal'mon [oppressed].

A porter, and the family which he founded (1 Chron. ix. 17). Members of the family returned from exile with Zerubbabel (Ezra ii. 42 ; Neh. vii. 45), and served as porters at the new temple (xi. 19 ; xii. 25).

Ta'mah. See TEMAH.

Ta'mar, in A. V. of N. T. **Thamar** [a palm tree, specially a date palm].

1. The wife of Er, son of Judah. When left a widow, she became the mother of Perez and Zerah by Judah (Gen. xxxviii. 6–26), and thus the ancestress of several tribal families (Num. xxvi. 20, 21).

2. Absalom's beautiful sister, ill-used by her half-brother Amnon (2 Sam. xiii. 1–39 ; 1 Chron. iii. 9).

3. A daughter of Absalom, named doubtless after his sister (2 Sam. xiv. 27). Perhaps she became Uriel's wife and the mother of Maacah, Rehoboam's wife (2 Chron. xiii. 2; Antiq. viii. 10, 1). See MAACAH 9.

4. A town in the desert (1 Kin. ix. 18). The Hebrew K'ri, or preferred reading, the A. V., the margin of the R. V., and 2 Chron. viii. 4 have Tadmor ; see TADMOR.

5. A place at the eastern end of the promised southern frontier of Palestine (Ezek. xlvii. 19 ; xlviii. 28). It would lie south of the Dead Sea ; and perhaps is identical with the village Tamara, located by Eusebius on the road between Hebron and Elath.

Tam'a-risk Tree.

The tamarisk (*Tamarix articulata*) is called *'athl* in Arabic, *'athla'* in Aramaic ; and accordingly the cognate Hebrew word *'eshel* doubtless likewise denotes the tamarisk. Abraham planted one in Beer-sheba (Gen. xxi. 33 ; in A. V. grove), Saul dwelt beneath one in Ramah (1 Sam. xxii. 6 ; in A. V. a tree), and the bones of Saul and his sons were buried beneath one in Jabesh-gilead (xxxi. 13 ; in

Tamarisk tree.

A. V. a tree). The chronicler states that the bones of the king and his sons were interred beneath the *'elah* in Jabesh (1 Chron. x. 12 ; in E. V. oak, R. V. margin terebinth). He may, however, use the term *'elah* in its broad signification of strong tree; see OAK. The tamarisk is a small tree, with durable wood, deciduous branches, and minute, scale-like, evergreen leaves. Nine species occur in Palestine. The most widely distributed is *Tamarix pallasii*, which attains a height of from 10 to 20 feet. The largest species is *Tamarix articulata*, from 15 to 30 feet. It is found along the western border of the desert of the wandering. *Tamarix mannifera*, from 10 to 15 feet in height, growing in ancient Moab, Edom, and the peninsula of Sinai, yields the substance popularly known as manna; see MANNA.

Tam'muz.

A deity of the Babylonians, called by them *Dumu-zi* or *Du-zi*, probably meaning son of life, from which the name Tammuz is derived. He was worshiped throughout Babylonia, and in Assyria, Phœnicia, and Palestine; and he gave name to the fourth month of the Semitic year; see YEAR. He was the husband of the goddess Ishtar, and king of the nether world. He was also god of the pasture, the patron of flocks and their keepers, and hence was himself entitled shepherd. He was represented as dying annually and returning to life with each recurring year. It was understood, by some at least, that he was slain by the sun-god Shamash. The story is confessedly a nature myth. However its details may be explained, it symbolizes more or less inclusively the annual withdrawal and invariable return of the sun, and the death and revival of vegetation. Ezekiel in vision saw the worship of Tammuz in favor among the Jews, and women sitting at the northern gate of the temple weeping for the god (Ezek. viii. 14). Cyril of Alexandria and Jerome identified him with the Phœnician Adonis. Though not proven, their conjecture has found much favor. Jerome says that the Syrians celebrated an annual solemnity to Adonis in June, when he was lamented by the women as dead, and afterwards his coming to life again was celebrated with songs. From other sources it appears that Byblos in Phœnicia was the headquarters of the Adonis worship. The annual feast in his honor was held at the neighboring temple of Aphrodite in mount Lebanon, and lasted seven days. It began with a commemoration of the disappearance of the god. Vessels filled with mold and containing stalks of wheat, barley, lettuce, and fennel, and called gardens of Adonis, were exposed to the heat of the sun. The withering of the plants symbolized the slaughter of the youth by the fire-god Mars. Then followed a search for Adonis by the women. At length his image was found in one of the gardens. The finding was celebrated by lewdness and song. The image was then coffined, and the wound made by the symbolical boar which slew the young god was shown on his body. The people sat on the ground around the bier with their clothes rent, and the women raised loud lamentation. Sacrifice was offered for the dead god, and the image was buried.

Ta'nach. See TAANACH.

Tan'hu-meth [consolation].

A Netophathite (2 Kin. xxv. 23; Jer. xl. 8).

Tan'ner.

A dresser of hides (Acts ix. 43), who removes the hair by means of lime or other agent, steeps the skins in an infusion of bark, especially of oak bark, in order to impregnate

them with the acid juice of the plant and render them firm, pliable, and durable, and thus converts the hide into leather. At Joppa Peter lodged with a tanner (x. 6). See LEATHER.

Ta'phath [a drop].

A daughter of Solomon, and wife of Abinadab's son (1 Kin. iv. 11).

Ta'phon. See TEPHON.

Tap'pu-ah [apple or, perhaps, quince or apricot].

1. A town in the lowland of Judah (Josh. xv. 34). Site unknown.

2. A town of Manasseh west of Shechem and on the boundary of Ephraim (Josh. xvi. 8; xvii. 7, 8).

3. A son of Hebron (1 Chron. ii. 43).

Ta'rah. See TERAH.

Tar'a-lah [staggering, reeling].

A city of Benjamin (Josh. xviii. 27). Site unknown.

Ta're-a. See TAHREA.

Tares.

The rendering of the Greek *Zizanion* in Mat. xiii. 25–27, 29, 30; on R. V. margin darnel. The tare (*Vicia sativa*), a vetch, with pinnate leaves and purple-blue or red papilionaceous flowers, would be easily distinguished from the wheat. The Greek word

Tares, left, compared with wheat, right.

zizanion corresponds to the Arabic *zuwân*, which denotes *Lolium*, and to the talmudic *zonin*. The bearded darnel (*Lolium temulentum*) is a poisonous grass, almost undistinguishable from wheat while the two are only in blade, but which can be separated without difficulty when they come into ear (cp. ver. 29, 30).

Tar'get. See ARMOR.

Tar'gum. See VERSIONS.

Tar'pel-ites.

The inhabitants of a place, presumably called Tarpel and situated near Babylonia or Elam (Ezra iv. 9).

Tar'shish, in A. V. four times **Tharshish** (1 Kin. x. 22; xxii. 48; 1 Chron. vii. 10).

1. A people descended from Javan (Gen. x. 4) and their country. As Jonah entered a ship at Joppa in order to flee thither, the route to it was evidently across the waters of the Mediterranean. It was a distant land (Is. lxvi. 19). Tyre was the "daughter" of Tarshish (xxiii. 10), perhaps in the sense that the commerce with Tarshish was the making of Tyre. The imports from Tarshish were silver beaten into plates (Jer. x. 9), also iron, tin, and lead (Ezek. xxvii. 12). It is believed that Tarshish was Tartessus, in the south of Spain, near Gibraltar (Herod. iv. 152), and the country of the Turti or Turditani, to which the town belonged. The mineral wealth of the region attracted the Phœnicians, who established a colony there and Semitized the name. Spain has long been noted for its mineral wealth.

Ships of Tarshish were originally ships trading to and from Tarshish, but ultimately ships of first-rate magnitude to whatever place their voyages may have been made (Ps. xlviii. 7; Is. ii. 16; xxiii. 1, 14; lx. 9; Ezek. xxvii. 25). Such vessels, built by Jehoshaphat to go to Ophir, lay in the harbor at Ezion-geber on the Red Sea (1 Kin. xxii. 48). The term Tarshish ship is paraphrased as "ship going to Tarshish" (2 Chron. ix. 21, Hebrew text; cp. 1 Kin. x. 22) and "ship to go to Tarshish" (2 Chron. xx. 36).

2. A Benjamite, son of Bilhan (1 Chron. vii. 10).

3. One of the seven highest princes of Persia (Esth. i. 14).

Tar'sus [not from Greek *tarsos*, a crate of wickerwork, any broad, flat surface]. The name was pronounced Tarzi by the Assyrians, and appears written on coins in Aramaic character as Trz.

The chief city of Cilicia, in the eastern part of Asia Minor. It was situated on both banks of the river Cydnus, about 12 miles from the sea. About 833 B. C. it is mentioned by Shalmaneser, king of Assyria. When the Romans formed the province of Cilicia in 64 B. C., they made Tarsus the residence of the governor. To compensate it for the sufferings it endured in its allegiance to the party of Cæsar, Marc Antony granted it freedom and exemption from taxation. It was famed for its schools, which almost rivaled those of Athens and Alexandria. It was the birthplace of the apostle Paul (Acts xxi. 39; xxii. 3), and he revisited it at least once after his conversion (ix. 30; xi. 25). It is still a considerable town.

Tar'tak.

An idol set up by the Avvites in Samaria (2 Kin. xvii. 31).

Tar'tan.

The title of the commander-in-chief of the Assyrian army (2 Kin. xviii. 17; Is. xx. 1). The name was pronounced by the Assyrians both *tartanu* and *turtanu*.

Tat'te-nai, in A. V. **Tatnai.**

A Persian governor west of the river Euphrates, who opposed the rebuilding of the temple (Ezra v. 3; vi. 6; in 1 Esdr. vi. 3, etc., Sisennes). He is mentioned as Ushtanu, governor of Babylon and Syria, in Babylo-

Ruins of the ancient city wall in Tarsus

nian contracts of the first and third years of Darius.

Tau, in A. R. V. **Tav.**

The twenty-second and last letter of the Hebrew alphabet, pronounced t or th according to position. English T comes from the same source, and with th represents it in anglicized Hebrew names; as Tamar, Nathan. It heads the twenty-second section of Ps. cxix., in which section each verse of the original begins with this letter.

Scribes occasionally confused tau and he (q. v.).

Tax'es.

Under the judges the regular payments obligatory on the Israelites were for the worship of Jehovah. There was as yet no army and no royal court to support. But there was a tabernacle and a priesthood, and these were maintained by the tithes and other offerings, and by the land which was permanently placed at the disposal of the Levites.

After the establishment of the kingdom, revenue for its support was obtained from various sources: 1. Taxes in kind were levied by Solomon on the produce of the field and the flock (1 Kin. iv. 7-28; cp. Amos vii. 1). 2. Special gifts were brought to the king at the commencement of his reign (1 Sam. x. 27) or in time of war (xvi. 20; xvii. 18). 3. Tribute was rendered by subject peoples (2 Sam. viii. 6, 14; 1 Kin. x. 15; 2 Kin. iii. 4), and service was exacted of the Canaanites who dwelt in the midst of Israel (Judg. i. 28, 30; 1 Kin. ix. 20, 21). When the Hebrews were subject to a foreign prince, they had to pay tribute to him in addition to taxes for the support of their own government. 4. Duties were paid by tradesmen and merchants (1 Kin. x. 15). Without levying taxes in money or produce, and with little expense to himself, David attained the object of a standing army by dividing the men of military age into brigades of 24,000 men, and requiring each brigade in turn to hold itself in readiness during one month for instant service (1 Chron. xxvii. 1). Under Solomon the people were oppressed by taxation, and this grievous burden was an immediate cause of the disruption of the kingdom (1 Kin. xii. 4). Exemption from taxation was a reward for service (1 Sam. xvii. 25; Antiq. xvii. 2, 1).

Under the Persian empire, by decree of Darius Hystaspis the satraps of each province paid a fixed sum into the royal treasury (Herod. iii. 89). The inhabitants had to provide for the maintenance of the governor's household also. This provision was called the bread of the governor, and so far as Judah was concerned included food and forty shekels daily in money (Neh. v. 14, 15). The revenue was derived from tribute, customs, and toll (Ezra iv. 13, 20). Priests, Levites, and Nethinim were exempted from these taxes in Judah (vii. 24); but the burdens pressed heavily on the great body of the people, who had the sanctuary likewise to support, and many were forced to mortgage their fields and vineyards to raise money for the tribute (Neh. v. 4; ix. 37).

Under the Egyptian and Syrian kings, instead of a fixed amount being levied by the crown on the people, the privilege of collecting the taxes of a district was put up at auction and sold to the highest responsible bidder. The party who promised the most revenue from a province was authorized to collect it and was furnished with military power sufficient to enable him to enforce his demands (Antiq. xii. 4, 1-5). The Syrian kings imposed a poll tax and a duty on salt, exacted a sum of money in lieu of the annual present of a crown of gold, which it had become customary to demand, took one-third of the grain and one-half of the fruit, and in addition levied on the tithes and tolls paid into the temple at Jerusalem (1 Mac. x. 29-31; xi. 34, 35; xiii. 37, 39; Antiq. xii. 3, 3).

When the Romans under Pompey took Jerusalem in 63 B. C., tribute was imposed on the Jews which in a short time amounted to more than 10,000 talents (Antiq. xiv. 4, 4, and 5). Julius Cæsar decreed that the tribute should not be farmed, that it should not be levied in a Sabbatic year, and that in the year following a Sabbatic year only one-fourth of the usual amount should be collected (10, 5 and 6). Herod the Great taxed the produce of the field (xv. 9, 1), and levied duties on commodities bought and sold (xvii. 8, 4). When Judæa was placed under procurators, the financial system of the empire was introduced. The revenues were farmed; see PUBLICAN. There were levied: 1. Tribute of the soil, paid either in kind or in money. 2. A poll tax (Mat. xxii. 17) and, under the same name, a tax on personal property. 3. Export and import duties, collected at seaports and at the gates of cities. In Jerusalem a house duty was paid by the inhabitants (Antiq. xix. 6, 3).

After the exile a temple tax of half a shekel was imposed on every Israelite who had reached the age of twenty years (Mat. xvii. 24). The collectors visited each town of Judæa annually at a fixed time, and in foreign countries places were designated where it might be paid. See TRIBUTE 2.

Tax'ing.

An enrollment, ordered by the Roman emperor Augustus, which in the providence of God brought Joseph and Mary to Bethlehem, and led to the fulfillment of the ancient prophecy that the Messiah should be born in that town (Mic. v. 2; Mat. ii. 5, 6; Luke ii. 1-20). A later enrollment led to tumults among the Jews (Acts v. 37). See QUIRINIUS.

Te'bah [slaughter (specially of cattle)].

A son of Nahor by Reumah, his concubine

(Gen. xxi:. 24), and the tribe descended from him. The name is found in 2 Sam. viii. 8, according to the Septuagint and the Syriac version, and also in 1 Chron. xviii. 8 in the form Tibhath, and denotes a town of Aramzobah.

Teb-a-li'ah [Jehovah hath immersed, *i. e.*, ceremonially purified].

A Merarite Levite, the third son of Hosah (1 Chron. xxvi. 11).

Te'beth.

The tenth month of the Semitic calendar (Esth. ii. 16). See YEAR.

Te-haph'ne-hes. See TAHPANHES.

Te-hin'nah [grace, supplications].

A man of Judah, descended from Chelub, and ancestor of the inhabitants of Ir-nahash (1 Chron. iv. 12).

Teil Tree.

The linden, a tree of the genus *Tilia*. The Hebrew word *'elah* is once translated thus in A. V. (Is. vi. 13; in R. V. terebinth); see OAK 1 and TEREBINTH. The teil tree does not grow in Palestine.

Te'kel. See MENE.

Te-ko'a, in A. V. thrice **Tekoah** (2 Sam. xiv. 2, 4, 9), and so in R. V. of 1 Mac. ix. 33, where A. V. has **Thecoe.**

A town in Judah (1 Chron. ii. 24; iv. 5; Septuagint of Josh. xv. 60), in the wilderness toward En-gedi (2 Chron. xx. 20; cp. 2, 16). It was fortified by Rehoboam (2 Chron. xi. 6). It was the home of the prophet Amos (Amos i. 1). In Nehemiah's time the common people of Tekoa helped to rebuild the wall of Jerusalem, while the nobles of the place showed indifference to the work (Neh. iii. 5, 27). The name still lingers as Tekû'a, a ruined village 5 miles south of Bethlehem. It is on a hill broad at the top, where are found the remains of the foundations of houses, often with beveled stones, the whole occupying an area of 4 or 5 acres. There is also a castle, but of more modern date.

Te-ko'ite.

A native or inhabitant of Tekoa (2 Sam. xxiii. 26).

Tel-a'bib [heap, or hill of ears of grain].

A place in Babylonia, near the river Chebar. Jewish exiles were located there (Ezek. iii. 15). Situation unknown.

Te'lah [fracture].

A descendant of Ephraim, probably through Beriah (1 Chron. vii. 25).

Tel'a-im [little lambs].

A place where Saul assembled his army to war against the Amalekites (1 Sam. xv. 4; and xxvii. 8, Septuagint). It may be Telem of Josh. xv. 24; but the two names, as traditionally pronounced, have a different meaning.

Te-las'sar, in A. V. once **Thelasar** (2 Kin. xix. 12) [probably, hill of Asshur].

A place inhabited by the children of Eden

(2 Kin. xix. 12; Is. xxxvii. 12), presumably in northwestern Mesopotamia. Til-ashûri, if identical with Telesaura, now Mar'ash, seems remote from Beth-eden.

Te'lem [perhaps, oppression].

1. A town in the extreme south of Judah (Josh. xv. 24). Site unknown. See TELAIM.

2. A porter, whom Ezra induced to put away his foreign wife (Ezra x. 24).

Tel-har'sha, in A. V. **Tel-har'sa** and **Tel-har'e-sha** [in Hebrew and Assyrian, mound of the artificer's work or of enchantment].

A place in Babylonia whence certain people who claimed to be Israelite exiles returned with Zerubbabel to Jerusalem (Ezra ii. 59; Neh. vii. 61). Situation unknown.

Tel-me'lah [hill of salt].

A place in Babylonia, whence certain people who claimed to be Israelite exiles came to Jerusalem with Zerubbabel (Ezra ii. 59; Neh. vii. 61). Situation unknown.

Te'ma.

A tribe of Ishmaelites and the district they inhabited (Gen. xxv. 15; Is. xxi. 14). Their caravans were well known (Job vi. 19). Tema is often identified with Taima in the Hauran; but it rather denotes the important people who dwelt in and about Taima, east of the Ælanitic gulf of the Red Sea and midway between Damascus and Medina.

Te'mah, in A. V. **Tamah** and **Thamah** [perhaps, laughter].

Founder of a family of Nethinim, members of which returned with Zerubbabel from the captivity (Ezra ii. 53; Neh. vii. 55).

Te'man [southern].

A tribe descended from Esau, and the district they inhabited (Gen. xxxvi. 11, 15, 34). The territory was in Edom (Jer. xlix. 20; Amos i. 12), apparently in the northern part (Ezek. xxv. 13). Its inhabitants were noted for their wisdom (Jer. xlix. 7).

Te'man-ite, in A. V. once **Tem'a-ni** (Gen. xxxvi. 34).

A member of the tribe of Teman (Gen. xxxvi. 34), or of Tema. It is not certain in which sense Eliphaz, Job's friend, was a Temanite (Job ii. 11).

Tem'e-ni.

A son of Ashhur (1 Chron. iv. 5, 6).

Tem'ple [in Hebrew, large house, palace, as 1 Kin. i. 21; 2 Kin. xx. 18; Dan. i. 4; iv. 4].

A building dedicated to the worship of a deity (Joel iii. 5; Ezra v. 14 with i. 7; Acts xix. 27). In three passages it is applied to the tabernacle (1 Sam. i. 9; iii. 3; 2 Sam. xxii. 7; cp. Rev. xv. 5); but generally the reference is to some one of the temples successively erected to Jehovah at Jerusalem.

1. *Solomon's Temple.* The erection of a permanent house of the Lord, instead of the movable tabernacle, was proposed by David, and the necessary materials were largely

amassed by him (2 Sam. vii. ; 1 Kin. v. 3-5 ; viii. 17 ; 1 Chron. xxii. ; xxviii. 11-xxix. 9). He gathered 100,000 talents of gold and 1,000,000 talents of silver for the prospective structure and its furnishings (1 Chron. xxii. 14), and added from his own private fortune 3000 talents of gold and 7000 talents of silver, and the princes contributed 5000 talents of gold, 10,000 darics of gold, and 10,000 talents of silver (xxix. 4, 7), making a total of 108,000 talents of gold, 10,000 darics of gold, and 1,017,000 talents of silver. This sum is equivalent to nearly 4900 million dollars or, if it may be legitimately reckoned by the lighter system of weights, nearly 2450 million dollars. This latter amount is perhaps not incredible, in view of the booty which David brought home from his wars and received as tribute. Still the sum is very large, and it is well to admit the probability of the text being corrupt. This store of precious metals was placed at the disposal of Solomon for the use of the temple, but it was not all expended (1 Kin. vii. 51 ; 2 Chron. v. 1). Solomon began the work in the fourth year of his reign, and it was completed in seven years and six months (1 Kin. vi. 1, 38). The alliance with Hiram, king of Tyre, rendered it easy to obtain timber from Lebanon, and skilled Phœnician artificers. 30,000 Israelites were levied, and sent in detachments of 10,000 for a month to the Lebanon mountains (1 Kin. v. 13), and the remnant of the Canaanites was impressed to the number of 150,000 to serve as hewers of stone and carriers (1 Kin. v. 15 ; ix. 20, 21 ; 2 Chron. ii. 2, 17, 18). Overseers were appointed, apparently 550 chiefs and 3300 subordinates (1 Kin. v. 16 ; ix. 23), of whom 3600 were Canaanites and 250 Israelites (2 Chron. ii. 17 ; viii. 10). The building was erected on mount Moriah, at the spot where the threshing floor of Ornan, or Araunah, the Jebusite, had stood (2 Chron. iii. 1). Its general plan was that of the tabernacle, but the dimensions were double and the ornamentation was richer. The interior of the edifice measured 60 cubits in length, 20 in breadth, and 30 in height, in this last particular deviating from the proportions of the tabernacle (1 Kin. vi. 2). The walls were built of stone made ready at the quarry (7). The roof was constructed of beams and planks of cedar (9), the floor was laid with cypress, and the walls from the floor to the ceiling were lined with cedar (15 ; and 2 Chron. iii. 5, where the Greek translators read cedar, not fir). The whole interior was overlaid with gold (1 Kin. vi. 20, 22, 30 ; 2 Chron. iii. 7 et passim), and its walls were carved not only with cherubim, but also with palm trees and flowers. The holy of holies was a cube. Each side measured 20 cubits (1 Kin. vi. 16, 20). The space, nearly 10 cubits high, between its ceiling and the roof was probably occupied by upper chambers, gold lined (1 Chron. xxviii. 11 ;

2 Chron. iii. 9). In the holy of holies itself was placed the ark (1 Kin. viii. 6), under the wings of two colossal cherubim of olive wood overlaid with gold. Each cherub was 10 cubits in height, and had wings 5 cubits long. With the tip of one wing it touched a side wall, and with the other wing it reached forward to the center of the room and touched the corresponding wing of its companion. The four wings thus extended across the width of the house, while the cherubim turned their faces toward the sanctuary (1 Kin. vi. 23-28 ; 2 Chron. iii. 13). Under their wings the ark was placed (1 Kin. viii. 6). The partition between the holy and the most holy place was of cedar boards, overlaid on both sides with gold, and it had two doors of olive wood, decorated with palm trees, flowers, and cherubim, and overlaid with gold ; see LEAF. This was hung, toward the sanctuary, with chains of gold and a curtain patterned after that of the tabernacle (1 Kin. vi. 16, 21, 31, 32 ; 2 Chron. iii. 14 ; cp. Antiq. viii. 3, 3 and 7).

The holy place or sanctuary was 40 cubits long, 20 wide, and 30 high. Its walls were pierced by latticed windows ; probably near the roof, above the top of the exterior building, and intended for ventilation and the escape of smoke (1 Kin. vi. 4). The altar of incense was made of cedar, instead of acacia, and overlaid with gold (20, 22 ; vii. 48). It belonged to the holy of holies (22, R. V. ; Heb. ix. 3, 4), but stood in the holy place, doubtless because the priest, who might enter the holy of holies but once in the year, had occasion to offer incense daily. There were ten golden candlesticks instead of one, and likewise ten tables, although doubtless the showbread was displayed on but one ; see CANDLESTICK and SHOWBREAD. The entrance to the sanctuary from the court had doors of cypress (vi. 33, 34).

Against the two exterior sides and the rear of the temple a three-story building was erected, containing chambers for officials and for storage (vi. 5-10). Before the front entrance a portico was built, 10 cubits wide, 20 long, and 20 or more probably 20 high (3 ; 2 Chron. iii. 4 ; cp. Septuagint ; Syriac). By it stood the two brazen pillars, Boaz and Jachin, each 18 cubits high, and richly ornamented (1 Kin. vii. 15-22 ; 2 Chron. iii. 15-17).

The courts of the temple were two ; the inner, upper court of the priests, and the great court (2 Kin. xxiii. 12 ; 2 Chron. iv. 9 ; Jer. xxxvi. 10). They were separated from one another, both by the difference of level and by a low wall, consisting of three courses of hewn stone and one course of cedar beams (1 Kin. vi. 36 ; vii. 12). In the court of the priests were a brazen altar for sacrifice (viii. 64 ; 2 Kin. xvi. 14 ; 2 Chron. xv. 8), in size nearly four times that used at the tabernacle (iv. 1) ; and a brazen sea and ten brazen lavers (1 Kin. vii. 23-39). The sea was for the priests to wash at ; the lavers were for washing such things as belonged to the burnt offering (2 Chron. iv. 6) ; see ALTAR, MOLTEN SEA, LAVER. The great outer court was for Israel (cp. 1 Kin. viii. 14). It was paved. (2 Chron. vii. 3) ; and it was surrounded by a wall, for it had gates (iv. 9 ; cp. Ezek. xl. 5).

This temple was plundered and burned by the Babylonians when they captured Jerusalem in 587 B. C. (2 Kin. xxv. 8–17).

2. *Zerubbabel's Temple.*—Cyrus authorized the erection of a temple 60 cubits in breadth and height (Ezra vi. 3 ; Antiq. xi. 4, 6). The limits which Cyrus set may have been attained by the exterior of the new building ; for Herod the Great, with 2 Chron. iii. 4 in mind, assigns 60 cubits to the height (xv. 11, 1). It was begun in the year 537 B. C., the second year after the return from captivity ; and, after much opposition from the inhabitants of Samaria, was completed in the sixth year of Darius, 515 B. C. (Ezra iii. 8 ; vi. 15 ; con. Apion. i. 21). The dimensions of the several parts are not known. The plan of Solomon's temple was, however, followed ; though the new building was projected on a scale of far less magnificence. In the construction of the house, cedar from Lebanon was used (Ezra iii. 7) ; and precious metals, which were provided, as in the wilderness, by the freewill offerings of the people (i. 6 ; ii. 68, 69). Many of the vessels used in the former temple were restored (i. 7–11). The interior walls were overlaid with gold ; and the house was divided, as usual, into the holy of holies and the sanctuary, apparently separated from each other by at least a veil (1 Mac. i. 21, 22 ; iv. 48, 51). The holy of holies was empty, for the ark of the covenant had disappeared (Cicero, pro Flac. 28 ; Tacitus, Hist. v. 9). The sanctuary was furnished with an altar of incense, and, like the tabernacle, with only one candlestick and one table for show-bread (1 Mac. i. 21, 22 ; iv. 49). Exterior chambers were attached to the building (Neh. x. 37–39 ; xii. 44 ; xiii. 4 ; 1 Mac. iv. 38) ; and the whole was surrounded with courts (Neh. viii. 16 ; xiii. 7 ; Antiq. xiv. 16, 2). A brazen sea (Ecclus. l. 3) and an altar for sacrifice were used (Ezra vii. 17). The altar was built of stones (1 Mac. iv. 44–47). The court of the priests was eventually separated from the outer court by a wooden railing (Antiq. xiii. 13, 5). The temple and its precincts were closed by doors and gates (Neh. vi. 10 ; 1 Mac. iv. 38).

3. *Herod's temple* superseded Zerubbabel's. It is fully described by Josephus, who was thoroughly familiar with the building (Antiq. xv. 11 ; War v. 5), and in the Mishna (*Middoth*). The materials were brought together before the old structure was taken down. Work was commenced in the eighteenth year of Herod's reign, 19 B. C. The main edifice was built by priests in a year and a half, and the cloisters were finished in eight years, either in 11 or 9 B. C.: but the work on the entire complex of courts and buildings was not completed until the procuratorship of Albinus, A. D. 62–64 (Antiq xv. 11, 5 and 6 ; xx. 9, 7 ; cp. John ii. 20). The old area was enlarged to twice its former dimensions (War i. 21, 1). The temple proper stood upon the highest ground in the inclosure. It was built of great blocks of white stone. Its interior had the length and breadth of Solomon's temple ; but a height of 40 cubits, exclusive of an upper chamber, instead of 30 cubits. It was divided into the holy of holies and the sanctuary on the customary lines. The holy of holies was empty. It was separated from the holy place by a veil (War v. 5, 5). The rending of this veil by an earthquake at the death of Christ signified that the way to the mercy seat is no longer closed to all save the mediating high priest, but is at all times open to the sincere worshiper (Mat. xxvii. 51 ; Heb. vi. 19 ; x. 20). The holy place contained, as usual, a golden altar for incense, a table for show-bread, and a candlestick. It was entered from the east by a great doorway closed by golden doors, each 55 cubits high and 16 broad ; hung with a veil of blue, purple, scarlet and fine linen ; and er compassed on the outer or court side by a golden vine from which depended immense clusters of golden grapes. Against the two sides and rear of the temple, a three-story building, 40 cubits high, containing chambers, was constructed (cp. War vi. 4, 7), and in addition two wings, one containing winding stairs, sprang from the front corners. The building measured externally 100 cubits in length and 54 or, including the two wings at the front, 70 cubits in width. Over the holy place and the holy of holies was an attic, which had the same dimensions as the sacred apartments beneath. This attic, together with its floor and the roof, increased the height of the sacred edifice to over 90 cubits. A vestibule or porch ran along the entire front of the house, 100 cubits long and high and 20 broad. Its portal was 70 cubits high by 25 broad (or, according to the Mishna, 40 and 20), without doors, allowing the great doorway of the sanctuary to be seen from without. Above this porch Herod erected the celebrated golden eagle (Antiq. xvii. 6, 2 and 3 ; War i. 33, 2 and 3). Twelve steps descended from the vestibule to the court of the priests. This court surrounded the sacred edifice. It contained the altar for burnt offerings, of which the height was 15 cubits, and the base a square measuring 50 cubits to the side. According to the Mishna, it was built of unhewn stones ; and contracted from a base 32 cubits square to a top 24 cubits square. It was reached by an inclined plane. A brazen sea or laver was also in use (Mishna). This court was encompassed by a wall or coping, about a cubit in height. All around the court of the priests lay, as of old, the great court, now double. It was inclosed

by a wall, whose top was 25 cubits higher than the pavement. Against the inner side of this wall storage chambers were built (War vi. 5, 2), and in front of these, that is, on the temple side, ran a covered colonnade. This court was divided into two parts by a gate in the center of the partition wall and by a descent of fifteen steps. Only Israelites might enter this court, and women might not advance farther. These three courts and the temple were embraced in the *chel*, or sacred inclosure. The inclosing barrier was

Model of Herod's temple constructed by Dr. Conrad Shick.

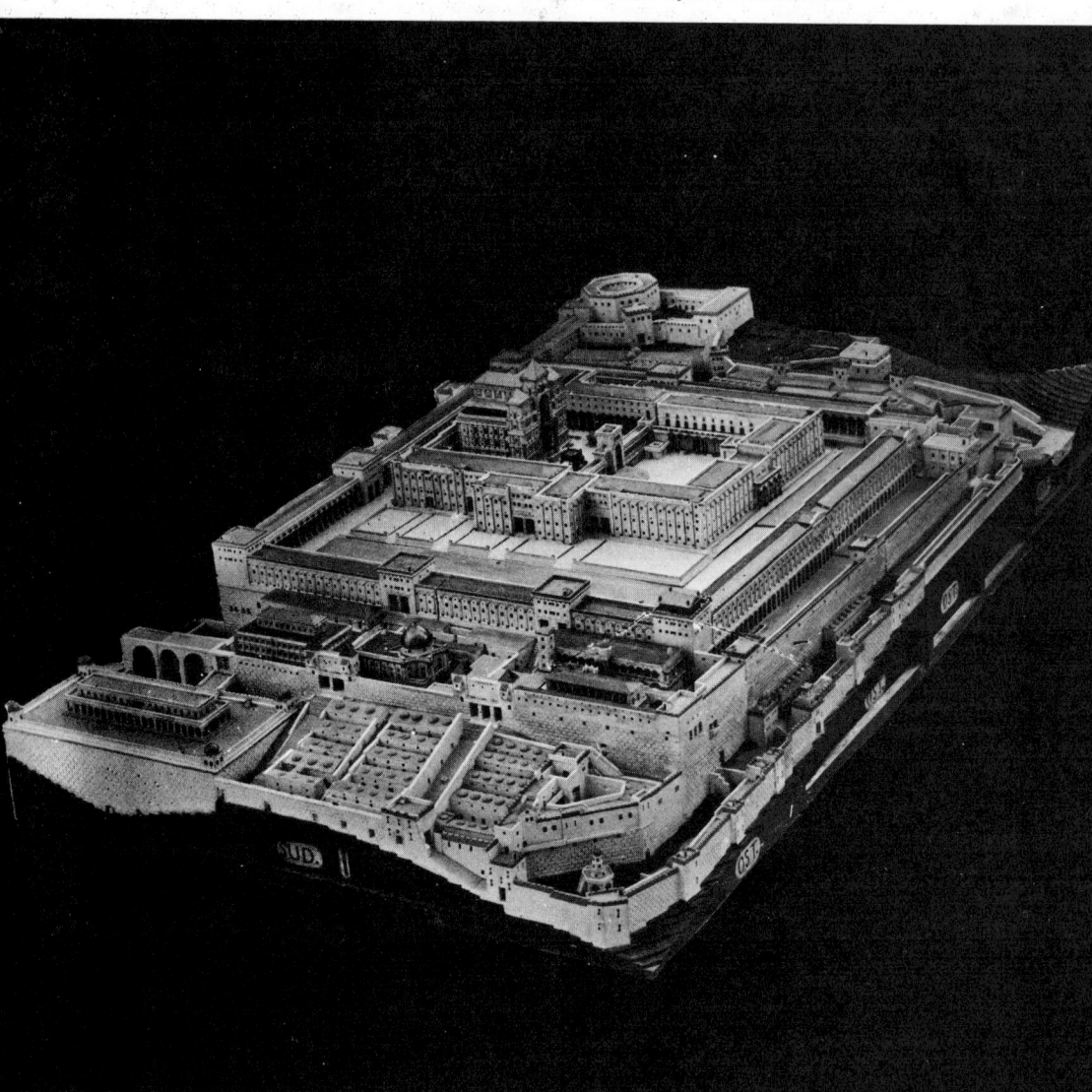

wall. The western portion, that encompassing the court of the priests, was the court of Israel. Only the men of Israel were allowed within it. The court of the women was the eastern and lower portion. It was reached from the court of the men through a great triple: the wall of the courts of Israel and the women, which has been already mentioned, and which was very thick, like the walls of a fortress (cp. War vi. 4, 1); a terrace, of which the top was level and 10 cubits broad; and at the foot of the terrace a wall

3 cubits in height, surmounted by pillars, on which were inscriptions forbidding all persons save those of the commonwealth of Israel, from entering the inclosure. "Let no gentile," so ran the Greek inscription, "enter inside of the barrier and the fence around the sanctuary. Anyone trespassing will bring death upon himself as a penalty." This triple wall of partition (Eph. ii. 14) was pierced by nine gates. These tower-like structures were sheathed with gold and silver. Four were on the northern, and four on the southern side. Of these, one on each side led into the court of the women and three into that of Israel. The ninth was the great eastern gate, the only one on that side, probably the gate Beautiful (Acts iii. 2, 10). The difference of level between the vestibule of the temple within the inclosure and the court of the gentiles without appears to have been about 15 cubits. From the vestibule to the court of the priests were 12 steps; from the court of Israel to that of the women 15; thence to the terrace 5, and thence to the court of the gentiles 14. This court of the gentiles occupied the remainder of the temple yard and completely surrounded the sacred inclosure. It was foursquare (War vi. 5, 4), and measured fully 6 stades, or three-quarters of a mile, in circuit (War v. 5, 2). It was paved throughout. At the northwestern corner stood the castle of Antonia (q. v.). Except perhaps at that point, it was bordered on all sides by magnificent, covered colonnades or cloisters (Antiq. xvii. 10, 2; cp. War vi. 3, 2). Those on the south were the finest. They contained 162 columns, arranged in four rows, forming three aisles. Each column was a monolith of white stone, 25 cubits high. The roof was ceiled with cedar, curiously carved and carefully polished. The other colonnades consisted of two rows of columns. That along the eastern side of the court was regarded as a remnant of the first temple, and was called Solomon's porch (John x. 23; Acts iii. 11; Antiq. xx. 9, 7; War v. 5, 1). It was this court which was so far abused that money changers were allowed to set up their tables and traders were permitted to expose cattle for sale there (Mat. xxi. 12; John ii. 14). Finally the sacred area was surrounded by massive walls. The western wall was pierced by four gates: the two more northerly ones led to the suburbs; the third crossed the Tyropœon valley at a point now marked by Wilson's arch; and the fourth still farther south, opened into the valley, and was reached by steps from the temple yard (Antiq. xv. 11, 5). In the southern wall were two gates, known by the name of Huldah. In the eastern wall was the Shushan gate. One is mentioned in the northern wall (War vi. 4, 1).

During the siege of Jerusalem by the Romans in A. D. 70, the Jews themselves, who were using the temple yard as a fortress, set fire to the outer cloisters; but the temple itself was fired by a Roman soldier contrary to the orders of Titus, and all that was combustible was destroyed (War vi. 3, 1; 4, 5; cp. 5, 1; 9, 2). Afterwards the conquerors threw down the walls (vii. 1, 1). On its site the emperor Hadrian dedicated a temple to Jupiter Capitolinus in A. D. 136 or earlier.

Stones in the western wall of the temple, known as the wailing wall.

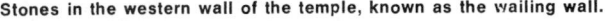

Greek inscription in the temple forbidding Gentiles to enter the inner court under penalty of death. The inscription dates from about A.D. 30

In A. D. 363 the emperor Julian, in order to defeat the prophecy of Christ (Mat. xxiv. 1, 2), undertook to rebuild the temple; but his plans were frustrated by flames which burst from the foundation. The Dome of the Rock, generally called the Mosque of Omar, now occupies the place where the old temples stood. Warren between February, 1867, and April, 1870, sunk shafts in the rubbish, in some places 100 and in one place 125 feet deep, which now covers portions of mount Moriah. The corner stones of the foundations, which still remain, are 14 to 15 feet long, and from 3½ to 4½ feet high. Some of those at the southeast angle have on them Phœnician characters, coming down at least from Herod's, and perhaps from Solomon's time. The walls surrounding the temple area were found to have been 1000 feet long, and the platform on which the holy place stood to have been supported by a buttress 200 feet high from the valley beneath. Finally, one of the inscriptions has been recovered which forbade any foreigner to enter the second court.

Ten Com-mand'ments.

The fundamental law of the Hebrew state; see THEOCRACY. The Hebrews called them the ten words (R. V. margin of Ex. xxxiv. 28; Deut. iv. 13; x. 4). They were spoken by God at Sinai, and written by him on two tables of stone (Ex. xxxi. 18). The engraving was on both front and back surfaces (xxxii. 15). The laws appear in two forms: the original form, contained in Ex. xx., and

the free citation of the words by Moses in Deut. v. 6-21. The principal difference is that the law of the Sabbath is enforced, in the original law, by reference to God's resting on the seventh day from the work of creation; whereas when Moses cites the law in his public address, he omits this fundamental basis of the command and urges the deliverance from Egypt as the reason why Israel should remember the day. Another difference, and one upon which undue stress has been laid, is that when Moses repeats the tenth commandment, he uses the word covet in one clause only and employs desire instead of covet in reference to a neighbor's house, field, etc. (R. V.). These differences are not contradictions, and they are fully explained by the character of Deuteronomy. See DEUTERONOMY, SABBATH.

The ten commandments are not individually numbered in the Bible. Later Jews regarded the words " I am the Lord thy God, which have brought thee out of the land of Egypt, out of the house of bondage" (Ex. xx. 2) as the first commandment. These words, however, are not in the form of a command. They constitute the preface to the ten laws which follow. Omitting the preface, there are two methods of enumeration: 1. According to the received teaching of the Roman Catholic and Lutheran churches, based on Augustine, the first table contains three commandments and the second table

Bedouin tent encampment near the Dead Sea.

seven. Augustine adopted this classification because it exhibits the symbolical numbers three, seven, ten and represents a real difference in the nature of the commands, the first three being duties toward God and the last seven duties toward man. The first division included the command to remember the Sabbath; and to make out three commands in this table, Augustine joined into one the commands to have no other gods and to make no graven image; and to secure seven in the second table he divided the command against covetousness into two laws. He followed the text of Deuteronomy, and made the command not to covet a neighbor's wife the ninth commandment, and that against desiring a neighbor's property the tenth. The Roman Catholic church follows the text of Exodus, and makes the command not to covet a neighbor's house the ninth, and that against coveting a neighbor's wife, manservant, etc., the tenth. The great objections to this method of enumeration are that it makes no distinction between polytheism and idolatry, and introduces an arbitrary distinction regarding kinds of covetousness. 2. The division which numbers the command against polytheism as the first, that against idolatry as the second, and that against covetousness as the tenth. This division is the oldest that is known. It was recognized by Josephus (Antiq. iii. 5, 5), by Philo (de Dec. i.), and by Origen; and it was adopted by the Reformed churches at the Reformation. But there are two methods of distributing the ten between the two tables: (1) They are ordinarily grouped as four relating to man's duty toward God and six to his duty to his fellows. This division is simple enough, and it is ethically correct; but it lacks symmetry. (2) Five are as-

signed to each table (Antiq. iii. 5, 8). This arrangement preserves the grouping of laws into decads, subdivided into pentads, which characterizes much of the legislation. And from the Jewish point of view, doubtless, the division is ethically correct; for the first table includes duties of piety, which imply no corresponding rights, and the second table embraces duties of justice, which involve rights. The duty of honoring parents to the extent of maintaining them if need be, was regarded as absolute and unconditional (Mark vii. 10–13). It was a pious duty, a religious duty, and properly belonged to the first table. Paul is sometimes cited as lending countenance to this division; for when summing up the duties which are comprehended in the command to love one's neighbor as one's self, he enumerates the last commandments, and makes no mention of honoring parents (Rom. xiii. 9). But Paul's enumeration is not intended to be complete. He omits the ninth commandment. Jesus placed the fifth commandment in the same group with the last five (Mark x. 19).

Tent.
1. A movable habitation; such as is used by nomads, shepherds, and soldiers (Gen. iv. 20; xxv. 27; Judg. viii. 11). The tent was frequently made of black cloth woven from goats' hair (Song i. 5), fastened with cords and stakes (Ex. xxxv. 18; Is. liv. 2). There were both round and tapering tents; and flat, oblong tents.
2. A habitation generally: a part of the dwellings being put for all, or one kind for another, according to circumstances (Gen. ix. 27; 1 Kin. viii. 66; 2 Kin. xiii. 5; Job viii. 22, R. V.; Ps. lxxxiv. 10; Jer. xxx. 18;

Lam. ii. 4, R. V.; Zech. xii. 7; Mal. ii. 12, R. V.).

Tent of the Con-gre-ga'tion. See next article.

Tent of Meet'ing, in A. V. **Tent** or **Tabernacle of the Congregation** [tent where Jehovah meets his people].

1. A provisional tent where Jehovah met with his people (Ex. xxxiii. 7–11; xxxiv. 34, 35). After the golden calf was made, Jehovah refused to acknowledge Israel any longer as his people and to dwell in their midst. He was estranged and distant. Because of this fact and to symbolize it, Moses used to pitch the tent outside the camp (xxxiii. 7, R. V.), probably until God again promised to go in the midst of Israel (xxxiv. 9). What tent this was is uncertain. But a tent unquestionably formed the headquarters of the camp. It was the place of judicial proceedings, where Moses sat to judge the people (Ex. xviii. 13). And it was the high tribunal after the administration of justice had been organized (21–26). Naturally it was for the time being the depository of the book of the covenant (xx.–xxiii.), which was at once a sacred volume of the statutes of God (xviii 16) and the book containing the civil laws for the government of Israel. It was probably this tent (the Greek translators read "his tent") which Moses now pitched without the camp. He called it the tent of meeting (1) because it was the tribunal of justice, whither everyone went that sought the Lord (xxxiii. 7); for the matter in dispute or doubt was laid before God or, to use their phrase, the party sought Jehovah's face (2 Sam. xxi. 1, R. V.), inquired of God (Ex. xviii. 15), brought the cause to God (19; Num. xxvii. 5), came unto God or came before him (Ex. xxi. 6; xxii. 9, R. V.). stood before Jehovah (Deut. xix. 17); and (2) because it was a place of revelation: there Jehovah met his people in their representative, when the pillar of cloud descended to the door of the tent (Ex. xxxiii. 9). It may have borne its appropriate name from the first; if not, Moses borrowed the name from the instructions which he received regarding the permanent tabernacle, since it represented the same truth (xxvii. 21). An altar may have stood near it (xviii. 12), but the tent was not a national sanctuary, did not contain an ark or paraphernalia for worship, did not possess a priesthood. This tent was cared for by Joshua (xxxiii. 11, E); the tabernacle, by Aaron (Deut. x. 6, E). The cloud descended upon this tent when Moses entered it to inquire of God; but the cloud abode on the permanent tabernacle and the glory of the Lord filled it, and Moses could not enter it (Ex. xl. 34, 35, 38).

2. The tabernacle (q. v.).

Tent of the Tes'ti-mo-ny (Num. ix. 15). See TABERNACLE.

Te'phon, in A. V. **Taphon.**

A town of Judæa fortified by Bacchides (1 Mac. ix. 50). Tephon is perhaps a modification of Tappuah, a name which was borne by several towns.

Te'rah, in A. V. twice **Tarah,** (Num. xxxiii. 27, 28) once **Thara** (Luke iii. 34) [probably, wild goat].

1. The son of Nahor, and the father of Abraham, another Nahor, and Haran. He was a resident at Ur of the Chaldees during the greater part of his life; serving other divinities than Jehovah (Josh. xxiv. 2), probably among the rest the moon-god, who had a celebrated temple at Ur. With Abraham and Lot, he removed to Haran, where he died, at the age of 205 (Gen. xi. 25–32).

2. An encampment of the Israelites in the wilderness (Num. xxxiii. 27, 28).

Ter'a-phim.

Images, but not of a particular deity, which were used in the household and by private individuals, and which varied in size from such as were small enough to be easily carried in hasty flight and concealed in the furniture of a camel (Gen. xxxi. 19, 30, 34, R. V.) to one apparently large enough to represent a man (1 Sam. xix. 13, R. V.). They were probably regarded as bringers of good luck. They were consulted with respect to the advisability of proposed actions (Ezek. xxi. 21; Zech. x. 2, both R. V.). The word, like the usual word for God, is plural in form, but may be singular in signification (1 Sam. xix. 13). Teraphim were employed in Babylonia (Ezek. xxi. 21). Laban used them in Haran, and his daughter Rachel stole them and carried them with her to Canaan (Gen. xxxi. 19, 34). This was done without Jacob's knowledge (32). When he reached Shechem, he demanded the surrender of all the strange gods which members of his company had brought with them, and he removed them from his people (xxxv. 2–4). In the days of the judges Micah of mount Ephraim had a private sanctuary with priest, ephod, and teraphim (Judg. xvii. 5), and eventually a molten image and a graven image (4; xviii. 14). Through them probably the Lord was consulted (5, 6). All these idols the band of Danites carried off for their own use (17–20). Samuel the prophet classed teraphim with witchcraft and rebellion (1 Sam. xv. 23, R. V.); nevertheless, there was one in David's house, doubtless belonging to his wife (xix. 13, R. V.). Teraphim figured largely in the corrupt religion of the northern Israelites (Hos. iii. 4). The teraphim were condemned with other idols as abominations, and were destroyed by Josiah in his work of reformation (2 Kin. xxiii. 24, R. V.); but they still found favor with a part of the people after the exile (Zech. x. 2).

Ter'e-binth.

The rendering of the Hebrew 'Elah, a robust tree, on the R. V. margin with oak in the text. Twice, when it is associated with another word, which is rendered oak, it appears in the text of the R. V. (Is. vi. 13; Hos. iv. 13). *'Elah* is probably the terebinth. The terebinth or turpentine tree (*Pistacia terebinthus*) is a small tree with pinnate leaves, inconspicuous flowers, with the sexes separated, and little roundish dark-purple fruit. It is a native of southern Europe, northern Africa, and western Asia, including Palestine. The turpentine is obtained by making incisions in the trunk. It merges into *Pistacia palæstina*, which is also found in Palestine, and is but a variety of the species.

Te′resh [perhaps Persian, austere].

A chamberlain who kept a door in the palace of king Ahasuerus, and plotted the murder of his master and king, a crime for which he and an accomplice were executed (Esth. ii. 21–23; vi. 2).

Ter′ti-us [third].

Paul's amanuensis, who wrote for him the Epistle to the Romans (Rom. xvi. 22).

Ter-tul′lus [diminutive of Tertius].

A Roman advocate, employed by the Jewish authorities to prosecute Paul before the tribunal of Felix, the Roman procurator (Acts xxiv. 1–8). His rhetorical address is thoroughly in the style affected by Roman advocates of the time.

Tes′ta-ment.

The rendering of the Greek *Diathēkē*, a will, a covenant. A third meaning has no bearing on the present subject. In Heb. ix. 16, 17 *diathēkē* is clearly a will. But in viii. 6–10, 13 and ix. 1, 4 the meaning is evidently covenant, and the term is so translated in the text. The Old Covenant and the New Covenant would be more accurate designations of the two parts of the Bible than the Old Testament and the New Testament. See HEIR, NEW TESTAMENT, OLD TESTAMENT.

Teth.

The ninth letter of the Hebrew alphabet. Greek theta comes from the same source; but the Greek versions represent it in Hebrew names by tau, reserving theta for the aspirated Hebrew tau. In the English versions teth is represented by t. It stands at the beginning of the ninth section of Ps. cxix. in several versions, in which section each verse begins with that letter.

Te′trarch.

One who rules over the fourth part of a kingdom or province. Philip of Macedon divided Thessaly into four districts called tetrarchies. Eventually the word was used loosely for a petty subject prince, even though the land was not divided among four such rulers. The Romans adopted the term, and used it as a convenient title for a prince to whom they granted a small territory only, and whom they were unwilling to dignify with the authority and rank of a king. The N. T. names three of these pretty dignitaries: Herod, tetrarch of Galilee, Philip, tetrarch of Ituræa and Trachonitis, and Lysanias, tetrarch of Abilene (Luke iii. 1). In the case of the tetrarchs Herod Antipas and Philip the title was appropriate; even in its original sense, for Augustus gave one-half of the kingdom of Herod the Great to Archelaus, with the title of ethnarch, and divided the remainder into two tetrarchies, which he gave to them (Antiq. xvii. 11, 4; War ii. 6, 3). A tetrarch was sometimes in courtesy called a king (Mat. xiv. 1 with 9; see also Mark vi. 14).

Thad-dæ′us. See JUDAS 8.

Tha′hash. See TAHASH.

Tha′mah. See TEMAH.

Tha′mar. See TAMAR.

Tham′na-tha. See TIMNAH.

Thank Of′fer-ing. See OFFERINGS.

Tha′ra. See TERAH.

Thar′shish. See TARSHISH.

The′a-ter.

A place where dramatic performances are given. The theater, with its auditorium, orchestra, and stage, and capable of seating immense throngs (see EPHESUS), was admirably adapted for large public meetings and the transaction of public business, and in Greek cities was often put to that use (Acts xix. 29, 31; Antiq. xix. 8, 2).

Thebes. See NO.

The′bez [perhaps, brightness or splendor].

A town near Shechem, having in it a strong tower, in besieging which Abimelech was killed (Judg. ix. 50–55; 2 Sam. xi. 21). It continues to exist in the large village of Tûbâs, 9½ miles northeast of Shechem, on the road to Beth-shean.

The-co′e. See TEKOA.

The-la′sar. See TELASSAR.

The-oc′ra-cy.

Josephus coined the word theocracy to describe the government instituted at Sinai. "Our legislator . . . ordered our government to be what I may call by a strained expression a theocracy, attributing the power and the authority to God" (con. Apion. ii. 17). Jehovah was the head of the nation, dwelling in its midst between the cherubim (Ex. xxv. 22). In him all the powers of the state, legislative, executive, judicial, were united. As legislator, he announced the fundamental law of the state in the hearing of the congregation. After that immediate presentation of himself to the nation, he exercised his governmental offices for the most part through men whom he raised up. Like all potentates, he delegated the judicial function for the most part to judges; only the most difficult matters were referred to Jehovah (Ex. xviii. 19); see URIM AND THUMMIM. His legislative function he exercised through Moses and through prophets (Deut. xviii. 15–19). Legislation was intermittent; the given body of laws was a sufficient rule, and seldom required modification or enlargement. The executive function was likewise exercised for many years intermittently through leaders, called judges, who were raised up from time to time, and who, accredited by the great deeds which were wrought by their hands, secured public confidence and became the acknowledged head in state affairs.

The theocratic government was proposed by God at Sinai on condition of obedience (Ex. xix. 4–9). The terms were accepted by the elders of the people (7, 8). The ten commandments, which formed the basis of the covenant, were proclaimed by Jehovah himself in such a manner that all the people could hear (xx. 1, 19, 22; Deut. iv. 12, 33, 36; v. 4, 22), in order that they might believe (Ex. xix. 9). At the people's request, the remaining laws, which are a practical application and interpretation of the ten commandments, were not spoken directly to them, but through Moses (xx. 18–21). Then the covenant was ratified. Moses wrote all the words of the Lord, erected an altar and twelve pillars, ordered a sacrifice, and sprinkled the altar with half the blood. He read the book of the covenant in the audience of the people, and, on their formal acceptance of it, sprinkled the remaining portion of the blood upon the people, saying: "Behold the blood of the covenant, which the Lord hath made with you concerning all these words." Finally the covenant meal of the contracting parties was eaten (xxiv. 3–11). Thus the theocracy was established. This book of the covenant contains the constitution and earliest laws of Israel. The ten commandments formed the fundamental law of the state. In modern mode of thought and expression, they would be called the constitution; in Hebrew conception and as a matter of fact, they were a covenant between God and the nation. There was a treaty, not between several communities, but between the community and God. Being fundamental law, they were engraven on stone, and deposited in the ark; they were known as the covenant (Deut. iv. 13; ix. 9, 11; 1 Kin. viii. 9–21; see also Num. x. 33; Judg. xx. 27; 1 Sam. iv. 3); or the testimony (Ex. xxxi. 18; xxxii. 15, etc.). The laws which follow the ten commandments are by-laws or statutes. They are constitutional, involving no principle contrary to the organic law of the state; they are expository, being the application of the doctrines of the constitution to the affairs of daily life; they are temporary, liable to abrogation and amendment and numerical increase to meet the new conditions and peculiar needs of each age. They are presented in the form of a code; they are not a loose aggregation of statutes, but are disposed in orderly arrangement, mostly in groups of ten or half of ten, and are usually

introduced by the word if: 1. Laws relating to the form of worship (xx. 23–26). 2. Laws to protect the rights of man. (a) To protect liberty (xxi. 2–11). (b) Concerning injury of person (12–36). (c) Concerning property rights (xxii. 1–17). 3. Laws to govern personal conduct (18–xxiii. 9). 4. Laws concerning sacred seasons and sacrifice (10–19). 5. The promise annexed (20–33). Regarding the antiquity, character, and codification of these laws, see AMRAPHEL and MOSES; and for the process of annulment and enactment during the ensuing forty years, see ZELOPHEHAD and DEUTERONOMY.

At the institution of the theocratic government at Sinai, the idea before the people was simply that God was ruler and Moses his accredited representative through whom he exercised the legislative, judicial, and executive offices. Moses already had subordinate judges to assist him (Ex. xviii. 21–26); and at the end of the wilderness period, promise was made of future legislation, that is, the continued revelation of the will of God (Deut. xviii. 15–19). The expectation was also entertained by Moses that God would appoint leaders to succeed him, and that eventually, on account of the people's lack of faith, a king would be needed as earthly, visible representative of the executive power when the people should be settled in Palestine. Accordingly a general law of the king was framed (xvii. 14–20).

The stability of the state under theocratic form of government depended in the first instance and ultimately on the faithfulness of God to his election and his promises; but the success of the theocracy at any given period was conditioned by the attitude of the people toward God and toward the provisions of the covenant. Their obedience to God and reliance on him were requisite. The theocracy was based on the conception of Israel as a community, and it is well to note the weakness of the bond which at the first bound Israel into a community. The children of Israel were divided into twelve tribes; they were bound together by common blood and common language, by common misfortune and common need. They were held together in pursuit of a great end by the enthusiasm and expectation which one man had awakened, by the hope of freedom and a country, by the promise and evidence of God's protection. They were kept together by providence. All these unifying elements save the last were weak. They were bonds that might easily be, and constantly were, broken. This lack of communal strength was an obstacle to the theocracy, which even the establishment of the monarchy did not rectify.

The-oph′a-ny.
A manifestation of God to man by actual appearance. It was not an immediate revelation of God the Father (John i. 18; 1

Tim. vi. 16) ; but a manifestation of Jehovah in the person of the angel of the Lord (Gen. xvi. 7), the angel of the presence or the Lord's presence (Ex. xxxii. 34; xxxiii. 14), the angel of the covenant (Mal. iii. 1), or Christ. A common classification is : 1. The O. T. theophany, an epiphany of the future Christ. 2. The incarnation of Christ, as the revelation of God in the flesh. 3. The second coming of Christ.

The O. T. theophanies were transient manifestations and permanent localization. They were temporary manifestations to the patriarchs, and became abiding in the shekinah. The theophanies which were granted to the patriarchs may have been unsubstantial manifestations, incorporeal and merely the appearance of the human form. Some interpreters, like Tertullian, believe that occasionally at least there was actual flesh, not putative flesh ; real and solid human substance ; just as Christ, who was God manifested in the flesh, had flesh and blood both before and after his resurrection, and could be seen and handled (Luke xxiv. 30–43 ; John xx. 27). If the angel of the Lord assumed an actual body, he did so miraculously, as Christ made the water wine ; and it disappeared miraculously, as Christ who possessed a human body of flesh and blood vanished from men's sight. In the O. T. theophany the angel of the Lord ate actual food (Gen. xviii. 1–8). Does this prove that the angel had assumed an actual body ? 1. Josephus interprets the eating as mere appearance (Antiq. i. 11, 2) ; so also Philo (Op. ii. 18) and the writer of Tobit (Tob. xii. 19). 2. Justin Martyr speaks of the angel as consuming food "as fire consumes" (Dial. c. Tryph. xxxiv.). The angel of the Lord who appeared to Manoah, touched the food, and it was burnt. "The thirsty earth absorbs water in one manner, the hot ray of the sun in another" (Augustine).

The transient manifestations gradually gave place to the permanent localization. The shekinah was the visible majesty of the divine presence, especially when dwelling between the cherubim in the tabernacle and temple in the midst of God's people Israel. It first appeared at the exodus. The Lord went before the Israelites in a pillar of cloud by day, and by night in a pillar of fire to give them light (Ex. xiii. 21, 22). A thick cloud rested upon mount Sinai, and the mountain was altogether on smoke, because the Lord descended upon mount Sinai in fire (xix. 16, 18). Later the glory of the Lord abode on mount Sinai, and the cloud covered it six days ; and the seventh day he called unto Moses out of the midst of the cloud, and the appearance of the glory of the Lord was like devouring fire on the top of the mount in the eyes of the children of Israel (xxiv. 16, 17). When Moses entered the first tent of meeting the cloud descended and hovered at the door, and the Lord talked with Moses face to face (Ex.

xxxiii. 11 ; cp. Deut. v. 4). When the tabernacle was erected, the Lord took possession of it. The cloud, dark by day and luminous by night, covered the tent, and the glory of the Lord filled it (Ex. xl. 34, 35 ; Num. ix. 15, 16). When Moses appeared before the Lord in the tabernacle, he heard the voice of one speaking unto him from off the mercy seat (Num. vii. 89 ; cp. Ex. xxv. 22 ; Lev. xvi. 2). Probably the glory was not seen constantly, but gleamed forth occasionally from the cloud which concealed it (Ex. xvi. 7, 10 ; Lev. ix. 6, 23 ; Num. xiv. 10 ; xvi. 19, 42 ; xx. 6). From frequent references, it seems that God continued to manifest his presence between the cherubim on the ark. At length, when the temple of Solomon was dedicated, the cloud filled the house of the Lord, so that the priests could not stand to minister by reason of the cloud ; for the glory of the Lord filled the house (1 Kin. viii. 10, 11).

The temporary manifestations had given place to the abiding presence in the tabernacle and Solomon's temple : and finally the Word became flesh and dwelt among men ; and men beheld his glory, glory as of the only begotten from the Father (John i. 14). The latter glory of the house was greater than the former (Hag. ii. 9, R. V.). The divine presence dwelt in Christ's body as in the temple.

The-oph'i-lus [loved by God].

The Christian to whom Luke addressed his Gospel (Luke i. 3) and The Acts of the Apostles (Acts i. 1). See ACTS OF THE APOSTLES, THE.

Thes-sa-lo'ni-ans, Epistles to the.

The First Epistle of Paul the Apostle to the Thessalonians is the earliest of Paul's epistles. It was written by the apostle in conjunction with Silvanus (Silas) and Timothy, to the church at Thessalonica. Paul had founded this church on his second missionary journey, and had been driven from Thessalonica to Berœa and from Berœa to Athens by the persecuting Jews ; see PAUL. The epistle contains allusions (1 Thes. ii.) to his life at Thessalonica. It also relates that, when at Athens, he had sent Timothy back to Thessalonica to encourage the Christians amid their persecutions (iii. 1–3) and that Timothy had recently brought him good news of their steadfastness. In Acts xviii. 5 we learn that Silas and Timothy rejoined the apostle at Corinth. Hence the epistle was written from that city, probably in the year A. D. 52. The allusions which the epistle contains to Paul's life in Thessalonica and to the distress felt by the Thessalonians over the death of their friends, as well as the elementary character of the instruction given, confirm this date. There appear to have been three special features in the condition of the Thessalonians which occasioned anxiety to the apostle, and led him to write this epistle : (1) a tendency to neglect their daily work, probably under the idea that the second advent would soon take place,—and with this was sometimes found a failure to preserve moral purity of life; (2) distress lest their Christian friends who died would fail to enjoy the glories of the kingdom which the returning Christ was to establish; (3) friction between the regular officers of the church and those who possessed miraculous endowments of the Spirit. Hence the analysis of the epistle: 1. A grateful statement of their Christian earnestness, their endurance of trial, and the influence they had already exerted over others (i.). 2. A reminder of the uprightness and industry with which he had lived among them, and of the enthusiasm with which they had received his preaching even in the face of persecution from the Jews (ii.). 3. A recital of the joy he had had in Timothy's good report of their condition (iii.). 4. Instruction on special points (iv. 1–v. 24): (a) Concerning purity in the relation of the sexes (iv. 3–8). (b) Concerning a life of mutual love and orderliness (9–12). (c) Concerning dead believers, declaring that at the advent they will rise first and be caught up with the living to meet the Lord in the air, and thus will not fail of their reward (13–18). (d) Concerning watchfulness and sobriety of life (v. 1–11). (e) Concerning respect for officers of the church, consideration for those in need, cultivation of spiritual gifts, and other duties of the Christian life (12–24). 5. Closing words (25–28).

The epistle strikingly illustrates the difficulties natural to a newly formed gentile church and the breadth and practical wisdom of the apostle's instructions.

The Second Epistle of Paul the Apostle to the Thessalonians evidently followed the first after but a short period. It too, therefore, is to be assigned to A. D. 52, and was written from Corinth. We learn from it that the difficulties of the Thessalonians had become more serious, but were still of the same general character as those dealt with in the first epistle. Like the first, this was written by Paul in conjunction with Silvanus (Silas) and Timothy; it deals largely with the second advent and misconceptions about it; and refers again to the tendency of some to disorderly living (2 Thes. iii. 6–12). If, however, the first epistle treated of the relation of the advent to believers, the second treats of its relation to the wicked (i. 5–10). Further the apostle warns them not to suppose that "the day of the Lord is now present" (ii. 2, R. V.), and that the visible advent would therefore soon come; for, before that happens, there must be the apostasy (predicted by Christ, cp. Mat. xxiv. 9–12; and referred to by Paul in Acts xx. 29, 30; Rom. xvi. 17–20; 2 Cor. xi. 13–15; 1 Tim. iv. 1) and the revelation of the man of lawlessness (2 Thes. ii. 3, 4, R. V.; Dan. vii. 25; xi. 36; 1 John ii. 18; see ANTICHRIST), whom the Lord will destroy at his coming.

He had, when with them, told them of these things (ii. 5).

The epistle may be divided as follows: 1. Thanksgiving for their fidelity amid persecution, and assurance that persecution should only make stronger their faith in the vindication of the saints and in the punishment of the ungodly which will take place at the second advent (i.). 2. Warning against supposing that "the day of the Lord is now present," and description of the apostasy and rise of the man of lawlessness, which must precede the coming of the Lord (ii. 1–12). 3. Expression of his confidence in their election and fidelity (13–17). 4. Concluding exhortations,—that they pray for him, that they avoid those who are disorderly, that they be industrious and faithful, that they all subject themselves to the authority which he as an apostle exercised, etc. (iii.). From ii. 2 it appears that a forged letter of Paul's had been circulated; hence in iii. 17 he appends his signature. We thus see also that from the beginning the same authority was attached in the church to the apostle's letters as to his oral teaching. The statements concerning the apostasy and the man of lawlessness have been variously interpreted. We think it most probable that the apostasy was contemplated by Paul as arising within the church; the man of lawlessness as the culmination of the apostasy in a personal antichrist; and he or that which hindereth (ii. 7) as either the civil power or else, and with much probability, the Holy Spirit.   G. T. P. (supplemented).

The First Epistle to the Thessalonians is included in the Old Latin version; is listed in the Muratorian fragment; is quoted by Irenæus, attributed by him to Paul, and designated the first letter to the Thessalonians; is quoted by Clement of Alexandria also and assigned to Paul; and is cited by Tertullian under the name of Thessalonians. Undoubted quotation from the Second Epistle is found earlier still, occurring in the writings of Polycarp about the beginning of the second century and possibly in the works of Justin Martyr.

Thes-sa-lo-ni'ca [conquest of Thessaly].

A city on the Thermaic Gulf, now called the gulf of Saloniki. The city was first called Therme, or Therma, hot spring; but Cassander, one of the successors of Alexander the Great, made it his residence and renamed it Thessalonica, after his wife Thessalonike, a daughter of the conqueror of the Chersonesus and sister of the great Alexander. Under the Romans it was the capital of the second district out of four into which they had divided Macedonia. It was a military and commercial station on the Via Egnatia; and was made a free city in 42 B. C. Its civil magistrates were called politarchs, rulers of the city (Acts xvii. 6, Greek text; inscription on arch in Thessalonica); see RULER.

Thessalonica.

The Jews had a synagogue in the city. Paul preached there and made converts, who became the nucleus of a Christian church (Acts xvii. 1–13; cp. Phil. iv. 16). To this church Paul sent two letters. Two of his co-workers, Aristarchus and Secundus, were men of Thessalonica (Acts xx. 4; xxvii. 2). Thessalonica was taken by the Saracens in A. D. 904. After various vicissitudes, it was captured by the Turkish sultan Amurath II. in 1430. It still exists as Saloniki, with a population of about 100,000 Mohammedans, Christians, and Jews.

Theu′das.

Gamaliel, in his speech before the sanhedrin, about A. D. 32, referred to Theudas, who gave himself out to be somebody, to whom a number of men, about 400, joined themselves, who was slain, and all, as many as obeyed him, were dispersed and came to nought, and after whom Judas of Galilee rose up in the days of the enrollment (Acts v. 36, 37). There can be no doubt that the Judas here spoken of was Judas the Gaulonite of Gamala, who, in the times of Quirinius, during the procuratorship of Coponius, raised an insurrection by opposing the enrollment (Antiq. xviii. 1, 1; War ii. 8, 1). Theudas accordingly arose sometime before A. D. 6. Now Josephus mentions a magician named Theudas, who, while Fadus was procurator of Judæa, A. D. 44–46, persuaded a great part of the people to follow him to the river Jordan, for he told them that he was a prophet, and that at his command the waters would divide and allow them a passage. But Fadus sent a troop of horse against him, who fell upon the people unexpectedly, slew many and took many others alive, and secured Theudas, cut off his head, and carried it to Jerusalem (Antiq. xx. 5, 1).

The question is, Do Luke and Josephus refer to the same person? Some answer that they do, and say that either Luke or Josephus errs. Josephus scarcely is mistaken, for he gives details. But Luke has fully established his credibility as a historian, and it is a rash thing to accuse him of an error. Accordingly other interpreters believe that it is quite probable that two persons by the name of Theudas, at a distance of forty years or more from each other, laid themselves open to the just vengeance or justifiable suspicions of the Romans and were punished. It is not at all clear that Theudas the magician was an insurgent of the same class as Theudas whom Gamaliel cites. The one was an impostor, a pretended prophet, who, on the faith of the people in his supernatural powers, drew crowds of followers after him. The other made some sort of claim to greatness, gained a following of 400 men, and came to naught. Who then was Theudas to whom Gamaliel refers? He was probably one of the insurrectionary chiefs, who led belligerent bands in the closing year of Herod the Great. That year was remarkably turbulent. Josephus mentions three disturbers by name, and makes general allusion to others. Theudas was either 1. One of these unnamed insurrectionists, whom Gamaliel cites to show that a bad cause and its leaders come to grief. Theudas was a common name, and within a period of half a century, might be borne by two persons of some prominence and somewhat similar in their career. Analogously Josephus gives an account of four men named Simon, who followed each other within forty years, and of three named Judas, within ten years, who were all instigators of rebellion. Or 2. One of the three insurgents who are named by Josephus. Two are advocated as identical with Theudas. (1) Simon (Antiq. xvii. 10, 6; War ii. 4, 2), a slave of Herod, who attempted to make himself king when Herod died. He was noted as a disturber of the peace at this time and his name would be apt to occur to Gamaliel; he was a man of lofty pretensions; he died a violent death; he appears to have had comparatively few adherents; he was a slave, and it was quite common among the Jews to assume a new name on changing occupation or mode of life. Gamaliel speaks of him as Theudas, the name he had borne longest, and by which he was best known in Jerusalem and to the members of the sanhedrin, while Josephus calls him by the name Simon, which he had adopted when appearing as king of the Jews and by which he was naturally known to the Roman government and people. (2) The man called Matthias by Josephus (Antiq. xvii. 6, 2; War i. 33, 2). Matthias is a Greek form of the Hebrew *Mattanyah*, gift of God, and is equivalent to the Greek name Theudas, which, it is urged, is the same as *Theodas*, shortened from *Theodōros*, gift of God. Matthias was an eloquent teacher, who with another teacher headed a band in the days of king Herod, and destroyed the golden eagle set up by the king over the great gate of the temple. He was caught and burnt alive with some of his companions, and many of the rest were put to death by other means.

Thief.

In a broad sense, anyone who appropriates what is not his own, as the petty pilferer (John xii. 6), the robber or highwayman (Luke x. 30, R. V. robber), the burglar (Mat. vi. 20). The highwayman was often a rebel against Roman rule and a fomenter of strife, like Barabbas (Mark xv. 7), who was compelled by the exigencies of the case, as much as by the lust of plunder, to flee from the soldiers and adopt the wild, robber life. Under the Mosaic law a thief caught had to make restitution of twice the amount he had taken, and if he were unable, could be sold into temporary servitude till he had earned the requisite amount. If a thief entered a house and, coming into contact with the owner in the dark, was killed, the homicide was not to be charged with blood-guiltiness; but if the sun had risen, the householder was held to be guilty if he killed the intruder (Ex. xxii. 1-4). That the thieves on the cross were something far beyond petty pilferers is plain from the Greek term applied to them, the severity of their punishment (War ii. 13, 2), and the fact that one of them acknowledged the justice of the death pen-

alty inflicted on him (Luke xxiii. 41); he must have been a robber at the least (Mat. xxvii. 38, R. V.), and quite possibly even a brigand. Both reviled Jesus on the cross (44), but subsequently one was touched with awe at the meekness and forgiving spirit of Jesus, and with the fear of God in his heart, the confession of the sinfulness of his past life, the acknowledgment that Jesus had done nothing amiss, and was the true King, and would reign in power after the death on the cross, turned to Jesus for acceptance after death (Luke xxiii. 39-43).

Thim′na-thah. See TIMNAH.

This′tle. See THORNS AND THISTLES.

Thom′as [Greek, from Hebrew *ta'om*, a twin].

One of the twelve apostles (Mat. x. 3). He was also called Didymus, a Greek name, meaning, like Thomas, a twin. When the disciples were astonished that Jesus intended going again to Judæa, where a little before the Jews had threatened to stone him (John xi. 7, 8), Thomas, in devotion to Jesus, determined to share the peril, and said to his fellow-disciples: "Let us also go, that we may die with him" (16). When Jesus, in anticipation of his departure, spoke of going to prepare a place for them, and added that they knew whither he was going and the way, Thomas said: "Lord, we know not whither thou goest; and how can we know the way?" To which the reply commenced with the well-known words: "I am the way, the truth, and the life" (xiv. 1-6). Thomas was not at the first meeting at which the privilege was granted of seeing the risen Lord, and when he heard that Jesus had been present he said: "Except I shall see in his hands the print of the nails, and put my finger into the print of the nails, and thrust my hand into his side, I will not believe" (xx. 24, 25). This incident has given rise to his designation, "doubting Thomas." But God turned the doubt of Thomas to the good of others. "He doubted that we might not doubt" (Augustine), and eight days later Jesus gave him the evidence he required, and elicited from him the adoring exclamation: "My Lord and my God!" (26-29). He was on the sea of Galilee with six other disciples when Jesus hailed them from the beach and told them where to cast the net (xxi. 1-8); and was with the rest of the apostles in the upper room at Jerusalem after the ascension (Acts i. 13). Tradition makes Thomas afterwards labor in Parthia and Persia, dying in the latter country. At a later period India was named as the place where he had preached and suffered martyrdom, and a place near Madras is called St. Thomas' mount.

Thorns and This′tles.

In most passages where these words occur the terms are generic rather than specific. Thorny weeds, bushes, and small trees of

Threshing floor.

various kinds are abundant in Palestine. Among them may be mentioned the thorny burnet (*Poterium spinosum*), which is burnt as fuel in lime kilns and ovens; the thorny caper (*Capparis spinosa*), seen everywhere hanging from rocks and walls; the Jamestown or jimson weed (*Datura stramonium*) by the roadside and in waste places; the artichoke (*Cynara syriaca*); and in the uplands the acanthus with its whitish flowers. The prickly pear (*Opuntia ficus indica*), a cactus with yellow flowers, is the characteristic hedge plant of modern Syria; but it was introduced from America and was unknown in ancient times. For hedge purposes there are also used the box thorn (*Lycium europæum*) and the bramble (*Rubus discolor*). Various hawthorns are found, *Cratægus azarolus*, *C. monogyna*, and east of the Jordan *C. orientalis*. Numerous thistles grow in the fields and waste places: such as *Cirsium acarna* with its leaves tipped with long, yellow spines; *Carthamus lanatus*, with yellow flowerets, *C. glaucus*, with purple, *C. cæruleus*, with blue, and *C. tinctorius*, with red flowerets, which are used as a red dye; *Carduus pycnocephalus* and *argentalus*; *Echinops viscosus*; the tall *Notobasis syriaca*, with pink flowers and powerful spines; cotton thistles (*Onopordon illyricum* and *cynarocephalum*); the milk thistle (*Silybum marianum*); sow thistles (*Sonchus oleraceus* and *glaucescens*); star thistles (*Centaurea calcitrapa* and *verutum*), the former with purple, the latter with yellow flowers. The cocklebur (*Xanthium*) is common, as is also teasel (*Dipsacus sylvestris*).

Several words rendered thorn or thistle appear to be used specifically: 1. Hebrew *dardar*, Greek *tribolos*, which grows in fields (Gen. iii. 18; Hos. x. 8; Mat. vii. 6; all in E. V. thistle; and Heb. vi. 8. in A. V. brier) is probably a species of *Tribulus*, perhaps *T. ter-* *restris*, one of the plants called caltrop. It is common in the fields and by the roadside. The fruit is composed of bony cells armed with prickles on the back. It does not belong to the *Compositæ*, as do the thistles. 2, 3, and 4, see BRAMBLE, BRIER 5, 6, NETTLE 2.

The crown of thorns, which was plaited by the Roman soldiers and placed on the head of Jesus to torture and insult him (Mat. xxvii. 29), is generally believed to have been made of the *Zizyphus spina Christi*, a species of jujube or lotus tree, with soft, round, pliant branches, and with leaves resembling the ivy with which emperors and generals were wont to be crowned. See BRAMBLE.

The thorn in the flesh was some bodily pain or infirmity, sent as a messenger of Satan to buffet the apostle Paul and keep him humble amid all his spiritual triumphs (2 Cor. xii. 7). Its nature is unknown.

Thou'sand.

A division of the tribe (Num. xxxi. 5; Josh. xxii. 14); consisting nominally of a thousand persons, but through birth and death ever varying and doubtless falling far short of the standard number; used for military and judicial purposes (Ex. xviii. 21, 25; and Num. xxxi. 14; 1 Sam. viii. 12; xxii. 7; 2 Sam. xviii. 1); and practically, perhaps exactly, equivalent to the subdivision of the tribe which was technically known as a father's house (Num. i. 2, 4 with 16, R. V.; Judg. vi. 15, cp. R. V. margin; 1 Sam. x. 19 with 21).

Three Tav'erns.

A small station on the Appian Way, about ten miles from Appii Forum, and 30 miles from Rome, where a number of Roman Christians met Paul on his way to Rome (Acts xxviii. 15).

Thresh'ing.

The process of separating grain from the straw. Small quantities of grain were beaten out with a stick or flail (Judg. vi. 11 ; Ruth ii. 7), and this was the customary method of hulling fitches and cummin (Is. xxviii. 27) ; but when much work was to be done, oxen and threshing floors were employed. The weather of Palestine permits the threshing floor to be under the open sky (Judg. vi. 37). It is generally common to the whole village, but may have a private owner (2 Sam. xxiv. 16). If possible, it is the surface of a flat rock on the top of a hill, exposed to any wind that blows. If such a natural floor is not available, an artificial floor is laid out by the roadside, and soon assumes a circular shape, about 50 feet in diameter, and becomes firm and hard under the trampling of the oxen. The sheaves are loosened and arranged in a circle on the floor ; or, if the straw is to be preserved whole, the ears are cut from the stock and cast on the floor. Oxen, which to this day are unmuzzled except by the niggardly (Deut. xxv. 4), are driven round and round to trample out the kernels ; or else are made to drag a sled or cart, weighted by a heavy stone or the driver, to facilitate the operation. The sled is made of two heavy planks, curved upward at the front and fastened side by side. Sharp pieces of stone are fixed in holes bored in the bottom. The cart, at least as used in Egypt, consists of a frame containing three wooden rollers set with sharp iron knives. If there is any wind, the threshed grain is tossed high in the air with a shovel or a fork (Is. xxx. 24 ; Mat. iii. 12; Iliad xiii. 588), when the chaff is blown away and the clean grain falls to the ground ; but if there is no wind, a large fan is plied by one man, while another tosses the grain with his shovel. The fan, however, is seldom used except to purge the floor of the refuse dust. Winnowing is done in the evening for the sake of the wind ; and it is customary for the owner of the grain to spend the night at the floor during the time of threshing to prevent stealing (Ruth iii. 2 seq.). The grain is finally passed through a sieve to cleanse it from dirt, after which it is ready for grinding (Amos ix. 9).

Thresh'olds of the Gates.

A building, in Hebrew '^asuppim, which was intended for the storage of temple goods (Neh. xii. 25, A. V.). See ASUPPIM.

Throne.

A chair of state, in Hebrew kisse', in Greek thronos, which was occupied by a person of authority, whether high priest, judge, military leader, governor, or king (Gen. xli. 40; 1 Sam. i. 9; 2 Sam. iii. 10 ; Neh. iii. 7; Ps. cxxii. 5 ; Jer. i. 15; Mat. xix. 28). Royal thrones were often portable, like those of Ahab and Jehoshaphat (1 Kin. xxii. 10), and the one used by Sennacherib at Lachish ; see

SENNACHERIB. Solomon's throne was an elevated seat reached by six steps. Its frame was probably made of cedar. It was inlaid with ivory, and elsewhere overlaid with gold ; the back of it was arched or rounded off ; it was furnished with arms and was provided with a footstool. A lion stood at each side, ornamenting the arms, and on each end of each of the six steps (1 Kin. x. 18–20 ; 2 Chron. ix. 17–19). It resembled the thrones of the Assyrian and Egyptian monarchs, but with its dais was the most magnificent royal chair of the time.

The king, arrayed in his royal robes, regularly sat on his throne when granting audiences, receiving homage, administering justice, or promulgating commands (1 Kin. ii. 19 ; vii. 7; xxii. 10; 2 Kin. xi. 19 ; Jon. iii. 6).

The throne symbolized supreme power and authority (Gen. xli. 40). It is constantly attributed to Jehovah.

Thum'mim. See URIM AND THUMMIM.

Thun'der.

The noise which follows a flash of lightning. It intensifies the awfulness of a terrific storm (Ex. ix. 23). Thunder is an unusual event during summer, which is the dry season in Palestine (Prov. xxvi. 1) ; and hence, when it occurred at that time of year after prayer for it, it was an evident answer and served as a sign (1 Sam. xii. 17). It was often called simply ḳol, voice, sound, noise ; and was poetically described as the voice of Jehovah (Job xxxvii. 2–5 ; xl. 9 ; Ps. xxix. 3–9), who sends and directs the storm (Job xxviii. 26). It accompanied manifestations of God's presence when he came in dread majesty (Ex. xix. 16 ; Rev. iv. 5) ; it was an indication of divine power at work in nature (Ps. xxix. 3–9) ; and as thunder is a precursor of the destructive storm, it symbolized divine vengeance (1 Sam. ii. 10 ; 2 Sam. xxii. 14, 15 ; Ps. lxxvii. 18).

Thy-a-ti'ra.

A city of Asia Minor, in Lydia, near the boundary of Mysia. It was on the road from Pergamos to Sardis. It had already come into existence and been known as Pelopia and Euhippia when Seleucus Nicator about 280 B. C. colonized it with Greeks, giving it the name of Thyatira. Its inhabitants were famed for their skill in dyeing purple ; and Lydia, the seller of purple at Philippi, came from Thyatira (Acts xvi. 14). It contained one of the seven churches in Asia (Rev. i. 11; ii. 18–24). Traces of its existence remain in fragments of columns built into the streets and edifices of its modern successor, Ak Hissar. Christians still live in the place.

Thy'ine Wood.

An article sold in the markets of the mystic Babylon (Rev. xviii. 12). It was the wood of Callitris quadrivalvis, a large tree of the cypress family. It is reddish-brown, hard, and fragrant; and was greatly prized by the

Romans for ornamental purposes. They ran it up to a high price. The resin which exudes from the tree is gum sandarac.

Tiberias.

Ti-be′ri-as.

A city on the sea of Galilee (John vi. 23), built by Herod the tetrarch, and named by him after the then reigning Roman emperor, Tiberius Cæsar (Antiq. xviii. 2, 3; War ii. 9, 1). Tiberias was fortified by Josephus during the Jewish war (Life 8; War ii. 20, 6). It opened its gates to Vespasian. A number of the inhabitants of Taricheæ, a neighboring town, whom he had assured of their lives, were afterwards slain in cold blood in the race course of Tiberias (War iii. 10, 1–10). After the destruction of Jerusalem and after the expulsion of the Jews from Judæa, consequent on the failure of Barcocheba's rebellion, Tiberias became the virtual metropolis of the Jewish nation, and coins of the city have been found, bearing the names of Tiberius, Claudius, Trajan, Adrian, and Antoninus Pius. The sanhedrin was transferred to Tiberias about the middle of the second century, and the city became the center of Jewish learning. A celebrated school was established in it, which produced the volume of Scripture tradition called the Mishna about A. D. 190 or 220, and its supplement, the Gemara, which was codified in the fourth century. The Masorah, or body of traditions which transmitted the details of the Hebrew text of the O. T. and preserved its pronunciation by means of vowel signs, originated in a great measure at Tiberias; see OLD TESTAMENT. The Jews regard Tiberias as one of their four sacred cities, Jerusalem, Hebron, and Safed being the others, in which prayer must be offered continually, or the world will instantly fall back into chaos. It still exists under the name of Tubarîya, on the western shore of the sea of Galilee, 11½ miles from the entrance and

The famed hot springs at Tiberias.

6 from the exit of the Jordan. At that place
the steep mountain ridge does not closely
approach the lake, but leaves on its margin
a narrow strip of undulating land, at the
northern part of which Tiberias stands. It
extends about half a mile along the shore,
and is defended on the land side by a wall,
towers, and a castle. The houses are mostly
of black basalt. On January 1, 1837, it suffered severely from an earthquake, but has
since in a large measure been rebuilt. The
Jewish quarter is near the lake.

The sea of Tiberias is more commonly
called the sea of Galilee (John vi. 1; xxi. 1).

Ti-be′ri-us Cæ′sar. See CÆSAR.

Tib′hath [slaughter].

A town of Aram-zobah (1 Chron. xviii. 8).
Site unknown. See BETAH and TEBAH.

Tib′ni.

A son of Ginath, and the unsuccessful
competitor for the throne of Israel with
Omri (1 Kin. xvi. 21, 22).

Ti′dal.

King of Goiim and one of Chedorlaomer's
confederates (Gen. xiv. 1, 9, R. V.). He was
Tudḫul, king of Gutium, northeast of Babylonia.

Tig-lath-pi-le′ser, in Chronicles **Tilgath-
pilneser** [Assyrian *Tukulti-apil-Eshara*, my
strength is the god Ninib].

A king of Assyria, who reigned from 745 to
727 B. C. Tiglath-pileser is but another name
for Pul, as appears from the fact that where
Ptolemy's list of Babylonian kings gives
Poros, and the so-called dynastic tablets of
the Babylonians give Pulu, the Babylonian
chronicle gives Tiglath-pileser. Probably Pul
was his original name, and when he secured
the throne he assumed the grander title of
Tiglath-pileser, which had already been made
famous by a great king of the past. There
is reason to believe that he owed his elevation to the throne to the disturbances in
Calah, which are recorded for the year 746 B. C.
He seated himself upon the Assyrian throne
on the thirteenth day of the second month
and in the seventh month was marching
against Babylonia. He first became known
to the Israelites as Pul. During the years
743–740 his military headquarters were at
Arpad in northern Syria, not far from the
site of the later Antioch; but he found opportunity to send or lead expeditions and
terrify the country within a radius of 100
miles or more. Among other places against
which he came at that time or a little later
was the land of Israel, but Menahem paid
him tribute and the Assyrian confirmed the
kingdom to Menahem and left the country
(2 Kin. xv. 19, 20); see PEKAH. Tiglath-
pileser records the names of kings who about
738 B. C. paid him tribute, and among others
the name of Menahem of Samaria. During
the next few years he was conducting war
first in the far east, and then in the country

north and northwest of Nineveh; but in
734 he was again in the west. The alliance
of Pekah and Rezin against Ahaz of Judah
impelled Ahaz, contrary to the exhortation
of the prophet Isaiah, to turn for help to a
human potentate. Tiglath-pileser was induced by large money (xvi. 7, 8), and by the
favorable opportunity afforded him of extending his authority, to side with Ahaz.
He marched against Philistia, capturing cities
on the Phœnician coast as he proceeded. He
apparently records the seizure of towns in
northern Israel; but whether he makes the
record or not, it was during his advance
south or as he returned north that he took
Ijon, Abel-beth-maacah, Janoah, Kedesh,
Hazor, Gilead, and Galilee, all the land of
Naphtali, and carried them captive to Assyria
(xv. 29). He captured Gaza. Thus he punished the Philistines, who had taken advantage of Judah's straits to pillage (2 Chron.
xxviii. 18). In the years 733 and 732 he
was at Damascus, according to the Assyrian
records. During the siege or immediately
after the capture of the city, he ravaged
sixteen districts of Damascus; leaving them,
as he says, like ruins after a flood-storm.
He slew Rezin king of Damascus. At this
time God stirred up the spirit of Pul king
of Assyria and (or rather, as it may equally
well be translated, even) the spirit of Tiglath-
pileser king of Assyria, and he carried them
away, even the Reubenites and the Gadites,
and the half tribe of Manasseh (1 Chron. v.
26). He reports his reception of tribute
from many kings, among others from the
kings of Ammon, Moab, and Edom, and
from Jehoahaz of Judah. This statement
agrees with the biblical record that king
Ahaz went to Damascus to meet Tiglath-
pileser (2 Kin. xvi. 10). In 730 B. C., according to biblical chronology, Hoshea revolted
against Pekah. The revolt was instigated
or assisted by Tiglath-pileser, who may have
been in Nineveh at the time, for he says:
" Pekah I slew and appointed Hoshea to rule
over them." After the fall of Damascus in
733 or 732 Tiglath-pileser returned to Nineveh. During the remainder of his life he
was much engaged in building operations;
but he found time for war, and among other
expeditions he conducted an army into Babylonia and made himself king of Babylon.
He died in the tenth month, Tebeth, 727
B. C., after having occupied the throne for
eighteen years and having raised the Assyrian empire to a power and glory unknown
to it under any of his predecessors.

Ti′gris. See HIDDEKEL.

Tik′vah [expectation].

1. The father of Shallum, the husband of
Huldah the prophetess (2 Kin. xxii. 14). In
2 Chron. xxxiv. 22 the name appears as
Tokhath, in A. V. Tikvath; but the Hebrew
form is probably a corruption of Tikvah (cp.
Lucian's Septuagint).

2. The father of a certain Jahaziah (Ezra x. 15).

Tik'vath. See preceding article.

Tile.
A slab or plate of baked clay. Tiles were the common writing material of Babylonia (Ezek. iv. 1). The characters were impressed on the surface while it was yet soft, and the clay was then baked to render the writing indelible. Tiles were used in many countries as roofing material (Luke v. 19), but not, or not commonly, in Palestine. Probably either Luke, accustomed to the tiled roofs of Greek houses, uses the expression "through 'the tiles" for through the roof, without reference to the material of the roof in question, or else in this particular house there was an opening in the roof to permit the inmates to ascend from the room to the coolness of the outer air, but which during the winter was closed with a frame and bricked over.

Til-gath-pil-ne'ser. See TIGLATH-PILE-SER.

Ti'lon.
A son of Shimon, whose registry was with the tribe of Judah (1 Chron. iv. 20).

Ti-mæ'us [highly prized].
Father of the blind beggar of Jericho (Mark x. 46).

Tim'brel or **Tab'ret.**
An humble kind of drum, which has developed into our modern tambourine. By the Hebrews it was called *toph,* an in-

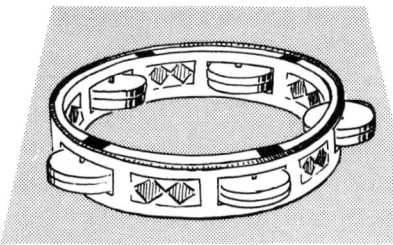

Timbrel.

strument that is beaten. It was much used in domestic festivities, was often played by women to accompany song and beat time for dances, and was employed alone or in orchestra in the worship of God (Gen. xxxi. 27; Ex. xv. 20; Judg. xi. 34; 1 Sam. x. 5; xviii. 6; 1 Chron. xiii. 8; Job xxi. 12; Ps. lxxxi. 2; Is. v. 12).

Tim'na, in A. V. twice **Timnah** (Gen. xxxvi. 40; 1 Chron. i. 51), and so once in R. V., oddly enough (Gen. xxxvi. 40) [restraint, inaccessible].

1. Daughter of Seir and sister of Lotan. She became a concubine of Eliphaz, Esau's eldest son, and the mother of Amalek (Gen. xxxvi. 12, 22; 1 Chron. i. 39). In interpreting these statements, it must be remembered that terms of relationship are used in describing tribes as well as individuals.

2. A duke of Edom (Gen. xxxvi. 40; 1 Chron. i. 51).

Tim'nah, in A. V. eight times **Timnath** (Gen. xxxviii. 12–14; Judg. xiv. 1–5), once **Thimnathah** (Josh. xix. 43), and once **Thamnatha** (1 Mac. ix. 50) [an assigned portion].

1. A town on the border line of the territory assigned to Judah, and not far from Beth-shemesh (Josh. xv. 10). It was subsequently given over to the tribe of Dan (xix. 43). It was occupied by the Philistines in the days of Samson (Judg. xiv. 2), and was captured by them in the reign of Ahaz (2 Chron. xxviii. 18). Its site is at Tibnah, about 3 miles west by south of Beth-shemesh, 15½ west by south of Jerusalem, and 16 east of Ashdod.

2. A town in the hill country of Judah (Josh. xv. 57), probably the place referred to in Gen. xxxviii. 12, 14; cp. 1. On the survey map it is placed at Tibna, 9 miles west by south of Bethlehem; but this site appears to be too remote from Maon, Carmel, and Ziph.

3. A town enumerated after Emmaus, Beth-horon, and Bethel, and before Pharathon (1 Mac. ix. 50). It was fortified by Bacchides. The data point to Thamna, chief city of a toparchy (War iii. 3, 5), which bordered on the toparchies of Gophna, Lydda, and Emmaus (ii. 20, 4), and lay between Antipatris and Lydda (iv. 8, 1). Its site is probably marked by the ruins Tibneh, 7½ miles west-northwest of Jufna (Gophna), on the old road from Antipatris by way of Gophna to Jerusalem. See TIMNATH-SERAH.

4. An improper spelling, found in both versions, of the name of Timna, daughter of Seir.

Tim'nath. See preceding article.

Tim-nath-he'res. See TIMNATH-SERAH.

Tim-nath-se'rah [superfluous or extra portion].
A village in the hill country of Ephraim, on the north side of the hill of Gaash. It was given to Joshua as an inheritance, and there he was buried (Josh. xix. 50; xxiv. 30). It is once written Timnath-heres, portion of the sun (Judg. ii. 9), but heres is probably serah accidentally written backwards. Conder locates it at Kefr Hâris, which might be an echo of Heres, and where Samaritan tradition locates the graves of Joshua and Caleb. It is rather 8½ miles south by west of this village, at Tibneh. See TIMNAH 3.

Tim'nite.
A native or inhabitant of Timnah (Judg. xv. 6).

Ti'mon [deeming worthy].
One of the seven men chosen to relieve the apostles from semisecular work in the primitive church (Acts vi. 5).

Ti-mo'the-us [worshiping God].
1. Leader of a large body of Ammonites,

with whom Judas Maccabæus fought several battles (1 Mac. v. 6, 40).

2. Paul's convert and fellow-worker. See TIMOTHY.

Tim'o-thy, in A. V. usually **Timotheus** [venerating or worshiping God].

The well-known companion and assistant of Paul. The terms which the apostle applies to him, "my beloved and faithful child in the Lord" (1 Cor. iv. 17, R. V.), "my true child in faith" (1 Tim. i. 2, R. V., etc.), seem to indicate not only the apostle's love for his youthful friend, but also that he had been the means of Timothy's conversion. At any rate it is clear (2 Tim. i. 5; iii. 11) that when on his first missionary journey Paul visited Lystra in Lycaonia Timothy's mother Eunice and grandmother Lois were led to Christ, and that Timothy was old enough to be instructed in the new faith which his mother had adopted. Though his mother was a Jewess, his father was a gentile (Acts xvi. 1). On the one hand, he had from a child been instructed in the O. T. (2 Tim. iii. 15); yet, on the other he had not been circumcised (Acts xvi. 3). But, whether converted through Paul, or afterwards through the instruction of his mother, Timothy soon became active in Christian work, so that when, a few years later, Paul on his second journey again visited Lystra he found the young man well reported of by the brethren both at Lystra and Iconium (xvi. 2). Already the voice of prophecy had indicated that Timothy was destined for special service (1 Tim. i. 18; iv. 14). Paul therefore determined to take him with him; and the young man was set apart to the work of an evangelist by the laying on of the hands both of Paul and of the presbytery (iv. 14; 2 Tim. i .6). In order also not to offend the Jews, Timothy was circumcised; the apostle thus indicating his wish, where no principle was involved, to conciliate those among whom in nearly every place he would have to begin work. Thereafter Timothy's fortunes were united with Paul's. He evidently accompanied the apostle through Galatia, then to Troas and Philippi, and then to Thessalonica and Berœa, for it is mentioned (Acts xvii. 14) that he and Silas remained in Berœa when Paul went on to Athens. Paul sent word for them to follow him to Athens speedily (15); but from 1 Thes. iii. 1, 2 it appears that he sent Timothy back to Thessalonica, and that Silas and Timothy did not rejoin him until he had reached Corinth (Acts xviii. 5; 1 Thes. iii. 6). Timothy then remained with Paul in Corinth (1 Thes. i. 1; 2 Thes. i. 1) and probably, though his name is not mentioned, accompanied the apostle on his return voyage. We next hear of him during Paul's ministry in Ephesus. Paul informs us in 1 Cor. iv. 17 that, before writing that epistle, he had sent Timothy to Corinth to correct abuses there. Yet for some reason, as 1 Cor. xvi. 10 inti-

mates, there was a possibility that Timothy might not reach Corinth, and in fact we do not know whether he did so or not. At any rate he seems to have returned to Ephesus, for shortly before Paul left that city Timothy and Erastus preceded him into Macedonia (Acts xix. 22), where Paul soon joined his young friend (2 Cor. i. 1). Together they went to Corinth (Rom. xvi. 21), and Timothy is mentioned as one of the company who escorted the apostle on his return from the third journey toward Jerusalem (Acts xx. 4). Whether Timothy went with the apostle to Jerusalem does not appear. No mention of him occurs during the imprisonment at Cæsarea or the voyage to Rome. But in the epistles written from Rome his name occurs (Phil. i. 1; ii. 19-22; Col. i. 1; Philem. 1). He had evidently followed the apostle to the capital, and was his devoted coworker. After the apostle's release, he seems to have more than ever intrusted important duties to Timothy. In 1 Tim. we find that he had been left in charge of the church at Ephesus. It was a post of responsibility and difficulty, especially for one who was still a young man (1 Tim. iv. 12). False teachers were to be combated, officials were to be appointed, church customs were to be organized or regulated. The position of Timothy appears to have been that of an apostolic deputy, and it is not surprising that Paul wrote to him a special epistle with regard to his task. To Timothy he also wrote his last epistle shortly before his death (2 Tim.). Almost alone, and with death impending, Paul desired ardently the presence of his "child" (iv. 9, 21), and to him he laid bare his whole heart. It is probable that Timothy reached Paul before the latter's death, but we do not know. The only further reference to him is Heb. xiii. 23. From it we learn that Timothy had suffered imprisonment, but had been set at liberty again. If that epistle was written by Paul, Timothy's imprisonment must have occurred during the period between Paul's release and his second arrest; see PAUL. If the epistle to the Hebrews was not by Paul, then we may believe that Timothy joined Paul and for a while shared his imprisonment. This, however, is mere conjecture. We know nothing certainly of Timothy's last years.

The First Epistle of Paul the Apostle to Timothy was written after the apostle's release from his first Roman imprisonment and resumption of missionary work (cp. above; also PAUL). Timothy had been left in charge of the church of Ephesus while Paul went into Macedonia (1 Tim. i. 3). Many suppose that the epistle was written from Macedonia, but that is by no means clear. It should probably be assigned to A. D. 64 or 65. It deals with the ecclesiatical difficulties which confronted Timothy, and gives him personal advice. It evinces the interest of the apostle in the practical working of the church and his personal interest in Timothy's own welfare and success. Its contents may be arranged as follows: 1. Instructions concerning the church (i.–iii.); including warnings against false teachers (i.), instructions concerning worship (ii.), instructions concerning church officers, closing with a brief statement of the dignity of the church and the fundamental truths on which it rests (iii.). 2. Advice for Timothy's own guidance (iv.–vi.), with respect to the false doctrines and practical errors which he had to meet (iv.), and with respect to his treatment of various classes in the church (v. 1–vi. 2), followed by concluding exhortations partly of a personal character and partly to reinforce the previous instructions (vi. 3–21).

The Second Epistle of Paul the Apostle to Timothy was written from Rome after the apostle had been arrested the second time, A. D. 67. It is the last product of his pen. He speaks of himself as a prisoner (2 Tim. i. 8, 16; ii. 9), charged with being an evildoer (ii. 9), and he expected soon to suffer martyrdom (iv. 6). Many of his friends had left him (i. 15; iv. 10, 12). Luke only, of his former friends, was with him (iv. 11), though other friends had gathered round him (21). He had already had one trial, at which he had not been condemned (16, 17), but he was still held on some other charge. In his loneliness and danger his heart turned to Timothy, and this letter was written partly to encourage Timothy in his work as an evangelist and partly to urge him to hasten to Rome and to perform some personal services for the apostle. It may be divided as follows: 1. After a brief introduction, expressive of his wish to see Timothy and his confidence in him (i. 1–5), he urges him to be courageous in spite of existing trials (6–12), and to be faithful to the truth he had received in spite of all opponents (13–18). 2. He charges Timothy to be strong; to secure the preservation of the truth; to be a good soldier; to bear in mind the imperishable foundation of fact and truth on which the gospel rests; to avoid false teaching; and to take heed to his own spiritual life (ii.). 3. He warns him that errors will increase, and bids him remember the example of steadfast endurance which Paul himself had shown him and the teaching of inspired Scripture in which he had been trained (iii.). 4. As his last direction, he bids him preach the word and make full proof of his ministry (iv. 1–5), solemnly adding that he, on the verge of death, rejoiced that he had been able to do the same (6–8). The epistle then closes with some personal directions (9–22).

The epistles to Timothy and Titus are called, from their contents, the Pastoral Epistles. Rationalistic critics refuse to believe that Paul wrote them, at least in their present form; but the external evidence that the church of the post-apostolic age received them as Pauline is abundant, and it is most natural that the closing years of the apostle's ministry should be occupied with the practical affairs of the churches. These epistles teach the same doctrines which are found in Paul's other writings, with only such an added emphasis on the practical aspects of Christian faith as the situation called for; and Paul would not be the large-minded man that we know he was if he had not dealt, as he does in these epistles, with the organization of the churches which he was so soon to leave.   G. T. P.

Tin.

A metal, in Hebrew *b⁽e⁾dil*, separated, alloy. It was obtained from its ore by smelting; and was sometimes refuse from silver ore (Ezek. xxii. 20). It was in use in Palestine and neighboring countries before the exodus (Num. xxxi. 22), in Egypt as early as the sixth dynasty at least. Its principal use was in making bronze, which is an alloy of copper and tin. The Tyrians got their supply from Tarshish (Ezek. xxvii. 12). Tin was obtained in Spain, but the most of it came from islands in the western ocean (Pliny, Hist. Nat. xxxiv. 47; Herod. iii. 115). There is little doubt that these islands were the isles of Scilly, off the Cornwall coast, and that the mines of Britain were the chief source of supply to the ancient world, and that Phœnician mariners made direct voyages from Gades in Spain to Cornwall for the metal (Strabo iii. 175). Later it was transported across France to the mouth of the Rhone by a thirty days' journey (Diodorus Siculus v. 21, 22). The same word signifies the base metal existing in combination with silver in the ore (Is. i. 25), and is supposed to denote the slag which separates from the lead when silver is being smelted from the ore.

Tiph'sah [a passage].

1. A town at the extreme limit of Solomon's dominions, in the direction of the Euphrates (1 Kin. iv. 24). It is generally identified with Thapsacus, a large city on the Euphrates, near the modern Rakka, by a ford. The ford was used by the armies of Cyrus the Younger and Alexander the Great.

2. A place on the inhabitants of which Menahem inflicted barbarous cruelties (2 Kin. xv. 16). It is mentioned in connection with Tirzah, from which it would seem not to have been far distant. Conder identifies it with the ruined village Ṭafsah, 6½ miles southwest of Shechem.

Ti'ras.

A land and its inhabitants, who were a Japhetic people (Gen. x. 2). Ancient opinion identified it with Thrace (Antiq. i. 6, 1), from slight similarity of sound. The river Turas, the modern Dneister, and the Turitai, who dwelt on its banks (Herod. iv. 51), have also been suggested. The conditions are best met by the Tursenoi, an ancient Pelasgic people who occupied islands and coast lands of the

Ægean Sea (Herod. i. 57, 94), probably the piratical Turusha who invaded Syria and Egypt in the 13th century B. C. *Tursēnos* is the Ionic and old Attic form of *Turrēnos*, Tyrrhenian.

Ti'rath-ites.

A family of scribes, Kenites from Tirah, dwelling at Jabez (1 Chron. ii. 55).

Tire.

The rendering of the Hebrew *Pe'er*, ornamental. It means an ornamental headdress (Ezek. xxiv. 17, 23). Aaron in his priestly capacity wore one of fine linen (Ex. xxxix. 28; in A. V. bonnet). Women used them (Is. iii. 20; in A. V. bonnet). The bridegroom decked himself with it (Is. lxi. 10; in A. V. ornaments, R. V. garland).

Tir'ha-kah. See PHARAOH.

Tir'ha-nah.

A son of Caleb, the brother of Jerahmeel, by Maacah, his concubine (1 Chron. ii. 48).

Tir'i-a.

A son of Jehallelel (1 Chron. iv. 16).

Tir-sha'tha.

The Persian title of the governor of Judah under the Persians. It is borne by Zerubbabel (Ezra ii. 63; Neh. vii. 65, 70), and Nehemiah (Neh. viii. 9; x. 1). In xii. 26 the latter ruler is called *peḥah* or governor, to which Tirshatha, therefore, must have been practically equivalent.

Tir'zah [pleasantness, delightfulness].

1. The youngest among the five daughters of Zelophehad (Num. xxvi. 33; xxvii. 1; xxxvi. 11; Josh. xvii. 3).

2. A town noted for beauty (Song vi. 4), which belonged originally to the Canaanites, but was captured by Joshua (Josh. xii. 24). Jeroboam I. took up his residence in Tirzah (1 Kin. xiv. 17), and it became the capital of the ten tribes (xv. 21, 33; xvi. 6, 8, 9, 15, 17) till Omri built Samaria (23, 24), after which it sank into a provincial but still important town (2 Kin. xv. 14, 16). Robinson, with much doubt, suggests as its site Ṭullûza, 6 miles east, very slightly south, of Samaria. Conder, with no hesitation, fixes it at Teîasîr, with ancient ruins, 13 miles east-northeast of Samaria, on a table-land where the valleys begin to dip suddenly toward the Jordan.

Tish'bite.

A member of the family, or native of the town, called Tishbeh or something similar (1 Kin. xvii. 1). A family of the name is unknown. Towns only claim attention. One is mentioned by Tobit (i. 2), "Thisbe on the right [south] of Kydios of Naphtali," *i. e.*, Kedesh of Naphtali (R. V.). Another is discerned by the Septuagint and Josephus in the text of 1 Kin. xvii. 1, lying east of the Jordan, in Gilead. The construct plural before Gilead in the Hebrew text, which is rendered sojourners in the E. V., the makers of the Septuagint regarded as a local name, and transferred it to their pages as a genitive

plural, Thesbon or Thessebon, of Thesbeh. Josephus prefixed the word city and added a singular termination to the name (Antiq. viii. 13, 2, Niese's text).

Tithe.

A tenth part of one's income consecrated to God. The separation of a certain proportion of the products of one's industry or of the spoils of war as tribute to their gods was practiced by various nations of antiquity. The Lydians offered a tithe of their booty (Herod. i. 89). The Phœnicians and Carthaginians sent a tithe annually to the Tyrian Hercules. These tithes might be regular or occasional, voluntary or prescribed by law. The Egyptians were required to give a fifth part of their crops to Pharaoh (Gen. xlvii. 24). Before the days of Joseph and Pharaoh, Abraham, returning with spoil from his victory over the confederate kings, gave to Melchizedek, priest-king of Salem, a tenth part of all (xiv. 20). Jacob said that if God conferred on him certain specified benefits, he would surely give the tenth of it unto God (xxviii. 22). Under the Mosaic law the fruits of the ground and cattle were subject to tithing (Lev. xxvii. 30, 32). The tithe of grain and fruit need not be paid in kind. The owner might redeem it by purchasing it at one-fifth more than its market value (31). But the tithe of the herd and flock might not be redeemed. This tithe was separated by causing the cattle to pass under the rod, and every tenth animal was taken, whether it was defective or without blemish. The choice had been committed to God, and the beast might not be exchanged (32, 33). Grain was threshed before it was tithed, and the fruit of vineyard and oliveyard was converted into wine and oil before the tenth was taken (Num. xviii. 27). All the tithe of Israel, which they offered as a heave offering, was given unto the Levites (21, 24). It was given to them as an inheritance in return for the service which they rendered at the sanctuary (21), and as compensation for their lack of landed possessions. They paid a tithe of it to the priest (26, 27), and freely ate the rest anywhere (31). On the eve of entering Canaan, where many of the Israelites would obtain homes far from the sanctuary, it was necessary to insist that the people should bring all prescribed sacrifices and freewill offerings, and all tithes, to the sanctuary (Deut. xii. 5, 6, 11). They might not eat at home the tithe of their grain, wine, or oil, nor any offering, but before the Lord (17, 18). They must tithe all the increase of the field, and eat before the Lord the tithe of grain, wine, and oil, and the firstlings of flock and herd; but if the distance to the sanctuary was great, they might convert the offering into money, carry that to the sanctuary, and there buy what they chose for the eucharistic meal (xiv. 23-27). Every third year each man's tithe should be laid up in his town.

and the Levite, the stranger, the widow, and the fatherless should go to the store and eat (28, 29). After tithing the tithe in this third year, which was distinguished as the year of tithing, and reminded the people that the tithe was to be kept in the town, it was put at the disposal of those for whom it was intended (xxvi. 12). There were two third-year tithings between Sabbatic years, when there was no tithe.

Inconsistencies between these laws do not exist, although interpreters often force them into contradiction. The Israelites took the tithe to the sanctuary both during the sojourn in the wilderness and after the settlement in the land (Num. xviii. 24; Deut. xii. 6). There was a portion eaten by the offerer and the Levites in a eucharistic feast, and the rest was given to the Levites. The law was slightly modified in anticipation of the settlement of Canaan, and the residence of Levites and producers in many cases far from the sanctuary. Every third year they should store the tithe in the town where they dwelt, dispense with the eucharistic meal, place all the tithe at the disposal of the Levites and other dependent persons, and make solemn protestation before the Lord to having done this (Deut. xxvi. 12-15). This asseveration before the Lord may have been made in the town, or at the sanctuary on occasion of attending one of the annual festivals. It is sometimes asserted that Deuteronomy is peculiar in two respects: it prescribes vegetable tithes only, and enjoins that they shall be eaten at the altar by the offerer and the Levites in company. If Deuteronomy does actually differ from the law of Leviticus and Numbers in these points, it is a modification of the law forty years after its first enactment and in view of new circumstances. In the later history, even when the Levitical legislation was in full force, the vegetable tithe alone is often mentioned (Neh. x. 37; xii. 44; xiii. 12). It was the more prominent, since agriculture and horticulture were the chief industries of the people. The tithe of the cattle is, however, referred to (2 Chron. xxxi. 6). It would be in itself natural, if the eucharistic feast did not already exist, for Moses to introduce it in connection with tithes and firstlings, in view of the fact that the offerer frequently came from a distance, and naturally required at least one meal at the sanctuary before returning. Still the omission of all mention of the feast in Leviticus and Numbers may be due to the feast's being regarded as a matter of course, a meal having been customary from time immemorial in connection with certain kinds of sacrifices and offerings; and the tithe on agricultural and horticultural products alone is mentioned in Deuteronomy, because among tithes it was with them only that a meal at the sanctuary was connected, and the legislation in question is treating of eucharistic meals.

Another interpretation of the tithing laws requires mention. Not a few scholars have believed that the setting apart of one-fifth for Pharaoh, to which the Israelites had been accustomed in Egypt, was perpetuated by the Mosaic law as tribute to Jehovah. This fifth was made up of two tithes. The first went to the Levites, the second was taken to the sanctuary and consumed there (Antiq. iv. 8, 8), but in the third year was given to the Levites in addition to their own tithe. Some interpreters have even thought of three tithes. They regard the tithing of the third year as additional to the two others. This interpretation is as old as Josephus at least (8, 22), but it is unnecessary, and was scarcely the original intention of the law. The law is satisfied by the theory of one tithing.

In times of religious declension the people neglected to pay tithes. Hezekiah found it necessary to call authoritatively for their payment (2 Chron. xxxi. 4-12), and the prophet Malachi was obliged to rebuke the people of his day for robbing God by withholding tithes and offerings (Mal. iii. 7-12). The response of the people to Hezekiah's appeal was so hearty that he had to prepare chambers in the temple precincts for storing the tithes (2 Chron. xxxi. 11). Whether he built additional quarters or cleared out old storehouses is not stated. The second temple was likewise provided with storehouses (Neh. xiii. 10-14; Mal. iii. 10), and Levites under the superintendence of a priest gathered the tithes into the towns and tithed them for the sanctuary (Neh. x. 37, 38). The payment of tithes continued (Ecclus. xxxv. 8; 1 Mac. iii. 49; Luke xi. 42; xviii. 12); but by the time of Christ changes had occurred. The tithe went to the priests (Antiq. xi. 5, 8; con. Apion. i. 22; cp. Heb. vii. 5), and was collected by them (Life 12, 15). Later the ordinary priests suffered from the cupidity of the chief priests, who forcibly took possession of the tithes (Antiq. xx. 8, 8; 9, 2).

Tit′tle, in A. V. of 1611 **Title** [late Latin *titulus*, in the sense of a mark made above a letter to distinguish it from another letter of similar form].

A point or small line used to distinguish one letter of the Hebrew alphabet from another, as שׁ from שׂ, or ר from ד; hence a minute requirement of the law (Mat. v. 18, in Greek *keraia*, little horn).

Ti′tus.

1. A godly man of Corinth who was surnamed Justus (Acts xviii. 7, R.V.); see JUSTUS.

2. A trusted companion of Paul. He is not mentioned in The Acts, but is frequently referred to in Paul's epistles. He was born of gentile parents (Gal. ii. 3), and was one of the delegation from Antioch (Acts xv. 2) who accompanied Paul and Barnabas to Jerusalem at the time of the council (Gal. ii. 3). It is possible that he was a native of Antioch, and, since Paul calls him "my true child after a common faith" (Tit. i. 4, R. V.), he

may have been converted through the instrumentality of the apostle. He was evidently also much younger than Paul. His presence at the council gave offense to the Judaizers, but the church refused to compel him to be circumcised, thus siding with Paul in his advocacy of the freedom of gentiles from the Mosaic law (Gal. ii. 3–5). Titus next appears during and after Paul's residence in Ephesus. We learn from 2 Cor. ii. 13; vii. 6, 13; viii. 6, 16; xii. 18 that Titus had been sent to Corinth to correct certain abuses there which caused anxiety to the apostle. Some suppose that he was one of the brethren who carried the first epistle to the Corinthians (1 Cor. xvi. 12). It is more probable, however, that he and another (2 Cor. xii. 18) were dispatched after 1 Cor. had been sent, on account of later reports which the apostle had received. His task was a delicate one, and Paul awaited his return with much solicitude (2 Cor. ii. 13). When the apostle left Ephesus, he expected to meet Titus at Troas (12, 13), and, failing in this, went to Macedonia. There Titus rejoined him with good news (vii. 6, 13, 14), and was forthwith sent back to Corinth with our Second Epistle to the Corinthians (viii. 6, 18, 23). We do not read again of Titus until after Paul's release from his first Roman imprisonment; see PAUL. The Epistle to Titus informs us that he had been left in Crete to superintend the organization of the churches in that island. He seems to have been, like Timothy in Ephesus, an apostolic deputy. His mission, however, was but a temporary one, and he was told to rejoin the apostle in Nicopolis. The only remaining notice of him is in 2 Tim. iv. 10, where he is said to have gone to Dalmatia.

The Epistle of Paul to Titus was written after Paul's release from his first Roman imprisonment and resumption of missionary work. It may be assigned to A. D. 65 or 66. Titus had been left as superintendent of the churches in Crete, and the epistle, like the First Epistle to Timothy, was intended to direct him in the performance of his difficult task. It may be divided as follows: 1. Salutation, particularly describing the dignity of the apostolic message (i. 1–4). 2. Instructions concerning the character of those selected for bishops or elders, especially in view of the many false disciples whom Titus would be likely to meet and by whom he might be imposed upon (5–16). 3. Instructions which Titus should give to various classes in the church, all to the effect that Christians should be "zealous of good works" (ii.). 4. Directions concerning the duty of Christians to society, bidding them emulate the love of man which God has shown in Christ (iii. 1–8). 5. Warnings against false teaching and heretics (9–11). 6. Personal directions and closing exhortation and benediction (12–15). The leading thought of the epistle is the importance of good works in all those representing or professing Christianity. On the

pastoral epistles see remarks at close of the article on TIMOTHY.   G. T. P.

Ti′zite.

The designation of a certain Joha (1 Chron. xi. 45), probably derived from the place of which he was a native.

To′ah [perhaps, low].

A Kohathite Levite (1 Chron. vi. 34); see NAHATH.

Tob [good].

A region east of the Jordan, to which Jephthah fled when disowned by his brethren (Judg. xi. 3, 5). When Hanun, king of Ammon, gave David just offense, he drew soldiers from Tob, among other places (2 Sam. x. 6, R. V.), which indicates that it was beyond the borders of Israel. It was probably the district of Gilead known in Greek as the land of Tubias (1 Mac. v. 13; cp. 2 Mac. xii. 17). Exact situation is debatable.

Tob-ad-o-ni′jah [good is my Lord Jehovah].

One of the Levites sent by Jehoshaphat to teach in the cities of Judah (2 Chron. xvii. 8).

To-bi′ah [Jehovah is good].

1. Founder of a family, members of which, coming to Jerusalem after the captivity, failed to prove their descent (Ezra ii. 60; Neh. vii. 62).

2. An Ammonite servant who ridiculed the effort of the Jews to rebuild the wall of Jerusalem (Neh. ii. 10; iv. 3, 7).

To′bie. See TUBIAS.

To-bi′jah [Jehovah is good].

1. One of the Levites sent by Jehoshaphat to teach in the cities of Judah (2 Chron. xvii. 8).

2. A Jew, one of those of the captivity from whom the prophet Zechariah obtained gold and silver to make crowns to put on the head of Joshua, the high priest (Zech. vi. 10, 14).

To′bit. See APOCRYPHA.

To′chen [a weight, a measure].

A city belonging to the tribe of Simeon (1 Chron. iv. 32). Site unknown.

To-gar′mah.

A country of the far north (Ezek. xxxviii. 6), inhabited by a people descended from Japheth through Gomer (Gen. x. 3). They traded in horses and mules (Ezek. xxvii. 14). It is generally identified with Armenia. Friedrich Delitzsch, however, believes that the name appears in Til-garimmu, a city in the extreme east of Cappadocia, mentioned in the Assyrian inscriptions.

To′hu [perhaps, low].

A son of Zuph (1 Sam. i. 1); see NAHATH.

To′i and To′u [wandering, error].

A king of Hamath, probably a Hittite, who was at war with Hadadezer, king of

Zobah, a Syrian. He sent to congratulate David on his victory over their common foe (2 Sam. viii. 9-12; 1 Chron. xviii. 9-11).

Tok'hath. See TIKVAH.

To'la [worm, scarlet].

1. A son of Issachar, and founder of a tribal family (Gen. xlvi. 13; Num. xxvi. 23; 1 Chron. vii. 1).

2. Son of Puah, of the tribe of Issachar, who judged Israel twenty-three years. He lived, died, and was buried at Shamir, on mount Ephraim (Judg. x. 1, 2).

To'lad. See ELTOLAD.

Tomb. See SEPULCHER.

Tongue.

An organ of the body (Ex. xi. 7; Jas. iii. 6), situated in the mouth (Job xxix. 10), and much used in speaking (Ps. xxxix. 3; lxxi. 24; Mark vii. 35).

A bar of gold (Josh. vii. 21, 24, literally tongue, but translated wedge). The Babylonians also spoke of tongues of gold, and a gold bar resembling a tongue has been found in the mound of ruined Gezer.

Figuratively, speech or language (Gen. x. 5; Acts ii. 8 with 11). The descendants of Noah inherited, and for a long time after the flood spoke, one language (Gen. xi. 1). Differences of speech were produced by divine judgment at Babel, which resulted in scattering the people who had gathered there abroad, to all parts of the known world (2-9); see BABEL. This event, which is known as the confusion of tongues, may have occurred among the Semites alone, after the rise of the family of Eber (x. 25). In process of time the descendants of Noah came to speak several distinct languages and many different dialects. The Japhetic peoples largely used the languages now classed as Indo-Germanic (x. 2-5), including the languages spoken in Media and Ionia (ver. 2). The Semitic peoples generally spoke various dialects of the Semitic group (21-31), embracing Assyrian, Aramaic (22), Arabic (26-29), and Hebrew; but the Elamites (22) used an agglutinative language, which is supposed to be akin to the Finnish. Many of the descendants of Ham also spoke Semitic; as, for example, Cush in Assyria (11), Arabia (6, 7), and Africa, and Canaan in Palestine and Phœnicia (15); but the old inhabitants of Mizraim (6, 13), better known as Egypt, used an agglutinative language, although many Egyptologists of the first rank believe in its descent from the same stock as the Semitic. It must be remembered that tribes which migrate to a new locality frequently adopt the language of the people among whom they have taken up their residence.

The gift of tongues was granted on the day of Pentecost which followed the feast of the passover at which Jesus suffered. The disciples being assembled together, suddenly there came from heaven a sound like that of a rushing, mighty wind, and visible tongues, having the appearance of fire, were distributed to each, and they were all filled with the Holy Spirit (Acts ii. 1-4). The church was qualified and symbolically commissioned by the Spirit to declare the gospel to all men. Two general theories exist as to the nature of this gift. 1. The gift of tongues was manifested in ecstatic or elevated praise of God (Acts x. 46), but which was unintelligible to man. The tongue was the organ of the Holy Spirit, and not of the person to whom the gift was given; and the words spoken were devotional and not for the instruction of the church. In defense of this view it is urged that: (1) Paul makes no mention of foreign languages having been introduced at Corinth; and if tongues were referred to in 1 Cor. xiv. only, the impression would never have been made that they denote foreign languages. (2) Paul teaches that the understanding was not engaged (1 Cor. xiv. 2). (3) The multitude could not understand them at Pentecost, and accused the speakers of being drunken. It was necessary for Peter to interpret to the multitude what had taken place (Acts ii. 13-17). Or if the disciples used foreign languages on the day of Pentecost, this was a temporary form in which the gift of tongues was manifested and did not appear again. 2. The gift of tongues was manifested in intelligible discourse in tongues before unknown. (1) Luke's language clearly implies this (Acts ii. 6-12). (2) Anybody could babble hysterically; only when the speakers used languages which they did not know before could the gift of tongues be recognized as miraculous. (3) The whole argument in 1 Cor. assumes that the gift was speech in a foreign language, Paul contrasting speech and prayer in a foreign language uninterpreted with speaking and praying so as to be understood (xii. 10, 30; xiv. 13-16, 27, 28). Christians who had the gift should use it for missionary purposes, and not exhibit their skill before their brethren, who did not understand what they said unless an interpreter were present.

Tongues were a sign that followed them that believed (Mark xvi. 17). They were a visible gift of the Holy Spirit bestowed in connection with the preaching of the apostles, or by the apostles through laying on of their hands (Acts x. 44-46; xix. 1-7; cp. viii. 14-24). They were a phenomenon of the apostolic age, and gradually disappeared afterwards. In the next century, perhaps fifty or sixty years after the death of the last apostle, Irenæus can still report that he had "heard many brethren who had prophetic gifts and spoke through the Spirit in all kinds of tongues" (adv. Haer. v. 6, 1).

In 1830 some people in Scotland, and in 1831 others in London, chiefly females of excitable temperament, believed that they had received the gift of tongues. They persuaded the Rev. Edward Irving to embrace their opinions, but failed to convince his brethren in the ministry. The movement led to the creation of the Catholic Apostolic Church.

To'paz

A precious stone, called by the Greeks *topazion*, and generally believed to be denoted by the Hebrew *pit^edah*. It was the second stone in the first row of the high priest's breastplate (Ex. xxviii. 17; cp. the Greek version and Antiq. iii. 7, 5). It was found in Ethiopia (Job xxviii. 19) and on an island in the Red Sea (Diodorus Siculus iii. 38; Pliny, Hist. Nat. xxxvii. 9), and was known at Tyre (Ezek. xxviii. 13). It adorns the ninth foundation of the New Jerusalem (Rev. xxi. 20). The topaz of the ancients was a yellow variety of corundum. The Romans seem to have transferred the name chrysolite to topaz, and called both chrysolite and precious stones resembling it topaz.

To'phel [perhaps, untempered mortar].

A place, perhaps once a station of the Israelites in the wilderness (Deut. i. 1). Robinson and others have identified it with Ṭufîleh, about 14 miles southeast of the southeastern curve of the Dead Sea. The consonants, however, are different, teth instead of tau, which raises a doubt as to the correctness of the identification.

To'pheth, in A. V. Tophet (except 2 Kin. xxiii. 10) [spitting out, abhorrence].

Certain high places built in the valley of the son of Hinnom, on which the people of Jerusalem in the times of Isaiah and Jeremiah were accustomed to burn their sons and their daughters in the fire (Jer. vii. 31), as offerings to Molech (2 Kin. xxiii. 10). Apparently on the top of the high place there was a deep and large hole, in which much wood was piled, ignition being produced by a stream of brimstone (Is. xxx. 33). Josiah defiled it (2 Kin. xxiii. 10), and Jeremiah prophesied that such a number of people should be killed there that the name Topheth should disappear, and the valley where it stood be called the valley of slaughter (Jer. vii. 32, 33; xix. 6). A Topheth, apparently of the same type, was to be prepared for the king of Assyria (Is. xxx. 33). See HINNOM.

Torch.

A flambeau, giving a flaring light, and often portable (Judg. vii. 16, R. V.; Mat. xxv. 3, R. V. margin; John xviii. 3, R. V.; cp. the proper name Lappidoth); primitively, merely a piece of resinous wood, or a bunch or twist of absorbent material soaked in oil and borne on a rod or carried by some other form of holder or incased in a narrow, conical clay wrapping or vase.

Tor'mah [fraud].

A town in which Abimelech was once found (Judg. ix. 31, margin). More probably the word means craftily, as it is rendered in the R. V.; in which case the town of Tormah disappears.

Tor-ment'ors.

The jailers who were to keep the debtor safe and make his life miserable by chains, stocks, and doubtless other means of distress and torture until his debts were paid (Mat. xviii. 34). Torture was often applied to extort confessions (Acts xxii. 24; Antiq. xvi. 8, 4; 11, 6).

Tor'toise. See LIZARD.

To'u. See TOI.

Tow'er.

A lofty building, much higher than broad. A booth was sufficient to shelter the watchman placed to guard a vineyard (Is. i. 8); but a tower, being more permanent and ornamental, indicated the owner's interest in his vineyard and his expectation of many seasons of fruitfulness (v. 2; Mat. xxi. 33; Mark xii. 1). Stronger towers were built for defense. They were erected in the wilderness for the security of the shepherds and to keep marauders away (2 Kin. xvii. 9; 2 Chron. xxvi. 10). They formed part of the defenses of fortified cities (xiv. 7; Neh. iii. 1). They were erected beside the city gates, at the corners of the walls, and at intervals in the intervening space (2 Chron. xxvi. 9); see illustrations, LACHISH, RAM. Watchmen were stationed on them (2 Kin. ix. 17), military engines for shooting arrows and stones were mounted on them (2 Chron. xxvi. 15), and the citizens found refuge in them when sore pressed by the enemy (Judg. ix. 51, 52; Ps. lxi. 3). Within their massive walls the inmates were secure; their height allowed openings for light and air, out of reach of the adversary; and from their top missiles could be advantageously discharged at the foe.

Town Clerk.

An official with the title of *grammateus* or scribe (Acts xix. 35). Probably the duties of a *grammateus* originally were to record the laws and read them in public, but in course of time other functions were added to the office. Coins show that in the several cities of Asia Minor the town clerk presided in popular assemblies, and was the virtual, or in some cases the actual, head of the municipal government.

Trach-o-ni'tis [rough, stony].

A region which at the appearance of John the Baptist as a preacher constituted, with Ituræa, a tetrarchy, ruled over by Philip, the brother of Herod, the tetrarch of Galilee (Luke iii. 1). It lay behind Damascus (Strabo xvi. 2, 20), and comprehended the stretch of volcanic rocks now called el-Lejjah, and extended westward to Ulatha and Paneas, and southward to the borders of Batanea and Jebel Hauran (Antiq. xv. 10, 3; xvii. 2, 1 and 2; Ptolemy v. 15, 4).

Trag'a-canth.

A gum (Gen. xxxvii. 25; xliii. 11, R. V. margin), produced by several low, spiny shrubs of the genus *Astragalus*, especially from *Astragalus gummifer*. The plant is leguminous. Those from which gum is obtained are dwarf shrubs, protected by a dense mass of long thorns. The flowers are axillary; and in most species are yellow, but in some are white or purple. Under the heat of the sun the gum exudes from the trunk, branches, thorns, and leaves; and is collected in Palestine by passing over the shrub a cloth or bunch of threads to which the viscous exudation adheres. It is used to impart firmness to pills, to marble books, and to stiffen crapes and calicoes.

Trance.

A state in which the functions of the senses are suspended and the soul seems to be liberated from the body while it contemplates some extraordinary object; ecstasy Peter on one occasion (Acts xi. 5), and Paul on another, fell into such a trance (xxii. 17). See VISIONS.

Tres'pass Of'fer-ing. See OFFERINGS.

Tribe. See EGYPT III. 7.

Trib'ute.

1. Money, goods, or service exacted by a nation or king from foreign subjects (Deut. xx. 11, R. V. margin taskwork; Judg. i. 28; Ezra iv. 13; Neh. v. 4; Esth. x. 1; Mat. xvii. 25). The Pharisees endeavored to put Jesus in a dilemma by asking him whether it was lawful to pay tribute to the Roman emperor (Mat. xxii. 17). If he answered in the affirmative, he would offend the people, since with them independence was a matter of religion and they paid the foreign tax with undisguised reluctance. The Pharisees expected him to declare that tribute to the Romans was unlawful, for they knew that he had publicly announced his claims to the throne of David; and an answer of this sort would justify a charge of rebellion against him. He replied by calling for a coin. The coinage of money is the prerogative of the ruler. Pointing to the image of the Roman emperor which it bore, he said: "Give to the ruler whom you acknowledge whatever belongs to him, and to God whatever belongs to God." Jesus recognized the distinction between the two spheres of duty.

2. The didrachma or half shekel paid for the expenses of the temple worship (Mat. xvii. 24, in R. V. half shekel). This payment was suggested at first by the half shekel which each male Israelite above twenty years of age paid as atonement money when he was numbered in the census (Ex. xxx. 11–16). In the time of Nehemiah the Israelites voluntarily assumed an annual payment of the third part of a shekel toward defraying the cost of the temple service (Neh. x. 32, 33). Later the third part of a shekel was changed to half a shekel, and was made an annual tax collected from every Jew of twenty years of age and upward throughout the world (Antiq.

xviii. 9, 1). The collector at Capernaum asked Peter whether his Master paid this half shekel, and Peter impulsively answered that he did (Mat. xvii. 24, 25). Jesus did indeed pay it; but it was incongruous for him to do so, and he drew Peter's attention to the matter. He pointed out to him that earthly kings exact tribute from aliens, not from their own children. Peter had recently confessed Jesus as the Son of God. It was for God's house and worship that this tax was levied, and it was scarcely proper for God's Son to be required to pay it. Such is the common interpretation of Christ's words on this occasion. After the fall of Jerusalem the Roman emperor Vespasian enjoined the Jews throughout the empire to bring to Jupiter Capitolinus in Rome the two drachmas which they had formerly paid to the temple (War vii. 6, 6).

Tro'as [the Troad, region around Troy].

A seaport (Acts xvi. 11) of Mysia; where Paul saw in vision a man of Macedonia inviting him to Europe (Acts xvi. 8–10; 2 Cor. ii. 12). The apostle tarried there a week while returning from his third journey (Acts xx. 6). On one occasion he left his cloak, books, and parchments there (2 Tim. iv. 13). It was founded by Antigonus, one of Alexander's successors, who called it Antigonia; but after his death his opponent Lysimachus, king of Thrace, altered its name to Alexandria, and Troas was added to distinguish it from Alexandria in Egypt. It was situated some distance south of Homer's Troy, which furnished the name Troas to the district. Its ruins, which are extensive, are now called Eski Stamboul.

Tro-gyl'li-um.

A town and a promontory on the western coast of Asia Minor, opposite the island of Samos. Paul tarried there on the return to Jerusalem from his third journey (Acts xx. 15; see R. V. margin). An anchorage at the place is called St. Paul's Port.

Troph'i-mus [nourishing].

A gentile Christian of Ephesus, who was with Paul for a time on his missionary travels, and whom he was falsely accused of having brought into the temple in defiance of the law (Acts xx. 4; xxi. 29). The last we hear of him is that he was left by the apostle at Miletus sick (2 Tim. iv. 20, in A. V. Miletum).

Trump'et.

1. A wind instrument, made of the horn of an animal or in imitation of it (Josh. vi. 5; cp. Dan. iii. 5, where *ḳeren*, horn, is rendered cornet), and called in Hebrew *shophar*. The word is rendered cornet in four passages where the *ḥaṣoṣerah* is mentioned with it and rendered trumpet (1 Chron. xv. 28; 2 Chron. xv. 14; Ps. xcviii. 6; Hos. v. 8). Its sound was loud, and audible at a great distance (Ex. xix. 16, 19); and was well adapted to increase the noise of shouting (2 Sam. vi.

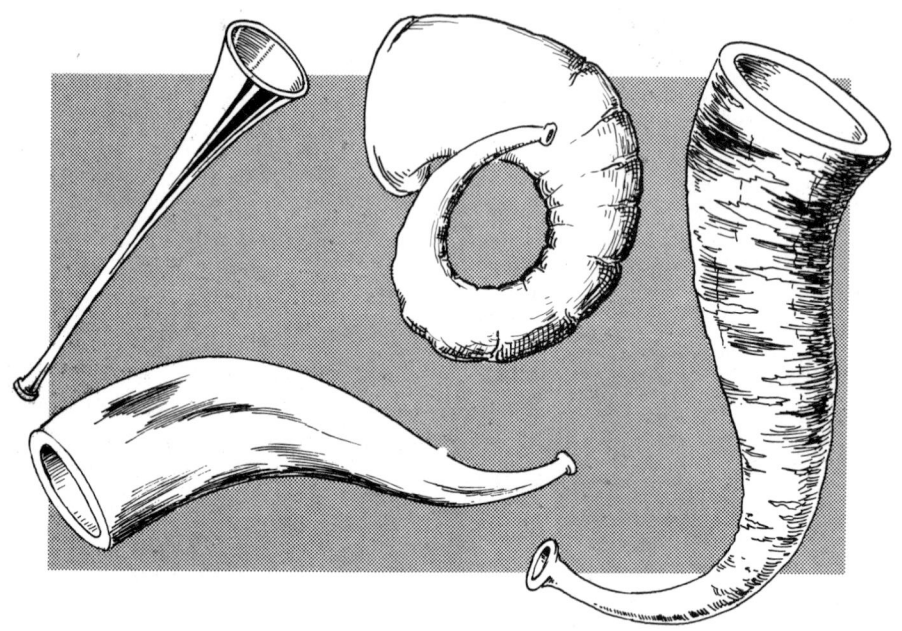

Ancient horns and trumpets.

15; 2 Chron. xv. 14; Ps. xcviii. 6), but was ill-suited to be played with harps and pipes in an orchestra. It was used in war to assemble the army (Judg. iii. 27; vi. 34; 1 Sam. xiii. 3), to sound the attack (Job xxxix. 24), to signal the cessation of the pursuit (2 Sam. ii. 28; xviii. 16), and to announce the disbanding of the army (xx. 1, 22). Watchmen blew it to sound the alarm (Jer. vi. 1; Amos iii. 6). Its blast proclaimed the accession of the king (2 Sam. xv. 10; 1 Kin. i. 34; 2 Kin. ix. 13), and the commencement of the year of jubile (Lev. xxv. 9). The first day of the seventh month was celebrated by solemn rest from ordinary labor, a holy convocation, and the offering of special burnt offerings (xxiii. 24, 25; Num. xxix. 1–6), because the day marked a recurring seventh portion of time. It was a day or memorial of blowing of trumpets, designed to bring the people into remembrance before the Lord (cp. Ex. xxviii. 12, 29; xxx. 16). The Jewish tradition is doubtless correct which states that the trumpet used was the *shophar* (cp. Lev. xxv. 9).

2. The invariable rendering of the Hebrew *Ḥᵃṣoṣᵉrah*. Two were made for use at the tabernacle (Num. x. 2); but the number was increased as time went on (2 Kin. xii. 13). One hundred and twenty were blown at the dedication of the temple (2 Chron. v. 12). Those used at the sanctuary were of silver (Num. x. 2). They were a little less than a cubit in length. The tube was narrow, somewhat thicker than a flute, and ended in the form of a bell, like common trumpets (Antiq. iii. 12, 6); see illustration under SHOW-BREAD. They were used by the priests to announce festivals, to call the congregation, and on advancing to battle (Num. x. 1–10; xxxi. 6). Rarely is mention made of their being blown by laymen in war (Hos. v. 8). Priests may have blown them at the coronation of Joash (2 Kin. xi. 14; 2 Chron. xxiii. 13). For their use in the temple orchestra see MUSIC.

3. Trumpet is expressed by the Greek word *salpigx* in N. T. It was used in war (1 Cor. xiv. 8), and will announce the second advent of Christ (Mat. xxiv. 31), and the resurrection of the dead (1 Cor. xv. 52). Seven trumpets were sounded to introduce as many apocalyptic visions (Rev. viii.–xi. 19). By *salpigx* the *hᵃṣoṣᵉrah* or sacred trumpet is meant in Ecclus. l. 16; 1 Mac. iii. 54; and probably iv. 40; v. 33; xvi. 8.

Try-phæ′na, in A. V. **Tryphena** [delicate, dainty].

A woman at Rome to whom Paul sent his salutation, commending her for laboring in the Lord (Rom. xvi. 12).

Try′phon [luxurious].

A general of Alexander Balas (1 Mac. xi. 39). He was a native of Casiana near Apamea in Syria, and originally bore the name of Diodotus (Strabo xvi. 2, 10). After the death of Balas and the recognition of

Demetrius II., as king of Syria, 146 B. C., Tryphon set up Antiochus VI., the infant son of Alexander Balas, as a rival to Demetrius (xi. 39, 40), and with the help of the Jews was rapidly conquering the country. His treachery to Jonathan Maccabæus, however (xii. 39-50; xiii. 23), caused his Jewish allies to go over to the side of Demetrius. Tryphon meantime had murdered young Antiochus and declared himself king (xii. 31, 39). The capture of Demetrius by Arsaces, the Parthian king, left Tryphon to his own schemes for a while, but Demetrius' brother, Antiochus VII., opposed him and succeeded in besieging him, first in Dor on the Phœnician coast (xv. 10-14, 37), and afterwards in Apamea, where Tryphon lost his life in 138 B. C. (Antiq. xiii. 7, 2).

Try-pho'sa [delicate].
A woman at Rome whose name is coupled with that of Tryphæna in the list of those Romans to whom Paul sent his salutation. They may have been sisters or fellow-deaconesses. They are mentioned as laboring in the Lord (Rom. xvi. 12).

Tsa'dhe. See TZADE.

Tu'bal.
A tribe descended from Japheth (Gen. x. 2). It is mentioned with Javan (Is. lxvi. 19) and with Meshech (Ezek. xxxii. 26) as trading in the Tyrian markets with slaves and vessels of brass (xxvii. 13). Gog was prince of Meshech and Tubal (xxxviii. 2, 3; xxxix. 1). The descendants of Tubal are the Tublâ of the Assyrian inscriptions and the Tibareni or Tibarenoi of the classical writers. For their country and history, see MESHECH.

Tu'bal-cain [possibly, production of forged work].
A son of the Cainite Lamech, by his wife Zillah. He was the forger of cutting instruments of brass and iron (Gen iv. 22).

Tu'bi-as, in A. V. **To'bie.**
A district east of the Jordan (1 Mac. v. 13; cp. 2 Mac. xii. 17), probably the land of Tob; see TOB.

Tur'ban. See DIADEM.

Tur'tle and **Tur'tle-dove.**
A species of pigeon. It is gentle and harmless, fit emblem of a defenseless and innocent people (Ps. lxxiv. 19). It is migratory (Jer. viii. 7), and a herald of spring (Song ii. 12). Abraham sacrificed a turtledove and other victims when the Lord's covenant was made with him (Gen. xv. 9). Under the law it served as a burnt offering (Lev. i. 14) and for a sin offering; and two turtledoves were prescribed for these two sacrifices in case a poor person was obliged to make a guilt offering, and for the purification of a woman after childbirth if she was poor, of a man or woman with an issue, and of a Nazirite (v. 7; xii. 6, 8; xv. 14, 29, 30; Num. vi. 10, 11). It was readily obtainable by the poor, for it abounds

in Palestine and is easily trapped. Three species of turtledove are described by Tristram as occurring in Palestine. The most abundant is the common turtledove (*Turtur vulgaris*), which reaches Palestine from the south in countless numbers at the beginning of March, and departs again at the approach of winter. The second is the collared turtledove (*Turtur risorius*). It is a summer migrant, breeding in Palestine in trees and bushes. The third species, the palm turtledove (*Turtur senegalensis*), does not migrate, but remains permanently in the Dead Sea valley, which has a tropical climate.

Tu'tor. See SCHOOLMASTER.

Twin Broth'ers. See CASTOR and POLLUX

Tych'i-cus [fortuitous].
A Christian of the province of Asia who, with others, traveled on in advance of Paul from Macedonia to Troas, and awaited the apostle's arrival in that city (Acts xx. 4). He was a beloved brother and faithful minister in the Lord, and was sent by Paul to carry to their destination the Epistles to the Ephesians and Colossians (Eph. vi. 21; Col. iv. 7). Paul proposed also to send him as a messenger to Titus in Crete (Titus iii. 12). Afterwards he was dispatched to Ephesus (2 Tim. iv. 12).

Ty-ran'nus [an absolute sovereign, a tyrant].
A man at Ephesus who was either a teacher of philosophy or rhetoric, or else a Jewish scribe who gave instruction in the law. In his school Paul disputed with the view of making Christianity known after he no longer had access for the purpose to the Jewish synagogue (Acts xix. 9).

Tyre, in A. V. often **Ty'rus** [a rock].
An important city of Phœnicia. It was a place of great antiquity (Is. xxiii. 7; Antiq. viii. 3, 1); but it was founded or attained to importance after Sidon (Gen. x. 15; Is. xxiii. 12). The priests of Melkarth told Herodotus that it was founded 2300 years before his visit, which would make the city come into existence about 2750 B. C. (Herod. ii. 44). According to ancient testimony, Tyre originally stood on the mainland; but in course of time, for safety against besiegers, it was transferred to the neighboring rocky island which gave name to the locality. Ancient writers frequently allude to its situation in the sea (Ezek. xxvi. 17; xxvii. 32). The town on the mainland became known as Palætyrus or Old Tyre. Tyre was nearer to the Israelites than Sidon, and this fact, with the increasing greatness of Tyre over Sidon, established the constant order observed in speaking of the two cities, Tyre and Sidon. Tyre was subject to Egypt in the fifteenth century B. C. (Tell el-Amarna tablets). In the time of Joshua, it was a strong place (Josh. xix. 29). It lay on the border of Asher, but was not assigned to that or any

other tribe (xix. 29; Judg. i. 31, 32), nor do the Israelites appear to have possessed it at any period of their history. In the time of David it was regarded as a stronghold (2 Sam. xxiv. 7). Hiram, king of Tyre, was friendly with David and Solomon, and aided them with materials for the erection by the former of his palace (v. 11; 1 Kin. v. 1; 1 Chron. xiv. 1) and by the latter of the temple and the other edifices which he built (1 Kin. v. 1; ix. 10–14; 2 Chron. ii. 3, 11; cp. Ps. xlv. 12). Another Hiram, a brass founder, who cast pillars and other work for the temple, was of mixed Tyrian and Hebrew parentage (1 Kin. vii. 13, 14, 40, 45). The taste of the Tyrians was not for war, but for manufacture, commerce, money-making, sea voyages, and colonization. They produced purple dyes, metal work, and glass ware; and they trafficked even with remotest peoples (cp. 1 Kin. ix. 28). Their merchants were princes, the honorable of the earth (Is. xxiii. 8). In the ninth century B. C. a colony from Tyre founded Carthage, which became a formidable rival to Rome. Still, though by taste a commercial people, they were often forced into war. Early in the ninth century they purchased immunity from Ashurnaṣirpal, king of Assyria, and later were represented in the alliance, which included Ahab, formed to resist Ashurnaṣirpal's son and successor Shalmaneser. But at length Tyre with others paid him tribute. About 724 B. C. Shalmaneser, king of Assyria, called the Fourth, after receiving the submission of old Tyre, laid siege to island Tyre, but he died in 722 without effecting its capture (Antiq. ix. 14, 2; cp. probably Is. xxiii.). It yielded to his successor Sargon. The friendliness of the Tyrians toward Israel had ceased by this time. The prophets denounced the Tyrians for delivering Israelites to the Edomites (Amos i. 9), and despoiling them of goods and selling them as slaves to the Greeks (Joel iii. 5, 6). The city was not plundered, as were the neighboring towns by Sennacherib, but was besieged by Esarhaddon, and yielded on honorable terms to Ashurbanipal in 664 B. C. In the next century it enjoyed great commercial prosperity, and its merchants traded with all the countries of the known world (Ezek. xxvii.). Jeremiah prophesied Tyre's subjection (Jer. xxvii. 1–11). The classic prophecy against Tyre, entering into more details, is that of Ezekiel (Ezek. xxvi.–xxviii. 19; xxix. 18–20). These prophecies of Jeremiah and Ezekiel refer largely to a siege of Tyre by Nebuchadnezzar, lasting thirteen years (con. Apion. i. 21). It is not certainly known whether he actually captured any part of the two cities (cp. Ezek. xxix. 18–20); if he did, it was probably only the one on the shore (xxvi. 7–11 and perhaps 12), and the result did not compensate the besiegers for their toil. However, Tyre finally made terms and acknowledged Nebuchadnezzar's suzerainty (as indicated by the date of a contract tablet). In 332 B. C. Alexander the Great took the city on the island after a siege of seven months, having made his way to it by building a mole from the mainland across the narrow strait. But it soon recovered considerable prosperity (cp. Is. xxiii. 15–18). Our Lord once visited the coasts of Tyre and Sidon (Mat. xv. 21–31; Mark vii. 24–31), and people from the region occasionally attended on his ministry (Mark iii. 8; Luke vi. 17). He pointed out that the responsibilities of those heathen cities were much less than those of the places around the sea of Galilee, which constantly heard his preaching and saw his miracles (Mat. xi. 21, 22; Luke x. 13, 14). A Christian community existed there in the first century (Acts xxi. 3–6). The scholar Origen, who died about A. D. 254, was buried in the Christian basilica. A larger and grander basilica was erected by bishop Paulinus, and at its consecration in 323 the church historian Eusebius, bishop of Cæsarea, preached the sermon. In 638 the city was captured by the Mohammedans. The lives and property of the citizens were spared on the humiliating condition that no new churches be built, no bells be rung, no horses be ridden by Christians, no insults be offered to the Mohammedan religion. On the 27th of June, 1124, Tyre was taken by the crusaders. The German emperor Barbarossa, who was drowned on his crusade in 1190, was buried in their cathedral. They lost the city again in March, 1291, when it was reduced almost to a heap of stones. Since then it has nearly always been in Mohammedan hands. Quantities of its stones have been carried away to Beirut, Acre, and Joppa, for building purposes. The walls are in ruinous condition, and have in part disappeared or been covered with sand. Formerly there were two harbors; now only the old Sidonian port is in use. It is on the northeast side of the island; the other, or the Egyptian port, has been filled with sand. Alexander's mole still remains; its breadth is nearly half a mile. Most of the ruins, including the cathedral, are of Crusading times. The fountains and reservoirs called Râs el-'Ain supplied the city with water by means of an aqueduct starting 15 or 20 feet above the level of the ground, so as to give a sufficient slope for its descent. Tyre was for a considerable period all but destitute of inhabitants. In the present century it has slightly revived, so that it may have at present about 6500 inhabitants. It is called eṣ-Ṣûr, the old name in Arabic form. Its houses are chiefly on the eastern part of what was once the island, but the former island has been converted by Alexander's mole and accumulated sand into a promontory jutting out from the shore.

The ladder of Tyre is a high mountain on the coast of Syria, 100 stades or about 11 miles north of Ptolemais (War ii. 10, 2). This statement of distance and direction identifies it with a part or the whole of the massive, mountainous promontory, 7 miles in width, which thrusts itself into the sea and forms the natural boundary between Palestine and Phœnicia (1 Mac. xi. 59). At its southwestern angle Râs en-Nâkûrah, a bold headland, projects, leaving no beach between its base and the water, and forcing the coast road to ascend and cross it. This part of the great promontory is commonly identified with the Ladder. Some travelers, however, localize the Ladder at the northwestern angle, where Râs el-'Abyad, the white promontory, stands. In its precipitous cliffs the road is cut for about a mile, overhanging the sea and rising at points to the height of 200 feet above the water.

Tza′de, in A.V. **Tzaddi**, in A. R. V. **Tsadhe.**
The eighteenth letter of the Hebrew alphabet. No letter in the English alphabet corresponds to it. In anglicizing Hebrew names, s, t, or z is used to represent it. It heads the eighteenth section of Ps. cxix., in which section each verse of the original begins with this letter.

U

U′cal [I am strong].
One of two sons, pupils, or contemporaries, to whom Agur addressed his prophecy or proverbs (Prov. xxx. 1). This interpretation represents the traditional Hebrew punctuation, and derives support from ver. 4, where a person is addressed and asked to answer, if he knows. Another interpretation, which, however, neglects the punctuation, is given on the margin of the R. V.

U′el [will of God].
A son of Bani, induced by Ezra to put away his foreign wife (Ezra x. 34).

Uk′naz.
The marginal reading at 1 Chron. iv. 15, A. V.; but a Hebrew proper name would not begin as this word does. In the text it is properly regarded as two words, and the R. V., correctly renders it "and Kenaz."

U′lai.
A river on the banks of which Daniel was in vision when he saw the prophetic ram, the he goat, etc. (Dan. viii. 2, 16). The Ulai is undoubtedly the Eulæus; identified both with the Kerkha, which washes the walls of Susa, that is Shushan, and the Karun, which flows considerably eastward of the city. The conflicting views have been reconciled by the apparently well-founded supposition that the Kerkha sent out a branch from a spot 20 miles northwest of Susa, which joined the Karun, so that the name Ulai might be applied to both rivers.

U′lam [front].
1. A Manassite (1 Chron. vii. 16, 17).
2. A son of Eshek, a Benjamite descended from Saul through Jonathan (1 Chron. viii 39, 40).

Ul′la [a yoke].
An Asherite (1 Chron. vii. 39), probably descended from Helem (35).

Um′mah [conjunction].
A town of Asher (Josh. xix. 30). Not identified. Thomson proposes 'Alma, about 5 miles from the shore at Râs en-Nâkûrah. Some considerations suggest that Akko may be the original text. Caph was not infrequently mistaken for mem, i. e. k for m; see BETH.

Un′cle.
The brother of one's father (2 Kin. xxiv. 17, Hebrew). The Hebrew word is *dod*, which is of broader meaning than uncle and denotes any kinsman on the father's side (Lev. x. 4; Amos vi. 10); as a cousin (Jer. xxxii. 12 with 8, 9), or a member of the same tribe (Num. xxxvi. 11).

Un-clean′ An′i-mals.
A general distinction between clean and unclean meats was made by the nations of antiquity. Some animals were recognized as fit for food and sacrifice, while others were not. The distinction was based partly on the discovered unsuitableness or unwholesomeness of the flesh for food, partly on habits and prey, and partly on an inexplicable natural abhorrence to certain animals. Regard was paid in the Mosaic legislation to this customary attitude of the men of the age, and the distinction between clean and unclean meats was incorporated in the law. Other animals were added to the list of the unclean, out of special considerations involved in the religion of the Israelites. Unclean animals were classified as follows: 1. Beasts that do not both part the hoof entirely and chew the cud (Lev. xi. 3, 4), including all that go on four paws (27). The law accordingly allows only animals of the ox, sheep, and goat kind, and deer and gazelles (Deut. xiv. 4, 5). It excludes among other animals all carnivorous beasts. They eat blood or carrion, and were therefore intolerable to the Israelite. 2. Carnivorous birds, of which twenty or twenty-one are specially named (Lev. xi. 13-19; Deut. xiv. 12-18). The enumeration included the bat, which was classed as a bird. They eat blood or carrion. 3. Winged insects which do not have in addition to the four legs two hind legs for leaping (Lev. xi. 20-23). All insects are excluded except the locust (grasshopper). 4. Whatever in the water had not both fins and scales (9, 10). This prohibition left for use the most wholesome varieties of fish found in the waters of Palestine. It excludes eels, and water animals which are not fish, such as crabs. Numa forbade the Romans to offer scaleless fish in sacrifice (Pliny, Hist. Nat. xxxii. 10); and the modern Egyptians are said to regard such fish as unwholesome. Some of these scaleless and finless creatures

were snakelike, and recalled the first sin and its curse. 5. Small creeping things (Lev. xi. 29, 30); every creeping thing that goeth upon its belly or upon all fours, or has many feet (41, 42). Some were unwholesome. Others crept in the dust or through slime. Others still were snakelike. Not improbably there was a religious repugnance to creeping things in general, because their mode of locomotion was a reminder of the serpent and the curse on the tempter.

These animals were unclean under any circumstance. But the flesh of even clean animals might become unclean. The law forbade the eating of things offered in sacrifice to idols, things strangled or dead of themselves or killed by beast or bird of prey. Blood and fat of bird and beast were sacred to the Lord. None might eat of the blood, not even the stranger that sojourned in Israel (Lev. xvii. 10–14). The violator of the law respecting blood was cut off from his people (vii. 27; xvii. 10, 14). The offender against the laws regarding unclean animals was unclean until the evening (xi. 24, 40; xvii. 15). Animals that died of themselves might be sold to strangers and eaten by them (Deut. xiv. 21).

Un-clean'ness.

The law distinguished between clean and holy (Lev. x. 10); for example, animals are clean or unclean, not holy or unholy. Uncleanness, when not presumptuously incurred, was ceremonial, not moral defilement. It excluded man from the sanctuary (vii. 20, 21) and from fellowship with members of the commonwealth of Israel, but it did not interrupt spiritual communion with God in prayer. At the same time, the laws that defined uncleanness were in some cases enforced by the injunction, " Be ye holy, for I am holy" (xi. 44, 45). In keeping himself from the unclean, man had regard to the fact that he was set apart from a common to a sacred service, and that as a man of God he was holy unto the Lord and must be separate and touch no unclean thing. Furthermore, ceremonial uncleanness was typical of sin. Physical cleanliness also is different from ceremonial cleanness. The two were not synonymous, although the two conditions sometimes coincided. Comfort and the demands of society required bodily cleanliness on the part of the Hebrews. There were divers washings which had nothing to do with ceremonial purity. The laws of cleanliness which governed men in their intercourse with each other were instinctively observed by reverent persons in their approach to God, and found expression in commands and institutions (Ex. xix. 12, 14; xxx. 18–21; Josh. iii. 5). Ceremonial defilement, for which purification was provided, was incurred in a special manner and was restricted to certain acts and processes. It was acquired by—1. Contact with a human corpse (Num. xix. 11–22). This defilement was the gravest, for the effect of sin is revealed in strongest light in the death of man and the dissolution of the body. Uncleanness arising from this cause continued seven days, and was removed by the water of separation. Even the necessary handling of the ashes of the red heifer, which were used to cleanse from defilement by contact with the dead, rendered unclean (7–10); and contact with the unclean person rendered the clean person unclean until evening (22). 2. Leprosy in man, clothing, or building (Lev. xiii., xiv.). The leper was excluded from human society (xiii. 46), and for his cleansing he required special ablution and sacrifice. 3. Natural and morbid issues from the generative organs (xv.), including puerperal uncleanness (xii.). Generation and parturition were not sinful in themselves; they were ordained by the Creator (Gen. i. 27, 28). The bodily issues connected with them, however, in man or woman, whether voluntary or involuntary, defiled; man's affinity to the lower animals is apparent in reproduction, for right though it is, in heaven they neither marry nor are given in marriage; and probably the divine judgment pronounced on Eve for sin was remembered in connection with childbirth. 4. Eating the flesh of an unclean animal, or contact with its carcass or with that of a clean animal not slain for food and which had thus become subject to the corruption of death (Lev. xi.). See Unclean Animals; Purification.

U'ni-corn.

Any one-horned animal, as the rhinoceros (Is. xxxiv. 7, A. V. margin). The biblical animal, however, was two-horned (Deut. xxxiii. 17, where the word is singular, and not plural, as in A. V.). It was possessed of great strength (Num. xxiii. 22; xxiv. 8), but was too untamable to bend its neck to the yoke, or assist man in his agricultural labors (Job xxxix. 9–12). It was frisky in youth (Ps. xxix. 6). It was not the wild buffalo, for this beast is quite tamable. The R. V. margin (Num. xxiii. 22) renders it by ox-antelope, meaning the oryx (Antilope leucoryx); see Antelope. This interpretation is supported by the analogy of the Hebrew re'em to the Arabic rîm, which is now used in Syria for the white and yellow gazelle; but the oryx is timid and in ancient Egypt was frequently tamed and used in the plow. There is every reason to believe that the Hebrew word signifies the wild ox (R. V.); for this animal is denoted by the corresponding Assyrian word rîmu. Admirable representations of it by Assyrian artists show it to be the aurochs (Bos primigenius). Tiglath-pileser about 1120 to 1100 B. C. hunted it in the land of the Hittites, at the foot of Lebanon. It is now extinct, and its name has been transferred in Syria to another animal; but its previous occurrence on and around Lebanon is independently proved by the fact that Tristram discovered its teeth in the bone caves of Lebanon. Julius Cæsar, who met with it in Gaul, described it as the *Bos urus* (Bello Gallico vi. 28). Independently of its size, it is distinguished from its descendant, the common ox, by having a flatter forehead and large horns with double curvature.

Un'ni [oppressed, afflicted].

1. A Levite of the second degree in David's reign, who played the psaltery (1 Chron. xv. 18, 20). It is doubtful whether the word doorkeepers (18) is intended to include him.

2. A Levite in the time of Zerubbabel (Neh. xii. 9, A. V.); see UNNO.

Un'no, in A. V. **Unni**, which was substituted by the Hebrews in reading the text [oppressed, afflicted].

A Levite who was a contemporary of the high priest Jeshua (Neh. xii. 9).

U-phar'sin. See MENE.

U'phaz.

A place from which gold was brought (Jer. x. 9; Dan. x. 5). The same, apparently, as Ophir, though the difference in form has not been satisfactorily explained.

Ur, I. [perhaps, settlement].

A city of the Chaldees, the birthplace of Abraham (Gen. xi. 28, 31; xv. 7; Neh. ix. 7). Its site is now generally held to have been at Mugheir or Um-mugheir, Bitumened or the Mother of Bitumen, in Lower Babylonia, on the western bank of the Euphrates. It is called on inscribed tablets Uru; was in a district which, according to inscriptions, was

called Kaldu as early as at least the ninth century B. C.; and was a seat of the worship of the moon-god. Considerable ruins are still found on its site.

Ur, II.

Father of one of David's mighty men (1 Chron. xi. 35). The transcriber perhaps made two heroes, Ur and Hepher, out of one whose name was Ahasbai or something similar (cp. 2 Sam. xxiii. 34).

Ur-ba'nus, in A. V. **Ur'bane** [urbane, polite].

A Christian to whom the apostle Paul sent his salutation (Rom. xvi. 9).

U'ri [fiery, or, perhaps, light of (Jehovah), being an abbreviation of Urijah].

1. Father of Bezalel, the craftsman (Ex. xxxi. 2).

2. Father of Solomon's taxgatherer Geber (1 Kin. iv. 19).

3. A porter whom Ezra induced to put away his foreign wife (Ezra x. 24).

U-ri'ah, in A. V. of N. T. **Urias** [light of Jehovah]. The Hebrew name is often rendered Urijah.

1. A Hittite, one of David's mighty men (2 Sam. xxiii. 39; 1 Chron. xi. 41), whom the king arranged to have placed at an exposed point in a battle with the Ammonites and lose his life, to prevent his discovering an intrigue which his sovereign had been carrying on with the faithful soldier's wife (2 Sam. xi. 1–27; Mat. i. 6).

2. A priest, one of two witnesses to a tablet written by Isaiah (Is. viii. 2); see URIJAH 1.

Fragment of limestone relief from royal tombs at Ur, dating back to twenty-sixth century B.C.

3. A prophet, the son of Shemaiah of Kir-jath-jearim. He predicted that the kingdom of Judah was about to be temporarily destroyed, which so enraged king Jehoiakim that he sought to kill the prophet of evil. Uriah fled to Egypt, but was brought back and slain (Jer. xxvi. 20-23; in A. V. Urijah).

4. A priest, father of a certain Meremoth (Ezra viii. 33). Called in Neh. iii. 4, 21 Urijah.

5. One of those, probably priests, who stood by Ezra while he addressed the people (Neh. viii. 4; in A. V. Urijah).

U′ri-el [light of God].

1. A Levite, family of Kohath, house of Izhar, descended through Korah, Abiasaph, and Tahath (1 Chron. vi. 24). He is probably a different person from Zephaniah (36), and belonged to the collateral line which sprang from Tahath. The head of the Kohathite family in David's reign bore this name (xv. 5, 11), and is conceivably the same person.

2. A man of Gibeah whose daughter Micaiah was Abijah's mother (2 Chron. xiii. 2).

U-ri′jah [light of Jehovah].

1. The high priest in Ahaz' reign who was directed to make an altar like that which caught the king's fancy at Damascus (2 Kin. xvi. 10-16). He was probably one of the two witnesses to the enigmatical inscription written by Isaiah (Is. viii. 2, in E. V. Uriah).

2. A prophet (Jer. xxvi. 20, A. V.); see URIAH 3.

3. A priest (Neh. iii. 4, 21); see URIAH 4.

4. One who stood by Ezra while he addressed the people (Neh. viii. 4; in R. V. Uriah); see URIAH 5.

U′rim and Thum′mim [lights and perfections]. The order is once reversed (Deut. xxxiii. 8), and twice Urim alone is used (Num. xxvii. 21; 1 Sam. xxviii. 6).

One or more objects belonging to the ephod of the high priest, put in the breastplate of judgment so as to be on the high priest's heart when he went in before the Lord (Ex. xxviii. 30; Lev. viii. 8). The receptacle was probably a fold of the breastplate or the space underneath it. In connection with the Urim and Thummim, the high priest learned the will of God in doubtful cases. This method was not adopted for inquiring the divine will concerning private individuals or private matters, but was only employed in behalf of the nation; hence the required place for the Urim and Thummim was in the breastplate of judgment, which bore the names of the twelve tribes of Israel on twelve precious stones. With the Urim and Thummim, the will of Jehovah, the judge, concerning judicial matters, and the royal desire of Jehovah, the king, were learned (Num. xxvii. 21; cp Josh. ix. 14; Judg. i. 1; xx. 18, 23, 27, 28; 1 Sam. x. 22; xiv. 36-42; xxii. 10, 13; xxiii. 9-12; xxviii. 6; xxx. 7, 8; 2 Sam. ii. 1; v. 19, 23, 24). The will of Jehovah was inquired with Urim and

Thummim, not only in the sanctuary or where the ark was (Judg. xx. 27, 28; 1 Sam. xxii. 10), but in any place, provided the authorized priest with the ephod was present. The answer was usually quite simple, often a mere affirmation or denial, or a choice of one tribe or place out of several; but it was not always so (1 Sam. x. 10; 2 Sam. v. 23, 24). Occasionally, also, when sin had interrupted communion with God, no answer was granted (1 Sam. xiv. 37; xxviii. 6). There is no reference to the use of Urim and Thummim after the reign of David, and at the time of the return from exile there was no priest with Urim and Thummim (Ezra ii. 63; Neh. vii. 65); hence Josephus is probably wrong in saying that the virtue or use ceased 200 years before his time (Antiq. iii. 8, 9). The use of this method was a prerogative of the high priest alone; and, since he belonged to the tribe of Levi, the possession of the Urim and Thummim was a glory of that tribe (Deut. xxxiii. 8).

Different explanations of the Urim and Thummim have been offered. For example, an analogue has been sought in the badge of office which the Egyptian high priest, as supreme judge, is reported by classical writers to have worn, consisting of an emblem of truth suspended from his neck on a golden chain; but the Egyptian high priest carried this official token during the judicial proceedings only, and hanged it on the person in whose favor judgment was pronounced; and there is no evidence that it was ever used as a means for inquiring the divine will. Other interpreters have supposed that when to the high priest, clad in the ephod with the Urim and Thummim and offering prayer, an idea occurred, its divine origin and truth were confirmed by the unwonted gleaming of the gems in the breastplate. From this phenomenon was derived the name Urim, lights. It has been suggested that the answer was spelled out by the successive gleaming of the letters which composed the proper names on the stones; but to say nothing of the fact that the complete alphabet is not yielded by these names, and that in several of the recorded responses letters occur which are not found on the stones, the whole idea smacks of the feigned miracles of Greek and Roman priests, and is foreign to the methods and conceptions of the Hebrew ritual.

Only two theories are important. 1. The Urim and Thummim were one or more appendages of the ephod and detachable, and were used as the lot, cast like dice, and by their fall revealed the divine will. This is, indeed, a possible conception, but it lacks proof. Support is sought for it in the fact that the casting of the lot is twice referred to in close association with seeking revelation through Urim and Thummim (1 Sam. x. 19-22; xiv. 37-42). In the latter case, Saul prayed : "Give a perfect lot" (41, R. V. margin). The word *thamim* is used, which it is proposed to pronounce *thummim*, and thus make the Urim and Thummim to have been a kind of sacred lot. But in the two cases mentioned, the casting of lots was a distinct act from inquiring of the Lord, and was undertaken for a different purpose from that for which counsel was asked. 2. The Urim and Thummim gave no outward manifestation, but served as a symbol. The high priest arrayed himself in the ephod with Urim and Thummim, which betokened his authority to obtain light and truth, as the name indicates, in order that he might seek counsel of Jehovah in the divinely appointed manner. He laid the matter humbly before God in prayer; the answer dawned in his mind; he believed that the response was correct, because he had made his request in the manner of God's appointment, and because he had God's promise that he should receive light and truth. Faith in God was the evidence of things not seen. This interpretation of the use of the Urim and Thummim accords with the spirituality of the entire ritualism of the tabernacle. The answer was inward illumination, without any external sign, and finds its parallel in the revelations granted to the prophets.

U'su-ry.
Interest on loaned money, the word being used in its primary sense, without any imputation that the interest is extortionate in amount. See LOAN.

U'thai [probably, helpful].
1. A man of Judah, family of Perez, and son of Ammihud. He was the head of the father's house to which he belonged, and dwelt at Jerusalem (1 Chron. ix. 4).
2. A descendant of Bigvai. He accompanied Ezra from Babylon (Ezra viii. 14).

Uz, in A. V. once **Huz** (Gen. xxii. 21).
A tribe of the Aramæans (Gen. x. 23), able to trace their descent partly from Nahor (xxii. 21), and connected by blood or political ties with Dishan the Horite (xxxvi. 28). Job resided in the land of Uz (Job i. 1), and was exposed to attack from the Sabeans and Chaldeans (15, 17). At the time of Jeremiah, Edomites dwelt in the land of Uz (Lam. iv. 21). Josephus regarded Uz as the founder of Trachonitis and Damascus (Antiq. i. 6, 4). Ptolemy locates the Ausitai in the desert west of the Euphrates. Uz, according to these data, was in the Syrian desert between the latitudes of Damascus and Edom.

U'zai.
Father of one who helped to rebuild the wall of Jerusalem (Neh. iii. 25).

U'zal [possibly, travel or wandering].
A people of Arabia descended from Joktan (Gen. x. 27; 1 Chron. i. 21; Ezek. xxvii. 19, R. V. margin). The kindred name Azal was, according to Arabian tradition, the ancient name of Sana, the capital of Yemen, in Arabia.

Uz'za [strength]. The orthography is Aramaic.
1. A Benjamite, a son or a descendant of Ehud (1 Chron. viii. 7).
2. The founder of a family of Nethinim, members of which returned from captivity (Ezra ii. 49; Neh. vii. 51).
3. A man known only as the original owner of a garden. This garden ultimately passed into the hands of Manasseh, king of Judah, and was within the precincts of his palace. Both Manasseh and his son Amon were buried in it (2 Kin. xxi. 18, 26; cp. 2 Chron. xxxiii, 20). The garden was apparently at or near Jerusalem, but the exact spot is undetermined.
4 and 5. Two men otherwise called Uzzah.

Uz'zah, and **Uzza** in 1 Chron. xiii. 7–11 and A. V. of vi. 29 [strength].
1. A son of Abinadab, of what tribe is unknown. When the ark had reached the threshing floor of Nacon, or Chidon, on its way to the city of David, the oxen stumbled, and Uzzah, putting forth his hand to support the sacred symbol, was struck dead. The place was therefore called Perez-uzzah, breach of Uzzah, or breaking out against Uzzah, and long retained the name (2 Sam. vi. 3–11; 1 Chron. xiii. 7–14).
2. A son of Merari (1 Chron. vi. 29).

Uz-zen-she'e-rah, in A. V. **Uzzen-sherah**.
A village built by Sheerah, daughter of an Ephraimite named Ephraim (1 Chron. vii. 24). It is mentioned in connection with the two Beth-horons, and is considered to have been at Beit Sira, 3 miles west by south of the nether Beth-horon, and 13 west by north of Jerusalem.

Uz'zi [my strength, or might of (Jehovah)].
1. A man of Issachar, family of Tola, and head of a father's house (1 Chron. vii. 2, 3).
2. A priest, son of Bukki, and father of Zerahiah, of the line of Eleazar (1 Chron. vi. 5, 6, 51). He was an ancestor of Ezra (Ezra vii. 4).
3. A Benjamite, family of Bela, and head of a father's house (1 Chron. vii. 7).
4. Another Benjamite, son of Michri, and father of Elah (1 Chron. ix. 8).
5. A Levite of the sons of Asaph. He was son of Bani, and overseer of the Levites at Jerusalem (Neh. xi. 22).
6. A priest, head of the house of Jedaiah in the days of the high priest Joiakim (Neh. xii. 19).
7. A priest, one of those who assisted at the dedication of the rebuilt wall of Jerusalem (Neh. xii. 42).

Uz-zi'a [probably, Aramaic spelling of *'Uzziyyah*, might of Jehovah].
A man from the town of Ashtaroth, and one of David's mighty men (1 Chron. xi. 44).

Uz-zi'ah, in A. V. of N. T. **Ozias** [might of Jehovah].
1. A Kohathite Levite, the son of Shaul (1 Chron. vi. 24).

2. The father of a certain Jehonathan in David's time (1 Chron. xxvii. 25).

3. A king of Judah (2 Kin. xv. 13, 30–34; 2 Chronicles and Isaiah; Hos. i. 1; Amos i. 1; Zech. xiv. 5; Mat. i. 9); called Azariah in 2 Kin. xiv. 21; xv. 1–8, 17–27; 1 Chron. iii. 12 (see AZARIAH). He succeeded his father Amaziah about 786 B. C. during the latter's lifetime, a few years after the crushing defeat was inflicted on Amaziah by the king of Israel. That he reigned during his father's lifetime is evident from the statement made in connection with the record of his reign, that he built Elath after the death of the king (2 Kin. xiv. 22). He was sixteen years old when he ascended the throne (21). After conducting the government for twenty-four years, it is recorded that "he reigned in the twenty-seventh year of Jeroboam" (xv. 1; the word "began" is not in the Hebrew text). This statement "is most easily explained," says Kleinert, "by the assumption that in this year the kingdom of Judah had regained the full sovereignty;" freeing itself from vassalage to Jeroboam, in which it had been held since the overthrow of Amaziah, the capture and dismantlement of Jerusalem, and the enforcement of hostages. Uzziah organized the army; and he improved the fortifications of Jerusalem, and the weapons and military engines of his troops. He gained important victories over the Philistines and Arabs razed the walls of Gath, Jabneh, and Ashdod, and received tribute from the Ammonites and other foes (2 Chron. xxvi. 6–8). So strong did Judah become. Uzziah promoted agriculture by building towers in the desert and digging wells. Uzziah himself worshiped Jehovah, but did not take away the high places at which his people sacrificed to other gods. At length, elated by his prosperity, he entered the temple against priestly remonstrance, and attempted to offer incense, but was struck with leprosy, from which he never recovered. He had therefore to associate his son Jotham with him in the government. A notable earthquake occurred during his reign (Amos i. 1; Zech. xiv. 5), which took place near enough to his attempt to invade the priest's office to be connected with it in the popular memory (Antiq. ix. 10, 4). His reign extended to fifty-two years. He died about the year 735 B. C. (2 Kin. xv. 1–7; 2 Chron. xxvi. 1–23). Before his decease the prophets Isaiah, Hosea, and Amos had begun their public career (Is. i. 1; vi. 1; Hos. i. 1; Amos i. 1).

4. A priest, son of Harim. He was induced by Ezra to put away his foreign wife (Ezra x. 21).

5. A man of Judah, family of Perez (Neh. xi. 4).

Uz′zi-el [might of God].

1. A Levite, son of Kohath, and founder of a tribal family (Ex. vi. 18, 22; Num. iii.

19, 27, 30). He was a kinsman of Aaron on the father's side (Lev. x. 4). Amminadab, the chief of the Uzzielites, and 112 of his brethren, were organized by David for service when he brought up the ark to the city of David (1 Chron. xv. 10).

2. A Benjamite, family of Bela (1 Chron. vii. 7).

3. A Levite, instrumentalist in David's reign (1 Chron. xxv. 4). Called in verse 18 Azarel; see AZAREL 2.

4. A Levite, son of Jeduthun. He assisted king Hezekiah in his work of reformation (2 Chron. xxix. 14).

5. A Simeonite captain, one of those who, in Hezekiah's reign, led a successful expedition against the Amalekites of mount Seir (1 Chron. iv. 41–43).

6. A goldsmith, son of Harhaiah. He helped to rebuild the wall of Jerusalem (Neh. iii. 8).

V

Va′heb.
A place near the Arnon (Num. xxi. 14, 15, R. V.), otherwise unknown. See DI-ZAHAB.

Va-iz′a-tha, in A. V. **Va-jez′a-tha** [Persian, perhaps meaning strong as the wind].
A son of Haman (Esth. ix. 9).

Vale and **Val′ley.**
The vale or the valley, *par excellence,* is in A. V. the Shephelah or lowland (q. v.).

Va-ni′ah [perhaps, distress].
A son of Bani, induced by Ezra to put away his foreign wife (Ezra x. 36).

Vash′ni.
According to 1 Chron. vi. 28 (A. V. following the Hebrew text), the eldest son of Samuel, in which case he would be the same as Joel of verse 33, and of 1 Sam. viii. 2. But the text is corrupt. Joel has accidentally slipped out, the conjunction *vau* before Abiah has crept in, and *vashni* should be rendered "and the second." (R. V. following Syriac and 1 Sam. viii. 2).

Vash′ti.
The queen of the Persian sovereign Ahasuerus. For refusing to show herself to the king's guests at a feast celebrated in his third year, she was divorced and deposed (Esth. i. 3 and 9–ii. 1). Vashti may be a title, old Persian *vahishti,* sweetest; or it may be connected with the name of an Elamite deity called Washti (see discussion, article ESTHER); or it may be the Hebrew reproduction of the Persian name which the Greeks pronounced Amestris. Amestris, daughter of Otanes, was the wife of Xerxes (Herod. vii. 61, 114). If she was Vashti, Vashti was ultimately restored to favor; for Amestris was the recognized wife of Xerxes about 479 B. C., at the end of his eighth or in his ninth regnal year (ix. 109).

Vav, in A. V. and E. R. V. **Vau.**

The sixth letter of the Hebrew alphabet The English F. through the Greek digamma or fau, has the same origin. Where it is a consonant in Hebrew names, it appears as v in the anglicized form.

It stands at the head of the sixth section of Ps. cxix. in several versions, in which section each verse begins with this letter.

At several different periods in the development of the Hebrew alphabet it has had similarity with other letters. On the tomb of James, dating from the first century before Christ, vau and zain are scarcely distinguishable from one another, and jod differs only by a hook at the top and a slope; thus, in the order named, ٦, ١, ٦ .

In the inscription on the synagogue at Kefr Bir'im the difference between vau and jod has disappeared.

Ve'dan.

A place with which Tyre traded (Ezek. xxvii. 19, R. V.); possibly either Adin or Weddân, between Mecca and Medina. But the text may be corrupt. The A. V. has the rendering "Dan also," the first syllable being regarded as the Hebrew conjunction vau.

Veil, in A. V. often **Vail.** See CLOTHING, TABERNACLE, and TEMPLE, HEROD'S.

Ver-mil'ion.

A red pigment obtained by grinding the mineral cinnabar (Pliny, Hist. Nat. xxxiii. 38). It was called *shashar* in Hebrew, *miltos* in Greek; and was used to paint walls, mural decorations, and idols (Jer. xxii. 14; Ezek. xxiii. 14; Wisd. xiii. 14). Vermilion is a satisfactory translation of the word in these passages; but *miltos* was of broader meaning and denoted any red, mineral, coloring matter; as red lead, or clay mingled with the oxide of iron and known as ocher. Rude Africans bedaubed the body with it (Herod. iv. 191, 194), and certain tribes used it as war paint (vii. 69).

Ver'sions.

Translations of the Bible or of any portions of it into vernacular tongues, for the benefit of those who understand the original imperfectly or not at all.

Versions are immediate or mediate, according as they are made directly from the original text or through the medium of other translations. Four ancient immediate versions of the O. T. have come down to modern times: the Septuagint, the Targums of Onkelos and Jonathan ben Uzziel, the Syriac Peshito with a considerable portion of its predecessors, and the Latin Vulgate. They derive special value from the fact that they were made before the Hebrew text of the Masoretes was established.

The Samaritan Pentateuch is not a version; it is the Hebrew text written in Samaritan or old Hebrew characters, with various divergences from the Hebrew text of the Masoretes (see SAMARITAN PENTATEUCH); and the Samaritan version of the Pentateuch is a translation of this divergent text into the Samaritan dialect.

I. *Ancient Versions of the O. T., made for the use of Jews.*

1. *The Septuagint.* The most celebrated Greek version of the Hebrew Scriptures and the oldest complete translation of them. It was called the Septuagint, commonly designated by LXX., after the seventy translators reputed to have been employed on it in the time of Ptolemy Philadelphus, 285–247 B. C. Aristobulus, a Jewish priest who lived in Alexandria during the reign of Ptolemy Philometor, 181–146 B. C., and who is mentioned in 2 Mac. i. 10, is quoted by Clement of Alexandria and Eusebius as stating that while portions relating to Hebrew history had been translated into Greek previously, the entire law was translated from the Hebrew in the reign of Ptolemy Philadelphus under the direction of Demetrius Phalereus. The same tradition, but considerably embellished, is contained in a letter purporting to have been written by Aristeas to his brother. This letter is condemned by modern scholars as spurious. The same story as that told by Aristeas is repeated with slight variations by Josephus, who may have had the letter before him. Josephus relates that Demetrius Phalereus, librarian to Ptolemy Philadelphus, who reigned alone from 283–247 B. C., wished to add to the 200,000 volumes in the library a copy of the Hebrew books of the law, and to have them translated into Greek, as they were unintelligible in the original. The king consented, and made application to Eleazar the high priest at Jerusalem for seventy-two aged and skillful interpreters, six from each tribe, to make the translation. They arrived in Alexandria, bringing the law written in golden letters on books of parchment. They were hospitably received, were assigned a quiet house on the island of Pharos in the harbor of Alexandria, and transcribed and interpreted the law in seventy-two days (Antiq. xii. 2, 1–13; con. Apion. ii. 4).

These ancient reports concerning the origin of the Septuagint have great value, although reliance cannot be placed on the details, and the statements regarding the scope of the work are difficult of interpretation. It is, however, commonly agreed that the Septuagint originated in Egypt, that the Pentateuch was translated into Greek in the time of Ptolemy Philadelphus, that the other books followed gradually, and that the entire work was completed by 150 B. C. Reference to a Greek version of the law, the prophets, and the other books is made by Jesus, son of Sirach, as early as 132 B. C. (Ecclus. prologue). It is possible that the work was revised in the Maccabæan period. The version is the work of many translators, as differences in style and method show, and its quality is unequal in different parts; it is also much corrupted. The translation of the Pentateuch, except poetic portions (Gen. xlix.; Deut. xxxii. xxxiii.), is the best part of the work, and on the whole is well executed, although not literal. The translators of The Proverbs and Job were masters of a good Greek style, but were imperfectly acquainted with Hebrew and handled the original arbitrarily. The translation of The Proverbs is based on a Hebrew text that varied considerably from the present Masoretic text. The general sense of the Psalms is fairly well reproduced. Ecclesiastes is rendered with slavish literalness. The translation of the prophets is unequal in quality. That of Amos and Ezekiel is tolerably well done, but that of Isaiah is quite inferior. The version of Jeremiah was possibly made from a different form of the Hebrew text than the Masoretic. Of all the O. T. books, Daniel is the most poorly translated, so much so that the early Christians, since the time of Irenæus and Hippolytus, substituted for it the version of Theodotion.

Christ and his apostles used the Septuagint frequently. In quoting from the O. T. sometimes they cited the Septuagint verbatim, or with unimportant verbal changes; at others, they apparently themselves translated from the original Hebrew. There are about 350 quotations from the O. T. in the gospels, The Acts, and the epistles, and only about fifty materially differ from the Greek version. The Ethiopian eunuch whom Philip met was reading the Septuagint (Acts viii. 30–33).

Three main recensions of the Septuagint were made. One was issued about A. D. 236, and the others previous to A. D. 311. They were that of Origen in Palestine, of Lucian in Asia Minor and Constantinople, and of Hesychius in Egypt. The Vatican manuscript of the Septuagint is acknowledged to exhibit relatively the purest and most original text, and it probably descended from that upon which Origen based the text of the Septuagint given in the fifth column of his Hexapla; see I. 2. Lucian's recension has been edited in part by Lagarde and by Oesterley. Lucian was a presbyter of Antioch, and died a martyr's death at Nicomedia in A. D. 311 or 312. He issued a revised text of the Septuagint based on a comparison of the common Greek text with the Hebrew text, which proves to have been a good text, but different from that of the Masoretes. Hesychius was bishop of Egypt, and suffered martyrdom A. D. 310 or 311; his text has been lost; but a codex, known as Q, preserved in the Vatican library, and containing the Prophets, is believed to show it for these books.

2. *Minor Greek Versions.* After the destruction of Jerusalem in A. D. 70, the Septuagint lost favor among the Jews, partly because of the successful use made of it by the Christians in establishing the claims of Jesus, and partly because they discovered that its style lacked elegance. Accordingly three translations of the canonical books of the O. T. were made by Jews in the second century. 1. The translation by Aquila, a native of Pontus and a proselyte to Judaism. He lived in the time of the emperor Hadrian, and he undertook to make a literal version of the Hebrew Scriptures in order to counteract the use of the Septuagint made by the Christians in advancing their doctrines. It was so slavishly literal as often to be unintelligible to readers who did not know Hebrew as well as Greek. 2. The revision of the Septuagint by Theodotion, a Jewish proselyte of Ephesus according to Irenæus, and according to Eusebius an Ebionite, believing in the Messiahship, but not in the divinity of Christ. He lived before A. D. 160, for he is mentioned by Justin Martyr. In his revision of the Septuagint he made use both of Aquila's translation and of the Hebrew original. 3. The elegant, but periphrastic, translation by Symmachus, a Samaritan Ebionite.

Origen arranged the Hebrew text and four different versions in six parallel columns for purposes of comparison. In the first column he put the Hebrew text, in the second the Hebrew written in Greek letters, in the third the version of Aquila, in the fourth that of Symmachus, in the fifth the Septuagint, in the sixth the revision by Theodotion. From these six columns his work takes its name of Hexapla. In the column devoted to the Septuagint he marked with obeli words which were not in his Hebrew text. He emended the Greek text by supplying words lacking in it, but found in the Hebrew. These he indicated by asterisks. He conformed the spelling of proper names to the Hebrew. Origen prepared a smaller edition containing the last four columns only, and hence called the Tetrapla. These two works were deposited in the library founded by Origen's disciple, Pamphilus, at Cæsarea in Palestine. They were consulted by Jerome in the fourth century, and were still in existence in the sixth century. It is thought that they were destroyed when the Mohammedans took the town in A. D. 638. Fragments of Origen's great work are preserved in quotations made by the fathers. The Septuagint column was separately published by Pamphilus and Eusebius; and it was translated into Syriac by Paul, bishop of Tella, in A. D. 617–18. Origen pursued an unfortunate method when he conformed the text of the Septuagint to the Hebrew text of his day; since the great desideratum of scholars is the Greek text as it left the translators' hands, for that text would throw light on the Hebrew text which they used. Moreover, the obeli and asterisks, which Origen used, were often neglected or carelessly employed by copyists, so that the additions which he made to the Septuagint and the portions of the Septuagint which he did not

Facsimile pages from the Codex Sinaiticus.

Facsimile page from the Gutenberg Bible.

The Wyclif Bible.

The King James Version.

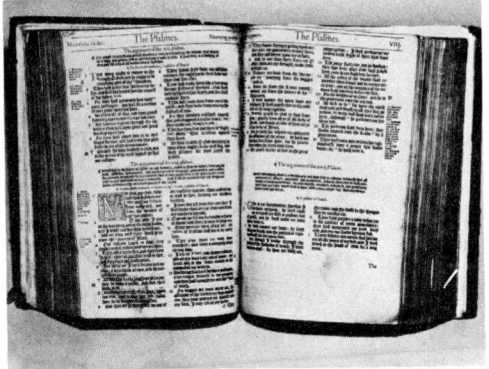

The Bishop's Psalter.

The Rheims-Douai Version.

The Tyndale Version.

The first Hebrew Bible published in America, 1814.

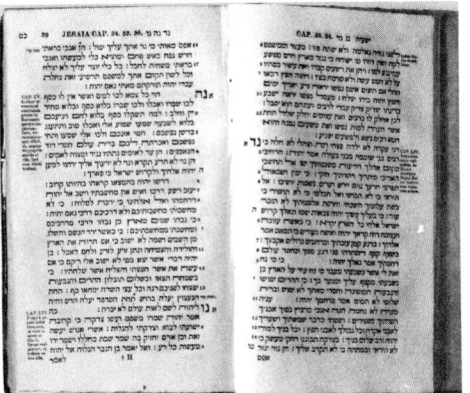

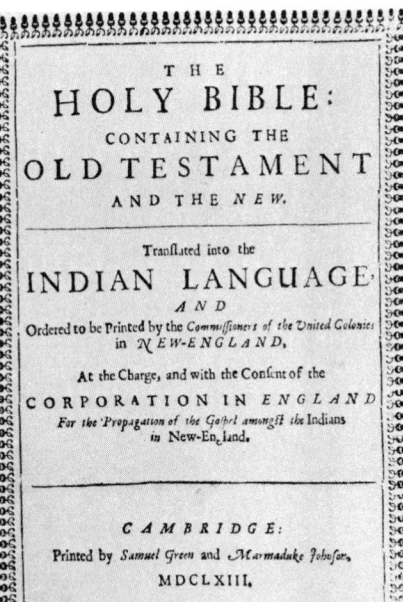

Title page of the Eliot Bible, translated by the Reverend John Eliot to assist in the "propagation of the Gospel among the Indians in New England." The Bible was printed in Utrecht in 1668.

find in his Hebrew text cannot always be discovered.

3. *The Targums.* When the Jews returned from the Babylonian exile, the Hebrew of their forefathers ceased to be their ordinary speech, and Aramaic, misnamed Chaldee, took its place. It soon became necessary at the public reading of the Scriptures for the reader or his assistant to translate the passage orally that the people might understand. The custom of explaining obscure words and phrases at the public reading was in vogue in Ezra's time (Neh. viii. 8). The event referred to has been cited as evidence that the words read were translated; but this is more than the statement warrants, and depends upon the answer to the question whether the Hebrews had adopted a foreign language during the exile. The oral targum—that is, interpretation or translation—which became necessary, was at first a simple paraphrase in Aramaic; but eventually it became elaborate, and in order to fix it as a translation and render it authoritative as an interpretation, it was reduced to writing. These written Targums are a valuable aid in determining the text as read in the early synagogues and in discovering the meaning which the Jews attached to difficult passages. The principal Targums are the Targum of Onkelos on the Pentateuch and the Targum of Jonathan ben Uzziel on the prophets. According to the Talmud, Onkelos was the friend of Gamaliel and a fellow-pupil of Paul, and therefore lived about A. D. 70. His Targum would then antedate the beginning of the second century; but it is generally regarded as a later production, perhaps as early as the second century. It is quite literal. The Targum of Jonathan ben Uzziel, on the other hand, is periphrastic; and it is of later date. The Targums on the Hagiographa date from the eleventh century.

II. *Ancient Versions of a part or the whole of the Bible, and intended chiefly for Christians.*

1. *Syriac Versions.*

(1) *The Old Syriac Version of the N. T.* This is represented by the gospels discovered by Mrs. Lewis in the convent of St. Catherine on mount Sinai in 1892, and by the closely related fragments found by Cureton in a Syrian convent in the Nitrian desert in 1841–43.

(2) *The Peshito.* Peshito means simple or vulgate. The O. T. was made directly from the Hebrew, and in the first instance was probably prepared for the use of Jewish proselytes. It was made as early as the first century. The N. T. is a revision of the old Syriac in order to bring it into closer agreement with the Greek text and improve its diction and style. The Peshito seems to have been in circulation in the second century. By reason of its elegance it has often been called the queen of versions.

(3) *The Philoxenian Version of the N. T.* This is so called because it was translated in A. D. 508 by Philoxenus, bishop of Hierapolis, in Asia Minor.

(4) *The Jerusalem or Palestinian Syriac Version of the N. T.* is but little known as yet, but promises to be of critical value.

2. *Latin Versions.*

(1) *The Old Latin or North African Version.* By the end of the second century a Latin version of the Scriptures was in circulation in northern Africa. It was used by Tertullian, who died about A. D. 220, and by Cyprian and Augustine. The O. T. was not translated immediately from the Hebrew, but was based on the Greek version.

(2) *The Itala or Italian Version.* Augustine testifies that a translation of the N. T. was made by any one who had sufficient knowledge of Greek. The North African version of the O. and N. T. was provincial in its language and offensive to the ears of the Latin-speaking Romans of the capital. In the fourth century, therefore, a recension of the text took place, which, from being made in Italy, was called the Itala.

(3) *The Vulgate.* The issue of the Itala was followed by other recensions, of which almost the only effect was to bring the text into confusion; till at length in A. D. 383 a Christian father, Jerome or Hieronymus, A. D. 329 or 331 to 420, the most learned scholar of his day and a man of moral earnestness and piety, was requested by Damasus, bishop of Rome, to undertake a revision of the Latin N. T. The gospels were compared with the original Greek, interpolations were removed, and gross errors were corrected. He also made two revisions of the old Latin version of the Psalms by comparing it with the Septuagint. These are known as the Roman and Gallican psalters, because introduced into Rome and Gaul respectively. Jerome then designed a revision of the entire O. T. In 387 he took up his residence in a monastery at Bethlehem. He began and completed a revision based on the hexaplar text of Origen; but ultimately he made a version immediately from the Hebrew, with constant reference to the Greek versions and with special respect for Symmachus. As a youth he had pursued the study of Hebrew, and after his removal to Bethlehem he resumed it with the aid of Jewish teachers. Samuel and Kings, prefaced by the famous *Prologus galleatus* giving an account of the Hebrew canon, were issued in 392, and the entire work was completed in 405. His own generation gave him abuse rather than gratitude for the very important service he had rendered it; and the eminent father, whose temper was none of the best, retorted by expressing the contempt which knowledge feels for blatant and aggressive ignorance. As the ages rolled forward, his work, which was done not for one generation, but for all succeeding time, was more and more appreciated. The Vulgate became the Bible of the whole western church in

the Middle Ages, and notwithstanding vernacular translations, remains the Bible of the Roman Catholic church still. A recension of the text was made by Alcuin, at the instance of Charlemagne, about 802. The Latin Vulgate was the first book ever printed, having been issued from the press about 1455, soon after the invention of printing. On April 8, 1546, the Council of Trent made a decree which expressed the wish for a fresh revision. Scholars were dilatory about undertaking the duty, till a pontiff of iron will, Sixtus V., urged on the work and even took a personal part in its accomplishment. The revision was published in 1590. A different one came forth under the auspices of pope Clement VIII. in 1592. It was an improvement on the Sixtine edition, but did not quite render it obsolete. Both editions are still in use. The Clementine text of the Vulgate of the O. T., with the various readings of the codex Amiatinus, has been edited by Heyse and Tischendorf, and the N. T. according to the codex Amiatinus by Tischendorf. It is from the Vulgate that a large part of the technical language used in theology is derived. For instance, sacrament, justification, and sanctification are simply the anglicized forms of *sacramentum, justificatio,* and *sanctificatio,* occurring in the Vulgate.

3. *Coptic Versions of the N. T.* They appear principally in two dialects, Memphitic and Thebaic. The Memphitic version is supposed to date from the close of the second century. It is for the most part faithful, and preserves the best text as current among the Alexandrian fathers, free from the corruptions that prevailed in the second century. The Thebaic version is believed to be slightly later in date, and it is less faithful to the original.

4. *The Ethiopic Version of the Bible* was made some time between the fourth and sixth centuries A. D.; it is the oldest monument as well as the foundation of the whole Ethiopic literature. Its translators were not learned men, nor entirely familiar with Greek, but the rendering is faithful and has preserved peculiarities. The O. T. portion was not translated immediately from the Hebrew, but was made from the Greek version, and is therefore valuable as an aid in determining the text of the Septuagint.

5. *The Gothic Version* was made in the latter half of the fourth century by Ulphilas, bishop of the West Goths. It embraced the whole Bible except the books of Samuel and Kings, which the bishop omitted, because he thought it would be dangerous to place them, with their warlike spirit and opposition to idolatry, in the hands of the Goths. Most of the N. T., but little of the O. T. in this version is extant. The translation is faithful and skillful.

6. *The extant Arabic Versions* are late, and of no critical importance.

III. *English Versions.*

1. *Early English Versions.* In Anglo-Saxon times portions of Scripture, especially the Psalms, the ten commandments, and portions of the gospels, were translated into the vernacular tongue. After the language had been modified by the Norman conquest, various portions of Scripture, especially the gospels, were rendered into the language of the nation. But no effort was made similarly to treat the Bible as a whole.

2. *Wycliffe and Purvey's Bible.* Of this there are two versions: the first apparently between 1382 and 1383, and the second about 1388. The first, which was robust and terse, but unpolished in language, was mainly Wycliffe's; the second, which was more refined, emanated chiefly from Purvey, for Wycliffe, who was born about A. D. 1324, had died on December 31, 1384. The best-known version is Purvey's. Here are specimens of both versions. Gen. i. 1: "In the firste made God of nou3t heuene and erthe." In the later version this reads: "In the bigynnyng God made of nou3t heuene and erthe." In the older version John iii. 16 is: "Forsothe God so loued the world, that he gaf his oon bigetun sone, that ech man that bileueth in to him perische not, but haue euere lasting lyf"; but in the later version it is changed to: "For God louede so the world, that he gaf his oon bigetun sone, that ech man that bileueth in him perische not, but haue euerlastynge lijf." Both versions were made from the Latin Vulgate. Wycliffe's version was the first rendering of the Scriptures into any form of modern English, and it helped to mold the language; it also exerted great influence on the national life; but it was circulated in manuscript copies only, and was not printed until 1848.

3. About 1526 there arrived from abroad a translation of the N. T. from the original Greek by the reformer William Tyndale who had left his native England to escape persecution. It was published at Worms, and was made from the Greek of Erasmus probably from the edition of 1519, although the edition of 1522 was consulted. Tyndale translated immediately from the Greek, using the German N. T. of Luther and the Vulgate as aids. His work excited great opposition from the leading dignitaries of the then dominant church, though many of the common people received it gladly. The book was pronounced full of pestilent errors, and was burnt at Paul's Cross. In 1530, and again in 1534, he published a translation of the Pentateuch, and in 1531 of the book of Jonah. They were made immediately from the original Hebrew, Luther and the Vulgate being used as aids. In 1534 a fresh edition of his N. T. was issued from Antwerp. There is evidence that he translated other portions of the O. T. besides those already mentioned, most probably to the end of Chronicles with several prophetical books; but he did not

live to publish them. He was arrested on the 23d or 24th of May, 1535, at Antwerp, where he had permanently settled, and on the 6th of October, 1536, was first strangled and then burnt as a heretic. But his work remained. It fixed the English standard of Bible translation, and its diction and style still live in the English version and lend it literary charm and character.

4. *Coverdale's Bible.* This work was published in 1535, with no mention who the printer was nor from what city or town it issued. Probably Zurich is entitled to the honor, but possibly Frankfort or Cologne. It was the first complete English Bible issued from the press. The N. T. and much of the O. T. are practically Tyndale's. Only the portion from Job to Malachi was translated independently by Miles Coverdale, and he used not the original Hebrew, but a Swiss-German Bible printed at Zurich in 1527–29. He describes the book as "translated out of Douche and Latyn in to Englishe." Coverdale's version of the Psalms, virtually unchanged, is still used by the church of England in its Book of Common Prayer.

5. *Matthew's Bible.* Thomas Matthew is believed to have been only a name assumed by John Rogers, successor to Tyndale as chaplain to the English merchants of the Steelyard at Antwerp, the first martyr in the persecution under Mary Tudor. In 1537 he printed an edition of the Bible, perhaps at Antwerp. It contains Tyndale's translations in their latest form. For books not translated by Tyndale, the text is taken from Coverdale's version. It had bold annotations, yet it was the first Bible licensed by public authority.

6. *Taverner's Bible.* This was published in the year 1539, and was designed to counteract the influence of Matthew's Bible, and especially of his daring explanatory notes.

7. *The Great Bible;* called also *Cranmer's Bible.* The first name was given it on account of its size, the page of type measuring 13¼ by 7½ inches, and the second name came into use because Cranmer wrote the introduction to it. It was undertaken by Coverdale at Cromwell's suggestion, was produced mainly by the revision of the text of Matthew's Bible, and appeared in 1539–41. It was warmly welcomed, and seven editions of it ere long appeared.

8. *The Geneva Bible.* This revision was the work of three exiles, who had taken refuge in Geneva during the Marian persecution, Whittingham, Gilby, and Sampson. It was a revision of Tyndale, collated with the Great Bible. From the occurrence of the word breeches in Gen. iii., where the A. V. was subsequently to have aprons, it is sometimes called the Breeches Bible. The N. T. appeared in 1557, and the whole Bible in 1560. These two editions were the first English translations to use the division into verses. The translators availed them-

selves of the aids furnished by the best biblical scholarship of the age, and it is itself the most scholarly of the early English versions. It was a handy volume, being small quarto in size. It was well received among the common people, especially those of Puritan tendency, and for seventy-five years was the Bible in current use. It was provided with notes, which form a sound and helpful commentary along practical, expository, and doctrinal lines, and was the first Bible printed in Scotland.

9. *The Bishops' Bible.* The popularity of the Geneva Bible was not acceptable to the bishops, and in 1568 they issued one of their own. It borrowed from the Geneva version the division of the chapters into verses. In 1571 Convocation pronounced in its favor, and ordered copies to be placed in all the churches. It was founded chiefly on the Great Bible, though borrowing a few variations from the Geneva version.

10. *The Rheims and Douay Bible.* This is the Roman Catholic version of the Scriptures into English. It was made from the Vulgate, and published, the N. T. at Rheims in 1582, and the O. T. at Douay in 1609–10. It contains a highly controversial commentary. Its language and style smack more of Latin than English; but it gave currency to many words borrowed from the Latin, and not a few of them, such as impenitent, propitiation, remission, found a place in the A. V.

11. *The Authorized Version.* The proposal to make this version came, apparently on the spur of the moment, from Dr. Reinolds, or Reynolds, president of Corpus Christi College, Oxford, during the discussion between the Anglicans and the Puritans at the Hampton Court Conference, on the 14th, 16th, and 18th of January, 1604. King James I., whose interest in theology is well known, was pleased by the proposal, and on the 10th of February, 1604, he ordered, among other things, "that a translation be made of the whole Bible, as consonant as can be to the original Hebrew and Greek; and this to be set out and printed, without any marginal notes, and only to be used in all churches of England in time of divine service." The king appointed fifty-four translators, but only forty-seven took part in the work. They were formed into six companies, two of which met at Westminster, two at Oxford, and two at Cambridge. The work was issued in 1611, with a fulsome dedication to king James. It was not a new translation, but a scholarly revision of a good version. It has endeared itself to all English-speaking Christians, and is the translation now in common use.

12. *The Revised Version.* A revision of the A. V. became necessary because in the course of more than two centuries and a half through new manuscripts and careful study corruptions had been discovered in the text of the Greek Testament which had been

used for the English version, and a superior text had been provided. Greek and Hebrew scholarship had also made great advances during the same period. In February, 1870, the Convocation of the Province of Canterbury planned, not a new translation, but a fresh revision of the time-honored version. Two companies were formed for the purpose, one for each Testament. That for the O. T. consisted of twenty-seven members; and that for the N. T. likewise of twenty-seven members at first, but for the greater part of the time of twenty-four. Two-thirds of these belonged to the church of England. Two companies of scholars in America cooperated, fourteen for the O. T. and thirteen for the N. T., representing the different Protestant churches. The work was begun on the 22d of June, 1870. The N. T. took ten and a half years, and was published in May, 1881. The revision of the O. T. was commenced on the 30th of June, 1870, and was completed in fourteen years, on June 20th, 1884. The American Revised Version is the Revised Version of 1881 and 1884 newly edited, the N. T. in the year 1900, and the O. T. in 1901. The American edition incorporates in the text the readings and renderings preferred by the two American committees, adds references to parallel and illustrative passages, provides a running headline to indicate the topics in the page, removes the verse numbers from the margin to the text, substitutes the name Jehovah for LORD and GOD, wherever it is found in the original, and increases the number of changes made for the sake of euphemism. The Revised is inferior to the Authorized Version in felicity of expression, and the sentences are less perfect in their rhythm and their cadence. But as a work of science it is a great improvement on the A.V. Especially in the poetic and prophetical portions of the O. T. and in the epistles of the N. T. has the true meaning been made clear. The orthography also of the proper names has been vastly improved.

Vine.

Any plant with a long, slender, prostrate or climbing stem, with tendrils, as a gourd (2 Kin. iv. 39). The word usually denotes the common or grape vine (*Vitis vinifera*). It is believed to be indigenous in western Asia south of the Caspian Sea (cp. Gen. ix. 20, 21). It was largely cultivated in Egypt (xl. 9–11; Ps. lxxviii. 47); and Egyptian sculptures of the Old Empire, before the time of Joseph, represent vineyards, vines laden with grapes, presses, and the manufacture of wine. The soil and climate of Palestine were favorable to the vine, and it was early cultivated in Canaan (Gen. xiv. 18). It is incidentally referred to as growing in the lowland of Philistia, at Jezreel, and in the plain of Gennesaret (Judg. xv. 5; 1 Kin. xxi. 1; War iii. 10, 8), and especially in the mountainous districts, as near Hebron, Shiloh, and Shechem

Vineyard on the Mount of Olives.

(Num. xiii. 23; Judg. ix. 27; xxi. 20; Jer. xxxi. 5). Especial mention is made of the vines of Eshcol in the hill country of Judah (Num. xiii. 23), of En-gedi in the valley of the Dead Sea (Song i. 14), of Heshbon, Elealeh, and Sibmah beyond Jordan (Is. xvi. 8–10; Jer. xlviii. 32), and of Lebanon (Hos. xiv. 7). There was great difference in value between the choicest, noble vines and the degenerate plant of a strange vine (Is. v. 2; Jer. ii. 21). Israel is compared to a vine (Ps. lxxx. 8–16), and our Lord to the stem of a vine, and his true followers to the branches (John xv. 1–8).

The vineyard was frequently on a hillside or peak (Is. v. 1; Joel iii. 18), which was terraced when necessary. It was surrounded by a hedge or a stone wall to keep out destructive animals (Num. xxii. 24; Ps. lxxx. 8–13; Prov. xxiv. 31; Song ii. 15; Is. v. 5). The ground was cleared of stones, the vines were planted, a booth or tower was erected for the watchman, a press was constructed, and a vat was hewn in the rock (Is. i. 8; v. 1–7; Mat. xxi. 33–41). Laborers were sometimes hired to work in it (xx. 1–16), for it was necessary to prune the vines, dig about them, and keep the ground free from weeds (Lev. xxv. 3; Prov. xxiv. 30, 31; Is. v. 6; John xv. 2). The vines were allowed to spread on the ground, the stock not being supported, only the fruit-bearing branches being slightly raised from the earth (Is. xvi. 8; Ezek. xvii. 6; Pliny, Hist. Nat. xvii. 35, 15). Other vines were doubtless trained to trees; and yet others were probably planted, as at present in Palestine, in rows, 8 to 10 feet apart, the stock being allowed to grow 6 or 8 feet high and then fastened to stout stakes and the branches trained from stock to stock.

The grapes ordinarily grown were red (Is. lxiii. 2; Rev. xiv. 19, 20); but at the present day a white variety is almost exclusively raised at Bethlehem and Hebron. The grapes began to ripen about August, in favored localities somewhat earlier. They were eaten both fresh and dried (Num. vi. 3; Deut. xxiii. 24). The dried grapes or raisins were preserved in clusters or pressed into cakes, and were esteemed as food (1 Sam. xxv. 18; 1 Chron. xvi. 3). The juice of grapes was expressed, and was drunk fresh and fermented ; see WINE.

The vintage began in the middle of September and continued into October. It was a season of festivity. In the vineyards there were singing and joyful noise, and the treaders in the press kept time by shouting as they trod the grapes (Judg. ix. 27; Is. xvi. 10; Jer. xxv. 30; xlviii. 33).

Vine of Sod'om.

A plant growing near Sodom, and bearing clusters of bitter fruit (Deut. xxxii. 32). But the language may be figurative. Josephus describes fruits growing near the site of Sodom, which bear a color as if they are fit to be eaten; but contain ashes, and if plucked with the hands, dissolve into smoke and ashes (War iv. 8, 4; cp. Tacitus, Hist. v. 6). This fruit does not correspond to the grapes of gall and bitter clusters which apparently characterize the vine of Sodom. It is often assumed, however, that the plants are one, and the effort is made to identify it. Excluding plants which are common elsewhere in Palestine, the principal claimants are: 1. What the Arabs call the *'ushâr*, an asclepiadaceous plant (*Calotropis gigantea* or *procera*), a native of Upper Egypt, Arabia, and India. It grows at En-gedi and other parts of the tropical Dead Sea valley, is a tree 10 or 15 feet high, and bears a fruit resembling an apple or orange, three or four of them in a cluster. They are pleasant to the eye and to the touch ; but if pressed or struck they explode like a puff ball, leaving only fragments of the rind and a few fibers in the hand. A formidable objection to the identification is the difficulty of seeing how the term vine can be applied to a small, erect tree. 2. The colocynth (*Citrullus colocynthus*), a trailing plant. Its fruit is "fair to look upon ; but when fully ripe, merely a quantity of dusty powder with the seeds inside its beautiful orange rind" (Tristram); see GOURD, WILD.

Vin'e-gar.

Wine or other strong drink turned sour by acetous fermentation (Num. vi. 3). If vinous fermentation was pushed too far, or if the wine was kept too long, it became vinegar. Vinegar is acid, setting the teeth on edge (Prov. x. 26), and hardening soap or neutralizing its alkali (xxv. 20). In itself it is unfit to drink (Ps. lxix. 21); but mingled with a little oil it is drunk by the common people in the East to quench thirst when fresh water is not obtainable; and it was used at meals in the heat of harvest, bread being dipped in it, as it brought grateful refreshment to the system (Ruth ii. 14). The vinegar used by Boaz' reapers is, however, regarded by many

interpreters as sour, not soured, wine. The Roman soldiers when in camp drank a thin, sour wine called *acetum*, vinegar, both in its pure state and diluted with water. In the latter condition it was termed *posca* (Pliny, Hist. Nat. xix. 29). It was probably a drink of this sort which the Roman soldier offered to Jesus on the cross to quench his burning thirst (Mark xv. 36; John xix. 29, 30). This draught, which Jesus accepted, was different from the sour wine, previously offered and refused, which was mingled with a bitter substance or more definitely with myrrh, which is astringent (Mat. xxvii. 34; Mark xv. 23).

Vine'yard. See VINE.

Vine'yards, Plain of. See ABEL-CHERAMIM.

Vi'ol. See PSALTERY.

Vi'per.

1. The rendering of the Hebrew *'Eph'eh*, blowing, hissing ; a venomous serpent referred to as inhabiting the south country (Job xx. 16; Is. xxx. 6; lix. 5). The species is not properly determined.

2. A poisonous reptile, in Greek *echidna*, incidentally mentioned as found on the island of Melita (Acts xxviii. 3) and familiar to the Jews (Mat. iii. 7); probably the common viper (*Vipera communis* or *Pelias berus*), which is common on the Mediterranean coast.

Vi'sions.

No sharp line of demarcation is discernible between visions and dreams (q. v.). The one shades into the other. The Bible recognizes —1. Vain visions (Job xx. 8; Is. xxix. 7). 2. Visions of the prophets. These were for the most part private ; they were apprehended by the individual, not by his companions. A natural cause sometimes cooperated in producing the vision : the vision of the great sheet let down from heaven, which Peter saw, and the voice heard saying "Rise, Peter; kill and eat," stood in some relation to his bodily hunger, as the account in the book of The Acts clearly intimates (x. 9 seq.). Thus far the visions of the prophets have points in common with visions begotten of an abnormal mental condition, and to this extent are to be classed as mental phenomena. These facts are only additional proofs of what might be expected, namely, that God, in holding communication with men, works in accordance with the laws of man's mind. The visions of the prophets, however, form a unique class. With perhaps one exception (Num. xxiv. 4), they were granted to holy men only, men who were surrendered to God's service, men between whom and their divine sovereign there "had arisen an understanding." These visions, again, were clearly distinguished, by those who saw them, from ordinary visions and were recognized as proceeding from God. They were cautiously accepted by the church ;

by law they were not received as genuine until their teaching and their credentials had been subjected to tests (Jer. xxiii. 16, 21, 22, 27; cp. Is. viii. 20; Deut. xviii. 10 seq.). The visions recorded in the Bible stand alone, in the history of religions, for purity and righteousness. They were never vain; never meaningless vagaries or lying wonders. They always have a clearly discernible moral and didactic content. They were often predictive, upon which fulfillment has set the seal of truth. They belong to an age of revelation and came to men who in manifold manner proved themselves to be vehicles of revelation.

Because there were genuine visions, false prophets feigned visions. These men are denounced and their destruction is foretold (Jer. xiv. 14; xxiii. 16; Ezek. xiii. 7 seq.).

Voph'si.

Father of Nahbi, the Naphtalite spy (Num. xiii. 14).

Vow.

A voluntary obligation to God, generally assumed on condition of his bestowing certain specified blessings. Man has shown a tendency during sickness or any other affliction, or in time of anxiety or earnest desire, to make a vow to God to be fulfilled when the calamity is over or the desired object obtained (Gen. xxviii. 20-22; Num. xxi. 2; 1 Sam. i. 11; 2 Sam. xv. 8). The vow sprang primarily from the consciousness of entire dependence on the will of God and of the obligation of thankfulness. Vows were taken by persons of every nation (Jonah i. 16), and not by the Jews only. The earliest mention of a vow in Scripture, and a typical case, is that of Jacob at Bethel, who promised that if God would care for him and bring him again to his father's house, the place where he was should be a sanctuary and the tenth of his income should be the Lord's (Gen. xxviii. 18-22).

The Mosaic law did not prescribe vows, it only regulated them. Three kinds were the subject of legislation. Vows of devotion, of abstinence, and of devotion to destruction. 1. By the vow of devotion, any person or possession, not already set apart for sacred uses, or otherwise removed from the legal control of the devoter, might be devoted and turned over to the sanctuary; but anything thus devoted to the service of God was redeemable, except a sacrificial animal (Lev. xxvii. 1-27), usually at one-fifth more than its assessed value. Devoted land sold by the owner, without having been first redeemed, was retained by the buyer, but at the year of jubile did not return to the seller, but became the possession of the sanctuary (20, 21). Persons devoted to God served at the sanctuary (1 Sam. i. 11, 24, 28), but were usually redeemed (2 Kin. xii. 4), especially as the service of the Levites rendered such devotion as a rule useless. The price of re-

demption varied with age and sex. 2. The vow of abstinence involved a renunciation of some enjoyment, otherwise allowable, for the glory of God. It included such acts as fasting, in testimony of penitence, and such obligation as was assumed by the Nazirite. 3. It has been inferred from Ex. xxii. 20; Deut. xiii. 16, that only what was under judgment for idolatry could be devoted by a vow of destruction. Nothing devoted by such a vow was redeemable (Lev. xxvii. 28, 29).

General principles applying to vows were: 1. Vows were assumed voluntarily, but once made were regarded as compulsory (Num. xxx. 2; Deut. xxiii. 21-23); only in exceptional cases as in those of Samson, Samuel, and John the Baptist, who had a special mission to fulfill, was the Nazirite vow prescribed. 2. A vow, especially a vow of abstinence, made by an unmarried daughter or a wife, was void if disallowed by the father or husband (Num. xxx. 3-16). 3. The produce of sinful traffic could not be devoted (Deut. xxiii. 18); see DOG. 4. Vows must not be taken rashly. This principle was enforced by the example of Jephthah, and inculcated by proverb (Prov. xx. 25).

Vul'gate. See VERSIONS.

Vul'ture.

A bird of prey, which has the head naked or but thinly covered with feathers, and feeds largely or wholly on carrion. It is employed in the A. V. to render the Hebrew words 'Ayyah (Job xxviii. 7, elsewhere kite; in R. V. always falcon), Da'ah (Lev. xi. 14; in R. V. kite), and Dayyah (Deut. xiv. 13; Is. xxxiv. 17; in R. V. kite). In the R. V. it is used to translate Raḥam (Lev. xi. 18; in A. V. gier eagle); and frequently on the margin, where the text has eagle, to render the Hebrew Nesher, Greek Aetos.

The great vulture (Lev. xi. 13, R. V. margin) is the fulvous or tawny vulture, generally called the griffin (Gyps fulvus). The neck and head are bald, covered with down. The whole of the body, the wings, and the back on to the tail are yellowish-brown. It is about 4 feet high. Its talons are not formidable, but its bill is. "The griffon," says Tristram, "is the most striking ornithological feature of Palestine. It is impossible in any part of the country to look up without seeing some of them majestically soaring at an immense height, and their eyries abound in great colonies in all the ravines of the country."

W

Wa'ges.

In early times and not infrequently at a comparatively late date wages were paid in kind (Gen. xxix. 15, 20; xxx. 28-34). In Egypt money or goods were given as hire at the time of the sojourn of the Israelites there (Ex. ii. 9). By the law of Moses, wages were to be paid each evening (Lev. xix. 13; Deut. xxiv. 14, 15), and the withholding of wages due was severely denounced by religious teachers (Jer. xxii. 13; Mal. iii. 5; Jas. v. 4). Tobit offered a drachma, or 16 cents, a day and food as wages (Tob. v. 14). When our Lord was on earth the rate for a day's labor was a denarius, worth about 17 cents (Mat. xx. 2, in E. V. penny). What the purchasing power of that amount was is, however, unknown; it was evidently great (cp. Luke x. 35). In the later days of the Roman republic, the usual pay of a Roman soldier was 10 asses, or about a dime, a day (Tacitus, Annal. i. 17).

Wag'on. See CART.

Wal'let. See SCRIP.

War.
Before engaging in aggressive war, the Israelites consulted God's will in the matter (Judg. xx. 23, 27, 28; 1 Sam. xiv. 37; xxiii. 2; 1 Kin. xxii. 6) or, when conflict was unavoidable, invoked God's help by prayer and sometimes by sacrifice (1 Sam. vii. 8, 9; xiii. 12; 2 Chron. xx. 6–12; 1 Mac. iii. 47–54). The heathen had recourse to divination for the same purpose (Ezek. xxi. 21), and were careful to set forth on a day pronounced to be propitious. Frequently before entering a hostile country or engaging in battle spies were sent forward to obtain information regarding the country, and the preparation for resistance (Num. xiii. 17; Josh. ii. 1; Judg. vii. 10; 1 Sam. xxvi. 4); and, when captives were taken, they were questioned with the same intention (Judg. viii. 14; 1 Sam. xxx. 11). When the host drew nigh unto battle, a priest or the commander encouraged the people by reminding them of God's presence and help; and the officers exempted from service those who were faint-hearted and those who had built a new house but not inhabited it, planted a vineyard but not enjoyed the fruit of it, betrothed a wife but not married her (Deut. xx. 2–9; 2 Chron. xx. 14–20; 1 Mac. iii. 56; iv. 8–11). Various stratagems were practiced, such as surprise, ambush, pretended flight, circumvention (Gen. xiv. 15; Josh. viii. 2, 5; Judg. vii. 16; 2 Sam. v. 23). Occasionally when the opposing armies were drawn up in battle array, a champion was chosen by each party (1 Sam. xvii.). Otherwise the battle was joined. A trumpet sounded the attack, the blast being both a signal to advance and an appeal to God (Num. x. 9; Josh. vi. 5; Judg. vii. 20; 2 Chron. xiii. 12; 1 Mac. iv. 13; v. 33). The host pressed forward with shouting (Josh. vi. 5; 1 Sam. xvii. 52; Jer. l. 42; Ezek. xxi. 22; Amos i. 14), and engaged in hand to hand conflict. The pursuit was bloody. Like other nations of their time, the Israelites when victorious pillaged the camp of the enemy, robbed the dead (Judg.

viii. 24–26; 1 Sam. xxxi. 9; 2 Chron. xx. 25; 1 Mac. iv. 17–23), and sometimes killed or mutilated the prisoners (Josh. viii. 23, 29; x. 22–27; Judg. i. 6; viii. 21; 2 Sam. viii. 2), but more frequently reduced them to slavery.

When a city was besieged, the besiegers fortified their own camp against attack (War v. 2, 3); if possible, they cut off the water supply from the city (Judith vii. 7). In order to bring their engines into play they cast up mounds in the direction of the city (2 Sam. xx. 15; Ezek. iv. 2). The mound gradually increased in height until it was sometimes half as high as the city wall. Upon this inclined plane the battering-ram was rolled into position; from its roof and from the mound, archers and slingers discharged their missiles, and from the summit of the mound scaling-ladders were leaned against the wall; see illustrations LACHISH, RAM. Sometimes fuel was laid against the gates and fired in order to burn them and afford ingress (Judg. ix. 52); and often the defenders of the wall were attacked by archers posted, not on the mound, but at the base of the wall. The besieged were not idle: they prepared for the investment by protecting their water supply, and repairing and strengthening the fortifications (2 Chron. xxxii. 3–5); they harassed the enemy and attempted to drive them off by sallies; they repelled attack and hindered the besiegers in their aggressive operations by casting darts and stones and shooting arrows at them from the walls; and they destroyed, or attempted to destroy, the military engines by hurling burning torches at them and by undermining the banks on which the battering-rams stood (2 Sam. xi. 21, 24; 2 Chron. xxvi. 15; 1 Mac. vi. 31; War v. 2, 2 and 4; 6, 4; 11, 4). Captured cities were often destroyed and their inhabitants slaughtered, neither age nor sex being spared (Josh. vi. 21, 24; viii. 24–29; x. 22–27; 2 Kin. xv. 16). Victory was celebrated with song and dance (Ex. xv. 1–18; Judg. v.; 1 Sam. xviii. 6; 2 Chron. xx. 26–28; 1 Mac. iv. 24). See ARMY.

Wash'ing. See BATHING.

Watch. See NIGHT.

Wa'ter of Bit'ter-ness.
Holy water in an earthen vessel, mingled with dust from the floor of the sanctuary (Num. v. 17), intended to reveal the innocence or guilt of a woman accused of adultery by her husband, when there were no witnesses. The charge was perhaps only brought when suspicion was aroused by the woman's being found with child. The accused woman, with loosened hair, sat before the Lord in the sanctuary, and held an offering of dry, unscented, barley meal in her hand (18, R. V.). The priest, taking the water of bitterness, asked that it have no effect upon the woman, if she were innocent, but that God would cause her body to swell and her thigh to fall away, if she were guilty. The

woman responded, Amen. The priest wrote the imprecation in a book, and washed it out into the water ; and having waved the meal offering before the Lord and thrown a handful of it on the altar, he gave the water of bitterness to the woman to drink. If guilty, it became bitter within her and the curse went into effect; if innocent, the potion remained inoperative, and the woman was pronounced clean and received or retained ability to conceive. The essential part of this procedure was the oath, the ritual was symbolical, the effect was left to God. It is probable that this ordeal was an old custom, which the Mosaic law took up in order to regulate and elevate it.

Wa′ter of Sep-a-ra′tion. See PURIFICATION 1.

Wa′ter-pot. See PITCHER, POT.

Wave Of′fer-ing.

The rite of waving was regularly performed in connection with—1. Peace offerings : the right thigh or shoulder was heaved and the breast was waved before the Lord and, having been thus consecrated, were eaten by the priest. 2. The sheaf of first ripe grain on the second day of the passover, whereby the harvest was consecrated to the Lord (Lev. xxiii. 10, 11). 3. The two loaves made from the new grain and the two lambs for a peace offering at Pentecost, fifty days from the waving of the sheaf at the passover (15, 20). 4. The guilt offering of the leper (xiv. 12, 21), whereby the offerer represented by it was consecrated again to the service of God. 5. The meal offering of jealousy (Num. v. 25).

When the peace offering was private, the wave breast and the heave shoulder or thigh went to the priest, and the rest of the flesh was eaten by the offerer and his friends before the Lord at the sanctuary (Lev. vii. 30–34 ; x. 14, 15; Num. xviii. 18). Of the peace offering brought by the Nazirite, the sodden shoulder of the ram went to the priest, in addition to his regular perquisites (Num. vi. 17–20). At Pentecost, the whole of the two lambs of the peace offering and the loaves went to the priests (Lev. xxiii. 20), since they were offered in behalf of the nation.

In performing the rite the priest laid the matter to be waved upon the hands of the offerer, probably placed his own hands under the hands of the latter, and moved them (Ex. xxix. 24, 25; Num. vi. 19, 20). The motion was horizontal backward and forward (Talmud), and toward the right and left (Rabbis), that is, toward the four cardinal points ; but this fourfold movement may have been a late refinement of the original waving.

Wea′sel.

The rendering of the Hebrew *Holed*, glider or burrower, applied to an unclean quadruped (Lev. xi. 29). It is confessedly either a weasel or a mole. The corresponding word

in Arabic and Syriac signifies a mole : but probably the former meaning is intended by the Hebrew word, as the ancient versions, followed by the A. V. and R. V., render it by weasel ; in the Talmud the *ḥul′dah* is often mentioned as an animal that captures birds and creeping things, like the mouse, can run with such prey in its mouth, and that can lap water out of a dish ; and, finally, the typical mole genus *Talpa* is not believed to occur in Palestine (see MOLE 2), while the weasel (*Putorius vulgaris*) and the polecat (*Putorius fœtidus*) are found throughout the country.

Weav′ing.

The Egyptians practiced the art of weaving before the arrival of the Israelites in their midst, producing woven goods, such as linen (Gen. xli. 42). The work was usually done by men (Herod. ii. 35), but not exclusively, for women appear at the loom in ancient Egyptian delineations. At the time of the exodus the Hebrews understood both simple and elaborate weaving (Ex. xxxv. 35). They produced various textures on the looms. Coarse kinds, such as tent cloth and rough garments for the poor, were made of goats' and camels' hair (xxvi. 7 ; Mat. iii. 4) ; finer goods were woven of flax and wool (Lev. xiii. 47) ; chequered and figured patterns, as well as variegated stuffs, were made by the use of differently colored threads (Ex. xxvi. 1 ; cp. xxviii. 39, R. V. ; cp. Herod. iii. 47), and gold threads were even woven in (Ex. xxxix. 3) ; cloth was also embroidered with figures or patterns (xxvii. 16 : xxxviii. 23) with the needle (ibid., Septuagint) ; see EMBROIDERY. Many interpreters, however, believe that the Hebrew word rendered embroiderer denotes one who inweaves designs, as the modern Arabic *marḳum*, from the same root, signifies the curtain with inwoven flowers or other patterns which is used to partition off apartments in a tent. Among the Hebrews, the weaving as well as the spinning was usually done by the women (2 Kin. xxiii, 7 ; cp 1 Sam. ii. 19 ; Prov. xxxi. 22, 24 ; Acts ix. 39). Mantles and even tunics came from the loom ready for use ; the latter, when thus woven complete, required no seam. Such tunics were prescribed for the priests (Ex. xxviii. 6, 8 ; Antiq. iii. 7, 4) ; and one was worn by Jesus previous to his crucifixion (John xix. 23), perhaps not without symbolical purpose.

The loom in Egypt was placed either vertically or horizontally. The accompanying illustration is intended to represent a loom in the latter position. The frame is but slightly raised above the ground, the weaver squats at his work and apparently treads on the threads. The warp threads run in parallel relation and extend between the two beams to which they are attached ; heddles of primitive sort, which separate the warp threads into two series and form a shed for the passage of the shuttle or other bearer of the woof threads, are next to him, between him and the woven cloth. With a reed he strikes the last thread which he shot through against the woof, pressing it close.

The Hebrew loom likewise had its beam

Weaving loom.

and shuttle (1 Sam. xvii. 7; 2 Sam. xxi. 19; Job vii. 6). The pin of the beam, or rather weaving pin, for a different Hebrew word is used from that elsewhere rendered beam, may have been the slay or reed by which the thread of the woof was struck home (Judg. xvi. 13, 14). The web was cut off from the thrum (Is. xxxviii. 12, R. V. margin), or to speak more generally from the loom (R. V. text).

Wed′ding. See MARRIAGE.

Wedge. See TONGUE.

Week.

The division of time into periods of seven days appears in Scripture in connection with the institution of the Sabbath (Gen. ii. 1–3), and according to both the Hebrew and Babylonian account was in vogue at the time of the flood (vii. 4, 10; viii. 10, 12); see FLOOD. In the Babylonian legend of Adapa, which was current fifteen centuries and more before Christ, it is mentioned that the wind ceased to blow for seven days. There is reason to believe that the reference to its cessation for seven days is more than the mere note of a chance fact. Izdubar's sleep lasted six days and seven nights; and this peculiar phrase was the familiar designation for a week. Gudea, prince of Lagash, celebrated the completion of a temple by a festival of seven days' duration. Seven days was the conventional period for marriage festivities in Syria at the time of Laban and Jacob (Gen. xxix. 27, 28); and the same custom prevailed among the Philistines in the days of Samson (Judg. xiv. 12, 17). Funeral obsequies also, like those of Jacob and others, were conducted for seven days (Gen. l. 10; 1 Sam. xxxi. 13). Weeks constantly entered into all the arrangements of the ceremonial law (Ex. xii. 15; xiii. 6, 7; xxii. 30; xxix. 30, 35, 37; Lev. xii. 2; xiii. 5; xiv. 8, etc.). A week with a fixed beginning, which everybody reckoned as the first day, is, of course, not intended in all or even in the

majority of these cases. The week of nuptial festivities, for example, began on the day of the wedding on whatever date it occurred. Nevertheless these numerous instances show that the seven-day period was a standard in common use; and it is worthy of notice that the periods are consecutive in the narrative of the flood (see FLOOD), as well as later, in determining the date of Pentecost. For the origin of the week, see SABBATH.

The ancient Hebrews named none of the days of the week except the seventh day, which they called the Sabbath. They numbered the days of the festivals, and the Babylonian narrator enumerates each of the seven days during which the ark lay stranded. In the N. T. period the Hebrews numbered the days of the week (Mat. xxviii. 1; Acts xx. 7), and besides the seventh day named also the preceding day, which they called the preparation (Mark xv. 42).

The week and the names of its days were introduced at a comparatively late period into the Roman empire. The ancient Romans had a week of eight days. The Greeks divided the month into three periods. The Egyptians, as early as the time when the pyramids were built, had a ten-day period, each one of which began with the rising of one of thirty-six constellations in succession. Dio Cassius, who wrote in the second century A. D., speaks of the hebdomadal division of time being universal in his day in the Roman empire and a recent introduction. He represents it as borrowed from the Egyptians, and as based upon astrology. Of the two schemes, by one or the other of which he considers that the planetary names of the different days were fixed, only one has plausibility: each day in succession was assigned to one of the planets as regent, and the hours were also allotted to the planets. If the planets are arranged in the order of their distance from the earth, as believed at the time of Dio Cassius, Saturn, Jupiter, Mars, Sun, Venus, Mercury, Moon, and if, further, the first hour is allotted to Saturn, the second to Jupiter, and so on, the twenty-fifth hour, or the first hour of the morrow, will fall to the sun and on the following morning to the moon, and so on to Mars, Mercury, Jupiter, and Venus. If the planet to which the first hour of the day belongs be reckoned as the regent of the day, the days of the week will be, Saturn's day, Sun's day, Moon's day, and so on. This theory must be held with cautious reserve. There may be an entirely different reason from that given for the order of the planets, although the effort to explain satisfactorily the names from

Babylonian astronomy has not been successful as yet. The names passed from Roman to European use, both in their Latin form, and also, when translated into the Germanic languages, with the names of Germanic deities substituted for the corresponding Roman ones. They are found also in India, which is believed to have received them with astronomy and astrology from Greece and Rome. The names are of heathen origin, and originated in superstition, but no associations of any kind are now connected with them any more than with January, the month of Janus, god of the sun and the year, or with March, month of Mars, god of war, or with June, which was sacred to the goddess Juno.

The Hebrew word for week, *shabua'*, hebdomad, might of itself refer to a period of seven years as well as to one of seven days. The existence of the Sabbatic year would tend to produce this usage. It is therefore not surprising to find the Hebrew word for week used by Daniel for a period of seven years, as interpreters commonly understand (Dan. ix. 24–27; cp. Lev. xxv. 8).

Weeks, Feast of.

The second of the three annual festivals at which every male Israelite was required to appear before the Lord at the sanctuary, and the first of the two agricultural festivals (Ex. xxxiv. 22, 23; 2 Chron. viii. 12, 13; cp. 1 Kin. ix. 25). It was so called because its date was set seven complete weeks after the consecration of the harvest season by the offering of the sheaf of the first ripe barley (Lev. xxiii. 15, 16; cp. Deut. xvi. 9, 10). This sheaf was waved on the morrow after the Sabbath (Lev. xxiii. 11). The Baithoseans (Sadducees) interpreted this Sabbath as meaning the weekly Sabbath which occurred during the festival of unleavened bread; and some modern scholars have adopted this view. The opinion has even been held that it denoted merely the weekly Sabbath which fell immediately before the harvest. The older and better opinion is that it denotes the first day of the festival of unleavened bread. The Greek translators understood it so (Lev. xxiii. 7, 11, Septuagint), as did also those who directed the services of the second temple (Antiq. iii. 10, 5); this first day was kept as a Sabbath, no work was done on it and there was a holy convocation; and such rest days, not less than the seventh day of the week, were called Sabbath (Lev. xxiii. 32; xxv. 2); on the morrow after the passover the new grain was used, which could not be eaten until the sheaf had been waved before the Lord (Lev. xxiii. 14; Josh. v. 10, 11, R. V. margin). The festival fell on the fiftieth day after the waving of the sheaf, which gave rise to the name Pentecost or fiftieth day (Acts ii. 1). It was also called the feast of harvest or day of firstfruits, because the firstfruits of the

wheat harvest, then ended in most districts, were presented (Ex. xxiii. 16; xxxiv. 22; Num. xxviii. 26). It celebrated the close of the grain harvest. It was bound up with the cycle of religious feasts by the number seven. It was observed as a Sabbath, ordinary labors were suspended and there was a holy convocation (Lev. xxiii. 21; Num. xxviii. 26); two loaves of leavened bread, such as was used in the household, representing the firstfruits of the grain harvest, were offered to the Lord (Lev. xxiii. 17, 20; cp. Ex. xxxiv. 22; Num. xxviii. 26; Deut. xvi. 10); and with them ten proper animals were sacrificed for a burnt offering, a kid for a sin offering, and two lambs for a peace offering (Lev. xxiii. 18, 19). The sacrifices for the entire day were distributed into—1. The regular daily burnt offering of two lambs (Num. xxviii. 3, 31). 2. The special sacrifices for the feast day (27–30), which were the same as on the day of the new moon and each day of unleavened bread (ver. 11, 19). 3. The sacrifices connected with the offering of the loaves and the two lambs (Lev. xxiii. 17–19). Josephus correctly sums up the offerings additional to the daily burnt offering, except that he or his text as transmitted mentions two instead of three rams (Antiq. iii. 10, 6). As at the culminating agricultural festival, so at this the people were urged to remember the needy (Deut. xvi. 11, 12). Pentecost came to be regarded in later times, especially in the early Christian centuries, as the commemoration of the giving of the law on mount Sinai; but there is no authority for this belief in the O. T., and it cannot be shown that the law was given exactly fifty days after the passover.

The most notable Pentecost was the first which occurred after the resurrection and ascension of Christ (Acts ii.). From it dates the founding of the Christian church. The essential traits of an institution are seen in the history of its establishment. At the institution of the church, the Holy Spirit descended into all believers, without distinction of age, sex, or class (1–4, 14–21); see TONGUE. Life had been imparted. The Spirit had been given to men before, but now the church entered upon what is characteristically the dispensation of the Spirit. The Spirit is now given in full measure to all believers without the intervention of prescribed rites. He had preserved a people of God on earth; in this new era of his power he devotes his divine energy to enlarging, perfecting, and edifying the church.

Weights.

The Hebrews used scales and weights (Lev. xix. 36), and they weighed money as well as other commodities (Jer. xxxii. 10). The denominations were talent (circle), maneh (part), shekel (weight), gerah (grain), and beka (half [shekel]).

20 gerahs = 1 shekel
60 shekels = 1 maneh
60 manehs = 1 talent.

It is important to observe that the table for gold and silver is different from the table for commodities, and is—

20 gerahs = 1 shekel
50 shekels = 1 maneh
60 manehs = 1 talent.

Pound is the rendering of 1. Hebrew *Maneh* (1 Kin. x. 17); 2. Greek *Mna* (1 Mac. xiv. 24; xv. 18), which is generally believed to be reckoned on the basis of the Attic talent, and hence a little more than half as heavy as the Hebrew maneh; and 3. *Litra* (John xii. 3; xix. 39), equivalent to the Roman *libra*, of which two and a half equaled a Hebrew maneh of gold. Pound as a sum of money was equivalent to 100 drachmas and worth about sixteen dollars (Luke xix. 13, R. V. margin); see MONEY.

In weight a shekel equaled 20 gerahs, and a maneh was 20 + 25 + 15 = 60 shekels (Ezek. xlv. 12). This interpretation is confirmed by the Assyrian and Babylonian division of their maneh into sixty parts. Weights of the denomination of maneh have been discovered in Nineveh and Babylonia, and show that a heavy and a light talent were used, the former weighing 60.6 kilogrammes and the latter exactly one-half or 30.3 kilo-grammes. The heavy and light manehs weighed 1010 and 505 grammes respectively, and the shekels 16.83 and 8.41 grammes. According to Josephus, the Hebrew maneh of gold equaled two and a half Roman pounds (Antiq. xiv. 7, 1) or 818.57, according to Madden, 819.538 grammes. It appears from this that the Jewish maneh of gold was reckoned at 50 shekels, that the shekel of gold was a trifle lighter than the Assyrian shekel of weight, being 16.37, according to Madden 16.39, grammes, and that the shekel of gold and the shekel of weight were intended to be identical. The difference between this Hebrew shekel and the Assyrian shekel was about seven troy grains. A comparison of 1 Kin. x. 17 (R. V. margin maneh) with 2 Chron. ix. 16, if the text is pure, probably indicates that a maneh of gold was sometimes reckoned at one hundred light shekels, instead of at fifty normal shekels.

Three thousand shekels of silver equaled one talent. This appears from the fact that 603,550 half shekels or 301,775 shekels of the sanctuary equaled 100 talents and 1775 shekels (Ex. xxxviii. 25, 26). It may justly be concluded that the talent of silver was reckoned at sixty manehs of fifty shekels each. The shekel equaled twenty gerahs (Ex. xxx. 13). The shekel of silver, however, was lighter than the shekel of gold and weight, the average weight of the extant silver shekel coins being only 14.5565, according to Madden 14.5668, grammes.

Stone weights used by ancient tradesmen in Nineveh. Often weights were made in the shape of a duck or a lion.

TABLE OF WEIGHT.

		Avoirdupois.			Troy.			
		lb.	oz.	grains.	lb.	oz.	pwt.	grains.
Talent = 909,438.48	grains =	129	14	313.48	157	10	13	6.48
Maneh = 15,157.308	" =	2	2	282.308	2	7	11	13.308
Shekel = 252.6218	" =			252.621			10	12.621

TABLE OF GOLD.

		Troy.			
		lb.	oz.	pwt.	grains.
Talent = 757,865.4	grains =	131	6	17	17.4 = $29,374.50
Maneh = 12,631.09	" =	2	2	6	7.09 = 489.577
Shekel = 252.6218	' =			10	12.62 = 9.791

The dollar containing 25.8 grains.

TABLE OF SILVER.

		Troy.			
		lb.	oz.	pwt.	grains.
Talent = 673,907.724	grains =	116	11	19	11.724
Maneh = 11,231.7954	" =	1	11	7	23.795
Shekel = 224.6359	" =			9	8.6359

The value of the silver shekel was one-fifteenth that of the gold shekel, or about 65 cents.

Well.

A pit sunk in the earth to reach a supply of water. It was called in Hebrew *b'er*, a word often used in compound names like Beer-sheba. The water reached was found collected in a depression, or slowly percolating through the sand on its way to a lower level, or flowing as an underground stream (Gen. xvi. 7 with 14 ; xxiv. 11 with 13). Wells were often scooped in the sandy soil by those who knew of the presence of water. They were dug in the wadies and fed by an underflow, even when the bed of the torrent was dry, as at Beer-sheba and in the valley of Gerar (xxi. 30, 31 ; xxiv. 19). They were sunk far and wide through the surface soil of the Philistine plain into the lower sand, where an inexhaustible stream makes its way to the sea. In hilly Palestine they were dug in the limestone rock. The well did not essentially differ in outward appearance from a cistern. The mouth was protected by a stone curb (John iv. 6), and to prevent accidents to man or beast was covered by a stone or plank (Ex. xxi. 33 ; 2 Sam. xvii. 19 ; Antiq. iv. 8, 37). When the well was shallow, steps were cut in the rock which led down to the water. Troughs of wood or stone were placed near the mouth for the benefit of the cattle (Gen. xxiv. 30). The water was dipped with the pitcher (16), or, when the well was deep, was drawn by a rope with bucket, jar, or waterskin attached (John iv. 11). The rope was either dragged over the curb by the person getting the water, or perhaps an ox or ass was sometimes employed, as now, for the purpose, and occasionally a wheel was, as now, fixed over the well to assist in the work.

The *shaduf* is common in Egypt for raising water from the Nile, and it was used there in antiquity. It is not employed in Palestine, but its counterpart, the well sweep and bucket, is used. In the Philistine plain, the Persian wheel, called *na'ura*, is employed by the hundred. It consists of a tall upright axle, bearing a horizontal cogwheel, and turned by a mule attached to a sweep; this turns a vertical wheel which is directly over the mouth of the well. Over this pass two thick ropes, made of twigs twisted together and carrying jars or wooden buckets. The ascending buckets come up full of water, which they empty into a spout as they pass over the wheel; this spout conducts the water to a reservoir. See CISTERN, FOUNTAIN.

Whale.

The word rendered whale in the A. V. of the O. T. denotes any great animal of the sea, except in Ezek. xxxii. 2, where the Hebrew text must be emended and translated dragon (R. V.) ; see DRAGON.

The Greek word *kētos*, which is used in Mat. xii. 40 and rendered whale in the E. V., means any huge fish or other large animal of the sea, such as the dolphin, sea dog, and seal, and later whale, shark, tunny. The Septuagint employs *kētos megalos* in Jon. i. 17 (in Septuagint ii. 1) to render the two words "great fish" of the Hebrew text, and thus the word *kētos* passed into Mat. xii. 40.

Wheat.

Wheat was cultivated in Babylonia (Herod. i. 193), in Mesopotamia (Gen. xxx. 14), in Egypt (Ex. ix. 32), in Palestine (xxxiv. 22 ; Deut. viii. 8 ; Judg. vi. 11), and elsewhere, from a very early period.

In Palestine wheat was sown in November or December, after the rains began. It was thought that the best manner of planting it was in rows (Is. xxviii. 25, R. V.). The harvest was in April, May, or June in Palestine, varying according to the locality, the soil at the place, and the weather at the time; see YEAR.

The ordinary bread of the Hebrews was made of the flour of wheat (Ex. xxix. 2). The ears were also roasted and eaten (Lev. ii. 14; Ruth ii. 14); see PARCHED CORN. The wheat, bruised and crushed, was also used as food (Lev. ii. 14, 16). New wheat thus prepared, or else the fresh ear, is mentioned as eaten (xxiii. 14; 2 Kin. iv. 42).

Egypt was the granary of the Mediterranean region, and vast quantities were shipped annually to Rome from Alexandria (Acts xxvii. 6, 38). The best quality, according to Pliny, was grown in Upper Egypt, in the Thebaid (Hist. Nat. xviii. 47). The Egyptian wheat was a bearded variety, with many ears on the head (*Triticum compositum*). It is mentioned in Gen. xli. 22, is depicted on the ancient monuments, and is still grown. The wheat commonly cultivated in Palestine is *Triticum vulgare*, with a simple head.

Wheel. See GARDEN, WELL.

Whore. See HARLOT.

Widow.

A widow from early times wore an appropriate garb (Gen. xxxviii. 14, 19); she laid aside her ornaments, clothed herself in sackcloth, let her hair hang unbound, and did not anoint her face (Judith x. 3, 4; xvi. 8). God shows special compassion to the more helpless classes, among whom he reckons widows (Deut. x. 18; Ps. lxviii. 5; cxlvi. 9; Prov. xv. 25; Jer. xlix. 11). Under the Mosaic law, and subsequently, the Hebrews were enjoined to treat widows with justice and consideration, threatening judgment on those who did differently (Ex. xxii. 22; Deut. xiv. 29; xvi. 11, 14; xxiv. 17–21; xxvi. 12, 13; Is. i. 17; Jer. vii. 6; xxii. 3; Zech. vii. 10; Mal. iii. 5), as our Lord also did in his preaching (Mark xii. 40). The apostolic

church looked after poor widows (Acts vi. 1; Jas. i. 27). In the churches under Timothy's care certain widows, who were widows indeed, and had neither children nor grandchildren to provide for them (1 Tim. v. 4), were enrolled and cared for by the church (16). To obtain enrollment it was required that they be at least sixty years of age, have been married but once, and be well reported of for good works (9, 10). Here are the beginnings of an institution. From the end of the second century to the fourth they are mentioned by ecclesiastical writers as elder widows or the order of widows. Their duty was to serve the church, and they had oversight over the women of the congregation, especially over widows and orphans. The office was abolished by the synod of Laodicea, A. D. 364.

For the enactment as to marriage in certain circumstances to a deceased husband's brother, see MARRIAGE.

Wife. See MARRIAGE.

Wild Ass, Bull, Goat, etc. See Ass and the other nouns; but for **Wild Ox** see both Ox and UNICORN.

Wil′der-ness. See DESERT.

Wil′der-ness of the Wan′der-ing.

1. *Boundaries and Extent of the Wilderness.* Nature has defined a large inverted triangle, having for its base the southeastern shore of the Mediterranean Sea and the southern boundary of Palestine, for its western side the depression in which the gulf of Suez and the Bitter Lakes lie, and for its eastern side the depression occupied by the gulf of Akaba and the gorge of the Arabah. The base of this triangle measures 200 miles, and its area about 22,000 square miles. This district may be called the wilderness of the wandering; but this designation in Arabic, Badiet et-Tîh, is restricted to the table-land north of Sinai. The region is barren, little desired by man; and the great nations of antiquity accordingly left it virtually to

A scene in the Wilderness of the Wandering.

itself. The Israelites pushed their southern boundary but a short distance into its limits, and the Egyptians fortified a frontier for themselves where its sands began.

2. *Physical Features of the Wilderness.* The chief features of the territory are four: a region of sand, or the northern and north-western coast; a region of limestone, or the table-land; a region of sandstone, or the low mountains; and a region of granite, or the high mountains. (1) The region of sand extends in a broad band from Philistia along the shore of the Mediterranean Sea to the boundary of Egypt and beyond, bending to the south and continuing in a strip about 10 miles wide past Suez to a point one-third of the way down the coast. This sandy region is more or less coextensive with the wilderness of Shur (Saadia, quoted by Delitzsch, Gen. xvi. 7). (2) The northern and central portion of the triangle is a sterile table-land of limestone, from 2000 to 2500 feet high; sloping down on the north to the sandy region on the Mediterranean; swelling in the northeast into a mountainous country; and confined on the other sides by an encircling chain of mountains, 4000 and more feet high, now called Jebel et-Tîh. The middle of this desert is occupied by a long central basin, which is drained into the Mediterranean by the wady el-'Arîsh and its tributaries. These water courses are dry most of the year, but filled by the rains with raging torrents. West of this basin, other wadies run by themselves down to the sea. On the east of the same central basin, between it and the Arabah, is another similar and parallel one, extending from Jebel et-Tîh nearly to Jebel 'Arâif and the mountainous country of the northeast, and drained throughout by the wady el-Jerâfeh. The table-land proper, with its continuation in the adjacent clusters of mountains in the northeast as far as the cleft of the wady el-Fikreh, was the wilderness of Paran (Num. x. 11, 12; xiii. 26; 1 Sam. xxv. 1, 2), in which the Israelites wandered for 38 years, and of which the portion lying between Horeb and Kadesh was remembered by them as "the great and terrible wilderness" (Deut. i. 19). This plateau is mostly naked of vegetation, and has a gravelly surface. The wadies, however, seldom fail to show vegetation of some sort, and after the rainy season are covered with a thin herbage. The springs are few, and generally send forth impure water; but in the region about Kadesh and along the border of the Arabah there is a considerable number of living fountains, and near Kadesh and even at other places in the very heart of the desert water is obtainable by digging. (3) The sandstone formation crosses the peninsula in a broad belt immediately south of Jebel et-Tîh and extends nearly from shore to shore, separating the limestone table-land from the granite mountains. It is rich in mineral wealth. It may

be compared to a dumb-bell in shape; for it consists of two groups of mountains connected by a central plateau. This sandy table-land has an altitude of about 1500 feet. (4) The region of granite consists of the groups of mountain ranges about mount Sinai. The watershed runs north and south, and lies just east of wady esh-Sheikh.

3. *Possibility of a Sojourn of Forty Years in the Wilderness.* The Israelites numbered 600,000 men from 20 years old and upward, according to the repeated testimony of the Hebrew records. According to statistics of population, which yield the proportion of four to five between those under and those above 20 years of age in a given community, the whole body of fugitives from Egypt numbered 2,100,000. The Bible, as well as exploration, teaches that this great host could not have survived for any great length of time in the wilderness save by the providence and miracles of God. Moses reminded the people that in the wilderness they had seen how that the Lord their God did bear them, as a man doth bear his son, in all the way that they went (Deut. i. 31). The recorded miracles of sustenance are few. In the wilderness of Sin, at the beginning of their journey, to the children of Israel manna was given, of which they continued to eat for forty years, until they came into the borders of Canaan (Ex. xvi. 1, 4, 14, 15, 35). This was the permanent provision for their needs. The occasional supplies were the quails, given at the same time as the manna, but apparently only as a sign and temporarily, for they are not again mentioned (xvi. 12, 13); the water provided shortly afterwards from the rock near Rephidim (xvii. 3–7); the quails given in the second year for a month (Num. x. 11; xi. 4–6, 31); and the water caused to gush from the rock at Kadesh toward the end of the forty years' sojourn (xx. 2–11). The Bible teaches further that, notwithstanding these miracles, certain periods of the sojourn remained a horrible memory (Deut. i. 19; viii. 15); that though it could be said "Thou hast lacked nothing" (ii. 7), yet the life in the wilderness was one of repeated privation and hardship. The water was insufficient at Rephidim and Kadesh (Ex. xvii. 1; Num. xx. 2); the people were murmuring three days after leaving Sinai before reaching Hazeroth (x. 33; xi. 1, 35) and as they journeyed from mount Hor toward the Red Sea (xxi. 4, 5); and the wilderness was found to be terrible (Deut. viii. 15).

It appears from the biblical narrative that the manna sufficed as staple fare, though the people grew weary of it; and that the water supply, though scanty often to distress, was ordinarily sufficient. Food was furnished continuously. In regard to the supply of water in this region of desolation, there are two considerations of importance: (1) The ability of the people to alleviate the distress of the desert journey arising from the scarcity of water. The power of man and beast to endure thirst is great in these dry countries. The camel drivers of Egypt, both men and boys, escort travelers across scorching sands and under a burning sun without tasting a drop of water from early morning until after nightfall, because unable to obtain it. Dr. Robinson relates that his Arab guide spent a fortnight on the Sinaitic peninsula near mount Serbâl pasturing his camels, without a drop of water for himself or them. He drank the milk of the camels; and they, as well as sheep and goats, when they have fresh pasture, need no water, sometimes going three or four months without it (*Researches* i. 150). Again, like other travelers in the desert, the Israelites undoubtedly carried a supply of water with them, which they replenished at every opportunity. It is evident from the narrative that at the beginning of their journey they provided water sufficient for a march of at least three days into the wilderness (Ex. xv. 22). Again, the Israelites discovered hidden natural supplies. Frequently when the bed of the wady or the surface of the plain is dry, a stream flows or water lies in a basin underground. According to the geologist Fraas, the so-called wells of Moses, which bubble up in the desert a short distance from Suez, are fed by a subterranean stream which flows from the mountains of er-Raḥah, 10 or 14 miles away (Baedeker, *Lower Egypt*, 421). In the wady Ghurundel, which is commonly identified with Elim, there is a subterranean stream which the Arabs open when the upper water course is dry. Though the rains fail for two or three years, water is always to be found by digging a little below the surface (Robinson, *Researches* i. 69). Back of Tur, at Mabuk, at Kubab, and elsewhere, water collects beneath the surface and may be reached with slight effort (Ritter, *Erdkunde* xiv. 161, 185; Robinson, *Researches* i. 167). The Hebrews understood this fact and took advantage of it during their sojourn in the wilderness, as the song of the well testifies (Num. xxi. 17, 18). Again, if the manner of travel was like the migrations of other large bodies of people, the Israelites scattered in order to utilize for man and beast all the soil and herbage and water. Again, the Israelites husbanded the resources of water. The rainfall is considerable; the wadies bear evidence of the torrents which at times sweep down their courses. The early Christian monks who dwelt in the mountains of Sinai and the former inhabitants and cultivators of the district about Kadesh built dams across the ravines and dug cisterns, and thus secured water for themselves, their cattle, and their gardens. Abraham, Isaac, and Jacob, the forefathers of these Israelites of the exodus, had likewise husbanded the rainfall, and the descendants of these Israelites dug trenches in

the valleys and built reservoirs for a like purpose; and doubtless so did the Israelites during their sojourn of 30 and 8 years in the wilderness. (2) A second important consideration is the evidence that the country was better wooded in former times. Charcoal has been made in the peninsula from the acacia tree for ages, but the improvident Arabs have never been wont to replace the destroyed timber by replanting. Bartlett in 1874 mentions seeing stumps where the Arabs had burned down the trees, and acacias with the boughs lopped off for the camels to eat (*From Egypt to Palestine*, pp. 225, 300, 301). Burckhardt, one of the earliest travelers to explore Sinai, in his journey across the country in 1812 came across charcoal burners (*Erdkunde* xiv. 183); and Rüppell in 1822 mentioned the burning of charcoal for sale in Egypt as an immemorial industry of the Bedouin, and ascribed the nakedness of the valleys to the neglect of the Arabs to replant the ground which they had denuded (*Erdkunde* xiv. 274, 342). A tribute in charcoal has also been imposed on the Arabs of Sinai by Egypt since 1823. But charcoal burning for domestic purposes and export has not been the only means whereby the peninsula has been impoverished of wood; mining and smelting have also caused the destruction of great quantities of timber. The ancient Egyptians worked copper mines in the sandstone mountains of the west intermittently from a very early period, and were still operating them subsequently to the exodus. Acacia wood was sometimes used as supports for the roofs of the mines (Palmer, *Desert of the Exodus* i. 205), and the smelting operations, which were of magnitude, demanded large quantities of timber for fuel (ibid. 26, 43, 231–235; *Erdkunde* xiv. 786, 787). One should recall the disappearance of the cedars of Lebanon and of wide stretches of forest in America. It is clear that, beginning long before the exodus and continuing down to the present day, causes have been at work reducing the timber in the region traversed by the Israelites. This fact has a direct bearing on the question of the water supply in earlier times; for the country being better wooded, there was a natural preservation of the rainfall. As always where there is vegetation, the rain fell more regularly; the water was absorbed by the wadies more slowly and gently; soil and vegetation were less ruthlessly swept away; springs were more numerous and flowed more copiously; and streams endured longer into the dry season and were more frequently perennial.

Under an energetic, competent, and provident leader who was acquainted with the desert and its resources, by husbanding the supply, by extending the bounds of the encampment, and by scattering from the central camp in groups of various size, and with no failure of the annual rains, it is not to be doubted that a large host could have secured a sufficient though scant supply of water for man and beast.

4. *The Route of the Israelites through the Wilderness.* Certain sites have been identified: Succoth in Egypt at the beginning of the journey, the river Arnon which was reached at the close of the forty years, when the wilderness was left, and the encampments beyond the Arnon which are mentioned in the itinerary; Kadesh, with which there is reason to believe Rithmah was practically equivalent, where the camp was twice pitched, and whence the Israelites expected to march directly into the promised land, and Ezion-geber, where the camp was located just before the second march to Kadesh, and near which they afterwards passed on their way to the Arnon. Mount Sinai is almost universally located in the peninsula, which is accordingly called the peninsula of Sinai. The camp at Moserah was hard by mount Hor, on the border of Edom; and the wells of Bene-jaakan and Hor-haggidgad were also near the boundary of Edom. Punon was east of Edom and northeast of Petra. With a knowledge of the location of these places, one may readily trace the general route. See maps, ABRAHAM, EGYPT.

An itinerary covering the journey from Rameses and Succoth to the camp opposite Jericho was drawn up by Moses (Num. xxxiii.). The encampments recorded in it

after Sinai represent the movements of the tabernacle. The people were, however, doubtless often dispersed through the wilderness, tending their flocks wherever herbage and water were found. When they were collected and encamping in a body, their camp was very large and, in a settled country, covered the distance between several towns; hence the same encampment may be differently described or designated (49 with xxv. 1). Besides the itinerary there is the narrative of the journey (Ex. xii.–Num. xxv.), and there are also scattered allusions in the address of Moses to various incidents that occurred on the way. It is important to remember that each of these three recitals was prepared for a special purpose of its own. The itinerary records formal encampments, and does not mention every halting place and every place of spending the night (Ex. xv. 22; Num. x. 33). It is doubtful whether it omits a single encampment where the tabernacle was set up. The narrative is apt to mention an encampment or even a stopping place where an important event occurred, and to pass over the others. In the address events are cited as illustrations or to enforce the argument; and of course they are chosen at random, without reference to chronological sequence, and they are frequently alluded to broadly and by comprehensive statement.

ITINERARY.		NARRATIVE.	ALLUSIONS IN MOSES' ADDRESS.
From Rameses to mount Sinai.			
Rameses, left in 1st month, 15th day . . Num. xxxiii. 3, 5		Night after 14th day of 1st month . . . . Ex. xii. 18, 34, 37	. . . . Deut. xvi. 1
Succoth	5	 37	
Etham, in the edge of the wilderness	6	. . . . xiii. 20	
Pi-hahiroth	7	. . . . xiv. 2	
Passage of the Red Sea .	8	 22	. . . . xi. 4
Went three days' journey into the wilderness of Etham and pitched at		Went out into the wilderness of Shur, and went three days in the wilderness and came to	
Marah	8	Marah xv. 23	
Elim	9	 27	
By the Red Sea	10		
Wilderness of Sin . . .	11	2d month, 15th day . . . xvi. 1	
Dophkah	12		
Alush	13		
Rephidim, where was no water for the people to drink	14	. . . . xvii. 1	. . . . vi. 16; xxv. 17
Wilderness of Sinai . . .	15	before the mount . . . xix. 2 in 3d month 1	. . . . iv. 10, 11; v. 2
From mount Sinai to Kadesh-barnea.			
Wilderness of Sinai . .		. . . . Num. x. 12 in 2d year, 2d month, 20th day . 11; cp. i. 1; ix. 5	Horeb
Kibroth-hattaavah . .	16	Three days' journey . . x. 33 . . . the outermost part of the camp where the fire devoured being called Taberah . . . . . xi. 1, 3, 34 Apparently remained 30 days 21	through all that great and terrible wilderness by the way to the hill country of the
			. ix. 22

ITINERARY.	NARRATIVE.	ALLUSIONS IN MOSES' ADDRESS.
Hazeroth . . . Num. xxxiii. 17	. . . . .Num. xi. 35	Amorites
	Remained at least 7 days . xii. 15	Deut. xxiv. 9 to
Rithmah 18	Kadesh, in the wilderness	Kadesh-barnea . . . . i. 19
	of Paran . . . xii. 16; xiii. 26	It is 11 days' journey from
	About the time of the	Horeb by the way of
	first ripe grapes, *i. e.* in	mount Seir to Kadesh-
	the latter part of the 5th	barnea 2
	month . . . . xiii. 20	 25
	Discouraged by the spies'	
	report, the Israelites re-	
	fused to advance. After	
	being condemned to	
	wander in the wilder-	
	ness 40 years and or-	
	dered to turn back into	
	the wilderness by the	
	way to the Red Sea, the	
	people attempted to en-	
	ter Canaan, and went	
	up into the mountain,	
	but were smitten, even	
	unto Hormah. Moses	
	departed not from the	
	camp . . . . xiv. 25, 33–45	. . . . i. 40–45 ; ix. 22
From Kadesh to Ezion-geber and Return, until the men of that generation died.		
Rithmah	. . . .	At Kadesh many days . i. 46
Rimmon-perez 19		Turned and took their
		journey into the wilder-
Libnah 20		ness by the way to the
Rissah 21		Red Sea, as God had
Kehelathah 22		commanded . . . . . ii. 1
Mount Shepher 23	In the wilderness . . . xv. 32	
Haradah 24		
Makheloth 25		
Tahath 26		
Terah 27		
Mithkah 28		
Hashmonah 29	In the wilderness . . xvi. 13	
Moseroth 30		
Bene-jaakan 31		
Hor-haggidgad 32		Compassed
Jotbathah 33		
Abronah 34		
Ezion-geber 35		mount
Wilderness of Zin, *i. e.*		
Kadesh 36	Wilderness of Zin at Ka-	
	desh, in 1st month [of	Seir
	40th year] . . . . . . xx. 1	. cp. xxxii. 51
	Moses and Aaron sinned	
	against God when	many
	smiting the rock . . . 2–13	. iii. 26 ; iv. 21
	Messengers were sent	
	to the king of Edom,	
	asking permission for	days, ii. 2
	Israel to cross his terri-	
	tory 14–17	
From Kadesh to the Jor-dan.		until
		finally
Kadesh	Kadesh 22	
	Journey toward Edom by	toward
	the way of Atharim or	
	the spies . . . . . . xxi. 1	Wells of Bene-jaakan. x. 6
Mount Hor, in the edge of	Mount Hor, by the border	Moserah, x. 6
the land of Edom . . 37	of the land of Edom xx. 22, 23,	
In 40th year, 5th month,		the
1st day 38		
Aaron ascended the		
mountain and died . . 39	 24–29	where Aaron died. x. 6
The king of Arad heard of	. The king of Arad heard	
the coming of the Israel-	of their coming, fought	close
ites 40	against them, and took	
	some of them captive . xxi. 1	of the

ITINERARY.	NARRATIVE.	ALLUSIONS IN MOSES ADDRESS.
	At mount Hor the Israelites probably received the answer of the king of Edom, and found his army drawn up to oppose them, wherefore Israel turned away from him . . Num. xx. 18–21	forty years Deut. ii. 7; xxix. 5 they peace-
	From mount Hor they journeyed, by the way to the Red Sea, to compass the land of Edom xxi. 4	Gudgodah. x. 7 fully Jotbathah. x. 7
Zalmonah . . Num. xxxiii. 41 Punon . . . . 42 Oboth . . . . 43 Iye-abarim, in the border of Moab 44	Fiery serpents hereabouts . 6–9 . . . . 10 . . . in the wilderness east of Moab . . . . 11 Valley of Zered 12	crossed the southern end of Edom, near Elath and Ezion-geber, and turned northward, Deut. viii. 15 journeying by the way of the wilderness of Moab . ii. 4, 5, 8 and Crossed the brook Zered 13 38 years after their condemnation at Kadesh-barnea 14
	In the wilderness on the other, i. e. the south, side of the [upper] Arnon 13	Crossed the [upper] Arnon, perhaps the tributary known as wady es-Saideh, and so were in the neighborhood of the Ammonites . . . . ii. 18, 19 and on the borders of the Amorite kingdom . 24
	Beer, in the wilderness 16, 18	From the wilderness which took its name from Kedemoth, the Israelites sent messengers to Sihon 26
	Sihon went against Israel into the wilderness, and the battle was fought at Jahaz . . . . 23 Mattanah, not in the wilderness. . . . . 18 Nahaliel 19	 32
Dibon-gad, the camp probably extending to Nahaliel . . . . 45 Almon to Diblathaim and probably to Bamoth 46 In the mountains of Abarim, before Nebo . 47 Plains of Moab, opposite Jericho, from Beth-jeshimoth to Abel-shittim 48, 49	Bamoth . . . . 19 Valley at the top of Pisgah . . . . 20 . . . . xxii. 1 at Shittim . . . . . xxv. 1	In the valley over against Beth-peor . . . iii. 29; iv. 46 In the 40th year, before the 11th month . . . . . . i. 3

Wil'low, Willow Tree.

1. Any tree of the genus *Salix*. It was called *ṣaphṣᵉphah* in Hebrew (Ezek. xvii. 5), *ṣafṣâf* in Arabic. Several species are common in Palestine.

2. The rendering of the Hebrew *ᵃrabah*. The Israelites were directed to take branches from it, as well as from other trees, to make booths at the feast of tabernacles (Lev. xxiii. 40). It grew beside brooks or water courses (ibid.; Is. xliv. 4), and afforded cover even to the bulky behemoth (Job xl. 22). It was the tree on which the Hebrews hung their harps when exiles at Babylon (Ps. cxxxvii. 2). The Septuagint and Vulgate render the Hebrew word by willow, and they are followed by the English version. It may have been the weeping willow (*Salix babylonica*), which is found abundantly on the Euphrates, and is cultivated in Palestine. But leading interpreters, following Wetzstein, understand the Arabic *gharab*,

and consequently its etymological equivalent, the Hebrew *'rabah*, to denote the Euphratean poplar (*Populus euphratica*).

Wil'lows, Brook of the.

A willow-fringed brook in Moab (Is. xv. 7), probably wady el-'Aḥsy, the upper course of wady Kurahi, the boundary between Moab and Edom. It may be identical with the brook of the Arabah (Amos vi. 14, R. V.).

Wim'ple.

An article of woman's attire, made of silk or linen, and worn as a covering for the neck, chin, and sides of the face. In A. V. of Is. iii. 22, it is the rendering of the Hebrew *Miṭpaḥhath*, a shawl or mantle (ibid.; Ruth iii. 15, both R. V.).

Wind.

The Hebrews, who did not define direction with the minuteness customary in modern times, recognized four winds: the east, the west, the north, and the south winds (Jer. xlix. 36; Ezek. xxxvii. 9; Rev. vii. 1). God created the wind (Amos iv. 13); and it stands at his summons, is under his control, and performs his pleasure (Job xxxviii. 25; Ps. lxxviii. 26; cvii. 25; cxxxv. 7; cxlviii. 8; Mat. viii. 26). The wind that blew from the west, southwest, and northwest brought rain to Palestine, and accompanied the storm (1 Kin xviii. 43-45; Ps. cxlvii. 18; Prov. xxv. 23, R. V.; Ezek. xiii. 13). Wind was often destructive to houses and shipping (Job i. 19; Ps. xlviii. 7; Mat. vii. 27). The scorching wind dried up streams, and blasted vegetation (Gen. xli. 6; Is. xi. 15; Ezek. xix. 12; Jon. iv. 8); see EAST WIND. The south and southeast winds traversed the Arabian desert, and were dry and hot (Job xxxvii. 17; Luke xii. 55). The north wind was cooler (Ecclus. xliii. 20), and was favorable to vegetation (Song iv. 16). Wind was taken advantage of by the thresher to blow away the chaff and broken straw (Job xxi. 18; Ps. i. 4); see THRESHING. The mariner also availed himself of the wind (Acts xxvii. 40). The words which are rendered whirlwind in the E. V. do not denote a rotary wind specifically, but signify a violent storm of any kind.

Win'dow.

An aperture especially in the wall of a building (Gen. xxvi. 8; 1 Kin. vi. 4; Jer. xxii. 14), which was opened and closed at convenience by means of a movable shutter of some sort (Gen. viii. 6; 2 Kin. xiii. 17; Dan. vi. 10), generally a lattice (Judg. v. 28; 2 Kin. i. 2; Prov. vii. 6; Song ii. 9); but a window on the ground floor, that looked into the street, was doubtless in ancient as in modern times small, high up in the wall, and strongly barred. In the better class of houses most of the windows faced the court. Houses that abutted on the town wall usually had windows looking toward the country (Josh. ii. 15; 2 Cor. xi. 33).

Wine.

Wine was made from grapes. The ripe clusters were gathered in baskets (Jer. vi. 9), carried to the press, and thrown into it. The press consisted of a shallow vat, built above ground or excavated in the rock (Is. v. 2) and, through holes in the bottom, communicating with a lower vat also frequently excavated in the rock (Joel iii. 13). An upper vat measuring 8 feet square and 15 inches deep had at times a lower vat 4 feet square and 3 feet deep. The grapes were crushed by treading (Neh. xiii. 15; Job xxiv. 11), one or more men being employed according to the size of the vat. In Egypt, and probably in Pales-

An ancient winepress located on a hillside in Gilead.

tine, the treaders held to ropes overhead to keep from falling; they sang at their work and shouted, doubtless to keep time (Is. xvi. 10; Jer. xxv. 30; xlviii. 33); and the red blood of the grapes flowed around them and stained their skin and their garments (Is. lxiii. 1-3). From the upper vat the juice trickled into the lower. From this receptacle the juice was put in bottles of skin (Job xxxii. 19; Mat. ix. 17), or in large earthenware jars, where it was allowed to ferment. When fermentation had proceeded far enough the wine was drawn off into other vessels (Jer. xlviii. 11, 12).

The juice of the grape when expressed was used in various conditions: as must, fresh from the press; as wine, which was produced by vinous fermentation; and as vinegar, which resulted when the fermentation was continued too long. Probably in ancient times, as at the present day, some of the must was reduced to a syrup or honey by boiling; see HONEY. As vinegar it was called ḥomes, in Greek, *oxos*; see VINEGAR. Various names were applied to it in the other states:

The Hebrew *tirosh*, that which takes possession of, intoxicates: or better, possession, product of labor. The R. V. sometimes renders this word by vintage (Num. xviii. 12; Neh. x. 37, margin); and the attempt has been made by some interpreters to limit the meaning to this sense, and to deny that it ever signifies new wine or must. It means juice of the grape or must in Joel ii. 24: "The floors shall be full of wheat, and the fats shall overflow with wine and oil;" cp. iii. 13: "Put ye in the sickle, for the harvest is ripe: come, tread ye; for the wine press in full [of grapes], the fats [both of them] overflow." It also means juice of the grape or new wine, as it is rendered in the E. V., in Hos. iv. 11: "Whoredom and wine and new wine take away the understanding;" for the exegesis is forced and invalid which interprets this verse as meaning that whoredom proceeds from the abuse of wine, and wine is connected with the abuse, that is, the fermentation, of tirosh or must The passage affirms that all three take away the understanding. There is no need to depart from this meaning of tirosh anywhere, and render it vintage; for example: 1. Not in Is. lxii. 8, 9: "Surely I will no more give thy corn to be meat for thine enemies; and strangers shall not drink thy wine [on margin, vintage], for the which thou hast labored: but they that have garnered it shall eat it, and praise the Lord; and they that have gathered it shall drink it in the courts of my sanctuary" (R. V.). There is no need to give tirosh the meaning of vintage here, as the R. V. shows by placing wine in the text, as the A. V. did. It is said indeed to be gathered; but this is a proleptic form of speech, and elsewhere wine and oil are said to be gathered (Jer. xl. 10; the Hebrew word for wine being yayin). 2. Not in Is. lxv. 8: "As the new wine is found in the cluster, and one saith, Destroy it not, for a blessing is in it." Cheyne renders "As when [a few good] grapes are found in the cluster, and one saith [to the other gleaners] destroy it not, for a blessing is in it." But the same meaning exactly is yielded by rendering: "As when the juice is found in the cluster," etc. (Alexander, Delitzsch, Dillmann). 3. Not in Mic. vi. 15: "Thou shalt sow, but shalt not reap: thou shalt tread the olives, but shalt not anoint thee with oil; and the vintage [in A. V. sweet wine], but shalt not drink the wine." The Hebrews spoke of treading grapes (Amos ix. 13) and of treading wine (Is. xvi. 10; yayin being used, and the word "out" not being found in the original). 4. Not even in those numerous passages where the fruits of the ground are mentioned comprehensively as corn, wine, and oil (Num. xviii. 12, R. V. vintage; Deut. vii. 13; xi. 14; xii. 17; Hos. ii. 8, 22; Joel i. 10; ii. 19, in all 18 times). In many of these passages the tithe of the corn, wine, and oil is spoken of. Since yishar denotes the oil which is found in the olive (2 Kin. xviii. 32; Zech. iv. 14), tirosh may denote the juice which is found in the grape; and as the grain was thought of as threshed, the tirosh and the oil may be thought of as expressed. Indeed the threshed grain rather indicates that the grape juice and the oil were expressed. The only question then is: Were not firstfruits and tithes brought from the other produce of the vineyard which was not reduced to wine? They were; but they are not specifically included in the threefold designation so often employed. The firstfruits of all that was in the land were presented to the Lord, as is more explicitly stated in Num. xviii. 13; and mint and anise were tithed, although the threefold designation does not when interpreted literally embrace them. Grain, must, and oil were prominent enough to stand for all.

The Hebrew 'asis, something trodden out; hence grape juice, must (Is. xlix. 26; Amos ix. 13). It does not denote the expressed juice of the grape only, but of other fruits as the pomegranate.

The Greek gleukos is used by Josephus in speaking of the grape juice squeezed into Pharaoh's cup (Gen. xl. 11; Antiq. ii. 5, 2). It is explained by Hesychius as the juice that flowed spontaneously from the grapes before the treading commenced. It was drawn off and kept separate from the juice which flowed under pressure. It was with this that the apostles were accused of being filled on the day of Pentecost (Acts ii. 13).

Must was drunk; and, after fermentation had set in, was intoxicating (Hos. iv. 11, tirosh; Acts ii. 13, gleukos; and probably Is. xlix. 26, 'asis). But although must was used as a drink, the old wine was preferred (Ecclus. ix. 10; Luke v. 39). Pliny regarded must as hurtful to the stomach (Hist. Nat. xxiii. 18).

The Hebrew yayin is undoubtedly the same word etymologically as the Greek oinos and the Latin vinum. Ḥᵃmar is the Aramaic name for the same thing; and ḥemer is the etymological equivalent of the Aramaic word, and is occasionally used in Hebrew poetry. When the Hebrew word yayin first occurs in Scripture, it is the fermented juice of the grape (Gen. ix. 21), and there is no reason to believe that it has a different meaning elsewhere. The Greek oinos also means the fermented juice of the grape, except when it is qualified by the word new, and even then there are not two wines, one fermented and the other unfermented. New wine is must, which only becomes wine by fermentation. An argument for the use of the term wine for unfermented grape juice has been sought in the fact that wine was used in later times at the passover, and yet leaven was strictly forbidden during the seven days of the paschal festival; hence the term wine, it has been argued, must have been applied to unfermented juice. But the reason is invalid. Vinous fermentation was not regarded as leaven. During the passover it was fermented drinks into which grain and hence the leaven of bread, had entered that the Jews would not taste or touch (Mishna, *Pesachoth* ii.). There were numerous varieties of wine which differed in body and flavor, such as the wine of Lebanon, the wine of Helbon. See VINE.

Fruit of the vine, the designation used by Jesus at the institution of the Lord's Supper (Mat. xxvi. 29), is the expression employed by the Jews from time immemorial for the wine partaken of on sacred occasions, as at the passover and on the evening of the Sabbath (Mishna, *Berakoth* vi. 1). The Greeks also used the term as a synonym of wine which was capable of producing intoxication (Herod. i. 211, 212). The juice of the grape

An ancient winepress in Jerusalem.

which was ordinarily planted was red (Is. lxiii. 2; Rev. xiv. 19, 20) and was called the blood of the grape (Gen. xlix. 11; Deut. xxxii. 14; 1 Mac. vi. 34). It was wine (Ecclus. l. 15).

Mixed wine was known by the specific names of *mesek* (Ps. lxxv. 8), *mimsak* (Prov. xxiii. 30; Is. lxv. 11), and *mezeg* (Song vii. 2), each of which means mixture and denotes wine mixed with spices to give it a pleasant flavor (Song viii. 2; Pliny, Hist. Nat. xiv. 19, 5), or with water to diminish its strength (Herod. vi. 84; see below).

Wine differed from *shekar*, rendered strong drink in E. V., in that wine was made from the juice of the grape, and *shekar* from the juice of other fruits and of grain. It was fermented, for it was capable of producing intoxication (Is. xxviii. 7; xxix. 9). It was prepared from barley (Herod. ii. 77), from honey, or from dates (i. 193; ii. 86; Jerome, *Epist. ad Nepotianum*), or from the lotus (Herod. iv. 177). The drink made from dates is wholesome and refreshing, but in one day's heat it undergoes rapid fermentation, effervesces, and produces intoxication if taken immoderately. *Shekar* is once used in a broad sense for strong drink generally in distinction from water, and refers to the drink offering, which consisted of wine exclusively (Num. xxviii. 7).

Other words are *sobe'*, a name derived from a root which signifies to soak or drink to excess (Is. i. 22; Nah. i. 10); and *sh°marim*, which strictly denotes the lees of wine and then is used for wine kept long on the lees, and hence, old.

Wine was employed medicinally (Prov. xxxi. 6; Luke x. 34; 1 Tim. v. 23); was used in the service of God (Ex. xxix. 39-41;

Lev. xxiii. 13); and light wine was a staple article of diet in Palestine, as it has been in other Mediterranean lands from time immemorial (Num. vi. 20; Deut. xiv. 26; 2 Chron. ii. 15; Neh. v. 18; Mat. xi. 19; 1 Tim. iii. 8). Palestine was a country where meat was difficult to obtain and vegetables were rare; and wine supplied the lack. It would be a mistake, however, to suppose that wine was the invariable accompaniment of a meal; many a repast was partaken of without it; see FOOD. Still wine was in common use. Bread and wine signified the staples of life (Ps. civ. 14, 15; Prov. iv. 17). Wine was offered as an ordinary hospitality (Gen. xiv. 18) and was served at festivities (Job i. 13, 18; John ii. 3). The Hebrew people were, as a rule, simple in their mode of living, and temperate; but the danger of excess in the use of even light wine, especially at feasts, was clearly discerned. Its use was accordingly forbidden to priests when ministering at the sanctuary (Lev. x. 9), and was declared to be improper for those about to sit on the judgment seat (Prov. xxxi. 4, 5; cp. Ecc. x. 17; Is. xxviii. 7); and precautions were taken to guard all men against excess. The means employed to prevent the danger line from being crossed were: 1. The weakening of the wine with water (2 Mac. xv. 39; Herod. vi. 84). That this was done further appears, for example, in connection with the kettle of warm water and the servants to mix the wine, which were employed at the passover (Mishna, *Pesachim* vii. 13; x. 2, 4, 7); hence in the early Christian church it was customary to mix the sacramental wine with water (Justin Martyr, Apol., i. 65). 2. The governor of the feast (Ecclus. xxxii. 1, 2; John ii. 9, 10), one of whose duties, at least where Greek customs were observed, was to fix the proportion in which the wine and water should be mixed and to determine how much wine each guest might drink; see MEALS. 3. Warnings against the danger of lingering over the wine, of tampering with the cup when it delights the eye, and of making strong intoxicants were urgently given, and the degradation of the drunkard was pointed out by sad example (Gen. ix. 21; Prov. xxiii. 29-35; Is. v. 22). 4. The folly of excess even from a worldly standpoint was emphasized and expressed in proverbs, and put on record in the religious literature of the people (Prov. xx. 1; xxi. 17; xxiii. 20, 21; Hab. ii. 5; Ecclus. xxxi. 25-31). 5. The sinfulness of drunkenness was earnestly taught and the condemnation of the drunkard by God the Judge was fully known (1 Sam. i. 14-16; Is. v. 11-17; 1 Cor. v. 11; vi. 10; Gal. v. 21; Eph. v. 18; 1 Pet. iv. 3).

Wine Press. See WINE.

Win'now-ing. See THRESHING.

Wis'dom.

One of the three departments of knowledge among the Hebrews, the other two being the law and prophecy. The law presents the commandments and claims of Jehovah to man; prophecy passes judgment on conduct in the light of God's revealed will and explains the object of God's dealings with men; wisdom seeks by observation, experience, and reflection to know things in their essence and reality as they stand related to man and God. The law and prophecy proceed directly from God, and in the highest sense are the word of God. Wisdom proceeds from man, and is the product of his own experience and observation. But while it is a human effort, it recognizes that a good understanding is the gift of God, and it postulates the fear of God and obedience to his commands as its first principle (Ps. cxi. 10; Prov. ix. 10; Ecc. xii. 13). In the earlier chapters of The Proverbs, in the Book of Job, and in the Wisdom of Solomon, wisdom is personified. See PHILOSOPHY.

The wise in counsel (Jer. xviii. 18) are met with from time to time during Israel's national history; as the wise woman of Tekoa (2 Sam. xiv. 2), the wise woman of Abel-beth-maacah (xx. 18), the four celebrities Ethan, Heman, Calcol, and Darda (1 Kin. iv. 31). Their utterances took the form of parable (2 Sam. xiv. 4-11), precept (Prov. xxiv. 27-29), proverb (23-26), riddle (i. 6), the story of real life and its lesson (xxiv. 30-34); and it is customary to see specimens of their keen observation, method, and shrewd sayings in Jotham's fable (Judg. ix. 7-20), Samson's riddle or dark saying (xiv. 14), Nathan's parable and those enacted by the wise woman of Tekoa and a certain prophet (2 Sam. xii. 1-7; xiv. 4-17; 1 Kin. xx. 35-43), and the fable uttered by king Jehoash (2 Kin. xiv. 9, 10). But the great books of Hebrew wisdom are Job, Proverbs, Ecclesiastes, Ecclesiasticus, and the Wisdom of Solomon.

Wis'dom of Solomon. See APOCRYPHA.

Witch and Witch'craft. See SORCERER.

Wit'ness.

Evidence which could be appealed to in the future was secured by some tangible token or memorial, as a heap of stones (Gen. xxxi. 46-52), or by calling in men to witness the event (xxiii. 10-18), by a written document, as a deed or a letter of divorce (Deut. xxiv. 1, 3; Jer. xxxii. 10).

The concurrent testimony of at least two witnesses was required under the Mosaic law to establish guilt of a capital crime (Num. xxxv. 30; Deut. xvii. 6; Heb. x. 28; cp. 1 Kin. xxi. 10, 13; Mat. xxvi. 60). This principle was a general rule in all judicial procedure (Deut. xix. 15). The Mosaic law did not sanction the use of torture to extract testimony; see PUNISHMENT. The witness, before his testimony was given, was adjured to tell the truth and to conceal nothing; and

then it was sin for him to withhold evidence in his possession (Lev. v. 1; Prov. xxix. 24). False witness bearing was denounced in the decalogue (Ex. xx. 16), and when detected, it drew upon the false witness the same penalty that he had attempted to get imposed on the accused (Deut. xix. 16, 19). The witnesses aided in executing a sentence of death; see STONING. Josephus asserts that women and children were excluded from giving testimony by the Mosaic law (Antiq. iv. 8, 15). The law itself says nothing on the subject; but the participation of the witnesses in the execution of the death penalty would make the exclusion of women and children from witness bearing expedient. Josephus' statement evidently represents the current interpretation of the Mosaic law in his day.

The excellent principle involved in having at least two witnesses is capable of broad application in the dealings of man with man (Is. viii. 2; Mat. xvii. 1, 2; xviii. 16; John viii. 17, 18; 1 Tim. v. 19).

Those who in the face of danger and distress testify to the truth of God are witnesses in the highest sense (Heb. x., xi., xii. 1). Martyr is a Greek word meaning witness, and it came to signify one who sealed his testimony with his blood, as Stephen and Antipas (Acts xxii. 20; Rev. ii. 13).

Wiz'ard.

A professed possessor of supernatural knowledge derived, in the form of wizardry referred to in the Bible, from the pretended ability to converse with the spirits of the dead (Is. viii. 19). The wizard chirped and muttered (ibid.) in imitation of the voice of the spirit (cp. xxix. 4). The wizard is never mentioned alone, but always in connection with them that have familiar spirits, because he belonged to the same class of questioners of the dead. The Canaanites consulted wizards (Deut. xviii. 9-12), so did the Egyptians (Is. xix. 3); but for a Hebrew to go to such an oracle defiled him, and was apostasy from Jehovah (Lev. xix. 31; xx. 6; Is. viii. 19). The offense of wizardry was punished with death (Lev. xx. 27). Saul, and subsequently Josiah, put the law in force (1 Sam. xxviii. 3, 9; 2 Kin. xxiii. 24); whilst Manasseh violated it shamelessly (2 Kin. xxi. 6).

Wolf.

1. A carnivorous animal, wild and fierce (Is. xi. 6; Hab. i. 8), that kills sheep (Ecclus. xiii. 17; John x. 12), and is accustomed to remain in hiding by day and seek its prey in the evening (Zeph. iii. 3). Benjamin was compared to the fierce and dreaded wolf (Gen. xlix. 9, 27; cp. the warrior Zeeb). But comparison with the wolf was not always intended as an honor. Violent princes who prey upon the helpless are likened to ravening wolves (Ezek. xxii. 27); and so are false teachers (Mat. vii. 15; Acts xx. 29), and enemies of the flock of

God (Mat. x. 16). The wolf of Palestine is a variety of the European species (*Canus lupus*), and is diffused throughout the country. Owing to the ease with which food is obtained and the mildness of the winter, they do not hunt in packs, as in the colder north, but prowl alone.

2. The rendering of the Hebrew '*Iyyim*, howling creatures (Is. xiii. 22; xxxiv. 14; Jer. l. 39; in A. V. wild beasts of the islands). The wolf belongs to the same genus as the dog; but it cannot bark, it can only howl.

Wom'an.

The counterpart of man, made to be his helpmeet and social equal (Gen. ii. 21–24; see EVE); and monogamy, or the marriage of one man and one woman, was the Creator's intention; see MARRIAGE.

The younger women of the family, especially in the earlier times and among the nomads, tended the sheep (Gen. xxix. 6; Ex. ii. 16), and they went to the harvest field and gleaned (Ruth ii. 3, 8); but the main duties of women were about the household. They brought water from the well (Gen. xxiv. 13; John iv. 7), ground the grain for daily use (Mat. xxiv. 41), prepared the meals (Gen. xviii. 6; 2 Sam. xiii. 8; Luke x. 40), spun wool and made clothing (1 Sam. ii. 19; Prov. xxxi. 13, 19; Acts ix. 36–39), taught the children religious truth (Prov. i. 8; xxxi. 1; cp. 2 Tim. iii. 15), and directed the household (Prov. xxxi. 27; 1 Tim. v. 14).

The Mosaic law and also public opinion among the Hebrews secured to women the enjoyment of many rights; see CONCUBINE, DIVORCE, MARRIAGE. Marriage was regarded by the Hebrews as a sacred relation (Mal. ii. 14–16). The wife was spoken of with respect and accorded honor (Prov. v. 18; xviii. 22; xxxi. 10–12; Ecc. ix. 9). To the mother honor was due, and her law had authority (Ex. xx. 12; Prov. i. 8). The capable woman was highly praised (xxxi. 10–31), and examples of noble womanhood were freely and purposely admitted to the sacred writings. The spirit of the N. T. was equally hostile to woman's degradation. It insisted that man and woman shall occupy their respective spheres as indicated by the Creator in mutual respect and dependence (Mark x. 6–9; Eph. v. 31; 1 Tim. ii. 12–15). The sanctity and permanence of the marriage relation were taught, and divorce permitted only for extreme causes (Mat. xix. 8, 9; 1 Cor. vii. 15; Eph. v. 22–33). Woman was made the recipient of the same grace as man, and heir of the same promises (Gal. iii. 28); she was accorded honorable position in the church, and her services in the cause of Christ were fully appreciated and acknowledged (Rom. xvi. 1–4, 6, 12). The practical precepts in the epistles were calculated, whether addressed to saints generally or to woman in particular, to refine and ennoble her, and to bring her best qualities into exercise (1 Tim. ii. 9, 10; iii. 11).

Wool. See SHEEP, SPINNING, WEAVING.

World.

The world as known in the Mosaic age was small (Gen. x.). On the south it extended from the mountains east of the Persian Gulf to the Nile; and on the north, from the Caspian Sea to the Grecian islands: in other words, it measured about 1500 miles from east to ِt, and 900, or including southern Arabia aجout 1500, miles from north to south. The area was about 2,250,000 square miles; but a large part of the surface was occupied by sea, so that the land was scarcely two-thirds of the extent of the United States, excluding Alaska. The history which is recorded in the Bible, and the great events of the world's history, were enacted in the northern portion of this region, in an area about one-third that of the United States.

During O. T. times these limits remained essentially unchanged, although the geographical horizon widened a little. Media and Persia rose to importance before the close of this period, making themselves known as never before and taking the first place among the nations. India became a boundary (Esth. i. 1). The existence of the Sinim was known (Is. xlix. 12). In the west Africa was circumnavigated during the reign of Pharaoh-necho, but without increasing geographical knowledge. The navigators did not realize the meaning of their achievement. They had spent more than two years on the voyage, and what appeared most noteworthy to them was that the sun, which rose upon their left hand when they sailed south from Egypt, rose on their right before they returned (Herod. iv. 42, 43). In Italy and on the opposite coast of Africa population was increasing and civilization was slowly developing; but these facts seldom reached the ears of men in the east, and then only through the reports of traders. Almost at the close of the O. T. period Greece emerged from obscurity by the vigorous resistance which it offered to the Persians.

Alexander the Great conquered the world. He extended its eastern limits, and added immensely to geographical knowledge, by carrying his arms across the Oxus into modern Turkestan, eastward beyond the bounds of modern Afghanistan, and southward into northern India. The Romans followed him. In the time of Christ the world, as currently thought of by men, extended from Spain and Britain to the plateau of Iran and India, and from the desert of Sahara on the south to the forests of Germany and the steppes of Russia and Siberia on the north. Knowledge of inhabited regions beyond these limits existed; but there was little contact with this outside world, it seldom engaged men's attention, and the ideas of its geography were confused.

World is frequently put for the inhabitants of the world (Ps. ix. 8; Is. xiii. 11; John iii. 16; vii. 7; Rom. iii. 19), and in the N. T. for that which pertains to the earth and this present state of existence merely (1 Cor. vii. 31; Gal. vi. 14; Eph. ii. 2; Jas. i. 27; iv. 4; 1 John ii. 15).

Worm.

Any small, creeping animal, whose body is boneless and consists of a number of movable joints or rings, and which has no limbs or only very short ones. It was generically called *tola'ath* or *tole'ah* in Hebrew, *skōlēx* in Greek; and it is mentioned as destroying grapes and the gourd vine (Deut. xxviii. 39; Jonah iv. 7), being bred over night in manna (Ex. xvi. 20), consuming the corpse (Is. xiv. 11; cp. lxvi. 24 with Mark ix. 48), and causing death to the living (Acts xii. 23). Man as feeble and despised is likened to a worm (Job xxv. 6; Is. xli. 14).

Specific worms referred to are :

1. Maggots, in Hebrew a collective term *rimmah*, putridity and the worm bred in it. They feed on corpses (Job xxi. 26; xxiv. 20; Is. xiv. 11), and might be expected in putrid manna (Ex. xvi. 24). Man as very small and despicable is likened to the maggot (Job xxv. 6). In all these passages the E. V. uses the general term worm.

2. The larva of the moth, in Hebrew *sas* (Is. li. 8); see MOTH.

3. The coccus worm, *tola'ath shani*, which, however, is not a worm, but an insect, according to modern classification; see SCARLET.

The Hebrew word *zaḥal*, creeper, denotes something that crawls on the ground, and is rendered by worm in A. V. (Mic. vii. 17; in R. V. crawling things).

Worm'wood.

A plant, ranked with gall, having very bitter juice (Deut. xxix. 18; Prov. v. 4), unpalatable and, when exclusively drunk, noxious (Rev. viii. 11); called in Hebrew *la'anah*, in Greek of N. T. *apsinthos*. It is used figuratively for injustice (Amos v. 7; vi. 12; in latter passage rendered hemlock in A. V.), for sore punishment (Jer. ix. 15), for bitter suffering (Lam. iii. 19) with which one is sated, not intoxicated (15). It seems to be some species of the great composite genus *Artemisia*. About 180 species are known. Post enumerates five species and several varieties as occurring in Palestine or the adjacent regions. The type is the common wormwood (*Artemisia absinthium*), cultivated in gardens.

Wor'ship.

Respect and honor shown to a person (Luke xiv. 10, in R. V. glory). This sense of the word worship has become obsolete. Respect which implies that the object thereof possesses divine attributes (Mat. xiv. 33; xv. 25; Rev. xiv. 7). Man is forbidden to give this worship to any but God alone (Ex. xxxiv. 14; Mat. iv. 10; Acts x. 25; Rev. xix. 10). The same outward act may be civility shown to man, as when people bowed down to Esau, to Joseph, or to the king

(Gen. xxxiii. 3; xlii. 6; 2 Sam. xxiv. 20), or worship rendered to God (Gen. xxiv. 52, R. V.; Ps. xcv. 6), the same Hebrew word being used in all these passages. The performance of this outward act to idols was strictly forbidden (Ex. xx. 5).

For public worship in apostolic times see CHURCH.

Writ'ing.

The Hebrews, or rather some of them, were able to write (Ex. xvii. 14; xxiv. 4; Num. xxxiii. 2). The art had been practiced in Babylonia centuries before Abraham left Ur of the Chaldees, and in Egypt centuries

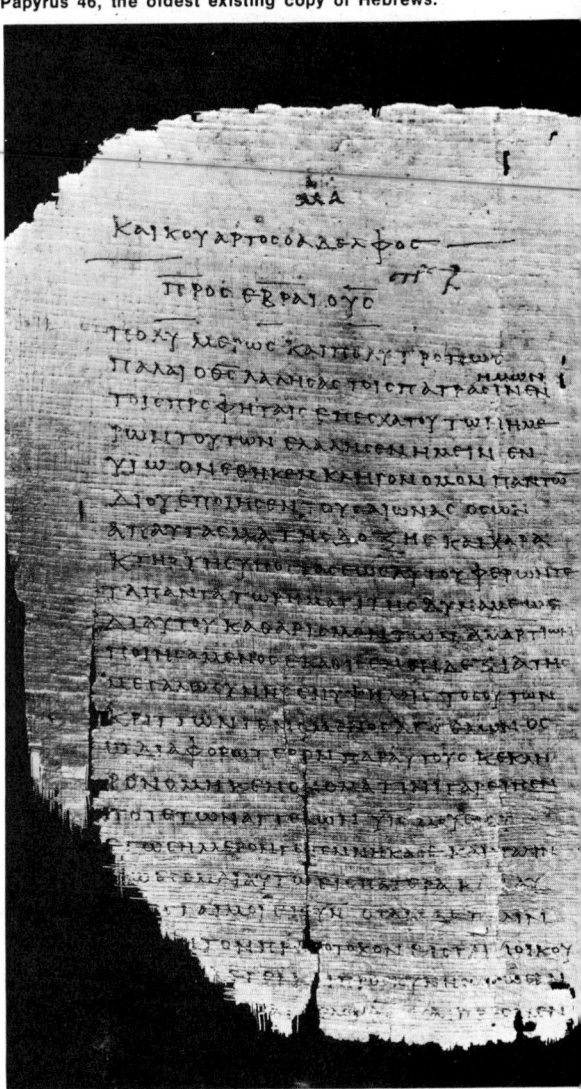

Papyrus 46, the oldest existing copy of Hebrews.

before the Israelites sojourned on the Nile. It was in use in the towns of Canaan before the conquest of the country by the Hebrews. It is recorded that the Hebrews at the time of the exodus wrote documents (ibid. ; Deut. xxxi. 24), inscribed the law on the plaster of an altar (xxvii. 4, 8 ; Josh. viii. 32), and engraved words on gems and metallic plates (Ex. xxxix. 14, 30). The ancient inscriptions of Babylonia were impressed on soft clay, afterwards baked ; and were engraven on stone tablets, on the surface of stone statues, on metal, and on the gem of which the seal was made. The letters sent from Canaan to Pharaoh previous to the exodus were written on clay tablets. The Egyptians, long before the sojourn of the Israelites among them, cut records in stone and wrote on papyrus. See BOOK, INK-HORN, PAPYRUS, PARCHMENT, TILE.

Y

Yarn. See LINEN 6.

Year.

The year of the Hebrews consisted of twelve months (1 Kin. iv. 7 ; 1 Chron. xxvii. 1–15). These appear to have been lunar (see MONTH), and the year would accordingly contain 354 days, 8 hours, 48 minutes, 32.4 seconds.

The annual festivals were inseparably connected with the agricultural seasons. A strictly lunar year would cause these festivals, as fixed by the calendar, to constantly recede from their appropriate season. It was necessary to bring the lunar year into correspondence with the solar year of 365 days. This was doubtless accomplished by the intercalation of an additional month every three or four years, although the custom is not mentioned in the Bible. The year began with the month Abib or Nisan (Ex. xii. 2 ; xxiii. 15 ; Esth. iii. 7), with the new moon next before or next after the vernal equinox, when the sun is in Aries (Antiq. iii. 8, 4 ; 10, 5) ; but there was from the earliest times a civil, or rather agricultural, year which began in the autumn (cp. Ex. xxiii. 16 ; xxxiv. 22 ; Lev. xxv. 4, 9, seq.). It was convenient for a people devoted to horticulture and agriculture to begin the year with the season of plowing and sowing, and to close it with harvest. In practice they frequently preferred to indicate the time of year by the particular harvest or agricultural occupation than by the number or name of the month (e. g. Num. xiii. 20 ; Ruth i. 22). Sometime after the exile the new moon of the seventh month came to be kept as new year's day. The custom was probably not started by the events recorded in Ezra iii. 6 and Neh. viii. 2, but was yet favored by them.

Month.	Approximation.	Festival.	Season.
1. **Abib** or **Nisan.** Ex. xxiii. 15; Neh. ii. 1; Antiq. iii. 10, 5.	April.	14. Passover in the evening, the beginning of the 15th day (Ex. xii. 18, 19 ; xiii. 3–10), introducing 15–21. Feast of Unleavened Bread (Lev. xxiii. 6). 16. Sheaf of firstfruits of the harvest presented (Lev. xxiii. 10–14; cp. Josh. v. 11 ; Antiq. iii. 10, 5).	Latter or spring rains. Flax harvest at Jericho (Josh. ii. 6). Jordan at flood (Josh. iii. 15; 1 Chron. xii. 15; Ecclus. xxiv. 26). Barley harvest in the maritime plain. Wheat ripe in hot Jordan valley. Pods on the carob tree. Dry season begins, continuing to early October, with prevailing wind from the northwest.
2. **Ziv** or **Iyar.** 1 Kin. vi. 1, 37; Antiq. viii. 3, 1.	May.	14. Passover for those who could not keep regular one (Num. ix. 10, 11).	Barley harvest in uplands. Wheat harvest in lowlands.
3. **Sivan.** Esth. viii. 9.	June.	6. Pentecost, or Feast of Weeks or of Harvest, or Day of Firstfruits. Loaves as firstfruits of gathered harvest presented (Ex. xxiii. 16 ; xxxiv. 22 ; Lev. xxiii. 15–21 ; Num. xxviii. 26 ; Deut. xvi. 9, 10).	Apples on sea coast. Early figs general. Oleander in bloom. Almonds ripe. Intense heat (War iii. 7, 32).
4. **Tammuz.**	July.		Wheat harvest in high mountains. First grapes ripe.

Month.	Approximation.	Festival.	Season.
5. **Ab.** Antiq. iv. 4, 7. 6. **Elul.** Neh. vi. 15. 7. **Ethanim** or **Tishri.** 1 Kin. viii. 2; Antiq. viii. 4, 1.	August. September. October.	1. Memorial of Trumpetblowing (Num. xxix. 1). 10. Day of Atonement (Lev. xvi. 29). 15–21. Feast of Ingathering or Tabernacles. Firstfruits of wine and oil (Ex. xxiii. 16; Lev. xxiii. 34; Deut. xvi. 13). 22. Solemn Assembly (Lev. xxiii. 36; Num. xxix. 35; Neh. viii. 18; cp. John vii. 37).	Olives in lowlands. Dates and summer figs. Vintage general. Pomegranates ripe. Season changing to the winter (Antiq. iii. 10, 4) or rainy season, with prevailing wind from west and southwest. Former or early rains. Pistachio nuts ripe. Plowing. Barley and wheat sown.
8. **Bul** or **Marcheshvan.** 1 Kin. vi. 38; Antiq. i. 3, 3. 9. **Chislev.** Zech. vii. 1; cp. Antiq. xii. 5, 4; 7, 6. 10. **Tebeth.** Esth. ii. 16; Antiq. xi. 5, 4.	November. December. January.	25. Feast of Dedication (1 Mac. iv. 52; John x. 22).	Olives gathered in northern Galilee. Winter figs on trees. Rainfall increases (cp. Ezra x. 9, 13). Hail; snow on higher hills and occasionally at Jerusalem. In lowlands grain fields and pastures green, wild flowers abundant.
11. **Shebat.** Zech. i. 7; 1 Mac. xvi. 14.	February.		Almond trees in blossom. Appearance of young fruit, or rather blossom, of the fig. Carob tree in blossom.
12. **Adar.** Esth. iii. 7; Antiq. iv. 8, 49.	March.	14, 15. Feast of Purim (Esth. ix. 21–28).	Oranges and lemons ripe in the lowlands. Storax blossoming and pomegranates showing their first flowers. Barley harvest at Jericho.

Yoke.

A small transverse bar of timber, generally with two portions of the lower surface hollowed so as to rest on the necks of two oxen, used to draw a cart or a plow (Num. xix. 2); see illustration, PLOW. Two oxen thus held together were also called a yoke (1 Kin. xix. 19), and so, figuratively, was any burden imposed on one as a token and means of subjection (xii. 4; Mat. xi. 30; Acts xv. 10).

Z

Za-a-na′im. See ZAANANNIM.

Za′a-nan [place of flocks].

A town (Mic. i. 11), perhaps the same as Zenan.

Za-a-nan′nim, in A. V. once **Zaanaim** (Judg. iv. 11), the Hebrew text being preferred to the traditional reading [departures].

A frontier town of Naphtali (Josh. xix. 33), near Kedesh (Judg. iv. 11). Conder follows Septuagint which has Besemiin, having made one word of "in Zaanannim" (so Josh. xix. 33, R. V. margin), and he believes it to have probably been near Bessûm, on the table-land west of the sea of Galilee.

Za′a-van, in A. V. once **Zavan** [unquiet].

A son of Ezer the Horite (Gen. xxxvi. 27; 1 Chron. i. 42).

Za′bad [he hath given or endowed].

1. A descendant of Ephraim, family of Shuthelah (1 Chron. vii. 21).

2. A man of Judah, family of Hezron, house of Jerahmeel, descended through Sheshan, and a great-grandson of Ahlai (1 Chron. ii. 31, 34–37). Possibly he was David's mighty man of this name (xi. 41).

3. Corrupt form of Jozacar (2 Chron. xxiv. 26); see JOZACAR.

4, 5, 6. Three Hebrews, each of whom was induced by Ezra to put away his foreign wife (Ezra x. 27, 33, 43).

Zab-a-dæ′ans, in A. V. **Zabadeans**.

An Arabian tribe which dwelt between the river Eleutherus, Hamath, and Damascus (1 Mac. xii. 30–32; cp. 25), and hence probably occupied that part of the Anti-Lebanon mountains where the villages of Zebedani and Zebad are situated, on the route from Ba'al-bek to Damascus.

Zab′bai [humming].

A son of Bebai. He was induced by Ezra to put away his foreign wife (Ezra x. 28). He was the father of a certain Baruch (Neh. iii. 20).

Zab'bud [endowed].

Head of a family among the sons of Bigvai, who accompanied Ezra from Babylon (Ezra viii. 14).

Zab'di [gift of (Jehovah)].

1. A man of Judah, family of Zerah, and founder of a house (Josh. vii. 1). Called in 1 Chron. ii. 6 Zimri. For the confusion of b and m, d and r, see BETH, DALETH.

2. A Benjamite (1 Chron. viii. 19).

3. A Shiphmite, David's officer over the increase of the vineyards for the wine cellars (1 Chron. xxvii. 27).

4. A Levite, son of Asaph (Neh. xi. 17); see ZICHRI 5.

Zab'di-el [gift of God].

1. Father of Jashobeam (1 Chron. xxvii. 2).

2. Son of Haggedolim (Neh. xi. 14), or one of the great men (A. V. and margin of R. V.).

3. An Arabian prince who treacherously decapitated Alexander Balas and sent the head to Ptolemy Philometor (1 Mac. xi. 17; Antiq. xiii. 4, 8). He is probably the person referred to by Diodorus Siculus as Diocles, ruler of Abæ, to whose care Alexander committed his infant son, and while sojourning with whom Alexander was murdered by two of his own officers.

Za'bud [given, endowed].

Son of Nathan and chief minister in Solomon's reign (1 Kin. iv. 5, R. V. margin).

Zab'u-lon. See ZEBULUN.

Zac'cai [pure, innocent].

Founder of a family, members of which returned with Zerubbabel from the captivity (Ezra ii. 9; Neh. vii. 14).

Zac-chæ'us [Greek from Hebrew *Zakkay*, pure].

A wealthy man of Jericho who farmed the revenue for the Roman government. He became a disciple of Christ (Luke xix. 1–10).

Zac'cur, in A. V. once **Zacchur** (1 Chron. iv. 26) [mindful].

1. A Reubenite (Num. xiii. 4).

2. A Simeonite, descended through Mishma (1 Chron. iv. 26).

3. A Merarite Levite, a son of Jaaziah (1 Chron. xxiv. 27).

4. A Gershonite Levite, a son of Asaph, and head of a course of musicians in David's reign (1 Chron. xxv. 2, 10; Neh. xii. 35). See ZICHRI 5.

5. A son of Imri, who helped to rebuild the walls of Jerusalem (Neh. iii. 2).

6. A Levite, who sealed the covenant (Neh. x. 12).

7. Son of Mattaniah and father of Hanan (Neh. xiii. 13).

Zach-a-ri'as, in R. V. twice **Zachariah** (Mat. xxiii. 35; Luke xi. 51) [Greek form of the Hebrew *Z°karyah*, Jehovah hath remembered]

1. Father of the captain Joseph (1 Mac. v. 18).

2. Father of John the Baptist. He was a priest of the course of Abijah (Luke i. 5); see ABIJAH. He and his wife were godly people, and she was related to Mary of Nazareth (6, 36). Their home was in the hill country of Judæa (39, 40.) It was customary to allot to the members of the course on duty at the sanctuary the several parts to be performed in the daily ministrations. When Zacharias' course assembled at Jerusalem the lot fell to him to burn incense; and while he was discharging this service at the hour of prayer, an angel appeared to him and announced that his supplication was heard. His old prayer for a son, although long abandoned as denied by God (18), and the prayer which he continually offered for the advent of the Messiah (68–75), were heard; and he was told that his wife should bear a son who should go before the face of the Lord to make ready for the Lord a people prepared for him (13–17). Zacharias questioned the promise on account of the advanced age of himself and his wife, and asked for a sign. The sign was granted in the form of a punishment. Zacharias was smitten with dumbness until the promise was fulfilled (18–22; 62–64). When the child was born, not only was the tongue of Zacharias released from its speechlessness, but he himself was filled with the Spirit and prophesied in words of thanksgiving and praise (67–79).

3. A righteous man who was murdered in the court of the temple, between the sanctuary and the house (Mat. xxiii. 35; Luke xi. 51); see ZECHARIAH 11.

Za'cher. See ZECHARIAH 1.

Za'dok [just, righteous].

1. A descendant of Eleazar, the son of Aaron (1 Chron. xxiv. 3). He was the son of Ahitub (2 Sam. viii. 17). He was doubtless the young man, mighty of valor, who went with the chief men of the tribes of Israel to David at Hebron to turn the kingdom of Saul unto him (1 Chron. xii. 27, 28). Early in David's reign he was joint high priest with Abiathar (2 Sam. viii. 17). During the rebellion of Absalom the two colleagues joined in David's flight from Jerusalem, carrying with them the ark, but the king desired them to return to the capital, and there await the issue of the contest (xv. 24–29). After the death of Absalom, a message, on which they acted, was sent by David to Zadok and Abiathar, requesting them to suggest to the people that the king should be called back (xix. 11). When, in David's old age, Adonijah plotted to usurp the throne, Zadok remained faithful, while his colleague Abiathar went with the usurper (1 Kin. i. 7, 8). When the plot was discovered to David, Zadok, with Nathan the prophet, received instructions immediately to anoint Solomon king (32–45). Abiathar was deposed from the priesthood, and Zadok was the sole occu-

pant of the high office till his death, during the reign of the new monarch (ii. 26, 27; cp. iv. 4). The office of the high priest was thus restored to the line of Eleazar; see HIGH PRIEST.

2. A priest in the line of high priests, father of Shallum (1 Chron. vi. 12). He was descended from the second Ahitub (ibid.; Ezra vii. 2) through the second Meraioth (1 Chron. ix. 11; Neh. xi. 11).

3. Father of Jerusha, king Uzziah's mother (2 Kin. xv. 33).

4. A son of Bani. He repaired part of the wall of Jerusalem (Neh. iii. 4), and was perhaps the person of the name who sealed the covenant (x. 21).

5. A priest, son of Immer. He repaired the city wall opposite to his house (Neh. iii. 29), and was perhaps the scribe who was made a treasurer (xiii. 13).

Za'ham [loathing].
A son of Rehoboam (2 Chron. xi. 19).

Za'in, in A. R. V. **Zayin**.
The seventh letter of the Hebrew alphabet. English Z, which had the same origin, represents it in Hebrew names in the English version. It heads the seventh section of Ps. cxix. in several versions, because each verse of the section begins with this letter.
For possibility of confusing it with other letters, see VAU.

Za'ir [little].
A place in or near Edom, where king Joram, of Judah, encamped before making a night attack on the Edomites (2 Kin. viii. 21; cp. the different text in 2 Chron. xxi. 9). Conder proposes Zuwêra, a double town near the Dead Sea, on the road from the southern end of the sea to Hebron.

Za'laph [fracture].
Father of a certain Hanun (Neh. iii. 30).

Zal'mon, in A. V. once **Salmon** (Ps. lxviii. 14) [shady].
1. An Ahohite, one of David's mighty men (2 Sam. xxiii. 28). Also called Ilai (1 Chron. xi. 29).
2. A wooded mountain near Shechem (Judg. ix. 48; cp. Ps. lxviii. 14).

Zal-mo'nah [shady].
An encampment of the Israelites (Num. xxxiii. 41, 42), either west or east of Edom.

Zal-mun'na [perhaps, shelter is denied].
One of the two kings of Midian slain by Gideon (Judg. viii. 4-28; Ps. lxxxiii. 11).

Zam'bri. See ZIMRI 2.

Zam-zum'mim, in A. V. **Zamzummims** [murmurers, makers of noise].
A tribe of Rephaim, who in ancient times inhabited the region east of the Jordan, afterwards occupied by the Ammonites (Deut. ii. 20); probably the same as the Zuzim.

Za-no'ah [foul water].
1. A town in the lowland of Judah (Josh. xv. 34). It was inhabited after the captivity (Neh. xi. 30), and seems to have been the Zanoah whose inhabitants restored the valley gate of Jerusalem (iii. 13). Robinson plausibly identified it with Zânûa, nearly 3 miles southeast by south of Beth-shemesh.

2. A town in the hill country of Judah (Josh. xv. 56; and probably 1 Chron. iv. 18). Zânûta about 12½ miles southwest by south of Hebron, 2½ south of Shuweikeh, and 5 southwest by west of es-Semua, is scarcely the site; for it belongs to the group of Josh. xv. 48-51 rather than to that of 55-57.

Zaph'e-nath-pa-ne'ah, in A. V. **Zaphnath-paaneah** [God speaks, he lives (Steindorff); or, the giver of the nourishment of life (Lieblein)].
Joseph's name, given him by Pharaoh (Gen. xli. 45). From the sound of the name, the Jews guessed that it meant revealer of secrets (Targum Onkelos; Antiq. ii. 6, 1).

Za'phon [concealment, north].
A town of the Gadites in the Jordan valley (Josh. xiii. 27; cp. Judg. xii. 1, R. V. margin). The Talmud calls it 'Amatho. If this is correct, it is Amathus (Antiq. xiii. 13, 5; xiv. 5, 4), and its site is Tell Ammete, in the Jordan valley, east of the river and 8 miles north by east of the mouth of the Jabbok.

Za'ra and **Zarah.** See ZERAH.

Za're-ah. See ZORAH.

Za're-ath-ite. See ZORATHITE.

Za'red. See ZERED.

Zar'e-phath, in A. V. of N. T. **Sarepta** (Luke iv. 26) [perhaps, smelting furnace].
A town belonging to Sidon (1 Kin. xvii. 9; Luke iv. 26; Antiq. viii. 13, 2). Thither Elijah repaired when the brook Cherith dried up. Trusting his word, spoken in the name of Jehovah, a widow of Zarephath gave him a home while the famine lasted. As a reward of her faith her oil and meal failed not, and her boy was brought back to life (1 Kin. xvii. 8-24). The town yielded to Sennacherib in 701 B. C. Its future possession by Israel is announced (Obad. 20). The name still lingers in the form of Surafend, a large village on a hill near the sea, 14 miles north of Tyre, and 8 south of Sidon. The ancient city was, however, on the shore, along which the ruins extend for a mile or more.

Zar'e-than, in A. V. **Zaretan** (Josh. iii. 16), and **Zartanah** (1 Kin. iv. 12), and **Zarthan** (1 Kin. vii. 46).
A village beneath Jezreel near the towns of Beth-shean and Adam (Josh. iii. 16; 1 Kin. iv. 12); evidently in the territory of Manasseh. In clayey ground between Succoth, east of the Jordan, and Zarethan, west of the river, bronze work for the temple was cast (vii. 46). In 2 Chron. iv. 17 the name is given as Zeredah in the form *sᵉredathah*; perhaps for *sᵉrerathah*, by confusion of the letters d and r, *i. e.*, daleth and resh. See DALETH.

Zar'hite, in R. V. **Zerahite**.

A person belonging to the family of Zerah. There was a family of this name in the tribe of Simeon and another in Judah (Num. xxvi. 13, 20; Josh. vii. 17; cp. 1; 1 Chron. xxvii. 11, 13).

Zar'ta-nah. See ZARETHAN.

Zar'than. See ZARETHAN.

Zat'tu, in A. V. once **Zatthu** (Neh. x. 14). Founder of a family, members of which returned from the captivity (Ezra ii. 8; Neh. vii. 13). Some of them married foreign wives, but were induced to put them away (Ezra x. 27) The representative of the family sealed the covenant (Neh. x. 14).

Za'van. See ZAAVAN.

Za'yin. See ZAIN.

Za'za [movement, abundance].

A man of Judah, family of Hezron, house of Jerahmeel (1 Chron. ii. 33).

Zeal'ot, in A. V. **Zelotes** [zealous one]; Greek equivalent of Cananæan (q. v.).

A member of a Jewish patriotic party (War iv. 3, 9; vii. 8, 1). Simon the apostle was distinguished from Simon Peter and others by this epithet (Luke vi. 15; Acts i. 13). The party was started into being by Judas the Galilæan in the time of Cyrenius to resist Roman aggression. Its increasing fanaticism contributed to provoke the Roman war. Ultimately it degenerated into a body of mere assassins, called Sicarii (Antiq. xviii. 1, 1 and 6; War ii. 8, 1; 17, 8; iv. 3, 9 seq.).

Zeb-a-di'ah [Jehovah hath given or endowed].

1. A Benjamite, of the house of Beriah (1 Chron. viii. 15, 16).

2. A Benjamite, descended from Elpaal (1 Chron. viii. 17, 18).

3. A son of Jeroham of Gedor. He joined David at Ziklag (1 Chron. xii. 7).

4. Son of Asahel, Joab's brother (1 Chron. xxvii. 7).

5. A Korhite Levite, a son of Meshelemiah, in David's reign (1 Chron. xxvi. 1, 2).

6. One of the Levites sent forth by Jehoshaphat to teach the law (2 Chron. xvii. 8).

7. A prince of Judah, who was the chief judicial functionary for civil cases in the court which Jehoshaphat established at Jerusalem (2 Chron. xix. 11).

8. A descendant of Shephatiah. He was one of those who accompanied Ezra from Babylon (Ezra viii. 8).

9. A priest of the house of Immer. He was induced by Ezra to put away his foreign wife (Ezra x. 20).

Ze'bah [slaughter, sacrifice].

One of the two kings of Midian pursued and slain by Gideon (Judg. viii. 4–28; Ps. lxxxiii. 11).

Ze-ba'im. See POCHERETH-HAZZEBAIM.

Zeb'e-dee [Greek form of Hebrew Zᵉbad-yah, Jehovah hath endowed].

The husband of Salome (q. v.), and father of James and John. Like his sons, he was a fisherman on the sea of Galilee (Mat. iv. 21, 22), and was a man of some substance, for he had hired servants (Mark i. 19, 20). He raised no obstacle to his sons following Jesus.

Ze-bi'dah, in A. V. **Zebudah**, the traditional pronunciation [given, bestowed].

A daughter of Pedaiah of Rumah, and mother of king Jehoiakim (2 Kin. xxiii. 36).

Ze-bi'na [acquired].

A descendant of Nebo. He was induced by Ezra to put away his foreign wife (Ezra x. 43).

Ze-boi'im and **Zeboim, I.** [gazelles]. In Hebrew text and R. V. the first form is used in the Pentateuch, the second in Hosea.

One of the five cities of the plain (Gen. x. 19). Its king was defeated by Chedorlaomer (xiv. 2, 8, 10). It was destroyed with the other cities of the plain by fire from heaven (xix. 17–29; Deut. xxix. 23; Hosea xi. 8).

Ze-bo'im, II. [hyenas].

1. A valley in the territory of Benjamin, between Michmash and the wilderness on the east (1 Sam. xiii. 16–18). A cliff just above the Jordan plain, near Jericho, is called Shukh ed-Duba, lair of the hyena, and perhaps indicates the locality.

2. A town occupied by Benjamites after the captivity (Neh. xi. 34). It is evidently to be sought in the hills bordering the plain of Sharon, near Lydda.

Ze-bu'dah. See ZEBIDAH.

Ze'bul [habitation].

The governor of the city of Shechem in the time of Abimelech, to whom he showed unswerving fidelity (Judg. ix. 28, 36–39).

Zeb'u-lon-ite. See ZEBULUNITE.

Zeb'u-lun, in A. V. of N. T. **Zabulon** [habitation, dwelling].

1. The tenth son of Jacob, and the sixth by Leah (Gen. xxx. 19, 20). He went down with his father into Egypt (Ex. i. 3). He had three sons: Sered, Elon, and Jahleel (Gen. xlvi. 14). Jacob, in his farewell address, blessing his sons, pictured Zebulun as dwelling at the haven of the sea, being a haven of ships, and having his border on Zidon (xlix. 13). This picture was realized in its essentials, but not in its details. Zebulun was allotted territory in the vicinity of the sea, and enjoyed the markets of the towns on the coast; but it was itself separated from the sea of Galilee by Naphtali and Issachar, and from the Mediterranean Sea and the city of Zidon by the tribe of Asher. This lack of agreement between the picture drawn in Jacob's address and the actual state of the tribe in Palestine is a strong argument that the address was not composed after the settlement of the tribes, but is genuine.

2. The tribe of which Zebulun was the

progenitor. From his three sons sprang the great families into which the tribe was divided (Num. xxvi. 26, 27). The prince of the tribe early in the wilderness wanderings was Eliab, son of Helon (i. 9; x. 16), and at a later period Elizaphan, son of Parnach, was a prince (xxxiv. 25). The spy from the tribe was Gaddiel, son of Sodi (xiii. 10). At the first census it contained 57,400 fighting men (i. 30, 31); at the second 60,500 (xxvi. 27). It was one of the six tribes the representatives of which stood on mount Ebal to pronounce curses on transgressors (Deut. xxvii. 13; cp. Josh. viii. 32-35). Moses before his departure, associating the two brothers, later sons of Leah, and with the prophecy of Jacob in mind, thus indicated their future history: "Rejoice, Zebulun, in thy going out; and, Issachar, in thy tents. They shall call the peoples unto the mountain; there they shall offer sacrifices of righteousness: for they shall suck the abundance of the seas, and the hidden treasures of the sand" (Deut. xxxiii. 18, 19, R. V.). In the mountain of Jehovah's inheritance (Ex. xv. 17), where he will establish his chosen people, Zebulun and Issachar will bring rich offerings to their bountiful Benefactor. After the conquest of Canaan, Zebulun was allotted territory in the northern part of the country. It lay north of Issachar, east of Asher, and south and west of Naphtali (Josh. xix. 27, 34). Its southern boundary ran by Daberath on the western foot of mount Tabor, passed Chisloth-tabor, and after skirting the plain of Esdraelon and then crossing it reached the brook that is before Jokneam (11, 12), probably the wady el-Milh, a southern tributary of the Kishon. Its eastern boundary went to Gath-hepher, which was probably 3 miles north by east of Nazareth, and on to Rimmon, 6 miles almost due north of Nazareth (13, R. V.). At the northwestern corner of the territory was the valley of Iphtah-el (14), probably about 9 miles north by west of Nazareth, and leaving the fertile plain of el-Buttauf within the bounds of Zebulun. Since Bethlehem, 7 miles west-northwest of Nazareth, belonged to Zebulun (15), the western boundary was doubtless in part the wady el-Khalladîyeh. The region possessed by Zebulun was fertile. It embraced a part of the mountainous country of lower Galilee and the northwestern corner of the plain of Esdraelon. The Zebulunites constituted an important part of Barak's force in the fight with Sisera (Judg. iv. 6-10; v. 14, 18), and of Gideon's army in the war with Midian (vi. 35). Deborah sang that there were in the tribe they that handle the marshal's staff, or the staff of the scribe (v. 14, R. V. text and margin), meaning the scribes who gathered and mustered the army (2 Kin. xxv. 19). The judge Elon was a member of the tribe, exercised his office, died, and was buried at Aijalon, within its territory (Judg. xii. 12). Fifty thousand

warriors of the tribe, with skillful and faithful commanders, went with the other tribes to Hebron to make David king (1 Chron. xii. 33, 40). Ishmaiah was the ruler of the Zebulunites in David's reign (xxvii. 19). The tribe with the rest of Galilee suffered severely during the Assyrian wars, but Isaiah prophesied that it would obtain compensatory blessings in Messianic times (Is. ix. 1, 2; Mat. iv. 12-16). Some men of the tribe accepted Hezekiah's invitation to come to Jerusalem for his great passover (2 Chron. x. 10, 11, 18). Ezekiel, of course, assigns a gate for the Zebulunites in the Jerusalem which he describes (Ezek. xlviii. 33), and of the tribe there were sealed in the apocalyptic vision the normal number 12,000 (Rev. vii. 8).

Zeb'u-lun-ite, in A. V. in Judges **Zebulonite.**

One belonging to the tribe of Zebulun, or resident within its territory (Num. xxvi. 27; Judg. xii. 11, 12).

Zech-a-ri'ah, in A. V. four times **Zachariah** (2 Kin. xiv. 29; xv. 8, 11; xviii. 2) [Jehovah hath remembered].

1. A Benjamite of the family of Jeiel of Gibeon (1 Chron. ix. 37); called in 1 Chron. viii. 31 Zecher (in A. V. Zacher). If the traditional vocalization is correct, Zecher is a synonymous name meaning memory. Perhaps, however, it was an abbreviation of Zechariah, as Ahaz is of Ahaziah, and was pronounced Zachar, meaning he hath remembered.

2. A Levite, family of Kohath, house of Izhar, descended through Ebiasaph. He was the eldest son of Meshelemiah. He was porter of the door of the tent of meeting in David's reign (1 Chron. ix. 21, 22; xxvi. 2). He was a discreet counselor (14).

3. A Levite of the second degree who played a psaltery in the procession that escorted the ark to Jerusalem, and afterwards was permanently employed in the tabernacle which David pitched for the ark (1 Chron. xv. 18. 20; xvi. 5). It is doubtful whether the word doorkeepers (xv. 18) is intended to include him.

4. A priest who blew a trumpet when the ark was brought up from the house of Obed-edom (1 Chron. xv. 24).

5. A Levite, family of Kohath, house of Uzziel. He was a son of Isshiah and lived in the reign of David (1 Chron. xxiv. 25).

6. A Levite, family of Merari, and fourth son of Hosah. He was one of the doorkeepers in David's reign (1 Chron. xxvi. 11).

7. A Manassite of Gilead and father of Iddo, who lived in David's reign (1 Chron. xxvii. 21).

8. A Levite, of the sons of Asaph, and hence of the family of Gershom (2 Chron. xx. 14).

9. One of the princes whom Jehoshaphat sent to teach the people of Judah (2 Chron. xvii. 7).

10. Fourth son of king Jehoshaphat (2 Chron. xxi. 2).

11. Son of Jehoiada, the high priest, and a righteous man like his father. He lived in the reign of king Joash of Judah. The Spirit of God came upon him and he remonstrated with the people on their apostasy from Jehovah which ensued on the death of Jehoiada. At the instance of the king he was stoned to death in the court of the temple (2 Chron. xxiv. 20-22). It is commonly believed that he is referred to by our Lord when speaking of the righteous blood shed on earth, from the blood of Abel unto the blood of Zechariah, who perished between the altar and the sanctuary (Luke xi. 51). Zechariah, son of Jehoiada, is the only person mentioned in Scripture as being thus slain; his violent death was memorable and was familiar to succeeding generations; and he is the last of the righteous men wickedly slain, as Abel was the first, who are mentioned in the Hebrew Scriptures, Chronicles being the last book in the Hebrew Bible. He is called the son of Barachiah in the parallel passage (Mat. xxiii. 35, in A. V. Barachias), which naturally identifies him with the well-known prophet who lived after the exile. But this explanatory clause in Matthew is not improbably a gloss which was written on the margin by a reader and afterwards crept into the text.

12. A man who had understanding in the vision of God, and gave wise counsel to king Uzziah, which for a time he followed (2 Chron. xxvi. 5).

13. A king of Israel and last ruler of the dynasty of Jehu. He came to the throne of Samaria in the thirty-eighth year of Azariah, king of Judah, and reigned six months, about 749 B. C. He was the son of Jeroboam II, and was murdered at Ibleam by Shallum, who succeeded him as king (2 Kin. xiv. 29; xv. 10, Lucian). By his occupancy of the throne the prediction was fulfilled that the fourth generation of Jehu's sons should sit on the throne (x. 30).

14. A Reubenite chief (1 Chron. v. 7).

15. Son of Jeberechiah. He was a witness that Isaiah wrote certain enigmatical words about a year before their meaning was explained by a prophecy (Is. viii. 2).

16. Maternal grandfather of Hezekiah (2 Kin. xviii. 2).

17. A Levite descended from Asaph. He took part in the cleansing of the temple during the reign of Hezekiah (2 Chron. xxix. 13).

18. A Kohathite Levite, overseer of the workmen employed to repair the temple in Josiah's reign (2 Chron. xxxiv. 12).

19. A ruler of the house of God in Josiah's reign and doubtless a priest (2 Chron. xxxv. 8).

20. A man of Judah, family of Shelah (Neh. xi. 5).

21. A man of Judah, family of Perez (Neh. xi. 4).

22. A priest descended from Pashhur of the house of Malchijah (Neh. xi. 12).

23. A descendant of Parosh. He returned from Babylon with a party along with Ezra (Ezra viii. 3).

24. A son of Bebai who did likewise (Ezra viii. 11.)

25. One of the chief men whom Ezra sent to secure Levites and Nethinim to accompany the returning exiles (Ezra viii. 16).

26. One of the men, probably priests, who stood beside Ezra at the public reading of the law (Neh. viii. 4).

27. A son of Elam, induced by Ezra to put away his foreign wife (Ezra x. 26).

28. A Levite, son of Jonathan, and a descendant of Asaph. He led a division of Levitical musicians at the dedication of the rebuilt wall of Jerusalem (Neh. xii. 35, 36).

29. A priest who blew a trumpet at the dedication of the rebuilt wall of Jerusalem (Neh. xii. 41).

30. A priest, head of the father's house of Iddo in the days of the high priest Joiakim (Neh. xii. 16). See the following.

31. A prophet, son of Berechiah, and grandson of Iddo (Zech. i. 1). His first recorded prophecy was delivered in the second year of Darius Hystaspis, 520 B. C., ibid., Ezra iv. 24 with v. 1.). He was a contemporary of Zerubbabel the governor, Jeshua the high priest, and Haggai the prophet (Zech. iii. 1; iv. 6; vi. 11; Ezra v. 1, 2), and united with Haggai in exhorting the leaders of the Jewish colony to resume work on the house of God. It scarcely admits of question that he was born in Babylonia, for the exiles had been back in Palestine eighteen years only and Zechariah hardly began to prophesy before he was eighteen. Not improbably Zechariah belonged to the tribe of Levi, and, like Jeremiah and Ezekiel, was a priest as well as a prophet; for, according to Nehemiah (Neh. xii. 1, 4, 7) Iddo was head of a priestly family and one who returned from Babylonia with Zerubbabel; and a descendant of his, Zechariah by name, was head of the priestly house of Iddo during the high-priesthood of Joiakim, son of Jeshua (10, 12, 16). It is true that the lineage, which is involved in Nehemiah's statements, may be quite distinct from the genealogy of the prophet, although it contains the same names in the same order, but the theory which identifies the two has not a little confirmation. 1. Since Iddo had attained to the headship of a priestly family, he is rightly judged to have been an elderly man in the year of the return, 538 B. C. His descendant, Zechariah, attained to the same position in the next generation, which would naturally involve his being of such an age in 520 B. C., that he could he called a young man. The prophet Zechariah is called a young man (though by an angel it is true), in the year 520 B. C. (Zech. ii. 4). 2. Assuming that the prophet's father Berechiah was the son of the

priest Iddo and died prior to 520, without attaining to the headship of the family, then the prophet Zechariah was left next in the line of succession, and this would lead Ezra to call him the son of Iddo, naming him both as descendant and successor of Iddo. But even if Berechiah were alive, his name might be omitted; for it was only necessary to name the father's house to which a man belonged, in order to locate him among the tribes and families of Israel. The assumption of Berechiah's death would also account for the fact that in the generation after the return, Zechariah was head of the father's house. 3. The theory that the prophet Zechariah was a priest accounts for his familiarity with priestly functions and ideas (iii.; iv.).

Another view is that favored by Kimchi. According to him, the term prophet in i. 1 and 7 refers to Iddo (for position of the title, cp. Ezra vi. 5), and the latter is the seer who prophesied in the reign of Rehoboam (2 Chron. xi . 15; xiii. 22). The theory is improbable, but it is not to be rejected because four centuries intervened between the seer Iddo and the prophet Zechariah.

The book of Zechariah is the eleventh of the minor prophets. It may be divided as follows:

I. Introduction to the book and a series of eight visions. The introduction (i. 1-6) strikes the keynote, not to these visions only, but to the whole book. Learn the lesson of the past: "Return unto me and I will return unto you." Vision 1: the drove of horses (7-17), fleet, tireless messengers. By this picture it is shown that God is watching the events of earth; there is no sign of relief for God's people or of the punishment of their oppressors; the nations are at rest. Yet God is jealous for Zion and sore displeased with its oppressors; therefore, he is returned to Jerusalem with mercies; his house and his city shall be built, the land shall greatly prosper. The first vision is introductory to the seven that follow. Vision 2: the four horns and the four smiths (18–21). The vision means that for each of the horns, *i. e.* nations that scattered Judah, destruction is appointed. Vision 3: the man with a measuring line (ii.). The comfortable message of the first vision is unfolded, namely, the rebuilding of the city. The idea is expanded, however. Jerusalem shall not be measured, as cities usually are, by the extent of its walls; for, enjoying unbounded prosperity, it shall spread abroad without walls. It will not be insecure, however; Jehovah will be a wall of fire about it. Vision 4: Joshua, the high priest (iii.). The priesthood, although human and defiled, a brand consuming in the fire of God's wrath, is by grace plucked forth, cleansed, and, on condition of obedience, promised continuance. Then the fact is emphasized that the priests are types of the Messiah, and by a symbolical

action it is declared that God has a purpose which he will accomplish; the one typified will be raised up. Vision 5: the golden candlestick and the two olive trees (iv.). It seems as though the light of the church burning feebly after the exile must needs go out; not so, God has provided an abundant, unfailing, self-furnishing supply of oil. Vision 6: the flying roll (v. 1-4). God has pronounced a curse for the destruction of wickedness. Vision 7: the departing ephah (5–11). This is the sequel of the sixth vision. Wickedness, personified as a woman and imprisoned, is removed from the land. Vision 8: the four chariots issuing from the presence of the Lord of all the earth (vi. 1-8). The four chariots are declared to represent the four winds, which commonly denote the unseen power of God; and the vision is a promise that the entire plan outlined in the preceding series will be executed by the Lord of all the earth.

II. Symbolic action: crowning of the high priest (vi. 9-15). This procedure is expressly declared to belong to the future and to relate to the well-known Branch who was the expected king of David's line.

III. Deputation from Bethel to inquire whether the fasts shall still be kept, now that the disasters which they commemorated have been in part retrieved, and the prophet's four answers (vii.; viii.). 1. Fasts terminate on the faster; they do not affect God; obedience is the one thing God requires (vii. 4-7). 2. Justice and truth are the will of God, which is to be obeyed. The desolation of the land and dispersion of the people were not a calamity to be bewailed; they were a punishment for disobedience and intended to work reform (8-14). 3. God returns to Zion in jealousy, and will secure truth and holiness (viii. 1-17). 4. The fasts will become festivals (18–23).

IV. Burdens naturally follow the visions which revealed God's purpose to destroy the oppressors of Judah and bring many nations into the kingdom. Burden 1: Jehovah's overthrow of the enemies of God's kingdom. Punishments are impending which shall bring the surrounding nations low. A remnant of Philistia, however, shall be incorporated in God's kingdom; and Jerusalem shall be safe amid the widespread desolation, for God shall encamp about Judah and Judah's king shall come (ix.). Episode: exhortation to look to the Lord for promised blessings; and not to idols and soothsayers, who only cause the flock to err (x. 1, 2). Resumption of the prophecy. The Lord, however, as already said, hath visited his flock, and because of his wrath will make it as his goodly horse in battle, free Judah from all oppressors, gather both Judah and Ephraim, and make Ephraim joyful in his former habitation (3-12). These promised blessings, however, will not be enjoyed for some time to come. Desolation to the land! is the prophet's cry (xi. 1-3). The reason for this desolation is explained by the parable of the rejected shepherd (4-17) : because of the continued rejection of God's righteous government, the covenant with the nations is broken, and Israel is open to desolation ; because of the same sin, the unity of Judah and Ephraim remains unaccomplished, and weakness, discord, and desolation result. Burden 2 : the conflict and final triumph of the kingdom of God. The nations of the earth are arrayed against Jerusalem and Judah, which at the time of the prophet Zechariah were coextensive with the visible church of Jehovah ; but Jehovah makes it a cup of reeling and a burdensome stone to the nations, smiting the enemy with madness, and revealing the fact that the citizens of Zion are strong in the Lord (xii. 1-8). The preparation of Jerusalem (9-xiv. 5) : God will prepare Jerusalem, first, by gracious spiritual change wrought by God (xii. 10-xiii. 6) ; second, by purifying chastisement (7-xiv. 5ᵃ). The final triumph (5ᵇ-21). The Lord shall come ; it shall be a time of darkness and judgment, both for the church and the nations ; but at a time appointed of God, at eventide there shall be light. The church shall flourish, and a remnant of the nations shall go up from year to year to worship Jehovah, the king. Then shall the idea of the kingdom of God be realized, the church shall be holy.

The first to hint that the book of Zechariah did not proceed in its entirety from the pen of the prophet whose name it bears was Joseph Mede, of Christ Church college, Cambridge, in 1653. He argued that chapters ix. to xi. were written by Jeremiah, because Matthew in quoting Zechariah xi. 13 refers it to Jeremiah (Mat. xxvii. 9). This argument has no longer weight in the estimation of critics. Some would say that the mention of Jeremiah is an error by Matthew, while others believe that it is probably an early corruption of Matthew's text. It has even been suggested that since the Hebrews in their arrangement of the Scriptures at one time began the latter prophets with Jeremiah, observing the sequence Jeremiah, Ezekiel, Isaiah, instead of the present order, Isaiah, Jeremiah, Ezekiel (see CANON), this prophetic section was sometimes referred to as Jeremiah, just as The Psalms and The Proverbs are referred to as the Psalms of David and the Proverbs of Solomon, although David was not the sole author of The Psalms nor Solomon of The Proverbs. Since Mede's day many critics have held that in the present book of Zechariah there are the writings of two, three, or more prophets. The principal views are : 1. Chapters ix. to xi. were written shortly before the fall of Samaria in 722 B. C., and chapters xii. to xiv. shortly before the destruction of Jerusalem in 587 B. C. 2. Chapters ix. to xiv. were written in the late Persian period more than a century and a half after the death of Zechariah, or in the

Maccabæan period. 3. Chapters ix. to xiv., as well as chapters i. to viii, proceeded from Zechariah. The debate, it will be seen, concerns chapters ix. to xiv. only. All critics confess that Zechariah wrote the first eight chapters. The debated section contains the two burdens. What then is the date of these burdens ? In regard to the first burden, when it was written the house of the Lord was standing (ix. 15 ; xi. 13) : but from this fact no argument as to the date of the burden can be drawn ; for Solomon's temple was standing down to the exile, and the new temple, built after the return, was in use after the year 515 B. C. The reference in x. 10, 11 has been cited to prove that Egypt and Assyria were great powers at the time that this prophecy was delivered, and it was delivered after Israel had been carried captive (6), hence after the capture of Samaria but before the fall of Nineveh, about 606 B. C. But a prophet after the exile, as well as a prophet of an earlier date, could foretell that the Israelites would be restored to the lands from which they had been carried, namely, from Egypt and Assyria ; and although Assyria had succumbed to a later world empire, he could still say that the pride of Assyria, the power by which the Israelites were still kept in captivity, should be brought down ; or Assyria may be used of a geographical region, including Babylonia, just as the term is employed by Ezra (Ezra vi. 22), although the region was then under the government of Persia. Accordingly, the first burden may have been delivered either before the fall of Nineveh, while Assyria was still a power, or else after the exile when the Assyrian empire had given place to other empires, and since the temple is standing, after the sixth year of Darius king of Persia. Another datum which contributes to the solution of this question is obtained from the statement that God will break the brotherhood between Judah and Israel (Zech. xi. 14). The brotherhood existed until the reign of Rehoboam, when it was broken by the refusal of the northern tribes to render further allegiance to the throne of David. It might also be said to have been broken when Samaria fell, and the northern tribes were scattered. The brotherhood existed once more after the Babylonian exile. Now this burden was pronounced after the fall of Samaria and the captivity of Ephraim (x. 6) ; and therefore it properly dates from the time after the exile, when the current conception was that Ephraim and Judah were reunited in the brotherhood. In point of fact they were reunited : many members of the ten tribes had joined themselves to Judah ; and the existing nation was universally regarded as the representative of the twelve tribes, and in Ezra's day accordingly twelve goats were offered as a sin offering at the dedication of the temple, and a second sin offering of twelve bullocks was made for all Israel

(Ezra vi. 17; viii. 35; cp. Mat. xix. 28; Luke ii. 36; Acts iv. 36; xxvi. 7; Phil. iii. 5). It is true that the prophet frequently uses the old terms Judah and Ephraim, and this fact has been urged to prove that the prophecy was uttered long before the time of Zechariah, but many people living after the exile used the old terms. Zechariah himself in the first eight chapters employs them. He addresses the "house of Judah and house of Israel" (Zech. viii. 13). It is to this post-exilic period accordingly that the references to the brotherhood of Ephraim and Judah point. There is a further mark. It is declared that God will raise up Judah against the distant sons of Javan, or the Greeks (ix. 13). It will be observed that the Greeks are chosen for two reasons: (1) Because the prophet descries the conflict of the church with the most distant nations of the world. Javan and the isles were at this time within the geographical horizon of the Hebrews, and they were used as types of the remotest heathen nations (Gen. x. 4, 5; Is. xli. 5; lix. 18; lxvi. 19; Ezek. xxvii. 13). (2) The novel feature here is that Javan looms up as the world power of heathenism. The earliest date when the coming power of Greece became evident to observers in the Persian empire was during the years from 500 to 479 B. C., and the coming greatness of Greece as the successful antagonist of Persia was clearly evident. Greece had successfully checked the advance of Persian arms, and the Grecian cities of Asia Minor were in open revolt against their Persian lords during the years 500 to 495 B. C.; the Persians were defeated at Marathon in 490 and, after their victory at Thermopylæ, were crushingly defeated by the Greeks at Salamis, 480, Platæa and Mycale, 479. Zechariah, there is reason to believe on considerable and varied evidence, was a young man, say twenty or twenty-five, when in 520 B. C. he exhorted Zerubbabel to the work of rebuilding the temple, and consequently these stirring events which revealed the unsuspected greatness of Greece and opened the prospect that it would successfully intermeddle in oriental affairs occurred during the years which were Zechariah's prime of life.

The second burden, chapters xii. to xiv., is also shown by its contents to belong to the post-exilic period. The writer refers to the terror of the people when the earthquake in the days of Uzziah occurred. He refers to it as an event living vividly in the consciousness of the people. It was vivid to them either because of recent occurrence or because it had made a lasting impression on their minds. It certainly had made this lasting impression; it is treated as an epoch by the people of the generation in which it occurred (Amos i. 1), and in the first century of the Christian era it was still remembered as a solemn and striking event (Antiq. ix. 10, 4). There is another historical mark in this second burden, the reference to the mourning of Hadadrimmon in the valley of Megiddon (Zech. xii. 11). The only natural reference here is to the killing of Josiah who opposed Pharaoh-necho at Megiddo, was mortally wounded there and soon died, and his death was mourned by the singing men and singing women, and a lamentation was composed by the prophet Jeremiah. Accordingly the second burden was delivered not earlier than the eve of the exile.

Not only do the historical references in the two burdens point to late times, but the literary characteristics of these burdens proclaim them to have proceeded from the same source as the first eight chapters. This is strenuously denied by certain critics. It is urged that a difference of style is discernible between the burdens and the visions. This is true, but it is a cardinal doctrine of literary criticism that the style of an author differs at various periods of his literary career, and when he essays different forms of literature. Zechariah's style naturally underwent change during a period of thirty or forty years and differed when he depicted visions and symbolical actions from the style in which he set forth solemn warnings. Still, in the parable or the symbolic representation of the good shepherd, there are traces of the same literary hand as that which portrayed the visions and the crowning of the high priest. And the more subtle marks of the same hand are seen in the unique usage of certain words and expressions which characterize the first eight chapters in common with the last six. A few of these are the Qal of *yashab* in a passive sense (ii. 8; ix. 5; xii. 6), *me'ober umishshab* (vii. 14; ix. 8), *'ehad* for the indefinite article (v. 7; xii. 7), *'al-yamin w^e'al-s^emol* (iv. 11; xii. 6), *'ᵃdamah* (ii. 16; ix. 16; xiii. 5). The employment of the same word in different senses is also a characteristic both of the section which is acknowledged to be genuine and of the section which is disputed. These reasons afford proof that Zechariah was the author of the entire book, and that his mature life was passed between the years 520 and 479 B. C.

Ze'cher. See ZECHARIAH 1.

Ze'dad.

A place, probably a tower, on the northern boundary line of Palestine (Num. xxxiv. 8; Ezek. xlvii. 15). Sudud or Sadad, in the desert east of the road from Damascus to Hums, is believed by many to be the site.

Zed-e-ki'ah, in A. V. once **Zidkijah** (Neh. x. 1) [righteousness of Jehovah].

1. A son of Chenaanah. Having joined with other false prophets in encouraging Ahab to attempt the capture of Ramoth-gilead, and having predicted that Ahab would defeat the Syrians, he was so excited when Micaiah, a prophet of Jehovah, made a contrary prediction, that he struck the man of God upon the cheek, accompanying the

blow with words of insult. Micaiah told him that he would have cause to acknowledge his error (1 Kin. xxii. 11–25).

2. A lying and immoral prophet, the son of Maaseiah. Jeremiah predicted that Nebuchadnezzar would roast him in the fire (Jer. xxix. 21–23).

3. A son of Hananiah. He was a prince of Judah in the reign of Jehoiakim (Jer. xxxvi. 12).

4. The name given by Nebuchadnezzar to Mattaniah, one of Josiah's sons, on appointing him vassal-king of Judah in the room of his nephew, Jehoiachin (2 Kin. xxiv. 17; 1 Chron. iii. 15). In 2 Chron. xxxvi. 10 he is called Jehoiachin's brother, i. e., kinsman of the same ancestry; see BROTHER. He was the younger of Josiah's two sons by Hamutal (2 Kin. xxiii. 31 with xxiv. 18). He was twenty-one years old when he ascended the throne, and reigned eleven years, from about 598 to 587 B. C. Neither he nor his people gave heed to the word of the Lord which was spoken by Jeremiah (2 Chron. xxxvi. 12; Jer. xxxvii. 2). The temple was polluted with idolatry (2 Chron. xxxvi. 14), and justice was not executed (Jer. xxi. 11, 12). A strong party in the state, assisted by false prophets, urged the king to throw off the foreign yoke (xxvii. 12–22). At the beginning of Zedekiah's reign (1, R. V. margin) messengers from Edom, Moab, Ammon, Tyre, and Zidon came to him at Jerusalem to plan a united revolt from the king of Babylon; but Jeremiah was divinely instructed to condemn the purpose (2–11). Zedekiah sent an embassy to Nebuchadnezzar, probably to assure the great king of his fidelity (xxix. 3), and in his fourth year he himself visited Babylon (li. 59). Ultimately he was rash enough to rebel. On the tenth day of the tenth month, in the ninth year of Zedekiah's reign, the Babylonian monarch took post against Jerusalem, and began to erect forts around the city. It was too strong to be taken by assault; and the Babylonians held it in siege. The advance of the Egyptians compelled the Babylonians to withdraw for a time (Jer. xxxvii. 5), but they soon returned. By the ninth day of the fourth month, in the eleventh year of Zedekiah's reign, the food in the beleagured capital was exhausted. That night Zedekiah, with all the men of war, secretly quitted the stronghold, and, passing as noiselessly as possible between the Babylonian forts, fled in an easterly direction toward the Jordan. On learning that the king was gone, the Babylonian army pursued and overtook him in the plain of Jericho, his soldiers having fled in all directions, leaving him nearly alone. He was brought a prisoner to Nebuchadnezzar, who had retired to Riblah, a little north of Palestine. There, after he had been tried and condemned, his sons were put to death in his presence, and his own eyes put out; after which he was bound

in fetters, carried to Babylon (2 Kin. xxiv. 17–20; xxv. 1–7; 2 Chron. xxxvi. 11–21; Jer. xxxix. 1–14), and put in prison till the day of his death (Jer. lii. 11). Jeremiah prophesied during the whole of Zedekiah's reign.

5. A son of Jeconiah (1 Chron. iii. 16); but some expositors assume that son is used here in the sense of successor.

6. A high official who set his seal to the covenant immediately after Nehemiah the governor (Neh. x. 1).

Zeeb [wolf].

A Midianite prince captured and put to death by Gideon. He was slain at a wine press, which was afterwards called that of Zeeb (Judg. vii. 25). Its exact situation is unknown, but it was doubtless west of the Jordan, near the river.

Ze'la, in A. V. **Zelah,** and so once in R. V. erroneously (Josh. xviii. 28) [rib, side].

A town allotted to Benjamin (Josh. xviii. 28). It contained the sepulcher of Kish; and thither the bones of Saul and Jonathan were carried from Jabesh in Gilead and buried (2 Sam. xxi. 14). Site unidentified.

Ze'lek [a cleft].

An Ammonite, one of David's mighty men (2 Sam. xxiii. 37; 1 Chron. xi. 39).

Ze-lo'phe-had.

A Manassite, family of Machir, subfamily of Gilead, house of Hepher. He had no sons, but five daughters (Num. xxvi. 33). This condition of affairs gave occasion for enacting the law that if a man die and have no son the inheritance pass to his daughter (xxvii. 1–8). The law was soon afterwards developed by the addition of the provision that the daughter must marry within her father's tribe in order that no part of the tribal possession be transferred to another tribe (xxxvi. 1–12). The inheritance of the family was east of the Jordan (Josh. xvii. 1–6).

Ze-lo'tes. See ZEALOT.

Zel'zah [perhaps, shadow in the heat of the sun],

A frontier town of Benjamin, near Rachel's sepulcher (1 Sam. x. 2). Exact situation unknown.

Zem-a-ra'im [two cuttings].

1. A town of Benjamin (Josh. xviii. 22). Es-Sumrah, a large ruined village about 3 miles west of the river Jordan, and 4 northnortheast of Jericho, and less appropriately the ravine es-Sumra, about 5½ miles west of Jericho on the road to Jerusalem, have been suggested.

2. A mountain in the hill country of Ephraim, on which Abijah, king of Judah, stood to address the ten tribes before encountering them in battle (2 Chron. xiii. 4). Perhaps it was south of Bethel (19). Probably it lay not far from the city of Zemaraim.

Zem'a-rite.

A Canaanite tribe (Gen. x. 18; 1 Chron. i

16). They are enumerated between the Arvadite and Hamathite; and were the inhabitants of Simura, Ṣumura, now Sumra, on the coast between Arvad and Tripolis.

Ze-mi′rah, in A. V. **Zemira** [melody, a song].

A Benjamite, family of Becher (1 Chron. vii. 8).

Ze′nan [point or, perhaps, a place of flocks].

A town in or west of the lowland of Judah (Josh. xv. 37). Perhaps the same as Zaanan (Mic. i. 11). Site unknown.

Ze′nas [contraction of Greek *Zēnodoros*, gift of Zeus].

A lawyer, journeying in Crete with Apollos, whom Titus was enjoined by Paul to set forward on their journey (Titus iii. 13).

Zeph-a-ni′ah [Jehovah has hidden].

1. A Levite of the family of Kohath and house of Izhar (1 Chron. vi. 36–38).

2. A priest, the son of Maaseiah. He was one of those who carried messages between Zedekiah and Jeremiah (Jer. xxi. 1; xxxvii. 3). A certain false prophet who dwelt in Babylon, Shemaiah by name, having sent him letters directing him to punish Jeremiah for his discouraging predictions, he showed the missive to the prophet (xxix. 24–32). He had the oversight of the temple, and was second priest under the chief priest Seraiah. After the capture of Jerusalem by the Babylonians, Zephaniah was put to death at Riblah (2 Kin. xxv. 18-21; Jer. lii. 24-27).

3. A man whose son Josiah lived in the days of Zerubbabel and the prophet Zechariah (Zech. vi. 10, 14).

4. A prophet, whose descent is traced through four degrees to Hezekiah (Zeph. i. 1). This ancestor is probably the king, from the fact that so remote a descent is traced and because the time suits. The prophet himself lived and labored in the reign of Josiah (ibid.).

The book of Zephaniah is the ninth among the minor prophets. The date given in its title (i. 1) is confirmed by the omission of Gath in the enumeration of Philistine cities (ii. 4), by Nineveh being still in existence (13), and by the absence of allusion to the Chaldeans. The basis of the prophecy is the great doctrine of God's universal judgment. 1. A universal judgment, like the deluge in destructiveness (i. 2, 3). Idolatry will be overthrown in Jerusalem (4-6), and the sinners of Judah visited with judgment, as though Jehovah conducted a great sacrifice (7-13); and it will be a day of wrath upon men because of their wickedness (14-18). 2. A call to repentance as the only possible means of escape (ii. 1, 2), especially a summons to the humble and God-fearing to seek Jehovah and perhaps obtain deliverance (3); enforced by the certainty that God will punish other nations for their wickedness (4-15), and Jerusalem shall not escape, for it does

not repent and the Lord in the midst of her is righteous (iii. 1-8). 3. The blessed result of the judgment. The nations shall turn to the Lord (9, 10), the remnant of Israel shall trust in the Lord and be holy (11-13), and the Lord shall reign gloriously and beneficently as king in the midst of his people (14-18), who shall be gathered from captivity and be a praise in the earth (19, 20).

Perhaps the prophecy was delivered before the religious reformation inaugurated by Josiah in 622 B. C. (2 Kin. xxii. 3; 2 Chron. xxxiv. 8-xxxv. 19). But a later date is possible, during the years of sin just before the advent of Nebuchadnezzar (Jer. xxv. 3; xxvi. 1-6, 12, 13, 20; 2 Kin. xxiii. 32, 37).

Ze′phath [watchtower].

A Canaanite town in the south country toward the border of Edom, assigned to the tribe of Simeon. The Simeonites, assisted by their brethren of Judah, captured the place and changed its name to Hormah (Judg. i. 17); see HORMAH. Robinson suggested that the name is perhaps retained in es-Sufah, the name of a pass leading up from the Arabah to the south of Judah; but the general opinion is in favor of S'baita, discovered by Rowlands and rediscovered by Palmer, 24 miles north by east of Kadesh-barnea, and 26½ south by west of Beer-sheba. The ruins cover an area of 1500 yards. The identification is philologically doubtful.

Zeph′a-thah [watchtower].

A valley near Mareshah, in the tribe of Judah (2 Chron. xiv. 10). Conder proposes the wady Safieh, which, commencing about a mile northeast of Mareshah, near Beit Jibrin, runs for a short distance in that direction.

Ze′phi and **Zepho** [watch].

A son of Eliphaz, and grandson of Esau. He founded a tribe (Gen. xxxvi. 11, 15; 1 Chron. i. 36). For the difference in spelling see VAU.

Ze′phon [watching, expectation.]

A son of Gad, and founder of a tribal family (Num. xxvi. 15). Called in Gen. xlvi. 16 Ziphion, a synonym having the form usually assumed by similar derivatives.

Zer [flint].

A fortified city of Naphtali (Josh. xix. 35). Site unidentified.

Ze′rah, in A. V. twice **Zarah** (Gen. xxxviii. 30; xlvi. 12); once **Zara** (Mat. i. 3) [springing up of light, dawn].

1. A duke of Edom descended from Esau and also from Ishmael (Gen. xxxvi. 3, 4, 13, 17; 1 Chron. i. 37, and perhaps 44).

2. One of twins borne to Judah by Tamar, and the founder of a tribal family (Num. xxvi. 20; Josh. vii. 1, 17).

3. A son of Simeon, and founder of a tribal family (Num. xxvi. 13). He is called in Gen. xlvi. 10 and Ex. vi. 15 Zohar, which means dazzling whiteness or brightness.

4. A Levite, of the family of Gershom (1 Chron. vi. 21, 41).

5. An Ethiopian who led a vast army to attack king Asa, but was defeated with great slaughter in a battle at Mareshah (2 Chron. xiv. 8–15). See PHARAOH 4.

Zer-a-hi'ah [the Lord is risen (cp. Is. lx. 1, 2)].

1. A priest, son of Uzzi, and a descendant of Phinehas (1 Chron. vi. 6, 51 ; Ezra vii. 4).

2. One of the children of Pahath-moab (Ezra viii. 4).

Ze'red, in A. V. once **Zared** (Num. xxi. 12) [exuberant growth].

A brook and valley, which the Israelites crossed 38 years after being turned back into the wilderness at Kadesh-barnea, and which constituted the farthest limit of the wanderings in the wilderness (Num. xxi. 12 ; Deut. ii. 13, 14). It was south of the Arnon ; not, however, on the southern boundary of Moab, but somewhere along its eastern border (Num. xxi. 11, 13). Hence not the wady el-'Ahsy, which was the boundary between Moab and Edom. It may be either the Sail Sa'ideh, a southeastern branch of the Arnon, or the upper course of the wady Kerek.

Zer'e-dah, in A. V. **Zereda**, and with the unaccented vowel of the old case-ending **Ze-red'a-thah** [cooling, coolness].

A village whence came Nebat, an Ephraimite, the father of Jeroboam, and apparently also Jeroboam himself (1 Kin. xi. 26) ; but the village itself may have been elsewhere than in the territory of Ephraim (cp. Josh. xvi. 9 ; xvii. 9). The exact equivalent of the name is found in 'Ain Seredah, the fountain of Khurbet Balâtah, in mount Ephraim, 15 miles southwest of Shechem, at a bend of the wady Deir Ballût (Albright). The Septuagint and Lucian, however, invariably call the city and home of Jeroboam Sareira, i. e., Zererah (1 Kin. xi., 26 Sept., 24 Luc.), and locate it in mount Ephraim (xi. 43 S., 42 L. ; xii. 24b S., 28, 29 L. ; 24f S., 39 L.) ; perhaps confusing it with Tirzah in xiv. 17 (Heb. and S., and 7, 10, 13 L.).

Zer'e-rah, in A. V. **Zererath**, as in the present Hebrew text.

A town in the Jordan valley (Judg. vii. 22, in the form Sererathah), apparently the same as Zarethan (1 Kin. iv. 12) ; and if so, indicative that two r's are blended in Zarethan.

Ze'resh [probably, gold].

The wife of Haman (Esth. v. 10 ; vi. 13).

Ze'reth [perhaps, fissure or brightness].

A son of Ashhur, of the tribe of Judah, by his wife Helah (1 Chron. iv. 5–7).

Ze-reth-sha'har, in A. V. **Zareth-shahar** [brightness of the dawn].

A town of Reuben, on a mountain which overlooks a valley, doubtless that of the Dead Sea (Josh. xiii. 19). Seetzen suggested Sara, or Zara, near the mouth of the Zerka Ma'în. The names, however, are not identical.

Ze'ri.

A son of Jeduthun (1 Chron. xxv. 3). In ver. 11 he is called Izri, which is doubtless the correct form, the initial jod having been lost in course of transcription.

Ze'ror [a bundle].

A Benjamite, an ancestor of king Saul (1 Sam. ix. 1).

Ze-ru'ah [smitten, leprous].

The widowed mother of Jeroboam I. (1 Kin. xi. 26).

Ze-rub'ba-bel, in A. V. of N. T. **Zorobabel** [probably, begotten in Babylon].

A son of Pedaiah, and heir to the throne of Judah (1 Chron. iii. 17–19). But he is constantly called the son of Shealtiel, who was the brother of Pedaiah, quite improbably his son (Ezra iii. 2, 8 ; Neh. xii. 1 ; Hag. i. 1, 12, 14 ; ii. 2, 23 ; Mat. i. 12, 13 ; Luke iii. 27). Shealtiel doubtless died childless ; and either his nephew was his legal heir, and hence called his son (Ex. ii. 10), or else Pedaiah married his widow, in which case the first child would be considered that of the deceased brother (Deut. xxv. 5–10, etc.). When Cyrus, after the conquest of Babylon, adopted the wise political policy of allowing the Jews to return to their own land, he appointed the prince of Judah, whose name Sheshbazzar was perhaps the name given to Zerubbabel by the Babylonians and used when acting as representative of Cyrus, to be governor of the colony (Ezra i. 8, 11 ; v. 14). The returning exiles were led by Zerubbabel and the high priest Jeshua, with other princes (ii. 1–64 ; Neh. vii. 5–7 ; xii. 1–9) ; and reached Jerusalem in 538 B. C. Arrived at the ruined city Jeshua as head of the priesthood and Zerubbabel as head of the civil administration, acting together, reared an altar and restored the worship (Ezra iii. 1–9). The foundations of the temple were next laid by Sheshbazzar as Persian governor, acting in his official name (i. 2 ; v. 16 ; and iii. 6, 10–13). But adversaries, failing to make Zerubbabel stop proceedings, appealed to successive Persian kings, so that building operations ceased until 520 B. C., the second year of Darius Hystaspis (iv. 1–24). In this year, urged by the prophets Haggai and Zechariah, Zerubbabel, now Persian governor under Darius, and Jeshua resumed the work ; and under the constant encouragement of the prophets brought the building to completion in the early spring of 515 B. C. (vi. 14, 15 ; Hag. i. 1–ii. 23 ; Zech. iv. 1–14). From the office Zerubbabel held when the second temple was built, and the personal interest he took in its erection, it is often called Zerubbabel's temple. His governorship continued at least till 515 B. C. How much longer it lasted is unknown. Zerubbabel was in his day the representative of the Davidic monarchy (Hag. ii. 20–23). He was also in the direct line of ancestry of our Lord (Mat. i. 12, 13 ; Luke iii. 27).

Ze-ru'iah [cleft, divided].

A sister of David (1 Chron. ii. 16), but probably, like her sister Abigail, not a daughter of Jesse, but a daughter of David's mother by an earlier marriage with Nahash (2 Sam. xvii. 25). She was the mother of Abishai, Joab, and Asahel (ii. 18; 1 Chron. ii. 16).

Ze'tham.

A Gershonite Levite, house of Laadan and son of Jehiel (1 Chron. xxiii. 8 and xxvi. 22).

Ze'than [olive tree or place of olives].

A Benjamite, family of Jediael (1 Chron. vii. 10).

Ze'thar.

A chamberlain at the court of Ahasuerus (Esth. i. 10).

Zi'a [motion, terror].

A Gadite, probably head of a father's house (1 Chron. v. 13).

Zi'ba.

A servant or slave of king Saul's. He had been set free (Antiq. vii. 5, 5), perhaps at the time of Saul's overthrow by the Philistines, and he was father of a large family and had acquired slaves (2 Sam. ix. 10). David made him and his sons and slaves servants to Mephibosheth, Saul's son, and ordered them to till Mephibosheth's lands (9–12). When David was compelled to flee from Jerusalem because of Absalom's rebellion, Ziba appeared with a couple of asses laden with provisions for the king, and stated that Mephibosheth was expecting Israel would restore Saul's kingdom to him. Thereupon David transferred Mephibosheth's estates to Ziba (xvi. 1–4). After the death of Absalom, when the king was returning to Jerusalem, among those who went to the Jordan to welcome him back was Ziba with his sons and slaves (xix. 17). Mephibosheth also went to meet the king. He had neglected his person, as a sign of sorrow, during the king's absence, and now he declared that he had ordered his ass to be saddled in order to accompany David on his flight; but Ziba had disobeyed his orders and had also slandered him to the king, and he asked David to do what seemed right. David replied somewhat crustily, and ordered half of the estates to be restored to Mephibosheth, and the rest left in the possession of Ziba (24–30).

Zib'e-on [dyed or, perhaps, seizing prey].

A Hivite (Gen. xxxvi. 2; if the text should not be amended to Horite), who perhaps migrated with his family to mount Seir and became a Horite tribe (20, 24), organized under a chief (29). He was ancestor of a wife of Esau (2, 25).

Zib'i-a [a female gazelle].

A Benjamite, son of Shaharaim and head of a father's house (1 Chron. viii. 9).

Zib'i-ah [a female gazelle].

A woman of Beer-sheba, wife of Ahaziah, and mother of Jehoash, king of Judah (2 Kin. xii. 1).

Zich'ri [mindful, famous].

1. A Levite, family of Kohath, house of Izhar (Ex. vi. 21). Zithri in this verse in many editions of the A. V. is a modern misprint.

2. A Benjamite, son of Shimei (1 Chron. viii. 19).

3. A Benjamite, son of Shashak (1 Chron. viii. 23).

4. A Benjamite, son of Jeroham (1 Chron. viii. 27).

5. A Levite, son of Asaph (1 Chron. ix. 15). In all probability he is the person called Zaccur, a synonymous name, in xxv. 2, 10; Neh. xii. 35; and also the person called Zabdi in xi. 17, in the latter instance the letters k, anglicized ch, and r having been misread as b and d; see BETH, DALETH.

6. A Levite, descended from Moses' son, Eliezer (1 Chron. xxvi. 25).

7. A Reubenite (1 Chron. xxvii. 16).

8. A man of Judah, and father of Amasiah, a captain in the army of Jehoshaphat (2 Chron. xvii. 16), and quite possibly of Elishaphat who aided Jehoiada in overthrowing Athaliah (2 Chron. xxiii. 1).

9. A valiant Ephraimite in Pekah's army, who slew Maaseiah, a royal prince, and two of Ahaz' chief officers (2 Chron. xxviii. 7).

10. A Benjamite (Neh. xi. 9).

11. A priest, head of the father's house of Abijah. He lived in the days of the high priest Joiakim (Neh. xii. 17).

Zid'dim [sides].

A fenced city of Naphtali (Josh. xix. 35). The Talmud calls the place Kefar Chittai, which has led to locating it at Hattin, about 5½ miles west by north of Tiberias, and less than a mile north of the celebrated Horns of Hattin.

Zid-ki'jah. See ZEDEKIAH.

Zi'don. See SIDON.

Zif. See ZIV.

Zi'ha [sunniness, drought].

Founder or possibly only the head of a family of Nethinim, members of which returned from the captivity (Ezra ii. 43; Neh. vii. 46). If he was identical with Ziha, an overseer of the Nethinim, who is named in Neh. xi. 21, the family was of recent origin among the Nethinim, and small, or else it was an older family named from its present chief.

Zik'lag.

A city in the extreme south of Judah (Josh. xv. 31), assigned to the Simeonites (xix. 5; 1 Chron. iv. 30). In the time of Saul it was in the hands of the Philistines, and at one time David held it as the vassal of their king, Achish (1 Sam. xxvii. 6; 1 Chron. xii. 1–22). It was captured, plundered, and burnt by the Amalekites, but David pursued them, recovered the spoil, and sent portions of it to many other towns (1 Sam. xxx. 1–31; 2 Sam. i. 1; iv. 10). The connection of David with Ziklag detached it permanently from the Philistines, and placed it under the kings of Judah (1 Sam. xxvii. 6). It was inhabited after the captivity (Neh. xi. 28). Not identified; unless its site is Zuheilikah, a ruin discovered by Conder 11 miles east-southeast of Gaza. Identification with 'Asluj, 32 miles south of Gaza, has nothing in its favor.

Zil'lah [a shadow].
One of Lamech's wives, and the mother of Tubal-cain (Gen. iv. 19, 22, 23).

Zil'le-thai, in A. V. **Zilthai**.
1. A Benjamite, son of Shimei (1 Chron. viii. 20).
2. A Manassite, captain of a thousand men, who joined David at Ziklag (1 Chron. xii. 20).

Zil'pah [dropping, a drop].
A maidservant, given by Laban to Leah on her marriage with Jacob (Gen. xxix. 24). At Leah's request, she became his secondary wife, and bore to him Gad and Asher (xxx. 9–13).

Zil'thai. See ZILLETHAI.

Zim'mah [counsel, device].
A Gershonite Levite, son of Shimei, and grandson of Jahath (1 Chron. vi. 20, 42, 43; and perhaps 2 Chron. xxix. 12).

Zim'ran [probably connected with the name for antelope].
A son or rather tribe descended from Abraham and Keturah (Gen. xxv. 2; 1 Chron. i. 32). An echo of the name has been surmised either in Zabram, a town west of Mecca, on the Red Sea (Ptol. vi. 7, 5), or in Zamareni, an Arabian tribe (Pliny, Hist. Nat. vi. 32, 5).

Zim'ri [pertaining to an antelope].
1. Son of Zerah, and grandson of Judah (1 Chron. ii. 6); called in Josh. vii. 1, 17, 18 Zabdi (q. v.).
2. A prince of the tribe of Simeon. He was slain at Shittim for participating with the Midianites in licentious idolatry (Num. xxv. 14; 1 Mac. ii. 26, in A. V. Zambri).
3. A Benjamite, a descendant of Jonathan, Saul's son (1 Chron. viii. 36; ix. 42).
4. A military officer who commanded half the chariots of Elah, king of Israel, whom he assassinated, fulfilling the denunciation against Baasha's house by exterpating it. Then he set up for himself as king in Tirzah. Israel at once proclaimed Omri, the commander-in-chief, king. He marched against the usurper, and captured his capital, Tirzah. When Zimri saw that the city was taken he set the palace on fire and perished in the flames. His reign, which lasted only a week, fell within the year 885 B. C. (1 Kin. xvi. 8–20). It has been suggested that he may have been Saul's descendant (1 Chron. viii. 36), seeking to regain the throne.
5. A people (Jer. xxv. 25), not otherwise known. They may have been descended from Zimran, but there is no certainty in the case.

Zin [dwarf palm].
A wilderness traversed by the Israelites on their way to Canaan. It was close to the southern boundary of that land (Num. xiii. 21). Kadesh-barnea was within its limits (xx. 1; xxvii. 14; xxxiii. 36; Deut. xxxii. 51). It constituted the limit of Edom on the west and of Judah on the southeast (Josh. xv. 1–3). It was either a part of the wilderness of Paran or marched on that wilderness at Kadesh. It is not the same place as the wilderness of Sin, the Hebrew words for the two being quite different.

Zi'na. See ZIZAH.

Zi'on; in Maccabees **Sion**, and so in A. V. of N. T. always, and in O. T. once (Ps. lxv. 1) [a dry, sunny place or a mound or even a defense].
1. One of the hills on which Jerusalem stood. It is first mentioned in the O. T. as the seat of a Jebusite fortress. David captured this stronghold and changed its name to the city of David (2 Sam. v. 7; 1 Chron. xi. 5). Hither he brought the ark, and the hill from that time forth became sacred (2 Sam. vi. 10–12). The ark was afterwards removed by Solomon to the temple which he erected on mount Moriah (1 Kin. viii. 1; 2 Chron. iii. 1; v. 2). From the last two of these passages it is plain that Zion and Moriah were distinct eminences. For the question which hill was known as Zion see Jerusalem, paragraph on topography.
2. After the building of the temple on mount Moriah and the transfer of the ark to it, the name Zion was extended to comprehend the temple (Is. viii. 18; xviii. 7; xxiv. 23; Joel iii. 17; Mic. iv. 7). This accounts for the fact that while Zion is mentioned between one hundred and two hundred times in the O. T., mount Moriah is named only once (2 Chron. iii. 1), or at most twice (Gen. xxii. 2).
3. Zion is often used for the whole of Jerusalem (2 Kin. xix. 21; Ps. xlviii.; lxix. 35; cxxxiii. 3; Is. i. 8; iii. 16; iv. 3; x. 24; lii. 1; lx. 14).
4. In the Maccabæan period the hill on which the temple stood, as distinct from the city of David (1 Mac. vii. 32, 33).
5. The Jewish church and polity (Ps. cxxvi. 1; cxxix. 5; Is. xxxiii. 14; xxxiv. 8; xlix. 14; lii. 8).
6. Heaven (Heb. xii. 22; cp. Rev. xiv. 1).

Zi'or [smallness].
A town in the hill country of Judah, near Hebron (Josh. xv. 54). Robinson suggested Sia'îr, 4½ miles north-northeast of Hebron.

Ziph.
1. A town in the extreme south of Judah (Josh. xv. 24). Site unknown.
2. A town in the hill country of Judah (Josh. xv. 55), near a wilderness and a forest

(1 Sam. xxiii. 14, 15). It was fortified by Rehoboam (2 Chron. xi. 8). The ruins, called Zif, are on a low ridge between two small valleys, 4 miles south by east of Hebron. To the east is a wilderness, very hilly, with narrow valleys of rich loam. A woods existed at the time of the Crusaders, but only a few straggling trees remain.

3. A man of Judah, house of Jehallelel (1 Chron. iv. 16).

Zi'phah.

A man of Judah, house of Jahallelel (1 Chron. iv. 16).

Ziph'ims. See ZIPHITE.

Ziph'i-on. See ZEPHON.

Ziph'ites, in A. V. once **Ziphims** (Ps. liv. title).

Natives or inhabitants of Ziph 2 (1 Sam. xxiii. 19; xxvi. 1; Ps. liv. title).

Ziph'ron [fragrance].

A place on the northern boundary line of the promised land (Num. xxxiv. 9). Not identified.

Zip'por [a small bird, a sparrow].

Father of Balak, king of Moab (Num. xxii. 4, 10).

Zip'po-rah [a small bird, a sparrow].

A daughter of Jethro, priest of Midian. She became the wife of Moses (Exod. ii. 21, 22). She evidently opposed the circumcision of their second son; but when the family was journeying to Egypt and her husband's life was in danger on account of that breach of the covenant, she acquiesced (Ex. iv. 18–26); see MOSES. She may have returned with her sons to her father at this time; but quite probably they accompanied Moses to Egypt, and after the exodus, when the host of Israel was slowly approaching mount Sinai, were sent forward to visit Jethro and inform him of all that God had done for Moses and for the Israelites, how the Lord had brought Israel out of Egypt (Ex. xviii. 1). Jethro returned with them to the camp at Rephidim (2–6).

Zith'ri. See SITHRI and ZICHRI 1.

Ziv, in A. V. **Zif** [splendor (of flowers in bloom)].

The second month of the Jewish year (1 Kin. vi. 1, 37), approximately May. Later it was commonly called Iyar. See YEAR.

Ziz [brightness, burnished plate, flower].

A cliff or ascent by which the Moabites and Ammonites ascended from En-gedi toward the wilderness of Jeruel and Tekoa (2 Chron. xx. 16; cp. 2, 20). Robinson believes it to be the pass up from En-gedi; Tristram and Conder the table-land west of En-gedi, to which the pass leads up, and by which it is commanded.

Zi'za [plenty, fertility].

1. A Simeonite, descended from Shemaiah (1 Chron. iv. 37).

2. A son of Rehoboam, by his queen Maacah (2 Chron. xi. 20).

Zi'zah [plenty, fertility].

A Levite, family of Gershom, house of Shimei (1 Chron. xxiii. 11). In ver. 10 the name is mistranscribed Zina.

Zo'an [Egyptian *T'a*, early changed to *T'an*].

An Egyptian city of the eastern part of the delta, on the Tanitic branch of the Nile, near the 31st degree of north latitude. It was built seven years later than Hebron, which was in existence in Abraham's lifetime (Num. xiii. 22). Zoan existed at least as early as Rameri Pepi of the sixth dynasty, whose pyramid remains. The earliest kings of the twelfth dynasty made it their capital in order to check invasions from the east. The shepherd kings fortified it and retained it as the capital. After their expulsion the city was neglected for several centuries; but it was again raised to importance by Ramses II. and other kings of the nineteenth dynasty, who erected buildings and frequently held court there. The new town which thus grew up adjacent to the ancient fortress was called Pa-Ramses, that is the city of Ramses. Zoan was the place of meeting between Moses and Pharaoh (Ps. lxxviii. 12, 43). It was still an important city in the time of Isaiah and also of Ezekiel (Is. xix. 11, 13; cp. xxx. 4; Ezek. xxx. 14). Between the days of Isaiah and Ezekiel, it was captured by the Assyrians. The city was known to the Greeks as Tanis. It has lingered on to modern times, and is now called San. The site has been explored under the auspices of the Egyptian Exploration Fund. The remains consist of a temple surrounded by a great ring of mounds. A colossal statue of Ramses II. was exhumed.

Zo'ar [littleness, smallness (Gen. xix. 20, 22)].

One of the cities of the plain, and apparently the smallest of the five (Gen. xix. 20, 22). The plain was visible from mount Nebo as far as Zoar (Deut. xxxiv. 3). Its original name was Bela, and it had a king, one of those defeated by Chedorlaomer (Gen. xiii. 10; xiv. 2, 8). When threatened judgment was about to descend on the guilty cities, Lot successfully interceded for Zoar, and fled thither from the catastrophe (xix. 20–23). A mountain (or at least high land) rose immediately behind it, with a cavern, in which Lot and his two daughters dwelt for a time (30). Zoar still existed in the days of Isaiah and in those of Jeremiah, and, from their mentioning it in connection with Moab, it may be presumed that it was on the Moabite or eastern side of the Dead Sea (Is. xv. 5; Jer. xlviii. 34; cp. also Gen. xix. 37). In the Maccabæan period it belonged to an Arabian kingdom of which Petra was the capital (Antiq. xiii. 15, 4; xiv. 1, 4). It stood at the southern end of the Dead Sea (War iv.

8, 4). In the Middle Ages it was an important point on the road from Elath to Jerusalem, three days' journey from the latter city via Hebron. These data are satisfied by assuming that Zoar was situated near where the wady el-'Ahsy opens through the Moabite mountains into the plain, about 2 miles from the southern end of the sea (Wetzstein), at the ruins el-Ķeryeh. This was the later settlement, whither the people of Zoar moved and to which they gave the old name. The original site doubtless now lies beneath the waters of the sea.

Zo'bah, in A. V. and Hebrew text twice **Zoba** (2 Sam. x. 6, 8); see ARAM 2 (3).

Zo-be'bah [gentle movement].
Son of Hakkos, a man of Judah (1 Chron. iv. 8).

Zo'har [brightness, whiteness].
1. Father of Ephron the Hittite (Gen. xxiii. 8).
2. Son of Simeon (Gen. xlvi. 10). Called also Zerah (Num. xxvi. 13); see ZERAH.
3. A man of Judah (1 Chron. iv. 7, R. V. margin); see IZHAR.

Zo'he-leth [a serpent or other creeper].
A stone beside En-rogel (1 Kin. i. 9). Not identified. Clermont-Ganneau pointed out that the ledge of rocks, on which the village of Silwan stands, is called by the Arabs Zehwele or Zahweileh, which is like an altered form of Zoheleth. But the Arabic and Hebrew words have no real affinity, it is questionable whether the term stone would have been applied to a cliff, and the distance of the ledge from En-rogel seems too great.

Zo'heth.
A son of Ishi, registered with the tribe of Judah (1 Chron. iv. 20).

Zo'phah [expanse, a flask].
An Asherite, son of Helem (1 Chron. vii. 35, 36).

Zo'phai. See ZUPH.

Zo'phar [chirper].
A Naamathite, one of Job's friends (Job ii. 11; xi. 1; xx. 1; xlii. 9).

Zo'phim [watchers].
A field on the top of Pisgah, from which Balaam could see a part of the encampment of the Israelites at Shittim (Num. xxiii. 14). Conder places it at Tal'at es-Safa, in the valley separating the southeastern point of Pisgah from Luhith.

Zo'rah, in A. V. once **Zoreah** (Josh. xv. 33), once **Zareah** (Neh. xi. 29) [perhaps, stroke or scourge].
A town in the lowland of Judah (Josh. xv. 33), inhabited by the Danites (xi⁻. 41).

Manoah, Samson's father, belonged to the place (Judg. xiii. 2), and Samson was buried near the town (xvi. 31). Some of the five Danite spies and of the warriors who subsequently took Laish were from Zorah (xviii. 2, 8, 11). The town was fortified by Rehoboam (2 Chron. xi. 10). It was inhabited after the captivity (Neh. xi, 29). Its site is doubtless Sur'ah, on the north side of the valley of Sorek, 2 miles west-southwest of Eshtaol.

Zo'rath-ite, in A. V. once **zareathite** (1 Chron. ii. 53).
A native or inhabitant of Zorah (1 Chron. ii. 53; iv. 2).

Zo're-ah. See ZORAH.

Zo'rite.
Either the same as Zorathite, or a citizen of some unknown place (1 Chron. ii. 54).

Zo-rob'a-bel. See ZERUBBABEL.

Zu'ar [smallness].
Father of that Nethaneel who was prince of the tribe of Issachar in the wilderness (Num. i. 8; ii. 5; vii. 18, 23; x. 15).

Zuph [honeycomb].
1. A Levite, descended from Kohath, and an ancestor of the prophet Samuel (1 Chron. vi. 35). A variant form, of similar meaning, is Zophai (26).
2. A district beyond the borders of Benjamin and apparently lying to the south of the territory of that tribe (1 Sam. ix. 4–6; x. 2). It may have received its name from the settlement of the family of Zuph there. See further in connection with RAMAH 2.

Zur [a rock].
1. A king of Midian, ally or vassal of Sihon, and the father of the woman Cozbi (Num. xxv. 15). He was killed in the war of extermination waged by Moses against the Midianites for their seduction of the Israelites to licentious idolatry (Num. xxv. 15, 18; xxxi. 8; Josh. xiii. 21).
2. A Benjamite, son of Jeiel (1 Chron. viii. 30).

Zu'ri-el [God is a rock].
A Levite, chief of the Merarites in the wilderness (Num. iii. 35, R. V.).

Zu-ri-shad'dai [the Almighty is a rock].
Father of the prince of the Simeonites in the wilderness (Num. i. 6; ii. 12; vii. 36, 41; x. 19).

Zu'zim, in A. V. **Zuzims.**
A tribe occupying a district called Ham, east of the Jordan, conquered by Chedorlaomer (Gen. xiv. 5). Apparently the same as Zamzummim.

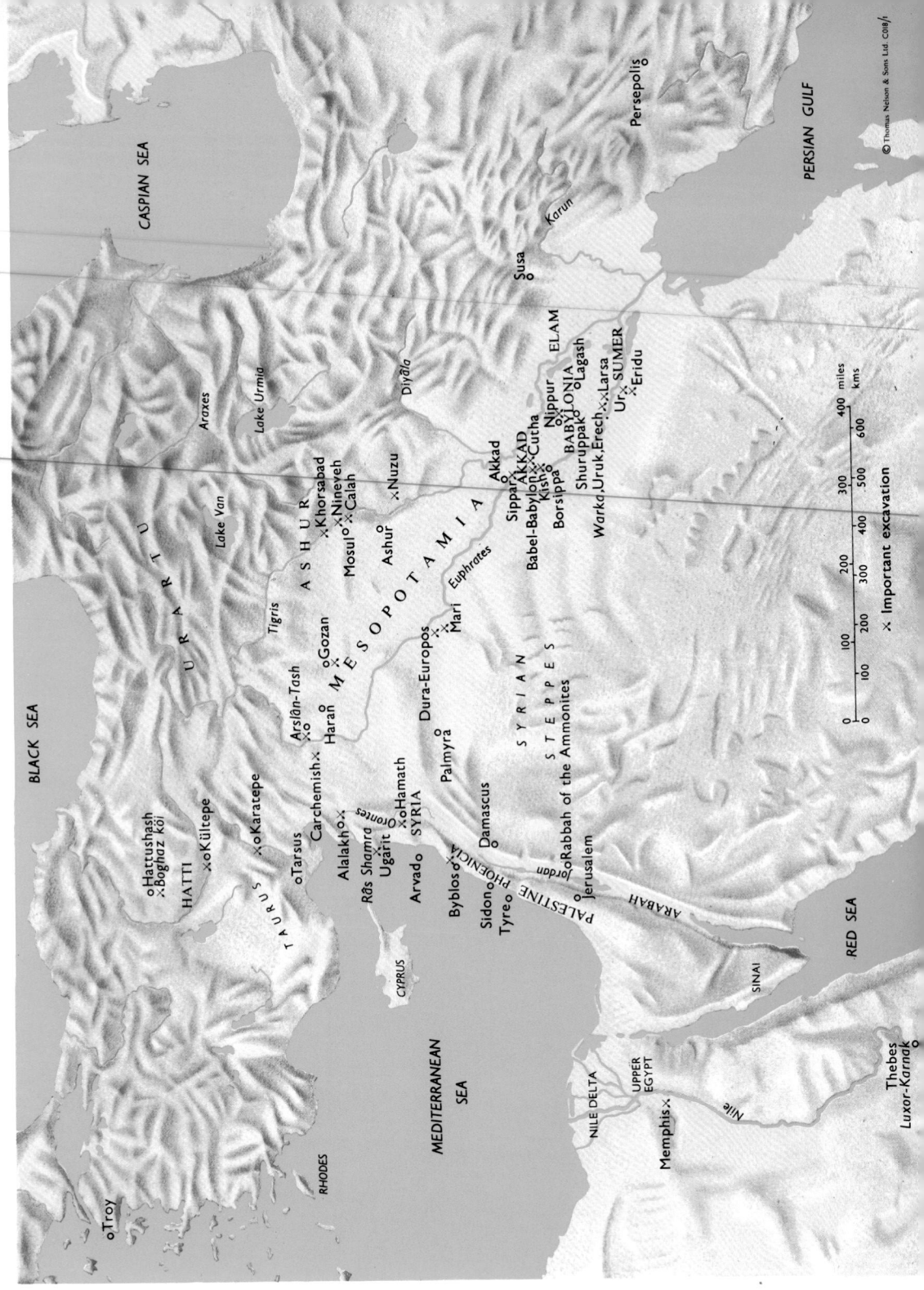

THE FERTILE CRESCENT

1

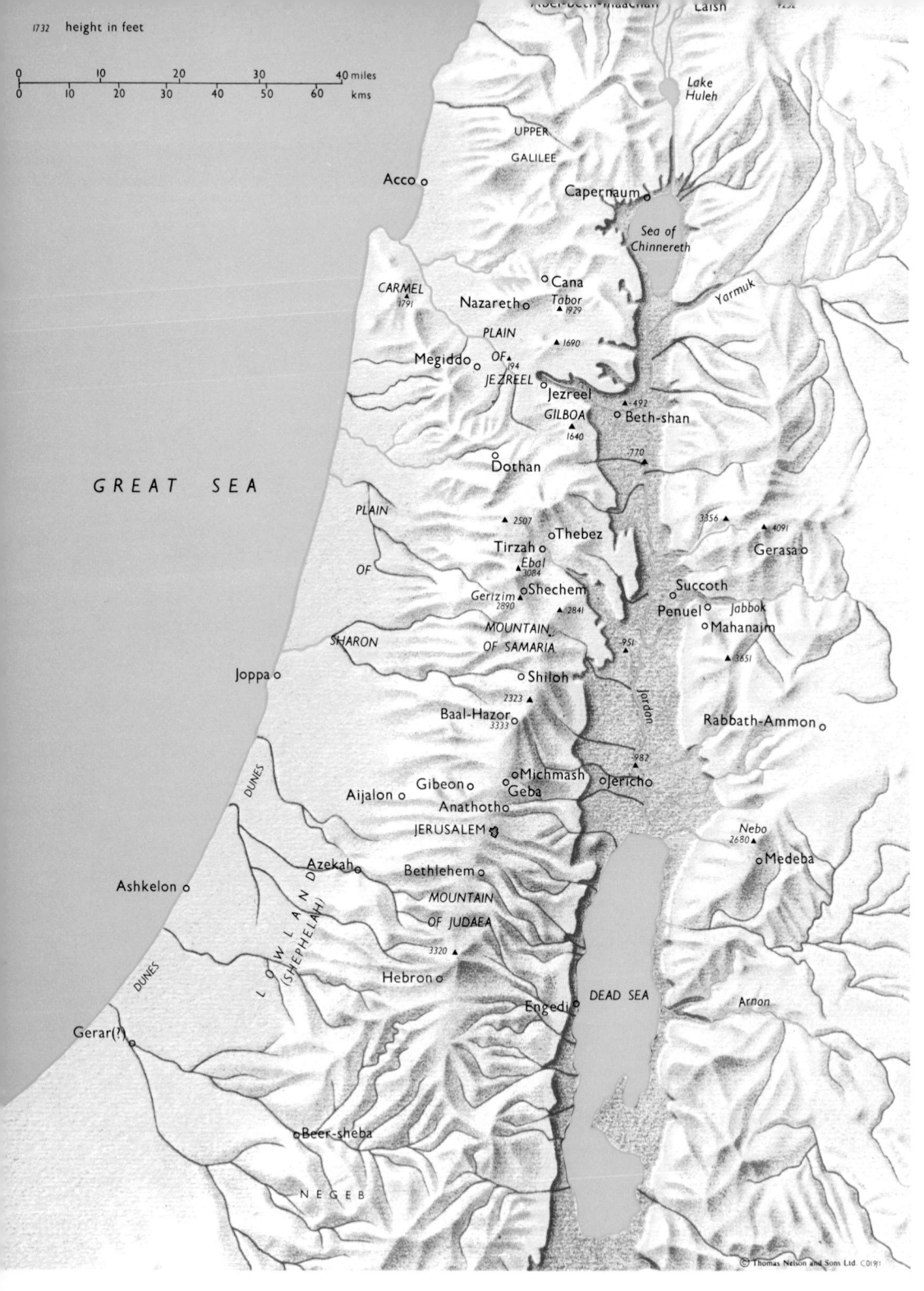

1732   height in feet

Laish

ABEL-BETH-MAACHAH

Lake
Huleh

UPPER

GALILEE

Acco ○

Capernaum ○

Sea of
Chinnereth

Cana ○
Nazareth ○   Tabor
▲ 1929

Yarmuk

CARMEL
1791

PLAIN
OF ▲ 1690

Megiddo ○

194 ▲

JEZREEL

Jezreel ○
GILBOA   ▲ -492
▲   ○ Beth-shan
1640

GREAT   SEA

Dothan ○   -770 ▲

PLAIN

3356 ▲   ▲ 4091

▲ 2507

Thebez ○

Gerasa ○

OF

Tirzah ○
Ebal
▲ 3084

Gerizim ▲   Shechem ○
2890   ▲ 2841

Succoth ○

Penuel ○   Jabbok

SHARON

MOUNTAIN
OF SAMARIA

▲ 951

Mahanaim ○

▲ 3651

Joppa ○

Shiloh ○

Jordan

2323 ▲
Baal-Hazor ○
3333

Rabbath-Ammon ○

DUNES

-982 ▲

Gibeon ○   ○ Michmash
Aijalon ○   Geba ○   ○ Jericho

Anathoth ○

JERUSALEM ◉

Nebo
2680 ▲

Azekah ○
Ashkelon ○

Bethlehem ○

○ Medeba

L
O
W
L
A
N
D
(SHEPHELAH)

MOUNTAIN
OF JUDAEA

3320 ▲

DUNES

Hebron ○

Engedi ○   DEAD SEA

Arnon

Gerar(?) ○

Beer-sheba ○

N E G E B

© Thomas Nelson and Sons Ltd. C0191

THE LAND OF PROMISE

2

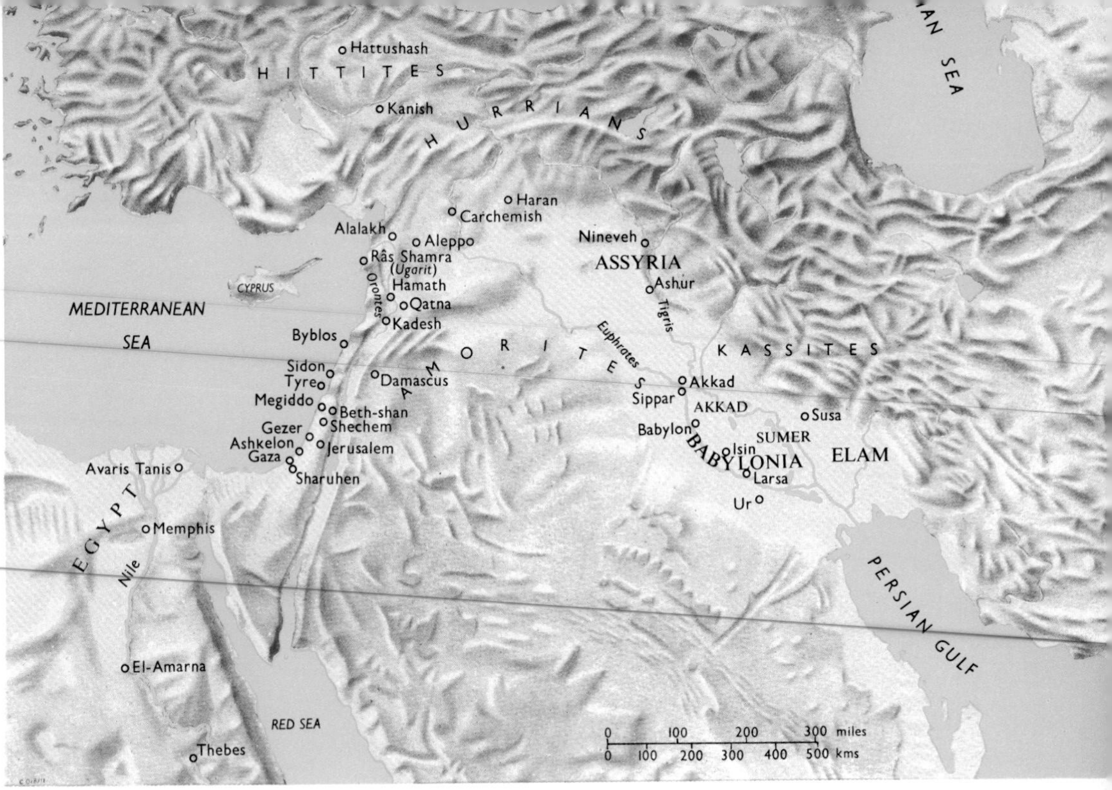

THE ANCIENT NEAR EAST (1500 TO 600 B.C.)

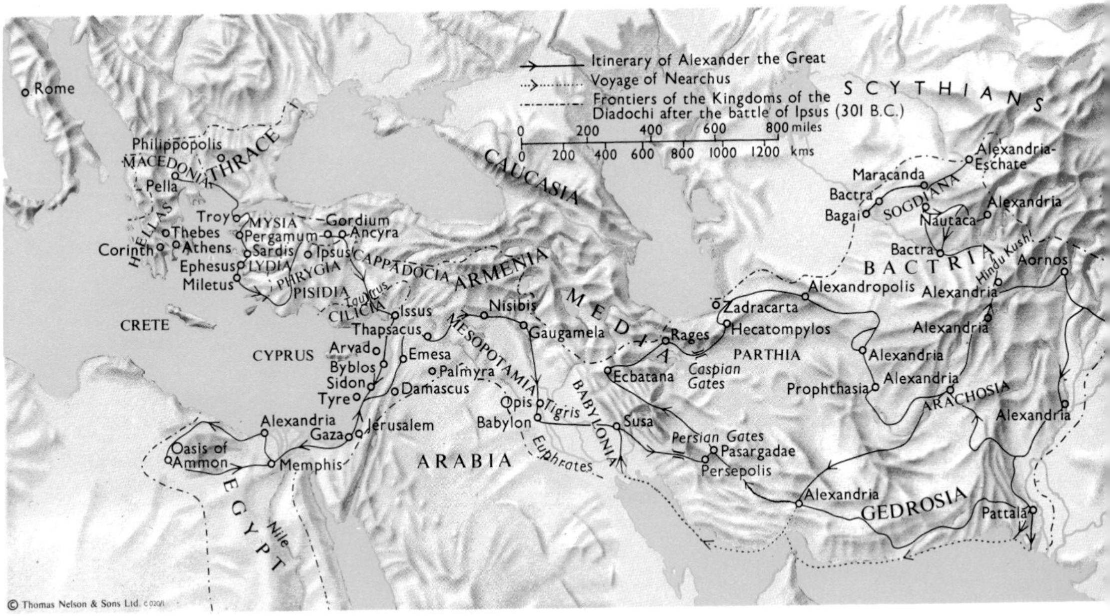

THE EMPIRE OF ALEXANDER

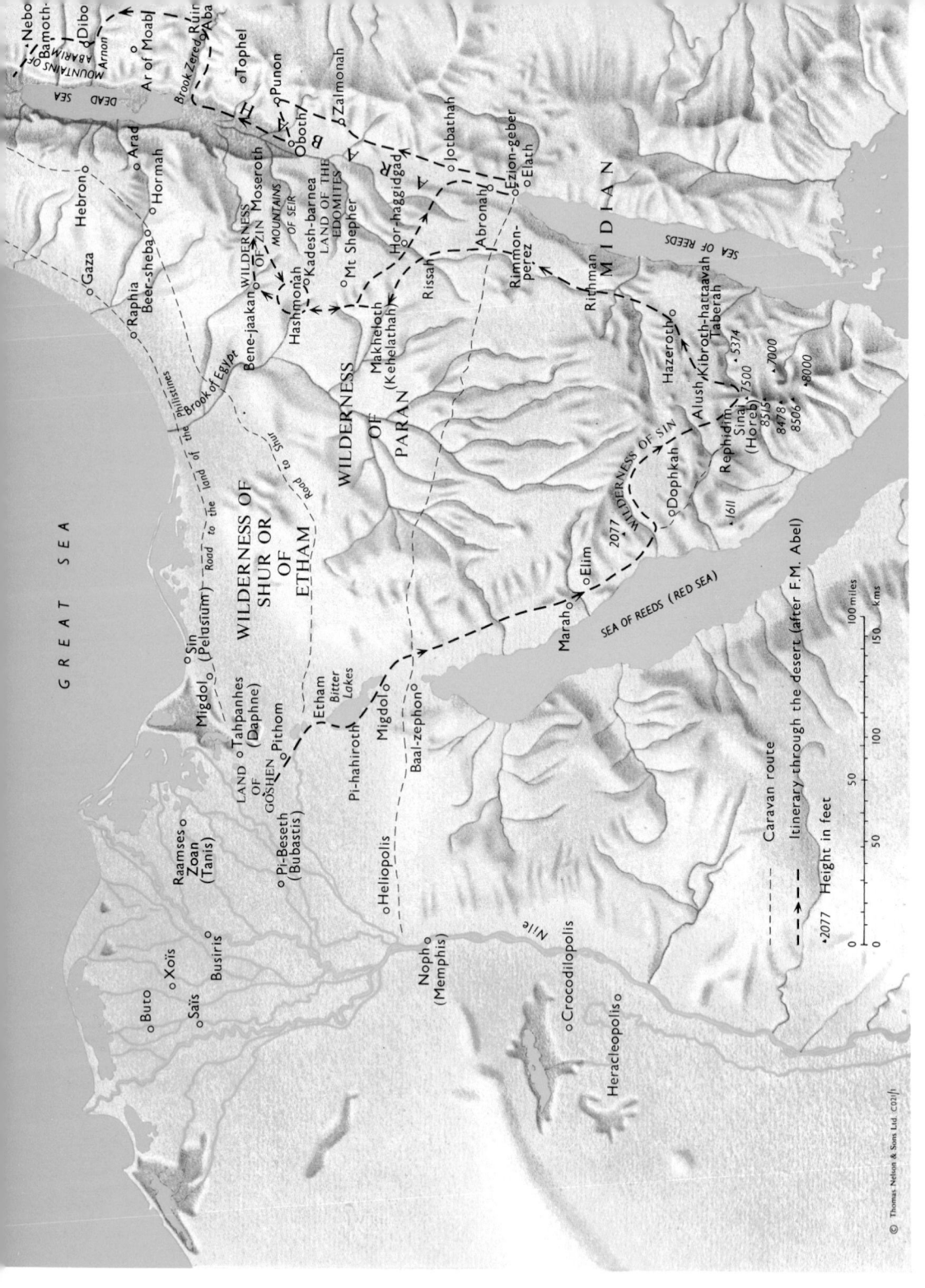

THE WANDERING IN THE WILDERNESS

THE SETTLEMENT IN CANAAN

5

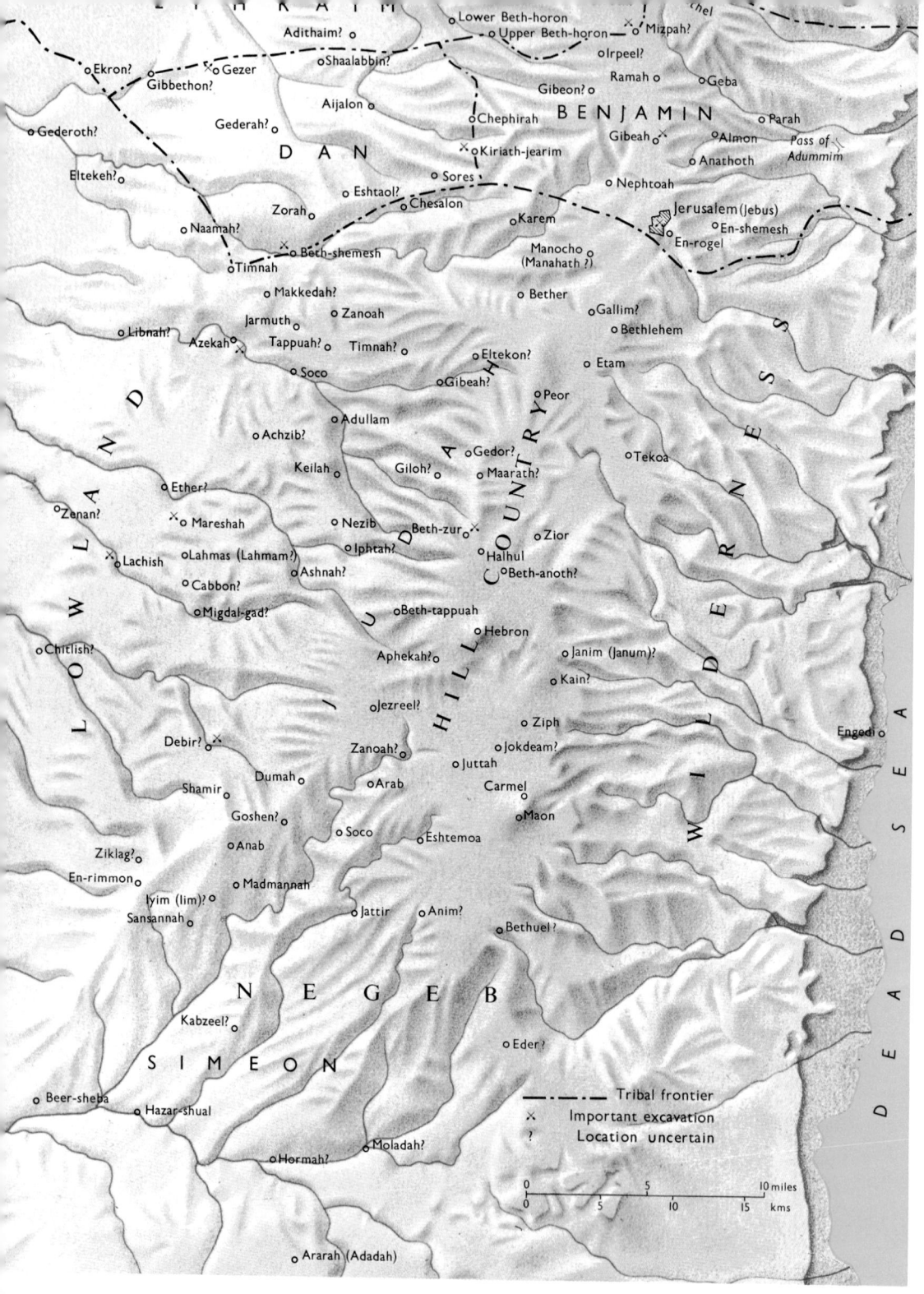

EPHRAIM

oLower Beth-horon
Adithaim? oUpper Beth-horon ×oMizpah?
oEkron? oIrpeel?
oGezer oShaalabbin?
Gibbethon? Ramah oGeba
Aijalon o Gibeon?
Gederah? BENJAMIN oParah
DAN oChephirah Gibeah oAlmon
oGederoth? ×oKiriath-jearim oAnathoth Pass of
Adummim
Eltekeh? oSores oNephtoah
Zorah oEshtaol oChesalon
oNaamah? oChesalon Jerusalem (Jebus)
×Beth-shemesh oKarem oEn-shemesh
oTimnah En-rogel
oMakkedah? Manocho
(Manahath?)
Jarmuth oZanoah oBether
oLibnah? oTappuah? Timnah? Eltekon? Gallim?
Azekah×o oSoco oGibeah? Bethlehem
oAchzib? Adullam oPeor Etam
Keilah oGiloh? Gedor? oTekoa
Ether? oMaarath?
Zenan? ×oMareshah oNezib Beth-zur oZior
×Lachish oLahmas (Lahmam?) oIphtah? Halhul
oAshnah? Beth-anoth?
oCabbon? oBeth-tappuah
oMigdal-gad? Hebron
Chitlish? Aphekah? oJanim (Janum)?
oKain?
oJezreel?
Debir?× oZiph Engedi
Zanoah? oJokdeam?
Dumah oArab Juttah
Shamir Carmel
Goshen? oSoco Eshtemoa oMaon
Ziklag? oAnab
En-rimmon oMadmannah
Iyim (Iim)? Jattir oAnim?
Sansannah oBethuel?

NEGEB

Kabzeel?
SIMEON oEder?
oBeer-sheba
Hazar-shual

—·—·— Tribal frontier
× Important excavation
? Location uncertain

oHormah? oMoladah?

0   5   10 miles
0   5   10   15 kms

oArarah (Adadah)

JUDAH

6

THE DIVIDED MONARCHY

PALESTINE IN THE TIME OF THE MACCABEES

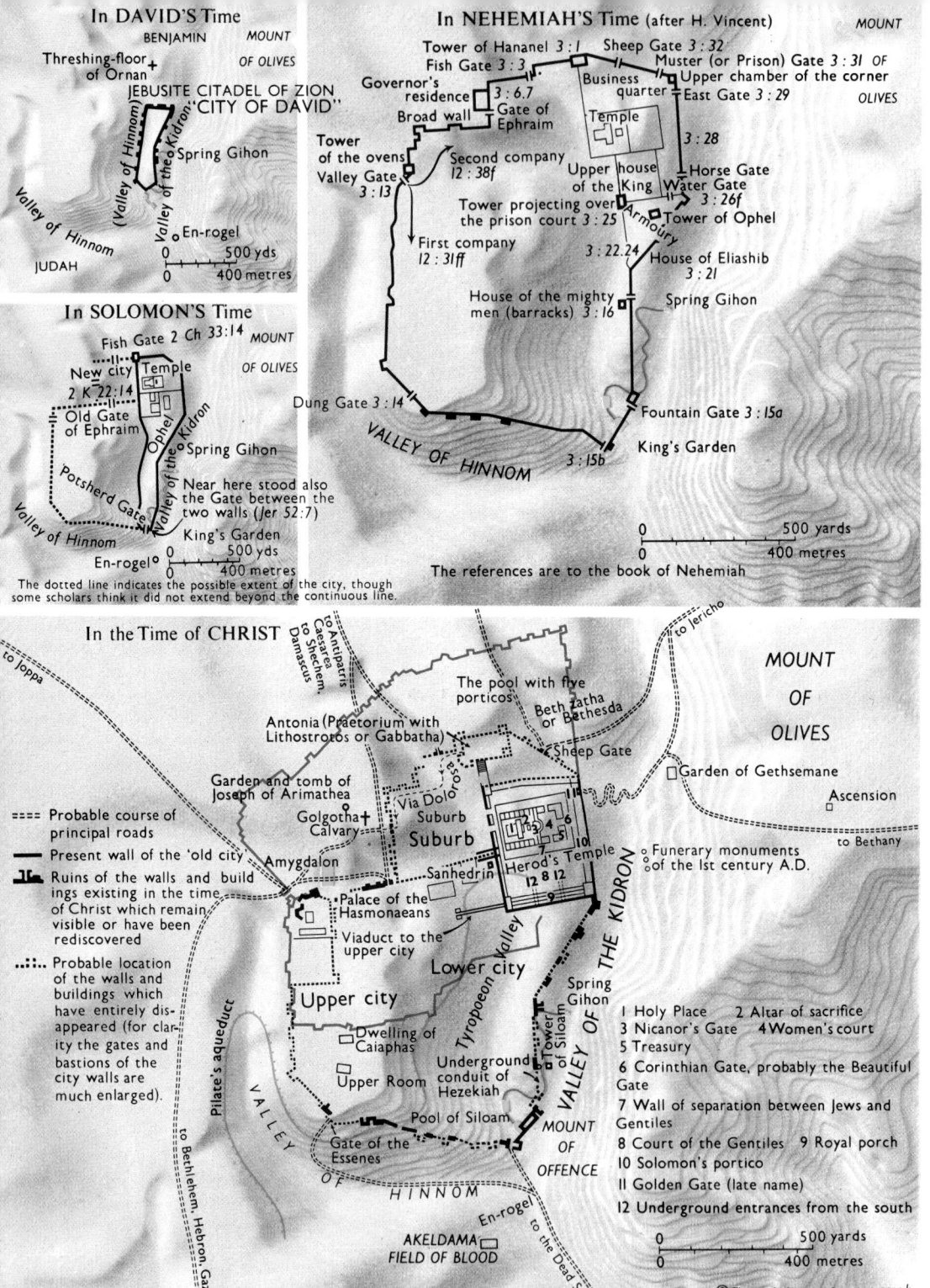

In DAVID'S Time

BENJAMIN — MOUNT OF OLIVES

Threshing-floor of Ornan

JEBUSITE CITADEL OF ZION "CITY OF DAVID"

(Valley of Hinnom)

Valley of the Kidron

Spring Gihon

En-rogel

Valley of Hinnom

JUDAH

0 — 500 yds
0 — 400 metres

In SOLOMON'S Time

Fish Gate 2 Ch 33:14 — MOUNT OF OLIVES

New city — Temple — 2 K 22:14

Old Gate of Ephraim

Ophel

Valley of the Kidron

Spring Gihon

Potsherd Gate

Near here stood also the Gate between the two walls (Jer 52:7)

Valley of Hinnom

King's Garden

En-rogel

0 — 500 yds
0 — 400 metres

The dotted line indicates the possible extent of the city, though some scholars think it did not extend beyond the continuous line.

In NEHEMIAH'S Time (after H. Vincent)

MOUNT OF OLIVES

Tower of Hananel 3:1   Sheep Gate 3:32
Fish Gate 3:3   Muster (or Prison) Gate 3:31
Governor's residence   Business quarter   Upper chamber of the corner
Broad wall   Temple   East Gate 3:29
3:6.7   Gate of Ephraim   3:28
Tower of the ovens   Second company 12:38f   Upper house of the King   Horse Gate
Valley Gate 3:13   Water Gate 3:26f
Tower projecting over the prison court 3:25   Armoury   Tower of Ophel
First company 12:31ff   3:22.24   House of Eliashib 3:21
House of the mighty men (barracks) 3:16   Spring Gihon
Dung Gate 3:14   House of Eliashib
VALLEY OF HINNOM   Fountain Gate 3:15a
King's Garden
3:15b

0 — 500 yards
0 — 400 metres

The references are to the book of Nehemiah

In the Time of CHRIST

to Joppa
to Antipatris, to Caesarea, to Sichem, Damascus
to Jericho

MOUNT OF OLIVES

The pool with five porticos
Beth zatha or Bethesda
Antonia (Praetorium with Lithostrotos or Gabbatha)
Sheep Gate
Garden and tomb of Joseph of Arimathea
Garden of Gethsemane
Golgotha Calvary
Via Dolo Suburb
Ascension
Suburb
Amygdalon
to Bethany
Sanhedrin
Herod's Temple
Funerary monuments of the 1st century A.D.
Palace of the Hasmonaeans
Viaduct to the upper city
Lower city
Upper city
Spring Gihon
Dwelling of Caiaphas
Tower of Siloam
Upper Room
Underground conduit of Hezekiah
Pool of Siloam
Gate of the Essenes
MOUNT OF OFFENCE
Pilate's aqueduct
VALLEY OF HINNOM
En-rogel
to Bethlehem, Hebron, Gaza
to the Dead Sea
AKELDAMA FIELD OF BLOOD

VALLEY OF THE KIDRON

==== Probable course of principal roads

—— Present wall of the 'old city'

Ruins of the walls and buildings existing in the time of Christ which remain visible or have been rediscovered

Probable location of the walls and buildings which have entirely disappeared (for clarity the gates and bastions of the city walls are much enlarged).

1 Holy Place   2 Altar of sacrifice
3 Nicanor's Gate   4 Women's court
5 Treasury
6 Corinthian Gate, probably the Beautiful Gate
7 Wall of separation between Jews and Gentiles
8 Court of the Gentiles   9 Royal porch
10 Solomon's portico
11 Golden Gate (late name)
12 Underground entrances from the south

0 — 500 yards
0 — 400 metres

© Thomas Nelson and Sons Ltd. C023/1

JERUSALEM

GREAT

SEA

SYRO-PHOENICIA

Tyre

Caesarea Philippi

▲9252

Ptolemais

Chorazin
Capernaum
Beth-saida
Magdala
Lake of
Gennesaret
Tiberias
Hippos

Cana

Nazareth

Abila

Nain ▲1690
194▲
Gadara

DECAPOLIS

Caesarea

1640 ▲
Scythopolis
Pella

Plain of Sharon

Aenon near
Salim

SAMARIA

Sebaste
(Samaria)
2507▲
3356▲
4091▲
Gerasa

GALILEE

Shechem
Gerizim
Sychar
Jacob's Well
2841▲

3651▲

Antipatris
Alexandrium
▲2323
Philadelphia

Joppa

Arimathaea

Ephraim

PERAEA

Lydda

Emmaus

Jericho

Jamnia

Jerusalem
Bethany
(Bethabara)

Azotus

Bethany
Kh. Qumrân

Ashkelon

Bethlehem
Herodium

JUDAEA

DEAD

Hebron ▲3320
Machaerus

Gaza

Engedi

SEA

A

B

Beer-sheba

IDUMAEA

N

A

▲ 2323   Height in feet

———   Main road

–·–·–·–   Provincial boundary

0   10   20   30   40   50 miles
0   10   20   30   40   50   60   70   80 kms

PALESTINE IN NEW TESTAMENT TIMES

11

THE JOURNEYS OF ST PAUL

Legend (from map):

- ·—·—·— First journey
- ·····— Second journey
- ——— Third journey
- ——— Journey to Rome
- - - - - Journeys planned but thwarted
- ——— alternative route
- Places where his addresses in synagogues are mentioned
- ——— Frontiers of the Roman Empire

Scale: 0 100 200 300 400 500 600 kms
0 100 200 300 400 miles

Labels on map:

PONTUS, BITHYNIA, GALATIA, LYCAONIA, PHRYGIA, CILICIA, SYRIA, Damascus, Antioch, Seleucia, Tarsus, Derbe, Lystra, Iconium, Pisidian Antioch, CYPRUS, Salamis, Paphos, Sidon, Tyre, Ptolemais, Caesarea, Jerusalem, Attalia, Perga, PAMPHYLIA, LYCIA, CARIA, Patara, Myra, Cnidus, Cos, Rhodes, Colossae, Laodicea, Hierapolis, Philadelphia, Sardis, Thyatira, LYDIA, Adramyttium, Pergamum, Ephesus, Miletus, Samos, Patmos, ASIA, Smyrna, Chios, Lesbos, Mitylene, Assos, Troas, Samothrace, MYSIA, THRACE, Neapolis, Philippi, Amphipolis, Apollonia, Thessalonica, Beroea, MACEDONIA, ATHENS, Corinth, Cenchreae, ACHAIA, Nicopolis, CRETE, C. Salmone, Phoenix, Lasea, Fair Havens, Cauda, Alexandria, Syrtis, ILLYRIA, DALMATIA, ADRIATIC SEA, ITALY, ROME, Three Taverns, Forum of Appius, Puteoli, Rhegium, Syracuse, SICILY, Malta

© Thomas Nelson and Sons Ltd. B076/1

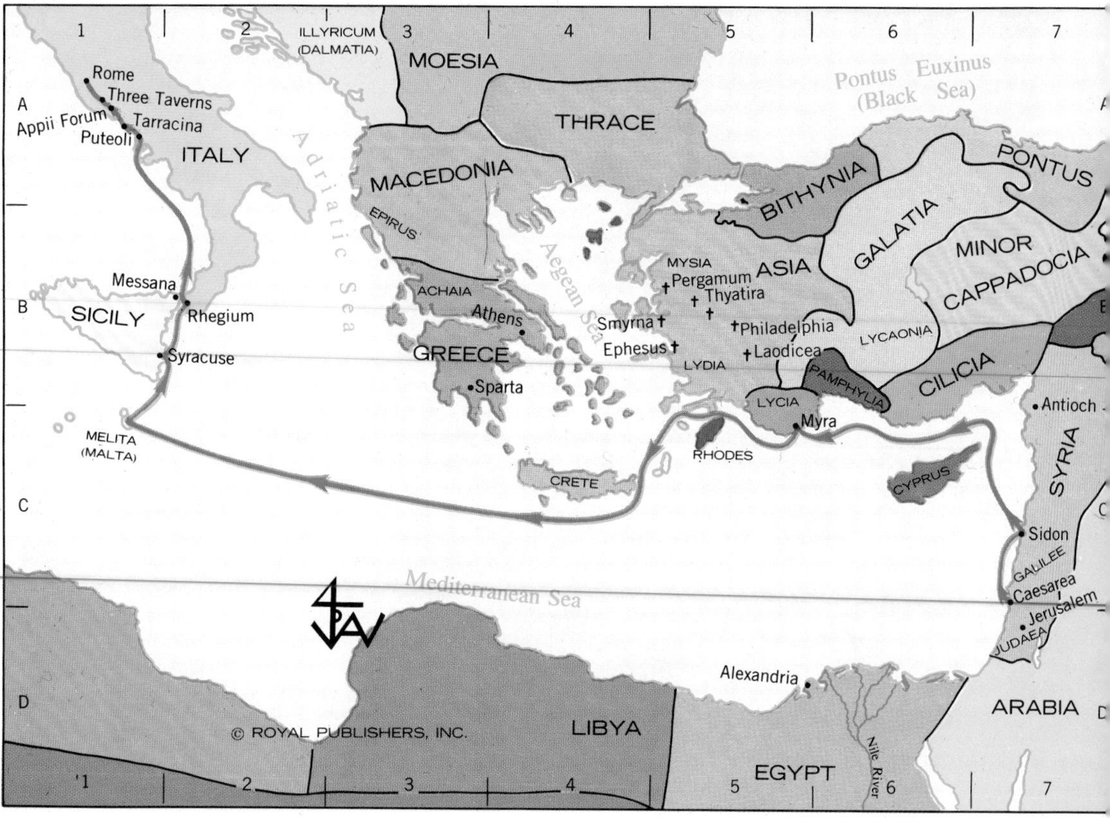

PAUL'S JOURNEY TO ROME

AND THE SEVEN CHURCHES OF ASIA
Revelation 1:19–3:22

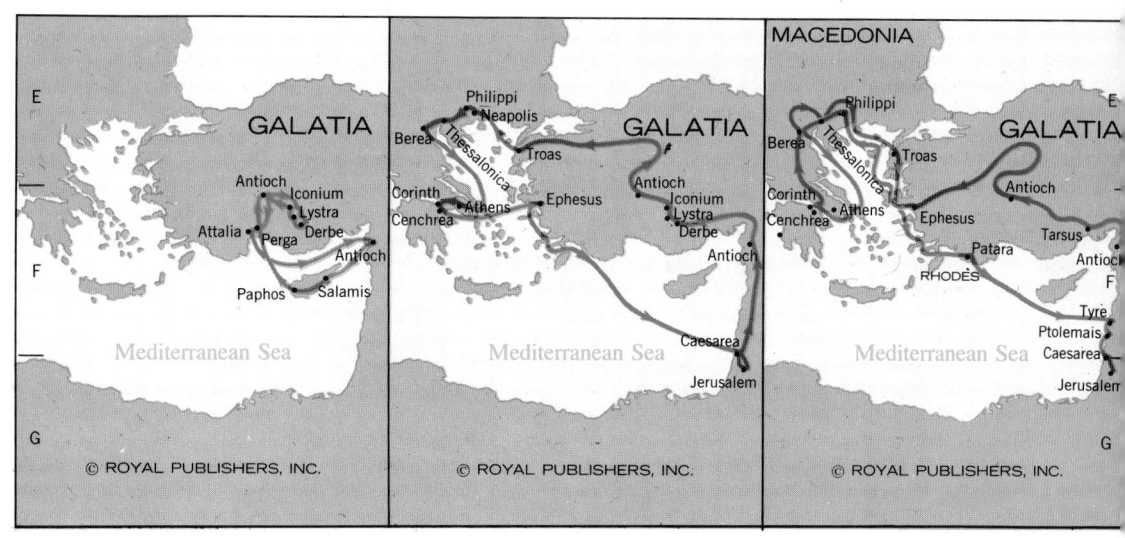

| PAUL'S FIRST MISSIONARY JOURNEY | PAUL'S SECOND MISSIONARY JOURNEY | PAUL'S THIRD MISSIONARY JOURNEY |

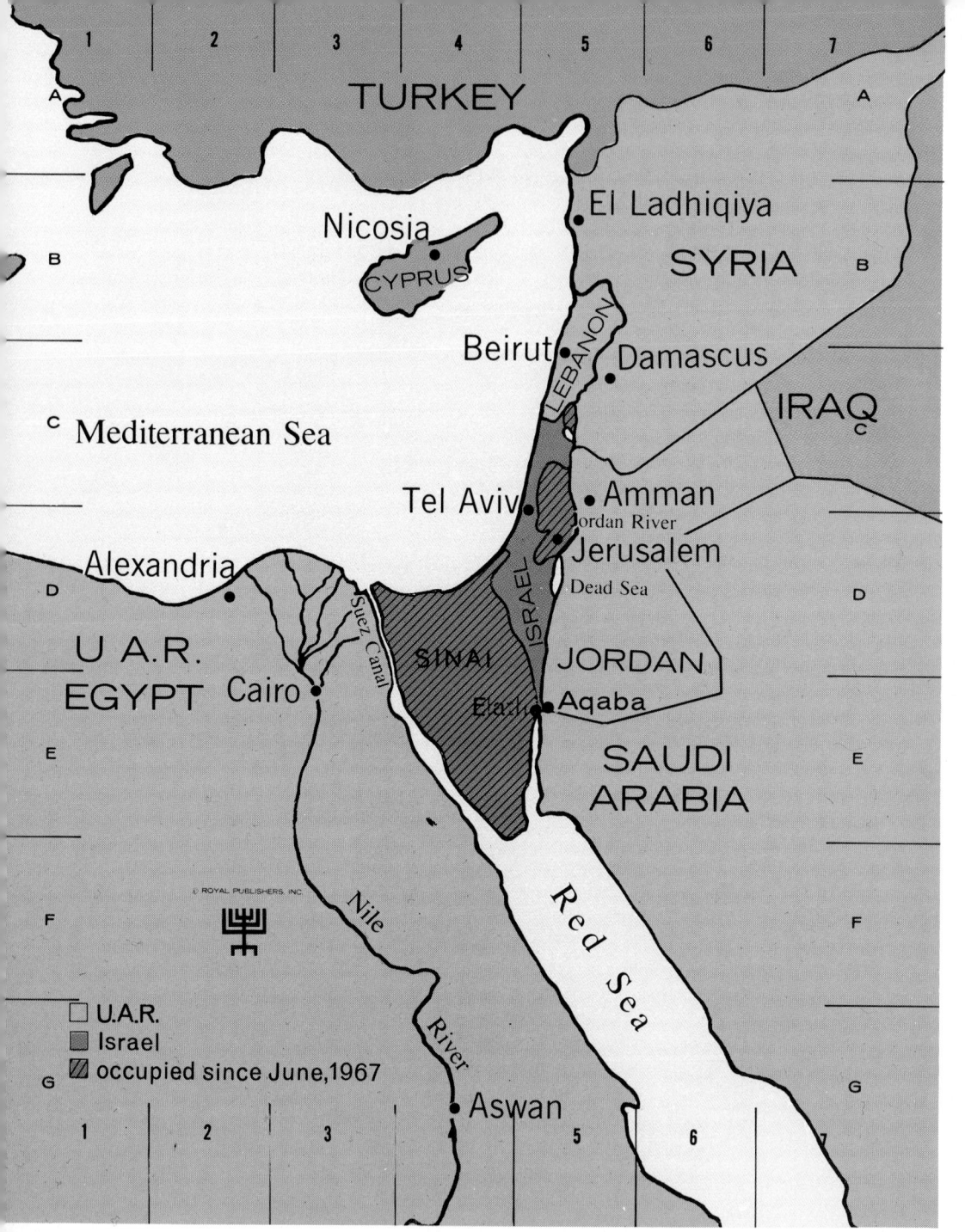

THE MIDDLE EAST AND
THE HOLY LAND AT PRESENT

14

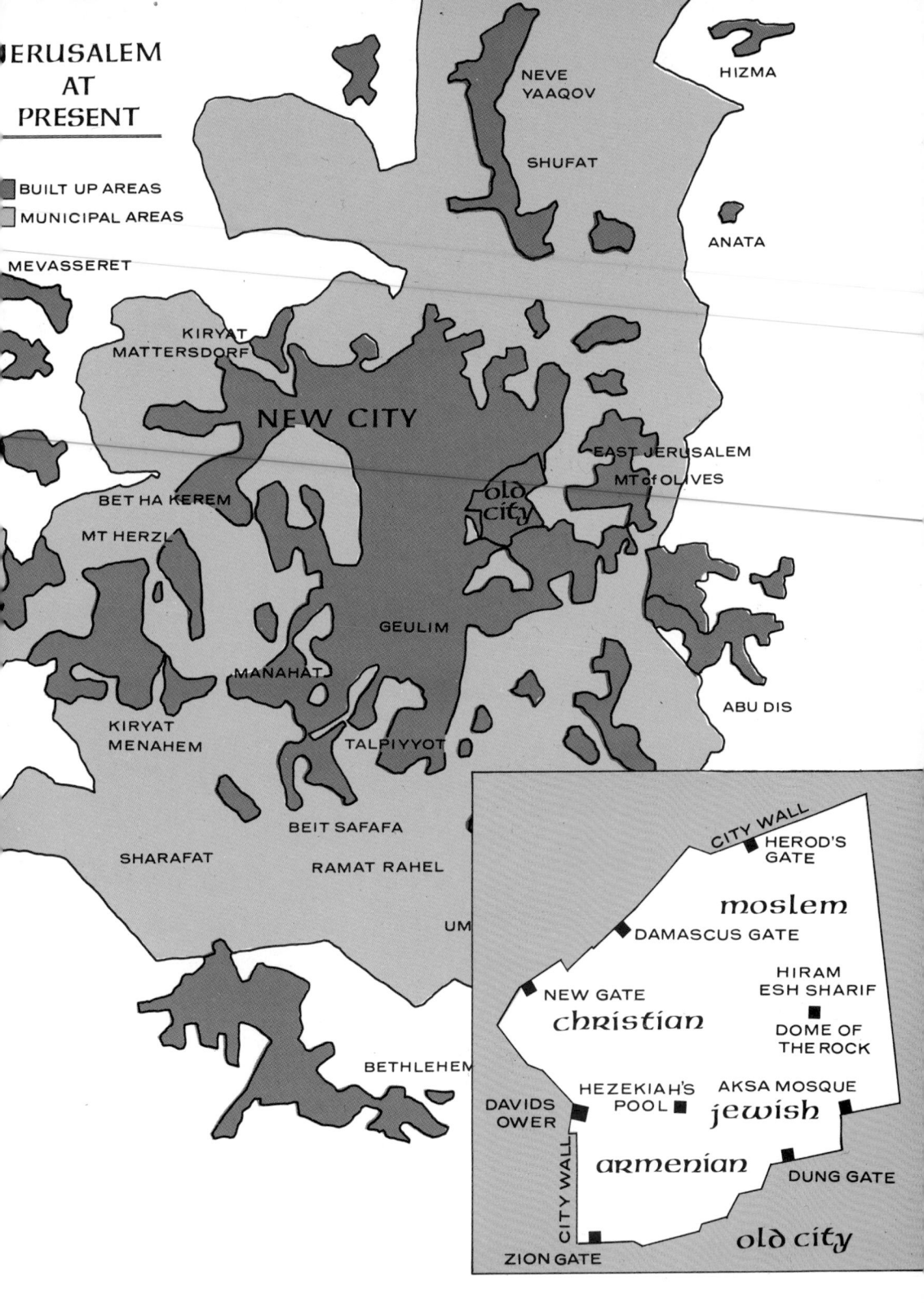

JERUSALEM
AT
PRESENT

- BUILT UP AREAS
- MUNICIPAL AREAS

HIZMA

NEVE
YAAQOV

SHUFAT

ANATA

MEVASSERET

KIRYAT
MATTERSDORF

NEW CITY

EAST JERUSALEM
MT of OLIVES

old
city

BET HA KEREM

MT HERZL

GEULIM

ABU DIS

MANAHAT

KIRYAT
MENAHEM

TALPIYYOT

BEIT SAFAFA

SHARAFAT

RAMAT RAHEL

UM

BETHLEHEM

CITY WALL

HEROD'S
GATE

moslem

DAMASCUS GATE

HIRAM
ESH SHARIF

NEW GATE

christian

DOME OF
THE ROCK

HEZEKIAH'S
POOL

AKSA MOSQUE

jewish

DAVIDS
OWER

armenian

DUNG GATE

CITY WALL

ZION GATE

old city

15

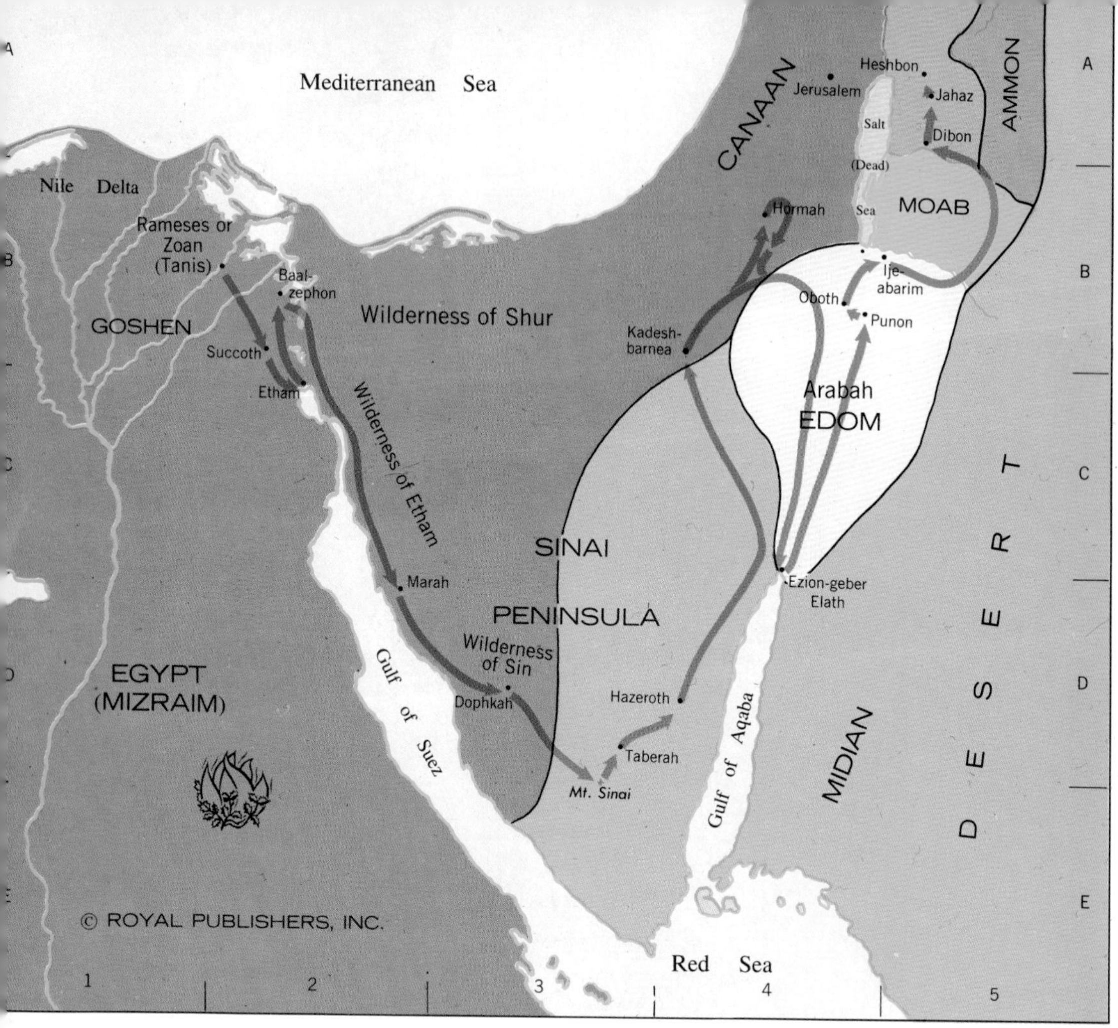

Mediterranean   Sea

CANAAN

A

Heshbon
Jerusalem
Jahaz
AMMON
Salt
Dibon
(Dead)
MOAB
Hormah
Sea

Nile   Delta

Rameses or
Zoan
(Tanis)
Baal-
zephon
Wilderness of Shur
Ije-
abarim
B

GOSHEN
Oboth
Punon
Kadesh-
barnea
Succoth

Etham
Arabah
EDOM

Wilderness of Etham

Gulf of Suez

C

SINAI

Marah
Ezion-geber
Elath

EGYPT
(MIZRAIM)
PENINSULA
Wilderness
of Sin
D
Dophkah
Hazeroth
MIDIAN
DESERT

Taberah

Mt. Sinai

Gulf of Aqaba

© ROYAL PUBLISHERS, INC.
E

Red   Sea

1   2   3   4   5

THE EXODUS

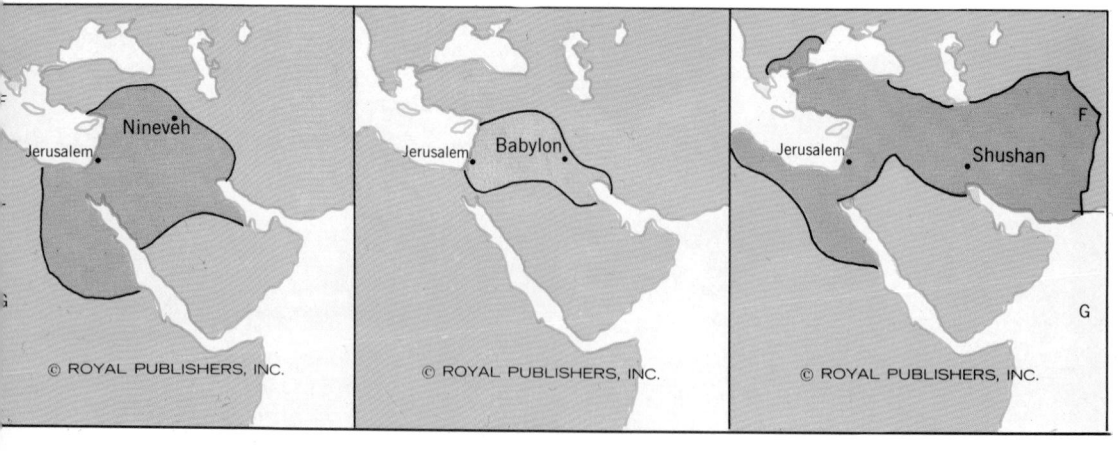

Nineveh
Jerusalem

Jerusalem
Babylon

Jerusalem
Shushan

F

G

ASSYRIAN EMPIRE
c. 725 B.C.

BABYLONIAN EMPIRE
c. 575 B.C.

PERSIAN EMPIRE
c. 525 B.C.

16